The Dante Encyclopedia

Garland Reference Library of the Humanities (Vol. 1836)

Advisory Board

The Dante Encyclopedia

Editor
Richard Lansing
Brandeis University

Associate Editors

Teodolinda Barolini
Columbia University

Joan M. Ferrante
Columbia University

Amilcare A. Iannucci
University of Toronto

Christopher Kleinhenz
University of Wisconsin, Madison

GARLAND PUBLISHING, INC.
A MEMBER OF THE TAYLOR & FRANCIS GROUP
NEW YORK & LONDON / 2000

Published in 2000 by
Garland Publishing, Inc.
A member of the Taylor & Francis Group
29 West 35th Street
New York, NY 10001

10   9   8   7   6   5   4   3   2   1

Library of Congress Cataloging-in-Publication Data
The Dante encyclopedia / editor, Richard Lansing ; associate editors, Teodolinda
Barolini . . . [et al.] ; advisors, Steven Botterill . . . [et al.].
     p. cm. — (Garland reference library of the humanities ; vol. 1836)
    Includes bibliographical references and index.
    ISBN 0-8153-1659-3 (alk. paper)
    1. Dante Alighieri, 1265–1321—Encyclopedias.   I. Lansing, Richard H.   II. Barolini,
Teodolinda, 1951–   III. Botterill, Steven.   IV. Series.

PQ4333. D36 2000
851'.1—dc21
[B]

                                      00-021203

Acknowledgments

Translation by Robert M. Durling, copyright © 1996 by Robert M. Durling from *The Divine Comedy of Dante Alighieri*, edited by Robert M. Durling, translated by Robert M. Durling, translation copyright © 1996 by Robert M. Durling. Used by permission of Oxford University Press, Inc.

Illustrations by Robert Turner, copyright © by Robert Turner from *The Divine Comedy of Dante Alighieri: Inferno*, edited by Robert M. Durling, translated by Robert M. Durling, translation copyright © 1996 by Robert M. Durling. Used by permission of Oxford University Press, Inc.

For use of the two illustrations (of Purgatory and of Paradise) by Robert Turner contracted for and made especially for this encyclopedia: Copyright © 1999 by Robert Turner.

Map of Florence adapted from William Anderson, *Dante the Maker,* Crossroad, NY, 1982; original from Toynbee's *A Dictionary of Proper Names and Notable Matters in the Works of Dante* (Oxford, 1968).

Printed on acid-free, 250-year-life paper
Manufactured in the United States of America

Contents

Preface

This encyclopedia assembles in a single volume a wealth of information and critical opinion concerning the life and works of Dante. Its primary goal is to provide readers with a broad base of knowledge elucidating not only the full corpus of the poet's literary and expository achievement but also the cultural and intellectual context in which it is set, in an easily and rapidly accessible format. Its compact form permits convenient reference to an extensive range of information relevant to Dante that cannot be found elsewhere in a single location in the English language. For many years the only comprehensive reference tool available to an English-speaking readership was Paget Toynbee's *A Dictionary of Proper Names and Notable Matters in the Works of Dante,* first published in 1898 and revised by Charles S. Singleton in 1968. But that volume has long been out of print, and, unlike the present text, it was a dictionary and not an encyclopedia. It limited itself by and large to proper nouns at the expense of notable matters: absent are entries on even major topics relating to the intellectual property of Dante's imagination. The only other reference tool, the monumental six-volume *Enciclopedia dantesca* published by Treccani in Rome (1970–75), has the advantage of presenting a prodigious amount of information, referencing virtually every word used in Italian by Dante. Its benefits, however, are reserved for those who possess a secure reading knowledge of Italian. Moreover, Dante criticism over the past quarter century has made significant advances. The present *Dante Encyclopedia,* therefore, provides an English-based readership with a body of knowledge founded on the most recent scholarship and up-to-date bibliographical data.

Entries are arranged alphabetically and are keyed to the English language. Forms of Italian proper names that do not typically undergo anglicization appear in Italian, with the exception of the titles of Dante's own works and special terminology. There are entries for every named character appearing in Dante's otherworld (historical and mythological) and for nearly all those that are referred to indirectly, as well as for geographical locations, topographical features, and titles of works cited or alluded to in the *Commedia.* The same is true for each of Dante's minor works. Very minor references of a tangential nature, listed in the Index of Italian and Latin Proper Names at the end of the volume, provide locus references to Dante's works. While accounting for a storehouse of factual information based on persons and places, the encyclopedia accords a large space to entries focusing on a wide array of topics and subjects aimed at providing an understanding of the intellectual and cultural groundwork underlying Dante's creative enterprise as well as his critical heritage. Here one will find informative articles on fields of human thought and activity, places, commentators and eminent past Dante scholars (limited to those who are deceased), language and poetics, institutions, documents, philosophical and theological concepts, categories of vice and virtue, and literary criticism. Attention has been paid not only to the tradition behind the poet's individual talent, the classical and medieval worlds, but as well to his afterlife, in the reception accorded him by successive generations of readers and critics. Every effort has been made to convey an understanding of the most authentic Dante that we possess. Consequently, passages from the original

Italian and Latin texts are cited from the most authoritative editions and are accompanied by translations of recent vintage; all foreign terms, except those in common use, have been translated. Like Dante's poem, this work seeks totality. And since Dante's imagination is so fundamentally encyclopedic in nature, it is only fitting that this volume reflect the poet's demiurge by taking the form of an encyclopedia.

Editions Cited

All cited references to the works of Dante are based on the following editions: *La Commedia secondo l'antica vulgata,* edited by Giorgio Petrocchi, Società Dantesca Italiana, Edizione Nazionale, 4 vols., Milan, Mondadori, 1966–1968; *Vita Nuova,* edited by Domenico De Robertis, in *Opere minori,* vol. 1/1, Milan-Naples, Ricciardi, 1984, pp. 3–247; *Il Convivio,* edited by Maria Simonelli, Bologna, Pàtron, 1966; *De vulgari eloquentia,* edited by Pier Vincenzo Mengaldo, in *Opere minori,* vol. 2, Milan-Naples, Ricciardi, 1979, pp. 3–237; *Egloge,* edited by Enzo Cecchini, in *Opere minori,* vol. 2, Milan-Naples, Ricciardi, 1979, pp. 645–689; *Epistole,* edited by Arsenio Frugoni and Giorgio Brugnoli, in *Opere minori,* vol. 2, Milan-Naples, Ricciardi, 1979, pp. 505–643; *Il Detto d'Amore,* edited by Gianfranco Contini, in *Opere minori,* vol. 1/1, Milan-Naples, Ricciardi, 1984, pp. 799–827; *Il Fiore,* edited by Gianfranco Contini, in *Opere minori,* vol. 1/1, Milan-Naples, Ricciardi, 1984, pp. 553–798; *Monarchia,* edited by Bruno Nardi, in *Opere minori,* vol. 2, Milan-Naples, Ricciardi, 1979, pp. 239–503; *Questio de aqua et terra,* edited by Francesco Mazzoni, in *Opere minori,* vol. 2, Milan-Naples, Ricciardi, 1979, pp. 691–880; *Rime,* edited by Gianfranco Contini, in *Opere minori,* vol. 1/1, Milan-Naples, Ricciardi, 1984, pp. 251–552.

Translations Cited

Editions containing the Italian or Latin text on the facing page have generally been preferred because they afford direct access to the original language. All translations of passages from Dante's works, which are based on the editions listed above, are taken from the following versions: *The Divine Comedy of Dante Alighieri,* translated by Robert Durling (New York and Oxford: Oxford Univer-

sity Press, 1996–); *Dante's Vita Nuova,* translated by Mark Musa (Bloomington and London: Indiana University Press, 1973); *Il Convivio (The Banquet),* translated by Richard Lansing (New York: Garland Publishing, Inc., 1990); *Dante: De vulgari eloquentia,* translated by Steven Botterill (Cambridge: Cambridge University Press, 1996); *Dantis Alagherii Epistolae: The Letters of Dante,* second edition, translated by Paget Toynbee (Oxford: Clarendon Press, 1966 [1920]); *Dante's Lyric Poetry,* two volumes, translated by Kenelm Foster and Patrick Boyde (Oxford: Clarendon Press, 1967); *Dante, "Monarchia,"* translated by Prue Shaw (Cambridge: Cambridge University Press, 1995); *Quaestio de aqua et terra,* translated by Alain Campbell White (Boston: Ginn & Company, 1903). (Note: In the Ricciardi Italian edition edited by Bruno Nardi, book 3 contains 15 chapters. Shaw's translation, following an alternative tradition, contains 16. In her volume, chapter 11 begins with the closing paragraph of chapter 10 in the Nardi edition. Locus references to the *Monarchia* in this volume are to the text in translation.)

Three recent translations of Dante's minor works not cited here but which should be borne in mind are Marianne Shapiro's *De vulgari eloquentia: Dante's Book of Exile* (Lincoln: University of Nebraska Press, 1990); *Dante's Monarchia,* translated, with a commentary by Richard Kay (Toronto: Pontifical Institute of Mediaeval Studies, 1998); and *Vita nuova / Dante Alighieri,* Italian text with facing English translation by Dino S. Cervigni and Edward Vasta (Notre Dame: University of Notre Dame Press, 1995). Shortly to appear in print is the first translation into English of two of Dante's early vernacular works, *The Fiore and the Detto d'Amore,* a translation with introduction and notes by Santa Casciani and Christopher Kleinhenz (Notre Dame, Ind.: University of Notre Dame Press, 2000).

Other Texts Cited

The following two texts are frequently cited in entries and bibliographies: Giovanni Villani, *Nuova cronica / Giovanni Villani,* 3 vols., edited by Giuseppe Porta (Parma: U. Guanda, 1991); *Enciclopedia dantesca,* 6 vols., directed by Umberto Bosco (Rome: Istituto dell'Enciclopedia Italiana, 1970–1978). Entry bibliographies in this volume generally omit reference to the corresponding entry in the *Enciclopedia dantesca,* since they are self-evident and for reasons of space. An exception is made for those entries where the entry name in Italian is not self-evident, or when reference is made to entries collateral to the main entry.

Acknowledgments

The Dante Encyclopedia, a project that began in 1994, contains nearly 1,000 entries written by outstanding scholars from around the world, many with extensive bibliographies designed to guide the reader toward further research. It is the product of a truly collective effort and represents the intellectual charity of 144 scholars from 12 countries around the world. A work of this size and scope would not have been possible without the indispensable assistance of each individual author, translator, associate editor, and advisor who in some way has been responsible for making Dante accessible to an ever-larger audience of readers. A special expression of gratitude, however, is due many who provided invaluable advice and assistance along the way. I wish to thank Angelo Mazzocco for having arranged with Mount Holyoke College to make available illustrations from the volumes of the Valentino Giamatti Dante Collection, courtesy of the Mount Holyoke College Archives and Special Collections. I am grateful in particular to Nancy Birkrem, Rare Books Librarian, and Peter Carini, Director of Archives and Special Collections, for their kind assistance in facilitating access to the collection. In like manner I am grateful to Christopher Kleinhenz for the photographic reproductions he made of illustrations contained in the John A. Zahm Dante Collection at the University of Notre Dame, and to Theodore J. Cachey, Jr., Director, and Louis E. Jordan III, Associate Director, of the William and Katherine Devers Program in Dante Studies at the University. Finally, I wish also to thank Brandeis University and, in particular, Charles Cutter, University Archivist, Director of the Special Collections Department for allowing me to make use of images from early editions of Dante's *Commedia.*

The "Chronology of the Life of Dante" that appears as an appendix to this volume is chiefly the work of Todd Boli, without whose unflagging dedication it would not have achieved its final state of precision. I am indebted to Maria Ann Roglieri, who has for many years been studying the relation of Dante to music, for two tables of information,

"Musical Settings of the *Commedia,*" which details compositions from the sixteenth century to the present, and "Recorded Musical Settings of the *Commedia,*" which provides a useful list of available recordings. Part of the personal joy of the editor in putting together this volume was derived from reproducing images that reflect the cultural reality of the world of Dante's Florence and Tuscany. I am speaking here not only of panoramas, statues, and buildings, photographs of which are linked to the relevant entries throughout the volume and are the result of my own inexpert hand, but more particularly of those who assisted in helping me realize these illustrations. Special thanks in this regard are due Vieri Wiechmann, who arranged for me to photograph the celebrated gold florin, held in utter contempt by Dante, whose obverse sports the image of the patron saint of Florence, St. John the Baptist, and whose reverse shows the *giglio,* or fleur-de-lis, symbol of the city of Florence. The actual coin whose image is shown was struck by the Peruzzi house and dates from 1306, so it is physically possible for that coin to have passed through the hands of the poet. Another image that inspired Dante's contempt is that of Boniface VIII, exemplified in Arnolfo di Cambio's marble statue of the pope; I am grateful to the director of the Museo dell'Opera del Duomo in Florence for granting permission to make a reproduction. Many thanks are also due the staff of Goldfarb Library at Brandeis University, and especially the assistance of Sue Swanson, Anthony Vaver, and Susan Pyzynski.

I wish to express my special gratitude to those whose labors frequently went beyond the call of duty and the pall that marks the norm: to Robert Durling not only for providing the text of his translation but for keyboarding significant parts of it into the textual body of the encyclopedia; to John Scott in Australia and Amilcare Iannucci in Canada, who responded graciously on more than one occasion to the plight of an editor in search of a new author who would take on yet another entry to fill a lacuna created by another; to Robin Treasure and Alison MacAdams, and to Todd Boli again, who took on, respectively, the task of keyboarding and verifying the lion's share of the Index citations, and of reviewing that work with a critical eye; to Zygmunt Barański for generously responding to all calls that went in the direction of the British Isles; to Teodolinda Barolini, Anthony Oldcorn, and Rachel Jacoff for assuming extra burdens at important junctures; to Lino Pertile and John Barnes for uncommon advice and assistance; to Chris Kleinhenz, for our almost daily email correspondence on issues major and minor; and I suppose as well to the inventors of the Internet and email, a vehicle of communication without which this project would have seen its period of genesis doubled. In the domain of original artwork prepared especially for this volume, I am indebted to Robert Turner for providing several new illustrations of Dante's cosmography, and to Oxford University Press for granting permission to reprint maps and charts by his hand which appeared earlier.

Last but of course not least, the editorial staff of Garland Publishing deserves hearty thanks for their guidance, helpfulness, and expertise in bringing this encyclopedia to the light of day. This project has seen three editors, to all of whom I am indebted for good cheer as well as good advice: to the encouragement of the original editor, Gary Kuris, who has conceived so many projects in the medieval series of encyclopedias; to Joanne Daniels, who took over in mid-stream; and finally to Richard Steins, the present Encyclopedia Development Manager, who has seen the ship into port.

Abbreviations

Ad Her.	Pseudo-Cicero, *Ad Herennium*
Acad.	Cicero, *Academica*
Aen.	Virgil, *Aeneid*
Comm. in Vergilium	Servius, *Commentarii in Vergilium*
Consol. philos.	Boethius, *Consolatione philosophiae*
Contra Gent.	Thomas Aquinas, *Contra Gentiles* (also *Summa Contra Gentiles*)
Conv.	Dante, *Convivio*
DVE	Dante, *De vulgari eloquentia*
Dec.	Boccaccio, *Decameron*
De civ. Dei	Augustine, *De civitate Dei*
De const. sap.	Seneca, *De constantia sapientis*
De divers. quaest.	Augustine, *De diversis quaestionibus*
Egl.	Dante, *Egloge*
Epist.	Dante, *Epistole*
Etym.	Isidore of Seville, *Etymologiae*
Fact. Dict. Mem.	Valerius, *Factorum et dictorum memorabilium libri IX*
Hist.	Orosius, *Historiarum adversus paganos libri VII*
Hom. in Ev.	Gregory the Great, *Homiliae in Evangelia*
Inf.	Dante, *Inferno*
Instit. Orat.	Quintilian, *De institutione oratoria*
Meta.	Ovid, *Metamorphoses*
Mon.	Dante, *Monarchia*
Nat. hist.	Pliny, *Natural History*
Nic. eth.	Aristotle, *Nicomachean Ethics*
Ody.	Homer, *Odyssey*
Par.	Dante, *Paradiso*
PL	*Patrologia latina*
Phars.	Lucan, *Pharsalia (De bello civili)*
Purg.	Dante, *Purgatorio*
Quest.	Dante, *Questio de aqua et terra*
Sat.	Juvenal, *Satires*
ST	Thomas Aquinas, *Summa Theologiae*
Theb.	Statius, *Thebaid*
Theog.	Hesiod, *Theogony*
Tusc. Disp.	Cicero, *Tuscalan Disputations*
VN	Dante, *Vita Nuova*

Contributors

John Ahern
Vassar College

Suzanne Conklin Akbari
University of Toronto

Maria Luisa Ardizzone
New York University

Peter Armour
Royal Holloway, University of London

Albert Russell Ascoli
University of California, Berkeley

Lawrence Baldassaro
University of Wisconsin, Milwaukee

Mark Balfour
Royal Holloway, University of London

Zygmunt G. Barański
University of Reading, England

John C. Barnes
University College Dublin

Teodolinda Barolini
Columbia University

†Jean-Pierre Barricelli
University of California, Riverside

Fiora A. Bassanese
University of Massachusetts, Boston

Rebecca S. Beal
University of Scranton

†Ernst Behler
University of Washington

V. Stanley Benfell
Brigham Young University

Pamela J. Benson
Rhode Island College

Todd Boli
Framingham, Massachusetts

Steven Botterill
University of California, Berkeley

Kevin Brownlee
University of Pennsylvania

Marina S. Brownlee
University of Pennsylvania

Michael Caesar
University of Birmingham, England

Gino Casagrande
University of Wisconsin, Madison

Anthony K. Cassell
University of Illinois, Champagne-Urbana

Jo Ann Cavallo
Columbia University

Dino Cervigni
University of North Carolina, Chapel Hill

Gary P. Cestaro
DePaul University

Paolo Cherchi
University of Chicago

Marguerite Chiarenza
University of Vancouver

Anna Maria Chiavacci Leonardi
University of Florence

Massimo Ciavolella
University of California, Los Angeles

†Vincenzo Cioffari
Boston University

Caron Ann Cioffi
University of California, Davis

Paul Colilli
Laurentian University

Thomas L. Cooksey
Armstrong Atlantic State University

Alison Cornish
University of Michigan, Ann Arbor

Gustavo Costa
University of California, Berkeley

†Charles T. Davis
Tulane University

Yolande de Pontfarcy
University College Dublin

Dante Della Terza
University of Naples

John G. Demaray
Rutgers University, Newark

Giuseppe Di Scipio
Hunter College, CUNY

Paul A. Dumol
Makati, Philippines

Robert M. Durling
University of California, Santa Cruz

Nancy Vine Durling
Berkeley, California

George D. Economou
University of Oklahoma

Steve Ellis
University of Birmingham, England

Richard K. Emmerson
University of Washington

Joan M. Ferrante
Columbia University

William Franke
Vanderbilt University

Warren Ginsberg
State University of New York, Albany

Diana Cavuoto Glenn
The Flinders University of South Australia

Michael Haren
University College Dublin

Nicholas Havely
University of York, England

Peter S. Hawkins
Boston University

Denise Heilbronn-Gaines
Earlysville, Virginia

Peter Herde
Julius Maximilians University, Wurtzburg

Ronald B. Herzman
State Univerity of New York, Geneseo

Robert Hollander
Princeton University

Olivia Holmes
Yale University

Claire Honess
University of Reading, England

Amilcare A. Iannucci
University of Toronto

Antonio Illiano
University of North Carolina, Chapel Hill

Charles Isenberg
Reed College

Rachel Jacoff
Wellesley College

Virginia Jewiss
Rome, Italy

Craig Kallendorf
Texas A&M University

Richard Kay
University of Kansas

Andreas Kiesewetter
University of South Africa, Pretoria

Robin Kirkpatrick
University of Cambridge

John Kleiner
Williams College

Christopher Kleinhenz
University of Wisconsin, Madison

Louis M. La Favia
The Catholic University of America

Richard Lansing
Brandeis University

Carol Lansing
University of California, Santa Barbara

Jessica Levenstein
Princeton University

Ernesto Livorni
Yale University

Carolynn Lund-Mead
University of Toronto

Donald Maddox
University of Massachusetts, Amherst

R. A. Malagi
Gujarat University, Ahmedabad, India

Ronald L. Martinez
University of Minnesota, Twin Cities

Angelo Mazzocco
Mt. Holyoke College

Francesco Mazzoni
University of Florence

Giuseppe Mazzotta
Yale University

Angela G. Meekins
University of Reading, England

Robert C. Melzi
Widener College

Giuseppina Mezzadroli
University of Bologna

Christian Moevs
University of Notre Dame

Leslie Zarker Morgan
Loyola College in Maryland

Molly G. Morrison
Ohio University

Sally Mussetter
University of Washington

John M. Najemy
Cornell University

Eugene Paul Nassar
Utica College of Syracuse University

Susan Noakes
University of Minnesota, Twin Cities

Anthony Oldcorn
Brown University

Frank B. Ordiway
Princeton University

Pina Palma
Southern Connecticut State University

Michael Papio
College of the Holy Cross

Deborah Parker
University of Virginia, Charlottesville

Anthony L. Pellegrini
State University of New York, Binghamton

Joseph Pequigney
State University of New York, Stony Brook

Lino Pertile
Harvard University

Edward Peters
University of Pennsylvania

Jennifer Petrie
University College Dublin

Michelangelo Picone
University of Zurich

Gabriella Pomaro
University of Tuscia, Viterbo

F. Regina Psaki
University of Oregon

Ricardo J. Quinones
Claremont McKenna College

Guy P. Raffa
University of Texas, Austin

Claudia Rattazzi Papka
University of Massachusetts, Amherst

David Robey
University of Manchester

Maria Ann Roglieri
St. Thomas Aquinas College

Roy Rosenstein
American University of Paris

Luca Carlo Rossi
University of Milan

Rinaldina Russell
Queens College

Aldo Scaglione
New York University

Brenda Deen Schildgen
University of California, Davis

Jeffrey T. Schnapp
Stanford University

John A. Scott
University of Western Australia

Marianne Shapiro
New York, New York

Laurie Shepard
Boston College

Michael Sherberg
Washington University

R. Allen Shoaf
University of Florida, Gainesville

Madison U. Sowell
Brigham Young University

Ruggero Stefanini
University of California, Berkeley

William A. Stephany
University of Vermont

Dana E. Stewart
State University of New York, Binghamton

H. Wayne Storey
Fordham University

Sara Sturm-Maddox
University of Massachusetts, Amherst

John Took
University of London

Robin Treasure
Rome, Italy

Alfred Triolo
Pennsylvania State University

George Andrew Trone
Yale University

Mario Trovato
Northwestern University

Aldo Vallone
University of Naples

Kathleen Verduin
Hope College

Alessandro Vettori
Rutgers University, New Brunswick

David Wallace
University of Pennsylvania

Winthrop Wetherbee
Cornell University

James J. Wilhelm
Rutgers University, New Brunswick

William Wilson
University of Virginia, Charlottesville

Donna Yowell
University of Washington

Translators

Susan Gaylard
University of California, Berkeley

Richard Lansing
Brandeis University

Tamao Nakahara
University of California, Berkeley

Robin Treasure
Rome, Italy

Maps and Illustrations

Italy, around 1300.

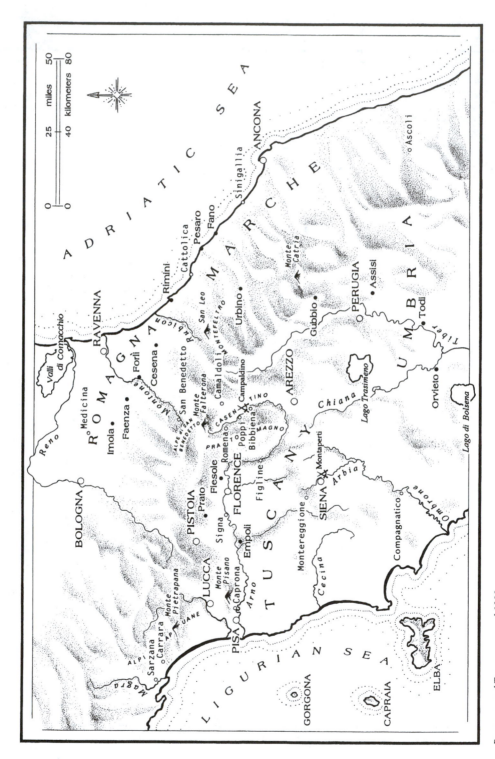

Romagna and Tuscany, around 1300.

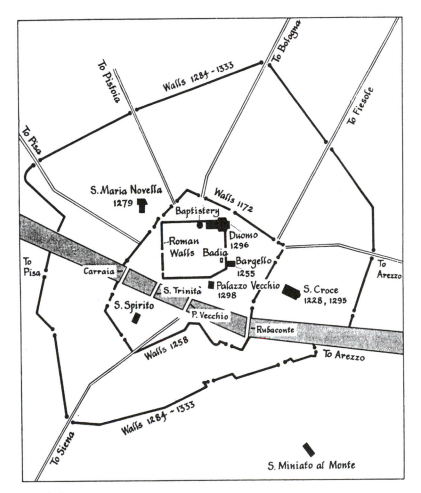

Map of Florence.

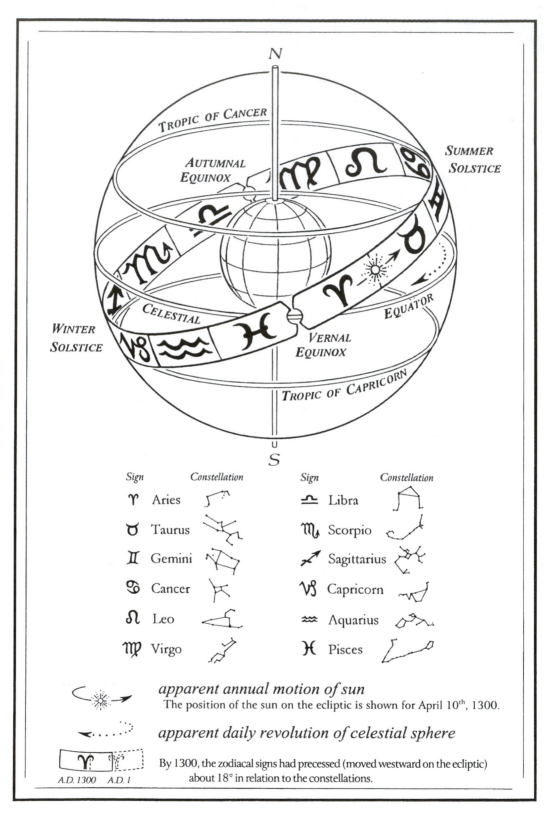

The Celestial Sphere and the Zodiac.

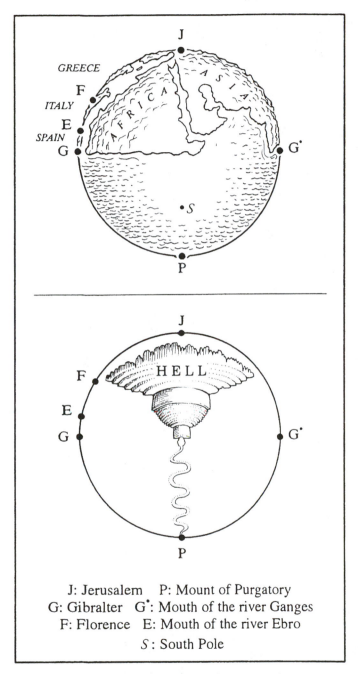

J: Jerusalem   P: Mount of Purgatory

G: Gibralter   G˙: Mouth of the river Ganges

F: Florence   E: Mouth of the river Ebro

S : South Pole

The Relative Positions of Gibraltar, Jerusalem, the Ganges, and Purgatory.

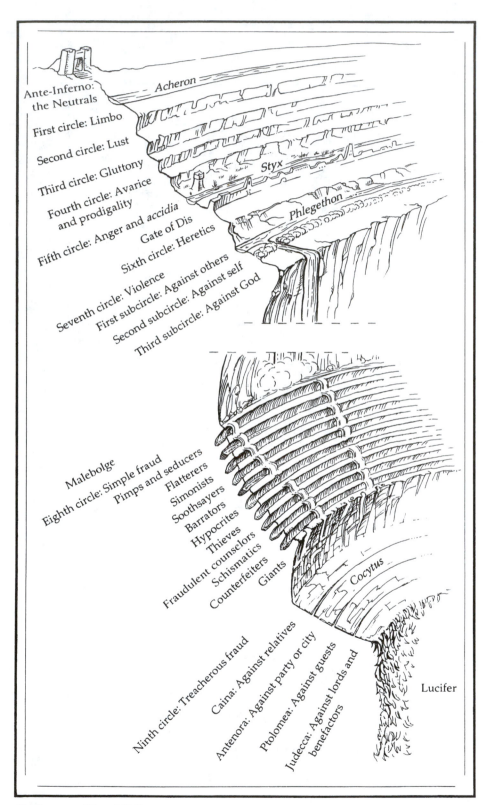

Ante-Inferno: the Neutrals

First circle: Limbo

Second circle: Lust

Third circle: Gluttony

Fourth circle: Avarice and prodigality

Fifth circle: Anger and *accidia*

Gate of Dis

Sixth circle: Heretics

Seventh circle: Violence

First subcircle: Against others

Second subcircle: Against self

Third subcircle: Against God

Acheron

Styx

Phlegethon

Malebolge

Eighth circle: Simple fraud

Pimps and seducers

Flatterers

Simonists

Soothsayers

Barrators

Hypocrites

Thieves

Fraudulent counselors

Schismatics

Counterfeiters

Giants

Cocytus

Ninth circle: Treacherous fraud

Caina: Against relatives

Antenora: Against party or city

Ptolomea: Against guests

Judecca: Against lords and benefactors

Lucifer

The Structure of Dante's Hell.

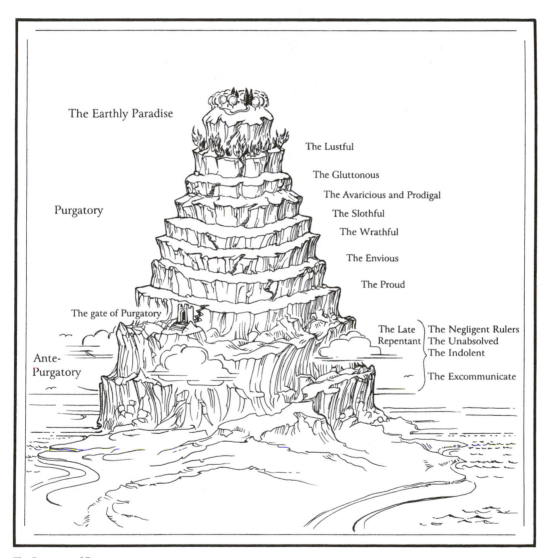

The Earthly Paradise

The Lustful

The Gluttonous

The Avaricious and Prodigal

The Slothful

The Wrathful

Purgatory

The Envious

The Proud

The gate of Purgatory

The Late Repentant

The Negligent Rulers
The Unabsolved
The Indolent

The Excommunicate

Ante-Purgatory

The Structure of Purgatory.

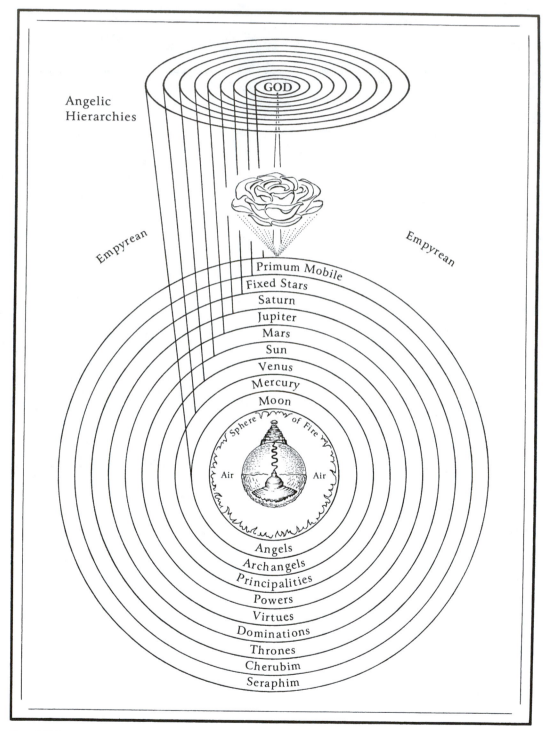

Angelic
Hierarchies

GOD

Empyrean

Empyrean

Primum Mobile
Fixed Stars
Saturn
Jupiter
Mars
Sun
Venus
Mercury
Moon
Sphere of Fire
Air
Air
Angels
Archangels
Principalities
Powers
Virtues
Dominations
Thrones
Cherubim
Seraphim

Dante's Universe.

The Dante Encyclopedia

A

Abati, Bocca degli

Punished in Antenora, in the ninth circle of Hell, among the traitors to one's country or cause (*Inf.* 32.78). Serving with the Guelf cavalry at the battle of Montaperti in 1260, he treacherously turned against their standard-bearer, Jacopo Nacca de' Pazzi, lopping off his hand and provoking a Guelf rout. Seeking oblivion, he refuses to respond to Dante's questioning, but his identity is betrayed by his fellow traitor Buoso.

Roy Rosenstein

Abel

Second son of Adam and Eve, keeper of sheep, killed in anger by his brother Cain (Gen. 4:1–10). Abel *(Abele, Abèl)* is named by Jesus as the first martyr (Matt. 23:34–36; Luke 11:49–51) and by the author of Hebrews as the first exemplum in a roll call of faith (Heb. 11:4). His is the first name pronounced by Virgil in the list of souls liberated from Limbo: *Trasseci l'ombra del primo parente, / d'Abèl suo figlio . . .* ("He led forth from here the shade of our first parent, of Abel his son . . ." *Inf.* 4.55–56).

Carolynn Lund-Mead

Abraham

The first patriarch of Israel and progenitor of the Hebrews, Abraham *(Abramo)* is named by Virgil among the souls drawn out of Limbo (*Inf.* 4.58). The designation *Abraàm patriarca* ("Abraham the patriarch") alludes to God's covenant with Abraham in the Old Testament: "No longer shall your name be Abram, but your name shall be Abraham; for I have made you the father of a multitude of nations" (Gen. 17:5). When God promises that Abraham's descendants will be as numerous as the stars of heaven, Abraham "believed the Lord; and he reckoned it to him as righteousness" (Gen. 15:6). "Through the righteousness of faith," according to the apostle Paul in the New Testament, Abraham becomes "the father of us all" (Rom. 4:13, 16), both Jews and non-Jews. In Luke 16:19–31, Jesus tells the Pharisees the story of a rich man who calls fruitlessly upon "Father Abraham," when in the torment of Hades he sees "Abraham far off and Lazarus [a poor man] in his bosom."

Carolynn Lund-Mead

Academics

The school of philosophers founded by Plato near Athens (c. 387 B.C.E.), known as the Academy *(Academia)*. In *Conv.* 4.6.14, Dante refers to the Academics *(Academici),* specifically mentioning Plato and his nephew Speusippus, while distinguishing the basis of their moral philosophy from that of the Stoics, who preceded them, and the Peripatetics, who later superseded them. Dante's source for this passage is Cicero's *Academia* 1.4.17.

Richard Lansing

Accident

In Aristotelian-Scholastic philosophy, "accident" means a nonessential characteristic inherent in a substantial reality. Thus, an artistic figure carved in marble is an accidental form that does not change the nature of the marble, which remains essentially a stone. Medieval philosophers would define a form sculpted in the marble as a "predicamental accident" *(accidens praedicamentale)*, which has two specific properties: (1) to be dependent on the substance of others (the marble) and (2) to provide this substance with a secondary mode of existence (the artistic work). On the contrary, a "predicable accident" *(accidens praedicabile)* has a broader meaning. The term refers to anything that may be predicated of a subject, like a title (judge, lawyer); or a quality strictly related and inseparable from the subject (masculine or feminine); or any kind of intellectual or moral activity performed by a subject. In this case, an accident is not different from a habit (see "Habit"). Thus, science is an accident, and so is love: *Amore non è per sé sì come sustanzia, ma è uno accidente in sustanzia* ("Love does not exist in itself as a substance, but is an accident in a substance," *VN* 25.1); however, it is important to understand that in God knowledge and love are not accidents but are consubstantial. Any ontological thing, therefore, is considered to be a potential unity made of both a substantial nucleus and a combination of qualities determining the modalities of the substantial being *(modi essendi)*. In this sense, even the universe may be seen as a potential unity. Dante contemplates the cosmos in God as a sum of all existing realities: *Nel suo profondo vidi che s'interna, / legato con amore in un volume, / ciò che per l'universo si squaderna; / sustanze e accidenti e lor costume / quasi conflati insieme* ("In its depths I saw internalized, bound with love in one volume, what through the universe is scattered quires: substances and accidents and their relations as it were conflated together" *Par.* 33.85–89).

From this theory, it follows that any ontological reality or any concept expressing it is a divisible unity, made of elements pertinent *per se* ("by itself") to a thing as well as of elements related only *per accidente* ("by accident"). The *per se* denotes the substance, the true nature of a thing; the *per accidente* regards anything added or related (like qualities or particular situations and circumstances) to the true nature of a thing. Dante often makes use of this distinction in order to point out the difference between an absolute, categorical statement and a relative one: *Dispregiare sé medesimo è per sé biasimevole* ("To disparage oneself is in itself blameworthy," *Conv.* 1.2.5); on the contrary, *Lodare sé è da fuggire sì come male per accidente* ("Self-praise is to be avoided as an

incidental evil," *Conv.* 1.2.7). The former is intrinsically *(per se)* evil; but *lodare sé* is not. Circumstances, however, may turn *lodare sé* into an evil behavior. Dante also applies this theory in his definition of the true concept of philosophy: *E sì come l'amistà per diletto fatta, o per utilitade, non è vera amistà ma per accidente . . . così la filosofia per diletto o per utilitade non è vera filosofia ma per accidente* ("And just as friendship founded on pleasure or utility is not true friendship but friendship by accident, . . . so philosophy founded on pleasure or utility is not true philosophy but philosophy by accident," *Conv.* 3.11.9). In this example, the pleasure and utility derived from learning are deemed accidental or incidental to the true objective and purpose of philosophy, which is the love of truth.

Bibliography

McCall, R. E. "Accident." In *New Catholic Encyclopedia.* Vol. I. New York: McGraw-Hill, 1967, pp. 74–79.

Stabile, Giorgio. "Accidente." *Enciclopedia dantesca,* 1:25–26.

Mario Trovato

Accorso, Francesco d'

D'Accorso (1225–1293) was a distinguished doctor of civil law at Bologna, where he was born. In 1173 he accompanied Edward I, who was returning from travel in Palestine, to England, where he assisted the king in the reorganization of the English judicial system. He may have lectured at Oxford and the Sorbonne before returning to Italy in 1281. Dante places d'Accorso among the sodomites, together with Brunetto Latini and Priscian, in the third ring of the seventh circle of Hell (*Inf.* 15.110). Interestingly, the fact that Pope Nicholas IV had granted d'Accorso complete absolution in 1291 was either unknown to Dante or, as in the case of Guido da Montefeltro, simply presented no obstacle to his fictional damnation. Francesco d'Accorso appears as well in tale 50 of the anonymous *Novellino.*

Michael Papio

Aceste

Cited in the description of the virtue of modesty on the part of Argia and Deiphyle, daughters of King Adrastus (*Conv.* 4.25.8). As their nurse,

Aceste *(Aceste)* led them to meet guests Polynices and Tydeus (Statius, *Theb.* 1.529).

Leslie Zarker Morgan

Acheron

In classical mythology and ancient literature, Acheron *(Acheronte)* is one of the five rivers of Hades, together with Styx, Phlegethon, Cocytus, and Lethe. In antiquity and the Middle Ages, Acheron was described variously as a pond, a lake, "the river of woe," and, within a Christian perspective, as "gloomy and hopeless." Dante the narrator calls the shore of Acheron—the first of four infernal rivers—a *riva malvagia* ("evil shore," *Inf.* 3.107), and Cato refers to it as the *mal fiume* ("the evil river," *Purg.* 1.88). Virgil identifies Acheron with Styx, the traditional entrance into the underworld in classical tradition *(Aen.* 6.296–297), Charon being the ferryman who bears souls across it in his ship. In Dante the Acheron likewise lies near the boundary of Hell, just within its Gate *(Inf.* 3.1–9), beyond the vestibule of Hell, where the Neutrals are punished *(Inf.* 3.23–69). As Virgil explains to the pilgrim, all those who die in God's wrath gather along the bank of the river to be ferried across by Charon *(Inf.* 3.121–129), who, contrary to pagan tradition, transports them over, requiring neither their bodies' burial nor an obol, or a piece of money. Here, however, Charon refuses to transport the pilgrim because he is an *anima viva* ("living soul," *Inf.* 3.88). Dante's actual crossing is never described. A sudden earthquake causes him momentarily to lose consciousness *(Inf.* 3.130–136), and upon his recovery he discovers himself on the other side of the Acheron. This mysterious crossing contrasts with that of his classical counterpart Aeneas, who is ferried by Charon after the Sibyl displays a golden bough and who never loses consciousness. The pilgrim's loss of consciousness may find a parallel in the event that preceded Christ's descent into Hell (according to the Apostles' Creed), namely, his death. If so, the pilgrim's swoon would suggest that his voyage through the Christian afterlife occurs by virtue of Christ's Redemption.

Dino Cervigni

Achilles

Principal Greek hero in the Trojan War, son of Peleus. His mother, Thetis, dipped him in the river Styx, rendering him invulnerable except at his heel. According to medieval accounts, Achilles was lured into the Temple of Apollo with promises of meeting with Priam's daughter Polyxena; Paris then struck him fatally in the heel. Because he dies for the love of Polyxena, Achilles *(Achille)* is placed in the second circle of Hell among the lustful *(Inf.* 5.65). His rearing by the centaur Chiron is mentioned *(Inf.* 12.71), as well as his desertion of Deidamia *(Inf.* 26.62) and his spear's healing properties *(Inf.* 31.5). *Purg.* 9.34 recalls Achilles' transport to Scyros by his mother, and *Conv.* 4.27.20 records his descent from King Aeacus. Statius mentions his own unfinished poem, the *Achilleid,* in *Purg.* 21.92.

Robin Treasure

Achitophel

The most trusted advisor to King David, Achitophel *(Achitofèl)* encouraged the king's son Absalom to rebel against his father. After David's advisor Chusai persuaded him to abandon his efforts on Absalom's behalf, Achitophel returned home and hanged himself. Dante parallels Achitophel's betrayal of David with Bertran de Born's instigation of Prince Henry to rebel against his father, King Henry II of England *(Inf.* 28.137).

Pina Palma

Acre

The largest city in the Latin kingdom of Jerusalem. Its fall to the Mamluks in 1291 marked the end of Christian rule in the Holy Land. Contemporary chroniclers, especially those from Italy, cite discord among the Italian merchants and colonizers as one of the reasons the city was lost. Guido da Montefeltro refers to the fall of Acre *(Acri)* when criticizing Pope Boniface VIII's crusade against the Colonna: *ché ciascun suo nimico era Cristiano / e nessun era stato a vincer Acri* ("for each of his enemies was a Christian, and none had been to take Acre," *Inf.* 27.88–89).

Mark Balfour

Active Life

Within the Christian tradition, the active life represents one of two ways of pursuing a virtuous life, the other being the contemplative life. These two models of Christian life are associated with the two

A greatest commandments, identified as such by Christ in the New Testament: "Thou shalt love the Lord thy God with all thy heart, and with all thy soul, and with all thy mind. This is the first and great commandment. And the second is like unto it, Thou shalt love thy neighbor as thyself" (Matt. 22:37–39). While the contemplative life enables its practitioner to observe the first commandment most thoroughly, the active life provides the more direct route to observance of the second commandment.

The concepts of active life and contemplative life as the best ways of living a happy and virtuous life predate Christianity. Aristotle, for example, makes the distinction in *Ethics* 10.7–9. While Christian exegetes interpreted Aristotle's words in the context of Christianity, they also found authoritative models for the active and contemplative lives in biblical texts. In the *Convivio,* Dante follows both Aristotle and the Christian tradition in affirming that the active life and the contemplative life are both virtuous ways of living that lead to happiness: *Veramente è da sapere che noi potemo avere in questa vita due felicitadi, secondo due diversi cammini, buono e ottimo che a ciò ne menano: l'una è la vita attiva, e l'altra la contemplativa* ("We must know, however, that we may have two kinds of happiness in this life, according to two different paths, one good and the other best, which lead us there," *Conv.* 4.17.9–10).

Despite his assertion that the contemplative life was the superior of the two, Dante chose to follow the active life. As poet, thinker, and writer, he took an active part in the intellectual debates of the time. In the medieval view, however, the active life also comprised the responsibility to be involved in civil affairs. Thus for Dante the active life was directly associated with civil or political life: *la vita attiva, cioè civile, nel governare del mondo* ("the active, that is the civil, life, in governing the world," *Conv.* 2.4.10). His role in the political and civil affairs of Florence, before his exile and afterwards, can thus be seen as part of the poet's attempt to live the active life.

In the *Convivio,* Dante associates the Moral Virtues with the active life, adopting Aristotle's schema and definitions of eleven virtues: *Fortezza, Temperanza, Liberalitade, Magnificenza, Magnanimitade, Amativa d'onore, Mansuetudine, Affabilitade, Veritade, Eutrapelia, Giustizia* ("Courage, Temperance, Liberality, Munificence, Magnanimity, Honor, Gentleness, Affability, Truth, Good Disposition, Justice"; see *Conv.* 4.17.4–6). Similarly, the contemplative life is associated with the Intellectual Virtues, which are less well known and thus more difficult to follow. Living the active life in accordance with the Moral Virtues can also therefore be seen as a necessary preparatory stage for living the contemplative life. In *Conv.* 2.4.9–12, Dante remarks that the angels, like their human counterparts, also follow either the contemplative life or the active life. Those angels responsible for moving the spheres are identified with the active life.

Dante's distinction between the two lives employs the typical personification allegories of the Scholastic and theological tradition. In *Conv.* 4.17.10, the distinction is embodied by the sisters Martha and Mary, representing respectively the active and the contemplative lives (Luke 10:38–42); in *Conv.* 4.22.14–15 Dante's gloss of Mark 16 associates three Marys (Mary Magdalene, Mary of James, and Mary Salome) with three schools of philosophy (the Epicureans, the Stoics, and the Peripatetics); in *Purg.* 27, the traditional exempla are the figures of Leah and Rachel, who appear in the pilgrim's third dream and are generally taken as prefigurations of the appearance of Matelda and Beatrice in the Earthly Paradise. The moral structure of Paradise as well reflects the superior status of the contemplative life, whose followers reside in the highest planetary heaven, Saturn, far above the souls of the active life in the heaven of Mercury.

Angela G. Meekins

Adam

Dante encounters the first human being, the father of all humanity, in *Par.* 26.80–142, where Adam answers questions that had long puzzled medieval Christians: the length of his stay in Eden (seven hours), the years he lived subsequently on earth (930), and his sojourn in Limbo before Christ's harrowing of Hell (4,302 years). Adam also reveals a number of facts about the origin of language that contradict what Dante wrote earlier in *DVE* 1.4–6. Whereas the poet formerly maintained that God gave Adam a language that humankind continued to speak until the confusion of tongues at Babel, Adam says in *Par.* 26 that his speech was his own creation, was extinct long before Babel, and, like any other human production, was subject to change and even death. In essence, Adam authorizes Dante's own vernacular by establishing that there is no God-given or normative speech.

Adam's placement in the celestial rose next to the Virgin Mary could not be more exalted. Yet he is specifically remembered there (*Par.* 32.121–123) not only as the progenitor of the human family but also as the perpetrator of the "original sin" of disobedience to the divine will, the "going beyond the mark" (*Par.* 26.117) established by God in Eden. This moral ambiguity characterizes Adam throughout the poem. While created directly by God, and therefore "made worthy of all the perfection brought by soul" (*Par.* 13.82–83), he is also the source of human imperfection and mortality.

Dante alludes a number of times to the typological relationship between the Old Adam and the New (Christ) formulated by St. Paul in Rom. 5: the sin of the one is contrasted to the Redemption of the other. This theology is evoked in *Purg.* 32, when the Griffin restores the barren tree associated with "Adamo" (32.37), as well as in *Par.* 7, when Beatrice explains the incarnation of Christ as God's response to Adam's sin.

Bibliography

Brownlee, Kevin. "Language and Desire in *Paradiso* XXVI," *Lectura Dantis* 6 (Spring 1990), 45–59.

Daniélou, Jean, S.J. "Adam and Paradise." In *From Shadow to Reality: Studies in the Biblical Typology of the Fathers*. Translated by Wulstan Hibberd. London: Burns and Oates, 1960, pp. 11–65.

Peter S. Hawkins

Adolf of Nassau

Cited in *Conv.* 4.3.6 with Rudolf and Albert as elected Roman emperors unworthy of the title because they had not been officially crowned. This distinction allows Dante to consider Frederick II "the last of the Roman emperors." Born c. 1255, elected king of Germany in 1291, Adolf *(Andolfo)* was defeated and killed in 1298 by Albert I of Hapsburg.

Leslie Zarker Morgan

Adrastus

King of Argos, father of Argia and Deiphyle. He married Argia to Polynices and, seeking to restore him to the throne of Thebes, led the war of the Seven against Thebes along with Polynices, Tydeus, Amphiaraus, Capaneus, Hippomedon, and Parthenopaeus. In *Conv.* 4.25.6, 8, 10, Adrastus *(Adrasto)* is cited as exemplifying the three emotions necessary for acting with nobility in the age of adolescence, namely *stupore* ("awe"), *pudore* ("modesty"), and *verecundia* ("sense of shame"). Dante illustrates these emotions with reference to three events in Statius' *Thebaid* (1.482–497, 527–539, 671–690).

Richard Lansing

Adrian V, Pope

Born Ottobono de' Fieschi of Genoa between 1210 and 1215, Pope Adrian V descended from a wealthy Genoese family that possessed extensive land holdings between Sestri and Chiavari. His uncle, Pope Innocent IV, had him elected a cardinal in 1251, in which office he served as a papal legate and represented Genoa's interests to the papal curia. He was elected pope, succeeding Innocent V, on July 11, 1276, but died at Viterbo only a few weeks later, on August 18, before being officially crowned.

Adrian V appears prostrate and face down on the fifth terrace of the avaricious in Purgatory (*Purg.* 19.79–145), where circumlocutions unveil both his papal identity as *successor Petri* ("Peter's successor," 99) and *roman pastore* ("Roman shepherd," 107) and his family title. No historical records document avarice in this particular pope, who symbolizes the medieval papacy's preoccupation with worldly power and earthly goods and the consequent need to repent. Dante's attribution of avariciousness to him evidently derived from a misreading of an excerpt from John of Salisbury's *Policraticus,* which circulated anonymously and assigned this trait to an earlier pope, Adrian IV.

Bibliography

Bosco, Umberto. "Adriano IV e V." In *Dante vicino.* Caltanissetta-Rome: Salvatore Sciascia, 1972, pp. 378–391.

Soave Bowe, Clotilde. "*Purgatorio* 19: Adrian V." In *Dante Readings.* Edited by Eric Haywood. Dublin: Irish Academic Press, 1987, pp. 123–142.

Madison U. Sowell

Aeacus

King of Aegina; son of Zeus and Aegina; father of Telamon, Peleus, and Phocus; and grandfather of Ajax and Achilles (Ovid, *Meta.* 7.476–657). For his high integrity, Zeus made him a judge of Hades, along with Minos and Rhadamanthus. Dante cites Aeacus *(Eaco)* in *Conv.* 4.27.17–20 as an example of four virtues: prudence, justice, liberality, and affability.

Leslie Zarker Morgan

Aeneas

Leader of the Trojans and founder of Italy, Aeneas is a resident of Limbo in *Inferno* and one of Dante's models for his otherworld journey. In *Inf.* 2.32 Dante-pilgrim declares, in response to Virgil's invitation that he accompany him into the otherworld on a journey, *"Io non Enëa, io non Paulo sono"* ("I am not Aeneas, I am not Paul"), an utterance that reveals both a bit of trepidation and a sense of modesty, not to mention also a lack of understanding. For ultimately Dante will discover his relation to these two other figures who have done what he claims, as poet, to have done as well: Aeneas has descended into the underworld and been rewarded with knowledge, while Paul has ascended to Heaven and been rewarded with a direct vision of God. Aeneas, therefore, is an important model for the heroic journey of Dante-pilgrim.

A key question, however, centers on which Aeneas served as Dante's model—Virgil's Aeneas or the Aeneas of his medieval allegorists. Fulgentius, Bernardus Silvestris, and John of Salisbury allegorized the *Aeneid* as a journey of the soul through the successive ages of life, and in *Conv.* 4.26 Dante cites Aeneas as his model in discussing the virtues of the age of maturity (see also 2.10.5, 3.11.16, and 4.5.6). In the *Commedia,* however, few traces of this approach remain, and the allegorists are never cited.

Virgil's Aeneas, on the other hand, is referred to throughout the *Commedia.* He appears among the pagans in Limbo (*Inf.* 4.122) and is mentioned periphrastically at the beginning of Justinian's history of the empire in *Par.* 6.3, but he tends more often to lurk behind the text for the reader who knows Virgil's poem. This relationship is present from the very beginning of the *Commedia,* for Dante-pilgrim follows Aeneas in seeking and obtaining divine help to move his earthly wanderings toward their appointed goal. Dante's story, however, is not a slavish imitation of Aeneas'. Like Aeneas, Dante-pilgrim meets Charon (*Inf.* 3.82ff.),

for example, but later in *Inf.* 8.1–30 he also meets Phlegyas, another obstructing boatman who takes on some of the characteristics of Charon in the *Aeneid.* Both pilgrims also yield to the temptation to lose themselves in artistic representations of their past, but for Dante it is Casella's setting of his second canzone from *Conv.* 3 (*Purg.* 2.106ff.), while for Aeneas the temptations were visual (*Aen.* 1.446–497, 6.14–41). Moreover, while Virgil disappears from the poem in *Purg.* 30, Aeneas continues to resurface in the text. Just as Aeneas was welcomed by his father, Anchises, in Elysium, so Dante-pilgrim is welcomed in Heaven by his ancestor Cacciaguida, who even greets him with the Virgilian expression *sanguis meus* ("my blood," *Par.* 15.28 = *Aen.* 6.835). Indeed at the very end of the poem (*Par.* 33.58–66), just before his final enlightenment, Dante-pilgrim is, like Aeneas, about to consult the Sibyl, with the phrasing echoing *Aen.* 3.448–452.

Typologically Aeneas figures Dante-pilgrim's journey *in bono,* but Dante-poet handles this relationship with considerable sophistication. In *Inf.* 26, for example, Ulysses attempts to define himself as a new Aeneas, first by boastfully comparing himself to the Roman hero (90–93), then by giving a speech to his men modeled on *Aen.* 1.198–207 (112–120). The canto ends, however, with Ulysses' ship whirling around and sinking in imitation of the ship of Aeneas' unsuccessful companions (*Aen.* 1.116–117), confirming Ulysses' rejection of Aeneas' *pieta* ("compassion," 94) and leaving him as a type *in malo* for Dante-pilgrim. Furthermore, there are places where the actions of Dante-pilgrim serve as a critique of the actions of Aeneas on which they are modeled. When Dante-pilgrim sees Beatrice again in *Purg.* 30 and responds to her in a translation of Dido's words (48 = *Aen.* 4.23), we realize that this is the Christian correction of Aeneas' love affair in Carthage. Because he was unknowingly chosen by God and lacked the grace by which he could be saved, Aeneas' actions can assume significance only in reference to the larger providential plan of which they are part.

Bibliography

Jacoff, Rachel, and William A. Stephany. *Inferno II.* Philadelphia: University of Pennsylvania Press, 1989.

Padoan, Giorgio. "Enea." *Enciclopedia dantesca,* 2:677–679.

Shapiro, Marianne. "Virgilian Representation in Dante." *Lectura Dantis,* 5 (1989), 14–29.

Craig Kallendorf

Aeneid

Epic poem by the Roman poet Virgil, in twelve books, recounting the story of Aeneas' journey from fallen Troy to his founding of a new civilization in Italy. When Dante-pilgrim first meets Virgil in the *Commedia,* he exclaims that Virgil has already been his *maestro* ("master") for many years and that he has studied his poetry and taken from Virgil *lo bello stilo* ("the pleasing style") which has brought him honor (*Inf.* 1.82–87). By this phrase Dante means the "noble" or "tragic" style, one that is evident in a number of his canzoni written well before the *Commedia.* But the *Commedia* will be the major expression of Dante's imitation of this style. In it one finds over two hundred direct citations, references, and allusions to Virgil's poetry, almost all of them to the poem Dante knew as the *Eneide.* Some of these citations are verbal: *carcere cieco* ("dark prison") in *Purg.* 22.103 is taken from *Aen.* 6.734; *selva antica* ("ancient wood") in *Purg.* 28.23 is taken from *Aen.* 6.179; and so forth. Other references involve details of plot which originated in the *Aeneid:* the reed with which Cato girds Dante-pilgrim in *Purg.* 1.94–95 renews itself spontaneously just like the golden bough in *Aen.* 6.143–144, and Dante-pilgrim tries three times in vain to embrace the shade of the musician Casella (*Purg.* 2.80–81) just as Aeneas tried to embrace Anchises in *Aen.* 6.700–702. In the sphere of Mars, Cacciaguida welcomes Dante-pilgrim just as Anchises welcomed Aeneas in the underworld, with the same greeting, *"O sanguis meus"* ("O my blood," *Par.* 15.28). In many cases, however, the allusions are more general. Characters like Sinon and Amata, demonic figures like Charon and Cerberus, and topographical features like the rivers of Hell (Acheron, Styx, Phlegethon, Cocytus) are found in the *Commedia* as well as in the *Aeneid,* suffusing Dante's poetry with a discernibly Virgilian air.

The relationship between the *Aeneid* and the works of Dante, however, is more complex than this simple inventory suggests. Throughout most of the *Convivio* and all of *De vulgari eloquentia,* Virgil is quoted as perfunctorily as the other Latin poets. But beginning with *Conv.* 4.26 Dante provides more detailed references from sections of the *Aeneid* he had not cited earlier, referring to Virgil with a new personal warmth as *lo maggiore nostro poeta* ("our greatest poet," *Conv.* 4.26.8). In *Inf.* 1.85 Dante refers to Virgil as an *autore* ("author"), a term which is reserved in the *Commedia* for writers who are major authorities, like the authors of the *Aeneid* and Scripture, and it is clear that in his later works Dante has come to see Virgil's epic as almost parallel to the Bible. Here he treats the *Aeneid* as quasi-historical, a poem with a literal sense that is historically true and assumes importance because it is the history of Rome, founded according to God's will to become the seat of the papacy (*Inf.* 2.13–27). Thus when Justinian traces the history of the Roman Empire and its *sacrosanto segno* ("sacrosanct emblem," *Par.* 6.32), he relies on the *Aeneid,* and when Dante defends the argument that Rome attained its hegemony by law rather than by force in *Mon.* 2, he draws on the *Aeneid* for historical support.

In the final analysis, however, the *Aeneid* is not the Bible, and recent scholarship has made significant progress in revealing how Dante also invites his reader to challenge a work he valued almost as much as Scripture. Many of Dante's allusions are in fact confrontational, setting up a dialogue of sorts with their source. In *Inf.* 1.106, for example, the reference to *umile Italia* ("humble Italy") recalls Virgil's *humilem . . . Italiam* (*Aen.* 3.522–523), but the contrast it evokes with *superbo Ilïon* ("proud Ilion," *Inf.* 1.75) infuses a new moral meaning into that phrase, thereby revealing an ethical dimension to Dante's reading of the *Aeneid.* Dante-pilgrim's meeting with Brunetto Latini in *Inf.* 15.79–85 symbolizes what is happening here. Dante-pilgrim greets his old teacher with an echo of Aeneas greeting Anchises in *Aen.* 6.695–696, for Brunetto has served as a father of sorts, teaching Dante to make himself immortal through his skill with words. The *parola ornata* ("ornamented speech," *Inf.* 2.67) which Virgil and Brunetto have taught Dante, however, will not fill his spiritual void, for the language of *l'alta . . . tragedia* ("high Tragedy," *Inf.* 20.113) has led these two figures to error and condemnation.

The problem, of course, is that Virgil was not a Christian, though Brunetto was; as he explains in *Purg.* 6.34–48, his exclamation in *Aen.* 6.376 (in words spoken by the Sybil) that prayer does not bend the will of God is true only for pagans like himself to whom no more than partial understanding had been given. Indeed there are several remarkable passages in which Dante-poet has Virgil correct his own text on the basis of information he has received after his death. In *Inf.* 20, for example, Dante-poet puts into the mouth of Virgil an account of the founding of Mantua that contradicts the account in the *Aeneid*, along with a warning to accept only this revised version. Even as a character in the *Commedia*, however, Virgil remains a fallible guide—he falters at the Gate of Dis in *Inf.* 8–9, for example, and reacts foolishly to the demons in *Inf.* 21–23. In *Purg.* 30 he finally withdraws from the poem, first by quoting a line from his *Aeneid* (6.883), then by translating another line (*Aen.* 4.23), and finally by echoing a passage from his *Georgics* (4.525–527). Indeed Virgil must disappear from the poem, for on Earth he remained a pagan even though his poetry should have led him to salvation. His poetry did just that for Statius, who is purging himself of prodigality in *Purg.* 22. Statius' repentance in *Purg.* 22.40–41 rests on what appears to be a misunderstanding of *Aen.* 3.56–57, but in the value scheme of the *Commedia* the text of the *Aeneid* becomes only an instrument, a tool for conversion whose meaning ultimately depends on God's providential plan. And it is this inscrutable providence that finally offers salvation to Ripheus, a minor figure mentioned in *Aen.* 2.426–428, and eternal condemnation to the author of the poem which represents the best that humanity can achieve without the illumination of grace.

Bibliography

Barolini, Teodolinda. *Dante's Poets: Textuality and Truth in the Comedy.* Princeton, N.J.: Princeton University Press, 1984, pp. 201–256.

Hollander, Robert. "Le opere di Virgilio nella *Commedia* di Dante." In *Dante e la "Bella Scola" della poesia: autorità e sfida poetica.* Edited by Amilcare A. Iannucci. Ravenna: Longo, 1993, pp. 247–343.

———. *Il Virgilio dantesco: tragedia nella "Commedia."* Florence: Leo S. Olschki 1983.

Jacoff, Rachel, and Jeffrey T. Schnapp (eds.). *The Poetry of Allusion: Virgil and Ovid in Dante's "Commedia."* Stanford, Calif.: Stanford University Press, 1991, pp. 1–156.

Whitfield, J. H. *Dante and Virgil.* Oxford: Blackwell, 1949.

Craig Kallendorf

Agathon

Athenian tragic poet (c. 448–402 B.C.E.), friend of Euripides and Plato, and student of Socrates. Dante did not know Plato's *Symposium,* which is set in Agathon's house. Fewer than forty lines of his work have survived. Virgil refers to him in *Purg.* 22.107 as one of the Greek poets residing in Limbo. Dante also cites Agathon *(Agatone)* on the nature of impossibility in *Mon.* 3.6.7.

Nancy Vine Durling

Ages of Life

At *Conv.* 4.23.4, Dante lists *quattro etadi,* or four "ages," into which a person's life is divided if he or she does not die prematurely: *adolescenza* ("adolescence"), *gioventute* ("maturity"), *senettute* ("old age"), and *senio* ("senility"). These four ages correspond to four divisions of an arc (23.6), of which the pinnacle would be the perfect age of 35 years, a fact significant for Dante's setting of his journey in the *Commedia* in his thirty-fifth year. Although the actual duration of each of these ages is dependent upon the specific length of any given individual's life span, Dante asserts a parallelism among them whereby adolescence and old age both last twenty-five years, or from birth to age 25 and from age 45 to 70, respectively (24.4). Between these lies the age of maturity. In his effort to assert a counterpart at the beginning of life for senility at its end, Dante also describes a period of eight months before adolescence (24.5), which most likely is to be understood as the period of gestation in the womb before birth. This period does not figure otherwise in Dante's schema, as he consistently speaks of four, and not five, ages; and since Plato, who possessed "a supremely excellent nature," died in his eighty-first year—the same age at which Dante postulates Christ would have died had he not been crucified—senility is assumed to last for a period of about ten years, or from age 70 until death (24.6). Dante finds natural correspondences to the division of life into four ages in the possible combinations of the four "qualities that comprise our composition"—heat, coldness, dryness, and moisture—as well as in the four seasons and the four parts of the day (23.13–14). Dante's treatment of the four ages of humankind is largely dependent on Albertus Magnus' *De aetate sive de iuventute et senectute* 1.2, where the ages are listed as *pueritia; iuventus* or *virilis; senectus;* and *senium* or *aetas decrepita*. (The citation of Albertus' *De meteoris* at 23.13 in place of *De aetate* is taken by many critics as Dante's error; Nardi, however, argues for its relevance in "L'arco della vita," pp. 125–126, n. 55.)

The delineation of the four ages of man appears in Dante's commentary on verses 121–140 of the third canzone of the *Convivio,* "Le dolci rime d'amor ch'i solia" ("The tender rhymes of love"), where he discusses the manifestations of nobility in a person of each of these different ages. "Adolescence," which means "increase in life" (24.1), and which corresponds to the "hot and moist," is endowed with "four things necessary for entering into the city of the good life" (24.11): *obedienza* ("obedience"), *soavitade* ("sweetness"), *vergogna* ("a sense of shame"), and *adornezza corporale* ("loveliness of being"). "Maturity," which corresponds to the "hot and dry," means "the age that can be helpful" since it "can give perfection"; it, thus, can be considered a "perfect age" (24.1) with reference to the person himself or herself, since it is *colmo de la nostra vita* ("the fullness of our life"). During this age, a noble nature shows itself to be *temperata* ("self-restrained"), *forte* ("strong"), *amorosa* ("loving"), *cortese* ("courteous"), and *leale* ("honest")—five qualities necessary for a person's perfection (26.2–3). In old age, which is "cold and dry," the noble soul is *prudente* ("prudent"), *giusta* ("just"), and *larga* ("liberal"), in addition to being *affabile* ("affable") insofar as "it takes delight in speaking well of others' virtues, and of hearing them well spoken of" (27.2). It is during old age that a person's perfection with respect to others arises in which one may be useful not only to oneself but to others as well (26.4; 27.3–4). Senility is the period which corresponds to the "cold and moist"; during this age the soul returns to God and "blesses the journey that it has made, because it has been straight and good and without bitterness of storm" (28.2).

Notable in this discussion of the four ages and their virtues is the allegorization of Marcia's life and return to Cato as it is narrated in Lucan's *De bello civile* 2.326–349. In Dante's apparently original reading, adolescence is represented by Marcia's virginity, while her first marriage to Cato represents maturity; her divorce from Cato and marriage to Hortensius signifies the passage into old age, and her widowhood resulting from Hortensius' death signifies senility. Marcia's return to Cato at the end of her life signifies "that the noble soul returns to God at the beginning of old age" (18.13–19).

Bibliography

Nardi, Bruno. "L'arco della vita." In *Saggi di filosofia dantesca.* 2nd ed. Florence: La Nuova Italia, 1967, pp. 110–138.

Frank B. Ordiway

Aghinolfo da Romena

Brother of Guido and Alessandro da Romena, of the Conti Guidi, one of the most wealthy and powerful families in northern Italy in Dante's day. In the last bolgia of Malebolge, Master Adam refers to the first two by name, and to Aghinolfo indirectly, blaming them for having induced him to counterfeit the Florentine gold florin (*Inf.* 30.77).

Richard Lansing

Aglauros

The daughter of Cecrops, king of Athens, a figure in mythology presented as an exemplum of envy on the second terrace of Purgatory (*Purg.* 14.139). When told about Mercury's passion for her sister Herse, Aglauros *(Aglauro)* attempted to end the love between the two. Because of her jealousy, Mercury turned her into stone (see Ovid, *Meta.* 2.737–832).

Paul Colilli

Agnello de' Brunelleschi

One of the five Florentine thieves whose metamorphoses from and into serpent form are described in *Inf.* 25. Dante and Virgil witness his waxlike meltdown and horrendous fusion—the paradoxically erotic Ovidian subtext is that of the froward Hermaphroditus with the enamored nymph Salmacis (*Meta.* 4.285–388)—with his previously transformed companion Cianfa into a perverse hybrid shape, neither man nor serpent. That the "Agnel" (a variant of "Agnolo" or "Angelo") named in *Inf.* 25.68 was a member of the prominent Brunelleschi family is a hypothesis of the early commentators neither contradicted nor confirmed by modern archival research.

Anthony Oldcorn

A

Air

One of the four sublunar elements in Aristotle's physics, air unites the primary qualities hot and wet. It is the second-lightest of the elements and therefore finds its proper place above the level of aqueous matter and below the level of fiery matter. Air rises or falls to this level on its own accord. Like the other three elements, air is mutable. If cooled, it can be transformed from a hot-wet element into a cold-wet element. Air can, in other words, condense into water. The pure elements air and water are not identical with the air and water that we breath and drink, but the behavior of our air and water are nonetheless to be understood in the same terms. Thus, as Dante points out in the *Questio de aqua et terra,* water is "generated" on mountaintops from the condensation of vapor—an aerial body *(Quest.* 83).

John Kleiner

Alberigo, Fra

Member of the prominent Guelf Manfredi family of Faenza who were banished in 1274 by their long-standing rivals, the Accarisi. After repeated attempts to return, the Manfredi succeeded on November 13, 1280, with the treacherous aid of the Ghilbelline Tebaldello dei Zambrasi, *ch'aprì Faenza quando si dormia* ("who opened Faenza when it slept," *Inf.* 32.123). Though the dates of his birth and death are uncertain, according to references in the early commentaries, at an advanced age Alberigo entered the order of the Jovial Friars, constituted in Bologna in 1261 (*Inf.* 23.103–108). It is clear from the pilgrim's astonishment upon finding him in Hell that he was still alive in April 1300, the fictive date of the journey; he in fact executed a will in Ravenna in 1302 and seems to have died around 1307. Dante refers to Alberigo's son, Ugolino Bucciola, as a poet who chose not to write in his Romagnole dialect (*DVE* 1.14.3).

Alberigo resides in Ptolomea, the third ring of the ninth circle of Hell reserved for traitors of guests (*Inf.* 33.109–150). On May 2, 1285, Alberigo had his cousin Manfredus de Manfredis and his son Albergittus killed during a banquet in his home, signaling the hired assassins with an order to bring the fruit. Records in the archives of Bologna suggest the web of economic and political interests that motivated the murder. Aware of the sizable inheritance due a young nephew and the political preeminence it would guarantee, in

1277 Alberigo required his cousin to legally recognize his role as guardian, a position Manfred apparently coveted for himself.

In *Inferno* Alberigo reveals startling information about Ptolomea (in one of the poet's most audacious departures from the canonical theology of his day): that certain of the souls it houses reside in Hell while their bodies continue to inhabit Earth. Though devils occupy human bodies in the Judeo-Christian folklore of the period, the idea is theologically suspect, at best. Alberigo provides support in the person of Branca d'Oria for what he terms the zone's "advantage" and the unorthodox doctrine it dramatizes.

Readers have speculated on the significance of the pilgrim's cold imperviousness to Alberigo, evident in the clever though deceitful bargain that he strikes with him and in his refusal to grant Alberigo's request that he alleviate his suffering. The poet's editorial comment on the pilgrim's refusal has elicited a fair amount of critical attention. The neatly expressed oxymoron *e cortesia fu lui essere villano* ("and it was courtesy to treat him boorishly," *Inf.* 33.150) reflects the ethics of Hell and the divine justice that engineered it, while also providing a formula (courtesy = villainy) for the verbal irony whereby words connote their opposites, which is employed in the final cantos of the *Inferno.*

Bibliography

Ferrante, Joan M. *The Political Vision of the "Divine Comedy."* Princeton, N.J.: Princeton University Press, 1984, especially pp. 191–193.

Triolo, Alfred A. "*Inferno* XXXIII: Fra Alberigo in Context." *L'Alighieri* 11.2 (1970), 39–70.

Donna Yowell

Albero da Siena

Mentioned by Griffolino (*Inf.* 29.109), who reports that he convinced Albero that he could teach him to fly. But when Griffolino failed to "make him Daedalus," Albero persuaded the bishop of Siena (his father, some say; his protector only, according to others) to burn Griffolino at the stake on a charge of heresy for having duped him.

R. Allen Shoaf

Albert I

The son of Rudolph of Habsburg, Albert ruled as king of Germany from 1285 to 1308, at which time he was assassinated by his nephew, John of Sweden. He was elected emperor in 1298 but was never crowned.

Albert I features prominently in Dante's blistering invective against Italy and Florence (*Purg.* 6.76–151). Inveighing against him in the pivotal apostrophe that opens *O Alberto Tedesco* (97–117), Dante rebukes him for his neglect of Italy; calls for divine justice to strike his dynasty and to put fear in his successor (a likely allusion to the untimely death of Albert's son Rudolph in 1307 and to the emperor's own tragic demise the following year); points to his and his father's greedy involvement in German politics as the cause of the desolation of the "garden of the empire"; and taunts him with a sarcastic invitation to come witness the extent of Italy's troubles. Another significant reference to Albert I appears in the Heaven of Jupiter, where Dante has the Eagle voice his disapproval of the emperor's invasion of Bohemia (*Par.* 19.115–119). In *Conv.* 4.3.6, he refers disparagingly to Albert as a non-Roman emperor, because he was never crowned in Rome.

Antonio Illiano

Albert the Great

Albert of Cologne, known as Albertus Magnus (1193–1280), renowned theologian known in his day as "doctor universalis" for the staggering range of his knowledge monumentalized in the thirty-eight volumes of his *Opera omnia* (Paris: Bibliopolem, 1890–1899). St. Albert *(Alberto)* played a leading role in introducing Aristotle's thought in its full amplitude into the mainstream of philosophical thought and speculative theology in medieval Europe. He thereby gave significant impetus to the new thinking called Scholasticism that dominated the thirteenth century. This period is commonly seen as culminating in St. Thomas Aquinas, who studied with Albert, probably in Paris, where he taught from 1245 to 1248, and certainly back at Cologne, where he taught until 1254, before becoming provincial of the Dominican order in Germany and eventually bishop of Regensburg.

Beyond his connection with Thomas Aquinas, Albert had an originality of his own and an importance for Dante that has emerged in recent decades as preempting that of the "angelic doctor" on many crucial points. Bruno Nardi has demonstrated that passages in Dante previously thought to be based on the system of Aquinas probably depend instead directly on works of Albert. In particular, the Neoplatonic cast of Dante's metaphysical assumptions derives more from Albert than Aquinas. This can be seen with regard to the doctrines of the nature and origin of the soul, as well as its prophetic powers of receiving revelation in dreams; the progressive derivation, basically emanationist in character, of intelligence and light from a divine source; and the notion of a deification *(deificatio)* involving union with a higher intellect through knowledge of forms of the celestial sphere.

Dante places Albert at the right side of Thomas—both were Dominicans—who introduces him as his brother and teacher *(frate e maestro fummi)*, among the wise spirits *(spiriti sapienti)* of the Heaven of the Sun (*Par.* 10.98–99). Albert's works, furthermore, are cited in connection with the theory of light, of the rarity and density of bodies and vapors, the necessary postulation of a ninth heavenly sphere, and the cold and damp humors of old age, in *Conv.* 2.13.21–22, 3.5.12, 3.7.3, and 4.23.12–13.

It is particularly in maintaining Platonic ideas within the new Aristotelian framework, as well as in the cultivation of the physical sciences as independent sources of knowledge rather than merely as instruments for theology, that Albert's thought distinguished itself and became massively influential. All reality became open to investigation—the physical realm, even by direct empirical methods. He is a great representative of the Gothic Age, an age that is endowed with a new sense of a directly observable nature and one that is brought to consummate expression by Dante.

Bibliography

Nardi, Bruno. *Saggi di filosofia dantesca.* 2nd ed. Florence: La Nuova Italia, 1967.

———. "L'origine dell'anima umana secondo Dante." In *Studi di filosofia medievale.* Rome: Edizioni di Storia e Letteratura, 1960, pp. 9–68.

———. *Dante e la cultura medievale: Nuovi saggi di filosofia dantesca.* 2nd ed. Bari: Laterza, 1949.

Toynbee, Paget. "Some Unacknowledged Obligations of Dante to Albertus Magnus." *Romania* 24 (1895), 399–422.

William Franke

Alberto degli Alberti

Count of Mangona whose two sons, Alessandro and Napoleone, having quarreled over their

A inheritance, killed each other. They are placed among the treacherous in Caina and are referred to by Camiscion de' Pazzi (*Inf.* 32.57), who names only the father.

Richard Lansing

Alberto della Scala

Lord of Verona between 1277 and 1301; succeeded by his sons Bartolommeo, Alboino, and, lastly, Cangrande, who hosted Dante at Verona. According to the unknown Abbot of San Zeno, he will soon die and repent the appointment of his physically and mentally deformed illegitimate son Giuseppe as abbot (*Purg.* 18.121).

Pamela J. Benson

Alberto di Casalodi

Guelf lord of Mantua ill-advised by the Ghibelline Pinamonte dei Bonacolsi in 1272 to exile the nobles and to side with the populace. He was in turn exiled by Pinamonte. Virgil mentions his fate in recounting the founding of Mantua (*Inf.* 20.95).

Pina Palma

Albumassar

Leading ninth-century Arab astrologer-astronomer. Dante's reference to Albumassar (*Albumasar;* Abū Ma' shar) in *Conv.* 2.13.22 appears to be taken from Albertus Magnus (*De Meteoris* 1.4.9).

Angela G. Meekins

Alchemy

Usually associated by modern readers with the search for a means of transforming base metals into gold, medieval alchemy in fact constituted a subtle and wide-ranging approach to what would today be thought of as the science of matter. By the fourteenth century it was customary to divide the subject into two branches: theoretical *(alchimia speculativa)* and practical *(alchimia operativa).* Many late medieval thinkers followed the thirteenth-century Franciscan Roger Bacon in distinguishing sharply between the former, as an honorable field of philosophical knowledge *(scientia);* and the latter, as a mundane, ignoble, physically and morally grubby occupation *(ars)* aimed exclu-sively (and literally!) at making money. Yet, however sordid the motivation, it was practical alchemy—through its dedication to experimental research and its progressive refinement of scientific techniques—that laid the foundations for the later discoveries that established the modern science of chemistry.

Dante mentions alchemy only twice, in the space of a single canto of the *Commedia* (*Inf.* 29), where the term "alchímia" occurs as part of the self-definitions offered by the falsifiers Griffolino and Capocchio. Griffolino tells the story of his death at the instigations of the vengeful Albero da Siena, whom he had attempted to deceive, but goes on: *Ma ne l'ultima bolgia de le diece / me per l'alchímia che nel mondo usai / dannò Minòs, a cui fallar non lece* ("But to the last pocket of the ten, for the alchemy I practiced in the world, Minos damned me, who may not err," *Inf.* 29.118–120). Capocchio, meanwhile, asking Dante if he recognizes him, boldly declares: *sì vedrai ch'io son l'ombra di Capocchio, / che falsai li metalli con l'alchímia* ("then you will see that I am the shade of Capocchio, who falsified metals with alchemy," *Inf.* 29.136–137). It should be noted, however, that Dante, in accordance with the teaching of several major late medieval theologians, including Thomas Aquinas (*ST* 2.2.77.2), appears not to see alchemy as inherently sinful. What condemns Griffolino and Capocchio is that they practiced their alchemical science in fraudulent and deceitful ways, laying claim to powers they did not in fact possess (as the tale told by Griffolino in lines 112–117 and Capocchio's stress on the falsity of his practice—*falsai*—both suggest). Dante's text pronounces no judgment, positive or negative, on the moral status of alchemy itself; but neither does it deny the validity, let alone the existence, of *genuine* alchemical knowledge—if there is such a thing—as opposed to the spurious kind exemplified in the careers of the infernal spokesmen in canto 29. Griffolino and Capocchio, in short, are seen to be condemned as falsifiers, not simply as alchemists.

This is interesting because, precisely in the years in which Dante was at work on the *Commedia*—the first two decades of the fourteenth century—alchemy and its moral legitimacy had become the subject of intense debate within the church, particularly in the context of the growing institutional rivalry between the Franciscan and

Dominican orders. The Franciscans—especially their radical "Spiritual" wing—were celebrated proponents of alchemical research and theorizing, whereas the Dominicans, in an increasingly severe set of official pronouncements from 1273 onwards, came to oppose it, even in its comparatively respectable "speculative" form. The culmination of this debate was the stern condemnation of alchemy and alchemists alike, issued in 1317 by Pope John XXII (of whom Dante, incidentally, had no very high opinion, as is clear from *Par.* 27. 58–60). This papal document is the first to include practical alchemy among its targets; previously the debate had extended only to alchemy in its speculative varieties. Pope John (who seems to have been inspired by his own personal fear and detestation of "magic" in all its forms) firmly and explicitly states that the practical alchemist's quest for the key to changing base metals into gold is pointless, because there is no such possibility in nature, and that those who claim to have succeeded in it are, therefore, necessarily liars and deceivers—so many counterparts, in fact, of Dante's Griffolino and Capocchio.

Yet, despite Dante's keen and documented interests in both scientific discussion and relations between the great religious orders, none of this debate has left obvious traces on the text of the *Commedia.* The distinction between the speculative and practical forms of alchemy is not spelled out by Dante, and indeed he never mentions speculative alchemy as such at all; Griffolino and Capocchio are clearly practitioners, not theorists. It is thus not easy—and would anyway probably be unwise—to try to move beyond the *Inferno*'s clear condemnation of false alchemy and deceptive alchemists in order to define its author's attitude toward alchemical science in general; but it remains tempting to see Dante's fierce condemnation of alchemical charlatans as coexisting with the kind of tolerant curiosity about the science's theoretical possibilities that is displayed by several of his intellectual mentors—Aquinas in particular.

Bibliography

Botterill, Steven. "Dante e l'alchimia." In *Dante e la scienza.* Edited by Vittorio Russo and Patrick Boyde. Ravenna: Longo, 1995, pp. 203–211.
———. "*Inferno* XXIX: Capocchio and the Limits of Realism." In *Italiana 1988.* Edited by Albert N. Mancini, Paolo A. Giordano, and Anthony J. Tamburri. River Forest, Ill.: Rosary College, 1990, pp. 23–33.
Holmyard, E. J. *Alchemy.* Harmondsworth, UK: Penguin, 1957.
Multhauf, Robert P. "The Science of Matter." In *Science in the Middle Ages.* Edited by David C. Lindberg. Chicago: University of Chicago Press, 1978, pp. 369–391.

Steven Botterill

Aldobrandesco, Guglielmo

Count of Santafiora and one of the powerful Aldobrandeschi lords of the Sienese Maremma, Guglielmo spent his life fighting Siena. A fierce foe of the emperor and a papal ally, he participated in the anti-imperial insurrection of 1243 and in the consequent defeat of Frederick II. His son Omberto speaks of him proudly as "a great Tuscan" in *Purg.* 11.58.

Pamela J. Benson

Aldobrandi, Tegghiaio

A member of the aristocratic Adimari, one of the most powerful Guelf clans in Florence. Tegghiaio was a responsible adult by 1236, when he was one of four citizens placed in charge of hostages from San Gimignano. Twenty years later he was podestà of Arezzo. In 1260 he advised his fellow citizens against the Sienese campaign, which was to culminate in the Battle of Montaperti; nonetheless he was one of the captains of the Florentine army in that campaign. Having survived Montaperti and taken refuge in Lucca, he died before 1267.

Dante places him among the sodomites (*Inf.* 16.41), although we have no independent evidence of such a vice on Tegghiaio's part. As a citizen and a politician, however, Tegghiaio commands Dante's respect. He is one of five prominent Florentines of the past about whom Dante asks Ciacco for information, calling them *sí degni* ("so worthy") and men who *a ben far puoser li 'ngegni* ("turned their wits to doing well," *Inf.* 6.79–82). On the burning sands of the seventh circle, Iacopo Rusticucci introduces him as one whose words *dovria esser gradita* ("should have been pleasing," 16.40–42) during his mortal life—presumably a reference to Tegghiaio's prescient counsel regarding the campaign against Siena.

John C. Barnes

The proud learning humility on the first terrace of Purgatory. Invenzioni di Giovanni Flaxman sulla Divina commedia, *illustrated by John Flaxman and Beniamino del Vecchio, Rome, 1826. Giamatti Collection: Courtesy of the Mount Holyoke College Archives and Special Collections.*

Alecto

Daughter of Night and Pluto or Acheron and second named of the three Furies threatening Dante at the Gate of Dis: *quella che piange dal destro è Aletto* ("she who weeps on the right there is Alecto," *Inf.* 9.47). Alecto's weeping follows Virgil's account (*Aen.* 7.324).

Rebecca S. Beal

Alessandro da Romena

One of the powerful Conti Guidi and leader of the exiled White Guelfs with whom Dante was allied at the beginning of his exile from Florence. Master Adam, condemned to Malebolge for fraud, blames Alessandro and his brothers Guido and Aghinolfo for having persuaded him to counterfeit the Florentine gold florin (*Inf.* 30.77). Dante had expressed a radically different view of Alessandro earlier in a letter of condolence sent to his nephews

Oberto and Guido upon his death in 1304, in which he had praised him highly (*Epist.* 2).

Richard Lansing

Alessandro degli Alberti

A son of Count Alberto, who in 1248 allied himself with Bologna, becoming a Guelf. When he and his Ghibelline brother, Napoleone, fought over their father's estate, they killed each other. Dante relegates both to Caina in the ninth circle of Hell (*Inf.* 32.57) among the traitors to kin.

Pina Palma

Alessandro Novello

Bishop of Feltre (1298–1320). His betrayal of several exiled Ferrarese whom he had promised to protect resulted in their execution. Cunizza, in the Heaven of Venus, speaks of the sorrow he will bring to Feltre (*Par.* 9.52).

Pamela J. Benson

Alexander the Great

King of Macedonia, celebrated military leader, and conqueror of the Persian Empire (356–323 B.C.E.). He may be the *Alessandro* punished among the tyrants in the first ring of the seventh circle in Hell (*Inf.* 12.107; see also 14.31), although Alexander of Pherae, a tyrant of Thessaly who ruled c. 368–359 B.C.E., is a possible candidate. Alexander the Great is perhaps the more likely person here, since Orosius, one of Dante's chief historical authorities, describes the Macedonian conqueror as being especially bloodthirsty (*Historia adversus paganos,* 3.7.5), and Lucan, another of Dante's authorities, depicts him as a mower of mankind (*Phars.* 10.20–36). Dante acknowledges the hero's munificence (*Conv.* 4.11.14), a virtue not only for which he was renowned throughout the Middle Ages but also of which he was considered to be the prime exemplum. In Dante's discussion of rulers who sought to establish a universal world monarchy, he observes that no other ruler came closer to realizing this goal (*Mon.* 2.8.8, 10). Alexander is also mentioned in *DVE* 2.6.2.

R. A. Malagi

Alfraganus

Early ninth-century astronomer (full name: Abū 'l-'Abbas Ahmad ibn Muhammad ibn Kathir al-Farghani). His astronomical treatise—based on Ptolemy's *Almagest,* but shorter and simpler—was translated from Arabic into Latin by John of Seville in 1137 and by Gerard of Cremona before 1175, and it circulated widely in the West under the titles *Elementa astronomica* and *Liber de aggregationibus scientiae stellarum.* This seems to have been Dante's principal source for astronomical data. Dante names Alfraganus *(Alfragano)* once, as his authority for the size of Mercury and of Earth (*Conv.* 2.13.11); in *Conv.* 2.5.16 he mentions the *libro de l'Aggregazion[i] de le Stelle* ("book of the *Constellations of the Stars*") in reference to the motion of Venus.

Christian Moevs

Algazel

Islamic philosopher, theologian, and mystic (full name: Abū Hamid Muhammad ibn Muhammad al-Tusi al-Ghazali), born at Tus in Iran (c. 1058–1111). In his *Intentions of the Philosophers,* he objectively expounded the theories of the Aris-totelian Neoplatonists, especially Ibn Sina (Avicenna) and al-Farabi, in order to destroy them in the *Incoherence of the Philosophers.* The first work, translated into Latin in 1145 as *Logica et Philosophia Algazelis Arabis,* led the Scholastic philosophers to attribute to him the views he was attacking. Thus both of Dante's references to Algazel (regarding the generation of substantial forms in *Conv.* 2.13.5 and the nobility of the soul in *Conv.* 4.21.2) pair Algazel with Avicenna; both references probably derive from Albert the Great.

Christian Moevs

Ali

Located in the ninth bolgia of Malebolge, among the creators of strife, Ali *(Alì)* embodies the bloodshed and dissension resulting from schism. Cousin of Muhammad and married to the Prophet's daughter Fatima, Ali ibn Abu Talib was the first convert, after Muhammad's wife Khadijah, to Islam. In 656, Ali was elected as the fourth caliph of the Muslim community. His succession was disputed, however, leading after Ali's assassination in 661 to the separation of Muslims into Sunni and Shi'i (literally, "partisans" of Ali). Dante depicts him *Inf.* 28.32–33 as split from chin to forehead. His wound complements the one that sunders Muhammad's body from chin to anus, symbolizing the split in the headship of the Muslims under Ali.

Fiora A. Bassanese

Alighieri, Dante

Although few facts of Dante's early life are available to us, we know that he was born in Florence sometime between May 14 and June 13 of 1265. He was given the name Durante (of which "Dante" is a contracted form) and was christened in a general public ceremony in the baptistry of San Giovanni on March 26, 1266, the Saturday before Easter.

Dante's father was called Alighiero. He does not seem to have earned any position of social distinction, nor was he a member of any of Florence's arts or Florence's guilds; if anything, there floated in his own lifetime suspicions that he may have been involved in the shady business of moneylending. Dante's mother, Bella, who belonged to the Abati family, bore her husband two children and died when Dante was 6 years old. At her death,

A

Portrait of Dante in the Lodovico Dolce edition of the Commedia *published in Venice in 1555.* La divina comedia di Dante, *edited by Lodovico Dolce and published by Gabriel Giolito de Ferrari in Venice in 1555. Giamatti Collection: Courtesy of the Mount Holyoke College Archives and Special Collections.*

Alighiero took a second wife, Lapa Cialuffi, by whom he had two other children, Francesco and Tana. Alighiero himself died sometime between 1281 and 1283.

Around 1285 Dante set up house with Gemma Donati, whom he had legally married on February 9, 1277. Four children were born from this union: three boys (Giovanni, Pietro, and Iacopo) and a girl (Antonia), who later reentered the aged poet's life in Ravenna, where she became a nun, taking the name Sister Beatrice.

Very little is also known of Dante's early education. The year 1250 marks a watershed for the emergence of universities and technical organizations of teaching in many European cities, such as Salerno, Bologna, Paris, and Oxford. In Florence, however, schools became centralized secular institutions only somewhat later. There were public grammar schools, but higher learning continued to take place around ecclesiastical centers (the Dominican Church of Santa Maria Novella, the Fran-

ciscan Church of Santa Croce, and the Augustinian Church of Santo Spirito).

By and large, Dante's early schooling followed an ordinary pattern. Like about ten thousand other Florentine children, he attended grammar school, where he learned reading and writing using textbooks that ranged from the classical works of Virgil, Cicero, and Horace to the medieval *Liber Aesopi,* the *Disticha Catonis,* and the dictionary of the time, the *Magnae Derivationes* of Uguccione de' Bagni of Pisa.

Our knowledge of Dante's intellectual development is less generic when he enters the circle of Brunetto Latini's disciples. Brunetto had returned to Florence from his exile in France in 1266. While in France, he had written didactic poems as well as the *Tesoretto* and, in French, *Li Livres dou Tresor.* Both texts are essentially parables of humanistic and civil education that are woven with several strands of tradition. Chief among them in the curriculum of the trivium (grammar, rhetoric, and dialectic) and the quadrivium (arithmetic, music, geometry, and astronomy) were the naturalistic philosophic doctrines current among the Italians (i.e., Bernard Silvester, Guillaume de Conches, and Alain de Lille). But the overarching concern of Brunetto's texts is the question of "science," by which one is to understand "natural philosophy" as the foundation of ethics, law, and political theories.

Dante pursued these grammatical-rhetorical studies, which climaxed in Brunetto's teaching, until 1286. By this time, and thanks in no small measure to Brunetto's influence, he became familiar with Provençal and French literature (the Carolingian and the Arthurian cycles), the didactic poetry of Guittone di Arezzo, and love treatises, as well as with the rhetorical-legal traditions that were vitally debated in Bologna. During this early period, however, Dante devoted himself exclusively to writing lyric poetry *(rime),* in a variety of traditional forms (though predominantly sonnets and canzoni), and those lyrics took their inspiration from his love for a woman named Beatrice, who was to remain for virtually his entire life the creative force of his imagination.

Dante himself records in his *Vita Nuova* that when he was 8 years old, he met Beatrice Portinari, also 8 years of age. He saw her again nine years later, in 1283, and his love for her acquired an absolute privilege. He defines it as a fundamental encounter that imaginatively turned into a radical beginning and revealed to his mind the existence of the realm of love and poetry. Under the powerful compulsion of this love for Beatrice, Dante entered into a new apprenticeship, an apprenticeship in the art of poetry as the path to reach the truth about their love. The story of their love is told in the *Vita Nuova,* which he began writing between 1292 and 1294 (although the lyrics themselves date from earlier). But his poetic education began earlier. The death of his father in 1283 forced him to take legal charge of his family. As the head of a household Dante could not but be involved in the demanding realities of public life and the political currents swirling in the city of Florence. But his first public acts were literary.

Around 1285–1286 he wrote *Il Detto* and *Il Fiore,* which are poetic exercises marking the progress of his apprenticeship. The language of the *Roman de la rose*—its concerns with nature, love and profanation—is translated into a rich medley of garrulous voices from the "realistic" school of

poetry rampant in Florence and all over Tuscany. To "translate," for the young poet, meant to decipher a natural passion that transcends states of subjectivity and rational deliberations. With an extraordinary energy and playfulness that spoof any frigid esthetician about love and go beyond doctrinal formulas, Dante centers the *Fiore* on desire as a rush of passion, as transgression that remains within the bourne of nature.

In 1287, Dante entered into a relationship with the poet Guido Cavalcanti that was to last until 1294. Their friendship was triggered by the sonnet "A ciascun' alma," which Dante had written for Beatrice. In the shadow of Cavalcanti a rigorous philosophic-poetic training began to take shape for Dante. He read the Sicilian poets and traveled to Bologna, where he came in contact with the poetry of Guido Guinizzelli. Cavalcanti became the means of gaining access to an elegant and prestigious circle of high-cultured Florentine intellectuals.

In 1283 Florence was not an intellectual center such as Paris and Bologna, but it was enjoying a rare period of tranquility and growing prosperity that lured to the city a host of jurists, notaries, and physicians from all over Tuscany (among whom were Dino Frescobaldi, Guido Orlandi, Gianni Alfieri, Lapo Gianni, Dante da Maiano, Cino da Pistoia, Ricco da Varlunga, etc.). For the writers poetry was a passion and a fashion. This is the group within which the so-called *dolce stil novo* ("Sweet New Style") was forged. The new poetic taste conveyed the view that the sensuous, material qualities of love are nothing without an ideal essence that incarnates it. These poets—and among them chiefly Dante—explore love's effect on the consciousness; how psychology shades into philosophy; and how poetry, at the deepest level, reveals the essence of love as a conjunction of material signs, impressions, and essences. Because they view consciousness as being of supreme value, Dante, Guido Cavalcanti, and Lapo Gianni scorn the practice of mindless verification and prize design and deliberateness in poetic language. The *Vita Nuova,* which was compiled in 1294, is a product of this intellectual experience. Confining himself to a detailed scrutiny of the soul and narrowly focusing on the vast phenomenology of love, Dante shows himself to be a metaphysician, an epistemologist, and a stylist of love.

This poetic-philosophical education changed direction in 1290. In June 1289 Dante served in the Florentine cavalry in the military campaign

Portrait of Dante. Comedia di Danthe Alighieri poeta divino, *with commentary by Cristoforo Landino, published by Jacob del Burgofra[n]co, Venice, 1529. Giamatti Collection: Courtesy of the Mount Holyoke College Archives and Special Collections.*

A against the Aretines at Campaldino. The event did not become an overt object of reflection for him for some time. In 1290 (on either June 8 or 19) Beatrice died. Her death—as Dante reports in the *Convivio*—marked the inception of a rigorous, if unsystematic course of studies in both philosophy and theology for a period of almost three years (between 1291 and 1294). Remigio de' Girolami, who had been a disciple of Thomas Aquinas in Paris, was teaching logic and ethics at the convent of Santa Maria Novella. At the same time, Giovanni Olivi (Peter of John Olivi), a representative of the Spiritual Franciscans, was disseminating his theological-political speculations at the Church of Santa Croce. The burden of his teaching centered on a plan of radical ecclesiastical reform of the *ecclesia carnalis*. His theories combined the symbolic and incarnational theology of Bonaventure with the prophetic theology of Joachim of Fiore, which issued in a critique of institutions. At the same time, at the Augustinian Church of Santo Spirito, Dante had an opportunity to study the theological-esthetic works of St. Augustine (from *Confessions* to *De Musica*) and of the neo-Augustinians (the Victorines and St. Bonaventure).

No doubt, these rhetorical, poetic, philosophical, and theological studies allied Dante to the wide spectrum of the city's "intelligentsia." They also held out to him the promise that he might excel in public life. From this point of view, in 1294, there was an event that ranked as most important. In March of that year Charles Martel, titular king of Hungary and son to Charles II of Anjou, passed through Florence, where he was to meet his father, who was returning to Naples. The Dominican Remigio de' Girolami welcomed him officially to the city. Charles, a lover of the arts and poetry, visited Cimabue's shop and met Dante, who recited to him his canzone "Voi che 'ntendendo il terzo ciel movete."

The encounter with Charles Martel, to whom Dante devotes the entire eighth canto of *Paradiso,* may have given rise to dreams of forging a bond between intellectuals and the court, as had happened at the court of Frederick II. The temporary proximity to Charles, however, must also have opened his eyes to the high stakes of imperial and Church politics. After the death of Pope Nicholas IV, the papal seat remained vacant for two years. On July 5, 1294, Pietro da Morrone was elected pope and took the name of Celestine V. Pope Celestine—who distrusted the cardinals, favored the Spiritual Franciscans' plans for ecclesiastic reform, and was dependent on the support of King Charles II of Naples—abruptly resigned on December 13 of that same year. He was succeeded by Boniface VIII, a man of superior intellect, who reigned from 1294 to his death in 1303 and who embodied all the principles Celestine opposed, which earned him the hatred of the Spirituals (among whom principally Iacopone da Todi). Boniface began to assert forcefully the doctrine of the Church's plenitude of power, which culminated in his bull *Unam Sanctam* (1302). He undertook to negotiate peace between the Angevins and the Aragonese as well as between Philip IV of France and Edward I of England, and he entertained a plan for absorbing the whole of Tuscany into the patrimony of Saint Peter.

Boniface's theocratic and hegemonic claims over Tuscany were strongly resisted by Florence, which was simultaneously asserting its own claims over other Tuscan cities. Florence's victory over the Aretines at Campaldino in 1289 reversed the mood of the city and mitigated the memory of the defeat at Montaperti in 1260; but it also unsettled the balance of power in the city. The Ghibellines underwent defeat at the hands of the Guelfs. The popular class, emboldened by Giano della Bella and by their decisive role in the city's military victory over Arezzo, sought to limit the power of the magnates. In 1293 the *Ordinamenti di Giustizia,* the new constitution conceived by Giano, codified the rules for participating in the government of the city: to aspire to the role of magistrates, one had to be a member of various guilds or corporations. The measure granted de facto recognition to the new social order of arts from three classes, ranging from judges to merchants of wool and silk. The government of the republic would be chosen from their rank.

It is within this turbulent context of social, political, and theological cross-currents that Dante launched his political career. His career reached its pinnacle in 1300 (between June 15 and August 15), when Dante, who had enrolled in the guild of the *Medici e speziali* ("Physicians and Apothecaries") in 1295, was elected one of Florence's seven priors. This experience was also the beginning of his grievous personal misfortunes. His tenure as a prior saw the city crippled by a steady increase in violence that involved the magnates and the representatives of the popular government. As a punitive measure for continuing acts of violence, the priors agreed to send the leaders of the Black Guelfs and the White Guelfs (the Donati and the Cerchi families) into exile. Among the exiles was Dante's own friend and White Guelf Guido Cavalcanti, who fell ill at Sarzana late in August of that year and died shortly upon his return to Florence.

When Dante's tenure as a prior expired, his immediate successors recalled the Whites from the exile, a decision that angered Pope Boniface. For the centenary year of 1300 he had proclaimed a Jubilee, or Holy Year—a special time of observance when indulgences would be granted, censures lifted, property restored. The return of Whites who were suspected of being Ghibellines in that very year seemed to the pope an act of open hostility toward him. Boniface called upon Charles of Valois, the brother of King Philip IV of France, to intervene militarily in Florence. The Florentines dispatched three emissaries to Rome to persuade the pope to keep the French from entering Tuscany. One of these ambassadors was Dante, who, while in Rome, was sentenced first to exile, on January 27, 1302, and later, on March 10, 1302, to death should he ever return to his native city. Dante went into exile, which was to last until his death in 1321.

At the beginning of his exile Dante remained within Tuscany. He joined other exiles at San Godenzo on June 8, 1302, where they met and planned to wage war against the Blacks. After roaming from city to city—the only contact with his family being his stepbrother Francesco—he settled briefly in Verona at the court of Bartolomeo della Scala. Pope Benedict XI, succeeding Boniface VIII (who had died in 1303), sought in vain to bring about a reconciliation of the various Florentine factions. Disillusioned and embittered by this turn of events, Dante broke away from compatriots whom he would call the *compagnia malvagia e scempia* ("wicked, dimwitted company," *Par.* 17.62) to become a party unto himself.

The pain of this ordeal lodged forever in his memory and became the core of his future works. Almost in overt contrast to the desolation, monstrosity, and madness brought about by the contingencies of political passions, he began highlighting the universal pattern and order of history. While writing the *Vita Nuova* he had been entranced and puzzled by the hidden, harmonious design he would discover at the heart of his own amatory experiences. The reality of exile—with its dangerous decisions and selfish entrapments—

instilled in him a need to transcend the barriers of contingency, the patrial and partisan viewpoints, and the limits of the here and now in which humanity is trapped.

In the early years of this new phase of his life he wrote the *De vulgari eloquentia,* begun around 1303 and never finished. Written in Latin, it argues, paradoxically, for the nobility of the vernacular tongue. As if to stress his transcendent, universal perspective, Dante recounts the history of language from Adam, which he spoke in the Garden of Eden, to the erection of the Tower of Babel, and, finally, to the fourteen Italian dialects, out of which the new vernacular language had to be forged. The treatise ends with the second book, which is dedicated to rhetoric and poetics.

Between 1304 and 1307 he wrote the *Convivio,* which was to be composed of fourteen canzoni accompanied by fourteen commentaries, with an introduction. Only four of the fifteen books were ultimately written. Conceived as a treatise on ethics and the value of philosophy, the *Convivio* begins with a reflection on the *Vita Nuova* and its limits. The new intellectual direction Dante undertakes here is revealed by the inclusion of his poem "Voi che 'ntendendo il terzo ciel movete"—the doctrinal canzone he had recited to Charles Martel. Philosophy (love of knowledge and not love of woman) is here conceived as enabling mankind to perfect the innate power of human reason. This is also the theme of the second canzone, "Amor che ne la mente mi ragiona." The third, "Le dolci rime d'Amor," focuses on defining the true concept of nobility, the role of the virtues in creating nobility, the authority of the emperor and the philosopher, and providential role of Roman history.

These two treatises, taken together, can be seen as dismissive of the restricted esthetics and the playful ideas about love that Dante had dramatized in the past. But they are not purely metaphysical speculations about the necessity of seeing the world as a whole from a universal standpoint. They are also political texts in which claims for the authority of the intellectual are staked out. That Dante had not abandoned his political dreams is made evident by the epistles he wrote during this same period. Some of them, such as "Popule mee," addressed to the Florentine people, are lost. In 1310, he composed the "Epistle to the Princes and Peoples of Italy" (*Epist.* 5); in 1314, he wrote the "Epistle to the Italian Cardinals" (*Epist.* 11), in which he expresses the hope that the Babylonian

A captivity of the Church be brought to an end. More importantly, in 1316, he composed a political tract, the *Monarchia*.

The inspiration for this treatise, in which Dante argues for the necessity of a universal empire, came to him from a momentous event that took place on the stage of European history. In November 1308, the electors of Germany had agreed to have Henry VII of Luxemburg crowned emperor. Henry, who would have to wait until June 1312 to be crowned by the pope, was expected to redress the political disorder in the various Italian cities of the north and of Tuscany. Dante hails Henry's arrival in Italy, celebrating him as a new messianic leader and exhorting him (particularly in *Epist.* 7) to rescue Italy from the political quagmire in which it found itself. The *Monarchia* elaborates this faith in a political order founded on the authority of a single ruler who is independent of the church, yet rules by the will of God and the providential history of the Roman Empire.

During these years, Dante had been writing the *Commedia*. By the time of Henry's descent to Italy, he had finished writing both the *Inferno* and most of the *Purgatorio*. In 1312, he moved back to the Court of Cangrande della Scala in Verona, where he began the *Paradiso*. When he had completed half of the last canticle, he accepted the invitation from Guido Novello of Polenta to move to Ravenna. He returned briefly to Verona on January 20, 1320, in order to deliver his *Questio de aqua et terra*. His last years in Ravenna, however, were serene. His material needs were generously met by Guido Novello, on whose behalf Dante undertook a number of diplomatic missions. His children, and possibly his wife, Gemma (who died in Florence in 1342), were with him. He was surrounded by devoted disciples. And the academicians from the nearby University of Bologna (such as Giovanni del Virgilio, with whom Dante had exchanged *Eclogues*) showed him marked admiration. Above all, however, while in Ravenna—where he died on September 13, 1321, after returning from an embassy to Venice—he completed his *Commedia*.

The *Commedia* constitutes an encyclopedic poem that brings together the moral, political, philosophical, linguistic, and theological truths and questions with which Dante had grappled all his life. And yet it is a totally new imaginative construction. It summons the reader to a spiritual conversion; it promotes the vision of human life as a morally unified journey toward the divine; it searches for a reconciliation of all sects and factions; it prophetically announces a new order within the Christian redemption of history; it retrieves Dante's own life and rediscovers the providentiality of his love for Beatrice; and it reminds us relentlessly of the scandal of evil that has the power to impede the journey toward the spiritual good.

Bibliography

Barbi, Michele. *Life of Dante.* Translated and edited by Paul Ruggiers. Berkeley: University of California Press, 1954.

Bemrose, Stephen. *A New Life of Dante.* Exeter: University of Exeter, 1999.

Bergin, Thomas G. "Dante's Life." In *An Approach to Dante.* New York: Orion Press, 1965, pp. 30–44.

Boccaccio, Giovanni. *Trattatello in laude di Dante.* Edited by Luigi Sasso. Milan: Garzanti, 1995.

The Early Lives of Dante. Translated by Philip H. Wicksteed. London: Alexander Moring Limited, 1904.

Petrocchi, Giorgio. *Vita di Dante.* Bari: Laterza, 1983.

———. "Biografia: Attività politica e letteraria." *Enciclopedia dantesca,* 6:3–53.

Giuseppe Mazzotta

Alighieri, Pietro

Second son of Dante and of Gemma Donati; followed his father into exile, accompanied him on his travels, and was very likely present at his death in Ravenna in 1321. Shortly after this Pietro returned to Florence in order to sort out a complex tangle of family affairs, debts, and rights of inheritance. Pietro had been included in the death sentence passed *in absentia* on Dante at Florence in 1315; this sentence was suspended (but not annulled) after Dante's death. Pietro traveled on to Bologna and studied law before settling at Verona in 1331. He developed a successful legal career at Verona, married Iacopa di Dolcetto Salerni (from Pistoia), and had at least seven children. His daughters Alighiera, Gemma, and Lucia became nuns at San Michele in Campagna. Pietro may have been visiting his illegitimate son Bernardo when he died at Treviso on April 21, 1364; his legitimate son Dante inherited considerable property. Pietro's links with Florence had greatly weakened over the years; at his death he willed half of his father's house in the S. Martino del Vescovo district to the charitable foundation of Orsanmichele and the Misericordia hospital. A funeral monument at Treviso, depicting Pietro sitting *in cathedra ad modum doctoris,* was commissioned from the Venetian sculptor Zilberto Santi. Taken apart early in the nineteenth century, it was reassembled in 1935 and placed in the Church of S. Francesco.

Pietro's earliest surviving works attest to his lifelong dedication to the study, clarification, and defense of his father's writings. A sonnet exchange with Jacopo dei Garatori da Imola offers to provide understanding of free will: *La vostra sete, se ben mi ricorda, / Par saziar Dante* ("Your thirst [for understanding], as I recall, Dante can satisfy"). A poem addressed as "Satira mia chanzon" in its final stanza and directed heavenward to God ("Since there is nobody down here who might answer you," 103–104) owes much to Dantean phrasings and to the thought of the *Monarchia;* another canzone offers a *nuova visione* of the seven sister Liberal Arts as they lament the death of Dante. But it is in his mature Veronese writings that Pietro assumes preeminent importance as a Dante commentator. Where his brother Iacopo slips back into forms and mental habits from the Duecento, Pietro pioneers new standards of neo-humanist commentary. Petrarch may have met Pietro during his student days at Bologna (1320–1326). They must have met at Verona (where, in the famous cathedral library, Petrarch discovered Cicero's *Letters to Atticus* in 1345); Petrarch favored Pietro with a metrical letter (III.vii). Pietro produced three recensions of his *Commentarium* (1340–1341, 1350–1355, c. 1358). In humanist fashion, he concentrates upon the letter of Dante's poetic text (rather than upon extraliterary sources of inspiration). Pietro's very modernity, however, often unwittingly assigns Dante to a vanished world: the spirit of the *stil nuovo* underpinning *Inf.* 5, with its talk of the *cor gentile* ("noble heart"), is foreign to him.

Bibliography

Alighieri, Pietro. *Il "Commentarium" di Pietro Alighieri nelle redazioni Ashburnhamiana e Ottoboniana.* Edited by Roberto della Vedova and Maria Teresa Silvotti. Florence: Olschki, 1978.

———. *Quelle sette arti liberali, in versi* (canzone). Edited by Domenico de Robertis. In *Studi danteschi* 36 (1959), 196–205.

———. *Le rime di Pietro Alighieri.* Edited by Giovanni Crocioni. Collezione di opuscoli danteschi. Città di Castello: S. Lapi, 1903.

———. *Commentarium.* Edited by Vincentio Nannucci. Florence: Apud Angelum Garinei, 1846.

D'Addario, A. "Alighieri, Pietro." In *Dizionario biografico degli italiani.* Rome: Istituto della enciclopedia italiana, 1960–, II, 453–454.

Minnis, A. J., and A. B. Scott, with the assistance of David Wallace. *Medieval Literary and Criticism, c. 1100–c. 1375. The Commentary Tradition.* Revised edition. Oxford: Clarendon Press, 1991, pp. 450–453, 476–491.

David Wallace

Alighieri Family

Of the many attested forms of his family name, "Alaghieri" was the one Dante preferred. "Alighieri" represents its Florentine pronunciation and has prevailed because it was used by the influential Boccaccio.

The name evidently originated as a patronymic. Dante says it derives from the baptismal name of his great-grandfather, Alaghiero di Cacciaguida, *da cui si dice / tua cognazione* ("from whom you take your family name," *Par.* 15.91–92). Looking further back, he says the name came from the Po Valley (*Par.* 15.137–138). There were, however, at least three other Aldighieri/Alighieri families, with no known connection to Dante, living in thirteenth-century Florence.

Although it is clear that Alaghiero's father was the Cacciaguida who occupies the central cantos of *Paradiso,* the family's remoter origins are obscure. Dante, our only source of information, seems to believe it derived from the ancient, aristocratic Elisei family. In the poem Cacciaguida says he had a brother who "was" Eliseo (*Par.* 15.136 could mean either that the speaker had two brothers, Moronto and Eliseo, or that he had a brother called Moronto who, unlike him, maintained the Elisei family name); and in *Par.* 16.40–42 he states that his family's houses were at the beginning of Via degli Speziali—which is where the Elisei lived, whereas the Alighieris' houses were in the parish of San Martino al Vescovo. On the other hand, a surviving document shows that Alaghiero and his brother Preitenitto had houses in the San Martino parish as early as 1189; to which Leonardo Bruni (c. 1374–1444), who wrote a biography of Dante partly based on materials which are now lost, adds that it was Cacciaguida himself who, on his marriage, moved from the Elisei houses to the San Martino area. One of the functions of the character Cacciaguida's giving the precise location of his ancestral home is to make the point that, unlike the Alighieri houses, it was within the *cerchia antica* (the "ancient circle" of city walls: *Par.* 15.97); this strengthens the suggestion that Cacciaguida's forebears had had a distinguished place in Florentine society since time immemorial.

Certainly the *Commedia*'s protagonist glories in his nobility of blood in *Par.* 16.1–9. And in *Inf.* 15.61–78 he apparently implies that he is part of the original Roman stock that colonized Florence at the time of its foundation in the first century B.C.E.: *la pianta, / . . . / in cui riviva la sementa santa / di que' Roman che vi rimaser quando / fu fatto il nido di malizia tanta* ("the plant . . . in which may live again the holy seed of the Romans who remained there when that nest of so much malice was built," 74–78). We are in no position to corroborate or refute such a claim; neither, we may surmise, was Dante. But what may be gathered from the available evidence is that the socioeconomic status of Dante's ancestors was more mundane than the *Commedia* intimates; not one of them is recorded among the makers of Florentine history.

According to Dante (*Par.* 15.137–138) Cacciaguida married a lady from the Po Valley, who brought the name Alighiero or Alighieri with her. The *Commedia*'s early commentators say she was from Ferrara, and an Aldighieri family is indeed evidenced in Ferrara from the eleventh century onwards. As far as we know, Alaghiero and Preitenitto, mentioned in the 1189 document, were the only offspring of Cacciaguida and his northern Italian consort.

Dante associates his great-grandfather with the sin of pride: Cacciaguida the character tells the protagonist that his son Alaghiero *cent' anni e piúe / girato ha 'l monte in la prima cornice* ("for a hundred years and more has been circling the mountain on the first ledge," *Par.* 15.92–93), even though the historical Alaghiero is recorded as still alive in 1201. From an independent source we learn that he married a sister of *la buona Gualdrada* ("the good Gualdrada," *Inf.* 16.37), that is,

a daughter of Messer Bellincione Berti dei Ravegnani (see *Par.* 15.112–113 and 16.94–99), thus linking himself with another of Florence's great families, as well as other families with which the Ravegnani had marriage connections, such as the Conti Guidi, the Adimari, and the Donati.

Alaghiero and his noble wife had two sons, Bello and Bellincione, who came to be seen as the founders of distinct branches of the family. Dante, as a grandson of Bellincione, belonged to the junior, nonaristocratic branch, while Bello's branch preserved the family's aristocratic status. The latter branch is best known to readers of the *Commedia* in the person of Messer Geri del Bello, of whom Dante the character speaks with Virgil in *Inf.* 29.18–36.

Both branches of the family threw in their lot with the Guelf faction, and Bellincione was a member of the council which in 1251 approved the formation of the Guelf league consisting of Florence, Genoa, and Lucca. He appears to have been quite deeply involved in Florence's internal strife, since he was one of the Guelf exiles both from 1248 to 1251 and from 1260 to 1267. Hence the Ghibelline leader Farinata degli Uberti can taunt Dante the character by saying of Dante's ancestors, *"per due fiate li dispersi"* ("twice I scattered them"), though Dante is able to retort that, unlike the exiles of his interlocutor's faction, *"ei tornar / . . . l'una e l'altra fiata"* ("they returned . . . the first time and the second," *Inf.* 10.48–50).

Bellincione had six sons, of whom Dante's father, another Alaghiero, may have been the eldest. All six of them, together with their father, were active in business, especially, it seems, in Prato. Bellincione probably died in 1269.

One of Bellincione's sons—and hence one of Dante's uncles—another Bello, known as Belluzzo, is mentioned by Forese Donati in "Va rivesti San Gal prima che dichi," the fourth of the six sonnets forming the *tenzone* between him and Dante (*Rime,* 76). Forese writes: *Dio ti salvi la Tana e 'l Francesco, / che col Belluzzo tu non stia in brigata* ("God keep Tana and Francesco for you, that you may find it possible to escape Belluzzo's company!"). Commentators interpret this as meaning that Belluzzo has fallen on hard times, so that Dante—himself impecunious according to Forese's sonnets—will want to avoid depending on him for financial support. Finance was a prominent concern in Bellincione's branch of the family, as several of its members made their living from

Tower of Dante's house. Public domain. Richard Lansing.

moneylending, a business practically indistinguishable from usury. This applies to Bellincione himself and to at least two of his sons, including Dante's father, Alaghiero di Bellincione.

Dante never mentions his father (who was born around 1210 and died in or before 1283) in any of his writings, but Forese names him, as a dealer in money, in both the other sonnets he contributed to the *tenzone*. In "L'altra notte mi venne una gran tosse" (*Rime*, 74) we read: *i' trovai Alaghier tra le fosse, / legato a nodo ch'i' non saccio 'l nome, / se fu di Salamone o d'altro saggio. / . . . / e que' mi disse: "Per amor di Dante, / scio'mi"* ("I found Alighieri among the graves, tied by some knot—I don't know if the one called Solomon's, or some other sage's. . . . And he said to me: 'For the love of Dante release me'"). Forese, in order to defame Dante, here alludes to some dishonor incurred by Alaghiero or by Dante in respect of Alaghiero. Perhaps Dante's father had died without repaying money earned by usury, in which case he would have failed to qualify for sacramental absolution; or he may have suffered some injury which his son had not avenged. The latter possibility is supported by the opening lines of the other sonnet (*Rime*, 79): *Ben so che fosti figliuol d'Alaghieri, / ed accorgomen pur a la vendetta / che facesti di lui sí bella e netta / de l'aguglin ched e' cambiò* ("I know you're Alighieri's son all right—I can tell that by the fine clean vengeance you took on his behalf for the money he exchanged"). Here Forese plainly (but sarcastically) charges Dante with inadequacy for not avenging an offense committed against his father in the course of some monetary transaction. (The *aguglione* was an old imperial coin used by money changers.) It should be noted, however, that considerable doubt has recently been cast on the authenticity of the *tenzone* by Mauro Cursietti.

In any case, by the time of the poet's birth the family had adjusted to quite a lowly status within the magnate class. Alaghiero di Bellincione seems to have been an unremarkable sort of man, a small-scale businessman and not particularly well off, though in addition to his house in Florence he did own two large estates near Fiesole and two plots of land just outside the city's second circle of walls. This was enough for his family to be self-sufficient in corn, wine, and firewood along with the livestock they raised.

Alaghiero's first wife, whose name was Bella, may have been a member of the Abati, a powerful Ghibelline family of Florence. And it could be for this reason that Alaghiero was not exiled after the Guelf collapse of 1260; alternatively, he may have been allowed to remain in the city because his Guelf sympathies had not been translated into action. Whatever the explanation, the fact that Alaghiero was not exiled meant that in 1265 Dante, unlike many of his Guelf contemporaries, was born in his ancestral home. As far as we know he was Bella's only offspring. The Francesco and Tana (Gaetana) mentioned by Forese in the *tenzone* are Dante's half-brother and half-sister, brought into the world by Alaghiero's second wife, whom he married in 1270 or 1271. Tana, who married a money changer, was still alive in 1320, while Francesco, a businessman, lived until at least 1340. Together with Dante's sons Pietro and Iacopo, he was the family's main representative after the poet's death.

Dante married the aristocratic Gemma di Manetto Donati, who is thought to have given him four children. The youngest, Antonia, became a nun and died no later than 1371. The other three were all sons. The eldest is likely to have been Giovanni, recorded as being in Lucca (with his father?) in 1308. It may be supposed that Giovanni was dead by 1332, when a document concerning Dante's sons makes no mention of him; nor is anything further known about him. The remaining sons are best known for their commentaries on the *Commedia.* Iacopo, who was probably the younger of the two and appears to have died in 1349, had three illegitimate offspring by two different women (with whom, however, he evidently lived in fixed liaisons), but his progeny had disappeared by the mid–fifteenth century. The most durable part of Dante's family proved to be that descending from Pietro, probably his second son. Pietro married between 1332 and 1335, moved to Verona, and by the time of his wife's death in 1358 had seven offspring including one named Dante, who further continued the line.

The family was still living in Verona in 1562 when the male line of descent from this later Dante became extinct with the death of a Francesco Alighieri. The daughter of one of Francesco's brothers, Ginevra, had married Count Marcantonio di Serego and borne him Pieralvise, the first of at least five children. Rather than allow the Alighieri line to be lost without trace, Francesco made his great-nephew Pieralvise his heir on condition that he and his descendants add Alighieri to their own surname—a condition which was accepted. Today the Serego Alighieris, in the person of another Count Pieralvise, still own the estate at Casal dei Ronchi in Gargagnago, near Verona and Lake Garda, which was bought by Pietro di Dante in the 1350s and is known for an impressive and expensive Amarone wine, Vaio Armaron.

In Dante's day the Alighieri coat of arms was per pale or and sable a fess argent. From Pietro di Dante onwards, however, this blazon was replaced by designs which included either one or two wings, presumably because a Latin form of the family name, *Alagerius,* puns on Virgil's *aliger* ("wing-bearing").

Bibliography

Codice diplomatico dantesco. Edited by R. Piattoli. 2nd edition. Florence: Gonnelli, 1950.

Apollonio, Mario. *Dante: storia della "Commedia."* 2 vols. Milan: Vallardi, 1951, II, 1327–1351.

Barbi, Michele. *Problemi di critica dantesca: prima serie (1893–1918).* Florence: Sansoni, 1965, pp. 157–188.

———. *Problemi di critica dantesca: seconda serie (1920–1937).* Florence: Sansoni, 1964, pp. 329–370.

Chimenz, S. A. "Alighieri, Dante." In *Dizionario biografico degli italiani.* Vol. 2. Rome: Istituto della Enciclopedia italiana, 1960–, pp. 385–451.

Cursietti, Mauro. *La falsa tenzone di Dante con Forese Donati.* Anzio: De Rubeis, 1995.

Zingarelli, Nicola. *Dante.* Milan: Vallardi, 1899. Especially Chaps. 1, 2, and 10.

John C. Barnes

Allegory

A technique both of composition and interpretation, allegory is found throughout the Western tradition from Homer to the present. If we understand allegory as medieval writers did—that is, as verbal expression in which "one thing is said, another signified"—then allegory is employed in nearly all of Dante's works, from the *Vita Nuova* and the lyrics to the *Monarchia;* Dante's masterpiece in the mode, the *Commedia,* is arguably one of the most compelling instances ever wrought. In the long history of study of Dante, scrutiny of the poet's allegory has raised fundamental questions, from the status of truth-claims for the *Commedia* to the problematics of representation inherent in language.

Medieval Traditions of Allegory

The word *allegoria* comes from the Greek *allos-agoeurein,* "to speak elsewhere than in the agora"—thus to speak secretly or obliquely. It first appears in Latin in rhetorical treatises around the beginning of the Christian Era, where it refers to extended metaphor: Quintilian's example is Horace's "ship of state" (*Odes* 1.14.1ff.; cf. *Purg.* 6.76). Not long before (first century B.C.E.), the term had been adopted by Hellenistic literary critics for philosophical interpretation of the Homeric narratives, a practice that antedated Plato and that served, early in the first century C.E., as the model for the platonizing interpretations of the Old Testament by Philo of Alexandria. By the early centuries of the Christian Era, the term is used to describe hidden meanings of the Bible, especially prefigurations of Christ and Christianity held to be implicit in the Old Testament, following numerous gospel passages (e.g., Luke 24:44; John 5:38) and following Paul's account of the consorts of Abraham in Gal. 4.21–26, where the slave Hagar and the freewoman Sarah are said to represent, "by allegory" *(per allegoriam)* Jews under the Law and Christians free of the Law (this is the sole occurrence of the word in the New Testament).

The vast Greek exegetical legacy of Origen (second to third centuries)—especially his threefold division of scripture into historical, moral, and spiritual senses—was shaped for Latin Christians by Jerome and Augustine into a "figural" or "typological" system (fourth to fifth centuries). The text of the Bible narrated historical events and referred to things in the created world themselves significant: Christ is adumbrated by such Old Testament patriarchs as Adam, Abel, and Isaac, as well as by the brazen serpent raised aloft by Moses (Num. 21:8–9). Thus scriptural allegory was of events ordained and things made by God *(in factis),* not merely things said, as in human speech or writing *(in verbis).* John Cassian (fourth to fifth centuries) standardized the identification of historical fact with the literal sense of the Bible (thus, Jerusalem is the city in Judaea), while the allegorical or mystical or spiritual senses were arranged in a threefold scheme that expressed a historical progress: Jerusalem as the Christian community (allegorical sense proper, the faith that was established with the life of Christ); as the human soul (tropological sense, expressing moral choice); and as the celestial city (spiritual or anagogical sense, the destination of the elect). In Dante's day students learned this system using a mnemonic composed by the late-thirteenth-century philosopher Augustine of Dacia: *Littera gesta docet / Quid credas allegoria / Moralis quid agas / Quo tendis anagogia* ("The letter indicates the deed; allegory, what you should believe; the moral teaches what behavior's sound; anagogy where your soul is bound"). Application of this scheme to Dante's *Commedia,* initiated by fourteenth-century commentators, was decisively refreshed in the mid–twentieth century, especially with Auerbach's view that Dante's representation of his characters in the afterlife is a fulfillment of their historical existence.

The influential seventh-century definition of allegory as *alieniloquium* ("other-speech") by Isidore, Bishop of Seville, also reiterates the formula of the ancient grammarians: *aliud dicitur, aliud intelligitur* ("one thing is said, another signified"; cf. *Epist.* 13.22). But Isidore's illustration from Virgil's *Aen.* 1.191 is more than rhetorical, taking the three stags seen by Aeneas as the three Punic

wars destined to be fought by Rome. Isidore's example places him in the tradition of allegorical interpretation of Virgil's narrative that sprang from the commentaries of Servius (fourth century) and Fulgentius (fifth to sixth centuries); for the Middle Ages, Virgil's poem was an encyclopedia of science, history, morality, and politics—itself, moreover, "figural" in its structure, with Aeneas' victory prefiguring Augustus' establishment of an imperial line. Courcelle has shown that the sixth book, recounting Aeneas' journey through the underworld, was especially congenial to Christian exegetes with Neoplatonizing tendencies, from Macrobius (fourth to fifth centuries) to Bernard Silvestris (twelfth century). Fulgentius' moralized collection of pagan myths nourished allegorical interpretation of Ovid, Lucan, and Statius as well—the writers found in Dante's list of "regular poets" *(DVE* 2.6.7; see also *VN* 25). This tradition also influenced Dante's own allegoresis of the *Aeneid (Conv.* 4.26), but the allegorical use of Virgil in the *Commedia* transcends all known models (Hollander 1969).

Prosopopeia, or personification—treated by the ancients not as allegory but as a trope, or figure of speech—has nevertheless been for modern critics typical of medieval allegory generally, from Prudentius' *Psychomachia* (early fifth century), the "mental battle" of Christian virtues with the vices (e.g., Pride, Lust), to the thirteenth-century Old French vernacular *Roman de la rose* by Guillaume de Lorris and Jean de Meun, in which personified agents such as Reason, Nature, and Fair Welcome discourse with the protagonist-lover. Personification allegory could work with other kinds of allegory: in Prudentius' poem, the personification of *Fides* ("faith") is accompanied by its biblical exemplar (cf. Heb. 11:8). Indeed, Paul's having Hagar and Sarah signify two communities also works as personification allegory; Christian iconography would later personify both *Synagoga* and *Ecclesia* (the Church) as female figures. Prosopopeia is conspicuous in Dante's work, which inherited the tradition of the twelfth-century personification allegories of Bernard Silvestris and Alain de Lille (see below, "Kinds of Dantean Allegory," and Dronke), as well as of the *Roman de la rose.*

Along with the text of the Bible, or "book of Scripture," medieval theologians were inspired by Ps. 18:2–3 and Rom. 1:20 to consider the Creation—insofar as it resulted from divine utterance (cf. Gen. 1:3)—as a "book of creatures," which might be read allegorically to find the vestiges of its divine maker. Buttressed by the text of Wisd. of Sol. 11:21, this method gave rise to bestiaries and lapidaries, their animals and gems decoded as signs of Christ. Classical and Jewish traditions that descried secret meanings in letters and numbers *(gematria)* also informed Christian interpretive practices, especially those of Franciscans like Bonaventura (cf. *Par.* 12.46–105). Such use of the cosmos and its creatures to signify the Creator also informs, if in complex ways, the mystical theology of Pseudo-Dionysius the Areopagite (in reality a Christian Neoplatonist of the fifth to sixth centuries), whether in naming God analogically (for example, "God is a strong right arm" and "Christ the sun of justice") or negatively and by unlikeness ("God is indefinable" or "God is like a lowly worm"). A Pseudo-Dionysian understanding of allegory—highly influential in thirteenth-century discussions of figurative language in the Bible— emerges most forcefully in Dante's work in the *Paradiso* and its partial commentary, the "Letter to Cangrande" (*Epist.* 13.60; cf. *Par.* 4.40–48, 30.76–81; Mazzeo 1958; Minnis et al.). Although the attribution of the *Epistle* to Dante is still disputed, it will here be treated as his.

Although distinctions among various forms of allegorical composition and allegorical interpretation were possible for medieval thinkers, in practice the nomenclature and uses of allegory were freely transposed: "allegory" continues to refer to scriptural exegesis, to fictions using personifications, and to the moralization of classical fables and secular texts, as well as to riddles and emblems—in short, to all the ways in which "one thing is said, another signified." All of the following Latin terms can and do refer to allegory (most are in Paul's letters): *figura, forma, velamen* ("veil"); *mysterium, umbra* ("shadow"); *symbolum, sacramentum, typus, exemplarium, parabola, signum, imago, enigma.* The early-fourteenth-century Old French *Ovide moralisé* uses *sentence, sen, exemple, entendement* ("understanding"), and *allegorie* without distinction to refer to the "truth" *(veritez)* under the lying surface *(mencoignable matire;* cf. *Conv.* 2.1.3). Nor is Dante more consistent: in the *Monarchia,* taking the Sun and the Moon as representing Church and empire is *allegorice* (3.4.2), while explaining the "two swords" that Christ offers his disciples as representing the spiritual and temporal powers

is *typice* (3.9.18); in the *Monarchia, figurare* is used for how the sons of Jacob, Levi and Juda, "figure" Church and empire (3.5.2), but the same word serves for the Ovidian characters Atalanta and Hippomenes and for Lucan's Hercules and Antaeus—pairs who "figure" the struggle for empire (2.7.10–11).

Dante on Allegory

There are two sustained discussions of allegory in Dante's writings. The first appears in the *Convivio* (1304–1307), which contains a prose exposition of three canzoni, the first two of which, Dante claims, have allegorical senses. The love sung in these poems is not, he insists, for a real lady but for Lady Philosophy *(filosofia),* for the love of Wisdom. As a propaedeutic for reading the canzoni (*Conv.* 2.1), Dante sets out an analysis of allegorical *scritture* ("writings" in general), which are to be expounded according to four senses. The first, literal sense "does not go beyond the surface of the letter, as in the fables of the poets." The second, allegorical sense "is hidden beneath the cloak of these fables, and is a truth hidden beneath a beautiful fiction." As an example, Dante offers the tale of Orpheus, whose movement of rocks, trees, and wild beasts with his music signifies the truth that the wise man, with his voice, tames the proud and influences the untutored, whose lack of art or science makes them like stones. Dante avers that although theologians take the second sense differently, he will follow the use of the poets. The third, moral level—concerning ethical instruction discernible in writings *(scritture)*—Dante illustrates with the Transfiguration (Matt. 17.1–8), which Dante suggests means that few should be present at secret events. The fourth sense is anagogic: when a writing is interpreted spiritually and is true (that is, historical) in its literal sense, then by the things signified it also means the supreme things of eternal glory. Dante's example is Ps. 113, "In exitu Israel de Aegypto," referring to the Exodus but also meaning "the exit of the soul from sin."

The second of Dante's discussions of allegory appears in the "Letter to Cangrande" (*Epist.* 13; 1317–1320?). The *Epistle* has three parts: the letter proper, an *accessus* to the *Paradiso,* and a literal exposition of the first fifteen lines of the work. The *accessus,* which is an introduction to a sacred or secular work, calls for identifying six "parts": subject, author, form, aim, title, and branch of philosophy. Somewhat unconventionally, Dante's discussion of allegory (*Epist.* 13.20–25) prefaces his discussion of the subject matter of his work, which he says is twofold: literally, the state of souls after death; allegorically, man's exercise of free will, by which he merits eternal punishment or reward. Dante claims that the meaning of his poem is "polysemous"; that is, that it has several meanings: the first is the literal, and the second is the allegorical or moral. This severalness is exemplified by Ps. 113, "In exitu Israel de Aegypto," which Dante conventionally interprets as signifying the Exodus of Israel on the literal level, followed by the allegorical, moral, and anagogical senses (see Sarolli, who has noted parallels in the thirteenth-century commentary of Hugh of St. Cher). Dante observes that "although these mystical meanings are called by various names, they may one and all be termed allegorical, inasmuch as they are different" *("diversi")* from the literal or historical; for the word "allegory" is so called from the Greek *alleon,* which in Latin is *alienum* (strange) or *diversum* (different; *Epist.* 13.22). As in the *Convivio,* Dante's example potentially has four senses, but the etymological analysis distinguishes only two: one literal (sometimes also historical), the other allegorical or mystical, which includes subspecies (e.g., moral, anagogical). This emphasis on the basic doubleness of allegory—much clearer than in the *Convivio*—seems to resonate with the previous presentation of the subject of the poem as double, a presentation that tends to underscore the moral sense. Indeed, for many critics the proper purpose of medieval allegory was the formation of its reader, and it is striking that the *Epistle* suggests a similar close connection between the moral sense, which portrays examples of moral choices good and bad, and what Dante says later is the practical end and moral purpose of his poem, that of removing souls from a state of sin to a state of grace (*Epist.* 13.39).

Generations of readers have struggled over these two passages, the interpretation of the *Convivio* being rendered more difficult by a substantial textual lacuna, and that of the *Epistle* by disputes over its authenticity. Students from Bruno Nardi to Peter Dronke have objected, too, that the theory of the letter does not seem to account for the practice of the *Commedia.* In both the *Convivio* and the *Epistle* the rhetorical purposes of the text framing the discussions of allegory dictate specific emphases, which should probably temper use of them as guides to Dante's thinking. In the *Con-*

vivio, for example, the charming of stones by Orpheus is exquisitely self-referential, given that Dante's purpose is to illuminate those who, having no leisure for liberal studies, are as insensible as rocks (although several critics, including John Scott and Albert Ascoli, have also called attention to the medieval roles of Orpheus as a philosophical, even "theological," poet often also taken as a figure of Christ). But there is a more fundamental rhetorical imperative: the writer requires a fictional literal sense of the canzoni to blunt attacks based on the assumption that the lady is a real one and thus that the courting of her is a betrayal of Beatrice (Scott 1973). This imperative informs much of the work (note the allegorical battle of the "old thought in opposition to the new" in *Conv.* 2.9–10).

In the *Epistle,* the rhetorical purpose is to offer, in exchange for patronage already granted (and in quest of more), a magnificent gift to Cangrande della Scala, *signore* of Verona, and to unfold for him the text of the *Paradiso.* To this munificent end the author of the letter displays mastery of the principal authoritative discourses of his day—the theological-exegetical, the poetic, and the philosophical. The marking of the two latter discourses is explicit: Dante's description of the "form of treatment" of the *Paradiso* consists of a double set of adjectives, listing the work as fictive, poetic, and metaphorical; as well as digressive, descriptive, and probative—categories associated, respectively, with poetic (but also biblical) and philosophical works (*Epist.* 13.27). Similar emphases recur throughout: Dante begins comparing his curiosity about Cangrande to the Queen of Sheba's about Solomon and to Pallas Athena's about Helicon (Solomon was renowned for sacred wisdom and poetry; Pallas signifies pagan wisdom, Mount Helicon, and the Muses of poetry; see *Epist.* 13.3). Very near the conclusion, he refers to Plato's use of *metaphorismus*—what we now call myths—to express difficult truths (cf. *Par.* 4.49–60), which for Dante is an explicit task of allegory (*Epist.* 13.84; see also 44–52, 57, 60, 61, 79). Although theological exposition predominates, as is consistent with glossing a journey to God, Dante's exposition balances poetic, philosophical, and theological discourses, and it suggests a key role for allegory in all three.

Dante's Allegory and the Critics
The history of criticism of Dante's allegory can seem one of important distinctions pressed too far.

A Although the preference of Romantic critics for symbolism over allegory has been largely superseded, the distinction has persisted in Singleton's view that when the *Commedia* reenacts the Exodus, it should be taken as allegory, whereas its use to signify the creatures (the "book of the world") should be considered symbolism. But Singleton's terminology is arbitrary: the two "books" are closely correlated by medieval writers, as in Bonaventura's *Journey of the Mind to God,* where the soul's path of return to God is illustrated by pairing Jacob's Ladder, a spatial vision of the spiritual cosmos, with the historical narrative of Exodus—a conflation assimilated as such by Dante (*Par.* 22.70, 94).

Nor does it seem useful to sharply distinguish personification from other types of allegory. In the *VN* 25, Dante discusses his use of the personified figure of Love *(Amore)* in his book, which he concedes might lead the reader to think love is a person, and thus a substance, rather than an "accident in a substance." But Dante's digression—sometimes unjustifiably taken as implying disapproval of personification—must be qualified in light of the preceding chapter, where Love shows the protagonist a waking vision of Beatrice and Giovanna: as Giovanna, the lady of Guido Cavalcanti, goes before Beatrice in their procession, so Giovanni (John the Baptist) was the forerunner of the true light (*vera luce, VN* 24.4). Love does not complete the proportion, saying only that Beatrice most resembles himself: but by establishing relations best described as figural, Dante suggests that Love and Beatrice both point to Christ. Taken as a whole, the text suggests that no sharp distinction can be drawn between Love as an accident (as might suit a merely rhetorical allegory) and Love as Beatrice or Christ, in which cases it would be a substance, in the latter case Being itself. In the end, all love participates in Love.

For Pépin, the distinction to make is between allegory as compositional method and allegorical reading, or allegoresis. Fair enough; but we should not let the distinction blind us to the "scenes of reading" that—from Francesca's fatal reading of the Old French *Lancelot* to Statius's famous "misreadings" of Virgilian passages—are among the richest episodes in the *Commedia:* nor, on the other hand, should we leave unread the allegorical dimensions of Dante's Latin treatises. Whitman has pointed out that the complexity of Western allegory owes much to the fact that the same term

describes both the divinely inspired *text* of the Bible, thought of as inexhaustible to human interpretation, and "philosophical" *meanings* read into pagan fables. Like reading and writing, allegory goes both ways; but whether spoken, written, or read, allegory remains a single habit of mind, best summarized with Isidore's formula.

Finally, for a number of influential critics (Singleton, Hollander), the *Letter to Cangrande* seems to ratify the distinction of two kinds of allegory supposed in the *Convivio,* but it decisively rejects the "beautiful fictions" of poetic allegory and adopts a figural "allegory of the theologians" as the key to decoding the *Commedia.* The view that the *Convivio* assumes two distinct kinds of allegory has dominated American Dante criticism but has not gone uncontested. Scott (1990), for example, observes that Dante never clearly distinguishes between two different fourfold systems and never employs the phrase "allegory of theologians" at all. The *Convivio* discussion might well be read as proposing one fourfold system of interpretation for all texts *(scritture),* with subdistinctions accounting for the different status of Scripture. Dante's separation of two kinds of allegory seems much less decisive, for example, than Bernard Silvestris' attempt to distinguish scriptural allegory from fables (*integumenta,* "coverings") with philosophical meanings and may signal the convergence of theological and poetic disciplines under way in the early fourteenth century (see next section).

With respect to the *Epistle,* many readers have felt that Thomas Aquinas' pronouncement (*ST* 1.1.10) that only God could write signification into history and into created things and that human writers could write only a literal sense that contained the whole intention of the author (including any figurative language) should have ruled out a "figurally" composed *Commedia.* But Dante's use in the *Epistle* of the fourfold interpretation of Ps. 113 has also appeared to many as a provocative appropriation by a human author of a technique Aquinas strictly reserved for Scripture. Early commentators, like Guido da Pisa and Dante's son Pietro, ratify the appropriation, if in different ways, and open the way to later assertions by Boccaccio and Petrarch that poetry is the peer of theology.

While for some (Hollander) Dante's use of the fourfold scheme marks his radical rejection of the use of the poets and announces the boldness and uniqueness of his claim to write in imitation of

God's way of writing, for others (Allen, Minnis et al.) Dante's gesture can be adequately situated within a broad, late Scholastic trend that saw techniques of scriptural interpretation and understanding of scriptural authors increasingly assimilated to the practices of an emerging vernacular literature and its newly prestigious authors. But even these critics would not deny to Dante an exceptional, indeed historically unparalleled, role in this process (see Ascoli).

In a famous attempt to elude Aquinas' strictures, Singleton suggested that "the fiction of the *Comedy* is that it is not fiction." But, as Scott has noted, this means only that the poem, like works of fiction in all ages, is convincing in its verisimilitude, and it leaves intact the poem's status as a fiction by a human agent. Is there then any point in debating whether the literal sense of the *Commedia* is "true," that is, historical? Many readers, Padoan and Dronke among them, continue to insist on the literal truth of the poem's vision, although both concede that the vision is necessarily mediated by human imagery and language.

Rather than locating the poem's vivid "realism" in the veracity of its narrated story, it might be useful to consider what meaning the terms "historical" and "fictional" would have had for Dante. Although medieval thinkers routinely distinguished *historiae* (real events) from *argumenta* (possible but fictional events) and *fabulae* (fanciful events), their sense of history did not correspond to a modern, positivist one. In fact, in some ways the medieval concept of the historical as a verbal construct, rhetorical and exemplary, is closer to the postmodern view of history as a construct calibrated by ideology. From this perspective, what is "true" is what fulfills preestablished exemplars, as a man or woman becomes a saint through imitation of Christ. Judson Allen's concept of *assimilatio* (thinking analogically) as the function by which the conceptual, the imaginative, the linguistic, and the "historical" or "real" are correlated rhetorically in an "ethical poetic" remains a promising model for understanding the poem's imaginative workings.

Yet the striking vividness of the poem in representing the afterlife is not without its own strong historical and cultural roots, and this has been a constant theme of critics. The identification of Dante's poem as a uniquely rich mixture of "history" and "allegory," of vital circumstance and theological system, goes back, at least, to F. W. J.

Schelling, and it informs Auerbach's influential documentation of the mixed style of Christian writing as manifesting the central paradox of Christianity: a God who is incarnated to suffer the fate of a criminal. For Auerbach this "creatural" aspect of divinity grounds Dante's ability to bring a secular, realistic vision into a systematic theological edifice (although for Auerbach the realism explodes the edifice, a debatable conclusion). In any case, the poem's prophetic urgency, its intricate contextualization within the history of its own epoch—something unmatched by any other poem of its time—would seem to have inevitable implications for its use of allegory. In the literal sense of an allegorical *Commedia*, where might the "historical" be located?

There is space here for but one hypothesis. To advance a suggestion by Joseph Mazzeo (1960), richly developed through much of Freccero's work, what is historically authentic about the poem's literal sense, the pilgrim's journey, is its autobiographical basis. Thus the *Commedia,* excerpted from the author's preexisting but wholly subjective "book of memory," like the *Vita Nuova,* also has an underlying, historical "literal sense." Prefigured throughout, this sense emerges explicitly in *Par.* 17.19–27, where the pilgrim is informed of his future exile by Cacciaguida. Often, however, the underlying autobiography is obliquely rendered, as in the pilgrim's escape from the devils in *Inf.* 21–22, a passage read by Pirandello—but the reading goes back to Rossetti, in the nineteenth century—as a fictionalized memory of the poet's near capture by the Black Guelfs, who condemned him to death. To cite Freccero's comparison of Dante's poem to Augustine's *Confessions:* "It [the *Commedia*] was meant to be both autobiographical and emblematic, a synthesis of the particular circumstances of an individual's life with paradigms of salvation history drawn from the Bible" (1993). Through allegory, the exile can fashion a poetic voice equal to the task of addressing his fellow creatures and thus intervene in the historical process. From this vantage, allegory has a direct role in making the poem's unique historicity possible.

Kinds of Dantean Allegory
The first book of the *De vulgari eloquentia,* Dante's treatise on language and poetry, defines itself as an allegorical hunt for a "panther" representing the ideal Italian vernacular (1.16.1), while

A the poet's political treatise, the *Monarchia,* has been seen quite conventionally as portraying an allegorical duel of syllogisms on the wrestling mat of discourse (*Mon.* 1.1.5–6, 3.1.3). But of course it is principally the allegory of Dante's major poem, the *Commedia,* that has interested most readers. Few students of the poem would now share the skepticism of Coleridge, Nardi, and Gilson and deny that Dante's *Commedia* is an allegorical poem. Near the end of the *Paradiso,* the pilgrim's voyage from Hell to Paradise is described as one "to the divine from the human, to the eternal from time, and from Florence to a people just and whole" (*Par.* 31.37–39), which is to say, to cite the *Epistle to Cangrande,* a journey from bondage to freedom. This is the basis of Singleton's formula juxtaposing the "journey there and the journey here": the coordination, through allegory, of the pilgrim's voyage with that of every soul through the moral dangers of life. More specifically, the descent into Hell and subsequent emergence on the shores of Purgatory imitates the descent and Resurrection of Christ—indeed, follows his very route. In these ways, the pilgrim's itinerary is part of a narrative allegorical pattern all but universal in the late Middle Ages, one that the Christian collectivity performed through the symbolic action of the Mass and the liturgy, which daily commemorate God's saving action in history. The individual, as we have seen, was called to take up the cross and follow the way of Christ, an invitation duly followed by Dante's pilgrim, whom Cacciaguida invests with his poetic task of retelling his experience for the profit of others, like a knight who takes up the cross.

Beyond this, the extent and specific uses of allegory in the *Commedia* are still much debated. Singleton's claim for a fourfold system of meaning in the *Purgatorio*—announced by the singing of "In exitu Israel de Aegypto" (Ps. 113) by the souls as they move, anagogically, from this life toward salvation—has been vastly influential, though Singleton limits himself to noting Exodus references scattered in the text (the ambitious reader may wish to tease out four senses from Dante's account of Statius, the Roman imitator of Virgil, as the risen Christ, *Purg.* 21.7–9). In this context, a number of readers (Charity, Allen) suggest that the literal sense of the poem is anagogy and that its principal additional level is the "moral," or ethical, given that Dante's otherworld archives the results of moral choices (tropology).

In addition to Dante's late medieval, syncretic use of "applied typology" (Charity), other allegorical species such as personification, metaphor, fable, emblem, enigma, and numerological and alphabetic figures are also indispensable to Dante's allegorical arsenal in the great poem, and they have received, comparatively speaking, much less discussion (but see Dronke). Dante makes vivid use of prosopopeia: Fortune (*Inf.* 7.62–96), historically the most banal instance of the trope, is transformed by Dante into an angelic intelligence controlling the sphere of the mutable. The figure is infused with angelic dynamism without ceasing to be a construct of Virgil's discourse (precisely the status she has in Boethius, where all of Fortune's words are related by Lady Philosophy). In the *Paradiso,* in an intentionally "obscure" passage, Thomas Aquinas unfolds the life of Francis of Assisi as an elaborate allegorical marriage: Poverty is personified as the spouse (recalling the Church as spouse of Christ), while Francis becomes a heavenly orb, the sun—a cosmic sign of Christ—as well as such a perfect embodiment of his virtues (and personification of them) that Francis comes to bear the stigmata of Christ.

Dante's use of "historical" figures to personify abstractions is, in fact, common in the *Commedia.* The cardinal virtues possessed by Cato make his face shine as if in sunlight; Matelda, Cato's counterpart on the other end of Purgatory, has been treated by Singleton as figuring Astraea, Justice personified, and by Armour as a compendium of biblical Wisdom. Even Dante's Virgil is a kind of personification, not so much of Reason, his traditional label, but of his *Aeneid,* its full voice reemerging to medieval readers through Dante's poem (a function linking him to the personified biblical books of the procession in *Purg.* 29). Key messages of the poem are voiced by personifications, such as at *Purg.* 6.72, where Rome, echoing the widowed Jerusalem of Lamentations, calls out to the emperor who neglects her; and in *Par.* 20, where the eagle personifies the collectivity of the Just as it inscribes the sixth heaven with the opening words of the book of Wisdom ("Love justice, you who judge the earth"). In Rome's cry of longing and in the eagle's imperative to rule justly, we hear in a sense the personified voice of the poem, or perhaps of its author, "a man preaching justice" (*Epist.* 12.7).

Inspired perhaps in part by Boethius's allegories of fables in the *Consolatio philosophiae,*

Dante's comparisons between the pilgrim and the personnel of pagan fables also point to key meanings in the poem. One example, recalled by Pépin as the object of Stoic allegoresis, is Phaëthon, the son of Apollo, who fails to control his father's solar chariot and, after setting fire to heaven and earth, is fulminated by Zeus' thunderbolt. In *Inf.* 17 the unruly Phaëthon is the inverse of the pilgrim, whose mount, Geryon, *is* bridled by Virgil; he returns allusively in *Purg.* 4.72, in a description of solar motion, and in *Purg.* 29.118–120, where his chariot is compared to that of the church, which for Dante was disastrously off its rails well before its removal to Avignon in 1309. In fact, the fable anchors the language of discipline and control in the *Purgatorio,* from the ship of state lacking a steersman in 6.94, to the bridles and lures of 14.143–151 (and 19.61–66), and to the bridle of poetic art itself in 33.141, thereby expressing the chief moral action of the whole canticle. In the *Paradiso,* Phaëthon is compared to the pilgrim about to meet his great-great-grandfather, in a comparison that becomes more resonant with the parallel Cacciaguida draws between the pilgrim's exile from Florence and the death of Hippolytus, also flung to his death from a runaway chariot. Tensions between the poet's ambition for vatic status, which the meeting with Cacciaguida is designed to confirm, and his fear of having undertaken a doomed "mad flight" like Ulysses', are, so to speak, funneled through the pagan fable of Phaëthon.

Dante's Allegory of Allegory

Recent accounts of allegory have emphasized the instability of the mode. For Whitman, allegory coordinates both the resemblance and dissemblance between a concept and a more complex reality or verbal expression (e.g., the virtue faith and a real woman or literary character named "Faith"). Consequently the difference established is constantly in tension with the resemblance that empowers the mode to create meaning in the first place. Van Dyke, with a similar analysis, points out that in Dante's poem the distance between concept and expression is never allowed to collapse, with the result that the meaning of the text seems inexhaustible. Of course, that Dante's poem enacts a passage from occulted to revealed meaning, a journey of interpretation, has long been argued in readings by Freccero and Mazzotta, whose views are ultimately informed by Augustine's account in

the *Confessions* of the human drive to return from this life—a place of exile and mere signs—to the fullness of meaning in the presence of God.

If the poem traces a journey of interpretation that is analogous to the act of decoding allegory, it also stages the process by which allegorical meaning comes about. When Dante adopts quasi-technical terms such as "veil" and "doctrine," he alerts us to an inquiry into allegory itself: he writes an allegory of allegory. The scene in which the wayfarers' entry into Dis is blocked (*Inf.* 8–9) suggests both the figural structure of the poem and Dante's self-consciousness regarding its use. Musa and others have pointed out the multiple adumbrations (the harrowing of Hell by Christ and the prophecy of its ultimate defeat, the descent of the spirit through grace, the transcendence of paganism) in the action of the "messenger" who descends to open the Gate of Dis, which the devils closed in Virgil's face. But an important dimension of the action is hermeneutic: the arrival of a messenger who releases the wayfarers from their impasse reenacts the descent of the Spirit at Pentecost (as well as that of Mercury, the gods' messenger, in Statius' *Theb.* 2.1ff.). This advent does not so much make language intelligible as reintegrate it: the messenger's "holy words" (*Inf.* 9.105) guaranteeing entry into Dis complete the "truncated words" (*Inf.* 9.14) of Virgil's speech, to which the pilgrim had given "a meaning . . . worse than they held" (*Inf.* 9.15) and which had created in him the fear that the wayfarers' hope, like that of the damned, might be "cut off" (*Inf.* 9.16)—in short, that the entire journey might be thwarted.

In an important essay, "Medusa: The Letter and the Spirit" (1986) Freccero associated the invitation of *Inf.* 9.63 to look "beneath the veil of the strange verses" with Paul's gloss on the veiled face of Moses, which only Christian truth could uncover (2 Cor. 3:13–16). Thus the messenger's "opening" of the Gate of Dis is comparable to the "opening" of meaning when Scripture is expounded spiritually, that is, allegorically. Such an opening of the way, and the emphasis on integrating speech, point to the "way" itself as one of interpretation. Thus the enigma of the "strange verses" must be read back into the whole text: capitalizing on medieval accounts of metaphor as the transfer of words from native to alien locations, Dante implies that all verses may be "strange" when infused with allegorical meaning ("other-meaning," *alieniloquium*) that literally descends

A from Heaven. And this descent of meaning from above is mirrored by the attention the passage demands from the reader: only when hidden meaning is sought are the poem's moral purpose and allegorical poetics satisfied.

Allegory in All Things

The prominence of allegory in Dante's work is, ultimately, a reflection of the prominence of allegorical thinking in general in the Middle Ages. The centrality of the notion of "book as symbol" to medieval culture was long ago pointed out in Curtius's great omnibus, and the centrality of both allegory and language to Dante's project is implicit in Dante's choice of a book to express how all Creation is held, in archetype, in the mind of God (*Par.* 33.84–87). Inevitably, the book in God's mind is the model for the two allegorical "books" that man was given to read, namely, the book of Scripture and the book of Creation. Inevitably, too, the book in God's mind is mirrored by Dante's poem, the book that records it—each being an allegory of the other. As Freccero (1986, 260) has noted, borrowing a concept of Kenneth Burke's, Dante's poem is at once theological and logological: in the beginning and in the end is the Word.

An implication of the principle that God's utterance, the cosmos itself, has an allegorical structure serves to organize the *Paradiso,* which, given that souls are located both in the Empyrean and in their specific planetary heavens, has a doubly mapped structure throughout (*Par.* 4.28–39). Thus in *Par.* 28.64–78, Beatrice describes the physical cosmos and the spiritual hierarchies of angels in a relation at once specular and chiastic: the nine spheres of the cosmos mirror the nine orders of angels, but by inversion—because the spheres increase in rank extensively as they embrace greater circumferences, but the angelic hierarchies increase in rank intensively as they approach the divine center. The pattern is a plausible model for allegory, in which signifier and signified are related through both similarity and dissimilarity. The human being, in turn, as the union of soul and material body, is the microcosm of the visible and the immaterial universes— indeed the horizon of the two (*Mon.* 3.16). For the Middle Ages, this doubleness of human nature expressed itself in the difference between the inner life of the soul and the exterior life of the body, between *intus* and *foris*—terms also used for the surface and depth of allegory, modeled on the book "written within and without" of Ezek. 2:9. But the soul–body relation can be also figured in the speech-act, as in *Purg.* 25.106–107, where the aerial "bodies" of the souls transmit emotions transparently, as if perfectly intelligible utterances. Is language, then, one might ask, allegorical as well?

At the extreme edge, recent literary criticism, spearheaded by Paul de Man, has proposed the idea that all language, indeed all representation, is allegorical. As Joel Fineman put it, "allegory acquires the status of the trope of tropes, representative of the figurality of all language, of the distance between signifier and signified." Such views, based on the rethinking of consciousness, intention, and language launched by thinkers such as Freud and Saussure, are anticipated by the explanation Dante's pilgrim gives of how his poetry is generated (*Purg.* 24.50–52): the breath of *Amor,* a name for the Holy Spirit, descends to the inner audition and notation of the poet ("dictates within"), and this dictation is then transcribed in the social medium of mutable, natural language ("I go signifying"). Because doubly translated, even the inspired word acquires that displacement between what is said and what is meant that is characteristic of allegory.

If recent literary theory assimilates allegory to irony as the modernist form of "saying one thing and meaning another" (and ancient rhetoric knew this species of allegory, too, calling it *inversio,* the "inversion" of meaning), Dante's view of language and poetry is no less radical in its registration of the homology between allegory and fraud. This possibility is dramatized—or, better, personified— by Geryon, the explicitly "imaginary" and fictional monster of the pilgrim's waking dream (*Inf.* 16.22). Describing the hybrid, multiple-bodied Geryon with a torrent of simile and metaphor, Dante unmasks the guises of fraud as Homer's Telemachus mastered the many shapes of Proteus. But as the famous paired, chiastic statements of 16.124 (the poet's "truth which has the face of falsehood") and 17.10 (Geryon's "face . . . of a just man") make clear, Dante is fully aware of the difficulty the reader faces in distinguishing what is allegorical from what is untrue. So dangerous is allegory that a Renaissance rhetorician would call it Falssemblant, the namesake of the fraudulent monk of the *Roman de la rose.*

In the *Commedia,* Dante archives the repertory of fraudulent semiosis with, among others, the panders, simonists, grafters, and thieves of Male-bolge. The last bolgia offers a quarrelsome pair, the counterfeiter Master Adam and the perjurer Sinon of Troy. As Durling (1981) argues, the structure of container and thing contained helps explain the swollen, deformed shape of Adam, Sinon's perjury, and the counterfeiter's coinage "with three carats of dross": that is, representations of the body (and "body politic"), legal instruments, and money. But "container and thing contained" also describes the structure of allegory. Durling's arguments make clear that the problem of allegory is not merely semiotic in nature but is also historical. Implicit in Dante's assaying of Adam's coinage is not only awareness of the generic danger to the body politic but also disapproval of the use by King Philip the Fair of France (1285–1314) of devalued coinage (*Par.* 19.118–119) and perjured testimony (*Purg.* 20.92–93) as instruments of policy, which marked for Dante a new, dreadful epoch in the misguidance of humankind. Gregory the Great (seventh century), at the beginning of his *Exposition on the Song of Songs,* writes that "for the soul placed far from God, allegory fashions a sort of stage-machine *(machina),* so that it might be raised up to Him" (cf. *Par.* 9.108). But in regard to the French monarchy, Dante's allegorical machinery excoriates Philip and thrusts, by means of prophecy, his compliant pope, Clement V, deep into the pits of Hell among the simonists (*Par.* 30.145–148). Many are the uses of allegory.

Bibliography

Allen, Judson B. *The Ethical Poetic of the Middle Ages.* Toronto: University of Toronto Press, 1982.

Armour, Peter. *The Door of Purgatory: A Study of Multiple Symbolism in Dante's "Purgatorio."* Oxford: Clarendon Press, 1983.

———. "Dante's Matelda." *Italian Studies* 34 (1979), 2–27.

Ascoli, A. R. "Access to Authority: Dante in the *Epistle to Cangrande.*" In *Seminario dantesco internazionale; International Dante Seminar 1.* Edited by Z. Barański. Florence: Le Lettere, 1997, pp. 309–352.

Auerbach, Erich. *Mimesis: The Representation of Reality in Western Literature.* Translated by Willard Trask. Princeton, N.J.: Princeton University Press, 1953.

———. "Figura." In *Six Scenes from the Drama of European Literature.* New York: Meridian Books, 1959, pp. 11–76. [Originally published in his *Neue Dantestudien,* Istanbul, 1944, pp. 11–71.]

Bloomfield, Morton W. (ed.). *Allegory, Myth, and Symbol* [Harvard English Studies, 9]. Cambridge, Mass.: Harvard University Press, 1981.

———. "Allegory and Interpretation." *New Literary History* 3 (1971–1972), 301–317.

Charity, A. C. *Events and Their Afterlife: The Dialectics of Christian Typology in the Bible and Dante.* Cambridge: Cambridge University Press, 1966.

Chydenius, Johan. *The Typological Problem in Dante: A Study in the History of Medieval Ideas.* Helsingfors, 1958.

Courcelle, Pierre. "Les pères de l'église devant les enfers virgiliens." *Annales d'histoire doctrinale et littéraire du moyenâge* 30 (1955), 5–74.

Curtius, Ernst Robert. *European Literature and the Latin Middle Ages.* Translated by Ralph Manheim. Princeton, N.J.: Princeton University Press, 1953.

Dronke, Peter. "Dante and the Medieval Modes of Reading." In *Dante and Medieval Latin Traditions.* Cambridge: Cambridge University Press, 1986, pp. 1–24.

Durling, Robert. "Christ in Hell." In *The Divine Comedy of Dante Alighieri.* Vol. 1: *Inferno.* Edited and translated by Robert M. Durling, introduction and notes by Ronald L. Martinez and Robert M. Durling. New York, Oxford: Oxford University Press, 1996, pp. 580–583.

———. "Deceit and Digestion in the Belly of Hell." In *Allegory and Representation.* Selected Papers from the English Institute, 1979–1980. Edited by Stephen Greenblatt. Baltimore: Johns Hopkins University Press, 1981, pp. 61–93.

Evans, Gillian. *The Language and Logic of the Bible: The Earlier Middle Ages.* Cambridge: Cambridge University Press, 1984.

Fineman, Joel. "The Structure of Allegorical Desire." In *Allegory and Representation.* Selected Papers from the English Institute, 1979–1980. Edited by Stephen Greenblatt. Baltimore: Johns Hopkins University Press, 1981, pp. 26–60.

Fletcher, Angus. *Allegory: The Theory of a Symbolic Mode.* Ithaca, N.Y.: Cornell University Press, 1964.

Freccero, John. *The Poetics of Conversion.* Edited by Rachel Jacoff. Cambridge, Mass.: Harvard University Press, 1986.

———. "Introduction to *Inferno.*" In *Cambridge Companion to Dante.* Edited by Rachel Jacoff. Cambridge: Cambridge University Press, 1993, pp. 172–191.

Green, Richard Hamilton. "Dante's 'Allegory of Poets' and the Medieval Theory of Poetic Fiction." *Comparative Literature* 9 (1957), 118–128.

Hollander, Robert. "Dante *Theologus-Poeta.*" In *Studies in Dante.* Ravenna: Longo, 1980, pp. 39–89.

———. *Allegory in the Commedia.* Princeton, N.J.: Princeton University Press, 1969.

Mazzeo, Joseph Anthony. *Medieval Cultural Tradition in Dante's Comedy.* Ithaca, N.Y.: Cornell University Press, 1960.

———. *Structure and Thought in Dante's Paradiso.* Ithaca, N.Y.: Cornell University Press, 1958.

Minnis, A. J., and A. B. Scott, with David Wallace (eds.). *Medieval Literary Theory and Criticism: The Commentary Tradition, c. 1100–c. 1375.* Oxford: Clarendon Press, 1988.

Mazzotta, Giuseppe. *Dante Poet of the Desert: History and Allegory in the "Divine Comedy."* Princeton, N.J.: Princeton University Press, 1979.

Lieberknecht, Otfried. *Untersuchungen zum Problem der Allegorie in Dantes "Commedia."* Inaugural-Dissertation, Freie Universität Berlin, 1996.

Musa, Mark. *Advent at the Gates: Dante's Comedy.* Bloomington, Ind.: Indiana University Press, 1974.

Padoan, Giorgio. "La mirabile visione di Dante e l'Epistola a Cangrande." In *Il pio Enea, l'empio Ulisse. Tradizione classica e intendimento medievale in Dante.* Ravenna: Longo, 1977, pp. 30–63.

Pépin, Jean. *Dante et la tradition de l'allégorie.* Paris: J. Vrin, 1970.

Sarolli, Gian Roberto. *Prolegomena alla "Divina Commedia."* Florence: Olschki, 1971.

Scott, John A. "Dante's Allegory of the Theologians." In *The Shared Horizon.* Edited by T. O'Neill. Dublin: Irish Academic Press, 1990, pp. 27–40.

———. "Dante's Allegory." *Romance Philology* 26 (1973), 565–591.

Singleton, Charles S. "The Vistas in Retrospect." *MLN* (1965), 55–80.

———. "In Exitu Israel de Aegypto." *Seventy-Eighth Annual Report of the Dante Society of America* (1960), 1–24.

———. *Dante Studies 2. Commedia: Journey to Beatrice.* Cambridge, Mass.: Harvard University Press, 1958.

———. "The Irreducible Dove." *Comparative Literature* 9 (1957), 129–135.

———. *Dante Studies 1. Commedia: Elements of Structure.* Cambridge, Mass.: Harvard University Press, 1954.

———. *An Essay on the "Vita Nuova."* Cambridge, Mass.: Harvard University Press, 1949.

Smalley, Beryl. *The Study of the Bible in the Middle Ages.* Notre Dame, Ind.: Notre Dame University Press, 1964.

Van Dyke, Carolynn. *The Fiction of Truth: Structures of Meaning in Narrative and Dramatic Allegory.* Ithaca, N.Y.: Cornell University Press, 1985.

Whitman, Jon. *Allegory: The Dynamics of an Ancient and Medieval Technique.* Cambridge, Mass.: Harvard University Press, 1987.

Ronald L. Martinez

Alliteration

In modern literary discourse, "alliteration" usually refers to the repetition of initial consonant sounds of words or stressed syllables in a neighboring sequence. The Latin word *alliteratio* was invented by Pontano in the fifteenth century, and thus it is in a sense anachronistic to speak of alliteration in Dante. Ancient and medieval rhetorical manuals employed other terms, however, for similar phenomena, principally *homoeoprophoron* (in Martianus Capella) and *par(h)omoeon* (or *paranomeon*). This latter occurs frequently in a wide variety of Latin treatises of the sort Dante might have known, including the *Rhetorica ad Herrenium* (4.12.18), Donatus's *Ars grammatica* (3.5.6), Isidore of Seville's *Etymologiae* (1.36.14), and Matthew of Vendôme's *Ars versificatoria* (3.10, 16), which specifies that true *paranomeon* repeats the initial consonant or syllable of no more or less than three contiguous words. Indeed, most medieval treatments warn against excessive use of this figure and repeat the same handful of illustrations from Virgil's *Aeneid* (1.294, 3.183, 4.526). Nearly all cite 1.113 of Ennius' *Annales,* often as an example of *paranomeon* run amuck: *O Tite, tute, Tati, tibi tanta, tyranne, tulisti.* In the *De schematibus et tropis,* the Venerable Bede offers scriptural exempla from Ps. 58 and Ps. 118. While not employing any specific term, both Geoffrey of

Vinsauf in the *Poetria nova* (vv. 1925–1930) and, within Dante's circle of intimates, Giovanni del Virgilio in his brief *Ars dictaminis* warn against excessive initial consonant repetition. Some rhetoricians distinguish letter-specific subcategories of alliteration: alliterative "m" constitutes *mytacismus;* "l," *lambdacismus;* and "s," *polysigma.*

It is important to think of a phonetic figure like *paranomeon* in terms of Dante's wider esthetic suppositions about poetry as a craft that relied on the liberal arts of grammar, rhetoric, and music (see *Conv.* 2.11.9 and *DVE* 2.4.2). Good poetry clothed virtuous ideas in appealing language by matching external *bellezza* ("beauty") to internal *bontade* ("goodness") (see *Conv.* 2.11.4, 4.6.3–5, 4.30.2 and *DVE* 2.1). In general, the musical pleasure produced by judicious use of alliteration might package difficult moral concepts so as to make them accessible and even attractive, thus fulfilling rhetoric's classical function of persuasion through eloquence.

According to Tateo, Dante employs alliteration sparingly in the *Rime,* somewhat more frequently in his vernacular prose and in the Latin epistles, and most frequently and imaginatively in the *Commedia.* Boyde concurs that Dante avoided most forms of repetition in his early lyrics but eventually developed a taste for simple alliteration, usually only two words. Tateo notes the prevalence of *mytacismus,* often revolving around the key substantive *amore,* in the love lyrics of the *Vita Nuova*: *si movea d'amoroso tesoro; / ond'io pover dimoro* ("which once came flowing from Love's treasure-store, / and I, now poor. . . ," 7.5.14–15).

There are instances of consonant repetition in Dante that seem plotted for specific effect related to the content of the period or verse. Tateo feels that the *polysigma* of *VN* 3.3 evokes sweet slumber: *mi sopraggiunse uno soave sonno* ("this marvel appeared before me"). The more formal Latin prose of the *Epistles* typically employs *paranomeon* to dramatize important moments and underscore key words (see the opening of *Epist.* 5 and *Epist.* 7.24).

As might be expected, the *Commedia* offers the most imaginative and widespread use of alliteration in Dante's works. Taylor has found 104 instances of alliteration in the *Commedia,* which is a relatively moderate quantity if one considers that the frequency of alliteration per verse in Petrarch is approximately double. These run the gamut from casual phonetic harmony to more strategic devices. We are tempted to discern echoes of a falling body in the stuttering velar occlusives of the end of *Inf.* 5: *e caddi come corpo morto cade* ("and I fell as a dead body falls"). Do not the sibilant/stop combinations of *Inf.* 6.18, *graffia li spirti ed iscoia ed isquatra* ("he claws the spirits, flays and quarters them"), call forth Cerberus' grating violence? The combined *paranomeon/polyptoton* of *Inf.* 13.68, *e li 'nfiammati infiammar sì Augusto* ("and those inflamed inflamed Augustus"), might be said to dramatize the perils of an excessive rhetoric that is in many ways the canto's theme, just as earlier at 13.42 Dante's description of the air forced from a burning green log, *e cigola per vento che va via* ("it . . . sputters as air escapes"), incorporates a rhythmic alliteration that invites us to sense escaping wind. A bowstring's snap resounds in the velar stops of *Inf.* 17.136: *si dileguò come da corda cocca* ("disappeared like the notch from the bowstring"). The taut dentals of *Par.* 28.129 describe a network of perfectly interdependent movement: *verso Dio / tutti tirati sono e tutti tirano* ("all are drawn, and all draw, toward God"). On an even grander conceptual scale, Virgil—Dante's poetic mentor and ersatz mother—consistently evokes the primal, bilabial phoneme (already associated in medieval grammars with an infant's desire for milk and first attempts at speech): *Dimmi, maestro mio, dimmi segnore* ("Tell me, my master, tell me, lord," *Inf.* 4.46) and *de l'Eneïda dico, la qual mamma / fummi, e fummi nutrice, poetando* ("of the *Aeneid,* I mean, which was my mama and was my nurse," *Purg.* 21.97–98).

Bibliography

Boyde, Patrick. *Dante's Style in his Lyric Poetry.* Cambridge: Cambridge University Press, 1971, pp. 237–361.

Tateo, Francesco. "Allitterazione." *Enciclopedia dantesca,* 1:168–169.

Taylor, R. L. *Alliteration in Italian.* New Haven, Conn.: Tuttle, Morehouse, and Taylor, 1900.

Valesio, Paolo. *Strutture dell'allitterazione: Grammatica, retorica, e folklore verbale.* Bologna: Zanichelli, 1968, pp. 32–38.

Gary P. Cestaro

Alpetragius

Spanish-Arab astronomer of Morocco (full name: Abu Ishak Nur al-Din al-Bitrudji; died c. 1204).

Named in *Conv.* 3.2.5 *(Alpetragio)* for the principle that every effect partakes of the nature of its cause.

Bibliography

Nardi, Bruno. "Dante e Alpetragio." In *Saggi di filosofia dantesca.* 2nd ed. Florence: La Nuova Italia, 1967, pp. 139–166.

Christian Moevs

Amphiaraus

Son of Oicles and Hypermnestra; poet, seer, and warrior from Argos; one of the seven kings in the war against Thebes. Initially Amphiaraus *(Anfiarao)* was reluctant to join the expedition because he foresaw his own death, but after his wife Eriphyle betrayed his hiding place to Polynices, he played a leading role in the fighting outside the gates of Thebes. He died when Zeus caused the earth to open up below him, and he plunged, with his horses and chariot, into the underworld. Dante places him among the soothsayers in the fourth bolgia of Malebolge and recalls—following Statius' *Theb.* 7.690–8.126, 225–226—his vivid and tragic end (*Inf.* 20.31–34).

Jo Ann Cavallo

Anastasius II

Beyond the walls of the cemetery reserved for heretics lies the tomb of the arch-heretic Pope Anastasius II (*Anastasio; Inf.* 11.1–9). According to medieval legend, he was entrusted to protect the orthodoxy of the church, but he betrayed that sacred trust when he persuaded the deacon of Thessalonica, Photinus, to deny the divinity of Christ. This heresy was associated with Acacius, Patriarch of Constantinople. Historically, Pope Anastasius II (496–498) was not guilty as charged in the legend: scholars explain Anastasius's reputation as a heretic on the basis of his controversial efforts—actively opposed by a faction of the Roman clergy—to end the schism between Rome and the Eastern Church caused by the followers of Acacius. The *Liber pontificalis* seems to be the source of Dante's error.

Bibliography

Bertolini, Paolo. "Anastasio II." In *Dizionario biografico degli Italiani,* 3. Rome: Istituto della Enciclopedia Italiana, 1961.

Nardi, Bruno. *Nuova "Lectura Dantis": Il canto XI dell'Inferno.* Rome: A. Signorelli, 1951.

Laurie Shepard

Anaxagoras

A pre-Socratic Greek philosopher (500–428 B.C.E.) born at Clazomenae in Ionia, Anaxagoras *(Anassagora)* is consigned to Limbo with the wise pagans (*Inf.* 4.137). Dante contrasts his explanation of the origin of the Galaxy, the Milky Way, in the sphere of the Fixed Stars, with that of the Pythagoreans in *Conv.* 2.14.6, a passage that derives from Aristotle's *Meteorologics* 1.8, 345a, 13-b, 12. Dante's sources include Cicero, *Acad.* 1.12.44, 2.31.100, 2.37.118; and *Tusc. Disp.* 1.43.104, 3.14.30.

Richard Lansing

Anchises

Father of Aeneas by Venus (*Inf.* 1.74; *Purg.* 18.137). Dante compares his encounter with Cacciaguida in the Heaven of Mars with Aeneas' meeting with the shade of his dead father in Hades (*Par.* 15.25; *Aen.* 6.236ff.), placing in Cacciaguida's mouth words that Anchises *(Anchise)* used in greeting Julius Caesar: *O sanguis meus* ("O my blood," 15.28). Aeneas' courage in undertaking his visit to meet his father in the underworld is referred to in *Conv.* 4.26.9, and Anchises' prophecy to Aeneas regarding the greatness of Rome is mentioned in *Mon.* 2.6.9 (cf. *Inf.* 2.13–27). His death is recalled in *Par.* 19.131–132.

Robin Treasure

Andrea dei Mozzi, Bishop

Member of the noble Florentine Mozzi family and bishop of Florence (1287–1295). In September 1295 he was deposed from the bishopric by Boniface VIII and transferred, because of his unseemly living, to the less important see of Vicenza, where he died a sodomite in February 1296. Benvenuto describes him as a simpleton and buffoon who betrayed his naivete ludicrously through trivial illustrations in his preaching. He is placed with the sodomites in the seventh circle of Hell (*Inf.* 15.112).

R. A. Malagi

Andreas Capellanus

Author of *De Amore* (or *De arte honeste amandi*), who has been identified with a chaplain of the same name who served at the court of Marie de Champagne in northern France in the late twelfth century (c. 1180). The work's first two books define the nature of love and articulate the rules of amatory conduct, the second introducing as well a series of judgments concerning cases involving lovers; but the third book strongly attacks the main assumptions of courtly love—namely, that love is the cause of virtue and nobility in the lover—while advancing antifeminist views and recommending love of God over erotic love. Dante never mentions the work, and it is not certain that he ever read it, but several concepts are common to each author. One of the laws of love invoked by Francesca, *Amor ch'a nullo amato amar perdona* ("Love, which pardons no one loved from loving in return," *Inf.* 5.103), seems to translate the phrase *Amor nil posset amori denegare* ("Love can refuse nothing to a lover," *De Amore*, 2.8), and similarities exist between parts of *De Amore* and *Conv.* 4 concerning the idea of nobility. But it is equally possible that these similarities are purely coincidental and stem from common sources.

Paolo Cherchi

Angels

The Paragon of Angels

The comparison of a lady to an angel is a standard trope in thirteenth-century Italian lyric poetry, found in phrases like *angelica figura, angelica sembianza, somiglianza d'angelo formata, angelicata criatura,* and most especially in the manifesto poem of the sweet new style, Guido Guinizzelli's "Al cor gentil," where the evidently blasphemous hyperbole of praise is justified by the lady's resemblance to an angel *(d'angel sembianza).*

In the *Vita Nuova,* Beatrice is reported to have been frequently taken for an angel: *Diceano molti, poi che passata era: "Questa non è femmina, anzi è uno de li bellissimi angeli del cielo"* ("Many would say after she passed: 'This is no woman, this is one of the most beautiful angels of Heaven,'" *VN* 26.2). In the sonnet "Tanto gentile e tanto onesta pare," the angelic quality is described as seeming to "come from Heaven / to earth, to manifest a miracle" *(e par che sia una cosa venuta / da cielo in terra a miracol mostrare).*

Similarly, angels clamor for Beatrice to join them while she is still alive, and they marvel at her beauty when death places her among them (*VN* 19.7, 31.10:16, 33.8:24). In "I' mi son parg letta bella e nova," a girl to whom Beatrice possibly refers in her rebuke to Dante in *Purg.* 31.59 is *un'angioletta* who comes from heaven to give evidence of its beauties. Remembering his beloved after her death, Dante records sketching angels on tablets (*VN* 34.1, 3). Another parallel between ladies and angels is evident in the shift from the first canzone of the *Vita Nuova,* "Donne ch'avete intelletto d'amore," addressed to ladies who have intelligence of love, to the first canzone of the *Convivio,* "Voi che 'ntendendo il terzo ciel movete," appealing to the angels whose understanding turns the Heaven of Venus, the planet of love.

The lady is likened to an angel because she surpasses all other creatures in beauty and perfection. The angels are the summit of creation (*Par.* 29.32). As the psalm (8.6) says, and as Dante reminds us in the *Convivio,* human beings were created just a little lower on the ladder of being than the angels *(poco minore che li angeli).* Yet human nobility, Dante makes bold to assert, might actually outdo that of the angels, because of the "multiplicity of its fruits" (*Conv.* 4.19.6–7). Human reason essentially belongs to angelic nature, the highest order of created things: *la quinta e ultima natura, cioè vera umana o, meglio dicendo, angelica, cioè razionale* ("the last and highest nature, that is the truly human, or better, angelic, that is rational," *Conv.* 3.3.11). Just as some men are so base as to be equivalent to beasts, so some people are so superior that they are virtually no different from angels (*Conv.* 3.7.7; cf. Brunetto Latini, *Et teus homes sont apelés angeliques, Tresor* 2.39.1–2). Thomas Aquinas would admit only that the rational part of men bore a certain resemblance to angels *(quasi ad similitudinem substantiarum separatarum)* and denied that an angel and a human soul were of the same species (*In decem libros Ethicorum* 7. lect. 1.1299; *ST* 1.75.7).

Angelic Nature

Much of the scholarly debate over Dante's angelology has been divided between those who want to see it as heterodox and Averroistic (as Bruno Nardi maintained) and others, such as Giovanni Busnelli and Attilio Mellone, who endeavor to reconcile it with the teaching of Thomas Aquinas.

Angel ferrying souls into Purgatory. Invenzioni di Giovanni Flaxman sulla Divina commedia, *illustrated by John Flaxman and Beniamino del Vecchio, Rome, 1826. Giamatti Collection: Courtesy of the Mount Holyoke College Archives and Special Collections.*

Angels differ essentially from human beings in that they are separated substances—separated, that is, from matter (*Conv.* 3.7.5). This separated state makes them purer and better receptors of intellectual substance. They are "intelligences" who feed on intellectual fare, namely, truth, and what Dante repeatedly calls the "bread of angels," to which they have direct access but to which the philosophically inclined may also aspire (*Conv.* 1.1.7; *Par.* 2.11). Whereas people come to know things only by abstracting from phantasms formed from sensory data, angels understand directly and immediately. In a vexed passage in the *Monarchia,* complicated by manuscript variants, Dante seems to have exceeded Aquinas' limits for separated substances, by claiming in *Mon.* 1.3.7 that their existence *(esse)* is nothing other than their understanding *(intelligere)*—a passage condemned by Guido Vernani in his 1329 attack on the *Monarchia,* since, as Aquinas teaches, only God is identical with his understanding. Dante's remark in the *Convivio* that angels' being is identical with their

operation is similarly open to a Thomistic critique (*Conv.* 2.4.4; cf. *ST* 1.54.2).

Another of Dante's startling assertions about the angels is that they are free not only from all matter but also from all potentiality, so that they are *puro atto* ("pure act," *Par.* 29.33). Aquinas repeatedly declares that *solus deus est actus purus* ("only God is pure act," *ST* 1.54.1). That an angel is pure act *(quod angelus est actio pura)* was a common "error" of thirteenth-century followers of Averroës (Mandonnet, 10). For Dante, the sempiternity (eternity since their creation) of the angels is guaranteed by their uninterrupted act of understanding—*sine interpolatione (Mon.* 1.3.7). According to Beatrice's exposition in *Par.* 29, the angels have never once turned away from the sight of God's face, since the moment it first gladdened them; thus their vision is "never interrupted by a new object" (*non hanno vedere interciso / da novo obietto, Par.* 29.79–80), which would seem to echo Thomas's statement that the angelic operation of understanding is continuous *et non intercisa*

(*Summa contra Gentiles* 2.97). Yet it also resembles the condemned proposition that angels never understand any new thing (*Quod angelus nichil intelligit de novo;* see Mellone 1974, 206), while Beatrice also energetically affirms, against prevailing opinion, that this continuous vision means that the angels have no memory (*Par.* 29.81; cf. *ST* 1.54.5r).

Light Metaphysics

Dante compares the angels' mode of understanding with the diffusion and refraction of light. Without the coarseness of matter, angels are almost perfectly diaphanous (*Conv.* 3.7.5). He explains that the First Good "paints" its power onto things by means, as it were, of a direct ray (*Conv.* 3.14.3–4). This divine light, elsewhere called the "Sun of the angels" (*Par.* 10.53), shines directly into the intelligences, without any intermediate filters, according to their own capacity to receive it, just as the sun also renders more or less diaphanous objects more or less luminous (*Conv.* 3.7.3–4; cf. Pseudo-Dionysius, *Divine Names* 4.1.693B; *Celestial Hierarchy* 13.3.301A–C). The simile of light is the standard Neoplatonic analogy used to explain the derivation of the One from the Many, the way a perfectly simple goodness flows out uniformly from the First Good but is received variously by different things (*Book of Causes* 20.157; *Liber de intelligentiis* 7). The quantity of light that each can reflect back, as Albert the Great says in his treatise on the intellect, is a measure of its nobility (*De intellectu et intelligibili* 1. tr. 3.2; *Liber de intelligentiis* 8.2). Angels are comparable to mirrors in the way they are superlatively transparent, posing no barrier to illumination but rather reflecting and multiplying the "reverberated splendor" so brilliantly that they become painful to the eye (*vincono l'armonia de l'occhio, Conv.* 3.7.3–4, 3.14.2–4; cf. Albert, *De intellectu et intelligibili* 1. tr. 3.2: *vincunt harmoniam oculi*). In the *Paradiso,* Beatrice also calls angels *tanti speculi* ("so many mirrors") in which Eternal Goodness is splintered while "remaining One in itself as before" (*uno manendo in sé come davanti, Par.* 29. 143–145); *Epist.* 13.21–23; *Celestial Hierarchy* 3.2.165A: *perlucida specula*). Because the human soul, as regards its capacity to reason, is also independent (literally, "denuded") of matter, like an angel it too can be divinely enlightened (*Conv.* 3.2.14; cf. 3.7.5, 3.14.9).

Finally, Dante's application of the principles of optics—the science of how light is reflected, which he calls *arte della perspectiva* (*Conv.* 2.3.6)—to the nature of angels as intermediaries and messengers of divine illumination informs an extended comparison in the *Purgatorio* of the approach of a dazzling angel to the refraction of a ray of light (*Purg.* 15.16–24).

Angelic Speech

Lack of material impediments enables angels to apprehend spontaneously not only the mind of God but also the minds of fellow angels. For this reason, as Dante explains in the beginning of his unfinished treatise on language, they have no need of speech or other manner of signifying *Cum igitur angeli ad pandendas gloriosas eorum conceptiones habeant promptissimam atque ineffabilem sufficientiam intellectus, qua vel alter alteri totaliter innotescit per se, vel saltim per illud fulgentissimum speculum, in quo cuncti representantur pulcerrimi atque avidissimi speculantur, nullo signo locutionis indiguisse videntur* ("Since the angels have a swift and ineffable capacity for expressing their glorious conceptions which is completely self-sufficient, whereby one makes itself known to the other either directly or by means of that resplendent mirror in which all are reflected in their beauty and in which all most eagerly gaze, they do not seem to have needed any speech signs," *DVE* 1.2.2–3). Mengaldo finds analogous discussions of angelic language in Vincent of Beauvais and William of Auxerre. Human beings, unlike angels, need sensible signs, because of the "grossness and opacity" of their mortal bodies, which block the transmission of spiritual understanding. Thomas Aquinas adduces similar arguments yet concludes on the contrary that angels do have a "tongue" of their own (*DVE* 1.3.1; *ST* 1.107.1 ad 1; *De veritate* 9.4).

Movers of the Spheres

Dante's doctrine of the angels comes from the amalgamation of traditions typified by thirteenth-century Scholastic angelology, whose two essential threads are the Judeo-Christian angels, or messengers, who intercede between God and man in the Bible; and Aristotle's "intelligences" responsible for the apparent motions of astronomical entities, in turn derived from Plato's Ideas. In his harmonization of these divergent traditions in the *Convivio,* Dante notes that the separated

PARADISO CANTO XXXI.

The ranks of the angels hovering above the White Rose. La comedia di Dante Aligieri, *with commentary by Alessandro Vellutello, published by Francesco Marcolini, Venice, 1544. Giamatti Collection: Courtesy of the Mount Holyoke College Archives and Special Collections.*

substances were recognized by Aristotle as mover-intelligences, by Plato as Ideas, and by less philosophically sophisticated pagans as gods and goddesses (*Conv.* 2.4.2–8; *Par.* 28.121). The identification of angels with gods and goddesses, which Edward Moore called "remarkable," is the basis of Renucci's thesis of Dante's accommodation of pagan religion to the Christian worldview, elaborated recently by Bemrose.

In *Metaphysics* 12, Aristotle ascribed to each sphere a wholly immaterial unmoved mover, or intelligence, that caused the heaven to move by being desired by it (see Weisheipl). It was widely understood in the Middle Ages that Aristotle's mover-intelligences had transformed Plato's Ideas, the separated and eternal species of all things, into the initiators of celestial motion (*Metaphysics* 12.8.1080; *ST* 1.115.3 ad 2; Thomas, *De substantiis separatis* 2.8). The resultant movements of stars and planets had a direct effect on the generation and corruption of elemental substances below the moon. The immutable realm was thus causally connected to the sensible world of flux and change through the medium of sphere-moving intelligences. For Plato, the separated substances

were the species or models of sensible things. For Aristotle, they were species of an altogether superior order, which nonetheless acted upon lower bodies, affecting their variety, mutations, and reproduction and bringing about their degradation. Because this plethora of unmoved-movers considered as the final causes of particular celestial movements seemed to contradict Aristotle's other tenet of a single Prime Mover, it fell to Neoplatonists to derive these multiple intelligences from the first in a series of "emanations," each the cause of subsequent, inferior beings. Arab philosophers who were heavily influenced by Neoplatonism, like Alfarabi and Avicenna, were the first to identify the Aristotelian intelligences with the angel-messengers of revealed religion. With the notable exception of Albertus Magnus, most Scholastic thinkers assumed that Aristotle's intelligences were in fact angels (Bemrose, 45–55).

There is no doubt that Dante emphatically subscribed to the notion of angels as movers of the astronomical spheres (*Conv.* 2.2.7, 2.4.2). As the intelligences responsible for the apparent motions of the stars and planets, angels explain celestial mechanics. They move the spheres, not by means of physical contact but by pure understanding, *solo intendendo*—by spiritual contact with their virtue, *tatto di vertù* (*Conv.* 2.5.18; cf. *Summa contra Gentiles* 2.92: *per intellectum movent; 2.56 tactus . . . virtutis*). In the *Convivio*, Dante assumes that there must be at least three movers of the Heaven of Venus in order to account for the three distinct proper movements discernible in the behavior of that planet. In that text, angels whose sole operation is to move the spheres seem to belong to a special class devoted to the active life, while the vast majority of these creatures are wholly engaged in pure contemplation (*Conv.* 2.4.9–12). In an effort to conform better to Aristotle, however, Dante goes on to make the apparently contradictory claim that even the sphere-movers contemplate, but that from their speculation results the circulation of Heaven (*Conv.* 2.4.13). Dante's assignment of angels from every hierarchy to the task of moving a planetary sphere is essentially unique. (Aquinas, for example, supposed such movers came only from the hierarchy called Virtues.) Dante may be reflecting a Thomistic distinction between ministers and contemplators when he claims that we receive gifts from the bottom hierarchy of angels because it is closest to us (*Conv.* 2.5.8).

In the *Paradiso,* the causal link between planets and angels is even stronger, as Beatrice denies (against Jerome) that the one could have preceded the other in the order of Creation, because the "perfection" of the "movers" is to turn the material heavens (*Par.* 29.44–45). Aquinas explicitly states that the moving of the spheres may be considered a ministry of angels, but it by no means constitutes the fulfillment of their nature (*De potentia Dei* 3.19 ad 3). Beatrice further seems to suggest that the whole array of angelic hosts, with the exception of those who sinned, are involved in the "art" of celestial circulation (*Par.* 29.52–54), although some scholars strenuously insist that this circling refers to their activity of contemplation, not sphere moving (Mellone 1974).

Angelic Influence

In the *Convivio* Dante characterizes the operation of the mover-angels as belonging to the active life, the government of the world, which is effected through the rotation of the heavens (*Conv.* 2.4.8). Natural laws prevail in the sublunar world, where God governs through these intermediaries, in contrast to the Empyrean, *dove Dio sanza mezzo governa* ("where God governs without intermediary") and natural laws are irrelevant (*Par.* 30.122–123).

Light is the principle of causality in the universe, making sensible bodies come into being and thrive, as the Neoplatonists taught (*Liber de intelligentiis* 6–7; *Divine Names* 4.4.697C). For Dante, the constant change and flux of bodily things on Earth is produced by the distribution of light effected by the heavens and their movers (*Inf.* 7.74–76). A ray of simple light from the Empyrean Heaven is transmitted downward from the Primum Mobile to the Heaven of the Fixed Stars, where it is first differentiated into a multitude of lights, and then further modified as it descends through each of the planetary spheres, which in turn pass their diverse characteristics onto sublunar things (*Par.* 2.118–120; cf. *Conv.* 2.6.9).

These astrological effects are all guided and caused, however, by the "blessed movers" *(beati motor),* who are themselves of different degrees of excellence, the way the human soul is differently distributed throughout the parts of the body (*Par.* 2.133–138). Dante's comparison of the angel-movers to the human soul comes perilously close to one of Bishop Tempier's condemned propositions in 1277 (No. 219) which holds that the celestial orbs are the organs of the intelligences. The

astronomical heavens are said to "receive from above and fashion below" (*di sù prendono e di sotto fanno, Par.* 2.123), just as the orders of angels who move them "all gaze upward and bind what is below, so that all are drawn, and all draw, toward God" (*Questi ordini di sù tutti s'ammirano, / e di giù vincon sì, che verso Dio / tutti tirati sono e tutti tirano, Par.* 28.126–129; cf. 1. *Liber de intelligentiis* 35).

Dante's emphasis on the angels' role as intermediary causes in the generation of elemental things is not easy to reconcile with Thomas Aquinas' condemnations of so-called mediated creation. In the *Convivio,* clearly echoing Neoplatonic emanationist philosophy, Dante asserts that every intellect knows what is above it—that is, God—as its cause and what is below it as its effect (cf. *Liber de intelligentiis* 35.2; *Book of Causes* 8–9). The mover-angels are said to be, moreover, *spezialissime cagioni* of the human form, since these angelic minds fabricate sublunar things by turning the heavens (*Conv.* 3.6.4–6). Aquinas, on the other hand, said that it was against the faith to assert that angels or the celestial bodies were intermediaries in the production of inferior forms (*De potentia* 3.4; *De veritate* 5.9, 23.5; *Summa contra Gentiles* 2.42, 2.98).

In the *Paradiso,* God's direct creative role is limited to the production of angels, the astronomical heavens, and prime matter—as well as the inspiration of each new human soul—all of which are thereby eternal (*Par.* 7.130–132, 142–144). Things made up of the four elements, from rocks to human bodies, as well as the souls of animals and plants, come to be and pass away through the "informing power" *(virtù informante)* that angels exert through the shifting rays of the stars (*Par.* 7.133–141; cf. *ST* 1.91.2: *angeli non possunt transmutare corpora ad formam aliquam:* "angels cannot change bodies into other forms"). Dante's explanation that the mortality or immortality of created things depends on whether they were created through the informing power of the angels via the heavens or directly by God *sanza mezzo* ("without intermediary") bears the traces of Avicenna's teaching that nothing variable or instable derives immediately from God (*Par.* 7.67–72).

Adopting the commonplace Aristotelian image of nature as the imprint of a seal on wax (*De anima* 2.4.416a–b), Dante identifies the angelic intelligences that cause the celestial wheels to move in a particular way not with the artisan himself but with the "art of the hammer" (*l'arte del martello, Par.* 2.126–129; cf. Albert, *De caelo* 2. tr. 3.14: *quo accipit malleus formam artificis ferrarii ad inducendum in ferrum*). The defects evident in the material world result not from these flawless ministers but rather from the changing readiness of material things to be informed by them (*Par.* 8.109–110). Nature works, Dante says, "like the artist who along with the habit of art has a hand that trembles" (*similemente operando a l'artista / ch'a l'abito de l'arte ha man che trema, Par.* 13.77–78). In this metaphor, angels correspond to the artist's technical competence, his art, and the astronomical bodies correspond to his trembling hand; the lamentable shortcomings of earthly reality are the result (cf. Albert, in *Metaphysica* 11 tr. 2. 13: *sicut manus artificis recipit formam artis, et sicut manus movetur per formam artis, ita movetur caelum per formam intellectus*). Another proposition condemned by Bishop Tempier (No. 61) epitomizes the influence of angels in Dante's cosmology: "that Intelligences move heavenly bodies by the power of their will and that they imprint forms into matter via the heavenly bodies, which are in this respect their instruments."

Number and Hierarchy

In the *Convivio,* Dante notes that even without benefit of revelation all the philosophers agreed that there are at least as many angels as there are celestial movements. Aristotle thought they were either forty-seven or fifty-five, depending on which astronomical model one accepted. Yet the Catholic Church teaches that they are in fact virtually innumerable or, as Beatrice puts it in the *Paradiso,* that their definite number is hidden (*determinato numero si cela, Par.* 29.135; *Conv.* 2.5.5; *Celestial Hierarchy* 14.321A; Thomas, *De substantiis separatis* 2.12; *Summa contra Gentiles* 2.68). In an argument that Nardi called far-fetched, Dante says that if we can in our own minds think of the possibility of almost innumerable orders of existence superior to us, then the divine intellect, which is the cause of our own and disproportionately superior to it, must have indeed created at least that many (*Conv.* 2.4.14; Nardi 1960, 61–62).

The distribution of the kinds of angels mentioned in various places in Scripture into nine hierarchies, or three triads, derives from the early-sixth-century Neoplatonic text *The Celestial Hierarchy,* carrying the pseudonymous authority of Dionysius the Areopagite, a disciple of Paul. The very term "hierarchy" is of Dionysian coinage; and it is from the same source that Dante derives his axiom that the order among things is what makes them similar to God (*Par.* 1.103–105; *Celestial Hierarchy* 3.1–2.164D–165A).

Dante is original in linking angelic hierarchies to Aristotle's mover-intelligences in *Conv.* 2.5.13, so that each astronomical sphere is moved by members of a different rank—a correlation that is maintained, despite an altering of their order, in *Par.* 28. Taking as an authority the words of Ps. 18, "the heavens narrate the glory of God," Dante says that it is "reasonable to believe" that the lowest order, the Angels, governs the movement of the lowly moon; the Archangels, Mercury; and the Thrones, Venus. Using Bonaventure's further distinction of the three angelic triads according to their triple contemplation of each person of the Trinity, he ingeniously connects the love of the Holy Spirit—special object of contemplation for the lowest angelic hierarchy—with the love that the ancients perceived to be caused by the Heaven of Venus (*Conv.* 2.5.12–14; Bonaventure, *In Hexaëmeron* 21.20; cf. Vincent of Beauvais, *Speculum historiale* 1.12; Pseudo–Hugh of St. Victor, *Summa Sententiarium* 2.5; Peter Lombard, *Sententiae* 2.9.1).

In assigning angels to spheres, Dante follows a hierarchical ordering different from that of Dionysius, which he may have found in Brunetto Latini, as follows: Angels, Archangels, Thrones, Dominations, Virtues, Principalities, Powers, Cherubim, Seraphim (*Conv.* 2.5.6; Latini, *Tresor* 1.12–13). In the *Paradiso,* he conspicuously changes his mind about this angelological point, shifting his allegiance to the authority of Dionysius and relating that Gregory the Great, who had also set forth a divergent arrangement, chuckled at his mistake when he came to Heaven. In Beatrice's exposition, the hierarchies are named in descending order as: Seraphim, Cherubim, Thrones, Dominations, Virtues, Powers, Principalities, Archangels, Angels (*Par.* 28.98–139; *Celestial Hierarchy* 6.2.201A; Gregory, 32.48). In contrast with Dante, medieval theologians generally diminished the importance of the discrepancy between Dionysius and Gregory (Lombard, *Sententiae* 2.9.1–2; Bonaventure, *In Hexaëmeron* 21.19–33; Thomas, *Summa contra Gentiles* 3.80; *ST* 1.108.1).

In *Par.* 8.34, when Charles Martel says that he and the other souls appearing in the Heaven of Venus are moved by the Principalities, he calls attention to the changed hierarchy by citing the first line of "Voi che 'ntendendo il terzo ciel movete," which in the *Convivio* was addressed specifically to the Thrones (*Par.* 8.34–37). The Thrones are nonetheless mentioned in the context of Venus by another of its representatives, Cunizza, who calls them mirrors reflecting God's judgment (*Par.* 9.61). As to the different activities of specific ranks, the Seraphim are said to "be most in God" (*Par.* 4.28); and Saint Francis, said to be "all Seraphic in love" *(tutto serafico in ardore)*, is distinguished from Saint Dominic, who, "in wisdom, was a splendor of Cherubic light" (*di cherubica luce uno splendore, Par.* 11.37, 39). The Seraphim were traditionally associated with the ardor of love; the Cherubim, with the fullness of knowledge (*ST* 1.63.7 ad 1; *Celestial Hierarchy* 8.1). Yet each of the zillions of individual angels differs from every other one in its own particular capability and art, as Dante says: *ciascun distinto di fulgore e d'arte* ("each one distinct in radiance and art," *Par.* 31.132).

The corrected order of the nine hierarchies is presented in the visual emptiness of the Primum Mobile, where the angels appear as nested wheels of sparks, orbiting an intense point of light, and spinning more rapidly the closer they are to it. Pseudo-Dionysius represented the prime mover as the center of an orb or circle, and the angels as flaming wheels, claiming that the name of the Seraphim evokes "their ever moving around things divine" (*Divine Names* 2.5.644A; *Celestial Hierarchy* 8.1.205C, 8.4.212A, 15.2.328C, 15.9.337D). Some have seen Dionysius' three movements of contemplation (circular, straight, and spiral) reproduced in Dante's fiery wheels, which transmit "Hosannas" from one chorus to the next and manifest their power on the lower world through the celestial spheres (*Divine Names* 4.8.704D; Thomas, *De substantiis separatis* 18.108; *ST* 2.2.180.6; Busnelli 1910, 101). Their song of "Osanna" is mentioned frequently in connection with the angels (*Par.* 28.94,118; *Purg.* 11.10–11; *VN* 23.7, canz., 61).

Dante's depiction of the nine angelic hierarchies greatly resembles a schematic illustration of the nine astronomical heavens derived from the planetary hypothesis of Alpetragius. The essential difference, as Dante remarks, is that in the visible universe the orbits are more sluggish the closer they are to Earth at the center. By having the smallest circle in the one system (the hierarchy of the Seraphim, which "loves most and knows most": *più ama e che più sape, Par.* 28.72) move the largest body in the universe (the Primum Mobile), Dante thus effects an inverse correlation between the celestial spheres and their movers, thereby synthesizing Dionysius' hierarchies with a simplified Aristotelian cosmology (*Par.* 28.70–78).

Ministers and Messengers

As we pass into the Empyrean Heaven the angels appear as ministers to the blessed rather than as engines of the material world. Heaven is defined as the "region of the angels" (*Par.* 20.102); God, as "lord of the angels" (*VN* 7.1), who are in turn called "celestial family members" (*Purg.* 15.28). The ecstatic festival of the angels in paradise is referred to as a perpetual wedding party, full of games and song (*Purg.* 32.72; *Par.* 31.133–135; cf. Daniélou, 52–53). The first vision of the supernatural Heaven is that of a river of light banked by a marvelous springtime of flowers and moving sparks and rubies (*Par.* 30.64–66), reminiscent of Saint Bernard's description of the Cherubim, who "pour forth a stream of knowledge to the citizens of heaven" (*On Consideration* 5.5). After drinking from this luminous flood, the pilgrim sees the great celebration of "both the courts of Heaven" more clearly (*Par.* 30.94–96). The saints become one huge flower, the celestial rose, and the angels are a multitude of bees, dipping in and out of it as they move incessantly between God and the happy human souls (*Par.* 30.94, 31.7). Their faces are living flame, their wings of gold, and the rest of them whiter than snow (31.13–15). Anselm compared the thousands of winged ministers shuttling between Heaven and Hell to bees between flowers and the hive. This up-and-down movement is also found in Jacob's vision of the ladder covered with angels descending and ascending (*Par.* 22.70–72). Among the swarm of angels centered on Mary at the lip of the celestial rose, the Archangel Gabriel, elsewhere called "angelic love," stands out, inflamed with love, engaged in his "game" of looking into her eyes (*Par.* 23.103, 31.130–132, 32.103–105; cf. *Conv.* 2.5.4; *Purg.* 10.34; *Par.* 14.34). No other angels taking an active role in the narrative are named, although

Beatrice alludes to Michael and Raphael, together with Gabriel, as examples of the church's iconographic "condescension" to human understanding (*Par.* 4.46–48).

Outside of Heaven, Beatrice herself is repeatedly represented in the company of angels. In Dante's dream presaging her death in the *Vita Nuova,* a multitude of angels sing "Hosanna" as they transport on high a little white cloud (*VN* 23.7, canz., 61). When she returns in the Garden of Eden in *Purg.* 30, Beatrice is greeted by a hundred "ministers and messengers of eternal life" rising off the processional chariot, covering her with a cloud of flowers, and answering her speech with Ps. 30: *"In te, Domine, speravi"* (*Purg.* 30.16, 22, 82).

In Purgatory, angels serve a variety of ministerial functions. The celestial helmsman of the boat bringing newly saved souls to the shore of the mountain is an angel (*Purg.* 2.27–29). Angels in green garments with blunted swords descend into the Valley of the Princes at sunset to scare off the serpent (*Purg.* 8.25, 106). An angel guards the door to Purgatory proper (*Purg.* 4.129, 9.104), and another (21.23) etches the seven "P"s onto the pilgrim's forehead, which seven more angels, one for each cornice, will erase (*Purg.* 12.79, 15.22, 16.144, 19.46, 22.1–2, 27.6). More often than not these are referred to as *angel di Dio,* recalling the biblical *angelus Domini* (*Purg.* 2.29, 4.129, 5.104, 9.104, 27.6).

The angels in Purgatory have direct parallels with the black angels, or devils, in Hell. The angelic helmsman steering souls to shore (*galeotto* and *celestial nocchier*) recalls the infernal boatmen, Phlegyas *(galeotto)* and Charon *(nocchier)* (*Purg.* 2.27, 43; *Inf.* 3.98, 8.17.80). The white "officials" appearing in the second realm are in opposition with the *angeli neri,* who administer the pains of Hell (*Purg.* 2.30; *Inf.* 23.131)—both of whom are sometimes called birds (*Purg.* 2.38; *Inf.* 23.96, 34.47). The descent of the angels into the Valley of the Princes before the gates of Purgatory proper is symmetrical with the descent of the celestial messenger *(messo celeste)* before the Gate of Dis in the *Inferno* (*Purg.* 8.25, 106; *Inf.* 9.85). The struggle between an angel and a devil for the soul of Buonconte da Montefeltro echoes the dispute between St. Francis and a black cherub for the soul of his damned father, Guido (*Purg.* 5.104; *Inf.* 27.113). Satan himself is a parody of the high Seraph he once was, now having three heads of three different colors and wings like a bat's (*Inf.* 34.28ff.).

The Fall

Dante says that the fall of Lucifer and his cohorts occurred "as soon as they were created" (*Conv.* 2.5.12) and "before you could count to twenty" (*Par.* 29.50). There has been some critical disagreement over which of the theories about the time of the angels' fall Dante thereby endorses: whether they sinned instantly or after a brief delay (Mellone 1974; Cornish). He describes their sin of *superbia* ("haughtiness") as the refusal to wait for light, which caused them to fall like unripe fruit (*Par.* 19.48). The angels who fell—perhaps a tenth of their total number—came from the entire spectrum of angelic ranks, not simply the lowest, and human souls were created to make up for their loss (*Conv.* 2.5.12).

In the *Commedia,* Dante also subscribes to an esoteric view of the existence of so-called neutral angels—derived from legend rather than doctrine—who earn his most acrid contempt in a vestibule just inside the Gate of Hell. In the primordial choice between good and evil, these neither rebelled against nor turned toward God but remained off by themselves, undecided (*Inf.* 3.8; Mellone, "Angelo"; Freccero).

Bibliography

Bemrose, Stephen. Dante's *Angelic Intellgences: Their Importance in the Cosmos and in Pre-Christian Religion.* Rome: Bulzoni, 1983

Boyde, Patrick. "The Angels." In *Dante Philomythes and Philosopher.* Cambridge: Cambridge University Press, 1981.

Busnelli, Giovanni. *Il concetto e l'ordine del paradiso dantesco.* Collezione di Opuscoli Danteschi. *Cosmogonia e antropogenesi secondo Dante Alighieri e le sue fonti.* Rome: Civiltà Cattolica, 1922.

———. Vol. 105. Città del Castello: S. Lapi, 1911.

Collins, James D. *The Thomistic Philosophy of the Angels.* Washington, D.C.: Catholic University of America, 1947.

Cornish, Alison. "Planets and Angels in *Paradiso* 29: The First Moment." *Dante Studies* 108 (1990), 1–28.

Daniélou, Jean. *The Angels and Their Mission.* Translated by David Heimann. Westminster, Md.: Christian Classics, 1976.

Freccero, John. "The Neutral Angels." In *Dante and the Poetics of Conversion*. Cambridge, Mass: Harvard University Press, 1986.

Mandonnet, Pierre. *Siger de Brabant et l'averroïsme latin au XIIIe siècle*. Part 2. 1908. Reprint, Geneva: Slatkine Reprints, 1976.

Matter, Ann. "Angel/Angelology." *Dictionary of the Middle Ages*, 1:249–250.

Mellone, Attilio. "Angelo." *Enciclopedia dantesca,* 1:268–271; "Dottrina della creazione," 2:251–253; "Gerarchia angelica," 3:122–124.

———. "Il canto XXIX del 'Paradiso'; (una lezione di angelologia)." *Nuove letture dantesche* VII (1974), 194–213.

Mengaldo, Pier Vincenzo. "Lingua degli Angeli," *Enciclopedia dantesca,* 1:271–272.

Moore, Edward. "Dante's Theory of Creation." *Studies in Dante*. Fourth Series. 1917. Reprint, New York: Haskell House, 1968.

———. "The Platonic Theory of Ideas." *Studies in Dante*. First Series. 1896. Reprint, New York: Haskell House, 1968.

Nardi, Bruno. "Il canto XXIX." *Convivium* 24 (1956), 294–302.

———. *Dal Convivio alla Commedia*. Rome: Istituto storico italiano per il Medio Evo, 1992, pp. 43–46.

Proto, Enrico. "L'ordinamento degli angeli nel *Co vivio* e nella *Commedia*." In *Studii dedicati a F. Torraca*. Naples: F. Perrella, 1912, pp. 17–28.

Renucci, Paul. *Dante disciple et juge du monde greco-latin*. Clermont-Ferrand: G. de Bussac, 1954.

Ricci, Pier Giorgio. "Un difficile e importante passo della 'Monarchia.'" *Studi danteschi* 42 (1965), 361–368.

Rorem, Paul. *Pseudo-Dionysius: A Commentary on the Texts and an Introduction to Their Influence*. Oxford: Oxford University Press, 1993.

Vacant, A., et al. "Anges." *Dictionnaire de Théologie Catholique*. Vol. 1, 1:1190–1271.

Vasoli, Cesare. "Intelligenza." *Enciclopedia dantesca,* 3:473–474.

Weisheipl, James A. "The Celestial Movers in Medieval Physics." *Thomist* 24 (1961), 286–326.

Zanini, Carlo. *Gli angeli nella "Divina Commedia."* Milan: L. F. Cogliati, 1908.

Alison Cornish

Angevin Dynasty

The term applied primarily to the cadet branch of the Capetian royal family of France, from which stemmed the monarchs of Sicily and Naples (1265–1282); of Naples as, in effect, a separate kingdom (1282–1435); of Hungary (1292–1295, in title only, and 1308–1392); and of Poland (1370–1399). The initial importance of this branch and its name derived from the apanage of Anjou and Maine, created by Louis VIII of France for his third son. After the latter's early death, it became the portion of Louis's seventh son, Charles (of Anjou). To these territories Charles added by marriage claims, which he vindicated and extended, in Provence (cf. *la gran dota provenzale* ["the great dowry of Provence"] of *Purg.* 20.61).

The Angevin intervention in Italy was by invitation of the papacy, which had faced the threat of political strangulation in the person of the Hohenstaufen emperor, Frederick II, created by a fusion between imperial power in Germany and northern Italy and Frederick's own tenure of the Kingdom of Sicily. The threat survived Frederick's death in 1250. It remained potent even when, on the death of his son, Conrad, in 1254, Frederick's illegitimate son, Manfred, assumed the throne of Sicily, and the northern and southern possessions were severed for the time being. In default of another champion, Urban IV in 1263 successfully approached Charles of Anjou with the offer of the Kingdom of Sicily as a papal fief. Urban and his successor, Clement IV, both French by origin, employed their authority heavily with Italian commercial and banking interests to secure funding for Charles and to deny it to Manfred. On January 6, 1266, Charles was crowned in St. Peter's, Rome, as king of Sicily. On February 26, he defeated and killed Manfred at Benevento. Frederick's legitimate son and heir, the 16-year-old Conradin, who attempted a counter-invasion, was defeated at Tagliacozzo on August 23, 1268, and was executed.

In the aftermath of conquest, Charles's rule was inevitably partisan, and he needed revenue both to meet standing obligations and to pursue expansion in the eastern Mediterranean. (He had secured within his family the French principality of Achaia in right of his daughter-in-law, and he nursed grandiose ambitions of conquering the Byzantine Empire itself, in right of his son-in-law, Philip de Courtenay, and the kingdom of Jerusalem, in right of a purchase in 1277.) Only in respect of these pressures might his government evidently warrant the judgment of *mala segnoria* ("ill government") applied to it by Charles's grandson, Charles Martel (*Par.* 8.73), to explain the revolt at Palermo, which began on Easter Monday, 1282. Known as the "Sicilian Vespers," this resulted in the establishment on the island of the Aragonese king, Peter, husband of Manfred's daughter, Constance. Though the Angevins maintained the traditional title and strove at great financial, political, and social cost to reintegrate Sicily and the Kingdom of Naples, they now ruled only on the mainland. Here, Charles I (d. 1285) was succeeded by his son, Charles II (1285–1309), who was in turn succeeded by his son, Robert (1309–1343).

It was from the marriage of Charles I's son, Charles (II), to Mary, daughter of Stephen V of Hungary, that their eldest son, Charles Martel (titular king of Hungary, 1290–1295), derived his claim to that kingdom—a claim made good by the latter's son, Charles Robert (king of Hungary, 1308–1342).

Dante conceived a deep antipathy to the effects that he judged to have been produced both in Italy and in the policy of the papacy by the Angevin intervention. The rival parties of Guelf and Ghibelline (pro-papal and pro-imperial factions, respectively) were of much older vintage. Indeed, it was the defeat of the Florentine Guelfs by the Ghibelline allies of Manfred at Montaperti in 1260 that set the conditions of the papal approach to Charles I. The latter was impelled, however, systematically to exploit the divisions, and the approximation of Guelf and Angevin interest was symbolized by the common emblem of the *gigli gialli,* or fleur-de-lis (*Par.* 6.100). The particularism militated equally against the ideal of universal government espoused in the *Monarchia* and against the spiritualized Christianity to which Dante aspired. In *Conv.* 4.6.17–20, he rebukes both Charles II and the Aragonese Frederick II of Sicily for the neglect of moral considerations on the part of their advisers, while in *DVE* 1.12.5 he contrasts the rapacity of their regimes with the nobility of the Hohenstaufen. His general disregard for the Angevins appears at various junctures of the *Commedia* (Charles I: *Purg.* 7.127–129, 20.67–69; Charles II: *Purg.* 20.79–84, *Par.* 6.106–111, 19.127–129, 20.63; Robert: *Par.* 8.76–84, 147). Only Charles Martel (*Par.* 8.31–148)—whom Dante probably knew and of whom he had entertained high expectations—and (in allusions) his

son, Charles Robert (*Par.* 9.1–3, 8.72, 19.142), are presented favorably.

Bibliography

Caggese, R. *Roberto d'Angio e i suoi tempi.* 2 vols. Florence: Bemporad, 1922–1931.

D'Alessandro, V. *Politica e società nella Sicilia aragonese.* Palermo: Manfredi, 1963.

Fawtier, R. *The Capetian Kings of France: Monarchy and Nation 987–1328.* London: Macmillan, 1960.

Fuiano, M. *Carlo I d'Angiò in Italia: studi e ricerche.* Naples: Liguori, 1974.

Jordan, E. *Les origines de la domination Angevine en Italie.* Paris: Picard, 1909.

Léonard, E. G. *Les Angevins de Naples.* Paris: Presses Universitaires de France, 1954.

Runciman, S. *The Sicilian Vespers. A History of the Mediterranean World in the Late Thirteenth Century.* Harmondsworth, Ind.: Penguin, 1960.

Smith, D. Mack. *A History of Sicily: Medieval Sicily 800–1713.* London: Chatto and Windus, 1968.

Michael Haren

Angiolello da Carignano

A leading noble of Fano. He and Guido del Cassero were drowned off the Adriatic coast at the command of Malatestino, lord of Rimini, as they journeyed to meet with him sometime after 1312. Pier da Medicina prophesies their death (*Inf.* 28.76).

Pamela J. Benson

Angiolieri, Cecco

Sienese poet and correspondent of Dante's who was born around 1260 and died not later than 1313. Cecco is the best-known satiric and "realistic" poet of his day. Ridicule of the elevation and spiritualization of women as practiced by Dante and the *stilnovisti* is a hallmark of Cecco's work. Two of Cecco's sonnets ("Lassar vo' lo trovare de Becchina" and "Dante Allaghier, Cecco tu' serv' amico") invite Dante to respond, and a third ("Dante Alleghier, s'i' so' buon begolardo") evidently responds to one of Dante's sonnets. Dante's corresponding poems, however, are unknown.

"Lassar vo' lo trovare di Becchina" reminds Dante that a certain *mariscalco* ("marshal") is not all that he seems. Identifiable as Amerigo di Narbona, the "marshal" was a veteran of the battle of Campaldino (1289) and was Charles II of Anjou's representative in Florence (1289–1291). The sonnet warns that the reputed military hero, who is apparently turning the heads of Florence's *donne e . . . donzelle* ("dames and damsels"), is in reality *una gallina* ("a chicken"). Cecco and Dante both fought in the battle of Campaldino, and Cecco probably trusted Dante to set the women straight, since, like Cecco, he had been able to appraise the marshal's performance firsthand.

In "Dante Allagier, Cecco, tu' serv' amico," Cecco cavils at the apparently self-contradictory claim of the *Vita Nuova*'s last sonnet. In the first tercet, or *muta* ("cubby") as Cecco calls it, Dante says he cannot understand the description of Beatrice given by his thought, which has been to Heaven to contemplate her: *io no lo intendo, sì parla sottile* ("I do not understand it, it speaks so subtly"). But in the second, Dante says he does understand it: *io lo 'ntendo ben* ("I understand it well"). That Cecco has not read the explanation given in the *Vita Nuova*'s "division" indicates that he read Dante's sonnet before it was set in the *Vita Nuova*'s framework of narrative and gloss. Some scholars believe it was in response to such cavils that Dante furnished the *Vita Nuova* with its divisions. They see both the *Vita Nuova*'s apparent answer to Cecco's argument and the *Convivio*'s defensive observations regarding the *Vita Nuova* as evidence of an "Angiolierian" phase in Dante's development.

With "Dante Alleghier, s'i' so' buon begolardo," Cecco answers Dante's apparent accusations of self-promotion and sycophancy by accusing him of practicing those vices in equal measure. The allusion to Dante's having made himself a *lombardo* ("Lombard," i.e., northern Italian) suggests that the sonnet was written during Dante's first residence in Verona, when Cecco was playing the *romano* ("Roman") at the court of a cardinal from Siena. The tone of the earliest sonnet is companionable; that of the second, mock-deferential; and of this, one of open antagonism: *E se di tal materia vo' dir piuè, / Dante, risponde, ch'i' t'avrò a stancare* ("And if you have more to say on this matter, Dante, answer, for I will tire you out"). Guelfo Taviani answered on Dante's behalf, calling Cecco a *musardo* ("complainer"), explaining that Dante's poverty was the result of his philosophic dedication to learning, and warning Cecco of seeming a fool in taking on Dante. Dante himself apparently declined to answer, and his relation with Cecco seems to have come to an end.

Bibliography

Angiolieri, Cecco. *Cecco, as I Am and Was: The Poems of Cecco Angiolieri.* Translated by Tracy Barrett. Boston: International Pocket Library, 1994.

Contini, Gianfranco. *Poeti del Duecento.* Vol. 2. Milan, Naples: Ricciardi, 1960, pp. 367–401.

Marti, Mario. *Cultura e stile nei poeti giocosi del tempo di Dante.* Pisa: Nistri-Lischi, 1953.

Todd Boli

Anna, St.

St. Bernard points out Anna to Dante in the Empyrean (*Par.* 32.133–135). The mother of the Virgin Mary, she sits in the white rose to the right of John the Baptist and directly across from St. Peter, next to whom sits her daughter, whom she gazes upon with a happy and contented air while singing hosannas.

Maria Ann Roglieri

Annas

Father-in-law of the high priest of the Jews, Caiaphas (John 18:13), Annas *(Anna)* is racked on the ground among the members of the Sanhedrin who ordered Christ's crucifixion (*Inf.* 23.121). Punished in the Valley of the Hypocrites in the sixth pouch of Malebolge, they bear the weight of those who have succeeded them in shame.

Roy Rosenstein

Anonimo Fiorentino

The name assigned to the anonymous Florentine author of a commentary on the *Commedia* dating to the fourteenth or early fifteenth century, as suggested by certain historical references it contains. Rather than offer a global interpretation of Dante's poem, the author glosses individual episodes, or *canti,* often with an eye to incorporating historical information about characters or events. The commentary evinces its author's broad preparation, even if the analyses themselves are not especially profound. The Anonimo had read the major commentaries on Dante—such as those of Jacopo Alighieri, Lana, Ottimo, and Benvenuto— as well as Boccaccio's *Esposizioni.* He also had read Boccaccio's *Decameron* and cites it in reference to characters who appear in both it and Dante's poem, and he knew Giovanni Villani's *Cronica* and Dino Compagni's historical writings. The commentary includes references to the Bible and mythology as well.

The Anonimo read Dante's poem as a poetic fiction in imitation of Virgil's epic, and he believed it could be read either historically or allegorically. The primary value of his commentary today remains its detailed attention to Dante's historical references and the information it provides to elaborate them.

Bibliography

Anonimo Fiorentino. *Commento alla "Divina Commedia" d'Anonimo Fiorentino del secolo XIV.* Edited by Pietro Fanfani. 3 vols. Bologna: G. Romagnoli, 1866–1874.

Mortari, Ileana. "Da Jacopo della Lana all'Anonimo Fiorentino." In *Psicanalisi e strutturalismo di fronte a Dante.* Florence: Olschki, 1972, pp. 471–501.

Parker, Deborah. *Commentary and Ideology: Dante in the Renaissance.* Durham, N.C.: Duke University Press, 1993.

Vallone, Aldo. *Storia della critica dantesca dal XIV al XX secolo.* 2 vols. Padua: Vallardi, 1981.

Michael Sherberg

Anonimo Latino

The *Anonymous Latin Commentary on Dante's Commedia,* which for convenience we call simply the *Anonimo Latino,* is a commentary compiled from systematic glosses appearing in substantially the same wording on the earliest existing manuscripts of the *Commedia.* A comparison of these Latin glosses reveals them to be a clarification of Dante's verses intended for those readers whose current language was Latin rather than Italian. The explanations emphasize that Dante's poem is a figurative representation of life in this world after the Fall. The explanation takes the form of glosses extending through the whole of the *Inferno* and the *Purgatorio* and including the first eleven cantos of the *Paradiso,* where they come to a sudden stop. The 1989 edition is based on sixteen of the earliest Dante manuscripts spread through various cities and countries: Munich, Seville, Florence, Geneva, London, Rome, Paris, Oxford, New York City, and Cambridge, Massachusetts.

The greatest number of glosses are in the *Inferno,* and we are able to group similar glosses into a shorter form and a longer one. In the *Purgatorio* the glosses are fewer and more or less of the same type. In the *Paradiso* the glosses are only in one manuscript, and they all appear to be by the same scribe. In some of the manuscripts the gloss follows a quotation from a verse in the poem; in others there is a letter over the word in the verse, with a corresponding letter introducing the gloss. The *Anonimo Latino* is not a critical edition of any one manuscript but a composite of the glosses occurring in the best known of the earliest manuscripts of the *Commedia* that contain glosses. It provides the basis for further study of the beginnings of commentaries on the poem.

Bibliography

Cioffari, Vincenzo. *Anonymous Latin Commentary on Dante's Commedia: Reconstructed Text.* Spoleto: Centro Italiano di Studi sull'Alto Medioevo, 1989.

———. "The *Anonimo Latino:* One of the Earliest Commentaries on Dante's *Commedia.*" *Mediaevalia* 12 (1989 for 1986), 127–153.

Vincenzo Cioffari

Anselm of Canterbury, St.

One of the theologians in the sphere of the Sun (*Par.* 12.137), named to Dante by St. Bonaventure. Born in 1033, Anselm *(Anselmo)* joined the monastery of Bec in Normandy (c. 1060–1061), where he studied logic with Lanfranc and developed remarkable dialectical and linguistic skills. In 1076 he began work on the *Monologion,* a work which *sola ratione* ("by reason alone") attempts to prove God's existence. King William Rufus appointed Anselm archbishop of Canterbury in 1093, but soon thereafter the relationship between the two deteriorated over the question of lay versus ecclesiastical investiture. After the coronation of Henry I, William's successor, Anselm renewed his battle against lay investiture, and after several years of exile, an acceptable compromise on the subject was finally reached in the spring of 1107—two years before Anselm's death. His *Cur Deus homo* (1094–1098), to which Dante owes much of his exposition on the nature of the Incarnation (*Par.* 7), explains the necessity of divine intervention in man's redemption and the manner in which Christ's death does justice and honor to

God. The *De similitudinibus,* a text attributed (wrongly) to Anselm and widely circulated in Dante's time, has been suggested by some as the principal model of the allegorical imagery of the *selva oscura* of *Inf.* 1.

Bibliography
Agresti, A. *Dante e S. Anselmo.* Naples: de Bonis, 1887.
Ryan, Christopher. "*Paradiso* VII: Marking the Difference between Dante and Anselm." In *Dante and the Middle Ages.* Edited by John C. Barnes and Cormac Ó Cuilleanáin. Dublin: Irish Academic Press, 1995, pp. 117–138.
Southern, R. W. *St. Anselm: A Portrait in a Landscape.* Cambridge: Cambridge University Press, 1991.

Michael Papio

Anselmuccio

Little Anselm shared the fate of his grandfather, Count Ugolino, when he was imprisoned in a tower in Pisa by Archbishop Ruggieri and starved to death (*Inf.* 33.50). Unlike his fellow prisoners, all of whom were adults, Anselm was perhaps 15 at most and is represented as innocently sustaining Ugolino, who fails to provide his offspring even with moral sustenance or verbal comfort.

Roy Rosenstein

Antaeus

Son of Neptune and the Earth goddess Terra, a giant and immensely strong wrestler from Libya. In Dante, Antaeus (*Anteo*) is one of four giants—together with Nimrod, Ephialtes, and Briareus—placed by Dante at the mouth of the ninth and lowest circle of Hell (*Inf.* 31.113–145). Acting at Virgil's request, he serves as a vehicle to deliver him and Dante down upon the ice of Cocytus from the eighth circle. Lucan's *Pharsalia* (4.590, 593–660)—Dante's main source for his character—portrays the giant as a monstrous enemy of humans and gods. Antaeus' absence during the battle against Olympus brings about the giants' defeat, and consequently, unlike the other giants, he is unfettered in the pit of Hell and speaks a comprehensible language. In *Inf.* 31.132 Dante makes a brief reference to Antaeus' fight against Hercules. The episode, drawn from *Phars.* 4.617, is recounted in greater detail in *Conv.* 3.3.7–8 and in *Mon.* 2.7.10, 2.9.11. Hercules defeats Antaeus after discovering that the giant can be overwhelmed only if kept aloft, for his mother, Earth, instills new strength in him each time he touches the ground.

Alessandro Vettori

Antenora

Antenora is the second of the four zones of Cocytus, in the ninth circle of Hell, set aside for political traitors and depicted in the second half of *Inf.* 32. Dante coined its name (oddly for us) after that of Antenor, the Trojan prince and mature counselor to Priam. Presented in the *Iliad* positively as a defender of Troy, albeit a realist, and neutrally in Livy and Virgil (*Aen.* 1.242–243), Antenor—later the fabled founder of Padua—came to be considered a traitor to Troy in one important strand of the Homeric tradition, perhaps because he advocated a final accommodation with the Greeks and the return of Helen. He was then implicated in the stratagem of the Trojan Horse and secret negotiations to open the city's gates by night in order to allow the entry of the Greek forces. This tradition was sponsored by Dictys of Crete in his *Ephemeris belli troiani* (5.4–17) and by Dares the Phrygian in *De excidio troiae* (39–44); it carried down to the romances of twelfth-century Troy and beyond. Benoit de Saint Maure calls Antenor a treacherous Judas in his *Roman de Troie* (v. 26135).

This tradition underlies Dante's labeling of traitors to political party associates and—ultimately, if at times unclearly—to the patria itself. Of special importance is Bocca degli Abati, betrayer of his fellow Florentine Guelfs at the bitterly remembered Battle of Montaperti (1260). Close by are Buoso da Duera, a Ghibelline and presumed traitor to Manfred; Tesauro dei Beccheria, abbot of Vallombrosa and a legate of Pope Alexander IV in Tuscany, who was apparently involved in intrigues between the Florentine Guelfs and Ghibellines and was beheaded in 1258; Gianni de' Soldanieri, a noble Florentine who went over to the Guelfs after 1266; and Tebaldello de' Manfredi, a Ghibelline of Faenza who betrayed his city to Bolognese Guelfs.

Located at the unmarked border between Antenora and Ptolomea, Dante and Virgil come upon by far the most famous and most discussed dwellers of Antenora: Count Ugolino della Gherardesca and Bishop Ruggieri degli Ubaldini of

Pisa. The ordinary posture of the Antenorans seems to be no different from that of the Caina denizens—head down, their color apparently shading from livid to a darkish purple, which is also the case of Bishop Ruggieri; but he is subjected to an additional punishment, an eternal gnawing at the nape of his neck inflicted by Count Ugolino, present here on his own account. A basic exegetical problem as to the precise nature of the treachery of each of them remains unresolved; there is no question, however, that Ruggieri is doubly culpable—most seriously in Dante's eyes for his barbarous consent to the death by starvation of Ugolino's innocent children. In this act of mad-bestial injustice he struck not only at the value of *pietas* ("loyalty to party and country") but also at *vindicatio* ("just punishment") by way of ferocious excess.

Bibliography

Triolo, Alfred A. "*Inferno* XXXIII: Fra Alberigo in Context." *L'Alighieri* 11 (1970), 39–70.

———. "Matta Bestialità in Dante's Inferno: Theory and Image." *Traditio* 24 (1968), 247–292.

Alfred Triolo

The arrival of the saved on the shores of Purgatory. La comedia di Dante Aligieri, *with commentary by Alessandro Vellutello, published by Francesco Marcolini, Venice, 1544. Giamatti Collection: Courtesy of the Mount Holyoke College Archives and Special Collections.*

Ante-Purgatory

As a geographical entity, the sloping region that lies at the base of the mountain of Purgatory and stretches from the seashore to the gate of Purgatory proper (*Purg.* 1.13–9.78). Dante imagines Ante-Purgatory as reaching to the limits of Earth's atmosphere and Purgatory proper as soaring above it, which accounts for the constantly changing sets of landscapes and environments that unfold as Dante and Virgil move from the beach area to the ridges and valleys of the uplands. Together with Purgatory proper and the Earthly Paradise at the top of the mountain, it is one of the three major areas of the *secondo regno* ("second realm," *Purg.* 1.4), a division that alludes symbolically, as does *terza rima,* to the Trinity.

Ante-Purgatory is a place that imposes punishment on those who for one reason or another delayed their penance until the very end of life. Individuals are divided into groups and are punished by confinement for a period suitably commensurate with the gravity and duration of their neglect. Ante-Purgatory is the realm *dove tempo per tempo si ristora* ("where they repay time for time," *Purg.* 23.84). After they have completed their period of detention, they will proceed to enter Purgatory proper and purge the stain of individual sin. The first area is inhabited by the excommunicate, whose shortcomings comprise not only their delayed repentance but also their excommunication from the Church, having refused to submit to its authority. They must delay their entrance into Purgatory for thirty times the number of years they lived in contumacy of the Church. The second area comprises *balzi* ("ledges") on which three other groups of negligent are confined for a period equal to the duration of their earthly lives: the indolent, whose apathy resulted in a deferral of repentance; those who died violently and repented only in the last moment of their lives, sometimes referred to as the unshriven or unabsolved; and the negligent rulers, those whose preoccupation with earthly affairs forced them to neglect their spiritual obligations. All four groups share the purgatorial need for human prayer as a means of shortening the terms of their detention.

The moral structure blends with the geographical and topographical configurations as the composition, following the prologue's interlocking of proposition and invocation, traces the

Virgil girding Dante with the reed of humility. Dante, with commentary by Cristoforo Landino and Alessandro Vellutello, published in Venice in 1564 by Marchiò Sessa & fratelli. Giamatti Collection: Courtesy of the Mount Holyoke College Archives and Special Collections.

pilgrims' upward progression. This progression begins with the emergence of Dante and Virgil from the deadly gloom of Hell into the lovely hues of the Southern Hemisphere's early morning skies on the shoreline of the mountain island of Purgatory and evolves in a complex narrative sequence that takes them to the doorsteps of Purgatory. Among the salient figures Dante meets along his ascent up the mountain are custodians like Cato (*Purg.* 1–2) and the guardian angels (*Purg.* 8–9) and numerous saved—Casella, Manfred, Belacqua, Jacopo del Cassero, La Pia, Buonconte da Montefeltro, Sordello, Nino Visconti, Currado Malaspina—who illustrate various kinds of negligent preparation for the afterlife.

The trajectory of ethical, theological, psychological, and structural notations is built by the narrative process. Thus, for instance, Virgil's exhortation to humanity not to attempt fathoming God's ways (*Purg.* 3.31–45) ensues from his explanation of the nature of shades, which in turn is prompted by Dante's seeing his own shadow. Similarly, the *contrapasso* is integrated into the compositive process so as to allow for the reader to learn, progressively and at times from the penitents themselves, not only the duration and implications of the waiting condition but also the way to ascend the mountain, and therefore also how moral progress can be realized.

Bibliography

Carroll, John S. *Prisoners of Hope: An Exposition of Dante's Purgatorio.* London: Hodder and Stoughton, 1906.

Fergusson, Francis. *Dante's Drama of the Mind: A Modern Reading of the Purgatorio.* Princeton, N.J.: Princeton University Press, 1953.

Illiano, Antonio. *Sulle sponde del prepurgatorio: Poesia e arte narrativa nel preludio all'ascesa (Purg. I-III 66).* Fiesole: Cadmo, 1997.

Pasquazi, Silvio. "Antipurgatorio." *Enciclopedia dantesca,* 1:304–306.

Antonio Illiano

Antigone

Daughter of Oedipus and Jocasta, she defied Creon's edict forbidding burial of her brother Polynices, and through Creon's revenge she was sealed in a tomb, where she hanged herself. Virgil mentions Antigone (*Antigone*) as one of the great women in Limbo (*Purg.* 22.109–114).

Nancy Vine Durling

Antiphon

Greek tragic poet (late fifth to early fourth centuries B.C.E.); only titles and fragments of three of his works survive. Virgil refers to Antiphon (*Antifonte),* together with Simonides and Agathon, as one of the Greek poets in Limbo (*Purg.* 22.106).

Nancy Vine Durling

Apocalypse

The Apocalypse, or Book of Revelation, is the last book of the Christian Bible. During the Middle Ages its author was universally identified as John, the beloved disciple and author of the Fourth Gospel (an identification not generally accepted by modern scholarship). Its rich symbolic and visionary character—communicating the absoluteness of the struggle between good and evil in a dramatically powerful way—made it a work of exceptional importance in its influence on medieval literature, art, and thought. Moreover, as the concluding book of the Bible, the Apocalypse was considered to be of especial importance. It was seen as a kind of summary, a work which contained or recapitulated the rest of the Bible. One of its most important (as well as most controversial) interpreters in the Middle Ages, Joachim of Fiore (d. 1204), called the work "the key of things past, the knowledge of things to come, the opening of what is sealed, the uncovering of what is hidden" *(Expositio in Apocalypsim).*

The word "Apocalypse" itself means a "revelation," or an "unveiling." But the word is used to refer both to a distinct literary genre and to a particular mentality. Thus the Christian Book of the Apocalypse belongs to a distinct genre with antecedents in Jewish apocalyptic writings. Among those, the most important is the Old Testament Book of Daniel, from which the Christian Apocalypse derives many of its images and much of its complex number symbolism. As a genre, an "apocalypse" can be defined succinctly but not inaccurately as a mediated revelation of heavenly secrets to a human sage, a revelation whose written and thus definitive character is highlighted (as opposed to the oral and traditional character of the Old Testament prophets). As a mentality, apocalypse entails above all a sense of imminence, that is, a sense in which present events must be seen and can be understood only in light of the events of the last times.

Not surprisingly—given its structural complexity, the density of its imagery, its highly symbolic character, and its complex number symbolism—a great many different interpretations of the biblical Book of the Apocalypse appeared throughout the Middle Ages. It was interpreted both as a revelation of the soul's relation to supernatural realities and as a prophecy of what is to come in human history. Augustine, whose view remained the most influential throughout the early Middle Ages, understood the book as a symbolic presentation of the conflict of good and evil within the contemporary Christian Church and a prophecy of the Church from the establishment of Christianity to Doomsday. But Augustine also believed that its prophetic symbols must not be interpreted literally or applied naively to contemporary events. Augustine was more interested in the larger patterns that represented the continuing battle between the City of God and the City of Man than he was in specific historical events. By the twelfth century, exegetes and commentators no longer shared Augustine's reluctance to apply specific symbols of prophecy to historical events. The various sequences of seven in John's vision were associated not only with the general pattern of history but also with specific events within that history. So, for example, the twelfth-century exegete Anselm of Havelberg interprets the opening of the seven seals (7, along with 3, being the most pervasive of the book's many numeric patterns; see Apoc. 6:1–8:2) as "seven successive states of the church from the Coming of Christ until all things will be consummated at the end" *(Dialogues* 1.7).

Dante accepts this interpretation in what is his own most complete evocation of the Apocalypse in the *Commedia,* the last cantos of the *Purgatorio.* Beginning in canto 29 with a pageant of the church and continuing through the coming of Beatrice, Dante presents what is surely one of the most concentrated and detailed appropriations of Apocalyptic imagery in all of literature. These images include the twenty-four elders, the four beasts, and the seven lamps of Apoc. 4. They include references to the whore of Apoc. 17 and the beast of Apoc. 13. They include a prophecy of the Second Coming of Christ in canto 33, which draws on references to the beast of Apoc. 17:8–9 and the rivers of Paradise of Apoc. 22. They include the appearance of Beatrice to Dante the pilgrim, fashioned by the poet in such a way as to evoke the Apocalyptic coming of Christ in Judgment. And they include, in canto 32, a seven-part history of the tribulations suffered by the church based on the exegesis of the opening of the seven seals of Apoc. 6–8, a history that moves through the calamities of the Church from early Christian times to Dante's contemporary world. Taken as a whole, these images are there to suggest Apocalyptic imminence; that is, they place Dante's personal drama of conversion within the wider frame of cosmic and universal history evoked by the Apocalypse.

A similar sense of judgment and imminence is evoked in other parts of the *Commedia* where apocalyptic imagery is present. This sense of cosmic judgment informing present-day events can be seen quite clearly in *Inf.* 19, for example, a canto rich with imagery taken directly from the Apocalypse. The denunciation of papal corruption in this canto is informed by the language of Apoc. 17:12: "Come, I will show thee the condemnation of the great harlot who sits upon many waters, with whom the kings of the earth have committed fornication." These words reappear in the mouth of the pilgrim Dante who castigates ecclesiastic degeneracy: *"Di voi pastor s'accorse il Vangelista / quando colei che siede sopra l'acque / puttaneggiar coi regi a lui fu vista, / quella che con le sette teste nacque, / e da le diece corna ebbe argomento / fin che virtute al suo marito piacque"* ("Of you shepherds the Evangelist took note, when he saw her who sits upon the waters whoring with the kings, she who was born with seven heads, and took strength from her ten horns as long as virtue pleased her husband" *Inf.* 19.106–111). The degeneration of the papacy in the present is meant to be seen as an adumbration of the evils of the last days, and the judgment that Dante places on these popes is meant to be seen as a foreshadowing of the Last Judgment.

Imagery from the Apocalypse plays an important part in other parts of the poem. The beast Geryon of *Inf.* 17 is clearly taken from the description of the locust beast of Apocalypse 9:7–10. The wondrous river of life of *Par.* 30:61–69 is derived from the paradisal river of Apoc. 22. The book of life of Apoc. 3:5, 20:12–15, 21:27, and 22:9 resonates with the *magno volume* ("great volume") of *Par.* 15.50, wherein his great-great-grandfather Cacciaguida reads of Dante's coming to him in the afterlife and of Dante's future beyond his journey. This *magno volume* is in turn linked with both the scattered leaves of the lost souls in *Inf.* 3—the poet playing on the analogue between leaves falling from a tree and the leaves of a book—and the description of the entire universe as a great volume bound together by love in the last canto of *Paradiso*. In the life of Francis of Assisi, which is told by Thomas Aquinas in the circle of the Sun, Francis—especially in his reception of the wounds of Christ, the stigmata—is compared to the angel of the sixth seal of Apoc. 6:12 and 7:2. These references, by no means exhaustive, suggest that the *Commedia* can be read as an "apocalyptic" text because they show that the events of the present are placed within a coherent scheme of history that gains meaning by its relation to the events of the last times. Like John the Revelator, who is both scribe and visionary, Dante, both poet and pilgrim, explores the relationship between his own personal drama and God's

plan for the governance of the cosmos. Appropriately, *Epist.* 13, Dante's *Letter to Cangrande,* concludes with a reference to Apoc. 21:6: God as the Alpha and the Omega. Finally, Dante's sense of prophecy may have been influenced in part by Joachim da Fiore's concept of spiritual *renovatio,* identified with the age of Holy Spirit in his *Liber Figurarum,* as Marjorie Reeves has argued.

Bibliography

Emmerson, Richard K., and Ronald B. Herzman. *The Apocalyptic Imagination in Medieval Literature.* Philadelphia: University of Pennsylvania Press, 1992.

———, and Bernard McGinn (eds.). *The Apocalypse in the Middle Ages.* Ithaca, N.Y.: Cornell University Press, 1992.

Herzman, Ronald B. "Dante and the Apocalypse." In *The Apocalypse in the Middle Ages.* Edited by Richard K. Emmerson and Bernard McGinn. Ithaca, N.Y.: Cornell University Press, 1992, pp. 398–413.

McGinn, Bernard. "John's Apocalypse and the Apocalyptic Mentality." In *The Apocalypse in the Middle Ages.* Edited by Richard K. Emmerson and Bernard McGinn. Ithaca, N.Y.: Cornell University Press, 1992, pp. 3–19.

Mineo, Nicolò. *Profetismo e Apocalittica in Dante: Strutture e temi profetico-apocalittici in Dante dalla Vita Nuova alla Divina Commedia.* Catania: Università di Catania, 1968.

Reeves, Marjorie. "Dante and the Prophetic View of History." In *The World of Dante: Essays on Dante and His Times.* Edited by Cecil Grayson. Oxford: Clarendon Press, 1980, pp. 44–60.

———. *The Influence of Prophecy in the Later Middle Ages.* Oxford: Clarendon Press, 1969.

Vallone, Aldo. "*La Divina Commedia* e L'Apocalisse." *Deutsches Dante-Jahrbuch* 65 (1990), 107–145.

Richard K. Emmerson and Ronald B. Herzman

Apollo

Apollo was the Greek and Roman god of light, healing, poetry, and oracular prophecy. Son to Jupiter and the nymph Leto (or Latona), Apollo was born with his sister, Diana, on the island of Delos, one of the Cyclades in the Ionia Sea. The island had been raised by Neptune from the sea to afford a refuge for Leto, persecuted by the jealous Juno, the wife of Jupiter. In gratitude to his birthplace, Apollo fixed the island with adamantine chains. After defeating the serpent Python, Apollo was made to desire Daphne, the daughter of the river-god Peneus, in retaliation for having mocked Cupid, the god of love (Ovid, *Meta.* 1.452–567). Daphne fled from Apollo and appealed to her father to preserve her virginity; he changed her into a laurel tree, which Apollo adopted, in the form of the crown of laurel, as a sign of love, glory, and victory, including victory in poetic competition (Statius, *Theb.* 1.21; Dante, *Par.* 25.7–9; *Egl.* 1.33–50).

As the patron of music and poetry and leader of the nine Muses (*Par.* 2.8–9) Apollo resided on twin-peaked Parnassus, in ancient Phokis (south-central Greece); he was also the tutelary deity of prophetic possession at his temple at Delphi, on the southern slope of Parnassus; the temple bore the admonition medievals knew as *nosce teipsum* ("know thyself"). In the wake of classical Latin and thus medieval uses, Apollo was for Dante also the sun, though Dante does not adopt the common Latin epithet of Phoebus (Italian = *Febo*) for the Sun; yet that form does appear in *Mon.* 2.8.13, where he cites Boethius, and in *Mon.* 1.11.6 (discussed below).

Medieval mythographers noted that Apollo's toponym "Delius," from Greek *delos* ("clear, manifest"), refers to the brightness of the Sun. Apollo is implicitly Delius at *Purg.* 29.78: *fa l'arco il Sole e Delia il cinto* ("the Sun makes his bow, and Delia her girdle"; see also *Purg.* 23.120); at *Purg.* 20.132: *li due occhi del cielo* ("the two eyes of Heaven"); and at *Par.* 29.1: *ambedue li figli di Latona* ("both Latona's children"). When an earthquake shakes Purgatory just prior to Statius' appearance as the risen Christ, Dante's reference to shaky Delos as the birthplace of Apollo and Diana (*Purg.* 20.130–132) implies that their birth heralded the peace and justice brought by Christ. In the *Monarchia,* when the fullness of justice is signified by Phoebe, the Moon—full because directly opposite the Sun (*frater Phoebe,* "brother of Phoebe," *Mon.* 1.11.5)—cosmic signification of the just balance of church and empire is probably implied. Dante's repeated pairing of solar Apollo with the Moon reflects longstanding concern with the traditional ecclesiological identification of the Sun with the church and of the Moon with empire (*Mon.* 3.4.2–3; *Epist.* 6.8).

In *Conv.* 4.25.6 Dante mentions the Oracle of Apollo which, in Statius' *Theb.* 1.491–492, astonished Adrastus *(Adrasto),* king of Argos, when fulfilled by the arrival of Tydeus and Polynices as fated husbands for Argia and Deiphile, the king's daughters. Apollo as both oracle and the inspirer of poetry dominates the exordium, or introduction, to the *Paradiso.* Dante appeals to Apollo as *padre* ("father") in presenting himself as a rare aspirant to the laurel crown of poetic achievement (*Par.* 1.22–33). To signify the violence of the divine inspiration he requires, Dante compares himself at *Par.* 1.19–21 to Marsyas, a satyr and devotee of Bacchus ordered flayed by Apollo for losing the contest between the rowdy panpipes and Apollo's temperate lyre (Ovid, *Meta.* 6.383–391). At *Par.* 1.36 Dante mentions Cirra, a port near Delphi and the name of one of the peaks of Parnassus, thus doubling his invocation of poetic inspiration with one to the god of prophecy ("happy Delphic deity," *Par.* 1.31–32). As both peaks of Parnassus are invoked (*Par.* 1.16–18), so both the poetic and prophetic gifts are necessary for Dante to manifest in poetry the *ombra del beato regno* ("shadow of the blessed kingdom," *Par.* 1.23).

Dante mentions Apollo *Timbreo* ("Thymbraeus," an epithet found in Latin epic)—so named from a shrine at Thymbra near Troy in Asia Minor—at *Purg.* 12.31, where Apollo joins Mars and Jupiter in defeating the attack on Olympus by the Earth-born giants: Dante's scene arrangement suggests that the pagan gods execute the will of the Christian deity, as the angels did in defeating the rebellion of Satan. In distinction to Augustine, for whom classical deities were demons (*City of God* 7.33), Dante treats pairings such as that of Apollo and Bacchus (*Par.* 13.25, where Apollo's epithet "Paean" means "victor" and "savior" because of his defeat of Python) as veiled foreshadowings of Christian mysteries: Apollo and Bacchus are mentioned with the Trinity, while Apollo's wearing of the laurel was sometimes interpreted as a fable of Christ's assumption of humanity in the Virgin Mary. Used alone, "Apollo" is a classicizing name for the angelic intelligences that move the celestial spheres, as in *Conv.* 2.4.1–7 and in the *Letter to Cangrande* (*Epist.* 13.48, 86). Such interpretations are consistent with the identifications by mythographers of Apollo with the Sun, with divine and human wisdom, and with the "spiritual light" (cf. *Conv.* 2.5.3), and they reflect traditions of

Christian Neoplatonism (e.g., Macrobius, *Commentary on the Dream of Scipio* 2.3.3).

Ronald L. Martinez

Appetite

The meaning that Dante assigns to the term "appetite" in its Italian *(appetito)* or Latin *(appetitus)* form varies from work to work, but in general it means "desire" or "the faculty of desire." The term *appetito* is used in both senses in the only chapter in the *Vita Nuova* where it appears: chapter 38. When Dante opposes appetite (by which he refers to his desire for the *donna gentile*) to reason (by which he refers to the thought of remaining faithful to Beatrice; 38.5–6), "appetite" may, not unreasonably, be taken to denote the faculty of desire and not merely desire. One use of the term in the same passage, however, clearly denotes desire. Appetite as faculty may follow or disobey reason; its disobedience to reason results in a "wicked [*malvagio*] desire" (39.2). As desire, appetite may grow, not necessarily with the consent or encouragement of the person in whom it takes shape; it is then a passion, something which *happens* to a person.

In the *Convivio,* Dante identifies two appetites in the human being, differing in origin (4.22.5): the *rational appetite,* which originates from the divine gift of nobility (4.21.13), and the *sense appetite* (4.22.10; see also 4.22.5, 4.26.5), which comes from the animal nature of the human being (cf. 3.3.10). Both are conceived of as natural appetites (4.22.4–5; see also 4.26.5), with the second being subordinate to the first (4.26.5–7).

The sensitive appetite has two operations, pursuit and flight (4.26.5), and moves on the basis of appearances (3.3.10). These two forms of appetite are called *concupiscible* (desire for something) and *irascible* (fear of something) and are spurred on and reined in by reason (4.26.6–7; cf. 3.8.19).

The rational appetite plays a central role in the *Convivio* as the common source of the desire for knowledge and virtue. At first indistinguishable from the sensitive appetite, it gradually awakens to the difference between the rational and nonrational parts of the human being, loving the former more than the latter and manifesting this love in the use of the rational part to contemplate and to act virtuously (4.22.7–11). Human beings with a vigorous rational appetite manifest virtues appropriate

to the successive stages of life at which they find themselves (4.23.4). The rational appetite for virtue of the noble human being, like desire for knowledge (1.1.1), is a natural inclination. This concept, taken from Aristotle, is the philosophical point of departure for the *Convivio* and for its opening sentence: *tutti li uomini naturalmente desiderano di sapere* ("all men by nature desire to know").

Two brief passages in *Conv.* 4.21 and 4.22 alter this concept of appetite as natural inclination in the process of qualifying it. The first (4.21.13–14; see also 4.22.11) clarifies that the rational appetite must be cultivated through good habits and must be kept firm in its rectitude by one's restraining the passions in order to bear fruits of virtue. With this clarification the appetite for virtue becomes a quality in potency that needs actualization, rather than a natural inclination: it becomes virtue in potency. The difference between this concept and the original one is that, following the latter, a person is good because his or her nature, his or her very constitution as an individual, is good; with the qualification, a person is judged to be good because he or she activates, sustains, and protects an innate inclination to perform good acts. The qualification makes room for merit. The second passage (4.22.12) observes that those who do not possess the gift of nobility (from which the rational appetite springs) in their very nature may nevertheless obtain it by imitating the way those blessed with this gift actualize virtue in themselves, that is, through much correction and through cultivation. Dante compares this to the engrafting of one nature onto another. The alteration that this passage works on Dante's concept of appetite is radical. It implicitly denies the relationship of appetite to nobility as effect to cause (cf. 4.16.10), since the appetite for virtue in this case precedes nobility. Appetite is here conceived as an indeterminate power to do either good or evil, to acquire either vice or virtue—not determined in any way by nature. This third concept opens the possibility of goodness to all, not just to those gifted with nobility. It underlies Dante's praise of the good man whose nature is defective (3.8.19). It is this concept of appetite which is compatible with the one extended passage about the will (4.9 passim) and the three passing references to it in the *Convivio* (1.12.9, 4.12.4, 4.22.10).

How does one account for the distinct and ultimately incompatible conceptions of appetite in the *Convivio*? One must hypothesize revisions to a first draft of the *Convivio,* with the revisions coming in two stages. Dante's revisions stopped, it would seem, at *Conv.* 4.22. Aside from the extended references to appetite in *Conv.* 4, there are passing references to it in the *Convivio* invariably linked either to the concept of rightness (as in *diritto appetito,* "right desire") or to the concept of virtue (3.8.16, 3.11.11, 3.11.13, 3.15.12, and 4.13.15, 16). The underlying assumption of such a link is the philosophical principle that there is only one end towards which human desires are rightly directed (4.6.8). Most if not all of these remarks would seem to be part of Dante's revision of his original conception of appetite.

The term *appetito* is used only three times in the *Commedia.* Two of the uses (*Purg.* 22.41 and 26.84) refer to sinful desire. *Purg.* 18:61–66 makes it plain that the appetite which the avaricious and the lustful repent for in Purgatory is not simply desire but desire to which the will has consented against the judgment of *la virtù che consiglia, / e de l'assenso de' tener la soglia* ("the power that gives counsel and must guard the threshold of assent"): in other words, *libero arbitrio* ("free will" or, literally, "free choice"). Free judgment assesses whether a concrete desire conforms or not to the primal act of the will (*Purg.* 18:61–63), which is to will the good. The latter is a natural inclination, devoid of merit (*Purg.* 18:55–60): it is consented desire, desire that conforms to or disregards free will, that wins Heaven or earns one a place in either Hell or Purgatory (*Purg.* 16:67–72). Dante is yet more precise in *Mon.* 1.12.3–5. Here he explains the concept of free will in terms of desire *(appetitus)* and the judgment of good and evil *(iudicium):* when the latter moves the former, not being anticipated by it in any way, then there is free judgment; when on the contrary the latter is moved or anticipated in any way by the former, then there is no free judgment. In either case, *appetitus*—understood as the actual pursuit of or flight from something—has the will's consent.

"Appetite" in *Par.* 16.5 may be understood in either sense, as desire or the faculty of desire. What matters is the point of the verse: that appetite cannot be twisted in Heaven, because the only object of cognition there is God and things divine. This underscores an essential characteristic of appetite and its specific difference from a natural inclination—that it is rooted in an apprehension representable by the imagination (*Purg.* 18.22–

33), to which apprehension appetite is a response (*Mon.* 1.12.3–4). A natural inclination, on the contrary, does not need an apprehension to come into being. Where God cannot be apprehended directly and the objects of apprehension are not limited to things divine—in *this* life, in short—there exists the possibility of a twisted appetite and, hence, the crux of the moral struggle: to ensure that one's desires, one's appetite, correspond to the natural inclination to the good (*Purg.* 18.61–69). The last three lines of the *Commedia* allude to this struggle, *velle* corresponding to the natural inclination of the will, and *disio* to appetite.

Bibliography

Albert the Great. *Opera omnia.* Vol. 14, 1. *Super Ethica: Commentum et quaestiones.* Edited by Wilhelm Kübel. Monasterium Westfalorum: Aschendorff, 1968.

Aquinas, Thomas. *Opera omnia: Iussu impensaque Leonis XIII P.M. edita.* Vol. 6. *Summa theologiae: Prima secundae: A quaestione 1 ad quaestionem 70.* Rome: Typographia Polyglotta, 1891.

———. *Opera omnia: Iussu Leonis XIII P.M. edita.* Vol. 47, 1. *Sententia libri Ethicorum.* Rome: Sancta Sabina, 1969.

Boyde, Patrick. *Perception and Passion in Dante's "Comedy."* Cambridge: Cambridge University Press, 1993.

Cicero, Marcus Tullius. *De finibus bonorum et malorum.* Edited by C. F. W. Müller. Leipzig: B. G. Teubner, 1908.

Paul A. Dumol

Aquinas, St. Thomas

Philosopher and theologian, for centuries (though not yet in Dante's time) the single most authoritative figure in the Catholic intellectual tradition. Born into the nobility c. 1225, Thomas studied at Monte Cassino and Naples and entered the Dominican order, despite intense familial opposition, in 1244. The rest of his life was spent teaching, studying, and above all writing for and on behalf of his order: first in Paris (1245–1248) and Cologne (1248–1252) with his master Albert the Great; then again in Paris (1252–1259), followed by various places in Italy (Anagni, Orvieto, Rome, Viterbo) between 1259 and 1269; in Paris once more (1269–1272); and finally in Naples (from 1272). In 1274 he died—some said, poisoned by Charles of Anjou, as Dante seems to accept at *Purg.* 20. 69—on his way to take part in the Council of Lyons.

Thomas's prodigious output in philosophy and theology belies the brevity of his life and shows a clear development from relatively conventional works of Scholastic commentary (e.g., on Peter Lombard's *Sentences*) to the groundbreaking masterpieces of his maturity. Among dozens of treatises and commentaries on biblical and Aristotelian texts his two great *summae* ("summaries") stand out: the early *Summa contra Gentiles,* a comprehensive handbook of natural theology designed for use by missionaries "against the nonbelievers"; and the *Summa theologicae,* unfinished at his death, which was immediately recognized as a magisterial achievement in the systematic exposition of Christian doctrine (though some individual propositions were rejected and even condemned by ecclesiastical authorities in the 1270s) and whose renown secured both Thomas's canonization (in 1323) and his work's later acceptance as the basis of orthodox Catholic theology, consecrated when Pope Pius V declared him *Doctor Angelicus* in 1567.

So vast and multifarious a body of work cannot be summed up in a few words, but it may be said that Thomas's thought centers on the relationship, and particularly the distinction, between reason and faith; the attempt to define their respective spheres of operation; and the consequences of such definition for the individual human being's understanding of self, the world, and God. Thomas stands in—indeed, incarnates—a tradition that may, loosely but usefully, be called "Christian Aristotelianism." Although he knew something of Plato and much of Neoplatonic thought (especially as embodied in Augustine and Pseudo-Dionysius), his basic concern is always to deepen the Christian community's understanding of its own faith by incorporating concepts and terminology derived from the Aristotelian corpus (rediscovered in the Latin West since the twelfth century) into mainstream theology. Hence his commentaries on Aristotelian texts (such as the *Ethics,* the *Politics,* the *Metaphysics,* and the *De anima*) stand beside his biblical commentaries, theological treatises, and spiritual writings not in contradiction (as an older Christian tradition of antipaganism would have wanted) but as part of an attempt at intellectual synthesis in the service of Christian truth.

Dante's Thomas appears both as a character in *Paradiso* and as a pervasive presence in the intellectual background of all his major works. Indeed, until recently it was common to see Thomas posited as the dominant or even exclusive influence on Dante's intellectual formation, to the point where caricatures of the *Commedia* as merely a versified *Summa theologiae* could be taken seriously by admirers and detractors alike. (Busnelli and Vandelli's edition of the *Convivio,* published in 1934, is often taken as representing the high-water mark of the neo-Thomist tide in Dante scholarship.) In the last fifty years, however, the monumental labors of a line of outstanding scholars, beginning with Étienne Gilson and Bruno Nardi (who stressed the extent of Albert the Great's influence on Dante), have established a much more accurate, detailed, and interesting version of Dante's philosophical and theological inheritance, in which Thomas continues to occupy a place of honor and immense significance, but in which Dante's many divergences from Thomism and frequent indebtedness to other authoritative individuals and traditions—not to mention his own consistently quirky independence of mind—can more readily be acknowledged. It is, for example, worth noting that Dante never actually quotes or even refers to the *Summa theologiae,* although the *Summa contra Gentiles* is quoted by name at *Conv.* 4.15.12 and 4.30.3 as well as at *Mon.* 2.4.1, while Thomas's commentary on Aristotle's *Ethics* is likewise quoted directly at *Conv.* 2.14.14 and 4.8.1.

Thomas appears in *Paradiso* in the Heaven of the Sun, alongside other great representatives of the tradition of Christian thought, including his teacher Albert. The voice that begins speaking at *Par.* 10.82, which eventually reveals itself as that of Thomas (10.99), identifies first Albert and then the other ten occupants of their celestial habitation. Most surprising in this speech is the respectfully irenic reference to the historical Thomas's bitter professional rival, Siger of Brabant (10.133–138). After a pause in which the heavenly spheres turn harmoniously, ending canto 10, and Dante's narrative voice initiates canto 11, Thomas resumes speaking. Explaining that Providence has established *due principi* ("two princes," 11.35) to guide an errant church—St. Francis and St. Dominic, founders of their respective mendicant orders—he recounts the life of Francis of Assisi in warmly encomiastic terms and denounces the corruption of his own Dominican order (11.13–139). (In the chiastic structure of cantos 11 and 12, the Franciscan Bonaventure will pronounce the eulogy of Dominic and utter an equally severe judgment on the Franciscans in canto 12.) Thomas returns to the foreground in canto 13, where he elucidates an earlier reference (10.112–114) to the unmatched wisdom of King Solomon (13.31–111) and issues a stern warning to Dante to avoid being misled by mankind's habitual but dangerous rush to judgment.

Throughout his involvement in the action of *Paradiso,* then, Thomas is presented in a manner wholly appropriate to his historical activity and stature: as a distinguished thinker in the Christian tradition, an exemplary member of the Dominican order, a figure deeply concerned with the proper use of the human intellect, and one who seeks to resolve differences of detail, approach, and conclusion in the celebration of fundamental Christian truth.

Bibliography

The Cambridge Companion to Aquinas. Edited by Norman Kretzmann and Eleonore Stump. Cambridge, New York: Cambridge University Press, 1993.

Davies, Brian. *The Thought of Thomas Aquinas.* Oxford: Clarendon Press; New York: Oxford University Press, 1992.

Foster, Kenelm. "St. Thomas and Dante." In *The Two Dantes and Other Studies.* Berkeley, Los Angeles: University of California Press, 1977, pp. 56–65.

———. *The Life of Saint Thomas Aquinas: Biographical Documents.* London: Longmans, Green; Baltimore: Helicon Press, 1959.

———. "Tommaso d'Aquino." *Enciclopedia dantesca,* 5:626–649.

Gilson, Étienne. *The Christian Philosophy of St. Thomas Aquinas.* Translated by L. K. Shook. Notre Dame, Ind.: University of Notre Dame Press, 1994.

———. *Dante and Philosophy.* Translated by David Moore. New York: Harper and Row, 1963.

Nardi, Bruno. *Dante e la cultura medievale.* Edited by Tullio Gregory and Paolo Mazzantini. Bari: Laterza, 1985.

Weisheipl, James A. *Friar Thomas D'Aquino: His Life, Thought, and Work.* Garden City, N.Y.: Doubleday, 1974.

Steven Botterill

Arachne

A weaver who, out of excessive pride in her work, challenged Minerva to a contest. Envious of the beauty and perfection of Arachne's tapestry, the goddess destroyed it, whereupon in despair Arachne hanged herself. But Minerva intervened to save her life, transforming the rope around her neck into a cobweb and Arachne herself into a spider (Ovid, *Meta.* 6.5–145). In *Inf.* 17.18, Dante draws on the medieval allegorical tradition that viewed Arachne *(Aragne)* as a figure of the devil; in *Purg.* 12.43–45, she is an example of punished pride.

Nancy Vine Durling

Arethusa

One of the Nereid nymphs *(Aretusa)* whom Diana transformed into a fountain so that she could escape the love of Alpheus, a river-god who had taken a human form. But by turning back into a river, he was able to merge his waters with hers. Dante refers to the myth *(Meta.* 5.572–641) in *Inf.* 25.97, where, describing the monstrous exchange of forms between a sinner and a serpent, he claims to surpass Ovid's fantastic metamorphosis of Arethusa and Cadmus.

F. Regina Psaki

Argenti, Filippo

In *Inf.* 8, as Dante and Virgil are traversing the marsh of the Styx in the boat powered by Phlegyas, they are suddenly accosted by the angry soul of Filippo Argenti, referred to here as the *fiorentino spirito bizzarro* ("wild Florentine spirit," 8.62). The Styx constitutes the fifth circle of Hell and contains those souls guilty of anger. Following Aristotle and Aquinas, some commentators divide these souls into three distinct classes (see Aristotle, *Nicomachean Ethics* 4.5; and Aquinas, *ST* 1.2.46.8, 2.2.158.5): the *acuti,* who are quick to anger; the *amari,* who are sullen; and the *difficiles* (or *graves*), who are vindictive. Argenti would appear to belong to the first category, since his words to Dante suggest an excitable person with a quick temper. He was a member of the Adimari family in Florence and appears to have received his nickname, "Argenti," because he had his horse shoed with silver, according to Boccaccio (*Dec.* 9.8), who describes him as being a very wealthy

Dante casting aside Filippo Argenti as he crosses the Styx. Opere di Dante Alighieri, *edited by Cristoforo Zapate de Cisneros, Venice, 1757–1758. Giamatti Collection: Courtesy of the Mount Holyoke College Archives and Special Collections.*

knight *(cavaliere ricchissimo)* and a member of the Cavicciuoli branch of the Black Guelf Adimari family. The early commentators allude to particular "historical" events that supposedly provide the motivational context for this encounter in the fifth infernal circle. Because they belonged to different political factions, Filippo once gave Dante a slap on the face; Filippo's brother obtained Dante's possessions that the commune had confiscated after the poet's exile; Filippo's family energetically opposed any possibility that the exiled poet might one day return to Florence. The antipathy between the two families may also lie behind the invective against the Adimari, who are referred to as *l'oltracotata schiatta* ("the presumptuous clan") in *Par.* 16:115–117.

In canto 8 we witness the first truly dramatic encounter in the *Commedia,* where three charac-ters are simultaneously on stage. One of the interpretive questions raised by this passage concerns the pilgrim's reaction to and apparent anger toward Filippo and whether that response is motivated by *ira bona* ("righteous indignation") or by *ira mala* ("sinful wrath"). Does the pilgrim demonstrate a properly contemptuous response to the sin of anger—*bona ira,* as St. Thomas calls it—by recognizing and rebuking it for the evil that it is? Or has he rather given himself over to wrath and thus become guilty of the very sin punished in this circle? This complex question admits of no easy answer and is perhaps left intentionally ambiguous by the episode. The final image of Filippo is one of self-destruction, for he begins to tear at his own flesh with his teeth: *in sé medesmo si volvea co' denti* ("turned on himself with his teeth," 8.63), which appears to symbolize the self-destructiveness of anger.

Bibliography

Bigi, Emilio. "Moralità e retorica nel canto VIII dell' *Inferno.*" *Giornale storico della letteratura italiana* 154 (1977), 346–367.

Borgese, Giuseppe Antonio. "The Wrath of Dante." *Speculum* 13 (1938), 183–193.

Casagrande, Gino. "Dante e Filippo Argenti: Riscontri patristici e note di critica semantica." *Studi danteschi* 51 (1978), 221–254.

Donno, Daniel J. "Dante's Argenti: Episode and Function." *Speculum* 40 (1965), 611–625.

Forti, Fiorenzo. "Filippo Argenti." *Enciclopedia dantesca,* 2:873–876.

Kleinhenz, Christopher. "*Inferno* 8: The Passage across the Styx." *Lectura Dantis* 3 (1988), 23–40.

———. "Dante and the Bible: Intertextual Approaches to the *Divine Comedy.*" *Italica* 63 (1986), 225–236.

Piemontese, Filippo. "Filippo Argenti fra storia e poesia." In *Studi sul Manzoni e altri saggi.* Milan: Marzorati, 1952, pp. 169–185.

Pietrobono, Luigi. "Il canto VIII dell' *Inferno.*" *L'Alighieri* 1.2 (1960), 3–14.

———. *Il poema sacro. Saggio d'una interpretazione generale della "Divina commedia": Inferno.* Vol. 2. Bologna: Zanichelli, 1915, pp. 13–37.

Pischedda, Giovanni. "Motivi provinciali nel canto VIII dell' *Inferno.*" *Dante e la tematica medioevale.* L'Aquila: Japadre, 1967, pp. 35–40.

A Sanguineti, Edoardo. "Dante, *Inferno* VIII." In *Il realismo di Dante*. Florence: Sansoni, 1966, pp. 31–63.

Christopher Kleinhenz

Argia

Daughter of Adrastus, king of Argos, and character in Statius' *Thebaid*. Her husband, Polynices of Thebes, gave her the golden necklace of Harmonia as a marriage gift. In *Purg.* 22.109–110, Virgil, responding to Statius, mentions Argia as being *de le genti tue* ("of your people"). Argia is among the noble women of antiquity residing in Limbo. In illustrating modesty, Dante mentions Argia in *Conv.* 4.25.8.

Molly G. Morrison

Ariosto, Ludovico

Ferrarese poet (1474–1533) who spent all his adult life in the employ of the Estense rulers of Ferrara, first in the entourage of Cardinal Ippolito d'Este, then transferring to the service of the latter's brother, Duke Alfonso I, as a court-sponsored poet and dramatist but also as a sometime diplomat and administrative official. In addition to a number of youthful lyrics and *capitoli,* he composed several "erudite comedies" (among the first and most influential in the spectacular "rebirth of drama" at the beginning of the Cinquecento); seven "satires" of obvious Horatian derivation; and, of course, the long chivalric poem for which he is best known—and which became the most widely circulated literary work in sixteenth-century Europe: *Orlando furioso.* Although he makes no explicit mention of Dante in any extant writings, Ariosto certainly ranks with Machiavelli as one of the "High Renaissance" authors most fascinated and influenced by him. In his *capitoli,* and especially in the *Satire,* Ariosto makes one of the more successful post-Dantean adaptations of the *terza rima* scheme. Still, it is primarily in the *Furioso* that one should look to appreciate Dante's importance for Ariosto, beginning with the famous first line of the poem, *Le donne, i cavallier, le armi, gli amori* ("Of ladies, knights, of love and war"), which, at least in the final edition, clearly alludes to two lines of the *Commedia* (*Inf.* 5.71 and *Purg.* 14.109). Italian scholars—particularly Luigi Blasucci, Cesare Segre, Carlo Ossola, and Emilio Bigi—have shown conclusively the high frequency of lexical echoes of the *Commedia* in the poem. There is, moreover, evidence to suggest that Dantean influence grew in the course of revising the poem from its first, 40 canto version (1516) to its final, 46 canto incarnation (1532). It has long been recognized that Ariosto "Italianized" the language of the poem as he revised, presumably under the influence of his friend Pietro Bembo's *Prose della Volgar Lingua* (1525), which established the classic Tuscan of Petrarch, Dante, and Boccaccio as a model for high vernacular culture; and recent work suggests that the addition of numerous Dantean echoes in the revisionary process may have had thematic as well as stylistic motivations. More recently, critics, including Parker and Ascoli, have argued that Ariosto undertakes an elaborate parody and critique of Dante's poetics in both thematic and structural terms. This is especially true in the two major allegorical episodes of the *Furioso.* In the so-called Alcina episode (cantos 6–8, 10), Ruggiero's voyage to the antipodes includes ample allusions to several Dantean episodes including those of Pier delle Vigne (*Inf.* 13), Ulysses (*Inf.* 26), and the *femina balba* ("stammering woman") of *Purg.* 19, whose larger purpose is to point out the failure of the young knight's allegorical education and of a poetics, like Dante's, which aspires to educate its readers through allegory. Similarly, the symmetrically placed lunar episode (cantos 34–35) offers an abbreviated and ironic tour of the three realms of the Dantean otherworld. In this case an Ariostan hero, now the Englishman Astolfo, descends into Hell, though only as far as the first circle, where one Lydia is punished for a sin antithetical to Francesca's: ingratitude to her lover. He then ascends to the Earthly Paradise (more conventionally located than Dante's, among the "mountains of the moon" at the source of the Nile), where he acquires the guidance of St. John, the evangelist and author of Revelations (John conflates elements of Dante's Virgil, Beatrice, St. Peter, and St. Bernard and may look back to several pointed analogies that Dante makes between himself and St. John precisely in the Earthly Paradise, e.g., *Purg.* 29.105, 32.76). With John's aid he then flies up to the Heaven of the Moon, where he finds Orlando's lost wits along with all the other items ever mislaid on earth, and then he listens as John expounds an allegory of the power of true poets to confer fame everlasting on their patrons—not based on historical merits but rather on their willingness to pay for services rendered. Just as Ariosto's Hell ends abruptly and travesties Dante's, so his Paradise extends no further than the first heaven of the *sacro poema* (whose thematics of broken vows and poetics of fictional accommodation he clearly evokes), and he ostentatiously substitutes the pursuit of the nominal eternity of a famous name on earth for Dante-pilgrim's quest for ontological glory in the Empyrean. In a strikingly anti-Dantean moment, St. John concludes the episode with a confession that his fondness for poets derives from the fact that *"fui scrittore anch'io"* ("I too was a writer") and that his "patron," Christ, rewarded him with eternal life—implying none too subtly that his Gospel is flattery purchased by patronage. If Dante represents himself as a "theologus-poeta," Ariosto implies that the "theologians" who composed the Bible, and perhaps Dante as well, were no better than lying poets. Though these and other allusions to the *Commedia* tend to transform, and at times to mock, Ariosto's great precursor, there is no doubt that they also acknowledge the power of his poetic vision and its shaping influence on the Italian vernacular tradition.

Bibliography

Ascoli, Albert R. *Ariosto's Bitter Harmony: Crisis and Evasion in "Orlando Furioso."* Princeton, N.J.: Princeton University Press, 1987. Bigi, Emilio (ed.). "Introduzione" and commentary in Ludovico Ariosto, *Orlando furioso.* 2 vols. Milan: Rusconi, 1982.

Blasucci, Luigi. "La *Commedia* come fonte linguistica e stilistica del *Furioso.*" In *Studi su Dante e Ariosto.* Naples, Milan: Ricciardi, 1969, pp. 121–162.

Johnson-Haddad, Miranda. "Gelosia: Ariosto Reads Dante." *Stanford Italian Review* 11 (1992), 187–201.

Ossola, Carlo. "Dantismi metrici nel *Furioso.*" In *Ludovico Ariosto: Lingua, Stile e Tradizione.* Edited by Cesare Segre. Milan: Feltrinelli, 1976, pp. 65–94.

Parker, Patricia. *Inescapable Romance: Studies in the Poetics of a Mode.* Princeton, N.J.: Princeton University Press, 1979.

Segre, Cesare. "Un repertorio linguistics e stilistico dell'Ariosto: La *Commedia.*" In *Esperienze Ariostesche.* Pisa: Nistri-Lischi, 1966, pp. 51–83.

Albert Russell Ascoli

Aristotle

Aristotle was born at Stagira in northern Greece in 384 B.C.E. At age 17, he went to study under Plato; after the latter's death, he became tutor to Alexander the Great. At 49, Aristotle founded his own philosophical school, the Lyceum. The term "Peripatetics" was applied to him and his followers from his habit of walking about *(peripatein)* while teaching and engaged in philosophical discussion. Aristotle died at Chalcis in 322 B.C.E. Few philosophers have ranged so widely, making important contributions to the study of logic, metaphysics, epistemology, physics, biology, meteorology, mathematics, psychology, rhetoric, dialectic, aesthetics, and politics. Aristotle can be credited with the invention of ethics as a branch of philosophy, and he was the first to develop the study of deductive inference.

After the closure of the philosophical schools at Athens by the emperor Justinian in 529 C.E., Greek thought was kept alive mainly at Byzantium but also in the Arab world, especially by the Persian Avicenna (980–1037; *Inf.* 4.143) and the Andalusian Averroës (980–1037; *Inf.* 4.144), who was often acclaimed as "the commentator" for his attempt to salvage "pure" Aristotelian doctrine. In the West, Aristotle was known for centuries solely through the Latin translation of the *Categories* and *On Interpretation,* made, with commentaries, by Boethius (c. 480–c. 525; *Par.* 10.124–129); these works, together with Boethius' commentary on Porphyry's *Isagoge* became known as the Old Logic *(logica vetus).*

The virtual rediscovery of Aristotelian thought is one of the major landmarks in the intellectual history of western Europe. It was a relatively rapid process that evolved during the one hundred years preceding Dante's birth, although already in 1114 a Pisan, Stephen of Antioch, translated Aristotle's medical works into Latin, and Western scholars in Constantinople translated his tracts on logic. By 1265, about fifty-five of Aristotle's works had been translated into Latin, with at least seventeen translators known to us by name. Some of the older translations were executed from Arabic texts (e.g., the partial translation of the *Metaphysics* executed by Michael Scot in Toledo, c. 1220–1235), while eventually there were no less than four translations of this same work made from the original Greek text. Various commentaries were supposed to guide students towards the text's authentic meaning, though all too often they were

A chiefly concerned with demonstrating that Aristotle's teachings were compatible with Christian doctrine. All of Aristotle's works on logic were now known and formed the core of the "New Logic" corpus, including his *Posterior Analytics,* which taught medieval thinkers two essential tools: the complementary processes of induction and deduction as well as the demonstrative syllogism. Logic now deposed grammar as the chief area of study. For the first time, Christians were confronted with an organic philosophical system of pagan origin, even as they attempted to assimilate its naturalistic view of the universe into the Christian vision of humanity's mission in this world.

The new university institutions played a fundamental role in this process of assimilation, with the University of Paris as its intellectual powerhouse, but the process was not without its pitfalls. Prohibitions were announced in 1210 (Sens), 1215 (Paris), and 1231 (Gregory IX, *Parens scientiarum*)—although after the death of Pope Gregory in 1241, the papal prohibitions of Aristotle lost their edge. In the period preceding Dante's birth, all of Aristotle's works were prescribed for the Faculty of Arts at Paris, and their author was commonly referred to as "the Philosopher." The new Dominican order—the first religious order to make study an essential part of its discipline (although its constitutions of 1228 had forbidden the study of profane sciences)—produced the two leading Christian interpreters of Aristotelian thought: Albert the Great (d. 1280; *Par.* 10.98–99), whose stay in Paris (1240–1248) marked a turning point in the history of Aristotelianism; and Thomas Aquinas (d. 1274; *Par.* 10.99). Both influenced Dante profoundly—especially Albert, for his vindication of the validity of natural knowledge as distinct from revealed doctrine or supernatural wisdom.

At about the time of Dante's birth, Averroës's interpretation of Aristotle's *De anima* as teaching monopsychism through the supposed unicity of the possible intellect had been winning over some of the leading scholars in the Faculty of Arts at Paris (including Siger of Brabant: *Par.* 10.133–138). Aristotle had attempted to explain the process of understanding by positing both an active, or abstractive, and a receptive faculty. He therefore introduced the "agent" or "active" intellect, capable of a separate existence, which acts upon intelligible notions in the way that light brings out the potentiality of color. Alexander of Aphro-

disias (c. 200 C.E.) transformed this active intellect into a transcendent divine being, which the Schoolmen took to be God. The Aristotelian active intellect was complemented by the "possible" intellect, which signified the human faculty of progressively acquiring knowledge by the light of the active intellect. Unlike angels, humans are not pure active intellect; instead, they are characterized by their rational faculties, among which the possible intellect actualizes the potentiality for understanding and knowledge found in the individual (cf. *Conv.* 4.26.5). Averroës had posited a single potential intellect, immortal, that was active in but remained separate from human beings only during their lifetime—a belief that denied the doctrine of individual human immortality (cf. *Inf.* 10.13–15). This heterodox interpretation of Aristotle's *De anima* 3.5.430a.17–23 also implied that the soul is not the substantial form of the human body. The Averroist view was attacked most forcefully by Aquinas in his *De unitate intellectus contra Averroistas* (1270); it was condemned by Stephen Tempier, bishop of Paris, in 1270 and again in 1277.

The first thirteen years of Dante's life were thus a period of great ferment in the leading intellectual center of Christendom. In 1270, Tempier condemned thirteen philosophical errors and excommunicated all those who taught them knowingly: the four principal ones were the eternity of the world (Aristotelian), the denial of universal providence, psychological determinism, and the unicity of intellectual souls (Averroist). Until 1270, the two mendicant orders had followed largely similar paths in their intellectual endeavors. At this point, however, Aquinas's far-reaching innovations and the radicalism of philosophers such as Siger of Brabant provoked the Franciscan Bonaventure into launching a fierce attack on Aristotle and the latter's failure to grasp exemplarism, which was at the source of all his errors. Stephen Tempier formed a commission of sixteen theologians in 1277 that hurriedly condemned a hotchpotch of 219 propositions, including Thomist theses on such matters as the localization of spiritual substances and voluntary operation. The golden age of Christian syncretism for which Albert and Thomas had worked so valiantly was over. Symptomatic of the reaction by conservative theologians is the following statement made by the Augustinian theologian Ugolino of Orvieto in the fourteenth century: "For the most part ethics is a false doctrine [. . .] Aristotle did not know virtue but only the shadowy semblance of the virtues [*simulacra virtutum*], nor did he give proper rules."

When we turn to Dante's intellectual career, we find that his first substantial work, the *Vita Nuova* (c. 1293) shows how right he was to claim later (*Conv.* 2.12.4) that "some time after" Beatrice's death (1290) his lack of philosophical training made it difficult for him to understand Cicero's *De amicitia* and Boethius' *De consolatione philosophiae*. One of the many riddles in Dante studies is his friendship with Guido Cavalcanti, who—a few months before his death in August 1300—seemed perhaps destined for the same punishment as his father, Cavalcante, among the heretics that denied the immortality of the individual human soul (*Inf.* 10, esp. 58–72). Guido's passionate interest in philosophy was proverbial (cf. Boccaccio, *Dec.* 6.9); a treatise on the beatitude offered by philosophy was dedicated to Guido by the radical Aristotelian, Giacomo da Pistoia; and yet, Dante's "first friend" (*VN* 3.14) does not seem to have led the younger poet to embark on the study of philosophy during the heyday of their friendship. Now, however, Dante decided to set about studying philosophy "where it was truly to be found, namely in the schools of the religious and the disputations of the philosophers" (*Conv.* 2.12.7). We thus know that, before embarking on his political career (1295), and at some time between the end of 1291 and 1294 or 1295, Dante acquired a sophisticated layman's knowledge of philosophy through the important Franciscan center at Santa Croce in Florence and the Dominicans at Santa Maria Novella, where weekly debates on philosophical and theological matters were open to laymen (and where Remigio dei Girolami was a key Aristotelian thinker and preacher). With probable visits to Bologna, where committed Aristotelians such as Gentile da Cingoli were teaching in a prestigious lay university, Dante acquired an eclectic body of philosophical knowledge based on medieval interpretations of Aristotle—but with important Neoplatonic elements derived from such sources as Boethius, Pseudo-Dionysius, the *Liber de causis* (often attributed to Aristotle, although composed in Arabic towards the middle of the twelfth century by the Jewish Ibn Daoud), Avicenna, and Albert the Great.

The first results in Dante's writings may already be found in the opening verse of the canzone "Voi che 'ntendendo" (1293–1294), in which the poet addresses the angelic intelligences that move the third heaven through purely intellectual energy and an understanding of God's purpose (*Conv.* 2.5.18). Some ten to twelve years later, the full flowering of Dante's passion for philosophy gave birth to the *Convivio,* where Aristotle is hailed as the "master and guide of human reason" who charted the way to humanity's goal on earth (*Conv.* 4.6.7–8). Although he followed the mistaken beliefs of the ancient astronomers (2.3.4), he is "that glorious philosopher to whom nature most opened up its secrets" (3.5.7), mentioned by name more than fifty times (and as "the Philosopher" some forty times), who is in fact "master of our life" (4.23.8). Aristotle's authority is definitively established in *Conv.* 4.6, where his "quasi-divine" intellect is said to have allowed him to bring the science of ethics to perfection.

The rejection of philosophy posited by some scholars is not in fact attested in Dante's writings. The dating of the *Monarchia* as contemporaneous with the first sections of the *Paradiso,* if accepted, is important in this regard. In the Latin work (*Mon.* 1.1.4), Dante scorns the idea of any attempt to define "the nature of happiness," which has already been shown by Aristotle to consist in intellectual activity and the practice of the moral virtues (cf. *Conv.* 4.17.8). The fundamental concept of greed (the she-wolf of the *Commedia*) as the greatest obstacle to justice is formulated in *Mon.* 1.11.11, with an appeal to Aristotle's *Ethics.* The whole argument threading its way through chapters 5–15 of *Mon.* 1 is largely inspired by the Greek philosopher's writings on physics, metaphysics, and ethics. A notorious *crux* is provided by the definition of nobility in *Mon.* 2.3.4 as consisting in "virtue and ancient wealth, according to the Philosopher in his *Politics,*" since this very same definition had been attributed to Emperor Frederick II—and rejected—in *Conv.* 4.3.6ff. Some scholars (e.g., Gilbert) have claimed that Dante had not read the *Politics,* although many now assume that he was acquainted with the text (as always, in Latin translation and with the aid of commentaries). If the author of the *Convivio* was already acquainted with Aristotle's definition of nobility, did he attribute this to the emperor in order to (1) define the limits of imperial authority? (2) safeguard the autonomy of philosophical enquiry? (3) avoid any lessening of Aristotle's authority (still to be investigated in *Conv.* 4.6)? Toward the end of the work (*Mon.* 3.10.13), Aristotle is press-ganged into proving that the church was not entitled to accept Constantine's donation, while in the final chapter (3.15.4) he is again pressed into service in order to confirm the belief that the human soul is incorruptible.

Which of Aristotle's writings did Dante know? We have specific references to the *Ethics, Metaphysics, Physics, De anima, De caelo et mundo, De sensu et sensato, De generatione et corruptione, De iuventute et senectute, De animalibus, Organon, Rhetoric* and *Politics.* For his favorite text, the *Nicomachean Ethics,* Dante seems to have turned to both Robert Grosseteste's celebrated translation from the Greek and the *Compendium Alexandrinum* (also known as *Liber Ethicorum*), a useful digest pillaged by Brunetto Latini in his *Tresor* (2.1–39). Grosseteste and the *Liber* were exploited by Dante particularly when he felt the need to synthesize highly technical passages. Albert the Great's commentaries were used (e.g., in *Conv.* 2.4.17, 4.19.8–10), and the hymn of praise to philosophy found in the last three chapters of *Conv.* 3 was inspired or encouraged by Albert's commentary on *Ethics* 10.7. Aquinas is quoted in *Conv.* 2.14.14 and 4.8.1, while the definition of happiness in *Conv.* 4.17.8 was probably derived from his commentary rather than from the stated "first book of the *Ethics.*" Brunetto Latini is the source that led Dante to suppose that Aristotle had stated of justice that even its enemies such as thieves and robbers "love it" (cf. Latini, *Tresor* 2.81.2; and Cicero, *De officiis* 2.11.40). Latini's *Tresor* is again the hidden text (2.21.7, 2.22.4) that sparks off a highly personal invective against the wicked ways of tyrants in *Conv.* 4.27.13–14.

In the *Commedia,* the vindication of Aristotle as a teacher of ethics is found in the startling fact that the overall moral order of the Christian *Inferno* is grounded in Aristotle's threefold division of sinful behavior, in what Virgil refers to as "your Ethics" (*Inf.* 11.80; cf. *Ethics* 7.1), with the idea of the golden mean particularly in evidence in the fourth circle of sinners (misers and prodigals). As a pagan, Aristotle is placed in Limbo, where he is found among the "great spirits" (*Inf.* 4.118–135), raised up and honored as "the master of those who know," while his Arab disciples, Avicenna and Averroës, are also found among the pagan elite "who did not sin" (*Inf.* 4.33, 143–144), although they lived after the Christian revelation. In the *Paradiso* itself, Aristotle is still recognized as "your master," even as

the fundamental Aristotelian view of man as a political animal is accepted without question by the pilgrim in *Par.* 8.115–117. The presence of the controversial radical Aristotelian philosopher Siger of Brabant among the wise saints (*Par.* 10.133–138; cf. *Fiore* 92.9–11) is as tantalizing as the reference to Averroës in conjunction with humanity's need to realize the full potential of the possible intellect, in *Mon.* 1.3.9. The former must surely be understood as vindication of the autonomy of legitimate philosophical speculation, while the latter must be interpreted in the light of *Purg.* 25.61–75, with its affirmation of the indissoluble unity of the possible intellect and the human soul, based on Albert the Great's Aristotelian embryology. Aristotle's inevitable limitations as a pagan are stressed in *Purg.* 3.34–35. Nevertheless, most commentators believe that it is Aristotle who demonstrated by philosophical reasoning the love of God felt by "the eternal beings," which, together with the Bible and other religious authorities, strengthened Dante's own love of God (*Par.* 26.25–48). Finally, and most significantly, it was Dante's passionate belief in the intellectual and political unity of humankind that led the poet of the *Commedia* to invent an Aristotelianized Virgil, the herald of the empire, whose task it was to lead the pilgrim to Eden, thereby illustrating Dante's conviction that it is the emperor who must lead humanity to terrestrial beatitude ("figured in the earthly paradise") by dispensing justice and following the teachings of philosophy (cf. *Mon.* 3.15.7–8).

Bibliography

Aristoteles Latinus. Edited by L. Minio-Paluello. Bruges, Paris: Desclée De Brouwer, 1953–1978.

Boyde, Patrick. *Perception and Passion in Dante's "Comedy."* Cambridge: Cambridge University Press, 1993.

———. *Dante Philomythes and Philosopher: Man in the Cosmos.* Cambridge: Cambridge University Press, 1981.

Corti, Maria. "La filosofia aristotelica e Dante." *Letture classensi* 13 (1984), 111–123.

———. "*L'amoroso uso di sapienza* nel *Convivio.*" In *La felicità mentale.* Turin: Einaudi, 1983, pp. 72–145.

Davis, Charles T. "Education in Dante's Florence." In *Dante's Italy.* Philadelphia: University of Pennsylvania Press, 1984, pp. 137–165.

——. "The Florentine *Studia* and Dante's 'Library.'" In *The Divine Comedy and the Encyclopedia of Arts and Sciences*. Edited by G. Di Scipio and A. Scaglione. Amsterdam, Philadelphia: John Betjemans, 1988, especially pp. 355–359.

Gilbert, Allan. "Had Dante Read Aristotle's Politics?" *PMLA* 43 (1928), 603–613.

Gilson, Étienne. *History of Christian Philosophy in the Middle Ages*. New York: Random House, 1955.

——. *Dante the Philosopher*. London: Sheed and Ward, 1948.

Minio-Paluello, Lorenzo, "Dante's Reading of Aristotle." In *The World of Dante: Essays on Dante and His Times*. Edited by Cecil Grayson. Oxford: Clarendon Press, 1980, pp. 61–80.

Moore, Edward. "Dante and Aristotle." In *Studies in Dante: First Series*. Oxford: Oxford University Press, 1896 [1969], pp. 92–156.

Nardi, Bruno. "La conoscenza umana." In *Dante e la cultura medievale*. 2nd ed. Bari: Laterza, 1983, pp. 135–172.

van Steenberghen, F. *Aristotle in the West: The Origins of Latin Aristotelianism*. 2nd ed. Louvain: Nauwelaerts, 1970.

John A. Scott

Arius

Condemned by Thomas Aquinas at *Par.* 13.127–129, along with Sabellius, as one who distorted the clear meaning of the Scriptures. Arius (*Arrio* or *Ario*) was a priest in the Alexandrian Church and either the author or early propagator of the Arian heresy, which asserts among its tenets that the Father and the Son of the Trinity are not of a single substance and that Christ and the Holy Spirit are "created" beings inferior to the Father. Arius and this heresy were condemned by the Council of Nicaea in 325; although Arius was able to achieve some form of rehabilitation in 327, he was once again condemned in 333 and again rehabilitated in 335. He died in 336.

In a passage from the *Summa contra Gentiles* (4.6–8), which may lie behind Dante's use of Aquinas' coupling of Arius with Sabellius and his condemnation of both, Aquinas lists a number of scriptural passages which the Arians had distorted in their arguments for Christ's "created" nature and their consequent denial of the orthodox understanding of the Trinity, in which the Father, Son, and Holy Spirit are of the same substance and nature, differing only in their persons. Aquinas provides the orthodox interpretation of these passages in chapter 8.

Frank B. Ordiway

Arnaut Daniel

Renowned Provençal poet from Ribérac in the Périgord born into a noble family (according to his medieval biography) whom Dante places in the seventh circle among the lustful in Purgatory (*Purg.* 26.140). Benvenuto da Imola claims that he lived in the time of "the good count of Provence, Raymond Berenger" (r. 1161–1181). If he was born in 1145 or 1150 his life would have overlapped the lives of Bertran de Born (*Inf.* 28) and Richard the Lionhearted. Arnaut himself affirms that he was present at the crowning of King Philip II of France. Of his extant eighteen compositions only one in a ribald vein is not a canto; the remainder are songs of courtly love for which Dante prized Arnaut above all other craftsmen of their mother tongue in the *Commedia*. The treatise *De vulgari eloquentia* cites him three times (2.2.56, 59; 2.6.39). Dante's opinion is seconded by Arnaut's abundance of references to his technical craftsmanship. Although Arnaut takes no part in controversies about style, he dwells upon the shaping, polishing, and ornamentation of his works, and he is justly believed to have followed the *trobar clus* ("closed poetics"). In a famous sestina, whose form he probably invented and which Dante adapted in the second of the *petrose,* "Al poco giorno e al gran cerchio d'ombra," Arnaut binds together the double themes of physical and spiritual love. A reminiscence of this poem appears at a turning point in *Purg.* 30.46–7: *Men che dramma / di sangue m'è rimaso che non tremi* ("Less than a dram of blood is left in me that is not trembling"; cf. Arnaut: *Non ai membre no.m fremisca, neis l'ongla*). Dante pays tribute to him by having him speak in Provençal (*Purg.* 26.140–147).

Bibliography

Barolini, Teodolinda. *Dante's Poets: Textuality and Truth in the "Comedy."* Princeton, N.J.: Princeton University Press, 1984.

Durling, Robert M., and Ronald L. Martinez. *Time and the Crystal: Studies in Dante's "Rime petrose."* Berkeley, Los Angeles: University of California Press, 1990.

Perugi, Maurizio (ed.). *Arnaut Daniel, Le canzoni.* 2 vols. Milan: Documenti di filologia, 1978.

———. "Arnaut Daniel in Dante." *Studi danteschi* 51 (1978), 59–152.

Shapiro, Marianne. "*Purg.* 30: Arnaut at the Summit." *Dante Studies* 100 (1982), 71–77.

Toja, Gianluigi (ed.). *Arnaut Daniel: Canzoni.* Florence: Sansoni, 1961.

Wilhelm, James J. (ed. & trans.). *The Poetry of Arnaut Daniel.* New York: Garland Press, 1981.

Marianne Shapiro

Arrigo

One of the five Florentines of whom Dante requests information from Ciacco the glutton (*Inf.* 6.80). His identity remains uncertain, despite his identification, by Benvenuto da Imola, as a member of the Fifanti family, and in particular as the son of Odarrigo (= Oddo di Arrigo) de' Fifanti, who was involved in the murder of Buondelmonte de' Buondelmonti on Easter Day 1216, an event that led to the creation of the Guelf and the Ghibelline factions in Florence.

Richard Lansing

Arrigo Mainardi

A descendent of an ancient family who settled in Bertinoro. Arrigo fought on behalf of the people of Forlì in 1170 against the Faentini in S. Varano, where he was taken prisoner with Pier Traversaro. Arrigo was a close friend of Guido del Duca, who, during his denunciation of corruption in the cities along the Arno and in Romagna, recalls Arrigo as one of the noble, civilized individuals who are now all too few (*Purg.* 14.97). Guido announces his praise of Arrigo to Dante (employing the *ubi sunt* topos) on the second terrace of Purgatory, where he undergoes penance for the sin of envy.

Paul Colilli

Aruns

Etruscan soothsayer who predicted the civil war and the victory of Caesar over Pompey, according to Lucan (*Phars.* 1.584–588). A native of the hills of Luni in western Tuscany, near Carrara (famous for its white marble quarries), Aruns *(Aronta)* is punished in Hell along with Amphiaraus, Manto, and Tiresias for the sin of divination (*Inf.* 20.46).

Richard Lansing

Asdente

Maestro Benvenuto, nicknamed Asdente ("Toothless"), a poor cobbler of Parma. Though simple and modest, he was famed as a prophet and soothsayer during the latter half of the thirteenth century. He is reported by Benvenuto to have foretold the defeat of Frederick II at the siege of Parma in 1248. He is placed among the soothsayers in the fourth bolgia of the eighth circle of Hell (*Inf.* 20.118). In *Conv.* 4.16.6 Dante cites him as an instance of a person who would be called noble, if notoriety constituted nobility.

R. A. Malagi

Astrology

In the Middle Ages, astronomy and astrology were the two branches of star science. Astronomy described the motions of the stars and planets, and astrology taught how things on Earth were affected by these movements. Both disciplines were thought to be based on scientific fact, both required a high degree of mathematical skill, and both were taught in university courses. No one doubted that the light from heavenly bodies (e.g., sunlight) effected changes in earthly things. Opinion was divided, however, as to whether these changes were inevitable. Theologians, especially, insisted that human free will could overcome astral influence.

Dante agreed both with the astrologers on the power of the stars and with the theologians on the power of free will. His works contain over thirty explicit references to astrology, from which his views on the subject have been reconstructed in detail without controversy (Moore, 19–21; *Enc. dant.*, 1:427–431; Kay, 1–12). Dante believed that God made his will manifest to humans through the heavens: "it is without doubt within the capacity of human understanding to comprehend the mover of the heaven [God], and his will, through the motion thereof" (*Epist.* 5.23). This is so because the heavens are God's "instruments" for distributing his goodness on Earth. Thus the stars are the means by which the ideas in the divine mind are transmitted to and embodied in matter. Insofar as physical things are good, this perfection is imparted by the stars. Such things are not always perfect, however, because the beneficent influence of the stars is often reduced by the matter receiving it.

Most frequently Dante links astrology with the generation of things. Although astral influence does explain the production of minerals and animals, Dante is chiefly interested in the way the stars affect human character. Their influence is imprinted on each human embryo in the course of its development. The human soul, however, with its capacity for reason and free will, is conferred on the embryo directly by God; consequently its fate is not determined by the stars. Still, astrology can tell us what strengths and weaknesses of character each individual is born with. It is up to the individual, exercising free will, to decide whether these innate talents are to be used for good or evil. This doctrine is expressed most clearly by Marco Lombardo: "The heavens begin your motions; I do not say all of them, but supposing I said it, a light [of reason] is given you to know good and evil, and free will [that enables you to decide how it shall be used]," *Purg.* 16.67–76).

In the *Commedia* Dante repeatedly refers to the role of the stars in shaping human character, but one passage is the key to all the others. In the Heaven of Venus (*Par.* 8.97–148), Carlo Martello explains that, although heredity is the basic influence that shapes human character, a second factor is often more influential, for the heavens can override heredity (*Par.* 8.133–135). Between them, these two factors account for the difference in human character, and the reason, Carlo explains, is because through such differentiation God provides the diversity of talents that are required by organized human society, which is based on specialization and exchange of services.

Moreover, God uses the stars to shape human history by distributing talents in accordance with mankind's future needs as anticipated by divine providence. For example, when God wills a period of warfare, in the preceding generation the influence of Mars will produce many fighters. Furthermore, the stars can subtly impose God's will on us by effecting long-term changes in the nonrational preferences of mankind, such as fashions in language (*Par.* 26.128–130). Thus, the stars provide an invaluable indicator of God's will concerning mankind as a whole. By studying the motion of the heavens, one not only can perceive God's providence working in past and present history but also can glimpse the future pattern of human events. Dante's prophecies of a great future reformer are probably based on such astrological projections (*Inf.* 1.101–111; *Purg.* 20.13; *Par.* 27.139–148). Similarly, in the *Monarchia* he argues that the stars produce both new political conditions and a leader appropriate to them, whom the electors of the Holy Roman Empire can identify by recourse to astrology (*Mon.* 3.15.12).

Although scholars have long acknowledged that Dante held most of the opinions summarized above, they have been slow to recognize that he also made tacit use of astrological materials in constructing his poetry. In 1940, Palgen pointed out a number of parallels between the *Commedia* and several astrologers, notably Firmicus Maternus, whom Dante is not likely to have read. More plausibly, Rabuse in 1958 traced the extensive influence of Mars on characters in the *Inferno*. But Dante's poetic use of technical astrology was first firmly established by Durling in his analysis of the canzone "Io son venuto" (1975), which he subsequently elaborated in collaboration with Martinez (1990). In 1994, Kay showed that the seven planetary heavens of the *Paradiso* are crammed with 1,431 allusions to the astrological effects, or properties, of those planets. For instance, nuns are astrologically appropriate to the Moon, and especially those who have broken their vows. Furthermore, Kay argued that Dante often Christianized the secular astrology found in his sources. Of these sources, Dante relied most heavily on Michael Scot and Guido Bonatti, both of whom are astrologers condemned in the poem (*Inf.* 20.115–118), but he also made substantial use of Alcabitius, Ibn Ezra, Albumasar, Haly, John of Seville, and Ptolemy.

These studies have established that astrology is an important source for Dante's poetry, but much remains to be done. It remains to be seen to what extent Dante, like Chaucer, made use of other, more technical, astrological doctrines. Nonetheless, it is already certain that astrology—like philosophy and theology and, to a lesser extent, law and medicine—is a medieval academic discipline from which Dante constructed his poem.

Bibliography

al-Biruni. *The Book of Instruction in the Elements of the Art of Astrology.* Translated by R. R. Wright. London: Luzac, 1934.

Capasso, I., and G. Tabarroni. "Astrologia." *Enciclopedia dantesca,* 1:427–431.

Durling, Robert M., and Ronald L. Martinez. *Time and the Crystal: Studies in Dante's "Rime petrose."* Berkeley: University of California Press, 1990.

Kay, Richard. *Dante's Christian Astrology.* Philadelphia: University of Pennsylvania Press, 1994, especially pp. 261–282.

Moore, Edward. *Studies in Dante: Third Series.* Oxford: Clarendon Press, 1903, especially pp. 19–21.

North, J. D. *Chaucer's Universe.* New York: Oxford University Press, 1988.

Palgen, Rudolf. *Dantes Sternglaube.* Heidelberg: Winter, 1940.

Rabuse, Georg. *Der kosmische Aufbau der Jenseitsreiche Dantes.* Graz: Böhlaus, 1958.

Tester, S. J. *A History of Western Astrology.* Wolfeboro, N.H.: Boydell Press, 1987.

Richard Kay

Astronomy

As the last of the seven liberal arts, astronomy was an integral part of medieval education. But Dante valued it even more highly, for he ended each part of his *Commedia* with the word "stars" in order to stress their role as the link between God and his creation on Earth. Dante was convinced that man could ascertain God and his will by studying the motions of the stars (*Epist.* 5.8.23), which is to say in modern terms that astronomy provided the basis for astrology. Consequently, in his efforts to make the essentials of Latin clerical culture available in Italian, Dante included many lessons in astronomy, most notably in *Purgatorio.* Indeed, his use of astronomy is so extensive that only a book-length study can do it justice; fortunately many such studies are available, both in English and in Italian, to which the curious reader is referred for details (see the bibliography). Instead, the present article will describe Dante's universe in a general way and identify the principal sources for this worldview.

Like all his contemporaries, Dante assumed that Earth was the center of the universe. Around it were ten concentric spheres, or heavens, the nine innermost being the subject of astronomy, while the tenth and outermost one was known only through revelation as the abode of God, his saints, and the angels. The nine lower spheres were themselves invisible, but they carried the visible heavenly bodies on their surface. Closest to Earth was the sphere bearing the Moon; next came the heavens of the other planets—Mercury, Venus, the Sun, Mars, Jupiter, and Saturn—followed by the eighth sphere, bearing the fixed stars, and finally the first moving body, the Primum Mobile. Because the Greeks believed that these heavens must be perfect, it was assumed, in accordance with the Pythagorean doctrine of perfection, that they were spherical and that their motion was circular and continuous.

Each of the nine heavens, however, had its own peculiar motion. For Dante, the invisible Primum Mobile, or crystalline sphere, had the simplest, most perfect motion because it was closest to God. It revolved once every day, communicating this motion to the eighth sphere, which passed it on to successively lower spheres. Without this diurnal motion, Dante explains, none of the heavenly bodies would rise and set every day (*Conv.* 2.14.16). Following his source (Albertus Magnus), Dante incorrectly states that Ptolemy was the first to add a ninth sphere to Aristotle's eight (2.3.5); rather that innovation seems to have been made by Thabit ibn Qurra (d. 901).

The eighth sphere is called the "starry heaven" because it bears the constellations and other stars whose mutual relations are fixed, unlike the planets, which instead are "wandering" stars. In contrast to the single, simple movement of the ninth sphere, the sphere of the fixed stars had two movements. One was its daily revolution around Earth, in 23 hours and 56 minutes (a sidereal, or star, day, as opposed to a solar day of precisely 24 hours), which was considered a "passive" motion because it was received from the Primum Mobile. The other was its "proper" motion, which causes the equinoxes to come slightly earlier every year—at the rate, Dante thought, of about one degree every century. The eighth sphere is impelled by the ninth to move from east to west, but its own motion is in the opposite direction, and it is a minute slippage between these contrary motions that causes the precession of the equinoxes. All the planetary spheres were similarly conceived as moving from west to east by their proper motion, although they were forced to move mostly in the opposite direction by the passive, diurnal motion imparted by the Primum Mobile.

Only the ninth heaven revolved on the same axis as Earth's. All the lower heavens revolved on an axis that is inclined 23.5 degrees from the "celestial" axis of the universe. In the case of the eighth heaven, midway between the poles of its axis lies the circular band (12 degrees wide) known as the zodiac, the midpoint of which is the circle called the "ecliptic." This band is the pathway followed by the Sun and the other planets.

For the Greek astronomers, the most challenging problem had been to construct a mathematical model that would accurately predict the irregular movements of the planets. Each of them moved relative to the fixed stars at a different rate, returning to a given star in a fixed period. Moreover, not all the planets (except the Sun and the Moon) always move in the same direction as the fixed stars. Mars, Jupiter, and Saturn occasionally reverse their course in a retrograde motion for some months, while Venus and Mercury oscillate from one side of the Sun to the other. These phenomena are more readily accounted for by a model in which the planets move around the Sun in elliptical orbits. Ptolemy, however, succeeded in constructing a geocentric model in which the same courses were described by a combination of circles. This could be done either by having the planet revolve on an epicycle—a smaller circle that had its center on the surface of the larger sphere that bore it (its "deferent")—or by offsetting the sphere's center from the axis of the universe, which produced an "eccentric deferent." Either way, the path of the planet then described an ellipse rather than a true circle. Moreover, Ptolemy accounted for the variable speed of some planets, such as Venus, by having the center of the epicycle revolve with uniform speed around a point called the "equant," which was offset from the center of the deferent sphere.

Dante was hardly concerned with these technicalities, however; they are mentioned rarely in the *Convivio* and only once in the *Commedia* (*Par.* 8.3). Like most learned medieval men, he did not need to puzzle through Ptolemy's complicated proofs in the *Almagest;* instead, he accepted the results, as summarized by Albertus Magnus, whose commentary on Aristotle's *De caelo* in turn depended on Alfraganus. Then as now, for the practical purpose of determining the position of planets, one needed only an accurate set of tables for the year in question. Almost certainly Dante used the Perpetual Almanac of Prophatius for the year 1300, but he may also have used the Marseilles Tables as well. Most of his remarkably accurate references to planetary positions, especially in connection with time-reckoning, could have been obtained readily by using these tabular data in conjunction with an astrolabe, which was in fact a two-dimensional model of the heavens that medieval scholars routinely employed to calculate

sidereal and solar time as well as the rising, setting, and position of the planets and major fixed stars.

In short, Dante's knowledge of astronomy was that of a well-educated man of his time (cf. Chaucer). What is remarkable, as Patrick Boyde has observed in detail, is not Dante's grasp of astronomy but his talent for converting it into poetry.

Bibliography

al-Biruni. *The Book of Instruction in the Elements of the Art of Astrology.* Translated by R. R. Wright. London: Luzac, 1934.

Albertus Magnus. *De coelo et mundo.* In *Opera omnia.* Edited by A. Borgnet. Vol. 4 (Paris: Vivès, 1890).

Alighieri, Dante. *Dante Alighieri, Opere minori 2.2.* Edited by Domenico De Robertis and Cesare Vasoli. Milan, Naples: Ricciardi, 1988.

Boyde, Patrick. *Dante Philomythes and Philosopher: Man in the Cosmos.* Cambridge: Cambridge University Press, 1981, pp. 132–171.

Buti, G., and R. Bertagni. *Commento astronomico della Divina Commedia.* Florence: Sandron, 1966.

Capasso, I., and G. Tabarroni. "Astronomia." In *Enciclopedia dantesca,* 1:431–435.

Dictionary of Scientific Biography. New York: Scribner's Sons, 1970–1980.

Moore, Edward. "The Astronomy of Dante." In *Studies in Dante: Third Series.* Oxford: Clarendon Press, 1903, pp. 1–108.

North, J. D. *Chaucer's Universe.* New York: Oxford University Press, 1988.

Orr, M. A. *Dante and the Early Astronomers.* London: Gall and Inglis, 1913.

Pecoraro, P. *Le stelle di Dante.* Rome: Bulzoni, 1987.

Pedersen, Olaf. "Astronomy." In *Science in the Middle Ages.* Edited by David C. Lindberg. Chicago: University of Chicago Press, 1978, pp. 303–337.

Prophatius of Montpellier. *Almanach Dantis Aligherii, sive Profhacii Judaei Mo tispessulani Almanach perpetuum ad annum 1300 inchoatum.* Edited by J. Bofitto and C. Melzi d'Eril. Florence: Olschki, 1908.

Thorndike, Lynn. *The "Sphere" of Sacrobosco and Its Commentators.* Chicago: University of Chicago Press, 1949.

Richard Kay

Atropos

Eldest of the three Fates (Parcae), Atropos *(Atropòs)* severs the thread of life that is wound by Clotho on Lachesis' distaff and is spun until Atropos' divine authority determines the moment of death for mortals. In *Inf.* 33.126 Dante learns that there are treacherous souls who are consigned to Ptolomea before the action of Atropos takes place.

Diana Cavuoto Glenn

Attila

King of the Huns (433–453) who invaded and ravaged Europe before being defeated by the Romans and Visigoths in 451 at Châlons-sur-Marne in France. Dante's description of him as *flagello in terra* evokes his reputation as the "Scourge of God" (*Inf.* 12.134). He is punished in the river Phlegethon, with other tyrants and murderers. In *Inf.* 13.149 Dante cites him as the destroyer of Florence, following a popular legend that confused his name with that of Totila, king of the Ostrogoths, who had attacked Florence in 542. But despite Villani's account (*Cronica* 2.1), which places the destruction of Florence in the year 440, no such event took place.

Richard Lansing

Auerbach, Erich

One of the two or three most important twentieth-century critics of Dante, born in Berlin (1892–1957). After an academic career that took him from Marburg, Germany, to Istanbul, Turkey, he taught for ten years, from 1947 to 1957, in the United States, first at Pennsylvania State University and later at Yale, where he became Sterling Professor of Romance Philology the year before he died. Dante is one of the authors to whom Auerbach devoted most of his attention, as in his major 1929 monograph, *Dante als Dichter der irdischen Welt (Dante: Poet of the Secular World)*. His seminal 1938 essay "Figura," first published in the Florentine periodical *Archivum romanicum,* provides a link between this early work and the methodological and exegetical conquests of his American years. In it Auerbach guides the reader with critical fervor and lucid intelligence through the complexities of the symbolic and poetic world of Dante's *Commedia.* Auerbach's criticism follows a twofold itinerary. On the one hand, it corroborates Hegel's assertion that "Dante plunges the living world of humankind, their destinies and their individual sufferings into a world of immutable existence." On the other, the critic identifies what he calls "the figural tradition" and situates Dante within it. This tradition considers the characters and events of the Old Testament as *umbrae futurorum* ("shadows of future things"), projections that will reach their destined fulfillment, their final realization, in the events of the Christian New Testament. The critic's task is to trace the development of the so-called *sermo humilis* ("humble style") of the Gospels until reaching the territory explored by Dante, in which the language of humility is exploited through the filter of the "comic style" of the new poem. An informed reader of Dante, however, must in Auerbach's view be capable of applying the principle of figural interpretation to the stages and episodes of the *Commedia.* Thus, Cato in the *Purgatorio* is seen as a *figura impleta*—a figure that has achieved fulfillment—because he is called on to represent for all eternity and on an absolute plane what he strove to be in the course of his life on Earth: a zealot and a champion of liberty. The cult of political freedom, which had been such a lifetime commitment for Cato that it led to his suicide, is translated in the world of the *Commedia* into freedom from sin. In the *Purgatorio* he becomes the authorized witness to this new kind of active Christian emancipation. Auerbach's later Dante criticism—the essays on Farinata and Ca alcante in *Mimesis* (1946) and on Saint Francis in the *Commedia* (1944); the notes on David "the humble psalmist," Raab, and Solomon (1946); the discussion of the prayer to the Virgin Mary (1949); "Dante's Addresses to the Reader" (1954)—is ever more bound to the dynamics of Dante's text. Although Auerbach's untimely death prevented him from synthesizing his insights in a second monograph, Dante criticism owes him an immense debt for the brilliantly innovative light he threw on the much-visited details of Dante's poem.

Bibliography

Auerbach, Erich. *Dante als Dichter der irdischen Welt* (1929). Translated by Ralph Maunheim as *Dante: Poet of the Secular World* (1961).

Della Terza, Dante. *Da Vienna a Baltimora. La dia pora degli intellettuali europei negli Stati Uniti d'America.* Rome: Editori Riuniti, 1987.

———. "E. A." *Belfagor* 18 (1963), 306–322.

Levin, Harry. "Two *Romanisten* in America: Spitzer and Auerbach." In *The Intellectual Migration:*

Europe and America, 1930–1960. Edited by Donald Fleming and Bernard Bailyn. Cambridge, Mass.: Harvard University Press, 1969, pp. 463–484.

Valesio, Paolo. "Foreword" to Erich Auerbach, *Scenes from the Drama of European Literature.* Minneapolis: University of Minnesota Press, 1984, pp. vii–xxviii.

Wellek, René. "The Scholar-Critics in the Romance Literatures: Erich Auerbach." In *A History of Modern Criticism: 1750–1950.* Vol. 7. *German, Russian, and Eastern European Criticism, 1900–1950.* New Haven, Conn.: Yale University Press, 1991, pp. 113–133.

Dante Della Terza

Augustine, Friar

One of the twelve residents of the second garland of souls in the sphere of the Sun, named by St. Bonaventure (*Par.* 12.130). A disciple of St. Francis (c. 1210), Augustine *(Agostino)* was named head of the order at Terra di Lavoro in 1216 and was reputed to have witnessed the ascension of Francis's soul to Heaven in 1226.

Michael Papio

Augustine, St.

No single individual has more profoundly shaped the Christian tradition of the West than Aurelius Augustinus (354–430). Trained as a pagan teacher of rhetoric, and driven by a restless desire for philosophical truth, he finally converted to the Christianity of his mother in 387. At first as monk and then as priest and bishop, Augustine led the diocese of Hippo, a city in northern Africa second only to Carthage in ecclesiastical importance. For thirty-five years there he taught, preached, and wrote, as well as engaging in many polemical struggles. His major works include his autobiographical *Confessiones* (397–401), with its now-famous account of his conversion; the *De Doctrina Christiana* (396, 426), in which he sets forth a Christian understanding of rhetoric centered on the Bible; the *De Trinitate* (399–422), his most profound theological work, with its subtle meditation on the Trinitarian structure of Creation; the *De Genesi ad litteram* (401–414), which provided an important discussion of different kinds of vision; and the *De civitate Dei* (413–427), written in response to the fall of Rome in 410 and a sustained examination of the tension between the City of Earth and the City of God. Together with his various writings on the Bible, these works were to exert an enormous influence on the theology of the Middle Ages, during which Augustine was perhaps the primary authority.

In accord with this prominence, Dante reveals a firsthand knowledge of Augustine's writings and, indeed, evokes the saint directly in many passages in the *Convivio,* the *Monarchia,* and the *Epistolae.* In the *Letter to Cangrande,* he appeals to the authority of Augustine as a warrant for his claims to the beatific vision, while in *Mon* 3.3, when speaking about those doctors of the church who were assisted by the Holy Spirit in writing their books, Augustine alone is cited by name. Given this, it is surprising that in the *Commedia,* where one might expect him to have a featured role in the *Paradiso* on the scale of those afforded Aquinas or Bonaventure, he should be mentioned only twice and then almost in passing. The first reference is in *Par.* 10.118–120, where Augustine is named by way of identifying someone else (Orosius); the second is in *Par.* 32.35, when St. Bernard points out various saints within the heavenly rose and notes, beneath John the Baptist, *"Francesco, Benedetto ed Augustino"* ("Francis, Benedict, and Augustine"). Whereas Francis is celebrated by Aquinas for almost an entire canto (*Par.* 11), and Benedict is encountered personally in the heaven of the contemplatives (*Par.* 22), Augustine is given nothing more.

Various reasons for this omission have been offered: the poet does not always reward important figures with an appearance in the *Commedia* (as witnessed by the absence of St. Paul, who is mentioned only in *Inf.* 2.32); Dante was marking a preference for the Aritotelian thought of the Scholastics over the Platonism of Augustine; he was expressing his radical dissent from the anti-Roman historical-political vision developed in the *De civitate Dei.* This latter possibility is perhaps the most likely, for both in the *Monarchia* and throughout the *Commedia* Dante not only takes issue with Augustine's negative assessment of pagan Rome but also argues for a more positive notion of the earthly city in general, whether he looks back to an earlier stage in the history of Florence (*Par.* 15) or calls for the renewal of a universal Christian empire.

Nonetheless, the *Commedia* is inconceivable apart from Augustine's thought, either encountered directly or through the mediation of subsequent theology. One sees this most evidently in Dante's civic imagination, the way he presents both Hell and Heaven according to Augustinian notions of *civitas,* or citizenship. Thus, while Dante rejected Augustine's near equation of Rome with the city of Satan, in the *Inferno* he drew heavily on the idea of the *civitas diaboli,* in which the lust for power and domination holding sway in fourteenth-century Florence is depicted as the *libido dominandi* described at length in the *De civitate Dei.* Likewise, Dante's idea of paradise, first presented in *Purg.* 15.49–57 as the eternal celebration of partnership, is almost a gloss on Augustine's description of God's city in *De civ. Dei* 15.5. The poet also reveals his debt when he has Sapia (*Purg.* 13.94–96) define life in the earthly city as a pilgrimage lived *in via,* en route to the heavenly realm where ultimately one belongs. Nor is Augustine's influence to be found only in Dante's thoughts about cities and citizenship. It has also been argued (Newman) that the three kinds of vision detailed in *De Genesi ad litteram* informed the way the poet imagines the three canticles: *Inferno* as the realm of materiality (Augustine's *visio corporalis*), *Purgatorio* as the space of dream and artistic representation *(visio imaginativa),* and *Paradiso* as unmediated vision *(visio intellectualis).* More fundamental still is the importance of Augustine's model of conversion presented in the *Confessiones,* where a writer looks back on his earlier self across the divide of a life-changing experience and recounts the painful journey between then and now precisely to bear witness to the goodness he discovered.

Bibliography

Calcaterra, Carlo. "Sant' Agostino nelle opere di Dante e del Petrarca." *Rivista di filosofia neoscolastica.* Special supplement to vol. 23 (1931), pp. 422–499. (Reprinted in *Nella selva del Petrarca.* Bologna: Capelli, 1942.)

Fallani, Giovanni. "Dante e S. Agostino." *L'esperienza teologica di Dante.* Lecce: Milella, 1976, pp. 185–203.

Freccero, John. *Dante: The Poetics of Conversion.* Edited by Rachel Jacoff. Cambridge, Mass.: Harvard University Press, 1986.

Hawkins, Peter S. "Divide and Conquer: Augustine in the *Divine Comedy.*" *PMLA* 106.3 (May 1991), 471–482.

Mazzotta, Giuseppe. *Dante, Poet of the Desert: History and Allegory in the "Divine Comedy."* Princeton, N.J.: Princeton University Press, 1979.

Newman, Francis X. "St. Augustine's Three Visions and the Structure of the *Commedia.*" *MLN* 82 (1967), 56–78.

Peter S. Hawkins

Augustus

The first Roman emperor, who lived from 63 B.C.E. to 14 C.E., and who was originally named Caius Octavius. He received a new name, Caius Julius Caesar Octavianus *(Ottaviano),* after his great-uncle, Julius Caesar, adopted him. The Roman senate and people conferred upon him the title of Augustus *(Augusto)* in 27 B.C.E. to signify their veneration. Dante employs this same honorific to refer to emperors Frederick II *(Inf.* 13.68) and Henry VII of Luxemburg (*Epist.* 5 and 7) and, in the feminine form, to refer to the Virgin Mary as Heaven's empress (*Par.* 32.119).

Positive references to Augustus occur both in Dante's prose writings (*Conv.* 2.13.22, 4.5.4; *Mon.* 1.16.1; *Epist.* 5.24) and in all three canticles of the *Commedia.* Virgil refers to the emperor as *'l buono Augusto* ("the good Augustus," *Inf.* 1.71) and as the one who buried the Latin poet's bones (*fur l'ossa mie per Ottavian sepolte, Purg.* 7.6). Dante-poet magnifies the splendor of the chariot in the Terrestrial Paradise by declaring that not even Augustus enjoyed one so beautiful (*Purg.* 29.116). But the key reference occurs in *Par.* 6.73–81, a passage lauding Augustus as the marshal *(baiuolo)* of the Roman peace *(pax romana)* that fostered the birth of Jesus in the meridian of time. Such high praise typifies the medieval view of Augustus' reign.

Bibliography

Davis, Charles T. *Dante and the Idea of Rome.* Oxford: Clarendon Press, 1957, especially pp. 58ff.

Hollander, Robert, and Albert L. Rossi. "Dante's Republican Treasury." *Dante Studies* 104 (1986), 59–82.

Madison U. Sowell

Authority

Throughout the Middle Ages, "authority" (Latin *auctoritas;* Italian *autorità* or *autoritade*) was a crucial concept in a range of fields, notably those of philosophy, theology, literature, and politics. And the "author" (Latin *auctor* or *autor;* Italian *autore*) who possessed it was a privileged cultural figure. In brief, "authority" refers to the legitimated or legitimating truth value or power or both accorded to a text or an official (both referred to as *auctoritates*). As Dante puts it , the "author" is one "worthy of faith [in his truth] and obedience [to the exercise of his powers]," and "authority" is the action of an author which commands such "faith and obedience" (*Conv.* 4.6). Thus Aristotle and Virgil and a restricted number of other classical figures are *auctores*, whose texts may be cited as *auctoritates*, carrying superior credibility with respect to later writings. Thus, *a fortiori,* the Scriptures and the Church fathers command the obedient attention of their readers. Thus, in the institutional domain, the pope and the emperor wield a supreme authority intrinsic to their respective offices.

In classical Roman times, the *auctor* was primarily a juridical witness defined by the rhetorical force and/or credibility of his testimony, which accrued to him through individual character and contingent circumstances (Cicero, *Topics* 20.73–78). Under the Christian dispensation *auctoritas* takes on an impersonal and transhistorical quality, in keeping with its ultimately transcendent source: God is the ultimate *Auctor* who combines absolute truth with absolute power, and from him, and in him, all human *authority,* both textual and institutional, derives and grounds itself. Medieval *auctoritas,* then—though expressed through fallible human writers and officials and their works—transcends the contingency and individuality of the Ciceronian witness (Curtius, 51–52, 464).

Into this pervasive "culture of authority" numerous typologies, distinctions, and qualifications were introduced. Much of the work of definition is done through etymological analyses of the two key words, and Dante too takes this route in his definitional treatment of the topic in the *Convivio.* As Chenu and others have shown, a range of competing etymologies were available in the Middle Ages. The most useful example, inasmuch as Dante's treatment in the *Convivio* derives directly from it, is in Hugutio of Pisa's early-thirteenth-century etymological encyclopedia, the *Magnae Derivationes,* where three separate etymologies are given to cover three different fields of authority.

The first of these is the political *auctor,* whose name is derived from *augere* ("to augment or expand"), because it is the office of *imperatores* to expand the state. The second definition, the one we have already seen Dante drawing upon, treats intellectual *auctores,* from Greek, *autentin* (that is, the "philosophers and the discoverers of the [liberal] arts" whose sayings are "worthy of imitation" and "should be believed"). Finally, Hugutio offers a third, much less common definition, *auctor* from *avieo* ("to bind"), which refers to poets, like Virgil and Lucan, who bind poems together with metrical feet. Again in *Conv.* 4.6, Dante gives, repeats, and expands this last definition as a secondary alternative to *auctor* from *autentin.* While he does not explicitly refer to the political *auctor,* from *augeo,* his discussion does distinguish the political authority of Frederick II from the philosophical authority of Aristotle in a way that recalls Hugutio's third type of *auctor* (Ascoli 1989). Noteworthy too is that, among nearly 120 uses of the Latin and Italian words for *author* and *authority* in the Dantean corpus, over half (65) are in the *Monarchia* and refer to the commanding authority of the political or spiritual leader. (The others are distributed as follows: *Convivio,* 31; *De vulgari eloquentia,* 6; *Commedia,* 5; and 10 spread over four *Epistles.*)

The *auctor* also is defined in relation to adjacent concepts and categories. Chenu (1927) notes the traditional opposition between the *auctor* as guarantor of a text's truth and the *actor,* who is the artisinal maker of a given object but confers no special status on it (Dante does not explicitly make this distinction, but he alludes to it: e.g., *DVE* 2.8; cf. Ascoli 1991). As A. J. Minnis (94) has shown, the *auctor* is also distinguished from other producers of texts: the *scriptor,* who physically produces a manuscript; the *compilator,* who assembles the texts of others into a new manuscript; the *commentator,* who creates his own text in explicating the text of an *auctor.* This typology emphasizes the radical separation between the authoritative past and the reverential modern culture that looks back to it for illumination. In the special case of the Scriptures there is more than one author, to whom differing degrees of "faith and obedience" are due: the human *auctores* and the divine *Auctor.* Finally, as an epistemological category, *auctoritas* is juxtaposed with two other potential, and potentially competing, sources of

A truth: reason and experience (cf. Aquinas, *ST* 1.1.8; Dante, *Mon.* 1.5, 2.1; *Conv.* 4.3).

Given the complex place of *auctoritas* in medieval culture, it is unsurprising to find important conceptual questions springing up around it or to note that its status is often quite problematic, increasingly so in the later Middle Ages. Peter Abelard's *Sic et Non* (twelfth century) explores at length the problem of reconciling frequently conflicting authorities on any given doctrinal question. Minnis observes a distinct trend in thirteenth- and fourteenth-century biblical exegesis, particularly in the academic prologues or *accessus ad auctores* to the works of *auctores,* toward redefining the respective roles of the two authors of the Bible, with increasing prominence given to the historical, human author. Minnis further argues that this trend is important for other types of late medieval writing, in effect tending to encourage the humanization and personalization of the writer. Related issues are raised by the major late medieval cultural project of the Scholastics, notably Aquinas, who, on the one hand, redefine the established canon of *auctores* by their reverential treatment of Aristotle and, on the other, make increasing claims for the power of individual human reason to define truth independent of *auctoritas* and for their own status as intellectual innovators (Chenu 1950). Similarly, the emergence of a rapidly growing vernacular philosophical and literary culture (e.g., the *Romance of the Rose,* Brunetto Latini's *Tresor,* and, of course, Dante) raised questions both about how to place modern writers vis-à-vis the ancient *auctores* and about the nascent vernaculars vis-à-vis the traditional vehicle of *auctoritas,* Latin (Ascoli 1991). In the domain of institutional authority, finally, there are repeated jurisdictional clashes between the papacy and secular powers, above all the Holy Roman emperors (especially, for Dante, Frederick II and Henry VII), which raise significant practical and conceptual issues about attempts of both sides to ground and legitimate their *potestas* in transcendent *auctoritas* (Tierney).

Numerous traditional means existed for resolving such conflicts and ambiguities. Temporal priority is usually taken as a defining attribute for establishing an effective hierarchy of authorities, as, for example, in Dante's description in *Mon.* 3.3.11–16 of the derivation of spiritual authority over time from the Scriptures to the councils and the fathers of the church and, finally, to the belated Decretalists, who gloss those who

came before. At the same time, as we have seen, divine authority always takes precedence over human and historical *auctoritates* no matter how venerable (*ST* 1.1.8; Chenu 1950), just as Christian truth supersedes pagan truth. As Hollander has shown, the latter principle is at work in Dante's best-known deployments of the language of *autore* and *autorità,* the complimentary references to Virgil as *lo mio maestro e 'l mio autore* ("my master and my author," *Inf.* 1.85) and to God as *verace Autore* of the Bible ("veracious author," *Par.* 26.40), and the small groups of references that cluster around them (*Inf.* 4.113; *Par.* 26.26, 47).

As the three examples cited from the *Convivio,* the *Monarchia,* and now the *Commedia* demonstrate, Dante operated well within the terms and the framework provided by the medieval culture of authority. He was concerned with all the three distinct types of *auctoritas* sketched by Hugutio: epistemological (whether philosophical or theological), institutional (whether spiritual or political), and poetic. At the same time, as befits a modern, vernacular author without official political or ecclesiastical standing, he scrupulously avoided attributing *auctoritas* directly to himself and his works: only one use of the word in his corpus is self-reflexive, and even then the authority attributed is only relative (in *Conv.* 1.4.13 he says he writes in a highly technical manner to acquire "greater authority" because of the degraded circumstances of his exile). Even in the *Epistle to Cangrande,* the writer who claims to be Dante, although following the form of an *accessus ad auctorem,* uses the unprecedented term *agens* rather than the normal *auctor* to designate the *Commedia*'s writer (para. 14), suggesting the *auctor* as mere "doer or maker" of a text.

At the same time, however, Dante's various works tend to make extraordinary de facto claims to authority, while, at the same time, his explicit treatments of the concepts of *auctoritas* and of individual *auctores* complicate and further challenge the already fluid and problematic situation of the culture of authority. The most typical strategies he uses are (1) delimiting the competence of two given authorities with respect to each other and (2) submitting one (human) authority to another (divine). And both strategies tend to increase the space in which his own implicit claims to authority can flourish. As Étienne Gilson (156) has noted, both the *Convivio* and the *Monarchia* pit two authorities against one another, attributing absolute competence to each, but within a clearly circumscribed field (in *Conv.* 4.3–9, the two are philosopher and emperor; in *Mon.* 3, the two are emperor and pope). In the *Commedia,* as just observed, the authority of the great pagan poets and philosophers is subordinate to the human authors of the Bible—and above all to God, the "truthful Author." This rhetorical and conceptual manuevering allows Dante to short-circuit, at least in part, the authorizing systems of political hierarchy and intellectual priority. In particular, his repeated stress on the ultimately divine origin of all historically exercised authority tends to humanize and hence to compromise even the most potent *auctores* (most notably Virgil), but it also allows for the possibility that even a modern writer whose claims on authority are as weak as his own could receive "authorization" directly from God. Illustrative is the passage from the *Monarchia* cited earlier, in which Dante discredits his opponents, the Decretalists, by invoking the traditional hierarchical model but implies his own absolute mastery of the issue, even though his place in the historical flow would make him more derivative and less credible than they.

The paradoxical results of this partial deconstruction of the medieval system of authority—which is, however, accompanied by a partial transfer of *auctoritas* to Dante, to modernity, and to the vernacular—can be registered in two later fourteenth-century developments. On the one hand is the increasingly prominent notion of a distinctly humanized authorship, found, for example, throughout the works of Francis Petrarch, which essentially rejects the impersonal medieval *auctor* (as, for example, in the highly personalized and sharply critical epistle addressed to Cicero, *Familiar Letters* 24.3). On the other hand is the spate of fourteenth-century commentaries and *accessus ad auctorem* which for the first time systematically treat a modern, vernacular writer, Dante Alighieri, with the same kind of reverence usually reserved for the classical *auctores.*

Bibliography

Ascoli, Albert Russell. "'Neminem ante nos': Historicity and Authority in the *De vulgari eloquentia.*" *Annali d'Italianistica* 8 (1991), 186–231.

———. "The Vowels of Authority (Dante's *Convivio* IV.vi.3-4)." In *Discourses of Authority in Medieval and Renaissance Literature.* Edited by Kevin Brownlee and Walter Stephens. Hanover: University Press of New England, 1989, pp. 23–46.

Chenu, M. D. *Toward Understanding St. Thomas.* Translated by A. M. Landry and D. Hughes. Chicago: Henry Regnery, 1964, especially pp. 128–138. First published in French, in 1950.

———. "Auctor, Actor, Autor." *Bulletin du Cange: Archivium Latinitatis Medii Aevi* 3 (1927), 81–86.

Curtius, Ernst Robert. *European Literature in the Latin Middle Ages.* Princeton, N.J.: Princeton University Press, 1953. First published in 1948.

Gilson, Étienne. *Dante and Philosophy.* Translated by D. Moore. New York: Harper and Row, 1949. Reprinted in 1963.

Hollander, Robert. *Allegory in Dante's "Commedia."* Princeton, N.J.: Princeton University Press, 1969.

Minnis, A. J. *Medieval Theory of Authorship: Scholastic Literary Attitudes in the Later Middle Ages.* 2nd ed. Philadelphia: University of Pennsylvania Press, 1988.

Stabile, Giorgio. "Autore"; "Autorità." *Enciclopedia dantesca,* 1:454–460.

Tierney, Brian. *The Crisis of Church and State, 1050–1300.* Englewood Cliffs, N.J.: Prentice-Hall, 1964.

Albert Russell Ascoli

Avarice

In Roman Catholic theology, one of the seven capital Sins. In its simplest definition "avarice" is an unchecked desire to have more than one needs. It is a sin because it goes beyond due measure in seeking or possessing material wealth, beyond what is necessary to a person's station in life. Taken specifically, and according to St. Thomas Aquinas, there are two ways in which this lack of measure or moderation may manifest itself.

First, *avarice* may mean lack of moderation regarding one's disposition toward worldly goods, such as an immoderate love, desire, or pleasure of having them. In this sense avarice is a sin against self and is the opposite of the sin of *prodigality,* which means going too far in giving. Both avarice and prodigality are opposed to the virtue of *liberality,* a golden mean that keeps the two extremes in check. In short the intrinsic meaning of avarice here is that of hoarding; and of prodigality, that of

A squandering. (Incidentally, it should be noted that souls guilty of prodigality must not to be confused with the so-called *squanderers* punished in the second ring of the seventh circle [*Inf.* 13]. The latter are really *violent destroyers of their own possessions.*)

Second, avarice may relate directly to the actual acquiring or retaining material possessions. This means going too far in getting or keeping them. In this sense avarice is a sin directed against one's neighbor. The wealth of this world cannot be possessed by many at one time. Therefore, it is sinful for a person to enjoy affluence beyond measure, while someone else suffers extreme want. But taken more broadly it is also sinful for anyone, including religious and political leaders of communities and states, to acquire or seize great riches or through violence to conquer lands and territories. The measure here is set by *justice.* Therefore, in this second case avarice is in direct opposition to justice and is a mortal sin.

In medieval times avarice was considered one of the gravest sins, indeed *the* gravest, against the Christian spirit of love. The concept took its impetus from St. Augustine's statement that "Greed is poison to charity" (*Quest.* 36.83), and it became a commonplace from the fifth century onward. The basis for this was the fact that during this time the meaning of avarice was broadened to include every sort of unchecked desire to possess any sort of things—including *avaritia . . . altitudinis* ("insatiable greed for high office," Gregory the Great, *Hom. in Ev.* 1.16.2). Thus the Pauline dicta that "avarice is the root of all evils" (1 Tim. 6:10) and that it is as "serving idols" (Ephes. 5:5) become fully justified within the long and rich tradition of avarice. In the thirteenth century the main authors and the basic ideas relating to avarice were discussed and formalized by St. Thomas Aquinas, as summarized above (see *ST* 2.2.118). Further, it is worth noting that St. Thomas, in discussing avarice in its role as opposing justice, invokes an animal image from Ezekiel in which the avaricious are compared to ravening wolves (Ezek. 22:27). This is interesting in the sense that it guarantees for us the symbolism that *lupa/lupo* ("wolf") acquires in the *Commedia.*

Dante inherited this tradition and made it his own. He is concerned with avarice taken in its first meaning, namely, as a sin against self, and with prodigality as its opposite. We find it punished in the fourth circle of *Inferno* (*Inf.* 7). But Dante's treatment of avarice here is only formal, and prodigality remains totally secondary. This, too, is strictly within tradition. Since early times avarice was considered as a more reprehensible moral fault than prodigality, for the latter was thought to be closer to, or to have greater affinity with, liberality. This is the reason for which in *Inf.* 7 Dante gives only marginal attention to prodigality, and in *Purg.* 19–22 he does not even mention it, only indicating indirectly that it was Statius' sin.

In reality Dante is much more concerned with the larger and more significant aspect of avarice. For him the gravity of the sin of avarice lies in its public dimension, namely, in the sense that it goes against the social order and hence against justice. This idea is expressed many times in his minor works as well as in the *Commedia.* In the *Convivio* Dante speaks of the psychological aspects of avarice: how it is born and what are its effects on the psyche of the avaricious. To support his argument he cites the Bible and classical authors: Cicero, Seneca, Horace, Juvenal, and Boethius as well (*Conv.* 4.12.4–8). But a reading of certain passages from the *Monarchia* and from the *Epistles* offers perspectives that help us understand the profound ethical and political reasons which motivate Dante in his approach to avarice. First and foremost in these two works greed is seen as the main obstacle to the realization of justice (*Mon.* 1.11.11–15), and hence to the realization of peace (*Mon.* 3.16.11) and of the empire as well (*Epist.* 6.22). According to Dante, avarice made Jewish priests abominable (*Epist.* 11.1), and now it blinds the clergy in general (*Mon.* 3.3.8) and cardinals in particular (*Epist.* 11.14ff.). From the *Commedia* we know that the infernal guardian of the avaricious and prodigal is Plutus, who is called "cursed wolf" (*Inf.* 7.8) and that in *Purg.* 20.10–12 the expression *antica lupa* ("ancient she-wolf") is a metaphor for avarice. According to the prophecy in *Inf.* 1, the *lupa* will be killed by a *veltro* ("greyhound"), and thus justice will be restored to humanity (*Inf.* 1.100–111). At the basis of contemporary corruption is the insatiable greed of the pope, who has assumed the power of the emperor, and now "the sword is joined to the shepherd's staff" (*Purg.* 16.109–110). Since Constantine's donation, popes have become idolaters of gold and silver (*Inf.* 19.112–115), and their avarice afflicts the world (*Inf.* 19.104). They deceive their flock by appearing as shepherds while operating as "rapacious wolves" (*Par.* 27.55), because the accursed florin (the most widely sought gold coin of the time, struck in Florence and, for Dante, the symbol of greed) has turned "the shepherd into a wolf" (*Par.* 9.131–132). In this connection, it must be remembered that in *Inferno* there is a particular place for a special kind of avarice—that practiced by some popes in Dante's time. It goes by the name of *simony* and is the subject of canto 19—a fundamental canto for the full understanding of the political aspect of avarice and of its consequences, as portrayed by Dante.

In addition to men of the church, Dante also accuses men of the state such as Rudolph of Habsburg (*Purg.* 6.103), King Frederick II of Sicily (*Par.* 19.130–132), and in particular the entire Capetian dynasty (*Purg.* 20.47ff.) of avarice. In this sense, entire collectivities are rebuked as avaricious, e.g., the Bolognese (*Inf.* 18.63), the Catalans (*Par.* 8.77), and especially the Florentines (*Inf.* 6.74, 15.68) who are themselves called "wolves" (*Purg.* 14.50) for their greed.

Dante's moral integrity on one side leads him to reproach vehemently avarice in all its forms and aspects, and on the other causes him to regret deeply the good old times when people were honest and despised material goods. And remember that this was a century in which commercial and financial systems had already been developed and operative for some time; when Florentine merchants and bankers had already been enjoying supremacy—and huge returns on their money—throughout northern Europe and elsewhere for many years, as the inscription placed in 1255 by the city fathers on the facade of the city hall (Bargello) bears witness, the same inscription that Dante will make his own in a bitter sarcastic rendering at the very beginning of *Inf.* 26: *Godi, Fiorenza, poi che se' sì grande / che per mare e per terra batti l'ali, / e per lo 'nferno tuo nome si spande!* ("Rejoice, Florence, since you are so great that on sea and land you beat your wings, and your name spreads through Hell!").

Bibliography

Bloomfield, Morton W. *The Seven Deadly Sins: An Introduction to the History of a Religious Concept.* East Lansing: Michigan State University Press, 1967.

Cassell, Anthony K. "Ed una lupa." In *Lectura Dantis Americana. Inferno* I. Foreword by Robert Hollander. Philadelphia: University of Pennsylvania Press, 1989, pp. 66–76.

Davis, Charles Till. "Dante's Vision of History." *Dante Studies* 93 (1976), 143–160. Reprinted in *Dante's Italy and Other Essays.* Philadelphia: University of Pennsylvania Press, 1984, pp. 23–41.

Ferrante, Joan M. *The Political Vision of the "Divine Comedy."* Princeton, N.J.: Princeton University Press, 1984.

Hyde, John Kenneth. "Social and Political Ideals of the *Comedy.*" In *Dante Readings.* Edited by Eric Haywood. Dublin: Irish Academic Press, 1987, pp. 47–71.

———. "Contemporary Views on Factions and Civil Strife." In *Violence and Civil Disorder in Italian Cities, 1200–1500.* Edited by Lauro Martines. Berkeley, Los Angeles: University of California Press, 1972, pp. 273–307.

Little, L. K. "Pride Goes before Avarice: Social Changes and the Vices in Latin Christendom." *American Historical Review* 76 (1971), 16–49.

Gino Casagrande

Avaricious and Prodigal, The

In the *Inferno* the avaricious and the prodigal, i.e., the misers and the spendthrifts, are placed in the fourth circle. They have as their guardian Plutus, the "cursed wolf" (*Inf.* 7.8), and are given one of the shortest descriptions of the entire *Commedia,* barely fifteen tercets (*Inf.* 7.22–66). In the description the two groups are together in the circle, indistinguishable and unrecognizable. They are separated only by the sign that distinguished them in life. They are compelled to push within their own semicircle large boulders: the avaricious in one half of the circle, the prodigal in the other. When they meet, they strike and reproach each other. Then they turn around, pushing the big weights in the other direction, until they meet again at the opposite end of the semicircle, and so on. The imagery of the semicircles is important. Avarice and prodigality may be thought as representing the opposite points of a circle's diameter, the center of which is the rational mean between the two extremes. The sinners are compelled to push around the huge boulders eternally without ever coming to the rational mean. This is their common punishment. In addition to the image of the circle, or two semicircles, we find here references to the whirlpool in the Straits of Messina and the specific mentioning of Charybdis and of the round dance (7.22–24). These, too, are also

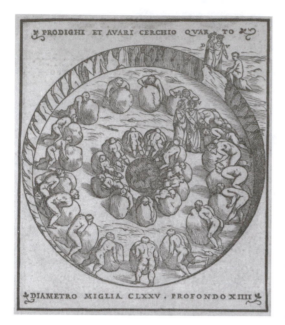

Dante among the avaricious and prodigal in the fourth circle of Hell. La comedia di Dante Aligieri, with commentary by Alessandro Vellutello, published by Francesco Marcolini, Venice, 1544. Giamatti Collection: Courtesy of the Mount Holyoke College Archives and Special Collections.

relevant, for in the Middle Ages "Charybdis" was commonly used as a synonym and personification of avarice. In addition, the imagery of circularity has the function of underlining the structure of the entire episode, and it ties in nicely with the other image of Lady Fortune and her wheel. Given the great multitude of people, individuals here are not identified. The distinguishing characteristic that separates the avaricious from the prodigal will be apparent only on Doomsday. The avaricious will rise from death with their fists clenched tight; the prodigal will rise with their hair cropped close. These are the symbols of their sin and the real sign of the *contrapasso*. In this circle Dante sees many tonsured people: these are priests and *papi e cardinali, / in cui usa avarizia il suo soperchio* ("popes and cardinals, in whom avarice does its worst," 7.47–48). This statement is noteworthy from at least two points of view. First, in the *Commedia* Dante is only marginally interested in the sin of prodigality. Second and more important, here at the beginning of the *Commedia* Dante, in a very indirect way, sets his aim against men of the church, particularly against cardinals and popes, because of their avarice. This will be one of the great motifs of the entire poem. In *Inferno* there is

a particular place for a special kind and a more sinful type of avarice (*Inf.* 19). It is reserved for some of the contemporary popes whose "avarice afflicts the world" (*Inf.* 19.104) and whose sin goes under the name of *simony*. They are Nicholas III, Boniface VIII, and Clement V. The last two in particular—according to Dante—are directly responsible for the political decadence and corruption of humanity.

In the *Purgatorio* the avaricious and the prodigal are atoning for their sins on the fifth terrace. The description of the terrace spans from the second half of canto 19 to most of canto 22. As made clear by Pope Adrian V (*Purg.* 19.115–126), here the punishment adheres very closely to the law of *contrapasso*. The sinners lie in prone position, face down upon the ground, with hands and feet tied, outstretched and motionless. They are weeping and, amid deep sighs, recite part of Ps. 119: *adhaesit pavimento anima mea* ("my soul clings to the dust"). Dante speaks only with two of the souls of this terrace, Adrian V and Hugh Capet. They are both avaricious. There is no mention by Dante that the prodigal are also here. We learn this later, when Virgil asks Statius how it could have been possible for him to be avaricious. To which Statius answers that in reality he was prodigal and as such he had to expiate his sin together with the avaricious (*Purg.* 22.19–54).

Dante's choice to place here Adrian V, a pope, and Hugh Capet, a king, acquires a deep political meaning. Here, on the Terrace of Avarice, are placed the highest representatives of the two powers on earth—the spiritual and the temporal. The two repentant sinners are the spokesmen for Dante's firm and unrelenting moral and political ideals against the two supreme guides of humanity—the pope and the emperor. To be sure, Adrian V was "entirely greedy" (*Purg.* 19.113), including avarice of honor and high position, as he himself admits (*Purg.* 19.109–110). This is Gregory the Great's *avaritia . . . altitudinis* ("insatiable greed for high office," *Hom. in Ev.* 1.16.2), commonly accepted throughout the Middle Ages. To become pope was to reach the highest position on Earth. On the other hand, Hugh Capet's dynasty had been ruthless in acquiring wealth, lands, and territories by force and violence. Here Dante wants to brand avarice and all the vices issuing from it, the so-called seven daughters of avarice (see St. Thomas Aquinas, *ST* 2.2.118.8). On this basis some critics, such as Scartazzini, point out that Dante exemplifies each daughter by the names of the seven examples of avarice that the souls on this terrace recite during the night (*Purg.* 20.103–117).

Bibliography

Casagrande, Gino, and Christopher Kleinhenz. "*Inferno* VII: Cariddi e l'avarizia." *Aevum* 54 (1980), 340–344.

Ciacone, Roberto. "Ugo Capeto e Dante." *Aevum* 49 (1975), 437–473.

Kaske, Robert E. "Dante DXV and Veltro." *Traditio* 17 (1961), 185–254.

Padoan, Giorgio. "Nella cornice degli accidiosi e degli avari (canti XIX–XX)." In *Lectura Dantis Modenese.* Modena: Banca popolare dell'Emilia, 1984–1986, pp. 83–99.

Paparelli, Gioacchino. "Adriano V e gli avari del Purgatorio." In *Ideologia e poesia di Dante.* Florence: Olschki, 1975, pp. 223–242.

Soave-Bowe, Clotilde. "Purgatorio 19: Adrian V." In *Dante Readings.* Edited by Eric Haywood. Dublin: Irish Academy Press, 1987, pp. 123–142.

Vallone, Aldo. "Canto VII." In *Lectura Dantis Scaligera: I, Inferno.* Florence: Le Monnier, 1971, pp. 221–244.

Gino Casagrande

Averroës (Ibn-Rushd)

Preeminent philosopher (c. 1126–c. 1198) of the Islamic world before Dante and esteemed commentator of Aristotle's works. Dante places Averroës *(Averois)* in Limbo as a pagan among those *di grande autorità* ("with . . . great authority," *Inf.* 4.113). Born in Córdoba, he was a jurist and a physician, but primarily a philosopher who was mainly concerned with defending the authority and the autonomy of philosophy against the absolute authority of theology. Against Algazel's *Destruction of Philosophers* he wrote *The Destruction of Algazel's Destructions.* Averroës believed that God is the author of both the natural and the supernatural revelation: the former is shown by the Aristotelian works; the latter, by the Koran *(On the Harmony of Religions and Philosophy).* He wrote three kinds of commentaries on Aristotle's works: the *Great Commentaries* (analysis and explanation of each paragraph of a work by Aristotle), the *Medium Commentaries* (syntheses of Aristotle's paragraphs), and finally *Commentaries,* which paraphrases the Aristotelian works and is followed by a personal conclusion.

Averroës attempted to resolve a seeming contradiction in Aristotle's *De anima.* The Greek philosopher states that the soul is the form of the body; but, being a substantial form, the soul is existentially conditioned by corporeal matter. Therefore, once separated from its partner, the soul itself will perish. On the other hand, in *De anima* 3.4.429a–b, Aristotle states also that human knowledge is abstract and independent of matter, its activity being spiritual in nature. In order to resolve the contradiction and defend the doctrine of the soul's immortality, Averroës conceived his famous Neoplatonic-inspired theory, according to which there is but one eternal active intellect for the human race, which is related to a passive one; both, however, are separated from human individuals whose proper form is an organic cogitative soul. The soul captures through the senses the external impressions or forms and transmits them to the passive intellect. The role of the active intellect is to join with the passive one and transfigure the material forms into intelligible ones. The active intellect, being the divine cause of the human species, makes the species, and not individuals, immortal. For all the philosophers of the Middle Ages, Averroës is known as the "Commentator" by antonomasia. Dante records his appreciation of the commentaries in the line *Averois che 'l gran commento feo* ("Averroës, who made the great commentary," *Inf.* 4.144). Even though in *Purg.* 25.63–67 Dante rejects the theory of a universal possible intellect—Averroistic theory—he resorts to citing the Arab philosopher's principles when they serve to corroborate his own demonstrative arguments, as in *Mon.* 1.3.9.

Bibliography

Davidson, Herbert. "Averroës on the Active Intellect as a Cause of Existence." *Viator* 18 (1987), 191–225.

Gilson, Étienne. *Dante and Philosophy.* Translated by David Moore. New York: Harper and Row, 1949.

Nardi, Bruno. *Dante e la cultura medievale. Nuovi saggi di filosofia dantesca.* 2nd ed. Laterza: Bari, 1949.

Vasoli, Cesare. "Averroe." *Enciclopedia dantesca,* 1:473–479.

Mario Trovato

Avicenna

Abū Ali al-Husain ibn Abd-Allah ibn Hasan ibn Ali ibn Sina—which by way of Hebrew became Europeanized as "Avicenna"—was the most renowned and influential philosopher-physician of medieval Islam. Born in August 980 (370 egira) in Kharmaithan, a village near Bukhara, of Persian parents (although little is known about his father, who had been governor of the town under the Samanid ruler Nuh), from an early age he became acquainted with every aspect of contemporary culture, studying philosophy, geometry, arithmetic, medicine, religion, literature, and natural science. He wrote his first book, a compendium entitled *Majmu (Compendium)* at the age of 21, and by his death in 1037 (426 egira) he had produced a phenomenal body of work. Over one hundred of his treatises have survived, ranging from encyclopedic books to brief works and covering philosophy, natural science, and religious and literary problems. Only a few of his works were written in Persian; most were written in Arabic. His principal medical work, *al-Qanun fi al-Tibb (The Canon of Medicine),* translated into Latin by Geraldo da Cremona (d. 1187), became the text on which medieval Scholastic medicine was based. Among his first works translated by various schools of translators were the principal parts of his most detailed and longest philosophical treatise, *Kitab al-Shifa (The Book of Healing).* Avicenna's philosophical system owes much to Aristotle's, although it cannot be called Aristotelian.

Although his works were already known in the West, it is generally believed that Dante knew Avicenna only indirectly, through Albertus Magnus and St. Thomas Aquinas. In *Inf.* 4.143, Avicenna is simply mentioned among the *spiriti magni* ("great spirits"), where he is placed between the two greatest physicians of antiquity, Hippocrates and Galen. In *Conv.* 2.13.5, Dante states that according to Plato, Avicenna, and Algazel, the generation of souls, both of animals and plants, results from the intelligences that move the heavens. In *Conv.* 2.14.5, Avicenna is mentioned with Aristotle and Ptolemy concerning the constitution of the Milky Way. In *Conv.* 3.14.5, he is mentioned for having clarified the difference between light, radiance, and reflected light. In *Conv.* 4.21.2, Dante distinguishes Avicenna's and Algazel's theories of the origin of nobility in the human soul from those of Plato and others.

More complex and problematic is the question of a possible indirect influence of Avicenna (probably via Albert the Great) on Dante concerning the nature of the *intelletto possibile* ("possible intellect," *Conv.* 4.21.5; but see also *Purg.* 25.37–75), a thesis proposed and strenuously defended by Bruno Nardi in his discussion of Dante's description of the origin of the human soul. Nardi's conclusion that Dante's philosophical view in this regard—revived recently by Maria Corti—was essentially heretical has not been shared by all critics. Avicenna's influence may also be present in Dante's discussion of the *divinatio in somnis* ("divination of dreams"), considered as a possible demonstration of the immortality of the soul (*Conv.* 2.8.13).

Bibliography

Afnan, Soheil M. *Avicenna: His Life and Works.* London: George Allen and Unwin, 1958.

Alverny, Marie-Thérèse D'. *Avicenne en Occident.* Paris: J. Vrin, 1993.

Corti, Maria. *La felicità mentale. Nuove prospettive per Cavalcanti e Dante.* Turin: Einaudi, 1983.

Nardi, Bruno. *Dante e la cultura medievale.* 2nd ed. Bari: Laterza, 1949.

Massimo Ciavolella

Azzolino

Ezzelino da Romano, born in 1194, was the leader of the Ghibellines in northern Italy and the son-in-law of Emperor Frederick II of Sicily. He was infamous for his cruelty. Villani remarks of him: *Questo Azzolino fu il più crudele e ridottato tiranno che mai fosse tra' cristiani* ("This Azzolino was the most cruel and feared tyrant who ever lived in Christendom," 7.73). So great were his atrocities that in 1255 Pope Alexander IV initiated a crusade against him. He is placed in the first ring of the seventh circle of Hell, among the tyrants (*Inf.* 12.109–110). His sister Cunizza alludes to the destruction he wrought on the March of Treviso in *Par.* 9.29–30. His death occurred shortly after he was wounded in battle by the Marquis of Este at Cassano in 1259.

Richard Lansing

B

Ballata

In the *De vulgari eloquentia* (2.3.5) Dante notes that the excellence of the canzone can be measured in part by the fact that it is complete in itself, requiring no external aids, unlike the *ballata,* which must have the accompaniment of dancers. He relegates the *ballata* and sonnet to the inferior ranks of poetry and promises to speak of them in the fourth book, which unfortunately was never written. The metrical form of the *ballata* was invented in the middle of the thirteenth century, and its basic strophic structure is very similar to that of the canzone, with one major difference: it begins with a refrain *(ripresa, ritornello)* of varying length that is then repeated (in performance) after every strophe. The number of lines in the refrain determines the nomenclature of the *ballata: stravagante* (five or more lines), *grande* (four lines), *mezzana* (three), *minore* (two), *piccola* (one), and *minima* (a single verse less than a hendecasyllable). The last verse (or verses) in each strophe contains a rhyme that recalls that of the refrain. For example, in the *Vita Nuova* Dante wrote a *ballata grande,* "Ballata, i' voi che tu ritrovi Amore," which has the following metrical structure: XYYXAbCAbCCDDX (the last rhyme in the stanza, X, recalling the final rhyme of the *ripresa*).

Of his six *ballate,* the one in the *Vita Nuova* is clearly reminiscent of those by Guido Cavalcanti. The other five are found among the *Rime.* One of Dante's earliest compositions, the *ballata mezzana* "Per una ghirlandetta," does not, however, follow Cavalcantian models but would appear to reflect in its shorter meters (combination of nine- or eight-syllable lines for the *fronte* and *settenari* for the *sirma*) the more popular style of the poems found in the *Memoriali Bolognesi.* The other four *ballate* are "I' mi son pargoletta," "Perché ti vidi giovinetta," "Voi che savete ragionar d'Amore," and "Deh, Violetta, che in ombra d'Amore" (the first two being *mezzana* and the last two, *grande*).

The hierarchy of styles formulated in *De vulgari eloquentia* would suggest, at least in the abstract, the superiority of the canzone over the *ballata* and of the *ballata* over the sonnet. In actual practice, however, Dante wrote many more—and often finer—sonnets than he did *ballate,* and thus readers must always seek to understand the poet's critical judgments within their original context.

Bibliography

Baldelli, Ignazio. "Ballata." *Enciclopedia dantesca,* 1:502–503.

Beltrami, Pietro G. *Metrica, poetica, metrica dantesca.* Pisa: Pacini, 1981.

Monterosso, Raffaello. "Ballata: musica." *Enciclopedia dantesca,* 1:503–504.

Fubini, Mario. *Metrica e poesia: Lezione sulle forme poetiche italiane.* Florence: Le Monnier, 1970.

Spongano, Raffaele. *Nozioni ed esempi di metrica italiana.* Bologna: Pàtron, 1974.

Christopher Kleinhenz

Bambaglioli, Graziolo de'

Graziolo (c. 1291–1343) was a notary in Bologna and author of one of the earliest commentaries on the *Commedia,* written in Latin in 1324. Unlike many fourteenth-century commentaries, there is no controversy surrounding its date of composition,

B which is recorded by the author himself in his gloss to *Inf.* 21.112–114.

Graziolo's commentary takes the form of an apotheosis of Dante. The *proemio* praises Dante exuberantly, proclaiming the poet a *philosophye verum alumpnum et poetam excelsum* ("a true pupil of philosophy and a distinguished poet"). The designation of Dante as poet and philosopher is a typical fourteenth-century tribute. Two scriptural citations provide a context for assessing Dante's accomplishments: the first compares Dante to the divinely inspired Solomon; the second, taken from Ezekiel, compares Dante to an eagle that has ascended to the heights of Mount Lebanon. Proof of Dante's scaling of such extraordinary heights is the *Commedia*, a vast repertoire of all sciences—theology, astrology, moral and natural philosophy, rhetoric, and poetry.

Graziolo's unqualified praise of Dante acquires greater resonance when seen against the criticisms launched by Cecco d'Ascoli, professor of astrology at the University of Bologna from 1322 to 1324; Cardinal Bertrando del Poggetto, who ordered the *Monarchia* to be burned; and Fra Guido Vernani, who wrote a treatise condemning the *Monarchia* in 1327, addressing his work to Graziolo. Although Dante had been dead only three years, his works had struck the world like a meteor, and observers had already begun arguing over what it was that had hit them.

Bibliography

Bambaglioli, Graziolo de'. *Il Commento dantesco di Graziolo de' Bambaglioli, dal "Colombino" di Siviglia con altri codici raffrontato.* Edited by Antonio Fiammazzo. Savona: D. Bertollotto e C., 1915.

Mazzoni, Francesco. "Per la storia della critica dantesca: Jacopo Alighieri e Graziolo Bambaglioli." *Studi danteschi* 30 (1951), 157–202.

Sandkühler, Bruno. *Di frühen Dantekommentare und ihr Verhältnis zur mittelalterlichen Kommentartradition.* Munich: Münchner romanistiche Arbeiten, 1967.

Vallone, Aldo. *Storia della critica dantesca dal XIV al XX secolo.* 2 vols. Padua: Vallardi, 1981.

Deborah Parker

Baptism

Baptism is the Christian rite of initiation, a ritual washing in the name of the Trinity that unites the believer to Christ in his death and Resurrection (Rom. 6:3–5). According to the Council of Florence (1438–c. 1445), it "holds the first place among all the sacraments because it is the door of the spiritual life. By it we are made members of Christ and of His body, the Church" (*New Catholic Encyclopedia* 2:62). Baptism takes away the original sin inherited from Adam and Eve and opens the believer to receive God's grace. It has therefore always been considered essential for salvation: "Unless a man be born again of water and the Holy Spirit, he cannot enter into the Kingdom of God" (John 3:5).

The importance of baptism to Dante is suggested by the personal and quite specifically Florentine contexts in which he alludes to it. In *Inf.* 19.16–21, he recalls the fonts *che son nel mio bel San Giovanni, / fatti per loco d'i battezzatori* ("those in my lovely San Giovanni, made as places for the baptizers"), which he was once accused of having desecrated. Likewise in *Par.* 25.1–12, when he imagines returning one day to Florence in order to be crowned as poet, he vows to receive this honor at the font of his baptism, because it was precisely there that he entered into the faith *che fa conte / l'anime a Dio* ("that makes souls known to God," 25.10–12). Here baptism becomes a way of speaking about his own identity as a Christian, a poet, and a citizen. The ancient baptistry of the cathedral of Florence—a city whose patron saint is none other than John the Baptist—is where he himself became (just as his great-great-grandfather became, at one and the same time) *"cristiano e Cacciaguida"* (*Par.* 15.135).

The *Commedia*'s most extensive treatment of Catholic baptismal theology is found in *Par.* 32, where St. Bernard discusses the infant souls that fill the lower reaches of the heavenly rose. Drawing on the authoritative teachings of Peter Lombard, Bonaventure, and Aquinas—not to mention those of Bernard himself—Dante presents baptism as both necessary and efficacious. As the very presence of the infants in Paradise attests, the sacrament confers grace even upon those who cannot choose it for themselves. In this case, it is the faith of those who administer the sacrament that matters, not the free will of the individual. Bernard also cites the principle of the three ages (32.73–84) by which the Church understood there to be a history of baptism even before Christ first instituted the sacrament. In the earliest ages, parental faith was sufficient for salvation; after the covenant with

Abraham (Gen. 18), circumcision in males became the sign of righteousness with God. With the coming of the "time of grace," however, these imperfect precursors of the sacrament gave way to *battesmo perfetto di Cristo* ("perfect baptism in Christ," 32.87). Without it, no one can hope to know God, experience the bliss of Heaven, or be freed from the power of sin to imprison even the apparently innocent souls of unbaptized infants from the infernal world *là giù* ("down below," 32.84).

Dante's primary concern in these matters, however, is not with those infants who died apart from baptism or its precursory rites but, rather, with the souls of the virtuous pagans, of whom Virgil is the prime example. In a highly unorthodox move, the poet opens up Limbo—the "place" theology had established for unbaptized infants—and makes it the afterlife home of those illustrious pagans who, though meritorious, had not experienced any form of baptism, *ch'è porta de la fede che tu credi* ("which is the gateway to the faith that you believe," *Inf.* 4.36). Deprived of grace, all the inhabitants of the first circle of Hell live in desire but without hope, in a twilight world that is forever cut off (as Virgil will say in *Purg.* 7.25–36) from the "sight of the high Sun" (7.26).

Long after Virgil vanishes from the poem, the fate of the unbaptized continues to be a preoccupation. In *Par.* 19.67–90 the Eagle of justice postulates the existence of a man born far outside the Christian world, whose wishes and acts are all good but who nonetheless dies *non battezzato e sanza fede* ("unbaptized and without our faith," 19.76). The eagle acknowledges the terrible difficulty posed by such a predicament but insists that no one was ever saved who did not believe in Christ, either before or after his crucifixion. Having laid down the law of orthodoxy, however, the Eagle continues in the next canto to describe two individuals who were saved through spectacular interventions of divine grace, one of whom (Ripheus) was so in love with righteousness that God opened his eyes to a still-future redemption (20.122–123). As a result, Dante affords Ripheus what the church refers to as a "baptism of desire," a remission of sin *dinanzi al battesar più d'un millesmo* ("more than a thousand years before baptizing began," 20.129) and one that, although without the sacrament itself, confers upon him the Christian virtues of faith, hope, and love.

Bibliography

"Baptism." In *The New Catholic Encyclopedia*. Vol. 2. New York: McGraw-Hill, 1967–1969, pp. 54–68.

Botterill, Stephen. "Doctrine, Certainty and Doubt: *Paradiso* XXXII, 40–84." *Italian Studies* 42 (1987), 20–36.

Freccero, John. "The River of Death: *Inferno* II, 108." Reprinted in *Dante: The Poetics of Conversion*. Edited by Rachel Jacoff. Cambridge, Mass.: Harvard University Press, 1986, pp. 55–69.

Marti, Kevin. "Dante's *Baptism* and the Theology of the Body in *Purgatory* 1–2." *Traditio* 45 (1989–1990), 167–190.

Paolini, Shirley J. *Confessions of Sin and Love in the Middle Ages: Dante's "Commedia" and St. Augustine's "Confessions."* Washington, D.C.: University Press of America, 1982. See chapter 5.

Tucker, D. J., O.S.B. "*In Exitu Israel de Aegypto: The Divine Comedy* in the Light of the Easter Liturgy." *American Benedictine Review* 11 (1960), 43–61.

Peter S. Hawkins

Barbi, Michele

Distinguished philologist and the leading Dante critic in Italy during the first half of the twentieth century. Barbi (1867–1941) was a student of Alessandro D'Ancona, completing his studies at the Scuola Normale Superiore in Pisa and publishing his thesis on *Della fortuna di Dante nel secolo XVI* (Pisa, 1890). He taught in the universities of Pisa, Messina, and Florence. Reacting against the prevailing positivistic ideology of his time, Barbi rejected the notion of absolute editorial impartiality in the field of philology and insisted that the reconstruction of a text required the critical examination of all available linguistic and historical information. More than any other critic of his time, Barbi defined the norms of modern Italian philology and the methodology of editing texts—the theoretical principles of which were established in *La nuova filologia e l'edizione dei nostri scrittori da Dante al Manzoni* (1938). So great was the influence of his method that it came to be known as the New Philology *(Nuova Filologia)*. His critical editions of the *Vita Nuova* (1907, 1932) and the *Rime* (1921) demonstrate the virtues of this method and remain fundamental contributions. He was an editor of the major critical edition of Dante's works sponsored by the Società Dantesca Italiana (*Le Opere di Dante,* 1921).

While Barbi's critical interests were broad and influenced every aspect of Dante criticism, he always stressed the importance of Dante's language within its historical context. His major contributions include the 1934 and 1941 collections of essays *Problemi di critica dantesca: Prima serie (1893–1918)* and *Problemi di critica dantesca: Seconda serie (1920–1937); Con Dante e coi suoi interpreti,* also of 1941; and *Problemi fondamentali per un nuovo commento della Divina Commedia,* published posthumously in 1956. While he was influenced by the work of Luigi Pietrobono, he entered into polemic with him in his important essay "Razionalismo e misticismo in Dante" (*Problemi* 2. 1–86), rejecting as exaggerated Pietrobono's thesis that the *Vita Nuova*—instilled with a mysticism that prepared for the *Commedia*—was written after the *Convivio,* a work Pietrobono characterized as devoted to exalting the power of philosophic rationalism beyond the power of faith. As a strenuous defender of Dante's indebtedness to Albert the Great's and Thomas Aquinas' theological imperatives, Barbi likewise attacked Bruno Nardi's claim that Dante's *Convivio* revealed strains of Averroistic philosophical influence that constituted the promotion of heretical views regarding the power of the faculty of human reason. He furthermore discountenanced the notion that Dante's works were significantly influenced by Augustinian and Neoplatonic thought, and he countered Benedetto Croce's schismatic reduction of the *Commedia* into *poesia* and *non poesia*—as though that text were a poem whose true poetic moments could be excised, and thereby saved, from the artifices of the allegorical structure. Barbi's Dantism emphasized the importance of determining meaning on the basis of the study of the letter of the text and on situating the text within its literary and cultural context.

Barbi edited the annual bibliography of the *Bullettino,* the early journal of the Società Dantesca Italiana, serving as its director from 1893 to 1905, and in 1920 he founded *Studi danteschi,* its successor, which he directed until his death.

Bibliography

Kleinhenz, Christopher. "Michele Barbi (1867–1941)." In *Medieval Scholarship: Biographical Studies on the Formation of a Discipline.* Vol. 2. *Literature and Philology.* Edited by Helen Damico. New York: Garland Publishing, 1998, pp. 325–338.

Mazzoni, Francesco. "Michele Barbi." In *Dizionario biografico degli Italiani.* Vol. 6. Edited by Alberto M. Ghisalberti. Rome: Istituto della Enciclopedia Italian, 1964, pp. 190–193.

Francesco Mazzoni
(translated by Richard Lansing)

Barrators

The sin of barratry *(baratteria),* synonymous with graft or corruption in public office, is punished in the fifth *bolgia* of the eighth circle of Hell, Malebolge. In *Inf.* 11.60 Virgil calls the sinners *baratti* (= *barattieri,* "barrators"). Barratry is the secular or civic equivalent of simony, the selling of church offices punished in the third bolgia of the eighth circle (*Inf.* 19). The *contrapasso* involves the immersion of the souls in boiling pitch. Whenever they emerge above the surface of the pitch in an attempt to find some relief from their suffering, they are hooked and mutilated by a host of devils, the *Malebranche,* who constantly patrol the banks of the ditch. The nature of the punishment appropriately mirrors the sin: on Earth, the barrators accepted bribes and committed other acts of civic fraud and corruption in secrecy, often under the cover of darkness, in what we might term today the "smoky back rooms of city hall" or the "dark alleys of the urban jungle." It is thus significant that, when the pilgrim first arrives on the scene, he sees the pitch but is unable to see into it: *I' vedea lei, ma non vedea in essa / mai che le bolle che 'l bollor levava* ("I saw it, but in it I saw no more than the bubbles that the boiling brought up," *Inf.* 21.19–20). The viscous quality of the black pitch also reflects the "sticky hands and fingers" of these sinners who, in life, were ready to engage in any sort of public fraud for money.

The introductory image of *Inf.* 21 presents the varied activities occurring at the Venetian shipyard, the Arsenal, during the winter season. At this time of year the ships are put in dry dock and repaired from stem to stern, including masts and sails, so that when spring comes, they will be seaworthy once again. The simile is pertinent to the events of the canto. In the first place, the bustling scene at the Venetian Arsenal contrasts dramatically with the momentarily calm and desolate atmosphere in the fifth *bolgia*. In the shipyard, the separate tasks of the various artisans are linked in a cooperative effort to repair the vessel—an effort that we may understand on the metaphorical level to be equivalent to keeping the "ship of state" afloat. In life the barrators engaged in a wide range of individual entrepreneurial activities, but without a common vision or goal; indeed, so focused were they on their own desires and interests that their actions often succeeded in causing great damage to the communal government—indeed, to the extent of "sinking" the metaphorical ship of state.

In this particular subdivision of the eighth circle (*Inf.* 21–22) the pilgrim encounters directly one soul, who is usually identified as Ciampolo (or Giampolo), an Italian grafter at the court of Thibaut II, king of Navarre. He sees an unnamed barrator from Lucca being unceremoniously thrown by a black devil into the pitch, and he hears the names of three others: Bonturo Dati, who, still alive in 1300, was supposedly the most notorious "boss" of Lucca; Fra Gomita of Gallura in Sardinia, who was reportedly hanged there, perhaps by Nino Visconti (cf. *Purg.* 8.53); and Michel Zanche, who, also from Sardinia, was the legate of King Enzo and governor of Torres and Logodoro and was murdered by Branca Doria (see *Inf.* 33.144).

Dante himself was accused of barratry by the Black Guelfs, and this charge was among those cited in the order of exile (January 27, 1302). The instinctive fear the pilgrim feels when confronted and threatened with bodily harm by the appropriately "black" devils (= the Black Guelfs) may be based on and reflect this autobiographical experience.

Bibliography

Chiappelli, Fredi. "Il canto XXII dell'*Inferno*." In *Letture dantesche*. Edited by Giovanni Getto. Florence: Sansoni, 1955, pp. 415–428.

Favati, Guido. "Il 'Jeu di Dante' (Interpretazione del canto XXI dell'*Inferno*)." *Cultura neolatina* 25 (1965), 34–52.

Kleinhenz, Christopher. "Deceivers Deceived: Devilish Doubletalk in *Inferno* 21–23." *Quaderni d'Italianistica* 10 (1989), 133–156.

Olschki, Leonardo. "Dante, i barattieri, i diavoli." *Giornale dantesco* 38 (1937), 61–81.

Pagliaro, Antonino. "La rapsodia dei diavoli." In *Ulisse: ricerche semantiche sulla Divina Commedia*. Vol. 1. Messina, Florence: D'Anna, 1966, pp. 311–324.

Sanguineti, Edoardo. *Interpretazione di Malebolge*. Florence: Olschki, 1962.

Scolari, Antonio. *Il canto XXI dell'Inferno*. Florence: Le Monnier, 1961.

Spitzer, Leo. "The Farcical Elements in *Inferno*, Cantos XXI–XXIII." *Modern Language Notes* 59 (1944), 83–88.

Christopher Kleinhenz

Beasts, The Three

The immediate cause of Dante's journey through the three realms of the afterlife is his inability to counter the threat of three beasts *(tre fiere)*—a leopard *(lonza)*, a lion *(leone)*, and a she-wolf *(lupa)*—who block his advance up the side of a mountain in *Inf.* 1. While each of these animals was known to inhabit Italy in the Middle Ages, commentators are in full agreement that their significance is entirely symbolic in nature. Although there is a broad diversity of opinion about what they signify, interpretations of the three beasts can be divided into four general categories.

The first group of interpreters, based on 1 John 2:16–17, held that the three beasts stood for the major lusts, desires, or temptations of man: "concupiscence of the flesh and the concupiscence of the eyes and the pride of life." Boccaccio's formulation in the *Esposizioni* (p. 73) is often cited to encapsulate the tradition: *Le quali [le tre bestie], quantunque a molti e diversi vizi adattare si potessono, nondimeno qui, secondo la sentenza di tutti, par che si debbano intendere per questi, cioè per la lonza il vizio della lussuria e per lo leone il vizio della superbia e per la lupa il vizio dell'avarizia* ("Although one could identify these [three beasts] with many different vices, nonetheless, according to the judgment of all, it here appears that they must be understood for the following: to wit, for the leopard the vice of lust, for the lion the vice of pride, and for the she-wolf the vice of avarice."). Thus, for most of the early commentators the beasts embodied, in order of appearance, the vices of lust, pride, and avarice; but this early consensus, despite its impressiveness, does not derive from a number of independent views but from the typical medieval and Renaissance tradition of plagiarizing encyclopedism.

The second group of interpreters asserted that the three creatures have an external political significance allied or not to the spiritual meanings within the pilgrim. Typical of the Risorgimento

B

Dante and the three beasts. Opere del divino poeta Danthe, ed. Pietro da Figino, Venice, 1520. *Giamatti Collection: Courtesy of the Mount Holyoke College Archives and Special Collections.*

was the view that the beasts represented corrupt contemporary political entities: the *lonza* was Florence (the spots, its factions); the lion, the king of France; the wolf, the pontifical curia.

The third category of interpreters urged, in the wake of Castelvetro's commentary (c. 1570), that *Inf.* 1 is to be viewed as symbolic of Dante's own experiences in Florence that led to his exile. They argue that the *lonza,* in particular, is envy. In corroboration they cite Ciacco in *Inf.* 6.49–50, 74 and Brunetto Latini in *Inf.* 15.68 for envy as Florence's besetting sin. In particular, Nardi (1963, 1966) emphasized a narrow, political, "exterior" interpretation, denying any relationship to the pilgrim's inner personal vices: the *lonza* signified fraud and the lusts of the world; the lion, the violent pride of Florentine factions; the avaricious wolf, Boniface VIII. Clearly, however, the distinction of "external" and "internal" in the realm of justice—

between the right ordering of the state and the right ordering of the soul—did not exist for Dante, as Plato's *Timaeus* and St. Thomas's *Commentary* on Aristotle's *Nichomachean Ethics* (5.11.2, 1138b [lecture 17.1106]) make clear: they are one. Of the microcosm's reflection of the macrocosm Dante knew from the writings of the Parisian theological School of St. Victor, with which he was intimately familiar. That devices such as governments were remedies for the infirmity of sin became a principle of his *Monarchia* (cf. 3.4). Ineluctably, the beasts symbolize both exterior and interior values.

The fourth group of interpreters squared the meaning of the beasts with the *Inferno*'s penal system, identifying them with the three dispositions "not wanted in heaven" (*Inf.* 11.81): malice, force (or "mad brutishness"), and incontinence. Giacinto Casella's thesis that the *lonza* was fraud, the *leone* violence, and the *lupa* incontinence has had the largest number of followers in Great Britain and America: the beasts adumbrate chiastically the three major divisions of Hell. In Italy, Flamini and Lajolo claimed perspicaciously that the beasts signified not the punishment *(pena),* which is unfathomably of God, but the guilt *(colpa)* of sin—that is, man's descent into evil, not of a specific kind, but of degree: incontinence, violence, and fraud. As species of sin, we find avarice, lust, and pride in all three divisions of Hell: for example, avarice is punished not only among the incontinent in *Inf.* 6 but also among the tyrants and their ilk in *Inf.* 12 and among the fraudulent simonists, barrators, thieves, and false counselors of Lower Hell. Pride stains not only Filippo Argenti (6.46) but also the violent Capaneus (14.64), the giants (31.91), and the fraudulent traitor, Lucifer. Lust damns not only Francesca, Cleopatra, Dido, and Semiramis but also the violent sodomites and Myrrha, who fraudulently lay with her father (30.38–39).

Logically the beasts embody external temptations that can affect the internal dealings of the state just as they affect the interior behavior of man; that is, they are symbolic of external lures or threats preying upon internal human weakness.

Dante taps the vast biblical precedence for the theme of "temptation with beasts in a desert." In Hos. 13:4–7, 14, for example, God threatens not only to punish the apostate Jews ("I knew thee in the desert, in the land of the wilderness . . . I will be to them as a lioness, as a leopard") but also to spare the repentant. Scholars have long noted that

Dante had chosen Jer. 5:6 as his major calque: "Therefore a lion from the forest hath slain them, a wolf in the evening shall despoil them. A leopard watcheth for their cities." But perhaps most important is the triple temptation of Christ as related in Mark 1:13: "And he was in the desert forty days and forty nights, and was tempted by Satan. And *he was with beasts* and the angels ministered to him." Clearly the pilgrim's experience in the prologue of the *Commedia* is *in imitatione Christi*.

The Beasts

1. *Lonza* ("pard"): from the earliest commentators, past the era of positivism, taxonomy has been the central crux in explicating the first of the beasts. The Florentine term can be found in no bestiary. Benvenuto da Imola (1373–1380) identified it in his *Comentum* (ed. Lacaita, p. 35) with the pard and noted, on the testimony of Boccaccio, that a "lonza" actually existed in Florence. Brunetto Latini translating Isidore's "pardus" from the *Etymologies* (12.2.8.9), also chose the word "lonce" (or "longe") in his *Tresor* 1.190.3. Contemporary Florentine city records note that a caged "leuncia" was kept at public expense as a mascot in a cage along with lions near the present Loggia del Bigallo. Among other church writers, Richard of St. Victor (particularly well known to Dante) identifies the speckled pard of the Bible with fraudulence in his *De eruditione interioris hominis* 3.11 (*PL* 196.1358). Dante's trenchant irony satirizes Florence's civic pride in using the animal and its very Florentine vernacular term for the temptation of the sin of fraud.

2. *Leone* ("lion"): besides being a Florentine mascot and heraldic device (viz. the *Marzocco; marzocchesco, "Florentine"*), the lion is typified in the bestiaries by its raging hunger (cf. Albertus Magnus, *De animalibus,* 22.107; Pseudo–Hugh of St. Victor, *De bestiis, PL* 177.150). In the poem, its upraised head signifies pride, a sin that also pertains to the irascible part of the soul (St. Thomas, *ST* 2.2.162.a3; cf. the unbent neck of Farinata in *Inf.* 10.75 and the bent necks of the proud in *Purg.* 11–12).

3. *Lupa* ("she-wolf"): Isidore derives the name "lupus" (Greek *lykos, Etymologiae* 12.2.23) from its "raging rapacity." Dante learned from medieval bestiaries and "scientific" treatises on beasts not only that the wolf eats dirt but that it is forever lean; it can never satisfy its hunger since it gulps its food without chewing (cf. *Inf.* 1.50, 98–99). He also exploits the fact that the papal curia had recently adopted the Capitoline statue of the Roman she-wolf as its own emblem, despite the negative association of the animal with whoredom (*lupa* was a Latin term for "harlot"; *lupanar* ["wolf den"], a brothel). Lactantius and St. Augustine had identified the nurse of Romulus and Remus as a prostitute (*Divine Institutes* 1.20; *City of God* 18.21). Since the animal was the mascot of Mars, the former patron of the city, the wolf is also another satirical symbol of Florence.

Dante associates the wolf in myriad negative ways with the Church and its Guelf followers (German *Welf* = "wolf"): the Guelf Count Ugolino and his "children" are wolves hunted by Archbishop Ruggieri (*Inf.* 33.29); Guido del Duca describes the Arno as a hellish river descending to the wolves of Florence (*Purg.* 14.49–51); the fiendish Florentine podestà, Fulcieri da Calboli, becomes one with the "ancient wolf" of avarice (*Purg.* 20.10), an *antica belva* (an "ancient wild beast," *Purg.* 14.62). Love of the florin has transformed the pope from shepherd into wolf (*Par.* 9.127–132, 27.55–57). Notably, Dante never uses the wolf emblem as a positive image of the empire anywhere in his works, ignoring Roman myth and history as well as Virgil's veneration (cf. especially *Aen.* 1.274–277).

Generally critics have recognized the striking oneiric, hallucinatory, even nightmarish quality of the vision conjured by the beasts—their liveliness contrasting with their unreality—despite the fact that the prologue scene is the only episode of the *Commedia* set in *this* world. The poet leads the reader repeatedly away from the literal actions of the animals to their possible spiritual "sovrasensi," forcing the reader to interpret the enigmas: How can the obstructing *lonza* be a cause for "good hope" (*Inf.* 1.41–42)? How can a she-wolf not only "cause many to live in wretchedness" (1.51) but also even push the pilgrim back "to where the sun is silent"? Such puzzles keep the images of the beasts hovering between reality and allegory in a poetic mode that differs from the concreteness typical of so much of the rest of the *Inferno*.

Bibliography

Apollonio, Mario. *Dante, storia della Commedia.* 2 vols. Milan: F. Vallardi, 1951; 3rd ed., 1964.

B

Bernardo, Aldo. "The Three Beasts and Perspective in the *Divine Comedy.*" *PMLA* 78, no. 1 (1963), 15–24.

Bonfante, G. "Ancore le tre fiere." *Italica* 23 (1946), 69–72.

Busnelli, Giovanni. *Il simbolo delle tre fiere dantesche: ricerche e studi intorno al Prologo della "Commedia."* Rome: Civiltà Cattolica, 1909.

Camus, Jules. "La 'lonza' de Dante et les 'léopards' de Pétrarque, de l'Arioste etc." *Giornale Storico della Letteratura Italiana* 53 (1909), 1–40.

Casella, Giacinto. "Della forma allegorica e della principale allegoria della Divina Commedia" (1865). In *Opere edite e postume di Giacinto Casella.* Vol. 2. Con prefazione del prof. Alessandro D'Ancona. Florence: G. Barbèra, 1884, pp. 369–396.

Cassell, Anthony K. "Three Beasts." In *Lectura Dantis Americana: Inferno I.* Philadelphia: University of Pennsylvania Press, 1989, pp. 45–76.

Chistoni, Paride. "La lonza dantesca." In *Miscellanea di studi critici edita in onore di Arturo Graf.* Bergamo: Istituto Italiano d'Arti Grafiche, 1903, pp. 817–848.

Cipolla, Francesco. "La lonza di Dante." *Rassegna bibliografica della letteratura italiana* anno III, no. 4 (April 1895), 103–114.

Del Lungo, Isidoro. "Canto I dell'*Inferno.*" Lectura Dantis Romana. Florence: G.C. Sansoni, 1901.

D'Ovidio, Francesco. *Studii sulla Divina Commedia.* Milan and Palermo: Remo Sandron, 1901.

Dozon, Marthe. "Le thème de la louve et des loups dans la *Divine Comédie: Echos d'un mythe étrusco-latin?*" *Revue des Études Italiennes* n.s. 15 (1969), 5–33.

Ferretti, Giovanni. "Le tre fiere" and "La matta bestialità." In his *Saggi danteschi.* Florence: F. LeMonnier, 1950, pp. 27–42, 77–112.

Filipponi, Osvaldo. *Le profezie di Dante e del Vangelo eterno.* Padua: MEB, 1983.

Flamini, Francesco. *I significati reconditi della Divina Commedia.* Part 2: *Il vero: L'allegoria.* Livorno: Raffaello Giusti, 1904. Revised and reprinted as *Il significato e il fine della Divina Commedia.* Part 2: *Il vero: L'allegoria.* Leghorn: Raffaello Giusti, 1916.

Getto, Giovanni. "Il canto 1 dell'*Inferno.*" *Lectura Dantis Scaligera.* Florence: F. LeMonnier, 1960. Reprinted in 1967. Reprinted in *Cultura e Scuola* 4 (1965), 406–415, as "Il canto introduttivo della *Divina Commedia*"; and reprinted in *Dante nella critica d'oggi.* Edited by Umberto Bosco. Florence: F. LeMonnier, 1965, pp. 406–415. Article reprinted in *Aspetti della poesia di Dante.* Florence: Sansoni, 1966, pp. 1–16.

Giglio, Raffaele. "Il prologo alla *Divina Commedia.*" *Critica letteraria* anno 1, no. 1 (1973), 131–160.

Guarnerio, P. E. "Ancora della Lonza di Dante." *Rassegna bibliografica della letteratura italiana* 3 (1895), 139–140, 203–204.

Lajolo, Gregorio. *Simboli e enigmi danteschi: esposizione ragionata delle allegorie più notevoli e controverse della Divina Commedia.* Vol. 1. Rome, Turin: Casa Editrice Nazionale Roux e Viarengo, 1906.

Mazzoni, Francesco. *Saggio di un nuovo commento alla "Divina Commedia": Inferno—Canti I–III.* Quaderni degli "Studi Danteschi" 4. Florence: Sansoni, 1967, pp. 109–111, 126–131.

McKenzie, Kenneth. "The Problem of the 'lonza' with an Unpublished Text." *Romanic Review* 1, no. 1 (1901), 18–33.

Nardi, Bruno. "Tre momenti dell'incontro di Dante con Virgilio." *L'Alighieri* 6, no. 2 (1965), 42–53. Reprinted in *Saggi e note di critica dantesca.* Milan, Naples: Ricciardi, 1966, pp. 220–237.

———. "Il preludio alla *Divina Commedia.*" *L'Alighieri* 4, no. 1 (1963), 3–17. Reprinted in *Lectura Dantis Romana.* Turin: SEI, 1964.

Nicosia, P. *Dieci saggi sull'Inferno dantesco.* Messina, Florence: D'Anna, 1969.

Parodi, Erenesto Giacomo. "Ancora della lonza." *Bullettino della Società Dantesca Italiana* 3 (1895), 24–26.

Pasquazi, Silvio. "Il primo canto della 'Divina Commedia.'" *Giornale italiano di filologia* 40 (1988), 177–199.

Pézard, André. *Tant que vienne le veltre: Enfer I: 100–101.* Paris: Chez Tallone Editeur-imprimeur, 1978.

———. "Les loups, Virgile et Dante." *Revue des Études Italiennes* n.s. 4 (1957), 5–30.

Proto, Enrico. "La lonza dantesca." *Giornale dantesco* 15 (1907), 1–16.

Ragonese, Gaetano. "fiera"; "le tre fiere." *Enciclopedia dantesca,* 2:857–861.

Renucci, Paul. "La 'lonza' dantesque est-elle un guépard?" *Revue des Études Italiennes* 2 (1937), 372–374.

Scrocca, Alberto. "Le tre fiere." In his *Saggi danteschi.* Naples: Perrella, 1908, pp. 1–50.

Singleton, Charles S. (ed. and trans.). *Dante. The Divine Comedy: Inferno.* Vol. 2. *Commentary.* Princeton, N.J.: Princeton University Press, 1970.

Torraca, Francesco. *Di un commento nuovo alla Divina Commedia.* Bologna: N. Zanichelli, 1899.

Triolo, Alfred A. "Matta Bestialità in Dante's 'Inferno': Theory and Image." *Traditio* 24 (1968), 247–292.

Vanossi, Luigi. "lupo e lupa." *Enciclopedia dantesca,* 3:742–743.

Anthony K. Cassell

with the verses *Beati cui alluma tanto di grazia . . . esuriendo sempre quanto è giusto* ("Blessed are they whom so much grace illuminates. . . , hungering always as much as is just!"); and "Beati mundo corde!" ("Blessed are the pure in heart," Matt. 5:8), on the terrace of lust (*Purg.* 27.8). In linking these seven beatitudes to the seven capital sins Dante may have been influenced by Hugh of St. Victor's *De quinque septenis,* a work that identifies five sets of seven elements in a pattern of conceptual correspondence and that explicitly opposes the Beatitudes to the seven capital sins.

Richard Lansing

Beatitudes

In the New Testament, the eight proclamations praising specific virtues, pronounced by Christ to his disciples and the multitudes in the Sermon on the Mount (Matt. 5:3–12). Some identify nine beatitudes, noting that the anaphoric repetition of "Blessed are they" occurs nine times in nine verses but that the last two verses (10–11) both refer to the same virtuous condition, the suffering of the persecuted. Dante makes use of the Beatitudes in *Purgatorio* as part of the ritual of purification. As the pilgrim completes his stay on a terrace and begins to ascend to the next terrace, an angel pronounces a beatitude, as a kind of benediction, and removes a "P" (for *peccatum*, "sin") from the pilgrim's forehead. The Beatitudes celebrate the seven virtues corresponding, by opposition, to the seven capital sins purged on the seven terraces. Dante varies from the biblical pattern, omitting from his scheme the second beatitude, "Beati mites" (Matt. 5:4), and dividing the fourth, "Beati qui esuriunt et sitiunt iustitiam," into two separate beatitudes. The correspondence is as follows: "Beati pauperes spiritu" ("Blessed are the poor in spirit," Matt. 5:3), on the terrace of pride (*Purg.* 12.110); "Beati misericordes" ("Blessed are the merciful," Matt. 5:7), on the terrace of envy (*Purg.* 15.38); "Beati pacifici" ("Blessed are the peacemakers," Matt. 5:9), on the terrace of wrath (*Purg.* 17.68–69); "Beati qui lugent" ("Blessed are they that mourn," Matt. 5:5), on the terrace of sloth (*Purg.* 19.50); "Beati qui . . . sitiunt," ("Blessed are they . . . that thirst," Matt. 5:6), on the terrace of avarice and prodigality (*Purg.* 22.6); "Beati qui esuriunt . . ." ("Blessed are they that hunger. . . , Matt. 5:6), on the terrace of gluttony (*Purg.* 24.151–154), where Dante paraphrases the Latin

Beatrice

The woman Dante loved and celebrated in the *Vita Nuova* and the *Commedia.* She is a dominant presence in both works, but very little is known about her outside that literary life. Dante uses only her first name, which—given its significance ("beatifier") and the prevalence of subterfuge in the lyric love game ("shield women" and pseudonyms to hide the identity of the actual beloved)—cannot be absolutely certain. But from everything else he tells of his love for her in the *Vita Nuova,* there can be no doubt that she came from Florence, that she was a member of the same social circle with whom he met at various gatherings and with whom he shared acquaintances if not friends, and probably that her father died shortly before she did.

Beatrice was identified by early commentators both as an allegory of theology and as a woman of Florence, a Portinari (according to Dante's son Pietro). Boccaccio identifies her specifically as the daughter of Folco Portinari (a respected citizen and benefactor of the city as well as several times its prior) and as the wife of Simone dei Bardi, from one of the major banking families *(Vita di Dante).* Boccaccio, who was born almost half a century later than Dante and could have known the details of his life only from the distant memories of those who knew him or from the hearsay of others (including a nephew of the poet and a cousin of Beatrice Portinari), tells of Dante's meetings with Beatrice as a child and young man as though these were biographical fact. They are probably based on the *Vita Nuova,* which is itself a revisionist history, an attempt by Dante to retell the story of his love and the poetry it inspired in the light of the significance he had come to impute to Beatrice. And that significance led some com-

PVRGATORIO

Beatrice descending on the Chariot drawn by the Griffin. La comedia di Dante Aligieri, *with commentary by Alessandro Vellutello, published by Francesco Marcolini, Venice, 1544. Giamatti Collection: Courtesy of the Mount Holyoke College Archives and Special Collections.*

mentators to interpret Beatrice as pure symbol with little or no basis in reality. It is probably impossible to disentangle the poetic fiction of the figure from historical fact; nonetheless Dante makes it clear that she is to be taken first as a real woman—by his own very physical reactions to her both in the *Vita Nuova* and in the *Commedia.*

The significance that Dante attributes to Beatrice, however, goes well beyond what is traditional in medieval lyrics, which might speak of women's powers to influence for good—might even identify them with stars or angels—but would not ordinarily make them a figure of Christ. The Christ connections are very strong in the prose narrative of the *Vita Nuova,* though they were not in the poetry it explicates (and may have been added or strengthened as Dante clarified his ideas for the *Commedia*). There are hints in her name, "beatifier"; in the number associated with her, 9, whose root is the Trinity; in the colors in which she first appears, red and white; and in the "new life" Dante is given by her death. But the identification becomes stronger with the intimations of her death—the portents in nature and the angels singing Hosanna as they accompany her in her ascension (*VN* 23)—and

then with her appearance preceded by Giovanna "Primavera," Cavalcanti's lady, as Christ was preceded by John the Baptist, and the suggestion of John in the name (Giovanni) and in the nickname (taking *primavera,* "spring," as a pun on *prima verrà,* "will come first," *VN* 24). In the *Commedia,* she descends to Hell, as Christ did—in her case, to bring out Virgil as Dante's guide, which Dante remembers in his final praise of her: *offristi per la mia salute / in inferno lasciar le tue vestige,* ("[who] deigned for my salvation to leave your footprints in Hell," *Par.* 31.80–81). One of the three cries that heralds her appearance in the Earthly Paradise recalls Christ's entry into Jerusalem: *Benedictus qui venis* (*Purg.* 30.19)—the surprising masculine form making the identification with Christ strikingly clear. Beatrice speaks Christ's words *Modicum et non videbitis me* to her attendants as Christ did to his disciples (*Purg.* 33.10); and the reference to her nickname, "Bice," in *Paradiso* (7.14) is given by its separate letters in a way which must evoke the abbreviations of Christ in manuscripts: "Be" (*beato,* "blessed") and "ice" (IC = *Iesu Cristo* = Jesus Christ).

Part of Beatrice's role as a Christ figure, a female in whom one can see God, is to help Dante see the female side of God. This is not unknown in medieval tradition (divine wisdom—Sophia or Sapientia—is a woman in the Old Testament; God and Christ are on rare occasions described as a mother; the Trinity and key divine attributes are feminine nouns), but Dante programmatically gives the female attributes of God alongside the male, showing that they are not determined by grammar but by conviction. For much of the poem Dante speaks of God in the masculine, but Beatrice speaks of *provedenza* (*Par.* 1.121), *la mente profonda* (2.131), *la verace luce* (3.32), *l'etterna luce* (5.8), and *la divina bontà* (7.64), using feminine adjectives and pronouns that emphasize the gender; and she describes the ultimate mystic union as the final salvation in which Dante will "inher" himself (*l'ultima salute . . . t'inlei, Par.* 22.124–127). Dante slowly moves into the feminine mode (*Par.* 13.26–27, 18.118–19), and by the last canto he describes his vision of God first in masculine terms and then in feminine (cf. *Par.* 33.115–120, and 124–132).

Beatrice's role as a female incarnation of the human incarnation of God is connected to the Virgin Mary's as the human mother of God, the one whose features most resemble Christ's

(*Par.* 32.85–86)—that is, the one who gave human features to Christ so that men could see him as one of them and who enables Dante to have the final vision of the human Christ within the circles of the Trinity. Beatrice is connected with the Virgin Mary early on, in the *Vita Nuova,* when Dante gazes at her in church while words are being spoken about the "queen of glory" (*VN* 5); Beatrice was first described by Dante as "the glorious lady of my mind" (*VN* 2). In the *Commedia,* it is the Virgin (unnamed but easily identified) who sends Beatrice to save Dante, and after Beatrice brings him to Mary's rose in the Empyrean, it is the Virgin who makes it possible for him to see the Trinity. Beatrice, Mary, and Lucy have been seen as a female trinity: Beatrice, the Christ figure; Mary, the counterpart of God, as queen of Heaven; Lucy, the saint of the Holy Spirit (although the association of a secular,

perhaps married, woman with two virgin saints is unusual).

While the Christ connections are most obvious in the *Vita Nuova*—and unsettling to some (suggestive religious language was edited out of the first printed edition in the post-Tridentine late sixteenth century)—Beatrice's more conventional role as an allegorical representation of theology, which is strongly hinted at in the *Commedia,* was pointed to by Dante's earliest commentators, including Dante's son Pietro (*qua mortua, ut eius nomen in famam levaret, in hoc suo poemate sub allegoria et typo theologie eam ut plurimum accipere voluit,* "after she died, to enhance the fame of her name, he wanted her to be taken as an allegory and type of theology in this poem," on *Inf.* 2.51ff.; cf. Benvenuto da Imola on *Inf.* 2.70–72); Jacopo Alighieri interprets her as divine scripture (on *Inf.* 2.70–72), which is the source of theology.

Beatrice in the Earthly Paradise. Invenzioni di Giovanni Flaxman sulla Divina commedia, *illustrated by John Flaxman and Beniamino del Vecchio, Rome, 1826. Giamatti Collection: Courtesy of the Mount Holyoke College Archives and Special Collections.*

B

Abstractions, because they are feminine nouns, were usually personified as women in medieval allegory, so the identification of a female figure with theology is not in itself surprising, even though a historical woman is; but while biblical women were often read as figures of the church—and some as the new covenant, or the contemplative life—it is extraordinary to find a contemporary (and secular) person cast in such a role. In any case, it is easier to accept theological teaching and even correction of great thinkers and fathers of the church by a woman, if that woman can be read as theology.

Beatrice's role as theology is implied by Virgil's frequent deferrals to her on religious questions: after a (self-corrective) explanation of his own position on prayers, Virgil tells Dante to suspend his doubt until he hears what Beatrice as the light between truth and the intellect tells him (*non ti fermar, se quella nol ti dice / che lume fia tra 'l vero e lo 'ntelletto. / Non so se 'ntendi; io dico di Beatrice,* "do not desist . . . until she tells you, she who will be a light between the truth and your intellect," *Purg.* 6.44–46); when he explains how sharing heavenly goods increases them, Virgil modestly says that if his argument *(ragion)* has not satisfied Dante's hunger, Beatrice will and more (*se la mia ragion non ti disfama, / vedrai Beatrice, ed ella pienamente / ti torrà questa e ciascun'altra brama,* "if my account does not take away your hunger, you will see Beatrice, and she will fully satisfy this and every other yearning," *Purg.* 15.76–78); and most suggestively when his discussion of human desire as love has led to new questions and doubts, Virgil admits the limitations of reason and commends Dante to the truth of faith from Beatrice (*Quanto ragion qui vede / dir ti poss'io; da indi in là t'aspetta / pur a Beatrice, ch'è opra di fede,* "As much as reason sees here, I can tell you; beyond that, wait still for Beatrice, for it is a matter of faith," *Purg.* 18.46–48; cf. 72–74).

Beatrice's significance as faith and theology is first suggested by contrast with Virgil's as reason and philosophy. Virgil, who guides Dante as Beatrice's agent, cannot take him beyond the realms of human error and correction; to perceive the visions and the sometimes paradoxical truths of Heaven, Beatrice, who like the other inhabitants of Paradise can see directly into the divine mind, must take over. Once she does, Beatrice does not defer to anyone; indeed she declares her judgment "infallible" (*secondo mio infallibile avviso,*

Dante, Virgil, and Beatrice. Opere del divino poeta Danthe, ed. Pietro da Figino, Venice, 1520. Giamatti Collection: Courtesy of the Mount Holyoke College Archives and Special Collections.

"according to my infallible view," *Par.* 7.19)—a word that is otherwise used only of God's justice in the *Commedia* (*Inf.* 29.56), and she promises to resolve his problem (about just punishment for just vengeance) swiftly with words of great significance (*Par.* 7.22–24). Beatrice does not hesitate to correct the writings of philosophers or theologians by name: she reinterprets Plato on souls returning to their stars (*Par.* 4.22ff.), rejects Gregory the Great on the orders of angels (*Par.* 28.133–135), and corrects Jerome on the creation of angels long before the creation of the world (*Par.* 29.37ff.). She teaches views that differ from those of Thomas Aquinas but without naming him: on mediated creation (*Par.* 2), on secondary creation of the elements (*Par.* 7), and on the memory of angels (*Par.* 29). Beatrice also discourses on universal order, free will, the sacredness of vows and valid dispensations, divine justice and revenge, and God's reason for creation. And she does all this in a heaven filled with learned doctors, several of whom had argued for Paul's injunction against women's speaking or teaching.

Though she is always the beautiful woman he loves, Dante seems to consciously cast Beatrice in male roles in the *Commedia:* when she appears in the Earthly Paradise heralded by three quotations, even though the first invokes the female bride of the Canticles, who represents the Church, the next two are Christ and his vicar, the emperor

(*Purg.* 30.11, 19, 21). Beatrice is like an admiral on the poop of the chariot that represents the Church (*Purg.* 30.58), and she serves as Dante's prosecutor, judge, and confessor of his past life (*Purg.* 30–31). In *Paradiso,* she teaches theology, in the formal mode of a master, getting Dante to give his answer and then correcting it (*Par.* 2.58ff.), presenting him for an examination and telling two of his examiners what to question him on and even answering one question for him (*Par.* 24.34–45, 25.29–33, 52–63). Why Dante has a (secular) woman play such male roles where there is no dearth of suitable males (in Heaven, at least) to perform them is a question that probably cannot be answered. But such a revolutionary reversal intensifies his criticism of the contemporary Church, strengthens his exaltation of human love as the most effective route to God, and marks the uniqueness of the message conveyed to and through him.

The problem arises because Beatrice is not simply a symbol. Certainly she seems to represent theology, revelation, faith, and perhaps contemplation (by virtue of her connection with Rachel) or grace (as the transmitter of divine light through the eyes), but she remains a real woman, even in death. When Dante sees her in the Earthly Paradise, his spirit feels the power of the "old love" (*d'antico amor sentì la gran potenza,* "[I] felt the great force of ancient love," *Purg.* 30.39), and he recognizes the signs of "the old flame" (*conosco i segni de l'antica fiamma,* "I recognize the signs of the ancient flame," 30.48), translating a line from the *Aeneid* in which Dido describes her feeling for Aeneas, as if to emphasize the physicality of Dante's response. The reaction is physical but not sinful because he has passed through the fire that cleanses lust. Beatrice herself reminds him of "the beautiful limbs" in which she was enclosed that so pleased him and that now are strewn about on Earth (31.50–51). To read Beatrice as Dante invites us to, as a (divinely ordained) figure for Christ and allegorical representation of theology, does not deny her historical reality; indeed, medieval exegesis demands the reality of a *figura,* the literal level of a sacred allegory, if we can only get over the fact that she is not a recognized saint but a secular woman.

Beatrice is a secular woman, but one destined virtually from birth for a special existence, as Dante takes pains to establish in the *Vita Nuova.* His first mention of her is as a woman in glory (*gloriosa donna, VN* 2.1) who was called "beatifier" *(Beatrice)* by those who did not know her name. He sees her at age 8 dressed in red, the color of love or charity, and his brain recognizes that this is his "beatitude." When he sees her again, in white, the color of faith and purity, and she greets him, he feels he has reached the limits of beatitude (*VN* 3.1–2), but the experience produces a disturbing dream which neither he nor his fellow poets can fully explain. Trying to hide his love for her (he claims), he showers such attentions on other women that Beatrice, "destroyer of all vices and queen of virtues," refuses to greet him (*VN* 10); that greeting had been so powerful and wondrous *(mirabile)* that even the expectation of it created a flame of charity in him which made him pardon any offender and respond to any request with love and humility (*VN* 11). If her reaction to his wandering attentions is touched with jealousy, Dante gives no hint of it. Indeed, he rarely allows Beatrice a normal human moment, such as when her unknown presence affects him physically and other women make fun of him with her (*VN* 14) or when she grieves at the death of her father (*VN* 22).

The first intimations of Beatrice's divine mission come in the poem Dante wrote to other women about her, "Donne ch'avete intelletto d'amor" (*VN* 19), in which Heaven requests her presence and God demurs because of one "who will say in Hell . . . I have seen the hope of the blessed" (*VN* 19:27–28); on Earth she has the power to disperse evil thoughts through love, to ennoble, even to save (*non pò mal finir chi l'ha parlato,* "he cannot finish evilly who has spoken with her," 19:42); God intends something extraordinary through her (*Dio ne 'ntenda di far cosa nova,* "God intends to make some wondrous thing of her," 19:46). The death of Beatrice's father leads to Dante's first (apparently subconscious) connection of Beatrice with Christ; he begins to fantasize about her death with strong echoes of Christ's death (*VN* 23); but then he sees her preceded by Giovanna Primavera just as John the Baptist preceded "the true light," and the connection is explicit (*VN* 24). Dante has already attributed to her the power to make pride and wrath flee before her (in the sonnet "Ne li occhi porta la mia donna Amore," *VN* 21); now other people recognize her as an angel, a marvel of God (who works through her), a miracle (*VN* 26.2 and "Tanto gentile e tanto onesta pare," line 8). And then the lord of justice calls her to glory with the Virgin Mary (*VN* 28).

B That is the end of her earthly story and the end of her role, such as it is, as an active if silent character in the *Vita Nuova.* Though Dante mentions her several times in the *Convivio,* it is not until the *Commedia* that she comes into her own as a speaking character. In the second book of the *Convivio,* Dante comments on a canzone, "Voi che 'ntendendo il terzo ciel movete," in which he is torn between the thought of (the dead) Beatrice and the attractions of the *gentile donna* whom he tries to explain away as Philosophy and who will ultimately be subsumed by Beatrice in the *Commedia;* he mentions that Beatrice is in Heaven with the angels and on Earth with Dante's soul (2.2.1), but it is not his intention to speak of the "living blessed Beatrice" in this book (2.8.7).

In the *Commedia,* however, she becomes a leading character with a large speaking role. Though she does not appear in person until the end of *Purgatorio,* she is a presence beginning with canto 2 of *Inferno,* where Virgil explains how she came for him and what she said, to reassure Dante that Heaven wills his journey. She begins as the lady of the *Vita Nuova,* in Virgil's description, blessed and beautiful, her eyes shining more than a star, her voice angelic and promising grateful (if puzzling) praise. But she quickly takes on new roles, speaking to Virgil, asking his help in rescuing the man she now speaks of as her friend and weeps for, and teaching Virgil what he does not know: why she is untouched by Hell. She establishes an important difference between herself and Virgil, whose "misery [as one of the damned] does not touch" her (*Inf.* 2.92)—a distinction that will be echoed at the beginning of *Purgatorio* when Cato accepts her authority for Dante's entry and rejects the thought of his former wife, Marcia, consigned now like Virgil "beyond the evil river" (*Purg.* 1.88).

Beatrice is invoked by Virgil several times in *Purgatorio* as a higher authority and finally, after all his arguments have failed, as the motivation to get Dante through the purifying fire (*Purg.* 27.36), but she does not appear until canto 30, after the procession. When she does, it is as a lyric lady, in a cloud of flowers, dressed in the colors Dante associated with her (white and red, under a green cloak), and Dante responds with the old feeling; but she breaks the spell quickly with her first words, the harsh, "Dante, though Virgil depart, do not weep yet" (30.55–56), for there is better reason to weep. If she seems like an admiral inspecting his fleet, regal in her pride, she is also like a

mother scolding her child. Once Dante has acknowledged his past errors, Beatrice reveals herself to him in her full beauty and then, reassuming her public role, leads him to the griffon and the tree, shows him the pageant of the history of the church (*Purg.* 32), makes a veiled prophecy (33.40–44), and gives him his assignment: to write everything he has seen and heard as a sign for the living, whether he understands it or not (33.52–78). Dante, who had acknowledged the influence of Virgil only in his style, credits Beatrice in *Paradiso* with his content—*Sì cominciò Beatrice questo canto* ("Thus Beatrice began this canto," 5.16); *Così Beatrice a me com'io scrivo* ("So Beatrice to me, as I write," 5.85)—and her final words to Dante in the poem are a prophecy of the seat for the emperor Henry in the celestial rose and of the hole awaiting popes Clement V and Boniface VIII in Hell (*Par.* 30.133–48).

But the character of Beatrice changes again in *Paradiso,* from the stern and mocking accuser to the helpful, informative, and even friendly teacher who takes pride in his achievements and smiles at his occasional lapses; to the concerned mother who comforts and nourishes him; to the lover who satisfies his desire. She is, curiously, more human in her relations with Dante in *Paradiso* than anywhere else in his writings. She draws him upward by the reflected light of the divine in her eyes—beautiful eyes which remain to the end the means by which Love caught him (*Par.* 28.11–12), in a fire that still burns (26.14–15). When he sees love in her holy eyes, his affection is free of any other desire (18.7–18), and she has to remind him that Paradise is not only in her eyes (18.21); when he looks down on Earth from the fixed stars, his mind, always in love and courting her, burns more than ever to bring his eyes back to her (27.88–90). Her beauty draws him, and her smile—denied here only once when its intensity would overwhelm him (21.4–6)—comforts and encourages him; the smile that burns in her eyes makes him feel he has plumbed the depths of Paradise (15.34–36). Even her corrections, such as "You are making yourself stupid with false imaginings" (1.88–89), are smiled words (*sorrise parolette brevi,* "her smiling brief words," 1.95) or silent smiles, as when he betrays family pride and affection in his response to Cacciaguida (16.13–15). She is pleased with him and "happy" (*lieta*), looking at him with eyes full of sparks of love (4.139–140), reassuring him when Charles Martel cites his poem ("Voi che 'ntendendo," 8.37), a poem in which the other woman seemed to win the competition for him in Dante's mind. Like a mother, she is pleased when his love for God makes him forget her momentarily (10.59–61); comforts him as one might a frightened child, when he hears the "thunder" of the saints ("Do you not know you are in Heaven? Do you not know that Heaven is all holy?" 22.7–9); and watches like a bird over its young, anxious to labor for their nourishment (23.1–6). But it is Beatrice as the beautiful woman who first attracted him, who has inspired his singing from that first sight to this moment, that Dante takes leave of when they reach the celestial rose—his poetic needs satisfied, his praise of her as complete as he can make it (30.28–36). His moral needs, however, continue; and so his final words to Beatrice thank her for descending to Hell in his cause and for doing whatever was needed to help save him, and they pray for her continued care, which she answers with a final smile (31.79–93).

Inspired by his love for Beatrice, Dante moves from the self-absorption of the lyric lover to the self-sacrifice of a public reformer. He sees her first as a beautiful and inaccessible woman, then as a Christ figure sent by God to give meaning to his life, and finally as a loving woman sent by Mary to save his soul (and his poetry) and to turn him into a willing instrument of the divine will. He imputes more and more meaning to her—as theology, revelation, faith, perhaps contemplation, and grace—but he never attempts, as he did with the *donna gentile,* to deny her reality as a woman he knew and loved. Those who would deny her historicity, like those who reject her allegorical significance, deny the fullness of Dante's poetry.

Bibliography

Allegherii, Petri. *Super Dantis ipsius Genitoris Comoediam Commentarium.* Edited by Vincentio Nannucci. Florence: Piatti, 1845.

Auerbach, Erich. *Dante: Poet of the Secular World.* Chicago: University of Chicago Press, 1961.

———. "Figura." In *Scenes from the Drama of European Literature.* New York: Meridian, 1959.

Boccaccio, Giovanni. *Vita di Dante.* Edited by Bruno Cagli. Rome: Anazini e Torraca, 1965.

De Robertis, Domenico. *Il libro della "Vita Nuova."* Florence: Sansoni, 1961.

Ferrante, Joan M. *Dante's Beatrice: Priest of an Androgynous God. CEMERS Occasional Papers,* 2. Binghamton, N.Y.: Medieval and Renaissance Texts and Studies, 1992.

Gilson, Étienne. *Dante and Philosophy.* New York: Sheed and Ward, 1949.

Harrison, Robert P. *The Body of Beatrice.* Baltimore: Johns Hopkins, 1988.

Jacoff, Rachel, and William A. Stephany. *Inferno II. Lectura Dantis Americana* 2. Philadelphia: University of Pennsylvania Press, 1989.

Nardi, Bruno. "Filosofia e teologia ai tempi di Dante." In *Saggi e note di critica dantesca.* Milan: Ricciardi, 1966.

Scott, John. "Dante's Admiral." *Italian Studies* 27 (1972), 28–40.

Singleton, Charles S. *An Essay on the "Vita Nuova."* Cambridge, Mass.: Harvard University Press, 1958.

———. *Dante Studies 2: Journey to Beatrice.* Cambridge, Mass.: Harvard University Press, 1958.

Williams, Charles. *The Figure of Beatrice.* London: Faber, 1943.

Joan M. Ferrante

Bede the Venerable, St.

English monk (c. 673–735), known as "the Venerable," who spent most of his productive scholarly career at the Benedictine abbey at Wearmouth-Jarrow in Northumbria, England. At 7 years of age Bede *(Beda)* was put in the care of the abbot of the monastery; he was ordained deacon at age 19, and priest the following year (703).

Bede's extensive scholarly output includes *De schematibus et tropis,* an examination of the tropes contained in Scripture; *De arte metrica,* on meter; as well as numerous other works on grammar, orthography, astronomy, chronology, and history. His formula for determining the date of Easter—a matter about which there were major disputes—became the dominant one. Bede's most influential work is perhaps his history of the English Church, *Historia ecclesiastica gentis Anglorum,* which he finished in 731 shortly before his death.

Bede assumes a minor role in Dante's works. In *Epist.* 11.16, Dante makes general reference to Bede's reputation as a learned scholar. Similarly, in *Par.* 10.131, Thomas Aquinas identifies Bede's spirit as being among the souls of the wise in the Heaven of the Sun. Isidore of Seville, Bede, and Richard of St. Victor are all named in the same verse.

Bibliography

Bede's Ecclesiastical History of the English People. Edited by Bertram Colgrave and R. A. B. Mynors. Oxford: Clarendon Press, 1991.

Blair, Peter Hunter. *The World of Bede.* Cambridge: Cambridge University Press, 1990.

Thompson, A. H. (ed.). *Bede: His Life, Times, and Writings.* Oxford: Oxford University Press, 1935.

Wallace-Hadrill, J. M. *Bede's Ecclesiastical History of the English People: A Historical Commentary.* Oxford: Clarendon Press, 1988.

George Andrew Trone

Beelzebub

One of four names attributed to Lucifer, *Belzebù* (of Hebrew origin) occurs once only in the *Commedia* and concludes the list of all recordings of Lucifer's names in the first canticle (*Inf.* 34.127). In the Bible, the term "Beelzebub," an ironic appellation, always designates a false god who is powerless before the true divinity of the Hebrews. No longer designated as "Baal the Prince" or "exalted Baal" (i.e., Baal Zebub), the false god is ironically called "Baal of the flies," or Beelzebub.

Dino Cervigni

Belacqua

The nickname of one Duccio di Bonavia, a Florentine maker of musical instruments who was famous for his indolence. That Dante had a fond and friendly relationship with him is suggested by early commentators. Benvenuto da Imola states that Dante, a lover of music, liked Belacqua especially because he was a musician as well as a maker of stringed instruments; and the Anonimo Fiorentino reports that Dante and Belacqua engaged in a witty exchange over the issue of his excessive laziness. Records show that Belacqua was still alive in 1299 but that he was dead by March 1302, so he may have died before 1300, the year of pilgrim Dante's journey through the otherworld. Dante's account of his meeting with Belacqua (*Purg.* 4.97–135) both conforms to a time scheme in which Belacqua would be a fairly recent arrival on the shores of Mount Purgatory and also confirms the friendly and humorous nature of their relationship.

As sole example of the indolent (spirits who bide their time in the Ante-Purgatory under a sentence that equals the duration of their spiritual negligence and delayed repentance in life), Belacqua reflects his legendary laziness in every aspect of his characterization. His manner of speech, pos-

ture, and dialogue with Dante are thoroughly imbued with his indolent personality, just as his interaction with the poet commemorates their affectionate, somewhat comical friendship. Thus, as Virgil leads Dante up the steep slope of the lower mountain, explaining to him that his climb will become easier as he nears the top and that once there he will be able to rest, a voice nearby sounds a gently ironic message, *Forse / che di sedere in pria avrai distretta!* ("Perhaps you will be obliged to sit before then!" *Purg.* 4.98–99), which causes the travelers to turn in its direction. They discover a large boulder, in the shade of which some spirits lazily lounge, among them one who sits clasping his knees and holding his face down between them. Overhearing Dante's remark to Virgil concerning his extremely slothful appearance, this spirit barely looks up and says, *Or va tu sù, che se' valente!* ("Now you go on up, you are so vigorous!" *Purg.* 4.114). The lazy sarcasm of this remark is all Dante needs to identify his old friend, and, though a little out of breath, he rushes up to him, providing a sharply contrastive picture of the two. For the remainder of their brief encounter, Belacqua characteristically shows no curiosity about the presence of a living person on the mountain, while Dante smiles at his old friend affectionately and asks him why he sits there: Does he wait for an escort, or has he resumed his old habits? Belacqua's answer to this question—that his wait below Purgatory's gate must be as long as his delay to repent in life was, unless one who lives in grace pray for him—explains the condition of the indolent in the scheme of divine justice. It also reminds us that within the warmth and humor of this episode there is established the first stage of the moral purification of the *Commedia*'s protagonist in this second realm of the dead, in which he is liberated from negligence and prompted to rise with diligence toward God.

George D. Economou

Benedict, St.

Known as "The Patriarch of Western Monasticism," St. Benedict (c. 480–c. 547; *Benedetto*) was born in Nursia and educated in Rome. Little is known of his life before his abrupt departure from Rome and general withdrawal from the world. Distraught and angered by the immorality and dereliction he found around him in those last days of the Roman Empire, he sought quietude and contemplation in a cave near Subiaco. There, at age 14, he took on the life of a hermit and remained one for many years. His complete devotion to the ascetic life, his spiritual self-control and discipline, and his knowledge of Scripture and allegiance to Christ's teaching attracted a large following. In imitation of Christ's choosing twelve apostles, Benedict established twelve monasteries; and as Christ chose his twelve to signal a rebirth of the ancient promise of God to the twelve tribes of Israel, Benedict appointed his twelve as a sign of the rebirth of Christendom in Europe. In 525 he moved his monastery from Subiaco to Monte Cassino, where he lived with his small band of monks until his death in c. 547.

Other than beginning the monastic movement in the West, Benedict's major influence was the rule he established by which monks should live. This "Rule of St. Benedict" (Regula Monachorum) borrows much from the teachings of the Desert Fathers—St. Basil, St. Augustine, and John Cassian—but is unique as a concise, clear account of both the demands of the Christian life and the administration of the monasteries in which the faith was to take new root, flourish, and spread.

Dante places Benedict in the Heaven of Saturn among the contemplatives (Par. 22.28). Dante's thoughts on the saint can be seen in his mixing together verses of serene contemplation and fiery anger at the derelict state of the church in Italy: contemplation and the ascetic life for Dante is a zeal for righteousness and restoration as well as peace gained in exercising the will of God. Dante's regard for Benedict can be seen (though this does not exhaust the meaning of the verse) in his request to be allowed to behold the saint in his true human form (Par. 22.58–60) behind the robe of light. This is the only such request in the entire Commedia. Benedict tells Dante that his wish will be granted when he reaches the Empyrean, where the pilgrim finds the saint seated between St. Francis and St. Augustine in the celestial rose (Par. 32.35).

William Wilson

Benevento

Town north of Naples and site of the battle where Charles of Anjou defeated Manfred, king of Sicily, whose body he buried along the river Calore under a pile of stones placed upon it one by one by each of Charles's soldiers. Later the archbishop of Cosenza, following the orders of Pope Clement IV,

disinterred the body and cast it unburied along the banks of the Verde.

Richard Lansing

Benincasa da Laterina

A renowned jurist of the thirteenth century who, during his tenure as acting judge in Siena, condemned to death a close relative of the notorious highwayman Ghino di Tacco. Ghino avenged that sentence by stabbing Benincasa in open court. Dante refers to Benincasa as "the Aretine who at the fierce hands of Ghino di Tacco met his death" (Purg. 6.13–14) and places him in the Ante-Purgatory, among those who died violently without absolution but who repented at the last moment.

Antonio Illiano

Benvenuto da Imola

Fourteenth-century commentator of the Commedia, born in Imola (c. 1320 or 1330) into a family of notaries. He probably received his early education from his father, who had a school in the city, and possibly he completed it in Bologna. From 1361 to 1364 his presence in Bologna is confirmed by the fact that he worked on the book Romuleon, a compendium of Roman history. In 1365 he was sent by the government of Imola to Avignon to plead with Pope Urban V for the preservation of the liberty of the Comune of Imola. When his mission failed, he chose to go into exile in Bologna (in his commentary he empathizes with Dante as exul immeritus). He remained there until the late 1370s. In Bologna, probably while commenting on Inf. 15, he accused some of his colleagues at the university of indecent actions. When they took retaliatory measures, he moved to Ferrara, under the protection of Niccolò II, to whom he dedicated his final commentary on the Commedia. He died in Ferrara sometime between 1387 and August 13, 1388. In Bologna and Ferrara he lectured and commented on the works of classical authors such as Virgil, Lucan, Seneca, and Valerius Maximus, as well as of his contemporaries Petrarch and Boccaccio. It is almost certain that his last work was the Augustalis libellus, an excursus on the Roman emperors from Caesar to Wenceslaus.

Benvenuto's fame, however, rests with his commentary on the Commedia, which comes to us in three different versions. The first is contained in

B a codex in Turin, under the name of Stefano Talice da Ricaldone (a copyist who lived a century later), which was published in 1875. A second version, written in Ferrara and presently at the Laurentian Library (Florence; in the Ashburnham Codex, no. 839), is still unpublished. The third version, contained in several codices, was published by G. F. Lacaita in 1887. The first two versions must be considered preparatory work—the final commentary being the first humanistic approach to the *Commedia* where rhetorical issues prevail over dialectics and where interest in the theological content of the poem is on the wane. Although in his commentary Benvenuto mentions that he has been in Florence in order to attend Boccaccio's lectures on the *Commedia* in 1373, his work reveals a greater dependence on Boccaccio's *Vita di Dante* than on Boccaccio's commentary. He was the first to comment on the poem verbatim—a critical practice still observed today—and it is in his commentary that we find the word *dantista* ("Dante critic") used for the first time.

Bibliography

Benvenuto da Imola. *Comentum super Dantis Aldigherij Comoediam.* Edited by G. P. Lacaita. 3 vols. Florence: 1887.

Benvenuto da Imola lettore degli antichi e dei moderni. Atti del Convegno Internazionale, Imola 26 e 27 maggio 1989. Edited by Pantaleo Palmieri and Carlo Paolazzi. Ravenna: Longo, 1991.

La Favia, Louis M. *Benvenuto Rambaldi da Imola: Dantista.* Madrid: Ediciones José Porrúa Turanzas, 1977.

———. "Benvenuto da Imola's Dependence on Boccaccio's Studies on Dante." *Dante Studies* 93 (1975), 161–175.

Louis M. La Favia

Berenger, Raymond IV

Last count of Provence in the court of Aragon-Provence, recalled by Emperor Justinian in the Heaven of Mercury (*Par.* 6.134). He reigned from 1209 to 1245 and was the first count in his line to reside in his domains. He married Beatrix of Savoy, by whom he had four daughters. Through the subtle diplomacy of his minister Romeo of Villeneuve he was able to marry each daughter to a king: Margaret became the wife of Louis IX of France, in 1234; Eleanor, the wife of Henry III of England, in 1236; Sancie, the wife of Richard, Duke of Cornwall (Henry III's brother), in 1241; and Beatrix, the wife of Charles I of Anjou (Louis IX's brother) in 1246. At the death of her father in 1245, Beatrix inherited the countship of Provence, which, upon the extinction of the house of Anjou-Sicily in 1481, was attached to the kingdom of France.

Justinian recalls how Count Raymond *(Ramondo Beringhiere)* was persuaded by a number of barons, acting out of jealousy, to submit his minister Romeo to questioning about his administration of the treasury (*Par.* 6.133). This act induced Romeo to leave his position, for which Justinian characterizes the count as ungrateful.

Yolande de Pontfarcy

Bernardin di Fosco

Believed to have been of humble origins, he nevertheless achieved high respect and prestige among the nobles of his community during his career. In 1240 he defended Faenza against Frederick II. Bernardin served as chief magistrate of Pisa (1248) and of Siena (1249). Guido del Duca, praising him as one of the noble figures of Romagna, calls him *verga gentil di picciola gramigna* ("noble shoot born of humble grass," *Purg.* 14.102) in his discourse on the second terrace of Purgatory.

Paul Colilli

Bernard Silvester of Tours

Twelfth-century philosopher best known for his work *De mundi universitate,* or *Cosmographia,* a Neoplatonic allegory of creation still circulating in Dante's time. Bernard may also have been the author of a commentary on the first six books of the *Aeneid,* in which the first half of Virgil's epic is read as a moral allegory of the five ages of man. Dante demonstrates his familiarity with this line of interpretation, if not specifically with Bernard's text, in *Conv.* 4.24.4–10, where he defines his concept of the four ages of man, and again in 4.26.8–15, where he interprets the moral allegory of Virgil's *Aeneid.* While this reading of the *Aeneid* is not itself important for the *Commedia,* the reputation of Virgil as a moral authority on which it is based is central to the *Commedia*'s concern with the Christian appropriation of pagan poetry and philosophy.

Claudia Rattazzi Papka

Bernard, St.

Born in Burgundy in 1090, Bernard *(Bernardo)* entered the Cistercian order in 1112 and rose rapidly to become founding abbot of Clairvaux in 1115. For the rest of his life he was tirelessly active, both in the everyday administration of his abbey and in a career as preacher, spiritual writer, and counselor to princes and prelates that took him far beyond the walls of Clairvaux and made him probably the most influential individual figure in the twelfth-century church. His fierce debates with theological radicals like Peter Abelard, his involvement on the side of legitimacy in the power struggle provoked by the election of the schismatic Pope Anacletus in 1130, his hugely successful preaching of the (ultimately disastrous) Second Crusade, and his mentorship of many leading figures in the ecclesiastical and secular worlds all contributed to his Europe-wide fame as a passionately eloquent spokesman for institutional and intellectual orthodoxy of the staunchest kind. He died in 1153.

Bernard's large and varied body of writings consists, amid much else, of numerous sermons (most famously a collection of eighty-six exegetical sermons on the Song of Songs); moral and theological treatises *(On the Steps of Humility and Pride, On Grace and Free Will);* devotional works *(On Loving God);* biography *(The Life of St. Malachy the Irishman);* essays on monastic discipline *(Apologia to William of St.-Thierry);* a "how-to" manual for the new pope, Eugenius III, who had been a monk at Clairvaux *(On Consideration);* a rule book for the Order of Knights Templar *(In Praise of the New Militia);* and hundreds of letters. Many of these works also circulated widely in the later Middle Ages in anthologies and selections, while many other writings, such as the famous hymn "Jesu dulcis memoria," were soon—wrongly but significantly—attributed to his authorship. Charismatic and controversial, a skilled polemicist, and by all accounts an astonishingly effective preacher (hence his popular title, "Mellifluous Doctor"), Bernard was also recognized even by his contemporaries as a man of unquestioned saintliness: he was canonized in 1174.

Bernard's influence on Dante's work has often been posited, but references to him there are few. Outside the *Commedia,* in fact, the only trace of Bernard is a mention of his *De consideratione,* as a fundamental work of contemplative mysticism, in the disputed *Letter to Cangrande (Epist.* 13.80). In *Paradiso,* however, a character bearing Bernard's name occupies a major role in the closing cantos, and this has often been held to justify the argument that the historical Bernard was among Dante's preferred authorities.

Bernard enters the text of *Paradiso* at 31.58, though his identity is not made clear until 31.102. He comes to preside over Beatrice's departure from Dante's side (31.58–93), to replace her as expositor of the wonders of the Empyrean (94–138), and to direct Dante's attention toward the new and more fitting object of his spiritual ardor, Mary (138–142). In canto 32 he undertakes a complex theological discourse describing the heavenly rose and its occupants and discussing the differential allocation of grace to those who were saved by repentance as adults and those who owe their salvation only to the fact of having been baptized into the Christian faith as infants. Finally, in canto 33 (1–39), he prays directly to Mary, on Dante's behalf, asking that Dante be allowed to proceed to the unmediated vision of God; after this (33.49) he slips, smiling, out of the text.

Since the earliest times, commentators on the *Commedia* have agreed that Bernard's surprising last-minute appearance in the poem's narrative as well as the crucial role he plays there are Dante's tribute to his historical renown in two main areas: contemplative mysticism and devotion to Mary. Both these aspects are duly highlighted in the text of *Paradiso.* Bernard is called *quel contemplante* ("that contemplative") at 32.1, and Dante-character's reaction to the discovery of Bernard's identity is to think of him as *colui che 'n questo mondo, / contemplando, gustò di quella pace* ("He who in this world, contemplating, had tasted of that peace," 31.110–111). As for Mary, Bernard describes himself as her *fedel Bernardo* ("faithful Bernard," 31.102), and the text repeatedly refers to his devotion thereafter (32.106–108, 33.28–30). More recently, it has been suggested that Bernard's thinking about relations between the temporal and spiritual powers, as expressed in *De*

B *consideratione,* may have had some influence on Dante's and also that his reputation for eloquence may have conditioned some details of his portrayal in *Paradiso.* But all these interpretations need to be viewed in light of the (perhaps surprising) fact that nowhere in the *Commedia* does Dante refer specifically or in detail to the historical Bernard's life and writings. Bernard's putative influence on Dante's work thus remains difficult to quantify using the traditional techniques of tracing literary or intellectual influence through quotation and allusion; but his importance in the narrative and thematic structures of the final cantos of *Paradiso* is obviously overwhelming, and the simple fact of his presence in so exalted a position may be the most telling evidence we have for Dante's high estimation of him.

Bibliography

Aversano, Mario. *San Bernardo e Dante: teologia e poesia della conversione.* Salerno: Edisud, 1990.

Botterill, Steven. *Dante and the Mystical Tradition: Bernard of Clairvaux in the "Commedia."* Cambridge: Cambridge University Press, 1994.

Gilson, Étienne. *The Mystical Theology of Saint Bernard.* London, New York: Sheed and Ward, 1955; Kalamazoo, Mich.: Cistercian Publications, 1990.

Petrocchi, Giorgio. "Dante e la mistica di San Bernardo." In *Letteratura e critica: studi in onore di Natalino Sapegno.* Edited by Walter Binni and others. 4 vols. Rome: Bulzoni, 1974. Vol. I, pp. 213–229.

Steven Botterill

Bertran de Born

Bertran de Born (*Bertram* or *Beltramo dal Bornio*) was born around 1450 and died before 1215. A nobleman from Altaforte in Périgord, he claimed to have played an important political role in the struggle that turned King Henry II of England against his sons (Henry the Young King in particular). Dante offers two sharply contrasting judgments of Bertran, with a positive, exemplary portrait contained in the *De vulgari eloquentia* and the *Convivio* giving way to a negative image in the *Commedia.* In *DVE* 2.2.8, Bertran is presented as the romantic model of the poetry that celebrates prowess of arms (*salus,* or *armorum probitas*). In *Conv.* 4.11.14 he is exalted along with other emi-

nent historical figures as the champion of the virtue of generosity *(liberalità).* But in *Inf.* 28 the early praise is transformed into open condemnation. Bertran is punished in the ninth bolgia of Malebolge as a sower of schism for having instigated Prince Henry to rebel against his father (*Inf.* 28.135), and is shown carrying his detached head "like a lantern" (28:122). The aptness of his punishment is evident to Bertran himself, who defines the general principle of retribution in Hell: *"Così s'osserva in me lo contrapasso"* ("Thus is observed in me the counter- suffering," 142). Most critics take the term *contrapasso,* expressing the idea that the punishment fits the crime, to refer to the condition of all sinners in Hell.

Michelangelo Picone
(translated by Robin Treasure)

Bible

The Bible undergirds the entire world in which Dante lived. Believed to be inspired by a God who chose human scribes to speak his Word, it had an authority quite beyond any human text. As the holy book of the church, it informed liturgy and preaching, art and architecture, thereby constituting a vast symbolic network intelligible to all classes of society. It is not surprising, then, that when Dante's writings are considered as a whole, the Christian Scriptures should be the source of more reference and allusion than any other work: by one count there are 575 citations of the Bible, compared with 395 references to Aristotle and 192 to Virgil.

Unlike the vast majority of laymen in the Middle Ages, who were more likely to hear or see representations from the Bible than ever to read it, Dante seems also to have studied the Scriptures and been exposed to the major interpretive traditions of his time and place. In *Conv.* 2.12.7 he speaks of having consoled himself after the death of Beatrice by going to the "schools of the religious and the disputations of the philosophers," referring presumably to the convent schools established by the Dominicans at Santa Maria Novella and by the Franciscans at Santa Croce. In both environments he would have come in contact not only with the *lectio divina* that was a traditional part of monastic life but also with lectures on the "sacred page" that were the final stage of theological study. Although the academic procedures of the two convents would no doubt have been similar—with an emphasis on parallel passages and chains of citations rather than on a more literary explication of the text itself—the exegetical atmosphere of each center was distinct. From the Dominicans Dante would have received the methodology of the *Summa,* whereby the words of Scripture and the Church Fathers serve to substantiate theological points. From the Franciscans, under the influence of Pietro Olivi (1248–1298) and Ubertino da Casale (1259–1325), he would have found a preoccupation with the Book of Apocalypse and its relevance to contemporary history. Both methods of interpretation can be found in the *Commedia*—the former in *Paradiso,* the latter in the closing cantos of *Purgatorio.*

By the year 1300 biblical scholars had access to many variant versions of St. Jerome's Latin (Vulgate) Bible, the most recent and important of which was the early-thirteenth-century edition prepared at the University of Paris. This *exemplar Parisiensis* was a compact, one-volume edition of the Scriptures popular not only with university students but also with the preaching orders. Medieval bibles typically presented the sacred text within a network of commentary, with citations both from the Church Fathers and from more recent exegetes filling the margins of the page and running between the lines. With the text literally surrounded by interpretation, there was no unmediated encounter with it. While it is thought that Dante largely made use of the "Paris edition" of the Vulgate (although there are other versions found in his writings), it is unknown if he owned such a bible himself. It is more likely that, whether in Florence or during the subsequent years of exile when he was actually at work on the *Commedia,* he relied on whatever manuscripts or scholarly resources were available to him, either in ecclesiastical libraries or through the private collections of the lords he served at Verona and Ravenna. Nor should we underestimate the degree to which the Scriptures he had at his disposal came to him through memory and, in particular, through a constant exposure to the liturgy, with its biblical readings, hymns, prayers, and sequences. The Scriptures Dante uses most often come precisely from those books that are privileged by the worship of the church: the Gospels, the Psalms, and the Epistles of Paul. (Genesis, Proverbs, and Isaiah are also important sources—but for Dante's prose treatises and epistles rather than for the *Commedia*).

While simple enumeration of biblical references is not in itself definitive, it is instructive to note patterns within the three canticles. Given Dante's overt dependence on classical sources in *Inferno,* it comes as no surprise that Hell should include the fewest direct citations of Scripture. Nor is it difficult to see why in *Paradiso* biblical allusion is far more common than actual citation. The blessed have become so completely one with God's Word as to assimilate it into their own speech, to pass beyond the mediation of the Scriptures and into the reality they signify—to be "ingodded" (to recall the neologism *"indiarsi"* which Dante invents in *Par.* 4.28 to describe the state of beatitude). Where the Bible plays its most important role in the poem, however, is in the middle space of *Purgatorio,* with its thirty direct citations and roughly forty allusions. In this realm of time and change, the souls have not yet reached an eternal destination. They remain *in via,* as needy of guidance and instruction as those who still live on Earth. Small wonder, then, that in the second canticle Dante should pay such sustained attention to God's Book, showing the power of its transforming word among the penitents and thereby suggesting its importance for the living.

It is in *Purgatorio,* moreover, that Dante stages a series of "meetings" with the Bible. The first of these is in *Purg.* 2.43–48, when a boatload of the blessed arrive on the shores of the mountain singing in unison Ps. 113/114, "In exitu Israel de Aegypto." This is the poem's first exact citation of the Vulgate; it also places this moment in the narrative (as the souls emerge from the "Egypt" of mortal life and as Dante-pilgrim issues forth from Hell) in the larger thematic context of Exodus, one of the great biblical paradigms that undergirds the entire *Commedia.* In addition, the introduction of the psalm text inaugurates a program of scriptural and liturgical reference that gives structure to the seven terraces of purgatory. On the terrace of pride (*Purg.* 10–12), for instance, Dante sees numerous biblical (as well as pagan) figures who either rejoice in humility or demonstrate the wages of arrogance. Signifying the virtue to be embraced, the biblical stories of Mary at the Annunciation (Luke 1:26–38) and David dancing before the Ark of the Lord (2 Sam. 6) are depicted as bas reliefs, along with the pagan figure of the emperor Trajan humbly acceding to the request of a commoner; likewise, representing the sin of pride (which the penitents are meant to reject), sculpted images

B

along the floor of the terrace show Satan, Nimrod, Saul, Rehoboam, and Holofernes among other nonbiblical figures.

The poet underscores the active participation of the souls in their own transformation not only by having them sing the psalms, hymns, or prayers of the church but also by having them paraphrase the Bible in their own language. Thus the proud pray a vernacular version of the Our Father, or Lord's Prayer, in *Purg.* 11.1–24, which represents a theological interpretation of the hallowed words. At the exit of each terrace, moreover, an angel speaks one of the Beatitudes from Christ's Sermon on the Mount (Matt. 5:3–12), sometimes giving the Latin text, sometimes offering an Italian translation, and sometimes offering a more elaborate interpretation of what the Beatitudes mean.

In *Purg.* 29, at the end of the penitential journey and within the Garden of Eden, Dante stages an allegorical presentation of the Bible itself—a pageant of Revelation. It begins with a file of twenty-four old men walking two by two. Behind them come four winged animals who escort a splendid griffin-drawn chariot. Following this ensemble there is yet another file of elders: first a pair of old men, then a quartet of males who appear "of lowly aspect," and finally a single old man with eyes closed. Once all these figures take their place, the canto ends. The stage is now set for the advent of Beatrice in *Purg.* 30. Drawing on a rich store of imagery found first in the prophet Ezekiel and then in the Revelation to John the Divine, this elaborate and quasi-liturgical procession not only rehearses visionary moments in both testaments but also gives us a vision of the Bible itself. For what Dante sees assembled before him is the Word of God made allegorical flesh; it is the canon of Scripture unfolding in time, from the alpha of Genesis to the omega of the Apocalypse. To begin, the twenty-four elders stand for the books of the Hebrew Scriptures, as they were enumerated by St. Jerome in his prologue to the Vulgate. The four winged animals who come next in line are a traditional representation of the Gospels, while the company that follows upon the chariot symbolizes the rest of the New Testament: the Pauline Epistles and the Acts of the Apostles paired together, the four Catholic Epistles (Peter, James, John, and Jude) walking behind them, and the Revelation to St. John the Divine at the very end, as the canon's last word.

How Dante saw himself in relationship to the Bible is suggested in *Par.* 25.64–78, where he describes himself ready to "rerain" the Holy Spirit's inspiration received by him through his reading both of the Psalms and of the Epistle of James. In his own work, therefore, he will pass on the overflow from the Old and New Testaments, as if he were himself writing a third testament in the *Commedia*. This claim to a kind of "scripturality" is also implicit in the *Letter to Cangrande*, which suggests that the way to read the poem is according to the fourfold interpretation reserved for Scripture alone. Indeed, the text used to explicate the multiplicity of the poem's "senses" or levels of meaning is none other than Ps. 113, "In Exitu Israel de Aegypto," the same stock example often chosen by the masters of the "sacred page" to demonstrate the principles of biblical exegesis. The implication is that, like God, Dante writes not only in metaphors but also in events: the journey he describes in his "sacred poem" is as historical as the Exodus itself.

So powerful is the force of Dante's claims in the *Commedia* that it is easy to forget that his authority is largely his own creation. As a layman, he had no particular standing within the church; as an exile from Florence, he had no base of power. Yet despite his worldly marginality, his conviction of a divine call resounds throughout his writings, enabling him to take every license. In *Inf.* 19.90–97, for instance, he delivers a scathing denunciation of the papacy in the person of Pope Nicholas III. This extended diatribe cites Matthew and Acts, Isaiah and the Apocalypse; it shows all the confidence of a preacher who not only knows the Scripture by heart but also recognizes that the hierarchy has abandoned the Gospel for silver and gold, its preachers given themselves over to vain inventions and "trifles" (*ciance, Par.* 29.110; see also *Par.* 11.133–135). With only his baptism as a Christian to show as his authorization to speak out, he appropriates for himself the boldness of apostolic speech, as if he were himself a successor to St. Peter.

One way to view the *Commedia*, in fact, is as an extended call narrative, a story (such as one finds at the beginning of Isaiah, or Jeremiah, or Ezekiel) about the making of a prophet. Like those Old Testament figures, Dante worries at first that he is not worthy of the calling (*Inf.* 2.10–42) but is emboldened after learning that he has been rescued by heavenly powers presumably for a higher purpose. In *Purg.* 32.103–105 Beatrice tells him that the visions that are about to be afforded him (like all that has happened to him thus far) are "for the good of the world that lives ill"; therefore, when he returns from the journey, he is meant (like John the Divine in Apoc. 1:11) to write it all down. Later in *Paradiso,* after having identified himself with St. Paul in the latter's rapture to the "third heaven" (*Par.* 1.73–75; cf. II Cor. 12:2–4), Dante is told by his ancestor Cacciaguida (*Par.* 17.133–135) to make manifest all that he has beheld, to let his cry be as the wind on the mountain top, like the prophet's voice in Isa. 40:9. Finally, no less than St. Peter himself commissions Dante to tell the whole story when he returns below: *apri la bocca, / e non asconder quel ch'io non ascondo* ("open your mouth and hide not what I do not hide," *Par.* 27.65–66).

To an extent unexampled in European literature, Dante reimagined the world of the Bible and turned its sacred figure into his own literary "fulfillment." What this entailed most obviously was the transformation of biblical character, narrative, and typology into the vernacular of his imagination: his reinvention of the Exodus, for instance, or his metamorphosis of the apostle Paul into himself over the course of *Paradiso.* One can also speak of how the *Commedia* revives the first-person discourse of biblical prophecy and apocalypse, or note Dante's aspiration to be another psalmist, "the highest singer of the highest Lord" (*Par.* 25.72). In all these ways the poet rewrites Scripture precisely by continuing to write it—not as a third testament, but as a sacred poem that is fully aware of itself as a work of literature.

Bibliography

Barblan, Giovanni (ed.). *Dante e la Bibbia.* Florence: Olschki, 1988.

De Lubac, Henri, S.J. *Exégèse médiévale: les quatres sens de l'écriture.* Vol. II, 2. Paris: Aubier, 1964.

Kleinhenz, Christopher. "Dante and the Bible: Biblical Citation in Dante's *Divine Comedy.*" In *Dante: Contemporary Perspectives.* Edited by Amilcare A. Iannucci. Toronto: University of Toronto Press, 1997, pp. 74–93.

———. "Dante and the Bible: Intertextual Approaches to the *Divine Comedy.*" *Italica* 63, no. 3 (Autumn 1986), 225–236.

Lampe, G. W. H. (ed.). *Cambridge History of the Bible.* Vol. II, *The West: From the Fathers to the Reformation.* Cambridge: Cambridge University Press, 1969.

Manetti, Aldo. "Dante e la Bibbia." *Bollettino della Civica Biblioteca.* Bergamo, 1984, pp. 100–128.

Penna, Angelo. "Bibbia." In *Enciclopedia dantesca,* 1:626–629.

Smalley, Beryl. *The Study of the Bible in the Middle Ages.* Notre Dame, Ind.: University of Notre Dame Press, 1964. Reprinted in 1951.

Spicq, C. *Esquisse d'une histoire de l'exégèse latine au moyen âge.* Paris: Vrin, 1944.

Peter S. Hawkins

Blacks and Whites

Designations for the two major political factions within the Guelf party, which struggled to dominate Florence at a critical period in Dante's life. Dante was among the most visible members of the White party when his exile from his native city began in 1302. During the years he spent composing the *Commedia,* however, he apparently reflected on intervening political events and came to write almost as critically of the Whites *(Bianchi)* as of the Blacks *(Neri)* in his poem. The very designations of these parties express metaphorically an absolute contrast, perhaps between two ideologies or two socioeconomic groups. But just as no serious student of American politics would be content to describe the Republicans merely as the party of big business and the Democrats as the party of working people, so no serious student of Dante can today accept what was once the standard characterization of the Blacks as the party of the aristocracy and the Whites as the party of the people. The scholarship of recent decades on Italian history indicates that the story of the Blacks and Whites must, paradoxically, be told in shades of gray which fluctuate with the passage of each of the eventful years of the late thirteenth and early fourteenth centuries. Careful attention to the dynamic character of this story, however, will reward the student of Dante, and especially of the *Commedia,* with a better understanding of why the nature of earthly politics constituted such an absorbing and difficult problem for him.

Because the Blacks and Whites originated in a split within the Guelf political party, one must

B understand something of the history of the Guelfs and their opponents, the Ghibellines, in order to follow their development and Dante's relation to it. The Italian Guelf and Ghibelline parties had, indeed, originated in eleventh- and twelfth-century Germany, in disputes over accession to the position of Holy Roman Emperor. Italians had a special interest in these disputes in Germany for two reasons: (1) the empire included large parts of northern Italy as well as Germany, and (2) the emperor, though chosen by German electors, had to travel through northern Italy to be crowned in the holy city of Rome in order to take full possession of this title. Italian political interests thus came to ally themselves with one or the other of the German parties in their quests for the imperial throne. The Ghibellines took their name from Waiblingen castle, which had belonged to an ancestor of the dukes of Swabia. Because the Swabian dynasty of the Hohenstaufens held the imperial throne during much of the high Middle Ages, the Ghibellines came to be understood as the party of the emperor. The Guelfs took their name from a dynasty of German dukes of Bavaria named Welf, from whose ranks the dukes of Bavaria had originated during the eleventh century. As sometime losers in the battle for the imperial throne, they came to champion the political cause of the pope and the role of the papacy in secular affairs, as a counterweight to imperial power and ambitions.

Some of the story of the introduction of the Guelf–Ghibelline conflict from Germany into Florence is told by Dante's ancestor Cacciaguida in *Par.* 16.66–147. Cacciaguida laments the expansion of Florence in the first half of the twelfth century because it caused the Buondelmonti, a family with Guelf sympathies, to move into the city from their castle in the Valdigreve. Buondelmonte de' Buondelmonti was then killed in Florence in 1216 in a feud with several other Florentine families, at least one of which, the Uberti, was Ghibelline. The animosity between two groups of Florentine families was thus intensified and broadened through association with these older, originally German, parties.

Struggles between Tuscan Ghibellines and Guelfs dominated the decades immediately preceding and following Dante's birth in 1265. In 1248, Emperor Frederick II helped the Ghibelline leaders, the Uberti, drive the Guelfs out of Florence—an event Dante the pilgrim discusses with Farinata degli Uberti in *Inf.* 10. In 1258, the Ghibellines were in turn driven out of Florence, taking refuge in Siena. From that base, they marched out to meet the Florentine Guelf forces at Montaperti in 1260 and defeated them decisively. In 1266 the Guelfs once again gained the upper hand in Florence, expelling the Ghibellines in the following year, their cause being further strengthened by the defeat of the Ghibelline Manfred, king of Sicily, at Benevento in February 1266 (see *Purg.* 3). The Ghibellines tried to reconquer Florence in 1289 at the battle at Campaldino, in the Casentino region east of Florence. The Guelfs, however— Dante probably among them (see *Inf.* 22.4–9)— defeated the Ghibellines definitively. After this Guelf victory, the Ghibellines were no longer in a position to play a significant role in Florentine affairs; yet the tensions that played out between them in Florence during much of the thirteenth century were given new life at the end of the century as the Guelf party split into two factions, the White Guelfs and the Black Guelfs. The names of these two Guelf factions arose during a conflict in late-thirteenth-century Pistoia, to which Dante alludes in *Inf.* 24.143. There the numerous Cancellieri family, all Guelfs, had split into two factions. Though this factionalization was precipitated by a violent quarrel between cousins in 1286, it was based in tensions which developed during the course of the thirteenth century in response to important changes in the social and economic organization of most cities in Tuscany. Certain families traditionally enjoyed knightly status: they and their ancestors trained their sons for military careers and had enough landed wealth to provide them with armor and warhorses, so that they could be *cavalieri* ("fighting horsemen"). These knightly families began to see their prestige threatened by others which, although of lower social origin, began to attain economic status superior to that of the knightly families. The success of these "upstart" families in the newly established banking industry and in international commerce put them in a position to challenge the feudal order, which had been in place in Tuscany for several centuries.

One branch of the Cancellieri family came to be called the Whites, perhaps because one of its female ancestors bore the name Bianca, and it happened that this branch had longstanding banking and commercial connections with knightly families and the remnants of the Ghibelline aristocracy.

The other branch, called, then, the Blacks, was more closely tied to the *popolani*. (This word literally means "the people" or "the popular class," but not in the sense in which these terms are commonly used in English, as rough equivalents for "the working class," "the poor," or, simply, "everyone.") Specifically, the *popolani* were the emerging mercantile class, people who did not have a knightly tradition but had enough wealth and prestige to be economically and, increasingly, politically influential. These *popolani* sometimes even were granted the title of "knight," though they lacked military training and tradition. They struggled politically to defend themselves and their commercial interests from the violent disruptions to which the knightly Whites of Pistoia were prone.

Both Cancellieri factions found allies in neighboring Florence, though, as often happens, the politics of the time made strange bedfellows. The cause of the Pistoiese Blacks, allied primarily with mercantile interests, was taken up by a Florentine group led by a representative of the old Florentine knightly class, Corso Donati. As the fourteenth century opened, the Donati and many of their Florentine allies had more inherited prestige than actual wealth. This discrepancy created a natural tension between the Florentine Blacks and the increasingly successful *popolani*. In Florence, the *popolani* allied themselves with the knightly Pistoiese Whites. The Florentine Whites were headed by the Cerchi, an enterprising and extremely wealthy family of nonknightly origins. Thus did Florence, around the turn of the thirteenth century to the fourteenth, reformulate its own internal tensions—formerly projected through the conflict between German Guelfs and Ghibellines—through the feud between Pistoiese Blacks and Whites.

The struggle for dominance between the two groups was most intense from 1300 to 1302, that is, just at the time Dante chooses for the fictive date of his journey to the otherworld. Moreover, it was a struggle which precipitated Dante's exile from his native city and thus his efforts to interpret his alienation from homeland within a broader political and spiritual context. Because of the importance of the conflict between Florentine Blacks and Whites in both Dante's biography and his imaginative life, any student needs not only to be aware of the major events in the conflict but also to recognize the wide range of forces underlying

its origin and development. The conflict reached a crisis in April 1300, when the Florentine government condemned for treason several Florentine bankers who had collaborated closely with the papal court. Pope Boniface VIII's reaction, to be sure, was quick and negative, especially after the condemnation was confirmed by the succeeding Florentine government. In this tense setting, Dante began, on June 15, a two-month term as a prior. In June, on the eve of the festival of Florence's patron saint, St. John the Baptist, a number of magnates (Blacks) attacked several prominent guildsmen (Whites), leading to the banishment of these magnates and a further deepening of resentments between the factions. Shortly after Dante completed his term as prior, the papal legate excommunicated those Whites who at the time held major government posts, confiscating their goods. As Dante was no longer a prior, he escaped this condemnation for the moment, but he continued to play a highly visible role in the standoff: from April 1 to September 30, 1301, he served on the Council of the Hundred, and in October of that year he was chosen as one of three ambassadors sent by Florence to Boniface to plead that Charles of Valois, brother of the king of France, not be allowed to enter Florence with his troops as the papal representative. Despite these pleas, Boniface allowed Charles to enter Florence in November 1301. Within a matter of weeks the banished Black leader, Corso Donati (referred to in *Purg.* 24.82–90), who had previously been exiled himself, returned to Florence by night with a small band of followers. They sacked the houses of the priors and began a reign of terror that Charles made no attempt to quell. The Blacks proceeded to install their own men as priors, so that the Ordinances of Justice could no longer be enforced. Early in 1302, the Black government began summoning leading Whites, group by group, to trial on various charges. Having failed to respond to a summons to appear before the podestà Cante de' Gabrielli of Gubbio, Dante together with several other Whites were sentenced, on January 27, to exile for a period of two years. As a result of Dante's having refused to meet the conditions of the sentence, a more severe penalty was imposed on him on March 10, condemning him to perpetual exile and to be burned alive at the stake if ever apprehended. The exiled Whites periodically mounted protests and considered forced reentry into Florence, but to build a sufficient base of

B power they were obliged to ally themselves with what remained of the Tuscan Ghibellines, which caused them to lose their distinct identity with the Guelf party.

Ideology—a certain rhetoric—was important to each of these factions, as it was to Dante, but any attempt to reduce either the Blacks or the Whites to a single ideological position encounters contradictions and inconsistencies which cause it to fail. Similarly, their conflicts were too multifarious to be reduced to "class struggle." As David Herlihy reminds us, "A faction was a vertical as well as a horizontal association, linking great men and small, cutting across class lines and working to obscure them" (199). Although it precedes by a few years the birth of the Black and White factions, a fundamental Florentine law, formulated between 1293 and 1295, sheds light on the underlying character of the conflict between Blacks and Whites. Sometimes compared to the Magna Charta, the Ordinances of Justice *(Ordinamenti di giustizia)* recognized two groups only as players in Florentine politics: the "magnates" and the "people." Contemporary documents indicate that both the Donati and the Cerchi (but not the Alighieri) were generally considered magnates. While scholars today still struggle to define just what a magnate was, the Ordinances of Justice make clear exactly what and who the magnates threatened: the "people," that is, the guildsmen, bankers, international merchants, judges, and notaries (this last, the influential profession of Dante's teacher, Brunetto Latini). The civil war between Blacks and Whites was but a symptom of a ruling culture in fragmentation, within which, as Carol Lansing explains, "it was not clear which ties had priority, how a man should choose a side" (232).

We cannot understand Dante if we imagine him as an inspired figure able to transcend this fragmentation; he played a part in it, using all his knowledge and imagination to respond to its surprises and pitfalls. How was he to choose a side? Through his wife, he was a distant cousin of Corso Donati, as well as a friend to Corso's brother Forese (see *Purg.* 23.40–24.97). His "first friend" Guido Cavalcanti was a notable magnate and bitter enemy to Corso. Dante was an enrolled guildsman, able to serve in the high office of prior, as no magnate could. He was a fellow spirit of the learned men of the town, the judges and notaries,

and the son of a man who was a part-time, rather unsuccessful banker. Efforts to pigeonhole his politics, to tie him during a given period to a settled ideology or class, have long dominated studies of his political thought and activities, including his relation to the conflict between Blacks and Whites. None is ultimately satisfying, because each produces a narrative which, however complex, remains too simple to capture its subject—even the narrative of Dante's successive political conversions. Recent historical scholarship which attempts to sort through this conflict and its setting should provoke readers of the *Commedia* to consider each of the poet's references to his native city, its woes and its sins, as evidence of his ongoing effort to understand—morally, politically, and spiritually—an extended crisis in that city which permeates his poem because it touched every aspect of his being.

Bibliography

Documents
Compagni, Dino. *Cronica.* Edited by Gino Luzzatto. Turin: Einaudi, 1978.
Ordinamenti di giustizia, 1293–1993. Florence: SP 44 Editore, 1993.
Villani, Giovanni. *Nuova Cronica.* Edited by Giuseppe Porta. Parma: Fondazione Pietro Bembo and U. Guanda, 1990–1991.

Studies
Ferrante, Joan M. *The Political Vision of the Divine Comedy.* Princeton, N.J.: Princeton University Press, 1984.
Herlihy, David. *Medieval and Renaissance Pistoia: The Social History of an Italian Town, 1200–1430.* New Haven, Conn.: Yale University Press, 1967.
Lansing, Carol. *The Florentine Magnates: Lineage and Faction in a Medieval Commune.* Princeton, N.J.: Princeton University Press, 1991.
Martines, Lauro (ed.). *Violence and Civil Disorder in Italian Cities, 1200–1500.* Berkeley: University of California Press, 1972.
Najemy, John M. *Corporatism and Consensus in Florentine Electoral Politics, 1280–1400.* Chapel Hill: University of North Carolina Press, 1982.
Passerin d'Entrèves, Alexandre. *Dante as a Political Thinker.* Oxford: Clarendon Press, 1952.

Scott, John. *Dante's Political Purgatory.* Philadelphia: University of Pennsylvania, 1996, pp. 85–95.

Susan Noakes

Blake, William

English poet, painter, and engraver (1757–1827). A visionary and a recluse who never left England, Blake used Michelangelesque and Mannerist motifs to suit his own fluid, dreamy style—some of which was influenced by his contemporary, the Swiss artist Johann Heinrich Füssli. An admirer of the Middle Ages, he fashioned a private, esoteric mythology that brought him, in an obscure and mystical way, closer to Jacob Böhme than to Emanuel Swedenborg. He liked to illustrate literary texts in series, among them Young's *Night Thoughts,* Blair's *The Grave,* Thornton's *Virgil,* the sequence entitled *Milton,* and (one of his best) *Inventions from the Book of Job.* One of his longest series—102 drawings, commissioned by John Linnell c. 1824–1825—was the *Commedia:* 72 for the *Inferno,* 20 for the *Purgatorio,* and 10 for the *Paradiso.* Most are unfinished (Blake never published the series because he died within two years of undertaking the project)—some sketched in pencil, some watercolor-tinted, some further elaborated with india ink, some touched with wash and others, finally, with full color. He learned Italian for the purpose, used Cristoforo Landino's and Alessandro Vellutello's 1564 Venice edition, but also relied on Henry Cary's 1814 English translation. This series, whose *Inferno* part T. S. Eliot referred to as a "continuous phantasmagoria," became for Blake a culminating labor of love; shortly before his death, he wrote to Linnell: "I am too much attach'd to Dante to think much of anything else."

Critics have found fault with incorrect proportions (Brunelleschi, *Inf.* 25), impossible postures (Antaeus, *Inf.* 31), or overdeveloped sinews (Bertran de Born, *Inf.* 28); and throughout, Dante's and Virgil's images never approximate portraiture. But as an illuminator more than as a painter, Blake emphasized rhythm and design, and especially his vivid and eccentric imagination. And he emphasized his own views, his own mythological ideas and mystical philosophy, which he deemed closer to the Bible than Dante's, who reminded him more of Homer and Aristotle. Dante, he believed, was a politician who stressed punishment and the forms it takes (retributive justice) more than moral grandeur: "Dante saw Devils where I see none— I see only good." As a result, Blake's tendency is to *use* Dante, partly as his illustrator, partly as his opponent who is uncomfortable with the glum tyrant Nobodaddy, the Angry God, Urizen. In this sense, we may speak less of "illustrations" as such than as "transformations" based on details of private significance. We study them for their intellectual content, not to envision Dante's scenes. For example, Blake did not care for the choice of Virgil as Dante's guide: the *Aeneid* extolled military valor too much; nor did he care for the choice of Beatrice: the "female will" for him was too debilitating and antisexual. Believing that man is always divided against himself, *Inf.* 1 depicts a fearsome, dark, oppressive right half with three snarling beasts and a protective, airy, serene left half made welcoming by the sea ("time and space") and the goddess Vala (nature), neither of which exist in Dante's text. Or we see Capaneus (*Inf.* 14) relaxed in proud insolence, scorning Nobodaddy's fire, and in so doing endorsing the human spirit.

But if politically and theologically divergent, Dante and Blake merged spiritually. Sometimes the latter wrote the former's text into the drawing, as if to stress the affinity. And Dante's triad of sin-suffering-redemption did parallel Blake's death-life-God. Although Blake may have been disaffected with Dante's punishments, he nonetheless mainly did scenes from the *Inferno,* and his drawings for the other two canticles—while spiritually moving and uplifting in their own right ("Dante Entering the Fire" [*Purg.* 27], for example, or "Dante Adoring Christ" [*Par.* 14])—do not possess the intensity and dynamism of those for the first canticle. His period's conception of the sublime—emotions of dread and terror in redoubtable landscapes that heighten a viewer's experience—surely promoted this inclination. Whatever the case, Blake admired Dante as an artist, mentioning him in other works alongside Shakespeare, Euripides, Virgil, and Milton. The *Commedia* drawings opened up new illustrational possibilities, away from the academic and stereotyped rehashings of Blake's predecessors.

Bibliography

Alighieri, Dante. *The Divine Comedy.* Translated and introduced by James Finn Cotter, with the complete illustrations (ninety-five black-and-white plates) by William Blake. Amity, N.Y.: Amity House, 1987.

Blake's Dante: The Complete Illustrations to the Divine Comedy. Edited by Milton Klonsky. New York: Harmony Books, 1980.

Blake's Illustrations for Dante. Selections from originals in the National Gallery of Victoria, Melbourne, and the Fogg Art Museum. Cambridge: Fogg Art Museum, 1953.

Blake's Illustrations to the Divine Comedy. Edited by Albert S. Roe. Princeton, N.J.: Princeton University Press, 1953.

Pite, Ralph. "Illustrating Dante." In *The Circle of Our Vision: Dante's Presence in English Romance Poetry.* Oxford: Clarendon Press, 1994, pp. 39–67.

Jean-Pierre Barricelli

Blasphemy

The term (Italian = *bestemmia,* Latin = *blasphemia*) derives from Greek and means "offensive sound," thus "offensive word" or "injurious word." In the Scriptures it refers to the uttering of injurious words against God (direct) and his creatures or Creation (indirect), or any action offensive to God, as in Tobias 13:16 ("They shall be cursed that shall despise thee; and shall be condemned that shall blaspheme thee") and in Titus 3:2 ("speaking evil of none, not quarrelsome, but moderate, showing all mildness to all men"). Theologically speaking, however, and following St. Augustine's teaching, blasphemy is an injurious expression against God (*blasphemia non accipitur nisi mala verba de Deo dicere, PL* 32, col. 1354). Furthermore, there are three types of blasphemy—oral *(blasphemia oris),* of the heart *(blasphemia cordis),* and of an action or gesture *(blasphemia operis)*—each of which is exemplified in Dante. The first consists of an injurious expression against God: *bestemmian quivi la virtù divina* ("there they curse God's power," *Inf.* 5.36) and *bestemmiavano Dio e lor parenti, / l'umana spezie e'l loco e 'l tempo e 'l seme / di lor semenza e di lor nascimenti* ("they cursed God and their parents, the human race and the place and the time and the seed of their sowing and of their birth," *Inf.* 3.103). The second is an offensive thought against God, as exemplified in *Inf.* 11.46–48, when Dante has Virgil define how one can be violent against God: *Puossi far forza ne la deitade / col cor negando e*

bestemmiando quella, / e spregiando natura e sua bontade ("One can use force against the Deity by denying it and cursing it in one's heart, or by scorning Nature and its goodness"). The third is an action likewise injurious to God which can take the form of a gesture, as in Vanni Fucci's vulgar act in *Inf.* 25.1–3: *Al fine de le sue parole il ladro / le mani alzò con ambedue le fiche, / gridando: "Togli, Dio, che a te le squadro!"* ("At the end of his words the thief raised his hands with both the figs, crying: 'Take them, God, I'm aiming at you!'"). God's revenge is immediate and devastating, and Dante compares Vanni Fucci to Capaneus for his pride and blasphemous behavior. While blasphemy may be considered a *vitium linguae* ("vice of the tongue"), it can indeed be also one of the pen, which would constitute heresy, for the written word equals the spoken one. It is in this sense that Thomas Aquinas speaks of it as a sin against the virtue of faith, because the blasphemer is asserting something contrary to the truth of the faith (*ST* 2.2.13.1). Blasphemy, therefore, can be heretical or nonheretical, and in the latter form it is simply an injurious expression against God.

In Dante we find blasphemy foremost as an offense or an act of violence against God punished in the seventh circle of Hell, where the blasphemers are subjected to the fiercest pain. They lie supine and naked under a rain of fire, a torment which fits their offense, the law of *contrapasso,* since when they blasphemed against God, they did so by arrogantly turning their face toward him. Dante also points out that of the three types of violence against God, while the blasphemers are the least numerous, they are most vociferous with their lament (*Inf.* 14.22–27).

Of those violent blasphemers Dante singles out Capaneus, one of the seven kings who besieged Thebes and proudly defied Jupiter before being destroyed by a thunderbolt. In Virgil's rebuke to Capaneus, the author alludes to the role of pride and anger as causal sources of blasphemy (*Inf.* 14.63–66), a sin traditionally punished by fire, as suggested by both the Apocalypse (16:8–9) and the myth of Jupiter's fulmination of the furious Capaneus. Another blasphemous character is Bocca degli Abati (*Inf.* 32.86), the infamous traitor of the Florentine Guelfs at the battle of Montaperti.

For Dante, *blasphemia operis* ("blasphemy of act against God") is a much graver offense than that of verbal blasphemy, for it is against faith and religion and may thus be an act of heresy. Dante was well aware of the gravity of blasphemy, since in the Old Testament it was punished by death: "whoever blasphemes the name of the Lord shall be put to death. The whole community shall stone him; alien and native alike must be put to death for blaspheming the lord's name" (Lev. 24:16).

Bibliography

Laraia, Vincenzo. "Bestemmia." *Enciclopedia dantesca,* 1:611.

New Catholic Encyclopedia. New York: McGraw-Hill, 1967. See G. A. Buckley, "Blasphemy," and J. A. Fallon, "Blasphemy (in the Bible)," pp. 606–607.

Reade, William Henry Vincent. *The Moral System of Dante's Inferno.* Oxford: Oxford University Press, 1909. Reprinted Port Washington, N.Y., and London: Kennikat Press, 1969.

Giuseppe Di Scipio

Bocca degli Abati

Noble Guelf Florentine reputed to have betrayed his party by severing the hand of the Guelf standard-bearer during the battle against Manfred and the Ghibellines of Siena at Montaperti (September 4, 1260), thereby causing the demoralization and defeat of the Guelf troops. Giovanni Villani provides a detailed account of the episode and identifies Bocca as the guilty party (*Cronica* 7.78).

In *Inf.* 32, a highly epigraphic canto, Bocca degli Abati emerges as the traitor at Montaperti and the most memorable among the traitors to political party and country submerged in the ice of Antenora, the second division of the ninth circle (*Inf.* 31.73–123). The pilgrim's participation as protagonist (he inadvertently stomps Bocca underfoot and aggressively yanks the traitor's hair in an attempt to extract his name) marks the episode as a culmination of expressive violence in the canticle. Noteworthy, too, is the pilgrim's dialogue with Bocca, comparable in its baseness to the crude debate between the falsifiers of word and coin in *Inf.* 30 and effectively matching Bocca's crude violence word for word. In the context of the pit of Hell—itself a mouth—Bocca's highly charged name (*bocca* = mouth) and the Scholastic doctrine expressed in the formula "names are the consequence of things" have been considered.

Donna Yowell

Boccaccio, Giovanni

Italy's first great master of vernacular prose (1313–1375) and Dante's first great promoter and apologist. Except perhaps for Dante's two sons, no one in the fourteenth century knew the poet's works more extensively or thoroughly than Boccaccio. No writer was ever more influenced by Dante, and none except Dante himself did more to establish the poet's reputation. Boccaccio saved works of Dante's that would otherwise have been lost, and he preserved crucial details of Dante's life and thought.

Boccaccio probably had his first systematic introduction to Dante in Florence when, at around age 9, he began attending the school taught by Giovanni Mazzuoli da Strada, an enthusiast of vernacular literature. Zanobi Mazzuoli, Giovanni's son and Boccaccio's schoolmate, would become Boccaccio's lifelong associate in the world of letters and a discerning reader of Dante in his own right.

When business took Boccaccio's father to Naples, around 1327, Boccaccio went with him. His father, who provided financial services to the Neapolitan kingdom on behalf of the Bardi bank, put Boccaccio to work in the bank as well. Although Boccaccio resisted his father's attempt to turn him into a merchant, he benefitted from his father's connections, which brought him into contact with the social and cultural elite who frequented the royal court. In that society Boccaccio could have met, for example, Graziolo de' Bambaglioli, who wrote one of the first commentaries on Dante's *Commedia.* Also present in Naples was Matteo Frescobaldi, a poet who imitated Dante and whose father, also a poet, had known Dante. From such acquaintances Boccaccio could have gleaned information about the poet's life and habits that he would later include in the *Trattatello in laude di Dante,* his "little treatise" on the poet's life and works, and in his commentary on Dante's *Commedia.*

When Boccaccio was about 18, his father revised his plans for his son and sent him to the university in Naples to study canon law. Although Boccaccio proved no more apt at religion than he had at business, university studies gave him the chance to meet Dante's friend and fellow poet, the jurist Cino da Pistoia. Cino visited the Neapolitan university to teach civil law from 1330 to 1332, and scholars think Boccaccio audited his courses.

B Some investigators believe that Boccaccio was one of several students who took turns making an early-fourteenth-century copy of Cino's commentary on Justinian's code. Boccaccio is also likely to have known Cino socially through Florentines who lived in Naples and whose relatives had known Dante and pursued vernacular poetry with him. In Boccaccio's first major work, the *Filostrato*—which was composed around 1335, while he was still in Naples—homage to both Cino and, particularly, Dante is evident.

Of the thirteen known surviving Latin epistles that are believed to be Dante's, Boccaccio is the unique source for three: the letters to Cino da Pistoia (*Epist.* 3), to the Italian cardinals (*Epist.* 11), and to the Florentine friend (*Epist.* 12). These epistles are all copied in Boccaccio's hand in one of his two surviving notebooks. The letters are accompanied by imitations which were composed by Boccaccio and suggest that he acquired their models while still a student. That the first letter is addressed to Cino further suggests that Cino himself was Boccaccio's source for it, and perhaps for the other two letters also. One of Boccaccio's exercises imitates a fourth letter of Dante's, the one to Moroello Malaspina (*Epist.* 4), but the letter is not included in the notebook and comes down to us from other sources.

It was most likely Cino who introduced Boccaccio to the poetry of his young friend Petrarch. Some years later, when Boccaccio had returned to Florence, he would meet the great poet, who was destined to become his closest friend. Until they met, however, Boccaccio seems not to have suspected that Petrarch's admiration for Dante was less enthusiastic than his own or that he would ultimately have to serve, much as Cino had done, as a bridge between the two poets.

Many believe that one of Boccaccio's notebooks is also responsible for all we know about Dante's Latin *Eclogues*. Boccaccio's treatment of Dante's *Eclogues* is invaluable in that it constitutes a genuine edition. His indication of textual variants shows that he examined several copies of the poems—copies whose only trace is now found here. The same notebook also includes Boccaccio's *Faunus*, the first of his own series of Latin eclogues. Although the *Faunus* was doubtless encouraged by the example of Petrarch's eclogues, its inclusion with Dante's suggests that the Renaissance interest in Latin pastoral, which flowered through the efforts of Petrarch and Boccaccio, had

Statue of Giovanni Boccaccio, Florence. Public domain. Richard Lansing.

an important source in Dante and in Giovanni del Virgilio.

The *Eclogues* had particular interest for Boccaccio in that they bear upon the question of Dante's use of the vernacular. In the *Eclogues,* Dante declines an invitation from the learned Bolognese professor of letters, Giovanni del Virgilio, to earn a poetic coronation by setting aside his work on the nearly completed *Commedia* and writing a poem in Latin instead. By resurrecting a genre used by Virgil, Dante's *Eclogues* show that, had he but chosen, he could well have contended for the laurel crown by writing in Latin. Once Petrarch had received the laurel for undertaking a Latin epic, such arguments on Dante's behalf took on added urgency for Boccaccio, and he campaigned strenuously against those who faulted Dante for his use of the vernacular.

Another document that appears in Boccaccio's notebook is a letter, or part of a letter, allegedly written at Dante's request by a certain Frate Ilaro to Uguccione della Faggiuola, tyrant of Pisa. Although some consider the letter to be Boccaccio's forgery, others argue persuasively for its authenticity. Ilaro relates how Dante had shown him a copy of *una pars operis mei, quod forte nunquam vidisti* ("a part of my work [the *Inferno*], which you perhaps have not seen"). Ilaro writes that Dante, finding the monk astonished to see such lofty themes expounded in the vernacular, explained how he had actually begun the work in Latin (the letter quotes the opening lines) but relented when he realized that his potential patrons would be unable to read it. Dante judged it "pointless," the letter continues, "to offer solid food to the gums of suckling babes" and began the work again in a manner better "suited to contemporary sensibilities."

Ilaro says Dante asked him to send a copy of what he had been shown to Uguccione and to convey Dante's offer to dedicate the first *cantica* of the poem to him. According to the letter, Dante directed the monk to tell Uguccione that the second *cantica* would be dedicated to Moroello Malaspina, lord of Lunigiana, and the third to the king of Sicily, Frederick of Aragon. If the letter is authentic, it must have been written soon after Emperor Henry VII's death in 1313, when Dante could still hope that Ghibellines like Uguccione, Moroello, and Frederick might carry forward the late emperor's political designs. That Dante may have had a favorable judgment of Frederick—which he then abandoned before publishing the *Purgatorio* with its condemnation of Frederick (7.112–127) and ultimately dedicating the *Paradiso* to Cangrande della Scala—suggests how dramatically the poet's ideas could change as his work on the *Commedia* progressed.

Boccaccio's activities as Dante's copyist, editor, and biographer were inseparable. Beyond simply copying the *Commedia,* Boccaccio made it part of a collection of the poet's vernacular verse. The collection typically consisted of the *Vita Nuova,* the *Commedia,* and fifteen of Dante's canzoni which Boccaccio had collected and arranged. Boccaccio then prefaced the resulting anthology with his *Trattatello in laude di Dante.* Two such anthologies in Boccaccio's hand are known to survive, each headed by a different version of the *Trattatello.* The survival of the *Trattatello* in as many as four versions suggests that Boccaccio made additional anthologies which have been lost.

The canzoni that Boccaccio collected represent nearly all that are known to have existed. Omitted are one canzone that was lost at an early date, one that seems to have had a limited circulation, and two that are known only from fragments. Boccaccio may have known another canzone but thought, like most modern scholars, that Dante did not write it. An important reason for collecting Dante's works, Boccaccio says in the *Trattatello,* was to make sure that *né alcuno delle sue s'intitolasse, né a lui fossero per avventura intitolate l'altrui* ("neither anyone should lay claim to his works, nor someone else's works should by chance be ascribed to him"). Dante's *De vulgari eloquentia,* which Boccaccio knew, treats the sestina as a variety of canzone, and accordingly Boccaccio's collection includes Dante's sestina and double sestina. Boccaccio's selection is the first to present the sestinas side by side and group the canzoni from the *Convivio* together and in the order in which they appear in Dante's work. In short, Boccaccio's selection is the first to treat Dante's canzoni systematically, and the care and good sense that the selection exhibits have given it an enduring authority.

By including the *Vita Nuova* in his Dante anthology, Boccaccio acknowledged it as more than just an early, uncertain version of the *Commedia.* The *Trattatello* may devalue the *Vita Nuova* by presenting it as little more than a love narrative, but its identification of Beatrice as a historical person and its insistence on the reality of Dante's experience rescued the work from purely allegorical interpretations and established its importance for understanding the *Commedia.* Boccaccio boldly places the explanatory divisions of the *Vita Nuova*'s poems in the margin and not *nel testo . . . come l'autore del presente opera le puose* ("in the text as the author of the work in question put them"). The divisions have seemed extraneous to other readers also, especially to those who have suggested that Dante added the divisions later in response to critics like the poet Cecco Angiolieri.

Boccaccio put the *Vita Nuova* in his anthology because he considered it to be primarily a book of poetry, a compilation of *certe operette, sì come sonetti e canzoni* ("certain brief works, such as sonnets and canzoni"). He left the *Convivio* out, except for its three canzoni, because he considered it to be mainly a work of prose, *uno commento in prosa in fiorentino volgare sopra tre delle sue canzoni distese* ("a prose commentary in Florentine

B vernacular on three of his extended *canzoni*"). Boccaccio's relegation of the *Vita Nuova*'s divisions to the margin may indicate that he thought so much prose was inappropriate in so poetic a work.

Boccaccio's edition of Dante's *Commedia* marks a watershed in the history of the work's text and reception. Boccaccio lacked the scientific approach to textual criticism that his friend and mentor Petrarch possessed. His interventions in the *Commedia*'s text were not devoted to the reconstruction of Dante's original; rather by reflecting Boccaccio's personal preferences and conjectures, they ended up blending textual traditions of varying authority. In a strict philological sense, Boccaccio's edition of the *Commedia* is more a hybrid of mutant strains than a restoration. Nevertheless, Boccaccio's adaptation of the *Commedia*'s text to his own cultural exigencies and to those of his time mirrors a similar intervention on his part in the general interpretation of the poem, one that was to help rescue Dante's masterpiece from its detractors and secure a position of eminence for it in the radically new cultural environment of humanism.

After Boccaccio had visited Petrarch in 1351 and discovered that his admired friend had no copy of the *Commedia*, he sent him one accompanied by a Latin metrical epistle ("Ytalie iam certus honos"), imploring him not to reject Dante but to read him and honor him as *concivem doctumque satis pariterque poetam* ("fellow citizen, fully learned, and equally a poet"). During his second visit to Petrarch eight years later, Boccaccio must have had fresh confirmation of the reserve with which his friend regarded Dante. In the letter he sent to Boccaccio not long after, Petrarch tries to explain his lack of interest in Dante and protests that it is not caused by envy.

Confronted anew by humanist resistance to Dante's merit, Boccaccio wrote the *Trattatello* and placed it at the beginning of his Dantean anthology. As before, Boccaccio's strategy of defending Dante's work and promoting it in the emerging humanist environment is twofold: let Dante's poetry speak for itself and add his own voice to speak on Dante's behalf. Part biography, part introduction to Dante's works, and part impassioned defense of the great vernacular poet, the *Trattatello* reinforces the plea of "Ytalie iam certus honos" with additional arguments and evidence.

To capture humanist approval, the *Trattatello* subjects Dante's character and works to revealing deformations. It contradicts what Dante says in the *Convivio* about not wanting to accuse the *Vita Nuova* of undue passion and claims instead that Dante *d'avere questo libretto fatto negli anni più maturi si vergognasse molto* ("was ashamed in his more mature years of having made this little book," 175)—precisely as Petrarch in his maturity affected embarrassment at having written the amorous "trifles" of his vernacular *canzoniere*. The *Trattatello* contradicts what Dante says in the *Vita Nuova* about the moral improvement he experienced through his love of Beatrice and claims instead that *tanto amore e sì lungo* ("so great and long a love") impeded Dante's *cibo, i sonni e ciascuna altra quiete* ("diet, sleep, and every other quiet") and constituted a harsh *avversario agli sacri studii e allo 'ngegno* ("adversary to sacred study and to his genius," 38)—precisely as Petrarch claimed his love for Laura caused him to lose appetite and sleep and kept him from completing important poetic works.

Perhaps the most significant of all the *Trattatello*'s deformations is its recasting of the *Commedia*'s divine mission in more earthly terms. For the *Trattatello*, the *Commedia*'s purpose is not so much "to lead those living in misery to blessedness" (*Epistle to Cangrande,* 21) as to secure earthly glory for the poet. Even Beatrice, who finds her apotheosis in the *Commedia* by guiding Dante to an understanding of his divine calling, is relegated to the poet's youthful biography and is never mentioned in connection with the great poem.

The *Trattatello* says that in the *Inferno* Dante composed *non miga come gentile, ma cristianissimo poetando cosa sotto questo titolo mai avanti non fatta* ("in no way like a pagan, but like one most Christian, poeticizing under this title something never done before," 179). By having Dante recover the ancient theme of the underworld from Homer and Virgil and deal with it in a Christian perspective, Boccaccio represents Dante as the quintessential humanist. Boccaccio further equates Dante to Homer and Virgil by having the biographical *Trattatello* precede his Dante anthology, just as lives of Homer traditionally preceded the *Iliad* and *Odyssey* and Donatus' life of Virgil preceded the *Aeneid*. Of course, by equating Dante to the ancient poets laureate, Boccaccio equates him by implication with the modern poet laureate, Petrarch.

No work on Dante has seen so many editions as Boccaccio's *Trattatello,* and its influence has been decisive. It has contributed to determining not only the conventional title of Dante's masterpiece but also the very name by which the poet is known. While the *Commedia*'s title was first printed with the honorific *"Divina"* in 1555, Boccaccio's *Trattatello* had referred to Dante's poem as his *"divina Comedia"* two centuries earlier. And while Dante always styled himself with the surname "Alaghieri" and his name always appears in contemporary records with its second syllable spelled with an "a," thanks to the *Trattatello*'s discussion of the origin of the poet's family name (13–15), which spells it with an "i," the poet has been known ever since as Dante "Alighieri."

As a poet in his own right, Boccaccio is the conscientious student of Dante, whom Boccaccio's *Filocolo* tells us he must *sì come piccolo servidore molto . . . reverente seguire* ("like a humble servant very reverently follow," 5.97.6). While still in Naples, Boccaccio programmatically follows Dante's suggestions and models in outlining works of his own. Just as Dante wrote, as he says in *VN* 6.2, a sirventes honoring the sixty most beautiful women of Florence, Boccaccio uses Dante's *terza rima* to write his own sirventes, the *Caccia di Diana*, honoring the sixty most beautiful women of Naples. Just as Dante invents his own verse form *(terza rima)* for the *Commedia*, so does Boccaccio for his *Filostrato* in inventing the narrative octave. Dante's *De vulgari eloquentia* says that no Italian has written a prose romance. Boccaccio fills the gap with his *Filocolo*. The *De vulgari eloquentia* says that no Italian has yet written verse on a military subject. Boccaccio writes his *Teseida*, and in its conclusion addresses his book as *primo a lor* [i.e., "alle Muse"] *cantare / di Marte . . . gli affanni sostenuti / nel volgar lazio più mai non veduti* ("the first to sing to the Muses of the sustained toils of Mars, never seen before in the Italian vernacular," 12.84.6–8).

After Boccaccio returns to Florence in 1341, he continues to use Dante as a source of literary recipes. Boccaccio's *Comedìa delle ninfe fiorentine* or *Ameto* mirrors Dante's *Vita Nuova* with its mixture of prose and verse, adheres to the *De vulgari eloquentia*'s stylistic program in presenting itself as a comedy, reflects the pastoral framework of Dante's *Eclogues,* and again, like Boccaccio's *Caccia di Diana,* uses the *terza rima.* The *Ameto,* however, shows that Boccaccio is beginning to respond to Dante's influence in a more poetically intimate and less programmatic way. The *Ameto*'s theme of personal conversion and its representa-tion through a series of concise illustrative narratives suggest that Boccaccio responds not just to the *Commedia*'s metrical form but also to its vital poetic core. The *Ameto* has been traditionally considered the forerunner of Boccaccio's *Decameron,* and it is in the *Decameron* that Boccaccio most thoroughly synthesizes Dante's influence and establishes himself as Dante's peer in the realm of Italian narrative.

The *Decameron*'s division into a hundred stories, like the *Commedia*'s division into a hundred cantos, is only the most obvious homage that Boccaccio's masterpiece pays to Dante's. More significant parallels are the *Decameron*'s use of the exemplary tale as a fundamental narrative constituent, its encyclopedic portrayal of Florence's rich cosmopolitan society, its rare insight into human motivation, its genius for capturing the exact flavor of Florentine speech, and its artful mixture of "high," "low," and "middle" styles. Also appearing in the *Decameron* are many of the *Commedia*'s characters, like Cangrande della Scala (1.7), Guiglielmo Borsiere (1.8), Frederick of Aragon (5.6), Giotto (6.5), Guido Cavalcanti (6.9), Ciacco dell'Anguillaia (9.8), Corso Donati (9.8), Filippo Argenti (9.8), Ghino di Tacco (10.2), and Charles I of Anjou (10.6). The *Decameron,* in answering Boccaccio's critics who declared it unseemly for a grown man to waste his time telling tales to please women, invokes Dante by name as one who even in his old age deemed it an honor and delight to serve women's pleasure (4. Intr. 33).

Boccaccio's *Amorosa visione*—with its fifty cantos, *terza rima,* and lady guide—is another work that owes much to Dante. As the *Visione*'s narrator dreams of the successive "triumphs" of wisdom, fame, wealth, love, fortune, and death (which are accompanied by the emblematic appearances of great figures from history and mythology) the work reveals its debt to the *Inferno*'s Limbo (4), the *Purgatorio*'s concluding mystical procession (29–33), and the *Paradiso*'s many exemplary tableaux. The first literary work to be devoted to a sequence of symbolic moral triumphs, Boccaccio's *Amorosa visione* was immediately imitated by Petrarch in his *Triumphs*—the only long work that Boccaccio's "preceptor" ever wrote in the vernacular. The *Amorosa visione* thus stands at the fountainhead of an important literary genre and serves to mediate Dante's influence and transmit it to such renaissance works as Politian's *Stanze per la giostra.* In *Amorosa visione*

B (5.67–6.18) Dante himself appears. Surrounded by the Muses, he receives the laurel that was denied him in life, and Boccaccio, thankful to see Dante so honored, acknowledges him as *il maestro dal qual io / tengo ogni ben, se nullo in me sen posa* ("the master from whom I have every good thing, if any in me is found").

Boccaccio portrays Dante in even more personal terms in his first major Latin composition, the *De casibus virorum illustrium.* The work is devoted to the fallen great from earliest times to the present, and in its final book Dante appears in a touching cameo. Boccaccio is surprised to recognize the docile poet in such sorrowful company and asks if Dante wants him to relate the poet's accomplishments and fortunes. *"Siste, fili mi"* ("Desist, my son"), Dante replies, asking Boccaccio to tell instead the story of Walter of Brienne, the tyrant who added so greatly to Florence's shame. The *De casibus* makes it clear that Boccaccio regarded Dante as his spiritual and poetic father and that he reserved the story of Dante's victory over misfortune for a work all its own, like the *Trattatello.*

Throughout his life, Boccaccio was in contact with people who had some connection with Dante. Boccaccio's stepmother's mother was a Portinari, and she furnished him with reliable information concerning Beatrice's identity and the part Beatrice played in the poet's biography. As a boy, Boccaccio knew Andrea Poggi, whose mother was Dante's sister. From Andrea, Boccaccio first heard the perplexing story of the rediscovery of the *Inferno*'s first seven cantos. Traveling often to Ravenna, where Dante spent his final years, Boccaccio met Pietro Giardini, who had been the poet's disciple and close friend. Pietro provided Boccaccio with crucial information about the date and circumstances of Dante's death and the presumed chronology of the *Commedia*'s action, and he told Boccaccio how Dante's son Iacopo discovered the *Paradiso*'s final thirteen cantos eight months after the poet died. In Ravenna, Boccaccio also met Dino Perini, a Florentine who had known the poet there and possibly had been his student. It is probably from Dino that Boccaccio learned the identification of persons and events alluded to in Dante's *Eclogues.* On his second visit to Ravenna, in 1350, Boccaccio conveyed—at the behest of the directors of Florence's Or San Michele—ten florins to Dante's daughter, Antonia, who as a nun had taken the name Sister Beatrice. (Boccaccio seems never to have met Dante's sons.)

The embassy to Sister Beatrice was probably a commission that Boccaccio himself prevailed on the venerable civic organization to give him. In a similar gesture, Boccaccio consented in 1373 to let his friends persuade the City of Florence to have him deliver a series of lectures on the *Commedia.* Thus would the city that had banished Dante receive him again for the first time. Boccaccio's *Esposizioni,* however, failed to satisfy either Dante's popular following or his learned critics. The *Esposizioni*'s relentless search for allegorical meanings and conventional moral messages may have diverted attention from the *Commedia*'s defiant and at times unorthodox views, but Boccaccio's religious critics still warned that the unlearned were being led by Dante's verse to accept a version of the afterlife that was condemned by the Church. For their part, Dante's sincere but less sophisticated admirers were bound to be disappointed by the *Esposizioni*'s marginalization of the *Commedia*'s literal story. The difficulty of Boccaccio's task and his own failing health brought the readings to an abrupt end, and he wrote bitterly (*Rime* 125.1–4) of the crowd who thought they were so wise and erudite, *l'ingrato vulgo* ("the thankless herd"), whom he had left adrift *senza biscotto . . . e senza alcun piloto* ("without biscuit and without any pilot"). Before abandoning the *Esposizioni,* however, Boccaccio returned for the last time to his cherished belief that vernacular Dante was in no way inferior to the learned Petrarch. Having briefly recapitulated the history of poetry from Orpheus through the poets of classical antiquity, he names Petrarch and Dante as the twin summits that mark poetry's glorious culmination in the present: "And so that I may come to our own day, has not Messer Francesco Petrarca filled every corner where the Latin language is known with his poetic teaching and put his name on the lips of not only princes but whoever excels in learning? And our present author [Dante], the light of whose worth was for some time hidden under the mist of the mother tongue—has he not begun to be desired and prized by literature's greatest students? And for how many centuries in the future do we believe their works will preserve their memory? I for one hope that their name will perish only when all other mortal things have passed" (15.96–97).

Bibliography

Bergin, Thomas G. *Boccaccio*. New York: Viking Press, 1981.

Boccaccio, Giovanni. *Amorosa visione*. Bilingual edition, translated by Robert Hollander, Timothy Hampton, and Margherita Frankel, with an introduction by Vittore Branca. Hanover, London: University Press of New England, 1986.

———. *Diana's Hunt: Caccia di Diana. Boccaccio's First Fiction*. Edited and translated by Anthony K. Cassell and Victoria Kirkham. Philadelphia: University of Pennsylvania Press, 1991.

———. *Esposizioni sopra la Comedia di Dante*. Edited by Giorgio Padoan. Milan: Mondadori, 1965.

———. *The Life of Dante (Trattatello in laude di Dante)*. Translated by Vincenzo Zin Bollettino. New York, London: Garland Publishing, 1990.

———. *Trattatello in laude di Dante*. Edited by Luigi Sasso. Milan: Garzanti, 1995.

Boli, Todd. "Boccaccio's *Trattatello in laude di Dante*, or *Dante Resartus*." *Renaissance Quarterly* 41.3 (1988), 389–412.

Dante, Petrarch, Boccaccio: Studies in the Italian Trecento in Honor of Charles S. Singleton. Edited by Aldo S. Bernardo and Anthony L. Pellegrini. Binghamton, N.Y.: Medieval and Renaissance Texts and Studies, 1983.

Grant, William Leonard. *Neo-Latin Literature and the Pastoral*. Chapel Hill: University of North Carolina Press, 1965.

Hollander, Robert. *Boccaccio's Dante and the Shaping Force of Satire*. Ann Arbor: University of Michigan Press, 1997.

———. "Boccaccio's Dante." *Italica* 63.3 (1986), 278–289.

Holme, Timothy. *"Vile Florentines": The Florence of Dante, Giotto, and Boccaccio*. New York: St. Martin's Press, 1980.

Larner, John. *Italy in the Age of Dante and Petrarch, 1216–1380*. London and New York: Longman, 1980.

Ruggiers, Paul G. *Florence in the Age of Dante*. Norman: University of Oklahoma Press, 1964.

Wallace, David. *Giovanni Boccaccio: Decameron*. Cambridge and New York: Cambridge University Press, 1991.

Todd Boli

Body, Human

The nature of the human body, its nexus with the soul, the question of its contribution—whether negative or positive—to the life and state of the soul, are all central concerns in Dante's oeuvre from the *Vita Nuova* onward. The Platonic and Neoplatonic traditions (and the various forms of gnosticism deriving from them) had defined the human being as a divine soul whose union with the body constituted a fall into materiality; but while the most radically Neoplatonic of the Greek fathers (Gregory of Nyssa, Maximus the Confessor, and others) accepted this negative view, the central tradition—and virtually all the Latin theologians (Erigena is the principal exception)—rejected it. They regarded the body as good because directly created by God (Gen. 2:7), and they defined the human being as essentially the *union* of soul and body. Dante accepted the medieval adaptation of Aristotle's doctrine that the soul is the form, the active shaping principle, of the body: every "physical" aspect of the body—from shape, skeleton, musculature, and physiological processes, to the senses and those organs of consciousness we share with the animals, such as sensation, imagination, and memory—is not only governed by the soul but created and shaped by it, matter being in itself a completely neutral receptivity to form and essentially nonexistent until united with form.

In the account of human embryology given in *Purg.* 25, which follows the opinions of Albert the Great, individuals inherit from the father a vital power that works on the mother's blood in the womb and governs the development of the fetus, becoming first a vegetative soul and then an animal soul as it organizes the various organs of the body; according to this doctrine there is nothing in the human body or soul different in kind from the bodies and souls of the other animals, which follow a similar process of natural development, until the articulation of the brain is complete. At this moment God directly infuses into the fetus a "new spirit, full of power" (*Purg.* 25.72), which subsumes into itself all the vegetative and animal powers of the existing soul and becomes one unified rational soul, capable not only of governing the body but also of conscious thought and reflection, all its faculties being summed up in the phrase *vive e sente e sé in sé rigira* ("[it] lives and feels and turns itself upon itself," *Purg.* 25.75). Except for intellect, then, all human mental processes depend directly upon the body. (The relation of *Purg.* 25 to the Neoplatonic account in *Conv.* 4.21 of the fashioning of the body and infusion of the "possible intellect"—the faculty that readies sense images for intellection—by the movers [angelic intelligences] governing the celestial spheres has not been adequately explored.)

Aquinas had argued that each successive stage of fetal development involved a direct, miraculous intervention of God which entirely replaced the previously existing soul with a new one appropriate to the new level, whether vegetative, animal, or rational. Albert's view, however, saw the human soul-body complex as a natural entity with a coherent development according to natural processes until the single miraculous event of the infusion of the rational soul. Albert's theory allowed a clearer explanation of human heredity and of the human embeddedness in nature—in particular, the part played by the changing influences of the heavenly bodies both on the development of the fetus and on the temperament of the individual after birth. The human intellect was indirectly influenced by the heavenly bodies, through the body's subjection to them, but was immune from direct influence.

For Christian thinkers, the source of evil was not the body, as it was for the Platonic tradition, but rather the soul—Adam's will to rebel against God. Punished with death (theologians were divided as to whether Adam and Eve had been immortal before the Fall), Adam's and Eve's sin infected the relation of body and soul: it subverted the natural order of the soul's higher and lower motives, so that, in St. Paul's terminology, "flesh"—the soul's attachment to bodily pleasure—warred against "spirit," its yearning for higher things (see Rom. 7:7–25). This wound in human nature, commonly referred to with the term "concupiscence," is inherited, along with Adam's guilt, by all humanity. Though the body is good in itself, the body of fallen humanity is mortal, and its relation with the soul is infected and problematic. In Christian belief, baptism released one from the divine punishment decreed on Adam's sin, but not from its natural consequences. Therefore the question of the relation of human freedom to the influence of the heavens can take on considerable urgency; it is central for Dante from the time of the petrose poems onward.

In the strictest medieval Aristotelian view, all human knowledge has its origin in sense perception, which the imagination, memory, and "possible intellect" developed in images, stored and purified to abstraction in preparation for the action of intellection ("active intellect") strictly understood. This is in the main Dante's view, though numerous passages follow a more Neoplatonic line in allowing for other sources of knowledge, including supernatural inspiration (*Par.* 33) and dreams resulting from planetary action upon the imagination (*Purg.* 17.13–18). The usefulness of the body is in fact one of Dante's major themes—for instance, in *Inf.* 21.127–135, where the pilgrim's fear of the demons (deriving from the faculty of *aestimatio,* shared with the beasts, which estimates whether a given object of sense perception is to be fled from or desired) is contrasted with Virgil's disembodied rationality; the contrast is developed further in *Inf.* 23.1–57, in which the pilgrim's (bodily) imagination accurately foresees the demons' pursuit of them. The *Purgatorio* sets forth a view of the integration of the human personality that gives bodily faculties like imagination an important role in moral development.

A major instance of the usefulness of the body is poetic *ingegno:* the faculties of sense perception, imagination, and memory—all crucial to the body—function through bodily organs. Obviously (nowhere more clearly than in Dante's own case) it was not only the strength and richness of these faculties but also their integration under the guidance of intellect that produced poetry. Nevertheless, they were gifts of nature that developed under the influence of the heavens and remained directly subject to stellar and planetary influence. Hence the passage in *Par.* 22.113–123 attributes his *ingegno* to the influence of the stars of Gemini and invokes their influence for help in writing of the *forte passo* ("difficult pass") that awaits him.

Central to the narrative of the *Commedia* is the idea that the pilgrim goes to the otherworld in the body and experiences it through his senses (except perhaps in the *Paradiso,* though the text does not resolve the issue). The souls encountered in the otherworld inevitably appear to the pilgrim as if they had bodies, and without exception in both Hell and Purgatory proper they undergo bodily torments that signify their spiritual states.

To a certain extent the increasing materiality of souls lower and lower in Hell corresponds to the

Neoplatonic conception of evil as immersion in matter, as well as to the Pauline conception of the "body of death." The representations are not reducible to merely general ideas, however. The question of the effect on the body of sin is ever-present. The principle can perhaps best be exemplified by Purgatory, especially by the five upper terraces, which purge the vices most obviously related to bodily impulse: anger, sloth, avarice, gluttony, lust. These vices, like others, inhere in the soul; the subjective inclination toward them, which may represent itself to the individual as originating in the body, in fact expresses the imbalance in the soul's governance of the body. The airy body radiated by the souls (*Purg.* 25) therefore permits them to experience the spiritual nature of their vice as such, since the airy body itself contributes nothing to the difficulty of acquiring self-mastery; in life, because of the materiality of the body and its immersion in secondary causes (climate, astrological influence, foods), there may be limits on the conquering of irrational impulse, but not so in Purgatory.

In the *Paradiso* the human outlines of the encountered shades—with the exception of Beatrice—gradually disappear behind the spiritual light of their happiness, so that, even as low as the sphere of Venus, they are no longer visible, until after the strengthening of the pilgrim's sight in the final cantos. The question is never raised whether the souls in Paradise have the airy bodies attributed to those in Purgatory. A recurrent theme is the nature of the "glorified body" that the redeemed will have after the Resurrection; much is suggested about its beauty and radiance, but little is said directly. The implication of the final cantos is that in Paradise people will have bodies that reflect the ages at which they died, whether infants, young adults, or the elderly.

The lower terraces of Purgatory, where pride and envy are purged, are less obvious in conception than the upper ones, and it is easy to mistake their modes of suffering as exclusively metaphorical: pride, as a weight on the soul; envy, as spiritual blindness. But in the realm of social life the desire to rise involved putting others down, imposing various kinds of spatial/physical lowering (including the definitive putting-down of killing). As Virgil's account of the two sins in *Purg.* 17 makes clear, they are versions of the same pattern: pride, focusing on one's own rise; envy, on others'

descent. Typical forms of posture are involved here, and the purgation involves practicing them. But the social interrelations are fundamental—although the purgation is always that of individuals' vices, the body that is to be reformed is also the body politic. In this perspective, it becomes clearer why on all the terraces of Purgatory the purgations have a strong collective dimension: the souls are purged *together,* albeit at differing rates.

For human beings are involved in larger structures—city, empire, church—that in antiquity and the Middle Ages were conceived on the analogy of the human body. The idea of the body politic goes back at least as far as to Plato's analyses of the structure of the *polis* as reflecting the structure of the human being. Christian thinkers, beginning with St. Paul, adapted that conception in thinking of the Church as the body of Christ—with Christ the head and believers the members. From very ancient times, also, the human being was thought of as a microcosm, a small model of the universe; Dante draws on this conception extensively in the petrose poems, as well as in the *Commedia.*

Dante's insistence on the inseparability of individual bodies from the body politic is most evident in the *Inferno,* where the traditional idea that the damned constitute the body of Satan (parodic of the body of Christ), provides Dante with an overall structure whereby Hell is a giant, distorted projection of the human body, disordered and perverted in function. Brain (memory and imagination), gullet, arms and hands, and spleen are correlated with Limbo and with the various sins of incontinence; sins of violence are related to the breast; sins of fraud are punished in the belly of Hell, because truth is the food of the soul and falsehood is its poison. Not only have the damned violated God's law, but their sins also express, and result in, distortion of their relation to their own bodies and to the great collective bodies. The bodily diseases and disorders represented in so many parts of the *Inferno* are diseases of the body politic as well as of the individual soul: sins are always committed in the context of society as a whole, and they affect it as a whole. Paolo and Francesca are fellow citizens with their murderer in Caina, subjects above rulers, both individually (*la ragion sommettono al talento,* "[who] subject their reason to their lust," 5.39) and socially: Gianciotto and Satan, rulers, have murdered the highest trust and are placed below all else.

B

Bibliography

Allers, Rudolf. "Microcosmus: From Anaximander to Paracelsus." *Traditio* 2 (1944), 319–407.

Barkan, Leonard. *Nature's Work of Art: The Human Body as Image of the World.* New Haven, Conn.: Yale University Press, 1975.

Bynum, Caroline Walker. *The Resurrection of the Body in Western Christianity, 200–1336.* New York: Columbia University Press, 1995.

Cornford, F. M. *Plato's Cosmology: The "Timaeus."* London: Routledge and Kegan Paul, 1937.

Durling, Robert M. "Deceit and Digestion in the Belly of Hell." In *Allegory and Representation: Selected Papers from the English Institute, 1979–80.* Edited by Stephen Greenblatt. Baltimore: Johns Hopkins University Press, 1981.

———. "Farinata and the Body of Christ." *Stanford Italian Review* 2 (1981), 5–35.

———, and Ronald L. Martinez. *Time and the Crystal: Studies in Dante's "Rime petrose."* Berkeley, Los Angeles: University of California Press.

Robert M. Durling

Boethius

Ancius Manlius Severinus Boethius *(Boezio)* was a noble Roman philosopher and statesman of the late fifth and early sixth centuries (480–520). He played an important role, as commentator and translator, in the preserving of Greek philosophy and science in the Roman world, and, under Ostrogoth King Theodoric, he rose to the powerful position of consul. Soon after, however, having been accused of plotting with Byzantine Trinitarians against the Arian king, he was imprisoned and, later, tortured to death. During his time in prison he wrote his most famous work, *The Consolation of Philosophy,* in which the allegorical Lady Philosophy comes to his cell to teach him to rise above his misfortunes by approaching them with a mind cleared of narrow, worldly values. By the end of her visit, she has persuaded Boethius that a perfect order reigns over all things and that, although fortune can do as it wills with his body and with his worldly goods, nothing can imprison his soul. Lady Philosophy teaches him that what seems cause for great despair is simply the loss of limited goods—such as riches, reputation, home, and family—which, unlike the truer and more permanent riches of the mind, were never, nor will ever be, secure. Dante places Boethius in the Heaven of the Sun as the one who taught of the fallaciousness of this world and who died a martyr and an exile (*Par.* 10.124–129). It is generally thought that Dante must have felt a special closeness to Boethius, both as a fellow victim of false accusations and political corruption and as an inspiration to turn the embittering events of his own life toward a great and positive goal.

Dante mentions Boethius frequently in his prose works, especially in the *Convivio,* and most notably in *Conv.* 1.2.13, where he compares his own reasons for writing about himself in order to protect his reputation with those of Boethius in the *Consolation.* The *Commedia* contains countless echoes of the *Consolation* and reflects its profound influence on Dante's philosophy, particularly with regard to the theme of fortune. In Lady Philosophy's teaching, what man calls fortune, or misfortune, is in reality simply his misinterpretation of events, which, if he could see them in the context of the whole divine plan, would have an entirely different meaning and an invariably benevolent purpose. *Inf.* 7.68–96, in which Virgil explains fortune as a misunderstood minister of the will of Providence, is the most clearly Boethian passage in the *Commedia.* Throughout the poem, however, Dante shows his philosophical allegiance to Boethius every time he represents Providence as incomprehensibly benevolent, that is to say, on all those occasions—from Virgil's reprimand of Dante's weeping over the contorted forms of the soothsayers (*Inf.* 20.28–30) to the Eagle's speech in the Heaven of Jupiter (*Par.* 19.40–90)—where the temptation to question divine wisdom is rejected in favor of trust in God's will. Finally, the figure of Lady Philosophy herself no doubt inspired some of Dante's own allegories. The lady personifying philosophy in the *Convivio* is often identified by critics with Lady Philosophy, as is the "holy lady" who appears in Dante's dream in *Purg.* 19. Moreover, there is a distinct kinship between Lady Philosophy and Beatrice herself, especially in the *Commedia,* where so much of Beatrice's role is to guide the pilgrim through the intricacies of philosophical and theological matters.

Bibliography

Chiarenza Marguerite. "Boethian Themes in Dante's Reading of Virgil." *Stanford Italian Review* 3, no. 1 (1983), 25–35.

d'Alverny, M. Th. "Notes sur Dante et la Sagesse." *Revue des Études Italiennes* 11 (1965), 5–24.

De Bonfils Templer, Margherita. "Il dantesco amoroso uso di Sapienza: sue radici platoniche." *Stanford Italian Review* 7, nos. 1–2 (1987), 5–27.

Freccero, John. "Casella's Song (*Purg.* II, 112)." *Dante Studies* 91 (1973), 73–80.

Mazzotta, Giuseppe. "A Pattern of Order: *Inferno* II and *Paradiso* VII." In *Dante: Poet of the Desert.* Princeton, N.J.: Princeton University Press, 1979, pp. 319–328.

Murari, Rocco. *Dante e Boezio.* Bologna: Zanichelli, 1905.

Marguerite Chiarenza

Bolgia

From a Tuscan word meaning "purse" or "pouch," bolgia is the term that identifies each of the ten concentric ditches, or ravines, that constitute Malebolge ("evil ditches"), the eighth circle of Hell, in which is punished the sin of fraud. Within each bolgia is punished a distinct category of the fraudulent sinners. The word appears eleven times in the thirteen cantos that compose Malebolge (18–30), twice each in cantos 18, 23, and 29 and once in cantos 19, 22, 24, 26, and 28. Only once does it appear in its plural form, *bolge* (*Inf.* 29.7).

The ten ditches of Malebolge are formed of *pietra di color ferrigno* ("stone the color of iron," 18.2) and are spanned by stone bridges. The whole slopes down toward the pit at the center of Hell, the circumference of each bolgia being smaller than that of the one above it, so as to resemble an amphitheater in shape. Each bolgia consists of an outer bank that slopes down to the bottom, or floor, of the ditch, where the sinners are punished, and an inner bank that is less steep than, and not as high as, the outer bank and that rises up to the margin of the next, lower, bolgia

Lawrence Baldassaro

Bonagiunta da Lucca

Bonagiunta Orbicciani da Lucca, son of Riccardo di Bonagiunta Orbicciani degli Averardi, was born as early as 1220 and died shortly before the end of the thirteenth century; he worked in Lucca, his native city, as a magistrate and notary (an expert in official documents). Dante mentions him in *DVE* 1.13.1 as a poet who resembled Guittone d'Arezzo in his use of the plebeian, "municipal" style. Dante's picture has been complicated by claims that Bonagiunta's adherence was, in fact, to Chiaro Davanzati or that Bonagiunta's work reflects a preference for Guittone's easy style *(trobar leu)* over his serried moralizing poems.

Bonagiunta speaks with Dante's pilgrim at *Purg.* 24.19–63, third of the poets (after Sordello and Statius, not counting Forese Donati) encountered in *Purgatorio*. That Bonagiunta, in an exchange of sonnets with Guido Guinizzelli, defended the poetic style of Guittone against perceived innovations by Guinizelli—whom Dante proclaims the father of poets using "sweet and graceful rhymes of love" (*Purg.* 26.99)—is widely understood to have motivated the palinode of earlier Italian poetic styles that Dante places in Bonagiunta's mouth in *Purg.* 24.49–63. Thus the role assigned Bonagiunta in *Purgatorio* tends to confirm Dante's judgment in the *De vulgari eloquentia,* with some qualifications.

Bonagiunta's remarks in the *Purgatorio* may be analyzed through his name and toponym, which Dante emphasizes by rhyme (Bonagi*unta,* L*ucca*) and repetition. Bonagiunta begins by predicting that a certain "Gentucca"—usually identified with Gentucca Morla—will receive the exiled Dante in Lucca and persuade him to revise his harsh judgment on that city (a probable reference to *Inf.* 21.40–42 and 18.123–126; the exiled Dante was in Lucca in 1311–1312). Bonagiunta, who appears never to have met the historical Dante, then asks the pilgrim if he wrote the canzone beginning *Donne ch'avete intelletto d'amore* (1290–1292), eliciting the pilgrim's self-definition as one who notes the inner dictation of love and signifies it outwardly (*Purg.* 24.52–54). This definition Bonagiunta embraces as a sufficient account of the *stil nuovo,* the "new style" (*Purg.* 24.55–57). Since Bonagiunta exchanged sonnets with an admirer who rhymed on *giunta* in its meanings of "juncture" and "knot," Bonagiunta's claim that he now perceives the "knot" which kept him and other poets (Guittone and Giacomo da Lentini, called *Il notaro,* "the notary") from understanding the new style may have been suggested by his name.

By placing the term *issa*—a Lucchesism for "now"—in Bonagiunta's mouth (*Purg.* 24.55), Dante's pilgrim alludes to Bonagiunta's use of this word in a *discordo* (a poem with a varying metrical scheme). Along with other echoes of Bonagiunta's work in *Purgatorio,* the citation, while reiterating Bonagiunta's "municipal" style, acknowledges Bonagiunta's historical role, perhaps in courteous exchange for Lucchese hospitality.

B

Regarding the choice of Bonagiunta as the herald of Dante's own poetics, Gianfranco Contini noted that Bonagiunta was old enough to have pioneered use, in central Italy, of conventions from the first Italian poetic school, the *Scuola siciliana*. Having composed work drawing from the Sicilian, Siculo-Tuscan, and Guittonian styles (one manuscript makes Bonagiunta a crow in borrowed plumage, a traditional figure for derivative poets), Bonagiunta suitably witnesses the pilgrim's proclamation of Dante's poetic credo; some of Bonagiunta's poems in the *trobar leu* have been read as anticipations of the *stil nuovo*.

Bibliography

Barolini, Teodolinda. *Dante's Poets: Textuality and Truth in the Comedy*. Princeton, N.J.: Princeton University Press, 1984, pp. 40–45, 85–89.

Ciccuto, Marcello. "Reperti allusivi nel canto XXIV del *Purgatorio*." In *Il restauro dell'Intelligenza e altri studi dugenteschi*. Pisa: Giardini, 1985, pp. 123–138.

Gorni, Guglielmo. *Il nodo della lingua e il verbo d'Amore. Studi su Dante e altri duecentisti*. Florence: Olschki, 1981.

Guittone d'Arezzo nel settimo centenario della morte. Atti del Convegno Internazionale di Arezzo (22–24 aprile 1994). Edited by Michelangelo Picone. Florence: Cesati, 1995.

Martinez, Ronald L. "The Pilgrim's Answer to Bonagiunta and the Poetics of the Spirit." *Stanford Italian Review* 3 (1983), 37–63.

Poeti del duecento. Edited by Gianfranco Contini. 2 vols. Milan, Naples: Ricciardi, 1960, Vol I., pp. 257–259.

Pertile, Lino. "Il nodo di Bonagiunta, le penne di Dante, e il Dolce Stil Nuovo. *Lettere italiane* 46 (1994), 44–75.

Simonelli, Maria. "Bonagiunta da Lucca e la problematica dello stil nuovo (*Purg.* XXIV)." *Dante Studies* 66 (1968), 65–75.

Varanini, Giorgio. "Dante e Lucca." In *Dante e le città dell'esilio*. Ravenna: Longo, 1989, pp. 91–114.

Wilkins, Ernest Hatch. "Guinizelli Praised and Corrected." In *The Invention of the Sonnet and Other Studies in Italian Literature*. Rome: Edizioni di storia e letteratura, 1959, pp. 111–114. First appeared as "Three Dante Notes," *44th Annual Report of the Dante Society* (1917), 30–32.

Ronald L. Martinez

Bonatti, Guido

A tiler by trade, born probably in Florence but perhaps in Forlì, Guido was a famous astrologer and soothsayer. Besides being at the court of Frederick II and several other princes, he seems to have served as domestic astrologer to Guido da Montefeltro (see *Inf.* 27.4–132), who through his aid is said to have won his crucial victory over the French papal forces at Forlì, on May 1, 1282. He claims in a treatise on astrology that in 1246 he disclosed the plot against Frederick II and that, as a follower of Guido Novello, he took part in the victorious battle at Montaperti—helped in both endeavors by astrological calculations. After the Ghibelline victory he became an astrologer of the republic at Florence. Dante boldly condemns Bonatti along with Asdente—the universally approved and admired astrologers of the day—to the fourth bolgia of Malebolge (*Inf.* 20.118), in order to reaffirm acceptance of the divine purpose as against the foolish knowledge of the diviners.

R. A. Malagi

Bonaventure, St.

Born around 1217 near Orvieto, Giovanni Fidanza entered the Franciscan order in 1243, studied in Paris with the theologian Alexander of Hales, and taught there—successfully if somewhat controversially—until being elected minister-general of the order in 1257. At some point he had acquired the nickname by which he is now known. As leader of the Franciscans he tried to steer a middle course between the growing moral laxity of the order's "Official," or "Conventual," wing and the increasing extremism and anti-intellectualism of its fundamentalist "Spiritual" members. His commentary on the Franciscan Rule and his biographical writings about Francis are important documents of his moderate position. He died in 1274, shortly after making a vital contribution to the attempt at the Council of Lyons to settle the schism between Eastern and Western Christianity.

Bonaventure appears in *Paradiso* (12.28–145) in the role he occupied in history: as spokesman for a moderate and spiritually pristine form of Franciscanism guaranteed by the authority of the order's founder. In an episode that parallels Thomas Aquinas' eulogy of Francis in canto 10, he first (31–105) speaks at length in praise of St. Dominic, founder of the Franciscans' great rival institution, and then (112–126) bitterly condemns the failings of his own order in the early fourteenth century, summed up in the Officials' dwindling devotion to Francis' Rule and the Spirituals' excessively rigorous application of it. Finally (127–145) he declares his own identity and goes on to list the other souls who appear alongside him: they include other early Franciscans (130–132) as well as an assortment of Jewish and Christian thinkers that includes—paradoxically and perhaps polemically—Joachim of Fiore, the intellectual patron of the Spirituals, whom the historical Bonaventure (unlike Dante) disparaged.

Bonaventure's voluminous writings circulated widely in the late Middle Ages, and some part of them may well have been known to Dante, even though there is no unambiguous allusion to them in his works. The biographical account of Francis in Bonaventure's *Legenda maior* and *Legenda minor* shares much with that in Aquinas' speech in *Par.* 11, and several attempts have been made to establish connections between Bonaventure's *Itinerarium mentis in Deum (Journey of the Mind toward God)*—which recounts a mystical ascent analogous to that of the *Commedia*—and the structure of Dante's poem. None of these is conclusive, however, and, in the absence of direct textual dependence, it remains no more than probable that Dante knew and used this celebrated text of medieval mysticism. The definitive edition of Bonaventure's prodigious writings is *S. Bonaventurae opera omnia* (Quaracchi, 1882–1902).

Bibliography

Freccero, John. "Dante's Pilgrim in a Gyre." *PMLA*, 76 (1961), 168–181.

Hagman, Edward. "Dante's Vision of God: The End of the *Itinerarium Mentis*." *Dante Studies* 106 (1988), 1–20.

Scrivano, Riccardo. "*Paradiso* 28." *Quaderni d'Italianistica* 10, 1–2 (1989), 269–285.

Steven Botterill

Bonconte da Montefeltro

Son of Guido da Montefeltro, the great Ghibelline captain featured in *Inf.* 27. Bonconte appears in *Purg.* 5, in Ante-Purgatory among those late repentant souls who died violent deaths. Born c. 1250, Bonconte followed in his father's footsteps to become a renowned Ghibelline champion in his own right. He led the campaign to expel the Guelfs from Arezzo in 1287; he successfully led the Aretines against the Sienese at Pieve del Toppo in the following year; and he again demonstrated valor as captain of the Aretine Ghibellines against the Florentine Guelfs in the famous battle of Campaldino on June 11, 1289. Dante numbered among the triumphant Florentines in that bloody skirmish in the Casentino Valley that cost Bonconte his life and from which his body was never recovered.

Bonconte refers to his wife and other members of his extended family at *Purg.* 5.89, where he claims: *Giovanna o altri non ha di me cura* ("Neither Giovanna nor another has any care for me"). *Altri* might include Guido's cousin, Galasso, who was podestà of Arezzo in 1290–1291 and again in 1297, and Bonconte's own brother, Federico, who was also podestà of Arezzo in 1300 and an important Ghibelline leader in Umbria and the Marche. (This Federico died in 1322 and must not be confused with his famous Renaissance namesake, the duke of Urbino, who lived from 1422 to 1482.) Bonconte had a daughter by Giovanna named Manentessa, who married into the illustrious dynasty of the Conti Guidi, age-old lords of the Casentino.

Bonconte's futile efforts to flee death at the hands of his Guelf pursuers at Campaldino provide the historical raw material (see Giovanni Villani, *Cronica* 7.120, 131; and Dino Compagni, *Cronica* 1.10) for the poignant account of his final hours in *Purg.* 5.85–129. Akin in some ways to Ulysses' unraveling of the enigma of his final days in *Inf.* 26, Bonconte illuminates the pilgrim and the reading public on the mystery of his death and missing body. Having fled the field—the blood spilling from a wound in his throat to merge with the waters of the Archiano and then the Arno—Bonconte died repentant *in extremis* with the Virgin's name upon his lips. Good and bad angels vied briefly for his soul, which wins salvation because of one final tear of repentance *(una lacrimetta)* in a parodic reversal of his father's fate (see *Inf.* 27.112–123). Even as his soul ascended, rain and river dragged his wounded body to eternal obscurity at the devil's spiteful bidding.

That single salvific tear participates in the larger fluvial thematics of *Purg.* 5, whereby Aristotelian naturalism merges with a more mystical, Neoplatonic notion of temporal and existential flow. Poetically, Bonconte's story joins with those of Jacopo (64–84) and la Pia (130–136) to draw the reader's attention to the inscrutable border

B between spiritual life and corporeal death within the flux of Creation.

Gary P. Cestaro

Boniface, Archbishop

From 1275 to 1294, Bonifazio dei Fieschi was archbishop of Ravenna. Dante places him among the gluttonous on the sixth terrace of Purgatory and identifies him as one *che pasturò col rocco molte genti* ("who pastured many people with his rook," *Purg.* 24.30)—an allusion to the shape of the archiepiscopal crosier of Ravenna, which, as Jacopo della Lana notes in his 1324 commentary on the *Commedia, è fatto di sopra al modo di rocco delli scacchi* ("is made at the top like the rook in chess"). Although Boniface was known for his wealth, there is no historical testimony to his having been gluttonous.

Claudia Rattazzi Papka

Boniface VIII, Pope

Born Benedetto Caetani, Boniface *(Bonifazio)* was trained as a lawyer, served as cardinal and papal legate, and had long experience in the papal curia before he was elected pope in 1294. Being an arrogant and irascible aristocrat who made enemies easily, his pontificate was marked by conflict from its beginning. Questions were raised about the legitimacy of his predecessor's resignation and therefore of his own accession—not helped by rumors that he had helped persuade, perhaps even trick, Celestine V to resign. His blatant nepotism exacerbated the hostility of the rival Colonna family, whose cardinals actively opposed his rule, and his worldly ambitions and machinations alienated the Spiritual Franciscans. His view of the papacy as the head of Christendom with authority over temporal leaders led him to interfere in local politics, particularly Italian and French. He tried but failed to make Sicily a part of a friendly Kingdom of Naples. Tuscany, for its banking interests and strategic position in central Italy, was another object of his attention; he tried but failed to get Albert of Habsburg to cede it to the papacy in return for recognition of Albert's election as emperor. He supported Corso Donati and the Black Guelfs, aided by Charles of Valois, against the Cerchi and the White Guelfs, and he was implicated in the successful coup that put the Blacks in power and that led to Dante's condemnation for

barratry and conspiracy. But it was his struggle with the powerful French monarchy and Philip IV that dominated Boniface's life and death.

In an attempt to settle the conflict between Edward I of England and Philip—both of whom were taxing their clergy to help pay for their war—Boniface in 1296 promulgated the bull *Clericis laicos,* reasserting the need for temporal rulers to have papal permission to tax clergy and for clergy to have permission in order to pay those taxes. Philip responded by cutting off all exports to Italy, creating a ripe situation for Boniface's enemies—particularly the Colonna, who demanded a council and accused the pope of tyranny, extortion, bribery, packing the curia, imprisoning and causing the death of his predecessor, and exercising powers he had de facto but not de jure. In an emergency the following year, Boniface conceded a king's right to tax without his permission. But when Philip arrested the bishop of Palmiers in 1301, tried and sentenced him in a secular court, imprisoned him, and then asked the pope's approval, Boniface called a council on the state of the French Church (November 1302). Fewer than half the French bishops attended, and Boniface promulgated *Unam Sanctam,* the bull that asserts the authority of the pope over the church and all its members, the predominance of spiritual over temporal rule (indeed, the ability of the spiritual to institute and to judge temporal power), and the necessity of subjection to the papacy for salvation. Before Boniface could promulgate a decree of excommunication against Philip in 1303, the king sent a royal minister who had denounced the pope, Guillaume de Nogaret, to seize him. The humiliating capture was effected at Anagni with the help of a Colonna, but while he and Nogaret argued over subsequent action, local forces came to the pope's rescue.

Boniface died shortly thereafter, but his struggle with Philip continued. A posthumous trial was held in France (1310–1311), with charges of every kind made against the pope—of heresies, simony, embezzlement of crusade funds, warmongering, assassination, idolatry, blasphemies, demon worship, fornication, and sodomy. Though the trial was connected with Philip's attack on the Templars, the extensive testimony about Boniface's crimes portrays him as an archvillain, just as the numerous references to him in the *Commedia* do. It is ironic that Boniface was at the center of the historic trial at which he could not be present clearly referred to in several other places which associate him with those sins as well. He is the *servo de' servi* ("Servant of the Servants [of God]," a traditional name for the pope) who transferred *(trasmutato)* a sodomite bishop from one see to another for political reasons *(Inf.* 15.112–113); the Jubilee he instituted is evoked in the circle of pimps and seducers *(Inf.* 18.29); and he is the "prince of the new Pharisees," who made war not on Saracens or Jews but on Christians at Rome and who had no regard for his office or sacred orders when he tricked Guido da Montefeltro into offering counsel against the Colonna with the false claim that he could open Heaven to Guido by absolving him of the sin he was asking him to commit *(Inf.* 27.85ff.).

Dante balances the negative view of Boniface to some extent in *Purgatorio* with sympathetic reference to the indulgences of the Jubilee *(Purg.* 2.98–99) and to the capture of Christ's vicar *(Purg.* 20.86–87)—the latter in the course of a condemnation of Philip's actions against pope and Templars. But Dante also intensifies his attack on Boniface. He has Marco Lombardo blame the papacy (under Boniface) for the evils of the world: the papacy has destroyed the power of empire and set an example of greed for its flock; the Church of Rome confuses the rules of church and state, falls in the mud, and soils itself and its burden *(Purg.* 16.100–129). The cart that stands for the church in the procession has become a monster because of its assumption of temporal wealth and power, and the curia is a whore vulnerable to abuse by the French king *(Purg.* 32).

In *Paradiso* Folquet of Marseilles condemns the greed of the pope and cardinals who study decretals rather than the Gospels in pursuit of gain, and he prophesies that the parts of Rome that were the burial grounds of Peter's army will soon be freed of that adultery *(Par.* 9.127–142). Cacciaguida, prophesying Dante's exile, implicates the papacy in it: *Questo si vuole e questo già si cerca / e tosto verrà fatto a chi ciò pensa / là dove Cristo tutto dì si merca* ("This is willed, this is already sought and soon will be done by him who thinks of it there where Christ is sold all day long," *Par.* 17.49–51). St. Peter, whose angry outburst may be read in part as an answer to Boniface's bull *Unam Sanctam,* cries out against the one who *usurpa in terra il luogo mio* ("on earth usurps my place") and who *fatt' ha cimitero mio cloaca del sangue e de la puzza* ("has turned my burial place into a sewer

Arnolfo di Cambio's statue of Pope Boniface VIII. Photo Richard Lansing, by courtesy of the Museo dell'Opera del Duomo, Florence.

because he was dead, just as he is a recurring motif in the fictional journey in which he cannot appear because he is alive when it is supposed to occur.

Leaving aside the many references to Florentine events which may have recalled Boniface and the part he played in them to Dante's audience, there are frequent references throughout the poem to the pope Dante saw as a personal and public enemy. In *Inferno,* Boniface is named where he is awaited in the circle of simony, by a predecessor who accuses him of seizing the church by deception and then violating it *(Inf.* 19.55–57), but he is

B

of blood and stench") to the devil's delight (27.22–26). The last reference to Boniface in the *Commedia* is almost offhand, but it is a chilling reminder of his fate and his lack of importance in the final scheme: when Beatrice shows Dante the rose of the saved souls and the empty seat that awaits the emperor, Henry VII, she prophesies that the one who opposes him (Clement V) will not long be suffered by God but will be sent to the circle of simony and thus will push "the one from Alagna" *(quel d'Alagna)* farther down *(Par.* 30.145–148).

Bibliography

Barraclough, Geoffrey. *The Medieval Papacy.* New York: Harcourt, Brace and World, 1968.

Boase, T. S. R. *Boniface VIII.* London: Constable, 1933.

Digard, Georges. *Philippe le Bel et le Saint-Siège de 1285 à 1304.* 2 vols. Paris: Sirey, 1936.

Dupuy, Pierre. *Histoire du Différend d'entre le pape Boniface VIII et Philippes le bel Roy de France.* Paris: Cramoisy, 1655.

Ferrante, Joan M. *The Political Vision of the Divine Comedy.* Princeton, N.J.: Princeton University Press, 1984.

Holmes, George. "Dante and the Popes." In *The World of Dante.* Edited by Cecil Grayson. Oxford: Clarendon, 1980.

Tierney, Brian. *The Crisis of Church and State, 1050–1300.* Englewood Cliffs, N.J.: Prentice-Hall, 1964.

Joan M. Ferrante

Bonturo Dati

The corrupt head of the popular party that controlled Lucca at the beginning of the fourteenth century. According to contemporary sources, he usurped his position through barratry. He was expelled from the city when Lucca returned to Ghibelline control in 1314, and he fled to Genoa and later to Florence, where he died. He is singled out among the corrupt public officials in the fifth bolgia of Malebolge when a devil remarks with sarcastic irony that in Lucca everyone is a *barattier* except for Bonturo *(Inf.* 21.41).

Jo Ann Cavallo

Bonvesin da la Riva

With a vernacular corpus of almost nine thousand alexandrines (all mono-rhymed quatrains) prestigiously crowned by a sizable Latin production, Bonvesin is fully entitled to appear on the map of European medieval literature, especially if we take into account the relevance of the subjects and the genres in which he engaged. His *Book of the Three Scriptures,* on the basis of its eschatological theme and tripartite structure, bears some resemblance to the *Commedia.*

Born probably in Milan around 1240, Bonvesin was a private teacher of *grammatica* (i.e., Latin) first in Legnano and later (from about 1285) in Milan, where he died between 1313 and 1315. A deeply religious person, Bonvesin belonged as a lay brother to the rich and influential order of the Humiliati and in this capacity exerted himself generously for the sake of the poor and the sick. Presumably in the last period of his authorial career, he wrote three Latin works: *Vita Scholastica,* a *vade mecum* for students and teachers (in 468 elegiac couplets); *De magnalibus Mediolani,* a panegyrical guidebook of the city of Milan (1288) whose prose is of great historical and rhetorical interest; and *Carmina de Mensibus,* a debate (430 hexameters) that has been considered either the first version or (preferably) the Latin translation by the author himself of the vernacular poem written on the same subject. The bulk of Bonvesin's production is written, however, in Old Milanese (apart from the titles of texts, for which Latin remains *de rigueur*) and can be divided into the following groups:

1. Lively debates devised not only to edify a religious audience ("Satan and the Virgin," "The Sinner and the Virgin," "Soul and Body") but also to promote civic virtues and subtly advocate the political interests of a wealthy and industrious bourgeoisie, ready, by then, to adjust to the authority of a signory ("The Fly and the Ant," "The Rose and the Violet," "The Debate of the Months").

2. Poems whose didactic concerns are expressed, as in religious sermons, through pressing exhortations and sequences of exempla. These narrative works (either miracles or parables) are remarkable for their vivid realism as well as for the awe of their prodigious denouements ("In Praise of the Virgin Mary," "On Almsgiving," "On Vain Things," plus a fragmentary "Legend of the Cross").

3. Two hagiographic compositions, "The Life of Saint Alexis" and "The Passion of Saint Job."

4. Merely didactic poems of either religious or secular content ("On False Excuses," "Judgment-Day," "An Exposition of Cato's Distichs," "Fifty Table-Manners").
5. *The Book of the Three Scriptures* (the Black, the Red, and the Golden), which contains a description of Hell and Paradise with an account of Christ's (and Mary's) Passion placed in between.

The Book of the Three Scriptures was probably written, as was the rest of the vernacular production, during the 1270s. Its division into three parts, which heralds the frame of the *Commedia*, derives from its tripartite subject matter, an eschatological vision of the afterlife centering on the figure of Christ, whose role as Judge is deeply rooted in the Passion he agreed to undergo. Hell (black) and Paradise (golden), the first and third parts, are treated by Bonvesin as strictly symmetrical, with a catalogue of twelve punishments and a corresponding list of twelve "glories." The Passion (red) forms the second part. The first item, in the black as well as in the golden series, provides the general setting, which for Hell is fire and for Paradise is the image of the precious Heavenly City. From number 2 to number 10, the two registers keep in close correspondence: stench vs. fragrance (2), sight of the damned and devils vs. sight of the angels and saints (5), groans and uproar vs. music and songs (6), torturing devils vs. Christ's loving attendance upon the blessed (7), hunger and thirst vs. the celestial banquet (8), harsh rags vs. sumptuous garments (9), and disfiguring maladies vs. the beauty of the glorious body (10). There are two exceptional instances, where the incredible cold (3) and the obnoxious worms (4) of Hell are oddly counterbalanced by the wealth and high rank of the blessed (a symptom of Bonvesin's social concern and self-consciousness) and by joy at having been released from the prison of earthly life (cf. *Purg.* 2.46–48). Numbers 11 and 12 are reserved, in both lists, for psychological reactions: rage at the foolish forfeiture of Paradise vs. the consoling thought of having escaped Hell, and the knowledge that pain/glory will endure forever.

As might be expected, the Golden Scripture is more static and stylized (Christ in waiting for the blessed is no match for the devils jeering at and pounding the damned), although some heavenly comforts (rich garments, elaborate feasts)—supposedly metaphorical—tend to become embarrassingly tangible, given the insistence on description. Certainly more appealing to the reader is Hell, where the vain lamentations of a representative sinner—which serve the purpose of conveying the principle of *contrapasso* that correlates mode of punishment with earthly misconduct—are not only pathetic but also intrinsically comic. The authorial voice enhances the vividness of the account by resorting to ingenious *exempla ficta* and to colorful glimpses of medieval daily life.

Bibliography

Bonvesin da la Riva. *Volgari Scelti (Selected Poems).* Edited by and translated by Ruggero Stefanini and Patrick S. Diehl. Bern, New York: Peter Lang, 1987.

———. *Le opere volgari.* Edited by Gianfranco Contini. Rome: Società filologica romana, 1941.

Ruggero Stefanini

Borsiere, Guiglielmo

Condemned for violence against nature and punished among the homosexuals in the seventh circle (*Inf.* 16.70–72). We have no firsthand information about him, not even whether his second name indicates his family or a trade ("purse maker"), although the statement that he *si duole [. . .] per poco* ("has been grieving . . . but a short time") indicates that he died in or just before 1300. Boccaccio, who describes him as an eloquent courtier with admirable manners, builds a story around him (*Dec.* 1.8) in which he wittily converts a Genoese aristocrat from avarice to liberality. Iacopo Rusticucci mentions him as a source of information on courtesy and valor (*Inf.* 16.67), for which function he would be well qualified if he was, in fact, a courtier.

John C. Barnes

Botticelli, Sandro

Florentine painter (1445–1510); original name Alessandro di Mariano Filipepi. He illustrated Cristoforo Landino's edition of the *Commedia* in the 1480s and became the first great serial artist of the poem to use the discursive method: following the text sequentially or episodically rather than approaching it synoptically. A master of graceful movement whose elegance relies on his sophisticated control of line, he enhanced the spiritual mood of his drawings by his preference of pen and ink to color (only rarely did he even begin to apply pigment, as in *Inf.* 10). Especially in *Inferno,* Dante's and Botticelli's styles differ considerably: the poet's hard scenes overcast with intense shadows contrasts with the illustrator's ubiquitous sense of delicate beauty. But Botticelli remains enchantingly Dantean in the way his diffuse outlines match the text's mystical overtones. The influence of Landino and of Florentine Neoplatonism is discernible in the overall absence of Gothic drama and what has been called his inclination toward purifying ecstasy. Throughout, there is a tendency to repetition, but any potential tediousness yields to an invitation to scrutinize the subtleties, and by the end of the final canticle the stylistic process has created a total coherence.

Botticelli likes to stress various moments successively (see *Purg.* 28, where he uses trees to separate the scenes). He seems to follow Virgil's and Dante's footsteps with the affection of a loyal narrator who will not mar the story with his own insights. He is as economical in his means as Dante is in his, and through it all he manages a fine rhythmic flow and considerable—however concealed—emotional intensity. Henry Fuseli did not care for Botticelli's manner ("culinary abominations," he called the drawings). But Bernard Berenson appreciated it, because he knew the artist's secret: the simple line. By hovering between dream and reality, the style acts as an abstraction of Dante's visual poetry.

The modalities of line enable Botticelli to distinguish among the three canticles. With the fantastic devils and monsters, medieval concepts persist in the *Inferno,* along with some indications of complexity and disarray (cantos 1, 9, and 13, for example). *Purgatorio* becomes more panoramic, on the whole, as in Botticelli's depiction of fire in cantos 24–27, though he still likes to focus on a central item (like the inverted tree in cantos 22–24). The spirituality of *Paradiso* inspires yet another manner, abandoning tableaux and discursiveness and concentrating on symbols, like the flame, the ladder, and flowers. What seems like little more than a series of ovals encompassing Dante and Beatrice in fact interiorizes the narrative, presenting changing states of mind through linear movements and expressions: aspiration (canto 1), surprise (2), love (7), wonder (10), bedazzlement (26), anticipation (27), joy (30), and so on. Because of what might be called his quiet inter-

pretation of the *Commedia,* there are those, like Giorgio Vasari, who considered Botticelli a commentator of the poem in his own right.

Bibliography

Batard, Yvonne. *Les Dessins de Sandro Botticelli pour la Divine Comédie.* Paris: Olivier Perrin, 1952.

Clark, Kenneth. *The Drawings of Sandro Botticelli for Dante's Divine Comedy.* New York, London: Harper and Row, 1976.

Jean-Pierre Barricelli

Branca d'Oria

Ser Branca d'Oria, born into the noted Genoese Ghibelline family around 1233, is sighted in Ptolomea in the ninth circle of Hell (*Inf.* 33.137), where he is punished for murdering his father-in-law, Michel Zanche (*Inf.* 22.88), the governor of Logudoro in Sardinia, whom he had invited to a banquet. As Fra Alberigo explains, such heinous traitors to their guests are sent into Hell to suffer immediate punishment even before they are dead, while their own bodies continue to live on Earth above, inhabited by devils. So despicable are the crimes of those in Ptolomea that Dante's treatment of them appears to contravene the fundamental doctrine of repentance.

Roy Rosenstein

Briareus

Son of Uranus and Earth, one of the mythological giants who attempted to conquer Heaven (Olympus). Virgil portrays him with a hundred arms and fifty heads (*Aen.* 10.565–568). In *Inf.* 31.98–105, however, Briareus (*Briareo*) resembles the other giants guarding the ninth circle of Hell (and thus has human features), though he is fiercer looking. He also appears as one of the examples of punished pride on the first terrace of Purgatory (*Purg.* 12.28–30).

V. Stanley Benfell

Brigata, Il

Ugolino (Nino) della Gherardesca, a moderate Ghibelline in the Pisan aristocracy. He was imprisoned with his grandfather, Ugolino della Gherardesca, in the tower of the Gualandi in Pisa in 1288, where he died of hunger, together with his younger brother, Anselmuccio, and his uncles Uguiccione and Gaddo. Dante recalls his fate in *Inf.* 33.89: *Innocenti facea l'età novella / . . . Uguiccione e 'l Brigata* ("Their young age . . . made Uguiccione and Brigata innocent").

Pina Palma

Brunetto Latini

Brunetto (Burnetto) Latini (or Latino) is encountered by Dante in Hell, where he is being punished among sinners against nature and its goodness: the sin of Sodom (*Inf.* 15.13–124; see *Inf.* 11.46–51). He was a Florentine, born c. 1220, the son of Bonaccorso di Latino. A notary, he is recorded as serving the *Primo Popolo* of 1250–1260, drawing up peace treaties (1254, 1257), acting as scribe to the *Anziani* (1254, 1259), and replying to Pavia on the execution of Tesauro dei Beccaria (1258). In 1260, he was sent on an embassy to Alfonso X of Castile, one of the imperial candidates, to ask for help against Manfred; during his absence and following the battle of Montaperti, the Ghibellines returned to power in Florence. Brunetto spent the next years in exile in France, principally in the regions of Artois and Picardy. From 1267, on his return to Guelf Florence, he resumed public service as protonotary to Charles of Anjou's vicar in Tuscany (1269), scribe to the Councils and Chancellor of the Commune (1272), consul of the Guild of Judges and Notaries (1275), one of the guarantors of the Peace of Cardinal Latino (1280), member of the war council and negotiator in the league against Pisa (1284–1285), prior (August–October 1287), and member of the war council against Arezzo (1289). He was married and had at least three, perhaps four, children. He died in 1294 (Florentine Style). A column, inscribed + *Latinorum,* which presumably had marked his grave, was later set up in the Church of Santa Maria Maggiore in Florence, with the coat of arms granted to one of his sons and the inscription *S[epulcrum] S[er] Burnetti Latini & filiorum.* Giovanni Villani describes him as "a great philosopher and a supreme master of rhetoric" who was the first to instruct and civilize the Florentines, making them "skilled in speaking well and in knowing how to guide and rule our republic according to Politics" (*Cronica* 9.10).

Apart from his surviving chancery and legal documents in Latin, Brunetto Latini wrote the following works in the vernacular.

Li Livres dou Tresor ("The Books of the Treasure") is written in French (with Picard forms) during Brunetto's exile and was completed after his return to Florence. It is addressed to a "fair, sweet friend" (variously identified as Charles of Anjou, Alfonso of Castile, or a patron). The metaphor of the title refers to the treasure of Wisdom, and the work's three books consist of the small change (the "theoretical" knowledge of things heavenly and earthly); the jewels (a "practical" discourse on vices and virtues); and the gold, the most precious part (rules for rhetoric and for civic government by a podestà). Drawing on a wide variety of sources—biblical, Christian, and classical (Aristotle, Cicero, and Pseudo-Seneca)—it is the first compendium of philosophy in a modern vernacular and hence an antecedent of Dante's *Convivio.* The attribution of an Italian version, the *Tesoro* ("Treasure"), to Bono Giamboni has been disputed, and it has been conjectured that it may be by Brunetto Latini himself.

La Rettorica ("Rhetoric") was written in Italian in exile for a rich Florentine patron (perhaps Davizzo della Tosa), who is called the author's refuge or harbor *(porto)*. An apparently unfinished translation and commentary on Cicero's *De inventione,* chapters 1–17, it expounds the context of Wisdom (Philosophy) and the Liberal Arts and then goes on to deal with the categories and purposes of rhetoric and the construction of speeches and letters, with discussion of some defects. Pertaining to the Ciceronian tradition underlying the medieval *ars dictandi* (the art of rhetorical composition), it is also a notable example of early Florentine civic prehumanism in the vernacular.

The *Tesoretto* ("Little Treasure"), with the internal title of *Tesoro* ("Treasure"), is an unfinished poem in Italian, composed of 2,944 *settenari baciati* (seven-syllable rhyming couplets), probably also written during its author's exile and showing the influence of the French allegorical romance tradition, to which the *Romance of the Rose,* written in octosyllabic rhyming couplets, also belongs. Originally planned as a *prosimetrum* (containing passages in prose), the *Tesoretto* consists of a dedication to a noble and virtuous lord (perhaps Charles of Anjou); an account of how, at Roncesvalles, its author heard of the Guelf defeat at Montaperti and became lost in a "strange forest"; his journey of instruction and education to Lady Natura, the realm of the Empress Virtù, and the garden of Love; his confession of his sins to a friar

B

in Montpellier; and the start of an episode in which Ptolemy is about to teach him about astronomy.

The *Favolello* ("Little Fable"), a poem in Italian, consists of 162 *settenari baciati* and was written during Brunetto's exile. In answer to a poem by Rustico Filippi (now lost), it expounds a doctrine of true moral and civic friendship, based principally on Cicero's *Laelius on Friendship* and its medieval successors.

A canzone, "S'eo son distretto inamoratamente" ("If I am constrained by Love"), was written in exile and perhaps sent to Bondie Dietaiuti in Florence. It is probably an expression of its author's love for Florence, the "white lily," now under Ghibelline control, and a request to his friends there to intercede for him so that he may return.

Dante meets Brunetto Latini in Hell in the third ring of the seventh circle in one of the groups of souls who must move around continuously on the burning sand beneath the rain of fire (*Inf.* 15.13–124). The episode consists of a scene of recognition (22–30) and a dialogue between Brunetto and Dante, his reverent "son," in which the principal themes are the eternal movement of the souls (34–42); Dante's journey home with the guidance of Virgil (46–54); Dante's stars and potentially glorious destiny (55–60); the corruption of the Fiesolan (non-Roman) Florentines, their future persecution of the innocent Dante, and his escape (by exile) (61–78); Dante's tribute to Brunetto's "dear, kind paternal image" when he taught Dante "how man makes himself eternal" and the permanent influence of this on Dante's own tongue or language (79–87); Dante's acceptance of whatever Fortune has in store for him and Virgil's confirmation of this (88–99); Brunetto's description of his group and naming of three of its members (100–114); his recommendation to Dante of his *Tesoro,* in which he still lives, and his running away like the winner of the annual race in Verona (115–124). The episode expresses Dante's positive affection for Brunetto as his "father," while indicating also the two men's contrasting destinies in relation to fame and immortality, both earthly and—for Dante but not for Brunetto—heavenly.

The exact nature of Dante's debt to Brunetto as a teacher is not known for certain, but the latter's works indicate that it was probably in the areas of philosophy and scholarship, of moral instruction and civic leadership, and perhaps also of rhetoric and versification (a possibility which might be supported by the attribution of the *Detto d'Amore* to Dante). However, it is not generally accepted that Brunetto Latini was the recipient of Dante's sonnet "Messer Brunetto, questa pulzelletta" (*Rime* 99); and later Dante included Brunetto among the Tuscan poets who wrote not in the illustrious, courtly vernacular but in a merely municipal language (*DVE* 1.13.1).

The sin of Dante's Brunetto and his group is apparently to be classified as a sin of Sodom (*Inf.* 11.49–51), and it has traditionally been assumed that Dante, perhaps learning about Brunetto Latini's private life in later years, is condemning him for sexual sin—and particularly for homosexuality, regarded as a sin against nature and condemned by Brunetto himself in the *Tresor* and *Tesoretto*. Ignoring the facts that Brunetto had a family and was a notable public servant, some critics have set this sin in a more general social context, as Brunetto's rejection of parental and therefore civic responsibilities. Some modern critics have detected gay imagery and language in *Inf.* 15. Alongside this interpretation, some of the early commentators state that Brunetto was an astrologer (and even that he cast Dante's horoscope), or that he unwittingly committed perjury, or that he was irreligious; in fact, admissions of worldliness and disrespect for the church are contained in Brunetto's confession in the *Tesoretto* (lines 2457ff., 2526ff.). In recent decades some critics have disputed the traditional identification of Brunetto's sin, arguing that it can be explained more satisfactorily as some sort of intellectual, rather than sexual, sin against nature: the rejection of his own language by writing the *Tresor* in French (Pézard); opposition to the empire (Kay); a quasi-Manichaean rejection of the doctrine of the goodness of human nature (Armour); or other errors connected with his professional life, his role as father figure and teacher, or his entirely worldly approach to fame.

Bibliography

Ahern, John. "*Nudi grammantes:* The Grammar and Rhetoric of Deviation in *Inferno* XV." *Romanic Review* 81 (1990), 466–486.

Armour, Peter. "Brunetto, the Stoic Pessimist." *Dante Studies* 112 (1994), 1–18.

———. "The Love of Two Florentines: Brunetto Latini and Bondie Dietaiuti." *Lectura Dantis* 9 (Fall 1991), 11–33.

———. "*Inferno* XV." In *Dante's Divine Comedy: Introductory Readings. I. Inferno.* Edited by T. Wlassics. *Lectura Dantis* 6: Supplement (Spring 1990), 189–208.

———. "Dante's Brunetto: The Paternal Paterine?" *Italian Studies* 38 (1983), 1–38.

Avalle, D'Arco Silvio. "Nel terzo girone del settimo cerchio." In his *Ai luoghi di delizia pieni.* Milan, Naples: Ricciardi, 1977, pp. 87–106, 191–197.

Bisson, Lillian M. "Brunetto Latini as a Failed Mentor." *Medievalia et Humanistica* 18 (1992), 1–15.

Bolton Holloway, Julia. *Twice-Told Tales: Brunetto Latino and Dante Alighieri.* New York: Peter Lang, 1993.

———. *Brunetto Latini: An Analytic Bibliography.* London, Wolfeboro: Grant and Cutler, 1986.

Ceva, Bianca. *Brunetto Latini: l'uomo e l'opera.* Milan, Naples: Ricciardi, 1965.

Costa, Elio. "From *locus amoris* to Infernal Pentecost: The Sin of Brunetto Latini." *Quaderni d'italianistica* 10 (1989), 109–132.

———. "Il *Tesoretto* di Brunetto Latini e la tradizione allegorica medievale." In *Dante e le forme dell'allegoresi.* Edited by M. Picone. Ravenna: Longo, 1987, pp. 43–58.

Davis, Charles Till. "Brunetto Latini and Dante." *Studi medievali,* 3rd ser. 8 (1967), 421–450; and in his *Dante's Italy and Other Essays.* Philadelphia: University of Pennsylvania Press, 1984, pp. 166–197.

Havely, Nicholas R., "Brunetto and Palinurus." *Dante Studies* 108 (1990), 20–38.

Kay, Richard. *Dante's Swift and Strong: Essays on Inferno XV.* Lawrence: Regents Press of Kansas, 1978.

———. "The Sin(s) of Brunetto Latini." *Dante Studies* 112 (1994), 19–31.

Latini, Brunetto. *Li Livres dou Tresor.* Edited by F. J. Carmody. Berkeley: University of California Press, 1948.

———. *La rettorica.* Edited by F. Maggini. Reprinted Bari: Laterza, 1968.

———. *Il Tesoretto; Il Favolello.* Edited by F. Mazzoni. Alpignano: Tallone, 1967. *Poeti del Duecento.* Edited by G. Contini. Milan, Naples: Ricciardi, 1960, vol. II, pp. 169–284.

———. *Il Tesoretto.* Edited by M. Ciccuto, Milan: Rizzoli, 1985.

———. *Il Tesoretto (The Little Treasure).* Translated and edited by Julia Bolton Holloway. New York, London: Garland, 1981.

———. *Il Tesoro di Brunetto Latini volgarizzato da Bono Giamboni.* 4 vols. Edited and revised by L. Gaiter. Bologna: Romagnoli, 1877–1883.

Mussetter, Sally. "'Ritornare a lo suo principio': Dante and the Sin of Brunetto Latini." *Philological Quarterly* 63 (1984), 431–448.

Najemy, John M. "Brunetto Latini's *Politica.*" *Dante Studies* 112 (1994), 33–51.

Nevin, Thomas. "Ser Brunetto's Immortality: *Inferno* XV." *Dante Studies* 96 (1978), 21–37.

Pequigney, Joseph. "Sodomy in Dante's *Inferno* and *Purgatorio.*" *Representations* 36 (1991), 22–42.

Pézard, André. *Dante sous la pluie de feu (Enfer, chant XV).* Paris: Vrin, 1950.

Sowell, Madison U. "Brunetto's *Tesoro* in Dante's *Inferno.*" *Lectura Dantis* 7 (Fall 1990), 60–71.

Sundby, Thor. *Della vita e delle opere di Brunetto Latini.* Translated by R. Renier. Florence: Le Monnier, 1884.

Vance, Eugene. "The Differing Seed: Dante's Brunetto Latini." In *Mervelous Signals: Poetics and Sign Theory in the Middle Ages.* London, Lincoln: University of Nebraska Press, 1986, pp. 230–255.

Witt, Ronald G. "Latini, Lovato and the Revival of Antiquity." *Dante Studies* 112 (1994), 53–61.

Peter Armour

Brutus, Lucius Junius

Son of Marcus Brutus, who murdered Julius Caesar. After the rape of Lucretia by Sextus Tarquinius, he drove Tarquin the Proud, the last of the Roman kings, from Rome in 510 B.C.E. Brutus *(Bruto)* is placed in Limbo along with the other pagan heroes of antiquity (*Inf.* 4.127). In *Conv.* 4.5.12, Dante mentions Brutus' becoming the first consul of the Roman republic, along with Lucius Tarquinius Collatinus. He twice celebrates Brutus' nobility for placing the welfare of his country above the lives of his own two sons, whom Brutus sacrifices when he discovers their involvement in a conspiracy: once in *Conv.* 4.5.14 and again in *Mon.* 2.5.13 (where he quotes *Aen.* 6.820–821).

Robin Treasure

Brutus, Marcus Junius

Son of a half-sister of Cato of Utica and married to Cato's daughter Portia. Although Brutus *(Bruto)* fought on the side of Pompey in the civil war of 49 B.C.E., he was pardoned by Julius Caesar after the

B

battle at Pharsalus in 48 B.C.E. and was entrusted with important political offices. Convinced by Cassius to join the conspiracy against Caesar and to aid in the reestablishment of the republic, Brutus participated personally in the assassination on March 15, 44 B.C.E. Dante condemns him as a traitor to a benefactor, placing him in Lucifer's black mouth in the last zone, Judecca, of the ninth and deepest circle of Hell (*Inf.* 34.65–66). He refers to Brutus' defeat by Augustus at Philippi in 42 B.C.E. in *Par.* 6.74.

Michael Papio

Bryson

Greek philosopher, said to be the son of Herodotus, who was criticized by Aristotle for his incompetence in attempting to square the circle (*De Sophisticis Elenchis* 11.171b16–17, 172a2–4; *Analytica Posteriora* 1.9.75b). Bryson *(Brisso)* is mentioned in the Heaven of the Sun, together with Parmenides and Melissus, as a philosopher whose reasoning was defective (*Par.* 13.125). Dante cites the squaring of the circle in several places as an example of a mathematical impossibility (*Conv.* 2.13.27; *Mon.* 3.3.2; *Par.* 33.133–135).

Bibliography

Herzman, Ronald B., and Gary W. Towsley. "Squaring the Circle: *Paradiso* 33 and the Poetics of Geometry." *Traditio* 49 (1994), 95–125.

Richard Lansing

Buiamonte, Giovanni

Gianni di Buiamonte de' Becchi (1260–1310); he took part in public affairs, was named Gonfaloniere di Giustizia in 1293, and was given the title of *cavaliere* (knight) in 1298. Early commentators identify him as the *cavalier sovrano* mentioned by Reginaldo degli Scrovegni in the third round of the seventh circle in Hell (*Inf.* 17.72). The Florentine usurers there are said to be still awaiting his arrival, because in 1300, the fictional time of the poem, he was still alive. He died in poverty in 1310. The meaning of his depiction through the heraldic metaphor of three eagle's beaks *(tre becchi)* has been the matter of some debate, but it is generally thought that Dante used it to call into question his family's banking practices. The Becchi, originally from an area between Florence and Pistoia, became one of the wealthiest families in

Florence through moneylending. Early commentators note that their family coat of arms bore three goats sable against a gold background.

Jo Ann Cavallo

Buondelmonte dei Buondelmonti

Though Buondelmonte is not himself a character in the *Commedia,* his catastrophic murder is recalled twice (by the guilty Mosca in *Inf.* 28.106–108 and by Cacciaguida in *Par.* 16.140), where it is presented, as it was by Dante's contemporary chroniclers, as the spark that touched off the political divisions within Florence's ruling class and the moment when the watchwords "Guelf" and "Ghibelline" were first taken up within the city's walls—the first by the Buondelmonti clan, the second by their Amidei rivals. In reparation for an offense done to Oddo Arrighi dei Fifanti, young Buondelmonte dei Buondelmonti first agreed to marry Arrighi's niece, the daughter of Lambertuccio degli Amidei. He was subsequently persuaded to break his promise (according to an anonymous chronicle falsely attributed to Brunetto Latini), by Gualdrada, wife of Forese di Vinciguerra Donati, who proposed he instead wed one of her own daughters. At a gathering of the slighted Amidei clan to discuss the form of their vendetta, Mosca dei Lamberti spoke out pithily against half measures: *Capo ha cosa fatta* ("A thing done is done"); and Buondelmonte was clubbed and knifed to death near the mutilated statue of Mars as he rode across the Ponte Vecchio from Oltrarno on Easter Sunday morning 1216 (Villani, *Cronica,* 6.38).

Bibliography

Schevill, Ferdinando. *History of Florence.* New York: Ungar, 1936. Reprinted in 1961.

Anthony Oldcorn

Buoso

One of the five Florentine thieves whose metamorphoses from and into serpent form are described in *Inf.* 25. With only a first name to go on (*Inf.* 25.140), early commentators variously identify him as Buoso degli Abati or Buoso dei Donati. Recent annotators follow Michele Barbi, whose archival research points to an uncle of Piccarda, Forese, and Corso Donati and a nephew to the other Buoso Donati explicitly mentioned in *Inf.*

30.44. Buoso's is the supreme metamorphosis, whose description outdoes both Lucan and Ovid: he exchanges forms at a distance with another thief, gradually becoming a serpent while the anonymous fellow Florentine he is paired with (identified by the same commentators as Francesco "Guercio" de' Cavalcanti) regains his human shape.

Anthony Oldcorn

Buoso da Duera

A politician condemned by Dante to Antenora, the second ring of the ninth and lowest circle of Hell, where those who were traitors to their homeland or party are buried in ice. Bocca degli Abati, another sinner condemned to this region of Hell, identifies him simply as *quel da Duera* ("him of Duera"), who *piange qui l'argento de' Franceschi* ("bewails the silver of the French here," *Inf.* 32.115–116).

Buoso was born to the lord of Soncino, but from 1247, together with Uberto Pallavicini, he was signore of Cremona and leader of the Ghibelline party there. In these capacities, he was entrusted by Manfred to block the passage of the French troops of Charles of Anjou as they marched south through Lombardy on their way to claim Naples in 1265. Buoso failed to oppose their progress, however. The precise nature of Buoso's treacherous behavior for which he is damned is somewhat obscure in its details, although Dante's reference to "the silver of the French" implies that he believed the stories that Buoso had accepted a bribe from the French. Buoso was exiled from Cremona in 1267. When he finally was able to return in 1282, he was imprisoned by Guelfs.

Frank B. Ordiway

Buoso Donati

Member of the important Florentine family of the Donati, Buoso is mentioned in *Inf.* 30.44 in connection with the fraud perpetrated by the mimic Gianni Schicchi, who is punished among the falsifiers of persons in the tenth pouch of Malebolge. According to Dante's early commentators, Buoso's death was concealed by his nephew (in some versions, his son) Simone Donati, who engaged Schicchi to impersonate him on his deathbed and to dictate a will in Simone's favor. Historical research has uncovered at least three members of the Donati family with the given name Buoso; the one Dante mentions should probably be identified with the earliest among them, the son of Vinciguerra di Donato del Pazzo, who lived in the first half of the thirteenth century. This Buoso died a widower without direct heirs and had a nephew named Simone (the father of Corso Donati). Another Buoso, who appears among the thieves in canto 25, may also be a Donati.

Olivia Holmes

C

Cacciaguida

Great-great-grandfather (and surrogate father) of Dante. Their meeting in the warriors' Heaven of Mars—explicitly inspired by and modeled on the encounter of Aeneas with the prophetic ghost of his father Anchises in the underworld (*Aen.* 6)—is one of the highlights of *Paradiso,* indeed, of the entire *Commedia.* The episode affords the poet Dante the opportunity to suggest that the nobility of his lineage matches the nobility of his character (all the while protesting modesty), as well as to express his nostalgia for a lost world of moral and political integrity and his defiant acceptance, given the corruption of his time, of a future of exile and his uncompromising mission as poet of moral rectitude in the *Commedia.* Almost all we know about Cacciaguida is derived from Dante's text. The two brothers mentioned there—Moronto and Eliseo (*Par.* 15.136)—are entirely unknown to history. External documentary evidence of Cacciaguida's own existence is at best indirect. Their late father's name appears in a legal instrument dated December 9, 1189, regarding his two sons (*filii olim Cacciaguide,* "sons of the late Cacciaguida"), Preitenitto and Alighiero (alternatively spelled "Alaghieri"). The latter, named after his mother, who came from the Po Valley, perhaps from Ferrara, bequeathed his name to Dante's family. Cacciaguida first appears in *Par.* 15 (symmetrically aligned with Brunetto Latini, the "father" of *Inf.* 15) and occupies center stage for three complete cantos (the most autobiographical and most political cantos of *Paradiso*), and so is accorded greater narrative space than any other dead soul, apart from Dante's guides. When asked by the pilgrim Dante

for details of his life, he alludes to the date of his birth in an aristocratic quarter of Florence through a complicated astronomical circumlocution (*Par.* 16.34–39), which most modern commentators interpret as referring to the year 1091. It is Cacciaguida, not Beatrice (as promised initially in *Inf.* 10.127–32), who prophesies Dante's earthly future. Before doing so and exhorting him to have no qualms about naming names in his account of the otherworld, this citizen of the City of God looks back with regret on the idealized, grassroots, hardcore, and pre-decadent "Roman" Florence that he was privileged to live in—a city with only one-fifth

Cacciaguida. From Opere del diuino poeta Danthe, *published by Bernardino Stagnino da Trino de Monferra, Venice, 1512. Reproduced by permission of the John A. Zahm Dante Collection in the Department of Special Collections, University Libraries, University of Notre Dame.*

the population it had accumulated by Dante's day—before the promiscuous immigration of men on the make from the surrounding countryside (the *gente nuova,* or "new people," of *Inf.* 16.73); and before the divisive clan warfare, sparked by the murder of Buondelmonte dei Buondelmonti and perpetuated in the ruinous factional rivalry, first between the Guelfs and the Ghibellines, later between the Black and the White Guelfs. Then Cacciaguida recounts how he died a crusader in the Holy Land, knighted for his services by the emperor Conrad III of Hohenstaufen (1138–1152).

Bibliography

Bergin, Thomas Goddard. "Light from Mars." *A Diversity of Dante.* New Brunswick, N.J.: Rutgers University Press, 1969, pp. 143–166.

Carpi, Umberto. "La nobiltà di Dante (a proposito di *Paradiso* XVI)." *Rivista di letteratura italiana* 8 (1990), 229–260.

Chiarenza, Marguerite M. "Time and Eternity in the Myths of *Paradiso* XVII." *Studies in Honor of C. S. Singleton.* Binghamton, N.Y.: SUNY Press, 1983, pp. 133–156.

Chiavacci Leonardi, Anna Maria. "*Paradiso* XVII." *Filologia e critica dantesca. Studi offerti a Aldo Vallone.* Florence: 1989, pp. 309–327.

Davis, Charles T. "Il buon tempo antico (The Good Old Time)." In *Dante's Italy and Other Essays.* Philadelphia: University of Pennsylvania Press, 1984, pp. 71–93.

Jacomuzzi, Angelo. "Considerazioni sopra i canti di Cacciaguida." In *L'imago al cerchio.* Milan: Franco Angeli, 1968, pp. 114–140.

Momigliano, Attilio. "La personalità di Dante e i canti di Cacciaguida." In *Dante, Manzoni, Verga.* Messina: G. D'Anna, 1944, pp. 33–57.

Pézard, André. "Les trois langues de Cacciaguida." *Revue des Études Italiennes* 13 (1967), 217–238.

Ramat, Raffaello. *Il mito di Firenze e altri saggi danteschi.* Florence, Messina: G. D'Anna, 1976.

Schnapp, Jeffrey T. *The Transfiguration of History at the Center of Dante's Paradise.* Princeton, N.J.: Princeton University Press, 1986.

Toscano, T. R. "Memoria storia e progetto politico nei canti di Cacciaguida." *Lectura Dantis.* Potenza: 1986–1987, pp. 57–93.

Anthony Oldcorn

Caccianemico, Venedico

A Guelf who distinguished himself fighting for his father, Alberto Caccianemico dell'Orso, in the civil wars that divided Bologna for many years. In 1274 Venedico defeated the adversary faction, exiling its leaders. He later governed Bologna and was himself exiled on at least two occasions for favoring the Este family of Ferrara, who had ambitions regarding Bologna. He appears among the panders and seducers in the first bolgia of Malebolge, where he accuses himself of procuring his own sister Ghisolabella for Obizzo d'Este, marquis of Ferrara, in exchange for money and favors (*Inf.* 18.55).

Pina Palma

Cacus

In the *Aeneid* (8.193–267), Virgil depicts Cacus as a half-human fire-belching monster who dwells in a cave under Mount Aventine and terrifies the countryside by stealing livestock and slaughtering men. When he steals some cattle from Hercules, he drags them to his cave by their tails so they cannot be tracked. Hercules, however, discovers the cattle and kills Cacus by strangling him.

Dante's Cacus *(Caco),* who appears in the seventh bolgia of the eighth circle among the thieves (*Inf.* 25.25), is a modified version of Virgil's half-human monster. Dante depicts him as a raging centaur, whereas Virgil explicitly identifies Cacus as a son of Vulcan—meaning that he cannot be one of the centaurs, who were the offspring of Ixion. And whereas Virgil's Cacus was himself a fire-breathing monster, Dante depicts him as having a fire-breathing dragon perched on his shoulders, along with snakes on his back. Finally, in Dante's account of Cacus' death, which apparently follows the version of either Livy (*Ab urbe condita,* 1.7.7) or Ovid (*Fasti* 1.575–578), Hercules kills Cacus with a club.

Virgil explains to Dante that Cacus is not with his "brother" centaurs who patrol the banks of Phlegethon in the first round of the circle of violence (canto 12) because of his cunning theft of Hercules' cattle (*Inf.* 25.29). At the same time, Cacus is like his "brothers" in that he serves as a guardian in the seventh bolgia.

Lawrence Baldassaro

Cadmus

Brother of Europa and father of Semele, Ino, and Polydorus, Cadmus *(Cadmo)* founded Thebes when he slew a dragon sacred to Mars and sowed its teeth to engender the Theban nation. As a punishment for this impiety, he was turned into a serpent at the end of his life, according to Ovid *(Meta.* 4.571–603), whose account of Cadmus' metamorphosis inspired Dante's depiction of the punishment of the thieves in *Inf.* 25.49–93. Dante makes the audacious claim, however, that he surpasses Ovid's portrayal, challenging his predecessor in *Inf.* 25.97 with the boast *Taccia di Cadmo e d'Aretusa Ovidio* ("About Cadmus and Arethusa let Ovid be silent")—an illustration of how the *Commedia* strives to transcend Ovidian material even as it emulates it.

Bibliography

Cioffi, Caron Ann. "The Anxieties of Ovidian Influence." *Dante Studies* 102 (1994), 77–100.

Hawkins, Peter S. "Virtuosity and Virtue: Poetic Self-Reflection in the *Commedia*." *Dante Studies* 98 (1980), 1–18.

Terdiman, Richard. "Problematical Virtuosity: Dante's Depiction of the Thieves." *Dante Studies* 91 (1973), 27–45.

Jessica Levenstein

Caecilius Statius

Major Roman comic poet (c. 220–166 B.C.E.), contemporary of Plautus and friend of Ennius, immediate predecessor of Terence. Titles of forty-two of his comedies are known, but only fragments have survived. He was praised by Cicero and Quintilian. Horace's reference to him in *Ars Poetica* 53–55 was Dante's source for *Purg.* 22.98, where Caecilius *(Cecilio)* is said to dwell with Virgil in Limbo.

Nancy Vine Durling

Cahors

A city in southern France that was renowned in the Middle Ages for the high interest rates imposed by its bankers. In Virgil's explanation of the structure of Hell, Cahors *(Caorsa)* is used to designate the sin of usury *(Inf.* 11.50). St. Peter's reference in the Heaven of the Fixed Stars to *Caorsini* ("Cahorsans") preparing to drink the blood shed by martyred popes of the early Church is a clear allusion to Pope John XXII, a native of Cahors *(Par.* 27.58).

Caiaphas among the hypocrites. Invenzioni di Giovanni Flaxman sulla Divina commedia, *illustrated by John Flaxman and Beniamino del Vecchio, Rome, 1826. Giamatti Collection: Courtesy of the Mount Holyoke College Archives and Special Collections.*

The pope's association with the city was, for Dante, fully in keeping with his natural cupidity.

Mark Balfour

Caiaphas

High priest of Jerusalem who advised the Hebrew priests and Pharisees that it was better for Jesus to die than for an entire nation to be lost (John 11:5). Dante places him in the sixth bolgia of Hell with the hypocrites *(Inf.* 23.115–126) but reserves for Caiaphas *(Caifa)*—along with his father-in-law Annas and the rest of the priests who condemned Christ—a singular punishment: he appears naked and crucified by three stakes on the ground. The other hypocrites, who wear heavy lead cloaks, must step on him as they pass. He represents the archetypical hypocrite who hid behind a feigned interest in the public good, but his hypocrisy assumes more gravity than other forms of the same sin because it had God as its victim. Virgil, who did not find salvation in Christ, marvels at this infernal likeness of the Crucifixion.

Olivia Holmes

Cain

Son of Adam and Eve and brother of Abel, whom he slew, thereby becoming the first murderer. He is presented as an example of envy in the second circle of Purgatory, where he cries out: *Anciderammi qualunque m'apprende* ("Whoever finds me will kill me," *Purg.* 14.133). In *Inf.* 20.126 the phrase *Caino e le spine* ("Cain with his thorns") refers periphrastically to the Moon with its spots. According to popular tradition, God punished Cain for his crime by burdening him with a bundle of thorns and exiling him to the Moon. Dante refers again to this tradition in Paradise when he asks Beatrice to explain the origin of the Moon's *segni bui* ("dark marks," *Par.* 2.49). The first zone of the lowest circle of Hell, Caina, where traitors to family are punished, bears his name.

Richard Lansing

Caina

Caina is the first of the four zones, or ghettoes, of the ninth circle, Cocytus, the lowest circle of Hell. Its name taken from the biblical Cain, modeled perhaps on that of Judecca (the real Venetian ghetto as well as the fourth zone), Caina partially recalls Gen. 4:17, where we are told that Cain built a city during his wanderings. St. Augustine made much of this first human city of evil throughout his *City of God,* Book 15. Cain, murderer of his brother Abel, is cited as an exemplar of the capital sin of envy, although not by name, as he shouts: *Anciderammi qualunque m'apprende* ("Whoever finds me will kill me," *Purg.* 14.133). Cain was also taxed with other root impulsions—injustice, pride, avarice, anger—during the millenia of exegesis and speculation on why precisely Yahweh was displeased with his offering, that of a farmer, which moved Cain to kill Abel, a shepherd. Any and all of these motives are operative in the moral psychology of the denizens of Caina, who are guilty of treachery against kin. It is clear that most of those mentioned in *Inf.* 32 murdered relatives within a political context, although some are so locally and biographically obscure that we cannot be certain who the victim was.

The damned of Caina protrude from the ice from (at most) the neck up; their teeth clacking with the cold, they are able to incline their livid faces down so as to prevent their tears from freezing in their eye sockets. Punished together are the nose-butting reciprocal fratricides Alessandro and Napoleone degli Alberti, counts of Vernia and Mangona (one a Guelf, the other a Ghibelline). Nearby are Vanni de' Cancellieri of Pistoia, nicknamed Focaccia; Sassol(o) Mascheroni, possibly a member of the noble house of the Toschi of Florence; Alberto Camicion (Camiscion) de' Pazzi, of the Ghibelline Pazzi family of Valdarno (he is the spokesman-informer here); and Mordred, who attempted to kill his father-uncle, King Arthur (who is the only non-Italian and nonhistorical figure included).

To these we may add at least four other figures mentioned by Dante elsewhere in the *Commedia,* the first of whom is specifically said to be damned in Caina: (1) Gianciotto, of the Malatesta of Rimini, who slew his wife, Francesca, and his brother Paolo, caught in the act of adultery—if we are to take Francesca's word in *Inf.* 5.107 as true. The rest are guilty of treachery against kin, if not placed in Caina: (2) the mythological Procne, who killed her son, Itys, and fed him to her husband, Tereus, in revenge for his violation (*impietas, Purg.* 17.19); (3) Alcmeon, who killed his disloyal mother, Eryphyle, at the behest of his father, Ampharaus—*per non perder pietà, si fé spietato* ("so as not to fail in piety, [he] made himself impious," *Par.* 4.105) nicely documents the special injustice and mad bestiality which underlie Caina and beyond (*spietato* blending lack of pity with the technical derogation of filial piety); and (4) Pygmalion, brother of Dido and slayer of her first husband, Sychaeus, for which Pygmalion is cited as an exemplar of the capital sin of avarice and is dubbed *traditore e ladro e paricida* ("traitor, thief, and parricide," *Purg.* 20.104)—"parricide" denoting a murder of any close relative (Sychaeus was Pygmalion's brother-in-law and perhaps his uncle as well).

Bibliography

Quinones, Ricardo. *The Changes of Cain: Violence and the Lost Brother in Cain and Abel Literature.* Princeton, N.J.: Princeton University Press, 1991.

Triolo, Alfred A. "Ira, Cupiditas, Libido: The Dynamics of Passion in the *Inferno.*" *Dante Studies* 95 (1977), 1–37; especially pp. 20–23, 28–33.

———. "Matta Bestialità in Dante's *Inferno:* Theory and Image." *Traditio* 24 (1968), 247–292.

Alfred Triolo

Calchas

The soothsayer who accompanied the Greeks to the siege of Troy, whom Dante associates with another soothsayer, Eurypylus. Both Calchas *(Calcanta)* and Eurypylus are damned in the fourth bolgia of the eighth circle of Hell (*Inf.* 20.110). There Dante's guide Virgil, referring to a passage in his *Aeneid,* speaks of their having foretold the time the Greek fleet would sail from Aulis to Troy. The *Aeneid,* however, makes no reference to this event (2.114–124), and it appears that Dante has conflated two events. Calchas, consulted in Aulis *before* the Greeks sailed for Troy, advised Agamemnon to sacrifice Iphigenia (cf. *Par.* 5.67–72) in order to placate the goddess Diana. But Eurypylus is referred to by Virgil *after* the siege of Troy, when the Greeks were preparing to return home. They send Eurypylus to consult the Oracle of Apollo about the favorable time for their departure.

R. A. Malagi

Calixtus I, Pope
Pope Calixtus *(Calisto),* who reigned from 217–222 and died a martyr. He is mentioned in *Par.* 27.44—together with Sixtus I, Pius I, and Urban I—in the recitation given by St. Peter of his own martyrdom.

William Wilson

Calliope
Muse of epic poetry, invoked by Dante the poet in *Purg.* 1.9, along with the other Muses, to assist him in elevating his song from the "dead poetry" of *Inferno.* Since Virgil had also called for Calliope's inspiration (*Aen.* 9.525), the invocation both aligns Dante with authoritative classical epic and subsumes that tradition into his salvific itinerary. It was Calliope (*Calïopè; Calliopè* in modern Italian) whom the Muses chose to represent them in a singing contest to which the Pierides—nine mortal women—had challenged them. The Pierides unwisely chose as their theme the rebellion of the giants; Calliope won the contest handily with a song about Ceres and Proserpina. The Pierides were punished for their insolence by being transformed into magpies (see Ovid, *Meta.* 5.290–678). In asking for Calliope's accompaniment, the poet implicitly distances himself from the Pierides' presumption.

F. Regina Psaki

Camilla
A resident of Limbo among the pagan spirits of renown who live in the noble castle (*Inf.* 4.124). A daughter of Metabus in the service of Artemis and queen of the Voscians, she fought with Turnus against Aeneas as a virgin warrior who died for Italy in the Trojan-Latin War (cf. *Aen.* 7.803–817, 11.759–835). In *Inf.* 1.107 Dante cites her first in a list of combatants who fell in the war on either side of the conflict.

Maria Ann Roglieri

Camillus, Marcus Furius
Hero of the Roman republic, consul in 403 B.C.E., six times consular tribune and five times dictator. He died in 365 B.C.E. Camillus *(Cammillo)* is cited in *Conv.* 4.5.15 and *Mon.* 2.5.12 as placing the good of his country before his own interests. Both passages refer to his voluntarily leaving Rome (after being recalled from exile to defeat the Gauls) until his return was legalized (Livy *Ab urbe condita* 5.32ff., 5.46; Virgil, *Aen.* 6.825).

Leslie Zarker Morgan

Camiscion de' Pazzi
A member of the Pazzi family of the Valdarno. Camiscion was reputed to have killed his kinsman Ubertino and seized property they held in common. Frozen in Caina among traitors to their families, he names nearby sinners and states that his crime will soon be eclipsed by that of his kinsman Carlino de' Pazzi (*Inf.* 32.68).

Pamela J. Benson

Campaldino
A Tuscan village and castle lying between Romena and Poppi in the Casentino, Campaldino is the site of a battle fought between the Florentine Guelfs and the Aretine Ghibellines on June 11, 1289. Then in the cavalry, Dante is believed to have participated with the Guelfs, who were victorious on this occasion. In *Purg.* 5.92, Campaldino is referred to in the story of Buonconte da Montefeltro, a Ghibelline leader who was slain on the bloody battlefield. The opening lines of *Inf.* 22 seem to recall, implicitly, Dante's participation in this battle.

Fiora A. Bassanese

Cangrande della Scala
Ghibelline lord of Verona (1311–1329) and one of Dante's patrons (1291–1329). Cunizza da Romano alludes to his military prowess in *Par.* 9.43–48,

while Cacciaguida tells Dante to look to Cangrande for future favors and protection in *Par.* 17.76–92.

Giorgio Petrocchi places the exiled Dante at the court of Verona from May 1303 to March 1304 during the lordship of Cangrande's older brother Bartolomeo, the *gran Lombardo* ("great Lombard") of *Par.* 17.71, and again from May 1312 to early 1318 during the lordship of Cangrande. Dante's sojourns in Verona isolated him from the petty feuds of other Guelf exiles (*Par.* 17.61–66). Dante's second sojourn was notable not only for the friendship but also for the literary encouragement he evidently received from Cangrande. In *Epist.* 13 (whose authenticity is questioned by some), Dante says he had doubted reports of Cangrande's generosity until he experienced it personally. In this epistle, Dante dedicates *Paradiso* to Cangrande. Petrocchi argues that the laudatory language of *Par.* 17 was inserted to express Dante's gratitude for Cangrande's patronage as the poet prepared to leave Verona for Ravenna. Boccaccio's *Trattatello in laude di Dante* relates how Dante would not let anyone see installments of the *Commedia* until he had shared them with Cangrande (183).

Dante's departure from Cangrande seems to have been prompted by the attractiveness of literary life at the court of Guido Novello da Polenta in Ravenna. The *Trattatello* celebrates Guido for his exceptional dedication to learning (80), while Petrarch's *Rerum memorandarum libri* suggests that a strain of Philistine coarseness may have blemished Cangrande's court (2.83–84). Nevertheless, Dante's friendship with Cangrande survived his departure from the court, for in January 1320 Dante returned to Verona to clarify an argument made in *Inferno* (see *Quest.* 24).

Cangrande is sometimes identified with the mysterious *Veltro* ("Hound") of *Inf.* 1.101–111, whose *nazion sarà tra feltro e feltro* ("birth will be between felt and felt") and who *Di quella umile Italia fia salute* ("will be the salvation of that humble Italy"). The identification is encouraged by his name, *Cane* in full, which, although it actually means "khan," is homonymous with the word for "dog." Some also discern an echo of *tra feltro e feltro* in Cunizza's prophecy in *Par.* 9.52–53: *Piangerà Feltro ancora la difalta / de l'empio suo pastor* ("Feltre will yet weep for the guilt of its wicked shepherd").

Todd Boli

Cantica

Cantica ("canticle") is the designation normally used to describe each of the three large narrative subsections—one for each of the three realms of the afterlife—into which the *Commedia* is divided. While Dante's poem totals one hundred cantos, each canticle is made up of thirty-three cantos (with the opening canto of the *Commedia,* even if nominally part of *Inferno,* serving as a prologue to the poem as a whole). Although *cantica* is now a neutrally descriptive tag, this should not conceal the important fact that its usage by the poet to refer to the organization of his poem is far from unproblematic. The Latin word *canticum* was not employed with the meaning given in the *Commedia* to its Italian variant, just as the vernacular feminine form *cantica* is not attested before Dante.

It comes as no surprise, therefore, that the *Commedia*'s first readers were left perplexed by the term's function and value. Their bafflement would have been increased by the fact that *cantica* was not the only name Dante adopted as a label for

The beginning of Paradiso. Comedia di Danthe Alighieri poeta divino, *with commentary by Cristoforo Landino, published by Jacob del Burgofra[n]co, Venice, 1529. Giamatti Collection: Courtesy of the Mount Holyoke College Archives and Special Collections.*

C his poem's three main subdivisions. In *Inf.* 20, when he first addressed the question of the *Commedia*'s unique structure, Dante employed the term "canzone," a designation which has been largely ignored because it appears to confuse the canticle with the much more famous and very different lyric form of the same name: *Di nova pena mi conven far versi / e dar matera al ventesimo canto / de la prima canzon, ch'è d'i sommersi* ("Of a strange new punishment I must make verses and take matter for the twentieth song of the first canticle, which is of [whose topic is] those submerged," 1–3). Dante utilized *cantica* only at the end of *Purgatorio,* when, for the second and final time, he drew explicit attention to his poem's partitioning into canticles: *ma perché piene son tutte le carte / ordite a questa cantica seconda / non mi lascia più ir lo fren de l'arte* ("but because all the pages are filled that have been laid out for this second canticle, the rein of art permits me to go no further," 33.139–141). From the two references he makes to the canticle, it is clear that Dante considered this to be a narrative (the allusion to *Inferno*'s subject matter) and structural metrical entity (the reference to *Purgatorio*'s preestablished limits). As a narrative-structural unit, the canticle has no obvious precursors in the epic tradition, though it does recall the tripartite divisions which biblical exegetes introduced into the organization of certain scriptural books such as Psalms.

In contrast to what might be imagined from today's highly restricted use, *cantica,* like all Dante's references to his poem, is richly allusive. Beyond its literal technical meaning, *cantica* establishes a series of quite precise correspondences between the *Commedia* and the Bible—correspondences which help to cast light on the poem's stylistic and ideological concerns. In particular, the term binds the *Commedia* to the Song of Songs—the *Cantica canticorum* or, quite simply and suggestively, the *Cantica,* to use the book's medieval titles (*cantica,* in this instance, is, of course, a Latin neuter plural). According to scriptural exegesis, the Song of Songs presented the account of the soul's spiritual progress to God in a literary form which underlined the *Cantica*'s comic characteristics. The relevance of all this for Dante's *comedía* is obvious; equally significant are *canticum*'s more general biblical connotations: its emphasis on praising God as well as its connections to scriptural poetry in general and to prophecy.

Inferno *1, from the Bartholomeo de Zanni da Portese edition of the* Inferno, *Venice, 1507. Reproduced by permission of the John A. Zahm Dante Collection in the Department of Special Collections, University Libraries, University of Notre Dame.*

Such interpretations of *canticum(a)* were widespread in the Middle Ages and would certainly have been familiar to Dante's thirteenth-century commentators. The reason why they failed to connect such meanings to the *Commedia* was probably because they found it difficult to accept Dante's claim that he, as a layperson, was writing a type of verse which owed substantial debts to the Bible. Yet, despite the daring of his position, there is no doubting Dante's intentions. *Cantica* clearly highlights the poem's ties to the Bible and its divine author. At the same time, however, "canzone" links it to secular literature, thereby restricting its dependence on Scripture. Thanks to their synonymous usage in Dante's poem, "canzone" and *cantica* join together to underline that the *comedía*'s singular character results not from its exclusive reliance on any single type of text or tradition but from its novel synthesis of sacred and profane writing.

Zygmunt G. Barański

Canto

Dante employed the vernacular locution "canto," and its Latin equivalent *cantus,* with a variety of meanings. In keeping with contemporary usage, he utilized it to refer to "poetry," "poetic composition," "song," and "singing." At the same time, and most famously, he gave it a new sense. He used "canto" to indicate each of the one hundred units into which the *Commedia* is divided (*Inf.* 20.2, 33.90; *Par.* 5.16, 5.139, though "canto" in this last instance could equally be said to refer to "song").

As well as partitioning his poem into cantos, Dante organized it into three large narrative subsections, one for each of the three realms of the afterlife: Hell, Purgatory, and Paradise. He labeled these subsections "canzoni" (*Inf.* 20.3), or *cantiche* (*Purg.* 33.140), and he distributed the 100 cantos equally among them. Dante was able to maintain a seeming numerical parity among the canticles, since, in line with medieval ideas on textual organization and exegesis, the opening canto of *Inferno,* despite its being a part of the first canticle, serves ideally as a general prologue to the poem as a whole. As a result, and as far as its division into cantos is concerned, the *Commedia* has the following basic structure: 1 + 33 + 33 + 33 = 100 cantos.

In contrast to the mathematical precision with which the poem as a whole is put together, the canto is an elastic structure whose length varies between 115 and 160 lines (the average length of a canto is just over 142 lines). The canto is made up of hendecasyllables which are laid out according to a fluidly interlacing triple rhyme scheme, the so-called *terza rima.* Unlike its flexibility of span and rhyme (and also of style and subject), the confines of the canto are rigidly fixed and clearly marked—first, by its opening and closing with a double rhyme *(rime rilevate)* rather than with a triple one and, second, by its ending with the single line of a new tercet. The canto is thus both a "closed" independent unit and an "open" one, since it unites with other cantos to form both canticles and a "comedy." It has been persuasively argued that one of the reasons why Dante invented the *terza rima,* the canto, and the canticle was to guarantee the integrity of his poem by creating highly determined structures which could resist the tamperings of copyists (Tatlock).

Both the particular units into which the *Commedia* is divided and the deliberately calculated manner of its organization have no obvious precedents in the literary tradition. The length and structure of the canto contrasts sharply with the very long classical epic *libri* (often not far short of a thousand lines), with the continuous unbroken flow of the Old French *romans* and of the Italian *poemetti,* and with the shortish *laisses* of the *chansons* (generally well under one hundred lines in length). By rejecting such forms, Dante perhaps wanted to suggest that none of these types of poetry, because of their conventionality, could provide a framework appropriate for his unique poem. Admittedly, the canto is closer in measure to some of Dante's own lyric *canzoni:* for instance, "Le dolci rime" (146 lines) and "Doglia mi reca" (158 lines). Although this association is noteworthy since it suggests a continuity among different moments of the poet's career—especially since in the Duecento canzoni of more than one hundred lines were extremely rare—what is much more significant is the contrast which emerges between the canzone's restrictions of style and content and the canto's formal and thematic freedom.

Even if no secular poem can serve as a model for the *Commedia*'s structure, there is a type of poetry with which it does have a noticeable affinity. The Bible, too, gathers up a considerable number of independent poetic texts into larger groupings, which then unite with other "books" to constitute the divine work as a whole. This arrangement is especially apparent in the Book of Psalms and the Song of Songs (see *Cantica*). More generally, the *Commedia*'s numerical balance and orderly design—the product of its division into cantos—are meant to highlight its "imitation" of the harmonious patterns of divine creativity. This feature is further underlined by the fact that, according to medieval symbolic thought, 1, 3, and 10—the numbers which control the basic distribution of the *Commedia*'s cantos—were closely associated with God.

Dante claimed God as his "authority" in order to legitimize the *Commedia*'s experimental stylistic and thematic variety, as well as its didactic intentions. The canto is where Dante put his new ideas about literature into practice. As a metrical and narrative unit, it is not tied to any one style or subject. Since it is without an effective precedent, the canto is able to establish its own rules of composition, performing stylistic and thematic switches and syntheses at will, unconstrained by traditional rhetorical notions of discrete "modes of

C writing," each with its own metrical forms. The canto is the fundamental artistic and ideological unit of the *Commedia*. Each canto, because of its versatility, stands as a microcosm of Dante's all-embracing "comedy." And this fact is confirmed by the designation "canto." Dante chose the term to describe the 100 parts of the *Commedia* precisely because of its traditional meaning as poetic composition and as poetry in general (the same reason also holds good for his choice of "canzone," *cantica,* and *comedía*). The all-embracing canto not only can contain any type of poetry and tell any kind of story but, because of its totalizing syncretism, also can give concrete expression to the abstract notion of "poetry." It is no exaggeration to say that, without the canto, there would be no *Commedia*.

Bibliography

Tatlock, J. S. P. "Dante's Terza Rima." In *American Critical Essays on the Divine Comedy.* Edited by Robert J. Clements. New York: New York University Press, 1967, pp. 26–36. Reprinted from *PMLA,* 51 (1936), 895–903.

Zygmunt G. Barański

Canzone

The canzone was developed in Italy under the direct influence of the Provençal *canso,* the Old French *chanson,* and the German minnesong. In the hands of the Sicilian poets, Guittone d'Arezzo, and the *Stilnovisti,* it became, over the course of the thirteenth century, the poetic vehicle par excellence for the treatment of various, particularly amorous topics. In *De vulgari eloquentia* Dante defines the canzone as the most excellent Italian verse form and the only one suitable for the expression, in the tragic style, of the three most noble topics: martial valor, love, and moral virtue (*salus. . . , venus et virtus,* or *armorum probitas, amoris accensio et directio voluntatis,* 2.2.7–8).

In his discussion of the canzone Dante presents a detailed picture of how the stanza functions as a poetic unit. The stanza is generally composed of the more noble verses—hendecasyllables, heptasyllables, and pentasyllables—and is divided into two parts, the *fronte* ("forehead") and the *sirma,* or *cauda* ("tail"). The *fronte* in turn is customarily divided into two equal metrical parts known as *pedes* ("feet"), while the *sirma* may also be divided into two parts, known as *versus* ("verses"). The passage from *fronte* to *sirma*—

which marks the change from one musical pattern to another—is generally known as the *diesis,* a term usually applied to this changeover and often to the first verse of the *sirma,* which introduces this new harmony. The sestina is the only exception to the rule of the divided stanza, and Dante cites his own "Al poco giorno e al gran cerchio d'ombra" as an example of this form (2.10.2). Some canzoni conclude with an envoi (*congedo* or *commiato* or *tornata*), that is, a short stanza generally having the same rhyme scheme as the *sirma* (or part of it), in which the poet addresses his composition and instructs it where it should go, with whom it should speak, what it should say.

According to Dante, an exceptionally fine canzone stanza either will consist of all hendecasyllables or will mix hendecasyllables and heptasyllables and will end each stanza with a rhymed couplet. In his treatise Dante cites many of his own canzoni as examples of stylistic and metrical excellence. One of these is "Donne ch'avete intelletto d'amore" (2.8.8), where we may observe the following structure of the strophe—abbc abbc cdd cee—and note that the *fronte* is composed of two *pedes* and the *sirma* of two *versus* with the *diesis* occurring between verses 8 and 9. This canzone is, notably, the first one of the *Vita Nuova* and the one in which the poet announces his intention to direct his poetry toward a different end, that of praising his lady.

After his invention of *terza rima* for the composition of the *Commedia,* Dante is primarily known as a writer of canzoni, from the first examples on amorous topics in the *Vita Nuova;* to the experimental, technical tours de force, the *rime petrose;* and, finally, to the more mature moral and doctrinal odes of the *Convivio* (i.e., both those included and those intended to be included in that work) and the period of exile. We may gain some insight on Dante's judging of his own compositions by observing which of his canzoni he cites in *De vulgari eloquentia* for their thematic, technical, and stylistic excellence: they are (in addition to the two already mentioned above) "Doglia mi reca ne lo core ardire," "Amor, che movi tua virtù da cielo," "Amor che ne la mente mi ragiona," "Donna pietosa e di novella etate," "Poscia ch'Amor del tutto m'ha lasciato," and "Amor, tu vedi ben che questa donna." We note in this list two canzoni from the *Vita Nuova,* one from the *Convivio,* and two of the *rime petrose,* while the other three would probably have been included in the *Convivio.*

Other of Dante's canzoni deserve mention here: the first and fourth of the *rime petrose,* "Io son venuto al punto de la rota" and "Così nel mio parlar voglio esser aspro"; the great allegorical canzone of exile, "Tre donne intorno al cor mi son venute"; and the canzone on nobility on which the fourth book of the *Convivio* is based, "Le dolci rime d'amor ch'i' solìa."

Bibliography

Beltrami, Pietro G. *Metrica, poetica, metrica dantesca.* Pisa: Pacini, 1981.

Boyde, Patrick. *Dante's Style in His Lyric Poetry.* Cambridge: Cambridge University Press, 1971.

———. "Dante's Lyric Poetry." In *The Mind of Dante.* Edited by Uberto Limentani. Cambridge: Cambridge University Press, 1965, pp. 79–112.

Cremante, Renzo, and Mario Pazzaglia (eds.). *La metrica.* Bologna: Il Mulino, 1973.

Fubini, Mario. *Metrica e poesia: Lezioni sulle forme poetiche italiane.* Milan: Feltrinelli, 1970.

Lisio, Giuseppe. *Studio sulla forma metrica della canzone italiana nel secolo XIII.* Imola: Galeati, 1895.

Pazzaglia, Mario. *Il verso e l'arte della canzone nel De vulgari eloquentia.* Florence: La Nuova Italia, 1967.

Spongano, Raffaele. *Nozioni ed esempi di metrica italiana.* Bologna: Pàtron, 1974.

Wilkins, Ernest Hatch. "The Canzone and the Minnesong." In *The Invention of the Sonnet and Other Studies in Italian Literature.* Rome: Edizioni di Storia e Letteratura, 1959, pp. 41–50. *Modern Philology* 12 (1914–1915), 527–558.

Christopher Kleinhenz

Capaneus

One of the seven mythical Greeks kings who attacked Thebes in support of Polynices, whose dispute with his brother Eteocles over the sovereignty of the city led to war. The war is the subject of Aeschylus' tragedy *The Seven against Thebes* and of Statius' epic poem the *Thebaid.* Upon scaling the walls of the city, Capaneus *(Capaneo)* madly challenged Jupiter, who struck him down with a thunderbolt. He is placed in the first zone of the seventh circle's third ring, where he is punished for blasphemy, which in Dante's scheme is a sin of violence against the Deity *(Inf.* 14.46).

Dante draws on Statius' description of Capaneus to create the character who foolishly and arrogantly refuses to accept God's omnipotence. Whereas in Statius, Capaneus is referred to as heroic and even magnanimous, in Dante his only greatness is that of physical proportion, for he lacks the dignity of such figures as Farinata degli Uberti *(Inf.* 10.73ff.) or Jason *(Inf.* 18.83–96). Dante sees in Capaneus the epitome of pride and presumption, and as such he is a *figura diaboli* or a *figura Luciferis* whose impious defiance of God represents an act of utter futility.

Bibliography

Bosco, Umberto. "Il canto XIV dell'*Inferno.*" In *Nuove Letture Dantesche.* Vol 2. Florence: Le Monnier, 1968, pp. 47–73.

Di Scipio, Giuseppe. "Inferno XIV." In *Dante's "Divine Comedy": Introductory Readings. I: "Inferno."* Edited by Tibor Wlassics. *Lectura Dantis* VI: Supplement (Spring): Special Issue: *Lectura Dantis Virginiana,* I, 173–188.

Paratore, Ettore. "Il canto XIV dell'*Inferno.*" In *Tradizione e struttura in Dante.* Florence: Sansoni, 1968, pp. 221–249.

Giuseppe Di Scipio

Capocchio

An important minor figure in *Inferno,* Capocchio ("Blockhead"), alchemist and falsifier of metals, represents himself as once acquainted with Dante *(Inf.* 29.135, 138), who should recall, he says, *"com'io fui di natura buona scimia"* ("how good an ape I was of Nature," 139). A Florentine, or perhaps a Sienese, he is damned as an alchemist. He thus emphasizes the problem of imitation in the bolgia of the falsifiers, the tenth pouch of Malebolge, suggesting to some recent commentators that Dante is making an oblique comment on his own involvement in imitation—a possibility reinforced perhaps by the story told by the commentator Benvenuto that one Good Friday Capocchio painted the entire story of Christ's Passion on his fingernails, only to erase it from them when Dante surprised him, and Dante thereupon reproached him for destroying something so wondrous.

R. Allen Shoaf

Caprona

A fortress located on a hill overlooking the river Arno, about five miles east of Pisa. In August 1289 Guelf forces, mainly from Lucca and Florence, attacked and captured several fortresses, including

Caprona, in response to the expulsion of Guelfs from Ghibelline Pisa. In *Inf.* 21.94–96, Dante compares the fear felt by the pilgrim—emerging from his hiding place to be confronted by menacing devils—to that which he saw in the faces of the soldiers surrendering at Caprona. Dante represents himself as an eyewitness to the event, and it is probable that he himself was a member of the victorious Guelf army.

Mark Balfour

Carlino de' Pazzi

Betrayed his people and three members of his own family by giving over to the Black Guelfs of Florence control of the castle of Piantravigne, thereby causing the capitulation of Pistoia. In *Inf.* 32.69, Carlino's kinsman, Camiscion de' Pazzi, foretells Carlino's act of treachery, which took place in 1302 and was therefore after the date of the pilgrim's journey. Camiscion, who resides in Caina among the traitors to kin, suggests that Carlino's sin will be far worse than his own, warranting his future placement in Antenora among the traitors to homeland or political party.

Pina Palma

Casalodi

The Guelf counts of Casalodi, a castle near Brescia, were nobles of Mantua until 1272, when Count Alberto was deceived by Pinamonte dei Bonaccolsi into removing his supporters from the city; there followed the massacre or exile of many of Mantua's nobility. For this reason Virgil terms Alberto *la mattia da Casalodi* ("the fool of Casalodi," *Inf.* 20.95).

Mark Balfour

Casella

Musician of Florence and friend of Dante who meets him on the shores of Ante-Purgatory in what is the poet-pilgrim's first encounter with souls who are saved, *la nova gente* (*Purg.* 2.58). According to contemporary records and the early commentators, Casella was famous for his singing voice and his ability to set poems to music. The Anonimo Fiorentino states that Casella was from Pistoia and that he composed music for many of Dante's songs and ballads, which the poet took great pleasure in hearing. A manuscript in the Vat-

ican also identifies him as a composer who set to music compositions by one Lemmo of Pistoia. Benvenuto da Imola says that Casella was from Florence and that Dante, when weary from study or excited by love's passion, used to revive his spirits by listening to him sing. An important, specific biographical fact survives in a document from Siena, dated July 13, 1282, which records a fine against Casella for wandering the streets at night; thus, the musician's death—the date of which is unknown—must have occurred between that date and the year 1300.

Though the specific Casella episode (*Purg.* 2.76–114) occupies center stage of the second half of the canto, the entire canto is its proper context. Casella, as yet unrecognized, is one of the hundred spirits Dante hears singing in unison the great Exodus psalm *"In exitu Israel de Aegypto"* (113 [114]) as they are being ferried to the shores of Purgatory by an angelic steersman (43–48). Thus, the singer and musician's initial appearance is counterbalanced by his final action in the scene in which Dante requests that he comfort his soul and his weary body by singing to him as he did in the past, and Casella complies by performing Dante's canzone from *Conv.* 3, "Amor che ne la mente mi ragiona" (106–114); the enraptured audience reaction of Dante, Virgil, and the other spirits elicits a harsh rebuke from Cato (115–123). Between these two songs—psalm and autocitation—the episode contains two more actions. The first is a dramatic event in which Casella draws forward from the group of new souls, who marvel at seeing a living man in this setting, and attempts to embrace Dante, who is moved to do the same; after three vain attempts to embrace, Dante recognizes his old friend, and they speak (76–87). This, in turn, evolves into a notably affectionate dialogue in which Casella, expressing his love—*Così com'io t'amai / nel mortal corpo, così t'amo sciolta: / però m'arresto* ("Just as I loved you in the mortal body, so do I love when loosed from it; therefore I stop")—asks Dante why he is going up the mountain (88–90). Responding in kind—*Casella mio, per tornar altra volta / là dov'io son, fo io questo vïaggio* ("My Casella, to return another time do I go on this journey")—Dante then, as though aware of the date of Casella's death, asks him why he has lost so much time in coming (91–93). Casella answers by saying that, having been denied passage many times, he was finally allowed, under an opportunity offered to all during the last three months, to embark from where the Tiber flows into the sea, where all the souls who do not sink to Acheron gather (94–105). Dante then asks him to sing.

Traditionally, this second canto of *Purgatorio* has been viewed as a major turning point in the *Commedia,* controlled as it is by the Exodus figure of conversion; and the encounter between Dante and Casella has been interpreted as the central episode, which conveys the meaning of this pivotal moment—although there are differing perceptions of the significance of the episode and its parts. The failed embrace has been taken as one of many contributions to a pattern of negative elements that, combined with Cato's sharp reprimand, remind the reader that Dante's responses to what he is experiencing are still flawed and inadequate; it has also been interpreted as an appropriation from the epic tradition (see *Aen.* 2.792–794, 6.700–702) in which the failed embrace between Dante and Casella emulates that of Aeneas and Creusa and of Aeneas and Anchises in order to draw attention to Dante's steady movement toward fulfilling the classical half of his destined role as visionary that he denied himself at the beginning of his journey: *Io non Enëa, io non Paulo sono* ("I am not Aeneas, I am not Paul," *Inf.* 2.32). Related to this view is the assertion that Casella's performance of Dante's canzone, which the composer previously might have set to music, successfully unites the two Christian souls, if only for a fleeting moment, in a way that the motif of the classical embrace cannot. Opinion about the import of Casella's song itself is basically divided between those who view it as primarily recreational and those who believe it offers an advance over the poetry of passion through the full force of its philosophical message. This latter view, in turn, has yielded a division of positions concerning the severity of Cato's rebuke of the song's listeners at the end of the canto into those who minimize it as a corrective to a minor fault and those who argue that it strongly repudiates the poem as a vain and tempting message of Lady Philosophy, to whom the song is dedicated in the *Convivio.* This latter position rejects Philosophy's message as a way of attaining happiness on various grounds, including one which explains this rejection in terms of medieval theories of profane and sacred music. As for the delay in Casella's arrival in Purgatory on Easter Sunday of 1300—a detail that has never been fully explained—there is some clarification in the recognition of its literary indebtedness to

two passages in the *Aeneid* (3.201–206, 6.315–330) and its historical relation to the plenary indulgence granted by Pope Boniface VIII on Christmas of 1299 (see "Jubilee"). Suffice it to say that even if Dante deliberately invented the delay, as has been suggested, it provided him with a rare opportunity to show for the first of several times in the remainder of this canticle his charity toward dear friends and his joy at their salvation.

Bibliography

Barolini, Teodolinda. *Dante's Poets: Textuality and Truth in the "Comedy."* Princeton, N.J.: Princeton University Press, 1984.

Economou, George D. "Self-Consciousness of Poetic Activity in Dante and Langland." In *Vernacular Poetics in the Middle Ages.* Edited by Lois Ebin. Kalamazoo, Mich.: Medieval Institute Publications, 1984, pp. 177–198.

Freccero, John. "Casella's Song: *Purgatorio* II, 12." In *Dante: The Poetics of Conversion.* Edited by Rachel Jacoff. Cambridge, Mass.: Harvard University Press, 1986, pp. 186–194.

Hollander, Robert. "*Purgatorio* II." In *Dante's "Divine Comedy": Introductory Readings.* Special issue: *Lectura Dantis Virginiana.* Vol. 2: *Purgatorio* (Spring 1993), 17–34.

Iannucci, Amilcare A. "Casella's Song and the Tuning of the Soul." *Thought* 65 (1990), 27–46.

George D. Economou

Cassino, Monte

Cassino is a mountain in Campania, between Rome and Naples, and site of a temple where Apollo was worshiped by *la gente ingannata e mal disposta* ("a people deceived and ill disposed," *Par.* 22.39). St. Benedict destroyed the temple and built a monastery in its place (c. 529), where he wrote his monastic rule *(Regula Monachorum)* and later died (c. 543). It is generally accepted that Dante derives the topographical detail of his description in *Par.* 22.37 from Gregory the Great's *Dialogues* (2.2).

Mark Balfour

Cassius, Gaius Longinus

One of the assassins of Caesar on the Ides of March in 44 B.C.E. Despite Cassius' alliance with Pompey at Pharsalia (48 B.C.E.), Caesar pardoned him and even promoted him to praetor.

Notwithstanding Caesar's magnanimity, Cassius (*Cassio*) remained bitterly opposed to him. He was the chief organizer of the plot to overthrow the emperor and is thought to have been personally responsible for convincing Brutus to participate in the conspiracy. For what Dante perceived as acts of treason against the Empire, he places Cassius in one of Lucifer's mouths, in the zone Judecca of the ninth circle of Hell (*Inf.* 34.67). He is mentioned as well by the emperor Justinian in *Par.* 6.74.

Michael Papio

Castelvetro, Lodovico

This native of Modena (c. 1505–1571) was one of Renaissance Italy's foremost and controversial literary critics. His formal education in some of the most prestigious universities was a stepping-stone to a career extending beyond his homeland and highlighting some of Italy's most famous poets. While Castelvetro's fame rests mainly on his commentary on Aristotle's *Poetics,* published in Vienna in 1570, his earlier works on Dante deserve equal attention. Soon after his university studies, Castelvetro became embroiled in a literary dispute with the poet Annibal Caro, a formidable opponent, who was then at the service of Cardinal Farnese. As a result of the dispute, Castelvetro was accused of heresy, summoned before the Tribunal of the Inquisition, and forced to seek refuge abroad. Before leaving Modena on the way to his exile, he annotated a volume of Dante's *Commedia* with the commentary by Cristoforo Landino, a volume which is known as the *Chiose.* In it, he tempered the Ficinian idealism of Landino's commentary with a great deal of realism. In a commentary on Petrarch's *Rime,* published posthumously, he tried to show Dante's superiority over the other major Italian poet. Castelvetro's perspective, articulated in the *Chiose,* resurfaced twenty-five years later in his *Sposizione a XXIX Canti dell'Inferno dantesco,* written around 1570, where he argued, in Aristotelian terms, that the *Commedia* is narrative and epic in form: Dante might have called it a "comedy" as a token of respect for Virgil, who had written his *Aeneid* in Latin, a language superior to the Italian in which the *Commedia* was written. Castelvetro, therefore, opposed the commentators who believed that the *Commedia* had been so named by Dante because it resembled a comedy and, as such, was divided into three acts: *Inferno, Purgatorio,* and *Paradiso.*

Bibliography

Castelvetro, Lodovico. *Le Rime del Petrarca brevemente sposte.* Basel: Pietro de Sedabonis, 1582.
———. *Sposizione a XXIX Canti dell'Inferno dantesco.* Edited by G. Franciosi. Modena: Tipi della Società Tipografica, 1886.
Melzi, Robert. *Castelvetro's Annotations to the Inferno.* The Hague: Mouton, 1966.
Parker, Deborah. *Commentary and Ideology: Dante in the Renaissance.* Durham, N.C.: Duke University Press, 1993.
Vallone, Aldo. *Storia della critica dantesca dal XIV al XX secolo.* Padua: La Nuova Libraria Editrice, 1981, vol. 1, pp. 423–428.

Robert C. Melzi

Catalano

Catalano de' Malavolti, or Catalano di Guido di Madonna Ostia (c. 1210–1285), was one of the original founders of the Confraternity of the Knights of the Blessed Virgin Mary, an organization formed in Bologna c. 1261 to protect widows and orphans and to assist in the mediation of civic disputes. Because of the members' predilection for sumptuous feasts, however, they soon came to be known as the *frati godenti* ("Jovial Friars"). After the battle of Benevento in 1266, Pope Clement IV had Catalano, a Guelf, and Loderingo, a Ghibelline, appointed as joint holders of the office of podestà in Florence (of which there had formerly been only one). Though such an arrangement was ostensibly meant as an attempt at political reconciliation, all the *frati godenti* had taken an oath of absolute allegiance to the pope and were therefore little more than minions in Clement's plot to oust the Ghibellines from the city. Soon after Catalano and Loderingo assumed office, they formed the "Council of Thirty-six," a governing panel that comprised members of both parties. Guido Novello and other Ghibellines who were bitterly opposed to the council were run out of Florence by the populace, and many of their homes (in the neighborhood known as Gardingo) were sacked. Having lost all appearance of impartiality, Catalano then returned to Bologna. Dante places him in the bolgia of the hypocrites (*Inf.* 23.76–144).

Michael Papio

Catello di Rosso Gianfigliazzi

In the seventh circle of Hell, among the violent against nature, the usurers are identified indirectly by the heraldic arms they wear. The coat of arms associated with one group of usurers—*in una borsa gialla vidi azzurro / che d'un leone avea faccia e contegno* ("on a yellow purse I saw blue that had the shape and bearing of a lion, *Inf.* 17.59–60)—is that of the Gianfigliazzi family of notable Black Guelfs. Catello, who was a money-lender in France and was knighted upon his return to Florence, is thought to be referred to here.

F. Regina Psaki

Cathars

Christian heretics who flourished, particularly in the twelfth century, in Languedoc, Lombardy, and central Italy. They were decimated in the four-teenth century as a result of the Crusade in Languedoc (1209–1229), the Inquisition, and the new attraction of the Dominican and Franciscan orders.

Their beliefs, based on the dualistic opposi-tion of good and evil, were inherited less from Per-sian Manichaeism than from Gnosticism and may be related to Bulgarian Bogomilism. Cathars believed that this world, in which evil is manifested through matter and time, was essentially a kind of hell and prison house that stood in opposition to the Kingdom of God. Therefore procreation—sig-nifying the creation of what amounted to a jail for the spirit—was considered an evil, and conse-quently marriage was forbidden. Cathars did not believe in the Incarnation (that God was made flesh), in the real presence of Christ in the Eucharist, in the redemptive value of Christ's Pas-sion, in the Last Judgment, or in the resurrection of the body. Salvation, which liberates the soul from this world (Hell), is obtained by the *conso-lamentum:* a baptism given by a "perfect" through the imposition of hands—a rite very often delayed until the time of death. The "perfects" practiced chastity and severe fasting, and they refused to take oaths and rejected the Christian sacraments.

Cathars called themselves "good men," or "God's Friends," a literal translation of the Slavonic "Bogomil" (equivalent to the Greek "Theophile"). They are referred to as "Albigen-sians," a name taken from the city of Albi in south-ern France to which St. Bernard went to preach against the heresy; as "Weavers," because of their association with the cloth trade; and in Italy as "Paterini" from the Pataria, an area in Milan asso-ciated with the secondhand clothes trade. Their adversaries named them "Cathars," from the Greek *katharoi* ("pure"), because of their ascetic ideals (although according to Alain de Lille the name derived from *cattus* ["cat"], the form under which the devil was worshiped in sorcery); and "bougres" ("Bulgares"), which became such an infamous term that it meant both a sodomite (in reference to their supposed antiprocreative sexual activity) and usurer (the other dreadful medieval insult).

Catharism is known through the works of the partisans of the Crusade and of Catholic theolo-gians who wrote against it, the reports of the Inqui-sition (1234–c. 1350), two treatises in Latin (one of which is in Florence and summarizes Jean Lugio of Bergamo's *Book of the Two Principles*), and two rituals (one in Latin, the other in Occitan).

Dante does not make direct mention of either the Cathars or the Albigensians, but he signals his approval of the ecclesiastic attack on the Albigen-sians by his placement of two crusaders in Par-adise. St. Dominic, appearing in the sphere of the Sun, is portrayed as a tireless militant against the *mondo errante* ("errors of the world," i.e., mainly, the Albigensians, *Par.* 12.94); and in the sphere of Venus, Dante sees Folco of Marseilles, troubadour love poet turned Cistercian monk and later appointed bishop of Toulouse, who was known to have been a vigorous and particularly merciless persecutor of heretics in southern France, although Dante makes no mention of this fact. Farinata, who is punished as a heretic in the sixth circle of Hell (canto 10), was a known Cathar, so it is conceiv-able that Dante meant to include the Cathars along with the Epicureans in this part of the underworld.

Bibliography

Armour, Peter. "Dante's Brunetto: The Paternal Paterine?" *Italian Studies* 38 (1983), 1–38.

Borst, Arno. *Die Katharer.* Stuttgart: Hiersemann, 1953.

Duvernoy, Jean. *Le catharisme.* Vol. 1: "La religion des Cathares." Vol. 2: "Histoire des Cathares." Toulouse: Privat, 1976, 1979.

Hamilton, Bernard. *The Medieval Inquisition.* Lon-don: Edward Arnold, 1981.

———. *Monastic Reform, Catharism and the Cru-sades (900–1300).* London: Variorum, 1979.

Lambert, Malcolm David. *Medieval Heresy: Popular Movements from Bogomil to Hus.* 2nd ed. London: 1977, 1992.

Lansing, Carol. *Power and Purity: Cathar Heresy in Medieval Italy.* New York: Oxford University Press, 1998.

Leff, Gordon. *Heresy in the Later Middle Ages, c. 1250–1450.* 2 vols. Manchester: Manchester University Press, 1967.

Manselli, Raoul. *L'eresia del male.* Naples: Morano, 1963.

Moore, Robert Ian. *The Origins of European Dissent.* Oxford: Blackwell, 1985.

Nelli, René (tr.). *Écritures cathares.* Paris: Planète, 1968.

Roquebert, Michel. *L'épopée cathare 1209–1229.* 3 vols. Toulouse: Privat, 1970, 1977, 1986.

Yolande de Pontfarcy

Cato of Utica

The historical Marcus Porcius Cato Uticensis (95–46 B.C.E.), descended from an old Roman senatorial family. His great-grandfather was Cato the Elder, the censor who promoted the destruction of Carthage at the end of the Punic Wars (*Conv.* 4.27.16). Like his ancestor, the younger Cato gained a reputation for strict moral discipline on Stoic principles (*Conv.* 4.6.10). Cato backed Cicero against Catiline; after Julius Caesar became consul in 59 B.C.E. with the support of Pompey and Crassus, Cato emerged as a leader of the aristocratic resistance to Caesar's autocratic tendencies. After Caesar crossed the Rubicon in 49 to precipitate the civil war (49–45 B.C.E.), Cato and Pompey joined to oppose him. Campaigning against Caesar's forces in North Africa after Pompey's defeat at Pharsalus (48 B.C.E.), Cato had initial success, only to be defeated at Thapsus. Rather than submit to Caesar—which for an aristocratic Roman of the republic was the equivalent of slavery—Cato withdrew to Utica and died a suicide there after reading Plato's *Phaedo* on the death of Socrates.

For treatments of Cato in the *Convivio* (4.5.16–17, 4.28.13–19, *Catone*), the *Commedia* (*Inf.* 14.13–15, *Caton; Purg.* 1.31–108, *un veglio* ["an old man"], 2.119–123), and the *Monarchia* (2.5.15–17, *Cato*), Dante drew from Roman imperial writers fascinated by Cato as a symbol of the political freedom and moral virtue lost with the passing of the republic: Cicero, Seneca, and Seneca's nephew Lucan, author of a historical epic on the civil war, the *Pharsalia,* in which Cato represents the last refuge of republican liberty. Virgil's cameo at *Aen.* 8.670 showing *secretos . . . pios his dantem iura Catonem* ("the just, off by themselves, and Cato giving laws to them") also helped authorize Dante's placement of Cato among the saved (*Aen.* 8.664–669). Medieval vernacular sources, e.g., the *Fet des Romans* and the *Disticha Catonis,* were probably less influential, but renewed interest in Roman history in Dante's day had made of Cato an exemplum for medieval defenses of the *bonum commune* ("common good"), or local communal government, against tyrannical overlords of all stripes—as in texts of Remigio de' Girolami, a Dominican preacher in Florence known to Dante. In this context, Cato's suicide, as Ernst Kantorowicz pointed out, exemplified the ideal—resurgent in the thirteenth century—of dying nobly for one's country (*pro patria mori*).

Ancient and medieval writers agreed that Cato had possessed the four cardinal virtues (prudence, fortitude, temperance, and justice) perfectively, which made him the living embodiment of virtue. But given that for Dante freedom consisted in uncoerced adherence to Roman law (*Epist.* 6.23), Dante's Cato, in his possession of justice, also embodies the moral freedom that Roman law—administered by the empire—was divinely appointed to foster in secular life. Thus, although the opponent of Caesar (whom Dante erroneously considered the first emperor), Cato represents the virtuous citizen that Dante's empire was designed to fashion: one who lived not for himself but for his fellow citizens and all the world (*Phars.* 2.380–383; *Conv.* 4.27.3).

The exaltation of Cato in the *Convivio* draws from Lucan in referring to the "most sacred breast of Cato" (*Conv.* 4.5.16; *Phars.* 2.285). In Dante's list of Romans "not just human, but divine citizens, inspired with a divine love for their city," it is with mention of Cato—indirectly compared to St. Paul (*Conv.* 4.5.16)—that Dante raises the level of praise, making him first among Roman citizens not only virtuous but recipients of an additional "light of divine goodness" and chosen to be direct instruments of God's providential design for Rome; Cato's suicide, however, is not mentioned. Near the end of the *Convivio* (4.21–28) Dante elaborates an allegorical treatment of the virtues appropriate for each stage of human life. To conclude the itinerary (*Conv.* 4.28.13–19), Dante

Cato beneath the four stars of the southern hemisphere. Opere di Dante Alighieri, *edited by Cristoforo Zapate de Cisneros, Venice, 1757–1758. Giamatti Collection: Courtesy of the Mount Holyoke College Archives and Special Collections.*

panding on *Conv.* 4.5.10–20), Dante not only makes Cato the "stern guardian" of liberty but also praises his suicide as an *inenarrabile sacrificium* ("indescribable sacrifice") for the common good, while pointedly grouping Cato with Romans like the Decii who gave their lives for their country. Unmentioned in the *Convivio*, Cato's self-sacrifice now reveals the hand of God shaping the providential history that endowed Rome with universal empire. With the clear implication that Cato's manner of death was sanctioned by God, Dante contradicts the skeptical account of its merit by Augustine (*De civ. Dei* 1.23). Cato's political martyrdom remained the basis of Dante's conception of Cato's suicide in the *Commedia,* whence it would descend to haunt both Renaissance writers on republican virtue and the martyrs of the Italian *Risorgimento,* including Foscolo's Jacopo Ortis.

In *Inferno,* Dante compares the desert sands the pilgrim traverses in the circle of the violent (*Inf.* 14.15) with the Libyan sands trod by Cato in Lucan's poem (*Phars.* 9.378, 394–395). As John A. Scott showed, the pilgrim's walk through Hell to the island of Purgatory in the Southern Hemisphere parallels Cato's march southward to evade Caesar's tyranny (cf. *Conv.* 3.5.12) and contrasts with the voyage of Ulysses to shipwreck off the mountain of Purgatory (*Inf.* 26.133–142). Dante juxtaposes Cato's prudence, Scott suggests, to Ulysses's *astutia,* which Thomas Aquinas identified as a specific perversion of prudence. As positive and negative exempla, Cato and Ulysses reflect aspects of the pilgrim himself, also on a dangerous journey toward salvation (the old commentator Benvenuto da Imola remarks Dante's esteem for a moral rigor, and one could add moral isolation, that mirrored Dante's own).

In canto 1 of *Purgatorio* Cato challenges the pilgrim and Virgil, whose arrival by subterranean passage—rather than angelic boat—seems to breach the law forbidding emergence from Hell (40–48). Cato's watchdog function and aged appearance echo the function and appearance of Charon in Hell (*Inf.* 3.83: "an old man"). Dante again follows Lucan (*Phars.* 2.372–376) in giving Cato a long, forked, grizzled beard; his face shines brightly as the Sun with the light of the four stars, symbolizing the cardinal virtues, which the pilgrim had just seen near the southern celestial pole (22–39). Cato's radiant visage recalls that of Christ (2 Cor. 3:18; Apoc. 1:16) and of figures in medieval vision literature who are custodians of

attributes to Lucan the allegorical construction of Cato's remarriage to his former wife Marcia, who begs to be taken back by him after the death of her husband Hortensius (*Phars.* 2.326–391): since Cato's perfect virtue makes him the human most suitable to stand for God (*Conv.* 4.28.15), Marcia's return to Cato signifies the return in old age of the human soul to its Creator, in preparation for death. Cato's role in the *Convivio* as the receiver of a virtuous soul in some respects anticipates the role Dante gives him subsequently as the guardian of Purgatory.

Cicero (*De officiis* 1.31) had reasoned that, given Cato's perfect probity, his suicide—unlike all other examples—lay beyond suspicion of cowardice or self-interest. Lucan for his part shows Cato wishing to shed his blood as an expiatory scapegoat who might spare Rome civil war (*Phars.* 2.306–313), a passage whose resemblance to the voluntary sacrifice of Christ did not escape medieval readers. Thus, in *Mon.* 2.5.15–16 (ex-

Hell and Purgatory; some readers have suggested a parallel between Cato and Moses, lawgiver to Israel and leader of the Exodus, whose face shone after speaking with God (Exod. 34.29)—a reading consistent with views of Cato as a Roman forerunner of the authentic moral freedom that St. Paul claimed was offered by Christianity (Rom. 8:21; Gal. 5:13). Cato does not name himself but is recognized by Virgil, who requests that the pilgrim, in his pursuit of freedom *(libertà),* be admitted to Cato's "seven realms" *(Purg.* 1.64–73, 82). Unless Virgil is mistaken, or exaggerates for the sake of obtaining Cato's favor, this suggests that Cato, the exemplum of moral freedom, is warden of Purgatory as a whole. Dante's initial description of Cato as "worthy, by his appearance, of so much reverence that never son owed father more" anticipates the language of *Mon.* 3.3.18 and 3.16.18, where Dante proclaims first his and then the emperor's duty of reverence for the papacy as an institution—and hints at how Cato, as guardian of the quest for moral virtue, might work in tandem with the angelic gatekeeper of the terraces of purgation *(Purg.* 9.104), who has his keys from St. Peter, like the pope.

Though mollified by Virgil's mention of the divine assistance offered by Beatrice, Cato is unmoved by Virgil's ingratiating reference to Marcia, for, as Cato explains, the worldly bond to his wife was broken when he departed Limbo *(Purg.* 1.76–93): the clear implication is that Cato, liberated during Christ's descent into Hell, is among the saved. Indeed, Virgil's reference to Cato's suicide as driven by love of liberty—because of which his body, shed at Utica, will one day be glorified (75: *ch'al gran dì sarà sì chiara* ["that will be so bright on the great day"])—strongly indicates that Cato is destined for Paradise and, indeed, that Cato's devotion to freedom anticipates St. Francis' devotion to poverty *(Par.* 11.58–84). However, if guardian of all or part of the island, Cato would probably remain in Purgatory until the Day of Judgment; to what extent this implies a penitential delay imposed on him remains controversial.

Virgil's mention of Utica, which serves to name Cato for *Purgatorio,* also indicates that Cato's salvation was not in spite of, but because of, his suicide: thus for Giuseppe Mazzotta Cato's suicide renders literally the ethical self-mortification by which the "new man" puts off the "old" (Paul, Eph. 4:22–24). Also dictated by Christian values is Cato's requirement that the pilgrim be girded with a rush and cleanse his face of tears and soot left by the passage of Hell *(Purg.* 1.93–99); following his instruction the wayfarers descend to the shore and use the humble dew collected there to wash the pilgrim's face, possibly invoking Christian humility as the "custodian of all the virtues" *(Purg.* 1.121–136).

In an episode often interpreted as a tropology (a moral lesson addressed to the reader and all the living), Cato returns to break up the rapt audition of a rendering by Casella of Dante's canzone "Amor che nella mente mi ragiona" *(Purg.* 2.120–123), recalling the souls—and the wayfarers—to their task. Cato neither reappears nor is mentioned again in the poem, though his monitory function is echoed in the "whips" and "bridles" of moral examples that reeducate the souls on the seven terraces *(Purg.* 13.39–40).

The presence of Cato in Purgatory has long challenged readers, since as an apparent pagan, a suicide, and an enemy of Caesar, founder of the empire, Cato would seem unfit for salvation by Dante. Most early commentators (Pietro di Dante and Bernardino Daniello are exceptions) evaded the difficulties by insisting that Dante thought of Cato merely as a symbol of human virtue; only in modern times did the consensus emerge that the moral exemplum and historical character coincide. But despite the implicit parallel between Cato's sacrifice and that of Christ, Cato's presence in *Purgatorio,* like that of the excommunicated Manfred two cantos later, was surely intended to surprise readers. Although other pagans (e.g., Ripheus and Trajan) are extraordinarily saved, they are not so prominent in the poem as Cato, nor is their acquisition of the faith necessary to salvation left inexplicit; and although other illustrious Romans of the republican era are mentioned (cf. Scipio Africanus), these had not opposed Caesar's interests in war. The greatest possible contrast is thus drawn between Brutus and Cassius—Cato's former allies and themselves suicides, punished deep in Hell as the murderers of Caesar *(Inf.* 34.64–67)—and Cato, found just a few lines later on the shore of Purgatory. Caesar himself remains confined to Limbo *(Inf.* 4.123), from which Cato has been freed. Placing Cato on the threshold between Hell and Purgatory, Dante has him mark the historical and cultural horizon where the moral and civic values sacred to Rome fuse with Christian humility and sacrifice. The fusion is remarkable; for Dante, Cato's salvation was a marvel of God's providential design for Roman history.

Constructing the relation of Cato's self-sacrificing love of political liberty to the moral freedom that is the goal of a Christian Purgatory is thus arguably central to Dante's conception of Cato. Erich Auerbach's view that Cato, as a figure who fulfills in the afterlife his historical existence on Earth, transposes a love of political freedom into one signifying not "civic virtue and the law" but the "freedom of the immortal soul in the sight of God" has been influential and summarizes the dominant view. But Auerbach too hastily transcends Cato's secular political meaning. Balance is offered by Scott's claim for Dante's Cato as the embodiment of the glorious tradition of republican Rome; along with Ripheus and Trajan, Cato was devoted to the justice and law that steered Dante's ideal, universal empire. For Christian souls who arrive in Purgatory to be purified, Cato's surprising example, no less than his admonitions, serves as an exhortation to the discipline of moral liberation that lies ahead; but for contemporary readers of the poem, Cato's salvation was evidence of the sacred task of Roman law in promoting that happiness in this present life which Dante saw figured in the Earthly Paradise at the summit of the mountain of Purgatory (*Mon.* 3.16.7).

Bibliography

Auerbach, Erich. *"Figura."* In *Scenes from the Drama of European Literature.* New York: Meridian, 1959, pp. 11–76. First published in German in *Neue Dantestudien* (Istanbul), 1944, pp. 11–71.

Beer, Jeanette. *A Medieval Caesar.* Geneva: Droz, 1976.

de Angelis, Violetta. *"'. . . e l'ultimo Lucano.'"* In *Dante e la bella scola della poesia.* Edited by Amilcare Iannucci. Ravenna: Longo, 1993, pp. 145–206.

Hollander, Robert. "The Figural Density of Francesca, Ulysses, and Cato." In *Allegory in Dante's Commedia.* Princeton, N.J.: Princeton University Press, 1969, pp. 104–135.

Kantorowicz, Ernst. *The King's Two Bodies: A Study in Medieval Political Theology.* Princeton, N.J.: Princeton University Press, 1957.

Mazzotta, Giuseppe. "Opus restaurationis." In *Dante, Poet of the Desert: History and Allegory in the Divina Commedia.* Princeton, N.J.: Princeton University Press, 1979, pp. 14–65.

Paratore, Ettore. "Lucano e Dante." In *Antico e nuovo.* Rome: Sciascia, 1965, pp. 165–210.

Raimondi, Ezio. "Rito e Storia nel I canto del *Purgatorio.*" In *Metafora e storia: Studi su Dante e Petrarca.* Turin: Einaudi, 1972, pp. 65–94.

Scott, John A. "Cato, a Pagan Suicide in Purgatory." In *Dante's Political Purgatory.* Philadelphia: University of Pennsylvania Press, 1995, pp. 69–84.

———. *"Inferno XXVI:* Dante's Ulysses." *Lettere italiane* 23 (1971), 145–186.

Silverstein, Theodore. "On the Genesis of *De Monarchia,* II, v." *Speculum* 13 (1938), 326–349.

Ronald L. Martinez

Cato the Elder

Born in Tusculum, 234 B.C.E., Marcus Porcius Cato (not to be confused with Cato of Utica) was censor in 184 and died in 149 B.C.E. Cato the Elder *(Catone)* is cited as an ideal of the republican past of Rome in *Conv.* 4.21.9, 4.27.16, and 4.28.6. All of Dante's references derive from Cicero. The first treats the source of divine nature in humans; the second, the enjoyment of discussion in old age; the third, to looking forward to seeing his ancestors after death (*De senectute* 21, 14, 23, respectively).

Leslie Zarker Morgan

Causes, The Four

Both ancient and medieval philosophy understood causation as the transformation of substance from one state of being to another. The law of sufficient reason dictated that substance could neither derive from nothing nor be reduced to nothing. Causation was therefore a movement from potentiality to actuality. Developing this concept, Aristotle argued in *Metaphysics* 1.3 that causation could be analyzed in terms of four causes: efficient, final, material, and formal. *Efficient cause* pertained to the labor necessary to produce something; *final cause,* to the purpose or goal; *material cause,* to the matter or material required; and *formal cause,* to the abstract principles governing the operation. Thus to provide an adequate explanation for what "causes" a house to come into being, one must account for the labor of the carpenters and masons, the kinds of building materials, the function or purpose for the house, and, finally, the constraints of architecture and engineering—each element contributing to the final outcome.

Most medieval philosophers accepted Aristotle's analysis, though often conflated the four causes under the term "efficient cause." This is the case in Aquinas' "proof from efficient cause," amid the five proofs for the existence of God in the *Summa Theologiae*. Later figures such as William of Ockham (1290–1349), who began to question the doctrine, considered the narrower concept of efficient cause the only valid one. Dante, however, accepted the doctrine and attributed his knowledge of the four causes *(quattro le cagioni)* to Aristotle and to a medieval compendium known as the *Liber de causis*. Also behind Dante was the influence of Guido Cavalcanti, who saw a parallel causal relationship between the astrological and mineralogical and the divine and human. Dante's interest in the doctrine—like that of many medieval theologians—related to First Cause, which linked all existence to divine potentiality: God as the first and ultimate cause of everything in the universe. The four causes thus provided a unifying concept that joined the moral and physical, the theological and the scientific, into a single whole and explained the substance, origins, purpose, and form of the cosmos.

The four causes are especially important for Dante in providing a theological and physical foundation to ethics. He illustrates this in his discussion of the virtue of nobility in the fourth book of the *Convivio*. Glossing a line of his canzone, he writes: *nobilitade umana non sia altro che 'seme di felicitade,' messo da Dio ne l'anima ben posta, cioè lo cui corpo è d'ogni parte disposto perfettamente* ("human nobility is nothing less than 'the seed of happiness,' *infused by God into the soul that is well placed,* that is, into the soul whose body is in every way perfectly disposed in this regard," *Conv.* 4.20.9 [emphasis added]). He then explains that this definition of nobility embraces the four causes. The "soul that is well placed" expresses for Dante the role of material cause. Since matter contributes to the outcome, a soul placed in poor matter will lack nobility, whereas good matter will allow its full expression. (In this way, Dante can also account for human imperfection without contradicting the premise that God has created a perfect soul.) In turn, "the seed" represents the formal cause, containing within itself the potentiality of happiness. Its infusion is the efficient cause, the means by which God acts to produce human happiness. Happiness itself, for Dante, is the final cause, the ultimate end or purpose of the divine activity, and in this he echoes Aristotle's contention that happiness is the highest realizable good. Such a process, he notes finally, is the same way that precious stones receive power from the heavenly bodies. Thus by appealing to the four causes, Dante demonstrates to his mind the integral harmony between God and the cosmos.

Bibliography

The Book of Causes. Translated by Dennis J. Brand. Milwaukee: Marquette University Press, 1984.

Courtenay, William J. *Covenant and Causality in Medieval Thought.* London: Variorum Reprints, 1984.

Gilson, Étienne. *History of Christian Philosophy in the Middle Ages.* New York: Random House, 1955.

Solmsen, Friedrich. *Aristotle's System of the Physical World.* Ithaca, N.Y.: Cornell University Press, 1960.

Wallace, William A. *Medieval and Early Classical Science.* Ann Arbor: University of Michigan Press, 1972.

Thomas L. Cooksey

Cavalcante de' Cavalcanti

Relatively little is known about Cavalcante, son of Schiatta de' Cavalcanti. A member of a leading Florentine Guelf family, he was podestà (chief magistrate) at Gubbio in 1257; after the Ghibelline victory at Montaperti in 1260, he went into exile at Lucca. Cavalcante returned to Florence in 1266 and married his son Guido to Farinata's daughter, Beatrice degli Uberti, in one of a number of political marriages that attempted to heal the Guelf-Ghibelline split (cf. Villani, *Cronica* 8.15). He died c. 1280.

Cavalcante plays an essential role in the drama portrayed in *Inf.* 10, although he is never identified by name. Instead, the narrator tells us that "His words and the manner of his punishment had already read to me his name" (64–65): his words, by revealing that he is the father of Dante's "first friend," Guido (*VN* 3.14); and the manner of his punishment, by his location in the sixth circle of Hell, indicating that the pilgrim could expect to find Guido's father damned for heresy, as one who had denied the soul's immortality (*Inf.* 10.15).

Cavalcante suddenly appears in the tomb next to the Ghibelline Farinata, on his knees (*Inf.* 10.52–54). The fact that a Guelf and a Ghibelline leader are neighbors in the same tomb is part of their *contrapasso,* for although in life they were neighbors, they had been relentless enemies whose bitter feuding was leading Florence to destruction. Here, instead, they are united in the tomb they had proclaimed to be the end of all life. Having recognized Dante, Cavalcante has only one thought: if his son's friend is journeying through Hell *per altezza d'ingegno* ("because of your high genius," 59), why is Guido not with him? Dante's reply highlights the damned soul's spiritual blindness, stressing the fact that it is not genius that has granted him this privilege but God's grace. The use of the past definite *ebbe* ("he had," 63) and the fact that the pilgrim does not answer make Cavalcante suppose that Guido is already dead. Cavalcante falls back into the tomb, his whole raison d'être destroyed, since this heretic, who had denied the immortality of his own soul, attempted to live in and through his son.

This highly dramatic episode is the finale to the troubled friendship between Dante and Guido Cavalcanti (cf. *Purg.* 11.97–99). Now, the latter's imminent death (in August 1300) is foreshadowed by Cavalcante's tragic misunderstanding, expressed in four staccato questions (61–63). We recognize the striking individuality conferred on the *Commedia*'s dramatis personae in the fact that Cavalcante's speech, made up solely of questions, is unique in the poem. In order to achieve this delineation, Dante uses with consummate mastery a variety of rhetorical devices and a stylistic palette which does not exist in European vernacular literature before him. Here, in *Inf.* 10, Farinata's total self-control is set off against the all-too-human vulnerability of his neighbor in the tomb. Another fascinating detail may be espied in the fact that Cavalcante's anguished questions are modeled both on Gen. 4:9–10 and on Andromache's outburst beside Hector's tomb: "Are you a real form? . . . are you alive? or if kindly light has fled, where is Hector?" (*Aen.* 3.310–312). The correspondences with Cavalcante's "where is my son?" and "Does the sweet light of day not strike his eyes?" (*Inf.* 10.60, 69) reveal the way in which Dante chose to weave into the vernacular texture of his Christian epic yet another poetic homage to his guide, precisely at the point (61–62) where Virgil is singled out as the representative of that divine grace necessary to accomplish the journey of redemption.

John A. Scott

Celestine V, Pope

Born Pietro da Morrone around 1215 in the province of Molise in central Italy, most probably at S. Angelo Limosano, the son of a family of peasants. He became a Benedictine monk in the monastery of S. Maria di Faifula before 1230, and then a hermit in the Morrone Mountains near Sulmona (c. 1235–1240), where he organized a community of hermits that was incorporated into the Benedictine order by Pope Gregory X in 1275. Pietro moved from S. Spirito del Morrone and his nearby cell at S. Onofrio to the hermitage of S. Spirito in the Maiella Mountains, farther to the east (c. 1240). He structured his community according to the model of the Cistercians, and although he had never received a formal education, he proved to be an efficient organizer who attracted many donors, so that his congregation soon spread from the Abruzzi to Rome and Apulia. He was said to heal the sick and work miracles, and his reputation was high at the papal court and at the Angevin court of Naples. When—after a vacancy of the papal throne of almost three years because of divisions in the College of Cardinals—King Charles II of Anjou mentioned Pietro's name to the cardinals, this eventually led to his election as pope by "inspiration" on July 5, 1294, at Perugia. Accepting the name of *Celestino* ("the heavenly one"), he was anointed and crowned at L'Aquila on August 29. Firmly under the control of King Charles II from the very beginning, he followed the king to Naples in October. On September 18 he created twelve new cardinals (the number of the apostles), among them five monks—as though he intended to initiate the age of the Holy Spirit, which was to be the age of the monks, according to the eschatological speculations of Joachim of Fiore. Soon corruption became widespread at the curia, and Celestine realized that he was not capable of governing the Church. He seriously considered abdicating, a possibility afforded him by canon law. Although the cardinals tried to persuade him not to renounce his office—fearing the consequences of such an unprecedented act—Celestine abdicated his position on December 13, 1294, after only five months in office. Shortly afterwards the cardinals elected as his successor Benedict Caetani, who took the papal name of Boniface VIII. Peter fled to his hermitage of S. Onofrio and from there to Apulia, where he tried to escape to Greece by following the example of the Franciscan

"Sciagurati che mai non fur vivi": Dante among the Neutrals. Dante, with commentary by Cristoforo Landino and Alessandro Vellutello, published in Venice in 1564 by Marchiò Sessa & fratelli. Giamatti Collection: Courtesy of the Mount Holyoke College Archives and Special Collections.

Church. Since Dante immediately recognizes him—as most scholars think, although the identification is hypothetical—in the vestibule of Hell among the neutrals as *l'ombra di colui / che fece per viltade il gran rifiuto* ("the shade of him who in his cowardice made the great refusal," *Inf.* 3.59–60; see also *Inf.* 27.104ff.), he may well have seen Celestine as a member of a Florentine delegation to Naples in November 1294. Dante thus was among the few who criticized his abdication, which opened the way to his unworthy successor, Boniface VIII. Although Dante did not contest the validity and legitimacy of Boniface's election, he despised Celestine's abdication as an act of pusillanimous irresponsibility. The fact that he does not identify the figure explicitly has led critics and commentators to assign various names to this *ombra,* among them Esau, Diocletian, Pontius Pilate, and Julian the Apostate; but his anonymity is also suggestive of his lack of character or strong identity. Not one of the neutrals in *Inf.* 3 is identified by name.

Bibliography

Dictionnaire historique de la papauté. Edited by Philippe Levillain. Paris: Fayard, 1994.

Herde, Peter. *Cölestin V. Der Engelpapst.* Stuttgart: Anton Hiersemann, 1981.

Nardi, Bruno. "Dante e Celestino V. 'L'ombra di colui che fece per viltà il gran rifiuto.'" *Lettere Italiane* 9 (1957), 225–238. Reprinted in *Dal "Convivio" alla "Commedia."* Rome: Istituto storico italiano per il Medio Evo, 1960, pp. 315–330.

Padoan, Giorgio. "'Colui che fece per viltà il gran rifiuto.'" *Studi danteschi* 38 (1961), 75–128.

Petrocchi, Giorgio. "Dante e Celestino V." *Studi romani* 3 (1955), 273–285. Reprinted in *Itinerari danteschi.* Bari: Adriatica, 1969, pp. 54–74.

Peter Herde

Spirituals, on whom he had conferred the status of an independent community bearing his name to protect them from the persecutions of the majority of the order. But in June 1295 he was arrested and returned to Boniface—then in residence at Anagni—who placed him in custody in the nearby castle of Fumone, where he died of natural causes a year later (May 19, 1296). He was buried in the Church of S. Maria di Collemaggio in L'Aquila. Through the efforts of his brethern, some Spirituals, and the French enemies of Boniface VIII, he was canonized on May 5, 1313, by Pope Clement V, but his name was canceled from the official calendar of saints of the Roman Church in 1969 because he had been venerated only locally in his Abruzzi homeland.

The simple hermit-pope, who was not however without harsh traits of character, soon became the object of eschatological speculations about the "angelic pope," and up to the present he has frequently served as the symbol of an "alternative" Church, even though his short pontificate had proved that he was not capable of reforming the

Centaurs

Mythological creatures—half man, half horse—most of whom were portrayed by Greek poets as violent and gluttonous. Some, however, were depicted as teachers of humans. Dante places centaurs in the first ring of the circle of violence (*Inf.* 12), where they serve as guardians of those guilty of violence against others. Armed with bows and

*E della schiera tre si dipartiro;
Con archi e asticciuole prima elette.*

Inferno Canto 12.

Three centaurs in the first ring of the circle of violence. Invenzioni di Giovanni Flaxman sulla Divina commedia, *illustrated by John Flaxman and Beniamino del Vecchio, Rome, 1826. Giamatti Collection: Courtesy of the Mount Holyoke College Archives and Special Collections.*

arrows, they patrol the banks of Phlegethon, the river of boiling blood in which the violent are submerged, shooting any sinner who attempts to emerge from his assigned place. When three of the centaurs approach Dante and Virgil menacingly, Virgil explains the nature of Dante's journey. Their leader, Chiron (who had served as tutor to Achilles and Hercules, among others), assigns one of his band, Nessus, to guide Dante and Virgil in their journey along the banks of Phlegethon. Like the Minotaur—the half man, half bull who serves as guardian of the circle of violence as a whole (*Inf.* 12.1–27)—the physical duality of the centaurs suggests the bestial nature of those sinners whose "mad rage" (*ira folle,* 12.49) drove them to their violent acts. At the same time, the poet establishes a curious distinction between the seemingly bestial centaurs and the sinners submerged in Phlegethon by focusing on the human attributes of

Chiron. In contrast to his rational behavior and speech, the sinners in this canto are deprived of speech; the only sounds they make are loud shrieks of pain (*alte strida,* 12.102). In this way Dante creates an ironic juxtaposition between the "human" sinners, who have sacrificed their humanity through their acts of violence, and the bestial-looking centaurs who hunt them. Centaurs are also among the examples of gluttony cited on the sixth terrace of Purgatory, where they are referred to as "the cursed ones formed in the clouds, who, gorged, fought against Theseus with their double breasts" (*i maledetti / nei nuvoli formati che, sattoli, / Teseo combatter co' doppi petti, Purg.* 24.121–123). The centaurs were said to have been born of a union between Nephele, a cloud-born woman, and Ixion, a king. The source for their being cited as examples of gluttony is Ovid, who relates that the centaurs, having become

Dante and Virgil with the centaurs in the first ring of the seventh circle of Hell. Opere di Dante Alighieri, *edited by Cristoforo Zapate de Cisneros, Venice, 1757–1758. Giamatti Collection: Courtesy of the Mount Holyoke College Archives and Special Collections.*

intoxicated with wine, attempted to seize the women at a wedding feast, whereupon they were engaged in battle by Theseus (*Meta.* 12.210–212).

Lawrence Baldassaro

Cerberus

The three-headed dog who guards the gluttons in the third circle of Hell and tortures them with his claws and barking (*Inf.* 6.13–33). His capture by Hercules is mentioned during the episode at the Gate of Dis (*Inf.* 9.98–99; cf. Virgil, *Aen.* 6.391–397; Ovid, *Meta.* 7.410–415).

In classical mythology Cerberus is the watchdog of the netherworld. Hesiod (*Theog.* 311) identifies him as a fifty-headed monster, the offspring of Typhon and Echidna. In Virgil's *Aeneid* a three-headed Cerberus with snakes entwined about his necks blocks the infernal entrance with his triple-throated barking and enormous bulk. The Sybil drugs Cerberus with honey cakes while guiding Aeneas into the lower regions (*Aen.* 6.417–423). Virgil briefly alludes to Cerberus' bloody cave strewn with half-gnawed bones (*Aen.* 8.297), and Ovid describes the effects of his poisonous slobber (*Meta.* 4.501, 7.416–424).

Dante's Cerberus—a grotesque, wildly agitated demon—has humanoid features suggestive of gluttony (large belly, greasy beard, clawed hands). Virgil subdues him with fistfuls of earth, possibly reflecting medieval allegorical commentaries on the *Aeneid* (cf. Servius, *ad Aen.* 6.395) that associate Cerberus with Earth. Like the three-headed Lucifer (*Inf.* 34.108), Cerberus is a "worm" (*Inf.* 6.22). His one truly canine characteristic is his barking, described in the striking construction *caninamente latra* ("[he] barks doglike") and echoed in the sinners' howling (*Inf.* 6.14, 19).

Cerberus threatening the pilgrim Dante. Opere di Dante Alighieri, *edited by Cristoforo Zapate de Cisneros, Venice, 1757–1758. Giamatti Collection: Courtesy of the Mount Holyoke College Archives and Special Collections.*

Bibliography

Dombroski, Robert S. "The Grain of Hell: A Note on Retribution in *Inferno* VI." *Dante Studies* 88 (1970), 103–108.

Heilbronn, Denise. "*Inferno* VI." In *Dante's "Divine Comedy": Introductory Readings. I: "Inferno."* Edited by Tibor Wlassics. *Lectura Dantis* 6: Supplement (Spring): Special issue: *Lectura Dantis Virginiana* I (1990), 71–80.

Kleinhenz, Christopher. "Infernal Guardians Revisited: 'Cerbero, il gran vermo' (*Inf.* VI, 22)." *Dante Studies* 93 (1975), 185–199.

Denise Heilbronn-Gaines

Chain of Being

Dante and the high Middle Ages inherited from Plato and Aristotle the concept that all things in the universe could be classified according to the degree of their innate perfection. Most commonly known as the *scala naturae* ("ladder of being") and later as the "chain of being" (Alexander Pope), the system aligns all forms of existence within a hierarchical order according to each being's capacity for reflecting the highest level of existence, the Divinity. Every inhabitant, organism, and element of matter in the universe is conceived as being characterized by some degree of imperfection with respect to the Deity: the less the approximation to the Deity, the inferior the position on the *scala naturae*.

The chain possesses in theory innumerable links interconnected one by one from the lowest form of mere existence to the sublime heights of the divine; but in practice, medieval philosophers, theologians, and poets refer only to several discrete major categories which become emblematic of the multiplicity of levels that make up the chain. This is the case with Dante, who explicates the chain of being in *Conv.* 3.7.5, identifying six levels of being below God: angelic, human, animal, vegetative, mineral, and elemental (see also 3.3.3–5). While man occupies a single rung on the ladder, it is an important aspect of his nature that he participates in all levels of being at once and incorporates the main features of the other levels of being, both higher and lower, so that he is quite literally to the medieval imagination a microcosm of the universe, reflecting the totality of its essence. This principle is most evident in the composition of man's soul, which subsumes the souls of all forms of living things. Following Aristotle's definition in *De anima* 2.2 (413b.10–13), Dante explicates in *Conv.* 3.2 the structure of the human soul, which is endowed with the separate powers of life, sensation, and reason. Having dominion over the animals, which lack the power of reason, and the plants, which lack both reason and sensation, man is closest to God among the beings that possess a physical form—lower only than the angels, which, being "separate substances," are immaterial beings of pure intellect. And at *Conv.* 4.7.11–15, Dante, again tracing Aristotle's discussion, emphasizes that each successively higher power cannot exist without the inferior powers: *le potenze de l'anima stanno sopra sé come la figura de lo quadrangulo sta sopra lo triangulo, e lo pentangulo, cioè la figura che ha cinque canti, sta sopra lo quadrangulo: e così la sensitiva sta sopra la vegetativa, e la intellettiva sta sopra la sensitiva* ("the powers of the soul stand one above another as the figure of the quadrangle stands above that of the triangle, and the pentagon [i.e., a figure having five sides] stands above the quadrangle: so the sensitive power stands above the vegetative power, and the intellectual power stands above the sensitive power," 14).

The concept of hierarchy at the heart of the chain of being, which derived principally from Aristotle and which Dante had access to primarily through St. Thomas, is the fundamental paradigm that underlies Dante's placement of individuals in one of the three realms of the otherworld. In effect, *Inferno*, *Purgatorio*, and *Paradiso* constitute a great ladder of degrees of excellence, from the greatest sinner in Hell (Judas) to the most blessed soul in Heaven (Virgin Mary). This kind of ranking of human beings according to personal virtue would not have been possible independently of the chain of being. He also employs the chain as a metaphor in *DVE* 1.16.5 and in *Mon.* 1.3.6 to support the argument that growth in intelligence is man's proper goal.

The notion of hierarchy so pervades all aspects of medieval thought that even the act of Creation—God's shaping of the material universe as it takes place over the period of the first six days—was deemed to contain the prescription of the chain's natural order from lowest to highest, for man was created last, after the dry land, the herbs, and the moving creatures. And the genesis of the human soul itself, passing through the lower stages to the higher as it develops in the fetus, replicates this evolutionary process in small. As Dante expounds it in *Purg.* 25.42–75, through the voice of his guide Virgil, the fetus acquires first the vegetative soul, only later the animal soul, and last—by an individual and direct act of God—the intellectual soul. The chain of being and the related concepts of the soul's entelechy and the notion of man as microcosm of the universe informed every area of medieval thought (see, for example, *Roman de la rose,* 19034–19050)—history as well as psychology, biology as well as philosophy—and were in currency until the end of the seventeenth century.

Bibliography

Boyde, Patrick. *Dante Philomythes and Philosopher.* Cambridge, New York: Cambridge University Press, 1981, pp. 128–131.

Lansing, Richard. "Dante's Concept of Violence and the Chain of Being." *Dante Studies* 99 (1981), 67–88.

Lovejoy, Arthur O. *The Great Chain of Being.* Cambridge, Mass.: Harvard University Press, 1936.

Mahoney, Edward. "Lovejoy and the Hierarchy of Being." *Journal of the History of Ideas* 48 (1987), 211–230.

Richard Lansing

Charity

The third of the three theological virtues—after faith and hope—charity (*carità, caritate; caritas* in Latin) is the supreme form of Christian love, the love of God. It embraces as well the fundamental attitude of love that the Father expresses toward his creatures: therefore charity has a divine origin, one whose deepest expression is the love that is bestowed on humankind by the sacrifice of Christ, the Son of God. The relationship between God and human beings is founded on a sense of brotherhood, and it comprises as well the love of others, having as its opposite cupidity, the love of temporal goods. The most striking aspect of charity is found in the evangelical message that love is owed even to one's enemies.

In Dante's works, charity is an important virtue from as early as the *Vita Nuova:* in reflecting on the effect of Beatrice's greeting, Dante stresses the power of forgiveness in the *fiamma di caritade* ("flame of charity," *VN* 11.1). The third canticle of the *Commedia* in particular, however, provides the most significant representation of charity—and the most significant references to the good effects of charity visible in the blessed souls. Charity is the love that the saved in Paradise express naturally for their maker and is the basis of their salvation: *Se tu vedessi / com'io la carità che tra noi arde, / li tuoi concetti sarebbero espressi* ("If you saw as I do the love that burns among us, your concepts would be expressed," *Par.* 22.31–33). The fount of charity is the Virgin Mary, the Queen of Heaven, as St. Bernard remarks: *Qui se'a noi meridïana face / di caritate, e giuso, intra 'mortali, / se' di speranza fontana vivace* ("Here to us you are a noon-bright torch of love and down below among mortals you are a lively fountain of hope," *Par.* 33.10–12). In the Heaven of the Fixed Stars Dante is examined on the nature of charity by St. John, where the pilgrim defines love as having its foundation in Christ's sacrifice: *la morte ch'el sostenne perch' io viva* ("the death that he underwent that I may live," *Par.* 26.59). For those critics who argue that the moral structure of Paradise is based on the virtues, both cardinal and theological, the Heaven of the Fixed Stars represents the perfection of the three theological virtues, of which the highest and last is charity.

Ernesto Livorni

Charlemagne

Charles the Great, king of the Franks, who restored the Roman Empire in the West, was born in Aachen, Germany, in 742 and crowned emperor in Rome in the year 800. In the Heaven of Mercury Emperor Justinian mentions Charlemagne (*Carlo Magno, Par.* 6.96) in connection with his defense of the church against Desiderius, the king of the Lombards in 773, when Pope Adrian I had invoked his aid (*Mon.* 3.11.1). Dante's claim in the latter passage that Charlemagne was crowned under Pope Adrian I is inaccurate, since he was crowned by Pope Leo III. Charlemagne is placed in the Heaven of Mars among those who fought for the faith (*Par.* 18.43). He is also mentioned at *Inf.* 31.17 in connection with the loss of his rear guard, under the command of his nephew Roland.

R. A. Malagi

Charles I of Anjou

The youngest child of Louis VIII of France and Blanche of Castile, Charles I of Anjou *(Carlo)* was born in March 1226. Through his marriage to Beatrice, daughter of Raymond Berenger IV, he became count of Provence in 1246. In the same year he was invested with his hereditary appanages Anjou and Maine by his brother King Louis IX of France. He reorganized the Provençal administration, and as a result of extensive negotiations with Pope Clement IV he was invested on June 28, 1265, with the Kingdom of Sicily and was crowned on January 6, 1266. After a successful campaign against the Hohenstaufen king of Sicily, Manfred, which culminated in the defeat and death of Manfred in the battle of Benevento (February 26, 1266), he was forced to defend his recently acquired kingdom against Manfred's nephew, Conradin. Charles succeeded in defeating the young Hohenstaufen in the battle of Tagliacozzo (August 23, 1268). Conradin was captured and executed by order of the king on October 19, 1268, in Naples. In order to stabilize his rule Charles exiled all Svevian partisans and nominated only Frenchmen for higher positions in the military and civil administration. Simultaneously, the king tried to extend Angevin domination of the Mediterranean by acquiring the principate of Achaia (1278) and the Kingdom of Jerusalem (1277). The ultimate aim of these acquisitions was the conquest of the Byzantine Empire. This ambition forced Charles to place an increasingly heavy burden on his subjects in the Kingdom of Sicily. This and other reasons (the Gallicization of the Regno, the restriction of the powers of the nobility, and the actions of the pro-Svevian exiles) led to the uprising of the Sicilian Vespers on March 30 or 31, 1282. This was followed by the secession of the entire island of Sicily from the Angevin rule and the intervention of Peter III of Aragon, who was recognized by the Sicilians as the new king of the island. In the last years of his life Charles tried in vain to reconquer his lost possession. He died January 7, 1285, at Foggia.

Although Dante places Charles in Purgatorio, his judgment of the king is highly unfavorable. He mentions none of Charles's military and political achievements but attributes the fortune and power of the king to his marriage to Beatrice of Provence, *la gran dota provenzale* ("the great dowry of Provence," *Purg.* 20.61). Because this dowry did not absolve the Angevin dynasty from the shame of being a collateral of the Capetian dynasty (*Purg.* 20.61–63), Charles had little interest in it. Compared with his rival for the rule of the island of

Sicily, Peter III of Aragon, Charles is inferior, and his wives (Beatrice and Margaret) have no reason to be proud of their husband (*Purg.* 7.128–129). After all, it was his wicked rule, the famous *mala Signoria,* that cried out for retaliation and resulted in the Vespers (*Par.* 8.73–75). In contrast to Dante's portrayal of the king's indifference to the great dowry stands his harsh judgment of him in *Purg.* 20.6–69, where Charles is accused of usurping the kingdom against the rights of the Hohenstaufen, of condemning Conradin to death, and even of poisoning Thomas Aquinas (the latter accusation being without historical foundation). Dante's judgment of Charles appears mildly positive only in comparison with his opinion of those toward whom he felt even greater hatred. The king is superior to his son Charles II (*Purg.* 7.127), and in judging Pope Nicholas III (who is despised by Dante) he is even characterized as *ardito* ("bold") because of his plans for world supremacy.

Bibliography

Arnaldi, G. "La maledizione del sangue e la virtù delle stelle. Angioini e Capetingi nella *Commedia* di Dante." *La Cultura* 30 (1992), 47–74, 185–216.

Brezzi, Paolo. "Dante e gli Angioini." In *Atti del II Congresso nazionale di studi danteschi: Dante e l'Italia meridionale.* Florence: Olschki, 1966, pp. 149–162.

Herde, Peter. *Karl I. von Anjou.* Stuttgart: Kohlhammer, 1979.

———. "Carlo I d'Angiò nella storia del Mezzogiorno." In *Unità politica e differenze regionali nel regno di Sicilia.* Galatina: Congedo, 1992, pp. 181ff.

Léonard, E. G. *Les Angevins de Naples.* Paris: Presses universitaires de France, 1954, pp. 36ff.

Tanzarella, A. "Dante e gli Angioini." *Archivio storico pugliese* 16 (1963), 150–162.

Andreas Kiesewetter

Charles II of Anjou

The eldest son of Charles I of Anjou and Beatrice of Provence, born in 1254, and king of Naples from 1285 to 1309. After the Sicilian Vespers massacre in 1282, he held the office of governor of the Kingdom of Naples for his father and tried to regain the confidence of his subjects with reforms, which resulted in the Capitula of San Martino (March 30, 1283), whereby he granted important privileges to the nobility, the clergy, and the citizens. Captured in the naval battle of Naples on June 5, 1284 by the Aragonese admiral Roger Lauria, he was released in November 1288 only after long negotiations. After his coronation as king of Sicily by Pope Nicholas IV (May 29, 1289), he attempted to resolve the Sicilian question by diplomacy. After these negotiations failed, he was forced by Pope Boniface VIII to play the military card once again after 1296. Recognizing that it was impossible to subject the Sicilians by military means and that a continuation of the fighting would ruin the finances of the Kingdom of Naples, Charles was ready to acknowledge the independence of the Kingdom of Sicily after 1299, which led to a conflict with the pope. After the failure of the last military campaigns against the Sicilians, Charles and Boniface were forced to ratify the treaty of Caltabellotta in 1303, which guaranteed the independence of Sicily under an Aragonese collateral line. The end of the first phase of the war of the Sicilian Vespers enabled Charles to restore Angevin hegemony in Piedmont and to secure the position of his family in Achaia (1303–1307). The climax of his foreign policy was the general acknowledgment of his grandson Charles Robert as king of Hungary (1308), which guaranteed the crown of St. Stephen for his dynasty. During his reign Charles II attempted to continue with the reform of the Regno, partially with negative results, because the power of the nobility and the centrifugal forces were strengthened. The financing of the war of the Vespers proved disastrous for the economy of the Kingdom of Naples because the king was forced to pawn numerous state revenues in order to procure loans from Florentine merchants who exploited the natural resources of southern Italy and prevented the rise of trade and industry. Much more successful were his reforms in the administration of the county of Provence, but his main achievement was to secure at least the continuation of Angevin rule in the continental part of the former Kingdom of Sicily. He died on May 5, 1309, in Naples.

The first references to Charles *(Carlo)* in the *Commedia* (*Purg.* 5.69, 7.127) reveal Dante's bias against him. This is even more apparent later, in Justinian's warning to Charles (*Carlo novello, Par.* 6.106) as leader of the Guelfs not to oppose the imperial eagle. Dante's judgment of him is generally severe and negative, because he regards the king above all as being subservient to the hated Boniface VIII and Charles of Valois. The passage in *Par.* 19.127–129 is especially famous, where Dante pours double scorn on the Angevin, calling him *Ciotto di Jerusalemme* ("the Cripple of Jerusalem"), thus alluding to Charles's physical handicap and his rule over a kingdom for which he maintained merely the title. One good deed stands opposed to a thousand bad deeds. Dante does not hesitate, of course, to emphasize the greatest disgrace in Charles's life: the disastrous naval battle of Naples and his subsequent captivity (*Purg.* 20.79). Twice he refers to the king's financial problems and avarice: Charles lures the Florentine merchants to his court by ringing a bell, and then he accepts their loans at usurious interest rates (*DVE* 1.12.5); and he sells his daughter to the highest bidder, just as the corsairs sold their slaves (*Purg.* 20.80–81)—alluding to the marriage of Charles's daughter Beatrice to Azzo VIII d'Este in 1304–1305, for which Azzo paid 51,000 florins to the king. Repeatedly Dante emphasizes the corrupt government of the Angevin, for which his subjects have every reason to complain (*Purg.* 7.126; *Par.* 20.62–63; *Conv.* 4.6.20). The king is judged to be more inferior than even his highly criticized father, Charles I (*Purg.* 7.127). The only reference seen by traditional scholarship as a positive reference to the king—the *natura larga* from which his son Robert descends (*Par.* 8. 82–83)—alludes most probably to Robert's elder brother Charles Martel, who died prematurely and was held in high esteem by Dante.

Bibliography

Arnaldi, G. "La maledizione del sangue e la virtù delle stelle. Angioini e Capetingi nella *Commedia* di Dante." *La Cultura* 30 (1992), 47–74, 185–216.

Brezzi, Paolo. "Dante e gli Angioini." In *Atti del II Congresso nazionale di studi danteschi: Dante e l'Italia meridionale.* Firenze: Olschki, 1966, pp. 149–162.

Kiesewetter, A. "Das sizilianische Zweistaatenproblem 1282–1302." In *Unità politica e differenze regionali nel regno di Sicilia.* Galatina: Congedo, 1992, pp. 247ff.

———. *Karl II. von Anjou, König von Neapel und Graf der Provence. Das Königreich Neapel und der Mittelmeerraum zu Ausgang des 13. Jahrhunderts.* Doctoral thesis. Würzburg: 1992 (in print).

Léonard, E. G. *Les Angevins de Naples*. Paris: Presses universitaires de France, 1954, pp. 161ff.

Tanzarella, A. *Dante e gli Angioini. Archivio storico pugliese* 16 (1963), 150–162.

Andreas Kiesewetter

Charles Martel

Carlo Martello (1271–1296) was the eldest son of Charles II, king of Naples (1248–1309), and Mary of Hungary, and he was the brother of Robert of Anjou, king of Naples (1309–1343). He served as regent of the Kingdom of Naples in 1285 and again in 1289, and he was heir to the county of Provence, the Kingdom of Naples, and the Kingdom of Hungary. With his marriage to Clemenza, daughter of Rudolph I of Habsburg, Charles joined the bloodlines of the two most eminent Guelf and Ghibelline families of his age. In March 1294, while Charles visited Florence for several weeks, he met Dante and apparently showed great admiration for the work of the poet. Dante's canzone, "Voi che 'ntendendo il terzo ciel movete" ("You whose intellect the third sphere moves," *Conv.* 2, canzone 1) was sung in Charles's presence, and all the sources agree upon the sumptuousness, civility, and obvious affection that Charles displayed for the city of Florence. Dante recalls this event when he meets Charles in the Heaven of Venus (the "third sphere"), where he appears among those whose love is marred by wantonness.

At the time of the events of the *Commedia* Charles had been dead for four years, and he serves as a type of the generous, affectionate prince who dies too young. In *Par.* 8 Charles also serves as the perfect example of male *adolescenza,* the second stage of life, turning into *giovinezza,* the third and ideal mature stage, characterized by temperance, strength, affection, courtesy, and legal-mindedness. Because of his own virtues, family circumstances, and early death, Charles becomes Dante's spokesman on the topics of human diversity, the necessity of civic life for human fulfillment, and the relations between individuals and the cosmos.

Edward Peters

Charles of Valois

Second son of King Phillip III of France and his wife Isabelle of Aragon, born in 1270, probably on March 12. Charles *(Carlo)* is mentioned twice by Dante, who refers to his inglorious appearance in Florence in the winter of 1301–1302, an event that ultimately led to the poet's exile from the city. The Capetian is compared to Totila (frequently confused with Attila in the Middle Ages, considered to be the destroyer of Florence) for having exiled the cream of the Florentine citizens and being unable to bring to an end the Sicilian war (*DVE* 2.6.4 as an example of *ars dictandi*). In another passage (*Purg.* 20.68–78) Charles is even compared to Judas with a reference to the Acts of the Apostles (1:18): he came to Florence without arms, and only through betrayal and insidiousness did he enforce the takeover of the Black Guelfs, resulting in killings, robbery, and exile. In this context Dante cannot resist strong sarcasm against the Valois, pointing out that instead of attaining his aspired kingdom, he reaped only destruction and disgrace. However, Dante's view of Charles is not so much that of the individual, responsible for the turmoil in Florence, but more that of an exponent of the hated Capetian dynasty and the Angevin collateral line, who, through their avarice and greed for power and money, were responsible for the political and social crisis in Italy. Thus Dante rises above his personal hatred for Charles and passes a wider verdict, which can be seen as the expression of an eternal judgment.

As a consequence of the papal-French-Angevin alliance during the war of the Sicilian Vespers, Charles was invested with the kingdoms of Aragon and Valencia on May 5, 1284, by Pope Martin IV. An attempt by his father to subject Aragon by force of arms ended in a complete disaster in 1285. In the course of the Angevin-Aragonese negotiations for a settlement, Charles of Valois married Margarethe, the daughter of Charles II of Anjou, at the end of August 1290. She brought the two paternal appanages of Anjou and Maine in France as dowry into the marriage in exchange for a possible renunciation by Charles of Valois of his pretensions on the Kingdom of Aragon. After the definite renunciation of his nominal Aragonese kingship in the Treaty of Anagni (June 20, 1295) and the death of his wife (May 2, 1299), he married Catherine of Courtenay, the heiress to the nominal pretensions on the Latin empire of Constantinople in January 1301. Before he could realize his plans for a military campaign against the Byzantine Empire, he was forced to move to Italy. The reason was that Pope Boniface

VIII had pressed King Phillip IV since 1298 for an intervention to end the war of the Sicilian Vespers and to subject the rebellious island. Charles came to Italy in the early summer of 1301 and was nominated on September 3, 1301, by Pope Boniface VIII as *vicarius et pacificator* in Tuscany, with the aim of supporting the struggle of the Black Guelfs against the White Guelfs. On November 1, 1301, he arrived in Florence, and after receiving the *signoria* of the city he embarked on a policy which unilaterally favored the Blacks. Numerous Whites—among them Dante—were banished on January 27, 1302, and were driven into exile. After the appointment of one of his followers as podestà he left the city in open turmoil on March 2 and entered the service of Charles II, who nominated him governor-general of the island of Sicily on March 10, 1302. At the end of that month he crossed the strait of Messina to Sicily. He recognized that a complete victory against the Sicilians was impossible, and when he was informed by his brother of the disastrous defeat of the French army by the Flemish at Kortrijk (July 11, 1302), he was constrained to sign the peace of Caltabellotta (August 29, 1302), which guaranteed the independence of the island of Sicily under the Aragonese king Frederick III. In the following years Charles of Valois pursued his dream of conquering Constantinople and therefore attempted to forge an alliance with Venice, the Catalan Company, and the Serb king Stephen II Uroš Milutin. But all these projects failed because of his financial difficulties. After the death of his second wife, Catherine of Courtenay (end of 1307 or beginning of 1308), he lost all interest in the affairs of the Latin Orient and concentrated his efforts—but also in vain—on the candidature for the German throne. During the reign of his nephew Louis X of France he succeeded in bringing down his greatest rival at the French court, Enguerrand de Marigny, a deed which strengthened his influence in the royal council. He was forced onto the sidelines under Phillip V but restored his influence during the reign of his godchild Charles IV, when he participated in various military campaigns against the Flemish and the English. Charles died on December 16, 1325, in Nogent, leaving enormous debts.

Bibliography

Davidsohn, R. *Geschichte von Florenz*. Berlin: E. S. Mittler, 1912.

Laiou, A. E. *Constantinople and the Latins: The Foreign Policy of Andronicus II, 1282–1328*. Cambridge, Mass.: Harvard University Press, 1972.

Neser, L. *Studien zur Biographie Karls von Valois*. Freiburg in Breisgau: Hammerschlag and Kahle, 1912.

Petit, J. *Charles de Valois (1270–1325)*. Paris: Picard, 1900.

Andreas Kiesewetter

Charon

The demon boatman (*Inf.* 3.82–129) who ferries the dead souls across Acheron, the infernal river marking the threshold of Hell. His character, name, role, and physical traits (a vigorous hoary man with red eyes) are taken from *Aen.* 6.298–304. Charon *(Caron, Caronte)* is the first of the demonized guardians Dante encounters on his journey, and the first to oppose the pilgrim's trip. Virgil neutralizes his opposition by invoking a kind of password-formula—*Vuolsi così colà dove si puote / ciò che si vuole* ("This is willed where what is willed can be done," *Inf.* 3.95–96)—which is repeated once verbatim and once in variation (*Inf.* 5.23–24, 7.11–12) to ward off opposition. Here, at the beginning of the poem, it underscores the fact that Dante's voyage is divinely ordained and cannot be checked.

Paolo Cherchi

Chaucer

Geoffrey Chaucer (c. 1340–1400) is important to Italian literary history as one of the first non-Italian European writers to acknowledge the achievement of the great Italian poets of the Trecento. As a member of the English royal household, and later an official of the Crown concerned with customs, he must have dealt with the Italian merchants and bankers, many of them men of culture and many of them Tuscan, who were establishing themselves in England in his day, and it was perhaps through them that he encountered the Italian language and Italian poetry. In 1372–1373 Chaucer traveled to Genoa and Florence, and in 1378 he visited the court of Bernabò Visconti at Milan. His poetry thereafter reveals an extensive knowledge of the writings of Boccaccio and Petrarch (both of whom he may conceivably have met on his first journey), and he becomes perhaps the first non-Italian—certainly the first major non-

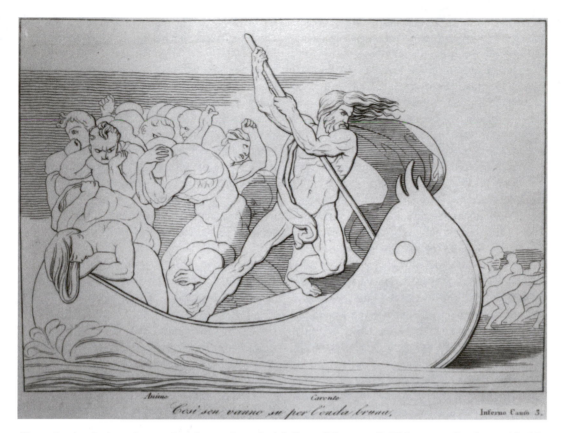

Charon ferrying the damned across the Acheronte. Invenzioni di Giovanni Flaxman sulla Divina commedia, *illustrated by John Flaxman and Beniamino del Vecchio, Rome, 1826. Giamatti Collection: Courtesy of the Mount Holyoke College Archives and Special Collections.*

Italian poet—to recognize the greatness of Dante's *Commedia* and the possibilities it had opened to poetry in the vernacular. He also knew the *Convivio,* possibly the *Vita Nuova,* and perhaps even the *De vulgari eloquentia,* but his long engagement with the *Commedia* affords a unique glimpse of one major poet's measuring his abilities and aspirations by the standard of another.

The unfinished *House of Fame,* usually dated 1378–1379, probably embodies Chaucer's first response to Dante. Its three books describe an encounter with Virgil's *Aeneid,* a journey through the universe on the back of an eagle, and a visit to the realm of Fame and Rumor. Each stage of the story has its Dantean aspect, but differences are as apparent as similarities. Where Dante had appropriated to his own use the *bello stilo* of Virgil, Chaucer's narrator undertakes to "sing" ("if I kan") the story of the *Aeneid* itself in English tetrameters, translating short passages with passable accuracy and deftly summarizing the rest. The

apparition of the eagle who carries the narrator through the heavens in Book II is modeled on the pilgrim's dream at the opening of *Purg.* 9, but the bird proves a loquacious pedant, and the revelation he promises is vaguely defined as "tidings" of love. The palace of Fame is adorned with the figures and words of poets and singers of all sorts, and in its great hall the poets of antiquity stand on massive pillars. But there is no coherent scheme, no clear standard for distinguishing truth and falsehood in the assigning of authority or renown to literature, and to the extent that it constitutes the "heaven" of the literary universe Chaucer has constructed, the palace amounts to a parody of the configuration of Christian truth in *Paradiso.* The poem includes striking invocations, to the Muses and to Apollo, clearly echoing those of *Inf.* 2 and *Par.* 1, which show Chaucer acknowledging, while distancing himself from, the vast ambition of Dante. Chaucer's mature poetry will maintain a submissive relation to the great poets of the classical past, accept the circumscribing authority of books, and quietly deprecate his own impulse to discover a transcendent meaning in human love.

The *Parlement of Fowles* (c. 1380) employs various Dantean motifs including a Virgil-like guide and a gate whose ominous inscription strongly recalls that over the *porta* of *Inf.* 3. *The Legend of Good Women* (1385–1390), whose Prologue contains a number of echoes of the canzone of *Conv.* 4, prefaces its artfully bungled version of the story of Dido with Statius' reverent but ambiguous image of Virgil as lantern bearer (*Purg.* 22). But the poem that reveals Chaucer's appreciation of Dante most fully is certainly *Troilus and Criseyde* (1385–1386), in which a historically localized story of earthly love (derived from Boccaccio's *Filostrato*) is played out against the background of the spiritual journey of the *Commedia*. The relationship is of course largely parodic: though the idealistic lover Troilus has much of the *buono ardor* of Dante's pilgrim, Criseyde is an all-too-worldly Beatrice—enmeshed in desire, politics, and history—and Pandarus, the guide who leads Troilus to the "hevene blisse" of sexual union, is a cynical and self-interested Virgil. Chaucer points to the parallels between his narrative and Dante's by a pattern of allusions to structurally significant moments in Dante's text. The most striking of these is Troilus' prayer to "Benigne Love" at the center of the consummation scene, which clearly echoes St. Bernard's address to the Virgin in *Par.* 33. The implications of the suggested comparison are complex. The barrier separating human from divine love is for a moment virtually translucent, but the context makes plain that Troilus is self-deceived and is destined in the end to be betrayed by the "grace" that seems to inform his experience.

The *Canterbury Tales* plainly recalls the *Commedia* at a number of points. The Knight quotes Virgil on Fortune (*Inf.* 7), at a crucial point in his story; the Wife of Bath cites "the wise poet of Florence" as authority for the long discourse on *gentilesse* (*Conv.* 4), which brings her tale to its climax; and the Monk contrasts his own pathos-ridden version of the story of Ugolino with Dante's fuller account. The movement of Chaucer's pilgrimage—its religious occasion notwithstanding—is resolutely horizontal; he, more truly than Dante, is Auerbach's "poet of the secular world." But the complexity of Chaucer's pilgrim characters is Dantean. The medium, both social and psychological, in which his figures move has the density of *Inferno,* and the characters' self-revelations are as powerful as those of Dante's sinners. Though Chaucer's pilgrims are not fixed forever in the attitudes defined by their besetting sins and often seem on the point of discovering new dimensions in their lives, they are close to Dante's characters in their embodiment of the reality of a fallen world, challenging us with the bodily, erotic reality of lives which refuse to be subsumed to allegory—a collective human drama for which the *Commedia* and Boccaccio's *Decameron* provide the only modern precedents.

Bibliography

Boitani, Piero. *Chaucer and the Imaginary World of Fame.* Cambridge: Cambridge University Press, 1984.

——— (ed.). *Chaucer and the Italian Trecento.* Cambridge: Cambridge University Press, 1983.

Neuse, Richard. *Chaucer's Dante: Allegory and Epic Theater in "The Canterbury Tales."* Berkeley, Los Angeles, Oxford: University of California Press, 1991.

Schless, Howard. *Chaucer and Dante: A Revaluation.* Norman, Okla.: Pilgrim Books, 1984.

Shoaf, R. A. *Dante, Chaucer, and the Currency of the Word: Money, Images, and Reference in Late Medieval Poetry.* Norman, Okla.: Pilgrim Books, 1983.

Taylor, Karla. *Chaucer Reads "The Divine Comedy."* Stanford, Calif.: Stanford University Press, 1989.

Wallace, David. *Chaucerian Polity: Absolutist Lineages and Associational Forms in England and Italy.* Stanford, Calif.: Stanford University Press, 1997.

Wetherbee, Winthrop. *Chaucer and the Poets: An Essay on "Troilus and Criseyde."* Ithaca, N.Y.: Cornell University Press, 1984.

Winthrop Wetherbee

Chiose all' "Inferno"

The shortest and possibly the earliest of all edited commentaries to the *Commedia,* written about 1322 by Jacopo Alighieri (c. 1300–1349). It consists of a *proemio* followed by a brief exposition of selected passages from every canto. Jacopo's objective is to explicate *parte del suo profondo e autentico intendimento* ("part of Dante's profound and authentic intention," 85). In practice this consists of a division of the poem's content *(divisio textus)* and an explication of its allegorical significance: these two emphases constitute the commentary's most distinctive features. For Jacopo, the *Commedia* is a work embracing all facets of learning. Dante's objective is to *dimostrare di sotto allegorico colore le tre qualitadi dell'umana generazione* ("to demonstrate through allegorical coloring the three qualities of human generation"). Jacopo's intended audience is implied in the first lines of the *proemio,* in which he refers to those unilluminated by *scientifica apprensione* ("scientific apprehension") suggesting that he has two readers in mind: those who can penetrate Dante's deeper meanings and those who require some assistance. This observation, coupled with the fact that the commentary is written in Italian, suggests that Jacopo is addressing the latter group.

Bibliography

Alighieri, Jacopo. *Chiose all' "Inferno."* Edited by Saverio Bellomo. Padua: Antenore, 1990.

Mazzoni, Francesco. "Per la storia della critica dantesca: Jacopo Alighieri e Graziolo Bambaglioli." *Studi danteschi* 30 (1951), 157–202.

Vallone, Aldo. *Storia della critica dantesca dal XIV al XX secolo.* 2 vols. Padua: Vallardi, 1981.

Wallace, David. "Assessing the New Author: Commentary on Dante." In *Medieval Literary Theory and Criticism c. 1100–c. 1375: The Commentary Tradition.* Edited by A. J. Minnis and A. B. Scott with the assistance of David Wallace. Oxford: Clarendon Press, 1988, pp. 439–519.

Deborah Parker

Chiron

The mythological figure Chiron *(Chirone),* son of Saturn and Philyra, was depicted by the classical poets as the wisest of all the centaurs, the tutor of Achilles and Hercules, among others. Accordingly, in *Inf.* 12, Dante depicts Chiron as the wise leader of the band of centaurs who, armed with bows and arrows, patrol the banks of Phlegethon, guarding the shades of the murderers, who are submerged in the river of boiling blood in the first ring of the seventh circle of Hell. He is mentioned as Achilles' tutor in *Purg.* 9.37 and is referred to in *Egl.* 3.79 (Giovanni di Virgilio's response to Dante).

Lawrence Baldassaro

Chivalry

Like others of his contemporaries, Dante saw chivalry as an institution and an ideology that, beyond investing modern mental attitudes, projected back into antiquity. The ancient Achilles, Hector, and Aeneas—like the medieval Tristan, Perceval, and Lancelot—were model heroes in the form of exemplary "knights" (cf. *le donne antiche e' cavalieri* ["the ancient ladies and knights"] *Inf.* 5.71). Similarly, Dante's supreme moral values—namely, valor *(valore),* courtesy *(cortesia/gentilezza),* measure *(misura),* wisdom *(senno),* good manners *(belli costumi),* and nobility *(nobiltà)* and the corresponding vices of avarice *(avarizia),* pride *(orgoglio),* envy *(invidia),* and immoderateness *(dismisura)*—were striking personal reinterpretations of much of the chivalric code.

Chivalry also found a strong echo in Dante's ancestry, which he traced back to Cacciaguida, "girded with knighthood in his service" for "just deeds" in the Crusade of 1147 by Emperor Conrad III *(Par.* 15.139f). The presence of this ancestor in *Par.* 15–16 introduces dramatic elements of intense loyalty even though Dante's milieu—the bourgeois mercantile republic of Florence—made him wary of excessive pride in social status. Conforming to the early chivalric ethics and with a conservative, sober moralism that characterizes Dante's aristocratic allegiance, Cacciaguida's discourse is also a denunciation of the bourgeois love of wealth and conspicuous consumption, which Cacciaguida contrasts with the good habits of days gone by. In the episode of Bertran de Born *(Inf.* 28), on the other hand, Dante condemns as "sowing of discord" the chivalrous appreciation of military prowess to the point of delighting in "private" warfare. This was part of Dante's firm espousal of the cause of peace—the supreme ideal of the universal empire he advocated for the worldly happiness of a just humankind.

Dante was familiar with the chivalric literature of France, though probably only with its thirteenth-century prose versions and without direct knowledge of the works of Chrétien de Troyes. His famous praise of "the beautiful tales of King Arthur" *(Arturi regis ambages pulcerrime, DVE* 1.10.2) shows his fascination with such readings, even while his references to Lancelot's adulterous tryst with Guinevere are charged with that moral disapproval that marks his critical stance vis-à-vis the medieval doctrine of "courtly love"

C

(think, first, of the episode of Paolo and Francesca, *Inf.* 5).

Bibliography

Ruggieri, Ruggero M. *L'umanesimo cavalleresco italiano da Dante all'Ariosto.* Napoli: Conte, 1977.

Scaglione, Aldo. *Knights at Court.* Berkeley, Los Angeles: University of California Press, 1991, especially pp. 188–204.

Aldo Scaglione

Christ

The life, death, and teachings of Christ *(Cristo)* permeate the *Commedia* and inform, to a greater or lesser extent, all of Dante's writings. The figure or image of Christ appears by direct and indirect means, by name and by periphrasis, by symbol and by theme. Indeed, taking Dante's works as a whole, one finds that references to Christ's birth, ministry, and Passion abound. They occur in the *Vita Nuova*'s hagiographic presentation of Beatrice as *figura Christi* ("figure of Christ"), discussed below, and in the *Convivio*'s citations of Christ's various roles, such as the Son of God and of the Virgin Mary (e.g., 2.5.2, 4.5.3–5) and as the Way, the Truth, and the Light (2.8.14). Even the allusion to Christ in *DVE* 1.1.1 pays homage to him as the Word, inspiring other words and setting the stage for Dante's remarks on the vernacular. In the *Monarchia,* the references to Christ tend to focus on him as peacemaker (1.4.3, 1.16.1–2) and as example of how to respond to civil authority (3.14.3). But in the *Commedia* Dante presents most fully his conception of Christ, from harrower of Hell to *Salvator Mundi* ("Savior of the World").

Already in the *Vita Nuova* Dante initiates his commentary on Christ by associating an idealized, perfected, ennobling Beatrice—whose name implies "one who confers blessedness" and in whose presence nothing vile can exist—with words, numbers, and events that point to Christ. Thus, Dante typically uses superlatives to describe his beloved's unique and lofty status: she is *gentilissima* ("the most gracious") and *nobilissima* ("the most noble"), the color of her dress is *bianchissimo* ("the whitest"), and her greeting is *dolcissimo* ("the sweetest"). Furthermore, the sacred numbers 3 and 9 (the square of 3), associated with the Trinity, accompany her: Dante first sees her when both are in their ninth year and then again

precisely nine years later; she appears in a threesome (in the midst of two other ladies); the time of day most often associated with her appearance is the ninth hour; and she dies in the ninth hour of the ninth month in the ninth decade of the thirteenth century (1290). Even the circumstances of her life and death are designed to remind us of Christ's. The companion who walks before Beatrice, for example, is named Giovanna, even as Giovanni (John the Baptist) preceded Christ—an analogy Dante makes explicit (*VN* 24). Similarly, pilgrims headed to Rome to view Christ's image in the Veronica first pass by Florence and see where Beatrice was born, lived, and died (*VN* 40).

One of the main messages of the *Vita Nuova* is that Dante receives "new life" through his love for and adoration of Beatrice, who among other things symbolizes Christ and like him represents a *miracolo* ("miracle") temporarily sent to Earth to inspire others but ultimately destined for the highest heaven. Though Dante's love for Beatrice begins as youthful eros, it eventually transforms itself into mature *caritas* ("charity"), the type of love embodied in Christ's atoning sacrifice and in the scriptural notion that God is love (1 John 4:8, *Deus caritas est*). The *Vita Nuova*'s descriptions of love in its various manifestations serve as a primer, a guide that introduces the potential relationship between earthly love (man for woman) and divine love (man for God), and in this context the author's concluding desire—*io spero di dicer di lei quello che mai non fue detto d'alcuna* ("I hope to write of her what has never been written of any other woman," *VN* 42)—can be interpreted as a proposal not only to compose the *Commedia,* in which Beatrice plays a key role, but also to write of Christ after the most innovative fashion possible.

Certainly, of all Dante's works, the *Commedia* best reflects, structurally and thematically, the author's focus on and devotion to Christ. The Christlike nature of this epic poem is embedded in its very structure, in which the form serves function in an unparalleled fashion. To understand this fact, the reader must appreciate the significance that Dante and medieval Christian writers in general conferred on numerology. As alluded to above, Christ is associated with various numbers throughout the Middle Ages. In addition to being one of *three* members of the Godhead, he began his ministry at the age of *thirty,* lived for *thirty-three* years, and died—as Dante underscores in *Convivio* 4.23.10—in his *thirty-fourth* year, after bleeding from *five* wounds on the cross. Similarly, Dante's poem is divided into *three* canticles (Hell, Purgatory, and Paradise); each canticle contains *thirty-three* cantos, except for the first canticle, which contains an introductory canto (for a total of *thirty-four*); each canto is made of tercets containing *three* hendecasyllabic verses, for a total of *thirty-three* syllables per tercet; and Beatrice makes her appearance in the *thirtieth* canto of *Purgatorio,* which canticle contains *five* references to Christ's name.

While Christ is not mentioned by name in *Inferno,* presumably out of respect for his holy person, references to him nevertheless figure prominently in the narrative. The second member of the triune Godhead that created Hell, he is the *somma sapïenza* ("highest wisdom") referred to in the carved inscription above the Gate of Hell (*Inf.* 3.6)—and possibly alluded to in an apostrophe in the canto of the simonists (*Inf.* 19.10). He is also the harrower of Hell, and *Inf.* 4.52–63 contains a description of the harrowing from Virgil's perspective, in which Christ is viewed as *un possente / con segno di vittoria coronato* ("a powerful one . . . crowned with a sign of victory," 53–54). Virgil again refers to this event in *Inf.* 12, when he refers to Christ by circumlocution as *colui che la gran preda / levò a Dite del cerchio superno* ("he . . . who took from Dis the great spoils of the highest circle," 38–39). He is the *nimica podesta* ("enemy governor," *Inf.* 6.96) who will judge the dead and, as Virgil reminds Dante at the end of the canticle, *l'uom che nacque e visse sanza pecca* ("the man who was born and lived without sin," *Inf.* 34.115).

Dante-pilgrim, in his invective against simoniacal popes, exalts Christ as *Nostro Segnore* ("our Lord," *Inf.* 19.91), the only epithet for Christ uttered by a saved soul in Hell. Images of Christ's Passion, however, are brought sharply and disturbingly to mind by means of the parodic iconography of various punishments, such as that of Caiaphas *crucifisso in terra con tre pali* ("crucified to the earth with three stakes," *Inf.* 23.111) and that of Satan, with his three faces and three bloody mouths, the middle of which contains Judas Iscariot (see *Inf.* 34.38ff.).

As mentioned earlier, Christ's name appears only *five* times in *Purgatorio:* 20.87, citing Boniface VIII as Christ's vicar; 21.8, making reference to the resurrected Christ's appearance on the road to Emmaus; 23.74, alluding to Christ's tree, mean-

The triumphs of Christ and Mary in the sphere of the Fixed Stars. La comedia di Dante Aligieri, *with commentary by Alessandro Vellutello, published by Francesco Marcolini, Venice, 1544. Giamatti Collection: Courtesy of the Mount Holyoke College Archives and Special Collections.*

ing the cross; 26.129, naming Christ the abbot of the college or brotherhood; and 32.102, referring to that Rome of which Christ is Roman, namely, Heaven. But even more than in *Inferno,* allusions to Christ pervade the second canticle, from the baptismal and resurrection imagery that refreshingly opens and also closes *Purgatorio* (e.g., the first canto's initial aquatic metaphors and the image of the regenerating reed; the final canto's depiction of the pilgrim immersed in Eunoe and the image of new plants renewed with new leaves).

The plan of Purgatory's seven terraces likewise recalls at the beginning of each purgation an event indirectly related to Christ via an exemplum taken from the life of the Virgin Mary. These events—the Annunciation (*Purg.* 10.34–35, 25.128), the marriage at Cana (13.29, 22.142–43), the child Jesus in the temple (15.88–92), the Visitation (18.100), and the Nativity (20.19–24)—constitute an essential part of the scourge of the penitents. Similarly, Christ's teachings are recalled at the end of each terrace via a beatitude pronounced to indicate the completion of that level's purgation (see *Purg.* 12.110, "blessed are the poor in spirit"; 15.38, "blessed are the merciful";

17.68–69, "blessed are the peacemakers"; 19.50, "blessed are they that mourn"; 22.6, "blessed are they that thirst"; 24.151–154, "blessed are they that hunger"; and 27.8, "blessed are the pure in heart").

Arguably, the chief image other than Beatrice that represents Christ in the second canticle is *un grifon* ("a griffin," *Purg.* 29.108), an animal that is half eagle and half lion and that has been traditionally taken to symbolize Christ's two natures, human and divine (alluded to in such later passages as *Par.* 2.41–42, 6.13–21, 7.35–36, and 13.26–27). Because the griffin pulls a two-wheeled chariot symbolic of the Church, Dante appears to make a strong iconographical and doctrinal statement on the close relationship that should exist between Christ and his church. However, the main message concerning Christ that *Purgatorio* seems to teach is that he was crucified for us (*per noi crucifisso,* 6.119) and that he liberated us with his blood (*ne liberò con la sua vena,* 23.75), meaning that his sacrifice on the cross takes away our sins (*le peccata leva,* 16.18).

The name of Christ appears in *thirty-four* verses but for a total of *thirty-five* times in *Paradiso* (appearing twice in 19.106): 6.14, Constantine alludes to the twofold nature of Christ; 9.120, Folco refers to the triumph of Christ, meaning his harrowing of Hell; 11.72, Thomas Aquinas states that Poverty accompanied Christ on the cross; 11.102, Francis preached of Christ before the sultan; 11.107, Francis received the stigmata from Christ; 12.37, Bonaventure refers to the army of Christ; 12.71, 73, 75, Bonaventure details Dominic's relationship to Christ; 14.104, 106, 108, Dante-poet describes the flaming cross of Christ in Mars; 17.51, Cacciaguida refers to Boniface VIII's buying and selling of Christ; 19.72, the Eagle speaks of the plight of the pagan who cannot know Christ; 19.104, 106, 108, the Eagle addresses the necessity of believing in Christ to gain salvation; 20.47, the Eagle talks of Trajan's failure to know Christ in life; 23.20, Beatrice enjoins Dante-pilgrim to behold the blessed host of Christ's triumph; 23.72, Beatrice refers to the rays of Christ, who is compared to the Sun; 25.15, Dante-pilgrim alludes to Peter as the first fruit of Christ's vicars; 26.53, Dante-pilgrim cites John the Evangelist as the eagle of Christ; 27.40, Peter refers to the church as the Bride of Christ; 29.98, Beatrice mentions Christ's Passion; 29.109, Beatrice speaks of Christ's preaching; 31.3, Dante-pilgrim refers to the blood of Christ; 31.107, a pilgrim gazing at the Veronica calls Christ his Lord and true God; 32.20, 24, 27, Bernard teaches of faith in Christ; 32.83, 85, 87, Bernard remarks on Christian baptism and the face most like Christ's, which is Mary's; 32.125, Bernard acknowledges Peter as the one to whom Christ gave the keys of the Church.

Together these *thirty-four* verses recall that Christ atoned for the sins of the world in his *thirty-fourth* year, while the *thirty-five* citations of his name recall both the perfect age of man (the midpoint of three score and ten years) and the age of Dante-pilgrim in the year he makes his pilgrimage to Christ. Furthermore, in the four cantos (sometimes grouped as *three* plus *one*) in which the name appears at the end of a line—cantos 12, 14, 19, and, much later, 32—Dante always rhymes the Italian word for Christ *(Cristo)* with itself, no other word being worthy. This practice also underscores the importance of understanding the name of Christ as the representation of the Word.

In *Paradiso* Christ is also referred to periphrastically by such standard epithets as the Lamb of God (*l'Agnel di Dio,* 17.33) and the blessed Lamb (*benedetto Agnello,* 24.2), Our Lord (*Nostro Segnor,* 24.35), the Word of God (*Verbo di Dio,* 7.30) and the Divine Word (*'l verbo divino,* 23.73), and the Light, accompanied by various adjectives such as "living" and "eternal" (see 13.55, 23.31, 33.116, 124). The message relating to Christ found in the central canto of the final canticle is that Christ "takes away our sins" (*le peccata tolle, Par.* 17.33), a statement that echoes *Purg.* 16.18, cited above.

The *Commedia* culminates in the vision of the triune Godhead (*Par.* 33.115ff.), in a contemplation of "three circles, of three colors and of one circumference" (*tre giri / di tre colori e d'una contenenza,* 116–117). The second circle (Christ the Son) reflects the first (God the Father), while the third represents the Holy Ghost. In presenting the members of the Godhead in this highly metaphorical fashion, Dante testifies to their eternal nature: like a circle, without beginning or end, they are eternal and endless. Christ, who condescended to come to Earth to effect the plan of salvation and to exist temporarily in time, now resides in more exalted spheres. The *Commedia*'s final commentary on the Word is that, having passed from time to eternity, he is now the object of celestial joy and awaits those who will repent and come unto him.

Bibliography

Baglivi, Giuseppe, and Garrett McCutchan. "Dante, Christ, and the Fallen Bridges." *Italica* 54 (1977), 250–262.

Cotter, James Finn. "Dante and Christ: The Pilgrim as 'Beatus Vir.'" *Italian Quarterly* 28, 107 (1987), 5–19.

Durling, Robert M. "Farinata and the Body of Christ." *Stanford Italian Review* 2, 1 (1981), 5–35.

Miller, Clarence H. "Hercules and His Labors as Allegories of Christ and His Victory over Sin in Dante's *Inferno*." *Quaderni d'italianistica* 5, 1 (1984), 1–17.

Sowell, Madison U. "*Paradiso* XIV." In *Dante's "Divine Comedy," Introductory Readings III: Paradiso*. Edited by Tibor Wlassics. *Lectura Dantis* 16–17 (Spring–Fall 1995), 198–212.

Madison U. Sowell

Chronicles, Florentine

The writing of Florentine chronicles evidently began as an exercise in "nationalist" propaganda. The earliest surviving exemplar is the anonymous Latin *Chronica de Origine Civitatis,* compiled by 1230. It has two main themes: Florence's essentially Roman character and the (imaginary) perennial antibiosis between Florence and Fiesole, culminated by Florence's destruction of its rival in 1125. The *Chronica* ends with this event, having prepared for it with a tapestry of legendary, mythological, and historical threads drawn from various classical sources and elsewhere. Opening with the city's supposed foundation (laid out in imitation of Rome) by Julius Caesar together with its colonization by the best of Roman society, Florentine history until 1125 is seen in two approximate halves, divided by the town's (fictitious) destruction by Totila and (equally fictitious) refoundation by the Romans, this time closely modeled on Christian Rome. Fiesole is denigrated as anti-Roman because Catiline made it his Tuscan headquarters (cf. *Par.* 6.53–54). But the two cities are also related, since Troy was supposedly a daughter of Fiesole; Rome, a daughter of Troy; and Florence, a daughter of Rome. These are the legends *d'i Troiani, di Fiesole e di Roma* ("about the Trojans, and Fiesole, and Rome") that Cacciaguida pictures twelfth-century Florentine matrons recounting to their households (*Par.* 15.124–126). Their function was to dignify a petty local rivalry.

No other Italian town made so much of its Roman connections; and the same theme is the leitmotif of the second extant chronicle, the *Gesta Florentinorum,* also in Latin, by Sanzanome, who draws on the *Chronica* and continues the narrative down to 1231. Here the conquest of Fiesole explicitly marks the dawn of the "modern" era in the *comune*'s history, an era of territorial expansion. There are verbal similarities between Sanzanome and Dante which suggest that the poet knew the *Gesta.*

Popular chronicles tended to be taken over as public property and revised with new emphases. This does not appear to apply to Sanzanome, but it does apply to the *Chronica,* of which at least four redactions survive, two in Latin (the second probably written in 1264) and two in Tuscan. One of the latter, the *Libro fiesolano,* written between 1284 and 1330, adapts and enlarges the original quite drastically. It also introduces a new theme: the influence of Mars, god of war, in the foundation of Troy.

Textual divergence apparently characterized just as extensively a second, anonymous chronicle entitled *Gesta Florentinorum,* which is lost but has been reconstructed (in Tuscan) from later works that used some version of it as a source. It seems to have covered the period from 1080 to 1278, though a redaction with those coordinates could itself have been an amplification of an older, slimmer text.

The earliest extant Florentine chronicle which was originally drafted in the vernacular is known as that of Pseudo–Brunetto Latini, because it was once erroneously attributed to Brunetto. It spans the years between 1180 and 1303, though with a gap from 1249 to 1285. Before the gap it merely elaborates Martin of Troppau's *Chronicon Pontificum et Imperatorum* with a Florentine slant, but the section starting at 1285 is genuinely focused on Florence and reveals the anonymous author as an able writer. His chronicle is the first to connect Florence with Mars: it mentions Mars's dilapidated statue by the Ponte Vecchio as the spot where Buondelmonte de' Buondelmonti was killed—the event which was seen as having launched Florence's factional strife (cf. *Inf.* 13.143–150; *Par.* 16.145–147).

Alongside two sets of Florentine annals (embracing, respectively, 1110–1173 and 1107–1247) and a list of consuls and podestà of Florence from 1196 to 1267, these works, in their various

C versions, are the only surviving Florentine chronicles before those of Compagni and Villani. Villani (5.30) states that many chronicles were destroyed by fire in 1115 and 1117, and even after those dates the extant specimens are presumably only a part of what once existed. The available evidence cannot fully account for Dante's knowledge of Florentine history and pseudo-history; nonetheless it does so in part, and to some extent illuminates his attitudes toward it. For instance, he calls Florence *la bellissima e famosissima figlia di Roma* ("the most beautiful and famous daughter of Rome," *Conv.* 1.3.4) and says that Rome made her *ad ymaginem suam atque similitudinem* ("in her own image and after her own likeness," *Epist.* 7.25).

It was formerly thought that the *Storia fiorentina* ascribed to Ricordano and Giacotto Malispini, which appears to stop at 1286 (though in one—truncated—manuscript it continues until at least 1317), was another thirteenth-century chronicle. It is now known, however, to be a late-fourteenth-century forgery copied from the *Libro fiesolano* and from an abridgement of Villani's *Nuova cronica,* with insertions designed to glorify certain Florentine families, especially the obscure Bonaguisi (another case of chronicles becoming quasi-public property).

Bibliography

Sources

Cronica fiorentina compilata nel secolo XIII. In *Testi fiorentini del Dugento e dei primi del Trecento.* Edited by A. Schiaffini [1926]. Florence: Sansoni, 1954, pp. 82–150.

Die Gesta Florentinorum von 1080-1278. Edited by B. Schmeidler. In *Die Annalen des Tholomeus von Lucca in doppelter Fassung.* Edited by B. Schmeidler (= *Monumenta Germaniae Historica: Scriptores Rerum Germanicarum, Nova Series,* 8). Berlin: Weidmann, 1930, pp. 243–277.

Quellen und Forschungen zur ältesten Geschichte der Stadt Florenz. 2 vols. Edited by O. Hartwig. Vol. 1, Marburg: Elwert, 1875; Vol. 2, Halle: Niemeyer, 1880.

Storia fiorentina di Ricordano Malispini, col seguito di Giacotto Malispini, dalla edificazione di Firenze sino all'anno 1286. Edited by V. Follini. Florence: Ricci, 1816. Reprinted in Rome: Multigrafica, 1976.

Studies

Aquilecchia, Giovanni. "Dante and the Florentine Chroniclers." *Bulletin of the John Rylands Library* 48 (1965–1966), 30–55.

Barnes, John C. "Un problema in via di chiusura: la *Cronica* malispiniana." *Studi e problemi di critica testuale* 27 (1983), 15–32.

Davis, Charles T. "Il Buon Tempo Antico." In *Florentine Studies: Politics and Society in Renaissance Florence.* Edited by N. Rubinstein. London: Faber, 1968, pp. 45–69. Reprinted in Davis's *Dante's Italy and Other Essays.* Philadelphia: University of Pennsylvania Press, 1984, pp. 71–93.

———. "The Malispini Question." In *A Giuseppe Ermini = Studi medievali,* third series, 10 (1970), iii, 215–254. Reprinted in Davis's *Dante's Italy and Other Essays.* Philadelphia: University of Pennsylvania Press, 1984, pp. 94–136.

———. "Recent Work on the Malispini Question." In *Dante's Italy and Other Essays.* Philadelphia: University of Pennsylvania Press, 1984, pp. 290–299.

———. "Topographical and Historical Propaganda in Early Florentine Chronicles and in Villani." *Medioevo e Rinascimento* 2 (1988), 33–51.

Rubinstein, N. "The Beginnings of Political Thought in Florence: A Study in Mediaeval Historiography." *Journal of the Warburg and Courtauld Institutes* 5 (1942), 198–227.

Santini, P. *Quesiti e ricerche di storiografia fiorentina.* Florence: Seeber, 1903.

John C. Barnes

Chrysostom, St. John

Early Greek Church Father, born in Antioch, Syria, c. 345 C.E., died near Comana, Helenopontus, 407. As a young man, he studied law and later became a monk before joining the priesthood, and in 398 he was appointed archbishop of Constantinople.

A highly skilled orator (hence his Greek surname, *Chrysostom,* meaning "golden-mouthed"), his eloquent speech and the enthusiastic nature of his preaching—together with his sense of humor and ability to apply the Scriptures to everyday life—made him popular with the common people. However, he was also the greatest moral theologian of the ancient church, and his castigation of the corrupt clergy and the profligate wealthy classes (in particular, he criticized Eudoxia, wife of Arcadius, the Eastern Roman Emperor) earned him many powerful enemies, leading to his banishment on two occasions, imprisonment, and eventual death in exile.

Chrysostom was a prolific writer of scriptural homilies and also produced sermons, treatises, and letters. While his work is not especially original, the intelligence of his biblical exegesis and his eloquent language and severe moral teaching made him an important source for later scriptural commentators.

Dante mentions Chrysostom *(Giovanni Crisostomo)* once, placing him in the second circle of wise souls in the fourth Heaven of the Sun and pairing him with the Old Testament prophet, Nathan, who also rebuked royal wickedness. He gives him the title *metropolitano* ("metropolitan"), which refers to his role as archbishop and patriarch of a major city and many dioceses (*Par.* 12.136–137).

Angela G. Meekins

Ciacco

A glutton who undergoes punishment in the third circle of Hell (*Inf.* 6.37–93). Nothing is known of his historical identity. According to Dante's text, he lived in Florence, was known there as "Ciacco," and was Dante's contemporary. Since he challenges the pilgrim to recognize him, they presumably knew each other.

Commentary on Ciacco focuses mainly on hypotheses concerning his identity and his name. It is doubtful that he was the thirteenth-century versifier Ciacco dell'Anguillaia, as one undocumented theory proposes. Boccaccio's story about a certain Ciacco, a witty and sociable glutton (*Dec.* 9.8), may be simply an imaginative elaboration of Dante's character. The name could be short for a given name (such as Giacomo) or a derogatory nickname meaning "hog."

The pilgrim asks Ciacco three questions. The central one elicits a recitation of civic turmoil, partisanship, and bloodshed in Florence, caused by envy, pride, and avarice. Ciacco's reply (*Inf.* 6.64–75) contains the first of several political prophecies throughout the *Commedia,* and it is the first of those with personal implications for Dante (cf. *Inf.* 10.79–81, 15.55–72; *Purg.* 8.133–139), whose exile results from Florentine partisan strife.

Dante's ancestor, Cacciaguida, spells out the precise meaning of these prophecies for the pilgrim in *Par.* 17.43–99.

Denise Heilbronn-Gaines

Ciampolo

Corrupt official of Navarre punished for barratry in the fifth bolgia of Malebolge. In *Inf.* 22.31–151, he is hooked out of the pitch like an otter; is played with like a mouse by the devils, who want to tear the flesh from his limbs; but in the end gets the better of his tormentors by tricking them into giving him just enough time to jump back into the boiling pitch. It is the early commentators who supply the name of the sinner, and they in turn rely on Dante for all the biographical information: Ciampolo's Navarrese origins, his wastrel father, his service in the household of "good king Thibaut," and his sin.

Michael Caesar

Cianfa

First to be named of the five all-but-anonymous Florentine thieves punished along with the Pistoiese Vanni Fucci in the seventh ditch of Malebolge (*Inf.* 25). Though Florentine archives mention a politically active Cianfa Donati who died before 1289, the early commentators' identification of the thief as a member of that prominent family is at best speculative, since—aside from the first name overheard by the pilgrim Dante (*Inf.* 25.43) and the fact that Cianfa and his companions are from Florence (*Inf.* 26.1–6)—the text provides no further clue to his identity. Another inference is that Cianfa has been transformed into the six-footed reptile which fuses with Agnello to produce a hybrid monster. To insist on attaching a historical identity to Cianfa and his fellows contravenes Dante's strategy of robbing the thieves of a perduring form and a name.

Anthony Oldcorn

Cicero, Marcus Tullius

Roman orator, philosopher, and statesman (106–43 B.C.E.), commonly referred to by Dante as *Tullio.* He is given a place of honor in Limbo among the great philosophers and writers of antiquity (*Inf.* 4.141). His writings transmitted Roman cultural values to European posterity and provided a model for Latin prose style for centuries to come. His philosophical essays, written during periods of enforced retirement from public life, passed Greek philosophy to western Europe. His political and literary activities were linked to the Roman republic and its principles. He was temporarily exiled by Caesar for his support of Pompey. After attacking Anthony in a series of speeches (the *Philippics*), he was beheaded in 43 B.C.E.

Cicero's extensive literary output can be divided into his orations, his treatises on rhetoric and philosophy, and his private correspondence. Dante was most familiar with his philosophical writings. Of the fifty quotations and references to Cicero that Moore has noted in Dante, over half come from the *De officiis* and the *De senectute,* with many others from the *De finibus bonorum et malorum* and the *De amicitia.* Moore further attributes features of Dante's classification of sins (e.g., the distinction between sins of violence and fraud) to Cicero. Andreotti sees Brunetto Latini as influential for Dante's use of Cicero, tracing some of his quotations of Cicero to Brunetto's *Tresor.*

In *Conv.* 1.11.14, Dante considers those who prefer Provençal to the Italian vernacular to be similar to those referred to by Cicero (in the opening of the *De finibus*) who preferred Greek to Latin culture. In *Conv.* 2.12.3, he credits Cicero's *De amicitia,* along with Boethius's *De consolatione philosophiae,* with having spurred his passion for philosophy after Beatrice's death.

Bibliography

Andreotti, Giulio. "Dante e Cicerone." *L'Alighieri* 1–2 (1993), 101–112.

Moore, Edward. *Studies in Dante. First Series: Scripture and Classical Authors in Dante.* Oxford: Clarendon Press, 1896. Reprinted in New York: Haskell House, 1968.

Renaudet, Augustin. *Dante humaniste.* Paris: Les Belles Lettres, 1952.

Renucci, Paul. *Dante: Disciple et juge du monde gréco-latin.* Paris: Les Belles Lettres, 1954.

Jo Ann Cavallo

Cimabue

Known today for his frescoes in Assisi as well as two important life-size crucifixes, Cimabue (c. 1240–1308) was a Florentine painter and Giotto's teacher. His significance in the history of Italian art lies not only in his works but also in his style: he was among the first to depart from the conventions of the Byzantine tradition, opting instead for a plasticity of figuration and a representation of emotion to which audiences could more easily relate.

Dante was probably familiar with Cimabue's *Maestà* in the Florentine Church of Santa Trinita, as well as with his crucifix in the Church of Santa Croce—one of the signal victims of the 1966 flood of Florence. The poet may also have visited Assisi and seen Cimabue's frescoes there, though no hard evidence exists to establish this. He apparently judged Cimabue to be the most significant artist of his youth, for in *Purg.*11.94 he cites the painter's displacement by Giotto as an example of the transitory nature of earthly fame: *Credette Cimabue ne la pintura / tener lo campo, e ora ha Giotto il grido, / sì che la fama di colui è scura* ("Cimabue believed he held the field in painting, and now Giotto has the cry, so that the fame of the first is darkened"). Dante's analysis appears to have been prescient, for Giotto remains today the more highly praised of the two painters.

Michael Sherberg

Cincinnatus, Lucus Quinctius

Roman general and statesman (519?–439? B.C.E.) cited in *Conv.* 4.5.15 *(Quinzio Cincinnato)* and *Mon.* 2.5.9–10 for his unselfish leadership and dedication to the common good. In *Paradiso* Justianian recalls his role in defending the Roman republic against the Aequians (6.46), and Cacciaguida refers to him as an example of virtue lacking in modern-day Florence (15.127). A farmer who was appointed dictator in 458 B.C.E., he resigned his office after his mission was accomplished. For Dante he exemplifies the right rule of the Romans, a people chosen by God to govern the world.

Richard Lansing

Cino da Pistoia

Cino (= Guittoncino) da Pistoia (1270–c. 1336) was an intimate acquaintance of Dante, a well-known jurist, teacher (in the studia of Bologna, Perugia, Siena, Naples, and perhaps Florence) and legal commentator (*Lectura in codicem,* on the first nine books of the Justinian code), and an active participant in the political events of his native city (from which he was exiled from 1303 to 1306). His lyric production is the largest of the *stilnovisti* (18 canzoni, 13 *ballate,* and 134 sonnets including fragments) and reflects virtually all their major themes, images, and concepts. In addition to the lyrics on amorous topics, Cino's *canzoniere* is especially rich in *tenzoni* and in poems inspired by local partisan strife and political exile.

Cino's acquaintanceship with Dante may have begun in Bologna in 1287, and he may have written one of the three extant responses to Dante's first sonnet in the *Vita Nuova* "A ciascun'alma presa e gentil core," if "Naturalmente chere ogni amadore" is by his hand (and not by Terino da Castelfiorentino's, as seems more likely). The first textual evidence we have of their friendship is Cino's canzone "Avegna ched el m'aggia più per tempo," written to console Dante on the death of Beatrice (1290). Their friendship flourished during the first decade of the Trecento, as several *tenzoni* on amorous topics attest. Dante praises Cino as the poet of love par excellence in *DVE* 2.2.8, citing the following canzoni for their excellence: "Digno sono eo di morte," "Non spero che giamai per mia salute," and "Avegna che io aggia più per tempo." Dante also addressed a letter (*Epist.* 3) to him, the *exulanti Pistoriensi* ("Pistoian in exile").

In addition to their literary affinities Cino and Dante were united in their fervent support of Henry VII of Luxemburg, whose death on August 24, 1313, put an end to Cino's and Dante's hopes for political peace and unity under the imperial aegis. The solemnity that characterizes Cino's canzone "Da poi che la natura ha fine posto," written on the occasion of Henry's death, conveys his keen sense of loss. Cino also wrote the moving canzone "Su per la costa, Amor, de l'alto monte" to commemorate the death of Dante.

Beyond his synthesis of various stilnovistic elements, Cino's basic contribution to the school lies in his objective psychological realism, which manifests itself in the intensely personal, almost confessional tone of his poems; and in this regard he serves as the bridge linking the *dolce stil nuovo* and Petrarch. Because of his extreme versatility as a poet, Cino was able to mediate among various "schools" and individual poets, to compose lyrics in a number of modes and styles and ultimately to derive profit from and contribute directly to the several major literary currents of his age. Cino enjoyed literary and personal friendships with the greatest contemporary Italian poets, all of whom regarded him with much admiration: in addition to Dante's praise in *De vulgari eloquentia,* Boccaccio pays him tribute by incorporating almost all his canzone "La dolce vista e 'l bel guardo soave" in the *Filostrato* (5:62–65), and Petrarch laments his death in the sonnet "Piangete, donne, et con voi pianga Amore."

Bibliography

Colloquio Cino da Pistoia (Roma, 25 ottobre 1975). Rome: Accademia Nazionale dei Lincei, 1976.

Corti, Maria. "Il linguaggio poetico di Cino da Pistoia." *Cultura neolatina* 12 (1952), 185–223.

De Robertis, Domenico. "Cino da Pistoia." In *I Minori.* Milan: Marzorati, 1961, pp. 285–306.

———. "Cino da Pistoia e la crisi del linguaggio poetico." *Convivium* (1952), 1–35.

———. "Cino e le 'imitazioni' dalle rime di Dante." *Studi danteschi* 29 (1950), 103–177.

Hollander, Robert. "Dante and Cino da Pistoia." *Dante Studies* 110 (1992), 201–231.

Kleinhenz, Christopher. "Cino da Pistoia and the Italian Lyric Tradition." In *L'imaginaire courtois et son double.* Edited by Giovanna Angeli and Luciano Formisano. Naples: Edizioni Scientifiche Italiane, 1992, pp. 147–163.

———. *The Early Italian Sonnet: The First Century (1220–1321).* Lecce: Milella, 1986.

Poeti del dolce stil nuovo. Edited by Mario Marti. Florence: Le Monnier, 1969.

Christopher Kleinhenz

Circe

Daughter of Helios, god of the Sun, and the sea nymph Perse. An enchantress on the island of Aenea, she is best known for her encounter with Ulysses, who is cast up on her island. Although she transforms his crew into swine, Ulysses escapes her curse and forces her to return the men to their previous state. He then succumbs to her charms and passes a year on the island (Ovid, *Meta.* 14.308). Ulysses, who is condemned as a fraudulent counselor in the eighth circle of Hell, recalls this episode (which occurs in *Ody.* 10) in his recounting of his final journey (*Inf.* 26.90–93). Circe is also referred to in *Purg.* 14.42 and *Par.* 27.137–138.

Virginia Jewiss

Clare, St.

St. Clare of Assisi (1194–1253; *Chiara*) was a disciple of St. Francis of Assisi. In 1212 she founded a female Franciscan order called the *Clarisse,* or "Poor Clares." The order quickly became popular in Italy. She is mentioned in the Heaven of the Moon (*Par.* 3.97–102) when Dante asks Piccarda to tell him what vow she broke during her lifetime. Piccarda relates how she fled from the world as a young girl and joined the order of St. Clare, later to be abducted from it against her will and forced to marry, thereby breaking the vow she made when she joined the order, namely, to be married only to Christ. In her story, Piccarda refers to St. Clare as a woman who lived a perfect life and who is assigned to a higher sphere in Paradise.

Maria Ann Roglieri

Classical Antiquity

One of the most famous scenes in the *Commedia* takes place in the first circle of Hell, where Dante-pilgrim and Virgil are met by *quattro grand'ombre* ("four great shades," *Inf.* 4.83) who come to greet them: *quelli è Omero poeta sovrano; / l'altro è Orazio satiro che vene; / Ovidio è 'l terzo, e l'ultimo Lucano* ("that is Homer, the supreme poet; the next is Horace the satirist; Ovid is the third; and the last, Lucan," *Inf.* 4.88–90). After a brief consultation, Dante-pilgrim is invited to join their company, and the great poets continue onward together.

As Dante-pilgrim learns, Limbo is populated by the great spirits of antiquity, primarily from the classical world. From myth and history Dante-pilgrim encounters Electra, Hector, Aeneas, Caesar, Camilla, Penthesilea, Latinus, Lavinia, Brutus, Lucretia, Julia, Marcia, Cornelia, and Saladin. Among the great sages of the past Aristotle reigns supreme, accompanied by Socrates, Plato, Democritus, Diogenes, Anaxagoras, Thales, Empedocles, Heraclitus, Zeno, Dioscorides, Orpheus, Cicero, Linus, Seneca, Euclid, Ptolemy, Hippocrates, Avicenna, Galen, and Averroës. In *Purg.* 22.97–114, Virgil will tell Statius of other souls who dwell in Limbo: Terence, Caecilius, Plautus, Varius, Persius, Euripides, Antiphon, Simonides, and Agathon join the sages of the past, while Antigone, Deiphyle, Argia, Ismene, Hypsipyle, Manto, Thetis, and Deidamia with her sisters join the figures from myth and history.

This was antiquity as Dante knew it—an antiquity about which it is difficult to generalize, because the poetry through which this vision reaches us requires careful attention to shifting nuance and context. For example, the list of master poets from antiquity in *VN* 25.9 is the same as the one in *Inf.* 4, but the one in *DVE* 2.6 is not. Here we find Homer and Horace omitted and Statius added, while in *Conv.* 2.13 Homer and Horace return, and Juvenal appears for the first time. At least in part the explanation for the changes seems to be that since *De vulgari eloquentia* presents models for rhetorical imitation, the context requires Statius rather than Homer, because Dante could not read Greek; the *Convivio,* in contrast, presents models for human behavior, so Dante selects a list of poets with primarily that end in mind.

To the extent that generalization is possible, Dante's vision of antiquity presents a number of surprising features. For one thing, it is intensely personal, a mental construct that constantly fragments itself into individuals who take on a life of their own in Dante's imagination. Second, his vision of antiquity privileges writers, especially authors of poetry. Aristotle may be *'l maestro di color che sanno* ("the master of those who know," *Inf.* 4.131), but Dante-pilgrim's guide through *Inferno* and *Purgatorio* is a poet, and the affective power of *Inf.* 4 rests in the encounter with the company of poets. What is more, notwithstanding what is implied by the number of individuals listed in *Inf.* 4.115–147, Dante's actual knowledge of antiquity turns out to derive from an intimate relationship with only a few key works. And finally, Dante's vision of antiquity is always tinged with sadness, for without the grace of God the best minds of the ancient world can never leave Limbo.

Since Dante's knowledge of antiquity derives from the texts he read, it is important to establish just which texts he knew. Edward Moore, whose hundred-year-old study remains the basic source on this question, counted almost a thousand citations, references, and reminiscences of classical authors that have left traces in Dante's choice of language. Of these the largest number—over three hundred—are to Aristotle, followed by Virgil with some two hundred references and Ovid with a hundred. Cicero and Lucan come next with around fifty each; then Statius and Boethius with thirty to forty each; and Horace, Livy, and Orosius with ten to twenty each. These are followed by scattered references to Plato, Homer, Juvenal, Seneca, Ptolemy, Aesop, and Augustine. It is possible that Valerius Maximus should also be added to the list.

Statistics, however, do not tell the whole story here, for even with Aristotle not all is as it seems, since in the Middle Ages he was read with a strongly Neoplatonic bias. On the one hand, Aristotle was *quello glorioso Filosofo, al quale la Natura più aperse li suoi segreti* ("that glorious philosopher to whom nature most revealed her secrets," *Conv.* 3.5.7). Although Cicero and Boethius were important, Aristotle was Dante's chief source in matters of ethics, physics, and physiology and an important guide in politics, psychology, and metaphysics as well. To him Dante was indebted for basic concepts, like the distinction between incontinence and malice, fundamental notions like the ethical mean and the relationship between virtues and vices, and curious details like the association between sodomites and usurers in *Inf.* 11.49–51 and 94–111 and 17.43ff. (cf. *Physics* 2.2. and 2.7). Yet Dante could not read Greek, which sent him scurrying through Latin translations that he himself complains do not always agree with one another (*Conv.* 2.14.6). And even though Moore claims that Dante drew freely from most of Aristotle's works, later research has shown that almost all of the exact references can be traced to the *Nicomachean Ethics, Physics, Metaphysics, De caelo,* and *De anima.* In other words, Dante saw much of his own world and that of the past in Aristotelian terms, but his vision in this area was limited.

Dante's knowledge of his other classical sources proves to be similarly restricted. Virgil was known mostly through the *Aeneid,* Ovid mostly through the *Metamorphoses,* Horace mostly through the *Ars poetica,* and Plato exclusively through the *Timaeus.* Dante seems to have known Cicero's *De officiis, De senectute, De amicitia,* and *De finibus;* there are a few citations to other works, but none to the speeches. Homer is cited only through intermediaries, and the references to Livy are sufficiently inexact that the same may be true for them as well.

In this area, Dante's limitations are simply those of his time. Before the age of printing, books were too expensive to be easily accessible, and the manuscripts that were available often lacked such basic reference aids as chapter divisions and indexes. Moving about as much as he did would have made it even more difficult for Dante to have

consistent access to the books he would have wanted. Then, as now, substitutes existed, and Dante appears to have taken advantage of a number of intermediaries when access to classical authors proved difficult: Albertus Magnus, Thomas Aquinas, and Giles of Rome in addition to Aristotle, for example, and John of Garland in addition to Ovid. With Ovid, Dante also used such scholarly aids as the prose summaries by Lanctantius Placidus and the later commentaries added in the margins of manuscripts. Dante is also known to have used *florilegia*—extracts from classical authors selected during the Middle Ages for their epigrammatic or sententious content. Such collections generally contained extracts from Horace's hexameter works but not from his odes, which probably explains why Dante cites the former rather than the latter, and Benvenuto da Imola explains that a reference in *Inf.* 23.4–6 to a nonexistent fable by Aesop also derives from a *florilegium.* Thus a variety of medieval filters stood between Dante and direct contact with the ancient world.

In time, however, Dante appears to have moved away from secondhand sources to direct study of a few favorite authors, and he transcends the usual limitations of his age in the depth and subtlety with which he ended up controlling these texts. In the discussion of the ages of man in *Conv.* 4.24–28, Dante appeals to the authority of the four poets prescribed in the Bologna arts curriculum: Statius, to illustrate adolescence; Virgil, whose Aeneas represents early manhood, or maturity; Ovid, whose Aeacus exemplifies old age, or full maturity; and Lucan, who describes in Cato and Marcia the return of the soul to God in one's later years. While Aristotle is an important guide in the *Convivio* and while other pagan figures like Trajan and Cato remain important models throughout Dante's work, the same four poets are privileged in *De vulgari eloquentia* and in the *Commedia.*

On the level of detail, Dante's use of these poets shows how deeply a few key authors dominated his imaginative picture of antiquity. From Ovid he reproduces rhetorical artifices (cf. *Purg.* 12.39 and *Meta.* 6.301–302); from Virgil, phrases (e.g., *lito rubro,* "the red shore," *Par.* 6.79 = *Aen.* 6.886) and similes (e.g., the comparison of generations of men to falling leaves in *Inf.* 3.112–120, taken from *Aen.* 6.309–312). It is worth noting that in this last example Dante has made a subtle but characteristic change, for the Virgilian amplification with reference to migratory birds is replaced

C by a reference to falconry—in other words, instinct yields to will. Anchoring the simile more firmly into a Christian afterlife driven by moral choice and its consequences, this change allows Dante to challenge his classical models in artistic terms as well.

Yet even these privileged authorities from the past are processed in different ways in Dante's creative imagination. In the case of Virgil, the author is damned, but the texts are salvific—provided we are willing to accept Dante's claim that Statius was saved by reading Virgil's *Ecl.* 4.5–6 and the *Aeneid.* With Statius, the situation is reversed; that is, the author is saved, but the poem itself serves as a textual model for Hell, in that the *Thebaid*'s account of the destructiveness of civil war becomes an exemplum for unredeemed violence and error. Ovid is different again: like Virgil, the author is not saved; but like Statius, he provides an important textual model for Dante and is the primary source of mythological exempla in *Purgatorio.* Lucan's *Pharsalia,* finally, serves as a source for information on Mediterranean geography in the time of Augustus, with the historical events portrayed being consistently corrected from the perspective of Dante's political vision.

Such an extensive reliance on classical antiquity has led a number of scholars, especially in Europe, to label Dante a humanist, the true initiator of the intellectual revolution which would lead to the "rebirth of antiquity" in the Renaissance. This claim cannot be dismissed out of hand. For one thing, Dante was unusually well versed for a writer of his age in the key disciplines of grammar, rhetoric, history, moral philosophy, and poetry— precisely the areas of study in which the humanist revolution took place. And the intensity with which Dante linked his civic feeling and his classical scholarship seems in many ways more typical of the generations to come than of his own.

Ultimately, however, there is one crucial step which Dante was not prepared to take, and that was to approach the ancient world on its own terms with a willingness to recognize and respect its differences from Christianity. That the two worlds could sometimes parallel one another, Dante acknowledged. In *Inf.* 2.32, for example, Dante-pilgrim defines himself in association with Aeneas and Paul, and in *Inf.* 30.97–98 Sinon is linked to Potiphar's wife. This parallelism extends to details of language as well (e.g., *Purg.* 30.19–21, which quotes both *Aen.* 6.883 and Matt. 21:9).

In the final analysis, however, the historical path which appeared independent to the partial vision of the pagans was incorporated by Dante into God's larger providential plan. The *Aeneid,* for example, preserves the record of how the Roman Empire was founded, but for Dante Rome *fu stabilita per lo loco santo / u' siede il successor del maggior Piero* ("[was] established to be the holy place where the successor of great Peter is enthroned," *Inf.* 2.23–24). Even Virgil, Ovid, and Lucan were able to see through the glass only darkly, for without the grace of God the literature produced by the best minds of antiquity still demands correction. Thus Virgil rewrites his *Aeneid* in *Inf.* 20, Dante-pilgrim casts himself as a new Phaëthon and a new Icarus in *Inf.* 17.106–111, and the Cato of the *Purgatorio* functions as a corrected reading of the *Pharsalia.* In short, Dante's conception of classical antiquity becomes clear only when he steps into the circle of great poets in *Inf.* 4, for the classical world as he sees it ultimately requires such mediation as this to be properly understood.

Bibliography

Barolini, Teodolinda. *Dante's Poets: Textuality and Truth in the Comedy.* Princeton, N.J.: Princeton University Press, 1984.

Bezzola, Reto. "L'opera di Dante, sintesi poetica dell'antichità e del medioevo cristiano." In *Atti del Congresso Internazionale di Studi Danteschi.* Florence: Sansoni, 1965, vol. 1, pp. 379–395.

Brownlee, Kevin. "Dante and the Classical Poets." In *The Cambridge Companion to Dante.* Edited by Rachel Jacoff. Cambridge: Cambridge University Press, 1993, pp. 100–119.

Hollander, Robert. *Il Virgilio dantesco: tragedia nella "Commedia."* Florence: Olschki, 1983.

Iannucci, Amilcare A. (ed.). *Dante e la "Bella Scola": autorità e sfida poetica.* Ravenna: Longo, 1993.

Jacoff, Rachel, and Jeffrey T. Schnapp (eds.). *The Poetry of Allusion: Virgil and Ovid in Dante's "Commedia."* Stanford, Calif.: Stanford University Press, 1991.

Martellotti, Guido. "Dante e i classici." *Cultura e scuola* 13–14 (1965), 125–137.

Minio-Paluello, Lorenzo. "Dante's Reading of Aristotle." In *The World of Dante: Essays on Dante and His Times.* Edited by Cecil Grayson. Oxford: Clarendon Press, 1980, pp. 61–80.

Moore, Edward. *Studies in Dante. First Series: Scripture and Classical Authors in Dante.* Oxford: Clarendon Press, 1896. Reprinted in New York: Haskell House, 1968.

Padoan, Giorgio. "Dante di fronte all'umanesimo letterario." In *Il pio Enea, l'empio Ulisse: Tradizione classica e intendimento medievale in Dante.* Ravenna: Longo, 1977, pp. 7–29.

Paratore, Ettore. "L'eredità classica in Dante." In *Dante e Roma: Atti del Convegno di Studi.* Florence: Le Monnier, 1965, pp. 3–50.

Renaudet, A. *Dante humaniste.* Paris: Les Belles Lettres, 1952.

Renucci, Paul. *Dante: Disciple et juge du monde gréco-latin.* Paris: Les Belles Lettres, 1954.

Ronconi, Alessandro. "Per Dante interprete dei poeti latini." *Studi danteschi* 41 (1964), 1–44.

Sowell, Madison U. (ed.). *Dante and Ovid: Essays in Intertextuality.* Binghamton, N.Y.: Medieval and Renaissance Texts and Studies, 1991.

Wetherbee, Winthrop. "*Poeta che mi guidi:* Dante, Lucan, and Virgil." In *Canons.* Edited by Robert von Hallberg. Chicago: University of Chicago Press, 1983, pp. 131–148.

Craig Kallendorf

Classical Canon

The classical canon refers to the list or catalogue of classical *auctores* whom Dante regards as preeminent in the field of poetry. In the *Commedia* the canon is closely associated with Dante's encounter with the great poets of antiquity in Limbo, which occupies the central portion of *Inf.* 4 (64–105). There in a dignified and solemn manner the following scene is developed. As Dante and Virgil move toward the noble castle illuminated by a blaze of light, Dante realizes that *orrerol gente possedea quel loco* ("people worthy to be honored possessed that place," 4.72). In answer to Dante's request to identify them, Virgil responds that honor and fame have won them a special place in the afterworld, a place separated not only from the damned of Hell proper but also from the unbaptized children and other virtuous souls of Limbo. Now the poets come forth to greet Virgil: *onorate l'altissimo poeta: / l'ombra sua torna, ch'era dipartita* ("Honor the highest poet: his shade returns, that had departed," 80–81). Homer appears first, bearing the symbol of epic poetry, a sword. He is followed by Horace, Ovid, and Lucan. These are the poets of *la bella scola* ("the lovely school"), who represent "timeless authority" (Curtius). After much ceremony, they welcome Dante into their midst, and he becomes *sesto tra cotanto senno* ("the sixth among so much wisdom," 102). They walk toward the castle, and, as Dante says, they speak of things that are pleasing but are now best left unsaid.

Thus in the *Commedia* does Dante establish his canon of classical poets. But this was not Dante's first attempt at establishing such a canon (Picone, 7 ff.). In Chapter 25.9 of the *Vita Nuova* Dante presents his first list of classical *auctores*. It begins with Virgil, whose *Aeneid* is cited twice; then comes Lucan, author of the *Pharsalia;* followed by Horace, with one verse quoted from the *Ars Poetica;* and last Ovid, whose treatment of love in the *Remedia amoris* will assume a central place in the *Vita Nuova* and will, in fact, drive Dante's own personification of love in that *libello.* In the sixth chapter of the second book of *De vulgari eloquentia* Dante provides a second canon, also consisting of four Latin epic masters (the *poeti regulati*), namely, Virgil, Ovid, Lucan, and Statius—the inclusion of whom will have consequences for the later establishment of the canon in the *Commedia.* Chapters 25 to 28 of the fourth book of the *Convivio* produce a third canon consisting of four Latin poets (Statius, Virgil, Ovid, and Lucan) associated with the different stages of human life which they examined. The *Commedia* then produces the list noted above. What then are we to make of this list—of its relation to earlier lists and of Dante's inclusion in it?

It is significant that Dante encounters the poets of *la bella scola* in Limbo. Dante's treatment of Limbo is unique in that it is peopled by virtuous pagans who share the abode with unbaptized children and who are forever excluded from eternal life with God because of their lack of faith. There is thus a poignant tragedy which is being played out in Limbo and against which Dante's encounter with the poets must be interpreted. An incompleteness characterizes the pagan poets, both spiritually (in that they are denied Heaven) and poetically (in that their poetry is shaped only by rational truth and not by the truth of the Word of God). Dante in Limbo is not concerned with the preservation of rational and classical truth (embodied by the ancient poets), as he was in the elaboration of his earlier canons, but with the reworking of that truth in the language of Christianity. Dante's poem will overtake the poetry of

C his predecessors, since Dante claims his authority—ideological and poetical—directly from God. This underlying attitude on Dante's part is likewise clearly seen in the Statius episode of *Purg.* 22, where the canon of *Inf.* 4 is both continued and completed. Statius had been omitted in *Inf.* 4 for one good reason, which now becomes apparent. He is saved, and, against the incompleteness of the pagan poets of antiquity, he alone has come to an experience of God (by reading Virgil's fourth Eclogue!). Statius thus stands as the proto-Christian poet who stands between Dante and Virgil, and through Statius Dante now positions himself within the Western literary tradition. Moreover, Statius in *Inf.* 4 is replaced by Horace who is given the epithet of *satiro*. This had led some commentators to conclude that the *bella scola* is symbolic of the medieval tripartite division of "styles" (Iannucci, 23–25). Homer, Virgil, Ovid, and Lucan represent the "tragic" register, while Horace stands for the "satirical." Thus the exclusion of Statius and the inclusion of Horace make it possible for Dante to claim the slot of "comic" poet. If this reading is accurate, it involves another exclusion from the canon, namely, Terence, who is considered to be the *comicus* par excellence. Dante's usurpation of that role signifies that Dante's poem will be a "comedy," but one which will resemble the old classical comedy only peripherally. Both structurally and stylistically its point of reference is the Bible and the "comic," or mixed, style. Thus is Terence excluded and replaced by Dante, whose *comedia* is pitted against Virgil's *alta tragedia*.

Dante's inclusion in the canon (the sixth in the *bella scola*) is an act of poetic self-definition. It declares both the scope of his literary ambition—he intends to write the as yet unwritten Christian epic of conversion—and the poetic models he will draw on in order to fulfill this ambition. It must be stressed that the meeting with the poets contains a double act of inclusion. As Dante the pilgrim-poet is being welcomed into the *bella scola* at the narrative level, Dante the poet is incorporating the works of the classical authors into his own poem. In other words, their generosity to him is matched by his to them. Through association with the poets of "timeless authority" Dante transfers that authority to himself. And Dante's authoritative text, based as it is on the Bible, forces a rethinking and a reposition of classical poetry which is now viewed in an anticlassical perspective: "The essential function of the canon of *auctores* in the *Commedia*

seems therefore to be that of demonstrating the incompleteness of the classical world—the absence of full meaning, which can only be granted by the Christian world" (Picone, 18).

Bibliography

Barolini, Teodolinda. *Dante's Poets: Textuality and Truth in the Comedy.* Princeton, N.J.: Princeton University Press, 1984.

Brownlee, Kevin. "Dante and the Classical Poets." In *The Cambridge Companion to Dante.* Edited by Rachel Jacoff. Cambridge: Cambridge University Press, 1993, pp. 100–119.

Curtius, Ernst Robert. *European Literature and the Latin Middle Ages.* Translated by Willard R. Trask. New York: Harper Torchbooks, 1963.

Iannucci, Amilcare (ed). *Dante e la "bella scola" della poesia.* Ravenna: Longo Editore, 1993.

Jacoff, Rachel, and Jeffrey T. Schnapp (eds.). *The Poetry of Allusion: Virgil and Ovid in Dante's "Commedia."* Stanford, Calif.: Stanford University Press, 1991.

Picone, Michelangelo. "Dante and the Classics." In *Dante: Contemporary Perspectives.* Edited by Amilcare Iannucci. Toronto: University of Toronto Press, 1996.

Amilcare A. Iannucci

Clemence of Habsburg

Daughter of Emperor Rudolf I and wife of Charles Mantel, titular king of Hungary. The verses *Da poi che Carlo tuo, bella Clemenza, / m'ebbe chiarito, mi narrò li 'nganni / che ricever dovea la sua semenza* ("After your Charles, beautiful Clemence, had enlightened me, he narrated the betrayals that his seed was to suffer," *Par.* 9.1–3) were thought by many to pertain to her daughter, Clemence of Hungary, wife of King Louis X of France, who died in 1328. According to more recent criticism, Dante can only be addressing the wife (c. 1272–1295), not the daughter, of Charles Mantel, who is referred to as *Carlo tuo*. Since Clemence was already dead at the fictional time of the poem, Dante may either be addressing her in memory or imagining her to be present at the side of her husband in the Heaven of Venus.

Jo Ann Cavallo

Clement IV, Pope

Pope Clement IV is mentioned only once by Dante, in a very negative sense (*Purg.* 3.124–129), for instigating the bishop of Cosenza to desecrate the corpse of Manfred after the death of the Hohenstaufen in the battle of Benevento (February 26, 1266). Thus he became for Dante the embodiment of utter disregard for the divine law, compassion, and love for one's neighbor. Simultaneously he became the symbol for the corrupt higher clergy.

Born in St. Gilles-du Gard (Languedoc) and baptized Gui Foucqois (Guy Foulques), he became legal counselor to Count Alphons of Poitiers and King Louis IX of France. He was repeatedly entrusted with *enquêtes* and so came into contact with the inquisitors in the Languedoc. For this reason he wrote a manual for the inquisitor around 1260, the *Questiones quindecim ad Inquisitores.* After the death of his wife he began an ecclesiastical career (1257 bishop of Le Puy, 1259 archbishop of Narbonne, 1261 cardinal bishop of Sabina). In 1265 he was elected pope. His pontificate stood under the shadow of having to resolve the question of succession of the Kingdom of Sicily. He succeeded in imposing more severe feudal obligations on Charles I of Anjou. Although his politics were crowned with success when he invested Charles with the Kingdom of Sicily (June 28, 1265), he was faced with several setbacks, because the king often did not meet his feudal obligations. He strengthened the ecclesiastical role of the papacy by reserving all vacant prebends for the pope (Constitution *licet ecclesiarum* of 1265). He died on November 29, 1268, in Viterbo, where he had ordered the building of the famous papal palace.

Bibliography

Dossat, Y. "Gui Foucois, enquêteur-réformateur, archevêque et pape (Clement IV)." *Cahiers de Fanjeaux* 7 (1972), 23ff.

Andreas Kiesewetter

Clement V, Pope

Pope from June 1305 until April 1314, Clement (*Clemente*) was born Bertrand de Got around 1260 in the Gironde of an influential Gascon family. Like many who ascended to the papacy in the thirteenth and fourteenth centuries, he studied canon law (as well as civil law). He was serving as archbishop of Bordeaux when elected pope on June 15, 1305, after months of intrigue and debate. The generally accepted belief is that his election resulted largely from the influence of the king of France, Philip IV, and was engineered in return for promises such as freeing Philip from the penalties of excommunication incurred by Pope Boniface VIII. The influence of Philip remained throughout Clement's papacy. Indeed, Clement seems to have been under constant pressure from Philip—pressure to which he invariably succumbed. The most far-reaching example of this was the Avignon papacy. The move to Avignon took place in 1309, and the papacy remained in France for the next seventy years. Before the move the College of Cardinals was 75 percent Italian; by 1316 it was less than 25 percent Italian. In 1312 Philip successfully pressured Clement to accept the suppression of the Templars (and the confiscation of their properties), which he had previously orchestrated without consulting Clement. In his treatment and support of the Holy Roman Emperor, Henry VII, Clement was at best lukewarm, constantly undercutting imperial claims. Indeed, soon after Henry's death, Clement issued the bull *Pastoralis Cura,* which went as far as any document of Boniface VIII in claiming papal superiority over imperial authority.

Dante's most elaborate reference to Clement occurs in *Inf.* 19. There, the current occupant of the inverted chair of Peter, Pope Nicholas III, prophesies to the pilgrim his own successors in simony. First will come Boniface VIII—the pope who is actually reigning in 1300, the fictional date of the pilgrimage. Then will come another even worse than he—Clement: *ché dopo lui verrà di più laida opra, / di ver' ponente, un pastor sanza legge, / tal che convien che lui e me ricuopra. / Nuovo Iasón sarà, di cui si legge / ne Maccabei; e come a quel fu molle / suo re, così fia lui chi Francia regge* ("for after him will come, from towards the west, a lawless shepherd of even uglier deeds, such that he will cover both him and me. He will be a new Jason, like the one we read of in Maccabees: and as his king was indulgent to the first one, so the ruler of France will be to him," *Inf.* 19.82–87).

The Jason referred to in this passage is the simoniacal high priest from the biblical Book of Maccabees, who bought his office from the dreaded King Antiochus Epiphanes (2 Macc. 4:7–26). Thus both Clement's simony and his willingness to turn the papacy into little more than a plaything for the French monarchy are underscored in this scathing prophecy. The relationship between Clement and the French monarchy is also condemned through the apocalyptic imagery of the whore and the giant at the end of *Purg.* 32, in the climax of the calamities of Church history presented there. The condemnation of Clement in *Par.* 27.58–60 is no less severe than in *Inf.* 19. This time, the condemnation comes not from a fellow simoniac pope but from no less a voice than the first pope, St. Peter himself: *o difesa di Dio, perché pur giaci? / Del sangue nostro Caorsini e Guaschi / s'apparecchian di bere* ("O divine protection, why are you still inert? Cahorsans and Gascons prepare to drink our blood," *Par.* 27.57–59). Clement's withdrawal of support from Henry VII's Italian campaign is listed as part of Cacciaguida's prophecy of exile to his great-great-grandson Dante in *Par.* 17.81. This withdrawal of support, as well as Clement's simony, is condemned once again at the end of *Par.* 30 (142–158). Dante also refers scornfully to Clement in *Epist.* 5.30 and 11.26 and in *Rima* 48, "Se vedi li occhi miei di pianger vaghi."

Ronald Herzman

Cleobulus

One of the Seven Sages of antiquity, Cleobulus *(Cleobulo)* is cited in *Conv.* 3.11.4—along with Solon, Chilon, Periander, Lindius, Bias, and Prieneus—in a discussion of the origins of philosophy. Dante's source is Augustine's *City of God,* 18.25, but he twice mistakes references to birthplaces for personal names, omitting Thales (commonly considered the first of the sages), who was born in Lindus, and Pittacus (Priene being the birthplace of Bias).

Richard Lansing

Cleopatra

Queen of Egypt (69–30 B.C.E.), who became the lover of Caesar and, after his death, Antony. Following the defeat at Actium and Antony's death, Cleopatra *(Cleopatràs)* committed suicide, by applying an asp to her breast, in order to avoid capture by Octavianus. Located with the carnal lovers in the second circle of Hell (*Inf.* 5.63), she is described as being *lussurïosa* ("lustful"), a word whose onomatopoeic quality accentuates her licentiousness. Justinian recalls her death when evoking the Roman eagle's victorious flight in history (*Par.* 6.76).

Diana Cavuoto Glenn

Cletus, Pope

Pope Cletus (or Anacletus, meaning "the blameless") was martyred under the persecution of Domitian. He was pope from 78–90. Dante mentions him in the Heaven of the Fixed Stars, in St. Peter's recitation on his own martyrdom (*Par.* 27.41). Cletus *(Cleto)* succeeded Pope Linus, who succeeded St. Peter.

William Wilson

Clio

One of the nine Muses and patron goddess of the arts. The daughter of Zeus and Mnemosyne, Clio *(Clìò)* is the Muse of history who records epic and heroic acts. Virgil mentions her when asking Statius about the moment of his conversion (*Purg.* 22.58). See also *Theb.* 1.41 and 10.630–631.

Virginia Jewiss

Clotho

At every mortal's birth, Clotho *(Cloto),* the youngest of the three Fates, places wool, representing the term of human life, on Lachesis' distaff. Lachesis spins the wool, which is cut by Atropos at the moment of death. Virgil evokes Clotho's role in human destiny, explaining that the course of Dante's life is not complete (*Purg.* 21.27).

Diana Cavuoto Glenn

Clymene

In *Meta.* 1.750–779, Ovid recounts how Phaëthon, taunted about the identity of his father, begs his mother, Clymene, to confirm that his father is the Sun god, Phoebus. Clymene then urges Phaëthon to visit his father and question him. During his visit, Phaëthon asks to drive his father's chariot, an undertaking that ultimately ends in his death. In *Par.* 17.1–6, Dante—responding to Beatrice's encouragement to seek clarification and reassurance from his ancestor Cacciaguida regarding his destiny—compares himself to Phaëthon, referring to him by circumlocution: *Qual venne a Climenè* ("As [one came] to Clymene," 17.1).

Diana Cavuoto Glenn

Cocytus

In rewriting and rationalizing the hazily integrated classical mythological river system of Hades, Dante made Cocytus *(Cocito)* the final dark confluence of the spillovers and cascades of the

Dante moving from Caina into Antenora. La comedia di Dante Aligieri, *with commentary by Alessandro Vellutello, published by Francesco Marcolini, Venice, 1544. Giamatti Collection: Courtesy of the Mount Holyoke College Archives and Special Collections.*

swampy waters of several rivers—Acheron, Styx, and Phlegethon. These waters apparently continue to fill the lowest Virgilian Tartarus, which is conflated with the Judeo-Christian pit, or abyss, and it takes on the image of a hard-frozen cistern. In neither classical nor biblical contexts is there any notion that the abyss is frozen, although Christian apocalyptical and vision literature on occasion offers such a description. In the Old Testament and in Virgil, giants and titans are present in the lowest Tartarus. Dante's Virgil has had occasion to travel to its very bottom, and he "now" knows its design (*Inf.* 9.19–30).

The waters of Hell, Dante tells us, originate in the tearful burden of postlapsarian human evil, resulting from unrepented sin or the consequences of sin in general. This is represented by Dante by means of the mythological figure of the Old Man of Crete in *Inf.* 14.94–120, whose tears feed all the rivers and descend to the bottom of Hell: *là dove più non si dismonta, / fanno Cocito* ("where there is no further descent, they become Cocytus," 118–119). This downward underground flow is

actually highly unnatural from the point of view of Aristotle's scientific philosophy, to which Dante generally subscribes (as Patrick Boyde reminds us). This unnaturalness is heightened by the fact that the freezing of the waters of Cocytus is caused by wind emanating from the six batlike wings of Satan, echoing a biblical notion that evil comes from the cold north (Jer. 1:14: *Ab aquilone pandetur malum super omnes habitatores terrae,* "From the north shall an evil break forth upon all the inhabitants of the land").

The Greek term "Cocytus" itself conveys the notion of wailing and groaning, but Dante's move to associate it with frozen water seems to stem chiefly from St. Isidore of Seville's placing it beside Tartarus, which he defines as denoting shivering and trembling; the Isidoran context includes Erebus and other underworld places in his *Etymologies,* Book 14. There are, of course, many other partial sources for punishing by cold as well as by fire.

Dante's Cocytus, the ninth circle, is divided into four unmarked zones: Caina, Antenora, Ptolomea, and Judecca. Their names are revealed almost casually as the two poets descend (we have heard two of these names earlier—Caina, in *Inf.* 5.107; and Judecca (in the form *cerchio di Giuda,* "the circle of Judas"), in *Inf.* 9.27. They house the traitors of various kinds and degrees: traitors to kin, to party and country, to guests (and perhaps hosts), and to benefactors, respectively. The zone names, we may note, move in what is for Dante a sacrohistorical time sequence, from the beginnings (Cain) down through the Troy crisis (Antenor) to Palestine just before Christ (Ptolemy) and finally to the center of time (Judas). Here both the Roman imperium and the salvific sacrifice of Jesus are in focus with the figures of Brutus, Cassius, and Judas, who are punished in the three mouths of Satan.

Bibliography

Greco, Franco Carmelo. "Tartaro." *Enciclopedia dantesca* 5:525–526.

Baldassaro, Lawrence. "Dante's Hardened Heart: The Cocytus Cantos." In *Lectura Dantis Newberryana.* Vol. 2. Edited by Paolo Cherchi and Antonio C. Mastrobuono. Evanston, Ill.: Northwestern University Press, 1990, pp. 3–20.

Boyde, Patrick. *Dante Philomythes and Philosopher: Man in the Cosmos.* Cambridge: Cambridge University Press, 1981.

Donno, Daniel J. "Moral Hydrography: Dante's Rivers." *MLN* 92 (1977), 130–139.

Presta, Vincenzo. "Nota sulla topografia morale del Cocito," *Convivium* 34 (1966), 353–361.

Triolo, Alfred A. "*Inferno* XXXIII: Fra Alberigo in Context." *L'Alighieri* 11 (1970), 39–70.

———. "Matta Bestialità in Dante's Inferno: Theory and Image." *Traditio* 24 (1968), 247–292.

Alfred Triolo

Coleridge, Samuel Taylor

English Romantic poet and critic (1772–1834). Deeply influenced by the German critics, especially the Schlegels, Coleridge was among the first English writers to offer a serious critical evaluation of Dante. His fullest treatment appeared in a lecture on the religious poets Donne, Milton, and Dante, delivered on February 27, 1818. Coleridge saw Dante as a Platonist and a Christian poet who unified art, philosophy, and religion more fully than any other poet, including Milton. This lecture, coupled with Henry Francis Cary's translation of the *Commedia* and Ugo Foscolo's review in the *Edinburgh Review,* played a pivotal role in popularizing Dante in the English-speaking world.

Thomas L. Cooksey

Comedy

Comedy and tragedy constituted the two major *modi scribendi* (modes of writing) practiced in the Middle Ages and recognized by medieval literary theory. Taken together, they were deemed to embrace the whole of literature. This view resulted from two principal factors. First, the Middle Ages had increasingly lost the sense of the dramatic dimension of both modes; and, second, definitions of the form and content of the two *genera stilorum,* and especially those pertaining to comedy, covered a rich variety of different types of writing and narrative situation. To stress the uniqueness of his poetic experience, Dante employed the terms with their totalizing meaning in *Par.* 30.22–24: *Da questo punto vinto mi concedo / più che già mai da punto di suo tema / soprato fosse comico o tragedo* ("At this pass I concede myself vanquished, more than any comic or tragic poet has ever been surpassed by a point of his theme").

Despite the dominant position of tragedy and comedy, the Middle Ages recognized, discussed, and composed in a whole range of other "styles." As the author of the disputed *Epistle to Cangrande*

noted at the end of his analysis of *comedia* and *tragedia* (13.32): *[s]unt et alia genera narrationum poeticarum, scilicet carmen bucolicum, elegia, satira et sententia votiva* ("there are other kinds of poetical narration, such as the pastoral poem, the elegy, the satire, and the votive song"). The most important of these *alia* was satire, which was often linked to tragedy and comedy, especially when equivalences were drawn between systems of "style." The Middle Ages had inherited from classical poetics and rhetoric a tripartite concept of "style"—which is not equivalent to our notion of "genre"—the weight of whose prescriptive influence cannot be exaggerated, given that it served as one of the bases of medieval schooling. These *stili*—contamination between which was normally discouraged and which, as a consequence, were defined in opposition to each other— were the "high," the "middle," and the "low" styles. Each *stilus* was assigned its own subject matter, language, rhetorical figures, and classical authors to serve as models. The *stilus sublimis/ gravis* (high style) was tied to tragedy, whose *auctor* was Virgil; the *mediocris* (middle style) was generally associated with satire, whose *auctoritates* were Juvenal, Persius, and Horace; while, under the aegis of Terence, comedy was frequently linked to the *humilis et communis* (low style). However, confusion between the latter two "styles" was far from uncommon, especially in light of the many different and competing descriptions of comedy that were in circulation.

Dante most famously accepted and drew on these distinctions in the *De vulgari eloquentia.* As part of his effort to elevate vernacular literature to the same status as literature written in Latin, Dante, in a move of some novelty, established a hierarchy for poetry in the "vulgar" tongue according to the basic framework of the three styles (2.4.5). However, given that the poet had only begun to assess the tragic "illustrious canzone" when he abandoned this treatise, it remains a matter of conjecture as to why in his tripartite scheme he substituted elegy for satire and placed comedy in an intermediate position which embraced the middle style (*mediocris quandoque humilis vulgaris,* 2.4.6). Adherence to conventional distinctions of "style" also helped Dante structure his catalogues of classical *auctores* in *VN* 25.9, *DVE* 2.6.7, *Inf.* 4.85–102, and *Purg.* 22.14, 97–108. In Limbo, the poet assigns to himself, as author of the Christian *comedìa,* the position of comic "authority" traditionally assigned to Terence (4.102), relegating the Roman dramatist to the canon of secondary writers presented in *Purgatorio,* where he appears with other comedians (22.97–98): *Terrenzio nostro antico / Cecilio e Plauto* ("our ancient Terence. . . , Caecilius, and Plautus").

In the *Commedia,* Dante rejected the long-established idea of separating the different *stili.* By exploiting comedy's traditional flexibility and by pushing conventional notions of "style" to their limits, his new vernacular poem, which he calls a *comedìa (Inf.* 16.128, 21.2; *Mon.* 1.12.6; *Egl.* 2.52–53), is made to embrace every form of linguistic and artistic utterance. One of the reasons why Dante's authorship of the *Epistle to Cangrande* has been questioned is because, in line with its normal literary conservatism, it clarifies Dante's radically experimental choice of genre and title in the light of the most traditional and restrictive contemporary definitions of comedy. Contrasting *comedia* with *tragedia,* the letter presents the comic as dealing realistically with low-class characters in a structure with a happy ending: *comedia dicitur a "comos" villa et "oda" quod est cantus, unde comedia quasi "villanus cantus." [. . .] Comedia [. . .] inchoat asperitatem alicuius rei, sed eius materia prospere terminatur, ut patet per Terentium in suis comediis. [. . .] in modo loquendi [. . .] comedia [. . .] remisse et humiliter* ("'comedy' is so called from *comos,* a village, and *oda,* a song; whence comedy is as it were a 'rustic song.'. . . Comedy begins with sundry adverse conditions, but ends happily, as appears from the comedies of Terence. . . . in [its] style of language . . . comedy is unstudied and lowly"). The *Commedia,* in both its form and content, markedly transcends such prescriptive definitions.

Bibliography

Barański, Zygmunt G. *"Libri poetarum in quattuor species dividuntur." Essays on Dante and "Genre."* Supplement 2. *The Italianist* 15 (1995).

Bareiss, Karl-Heinz. *Comoedia. Die Entwicklung der Komödiendiskussion von Aristoteles bis Ben Jonson.* Frankfurt am Main-Bern: Peter Lang, 1982.

Kelly, H. A. *Tragedy and Comedy from Dante to Pseudo-Dante.* Berkeley, Los Angeles, London: University of California Press, 1989.

Quadlbauer, Franz. *Die antike Theorie der "Genera dicendi" im lateinischen Mittelalter.* Vienna: Hermann Böhlaus Nachf., 1962.

Villa, Claudia. *La "Lectura Terentii."* Padua: Antenore, 1984.

Zygmunt G. Barański

Commedia

1. Introduction

The late medieval literary imagination is preoccupied with models of all kinds, whether literary, philosophical, or theological, and it is a preoccupation that lies at the heart of Dante's masterpiece, the *Commedia.* A poem of 14,233 eleven-syllable verses arranged in stanzas of three lines interlinked by a wholly original triple rhyme scheme *(terza rima),* it comprises one hundred cantos divided into three canticles. The poem takes as its literal subject the state of souls after death and presents an image of divine justice meted out as due punishment or reward. The poem's first-person narrative describes the poet's journey through the three realms of the afterlife, as a pilgrim accompanied by three guides—Virgil, Beatrice, and, to a lesser degree, St. Bernard—each of whom assists Dante in completing one stage of the providentially ordained mission to bring him into the presence of God and to the beatific vision of ultimate truth. Although the journey bridges the full dimension of the cosmological universe and has the purpose of educating the pilgrim about the ideal moral life, it has its origin in Dante's profound and enduring love of a Florentine woman named Beatrice, whom he first encounters, as he says in the *Vita Nuova,* in his ninth year. On the level of literature, Dante throughout the poem engages his most admired models: the poet Virgil, the philosopher Aristotle, and the theologian St. Thomas—to note only a few major instances of his intellectual and spiritual indebtedness. Although it is customary to think of Dante as one of the most original writers of all time, much of the intellectual content of his great poem is borrowed and redeployed. Dante is one of the most indebted of writers: his poem reveals the imprint of the literary and philosophical texts of classical antiquity (Virgil, Ovid, Statius, Lucan, Aristotle, Plato, Cicero); Holy Scripture (Old and New Testaments); philosophical and theological commentary (Thomas Aquinas, Albert the Great, Bonaventure, Bernard, Dionysius the Areopagite, William Peraldus, Hugh of St. Victor); historical texts (Orosius, Augustine, Livy); philosophical allegory (Macrobius, Boethius, Jean de

Meun, Brunetto Latini); and the recent vernacular literary traditions (Old French romances, Provençal and Sicilian lyrical poetry). His sources are virtually coextensive with the sum of accessible recorded human thought. Other putative "models" can at best be considered instances of cultural interaction: here one thinks of the age-old search for the poem's supposed Arabic roots (which began with Miguel Asín Palacios's work of 1919), not to speak of classical and Christian medieval visions of the otherworld.

In the early stages of his literary development Dante places himself on a level with Guinizzelli and Cavalcanti—or even slightly higher—regarding the relationship he establishes between the "new" *(dolce stil nuovo)* school of poetry to which he belongs and the "old" school, from which he distances himself. But when diversity and novelty are embraced (as when Dante envisions a yet nobler style, expressed in the last chapter of the *Vita Nuova*), even these relationships are redefined. He marks his separation from the other practitioners of the *dolce stil nuovo*—Cavalcanti in particular—although this does not signify a renunciation of the experience and poetic technique previously acquired. There are unmistakable signs of this disassociation in the *Commedia,* as, for example (leaving aside Beatrice's rebuke in the Earthly Paradise), the exchange between Guido Cavalcanti's father and Dante himself in *Inf.* 10; the heavily autobiographical sonnet 52, "Io mi credea del tutto esser partito" (perhaps written in 1303), in which Dante announces to Cino da Pistoia his decision to assume *omai altro ca mino* ("now a different path"), thereby bringing to an end the youthful period of *nostre rime* ("our rhymes"); and finally, in the *Convivio,* the attestation of experiences of an entirely new nature, of visits to places where philosophy was practiced—namely, *ne le scuole de li religiosi e a le disputazioni de li filosofanti* ("to the schools of the religious orders and to the disputations held by the philosophers," 2.12.7). These experiences result in the creation of works of a doctrinal cast, namely, the *Convivio* and *De vulgari eloquentia* (the *Monarchia* being of a later period, however it is dated). During his years in exile Dante already has a clear plan in mind and is intent on formulating broad structures to accommodate theological doctrine and science, politics and history (both past and present), ancient myth and popular legend, and personal experience

Portrait of Dante in Opere di Dante Alighieri, *edited by Cristoforo Zapate de Cisneros, Venice, 1757–1758. Giamatti Collection: Courtesy of the Mount Holyoke College Archives and Special Collections.*

charged with hope and burdened with ever-increasing disillusion. All of this is projected against a backdrop of places that he knew intimately through personal experience or that he learned about through sermons delivered by preachers or in tales told by merchants.

The author of the *Commedia* was almost immediately called a "divine" poet. The epithet would ultimately be applied to the poem itself for the first time in the Lodovico Dolce edition published in Venice by Giolito in 1555. Dante gives his poem the title *"Comedìa"* (spelled with a single "m"), a term he uses twice in *Inferno* (16.128, 21.2). In the third canticle, however, he speaks of his work as a "sacred poem" *(sacrato poema, Par.* 23.62; *poema sacro, Par.* 25.1). The various terms have raised the question of whether the title applies to *Inferno* alone or to the entire poem. A more important question—why Dante should have called his poem a "comedy" in the first place—preoccupied some of the earliest critics, among them Benvenuto da Imola and Boccaccio. A clear and concise answer may be found in the *Letter to Cangrande* (*Epist.* 13.28–29), even if it is not by Dante himself, where the term is explicitly defined: *Comedia [. . .] inchoat asperitatem alicuius rei, sed eius materia prospere terminatur* ("comedy . . . begins with sundry adverse conditions, but ends happily"). He derives the term etymologically from the combining of *comos* ("village") and *oda* ("song"), meaning "rustic song," so that he associates comedy with the middle or low level with respect to subject matter and style, as opposed to the high style of Virgil's epic, which he classes as a *tragedìa* ("tragedy," *Inf.* 20.113). Later (37) it is confirmed that this title applies to the whole poem. While *Epist.* 13 refers to two characteristic formal features of the work—one relating to genre (29) and the other regarding style (30)—in other places, namely, *Conv.* 1.5.8 and *DVE* 2.4.6, greater attention is focused on the aspect of style.

Another source of great controversy, perhaps today more than ever, concerns the chronological setting of the journey through the realms of the otherworld. Dante imagined it to take place over a period of seven days in the year 1300 (the year of the first Jubilee, proclaimed by Pope Boniface VIII), beginning on the eve of Good Friday, April 7–8 (others argue for March 25, the first day of the new year). Astronomical references interspersed throughout the poem, however, make it clear that the beginning of the journey coincided with a full moon (*Inf.* 20.127–129; *Purg.* 23.118–121, 10.14–16, 17.61–63, etc.). Moreover, as one of many mutually supporting facts, the Sun was already in the constellation of Aries (*Inf.* 1.38–40; *Par.* 1.37–45, 10.7–15, 27.86–87, etc.). If these references and others regarding the position of the stars are accepted as reliable indicators, they would associate the beginning of the journey with the period from March 25 to March 31 of the year 1301. Such a timeframe would set the beginning of the journey at the first hour of March 25 (*Temp' era dal principio del mattino* ["The time was the beginning of the morning," *Inf.* 1.37]) and the end in Paradise at 3 P.M. on March 31. But this hypothesis has not found wide currency.

Dante fixes Hell in the hemisphere of land (the Northern Hemisphere) at the center of the universe, in accord with the Ptolemaic system. He places Purgatory on top of a mountain in the hemisphere of water, which is the Southern Hemisphere. The ten spheres of Paradise comprise the nine concentric spheres that rotate around the Earth, and the tenth and final Heaven of the Empyrean, which, lying beyond time and space, is immobile. One therefore finds arranged along a single symbolic vertical axis the Holy City of Jerusalem, Lucifer at the center of Hell, the shores of the mountain Purgatory with the Earthly Paradise at its summit, and the Empyrean beyond the uttermost reaches of the physical universe. The movement from vice and sin to expiation and redemption and finally the state of beatitude lies along a single trajectory, symbolizing an individual's capacity to undergo conversion and ultimately attain to the vision of God.

The itinerary that takes Dante through the three realms of the otherworld is recorded in three canticles of similar length: *Inferno, Purgatorio, Paradiso.* The sins of Hell are divided into three major conceptual categories—incontinence, violence, and fraud—each of which comprises a subset of specific vices, assigned to nine circles. Despite the fact that they technically reside outside of Hell proper, the neutrals are traditionally counted as occupying a circle, so that the total number of circles in Hell is ten. Purgatory is likewise divided into three major areas: the Ante-Purgatory, where the late repentant undergo a process of preparation for purgation; Purgatory proper, where penitents cleanse themselves of their sinful dispositions on seven terraces (pride, envy, wrath, sloth, avarice and prodigality, gluttony, and lust); and the Earthly Paradise, where the redeemed soul rejoices in its redemption and prepares to ascend to Paradise. The ten heavens of Paradise, defining incremental degrees of perfection from the lowest to the highest heaven—the Moon, Mercury, Venus, the Sun, Mars, Jupiter, Saturn, the Fixed Stars, the Primum Mobile, and the Empyrean—appear to maintain a tripartite classification by lodging the blessed (temporally, for the pilgrim's benefit) according to the nature of their virtue. The first three heavens present souls whose virtue is in some way marred or deficient (inconstancy in vows, marred ambition, earthly lovers); the souls of the remaining four planetary spheres exemplify the proficiency of the four cardinal virtues (prudence, fortitude, justice, temperance); and the final three spheres are the abodes of those proficient, respectively, in the three theological virtues (Fixed Stars), of the angels (Primum Mobile), and of the Deity (Empyrean), who is the ultimate perfection. The tenth and final sphere of the Empyrean,

C

however, is the realm not only of God but also of his saved creatures, who display themselves in the petals of the great celestial rose and contemplate eternally the mystery of his being.

Critical problems surrounding the text and its manuscript tradition remain ever-present in Dante scholarship. The earliest commentators allude to interpretive challenges posed both by individual episodes in the poem and by textual variants contained in the plethora of manuscripts (in the fourteenth century the number had already approached four hundred), whose multitude principally arose from the poem's extraordinary proportions and the various interpretive strategies it gave rise to. After initial attempts in the sixteenth century (Bembo) and the nineteenth century (Karl Witte, Edward Moore), the Florentine school of textual philology achieved significant progress with the work of Michele Barbi and Giacomo Parodi and with the editions by Giuseppe Vandelli (1921), Mario Casella (1923), and Giorgio Petrocchi (1965–1966). Antonio Lanza's recent edition (1996) attests to the fact that the search for a better text remains unabated.

Originally composed in Verona and Ravenna, the *Commedia*'s early manuscript forms first circulated to Bologna and then throughout Tuscany. As its fame spread, allusions and references to the poem, paraphrases of cantos (even in Latin and dactylic hexameter), and groups of cantos or individual canticles multiplied and moved farther west and later to the east. The first complete translation of the poem is considered the Castilian version by Enrique de Villena of 1428, followed a year later by the Catalonian translation in tercets edited by Andreu Febrer. After the first editions printed in Foligno, Mantova, and Venice in 1472, the Italian horizon broadens in the sixteenth century with the development of new printed editions accompanied by commentaries. Nevertheless, in the world of printing, even outside Italy, Petrarch's *Canzoniere* reigns supreme. By the nineteenth and twentieth centuries, however—initially with the development of German philological methodology and the Romantic revival of interest in the poem—editions of the *Commedia* begin to multiply by the hundreds, with translations appearing in almost every modern language (and even in some dialects as well). The universal appeal of the poem derives in large measure from the unity of its thought and expression; the cohesion and fluidity of its interrelated parts; the power of the poet's

imaginative inventiveness in integrating history, politics, philosophy, and theology within a narrative framework; and the depth of his vision into the human condition.

Bibliography

Anderson, William. *Dante the Maker.* New York: Crossroad, 1982.

Bergin, Thomas. *Dante.* New York: Orion, 1965.

Chiarenza, Marguerite. *The Divine Comedy: Tracing God's Art.* Boston: Twayne, 1989.

Esposito, Enzo (ed.). *L'opera di Dante nel mondo.* Ravenna: Longo, 1992.

Fiaschini, Modesto (ed.). *Pagine di Dante. Le edizioni della Divina Commedia dal torchio al computer.* Perugia: Electa, 1989, especially the essay by Anna Maria Chiavacci Leonardi, pp. 51–74.

Mazzeo, Joseph. *Medieval Cultural Tradition in Dante's "Comedy."* Ithaca, N.Y.: Cornell University Press, 1960.

Pisanti, Tommaso. *"L'un lido e l'altro": circolazione dantesca ed altri saggi.* Naples: Liguori, 1995, pp. 5–30, 31–52.

Quinones, Ricardo. *Dante Alighieri.* Boston: Twayne, 1979; updated edition New York: Twayne, 1998.

Vallone, Aldo. *Dante.* 2nd ed. Milan: Vallardi, 1981.

——. *Storia della critica dantesca dal XIV al XX secolo.* Vol. 2. Milan: Vallardi, 1981.

——. "Modelli di interpretazione dantesca nel tempo." In *Medieval Culture: An Introduction to Dante and His Times.* Edited by Karl Vossler. Translated by William Cranston Lawton. 2 vols. 1929. Reprinted New York: Ungar, 1958.

Aldo Vallone
(translated by Robin Treasure)

2. Commedia: *Title and Form*

Evidence for the poem's title—*Comedìa* (the epithet *divina* was only added in the Venetian edition of 1555 printed by Gabriele Giolito and supervised by Ludovico Dolce)—comes from manuscript rubrics, its fourteenth-century exegetical tradition, the *Monarchia* (1.12.6), and two passages in *Inferno* (16.127–128, 21.1–2): *per le note / di questa comedìa, lettor, ti giuro* ("by the notes of this comedy, reader, I swear to you") and *altro parlando / che la mia comedía cantar non cura* ("speaking of other things my comedy does not record").

There is no doubting the importance of the *Commedia*'s title as a means to understanding the poem; just as there is little doubt that Dante's

The first appearance of the word divina *in the poem's title in* La divina comedia di Dante, *edited by Lodovico Dolce and published by Gabriel Giolito de Ferrari in Venice in 1555. Giamatti Collection: Courtesy of the Mount Holyoke College Archives and Special Collections.*

guishing it from tragedy, such definitions associate comedy with fraught beginnings and happy endings, with the low and occasionally the middle style, and with low-class characters and realistic situations—features which are patently inadequate to render justice to the variety of the *Commedia*'s novel form and content. To confound matters further, Dante seemingly made little direct effort from within the poem itself to explain his choice of title. As has already been noted, in *Inferno,* he twice refers to his work, almost *en passant,* as *"comedìa,"* while, in *Paradiso,* he distinguishes his comedy from the creations of traditional comedians and tragedians (*Par.* 30.22–24).

However, these difficulties should not encourage us to dismiss the poem's title as somehow flawed, eccentric, or even "unintelligible." Given the *Commedia*'s highly developed system of reflection on matters of literature and on its own literary novelty, it is reasonable to assume that Dante believed his idiosyncratic title to be both technically appropriate and accessible as such to his audience.

The abundance of critical proposals put forward to clarify Dante's designation of his poem as a *comedìa* is impressive, as is the sound documentary evidence on which these interpretations are based. Thus, his choice is deemed, *inter alia,* to be an act of humility; to provide the means by which he could underline the difference between his poem and the *Aeneid,* Virgil's *alta [. . .] tragedìa* ("high tragedy," *Inf.* 20.113); to allude to the *Commedia*'s bonds with satire; to indicate its allegory and structure; and to furnish proof of its veracity. It is clear that, in the Middle Ages, comedy was a wide-ranging "style"—in fact, the most wide-ranging. Thus, if one considers analyses of comedy from Cicero to the fourteenth century, the number and scope of competing definitions is striking; and most of these establish suggestive links with the *Commedia.* For example, in addition to the interpretations just mentioned, comedy is tied to the kind of narrative found in an *argumentum*—the account of something which is normally impossible but which becomes real as a result of an act of divine intervention (John of Garland, *Poetriae* 5.327–331); it is peopled by characters and emotions of every type (Quintilian, *Instit. Orat.* 1.7.7); it is associated with prose (John of Garland, *Poetriae* 1.51–52); it presents erotic situations (Servius, *Comm. in Vergilium* 1.459.2–5); and it includes a rich array of formal registers

choice of *"comedìa"* is deeply problematic. Thus, it is difficult to see how a term which refers to a specific "mode of writing" can describe a poem whose overwhelming literary characteristic, underpinned by a highly individual sense of style, is its formal and thematic all-inclusiveness and flexibility. More specifically, by being written in such a manner, the *Commedia* openly challenged the notion, deeply entrenched in the written culture of the Middle Ages, that each *modus scribendi* was essentially self-standing and limited in its subject matter and language. Indeed, not only was comedy one of the primary pillars supporting this doctrine of textual separateness, but also the standard medieval definitions of the *stilus* cast little light on the *Commedia*'s status as a comedy. While distin-

LA DIVINA COMMEDIA

DI DANTE ALIGHIERI
Nobile Fiorentino

RIDOTTA A MIGLIOR LEZIONE
dagli Accademici della Crusca.

CON PRIVILEGIO.

IN FIRENZE PER DOMENICO MANZANI 1595
Con licenzia de' Superiori.

Oldest edition of the Commedia *of the Accademia della Crusca (1595). Reproduced by permission of the John A. Zahm Dante Collection in the Department of Special Collections, University Libraries, University of Notre Dame.*

which span the "elegance" of tragedy and the rather more "pedestrian" conventions of the *mediocris* and *humilis* "modes," before descending to the plebeian crudities of spoken language.

Comedy thus seems to touch on every subject and style—to stand for literature in its entirety. It appears as the only manner of writing which, rhetorically, could offer Dante the space and liberty to accommodate a work as ambitious as his masterpiece. By the beginning of the fourteenth century, the concept of comedy embraced, albeit in a nonsystematic manner, the same all-inclusive and freewheeling viewpoint as that which characterized the *Commedia*'s form and content; and, in any case, the comic had long been deemed the traditional category for experimentation. What Dante did was to bring together in a single, tightly organized work that plurality of elements which his culture recognized as typical of the comic but which it never actually conflated. It needed the poet's great synthesizing ambition, as well as his encyclopedic imagination, to reveal and exploit comedy's true literary potential. If, as was his custom, Dante's aim was to offer a concise traditional

term through which to give a first impression of his new poetry and poetics, then he could not have found a more telling tag than *comedìa*. In addition, the title's very idiosyncrasy is meant to be a spur to its interpretation, not least because it was a basic medieval exegetical strategy to focus on the *titulus* when assessing a text in its entirety.

Crucial support for this interpretation of Dante's choice of title comes from two authoritative sources. That all-inclusiveness, literary freedom and comedy were synonymous for the poet is obvious when he states that there were "other things that his comedy was not concerned / to sing" (*Inf.* 21.1–2). Dante here implies that, if he had so wanted, he could have "sung" this *altro* but that, unfettered by conventional rhetorical requirements, he deliberately chose not to express these "things." Even more pointedly, when accounting for the *Commedia*'s title, Jacopo Alighieri gives this unprecedented definition of comedy: "the second style is called 'comedy,' under which generally and universally all things are treated, and hence the title of the present work stems from this" (*Chiose, Proemio* 17–19). One cannot help but wonder whether, behind the son's prose, we are not actually hearing the father's voice.

Although the poet could have found hints in authoritative sources and their *commentaria* to suggest that the division between "styles" was not necessarily an absolute (e.g., *Ad Her.* 4.11.6; Horace, *Ars Poetica* 9–11, 93–96), to legitimate his radical experimentation—which unquestionably did challenge the dominant literary dogma—Dante sought refuge in another, quite unimpeachable *auctoritas.* Throughout the *Commedia,* the poet claimed that, unlike other texts, his *poema sacro* (*Par.* 25.1) was written according to God's wishes. In order to fulfill its moral-didactic ends, its author had the divinely willed responsibility to provide as accurate an account as possible of his eschatological adventures (*Purg.* 33.52–57; *Par.* 17.127–129)—an experience which evoked every aspect of Creation. Dante could do this only if he were free to use those formal and linguistic solutions which his discrimination—sharpened by the journey and his artistic gifts (*Par.* 22.112–114)— suggested as most appropriate for his ends. The poem's hybrid "comic style"—its status as a new type of comedy—is thus presented as the direct consequence of its God-given mission to return humanity to the "straight way" (*Inf.* 1.3). To talk to everyone about everything, Dante needed not only the fullness of language and literature but also a means of communication: the vernacular, which, at least in abstract, would be accessible to every speaker. Human conventions, including those which artificially partitioned experience into different "styles" and which downgraded the vernacular in favor of Latin, made little sense for a literary enterprise such as his. Indeed, the poet leaves little doubt that, when he came to write the *Commedia,* his most direct literary models were also provided by God in the shape of *his* two "books": the universe, which embraces Creation "in a volume" (*Par.* 33.86), and the Bible, whose *sermo humilis* includes every style and subject and every type of knowledge. And it is a matter of some consequence (not least for appreciating the poem's title) that, of all the medieval literary types, comedy was the one most closely associated with ethics and with the "humble speech" of Scripture.

It is in divine art with its emphasis on the interrelationship between the one and the many that the ultimate source for both the *Commedia*'s variety and its structural cohesion should be sought. In imitation of the *Deus artifex,* Dante also strove to create a synthesis by constraining the different styles, modes, languages, and concerns of his culture within a mathematically harmonious structure of 3s (most notably, the *terza rima,* the three canticles, and the broad tripartite subdivision of each realm of the afterlife) and 10s (specifically, the 100 cantos and the more nuanced decimal organization of Hell, Purgatory, and Paradise). The *Commedia,* not least because both 3 and 10 were commonly interpreted as quintessentially divine numbers, stands as a textual exemplum of the principles, wealth, and *ordo* of God's Creation.

By claiming God as his model and by casting his divine poetry in the shape of a comedy, Dante was able to bring together his literary experimentation and his didactic aims as well as to account for his poem's heterogeneity and integrate its many discrete elements (additional support for his effort to create an all-encompassing work would have come from the tradition of medieval encyclopedism). The kind of story, and hence narrative structure, which could serve as the vehicle for Dante's artistic and ideological ambitions can also be said to owe its existence to God and the conventions of comedy.

The *Commedia* is the first-person account of the divinely sanctioned journey through the three realms of the afterlife which the Florentine poet,

Dante Alighieri, undertook in the thirty-fifth year of his life. The voyage, under the stewardship of three guides—Virgil, Beatrice, and St. Bernard of Clairvaux—begins in the spring of 1300 and lasts seven days. At the start of his adventure, as in any good comedy, the protagonist finds himself in serious trouble, lost in the "dark wood" (*Inf.* 1.2) of sin. His otherworldly voyage, during which he meets and converses with many spirits, provides him with the enlightenment he needs to reject evil and reach God—and so happily conclude his *quête.* Thus, two of the basic structural-ideological paradigms around which the poem is organized are salvation and the progressive acquisition of knowledge. In order to ensure a broad moral appeal for the *Commedia,* the protagonist has an exemplary function. He is both himself and the representative of humanity, the ordinary Christian faced with the concrete problem of saving one's soul. In the same way, the different shades whom he meets on his journey do not just symbolize a particular vice or virtue, as occurred in traditional moralizing and eschatological writing. Rather, by their behavior and speech and by their position in the otherworld, each dramatically enacts for eternity her or his individual attitude to salvation in life (see Contrapasso). This solution allowed Dante perfectly to mesh his stylistic, narrative, and ideological needs. The *Commedia*'s gallery of characters—another recognized feature of comedy—is a source of constant formal variety and narrative drama. With their different voices, different experiences, different personalities, different sensibilities, and different backgrounds, Dante's souls underpin the poem's universalizing form and breadth of vision.

As well as recounting the story of a voyage through the afterlife, the *Commedia* also tells of the "journey" of its own composition. The poem thus has two distinct yet closely interconnected protagonists, whom recent scholarship has respectively labeled "Dante-pilgrim" and "Dante-poet." In contrast to what happens to the *viator,* the greatest difficulties confronting the *auctor* occur in *Paradiso.* The obstacles which he faces in remembering and putting into language his supra-rational experience (see "Mysticism") provide the fundamental dramatic tension of the third canticle. In Hell and Purgatory, on the other hand, drama stems from the obstacles placed in the path of the pilgrim by the inhabitants and by the topographical configurations of the two realms.

Dante gave breadth and further structural cohesion to the *Commedia's materia* not only through the narrative complexity and variety of his story but also through the wealth and multiformity of his figurative imagination. Complementing the poem's literal level, Dante's inventive and rich use of imagery significantly augments the range of the *Commedia's* concerns beyond those normally associated with the afterlife. His recourse to tropes and similes introduces into the poem topics as diverse as animal behavior, urban and country living, warfare, science, classical mythology, and scatology.

The most interesting formal implications of Dante's comic experimentation, however, are probably evident in his choice of language. Its wealth and variety constitute the most direct challenge to medieval literary sensibilities. None of his other works is, linguistically, as Florentine as the *Commedia,* in which he utilized every register of his native tongue and further enriched the language with Latinisms, Gallicisms, neologisms, regionalisms, words associated with particular literary genres, other kinds of technical vocabulary—drawn, for example, from optics, astronomy, the commentary tradition, scholastic theology, mysticism, the language of merchants—invented languages, and foreign words (Hebrew, Greek, Latin, Provençal). Although Dante keenly felt the differences between one language and another, as the subtle ways in which he modulated his lexical choices in the poem reveal, his aim—in opposition to contemporary stylistic separatism—was to blend his babel of words into a single language. Even though, in the widest comparative rhetorical terms, Dante did conventionally "raise" his stylistic register across the three canticles, what is significant is the way in which each canticle incorporates all forms of utterance and ensures their constant interpenetration in tercet after tercet. Suggestively, one of the principal elements which helps to unite the *Commedia* is, in fact, its variety.

The poet was aware of the dangers which stemmed from his experimentation and the diffuseness of his vision. As bulwarks against these, first he invoked the example of the divine artist, and then he chose an overarching structure which, arguably, could accommodate his original narrative, formal, and ideological aspirations. In turning to an established *stilus,* Dante hoped not only to underline the continuity between his new poem and the literary tradition but also to clarify what it was that separated the *Commedia* from that tradi-

tion. The notion of comedy, because of its amorphousness and its all-pervasive presence in contemporary discussions of literature, could amply fulfill both these exegetical needs.

Bibliography

Auerbach, Erich. *Dante: Poet of the Secular World.* Chicago, London: University of Chicago Press, 1961.

Barański, Zygmunt G. *"Luce nuova, sole nuovo."* In *Saggi sul rinnovamento culturale in Dante.* Turin: Scriptorium, 1995.

———. "'Primo tra cotanto senno': Dante and the Latin Comic Tradition." *Italian Studies* 46 (1991), 1–36.

Barolini, Teodolinda. *The Undivine Comedy: Detheologizing Dante.* Princeton, N.J.: Princeton University Press, 1992.

Contini, Gianfranco. *Un'idea di Dante.* Turin: Einaudi, 1976.

Iannucci, Amilcare A. (ed.). *Dante e la "bella scola" della poesia.* Ravenna: Longo, 1993.

Mazzotta, Giuseppe. *Dante's Vision and the Circle of Knowledge.* Princeton, N.J.: Princeton University Press, 1993.

Mengaldo, Pier Vincenzo. "L'elegia 'umile' (*De vulgari eloquentia* II.iv.5–6)." In *Linguistica e retorica di Dante.* Pisa: Nistri-Lischi, 1978, pp. 200–222.

Munk Olsen, Birger. *I classici nel canone scolastico altomedievale.* Spoleto: Centro Italiano di Studi sull'Alto Medioevo, 1991.

Pertile, Lino. "*Paradiso:* A Drama of Desire." In *Word and Drama in Dante.* Edited by John C. Barnes and Jennifer Petrie. Dublin: Irish Academic Press, 1993, pp. 143–180.

Quadlbauer, Franz. *Die antike Theorie der "Genera dicendi" im lateinischen Mittelalter.* Vienna: Hermann Böhlaus Nachf., 1962.

Rajna, Pio. "Il titolo del poema dantesco." *Studi danteschi* 4 (1921), 5–37.

Segre, Cesare. *Fuori del mondo.* Turin: Einaudi, 1990, pp. 11–66.

Villa, Claudia. "Il lessico della stilistica fra XI e XIII sec." In *Vocabulaire des écoles et des méthodes d'enseignement au moyen âge.* Edited by Olga Weijers. Turnhout: Brepols, 1992, pp. 42–59.

Zygmunt G. Barański

3. Commedia: *Moral Structure*

The *Commedia* is divided into three parts, or canticles, representing sins *(Inferno),* sinful disposi-

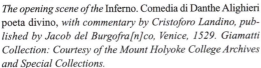

The opening scene of the Inferno. Comedia di Danthe Alighieri poeta divino, *with commentary by Cristoforo Landino, published by Jacob del Burgofra[n]co, Venice, 1529. Giamatti Collection: Courtesy of the Mount Holyoke College Archives and Special Collections.*

Inset of the opening scene [of previous image]. Comedia di Danthe Alighieri poeta divino, *with commentary by Cristoforo Landino, published by Jacob del Burgofra[n]co, Venice, 1529. Giamatti Collection: Courtesy of the Mount Holyoke College Archives and Special Collections.*

tions *(Purgatorio),* and examples of virtue *(Paradiso).* The placement of the souls in each of these otherworldly regions, directly and proportionally related to their individual earthly activities, determines whether they are condemned to eternal punishment, undergo purgation for a specific period of time, or experience eternal bliss. Their fate is ultimately governed by divine judgment, but it is the direct result of personal choice exercised through free will. The concept of divine justice is fundamentally and inescapably based on mankind's ability to perceive and distinguish between good and evil, by virtue of the faculty of human reason and the powers conferred by the three theological virtues (faith, hope, and charity). Individuals merit either just reward or punishment on the basis of their acts during life on Earth; in effect, each individual actively chooses his or her final destination.

The three canticles are related in many ways and reflect a coherent structural unity, which is achieved by means of numerous points of symmetry and symbolical correspondences that invest the moral structure of the otherworld realms. There are analogies which exist among the three canticles (mostly between *Inferno* and *Purgatorio,* in the distribution of sins and of punishments), although they are not rigidly precise. The numbers 3 and 10 (or multiples of 3 and 10)—considered perfect numbers in medieval tradition—dominate the poem's structure. *Purgatorio* and *Paradiso* contain thirty-three cantos each, while *Inferno* has thirty-four, the opening canto serving as an introduction to the entire *Commedia.* Thus the entire poem consists of 100 cantos. Each canticle is characterized by division into ten separate groupings of souls. *Inferno* is divided into nine circles of sin and the vestibule of the neutrals. *Purgatorio* comprises the Ante-Purgatory, divided into a lower level (the shore, where the excommunicates roam) and a higher level (where the late repentants reside); seven terraces; and the Earthly Paradise.

C *Paradiso* consists of the nine physical heavens and the Empyrean.

Dante envisions Hell as an immense conical cavity—spanning from a point directly below Jerusalem to the center of Earth—which was formed when Lucifer and his angels were thrown from Heaven. Here divine retribution assumes the form of the *contrapasso,* or the just punishment of sin effected by a process either resembling or contrasting with the sin itself. Hell's penal system punishes sinners according to their proximity to Lucifer, the king of evil, and their distance from God: those lodged deeper within the infernal pit are more severely punished by virtue of their greater distance from the Deity. The abyss comprises nine separate circles. In the vestibule that leads to Hell itself are found the neutrals *(ignavi),* who in life refused to perform meritorious acts but nevertheless committed no reprehensible deeds. They are therefore not "worthy" to reside in Hell proper. Among them are the neutral angels who sided neither with God nor Lucifer when he revolted. The first circle, Limbo, contains the souls of unbaptized infants and virtuous non-Christians. Unlike all other sinners in Hell, they are guilty of no personal sin, their only failing being that they were not cleansed of their original sin by the rite of baptism. These souls, which include Virgil, suffer no physical torment but live in a state of eternal desire, without the hope of ever seeing God.

Hell proper—which punishes sinful acts for which individuals are personally responsible—begins with the second circle and extends to the ninth circle at the bottom of the abyss. It is divided into two major divisions: Upper Hell, which has no name, and Lower Hell, called the City of Dis (*Dite* 8.68). Each division in turn comprises four circles. Upper Hell punishes the sins of incontinence, which originate from an inability to control the sensitive appetite, or from excessive adherence to natural instincts which are in themselves good. The second through fifth circles contain the lustful, the gluttons, the prodigal and miserly, and the wrathful and sullen—each group being guarded, respectively, by a separate monster (Minos, who also has the role of assigning each soul its proper place in Hell; Cerberus; Plutus; and Phlegyas, the ferryman of the river Styx). Within the City of Dis are punished the various sins of malice, sins that become increasingly grave and complex in nature, with the result that after the sixth circle, where the heretics are imprisoned in fiery tombs, each sub-

sequent circle subdivides into smaller sections. Thus malice—acts that do injury or harm—breaks down into the sins carried out by means of either force and fraud, the latter comprising both simple fraud and complex or aggravated fraud (treachery). Violence is punished in the seventh circle (guarded by the Minotaur) and comprises three classes of violent action, according to the specific person (and the person's possessions) against which injury is done: against another (murderers and tyrants); against self (suicides, spendthrifts); and against the Deity with respect to each of three aspects, namely, the person of God, God's offspring Nature, and Nature's offspring Art (blasphemers, sodomites, usurers). Simple fraud, presided over by Geryon, is punished in the eighth circle, Malebolge ("evil pouches"), which itself divides into ten separate *bolge* containing the seducers and panders, flatterers, simoniacs, soothsayers, barrators, hypocrites, thieves, false counselors, schismatics, and falsifiers. Simple fraud involves the use of deceit to perpetrate a crime against another human being or an institution. Treachery also employs deceit but is more serious because the individual breaks not only the natural bond of humanity that he or she possesses with others but also a special bond. The ninth and lowest circle, a frozen river named Cocytus *(Cocito)* presided over by Lucifer and the giants, houses the treacherous and is divided into four zones: Caina (traitors to kindred), Antenora (traitors to country), Ptolomea (traitors to guests), and finally Judecca (traitors to lords and benefactors). At the center of Cocytus, which is the centermost point of Earth and the lowest point in the universe, Lucifer is suspended silent and immobile, locked in ice and chewing mindlessly on three archsinners.

Dante's division of sins into the categories of incontinence and malice derives from Aristotle's *Nicomachean Ethics,* as commented upon and endorsed by St. Thomas Aquinas, but the Aristotelian concept incorporates Cicero's distinction between the sins of the lion and those of the fox, that is, of force and fraud, or *vis* and *fraus* (*De officiis* 1.13). But Dante's adoption of Aristotle's model is not entirely unproblematic, for his division of sins into incontinence, violence, and fraud is not easily equatable with Aristotle's threefold classification of the sins of into *malitia, incontinentia,* and *bestialitas* (the Latin translation of the Greek terms for malice, incontinence, and bestiality used by St. Thomas; see Aristotle's *Ethics* VII.1). Dante does not give bestiality its own place in Hell, and if it corresponds to the sins of violence in the seventh circle, as many critics argue, the term *malitia* then overlaps with violence, since it includes both force and fraud. At best Dante has remolded Aristotle and used him only selectively, inasmuch as several categories of sin—the neutrals, Limbo, the heretics—cannot be accounted for by reference to Aristotle. The neutrals are not in Hell proper, and both Limbo and the heretics are categories based on Christian doctrine entirely foreign to Aristotle. The heretics, who lie immediately inside the walls of Dis, are, in fact, in a kind of no-man's-land between the sins of incontinence and those of malice: their sin does not even fall technically under malice, because injury is not their goal.

Dante conceives of Purgatory as a steep mountain rising out of the southern sea on the opposite side of Earth from Jerusalem and having the form of an immense truncated cone. Dante imagines that the mountain of Purgatory, along with Hell, was formed when Lucifer and his angels rebelled and were cast out of Heaven. As he fell into the Southern Hemisphere and then to the center of Earth, the land in front of him, fearing contact with him, fled to the Northern Hemisphere; and the land at the center of Earth, to avoid contact with Lucifer, recoiled backwards to the surface of the southern side and piled up to form the island and mountain of Purgatory. The steepness of the mountain contrasts with the deepness of the pit of Hell, but the shape of both realms, a conical cylinder, is identical, the principal difference being that the cone of Hell comprises, topographically and tropographically, a vacuum.

The moral structure of *Purgatorio,* like that of *Inferno,* is determined by its topography. While in *Inferno* the sins being punished become more and more grave as one descends into the abyss, in *Purgatorio* the sinful tendencies being purified become less and less grave as one ascends the mountain: the closer to God, the greater one's degree of perfection. But whereas a sinner is eternally fixed in Hell in a single location, the penitent in Purgatory progress up the mountain in stages, which signifies an ongoing process of moral recovery and purification. In Hell the damned are judged according to the sinful acts they committed; in Purgatory repentant sinners are judged according to the tendencies that underlay the cause of their sins. Their penance is neither punitive or retributive, as it is for the damned in Hell, but rather is rehabilitative and remedial.

There are three main divisions on the mountain of Purgatory. The area from the seashore to the gate of Purgatory constitutes Ante-Purgatory, which is still subject to Earth's atmospheric changes. Inside the gate lies Purgatory proper, consisting of seven levels, or terraces, on each of which is purged one of the seven capital sins, beginning with the gravest: pride, envy, wrath, sloth, avarice, gluttony, and lust. At the top of the mountain lies the Earthly Paradise, the Garden of Eden, site both of the original Fall and of Redemption. The Ante-Purgatory detains the souls of those who died without having availed themselves of the means of penitence offered by the Church. These souls are lodged at the foot of the mountain and may not yet begin their ascent of the mountain, being forced to postpone the purgation they desire because while alive they put off repentance until the end. They are divided into four classes: the excommunicates; the indolent, who put off repentance through lassitude; the unshriven, who died a violent death yet managed to repent in their final moments; and, lastly, the negligent rulers, who deferred their repentance because of the pressure of temporal duties.

Purgatory proper is entered through a gate guarded by an angel and consists of seven terraces which rise in succession with diminished circuit as they approach the summit. The threshold of Purgatory consists of three steps whose different colors have been traditionally interpreted to symbolize the three stages of the sacrament of penitence: contrition of the heart *(contritio cordis),* oral confession *(confessio oris),* and satisfaction through the performance of good deeds *(satisfactio operis).* On the threshold of the gate sits a guardian angel with a sword who traces the letter "P" seven times on Dante-pilgrim's forehead, instructing him to "wash away" these wounds during his ascent up the mountain. These seven tracings ("P" for *peccatum,* the Latin word for "sin") represent the stains of the seven capital sins being purged by the souls in *Purgatorio.*

Each of the seven terraces corresponds to one of the seven deadly, or capital, sins, out of which, according to St. Thomas Aquinas, other vices spring. On each terrace Dante experiences a sequence of events that is liturgical in nature and symmetrically ordered from terrace to terrace

(Moore). This pattern, based on the trinitarian number 3, presents a set of virtues and a corresponding set of vices, between which the individual penitents of the capital vice being purged are introduced to the pilgrim. Dante almost certainly derived his symmetrical balancing of a set of virtues with a set of vices (which extends into the Earthly Paradise as well) from Conrad of Saxony's *Speculum* and from Hugh of St. Victor's *De quinque septenis,* and its effect is to emphasize the ritual nature of the penitential experience.

The pattern of the seven capital sins is subsumed into the larger and quintessentially positive concept that love is the motivating force of all human action. As Virgil explains to Dante—expounding principles taken from Aquinas' *Summa Theologiae*—there are two kinds of love: *naturale o d'animo* (natural love and rational love, *Purg.* 17.93). Natural love is instinctual love, a love innate in all humans, and includes the unerring predisposition to love God. It is a neutral factor, worthy of neither praise nor blame, and is unerring and never sinful, although it must be subjected to one's free will. In contrast, rational love (also called elective, or mental, love, being conceived by the faculty of reason) is the source of sin either when it is misdirected toward possessing the wrong object or when it lacks the proper measure, either through excess or through insufficiency. Wrong love comprises the sins of pride, envy, and wrath, which are purged on the first three terraces. Insufficient love, or sloth, is purged on the fourth terrace; while excessive love, in the form of avarice, gluttony, and lust, is purged on the highest three terraces. Dante's conception of misdirected or disordered love *(amor inordinatus),* with its bipartite categorization, derives either directly or indirectly from William Peraldus' *Summa de vitiis et de virtutibus* (c. 1250), a work Pietro di Dante relied upon in his commentary on *Purg.* 17.

Dante's *Paradiso* is modeled on the Ptolemaic system and consists of nine concentric heavens that revolve around Earth, which is fixed at the center of the universe. Surrounding these is a tenth motionless heaven lying beyond time and space, the Empyrean, the home of God and all the blessed souls in Heaven. In Dante's cosmos each of the nine angelic orders presides over one of nine heavens, each of which in turn exercises its specific influence on Earth and its inhabitants. The heavens move progressively faster and are larger the closer they are to the Empyrean. The seven lowest heavens contain the planets: the Moon, Mercury, Venus, the Sun, Mars, Jupiter, and Saturn. The eighth, or stellar heaven—the sphere of the Fixed Stars, or firmament—is the highest visible region of the celestial world. Above this visible firmament, the ninth, or crystalline heaven—the Primum Mobile—directs with its movements the daily revolution of all the other spheres. From this heaven proceed time and motion, and it communicates in different degrees some measure of the light of God to the spheres which it encloses and therefore to the entire universe. This heaven moves more swiftly than the others, because of its fervent desire to be united to the Empyrean, where God beatifies the blessed souls and all the angels by vouchsafing the vision of his essence. The Empyrean is the true Paradise, while the lower heavens illustrate various degrees of virtue. Each of the nine spheres represents a different degree of increased knowledge, love, and blessedness—in a word, virtue—until in the true Paradise (the Empyrean) all souls are displayed within the celestial rose, some higher and therefore closer to God, some lower and farther from God, each according to his or her individual merit.

While all the blessed dwell in the Empyrean, they manifest themselves to Dante in the various heavens in groups corresponding to their capacity for love of God. Although all souls in Paradise receive blessedness, their capacities vary both in quantity and in quality. Each heaven takes in a greater or lesser amount of the divine light that it is capable of receiving. Likewise, the souls that appear in the various heavens have a greater and lesser capacity to receive God's goodness, their merit being demonstrated by their propinquity to God. The concept that individual souls differ in their knowledge of God and in their capacity to love him is derived by church theologians—chiefly Augustine and Thomas Aquinas—from John 14:2: "In my Father's house are many mansions." Different degrees of virtue and excellence, however, mean different degrees of happiness; yet each individual is perfectly happy and perfectly satisfied with his or her degree of happiness. In canto 3 of *Paradiso,* the soul of Piccarda Donati explains to the pilgrim that all the souls are content wherever they find themselves in the hierarchy of Paradise. They do not desire to attain a higher place in the orderly arrangement of Heaven, since they all possess a perfected volition and take delight in accepting the will of God as their own.

Despite the many critical attempts to identify the underlying moral structure of the *Paradiso,* it is difficult to determine precisely how the souls are categorized in the various heavens. Unlike in Hell and Purgatory, the poet does not overtly specify the criteria for his partitioning of the souls into the separate heavens. The angelic intelligences exert their influence through the nine spheres, to stamp the divine imprint on the material Creation and carry out the divine plan in the governing of the universe. By means of the influence of the stars, the nine orders of celestial intelligences impress humankind with their own characteristics but do not interfere with an individual's free will. The influence of the heavens determines the initial movements of the soul but not all its movements, and this influence does not impede the use of reason nor the ability to distinguish good from evil. Some combination of individual disposition provided by angelic influence and personal achievement accounts for one's virtue, and individuals appear to be grouped, in what is perhaps the best analysis, according to traditionally identifiable virtues—each heaven representing a classification of virtue that stands as an ideal model. The most explicit linking of the planets to specific virtues appears in the heavens of the Sun, Mars, Jupiter, and Saturn, which traditionally have been seen as representing the four cardinal virtues. The theologians *(spiriti sapienti)* of the Sun, an emblem of enlightenment, have been associated with the virtue of prudence. The crusaders of Mars, who have given their lives to defend the faith, represent the virtue of courage. Jupiter is manifestly connected to the virtue of justice, as the souls in this heaven assemble themselves to spell out the phrase *Diligite iustitiam qui iudicatis terram* ("Love justice, you who judge the earth," *Par.* 18.91–93). The final letter "M," standing for *monarchia* ("monarchy")—representing the ideal form of government on Earth—then transforms itself into an eagle, the symbol of the Empire. Saturn, finally, is associated with temperance, being the abode of the contemplatives who have devoted themselves to the monastic life, which emphasizes heightened spirituality through abstinence and chastity. Less explicit is the pattern that defines specific virtues in the first three heavens, but a suggestive case has been made by several critics that these heavens represent a deficiency of the three theological virtues—faith, hope, and charity—because they fall within the shadow of Earth (Carroll, Ordiway).

The nuns of the Moon who abandoned their conventual vows lacked sufficient faith; the souls in Mercury fall short by placing their hope in earthly fame more than in the love of God (*Par.* 6.112–117); and the souls of Venus find their *caritas* (love of God) marred by their sexual wantonness *(cupiditas)*. The pattern is completed in the Fixed Stars, where the theological virtues are shown in proficiency, as Dante himself is examined on the nature of faith by St. Peter, on hope by St. James, and on charity by St. John. The Primum Mobile, the heaven of the angels, lies above the human virtues and represents angelic power.

The tenth and final heaven, the Empyrean, is the abode of the Deity and all the spirits of the blessed souls of Heaven. It is the true Paradise, where human will is set at rest in union with the universal Good and where intellect is in possession of universal Truth. Here the pilgrim sees the souls arranged in the petals of the vast, white, Celestial Rose, which resembles a kind of amphitheater and whose form is composed of the light of the Godhead reflected upward from the convex outer shell of the Primum Mobile. Within the celestial rose sit the Virgin Mary, John the Baptist, various saintly men and Hebrew women, the blessed souls of the Old Testament, the saints of the New Testament, and infants. In the Empyrean the pilgrim is accorded a direct vision of God, figured as three circles of different colors within a single light (the second circle reflected from the first, and the third emanating from both the first and the second), in an image of the miracle of the Trinity: the mysterious triune essence of God. In a final vision, before all sight is lost, the pilgrim perceives in the second circle the human form of Christ (*nostra effige, Par.* 33.131): the mystery of the Incarnation.

Bibliography

Busnelli, Giovanni. *Il concetto e l'ordine del "Paradiso" dantesco.* 2 vols. Città di Castello: S. Lapi, 1911–1912.

Carroll, John. *In Patria: An Exposition of Dante's Paradiso.* London: Hodder and Stoughton, 1911.

Cornish, Alison. "Dante's Moral Cosmology." In *Cosmology: Historical, Literary, Philosophical, Religious, and Scientific Perspectives.* Edited by Norris S. Hetherington. New York and London: Garland, 1993, pp. 201–215.

Hollander, Robert. "The Moral System of the *Commedia* and the Seven Capital Sins." In *Allegory in Dante's Commedia.* Princeton, N.J.: Princeton University Press, 1969, pp. 308–320.

Lansing, Richard. "Narrative Design in Dante's Earthly Paradise." *Dante Studies* 112 (1994), 101–113. Reprinted in *Dante: Contemporary Perspectives.* Edited by Amilcare A. Iannucci. Toronto: University of Toronto Press, 1997, pp. 133–147.

Moore, Edward. "Unity and Symmetry of Design in the *Purgatorio.*" In *Studies in Dante. Second Series: Miscellaneous Essays.* Oxford: Clarendon Press, 1899, pp. 246–268.

Ordiway, Frank. "In the Earth's Shadow: The Theological Virtues Marred." *Dante Studies* 100 (1982), 77–92.

Pietrobono, Luigi. *Dal centro al cerchio; la struttura morale della Divina Commedia.* Turin: Società editrice internazionale, 1923.

Reade, W. H. V. *The Moral System of Dante's Inferno.* Oxford: Clarendon Press, 1909.

Valli, Luigi. *L'allegoria di Dante secondo Giovanni Pascoli.* Bologna: Zanichelli, 1922.

Wenzel, Siegfried. "Dante's Rationale for the Seven Deadly Sins (*Purgatorio* XVII)." *Modern Language Review* 60 (1965), 529–533.

Molly G. Morrison and Richard Lansing

4. Commedia: *Allegory and Realism*

The terms "allegory" and "realism" are generally taken to refer to two different and often opposing poetic procedures. *Allegory* ("other speaking") denotes a method of composing literature which invokes a supplemental level of meaning distinct from the literal. *Realism,* on the other hand, describes the representation of experience in such a way that the image of reality fabricated by the words evokes a close resemblance to what we know about the world from sense data directly. Dante's Commedia poem has the special power of conveying realistic images of both the real world and human experience while simultaneously *empowering* that reality to suggest higher levels of meaning, so that we might characterize his narrative procedure as "allegorical realism."

In the doublet "allegory and realism," realism is, perhaps surprisingly, actually the more difficult concept. Because we are so used to the notion of realism, we need at first to estrange ourselves from it and to defamiliarize it.

Realism emerged and came to dominance in the genre of the novel during the nineteenth and early twentieth centuries in the advanced technological societies of the West. Realism depends for its effects above all on the effacement of the medium. Realism invites us to the window whose glass is invisible, whose frame is unobtrusive, and whose view onto experience is uninterrupted and verisimilar to what we know about the world. Realism, in short, is wholly dependent on artifice just because it must, to succeed, suppress or efface all signs of artifice—the ultimately artificial effect.

In this view, perhaps paradoxically, allegory is the more accessible and comprehensible concept. Allegory always betrays its artifice. If we posit for the moment an analogy with architecture, allegory is the Gothic cathedral of Dante's age, with flying buttresses everywhere in evidence. Allegory is always concerned to call attention to its disjunction from the real. Allegory, as Dante teaches us, is a darkened glass, interrupting and interfering with our view.

We might consider, in this light, the following four episodes in the Commedia. In *Inf.* 1, Dante tells us he cannot recall how he entered the dark wood because he was "full of sleep . . . at the point when [he] left the true way" (1.11). In canto 5, after hearing Francesca's story of her love affair, Dante faints out of pity for her condition, swooning as though in death *(com' io morisse)* and falling "as a dead body falls" *(come corpo morto cade,* 140–142). In *Purg.* 30, when Beatrice rebukes Dante the pilgrim for his apostasy, the poet recalls: "My eyes fell down to the clear spring, but, seeing myself there, I turned them to the grass, such shame weighed down my forehead" (76–78). Finally, in *Par.* 26, Dante meets the first man, Adam, who is described by means of a curious simile: "Sometimes a hidden animal stirs in such a way that its affect appears as its covering responds to it: similarly the first soul made me see through its covering how gaily it came to please me" (*Par.* 26.97–102).

In each of these episodes, there is an element we recognize as realistic—the state of sleepiness, for example, or fainting, or shame disfiguring the face of the embarrassed, or an animal's movement revealing its purpose. And yet, circumscribing that element in each episode is a much larger structure of allegory. And this is the poet's method: Dante intuits the allegorical within the real, and his writing repeatedly isolates that moment when the real issues into a different, larger, and more complicated vista. In Dante's writing, "this is how it happened" metamorphoses into "this is how it means" before our eyes. In this sense, Dante's writing is most accurately described as "allegorical realism."

Erich Auerbach, one of the greatest Romance philologists and literary critics of the twentieth century, is renowned in Dante studies especially for his notion of "figural realism." Based in Christian typology and exegesis, *figural realism* argues that "[b]oth figure and fulfillment possess . . . the character of actual historical events and phenomena. The fulfillment possesses it in greater and more intense measure, for it is, compared with the figure, *forma perfectior.* This explains the overwhelming realism of Dante's beyond" (*Mimesis* 197). Cato in Purgatory—one of Auerbach's favorite examples—is the fulfillment of the historical figure of Cato, his "finalized" identity in the otherworld constituting his greater and more intense reality. "Allegorical realism," as used in the present article, clearly depends upon Auerbach's notion of "figural realism." Thus, for example, the disjunctive force of allegory is implicit in Auerbach's comparatives, "greater and more intense . . . *forma perfectior,*" which acknowledge the gap between figure and fulfillment. At the same time, allegorical realism is a partial corrective to the deep bias in Auerbach's figural realism toward characterology—almost all his examples are characters. This bias betrays the dominance of the novel in his thought: Auerbach is very much a reader of the nineteenth century and of nineteenth-century realism (even if he flourished in the twentieth century). The epigraph to his earlier book *Dante, Poet of the Secular World,* taken from Heraclitus, "a man's character is his fate," is telling and reveals Auerbach's habitual focus on character as exemplifying figural realism (see especially *Mimesis* 200–201).

The term "allegorical realism," on the other hand, suggests a revision of the bias against allegory in Auerbach's ultimately Romantic and Goethean view that "medieval symbolism and allegorism are often . . . excessively abstract" (*Mimesis* 196). Such dismissal marks the history of all discourse about allegory since the late eighteenth century. The past two centuries have stigmatized allegory as the weak sibling of symbolism especially, and of realism as well. Dante's allegory, however, is a different mode. Not only in characters but also in events and images and even in abstractions Dante achieves "the overwhelming realism of [his] beyond," and he does so by virtue of the decorum of his style; and here Auerbach

remains a remarkably faithful guide for readers of Dante, especially in his earlier book.

The key to this decorum is *convenientia* ("convenience"). A term appearing frequently in Dante's writings and in those of his commentators, it is best translated for our purposes as "fittingness." Dante's writing astonishes us with its repeated success in "fitting" event with meaning—the concept of *contrapasso* being perhaps the most vivid example. The "fit" or "convenience" between Dante's faint at the end of Francesca's narration and our understanding of the pernicious effects of amorous rhetoric is an excellent example of a "realistic" event—that of fainting under great emotional stress—and its "allegorical" meaning, namely, that the rhetoric of *fin'amors* is as adulterating as the adultery itself. If Paolo and Francesca sinned because *quel giorno più non vi leggemmo avante* ("that day [they] read there no further," *Inf.* 5.138) in the pandering book recounting the story of Lancelot and Guinevere (5.137),

Dante, Virgil, and the three beasts. Opere di Dante Alighieri, edited by Cristoforo Zapate de Cisneros, Venice, 1757–1758. Giamatti Collection: Courtesy of the Mount Holyoke College Archives and Special Collections.

Dante guards against the possibility that we, his readers, will lapse into a similar sin with his text by interrupting our reading with the narration of the pilgrim's fainting: we are not overcome with pity because we see that the pilgrim is, and so we continue our reading.

We may test this sense of *convenientia* in the *Commedia* with reference to two justly renowned episodes—that of the peasant *(villanello)* at the opening of *Inf.* 24 and that of the appearance of Adam in *Par.* 26—and then consider one of the most famous episodes of the entire poem, that of Ugolino (*Inf.* 33), where allegorical realism is arguably more vivid than anywhere else in the *Commedia*.

Dante opens *Inf.* 24 with one of his most complex extended similes: "In that part of the youthful year when the sun tempers its locks under Aquarius and already the nights are moving south, when on the ground the frost copies the image of her white sister, but her pen retains its temper only briefly, the peasant, his provisions running short, rises to look, and sees the fields all white, and he strikes his thigh, goes back in his house, and complains here and there like a wretch who knows not what to do; then he goes forth again and stores hope in his wicker basket again, seeing the face of the world has changed in a short time; and he takes his crook and drives the little sheep forth to pasture" (1–15). The key here is the image of writing: we are presented with an image of the structure of writing which suggests that writing is mutable, temporal, and elusive, requiring always a second reading as a minimum toward comprehension of meaning. One moment the peasant sees (the image of) snow, but on second look (on rereading) he sees that "the face of the world has changed." Here the real itself behaves like the allegorical. So it is with Dante's allegorical realism throughout the poem: we look the first time and see episode after episode that impresses us with realism (especially by way of remarkable similes); but when we look again, when we reread (as Paolo and Francesca did not), we see realism (and the real) give way to a different vista, a "changed face," the true face, which is always there, even if not always visible to fallen eyes.

It is the changing of the face, as much as the changed face, that is the crucial effect of Dante's allegorical realism: what makes Dante's poem of such enduring value is the way in which his style moves us through the changing to the results of the change—the way it shows us the realization of the allegory as well as the allegorical meaning of the real. We might consider, in this light, the extraordinary moment of Adam's emergence; he appears like an animal that is covered but which so stirs that its reactions are evident, since what envelops it follows its movements. (*Par.* 26.97–102). It is an emergence in which the literal becomes the allegorical in its very unfolding. Adam, whose sin was *il trapassar del segno* ("the going beyond the mark," *Par.* 26.117), the transgression of the boundary marker, or sign, appears to the pilgrim in the sign of a sign: Dante's image of the covered animal (the sign of the animal's presence) is the sign of how a sign signifies. So much is confirmed, we should note first, by the extraordinary diction: *convien che* (98) is the lexical marker of *convenientia,* and *invoglia* (99) is a technical term in medieval literary theory for an allegorical image *(involucrum)*. We may translate then as follows: "sometimes a hidden animal stirs in such a way that it must be that [literally, "becomes fitting that" *(convien che)*] its affect makes itself appear [*si paia*] by means of the movement that the wrapping [also "image" *(involucrum)*] makes on it." This (necessarily) cumbersome translation exposes Dante's insistence on the allegorical already inherent within the real. The "other speaking" ("allegory" < Greek, *allos agoreuein;* medieval Latin, *alieniloquium*) of the animal's covering is (already) natural or, in our terms, real.

Moreover, Dante implies in this canto, this effect is the result of *il trapassar del segno:* the sign having been transgressed by the first user of signs, Adam, all signs henceforth function by the postlapsarian dialectic of revelation—concealment and exposure, revealing that is also re-veiling, uncovering *(si paia)* that depends necessarily on covering *(per lo seguir che face a lui la 'nvoglia).* And further, as the homophony between "animal" and "anima" *(primaia)* suggests, Adam can appear to Dante the pilgrim only in his *coverta:* he can appear only as appearance (Adam to the pilgrim's eyes is not visible; only that which covers him is visible), and he can show the pilgrim his pleasure only by the indirection of "other speaking." In a fallen world, in a world corrupted by Adam's sin, the real is always already allegorical; that is to say, the real is always first only the apparent, in need of reading, interpretation, investigation. And that, of course, is why, unlike Paolo and Francesca, we must always read further (if we would not be damned)—the real of our experience is rarely what it seems, precisely because it seems so real.

Dante's most telling and most moving figuration of this postlapsarian corruption of our intellect is his account of Ugolino, whose most famous line—*poscia, più che 'l dolor, poté il digiuno* ("then fasting had more power than grief," *Inf.* 33.75)—disturbs us so deeply because of its indeterminacy: it suggests that Ugolino committed cannibalism upon his children, although we can never know for sure, since the line can be read to mean simply that Ugolino's hunger, not his sorrow, brought about his death. In Ugolino the allegorical already in the real is so far corrupted, so infernal, that it becomes pure indeterminacy: we can, and we do, argue interminably about the line's meaning, without resolution, because the line is completely corrupted allegorical realism.

The measure of Dante's mastery of allegorical realism is evident in his ability to corrupt it in this line—and still to expect his reader to follow him to his meaning, to see the version of the truth of which the line is the perversion. It is now a commonplace of Dante scholarship that Ugolino's story is an allegory of the Eucharist; after the work of Freccero, Hollander, Mazzotta, and others, we know that the narrative very carefully maps images of and allusions to the Eucharist onto Ugolino's account of his and his son's deaths. We also know at the same time that the story as Dante tells it is largely his own invention. If based in the real, Dante's story is still very much fiction. But so much is what we expect from the style of allegorical realism. It is specific to Dante's realism that the edifice of fiction supporting his allegory should emerge into our view—like the flying buttresses of the Gothic cathedral. For Dante the real is already transubstantiated into the Word of salvation-history by the sacrifice of Jesus—the real is already fictive, made of words and the Word.

But this is precisely what Ugolino cannot or will not see: he sees his sons dying and nothing else—no story, none. Not even when Gaddo flings himself at Ugolino's feet and begs, "My father, why do you not help me?" (*Padre mio, chè non m'aiuti?* 33.69) can or will Ugolino see more than the real, through the real, and comfort his dying sons with the Word. Stonily, he rejects the hope of the salvation bought for them by the sacrifice of that other son (of man) who also cried out, "My God, my God, why hast thou forsaken me?" and

upon whom the faithful feed every time the Mass is celebrated. As Ugolino says earlier, *"sì dentro impetrai"* ("I so turned to stone within," 33.49). And this, we may propose, is his damnation: to be so turned to stone that he cannot read through the real to its eternal significance; to be so dehumanized that he can only riddle the reality of his and his sons' dying in a line that is, we see now, an infernal version of allegorical realism precisely in the corrupted way it evokes the Eucharistic "feeding" upon the flesh of Jesus only to revoke its sacramental and allegorical significance.

Bibliography

Auerbach, Eric. *Dante, Poet of the Secular World.* Translated by Ralph Manheim. Chicago: University of Chicago Press, 1961.

———. *Mimesis: The Representation of Reality in Western Literature.* Translated by Willard Trask. New York: Anchor Books, 1957.

Barolini, Teodolinda. *The Undivine "Comedy": Detheologizing Dante.* Princeton, N.J.: Princeton University Press, 1992.

Botterill, Steven. "*Inferno* XXIX: Capocchio and the Limits of Realism." In *Italiana 1988.* Edited by Albert N. Mancini, Paolo A. Giordano, and Anthony J. Tamburri. *Rosary College Italian Studies* 4. River Forest, Ill., 1990, pp. 23–33.

Durling, Robert M. "Ugolino." In *The Divine Comedy of Dante Alighieri: Inferno.* Edited and translated by Robert M. Durling. Introduction and notes by Ronald L. Martinez and Robert M. Durling. Oxford, New York: Oxford University Press, 1996, pp. 578–580.

Freccero, John. "Bestial Sign and Bread of Angels: *Inferno* 32 and 33." Reprinted in *Dante: The Poetics of Conversion.* Edited by Rachel Jacoff. Cambridge, Mass.: Harvard University Press, 1986, pp. 152–166.

Hollander, Robert. "*Inferno* XXXIII: 37–74: Ugolino's Importunity." *Speculum* 59 (1984), 549–555.

Mazzotta, Giuseppe. *Dante, Poet of the Desert.* Princeton, N.J.: Princeton University Press, 1979.

Shoaf, R. A. "The Crisis of Convention in Cocytus." In *Allegoresis: The Craft and Meaning of Allegory.* Edited by J. Stephen Russell. New York: Garland Publishing, 1988, pp. 157–169.

Trimpi, Wesley. *Muses of One Mind: The Literary Analysis of Experience and Its Continuity.* Princeton, N.J.: Princeton University Press, 1983.

R. Allen Shoaf

5. Commedia: *Manuscript Tradition*

The *Commedia*'s very form, as well as its twenty-year-long period of gestation, has from the beginning tainted the poem's textual tradition. While it is impossible to identify editorial stages in the making of the *Commedia,* there is, however, evidence about how the poet provided for the dissemination of individual groups of cantos and, later, of the first two canticles. The dating of these events has long been the subject of controversy, but it is certain that *Inferno* was published around 1315, and it is certain that the entire *Purgatorio,* which Giovanni del Virgilio attests to knowing well, was in circulation before 1320.

It is thus understandable that even the oldest extant copies of the poem—few in number and appearing relatively late, considering the work's long and laborious gestation period—display a textual corruption that is difficult to emend. This has been confirmed by the "National Edition" of the poem, edited by Giorgio Petrocchi, which we will consistently refer to as the most recent and the only systematic exploration of the manuscript sources (as well as the reference point for the manuscripts' sigla).

If we exclude the fragmentary texts of minimal philological importance—despite their being the earliest, such as citations found in Bolognese records between 1317 and 1321 (Bologna, Archivio di Stato, Curia del Podestà, *Accusationes,* 1317, citation of *Inf.* 3, etc.)—the earliest extant manuscript is ASH, which dates prior to 1335 (Florence, Biblioteca Medicea Laurenziana, *Ashburnham* 828). This manuscript originated in western Tuscany, an area that also gave birth ten years later to another important manuscript called HAM (Berlin, Deutsche Staatsbibliothek, *Hamilton* 203). The Hamilton manuscript was written in Pisa in 1348 by the eighteen-year-old Tommaso di Pietro Benetti. However, it is certain that Florence quickly assumed an indisputable centrality in the initial tradition of the work. It is thus not surprising that the oldest complete copy that is datable originated in Florence, although it is now lost and known only through indirect evidence. It was commissioned by Giovanni Bonaccorsi and copied in Florence between 1330 and 1331 by a certain Forese, who made use of many exemplars. In 1548 this manuscript passed through the hands of Luca Martini, who noted the variants of the *Commedia* on his own printed copy while also faithfully transcribing the colophon. Although Forese's manuscript has been lost, the printing with Martini's collation is extant: this text is known as MART, the Aldine edition of 1515 preserved in Milan (Biblioteca Nazionale Braidense, Aldina AP XVI 25).

The third manuscript whose date is certain, known as TRIV, is dated 1337 (Milan, Biblioteca Trivulziana, 1080). (The second, LA, dated 1336, warrants and will receive a separate discussion later.) TRIV—one of the few manuscripts that is not of anonymous origin—bears the signature of a Florentine named Francesco di Ser Nardo da Barberino. This manuscript and its contemporary, GV, which is dated 1338—or 1337 Florentine style—originated in Florence (GV was once in Florence at the Biblioteca dei Marchesi Venturi Ginori Lisci, 46; it is now in Ravenna at the Centro Dantesco dei Frati Minori). Finally, although slightly later but still originating from the same area, there is the manuscript known as GA (Florence, Biblioteca Medicea Laurenziana, Pl. 90 sup. 125), dated 1347–1348, also ascribed to Francesco di Ser Nardo da Barberino. This manuscript is textually independent from the aforementioned TRIV, despite being the work of the same scribe, to whom even a third Dantean undertaking is attributed. The text, now reduced to a few fragments, is known as MO (Modena, Archivio di Stato e Biblioteca Estense, fragments from *Inferno* and *Purgatorio*).

Just ten of the earliest *Commedia* manuscripts are dated, including the following four: PA (Paris, Bibliothèque Nationale, It. 538, year 1351); URB (Urbinate latino 366, year 1352); MAD (Madrid, Biblioteca Nacional, 10186, year 1354); and LAUR (Florence, Biblioteca Medicea Laurenziana, Pl. 40.22, from 1355). This number is trifling in comparison with the actual diffusion of the work. The number of manuscripts that are not dated but which are judged to be old enough—within or slightly later than the middle of the fourteenth century—for Petrocchi to include them in his analysis is not significant, so that the total number of manuscripts, both dated and undated, comes to barely thirty.

In fact, however, the public demand for the *Commedia* in Florence before the 1330s must have been very high. Vincenzo Borghini, a famous Florentine philologist, reported an anecdote that offers proof of a large-scale production at a professional level. He tells of a fourteenth-century scribe who built up his daughters' dowries by copying out one hundred manuscripts of the *Commedia*. This anecdote was well received by late-nineteenth-century philologists, since on one of the oldest (though undated) copies of the poem (LAU, Florence, Biblioteca Medicea Laurenziana, Pl. 40.16) the following annotation, inscribed by its sixteenth-century owner, was found: *Questo Dannte de ciento è di me . . .* ("This Dante of one hundred belongs to me . . ."). Many scholars, ranging from Täuber to Marchesini, have related similar manuscripts to this so-called *bottega del Cento* ("workshop of the one hundred").

This large-scale production is thought to have been directed by Francesco di Ser Nardo (of whom we otherwise know nothing) because of similarities of script, manuscript form, and textual format which it shares with the GA manuscript (Francesco's second signed copy, dating from 1347–1348). Petrocchi also accepts this hypothesis, although it has not been confirmed by an accurate scribal and paleographic examination of the original manuscripts, both because Francesco di Ser Nardo's works (among them a non-Dantean text, R.1523 in the Biblioteca Riccardiana in Florence) have proved to be more luxurious than the "standard" Florentine fare and because some of the manuscripts cited as belonging to that workshop are prior to GA, as Gabriella Pomaro has argued.

Beyond establishing that textual corruption is evident in even the oldest manuscripts in the tradition, Dantean philology has for some time (at least since Moore) acquired knowledge of various families of manuscripts that share textual similarities. A satisfactory survey of the entire manuscript tradition has never been completed. The existence of an extraordinary number of manuscripts—Roddewig has counted 827 individual manuscripts—has created a formidable challenge. Various scholars have suggested different approaches—the last being Petrocchi's *antica vulgata*—but all approaches are vulnerable to criticism. Nevertheless, the existence of these families of texts gives the philologist a point of reference, despite the ongoing need to examine the later tradition. We have already alluded to the "del Cento" group, which is said to have originated from a matrix of closely related manuscripts that were prepared at one or more workshops in early-fourteenth-century Florence and which continued to be circulated throughout the fourteenth century right up to the three *princeps* printed editions of 1472, and even later. Of the sixty-one manuscripts

recorded by Roddewig as members of this textual family, only ten definitely fall outside the limits of the *antica vulgata*. The majority of the others have generally been assigned to the Francesco di Ser Nardo school by late-eighteenth-century scholars. This leads us to appreciate the subtle relationship between this text and the Florentine *vulgata* of the mid-fourteenth century.

Earlier rather than contemporaneous with the "del Cento," a copy of the *Commedia* whose text was quite different in character seems to have circulated in Florence. This manuscript, referred to as PARM (Parma, Biblioteca Palatina, Parmense 3285; it lacks a precise date but falls within the fourth decade of the fourteenth century), had a greater diffusion than previously thought. Other textually related copies can also be attributed to this scribe, while the appearance of work by his hand in the "Statuti delle Arti di Firenze" of 1330 confirms their antiquity.

Meanwhile, the strong "Vatican family" would seem to be Tuscan, not Florentine, in origin. Through the auspices of Boccaccio this family of manuscripts was to have a wide diffusion, and through those of Bembo it made its way into the world of early-sixteenth-century printing presses. The family takes its name from a renowned manuscript copy (VAT, Vatican City, Vat. Lat. 3199), probably the dedicatory copy sent by Boccaccio to Petrarch. The work, dating from 1351, is by an anonymous copyist from western Tuscany who also produced the invaluable CHA manuscript (Chantilly, Musée Condé, 597). The Chantilly codex contains only the first canticle, in a format very similar to that of VAT, along with Guido da Pisa's Latin commentary, the *Expositio,* and his *Declaratio.* The CHA manuscript, which is the lone source text of Guido da Pisa's *Expositio* and *Declaratio,* likewise exhibits western Tuscan attributes and is richly decorated in a style typical of the school of Francesco Traini of Pisa. Roddewig has assigned thirty-five manuscripts to the Vatican family, including Bembo's autograph copy of 1502 (based on VAT), even though the textual context is broad and cross-contaminated.

According to Moore, we have the "Ashburnham" group, of fairly dubious consistency, as well as a richer group referred to as the "Sienese." There remains the Boccaccian *editio,* which merits a separate discussion. A true and distinct editorial plan for the works of Dante begins to emerge in the three copies (neither signed nor dated) that

C have long been recognized as in the hand of Giovanni Boccaccio over a twenty-year period (in the sequence TO, RI, CHIG: Toledo, Biblioteca del Cabildo 104.6; Florence, Biblioteca Riccardiana 1035; and Vatican City, Biblioteca Apostolica Vaticana Chig. L. VI.213.). Here Dante's masterpiece is accompanied by three brief introductions by Boccaccio placed at the head of each canticle; the *Vita di Dante,* which is also by Boccaccio, though in different versions; the *Vita Nuova;* and an anthology of fifteen canzoni. At present CHIG contains only Boccaccio's introductions to the *Commedia,* but as De Robertis has shown, the codex represents the final section of one of the other Boccaccio autographs, the CHIG. L. V.176, and the two pieces together make up the complete corpus. The *Commedia* text that Boccaccio followed is clearly similar to that of VAT, even though the three copies are never identical. The fidelity with which he constructed this text is remarkable. According to Billanovich's interesting hypothesis, the copy Boccaccio made and dedicated to Petrarch must have been delivered to Petrarch in Avignon in 1351 by Forese Donati, the scribe of MART, who went there in the company of the Florentine bishop Angelo Acciaioli. If this is true, the VAT/CHIG lineage would have to be characterized as more "cultured" and less direct than the *vulgata* text embodied in the decidedly Florentine "Cento." An analysis of the codices and paleography fully supports this interpretation of the age-old confrontation between the two textual families. Even throughout the sixteenth century, the "VAT family," embodied in Bembo's Aldine edition, was placed in opposition to the Florentine philological school. The "Cento" manuscripts adhere to a standardized line of production in both physical format and choice of script (Florentine chancery) as well as in ornamentation. Lacking a commentary and having less than a hundred pages, the product was clearly intended to satisfy the needs of the notary class and therefore of a bourgeoisie deeply involved in civic life. Conversely, at least the earliest manuscripts of the "Vatican family" are of superior, often deluxe quality, usually having been privately commissioned and produced by a learned scribe predisposed to using Latin idioms. He was also most likely a cleric active in Florence though not of Florentine origin, and he was certainly well known, especially if Boccaccio turned to him.

Isolated marginal manuscripts remain that are nevertheless of utmost importance with regard to the reconstruction of the text. They are very likely of Florentine origin but are not part of any "production series" and still require further analysis: PO (Florence, Biblioteca Nazionale Centrale, Pal. 313), which is certainly older than presently thought, and FI (Naples, Biblioteca dei Gerolamini, 4.20).

The textual history of Dante's poem is, however, not limited to Florence. The production of manuscripts emanating from the provinces, especially from the north, is less consistent but also less contaminated. The Petrocchi stemma, which is rigidly bipartite, postulates that LA derived from the subarchetype ß in the Po Valley region (Piacenza, Biblioteca Comunale Passerini Landi, 190). As one of the ten dated copies of the *antica vulgata,* this source text was written in 1336 by Antonius de Firimo for Beccaria de' Beccari, who was then chief magistrate of Genoa. The LA manuscript was corrected on an exemplar based on the "del Cento" text before 1356, the year of the owner's death. RB also stems from the ß branch (Florence, Biblioteca Riccardiana 1002; and Milan, Biblioteca Nazionale Braidense AG XII.2) and was written and illuminated between 1330 and 1340 by Maestro Galvano of Bologna.

The Petrocchi critical edition has discerned in Boccaccio's work a watershed between the older and more recent traditions of Dante's poem. Although the more recent tradition has still not been fully analyzed, it is well enough known to make it seem doubtful that further analysis could possibly produce any notable new readings in the text. Moreover, in 1955 Petrocchi had already demonstrated this hypothesis by using the late-fourteenth-century AN manuscript (Rome, Biblioteca Angelica, 1101) for comparative purposes. Subsequently Petrocchi devalued the importance of the LauSC manuscript (*Introduzione,* pp. 47–55) by demonstrating its link with Boccaccio's *editio.* The LauSC manuscript (Florence, Biblioteca Medicea Laurenziana Pl. 26 sin. 1) was too highly regarded by Witte, who used it as a foundation for his edition in 1862, and his successors, because it was in the hand of the renowned Filippo Villani, yet believed to be older than it really was. This is a excellent example of the process of contamination that pervades the poem's later manuscript tradition.

Any new analytical approach arising out of advances in the discipline of paleography will almost certainly not result in progress in the area of dating manuscripts, but it must clearly allow for a reevaluation of the texts that are chronologically older, with at least three positive results: it would enrich the current skeletal paradigm of the poem's stemma; it would also permit a better distribution of the undated texts along the chronological axis of the fourteenth century; and it would replace some problematic texts, such as CO (Cortona, Biblioteca dell'Accademia Etrusca, 88), whose dating is controversial, with manuscripts whose dating is more certain.

Bibliography

The bibliography that accompanies the description of every manuscript cataloged in Roddewig renders superfluous any reference to previous critical work. The following works are nevertheless listed for their historical import.

Alighieri, Dante. *La Commedìa. Nuovo testo critico secondo i più antichi manoscritti fiorentini.* Edited by Antonio Lanza. Nuova edizione. Anzio: De Rubeis, 1996.

———. *La Commedia secondo l'antica vulgata.* Edited by Giorgio Petrocchi. 4 vols. Milan: Mondadori, 1966. Reprinted in Florence: Le Lettere, 1994, especially Vol. I, pp. 57–91: *I manoscritti dell'antica vulgata.*

Barbi, Michele. *Problemi di critica dantesca. Prima serie 1893–1918.* Reprinted in Florence: Sansoni, 1975.

Billanovich, Giuseppe. *Petrarca letterato. I. Lo scrittoio del Petrarca.* Rome: Edizioni di "Storia e letteratura," 1947, especially pp. 161–164.

Borghini, Vincenzo. *Lettera intorno a' manoscritti antichi* (c. 1573). In *Opuscoli inediti o rari di classici o approvati scrittori.* Florence: Società Poligrafica Italiana, 1884, Vol. I, pp. 17–41.

De Batines, Paul Colomb. *Bibliografia dantesca ossia Catalogo delle edizioni, traduzioni, codici.* . . . Prato: Tipografia Aldina, 1846–1848; with the related *Giunte e correzioni inedite alla Bibliografia Dantesca.* . . , published by G. Giagi. Florence: Sansoni, 1888.

De Robertis, Domenico. *Il codice Chigiano L. V.176 autografo di Giovanni Boccaccio.* Rome, Florence: Fratelli Alinari, 1974.

Esposito, Enzo. *Bibliografia analitica degli scritti su Dante, 1950–1970.* Florence: Olschki, 1990.

Marchesini, Umberto. "I Danti del Cento." *Bullettino della Società Dantesca Italiana* 2–3 (1890), 21–42; 4 (1890), 19–26.

Moore, Edward. *Contributions to the Textual Criticism of the Divine Comedy.* Cambridge: Cambridge University Press, 1889.

Petrocchi, Giorgio. "La tradizione recenziore della Commedia." *Atti del Convegno Internazionale di Studi Danteschi.* Ravenna: Longo, 1979, pp. 167–171.

———. "Radiografia del Landiano." *Studi danteschi* 35 (1958), 5–27.

———. "Proposte per un testo-base della *Divina Commedia.*" *Filologia Romanza* 2 (1955), 337–365.

———. "L'antica tradizione manoscritta della '*Commedia.*'" *Studi danteschi* 24 (1947), 7–126.

Pomaro, Gabriella. *Frammenti di un discorso dantesco.* Nonantola: Comune di Nonantola, 1994 (Archivio Storico Nonantolano 3).

———. "Codicologia dantesca. I. L'Officina di Vat." *Studi danteschi* 58 (1990), 343–374.

Roddewig, Marcella (ed.). *Die Göttliche Komödie. Vergleichende Bestandsaufnahme der Commedia-Handschriften.* Stuttgart: Hiersemann Verlag, 1984.

Täuber, Carl. *I capostipiti dei manoscritti della Divina Commedia.* Winterthur: Tip. sorelle Ziegler, 1889.

Vandelli, Giuseppe. "Giovanni Boccaccio editore di Dante." *Atti della R. Accademia della Crusca* 1923, 63–95.

———. *Per il testo della "Divina Commedia."* Edited by Rudy Abardo. Florence: Le Lettere, 1989.

Gabriella Pomaro
(translated by Robin Treasure)

6. Commedia: *Editions*

The first editions of the *Commedia* have little in common with the criteria used for establishing the critical edition, for they more or less faithfully reproduce some exemplar chosen according to principles that were not always justifiable, even though the manuscripts chosen were authoritative if uncritically accepted. For instance, as Michele Barbi established, the three *princeps* editions of 1472 are based on a section of the tradition called "del Cento": Foligno, dated April 11, printed by Johann Numeister of Mainz; Mantova, whose date is uncertain but dated prior to the third edition,

C

Title page of the 1564 Sessa edition of the Cristoforo Landino commentary. Reproduced by permission of the John A. Zahm Dante Collection in the Department of Special Collections, University Libraries, University of Notre Dame.

printed by Georg and Paul Butzbach of Frankfurt; and Venezia (Jesi), dated July 18, printed by Federico de' Conti of Verona. In 1972, Casamassima definitively established the manuscript source of this text in a descendent of the codex Lo (Belluno, Biblioteca del Seminario, 35).

With variations based more on printers' assumptions than on the manuscript tradition, this version of the text is preserved in two later Neapolitan editions (reprints of the Foligno edition) and also in the Venetian edition of 1478. Similarly, its presence is noted in those editions of the poem accompanied by a commentary: the Venetian edition of 1477, accredited to Windelin of Speyer (with a Latin commentary by Jacopo della Lana, mistakenly attributed to Benvenuto da Imola); the Milanese edition of 1478, known as the Nidobeatina (mostly a copy of the Venetian edition); and finally Landino's monumental undertaking, which was printed four more times in the fifteenth century alone.

The "del Cento" text of the fifteenth-century editions, uncontroversial and reflecting the fourteenth-century Florentine "vulgate" text, was completely overshadowed by the appearance of the first "portable Dante": the Aldine edition in octavo edited by Pietro Bembo and published in Venice in 1502, to which Bembo assigned the title *Le terze rime di Dante*. The prestige of both the editor and the printer (Aldo Manuzio), whose influence was so great that their work was pirated in Lyons that same year, guaranteed the universal success of this edition, which was based on a version of the text that "official" culture has since then always preferred. Bembo confined himself in essence to following the manuscript held at the Vatican (Città del Vaticano, Biblioteca Apostolica Vaticana (Vat. Lat. 3199 = VAT), a copy that Boccaccio had given to Petrarch and that Bembo had probably found in the library of his father, Bernardo. Bembo used it to prepare an autograph copy (now Vat. Lat. 3197), which contained some differences resulting from either guesswork on his part or limited recourse to other manuscripts. The relation between the VAT text and the Aldine edition has been noted by Witte, Barbi, and, most recently, Roddewig. According to Barbi, the five editions printed in Lyons, the three Venetian editions of 1554, 1572, and 1575, and others with commentaries by Landino and Vellutello, all adhere to the Bembo text, with the odd result that the Dante text discussed in the commentary does not always correspond to the printed version of the text. It is interesting to note that the great success of the Bembo edition, reprinted in 1515, did not meet with much approval in Florence, not only because of a general hostility toward Bembo in Florentine circles but also for purely philological reasons. The leading authorities of the Florentine Accademia, from Varchi and Giambullari to Gelli, expressed numerous reservations, which resulted in a series of new collations. We know of two of these collation "campaigns": one in 1546 and another in 1548. The results of the second effort can be found in MART (Milan, Biblioteca Nazionale Braidense, Aldina AP XVI 25), which contains handwritten glosses in the margin of the Aldine edition of 1515 detailing variants found in a manuscript of 1330 that is no longer extant. Even Borghini, perhaps the foremost Florentine philologist of the time and librarian of the Biblioteca Rinuccini, scrupulously annotated his printed copies of the poem on the basis of manuscripts that passed through his hands. Thus in 1595, under the sponsorship of the Florentine Accademia della Crusca, the first truly critical edition of the poem appeared, based on an examination of forty manuscripts owned by the Laurentian Library, fifty-one that were privately owned, another owned by Luigi Alamanni (containing the results of his collation of seven others), and another owned by Cosimo Bartoli with other variants in the margins. However, this edition did not fully reflect the enormous effort of collation that had preceded it, and it did not meet with general approval, in part because of its 465 departures from the Aldine text, which nevertheless served as its basis (the manuscript selection process had not been meticulous), and also, it must be said, because interest in Dante was on the wane.

Only three editions were printed in the seventeenth century—two in Venice and a third in Padua—compared to thirty-five registered in the sixteenth century and thirty-two in the eighteenth century. But the eighteenth century opened with renewed interest in Dante. In 1716 the Crusca edition was reprinted (and it would undergo a third revision in 1837), although the numerous typographical errors that defaced the 1595 edition were only partially emended. The 1716 text, purged of its typographical errors, was then reprinted in 1726–1727 by Volpi, whose text was adopted in numerous other editions, including one in 1732 which put Pompeo Venturi's commentary into circulation for the first time. As a result, both without and with an accompanying commentary—especially Lodovico Dolce's (Venice 1555) or Venturi's, which was reprinted until 1850—the Crusca text was essentially the dominant one throughout the entire eighteenth century. Its influence would remain virtually unaffected by the appearance of Lombardi's pretentious work in 1791.

"Father Bonaventura Lombardi was the first to take up the critical study of Dante's *Commedia* in 196 years," Witte correctly asserts, yet the ambitious undertaking produced few positive results. Lombardi's advocacy of a renewed appraisal of the earliest editions, particularly the Nidobeatina, lacked valid theoretical motives. He consulted many manuscripts (most of them Roman), but only for isolated passages of the poem. Despite being a bit of a hodgepodge, this edition did elicit praise and more than a few reprints, primarily because competing editions were scarce.

In 1795 Dionisi engaged Lombardi in a lively public debate with his new edition. Returning to the old concept of the *codex optimus,* Gian Giacomo Dionisi produced a text that was indeed based on a direct examination of several Florentine sources but that was in fact strongly rooted in Filippo Villani's *Commedia,* LauSC (Florence, Biblioteca Medicea Laurenziana Pl. 26 sin. 1). Heavily burdened by negative assessments, particularly Foscolo's, the 1795 text was reprinted twice (at the Bodoni press in Parma), and for the last time in 1810. Much later Dionisi's philological endeavors (little esteemed even by Witte) underwent a reevaluation, thanks particularly to Carducci.

The nineteenth century was "Dantean" par excellence: its editions of the *Commedia* alone account for 410 entries in the Mambelli bibliography (nos. 88–497). The first to appear were editions with older commentaries: Dolce, Volpi, Venturi, Lombardi. Gradually, however, new commentaries were published, such as the very successful ones by Paolo Costa, Brunone Bianchi, and Pietro Fraticelli, in addition to those by Raffaele Andreoli, Niccolò Tommaseo, and Giosafatte Biagioli. Specific reference should also be made to the edition "illustrated by Ugo Foscolo and edited by an 'Italian,'" which appeared in London in 1842–1843 (thus after Foscolo's death) under the editorship of Giuseppe Mazzini. Lacking any great significance on the score of textual reconstruction—the Foscolo edition is based on earlier editions, with the support of several manuscripts, two of which were owned by Foscolo—this edition includes a clearly poetic interpretation that left a discernible mark on nineteenth-century literary circles.

There are also several diplomatic reproductions of important manuscripts, and in 1858 W. W. Vernon sponsored an edition that reproduced side by side the texts of the first four editions (Foligno, Jesi, Mantova, and Napoli). Yet the issue of Dante's text—complicated by the breadth of the manuscript tradition and by textual contamination, and inseparably linked to the progress of the science of philology—was not resolved. The various editors generally modified earlier editions without undertaking a systematic analysis of the manuscripts, performing only a haphazard or limited inspection of manuscripts whenever they were not consulting just a single text. Within this context, Karl Witte's edition of 1862 assumes a special importance. Although not supported by sufficient paleographic groundwork, it can truly be considered the first critical edition of the poem. Renouncing the possibility of a stemma, the Witte version is essentially based on four codices deemed "authoritative" and systematically follows the principle of *lectio difficilior.* Although this was not an innovative approach, it was amply set forth in an eighty-page introduction that summarized the *status quaestionis,* briefly reviewed the earlier editions, and thoroughly exploited the information on the manuscripts recently made available in the De Batines bibliography. As a result, textual debate, philological studies, and theoretical speculation took on new life: from Mussafia (1865) and Monaci (1888) in Italy, to the nearly contemporary Täuber (1889) and his efforts to identify the chief sources of the manuscript tradition, and finally to the indefatigable work of Michele Barbi. Meanwhile, in 1894, Moore published his *Contributions,* a masterly work still valid as a source of information: it examined hundreds upon hundreds of manuscripts, analyzing some in their entirety, others only in *loci selecti* ("selected passages"). Granting the impossibility of a comprehensive examination of the textual tradition, the "Florentine school" followed the *loci selecti* approach, which was institutionally formulated by the Società Dantesca Italiana (1888) in the *Bullettino degli Studi Danteschi.* Already in 1891 a canon of 396 *loci selecti,* established by Michele Barbi, had appeared in the *Bullettino* and was adopted as a practical tool by a number of Florentine critics, although they espoused divergent theoretical positions. This circle included Morpurgo, Fiammazzo, Marchesini, and also Vandelli (the finest connoisseur of the manuscript tradition of the *Commedia* that Dante studies have yet seen) who collated hundreds of manuscripts. The Società Dantesca Italiana entrusted Vandelli with the onerous task of preparing the centenary edition of 1921. Despite its lack of a critical apparatus and the fact that the title of "National Edition" had not yet been conferred upon it, the 1921 edition became the text par excellence and one that is still referred to by many scholars today—particularly now that dissatisfaction with the National Edition, edited by Giorgio Petrocchi, has emerged.

Reference has been made to the "divergent theoretical positions" of the Florentine circle. They are typified in Mario Casella's representation of

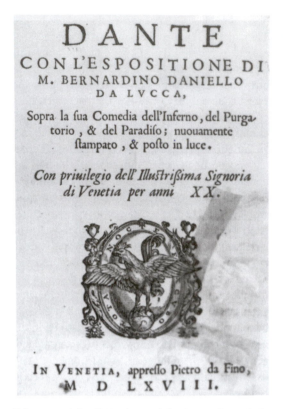

Title page of the 1568 edition of the Commedia *with the Bernardino Daniello commentary. Reproduced by permission of the John A. Zahm Dante Collection in the Department of Special Collections, University Libraries, University of Notre Dame.*

diverse, questionable positions that often were founded on weak paleographic skills but were nonetheless very productive. Although his text was immediately and widely criticized, his commentary was to enjoy a long life: it has been repeatedly reissued, at first with some revisions and later with the replacement of the Casella text with that of the Società Dantesca Italiana.

Breaking with the age-old *querelle* between full collation versus *loci selecti,* Giorgio Petrocchi's intervention brought about significant reform. Based on a series of previous theoretical studies by Petrocchi, the National Edition of the poem, *La Commedia secondo l'antica vulgata* ("The Comedy according to the early Florentine manuscript tradition") was published in 1966, based on an analysis of the oldest tradition comprising some thirty manuscripts and adopting the hypothesis, argued at some length, that the more recent tradition, from Boccaccio on, presents nothing useful for the study of the text. This theoretical proposition has been challenged in many sectors on the basis of the sound philological principle *recentiores non deteriores* ("the more recent manuscripts are not necessarily worse"). However, the proposition finds its defense in the subtitle "according to the earliest Florentine manuscript tradition," which leaves the door open to assessments of the later tradition. A weak point in the National Edition has been its reliance on a selection of codices that is too limited (especially for the non-Florentine tradition) to provide a reliable evaluation of the different families of manuscripts, which from the beginning have problematized the tradition. Nonetheless, we can assert that none of the various editions of the poem with commentary nor any of the translations following the 1966 edition has clearly departed from the Petrocchi edition, with the exception of the recent one by A. M. Chiavacci Leonardi. This edition of the *Commedia,* with commentary, incorporates a number of readings from the 1921 text, a sign of dissatisfaction with the Petrocchi text and a departure from it. This dissatisfaction is most apparent in another recent edition, by Antonio Lanza, who rejects Petrocchi's ranking of the manuscripts and argues for the superiority of the earliest Florentine and Tuscan manuscript, TRIV, dated 1337 (Milan, Biblioteca Trivulziana, 1080).

Bibliography

Bibliographies

Biagi, Guido. *Giunte e correzioni inedite alla Bibliografia Dantesca.* Florence: Sansoni, 1888.

De Batines, Paul Colomb. *Bibliografia dantesca ossia Catalogo delle edizioni, traduzioni, codici.* Prato: Tipografia Aldina, 1846–1848.

Koch, T. Wesley. *Catalogue of the Dante-Collection.* Ithaca, N.Y.: Cornell University Library, 1898–1900; and *Additions* edited by M. Fowler, 1921.

Mambelli, Giuliano. *Gli annali delle edizioni dantesche. Contributo ad una bibliographia definitiva.* Bologna: Zanichelli, 1931. Reprinted in Turin: Bottega d'Erasmo, 1965.

Manfre, Guglielmo. *Le edizioni della Divina Commedia nella storia dell'arte tipografica del secolo XV. I: Le edizioni del testo.* Naples: Libreria Scientifica Editrice, 1973.

Early Editions

Alighieri, Dante. Foligno text, edited by L. Sinisgalli (Foligno: Campi Grafica, 1973); Mantova text, edited by L. Pescasio (Mantova: Editoriale Padus, 1972); Venice (Jesi) text, edited by S. Ragazzini and L. Pescasio (Mantova: Editoriale Padus, 1974).

———. *La Divina Commedia.* Edited by Lodovico Dolce. Venice: Gabriele Giolito de' Ferrari, 1555.

———. *Le terze rime di Dante.* Edited by Pietro Bembo. Venice: Aldo Manuzio, 1502.

Witte, Karl. *La Divina Commedia di Dante Allighieri.* Berlin: R. Decker, 1862.

Later Editions

Alighieri, Dante. *Commedia.* Edited by Anna Maria Chiavacci Leonardi. Milan: Mondadori. *Inferno,* 1991; *Purgatorio,* 1994; *Paradiso,* 1997.

———. *La Commedìa. Nuovo testo critico secondo i più antichi manoscritti fiorentini.* Edited by Antonio Lanza. Nuova edizione. Anzio: De Rubeis, 1996.

———. *La Commedia secondo l'antica vulgata.* Edited by Giorgio Petrocchi. 4 vols. Milan: Mondadori, 1966. Reprinted in Florence: Le Lettere, 1994.

———. *La Divina Commedia.* Edited by Tommaso Casini. Florence: Sansoni, 1985.

———. *La Divina Commedia.* Edited by Emilio Pasquini and Antonio Quaglio. Milan: Garzanti, 1982.

———. *La Divina Commedia.* Edited by Mario Casella. Bologna: Zanichelli, 1923.

———. *Opere* (G. Vandelli text). Florence: Le Monnier, 1927.

Vandelli, Giuseppe. *Per il testo della Divina Commedia.* Edited by Rudy Abardo. Florence: Le Lettere, 1988, pp. 39–46.

Criticism

Barbi, Michele. *Della fortuna di Dante nel secolo XVI.* Pisa: Nistri, 1890, pp. 105–145: Chap. III, *Studi preparatori alla lettura della Commedia.*

Casamassima, Emanuele. *La prima edizione della Divina Commedia. Foligno, 1472.* Milan: Il Polifilo, 1972.

Folena, Gianfranco. "La tradizione delle opere di Dante Alighieri." In *Atti del Congresso Internazionale di Studi Danteschi.* Vol. 1. Florence: Sansoni, 1965, pp. 64–78.

Monaci, Ernesto. "Sulla classificazione dei manoscritti della *Divina Commedia.*" *Rendiconti dell'Accademia dei Lincei.* Series 4, iv (1888), 228–233.

Richardson, Brian. "Editing Dante's *Commedia, 1472–1629.*" In *Dante Now: Current Trends in Dante Studies.* Edited by Theodore J. Cachey Jr., Notre Dame, Ind., and London: University of Notre Dame Press, 1995, pp. 237–262.

Roddewig, Marcella. "Bembo und Boccaccio unter dem Diktat von Vat. 3199. Qualität und Textabhängigkeit der Aldina Ausgabe der *Commedia.*" *Deutsches Dante-Jahrbuch* 47 (1972), 125–162.

Täuber, Carl. *I capostipiti dei manoscritti della Divina Commedia.* Winterthur: Tip. sorelle Ziegler, 1889.

Vallone, Aldo. *La critica dantesca nel Settecento e altri saggi danteschi.* Florence, 1961, pp. 54–58.

Gabriella Pomaro
(translated by Robin Treasure)

7. Commedia: *Early Commentaries*

The Significance of the Earliest Commentaries

At its first appearance, Dante's *Commedia* had an extraordinary effect on literati, brought about by its contents, its structure, and its language: theology, philosophy, and the classical Latin tradition were transferred into a narrative poem written in the vernacular and addressed to a popular audience. Nevertheless, its success was immediate and widespread (only the Bible was read or cited more frequently in fourteenth-century Italy) and overwhelmed skeptical critics. The main goals for the first production of commentaries were to defend Dante against the attacks of the official cultural establishment and to help readers understand the deeper meanings of Dante's book. Moreover, the unique value set on this unprecedented work—a sort of crucible of biblical, classical, and medieval traditions—required the use of a commentary, a procedure previously employed only for the Bible and classical authors (the case of juridical and medical texts being totally different).

Difficulties in Studying Commentaries

Difficulties in studying early commentaries on Dante center on their uncertain chronology, the various versions of the same commentary, and the complex relationships among commentaries. Moreover, since the commentary was considered *res nullius* in the Middle Ages and was not protected by literary copyright, every scribe tended to modify this text in a personal way with additions and/or deletions. This explains the lack of modern critical editions, except in a few instances, as well as the relative uncertainty of some information and conclusions. The following checklist is meant to illustrate the main fourteenth- and fifteenth-century commentaries on Dante's *Commedia* and describe their characteristics.

A Checklist of Commentaries

The author of the first commentary is Iacopo Alighieri, one of Dante's sons. In his work, written in the vernacular in 1322, Iacopo explicates only *Inferno* and, insisting on the allegorical meaning of poetry, tries to defend his father against charges of heresy. The attacks on Dante had come especially from Bologna, a lively cultural center where vernacular poetry was cultivated alongside the traditional Latin culture: polemical writings against Dante were motivated by both cultural reasons (his choice of Italian instead of Latin for such elevated subject) and political reasons (Bologna was a Guelf stronghold). Iacopo's commentary is connected to Bologna (he sent it to Guido Novello da Polenta, the Capitano del Popolo in Bologna), as is Graziolo Bambaglioli's Latin exegesis on *Inferno* (1324). "Cancelliere" of Bologna, Graziolo wrote in Latin to emphasize the high cultural, moral, spiritual, philosophical, and theological value of the *Commedia* to literati, specifying a fundamental allegory of the poem much simpler than Iacopo's: Dante's journey is an allegory of moral and spiritual process of purification achieved by the strengthening of reason in support of Christian virtues.

Another commentary of the same period, written between 1324 and 1328 by Iacopo della Lana, also of Bologna, is completely different in nature. His is the first to cover the whole *Commedia.* Lana, who held the academic title of *licentiatus in artibus et teologia,* considers the poem from a scholastic point of view as a sort of didactic encyclopedia and not only illustrates its most important allegories and its doctrinal contents but also describes the principal situations and characters. Lana's commentary and its wide diffusion show that, in spite of a resistance to Dante's novelty, his poem was read and required a "professional" commentary constructed exactly like those used by the academic culture that reacted against the *Commedia.*

Very peculiar and, indeed, in many ways unique, is the set of Guido da Pisa's glosses in Latin on *Inferno.* His interpretation postulates that Dante's journey is a true *visio per somnium* ("dream vision") and presents Dante as a prophet. Although the identity of the author and the date of his work (between 1327 and 1340) are uncertain, Guido da Pisa is in full possession of the medieval encyclopedic culture: his interpretation was discussed by subsequent commentators and was usually rejected as dangerous.

In 1333 the first Florentine commentary on the *Commedia* made its appearance and came to be known as the *Ottimo* ("the Best"), a designation conferred by the Accademia della Crusca at the beginning of the seventeenth century for the highly esteemed quality of its "Florentine" vernacular. Andrea Lancia, the author, a notary who devoted himself to the development of the literary qualities of the Italian vernacular (he had translated the *Aeneid* into vernacular prose), had met Dante and quoted from a number of his works. Lancia's exegesis uses Lana's glosses as basic subject matter, discusses ideas coming from various commentators, and reduces the allegorism in his interpretation. The *Ottimo commento* was widely circulated, but not as widely as Lana's commentary.

The Latin commentary on the entire *Commedia* by Pietro Alighieri, the oldest of Dante's sons, who lived in the area of Veneto, was written about 1340 (perhaps two later versions exist). In this work, he considers the poem as pure *fictio* and is interested in the Dantean spiritual world. His juridical culture is quite evident, for it is there that he derives most of his classical and patristic quotations.

Beyond this core of commentaries there are some anonymous glosses, whose general mapping needs still to be done. The cases of the *Anonimus lombardus* (Latin glosses to *Inferno* and *Purgatorio,* written before 1326) and of the *Anonimus theologus* (Latin glosses to *Inferno* and to *Paradiso* from canto 1 to 11, written about 1334)—although still not fully resolved—have recently been united under the name of *Anonimous latinus* (1989). On the other hand, we know that the Latin *Chiose Ambrosiane* to the entire poem were composed in the area of Romagna in 1355 and that they were connected with a group of Dante scholars. More work remains to be done on the *Chiose Selmi* (to *Inferno,* before 1337, from Florence or Siena) and the *Chiose Cagliaritane* (to the *Commedia,* after 1345, from the area of Arezzo), both in the vernacular.

There is a sort of exegetical blackout from the 1350s through the 1370s, which could be explained as the result of the influence of the new cultural wave, based on the cult of Latin classical authors and on an aristocratic idea of culture, initiated by Petrarch. This initial silence, however, was followed by the works of Giovanni Boccaccio and Benvenuto da Imola, both of whom were in personal contact with Petrarch. Their exegesis, undoubtedly influenced by the humanistic mentality, introduces new topics of discussion that celebrate the fundamental literary, rhetorical, and poetic character of the *Commedia* and emphasize the great distance that separates them from the Scholastic world of Dante. Moreover, they inform us that the *Commedia* was read and explained to public audiences and featured in school activities. Boccaccio's *Esposizioni sopra la Comedia di Dante* contains the text on which he based his public lectures, given in Florence between 1373 and 1374, and conclude with the beginning of *Inf.* 17; he pays great attention to technical aspects of Dantean poetry, to every nuance of the text, and to an explanation of the "sublimity of the meaning hidden under the poetic veil" with some moralistic interest.

The dating of the vernacular commentary on the *Commedia* called "Falso Boccaccio" should be the same as Boccaccio's *Esposizioni* (1373–1374): its author is a Florentine who shows his interest in history and mythology and who quotes a sonnet of *Il Fiore* as if it were Dantean; there may be also some points of contact with Francesco da Buti's later glosses (but this remains conjecture).

Benvenuto da Imola wrote his elaborate Latin *Comentum* on the *Commedia* about 1380, after lecturing on it at least twice (in Bologna in 1375, then in Ferrara in winter 1375–1376). The characteristic features of this lively work, defined as "late Gothic," are an attention to the formal aspects of Dantean poetry, a sensitivity to historical issues far removed from Dante's theological "pathos," an awareness of the Aristotelian critical criterion used in evaluating the poem's quality, and the pleasure that Benvenuto evinces in reading the text and in comparing different interpretations of it, while introducing a number of interesting autobiographical recollections. The *Comentum* is written in a spoken Latin, typical of oral expositions at school.

Francesco da Buti's exegesis also is connected with the school circle, for this *magister* of rhetoric taught at the Pisan University between 1370 and 1395, and his work on the whole *Commedia* is the result of his teaching. His interpretation, written in the vernacular, concentrates on technical aspects of Dante's poetry and reiterates some previously articulated allegorical views, but he tends to stress his concern with the abstract symbolism of the poem.

The Latin *Expositio* on *Inf.* 1 by Filippo Villani, written at the end of the fourteenth century, is an extended analysis of the figural meaning of Dante's text, a continuous search for allegory: the *Commedia* is read as an allegory of the destiny of mankind, culminating in Christian redemption. Villani's attitude can be understood if we consider that his commentary was written during a polemic between supporters and detractors of the first period of humanism in Florence: he tried to defend poetry in general against the charge of paganism, and Dante's poem was his main case in point.

The so-called Anonimo Fiorentino should perhaps be considered to belong to the same milieu. In his vernacular commentary on the entire poem—mostly derived from Lana's and written between the end of the fourteenth and the beginning of the fifteenth centuries—the author makes recourse to the Florentine vernacular tradition and quotes liberally from the chronicles of Giovanni Villani and Dino Compagni and, as well, from the works of the "three crowns" (namely, Dante, Petrarch, and Boccaccio).

At the beginning of the fifteenth century the *Commedia* is at the peak of its fame and circulation. It is studied at school and read in public. Most of the surviving manuscripts containing the poem are written between 1380 and 1450; and, in spite of a few humanists' reservations about Dante's *latinitas,* the poem is at the center of a number of cultural and political discussions, especially in Florence during the republic (e.g., Coluccio Salutati, Leonardo Bruni). The Trecento commentaries are still used (Lana, Benvenuto, and, less frequently, Francesco da Buti) and are the basis on which some scholars prepare their exegeses. Among them, Giovanni da Serravalle, bishop of Fermo, undertakes a Latin translation of the poem with a partial revision of Benvenuto da Imola's glosses on the occasion of the Council of Konstanz in 1416–1417, in order to confirm the ecclesiastical reforms being discussed there. Guiniforte Barzizza, son of the well-known humanist Gasparino, wrote a vernacular commentary on *Inferno*—copied in great part from those of Francesco da Buti, Boccaccio, and Benvenuto—

for the Milanese ducal court of Filippo Maria Visconti before 1438. The production of glosses, though not as intense as it was during the previous century, merits further attention; however, it is possible to cite the examples of the Franciscan friar Stefano (Latin glosses to the poem, written in Castel Bolognese, 1408); the *Chiose Oratoriane* (Latin glosses to the poem, written at the beginning of the fifteenth century); the Romagnolo humanist Matteo Chiromono (Latin glosses to the poem, written in 1461); and the Paduan poet Niccolò Lelio Cosmico (fragments, in the vernacular, before 1475).

After the invention of printing the majority of printed books are in Latin, but in Italy incunabula already contain 20 percent of the disseminated vernacular literature—a percentage that will increase by the end of the fifteenth century. Between 1470 and 1500 the vernacular authors whose works were most frequently published are Petrarch (forty-eight incunabula) and Boccaccio (thirty-eight); Dante appears in only sixteen incunabula. Printing gives value to commentaries by making them available to a larger audience than that of students and scholars. The first printed commentary written by a Quattrocento commentator (1476–1477) is that of Martino Paolo Nibia, an important and cultivated officer of the Milanese court of the Sforza family. In his vernacular glosses, based mainly on those of Lana's, he inserts notes on contemporary history and reads the *Commedia* according to the milieu of new courtly culture in which he found himself. Nevertheless, these works are not particularly original. The commentary in this period that offers a totally new interpretation of the poem comes from Florence and was written in the vernacular by Cristoforo Landino. In his edition of 1481—accompanied by some of Botticelli's illustrations and an epistle by Marsilio Ficino—Landino presents a Neoplatonic interpretation of Dante's mission as the journey of the soul as a spark of God's universal light that, released by death from the prison of the body, returns to the original source of light. Landino's work brings the fifteenth century to a close and remains throughout the Renaissance the most significant and influential commentary on the *Commedia.*

Bibliography

Editions
(*Note:* Commentaries cited above but not listed below lack a modern or a critical edition.)

Alighieri, Jacopo. *Chiose all' "Inferno."* Edited by Saverio Bellomo. Padua: Antenore, 1990.

Alighieri, Pietro. *Il "Commentarium" di Pietro Alighieri nelle redazioni Ashburnhamiana e Ottoboniana.* Edited by Roberto Della Vedova and Maria Teresa Silvotti. Florence: Olschki, 1978.

———. *Petri Allegherii Super Dantis ipsius genitoris Comoediam commentarium. . . .* Edited by Vincenzo Nannucci. Florence: Piatti, 1845.

Anonimo fiorentino. In *Comento alla divina Commedia d'Anonimo fiorentino del XIV secolo.* Edited by Pietro Fanfani. 3 vols. Bologna: Romagnoli, 1866–1874.

"Anonimus latinus." In *Anonymous Latin Commentary on Dante's Commedia. Reconstructed Text.* Vincenzo Cioffari. Spoleto: Centro italiano di studi sull'Alto Medioevo, 1989.

Bambaglioli, Graziolo. *Commento all' "Inferno."* Edited by Luca Carlo Rossi. Pisa: Scuola Normale Superiore, 1998.

Barzizza, Guiniforte. *Lo Inferno della Commedia di Dante Alighieri col commento di Guiniforto delli Bargigi. . . .* Edited by Giuseppe Zaccheroni. Marseille, Florence: Mossy-Molini, 1838.

Benvenuto da Imola. *Comentum super Dantis Aldigherii Comoediam.* Edited by J. Lacaita. 5 vols. Florence: Barbèra, 1887.

Boccaccio, Giovanni. *Esposizioni sopra la Comedìa di Dante.* Edited by Giorgio Padoan. Milan: Mondadori, 1965.

Chiose Cagliaritane. *Le Chiose Cagliaritane scelte e annotate da Enrico Carrara.* Città di Castello: Lapi, 1902.

Chiose Selmi. *Chiose Anonime alla prima Cantica della Divina Commedia.* Edited by Francesco Selmi. Turin: n.p., 1965; *Le antiche Chiose anonime all'Inferno di Dante secondo il testo Marciano.* Edited by G. Avalle. Città di Castello: Lapi, 1900.

Falso Boccaccio. In *Chiose sopra Dante. Testo inedito ora per la prima volta pubblicato.* Florence: Piatti, 1846.

Francesco da Buti. In *Commento di Francesco da Buti sopra la Divina Comedia di Dante Allighieri.* Edited by Crescentino Giannini. 3 vols. Pisa: Nistri, 1858–1862. Reprinted in Pisa: Nistri-Lischi, 1989.

Giovanni da Serravalle. *Fratris Johannis de Serravalle ord. min. . . . translatio et comentum totius libri Dantis Aldigherii. . . .* Prato: n.p., 1891. Reprinted in San Marino, 1986.

Guido da Pisa. *Expositiones et glose super Comediam Dantis or Commentary on Dante's Inferno.* Edited by Vincenzo Cioffari. Albany: State University of New York Press, 1970.

Iacopo della Lana. *Comedia di Dante degli Allagherii col commento di Jacopo della Lana bolognese.* Edited by Luciano Scarabelli. 3 vols. Bologna: Tipografia regia, 1866–1867.

Lancia, Andrea *(Ottimo). L'Ottimo commento della Divina Commedia. Testo inedito d'un contemporaneo di Dante citato dagli Accademici della Crusca.* Edited by Alessandro Torri. 3 vols. Pisa: Capurro, 1827–1829. Reprinted in Bologna: Forni, 1995.

Le Chiose Ambrosiane alla "Commedia." Edited by Luca Carlo Rossi. Pisa: Scuola Normale Superiore, 1990.

Villani, Filippo. *Expositio seu comentum super "Comedia" Dantis Allegherii.* Edited by Saverio Bellomo. Florence: Le Lettere, 1989.

Criticism

Mazzoni, Francesco. "La critica dantesca del secolo XIV." *Cultura e scuola* 13–14 (1965), 285–297.

Parker, Deborah. *Commentary and Ideology: Dante in the Renaissance.* Durham, N.C.: Duke University Press, 1993.

Rigo, Paola. "Commentatori danteschi." *Dizionario critico della letteratura italiana.* Vol. 2. Turin: UTET, 1896, pp. 6–22.

Rocca, Luigi. *Di alcuni commenti della Divina Commedia composti nei primi vent'anni dopo la morte del poeta.* Florence: Sansoni, 1891.

Sandkühler, Bruno. *Die frühen Dantekommentare und ihre Verhältnis zur mittelalterlichen Kommentartradition.* Munich: Hueber Verlag, 1967.

Vallone, Aldo. *Storia della critica dantesca dal XIV al XX secolo.* 2 vols. Padua: Vallardi, 1981.

Luca Carlo Rossi

8. Commedia: *Renaissance Commentaries*

Medieval commentators, by adding a commentary to the poem—an apparatus previously accorded only Scripture and classical texts—conferred upon the *Commedia* a status previously enjoyed by only an established canon of *auctores.* As readers became further removed from the sensibilities and political and religious circumstances which informed the composition of the poem, their interpretive concerns changed. Renaissance commentators who no longer needed to establish Dante's authority introduced into their discussions of the

Commedia contemporary philosophical, literary, linguistic, and political concerns.

The commentaries assume a wide range of forms: we have commentaries that offer a line-by-line exposition of the entire poem, marginal glosses culled from these larger commentaries, editions of the poem which feature two commentaries, and extended discussions of particular passages. Among the commentaries written between 1400 and 1600 are those of Fra Giovanni da Serravalle (1373–1380), Guiniforte Barzizza (whose exposition is limited to *Inferno,* c. 1438), Nidobeato (1477), Cristoforo Landino (1481), Trifone Gabriele (1526–1527), Alessandro Vellutello (1544), Bernardino Daniello (1568), and Lodovico Castelvetro (who commented on the first twenty-nine cantos of *Inferno,* c. 1570). (Serravalle's, Barzizza's, and Nidobeato's commentaries will not be discussed in this entry, as they are little more than reworkings of medieval commentaries to the poem.)

The majority of the Renaissance commentators were either professional commentators or aristocratic intellectuals. They moved in distinguished social circles and participated in literary debates with other writers: Landino held the chair of rhetoric and poetry at the University of Florence and wrote his commentary under the patronage of the Medici; Trifone Gabriele was among an elite group of Venetian intellectuals in Pietro Bembo's circle; Daniello was a student of Gabriele's; Vellutello wrote his commentary in opposition to Bembo's ideas on language.

Critical exposition of Dante was based in the two leading cultural centers, Florence and Venice. As the place of Dante's birth Florence had a long tradition of Dante studies; Venice, the center of Renaissance printing, assumed the lead in the printing of editions of the *Commedia.* Between 1472 and 1595 fifty-two editions of the poem appeared, the majority of which were printed in Venice. Explications of the poem reflect the cultural concerns of these two cities. In Florence, for example, Landino interpreted Dante's poem in the light of Neoplatonic philosophy, while in Venice commentators evaluated the work according to Bembo's linguistic criteria.

Cristoforo Landino's commentary constitutes the most influential and widely diffused commentary of the Renaissance. Presented to the Florentine *signoria* on August 30, 1481, in a sumptuous folio edition with engravings now attributed to Sandro Botticelli, Landino's commentary is a

Title page of the Commedia. Opere del divino poeta Danthe, *ed. Pietro da Figino, Venice, 1520. Giamatti Collection: Courtesy of the Mount Holyoke College Archives and Special Collections.*

monument to Florentine nationalism, culture, and Neoplatonism. Landino's commentary was printed sixteen times between 1481 and 1596—more often than any other commentary to the poem. A number of factors underlie the commentary's immense success: it was the first printed edition of the poem which featured illustrations; it synthesized the contributions of Dante's fourteenth-century commentators; it presented as an exemplary exponent of Neoplatonic ideals; it introduced a discussion of the dimensions of Hell based on Antonio Manetti's calculations; and it offered the most thorough explication of the poet's language to date. Landino considers the poem, with its unrivaled wealth of learning, equal to that of classical works: Dante is *vero imitatore di Virgilio* ("true imitator of Virgil"), extols Landino, *ma di più alta dottrina* ("but possesses superior doctrine"), and the poet is unsurpassed in his *divinità dello ingegno* ("divinity of genius"). Landino lavishes particular attention

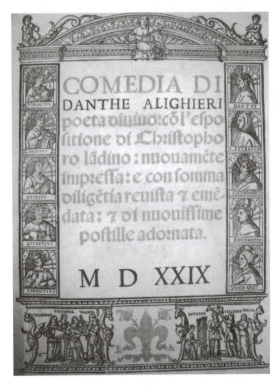

COMEDIA DI DANTHE ALIGHIERI poeta diuino: cõl'espo sittione di Christopho ro lãdino: nuouamẽte impressa: e con somma diligẽtia reuista 7 emẽ data: 7 di nuouissime postille adornata.

M D XXIX

Title page of the 1529 edition of the Commedia *with commentary by Cristoforo Landino.* Comedia di Danthe Alighieri poeta divino, *with commentary by Cristoforo Landino, published by Jacob del Burgofra[n]co, Venice, 1529. Giamatti Collection: Courtesy of the Mount Holyoke College Archives and Special Collections.*

on Dante's use of the Florentine dialect: the poet is the *primo splendore del nome fiorentino e d'eloquenzia* ("the first splendor of the Florentine name and of eloquence").

The Neoplatonic tenor of the commentary is most evident in Landino's grandiloquent *proemio*. In the section entitled *Che cosa sia poesia e poeta e della sua origine divina et antichissima* ("On poetry, the poet, and their divine and ancient origin"), Landino develops Ficino's conception of poetry as an earthly image of *divina armonia* ("divine harmony"); poets can convey this image by relaying *gli intimi sensi della mente loro* ("the innermost perceptions of their minds"). Not all of the poem is filtered through a Neoplatonic lens. Landino also derives much theological and historical information from earlier commentaries, notably, those of Francesco da Buti and Benvenuto da Imola. The practice of incorporating earlier readings is typical of the cumulative and repetitive nature of the commentaries: each exposition conserves traces of readings and interpretive procedures developed over extended periods of time. Notwithstanding his debt to medieval commentators, Landino's work constitutes a significant departure from earlier explications in its presentation of Dante as an exponent of humanist culture.

Whereas Landino tends to emphasize philosophical concerns, Trifone Gabriele and Bernardino Daniello are more concerned with explicating Dante's language. Inasmuch as Daniello had attended Gabriele's lectures on the *Commedia,* the two commentaries are fairly similar. Gabriele's contemporaries commonly referred to him as *il Socrate veneziano,* largely because of his preference for direct, informal teaching. Daniello envisioned himself as a kind of Plato to Gabriele's Socrates—a faithful transcriber and circulator of his teacher's ideas. There is no evidence that Gabriele ever published or even wrote down his ideas. His annotations were dictated to one of his students, Vettor Soranzo, who contributed to the work's composition. Gabriele's *Annotationi* do not provide a full line-by-line commentary; as the title suggests, the exposition consists of annotations to certain passages and words from each canto. Gabriele's comments are often brief and rather schematic; many observations are reminiscent of personal musings. Daniello often expands observations and analyzes in greater detail the scientific, theological, and philosophical aspects of the poem. Both commentaries encompass a wide range of subjects, including scientific, literary, philosophical, and geographical matters. The most distinctive feature of both commentaries, however, is the thorough analysis of Dante's language and style. Bembo's treatment of the vernacular in the *Prose della volgar lingua* influenced both commentators' approaches to the *Commedia.*

Alessandro Vellutello's commentary represents a significant departure from Landino's and Gabriele's commentaries. Printed by Francesco Marcolini in 1544, the commentary features the most beautiful illustrations of the poem after those of Botticelli. In his *proemio* Vellutello calls into question many of Landino's premises and conclusions. For example, Vellutello disputes Landino's calculations on the dimensions of the *Inferno* and his dependence on Boccaccio's biography of Dante; Vellutello considers Leonardo Bruni's life of Dante far more reliable. Vellutello's most severe criticisms are leveled against Aldus Manutius'

C 1502 edition of the poem. These remarks are very likely directed at Pietro Bembo, who edited the poem for this production. Students of the commentary tradition have long noted Vellutello's disagreements with Bembo on literary matters. Vellutello did not share Bembo's emphasis on purity of diction, nor did he accept Petrarch's works or the classics as models for imitation. Vellutello sought to provide a more reliable text of the *Commedia* and offered a more thorough discussion of the poem's historical allusions. Francesco Sansovino published Landino's and Vellutello's commentaries together in 1564; this edition was reprinted in 1572 and 1596.

Lodovico Castelvetro's exposition of the first twenty-nine cantos of *Inferno* constitutes one of the most polemical commentaries to the poem. Castelvetro's critical views are largely informed by his admiration for Aristotle's philosophy and Petrarch's poetry. This orientation makes for a lively, at times pugnacious treatment of the poem. Castelvetro often faults Dante for what he sees as unrealistic, illogical, and incoherent images and situations. The commentary offers a continual comparison of Dante's and Petrarch's poetry—often to the detriment of the former. Notwithstanding Castelvetro's emphasis on rationality, his commentary is widely considered one of the most original expositions of the period.

In addition to the aforementioned commentaries, the sixteenth century also witnessed the publication of a number of expositions on specific passages or cantos. The majority of these explications were based on public lectures given at the Accademia Fiorentina, a literary academy devoted to the elevation of vernacular literature which flourished from 1540 to 1589. Among the more well known Academicians who gave lectures on Dante are Benedetto Varchi, Pier Francesco Giambullari, and Giovan Battista Gelli. Many of these critics sought to mitigate Bembo's harsh valuation of Dante. While each critic emphasizes different issues—Giambullari sought to illustrate the richness of Dante's language, Varchi analyzed the poem's moral and philosophical dimension, and Gelli underscored the poet's scientific and ethical concerns—these men shared a moral and philological approach to the poem.

Commentators in the Renaissance continuously adapted Dante's poem to the concerns of their own period. If one of the most salient features of a masterpiece is its productivity—a text's ability to assume a new life in different literary and social environments—one would be hard-pressed to find a period that offers a more complex interpretive history of the *Commedia* than the Renaissance.

Bibliography

Editions of Commentaries

Barzizza, Guiniforte. *Lo Inferno della Commedia di Dante Alighieri col comento di Guiniforto delli Bargigi.* Edited by G. Zac[c]heroni. Marseille: L. Mossy; and Florence: G. Molini, 1838.

Castelvetro, Lodovico. *Sposizione di Lodovico Castelvetro a XXIX Canti dell'Inferno dantesco.* Modena: Società tipografica, 1886.

Daniello, Bernardino. *Dante con l'espositione di M. Bernard[in]o Daniello da Lucca con la sua Comedia dell'Inferno, del Purgatorio, & del Paradiso.* Venice: Pietro da Fino, 1568. Reprinted by University Press of New England, 1988.

Gabriele, Trifone. *Annotationi nel Dante fatte con M. Trifon Gabriele in Bassano.* Edited by Lino Pertile. Bologna: Commissione per i Testi di Lingua, 1993.

Gelli, Giovan Battista. *Comento edito e inedito sopra la Divina Commedia.* Edited by C. Negroni. Florence: Bocca, 1887.

Giovanni da Serravalle. *Fratris Johannis de Serravalle Ord. Min. Episcopi et Principus Firmani Translatio et Comentum totius libri Dantis Aldigherii.* Edited by Marcellino da Civezza and Teofilo Domenichelli. Prato: Giachetti, 1891.

Landino, Cristoforo. *Comento di Christophoro Landino fiorentino sopra la Comedia di Danthe Alighieri Poeta fiorentino.* Florence: Nicholò di Lorenzo della Magna, 1481.

Nidobeato, Martino Paolo. *La Comedia di Dante Aldighieri, excelso poeta fiorentino.* Milan: Lodovico and Alberto Piedimontani, 1477–1478.

Vellutello, Alessandro. *La Comedia di Dante Alighieri con la nova espositione di Alessandro Vellutello.* Venice: Francesco Marcolini, 1544.

Critical Bibliographies

Barbi, Michele. *Dante nel Cinquecento.* Avezzano: Polla, 1983. Reprint of the 1890 edition published in: Annali di R. *Scuola normale superiore di Pisa,* vol. 7. Pisa, 1890.

Bigi, Emilio. *Forme e significati nella "Divina Commedia."* Bologna: Capelli, 1981.

Cardini, Roberto. *La critica del Landino.* Florence: Sansoni, 1973.

Dionisotti, Carlo. "Dante nel Quattrocento." In *Atti del congresso internazionale di studi Danteschi.* Florence: Sansoni, 1965.

Parker, Deborah. *Commentary and Ideology: Dante in the Renaissance.* Durham, N.C.: Duke University Press, 1993.

———. "Bernardino Daniello and the Commentary Tradition." *Dante Studies* 106 (1988), 111–121.

Pertile, Lino. "Trifone Gabriele's Commentary on Dante and Bembo's *Prose della volgar lingua.*" *Italian Studies* 40 (1985), 17–30.

Procaccioli, Paolo. *Filologia ed esegesi dantesca nel Quattrocento: L'"Inferno" nel "Comento sopra la Comedia" di Cristoforo Landino.* Florence: Olschki, 1989.

Vallone, Aldo. *Storia della critica dantesca dal XIV al XX secolo.* 2 vols. Padua: Vallardi, 1981.

Deborah Parker

Commutative Justice

In defining the notion of justice, St. Thomas Aquinas refers to the definition provided by the *Iustiniani Digesta: iustitia est perpetua et constans voluntas ius suum unicuique tribuens* ("Justice is a permanent and unchangeable will to give each his due," *ST* 2.2.58.1). He argues that the concept of justice "denotes a balance of equity" between two parties (*cum nomen iustitiae aequalitatem importet, ST* 2.2.58.2). Arithmetical equality constitutes the essence of commutative justice, meaning that in an exchange (selling and buying) each party is bound by justice to give the other party its due, that is, to return equal value for value received. Since commutative justice implies a transaction, moralists distinguish between a voluntary, or just, transaction and an involuntary, or unjust, one; the former calls for one exclusive unit of measurement corresponding to both buyer and seller. Involuntary transactions, however, "are done by manifest violence . . . either upon a person . . . or by robbing another of his goods" (*Commentary on the Nichomachean Ethics,* 401). In his works Dante does not explicitly mention this specific kind of justice; he presents, however, examples and cases of involuntary transaction that constitute unjust commutations. According to Dante, those who judge themselves must not use *le misure del falso mercante, che vende con l'una e compera con l'altra* ("the measures of a dishonest merchant who buys using one measure and sells using another," *Conv.* 1.2.9) in order to inflate their sense of self-worth. Moreover, in his interpretation of Aristotle's *Ethics* and Cicero's *Offices* regarding *larghezza* ("generosity," *Conv.* 4.27.13), Dante presents another case of commutative injustice perpetrated by those who defraud *vedove e pupilli* ("widows and wards") in order to deploy their gains for arranging *conviti* ("banquets") and for making gifts of *cavalli e arme, robe e denari* ("horses and arms, goods and money," *Conv.* 4.27.14).

Bibliography

Delhaye, Philippe. "Giustizia." *Enciclopedia dantesca,* 3:233–235.

Häring, B. "Justice." *New Catholic Encyclopedia.* New York: McGraw-Hill, 1967, pp. 70–71.

Mario Trovato

Compagni, Dino

A Florentine merchant and politician who wrote an important chronicle of Dante's Florence, the *Cronica delle cose occorrenti ne' tempi suoi.* A White Guelf like Dante, Compagni was born in about 1246–1247 and well educated. He was a member of the Silk Guild by 1269 and served as a consul of that body six times between 1282 and 1299. At the same time he served the *comune* as a member of various councils, and in 1282 and 1294 he contributed to the reform of the Florentine constitution; he was tried and acquitted after the expulsion of Giano della Bella, whom he had supported to the end. He was one of the priors in 1289, *gonfaloniere di giustizia* in 1293, and in 1301 a member of the last White Guelf priorate. When Corso Donati took over the city with papal protection, Compagni left public life both at city-state level and within his guild. He was fortunate in avoiding the fate which befell Dante—exile—partly at least because of a law exempting recent priors from prosecution. He died in 1324 and is buried in his parish church, Santa Trinita.

The *Cronica,* evidently written between 1310 and 1312, focuses on the period from 1280 to 1312 and is a rich source of illumination on people and events alluded to by Dante. It was presumably intended for semi-clandestine circulation, though the Anonimo Fiorentino commentator on the *Commedia* (c. 1400) certainly read it. In one respect Compagni's outlook diverges radically from

Dante's: whereas Dante sees the seeds of a Florentine decline in the territorial and economic expansion of the thirteenth century, Compagni is with the majority in understanding the city's development throughout that century as a success story. Otherwise, to a large extent the two writers—who had much in common and must have known each other—see events from the same viewpoint (but Compagni, writing before Dante, became famous and mentions him only once, fleetingly: 2.25). The *Cronica* has been called a diary of the White Guelf defeat. Rather than identifying broad historical forces, it somewhat naively sees the course of events as propelled by wicked, overbearing individuals, abetted by the cowardice and weakness of those who had an interest in obstructing them. With Henry VII (apparently, at the time of writing) on the point of extinguishing Florence's independence, it reads like a parable about what happens to a free, happy city when it gives in to unwholesome interests.

Bibliography

Arnaldi, G. "Dino Compagni cronista e militante 'popolano.'" *La cultura* 21 (1983), 37–82.

Bec, Christian. "Sur l'historiographie marchande à Florence au XIVe siècle." In *La Chronique et l'histoire au Moyen-Age.* Edited by Daniel Poirion. Paris: Presses de l'Université de Paris-Sorbonne, 1984, pp. 45–72. Also published as Chap. 5 of Bec's *Florence 1300–1600: histoire et culture.* Nancy: Presses Universitaires de Nancy, 1986, pp. 129–153.

Compagni, Dino. *Cronica delle cose occorrenti ne' tempi suoi.* Edited by G. Bezzola. Milan: Rizzoli, 1982.

Del Lungo, Isidoro. *Dino Compagni e la sua "Cronica."* 3 vols. in 4. Florence: Le Monnier, 1879–1887.

Dino Compagni's Chronicle of Florence. Translated with an introduction and notes by Daniel E. Bornstein. Philadelphia: University of Pennsylvania Press, 1986.

Luzzatto, Gino. "Introduzione" to his edition of D. Compagni, *Cronica* [1906]. Turin: Einaudi, 1978, pp. vii–xli.

Pirodda, Giovanni. "Per una lettura della *Cronica* di Dino Compagni." In *Filologia e letteratura* 13 (1967), 337–393.

Ricci, Pier Giorgio. "Compagni e la prosa storica del '300.'" In *Orientamenti culturali: letteratura italiana: i minori.* 4 vols. Milan: Marzorati, 1969, Vol. 1, pp. 201–216.

Tartaro, Achille. "Delusione e moralismo del Compagni." In *Il manifesto di Guittone e altri studi fra Due e Quattrocento.* Rome: Bulzoni, 1974, pp. 103–109.

John C. Barnes

Confession

Confession, or penance, is a sacrament of the Roman Catholic Church. While the terms are synonymous, confession—the private oral acknowledgment of one's sins to a priest—is itself one of three steps of penance. Confession takes its biblical warrant from the words Christ uttered to the Twelve Apostles in the Gospel ("If you forgive anyone his sins, they are forgiven; if you do not forgive them, they are not forgiven," John 20:23). Private confession of sins was treated as a sacrament as early as the sixth century, but it was only officially instituted as one of the seven sacraments at the Fourth Lateran Council of 1215. In this sacrament, the priest, by virtue of the power given to him by Jesus, "absolves" the sinner. This freedom from sin can take place only if the sinner declares guilt, repents, and begs the forgiveness of God. A Christian can merit salvation at the point of death on the condition that all sins have been confessed, which is why Peter and successor popes are said to hold "the keys" to Heaven.

This sacrament has had various ritual modalities over the long history of the church. In Dante's time it was practiced in a manner that has remained the norm. The three conditions required of the penitent—codified by St. Thomas Aquinas in the *Summa Theologiae* (3.86.6)—are contrition, or the feeling of sorrow for having committed sins; oral confession to a priest; and "satisfaction," or a penitential act of compensation for the offense committed against God, one's self, or one's neighbor. If for any reason satisfaction is not fully realized during life on Earth, it must be completed after death, in Purgatory (cf. *Purg.* 11.70–72; *ST* 3, Suppl. 71.6r). We see the sacrament presented in the *Commedia* in two different modes: in *Purgatorio* the ritual of penance is represented in symbolic form at the moment when Dante-pilgrim enters the door of Purgatory, while in *Inferno* Dante records a historical instance of improper, and therefore invalid, confession.

The entrance into Purgatory proper is achieved by ascending three steps made of three stones of different colors (resplendent white marble, a rough stone of dark purple, and blood-red porphyry). The three steps have traditionally been interpreted as representing the three parts of the sacrament of confession as it was codified in scholastic theology (*ST* 3.90.2): *contritio cordis* ("contrition"), *confessio oris* ("spoken confession"), and *satisfactio operis* ("satisfaction"). An alternative reading that perhaps more closely adheres to the text takes the reflective first step to symbolize the conscious recognition of one's sins (*mi specchiai in esso,* "I was mirrored in it," 9.96) and probably also, therefore, the denunciation or confession of them; the cracks in the form of a cross (*crepata per lo lungo e per traverso,* "cracked both lengthwise and across," 9.99) in the second step to denote the pain caused by the experience of contrition; and the red-blood color of the third step to represent the ardor and passion of restorative acts of charity. By climbing these steps and approaching the angelic guardian of the gate, Dante then proclaims himself to be a sinner, beats his chest three times, and humbly begs forgiveness. These gestures and words were traditionally performed in the sacramental rite of the time, even as they are today. The angel, clearly fulfilling the office of the priest, opens the gate with the two keys. The gold key represents God's power to absolve, and the silver symbolizes the pastoral discernment and judgment needed in a proper confessor (*Purg.* 9.124–126; cf. *ST* 3.17.3).

The scene depicting a false confession occurs in *Inf.* 27, where Guido da Montefeltro recounts the drama of his eternal perdition. Having repented of his past life of violence and retired to a monastery, he is called upon by Pope Bonifazio VIII to provide advice on how to defeat his political adversaries, the Colonna faction with whom the pope was at war. When Guido hesitates, the pope promises to absolve him in advance for his wrongdoing. Guido, caught between his fear of committing the sin of "fraudulent counsel" and his fear of displeasing the pope, decides to put his trust in the absolution that has been granted to him. But at the moment of death, a devil comes to take his soul and declares that *ch'assolver non si può chi non si pente* ("for he cannot be absolved who does not repent," *Inf.* 27.118), thus denying him the salvation he thought he had won. The inverse of this

scene is dramatized in *Purg.* 5, where Guido's son, Buonconte, experiences precisely the opposite fate. Mortally wounded on the battlefield, Buonconte repents his sins at the very moment of death, uttering the name of the Virgin Mary in his last breath. As his soul is carried heavenward by an angel, a dejected devil laments having lost a victim *per una lagrimetta* ("because of a little teardrop," *Purg.* 5.107). These two episodes illustrate the central Christian doctrine that it is the true condition of the heart that determines the soul's fate. The sinner who is absolved by the pope without having repented is, in fact, condemned, while the sinner who directs a single breath of repentance to God is saved, even though he has not participated in the sacrament of confession. The episode of the excommunicate Manfredi, who is saved for his sincere act of repentance at the point of death (*Purg.* 3.118–135), makes the same theological point: salvation is determined by God alone on the basis of his knowledge of the sinner's true moral state, not by a priest, the pope, or the Church—which serve only as an intermediary whose office is to facilitate the soul's reconciliation with God.

Bibliography

Fallani, Giovanni. "Penitenza." *Enciclopedia dantesca,* 4:375–376.

Meerssemann, Gilles. "Penitenza e penitenti nella vita e nelle opere di Dante." In *Atti del Convegno di studi Dante e la cultura veneta.* Florence: Olschki, 1966, pp. 229–246.

Vazzana, Steno. "Il canto IX del *Purgatorio.*" In *Purgatorio: letture degli anni 1976–79.* Casa di Dante in Roma. Rome: Bonacci, 1981, pp. 175–198.

Anna Maria Chiavacci Leonardi
(translated by Tamao Nakahara)

Conrad I

Founder of the "Spino Secco" branch of the Malaspina family, Conrad I *(Currado),* referred to as *l'antico* ("the Elder") by his grandson Conrad II (*Purg.* 8.119). He was a staunch supporter of Emperor Frederick II, having married one of his daughters. After Conrad's death (c. 1254), the family aligned itself with the Guelfs. His grandson Franceschino hosted Dante in Lunigiana in 1306.

Pamela J. Benson

C

Conrad II

Grandson of the older, more famous Conrad Malaspina (*l'antico* ["the Elder"] of *Purg.* 8.119), and known as "the Younger"; belonged to a great Ghibelline family. Conrad (*Currado*) appears as one of the negligent rulers in the Ante-Purgatory (*Purg.* 8.65), where he purifies the love he bore his family (8.120), since that love caused him to defer his repentance until the last moment. Dante tells him that he knows his family for its "honor of purse and sword" (*Purg.* 8.129). Conrad predicts that before seven years will have passed, Dante will take refuge with the Malaspina family during an early period in his exile. Dante's praise here is a grateful thanksgiving to Conrad's cousin Franceschino, whose hospitality in Lunigiana he had enjoyed in 1306. Conrad II died about 1294.

R. A. Malagi

Conrad III

Son of Frederick, duke of Swabia, Conrad III (*Currado*) lived from 1093 until 1152 and was emperor from 1138 to 1152. In 1147, at the instigation of St. Bernard, he undertook the ill-fated Second Crusade, along with Louis VII of France. He is mentioned in the Heaven of Mars by Cacciaguida, the crusader and great-great-grandfather of Dante who had followed the emperor and had been knighted by him (*Par.* 15.139).

R. A. Malagi

Conradin

Grandson of Frederick II, Conradin (*Curradino*), who lived from 1252 until 1268, inherited the crown of Sicily and Naples at the age of three from his father, Conrad IV, in 1254 but claimed it only in 1266 after the death of his uncle Manfred, who had usurped his right to the throne. Defeated by Charles of Anjou at Tagliacozzo while attempting to free Sicily from the grip of French rule, Conradin was captured and executed after a trial that was considered illegal by many. He was 16 years old. Dante mentions Conradin in *Purg.* 20.68 to underscore the perversity of the Capetian kings.

Rinaldina Russell

Constance

Daughter of Roger II, king of Sicily; wife of Emperor Henry VI; mother of Frederick II (*Inf.* 10); and grandmother of Manfred (*Purg.* 3.112–113). Empress Constance (*Costanza*), who lived from 1152 until 1198, appears in the Heaven of the Moon as one who failed to observe her religious vows (*Par.* 3.109–120). She had become a nun but was later removed from the convent by the archbishop of Palermo and was forced to marry in order to produce a royal heir.

Virginia Jewiss

Constantine

Constantine the Great (*Costantino*) was celebrated during his own lifetime (288–337) by Lactantius and Eusebius of Cesarea for his central role in history as the first Christian emperor of Rome. Together with Licentius, emperor in the East, Constantine promulgated the Edict of Milan (313), granting official recognition to the Christian Church and general religious toleration (Christianity became the official state religion only in 381). In 323, he defeated Licinius and became the sole master of the empire. He transferred its capitol from Rome to Byzantium, thereafter "Constantinople" (founded in 330)—which Dante regrets as a retrograde step, against the providential westward course of empire, the *translatio imperii*, carried forward heroically by Aeneas: *Poscia che Costantin l'aquila volse / contr' al corso del ciel, ch'ella seguìo / dietro all'antico che Lavina tolse* ("After Constantine turned the eagle back against the course of the heavens, which it had followed after the man of old who wedded Lavina," *Par.* 6.1–3).

Constantine, in fact, is an ambivalent and problematic figure for Dante. Hallowed in an aura of sanctity by legend, he is presented by Dante, too, as an exemplar of the Christian monarch. He is placed among the just rulers round the eye of the imperial eagle that dominates the Heaven of Jupiter, and he is exalted to the crest of the eagle's brow (*Par.* 20.55–60). Yet, despite this traditional reverence, Constantine is implicated in what for Dante was the disastrous conflation of temporal with spiritual power in the church. Though proved to be a forgery by Lorenzo Valla in the fifteenth century, the so-called Donation of Constantine—in which the emperor, in 314, would have ceded to the popes civil jurisdiction over Rome, the cities of Italy, and the entire Occident—was accepted by Dante and the whole of the Middle Ages as authentic. Dante, in the voice of the golden eagle, emblem of the empire, excuses Constantine for having meant well, but he laments the bitter fruit of this well-intentioned folly, which is bound up with the transfer of the imperial seat east to Greek Byzantium: *L'altro che segue, con le leggi e meco, / sotto buona intenzion che fé mal frutto, / per cedere al pastor si fece greco* ("The next who follows, with good intention that bore evil fruit, made himself Greek, along with the laws and me, in order to give precedence to the shepherd," *Par.* 20.55–57). This abdication Dante relentlessly deplores throughout the *Commedia* (see especially *Purg.* 16.106–129), and in the *Monarchia* he argues that it was illegitimate and juridically impossible (see, for example, 2.12.8 and 3.10.14).

Eusebius transmits the legend of Constantine's conversion to Christianity as occasioned by the vision of an illuminated cross over the Eternal City with the inscription "In hoc signes vinces" ("In this sign you will conquer") on the eve of his battle against Maxentius, son of Maximianus (joint emperor with Diocletian) at Pons Milvius near Rome in 312. Dante, however—preoccupied by the relations between empire and papacy—concentrates on another tradition: Constantine's having been cured of leprosy and baptized by Pope Silvester I (*Inf.* 27.94–95; *Mon.* 3.10.1). It is in gratitude for this healing that Constantine donates to the papacy authority over the western provinces of the Roman Empire. This event leads to compromising the unrestricted sovereignty of the emperor in the temporal sphere, causing in Dante's view the second great catastrophe of the human race after the Fall of Adam (*Purg.* 32.124–129, 33.55–57)—though once again allowance is made for Constantine's good intentions (*forse con intenzion sana e benigna* ("perhaps with healthy and benign intention," *Purg.* 32.138).

William Franke

Contemplative Life

In the most extreme and complete sense, contemplative life is a way of living in which the desire to love and know God through contemplation and prayer excludes most active concerns and temporal occupations. It can therefore usually be followed only by those with a vocation to a religious life, often as a member of a religious order. Contemplative life is thus a Christian way of living composed mostly of prayerful contemplation, whereas active life—the opposite aspect of Christian life—seeks to supplement prayer with virtuous acts combined with manual or intellectual labor. Religious life can be active or contemplative or a mixture of the two. Those who desire to live a contemplative life usually withdraw from society to an environment characterized by solitude and silence, and they abandon worldly pursuits.

The chief motivating factor for those who choose the contemplative life is love of God and spiritual concerns, together with admiration for his works. Contemplation is thus also a joyful act of worship as a means of expressing that love. The object of contemplation can be anything to do with God or his Creation.

Contemplative life is closely linked to mysticism and to contemplative religious orders—although not all contemplatives are mystics and not all contemplation is mystical. The aim of mystical contemplation is to attain an experiential knowledge of God through mystical union with the divine, which is achieved through passive prayer and intuition, rather than by speculative thought or reasoning.

Christian writers who wrote about contemplation before Dante's time include Gregory of Nyssa, Pseudo-Dionysius, Augustine, Cassian, St. Benedict, Gregory the Great, St. Bernard, Hugh of St. Victor, Richard of St. Victor, and Albertus Magnus. The great thirteenth-century theologians, St. Thomas Aquinas and St. Bonaventure, also wrote on this subject. St. Bonaventure's ideas were especially influential in the medieval period and up until the sixteenth century, when those of Thomas Aquinas became more popular and pervasive.

The Bible provided authoritative models for both the active life and the contemplative life. Allegorical interpretation of the story of the Old Testament patriarch, Jacob, identified his first wife, Leah, who bore him six sons, with the active life; her sister, Rachel—Jacob's second and most loved wife, who gave birth to only two sons—was seen to symbolize the contemplative life (Gen. 29–35). References to this interpretation of the roles of Leah and Rachel occur frequently in religious writing (see, for example, Aquinas, *ST* 2.2.179.2). New Testament models include St. Paul, whose works show that he pursued the active life but whose experience of being taken up into Heaven while still alive indicates that he also excelled in prayerful contemplation (2 Cor. 12:3–4). Christ himself, whose life embodied perfection in both the contemplative life (through perfect prayer and communion with the Father) and the active life (his teaching and miracles), served as the ultimate model. Another story which was commonly used to illustrate these concepts was that of Martha, who looked after Christ when he visited her home, and her sister Mary, who sat at his feet and listened to his words (Luke 10:38–42).

Dante comments on the active life and the contemplative life, stating that while both are good ways to live, the contemplative life is superior (*Conv.* 2.4.10, 4.17.9, 4.22.10–11). He also refers to the story of Martha and Mary, and to Christ's confirmation that Mary had made the better choice (*Conv.* 4.17.10). In the pilgrim's third and final dream in *Purgatorio* (27.94–108), before he reaches the Earthly Paradise, he sees Leah weaving a garland of flowers. She explains to him that while she prefers the act of adorning herself with flowers, Rachel chooses to contemplate her own reflection. This recalls Dante's comment in the *Convivio* that *l'anima filosofante non solamente contempla essa veritate, ma ancora contempla lo suo contemplare medesimo e la bellezza di quello, rivolgendosi sovra sé stessa e di sé stessa innamorando per la bellezza del suo primo guardare* ("the philosophic soul not only contemplates the truth but, moreover, contemplates its own contemplation and the beauty of that act as well, by turning back its glance upon itself and becoming enamored of itself by reason of the beauty of its first contemplation," *Conv.* 4.2.18).

The pilgrim's dream of Leah and Rachel is generally interpreted as prefiguring, respectively, the appearance of Matelda (also seen gathering flowers, who represents the joy attainable through virtuous acts of Christian living) and of Beatrice in her guise as revealed knowledge of God, which is the goal of contemplation. Rachel's mirror reminds us not only that God's created universe acts as a mirror in which we can see evidence of the Creator but also that the mind of God functions as a mirror (*Par.* 15.61–63), to which the souls in Paradise as well as those on Earth who choose the path of mystical contemplation all have recourse.

We see Rachel again in Paradise, in the celestial rose, where—as the type for the contemplative life—she is placed next to Beatrice and opposite the great contemplative St. Benedict (*Par.* 32.7–9). The pilgrim had previously met St. Benedict and Peter Damian (a Benedictine abbot) in the sphere of Saturn, the Heaven of the contemplatives (*Par.* 21.1–22.102), where the souls are seen ascending and descending a ladder—an important symbol, already seen by Jacob, representing the steps leading to mystical union with God (*Par.* 21.28–42, 22.68–74). Beatrice and the pilgrim follow the souls up the ladder to the next sphere, suggesting that the true nature of the pilgrim's journey to God is one of mystical contemplation (*Par.* 22.100–102).

Bibliography

Cervigni, Dino S. *Dante's Poetry of Dreams.* Florence: Olschki, 1986, pp. 156–165.

Consoli, Domenico. *Il Canto XXVII.* In *Purgatorio: Letture degli anni 1976–79.* Casa di Dante in Roma. Rome: Bonacci, 1981, pp. 627–655; especially pp. 643–646.

Frattini, Alberto. *Canto XXVII.* In *Lectura Dantis Scaligera: Purgatorio.* Florence: Le Monnier, 1967, pp. 995–1031; especially pp. 1018–1023.

Gardner, Edmund G. *Dante and the Mystics.* London: Dent and Sons, 1913, pp. 314–320.

Mazzeo, Joseph A. *Structure and Thought in the Paradiso.* New York: Greenwood Press, 1968, pp. 84–110.

Mazzotta, Giuseppe. *Dante's Vision and the Circle of Knowledge.* Princeton, N.J.: Princeton University Press, 1993, pp. 154–173.

Niccoli, Alessandro. "Vita." *Enciclopedia dantesca,* 5:1081–1085; especially 1083.

Angela G. Meekins

Contini, Gianfranco

Dominant Italian romance philologist and literary critic, born in Domodossola in 1912. Contini held the chair of romance philology at the University of Fribourg (Switzerland) from 1938 to 1953, carrying on a tradition established by the legendary Joseph Bédier, the university's founding philologist (1889). He later taught philology at the Scuola Normale in Pisa and at the University of Florence, where he remained until his death in 1990. From 1957 through 1981 he was president of the Società Dantesca Italiana and, until 1968, director of *Studi danteschi,* its official publication. He also presided as director of the Centro di filologia italiana at the Accademia della Crusca. During the 1960s he revitalized interest in completing the *Edizione nazionale* of Dante's works—a project which was begun in the 1920s under the sponsorship of the Società Dantesca Italiana and which remains to be completed.

Contini's central interest and contribution to Dante studies lay in his commitment to a systematic, scientific study of the formal properties of Dante's literary process and, in particular, of the stylistic and linguistic properties of the text—a conviction informed by his adherence to Saussurean semiotic principles. The analysis of the technical aspects of linguistic expression might have been, for some critics, an end in itself, but for Contini it was the first stage of literary criticism, the foundation upon which all interpretation of the text rested. Although he believed in the absolute cohesiveness of form and content, he always insisted that the proper understanding of a text required that it be situated within its historical context. While independently sharing with the American New Critics a rejection of the relevancy of biographical, psychological, and ideological considerations, Contini always insisted on the importance of the text's historical dimension: its roots in the language of its affiliated and predecessor texts and its relation to prior linguistic expression.

Contini's method is best illustrated by his collection of essays *Un'idea di Dante: Saggi danteschi* (1976), which contains two fundamental studies: "Un'interpretazione di Dante" and "Dante come personaggio-poeta." The former in particular demonstrates Contini's interest in intertextual analysis, in the detection of uses of the same word in different vernaculars, in the "plurilinguistic, composite character" (18) of the poet's use of language, and in the suggestiveness of "semantic interplay" among texts (26). Since such interplay was a salient characteristic of Dante's own works, Contini insisted on the importance of "explicating Dante with Dante"—of analyzing internal verbal echoes *(echi di Dante in Dante)* within his texts and from one text to another for their power to create a context of meaning.

Contini's dominance as a philologist was established with his magisterial edition of Dante's *Rime* (1939; second edition, 1946) and an edition of Bonvesin da la Riva's works in the vernacular, *Le opere volgari* (1941). In 1960 he published a two-volume edition of lyric poems of the thirteenth century, *I Poeti del Duecento;* and his edition of *"Il Fiore" e "Il Detto d'amore" attribuibili a Dante* appeared in 1984.

Bibliography

Breschi, Giancarlo (ed.). *Bibliografia degli scritti di Gianfranco Contini.* Florence: Società Dantesca Italiana, 1973.

Contini, Gianfranco. *Un'idea di Dante: Saggi danteschi.* Turin. Einaudi, 1976. Revised edition of *Varianti ed altra linguistica: una raccolta di saggi (1938–1968).* Turin: Einaudi, 1970.

———. "Philology and Dante Exegesis." *Dante Studies* 87 (1969), 1–32.

Diligenza e voluttà. Ludovica Ripa di Meana interroga Gianfranco Contini. Milan: Mondadori, 1989.

Filologia e critica 15.2–3 (1991), 165–661; issue dedicated to G. Contini.

Richard Lansing

Contrapasso

Two of the general conditions that apply to all souls outside Dante's Paradise are the deprivation of the sight of God *(poena damni)* and the suffering, either permanent (Hell) or transient (Purgatory), which each soul (excepting those in Limbo) must undergo as punishment or therapy for a particular sin *(poena sensus)*. These conditions are theologically normative and are best articulated by St. Thomas Aquinas (*ST* 1.2.87.4, 2.2.79.4). The principle of justice that determines the precise form which this second type of suffering takes in Hell and Purgatory is called *contrapasso,* a term Dante borrows from Aquinas to express the logic that fits a specific mode of punishment for each sin.

The concept is illustrated in exemplary fashion in *Inf.* 28 by the sinners of the ninth bolgia of Malebolge. Those who while alive sowed scandal and division in communities and among previously united individuals are punished for eternity by a devil who slashes them with his sword each time they pass by him. Thus Muhammad is shown split from chin to anus; Ali is sliced from chin to hairline; various parts of Pier da Medicina are pierced or severed; Curio has his tongue cut off; Mosca has both his hands amputated; finally, the decapitated Bertran de Born walks holding up his head by the hair like a lantern. The same Bertran explains that, just as he "parted" those who were joined (in that he caused division between the king of England, Henry II, and his son, Henry III), he now carries his own head "parted" from his trunk:

C *Così s'osserva in me lo contrapasso* ("Thus you observe in me the counter-suffering," *Inf.* 28.142).

With the term *contrapasso* (from the Latin *contra* ["in return"] *pati* ["to suffer"]), which he uses only in this episode—though the concept is clearly alluded to also on other occasions (see *Inf.* 13.105, 20.38–39; *Purg.* 11.52–54)—Dante sums up the retributive principle which establishes that every soul must suffer in the afterlife according to the sin he or she has committed on Earth. This suffering is retributive and eternal in Hell, whereas in Purgatory it is remedial, lasting only as long as it takes for the soul to rectify its sinful disposition. In Paradise, too, the situation of the blessed appears to be closely related to their behavior on Earth. Thanks to God's "condescension" to the pilgrim's human faculties (*Par.* 4.43–44), the souls of the blessed, by appearing in different spheres, are shown to receive the quality and measure of reward appropriate to each of them. Thus God's infallible justice is done, and is seen to be done, in all three realms of the afterlife. At the same time, for the poet, this justice acts as a magnificent structuring device whereby, at the narrative level, the three *cantiche* naturally acquire both order and variety.

As a principle of justice, the *contrapasso* derives from the biblical law of retaliation *(lex talionis),* which required that every sinner should be punished in the same manner in which he or she had sinned (see Ex. 21:23ff.; Lev. 24:17–20; Deut. 19:21; but see also Matt. 5:38, 7:1–2, 12). However, a similar concept is present also in classical authors such as Virgil (*Aen.* 6.654) and especially Seneca (*Hercules furens* 735–736): *Quod quisque fecit patitur; auctorem scelus / repetit suoque premitur exemplo nocens* ("What each has done, he suffers; upon its author the crime comes back, and the guilty soul is crushed by that of which he has himself given the example"). The word *contrapassus,* with the same meaning as Dante's, existed already in Latin as a translation for the Aristotelian *antipeponthòs,* and as such it had already been used by Scholastic theologians (e.g., *ST* 2.2.61.4). Dante probably transposed it into Italian from Thomas Aquinas, who writes: *Judicium enim divinum est simpliciter justum. Sed haec est forma divini judicii, ut secundum quod aliquis fecit, patiatur, secundum illud Matt. [7:2],* "In quo judicio judicaveritis judicabimini et in qua mensura mensi fueritis remetietur vobis." *Ergo justum est simpliciter idem quod contrapassum* ("For the divine judgment is purely and simply just, and this is the form it follows, that as a person does so shall he suffer; according to Matthew, *'With the judgment you pronounce you will be judged, and the measure you give will be the measure you get.'* Therefore the just simply is the same as the reciprocal," *ST* 2.2.61.4). But the idea of a divine punishment befitting the crime can also be found, albeit in a rudimentary form, in other, less learned Christian as well as non-Christian narratives of the Middle Ages describing visions of the other world—for instance, in the Irish *Vision of Tundale* (vv. 290ff.) and in the Islamic *Book of the Ladder of Muhammad* (§§ 199–201).

In this popular tradition the *contrapasso* responds, as it does in Dante, to the universal desire to see justice done and the wicked suitably punished. What distinguishes its appearance in the *Commedia* is that, in the poem, it does not function merely as a form of divine revenge but, rather, as the fulfillment of a destiny that is freely chosen by each soul during his or her life. In this light, Minos' role in Hell can be viewed as being "administrative" rather than judgmental: he does not sentence the sinners but places them exactly where he knows they belong on the basis of their freely committed sins (*Inf.* 5.9–10). The state of the souls after death does not seem to be devised and enforced by an external agent; rather, it seems to be "a continuation, intensification and definitive fixation of their situation on earth" (Auerbach 88). The souls inherit their particular characteristics from their former lives, but they manifest them "with a completeness, a concentration, an actuality, which they seldom achieved during their term on earth" (134).

Thus, in Dante's afterlife, far from being canceled or diminished or even altered, the historical identity of each soul is revealed in its very essence and intensified. Each individual is fixed in the otherworld as he or she really was, beneath all appearances, in this. Such realism has a definite didactic purpose. The more convincing the representation, the more effective it will be as an exemplum for the moral education of the reader. This is why, we are told, Dante the pilgrim is shown only the souls of well-known people, for the readers of the poem will not profit unless its examples are manifestly clear and rooted in the reality of life (see *Par.* 17.136–142). In Dante's use of *contrapasso,* imagination, poetic skill, and didactic purpose combine to serve the poem's fundamental aim: the reformation of a society on the brink of eternal ruin (see *Purg.* 32.103).

The *contrapasso* is traditionally said to function either by analogy or by contrast or by a combination of the two. In fact, if the basic doctrinal principle is the same throughout Dante's afterlife, the ways in which it works in the narrative are as many as the sins, if not actually the sinners, to which it is applied. It is true that there are categories of sinners who are not seen as individuals. But this, in turn, is a reflection of their particular sin and therefore part and parcel of the *contrapasso* itself. For example, if the neutrals of *Inf.* 3 are not singled out individually, that is because, by avoiding commitment in this life to any cause, either good or evil, they themselves chose not to be individuals; in Hell, therefore, their neutrality reveals itself for what it was, namely, the obsessive pursuit of a non-choice. Far from being in opposition to their former existence, their present endless running after a nondescript banner captures and fixes forever the essence of that existence.

There are a number of interesting cases in which the *contrapasso* seems to function as the tragic fulfilment and realization of metaphorical discourse, that is to say, as the conversion to eternal "reality" of ordinary metaphors which in this life are employed to describe the inner, spiritual condition of certain sinners. For example, the metaphorical storm of passion that possessed the lustful while alive is turned in Hell into a "real" storm that will torment them forever (*Inf.* 5.31–45); the wasting and scattering of their substance, which marked the behavior of the spendthrifts on Earth, is now inflicted literally upon them by the hounds which hunt and tear them apart, scattering the pieces of their bodies through the forest (*Inf.* 13.109–129); the unnatural distortion whereby the diviners, while looking into the past, fraudulently claimed to be seeing the future, has now become the eternal condition of their bodies (*Inf.* 20.10–15); and the cloak that figuratively masked the hypocrites in this life is now converted, following a well-known gloss of the word "hypocrite" as meaning *supra-auratus* ("gilded over"), into a cape of lead covered by a thin layer of gold (*Inf.* 23.58–66). In other cases the literal condition of the sinners after death appears to be a continuation of a real choice made by them while alive. For instance, the momentary act with which the suicides violently renounced their bodies is extended to last forever, even beyond the day of

Resurrection (*Inf.* 13.106–108). However, the relationship between crime and punishment does not always stand out in such a clear and direct manner. For example, panders and seducers are incessantly whipped by demons (18.34–39); flatterers are plunged in human excrement (18.112–114); and fraudulent counselors are enveloped in tongues of fire (26.40–42, 27.7–15). We assume that some compelling reasons must dictate these particular forms of punishment, though what they might be remains a matter for speculation.

Although the principle is the same, the scope of the *contrapasso* in Purgatory is considerably restricted, for here the actual sin no longer exists; what is left, and needs purging, is the general inclination that brought the soul to sin. In addition, however, the souls undergoing purgation feel with great intensity the pain of being separated from God. It is this sense of separation and exile which, like a reversed nostalgia, makes them behave as pilgrims longing to reach their heavenly home. Indeed, this is the only pain the souls feel in the Ante-Purgatory, where they pay for their tardiness in repenting by being kept back from their longed-for purgation—a perfect *contrapasso* for those who had paid scant attention to the needs of salvation while on Earth. As a result, the *poena damni,* hardly evident in *Inferno* outside Limbo (see, for example, Francesca, *Inf.* 5.91), is so foregrounded in *Purgatorio* as to become one of its major themes. There is one further difference with Hell, in that the penitents, though still suffering for their sins, reveal their saved natures by speaking words of justice.

As for the *poena sensus,* whereas the damned are fixed forever in that part of Hell where the sin which most characterized them in life is punished, the penitents progress up the mountain of Purgatory and undergo penance on each terrace for which they have a need to cleanse themselves of a specific sinful disposition, for an amount of time corresponding to the degree of their guilt. Thereby, they continue and fulfill in Purgatory the process of repentance that they began on Earth. Contrary to the great variety of Hell, in Purgatory there are only seven categories of sinners and seven forms of purgation (even though internal distinctions are implied between the avaricious and the prodigal and are made explicitly between heterosexual and homosexual lovers). The *contrapasso* is thus generally clear and precise. Once they reach Purgatory proper, the proud walk in a bent position under the

C crushing weight of huge stones; the envious have their eyelids sewn up with wire; the wrathful walk blinded by thick smoke; the slothful make haste frantically; the avaricious and prodigal lie face down on the ground, motionless and outstretched; the gluttonous are subjected to extreme hunger and thirst but are allowed neither food nor drink; finally, the lustful walk inside a wall of fire. In most of these cases, too, as in Hell, a metaphor can be seen to have become, by analogy or antithesis, painfully "real"; and that is how the individual experience of purgation acquires its universal value as exemplum.

Strictly speaking, there is no *contrapasso* in Paradise. Nevertheless, the principle can be invoked insofar as the blessed, too, appear to be placed in various degrees of proximity to the Godhead according to an order that corresponds to their individual capacities and inclinations: venereal souls in Venus, martial in Mars, saturnine in Saturn, and so on. However, this distribution does not correspond to the "reality" of Paradise; it is an appearance—we are told (*Par.* 4.28–48)—which is rendered necessary by the limits and constraints of the poet's mind and language. The souls whom Dante meets in the different heavens are visible and temporal manifestations of spiritual realities that are eternal, intangible and ineffable, and that reside in the Empyrean; in other words, they are metaphorical enactments of their true selves. Only by presenting themselves in this way can the correspondence between their former reality on Earth and their present blissful state be fully appreciated—and so become an example which can benefit Dante the pilgrim-poet and his future readers. Thus, thanks to the *contrapasso*, in Hell and Purgatory earthly metaphors become real; in Paradise reality becomes metaphorical. In either case the overriding rule—as Cacciaguida explains (*Par.* 17.136–142)—is that what the pilgrim "finds" must be clearly exemplary. This of course requires that it be both significant and amenable to poetic representation. Ultimately, therefore, through the *contrapasso*, language makes a virtue of its own shortcomings by ensuring that even the state of the souls after death remains within the scope of human discourse.

Bibliography

Auerbach, Eric. *Dante, Poet of the Secular World.* Translated by Ralph Manheim. Chicago: University of Chicago Press, 1961.

D'Ovidio, Francesco. *L'ultimo volume dantesco.* Rome: A.P.E., 1926; see pp. 121–140.

Gross, Kenneth. "Infernal Metamorphoses: An Interpretation of Dante's 'Counterpass.'" *MLN* 100 (1985), 42–69.

Pasquazi, Silvio. *"Contrapasso."* Enciclopedia dantesca, 1:181–183.

Vazzana, Steno. *Il contrapasso nella Divina Commedia.* Rome: Editrice Ciranna, 1959.

Lino Pertile

Conversion

Conversion signifies a radical change of life, always from a state of sinfulness to one of goodness—the spiritual change implied in the New Testament word *metanoia.* In the *Commedia,* the word *conversione* is used three times. Two of these refer to a conversion from a non-Christian religion to Christianity: in the case of Constantine in *Inf.* 19.115–117; and in *Par.* 11.103–104, the unsuccessful attempt of St. Francis to convert the Muslims. In *Purg.* 19.106, the word is used in the sense of a moral or spiritual redirection of life, as the formerly avaricious Pope Adrian V came to realize the deceitfulness of worldly goods. It is mainly in this second sense—taken broadly to mean a radical change of outlook from some form of worldliness or pride to a life governed by the Christian faith—that conversion may be seen as a major theme in Dante's works.

For a substantial body of Dante criticism, especially in America, conversion is a key topic in Dante. This can be seen in the work of Charles S. Singleton and, more recently, in that of John Freccero. Conversion is seen not merely as a topic forming part of the content of Dante's works but as structurally significant and bound up with the literary forms Dante uses, especially those of autobiographical narrative and of figural allegory.

The use of autobiographical narrative characterizes all Dante's extended vernacular works. First-person narrative is conventionally present in lyric poetry and perhaps particularly evident in that of Dante, but what is original about him is his desire to incorporate his lyrics into an autobiographical framework, as he does in the *Vita Nuova* and to a lesser extent in the *Convivio.* A study of Dante's use of autobiographical narrative offers a particularly promising basis for discussing the topic of conversion, as Freccero especially shows. The most outstanding and influential autobiographical work in the Christian tradition is Augustine's *Confessions,* in which the protagonist's conversion to Christianity completes and in a sense closes the story, while at the same time the radical change brought about by this conversion—the death to the old self bringing into being a new person—creates a distance between the narrator (writing after the conversion) and the "I" of the narrative, the changing protagonist. Behind this it is possible to see the story of the conversion of St. Paul (told in the first person in Acts 22 and Acts 26; Gal. 1:11–24 and 2 Cor. 11, 12 should also be noted) with its distinction between Saul and Paul. A number of references to Paul in the *Commedia* serve to relate Dante's story to the biblical one, thus suggesting that this is an exemplary Christian tale of conversion and revelation. The question of the importance of Augustine for Dante's work as a whole is much debated, and the differences between Augustine and Dante are considerable; but the significance of the *Confessions* precisely as a conversion narrative written in the first person seems highly plausible.

On this view, the most significant texts for the topic of conversion are the *Vita Nuova* and the *Commedia.* For Singleton, in his important work on the *Vita Nuova,* the early work is an account of a conversion from a secular and in many ways self-regarding love to a selfless love akin to the Christian love of God, associated with the disinterested poetry of praise. Beatrice comes to be seen, by analogy, as a grace-giving Christ-like figure. This highly influential reading has considerable force, although there have been others which tend to qualify it. Domenico De Robertis, for example, while not denying the progression from *amor* to *caritas,* sees the work as a treatise on love in which Dante distances himself from the position of Cavalcanti, rather than as an account of a Christian conversion, whether in personal or general terms. More recently Robert P. Harrison has placed the emphasis on Beatrice's physical presence or absence and has noted narrative discontinuities rather than a clearly structured conversion narrative.

It would be difficult to deny the importance of conversion in the *Commedia.* Indeed the poem as a whole may be read as a conversion narrative. The pilgrim is converted from a state of error or sinfulness (presumption, in Freccero's view) and alienation from God, represented by the dark wood. He undergoes an awakening in the wood and the obstruction by the three beasts, and he undertakes the journey guided by Virgil, at Beatrice's behest, through the encounter with the evil of his own world represented in Hell, and the visions of penitence in Purgatory, until he meets Beatrice in the Earthly Paradise, hears the accusations she levels at him, admits his guilt, and is purified by his immersion in Lethe and drinking of Eunoe, so that he can participate in the vision of Heaven. There is, it seems, a new conversion to Beatrice and all she stands for after a period of worldly infidelity.

The distance between poet and pilgrim is a commonplace of Dante criticism, and this may be seen as constituted not merely by distance in time, or the biographical fact of exile, but also by the experience (real or fictional) of conversion. It is possible then to find in the narrative a certain ironic detachment from the still worldly attitudes of the pilgrim in the *Inferno.* It is in the *Purgatorio,* however, that conversion can be said to be thematized. Various episodes in this *cantica* involve an enactment or ritualization of conversion, at least in the sense of repentance: for example, the engraving of the seven "P"s on the pilgrim's forehead by the angel at the door of Purgatory. The hymn of the redeemed souls in *Purg.* 2.45, "In exitu Israel de Aegypto"—which is used in the *Letter to Cangrande* (*Epist.* 13.21) to illustrate the fourfold allegory, in its moral sense, according to the writer—refers to the conversion of the soul from the wretchedness of sin to the state of grace (the other two senses, redemption through Christ and the departure of the soul to eternal glory, are also of course relevant here). *Purgatorio* also contains an explicit story of a conversion: that of Statius, which combines a religious change from paganism to Christianity with a moral repudiation of prodigality. Both forms of conversion are at least partly motivated by a reading of Virgil; this may serve to link the conversion of Statius with that of Dante himself.

It is possible to understand conversion in the *Commedia* as a general theme of which the poet-pilgrim is to be seen mainly as a type or example, converted from sin in order to speak convincingly to his world, or it is possible to understand it as a biographical fact. In the latter case there follows the question of what precisely constituted Dante's sin: whether it was a matter of general worldliness, or perhaps intellectual pride and presumption, or whether it involved a measure of philosophical

C heterodoxy. This issue has been debated in studies of Dante's thought, with scholars such as Bruno Nardi arguing for a secular, even heterodox orientation in the *Convivio*, while Étienne Gilson and Kenelm Foster tend to see greater continuity in Dante's thought. Given a substantial intellectual continuity, the conversion would be of a more moral and more personal and less intellectual kind.

Bibliography

Augustine, Saint. *Confessions.* Translated by Henry Chadwick. Oxford: Oxford University Press, 1986.

———. *S. Augustini Confessionum libri xiii.* Edited by L. Verheijen. Corpus christianorum series latina. Turnhout: Brepols, 1981.

Armour, Peter. *The Door of Purgatory: A Study of Multiple Symbolism in Dante's "Purgatorio."* Oxford: Oxford University Press, 1983.

De Robertis, Domenico. *Il libro della Vita nuova.* 2nd ed. Florence: Sansoni, 1961, 1970.

Foster, Kenelm. *The Two Dantes and Other Studies.* London: Darton, Longman and Todd, 1977.

Freccero, John. *Dante: The Poetics of Conversion.* Cambridge, Mass.: Harvard University Press, 1986.

Gilson, Étienne. *Dante and Philosophy.* Translated by D. Moore. New York: Harper and Row, 1963.

Harrison, Robert Pogue. *The Body of Beatrice.* Baltimore: Johns Hopkins University Press, 1988.

Meersseman, Gilles Gérard, "Conversione." *Enciclopedia dantesca,* 2:190–191.

Nardi, Bruno. *Dante e la cultura medievale. Nuovi saggi di filosofia dantesca.* 2nd ed. Bari: Laterza, 1949.

———. *Nel mondo di Dante.* Rome: Storia e letteratura, 1944.

Singleton, Charles. *Dante Studies 2: Journey to Beatrice.* Cambridge, Mass.: Harvard University Press, 1958.

———. *Dante Studies 1: "Commedia": Elements of Structure.* Cambridge, Mass.: Harvard University Press, 1954.

———. *An Essay on the "Vita Nuova."* Cambridge, Mass.: Harvard University Press, 1949.

Jennifer Petrie

Convivio

In the early years of his exile from Florence and some ten years after completing the *Vita Nuova,* Dante begins composing the *Convivio* ("The Banquet"), only to set it aside unfinished by late 1307, very likely in order to embark on a new and more elaborate artistic project, the *Commedia.* Most simply and succinctly described as an encyclopedia of knowledge, the *Convivio* occupies therefore a middle position between the two works in the vernacular devoted to the celebration of Beatrice, the miraculously beautiful young woman of Florence presented as a *figura Christi* who is invested with the mission of representing divinity on Earth and of rescuing the poet from a set of personal disasters. As the successor work to the *Vita Nuova,* the *Convivio* charts a new course, announcing the end of the poet's preoccupation with Beatrice and the inception of his love for another lady, Lady Philosophy, whom the poet exalts as an allegorical figure personifying human knowledge *(scienza)* and wisdom *(sapienza),* in the broadest and most ideal sense. This new savior, however, will soon yield to the return of Beatrice in the *Commedia,* who is reconceived and revitalized and given a fully developed eschatological role that transcends Dante's conceptions of both the early Beatrice and Lady Philosophy. The *Convivio* marks a middle, almost experimental stage between the two works. While it is written in the vernacular and shares with them the theme of salvific love of woman, it differs by being a work of (chiefly) expository prose. In fact, it is the first extended piece of original expository prose in the Italian vernacular. But for whatever reason, it nevertheless constitutes a false start, for Dante abandons his undertaking after completing only the first four of a projected fifteen books, without ever returning to it and without making what he had written available to the public.

Origins

The first book of the *Convivio* serves as an introduction to and undertakes to justify the projected additional fourteen books (called *trattati*), only four of which were completed. The second, third, and fourth are each preceded by a canzone, which is then subjected to explication in the prose commentary that follows. The canzoni for these books—"Voi che 'ntendendo il terzo ciel movete," "Amor, che ne la mente mi ragiona," and "Le dolci rime d'amor, ch'i' solìa"—had been written sometime earlier, and others already in circulation were projected for the remaining books. The work was conceived and written not long after Dante's discovery of philosophy between the years 1291 and

1529 edition of the Convivio *published in Venice by Niccolo di Aristotile detto Zoppino. Reproduced by permission of the John A. Zahm Dante Collection in the Department of Special Collections, University Libraries, University of Notre Dame.*

parallel with Boethius' similarly unjust fate, his imprisonment under King Theodoric on a charge of treachery. He explicitly refers to Boethius' *Consolation* by way of apologizing for speaking of himself in his own work (a practice deemed impermissible by medieval rhetoricians) on the model of Boethius himself, who had justified speaking of the self on the grounds that, in Dante's words, no one else would defend him against *la perpetuale infamia del suo essilio* ("the perpetual infamy of his exile," *Conv.* 1.2.13). Dante cites as well the example of Augustine's *Confessions* in defending his adoption of an autobiographical voice. His sudden reversal of fortune and ensuing emotional despondency constitute the background to the *Convivio* and are events that occasion his most personal remarks in the work: "Since it was the pleasure of the citizens of the most beautiful and famous daughter of Rome, Florence, to cast me out of her sweet bosom—where I was born and bred up to the pinnacle of my life, and where, with her good will, I desire with all my heart to rest my weary mind and to complete the span of time that is given to me—I have wandered like a stranger, almost like a beggar, through virtually all the regions to which this tongue of ours extends, displaying against my will the wound of fortune for which the wounded one is often unjustly accustomed to be held accountable" (1.3.4). His exile and poverty are, however, but one cause of his infamy, the other which he feels obliged to excuse being the image he had projected of himself earlier in the *Vita Nuova* and in other lyrics, as a thrall to love's passion. Important as the political element might be, Dante is clearly more concerned with reestablishing himself in the *Convivio* as a poet of moral rectitude, as a mature man who has set aside youthful folly. His motivation now is not *passione,* by which he means amatory passion, but *virtù* ("virtue," 1.2.16). His focus is on the pursuit of philosophical wisdom, idealized in the figure of Lady Philosophy, and the goal of his acquisition of knowledge is earthly happiness.

1295, a time when he began to frequent, as he says, "the schools of the religious orders and . . . the disputations held by the philosophers" (*Conv.* 2.12.7). Since at this time convent schools in Florence were open to the public at no charge, Dante more than likely attended lectures and discussions among the Dominicans at Santa Maria Novella, the Franciscans at Santa Croce, and the Augustinians at Santo Spirito. During this period, which he indicates lasted thirty months, Dante read and was particularly inspired by Boethius' *Consolation of Philosophy,* an autobiographical work whose formal structure and basic allegory he mirrors in the *Convivio.* Both are examples of the prosimetrum genre (prose mixed with poetry), both revere Lady Philosophy as the allegorical embodiment of human knowledge, and both conceive of the pursuit of knowledge as having the power to liberate the soul from human affliction and to generate human happiness. Dante, who bitterly condemns as unjust his own political exile from Florence in 1302 (*Conv.* 1.3.4), must have been particularly struck by the

Dating

Evidence internal to Dante's works suggest that the *Convivio* was begun sometime in the year 1304 and abandoned by late 1307, possibly early 1308. Since in *DVE* 1.12.5 he refers to Giovanni di Monferrat, who died in 1305, as being alive, and since in *Conv.* 1.5.10 he describes the *De vulgari eloquentia* as a work yet to be undertaken, the

Convivio could not have been begun later than 1304, and possibly as early as 1303. On the basis of the reference in *Conv.* 4.14.12 to Gherardo da Camino, who died in March 1306, as deceased, we can be virtually certain that the rest of Book 4 could not have been completed prior to that date. It is also likely that he broke off at the end of Book 4 before the close of 1308, since his description of Frederick II as "the last of the Roman emperors" and mention of Rudolf, Adolf, and Albert at *Conv.* 4.3.6 omits any reference to Henry VII of Luxemburg, who was elected emperor in November 1308. The dating of the text to 1304–1307, established by Michele Barbi, has long been embraced by almost all critics, but in 1983 Maria Corti argued, on the basis of stylistic and linguistic evidence, that the composition took place in two distinct periods (*La felicità mentale*, 72–155). Her theory that the first three books belong to the period 1303–1304, and the last to the years 1306–1308, does not, however, differ radically from the conventional view, and it has been disputed by Franca Ageno (1986). More recently A. Longoni has contended that Dante composed the second and third books before the first. But there is little doubt that he broke off Book 4 only shortly before beginning the *Commedia,* which almost all critics assign to late 1307 or early 1308.

Philosophical Allegory

The *Convivio* is a hymn of praise to divine wisdom and human knowledge under the guise of allegory. It celebrates the sanctity of human reason as a faculty endowed with sufficient intellective power to enable the individual to achieve happiness in the present life. Indeed, this is the point of departure for the entire work and the basis for the structure of knowledge deployed in it. The very opening sentences establish two fundamental propositions, that "all men by nature desire to know" and that "knowledge is the ultimate perfection of our soul, in which resides our ultimate happiness." Consequently, by simple deductive logic, all men desire their "ultimate happiness," which is the ultimate perfection of their being in life. For Dante, such knowledge could only be a full and all-embracing understanding of the nature of man and of the universe in which he resides. Because this body of knowledge is the gift of God, created by him so that mankind might have a means to come to know his being and thereby gain salvation, it necessarily reveals the beauty, coherence, harmony, and total-

ity of the divine mind. The *Convivio* seeks to be a kind of *summa* of secular knowledge about the nature of the created universe, a record of all that the human mind has learned is true and valuable from ancient times to the present, presented in an orderly fashion for the moral improvement of the reader.

Dante's praise of knowledge, however, is more than simply praise; it is an expression of a deep and binding love. The work's formal allegory (a narrative device familiar to much of medieval literature) presents Dante as a lover enamored of Lady Philosophy, whose bright eyes graciously shine upon him, instilling in him a desire to achieve spiritual union with her, for by definition "love is nothing but the spiritual union of the soul and the thing which is loved" (*Conv.* 3.2.3; see also 4.1.1). She is the most noble thing in the universe, *la sposa de lo Imperadore del cielo . . . e non solamente sposa, ma suora e figlia dilettissima!* ("the bride of the Emperor of heaven, and not the bride alone but the sister and the most beloved daughter!" 3.12.14), and *regina di tutto* ("queen of all things," 2.12.9). Her perfection is supreme, her relationship to God one of marriage: "She is most noble because the divine essence is most noble; and she exists in him in a true and perfect manner, as if by eternal marriage" (3.12.13). It is apparent that Dante conflates all sources of authoritative knowledge into one allegorical figure, Lady Philosophy, who is and was the lady of all men who have sought to possess a true understanding of the nature of man, the cosmos, and knowledge itself. Knowledge, wisdom, learning: Lady Philosophy is a woman of many names, though all signify one and the same essence. She is what she represents, love (*philo*) of wisdom (*sophia*). Because love of philosophy is not complete unless it leads to virtuous action, *filosofia* in its truest sense is said to be *uno amoroso uso di sapienza,* "a loving use of wisdom" (3.12.12). Such love ennobles and perfects the mind, defines our nobility of being—"the word 'nobility' means the perfection of the nature proper to each thing" (4.16.4)—and is the source of all our virtues and the cause of our happiness. Book 4 in particular will expand upon the nature of the Moral Virtues—specifically, eleven virtues that Dante identifies as deriving from Aristotle—which must be acquired as a habit and are the goal of the active life (as opposed to the contemplative life), whose path leads to happiness in this world.

The *Convivio,* like the *Vita Nuova* and the *Commedia,* is founded on a love story, although unlike either of those works there is little story, and what there is serves only as a vehicle for conveying a body of philosophic knowledge. Dante's Lady Philosophy, unlike Boethius', never has a speaking part, and hence proves to be less than even a true personification of an abstract notion. She remains an idea addressed by Dante's mind, and only a few specific features of her beauty—namely, her eyes and her smile—are allegorized. The allegory of the *Convivio* qua event remains occasional, indeed rare, whereas allegorical explication abounds in the commentary to the first two canzoni, "Voi, che 'ntendendo il terzo ciel movete" and "Amor che ne la mente mi ragiona." Dante subjects the text of each poem to twofold analyses in succession, explicating first the literal and then the allegorical meaning, in most instances line by line. (In the third canzone, "Le dolci rime d'amor, ch'i' solìa," Dante claims to have abandoned allegory altogether.) Dante's deployment of the metaphor of the banquet at the opening of his work is yet another example of artificial and occasional use of allegory. The "meat" and "bread" of the banquet, symbolizing respectively the projected fourteen canzoni and their accompanying commentaries, will nourish those in need of the spiritual food of true knowledge, *lo pane de li angeli* ("the bread of the angels," 1.1.7). This is a banquet at whose table Dante, in an act of modesty, claims not to be truly present; rather, as he states, he sits near the table, collecting the crumbs that fall from the plates of those wise enough to attend it. His act will be one of service on behalf of those lacking a formal education, to arrange and convey what knowledge he is able to gather from his learning for the benefit of his fellow countrymen who have little time or capacity to undertake the study of philosophy on their own. At the heart of the *Convivio,* then, is a passionate desire to educate as wide an audience as possible, one that included women as well as men, and it is for this reason that he writes in the vernacular and not in Latin.

The Structure of the Convivio

Dante's most important philosophic authority in the *Convivio* is Aristotle, whose fundamental role as guide is apparent from the opening sentence: *Sì come dice lo Filosofo nel principio de la Prima Filosofia . . .* ("As the Philosopher says at the beginning of the First Philosophy. . . ," 1.1.1). Aristotle's influence and authority are so pervasive in the Middle Ages that Dante, following established convention, refers to him simply as "the Philosopher." He is *maestro e duca de la ragione umana* ("the master and leader of human reason," 4.6.8), and he serves as Dante's moral guide in the work, a role that Virgil and Beatrice will have in the *Commedia.* Indeed, Aristotle's identification with the faculty of human reason as its greatest exemplar is so profound that his opinions are considered divine. Dante had, however, only indirect access to his works, since he knew no Greek. His knowledge of Aristotelian thought derives from Latin commentaries on translations from the Greek (for example, St. Thomas' *Commentary on the Nicomachaean Ethics* and his *Commentary on the Metaphysics*). Dante's goal in the *Convivio* is to present a complete body of knowledge about the universe, the individual's place in it, and the means by which one can realize happiness in this life. His procedure is to deploy a highly organized and rigorously schematized series of assertions of truths followed by argumentation, proofs, or demonstrations, which are conducted according to the principles of Scholastic logic. These truths are already said to be incorporated, in condensed form, in the poetry written in praise of Lady Philosophy, which is then explicated, elucidated, and expanded upon in the prose commentaries that make up the substance of each of the three books following the first, introductory book.

The first book, which serves to introduce and justify Dante's project, is remarkable chiefly for the poet's impassioned defense of the Italian vernacular, which reaches full pitch in the closing chapters. The vehemence of his attack falls on those who write in other languages and despise their own vernacular. They are *malvagi uomini* ("contemptible men," 1.11.1) and *abominevoli cattivi* ("detestable wretches," 1.11.21), their abandonment of Italian being portrayed as an act of meretricious adultery. This tone may strike one as excessively shrill, all the more so because these detractors of Italian remain anonymous—Pézard's theory that Dante is referring to Brunetto Latini, who wrote in French during his exile, has generally been discredited—but beneath the stridency one detects a tenacious commitment to the diffusion of knowledge. The food of the banquet is expressly prepared for a lay, not a learned, audience. Italian, not Latin, is to be the language of communication because that is the language that can reach the greatest number: it is language of the *molti* (1.9.4). Dante casts himself as an anti-elitist and a rebel against the established values of the professional world, which are founded on a desire for fame or monetary gain. He embraces goals that are at once altruistic and practical in nature: first, to improve the intellectual and moral life of the individual and, second, to improve the quality of civic government.

Each of the three succeeding books reveals a defined conceptual structure and possesses an inherent thematic logic. The first canzone, "Voi che 'ntendendo il terzo ciel movete" ("You whose intellect the third sphere moves"), opening the second book, identifies and describes the source of the spirit of his love for Lady Philosophy, the influence which rains down from the third heaven, governed by the angelic intelligences who reside in the highest material heaven. After defining (somewhat ambiguously and incompletely) his allegorical method and purpose (2.1.1), Dante proceeds to explicate the poem on two levels, first the literal and then the allegorical. The description of the third heaven, Venus, becomes a pretext for mapping out the entire cosmos, the nine heavens familiar to Aristotle and the tenth and Christian heaven, the Empyrean, which lies beyond time and space. The number, hierarchy, and allegorical significance of each heaven is then carefully explicated, on both the literal and the allegorical level. Each heaven is associated allegorically with one of the major disciplines of learning taught in the universities, that is, with one of the seven liberal arts (the trivium and quadrivium). The Moon is aligned with grammar, Mercury with dialectic, Venus with rhetoric, the Sun with arithmetic, Mars with music, Jupiter with geometry, and Saturn with astrology. The highest three heavens are then associated with the higher sciences. The Fixed Stars correspond with physics and metaphysics—the "natural sciences" of Aristotle, both of which deal with first principles. The Primum Mobile is linked to moral philosophy (ethics) and is conceived to govern and dispose all the lower sciences. The Empyrean, which transcends and embraces all the physical heavens, is associated with theology, the *divina scienza* ("divine science," 2.14.19), which is founded on revelation and which deals with truths that lie beyond the reach of human reason.

The cosmological model of Book 2 provides a logical and natural introduction to the subject of the third book, which examines how the object of the poet's love, Lady Philosophy, manifests within herself the presence and the majesty of the Divine Creator as they are manifest in the things that exist on Earth. At the heart of the commentary on the second canzone, "Amor, che ne la mente mi ragiona" ("Love, that speaks to me within my mind"), Dante expounds the chain of being, the *scala naturae* or ladder of perfection delineating the degree of moral excellence of all inhabitants, organisms, and matter within the universe according to each being's capacity to reflect the perfection of the Divinity. As a paradigm, the hierarchy of being originates with the Greeks, chiefly Plato and Aristotle, but it survives virtually unchanged until well into the eighteenth century. Dante distinguishes six levels of being below God—the angelic, human, animal, vegetative, mineral, and elemental—and identifies the nature of their love, which draws them closer or less close to God according to the measure of their perfection. Man is naturally drawn to God, but the beauty of Lady Philosophy, who reflects the image of God, has the power to draw him even closer, if not into the direct presence of the Divine Being.

The nobility of man, the subject of the fourth book, derives naturally from the preceding arguments, for the love of Lady Philosophy which draws the lover closer to God perfects his being, thereby ennobling his soul. Dante's disquisition on the nature of nobility is founded on an attack on Emperor Frederick II's notion that nobility consists of ancestral wealth accompanied by fine manners. In keeping with the views expressed by many medieval writers (from Jean de Meun to Chaucer), Dante defines nobility as a quality that derives from moral worth, not accident of birth. Wealth, which can be inherited, can play no role in determining true nobility, which cannot be passed from generation to generation by means of procreation. This theme reaches the pinnacle of artistic refinement in the magnificent canzone "Le dolci rime d'amor" ("The tender rhymes of love") and becomes the subject of an impassioned disquisition in which the poet condemns the spirit of acquisition, arguing that reason and wealth are virtually incompatible (chaps. 11–13). (In the *Commedia* the attack on avarice, seen as the root cause of political instability in Italy, will become even more scathing.)

Dante divides the fourth book into two halves of fifteen chapters each, the first devoted to dismantling the archaic conception of nobility espoused by Frederick II (4.3.9), the second to defining its true nature. That definition, which has its roots in Aristotle's thinking as well as Solomon's wisdom, establishes nobility as "the perfection of the nature proper to each thing" (*perfezione di propria natura in ciascuna cosa,* 4.16.4) and bases the achievement of perfection on the acquisition and fortification of virtue, and specifically on eleven Moral Virtues espoused by Aristotle. These virtues—courage, temperance, liberality, munificence, magnanimity, love of honor, gentleness, affability, truth, good disposition, and justice—enable the individual to reach the highest degree of happiness in this life, following the path of the active life. Dante clearly recognizes the superiority of the contemplative life, based on the three Intellectual Virtues, but argues that because the Moral Virtues are more common, better known, more sought after, and more imitated, his treatment of virtue must begin with and emphasize them (4.17.12). After all, in light of his desire to educate and empower a broad class of nonprofessional individuals in order to promote civic stability and universal peace (1.7.12, 1.9.5, 4.4), the core of his program of learning had to center on the virtues of the active life. The Moral Virtues are a gift of God and are instilled in the intellectual soul, and so constitute an individual's *bontade divina* ("divine goodness," 4.23.4), or personal nobility. While Dante also lists here the seven gifts of the Holy Spirit, which are likewise instilled in the individual by the Creator as a gift (*Conv.* 4.21.12), his interest in the Moral Virtues is paramount. The last third of Book 4 is devoted to describing the signs of nobility in an individual deriving from the Moral Virtues, a discussion that employs the paradigm of the four ages of life (adolescence, maturity, old age, senility).

There is a suggestion that each of the eleven remaining unwritten books of the *Convivio* was to be devoted to one of the eleven Moral Virtues. Since the work was never completed, such a conceptual structure must remain pure hypothesis. Nevertheless Dante clearly divides the fourth book of thirty chapters into two parts, the second of which begins with Chapter 16, precisely the first of the remaining fifteen chapters, and the chapter in which he introduces the true definition of nobility. The fourth book, then, is a kind of double book, for Books 2 and 3 each contain fifteen chapters.

The thesis gains some weight from the fact that Dante appears to assign treatment of three of the virtues to specific books: justice to the fourteenth book (1.12.12, 4.27.11), temperance to the seventh book (4.26.8), and liberality to the last book (1.8.18). Antonio Biscioni first advanced this idea in his edition of 1741, and a century later Antonio Selmi endorsed it. But it has found little critical favor after Michele Barbi's remark that, had Dante had a thematic pattern in mind for the remaining books, he would have announced it (Busnelli-Vandelli, xiv). It should nevertheless be recalled that the moral structure of the *Commedia* depends for its formal order on the traditional vices and virtues, just as did many other medieval works, among them William Peraldus' *Summa de vitiis et de virtutibus* and Brunetto Latini's *Tresor,* and that a similar patterning in the *Convivio* would be entirely conventional. The schema of the vices and virtues would have a long life as an organizing principle of a literary or expository text, as Spenser's *Faerie Queene,* based as well on the Aristotelian Moral Virtues, attests to.

The *Convivio's Relation to the* Vita Nuova *and the* Commedia

In the closing chapters of the *Vita Nuova,* Dante proclaims the triumph of his love for the memory of Beatrice over his affection for a rival love, an unnamed young lady referred to simply as *donna gentile* and *donna pietosa.* The *Convivio,* however, tells the same story to opposite effect—the *donna gentile,* now baptized Lady Philosophy, emerging victorious over Beatrice. That victory is recorded and celebrated in the first of the three canzoni, "Voi, che 'ntendendo il terzo ciel movete," and elucidated in the ensuing commentary. Dante's apparent rewriting of his amatory experience creates serious interpretive problems, because in the closing lines of the *Vita Nuova* Dante seems to anticipate the germination of the *Commedia* when he says that he intends to write of Beatrice "what has never been said of any woman." The blatant inconsistency created by this remark has induced some critics to formulate speculative hypotheses designed to minimize or even suppress the obvious contradiction between the works in order to preserve their harmony. These attempts to preserve the appearances, to save the phenomena, however, are not unlike what medieval astronomers were required to hypothesize in order to accommodate the observed events of the heavens to the imperative of their belief in an Earth-centered universe. It has been suggested, for example, that the *Vita Nuova* originally concluded with the victory of the *donna gentile* over Beatrice but that the ending of the text was later revised by Dante to accommodate the *Commedia* (Pietrobono and Nardi). But, as others have observed, there is no manuscript evidence in support of such a thesis (De Robertis). Whether we endorse the argument that the problem of inconsistency is insoluble (Corti) or the assertion that it is nonexistent because what we have is simply two different interpretations of the same experience (De Robertis), we are still left with the realization that the *Convivio* represents a kind of cul-de-sac for Dante, a work he chooses to abandon and which he chooses to leave in many respects outside his official oeuvre. Unlike all his other works, including the unfinished *De vulgari eloquentia,* the *Convivio* was subjected by the poet to a kind of house arrest: he never disseminated the text; its existence did not come to light until after the poet's death. The first printed edition, by Francesco Bonaccorsi of Florence, would not appear until 1490.

A related critical problem has been Dante's exceptional praise of secular knowledge in the *Convivio.* A number of critics have charged that by embracing Lady Philosophy Dante sought to posit extraordinary claims for the power of reason as a human faculty and for philosophy as an intellectual domain, namely, the power to bring man into a state of happiness sufficient to ensure the salvation of the soul. Certainly Dante's exaltation of philosophy toward the close of Book 3, where he speaks of philosophy as divine and as united with God in eternal marriage, rings with such an intense enthusiasm that it seems to obtrude upon, or at the very least exclude, the sphere of theology. Alluding to the traditional theological concept of the Church as bride of Christ and echoing in particular the language of the Song of Solomon (4:10), he even promotes Philosophy as *sponsa Dei:* "O most noble and excellent is that heart which directs its love toward the bride of the Emperor of heaven, and not bride alone but sister and most beloved daughter!" (3.12.13). For critics like Pietrobono and Nardi, Dante's love of philosophy constitutes a kind of heretical, secular philosophism based on reason and not revelation, amounting to a sinful straying from the right way. For some, indeed, the image of the *selva oscura* in the opening lines of *Inferno* records the poet's crisis of pure philosophism, his error in aban-

doning Beatrice for Lady Philosophy, and his ultimate rejection of his moral lapse (*Purg.* 30–31). But it should be stressed that in the *Convivio* Dante never explicitly sets reason in opposition to faith or philosophy against theology. His goal, as the spirit and letter of the passage cited above indicate, is forever one of synthesis, of bringing together, or at least correlating, diverse systems of thought. As Gilson observed, Dante "seems in the *Banquet* to profess not a philosophical rationalism directed against theology, but a doctrine of the autonomy and the adequacy of the aims of philosophy viewed in its proper setting" (159). The debate between those who view the road from the *Vita Nuova* to the *Convivio* and finally the *Commedia* as continuous and those who view each successive work as a palinode to the previous one is not, however, likely to be easily resolved.

Another issue of critical debate concerns the degree to which the exposition of philosophical and theological ideas in the *Convivio* reflects instances of "radical Aristotelianism" or Averroistic thinking, of the kind found in thinkers like Boethius of Dacia or Siger of Brabant. But few would deny that the ideas, issues, and concepts Dante addresses in the *Convivio* return in the *Commedia,* sometimes more fully developed, sometimes transformed. The three canzoni that introduce the commentaries present established truths regarding universal principles of reality and ethical conduct that inform the moral structure of the *Commedia.* Dante's analysis of the ten heavens, in the second book of the *Convivio,* develops into the cosmological structure of *Paradiso.* The chain or levels of being *(scala naturae),* described in the third book, becomes the conceptual basis for the hierarchic distribution of the dead souls in Hell, Purgatory, and Paradise according to their various degrees of moral excellence. And his concept of a providentially ordained world government, established to provide universal human happiness by creating peace out of discord (outlined in 4.4–6), sets the stage for the separate treatise *Monarchia* and the exaltation of Henry VII as the ideal emperor. All the seeds are here: the notion that human society requires government in the form of a monarchy with a single strong ruler (4.4.4), that the ruler must be the emperor of the Roman Empire (4.4.8), that God chose the Roman people to provide this government for the benefit of all (4.4.10). It is precisely at this point that the role of Virgil—in particular,

Virgil the author of the *Aeneid*—begins to take hold of Dante's imagination. It is but a step to the Virgil of the *Commedia,* Virgil as guide through the otherworld.

Editions

The *Convivio,* of which there are forty-six extant manuscripts (none of which is the original text), was never disseminated by Dante and never appeared during his lifetime. Some early commentators of the *Commedia* (L'Ottimo, Pietro Alighieri) refer to it, but it is not until 1490 that the first printed edition is published by Francesco Bonaccorsi of Florence, on the basis of a single manuscript chosen at random (Vasoli, lxxxi). The text was reprinted three times during the sixteenth century in Venice, each time under the title *L'amoroso convivio di Dante,* but not again until the eighteenth century in Anton Maria Biscioni's edition of 1723. Numerous advances in textual editing, resulting in numerous new editions, took place throughout the nineteenth century, but the first modern edition based on an attempt to construct a critical edition is found in the edition of Ernesto Giacomo Parodi and Flaminio Pellegrini, published in 1921. This text has been chosen by virtually all editors who have published an edition with commentary during this century, including both the Busnelli-Vandelli edition of 1934–1937, which is heavily invested in establishing the primacy of Thomistic doctrine in Dante's philosophic thought, and the De Robertis-Vasoli edition of 1988, containing Vasoli's massively erudite and more balanced commentary. In 1966 Maria Simonelli published the first critical edition of the *Convivio,* accompanied by scrupulous textual notes, and in 1995 the long-awaited critical edition of Franca Brambilla Ageno, based on a complete study of the extant manuscripts, appeared as part of the Edizione Nazionale of Dante's works. It is now universally accepted that all manuscripts derive from a single lost copy of the *Convivio* which was exceptionally corrupt and unreliable. While much of the text is certain, there remain many areas of insurmountable lacunae and many issues of critical disagreement.

Bibliography

Editions

Alighieri, Dante. *Il Convivio.* Edited by Franca Brambilla Ageno. Florence: Le Lettere, 1995.

———. *Dante's Il Convivio (The Banquet).* Translated by Richard Lansing. New York: Garland Publishing, 1990.

———. *The Banquet.* Translated by Christopher Ryan. Saratoga, Calif.: ANMA Libri, 1989.

———. *Il Convivio.* Edited by Domenico De Robertis and Cesare Vasoli. In *Opere minori,* vol. I, pt. 2. Milan, Naples: Ricciardi, 1988.

———. *Il Convivio.* Edited by Maria Simonelli. Bologna: Pàtron, 1966.

———. *Il Convivio.* Edited by Giovanni Busnelli and Giuseppe Vandelli. Introduction by Michele Barbi. Vol. I. Florence: Le Monnier, 1934; Vol. II, 1937, 1964.

———. *Il Convivio.* In *Opere di Dante della Società Dantesca Italiana.* Edited by Parodi, Ernesto Giacomo, and Flaminio Pellegrini. Florence: Bemporad, 1921.

Criticism

Ageno, Franca Bambilla. "La funzione delle fonti e dei luoghi paralleli nella fissazione del testo critico: Esperienze di un editore del *Convivio.*" *Studi danteschi* 58 (1986), 239–273.

Ascoli, Albert Russell. "The Unfinished Author: Dante's Rhetoric of Authority in *Convivio* and *De vulgari eloquentia.*" In *The Cambridge Companion to Dante.* Edited by Rachel Jacoff. Cambridge: Cambridge University Press, 1993, pp. 45–66.

Boyde, Patrick. *Dante, Philomythes and Philosopher: Man in the Cosmos.* Cambridge: Cambridge University Press, 1981.

Corti, Maria. *La felicità mentale. Nuove prospettive per Cavalcanti e Dante.* Turin: Einaudi, 1983.

De Robertis, Domenico. "Il libro della 'Vita Nuova' e il libro del 'Convivio.'" *Studi urbinati* 25 (1951), 5–27.

Dronke, Peter. *Dante's Second Love: The Originality and the Contexts of the Convivio.* Leeds: Manley and Son, 1997.

Gagliardi, Antonio. *La tragedia intellettuale di Dante: Il Convivio.* Catanzaro: Pullano, 1994.

Gilson, Étienne. *Dante and Philosophy.* Translated by David Moore. New York: Harper and Row, 1949. Reprinted in 1963.

Lanza, Antonio. *Dante e la Gnosi. Esoterismo del Convivio.* Rome: Edizioni Mediterranee, 1993.

Leo, Ulrich. "The Unfinished *Convivio* and Dante's Re-Reading of the *Aeneid.*" *Medieval Studies* 12 (1951), 41–64.

Longoni, A. "La travagliata struttura del *Convivio.*" *Strumenti critici* 65 (1991), 147–170.

Nardi, Bruno. *Dal "Convivio" alla "Commedia."* Rome: Nella sede dell'Istituto, 1960.

Pietrobono, Luigi. "The Unfinished *Convivio* as a Pathway to the *Comedy.*" *Dante Studies* 113 (1995), 31–56.

———. *Nuovi saggi danteschi.* Turin: SEI, 1954.

Scott, John. "Dante and Philosophy." *Annali d'Italianistica* 8 (1990), 258–277.

Simonelli, Maria. *Materiali per un'edizione critica del "Convivio" di Dante.* Rome: Ateneo, 1970.

Took, John F. *Dante: Lyric Poet and Philosopher.* Oxford: Clarendon Press, 1990, pp. 81–122.

Vallone, Aldo. *La prosa del 'Convivio.'* Florence: Le Monnier, 1967.

Vasoli, Cesare. "Dante e la scienza dei 'peripatetici.'" In *Dante e la scienza.* Edited by Patrick Boyde and Vittorio Russo. Ravenna: Longo, 1995, pp. 55–70.

———. "Il *Convivio* di Dante e l'enciclopedismo medievale." *L'enciclopedismo medievale.* Edited by Michelangelo Picone. Ravenna: Longo, 1994, pp. 363–381.

Richard Lansing

Cornelia

Roman matron of the second century before Christ, daughter of Scipio Africanus the Elder, and mother of the tribunes Tiberius and Gaius Gracchus. Cornelia *(Corniglia)* was celebrated for her strength of character and total dedication to her family. She resides in Limbo (*Inf.* 4.128) and is mentioned by Cacciaguida as an example of womanly virtue likely to astonish contemporary Florentines (*Par.* 15.129).

Rinaldina Russell

Corso Donati

Leader of the Black Guelfs in Florence, brother of Forese and Piccarda, and bitter enemy of Dante. He is never mentioned by name in the poet's works, but direct allusions to him appear in *Rime* 77 (*Bicci novel, figliuol di non so cui,* vv. 12–14) and in the "prediction" of his death in *Purg.* 24.82–87 (cf. Villani, *Nuova cronica,* 8.96), where he is referred to as the one *che più n'ha colpa* ("who is most to blame," 82). The chief magistrate of Bologna in 1283 and 1288 and of Pistoia in 1289, Corso became a ruthless Florentine knight and politician who initially made a name for himself through an act of reckless courage against Arezzo in the Battle of Campaldino (1289), in which Dante may have participated (cf. *Inf.* 22.4–5; *Purg.* 5.94–95). He is remembered in *Par.* 3.106–108 for having forcibly removed his sister Piccarda from a convent around 1288 and insisting that she marry one of his political allies. He was the leader of the Black Guelfs during the political strife of the 1290s and the target of Guido Cavalcanti's failed assassination attempt in 1296. Shortly after the May Day brawl of 1300 he was banished from Florence and sentenced to death. But Corso enjoyed the political favor of Boniface VIII and Charles of Valois, with whose support he reentered the city and quickly assumed power. More than six hundred White Guelfs, including Dante, were condemned to exile by early 1302. Over the next six years, Corso's popularity gradually waned, and his association with his father-in-law, the Ghibelline leader Uguccione della Faggiuola, left him with few allies. While attempting to escape from Florence in 1308 he was seized by Catalan mercenaries and murdered in a fashion perhaps not too dissimilar to what Dante described, in the voice of Forese, in *Purg.* 24.82–87: *"Or va," diss'el: "ché quei che più n'ha colpa / vegg' ïo a coda d'una bestia tratto / inver' la valle ove mai non si scolpa. / La bestia ad ogne passo va più ratto, / crescendo sempre, fin ch'ella il percuote, / e lascia il corpo vilmente disfatto"* ("Now behold": said he, "the one most to blame for it I see dragged at the tail of a beast toward the valley where guilt is never forgiven. The beast goes faster with each step, ever growing, until it tramples him and leaves his corpse basely disfigured").

Michael Papio

Cosmology

The cosmology adapted and elaborated by Dante in the *Commedia* and in other writings is based on Platonic-Aristotelian cosmological conceptions modified in special ways by the Church Fathers' theological-metaphysical view that matter necessarily conforms to the truths of spiritual reality. Dante depicts the heavens as a cosmic temple constructed of circles within nested circles, a temple through which the guided pilgrim moves from lower regions to the highest realms. The heavens, which are ten in number, comprise the seven planetary spheres (the Moon, Mercury, Venus, the Sun, Mars, Jupiter, Saturn), the Fixed Stars, the Primum Mobile, and the Empyrean, which is immaterial and lies beyond time and space. The circular Earth takes its form after the pattern of the heavens, but it contains an interior Hell that is viewed by the traveler and an external Mount Purgatory on whose circular terraces the traveler becomes a pilgrim. The cosmological structure of the universe is everywhere, in each of its realms and parts, fundamentally based on the image of the perfect circle.

The circular court of the true Heaven, a vast white rose filled with the ordered ranks of the blessed in the eternal Empyrean, is called by Beatrice *nostra basilica* ("our kingly court," *Par.* 25.30). The Primum Mobile, or first moving circle and the first material heaven, is referred to by Dante as an *angelico templo* ("angelic temple," *Par.* 28.53), and this temple, the abode of the angels, in turn is a part of the "copy" (*essemplare,* 56) of which the Empyrean is the "model" (*essemplo,* 55). This heavenly theological-metaphysical temple with its earthly counterpart is "operational," with each virtuous being in life seeking its highest appropriate place within the universal order. All beings beyond earthly existence move, unless otherwise permitted by divine dispensation, in restricted ways within a fixed hierarchy defined by the heavenly spheres.

The ultimate fulfilling and sustaining point of reference for beings is the all-containing *volume,* or Book of the Cosmos (*Par.* 33.86)—the *volume* toward which all virtuous beings in *Paradiso* are upwardly drawn, and the one that is seen by Dante during beatific vision. This *volume* binds together in love and in-gathers in Godhead all the scattered leaves of the universe (85–95). And this *volume* appears as a simple flame, a *forma universal* ("universal form") that transfigures in Dante's view into one paradoxical *semplice sembiante* ("one simple aspect," 109) that appears as three rotating *giri* ("circles") of light that finally reflect within themselves *nostra effige* ("our image," *Par.* 33.131).

Lesser luminous icons of these ultimate wheels of the Godhead in the eternal Empyrean extend downward in spheres of increasing imperfection, from the Primum Mobile (or Crystalline), to the Fixed Stars (also called the Galaxy in *Conv.* 2.14), to the seven spheres of the planets, and finally to the grossly material circular Earth. The blessed souls of Heaven have their seat in the white rose of the Empyrean, but they are manifested to Dante in the different planetary spheres below the Primum Mobile (which is reserved for the angels) and the Fixed Stars (the sphere of triumphs) in ordered iconographic formations. Critical interpretation commonly associates these seven spheres, respectively and in descending order, with each of the four cardinal virtues—temperance (Saturn), justice (Jupiter), fortitude (Mars), and prudence (the Sun)—and with a holiness marred by earthly love (Venus), ambition (Mercury), and inconstancy (the Moon).

Dante's universe, beyond its fundamental indebtedness to Aristotelian and Ptolemaic thought, reflects in its general form medieval conceptions on the order of the cosmos advanced by St. Augustine in *De ordine* 2.39. Macrobius, remarking on that order in *Somnium Scipionis* 1.14, describes the universe as a "cosmic temple." Medieval numerological interpretations of the ordered universe accordingly were developed by using cosmic proportions cited in Plato's *Timaeus* and supposedly advanced by Pythagoras, and by employing passages in the Bible on the size of Solomon's temple. Such numerology, governed by Trinitarian mathematical theories developed particularly in the late Middle Ages at the Cathedral School of Chartres, influenced the design of literary and artistic works, of circular cathedral rose-wheel stained-glass windows and corresponding circular labyrinth nave floors, and of the numerous Knights Templars' and Hospitallers' round temples in the Near East, Italy, and throughout Europe. Yet the key medieval model for the cosmic round temples was Constantine's fourth-century iconographic Temple of the Holy Sepulchre located at the supposed geographic center of the world at Jerusalem, a temple with a perfect-circle Resurrection building, or Anastasis; an Anastasis hemisphere covering, or dome; and the central tomb of Christ surrounded by twelve pilasters. Thirteenth-century illustrations often depicted the Holy Sepulchre as a circle enclosing a cross, marking the supposed center of the geographic world, within the wider circle of the Holy City.

The general universal cosmology mirrored in the *Commedia* is well illustrated in a manuscript, of a kind that would have been available to Dante in Florence, now in the Laurentian Library, namely, a copy of Sallust's widely circulated *Bellum Iugurthinum* (c. 1160). The illustration on an unnumbered page shows two simple circular diagrams: the upper one consists of lined circles within circles signifying the seven spheres labeled with the names of the planets; the lower one is a traditional T-O map, consisting of a drawing of Earth as a circular land mass surrounded by an ocean, with a dark T-shaped area representing the Mediterranean Sea and the Danube and Nile Rivers interposed upon one half of the land mass.

While the images of Dante's *Paradiso* refer ultimately to the transcendent light and wheel icons signifying Godhead, those relating to Earth—through an ingenious inversion and preservation of figural bonds joining earthly and heavenly types—refer both to the transcendent center above but also to figured "centers" of this world. The icon of the Godhead sustains, fulfills, and synthesizes even these antithetical or complementary earthly centers: the *tomba* of Satan at the lowest point of the poet's universe at the inner core of Earth (*Inf.* 34.128); the tomb and cross of Christ, the second Adam, at the summit and center of Earth's circular external land mass on the Northern Hemisphere in Jerusalem (*Inf.* 34.1–3, 112–117); the nest *(nido)* of the human race and the traditional tomb of Adam in Eden at the island-mountain summit and center of the great ocean covering the Southern Hemisphere (*Purg.* 28.78, 32.37); and the tomb and Temple of St. Peter, the Father of the Church, in the earthly Eternal City of Rome that is the foreshadowing type of the circular heavenly city in which the saint appears enthroned on high (*Par.* 27.22–27, 32.124–130). By means of this typology Dante becomes a prime exponent of a medieval architectural mode, namely, the Martyrium temple-tomb marking a spiritual geographic center and related through earthly types and anti-types to Christ's tomb in Jerusalem.

The souls in *Inferno* are placed in nine major circles, divided into three categories corresponding to the three major classifications of sin—incontinence, violence, and fraud—which lead down to Satan, entombed in ice at Hell's center. Satan's fall to the core of Earth, Virgil explains in *Inf.* 34.124–129, caused the land of the Southern Hemisphere to flee from his sinful being; this land, in turn, gathered in the Northern Hemisphere where the temple and tomb of Christ mark its geographic center. Dante, in turning from the Northern Hemisphere to the Southern Hemisphere on the hairy sides of Satan, is informed by Virgil that,

though in Hell, he is under Jerusalem, where Christ was *consunto* ("consumed") on the cross of Redemption (114).

At the antipodal center of the Southern Hemisphere directly opposite Jerusalem at the center of the Northern Hemisphere, Mount Purgatory rises in seven major terraces on which souls are purged, respectively, of each of their sinful dispositions, based on the seven capital sins. In Eden at the mountain's summit, the point on Earth farthest from Satan and closest to God, Dante views the second "true" medieval source work that complements the "volume" of the cosmos seen in beatific vision, namely, the Bible, or God's Book of Words, represented by an allegorical procession that culminates in the appearance of Beatrice, who replaces Virgil as his mentor and becomes his guide through the ten spheres of Paradise.

In his depiction of solely the symbolic topography of the physical Earth, Dante reflects a biblical world iconography that first emerged in the fourth and fifth centuries from pilgrim tracts and from the writings of clerics such as St. Jerome and Paul Orosius. In the sixth century the Sinai monk Cosmas Indicopleustes in his influential *Topographica Christiana* interpreted supposed geographic passages in the Bible as literal "truths" and so placed Jerusalem at the geographic center of the world with the Sinai sites near to that center. By the eighth century, biblical commentaries were regularly illustrated by maps of the Beatus and Sallust types, which placed Sinai sites close to the central Holy City. From the tenth through the thirteenth centuries, world T-O maps (culminating in the detailed projections of Isidore of Seville, Henry of Mainz, Richard of Haldingham, and the creator of the Epsdorf world chart) regularly included triangular drawings of Mount Sinai on the sometimes-marked Exodus path leading through the Red Sea to Jerusalem at the center. This world iconography was disseminated in the thirteenth and fourteenth centuries by, among others, Italian Franciscans, who established chains of pilgrim hostels in the Holy Land, and by the international orders of knights. This biblical world iconography was also incorporated into Brunetto Latini's encyclopedic *Tresor,* mentioned by name in *Inf.* 15.119.

The elaborated T-O *mappaemundi* of the eighth and later centuries were flat projections with the land masses of Europe, Africa, and Asia—the then-known world—contained usually in a circle, but on occasion in an ellipse or even a rectangle, with the Garden of Eden at the top center of the circle at the farthest point east. Asia, harboring sites including Mount Sinai, the Dead Sea, and Jerusalem, was located in the upper half of the circle; Africa and the City of Babylon, modern Cairo, and the Nile River and Red Sea sites were in the lower right quadrant; and Europe containing Rome on the river Tiber was in the lower left quadrant. The medieval *Mare Internum,* the present Mediterranean Sea, divided the lower half of the circle in the form of an altarlike "T." The Pillars of Hercules—modern Gibralter in Europe and Abyla in Africa—which gave access to the Great Ocean surrounding the entire circular land mass, were situated in a low position at the base of the "T," while holy Jerusalem was placed, as might be expected, just above the "T" crossbar, near or at the spiritual-physical center of Earth's round land mass. The Holy City was in turn regularly drawn as a circle, bisected by two key streets in the form of a cross, nested within the wider circle of the world.

On the Hereford world map (c. 1285), which appears to have been in part based on earlier projections of routes to the Holy Land, the labyrinthine line of the Exodus leads from Babylon (modern Cairo) in the lower right African quadrant, across the Red Sea to the triangular drawing of Mount Sinai in the upper semicircle of Asia, and on in a winding manner past the Dead Sea to a terminus near Jerusalem at the middle. Mount Sinai, given its position on the Exodus pilgrimage route of spiritual "conversio," has for this and other figural reasons been suggested as an earthly type for Dante's Mount Purgatory.

In adapting this Latin-Byzantine medieval world perspective to the iconography of the *Commedia,* Dante—accepting a common medieval belief advocated by Brunetto Latini and others that Earth is a globe—can be seen to have depicted the circular land mass as bent like a concave shell over the Northern Hemisphere with Jerusalem at the center and summit, the "podes"; and the Great Ocean as extending over the convex Southern Hemisphere with Eden now an island at the bottom center, the "antipodes." Other places mentioned by Dante such as Rome, Gibraltar, and Exodus locales are in accord with their iconographic representation in early tracts, world icons, and the *Tresor* of Latini.

Bibliography

Armour, Peter. "Dante e l'*imago mundi* del primo Trecento." In *Dante e la scienza.* Edited by Patrick Boyde and Vittorio Russo. Ravenna: Longo, 1995, pp. 191–202.

Bagrow, Leo. *History of Cartography.* Revised by R. A. Skelton; translated by D. L. Palsey. Cambridge, Mass.: Harvard University Press, 1964.

Crone, G. R. *The Hereford World Map.* London: Royal Geographical Society, 1951.

Demaray, John G. *Dante and the Book of the Cosmos.* Philadelphia: American Philosophical Society, 1987.

Doob, Penelope Reed. *The Idea of the Labyrinth from Classical Antiquity through the Middle Ages.* Ithaca, N.Y., and London: Cornell University Press, 1960.

Fallani, Giovanni. *Dante e la cultura figurativa medievale.* Bergamo: Minerva italica, 1971.

Graf, Arturo. *La leggenda del Paradiso Terrestre.* Turin: E. Loescher, 1878.

Grant, Edward. *Planets, Stars, and Orbs: The Medieval Cosmos.* Cambridge: Cambridge University Press, 1994.

———. *A Source Book in Medieval Science.* Cambridge, Mass.: Harvard University Press, 1974.

Kaske, Carol V. "Mount Sinai and Dante's Mount Purgatory." *Dante Studies* 79 (1971), 1–18.

Kern, Hermann. *Labyrinthe.* Munich: Prestel-Verlag, 1982.

Moore, Edward. *Time-References in the Divina Commedia and Their Bearing on the Assumed Date and Duration of the Vision.* Oxford: D. Nutt, 1887.

———. "The Astronomy of Dante." In *Studies in Dante. Third Series: Miscellaneous Essays.* Oxford: Clarendon Press, 1903, pp. 1–108.

Latini, Brunetto. *Li Livres dou Tresor.* Edited by Francis J. Carmody. Berkeley, Los Angeles: University of California Press, 1948.

Orr, M. A. *Dante and the Early Astronomers.* London, Edinburgh: Gall and Inglis, 1913.

Revelli, Paolo. *L'Italia nella Divina Commedia.* Milan: Fratelli Treves, 1922.

John G. Demaray

Courtly Love

Dante defined his personality as an author by the "school of love poetry" of which he declared himself a member: *I' mi son un che, quando / Amor*

C *mi spira, noto, e a quel modo / ch'e' ditta dentro vo significando* ("I myself am one who, when Love breathes within me, take note, and to that measure which he dictates within, I go signifying," *Purg.* 24.52–54). He thus made love the center of his poetic inspiration and, given the context of the episode, somewhat polemically stated that the way he expressed his love experience was unique. Indeed, Dante's "theologized" love for Beatrice was undoubtedly a central experience and a novel one, which meant, first of all, that it distinguished itself not only from that of his Italian predecessors but also from the kind of love that had been "invented" and broadly diffused throughout medieval Europe by the great tradition of love poetry of the twelfth and thirteenth centuries, namely, that of the Provençal lyric in southern France and of the Old French romances in the north, chiefly those of Chrétien de Troyes and his successors.

This is largely what was later called "courtly love," to use the expression invented by the nineteenth-century French philologist Gaston Paris. This convenient term of reference is not easy to define, since it designates a variable phenomenon, individually circumstantiated in time and place, and even admitting of some broad contradictions. For the purpose of this discourse it may be expedient to begin by turning directly to how Dante dealt with the doctrine of love he received from his predecessors and what objections he raised to it. The first text that comes to mind is the celebrated episode of Paolo and Francesca in *Inf.* 5.

"Courtly love" was related to courtliness and to courtesy or courteousness—the former being a pattern of behavior for people living and acting at court, and the latter referring to a degree of "civilization" that refined interpersonal relations and made its practitioners worthy of being regarded as "noble" or "gentle." Dante identified courtliness *(curialitas)* and courtesy *(cortesia)* with virtue and moral dignity *(honestas): Cortesia e onestade è tutt'uno; e però che ne le corti anticamente le vertudi e li belli costumi s'usavano, sì come oggi s'usa lo contrario, si tolse quello vocabulo da le corti, e fu tanto a dire cortesia quanto uso di corte* ("Courtesy and dignity are one and the same; and because in the courts in times past virtue and fine manners were practiced, just as the contrary is now the case, this word was derived from courts and 'courtesy' was as much as to say 'the custom of the court,'" *Conv.* 2.10.7–8). In *DVE* 1.18.4 he specif-

ically defined *curialitas* as *librata regula eorum quae peragenda sunt*—a balanced rule of behavior and, hence, *mensura* or *ordo,* "measure" or "order." In portraying Francesca, however, he dealt quite differently with the refined type of "courtly love" that had flourished in medieval courts, condemning it as sinful and immoral. In this episode, the courtly literary example of the adulterous love between Lancelot and Queen Guinevere, derived from the prose romance of *Lancelot du Lac,* is introduced as a corrupting element that contributed to the adulterous lovers' fall and consequent human and divine punishment. Dante resolved the apparent conflict by embracing courtesy without the "adulterous" kind of love it had often postulated, and by grafting his own theologized, Beatrice-centered love onto the old-fashioned knightly kind of courtliness: see the episodes of Guglielmo Borsiere (*Inf.* 16) and Cacciaguida (*Par.* 15) for praises of the good court habits of times gone by.

Dante's stand was, in its unique way, the culmination of a revisionary process that had begun in the literature of northern France. Provençal troubadours had sung a form of love that, for all its individual variations (even considering its potential for self-denial in the name of a total dedication to an unreachable ideal of sublime perfection and purest beauty), was a profoundly secular form of self-gratification that flouted the received standards of Christian morality and the church's social and institutional demands of personal loyalty and fidelity within marriage. Love of a courtly nature was a form of self-assertion that was typical of the social status of (poor) knights at court, professing devotion to their lady as a substitute for their supporting lord. But in the north, Chrétien de Troyes had earnestly examined the moral issues that arose from a doctrine that always raised the question of possible conflict between dedication to a lady and dedication to a selfless life of knightly service to a king and society—even if it did not specifically postulate adultery, as apparently predicated in the famous *De amore* of Andreas Capellanus, as the only form of free, pure love beyond the performance of unfree, contractual, socially bound duties between spouses. After Chrétien, the thirteenth-century prose versions of the Arthurian romances (the only ones probably accessible to Dante)—most typically, the tale known as the *Queste del saint Graal,* or "Quest for the Holy Grail"—had systematically proposed an austere ideal of ascetic dedication to knighthood in search of spiritual perfection, climaxing in the triumph of Sir Galahad, the pure at heart, the only man fit enough to conquer the Grail, which had been denied even to the likes of Perceval, Gawain, and Lancelot. This type of chivalric career demanded complete transcendence of the erotic instincts. Dante's Beatrice was Dante's Grail.

Because the notion of courtly love is so extensive and in some of its aspects both vague and contradictory, it is useful to place Dante within precise parameters of the literary tradition that is usually covered by that term. In this sense it has been said that, while, as already suggested, he opposed and condemned the notion and practice of courtly love advocated or at least defined by Andreas Capellanus, Dante was part of the trend that was started by the first troubadour, William IX of Aquitaine. William IX was the first to place the relationship between the lover and the lady in terms of feudal vassalage, the lady being put on a pedestal of superior nobility that by its own nature increases the lover's nobility.

This paradigm had been absorbed by most of the Provençal and French lyrical poets, followed closely by the Germans and then the Italians. But the Italian lyrical schools, starting with the Sicilians, reduced the feudal connotations and shifted their matter to a level of metaphysical, moral, and psychological nobility. In particular, the school of Guinizzelli and the subsequent *stil nuovo* replaced the lady-lord (Provençal: *midons*) with the *donna-angelo,* the lady-angel who appears to lead to God. It was left for Dante to develop this theme to its most radical consequences by making Beatrice his guide to Paradise. Courtly love thus became theologically based love.

When compared with the way the lady had tended to be treated by the other Italian poets, it must be noted that—differently from the ladies of the Sicilians, the *stil nuovo*, and specifically Cavalcanti (monna Giovanna)—Beatrice is, indeed, a personification of the church and divine grace, even in a Christological light; but she is also endowed with a full-bodied human personality, far from being an evanescent symbol of total dedication and supreme, abstract beauty. The *Vita Nuova* already described her clearly as an earthly presence who affected the lover by the unparalleled beauty of her limbs, and this would be confirmed by Beatrice's own words about herself in the *Commedia*'s Earthly Paradise, where she spoke of her body as a unique masterpiece of nature. Despite its ostensible, exquisitely medieval references, this adaptation of courtly love prepared the way to the more realistic elements of Petrarch's Laura and the subsequent lyrical tradition.

Famous is Cino da Pistoia's canzone "Avegna ched el m'aggia piú per tempo," written to Dante in consolation for the death of Beatrice (1290). The consolatory arguments fit admirably with Dante's own transformation of courtly love psychology. Just as Dante had professed (also through Beatrice's mouth in the Earthly Paradise), that the lady had become worthier of being loved after dying, because then she had divested herself of her earthly imperfections and attained celestial beatitude, so does Cino suggest that Dante should rejoice at the prospect that Beatrice is now waiting to meet with him again in all her glory. This triumph of pure love, which comes to fruition in Dante's *Paradiso,* was darkly announced at the end of the *Vita Nuova,* and it marked the accomplished transition from the lady of courtly love, who ennobled the lover, to a Beatrice who literally and effectively guides Dante to God and Paradise through and after her own death—an apotheosis that is analogous to Christ's Resurrection and Ascension.

Bibliography

Boase, Roger. *The Origin and Meaning of Courtly Love.* Manchester: Manchester University Press; Totowa, N.J.: Rowman and Littlefield, 1977.

Busby, Keith, and Erik Kooper (eds.). *Courtly Literature: Culture and Context.* Papers from the 5th Triennial Congress of the International Courtly Literature Society, Dalfsen, The Netherlands, 1986. Amsterdam: John Benjamins, 1990.

De Robertis, Domenico. *Il libro della "Vita Nuova."* Florence: Sansoni, 1961.

Di Giovanni, Alberto. *La filosofia dell'amore nelle opere di Dante.* Rome: Abete, 1967.

Dragonetti, Roger. "Aux frontières du langage poétique (Études sur Dante, Mallarmé, Valéry)." *Romanica Gandensia* 9 (1961), 93–116.

Gilson, Étienne. *Dante et la philosophie.* 2nd ed. Paris: J. Vrin, 1953.

Kelly, F. Douglas. *Medieval Imagination: Rhetoric and the Poetry of Courtly Love.* Madison: University of Wisconsin Press, 1978.

Lo Cascio, Renzo. "Le nozioni di cortesia e nobiltà dai Provenzali a Dante." In *Atti del Convegno di Studi su Dante e la Magna Curia.* Palermo: Centro di Studi Filologici e Linguistici Siciliani, 1967.

Nardi, Bruno. *Saggi di filosofia dantesca.* 2nd ed. Florence: La Nuova Italia, 1967.

Poggioli, Renato. "Tragedy or Romance? A Reading of the Paolo and Francesca Episode in Dante's *Inferno.*" *PMLA* 22 (1957), 313–358.

Topsfield, L. T. *Troubadours and Love.* London, New York: Cambridge University Press, 1975.

Vallone, Aldo. *La "cortesia" dai Provenzali a Dante.* Palermo: Palumbo, 1950.

Aldo Scaglione

Crassus

Marcus Licinius Crassus, surnamed *Dives* ("the wealthy") because of his love of money, was consul with Pompey, 70 B.C.E., and triumvir with Caesar and Pompey in 60. He was defeated and beheaded by the Parthians. Their king, mocking his passion for wealth, poured molten gold down his throat. Dante includes Crassus *(Crasso)* among the examples of avarice in *Purg.* 20.116.

Molly G. Morrison

Croce, Benedetto

An Italian philosopher, statesman, critic, and literary historian, Benedetto Croce (1870–1952) is the dominant figure of modern Italian philosophy and one of the most significant estheticians of the twentieth century, influencing thinkers such as R. J. Collingwood, René Wellek, and John Crowe Ransom, as well as the work of the romance philologists Erich Auerbach, Leo Spitzer, Karl Vossler, and Ernst Robert Curtius. Croce was a prolific writer as well as the editor of the journal *La critica.* His collected works fill over sixty-seven volumes, ranging widely over philosophy, logic, aesthetics, economics, literary criticism, and history.

Influenced by the Hegelianism of the nineteenth-century Italian literary historian Francesco De Sanctis, which led to an extensive reexamination of Hegel, and the historicism of Giambattista Vico, Croce developed his esthetics as a foundation to a metaphysical idealism. In his 1902 book, *Estetica come scienza dell'espressione e linguistica generale* (translated in 1922 as *Aesthetics*) and the 1913 *Breviario di estetica* (translated in 1921 as *The Essence of Aesthetics*), and later in the 1928 *Aesthetica in nuce,* which appeared as the article "Aesthetics" in the fourteenth edition of the *Encyclopaedia Britannica,* Croce developed the doctrine that esthetic intuition was a primitive cognitive experience which occurs prior to any conceptual awareness or intellectual differentiation. This intuition is objectified into an expression representing a fundamental awareness that in turn becomes the basis of concepts and the distinction between the real and the unreal. Out of this Croce argues that all intuition is lyrical, understood as a nonconceptual communication expressing the underlying mood or emotion. Art, in turn, is an expression of the emotion. By "expression," Croce means not a romantic evocation but form given to the intuition: the work of art exists not in the object itself but in its ability to create and evoke the emotion and, thereby, the underlying intuition of the artist in the mind of the observer. In this regard all art is poetry—literally, that which puts things together. In *La poesia* (1936), Croce develops the implications of this doctrine. If art is an expression of the intuition, then those features attributed to art such as entertainment or moral instruction are not art. Indeed bad art represents a work artificially constructed out of rules or concepts rather than intuitions and therefore is devoid of emotion. Croce's esthetic theories shape his critical response to Dante.

Croce frequently refers to Dante in numerous articles on literature. His fullest treatment is found in *La poesia di Dante* (1921). On an esthetic level, he argues for the lyrical nature of Dante's poetry and how, in his greatest works, he achieves it. Much of his concern, however, is polemical, directed against those *Dantisti* who focus on the extrinsic or "allotrious" features rather than the poetic. Looked at from the perspective of its intellectual doctrines, the *Commedia* is merely a "theological romance." Dante's biography, Scholasticism, or other doctrines are external to the esthetic foundations of his work. If the poetic were related to the intellectual content or doctrine, then, as Croce observes, Aristotle's *Metaphysics* would be considered a great work of poetry. As a consequence of this, Croce rejects all allegorical readings of Dante, or any that focus on Dante's "moral geography"—the elaborate hierarchies of sins, sinners, and their relationship to the physical topography found in the *Commedia.* Dante, Croce argues, is simply not always clear or even consistent, and for the critic to fill in gaps or posit some intellectual framework falsifies the text. Similarly, while some biographical, historical, and philological interpretation is necessary to clarify ambiguities in Dante's words, it merely represents the substitution of one set of words for another and gets no closer to the underlying lyrical and emotional character of the poetry itself. As Croce notes in *La poesia,* when Dante describes the Sun, it is irrelevant whether he means a medieval or a modern sun. What Dante describes is Dante's sun, the product and expression of his poetic imagination. In summary, the poetic unity of the *Commedia* is not in its intellectual structure or theological doctrine but in the relationship and intensities among its lyric episodes.

Bibliography

Croce, Benedetto. "The Character and Unity of Dante's Poetry"; "Dante: The Concluding Canto of the *Commedia.*" In *Benedetto Croce: Essays on Literature and Literary Criticism.* Annotated and translated from the Italian with an Introduction by M. E. Moss. Albany: State University of New York Press, 1990, pp. 69–74, 208; 75–82, 209–210.

———. *The Poetry of Dante.* Translated by Douglas Ainslie. Mamaroneck, N.Y.: P. P. Appel, 1971.

Caserta, Ernesto G. "Croce critico di Dante." *Dante Studies* 106 (1988), 61–79.

Contini, Gianfranco. *L'influenza culturale di Benedetto Croce.* Milan, Naples: R. Ricciardi, 1967.

Moss, M. E. *Benedetto Croce Reconsidered.* Hanover: University Press of New England, 1987.

Orsini, Gian N. G. *Benedetto Croce: Philosopher of Art and Literary Critic.* Carbondale: Southern Illinois University Press, 1961.

Verdicchio, Massimo. "Croce Reader of Dante." *Dante Studies* 108 (1990), 97–112.

Wellek, René. *Four Critics.* Seattle: University of Washington Press, 1981.

Thomas L. Cooksey

Crusades

The fall of the City of Acre in 1291 brought an end to Christian rule in the Holy Land, but not to crusading enthusiasm. The crusade to the Holy Land continued to be the subject of discussions and plans, dreams and visions, and the next few decades saw a proliferation of treatises on its recuperation. In 1300 there was a widespread rumor that the Mongols had recaptured the Holy Land and had handed it over to the Christians: an inscription in Florence records the belief that Boniface VIII proclaimed the Jubilee as a response to the good news. Neither Boniface nor Benedict XI launched a Holy Land crusade: Clement V and John XXII were more committed, with the French monarchy the main focus of crusading plans. Throughout this period the accusation that the actions of a political foe were hindering a Holy Land crusade remained an important feature of polemical exchanges between Western powers.

Crusades continued to be waged in Italy itself, often with widespread support from the Guelf allies of the papacy. In 1297 Boniface VIII proclaimed a crusade against his personal enemies, the Colonna. The crusade against the Sicilians was renewed several times, until the treaty of Caltabellotta in 1302. Boniface consistently presented the defeat of the Sicilian rebels and the pacification of Italy by Charles of Valois as necessary prerequisites for a crusade to the east. The early fourteenth century saw further crusades in Italy: in 1306–1307, against the heretic Fra Dolcino and his "Apostolics"; in 1309, against the Venetians; and in 1321, against Ghibelline *signori.*

It would be fair to say that Dante's references to crusade in the *Commedia* have received little attention from commentators. For Dante, it would be the task of the Roman emperor to recover the Holy Land as a necessary part of the establishment of a worldwide Christian imperium, thereby "healing" the schism brought about by Muhammad and his followers. Indeed, Henry VII, upon whom Dante's political hopes rested until the emperor's untimely death, is recorded as being convinced that it was his eventual mission to liberate the Holy Land. However, the proclamation of a crusade, which involved the making available of spiritual benefits to those taking the cross, would be under the jurisdiction of the papacy. Without that proper exercising of the papacy's spiritual authority, a crusade could not take place: it would remain undifferentiated from secular warfare. Thus it is the papacy, not the secular powers, that bears the brunt of Dante's criticism for its neglect of the Holy Land.

In *Inf.* 27.87–90 Guido da Montefeltro criticizes Boniface VIII's crusade against the Colonna: *non con Saracin né con Giudei, / ché ciascun suo nimico era Cristiano, / e nessun era stato a vincer Acri / né mercatante in terra di Soldano* ("not against Saracens or Jews, for each of his enemies was a Christian, and none had been to conquer Acre, nor a merchant in the Sultan's land"). It is reasonable to take this passage to be an indication of Dante's own view concerning who constituted a legitimate crusade enemy: Saracens (the constructed and undifferentiated figure of the Muslim in Western medieval discourse), Jews, and Christians in some form of alliance with the Saracens. In naming the Jews as a legitimate enemy, Dante diverges from "official" crusading discourse, for the papacy consistently stressed that Jews should not be attacked by crusaders. However, the common presentation of crusade as an act of vengeance against the Saracens frequently led also to the crusaders' wreaking vengeance upon the Jews. In this passage Dante echoes the widespread condemnation of those Christians who continued to trade with the Saracens: the maintenance of economic sanctions against Egypt was thought to be vital to the success of any future crusade.

It would be wrong to infer from Dante's harsh judgment of the war on the Colonna that he similarly condemned all crusades proclaimed against heretics and schismatics. Indeed, Muhammad's warning to Fra Dolcino establishes a connection between the originary schismatic and the contemporary heretic (*Inf.* 28.55–60). Moreover, it has been argued that the wounds which Manfred still bears in the afterlife, inflicted at the hands of a crusading army led by Charles I of Anjou, signify the Hohenstaufen ruler's participation in the sin of schism (*Purg.* 3).

Dante chooses Folquet of Marseilles, a troubadour turned bishop, as mouthpiece for his fiercest condemnation of the papacy's lack of interest in the Holy Land (*Par.* 9.121–138). While a troubadour, Folquet had written three, possibly four crusade songs, but it is his ecclesiastical activities that more probably recommended him to Dante for such a role: as bishop of Toulouse, Folquet was one of the main preachers of the Albigensian crusade, waged against Cathar heretics in the Languedoc in the early thirteenth century. Folquet attacks the cupidity of the church's leaders, which causes them to forget Christ's homeland— their desire for *il maladetto fiore* ("the cursed flower," i.e., the florin) taking precedence over Nazareth, the town whose Hebrew name was conventionally interpreted to mean "flower."

The crusading theme of *Par.* 9 foreshadows that of the Heaven of Mars, which is populated by the souls of holy warriors and dominated by the

sign of the cross. Dante's ancestor Cacciaguida tells of how he, a knight in the army of Emperor Conrad III, followed the emperor on crusade against the Saracens, who still hold the Holy Land *per colpa d'i pastor* ("through the fault of your shepherds," *Par.* 15.139–144). It was on crusade that he died, *e venni dal martiro a questa pace* ("and I came from martyrdom to this peace," 148). Cacciaguida here refers to the indulgence promised to crusaders, which meant that if they confessed, were absolved, and died, they would be accorded the status of martyr and would go straight to Paradise, without first spending time in Purgatory. It is noteworthy, given the Francocentric crusading plans of his contemporaries, that Dante should present as his exemplary crusader a Florentine serving in the army of a Roman emperor. The heroes in the cross of Mars, whom Cacciaguida later points out to the pilgrim, reflect the use made in crusading discourse of Old Testament heroes, past crusaders, and, to a lesser extent, heroes of the *chansons de geste,* who fought Saracens in Spain, as exempla for later crusaders to follow (*Par.* 18.37–48).

Bibliography

Armour, Peter. *Dante's Griffin and the History of the World.* Oxford: Clarendon Press, 1989.

Balfour, Mark. "'Orribil furon li peccati miei': Manfred's Wounds in *Purgatorio* III." *Italian Studies* 68 (1993), 4–17.

Cardini, Franco (ed.). *Toscana e Terrasanta nel Medioevo.* Florence: Alinea, 1982.

Housley, Norman. *The Later Crusades, 1274–1580: From Lyons to Alcazar.* Oxford: Oxford University Press, 1992.

———. *The Avignon Papacy and the Crusades, 1305–1378.* Oxford: Clarendon Press, 1986.

———. *The Italian Crusades: The Papal-Angevin Alliance and the Crusades against Christian Lay Powers, 1254–1343.* Oxford: Clarendon Press, 1982.

Kedar, Benjamin Z. *Crusade and Mission. European Approaches toward the Muslims.* Princeton, N.J.: Princeton University Press, 1984.

Riley-Smith, Jonathan. *The Crusades: A Short History.* London: Athlone, 1987.

———. *What Were the Crusades?* London: Macmillan, 1977.

——— (ed.). *The Oxford Illustrated History of the Crusades.* Oxford, New York: Oxford University Press, 1995.

Schein, Sylvia. *Fideles Crucis: The Papacy, the West, and the Recovery of the Holy Land, 1274–1314.* Oxford: Clarendon Press, 1991.

———. "*Gesta Dei per Mongolos* 1300. The Genesis of a Non-Event." *English Historical Review* 94 (1979), 805–819.

Siberry, Elisabeth. *Criticism of Crusading, 1095–1274.* Oxford: Clarendon Press, 1985.

Mark Balfour

Cunizza da Romano

Youngest daughter of Ezzelino II and Adeleita dei Conti di Mangona, sister to Alberico of Treviso and Ezzelino III, who was born c. 1198. For political reasons she was married to Count Riccardo di San Bonifazio of Verona, a Guelf captain. However, when a liaison developed between her and Sordello (the Mantuan poet whom Dante encounters in Ante-Purgatory, *Purg.* 6:74), her brother Ezzelino had her abducted and brought back to Treviso. She then went to Alberico's court, where she entered an amorous relationship with the knight Bonio, with whom she traveled extensively. When Bonio was killed in a battle between Ezzelino and Alberico, the victorious Ezzelino wed her to Aimerio, count of Breganze. After the count's death, which resulted from a disagreement with Ezzelino, she married a Veronese—and later a fourth husband, Salione Buzzacarini of Padua, Ezzelino's astrologer. Around 1260, after the death of her brothers, she took up residence in Florence and granted freedom to all her father's and brothers' slaves who were not involved in the betrayal of Alberico. These emancipation documents were signed in the house of Cavalcante de' Cavalcanti (*Inf.* 10). In 1279, she drew up her will, in which she left her property to her nephews, the sons of Count Alessandro degli Alberti of Mangona. She died shortly thereafter in the same year.

Dante places her in the Heaven of Venus, the celestial realm of lovers. Commentators have stumbled over her placement here; however, Dante clearly finds redeeming her relentless pursuit of love. Her speech demonstrates her concern for Italy and her interest in politics, a rhetorical strategy which deliberately counters the neglect of such issues by the lustful condemned in *Inf.* 5. She forgives herself her past excesses, noting that they have brought her to salvation (*Par.* 9.34–36); Dante emphasizes her kindness and her rejoicing in her blessedness (23–24). She pairs herself geographically with her warring brother, of whose cruelty she was well aware, but then notes that she was vanquished by another source, Venus. Cunizza identifies the flame of the troubadour poet Folquet de Marseille and remarks on the importance of good fame. Her speech bears a prophetic tone regarding the war between Padua and Vicenza, the assassination of Riccardo da Camino, and Alessandro Novello's betrayal of Ferrara's Ghibellines. She concludes with a reference to the Thrones, the order of angels associated with justice.

Virginia Jewiss

Cupid

According to classical mythology, the son of Venus; the winged child armed with bow and arrows, also called Love (see *Conv.* 2.5.14), and representative of the carnal aspect (*Par.* 8.7). In his comparison of Matelda to Venus in the Earthly Paradise (*Purg.* 28.66), Dante recalls the mythological episode in which Venus fell in love with Adonis after one of Cupid's arrows accidentally struck her (*Meta.* 10.525ff.).

Ernesto Livorni

Cupidity

Cupidity (*cupidigia, cupidità; cupiditas* in Latin) is the excessive desire for earthly possessions, or covetousness, and as such, it stands as the opposite of charity, according to Augustine's distinction between *uti* and *frui*. It is one of the central motives of Dante's ethical polemics, and it is conceived by him as the chief source of evil in the world, a view that is consistent with the traditional medieval characterization of cupidity as the root of all evil: *cupiditas radix malorum est* (1 Tim. 6:10; and see, for example, *ST* 1.2.84.1). Dante's *Letter to the Italian Cardinals* provides a succinct statement of the opposition of cupidity and charity: *Cupiditatem unusquisque sibi duxit uxorem, quemadmodum et vos, que nunquam pietatis et equitatis, ut caritas, sed semper impietatis et iniquitatis est genitrix* ("Each one has taken avarice to wife, even as you yourselves have done; avarice, the mother never of piety and righteousness, but ever of impiety and unrighteousness," *Epist.* 11.14). In *Conv.* 4.12.6 Dante, citing Cicero (*Paradoxa stoicorum* 1.1.6), condemns the desire for wealth because acquisition only begets renewed desire to acquire yet more wealth: "For never is the thirst of cupidity satisfied or satiated." Dante's attack on cupidity here is designed to refute Frederick II's belief that *di gentilezza / sia principio ricchezza* ("riches are the source of nobility," *Conv.* 4, canzone 1.16–17). In *Mon.* 1.11.11–12 and passim Dante bolsters his argument in favor of a single universal ruler, a prince, on the basis that a prince would be immune to the seductive power of cupidity, since in being ruler of the world he would already possess all things and could not then suffer the need to desire to possess more.

In all cases the terms *cupidigia* and *cupidità* are virtually synonymous with the word *avarizia* ("avarice"). Hence it is this desire which motivates the *lupa* ("she-wolf") in *Inf.* 1.49 and the *antica lupa* of *Purg.* 20.10, underlies the evils engendered by the Donation of Constantine, and constitutes the essence of avarice as a sin punished in Hell (the fourth circle) and purged in Purgatory (the fifth terrace). Specific use of the terms for cupidity, however, is made in each of the three canticles, frequently in the rhetorical form of an apostrophe or an invective. In *Inf.* 12.49, cupidity is the source of violence in the murderers and plunderers: *Oh cieca cupidigia e ira folle* ("Oh blind cupidity and mad rage"). In *Purg.* 6.103–105, Sordello inveighs against the thirst for power and possession that drove Emperor Albert and his father, Emperor Rudolph I of Habsburg, to ruin Italy: *Ch'avete tu e 'l tuo padre sofferto, / per cupidigia di costà distretti, / che 'l giardin de lo 'mperio sia diserto* ("For you and your father, held by your avarice up there, have suffered the garden of the empire to be laid waste"). In *Par.* 27.121–123, Beatrice inveighs against cupidity as a form of blindness: *La cieca cupidigia che v'ammalia / simili fatti v'ha al fantolino / che muor per fame e caccia via la balia* ("The blind greed that bewitches you has made you like the little child that is dying of hunger but drives away his wet-nurse"). (Dante frequently links cupidity to blindness: see, for example, *O mira cupidine obcecati*—"Oh you blinded by wondrous greed," *Epist.* 6.12.) And in *Par.* 30.139–141, Beatrice reiterates her attack on blind cupidity in her praise of Emperor Henry VII, who succeeded Albert I of Austria: *Oh cupidigia, che i mortali affonde / sì sotto te, che nessuno ha podere / di trarre li occhi fuor de le tue onde!* ("Oh greed, that so submerge mortals that none has the power to raise his eyes above your waves!"). Just as the destruction of the *lupa* of *Inf.* 1 will require the advent of the *veltro* ("greyhound"), so will universal greed require a universal savior, in the person of Henry. Dante had great hopes for the emperor, but they were cut short by his unexpected death near Siena, in 1313. Dante clearly sees Henry as the adversary of cupidity and greed, for Henry's opponent, Clement V, whose fate is referred to in the verses that follow (*Par.* 30.142–148), is destined to join Boniface VIII among the simonists in Hell.

Ernesto Livorni

Curio

First a follower of Pompey and later an adherent of Caesar in the civil war against the Roman republic, Gaius Scribonius Curio (*Curio* or *Curione*) is damned among the schismatics in the ninth bolgia of Malebolge (*Inf.* 28.96), where fellow schismatic Pier da Medicina points him out to Dante, observing that Curio urged Caesar to cross the Rubicon and attack Rome. Dante's source for this scene is *Phars.* 1.269ff. In the *Letter to the Emperor Henry VII* (*Epist.* 7.16), Dante borrows from the same passage in exhorting Henry to enter Tuscany, using words echoing Curio's entreaty to Caesar not to delay his advance.

Richard Lansing

Curius

Curius Manius Dentatus *(Curio)*, a model of Roman civic virtue known especially for his indifference to wealth, is cited in *Conv.* 4.5.13. Consul in 290 and in 275 B.C.E., and censor in 272, he declined monetary gifts from the Samnites, saying that he would rather rule over those who owned gold than own it himself (Cicero, *De senectute* 6.15; Valerius Maximus, *Factorum et dictorum inemorabilium libri novem,* 4.3.5).

Leslie Zarker Morgan

Currado da Palazzo

A noble Guelf from Brescia, praised by Marco Lombardo, along with Gherardo da Camino and Guido da Castello, for his great virtue as a leader (*Purg.* 16.124). In 1276 he served as vicar to Charles I of Anjou in Florence, was captain of the Guelfs there until 1277, and became, in 1288, the podestà (chief magistrate) of Piacenza.

Richard Lansing

Curtius, Ernst Robert

Born in Thann, Alsace, Curtius (1886–1956) studied with the distinguished German medievalist Gustav Gröber, who steered him toward philological studies. Curtius's academic career took him from Bonn to Marburg to Heidelberg and back to Bonn. His interest in Dante was directed in the first instance toward the theological background of the poet's ethical and philosophical commitment, as well as the medieval Latin sources of his culture. Dante's rhetorical approach to poetry is at the center of the 1948 classic (and controversial) *Europäische Literatur und lateinischen Mittelalter* (*European Literature and the Latin Middle Ages,* translated into English by Willard Trask, 1953)—the critic's crowning achievement and a sort of compendium of his research. A number of its chapters are dedicated to the ways Dante revives the *topoi* of medieval Latin literature and to his mentality as a man of the Middle Ages. Particularly noteworthy are his symbolic-descriptive analysis of Dante's use of the notion of the "Book of Memory" from the *Vita Nuova* to the *Commedia,* and his account of the evolving generational stances that led readers, from the Weimar classicists to the Pre-Raphaelites, to see Dante as a poet at once problematic and irreplaceable. Curtius maintains a skeptical attitude toward Auerbach's "figural" interpretation. He is not convinced, for example, by the parallel drawn by Auerbach between Dante's figural approach and the Christian evangelical heritage of the *sermo humilis* (sermons preached to the people). For Curtius, a classical author like Cicero had already evolved techniques that go far beyond the "separation of styles."

Bibliography

Della Terza, Dante. "E. R. C." *Belfagor* 22 (1967), 166–185.

Petronio, Giuseppe. "E. R. C. o la critica del luogo comune." *Società* 14 (1958), 781–799.

Rizzo, Gino. "Valore e limiti del contributo di E. R. C. agli studi danteschi." *Italica* 37 (1960), 277–286.

Dante Della Terza

Cyrus

Founder of the Persian Empire, Cyrus (*Ciro*) was slain by the Massegetae, whose queen, Tomyris, according to Orosius (*Hist.* 2.7.6), mocked his decapitated head with the words paraphrased by Dante in *Purg.* 12.57: *Sangue sitisti, e io di sangue t'empio* ("You have thirsted for blood, and with blood I will fill you"). An exemplum of pride sculpted on the marble pavement of the first terrace in *Purgatorio,* Ciro is punished for his refusal to release Tomyris' son from prison and choosing instead to kill him. He is also mentioned in *Mon.* 2.8.6, as the third ruler to attempt to conquer the world—a mission, in Dante's view, destined to be accomplished according to providential design by the Romans.

Jessica Levenstein

D

Dalí, Salvador

Spanish painter born in Figueras (1904–1989). Before Dalí affiliated himself with the Paris Surrealists in 1929, his early influences included Italian Futurism, Cubism, and the Italian "Metaphysical Painters" like de Chirico and Carrà with their opposition to Futurist machine fascination and their stress on incantation and inner perception. Although Dalí disavowed the Metaphysical school around 1950, as he did abstract art in favor of more objective representation, some tenets of his earlier influences remained with him. But the sense of the hallucinatory and the oneiric—dreams flowing from the subconscious—and its Freudian implications (he met Freud in 1939) became the hallmark of his esthetic, which he distinguished with superb draftsmanship, an impeccable sense of color, and a private vocabulary of iconographical devices. Among these appear crutches, bones, insects, an eerie lyrical light, cannibalistic and mandibular emphases, elongations, fatty roundnesses, and grotesque juxtapositions (especially involving the female bosom).

This manner fits Dante's poem well, to the extent that it has dream-vision qualities, and its first canticle may be described as a nightmare. From 1951 to 1952, Dalí issued a series of 100 lithographs, one for each canto, ranging from sketches and anatomical exercises to watercolor figures and scenes. A portfolio containing plates and text was issued in 1954, and in 1960, under the auspices of Joseph Forêt, the entire series of woodblock prints appeared in Paris as *La divine Comédie*. The artistic style changes from one canticle to the next: on balance, the *Inferno* is surrealistic, the *Purgatorio* expressionistic, and the *Paradiso* more along the lines of traditional religious iconography. The movement is from what is warped, to what is palpable, to what is ideal.

Dalí's true oneiric style is most apparent in the *Inferno*. At first it may seem that, in the *Inferno* particularly, Dalí sets up his own fantastic world, giving free play to his delight in chance effect, disorder, and random sequence (indeed, were it not for his own titles, some illustrations might seem better suited to different cantos). Ultimately, however, he does not subvert the text. For example, crutches (symbols of social weakness and vulnerability) may appear out of place in Dante, but they relate both to the failings of blasphemers and flatterers (*Inf.* 14, 18), and to the arduousness of Purgatory's ascent (*Purg.* 7). Similar associative cases may be made for the bone theme in relation to Limbo (*Inf.* 4), cannibalism in relation to Lucifer (*Inf.* 34), and even the very geological surroundings of the grafters (*Inf.* 22). The presentation is diversified. Often, through the use of recessive planes, an eerie lyrical light works technically to produce sharply lucid details and spiritually to impart a sense of estrangement or existential loneliness (*Inf.* 1, 32 [Antenora]). In these images Dalí's manner becomes expressionistic. Elsewhere it can be strictly classical and academic: Farinata and Cacus the Centaur (*Inf.* 10, 25); the ascent, the Angel of Mercy, and the Siren (*Purg.* 4, 15, 19); or the Cross of Mars, St. Peter, and the Archangel Gabriel (*Par.* 14, 27, 32).

Not surprisingly, his *Inferno* has attracted the greatest degree of attention. Hell, said Dalí, represents a psychic disturbance, a "paranoiac" process of thought by which "irrational knowledge" leads to the "dreamed itinerary of paranoic phenomena." Here one might put the sowers of discord or the sodomites (*Inf.* 28, 15–16). Orality and suggestions of mandibular activity may be discerned in *Inf.* 11 (the topography of Hell) and in the Gianni Schicchi and Lucifer cantos (*Inf.* 30, 34); sexuality, with appurtenant scrota and penises, may be discerned in the cantos of Charon, Minos, the hoarders, and Manto (*Inf.* 3, 5, 7, 20). Only rarely do such motifs appear in *Purgatorio* (the violently dead of 5, the Angel Guardian of 9, or the prodigal of 22). And, of course, no phallic, crutched, oral, osseous, or cannibalistic motifs appear in *Paradiso,* which is airy, serene, meditative, and imbued with a genuine Christian spirit.

All in all, there is more evocation than description in Dalí's renderings. They present three different modes which are in their own perhaps eccentric way perfectly consistent with the modes of the text. Nevertheless he has managed to create a cohesiveness out of these disparate styles of representation.

Bibliography

Alighieri, Dante. *La divine Comédie.* Translated by Julien Brizeux. Illustrated by Salvador Dalí. Paris: Éditions d'Art les Heures Claires, 1959–1963.

———. *La divina commedia.* Illustrated by Salvador Dalí. Rome: Arti e Scienze; Florence: Salani, 1963.

Forêt, Joseph. *Illustrations pour La divine Comédie.* Paris: 1960.

Isteni szinjatek. Salvador Dalí festmenyeivel. Budapest: Helikon Kiado, 1987.

Jean-Pierre Barricelli

Damian, St. Peter

Bishop and church reformer (1007–1072). Orphaned at a young age, Peter Damian *(Pietro Damiano)* came under the guardianship of his brother Damian and thenceforth assumed his brother's name. After studying in Faenza and Parma and teaching rhetoric in Ravenna, he entered the monastery at Fonte Avellana, which observed an austere variation of the Benedictine Rule introduced by St. Romauld (referred to by St. Benedict in *Par.* 22.49). In 1043 he was elected prior and undertook needed reforms and improvements at the monastery, including an expansion of its library.

During this time Peter Damian became involved in the workings of the papal curia. He wrote tracts condemning its excesses and called for a renewal of both lay and clerical spirituality. In 1057 Pope Stephen IX appointed him cardinal bishop of Ostia, a post which he accepted only reluctantly. In that position Peter Damian continued to fight for reform, addressing such issues as the married clergy and simony.

His writings consist of 180 letters, some of which have been treated separately as short books or treatises. A few of his notable works are the *Book of Gomorrah,* a treatise against sodomy; *Liber gratissimus,* in which he argues for the validity of the ordinations of simoniacal clerics; *On Divine Omnipotence,* addressed to Abbot Desiderius and the monks at Monte Cassino; and *Dominus vobiscum,* in which he makes use of the image of the ladder of contemplation.

The image of the ladder is likewise deployed by Dante in the Heaven of Saturn, where Peter Damian and the rest of the contemplatives appear. The saint's conversation with the pilgrim centers on three topics: the silence of the seventh heaven, the mysterious nature of predestination, and Peter Damian's description of his life and his denunciation of the corruption of the clergy.

Much critical attention has been paid to *Par.* 21.121-123: *"In quel loco fu' io Pietro Damiano, / e Pietro Peccator fu' ne la casa / di Nostra Donna in sul lito adriano"* ("In that place was I Peter Damian, and I was Peter the Sinner in the house of Our Lady on the Adriatic shore"). The difficulty stems from the ambiguity of the verb *fu'* in verse 122, which could be either first or third person. The consensus of critical opinion now tends to support reading the verb as first person, as in the above translation.

Bibliography

Damian, Peter. *Letters.* Translated by Owen J. Blum. The Fathers of the Church, Mediaeval Continuation, vols. 1–3. Washington, D.C.: The Catholic University of America Press, 1989–1992.

———. *Book of Gomorrah. An Eleventh-Century Treatise against Clerical Homosexual Practices.* Translated by Pierre J. Payer. Waterloo, Ont.: Wilfrid Laurier University Press, 1982.

Barbi, Michele. "Pier Damiano e Pietro Peccatore." In *Con Dante e coi suoi interpreti.* Florence: Felice Le Monnier, 1941, pp. 255–296.

Blum, Owen J. *St. Peter Damian: His Teaching on the Spiritual Life.* Washington, D.C.: The Catholic University of America Press, 1947.

Dressler, Fridolin. *Petrus Damiani: Leben und Werk.* Rome: Herder, 1954.

Hawkins, Peter. "Dante's Lesson of Silence: *Paradiso* 21." *Lectura Dantis* 11 (1992), 42–51.

Leclercq, Jean. *Saint Pierre Damien: Ermite et homme d'église.* Uomini e dottrine 8. Rome: Edizioni di Storia e Letteratura, 1960.

Resnick, Irven Michael. *Divine Power and Possibility in St. Peter Damian's* De Divina Omnipotentia. Leiden: E. J. Brill, 1992.

George Andrew Trone

Daniel

One of the noble young Israelites exiled to Babylon (605 B.C.E.), Daniel *(Daniele, Danïello)* is named by a voice from the inverted tree on the sixth terrace of Purgatory as an example of temperance (*Purg.* 22.146–147). Having refused the rich food and wine offered to him from King Nebuchadnezzar's table in favor of vegetables and water, Daniel received wisdom and learning from God, as well as the understanding of visions and dreams (Dan. 1:8–17). Beatrice's response to Dante's unspoken questioning (*Par.* 4.13–15) is compared with Daniel's revelation and interpretation of Nebuchadnezzar's forgotten dream (Dan. 2:1–45). Virgil's description of the Old Man of Crete (*Inf.* 14.106–110) makes allusion to Daniel's delineation of the "great image" in this dream (Dan. 2:32–33). In *Par.* 29.133–135, Beatrice alludes to Daniel's phrase, "a thousand thousands served him, / and ten thousand times ten / thousand stood before him" (Dan. 7:10), as evidence of the innumerability of the angels. In *Mon.* 3.1.1, 3, the example of Daniel's response to King Darius from the lion's den (Dan. 6:22) gives Dante courage to speak the truth in spite of his detractors.

Carolynn Lund-Mead

Daniello, Bernardino

Born in Lucca in the early years of the sixteenth century, Daniello ranks fourth both in fame and reputation (after Landino, Vellutello, and Castelvetro) among the major Renaissance commentators of Dante's *Commedia.* His commentary, entitled *Dante con l'espositione . . . sopra la sua Comedia,* was published posthumously in 1568 and represents the climax of a lifetime devoted to letters: vernacular poetry (he was the author of a body of now-forgotten sonnets and canzoni); poetics (*Della Poetica,* 1536); translation (*La Georgica di Virgilio,* 1545); and commentary (*Sonetti, canzoni e triomphi di F. Petrarca,* 1541). Daniello's text is heavily dependent on that of his teacher Trifone Gabriele, to the point that its originality has sometimes been called into question. Nonetheless, his work as a Dante scholar has gained special recognition in the Anglo-American context because of the fact that it was known to the great seventeenth-century English poet John Milton, author of *Paradise Lost.*

Bibliography

L'espositione di Bernardino Daniello da Lucca sopra la Comedia di Dante. Edited by Robert Hollander and Jeffrey Schnapp, with Kevin Brownlee and Nancy Vickers. Hanover, N.H., and London: University Press of New England, 1989.

Parker, Deborah. "Beyond Plagiarism: New Perspectives on Bernardino Daniello's Debt to Trifone Gabriele." *MLN* 104.1 (1989), 209–218.

———. "Bernardino Daniello and the Commentary Tradition." *Dante Studies* 106 (1988), 111–121.

Jeffrey T. Schnapp

Dante and Film

The *Commedia* is, to use a term coined by John Fiske (95), a "producerly" text that simultaneously encapsulates characteristics both readerly (it has great popular appeal and is an easy read) and writerly (it is designed for the refined reader and can be read as multiple, difficult, and self-reflexive). Consequently it appeals to the widest possible audience, and therefore it is highly appropriate that this producerly quality has been manipulated by cinema throughout its history and that this has resulted in myriad diverse cinematic treatments, running the gamut from high-brow, artistic attempts to capture the classical status of Dante's poem to more popular forms of cinematic incorporation, such as adapted reuse and downright parody.

Early Silent Films (1895 to the Mid-1920s)

Early silent-film makers, both in Italy and abroad, made extensive use of Dante's poem. They appreciated that its particular material—its episodically arranged and compellingly dramatic stories—was ideal for their cinematic purposes: the dramatic and often cinematically novel retelling of a classic tale in a few brief scenes aimed at the widest possible audience. In addition, they desired to legitimize the new medium of cinema by anchoring it in one of the seminal works of literature. Silent-film treatments of the Dantean material took one of three forms.

First, a number of individual episodes from the *Commedia* were filmed as part of a cinematic cultural series. In the United States, for example, one of the most important pre-Hollywood companies, Vitagraph, included among its "quality films" the release of *Francesca da Rimini* (1908), a film reflecting the American Dante craze that existed at the turn of the century; it has obvious similarities with the popular theatrical treatment of the Francesca story during the same period (see Uricchio and Pearson, 95ff.). In Italy the so-called *cinema d'arte* used Dante as one of its mainstays; favorite episodes were those of Pia de' Tolomei (filmed by Casini, 1908; Lo Savio, 1910; Zannini, 1921; and Volpe and Dalbani, 1922); Count Ugolino (Liguoro, 1909); and Francesca da Rimini (Morais, 1908; Falena, 1910).

Second, there were more audacious and exclusively Italian attempts to film an entire canticle. Most notable among these early holistic treatments is the *Inferno* of Milano Films (1911), directed by Francesco Bertolini and Adolfo Padovan with the participation of Giuseppe di Liguoro. Deliberately high-brow, the film progresses in linear fashion from the pilgrim's meeting with Virgil and descent into the underworld to their reemergence into the starry sky at the end of the *Inferno*. The film displays a high degree of technical sophistication. Its hand-tinted images were inspired by the engravings of Gustave Doré, as was its use of light, and a hand-held camera led to a proliferation of new camera angles and trick shots that were accompanied by state-of-the-art special effects. The film achieved great popularity both in Italy and abroad, although Milano only produced an *Inferno*. The Helios of Velletri, which also released an *Inferno* in the same year, produced a *Purgatorio* as well. Two other smaller, more scholarly film houses, Torino's Società Anonima Ambrosio and Rome's Psiche, produced more high-brow if very limited treatments of *Purgatorio* and *Paradiso* in 1911 and 1912 respectively; the latter was scripted by Giovanni Pettine. More in keeping with popular presentation were Franco Liberati's comedy of the *Inferno,* produced in 1914, and the German *Inferno* of the Austrian director Paul Czinner (1920), entitled *Das Spiel mit dem Teufel.*

Third, early silent cinema turned to Dante for cinematic incorporation of his life set against the historical and political reality of his times. The two best examples are Luigi Sapelli's *La mirabile visione* (1921) and Domenico Gaido's *Dante nella vita dei tempi suoi* (1922). Both films were produced to celebrate the six-hundredth anniversary of the death of Dante; both were historical in nature; and both, because of their great political themes, were immediately adopted by the fascist regime, accorded cult status, and introduced into the curricula of universities and schools. Of the two films, Gaido's is the more dramatically engaging. Here Dante's life unfolds against a backdrop of political intrigue and romantic tragedy, and his poetry is interpreted primarily along autobiographical lines.

Late Silent Cinema and the Advent of Sound: Mid-1920s through the Postwar Period

In this period one detects a marked shift in the way in which Dante's *Commedia* is used cinematographically. To be sure, there is continuing preoccupation with filming individual episodes, especially the tragic ones, as can be seen in the examples of the sound versions of *Pia de' Tolomei* (1941, reissued in 1958), *Il Conte Ugolino* (1949), and *Paolo e Francesca* (1949, reissued in 1971). But the striving after artistically conceived film versions of episodes and whole canticles along deliberately high-brow lines comes to a decisive close. In its place, the Dantean material does not so much stand on its own but now is inserted into a script aimed at a popular audience and becomes the frame for the main unfolding of the film. This is done for two reasons: to confer moralistic purpose on the story line, and to introduce parody into the Dantean material.

We see the moralizing impulse prominently at work in Henry Otto's *Dante's Inferno* (1924), the product of America's Fox Film Corporation. Here the staging of the Dantean *Inferno* according to the illustrations of Doré is used as a backdrop to a contemporary story which concerns the unscrupulous workings of Mortimer Judd, a millionaire who is responsible for the financial ruin of Eugene Craig. Craig pens his own curse in a copy of the *Inferno* ("If there is Hell, this, my curse, will take you there") and sends it to Judd, who takes up reading it and so enters a lengthy dream, at the center of which is the Dantean vision of Hell. The journey through the underworld is telescoped into select scenes, and everything associated with it, especially its punishments, is put to moralistic use to remind the millionaire that his wicked ways will lead him to perdition if he does not reform. The kind of moralizing exemplified in Otto's *Inferno* was taken up anew in the sound era with the 1935 production of 20th Century Fox's *Dante's Inferno,* a film directed by Harry Lachman. Like Otto's, it is a modern morality play depicting the story of the ruthlessly ambitious Jim Carter (Spencer Tracy), who inherits a fairground concession known as "Dante's Inferno." He brings about its eventual collapse, escapes prosecution on charges of perjured testimony, and then turns his efforts to establishing a floating pleasure palace laden with sin and shameless revelry. But when the pleasure palace becomes engulfed in flames, Carter heroically saves as many passengers as he can and comes to realize as a consequence that money isn't everything. Once again, the Dantean material serves as the moralizing adhesive that holds together the entire narrative.

In addition to inculcating a moral principle, the Dantean material is also used throughout this period as a vehicle for parody. In both cases an added incentive to incorporate Dante lies in the *Commedia*'s power to inspire creative use of state-of-the-art special effects. One example is Guido Brignone's *Maciste all'Inferno* (1926). Maciste was brought to life as a character in Giovanni Pastrone's *Cabiria.* On the strength of that film and many others that followed, he became ingrained in the popular imagination as a mythological hero of great prowess, the proverbial breaker of chains. It is his value as a creature of parody, however, that Brignone exploits. Maciste, portrayed by Bartolomeo Pagano, the docker from Genoa whom Pastrone had groomed for the same role in *Cabiria,* accentuates the role's comedic possibilities. His underworld transformation is one of the comic highlights of the film and constitutes—in what was to become the mainstay of the *cinema popolare* of the late 1920s to the late 1940s—a parody of everything held sacred, both in this world and in the world beyond. The original *Maciste* was rereleased in 1940 in a sound version and again enjoyed great popularity. The 1962 full-sound remake by director Riccardo Freda was, however, nothing more than a cheap melodrama.

It would be left to another popular cinematic icon, a comic of unsurpassable genius, to leave his mark on the Dantean material during the period of Italian cinema immediately after the war. Antonio de Curtis, alias Totò, was one of the most popular comic actors of Italy in the 1940s and 1950s, and his comedic talents served as the basis for a series of Totò adventures. Two of these are Mario Matoli's *Totò al giro d'Italia* (1948) and Camillo Mastrocinque's *Totò all'Inferno* (1954). The plot lines of both films are downright silly and are a far cry from the early silent cinema's attempt to present Dante along artistically engaging lines. Now Dante and his material have become marginalized and serve as the cinematic backdrop for the display of Totò's comedic gifts. But however secondary, Dante and his text still provide the impetus for these cinematic comic retellings or incorporations. These films, in turn, not only reinforce the broad popular appeal of Dante and his text in Italy but also highlight the prominence that Dante retained in postwar Italian culture.

Modern Cinema: From the Postwar Period to the Present

Throughout this period the principal means of incorporating Dante into film is cinematic allusion. On occasion the allusion is visible throughout a director's entire cinematic career; in other cases it is limited to one or a few movies by a particular director. Among the directors whose preoccupation with Dante spanned an entire career are Federico Fellini and Pier Paolo Pasolini, and, outside Italy, the experimental British director Peter Greenaway.

It can be said that without Dante, there would have been no Fellini. His entire cinematic output reveals him as an avid appropriator of Dantean ideas. For example, the opening shot of *8½* admirably translates the idea of an infernal journey into the cinematographic terms of the protagonist's being gridlocked in a traffic jam. The salvific power of the pure and innocent female figure, echoing Beatrice, appears in numerous films, including *La strada,* which portrays the sacrificial love of Gelsomina for Zampano, who fails to respond to that love until too late. Many critics have suggested that Fellini's characteristic preoccupation with grotesque and hellish characters derives from Dante, a perception that Fellini himself validated in *Block-Notes di un regista.*

In a similar vein, Pasolini appropriated Dante in a holistic manner for reasons of cinematic structure. In his first film, *Accattone,* the sordid world of the Roman *borgate* is modeled on the Dantean vision of the netherworld *bolgias,* as is the spiral descent of the film's hero, whose spiritual and physical death are mirrored in the film's opening quotation from *Purg.* 5. In his last film, *Salò,* Pasolini employs the structure of the *Inferno,* beginning with an Ante-Inferno and proceeding through three circles of perversions, excrement, and blood, where cruel punishments are meted out to the hapless victims of Salò's hellish villa.

Peter Greenaway has based many of his ideas on Dante and his world. Two of his early films, *The Draughtsman's Contract* and *Drowning By Numbers,* are overtly Dantean: the first is concerned with the fine art of depicting reality and the elusive power of the imagination, while the second shares Dante's preoccupation with numerology. In his *A TV Dante Cantos 1–8,* the depiction of the science of numbers is likewise important, but the two most fundamental themes concern the power and sacredness of the *Commedia* as written word or text, and the power and sacredness of the individual imagination's response to it. For this reason Greenaway not only includes in his filming of the first eight cantos of the *Inferno* numerous examples of words and text, but he also employs multiple experimental filming techniques, from pictures within pictures to juxtaposition of images suggestive of every conceivable time period and intellectual discipline. Greenaway thus underscores the power of Dante's text *qua* text and invites his audience through his often lurid and violent images to respond to the writerly quality of Dante's poem—a quality that compels the individual's imagination to participate in the discovery of meaning.

More limited cinematic allusion to Dante has been employed selectively throughout the modern era to promote characterization (as in William Dieterle's *The Devil and Daniel Webster*), plot development (as in the sinister *Inferno* of Dario Argento), or background environment and tone (as in Ken Russell's *The Devils*). Moreover, Dante has served as the basis of a host of experimental films, including *Dante's Inferno* of Ken Russell (1968), *Cants from Natural History Works* of Gary Adkins (1975), *The Dante Quartet* of Stan Brakhage (1987), and *Paradiso/Dante's Dream* of David E. Simpson (1990). In Hollywood since the 1970s, the fascination with Dante's world has increased to become a major source of cinematic allusion for directors as diverse as Martin Scorsese *(Taxi Driver),* Francis Ford Coppola *(Apocalypse Now),* Alan Parker *(Angel Heart),* Tim Burton *(Batman),* and David Lynch *(Blue Velvet);* all of these, especially Lynch, have employed Dantean ideas and images to energize their particular cinematic visions. Most recently, cinematic allusion has become less structured and more approximate in Hollywood's hands. In David Fincher's *Seven,* for example, Dante and his presentation of the seven deadly sins are used in a facile manner as the source for unraveling a gruesome series of murders. In *Dante's Peak* the engagement of Dante is even more casual: the film reverses the poem and its structure by beginning with an idyllic Edenic scene that is transformed into a raging Inferno, although the movie still manages to achieve a happy ending.

Conclusion

The polysemous text of Dante's *Commedia* has been a fundamental source throughout the history of cinema. Filmmakers have turned repeatedly to Dante for cinematic ideas and images, and for visual assistance in recreating the vastness and hypnotic spell of Dante's world in all of its myriad complexity. The title Gian Piero Brunetta (see Casadio, 21–28) assigns to his survey of the importance of Dante for cinema seems especially apt: *Padre Dante che sei nel cinema* ("Father Dante, who art in film").

Bibliography

Barbina, Alfredo. "Cinema." *Enciclopedia dantesca,* 2:4–5.

Bernardini, Aldo. *Cinema muto italiano.* 3 vols. Bari: Laterza, 1980–1982.

Casadio, Gianfranco (ed.). *Dante nel cinema.* Ravenna: Longo, 1995.

Fiske, John. *Television Culture.* London: Methuen, 1987.

Iannucci, Amilcare A. "Dante, Television and Education." *Quaderni d'Italianistica* 10 (1989), 1–33.

Uricchio, William, and Roberta E. Pearson. *Reframing Culture: The Case of the Vitagraph Quality Films.* Princeton, N.J.: Princeton University Press, 1993.

Vickers, Nancy J. "Dante in the Video Decade." In *Dante Now: Current Trends in Dante Studies.* Edited by Theodore J. Cachey. Notre Dame, Ind.: University of Notre Dame Press, 1995, pp. 263–276.

Welle, John P. "Dante in the Cinematic Mode: An Historical Survey of Dante Movies." In *Dante's*

D

Inferno: The Indiana Critical Edition. Translated and edited by Mark Musa. Bloomington: Indiana University Press, 1995, pp. 381–395.

Amilcare A. Iannucci

Dante and the Arts

Dante's years fall squarely inside the 400–year span usually attributed to Gothic art, primarily in its architectural manifestation (for which the term was coined), although the age of the great cathedrals, 1150 to 1250, just preceded him. The designation "Gothic," however, applies largely to Europe outside Italy, if one thinks of St.-Denis and Notre Dame (Paris), Chartres, Amiens, Reims, St. Urbain (Troyes), St. Maclou (Rouen), Salisbury, Gloucester, and Nuremberg's St. Sebald. Italian Gothic demands a category apart because it is not a continuation of the Romanesque. The brighter Mediterranean tradition stood strong, even in the twelfth century. The Cistercian austerity of the Abbey Church at Fossanova (1208) may relate superficially to Burgundian or English Gothic, and Dante's sensitivity to St. Francis may well have brought him to appreciate its simplicity; but with equal openness of spirit he was drawn to the more emotional Arnolfo di Cambio's Santa Croce (1296), a seminal example of Mediterranean Gothic. From there, the step to the lightness of Lorenzo Maitani's Orvieto Cathedral (1310)—where on the fourth facade pillar is sculpted a Dantean scene of Hell—seems predictable. But secular buildings, like Florence's Palazzo Vecchio (begun 1298), reflect a darker, fortress-like need for defense in the strife-riddled life of the city-states—something to which Dante the politician and exile was particularly sensitive.

Sculpture naturally accompanied architecture, and if there was severe Gothic, it was to be found in German Emperor Frederick II's south, though he encouraged Classic tendencies. The southerner Nicola Pisano, who settled in Florence around 1250 and completed the Pisa Baptistry five years before Dante was born, inherited this taste. As Dante may be called a medieval classicist, so may Pisano. Half a century later, as Dante approached his writing of the *Commedia,* Nicola's son Giovanni created the marble pulpit (1302–1310) of Pisa's cathedral in a more elegantly flowing style. His *Madonna* (c. 1315) says as much, and Maitani's *Last Judgment* (c. 1320), though composed while Dante was finishing his epic, evidences the same fluidity.

It was Italian painting, however, that ultimately dominated the artistic scene of Europe during Dante's day, and this was derived less from the Gothic than from the Byzantine manner. Panel paintings, mosaics, and murals resurfaced, and the admixture produced the revolutionary style of Giotto. Giotto's presumed teacher, Cimabue, had rendered a severe—meaning closed—architectural perspective (see his *Madonna Enthroned,* c. 1280–1290, today in Florence's Uffizi Gallery), which Duccio of Siena had opened up, as it were, if one observes his own *Madonna Enthroned* or his *Annunciation of the Death of the Virgin,* both part of the Maestà Altar (1308–1311) in Siena's museum. Around this time—in 1305 and 1306— Giotto did a series of esthetically bold fresco representations in Padua's Arena Chapel which bring the viewer inside the scene synoptically, thanks to his lifelike three-dimensionalism. As he composed *Purg.* 32, Dante could not have failed to appreciate the symbolic tree of knowledge that appears in the *Lamentation* panel. As Dante foresaw, a new future in art was developing: the road to Simone Martini and Pietro Lorenzetti was now paved.

That Dante appreciated art or had artistic tendencies of his own cannot be disputed. As the *Commedia* illustrates time and again, he was a visual poet; his notion of poetry as *visibile parlare* must be taken seriously, and for several reasons—including his adumbrations of Renaissance painterly esthetics—he has been called "the Michelangelo of poetry." Supposedly he drew: Leonardo Bruni said that he sketched marvelously, and Dante himself alluded to his "outlining an angel on some drawing tablets" (*VN* 34). He knew a number of painters, among them the famous manuscript illustrator and miniaturist Oderisi da Gubbio, who is depicted atoning for his sin of pride in Purgatory, and his student, the little-known Franco Bolognese. Above all, he admired the young Giotto, who supposedly did the Bargello portrait of him; we recall Mochi's nineteenth-century oil of Dante presenting Giotto to Guido Novello da Polenta. He admired Cimabue too, but declared Giotto superior (*Purg.* 11.94–96).

As expressed variously in the *De vulgari eloquentia* and the *Convivio,* the act of the artist resembles the act of God. Beauty on Earth derives from God's harmony (more than a musical term here) and from identity with the truth, both of which are the painter's goals. And as nature and art paint in their *pitture,* so, by implication, has Dante set out "to capture the eyes and so gain the mind" in portraying Beatrice (*Par.* 27.91–93). This painterly disposition pervades the *Commedia,* which becomes a rigorously self-sufficient esthetic system. Dante's esthetic is free of the medieval, northern Gothic tension between the realistic and the symbolic, and it shapes a vision that is both naturalistic and lyrical. He is not a poet of death in the mode of his northern contemporaries (and subsequent poets, if one thinks of Villon), but, as befits the Mediterranean style, a poet of life. Not surprisingly, he draws many metaphors and similes from the world of art, and he knows how to handle space and light (along with color), two of the basic ingredients of painting. Even in the closed system of Hell, his vistas extend beyond the potential of the human eye, and far more in the spaciousness of Purgatory and the spacelessness of Paradise. His landscapes and vanishing points outdo Giotto in the matter of perspective; and in the stereoscopic ("transhumanizing," *trasumanar, Par.* 1.70) ultra-perspective that brings all the blessed—wherever placed in Heaven—close to God, his vision outdistances even the Renaissance. Like a post-Giottoan, Dante's sense of light is no longer linear but tonal, leading toward a new realism that tends to an organic rather than a static interpretation of the human body. Chiaroscuro, like looking at someone at night under the moon (*Inf.* 15.17–19), has its place, as does tenebrism, so strikingly conceived in the Ugolino episode (*Inf.* 33). And every conceivable intensity of brightness is presented visibly in the *Paradiso.*

One may also speak of Dante's sculptural vision, if only by considering the statuesque trio of centaurs in *Inf.* 12, and the bas-reliefs, lifelike effigies of humility in which the proud are cast down (*Purg.* 10, 12) and, surpassing Polyclitus (10.29), "dead seemed the dead and the living living" (12.67). Dante's is truly *visibile parlare*—the poet's delight in creation that fashions a mindscape in which, if the characters' essence is moral, their existence is pictorial.

During the time of the great Gothic cathedrals that just preceded Dante, music began to undergo important changes that added a secular option to the religious. Polyphony, in the form of organum and descant (parallel additions in 4ths or 5ths above the plain chant's single melodic line, and ornamental counterpoint to it, respectively), had revitalized the art and removed it from the exclusive domain and control of the Church. Qualitatively, the Church profited as well, since the motet, one of the most important forms of sacred music, made possible the inclusion of an instrument for the single line (previously, church music was sung and not played). The step to the development of the secular instrument-accompanied song of the troubadours, trovatori, and Minnesänger was but a short one.

It was also a step from the more somber expression of the Mass to the brighter expression of the coming madrigals. Generally, the movement of musical influence in the thirteenth century went southward, from France to Italy. One of the topics exploited by poets and musicians preceding Dante's time was love, and during his time it flowered unabated in the form of songs and ballads. Dante must have been impressed by the way that organum polyphony allowed a hymn in Latin and a love lyric in French to be sounded simultaneously, and on an elaborated melody derived from the melismas of Gregorian chant! The music Dante heard was heading for the Ars Nova, a free system of rhythmic notation which a few years after his death became recognized more broadly as a new style, thanks to composers like Guillaume de Machaut (1304?–1377) and Francesco Landini (1325–1397). The new naturalistic style shaped by Giotto in painting was reflected in the new, freer, more intensely melodic style that evolved in music—and all these qualities permitted the musician to establish himself as an independent, creative artist.

Dante was sensitive to the new situation. He had Casella, who had set music to poems by Lemmo Orlandi, set his own canzone "Amor che nella mente mi ragiona" to music, undoubtedly in a melodic rather than polyphonic manner, since the composer sings it to him beautifully as the poet reflects on how music "used to quiet all my desires" (*Purg.* 2.108). Dante was certainly aware of the place of music as a theoretical discipline, in numerical Pythagorean fashion (as reported in psycho-physiological terms in *Conv.* 2.13.23–24), among the mathematical categories of the Quadrivium, but he also saw music involved in the *human* activities of singing, playing, and dancing. He saw music in the macrocosm and the

D microcosm, hence his *musica mundana (coelestis), musica humana,* and *musica instrumentalis,* to which he adds *musica rhythmica,* the art of singing poetically (*DVE* 2.3.8). This is the art of melodic diction and linguistic modulation (*DVE* 2.8.4–6). He therefore favored Casella's able efforts as enthusiastically as Amore encouraged him (*VN* 12) to write a ballad for Beatrice to be put to music.

Chapters 5, 7, 8, 9, 11, and 12 of *Conv.* 1 all deal seriatim with music. They allude to its prevalence over all things: the union of body and soul; the harmonious disposition of bodily structures considered analogous to the balance evident in pleasant song, which in turn is tantamount to harmonious dispositions in nature; the ineffable communicative power of music through tone or rhythm, and the emotional beauty of sound combinations; the inalienable conjunction of poetry with music, such that all translations become vitiated; the audible individuality of instruments; and the fraudulence of talking about music without knowing it ("leave music to the musician"). In other words, Dante here emerges as a music theorist.

In addition, he becomes its philosopher and psychologist. His canzone "Voi che 'ntendendo il terzo ciel movete," in *Conv.* 2, places music in the sphere of Mars—the fifth and thus centermost of the nine physical spheres. And as we know, the 5th is the dominant in the diatonic scale, the moving determiner. Beauty, in poetry (*parole armonizzate e . . . canti,* "harmonized words and . . . songs," *Conv.* 2.13.23) among other human expressions, resides in harmonious relationships, for which music is the functioning metaphor. Concept itself, to be convincing, must be clad in assuring sound. But more than a metaphor, psychically music not only stirs human activity but often quiets it. Hence the rapt attention of the souls listening to Casella in *Purg.* 2—which causes the mind "to heed no other [of its] power[s]" (*Purg.* 4.4).

The *Commedia* abounds in musical references, from the vulgar trumpeting of the devils in Hell (*Inf.* 21–22) to the beatified music of the spheres in Heaven. There are no fewer than 146 references to music (29 in *Inferno,* 59 in *Purgatorio,* and 57 in *Paradiso*). There are hymns, chants, and liturgical songs (*Regina Coelis, Gloria, Sanctus, Miserere, Agnus Dei, Te Deum Laudamus, In Exitu Israel*), instruments of all kinds (drums, horns, trumpets, harps, kitharas, lutes), choirs and even a nine-part polyphonic chorus (*Par.* 10.139), and many dances, from the fickleness of Dame Fortune (*Inf.* 7) to the joyful symmetries of the blessed (*Par.* 8) and beyond.

The *Commedia* is a phonic structure whose mortar is music. In its most rarefied expression, music corresponds to the essence of the luminosity of Paradise. Historically, composers of Dante's day may not have enjoyed the recognition they were to receive in later centuries, but long before the Romantics and Schopenhauer, Dante seemed to sense music's coming dawn and its autonomy in the world of the arts. Not surprisingly, just as some have referred to his poem as a grand piece of architecture, there are those who have visualized it as a vast painting, and also those, like Tieck, who have heard it as "essentially a song."

Bibliography

Barricelli, Jean-Pierre. *Dante's Vision and the Artist: Four Modern Illustrators of the "Commedia."* New York: Peter Lang, 1992.

Bassermann, Alfred. *Dantes Spuren in Italien.* Munich: R. Oldenbourg, 1898.

Bonaventura, Arlando. *Dante e la musica.* Livorno: R. Giusti, 1904.

Kraus, Franz Xavier. *Dante, sein Leben und sein Werk, sein Verhältnis zur Kunst und zur Politik.* Berlin: G. Grote, 1897.

Loos, Erich. *Die Bedeutung der Musik im Werk Dantes.* Stuttgart: F. Steiner, 1988.

Panofsky, Erwin. *Gothic Architecture and Scholasticism.* Latrobe, Penn.: Archabbey, 1951.

Pazzaglia, Mario. "L'universo metaforico della musica nella *Divina Commedia.*" *Letture Classensi* 15 (1986), 79–97.

Pirrotta, Nino. "Poesia e musica." *Letture Classensi* 16 (1987), 153–162.

Pistelli-Rinaldi, Emma. *La musicalità di Dante.* Florence: Le Monnier, 1968.

Schlosser, J. "Della dottrina artistica di Dante." In *La letteratura artistica.* 2nd ed. Florence: Nuova Italia, 1956.

Jean-Pierre Barricelli

Dante and the Classical Tradition

Dante's works give the impression of great familiarity with the classical tradition, at least in its Latin form, but a precise account of his classical reading presents problems. It is not always easy to say what texts he knew at first hand and what at second hand through the anthologies or collections of excerpts known as *florilegia,* through quotations in other writers or marginal glosses on their works, or through textbooks and works of reference such as manuals of rhetoric and encyclopedias. In general, his exile from Florence meant difficulty in obtaining books, although at times it may have facilitated access to a number of libraries with a wide range of material. Dante's memory was impressive, if sometimes inaccurate, and all in all, his classical knowledge compares very favorably with that of his contemporaries.

Higher education was not available in Dante's Florence except in the houses of study belonging to the religious orders, and Dante describes in *Conv.* 2.12.7 how he attended these to study philosophy. His schooling would have included Latin grammar (based on the standard Latin texts of Donatus or Priscian) and rhetoric. Brunetto Latini's circle had promoted the study of rhetoric in Florence; important texts were Cicero's *De inventione,* the pseudo-Ciceronian *Rhetorica ad Herennium,* and medieval works on rhetoric and poetics. On the whole, however, a careful study of classical texts according to humanistic pedagogical principles would not have been part of the educational system of the time. Virgil's hoarseness at the beginning of the *Inferno* might be read as an indication of such neglect (*Inf.* 1.63). Greek was not studied or widely known, and apart from the works of Aristotle, very little Greek literature was available in translation.

However much or little they were studied, there can be no doubt of the respect in which the ancient writers were held as authorities, *auctores.* This is evident in chapter 25 of the *Vita Nuova,* where Dante provides a series of classical precedents from Virgil (*Aen.* 1, 3), Lucan (*Phars.* 1), Horace *(Ars poetica),* and Ovid (*Remedium amoris* 2), in order to justify his use of personification. It is hard to say to what extent this represents the young Dante's reading and to what extent it comes at second hand from textbooks of rhetoric, but it indicates the respect and authority enjoyed by these writers, at least in theory. It is also noteworthy that these four poets, together with Homer, form the *bella scola* in Dante's Limbo (*Inf.* 4.86–96). They constitute his classical poetic "canon" from the beginning.

The *Convivio* speaks of the consolatory power that Cicero's *De amicitia* and Boethius's *De consolatione philosophiae* had upon Dante after Beatrice's death, works that stimulated his interest in philosophy (*Conv.* 2.12.3–4). Dante remarks that he found them quite difficult, which suggests that his classical reading at that time was still fairly limited. The *Vita Nuova* shows the impact of these two works in its structure and in its treatment of love, while the *Convivio* reveals evidence of a much wider awareness of classical texts, especially of Cicero's moral works and Aristotle's *Nicomachean Ethics.* Aristotle, *the* philosopher for Dante and his contemporaries, was the ancient Greek writer best known (in Latin translation) to Dante. Of Plato, he appears to have known part of the *Timaeus* (referred to in *Par.* 4.49), the only work of this Greek philosopher then widely available, though only in part; his access to it may have been at second hand. In the case of Cicero, Dante seems to have been particularly interested in the moral works: the *De officiis,* the *De finibus,* the *De amicitia,* and the *De senectute* are those most cited in both the *Convivio* and in the *Commedia.* Seneca, the other Latin moralist widely read in the Middle Ages, is less obviously present in Dante: there are some citations, not always accurate.

In the *Convivio,* classical poets are seen to convey truth beneath the guise of allegory. Ovid's account of Orpheus in the *Metamorphoses* contains as its allegorical meaning (the truth hidden beneath a beautiful lie) the soothing and edifying effect of the words of a wise man (*Conv.* 2.1.3). Dante's account of the stages of man's life (*Conv.* 4.23–28) draws in part on the allegorizations of Virgil's *Aeneid,* particularly that of the sixth-century writer Fulgentius. It is a view of Virgil's poem that will later yield to a reading which places far greater emphasis on history.

This shift in emphasis is also apparent in the *Monarchia* and the *Commedia.* In book 2 of the *Monarchia,* where Dante sets out to show the providential nature of Rome's rise to power, the *Aeneid* is a major authority. Of the historians whom he cites, Orosius, the fifth-century historian of Rome, probably influenced Dante's view of Roman history more than did classical historians like Livy. Dante does refer to Livy a number of times and with great respect (see, for example, *Mon.* 2.3.6 and *Inf.* 28.12), but the extent of his knowledge of this historian is limited and uncertain. Before the time of Petrarch a satisfactory text of Livy would have been difficult to obtain, but Dante may have had access to the early books of his *History of Rome.*

D   A consideration of Dante's use of the classical tradition in the *Commedia* can well begin with the two passages on the virtuous pagans in Limbo, in *Inf.* 4.82–144 and *Purg.* 22.97–114. In the first of these Dante begins with an encounter with the four great poets Homer, Horace, Ovid, and Lucan, who greet him and Virgil. Dante had no direct knowledge of Homer but would have grasped his importance through his classical reading—for example, from Horace's *Ars poetica* or from Aristotle. Virgil stands on his own, chosen as Dante's guide through the other world. He is presented as the major representative of the ancient world, and it is significant that Dante has chosen a poet for this role. Virgil qualifies because of his literary greatness and his elevated "tragic" style, because he is the poet of the other world in *Aeneid* 6, and because he is the poet who celebrates the founding of Rome. In *Purgatorio,* he is also the poet of the *Eclogues* (*Purg.* 22.57), who anticipated Christianity without ever becoming Christian (*Purg.* 22.64–72). It is not certain that Dante knew the *Georgics,* unless the repetition of Virgil's name on his departure in the Earthly Paradise (*Purg.* 30.49–51) is seen to reflect the iterated call of the name of Eurydice by the dying Orpheus in *Georgics* 4.525–527.

Horace follows Homer in the series of four poets (*Inf.* 4.89). His title of "satirist," *Orazio satiro,* owes more to convention than to Dante's privileging of the *Satires.* In fact, the work of Horace most cited by Dante is the *Ars poetica,* or the *Poetria,* as Dante called it. It is likely that an appreciation of this work, whose flexibility is so distinct from the rigid rules of medieval works of rhetoric, helped Dante to develop his own varied "comic" style.

Ovid follows, and in the *Commedia* he is mainly the poet of the *Metamorphoses.* Although some of his characters appear in Dante's other world and are treated as if they were historical, Ovid is treated mainly as a source of mythology. In many cases Dante the pilgrim is compared to the protagonist of the *Metamorphoses,* providing—as Kevin Brownlee has suggested—a Christian "correction" of the model offered by the myth: pagan metamorphosis becomes Christian conversion (like the *trasumanar* represented by Glaucus, *Par.* 1.67–72).

Lucan comes last, in an order that is most likely chronological but possibly hierarchical. Dante seems to have admired the *Pharsalia* as a historical poem, perhaps with some reservations, since its anti-imperial ideology conflicts with Dante's political imperatives. In *Inf.* 25.94–102 Dante speaks of outdoing Lucan as well as Ovid in describing snakes and metamorphoses. Of the characters from Lucan present in the *Commedia,* the most remarkable is Cato, chosen (despite his antipathy to Caesar) as an example of high virtue and self-sacrifice in the cause of liberty. He is made the guardian of Purgatory and is destined ultimately to be saved (*Purg.* 1.31–108 and especially 70–75) even though a suicide.

Statius, the other Latin poet of great significance for Dante, appears in Purgatory as a secret Christian (*Purg.* 22.90). As with Virgil and Lucan, Dante treats his poems as historical. The *Thebaid* is particularly important in the *Inferno,* where its rendering of Thebes serves as a correlative both to the infernal city and to the evils of Italy in Dante's own time (*Inf.* 30.1–12, 32.11, 33.89). For Dante, who was unacquainted with Greek tragedy, Statius provided something of the impact of the Theban story.

Dante's preference is for narrative—indeed, epic—poets. There is little indication of any familiarity with Horace's *Odes,* the Roman elegists, or Lucretius, all of whom were virtually unknown in Dante's day. Roman drama does not fare much better. Neither Terence nor Seneca has an obvious presence in Dante's work. Seneca the moralist (*Seneca morale, Inf.* 4.141) is present in Limbo, but the epithet serves to distinguish him from "Seneca the tragedian," who was then regarded as another person. Both are referred to in the *Letter to Cangrande,* (*Epist.* 13.29). And Statius asks after Terence, who is placed in Limbo along with the other dramatic writers Plautus and Caecilius (and also Varius, if that reading is to be preferred to Varro), whose names Dante probably learned at second hand (*Purg.* 22.98). This catalogue in itself is a sort of tribute to Roman drama, but it does not imply direct knowledge on Dante's part. Taide (*Inf.* 18.133–135), or Thaïs, is a character from Terence's *Eunuchus,* but Dante misquotes the text, and his immediate source is probably Cicero's *De amicitia,* not the Roman dramatist.

The only Latin prose writers in Limbo are Cicero and the moralist Seneca (unless *Purg.* 22.98 refers to Varro, which seems unlikely). The remaining poets are the satirists Persius (*Purg.* 22.100) and Juvenal (*Purg.* 22.14). It is possible but not certain that Dante knew Persius; he does quote Juvenal in the *Convivio* and the *Monarchia,* but he could not be said to have a significant presence in the *Commedia.*

The remaining figures identified as being present in Limbo are Greek and Arab philosophers (in *Inferno*) and Greek poets (in *Purgatorio*), virtuous men and women from Trojan and Roman history, Saladin, and virtuous Greek women from the two poems of Statius. As these figures show, the ancient world is for Dante a source of philosophical wisdom and of exemplary historical characters who serve as a guide to virtue and good government and even point the way toward Christianity; the turning point is marked by Virgil's role in the conversion of Statius (*Purg.* 22.34–87). In *Inferno* pagans are often condemned side by side with Christians as offending against natural justice and in some cases, it would seem, against natural religion: Epicurus is damned as a heretic (*Inf.* 10.14) and Capaneus as a blasphemer (*Inf.* 14.43–72). In *Purgatorio* there are parallel Christian and pagan examples of vice and virtue on each of the seven cornices of the mountain. The moral scheme of Hell as set out in *Inf.* 11 draws on Cicero's *De officiis* for the distinction between violence and fraud, and on Aristotle's *Ethics* for the concepts of *incontinenza* (incontinence) and *malizia* (malice).

One case in which the balancing of pagan and Christian examples is not operative is the category of suicide: no pagans are mentioned in *Inf.* 13, while Lucretia (*Inf.* 4.128) remains in Limbo and Cato is destined for salvation (*Purg.* 1.75).

The case of Cato is but one instance of Dante's "saving" a pagan figure. Other instances include pagans who undergo conversion in one manner or another: Statius, presented as a hidden Christian; Trajan, who according to legend was brought back to life so that he might undergo baptism (*Par.* 20.112–117); and Ripheus, a Virgilian character treated as a historical figure, who was granted a special revelation in life (*Par.* 20.118–129). These characters, however, are exceptions. In general, classical culture as a whole symbolizes the approach to and anticipation of—indeed, the preparation for—Christianity, without the benefit of attaining salvation. Although the pagan poets on Parnassus may have been dreaming of the Earthly Paradise (*Purg.* 28.139–141), Virgil is but a traveler by night who lights the way for others and not for himself (*Purg.* 22.67–69).

Bibliography

Barański, Zygmunt. "Dante and the Latin Comic Tradition." *Italian Studies* 46 (1991), 1–36.

Barolini, Teodolinda. *Dante's Poets: Textuality and Truth in the "Comedy."* Princeton, N.J.: Princeton University Press, 1984.

Brownlee, Kevin. "Dante and the Classical Poets." In *The Cambridge Companion to Dante.* Edited by Rachel Jacoff. Cambridge: Cambridge University Press, 1993, pp. 100–119.

Hollander, Robert. *Il Virgilio Dantesco: Tragedia nella "Commedia."* Florence: Olschki, 1983.

Iannucci, Amilcare A. (ed.). *Dante e la "bella scola" della poesia: Autorità e sfida poetica.* Ravenna: Longo, 1993.

Jacoff, Rachel, and Jeffrey T. Schnapp (eds.). *The Poetry of Allusion: Virgil and Ovid in Dante's "Commedia."* Stanford: Stanford University Press, 1991.

Moore, Edward. *Studies in Dante, First Series: Scripture and Classical Authors in Dante.* New introductory matter edited by C. Hardie. Oxford: Clarendon Press, 1969.

Pastore Stocchi, Manlio. "Cultura classica." *Enciclopedia dantesca* 2:30–36.

Picone, Michelangelo. "Dante and the Classics." In *Dante: Contemporary Perspectives.* Edited by Amilcare A. Iannucci. Toronto: University of Toronto Press, 1997, pp. 51–73.

Sowell, Madison U. (ed.). *Dante and Ovid: Essays in Intertextuality.* Medieval and Renaissance Texts and Studies 12. Binghamton, N.Y.: 1991.

Jennifer Petrie

Dante da Maiano

Poet who exchanged sonnets with Dante and other contemporaries such as Chiaro Davanzati and Guido Orlandi. His identity is disputed, but the tone of deference that the youthful Dante Alighieri uses toward him, as well as the traditional themes and language of his poetry, would place him in the school of Guittone d'Arezzo. His four poems to Dante da Maiano are among the earliest he wrote (*Rime* 1a, 2a, 3a, 4a).

Jo Ann Cavallo

Dante in England

Dante's earliest relationship with an English writer is a complex and uneasy one: Chaucer's *House of Fame* (written c. 1380) has been read both as a

D tribute to the *Commedia* (for example, in its use of invocations to the Muses that imitate those at the opening of Dante's *cantiche,* and in its central episode of the protagonist's heavenward flight in the claws of an eagle, based on *Purg.* 9.19–33), and also as a critique of Dante's system of divine judgment in its highlighting of the arbitrary basis of moral reputation. Although Dante's use of the vernacular (in both a colloquial and a lyrical mode) and his elevation of the status of the vernacular poet clearly inspired Chaucer to emulation, notably in *Troilus and Criseyde,* Chaucer's work as a whole embraces personae who evade unambiguous moral categorization: not a vision of judgment, as in Dante's case, but a statement of the difficulties of judging. Such a response practically sets the agenda for Dante's absorption into the English tradition, in that a fervent admiration for Dante's "poetry" has often gone hand in hand with a rejection of his didacticism; indeed, many later interpretations of him suggest that the latter was merely a convention of his age to which Dante gave lip service, while simultaneously promoting figures like Francesca and Ulysses to heroic status within Hell.

The sense of the *Commedia* as a synthesis of outmoded "medieval" morality and design, and one moreover written in a vulgar and barbarous style, is responsible for the devaluation that overtook Dante's work across Europe in self-consciously enlightened periods like the Renaissance that followed. Only in the mid-eighteenth century when so-called Gothic values were revived did Dante enter on wide popularity in England. There are occasional references to Dante's antipapal invective in English Protestant writing of the sixteenth and seventeenth centuries, notably in Milton's *Of Reformation* (1641) and in "Lycidas" (1638), where St. Peter's famous attack on the clergy for not feeding their wind-swollen sheep (ll. 125–127) closely resembles *Par.* 29.106–107. Milton was well acquainted with the range of Dante's work, and there are echoes of the *Commedia* in *Paradise Lost* (1667), though the baroque grandeur of Milton's epic topography shows a marked difference from the human scale of Dante's journey.

Many readers in the Romantic period conceived an enthusiasm for a Dante of gloom and horror, based solely on a few celebrated passages in the *Inferno*—notably the episode of Ugolino, a figure whose satanic hatreds are fueled by the indignity of political exile and the thirst for revenge against Florence. This is essentially the Dante of Byron's poem "The Prophecy of Dante" (1821) and of the famous essays by Macaulay (in *Knight's Quarterly Magazine,* 1824) and Carlyle ("The Hero as Poet," in *On Heroes,* 1841), a figure further poisoned by the tragedy of Beatrice's early death. Poets of this period like Shelley and Arthur Hallam do, however, show an untypical interest in other areas of Dante's work, like the *Vita Nuova* and *Paradiso;* the images of light and cosmic harmony in the latter powerfully influenced Shelley's allegory of political revolution in *Prometheus Unbound* (1820). Indeed, Dante as the "poet of liberty," whose *Commedia* casts off centuries of darkness and superstition and inaugurates the modern world via the individualism of its free-thinking protagonist and his bold attacks on papal corruption, is a central figure in Shelley's *Defence of Poetry* (written 1821): Dante is "the first awakener of entranced Europe." Shelley's homage to Dante is most explicit in his unfinished *terza rima* poem *The Triumph of Life* (1824), in which the narrator is introduced to an *Inferno*-like vision of the "captive multitude" led in triumph by Life's chariot.

H. F. Cary's translation of the *Commedia* (1814) deservedly enjoyed constant popularity during the nineteenth century and since, though it turned Dante's concise and colloquial style into orotund Miltonics. As we move into the Victorian period, many more translations of this and many of Dante's other works start to be produced—notably of the *Vita Nuova,* first by the American Joseph Garrow (1846), followed by the well-known version of D. G. Rossetti (1861, though begun much earlier) and by that of Theodore Martin (1862). A switch of interest to this text, and to those parts of the *Commedia* concerned with the Dante–Beatrice relationship, characterizes much of the art and writing of the mid-nineteenth century, above all in the work of the Pre-Raphaelites. They celebrated *Vita Nuova* as an initiates' text full of esoteric vision and numerology; Rossetti's work in particular evokes a Dante concerned primarily with the ritualistic mysteries of love and sexuality.

Dante's work at this stage was becoming more widely known in America too, with the publication of Longfellow's translation of the *Commedia* (1867) and of a growing mass of critical writing, including Charles Eliot Norton's *Essay* on and translation of the *Vita Nuova* (1859, 1867). Norton was a regular correspondent on Dante matters with John Ruskin, who counteracted any tendency to stress the arcane Dante of the *dolce stil nuovo* (as in Rossetti's "Brotherhood") by insisting fully on Dante as a public man with a keen and active sense of political and moral rectitude. For Ruskin, Dante was "the central man of all the world, as representing in perfect balance the imaginative, moral, and intellectual faculties, all at their highest" (*Stones of Venice,* 3.3.67). Ruskin stresses particularly Dante's social concerns in the *Commedia*'s attacks on financial corruption and materialism, which chime with Ruskin's own onslaughts on the malpractices of modern society. In this, and in his admiration for Dante's system-building in the *Commedia,* he anticipates Ezra Pound, who in the following century attempted to diagnose the mercenary ills of an era in his own poetic summary of an entire civilization, the *Cantos* (1917–1970).

For the modern reader, the prestige and popularity of Dante's work in the twentieth century is likely to be associated with Pound's writings and with those of T. S. Eliot, James Joyce, and Samuel Beckett. Dante was one of the main weapons in modernism's assault on the insularity of the English tradition. The precision and vivacity of his imagery is used to challenge Miltonic "obscurity," or what Eliot called the "mistiness" and "vagueness" of late Victorian poetry. Pound's early concerns were largely with Dante as a stylistic exemplar, though as indicated above, his own interests later widened to include economics and the concept of the just state, and Dante's polemic (notably in *Inf.* 17.43–75 against the usurers) becomes a central focus in the *Cantos* (see especially canto 45 and the so-called Hell cantos, 14–15). Eliot was from an early stage interested in what he saw as Dante's anti-individualism and submission to authority; in the final two essays of *The Sacred Wood* (1920) he compares the private and cranky nature of Blake's mythological systems with Dante's Catholic orthodoxy, which puts the latter at the heart of Europe and the European tradition. In his later writing he stresses the Dante–Virgil connection as an encapsulation of the writer's duty to constrain individual talent within the piety due to tradition. In his well-known essay on Dante of 1929 he also sees what he calls the "economy" and "austerity" of Dante's style as a useful corrective to the tendency of English poets toward an excessive and "too poetical" indulgence in descriptive effects, and again toward a self-conscious individualism. The fruits of this can be seen in Eliot's own *Four Quartets* (1936–1942).

The exactness with which Joyce plots the time and place coordinates of his Dublin setting in *Ulysses* (1922) is arguably indebted to Dante's similar attention to these features in the *Commedia*'s topography, and it has often been maintained that the increasing somberness of the story-sequence in *Dubliners* (1914) deliberately parallels Dante's descent into Hell. Joyce's attitude to Dante seems to have been a mixture of admiration and exasperation, encapsulated in Stephen Dedalus's sardonic comment, with regard to relations between the sexes, on "the spiritual-heroic refrigerating apparatus, invented and patented in all countries by Dante Alighieri" at the end of *A Portrait of the Artist* (1914–1915). Joyce's foregrounding of sexuality throughout his work might be seen as his major revision in incorporating into his work Dantesque structures and positions, such as an anticlericalism that is indebted to Dante's invective.

Although the title and scope of Pound's *Cantos* allude to the *Commedia,* and its loose progression along an *Inferno–Purgatorio–Paradiso* sequence struggles out of the corruption of modern Europe and "ends in the light," in Pound's phrase, a stricter imitation of some of the narrative or formal qualities of Dante's poem can be found in other modern works like W. H. Auden's "In the Year of my Youth" (written 1932–1933, published in the *Review of English Studies,* 1978) and Louis MacNeice's *Autumn Sequel* (1954). The former, left unfinished and not published in Auden's lifetime, is a dream-vision journey through the slump of 1930s Britain, complete with a Virgil-type escort. The latter is a sustained exercise in hendecasyllabic *terza rima,* amounting to 26 cantos of 140 to 160 lines each. Largely an autobiographical memoir, it adopts a Dantesque framework to pursue deeply un-Dantesque concerns, arguing for a philosophical and political relativism and agnosticism that contest hierarchy and authority.

If this last poem is one that takes Dante to undo Dante, we can regard this as typical of the stimulus and dissent that Dante has provoked in many of his followers, often in equal measure: a desire to preserve the "poetry" while rejecting much of the content. This reaction, arguably initiated by Chaucer, is recurrent in the modern period; Benedetto Croce's criticism and Wallace Stevens's

D poetics also display this dual response to an author who influenced both writers deeply. The *Commedia* is a work projected on so vast a scale and encompassing so many interests, political, theological, linguistic, and autobiographical, that it is no surprise that many modern writers can somehow claim to align themselves with Dante while representing utterly diverse positions. Thus Shelley finds fuel for his radicalism in Dante, whom he sees as essentially a rebel against his age, while for Eliot Dante exemplifies submission to authority on both a poetic and a moral plane. Such views are often underwritten by the authors' responses to the relation between the medieval and the modern periods generally; to some Dante's period and his poetry represent a lost order and unity nostalgically evoked, while to others, like Shelley and Pound, Dante is a progressive casting off of the religious obscurantism of his age—essentially a social and political thinker and troubleshooter. This latter interest also features in Seamus Heaney's ongoing immersion in Dante; the latter's encounters in the *Commedia* with the victims and protagonists of the political strife of his period inspire the troubled elegiac landscape of "Station Island" (1984) and other poems.

The "romance" interest in Dante's life and work has also exercised much fascination. The relationship and reunion with Beatrice and the discourse that invests it have influenced a whole range of writing, from Shelley's *Epipsychidion* (1821) to Browning's love lyrics and the narrator's communications with the dead Hallam in Tennyson's *In Memoriam* (1850); and from Keats's description of the mystical priestess Moneta in "The Fall of Hyperion" (written 1818–1819) to Yeats's elaborate theorizing of the "anti-self," with the purity of Dante's love for Beatrice representing the struggle away from the lust-consumed self proper (see in particular *Per Amica Silentia Lunae*, 1917).

While it is poets who have taken most interest in Dante and have occasionally risen to the challenge of reproducing the scale and formal properties of the *Commedia* itself, any number of novelists, essayists, and playwrights have fastened on particular parts of Dante's work for comment or quotation; notable among them are George Eliot, Forster, and Beckett. It has been argued, for example, that the Ante-Purgatory, and especially Belacqua's enforced wait there in 4.106–135, is some sort of model for the situation in which the stranded and "waiting" protagonists of Beckett's plays find themselves. The difficulty with an author who has written on such a scale as Dante is not to find writers, at least in the modern period, who have been influenced by him, but writers who have not.

Bibliography

Brand, C. P. *Italy and the English Romantics*. Cambridge: Cambridge University Press, 1957.

Caesar, Michael. *Dante: The Critical Heritage 1314(?)–1870*. London: Routledge, 1989.

Ellis, Steve. *Dante and English Poetry: Shelley to T. S. Eliot*. Cambridge: Cambridge University Press, 1983.

Friederich, Werner P. *Dante's Fame Abroad 1350–1850*. Chapel Hill: University of North Carolina Press, 1950.

Giovannini, Giovanni. *Ezra Pound and Dante*. Nijmegen: Dekker and Van de Vegt, 1961.

Gray, Nicolette. *Rossetti, Dante and Ourselves*. London: Faber, 1947.

La Piana, Angelina. *Dante's American Pilgrimage*. New Haven: Yale University Press, 1948.

Manganiello, Dominic. *T. S. Eliot and Dante*. Basingstoke: Macmillan, 1989.

McDougal, Stuart Y. *Dante Among the Moderns*. Chapel Hill: University of North Carolina Press, 1985.

Neuse, Richard. *Chaucer's Dante: Allegory and Epic Theater in the Canterbury Tales*. Berkeley: University of California Press, 1991.

Payne, Roberta L. *The Influence of Dante on Medieval English Dream Visions*. New York: Peter Lang, 1989.

Pite, Ralph. *The Circle of Our Vision: Dante's Presence in English Romantic Poetry*. Oxford: Clarendon Press, 1994.

Reynolds, Mary T. *Joyce and Dante: The Shaping Imagination*. Princeton, N.J.: Princeton University Press, 1981.

Samuel, Irene. *Dante and Milton: The Commedia and Paradise Lost*. Ithaca, N.Y.: Cornell University Press, 1966.

Schless, Howard H. *Chaucer and Dante: A Revaluation*. Norman, Okla.: Pilgrim Books, 1984.

Shoaf, R. A. *Dante, Chaucer and the Currency of the Word: Money, Images and Reference in Late Medieval Poetry*. Norman, Okla.: Pilgrim Books, 1983.

Taylor, Karla. *Chaucer Reads the Divine Comedy*. Stanford: Stanford University Press, 1989.

Toynbee, Paget. *Dante in English Literature: From Chaucer to Cary (c. 1380–1844)*. 2 vols. London: Methuen, 1909.

Wilhelm, James J. *Dante and Pound: The Epic of Judgement*. Orono: University of Maine Press, 1974.

Steve Ellis

Dante in France

The first, brief reference to Dante's work in French literature appears in *Espinette amoureuse* by Jean Froissart (c. 1337–c. 1410): two lovers become aware of their love while reading a romance (cf. *Inf.* 5.138). The first writer to reflect Dante's influence to any extent is Christine de Pisan (1364–1429), who recommends "the book called Dante . . . where you will draw greater profit than from your *Roman de la rose*." Her *Livre du chemin de long estude* (1402) takes its title from *Inf.* 1.83; it narrates an allegorical pilgrimage culminating in an ascent to Heaven, where the Sibyl Almethea takes on the role of Dante's Virgil. Christine also echoes Dante's censure of Florence (*Inf.* 26.1–6) in her *Livre de la mutacion de la fortune* (ll. 4643–4670).

Although Dante was known by name in fifteenth-century France, his influence was scant. The French invasion of Italy (1494) signaled a turning point: Charles VIII brought back to France Dante's lyric poems as well as Bruni's *Life of Dante*. By 1496 an important manuscript of the *Commedia*— "in Italian and in French" (the first known translation, now lost)—was in the library of the father of Francis I and Marguerite of Navarre. Francis's court fell under the spell of Italian culture (Leonardo da Vinci died an honored guest at Amboise in 1519): a courtier presented the king with a manuscript of the *Inferno* in 1519; another courtier, François Bergaigne, dedicated his translation of the *Paradiso* to Queen Claude. Francis's sister Marguerite incorporated into her writings a number of passages from the *Commedia*'s first five cantos, especially *Inf.* 5.121–123. Luigi Alamanni and others discussed Dante at court; an anecdote relates that the king became violently angry when Alamanni read out *Purg.* 20, with its assertion that Hugh Capet was the son of a butcher (52). The first printed editions of the *Commedia* were published at Lyons by Baldassarre da Gabiano beginning in 1502; counterfeits of the Aldine editions, their quality is superior to the originals. The first published French translation of the *Commedia,* by Balthasar Grangier, appeared in 1596 (cf. 1513 for Petrarch and 1543 for Ariosto). The first French biography of Dante, Papire Masson's *Vitae trium Hetruriae procerum, Dantis, Petrarchae, Boccacci* (1587), seized on the idea that Dante stayed in Paris during his exile and thus gained a thorough grounding in theology.

With the triumph of Petrarchism and the Pléiade school of poets, Dante's influence waned, although the *editio princeps* of the *De vulgari eloquentia* was published in Paris by Iacopo Corbinelli in 1577, accompanied by two poems in praise of Dante. The religious wars and controversies also affected Dante's reputation, with both Huguenots and Gallicans exploiting the Italian poet's attacks on a corrupt papacy (already in 1434, Alain Chartier had mentioned Dante in regard to the highly controversial Donation of Constantine, as did Philippe Duplessis-Mornay in 1611).

The tidal wave of French classicism drowned all interest in the medieval Italian poet. René Rapin (1674) expressed the general view that Dante's poem was too depressing and his theme often too complex for poetic expression. Another Jesuit, Jean Hardouin, claimed in 1727 that the *Commedia* had been written in 1412 and by a disciple of Wycliffe.

The Age of Enlightenment found in Dante the typical representative of an epoch blighted by religious superstition and obscurantism, although travelers to Italy began to acquire some acquaintance with his writings and reputation. An unusual event was the publication of translations of the odes from the *Convivio* in La Touche-Loisi's *Consolations chrétiennes* (1744). Three years later Louis Racine cited Dante as a Christian poet, despite his tendency to condemn popes to Hell and his appointment of a pagan suicide as guardian of Purgatory. Voltaire, in his speech to the French Academy (1746), included Dante in his appeal to broaden the scope of French poetry; he incorporated a free translation of *Purg.* 16.106ff. into his *Essais sur les moeurs* (1756), describing Dante's poem as "bizarre, but brilliant with natural beauties." However, he later created a furor with his travesty of the Guido da Montefeltro episode (*Inf.* 27), his dismissal of the whole *Commedia* as a "hotchpotch," and his claim in the *Dictionnaire philosophique* (1764) that the Italian poet's "reputation will always assert itself, because hardly

D anyone reads him," accompanied by factual inaccuracies. Even Voltaire admitted that he knew some twenty passages from the *Commedia* by heart; however, although "a volume of Ariosto is always being stolen from me, no one has ever stolen a Dante from me." In *Jacques le fataliste* (1772–1775), Diderot quoted the chrysalis image of *Purg.* 10.124–126; and Dante's celebrated line *Lasciate ogne speranza, voi ch'ntrate* ("Abandon every hope, you who enter," *Inf.* 3.9), even found its way into *Le Mariage de Figaro* (1784) by Beaumarchais. The best-known episode, that of Ugolino (*Inf.* 32.124–33.90), was translated into Latin by Charles Lebeau (1782) and was praised by Chénier as an example of the sublime that offset the poem's absurdities.

Antoine de Rivarol's prose translation of the *Inferno* appeared in 1785; somewhat bowdlerized, it was appreciated by such literary stars as Chateaubriand, Hugo, and Sainte-Beuve, and was last reprinted in 1955. It thus prepared the way for the high noon of Dante's reputation, sparked by the movement of Romanticism with its interest in the Middle Ages, the myth of the Romantic hero, and the idealized beloved. In *Racine et Shakspeare* (1823–1825), Stendhal claimed "Dante is the supreme Romantic poet," in that he was guided by the interests and beliefs of his own age. Already in Madame de Staël's *Corinne* (1807) Dante was hailed as the "Homer of modern times . . . a hero of thought"; and in 1861 Alexandre Dumas nominated Dante as one of three poets constituting "the world's literary trinity" *(Une nuit à Florence).*

In 1813 Sismondi translated the Ugolino episode into *terza rima,* a verse form abandoned by French poets since the Renaissance but now resuscitated, especially by Gautier and the Parnassians. Dante scholarship was inaugurated in France by the work of Villemain and Fauriel; the latter—a friend of Manzoni—reversed the popular trend by extolling the *Purgatorio* and *Paradiso* above the *Inferno.* Fauriel's lectures were attended by Ampère, Sainte-Beuve, and Renan, as well as by Frédéric Ozanam, whose *Dante et la philosophie catholique au treizième siècle* (1839) saw in the Italian poet a glorious expression of medieval philosophy. Ozanam, Wilhelm Schlegel, and others set out to refute Gabriele Rossetti's bizarre interpretation (1832) of the *Commedia* as a work written in a secret code for a heretical movement bent on overthrowing the church. A similar aberration is found in *Dante hérétique, révolutionnaire*

et socialiste (1853), in which Eugène Aroux dedicated his book to Pius IX and denounced Dante's genius as that of a heretic and an atheist, "one of those men devoid of both faith and honor who dream and plot revolutions."

The extent of fashionable interest in Dante is illustrated in various ways. Stendhal boasted that he knew Dante virtually by heart. In a letter to his sister (July 1804), he claimed that even "divine Homer has nothing to compare" with the Ugolino episode; for him, Dante personified the genius of Italian poetry, as Raphael did that of painting. Madame d'Agoult read Dante with Liszt by the shores of Lake Como and quoted him in her letters to the composer. George Sand nicknamed a friend "Graffiacane" after the demon of Malebolge (*Inf.* 21.122, 22.34–36). Delacroix had Dante ("the first of poets") read out to him while he worked at his easel; he attended a fancy-dress ball disguised as the medieval Italian poet, and in 1849, on the evening after Chopin's funeral, he paid homage to the composer's genius by sketching him in the guise of Dante. Gautier's sonnet "Ambition" (1844) managed to encapsulate the entire pantheon of French Romanticism in two verses: "To be Napoleon, to be even greater! / What then? to be Shakespeare, to be Dante, to be God!"

In his preface to *Cromwell* (1827) Victor Hugo praised Dante and Milton as artists who had understood that the sublime in life and art necessarily entailed the grotesque. Dante is coupled with Napoleon as an example of greatness in *Les Feuilles d'automne* (1831). Two chapters of *Notre-Dame de Paris* (1831) have titles taken from Dante: *Lasciate ogni speranza* ("Abandon all hope," book 8, chap. 4) and *La creatura bella bianco vestita* ("The beautiful creature clothed in white," book 11, chap. 2, adapted from *Purg.* 12.88–89). In *Après une lecture de Dante* (1836), references are made to Francesca and Paolo, the hypocrites' leaden cloaks, and the figure of Satan. Virgil and Dante are acclaimed as the poet's "divine masters" in his preface to *Les Rayons et les ombres* (1840), the collection which first expresses his view of the poet as prophet. Hugo's political writings in exile, such as *Les Châtiments* (1853), were placed under the aegis of Juvenal and Dante. *La Vision de Dante* (not published until 1883) is the poem most concerned with the exiled Florentine poet, who is awakened in the tomb and presented with a vision of the Last Judgment whereby the ultimate responsibility for suffering and oppression is laid on the figure of Pope Pius IX, condemned by the voice of God himself, who says to Dante, "Put him in your hell, I put him in mine." In spite of these and other references, Hugo's knowledge of Dante was patchy: he attributed to him a fascination with the great empires of the Orient, and he wrote of seven (instead of nine) circles in Dante's *Inferno*. Hugo's convictions that the idea of Hell was a survival from pagan superstition and that even Satan would eventually be forgiven by God, and his anticlericalism all made it difficult for the nineteenth-century French writer to acquire a better understanding of Dante's work. Nevertheless, Hugo deserves special mention for his anticipation of one of the key concepts in modern Dante scholarship: in *William Shakespeare* (1864), he referred to Dante's dual personality *(dédoublement)* as both author and protagonist of his great epic.

In 1840 Pier Angelo Fiorentino's prose translation of the whole *Commedia* appeared, the most popular of the century (sixteen editions), and was welcomed by Baudelaire as "the only good translation for poets and men of letters who do not know Italian." The *Vita Nuova* was first translated into French by Delécluze in 1841; it was followed in 1843 by the translation by Sébastien Rhéal, who now began to translate the *Oeuvres complètes de Dante* (1843–1856).

The influential writer and critic Sainte-Beuve had a knowledge of the whole *Commedia* shared by few of his French contemporaries: he quoted Oderisi's lines on artistic fame (*Purg.* 11.94–95), the appearance of Statius in *Purg.* 21, *Par.* 2, 13.130–138, and the prayer to the Virgin in *Par.* 33. Two of his poems have epigraphs taken from the *Vita Nuova,* and he incorporates a substantial passage from its twenty-third chapter into the poem dedicated to Antony Deschamps in *Les Consolations* (1830). Sainte-Beuve held up Dante's love for Beatrice as the supreme example of spiritual love; in 1854, he pointed to Beatrice's return in *Purg.* 30–33 as the kernel of the whole poem, which initiates its "hymn of love" and joy.

Balzac chose Dante as the protagonist of his short story *Les Proscrits* (1831), based on the legend of the exiled poet's stay in Paris (where Dante supposedly attended a lecture given by Siger of Brabant [*Par.* 10.133–138]). In 1846 Balzac claimed that *Paradiso* was "far superior to the *Inferno.*" He used the abbreviated form *Bice* for Beatrice (*VN* 24.8) in *Les Illusions perdues* (1837–

1843) and *Massimilia Doni* (1839). Balzac even quoted *Par.* 27.9 *(oh sanza brama sicura ricchezza!)* in *Béatrix* (1839) and in letters to Madame Hanska. However, he never referred to the title of Dante' s poem in connection with his own *Comédie humaine,* though the shift in epithet clearly reveals the novelist's intentions.

Other names, such as those of Musset and especially Nerval, could be added to the list of French writers attracted by Dante. From 1848 to 1851, Baudelaire intended to give the title *Les Limbes* to his collected poems; he used the title "La Béatrice" at least three times in his career. In 1857, in the first series of proofs for the poem that finally appeared with this title in *Les Fleurs du Mal,* Baudelaire wrote that "Beatrice" (and not the gallicized "Béatrix") was the correct title, since it was the Italian form signifying "the deity, the poet's mistress." The poem can in fact be read as an infernal parody of Dante's vision of Beatrice's death and assumption into heaven (*VN* 23).

With the waning of Romanticism, however, the Italian poet's fortunes ebbed. Auguste Rodin appears as a solitary giant, struggling with the *Gates of Hell* (commissioned in 1880) until his death in 1917. "I lived a year with Dante, drawing the . . . circles of his hell" and producing numerous sketches of figures locked in passionate embrace, sinners attacked by serpents, and Ugolino weeping over his sons and then devouring them. His final sculpture of Ugolino (1882) was placed on the left-hand door, which also portrayed Francesca and Paolo. The image of the humble sheep (*Purg.* 3.79–84) is found in Verlaine ("Sagesse," 1881), and echoes of Dante may be perceived in the writings of Arthur Rimbaud, who attempted to "invent . . . new stars . . . new languages" (*Une saison en enfer,* 1873). Nevertheless, Dante no longer inspired leading French writers.

In the twentieth century, Paul Claudel honored Dante as one of the five great masters who had taught him the art of poetry. Marcel Proust was probably inspired by Dante's narration of a guided journey in his structural use of the Narrator of *À la Recherche du temps perdu* (1913–1922). In 1922, Paul Valéry declared that he had discovered the *Paradiso* with its "manner of versifying abstractions that I used a little in my *Cimetière marin.*" The year before, Claudel had written an ode for the anniversary of Dante's death, which praised the poet for his unique, "divine" vision of

D the human comedy and for possessing the rarest of poetical virtues: inspiration, intelligence, and universality. In 1865 Victor Hugo had sent a speech to be read in Florence at the first international congress to honor Dante, the "incarnation of Italy" and Italian unity. This tradition was continued in 1965, when Saint-John Perse broke his rule of never speaking in public in order to deliver the inaugural address to the International Dante Congress in Florence. He praised the medieval poet for having forged the Italian people's soul by forging their literary language: "alien to the ways of mysticism," Dante combined a dual destiny as both dreamer and man of action. *La Peste* (1947) and *La Chute* (1956) by Albert Camus both display certain parallels with Dante's underworld, in spite of the author's "passionate unbelief." More recently, Yves Bonnefoy and Jean-Charles Vegliante have turned at times to the Italian poet. Vegliante in *Vers l'amont Dante* (1986) combines translated fragments of the *Inferno* with his own verse; he published the first part of his translation of the *Commedia* in 1995. Bernard Buffet produced a series of illustrations for his *L'Enfer de Dante* (1977).

The fine tradition of Dante scholarship, which began at the height of his French fortunes with the writings of Ozanam and the extraordinary *Bibliografia dantesca* published in 1846 by the Viscount Colomb de Batines, has been proudly maintained in the twentieth century by such eminent scholars as Étienne Gilson, Augustin Renaudet, Paul Renucci, and André Pézard. The last set a record in 1965 by publishing his translation of all of Dante's extant works. For the *Commedia,* Pézard chose the unrhymed decasyllable of the medieval French epic and selected wherever possible words recognizable despite their ancient patina ("old jewels rediscovered"). For her equally successful translation (1985–1990), Jacqueline Risset took the opposite, "utterly modern" approach in her blank verse in tercets. In 1996 translations of Dante's collected works were published in paperback under the editorship of Christian Bec.

Dante is still an important figure on the French cultural scene, although he is no longer the (often mythical) lodestar that inspired Romantic writers and artists. France has not produced a leading writer influenced by Dante to the same extent as Chaucer or Eliot; nevertheless, Dante's presence over the centuries has been a significant one, and few artists have produced works as important as the Dantesque creations of Delacroix and Rodin.

Bibliography

Bec, Christian. "'Le Dante' en langue française au XXe siècle: essai de synthèse." *Letture Classensi* 19 (1990), 105–116.

Ceserani, Remo. "Fortuna di Dante in Francia." *Enciclopedia dantesca,* 3:29–46.

Friedrich, Werner P. *Dante's Fame Abroad (1350–1850).* Chapel Hill: University of North Carolina Press, 1950.

Pitwood, Michael. *Dante and the French Romantics.* Geneva: Droz, 1985.

Rigolot, Carol. "Victor Hugo et Saint-John Perse: *Pour Dante.*" *French Review* 57 (1984), 794–801.

Risset, Jacqueline. "Dante nella poesia francese contemporanea." *Letture Classensi* 19 (1990), 15–22.

Simone, Franco. *Umanesimo, Rinascimento, Barocco in Francia.* Milan: Mursia, 1968, pp. 59–74, 151–168.

Strauss, Walter A. "Proust–Giotto–Dante." *Dante Studies* 96 (1978), 163–185.

Vickers, Nancy J. "Claudel's Delectation in Dante." *Claudel Studies* 8 (1981), 28–41.

John A. Scott

Dante in Germany

The history of Dante in Germany has been explored by Karl Witte, Wilhelm Freiherr von Locella, Johann Andreas Scartazzini, and Emil Sulger-Gebing and forms an important and interesting part of German literature and criticism. The following account divides this history into three parts: (1) from the Renaissance to the rise of Romanticism; (2) the period of Romanticism and German Idealism; and (3) the later nineteenth and the twentieth centuries.

From the Renaissance to the Rise of Romanticism

The first recorded mention of Dante on German territory occurred at the Council of Constance (1414–1418), when the Bishop of Fermo, Giovanni Bertoldi da Serravalle, presented the *Divina Commedia* in lectures from 1 February 1416 to 16 February 1417. A copy of these lectures has been preserved at the Vatican Museum. The first printed source on Dante can be found in the comprehensive historical work *Chronicon sive opus histori-arum* by the Florentine Archbishop Antoninus (1389–1459), which appeared in three folio volumes in Nuremberg in 1484. The third volume contains an informed section on Dante which focuses more on the political issues in his writings, especially in *Monarchia,* than on his poetry. Dante's adversarial attitude toward the pope forms the center of interest. This particular aspect determined the German view of Dante for a long time. The famous jurist Bartolus of Sassoferrato (1313–1359) discusses Dante's canzone *Le dolce rime d'amor* as an example of poetry *in vulgari* in his *Tractatus de dignitatibus* (Leipzig, 1493), but mostly in a polemical manner. He also mentions his *Monarchia* as a heretical writing expressing a wrong attitude toward *imperium* and *sacerdotium.*

The first German author to mention the life and writings of Dante is the Benedictine abbot of Sponheim, Johannes Trithemius, author of *Liber de scriptoribus ecclesiasticis* (Basel, 1494)—which despite its title also includes secular authors. Here again, emphasis is on the philosopher and not on the poet. Trithemius' information is mostly borrowed from *Supplementum chronicarum* by Jacobus Philippus Bergomensis (or Bergomas), which appeared shortly before in Venice. Jakob Lochner (1470–1528), a disciple of Sebastian Brant, produced a Latin translation of the latter's *Narrenschiff* ("Ship of Fools") under the title *Stultifera navis* (Basel, 1497). In his prologue, Lochner refers to Plato, Socrates, Lucilius, Horace, Persius, and Juvenal, but also to Dante and Petrarch. He thereby raises them to the rank of classical authors and regards them as models for those who want to write poetry in their native dialect. Lochner also introduced, along with Sebastian Brant, Ulrich Tengler's *Layenspiegel* (Augsburg, 1509) by writing a longer poem on what Dante, Boccaccio, and Petrarch had accomplished in the vernacular. This poem shows that he knew more about Dante than merely the name.

Meanwhile, the critique of the *Monarchia* continued. Johannes Nauclerus Verge (1430–1510) articulated a critique in Catholic style in his *Chronica ab initio mundi usque ad annum Christi nati MCCCCC* (Tübingen, 1501) by characterizing the work as an attempt to prove *"monarchiam esse in imperio Romano et rege Romanorum quod nullam dependentiam habet a papa sed a solo Deo"* ("that the monarchy is in the Roman Empire and under the government of the Romans and has no dependency from the Pope but only from God"). Josias Simler (1530–1576) offers little more than brief bibliographical notes in his *Epitome bibliothecae Conradi Gesneri* (Zürich, 1555). Mathias Flaccius, however, views Dante as a "witness of Protestantism before Protestantism" (Emil Sulger-Gebing) by claiming that in his *Monarchia* he proved *Papam non esse supra Imperatorem, ne habere aliquod jus in Imperium* ("that the Pope was not above the Emperor and had no jurisdiction whatsoever in the Empire"). He does this in his *Catalogus testium veritatis qui ante nostram aetatem reclamarunt Papae* (Basel, 1556). In the same year, a *Catalogus haereticorum* appeared in Königsberg, authored by Peter Paul Vergerius, a Lutheran, who defends Dante's *Monarchia* against its condemnation as a heretical book. Vergerius is also the author of *Annotationes* for this catalogue of 1560 which give a much more detailed account of the *Monarchia* and quote some of Dante's most explicit pronouncements against the pope and the secularization of the church. In 1559 the first German translation of this book, by Basilius Herold, appeared in Basel, as well as the first Latin edition of it, published by Joannes Oporinus; these editions were printed in Protestant territories because the *Monarchia* was still on the list of heretical books in Catholic lands. In 1600 the jurist Johannes Wolfius (1537–1600) published his voluminous *Lectionum memorabilium et reconditarum centenarii XVI,* a summary chronicle of sixteen centuries. The year 1321 is devoted to Dante's *Monarchia* and presents all his arguments for the autonomy of the Empire, high praise of Dante's courage in voicing such dangerous opinions despite the great power of the pope. Wolfius adds translations not only from the *Monarchia* but also from Dante's *Commedia* in Latin, which he renders line by line in prose (*Par.* 9.126–142, 18.127–136, 29.88–126). Dante is one-sidedly seen from a Protestant perspective as an enemy of the pope and the Catholic clergy. There is no awareness of his "Catholic" attitude. This is also the case in Matthias Bernegger's (1582–1640) *Hypobolymae divae Mariae deiparae seu idolum lauretanum* (Argentorati, 1619) and Johann Gottfried Olearius's (1635–1711) *Abacus patrologicus sive ecclesiae christianae patrum atque doctorum alphabetica enumeratio* (Jena, 1673).

Another important source for Dante in German literature consists in anecdotes, witty answers, and remarks on his part which had been transmitted in Italian literature (Domenichi, *Detti e fatti di diversi signori,* Venice, 1562) and now made their appearance in German literature—for example, in Sebastian Brant and Hans Sachs. One of these is of particular prominence. Cangrande's court jester once observed that Dante, with all his wisdom, remained poor and needy, whereas he outdid him by far in terms of wealth. Dante is reported to have answered that if he found a master equal to himself and who conformed with his own habits, this would also make him rich. We find this anecdote in several writings of this time, but it is most prominent, and combined with a description of Dante's life and writings, in Hans Sachs's *Historia.* From 1565 to 1586, Theodor Zwinger (1533–1588), a professor of medicine from Basel, published his *Theatrum sitae humanae,* which frequently mentions Dante in anecdotes. Nicolaus Reusnerus (1545–1602), a jurist from Strasbourg and Jena, published a booklet titled *Icones sive imagines vivae literis cl. virorum Italiae, Graeciae, Germaniae, Galliae, Angliae, Ungariae,* containing many portraits including one of Dante. Prince Ludwig of Anhalt-Cöthen (1579–1650) composed a rhymed description of his journey to Italy during the last years of the sixteenth century (Zerbst, 1716) and mentions Dante as a poet, with high praise and direct reference to the *Commedia.*

During the seventeenth century the first translations from the *Divina Commedia* appeared. At first only particular sections were translated in the context of larger books in which they were quoted. For instance, in Markward Freher's historical account of Constantine the Great's supposed donations, which appeared anonymously as *Constantini M. Imp. Donatio Sylvestro Papae Rom. inscripta* (Augsburg, 1610), the last pages quote in the original those *terze rime* that relate to this event (*Inf.* 19.115–117, *Par.* 6.1–9). Aegidius Albertinus (1560–1620) published a type of chronicle on the most famous men and women since the creation of the world (Munich, 1612) mentioning Dante's *Commedia* and its three parts. Georg Friedrich Messerschmid's *Sapiens stultitia* ("Wise Foolishness," 1615) includes distorted translations from *Inferno* (5.115–117) and *Purgatorio* (10.121–129). Other translations of sections from the *Commedia* can be found in the anonymous translation of Tommaso Garzoni's (1549–1589) *Piazza universale* (Frankfurt, 1619), a collection of quotes from many sources. The Dante quotes in this book relate to his conception of theology in the image

of Beatrice, a relationship not previously noted in Germany, and to the slanderers and loafers punished in Hell.

Subsequent references to Dante and his poetry increased rapidly in Germany. The great Baroque poet Martin Opitz (1597–1639) mentions Dante in the preface of his *Weltliche Poemata* (1628) in the context of a condensed history of Roman literature. The Austrian Jesuit Melchior Inchofer (1584–1648), in his *Historiae sacrae latinitates libri VI* of 1635, refers for the first time in Germany to Dante's treatise *De vulgari eloquentia* and distinguishes between the *vulgare latinum* and the *vulgare proprium,* as well as between the *vulgare illustre, aulicum,* and *curiale.* When Christian Brehme of Leipzig published his poetry (*Gedichte,* 1639) he included a translation of *Purg.* 3.34–39. Georg Philipp Harsdörffer (1607–1658) criticizes Dante for his use of poetic language in a 1643 book on *Gesprächsspiele,* or puns and word games. David Schirmer's *Poetische Rosengebüsche* ("Poetic Rosebushes," 1657) praises the German poets above foreign poets, among whom Dante is expressly mentioned. Andreas Gryphius (1616–1664), in his tragedy *Grossmütiger Rechtsgelehrter oder Sterbender Aemilius Paulus Papinianus* (1659), quotes in his annotations a passage from the *Inferno* describing brutal men and tyrants (*Inf.* 12.46–48, 100–102).

A longer seventeenth-century article on Dante appears in Johann Jakob Hoffmann's (1635–1706) *Lexicon universale,* which ignores the *Divina Commedia;* a much shorter entry on Dante in Daniel Georg Morhof's (1639–1691) *Unterricht in der Teutschen Sprache und Poesie* (Kiel, 1682) contains a section on the Triumviri of Italian poetry—Dante, Boccaccio, and Petrarch. The folio volume *Theatrum virorum eruditione clarorum* (1688), by Paul Freher (1611–1682) of Nuremberg, includes a long article on "Dante Aligerus." Dante's fame as a scholar is complemented by his even wider fame as a poet in his own language: *"erat enim non tantum Graece et Latine peritus, sed etiam in lingua Hetrusca fecundus"* ("he was not only experienced in Latin and Greek, but also prolific in the Tuscan language"). This long, informed article is the last major piece on Dante from the seventeenth century.

Dante became a topic in the great encyclopedias of the eighteenth century, most of which follow the entry on Dante in Pierre Bayle's famous *Dictionnaire historique et critique* (1659–1697).

This is the case in Johannes Francescus Buddeus's (1667–1729) *Allgemeines historisches Lexikon* (Leipzig, 1709), Benjamin Hederich's (1675–1748) *Notitia auctorum antiqua media* (Wittenberg, 1714), Johann Burckhard Menke's (1675–1732) *Kompendiöses Gelehrtenlexikon* (Leipzig, 1715), and Johann Heinrich Zedler's *Universallexikon* (Halle and Leipzig, 1732). Joannes Albertus Fabricius' (1668–1736) *Bibliotheca latina mediae et infimae aetatis* (Hamburg, 1734) has a more comprehensive entry on Dante that also relies on Italian sources. Christian Gottlieb Jöcher (1694–1758) largely follows Fabricius in his *Allgemeines Gelehrtenlexikon* (Leipzig, 1750).

Dante also occurs in poetic works of this century by way of comparison or reference. When Christian Heinrich Postel (1658–1705), a Hamburg author of opera texts, wanted to describe the fright of his protagonist Wittekind, he referred to Niobe in *Purg.* 12.37–39. When Georg Wilhelm Reinbaben (died 1739) defended Tasso in the long preface to his *Poetische Übersetzungen und Gedichte* (Weimar, 1711), he suggested that everyone who read Tasso's *Aminta* would say about this work what Dante had said about Beatrice: that whenever he had seen her, she had inspired him through her beauty with renewed vigor. The anonymous *Anleitung zur Poesie* (Breslau, 1725) has only very general references to Dante. Dante is also frequently mentioned in academic and bibliographical journals of these years, but according to Sulger-Gebing, these notes only show "how far removed scholars of that time were from the poet Dante."

This situation changed toward the middle of the eighteenth century, when controversy arose between the adherents of a classicist conception of poetry and the proponents of a more imaginative conception, and Dante was drawn into the debate. Johann Christoph Gottsched, the fiercest advocate of classicist taste, was the editor of a number of critical journals in which the name of Dante occasionally occurs—usually associated with the "mad" and "excessive" conception of poetry which Gottsched opposed. Dante is also reproached for having inspired Milton to extravagances. Gottsched wrote the article on Dante in his *Handlexikon oder kurzgefasstes Wörterbuch der schönen Wissenschaften und freien Künste* (Leipzig, 1760); this shows that despite his enmity he considered Dante important enough to rank among the great poets of history. Gottsched's

opponent in this battle, the Swiss critic Johann Jakob Bodmer (1698–1783), had a much more profound knowledge of Dante. He refers to Dante in some of his poems, mentions him in his *Critische Abhandlung von dem Wunderbaren in der Poesie* (1740)—a defense of Milton against Gottsched—and speaks more concretely about the Ugolino and Francesca da Rimini episodes in his *Critische Betrachtungen über die poetischen Gemälde der Dichter* (Zürich, 1741). Bodmer's most detailed discussion of Dante occurs in letter 29 of his *Neue kritische Briefe* (Zürich, 1749), bearing the title "Von dem Werthe des dantischen, dreyfachen Gedichtes." He emphasizes that Dante knows how to use all manners of writing—the tragic, comic, satirical, and lyrical. Bodmer also translated several scenes from the *Commedia* and composed a drama, *Der Hungerturm zu Pisa,* using the Ugolino scene in free adaptation. He was the first in the German-speaking world to sense Dante's greatness and universality as a poet.

With Bodmer, the debate about Dante moved closer to the apex of German literature in the eighteenth century, to authors like Klopstock, Lessing, Herder, and Goethe. The outcome of this phase in terms of real knowledge and understanding of Dante, however, was surprisingly meager. Klopstock had no relationship to Dante. Lessing knew him but had no appreciation of the enormous range of Dante's imagination: when he discusses the use of the ugly and the repulsive in poetry in his *Laokoon* (1766), he refers to the Ugolino scene and finds the height of the repulsive in the instance when the sons offer themselves to their father as food (chap. 25). When Heinrich Wilhelm Gerstenberg published his drama *Ugolino* (1767), Lessing sensed a Shakespearean spirit in it. This coordination of Dante and Shakespeare is important because of Lessing's attempt to establish Shakespeare, rather than French classicist tragedy, as the model for German dramaturgy. This association was taken up by other critics—for example, Johann Jakob Dusch (1725–1787) in his *Briefe zur Bildung des Geschmacks* (1765–1773)—but was of no importance for Lessing. Nor did Dante have any significance for Herder; he occasionally mentions him, mostly in reviews, but never makes a major pronouncement. The same applies to Goethe, although he occasionally mentions Dante in his conversations and letters, especially during his later period. He even translated various scenes in 1826 (*Inf.* 12.1–9, 28–45, 79–81)

D and used others in free adaptions. He also reviewed Böhlendorf's adaption of Ugolino in the *Jenaer allgemeine Literaturzeitung* of 1805, but he never gave any particular weight to the Italian poet.

The eighteenth century is also the time when the first comprehensive German translations of the *Commedia* originated. In 1755 Nicolo Ciangulo published the first German edition of Dante's *Inferno* (Leipzig, 1755). The first complete edition of the *Divina Commedia* appeared in Nuremberg from 1788 to 1804. When Moses Mendelssohn published an excerpt from Joseph Warton's *Essay on the Genius and the Writings of Pope*, he was faced with the Ugolino episode, which forms an important section in its fifth part as an example of pathetic poetry. Mendelssohn translated the entire text from Warton's English and produced, in spite of some omissions, a readable prose version. In 1763 Johann Nikolaus Meinhard published his *Versuche über den Charakter und die Werke der besten italiänischen Dichter* in Braunschweig. The first volume is devoted to Dante and Petrarch but conveys more about the former than the latter. Meinhard does not present a complete translation of the *Commedia,* but rather a condensed account of all three parts with long sections in prose translation. His rendering is the work of an enlightened person professing a moderate rationalism; when confronted with the daring turns of Dante's imagination, he withdraws and refuses imitation. He opposes Voltaire's critical view of Dante in the *Dictionnaire philosophique* of 1764 but approves of Voltaire's criticism on the whole. One year after Meinhard's translation, Johann Georg Jacobi (1740–1814) published his *Poetische Versuche* (Düsseldorf, 1764), a small, elegant volume of his own poetry which also contains the first translation of the Ugolino episode in German verse. It is obvious that German interest focused on the *Inferno,* and that the two scenes that aroused the greatest attention were the Ugolino and the Francesca episodes, especially the former. Jacobi translated Dante in unrhymed iambic pentameter. This was also the form into which Jagemann cast his metrical translation of the entire *Inferno* in his *Magazin der Italiänischen Literatur und Künste* (Weimar, 1780–1782). The first complete translation of the *Commedia* into German prose, by Leberecht Bachenschwanz (1729–1802), appeared in three parts in 1767, 1768, and 1769 in Leipzig. The first volume, containing the *Inferno,* was followed by a second edition in the same year. The

translation has been severely criticized, but it remains Bachenschwanz's merit to have provided his country with the first complete translation. This concludes the first part of the German reception of Dante, a phase of exploration and progressive discovery. The next phase, one of esthetic understanding and evaluation, began with the period of early Romanticism.

Romanticism and German Idealism

When August Wilhelm Schlegel focused his critical studies on the *Commedia* in 1790, a new phase in the German engagement with Dante began, and interest shifted from the political, theological, and historical aspects of the work to its poetry and poetic structure. Schlegel was twenty-four at that time and obviously on his way to creating an adequate German translation of the work as well as a historically correct image of Dante. He first wrote a comprehensive essay on Dante and the nature of his poetry for the Göttingen *Akademie der schönen Redekünste* in 1791; he illustrated this with sample translations, first from the *Inferno* and later also from the *Purgatorio* and *Paradiso.* His brother Friedrich urged him to continue this work, which Friedrich compared to the "discovery of a hidden sanctuary." Through his efforts, Dante became a guiding figure for early German Romanticism and the attempt to develop a self-conscious modern style of literature. Schlegel had a particular talent for the forms of poetry and considered it important to follow the *terza rima* of the original in his translation. At that time, however, he believed that the German language would not permit a full imitation of *terza rima,* and he therefore resigned himself to rhyming the first and third lines; he sacrificed the rhyming of the middle line with the following first and third lines that gives Dante's original its smooth transitions. Later, however, he utilized the full form of *terza rima* perfectly in his *Prometheus* and in his translation of Boccaccio's *Ameto.* Through Schlegel's knowledge of Italian Renaissance poetry and Dante in particular, as well as through his translations, Dante scholarship was rapidly raised to a new level. Schlegel continued his work as a translator and published selected scenes from the *Commedia* in German in a great variety of journals and magazines. He published some pieces more than once, but always with improvements.

In 1794 Schiller founded two new journals, the *Horen* and the *Musenalmanach;* the former became the organ for the type of classicism Schiller and Goethe pursued in Weimar. Schiller asked Schlegel to become a member of the exclusive group of collaborators, and, in addition to critical essays, he contributed his translations and annotations of scenes from Dante's *Inferno,* which caused a sensation in literary circles. During the same period, Schlegel began to translate scenes from Shakespeare for journals, including *Horen.* For a while he wavered between Dante and Shakespeare, but he eventually chose the latter and became nineteenth-century Germany's most successful Shakespeare translator and critic. His Dante translations remained unfinished, but Schlegel later polished them and organized them according to their sequence in the original, filling the gaps with transitions and explanations in prose. His *Dante: Über die göttliche Komödie* provides a complete overview of the work, including superb translations of individual scenes. He did not publish this manuscript, but it was included in his *Sämtliche Werke* of 1846. Schlegel displayed his Dante criticism in his lectures on *Schöne Literatur und Kunst,* presented in Berlin from 1801 to 1804, especially in the third section, "Romantic Literature" (1803–1804). Schlegel ranks Dante with Boccaccio and Petrarch as the beginning of modern literature, and with Cervantes and Shakespeare as one of the triumvirate of Romantic literature. Of particular importance is his discussion of allegory and symbol in the *Divina Commedia,* which permits him to view the more historically oriented parts in a new light and to open new vistas on the relationship of poetry and philosophy in this work.

His brother Friedrich Schlegel is of equal importance for Dante criticism. He places Dante right at the beginning of modern poetry and views him, together with Cervantes and Shakespeare, as a founder of a type of poetry that was not imaginable within the confines of classical poetry. Dante is thereby drawn into the struggle between the ancients and the moderns and becomes one of the most prominent figures of the Western tradition. This is noticeable in Schlegel's early essay *Über das Studium der griechischen Poesie* (1795) and determines his view of Dante as one of the main representatives of world literature. He expresses this opinion in fragment 247 of the periodical *Athenaeum,* the main literary organ of early Romanticism, where he sees in Dante, Shakespeare, and Goethe "the great triple accord of modern poetry, the inmost and holiest circle among all the broad and narrow spheres of a critical anthology of the classics of modern poetry."

This romantic view of Dante had an impact on German Idealism. The philosopher Schelling follows August Wilhelm and Friedrich Schlegel in his essay of 1803, *Über Dante in philosophischer Beziehung,* and augments their views about an inner relationship between poetry and philosophy in Dante's *Commedia.* Since then, the relationship of the *Commedia* to philosophy has been a major argument in Dante scholarship; see Étienne Gilson's *Dante et la philosophie* (Paris, 1939). A particular point in Schelling's interpretation is the relationship of allegory to history in Dante. The great figures of his poem have both an allegorical and a historical dimension. They thereby assume a mythological expression which is valid not just for a particular age but for all time. The same applies to the succession of the three realms, which relate to three realms of human experience: nature, history, and art. Nature is "eternal night" and "distance from God"; life and history are in a continual progression; and art is the "paradise of life." Nothing should be interpreted in isolation, according to Schelling, but only in relationship to the entire work. Dante's *Commedia* presents a poetic unity that has no equal in the history of poetry. Poetry and philosophy are so intimately related that they cannot be separated, as they later would be in Benedetto Croce's view (*La poesia di Dante,* 1920). Hegel intensified these views in his *Lectures on Aesthetics* by stating: "Here everything individual and particular in human interests and goals disappears before the absolute greatness of the final goal and purpose of all things; yet the merely transitory and fleeting quality of the living world simultaneously stands up in an epical manner, objectively explored in its inner value and judged in its worth and lack of by the highest concept, by God."

Later Nineteenth and Twentieth Centuries

From this period to the present, Dante has remained an important figure in Germany's literary consciousness and one of the main representatives of world literature. Several translations testify to his continuing presence in German literature. From 1839 to 1849 an annotated prose translation appeared under the pseudonym Philalethes ("Friend of Truth"), the name under which Johann Nepomuk, later king of Saxony, published his work on Dante. And his mother, Caroline of

D Parma, had instilled in him a predilection for the Italian language and Italian literature. Johann of Saxony collaborated in his work on Dante with Karl Witte (1800–1883), a famous jurist at the University of Halle, a genius in his command of languages, and the most distinguished Dante scholar of his time. In his youth he spent two years in Italy, where he acquired the foundations of his Dante scholarship. Parallel to his distinguished career in law, he published German translations of Boccaccio's *Decameron* (Leipzig, 1859) and Dante's *Lyrische Gedichte* (together with Kannegiesser, 1842). In 1862 he edited a scholarly annotated edition of Dante's *Commedia* which surpassed all previous textual criticism of this work and laid the foundation for true Dante scholarship. To be sure, Witte applied the norms and rules of classical philology too severely to a modern author; moreover, his edition is based on only four manuscripts and was outdone by the editions of Vandelli (1921), Casella (1923), and Petrocchi (1966). But he has the merit of having founded a methodologically self-conscious and self-critical Dante scholarship in the modern sense of the word. In 1865 Witte published his own metrical but unrhymed translation of the *Divina Commedia* with annotations, followed by editions of the *Monarchia* (Vienna, 1874) and *Vita Nuova* (Leipzig, 1876). His own two volumes of *Dante-Forschungen* appeared 1869 in Halle and 1879 in Heilbronn. Witte in 1865 founded both the Deutsche Dante-Gesellschaft and the *Deutsches Dantejahrbuch,* two institutions that still exist today. He also reedited the fifth edition of Karl Ludwig Kannegiesser's (1781–1861) translation of the *Commedia* (Leipzig, 1809–1821) in 1873. This was an enormously popular translation in the nineteenth century, and Kannegiesser is a truly meritorious translator; his translations from the Italian also include Dante's *Lyrische Gedichte* (together with Witte, 1827) and *Leopardis Gesänge* (Leipzig, 1832).

Johann Andreas Scartazzini (1837–1901) is next in the line of distinguished Dante scholars in the German-speaking world. He grew up in the Swiss canton of Graubünden with German and Italian as his native tongues and published in both languages. Scartazzini studied theology and became a pastor in Bern, and later (1871) a professor of Italian in Chur. His most important works deal with Dante: *Dante Alighieri, seine Zeit, sein Leben, seine Werke* (Biel, 1869; 2nd ed., Frankfurt,

1879); *Abhandlungen über Dante Alighieri* (Frankfurt, 1870); *Dante in Germania* (Milan, 1881–1883, 2 vols.); *Dante: Vita ed opere* (Milan, 1883, 2 vols.; 2nd ed., 1 vol. under the title *Dantologia,* Milan, 1894; 3rd ed. by Scarano, 1906). Scartazzini also published a critical edition of the *Commedia* with comprehensive annotations (Leipzig, 1874–1882, 3 vols.) and later added his *Prolegomeni della Divina Commedia* (Leipzig, 1890) to this edition. His *Dante-Jahrbuch,* a second yearbook on Dante in Germany, developed out of these *Prolegomeni.* Most useful is also his "small" edition of the *Divina Commedia* (Milano, 1893; 5th ed., 1907). He finally published his *Enciclopedia dantesca,* which appeared in Milan from 1896 to 1904; the last volumes were edited by Fiammazzo. Even today, after a century, one consults Scartazzini with profit and pleasure.

After Scartazzini, Karl Vossler (1872–1949) emerged as a prominent Dante scholar. Best known as a professor of Romance literature at the University of Munich, he mastered the entirety of that field and gave new impulse to the study of French, Italian, Spanish, and Portuguese literatures. He approached literature from a formal and purely esthetic point of view comparable to the New Criticism in North America and the concept of poetry established by Benedetto Croce, with whom he maintained a lively intellectual relationship. This is a view of poetry independent of philosophical, theological, social, political, and autobiographical considerations—a belief in the possibility of separating, as in Croce's *La poesia di Dante,* the merely didactic parts of the *Commedia* from its truly poetic ones. Vossler was also actively engaged in the study of language and wrote a number of books and essays on language theory. He conceived of language as "creation" and "evolution" (1905). In this sense, he studied, e.g., the culture of France in its relationship to the development of the French language (1913). His great work on Dante appeared during the first decade of the twentieth century: *Die göttliche Komödie: Entwicklungsgeschichte und Erklärung* (1907–1910). His translation of the *Divina Commedia* appeared in 1942. Vossler is also the author of *Dante als religiöser Dichter* (1921). He made the study of Dante an academic discipline and thereby exposed it to the fluctuating trends of academic criticism. All subsequent Dante interpreters were university professors and worked from within a particular critical framework. The great exception is Stefan George (1868–1933), who approached Dante as a poet in his own right and created a renowned translation of the *Divina Commedia*—which, however, exhibits the idiosyncrasies of the George Circle.

Erich Auerbach's (1892–1957) approach to Dante can best be described in relation to his general attitude toward the world of literature, as historical perspectivism or perspectivistic historicism which sees singular phenomena in a given epoch and simultaneously discovers a universal meaning in them—a meaning, however, that is hard to articulate and is best left vague. This approach is certainly an outcome of Auerbach's intense study of Vico and his translation of Vico's *Principi di una scienza nuova d'intorno alla commune natura delle nazioni* (Munich, 1925). It informs such essays as "Franz von Assisi in der Komödie," "Stefan Georges Danteübertragungen," "Entdeckung Dantes in der Romantik," "Dante und Vergil," "Figura," "Dante's Prayer to the Virgin (*Par.* XXXIII)," and "Dante's Addresses to the Reader." Many of his shorter works on Dante are collected in his *Neue Dantestudien* (Zürich, 1944), *Studi su Dante* (Milan, 1963), *Maestro Dante: Saggi e testimonianze di Erich Auerbach* (Milan, 1962), and *Gesammelte Aufsätze zur romanischen Philologie* (Bern, 1967). At the beginning of this rich scholarly work stands Auerbach's *Dante als Dichter der irdischen Welt* (Berlin, 1929), which emphasizes the earthly side of existence in Dante's interplay of the historical and the eternal, the individual and the universal, earth and heaven.

Ernst Robert Curtius's Dante interpretation is marked by his particular understanding of the relationship between the modern age and the Latin Middle Ages. He is of the opinion that the strong presence of classical antiquity in Dante's writings has to be seen as a mediated antiquity, shaped and reshaped during the Latin Middle Ages. Dante was a person of his time who lived and wrote under its aegis, and that period was the Middle Ages. In a certain sense Curtius developed these ideas parallel to Bruno Nardi (*Dante e la cultura medievale,* 1942), but he understands them from a much wider perspective. This relationship is not limited to medieval Aristotelianism and has a broader aspect deeply related to literature; nor is it limited to works that Dante wrote in Latin but includes his works in the vernacular, especially the *Commedia.* The poetics that stands behind this text cannot be found in ancient rhetoric nor in the *ars dictaminis;*

it has its own medieval origin. Curtius refers to Dante's famous letter to Cangrande della Scala and the particular way of allegorizing that it reveals. Curtius's study of Dante thereby becomes a case study for his monumental *European Literature and the Latin Middle Ages* (1948).

The period from the end of World War II to the turn of our century will be characterized here only by names and titles. Germany's interest in Dante has by no means decreased during this time, but its focus has shifted. The following authors and book titles may indicate its direction: August Rüegg, *Die Jenseitsvorstellungen vor Dante und die übrigen Voraussetzungen der Divina Commedia: Ein quellenkritischer Kommentar* (Einsiedeln, 1945); Hermann Gmelin, *Die göttliche Komödie: Kommentar* (Stuttgart, 1954–1957, 3 vols.); Ulrich Leo, *Sehen und Wirklichkeit bei Dante* (Frankfurt, 1957); Theophil Spoerri, *Dante und die europäische Literatur* (Stuttgart, 1963); Wilhelm Theodor Elwert, "Zur Frage der Dante-Übersetzung," in his *Italienische Dichtung und deutsche Literatur* (Wiesbaden, 1969); Hans Rheinfelder, *Dante-Studien* (Cologne: Böhlau, 1975).

Bibliography

Locella, Wilhelm Freiherr von. *Zur deutschen Dante-literatur mit besonderer Berücksichtigung der Übersetzungen von Dantes Göttlicher Komödie.* Leipzig: Teubner, 1889.

Scartazzini, Johann Andreas. *Dante in Germania.* 2 vols. Milan: Hoepli, 1881–1883.

Sulger-Gebing, Emil. "August Wilhelm Schlegel und Dante." In *Germanistische Abhandlungen: Hermann Paul dargebracht.* Strassburg: K. J. Trubner, 1902, pp. 99–134.

———. "Dante in der deutschen Literatur." *Zeitschrift für Vergleichende Literaturgeschichte* n.f. 8 (1895), 221–253, 453–479; 9 (1896), 457–490; 10 (1896), 31–64.

Witte, Karl. *Dante-Forschungen.* 2 vols. Halle: G. E. Barthel, 1869; Heilbronn, 1879.

Ernst Behler

Dante in Italian Literature

There are two histories of Dante's presence in Italian literature to be written. The first tells of the ineluctability of his work, especially the *Commedia,* from the fourteenth century to the present, in the minds and memories of Italian writers and, no less importantly, in those of readers and the whole educated public who are potential readers. This is the Dante who forms a necessary part of the written culture of Italy—who is a given point of reference, and not only in periods of powerful ideological consensus. Even at those moments when active interest and admiration are at their feeblest, as notoriously in the seventeenth century, a residual collective memory recognizes Dante's language as the foundation of what the culture has become. Seen from this perspective, Dante is ubiquitous in Italian literature; such ubiquity, however, should not be taken to mean that the memory of Dante is constant through time or preeminent in any individual case. Cultural memory is selective: parts of Dante are remembered, others forgotten or suppressed; parts are taken out of context, misremembered, recontextualized; the memory is frequently indirect, received via quotation, commentary, compendium, school or university exercise. Dante is everywhere in the writing of his successors, but more often than not the encounters are fleeting and strictly functional: Dante serves for a certain time, for a certain purpose, and then fades from center stage.

An exemplary case might be that of Giacomo Leopardi. Explicit references to Dante are numerous in his early writings, notably in the poem "Appressamento della morte" (1816) and in the strongly political references of his first three *canzoni,* as well as in the reflections of the *Zibaldone* devoted to the history of the Italian language. In 1823 Leopardi wrote his most "stilnovistic" ode, "Alla sua donna," the platonizing argument of which is distinctly non-Dantean, and in the same year he lauded the "amiability" of Tasso over the "admirability" of Dante. Thereafter, although Dantean echoes continue to be heard throughout the *Canti,* and the cosmic sweep of the *Commedia* is recognizable in late compositions such as "La ginestra" and the *Paralipomeni della Batracomiomachia,* Leopardi's attention is directed elsewhere, to other models and interlocutors.

This first history cannot in reality be other than a series of micro-histories, like that just sketched for Leopardi: a history of readings, reminiscences, and recyclings of Dante on the part of later generations, which vary in intensity, duration, and effect. Any individual mention, or simple echo, of Dante may be presumed to be determined by broader, general movements in the culture; but each occasion is so specific, and in a sense so random or accidental, as to be capable of yield-

ing meaning only under the most minute analysis. Such an analysis is beyond the scope of this article.

There is, instead, a larger story to be told. The reception of Dante in Italian culture over the past 700 years is marked by two long periods of strong consensus around Dante, or at least a part of his work: in broad terms, his own lifetime and the forty years or so after his death; and the high nineteenth century, particularly the years of nation-building between the defeat of Napoleon and the unification of Italy in 1861, followed by the celebration in 1865 of the sixth centenary of Dante's birth. The periods of consensus are notable for the variety, originality, and detail of the critical interpretations which they stimulate and which in turn feed into the collective literary imagination, as well as for the fair dose of hagiographic nonsense with which they are laced. Each was followed by an even longer period of disintegration, often prefigured in the consensus itself. The first of these takes on in retrospect the appearance of an accelerating withdrawal from the territory mapped out around Dante by his contemporaries; the second, which marks the twentieth century, is more remote from Dante and less directly concerned with the substantial issues that preoccupied him and his immediate successors, and it seems more fragmented and sporadic. The disintegration of consensus does not of itself lead necessarily to an abandonment or ignoring of Dante; on the contrary, it may produce new perspectives and fresh responses.

From an early stage, within a few years after Dante's death, the poet's name came to be associated first and foremost with the *Commedia.* Dante's beginnings as a love poet (pointedly recalled in *Purg.* 26)—and hence some of the scattered lyrics and, above all, the *Vita Nuova*—were not forgotten and would provide material for the *Life of Dante* of which Boccaccio wrote the first draft in the 1350s. The *Monarchia* and the public, political letters had an afterlife of their own, surfacing at different moments of antipapal tension from the 1320s on and attracting the censure of the ecclesiastical authorities. The other, uncompleted works, the *De vulgari eloquentia* and the *Convivio,* were rarely referred to in the fourteenth century, and the manuscript tradition is sparse. The *Commedia,* in contrast, commanded immediate and constant attention; this is attested by the extensive manuscript tradition, which includes many examples owned by private citizens, and by the commentaries on all or part of the poem, of which the earliest may well be that by Dante's son Jacopo, probably written before 1324 and followed by another ten in the next thirty years. This immediate focus on Dante's great vernacular work confirms Erich Auerbach's observation that by choosing the vernacular rather than Latin, Dante created a public for himself and his successors, and "molded, as potential readers of his poem, a community which was scarcely in existence at the time when he wrote and which was gradually built up by his poem and by the poets who came after him."

There is an essential agreement among all the early fourteenth-century commentators, the author (whoever he is) of the *Epistle to Cangrande,* and, presumably, the poem's readers that the primary interest of the *Commedia* is doctrinal and moral; as possessors of *'ntelletti sani* ("sound intellects") they must keep focused on *la dottrina che s'asconde / sotto 'l velame de li versi strani* ("the teaching that is hidden beneath the veil of the strange verses," *Inf.* 9.61–63). The biggest problem of reading it comes in determining the relation between the "strange verses" and the "teaching": if, as the *Epistle to Cangrande* states, the subject of the work, taken in the literal sense only, is "the state of souls after death, pure and simple," what weight is to be given to the pilgrim-protagonist who occupies the narrative throughout? And in what sense is that pilgrim experience to be understood as "true"? Beyond that, what allegorical meanings are to be attributed to particular figures in the poem, such as Beatrice or Virgil, or to crucial episodes in the narrative? On the whole, the early fourteenth-century commentators tend to focus on allegorical interpretations at the expense of the journey's experiential nature on which Dante insists so strongly throughout; and there is an inherent temptation to read the *Commedia* as an encyclopedia and to accumulate more and more extraneous matter around it.

Despite the varieties of interpretation which the text generates even in these early readers, there is essential agreement about the conventions of interpretation itself, and these are consonant with Dante's own ideas, even if they do not do full justice to his achievement. By the middle of the century, this consensus is crumbling. The kind of synthesis represented by the *Commedia* and the unitary conception of life which Dante so strongly propounded—the links between idea and symbol,

faith and reason, this world and the next—is disintegrating. The notion that reason can provide access or approach toward metaphysical truths is questioned; a different, less practical kind of ethics prevails. The theology and scholastic philosophy which had dominated intellectual life in the thirteenth century and the early part of the fourteenth are now challenged by new interests in which the study of classical literary texts plays a central role, and the relations between the two spheres that Dante strove to keep united become strained: poetry and theology assert control in their respective territories. The consensus around a culture that, at least theoretically, sought to achieve supreme syntheses starts itself to come under strain. The strain is most apparent in Boccaccio. In his *Life* he calls theology "the poetry of God" and lauds Dante as a *poeta cristianissimus,* but near the end of his life he is regretting that Dante wrote in the vernacular and that he, Boccaccio, has spent his time expounding Dante to the vulgar (in his public lectures of 1373–1374).

Boccaccio's later opinion was colored by his friendship with and admiration for Petrarch, who had taken his distance from Dante in a letter of 1359 in which he had made little concession to Boccaccio's claims that Dante should be treated as a classic on a par with the masters of antiquity. Petrarch's letter, in one reading at least, is a statement of achieved independence, first in an anti-Dantean use of the vernacular, and then in a no less anti-Dantean rejection of the vernacular altogether. He is the proponent of a poetry that must have nobility, polish, and charm, and he undoubtedly regarded the *Commedia* as a kind of versified theology lacking at least the last two qualities. But beyond that, it is as a cultivator of the classics, a humanist, a refined and aristocratic Latinist, that Petrarch wishes to establish his distance from— and his superiority over—his predecessor, and this is the distinction which is seen and recognized by his contemporaries and their immediate successors. The idea of a Petrarch supreme in Latin and a Dante supreme in the implicitly lowlier vernacular gradually took root; 150 years later Petrarch was awarded primacy over Dante even as a vernacular poet by generations of Italian, and other European, readers.

Petrarch's respectful but unambiguous demurral (in practice too, even in the supposedly Dantesque *Trionfi,* the Dantisms discernible in his language are a kind of lowest common denominator of influence) and Boccaccio's clear discomfort signal the start of a process which was as inevitable as it was unpredictable in its outcome. Itself the victim of a massive cultural shift, the consensus around the moral and doctrinal system of the poem no longer exists. That does not mean that Dante was simply swept away in the minds of readers (or writers); he had to be rethought, recodified. This is particularly the case in fifteenth-century Florence, heart of a politically and culturally assertive Tuscany, where Dante was recast first as a patriotic citizen (his vituperations against his native city largely forgotten) and then as a Ficinian Platonist in Cristoforo Landino's splendid edition of 1481, illustrated by Botticelli. Of no less importance to the developing history of "Italian" literature was the continuing challenge posed by Dante's language. Carlo Dionisotti has observed, writing of Dante and the Quattrocento, that while "the imitation of Petrarch was easier and more profitable [for the nascent printing industry], the *Commedia* was still linguistically fundamental, because of its enormous wealth and variety."

But the beginning of the sixteenth century was precisely the moment when serious systematizations of the Italian language and its written tradition were being attempted, for the first time perhaps since Dante himself. The rediscovered *De vulgari eloquentia* was used by the Vicentine G. G. Trissino to support the idea of a common national language, to the dismay of Florentine patriots like Machiavelli, some of whom thought that the treatise must be a fake. Of still greater significance for the reception of Dante was the publication of Pietro Bembo's *Prose della volgar lingua* in 1525. In arguing for the validity of Italian as a literary language and for Florentine writing of the fourteenth century as the basis of that writing (linked to his conviction that no speech [*favella*] can become a language [*lingua*] unless it has a written literature), Bembo argues primarily as a writer addressing an audience of actual or potential users of the written language. From this practical point of view, he is particularly concerned to establish norms of writing and to propose models that could be imitated. The attraction of the Florentine Trecento—or rather, of the two writers whom he thought particularly appropriate as models, Petrarch in verse and Boccaccio in prose—lay in their transposition into modern literature of the poise, decorum, grace, and charm of classical writing. Measured with this Horatian rule, read against

an ideal of literature as matching inner feeling with outer expression, and obliged to find a home in the courtly entertainments of princes and *signori,* Dante appeared too excessive, too extreme. He exaggerated, in the vastness of his ambition to say everything and in the baseness of the language he had to use to do so. He marks the outer limits of the language, reached in an early, experimental stage; Petrarch, in contrast, establishes the middle ground, the proper range of poetry that should not be overstepped.

Bembo underpins his condemnation of Dante's language and style with a methodological choice that appealed greatly to many of his contemporaries and was to exercise great influence: the decision to focus on the linguistic, rhetorical features of writing—Dante's as well as others'—to the exclusion of other criteria. This opens the way to an assessment of the *Commedia* uncluttered by any consideration of its value as theology, speculative philosophy, practical ethics, political ideology, or historical information. The assessment is of course generally, though not universally, negative in the long shadow now cast by Petrarch, and there was an increasing tendency in the later sixteenth century and in the seventeenth for the reading of Dante to become the preserve of specialist academies which produced immense expositions, first delivered orally, then transcribed; the main feature of these was that they were never completed. The apparent deafness to Dante of Torquato Tasso, the late sixteenth-century poet who might seem to have most affinity with Dante and the most to learn from him, may be due simply to the fact that the older poem, where neither the nature of the subject matter nor the particular position of the narrator-protagonist facilitates a naturalistic reading in terms of acceptable epic conventions, did not and could not provide him with the answers he was seeking as a Christian epic poet. And yet, the focus on the language also had a contrary effect. Bembo's concerns were normative, but there were others, such as Trifone Gabriele and Carlo Lenzoni, who pointed out that Dante was a master in using language appropriately to his purpose and need. It is true that during the sixteenth century the readership of the *Commedia* appears to have become an increasingly professional and learned one, but at the same time, the emphasis on language and style made the poem paradoxically more accessible to the reader who did not possess specialized exegetical skills. Readers and writers of the seventeenth century had strong ideological reasons as well as reasons of fashion for dismissing Dante: his orthodoxy appeared suspect in the wake of the Counter-Reformation; his poetry was found to be neither pleasurable nor polished; and above all, in a period of innovation and invention, Dante was considered anything but modern. But just as the casting off of the ideological structures of the poem left the text open to a linguistic inquisitiveness which did not have to be bound by the normative Petrarchism of high-Renaissance literary orthodoxy, so the collapse in the Baroque of sixteenth-century aspirations to overriding literary models or regularity (which in the case of Dante produced a long *querelle* on the genre of the *Commedia*) made possible the appreciation within a historical perspective of aspects of Dante's output which the concern with structures had tended to obscure (Chiabrera's reading of Dante's lyrics, for example). Without realizing or intending it, Bembo had pushed ajar the door to an esthetics of personal taste which the Baroque, in all its hostility or indifference to Dante, opened farther still.

The second great moment of consensus around Dante came in the first half of the nineteenth century. Like the early fourteenth-century view, of which it was profoundly conscious, the Romantic cult of Dante depended on a powerful synthesizing vision, a "master discourse" capable of organizing around itself many and various particular perceptions. In the fourteenth century, this discourse had been doctrinal or theological; in the nineteenth, it was historical. The historicization of Dante was not all one-way: if history enabled the modern reader to get closer to Dante than ever before, it also measured the distance which separated the nineteenth century from the fourteenth. Reading Dante in history meant opening oneself to the contrary pulls of the "primitive," of which the eighteenth century had already been aware and which thinkers from Gravina and Vico to Cesarotti had theorized: the early time, the beginning, the origin, as possessed of a particular energy and imaginative authority against which the present is registered as loss or decline—but also as that which is destined to be superseded in later time. And despite (perhaps because of) the Romantic drive toward totalization, readers were also aware that the meaning of the remote text could not be supplied by historical information alone: understanding and interpretation required a leap of the imagination, a readiness to enter into the spirit of the work, a sharpening of one's private sensibility to the nuance of the linguistic matter of the poem. The development of an esthetics of taste or sensibility (which in the eighteenth century had allowed readers to appreciate certain parts of the *Commedia* while rejecting others) combined with the foregrounding of history to produce the distinctively Romantic reading of Dante. The *Commedia* is not only a poem *by* an individual perfectly attuned to his own civilization—"the artistic epic proper of the Christian Catholic Middle Ages," as Hegel described it—but it is also a poem *of* the individual. Its very subject matter is the eternal fate of the individual rooted in the earthly here-and-now; it raises ultimate questions in the language of myth, symbol, and allegory yet is based on a real sense of concrete, historical existence. All of this makes it supremely accessible to the individual suffering, aspiring Christian reader. Those readers do not have to pursue every little detail in order to understand and appreciate the whole, and yet they do need to have their sense of their own historical existence constantly confirmed by the reconstruction, in the greatest possible detail, of that of others.

The two-way process of reading Dante historically is first and best expressed by Ugo Foscolo in two essays written for the *Edinburgh Review* in 1818. Foscolo's relation to Dante as a creative writer was personal and complex. As a young man, Foscolo celebrated Dante as a "father," as Alfieri had done, and he revered the same qualities of mind, love, and proud independence (not to say political intransigence) which had entranced the older playwright. This admiration for the personality of the poet was linked to a Vichian perception of the commanding position he occupied in European literature as a "primitive" poet, equivalent to Homer and (in Foscolo's view) Shakespeare. Foscolo's own poetry is not "Dantesque"—the molding of strong feeling into classical form owes more to Petrarch and Tasso than to Dante—but in poems written during his years of exile in England, Foscolo feels increasingly close, as many other political refugees later would, to the *ghibellin fuggiasco* (the "fugitive Ghibelline") whom he invoked in the great ode "Dei sepolcri" of 1807. His critical writing, however, does not depend on mere sentimental identification. "Dante's whole work," he writes, "though founded on what may be considered an extravagant fiction, is conversant only with real persons." This directness and actuality imparts to

D Dante's narrative an extraordinary degree of familiarity: there is in Foscolo's characterization the analogy with the experience of any one of us ("he takes all his characters from among his countrymen, his contemporaries, his hosts, his relatives, his friends, and his enemies"). But it also makes the text extraordinarily allusive and dependent on commentaries, for "he often speaks of anecdotes, of men and of crimes not mentioned by any contemporary writer." This dialectic between the poet's direct grasp of reality and the obscurity to the modern reader of his allusions may also be expressed in other terms. As material the poet uses the particular, the day-to-day, the small incidents of ordinary living which but for him would be entirely forgotten, and these he preserves and makes universally interesting; yet his subject is nothing less than the entire history of his age, and this he treats with a concision and compression which Foscolo regards as one of the great stylistic beauties of the *Commedia*. The job of the critic-historian, therefore, is both to recognize what Dante is alluding to and to provide the information necessary to complete it.

History is a universalizing discourse: it wants to see Dante whole, at every level. It wants to see the whole of Dante, all his works (it is now that there is not only a rediscovery of the "minor" works, but also a concerted effort to put them into relation with one another and with the *Commedia*); it wants to see all the literature around Dante (and in the first half of the nineteenth century, the early commentaries and chronicles were published for the first time in modern editions); it wants to see Dante on a global scale, as a founder not only of Italian literature but of European or "world" literature too; and it wants to celebrate not only this universality in space but also the continuity in time that links past to present. This continuity was differently defined as the 1820s and 1830s gave way to the 1840s and 1850s. According to Foscolo, influenced by Vico here, Dante is the first of the moderns, the figure from whom "we may date the commencement of the literary history of Europe." But increasingly this figure of the father or the origin gives way to that of the prophet. In this view, Dante gave voice to something that continued beyond him and that was to be fulfilled subsequently. Most frequently this larger entity was conceived to be a political one, and Dante was seen either as a religious reformer foretelling the Reformation or as a patriot reaching forward to the future unification and independence of Italy—or as an agglomeration of the two. Thus, when Cesare Balbo in his biography of 1839 describes Dante as "the most Italian Italian there has ever been," it is not for purely hyperbolic effect. What he means is something like "This idea of 'Italianness' which we are bringing to realization here and now in our Risorgimento was already prefigured and in a sense embodied in our great national poet." Or, as Mazzini put it in 1844, "The secret of Dante is a thing which concerns the present time."

The consensus around Dante of the first generations after the poet's death had given way to a kind of "forgetting" in the centuries that followed. Dante was pushed farther and farther back in time; much of the substance of the major poem was bracketed out as being irrelevant to an educated appreciation of the poet's language; and in the eyes of much of cultured Italy, then Europe, Dante's work had greatly shrunk in value. The dissolution of the early nineteenth-century synthesis based on history led not to the complete or even partial erasure of Dante from the literary memory, but to a scattering of the pieces from which that synthesis had been built. Italian writing of the twentieth century does not deny the actuality of Dante, and in this respect it both continues and exacerbates the historicism of the nineteenth, to the point of eroding its historical base. Mazzini's position was in a way itself prophetic, not so much because of its crude "nationalization" of Dante (a political use of the literary ancestor which recurred toward the end of the century in Carducci and particularly in Pascoli), but because of its firm location of Dante in the present. The personal rapport which pre-Romantic and Romantic readers felt with Dante (as with other great modern writers, notably Shakespeare) was institutionalized later in the nineteenth century through the key role ascribed to Dante in the national school and university curriculum. This position ensured the permanent presence of Dante's writing in the formation of educated Italians and the memorability of his text as a reservoir of quotation, allusion, reference, echo, and indeed pastiche and parody, particularly to those most attuned by personal taste and talent to hear it.

In fact, outside the world of academic specialists and scholars, readers and writers of the twentieth century share with their predecessors of the nineteenth a common currency, the only language in which it is now possible to read Dante, that of contemporaneity. Dante has become legible, and usable by other writers, only by reference to the personal and historical experience of the present; and for the present-day reader, as Foscolo foresaw, the need to have the text made intelligible by adequate explanation of its obscurities is balanced by the openness to that in the text which seems to speak to one's own experience. For Croce this was an esthetic experience, an intuition of the (universally) poetic qualities of the text to the exclusion of its nonpoetic ones. But a sense of shared passions, or a common ethical or political stance, has proved equally potent. For many readers of the past 200 years, unlike many of their predecessors (Boccaccio notwithstanding), the point of contact has been through the story of Dante's love for Beatrice, extending from the *Vita Nuova* to the *Paradiso* (or at any rate to the last *canti* of the *Purgatorio*). The *Vita Nuova* itself, insofar as it can be read as an autobiographical fiction, the story of a sentimental education, or a kind of *Bildungsroman,* has proved as suggestive to post-Romantic writers as the *Commedia;* one critic, for example, has suggested a radically transformed *Vita Nuova* as a model for Montale's collection *La bufera e altro,* despite the allusion to the *Inferno* of the latter's title. For other readers, particularly in the depths of the European catastrophe of the 1930s and 1940s, specific episodes or characters of the *Commedia* have served to bolster writers' confidence in human dignity—a humanism paradoxically sustained by a Dante shorn of any religious belief (one thinks of Vittorini's *gran Lombardo* or Primo Levi's citation of Ulysses' speech in Auschwitz in *Se questo è un uomo*). In another strain, Pasolini formed his approach to the problems confronting a *piccolo poeta civile degli Anni Cinquanta* ("little civic poet of the Fifties," *La Divina Mimesi,* 1975) in part by meditating on formally analogous problems in Dante: the poet's practice in the *Commedia,* especially in the light of the Continian distinction between (Dantean) "plurilinguism" and (Petrarchan) "monolinguism"; the combination of his "theological" and his "sociological" points of view; and the balance between *Dante narratore* and *Dante personaggio.* Examples of such readings—less personally committed perhaps than Pasolini's, but all more or less significant—could be multiplied many hundreds of times, and as they proliferate, they take us further into those micro-histories of which we spoke at the beginning of this article. The circulation of Dante within the Italian literary world, among the readers as well as the writers of Italian literature, depends on the openness of the text to many diverse encounters—a condition which at the same time makes any future interpretive synthesis appear for the moment unlikely.

Bibliography

Auerbach, Erich. *Literary Language and Its Public in Late Latin Antiquity and in the Middle Ages.* London: Routledge and Kegan Paul, 1965.

Barański, Zygmunt. "The Power of Influence: Aspects of Dante's Presence in Twentieth-Century Italian Culture." *Strumenti critici* n.s. 1 (1986), 343–376.

Caesar, Michael (ed.). *Dante: The Critical Heritage.* London and New York: Routledge, 1989.

Cavallari, Elisabetta. *La fortuna di Dante nel Trecento.* Florence: Società anonima editrice F. Perrella, 1921.

Consoli, Domenico. "Leopardi e Dante." In *Leopardi e la letteratura italiana.* Florence: Olschki, 1978, pp. 39–90.

Contini, Gianfranco. "Preliminari sulla lingua del Petrarca." In *Varianti e altra linguistica.* Turin: Einaudi, 1970, pp. 169–192.

Da Pozzo, Giovanni. "Dante e Foscolo." *Belfagor* 33 (1978), 653–679.

Dionisotti, Carlo. "Dante nel Quattrocento." In *Atti del congresso internazionale di studi danteschi.* Florence: Sansoni, 1965, vol. 1, pp. 333–378.

Dolfi, Anna. "Dante e i poeti del novecento." *Studi danteschi* 58 (1986), 307–342.

Grayson, Cecil. "Dante and the Renaissance." In *Italian Studies Presented to E. R. Vincent.* Edited by C.P. Brand et al. Cambridge: Cambridge University Press, 1962, pp. 57–75.

Kates, Judith A. *Tasso and Milton. The Problem of Christian Epic.* Lewisburg, Penn.: Bucknell University Press, 1983.

Martinelli, Luciana. *Dante.* Palermo: Palumbo, 1966.

Petrocchi, Giorgio. "Dante in Manzoni." In *L'ultima Dea.* Rome: Bonacci, 1977.

Scorrano, Luigi. *Modi ed esempi di dantismo novecentesco.* Lecce: Adriatica Editrice Salentina, 1976.

———. *Presenza verbale di Dante nella letteratura italiana del Novecento.* Ravenna: Longo, 1994.

Tavani, Giuseppe. *Dante nel Seicento: Saggi su A. Guarini, N. Villani, L. Magalotti.* Florence: Olschki, 1976.

D

Trovato, Paolo. *Dante in Petrarca: Per un inventario dei dantismi nei 'Rerum vulgarium fragmenta.'* Florence: Olschki, 1979.

Vallone, Aldo. "Dante e la *Commedia* come tema letterario dell'Ottocento." In *Studi sulla Divina Commedia.* Florence: Olschki, 1955, pp. 129–166.

Zennaro, Silvio (ed.). *Dante nella letteratura italiana del Novecento: Atti del Convegno di Studi, Casa di Dante, Roma, 6-7 maggio 1977.* Roma: Bonacci, 1979.

Michael Caesar

Dante in Russia

Dante's presence in Russian literature is chiefly a topic pertaining to the nineteenth and twentieth centuries. It can be studied in various registers: translations of Dantean texts into Russian; particular citations, especially in the form of epigraphs; formal borrowings, such as imitations of *terza rima;* and finally, the evolution of the "Dante theme" in the creation of a Russian Dante, who takes shape and metamorphoses within modern Russian literature.

According to Golenishchev-Kutuzov (1971), the first fragmentary translation (*Purg.* 28.1–75) appeared only in 1798. D. E. Min's verse translation of the *Commedia,* for nearly a century the standard edition, began publication in 1853.

Many of the writers who reflect a Dantean influence read him in the original. Nevertheless, as Iliushin (1968) shows in his study of the reception of Dante in Russia, writers tended not to expand their sources in the Dantean corpus but rather to keep reworking a restricted number of loci, chiefly from the *Commedia* and especially from *Inferno.* Hence, the process of poetic appropriation has primarily taken the form of finding original ways to use the most popular of Dante's verses.

Iliushin gives the following catalogue of what the nineteenth-century Russian reader knew of the *Commedia:* the tripartite plan and the triadism of its components; the main characters, Virgil and Beatrice, and their roles; and the celebrated passages from the *Inferno,* chiefly cantos 1–3 (in particular, the inscription over the Gate of Hell), the figure of Francesca from canto 5, and the Ugolino episode from cantos 32–33. A few readers would know the verses from *Par.* 16 about the bitterness of the poet's exile, which are alluded to, for instance, in Alexander Pushkin's short story "Piko-vaia dama" ("The Queen of Spades," 1833): *Gorek chuzhoi khleb, govorit Dante . . .* ("Bitter is the bread of exile, as Dante says . . ."). Professional writers also drew from the *Vita Nuova,* but rarely before the twentieth century.

Dante was essentially discovered by Russian writers in Pushkin's (1799–1837) day. Pushkin was the first Russian poet seriously to study and adapt Dante. His Dante is colored by European and Russian Romanticism and is associated with Byron, with Goethe's *Faust,* and with the figure of Ovid in exile. Indeed, in the wake of Pushkin's own exile to southern Russia (1820–1824), Dante became the focus uniting the themes of exile, the descent into Hell, and the poet's sacred mission (Gasparov, 1983). Moreover, Pushkin found in Dante the inspiration for the theme of "bookish love"—the love of a woman or couple seduced by the act of reading, first embodied in Tatiana, the heroine of his verse novel *Evgenii Onegin* (Eugene Onegin, 1823–1831); in a draft version, an epigraph consisting of *Inf.* 5.118–120 precedes the story of Tatiana's love in chapter 3. Other Russian refractions of Dante's Francesca da Rimini include Ivan Turgenev's Vera (in his short story "Faust," 1856) and Leo Tolstoy's Anna Karenina (1873–1877), as well as three lyrics by the Symbolist poet Alexander Blok. The Pushkin–Dante connection has been a scholarly topic since the posthumous publication of three verse fragments from 1830–1832 under the title "Imitations of Dante."

After Pushkin, Nikolai Gogol (1809–1852) is the next major contributor to the Russian Dantean tradition. From the *Vita Nuova* and the *Commedia* Gogol takes the theme of purification and spiritual rebirth. While scholars have found echoes of Dante in several of Gogol's stories and essays, the main work of appropriation can be seen in *Dead Souls* (1842), which the author labeled a *poéma* (a cognate with the Italian, the Russian word conventionally refers to a large-scale work of narrative verse); as contemporary readers like Aleksandr Herzen and P. A. Vyazemsky noted, *Dead Souls* seems to have been intended as a modern *Commedia,* with a tripartite plan. Modern Russian critics have also seen Dante as Gogol's model for the narrative of purification and rebirth. Iurii Mann (*Poétika Gogolia* [Gogol's Poetics], 1978) bases his interpretation on an explicitly Dantean allusion, a passage in chapter 7 in which a bureaucrat is characterized as a "new Virgil," serving Gogol's hero Chichikov "as Virgil had once served Dante."

Recent Western scholarship has focused on the Dantean implications of the title of Gogol's novel and the attendant paradox of dead souls in living bodies, which Donald Fanger (*The Creation of Nikolai Gogol,* 1979) links to *Inf.* 3.36, 64, 65. Marianne Shapiro (1987) sees in Gogol's novel a meditation on the *Commedia* and a transformation of the image of Dante taken over by Russian writers from German Romanticism: *Dead Souls* is indebted to the *Commedia* in its ethical schema, mystical overtones, and drive toward redemption. Moreover, Dante's use of the scheme of the seven capital vices in the *Purgatorio* finds stylistic echoes in Gogol's satirical treatment of the landowners encountered by Chichikov.

Dantean allusions have also been found in Gogol's "The Portrait" (1835), *The Inspector General* (1836), and "Rome" (1842). Annunziata, the heroine of "Rome," is modeled on the Beatrice of the *Divina Commedia* and the sonnets of the *Vita Nuova,* with one striking difference: whereas Beatrice in the *Commedia* becomes the embodiment of mystical religious truth, Gogol's heroine embodies the salvific power of the work of art (Baroti, 1983).

The image of Dante has been especially important to the Symbolist and Acmeist branches of Russian Modernism. In the epoch of Modernism (roughly 1890–1930), Dante's Beatrice becomes a figure for the tension between mystical divine truth and more secular conceptions of poetic art. The Modernists who show the deepest affinities with Dante are the poets Aleksandr Blok (1880–1921), Vyacheslav Ivanov (1866–1949), Osip Mandelstam (1891–1938), and Anna Akhmatova (1889–1966). Blok's poem "Dvenadsat'" ("The Twelve," 1918), which follows a detachment of Red Guards as they prowl about revolutionary St. Petersburg, is his culminating response to the *Inferno.* Thus, as McCarey and Cardines (1985) have suggested, the storm in the opening lines, a symbol of the revolution, is connected to *Inf.* 5.28-36, which pictures spirits cursing God's power as they are buffeted about by a hellish storm (both image of and punishment for their carnal passions). There are also extensive parallels between the Red Guards and the squad of devils in *Inf.* 21–22, and the Christ who appears at the end of "The Twelve" is connected with Christ's descent into Hell, referred to in *Inf.* 4, 12, 22. Blok's poem introduces Dantean overtones into Russian literature's treatment of the themes of the October Revolution, as later poems by Akhmatova and the prose of Aleksandr Solzhenitsyn would use Dante to treat the Stalinist terror.

The two most significant Modernist exponents/appropriators of Dantean poetics are the Symbolist Vyacheslav Ivanov and his one-time student, the post-Symbolist Osip Mandelstam. The centrality of Dante to the outlook of Ivanov, the most learned of the Symbolists, is already evident in his use of *Purg.* 27.88–90 as the epigraph to his first collection of poetry, *Kormchie zvezdy (Pilot Stars,* 1903). Ivanov's major theoretical statement on Dante comes in his essay "On the Boundaries of Art" (1913). Ivanov's essay includes his translation of most of the third chapter of the *Vita Nuova,* which he uses as his warrant for a religious Symbolist art.

Pamela Davidson, who has made Ivanov's affinity with Dante the focus of several studies (1982, 1986, 1989), focuses on the poets' shared intellectual and philosophical turn of mind and their perception of human experience within the framework of a religious worldview. From her close study of the manuscript sources (especially Ivanov's project of translating the *Convivio,* the *Vita Nuova,* and the *Commedia*), Davidson demonstrates how Ivanov transforms Dante into a proto-Symbolist, an exponent of Ivanov's own fusion of mystical Christianity with a Dionysian ecstatic religion containing transgressive and erotic overtones. These overtones color the image of Beatrice, who also remains a symbol of mystical wisdom. The transcendent realm, too, becomes heavily symbolic and abstract, and Dante is celebrated as a precursor poet who likewise wrote in an opaque and complex style.

For readers both in Russia and elsewhere, Osip Mandelstam's essay "Razgovor o Dante" ("Conversation about Dante," 1933) has become perhaps the best-known contribution to the creation of a Russian Dantean tradition. For the circle of young poets (later known as the Acmeists) from which Mandelstam and Anna Akhmatova emerged, an interest in Dante was one legacy of Symbolism they were far from rejecting. For Nikolai Gumilev (1886–1921), Dante was the great prototype of the poet as romantic exile; Mikhail Lozinskii (1886–1955) later became an outstanding translator, whose rendering of the *Commedia* (1939–1945) is considered his masterpiece.

Mandelstam's interest in Dante became incandescent in the early 1930s. So inspired was he by

D the *Commedia* that he twice took it to prison with him. Like his mentor Ivanov, Mandelstam in his "Conversation" uses Dante's text (in the final version, chiefly the *Commedia*) to illustrate his own poetics. Whereas Ivanov sees in Dante's works the embodiment of an esoteric, abstract theological system, Mandelstam's Dante is much more down to earth; his cosmos is a concrete experiential reality, not an intellectualized invention of the poet's imagination. In place of the Symbolist view of Dante as poet-theurge and summit of the medieval *forma mentis,* Mandelstam celebrates Dante as the prototype of all poet-outlaws and the greatest master of poetic language, as one whose mastery shows itself in his exploitation of the tactile, material qualities of language and its dynamism— qualities summed up by Mandelstam as "the transformability of poetic raw material." He is the creator of a "thirteen-thousand-faceted form," which is grasped only in process and performance. Far from being of antiquarian interest, Mandelstam's Dante is represented as being more avantgarde than the literature or science of the 1930s.

Mandelstam and Akhmatova read Dante together, and their verse contains many allusions to him. Given their experience of exile and repression under Stalin, it is natural that Dante's exile and his subsequent wanderings would figure prominently in these Dantean references. Thus, both poets have verses in which Dante's Florence is associated with their Petersburg; the motifs of dead or poisoned air (as in *Purg.* 1. 17, for instance) signal the connection. Mejlax and Toporov (1972) have identified *Par.* 17.55–60 as the locus classicus for the motif of Dantean exile and have traced its refractions in Mandelstam's "Otravlen khleb i vozdukh vypit" ("The Bread Has Been Poisoned and the Air Drunk Up," 1913), "Slyshu, slyshu rannij led" ("I Hear, I Hear the Early Ice," 1937); and in Akhmatova's "Ne s temi ja, kto brosil zemlju" ("Not with Those Who Have Abandoned the Land Am I," 1922), "Dante" (1936), and *Poéma bez geroja* (*Poem without a Hero,* written 1940–1962).

Akhmatova's extensive notations on her copy of the *Commedia* substantiate the importance of Dante's influence on her poetics from the 1930s on, and they also clarify the many oblique references to Dantean texts in her lyrics and poems. In her poem *Requiem* (1935–1961), for example, those standing in the prison lines of Leningrad resemble the dead of the *Inferno,* and the poet, like Dante, takes on the task of describing their experience. Moreover, as Amert (1990) points out, Akhmatova's aim is akin to Dante's: both poets seek to keep the memory of the dead alive for the living.

Dantean echoes may also be found in the prose of Mikhail Bulgakov (1891–1940) and Aleksandr Solzhenitsyn. Beatie and Powell (1981) have demonstrated a Dantean influence on the nature of time and space in Bulgakov's satirical masterpiece *The Master and Margarita* (written 1928?–1940). The ending of Bulgakov's novel, and especially the assigning of fates to its heroes, reflect the chronotope of *Purg.* 28, which describes Dante's entry into Eden.

Solzhenitsyn's novel *The First Circle* draws a parallel between the first circle of Hell and the *sharashka,* a relatively privileged form of prison in which Soviet scientists and technicians were forced to labor for the Soviet state. Some scholars have argued that Solzhenitsyn's history of the Stalinist camps, *The Gulag Archipelago,* not only contains scattered hints (e.g., reference to I. L. Auerbach in part 3 as "our Virgil") but even reflects the salvific plot of the *Commedia.* According to Matual (1982), some characters—especially Solzhenitsyn himself—undergo a journey through an inferno and a purgatory, arriving finally at a paradise. While Solzhenitsyn's inferno can be situated (its limits are coextensive with the boundaries of the Soviet Union), his purgatory and paradise are inward states: the pilgrim enters paradise when he accepts his sinfulness and renounces his desires. The sinners' guilt is the postlapsarian guilt of all who find themselves in the Soviet Union after the Revolution, presented as a Luciferian fall. Thus, Solzhenitsyn has an affinity with Dante's Christian worldview, but his theology and poetics are distant from the poet's.

In sum, each Russian writer or school finds something different in the Dantean legacy: a "medieval" ideal of beauty for Romanticism; an avatar for the life of the poet as prophet and exile for Pushkin; an epic and salvific potential for Gogol; a theology and theory of the symbol for the Symbolists (Ivanov, Blok); the representative of an organic worldview and a semantic poetics for the Acmeists (Mandelstam and Akhmatova); and a model for the geography and metaphysics of Hell—a Hell which writers have identified, variously, with nineteenth-century Russia (Alexander Herzen) and the Soviet Union (Solzhenitsyn and other chroniclers of the Gulag).

Bibliography

Amert, Susan. "Akhmatova's 'Song of the Motherland': Rereading the Opening Texts of *Rekviem*." *Slavic Review* 49 (1990), 374–389.

Asoian, A. A. *Dante i russkaia literatura*. Sverdlovsk: Izdatel'stvo Uralskogo Universiteta, 1989.

Baroti, T. "Traditsiia Dante i povest' Gogoliia 'Rim.'" *Studia Slavica* 29 (1983), 171–183.

Beatie, Bruce. A., and Phyllis W. Powell. "Bulgakov, Dante, and Relativity." *Canadian-American Slavic Studies* 15 (1981), 250–270.

Cavanagh, Clare. "The Poetics of Jewishness: Mandelstam, Dante and the 'Honorable Calling of Jew.'" *Slavic and East European Journal* 35 (1991), 317–338.

Colucci, Michele. "Dante in Russia e nella russistica occidentale negli ultimi venticinque anni." In *Dalla bibliografia alla storiografia: La critica dantesca nel mondo dal 1965 al 1990*. Edited by Enzo Esposito. Ravenna: Longo, 1995, pp. 177–184.

Crone, Anna Lisa. "Wood and Trees: Mandel'stam's use of Dante's *Inferno* in 'Preserve My Speech.'" In *Studies in Russian Literature in Honor of Vsvevolod Setchkarev*. Edited by Julian Connolly and Sonia Ketchian. Columbus, Ohio: Slavica, 1986, pp. 87–101.

Davidson, Pamela. *The Poetic Imagination of Vyacheslav Ivanov: A Russian Symbolist's Perception of Dante*. Cambridge: Cambridge University Press, 1989.

———. "Vyacheslav Ivanov and Dante." In *Vyacheslav Ivanov: Poet, Critic, and Philosopher*. Edited by Robert Louis Jackson and Lowry Nelson, Jr. New Haven: Yale Center for International and Area Studies, 1986, 147–161.

———. "Vyacheslav Ivanov's Translations of Dante." *Oxford Slavonic Papers* 15 (1982), 103–131.

Étkind, E. "'Ten' Danta.'" *Voprosy literatury* 14 (1970), 88–106.

Gasparov, B. "Funktsii reminiscentsii iz Dante v poézii Pushkina." *Russian Literature* 14 (1983), 317–349.

Golenishchev-Kutuzov, I. N. *Dante i mirovaia kul'tura*. Moscow: Nauka, 1971.

Guidubaldi, Egidio, S. J. (ed.). *Dantismo russo e cornice europea. Atti dei convegni di Alghero–Gressoney (1987)*. 2 vols. Florence: Olschki, 1989.

Iliushin, A. A. "Reministsentsii iz 'Bozhestvennoi kommedii' v russkoi literature XIX veka." In *Dantovskie chteniia*. Edited by Igor' Bel'za. Moscow: Nauka, 1968, 146–168.

Kopper, John M. "Dante in Russian Symbolist Discourse." *Comparative Literature Studies* 31 (1994), 25–51.

Jackson, R. L. "Vzaimosviaz' 'Fausta' Gete i 'Komedii' Dante v zamysle rasskaza Turgeneva 'Faust.'" In *American Contributions to the Ninth International Congress of Slavists,* vol. 2. Edited by Paul Debreczeny. Columbus, Ohio: Slavica, 1983, pp. 239–249.

Levin, J. "Zametki k 'Razgovoru o Dante' O. Mandel'shtama." *International Journal of Slavic Linguistics and Poetics* 15 (1972), 184–197.

Lotman, M. I. "Istoriko-literaturnie zametki. 1. Tiutchev i Dante. K postanovke problemy." *Uchenye zapiski tartusskogo gosudarstvennogo universiteta, Trudy po russkoi i slavianskoi filologii, Literaturovedenie* 620 (1983), 31–35.

Matual, D. "The Gulag Archipelago: From Inferno to Paradise." *Studies in Twentieth Century Literature* 7 (1982), 35–43.

McCarey, Peter, and Mariarosaria Cardines. "The Harrowing of Hell and Resurrection: Dante's *Inferno* and Blok's 'Dvenadtsat.'" *Slavonic and East European Review* 63 (1985), 337–348.

Mejlax, M. B., and V. N. Toporov. "Akhmatova i Dante." *International Journal of Slavic Linguistics and Poetics* 15 (1972), 29–75.

Shapiro, M. "Gogol and Dante." *Modern Language Studies* 17 (1987), 37–54.

Charles Isenberg

Dante in Spain

The legacy of Dante in Spain is both rich and varied, yet its history of scholarly appraisals seems, in large measure, to belong to either of two extreme views. Arturo Farinelli, for example, concludes that Spain produced no significant rewritings of the Florentine poet, whereas the Spanish critic Agustín de Amezúa represents the group of critics who find an extensive and profound presence of Dante in Spain. Several of the critics conforming to the latter view can perhaps be taken to task for a lack of specificity, in that they frequently identify much medieval Spanish allegory necessarily with Dante despite the extended presence of allegorical discourse long before his dissemination in Iberia. Nonetheless, his impact on the peninsula is indisputable.

During the century after Dante's death, seven translations of the *Commedia* were undertaken, some in prose and others in verse, Castilian as well as Catalan. In addition, the most important commentaries—those of Pietro Alighieri, Benvenuto da Imola, and Jacopo della Lana—circulated in Iberia not only in their original Latin or Italian form but also in Castilian translation. The sizable number of extant manuscripts and translations of the text as well as of its most influential contemporary commentaries reflects the poem's undeniable importance, which extended until the mid-seventeenth century.

Three principal categories of Dantean influence have been the object of scholarly investigation: adaptations of the *Commedia* as a whole or of selected parts of it (especially the Paolo and Francesca episodes of *Inf.* 5 or, more broadly, the experience of the *Inferno*) in the form of verbatim citations or Spanish translations of Dante's words; verbal resonances; and generalized use of allegorical journeys focusing on issues of ethical behavior and its consequences. For example, Juan Rodríguez del Padrón's *Siervo libre de amor* (1440) and the *Triste deleytación* (1460s, attributed only to "F.A.D.C.") exploit the *Commedia's* tripartite division to ponder the limits of courtly love. The tremendous prestige of Dante as the consummate Christian poet explains a good deal of his impact in Spain. His depiction of civil discord was equally appealing among the strifetorn political realities of fifteenth-century Spanish life.

Although Dante's poem was known in Spain sixty years after his death, the person who first promoted serious literary consideration of the Florentine master and his text was the proto-Humanist soldier-poet, the Marqués de Santillana, Iñigo López de Mendoza (1398–1458). Known not only for his military prowess but also for his passion for books, Santillana is recognized for having collected an impressive private library, for having written the first work of literary criticism in modern Spanish (the *Prohemio e carta al condestable de Portugal,* 1449), and also for having commissioned a fellow author, Enrique de Villena, to translate the *Commedia* into Castilian prose (finished in 1428). The influence of Dante extended to Santillana's own literary output, most visibly in his *Comedieta de Ponça* and the *Infierno de los enamorados.* While the first text reveals an understanding of *comedia* and *tragedia* as complementary opposites (a generic conception he accurately attributes both to the Latin comedy and to Dante),

the *Infierno* is a case of an allegorical vision modeled on Dante's first *cantica.*

Santillana is explicit in establishing Dante as the unparalleled model of vernacular *auctoritas:* both the implicit commentary he makes in the form of annotations to his own copy of the *Commedia* and the explicit assertions made in the *Prohemio* offer evidence to this effect. Yet to appreciate his work fully, we must bear in mind that the *Prohemio* was written at a time when there existed considerable skepticism about both the inherent value of poetry and the degree to which it was a meaningful pursuit for the nobility. By contrast with critics like Fernán Pérez de Guzmán, who wrote that poetry was *más graciosa / que útil nin honorable* ("more enjoyable than useful or honorable"), Santillana argued that the prestige of poetry is amply demonstrated as early as the eloquent example of the Bible, and that its finest expression has traditionally been found among the intellectual and social elite. Poetry is, in his estimation, also a means of achieving eternal fame.

The reverential views expressed by Santillana toward Dante and toward Latin *auctores* as well, along with the exegetical and reflective reading he advocated, were symptomatic of important developments in Spanish readership, and these were tied to further manifestations of Dante's impact. Juan II's reign (1419–1467) was a time of social turmoil during which a generalized spread of lay literacy led to a striking increase in reading among the nonclerical classes. Reading and exegesis became viewed as a source both of esthetic pleasure and of models of social ideals to be emulated. And Dante—along with the classical *auctores*—provided an illustrious paradigm on both counts.

Other European countries had, in the fourteenth century, already begun to articulate their national literatures: France with Jean de Meun and Machaut, Italy with Dante and Petrarch, and England with Chaucer. Yet it was not until the fifteenth century that Spain began to forge its own literary lineage. Although Dante could not be claimed as a native son, he could certainly be appropriated to dignify the new Spanish vernacular enterprise, as the work of Juan de Mena (1411–1456) and Francisco Imperial (late fourteenth century–early fifteenth century) boldly attest.

Juan de Mena, like Dante, strove to create an illustrious vernacular, the first "pure" poetry in Spanish that would rival the prestige and learnedness of Latin. In his learned syntax, lexicon, and predilection for mythological allusion Mena also resembles two other writers from his native Córdoba, Lucan and Góngora. He writes for a minority of highly educated readers who will gloss the text of this new Iberian poet-sage. Mena boldly represents himself in that guise in *La Coronación* (1438).

Santillana's commitment to learned literature and its salutary effects for both writers and meditative readers, as well as his admiration for the great writers of classical antiquity and medieval Italy and France, had earned him widespread recognition as a humanist exemplar in Spain's "fifteenth-century Renaissance." Although he modestly represented himself as *compilador* ("compiler") and connoisseur of the classics both ancient and modern, his disciple Juan de Mena elevated him to the status of *auctor* in his elaborately conceived *Coronación*—subtitled *Calamicleos,* a neologism conflating Latin *calamitas* with Greek *cleos,* "misery" and "glory," a way of expressing the double perspective of his text. Wandering alone in the month of April in search of Parnassus, the poet-protagonist loses his way. He beholds a terrifying spectacle: a gorge which he identifies as Hell, in which people are being devoured by serpents. Fainting from fear, he awakens after an undetermined period of time at Parnassus. There he beholds a group of unnamed sages and illustrious men seated on thrones. The one empty throne is suddenly occupied by a distinguished man—Santillana—whom the nine Muses crown with laurel. Yet, in a scene reminiscent of the double crowning of Dante by Virgil, first with crown and then with a miter (*Purg.* 27), Santillana is also honored by a second wreath, made of oak leaves to symbolize his military prowess, specifically his recent decisive victory at Huelma (1436) against the Moors, a battle which rekindled the stalled effort of the reconquest. In this way he is presented as the doubly exemplary scholar-hero.

Mena's more famous work, the *Laberinto de Fortuna* (1444), reflects a different kind of debt to Dante. This work was written not only to present himself as a polymathic poet-sage as in the *Coronación* but also to influence King Juan II and his citizens to follow the lead of Alvaro de Luna, his powerful advisor, who was beheaded in 1453. Designed to turn the attention of the warring nobles away from civil war and toward the constructive goal of the reconquest of Spain from the infidel, this poem, like the *Commedia,* offers a pageant of historical figures as well as mythological ones, with the poet (like Dante) depicting himself as both Aeneas and Virgil. Although the 300-stanza poem is intended to praise Juan II and motivate him to action, Mena characterizes him with some surprising Dantean resonances, as when he likens the monarch to Geryon (stanza 272). This is a rather bold and ambiguous analogy, given Geryon's monstrous nature, whether or not Mena is recalling his fraudulent Dantean persona or the other mythographic tradition in which he is killed by Hercules in his final labor. The appearance of Providence in the poem is reminiscent of Beatrice (*Purg.* 30), and Mena also recalls Dante when he attempts to embrace his guide who has suddenly disappeared, just as Dante vainly tries to embrace Virgil (*Purg.* 30, a calque on *Aen.* 6.700–702, when Aeneas also tries to embrace his paternal guide in the Elysian Fields).

These and other of Mena's strategic recollections of Dante bespeak his profound knowledge and appreciation of the *maestro.* Yet his contemporary, Francisco Imperial (late fourteenth–early fifteenth century) produced a 464-verse poem, the *Dezir a las siete virtudes,* which offers an even more dazzling recasting of Dante. This learned work begins with a conflation of the first and last invocations of *Paradiso,* but it significantly omits the Pauline allusion of *Inf.* 2.28, thereby signaling to the reader that Imperial will not attain the type of unmediated spiritual vision experienced by his illustrious predecessor. This is an essential difference, since for Dante-protagonist the *Paradiso* involves experiences that are clearly beyond the bounds of human perception and articulation. Imperial considers Dante's celestial voyage not as the literal fact that Dante claims, but as a dream—albeit the most exalted one.

That Imperial's remotivation of Dante is carefully wrought is also borne out by his calculated omission of Beatrice. Imperial signals to his reader that he can undergo the Ovidian transformation without need of an explicit guide, by contrast with Dante's reliance on Virgil, Beatrice, and ultimately St. Bernard. Further remotivations with profound and programmatic implications are evident when, for example, Imperial witnesses the stars shining down not upon Cato's face (*Purg.* 1) but upon his own (stanzas 47–48). This figuring of himself as Cato is intimately linked to his specifically Iberian concern—the desire to counter corruption at home by recalling for his readers the Roman exemplar of civil integrity. In this departure, Imperial reveals that he is not interested in retracing Dante's transhumanation (his literal *raptus* into the heavens, with all the spiritual implications it entails) but rather in forging a literary journey with an immediate and profound terrestrial message.

Dante as guide will remain at his disciple's side until the moment when Imperial awakens at the end of the poem with a copy of the *Commedia* in his hands (open to the "Hymn to the Virgin" of *Par.* 33.1). Imperial not only valorizes Dante as the consummate guide; he also endows him with the novel attribute of a passionate interest in Iberia. More precisely, he will explain to his disciple why the stars never appear in the skies over the peninsula (vv. 280ff.). The Seven Virtues are depicted in the Spanish poem not as Beatrice's handmaidens but as beings important in and of themselves, not subservient to anyone else. The seven serpents depicted by the *Dezir* also refer to the *Commedia*—to its longest canto (*Purg.* 32), where the serpent represents the Devil in the form of the seven historical heresies against the church. This interpretation of the serpents is a compelling one because the entire thrust of the *Dezir* is historical: the timely political and personal castigation leveled by Imperial against Seville recalls Dante's rebuke of his native Florence.

The final major Dantean nexus in Imperial focuses on the Celestial Rose. Though aware of its key metaphorical function for the *Commedia* and its epistemology, Imperial offers his readers literal roses instead. This moment in the Italian text (*Par.* 33), at which Dante begins to see God face to face, is thus radically altered by Imperial. In the *Dezir,* the pilgrim encounters literal roses and mediated angels—a striking inversion of Dante's metaphorical roses and literal angels. Dante is thus rewritten as a more limited form of allegoresis, representation, and language.

Imperial crystallizes this daring *mise en abîme* of Dante's celestial voyage by ending his poem with a reference to the first verse of *Par.* 33: *Vergine Madre, figlia del tuo figlio.* But instead of referring to canto or verse, Imperial speaks of *"el capítulo que la Virgen salva"* ("the chapter which praises the Virgin," v. 464). This prose marker, "chapter," distinguishes the second text from the first, reminding the reader of the two very different literary projects that the *Commedia* and *Dezir* represent. The Spanish protagonist, in the last two verses of the poem, awakens holding a copy of the *Commedia*—the book itself as object, not the vision or experience it depicts. In this way, and by his extraordinarily dense recasting of his model, Imperial eloquently remotivates Dante for his own uniquely Iberian literary and political purposes. By virtue of its dense and profound understanding of the *Commedia,* this text constitutes perhaps the most extended programmatic rewriting of Dante in the Western tradition.

The influence of Dante continues to be felt in such texts as Cervantes's *Don Quijote,* part 2, chapter 69 (1615), and in the very conception of the *Sueños* of Francisco de Quevedo (1627). Quevedo's narrator-protagonist claims to have experienced his visions *habiendo cerrado los ojos con el libro de Dante* ("having closed his eyes with Dante's book").

The second half of the nineteenth century saw a resurgence of interest in Dante with such works as Gabriel García y Tássara's *A Dante* and Gaspar Núñez de Arce's symbolic *La selva oscura* (1870s). In general, however, serious interest in Dante was not revived in Spain because models for literary inspiration were sought in the autochthonous authors of the Golden Age rather than in other national literatures. It is unquestionably fifteenth-century Spain, in its obsession with the need to forge a prestigious Spanish vernacular tradition, that looks most intensely to Dante for inspiration.

Bibliography

Amezúa, Agustín de. *Fases y características del Dante en España.* Madrid: Editorial Reus, 1922.

Farinelli, Arturo. *Dante in Ispagna—Francia—Inghilterra—Germania.* Turin: Fratelli Bocca, 1922.

Friedrich, Werner P. *Dante's Fame Abroad 1350–1850.* Rome: Edizioni di Storia e Letteratura, 1950.

Lida de Malkiel, María Rosa. *Juan de Mena, poeta del prerrenacimiento español.* Mexico, D.F.: UNAM, 1950.

Morreale, M. *Apuntes bibliográficos para el estudio del tema "Dante en España hasta el s. XVII."* Bari: Editoriale Universitaria, 1967.

Post, Chandler R. *Medieval Spanish Allegory.* Cambridge, Mass.: Harvard University Press, 1915.

———. "The Beginnings of the Influence of Dante in Castilian and Catalan Literature." *Twenty-Sixth Annual Report of the Dante Society of America,* 1908.

Weiss, Julian. *The Poet's Art. Literary Theory in Castile (c. 1400–1460).* Oxford: Medium Aevum Monographs, 1990.

Marina Brownlee

Dante and Television

Dante's *Commedia* possesses the qualities of a "producerly" text (Fiske 95): that is, it is a text that commands great popular appeal while simultaneously manifesting complex narrative strategies accessible only to the well-informed reader. Given the polysemous and image-based nature of the poem and the importance that orality plays in its genesis and reception, it is not surprising that Dante should "produce" television (for television as an auditory-based medium, see Marshall McLuhan, *The Gutenberg Galaxy*). What is surprising is that Dante has been a relatively late subject for televisual treatment and that little of what has been produced has managed to rise above the mediocre.

Programs on Dante Produced by Italian Television (RAI)

The first twelve years of Italian television produced only two documentaries on Dante of cinematographic origin: a series of dramatic readings of selected verses by Vittorio Gassman as part of the program *Lettere poetiche* (1955), and another program devoted to episodic readings from the *Commedia*. The seventh centennial of Dante's birth saw a much more concerted effort, the greater part of which was documentary in nature. The most successful work in this genre is Vittorio Cottafavi's *Vita di Dante* (1965). Filmed in an opaque style by Cesarini da Senigallia and with Giorgio Albertazzi as Dante and Loretta Goggi as the silent and symbolic presence of Beatrice, this is a docudrama that dramatizes Dante's life and intersperses into the narrative both documentary materials and passages from Dante's works. Also documentary in nature is *Dante, uomo e poeta,* televised under the direction of G. Betti in 1966; it traces the human and artistic evolution of Dante and makes much use of the illustrations of Gustave Doré.

A much more ambitious project and one focused on Dante's work is the 100-part prime-time series on the *Commedia* telecast in 1988, produced by the Dipartimento Scuola Educazione of RAI and directed by Marco Parodi. Each canto is introduced by Giorgio Petrocchi, the project's aca-demic coordinator, and then read by a well-known actor. Finally, a commentary is provided in the form of an artificially constructed dialogue between two distinguished scholars (for *Inf.* 5, for example, Giorgio Petrocchi and Ignazio Baldelli). From an academic point of view, these programs are impeccable in their fidelity to scholarship, which is a tribute to Petrocchi, one of the foremost Dante scholars of the past century. From an artistic point of view, however, much can be said to be lacking. Designed as an academic enterprise, the programs are sensitive neither to the language of television nor to the telepotential language of Dante's *Commedia.* The interpretive readings are too theatrical for the medium; the commentary is basic, but still too learned for the intended audience. The series amounts to little more than a televised *lectura dantis* and succeeds, in fact, in excluding the very audience it intended to address.

Equally lacking balance from an artistic point of view is Vittorio Gassman's series of dramatic readings of forty cantos of the *Commedia* (the whole of the *Inferno,* four cantos of the *Purgatorio,* and two of the *Paradiso*), produced by RAI in 1993 and directed by Rubino Rubini. The installments begin with short introductions by Gassman, followed by dramatic readings set in various opulent Italian locales such as public squares and theaters. The readings are a tribute to both the vocal range and thespian talents of Gassman, but ultimately this series amounts to little more than recorded readings and fails, like the preceding series, to realize the potential of the medium and the telepotential language of Dante's text.

Of far greater impact on the popular reception of Dante than the carefully planned RAI Dante projects, and the most interesting "performance" of Dante on Italian television, has been a chance occurrence on *Babele,* a live-transmitted RAI program dedicated to books and hosted by Corrado Augias. One evening in 1995 the program introduced as its guest the comic actor Roberto Benigni, star of such popular films as *Il mostro* and *Johnny Stecchino.* Benigni, who is Tuscan in origin, decided on the spur of the moment to recite from memory *Inf.* 5. The results were magical: Benigni's bravura—his language is the language of Dante—approximated an oral performance of Dante's poem using the "secondary orality" (Ong) of television. The fact that it was live and impromptu helped to recreate the aura of an early oral performance of Dante. Benigni's success lay

D perhaps in his exploitation of the telepotential aspect of Dante's text—its power to grasp the imagination.

Programs on Dante Produced Outside Italy

Early and cursory attempts at presenting Dante and his world include *Dante's Inferno* (United States, 1960), directed by Michael Meshekoff and starring (improbably) Howard Duff as Dante; *Beatrice, visage d'un mythe* (Belgium, 1963), directed by Emile Degelin; and *Dante: Inferno* (Hungary, 1974), directed by Andreas Rajanai. Much more ambitious in scope and more audacious in presentation is Britain's *A TV Dante,* begun in the late 1980s, although the pilot of *Inf.* 5 was completed in 1984. Produced by Channel Four Television with Bob Peck as Dante and John Gielgud as Virgil, the series will eventually contain thirty-four episodes, one on each canto of the *Inferno,* and will involve directors as diverse as Peter Greenaway, Terry Gilliam, and Nagisha Oshima. The first fourteen cantos were completed by 1991: cantos one through eight are directed by Tom Phillips, a well-known experimental artist, novelist, and maker of books, and by Peter Greenaway, one of Britain's foremost contemporary intellectual and experimental filmmakers; cantos nine through fourteen are directed by the South American avant-garde and socially committed director Raul Ruiz. The two sets of cantos reveal diverse responses to Dante's poem. Phillips and Greenaway focus on the writerly aspects of the text, highlighting Dante's discursive strategies and metaliterary discourse. To achieve this effect, and to bridge the seemingly inaccessible gap between the world of Dante (with its complexity of historical, theological, philosophical, and cosmological allusions) and that of modern viewers, the directors deployed television technology in new and daring ways. The television screen is made to explode with a host of images—visual plays on words, geometric constructs, radar screens, weather graphs, cardiographs, Muybridge animations, the Luftwaffe's bombings of London—many of which are presented as stacked or appear on a split screen or a screen within a screen. Accompanying the presentation of an arsenal of visual images is an equally impressive array of experts (on numerology, mythology, ornithology, stock-broking) who are called into play at key moments to explain the subtleties of Dante's immense learning. The net effect is a foregrounding of stylistic

and technical virtuosity and a televisual bombardment of the senses which aims both at exposing the primacy of Dante's text and at forcing a response from the modern imagination. It is for this reason that so many of the images are violent, brutal, and disturbing.

Inf. 5, which served as a pilot for the project, is indicative of the overall approach. The first part of the segment moves at a feverish pace—a Felliniesque Minos is followed by a televised weather warning about an approaching tornado in the southern United States for the *bufera infernale,* and the distinctive, snapshot style of British documentary for the epic catalogue. Throughout we are forced by the proliferation of repulsive sounds and images, by the split screen, and by the altering of sound and color, to enter the episode's underworld setting. The segment is framed by the word "LUSTFUL" (the opening introduces a visual word play on "LUSTFUL," "LUST," "US") and its representative Francesca, whose illicit love is presented through the imagery of the words themselves: the word "LOVE" is literally branded in fire onto the screen each time Francesca utters it in the three famous tercets, while during the Galeotto passage the camera focuses on her sensuous mouth, which takes on a vaginal form and the shape of the letter V in "EVE." This framing device successfully conveys the nature of lust and the episode's *contrapasso* and also roots the televisual spectacle in the power of Dante's text. Although these first eight cantos have not been embraced enthusiastically by Dante scholars, and although the readerly quality of Dante's poem—its easy accessibility—has been downplayed at the expense of the writerly, they are to this date the most stunning and compelling translation of Dante from poem into video.

A far different approach is employed by the series's second director, Raul Ruiz, for cantos nine through fourteen. Ruiz, the most prolific Chilean filmmaker, has been concerned with the artistic themes of the evocation of memory and the possibility of life after exile. Himself an exile, he has observed that he chose Chile as a locale for *A TV Dante* as a way of establishing a correspondence with Dante as exile. His interest in a radically politicized filmmaking process is evident in his segment of *A TV Dante,* which is grounded in a politicization of the text. He creates an urban Hell on Earth by recording the journey of the pilgrim and his guide against the everyday reality of the inhabitants of Santiago, (emphasized through-out by the opening text of each canto, "Santiago de Chile"). The landscape is barren, sparse, and threatening, and the pilgrims (Dante clad in jacket and tie with a copy of the *Codex civilis* in one hand, and Virgil in a camel's-hair coat) traverse this landscape in virtual silence. Against a background narration spoken by John Gielgud and Bob Peck, they move from an antechamber (canto 9) to the City of Dis; the Furies are presented as three inter-woven women with a huge spider writhing in front of them, and the celestial messenger as a faceless businessman. The claustrophobic hellish city, a great desertlike necropolis (canto 10), is figured as a series of contemporary modern images from everyday life in Santiago—Farinata appears as a relaxed figure sipping a drink in a huge funereal urn. This gives way to Virgil's explanation of the lower circles (canto 11), where the violent are seen sharpening bloody implements in the context of images of suspended carcasses of slaughtered ani-mals, followed by a set of images of slaughtered humans. The violent against their neighbors are represented, in a basement chamber, by mutilated body parts into which are inserted various country flags (canto 12); the suicides by a forest of human trees surrounding people celebrating the joys of life (canto 13); and the blasphemers by a pan of eyeballs frying in hot grease (canto 14). Through-out the style is surreal, layered in the grotesque with a proliferation of repulsive images. The effect is one that sacrifices the narrative power of Dante's text in order to promote a decidedly Marxist ide-ology focused on issues of class struggle and the oppression of the proletariat. (Peter Greenaway will return to direct the last cantos of the *Inferno,* those of Cocytus.)

Educational Programs Not Intended for Public Broadcast

Programs dealing in general with Dante's life and works have been designed for presentation to students (primarily undergraduates) in a class-room setting. One such example, produced by Educational Filmstrips and Video of Huntsville, Texas, in 1987, is *Dante: Divine Poet and Wander-ing Exile.* It traces the route Dante took following his exile from Florence and documents the land-scapes he later used in the *Commedia.* It also attempts to show how the poet's experiences in exile shaped his vision of the otherworld. The result is a kind of biographical travelogue. Much

of the visual material used is anachronistic, and no serious attempt is made to engage it to evoke Dante's powerful verbal imagery or to comment on the poem's textuality. The same may be said of *Dante: The Journey of Our Life,* made in 1991 by Roger McCarthy Productions of Princeton, New Jersey. It too is visually static and technically unimaginative, but the text, written by Robert Hol-lander, is adept and critically sophisticated, intro-ducing students not only to Dante but to the "American" allegorical interpretation of Dante. Hollander's discourse is essentially Singletonian in perspective: Dante the pilgrim's journey of redemption through the three realms of the after-life is potentially our journey through this life.

Dante's Divine Comedy: A Televisual Com-mentary, coordinated by Amilcare A. Iannucci and produced by the Media Centre at the University of Toronto, constitutes the most recent ongoing attempt to present Dante's *Commedia* in a visual format. Two programs have been completed, one on *Inf.* 5—"Vulcan's Net: Passion and Punish-ment" (1987)—and the other on *Inf.* 26, "Dante's Ulysses and the Homeric Tradition" (1985); others are in progress. Though intended for use in the classroom like the American videotapes referred to above, the University of Toronto videos ap-proach the subject in a completely different way. They attempt to reconstruct televisually the iconography of damnation and salvation which Dante's powerful verbal imagery would trigger in the minds of his contemporaries. This effect is achieved by using manuscript illuminations and other kinds of visual images, even from late sources, which belong to Dante's and his original public's cultural patrimony and memory. Manu-script illuminations have been privileged because they are small, flat, and often ill-defined, charac-teristics that make them ideally suited for the medium of television with its small screen and rel-atively low definition. The primary purpose of the University of Toronto Dante video series is, there-fore, to reposition students historically in a pre-humanistic setting and make them conscious of the artistic process, so that the visual and aural contexts of the *Commedia* may be critically re-experienced. The perspective and imagery thus re-claimed are used to illustrate key aspects of Dante's poem, whether thematic or structural. This particular approach is exemplified by the synopsis of "Vulcan's Net." The video retells the story of Paolo and Francesca, setting it against the broader theme of love and war. Its archetype is traced to the adultery of Venus and Mars, which Ovid characterizes as "the best-known story in all Heaven." Images of Venus thus dominate the screen, but near the end of the program, at the moment when Dante the pilgrim swoons, the image of Venus slowly dissolves and is replaced by one of the Trinity. This technique, reinforced by the narration of the closing verses of the canto, suggests that the pilgrim in this crucial episode is coming to terms with the destructive consequences of lawless love, and that his *poema sacro* celebrates not *folle amor* but *caritas*—not Francesca but Beatrice.

Tom Phillips remarks that "Dante, with his apocalyptic vision, belongs as much to us as to his contemporaries; and television is the medium of our time. So, why not bring the two together?" (*The World of Peter Greenaway,* 80). The history of Dante in television is a series of televisual attempts to do just that, and even though the results have been mixed, Dante still remains an inexhaustible source for television treatment.

Bibliography

Antonucci, Giovanni. "Televisione." *Enciclopedia dantesca,* 5:538.

Casadio, Gianfranco (ed.). *Dante nel cinema.* Ravenna: Longo, 1995.

Fiske, John. *Television Culture.* London: Methuen, 1987.

Iannucci, Amilcare A. "Dante Produces Television." *Lectura Dantis* 13 (1993), 32–46.

———. "Dante, Television and Education." *Quaderni d'Italianistica* 10 (1989), 1–33.

McLuhan, Marshall. *The Gutenberg Galaxy: The Making of Typographic Man.* Toronto: University of Toronto Press, 1968.

Ong, Walter J. *Orality and Literacy: The Technologizing of the Word.* London: Methuen, 1984.

Phillips, Tom. "Dante's *Inferno.*" In his *Works and Texts.* London: Thames and Hudson, 1992, pp. 219–251.

Steinmetz, Leon, and Peter Greenaway. "Frames: *A TV Dante.*" In his *The World of Peter Greenaway.* Boston: Journey Editions, 1995, pp. 76–93.

Vickers, Nancy J. "Dante in the Video Decade." In *Dante Now. Current Trends in Dante Studies.* Edited by Theodore J. Cachey. Notre Dame, Ind.: University of Notre Dame Press, 1995, pp. 263–276.

Amilcare A. Iannucci

Dante Society of America

Second oldest of the great Dante societies, after the Deutsche Dante-Gesellschaft (1865), but the longest-lived by continuity (1881–present), the Society originated from a small group of friends with a common interest in Dante who met regularly during the 1860s in Cambridge, Massachusetts, with Henry Wadsworth Longfellow to critique his translation of the *Commedia* as he completed it canto by canto. From "Mr. Longfellow's Dante Club" the Dante Society was formally constituted at an initial meeting in 1881, with the stated purpose, "the encouragement and promotion of the study of Dante's life and works." Appointed as the first president, Longfellow was succeeded after his death in 1882 by a series of other notable Harvard professors, including James Russell Lowell (1882–1892) and Charles Eliot Norton (1892–1908).

In keeping with the society's purpose, from the start much effort went into building a Dante collection in the Harvard College Library and into sponsoring the publication of a series of concordances to Dante's works: E. A. Fay, *Concordance of the Divina Commedia* (1888); E. S. Sheldon and A. C. White, *Concordanza delle opere italiane in prosa e del canzoniere di Dante Alighieri* (1905); E. K. Rand, E. H. Wilkins, and A. C. White, *Dantis Alagherii operum latinorum concordantiae* (1912); L. H. Gordon, *Supplementary Concordance to the Minor Works of Dante* (1936); and E. H. Wilkins and T. G. Bergin, *A Concordance to the Divine Comedy* (1965). Over the years the society has, occasionally, also published a number of short studies, signal among them C. S. Singleton's *Essay on the "Vita Nuova"* (1949). A regular, ongoing feature has been its yearbook, beginning in 1882 as the *Annual Report of the Dante Society, with Accompanying Papers;* many issues, reflecting intervals of diminished activity of the society, were published in multiple numbers after 1921 and especially between 1936 and 1954.

Under the presidency of E. H. Wilkins (1954–1959), the Society was incorporated and expanded from a Boston-Cambridge coterie to a national and international entity as the Dante Society of America; of additional significance, the *Annual Report* was restored to regular yearly publication, with an annual annotated "American Dante Bibliography" as an integral feature (continuous since 1953). In 1966 a new office of editor was established to handle the yearbook, which, under the "founding editor," Anthony L. Pellegrini, was transformed, with a new and much expanded format, from a spare house organ to a full-fledged scholarly journal: *Dante Studies, with the Annual Report of the Dante Society.* In a more recent publishing development, as part of its centenary activities the Dante Society conceived and sponsored the *Lectura Dantis Americana*, a series of volumes to be prepared by prominent scholars, analyzing individual cantos of the *Commedia,* initially under the general editorship of Robert Hollander; the first volume, on *Inf.* 1, was published in 1989, and additional volumes on successive cantos have followed. In 1994, under the direction of Richard Lansing, the complete *American Dante Bibliography (ADB)* from 1953 to the present was made available in electronic format on computer disk and later placed on the Web, and in 1996, also under his direction, the society published the first *International Dante Directory.* In 1996, under the guidance of Robert Hollander, the society established the *Electronic Bulletin of the Dante Society of America (EBDSA),* a scholarly electronic journal on the Web.

The society in 1998 had 430 members, including a number of internationally renowned honorary members. From the Society's founding in 1881 (with the one exception of 1939) the annual meeting has taken place each May in Cambridge, with a paper or panel discussion on a Dantean topic following the short business proceedings. Beginning in 1965, a secondary meeting has been held in conjunction with the annual December meeting of the Modern Language Association of America. Since 1887 an annual Dante Prize has been administered by the society for the best student essay submitted at the undergraduate level, and since 1965, the Charles Hall Grandgent Award at the graduate level. The society was incorporated in the state of Massachusetts in 1954.

A. L. Pellegrini

Dardanus

Son of Jupiter and Electra, the mythical ancestor of the Trojans, and therefore of the Romans, named *(Dardano)* in *Conv.* 4.14.14 and *Mon.* 2.3.11 (see *Aen.* 8.136–137).

Richard Lansing

Dark Wood

The introductory canto of the *Commedia* finds the protagonist Dante having strayed into a *selva oscura* ("dark wood") where he has lost the *diritta via* ("straight way," *Inf.* 1.3). Whatever specific allegorical meaning the image might contain, its general intent is clear: the lost way represents a departure from virtue and truth into the chaos of sin, which corrupts the individual's mind and spirit. The wood's darkness is generally taken to denote error and is associated with evil, while the wood itself has been interpreted as the human condition of worldliness, corruption, and ignorance. The early commentators (Jacopo Alighieri, the Ottimo, Benvenuto, and the Anonimo Fiorentino) equate the *selva* with the sinful aspects of earthly life itself. The lost path prefigures the textual journey out of sin into goodness, as the wayfarer moves from confusion and evil to knowledge and redemption.

As a prologue, *Inf.* 1 symbolically sets the scene for the journey that the protagonist Dante will take through the other world. The literal voyage through its three realms represents the journey of the soul that seeks to return to its maker, and its symbolism borrows from the traditional Christian conception of life as a pilgrimage. Like many a medieval traveler, Dante's pilgrim is waylaid by dangers within the forest. The literal wood is *selvaggia, e apra e forte* ("savage and harsh and strong," 5), connoting its power to bewilder the senses and cause the soul to stray from the path of righteousness. Dante operates within a familiar ideological and intellectual culture for his time, which viewed natural phenomena as appearances veiling truer realities or as projections of a transcendent universe. The motif of being lost in the woods was frequently employed in allegorical writing throughout the Middle Ages: one of Dante's mentors, Brunetto Latini, in his *Tesoretto* describes a fantastic voyage which is begun in a forest. A classical source for the image of the dark woods is Virgil's *Aen.* 6.179 (*antiquam silvam,* "ancient wood"), in which the entrance to Hades is hidden by the trees and vegetation of a vast forest. In *Conv.* 4.24.12, Dante himself employs the image of the "meandering forest" as a metaphor for deviation from the good or desirable *(la selva erronea di questa vita)* when he describes the difficulties encountered by an adolescent who requires the assistance of a guide lest he stray from

D

Dante in the dark wood. La comedia, *ed. Piero da Fighino, 1491. Giamatti Collection: Courtesy of the Mount Holyoke College Archives and Special Collections.*

From Opere del diuino poeta Danthe, *published by Bernardino Stagnino da Trino de Monferra, Venice, 1512. Reproduced by permission of the John A. Zahm Dante Collection in the Department of Special Collections, University Libraries, University of Notre Dame.*

the *buono cammino* ("right way"). The wood is associated with the vegetative world, which has led some critics to speak of being lost in the wood as symbolizing a descent on the chain of being from the rational level to the vegetative (Pagliaro 11).

The lack of an exact geographical locus for the dark wood has led some commentators, both medieval and modern, to see it as an oneiric image, a powerful dream, rather than as an actual (albeit fictional) place. The narrator's confusion as to how he entered the wood, explained as a state of sleep "at the point when I abandoned the true way," 11–12), suggests a dormant state of moral awareness, a state of unconsciousness, or more exactly a loss of conscience, which leads to spiritual death. Although Dante's poem is generally not considered a dream-vision, there are several references in *Inf.* 1 to a dreamlike state of being in which the wood functions as a typological dreamscape which oppresses and confines the dreamer. In the Bible and in early Christianity, sleep was associated with both spiritual disorder and a condition of sinfulness. The canto's emphasis on emotions and reactions supports a psychological reading of the space as a projection of Dante's state of mind.

The allegory of *Inf.* 1 is extensive and has been criticized by some as lacking in true poetry. The image of the dark wood itself is part of a larger metaphorical sequence that includes a hill and three beasts. The hill, whose summit is lit with the rays of the Sun, constitutes a symbolic antithesis to the wood: the light of God's illuminating grace fosters hope and contrasts with the fearsome darkness of the wood. Blocking access to the hill, three beasts—leopard, lion, and she-wolf—are related to the physical and spiritual environment of the wood. While debate over the specific allegorical meaning of the animals has continued unabated for centuries, nearly all critics agree that they represent different types of sinfulness. The beasts block the pilgrim's ascent up the hill and ultimate access to God's light. Within the imagery of the canto, they drive the pilgrim back into the darkness of the wood, back into worldliness and sin. It is only with the arrival and assistance of Virgil, who is often taken as the symbol of human reason (especially among the early commentators), that the pilgrim is able to escape from the wood and the beasts.

The introductory allegory also denotes the age of the wayfarer. Given the biblically allotted term of life as threescore years and ten, the *mezzo del cammin* ("middle of the journey") marks the midpoint, the thirty-fifth year, in the life of the pilgrim, and it suggests the ideas of human maturity and midlife crisis. Since Dante was born in 1265, the opening scene places the action in the symbolic year 1300. Astronomical references in the canto to the Sun in Aries (37–40) indicate that the opening action takes place during the week of Easter, and the pilgrim meets Virgil on Good Friday, a day that commemorates the death of Christ and, symbolically, all of humanity. Although the dark wood suggests sin and evil, it also prefigures another, positive, forest in the *Commedia:* the divine forest of Eden. If the wood of *Purgatorio* is the locus of man's prelapsarian state of grace, to which he ultimately returns through the process of redemption, the dark wood of the prologue represents man's postlapsarian condition. By the same allegorical token, the hill of the first canto anticipates and corresponds to the mountain of Purgatory which the pilgrim will ascend after completing his journey through Hell.

Some biographical readings of the canto have focused on the description of the pilgrim astray in the dark wood as a fictional allusion to Dante's youthful period of error. An exclusively biographical reading, however, would diminish the universal implications of the episode. The wayfarer's wandering in the dark wood is ultimately best understood as a paradigm of a world that has lost its moral purpose and its spiritual goal.

Bibliography

Cassell, Anthony K. *Lectura Dantis Americana: Inferno I.* Philadelphia: University of Pennsylvania Press, 1989.

Freccero, John. "The Prologue Scene" and "The Firm Foot on a Journey Without a Guide." In *Dante: The Poetics of Conversion.* Cambridge and London: Harvard University Press, 1986, pp. 1–28, 29–54.

Getto, Giovanni. "Canto I dell'*Inferno.*" In *Lectura Dantis Scaligera: Inferno.* Florence: Le Monnier, 1967, pp. 1–20.

Masciandaro, Franco. "The Prologue: The Nostalgia for Eden and the Rediscovery of the Tragic." In his *Dante as Dramatist: The Myth of the Earthly Paradise and Tragic Vision in the Divine Comedy.* Philadelphia: University of Pennsylvania Press, 1991, pp. 1–35.

Nardi, Bruno. *Il preludio alla Divina Commedia.* Turin: SEI, 1964.

Pagliaro, Antonino. "Il proemio" and "Il prologo." In his *Ulisse: Ricerche semantiche sulla Divina Commedia.* 2 vols. Messina and Florence: G. D'Anna, 1967, pp. 1–69, 71–114.

Pietrobuono, Luigi. *Il Canto I dell'Inferno.* Turin: SEI, 1959.

Fiora A. Bassanese

David

One of the most important figures of the Old Testament, where he is portrayed as a king, prophet, poet, and both ancestor and figure of Christ. He was the second king of Israel, the successor of Saul and the father of Solomon. According to the Bible (1 Sam. 16–1 Kings 2), David was a young shepherd, the youngest son of Jesse, when the prophet Samuel anointed him to be the next king of Israel. Shortly thereafter, David fought the Philistine giant Goliath and defeated him. King Saul initially favored David but later came to envy him because of his talents and his popularity with the people and with Saul's son Jonathan. David was forced to flee from Saul, but after the king's death he became king of Judah and eventually united all the twelve tribes under his rule. During his reign he was guilty of two grievous sins: he committed adultery with Bathsheba and then arranged for the death of her husband, Uriah; and, toward the end of his life, he conducted a census of Israel in opposition to the wishes of the Lord. His reign was marked by great triumphs but also by personal tragedy and (when his son Absalom rebelled against him) by civil war. He was Israel's greatest king and their model for the ideal king: biblical prophets, in fact, later foretold the return of a "Davidic" king who would restore Israel to greatness. Christians interpreted this prophecy as referring to Christ, and David was often seen as a type of Christ. He was also a poet and musician, and most of the book of Psalms has been attributed to him in the biblical tradition.

Dante refers to virtually all of David's roles. He is first mentioned in the *Commedia* as one of the Hebrews rescued from Limbo by Christ and is there called *Davìd re* ("King David," *Inf.* 4.58). In the *Monarchia,* Dante mentions David's victory over Goliath (*Mon.* 2.9.11), designating him *rege illo sanctissimo* ("that most holy king"). Dante further underscores David's kingship in the *Paradiso,*

D

where he portrays David as the pupil of the eagle's eye in the heaven of Jupiter, the heaven devoted to justice (*Par.* 20.37-42). On the first terrace of the *Purgatorio,* David appears in one of the three relief sculptures that depict exemplary figures of humility, where he is shown dancing before the Ark of the Covenant as his wife Michal scornfully looks on (*Purg.* 10.55–69; the biblical story is found in 2 Sam. 6). In his role of the paradoxically humble king—*e più e men che re era in quel caso* ("and he was both more and less than king on that occasion")—David anticipates Christ himself. David's willing humiliation enacts the fundamental antithesis of Christ's incarnation: sublimity through humility *(humilitas-sublimitas).* Dante thus portrays David here as a figure of Christ *(figura Christi).* Dante also mentions David's identity as an ancestor of Christ at *Conv.* 4.5.5–6.

Dante most frequently mentions or cites David as an inspired poet and prophet. He calls David the *Profeta* ("Prophet") in the *Convivio* (2.1.6), cites the Psalms more than any other scripture, and refers to David as *l'umile salmista* ("the humble psalmist," *Purg.* 10.65) as he dances before the ark in *Purg.* 10. And indeed, in the heaven of Jupiter, where his justice as king should be at issue, Dante calls him not king but *il cantor de lo Spirito Santo* ("the singer of the Holy Spirit," *Par.* 20.38), and states that David's merit derives from *suo canto* ("his singing"). At a number of places in the *Commedia* and in his minor works Dante emphasizes that this singer of the Holy Ghost was inspired. Dante asserts in the *Monarchia* that those who misinterpret scripture err not only against the human authors of the Bible (among whom he mentions David), but also against the Holy Spirit *qui loquitur in illis* ("who speaks through them," 3.4.11). And in the heaven of the fixed stars, Dante tells the Apostle James that it was David, *sommo cantor del sommo duce* ("highest singer of the highest Lord," *Par.* 25.72), who—through his *tëodia* ("divine song")—first taught him to hope for eternal salvation.

Dante, moreover, finds a parallel between his own erring journey toward God and attempt to render it into verse, and David's identity as a sinner who nevertheless finds salvation and tells of it in the Psalms. Dante's own first spoken words in the *Commedia, "Miserere di me"* ("Have pity on me," *Inf.* 1.65), cite Psalm 50, in which David laments his sin with Bathsheba and asks the Lord's forgiveness: *Miserere mei* ("Have mercy upon me").

Toward the end of the poem, Dante names Ruth through a periphrasis that refers to her as David's ancestor, *bisava al cantor che per doglia / del fallo disse "Miserere mei"* ("great-grandmother to the singer who, grieving at his sin, cried 'Miserere mei,'" *Par.* 32.11–12), which both cites David's Psalm and recalls Dante's own words at the opening of the poem.

David's repentance and inspired songs therefore come to prefigure Dante's turning from the sin of the *selva oscura* ("dark wood") and his writing of the *Commedia,* as he consistently links the prophet-poet David to himself and his poem to David's biblical poetry. Just as David was both more and less than king when he danced before the Ark of the Covenant, so Dante's poem, a lowly comedy, becomes greater than the works of antiquity and takes its place beside David's *tëodia* as a modern, vernacular, divine song.

Bibliography

Auerbach, Erich. "Figurative Texts Illustrating Certain Passages of Dante's *Commedia.*" *Speculum* 21 (1946), 476–477.

Barolini, Teodolinda. *Dante's Poets: Textuality and Truth in the Comedy.* Princeton: Princeton University Press, 1984, pp. 275–279.

Battaglia Ricci, Lucia. "Scrittura sacra e 'sacrato poema.'" In *Dante e la Bibbia. Atti del Convegno Internazionale promosso da "Biblia."* Edited by Giovanni Barblan. Florence: Olschki, 1988, pp. 295–321.

Hollander, Robert. "Dante's Use of the Fiftieth Psalm." In *Studies in Dante.* Ravenna: Longo, 1980, pp. 107–113.

V. Stanley Benfell

De Sanctis, Francesco

A patriot of the Risorgimento and a literary scholar, De Sanctis (1817–1883) was one of the leading Italian literary historians of the nineteenth century. While teaching in Naples, De Sanctis became an exponent of Hegel; he translated Hegel's *Logik* while in a Bourbon prison following the failure of the Neapolitan Revolution of 1848. Eventually he transformed Hegelian esthetics according to the needs and conditions of realism, while preserving the doctrines that art creates its own autonomous world, that it is organic, and that it creates a concrete form. As an exile he continued his literary and philosophical studies and lectured on Ariosto, Petrarch, and Italian literature at Turin and the Zürich Polytechnic. De Sanctis returned to Naples with the establishment of the Kingdom of Italy in 1861, becoming a member of the first Italian parliament and the first minister of education. He published *Saggi critici* (*Critical Essays,* 1865), *Saggio critico sul Petrarca* (1869), and *Nuovi saggi critici* (1872). These works comprise collections of his essays on individual writers, poems, or individual cantos of the *Commedia.* In 1870 and 1871 he brought out his masterpiece, *Storia della letteratura italiana (The History of Italian Literature),* widely regarded as one of the best literary histories ever written.

Underlying De Sanctis's critical views is the concept that art is distinct from emotion, science, philosophy, or politics: art creates an autonomous, organic world of its own that should be judged according to its own truth and not by criteria extraneous to it. Because a work of art forms a concrete organic unity, each work is individual, so questions of literary genre or type are of little importance. Such distinctions are external. This being the case, matters such allegory, symbolism, and personification which subordinate the organic life of the form to some intellectual structure are not art. "Allegory dies and poetry is born," De Sanctis declared in the *History.* The power and greatness of art reside in its spontaneity and potential for growth according to its internal logic.

De Sanctis argued that the concept of the *Commedia* was neither original nor extraordinary. Dante's greatness and inspiration were to take the ordinary folk tradition and fill it with the high culture of the day. Thus, the mystery of popular legend was elevated by the conceptions of science and philosophy, and science and philosophy were given a dimension of mystery. For De Sanctis, Dante was the first modern poet to exercise the faculty of fantasy *(fantasia),* an organic synthesis that allows the work to develop according to its inner logic. He contrasts this with *immaginazione,* a mechanical manipulation of external features. (De Sanctis's terms reverse those in Coleridge's distinction between imagination and fancy.) Thus, where Guinizzelli and Cavalcanti generate their poetry by manipulating conventions, Dante creates living figures who go beyond his intellectual conception. Figures such as Satan and Geryon have little power or originality because they conform to the allegorical type. By contrast, figures such as Beatrice, Francesca da Rimini, and Farinata are great because Dante has allowed them to grow beyond the type of a morality figure into creations that make him one of the first psychological realists.

Bibliography

De Sanctis, Francesco. "The Subject of the Divine Comedy." In *Critical Essays on Dante.* Edited by Giuseppe Mazzotta. Boston, Mass.: G. K. Hall, 1991, pp. 60–81.
———. *History of Italian Literature.* 2 vols. Translated by Joan Redfern. New York: Barnes and Noble, 1968.
———. *De Sanctis on Dante.* Essays edited and translated by Joseph Rossi and Alfred Galpin. Madison: University of Wisconsin Press, 1957.
———. *Lezioni e saggi su Dante.* Edited by Sergio Romagnoli. Turin: Einaudi, 1955.
———. *Lezioni sulla "Divina Commedia."* Edited by Michele Manfredi. Bari: Laterza, 1955.
Wellek, René. "Francesco De Sanctis." *Italian Quarterly* 1.1 (1957), 5–43.

Thomas L. Cooksey

De vulgari eloquentia

Begun in the immediate aftermath of Dante's exile from Florence, perhaps as early as 1302, and apparently abandoned some time before the end of 1305, Dante's treatise on vernacular language and its use in lyric poetry remained largely obscure for several centuries after its composition. Only three medieval manuscripts survive, and even after the first printed edition appeared in 1577, evidence for its circulation is scanty. Shifting priorities among scholars finally brought it to the forefront of critical attention in the second half of the twentieth century. The renewal of interest in Dante's poetics that has generated much of the best Dante scholarship of the last few decades has made study of the *De vulgari eloquentia* indispensable to a fully nourished understanding of Dante's work as a whole.

The text of *DVE* that has reached us is a short prose treatise in elegant scholastic Latin, divided (apparently by Dante himself) into two books, the first of nineteen chapters and the second of fourteen. Despite its brevity, it is a work of considerable range and ambition. The first chapter announces its subject: "the language of people who speak the vulgar tongue," the vernacular which "infants acquire from those around them

D when they first begin to distinguish sounds" (1.1.1). This natural and spontaneously evolving language is distinguished by Dante from another kind of language—artificial, static, rule-governed, and acquired only through lengthy and painful study—which he calls *gramatica;* the relevant instance, in the Italian peninsula, is Latin, though it is important to note that for other vernacular communities another language might fill this role, and thus, *gramatica* is not to be equated with Latin. And in a modest but momentous phrase Dante concludes that, of these two kinds of language, "the more noble is the vernacular" (1.1.4). The death knell of Latin's age-old and unchallenged predominance in European culture resounds in those words.

After this statement of intent, *DVE* proceeds to offer first a philosophical explanation of language as a concept (1.2–3) and then (1.4–9) a history of linguistic change, along a timeline that runs from the Garden of Eden through the Tower of Babel, then down (with somewhat startling rapidity) to the Italy of Dante's own time. For Dante language is, in principle, a supremely and uniquely human attribute, given by God to his human creatures and to no others—not to animals or angels—in order that they might express to each other the concepts formed in their equally God-given minds; and language is thus, as the *Commedia* will also repeatedly if indirectly insist, the vital basis of the ordering of human living that constitutes society. In practice, it is above all a system of signs, in which a conventional or arbitrary sign or image is accepted by users of a given language as representing a particular mental construct (*DVE*'s affinities on this point with modern semiotics are obvious but surprisingly little studied). Dante's historical account begins with sometimes controversial questions of biblical exegesis: Who was the first speaker (Adam)? What language did he speak (Hebrew)? And so on. It proceeds to consider how the originary linguistic conformity of Eden was replaced by the *confusio linguarum* or scattering of tongues imposed at Babel and perpetuated in the modern world.

Dante retells the Babel story from Gen. 11 with detailed and almost novelistic relish (1.7), but he quickly moves on to his contemporary situation. The dispersal of populations after Babel's fall sent settlers into Europe, and they brought with them a threefold language which Dante calls *ydioma tripharium* (1.8). Each of this language's three varieties was spoken in a particular area: roughly speaking, northern, southern, and eastern Europe. The variety spoken in southern Europe has itself become threefold—divided according to the words used as affirmatives, *oc, oïl,* and *sì*—and these belong to the particular regions of Provence (and modern Catalonia), northern France, and Italy.

At this point Dante breaks off his narrative to insert a remarkably interesting chapter (1.9) on linguistic change and the diversity it produces, which he identifies as ubiquitous and as affecting not only large political and geographical units but also jurisdictions as small as a single city or even neighborhood. He attributes the universality of this phenomenon to an underlying cause equally universal, not to say inescapable: the imperfection of human affairs consequent upon the fallen state of humanity. We speak different languages because we are sinners; and we speak different languages from those our ancestors spoke because they were sinners too. Change—and decay—are thus inevitable, even if undetectable within a single lifetime because of the slow rate at which they take place; and so, says Dante, with a historicist confidence and a perceptive realism not always found in medieval thinking about language, "If the ancient citizens of Pavia were to rise from the grave, they would speak a language distinct and different from that of the Pavians of today" (1.9.7). (It is worth noting that one of the advantages of Latin, or any other *gramatica,* is its ability to withstand the pressures of mutability that affect the vernacular, precisely by virtue of its being an artificial construct.)

Building on these historical, philosophical, and theological approaches to language, Dante turns dialectologist in 1.1–15, passing in often acridly witty review fourteen major and several minor varieties of Italian vernacular. This is part of the quest—the metaphor is Dante's own—that the rest of book 1 will undertake: a hunt for a form of Italian that will be a worthy vehicle not only for the noblest kinds of poetry in the vernacular, but also for the redemption of Italy's secular institutions and the activities of its yet nonexistent imperial court. This is a crucial point in Dante's thinking: the *vulgare illustre* ("illustrious vernacular") that he is trying to identify and define will not only be used to improve the standards of Italian poetic practice, though it will certainly have that effect; it will also have the power to transform

Giovanni di Boccaccio da Certaldo, ne la vita di Dante.

Appresso gia vicino a la sua Morte compose un Libretto in prosa latina, il quale elji intitulo. De vulgari Eloquentia; E come che per lo detto libretto apparisca lui havere in animo di distinguerlo, e di terminarlo in quattro libri, o che piu non ne facesse da la Morte suo prospresso, o che perduti sianno lj'altri, piu non ne appariscono, che i dui primi.

Title page of the 1529 Italian translation of the De vulgari eloquentia *published by Ianiculo in Vicenza. Reproduced by permission of the John A. Zahm Dante Collection in the Department of Special Collections, University Libraries, University of Notre Dame.*

the ways in which the inhabitants of the Italian peninsula engage directly with the agonies and ambiguities of life in the world. The role of language and the argument of *DVE* itself are conceived by Dante as much in political and moral terms as in esthetic ones, though it is equally important that these differing aspects of his thinking about language and its use be seen as necessarily conjoined and not artificially dissevered.

The Italian vernacular for which Dante is hunting, and which the tongues spoken in his own Italy so signally fail to supply, will be "illustrious," but it will also be "cardinal," "aulic," and "curial"; and these idiosyncratically chosen terms, frequently deployed in the last four chapters of book 1, clearly point toward the political dimension of Dante's argument. The political preeminence enjoyed by a court is intimately connected with the poetic supremacy to be enjoyed by the "illustrious vernacular"; but it is central to Dante's thinking in *DVE* that, so far at least, neither court nor vernacular exists. Early Trecento Italy has no central

or monarchical authority, and none of the existing Italian vernaculars is worthy of assuming the lofty position reserved in Dante's scheme for the *vulgare illustre*—however clearly the poetry of Dante and some of his associates may already have begun to point in the right direction.

Book 2 of *DVE* proceeds logically from book 1, but it is more narrowly focused on technical aspects of poetic composition, while remaining no less fascinating as a repository of factual evidence and critical evaluation. Beginning from the absence of an illustrious Italian vernacular he has identified at the end of book 1, Dante sets out to show how such a vernacular, when finally brought into being, will be adapted to the nature and requirements of lyric poetry. The treatise thus continues its progression from general to particular: from the themes of enormous scope that were its starting point, through sweeping historical and geographical treatments on a global scale, to the specific situation of contemporary Italy and its elusive *vulgare illustre*. Now Dante undertakes to examine a single—though for him immensely important—area in which that vernacular will be used, albeit only by a tiny minority of exceptionally gifted poetic practitioners.

In the second book of the treatise, then, Dante offers instruction in the art of poetic composition, from the viewpoint of an acknowledged expert. He can cite his own work in illustration of his technical and critical points, though he never directly uses his own name; indeed, his own expertise is implicitly called upon to justify both his frequent disparagement of the poetic efforts of others and his rather more sparing distribution of praise to the lucky few. First (2.2.7), he establishes the most legitimate subject matter for lyric poetry—"prowess in arms, ardor in love, and control of one's own will" (or "integrity")—and names the poets who have achieved most in each of these respective fields: Bertran de Born for arms, Arnaut Daniel and Cino da Pistoia for love, Giraut de Borneil and "Cino's friend" (surely Dante himself) for integrity. (This is an interesting expansion, for Dante, of lyric's area of interest; before his exile he had held that its only justified preoccupation was love.) Then, in successive chapters (2.4–7), he discusses metrical forms (canzone, sonnet, *ballata*); styles (tragic, elegiac, comic); types of line (hendecasyllable, heptasyllable, pentasyllable); levels of "construction" or register ("flavorless," "flavored," "graceful

D and flavored," "graceful, flavored and striking"); categories of word ("infantile," "womanish," "virile," "rustic," "urbane," "combed," "glossy," "shaggy," "unkempt"); and the ways in which all these elements may be combined to create either a whole canzone (2.8) or a single stanza (2.9–11), through the disposition of lines of differing lengths (2.12) and the distribution of rhymes (2.13).

Throughout this treatment of what vernacular lyric is and, more important, what it should be, Dante's evaluation of his own and his contemporaries' poetic practice is based on two principles that can be seen to underlie not only the theory of *DVE* but also the (albeit chronologically later and generically distinct) practice of the *Commedia:* hierarchy and appropriateness. Some kinds of poem, or line, or style, or construction, or word, are simply better (conceptually nobler, rhetorically more effective, technically more difficult) than others; and the best poets are those who habitually and with the most success deal in the best poems (or lines, styles, constructions, etc.). However, the principle of hierarchy must coexist with that of appropriateness. A word that is right in a canzone may be wrong in a *ballata,* but the converse is also true; and the ability both to understand and to practice distinctions of this kind is another mark of the successful poet, as well as the best use of the *vulgare illustre* for poetic purposes.

The *DVE* as we have it peters out, not merely in mid-chapter but in mid-sentence; whimsical scholars with time on their hands have often wondered what the finished work would have become. Some clues are afforded by Dante's mentions within the text of his own plans for later books. (Few scholars have accepted Warman Welliver's suggestion that the work is *deliberately* unfinished in order to inculcate a lesson about the inadequacy of human language for Dante's purpose.) We may certainly regret the treatise's truncation: how much of the scholarly energy spent in discussing the implications of the title of the *Commedia,* for instance, would have been saved if Dante had fulfilled his promise (2.4.6) to discuss the comic style in Book 4 of *DVE*! Nonetheless, more than enough remains to guarantee *DVE*'s continued relevance not just to our understanding of Dante's work as a whole, but also to our steadily growing appreciation of the depth and resonance of late medieval thinking about language and poetry in general. None of Dante's so-called *opere minori* less deserves that sadly belittling epithet.

Bibliography

Alighieri Dante. *De vulgari eloquentia.* Edited and translated [into English] by Steven Botterill. Cambridge: Cambridge University Press, 1996.

———. *De vulgari eloquentia.* Edited and translated [into Italian] by Pier Vincenzo Mengaldo. In Dante Alighieri, *Opere minori,* vol. 2. Milan and Naples: Riccardo Ricciardi, 1979.

Ascoli, Albert Russell. "'Neminem ante nos': History and Authority in the *De vulgari eloquentia.*" *Annali d'italianistica* 8 1990, 186–231.

Grayson, Cecil. "'*Nobilior est vulgaris*': Latin and Vernacular in Dante's Thought." In *Centenary Essays on Dante by Members of the Oxford Dante Society.* Oxford: Clarendon Press, 1965.

Pagani, Ileana. *La teoria linguistica di Dante. "De vulgari eloquentia": Discussioni, scelte, proposte.* Naples: Liguori, 1982.

Peirone, Luigi. *Il "De vulgari eloquentia" e la linguistica moderna.* Genoa: Tilgher, 1975.

Shapiro, Marianne. *"De vulgari eloquentia": Dante's Book of Exile.* Lincoln and London: University of Nebraska Press, 1990.

Welliver, Warman. *Dante in Hell: The "De vulgari eloquentia."* Ravenna: Longo, 1981.

Steven Botterill

Decretalists

Canon lawyers, usually professors of law, who commented on the official collections of canon law, beginning with the *Liber Extra* of Pope Gregory IX, issued in 1234. Since the publication of Gratian's *Decretum* around 1140, decretals—papal letters issuing judicial decisions—had reflected a greater legal precision than earlier papal documents, and lawyers had begun to collect them into books that they used to supplement Gratian's work. The first such collection issued by a pope was the *Compilatio Tertia,* issued by Innocent III in 1210. Such early compilations, however, were replaced by the *Liber Extra* and by later official collections, such as the *Liber Sextus* of Boniface VIII, issued in 1298, and the *Extravagantes* of Clement V, issued in 1317. The *Liber Extra* was so called because it went beyond the collection of Gratian; the *Liber Sextus* because it offered a "sixth book" to the five books of the *Liber Extra* (although the *Liber Sextus* was itself divided into five books paralleling the structure of the *Liber Extra*). The decretal collections contained edited versions of original papal legal decisions, often in official communications to papal judges delegate, and they distributed different parts of individual papal letters that dealt with more than one legal issue among different titles that treated different sections of the law.

The decretalists began teaching the law in the decretals as early as the 1180s in northern France and by 1190 at Bologna, the center of legal study. This law was more recent than the work of Gratian and hence had a wide and immediate appeal. The collections were topically organized into five books, whose order students learned by the mnemonic device: *judex, judicium, clerus, connubia, crimen*—"the judge, the judgment, the clergy, marriage, crime." The law of the decretals was common to all Christians, and it was imposed by the increasingly sharply defined legal authority of the popes. Canon law covered an enormous range of human activity, since, as one lawyer observed, "The lord pope may intervene in every matter where sin may be involved." There also emerged considerable opposition to both the scope and the authority of canon law.

The *Liber Extra* acquired an ordinary commentary by the decretalist Bernard of Parma in 1241, and both text and commentary were regularly taught in the law schools. Three of the most influential legal minds in European legal history were among the most influential decretalists: Henry of Susa, Cardinal Bishop of Ostia (hence called *Hostiensis*), who is cited in *Par.* 12.83 and *Epist.* 11.16; and Wilhelmus Durantis and Sinibaldo Fieschi, later Pope Innocent IV, who are also referred to in *Epist.* 11.16. The decretalists continued their work down to the end of the classical period of canon law in 1378.

Dante knew a great deal of law, but his ideal was Roman law, which he and the jurists called "written reason." Dante accused the decretalists, somewhat inaccurately, as being ignorant of both theology and philosophy, and thereby creating false and misleading law (*Mon.* 3.3.9). In *Par.* 9.133–135, Folco of Marseilles denounces the avarice that has turned scholars away from the Gospels and the writings of the Doctors of the Church so that they now study only the decretals, as can be seen by the marginal notations that cover the manuscripts of the law. The decretals have made the pope, who ought to have been the "shepherd" of all Christians, a wolf.

Edward Peters

Deianira

Wife of Hercules, loved by the centaur Nessus. Fatally wounded by Hercules' poisoned arrow, Nessus gave Deianira his blood-soaked shirt as a love charm. She later gave it to Hercules, who had taken Iole as his lover, in an attempt to win back his affection. But the shirt, being poisoned, drove him mad and caused him to incinerate himself. Dante refers to the myth, taken from Ovid (*Meta.* 9.127ff.), in describing the centaur Nesso (*Inf.* 12.67-69), who guards the violent against others in the seventh circle.

F. Regina Psaki

Deidamia

Mother of Pyrrhus (Neoptolomus) by Achilles in Statius' *Achilleid.* She died of grief when Achilles was lured from Scyros by Ulysses, an act that is counted as one of Ulysses' sins in *Inf.* 26.61-63. Virgil refers to her in *Purg.* 22.114 as a resident of Limbo.

Nancy Vine Durling

Deiphyle

Wife of Tydeus, one of the Seven against Thebes in Statius' *Thebaid,* and mother of Diomedes. Dante mentions Deiphyle *(Deifile)* as an example of modesty in *Conv.* 4.25.8; in *Purg.* 22.110, Virgil, addressing Statius, says that she resides in Limbo.

Nancy Vine Durling

Delacroix, Eugène

French painter (1798–1863), son of an ardent revolutionary whose spirit abided in him. He studied at the Atelier Guérin in Paris, and literary inspirations informed some of his best art—he drew from the Bible, Homer, Aeschylus, Virgil, Shakespeare, Ariosto, Goethe, Scott, and Byron—but it was Dante, always an inspiration to him, who launched him. He did primarily easel paintings, and his first such painting, the one that called immediate attention to him, was his *Dante and Virgil in the Infernal Regions* (1822), subsequently known as *Dante's Bark* (an illustration of *Inf.* 8). While he was painting it, a friend read the canto over and over to him.

It may be argued that all of Delacroix is in this early painting. His was a Romantic response to the

D

hard, cold, academic Classicism of Jacques-Louis David, an emotion-filled esthetic that thrived on narrative emphasis and on the representation of the human figure. His father was an ardent revolutionist, and Delacroix inherited much of his spirit, as his *Liberty at the Barricades* (1830) suggests. Yet, given his love of the Italian Renaissance and of Michelangelo's combination of fiery vigor and balanced proportions, there is much reserve and control in his work, such as the *Massacre at Chios* (1824) and the many Oriental paintings after 1831. Sonorous color and loose paint create a classic sense of the well-set and well-proportioned. The poet Baudelaire described his painting manner aptly: "a volcano artistically hidden by bouquets of flowers."

Apart from his imposing fresco *Dante and Virgil with the Poets in Limbo,* inspired by *Inf.* 4 and adorning the cupola of the library of Paris's Chamber of Deputies, and such minor works as a *Paolo and Francesca* (a coy couple unsuspecting the tragic violence about to befall them), it is *Dante's Bark* that holds the spotlight for Dantean scholars. In the circle of wrath, Dante and Virgil are being ferried across the River Styx, in which the rabid souls are raging against one another. Contrasts of mood and mode define it: the walls of the City of Dis brightly aflame in the dark regions of the upper left; the sinner who rises from the river to bite the boat's bow at the left and the sinners who wrestle each other angrily on the lower right contrasting with the resignation of the woman on the right and the agony of the man on the left; the oarsman Phlegyas' powerful movements to check the powerless souls attacking the boat; and above all—so centrally placed that the canto's protagonist, Filippo Argenti, may not be identified—Dante and Virgil standing. Here a Romantic figure, Dante extends his arms high and low in fear and alarm, while Virgil, here a Classical figure, is poised in guardianship though not entirely serene. The painting aroused both enthusiasm and contempt, and it set a course for future painting.

There are no editions of Delacroix's Dante work, because his output in this area is minimal.

Bibliography

Bishop, Morris. "Dante's Pilgrimage." *Horizon* 7.3 (1965), 4–15.

Nassar, Eugene Paul. "Illustrations to Dante's *Inferno:* A Critical Perspective." *Bulletin of Research in the Humanities* 87 (1986–1987), 440–461.

Jean-Pierre Barricelli

Del Cassero, Guido

Guido del Cassero and Angiolello da Carignano, the *due miglior da Fano* ("the two best men of Fano," *Inf.* 28.76), were victims of Malatestino Malatesti, lord of Rimini, who invited them to a party with the intention of slaying them. The treacherous host arranged to have his guests drowned in the Adriatic on their journey and thereby gained control of the city of Fano. Pier da Medicina foretells this crime in the ninth bolgia of Malebolge, bidding Dante warn the two and thus perhaps forestall an event which was supposed to take place in 1312.

Roy Rosenstein

Del Cassero, Jacopo

A nobleman from Fano, del Cassero (pronounced *Càssero*) figures among the tardily repentant victims of violence in the Ante-Purgatory (*Purg.* 5.64). As governor of Bologna, he quarreled with Azzo VIII, marquis of Este, who had him murdered in the marshes at Oriago in 1298. He was presumably a relative of Guido del Cassero (*Inf.* 28.77), also slated to die in an ambush.

Roy Rosenstein

Delight

The terms for "delight" (*diletto, dilettazio,* and *delettazio*) as a philosophical concept are not used in the *Vita Nuova.* In the *Convivio,* however, Dante employs "delight" repeatedly and links its essence to desire: delight follows the fulfillment of desire, and perfect delight follows the perfect fulfillment of the desire for perfection (3.6.7). If desire is the movement of the soul toward the object of desire (see *Purg.* 18.31–33), then delight is the repose of the soul in its possession of the object of desire. The species of delight follow the cognitive powers of the soul: senses (1.2.17, 1.4.5, 3.3.10, 3.3.12, 4.26.8) and intellect (2.3.2, 2.11.4, 3.6.8). Vicious delight may suffocate the desire for knowledge (1.1.3; cf. 2.15.8).

There is no essential difference between the concepts of delight in the *Convivio* and the *Commedia,* but a change is noticeable in the *Comme-*

dia in Dante's understanding of what constitutes human delight. In the *Commedia,* only one (*Par.* 11.8) of the references to the delight of the senses (*Purg.* 1.13–16, 4.1–2, 7.62–63, 15.31–33, 23.10–12; *Par.* 23.127–129, 26.112) expresses disapproval of the delight referred to, in contrast to the *Convivio,* in which all but one (1.2.17) of the references to the delight of the senses express disapproval of some sort. This reflects Dante's new view in the *Commedia* of the relationship of body to soul. In the *Convivio,* the body is in the case of most individuals an impediment to the operations proper to the human soul (4.21.7–10, and see 3.7.6–7); in the *Commedia,* on the contrary, the souls of the blessed will know God more and delight in this knowledge more perfectly once they are reunited to their bodies at the end of time (*Par.* 14.43–60). The point is that delight follows upon the attainment of perfection, and perfection for the human being includes the union of body and soul.

The *Commedia* has references as well to the delight that attends the practice of virtue (*Par.* 18.58–60) and the struggle to rid oneself of vice (*Purg.* 12.121–126 and 27.74–75). Delight is good or evil depending on the goodness or evil of the action that brings it about (*Purg.* 17.97–99). The goodness or evil of a human action, however, depends ultimately on its harmony with the divine will. Thus, the delight of the soul described in *Conv.* 4.23, a delight in knowledge and virtuous action, is inadequate (as the cases of Farinata and Ulysses in the *Inferno* imply); perfect delight resides in acceptance of the divine will (*Par.* 3.85).

Two explicit references to delight in the *Monarchia,* 1.13.2 *(delectatio)* and 15.9, repeat points made in the *Convivio* and maintained in the *Commedia. Diletto* is personified in the *Fiore* (79.5), in the service of the God of Love.

Bibliography

Cogan, Marc. "Delight, Punishment, and the Justice of God in the *Divina Commedia.*" *Dante Studies* 111 (1993), 27–52.

Paul A. Dumol

Democritus

A Greek philosopher from Thrace (c. 460 B.C.E.–c. 370 B.C.E.), Democritus *(Democrito)* advanced the theory of atomism and believed that the world was created by the random assemblage of atoms (*che 'l mondo a caso pone,* "who assigns the world to chance"). He is a resident of Limbo (*Inf.* 4.136) with other pagan philosophers. In *Conv.* 2.14.6, Dante cites his theory that the Galaxy (Milky Way) can be explained as the Sun's reflected light, and in 3.14.8 he describes the philosopher's indifference to all things except wisdom.

Bibliography

Lucchesi, Valerio. "Epicurus and Democritus: The Ciceronian Foundations of Dante's Judgement." *Italian Studies* 42 (1987), 1–19.

Richard Lansing

Demonology

Lucifer, the rebellious angel, is the king of Hell, and, fittingly, his ministers are devils and demons. Devils are, like their king and leader, either rebellious or neutral angels; demons, however, are figures of ancient mythology transformed into demonic or infernal semigods, who have the function of judging or transporting the damned souls or of guarding a circle. Nevertheless, in the popular imagination devils and demons are considered to be one and the same. Dante uses the terms *demonio* and *diavolo* interchangeably for his devils, but he refers to his mythological monsters only as demons (e.g., *Inf.* 3.109, 6.32).

Dante deals with the problem of the rebel angels in *Conv.* 3.12 and in *DVE* 1.2.4. In accord with orthodox theology, he maintains that they rebelled before occupying the place in the universal order assigned to each one of them. In this way theologians were able to deny that God had created good and wicked angels and to affirm that their rebellion was an act of pride (see also *Par.* 19.48, 29.55–56).

Fallen angels are first found in the vestibule of Hell among the lukewarm or pusillanimous souls. They are the neutral angels *che non furon ribelli / né fur fedeli a Dio, ma per sé fuoro* ("who were not rebels yet were not faithful to God, but were for themselves," *Inf.* 3.38–39). Their existence has no basis in scripture, but some theologians, such as Clement of Alexandria, make reference to them, and there are likewise legends about them. They are not described further, just as no other neutral is. The first group of rebellious devils appears at the Gates of Dis, where they confront Dante and Virgil and block their advance. Their attempt to repel the two wayfarers, reinforced by the appearance of the Furies and the

D threat of Medusa's assistance, ultimately fails, but their stand at this point of the poem demonstrates that they are rulers of the City of Dis. They receive no description, but later on, in reference to this particular episode, they are called *demoni duri* ("hard demons," *Inf.* 14.44), emphasizing a quality traditionally associated with heresy, which suggests that they may be serving as guardians of the circle of heretics. Only in the eighth circle, Malebolge, do we encounter devils taking on the role of tormentors long assigned to them by tradition. In the first bolgia, horned devils whip ruffians. In the fifth bolgia, they become protagonists in one of the most "comic" episodes of the *Commedia,* and here they are given individual names. Their image, created in opposition to that of the angels, is traditional: ugly, dark, sharp-toothed, winged, tailed, vulgar, deceitful, and cruel. In the ninth bolgia, a devil maims the scandalmongers. Finally, alone in his infinite ugliness, powerlessness, and ignorance, stands Lucifer, locked in the lake of ice, Cocytus, at the very bottom of his kingdom. Devils have *scientia*—that is, knowledge—but not *sapientia,* or knowledge through virtue. They may be found outside of Hell, debating with a saint or an angel over the soul of a dead person (for example, Guido da Montefeltro and Bonconte da Montefeltro), and sometimes they keep a body alive whose soul is already in Hell (for example, that of Alberigo), but primarily we find them in the act of punishing damned souls.

Demons have a different origin and present problems that are not strictly theological in nature. Charon, Minos, Cerberus, Pluto, Phlegyas, the Furies, Medusa, the Centaurs, the Harpies, Geryon, and Cacus (the giants of Cocytus constitute a significant exception) are ancient mythological figures, some of whom are found in the *Aeneid.* Why, it might be asked, are these pagan demons in a Christian Hell? Because Dante read the *Aeneid* as a "truthful" work? Perhaps, but equally important must have been the fact that the Church Fathers (for example, St. Augustine, *De civitate Dei* 8) believed the pagan gods to be demons, although twelfth- and thirteenth-century theologians considered Jupiter and the highest gods as prefigurations of the Christian God (*sommo Giove, Purg.* 6.118), and the lesser divinities or semigods as prefigurations of the bad demons (the function of the good demons being taken over by the angels).

There are other beings whom one might locate among the devilish forces, such as the dogs that hunt the spendthrifts, or the snakes that tie the hands of the thieves. These animals torture the damned as do the devils, but they do not possess any of the "rational" traits which place devils, demons, and their victims on a completely different level. The presence of these beasts, however, corresponds to folkloric traditions in which some animal (a snake, wolf, lion, etc.) was deemed to signal the presence of the devil. Their inclusion in Dante's demonological system responds to the need for stark and brutal realism which has made the *Commedia* so popular.

Bibliography

Freccero, John. "The Neutral Angels." In *Dante: The Poetics of Conversion.* Edited by Rachel Jacoff. Cambridge and London: Harvard University Press, 1986, pp. 110–118.

Grabher, Carlo. "Mostri e simboli nell'Inferno dantesco." *Annali della Facoltà di Lettere e Filosofia dell'Università di Cagliari* 21 (1953), 47–66.

Graf, Arturo. "Demonologia di Dante." In *Miti, leggende e superstizioni del Medievo.* Turin: Loescher, 1893, pp. 289–335.

Padoan, Giorgio. "Demonologia." *Enciclopedia dantesca,* 2:368–374.

Russell, Jeffrey Burton. *Satan: The Early Christian Tradition.* Ithaca, N.Y.: Cornell University Press, 1981.

———. *The Devil: Perceptions of Evil from Antiquity to Primitive Christianity.* Ithaca, N.Y.: Cornell University Press, 1977.

Sanguinetti, Edoardo. *Interpretazione di Malebolge.* Florence: Olschki, 1961.

Seznec, Jean. *The Survival of the Pagan Gods.* New York: Pantheon Books, 1953.

Paolo Cherchi

Demophoön

Mentioned by Folquet de Marseille (*Par.* 9.101), Demophoön (*Demofoonte*), son of Theseus and Phaedra, was the lover of Phyllis, who killed herself when he failed to return to her. Folquet declares that although his love burned stronger than that of Phyllis, his repentance for his sin of lust has brought him to salvation.

R. Allen Shoaf

Despair

According to Roman Catholic doctrine and moral teaching, despair is a fatal sin resulting from an act of turning from God and the hope of salvation to the love of worldly objects as the preeminent good. Thus, despair is the exact opposite of Christian hope and is evidenced by the believer's repeated attempts to find an eternal and final satisfaction in what can give only mundane and temporary satisfaction.

Dante's damned find themselves in the eternal pit of the Inferno precisely because they have chosen to practice the words over the entrance gate: *Lasciate ogne speranza, voi ch'intrate* ("Abandon every hope, you who enter," *Inf.* 3.9). Each suffering citizen of Hell attempts to find, over and over again, a lasting good in what is only temporary, be it sexual lust, worldly gain, self-esteem, or proud defiance toward God and all others. In doing this they "abandon every hope." Dante inherited the teaching that avarice, the turning from God to the world, is the root of all sin (pride is the cause), and thus an element in all sin; and so, from the sighs of those in Limbo to the tears of Lucifer, the damned lament in despair as they feel the pain of returning constantly to the object of their false hope.

The difference between this notion of despair and what we would think of as an attitude or mood from which we can quickly recover once circumstances and outlook change can be found in the fact that, for Dante, an attitude or mood (anger, joy, lassitude, despair) is a state in which we are being acted upon from the outside. He would explain that to be in such a state is to be "passionate," and that word connotes "passivity." After all, we do not choose these states of mind; rather, we are overcome by them.

Dante, following Aristotle, held that there is a *ben de l'intelletto* ("good of the intellect," *Inf.* 3.18), a goal which the intellect might not choose to seek. Such an act would by necessity leave the mind wounded and helpless, prey to any immediate desire. In *Purg.* 13–18, Virgil teaches that the freedom of the human mind and will is subject to an ordered love. God must be loved preeminently; if not, the good things of life will not be loved according to their nature. Love will then be irrational, and the soul subject to the passions of all immediate desires. Objects whose nature should instill courage will bring on fear; objects whose nature should instill beatitude will bring on envy.

Hope, then, is the virtue of knowing that though we are still pilgrims and the goal of faith is not yet realized, nothing in the world can defeat the stalwart, because the love for the goal—the love of God, as the true measure of all we encounter—transcends all. Despair, by contrast, is the shrinking from all challenges and joys in an avaricious taste for the world and the immediate, and a suffering of the passions of fear, dalliance, turpitude, and temporary pleasure.

The sin of despair is dramatized, according to a number of critics from the early commentators to the present, in *Inf.* 9, when the devils temporarily block Dante's and Virgil's progress through Hell. This interruption, coupled with Virgil's initial inability to negotiate an entrance into the City of Dis, instills in the pilgrim a fear so great that it verges on despair. This fear is compounded by the appearance of the Furies, traditionally taken to symbolize remorse, who invoke Medusa, an allegorical figure whose power to turn anyone to stone is suggestive of the spiritual paralysis brought on by despair.

William Wilson

Detto d'Amore

The designation given to a late thirteenth-century Tuscan, almost certainly Florentine, short narrative poem based on the *Roman de la rose*. The poem, which survives in a single manuscript (Laur. Ashb. 1234), was discovered and published in 1888 by Salomone Morpurgo. The early fourteenth-century manuscript copy lacks a title; Morpurgo coined the name *Detto d'Amore* for the poem on the basis of two internal references to its genre: *Amor sì vuole [. . .] ched i' faccia un detto* ("Love wants me to compose a *detto*," 1–3; cf. 490). The term *detto* ("tale") appears to be the Italian equivalent of the Old French *dits,* the label often assigned to poetic texts that blended narrative and didactic elements.

The *Detto* is both a love story and a meditation on love. Although it draws on the *Rose,* especially in its composition of the episodes involving the allegorical figures Ragione ("Reason") and Ricchezza ("Wealth"), it makes no overt reference to the French work. It is a powerful expression of the ideology of courtly love, centered on a lover who declares his absolute fidelity to Love despite the opposition of Reason, Jealousy, and Wealth. Within this basic narrative framework, there is also a detailed, albeit conventional, *descriptio* of the beauty and nobility of the woman, as well as a list of Love's commandments on how the lover should

D

behave. The extant version of the poem closes with these directives; nevertheless, most scholars agree that line 480, its last verse, does not constitute the actual end of the poem (there is another lacuna in the text between lines 360 and 361).

Although in its content the *Detto* is unremarkable, in its form and its standing in the Romance tradition it is a work of bold experimentation. While its choice of meter—seven-syllable couplets—is based on the *Rose*'s octosyllabic couplets, it clearly challenges its source's unadventurous use of rhyme by transforming all its own rhymes into "equivocal" ones. The poet's skill in sustaining such a difficult scheme is a mark of his artistic seriousness and of his independence from the *Rose*. The same may be said of his decision to abridge radically the French text. His aim was to "translate" his source creatively rather than to "imitate" it mechanically. In the Middle Ages, *translationes* were one of the means by which authors could establish their autonomy from their models and assert the importance of their own language and cultural milieu. It is noteworthy, therefore, that despite its basic links to the *Rose,* the *Detto* should also skillfully synthesize a wide variety of Italian sources, from the Sicilians to Guinizzelli and from Brunetto to Guittone and the *siculo-toscani.*

The *Detto* is thus a poem of some importance, and its significance is considerably increased by the fact that scholars of the caliber of Gianfranco Contini have suggested that it could be by Dante. Textual critics have irrefutably demonstrated that the copy of the poem found in the Biblioteca Laurenziana in Florence was originally part of the same manuscript as that which now contains the *Fiore*. This important detail takes on additional meaning in view of the widespread agreement that the *Fiore* and the *Detto* were written by the same author (though one or two critics have recently questioned this claim). Given the ever-growing amount of textual evidence to suggest that Dante was indeed the author of the *Fiore,* then by extension the *Detto,* which has many fewer ties with the poet's *oeuvre,* must also have come from his pen. If this is the case, the *Detto* would fit in well with Dante's early interest in the recherché conventions of the *siculo-toscani.* Equally, the poem is characterized by an experimental vigor and a self-confidence which are hallmarks of the poet's *modus operandi.*

Bibliography

Alighieri, Dante. *Il Fiore. Detto d'Amore.* Edited by Luca C. Rossi. Milan: Mondadori, 1996.

Peirone, Luigi. *Il "Detto d'Amore" tra "Il Fiore e Dante."* Geneva: Tilgher, 1983.

Picone, Michelangelo. "Glosse al *Detto d'Amore.*" *Medioevo Romanzo* 3 (1976), 394–409.

Took, John. *Dante, Lyric Poet and Philosopher: An Introduction to the Minor Works.* Oxford: Clarendon Press, 1990.

Vanossi, Luigi. *La teologia poetica del "Detto d'Amore" dantesco.* Florence: Olschki, 1974.

Zygmunt G. Barański

Deutsche Dante-Gesellschaft

The German Dante Society evolved from a number of small-group initiatives, dating from 1819–1820, into its formal organization in 1865, thanks to the efforts of Karl Witte and the patronage of Prince John of Saxony. With the death of several key scholars, the Society went into suspension between 1883 and 1914, when Hugo Daffner with other scholars, particularly Karl Vossler, relaunched the organization as the Neue Deutsche Dante-Gesellschaft. It then met sporadically, given the interruption of World War I, in Weimar, Dresden, and other German cities, until 1927. In that year the Society was completely reorganized with Walter Goetz (of Leipzig) as president; it entered a very productive period until 1939, followed by another period of inactivity owing to World War II. In 1949 Hans Rheinfelder became president, and meetings were held in Weimar until 1954. During the east-west division of the country, the East German members continued to meet in Weimar and the West German members in various West German cities, but every two years in Krefeld. In the reunited Germany after 1990, the seat of the Society has remained in Weimar. After his death in 1971, Rheinfelder was succeeded by August Buck, who retired in 1993, assuming the position of honorary president and turning the Society's direction over to Bernhard König.

The Society initially favored critical editions of works of Dante and the early commentators, but it has catered in varying degrees and at various times to the interests of both the specialized scholar and the amateur or the wider educated public. Membership has run as high as 400, in 1922;

more recently it has hovered around 300. In keeping with the fortunes of the Society, publication of its annual journal has been somewhat irregular, particularly in the earlier years: four volumes as *Jahrbuch der Deutschen Dante-Gesellschaft* (1867–1877); volumes 5–9 as *Deutsches Dante-Jahrbuch* (1920–1925); and continuing thereafter fairly regularly (with occasional combined volumes) in a new series (neue Folge), beginning with volume 10. The two most important editors of the *Deutsches Dante-Jahrbuch* since Hugo Daffner's tenure (1920–1925) have been Friedrich Schneider (1928–1961) and Marcella Roddewig (1972–present); the latter has done significant work on the Dante manuscript tradition. In addition, the Society launched a monograph series, *Schriften der Deutschen Dante-Gesellschaft*, in 1937. Beginning in 1953, it has also published a bulletin, *Mitteilungsblatt der Deutschen Dante-Gesellschaft*.

Bibliography

Buck, August. "Saluto della 'Deutsche Dante-Gesellschaft.'" In *La Società Dantesca Italiana 1888-1988: Convegno internazionale.* Edited by Rudy Abardo. Milan: Ricciardi, 1995, pp. 3–8.

———. "125 Jahre 'Deutsche Dante-Gesellschaft.'" *Deutsches Dante-Jahrbuch* 66 (1991), 7–24.

Goetz, Walter. "Geschichte der Deutschen Dante-Gesellschaft." In *Dante: Gesammelte Aufsätze.* Münchner Romanistische Arbeiten, 13. Munich: Max Hueber, 1958, pp. 103–142.

Rheinfelder, Hans. "Nascita e sviluppo della Società Dantesca Germanica." In *Dante e la cultura tedesca.* Edited by Lino Lazzarini. Padua: Università degli Studi, 1967, pp. 27–38.

A. L. Pellegrini

Devils

Devils have a less visible presence in Dante's Hell than many modern readers might think. Indeed, they are found in only five specific locations in the *Inferno*: a group of the rebellious angels who fell from heaven (*da ciel piovuti,* 8.83) attempts to obstruct Dante's and Virgil's entry to the City of Dis; in three places in Malebolge they torment sinners (the panders and seducers, canto 18, the barrators, 21–22, and the schismatics, 28); and in Cocytus, Lucifer, the "emperor of the dolorous kingdom" (*Lo 'mperador del doloroso regno,*

34.28), is punished for his treachery and serves as the tormentor of the traitors Judas, Cassius, and Brutus. Dante also refers to "one of the black cherubim" (*un d'i neri cherubini,* 27.113), who contests the soul of Guido da Montefeltro with St. Francis, but this dispute between the devil and the saint does not occur within the confines of Hell.

The devils assigned to patrol the fifth ditch of the eighth circle (cantos 21–23)—the Malebranche ("Evil Claws")—are especially worthy of note because they appear to represent in both semblance and behavior those characteristics that many people, both now and in the Middle Ages, associate with the demonic world. In this episode, one of the most dramatic in the *Inferno,* the pilgrim and his guide Virgil are searching for a bridge that will allow them passage over the sixth ditch of the Malebolge (that containing the hypocrites). Intending to entrap the innocent wayfarers, the head devil, Malacoda ("Evil Tail"), constructs an elaborate but convincing lie about the existence of such a bridge and then assigns them to his troop of ten demons, thus "guaranteeing" their safe passage. This platoon of devils is headed by Barbariccia ("Curly Beard").

Throughout this entire episode (cantos 21–23) a superficial atmosphere of playfulness prevails, belying the darker, ever-present threat of real danger posed by the devils not only to the sinner but also to the wayfarers. It is here that grotesque and comic elements come to the fore and medieval theater intrudes into the fabric of Dante's *Commedia.* Farcical elements abound, such as the unexpected "trumpet blast" (21.139) that occasions the mock-epic description with which canto 22 begins. The pilgrim's summary comment about their traveling in the company of the devils discloses the nature and mood of the episode: *"Ahi fiera compagnia! Ma in chiesa / coi santi, ed in taverna co' ghiottoni"* ("Ah, fierce company! but in church with the saints, in the tavern with the gluttons," 22.14–15). These elements of black humor only barely mask the fear and dread that the protagonists experience—the pilgrim Dante in particular.

Part of the humor of the episode is conveyed by the colorful names of the devils: in addition to those mentioned above, we find Cagnazzo ("Nasty Dog"), Graffiacane ("Dog Scratcher"), Ciriatto ("Wild Hog"), and Draghignazzo ("Big Nasty Dragon"). Other names suggest pertinent diabolical associations, such as Alichino (from Harlequin,

D

The Malebranche devils attacking the barrators. Invenzioni di Giovanni Flaxman sulla Divina commedia, *illustrated by John Flaxman and Beniamino del Vecchio, Rome, 1826. Giamatti Collection: Courtesy of the Mount Holyoke College Archives and Special Collections.*

the typical name of a devil). Others are not easily interpreted: Calcabrina may mean something like "Grace Stomper"; Scarmiglione, "Trouble Maker"; Rubicante, "Red-faced Terror"; Libicocco, "Libyan Hothead"; Farfarello, "Goblin"; but these meanings remain hypothetical.

It has been proposed that some of the devils' names are playful adaptations or corruptions of the names of prominent families in Lucca (a city notorious for its barrators), Florence, and other medieval Italian cities. Scarmiglione is the name of a family in Lucca; Barbariccia might suggest the Ricci family of Florence or the Barbarasi of Cremona, as well as Emperor Frederick I "Barbarossa"; Cagnazzo might be the Tuscan family Canasso or the Cagnasso from Lucca; Calcabrina could suggest the Florentine families of Scaldabrina, Falabrina, and Lanciabrina; Ciriatto would seem to be associated with the Tuscan Ciriolo and Cerviatto; and Draghignazzo would recall the Florentine families Dragondello and Dragonetto, just as Graffiacane would recall the Raffacani family of Florence and Rubicante the Florentine podestà

Rubaconte (whose name is also attached to a bridge; see *Purg.* 12.102).

The souls of the sinners, the barrators, must remain beneath the boiling pitch or risk mutilation by the hooks of the devils. One particular sinner, Ciampolo, comes to the surface of the boiling pitch to find some momentary relief from his punishment and is immediately captured by two devils, Alichino and Calcabrina. True to his maliciously clever ways, Ciampolo devises an intricate ruse to gain his "freedom": he tells the devils of a system developed by the sinners by which they are able with a particular signal (a whistle) to notify one another that it is safe to come to the surface. In exchange for his release, Ciampolo offers to betray his fellow sinners by giving that signal: thus, he argues, since many souls will come to the surface, the devils will have more souls to torment than his alone. In short, as one versed in the ways of civic corruption, Ciampolo offers a handsome bribe to the devils, who after some discussion accept it and release him. Once free, Ciampolo immediately dives back to the relative safety of the boiling pitch. Enraged over their loss, the two devils begin to fight with each other in midair and fall into the pitch; in their malicious, deceptive ways, they are essentially no different from the barrators. This unexpected turn of events infuriates the devils, who then energetically pursue Dante and Virgil with the idea of capturing them, as they apparently had intended to do all along. The two wayfarers escape this very real danger by sliding down into the next bolgia (canto 23), where, by Divine decree, the devils cannot go.

Bibliography

Favati, Guido. "Il 'Jeu di Dante' (Interpretazione del canto XXI dell'*Inferno*)." *Cultura neolatina* 25 (1965), 34–52.

Graf, Arturo. "Demonologia di Dante." In *Miti, leggende e superstizioni del Medio Evo,* vol. 2. Turin: Loescher, 1892–1893; reprinted, New York: Burt Franklin, 1971, pp. 79–139.

Kleinhenz, Christopher. "Deceivers Deceived: Devilish Doubletalk in *Inferno* 21–23." *Quaderni d'italianistica* 10 (1989), 133–156.

Olschki, Leonardo. "Dante, i barattieri, i diavoli." *Giornale dantesco* 38 (1937), 61–81.

Pagliaro, Antonino. "La rapsodia dei diavoli." In his *Ulisse*: *Ricerche semantiche sulla Divina Commedia,* vol. 1. Messina and Florence: D'Anna, 1966, pp. 311–324.

Spitzer, Leo. "The Farcical Elements in *Inferno,* Cantos XXI–XXIII." *Modern Language Notes* 59 (1944), 83–88.

Christopher Kleinhenz

Diana, the Goddess

Daughter of Jupiter and Latona and twin sister of Apollo, goddess of the Moon and the hunt, and queen of the underworld. Dante calls her *Diana* only in *Purg.* 25.130–132, where she is named as a paragon of chastity. Elsewhere he uses her other names (*Delia, Purg.* 29.78; *Phoebe, Mon.* 1.11.5; *Hecate, Inf.* 10.80; *Trivia, Par.* 23.26) or refers to her indirectly. *Epist.* 6.8 mentions Delia in connection with the Guelf theory, rejected by Dante, that likens the Church to the Sun and the Empire to the lesser Moon. That *Purg.* 20.132 refers to Diana as one of the *due occhi del cielo* ("two eyes of heaven") may reflect Dante's insistence on the equality of Church and Empire. Dante invokes Diana in some instances to indicate chronology by way of astronomical reference. For example, in *Inf.*

10.79–80, Dante is told that *non cinquanta volte fia raccesa / la faccia de la donna che qui regge* ("not fifty times will be rekindled the face of the lady [Proserpina or Diana, i.e., the Moon] who reigns here [in Hell]") before he experiences the difficulty of returning from exile.

Todd Boli

Dido

Queen and founder of Carthage and a competent ruler until she fell in love with Aeneas, then an impassioned lover and suicide, as recounted in the fourth book of Virgil's *Aeneid.* She appears three times in the *Commedia* as an example of lust (cf. *Conv.* 4.26.6–8). She is described among the lustful in Hell as the one who killed herself for love and broke faith with the ashes of Sychaeus, her dead husband (*Inf.* 5.61–62); Folquet, in the Heaven of Venus, compares himself in his burning passion to the daughter of Belus who harmed both Sychaeus and Creusa (*Par.* 9.97). She is named *(Didone),* however, only by Charles Martel in connection with Cupid, Venus's son, who was said to have sat in Dido's lap (*Par.* 8.9). In the *Monarchia,* she is instead called the second of Aeneas's three wives (2.3.15); there she represents the continent of Africa in an allegory that defines Aeneas' nobility, and hence the hereditary nobility of the Roman people, on the basis of his having had three wives on the three different continents of Asia, Africa, and Europe.

Joan M. Ferrante

Diogenes

One of the ancient philosophers *(Dïogenès, Diogene)* consigned to the *nobile castello* of Dante's Limbo in the first circle of Hell (*Inf.* 4.137). Most commentators (including the earliest ones) identify him with Diogenes the Cynic (c. 400–c. 325 B.C.E.), often mentioned by Aristotle and Aquinas as one who reportedly scorned the normal amenities and customs of life.

V. Stanley Benfell

Diomedes

Hero of Greek mythology, son of Tydeus and Deiphyle, and king of Aetolia. A fearless warrior, Diomedes (also Diomed) fought bravely in the Trojan War, engaging Hector and Aeneas and even wounding Venus in battle (*Iliad* 5.318–351). Dante would have known him from Virgil, Ovid, Statius, and probably the mythographer Hyginus. In the *Commedia,* Diomedes *(Dïomede)* appears as Ulysses' silent companion in the bolgia of the fraudulent counselors (*Inf.* 26.52–63), where the two heroes are enveloped by the same twin-peaked flame. They are punished together just as together they committed their sins, among which a medieval tradition—Benoît de Sainte-Maure's *Roman de Troie,* Guido delle Colonne's *Historia destructionis Troiae,* Dictys of Crete's *De bello Troiano,* and Dares the Phrygian's *De excidio Troiae*—included the deceit of the wooden horse by which the Greeks conquered Troy.

Lino Pertile

Dionysius Agricola, or Diniz

Born in 1261, Diniz succeeded his father, Alfonso III, to the Portuguese throne in 1279. Over the course of his long reign he proved himself a wise and able ruler, promoting the economic growth of Portugal, encouraging the development of industry and commerce, and doing much to prepare the country for its future glory as a seagoing nation. His efforts at promoting agricultural development earned him his nickname. He brought corrupt nobles and clergy into line and restored relations with the Church. In addition, he reformed legislation and insisted that laws should be written in Portuguese rather than in Latin.

His impact on the culture of his country was notable. He founded the University of Lisbon in 1290; it transferred to Coimbra in 1308. Diniz also ordered the translation into Portuguese of many Latin, Arabic, and Spanish works. The royal court was a center for poets and musicians, and Diniz and his sons themselves wrote poetry in the style of the troubadours, with some success. He died in 1325.

Surprisingly, Dante includes Diniz (*quel di Portogallo,* "he of Portugal," *Par.* 19.139) in a list of princes condemned by the Eagle in the Heaven of Jupiter. There are several possible reasons for Dante's condemnation of Diniz. Dante may have disapproved of the king's involvement in civil wars with his heir, his suppression of the Templars, the effort he expended in developing his country rather than fighting the Moors, or even his infidelity to his wife. However, it is likely that Dante knew little about Diniz or his achievements, except for the fact that he had not been involved in any great religious wars.

Angela G. Meekins

Dionysius the Academician

Plato's teacher, referred to by Dante in *Conv.* 2.13.5 as believing, with Socrates and Plato, that the form of each human soul is generated directly by the stars (see also *Par.* 4.52–56). He is not to be confused with Pseudo-Dionysius the Areopagite, author of the *Celestial Hierarchy.*

Richard Lansing

Dionysius the Areopagite

"Pseudo-Dionysius" *(Dionisio),* as he is generally called today, is known only as the author of a body of writings fundamental to Christian mystical tradition, the *Corpus Areopagiticum.* For centuries these writings were accepted, according to their identification of themselves, as works of the Dionysius converted at Athens by Paul, speaking before the Areopagus (Acts 17:16–34). Tradition held him to have been the first bishop of Athens. The same personage was claimed by the French to have brought the Christian faith to the Gauls and to have become the first bishop of Paris before dying a martyr. He was thereafter made the patron of the Abbey of St. Denis, the site to which his decapitated body was believed to have carried its severed head before finally lying down to rest.

The attribution of the writings to Paul's convert had already been questioned in antiquity and was further challenged by Peter Abelard before it was shown by Renaissance scholars to be highly unlikely. Though much mystery remains, modern research has determined—principally on the basis of the author's dependence on Neoplatonic writers, especially Proclus—that the writings originated in the late fifth or early sixth century (Koch).

In the probable order of their composition, inferred from internal references among them, the treatises comprise the *Divine Names,* which probes the grounds and limits of meaningfulness for the scriptural terms predicated of God; the *Mystical Theology,* which concerns the experience of God beyond all words and symbols; the *Celestial Hierarchy,* which deals with the orders of the angels, their different offices, and purely spiritual nature, and considers the symbolic value that imagery drawn from the world of the senses can have for describing them; and the *Ecclesiastical Hierarchy,* which interprets theologically the rites and ceremonies of the Church. In these four extant treatises addressed to a certain Timothy, evidently supposed to be the one Paul writes to, and ten letters, seven other titles of works that have been lost are mentioned.

Pervasively influential, Dionysius is generally acknowledged to be the fountainhead of Negative Theology in his postulation of the impossibility of making any positive affirmations about God. Nevertheless, his theology is distinguished by an infectious sense of all creation and of all the structures and rites of the church, as manifesting God—as theophany. Hierarchy is understood by him as a principle not of separation and domination but rather of communication and revelation; that is, all orders of being are linked together in a structure of unified communication with the Supreme Being, and this hierarchy delineates a graduated approach to God, culminating in the experience of ecstatic union beyond all powers of knowing.

In the Middle Ages, Dionysius' writings, reputed to be of nearly apostolic origin, enjoyed an authority hardly exceeded by that of scripture. This conviction registers in Dante's allusion to Dionysius in *Par.* 28.130–139, which attributes to his ordering of the angelic ranks the direct authority of St. Paul, who had been to Paradise, according to the tradition of his *raptus* (2 Cor. 12:2–4). This passage constitutes a palinode correcting Dante's own earlier ordering of the angelic ranks in *Conv.* 2.5.6, based on Gregory the Great, *Moralia in Job* 22.48.

Dionysius appears in person in the heaven of the Sun as the sixth of the twelve theologians, the *spiriti sapienti,* including Thomas Aquinas, who form a garland around Dante and Beatrice. He is identified as *il lume di quel cero / che giù, in carne, più a dentro vide / l'angelica natura e 'l ministero* ("the light of that candle which below, in the flesh, saw deepest into the nature and ministry of angels," *Par.* 10.115–117). Dionysius is also mentioned by Dante in his letters to the Italian cardinals (*Epist.* 11.16) and to Cangrande della Scala (*Epist.* 13.60); the latter refers specifically to the office of the angels to communicate light received from God to lower creatures.

Although these references all seem to revolve around the *Celestial Hierarchy,* which had been translated into Latin by John Scotus Erigena in the ninth century, Dionysius' significance for Dante

has been explored in broader terms by modern scholars. As a mystic theologian of the ineffable, Dionysius is considered fundamental to the whole project of the *Paradiso* by recent critics such as Giuliana Carugati and Manuela Colombo.

Bibliography

Carugati, Giuliana. *Dalla menzogna al silenzio: La scrittura mistica della "Commedia" di Dante.* Bologna: Mulino, 1991.

Colombo, Manuela. *Dai mistici a Dante: Il linguaggio dell'ineffabilità.* Florence: La Nuova Editrice, 1987.

Koch, Hugo. *Pseudo-Dionysius Areopagita in seinen Beziehungen zum Neoplatonismus und Mysterienwesen.* Mainz: Kirchheim, 1900.

———. "Proklus als Quelle des Ps-Dionysius Areopagita in der Lehre von Bösen." *Philologus* 54/1 (neue Folge, 8/1, 1895), 438–454.

Louth, Andrew. *Denys the Areopagite.* Wilton, Conn.: Morehouse-Barlow, 1989.

Pseudo-Dionysius: The Complete Works. Translated by Colm Luibheid and Paul Rorem. Mahwah, N.J.: Paulist Press, 1987.

Roques, R. *L'Univers dionysien. Structure hiérarchique du monde selon le Pseudo-Denys.* Paris: Cerf, 1983.

William Franke

Dionysius the Elder

Ruler of Syracuse from 430 to 367 B.C.E., who enforced a program of Sicilian unification by military strength. His cruelty was made proverbial by Cicero (*De off.* 2.7.25) and, in Dante's time, by Brunetto Latini (*Tresor,* 2.119.6). Dionysius (*Dionisio*) is found in the first ring of the seventh circle of Hell, among the violent against their neighbors (*Inf.* 12.107), together with Alexander the Great, Azzolino, and Opizzo da Esti. Some believe the reference is to Dionysius the Younger, who was a tyrant like his father, although the people succeeded in expelling him in 356.

Rinaldina Russell

Dioscorides

Greek natural scientist and physician of the first or second century C.E. His *De materia medica* (translated from the Greek in the sixth century), a study of the medicinal properties of herbs, was highly influential. Dante refers to him (*Dïascoride*) only once in his works, as a resident of Limbo with the wise pagans (*Inf.* 4.140).

Richard Lansing

Dis

Taking its name from its ruler (Dis being the Roman name for Pluto, king of the underworld; see, for example, *Aen.* 6.127), the city of lower Hell spans the *Inferno* from 9.106 to 34.81 and embraces circles six through nine, in which the graver sins of heresy, violence, fraud, and treachery are punished. Like a city, Dis *(Dite)* has a name, as do its last two circles, Malebolge and Cocytus. The first reference to Dis as a city, *la città ch'ha nome Dite* ("the city whose name is Dis"), occurs while Virgil and Dante are crossing the Styx in Phlegyas' boat (*Inf.* 8.68). The rapid description in *Inf.* 8.70–78 recalls Virgil's *Aen.* 6.541 and 548–556, but it focuses on the architectural structure of the city, developing Virgil's repeated suggestion of Hell's city buildings *(moenia)* and the surrounding walls. However, Virgil never defines the nether world as a "city" *(civitas).* Nevertheless, this strong cultural association of Hell with the architectural features of the city and the fortress (cf. also Andrea Lancia's 1316 translation of *Aen.* 6.541–555) figures heavily as a structuring device throughout the rest of the *Inferno*. The city's towers, gates, walls, ramparts, bridges, and moats become important geographical elements in the narrative of the pilgrim's journey. But Dante's use of *città* (city) and its synonyms (especially *terra*) often leads to imprecise definitions. Is the *città dolente* which Dante describes as the City of Dis (*Inf.* 9.32) the same *città dolente* noted above the Gate of Hell in *Inf.* 3.1? During the tense negotiations with the multitude of devils who guard the city's gate, Virgil suggests (*Inf.* 8.124–126) that the devilish guardians demonstrated the same insolence when Christ descended through the first gate to Hell, now unbolted, mentioned in *Inf.* 3. Farinata's reference to the "city of fire" (*Inf.* 10.22) seems to indicate only the circle of the heretics, while the "ruddy city" (*città roggia, Inf.* 11.73) is usually taken to refer to the City of Dis.

Equally suggestive for Dante and his culture must have been the counterpart to Augustine's City of God, defined in the exegete's *City of God* 18.51 by reference to its leader: "the Devil, the prince of that irreligious city." The contrast between the

El terzo difegno (fe bene ui ricorda)fi rimafe che figuraffi lo octauo cerchio cioè laualle dima lebolge fola. Ma io ci ho uoluto agiugnere en chora elpozzo de Giganti. Perche nel difegna re mi parue che ueniffi bene cofi. El difegno è quefto.

The City of Dis, from Commedia di Dante, *published by Filippo Giunti, Florence, 1506. Reproduced by permission of the John A. Zahm Dante Collection in the Department of Special Collections, University Libraries, University of Notre Dame.*

heavenly city, characterized "by the love of God carried as far as contempt for self," and the earthly city, "created by self-love reaching the point of contempt for God" (*City of God* 14.28), forms the basis for the still debated moral order of Dante's *Inferno*.

It is critical to understand that Dante's definition of "city" is both religious and political, and that humankind, naturally civic in its associations for a common good, must conduct itself morally as a first, earthly step toward eternal happiness (*Mon.* 3.15). This step can be subverted by human desire (*humana cupiditas, Mon.* 3.15.9)—that is, by the "standard of the flesh" (*City of God* 14.4) rather than of the spirit. Thus, as Virgil explains in *Inf.* 11.79–90, recalling Aristotle's *Nicomachean Ethics* (7.1.1145a.15ff.), those who are unable to control their passions—the incontinent, the souls in circles two through five—offend God less and are not condemned to lower Hell, while those who have lived by *malizia* (from *malus,* "wickedness" [cf. *Conv.* 4.15.17], rather than the more limited "deceptiveness" [*astuzia, astuto,* cf. *Conv.* 4.27.5]) and by *matta bestialitade* ("crazed bestiality") are punished in the last three circles of Hell. While some critics have seen a direct correspondence between the violent of the seventh circle and *matta bestialitade,* as well as between the fraudulent and treacherous of the eighth and ninth circles and *malizia,* other scholars have concentrated on the reference to Aristotle's *Ethics* as a demonstration that the sins of incontinence are simply lesser transgressions than those of the wickedness of lower Hell, and that *matta bestialitade* does not correspond to any of Dante's categories. Still other scholars have argued—against Aristotle's cultural understanding of morality—that heresy, the sixth circle (often ignored in discussions of the moral order of the City of Dis), corresponds to Virgil's designation of *matta bestialitade.* Another group of critics believes that *malizia* should be identified with circles seven and eight, while *matta bestialitade* describes an "inhuman wickedness" with which the sinner destroys the most basic civic, familial, and religious foundations of happiness, and this is punished in the ninth circle of Hell. The last interpretation is supported by Virgil's general moral definition of *malizia* in *Inf.* 11.22–24, especially by the construction "either by force or by fraud" (v. 24). However, his similarly binary treatment of fraud (*Inf.* 11.52–54) suggests a strong link between the sins of simple fraud and treachery (eighth and ninth circles); both, according to v. 25, are "proper to man" but distinguished by the confidence (v. 54), or special faith (v. 63) which the victims would have bestowed upon their deceivers.

Two points in Virgil's exposition in *Inf.* 11 help to clarify the moral order of the City of Dis. The first occurs in Virgil's use of *ingiuria* to elucidate the meaning of *malizia:* "Of every malice *(malizia)* gaining the hatred of Heaven, *injustice* is the goal; and every such goal injures someone either with force or with fraud" (vv. 22–24). In spite of efforts to trace Dante's usage to the technical legal term *iniuria* in the *Institutiones,* the poet's command of the *Corpus iuris civilis* was not systematic, like that of a legal specialist, but more generically oriented toward widely circulated philosophical and moral principles. Verses 22–24 are actually a fair translation of Cicero's *De officiis* 1.13.41, an ancient authority—in this canto of authoritative proofs—on exactly why *willful harm* (Aquinas's *ex intentione*) constitutes a graver

moral transgression than the inability to control one's passions (incontinence). The second point of clarification occurs in Virgil's enumeration of the circles Dante has yet to see ("the first circle," 27; the "second circle," 57). Virgil's numbering excludes the first six circles of Hell and starts with the seventh (the violent) as the first. Throughout most of the canto, his explanations are designed to distinguish between the four circles of the incontinent and the last three circles (*Inf.* 11.16–18), where the willfully evil and injurious are punished in the City of Dis. Only his brief philosophical synopsis (11.79–90) gives the authoritative—but general—foundations for the entire moral order of Hell.

The most problematic aspect of the City of Dis remains the sixth circle (heretics), which Dante has already seen in *Inf.* 10, when Virgil pauses to acclimate him to the stench of lower Hell and to outline the ordering of the rest of Lucifer's evil city. Virgil neither names nor numbers the circle in *Inf.* 11. Most commentators are silent on the place of heresy, except to note that Aristotle's *Ethics,* Virgil's authority on the "three dispositions that Heaven refuses," could not have treated the Christian notion. Only vv. 85–90 offer, again, the distinction between those sinners who "suffer punishment above, outside [the walls of Dis]" and the willfully wicked souls (*felli,* 88) of Dis. However, Dante's consistent use of *fello,* along with Francesco da Buti's fourteenth-century glosses of *fellonia (Par.* 16.95) as *malizia e falsità* (wickedness and falsehood) and of *fello* as "one who thinks of doing evil to another," suggests that the heretics, characterized by Augustine (*City of God* 18.51) as willfully injurious to other Christians in their "deadly dogmas," fall under the general category of *malizia.* Thus, as Phlegyas races across the Styx to collect another soul destined for the City of Dis, he cries out "Now you are caught, wicked soul!" (*anima fella, Inf.* 8.18).

Bibliography

Durling, Robert M. "Farinata and the Body of Christ." *Stanford Italian Review* 2 (1981), 5–35.

Filomusi-Guelfi, Lorenzo. "La città di Dite." In *Nuovi studi su Dante.* Città di Castello: S. Lapi, 1911.

Pietrobono, Luigi. "La città di Dite." In *Il poema sacro: Saggio d'una interpretazione general e della Divina Commedia. Inferno,* part 2. Bologna: Zanichelli, 1915.

H. Wayne Storey

D

Distributive Justice

In his *Commentary on the Nichomachean Ethics* (Book 5, lect. 4, n. 927 seq.), St. Thomas underlines the distinction between justice in its broad meaning (*iustitia legalis,* or justice understood as a common virtue), and justice in its special sense *(iustitia particularis),* which is subdivided into distributive justice and commutative justice. The latter denotes a balance of equity between two parties. Distributive justice is defined as "the distribution of certain common goods . . . whether honor or money, or any other thing belonging to external goods or even to external evils, like labor, expenses and so on." Distributive justice is the responsibility of the leader of a community, who, in distributing rewards and punishments, has the duty to observe the rule of relational proportionality based on the real and personal merits of each member of the community.

Dante refers to distributive justice in *Conv.* 4.11.6, where he is concerned with the origin of riches: *dico che la loro imperfezione primamente si può notare ne la indiscrezione del loro avvenimento, nel quale nulla distributiva giustizia risplende* ("I say that their imperfection may be observed first in the lack of discretion attending their appropriation, in which no distributive justice is present"). Dante's attack on society's "evil habit and lack of intelligence" in judging the worth of individuals (*Conv.* 4.1.6–7), which derives from conceiving nobility on the basis of birth and not personal merit, is fundamentally an attack upon a defective system of distributive justice. Since this kind of justice calls for an impartial and prudent authority, Dante suggests that only men of "the third age of life, namely old age" should be chosen to govern societies: *E perché questa singolare virtù, cioè giustizia, fue veduta per li antichi filosofi apparire perfetta in questa etade, lo reggimento de le cittadi commisero in quelli che in questa etade erano* ("Because this singular virtue, namely justice, was perceived by philosophers in ancient times to display itself to perfection in this age of life, they entrusted the rule of the cities to those who were in this age of life," *Conv.* 4.27.10).

Bibliography

Mazzotta, Giuseppe. "Metaphor and Justice." In *Dante's Vision and the Circle of Knowledge.* Princeton: Princeton University Press, 1993, pp. 75–95.

Mario Trovato

Divine Comedy. See *Commedia.*

Dolce stil novo

The phrase *dolce stil novo* ("sweet new style") occurs once in Dante's *oeuvre.* It is uttered on the sixth terrace of Purgatory (*Purg.* 24.57) by the glutton and poet, Bonagiunta da Lucca, during a brief discussion with the pilgrim on the history and achievements of Italian vernacular lyric poetry, and on the contribution that the two of them had made as poets to this tradition (49–62). The exchange is divided into three parts. First (49–51), Bonagiunta describes Dante-character as the author of "the new rhymes" (50) which began with "Donne ch'avete intelletto d'amore" ("Ladies that have intellect of love," the canzone that, in the *Vita Nuova,* marks the shift to poetry written in praise of Beatrice). Second (52–54), the wayfarer describes himself as someone who gives accurate formal expression to Love's inspiration. Third (55–62), Bonagiunta acknowledges that, in contrast to the kind of poet who is able to match his style closely with the source of his subject matter, he and other poets belonging to generations older than the pilgrim's had failed to achieve such a synthesis in their verse. This failure, Bonagiunta concludes, irrevocably separated him and his peers from poets of Dante's ilk: it imprisoned them with *il nodo / che 'l Notaro e Guittone e me ritenne / di qua dal dolce stil novo ch'i' odo!* ("the knot that held the Notary and Guittone and me back on this side of the sweet new style I hear," 56–57).

As used by Bonagiunta, the phrase *dolce stil novo* echoes similar, albeit not identical, formulae employed in the Middle Ages to speak of literary matters. Indeed, each of the three words making up the phrase was widely used in classical and medieval writing on literature. *Novus* highlighted the innovative traits of a text, whether in form or in subject matter; *stilus* either was equivalent to the modern notion of "style," or it designated the relationship between form and content. The adjective *dulcis* described the aurally pleasing phonic qualities of a composition (in contrast to works characterized by the "harshness" of their sound structure); alternatively, it attested to the clarity and accessibility of a work's manner of expression (in contrast to "obscure" forms of writing); or it indicated that a text belonged to the "comic" tradition, since "sweetness" was deemed a particular attribute of "comedies." In addition, both "sweet" and "new" had important connotations for religious authors. As well as defining the positive formal characteristics of sacred modes of communication, they referred to spiritual renewal and to the wondrous nature of the relationship with God—topics which were often celebrated in texts that themselves were both "sweet" and "new."

The rich allusiveness of the phrase *dolce stil novo* is typical of the way Dante constructs the whole encounter between Bonagiunta and the pilgrim. Their meeting is one of the most densely complicated moments in the *Commedia*. Thus, the reference to the "sweet new style" has a direct bearing on at least two highly complex and wide-ranging issues, each of which raises its own host of difficulties. These issues relate first to Dante's views of poetry (his own, that of others, and in general); and second, to the extent to which Dante meant the fictional conversation between Bonagiunta and the pilgrim to stand as an objective assessment of the history of the early Italian lyric. More specifically, semantic ambiguity not only surrounds the expression *dolce stil novo* but is also a feature of several other key terms that make up the exchange between the two poets. For instance, is the *Amor* which "inspires" (53) Dante-character meant to designate Love or God (and in particular the Holy Spirit)? What is the nature of the "knot" (55) which restrained *'l Notaro e Guittone e me?* Is the *vostre* ("your") of *le vostre penne* ("your pens," 58)—used by Bonagiunta in his description of poetry which successfully follows its *dittator* ("him who dictates," 59)—an honorific plural referring solely to the pilgrim, or an ordinary plural applied to a community of poets of which Dante-character is a member? And in regard to the last phrase, it is equally open to dispute whether *penne* means "pens" or "feathers," and hence "wings."

The manner in which one interprets Bonagiunta's and the pilgrim's polysemous words fundamentally alters one's reading of the broader issues raised by their encounter. Consequently, and not surprisingly, the significance of the *dolce stil novo* (and the whole episode of which it is part) has long been the source of scholarly controversy. Nonetheless, it is possible to discern some general interpretive trends.

Most Dantists read the exchange between Bonagiunta and the wayfarer as a single, seamless statement which reflects the historical Dante's opinions. According to this view, in *Purg.* 24

Dante states that until the appearance of the "sweet new style," the Italian love lyric had revealed serious literary flaws. The two major established traditions, the "Sicilian School" headed by Giacomo da Lentini, the "Notary," and the "Sicilian-Tuscan" movement, whose most influential figures were Guittone d'Arezzo and Bonagiunta, had signally failed to find artistic means adequate to express the substance of their inspiration; to put it in more modern terms, they had failed to harmonize form and content. This was a capital charge which accused them of incompetence both as lovers and as poets. It was generally held in the Middle Ages that the quality of an erotic poet's verse reflected the quality of his love, while, according to the doctrine of "fittingness" *(convenientia),* it was an author's basic duty to match his rhetorical choices to his subject matter. In contrast, the "sweet new style" showed no such flaws.

It is at this juncture that several important exegetical problems emerge. The first involves the status of the *dolce stil novo.* In light of Bonagiunta's seeming reference to poetic movements, most scholars assume that by "sweet new style," Dante intended to designate a specific "school" of poetry. They disagree, however, as to its possible composition. Some have drawn a close equation between *le nove rime* of "Donne ch'avete" and the *dolce stil novo,* and thus they have maintained that Dante meant to limit membership of the new "school" to himself. Others—a majority—have drawn on the positive assessments Dante makes elsewhere of Italian lyric poets (for instance, *VN* 3.14, 20.3; *DVE* 1.10.3, 13.3, 17.3, 2.2.9; *Purg.* 11.97–98, 26.97–99, 112–114), as well as on the evidence provided by thirteenth-century poetic disputes regarding the correct way to write (such as the polemical exchange of sonnets between Bonagiunta and Guido Guinizzelli, echoes of which can be clearly heard in lines 49–63), in order to claim that Dante saw in the "sweet new style" a fellowship of like-minded poets. Considerable disagreement has arisen, however, on the make-up of this group. In keeping with Dante's own declared, albeit shifting, sympathies, the names most commonly mentioned are those of Guido Guinizzelli, Guido Cavalcanti, and Cino da Pistoia. A third set of scholars has attempted to reach a compromise between the two interpretations presented above by arguing that Dante, while referring to a community of poets of the "sweet new style," was also highlighting a uniquely personal version of this style.

D The artistic characteristics of the *dolce stil novo* have been defined by relating the epithets *dolce* and *novo* to the love poetry written by Dante (up to and including the *Vita Nuova*) and by poets such as the two Guidos and Cino. In addition, their verse is contrasted with that of the Sicilian School and of the Sicilian-Tuscans. As a result, the "sweet new style" is normally described as a kind of lyric verse which is formally elegant, linguistically refined, and aurally attractive, and which presents a view of love as intellectually and spiritually ennobling. Indeed, for those critics who see in *Amore* a personification not of Love but the Christian God, the *dolce stil novo* has explicitly religious aspirations—a view which is strongly supported at least by the *Vita Nuova*. Conversely, some or all of these features are missing from the work of the Sicilians and the Sicilian-Tuscans, and their lack constitutes the "knot" which ensures the literary failure of these schools (critics disagree, however, on which particular features cannot be found in their poetry).

The above interpretations of the "sweet new style" are fundamentally predicated on the belief that Dante viewed the history of the Italian love lyric in the light of distinct movements or "schools." However, there is no evidence that the phrase *dolce stil novo* would have been read in this way in the Middle Ages. The words that constitute it were much too generic and amorphous to have been recognized as referring to a particular artistic movement. Nor is it even clear that Dante thought of the literary tradition in terms as precise as that of "schools." He often changed his mind about the status of other poets, and, rather than "schools," he tended to categorize writers into loose, overlapping groupings based on geography, subject matter, and rhetorical practice. It was, in fact, the historiographic and taxonomic ambitions of the nineteenth century that introduced the idea of a *dolce stil novo* "school" of poetry in opposition to other "schools." Indeed, to distinguish between Dante's specific use of the phrase in the *Purgatorio* and the general poetic movement, scholars, omitting the epithet *dolce,* normally designate the latter as the *Stil nuovo* or, less commonly, the *Stil novo.* Such a distinction is crucial. In his *oeuvre,* Dante was not so much interested in presenting balanced critical assessments of his fellow writers as he was intent on using them to define his own literary identity.

By wanting to see in *dolce stil novo* a precise literary tag under which particular poets and poems can be subsumed, scholars have not paid enough attention to Dante's actual words in *Purg.* 24. They have also restricted the potential meaning of the key word *dolce.* In order to define the "sweet new style" in exact formal and ideological terms, Dantists have relied on external evidence coming from the thirteenth-century lyric corpus. They have paid little attention to the fact that in lines 52–62, Dante is simply stating that the *dolce stil novo* is a way of writing in which form and content are in harmony. This confluence is the source of the poetry's "sweetness," namely—remembering another of the meanings of *dulcis*—its clarity (an attribute which was regularly associated with phonic "sweetness"). In contrast, according to medieval literary theory, obscurity was the inevitable result of the disjuncture between form and content. In *Purg.* 24, Dante is asserting the need for literature to be as intelligible as possible, and for poets to avoid the kind of rhetorical excess that conceals meaning and is an end in itself. Both the Sicilian and the Sicilian-Tuscan poets were well known for their formal bravado. On the other hand, in "Donne ch'avete"—the only lyric composition specifically mentioned in *Purg.* 24—Dante states in the proemial stanza that he will not *parlar sì altamente* ("attempt a style so lofty," l.9), or use recherché rhetorical forms, but will instead write about Beatrice *leggeramente* (l.12), "lightly" and hence "sweetly"; the two words were technical synonyms. In keeping with medieval literary usage, with Dante's own words in *Purg.* 24, and with the context of the exchange between the pilgrim and Bonagiunta, the phrase *dolce stil novo* would seem to mean "the new lyric poetry written in the 'clear' style." Dante is not distinguishing between poetic "schools," but, in line with one of the principal tenets of classical and medieval literary theory, he is discriminating between two ways of writing.

Beyond its local narrative concerns, and like the *Commedia*'s other discussions of literature, *Purg.* 24 also casts light on the poetics of Dante's masterpiece. The link between *dulcis* and "comedy," as well as the term's ties with religious writing, points to this fact. The verb *spirare* serves a similar function. It was traditionally associated with writers, such as Biblical authors, who were divinely inspired, and was not used in relation to secular authors or the influence of the God of Love. Thus, the pilgrim's artistic self-description in lines 52–54 has been interpreted as alluding to the *Commedia*'s heavenly origins; and the entire episode has been seen as elucidating Dante's aim, sanctioned by Cacciaguida (*Par.* 17.124–142), to recount his marvelous experiences as lucidly as possible. Tying *Purg.* 24 to the poem as a whole has led to a further set of queries. In particular, it has raised two questions: first, whether Dante intended to connect the *Commedia* to his lyric verse and the *Vita Nuova,* or whether he drew a distinction between them and hence was criticizing his earlier work; and, second, the extent to which the otherworldly meeting between the two poets reflects, on the one hand, the historical Dante's views on the vernacular lyric when he wrote *Purgatorio,* and, on the other, the views he may have held in 1300, the date of the supposed journey.

As with other questions relating to the *dolce stil novo,* straightforward answers to these problems are not forthcoming. It is a feature of the *Commedia* that Dante constructed its key moments in such a manner that it is ultimately impossible to provide univocal and definitive interpretations of their significance. When it came to the nodal points of his great poem, Dante wanted to involve his readers' exegetical abilities to the utmost. Thus, in *Purg.* 24, he wanted them to appreciate the novel "sweetness" of the *Commedia* in the light of the traditional "sweetness" of poetry.

Bibliography

Barański, Zygmunt G. "*'Nfiata labbia* and *dolce stil novo:* A Note on Dante, ethics, and the technical Vocabulary of Literature." In *Miscellanea Mazzoni.* Edited by Domenico De Robertis and Leonella Coglievina. Florence: Le Lettere, 1998.

Barolini, Teodolinda. *Dante's Poets: Textuality and Truth in the "Comedy."* Princeton, N.J.: Princeton University Press, 1984, pp. 40–57, 85–153.

Durling, Robert M., and Ronald L. Martinez. *Time and the Crystal: Studies in Dante's "Rime petrose."* Berkeley: University of California Press, 1990, pp. 53–70.

Favati, Guido. *Inchiesta sul dolce stil novo.* Florence: Le Monnier, 1975.

Marti, Mario. *Storia dello stil nuovo.* 2 vols. Lecce: Milella, 1973.

———. "Stil nuovo." *Enciclopedia dantesca,* 5:438–444.

Martinez, Ronald L. "The Pilgrim's Answer to Bonagiunta and the Poetics of the Spirit." *Stanford Italian Review* 3 (1983), 37–63.

Mazzotta, Giuseppe. *Dante, Poet of the Desert.* Princeton, N.J.: Princeton University Press, 1979, pp. 192–226.

Pertile, Lino. "Il nodo di Bonagiunta, le penne di Dante e il dolce stil novo." *Lettere italiane* 46 (1994), 44–75.

Russo, Vittorio. "Il 'nodo' del Dolce Stil Novo." *Medioevo Romanzo* 3 (1976), 236–264.

Zygmunt G. Barański

Dolce, Lodovico

Venetian author of tragedies and comedies in the classical style, essayist, and editor of fourteenth-century Italian texts. He served as managing editor of the famous Venetian printing establishment of the Giuntis. He is credited with having added the descriptor *divina* to the title of Dante's *Comedia* in his edition and commentary of the poem, *La Divina Commedia di Dante con gli argomenti, allegorie e dichiarazione di Lodovico Dolce* (Venezia: G. Giolito de Ferrari et fratelli, 1555). He lived from 1508 to 1568.

Bibliography

Parker, Deborah. *Commentary and Ideology: Dante in the Renaissance.* Durham: Duke University Press, 1993, p. 148.

Vallone, Aldo. *L'interpretazione di Dante nel Cinquecento.* Florence: Olschki, 1989, pp. 90–93.

Robert C. Melzi

Dolcino, Fra

Dolcino de' Tornielli of Novara was associated with the sect of the Apostolic Brothers, founded in 1260 by Gerardo Segarelli of Parma. He became its head in 1300 and was charged by his opponents with holding heretical views, especially his advocacy of the community of goods and women. When Clement V proclaimed a crusade in 1305 to extirpate this sect, Dolcino withdrew to the hills of Novara and Vercelli along with his followers and held his own for more than a year. He was finally taken prisoner, along with his alleged mistress Margaret, and was burned alive at Vercelli in June 1307 after being paraded through the streets, horribly tortured and mangled. Dante considers him a schismatic and punishes him in the ninth bolgia of the eighth circle in Hell (*Inf.* 28.55).

R.A. Malagi

D

Dominic, St.

Dominic (*Domenico,* b. Domingo de Guzmán) was born in Caleruega, Castile, in 1170 and died in 1221. He established the Order of the Friars Preachers (1215), which received official confirmation from Pope Honorius III in 1216. As a founder of the mendicant movement he is often paired with St. Francis in early texts and iconography. Gregory IX's bull promoting Dominic's canonization (3 July 1234) stressed what Di Biase calls "the providential complementarity of the two saints" (pp. 25–26); so did Celano (*Vita secunda* of St. Francis, 2.109–110) and Bonaventura (sermon on Dominic, *Opera omnia* 9, p. 565b). He was a vigorous opponent of the Cathars in Languedoc in the first decade of the thirteenth century.

Dante mentions Dominic alongside Benedict, Augustine, and Francis as a founder of one of the main religious orders in *Conv.* 4.28.9. More importantly, he also associates the two mendicant "patriarchs" closely through the structure, narration, and imagery of the cantos devoted to them in *Paradiso* (11 and 12). Here the life of St. Francis is narrated by the leading Dominican theologian, Aquinas, and that of St. Dominic is described by the leading Franciscan, Bonaventura, who had linked the two saints in his own writing (see above; also *Opera* 5, p. 440b). Dominic is also here represented, with St. Francis, as a fellow helmsman of the "ship of St. Peter" (*Par.* 11.118–120) and as one of the twin wheels of the chariot of the Church (*Par.* 12.106–111).

The account of St. Dominic's life and mission in *Par.* 12 alludes to the hagiographic tradition that had developed during the previous century through the canonization process and the early Lives, particularly those by Dominic's successor as master-general, Jordan of Saxony, and other Dominicans such as Peter Ferrand, Constantine of Orvieto, Humbert of Romans, and Dietrich of Apolda. Such sources give details of the visions that his mother and godmother are said to have been granted before the saint's birth (*Par.* 12.58-66). The first of these visions indicates Dominic's role as a bearer of fire (*MOPH* 16 [1935], 16, 27–28, 210–211, 288–289, 371), and the second as a bearer of light (*MOPH* 30, 212, 289, 372).

When granting confirmation to the Order of Preachers in 1216, Honorius III saw them as not only "lights of the world" but also as "future fighters for the faith" (*futuros pugiles fidei,* Potthast vol. 1, p. 476). The militancy of the order is a feature

that Dante's imagery also recognizes. Dominic is represented in *Par.* 12 as a rather more aggressively warriorlike figure than St. Francis. The order sprang from his mission against the heresy of the Cathars in Languedoc, and Lawrence suggests that "some of the combative fervour of the Crusader that marked his missionary activities derived from his Spanish upbringing in a society preoccupied with the *reconquista*"(67). Dante acknowledges Dominic's role as a champion of orthodoxy by representing him as *gran dottor* ("great teacher," *Par.* 12.85), as the cultivator of the Church's "vineyard" (86–87) and "orchard" (72, 103), and as a mountain torrent forcefully uprooting the "thickets of heresy" (99–102). Dominic's ally in this campaign (and one of the most active patrons of the order), Bishop Foulques *(Folco)* of Marseille, is also a prominent presence in the previous sphere of *Par.* (9.67–142).

The importance of learning *(dottrina)* to Dominic's apostolic mission is stressed in *Par.* 12.97–98, and through Dante's choice of the Dominican Aquinas as the dominant voice in this sphere (*Par.*10, 11, 13). The need of the Order of Preachers for a core of highly trained theologians led them to establish themselves early on in Paris and Oxford; and the intellectual preeminence of Bologna seems to have induced Dominic to make it his headquarters and the site of the order's first general chapter in 1220 (see Lawrence 72–75, 79). Unlike the Franciscans, who because of their founder's strong reservations about academic learning were late developers in this field, the Dominicans were thus from the start "an order of students" (Lawrence 84–88, 127–151).

Dante's Aquinas announces himself first of all as one of "the holy flock which Dominic leads along [the] path" (*Par.* 10.94–95), and he identifies his closest companion, "a brother and my master," as one of the leading early Dominican teachers, Albertus Magnus (*Alberto . . . di Cologna,* 98–99). The respect for the tradition of Dominican learning here is perhaps qualified by the warning about the order "wandering" (*Par.* 10.96) in quest of "new foods" (*Par.* 11.124). This "straying" could represent the pursuit of material goods or worldly offices, but several *trecento* and modern commentators (Pietro di Dante, Buti, Bosco and Reggio) construe it as a kind of intellectual gluttony for speculative or nontheological learning, possibly of the kind that Beatrice associates with vain preachers in *Par.* 29.94–126. Dante may have had in mind here the extravagant use of exempla by popular Dominican preachers such as Giordano da Rivalto. If so, he would have been biting the hand that fed him, since he may well have attended lectures at the *studium* of S. Maria Novella in Florence, which during his time was one of the leading Dominican schools (*Conv.* 2.12.7; Davis 156, 158).

There is reference to at least one other known Dominican figure in the *Commedia:* Bonifazio Fieschi, archbishop of Ravenna from 1274 to 1295 (*Purg.* 24.29–30), and the notion of pasturing a flock occurs ironically in this context (the terrace of the gluttons) as well. More significant in the end, however, is the intellectual nourishment that Dante probably derived from the Dominicans. The teaching of Remigio Girolami (lector at S. Maria Novella during the 1280s, 1290s, and early 1300s) is one of the most immediate channels through which Aristotelean ideas on, for example, the desire for knowledge and the nature of citizenship are likely to have reached him (see Davis 163–165, 199–202); and Remigio's political theory, as Davis has shown (202–207), also anticipates Dante's in several respects.

Bibliography

Biase, Carmine di. *Il canto XII del Paradiso.* Naples: Cassitto, 1992.

Bosco, Umberto, and Giovanni Reggio. *Dante Alighieri, "La Divina Commedia: Paradiso."* Florence: Le Monnier, 1979, pp. 172–180, 193–206.

Davis, Charles T. "Education in Dante's Florence" and "An Early Florentine Political Theorist: Fra Remigio de' Girolami." In his *Dante's Italy and Other Essays.* Philadelphia: University of Pennsylvania Press, 1984.

Kaske, Robert. "Dante's 'DXV' and 'Veltro.'" *Traditio* 17 (1961), 185–254.

Lawrence, Clifford. *The Friars: The Impact of the Early Mendicant Movement on Western Society.* London and New York: Longman, 1994.

Lehner, Francis C. S. *Dominic: Biographical Documents.* Washington, D.C.: Thomist Press, 1964.

Monumenta Ordinis Fratrum Praedicatorum Historica [*MOPH*] 16 (1935) [for Latin texts of the early *Lives* of *St. Dominic*].

Potthast, Augustus. *Regesta pontificum romanorum (1198–1304).* 2 vols. Berlin: Decker, 1874–1875, vol. 1, p. 476, item 5402.

Nicholas Havely

Dominicans

Friars of the Dominican Order are named after their founder, St. Dominic, but are officially known as members of the Order of Preachers (Ordo Predicatorum, OP), or in England as Blackfriars, from the color of their mantle and cowl. The Dominican Order was founded by the Spaniard Dominic of Caleruega (Domingo de Guzmán) during the second decade of the thirteenth century and officially recognized by Pope Honorius III in 1216. The occasion for its foundation came when Folquet of Marseille, a former Provençal poet and then bishop of Toulouse (1215), invited Dominic to southern France to combat the Cathar heresy with his preaching and deeds. The Dominican Order developed from the small group of volunteering brothers gathered around Dominic. The order flourished and greatly expanded in the course of the thirteenth century, side by side with the other great mendicant movement, the Franciscan Order. In the history of the church, the Order of Preachers is traditionally associated with the Inquisition.

As shown by the abundant references in his work, Dante was strongly influenced by the Dominican Order, which was immensely popular during his lifetime. Dante almost certainly had contacts with the Florentine Dominican convent of S. Maria Novella. He may also have had direct contact with Dominicans at the *studio di teologia* in Florence, where eminent Dominican scholars such as Remigio de' Girolami and Giordano da Pisa were teaching. A vague reference to the philosophical teaching acquired in this religious institution occurs in *Conv.* 2.12.7. With the exception of that and another general reference to the religious life instituted by St. Dominic in *Conv.* 4.28.9, all references to the Dominican Order in Dante occur in the *Commedia.*

In *Purg.* 24.29–30, Boniface Fieschi, bishop of Ravenna, is placed among the gluttons, following a widespread contemporary legend about his prodigality and gluttony. Dante's high esteem of the Dominican Order would seem to preclude any direct reference to this prelate's association with it. In *Paradiso,* Dante traces the order's history and fortune in three consecutive cantos. St. Thomas Aquinas first introduces the Dominican Order, to which he belongs, in the Heaven of the Sun. While pointing at the twelve wise spirits that make up the first crown, Thomas mentions himself and Albert the Great as belonging to the Dominican Order, and he obscurely criticizes the

D

Santa Maria Novella, Florence. Christopher Kleinhenz.

current reprehensible conduct of the order as a whole: *Io fui de li agni de la santa greggia / che Domenico mena per cammino / u' ben s'impingua se non si vaneggia* ("I was of the lambs of the holy flock which Dominic leads on the path where there is good fattening if they do not stray," *Par.* 10.94–96). The final line, which summarizes Thomas's bitter criticism of his own order, is diffusely explained later on and quoted again in a recapitulation of Thomas's entire speech in *Par.* 11.139. The pastoral metaphor employed here to refer to Dominic's mission is one of several different images which serve the purpose of telling the story of the order and Thomas's criticism of it. When Dominicans abandon the straight path of poverty and penance indicated by the founder, they do not grow in doctrine and spirit. Thomas's invective in *Par.* 11.124–132 is structured on a pastoral metaphor combined with an eating metaphor: the destiny of the order depends on the quality of food on which the flock feeds. Thomas maintains that the new sheep, the brothers of the order, stray away from their shepherd St. Dominic because they are attracted by more appealing pastures—material things rather than spiritual ones. When they return to the fold, they are bereft of milk, and milk is the depth of spiritual life. If the Dominicans abandon

the line of poverty, penance, and preaching set by their founder, they do not grow spiritually and doctrinally. St. Thomas's criticism of his own order (*Par.* 11.124–132) follows his long exaltation of Francis and the Franciscan Order (*Par.* 11.43–117) and a two-tercet praise of Dominic (*Par.* 11.118–123), and it matches the specular self-critical tirade by St. Bonaventure against the Franciscans (*Par.* 12.112–126), which follows a long exaltation of St. Dominic (*Par.* 12.31–105). The parallel accounts of the lives of the two most prominent founders of the mendicant orders comprise Dante's response to the competitive atmosphere of contention between the two orders. Dante intertwines the two lives, the two accounts, and the two orders so as to stress their peaceful collaboration in reforming the corrupt Church.

St. Thomas Aquinas's philosophy, adopted by the Church as its official dogma regarding revelation and commonly known as Thomism, exerted great influence on Dante. It has been noticed that Dante's concepts and vocabulary are structured on Thomism throughout the section dedicated to the Dominicans, beginning with *Par.* 10. Albert the Great, another Dominican philosopher and Thomas's teacher, also amply influenced Dante's theological thinking.

Bibliography

Needler, Howard. *Saint Francis and Saint Dominic in the Divine Comedy.* Krefeld: Scherpe, 1969.

Reeves, John B. *The Dominicans.* New York: Macmillan, 1930.

Alessandro Vettori

Domitian, Emperor

Titus Flavius Domitianus Augustus (51–96 C.E.), second son of Vespasian, became emperor in the year 81. He soon revealed himself a tyrant and was eventually assassinated. In *Purg.* 22.82–84, Statius recalls that the persecution of Domitian *(Domiziano)* made the Christians weep.

Nancy Vine Durling

Donation of Constantine

Manufactured at the papal court or in France, probably between 750 and 850, this document was believed to constitute the official act by which the Emperor Constantine donated the city of Rome and the entire Western Empire to the Church. According to a legend dating back to the fifth century, Constantine made his gift to Pope Sylvester in recompense for his having converted him to Christianity and then cured him of leprosy in the year 314. Forged perhaps deliberately to justify the Church's temporal claims, the document was at first either ignored or treated as a fraud. When in the twelfth century it found its way into the text of Gratian's *Decretum* (the official manual for the teaching of canon law), the document received a seal of authenticity which was to remain virtually unbroken until, three centuries later, the humanist Lorenzo Valla conclusively proved it to be a fake on the basis of philological and historical evidence. In the thirteenth and fourteenth centuries especially, the Donation was invoked by such popes as Innocent IV and Boniface VIII in the context of the power struggle between Church and empire—but also between Church and emerging national states, especially France—to affirm the temporal, as well as spiritual, supremacy of the pope over all earthly kings and kingdoms. Any political authority the emperor (or any king) might have had was conceived to have derived from the pope, who could extend or withdraw it at will. Indeed, since the imperial seat was deemed to have remained vacant after the death of Frederick II in 1250, Pope Boniface VIII, in his bull *Unam sanctam* (1302), could claim to be the sole head of the Christian world.

The Donation is at the very heart of Dante's interpretation of Christian history and of his political thinking. Several crucial passages in the *Commedia* are directly inspired by his profound aversion to its influence. In *Inf.* 19.106–117, he identifies it as the root of the sin of simony and the primary cause of papal corruption which transformed the Bride of Christ, the Church, into the Whore of Babylon: *"Ahi, Costantin, di quanto mal fu matre, / non la tua conversion, ma quella dote / che da te prese il primo ricco patre!"* ("Ah, Constantine, not your conversion, but that dowry which the first rich father took from you, has been the mother of so much evil!"). In *Purg.* 32.124–129, the Donation is represented allegorically as one of the seven calamities in ecclesiastic history that debase the Church. In *Par.* 20.55–60, it is an evil that has brought the whole world to ruin, despite the *buona intenzion* ("good intention") of the donor Constantine, who could not foresee the consequences of his act.

Only in the *Monarchia,* however, does Dante offer a systematic discussion of the Donation. Dante believed that God had providentially ordained two authorities, independent of each other, for the proper fulfilment of human destiny: the Roman Empire, which, owning everything on Earth, would restrain cupidity and lead the human race to earthly happiness; and the Church, which, being the sole and supreme repository of spiritual power, would guide the world to eternal salvation. By giving Peter's successors what belonged exclusively to Caesar's, the Donation had, in his view, gravely undermined God's plan. Although Dante, like many of his contemporaries, did not doubt the authenticity of the Donation, in keeping with a tradition widely supported by civil lawyers he denied that it had any juridical validity. On the one hand, he maintained that Constantine could not legally give away or divide the Empire, since such an act would go against the purpose of his office, whose primary duty was the preservation of the integrity of the Empire itself (*Mon.* 3.10.4–6). On the other hand, as many religious reformers insisted, even if Constantine had been entitled to give away the Empire, the pope was not entitled to accept it, for the Gospels (Matt. 10:9–10) explicitly prohibited the Church from having any material possessions (*Mon.* 3.10.13–15).

Dante goes so far as to curse the day of Constantine's birth (*Mon.* 2.11.8); and he seems to believe in the legend according to which, on the day of the Donation, angelic voices were heard saying "Today a poison is spread through the Church" (see *Purg.* 32.136–141). Nevertheless, although the emperor had erred, Dante never doubts his good intention, despite all the evil that had resulted from his action (*Mon.* 2.11.8; *Par.* 20.56). This is why Constantine is to be found in the eye of the Eagle in Paradise (*Par.* 20.55–60). Indeed, while maintaining that the Donation was illegal, Dante concedes that what Constantine could have given to the Church was not full possession of the property but merely a trusteeship of the imperial resources. And Pope Sylvester and his successors could have accepted such a gift, but only on condition that it be used for the benefit of the poor (*Mon.* 3.10.16–17). Subsequently, and thus betraying Constantine's *pia intentio* ("pious intention," *Mon.* 2.11.8), the popes claimed that the Donation entailed a renunciation on the part of the Empire of its earthly jurisdiction, thereby justifying the Church's claim to wealth and temporal power. Thus, for Dante the Donation was ultimately, though not intentionally, responsible for the contemporary union of temporal and spiritual power in the hands of the pope (*Purg.* 16.103–111)—something that he believed had devastating effects on the Church itself and on the whole of humankind, especially in Italy. In his view, the political and moral crisis in the world and the desperate state of Italy could therefore be remedied only by reversing the effects of the Donation. This fervent desire underlies the message of several prophecies in the *Commedia,* particularly those of Virgil (*Inf.* 1.100–111) and Beatrice (*Purg.* 33.37–51), in which Dante reveals his faith in the coming of a divinely appointed savior—an imperial agent, according to many commentators and critics—who would return the Church to its pristine poverty and restore universal earthly power to the Empire.

Bibliography

Fuhrmann, Horst (ed.). *Das Constitutum Constantini.* Hannover: Hahn, 1968; English text in *Church and State through the Centuries,* Sidney Z. Ehler and John B. Morrall (trans. and ed.). New York: Biblo and Tannen, 1967, pp. 16–22.

Nardi, Bruno. *Nel mondo di Dante.* Rome: Edizioni di Storia e Letteratura, 1944, pp. 109–159.

Pagliaro, Antonino. *Ulisse: Ricerche semantiche sulla Divina Commedia.* Messina and Florence: G. D'Anna, 1967, pp. 253–291.

Petrucci, Enzo. "Costantino." *Enciclopedia dantesca,* 1:236–239.

Ricci, Pier Giorgio. "Donazione di Costantino." *Enciclopedia dantesca,* 1:569–570.

Lino Pertile

Donatus

Donatus (fl. 350 C.E.)—*quel Donato / ch'a la prim'arte degnò porre mano* ("and that Donatus who deigned to put his hand to the first art," *Par.* 12.137–138)—was the major Latin grammarian of the Middle Ages. He is one of the twelve spirits in the second crown of great doctors of the Church in the Heaven of the Sun. A contemporary of St. Jerome, he was also considered "the grammarian" of the Church because Jerome claimed that he had learned Latin from Donatus. In the Heaven of the Sun (*Par.* 12), St. Bonaventure identifies Donatus as one among the central figures associated with various branches of medieval learning. Bonaventure follows the medieval tradition of identifying Donatus with grammar, the *prim'arte* ("the first art") in contrast to rhetoric and logic, the other two disciplines of the *trivium,* the three subjects that formed the foundation of medieval education. Both language and literature were included in the discipline of grammar in the Middle Ages. Donatus himself had produced works on grammar, the *Ars minor* and *Ars maior,* and on literature, including a now lost commentary on Virgil's *Aeneid* that is quoted in Servius' *Commentary on Virgil,* and a commentary on Terence, also lost.

Brenda Deen Schildgen

Donna gentile of the Vita Nuova

The episode of *una gentile donna giovane e bella molto* ("a gracious lady, young and exceedingly beautiful," *VN* 35.2), also called *pietosa donna* ("compassionate lady," *VN* 35.3), spans *VN* 35–38. While still mourning Beatrice's death, the first anniversary of which he has just commemorated (*VN* 34.1), the protagonist is struck by the sight of a lady full of pity for his state of sorrow (*VN* 35.1–3), and he resolves shortly afterward to write a sonnet to describe his experience (35.4–8). On successive occasions the lady takes on a compassionate look and a pale color, as if prompted by love, which the protagonist again describes in a second sonnet (*VN* 36). Dante begins to take such delight in the sight of this lady that a conflict, described in the third sonnet, develops between his old love for Beatrice and his new affection for the *donna gentile* (*VN* 37). The dominance of the new love over the old is described as an allegorical struggle between the heart, which defends the new love, and reason, which defends the old love for Beatrice (*VN* 38). A vision of Beatrice finally enables the protagonist to overcome the attraction of the new love (*VN* 39.1).

The influence of the compassionate lady on the protagonist is said to have lasted only several days. The text's scant chronological data make it impossible to situate the episode exactly in time. The episode begins "some time after" (*VN* 35.1) the first anniversary of Beatrice's death (June 8, 1290), that is, some time after June 8, 1291. The episode ends when a "powerful vision" of "the glorious Beatrice" takes place at the ninth hour (39.1), leaving the day, month, and year of that concluding moment unspecified. It is possible, however, that the episode takes the narrative to the second anniversary of Beatrice's death: June 1292. For just as the first appearance of *la gloriosa donna de la mia mente* ("the glorious lady of my mind") provides the narrative's beginning of the whole love story (*VN* 2.1), it may be argued that the vision of the "glorious Beatrice" (*questa gloriosa Beatrice,* 39.1), appearing in *quelle vestimenta sanguigne co le quali apparve prima* ("those crimson garments with which she first appeared," 39.1), may bring the episode to a close. Unquestionably, the episode refocuses on Beatrice by attributing to her the heavenly glory she has attained with her death, and it ends with Beatrice's victory over the compassionate lady and the protagonist's recovery from his temporary *smarrimento* ("wandering"), which he conceives as a moral lapse.

The *gentile donna* episode has been unduly complicated by the critics' attempts to interpret it not so much on the basis of the elements present in the *Vita Nuova* as through its re-elaboration in the first canzone of *Convivio* (*Voi che 'ntendendo il terzo ciel movete,* "You whose intellect the third sphere moves"), through its commentary (as far as the *gentile donna* is concerned) in *Conv.* 2.2 and 2.12, and finally through Beatrice's possible reference to it in *Purg.* 30.124–138. To be sure, Dante

himself suggests such a "contamination" by explicitly identifying the occasion of the *Convivio*'s first *canzone* with the *gentile donna* episode in the *Vita Nuova,* and also by equating the *Convivio*'s *gentile donna* (2.2.1; *donna gentile, Conv.* 2.12.6) with the lady—both are called *donna gentile.* Certain fundamental differences, however, distinguish the *Vita Nuova*'s *gentile donna* from the *gentile donna* of the *Convivio.* First, in contrast with the *Vita Nuova*'s *gentile donna,* who does not seem to be an allegory (but see Corti, *Felicità mentale* 148–150), the *Convivio*'s *gentile donna* is the allegorical figure of Philosophy, "daughter of God, queen of all things, most noble and most beautiful" (*questa donna fu figlia di Dio, regina di tutto, nobilissima e bellissima Filosofia, Conv.* 2.12.9). Second, whereas in the *Vita Nuova* Beatrice defeats this lady, the *Convivio*'s *gentile donna* has the upper hand over Beatrice (*Conv.* 2.2.3–4; 2.12). And third, whereas the *Vita Nuova*'s *gentile donna* episode offers scant chronological evidence, *Conv.* 2.2.1–2 dates the beginning of the episode with reference to the revolutions of Venus. Most critics interpret the chronological references of *Conv.* 2.2.1–2 as defining a period of three years and two months, so that the episode began in August 1293 (a chronology which seems to differ from that of the *Vita Nuova*).

The *gentile donna* episodes have been interpreted in three different ways. For some critics, all the texts concerning the *gentile donna* were first written for a woman, either real or imaginary, and only later did Dante transform that lady into the allegory for Philosophy in the *Convivio.* For other critics, such as Barbi, Gilson, and De Robertis, the *Vita Nuova* narrative, written for a real woman, must be clearly distinguished from that of the *Convivio,* where both the *canzone* and the commentary present the allegorical figure of Philosophy. Finally, some critics, including Corti, accept what Dante writes in the *Convivio* and hold that the *donna gentile* of both works represents Philosophy, and that all poems dealing with her are likewise allegorical in nature. To resolve the conflict between the two works, Pietrobono hypothesized a remaking of the *Vita Nuova*'s ending after Dante had written the *Commedia*—a hypothesis opposed by Barbi, accepted by Nardi, and successfully criticized by Marti. No critical position, however, has managed fully to resolve the inconsistencies created by Dante's treatment of the *donna gentile* in the two works.

Bibliography

Barbi, Michele. "Introduzione." In Dante, *Il Convivio.* Edited by G. Busnelli and G. Vandelli, vol. 1. 2nd ed. Florence: Le Monnier, 1968, pp. xv ff.

Corti, Maria. *Felicità mentale: Nuove prospettive per Cavalcanti e Dante.* Turin: Einaudi, 1983.

De Robertis, Domenico. "Introduzione." In Dante, *Opere minori* 1.1, *Vita Nuova.* Milan: Ricciardi, 1984, pp. 3ff.

Foster, Kenelm, and Patrick Boyde. "Appendix: The Biographical Problems in '*Voi che 'ntendendo.*'" In their *Dante's Lyric Poetry.* 2 vols. Oxford: Oxford University Press, 1967.

Marti, Mario. "Vita e morte della presunta doppia redazione della *Vita nuova.*" *Rivista di cultura classica e medievale* 7 (1965), 657–669.

Vasoli, Cesare. "Introduzione." In Dante, *Opere minori* 1.2, *Convivio.* Milan: Ricciardi, 1988, pp. lvii–lxi.

Dino Cervigni

Doré, Paul Gustave

French printmaker and painter, born in Strasbourg. Doré, who was born in 1832 and died in 1883, was first attracted to the *Commedia* at the age of twenty-three, and his woodblock engravings for it have remained very popular. In 1861 he published *L'Enfer, avec les dessins de G. Doré,* or the *Inferno* (75 plates), followed in 1864–1866 by the *Purgatorio* (42 plates) and *Paradiso* (18 plates). He illustrated other famous literary works (by, among others, Balzac, Montaigne, Cervantes, La Fontaine, Ariosto, Milton, and Rabelais), and the Bible, but, according to his brother Émile, the Dante effort was his masterpiece and his favorite. Indeed, he loved it so much that he repeated the subjects with oils and watercolors. He also did Dante drawings in watercolor, ink, and white gouache (*Inf.* 24), ink washes with white gouache (*Inf.* 5 and 34), a dramatic oil of Ugolino (*Inf.* 33), and more works that have remained obscure owing to the prominence of the engravings. His knowledge of the text was based on the Pier Angel Fiorentino's French version.

A good Romantic, Doré stimulates in the viewer a sense of awe before nature's mighty powers. Especially for Hell, he creates gloomy, rocky landscapes and enormous spaces, highlighted by textual elements like fire or his own symbolic bursts of light. In his visionary renderings, the Romantic sublime becomes mysterious majesty. He is less interested in understanding the poem in a critical sense than in moving the viewer's imagination in the direction of wonder. He chooses his subjects for their greatest effect: Bertran de Born speaking through his severed head; the descent on Geryon's back; Ulysses speaking through a flame; the thieves horrified in their reptilian transformations. For this reason, he likes to concentrate not synoptically on a whole canto, but specifically on a dramatized moment in it—a practice which led him to make several versions of a given canto, each depicting a different aspect of it.

Except from a technical point of view, Doré's illustrations for Purgatory and Heaven are less spectacular. A wondrous, almost fairyland quality prevails in the former (note the Angel Pilot of canto 1 or the ancient forest of 28), interrupted only by settings where atonement becomes graphic (the proud of canto 12 or the gluttons of 24). In depicting Heaven, Doré makes expert, albeit repetitious, use of light and resplendence (as with Cacciaguida in *Par.* 16 and the Heavenly Host in 27) in an attempt to reproduce Dante's ever more luminous ascent. The attempt is more admirable for its effort than for its success.

What gives Doré's illustrations stature is his technical dexterity. His woodcuts have tonal shading and depth, displaying a formidable ability to approximate painting more than drawing by handling sfumato and chiaroscuro as if to challenge the supremacy of other media. Some have praised him (Gautier, Dumas, Rodin), and others have maligned him (Yeats, Berenson). Whatever the case, he remains a representative of his era because he responds to its emotional demands.

Bibliography

Alighieri, Dante. *La divina commedia.* Illustrations by Gustavo Doré, preface by Francesco Flora, introduction by G. M. Boccabianca. Milan: Istituto Editoriale Italiano, 1954.

———. *La divina commedia.* Illustrations by Gustavo Doré. Edited by Eugenio Camerini. Milan: Casa Editrice Sonzogno, 1965/1971.

———. *The Divine Comedy.* Translated by John Ciardi, limited ed., with illustrations of Gustave Doré. Franklin Center, Penn.: Franklin Library, 1977.

Doré, Gustave. *The Doré Illustrations for Dante's Divine Comedy.* 136 plates. New York: Dover Publications, 1976.

Jean-Pierre Barricelli

Dramatic Arts

Dante's life and works, especially the *Commedia,* are inherently dramatic: the human drama of love, his exile, and the quest for artistic expression are played out on the stage of this life and the next. In his major work, Dante's highly developed dramatic sense and sensitivity to existing dramatic forms (both ancient and modern) are everywhere to be seen. The very title he gave the poem, *Comedía,* conjures up shades of Roman comedy (Armour, Barański). Its overall plan resembles a mystery play: set during Easter week in 1300, Dante's *poema sacro* unfolds like a *sacra rappresentazione* modeled on the "comic" structure of Christian history seen as providential drama (Iannucci, "Dante's Theory of Genres and the *Divina Commedia*"). The great battle between good and evil is played out not only at the macrotextual level (Masciandaro) but also, and, more poignantly, at the microtextual one, in the many episodes where the battleground is the individual human soul. And these mini-dramas, some disposed in a strikingly "theatrical" way (see Bosco and Iannucci on the battle before Dis in *Inf.* 8 and 9), are held together not so much by the metaphor of a pilgrimage through the three realms of the afterlife, as by Dante's life story, which intersects and comes into play in his dramatic encounter with many of the poem's vast cast of characters—with Virgil, Beatrice, Francesca, Farinata, the Montefeltros, the Donatis, Cacciaguida, and so on. Thus, the *Commedia* not only possesses a dramatic element in itself but also lends this dramatic element to many of its episodes, where the scene shifts back and forth between this life and the next. It is not surprising, therefore, that the poem and its author should have exerted a significant influence on the dramatic arts, and in numerous ways, from simple theatrical echoes, to entire plays based on Dante's life, works, and characters, and even to musical adaptations.

Echoes in Drama

There are numerous echoes of Dante in the religious drama and other dramatic forms of the later Middle Ages and early Renaissance (such as a *devozione* for Maundy Thursday, contained in a Venetian manuscript of the last quarter of the fourteenth century). Although the high Renaissance did not turn to Dante for inspiration, playwrights of the late Renaissance and successive periods did. Probably the earliest echo of the *Commedia* in Ital-ian secular drama occurs in the first modern tragedy, *Sofonisba* (1515) by Giangiorgio Trissino. Its final chorus employs a metaphor of the trembling sea, which recalls the pilgrim's *Conobbi il tremolar della marina* ("I could recognize the trembling of the sea," *Purg.* 1. 117) to describe the hellish chaos out of which he has emerged at the beginning of the *Purgatorio.* In the next century, Giovanni Briccio's bizarre comedy, *La Tartarea, Commedia Infernale* (1614), which takes place in the bowels of the Earth, borrows from Dante dramatic elements (the Gate of Hell bears the same inscription as in the *Commedia*), characters (e.g., Charon), its allegorical plot (the play's heroine Albinia represents Virtue, and Mercury divine kindness) and many of its lines, such as *tornare a vedere madonna Luna e messere Sole,* mirroring the pilgrim's *tornar a riveder le stelle* at the end of the *Inferno.* Not only seventeenth-century comedy but tragedy too echoed Dante: the first tragedy based on the *Inferno* was Giovanni Leone Semproni's *Il conte Ugolino* (not published until 1724, though its author died in 1646). Although the romantic subplot, which Semproni added, dominates, the play's theme is Dantean—the misery of civil strife—and many of its memorable lines, such as *vita ne desti già; vita ne togli* and the count's address to the three Pisans, echo similar lines in Dante's account in *Inf.* 33. Equally reminiscent of Dante is an eighteenth-century tragedy by Andrea Rubbi, *Ugolino Conte de' Gherardeschi* (1779). Although Rubbi cites Villani as the source for his play and, like Semproni, makes no mention of Dante, the final speeches of the tragedy—especially *Se tu mangi di noi; tu ne vestisti / Queste misere carni, e tu le spoglia*—clearly evoke Dante. Although nineteenth- and twentieth-century plays have made more explicit use of Dante, adopting his life and his characters as their bases, echoes of his work have continued to resonate into the twentieth century. In Italy one need think only of Dino Buzzati's clever structural appropriation of Dante in *Un caso clinico* (1953), while in the English-speaking world the late works of Beckett, such as *Waiting for Godot* (completed 1949, first performed 1953), reveal the influence of Dante.

Plays Based on Dante's Life

Plays based on Dante's life and works are a more recent phenomenon, the beginnings of which can be traced to the Romantic rediscovery of Dante and the Risorgimento's appropriation of him for

D patriotic and political reasons. This is especially true of plays about Dante's life.

Ferrigni, who deals with nineteenth- and twentieth-century adaptations of Dante, lists sixty-three Italian plays based on Dante's life or subjects (for a comprehensive list, see Antonucci). Of those devoted to Dante's life, some are comic, others are tragic, but almost all are minor, such as those of Pieracci (1820), Cosenza (1830), Tolli (1845), Gattinelli (1865), Fabbri (1874), Basile (1891), and Sardou (1903). Of greater note are one comedy and two tragedies. Written in 1853 but not performed until 1875, Paolo Ferrari's *Dante a Verona,* an ambitious comedy of precise detail, is a typically political Risorgimento vehicle (note the political manifesto of his preface), which was originally considered too dangerous for the stage. In it, Dante, whose enemies are bitterly satirized, is portrayed as a young man at the court of Cangrande. Dante at first is shown trying to persuade Cangrande to seize the crown and unite all of Italy under his rule, but he ultimately realizes that his appeal to the ineffectual leader is in vain and so accepts Guido da Polenta's invitation to Ravenna. An obvious appeal to the House of Savoy to play the part of the *Veltro,* the comedy fared badly because it lacked real theatrical vitality and was little more than *una lezione di ambiente storico e politico dialogata* (Del Balzo, 401). Far more successful was the drama by Pompeo di Campello, *Dante Alighieri* (1855). A tragedy in five acts, the play concentrates on the final twenty years of Dante's life, the period of his exile. A man of political action who knew at first hand of the heartless reversals of political life, Campello was able to evoke the harshness Dante endured during his exile. In a series of lyrically charged scenes, he exposes Dante's soul as he reflects on the loss of his native city, the lack of gratitude in his supporters, and, above all else, the thorns of exile which produce in him feelings of intense hatred and anger. No dramatist seems to have been as successful as Campello in plumbing the depths of Dante's tortured soul. Del Balzo considers it to be the best drama based on Dante's life (405). Of equal theatrical appeal was Tommaso Salvini's *Dante* of 1917, owing in no small measure to the spirited production directed by the author's father. Written in blank verse with a hendecasyllabic rhyming scheme, the play unfolds in three theatrical visions corresponding to three definitive moments in Dante's life: his love of Beatrice, his political activities, and his literary outpouring toward the end of his life. Not only was the play a popular success; it also received the praise of such leading *dantisti* as del Lungo, Passerini, and Flamini.

Plays Based on Dante's Works

There are very few plays based on the minor works. Two plays have been devoted to the *Vita Nuova,* by Monachelli (1899) and Ellero (1921). The first is merely a paraphrase of Dante's work, while the latter is based on Dino Compagni's *Cronica,* in which Dante is mentioned. However, the material of the *Vita Nuova* (i.e., Dante's love for Beatrice) is incorporated into many of the plays based on Dante's life.

Plays based on the *Commedia* as a whole or on one of the *cantiche* form a larger body of work. In 1966, Orazio Costa staged his *Divina Commedia.* Although Dante is named as author, the play presents a mystical/intellectual interpretation of the poem with Dante-poet reading from his poem while a series of dreary scenes depicts characters from Dante's work. The play was critically trashed as slipshod and hysterical in tone. On far sounder footing, but equally experimental, is Federico Tiezzi's production of the *Commedia.* Tiezzi chose three prominent Italian poets and playwrights to script each of the three *cantiche*: the *Commedia dell'Inferno* was adapted by Edoardo Sanguinetti (1989), the *Purgatorio* by Mario Luzi (1990), and the *Paradiso* by Giovanni Giudici (1991). Performed by the Teatro Metastasio di Prato, each work unfolds on an almost bare stage. Sanguinetti focuses attention on the textual component of Dante's work and its figural dimension, treating the characters as still-lifes and moving beyond them to get at a Dante capable of multilinguistic expression. Thus, Sanguinetti's "Dante in disguise" is the very opposite of a costumed staging of Dante. In Luzi's "dramaturgy of ascent," the stage dramatizes the existential condition of humankind trapped between the memory of the past and the hope of eternal liberation. Finally, Giudici's *Paradiso* is concerned with the spiral ascent from the world of human memory to the irreducible vision of God. The dramatic action thus drives a tight wedge between Dante as pilgrim *(viator)* and Dante as author *(auctor).* For while the *viator* is painfully aware of his own humanity as a limiting force in describing beatitude, the *auctor* realizes that he is the preexistent "expresser" of the inexpressible. In this tension Dante is revealed as a poet tormented by his own ambition and torn between pride in his accomplishment and fear of failure.

Plays Based on Dante's Characters

The nineteenth and twentieth centuries witnessed a plethora of dramas centered on Dante-based characters. Many of these—like *Pia de' Tolomei* by C. Marenco (1836), *Manfredo* by G. Checchetelli (1839), *Piccarda Donati* by L. Marenco (1855), *Pier della Vigna* by A. De Gubernatis (1860), and *Sordello* by P. Cossa (1872)—are today little more than names, as are the myriad productions of the Francesca story, including those of Edoardo Fabbri (1801), Silvio Pellico (1815), and Stephen Phillips (1902). The last two are somewhat more distinguished than the others. Pellico's lyrically romanticized version afforded the famed Italian actress, Adelaide Ristorie, then fourteen, her first stage role. Phillips' play, commissioned by no less a theatrical personage than Sir George Anthony, enjoyed revivals in 1924 and 1929. Of special note, however, are three dramatic incorporations of the Francesca material.

First among these is Gabriele D'Annunzio's *Francesca da Rimini,* first staged at Rome in 1901 and subsequently restaged in New York (1902) and Milan (1927). D'Annunzio wrote the play for the Italian actress Eleonora Duse (1858–1924), with whom he was involved romantically from 1897 to 1902. Duse was one of the foremost actresses of her day and had starred not only in such notable vehicles as Ibsen's *Ghosts* and *Lady from the Sea* but also in D'Annunzio's *La Giaconda* and *La Città Morta. Francesca* was to have been the first in a proposed trilogy on the Malatestas; the second, *Parisina,* appeared in 1913, but the third, *Sigismondo Malatesta,* was never performed. The five acts of *Francesca* portray her marriage to Gianciotto, her falling in love with his brother Paolo, and their ultimate betrayal by (in D'Annunzio's version) Malatestino, another brother of Gianciotto and the real villain of the play. There is very little action or characterization in the play; in fact, D'Annunzio set out chiefly to create a medieval spectacle. The result is an elaborately staged play (complete with huge sets, split levels, staircases, and ornate costumes) in which visual effects take precedence over action and characters function as still pieces in a series of *tableaux vivants*. It is a flamboyant set piece, "a melodrama of the thirteenth century," as one critic put it (*New York Times,* 12 Nov. 1902), that does nothing to capture the sense of lyricism or tragedy in Dante. Moreover, the play miscalculated audience sensitivities and was virtually doomed to failure before it opened. Hopelessly expensive, mismanaged by D'Annunzio (who assumed the roles of director, designer, and choreographer), the play was beset on opening night by technical difficulties and lasted six hours, and it had only a brief run.

Likewise significant for its leading lady is the production of the same story by Francis Marion Crawford (1854–1909). An American who lived most of his life in Italy, Crawford was one of the foremost advocates of Romanticism in fiction and a prolific author of forty-four novels, volumes of history and travel, and one play. He wrote *Francesca da Rimini* in 1901 for Sarah Bernhardt (1844–1923), the greatest actress of her day, at a time when her stage reputation was at its height.

Although Crawford's play was originally written in English, it was immediately translated into French by Marcel Schwob and was first performed in Paris in 1902 (repeated in the same year in London), with Bernhardt in the lead role and serving as the play's producer. Ironically, given Crawford's Romantic bias, the play introduced an unprecedented level of realism, not only in its costuming and staging (both predominantly Byzantine), but especially in its dramatic approach. Like Dante, Crawford treats the love of Francesca for Paolo as sinfully adulterous and perverted. Thus, although the prologue evokes some sympathy for Francesca with its description of the deceit practiced on the young girl (she is portrayed as having thought she was to be given in marriage to someone as handsome as Paolo, following the account in Boccaccio), in the four acts that follow that sympathy is eroded. We find her fourteen years later still bitterly harboring her resentment and still pursuing her affair with Paolo, who not only neglects his own wife and his children but also conspires against Gianciotto. This is a Francesca defiantly blind in her love for Paolo, just as Dante's Francesca was, for she refuses to acknowledge the pain that her blind love brings to Gianciotto and her daughter Concordia. This realistic portrayal of Francesca distanced audiences and doomed the play. Bernhardt, despite her skill, was not able to create support for the character of a notorious adulteress viewed in an entirely unsympathetic manner. As a result, the play ran for only twenty-five performances.

More noted for its dramatic scope and for the influence that it was to have on the fledgling film industry in the United States is a production by George Henry Boker (1823–1890). A distinguished man of letters and a diplomat, Boker was the author of several books of poetry, but he is best remembered for his plays, nearly all written in blank verse. Two of these, the tragedy *Calaynos* and the comedy *The Betrothal,* had popular appeal, but his best play as well as his most successful was *Francesca da Rimini,* produced on Broadway in 1855 and revived in 1882 and 1901, and more recently by the American repertory Company of Twelve at Lincoln Center in 1967. The play unfolds in five acts. Act I serves as exposition, introducing the arranged marriage, the journey of Paolo to Ravenna, and the continual taunts of the court jester Pepe, a character of Boker's invention. Act II portrays Francesca's transformation from a charming, dutiful daughter into a woman who is aware of the cruel trickery that her marriage with her husband (here named Lanciotto rather than Gianciotto) foists upon her. Act III enacts the first encounter between Lanciotto and Francesca: here there is an abundance of irony as Lanciotto suddenly feels that he can love and be loved, and as Francesca realizes that she must practice deceit in order to appear to love. Act IV opens with the lover's dream of Lanciotto, moves through his fears of never being loved, and ends with his leaving Ravenna to do battle. Act V portrays the betrayal of Paolo and Francesca by Pepe, Lanciotto's return, and his murder of the lovers. The play displays throughout an adroitly dramatic handling of the story which makes Lanciotto the main character of the play. Not only does he determine the play's major action, he is also, in Boker's sensitive portrayal, the preeminent tragic figure. His deformity is a controlling concept: he is aware of his "gnarled, blighted trunk" and extremely self-conscious of his marriage to one far more beautiful ("I, the great twisted monster of the wars / The brawny cripple, the herculean dwarf / I be a bridegroom!"). He thus has a vivid sense of reality, but it does not deter him from dreaming of love (". . .'tis sweet, / Sweeter than slumber to the lids of pain, / To fancy that a shadow of true love / May fall on this God-stricken mould of woe, / From so serene a nature"). In the end, when his appeal to the lovers to deny their love has failed, he responds to the claims of family honor and the "laws of Italy" and kills what he most loves. The play's ulti-

mate tragedy therefore arises out of Lanciotto's suffering, and this accorded it a degree of critical success: "In *Francesca da Rimini* Boker found his masterpiece. . . . He is the only [dramatist] to conceive the pathos of the deformed husband, Lanciotto, without sacrificing the enduring appeal of the young lovers, Paolo and Francesca, and to recognize that callous society, not fate, was the agent of the tragedy. . . . With this play, romantic tragedy in America achieved the dignity of art" (Spiller 1002–1003).

Surprisingly, however, the play's opening run was neither as successful nor as profitable as its revivals. Moreover, it was on the strength of those revivals that the play was converted into an early movie of the silent era. In 1908 the American company Vitagraph included among its "quality films" the release of *Francesca da Rimini;* indicative of the American Dante craze at the turn of the century, it reveals an obvious affinity with Boker's play (Uricchio and Pearson 95–99): the jester is retained (though renamed Beppe), the set designs are similar, there is a similar dramatic emphasis on Lanciotto, and the story line is almost identical. The film follows the story of Francesca and Paolo from the reception of Lanciotto's proposal of marriage through his departure for the wars, the lovers' infidelity, their betrayal by the jester, and their murder at the hands of Lanciotto, who closes the film by stabbing himself. The movie was a huge success and helped establish Vitagraph's reputation as one of the most important of the pre-Hollywood companies.

Musical Adaptations

Most of the numerous musicals, dances, and orchestral pieces based on Dante's life and characters, especially Francesca (even D'Annunzio's play was set to music by Riccardo Zandonai), are all but forgotten today, but there are two works of a more enduring nature. The Russian composer Peter Ilich Tchaikovsky began work on his *Francesca da Rimini* in 1876. Earlier in the same year, a libretto for an opera based on Dante had been sent to him by the music critic Hermann Laroche, but at the suggestion of his brother Modest, Tchaikovsky abandoned the idea of an opera and opted for an orchestral work instead. The result was the symphonic fantasy *Francesca da Rimini* (op. 32), first performed in Moscow in 1877; it received its English première in 1893 under the direction of Tchaikovsky himself. Tchaikovsky wrote to Modest that the work had been the result of reading Dante on a journey to Bayreuth and that he "had written it with love." The work, which matches the tripartite nature of Dante's story (whirlwind–story–whirlwind), has three parts: the two outer depict the storm, and the inner, a central *andante cantabile,* contains the love theme. Although Tchaikovsky lamented that the depiction of the whirlwind did not measure up to Doré's illustration, the *andante* has all of the composer's melodic mastery. However, the piece as a whole has been deemed less than successful, apparently because Tchaikovsky identified too closely with Francesca and therefore reduced all the musical elements to her consuming passion.

In the second decade of the twentieth century, Giacomo Puccini conceived of performing three short but sharply contrasting operas in one evening. The result was the *Trittico* of *Il Tabarro, Suor Angelica,* and *Gianni Schicchi.* The last was scripted by the Italian playwright Giovacchino Forzano and was first performed in New York in 1918. The germ of the opera comes from canto 30 of the *Inferno,* where Gianni Schicchi is portrayed among those damned as falsifiers. It is probable, though not certain, that it was Puccini who first conceived the brilliant idea of an opera based on these few lines of Dante's text and who suggested the idea to Forzano. The opera's plot, like that of Dante's tale, is extremely clever. Hired by the relatives of Buoso Donati, whose will, never made public, leaves everything to the church, Gianni Schicchi impersonates the deceased Donati and dictates a new will to a notary. But rather than leaving everything to the relatives, as they had intended, he arranges to leave everything to himself. At the conclusion of the opera, he claims to have perpetrated this fraud in order to aid his daughter Lucrezia and her young lover, Rinuccio. He also adds that he had been condemned to Hell for his crime, but, by permission of the "great father Dante," he begs the audience to grant him extenuating circumstances if they have enjoyed the show. The opera was and has continued to be a great success, often being performed on its own.

Conclusion

As he is for so many other media, Dante stands as an inexhaustible source for the dramatic arts. What has made so many radically different theatrical pieces possible is the inherently dramatic nature of Dante's life and work, the *Commedia* in particular.

Of equal importance to the influence of Dante on theater is the "producerly" quality of Dante's major work. The *Commedia*'s peculiar textual characteristics—its combination of relative stylistic simplicity, narrative linearity, and memorable characters and situations with densely allusive, complex, self-reflective discursive practices—make the poem appealing to a broad audience, from the unsophisticated to the refined. It is this "producerly" quality, this potential of the text to enable, that has allowed the *Commedia* to be interpreted theatrically in a host of different ways, and that has engaged the minds of myriad playwrights, directors, and composers who have reworked the text to make Dante appeal to both popular and avant-garde audiences.

Bibliography

Antonucci, Giovanni. "Teatro." *Enciclopedia dantesca,* 5:530–533.

Armour, Peter. "Comedy and Origins of Italian Theater around the Time of Dante." In *Writers and Performers in Italian Drama from the Time of Dante to Pirandello.* Edited by J. R. Dashwood and J. E. Everson. Lewiston, N.Y.: Edwin Mellen Press, 1991, pp. 1–31.

Balzo, Carlo del. "Dante nel teatro." *Nuova antologia* 189 (1903), 389–415.

Banham, Martin. *The Cambridge Guide to Theater.* Cambridge: Cambridge University Press, 1995.

Barański, Z. G. "Dante e la tradizione comica latina." In *Dante e la "bella scola" della poesia.* Edited by Amilcare A. Iannucci. Ravenna: Longo, 1993, pp. 225–245.

Bassnett, Susan. "*Francesca da Rimini* by Gabrielle D'Annunzio." In *International Dictionary of Theater,* vol. 1, *Plays.* Edited by Mark Hawkins-Dady. Chicago: St. James Press, 1992, pp. 270–271.

Bordman, Gerald. *The Oxford Companion to American Theater.* New York: Oxford University Press, 1984.

Bosco, Umberto. "Dante e il teatro medievale." In *Studi filologici letterarii e storici in memoria di Guido Favati.* Edited by G. Varanini and P. Pinagli. Padova: Antenore, 1977, pp. 135–147.

Bradley, Edward Sculley. *George Henry Boker: Poet and Patriot.* Philadelphia: University of Pennsylvania Press, 1927.

Corrigan, Beatrice. "Dante and Italian Theater: A Study in Dramatic Fashions." *Dante Studies* 89 (1971), 93–105.

Ferrigni, Mario. "Dante e il teatro." *Annali del teatro italiano* 1 (1901–1920), 1–23.

Iannucci, Amilcare A. " Dante's Theory of Genres and the *Divina Commedia.*" *Dante Studies* 91 (1973), 1–25.

———. "Dottina e allegoria in "*Inferno* VIII, 67–IX, 105." In *Dante e le forme dell' allegoresi.* Edited by Michelangelo Picone. Longo.

Masciandaro, Franco. *Dante as Dramatist: The Myth of the Earthly Paradise and Tragic Vision in the Divine Comedy.* Philadelphia: University of Pennsylvania Press, 1991.

Meserve, Walter J. "*Francesca da Rimini* by George Henry Boker." In *International Dictionary of Theater,* vol. 1, *Plays.* Edited by Mark Hawkins-Dady. Chicago: St. James Press, 1992, pp. 267–270.

———. "George Henry Boker." In *International Dictionary of Theater,* vol. 2, *Playwrights.* Edited by Mark Hawkins-Dady. Chicago: St. James Press, 1994, pp. 108–110.

Spiller, Robert E., et al. (eds.). *Literary History of the United States.* New York: Macmillan, 1974.

Uricchio, William, and Roberta E. Pearson. *Reframing Culture. The Case of the Vitagraph Quality Films.* Princeton: Princeton University Press, 1993, pp. 95–99.

Amilcare A. Iannucci

Dreams

Dreams, either as literary devices or poetic, speculative, or religious motifs, played a fundamental role in literature from classical antiquity through the Middle Ages. Dante evinced a keen interest in the visionary in his earliest writings, and in his masterpiece he fully exploited the states of sleep and dream. In the *Vita Nuova,* dream visions and imaginings govern the text's narrative structure and mark the various moments in the life of the youthful protagonist. In the *Commedia,* the pilgrim becomes lost in the dark forest when he is *pien di sonno* ("full of sleep," *Inf.* 1.11); two swoons mark the beginning of his descent into Hell (*Inf.* 3.135–136; 5.139–142); and three dreams symmetrically punctuate his ascent of Mount Purgatory (*Purg.* 9.13–33, 19.1–36, 27.94–108). In the Earthly Paradise, as the mysterious vision of the pageant unfolds before his eyes, the pilgrim first swoons (31.85–93) and later falls asleep (*Purg.* 32.61–72), bringing to culmination all previous sleep and dream experiences and preparing him for the heavenly experience, where neither swoon nor slumber will ever interrupt his vision.

In a poetic transformation of the youthful life of the narrator-protagonist, the *Vita Nuova* presents his actual encounters with his lady, Beatrice, together with several imaginings, dreams, or oneiric visions, as well as higher visionary experiences. Beatrice appears to the protagonist in *VN* 2.1–3 for the first time at the age of eight and then again at the age of eighteen (3.1–2). He sees her in church (5.1) and at an unspecified place where she denies him her greeting (10.2); he sees her again at a wedding (14.4–7), and in an open space as she follows after Giovanna (24.1–9). Intermixed with these real sightings of Beatrice are several imaginings: of Love personified (9.3–7 [9.9–12], 24.2–3 [24.7]), and of the glorious Beatrice in the same crimson garments in which she first appeared to him (39.1). Dreams likewise mark the protagonist's experience: in a dream he sees Love personified holding Beatrice in his arms (3.3–7 [3.11–12]), Love weeping (12.3–8), and, finally, in a nightmarish and fantastic dreamlike vision, the dead Beatrice being borne into Heaven (23.4–13 [23.21–28]). Two visions of a higher nature conclude the *Vita Nuova:* in *VN* 41.10–13 the protagonist's *sospiro* ("sigh") ascends to the highest heaven, the Empyrean, and sees Beatrice in glory; and in *VN* 42.1, a *mirabile visione* ("wonderful vision") appears to him, after which he decides to refrain from writing about Beatrice until he can treat of her more worthily. In the *Vita Nuova,* therefore, the worlds of physical reality, imagination, dream, and higher, spiritual visions intersect and nurture one another. Furthermore, Dante the author also proposes how these worlds should be interpreted: sightings of physical reality can be placed in relationship with *cogitatio* or vision of sensible things; dreams and imaginings with *meditatio,* or the understanding of the spiritual value inherent in them; and the two higher visions with *contemplatio,* which involves the highest understanding of things (Branca; Cervigni 58–62).

Swooning, sleeping, and dreaming have an important function in the *Commedia,* which is itself a *visio* or vision of the afterlife that the narrator-protagonist claims to have had while alive and awake. At the beginning of this experience, the poet relates that he was *pien di sonno* ("full of sleep," *Inf.* 1.11) when he went astray and entered the dark wood. Most commentators refuse to read this line as the indication that the *Commedia* represents a *visio in somniis* (a vision in a dream or dream-vision) and interpret this initial experience metaphorically to represent a sinful condition on the part of the protagonist. Along the River Acheron the pilgrim, frightened by an earthquake and a flash of blood-red light, falls *come l'uom cui sonno piglia* ("like one whom sleep is taking," *Inf.* 3.136) and is later startled back to consciousness by a thunderclap (*Inf.* 4.1–3). Like the purgatorial earthquake which heralds the soul's deliverance (*Purg.* 20.124–142, 25.1–72), these infernal phenomena can be related to the Passion of Christ, whose victorious descent into Hell, described by Virgil shortly afterward (*Inf.* 4.52–63), is the model for the pilgrim's journey. Christ's death, it should be observed, was followed by an earthquake (Matt. 25:51–52; Mark 15–38; Luke 23:45). Insofar as Christ's redemption makes it possible for the pilgrim to journey in the afterlife, he too, like Christ, must experience a kind of death, a parallel that is suggested by the protagonist's loss of consciousness and lack of awareness of how he has crossed the Acheron. He will swoon a second time at the end of *Inf.* 5, after hearing Francesca recount the story of her fall into sin. As we learn shortly thereafter, the pilgrim not only loses consciousness but also lacks an awareness of why he loses consciousness.

The pilgrim's ascent of Mount Purgatory lasts three days and three nights. Each night while sleeping, he experiences a dream. During the first night, just before entering Purgatory proper and commencing the true process of purification, he sees in a dream an eagle that hovers in the sky, descends rapidly and terrifyingly, and carries him aloft into a region of fire that engulfs both of them, thus interrupting the dream and sleep alike (*Purg.* 9.13–3). During the second night, the weary pilgrim is slowly lulled to sleep (*Purg.* 18.139–145). In his second dream (*Purg.* 19.1–36), a loathsome woman transforms herself into a singing, alluring siren before his enraptured eyes. A holy lady suddenly appears to bring to an end the evil fascination of the hag-siren, whose unmasking and attendant stench cause Dante to awaken. Finally, during the third and last night, the pilgrim dreams of a young lady, Leah, in the middle of a meadow of flowers, making a garland with which to adorn herself.

The three purgatorial dream accounts define the external structure of the second *cantica* according to a pattern centered on the numbers three (three dreams) and nine (*Purg.* 9, 18–19, 27), marking respectively the beginning, the middle, and the conclusion of the pilgrim's purgatorial experience. In its threefold repetition, the pilgrim's dream experience constitutes a ritual which depends first and primarily on the Divinity who sends oneiric visions to the seer during the night, when all souls in Purgatory are barred from climbing the mountain any farther (*Purg.* 7.43–60). Forced to rest owing to the weakness of human nature (*Purg.* 9.10), the pilgrim is visited by the Divinity, who sends him dream visions at dawn, the traditional time for truthful dreams (*Purg.* 9.16–18, 19.4–6, 27.91–93).

Finally, at the end of his purgatorial journey, in the Earthly Paradise Dante the pilgrim, after being reproached by Beatrice (*Purg.* 30.55–145, 31.1–84), becomes fully aware of his past sinful life and repents of it so deeply that he loses consciousness (*Purg.* 31.88–90). Contrary to what happens in *Inf.* 5.141, where he swoons in front of Francesca because of his inability to comprehend (*Inf.* 6.1–3), here he becomes unconscious precisely because the awareness of his sinfulness overwhelms him. Shortly after experiencing the effects of Lethe's waters (*Purg.* 31.91–96) and witnessing the reflowering of the withered tree (*Purg.* 32.49–57), the pilgrim falls asleep for the last time amid the singing of a hymn which he cannot understand and whose melody he cannot bear until the end (*Purg.* 32.61–63). The pilgrim's sleep can be likened to the sleep that God infused into Adam in order to create Eve from his side (Gen. 2:21). According to patristic interpretation, Adam's sleep and Eve's formation stand for the birth of the Church and prefigure the mystery of Christ and the Church. Likewise, Dante's final slumber cancels the negative effects of his sleep in the dark wood and the two infernal moments of slumber and marks the beginning of his journey among those who enjoy eternal happiness.

In brief, the poet's treatment of the oneiric evidences his poetic exploitation of all the experiences open to human beings. Following St. Augustine's paradigm for the three types of vision for seeing God, the poet defines three kinds of vision on the part of the pilgrim. He has *visio corporalis,* or knowledge through the senses, when he

D is awake; *visio spiritualis* (or *imaginativa*), or mental representation of corporeal things, when he has dreams; and finally *visio intellectualis,* or intellectual illumination, which he attains when he is illumined directly by the Divinity. Only upon the completion of his voyage, in fact, will the pilgrim both understand God's purpose in sending him prophetic dreams and comprehend their full meaning (*Par.* 33.140–42).

Bibliography

Augustine. *Oeuvres de Saint Augustin: La genèse au sens littéral en douze livres (De genesi ad litteram libri duodecim).* Translated by P. Agaësse. Vol. 49, ser. 7. Paris: Desclée de Brower, 1970.

Branca, Vittore. "Poetica del rinnovamento e tradizione agiografica nella *Vita nuova.*" In *Miscellanea in onore di Italo Siciliano.* Florence: Olschki, 1966, pp. 123–148.

Bundy, Murray Wright. "The Theory of Imagination in Classical and Medieval Thought." *University of Illinois Studies in Language and Literature* 12 (1927), 183–472.

Cervigni, Dino S. *Dante's Poetry of Dreams.* Florence: Olschki, 1986.

Newman, Francis X. "St. Augustine's Three Visions and the Structure of the *Commedia.*" *Modern Language Notes* 72 (1967), 56–78.

Dino Cervigni

E

Eagle

Dante uses two forms to designate the eagle in the *Commedia, aguglia* and *aquila,* the former far more frequently than the latter. In the literary and historical sources Dante knew, the eagle was associated with Jove (cf. *Purg.* 32.12) and was the symbol affixed to the standards of the Roman legions (cf. *Purg.* 10.80). In medieval bestiaries, the eagle is said to derive its name from the acuteness (*acumine* > *aquila*) of its vision; it was supposed to be able to stare unblinkingly at the sun (cf. *Par.* 1.48, 20.32). It was known to be a bird of great power, able to fly as high as "the circle of the sun" and swoop down like a thunderbolt (cf. *Purg.* 9.29–30); this attribute enabled the eagle to symbolize the regeneration of baptism and the resurrection. It was also famed for the rigorous way it educated its young. In exegetical texts, the eagle was sometimes associated with penance (e.g., Vincent of Beauvais on Psalm 102) or with the soul contemplating the Incarnation and Ascension (e.g., Richard of St. Victor, *On the Trinity*).

In the *Commedia,* the eagle appears as a local referent (e.g., the heraldic symbol on the coat of arms of the Polentas of Ravenna in *Inf.* 27.41); as a specific symbol (for the imperial Roman army in *Purg.* 10. 80; for the Ghibellines, who made it their ensign in *Par.* 6. 103–104; and for the evangelist John, who was commonly depicted as an eagle in *Par.* 26.53); or more generally as a symbol of the imperial authority that executes divine justice.

The three most significant appearances of the eagle in the *Commedia* are in Dante's dream before the gates of Purgatory (*Purg.* 9. 13–32); in Justinian's condensed history of the Empire's progress from the fall of Troy to the wars between the Guelfs and Ghibellines in thirteenth-century Italy (*Par.* 6.1–111); and in the final form in a series of transformations that the spirits of just rulers undergo in the Heaven of Jupiter (*Par.* 18–20). Each occasion stages a meeting between the orders of nature and grace and the discourses appropriate to them.

In the early morning of his second day in Purgatory, Dante dreams he sees "an eagle hovering in the sky, with golden feathers and open wings, intent to stoop." Dante imagines he is in Troy, "in the place where Ganymede abandoned his own company"; the eagle then swoops down and snatches Dante up as far as the fire, where he seemed to burn. On Dante's awakening, Virgil explains that while Dante was asleep, Lucy (*Inf.* 2.97–102) had borne him from the Valley of the Princes to the steps of the Gate of Purgatory.

Many readers agree with the earliest commentators, who identify Lucy as illuminating grace and connect her with the eagle (e.g., Anonimo Fiorentino). Others associate the eagle with Dante's idea of divine justice, which is realized on earth through the purifying power of the Empire (Kantorowicz). Some see the eagle as a biblical figure of penance, which is part of justice (Raimondi); in its swoop and ascent others think Dante saw a figure for the angels descending and ascending the ladder of Jacob's dream (Ginsberg).

In the Heaven of Mercury, Justinian traces the course of the Empire, which he symbolizes as the eagle's flight across time from Troy to Dante's own day. In a rehearsal of Roman history similar to the summaries Dante gives in the *Convivio* (4.5.11–19) and the *Monarchia* (2. 4.5–10; 10.2–7), Justinian says the "sacrosanct emblem" became

The Eagle in the Heaven of Jupiter. La comedia di Dante Aligieri, *with commentary by Alessandro Vellutello, published by Francesco Marcolini, Venice, 1544. Giamatti Collection: Courtesy of the Mount Holyoke College Archives and Special Collections.*

Jupiter. After the souls of the just have spelled out *Diligite iustitiam qui iudicatis terram* ("Love justice, you who judge the earth," Wisdom 1.1), the righteous remain in the shape of the final *M.* Most often interpreted as "monarchy" or "Mary," this golden letter (which looked more like a lower-case *m*) then undergoes a transformation. A form like a lily (interpreted variously as the emblem of the French monarchy or the Guelfs) appears over the central descender of the *m,* which then becomes the head and neck of an eagle seen in profile. The eagle tells Dante that God's justice is not man's. The damnation of those who never heard of Christ is entirely just; the evil princes of the world, though professed believers, may well be damned.

Traditionally this eagle has been seen as a symbol of empire, or earthly justice instituted by imperial authority, or as Christ as supreme judge or as eternal justice (see Chierici), or as some combination of these aspects (Pasquazi). But Dante's figure resists reduction; by continually pointing not only to its textuality but also to how it transcends all depiction bound by space and time, Dante assures its integrity even as he places it beyond human understanding.

Bibliography

Chierici, Joseph. *L'aquila d'oro nel cielo di Giove (Canti XVIII–XX del Paradiso).* Rome: Istituto Grafico Tiberino di Stefano De Luca, 1962.

Ginsberg, Warren. "Dante's Dream of the Eagle and Jacob's Ladder." *Dante Studies* 100 (1982), 41–69.

Kantorowicz, Ernst. *The King's Two Bodies.* Princeton, N.J.: Princeton University Press, 1957.

Mazzotta, Giuseppe. *Dante's Vision and the Circle of Knowledge.* Princeton, N.J.: Princeton University Press, 1993.

Pasquazi, Silvio. "L'aquila del cielo di Giove." *Giornale italiano di filologia* 23 (1971), 245–266.

Raimondi, Ezio. "Analisi strutturale e semantica del canto IX del *Purgatorio.*" *Studi danteschi* 45 (1968), 121–146.

Warren Ginsberg

worthy of reverence with Pallas' death. He then traces its progress from Aeneas through the Horatii to Augustus, the crucifixion of Jesus under Tiberius, and the revenge Titus exacted by sacking Jerusalem. The ensign then passed to Charlemagne; in Dante's lifetime, Justinian concludes, the Guelfs and Ghibellines, under their respective banners of lily and eagle, give equal offense to the justice they claim they fight for.

Justinian seems at once to endorse Rome's victories and to probe their relation to the laws he helped codify. As Dante says in *Mon.* 2.9.1, Roman conquests did not violate justice; they were instead part of a history of warfare in which God favored his chosen party. At the same time, however, laws are just because they determine what is equitable dispassionately; the acts of war and vengeance that legitimate the Empire as the proper executor of God's justice on earth seem outside the reasoned balance that is the very principle of law (cf. *Mon.* 1.1–5). Together with the dream of the eagle, this acknowledgment of the inevitable "violence that occurs when knowledge is turned into action" (Mazzotta) becomes the backdrop to the extraordinary eagle of spirits in the Heaven of

Earth, Globe

There are two earths in Dante's writings. The first is the conventional earth of medieval geography that is variously described in the *Convivio,* the *Monarchia,* and the *Questio de Aqua et Terra.* This earth is a solid sphere whose surface is entirely

Imaginateui che quefto tondo fia tutto el corpo
dello aggregato dellacqua et della terra, et
che quefto triangolo che occupa (come uoi uede
te) la fexta parte di decto aggregato, et che
O iiii

From Commedia di Dante, *published by Filippo Giunti, Florence. 1506. Reproduced by permission of the John A. Zahm Dante Collection in the Department of Special Collections, University Libraries, University of Notre Dame.*

covered by water except in the Northern Hemisphere, where three continents—Europe, Asia, and Africa—rise above the ocean's surface. The dimensions of these continents vary quite substantially from their dimensions on modern atlases. Land extends to the south only as far as the equator and to the north as far as the Arctic Circle. But while the continents are compressed latitudinally, they are considerably widened longitudinally. From east to west the continents extend a full 180 degrees. The earth as a whole is smaller, its circumference set at 20,400 miles as opposed to the modern figure of 24,800 miles. In *Conv.* 2.6.10 Dante speaks of the distance from the earth's surface to its center as being 3,250 miles; in 3.5.11 he states that half the earth's circumference is 10,200 miles, a figure he derives from Alfraganus.

Dante derived this picture of the earth from medieval encyclopedists like Brunetto Latini and Isidore of Seville, who, in turn, drew on classical authorities like Pliny and Strabo; it is thus an earth shaped less by direct observation than by a literary tradition. Within that tradition there is considerable agreement on some matters, such as the earth's spherical shape and its rough dimensions, while there is sharp disagreement on others. One question on which Dante was forced to take sides is the existence of land in the Southern Hemisphere and the possibility of its being inhabited. Cicero and Albertus Magnus both argue for life in the antipodes; Dante follows Augustine who argues vigorously against it.

Employing a convention derived from Ptolemy, Dante divides the habitable earth into seven zones, or climates, running parallel to the equator. In the extreme northern and southern climates live, he reports, the exotic Scythians and naked Garamantes, the one oppressed by almost intolerable cold, the other by unbearable heat (*Mon.* 1.14; *Conv.* 3.5). Following a tradition that goes back as far as Juvenal, Dante designates the eastern and the western margins by the mouth of the river Ganges and the city of Cadiz, which he associates with Hercules' pillars. In the center of the habitable earth, midway between the Scythians and the Garamantes, and midway between Ganges and Cadiz, stands Jerusalem.

Dante's other earth, the earth of the *Commedia,* shares most of the features of the first, but with two remarkable additions. Extending beneath Jerusalem is the great hollow cone of Hell, a subterranean cavern that reaches to the center of the earth. Though there are obvious classical and biblical precedents for an underworld populated by the dead, Dante's precise imagining of the infernal geography is essentially new. Standing exactly opposite Jerusalem in the midst of the southern ocean is Purgatory, a towering mountain capped by the garden of Eden. This representation of Purgatory seems very largely Dante's invention, as does his placement of Eden in the Southern Hemisphere. The closest that scholars have come to identifying a source is Bruno Nardi's suggestion that Dante's southern mountain draws together several threads of patristic speculation.

The precise form of Dante's geographical fantasy fixes for his journey a very specific trajectory. Throughout Inferno, Dante descends beneath the Northern Hemisphere. Then, in Purgatory, he climbs upward in the Southern. The point where these two movements meet is the dead center of the earth and Satan's groin. There Dante must literally turn himself upside down in order to move forward, an inversion that is clearly central to the poem's spiritual allegory. In Paradise, Dante twice

E looks back to view the earth, *l'aiuola che ci fa tanto feroci* ("The little threshing-floor that makes us so ferocious," *Par.* 22.151; see 27.86), as a small and, from the perspective of eternity, insignificant globe. Geographical lore also figures importantly in the *Commedia*'s elaborate chronology. Dante's preferred method for telling time is to fix astronomical events in relation to one or more reference points on the earth's surface. Making sense of such passages depends on knowing that Cadiz, Jerusalem, Ganges, and Mount Purgatory are all 90 degrees—or six hours—apart.

Bibliography

Armour, Peter. "Dante e l'*imago mundi* del primo Trecento." In *Dante e la scienza*. Edited by Patrick Boyde and Vittorio Russo. Ravenna: Longo, 1995, pp. 191–202.

Grant, Edward. *Planets, Stars, and Orbs: The Medieval Cosmos, 1200–1687*. Cambridge: Cambridge University Press, 1994, pp. 618–636.

Nardi, Bruno. "Il mito dell'Eden." In *Saggi di filosofia dantesca*. 2d ed. Florence: La Nuova Italia, 1967, pp. 311–340.

Orr, M. A. *Dante and the Early Astronomers*. London: Wingate, 1913.

John Kleiner

Earth, Element

One of the four sublunar elements in Aristotle's physics, Earth unites the primary qualities Cold and Dry. It is the heaviest of the elements and therefore finds its proper place at the center of the universe. Like the other three elements, Earth is mutable. If heated, it can be transformed from a Cold-Dry element into a Hot-Dry element. Earth can, in other words, ignite into Fire. The element Earth is not to be confused with earthy matter; still the behavior of common rock, soil, and other solids such as wood are to be understood in its terms. The nature of Earth is one of the principal subjects of the *Questio de Aqua et Terra*. In that treatise Dante tries to accommodate within Aristotelian theory the anomalous appearance of dry land in the Northern Hemisphere. Since the proper place of Water is higher than Earth, one would expect on the basis of Aristotle's physics that the surface of the earth should be uniformly covered by water. In the *Questio de Aqua et Terra* Dante entertains several possible explanations before finally invoking astral influences. Stars in the northern celestial hemisphere have drawn up the earthy matter of the continents.

John Kleiner

Earthly Paradise

Dante's earthly Paradise is situated on the summit of the mountain of Purgatory, and his description of it and of his experiences there occupies the final cantos of the *Purgatorio* (27.91–33.145).

The term "earthly Paradise" was widely used in the Middle Ages for the Garden of Eden, the "paradise [garden] of pleasure." Planted by God "from the beginning" *(a principio),* it is irrigated by a river divided into four streams (Phison, Gehon, Tigris, and Euphrates) and contains beautiful trees bearing sweet fruit and, in the middle, the tree of life and the tree of the knowledge of good and evil. God placed the newly created Adam in the garden to work and to guard it, commanding him not to eat of the tree of the knowledge of good and evil, "for on whatever day you eat of it, you shall die by death." After Eve was tempted by the serpent, and both she and Adam had eaten the forbidden fruit, God expelled them, ordering Adam henceforth to live off the earth with its thorns and thistles, to earn his bread by the sweat of his brow, and eventually to die, returning to the dust from which he had been made. To prevent his returning to eat also of the tree of life and so to become eternal, God set a cherub with a fiery two-edged sword in front of the garden "to guard the way to the tree of life" (Gen. 2:5–3:24). The rivers of the earthly Paradise are said to have poured forth from God's Wisdom (Ecclus. 24:35–37, 40), and the pleasures of the Paradise, set on "God's holy mountain," stood for the original wisdom and perfection of human beings before the coming of sin (Ezek. 28:12–15).

From an alternative reading of Gen. 2:8, in which God plants the garden in the east *(ad orientem),* medieval descriptions of the world and world-maps *(Mappaemundi)* located the earthly Paradise on the eastern edge of the inhabited dry land, in "furthermost India," which was famed also for its immensely tall and miraculous trees (see *Purg.* 32.40–42). Theologians conceived of it as inaccessible, cut off from human habitation by land or mountains or sea, or perhaps situated on a mountain so high that it reached the sphere of the Moon. However, since humans had lived there, it could not be excessively hot or cold but is always temperate, without clouds or storms or thunder, a place of incorruption and immortality. It was thought of as containing many trees and fruits—including not only the trees mentioned in Genesis but also a tall, bare tree—together with flowers, birds, and a spring divided into four streams. This image of the human race's original *locus amoenus* was developed principally from two apocryphal works: the *Vision of Paul* and the *Gospel of Nicodemus*. The latter contains the story of Seth's journey to the paradise from which his parents had been expelled, and gave rise to other legends, in particular that of the rood-tree, according to which a tree, deriving from the tree of the Fall, grew on Adam's grave and later provided the tree from which Christ's cross was made. Biblical exegesis, the Church's liturgy, and theologians established a series of relationships of prefiguration and fulfillment: between Adam and Christ, the new Adam (1 Cor. 15:21–22, 45–49); between the tree of the Fall and the cross, and between the fruit of the former and Christ hanging on the latter to redeem the human race from that sin; between Eve (formed from Adam's rib), Mary (the new Eve), and the Church (formed from the wounds in Christ's side); and between the earthly Paradise, lost by sin, and the heavenly Paradise, made accessible again to the saved by the merits of the Redemption.

Dante locates the earthly Paradise on the top of Mount Purgatory, the immensely tall island-mountain set in the middle of Occanus in the Southern Hemisphere at the antipodes of Jerusalem, where Christ died (*Inf.* 34.112–115; *Purg.* 2.1–3; see also *Par.* 1.43–45); this striking innovation may also be viewed from the other direction, as Dante's setting of Purgatory on the slopes and terraces of the mountain of the earthly Paradise. In either case, the ascent of purification from the effects of sin—for Dante and for the souls of the saved—culminates in the return to the place of the human race's original earthly happiness and innocence, which was lost by the first sin, before the ascent to the spiritual joys of the heavenly Paradise.

In Dante's doctrine of man's "double purpose" or "two goals," the earthly Paradise represents the "happiness of this life," which is acquired by human powers, by philosophy, and by the practice of the moral virtues; the directive guide to this earthly happiness of liberty and peace is the emperor. In contrast, the happiness of eternal life,

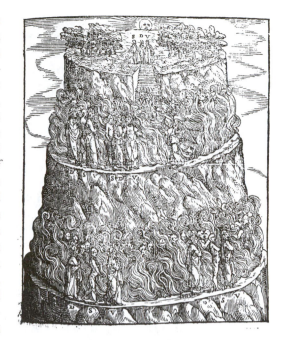

Dante ascending from the terrace of the lustful to the Earthly Paradise. La comedia di Dante Aligieri, *with commentary by Alessandro Vellutello, published by Francesco Marcolini, Venice, 1544. Giamatti Collection: Courtesy of the Mount Holyoke College Archives and Special Collections.*

represented by the heavenly Paradise, can be acquired only with the assistance of God's grace and revealed truth, with the practice of the three Theological Virtues and under the direction of the pope (*Mon.* 3.15.6–11). This passage contains the only occurrence of the phrase "earthly Paradise" in Dante's works; elsewhere, he refers to it as "Paradise" (*DVE* 1.4.2; 1.5.3; *Par.* 7.87), once as the high garden (*Par.* 26.110), and otherwise by specifying its position on the mountain (*Purg.* 6.47–48; 8.114) or its function as the place of pleasure and delights—the original, beautiful home of the human race, lost by sin (*DVE* 1.7.2; *Purg.* 28.77–78, 91–96; 29.29; 30.52, 75; 32.31–32; *Par.* 1.56–57; 26.139–140).

Dante's experiences in the earthly Paradise are introduced by his dream of Leah, by Virgil's promise that his hunger will today be sated by *Quel dolce pome che per tanti rami / cercando va la cura de' mortali* ("That sweet apple which the zeal of mortals goes seeking along so many branches," *Purg.* 27.115–116), and by Virgil's instructions to him that, now his will is restored to true freedom, he may choose either to sit and wait for Beatrice or to explore the miraculous

Enatural beauties of the place (*Purg.* 27.94–108, 115–117, 130–138). In *Purg.* 28, Dante gives his version of the Bible's original "paradise of pleasure" as a *divina foresta spessa e viva* ("divine forest, thick and alive") which delights his senses with its fragrance, gentle breeze, birdsong, and rustling leaves, and its visible beauties of colored flowers and blossoming trees; in this antithesis of the *selva selvaggia e aspra e forte* ("wood [. . .] savage and harsh and strong") of *Inf.* 1.5, nature is primordial, perfect, and unspoilt. It contains two streams flowing from a single source; named the Lethe and the Eünoè, they both have moral functions in relation, respectively, to the forgetting of sin and to the remembering of good. A beautiful lady, later called Matelda, who fulfils the dream of Leah and, gathering flowers, sings in praise of God's creation, is Dante's guide and teacher in the earthly Paradise and conducts him to the procession in which Beatrice will come from Heaven to meet him; later, she administers to him the waters of the two streams (*Purg.* 28.37–148; 29.1–15, 61–63; 31.91–105; 32.28, 82–93; 33.118–135). While critics debate whether she is the soul of a real person, the traditional candidate being the countess Matilda of Tuscany (1046–1115) or a purely allegorical figure (Active Life, perfect earthly happiness, natural justice, humanity restored in an image of an unfallen Eve, and so on), her actual functions in the narrative are a strong indication that she is to be associated above all with the biblical Lady Wisdom, who was with God and rejoiced at the creation (Prov. 8: 22–31; Ecclus. 24: 5–47) and who contributed to Dante's own presentation of Lady Philosophy and his love of the Wisdom poured by God into his creation (*Conv.* 3). Wisdom, as the perfection of the intellect, is an integral element in Dante's conception of earthly happiness.

Dante's earthly Paradise represents the summit of nature at its confines with the supernatural. As Matelda explains, the breeze is caused by the air revolving with the sphere of the Moon and broken by the peak of the mountain; it carries round the power of the trees and plants; and the spring which feeds the streams flows ceaselessly and unchangingly by the direct decree of God's will. As a corollary, she adds that pagan poets who wrote of the Golden Age (see especially Ovid, *Meta.* 1.89–112) perhaps had had an intuition of this biblical truth of humanity's original innocence in this place of eternal spring.

The procession in the Earthly Paradise. La comedia di Dante Aligieri, *with commentary by Alessandro Vellutello, published by Francesco Marcolini, Venice, 1544. Giamatti Collection: Courtesy of the Mount Holyoke College Archives and Special Collections.*

Dante's further experiences in the earthly Paradise consist of universalizing representations of the history of the human race, alternating and combined with episodes relating to the personal history of his love for Beatrice and his abandonment of her after her death. First, the triumphal procession, which is based principally upon passages in the Book of Revelation (the Apocalypse), represents the ideal state of the world, as it was in the past (at Christ's birth), as it should be in the present, and as it will be in the future, in the prophesied millennium which will precede Christ's Second Coming and then, forever, in the Church Triumphant of the saved in the heavenly Paradise (*Purg.* 29). Beatrice, appearing in the role of Christ, upbraids Dante for straying from her; when Dante confesses his error, Matelda takes him through the Lethe to wash away his memory of sin; the four lady-Virtues lead him to his vision of the griffin reflected in Beatrice's eyes, and the three others to his overwhelming vision of her eyes and smile (*Purg.* 30–31; 32.1–12). The procession then moves to the tall, bare tree of Adam, the prefiguration of the cross, where Dante is shown a dramatic representation of the Redemption: uttering

The historical calamities of the Church dramatized in the Earthly Paradise. La comedia di Dante Aligieri, with commentary by Alessandro Vellutello, published by Francesco Marcolini, Venice, 1544. Giamatti Collection: Courtesy of the Mount Holyoke College Archives and Special Collections.

words on justice, the griffin ties the chariot to the tree, which is renewed with leaves and blossoms; music lulls Dante into an enraptured sleep (*Purg.* 32.13–69). Awakened by Matelda, he then witnesses a second dramatized scene, which Beatrice instructs him to report back as a moral message to the living: a series of attacks on the tree and the chariot, culminating in the sight of the seven-headed, ten-horned beast, the prostitute, and the giant—prophetic symbols representing the corruption of the world and the Babylonian exile of the church in Avignon by means of images taken, once again, from the Book of Revelation and St. John's vision of the time of the Antichrist which will precede the Last Judgment (*Purg.* 32.70–160). Beatrice prophesies the certain and imminent arrival of a heaven-sent avenger, an heir of the eagle, encoded as the number 515 (DXV) in opposition to 666 (DCLXVI), the number of the beast in Revelation. No interpretation has convincingly identified this enigma with a historical person (such as Henry VII or Cangrande della Scala), and it is best viewed as a deliberately obscure prediction concerning a restoration of the Roman Empire which will itself prefigure or prepare for the Sec-

ond Coming of Christ at the end of the world. Matelda takes Dante to the Eünoè, whose waters renew him and prepare him for ascent to the stars (*Purg.* 33). Beatrice looks into the sun, and Dante, receiving the power to do so too, sees the whole sky joined in sunlight; he has already left the earthly Paradise for the heavenly (*Par.* 1.37–93).

Bibliography

Apocryphal New Testament, The. Edited by M. R. James. Oxford: Clarendon Press, 1924, pp. 126–128 ("The Gospel of Nicodemus"), 549–553 ("The Apocalypse of Paul").

Armour, Peter. *Dante's Griffin and the History of the World: A Study of the Earthly Paradise ('Purgatorio,' cantos xxix–xxxiii).* Oxford: Clarendon Press, 1989.

———. "L'Apocalisse nel canto XXIX del *Purgatorio.*" In *Dante e la Bibbia.* Edited by G. Barblan. Florence: Olschki, 1988, pp. 145–149.

———. "Matelda in Eden: The Teacher and the Apple." *Italian Studies* 34 (1979), 2–27.

Ciotti, Andrea. "Paradiso terrestre." *Enciclopedia dantesca,* 4: 289–291.

Coli, Edoardo. *Il paradiso terrestre dantesco.* Florence: Carnesecchi, 1897.

D'Ancona, Alessandro (ed.). *La leggenda d'Adamo ed Eva.* Bologna: Romagnoli, 1870.

Dronke, Peter. "L'Apocalisse negli ultimi canti del *Purgatorio.*" In *Dante e la Bibbia,* ed. G. Barblan, Florence: Olschki, 1988, pp. 81–94.

———. "The Phantasmagoria in the Earthly Paradise." In his *Dante and Medieval Latin Traditions.* Cambridge: Cambridge University Press, 1986, pp. 55–81.

———. "The Procession in Dante's *Purgatorio.*" *Deutsches Dante-Jahrbuch* 53–54 (1978–79), 18–45; also published as "*Purgatorio* XXIX" in *Cambridge Readings in Dante's "Comedy."* Edited by K. Foster and P. Boyde. Cambridge: Cambridge University Press, 1981, pp. 114–137.

Forti, Fiorenzo. "Matelda." *Enciclopedia dantesca,* 3: 854–860.

Foster, Kenelm. "*Purgatorio* XXXII." In *Cambridge Readings in Dante's 'Comedy.'* Edited by K. Foster and P. Boyde. Cambridge: Cambridge University Press, 1981, pp. 138–154.

———. *God's Tree.* London: Blackfriars, 1957, pp. 33–49.

Frugoni, Arsenio. "Il canto XXXIII del *Purgatorio.*" In *Nuove letture dantesche.* Vol. 5. Florence: Le Monnier, 1972, pp. 235–253.

E
Ghirardini, Giovanni. "Della visione di Dante nel paradiso terrestre." *Il Propugnatore* 10/2 (1877), 193–227, and 11/1 (1878), 27–76.

Giamatti, A. Bartlett. *The Earthly Paradise and the Renaissance Epic.* Princeton, N.J.: Princeton University Press, 1966, pp. 11–122.

Graf, Arturo. "Il mito del Paradiso terrestre." In *Miti, leggende e superstizioni del Medio Evo.* Vol. 1. Turin: Loescher, 1892–1893, pp. xi–xxiii, 1–238.

Kaske, Robert Earl. "Dante's *Purgatorio* XXXII and XXXIII: A Survey of Christian History." *University of Toronto Quarterly* 43 (1974), 193–214.

Lansing, Richard. "Narrative Design in Dante's Earthly Paradise." *Dante Studies* 113 (1995), 101–113.

Mazzamuto, Pietro. "Cinquecento diece e cinque." *Enciclopedia dantesca,* 2: 10–14.

Migliorini Fissi, Rosetta. "L'ingresso di Dante nell'Eden." *Studi danteschi* 58 (1986), 1–47.

Moore, Edward. "Symbolism and Prophecy in *Purg.* xxviii–xxxiii." In *Studies in Dante: Third Series.* Oxford: Clarendon Press, 1903, repr. 1968, pp. 178–283.

Nardi, Bruno. "Il mito dell'Eden." In *Saggi di filosofia dantesca.* 2d ed. Florence: La Nuova Italia, 1967, pp. 347–374.

Proto, Enrico. *L'Apocalissi nella 'Divina Commedia.'* Naples: Pierro, 1905.

Sabbatino, Pasquale. "L'Eden della nuova poesia: *Purg.* XXVIII–XXXIII." In his *L'Eden della nuova poesia: Saggi sulla 'Divina Commedia.'* Florence: Olschki, 1991, pp. 45–124.

Salvadori, Giulio. *La mirabile visione nel paradiso terrestre di Dante.* Turin: Libreria Editrice Internazionale, 1895.

Scartazzini, Giovanni Andrea. "Dante's Vision im irdischen Paradiese und die biblische Apokalyptik." *Jahrbuch der deutschen Dante-Gesellschaft* (= *Deutsches Dante-Jahrbuch*) 2 (1869), 99–150.

Singleton, Charles S. *Dante Studies II: Journey to Beatrice.* Cambridge, Mass.: Harvard University Press, 1958.

Wlassics, Tibor (ed.). *Dante's "Divine Comedy": Introductory Readings. II. "Purgatorio." Lectura Dantis,* 12: Supplement (Spring 1993), pp. 411–500.

Peter Armour

Eclogues

The *Paradiso* apart, two documents testify to Dante's disposition as a poet and philosopher in the final years of his life, the *Questio de Aqua et Terra* and the eclogues addressed in 1319 and 1320 to the Latin poet Giovanni del Virgilio associated with the studium at Bologna and himself the author of a number of poems in the Virgilian manner. But whereas the *Questio* has about it a certain ferocity as Dante confirms, over and against his detractors, his capacity, if and when he so chooses, to frame his argument philosophically, the eclogues bear witness altogether more genially—though no less unambiguously—to his capacity, again if and when he so chooses, to meet the new generation of (in this case) protohumanists on their own ground.

The context and substance of Dante's exchange with Giovanni del Virgilio are as follows. Dante, established in Ravenna under the patronage of Guido da Polenta and probably engaged in the teaching of rhetoric, is invited in the first of the poems addressed to him by Giovanni del Virgilio to turn his hand to a new and more fashionable species of literary enterprise consisting of Latin verses on a subject of—relative to the anagogical concerns of the *Commedia*—more immediate historical interest. On this basis, he (Dante) will not only speak more powerfully to the condition of Italy, but he will rightfully lay claim to the laurel crown which Giovanni del Virgilio, as a sincere and humble admirer of the great vernacular poet, will be privileged to place on his brow. This, at any rate, is the substance of Giovanni del Virgilio's opening eclogue, a piece testifying both to his mastery of the Virgilian pastoral style and to a deftness in exploiting its oblique discursive manner for the purposes of inviting Dante to look now in a fresh direction. Sensitive to the honor done him, and eager as always to meet his correspondent on his own technical ground, Dante takes up the pastoral fiction in the first and more engaging of his two eclogues. Anxious as he is, he says, to receive the laurel crown, he hopes this will come about, not in Bologna, but in Florence, and on the basis, not of a Latin epic, but of the *Commedia,* from the *Paradiso* of which he will now send Giovanni del Virgilio "ten pailfuls of milk" (ten cantos) in acknowledgment of the latter's generous expression of esteem. The tone throughout is elegantly bucolic, but the imaginative contrivance of the poem scarcely conceals its serious tone or its concern with matters of poetic glory, of the fate of poets and poetry in Dante's generation, and of homecoming from exile; so, for example, the following lines (1.36–44) on Giovanni del Virgilio's heroism and on Dante's determination to return to Florence in the twilight of his years there to enjoy proper recognition:

"O Moliboeus, the glory, nay, the very name of bard has vanished into the air. The muse has taxed her power to give us vigil-keeping Mopsus," I had replied, when thus did indignation give me voice: "What were the bleatings to which the hills and pastures would echo, were I to raise the paean on my lyre, when locks entwined with green! But let me dread the groves and countryside that know not the gods. Were it not better to trim my locks in triumph, and that I, who erst was auburn, should hide them, hoary now, under the twined leaves when, if it be so, I come again to my ancestral Sarnus?"

But Giovanni del Virgilio is insistent and, in a sturdier statement still of his combined admiration and sense of unworthiness in Dante's regard, returns to his theme. Dante, he says, taking up as he does so Alighieri's comments on the state of contemporary poetry, is himself the new Virgil, and should he come to Bologna, will most certainly be feted as such. To this Dante once more replies in kind, though with the substance of his answer already established in the first eclogue, with—if anything—a still greater concern for technical possibility. Thus the second eclogue, which at the level of content settles for emphasizing the danger of Dante's ever setting foot again in Guelf Bologna, witnesses to a further intensification of the pastoral metaphor, studiously enhanced in respect of its resourcefulness and allusiveness. Here as throughout—but in an altogether novel register—the poem presents itself as an opportunity for technical self-assertion, for an outdoing of his correspondents in point of poetic procedure.

But what matters about these eclogues, over and above their self-conscious *tecnicismo,* is their extraordinary blend of tenacity and graciousness as Dante affirms once more the *rationes* of his career as a visionary poet in the vernacular. Sensitive to the new emphases abroad in the art and esthetics of verse-making, he was no less sensitive to the challenge this represented to the shape and substance of his own activity as a poet. Part of him was eager to rise to the challenge and, in and through his mastery of the new style, to show himself equal to contemporary expectation. But such now is his sense of self and of what he has come to stand for that he is able at one and the same time both to acknowledge the challenge—and even, by way of elegantly declining it, to take it up—and yet to affirm the now settled pattern of his existence as a theological poet in the vernacular. For all their technical bravura, the eclogues witness in this sense to an extraordinarily seasoned state of mind.

Bibliography

Bolisani, Ettore, and Manara Valgimigli. *La corrispondenza poetica di Dante Alighieri e Giovanni del Virgilio.* Florence: Olschki, 1963.

Marigo, Aristide. *Il classicismo virgiliano nelle ecloghe di Dante.* Padua, 1910.

Martellotti, Guido. "Egloghe." *Enciclopedia dantesca,* 2: 644–646.

Padoan, Giorgio. *Introduzione a Dante.* Florence: Sansoni, 1975, pp. 113–118.

Reggio, Giovanni. *Le egloghe di Dante.* Florence: Olschki, 1969.

Took, John F. *Dante, Lyric Poet and Philosopher: An Introduction to the Minor Works.* Oxford: Clarendon Press, 1990.

Wicksteed, Philip H., and Edmund G. Gardner. *Dante and Giovanni del Virgilio.* Westminster: A. Constable, 1902.

John Took

Egypt

Country located to the east of the river Nile and so, according to Dante's geography, on the continent of Asia. Egypt *(Egitto)* is designated in *Inf.* 5.60 as *la terra che 'l Soldan corregge* ("the land the Sultan governs"), which the incestuous Semiramis had once governed, and in *Inf.* 24.90 as *ciò che di sopra al Mar Rosso èe* ("what lies beyond the Red Sea")—although some commentators take this to refer to Arabia, or in a more general sense. References are made, in the *Monarchia,* to the death and burial there of Alexander (*Mon.* 2.8.8) and to two kings of Egypt—Vesoges (*Mon.* 2.8.5) and Ptolemy (*Mon.* 2.8.9)—and in *Conv.* 2.14.2 to the astronomical calculations of *li savi d'Egitto* ("the wise men of Egypt").

Allegorically, Egypt stands for the earthly life of the *civitas terrena,* as opposed to the *civitas Dei* of Jerusalem; as in *Par.* 25.55–56, where the pilgrim's journey to heaven is portrayed as one *d'Egitto / [. . .] in Ierusalemme* ("from Egypt . . . to Jerusalem"). Similarly, in *Purg.* 2.46 the psalm "In exitu Isräel de Aegypto" (Psalm 113) is heard being sung by the souls arriving at the shores of Mount Purgatory. Here the slavery of the people of Israel in Egypt is likened to the spiritual slavery of sin, as Dante makes plain in *Conv.* 2.1.6–7: *in quello canto del Profeta che dice che, ne l'uscita del popolo d'Israel d'Egitto, Giudea è fatta santa e libera [. . .] spiritualmente s'intende [. . .] che ne l'uscita de l'anima dal peccato, essa sia fatta santa e libera in sua potestate* ("in the song of the Prophet which says that when the people of Israel went out of Egypt, Judea was made whole and free [. . .] that which is spiritually intended is [. . .] that when the soul departs from sin it is made whole and free in its power"). In the letter to Cangrande (*Epist.* 13.21) this same verse serves as an illustration of the fourfold system of allegorical interpretation.

Claire Honess

Electra

The daughter of Atlas and mother, by Jupiter, of Dardanus, the founder of Troy, Electra *(Elettra)* is named first among the company of great spirits gathered in the noble castle of Limbo (*Inf.* 4.121). Citing Virgil, Dante describes her in *Monarchia* as Aeneas' "most ancient ancestress" (2.3.2).

Virginia Jewiss

Elements

Borrowing from Aristotle, medieval philosophers maintained that all substances between the center of the earth and the orbit of the moon were composed of four elements. These elements—Earth, Water, Air, and Fire—were themselves thought to be composed of two pairs of contrary qualities: Hot/Cold and Wet/Dry. Unlike the elements of modern physics, the four Aristotelian elements could readily transmute into one another. Evaporation, for example, was explained as the transformation of Water (the Wet-Cold element) into Air (the Wet-Hot element). Each element was further held to possess a proper place in the cosmos and hence, also, a proper motion. Since earth's proper place is the center of the universe, substances in which Earth is the predominant element naturally fall downward toward the earth's center. Fire, by contrast, finds its proper place in the spherical region beneath the moon's orbit, and so fiery matter rises.

Dante's most extensive engagement with this doctrine is the *Questio de Aqua et Terra,* a work in which he sets out to explain the existence of dry land in the Northern Hemisphere. Such land is plainly puzzling because it appears to violate the theory that elements naturally seek out their own proper level. Since earthy matter should on its own accord seek out a lower level than water, one would expect the earth's surface to be ocean from pole to pole. The doctrine also features prominently in *Conv.* 3.2. As he glosses the first lines of "Amore che ne la mente mi ragiona," Dante is led to compare the natural love of the elements for their proper places to man's proper love for what is perfect and just.

In the *Commedia,* Dante engages the doctrine of the elements twice. Both discussions are provoked by apparent violations of established Aristotelian principles—a striking parallel with the *Questio*—and in both cases Beatrice explains away the apparent contradiction. In *Par.* 1 Dante marvels to find himself rising heavenward, drawn above the *corpi levi* ("light bodies") of Air and Fire. Beatrice answers Dante's surprise with an argument that has strong affinities with *Conv.* 3.2. All creatures—both material and intellectual—have a natural place in the cosmos, and man, freed of hindrances, finds his proper place with God: *Non dei più ammirar, se bene stimo, / lo tuo salir, se non come d'un rivo / se d'alto monte scende giuso ad imo* ("You should not wonder at your ascent, if I judge rightly, otherwise than at a stream, if from high on a mountain it descends to the base," *Par.* 1.136–138). In *Par.* 7, Beatrice observes that all things created directly by God are eternal, an observation that Dante has difficulty squaring with the fact that the elements are mutable. Beatrice resolves this contradiction by pointing out that the elements are not directly created by God, although he has created the primary matter from which they are formed.

John Kleiner

Elijah

Ninth-century Israelite prophet (1 Kings 17–19, 21; 2 Kings 1–2; 2 Chron. 21) identified with the messenger whom God will send to prepare his people for the day of judgment (Mal. 4:5) and believed to have returned in the figure of John the

Baptist (Matt. 11:14, 17:10–13; Luke 1:17). In the *Commedia*, Elijah *(Elia)* appears within extended similes describing Dante's experience. As the flame in which Elijah disappeared into heaven (in a chariot drawn by horses of fire) was manifest to his successor Elisha (2 Kings 2:11–12), so the flames in the eighth bolgia of *Inferno* reveal themselves to Dante (*Inf.* 26.35–39). And as Peter, James, and John were awakened at the Transfiguration to discover that Elijah (who along with Moses had appeared in conversation with Jesus) was no longer present (Matt. 17:1–8, Mark 9:2–8, Luke 9:28–36), so Dante is awakened from sleep to find that the griffin and his procession are departing upward into heaven (*Purg.* 32.70–90). In a demonstration of the apostle Peter's presumptuousness (*Mon.* 3.9.11), Dante mentions Elijah as a participant in the Transfiguration.

Carolynn Lund-Mead

Eliot, T[homas] S[tearns]

Poet (1888–1965) born in St. Louis, Mo., who became a British citizen in 1927. He was educated at Harvard, where he studied Dante, and went on to further study in philosophy at Oxford. In September 1914, as World War I was beginning, Eliot met Ezra Pound in London, who persuaded him to remain permanently in England. At their meeting, Pound was impressed with Eliot's knowledge of Dante and the Middle Ages, noting to the editor of *Poetry,* Harriet Monroe, that "he is the only American I know of who has made what I can call adequate preparation in writing."

In the early poems published in 1917 as *Prufrock and Other Observations,* Eliot expressed a view of the twentieth-century world as devoid of purpose and meaning. The epigraph for *The Love Song of J. Alfred Prufrock,* for example, is taken from *Inf.* 27.61–66. This view was made even more explicit in *The Waste Land* (1922), where lines from Dante underscored the notion of a modern *Inferno:* "I had not thought that death had undone so many" (63; cf. *Inf.* 3.56–57). The notes to the poem list other echoes or direct borrowings.

In 1925 Eliot became a director of the publishing firm of Faber and Faber, and in 1927 he joined the Anglican Church. From here on, his poetry began to acquire a more religious tone. Poems like "The Hollow Men" (1925) express important Dantesque images like the "multifoliate rose," and "Ash-Wednesday" (1930) shows an intertextual relationship with Guido Cavalcanti: "Because I do not hope to turn again."

From 1935 to 1942, Eliot composed his *Four Quartets,* which come as close to expressing a Christian notion of Paradise as any poet in the twentieth century has managed, although many people (like Pound) found the poetry and the feelings behind it artificial.

Eliot's most complete statement on Alighieri occurs in his essay "Dante," which appears in his *Selected Essays* (199–237), where he called the Italian the most "universal" of poets. He noted that Dante had a great poetic "lucidity" and a strongly "visual imagination," as Pound had stated in forming the Imagist school. He said that "more can be learned about how to write poetry from Dante than from any English poet" (213), and he cited Coleridge's well-known doctrine of "suspension of disbelief" (219), saying that one does not have to be Catholic to enjoy or even understand Alighieri. His greatest statement of praise was: "Dante and Shakespeare divide the modern world between them; there is no third" (225).

When Eliot died in 1965, the aged Pound flew from Venice to his gravesite in London. The following year in the winter issue of the *Sewanee Review,* he paid him a supreme compliment: "His was the true Dantescan voice—not honoured enough, and deserving more than I ever gave him."

Bibliography

Eliot, T. S. *Complete Poems and Plays, 1909–1950.* San Diego: Harcourt, Brace and Company, 1971.

———. "Dante." *Selected Essays.* San Diego: Harcourt, Brace and Company, 1950, pp. 199–237.

Ellis, Steve. *Dante and English Poetry: Shelley to T. S. Eliot.* Cambridge: Cambridge University Press, 1983.

Manganiello, Dominic. *T. S. Eliot and Dante.* New York: St. Martin's Press, 1989.

McDougal, Stuart Y. "T. S. Eliot's Metaphysical Dante." In *Dante among the Moderns.* Edited by Stuart Y. McDougal. Chapel Hill and London: University of North Carolina Press, 1985, pp. 57–81.

Wilhelm, James J. "Two Visions of the Journey of Life: Dante as a Guide for Eliot and Pound." *Dante's Influence on American Writers, 1776–1976.* New York: Dante Society of America, 1977.

James J. Wilhelm

Elisha

Prophet of Israel whom God instructed Elijah to name as his successor. When Elisha asked for a double portion of his spirit, Elijah promised that if Elisha should actually see him taken from him, his request would be granted (2 Kings 2.9–10). Dante captures the moment in which Elisha *(Eliseo)* stood watching Elijah disappear in flames *(Inf.* 26.35–39; 2 Kings 2:11–12). Dante identifies Elisha by means of a subsequent incident in which he cursed a group of boys who were mocking him, forty-two of whom were immediately torn to pieces by two she-bears *(Inf.* 26.34; 2 Kings 2:23–24).

Carolynn Lund-Mead

Elysium

Elysium *(Elisio, Eliso)* is the dwelling of the virtuous in the afterlife in classical mythology. In Virgil's *Aen.* 6.637–892, Aeneas meets the soul of his father Anchises in Elysium. Alluding to this episode in a simile, Dante likens Cacciaguida's greeting of Dante in the sphere of Mars to Anchises' recognizing Aeneas in *Eliso* (*Par.* 15.27).

Jennifer Petrie

Empedocles

Greek pre-Socratic philosopher and polymath born at Agrigentum in Sicily (c. 495–435 B.C.E.), particularly admired by Aristotle (*Metaphysics* 3.4). Only fragments of his work survive. Dante places Empedocles in Limbo with other philosophers of antiquity (*Inf.* 4.138); he later alludes to his theory of the universe as governed alternately by love and strife (*Inf.* 12.41–43).

Nancy Vine Durling

Empire

Dante advocated a revival of the Roman Empire, which he conceived to be divinely appointed to rule the whole world and which he insisted was not subject to the papacy. In adopting this position, he was attempting to solve Italy's current problems by an appeal to its past.

Under the republic, Rome had acquired hegemony—the right of "command" *(imperium)*—first over its Italian neighbors and then over the whole Mediterranean world. In 31 B.C.E. Rome's internal government changed from a republic to a military dictatorship under Augustus, the permanent commander in chief (*imperator* = emperor). Thus both Rome's allies and her citizens, being subject to one ruler, came to form a single empire *(imperium).*

In 395 C.E. the Empire was divided into a western and eastern half, the capital of the latter being Constantinople (Byzantium). By 500 C.E. the western half of this Empire, including Italy, was controlled by Germans, and there was no western emperor after 476. The title was revived by Charlemagne in 800, however, after his Franks had conquered Italy. With the breakup of the Frankish empire, the title of Roman emperor passed to the Germans in 962, who then ruled Italy for about a hundred years.

From 313 until 1076, the emperor was the effective head of the Christian church (caesaropapism), but during the Investiture Struggle (1076–1122) the pope won independence from imperial control both for himself and the other bishops of Italy. At the same time, in the cities of northern Italy local nobles and merchants allied in communes and seized control of city government. Thus by 1122 the German emperor had lost control of both church and state in Italy.

The cities were now independent states de facto, and they began to wage war against one another to secure commercial and territorial advantages. In 1158 the emperor Frederick I (Frederick Barbarossa) intervened in an attempt to restore peace and order, and many cities accepted his support against their enemies, forming a party that came to be known as the Ghibellines. But other cities preferred to continue their unrestrained aggression and resisted the emperor's efforts; eventually they were joined by the pope, whose independence was likewise threatened by the restoration of a strong central government in Italy. After a century-long struggle, this anti-imperial alliance, which eventually became the Guelf party, managed to baffle the attempts of Barbarossa and his successors—notably Frederick II—to reunite Italy. As a result, intercity and interparty warfare continued to plague Italy down to the time of Dante. Meanwhile, after the death of Frederick II in 1250, no new emperor was crowned until Henry VII (1311), largely due to the opposition of the papacy, which in 1298 secured the right to veto the emperor's election.

Thus history led Dante to believe that Italy needed a strong emperor to restore peace and tranquillity, and that the principal obstacle to such a restoration was the papacy. Furthermore, French and Aragonese intervention in Italian affairs since 1265 made it evident that with aggressive, independent neighbors, even a united Italy could not enjoy peace. Dante's ideal empire, therefore, would have to be universal, as the Roman Empire had, with exaggeration, claimed to be in antiquity. Unrealistic though this ideal might be, it greatly facilitated Dante's philosophic arguments for an empire that was the earthly reflection of a monotheistic cosmos.

Dante expounded his political vision most extensively in the *Monarchia,* though it was already present in the *Convivio* (4.4–5) and is reflected in the *Commedia.* He begins with a definition: "Temporal monarchy, which is commonly called 'empire,' is the political supremacy of one ruler, and it is over all things temporal, or more precisely, among and over all things that are measured by time" (*Mon.* 1.2.2). Hence it is the rule over the whole earth, as opposed to God's rule over the universe. "This pre-eminent office is called the Empire, without qualification, because it is the command of all other commands. And thus he who is placed in this office is called the Emperor, since he is the commander of all other commands; what he says is law for all and ought to be obeyed by all, and every other command gains strength and authority from his" (*Conv.* 4.4.7).

Dante proposes to prove three theses about this empire: (1) that it is necessary for the welfare of mankind; (2) that the Roman people lawfully acquired it; and (3) that the authority of the emperor comes to him directly from God, and not indirectly via the pope. Dante devotes a book to each of these propositions. His point of departure is the fundamental principle that mankind needs to live "in the quiet or tranquillity of peace" in order to realize its collective potentialities (*Mon.* 1.3–4). Dante marshals twelve arguments to prove his first thesis, that such peace can only be attained under a single world ruler, the monarch, or emperor *(imperator).* For example, since mankind has its own goal, so it should be guided to it by a single person, just as one ruler directs a family, a village, a city, or a kingdom to its proper goal (1.5; cf. *Conv.* 4.4.2–4). Again, in any human organization, the parts ought to be subordinated to a leader, so

mankind, like an army, ought to have a commander (*Mon.* 1.6; cf. *Conv.* 4.4.5–6). Moreover, mankind should imitate the cosmic order, which is ruled by God, the ultimate absolute monarch (1.7–9).

Nowhere does Dante indicate how his ideal empire should be organized: such constitutional arrangements are apparently to be devised by the emperor. Nonetheless, in the course of Book 1 he does make two of the emperor's functions perfectly clear. First, the emperor is the supreme judge, from whom there is no appeal (*Mon.* 1.10). He is best able to do justice because he alone among rulers is free from greed, since he already rules the entire world (1.11). Second, the emperor is the supreme legislator, who makes laws that apply to all men—Dante is thinking here of Roman law—whereas subordinate rulers may adapt these laws to the special needs of particular places (1.12). Although Dante never says so, papal government in his day suggests how this regime might have worked in practice, since it was founded on the pope's similar position as supreme judge and legislator for the Church.

The second stage of Dante's argument was to prove that the one and only ruler of the world must necessarily be Roman. A review of earlier aspirants to world rule, such as the Assyrians and Macedonians, shows that none of them attained the goal (2.8), but that Rome did is chiefly proved by revelation: according to Luke 2:1, the "whole world" *(universus orbis)* was subject to the emperor at Christ's birth (*Mon.* 2.8.14, 2.10.6). Dante regards world empire as a prize that Rome won in a contest with other powers, and that contest, which was over before the birth of Christ, is never to be repeated (2.7–9).

Dante therefore had no doubt that Rome was the only world empire. The question for him was whether that empire had been acquired justly, rightly, and lawfully *(de iure)* or simply by force (cf. *Conv.* 4.4.8–12). Book 2 of the *Monarchia* argues that Rome's conquests must have been just because God willed them, as Dante tries to prove (cf. *Conv.* 4.5.10–20). God's good will for the Roman people is shown by their nobility (*Mon.* 2.3), by miracles in their favor, such as the goose that saved the Capitol from the Gauls (2.4), and by their natural aptitude for rule (2.6). Above all, Dante insists that the Romans' struggle for empire was a contest that revealed the judgment of God (2.7–9). Finally, Dante argues that Christ would

E not have been born under an unjust rule and that his crucifixion would not have been a valid sacrifice if Roman rule were not legitimate (2.10–11; cf. *Conv.* 4.5.1–9).

The thesis of *Mon.* 3 is that the emperor's authority is derived directly from God. Unlike the theses of the first two books, this had immediate practical implications, both for the creation of emperors and for the authority of imperial vicars in Italy. Dante begins by insisting that the Empire is natural (*Mon.* 3.2) and goes on to refute nine objections to his thesis (3.4–11), most of which concern the papacy rather than the Empire, and hence are irrelevant here. He dismisses the Donation of Constantine as an invalid transaction and the papal coronation of Charlemagne as a usurpation (3.10). Having removed the objections, he goes on to prove that the Church cannot have authority over the emperor, especially because the Empire was prior in time to the Church (3.12).

Dante's view of the Empire, however, is stated most clearly in the climactic last chapter of the *Monarchia* (3.15). Mankind, he explains, has two goals—namely, happiness here on earth (symbolized by Eden, the earthly Paradise) and happiness in the afterlife (symbolized by the heavenly Paradise). Mankind can achieve its happiness here on earth by practicing the moral and intellectual virtues discovered by philosophy, but men are impeded from attaining this goal by greed *(cupiditas)*. It is the emperor's divinely appointed function as "caretaker of the world" *(curator orbis)* to restrain human cupidity so that mankind can live "freely in peace."

To do this effectively, the emperor must be the right man for his times. Especially, he must be able to apply the general principles of philosophy to times and places that alter according to the changing disposition of the heavens. Hence, Dante argues, the emperor must be chosen by one who knows all the dispositions of the heavens simultaneously, and that one can only be God, who ordained the movements of the stars.

Thus, properly speaking, only God elects and confirms the emperor, who has no superior on earth. Nonetheless Dante allows that the electors of the Holy Roman Empire participate in the process by announcing the will of God. Dante does not explain here how the electors discover God's will, but elsewhere he asserts that human reason can discover it from the motion of the heavens, i.e., by astrology (*Epist.* 5.23).

The papacy, on the other hand, has the function of leading mankind to eternal life in accordance with revealed truth. Since this goal is higher, the emperor owes the pope the same respect that a firstborn son owes to his father. By showing respect to the supernatural order, the emperor will receive grace, which will enhance his light of natural reason, just as sunlight enhances the moon's native light (cf. *Mon.* 3.4.20).

Dante's ideal of the Empire is best exemplified by Justinian in *Par.* 6. There the ex-emperor explains that his office gave him no competence in theology and that he was dissuaded from heresy by the preaching of a saintly pope, whom he simply believed. Once Justinian was in accord with the Church, God inspired him to codify Roman law, and the emperor delegated his military functions to a capable general. Thus Dante indicates that the emperor's chief concern is not with war but with peace. Above all, as the supreme legislator, he uses the truths of philosophy to make laws that will restrain human greed, while, like a dutiful son, he accepts the truths of revelation on faith from the Church.

Bibliography

Brooke, Z. N. *A History of Europe from 911 to 1198.* 3d ed. London: Methuen, 1951. [With Previté-Orton (below), the best English narrative of German imperial involvement in Italy.]

Davis, Charles. "The Middle Ages." In *The Legacy of Rome: A New Appraisal.* Edited by Richard Jenkyns. Oxford: Oxford University Press, 1992.

———. *Dante and the Idea of Rome.* Oxford: Clarendon, 1957.

Ferrante, Joan M. *The Political Vision of the "Divine Comedy."* Princeton, N.J.: Princeton University Press, 1984.

Gilson, Étienne. *Dante the Philosopher.* Trans. David Moore. New York: Sheed and Ward, 1949.

Maccarrone, Michele. "Papato e Impero nella *Monarchia.*" *Nuove letture dantesche* 8 (1976), 259–332.

———. "Il terzo libro della *Monarchia.*" *Studi danteschi* 33 (1955), 5–142.

Mancusi-Ungaro, Donna. *Dante and the Empire.* Peter Lang: New York, 1987.

Nardi, Bruno. [Commentary to the *Monarchia.*] In *Dante Alighieri, Opere minori,* 2. Milan and Naples: Ricciardi, 1979.

Previté-Orton, C. W. *A History of Europe from 1198 to 1378.* 3d ed. London: Methuen, 1951.

Ricci, Pier Giorgio, et al. "Impero." *Enciclopedia dantesca,* 3: 383–393.

Vinay, Gustavo. [Commentary to the *Monarchia.*] In Dante Alighieri, *Monarchia.* Florence: Sansoni, 1950.

Richard Kay

Empyrean

The tenth and highest heaven, encompassing all creation (< Greek *empyrios,* fiery). Unlike the other nine heavens, or moving celestial spheres, the Empyrean is immaterial, the ninth heaven or Primum Mobile being the *maggior corpo,* the "greatest body" (*Par.* 30.39; cf. 23.112–114; 28.53–54). The Empyrean is pure (intellectual) light, love, and joy (*Par.* 27.112; 30.39–42); the divine mind itself (*Par.* 27.109–111); and the abode of God, angels, and the blessed (*Par.* 30.43–44, 30.91–132, 31.1–27, 33.52–141).

The *Convivio* (2.3.8–12) reflects the tension between the purely theological (neoplatonic) origin of the concept of the Empyrean (divine reality as light, consciousness, fire of love), and its assimilation into Aristotelian cosmology as the outermost of the concentric heavenly spheres. Thus Dante notes, *fuori di tutti questi [cieli mobili], li cattolici pongono lo cielo Empireo, che è a dire cielo di fiamma o vero luminoso* ("outside all these [moving heavens] the Catholics place the Empyrean Heaven, which is to say, the 'heaven of flame,' or 'luminous heaven,'" 2.3.8). He also states both that the Empyrean is motionless because it has in each of its parts *ciò che la sua materia vuole* ("what its matter desires"), and that as the ever-quiet and peaceful abode of God and the blessed, containing all and contained by nothing, it is not in space, *ma formato fu solo ne la prima Mente* ("but was formed solely in the Primal Mind," 2.3.9–12). The tenth heaven *annunzia essa unitade e stabilitade di Dio* ("proclaims the very unity and stability of God," 2.5.12); in its peace it resembles theology (2.13.8, 2.14.19); for love of it, the Primum Mobile spins within it at almost inconceivable speed (*Conv.* 2.3.9; cf. *Par.* 1.123, 2.112–113, 27.109–111).

Glossing *Par.* 1.4–5, *Nel ciel che più de la sua luce prende / fu' io* ("In the heaven that receives most of his light have I been"), the Letter to Cangrande (*Epist.* 13.66–76) comments that this is a circumlocution for Paradise, or the Empyrean, *quod est idem quod celum igne sui ardoris fla-*

The White Rose in the Empyrean. La comedia di Dante Aligieri, *with commentary by Alessandro Vellutello, published by Francesco Marcolini, Venice, 1544. Giamatti Collection: Courtesy of the Mount Holyoke College Archives and Special Collections.*

grans; non quod in eo sit ignis vel ardor materialis, sed spiritualis, quod est amor sanctus sive caritas ("that is to say the heaven burning with the fire of its ardor; not that there is material flame or heat in it, but rather spiritual, in other words holy love or charity," 13.66–68). This is the highest heaven, containing all, contained by nothing, in whose eternal stillness all bodies move (13.67). The letter then offers two proofs that the Empyrean receives most of the divine light: (1) containing all, it is the formative cause of all; since this causative force is a divine ray emanating from God, the Empyrean is the most luminous heaven; (2) lacking nothing in any part, the Empyrean alone does not move; since all perfection is a ray of divine perfection, the Empyrean is most luminous.

In the *Commedia,* the word *empireo* occurs only once, in *Inf.* 2.21 (Aeneas was chosen as father of Rome and her empire *ne l'empireo ciel* ["in the Empyrean heaven"]), to be replaced by a breathtaking array of metaphors, in which any vestiges of a material astronomical object dissolve into a purely spiritual vision. Thus if the Empyrean is a *spera* ("sphere"), *non è in loco e non s'impola* ("it is not in space and turns on no pole," *Par.* 22.67); it is *il ciel de la divina pace* ("the heaven of God's peace," *Par.* 2.112), *fa 'l ciel sempre quieto* ("[makes] ever quiet that heaven," *Par.* 1.122; cf. *Conv.* 2.3.8–10, 2.13.8), *il ciel . . . ch'è pien d'amore e più ampio si spazia* ("the heaven . . . that is full of love and encloses the most ample space," *Purg.* 26.63), *il ciel più chiaro* ("the brightest heaven," *Par.* 23.102), *la spera supprema* ("the supreme sphere," *Par.* 23.108, *Purg.* 15.52), *il primo cielo* ("the first heaven," *Purg.* 30.1; cf. *Epist.* 13.70–72), *il primo giro* ("the first circle," *Par.* 4.34).

After arriving in the Empyrean (*Par.* 30.38), Dante is enveloped and blinded by a flash of light (30.46–54); his vision thus strengthened, he sees a river of light, from which sparks emerge to enter flowers on the banks and then return (30.61–69). When Dante dips his eyes into the river, it becomes a sea of light, and the sparks and flowers are revealed as angels and blessed souls (30.70–108). The souls are arranged in ascending tiers, forming a vast rose; the seats are nearly filled, one being reserved for the emperor Henry VII (30.109–148). The angels descend into the rose and re-ascend, but their multitude does not block Dante's vision (31.1–24). Dante gazes in wonder, and turning to address Beatrice, finds her replaced by St. Bernard, who directs his eyes to Beatrice, now in her place in the rose, and to Mary, surrounded by angels (31.25–142). Bernard explains the arrangement of the rose (32.1–84, 109–138): a vertical line of Old Testament women (Mary, Eve, Rachel, Sarah, Rebecca, Judith, Ruth) on one side, and of New Testament men (St. John the Baptist, St. Francis, St. Benedict, St. Augustine) on the other, divides the rose between those who believed in Christ to come, and those who believed in Christ already come. Among the former, Adam and Moses sit to Mary's left, St. Anne to the Baptist's right; among the latter, St. Peter and St. John the Evangelist are on Mary's right, Beatrice on Rachel's right, and St. Lucy on the Baptist's left. The lower half of the rose is filled with children, saved through baptism, circumcision, or their parents' faith. St. Bernard prays to the Virgin (33.1–39), and Dante looks into the light, which eclipses his speech, memory, and sight (33.49–105). In the light he sees three colored rings, the second inscribed with the human form (33.109–132); in a final flash of enlightenment, the poem ends (33.133–145).

Christian Moevs

England

There are only a few references to England, the English, and the English language in the works of Dante. In the course of his argument in favor of the vernacular over Latin as the appropriate language for the *Convivio,* Dante explains that knowledge of Latin does not guarantee the ability to distinguish one vernacular from another; for example, an Italian with perfect knowledge of Latin would not thereby know the difference between English and German (1.6.8). In the following chapter, Dante argues further that even though a commentary in Latin on his *canzoni* would be intelligible to learned Germans and English, such a commentary would constitute an attempt to convey the poems' meaning that cannot account for their beauty (1.7.13). In the *De vulgari eloquentia,* he refers to England as one of the western boundaries of Europe and to the English *(Anglici)* as speakers of one of the vernaculars into which the first European language divided (1.8.4).

There are two references and one allusion to persons and matters English in the *Commedia,* not counting the possibility that the counterfeiter Master Adam (*Inf.* 30.61) was an Englishman. When Bertran de Born, among the schismatics in Hell, explains the nature of his *contrapasso* (*Inf.* 28.133–142), he alludes, without naming names, to his bad counsel to young Henry, the second son of Henry II of England (1155–1183), and the consequent division between father and son. Henry II's grandson, Henry III, appears in the Valley of the Princes in the Ante-Purgatory, pointed out by Sordello: *Vedete il re de la semplice vita / seder là solo, Arrigo d'Inghilterra: / questi ha ne' rami suoi migliore uscita* ("See the king who lived simply, sitting alone there, Harry of England: he has better issue in his branches," *Purg.* 7.130–132). One of the kings Sordello reproached for their degeneracy in his famous lament *Planh de Ser Blacatz,* Henry was singled out for his cowardice and sloth. While this might explain Henry's presence among the negligent rulers, his characterization by Sordello sets him somewhat apart from the others. Though there is disagreement over the reasons for this, it is clear that Henry III, who ruled from 1216 to 1272, provides an exception to one of the themes of Sordello's catalogue of rulers, that virtue is not transmitted by bloodline; for his "better issue" is his son Edward I (1272–1307), who instituted extensive and enduring legal reforms during his own long reign. Yet it is to another, less positive, aspect of Edward's royal career that the Eagle in the sixth heaven and sphere of Jupiter refers during its denunciation of European rulers. In the third tercet of the letter *L* in the acrostic anaphora that spells out *LVE* ("plague" or "pestilence"), the Eagle says, *Lì si vedrà la superbia ch'asseta, / che fa lo Scotto e l'Inghilese folle / sì che non può soffrir dentro a sua meta* ("There will be seen the thirsty pride that so maddens the Scot and the Englishman that neither can bear to stay within his bounds," *Par.* 19.121–123). Since the Eagle's survey is limited to rulers in power during the year of Dante's journey, 1300, the Englishman must be Edward I, whose frequent engagement with the Scots in border warfare is described in Villani's *Cronica* (8.67).

Since most of Dante's adult life coincided with the reign of Edward I, it is not surprising that the poet was aware of the English monarch's reputation—as indicated by the two references to him in the *Commedia*. Edward's energetic and innovative overhauling of the feudal system under his royal control included the establishment of measures against administrative corruption, the growth and definition of the common law, the transition of the exchequer and chancery from functions of the king's curia to departments of the state, and the evolution of Parliament as a comprehensive and durable organ of government. While such accomplishments in national institutions and law have earned recognition of Edward's rule as a major turning point in England's political history, his great ambition and civil wars proved to be a disastrous strain on his country and brought dire consequences in the future.

Edward I is also remembered for his expulsion in 1290 of England's Jews, who had been impoverished for some years and were no longer a source of financial support. In fact, Edward had relied for loans for many years upon Italian merchant banking companies, whose founders arrived to trade in the early thirteenth century. By mid-century, the Italian companies, already papal bankers and successful wool merchants, were being drawn from many cities in Italy to England in considerable numbers by papal taxes and Europe's best wool. In a partnership between an agricultural country (whose expanding government needed greater and greater revenues) and an advanced industrial and financial organization, Italy invested her mobile capital in England for the raw material needed by her industries, wool to be woven in the factories of the Arno and Po valleys. Thus, the main connection between Italy and England during the century was through trade and banking, with Italy attaining a maximum influence on English economic affairs in the reign of Edward I, who relied systematically upon the credit facilities of the Italian *societates*. From 1272–1294, the first twenty years of his reign, Edward depended primarily upon the Riccardi of Lucca from among several "bankers to the crown." When the Riccardi began to fail, he used several companies from Florence, including the Bardi, but eventually filled the position vacated by the Riccardi with the Florentine Frescobaldi *societas*. Like their predecessors, the Frescobaldi also buckled under the weight of Edward's repudiation of his debts, a fate dealt to numerous other companies later in the fourteenth century by Edward I's son and grandson. Though there is no direct evidence for the nature or degree of Dante's knowledge of this international relationship, there can be no doubt he was aware of it.

Bibliography

Kaeupur, Richard W. *Bankers to the Crown.* Princeton, N.J.: Princeton University Press, 1973.

———. "The Frescobaldi of Florence and the English Crown." *Studies in Medieval and Renaissance History* 10 (1973), 41–95.

Lloyd, T. H. *Alien Merchant in England in the High Middle Ages.* New York: St. Martin's Press, 1982.

Previté-Orton, C. W. *The Shorter Cambridge Medieval History.* Vol. 2. Cambridge: Cambridge University Press, 1971.

George D. Economou

Envy

One of the Seven Capital Sins, and in Dante's categorical system a disposition corrected specifically on the second level of Purgatory. Dante's purposeful omission of a circle of envy *(invidia)* and, likewise, of pride, in Hell has precipitated much critical controversy. As the archetypal motivation of Satan himself (Wis. of Sol. 2:23–25, cf. *Inf.* 1.111), however, envy permeates the *Inferno*. In the *Conv.* 1.4.2, Dante had treated the sin as denigration: he gives it as one of three reasons why *la presenza fa la persona di meno valore ch'ella non è* ("why a man's presence makes him less worthy than he really is"). Envy-as-character-assassination (*Inf.* 13.64–66) is the motive for Pier della Vigna's low reputation, in his own words *"ancor del colpo che 'nvidia le diede"* ("languishing still beneath the blow that envy dealt it," *Inf.* 13.78). In the same way, Romeo di Villanova suffers from those who turn others' good deeds to evil (*Par.* 6.127–142). Florence, particularly, is viewed as a nest of envy through the *Inferno:* Ciacco scorns it as *"La tua città . . . piena / d'invidia sì che già trabocca il sacco"* ("Your city . . . so full of envy that the sack already overflows," *Inf.* 6.50), where pride, envy, and avarice have inflamed all hearts (*Inf.* 6.74–75). Brunetto Latini agrees: *"gent' è avara, invidiosa e superba"* ("they are a people avaricious, envious, and proud," *Inf.* 15.68).

The term *"invidia"* had a connotation wider than the English "envy" in the theology that Dante inherited: it signified not only jealousy of another's good fortune considered as detrimental to one's own, but pleasure in another's misfortune and a general will to harm (cf. the definition given in *Purg.* 17.118–120 and the sin of Guido del Duca over against the sin of Sapìa, *Purg.* 13.110–111). In a colloquial sense we might call *invidia* "bloody mindedness"; in its most serious form we would call it "psychopathy" (cf. *Purg.* 13.113). Envy violates the injunction of Rom. 13:15: "Rejoice with them that rejoice: weep with them that weep." The Fathers of the Church from St. Cyprian through St. Augustine saw envy as the supreme diabolical sin: Augustine identified it as a sin against the Holy Spirit, that is, against divine love (*De sermone Domini in monte* 1.22.75). Church writers conflated two biblical passages in particular in their discussions of envy (cf. St. Gregory, *Moralia in Job* 6:38 [*PL* 75.749–750]): "He that hateth his brother is in darkness and walketh in darkness and knoweth not whither he goeth, because darkness hath blinded his eyes" (1 Cor. 2:11), and "They shall meet with darkness in the daytime and grope in the noonday as in the night" (Job 5:14). Blindness was also present in the traditional etymology that deduced *invidia* from "in + video," "I do not see you." According to Christian doctrine, envy blinded the soul to charity or brotherly love. The concepts form the matrix of the events and imagery in the episode of envy in *Purg.* 13 and 14.

The souls of this cornice in their livid hairshirts are, appropriately, indistinguishable from the color of the livid rock (*il livido color della petraia,*

Purg. 13.9) upon which they lean and grope in the midday sun (*Purg.* 13.13–21; 43–72): *livor* and *livore* signify "envy" in Latin and Italian (cf. *Purg.* 14.82). The penitents' eyes are stitched shut with an iron wire that makes a hideous seam through which their tears ooze. In an age innocent of stainless steel the effect would have been clear to the reader: indeed, "rust" (*aerugo* or *ferrugo*) in the classics (in Horace and Martial, for example) also denoted "envy"; in Christian theology envy was the "rust" of the eyes and heart (cf. St. Augustine, *De beato Joseph, PL* 39.1769; St. Cyprian, *De invidia, PL* 4.615–616; Alain de Lille, *Contra invidiam, PL* 210.129). The verse *"Io sono Aglauro che divenni sasso"* ("I am Aglauros who became a stone," *Purg.* 14.139) relates not only to the idea of petrification *("la petraia")* but also evokes, via Ovid's *Meta.* 2.803–805, the metaphor of rust: Envy enters Aglauros' bedchamber and conjures up images to inflame the girl with jealousy against her sister Herse, who is about to wed Mercury: *Pectusque manu ferrugine tincta tangit* ("and she touched the girl's breast *with her rust-stained hand"*).

We can observe that Dante's strategy in describing the temporary expiatory suffering of the penitent in Purgatory consists mainly in the literalizing of classical, biblical, and theological metaphors concerning the nature of envy so that the universal "truth" of those texts may become the spiritual substance of his sacred poem's message.

Anthony K. Cassell

Ephialtes

One of the giants of classical mythology, the son of Neptune and Iphimedia, who joined his brother Otus in a failed attempt to conquer heaven and oust Jove by piling Mount Ossa onto Mount Pelion. In *Inferno,* Ephialtes *(Fïalte)* is one of the giants guarding the entrance to Hell's ninth circle (*Inf.* 31.91–96).

V. Stanley Benfell

Epic Poetry

Epic poetry in the Greek and Roman classical tradition is recast by Dante in the *Commedia* in the matrix of biblical, Latin, and Byzantine literary and iconographic culture, of visionary writing, and of the medieval pilgrimage tradition.

The oral Greek epic, as exemplified in the *Iliad* and *Odyssey* attributed in Dante's period to

Homer, and the Latin literary epic, dominantly represented by Virgil's *Aeneid,* were by the poet's period characterized by a number of established conventions. Dante, under the sway of the *Aeneid* and the classical epic tradition, employed and transformed epic devices and motifs—in particular the divine invocations, the heroic voyage-quest, the epic similes, the descent into the underworld, visions and prophesies, the encounters with monstrous and divine beings, and the arrival at a divinely ordained spiritual "home" or kingdom—but in the context of a sequential medieval otherworldly pilgrimage to the Godhead recounted in the Italian vernacular. Dante's knowledge of the tradition derives chiefly from Virgil's *Aeneid,* Statius' *Thebaid,* and Lucan's *Pharsalia;* he had no direct knowledge of Homer's works.

Two foreshadowing earthly types for the poet's otherworldly journey—one drawn from the pagan epic, the *Aeneid,* and the other from the Hebraic-Christian Bible—are mentioned in *Inf.* 2.10–30. Dante there learns that he must follow in the footsteps of Aeneas, underworld traveler and founder of Rome in Virgil's epic, and St. Paul, missionary and visionary who recounts his ascent into the third heaven in 2 Cor. 12:2–4. Similes repeatedly relate episodes in Dante's journey to those in classical epics or Hebraic-Christian source works. In *Inf.* 3. 112–117, for example, Dante describes a multitude of dead souls cringing before the Virgilian boatman Charon; but contexts are transformed by a comparison of the damned to falling leaves that have been seen as antitypes to fulfilled vernal icons in the Heavenly Rose.

With the exception of the poet Statius, who later enters in *Purg.* 21.10, the major classical writers influencing Dante appear in *Inf.* 4 as noble heathen authors who are confined to Limbo in Hell, a place to which even Dante's revered guide Virgil must eventually return. Homer, the *poeta sovrano* ("supreme poet"), stands before the assembly with sword in hand. And Dante, upon being greeted by one or more of the literary artists, boldly joins Homer and Virgil in the company of Ovid, Lucan, and Horace, thus formally associating himself and his work with classical epic tradition. Of this group, all but Horace wrote in the epic genre. But because Dante's new kind of heroic journey draws upon Hebraic-Christian scriptural and iconographic "source works," as well as upon Christian liturgical events, the poet's journey contrasts significantly with the voyage-quests of classical, or pagan, epic heroes.

In *Inf.* 26 the poet presents the *Odyssey*'s hero Ulysses, in keeping with Virgil's negative Roman estimate of his character, as a world traveler whose deceptiveness and fraudulent counsel condemns him to Hell. Ulysses, who made a proud and deadly voyage beyond the Pillars of Hercules to the base of Mount Purgatory, serves as an antitype to Dante, who makes a very different kind of journey. In the heaven of Mars (*Par.* 15–16), Dante patterns his encounter with his great-great grandfather, the crusader Cacciaguida, on Aeneas' underworld encounter with his father Anchises, thereby reinforcing the figure of Aeneas as a positive model for Dante as otherworld traveler. Ulysses defines the negative, forbidden journey; Aeneas, the positive and preordained.

In the instance of Ulysses as in many others, Dante compellingly treats both the fabulous or fictional figures of past epic poetry, as well as the historical figures, in medieval fashion as moral exempla. Cato, who in Lucan's Roman epic commits suicide rather than submit to Caesar (*Phars.* 2.373–379), is transformed in *Purg.* 1 into a figure

Statue of Dante Alighieri in Florence. Richard Lansing.

E of spiritual liberty. The wall separating the carnal lovers Pyramus and Thisbe, taken from Ovid's *Meta.* 4.65–66, is made analogous to the wall of virtuous flame in Purgatory, which purges the sin of lust (*Purg.* 27.37–39). And many of the powerful heroes of Virgil's *Aeneid,* and of Statius' *Thebaid* and in the surviving fragments of his *Achilleid,* are alluded to by Dante in varied depictions of the moral state of souls (*Inf.* 1. 23–26, 107–108; 4.121; 5.61–62; and *Purg.*18.136–138; 20, 102–106). Dante borrows heavily from the epic tradition, but re-presents and re-creates its historical and literary figures, its myths, images, similes, and its history, by placing them under the aegis of a Christian imperative.

Having written in the *Vita Nuova* of the earthly pilgrimages of Palmers and Romers as foreshadowing the heavenly pilgrimage toward Beatrice (Chapters 41–42), Dante has been interpreted in the *Purgatorio* and *Paradiso* as fulfilling *in figura* the pilgrimage of an earthly Palmer-Romer who, during the Jubilee pilgrimage of 1300, traces out the itinerary of pilgrimage stations linking worldly Egypt to Holy Jerusalem and eternal Rome, stations which in the pilgrimage tradition represent the most holy metaphoric "words" in God's Book of Nature. This Book of the World—together with the Bible, God's other book, his Book of Words—supersede for Dante the writings of the classical epic authors largely gathered in *Inf.* 4. The two Books of God have been seen to point in their actual events or their metaphoric "words" to spiritually heroic biblical pilgrimage events enacted sequentially by the poet; namely, the Exodus of conversion, beginning in *Purg.* 2.46–48 and continuing through canto 28; the Redemption and Regeneration in *Purg.* 29–33; and the Transfiguration in *Par.* 24–26 and alternately through canto 33. Images of the two Books of God are accordingly depicted at crucial, pivotal points along Dante's visionary journey: the Bible appearing as a procession of allegorical figures in *Purg.* 29–30, and the universal form of the "volume" of God's creation in a single flash of light in *Par.* 33.82–93.

In the *Commedia* Trinitarian and related "spiritual" numerology associated with the two Books of God govern formal divisions and structures, thus replacing the typical twelve-book poetic structure of the classical epic. True heroism is now represented, not as proud martial or adventurous action, but as the gaining of humility ultimately through the knowledge and practice of faith, hope, and charity, and in Dante's case, by a final, transcendent vision of the cosmic "volume" ingathered in the Godhead.

Although called a comedy by its author (*Inf.* 16.128; 21.2) in the medieval sense of a vernacular work with action leading from a low to a high spiritual state, Dante's work, with its deep seriousness of purpose, cosmic perspectives, spiritual journey theme, and visionary conclusion, exemplifies the epic tradition and, as the weight of critical opinion has generally held, constitutes in itself a new kind of epic poem. The *Commedia* is a singular encyclopedic example of classical epic transformed by a Christian ethos and ethical vision.

Bibliography

Bowra, Cecil Maurice. *From Virgil to Milton.* London: Macmillan & Co., 1945.

Dante e la "bella scola" della poesia: Autorità e sfida poetica. Edited by Amilcare A. Iannucci. Ravenna: Longo, 1993.

Demaray, John G. *Cosmos and Epic Representation: Dante, Spenser, Milton and the Transformation of Renaissance Heroic Poetry.* Pittsburgh, Pa.: Duquesne University Press, 1991.

Graf, Arturo. *Dell'epica neo-Latina primitiva. Studio. pt. 1.* Roma, 1876.

Hollander, Robert. "Dante and the Martial Epic." *Mediaevalia* 12 (1989 for 1986), 67–91.

Lansing, Richard. *From Image to Idea: A Study of Simile in Dante's Commedia.* Ravenna: Longo Editore, 1977.

Newman, John Kevin. *The Classical Epic Tradition.* Madison: University of Wisconsin, 1986, pp. 244–281.

Thompson, David. *Dante's Epic Journeys.* Baltimore and London: Johns Hopkins University Press, 1974.

Vossler, Karl. *Medieval Culture: An Introduction to Dante and His Times.* Translated by William Cranston Lawton. 2 vols. London: Constable & Co., 1929.

John G. Demaray

Epicureans

Followers of the philosopher Epicurus. In antiquity the Epicureans *(Epicurei)* were one of the largest and most influential philosophical sects. Dante's seemingly inconsistent references to them have occasioned puzzlement. In the *Commedia* the only doctrine identified as Epicurean is mortalism (the doctrine of the mortality of the soul), the featured mode of heresy in *Inf.* 10; its representatives, other than Epicurus, are all moderns: Farinata degli Uberti and Cavalcante dei Cavalcanti, both of whom appear and speak with the pilgrim, and Frederick II of Hohenstaufen and Cardinal Ottaviano degli Ubaldini, who are only mentioned. (It has been argued that Dante's real targets were the Averroists, who were mortalists, or the Cathars, who were not.) The treatment of Epicureanism in *Inf.* 10, drawing on Augustine's discussions of Acts 17:18, representing Epicurean mortalism among Christians as leading to a cult of bodily pleasure (derived from Is. 22:13 and 1 Cor. 15:32), is consistent with the bitter condemnation of mortalism in *Conv.* 2.8.7–12, where, however, neither Epicurus nor his followers are mentioned, and with *Conv.* 4.22.15, where the Epicureans, Peripatetics, and Stoics are identified as the "three sects of the active life," who must inevitably learn that happiness consists in contemplation, thus not in this life (a major theme in *Inf.* 10 as well, which, like *Conv.* 4.22, draws on the visit of the three Marys to the tomb of Christ in the Gospels).

The most puzzling reference to the Epicureans occurs in *Conv.* 3.14.15, part of the allegorical interpretation of the canzone *"Amor che ne la mente mi ragiona"* as written in praise of philosophy (the love of divine Wisdom): Dante imagines a "celestial Athens" *(quella celestiale Atene),* in which, thanks to the faith, hope, and love instilled by philosophy, "through the light of the eternal truth" *(per l'al[bo]re de la veritade eterna),* Stoics, Peripatetics, and Epicureans "concur harmoniously in one will" *(in un volere concordevolmente concorrono),* a syncretic optimism that hardly seems consistent with the harsh condemnations cited above. The apparent contradiction has been explained by supposing that when he wrote the *Convivio* Dante was unaware that Epicurus and his followers were mortalists, but this explanation seems unlikely.

Bibliography

Brown, Emerson, Jr. "Epicurean Secularism in Dante and Boccaccio: Athenian Roots and Florentine Revival." In *Magister Regis: Studies in Honor of Robert Earl Kaske.* Edited by Arthur Groos, with Emerson Brown, Jr., Giuseppe Mazzotta, Thomas D. Hill, and Joseph S. Wittig. New York: Fordham University Press, 1986, pp. 179–193.

Lucchesi, Valerio. "Epicurus and Democritus: The Ciceronian Foundations of Dante's Judgement." *Italian Studies* 42 (1987), 1–19.

Mazzeo, J. A. "Dante and Epicurus." *Comparative Literature* 10 (1958), 106–120.

Pézard, André. "Un Dante épicurien?" In *Mélanges offerts à Étienne Gilson.* Paris: Vrin, 1959, pp. 499–536.

Robert M. Durling

Epicurus

Greek philosopher (341–270 B.C.E.), born in Samos, resident mainly in Athens. Of the numerous works written by Epicurus *(Epicuro),* only a few have survived. None of them was known to Dante, whose knowledge of his teachings was derived from Aristotle, Cicero, Augustine, and others. Developing a form of atomism derived from the pre-Socratic Democritus, Epicurus held that the world was the product of chance combinations of atoms falling through the void. He denied the immortality of the soul and the interference in human affairs of the gods (who exist, but in serene detachment). Since the soul is itself a combination of atoms dispersed at death, hopes and fears for the afterlife are vain. Happiness is to live serenely, without passion and without pain: Epicurus defined pleasure as the highest good, but in terms of tranquillity, not sensuous pleasure. He avoided controversy, urging his followers to exist in harmonious friendship; his tranquil and virtuous existence was famous and much admired in antiquity.

The only explicit mentions of Epicurus himself (as opposed to the Epicureans) in Dante's works occur at *Inf.* 10.14, where he is condemned as a heresiarch (heretic) for his mortalism (belief in the mortality of the soul); in *Conv.* 4.6.11–12, where his doctrine of pleasure is summarized in relatively neutral terms, on the basis of Cicero's *De finibus bonorum et malorum,* Book 2; and in passing, in *Mon.* 2.5.10.

Robert M. Durling

Epicycle

In Greek astronomy, an epicycle is a small sphere that is "carried upon" (Greek *epikyklos,* Latin *epicyclus*) the circumference of a larger sphere, called the "carrier," or deferent. This arrangement was known to Apollonius of Perga (fl. 230 B.C.E.) and perhaps to earlier Greek astronomers, but it was Ptolemy (fl. 150 C.E.) who first used it extensively as a geometrical representation of certain irregular movements of the planets. Before Ptolemy, most astronomers had assumed that the seven planets were each borne on a single sphere, the center of the planet being located on the sphere's circumference. Instead, Ptolemy hypothesized that a smaller sphere was so located, with the planet on its circumference.

Ptolemy used epicycles to explain the retrograde movement of the superior planets—Mars, Jupiter, and Saturn—all of which occasionally reverse their periodic movement from east to west and move in the opposite direction from the motion of the fixed stars, sometimes for several months. Moreover, epicycles served to explain the oscillation of Mercury and Venus, which both accompany the Sun but move from one side of it to the other, appearing alternately as morning and evening stars. In the case of the Moon, Ptolemy used an epicycle to account for observed variations in her speed during the course of a lunar month. He decided not to give the Sun an epicycle, even though he was able to show that this could account for apparent variations in the speed of its annual progress through the zodiac. Instead, following the principle of economy, Ptolemy got the same results with a simpler equivalent device, namely, by assuming that the center of the Sun's rotation was offset from the axis around which the earth and the fixed stars rotate (*Almagest* 3.3).

Dante mentions the epicycle of Venus in *Par.* 8.3; he explains the concept in *Conv.* 2.3.15–16, and in *Conv.* 2.5.16–17 he declares that since an epicycle has its own movement, it must have its own mover, namely an angelic intelligence. Although Ptolemy considered both the epicycle and its deferent to be mathematical constructs, Dante and his contemporaries assumed that they were material bodies. Strange to say, Dante ignores the difficulty of having one solid, continually bearing another, pass through the surface of another solid.

Bibliography

Campanus of Novara. *Campanus of Novara and Medieval Planetary Theory: "Theorica planetarum."* Edited and translated by Francis S. Benjamin, Jr., and G. J. Toomer. Madison: University of Wisconsin Press, 1971.

Poulle, Emmanuel. "Epiciclo." *Enciclopedia dantesca*, 2: 697.

Ptolemy (Claudius Ptolemaeus). *The Almagest.* Translated by R. Catesby Taliaferro. In *Great Books of the Western World.* Edited by Robert M. Hutchins and Mortimer J. Adler. Vol. 16. Chicago: Encyclopaedia Brittanica, 1952, pp. ix–477.

Richard Kay

Epistle to Cangrande

1. Introduction

At the center of a series of philological and interpretive polemics over the last two centuries, the so-called *Epistle to Cangrande* is usually included as the thirteenth and last of the Latin letters attributed to Dante Alighieri. This practice continues despite the following significant obstacles: (1) the authenticity of the document's attribution to Dante has been seriously debated since early in the nineteenth century; (2) the document appears later in the early manuscript tradition than the other twelve epistles, and separate from them; and (3) at the most, six of the thirty-three paragraphs into which the document is conventionally divided by modern editors can reasonably be said to be written in the epistolary mode. The importance of the *Epistle* has been widely recognized in the modern critical tradition, especially certain of the individual topics it treats. Other significant aspects of the *Epistle* have received less extensive treatment, though the balance is now being redressed to some extent (cf. Minnis & Scott, Barański, Ascoli).

2. Description

The *Epistle to Cangrande* is composed of three, or four, major sections. The first four paragraphs are a formal letter composed according to the medieval *ars dictandi* and addressed to "The magnificent and victorious lord, Lord Cangrande della Scala, Vicar general of most holy Caesar in Verona and Vicenza" from his servant and friend, "Dante Alighieri, Florentine by birth but not in manners." This section culminates in the offer of the only gift worthy of such a friend, "the highest canticle of the *Commedia,* which is ornamented with the title of *Paradise.*" Having completed this dedication and "exhausted the formula of the epistle," the speaker then turns "in the office of *lector* [that is, reader or commentator]" to introduce the proffered work. The bulk of the text is then composed of two major sections. The first, covering para. 5 to 16, is a formal introduction to the *Commedia* as a whole and the *Paradiso* in particular, following a modified, and occasionally idiosyncratic, version of the academic prologue or *accessus ad auctorem* scheme used in conjunction with the study of literary and other authoritative texts in the later Middle Ages (cf. Moore, Curtius, Nardi, Minnis & Scott). It covers six basic topics—the subject, the form, the title, the "agent" or author, the purpose, and the philosophical genus of the work—all derived from the *accessus* tradition. The second, beginning in para. 17 and continuing through the end of the text, presents itself as a literal (as against an allegorical) commentary on the *Paradiso,* again modeled on the medieval exegetical tradition as it had developed during thirteenth-century Scholasticism. The commentator divides the canticle in two parts, the prologue (*Par.* 1.1–36) and the "executive part"— that is, all the rest. The commentary in fact treats primarily the first part of the prologue (1–12 [para. 18–30]), while the second part of the prologue receives one paragraph and part of a second (para. 31–32), and the executive part is treated summarily in the final paragraph. Only in the penultimate paragraph does the first-person address to Cangrande resume, immediately breaking off with a plea of poverty and for continued patronage, sometimes seen as reflecting an abjection unworthy of the "true" Dante.

3. Contexts

Dante criticism, especially American Dante criticism, has typically treated the *Epistle* in relative isolation and as a privileged key to interpretation of the *Commedia.* Nonetheless, recent scholarship has established that it is best understood in terms of three interlocking contexts which condition both its form and its content, and has begun to see it as work to be studied in its own right. The first context, noted above, is the twelfth- and thirteenth-century tradition of academic prologues (or *accessus*) and commentaries written in Latin upon authoritative Latin texts. The second is Dante's own well-established practice of self-reflective theorizing about his own language and poetics, and in particular his propensity (virtually unique among contemporary vernacular writers) for the formal device of self-commentary, as carried out in two hybrid vernacular works, *Vita Nuova* and *Convivio.* The *Epistle* presents itself at the outset as just such an authorial self-exegesis, and it contains numerous verbal and conceptual recalls of *Convivio*

(Brugnoli). The third context is the unprecedented series of Latin and Italian prologues and commentaries by various hands on the *Commedia* which emerged after Dante's death and grew rapidly over the course of the fourteenth century (other contemporary vernacular and Latin texts, like Cavalcanti's "Donna me prega" and Mussato's *Ecerinis,* received individual commentaries but did not generate a tradition). Though the *Epistle* has features which set it apart from other *Commedia* commentaries—notably, the claim to be written by the author himself; the hybrid combination of letter, accessus, and commentary; and the focus on the opening of *Paradiso*—it clearly belongs in this tradition, though where remains a matter of debate. Framed within these three contexts, the *Epistle* points to Dante's pivotal role in conferring on vernacular authors and works an intellectual and artistic standing approaching that of the Latin *auctores* (Ascoli).

4. Analysis

Despite its relative brevity, the *Epistle* has not, with a few extravagant exceptions, received the close critical scrutiny that one might expect for a Dantean, or even pseudo-Dantean text. One hopes that recent efforts in this direction (e.g., Costa, Botterill) will soon be joined by others, although in the present context, one can only signal a very few topics, those which have in fact attracted a preponderance of critical attention in the past. The first, epistolary, and third commentary sections have gone relatively unattended to. In the epistolary section proper, of greatest note may be the extended proof that an inferior (that is, Dante) can legitimately call himself the "friend" of a social superior (Cangrande). This passage (para. 2–3) recalls a series of authentically Dantean passages in which "friendship" is a crucial category (e.g., *VN* 3.24–25; *DVE* 1.10, 17; 2.2, 5–6; *Conv.* 1.12–13; 3.11–12; *Inf.* 2.61; etc.). The final, "commentary" section (para. 17–32) has attracted the least attention of all. Of note, in any case, are: (1) the scholarly debate over possible contradictions between the *Epistle*'s definition of the Empyrean heaven and that of the *Commedia* (para. 24; cf. Brugnoli); (2) the commentator's defense of "Dante's" apparently hubristic claim to have experienced the mysteries of heaven (para. 28), and in particular the triple citation of Richard of St. Victor, Augustine, and Bernard probed by Botterill; and (3) the extensive neoplatonic culture reflected

E throughout this section, notably in a series of allusions to the *Liber de Causis.*

The central *accessus* section has traditionally excited the most critical commentary because it addresses topics of greatest direct relevance to the *Commedia.* Most famously, the seventh paragraph illustrates the functioning of allegory with a four-fold scheme taken over from biblical exegesis. The basic literal or historical sense is set alongside three allegorical senses: (1) the allegorical proper, which pertains to the life of Christ (or, traditionally, the history of the Church) and thus to the ful-fillment of the Old Testament in the New; (2) the moral or tropological, which pertains to the actions of the individual soul in this life; and (3) the ana-gogical, which pertains to the life to come. All four senses are then illustrated with reference to the Old Testament story of Exodus. This passage has been cited by critics, notably Singleton and Hollander *(Allegory),* in support of the argument that the *Commedia* deliberately imitates "God's way of writing" in the Bible, rather than using the twofold "allegory of poets" where a fictive literal sense is accompanied by a subjacent moral allegory (cf. *Conv.* 2.1). Against this, one should note that: (1) the fourfold model had already been applied to "secular" texts (e.g., Conrad of Hirsau's late twelfth-century *Dialogus super auctores*); (2) no direct application of the fourfold scheme is made to the *Commedia;* (3) the passage is not directed specifically at defining the poem's subject, but rather at explaining the word "allegory"; and (4) the next paragraph defines the poem's subject in terms of a twofold model, the literal significance of the poem being "the state of the souls after death" and its allegorical significance being "man, in the exercise of his free will, earning or becom-ing liable to the rewards or punishments of jus-tice." Still, it is certainly the case that even this ambivalent and ambiguous invocation of the four biblical senses suggests a daring rapprochement of Dante's poetic opus to Scriptures.

A second notably controversial heading is that of the "title" where the term "comedy" is given two derivations, both ostensibly applicable to the poem (para. 10). In the first instance "comedy" is seen in dialectical relation with "tragedy," as describing a plot which "begins in misery and ends in happiness." In the second instance it is seen as describing the style of the work, which is "lowly and humble" because it is written in the inferior idiom of the Italian vernacular. The latter defini-tion in particular has been seen as inadequate, and possibly non-Dantean, because it is in clear con-tradiction with *DVE* 2.4, where the vernacular is assigned a greater nobility than Latin and allowed the full range of styles from "high" tragic style to "low" elegiac style, and because it seems to ignore both the ambitions of the *poema sacro* and its "plurilingual" stylistic range (Barański).

Finally, the brief heading of *agens,* or "agent" (para. 15) has generated a certain perplexity, though more in Italy than in the United States. The main problem is the unusualness of the word *agens* (the heading is usually *vita auctoris* or *causa effi-ciens*), the only other attested appearance being in Guido da Pisa's commentary to which it may have a direct genetic filiation (see the following section, "Authenticity"). This oddity has led Mazzoni to argue that the heading refers not to Dante as "author" of the *Commedia,* but rather to the char-acter Dante whose journey is described. Mazzoni's hypothesis, however, founders because this head-ing, whatever word stands before it, invariably refers to the writer of a work in the *accessus* tra-dition, and the *Epistle* makes no overt effort what-soever to redefine the term.

5. Authenticity

Over the last two centuries the authenticity of the *Epistle* has been questioned repeatedly. A few crit-ics insist that the document as a whole is a forgery; others, more numerous, accept the authenticity of the epistolary section (para. 1–4; cf. Nardi; Mancini), which appears separately in the earliest manuscript tradition, while contesting that of the rest. In what initially appears as a prima facie case for authenticity, several locutions from the *acces-sus* section of the *Epistle* are duplicated verbatim in major Trecento *Commedia* commentaries, notably Guido da Pisa's *Expositio,* usually dated to shortly after Dante's death (c. 1324), and Boccac-cio's *accessus* to his lectures on *Inferno,* written much later in the century (c. 1373; cf. Mazzoni; Jenaro-MacLennan). As opponents to authenticity have noted, however, the *Epistle* per se is not cited, nor, a fortiori, attributed to Dante, before Filippo Villani in the early fifteenth century, from which period the earliest manuscripts also date. With this excuse, ingenious though not fully convincing, arguments have been adduced for the *Epistle* deriving from Guido and the others, rather than the reverse (most elaborately by Kelly). Most discus-sions of the question, even those in which arguments concerning dating and textual filiation are prominent, are driven by interpretive concerns of content and style.

Arguments concerning content generally reflect the particular critic's sense of whether certain passages in the *Epistle* support his or her interpretation of Dante's poetics in the *Commedia*. Thus the first questioner of the *Epistle*'s authenticity, Filippo Scolari, saw its mystical, theological emphasis as incompatible with what he believed to be Dante's exclusive emphasis on neo-Ghibelline politics. Thus, more recently, Nardi argued that the definition of the poem's subject in para. 9 is non-Dantean because it does not specifically account for the centrality of the drama of Dante-pilgrim. And thus, as noted above, Mazzoni attempts to counter Nardi by arguing that Dante-pilgrim *is* present in the *Epistle* as the *agens*. None of these arguments is fully convincing. The debates over the appropriateness of the *Epistle*'s definitions of the poem's literal/allegorical subjects and its title (para. 7–8, 10) also tend to elicit corresponding affirmations or negations of authenticity. All of these debates have been fruitful at times, but they have not been resolved because: (1) they depend on complex, unverifiable interpretive judgments and personal taste; (2) they rarely take into account Dante's well-established propensity for changing his mind between works and over time; and (3) they almost always isolate single passages for discussion and rarely attempt to understand the role of these passages within the *Epistle* as a whole.

Stylistic concerns have been raised at times regarding a perceived lack of correspondence between the *Epistle*'s diction and that in the authenticated canon. Much recent discussion of style, however, has centered around claims that the quantity and quality of metered prose, or *cursus,* in the *Epistle* differ significantly from those in Dante's other letters and Latin writings (e.g., Dronke, Kelly; cf. Hollander *Dante's Epistle,* Ascoli). Though the question remains open, no convincing version of this argument has yet been made. Its proponents invariably fall into one or more of the following traps: (1) they treat the *Epistle* as a whole as if it were a letter, when it is not; (2) they do not compare the *accessus* and commentary sections with typical usage of *cursus* (or lack thereof) in contemporary examples of these genres by other hands; and (3) they note differences in use of the *cursus* between the *Epistle* and canonical Dantean works without noting that differences also exist among those works.

6. Conclusion

While the authenticity of the *Epistle to Cangrande* remains doubtful and, barring new manuscript evidence, will remain so, its importance as a document in the tradition of Dante criticism is certain, independently of who its author may have been. Unfortunately, focus on the empirically moot question of authorship has had the pernicious effect of distracting attention from several historically highly significant features of the *Epistle,* including these three: (1) its innovative juxtaposition of poetry with other modes of discourse, especially the Bible itself, in the *accessus* paragraphs on subject matter and form; (2) its symbolic importance in the process of "authorizing" vernacular poetry by conferring on it a cultural prestige and respect previously reserved for Latin works; (3) its deployment of a formal structure of self-exegesis which is clearly inspired by authentic works of Dante (notably, *Vita Nuova* and *Convivio*), whether or not it was actually written by him, and which points toward a self-reflexive modality of authorship that, from Petrarch forward, becomes a hallmark of the humanistic Renaissance. It is to be hoped that future studies of the text will be more open to explorations of it "on its own terms," rather than on its pertinence, or lack thereof, to an understanding of the *Commedia,* and in relation to the full range of cultural contexts from which it evidently emerges.

Bibliography

Alighieri, Dante. *Epistole.* Edited by Arsenio Frugoni and Giorgio Brugnoli. In Dante Alighieri, *Opere minori,* Vol. 2. Edited by Pier Vincenzo Mengaldo et al. Milan and Naples: Ricciardi, 1979.

Ascoli, Albert Russell. "Access to Authority: Dante in the *Epistle to Cangrande.*" In *Seminario dantesco internazionale / International Dante Seminar I.* Edited by Zygmunt Barański. Florence: Le Lettere, 1997, 309–352.

Barański, Zygmunt. "*Comedia.* Notes on Dante, the Epistle to Can Grande, and Medieval Comedy." *Lectura Dantis* 8 (1991), 26–55.

Botterill, Steven. "'Quae non licet homini loqui': The Ineffability of Mystical Experience in *Paradiso* 1 and the *Epistle to Can Grande.*" *Modern Language Review* 83 (1988), 332–341.

E

Costa, Dennis. "One Good Reception Deserves Another: The Epistle to Can Grande." *Stanford Italian Review* 5 (1985), 5–17.

Curtius, Ernst R. *European Literature in the Latin Middle Ages.* Translated by W. R. Trask. Princeton, N.J.: Princeton University Press, 1953, pp. 357–362.

Dronke, Peter. *Dante and the Medieval Latin Traditions.* Cambridge: Cambridge University Press, 1986.

Hollander, Robert. *Dante's Epistle to Cangrande.* Ann Arbor: University of Michigan Press, 1993.

———. *Allegory in Dante's "Commedia."* Princeton, N.J.: Princeton University Press, 1969.

Jenaro-MacLennan, Luis. *The Trecento Commentaries on the "Divina Commedia" and the "Epistle to Cangrande."* Oxford: Clarendon Press, 1974.

Kelly, Henry Ansgar. *Tragedy and Comedy from Dante to Pseudo-Dante.* Berkeley: University of California Press, 1989.

Mancini, Augusto. "Nuovi dubbi ed ipotesi sulla Epistola a Cangrande." *Atti del Reale Accademia d'Italia. Rendiconti, Classe di Scienze morali, storiche e filologiche.* Ser. 7, 4 (1943), 227–242.

Mazzoni, Francesco. "Per l'Epistola a Cangrande." In *Contributi di filologia dantesca.* Florence: Sansoni, 1966, pp. 7–37.

———. "L'Epistola a Cangrande." *Rendiconti della Accademia Nazionale dei Lincei. Classe di Scienze morali, storiche e filologiche.* Ser. 8, 10 (1955), 157–198.

Minnis, A. J., and A. B. Scott. *Medieval Literary Theory and Criticism, c. 1100–c.1375: The Commentary Tradition.* Oxford: Clarendon Press, 1988.

Moore, Edward. "The Genuineness of the Dedicatory Epistle to Can Grande." In *Studies in Dante, Third Series.* Oxford: Clarendon Press, 1903, pp. 284–369.

Nardi, Bruno. "Osservazioni sul medievale 'accessus ad auctor' in rapporto al *Epistola a Cangrande.*" In *Saggi e note di critica dantesca.* Milan and Naples: Ricciardi, 1966, pp. 268–305.

———. *Il punto sull'Epistola.* Florence: Le Monnier, 1960.

Paolazzi, Carlo. *Dante e la "Comedia" nel Trecento: Dall'Epistola a Cangrande all'età di Petrarca.* Milan: Pubblicazioni della Università Cattolica, 1989, pp. 3–110.

Scolari, Filippo. *Intorno alle epistole latine di Dante Allighieri.* Venice: Tipografia all' Ancora, 1844.

Singleton, Charles S. *Dante Studies 1. Commedia: Elements of Structure.* Cambridge, Mass.: Harvard University Press, 1954.

Albert Russell Ascoli

Epistles

Not all of the Latin epistles which Dante wrote throughout his life survive. Leonardo Bruni (1369–1444), chancellor to the Florentine republic, in his *Life of Dante* (1436) mentions seeing (probably in the archive of the Florentine chancery) many letters by Dante, some in his own "long, lean, and very correct" hand, and addressed to the rulers of Florence and to individual citizens, as well as to the people. Bruni cites the opening words of one, *"Popule mee, quid feci tibi?"* ("My people, what have I done to you?"), in which Dante asked to be allowed to return to Florence. Writing a century before, Giovanni Villani (*Cronica* 10.136) also mentions this epistle as well the present Epistles 7 and 11. In another epistle known to Bruni, Dante told of the Battle of Campaldino (1289) and his own part in it. Bruni also translates part of a letter in which Dante declares that all his troubles began with his term as prior in the summer of 1300. In another Dante defended himself against the charge of favoring the White Guelfs.

We know of other letters that did not survive. The poet Cecco d'Ascoli says that Dante had written to him from Ravenna, but we do not know if this was an exchange of poems or a Latin epistle with an Italian poem (*L'Acerba* II, 13), as in Dante's third epistle. Dante himself in *Vita Nuova* 30.1–2 mentions an epistle to the princes of the earth composed after Beatrice's death (1290) which has likewise vanished, if in fact it ever existed.

Of the thirteen surviving epistles the twelve that are accepted as authentic appear in two fourteenth-century Tuscan manuscript miscellanies. Giovanni Boccaccio's *Zibaldone* (1350), Laurenziano plut. 29, 8, provides the sole copy of epistles 3, 11, and 12. Vaticano Palatino 1729, which was composed in 1394 by Francesco Piendibeni, a friend and correspondent of another Florentine chancellor, Coluccio Salutati, contains the other nine epistles: 1, 2, 4, 5, 6, 7, 8, 9, 10, along with Dante's *Monarchia* and Petrarch's *Bucolicum Carmen.*

What is now called the thirteenth letter, the *Epistle to Cangrande della Scala,* stands in a separate category. It is first mentioned as written by Dante only in 1402 by Filippo Villani, although many earlier commentators referred to it without naming its author. It appears in neither of the two cited manuscript collections. It is found in nine fifteenth- and sixteenth-century manuscripts from northern Italy. The three oldest give just the strictly epistolary section (§§1–4) and the six later ones give the entire text—a fact which can be interpreted to mean that the remaining text, consisting of an *accessus* (§5–16) or introduction to the *Commedia* and exposition of *Par.* 1.1–38 (§17–31), is a later fabrication. Scolari (1819) thought it the forgery of an ancient commentator. Witte (1855), Giuliani (1882), and Torraca (1899) defended its authenticity. D'Ovidio's curt rejection (1899) reopened the question. Moore's vigorous defense (1903) prevailed well into the 1960s, particularly in the English-speaking world, despite the demurs of Pietrobono (1937) and Mancini (1943). Schneider (1957), Hardie (1960), and Nardi (1960, 1961) reopened the debate. Brugnoli's edition (1978) declared its status an open question. Dronke (1986) challenged the *Epistle* because its *cursus* (rhythmic endings for sentences and clauses) are frequent in the epistolary section but rare elsewhere in the document. Kelly (1989) rejected it on several grounds. Hollander (1993) in an overview of the entire controversy argued forcefully for its authenticity. Opinion remains divided: some accept the entire text as genuine, others just the opening epistolary section; and others reject the entire text as a forgery. The evidence is so problematical that probably no side will succeed in resolving the matter to the satisfaction of all. Nevertheless, it continues to be printed with the twelve indisputably authentic epistles.

Several epistles attributed to Dante have long been considered forgeries. G. M. Filelfo (1426–1480) mentioned epistles from Dante to the king of the Huns, Pope Boniface, and a son-in-law—all now lost and believed to be the work of Filelfo himself. A. F. Doni published in 1547 an epistle to Guido da Polenta, supposedly sent on March 30, 1314. Toynbee's demonstration that it is forgery has been universally accepted. The subsequent appearance of twenty manuscripts indicate that Doni may have published it in good faith. Thus it still appears to be a forgery but not by Doni.

The canon of Dante's epistles was established by two editions early in the twentieth century: Toynbee 1920, and Pistilli the following year for the Società Dantesca Italiana. The first twelve epistles vary greatly in subject and style. Unlike Petrarch's two collections of epistles, the *Familiares* and *Seniles,* composed later in the fourteenth century, Dante's epistles were never intended to be read together (or separately) as literary texts. Nor were they meant to shed light on the *Commedia,* with the possible exception of the letter to Cangrande, or on any of his other literary works.

Writing from Arezzo late in winter 1304 on behalf of fellow Florentine exiles, Dante addressed the first epistle to Cardinal Niccolò da Prato in Florence, thanking him for his peacemaking efforts and promising to refrain from acts of aggression.

He addressed the second epistle to the Counts Oberto and Guido da Romena, probably in the spring or early summer of 1304, consoling them on the death of their uncle Count Alessandro. After praising the deceased's virtues, Dante apologizes for not attending his funeral due to poverty—a veiled request, perhaps, for economic assistance. He later overturned his high opinion of Alessandro, assigning him to the circle of traitors (*Inf.* 30.76–77).

In the heading to the third epistle as it appears in Boccaccio's *Zibaldone,* Dante describes himself as "a Florentine in undeserved exile"—a formula which first appeared in the previous epistle and is repeated in epistles 5, 6, and 7. He sent this brief letter probably around 1305–1306 to his fellow poet, the jurist Cino da Pistoia, who had inquired in a sonnet whether the soul can "pass from passion to passion." In response Dante argues that reason and authority alike confirm that it can, as demonstrated by the tale of Apollo and Leucothoë (Ovid, *Meta.* 4.192–197, 204–208). He included a sonnet to Cino, *"Io sono stato con amore insieme."*

Dante spent the fall of 1309 as a guest of the Malaspina family in Lunigiana (*Purg.* 8.133–139), serving them as procurator in successful negotiations with the bishop of Luni. After his departure, but before 1310, he wrote the fourth epistle to a member of the Malaspina family usually identified as Moroello III (*Inf.* 24.145). In this epistle, Dante recounts how after he had left Moroello the appearance of a beautiful woman whom he had met in the valley of the Arno took possession of him and utterly subjugated his will, as recounted

E in the enclosed canzone, *"Amor, da che convien pur ch'io mi doglia."* In his *Trattatello in laude di Dante,* Boccaccio claimed that Moroello had persuaded Dante to continue the *Inferno,* which he had begun in Florence before exile in January 1302, and that consequently Dante dedicated the entire *Purgatorio* to him.

Dante composed the next three political epistles to gather support for the emperor Henry VII on his arrival in Italy in autumn 1310. These impassioned letters bristle with biblical (and to a lesser extent classical) quotations and allusions. He wrote the fifth epistle in the fall of 1310 after Pope Clement V's encyclical, *"Exultet in gloria,"* which approved Henry's election as emperor. Echoing the language and style of the papal letters, Dante addressed this political manifesto in the form of a circular letter to all the rulers of Italy, presenting Henry as a political messiah with universal sovereignty, a second Augustus, the bridegroom of Italy, the sun of justice, and a figure of Christ who will bring peace. The epistle enjoyed wide circulation. From the Casentino on March 31, 1311, Dante directed the sixth epistle to "the most iniquitous Florentines inside the city," informing them that God ordained the office of emperor just as he had that of the pope. Therefore those who, like the Florentines, oppose Henry also oppose God and risk destruction by divine vengeance. He likens Italy to a storm-tossed ship as he does in *Purg.* 6.77. Two weeks later on April 17, 1311, speaking like a biblical prophet, he sent the seventh epistle to Henry (whom he had met) and "all peace-loving Tuscans," comparing the emperor to Aeneas, Hercules, and David, and inviting him to enter Italy and especially Florence, the center of corruption.

The next three very short letters were thought to be forgeries until Moore (1914) proved their authenticity. They are so similar in content that some believe them to be versions of a single letter. Dante composed them in the Casentino at the Castle of Poppi in April and May 1311 in the name of the Gherardesca, Countess of Battifolle, the wife of Count Guido, whose secretary he was and who had just joined the Ghibelline cause. All three are addressed to the empress Margaret of Brabant, wife of Henry VII. In the eighth epistle the countess thanks the empress for her letter and prays for the emperor's success in reforming "the human family in this crazy age." In the ninth letter she thanks the empress for news of the emperor's

progress and asks her protection. In the tenth letter, dated May 18, 1311, she again thanks the empress for news of Henry's success and informs her that she and her family are in good health.

In the following three years the situation of both Empire and Church worsened dramatically from Dante's point of view. After being crowned emperor in Rome in June 1312, Henry VII died unexpectedly in August of the following year. The Gascon (or French) pope, Clement V (1305–1314), had transferred the papacy to Avignon in 1309 and appointed a large majority of French cardinals. Dante composed the eleventh epistle, more a lay sermon than a traditional missive, a month or two after Clement's death on April 20, 1314. In it he addressed the six Italian cardinals gathered, with eighteen others, at the conclave at Carpentras near Avignon to elect a new pope. He blames the cardinals for transferring the papacy from Rome to Avignon. They worship riches, not God, and study canon law, not church fathers. The cardinals should be ashamed that a private individual rather than they themselves has raised this issue. Dante opens this letter with the opening words of Jeremiah's Lamentations, *"Quomodo sola sedet civitas"* ("How solitary sits the city"), which he had also applied to Beatrice's death in the *VN* (28.1). This epistle was well known: Villani mentions it (*Cronica* 10.136), and Petrarch quotes one of its verses in his canzone "Spirto gentil, che quelle membra reggi," *Rerum vulgarium fragmenta* 53 (1336–1337). It had, however, no effect. The French party, fearing that an Italian pope might restore the papacy to Rome, broke into the conclave, weapons in hand, guided by the late pope's nephew, shouting, "Death to the Italian cardinals," and drove them out of the conclave. Of Dante's surviving epistles, this comes closest to the tone and style of the *Commedia.* Its intense prophetic language recalls that of certain passages in the *Paradiso,* such as St. Peter's diatribe against his successors (*Par.* 27.19–148).

Dante addressed the lucid and flowing Latin of the twelfth epistle to an unnamed friend in Florence, probably sometime after the amnesty of May 19, 1315. Dante and his correspondent are probably related, as they share a nephew (probably Filippo Donati, the son of the brother of Dante's wife, Gemma). His correspondent may also be a priest because Dante twice addresses him as "father," and says that he received his letter with "due reverence." Dante thanks him for the concern shown for his ongoing exile. He concludes from a letter which he has received from their common nephew that his return to Florence is possible provided he accept humiliating conditions—i.e., pay a fine and undergo the "stigma of oblation," a public ceremony in which the malefactor, dressed in sackcloth and wearing a paper mitre with his name and offense on it, was escorted from prison to the baptistery to be offered by a sponsor at the altar to God and St. John. Dante says that if an innocent man cannot return honorably, he will not return at all. He can contemplate the Sun and the stars and the most precious truths anywhere, not just in Florence. This is the only letter in which Dante names himself. In the six remaining years of his life, there is no trace of other epistles apart from the verse *Eclogues.*

Bibliography

Editions and Translations

Alighieri, Dante. *Epistole.* Edited by Arsenio Frugoni and Giorgio Brugnoli. In *Opere minori di Dante Alighieri,* II. Ed. P. V. Mengaldo et al. Milan and Naples: Ricciardi, 1979, pp. 507–563.

———. *Monarchy, and Three Political Letters.* Translated with an introduction by Donald Nicholl, and a note on the chronology of Dante's political works by Colin Hardie; with a new introduction for the Garland edition by Walter F. Bense. New York: Garland, 1972.

———. *Dantis Alagherii Epistolae: The Letters of Dante.* Edited by Paget Toynbee. Oxford: Clarendon Press, 1920.

Criticism

Ahern, John. "Come se fosse falso: Can the Epistle to Can Grande Be Read as a Forgery?" In *Atti del Primo Seminario Internazionale Dantesco.* Florence: Le Lettere, 1997, pp. 281–307.

Frugoni, Arsenio. "Dante tra due conclave. La lettera ai Cardinali italiani," *Letture Classensi* 2 (1969), 69–91.

———. "Le epistole." *Cultura e Scuola* 4 (1965), 739–748.

———. "Dante, *Epistola* XI, 24–25." *Rivista di cultura classica e medievale* 7 (1965), 477–486.

Hollander, Robert. *Dante's Epistle to Cangrande.* Ann Arbor: University of Michigan Press, 1993.

Kelly, Henry Ansgar. *Tragedy and Comedy from Dante to Pseudo-Dante.* Berkeley, Los Angeles, London: University of California Press, 1989.

Mazzoni, Francesco. "Le epistole di Dante." In *Conferenze aretine 1965.* Arezzo: Tipografia Zelli, 1966, pp. 47–100.

———. "Riflessioni sul testo dell'Epistola VII di Dante: vi fu un archetipo?" *Filologia e critica* 15 (1990), 434–444.

Migliorini Fissi, Rosetta. "La lettera pseudo-dantesca a Guido da Polenta: edizione critica e ricerche attributive." *Studi danteschi* 46 (1969), 101–272.

Moore, Edward. "The Battifolle Letters Sometimes Attributed to Dante." *Modern Language Review* 9 (1914), 173–189.

Morghen, Raffaelle. "La lettera ai cardinali italiani." *Bullettino dell'Istituto storico italiano per il Medio Evo* 68 (1956), 1–31.

Pastore Stocchi, Manlio. "Epistole." *Enciclopedia dantesca,* 2: 703–710.

Pézard, André. "Dante et l'Apocalypse de Carpentras *(Ep.* XI, 25: 1314–1316)." *Archives d'historie doctrinale et littéraire du Moyen Age* 50 (1983), 61–100.

John Ahern

Erard de Valéry

Famous crusader and knight, constable of Champagne, born around 1220 and exalted in the thirteenth-century French poetry of Rutebeuf. His military expertise was instrumental in the battle of Tagliacozzo (August 1268), for which Dante remembers him in *Inf.* 28.18: *Là da Tagliacozzo, / dove senz'arme vinse il vecchio Alardo* ("at Tagliacozzo where old Elard won without arms"). Serving as adviser to Charles I of Anjou, he devised the strategy of using fresh troops, held in reserve until the decisive moment, to overcome the disadvantage of having a smaller army and defeat the forces of Conradin. The phrase "without arms" refers to his use of cleverness in helping Charles achieve victory.

Pina Palma

Erichtho

A witch of Thessaly who figures prominently in Lucan's *Phars.* (6.507–830), Erichtho (*Eritòn, Inf.* 9.23) plays a crucial role in Dante's plotting of his and Virgil's itinerary through Hell since Virgil reports (9.22–30) that not long after his death she summoned his shade (her greatest power being the capacity to recall shades to their bodies) so that he might draw *"un spirto del cerchio di Giuda"* ("a spirit from the circle of Judas"). Thus Virgil can say to Dante the pilgrim that *"ben so 'l cammin; però ti fa sicuro"* ("well do I know the way, therefore be free of care"). In effect, then, this brief narrative serves to authorize Virgil as Dante's guide. Virgil is careful to describe the circle of Judas as *"'l più basso loco e 'l più oscuro, / e 'l più lontan dal ciel che tutto gira"* ("the lowest place and the darkest and the farthest from the sky that turns all things"). Virgil, in other words, has seen it all and can show it all to Dante.

It should be noted that most early commentators consider this account a fiction: Benvenuto, e.g., calls it a *fictio nova* ("a newly invented fiction"). It seems likely that Dante invented the story from his reading in Lucan, on the one hand, and on the other, from his familiarity with the ubiquitous medieval legends of Virgil as a magician.

It also seems likely that Virgil protests too much; i.e., the fiction participates in a pattern detectable elsewhere in *Inferno* (and *Purgatorio* too) that reveals definite limits on Virgil's capabilities. Moreover, Virgil's story is clearly crafted to allay the pilgrim's fear that Virgil will not succeed in overcoming the challenge of the devils who block their entrance into the City of Dis (9.1–3), which suggests that he may also be intending to provide a cover-up for his own failure as a guide at this point in the journey (cf. 9.10–12).

R. Allen Shoaf

Erysichthon

Son of King Triopas of Thessaly *(Erisittone)*. Impious and violent, he cut down trees in a sacred grove dedicated to Ceres, and was punished by the goddess with perpetual insatiable hunger. After having devoured all his possessions and allowed his daughter Mnestra to sell herself as a slave to procure funds for food, he finally died by eating his own flesh (Ovid, *Meta.* 8.738–878). Dante recalls his fate to describe the emaciated spirits who are expiating the sin of gluttony in the sixth terrace of Purgatory: *Non credo che così a buccia strema / Erisittone fosse fatto secco, / per digiunar, quando più n'ebbe tema* ("I do not think that Erysichthon was so dried up into a mere rind by his hunger, when it made him most afraid," *Purg.* 23.26–28).

Jo Ann Cavallo

Esau

Firstborn son of Isaac and Rebecca. Unlike his twin brother, Jacob, he was born red and hairy (Gen. 25:25). "A skillful hunter, a man of the field" while Jacob lived "in tents" (27), Esau became the father of the Edomites (Gen. 36:1, 9), who, as a rival people of the Israelites (descended from Jacob), suffered God's continued anger (Jer. 49:8, 10; Mal. 1:2–3). This supremacy of the younger over the elder brother was first signaled by their prenatal struggle (Gen. 25:22–23), an incident reinterpreted by the apostle Paul as a fulfillment of God's "purpose of election" (Rom. 9:10–13). Echoing Paul, Charles Martel attributes the differences or inequalities between the brothers, despite their shared parentage, to God's will, mediated through the Angelic Intelligences before birth. He observes that "A begotten nature would always take a path like that of the begetter, if God's Providence did not intervene" (*Par.* 8.133–135). Also following Paul (Rom. 9:19–24), St. Bernard confirms God's right to bestow grace diversely as he pleases (*Par.* 32.61–72). Benvenuto (contested by Boccaccio) associated the unnamed figure among the neutrals (who made the great refusal, *Inf.* 3.59–60) with Esau, who in Gen. 25:34 and Heb. 12:16–17 is criticized for having so despised his birthright that he refused it in giving it to his brother.

Carolynn Lund-Mead

Esther

Protagonist of a book of the Old Testament and Jewish queen of the Persian Ahasuerus, Esther *(Estèr)* saved the Jews from destruction by Haman, at the urging of her uncle Mordecai. An example of the faithful wife persuading her infidel husband to good in medieval teaching, as well as a figure for the Church in exegesis, she is mentioned by Dante simply as one of those looking at the crucified Haman, who is presented as an example of excessive wrath (*Purg.*17.29).

Joan M. Ferrante

Eteocles

Son of Oedipus and Jocasta, Eteocles *(Eteòcle)* and his twin brother, Polynices, kill each other over who was to succeed to the Theban throne, in the war depicted by Statius' *Thebaid,* the Seven against Thebes; hence Virgil's reference in *Purg.* 22.56 to the *doppia trestizia di Giocasta* ("Jocasta's two-fold sorrow"). The forked flame of their joint funeral pyre, alluded to in *Inf.* 26.52–54, indicates their lasting enmity. For Dante's sources see *Theb.* 12.429–432 and Lucan, *Phars.* 1.549–552.

Jessica Levenstein

Eternity

Eternity and time describe different measures of opposing realms. According to Aristotle, whose definition Dante cites in *Conv.* 4.2.6, time is a measure of movement, in particular of celestial movement. Eternity, properly speaking, is by contrast a timeless condition in which there is no movement or change. Near the end of the *Paradiso,* the poet, looking back upon his experience, characterizes his journey through the otherworld as a movement from time to eternity (*a l'etterno dal tempo, Par.* 31.38), from the secular world of evanescent value to those things of God that last. Eternity is enjoyed in the Empyrean heaven by the divine mind itself, by angels, and by blessed human souls. Yet the stars and the heavens are sometimes called eternal, although they were created and move (*etterne rote, etterna margarita, ninfe etterne; Par.* 1.64; 2.14; 23.26). So too is Hell, as its portal declares (*e io etterno duro),* alternately described as eternal sorrow, eternal darkness, eternal lamentation, eternal exile, and eternal prison (*etterno dolore, tenebre etterne, etterno pianto, etterno essilio, pregione etterna, Inf.* 3.2–8; 3.87; 9.44; 23.126; *Purg.* 1.41). These instances, implying an unlimited duration in time, would be more properly defined as "sempiternal" (cf. *Epist.* 13.71–74), especially since the unceasing flux that is part of the punishment of the damned is fundamentally different from the "complete possession all at once of illimitable life" (*Aeternitas igitur est interminabilis vitae tota simul et perfecta possessio, Consolation of Philosophy,* Book 5, Prose 6.8), as Boethius defined eternity for the Middle Ages. In his treatise on the Trinity (20.64ff), Boethius also compared eternity to a "now" that stands still *(nunc stans),* a present moment that endures, unlike the fleeting "now" of passing time. Although Dante makes no rigorous distinction in his use of "eternity" and "sempiternity," in many passages he alludes to the concept of eternity as a radically different mode of being. For example, in a summary of creation God is described as acting *in sua etternità di tempo fore* ("in his eternity, outside of time," *Par.* 29.16). In *VN* 12, Love's declaration that he, unlike the lover, resembles the center of a circle, equidistant from every part of the circumference, recalls a Boethian comparison of eternity's proportion to time with that of a point in relation to a circle (*Cons.* 4.6.17: *ad aeternitatem tempus, ad punctum medium circulus*). Similarly, in the pilgrim's final glimpse of divinity he sees everything that is spread out through the universe and through history reduced to a single point, or moment: *un punto solo m'è maggior letargo . . .* (*Par.* 33.94).

Alison Cornish

Euclid

Greek mathematician (c. 300 B.C.E.) who lived in Alexandria and is known for his *Elements.* Euclid *(Euclide)* assumes a character of unquestionable authority in the field of mathematics, particularly geometry, in the few times Dante mentions him. In *Mon.* 1.1.4 Dante groups Euclid, Aristotle, and Cicero together as three of the ancients with definitive and unassailable wisdom. In *Conv.* 2.13.26 Dante evokes the authority of Euclid who is reported to have held that the point is the principle of geometry. In *Inf.* 4.142 Euclid, identified as the *geomètra* ("geometer"), appears with the other virtuous pagans in Limbo.

Bibliography

Bulmer-Thomas, Ivor. "Euclid." In *Dictionary of Scientific Biography.* Vol. 4. New York: Charles Scribner's Sons, 1971, pp. 414–437.
Heath, Thomas L. *The Thirteen Books of Euclid's Elements.* 3 vols. New York: Dover, 1956.

George Andrew Trone

Eunoe

One of the two branches of the river that runs through the earthly paradise. The other branch, Lethe, removes the memory of sinful deeds; Eunoe *(Eünoè)* restores the memory of good deeds. The commentator Benvenuto remarks that, just as Eden was bounded by the Tigris and Euphrates, so Lethe girds Dante's terrestrial paradise on the left side, Eunoe on the right side. This is because the waters of forgetfulness carry away all memory of evil, which is always figured as on the left, or sinister side, in Christian thought. In contrast, Eunoe, whose etymology Benvenuto traces back to the Greek word meaning "favorable," flows to the right. The modern critic Charles Singleton more accurately locates its root in the Greek word for "well-minded," so that the neologism "Eünoè" is coined by Dante on the model of "Protonoè," a transliteration of an expression in Greek, taken from Uguccione da Pisa's *Magnae derivationes*. In the *Conv.* (2.3.11), Dante glosses Protonoè as *la prima Mente* ("the first [i.e., the divine] mind"). Unlike Lethe, which is mentioned in classical poetry, Eunoe is Dante's own poetic creation; drinking from the stream results in "eu + nous," thoughts and memories of the good.

In fashioning his Edenic hydrography, Dante rejects or at least revises the description of the earthly paradise found in Gen. 2:10: "And a river went out of Eden to water the garden; and from thence it was parted, and became into four heads," namely Pison (or Ganges), Gihon (or Nile), Hiddekel (or Tigris), and Euphrates." In an act of daring syncretism, Dante conflates the four biblical rivers into two classicized ones, thereby destroying any structural symmetry with the four infernal rivers: Acheron, Styx, Phlegethon, and Cocytus. Indeed, Dante emphasizes the numerical difference by referring to Lethe for the first time in the context of Virgil's explanation of the watering system of Hell (*Inf.* 14.131). Curiously, Eunoe is not mentioned at this point in the text. Matelda (*Purg.* 28.121–133) later explains that Lethe and Eunoe both issue from a single pure fountain, replenished constantly by the will of God. She also notes that the branch termed Lethe must be tasted first and Eunoe second; that is, the elimination of all memory of and remorse for sin must precede the remembrance of good deeds.

Dante reiterates the idea of a sole source in *Purg.* 33.112–114 and 116–117. After bathing and drinking in Lethe, he sees the two rivers issuing from one fountain and parting from one another, and he mistakes them for Euphrates and Tigris. Why this confusion? Both Pliny (*Nat. hist.* 6.9.25) and Boethius (*Consol. philos.* 5.1) point out that Euphrates and Tigris originate from the same fountain. Pliny later tells us that near the river Hercynnum in Boeotia are two springs; one brings remembrance, the other forgetfulness (*Nat. hist.* 31.2). Isidore of Seville (*Etym.* 13.18.4) repeats

Pliny's second assertion. In addition, Orphic mystery rites specify that there are two springs in Hades, Lethe on the left and Mnemosyne on the right, and that, while Lethe is to be avoided, it is necessary to drink from Mnemosyne to enter Elysium. Singleton argues persuasively that, regardless of the complex and often contradictory literary influences on Dante, the poet's motive in "creating" Eunoe and Lethe is clear: he intends to dramatize with them the superfluity of divine grace made available by Christ's Crucifixion and Resurrection. To do so, he must depart from the Old Testament description of Eden. It is thus fitting that Matelda, a nymphlike spirit who corresponds to the virgin Astraea, pagan goddess of justice and moral rectitude, administers the waters of Eunoe to Statius (*Purg.* 33.134–135), to Dante (*Purg.* 33.127–145), and presumably to all souls reaching the purgatorial summit. In this way, they can experience not only the penitential shame of recollected sin and the numbing oblivion of that sin by Lethe, but also the positive joy and the active remembrance of good deeds, of innocence and salvation regained.

Bibliography

Donno, Daniel J. "Moral Hydrography: Dante's Rivers." *MLN* 92 (1977), 130–139.

Singleton, Charles. *Dante Studies 2. Journey to Beatrice.* Cambridge: Harvard University Press, 1958, pp. 224–227.

Caron Cioffi

Euripides

Greek playwright, born at Salamis (c. 485–407 B.C.E.), who wrote some seventy-five tragedies, of which eighteen survive (including *Medea, Trojan Women, Electra, Iphigenia in Tauris, Orestes*). Dante knew of his work indirectly, through references in Aristotle, Cicero, Quintilian, and Macrobius. Virgil mentions Euripides *(Euripide)* to Statius in *Purg.* 22.106 as a resident of Limbo.

Nancy Vine Durling

Europa

Daughter of King Agenor, Europa is deceived by Jupiter, who is disguised as a bull, and carried away from the Phoenician coast, which Dante designates *il lito / nel qual si fece Europa dolce carco* ("the shore where Europa made herself a sweet burden," *Par.* 27.84) when he regards the earth from the Sphere of the Fixed Stars in Paradise. Raped by the god, she gives birth to Minos in Crete. Ovid, Dante's source, relates the story in *Meta.* 2.833–875 and again in *Meta.* 6.103–107 and *Fasti* 5.604–618.

Bibliography

Jacoff, Rachel. "The Rape/Rapture of Europa: *Paradiso* 27." In *The Poetry of Allusion: Virgil and Ovid in Dante's "Commedia."* Edited by Rachel Jacoff and Jeffrey T. Schnapp. Stanford, Cal.: Stanford University Press, 1991, pp. 233–246.

Jessica Levenstein

Europe

One of the three continents of the world according to Dante's geography. This envisaged the inhabited Northern Hemisphere as divided into three by a T shape, whose crossbar is made up of the rivers Tanais (or Don) and the Nile and whose stem is represented by the Mediterranean. Europe *(Europa)* is thus located between the Mediterranean and the Don, and is imagined as roughly triangular in shape—*tricornis* (*Epist.* 7.11). In *Par.* 12.46–48 Europe's western boundary is identified with the Iberian peninsula, the area from which the west wind first brings spring to the continent: *quella parte ove surge ad aprire / Zefiro dolce le novelle fronde / di che si vede Europa rivestire* ("In that direction where sweet Zephyr rises to open up the new leaves with which we see Europe clothed again"). In *Par.* 6.5 *lo stremo d'Europa* ("the edge of Europe") refers to Constantinople, where Europe meets Asia. Astronomically, the continent is referred to as the *paese d'Europa, che non perde / le sette stelle gelide unquemai;* ("the lands of Europe, which never once lose the seven cold stars," vv. 28–29 in the canzone *Io son venuto al punto de la rota*); that is, as the region where the constellation of the Great Bear is always visible.

The *De vulgari eloquentia* deals with the earliest history of Europe: its population by immigrants from the East, bringing with them an *ydioma* [. . .] *tripharium* ("a tripartite language," *DVE* 1.8.1–3), and the subsequent division and distribution of the European languages (*DVE* 1.8.4–9).

In a broader sense, "Europe" may indicate the civilized Christian world in general, as in *Purg.* 8.123, where the Malaspina family is said to be famous *per tutta Europa* ("in all Europe"), or may be used in combination with references to Africa and Asia to evoke the whole inhabited world. For example, in the *Monarchia,* Dante stresses the suitability of Aeneas to be the founder of a worldwide empire, since he is linked, through both ancestry and marriage, with each of the three continents. Europe is here represented by Aeneas's ancestor Dardanus (*Mon.* 2.3.11–12) and his third wife, Lavinia (*Mon.* 2.3.16). The reference to the latter, moreover, provokes the definition of Italy—the seat of the empire—as Europe's noblest region: *Que ultima uxor de Ytalia fuit, Europe regione nobilissima* ("This last wife was from Italy, the most noble region of Europe"). Elsewhere too, Europe is equated with the center of imperial jurisdiction. The passage cited from *Epist.* 7.11 asserts that imperial authority is not merely European but universal, while in *Mon.* 3.13.7 Dante claims that the majority of the inhabitants of Europe (as well as those of Africa and Asia) would refute the Church's claim to authority over the Empire: *Et quod etiam ab assensu omnium vel prevalentium non habuerit quis dubitat, cum non modo Asyani et Affricani omnes, quinetiam maior pars Europam colentium hoc aborreat?* ("And who can doubt that it did not receive it from the consent of all men or of the most exceptional among them, given that not only all Asians and Africans, but also the greater part of those who live in Europe, find the idea abhorrent?" *Mon.* 3.14.7).

Claire Honess

Euryalus

Young Trojan soldier who accompanies Aeneas to Italy. In *Aen.* 5, Euryalus participates in games honoring Anchises, an event to which Dante refers in *Mon.* 2.7.11–12. In *Aen.* 9, Euryalus and his beloved friend Nisus are slain as they attempt to loot the enemy camp in a night raid. Dante mentions Euryalus (*Eurialo*) in *Inf.* 1.108 among the warriors who died for Italy.

Nancy Vine Durling

Eurypylus

In *Aen.* 2.114–119, the Greek augur said by Sinon to have interrogated the oracle of Apollo and informed the Greeks that their return home from Troy required a human sacrifice in order to propitiate the winds, just as the journey from Aulis to

E Troy had required the sacrifice of Iphigenia. Eurypylus *(Euripilo)* is placed among the soothsayers in the fourth bolgia of Malebolge in Hell *(Inf.* 20.106–113), where Dante has Virgil associate him with Calchas in prophesying the Greek departure from Aulis—although he is not mentioned in that connection in Virgil's poem.

Pina Palma

Eve

The mother of the human race, Eve *(Eva)* is barely mentioned in the canonical books of the Old Testament, though later, in Sirach, she is called the beginning of sin and the cause of death (25.24). It is in the Pauline epistles that Eve's role in the Fall, which may have been nothing more than a reckless desire for wisdom (Gen. 3), along with her place in the order of creation (Gen. 2), becomes the excuse for mistrust and subordination of women: "Let a woman learn in silence with full submission. I permit no woman to teach or to have authority over a man; she is to keep silent. For Adam was formed first, then Eve; and Adam was not deceived, but the woman was deceived and became a transgressor" (1 Tim. 2:11–14, no longer attributed to Paul); cf. "man was not made from woman, but woman from man. Neither was man created for the sake of woman, but woman for the sake of man. For this reason a woman ought to have a symbol of authority on her head. . . ." (1 Cor. 11:8–10).

The treatment of Eve during the Middle Ages is somewhat ambivalent. Eve is usually a symbol of destructive female pride, deception, weakness, or greed in medieval misogyny—the source of sin and death for the human race—but she is also its mother, and among the first to be taken out of Hell at the harrowing. For Christianity, Eve (and women) were indispensable in procreation, but sex was sinful and connected with the seduction of the Fall. Eve represented the lower side of human nature, flesh, or the appetites which should be subject to the higher soul or reason, but she was also a symbol for the Church, drawn from the side of Christ; as Adam is fulfilled in Christ, Eve is fulfilled in Mary. Medieval women writers often had a more sympathetic view of Eve than traditional moralists, recognizing that if woman was subordinate to man, man should assume responsibility for his own actions.

Dante in *De vulgari eloquentia* takes a traditional misogynist position on Eve, calling her *praesumptuosissima* ("the most presumptuous") and even insisting that she could not have spoken before Adam no matter what the Bible records because such an important act must have been committed first by a man (1.4.2–3). Similarly, in the *Commedia,* as he climbs the mountain of Purgatory, Dante the pilgrim tends to blame Eve for man's problems and to connect the Fall exclusively with her: the serpent in the Valley of Negligent Princes may be the one who gave Eve the bitter food *(Purg.* 8.99); the proud are children of Eve (12.71); in gluttony he is told of the tree that Eve bit (24.116). As he sees the beginning of the miraculous procession in the earthly paradise, the personal resentment of Eve intensifies. He reproaches her *ardimento* ("boldness") for alone refusing to remain under a veil where earth and heaven obeyed—if she had not, "I would have felt those ineffable delights sooner, and for a longer time" (29.24–30). When, standing before Beatrice, he becomes aware that he has lost Virgil, "all our ancient mother lost" cannot keep him from weeping (30.52). And as he walks with Beatrice and Statius toward the tree of divine justice, he thinks of the wood "empty by the fault of her who trusted the serpent" (32.31–32). But the procession itself, the army from the heavenly kingdom, murmurs "Adam" (32.37), perhaps to remind Dante that every being has to assume responsibility for his sin.

In *Paradiso,* Thomas Aquinas, who took strong Pauline positions on the functions of women in the Church, speaks of the "beautiful cheek whose palate all the world pays for" (13.38–39), but when Bernard describes the figures in the rose, he speaks of Adam as the father through whose bold taste *(ardito gusto)* human kind tastes so bitterly *(Par.* 32.122–123). Shortly before, Dante had Adam himself explain that the cause of his exile was not eating the fruit (tasting the tree), but going beyond the limits set *(Par.* 26.115–117). In the course of *Purgatorio* and *Paradiso,* Dante seems to trace his own move from his earlier misogynist views of Eve (as expressed in *DVE*) to a more balanced sense of human responsibility, cf. a reference to the Fall of the first parents in a later work *(Mon.* 1.16.1).

Joan M. Ferrante

Excommunicates

The first group of souls encountered by Dante and Virgil as they enter the realm of Purgatory. They reside at the foot of the mountain on the lowest of four levels of the Ante-Purgatory, where those who delayed their repentance dwell until they are prepared to enter Purgatory proper. Not only have these souls delayed their repentance, they have committed sins so heinous that they have been excommunicated from the Church and died *in contumacia,* in a state of contumacy (*Purg.* 3.136). They are represented by Manfred, king of Sicily, the only individual of the group who is named, a man whose sins, as he himself admits, were horrible (3.121), although his excommunication, first by Pope Alexander VI and later by Pope Urban IV, had more to do with political factors than with his sins. Manfred recounts the story of his death in battle at Benevento, a victim of a betrayal by the Apulian barons, and how at the very instant of death, filled with sudden contrition, he turned to God and sought forgiveness for his sins. On the basis of this single, brief act of repentance, and without the benefit of the auspices of the Church, Manfred is granted salvation. That an individual should live a life in sin and yet merit salvation for so tardy and minimal, though sincere, an act of repentance marks the profound inscrutability of God's mercy. Manfred, more specifically, illustrates the efficacy of repentance even for those who have so strongly rebelled against God's will that they have merited excommunication from the Church. He is the image of one who, until the very moment of death, stood as far from God on earth as it was possible to be and still gained salvation. As the first soul in Purgatory, Manfred is an example of the power of God's forgiveness and an embodiment of the possibility of the moral reconstitution of the human spirit.

Excommunication constitutes a formal penalty in canon law that excludes a person from participating in the life of the Church, in particular in its sacraments. It does not signify expulsion from the Church, and it is not itself a sin, but rather a punishment. However, contempt for or rejection of excommunication was considered to be a sin as early as Gregory I. The doctrine of excommunication, which developed out of and was associated with the doctrine of anathema, especially reserved for heretics, was affirmed by Innocent IV and the Council of Lyon in 1245 (Vodola, 42). There is a special irony in this fact, since Innocent IV was an enemy of Manfred and had challenged, unsuccessfully, Manfred's campaign to become king of Sicily in the late 1250s.

Christian doctrine explicitly stipulates that excommunication from the Church does not prejudge or predetermine the fate of a soul (as Dante makes explicit in lines 133–135). In practice, however, the Church frequently diverged from its official doctrine and abused its power of excommunication by seeking to instill in the people a fear of inevitable damnation. One of the central purposes of this canto, therefore, is to exemplify the doctrine that each soul possesses an intimate and personal relationship with the Creator, and that the question of salvation hangs on the Creator's will, not on the will of the papacy or of any other Church official. And a collateral purpose comes in the form of a severe criticism of the papal practice of carrying out acts of excommunication purely for political motives. Yet, Dante disputes neither the validity of Manfred's excommunication nor the increased isolation between the sinner and God created by the state of contumacy. Such isolation, however, can be overcome by the individual who, through the grace of God, expresses sincere remorse and repents his or her sins.

The image of the excommunicates' earthly isolation undergoes a reversal in the Ante-Purgatory, where Manfred and his companions are described as sheep walking slowly and timidly, the one following in the steps of the other, *non sappiendo 'l perché* ("without knowing why," 3.93). Critics have been divided on whether the image of the *pecorelle,* the sheep, signifies a state of weak individual will, benign ignorance, and blind and servile submission to their leader, or an attitude of humility and newfound and deferential Christian respect for others. In a word, it is a question of whether the excommunicates display the same old delay and deferral that characterized their earthly behavior, or can be seen as atoning for their previous spirit of defiance of authority. The simile's symbolic allusion to the traditional image of Christ leading his flock of sheep strongly suggests that the excommunicates are engaged in reconciling themselves to the Christian ideal of *communitas.*

Unique among the four groups of late repentants in the Ante-Purgatory, the excommunicates must spend thirty years awaiting entrance into Purgatory proper for every year of their contumacy, unlike the indolent, the unabsolved, and the preoccupied rulers, whose penalty is one year for each year of delayed repentance. The term for each may be shortened by prayers said by the living (3.140–141).

E

Bibliography

Binni, Walter. "Il canto III del *Purgatorio.*" In *Letture dantesche.* Vol. II. Edited by Giovanni Getto. Sansoni: Florence, 1964 [1958]), pp. 723–745.

Lansing, Richard. "*Purgatorio* III." In *Dante's Divine Comedy: Introductory Readings, II: Purgatorio.* Edited by Tibor Wlassics. Charlottesville: University of Virginia, 1993, pp. 35–52 (rpt. 1991).

Scott, John. *Dante's Political Purgatory.* Philadelphia: University of Pennsylvania, 1996, pp. 85–95.

Vodola, Elizabeth. *Excommunication in the Middle Ages.* Berkeley: University of California Press, 1986.

Richard Lansing

Exile

Official court documents record the technical details of Dante's exile from Florence. On January 27, 1302, the Black Guelf government of Florence issued a judgment finding Dante and fourteen others guilty of barratry, extortion, and resistance to the pope. For each of the convicts, the court ordered future exclusion from politics, payment of a fine, and exile for two years. On March 10, 1302, apparently because of their disregard or defiance of the first court order, Dante and the others were condemned and were permanently banned from entering Florence under penalty of death. Dante's exact whereabouts at the time these sentences were handed down are unknown, although most commentators, following the lead of Compagni (*Cronica* 2.25), state that he was on an official Florentine embassy at the papal court in Rome.

Thus begins Dante's life as a political exile, wandering throughout the Italian peninsula and sojourning as the guest of patrons in cities such as Verona, Lunigiana, Lucca, and Ravenna. The precise itinerary of Dante's travels is uncertain, and scholarly attempts to reconstruct it, drawing mainly from references made in Dante's own works, have yielded conflicting scenarios. There is some speculation, based on the accounts of G. Villani and Boccaccio, that Dante may have traveled outside Italy, perhaps arriving as far away as Paris and maybe even Oxford. Notwithstanding so much uncertainty about the particulars of his exile, it remains certain that Dante never returns home to his native city.

In medieval legal terms the penalty of exile is almost equal in severity to capital punishment. By precluding the individual's participation in civic life, exile denies an integral part of human nature, which, according to Aristotle (*Politics* 1253a1), is political. The encounter between Dante and Charles Martel in the Heaven of Venus illustrates Dante's unquestioning acceptance of the Aristotelian definition of the political nature of human beings: *Ond'elli ancora: "Or dì: sarebbe il peggio / per l'omo in terra, se non fosse cive?" / "Sì," rispuos' io; "e qui ragion non cheggio"* ("Then he again: 'Now tell me, would it be worse for man on earth if he were not a citizen?' 'Yes,' I replied, 'and here I ask no proof,'" *Par.* 8.115–117). An exile, on the contrary, is not a citizen but an alien, and his native city is foreign soil. The etymology of the word "exile" offered by Isidore of Seville (*Etym.* 5.27.28) highlights precisely the territorial dimension of banishment outside the city walls: *Exilium dictum quasi extra solum. Nam exul dicitur qui extra solum est* ("Exile means, as it were, outside the soil, for one who is outside his soil is said to be an exile"). An exile, then, is literally an outlaw, cast into the wilderness and disorder of the no-man's-land outside the medieval city. The exile's desire to return to his homeland, therefore, is not only prompted by a longing to be reunited with family and friends but, more fundamentally, is stimulated by an existential need to participate in the life of the community.

With the despair and dismay of a disowned son, Dante describes the abandonment of his exile in *Conv.* 1.3.4:

Poi che fu piacere de li cittadini de la bellissima e famosissima figlia di Roma, Fiorenza, di gittarmi fuori del suo dolce seno—nel quale nato e nutrito fui in fino al colmo de la vita mia, e nel quale, con buona pace di quella, desidero con tutto lo cuore di riposare l'animo stancato e terminare lo tempo che m'è dato—per le parti quasi tutte a le quali questa lingua si stende, peregrino, quasi mendicando, sono andato, mostrando contra mia voglia la piaga de la fortuna, che suole ingiustamente al piagato molte volte esser imputata ("Since it was the pleasure of the citizens of the most beautiful and famous daughter of Rome, Florence, to cast me out of her sweet bosom—where I was born and bred up to the pinnacle of my life, and where, with her good will, I desire with all my heart to rest my weary mind and to complete the span of time that is given to me—I have wandered like a stranger, almost like a beggar, through virtually all the regions to which this tongue of ours extends, displaying against my will the wound of fortune for which the wounded one is often unjustly accustomed to be held accountable").

This frequently quoted passage powerfully captures the pain and alienation of Dante's life in exile and reminds us of the material poverty which renders him dependent on the charity of others. More spiritually, Dante's self-depiction as a stranger and weary traveler in search of repose, identifies him as a Christian *homo viator,* the terrestrial wayfarer struggling to regain the peace of his celestial home.

Christian tradition characterizes the earthly life after the expulsion of Adam and Eve from the garden as exile. Adam himself, in his exchange with Dante-pilgrim, refers to life after the Fall as *tanto essilio* ("so long an exile," *Par.* 26.116; cf. *DVE* 1.7.2). This echoes the earlier reference in *Par.* 23.134–135 to the *essilio / di Babillòn* ("exile of Babylon") and further recalls Beatrice's statement about Dante in *Par.* 25.55-56: *li è conceduto che d'Egitto / vegna in Ierusalemme* ("it is granted him that from Egypt he come to Jerusalem"). Exodus, the Jews' escape from exile in Egypt ("Babylon") to the peace of Jerusalem ("the promised land"), affords Dante, in keeping with Christian theology, a biblical typology of the ultimate recompense for the exile incurred by Adam. In his letter to Henry VII, Dante alludes to the exile lament of Psalm 136 [137] ("By the waters of Babylon . . .") and identifies himself as being an exile in Babylon (*Epist.* 7.4, 30). Furthermore, references to Psalm 113 [114] ("When Israel went forth from Egypt . . .") in *Conv.* 2.1.6–8, *Purg.* 2.146, and *Epist.* 13.21 attest to the importance of the theme of exodus in Dante's thought. Indeed, Dante's own pilgrimage from the dark wood of *Inf.* 1 to the beatific vision in *Par.* 33 is cast as reenacting in his own life the biblical pattern of exodus. In the Christian scheme of salvation, exile is the earthly condition, which nevertheless inspires hope in the future heavenly reconciliation with God.

The temporary duration of earthly exile is underscored by the eternal nature of its infernal counterpart. In an infernal parody of the Crucifixion in *Inf.* 23.126, the high priest Caiaphas lies stretched out on a cross *tanto vilmente ne l'etterno essilio* ("so basely . . . in the eternal exile"). In *Purg.* 21.16–18 Virgil recommends Statius to his future heavenly reward while lamenting his own eternal damnation: *Poi cominciò: "Nel beato concilio / ti ponga in pace la verace corte / che me rilega ne l'etterno essilio"* ("Then he began, 'May the true court soon give you peace in the blessed, though it binds me in eternal exile'"). Indeed, Dante's characterization of Hell as a place of exile adds a realistic political twist to his portrayal of the damned.

In addition to the political and moral dimensions of exile, Dante also accentuates the linguistic nature of exile. In a substantial revision of *DVE* 1.4.4, Adam reveals the connection between exile and language in his description of the Fall in *Par.* 26. At lines 115–117, he explains to Dante the pilgrim: *Or, figliuol mio, non il gustar del legno / fu per sé la cagion di tanto essilio, / ma solamente il trapassar del segno* ("Now, my son, not the tasting of the tree in itself was the cause of so long an exile, but only the going beyond the mark"). Adam's fall from eternity and unity into temporality and multiplicity is simultaneously a fall into linguistic flux, in which not even the name of God escapes mutation (*Par.* 26.124–138). According to Adam, language is the unstable instrument of fallen man. After the Fall man enters the realm of metaphors, he implies, one in which words lack a necessary or literal correlation to the things they signify. Originally, therefore, exile and poetry (i.e., metaphorical language) characterize man's fallen state. More concretely, in Dante's case, exile makes his poetic mission possible. His personal experience of exile exposes him to the injustice and decadence of Florence and compels him to voice his outrage.

Earlier in *Paradiso* Dante's ancestor, Cacciaguida, clarifies the ominous prophecies of exile given by Ciacco, Farinata, Brunetto, and others. In the Heaven of Mars, Cacciaguida flatly tells Dante of the pain and hardship he will have to endure as a result of his impending exile (*Par.* 17.46–93). At the same time, however, Cacciaguida admonishes Dante to have the courage to speak out truthfully: *Ma nondimen, rimossa ogne menzogna, / tutta tua visïon fa manifesta, / e lascia pur grattar dov' è la rogna* ("But nonetheless, putting aside every falsehood, make manifest all your vision, and just let them scratch where the itch is," *Par.* 17.127–129; cf. *Par.* 27.64–66). In truth, exile is the necessary precondition for the writing of the *Commedia,* which, in retrospect, would not have been possible without it. Cacciaguida's vindication of Dante's political individualism (*Par.* 18.69) baldly endorses the positive, indeed virtuous, aspect of exile.

In his minor works Dante reiterates the injustice and dishonor of his exile, while simultaneously implying a growth in his moral virtue as a result of it. Exile thus assumes an ambivalent status—both good and bad—throughout Dante's writings. In *Epist.* 2.7 Dante characterizes himself as an *exul inmeritus* ("undeservingly an exile"), a phrase that reappears in the titles of epistles 3, 5, 6, and 7. Likewise, in *DVE* 1.6.3 Dante writes *exilium patiamur iniuste* ("I suffer exile unjustly"). Although an eventual homecoming remains his constant hope, Dante obstinately refuses to return to Florence unless he can do so with honor.

In fact, in *Epist.* 12, "To a Florentine Friend," Dante rejects the opportunity to return to Florence after the general amnesty decreed in May 1315. In that letter, he ridicules the terms of the amnesty, which would have made him pay a fine as well as submit to the humiliation of an oblation, a ceremony in which Dante would have to admit guilt. Dante's dignity and sense of justice spur his categorical rejection of the offer of amnesty, to the point where exile itself becomes a badge of honor and righteousness, protecting him from the decadence and corruption of the city.

In the canzone, "Tre donne intorno al cor mi son venute," Dante most explicitly voices the transformation of exile from a sign of shame into one of honor: *l'essilio che m'è dato, onor mi tegno* ("I count as honor the exile imposed on me"). Moreover, Dante takes comfort in the historical precedents of other illustrious exiles, justifying, for instance, the self-defense and rehabilitation of his own name on the example of Boethius, whose imprisonment he takes metaphorically as a kind of exile (*Conv.* 1.2.13; cf. *Par.* 10.128–129).

In *Par.* 25.7–9, Dante expresses his hope of one day returning to Florence from exile to receive the laurel crown: *con altra voce omai, con altro vello / ritornerò poeta, e in sul fonte / del mio battesmo prenderò 'l cappello* ("with another voice by then, with other fleece, shall I return as poet, and at the font of my baptism I shall accept the wreath"). The repetition of the future tense (*ritornerò, prenderò*) hints at the remoteness of such a triumphant homecoming. Yet, the emphasis on the futurity of the event also illustrates the canto's theme of hope, a future-oriented virtue.

Unsurprisingly, the passage takes for granted the link between exile and poetry already noted in the cantos of Cacciaguida and Adam. The image in *Par.* 25 subtly suggests to the reader the paradox that a practical stranger, an exile of over ten years, is potentially the city's most cherished citizen. The reiteration of the adjective *altro* ("other") twice in the same verse seems to stress Dante's alien quality. He is nevertheless hopeful that, through his *poema sacro* ("sacred poem"), the factions splitting apart society will embrace peace and reunify the city.

Clearly, no matter how much distance—physical, moral, or intellectual—separates Dante from his homeland, he still maintains an intimate bond with his native city. In anthropological terms, Dante can be said to occupy a liminal and marginal position with respect to Florence. He is both an insider and an outsider, "betwixt and between," in Victor Turner's words. Dante's liminal perspective grants him a crucial insight into the artificial nature of the boundaries which continue to fragment Italy. Against the divisiveness of these boundaries, Dante offers a poetic alternative which transcends differences and envisions lasting peace and harmony.

Bibliography

Di Pino, Guido (ed.). *Dante e le città dell'esilio.* Ravenna: Longo Editore, 1989.

Ferguson, Margaret W. "Saint Augustine's Region of Unlikeness: The Crossing of Exile and Language." *Georgia Review* 29, 4 (1975), 842–864.

Iannucci, Amilcare A. "L'esilio di Dante: 'per colpa di Tempo e di Fortuna.'" In *Dal Medioevo al Petrarca.* Florence: Leo S. Olschki Editore, 1983, pp. 215–232.

Ladner, Gerhart B. "*Homo Viator:* Mediaeval Ideas on Alienation and Order." *Speculum* 42, 2 (1967), 233–259.

Mazzotta, Giuseppe. "Theology and Exile." In *Dante's Vision and the Circle of Knowledge.* Princeton, N.J.: Princeton University Press, 1993, pp. 174–196.

———. "*Communitas* and Its Typological Structure." In *Dante, Poet of the Desert.* Princeton, N.J.: Princeton University Press, 1979, pp. 107–146.

Paolucci, Anne. "Exile among Exiles: Dante's Party of One." *Mosaic* 8, 3 (1975), 117–125.

Petrocchi, Giorgio. *Vita di Dante.* Bari: Laterza, 1989.

Shapiro, Marianne. *De Vulgari Eloquentia. Dante's Book of Exile.* Lincoln and London: University of Nebraska Press, 1990.

Starn, Randolph. *Contrary Commonwealth.* Berkeley: University of California Press, 1982.

Turner, Victor. "Betwixt and Between: The Liminal Period in *Rites de Passage.*" In *The Forest of Symbols.* Ithaca and London: Cornell University Press, 1967, pp. 93–111.

George Andrew Trone

Exodus

The second book of the Pentateuch, traditionally believed to have been written by Moses, and one of the most important books of Scripture in the Hebrew and Christian traditions. Exodus tells of the liberation of the Israelites, under the leadership of Moses, from slavery in Egypt and their subsequent wanderings in the desert before their arrival in the promised land. It records the early life of Moses, the tribulations of the Israelites, the origins of Passover, the receiving of the law (in particular the Ten Commandments), and the idolatrous worship of the golden calf in the desert. From a Christian perspective, the historical account of the Israelites' emancipation is the prefiguration of the Incarnation, of human salvation through Christ, and the soul's spiritual journey from death to life. For Dante, the exiled poet journeying through the cosmos, it also speaks to his own trials and wanderings and grounds his hope both for a return to his beloved Florence and an arrival at his final home, the heavenly Jerusalem. The Book of Exodus can be read as the spiritual epic and journey of education for the Israelites. In the *Commedia,* it thus provides the theological counterbalance to and amplification of the strong resonances of the classical epic, in particular Virgil's *Aeneid.*

Dante uses the Exodus story to exemplify the various layers of theological allegory and the polysemous nature of the poem (*Epist.* 13.20–22). The poetic substance of this theory is demonstrated in the choice of song performed by the penitent souls on the banks of Purgatory (*Purg.* 2.46–48); they sing "In exitu Israel de Aegypto," Psalm 113, a hymn of thanksgiving sung by the Israelites. (For other allusions to Exodus see *Conv.* 2.1.6; *Epist.* 5.4; 13.21; *Par.* 25.55–57). Accordingly, critical readings, primarily that of Singleton as elaborated upon by Freccero and Mazzotta, identify the underlying structure and sustaining metaphor of the *Commedia* as a journey of exodus, a voyage patterned on the biblical account of liberation from the desert of sin to the heavenly city.

Dante quotes the Book of Exodus in *Par.* 26.42 and in *Mon.* 2.4.2 and 2.12.4. He refers to Exodus in *Par.* 32.131–132 and in *Mon.* 1.14.9 and 2.7.8. Furthermore, Exodus is figured by one of the twenty-four elders in the mystical procession in the earthly paradise (*Purg.* 29.83–84).

Virginia Jewiss

Ezekiel *(Ezechiele)*

Carried to Babylon with the first wave of captivity (598 B.C.E.), Ezekiel warned of the judgment of God against Israel up until the fall of Jerusalem (586 B.C.E.), after which he delivered oracles of salvation. For a depiction of the four animals (except for the number of their wings) which appear in the pageant of Revelation (*Purg.* 29.92–95, 100–105), Dante refers his readers directly to Ezekiel's vision of the four cherubim: *leggi Ezechïel* ("read Ezekiel"). This vision first signaled Ezekiel's call to become a prophet of God in Babylon (Ezek. 1:1–25) and then reappeared as a sign of the departure of God's glory from Jerusalem (Ezek. 10). In *Epist.* 11.6, Dante refers to an abomination which, in a vision, Ezekiel was shown in the temple of Jerusalem (Ezek. 8:16); in *Epist.* 13.76, Dante quotes Ezekiel's evocation of man's perfect beginnings in Eden embedded within his lamentation over the king of Tyre (Ezek. 28:12–13); in *Epist.* 13.80, Dante refers to Ezekiel's response to his vision of election (Ezek. 1:28).

Carolynn Lund-Mead

Ezzelino III da Romano

Son-in-law of the emperor Frederick II, lord of Vicenza, Verona, Padua, and the March of Treviso, Ezzelino *(Azzolino)* was a prominent Ghibelline and thus an enemy of the papacy. In 1255 Pope Alexander IV launched a crusade against him, and after a war of three years, he was captured and died shortly thereafter. Especially among the Guelfs, he had a reputation of being a horrible tyrant, and according to Villani, he was guilty of massacring the citizens of Padua. Villani refers to him as the "most cruel and feared tyrant who ever existed among Christians" (*Cronica,* 7.72), and a contemporary chronicler (Salimbene of Parma) wrote that he "was truly of the body of the devil and a son of iniquity." One legend even asserted that he was the son of the devil. Dante places him among the tyrants guilty of violence and cruelty in the river of boiling blood (the Phlegethon) in the first ring of Hell's seventh circle, where Nessus points out his conspicuous black hair to Dante and Virgil (*Inf.* 12.109–110). He is also mentioned in *Par.* 9.29–31 by his sister Cunizza da Romano, who refers to him as *una facella* ("a torch"), following a legend that Ezzolino's mother dreamed that she would give birth to a firebrand. Dante contradicts the rumor of Ezzelino's demonic birth, since Cunizza says that she and her brother are of *una radice* ("one root").

V. Stanley Benfell

F

Fabbro de' Lambertazzi

A Bolognese noble who lived during the first half of the thirteenth century, Fabbro was a man of politics (and a virtuous one in Dante's eyes) who belonged to a family associated with the Ghibelline party of the city, of which he was head at one time. He also held the position of chief magistrate in a number of different cities in Romagna. His death in 1259 signaled the downfall of the Ghibellines. He is mentioned by Guido del Duca on the second terrace of Purgatory as one of the noble figures of Romagna (*Purg.* 14.100).

Paul Colilli

Fabricius

Gaius Fabricius Luscinus, Roman consul in 282 and 278 B.C.E., and censor in 275, celebrated for his incorruptibility and personal austerity. In the fifth tier of Purgatory, Fabricius *(Fabrizio)* is presented as the second of three spoken examples of the virtue opposing avarice (*Purg.* 20.25). In the *Convivio* Dante cites his dedication to poverty and presents him as one of numerous models of civic virtue and, consequently, proof that Rome and her people received God's special favor: "Who will say that Fabricius was not divinely inspired when he refused to accept an almost infinite amount of gold because he would not abandon his country?" (4.5.13). He repeats his example in *Mon.* 2.5.11, together with many of the same Roman exemplars listed in the *Convivio* (taken from Augustine, *The City of God,* 5.18.2), and invokes Virgil's praise of his penury in the phrase *parvoque potentem / Fabricius* ("Fabricius, great with little," *Aen.* 6.843–844).

Richard Lansing

Fall of Man

In *Par.* 7.25–33 Beatrice recapitulates the essential points of the Christian doctrine of the Fall:

> *"Per non soffrire a la virtù che vole / freno a suo prode, quell'uom che non nacque, / dannando sé, dannò tutta sua prole; / onde l'umana specie inferma giacque / giù per secoli molti in grande errore, / fin ch'al Verbo di Dio discender piacque / u' la natura, che dal suo fattore / s'era allungata, unì a sé in persona / con l'atto sol del suo etterno amore"*
> ("By not enduring any rein upon the power that wills, though for his good, that man who was not born, in damning himself damned all his offspring; therefore the human race lay sick for many centuries in great error, until it pleased the Word of God to descend where he united with himself, in one Person, with the sole act of his eternal love, the nature that had gone far from its Creator").

Adam's transgression is an act of sinful disobedience, resulting from his pride and unrestrained will. Such unlawful insubordination condemns Adam and his posterity to suffer the punishment of exile, a forced expulsion and separation from the delights of Paradise (cf. Rom. 5:12; *Mon.* 2.11.1–3). Simultaneously, Adam's sin permanently debases the originally pure and good condition of human nature (*Par.* 7.36; cf. *Conv.* 4.5.3). As restitution for Adam's transgression, however, Christ's loving act of redemption atones for original sin, thereby reopening the gates of Paradise to Adam's children (cf. *Mon.* 1.16.1–3; 1 Cor. 15:21–22).

Dante follows the gist of Augustine's theology of the Fall, which emphasizes the importance

F of Adam's corrupted will. In book fourteen of *The City of God,* Augustine examines the issues surrounding the sin of Adam and concludes that love of self and contempt of God are the ultimate reasons for the Fall (14.28). This love of self over God instills a harmful pride in Adam, which corrupts his will and leads to his sinful act of disobedience (14.13). Moreover, because of the shame of nakedness Adam and Eve feel when their eyes are opened, Augustine infers that the first sin involves sexual perversion (14.17). According to Augustine, sex, the propagator of the human race, transmits original sin from one generation to the next. Hence, the immaculately conceived Jesus remains unblemished by the sinfulness of human nature (cf. *Inf.* 34.115), even though he paradoxically retains his full humanity.

While Dante accepts Augustine's basic argument regarding Adam's disobedience and pride, he nevertheless stops short of fully developing the sexual implications of the Fall. Commentators have noted allusions to the Fall in Dante's encounter with Paolo and Francesca in *Inf.* 5. In an apparent allusion to Eden, for instance, Francesca mentions *la prima radice* ("the first root," 124) of the couple's love. Moreover, the insistence on Dante's falling in the last verse of the canto—*E caddi come corpo morto cade* ("and I fell as a dead body falls," 142)—is said to reenact literally Adam's fall from grace. Notwithstanding these allusions to the bond between sex and the Fall in *Inf.* 5, Dante's specific treatment of the Fall in *Par.* 7 and 26 lacks a sustained emphasis on this sexual dimension.

Dante's examination on love conducted by St. John in the first half of *Par.* 26 sets the stage for Dante's encounter with Adam in the second half of the canto. Indeed, the first half of the canto depicts a return to the moral rectitude of Eden, a restoration of the integrity of the will, and the innocence of human nature before the Fall. In fact, Dante even seems to assume the status of a prelapsarian Adam. For instance, Dante is blinded during the examination on love. Unlike Adam's reaction of shame when his eyes are opened (Gen. 3:7), Dante experiences a feeling of awe and wonder—*stupefatto* ("stupified," *Par.* 26.80) and *stupendo* ("marveling," 89)—when his eyes are opened. Furthermore, the otherwise odd metaphor of biting used during the examination—St. John asks Dante to declare *con quanti denti questo amor ti morde* ("with how many teeth this love bites you,"

51)—makes sense when seen in connection with Adam's biting into the forbidden fruit (cf. *Par.* 13.39; *Par.* 26.115; *Par.* 32.122). In truth, Dante's first address to Adam as *O pomo* ("O fruit," 91), besides being ironic, evokes Adam's role as the "seed" or "root" of humanity (*Par.* 7.86; *Purg.* 28.142; cf. *Inf.* 3.115).

Perhaps more obviously, metaphors of foliage and gardening dramatically join together the seemingly disparate halves of *Par.* 26. With an unmistakable allusion to the Garden of Eden, Dante exclaims to St. John: *"Le fronde onde s'infronda tutto l'orto / de l'ortolano etterno am' io cotanto / quanto da lui a lor di bene è porto"* ("The leaves wherewith all the orchard of the eternal Gardener flourishes, do I love in the measure of the goodness that is conveyed from him to them," *Par.* 26.64–66). Not long after, when he first notices the presence of the spirit of Adam, Dante compares himself to a *fronda che flette la cima / nel transito del vento* ("branch that bends its tip as the wind goes by," 85–86). Finally, Adam concludes his reflections on the mutable nature of language by echoing Horace (*Ars poetica,* 60–63): *"l'uso d'i mortali è come fronda / in ramo, che sen va e altra vene"* ("the usage of mortals is like a leaf on the branch, which departs and another arrives," 137–138). The textual cohesiveness of *Par.* 26 implicitly suggests that, for Dante, Adam's sin and fall have to do with love which is misdirected and perverted. At the same time, however, the contour of Adam's discourse explicitly delineates the linguistic aftermath of the Fall.

Dante briefly traces the linguistic ramifications of the Fall in *DVE* 1.7. He begins by admitting the shame that swells within him as he recounts the ignominy of the human race (*DVE* 1.7.1). Then, after apostrophizing the forever sinful quality of human nature, Dante describes three falls: the Expulsion from Eden, the Flood, and the Tower of Babel. While each fall is an example of the pride or, as he puts it, presumption, of human beings, the third fall, the construction of the Tower of Babel, comes to epitomize the corruption of human nature. This third fall, instigated by the giant Nimrod, is punished by the confusion of languages and the accompanying dispersion of nations (*DVE* 1.7.6). Against the harmonious perfection of heavenly life, earthly life is instead characterized as a cacophony of foreign languages.

In *Par.* 26 Dante profoundly revises this early theory of linguistic mutability. In what seems to be an explicit reference to the above passage of *De vulgari eloquentia,* Adam says that his language was extinct by the time *"che . . . fosse la gente di Nembròt attenta"* ("that the people were tempted by Nimrod," *Par.* 26.126) and undertook their impossible task. The implications of Dante's shift in perspective are serious, for his revised opinion implies that language, by nature, is in constant flux. The news that not even the name of God can escape the flow of time (*Par.* 26.133–136) acknowledges the inherently unstable nature of language, whereby a word lacks any necessary correlation to the thing it signifies.

Dante's revised stance concedes the extreme difficulty, if not impossibility, of ever attaining knowledge of God through a linguistic medium. The inadequacy of language jeopardizes Dante's poetic attempt at fully recapturing the peace and harmony of the lost garden. Christ's act of redemption, however, rescues both language and human nature from its fallen state, thereby encouraging Dante's hope for the ultimate success of his project.

Bibliography

Jager, Eric. *The Tempter's Voice.* Ithaca and London: Cornell University Press, 1993.

Mazzocco, Angelo. " 'La lingua ch'io parlai fu tutta spenta.' Dante's Reappraisal of the Adamic Language (*Paradiso* XXVI, 124–138)." In *Linguistic Theories in Dante and the Humanists: Studies of Language and Intellectual History in Late Medieval and Early Renaissance Italy.* Leiden-New York-Köln: E. J. Brill, 1993, pp. 159–179.

Pagels, Elaine. *Adam, Eve, and the Serpent.* New York: Random House, 1988.

Ries, Julien. "The Fall." In *The Encyclopedia of Religion.* Edited by Mircea Eliade. Vol. 5. New York: Macmillan, 1987, pp. 256–267.

Singleton, Charles S. "Natural Justice." In *Journey to Beatrice.* Baltimore and London: Johns Hopkins University Press, 1977, pp. 222–253.

George Andrew Trone

Falsifiers

Dante's falsifiers are gathered in the tenth and last *bolgia* of Malebolge (*Inf.* 29.40–30.148). They fall into disparate groups united only by the fact that each particular sin depends on malicious pretense, the successful attempt, usually for purposes of financial gain, to pass something off as that which it is not.

The first group of falsifiers encountered by Dante and Virgil (29.40–139) is represented by the alchemists "Griffolino" and Capocchio, condemned for the falsification of metals on which rested their fraudulent claim to have turned base metal into gold, and now condemned to eternal torment by a loathsome skin disease whose effects are described (73–84) with the linguistic vivacity, derived from the contemporary tradition of *poesia giocosa,* that is characteristic of these cantos. These are followed (30.1–48) by the falsifiers of person, afflicted with a bestial madness akin to rabies—Gianni Schicchi, who pretended to be another man in order to falsify a will for his own benefit, and Mirra, who assumed her mother's identity in order to sleep with her own father. Third come the falsifiers of coinage, represented by the notorious English forger Master Adam (30.49–90), whose punishment is an acute form of dropsy; and finally (30.91–99) the falsifiers of words, stricken by an unbearably high fever, whose representatives are Potiphar's wife, false accuser of the biblical Joseph, and Sinon, who fatally persuaded the citizens of Troy to admit the wooden horse. A quarrel breaks out between Sinon and Adam (30.100–129); Dante's enjoyment of this comic spectacle is sternly reproved by Virgil, and the episode ends (30.130–148).

Dante's moral objection to the falsifiers' behavior is obviously connected with his condemnation of fraud in general: perversion of the good and real things of God's creation toward shabby and deceitful human ends is necessarily an offense against central principles of divine order and justice in the world. These sinners' consistent presentation in terms of bodily disease, however, strongly suggests the particular horror with which Dante regards a sin that makes impossible any kind of reliance on external appearances or any kind of trust among human beings that things (people, words) are indeed what they seem. The falsifiers thus strike at the heart of Dante's vision of the just society, by forcing dealings within that society to take place in an atmosphere of mistrust and suspicion; and the disease that is their punishment clearly stands, according to the principle of *contrapasso,* as an image of that which they engendered, during their lives, in the body politic.

Steven Botterill

Fantasy

The power or faculty of the mind which collects, retains, coordinates, and (re)combines the impressions entering into it from the outside world through the medium of the senses: the imagination, the picturing faculty in both passive (receiving) and active (representing) aspects. As Aquinas remarks, "the fantasy or imagination is like a treasure house of images received by the senses" (*est enim phantasia sive imaginatio quasi thesaurus quidam formarum per sensum acceptarum, ST* 1.78.4).

The "common sense" processes and synthesizes the sensory perceptions of experience as forms. The fantasy then is the faculty that retains or preserves these forms as the material of abstract thought, the "picture" that it calls to mind providing the "concrete" image from which a "concept" is formed (see Aristotle, *De anima* 3.427a3; Aquinas, *ST* 1.78.4, 1.84.7, and 1.88.1).

There are things (like immaterial substances) which through no fault of our own our fantasy cannot imagine (*Conv.* 3.4.9–11); the things we imagine are not always sufficient to the desires of the intellect (*Conv.* 3.15.8–10); our desire to know drives our fantasy toward ever farther ends (*Conv.* 4.13.6–9); and frivolous imaginations leap from conclusion to conclusion without understanding the truth of a thing (*Conv.* 4.15.15–16). But dependent as it is on the senses, limited by its own materiality and prone to error, the fantasy allows us to come as close as we can come to vision, knowledge, and insight. Yet it has its limits, as is clear from *Par.* 33.142, where the flash of light that grants the pilgrim his wish to perceive the Divinity in its truest essence exceeds his power of representing it in his mind: *A l'alta fantasia qui mancò possa* ("Here my high imagining failed in power").

The fantasy may "picture" interior experiences as well as exterior: love has been having such an effect on the lover of the *Vita Nuova* that when memory prompts his imagination to consider his feelings, he becomes even more distressed (16.2); later, his fantasy torments him with images of Beatrice's death and his own (23.4–6, 8, 13).

The "high imagining" can be so directly "rained into" us from the heavens that we are made oblivious to even the sound of a thousand trumpets (*Purg.* 17.13–30)—that is, we can reflect so intently on our mental pictures that we become "ecstatic," the body's senses being blocked temporarily by the power of contemplation and thought. And from the representations which such "fantastical" and/or sensory experiences impress into our picturing faculty comes the art of representation. Dante's "wit and art and practice" can never tell of the Sun so that it might be imagined by a reader (*Par.* 10.40–48); when he describes the Eagle, he has to tell of something which neither tongue nor ink ever brought forth—or fantasy ever conceived (*Par.* 19.9); but our imagination, like our speech, lacks the depths necessary to represent the divine song which Peter's fire sings as it encircles Beatrice (*Par.* 24.19–27).

Bibliography

Baldelli, Ignazio. "Visione, immaginazione e fantasia nella *Vita nuova*." In *I sogni nel Medioevo*. Edited by Tullio Gregory. Rome: Edizioni dell'Atene, 1985, pp. 1–10.

Bundy, Murry Wright. *The Theory of Imagination in Classical and Mediaeval Thought*. Urbana: University of Illinois, 1927.

Kardos, Tibor. "La fantasia creatrice di Dante." *Beiträge zur Romanischen Philologie* 3, 1, and 2 (1964), 30–53; 26–43.

Wolfson, Harry Austryn. "The Internal Sense in Latin, Arabic, and Hebrew Philosophic Texts." *Harvard Theological Review* 28 (1935), 69–133.

Sally Mussetter

Farinata degli Uberti

Farinata (or Manente) was born into the powerful Uberti family of Florence at the beginning of the thirteenth century. From 1239 on he was the head of both the Uberti clan and the Ghibelline party in the city. As he reminds Dante the pilgrim (*Inf.* 10.48), under his leadership the Ghibellines twice expelled the Guelfs, first in 1248 with the help of Frederick II and later, after the great victory of Montaperti in 1260 (*Inf.* 10.85–87), with the help of Florence's hated rivals, the Sienese and King Manfred. Farinata died in 1264. Some nineteen years later, on 16 October 1283, the Florentine inquisition, headed by the Franciscan Salomone da Lucca, posthumously condemned both Farinata and his deceased wife Adaletta as impenitent Cathars. Their remains were removed from their resting place in the Church of Santa Croce and deposited in unconsecrated ground.

Farinata degli Uberti. Invenzioni di Giovanni Flaxman sulla Divina commedia, *illustrated by John Flaxman and Beniamino del Vecchio, Rome, 1826. Giamatti Collection: Courtesy of the Mount Holyoke College Archives and Special Collections.*

Farinata is the first of the legendary Florentines judged by the pilgrim in his encounter with Ciacco to have been *degni* ("worthy," *Inf.* 6.79–81); and his judgment according to the ways of this world receives a rude correction in Ciacco's uncompromising reply informing him that God has in fact damned Farinata with those other famous Florentines *tra l'anime più nere* ("among the blacker souls," 85). It is therefore in the fiery cemetery at the entrance to the City of Dis that Farinata appears to Dante among a particular group of the heretics of the sixth circle, the followers of Epicurus, those *che l'anima col corpo morta fanno* ("who make the soul die with the body," *Inf.* 10.15). As Virgil points out with the pregnant word *cimitero* ("cemetery," 13), the heretics who denied the immortality of the human soul now have for all eternity what they proclaimed in life: the grave that they considered the ultimate destiny for humanity. Despite the poet's aversion to the denial of the soul's immortality (*Conv.* 2.8.8–16), his portrayal of Farinata recognizes the latter's greatness of character.

The dialogue between the pilgrim and Farinata, interrupted by Cavalcante's questioning (52–72), takes up most of canto 10. Out of the fiery darkness, a voice suddenly breaks through the silence of the open tombs, and in a few lines (22–27) the poet achieves a miracle of compression. In a mere thirty-eight words, the reader learns that the speaker has recognized the wayfarer as a Florentine (cf. Matt. 26.73), as a living person, and as someone of honorable and courteous speech; at the same time, the speaker signals his lifelong devotion to Florence by declaring himself (now a citizen of the Devil's city) to have been a native of that noble city which he had "perhaps" harmed by his actions, *a la qual forse fui troppo molesto* ("to which I perhaps was too harmful," 27). The nobility and gravity of Farinata's speech are evident in his choice of words and the rhythmic intensity of his utterance (e.g., the proparoxytone of *piacciati* ("let it please you") in verse 24, with the natural stress falling on the word *forse* ("perhaps") in verse 27, thereby emphasizing the psychological drama behind the damned soul's reluctant admission that he had in fact harmed his beloved native city, for which he would have gladly sacrificed his own life (91–93;

cf. John 15:13). Virgil therefore warns the pilgrim that his speech must be worthy of his noble interlocutor (39).

Virgil has—in some mysterious way—recognized the speaker, identifying him for the pilgrim and telling him to turn toward the fiery tomb, where he will see Farinata from the waist up. The stress apparent in *tutto 'l vedrai* ("you will see *all* of him," 33) has led critics to dwell on Farinata's imposing, statuesque appearance—especially, when contrasted with his neighbor (53–54). Two critics (Durling and Cassell) have, however, pointed to an irony implicit in Farinata's stance, which appears as an infernal parody of the *Imago pietatis,* where the upper portion of Christ's body was represented as both dead and yet vertical—a reminder of Christ's sacrifice on the cross and his promise of eternal life (cf. 1 Cor. 15:12–22). Christ ascended into Heaven from his open tomb; instead, after the Last Judgment, Farinata and his fellow heretics will be imprisoned for eternity in the tombs they had chosen as their final resting place (10–12). The irony is underscored by Farinata's posture and countenance, in his apparent contempt for Hell described (35–36).

Farinata's whole raison d'être is then revealed (42) in his question *Chi fuor li maggior tui?* ("Who were your forebears?"). Unable to recognize the wayfarer, born the year after his death, Farinata is not interested in the individual before him nor in the latter's extraordinary mission as a voyager through the afterlife; the Ghibelline leader has only one desire, to be able to place a political label on his interlocutor: "Friend or foe?" Again, Farinata's all-pervasive egotism is manifest in his declaration that Dante's ancestors had been bitter enemies *a me e a miei primi e a mia parte* ("to me and to my ancestors and to my party," 47), where the order *self-family-party* reflects Farinata's total absorption of clannish and party fortunes within the political microcosm of his own ego. Farinata's Ghibelline arrogance, his boast that he had twice exiled Dante's Guelf ancestors (who are thus elevated to an eminence they hardly enjoyed in reality), stings the pilgrim to the quick. It is essential to realize that the author of the *Commedia*—who denounced both Guelfs and Ghibellines (*Par.* 6.97–111)—portrays himself as he really was in the year 1300: elected prior of the Guelf commune in that year, totally enmeshed in the political struggles and factions afflicting the "divided city" (*Inf.* 6.61). And here we may discover the fundamental link uniting heresy and faction. Both destroy the life-giving unity of the city in its two essential manifestations: the universality of the City of God in the communion of the faithful on earth and the city-state on which Dante's universal empire rested (cf. *Par.* 8.115–117).

The pilgrim's taunt, that his ancestors twice returned from exile (in 1251 and 1267) whereas Farinata's family has never learned *"quell'arte"* ("that art," 51), goes straight to its mark. In an episode of twenty-one verses, played out between Dante and Farinata's Guelf enemy Cavalcante, Farinata remains silent and detached. With supreme dramatic skill, the poet contrasts Cavalcante's virtual annihilation at the news of his son's supposed death with the stoic self-control displayed by his neighbor (73–75). In his steely composure, Dante's Farinata reflects Aristotle's description of the great-souled or magnanimous man (*Ethics* 4.3). Indeed, the description of him as *magnanimo* ("great soul," 73) offers the reader a verbal microcosm reflecting the complexity of his personality, which combines great courage and composure with immense, unbending pride, while his motionless neck (75) may well remind us of Jehovah's anger against his stiff-necked people (Deut. 31:27). Also relevant is Dante's great sensitivity to the etymology of the words he uses: it is therefore difficult to imagine that he could have been blind to the terrible irony implicit in describing a damned soul as *magnanimo,* when that sinner had in fact denied the immortality—hence the true greatness—of his own soul.

The dramatic differentiation between Farinata and Cavalcante is an outstanding example of the way the author of the *Commedia* represented each soul portrayed as a discrete individual, in utter contrast to the general anonymity and universal monotony that characterize medieval visions of the afterlife. Nevertheless, Farinata, too, is overwhelmed by what the pilgrim has revealed: in verses 77–78 he admits that the news of the Uberti's failure to return to Florence torments him *più che questo letto* ("more than this bed"). As a statement, this is theologically absurd but profoundly human. Strictly speaking, the sinner's infernal bed must be the totality of his sufferings. As a great artist, however, Dante is bent on revealing the fragility of the surrogates for immortality sought by these heretics: for Cavalcante, his son; for Farinata, his family and his party.

Farinata then declares that before fifty months have passed, Dante will himself learn how difficult is the art of returning from exile—thus amplifying a "prophecy" made by Ciacco (*Inf.* 6.64–75), soon to be amplified in the encounter with Brunetto Latini (*Inf.* 15.61–96). It is Farinata, however, who is chosen by the poet to give the pilgrim his first clear warning of impending exile. The fifty months refer to the period in Dante's exile (1302–1304) when he joined the exiled White Guelfs and Ghibellines in their attempts to return to Florence (cf. *Epistle* 1). In 1304, Dante disassociated himself from the other Whites (*Par.* 17.61–69), while their ignominious defeat at La Lastra on July 20, 1304, highlighted yet again the difficulties of the "art" of returning to Florence from exile.

Farinata then asks the pilgrim why the Florentines are so pitiless in their persecution of the Uberti family (83–84). A similar fate awaited Dante Alighieri, whose sons were automatically sentenced to exile at the age of fourteen, and who, like their father, were excluded from the general amnesty offered by the hard-pressed Florentine commune in 1315. As a father, Dante must have struggled to justify within himself his actions and the fateful consequences they had for his children; as a poet, the moral and all-too-human dilemma he faced inspired some of his greatest poetic recreations: Farinata (whose son Lapo Dante met in exile), Cavalcante (father of Dante's "first friend"), Ulysses, Ugolino.

The pilgrim replies that it was the slaughter of the Florentine Guelfs, perpetrated at the battle of Montaperti in 1260, that motivated the commune's adamant refusal to allow the Uberti to return. Farinata's present anguish is now obvious: instead of his previous immobility, he sighs and shakes his head, declaring that he was not alone in inflicting the defeat that had made the River Arbia run red with Florentine blood. Instead, he was the only one who dared to defy the other Ghibellines at the Council of Empoli, when they proposed to raze Florence to the ground, thus saving his native city from destruction. It is interesting to note that the Guelf historian Giovanni Villani compares Farinata to Marcus Camillus, the savior of Rome, in *Cronica* 7.81, while in another passage (13.44) Farinata is listed with Dante and three Florentine Guelfs, together with Camillus, Scipio Africanus, and Julius Caesar, as outstanding examples of great citizens who received nothing but base ingratitude from their native cities. Even after Dante's death, Farinata's defense of his native city at Empoli would still be remembered as an act of heroism.

The pilgrim expresses the hope (93) that Farinata's descendants may finally find peace, and he goes on to ask about the sinners' knowledge of contemporary events on earth. Farinata replies (100–108) that they can only see things at a certain distance; when events are near or actually occur, they are quite outside the sinners' knowledge. The damned will therefore suffer from this mental void, after the Last Judgment, when there will be nothing but an eternal present—a punishment particularly fitting for the heretics who had taken inordinate pride in their intellectual prowess and knowledge (but cf. *Inf.* 16.67–72, 27.25–28).

Farinata's final words indicate not only that there he is surrounded by a multitude of heretics who had denied the soul's immortality but also that such a "bestial" belief has corrupted the pinnacles of both Church and state, *'l secondo Federico / e 'l Cardinale* ("the second Frederick, and the Cardinal," 119–120). Like Farinata, Frederick II proved that greatness of character and damnable heresy can coexist in the same individual.

Bibliography

Auerbach, E. "Farinata and Cavalcante." In *Mimesis*. New York: Doubleday, 1957, pp. 151–177.

Bosco, U. "Né dolcezza di figlio . . ." In *Dante vicino*. Caltanissetta-Roma: Sciascia, 1966, pp. 185–191.

Cassell, A. K. "Farinata." In *Dante's Fearful Art of Justice*. Toronto: University of Toronto Press, 1984, pp. 15–31.

Durling, R. M. "Farinata and the Body of Christ." *Stanford Italian Review* 2:1 (1981), 5–35.

Moleta, V. B. "Dante's Heretics and the Resurrection." *Medioevo Romanzo* 7 (1980), 247–284.

Petrocchi, G. "Tre postille in margine a Farinata." In *Itinerari danteschi*. Bari: Adriatica, 1969, pp. 276–294.

Scott, J. A. "Farinata as *magnanimo*." *Romance Philology* 15 (1962), 1–13.

John A. Scott

Federico Novello

Among the Late Repentant who died violently (with repentance *in extremis*) and who beg for prayers to hasten their departure from the Ante-Purgatory and admission into Purgatory (*Purg.* 6.17). The son of Guido Novello of the Counts Guidi of Casentino, he was a fervent Ghibelline, participating in a number of military actions.

According to early commentators, he was killed in 1289 by a member of the Guelf Bostoli of Arezzo, but other sources report that he died in 1291 while fighting to regain control of his family lands in the Casentino.

Antonio Illiano

Federigo Tignoso

A relatively obscure figure who probably lived in the first part of the thirteenth century. A member of the Tignosi of Rimini, although said to have lived in Bertinoro, he was renowned for his wealth and generosity, as Guido del Duca claims in his praise of him and of other worthy figures on the second terrace of Purgatory (*Purg.* 14.106).

Paul Colilli

Feltro

City in northeastern Italy whose modern-day name is Feltre, referred to prophetically by Cunizza da Romano in *Par* 9.52–53. In *Inf* 1.105, the phrase, *sua nazion sarà tra feltro e feltro* ("his birth will be between felt and felt") is used to refer prophetically to the birth of the Veltro, or "greyhound," a figure Dante believes will deliver Italy from corruption and evil. Many different interpretations of the line—depending, in a large part, upon the broader problem of the identification of the Veltro—have been proposed. For some, the line, read as *tra Feltro e Feltro* ("between Feltro and Feltro"), is interpreted as specifying the area in which the Veltro will be born. Most take the line as referring to the cities of Feltre and Montefeltro (in which case the Veltro would be identified with Cangrande or with Benedict XI); although, if the Veltro is identified with Uguccione della Faggiuola, San Leo Feltrio and Macerata Feltria may be intended. For others, the fabric, felt, is indicated, suggesting that the Veltro will be of humble origins, or that he will be a friar. Other interpretations include: a link with the Tartars, whose leaders were buried wrapped in felt; an indication that the Veltro will be born under a favorable constellation; a reference to the felt-lined urn used, in the communes, for the voting-in of magistrates; or an allusion to the traditional felt caps of Castor and Pollux, the twins of the sign of Gemini. In this case the Veltro would be identified with Dante himself, who was born under this sign, as he recalls in *Par.* 22.114.

Bibliography

Davis, Charles. T. "Il problema del Veltro nell'*Inferno* di Dante." *Enciclopedia dantesca,* 5: 908–912.

Getto, Giovanni. "Canto I." In *Lectura Dantis Scaligera: Inferno.* Florence: Le Monnier, 1967, pp. 3–24.

Olschki, Leonard. *Dante "Poeta Veltro."* Florence: Olschki, 1953.

———. *The Myth of Felt.* Berkeley and Los Angeles: University of California Press, 1949.

Petrocchi, G. "Il canto I dell'*Inferno*." In *Nuove Letture Dantesche.* Florence: Le Monnier, 1966. Vol. I, pp. 1–16.

Vallone, A. "Il veltro." In *Studi su Dante medievale.* Florence: Olschki, 1965, pp. 127–142.

Claire Honess

Ferdinand IV of Castille

Ferdinando, king of Castile and Leon (1295–1312). One of the negligent and irresponsible rulers referred to by the Eagle in the Heaven of Jupiter, blamed for his luxury and effeminacy (*Par.* 19.125). He is in office at the time that the poem's action is conceived to take place (1300).

R. A. Malagi

Fiesole

Etruscan city, situated on a hill close to Florence. More important, culturally and commercially, than its neighbor until the tenth century, its fortunes fell as those of Florence rose, culminating in the city's destruction at the hands of the Florentines in 1125.

Dante is concerned, above all, with the legendary history of the city, which attributed the foundation of Fiesole to Atlas, whose son Dardanus had founded Troy and thus set in motion the series of events which brought Aeneas to Italy to found the Roman Empire. According to these legends Catiline had held out against the Romans in Fiesole after his conspiracy against Cicero, and traditionally, it was to avenge this act that Julius Caesar had ordered the destruction of Fiesole, and the construction of a new city—Florence, the *bellissima e famosissima figlia di Roma* ("most beautiful and famous daughter of Rome," *Conv.* 1.3.4)—which was peopled by a mixture of Fiesolans and Romans.

It is to these legends that Cacciaguida alludes in *Par.* 15.125–126 in his depiction of the good

Florentine mother of his day, who *favoleggiava con la sua famiglia / d'i Troiani, di Fiesole e di Roma* ("told with her household tales of the Trojans, of Fiesole, and of Rome"). Here the passing on of civic history is presented as an important element of good citizenship.

In *Par.* 16.121–122 Cacciaguida refers to immigration to Florence from Fiesole—*Già era 'l Caponsacco [. . .] / disceso giù da Fiesole* ("Already Caponsacco had come down from Fiesole")—while in the encounter with Brunetto Latini, the factional conflicts in Florence are seen as deriving from the Fiesolan element within the city, and from the fact that Florence's Roman inheritance no longer serves as a model for its citizens. The Florentines are thus defined as *quello ingrato popolo maligno / che discese di Fiesole ab antico* ("that ungrateful, malicious people who came down from Fiesole of old," *Inf.* 15.61–62), and as *le bestie fiesolane* ("the Fiesolan beasts," *Inf.* 15.73), while Dante is *la sementa sante / di que' Roman che vi rimaser quando / fu fatto il nido di malizia tanta* ("the holy seed of the Romans who remained there when that nest of so much malice was built," *Inf.* 15.76–78).

The Fiesolan support for Catiline is referred to in *Par.* 6.53–54, when Justinian remarks that the imperial eagle *a quel colle / sotto 'l qual tu nascesti parve amaro* ("to that hill under which you were born [. . .] seemed bitter"); and in *Epist.* 6.24 the *miserrima Fesulanorum propago* ("most wretched offshoot of Fiesole"), which had opposed Rome at the time of Catiline, is seen as rebelling once more against the empire, this time in its resistance to Henry VII.

Claire Honess

Figuralism

In his groundbreaking essay "Figura" (1939), Erich Auerbach adopted the term "figuralism" in order to clearly distinguish Dante's realistic mode of representation in the *Commedia* from other modes of allegory and symbolism that were popular during the Middle Ages. Although like other modes it is used to signify one thing by another, figuralism always has to do with concrete, historical realities, not with abstractions, personifications, or mere analogical correspondences to an invisible, purely spiritual (Neoplatonic) universe. Modeled on the Bible, the characters and events represented by the method of figuralism are taken to have really existed or to have happened as recorded.

In figural representation in the Bible, historical realities are understood to be intrinsically related to each other by special correspondences. Specifically, persons and events of the Old Testament are taken to signify persons and events in the New Testament. Both members of the figural relation are equally real and historical, but the New Testament personality or event is considered to be the "fulfillment" of the corresponding "figure" in the Old Testament.

To the extent that in the figural relation one thing is signified by another, it can be called "allegorical" in a broad sense. This usage is in fact current in the literature of and on "biblical allegory" (see De Lubac). Nevertheless, the figural relations of prefiguration and fulfillment obtaining between what are reputedly real historical facts and individuals cannot be produced by allegory as a merely rhetorical technique. An allegory may refer to what is no more than a construction of figurative language, or it may be an elaborate metaphor for something more abstract or merely mythical or fictitious. In figural relations, on the other hand, it is not language but the realities themselves that signify, and what they signify is the reality in which they will ultimately be fulfilled and have their final meaning revealed.

This makes the figure an essentially relational reality. When presented as figures, personages or events are in specific relations and have determinate significances. For instance, Moses receiving the Law on Mount Sinai stands as a figure of Christ promulgating his new commandment in the Sermon on the Mount. Both individuals are taken as fully historical, but the meaning of each is understood as determined by the other. The figure of Moses handing down the Law to the Jews prepares the way for understanding the significance of Jesus' new teaching and his law of love. At the same time, the full significance of Moses is disclosed only retrospectively, when the Christian gospel appears as the fulfillment of the Old Testament Law. In a sense special to figuralism, Moses represents Christ in a preliminary, veiled, and incomplete form, while Christ's full historical reality and significance are achieved through his fulfilling the role of a new Moses.

In general, the figures of the Old Testament all point to or signify the central figure of the New Testament—namely, Christ—and other persons

F and things (like Rahab as a figure for the Church) related to him. This system of biblical figuralism is known alternatively as "typology," and the Old Testament figure is termed the "type," while its fulfillment in the New Testament goes by the name of "antitype." Abraham's setting about to sacrifice his only son, Isaac, who carries for his father the wood up the mountain of Moriah (recounted in Gen. 12), is a type for the sacrifice by God the Father of his only-begotten Son, who bears his wooden cross up Mount Calvary. Even Adam, in his created perfection, is a type or figure of Christ, the New Adam (1 Cor. 15:47), who has returned to pay the outstanding debt of the old one.

In the strict sense, then, figuralism concerns the relation of the Old Testament to the New. Its sources are in the Gospel of Matthew and St. Paul's interpretations of Old Testament events as being "types or examples for us." In what became a touchstone text for the Middle Ages and specifically for Dante, Paul interpreted the Exodus figurally as a type for the pilgrimage of the Church, and the saving of the Hebrews in the Red Sea served as a figure of baptism (1 Cor. 10:1–11). Paul similarly interpreted the two sons of Abraham, Ishmael and Isaac, as figures for the synagogue and the Church: the one born to Abraham's slave, Hagar, and the other to his wife, Sarah, prefigure, respectively, the old covenant of bondage to the Law and the new covenant of freedom offered to the children of God, heirs to the kingdom of Heaven (Gal. 4:21–31). Consistently, Paul saw in Jewish rites and religion "a shadow of things to come" (Col. 2:17)—that is, a figure of Christ and the Christian liberty that frees from the Law through grace. "The old law is a figure of the new law" (*Lex vetus figura est novae legis,* Heb. 7:19).

The early Church fathers followed Paul's lead in interpreting the Old Testament figurally, but at the same time they mixed figural interpretation with forms of interpretation based on various sorts of allegory. Origen, in particular, while not unimportant to the development of the figural interpretation of the historical realities of Scripture, tended to favor a more abstractly spiritual- or moral-allegorical method of exegesis in which the supposedly historical contents of Scripture were interpreted as signifying inner states of the soul or philosophical doctrines. In St. Augustine, however, these divergent exegetical tendencies are harmonized by according a clear priority to historical-figural—that is, real-prophetic—interpretation. In addition to relying on the Pauline source texts to validate figural interpretation, Augustine finds the method to be authorized by John 5:46, in which Christ says, "If you had believed Moses, you would have believed me, for he wrote of me" (see *City of God* 20.28). Accordingly, the Pentateuch, of which Moses was considered to be the author, and by extension the whole of the Old Testament, was held to be "about Christ"; that is, everything in it was held to signify him, in his various relations, figurally.

From such early interpretive practices emerged the fourfold method of scriptural exegesis that became canonical in the Middle Ages and which Dante outlines in *Conv.* 2.1, expressly applying it to the interpretation of his poem in *Epist.* 13.20–25 (assuming he wrote it). The method makes room for a moral-allegorical level of meaning alongside the literal-historical and strictly figural or typological meaning, and it includes as well an anagogical meaning by which history prefigures what is beyond history—the kingdom to come. The fourfold method of exegesis thus integrates figural with allegorical interpretation broadly considered, and this integration is especially suited to and evident in Dante's adaptation of these exegetical methods to his poetic project.

There is, however, a serious obstacle to taking Dante's poem as figural in the sense that is defined by the Bible and its exegesis. For Dante emphasizes that what he sees is damnation or salvation realized, not just prefigured. It is the state of souls in eternity (*status animarum post mortem, Epist.* 13.24) and not just a figure for this. Dante's souls do not signify anything beyond themselves, and nothing is going to come after to fulfill them. However, a qualification is necessary here, for the souls will be reunited with their bodies after the Last Judgment, and their state will then be perfected (*Inf.* 6.103–111; *Purg.* 1.73–75; and *Par.* 14.37–66). Nevertheless, this "perfecting" still does not involve a relation between two historical entities, but only the more intense realization of an existence itself already beyond history. The main point about the souls Dante sees in the afterlife is that they already have their fulfillment in themselves, and this is what so radically distinguishes them from all this-worldly, historical beings.

In order to understand the *Commedia* as basically figural, we need to consider the earthly existences of the individuals that Dante encounters in the otherworld. It is this historical life that is the figure of what Dante sees fulfilled in the afterlife. The historical life is not directly represented by Dante in his encounter with the souls in the afterlife but is generally related by the characters themselves or, at any rate, it "shows through" as the kind of life—in its decisive act or crucial moment—that would inevitably lead to such a state in eternity as Dante does see and represent. On this basis, if there is to be a figural connection, it must generally be established backward to the earthly existence that, while not necessarily represented in the poem, in fact constitutes the basis for Dante's representations of eternity. In other words, Dante indirectly represents human character as it was on earth, and this representation is the figure of what is fulfilled in the afterlife of Dante's poem.

This relation to historical reality is evident in the example on which Auerbach's exposition turns—namely, the historical Cato as figure of what he is to become in the afterlife. The pagan Cato, known to Dante from tradition for his unyielding integrity, is recognizable in the venerable, albeit rigid and unyielding, solitary old man *(veglio solo)* astonishingly revealed on the shore of Purgatory as its guardian. The historical Cato of Utica valued political freedom above his own life—which he himself took in order to avoid outliving the free Roman republic—making him an apt prefiguration of the watchman over Christian freedom that he becomes in the realm of the afterlife. Moreover, as a guardian of the Law, Cato shows up in the guise of a pagan Moses, as is also hinted at in his transfigured face. This sort of allusion to an Old Testament figure who parallels the figure evoked from ancient pagan history suggests that Dante's procedure constitutes an extension of figuralism from its originally biblical application to the wider field of universal history. Just as Christian interpreters had read the Old Testament, so Dante reads ancient history figurally.

Dante's representations, then, can be of figures taken from universal history. Yet still, the fulfillment of these figures seems not to be historical and hence not to fit exactly the definition of figuralism. For the souls as Dante sees them are in eternity. Here a somewhat more complicated model than one based simply on the relation between the Old and the New Testaments, which defines typology or figuralism in the strictest sense, becomes necessary.

The system of figural correspondences in the Bible itself was indeed not limited solely to relations between the Old Testament and the New, but could be extended further from the New Testament to subsequent history in such a way that events of Christ's life were taken to signify what was to happen in the age of the Church. Jesus' miracles—for example, the feeding of the five thousand—came to be read as figures of the sacraments, and his parables of the kingdom of Heaven were taken as prophecies of the establishment of the Church on Earth. Martha and Mary, themselves prefigured by the Old Testament sisters Leah and Rachel, were widely held to be figures, respectively, of the active and contemplative lives and callings of Christians. Peter's healing of a paralyzed man by the gate of the temple, as recounted in Acts 3, was read as a figure of baptism.

But a further step is nevertheless necessary to make Dante's new use of figuralism in representing the afterlife comprehensible in terms of its biblical precedent. Indeed, biblical figuralism, too, turns out to have a further, ultrahistorical dimension, to the extent that the historical events of the New Testament themselves figure something to be realized only at the end of time, in the *eschaton*. Christ incarnate and his actions on Earth prefigure what will be consummated at his Second Coming for all eternity. This is the "anagogical" sense in which Scripture represents what in fact exceeds history in fulfilling it.

This reference to what may be beyond history does not weaken the historical specificity—the reality of both figure and fulfillment—of figuralism, but rather raises it to another level. For the consummation of history in eternity reveals the final truth of history: making it even more real than historical reality itself. Dante's representation of the eternal states of souls thus comprehends their historical reality while projecting it into the suprareality of an eschatological existence where history is perfected and fulfilled.

Dante's realized eschatology, his representing the eternal states of souls in the shape of historical individuals, tends to blur the lines between figure and fulfillment, but in this it is actually consonant with the Christian theology of the Christ event. For the Resurrection of Christ is already the fulfillment of history, the *eschaton;* it is paradoxically the end of history within history, though its full implications are still to be worked out by the further development and consummation for all of what is definitively achieved already in Christ. To this extent, the relation of figure and fulfillment

F between the New Testament and subsequent history can even be reversed. All fullness is in Christ and the Christ event, of which subsequent Christian history is a "postfiguration."

Chief examples of the *Commedia*'s figuralism, taken by Auerbach and other interpreters as integral to the poet's method of representing the other world throughout the poem, are Virgil and Beatrice. For centuries, failure to clearly recognize the difference between figural, or real-prophetic, and other forms of allegorical representation, resulted in treating Virgil as only an allegory of Reason, rather than as a concrete, historical individual. As a figure, however, it is precisely the historical Virgil that signifies, prefiguring by his earthly life the Virgil in Limbo, who is likewise posited as a concretely real existence. Virgil the prophet of empire and the Roman poet who leads the likes of Statius to Christian salvation, prefigures the Virgil who guides Dante through the realm of the afterlife, just as the historical Rome prefigures the kingdom of God, the Rome in which Christ is a Roman (*Purg.* 32.102). The significance of Virgil in God's providential plan is thus represented as fulfilled in eternity, without in any way diminishing Virgil's historical reality, but rather precisely on that historical basis.

As for Beatrice, similar debates have stretched over centuries, attempting to resolve the question of her identity—as either a Florentine girl or an allegory for theology—one way or the other. But considered figurally, her historical reality does not exclude but rather grounds her theological meaning. Her apotheosis as an incarnation of divine revelation—that is, as a personal savior and beatifier, a *figura Christi* for Dante—brings to the highest imaginable consummation his real, historical relation to her as the object of his total love and devotion.

The figural relation between two concrete realities which makes one element (whether earlier or later) the figure for the other must not be understood as imposed externally by an arbitary act of interpretation. In the language of medieval exegesis, figural significances are *innatae* rather than *illatae,* not inferential but inherent in the things themselves. These are significances that history proves to realize and reveal. The figure of Joshua's leading the Israelites over Jordan into the promised land, for example, is not simply comparable or analogous to Christ's leading humanity out of sin into salvation but rather intrinsically related

to this later, culminating event. Although the figure is a real event in and for itself, its deepest reality, what it truly is and means, is revealed and realized only through the figural relation to the culminating historical reality, the fulfillment.

The significances embodied in figural relations, consequently, are established exclusively by the Creator and Lord of history, who alone determines what history definitively is and means. Indeed, figuralism presupposes a conception of history as guided teleologically, as *intended* in accordance with a providential plan that gives specific significance to each individual and event by reference to the final end of all things. Such significance can be disclosed only by revelation, in which history's final meaning is known—a conception that is alien to modern views of history, which are based rather on chronological and causal connections in a continuum of events without any known end.

The importance for Dante studies of figuralism, generally presumed to be fundamental to the composition of the *Commedia,* resides in its embodying what is ultimately a prophetic mode of writing that approximates the kind of writing employed, according to tradition, by God himself—in the Bible and even more fundamentally in authoring history, of which the Bible discloses the meaning. The keynote for Auerbach's theory of "figura," as well as for the great part of Dante criticism that follows him, is realism. And this certainly deserves the recognition it has achieved as an *aspect* of Dante's vision. But Dante's representations of historical reality were a figure of what was more real than "reality." Ultimately, realism is resolved by Dante into his vision of eternity. Indeed, the final insight encapsulated in the term "figuralism" is that Dante's representations in the *Commedia* purport to reveal in a definitive perspective, sub specie aeternitatis, the full historical meaning and reality of individuals and events.

Bibliography

Armour, Peter. "The Theme of Exodus in the First Two Cantos of the Purgatorio." In *Dante Soundings: Eight Literary and Historical Essays.* Edited by David Nolan. Dublin: Irish Academic Press, 1981.

Auerbach, Erich. "Figura." *Scenes from the Drama of European Literature.* New York: Meridian Books, 1959.

———. "Typological Symbolism in Medieval Literature." *Yale French Studies* 9 (1952), 3–10. Rpt. in *American Critical Essays on the "Divine Comedy."* Edited by R. J. Clemens. New York: New York University Press, 1967, pp. 104–113.

———. "Figurative Texts Illustrating Certain Passages of Dante's *Commedia.*" *Speculum* 21 (1946), 474–489. Rpt. in Auerbach, *Gesammelte Aufsätze zur romanischen Philologie.* Bern: Francke, 1967, pp. 93–108.

Charity, A. C. *Events and Their Afterlife: The Dialectics of Christian Typology in the Bible and Dante.* Cambridge: Cambridge University Press, 1966.

Chydenius, John. *The Typological Problem in Dante: A Study in the History of Medieval Ideas.* Commentationes Humanarum Litterarum 25/1. Helsingfors: Societas Scientiarum Fennica, 1958.

De Lubac, Henri. *Exégèse médiévale: Les quattre sens de l'écriture.* 4 vols. Paris: Aubier, 1959–1964.

Demaray, John. *Dante and the Book of the Cosmos.* Transactions of the American Philosophical Society 77, pt. 5 (1987).

Hollander, Robert. *Allegory in Dante's Commedia.* Princeton, N.J.: Princeton University Press, 1969.

Pépin, Jean. *Dante et la tradition de l'allégorie.* Paris: Vrin, 1970.

Sayers, Dorothy. "The Fourfold Interpretation of the Comedy." In *Introductory Papers on Dante.* New York: Barnes and Noble, 1954.

Schwietering, Julius. "Typologisches in mittelalterlicher Dichtung." In *Vom Werden des deutschen Geistes. Festgabe Gustave Ehrismanns.* Edited by Paul Merker and Wolfgang Stammler. Berlin: de Gruyter, 1925.

Singleton, Charles. *Dante Studies 1. Dante's "Commedia": Elements of Structure.* Cambridge, Mass.: Harvard University Press, 1954.

Thompson, David. "Figure and Allegory in the Commedia." *Dante Studies* 90 (1972), 1–11.

William Franke

Fiore

A minor work in the Italian vernacular attributed to Dante, *Il Fiore* ("The Flower") is a series of 232 sonnets that summarize the narrative of the *Roman de la rose,* the masterpiece of Old French allegorical literature. Contained in ms. H 438 of the Biblioteca Interuniversitaria of Montpellier, the poem was published for the first time in 1881 by its discoverer, Fernand Castets. This same manuscript also has a section containing the *Detto d'Amore* (Ashb. 1334, now located in the Biblioteca Laurenziana in Florence). The *Detto d'Amore* likewise attempts to adapt the *Rose,* in a much more condensed manner and with a very different metric form.

The first part of the *Rose* composed by Guillaume de Lorris, which is idealistic and courtly, had already served as a model for Brunetto Latini's *Tesoretto,* an allegorical-didactic poem in mono-rhyming couplets of seven-syllable lines written in France at the beginning of the 1260s. The *Detto* and the *Fiore* were composed in Florence in the 1280s and 1290s, and are true remakings of the *Rose* (to which Jean de Meun had by then added his own continuation emphasizing scholastic learning).

The question of Dante's authorship of the two works, particularly the *Fiore,* rests on arguments that have remained essentially the same since the time of Castets. The most important evidence of authenticity is provided by the internal signature: the author twice identifies himself as Durante, the diminutive of which is "Dante" (82.9 and 202.14). Even if the second instance occurs in a completely comical and insignificant context, the first instance corresponds to Jean de Meun's citation of Guillaume de Lorris in a part of the *Rose* that is primary for the identification of the two authors. "Durante" is thus the name of the first-person narrator, but also the name of the poem's author. Additional evidence appears in the first quarter of sonnet 97, where the poet employs the evangelic motif of the wolf disguised as a sheep (which reappears in the *Commedia*). The parallel reference to Frate Alberto in two of the *Fiore*'s sonnets (88.13 and 130.4) and in Dante's sonnet "Messer Brunetto, questa pulzelletta" (*Rime* 99.10) suggests a common origin for these two texts. Further evidence of Dante's authorship is the recollection of the violent death of Siger of Brabante (92.9–11), who will appear in *Par.* 10.133–138. In the *Fiore,* the Averroist philosopher and adversary of St. Thomas is exalted for his futile battle against the overwhelming power of Scholastic logic. In *Paradiso,* he is praised by St. Thomas himself for the significant way in which his philosophical truth coincided with theological truth.

Beyond evidence of a cultural nature external to the poem, recent critics have directed their attention to internal, textual evidence of the kind that Gianfranco Contini labels "echoes of Dante within Dante." Yet Francesco D'Ovidio had already argued that not only the *candida rosa* of *Paradiso*'s final cantos was a correction of the profane, sensual *rosa* hidden in the *Fiore,* but that the word *Cristo* rhyming with itself in *Paradiso* made amends for the *Fiore* (e.g., 104.9–13) in which *Cristo* was made to rhyme with *tristo* ("sad") and *ipocristo* ("hypocrite"). There is thus a set of significant examples of lexical and stylistic forms common to the *Fiore* and to Dante's known works (above all the *Commedia*). For example, the phrase "*con gli occhi tor*ti" in *Inf.* 33.76 and "*li occhi tor*si" in *Par.* 3.21 are derived from the same syntagmatic structure ("*gli occhi tor*na" in *Fiore* 26.9).

The attention that Contini and his followers have given to similar microstylistic features has obscured the macrotextual issues that still remain unresolved. The position the *Fiore* occupies within the Italian poetic tradition and within the Dantean corpus has yet to be fully determined. The recent initiative undertaken by a group of English scholars (Barański and Boyde), who focus on an analysis of the *Fiore* within its historical and cultural context and without regard to the question of its authorship, marks a new advance.

What most clearly defines the *Fiore*'s literary achievement is its author's ability to unite the two parts of the *Rose*. The first thirty-four sonnets condense the story told in the first 4,000 verses of the Guillaume de Lorris text, while the following 198 sonnets summarize the nearly 18,000 verses added by Jean de Meun. Thus on one hand, the *Fiore*'s author reintegrates the substantial encyclopedic and doctrinal treatment of the *Rose*'s second part with the fundamental narrative line, and on the other, he harmonizes the ideological and stylistic differences that exist between the two parts. The *Fiore* recounts the narrator's attempt to possess the object of his desire, the *fiore* ("flower"), which symbolizes the intimate being of the beloved. The narrator-lover, assisted by the God of Love, encounters various obstacles in his quest to realize his goal: the resistance deriving from the woman's own emotional reserve in the person of Schifo ("Disgust"), as well as the forces of social disapproval in Malabocca ("Evil Mouth"). The narrator-lover has his own supporters and defenders in the likes of Amico ("Friend"), who counsels the use of disguise and hypocrisy, personified by Falsembiante ("False Seeming"), who later defeats Malabocca. And he must accept assistance from the Vecchia ("Old Lady"), who, during a long discourse in sonnets 144–193, exhorts the beloved to yield to the narrator-lover's amorous proposals. The poem comes to a close with a description of the assault of the castle where the forces of the beloved have prepared their final defense; with the direct intervention of the goddess Venus, all resistance is overcome as the narrator-lover makes his entry and succeeds in plucking the flower from the rosebush.

The *Fiore*'s date is the subject of much controversy. Contini's dating of 1285–1290 is now generally accepted, although earlier views favored a later date of around 1295. The problem assumes a certain degree of importance if the text is attributed to Dante. The earlier date would be very problematic given the autobiographical context of the *Vita Nuova.* That work, centering on Beatrice as *donna angelicata,* projects a transcendental, spiritual concept of love, while the *Fiore* exalts an earthly, blatantly sexual love. The later dating, however, would fit into the context of the poet's straying from the right path, for which Beatrice will chastise Dante in the Earthly Paradise (*Purg.* 30.130–132). This would place the *Fiore* together with a number of other works (e.g., the dispute with Forese, the *rime petrose,* or the *Convivio*) for which the *Commedia* is a palinode.

Bibliography

Alighieri, Dante. *Il Fiore. Detto d'Amore.* Edited by Luca C. Rossi. Milan: Mondadori, 1996.

———. *The Fiore and the Detto d'Amore.* A translation with introduction and notes by Santa Casciani and Christopher Kleinhenz. Notre Dame, Ind.: University of Notre Dame Press, 2000.

Contini, Gianfranco. *Un'idea di Dante: saggi danteschi.* Turin: Einaudi, 1976, pp. 91–93, 153–154, 245–283.

Fasani, Remo. "L'attribuzione del Fiore." *Studi e problemi di critica testuale* 39 (1989), 5–40.

Lettura del "Fiore." Letture Classensi 22 (1993).

The Fiore in Context: Dante, France, Tuscany. Edited by Zygmunt Barański and Patrick Boyde. Notre Dame and London: University of Notre Dame Press, 1997.

Took, John. *Dante: Lyric Poet and Philosopher.* Oxford: Clarendon Press, 1990.

———. "Towards an Interpretation of the *Fiore*." *Speculum* 54 (1979), 500–527.

Michelangelo Picone
(translated by Robin Treasure)

Fire

One of the four sublunar elements in Aristotle's physics, Fire unites the primary qualities Hot and Dry. The lightest of the four elements, it rises naturally toward its proper place just beneath the lunar sphere where it forms a fiery shell. At the start of the *Paradiso*, Dante finds himself passing through this shell of Fire, and this passage triggers his first conversation with Beatrice. Dante is puzzled, initially, by the intense light and then by his ability to rise above the *corpi levi* ("light bodies") of Air and Fire. Beatrice explains this apparent violation

Dante with Beatrice, climbing through the circle of fire below the Heaven of the Moon. Dante, with commentary by Cristofo Landino and Alessandro Vellutello, published in Venice in 1564 by Marchiò Sessa & fratelli. Giamatti Collection: Courtesy of the Mount Holyoke College Archives and Special Collections.

of Aristotelian doctrine by reasserting its central principles in a new Christian form. The human soul, freed of hindrances, rises as naturally toward God as each element seeks out its proper place in the cosmos drawn there by its natural instinct (*Par.* 1.76–142).

John Kleiner

Five Hundred Ten and Five

The number 515 *(cinquecento e dieci e cinque)* announced at *Purg.* 33.43 symbolizes and conceals the identity of the future redeemer of Italy in Dante's prophetic view of history.

In the final stages of his allegorical representation of the historical relationship between the Church and the Empire, Dante describes the transformation of the chariot (the Church) into a hideous monster (*Purg.* 32.136–147). An "ungirt whore" (Pope Boniface VIII, or the corrupt papacy generally) then appears astride the beast, with a giant at her side (Philip the Fair), and the harlot and giant begin to kiss (148–153). When the harlot turns her lustful eyes on Dante, the giant beats his lover and, enraged, drags the monstrous chariot, together with the harlot, deep into the wood and out of Dante's vision (154–160). In the next canto, the last of *Purgatorio*, Beatrice answers Dante's unspoken desire to understand the significance of the violent scene he has just witnessed. Yet, far from clarifying matters, Beatrice's words constitute perhaps the most cryptic of all the prophecies of the *Commedia*:

> *Non sarà tutto tempo sanza reda / l'aguglia che lasciò le penne al carro, / per che divenne mostro e poscia preda, / ch'io veggio certamente, e però il narro, / a darne tempo già stelle propinque, / sicure d'ogn' intoppo e d'ogne sbarro, / nel quale un cinquecento diece e cinque, / messo di Dio, anciderà la fuia / con quel gigante che con lei delinque*
> ("Not for all time without heir will the eagle be who left his feathers on the chariot, whereby it became a monster and then booty, for I see clearly, and therefore I relate it, stars already near, safe from all obstacle and all barrier, that will give us a time in which a five hundred ten and five, messenger of God, will slay the thieving woman and the giant that transgresses with her," *Purg.* 33.37–45).

F Beatrice herself characterizes the prophecy as an *enigma forte* ("hard enigma") in verse 50, and it is surely that as revealed by the attempts of critics and commentators to decipher it over the past six and a half centuries. Despite the very real possibility that Dante may have well intended for his prophecy to be purposefully vague (and to thereby retain its enigmatic quality), numerous interpretations have been offered as to a specific solution, much as the apocalyptic number of the beast in the Book of Revelation (666) was thought to indicate the Emperor Nero.

As to the method of interpretation, the various attempts can be divided into three major types. The first and most common method, beginning with some of the earliest commentators (e.g., Lana, L'Ottimo, Benvenuto), converts the Hindu-Arabic number (515) to its Roman form (500=D, 10=X, 5=V). From here, the usual procedure is to reverse the position of the last two letters in order to obtain the Latin word "DVX," equivalent to "leader," generally understood in a political-military sense. The idea that Dante had in mind a secular ruler accords well with the episode of the Eagle and the chariot (and the giant and the harlot) in *Purg.* 32 that occasioned Beatrice's prophecy in the first place.

The most commonly offered candidates for the prophesied savior are Henry VII and Cangrande della Scala, with a few votes going to the Ghibelline leader Uguccione dalla Faggiuola and Ludwig IV of Bavaria. Support for Henry VII derives from Dante's praise, similar in tone to the present passage, in several of his *Epistles,* though a reference to Henry's future action would seem to imply that Dante wrote the scene before August 1313 when Henry died. Cangrande, on the other hand, emerges as a strong candidate based on Cacciaguida's praise, in nearly prophetic terms, of the young Ghibelline leader in *Par.* 17.76–93 as well as the possible association of Cangrande ("Big Dog") with the *veltro* ("greyhound") of *Inf.* 1. However, the regional sphere of Cangrande's influence perhaps makes him less attractive than Henry VII as the secular ruler Dante appears to invoke with his prophecy.

The second method, pursued independently by Kaske and Sarolli and producing similar results, is also based on converting the number 515 to Roman numerals. These scholars argue that Dante had in mind a well-documented Christological monogram based on prayers preceding the medieval canon of the Mass. These prefatory prayers begin with the words *Vere dignum et iustum est, equum et salutare, nos tibi semper et ubique gratias agere, Domine sancte, Pater omnipotens, eterne Deus* ("It is truly meet and just, right and availing unto salvation, that we at all times and in all places give thanks to Thee, O holy Lord, Father almighty, everlasting God"). As a shorthand liturgical formula for the prayers, the initial letters of the opening Latin words—(V from *Vere,* D from *dignum*)—were often joined with a horizontal line passing through the center. The figure that emerges comprises the letters V and D joined by a small crosslike X, thus producing the three Roman numerals (VXD) of Beatrice's numerical prophecy in reverse order.

The application of this figure to the prophecy is supported by twelfth- and thirteenth-century interpretations of the monogram as a symbol of Christ's incarnational union of divine and human natures (D=*Dio*="God"; V=U=*Uomo*="Man"). In this way, the enigmatic prophecy may be seen as an analogue to the Christlike griffin, while the destructive giant (usually associated with Philip the Fair), according to an exegetical tradition viewing the number of the beast in the Apocalypse (666) as a sign of a giant parodying Christ's dual nature, represents the Antichrist. Consistent with the apocalyptic tone and imagery of Dante's episode, Sarolli and Kaske align the "five hundred, ten, and five" with the final coming of Christ, who will defeat the Antichrist, much as the Hound will drive the she-wolf back into Hell (*Inf.* 1.109–111).

The third prominent type of solution to Dante's enigma is based on the process of gematria, often used in the kabbalah, whereby the letters of the Hebrew alphabet are assigned numerical values. For Moore, recourse to gematria does not offer a new solution to the riddle, only a new method of arriving at an old one. Firmly convinced that Beatrice's prophecy points unequivocally to Henry VII, Moore finds that a form of Henry's name, *Arrico,* a variant of the more common *Arrigo,* could yield the desired number 515 according to the following traditional values: a=aleph=1; r=resh=200 (two times); I=yod=10; c=koph=100; o=4 (this last letter, having no Hebrew equivalent, is assigned a value of 4 because it is the fourth of the five vowels in the sequence *aeiou*). Moore thus concludes that the specific reference to Henry VII based on the application of gematria to "Arrico" complements the more common, general interpretation of the prophecy as "DUX" ("leader"). More recently, Kearney and Schraer have argued that Dante's five hundred and fifteen, when expressed in corresponding Hebrew numbers (four hundred, one hundred, ten and five) produces a word whose sound ("tkeeyah") means the blast of a horn or shofar. This horn blast echoes Gabriel's trumpet at the Last Judgment and therefore reinforces the apocalyptic tone of Dante's prophetic riddle.

Still others, usually based on one of the three methods discussed above, think the prophecy refers to some future pope or to Dante himself. For those who interpret the "five hundred, ten, and five" as a measure of time (as opposed to a being, human or otherwise), the most common explanation is that Dante meant to indicate the year 1315, five hundred and fifteen years after the coronation of Charlemagne as Holy Roman Emperor in 800.

Bibliography

Davidsohn, Robert. "Il 'Cinquecento diece e cinque' del *Purgatorio.*" *Bullettino della Società Dantesca* 9 (1902), 129–131.

Fletcher, Jefferson B. "The Crux of Dante's *Comedy.*" *Romanic Review* 16 (1925), 1–42.

Kaske, R. E. "Dante's 'DXV' and 'Veltro.'" *Traditio* 17 (1961), 185–254.

Kearney, Milo E., and Mimosa S. Schraer. "A Better Interpretation of Dante's 'Cinquecento Diece e Cinque.'" *Italica* 59.1 (1982), 32–40.

Mastrobuono, Antonio C. "The Powerful Enigma." In *Lectura Dantis Newberryana.* Vol. 1. Edited by Paolo Cherchi and Antonio C. Mastrobuono. Evanston, Ill.: Northwestern University Press, 1988, pp. 153–198.

Mazzamuto, Pietro. "Cinquecento diece e cinque." *Enciclopedia dantesca,* 2:10–14.

Moore, Edward. "The DXV Prophecy." In *Studies in Dante, Third Series: Miscellaneous Essays.* 1903. New York: Haskell House, 1968, pp. 253–283.

Sarolli, Gian Roberto. "'DXV' e 'Veltro': simboli cristomimetici." In *Prolegomena alla "Divina Commedia."* Florence: Olschki, 1971, pp. 247–273.

Guy P. Raffa

Fixed Stars

The stars which, unlike the planets, never change their relative position. Aristotelian-Ptolemaic cos-mology considered each of the "wandering" stars (the planets, sun and moon) to be embedded in one of seven transparent concentric spheres rotating about the earth (*Conv.* 2.13.7; 2.3.7); all the fixed stars were embedded in an eighth sphere (*Conv.* 2.3.3,7; 2.13.8; *Par.* 2.64,115,130; *Quest.* 69), whose rotation, according to Aristotle, was responsible for the daily east-west movement of the heavens. The discovery of the precession of the equinoxes, a slight west-east "slippage" in the daily rotation of the stars, led Ptolemy to attribute the cosmic diurnal motion to an invisible, "Crystalline" ninth sphere, the Primum Mobile, or first moving heaven (*Conv.* 2.3.3, 5). In its own particular contrary motion, the eighth sphere was thus the slowest of the heavens (*Purg.* 11.108), completing one west-east rotation in 36,000 years (25,800 by modern calculations), or one degree per century (*Conv.* 2.14.1,10–13,16; 2.5.16; *VN* 2.2).

As the intermediary between the Primum Mobile and the planets, the sphere of fixed stars represents the source of multiplicity in the cosmos: it differentiates the divine light, or formative-generative influence, transmitted from the Empyrean by the Primum Mobile, into distinct formal principles, each embodied in a star (*Par.* 2.130–138; *Quest.* 69–73). Transmitted in turn through the planets to the earth, these specific stellar influences govern the generation and dissolution of all corruptible sublunar substances (*Par.* 2.112–123; 7.139–141; 13.52–66). These diverse influences, as they inhere in the Moon, are manifest as light and dark spots visible from Earth (*Par.* 2.49–148). In *Conv.* 2.3.15 Dante observes that the stars nearest the eighth sphere's equator have the greatest "virtue" or influence.

The light of the fixed stars derives from the sun (*Par.* 23.28–30; 20.1–6; 18.105; *Conv.* 2.13.15; 3.12.7). The stars are classified by size; according to Ptolemy and Alfraganus there are fifteen of the first magnitude (see *Par.* 13.4–6; 28.19). The fixed stars form the constellations visible in the Northern Hemisphere (see *Quest.* 71), those imagined to be in the unseen Southern Hemisphere (*Inf.* 26.127; *Purg.* 1.23; 8.91), and the twelve zodiacal constellations through which the sun moves as it travels along the ecliptic (e.g., *Inf.* 1.38; *Purg.* 32.57; *Par.* 1.40–41; 29.1–3).

In *Conv.* 2.13.8 and 2.14.1–13 Dante compares the eighth sphere to physics and metaphysics: for the number (1022) of its stars (*Conv.*

2.14.2–4); for its band of diffuse light (the galaxy or Milky Way) emanating from indiscernible stars (2.14.5–8); for its two poles, one visible and the other not (2.14.9); and for its double (diurnal and precessional) motion (2.14.10–13).

Dante enters the sphere of fixed stars from Saturn at *Par.* 22.100, and leaves it for the Primum Mobile at *Par.* 27.97. His stay, framed by glances back toward the earth (*Par.* 22.124–153; 27.76–87), is in the constellation of Gemini, the sign of his birth, to which he attributes his genius, and which he invokes for inspiration (*Par.* 22.110–123; 27.98–99). In the eighth heaven Dante is witness to the triumph of Christ and the coronation of Mary (*Par.* 23); after he is interrogated by St. Peter on faith (*Par.* 24), by St. James on hope (*Par.* 25), and by St. John on love (*Par.* 26.1–69), he meets Adam, and asks when and how man fell from grace (*Par.* 26.81–142). St. Peter then delivers an invective against the corruption of the Church, and a prophecy of divine retribution, which he charges Dante to relay (*Par.* 27.10–66); whereupon the blessed souls return to the Empyrean, and Dante and Beatrice ascend to the Primum Mobile.

Christian Moevs

Flatterers

Dante's description of the humiliating punishment of the flatterers (in Italian *adulatori* or *lusingatori*), whom he finds groveling in what looks and smells like a trough of human feces (*in uno sterco / che da li umani privadi parea mosso*, "in dung that seemed to have come from human privies," *Inf.* 18.113–114) in the second of the ten concentric ditches of Malebolge, the eighth circle of Hell, is an outstanding example of his uninhibited realism and his virtuoso matching of style to content. The deliberate use of a plebeian lexicon and the challenging deployment of harsh and difficult multiconsonantal rhyme-words add an expressionistic stylistic dimension to the sycophants' caricature. As much as in the "comic" language and the grotesque attitudes, the poet's contemptuous distance is reflected in the brief space allotted them— *Inf.* 18.100–136 (hardly more than a quarter of a canto)—and the brusque manner of their dismissal. In their commentaries to Ps. 140:5 ("let not the oil of the sinner [*oleum peccatoris*] fatten my head"), Augustine, Cassiodorus, and Thomas Aquinas all gloss the *oleum peccatoris* of the Latin Vulgate as signifying the false praise of the adu-

lator. From here it is a fairly logical step to the poet's parodic anointing of the head of Alessio Interminei with a new kind of chrism, and the excrement-encrusted fingernails of Thais are implicit in the Scriptures' prophecy of a coprophiliac embrace for arms that had valued worldly luxury over goodness (cf. Lam. 4:5: *Qui nutriebantur in croceis, amplexati sunt stercora* ["They that were brought up in scarlet have embraced the dung"]).

Bibliography

Durling, Robert M. "Deceit and Digestion in the Belly of Hell." In *Allegory and Representation: Selected Papers from the English Institute, 1979–80.* Edited by Stephen Greenblatt. Baltimore and London: Johns Hopkins University Press, 1981, pp. 61–93.

Rossi, Aldo. "Lusingatori." *Enciclopedia dantesca,* 3: 744.

Sanguineti, Edoardo. "Canto XVIII." In *Interpretazione di Malebolge.* Florence: Olschki, 1962, pp. 1–33.

Storey, Wayne. "*Inferno* XVIII." In *Lectura Dantis: Supplement.* Vol. 6. *Dante's Divine Comedy. Introductory Readings, I: Inferno.* Edited by Tibor Wlassics. Charlottesville: University of Virginia, 1990, pp. 235–246.

Anthony Oldcorn

Flaxman, John

English sculptor and illustrator (1775–1826). He learned modeling from his father, a plaster-case maker, and in 1770 began studying at the Royal Academy. From 1787 to 1794 he studied classical art in Rome, and he illustrated Homer, Aeschylus, and Dante, evincing praise in a number of countries. His well-known monuments (Robert Burns, Horatio Nelson, Joshua Reynolds) were executed later; he taught sculpture and produced, among other things, a notable relief of the "Shield of Achilles" and a set of Hesiod illustrations engraved by William Blake.

In fact, his 110 pieces (engraved by Tommaso Piroli in 1973 and reissued as *Compositions from the Divine Poem of Dante* in 1807) influenced Blake. But Flaxman was a sculptor; reminiscent of bas-reliefs, his "outline" contours on paper reveal no rounded substances or anatomical details. One cannot speak of a faithful Dantean characterization, if naturalistic musculature is the criterion. Though he influenced Romantic illustrators, his

Dante'   *Virgilio*

Allor si mosse ed io gli tenni dietro.   Inferno Canto 1.

Dante accepting Virgil as guide. Invenzioni di Giovanni Flaxman sulla Divina commedia, *illustrated by John Flaxman and Benia-mino del Vecchio, Rome, 1826. Giamatti Collection: Courtesy of the Mount Holyoke College Archives and Special Collections.*

figures were modeled on ancient statuary; a certain repetitiveness plagues his Dantean work, and, because his draftsmanship excels over his poetic interpretation, his drawings fall short of the poem's vigor and vitality.

Goethe was unsure of Flaxman's talent; A. W. von Schlegel admired it. But subsequent illustrators of the *Commedia* owed him much (Genelli, Pinelli, Girodet, Koch, even Goya who, like the others, greatly appreciated the style of the long-cowled hypocrites and Caiaphas of *Inf.* 23). Flaxman's version of Paolo and Francesca (*Inf.* 5) was echoed in Koch, Ingres, Dyce, and Scheffer, not to mention Carstens. Notable are his illustrations of the diseased falsifiers (*Inf.* 30), the deceptive Geryon (*Inf.* 17), the plight of Guido da Monte-feltro (*Inf.* 27), and Charon's boat (*Inf.* 3). Design supersedes expression. More than an emotion, Flaxman's drawings convey a mood: sulking (*Inf.* 24), resting (*Purg.* 17), dreaming (*Purg.* 28), or gentleness (*Par.* 23 and 33). Movement, too, is one of his fortes—the metamorphoses of thieves and snakes in *Inf.* 25, for example. At times, his representations seem to lack seriousness, like his grotesque Lucifer for *Inf.* 34, or his Dante exerting enormous leverage to snap a twig that will make the suicide, Pier delle Vigne, speak (*Inf.* 13).

Consistent with his sculptural background, Flaxman shaped drapery very economically and on the whole enhanced Dante's own pure-line simplicity. His overall grace and elegance are more eighteenth than nineteenth century, or to put it another way, his dramatic vision befits the *Paradiso* more readily than the *Inferno*. Whatever the case, his work deserves the credit of being the first fully illustrated edition of the *Commedia* since about the middle of the eighteenth century, and his 110 pieces occasioned the vogue of Dante illustrations which followed.

Bibliography

Alighieri, Dante. *The Divine Comedy.* Translated by Kenneth Mackenzie. With 111 engravings by John Flaxman. London: Folio Society, 1979.

Flaxman Designs for Dante: Inferno, Purgatorio, Paradiso. Edited by Bill Tate. Truchas, New Mexico: Tate Gallery, 1968.

Flaxman e Dante. Edited by Corrado Gizzi. Milan: Mazzotta, 1986.

Jean-Pierre Barricelli

Florence

Florence, the city of Dante's birth and the object of both his love and scorn in the *Commedia,* became in the decades before and during his lifetime one of the richest cities in Europe, the hub of a vast commercial and financial empire, the cornerstone of the Guelf alliance that expelled imperial power from Italy, and a self-governing republic that underwent severe factional and social conflicts, one phase of which led to Dante's exile in 1302. From the middle of the thirteenth century, the history of Florence produced dramatic political and military events central to the larger Italian and southern European theater of papal, imperial, and Angevin conflicts. Florence's importance in these struggles lay in its strategic location, its burgeoning population, and its unprecedented economic power. In the midst of this demographic and economic growth, two competing political cultures took shape. The first, an elite, was composed of powerful families organized as agnatic lineages for the accumulation of property and the control of churches, neighborhoods, and patronage systems, and frequently divided into factions that vied with each other for political power within the communal government. The second was a more numerous and socially heterogeneous guild community of local merchants, artisans, shopkeepers, notaries, and providers of services, organized into self-governing corporations, or guilds, whose legal structures and political union gave birth to a popular republicanism grounded in the notions of consent, law, and representation. Florentine history in the thirteenth and early fourteenth centuries was thus dominated by two sorts of conflicts: the civil wars fought between rival factions of upper-class families, and the challenges initiated by the guild community, or *popolo,* to tame the sometimes unruly elite families and bring them under the discipline of communal law. From this popular political culture came the earliest developments in Florentine political thought, historiography, and the nascent interest in classical history and rhetoric.

The house in Florence where Dante was born. Richard Lansing.

Demography and Urban Development

The population of Florence grew rapidly from perhaps 30,000 in 1200, and no more than 50,000 around mid-century, to 100,000 in 1300 and, according to some estimates, to as much as 120,000 by the first third of the fourteenth century. The chief cause of this expansion was the steady immigration to the city from the surrounding countryside *(contado)* under Florentine control, an area that originally corresponded roughly to the dioceses of Florence and Fiesole but which grew steadily as the city brought more territories into its sphere of influence. In 1300 the *contado* extended roughly twenty-five miles north to the Mugello valley, some fifteen miles northeast and east beyond Pontassiere almost to the northern end of the Casentino, thirty miles to the southeast in the upper Arno valley to Montevarchi, twenty-five miles southwest to Certaldo and Poggibonsi in the Valdelsa, twenty miles down the lower Arno valley to Empoli, but only some ten miles west by northwest beyond Signa and Campi. In the 1320s the Florentines pushed farther west and took control of the Monte Albano, but not until 1350 was even nearby Prato incorporated into the Florentine dominion. Before the mid-fourteenth-century plagues, the *contado* supported a huge population of between 280,000 and 320,000. Throughout the twelfth and thirteenth centuries, immigrants of all social groups—some wealthy landowners, hundreds of notaries, and thousands of skilled artisans and former agricultural workers seeking employment in the city's growing textile industries—poured into the city and swelled its population: the phenomenon lamented by Cacciaguida in *Par.* 16. Older immigrants, especially those belonging to prominent families, crowded into the city's center (the "cerchia antica") located entirely on the north side of the Arno. New neighborhoods, or *borghi,* grew up outside this original nucleus and were included within the new set of walls built in the 1170s, which enclosed an area of 197 acres, less than one square kilometer, and which reached, for the first time, across the river to the Oltrarno section to the south. Three new bridges were built across the Arno between 1220 and 1252, and an expansion of the Oltrarno walls in 1258 enclosed still more territory: clear indications that much of the population boom was occurring in the Oltrarno section. By the last quarter of the thirteenth century, as immigration peaked, still more *borghi* were spilling out in every direction beyond the twelfth-century walls, and in 1284 the government initiated the construction of a third set of walls around a vastly larger area. When the project was completed in 1334, the new walls, which followed the route of the modern *viali,* enclosed 1,556 acres, just over six square kilometers. The catastrophic occurrences of plague that began in the 1340s reduced the city's population to less than half its pre-plague size, and the large empty spaces that remained within the walls over the next two centuries served as dramatic testimony to Florence's spectacular growth in the thirteenth century.

Population expansion brought with it a building boom. Much of it, especially the building of residences for newly immigrated artisans and workers, was hurried construction in wood. Except for the townhouses of wealthy families and the great public and ecclesiastical monuments, thirteenth-century Florence was largely built in wood, and it was only after a great fire in 1304, which was set by one of the warring upper-class factions and

Baptistry of San Giovanni. Richard Lansing.

destroyed at least 1,700 houses in the center of town, that even modest building projects began regularly to be in brick or stone. Even in the first half of the thirteenth century, the private building of the upper classes must itself have supported a huge construction industry, as every elite family sought to advertise its power and wealth with a tall inner-city tower. But it was the huge public and ecclesiastical projects that dominated the building history of Florence from about 1250 through the early fourteenth century. The popular government of 1250–1260 built the Palazzo del Popolo, today the Bargello, as the seat and symbol of its authority, and in the 1290s another popular government began the construction of Palazzo Vecchio. In 1278 the Dominicans began work on the immense church of Santa Maria Novella, and in the 1290s across town the Franciscans initiated the construction of Santa Croce. At about the same time the most monumental project in the history of the city—the building of Florence's new cathedral, Santa Maria del Fiore—got underway. And to all

Fof this should be added the third set of walls. These are only the largest and best known of the dozens of major construction projects (and the hundreds of private buildings) that must have kept thousands of workers employed over many decades in the various building trades. These decades were the golden age of Florentine building, the time in which the city as we still know it—its major monuments and streets (but not yet all of its characteristic piazzas)—took shape.

Economic Growth and Social Organization

Dante's Florence generated its exceptional wealth in three principal ways: first, as a magnet for the surplus profits of a prosperous *contado* whose landowners, many of them city residents, also invested in lucrative forms of commerce; second, as the nerve center of long-distance commerce and deposit banking that attracted the wealth not only of hundreds of Florentines but of investors throughout Italy and Europe; and third, through its domestic textile industry and a wide variety of artisan trades and services.

The economic symbiosis of city and countryside was fundamental to Florentine economic growth, not simply because the countryside provided both the human resources and the food supplies necessary for urban expansion, but also because the countryside was a major source of capital. Wealthy Florentines owned huge amounts of land in the *contado,* typically entering into contracts with sharecroppers and directing the profits toward their city business interests. The significant holdings in rural property also became the foundation of the huge Florentine deposit-banking enterprises. Land, combined with the unlimited liability of the investing partners, constituted the crucial collateral—the tangible guarantee—that persuaded potential depositors to assume the risk of investing their money in a trading or banking company. Wealthy nobles and landowners, princes of the Church, and moderately wealthy townsmen from Florence and elsewhere became creditors of the companies and received a stipulated return on their investments whenever the partners closed the books and calculated the profits. The possession of large amounts of land by the partners was the material demonstration that, in the event of crisis or bankruptcy, the company had assets from which it could repay these creditors. Control, and indeed ownership, of the *contado* was thus motivated not only by the needs of defense and food supplies; it

Bargello, town hall of Florence, built in 1255. Richard Lansing.

was also the element that attracted so much capital from beyond Florence and Tuscany. The greatest of all the trading and banking firms in the early fourteenth century, the Bardi, owned vast amounts of land, which they were indeed forced to sell off at the time of their spectacular bankruptcy in 1346.

Long-distance commerce and banking were controlled by, and helped to define the circle of, Florence's elite families. Most of these families were not noble—in the strict sense that they lacked titles of nobility—and very few of them could trace their social prominence back more than a few generations. They were in the main fairly new families that rose to prominence in the late twelfth and thirteenth centuries by organizing themselves as agnatic lineages—descent groups limited to the male line—for the purposes of maintaining joint control over property and sharing the use of common resources, such as towers and family palaces and in some instances ecclesiastical patronage rights. Lineages sought to prevent the fragmentation and dispersal of patrimonies through a strategy of inheritance that included all sons in generally equal and undivided shares but excluded wives and daughters. Women were not legally barred from inheriting property, but it was common practice in upper-class families to provide daughters with dowries in lieu of a share of their fathers' estates, on the assumption that any property they inherited might be lost to the lineage once they married. Widows were allowed to remain in their husbands' households if they did not implement their legal right to restitution of their dowries; if they did reclaim their dowries, they either returned to their families of origin or remarried, but in either case generally left their children in their husbands' households. The lineage structure preserved property in male descent groups and fostered cooperation among their members. Lineages acquired a group identity and a history (sometimes an embellished one), and upper-class Florentines began to preserve the collective memory of their lineages quite as much as they did their joint property. They typically located their physical unity in jointly owned townhouses whose towers became both the symbol of their prestige and wealth and a source of physical security in times of conflict. The lineage also made marriage a crucial component of family inheritance strategies and of the inevitable competition among different lineages, or groups of lineages, for wealth, neighborhood power, and political influence.

The great Florentine commercial companies of this era were the creation of members of such upper-class families: the Bardi, Peruzzi, Acciaiuoli, Spini, Frescobaldi, Buonaccorsi, Alberti, Albizzi, Covoni, Scali, Dell'Antella, Mozzi, and several dozen others who became the economic wonder of Europe and the Mediterranean from the mid–thirteenth to the mid–fourteenth century. The majority of investing partners in a company were usually closely related members of one family, although partners from outside the family were also common. The partners pooled their investments, accepted a high level of liability, and thus attracted the deposits that swelled the company's assets to many times the original capital contributed by the partners. The companies invested these financial resources in several different ways: in long-distance trading throughout Europe and the Mediterranean, especially in wool, cloth, grain, and the famous "spices" and specialty items that came from the East; in loans to ecclesiastical, noble, and royal clients, including the papacy and the kings of England and Sicily; in the manufacture of woolen cloth in Florence itself; in loans to the Florentine government, an investment whose expected profits included some share of political influence; and in smaller loans to Florentines and others for a variety of purposes including both dowries and taxes. These giant companies thus linked the financial interests of wealthy foreigners to those of both individual Florentines and their government in a complex system in which the commune's fiscal policy and its ability to meet interest payments on the debt could seriously affect the financial health of the companies and its creditors. This made it imperative for the commercial elite to establish and maintain control over the institutions of government. For some eighty years from the 1260s to the 1340s, this system generated huge profits for both the elite families who controlled the companies and their depositors. The fortunes accumulated by the commercial elite made them not only the dominant class in Florence but also power brokers from the English court to the papacy, and from the south of Italy to many areas of the Mediterranean.

The third major producer of Florentine wealth was the vibrant manufacturing and artisanal economy, some of it owned by the great companies, but much of it in the hands of economically more modest guildsmen. The elite merchants of the Calimala guild imported cloth to the city to be finished and dyed, whereas the entrepreneurs of the Wool, or Lana, guild imported raw wool for the manufacture of cloth. Some producers in the Wool guild came from elite families and companies; they tended increasingly to specialize in the manufacture of luxury cloths made from high-quality English wool and then sold in foreign markets. But there were also hundreds of nonelite producers of cheaper-quality cloths destined for the local and regional markets. The Wool guild thus contained representatives of both the elite and the nonelite *popolo*. Thousands of unskilled workers, whose job it was to sort and beat the wool, were directly employed by the merchant entrepreneurs. But many of the specialized and skilled phases of work were performed by artisans—dyers, spinners, and weavers—who either owned their shops or worked at home, sometimes hiring their own laborers and accepting work from the merchant entrepreneurs for agreed upon piece-rates. Except for the brief period (1378–1382) that began with the rebellion of the Ciompi, the Wool guild always prevented these artisans and workers from organizing themselves into guilds of their own, and the guild itself claimed the right to regulate and discipline them.

The woolen cloth industry boomed in Florence between the second half of the thirteenth century and the 1340s. In 1300, according to the chronicler Giovanni Villani, 300 firms produced a total of 100,000 large rolls of cloth each year; for the late 1330s he estimated 200 firms and an annual production of 70,000 to 80,000 rolls, but of cloth of increasingly higher quality and value. He also estimated the total value of the cloth produced each year in Florence at 1,200,000 florins and the annual wage income at 400,000 florins, from which 30,000 people—nearly a third of the city's population (10,000 to 12,000 workers and artisans and their families)—were supported. And to these numbers should be added the hundreds of retail cloth dealers in the guild of Por Santa Maria and used-cloth dealers in the guild of the Rigattieri whose livelihoods also depended on the production and sale of woolen cloth.

Although in its various stages of production and distribution the woolen cloth industry employed more Florentines by far than any other economic activity, Florence was never a one-industry town. Other trades and commercial activities proliferated and became increasingly specialized in the thirteenth century. Among the most prominent—and these are only the main categories covering many hundreds of specialized artisan activities—were the building trades (masons, carpenters, and woodworkers), footwear manufactures (shoemakers and stockingmakers), the metalworking and iron industries (smiths, locksmiths, and makers of tools and implements), the provisioning trades (butchers, wine retailers, bakers, sellers of oil, cheese, and other foods), and leather manufactures (tanners and beltmakers). The vitality, diversity, and size of these artisan sectors of the economy were the foundation of the political strength of the minor guilds.

In the thirteenth century, scores of separate trades voluntarily organized themselves into self-regulating guilds: legal corporations (*universitates*) that could assume obligations on behalf of their members and in turn be represented by designated syndics or procurators. The Florentine guilds were in effect miniature republics: they elected their own executive consuls and deliberative assemblies; they passed laws and promulgated statutes; and they exercised jurisdiction over their members in matters of civil and commercial law. A guild's chief purpose was to guarantee the good standing of all its members and to avoid collective sanctions, or reprisals, against them by holding each member accountable for the observance of contracts and obligations assumed vis-à-vis clients, customers, and partners. To this end a guild functioned as a court to which members and nonmembers alike brought civil actions against any member who failed to honor stipulated agreements or to deliver products or services according to the minimum standards required by the statutes. Authority within guilds was delegated by the full membership to elected councils and executive committees whose membership was renewed every few months. Guilds were thus laboratories of participatory republicanism long before they united in a powerful political federation at the end of the thirteenth century and remade the government of the commune in their own image.

The oldest of the guilds was the elite association of Calimala merchants, which originally brought together traders of many kinds. But by the early or mid–thirteenth century the jurists and notaries (Arte dei giudici e notai), moneylenders and bankers (Arte del cambio), woolen cloth manufacturers (Arte della lana), retail cloth dealers (Arte di Por Santa Maria), doctors, "spice" importers, and apothecaries—soon to be joined by the dry-goods retailers (Arte dei medici, speziali, e merciai)—and furriers (Arte dei pellicciai) established independent associations of their own. Because these were among the economically most powerful guilds, several of which (in particular the Cambio and Lana guilds) had many members from elite families, they gained an early and important role in communal politics and became known as the major guilds. By the end of the century some powerful artisan guilds also achieved political recognition: first a group of five so-called middle guilds—the butchers, shoemakers, smiths, masons and builders, and used-cloth dealers—and slightly later a group of nine "minor" guilds—wine retailers, innkeepers, retailers of oil and cheese, tanners, armorers, locksmiths and ironworkers, manufacturers of harnesses and leather belts, woodworkers, and bakers. These were the twenty-one associations that formed the guild federation in the 1290s, but even this large community of guilds excluded many smaller artisan corporations that continued to exist outside the federation until they were either absorbed into the existing guilds or denied legal standing and prohibited. By the early fourteenth century the official guild community had a total population of perhaps seven to eight thousand, of which approximately five to six hundred major guildsmen came from the families of the elite—a majority of the members of the Calimala, large minorities in the Cambio and Lana, and smaller but important minorities in the other major guilds, including the jurists in the Giudici e Notai. The remainder, and vast majority, of the guild community—even most major guildsmen and certainly the near totality of minor guildsmen—constituted the *popolo:* citizens who did not come from families of great wealth or ancient lineage, who often lacked even surnames, who in many cases had recently immigrated from the *contado* and prospered as local or regional merchants, shopkeepers, artisans, and notaries, and whose sense of political identity was grounded in their professions and guilds. These nonelite guildsmen became the driving force of the political movement that repeatedly challenged the power of the elite in the second half of the thirteenth century.

Coat-of-arms of the Capitano del popolo, detail from Giotto's tower. Richard Lansing.

Politics and Political Ideas

Florence became a commune—a self-governing and originally sworn association of citizens, although still in theory subject to the overlordship of the Holy Roman Emperor—sometime in the early twelfth century. Until the middle of the thirteenth century, the upper class of elite families supplied most of the commune's governing consuls and controlled the two overlapping associations of the knights and the Calimala merchants whose own consuls regularly met with the communal consuls. For reasons that are still obscure, this consular aristocracy experienced a violent split in the early thirteenth century, as two groups of families fell into a series of conflicts that repeatedly engulfed the city in rituals of revenge and vendetta. Later chroniclers, mainly from the ranks of the *popolo,* dramatized, but also oversimplified, this civil war among the elite families by ascribing its origins to the murder in 1216 (evoked by Cacciaguida in *Par.* 16) of Buondelmonte de' Buondelmonti at the hands of elders from a group of families insulted by his failure to honor an agreement for a marriage alliance that was to have settled a dispute. The *popolo* looked back to this semilegendary event as emblematic of the irrational violence of an elite whose preferred methods of conflict resolution only and always made matters worse.

Due in part to their actual military service in the communal army, but also to their cultural identification with the ideals of knighthood and chivalry, in the thirteenth century the elite families styled themselves as a warrior aristocracy endowed with the privilege of ostentatiously displaying its wealth and power, including the right to control neighborhoods by force, to amass armed retinues, and to carry out vendettas and assaults in city streets and squares. The violence became much worse when, in the 1240s, these factional disputes became absorbed into the conflicts of the pan-Italian Guelf and Ghibelline parties and thus embroiled in the long war between the emperor Frederick II, who sought to extend imperial control over central and northern Italy, and a string of popes who, together with Guelf factions from many of the cities, fought to block Frederick's ambitions. Because of its already notable wealth and strategic position, Florence was crucial to this struggle, and by the 1240s Frederick and the Ghibellines assumed control of the city, sending

F large numbers of Guelf families into exile in 1248. The emperor even sent one of his sons, Frederick of Antioch, to preside over Florence as his representative.

In October 1250, after years of civil war between the imperial Ghibelline regime and the Guelf exiles, a popular revolution declared itself independent of both aristocratic parties and promulgated a republican constitution based on the representation of the city's twenty administrative and military subdivisions. Each of these zones contained a citizen militia in which all *popolani*—adult males who were not knights—owed service. The zones also elected representatives who appointed the Captain of the People, the *popolo's* military commander and judicial official, who had to be a foreigner. In place of the old consuls, a communal executive committee of twelve elders *(Anziani)* was elected twice a year, most likely by the representatives of the military companies and the guilds, who also met with the elders to take part in deliberations on matters of particular importance, especially war and taxes. The popular government attacked the power of the elite families in several ways. Knights were not only barred from membership in the military companies; the new government also abolished their formal association and thus their representation as a corporate body in the government. It restricted the participation in elective offices of members of both the Guelf and Ghibelline parties and nearly eliminated that of the knights: of the 176 *Anziani* whose names have been discovered for the decade 1250–1260, only two were knights. And it also ordered that all private towers be reduced to a height of no more than twenty-nine meters.

This government was subsequently known as the *primo popolo* because it was the first of a series of organized alternatives to the hegemony of the elite families. Under the *primo popolo* Florence enjoyed a decade of both economic expansion, marked by the minting of the gold florin, and military supremacy in Tuscany. Despite its initial intention to remain neutral between Guelfs and Ghibellines and to contain their costly factional wars, the *primo popolo* inevitably became identified with Guelfism as it fought to prevent revivals of imperial and Hohenstaufen power in central Italy. Toward the end of the decade, prominent Ghibelline families were forced out of the city, and in 1258 another of Frederick II's sons, Manfred, king of Sicily, rallied the Tuscan Ghibellines

and prepared for a showdown with the arrogant popular regime in Florence that had thrown off his father's rule. On 4 September 1260 at Montaperti near Siena, a combined Ghibelline-Sienese-imperial army, one of whose commanders was the Florentine Ghibelline Farinata degli Uberti, inflicted a bloody defeat on a larger Guelf army in which the Florentine contingent alone numbered 16,000: the "slaughter and the great loss that stained the Arbia red," as Dante-pilgrim reminds Farinata in *Inf.* 10. The Ghibelline aristocracy, under the overlordship of Manfred, took control of Florence, and fifteen hundred Guelfs were sent into exile (among them the chief notary and letter writer of the *primo popolo,* Brunetto Latini). Guelf property was confiscated and destroyed: the Ghibellines tore down more than 100 city palaces, nearly 600 other buildings, and 85 towers.

The Ghibellines ruled Florence for six years and removed all traces of the popular constitution. The guilds survived, but they were deprived of any political role. In these years the great families among the exiled Guelfs turned their attention to securing military backing for revenge against the Ghibellines. At least 146 Guelf bankers, including members of the Bardi, Frescobaldi, Cerchi, Scali, Spini, and Mozzi families, entered into a formal alliance with two successive French popes, Urban IV and Clement IV, who in turn invited Charles of Anjou, Count of Provence and brother of King Louis IX of France, to undertake a crusade against Manfred and to supplant him as ruler of southern Italy. The money for Charles's army came in the form of loans from the Florentine Guelf bankers and also from clerical taxes and crusading levies collected throughout Europe, but especially in France, paid in many cases again with loans from the same Florentine bankers, who were also appointed as depositaries of these ecclesiastical revenues. Charles promised his Guelf creditors economic privileges and exemptions in the southern Italian lands he was about to conquer, an arrangement that became one of the main sources of the huge fortunes made by the Guelf commercial oligarchy over the next eighty or so years. His army was ready at the beginning of 1266, and on February 26, at the battle of Benevento, the catastrophe of Montaperti was replayed in reverse as the Angevins and Guelfs emerged victorious. Manfred was wounded and died shortly thereafter, and the Ghibelline regime in Florence disintegrated by November. In April 1267 the Angevin army arrived in Tuscany to oversee the triumphant return of the Guelfs and the beginning of more than a decade of rule by the Guelf elite under the protection of the Angevins.

In the year between Benevento and the repatriation of the Guelfs, however, the *popolo* reasserted its own political agenda, this time under the banners of the guilds. The seven most powerful guilds organized themselves into a military federation for the defense of the *popolo,* elected representatives to a joint committee that they called the "priorate of the guilds," and attempted a revival of the constitution of 1250–1260. None of this lasted for more than a few months, but the brief popular revival of 1266–1267 became a bridge between the *primo popolo* and the popular movements of the 1280s and 1290s. For the first time the guilds functioned as the principal vehicles of the popular movement.

The Angevin-Guelf regime, dominated by the elite banking families, swept away the popular institutions just as its Ghibelline counterpart had done in 1260. The Guelfs, no less than the Ghibellines, conceived of the commune as an arena for the authority and privilege of the great families, including a certain tolerance for their easy recourse to vendetta and private violence. This regime was perhaps open to greater numbers of families from the economically powerful guilds than the Ghibelline regime had been, but it did not extend to the guilds the kind of institutional role in communal government that would later give nonelite guildsmen a political voice. This began to change toward the end of the 1270s. In 1279 Pope Nicholas III, aiming to reduce Angevin power in central Italy, sent the Dominican cardinal and papal legate, Latino Malabranca, to Florence to negotiate a formal reconciliation between Guelfs and Ghibellines. The Peace of Cardinal Latino, promulgated in 1280, brought some Ghibellines back into government, but the most significant aspect of the agreement was that eight guilds gave it their formal support by accepting to serve in the crucial role of legal guarantors of the observance of its terms by both parties. The eight included four major and four middle guilds, a clear sign that the nonelite *popolo* was returning to an active role in politics. Although the constitutional arrangements decreed by the Peace of 1280 did not last for more than a few years, an expanding guild community continued to assert itself in politics. In June 1282, in the wake of the anti-Angevin rebellion in Sicily

that caused Charles of Anjou to turn his attention away from Tuscany, a coalition of guildsmen, including nonelite members of the major guilds like the chronicler Dino Compagni, successfully lobbied for the creation of a new chief executive magistracy to be elected every two months from and by the guilds and to be called the "priorate of the guilds," a name that explicitly linked this popular reform to the brief government of 1266–1267. The first priorate of June–August 1282 consisted of only three members from the Calimala, Cambio, and Lana guilds. But the next priorate was composed of six members, and extant debates on electoral procedures reveal pressures from a much larger group of guilds for some share in the new office. The elite accepted the institution of the priorate and its link to the guild community, but for the next ten years it successfully resisted the pressures from the middle and minor guilds for broader participation. Although representatives of the seven major and five middle guilds were regularly convened to some of the commune's legislative assemblies between 1282 and 1292, the priorate was dominated in these years by elite members of the major guilds. But the price of acceptance by the wider guild community of a more limited role in the priorate than some had wanted may have been the passage of the early antimagnate laws that sought to control the unruly behavior of members of elite families, many of whom still flouted the authority of the commune with their armed retinues, youth gangs, and ritual violence.

The popular movement achieved its greatest success in 1293–1294, under the leadership of Giano della Bella. His stern and unyielding stance against the magnates and the rise and fall of the popular government are described by Compagni, who was evidently Della Bella's close confidant and loyal supporter. At the end of 1292 pressure from the nonelite guildsmen resulted in revised electoral procedures that gave each of the twelve guilds an equal and autonomous voice in the selection of the communal priors. Over the next several years nonelite guildsmen had a more prominent role in Florentine politics than ever before. The first of these popular priorates promulgated the antimagnate Ordinances of Justice in January 1293, and the second, the priorate of which Giano della Bella was a member, nearly doubled the list of elite families affected by the Ordinances. The first rubric of the Ordinances declared the guilds to be the "parts" of a political whole that is "considered perfect when it consists of all its parts and is approved by the judgment of them all"; it thus decreed a formal union of twenty-one guilds, each of which sent a representative to swear its loyalty to the "good, faithful, pure society and company of all the guilds." For the first time, no doubt in response to pressures from the wider guild community, the nine minor guilds were included in the corporate federation, and, although only the twelve major and middle guilds participated in the election of the priorate, members of all twenty-one guilds who were continuously active in their trades or professions, and who were not knights, were eligible for election. The exclusion of knights soon led to the explicit ineligibility of the magnates—a specific list of at first thirty-eight families, to which another thirty-four families were added during Giano della Bella's priorate—for both the office of prior and the consulates of the guilds. Magnates were required to post surety for good behavior, and their families were subjected to collective punishment, including heavy fines and the possible destruction of their houses, for crimes of violence committed by any of their number against non-magnates. The enforcement of these penalties was the responsibility of the newly added seventh member of the priorate, the Standardbearer of Justice, and his large armed internal security force.

Escutcheon of the lily, emblem of Florence, detail from Giotto's tower. Richard Lansing.

Although the magnates were not an entire social class, they constituted a large portion of the elite from both sides of the great factional divide. The list includes families from both the city and countryside; both older Guelf families (like the Donati, Buondelmonti, and Adimari) and older Ghibelline families (such as the Uberti, Amidei, and Lamberti), but also many newer families from the heart of the Guelf mercantile elite (e.g., the Bardi, Mozzi, Frescobaldi, Scali, Spini, Cerchi, and Franzesi). The Ordinances should not be seen as an assault by a rising merchant class against an older feudal nobility, but rather as the manifesto of the guild-based *popolo* against the *prepotenza* of the entire elite. But the *popolo*'s strategy was evidently to divide the elite and to allow some of its families to escape the punitive Ordinances and to retain their officeholding rights in the hopes that they would support the guild regime. Thus the Alberti, Peruzzi, Acciaiuoli, Altoviti, Albizzi, Covoni, Medici, Ricci, Baroncelli, Rucellai, Magalotti, Strozzi, Dell'Antella, Corsini, and many other families of great wealth, and in some cases of ancient lineage, were left off the magnate lists—

although the *popolo* subsequently made clear that repeated episodes of disruptive behavior by any of them could result in their inclusion at some later time. The ordinances were a frontal attack on the entire upper class of great families, a class defined more by its behavior and by attitudes of contempt for civil moderation and the discipline of law, by its military ethos, private armies, and by the codes of honor that made vendetta a duty, than by any specifically economic criteria or antiquity of lineage. The most famous example of the threat to civil peace that the *popolo* saw in the magnates was the charismatic and arrogant Guelf leader Corso Donati, described by Dino Compagni as "a knight in the mold of Catiline the Roman, but more cruel; noble of blood, handsome of body, a charming speaker, adorned with good breeding, subtle of intellect, with his mind always set on evildoing; one who gathered many armed men and kept a great entourage, who ordered many arsons and robberies and did great damage to the Cerchi and their friends. . . ; such was Corso Donati, who because of his pride was called the Baron. . . . He was led by vanity, and bestowed many favors" (translation by Daniel E. Bornstein, *Dino Compagni's Chronicle of Florence,* pp. 48–49).

No doubt because it sought to tame and discipline such overmighty citizens, even this broader and stronger popular government came under attack in the late 1290s by the great families who promptly proceeded, in the time-honored fashion of the aristocracy, to divide themselves, this time into the factions of the White Guelfs, led by the Cerchi, and the Black Guelfs, led by the Donati. The city was once again overrun by increasingly violent clashes between gangs from rival elite families. As chaos threatened and the factions attracted growing numbers of clients as much out of fear as any political preference, the supporters of the popular regime lost control of the institutions of government. In 1300 an increasingly desperate government banished several members from both parties, including Corso Donati and members of the Della Tosa, Pazzi, Spini, and Manieri families among the Blacks, and from the ranks of the Whites, several of the Cerchi and their partisans, including the poet Guido Cavalcanti. Both sides sought help from outside the city, the Cerchi from their allies in Pistoia, and the Donati from Pope Boniface VIII, who enlisted Charles of Valois, brother of the French king Philip IV, as the military arm of the Blacks in their effort to return from exile, overthrow the regime, and gain revenge against the Cerchi. As the city feared invasion by Charles's troops, the parties agreed to the selection of a priorate of neutral and respected citizens, including Dino Compagni, who, according to his own account of these events in the *Cronica,* attempted to reconcile the factions and thus prevent an attack on the city and preserve what he could of the constitution of the popular regime. But his exhortations to the parties failed, and in the end he appealed to the guild community for support against Charles of Valois's entry into the city. "Wishing to do nothing without the consent of their fellow citizens," he and his fellow priors turned to the full community of guilds—Compagni here speaks of seventy-two guilds, evidently including many beyond the federation of 1293—and asked each to express an opinion as to whether Charles of Valois should be permitted to enter Florence. But the demoralized guild community failed to respond as Compagni hoped it would: only one guild, the bakers, voted to defy the French prince. Charles and the Blacks entered the city in early November 1301; four days of violence

ensued, followed by many decrees of banishment against the Whites, including Dante. For several years the exiled Whites and the remnants of the old Ghibellines hatched plots and sought foreign support for their futile efforts to displace the Black Guelfs. In 1310 the new Emperor Henry VII entered Italy and rallied Whites and Ghibellines against the two chief Guelf powers of Italy, the Angevin kingdom of Naples and the Florentine republic. Despite Dante's high hopes, the emperor was no match for the alliance arrayed against him, and his death in 1313 brought to an end more than a decade of civil war, conspiracies, and threats of foreign intervention.

Over the next generation, the factional wars of Florence's upper class began to subside. Although the papal-imperial struggle was not quite finished, with the papacy in Avignon after 1309 and the empire in disarray, neither was able to intervene in Italian politics with the same influence that had been at their disposal during the thirteenth century. The foreign conflicts that had nourished and exacerbated divisions within the Florentine elite gradually became less important than they had once been. The Florentine elite was also changing, as it slowly shed the components of its old collective image rooted in military and chivalric ideals and institutions, and acquired a new sense of itself as an economic oligarchy and a republican ruling class. As the violent ideological fissures that had lacerated the elite for a century grew weaker, the oligarchy turned its attention to securing the economic, institutional, and political bases of its power. The creation in 1308 of the Mercanzia, an association of international merchants, bankers, and traders from the five major commercial guilds (Calimala, Cambio, Lana, Por Santa Maria, and Medici, Speziali, e Merciai) marks a crucial moment of this transformation. The Mercanzia organized this merchant elite, now explicitly defined by economic criteria, into a formal corporation with jurisdiction over bankruptcies, reprisals, and commercial law, and soon thereafter with considerable political power over the guilds. It thus gave this class an institutional expression and collective identity grounded, for the first time, in its economic hegemony and dominance within and over the guild community. The commune's formal recognition in 1309 of the Mercanzia's extensive competence as a commercial court was the first step in the effort, ultimately successful over the course of the fourteenth century, to undermine the autonomy that the guilds had previously enjoyed in their civil jurisdiction. The Mercanzia also gained significant regulatory power over a wide variety of economic and commercial activities, and by the 1320s and 1330s it had a major role in the election of the consuls of all the guilds. A series of reforms in the procedures for electing the communal priors similarly allowed the oligarchy to control the powerful executive office almost without interruption from about 1310 to 1340. In what may have been the generation of its greatest prosperity, the oligarchy combined growing political stability with economic power to dominate communal politics and deprive the nonelite guild community of much of the political strength it had had in the 1280s and 1290s. Not until the 1340s, when the oligarchy suddenly lost both its economic empire and its political dominance, did the popular movement revive. Dante died in exile excoriating this ruling class as it consolidated its power.

Culture, Education, and Literacy

In cultural matters, too, the thirteenth century was a time of growth and rapid change. Whereas in 1200 Florence did not loom large on the cultural and intellectual map of Italy, several factors help to explain the rise of its distinctive lay and civic culture during the next century. Florence did not yet have a university, and its intellectual life was never dominated by the philosophical culture of university cities like Bologna or Paris where law and theology were the chief disciplines. Perhaps the most pervasive influence on Florentine cultural life was the vitality of the professional cadre of notaries whose training in the practical rhetorical arts of official letter writing and the redaction of contracts in Latin created a large class of middle-brow intellectuals for whom the literary and republican legacy of ancient Rome became the focal point of their culture. (In 1280, a total of 374 notaries in the city and 204 in the *contado* were registered with the guild, and in 1338 the total was an astounding 880.) The most famous example is Brunetto Latini, chancellor of the *primo popolo* and a literary figure and teacher of notable influence until his death in 1295. While not all notaries matched his level of learning and fame, Latini reflected and promoted the general assumptions of his profession, both in the cultivation of an increasingly classicizing Latin style in the letters, treaties, and legislation that official notaries composed for

governments, and in the growing attention to Roman history and Latin literature as the privileged sources of moral philosophy and political education. Another Florentine notary worthy of note was the father of Francesco Petrarca, Ser Petracco from Incisa in the Valdarno, who, like hundreds of others of his profession in the thirteenth century, moved to the city where he became involved in politics (as suggested at least by his exile in 1302 following the Black Guelf coup d'état) and also developed a taste for classical learning. He revered Cicero, had a copy of Virgil made for himself, and not least, arranged for his son, although growing up in exile and even out of Italy in Provence, to study Latin with a well-known Tuscan teacher of grammar and rhetoric, Convenevole da Prato.

By the early fourteenth century, Florence was a remarkably literate city, thanks to a combination of extensive private education of the sort that Ser Petracco provided for his son and a variety of lay and religious schools. In the 1330s, according to Giovanni Villani, between eight and ten thousand boys and girls "went to reading school"; between one thousand and twelve hundred older boys studied commercial arithmetic in six schools; and 550 to 600 students learned Latin and logic in "four big schools." Some have doubted the reliability of these figures because of the extraordinarily high level of literacy that they imply: at least forty percent of the total population, and perhaps as much as two-thirds of the male population. But Villani's statistics are generally accurate, and it is known from other sources that the ability to read and write, at least in the vernacular, was universal in the upper classes, nearly so throughout the artisan community, and extended to many women and even to a portion of the working class. Florentines—and not only those of the upper class—were already beginning to write diaries, letters, account books, and civic chronicles in impressive numbers, and the high level of vernacular literacy was obviously an important enabling factor.

The knowledge of Latin was less widespread but on the increase. In addition to the notaries, jurists, and doctors whose professional activities required a mastery of legal and technical Latin, growing numbers of Florentines, from both the elite and the *popolo,* learned some literary Latin and read classical authors. The hundreds of office-holders in both the guilds and the commune, including the large legislative councils, debated

Porta alla Croce, eastern gate of Florence. Richard Lansing.

and approved laws, statutes, and ordinances that were written in Latin. And it was mainly from the *popolo,* from writers imbued with the traditions of Roman republican political culture and ancient models of historical writing, that the early achievements in Florentine political thought and historiography emerged. Florence's Roman origins and the expansion of its power against neighboring Fiesole are prominently featured in two early thirteenth-century works, the *Chronica de origine civitatis and the Gesta florentinorum.* In the generation around 1300, the expanding genre of civic chronicles reflected the main themes of the *popolo*'s political challenge to the elite: works like the anonymous chronicle once attributed to Brunetto Latini, the *Cronica* of Paolino Pieri, the dramatic and anguished *Cronica* of Dino Compagni, and the great history of Giovanni Villani.

Side by side with the emerging civic, rhetorical, and classical culture of the *popolo* was the elite's preference for a culture that emulated both the festive ritual and the literary genres of the courts and their chivalric codes. The popularity of the institution of knighthood no doubt nourished the elite's fascination with chivalry, jousting, and lavish festivities, as did the influence of the foreign courts with which they had regular contact, especially in periods of exile. In its literary tastes, this would-be courtly aristocracy cultivated both the witty love poetry of Provençal and Sicilian origin and the legends of crusade and war found in northern European chivalric literature, both in the vernacular. Even in naming their children, Florentine elite families often had recourse to chivalric literary and cultural models. Many of the tales included in the earliest important collection of Florentine vernacular "novelle," the *Novellino,* reflect this aristocratic culture of love and war, knights and ladies, courtesy and valor. The class dimension of these literary themes is evident in the unknown author's assertion that the stories deserve to be recorded because "persons of nobility and gentility are in their speech and actions almost like a model of perfection to those of lower social standing [*quasi com'uno specchio appo i minori*]."

The opportunity for advanced study in philosophy and theology came to Florence late in the thirteenth century. In the *studia* of the Franciscans and the Dominicans, lay students heard lectures on these subjects and could follow the great debates on poverty and ecclesiology, especially in the Franciscan order, which, by the end of the thirteenth century, was seriously divided over the interpretation and implementation of Francis's doctrine of apostolic poverty. Two prominent theorists of the strict interpretation promoted by the Spirituals, Ubertino da Casale and Pierre Jean Olivi, spent periods of time as lectors at Santa Croce in the late 1280s. Dante's critique of the Church's wealth and political power may have had roots in the teaching of these Spirituals. Many of the preachers and teachers assigned to Santa Croce and Santa Maria Novella had studied in Paris and thus had brought to Florence some of the philosophical culture of the northern universities. But this was never as pervasive a factor in Florentine intellectual life as were the rhetorical arts of notaries and protohumanists.

Religion and Charity

The religious history of Dante's Florence shared in the doctrinal and social turbulence characteristic of European society in this period. In the twelfth and early thirteenth centuries Florence was a major center of the rival dualist church of the Cathars. Florentine Catharism found significant support within the upper class, and especially among women, who may have been attracted to it as a way of escaping the restrictions of marriage and family life imposed by male-dominated lineages. The mendicants, at first the Dominicans and later the Franciscans, led the Inquisition's campaign to stamp out Catharism, which was largely successful by the last third of the thirteenth century. In the early fourteenth century only small cells of Cathars, or Patarines as they were now called, survived, and mostly in the *contado*.

After the decline of the Cathars the religious history of Florence was marked by an extraordinary flowering of a variety of forms of religious association, both clerical and lay, involving both men and women of all social levels, and ranging from the completely orthodox to the heretical—a phenomenon of spontaneous formation of communities around religious purposes that parallels and reflects the simultaneous formation of guilds and other professional associations. Certainly the major inspiration behind the formation of religious communities was the arrival of the mendicant orders, and especially the establishment in the city, as early as the 1220s at Santa Croce and Santa Maria Novella, respectively, of the Franciscans and

the Dominicans, who, here as elsewhere, through preaching and attention to the needs and problems of urban society, spread their sense of religious vocation as pastoral work in the world, imitation of Christ, sanctification of everyday life, and renunciation of wealth. Other mendicant orders were founded in the 1250s and 1260s (Augustinians at Santo Spirito, Servites at Santissima Annunziata, Humiliati at Ognissanti, Friars of the Sack at Sant'Egidio, and Carmelites at Santa Maria del Carmine). The location of all these orders either outside the walls of the 1170s or in the Oltrarno section, and thus in the rapidly expanding *borghi* then filling up with immigrants from the *contado*, suggests that the mendicants were especially popular among the newest elements of Florentine society in need of the kinds of community and social services that mendicants either provided or supported—care for the sick, alms for the poor, lodging for travelers, and honorable burials, but also preaching and organized devotion.

The leadership of the mendicants in the struggle against Catharism was only one of several areas in which they transformed urban religious life. Both Franciscans and Dominicans attracted large crowds from all social levels to their public preaching. The Franciscans may have been more popular among artisans and middle-rank merchants of the *popolo*, while the Dominicans cultivated ties to elite families as well. But preachers from both orders regularly addressed the concerns and dilemmas of an urban laity wrestling with the moral implications of rapidly and unevenly accumulating wealth, of changing economic practices and attitudes, and of social mobility and political tensions. The Dominican presence in Florence sometimes took explicitly political forms, as in the order's role in the Inquisition and the mediation performed by the Dominican cardinal in the 1280 reconciliation of Guelfs and Ghibellines. Two great Dominican preachers of the early fourteenth century, Giordano da Pisa and Remigio de' Girolami, openly preached on political themes. Girolami, who came from an upper-class family, several of whose members joined the popular movement of the 1290s, even wrote two treatises on civic peace, *De bono communi* and *De bono pacis*.

The impact of the Franciscans on Florentine and Tuscan religious history is of course inseparable from the dramatic division within the order between the Spirituals, who insisted on the literal observance of the vow of poverty, and the main branch of the order, known as the Conventuals or the Community, who were willing to accept the legal arrangements that allowed them to use property that, according to Francis's Rule, they were forbidden to own. The Spirituals combined their strict interpretation of the rule of poverty with a critique of the wealth of the entire Church and of the power and worldliness of the papacy. Among the more radical Spirituals, emotionally powerful strands of Joachite prophecy and eschatology led to openly heretical ideas about the role to be played by a corrupt papacy in what were believed to be the coming last days and the establishment of a new dispensation of the spirit. These Franciscan revolutionaries found much support in Tuscany, and, as the debates on poverty raged before Pope Clement V at the council of Vienne in 1312, groups of Tuscan Spirituals began to secede from the order. In the 1320s Pope John XXII declared the doctrine of apostolic poverty itself heretical; the Spirituals were driven underground and became known as the Fraticelli. The Tuscan inquisition turned its attention to these new heretics, but despite a small number of prosecutions in the 1320s and 1330s, it was not until later in the century that the Fraticelli emerged as a major movement in Florence among the woolworkers and artisans who were at the center of the social and political agitations of the 1370s. The prominence of radical Franciscanism in the second half of the century suggests that it had quietly put down deep roots in Florentine society in the first half. The ideas of the Spirituals had their defenders in Florence even after the condemnations of John XXII, among them the Augustinian friar Simone Fidati da Cascia, whose right to preach was protected by the Florentine government after a public disputation that pitted him against his Dominican critics.

The model of the Franciscans and Dominicans also generated a variety of mimetic responses of more orthodox stamp. The Franciscans accepted and supervised a separate order for women, the Clarisses, named for its founder and Francis's collaborator, Clare. The first nonclerical association to appear in the orbit of the mendicants was the Order of Penitents, groups of laypersons, including many from the middle orders of society, who wore a religious habit but lived at home and practiced their professions. They administered the property that the mendicants could not own and ran hospices for travelers and hospitals for the sick

Portrait of Dante by H. Robinson from an 1842 edition of the Commedia. La commedia di Dante Allighieri, *illustrated by Ugo Foscolo and edited by Giuseppe Mazzini (London, 1842). Giamatti Collection: Courtesy of the Mount Holyoke College Archives and Special Collections.*

and poor, including the Hospital of San Paolo, which became one of the city's largest. At the end of the thirteenth century they divided into two factions over the question of how much autonomy their association should have from ecclesiastical authorities. More closely supervised by the mendicant orders were the tertiaries, members of the so-called third orders of lay brothers and sisters, who, like the Penitents, wore a religious habit and observed an austere mode of life governed by a formal rule, although they were not required to renounce marriage or secular society. A notable number of tertiaries came from socially elevated families and typically used income from their property holdings to support hospitals and hospices for the poor.

Another manifestation of the enthusiasm for lay religious association, also inspired by the mendicants and the Penitents, were the lay confraternities that redacted formal statutes, elected officers, and met regularly for prayer, penitence,

Santa Maria del Fiore, the Duomo, or cathedral of Florence, begun by Arnolfo di Cambio in 1296. Richard Lansing.

Torre della Castagna, first residence of the Priori delle Arti. Richard Lansing.

philanthropy, and the singing of vernacular religious songs. From perhaps no more than a handful in the mid-thirteenth century, these associations multiplied rapidly, reaching at least twenty by 1300, and perhaps as many as forty by 1348. The documented existence of at least one confraternity of women and of a few artisan confraternities suggests that there may have been others. A majority of the early confraternities, like the mendicant houses, were located in the expanding *borghi;* here too some correlation between the growth of the confraternities and the arrival of so many immigrants from the *contado* seems likely. The spread of confraternal association in the city may in fact owe much to the religious culture of the *contado,* for which an astounding total of 180 confraternities have been counted for the period down to 1400.

Several of the earliest confraternities were founded in the high tide of the campaign against Cathar and Ghibelline heresy and were thus closely tied to the mendicants and organized around devotional activities, especially the singing

of hymns of praise *(laude)* to the Virgin. These *laudesi* companies were the most prevalent type until the middle of the fourteenth century when confraternities of flagellants, or *disciplinati,* with their emphasis on the imitation of the suffering Christ, in part perhaps because of the terrors of the plague, became more popular. Still other confraternities specialized in charitable activities; some assisted their own members by offering occasional financial help and guaranteeing decent burials, while others distributed alms to the poor, supported and administered hospitals and schools, and provided assistance to widows, foundlings, and prostitutes. Among the most prominent of the early confraternities were: the Bigallo, founded no later than the 1240s, which ran a number of small hospitals in the *contado;* the Misericordia, which administered bequests to the poor; the company of San Pier Martire of Santa Maria Novella, which met regularly to sing *laude* and, like some other *laudesi* companies, also ran a singing school; San Zanobi, founded in 1281, which combined processions, *lauda*-singing, and almsgiving; and

Orsanmichele, founded in 1291, which soon became a magnet for pious bequests and the major vehicle in the fourteenth century for the distribution of alms to Florence's poor.

From the combined philanthropy of religious orders and confraternities and the charitable initiatives of private individuals, early-fourteenth-century Florence could boast an extensive network of social services. Giovanni Villani counted no fewer than thirty hospitals and hospices with a total of a thousand beds for "the poor and the infirm," among them no doubt the hospital of Santa Maria Nuova, founded in 1288 by Folco Portinari, the father of Dante's Beatrice. But the dimensions of institutionalized philanthropy also highlight the incidence of poverty and the radically uneven distribution of Florence's great wealth—problems that contributed to the social tensions and political turbulence of the second half of the century.

Bibliography

Published Primary Sources

Bornstein, Daniel E. *Dino Compagni's Chronicle of Florence.* Philadelphia: University of Pennsylvania Press, 1986.

I capitoli del comune di Firenze: Inventario e regesto. Edited by C. Guasti and A. Gherardi. 2 vols. Florence, 1866–1893.

Consigli della repubblica fiorentina. Edited by B. Barbadoro. 2 vols. Bologna, 1921–1930.

Le Consulte della repubblica fiorentina dall'anno MCCLXXX al MCCXCVIII. Edited by A. Gherardi. 2 vols. Florence, 1896–1898.

Cronica fiorentina compilata nel secolo XIII. In *Testi fiorentini del dugento e dei primi del trecento.* Edited by Alfredo Schiaffini. Florence: Sansoni, 1954, pp. 82–150.

Del Lungo, Isidoro. *Dino Compagni e la sua Cronica.* 3 vols. Florence: Le Monnier, 1879–1887.

Documenti dell'antica costituzione del comune di Firenze. Edited by Pietro Santini. 2 vols. Florence: G. P. Vieusseux, 1895–1952.

Filippi, Giovanni. *L'arte dei mercanti di Calimala in Firenze ed il suo più antico statuto.* Turin: Fratelli Bocca, 1889.

Il libro di Montaperti. Edited by C. Paoli. Florence, 1889.

Novelle italiane: il Duecento, il Trecento. Edited by Lucia Battaglia Ricci. Milan: Garzanti, 1982.

Ordinamenti di giustizia. Introduction by Franco Cardini. Florence: SP 44 Editore, 1993. (Text reprinted from the edition by F. Bonaini in the *Archivio storico italiano,* new series, 1 [1855], 37–71.)

Pegolotti, Francesco Balducci. *La pratica della mercatura.* Edited by A. Evans. Cambridge, Mass.: Medieval Academy of America, 1936.

Pinto, Giuliano. *Il libro del biadaiolo: Carestie e annona a Firenze dalla metà del '200 al 1348.* Florence: Leo S. Olschki, 1978.

Statuti della repubblica fiorentina. Edited by R. Caggese. 2 vols. Florence: Tipografia Galileiana, 1910–1921.

Statuti dell'arte dei Legnaioli di Firenze (1301–1346). Edited by Francesca Morandini. Florence: Leo S. Olschki, 1958.

Statuti dell'arte dei Medici e Speziali. Edited by Raffaele Ciasca. Florence: Attilio Vallecchi, 1922.

Statuti dell'arte dei Rigattieri e Linaioli di Firenze (1296–1340). Edited by Ferdinando Sartini. Florence: Le Monnier, 1940.

Statuti dell'arte del Cambio di Firenze (1299–1316). Edited by Giulia Camerani Marri. Florence: Leo S. Olschki, 1955.

Statuto dell'arte della Lana di Firenze (1317–1319). Edited by Anna Maria E. Agnoletti. Florence: Le Monnier, 1940.

Statuti delle arti degli Oliandoli e Pizzicagnoli e dei Beccai di Firenze (1318–1346). Edited by Francesca Morandini. Florence: Leo S. Olschki, 1961.

Villani, Giovanni. *Nuova Cronica.* Edited by Giuseppe Porta. 3 vols. Parma: Fondazione Pietro Bembo/Ugo Guanda, 1990–1991.

Selected Secondary Sources

Barbadoro, Bernardino. *Le finanze della repubblica fiorentina. Imposta diretta e debito pubblico fino all'istituzione del Monte.* Florence: Leo S. Olschki, 1929.

Becker, Marvin B. *Florence in Transition, I: The Decline of the Commune.* Baltimore: Johns Hopkins University Press, 1967.

Benvenuti Papi, Anna. *"In castro poenitentiae": Santità e società femminile nell'Italia medievale.* Rome: Herder Editrice, 1990.

Corsi, Dinora. "Firenze 1300–1350: 'Nonconformismo' religioso e organizzazione inquisitoriale." *Annali dell'istituto di storia, Università di Firenze, Facoltà di Magistero* 1 (1979), 29–66.

Dameron, George W. *Episcopal Power and Florentine Society, 1000–1320.* Cambridge, Mass.: Harvard University Press, 1991.

F

Davidsohn, Robert. *Geschichte von Florenz.* 4 vols. Berlin, 1896–1927; reprint ed. Osnabrück, Germany: Biblio Verlag, 1969. Italian translation *Storia di Firenze.* 8 vols. Florence: Sansoni, 1972–1973.

Davis, Charles T. *Dante's Italy and Other Essays.* Philadelphia: University of Pennsylvania Press, 1984.

Del Lungo, Isidoro. *I Bianchi e i Neri.* Milan: Hoepli, 1921.

Del Monte, Alberto. "La storiografia fiorentina dei secoli XII e XIII." *Bollettino dell'istituto storico italiano per il medio evo* 62 (1950), 175–282.

De Rosa, Daniela. *Alle origini della repubblica fiorentina: Dai consoli al "primo popolo" (1172–1260).* Florence: Arnaud, 1995.

Doren, Alfred. *Das Florentiner Zunftwesen vom 14. bis zum 16. Jahrhundert.* Vol. 2 of *Studien aus der Florentiner Wirtschaftgeschichte.* Stuttgart, 1901, 1908; reprint ed. Aalen: Scientia Verlag, 1969. Italian translation by G. B. Klein, *Le arti fiorentine.* 2 vols. Florence: Le Monnier, 1940.

———. *Die Florentiner Wollentuchindustrie vom vierzehnten bis zum sechzehnten Jahrhundert.* Vol. 1 of *Studien aus der Florentiner Wirtschaftgeschichte.* Stuttgart, 1901.

Fiumi, Enrico. "Fioritura e decadenza dell'economia fiorentina." *Archivio storico italiano* 115 (1957), 385–439; 116 (1958), 443–510; 117 (1959), 427–502. Reprint ed. Florence: Leo S. Olschki, 1977.

Gehl, Paul. *A Moral Art: Grammar, Society, and Culture in Trecento Florence.* Ithaca, N.Y. and London: Cornell University Press, 1993.

Green, Louis. *Chronicle into History: An Essay on the Interpretation of History in Fourteenth-Century Florentine Chronicles.* Cambridge: Cambridge University Press, 1972.

Henderson, John. *Piety and Charity in Late Medieval Florence.* Oxford: Clarendon Press, 1994.

Holmes, George. *Florence, Rome and the Origins of the Renaissance.* Oxford: Clarendon Press, 1986.

Hoshino, Hidetoshi. *L'Arte della lana in Firenze nel basso medioevo: Il commercio della lana e il mercato dei panni fiorentini nei secoli XIII–XV.* Florence: Olschki, 1980.

Jones, Philip. "Economia e società nell'Italia medievale: la leggenda della borghesia." In *Storia d'Italia. Annali I: Dal feudalesimo al capitalismo.* Turin: Giulio Einaudi, 1978, pp. 185–372.

Lansing, Carol. *The Florentine Magnates: Lineage and Faction in a Medieval Commune.* Princeton, N.J.: Princeton University Press, 1991.

La Roncière, Charles M. de. *Religion paysanne et religion urbaine en Toscane (c. 1250–c. 1450).* Brookfield, Vt.: Variorum, 1994.

———. "Pauvres et pauvreté à Florence au XIVe siècle." In *Études sur l'histoire de la pauvreté.* Edited by M. Mollat. Paris: Publications de la Sorbonne, 1974, pp. 661–745.

Lesnick, Daniel R. *Preaching in Medieval Florence: The Social World of Franciscan and Dominican Spirituality.* Athens, Ga. and London: University of Georgia Press, 1989.

Najemy, John M. "Dante and Florence." In *The Cambridge Companion to Dante.* Edited by Rachel Jacoff. Cambridge: Cambridge University Press, 1993, pp. 80–99.

———. *Corporatism and Consensus in Florentine Electoral Politics, 1280–1400.* Chapel Hill, N.C.: University of North Carolina Press, 1982.

Ottokar, Nicola. *Il comune di Firenze alla fine del dugento.* Florence, 1926. Reprint ed. Turin: Giulio Einaudi, 1962.

Papi, Massimo D. "Confraternite ed ordini mendicanti a Firenze: Aspetti di una ricerca quantitativa." *Mélanges de l'École française de Rome* 89 (1977), 597–608.

Pirillo, Paolo. *Famiglia e mobilità sociale nella Toscana medievale: I Franzesi Della Foresta da Figline Valdarno (secoli XII–XV).* Florence: Opus Libri, 1992.

Plesner, Johan. *L'émigration de la campagne à la ville libre de Florence au XIII siècle.* Copenhagen: Nordisk Forlag, 1934. Italian translation, *L'emigrazione dalla campagna alla città libera di Firenze nel XIII secolo.* Florence: Francesco Papafava, 1979.

Raveggi, Sergio, Massimo Tarassi, Daniela Medici, and Patrizia Parenti. *Ghibellini, Guelfi e popolo grasso: I detentori del potere politico a Firenze nella seconda metà del Dugento.* Florence: La Nuova Italia, 1978.

Rubinstein, Nicolai. "The Beginnings of Political Thought in Florence." *Journal of the Warburg and Courtauld Institutes* 5 (1942), 198–227.

Salvemini, Gaetano. *La dignità cavalleresca nel comune di Firenze e altri scritti.* Milan: Feltrinelli, 1972.

———. *Magnati e popolani in Firenze dal 1280 al 1295*. Florence, 1896; reprint ed. Milan: Feltrinelli, 1966.

Santini, Pietro. *Studi sull'antica costituzione del comune di Firenze*. Reprint ed. Rome: Multigrafica Editrice, 1972.

Sapori, Armando. *Studi di storia economica*. 3 vols. Florence: Sansoni, 1955–1967.

Stephens, J. N. "Heresy in Medieval and Renaissance Florence." *Past and Present* 54 (1972), 25–60.

Sznura, Franek. *L'espansione urbana di Firenze nel Dugento*. Florence: La Nuova Italia, 1975.

Waley, Daniel. "The Army of the Florentine Republic from the Twelfth to the Fourteenth Century." In *Florentine Studies: Politics and Society in Renaissance Florence*. Edited by Nicolai Rubinstein. Evanston, Ill.: Northwestern University Press, 1968, pp. 70–108.

John M. Najemy

Focaccia

Vanni de' Cancellieri, an extremely violent White Guelf of the Pistoian nobility whose crimes included the murder of his relative Detto di Sinibaldo Cancellieri, a member of the Black Guelfs, in 1293. His numerous acts of revenge fomented chaos in the city of Pistoia, leading authorities to appeal for assistance from the city of Florence to reestablish civic order. The intervention of the Florentines in turn spread the turmoil to Florence itself, so that Focaccia is considered to have instigated the strife between the Blacks and the Whites. He is mentioned by Camiscion de' Pazzi as deserving of punishment in Caina (*Inf.* 32.63).

Richard Lansing

Folco of Marseilles

Folquet de Marselha, Troubadour poet active during the last quarter of the twelfth century. After withdrawing from the world in 1195 and becoming a Cistercian monk, he was elected bishop of Toulouse in 1205, an office he held until his death in 1231. He was a fierce opponent of the Catharist heresy and participated, along with Simon Montfort, in the crusade against the Albigensians. His Provençal *vida*, which provides a romanticized account of his life, identifies him as the son of a wealthy merchant from Genoa who fell in love with Adelais, the wife of his feudal lord Barral, Visconte of Marseilles. He wrote poetry in her praise, but his love was unrequited, and her death was the reason he abandoned secular life for the monastery. The itinerary of Folco's passage from *eros* to *caritas* and the importance he gave his lady's death have a close affinity with events in Dante's own amatory experience, as he describes it in the *Vita Nuova*.

In *DVE* 2.6.6 Dante cites Folco's canso *Tant m'abellis l'amoros pessamens* as an example of the highest level of rhetorical construction in Provençal poetry, and later uses it to inform the discourse (in Provençal) of Arnaut Daniel, who repents of his *passada folor* ("past folly," *Purg.* 26.143) among the lustful in Purgatory. This kind of homage to Folco helps to explain the extraordinary position he is accorded in the *Commedia:* he is, in fact, the only romantic poet deemed worthy of being placed among the saved in Paradise. When Dante encounters him among the amatory spirits in the Heaven of Venus (*Par.* 9.94–108), Folco not only justifies his eternal salvation because he abandoned earthly love to pursue divine love, but he also rebukes the corruption of the Church, singling out Boniface VIII for his failure to pursue the liberation of the Holy Land (126), condemns Florence, which he describes as a city born of the seed of Lucifer, and prophesies a time when the Vatican will be liberated from its "adulterous" practice of simony (139–142).

Michelangelo Picone
(translated by Robin Treasure)

Forese Donati

A friend to Dante, born perhaps around 1260, dead by 1296, Forese belonged to one of the most powerful Florentine families of the time. A distant cousin of Dante's wife Gemma Donati, Forese was overshadowed politically by his brother Corso, head of the Black Guelf party. He appears as a character in *Purg.* 23 and 24 among the gluttonous on the sixth terrace, where he condemns his brother's politics and its effect on Florence.

Forese wrote three sonnets in response to three bitterly comic poems, also sonnets, addressed to him by Dante, an exchange now known as the *Tenzone with Forese*. (A *tenzone* [*tenso*, Provençal] is a poetic debate between poets in the form of an invective.) Although we do not know just when

Dante and Forese had this poetic exchange, it was certainly before Dante began writing the *Commedia,* possibly around 1293–1296. Dante's attitude toward Forese in *Purgatorio* seems entirely different from—even the opposite of—his attitude toward him in these poems, a discrepancy which has occasioned much speculation about Dante's real relationship with Forese.

The six sonnets, laden with erotic and monetary double entendres, may, with some simplification, be summarized as follows:

1. Dante describes Forese's wife as suffering from cold, implying not only that Forese's economic resources are inadequate to maintain her properly, but also that he fails in the performance of his husbandly duties in the marriage bed.
2. Forese replies that one day he indeed arose with a cough because he had no covers in bed, went out to see what he could pick up, and found a container in a ditch. Hoping it contained pearls or gold, he was disappointed to find in it Alighiero, Dante's dead father. (Deceased usurers were commonly punished at the time by being cast into ditches outside city walls, rather than buried in hallowed ground.) Alighiero asks Forese to untie him, for the love of Dante, but Forese, unable to see how to do this, goes on his way.
3. Dante's rejoinder builds on the notion of debt, predicting that Forese's gluttony will cause him to incur so much debt he will likely end in prison. But, he concludes, because Forese is an accomplished thief, he will be able to pay his debts.
4. Forese taunts Dante with his poverty, asserting that Dante has received alms, eats food handed out to beggars, and will end in a poorhouse founded by the Donati family.
5. Asserting that no one but his mother knows who Forese's father is, Dante claims that people avoid Forese because he is a well-known thief. He depicts Forese's putative father Simone lying awake worrying about whether his thieving son will be arrested. Dante further insults Forese's brothers and their wives.
6. Forese concludes the exchange by affirming that it is well known that Dante is Alighiero's son and that the vendetta Dante therefore owed his father's memory has been inadequate, ironically implying a deficiency in Dante's man-

hood. Dante's friendship for those many who do him harm is further proof of his cowardice.

It should be noted, however, that the authenticity of the *tenzone* has recently been challenged by Mauro Cursietti, who argues that it is a parodic forgery produced by Florentine homosexual circles around 1400.

In the *Purgatorio,* on the other hand, Forese is one of the most prominent characters and he appears at length, filling multiple functions, learning the names of Dante's guides, separating from the pilgrim with deep pathos. Several allusions to the earlier comic poems in the Forese episode in *Purgatorio* seem to suggest that Dante is here purging himself of sins he committed in earlier writing about Forese so cruelly: in *Purgatorio,* for example, the great mutual love of Forese and his wife is emphasized. The Forese of *Purgatorio* is, moreover, a sympathetic character morally because he praises his sister Piccarda, now in Paradise, and predicts the horrible end of his evil brother Corso.

Bibliography

Barbi, Michele. "La tenzone di Dante con Forese." In *Problemi di critica dantesca. Seconda serie (1920–1937).* Florence: Sansoni, 1975, pp. 87–188.

Cursietti, Mauro. *La falsa tenzone di Dante con Forese Donati.* Anzio: De Rubeis, 1995.

Russo, Vittorio. "*Pg.* XXIII: Forese, o la maschera del discorso." *MLN* 94 (1979), 113–136.

Stefanini, Ruggero. "Tenzone sì e tenzone no." *Lectura Dantis* 18–19 (1996), 111–128.

Susan Noakes

Fortune

In *Inf.* 7.61–96 Fortune *(Fortuna)* is described by Virgil to the pilgrim as the "general minister and leader" who has been divinely entrusted with the duty of incessantly shifting the possession of earthly goods from person to person according to the providential plan. Before Dante, and among most of his contemporaries, medievals derived the personified figure of Fortune largely from the pagan notion of a minor goddess of chance, luck, and unforeseen events of all kinds. She is typically fickle, unwavering (as in Cicero, Alan of Lille, Boccaccio, Chaucer, and Dante's *Fiore*), and wholly invincible (as opposed to the concept of her developed during the Roman republic and renewed in the Renaissance).

Among Dante's sources of inspiration for Fortune's divine role in human affairs we must count above all Virgil—who, in the *Aeneid,* identifies the term "fortune" with the will of Jove whenever speaking of Aeneas' predestined task of nation building—and Boethius—who depicts fortune as an entity which operates beyond the ken of mortal man and yet which is also subordinated to a higher, divine power. The Church Fathers were, however, concerned about the common perception of fortune and went to great pains both to destroy the belief in a capricious goddess of chance and to delineate theologically the precise relationship of chance to providence. Augustine (*De Divers. Quaest.* 24) and Aquinas (*Contra Gent.* 3.74 and *ST* 1.116.1) prepared the way for Dante's exposition on Fortune in *Inf.* 7 by explaining that the cause of every event is known to God, though perhaps not to man, and that all things ultimately occur according to the divine plan. Given this conception, it is logical to conclude that, if Fortune exists and operates in the world, her efforts must be in harmony with providential order (cf. *Par.* 13.37–42 and *Consol. philos.* 5 pr. 4.28–91). By combining the Virgilian/Boethian literary figure of a personified Fortune with patristic teaching on the matter, Dante formulated the first representation of Fortuna as a Celestial Intelligence (cf. *Conv.* 2.4).

In *Inf.* 7, the first lengthy theoretical digression of the *Commedia,* Dante establishes an exacting description of Fortune's duties. She is the being in charge of distributing and redistributing *li ben vani* (7.79), "the empty goods," "from one people to another, from one family to another, beyond any human wisdom's power to prevent; therefore one people rules and another languishes, according to her judgment, which is hidden, like the snake in grass." It is within her power to grant as well as to withdraw her favors in spite of man's best attempts to understand her reasons. Fortune's effects on mortals' lives are hence cast as the mover of Aristotle's *causae per accidens.* For Dante, she is no longer fickle and unruly (though she may seem so to those of limited or unenlightened intellect), but is instead an integrated (even necessary) component of God's effectuation of providence among the affairs of men. Though we may rail against her (*Conv.* 4.12.7), she operates by a higher authority

and is deaf to both our complaints and our praises (cf. *Consol. philos.* 2, met. 1.5–7). Her famously Boethian wheel has become in Dante a heavenly sphere and, once a pagan goddess, she is now *beata* or "blest."

Throughout the rest of the *Commedia* and in many of the minor works, "fortune" (both personified and used as an inanimate noun) appears numerous times. In keeping with the semantic scheme set out in *Inf.* 7, Fortune, the Celestial Intelligence, is portrayed as the distributor of *beni vani* ("empty goods") in *Rime* 106.90 and *Epist.* 6.19. She is shown transferring goods from household to household in *Conv.* 4.8.9 and 4.12.7, and from nation to nation in *Inf.* 30.13–15, *Par.* 16.82–84, and *Epist.* 13.5. Dante alludes to her role as the active handmaiden of providence in *Mon.* 2.9.8–9 in quoting the words of Pyrrhus ("Here Pyrrhus called fortune 'Hera'; we call that same cause by the more appropriate and accurate name 'divine providence'"), in the somewhat enigmatic assertion of fortitude in *Inf.* 15.91–96, and in its counterpart of *Par.* 17.23–27. Very close to the connection between fortune and providence is that of fortune and destiny which is suggested in *Epist.* 13.5 and *Inf.* 15.46 (echoed again in the parallel construction of *Inf.* 32.76). Fortune's role in the poet's own personal destiny is often developed in relation to the recurrent theme of an unjustly imposed exile (cf. *Epist.* 2.3 and *Par.* 8.139–141), and it comes as no surprise that Dante has Cacciaguida expound in *Par.* 17 upon the divine intention which underlies the political persecution. In fact, Dante even refers to the edict of exile as the "wound of fortune" (*Conv.* 1.3.4) and as a "blemish," occasioned by fortune, upon his character (*Conv.* 1.4.8–9).

Although these several passages reflect a well-polished theological system, it must be noted as well that Dante does not at all times adhere to it as it is defined in *Inf.* 7. *Fortuna* can likewise connote "luck" or "chance" (e.g., *Conv.* 4.11, *Par.* 12.92, *Mon.* 2.10.5, and *Epist.* 8.5). There are, however, a number of additional occurrences (most notably *VN* 12.16, 18.1, *Inf.* 13.98, 30.146, and 32.76) which are not unequivocally identifiable as belonging either to fortune as "Intelligence" or to fortune as "chance" and must consequently be regarded as ambiguous (an ambiguity, as is often the case in Dante, which may be altogether intentional).

F

Bibliography

Cioffari, Vincenzo. *The Conception of Fortune and Fate in the Works of Dante.* Cambridge, Mass.: Harvard University Press, 1940.

———. *Fortune in Dante's Fourteenth Century Commentators.* Cambridge, Mass.: Harvard University Press, 1944.

Kirkpatrick, Robin. "Dante's Fortuna: *Inferno* VII." In *Dante Soundings: Eight Literary and Historical Essays.* Edited by David Nolan. Dublin: Irish Academic Press; Totowa, N.J.: Rowman and Littlefield, 1981.

Kleinhenz, Christopher. "Plutus, Fortune, and Michael: The Eternal Triangle." *Dante Studies* 98 (1980), 35–52.

Magee, John C. "The Boethian Wheels of Fortune and Fate." *Mediaeval Studies* 49 (1987), 524–533.

Patch, Howard R. *The Goddess Fortuna in Medieval Literature.* Cambridge, Mass.: Harvard University Press, 1927; New York: Octagon Books, 1967.

Michael Papio

Foscolo, Ugo

An Italian poet, novelist, soldier, and scholar, Foscolo (1772–1834) forms with Giacomo Leopardi (1798–1837) and Alessandro Manzoni (1785–1873) the great triumvirate of Italian Romanticism. Born on the Greek island of Zante and raised in the cosmopolitan atmosphere of Venice, Foscolo was caught up in the turbulence of the Napoleonic era and the struggles for Italian independence and unity, making him an important figure of the Risorgimento. As a soldier, he saw action at Centro and Genoa; as a scholar he was briefly an editor of the journal *Monitore* in Milan and later a professor of eloquence at the University of Pavia. After some initial notoriety as a playwright, Foscolo achieved his first major success with his novel *Ultime lettere di Iacopo Ortis* (1802, 1817), a work comparable in form and character to Goethe's *Sorrows of Young Werther* (1774, 1787). His poetic reputation rests on his masterpieces *I Sepolcri* ("The Sepulchers"), published in 1806, and *Le Grazie* ("The Graces"), published in 1813. With the Austrian occupation of Milan after Waterloo, Foscolo joined the ranks of the Risorgimento exiles in London, there contributing reviews and completing other scholarly projects, including his *Discorso sul testo della Commedia di Dante* ("On

the Text of the *Commedia* of Dante") and *Saggi sul Petrarca* ("Essays on Petrarch").

While Petrarch and Tasso were Foscolo's poetic inspiration, Dante nevertheless played a central role, symbolizing the spirit of Italian unity and patriotism, the poet of exile, and uncompromising idealism. In addition to an early ode, "A Dante" (1795), Foscolo frequently alluded to Dante in his creative works. More significant, however, were Foscolo's contributions to Dante scholarship. Foscolo was among the first Italian scholars to examine Dante's poetry critically, rather than with praise or censure. In *Dell'origine e dell'ufficio della letteratura* ("On the Origin and Function of Literature"), an inaugural speech delivered in Pavia, and later in the *Discorso* and *Saggi,* he developed the historicism of Vico to analyze Dante's poetic achievement. For Foscolo, Dante exemplified the "primitive poetry" of the Italian nation, just as Homer did for the Greeks, and Shakespeare for the English. Thus, while Petrarch and Tasso possessed greater eloquence and sophistication, Dante had greater power, emerging as the natural product of the spirit of the Florentine republic. In an influential review of Henry Francis Cary's translation of the *Commedia* for the *Edinburgh Review* (1818), Foscolo played an important role in popularizing Dante in the English-speaking world.

Bibliography

Cambon, Glauco. *Ugo Foscolo: Poet of Exile.* Princeton, N.J.: Princeton University Press, 1980.

Radcliff-Umstead, Douglas. *Ugo Foscolo.* New York: Twayne, 1970.

Vincent, E. R. *Ugo Foscolo, an Italian in Regency England.* Cambridge: Cambridge University Press, 1953.

Thomas L. Cooksey

Foster, Kenelm, O.P.

Lecturer and reader at the University of Cambridge until his retirement in 1978, and for many years the doyen of British Dantists, Foster (1910–1986) brought to the study of Dante a unique combination of theological and literary scholarship together with a way of writing marked at once by precision and accessibility. Among his publications on Dante (other areas of interest included Petrarch and Italian authors of the nineteenth century) are *God's Tree* (1957), *Dante's Lyric Poetry* (an edition of and commentary on Dante's lyric poetry written in collaboration with Patrick Boyde; 1967), *The Two Dantes,* (a mature expression of his long meditation on the nature of Dante's particular species of Christian humanism; 1977), and papers delivered before the London Aquinas Society and in Cambridge (especially "The Mind in Love," 1956, and "Religion and Philosophy in Dante," 1965).

Bibliography

Boyde, Patrick, and Kenelm Foster. *Dante's Lyric Poetry.* 2 vols. Oxford: Oxford University Press, 1967.

Foster, Kenelm. *The Two Dantes and Other Studies.* Berkeley and Los Angeles: University of California, 1977.

———. *God's Tree: Essays on Dante and Other Matters.* London: Blackfriars Publications, 1957.

John Took

France

The most explicit and sustained representation of France *(Francia)* in the *Commedia* involves its condemnation as a political and military danger to the empire and to the papacy, to Italy in general, and to Florence in particular. Hugh Capet's speech in *Purg.* 20.43–96 provides a historical, sequential account of the crimes of the Kingdom of France in terms of the rise of the Capetian dynasty after the extinction of the royal line of Charlemagne (considered by Dante to be the last legitimate Roman emperor; see *Par.* 6.94–96). France is here characterized as the *mala pianta / che la terra cristiana tutta aduggia, / sì che buon frutto rado se ne schianta* ("the evil plant that overshadows all the Christian lands, so that one rarely breaks good fruit from it," *Purg.* 20.43–45). Hugh presents himself as the ancestor of *i Filippi e i Luigi / per cui novellamente è Francia retta* ("the Philips and the Louis by whom France in recent times is ruled," *Purg.* 20.50–51).

Four royal French figures are singled out for special condemnation by Hugh. The first mentioned is Charles I of Anjou (King Louis IX's brother), who invaded Italy in 1265 at the invitation of Popes Urban IV and Clement IV to assume the crowns of Naples and Sicily. His defeats of Manfred at Benevento (1266) and of Conradin at Tagliacozzo (1268) effectively ended direct imperial (Hohenstaufen) rule in Italy (*Purg.* 20.67–68). Next, Hugh prophesies the coming of *un altro Carlo fuor di Francia* ("another Charles out of France," *Purg.* 20.71), Charles of Valois (King Philip IV's brother) who arrived in Florence in 1301, having been invited by Pope Boniface VIII to reconcile peacefully the conflict between the White Guelfs and Black Guelfs. Contrary to his public charge, however, Charles of Valois (who is compared to Judas in *Purg.* 20.74) supported the Black Guelfs in what quickly became an armed struggle leading to the expulsion of the White Guelfs from Florence, in April 1302 (with Dante named among those condemned to exile). Third, Hugh characterizes Charles II of Anjou (son of Charles I of Anjou and King of Naples from 1285 to 1309) as epitomizing the avarice that characterizes the entire Capetian family (*Purg.* 20.80–84).

Hugh concludes his negative treatment of the French royal line he himself founded by denouncing the future crimes of Philip IV (known as Philip the Fair, king of France from 1285 to 1314) against the papacy and the Knights Templars (*Purg.* 20.85–96). The imprisonment and mistreatment of Pope Boniface VIII at Anagni in September of 1303, by agents of Philip (initially referred to as *lo fiordaliso* ("the fleur-de-lis," *Purg.* 20.86), is presented as the equivalent of a second crucifixion (*Purg.* 20.86–90) with the French king playing the role of *il novo Pilato* ("the new Pilate," *Purg.* 20.91). His persecution of the Templars, initiated in 1307 and involving the suppression of the order in 1312, is presented as an impious looting motivated by greed (*Purg.* 20.91–93).

Philip the Fair is repeatedly denounced elsewhere in the *Commedia,* though he is never named explicitly. He is first mentioned in *Inf.* 19.87, where Pope Nicholas III refers to him as *chi Francia regge* ("he who governs France"), and condemns him for having effected the election of the French pope, Clement V, in 1305. Sordello refers to Philip as the *mal di Francia* ("plague of France") in *Purg.* 7.109, while indicating to Virgil and Dante how his father, Philip III, King of France (1270–85), and his father-in-law, Henry I, King of Navarre (1270–1274), both grieve over *la vita sua viziata e lorda* ("his vicious, filthy life," *Purg.* 7.110) from their places in the Ante-Purgatory. The eagle in the Heaven of Jupiter prophesies how France, identified by metonymy as *Senna* ("the Seine," *Par.* 19.118) will suffer from Philip's

F debasement of the coinage, at the same time predicting his death from a hunting accident in 1314 by referring to him as *quel che morrà di colpo di cotenna* ("he who will die from the blow of the boar's hide," *Par.* 19.120).

Dante's view of the ultimate French crime against the Church—the removal of the papacy from Rome to Avignon in 1309—is represented in *Purg.* 32.148–160, at the close of the pageant of the *carro* ("chariot") and its transformations as the seventh, last, and greatest calamity to befall the Church in history. The *puttana sciolta* ("ungirt whore," *Purg.* 32.149) figures the papacy (especially the French pope Clement V) and the *gigante* ("giant," *Purg.* 32.152) figures the French royal house (especially Philip the Fair), while Beatrice's prophecy of the DXV promises divine vengeance on this pair (*Purg.* 33.43–45). The corresponding French crime against Dante's vision of the Empire involves Philip's constant opposition to Henry VII of Luxemburg—first as candidate, then as emperor—a position which led the French king to use his power over Clement V to turn the pope secretly against Henry after having first supported his entry into Italy to be crowned emperor (cf. *Par.* 17.82). Beatrice denounces this treachery at the end of her final speech in the poem (*Par.* 30.142–148).

Other references to France and the French in the *Commedia* tend to be negative, dismissive, or pejorative. Speaking to Guido da Montefeltro about the condition of Romagna, Dante-protagonist characterizes Forlì as the city which once made *di Franceschi sanguinoso mucchio* ("a bloody heap of the French," *Inf.* 27.44), referring to the defeat inflicted by the Forlivesi on their besiegers in 1282. Commenting to Virgil on Albero of Siena's desire to fly, Dante-protagonist refers to *la francesca* ("the French," *Inf.* 29.122–123) as a standard of vanity against which the Sienese are measured. In Antenora, Bocca mockingly identifies Buoso da Duera to Dante as having betrayed Manfred's cause in Lombardy to the invading army of Charles of Anjou in 1265 for *l'argento de' Franceschi* ("the silver of the French," *Inf.* 32.115). Marco Lombardo emphasizes the virtue of Guido da Castel by explaining that his nickname, *il semplice Lombardo* ("the honest Lombard," *Purg.* 16.125), has been given *francescamente* ("in the French way," *Purg.* 16.126). Cacciaguida condemns the corruption of civic and family life in Dante's Florence as a result of that city's extensive commercial ties with France: he contrastively recalls the pre-mercantile virtuous simplicity of the earlier Florence of his own lifetime, before any Florentine wife had been *per Francia nel letto diserta* ("left alone in her bed because of France," *Par.* 15.120), before Franco-Florentine trade required significant foreign travel by Florentine husbands for business reasons.

The *Commedia's* few explicit allusions to French literature demonstrate Dante's familiarity with two of the major narrative genres of the medieval French canon. On the one hand, there is Arthurian romance (known as the *matière de Bretagne*) with its highly erotic content. In *Inf.* 5.67, Tristan is evoked, and the Old French *Prose Lancelot* plays a key role in the celebrated final sequence in which Francesca presents, as the immediate cause of her own adulterous love affair, her reading with Paolo of the scene in which Guinevere kisses Lancelot for the first time (5.127–138). In *Inf.* 5.137, Francesca compares both the French book and its author to the Arthurian knight Gallehault *(Galeotto)*, the character who acts as facilitator and go-between for the lovers in the romance. The conclusion of the *Prose Lancelot*, with Mordred's treacherous murder of King Arthur, is mentioned by Camiscione de' Pazzi (a traitor condemned to Caina) in *Inf.* 32.61–62, showing Dante-author's knowledge of the ultimate destructive consequences of the love between Lancelot and Guinevere. Implicitly foregrounded is the suggestion that Dante, unlike Francesca, continued to read this particular French book to its very conclusion. In *Par.* 16.13–15, Beatrice's smile, when Dante begins to speak to Cacciaguida, is compared to the cough of warning to Guinevere by one of her ladies.

On the other hand, there is the French *chanson de geste,* the epic cycle of Charlemagne and Roland (known as the *matière de France*), which Dante tends to treat as historical events rather than romance adventures. Ganelon is placed in Antenora (*Inf.* 32.122), along with the other traitors to country or cause. Roland and Charlemagne appear among the crusaders in the fifth Heaven (*Par.* 18.43), along with William and Renouard (*Par.* 18.46). There is also the comparison of Nimrod's horn in the ninth circle to Roland's horn at the defeat at Roncesvalles (*Inf.* 31.16–18), when Charlemagne lost *la santa gesta* ("the holy company," 31.17), as well as the Eagle's presentation of Charlemagne as the sixth and final Roman emperor in *Par.* 6.96 (relevant, as mentioned above, to Dante's devalorization of the "merely French" Capetians as lacking legitimacy in terms of the Roman imperium; cf. *Purg.* 20.52).

Dante locates France geographically and linguistically in *DVE* 1.8.5–6. He differentiates French from the two other Romance vernaculars ("Hispanic" and "Italian") in his taxonomic system, using its affirmative particle *(oïl)* as its identifying label (as opposed to *oc* and *sì,* respectively). He situates the territory of French speakers as bordered by the Germans to the east, by the sea to the north and west, and by the Aragonese mountains, Provence, and the Apennines to the south.

In *DVE* 1.10.2, Dante expounds in general terms the forms, subjects, and genres that he deems most appropriate to the particular qualities of the French vernacular: *Allegat ergo pro se lingua oïl quod propter sui faciliorem ac delectabiliorem vulgaritatem quicquid redactum est sive inventum ad vulgare prosaycum, suum est: videlicet Biblia cum Troianorum Romanorumque gestibus compilata et Arturi regis ambages pulcerrime et quamplures alie ystorie ac doctrine* ("Thus the language of *oïl* adduces on its own behalf the fact that, because of the greater facility and pleasing quality of its vernacular style, everything that is recounted or invented in vernacular prose belongs to it: such as compilations from the Bible and the histories of Troy and Rome, and the [very beautiful adventures] of King Arthur, and many other works of history and doctrine").

Bibliography

Brownlee, Kevin. "The Practice of Cultural Authority: Italian Responses to French Cultural Dominance in *Il Tesoretto, Il Fiore,* and the *Commedia." Forum for Modern Language Studies* 33 (1997), 258–269.

Hauvette, Henri. *La France et la Provence dans l'œuvre de Dante.* Paris: Boivin, 1929.

Maddox, Donald. "The Arthurian Intertexts of *Inferno V." Dante Studies* 114 (1996), 113–127.

Marti, Mario. "Il pianto de Ugo Capeto e il natalizio 'Gloria' nell'unità del XX del *Purgatorio." Giornale Storico della Letteratura Italiana* 162 (1985), 321–343.

Richards, Earl Jeffrey. *Dante and the "Roman de la Rose." An Investigation into the Vernacular Narrative Context of the "Commedia."* Tübingen: Niemeyer, 1981.

Vasina, Augusto. "Dante di fronte ad Avignone." *Letture Classensi* 9–10 (1982), 173–189.

Kevin Brownlee

Francesca da Rimini

The daughter of Guido Minore da Polenta (also referred to as Guido il Vecchio da Polenta), lord of Ravenna, and the aunt of Guido Novello da Polenta, Dante's host in Ravenna during the last years of the poet's life, Francesca married Giovanni Malatesta (called Gianciotto, "crippled John"), the second son of Malatesta da Verrucchio, lord of Rimini, circa 1275. The marriage, which testifies to the political alliance between the two principal incipient despotisms of Romagna (both Guelf), and which produced a daughter, Concordia, ended in tragedy. According to the stories that have accreted around *Inf.* 5, Francesca entered into an adulterous love affair with Paolo Malatesta, known as Paolo il Bello and third son of Malatesta da Verrucchio. She and Paolo were killed by Gianciotto, most likely between 1283 and 1286. The date of death must be inferred circumstantially, like every other event of Francesca's unrecorded life. Paolo, who in 1269 married Orabile Beatrice, countess of Ghiaggiolo (by whom he had two children), was in Florence as *capitano del popolo* ("commander of the local militia") in 1282; he tendered his resignation on the first of February, 1283, and returned to Rimini. By 1286 Gianciotto had remarried (his second wife, Zambrasina, daughter of the traitor Tebaldello de' Zambrasi of Faenza, bore him five children).

Dante condemns the two lovers to the second circle of Hell, reserved for the souls of the lustful, or carnal sinners: *i peccator carnali, / che la ragion sommettono al talento* ("the carnal sinners, who subject reason to desire," *Inf.* 5.38–39). Hardly prolix, the text of the *Commedia* offers only the following information, in this order: Francesca's birth place (*Siede la terra dove nata fui / su la marina dove 'l Po discende / per aver pace co' seguaci sui,* "The city where I was born sits beside the shore where the Po descends to have peace with its followers," *Inf.* 5.97–99), her Christian name (*Francesca, i tuoi martìri,* "Francesca, your sufferings," *Inf.* 5.116), the fact that she and her lover were killed by a relative (*Caina attende chi a vita ci spense,* "Caina awaits him who extinguished our life," *Inf.* 5.107), the fact that the lovers are in-laws (*i due cognati,* "the two in-laws," *Inf.* 6.2). This presentation is remarkably oblique, on a number of counts. First, it forgoes altogether the names of both Francesca's lover and her husband. Second, while Francesca's Christian name is registered, her family name must be inferred from her natal city, Ravenna, which in turn is never named but alluded to in an ambiguous geographical periphrasis. Third, the fact that she and her lover were killed by a relative is presented in one compact and elliptical verse that in itself requires glossing: "Caina awaits him who extinguished our life" implies that the lovers' murderer is a relative, destined for the zone of the ninth circle, named after Cain—the first fratricide—and reserved for the traitors of kin. It is information that is meaningless without a good commentary or prior knowledge of the *Inferno.* Fourth, the fact that the murderer is related to *both* lovers, in other words the fact that the lovers were themselves related, is given to us only after the encounter with Francesca has ended, at the beginning of canto 6 when the narrator refers to them as "the two in-laws."

In weighing the significance of Dante's intervention vis-à-vis Francesca, it is important to bear in mind that there is virtually no independent documentation of her story; we are indebted for what we know to Dante and to his commentators. The qualifier "virtually" in the preceding sentence is intended to leave space for the fourteenth-century historian Marco Battagli, whose passing reference in his history of the Malatesta (1352) serves as precious, plausibly independent (despite postdating the *Commedia*) confirmation of an occurrence that presumably lived in local memory and oral sources. Battagli alludes to the event in which Francesca died without naming her: *Paulus autem fuit mortuus per fratrem suum Iohannem Zottum causa luxurie* ("Paolo was killed by his brother Giovanni the Lame, *causa luxurie,*" *Marcha*). Like Battagli, the anonymous author of the fourteenth century *Cronaca malatestiana* (this author certainly knew the *Commedia,* which he cites elsewhere) refers to the killing of Paolo and Francesca in passing—though while he does accord Francesca a role in the drama, he too dispenses with her name, referring to her merely as wife, *la donna sua.* What is most noteworthy about the historical record regarding Francesca, then, is its silence. This silence was broken by Dante, who in

effect saved Francesca from oblivion, giving her a voice and a name.

Dante's commentators at first step into the information vacuum gingerly. Jacopo Alighieri (c. 1322), for instance, offers little more than the names of all the protagonists and a schematic rendering of events, summing up the "Paolo and Francesca plot" in four dry and unsensationalist consecutive clauses: "having carnal relations with her, that is she with her aforementioned brother-in-law, on a few occasions together, they were killed by the husband." Shortly afterwards, Jacopo della Lana (1324–1328) adds some color, including a first description of the death scene: "finally he found them while sinning, he took a sword and pierced them at the same time in such a way that locked together in an embrace they died." The *Ottimo Commento* (1333–1340) goes further, adding the dynastic frame, character sketches of the protagonists, and a servant who conveys the news of the adulterous liaison to Gianciotto. He also dwells at length on the *Commedia*'s scene of the lovers reading together about Lancelot and Guinevere. It is Boccaccio, the great raconteur, who elaborates Francesca's story to novella-like proportions and whose imprint on it is most indelible. Picked up by subsequent commentators, his melodramatic tale has achieved canonical status and has utterly contaminated the reception of Francesca's story. In Boccaccio's tale Francesca is effectively innocent of any misdeed, since her father deceives her into wedlock with the ugly Gianciotto through the use of the handsome Paolo as a proxy for his brother. One could say that Boccaccio thus initiates the romantic reading of Dante's Francesca, a reading that has been cultivated passively by commentators who have repeated Boccaccio's version of the story over the centuries, as well as actively by genuine romantics like Foscolo, or De Sanctis, who writes of Francesca's *Eternità d'amore, eternità di martirio* ("eternal love, eternal suffering"). However, the romantic reading has always coexisted with a moral interpretation of the canto (Boccaccio provides this too, in his *esposizione allegorica*), which views romance and eros as under the aegis and control of reason, an unabashed moralistic reading that not only has no sympathy for Francesca but even views her as manipulative and mendacious, and has come to the fore in our own century. Whatever the critical scenario, by now our cultural imagination has been for so long overstocked with commentaries

Paolo and Francesca. Invenzioni di Giovanni Flaxman sulla Divina commedia, *illustrated by John Flaxman and Beniamino del Vecchio, Rome, 1826. Giamatti Collection: Courtesy of the Mount Holyoke College Archives and Special Collections.*

that mechanically repeat their predecessors, not to mention the many paintings, dramas, tragedies, poems, and musical responses to Francesca, that we only with difficulty clear away the cultural underbrush and concentrate on Dante's story.

Dante's Francesca is, as is usually the case with his characters, less reducible and linear than his commentators find acceptable. She offers no extenuating circumstances to justify her behavior, no deceitful father or proxy marriage, just the overwhelming force of overriding passion. Desire compels her, and she sins. That is her story, and it is one that foregrounds the key philosophical issues at stake here for Dante, issues of compulsion and the will, already condensed in the key verse *che la ragion sommettono al talento:* reason struggles with desire, and in Francesca's case desire triumphs. Her discourse of justification engages a deeper logic than Boccaccio's circumstantial inventions: her point, reflected in her very syntax, is that desire cannot be withstood. Dante is passionately invested in the belief that desire can

be withstood, that reason can and must triumph, and it is this profoundly psychological and ethical drama, with deep roots in the courtly tradition, that is ultimately played out in his treatment of lust. Whereas vision literature (see Gardiner) emphasizes sex itself as sinful, subjecting carnal sinners to degrading and sexualized punishments, the contrapasso fashioned by Dante in *Inf.* 5—where the lustful are tossed by the hell-storm as in life they were buffeted by their passions—emphasizes the psychology of desire. For Dante, the issue is not fornication or adultery per se (after all, Cunizza da Romano, a scandalous adulterer, is in paradise, along with Rahab, a prostitute), but the sinful surrender to desire, a surrender with which the pilgrim so thoroughly identifies that he faints to the floor of Hell at the conclusion of Francesca's story.

In her famous tercets, each beginning with "Love" as subject, Francesca draws on the fundamental tenets of the established amatory code to tell her story in, precisely, coded form. The chosen code dictates biographical and historical opacity;

F in place of recognizable humans engaging in recognizable human behavior, the code renders the lovers as particles adrift in a force field governed by powers beyond their control: love, beauty, nobility. To the degree that other people enter the lovers' realm, they are rendered as demonized abstractions. Deftly and densely these verses weave a plot that contains no human agency. The first tercet goes to the heart of Francesca's story by placing her and her lover in a matrix of love and violent death, while at the same time evading all responsibility for either that love or that death. While fundamentally ahistorical, the tercet sketches the lineaments of a history that is initiated with the passions of the man. In this chronology, Paolo is the first to love: *Amor, ch'al cor gentil ratto s'apprende, / prese costui de la bella persona / che mi fu tolta; e 'l modo ancor m'offende* ("Love, which is swiftly kindled in the noble heart, seized this one for the lovely person that was taken from me; and the manner still injures me," *Inf.* 5.100–102). The syntactic density of this language creates a sense of tightly compacted ineluctability, of a destiny that cannot be escaped. Francesca tells us that love, which is quickly kindled in a noble heart, seized Paolo, that the love that seized him was for her beautiful body, the same body that was taken from her, and that the mode (of what? of loving? of being murdered?) still offends her. The agents of causality here are love (which the noble-souled are not able to withstand)—this precept recapitulates the poet Guido Guinizzelli, implicitly an authority, and thus another agent of causality), Francesca's physical beauty (which seizes Paolo), the unnamed agents that take Francesca's body from her, and the mysterious *modo*—the way, the modality—that still offends her. The next tercet is only somewhat less dense. She explains that, since reciprocity in love is obligatory (here she draws on the late twelfth-century treatise *The Art of Courtly Love* by Andreas Capellanus, another implicit authority, hence agent), love caused by his beauty bound her reciprocally—and eternally: *Amor, ch'a nullo amato amar perdona, / mi prese del costui piacer sì forte, / che, come vedi, ancor non m'abbandona* ("Love, which pardons no one loved from loving in return, seized me for his beauty so strongly that, as you see, it still does not abandon me," *Inf.* 5.103–105). Francesca's two-verse conclusion is less syntactically complex, more stark, still opaque however, and equally devoted to maintaining the role of object: *Amor*

condusse noi ad una morte. / Caina attende chi a vita ci spense ("Love led us to one death. Caina awaits him who extinguished our life," *Inf.* 5.106–107).

These abstract and codified declarations manage to reveal the speaker's identity to her interlocutor, causing him to speak to her by name: *Francesca, i tuoi martìri / a lagrimar mi fanno tristo e pio* ("Francesca, your sufferings make me sad and piteous to tears," *Inf.* 5.116–117). Once he knows her identity, the pilgrim formulates a query that is undeniably voyeuristic: how did love first permit the lovers to recognize their desires? Her response is classically Dantesque, in terms of poetic yield, that is, the ratio of poetic richness achieved (very great) to linguistic expenditure (very sparing). It introduces a new subtext, the romance *Lancelot du Lac,* to whose protagonists Francesca compares herself and Paolo. It brings the complicity of writing and literature ever more to the attention of the reader as a main theme of the canto, a theme that culminates in Francesca's indictment of the *Lancelot* and its author as the "go-betweens" who brought her and Paolo to the point of surrendering to passion. And Francesca responds to the implicit voyeurism of the pilgrim's request by providing a more detailed window onto her affair, portraying a scene that is powerfully specular, a *mise en abyme* where our passions are engaged as we read of passionate readers reading about passion.

Reading together one day for pleasure, *per diletto,* the couple read of how love seized Lancelot. The reading constrained their eyes to meet and their faces to pale, and finally—but only when they read of how Lancelot kissed Guinevere—Paolo kissed Francesca. But this account is brought up short by two remarkable consecutive statements. Francesca's famously elliptical conclusion, *quel giorno più non vi leggemmo avante* ("that day we read there no further," *Inf.* 5.138), leaves both pilgrim and reader to grapple with a declaration that suggests volumes but tells nothing, and whose very reticence has generated the voyeuristic fascination that we find in the commentaries. And her preceding statement, *Galeotto fu 'l libro e chi lo scrisse* ("Galeotto was the book and he who wrote it," *Inf.* 5.137), is an indictment that masterfully synthesizes the canto's fundamental questions about agency and art. The verse states that the Old French romance and its author occupied the same role—the role of go-between—

in the lives of Francesca and Paolo that the knight Gallehaut occupied in the lives of Guinevere and Lancelot. Thus, the *Lancelot* romance and its author—*'l libro e chi lo scrisse*—are responsible for bringing together Francesca and Paolo and causing them to sin. Does moral responsibility lodge with the author or the reader? In contemporary terms, does it lodge with the creator/producer of the violent film or with the viewer/consumer?

There is no doubt that, for Dante, Francesca has to bear responsibility for her own destiny; her syntactic passivity mirrors her sinful refusal of moral agency, of reason—indeed, in Dante's scale of values, of life itself. But the pilgrim's swoon marks the end of an episode that is deeply complicitous, for Dante as a love poet had himself once been under the sway of a dark and deadly eros. While the linking of love and death in *Inf.* 5 has classical antecedents, figured in Dido, *colei che s'ancise amorosa* ("she who killed herself for love," *Inf.* 5.61), the most powerful contemporary theorist of the death-love was Guido Cavalcanti, Dante's best friend of the *Vita Nuova*. When Francesca declares that *Amor condusse noi ad una morte,* she inscribes the true rubric of *Inf.* 5, whose topic is not just sinful love but the love that leads to death, the love of which one could say—with Cavalcanti—that *Di sua potenza segue spesso morte* ("From its [love's] power death often follows," "Donna me prega," 35).

Now, viewed teleologically, Dante's work and thought is governed by one principle: that love is a life force, and that the life force is love. Beatrice's salvific *amor mi mosse, che mi fa parlare* ("love has moved me and makes me speak," *Inf.* 2.72) is at the antipodes of Francesca's *Amor condusse noi ad una morte.* The bedrock principles of the *Commedia* are that love can save, love can beatify, love can give life. *Inf.* 5, which constitutes Dante's most synthetic and compelling meditation on love as a death force, on love as a power that is not death defying but death inducing, on love as a dark compulsion that leads not to salvation but to damnation, thus derives its extraordinary importance within the economy of Dante's oeuvre from its perverse mirroring of the poet's primal foundational belief. *Inf.* 5 is, moreover, concerned not just with love but with the linguistic means by which love is communicated: with speaking, writing, and reading, and with the modalities wherein speaking, writing, and reading about love occur, in particular the literary genres of lyric and romance. By enabling the canto's chief protagonist, Francesca, to draw with great precision on both lyric and romance registers in her speech, Dante raises the question of the complicity of language and literature in her damnation, thus broaching a topic of enormous relevance to himself and his own enterprise, which is after all nothing less than the construction of a literary text that self-consciously sets out to procure the salvation of its readers through the deployment of words and language.

Bibliography

Alighieri, Jacopo. *Chiose alla Cantica dell'Inferno di Dante Alighieri scritte da Jacopo Alighieri.* Cited from the Dante Dartmouth Database.

Avalle, D'Arco Silvio. ". . . de fole amor." *Modelli semiologici della Divina Commedia.* Milan: Bompiani, 1975, pp. 97–121.

Battagli, Marco. *Marcha.* Edited by Aldo Francesco Massra. *Rerum Italicorum Scriptores.* Vol. 16, part 3. Città di Castello: Lapi, 1913.

Boccaccio, Giovanni. *Esposizioni sopra la Comedia di Dante.* Edited by Giorgio Padoan. *Tutte le opere di Giovanni Boccaccio.* Vol. 6. Milan: Mondadori, 1965.

Caretti, Lanfranco. "Il canto V dell'*Inferno.*" *Nuove letture dantesche.* Vol. 1. Florence: Le Monnier, 1968, pp. 105–131.

Cavalcanti, Guido. *Guido Cavalcanti: Rime.* Edited by Marcello Ciccuto. Milan: Rizzoli, 1978.

Contini, Gianfranco. "Dante come personaggio-poeta della *Commedia.*" Originally in *L'Approdo letterario* 4 (1958). Reprint *Un'idea di Dante.* Turin: Einaudi, 1976, pp. 33–62.

Cronaca malatestiana. Edited by Aldo Francesco Massra. *Rerum Italicorum Scriptores.* Vol. 15, part 2. Bologna: Zanichelli, 1922.

Della Terza, Dante. "*Inferno* V: Tradition and Exegesis." *Dante Studies* 99 (1981), 49–66.

De Sanctis, Francesco. "Francesca da Rimini." *Nuova Antologia* 10 (1869), 34–46. Reprint, *Lezioni sulla Divina Commedia.* Edited by Michele Manfredi. Bari: Laterza, 1955, pp. 137–147.

Hatcher, Anna and Mark Musa. "The Kiss: *Inferno* V and the Old French Prose *Lancelot.*" *Comparative Literature* 20 (1968), 97–109.

Lana, Jacopo della. *Comedia di Dante degli Allaghieri col Commento di Jacopo della Lana bolognese.* Cited from the Dante Dartmouth Database.

Matteini, Nevio. *Francesca da Rimini: storia / mito / arte.* Bologna: Cappelli, 1965.

Noakes, Susan. "The Double Misreading of Paolo and Francesca." *Philological Quarterly* 62 (1983), 221–239.

Poggioli, Renato. "Tragedy or Romance: A Reading of the Paolo and Francesca Episode in Dante's *Inferno*." *PMLA* 72 (1957), 313–358.

Scott, John A. "Dante's Francesca and the Poet's Attitude towards Courtly Literature." *Reading Medieval Studies* 5 (1979), 4–20.

Tonini, Luigi. *Della storia civile e sacra riminese.* Vol. 3. Rimini: Malvolti ed Ercolani, 1862.

Torraca, Francesco. "Il canto V dell'*Inferno*." *Nuova Antologia,* 1902. Reprinted in *Studi danteschi.* Naples: Perrella, 1912, pp. 383–442.

Toynbee, Paget. "Dante and the Lancelot Romance." *Dante Studies and Researches.* London: Methuen, 1902.

Vasina, Augusto. "Malatesta"; "Maltesta, Giovanni, detto Gianciotto"; "Malatesta, Malatestino"; "Malatesta, Paolo (detto il Bello)"; "Malatesta da Verucchio." *Enciclopedia dantesca* 3:782–785.

Visions of Heaven and Hell before Dante. Edited by Eileen Gardiner. New York: Italica Press, 1989.

Teodolinda Barolini

Francesco da Buti

Francesco di Bartolo da Buti, known generally by the abbreviated form of Francesco da Buti, was born in Pisa in 1324 and died in his native city on July 15, 1405 of the Pisan calendar. A modest classroom teacher who spent his mature years as an instructor at the Studio di Pisa, Buti read and discussed with his students the Latin classics as well as Italian literature, the best example of which was Dante's *Commedia*. After years of commenting orally about this great poem with his students, he composed a formal, written commentary. This explication is divided in two parts: the first half is a literal paraphrase of the verses, the second half a cultural and allegorical interpretation. Buti was influenced by Guido da Pisa's *Expositio,* on the whole of the *Inferno,* and by Boccaccio's commentary on the first half of the *Inferno.* The first draft of Buti's explication was apparently written in 1385, but a full draft did not appear until 1395. Francesco da Buti's commentary has been published only once.

Bibliography

Giannini, Crescentino (ed.). *Commento di Francesco da Buti sopra la Divina Commedia di Dante Alighieri.* 3 vols. Pisa: Fratelli Nistri, 1858–1862.

Vincenzo Cioffari

Francesco de' Cavalcanti

The early commentators are all but unanimous in identifying Francesco (also named Guercio) as the last of the five noble Florentine thieves encountered in the seventh ditch of the eighth circle of Hell (Malebolge), who, first appearing in serpent form, exchanges shapes with Buoso, stealing the latter's human features. His name does not occur in Dante's text, although he is referred to obliquely by a circumlocution: *quel che tu, Gaville, piagni* ("the one that makes you, Gaville, weep," *Inf.* 25.151). His murder by men from Gaville, the commentators claim, led to savage reprisals by his family against the town. Although the text would seem to allude to an incident sufficiently well known to require no further elaboration, no historical record of it survives. History has conspired with Dante to condemn this particular member of the Cavalcanti clan to anonymity.

Anthony Oldcorn

Francis of Assisi, St.

Francesco Bernardone, Francis of Assisi, was born in 1182, the son of a prosperous merchant. Following a carefree youth he suffered an illness, after which deep religious feelings led to his renunciation of his earthly possessions. He began giving his money and some family belongings to the poor. Called to account by his father at the court of the bishop of Assisi, he stripped himself naked, returned his clothes to his father, and declared that henceforth he would be loyal only to his father in Heaven. He then settled in a small church called the Porziuncola (Santa Maria degli Angeli) and, together with a few other men from Assisi, lived a life of poverty, prayer, and good works. In 1209, he traveled to Rome to receive permission from Pope Innocent III to found an order dedicated to living a life of poverty and preaching repentance. The order grew rapidly after Innocent's approval. In addition, Francis established a female branch of the movement, called the Clares (after Clare of Assisi, the first woman converted to his way of life). A so-called third order was also formed for those in secular life who wished to practice Franciscan virtues as far as their station in life allowed.

Francis continued to lead a life that alternated between periods of solitary prayer and active ministry to the poor. He also traveled throughout Italy and as far away as Egypt in an attempt to convert Muslims to Christianity and (unsuccessfully) to find martyrdom for himself. The order continued to expand, and as it grew it required a more comprehensive rule than what it began with in 1209. In 1221, the so-called First Rule was published, but because its language was deemed imprecise or insufficiently legal, another Rule was promulgated in 1223. This Rule, which became the official Rule for the order, stressed obedience to the pope but also allowed concessions to the strict poverty which was Francis' original ideal. Francis' last years, however, saw a relaxation of the original rigor of the order and his *Testament,* written shortly before his death, implored the friars to preserve the simplicity of those earlier and, for him, happier times. Francis' deep contemplation and devotion to Christ culminated, according to tradition, in his reception of the wounds of Christ, the stigmata, on Mount La Verna in 1224. Francis' joy in creation and love for nature, detailed in an extraordinarily large number of stories written about the saint, can perhaps best be seen in a poem he himself composed toward the end of his life called the "Canticle of the Creatures." Often considered the earliest poem in an Italian dialect, the canticle expresses loving praise of God the creator for the gift of his creation. Francis died in 1226 and was canonized only two years later by Pope Gregory IX.

Francis is given an especially exalted place by Dante in *Paradiso.* In canto 32 he is placed just below John the Baptist and just above St. Benedict in the mystical rose, in a section reserved for the great founders of religious orders. His life is recounted in considerable detail by Thomas Aquinas in canto 11 of *Paradiso,* within the circle of the Sun. In this telling, Dante, through the figure of Thomas, follows fairly precisely the *Legenda maior,* or *Major Life,* the authoritative life of Francis by St. Bonaventure (published in 1263). As such, Dante's Francis is a model of clarity and compression. We are told of Francis' birth, of his marriage to Lady Poverty (an aspect of Francis' life taken not from Bonaventure but from the *Sacrum Commercium*), of the renunciation of his father, of his rules for the order, of his reception of the stigmata, and of his death. This retelling is faithful to the enormous poetic energy of its primary source, as well as to its vision, a vision in which Bonaventure sees Francis as a figure of *renovatio* in the Church, a herald of the last times, and a figure of apocalyptic significance. Indeed, in his reception of the stigmata Francis is explicitly compared to the angel of the sixth seal of Rev. 6:12 and 7:2, both by Bonaventure and by Dante. To Bonaventure, Francis was not simply a saint, but a saint among saints, a saint unique in Christian history. Bonaventure was concerned with Francis' place in a comprehensive scheme of history, and it is this vision of Francis which Dante emphasizes in his narrative of Francis' life.

This retelling of Francis' life in the circle of the Sun can also be seen as part of a larger movement in which Dante the poet presents a plea for reform and order in the Church and, in its complementary structure, the retelling is itself an example of what that order might look like. Just as Thomas Aquinas, the great Dominican theologian, praises the life of Francis, proposing it as a model for emulation, in the following canto the great Franciscan theologian Bonaventure presents the life of Dominic, the founder of the Dominican order. Francis and Dominic are thus praised as the twin agents of reform in the Church, and this intersection of Francis and Dominic, Aquinas and Bonaventure, foregrounding as it does the relationship between parts and the whole, can be related to other complementary models of harmony present in the circle of the Sun: the two concentric circles each made up of twelve wise and learned Christian sages (who comprise the totality of the inhabitants of the circle of the Sun), and the intersecting circles, described at the beginning of *Par.* 10, of the daily and yearly rotations of the universe itself.

But if the figure of Francis as portrayed by Dante can be seen as part of a larger cosmic whole, he is also a figure who may well be speaking to the pilgrim and his journey with a particular directness. This should not be surprising, since there are considerable biographical links between Dante and St. Francis. Dante was in all probability educated at the school at Santa Croce, the Franciscan church in Florence. There is also a widely accepted tradition (met with skepticism by some) that Dante was himself a third-order Franciscan. Of less importance individually but worth mentioning cumulatively are the facts that Dante was buried in the church of St. Francis in Ravenna, that his daughter became a Franciscan nun, and that he sometimes appears in crowd scenes in paintings in

Franciscan churches. Thus, Francis can be seen not simply as a model for emulation by everyone. He is an especial model for the pilgrim. In particular, what Dante the pilgrim needs to learn from Francis of Assisi is that the twin virtues embodied in Francis, poverty and humility, are the virtues that he will most need to take with him into exile. Like Francis, he will become a beggar, as he is about to learn from his great-great-grandfather in the circle of Mars in *Par.* 17. And if poverty is the Franciscan virtue that he needs to practice because of the circumstances of his exile, humility is the virtue that he needs by temperament to combat the sin of pride.

Francis of Assisi is also mentioned in *Inf.* 27. There, the condemned soul of Guido de Montefeltro tells Dante the pilgrim that when he died, Francis came to take his soul to Heaven, but he was rebuffed because Guido, who took the vows of a friar late in life, had fallen back to his old sinful ways before his death, and so his repentance was largely a sham. As in *Par.* 11, Dante contrasts the saintliness of Francis with the corruption that has overtaken his order in the time since his death. St. Benedict also refers to Francis in *Par.* 22.90 as the founder of a religious order which did not maintain its original purity in its subsequent history.

Bibliography

Armstrong, Regis, and Ignatius Brady (eds.). *Francis and Clare: The Complete Works.* New York: Paulist Press, 1982.

Auerbach, Erich. "St. Francis of Assisi in Dante's *Commedia.*" *Italica* 22 (1945), 166–179.

Bonaventure. *Bonaventure: The Soul's Journey into God, The Tree of Life, The Life of Francis.* Edited by Ewert Cousins. New York: Paulist Press, 1978.

Habig, Marion (ed.). *Francis of Assisi: Omnibus of Sources.* Chicago: Franciscan Herald Press, 1973.

Herzman, Ronald. "Dante and Francis." *Franciscan Studies* 42 (1982), 96–114.

Needler, Howard. *Saint Francis and Saint Dominic in the Divine Comedy.* Krefeld: Scherpe Verlag, 1969.

Ronald B. Herzman

Franciscans

The Franciscan order (or Order of Friars Minor) was founded by St. Francis of Assisi in 1209 when Pope Innocent III gave verbal approbation to its Rule. A revised Rule was confirmed in a papal bull by Honorius III in 1223.

St. Francis and the early Franciscans were not unique as a religious phenomenon. The increasingly secular nature of society in the century before Francis' birth, characterized by the growth of the economic and political power of the emerging city states, as well as a new emphasis on trade and wealth, had inspired a religious revival. Dissident religious groups, often with large popular followings, sprang up in many places. These included the Cathars in the Languedoc, the Umiliati in Lombardy, and the Waldensians in Lyons. Common factors uniting these movements were a desire to return to the simplicity of faith preached by Christ in the New Testament, and a commitment to poverty. Indeed, some reformers entirely rejected the established Church with its trappings of wealth, power, and privilege. The Church considered many of the new sects to be unorthodox and heretical, and severely persecuted them. Like some of the other groups, Francis embraced poverty, humility, and simplicity. He differed from them, however, in two important aspects: he was loyal to the Church, and he wanted to reform it from within.

Francis, whose vocation had been revealed to him by God in a series of mystical experiences, also started a tradition of mysticism within the order. The Franciscans' great emphasis on love for and communion with God led to their being associated with the Seraphim, the highest order of angels, who had the greatest love for God. Perfect love for God could be shown by perfect imitation of Christ in word and deed, and this was Francis' greatest desire for himself and his followers. His First Rule was based on the words of Christ recorded in the Gospels. Like the disciples in the New Testament who had been given instructions by Christ, the friars went preaching from town to town, taking with them no money or provisions (see Luke 9:2–3). In the *Inferno*, Dante evokes Franciscan friars, to describe the pilgrim and Virgil's characteristic way of traveling: *Taciti, soli, sanza compagnia / n'andavam l'un dinanzi e l'altro dopo, / come frati minor vanno per via.* ("Silent, alone, without companions, we were walking one before, the other after, as friars minor go their way," *Inf.* 23.1–3).

The Friars Minor were very popular. During Francis' lifetime, membership grew to more than

5,000 men. The movement's success owed much both to the personality of Francis and to his christocentric vision of the mission of the order. Yet, paradoxically, the success and rapid growth of the Franciscans led to the negation of the very concepts Francis held dear. Francis recognized that, simply to cater for such a large and ever increasing body of men, changes in the Rule were unavoidable. He drew up a revised Rule which was approved by the chapter of 1221. Francis did not have much say, however, in the drafting of the final Rule, a formal and legal document which received the solemn approbation of Honorius III in 1223 in the *regula bullata* but contained little of the saint's original vision. Thus, the Franciscans became assimilated into the structure of the Church, becoming more like the monastic orders. A more rigid organizational structure for the friars appealed to the Church authorities, since this allowed them a greater degree of control. Although, nominally, poverty was still a major commitment, and there was no individual or communal ownership, the friars were allowed the use of property—convents, churches, libraries—which was officially owned by the Church or other bodies. Moreover, they ceased being dependent on the general goodwill of the people for their day-to-day needs. While they no longer practiced absolute poverty, however, the friars remained committed to helping the poor, and their acts of charity ensured their continued popularity.

Francis had held that even intellectual pursuit should be abandoned so that the friars remained humble. However, many members wanted to study, and Franciscan schools of theology were established at the universities of Paris (1225–1229), Oxford (1229), and Cambridge (1230). There were also other important Franciscan schools, like that at the convent of Santa Croce in Florence.

It has been suggested that Dante studied at the Santa Croce convent, as well as at the Dominican school at Santa Maria Novella. Although he was certainly referring to these when he claimed to have gone to *le scuole de li religiosi* ("the schools of the religious orders," *Conv.* 2.12.7), it is far from clear what such attendance would have entailed for a layman such as Dante. The most likely scenario is that he would only have listened to lectures or sermons. It is much less likely that he would have had access to their libraries, since these were jealously guarded by the *religiosi* for their own use.

The fourteenth-century commentator Francesco da Buti claimed that Dante had been a Franciscan novice in his youth *(Commento sopra la Divina Commedia)*. This belief was apparently based on a passage in the *Inferno* (16.106–108) where the pilgrim says he is wearing a belt with which he had previously hoped to catch the leopard in the dark wood. The Franciscans wore a rough cord belt as a symbol of their humble state, and also to remind themselves that their body was like a wild beast which needed to be restrained. However, no contemporary evidence has been found to confirm that Dante took orders.

Departures from the original Rule of St. Francis led to serious disputes within the order. The friars were split into several factions, the two most important being the *Zelanti* (Zealots), later known as the Spirituals, who wanted to adhere to the original Rule and strictness of Francis' vision, and the moderates, known as the *Fratres de communitate* or Community, later called the Conventuals, who wanted some relaxations to the Rule and a more traditionally organized monastic life. Bitter disputes between the two groups continued for many

Santa Croce, Florence. Richard Lansing.

years, eventually resulting in severe persecution by the Church of some of the more extreme Spirituals. Dante makes Bonaventure criticize the degeneracy of the Franciscans, and also the extreme views of both factions (*Par.* 12.106–126), represented respectively by Ubertino da Casale and by Matteo d'Acquasparta, neither of whom could say, in the original spirit of the Franciscans, *I' mi son quel ch'i' soglio* ("I am still as I was," *Par.* 12.123).

The Franciscans were, as mentioned, not the only mendicant order established in the thirteenth century. In 1215, St. Dominic founded the Dominicans, who had a particular duty to preach and study, and who, initially, were also committed to poverty. St. Francis and St. Dominic, as well as their early followers, saw themselves as fulfilling a prophecy of the Cistercian monk and mystic Joachim of Flora that two new religious orders, practicing absolute poverty, would restore the Church to its original purity. Dante appears to have given credence to the prophecy, because he represents the two saints, and therefore their respective orders, as two champions supporting and guiding the Church (*Par.* 11.28–39; 12.37–45). He also

places Joachim in Heaven, and has St. Bonaventure retract the accusation he made in his lifetime that Joachim was a false prophet (*Par.* 12.139–141). In his portrayal of Joachim, Dante may have been influenced by two leading Spirituals who appear to have been influenced by Joachim, Pietro di Giovanni Olivi and his disciple, Ubertino da Casale. Dante probably heard them speak in Santa Croce: Olivi taught there in 1287–1289, while Ubertino was active in the convent from 1285 until at least 1289. This could account for the Spiritualist influence in the *Commedia*. That Dante was sympathetic to the Spirituals' viewpoint is evident, for instance, from his fierce condemnation of decadence among the clergy, religious orders, and church leaders throughout the *Commedia*.

Among Francis' followers, Dante most admired St. Bonaventure of Bagnoregio, an original thinker, theologian, and mystic who had been minister general of the order from 1257–1274. Bonaventure tried to find a middle path to unify the different factions within the order. He took a hard line with the Joachimite Spirituals, while also castigating the friars for their lax observance of the

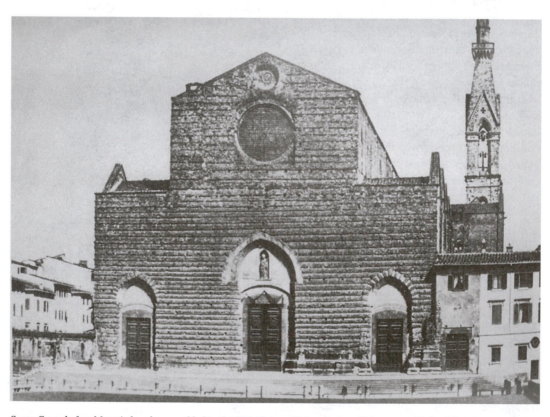

Santa Croce before Matas's façade was added in the 19th century. Unknown: late 19th century. Richard Lansing.

Rule. Dante's admiration for Bonaventure is shown by the fact that he pairs him with the Dominican theologian St. Thomas Aquinas in the fourth heaven of the Sun. These two great theologians represent the two main aspects of Scholastic theology: Bonaventure the intuitive, exegetical tradition of Christian Neoplatonism and mysticism, and Thomas the new rationalizing, speculative thought of Christian Aristotelianism. Each character tells the story of the founder of the other's order, and then criticizes the present state of their own order (*Par.* 11.28–139 and 12.31–126).

Several other Franciscans appear in the *Commedia.* Three companions of St. Francis—Bernardo, Egidio, and Silvestro—are mentioned in Thomas Aquinas' retelling of the saint's life (*Par.* 11.79–84). Illuminato and Agostino, two other early followers, appear among the souls of the wise in the Heaven of the Sun (*Par.* 12.130–132). Piccarda Donati, placed by Dante in the Heaven of the Moon with those who failed to keep their religious vows, had been a nun in the Franciscan Order of the Poor Clares founded in 1212 by St. Clare of Assisi, who is herself alluded to as having lived a perfect life and gained an even higher station in heaven (*Par.* 3.34–123). Pier Pettinaio, whose prayers Sapia claims have helped accelerate her journey through Purgatory, was a comb-maker in Siena (*Purg.* 13.125–129). A very virtuous man and mystic, he belonged to the Franciscan tertiary order for lay people of both sexes, founded in 1221. Among the deceivers in the eighth bolgia of the eighth circle of Hell is Guido da Montefeltro, the Ghibelline captain, whom Dante had praised in *Conv.* 4.28.8. After a violent and sinful life he became a friar, but he was tempted by Pope Boniface VIII to return to his sinful ways (*Inf.* 27.19–132). He refers to himself as *cordigliero* ("a cord-wearer," *Inf.* 27.67), because of the rough cord girdle worn by the Franciscans.

Dante also mentions the Franciscans, together with other religious orders, as examples of a good way of living in *Conv.* 4.28.9.

Bibliography

Baldi, Agnello et al. *Dante e il francescanesimo.* Lectura Dantis Metelliana. Cava dei Tirreni: Avagliano, 1987.

Barański, Zygmunt G. "Dante, commentatore e commentato: riflessioni sullo studio dell'*iter* ideologico di Dante." *Letture Classensi* 23 (1994), 135–158.

Bertoldi, Alfonso. "Il canto XII del *Paradiso.*" In *Letture dantesche.* Vol 3. Edited by Giovanni Getto. Florence: Sansoni, 1961, pp. 239–254.

Comollo, Adriano. *Il dissenso religioso in Dante.* Florence: Olschki, 1990.

Gardner, Edmund. *Dante and the Mystics.* London, New York: Dent, 1913.

Giannini, Crescentino (ed.). *Commento di Francesco da Buti sopra la Divina Commedia di Dante Alighieri.* 3 vols. Pisa: Fratelli Nistri, 1858–1862.

Gratien, Badin. *Histoire de la Fondation et de l'évolution de l'Ordre des Frères Mineurs au XIIIe siècle.* Paris: Société et librairie S. François d'Assise, 1928.

Lambert, M. D. *Franciscan Poverty: The doctrine of the absolute poverty of Christ and the apostles in the Franciscan Order, 1210–1323.* London: S.P.C.K., 1961.

Manselli, Raoul. "Dante e gli Spirituali francescani." *Letture Classensi* 11 (1982), 47–61.

———. "Il canto XII del 'Paradiso.'" In *Nuove letture dantesche.* Vol. 6. Florence: Le Monnier, 1973, pp. 107–128.

———. "Francescanesimo." *Enciclopedia dantesca.* 3:14–16.

———. "Spirituali." *Enciclopedia dantesca,* 5:392–393.

Moorman, C. *The History of the Franciscan Order.* Oxford: Clarendon Press, 1968.

Angela G. Meekins

Franco of Bologna

Manuscript illuminator whom Oderisi, in an act of humility, calls a better artist than himself in *Purg.* 11.82–84. Vasari, in his *Vite,* says that Franco of Bologna *(Franco Bolognese)* was employed in the Vatican Library. He may have been a pupil of Oderisi.

Bibliography

Fallani, Giuseppe. *Dante e la cultura figurativa medievale.* Bergamo: Minerva Italica, 1971.

Molly Morrison

Fraud

With incontinence and violence, fraud is one of the three major categories of sin in the *Inferno.* This broad tripartite division is based on Christian morality (including, for example, the sin of heresy), but it is heavily influenced by a study of Aristotle's *Ethics* 7.1.1145a (cf. *Inf.* 11.79–84). However, Aristotle did not deal with the question of whether fraud is worse than violence. In placing the sins of fraud at the bottom of Hell (where they occupy seventeen cantos [18–34], no less than precisely half of the *Inferno*), Dante went against the authoritative judgment of Aquinas, who declared that "other things being equal, it is a worse sin to harm someone openly, as if by violence, than secretly" (*ST* 2.2.116.2.1). As a true son of Florence, our poet also disagreed with Aquinas on the relative gravity of heresy and falsifying the coinage. For the Angelic Doctor, heresy was a sin far worse than forgery, since "it corrupts the faith, which gives [eternal] life to the soul," whereas money merely helps to sustain life in this world (*ST* 2.2.11.3). Instead, in Dante's Hell, the heretics are found in the sixth circle (*Inf.* 10), whereas the falsifiers of the coinage are at the very bottom of the eighth circle (*Inf.* 30), nearer to Satan, since their fraudulent activities threatened to destroy the very fabric of society.

It was this same obsession with the social and political consequences of sin that made Dante conceive of fraud as the worst category of sin in his Hell. And it was precisely society's need for mutual trust and good faith that led the poet to stress the fact that the Devil's City mirrors the results of fraud's actions by placing its perpetrators in nether Hell, which is utterly cut off from its upper reaches by a huge chasm. This topographical detail points to the moral degradation the pilgrim will encounter in its depths, while it illustrates the fact that fraud creates an unbridgeable gap in society through its destruction of the natural bonds that should unite all citizens.

The empire of fraud covers two circles of Dante's *Inferno:* the eighth, where fraud "simple" is punished, and the ninth or last circle, occupied by fraud "complex" (treachery), the latter committed against persons to whom the sinner is bound by ties of love and trust (*Inf.* 11.52–54). Reflecting the axiom that good is simple, evil complex, the eighth circle has the greatest number of subdivisions: ten in all, an infernal antithesis of the perfect number. Dante invented the term *malebolge* to describe the ten concentric ditches where those who committed various types of fraud are punished. The ditches, all made of dark rock, are—with one exception—joined together by bridges (*Inf.* 18.1–18): they thus guard the pit of Hell,

Satan's stronghold, even as the moats and drawbridges of a medieval castle formed a virtually impregnable approach to the fortress.

Before listing the sins punished in Malebolge, it must be pointed out that the sinners in the eighth *bolgia* have traditionally been identified as counselors of fraud (from *Inf.* 27.116). Recent scholarship has put forward an alternative hypothesis, based on the common denominator between Guido's sin and the sins for which Ulysses and Diomed are punished (*Inf.* 26.58–63): *astutia,* which is guile or cunning. Aquinas (*ST* 2.2.55.4.2) states that "The execution of cunning with the purpose of deceiving, is effected first and foremost by words . . . hence guile is ascribed chiefly to speech. Yet guile may happen also in deeds." Hence, in the ten ditches are punished: (1) seducers and pimps; (2) flatterers; (3) simoniacs; (4) soothsayers and magicians; (5) barrators; (6) hypocrites; (7) thieves; (8) the guileful; (9) sowers of schism and scandal; (10) falsifiers. It may be noted that the rock of Malebolge takes on especial significance in the third ditch, where popes and other leading churchmen are punished as simoniacs for their perversion of the rock on which Christ founded his church (Matt. 16:18). Even so, the fact that Dante was a poet and not a theological computer is evident in the fact that barratry—a lay version of simony (but a sin of which Dante was publicly accused)—is placed lower down, in the fifth *bolgia,* while it might surely be argued that simony perpetrated by a pope necessarily betrays trust and should therefore be assigned to fraud complex (treachery).

The essence of fraud as deception is conveyed by the allegorical figure of Geryon: with the face of a just man, the trunk of a serpent, and a scorpion's tail, this is truly the evil that *rompe i muri e l'armi . . . che tutto 'l mondo appuzza* ("pierces walls and armor . . . that makes the whole world stink!," *Inf.* 17.2–3). In order to summon this infernal helicopter, Virgil commands Dante to undo from his waist and hand over *una corda . . . con essa pensai alcuna volta / prender la lonza a la pelle dipinta* ("a cord . . . with it I had thought at times to capture the leopard with the spotted hide," *Inf.* 16.106–108). Both beasts—the leopard and Geryon—have "painted" skins, suggesting the outer appearance of the sins represented. If the first of the three beasts encountered by the pilgrim in the dark wood (*Inf.* 1.31–43) represents the sins of incontinence—lust, in particular—then the cord around Dante's waist would be similar to that worn by members of the Franciscan order, in imitation of their founder, who bound his body like a beast which had to be controlled by a halter. The polysemy of much of medieval allegory allows other explanations: perhaps the most convincing is that which sees the cord as symbolizing not only chastity (the antidote to lust) but also justice and good faith (opposed to fraud in general). Thus, in his youth, Dante had attempted to curb the temptations of lust, while at this juncture in the infernal descent Virgil needs a symbol of justice and faith in order to command the dangerous figure of Geryon.

The descent to the ninth circle (treachery) is accomplished by a different means of transport: the giant Antaeus, who picks up Dante and Virgil and sets them down in the pit of Hell (*Inf.* 31.142–143). Antaeus's ferocious nature had been graphically described by Lucan (*Phars.* 4.593–600), who nevertheless affirmed that Antaeus had not taken part in the giants' rebellion against Jove at the battle of Phlegra (*Inf.* 31.94–95; cf. 14.58): unlike his fellow monsters, who prefigure Satan, Antaeus is unfettered and retains the human faculty of language. The corruption of language, so characteristic of the sins of fraud, is in fact signified by the presence of Nimrod, whose gibberish (*Inf.* 31.67) is a just punishment for his hubris as the founder of the Tower of Babel (according to Augustine's reading of Genesis 11). For Dante, Babel represented virtually a second Fall. As an artist, the Florentine poet was obsessed with the mutability of language; as a political thinker, he yearned for the unity of humanity under the aegis of the emperor. Nimrod's treachery at Babel was therefore regarded by Dante as an act of treachery against both God and humanity. This interpretation is reinforced by the fact that the terrifying sound of Nimrod's horn is compared to that of Roland's in *Inf.* 31.16–18, where the reference to the destruction of the flower of Charlemagne's army at Roncevaux would have evoked for Dante's contemporaries the supreme act of treachery in the history of the Christian empire. Moreover, treachery is effected first and foremost by words, "which hold the chief place among those signs whereby a man signifies something to another man" (Aquinas, *ST* 2.2.55.4.2). Semiotic confusion thus destroys the very basis of human intercourse and society, transforming the earth into Satan's kingdom of absolute evil.

The ninth circle or Cocytus (from Greek "to lament") shares its name with that of a river of the underworld in Virgil (*Aen.* 6.296–297), while Dante's syncretism must have been overjoyed to find it mentioned in the Vulgate (Job 21:33), where it signifies the valley of death. The poet transforms Cocytus into a lake of ice, perpetually frozen by the icy blasts issuing from Satan's wings. In it are imprisoned the souls of the various traitors, who are set deeper and deeper according to the gravity of their sin. The first area, Caina, named after Cain (Gen. 4:1–13), contains the souls of those who betrayed their kin; the second, Antenora, named after Antenor of Troy (who, according to Servius, betrayed his city to the Greeks), houses the souls of the political traitors. The third region engulfs the traitors to hospitality and is probably named after Ptolemy, captain of Jericho, who invited Simon and the High Priest with his sons to a banquet at which he murdered them (1 Macc. 16). The last region is Judecca, named after Judas Iscariot, where we find the traitors to their lord. After the ingenuity displayed by the poet's imagination in inventing a veritable phantasmagoria of blood-curdling punishments—and after the ubiquitous image of hellfire in medieval iconography, reflecting the "everlasting fire" of Matt. 25:41—the use of ice for the punishment of the worst sinners in the universe, including Satan himself, may appear as something of an anticlimax. It is therefore necessary to imagine what ice could mean for a medieval Italian. In the world of nature, it was something essentially barren and utterly opposed to the life-giving heat of the Sun. Whereas fire could be seen as having purifying properties (*Purg.* 26.148) and could even be used as a metaphor for the Virgin Mary (*Par.* 23.90) or to indicate God's holy presence (Exod. 19:18; Matt. 3:11; *Par.* 33.119), no such ambivalence was possible in the spectacle of ice, which reflected the hardness of the sinners' souls. Dante's intention is to emphasize the essentially negative quality of evil: this negativity is pictured in the total sterility of the ice of Cocytus, which paralyzes this region of Earth and symbolizes the winter of the soul, on the one hand, and in the enormous mass of matter (the giants and Satan), unredeemed by spirit, on the other.

In upper Hell, sinners had been eager to make themselves known to the pilgrim, in the hope that he might keep their name alive on Earth. In the ninth circle, however, the traitors are unwilling to reveal their identity—although they are happy enough to betray their neighbors to the man who shall report the latter's infamy to the world of the living. The traitors continue in their sin. Even the pilgrim would seem to be caught up in the general atmosphere of treachery, when he tricks one of the traitors into revealing his name (*Inf.* 33.115–117, 148–150). Not only does treachery breed treachery; it also turns the whole moral code of the medieval world on its head: here, the villain is lord and courtesy is villainy (*Inf.* 33.150).

In general, the fraudulent are well differentiated. Although punished in the same ditch, Jason the seducer and Venedico Caccianemico the pimp are utterly different: the former retaining a regal aspect (*Inf.* 18.82–85), the latter's baseness well punished by the first typically medieval devils, equipped with whips, to appear in the *Inferno* (18.64–66). It would be difficult to find two sinners more disparate than the obscene thief, Vanni Fucci (*Inf.* 24.92–25.16), and the intrepid, crafty explorer, Ulysses (*Inf.* 26.88–142). Nothing could be farther removed from the monotony of medieval visions of Hell than the wealth of characterization and the narrative variety of Dante's *Inferno*. The biblical solemnity of the narrator's denunciation of the simoniacs, with its prophetic tones, in *Inf.* 19.90–117, is followed by the comic interlude of *Inf.* 21–22, where the poet-narrator is bent on highlighting the vulgarity of the sin for which he had been condemned to death while providing dramatic relief amid the growing intensity of absolute evil; similarly, the baseness of the thieves (*Inf.* 24–25) is set off against the intellectual cunning of the guileful (*Inf.* 26–27). Narrative variety is also created by the decision to devote more than one canto to the same sin.

Two final observations must be made. The first is that Dante's hatred of fraud leads him to contradict one of his sources, Cicero's *De officiis* 1.13.41, where fraud and violence are both vices "most foreign to man" *(utrumque homine alienissimum)*. Instead, Dante makes his Virgil declare that fraud is *de l'uom proprio male* ("an evil proper to man," *Inf.* 11.25). The second point is that treachery was so destructive of human society that it led the poet to express the quasi-heretical idea that certain of its manifestations are so evil that they cause the soul to be sent down to Hell, even before death overtakes the body, which is then governed by a devil for the time allotted to it on earth (*Inf.* 33.124–135; cf., however, John 13:27). It would be impossible to find more striking proof of Dante's abhorrence of fraud.

Bibliography

Barolini, Teodolinda. *The Undivine "Comedy": Detheologizing Dante.* Princeton, N.J.: Princeton University Press, 1992, pp. 48–98.

Ferrante, Joan. "*Malebolge (Inf. XVIII–XXX)* as the Key to the Structure of Dante's *Inferno.*" *Romance Philology* 20 (1967), 456–466.

Moore, Edward. *Studies in Dante. Second Series: Miscellaneous Essays.* Oxford: Oxford University Press, 1899, pp. 152–245.

Reade, W. H. *The Moral System of Dante's "Inferno."* Oxford: Oxford University Press, 1909, pp. 354–366.

Sanguineti, Edoardo. *Interpretazione di Malebolge.* Florence: Olschki, 1961.

Scott, J. A. "Treachery in Dante." In *Studies in the Italian Renaissance: Essays in Memory of Arnolfo B. Ferruolo.* Edited by Gian Paolo Biasin et al. Naples: Società Editrice Napoletana, 1984, pp. 27–42.

John A. Scott

Fraudulent Counsel

Although Dante never explicitly employs the term to refer to a category of sinners, fraudulent counsel is the term commonly applied to the sin punished in the eighth *bolgia* of the eighth circle of Hell. Virgil names each of the sins of the first seven ditches in his explanation of the structure of Hell in *Inf.* 11.16–66, but those punished in the last two ditches of the Malebolge are simply labeled *simile lordura* ("similar filth," 11.60). While Muhammad later provides the identity and *contrapasso* of the sinners of the ninth ditch (*Inf.* 28.30–45), no comparable classification is given for the sinners entrapped in flames: Ulysses, Diomedes, Guido da Montefeltro, and their companions. Early commentators, such as Dante's son Jacopo and the author of the *Chiose selmiane*, however, derived a designation from the black cherub's characterization of Guido da Montefeltro's evil advice to Boniface as *consiglio frodolente* ("fraudulent counsel," *Inf.* 27.116). But subsequent commentators rejected this reading, arguing that fraudulent or false counsel could not adequately be said to describe the sins of Ulysses.

Benvenuto da Imola (c. 1380) classifies the sin solely as *astutia* ("trickery" or "deceit")—a category that previously had been used to supplement the term "fraudulent counsel"—as does the Anonimo Fiorentino (1400). But other commentators, from Jacopo della Lana and Guido da Pisa to Francesco da Buti, employed the original appellation, often accompanied by explanations of Ulysses' shrewdness, and in so doing created an exegetic division that lasted into the sixteenth century. During the 1500s, the sin was thought to be an offense best understood as unethical trickery in general, of intelligence employed without the guidance of virtue. Modern editors and scholars of the *Inferno* have customarily returned to the original term, rather consistently referring to the sin of the eighth *bolgia* as "fraudulent counsel," despite occasional, and sometimes convincing, attempts to identify further parallels between the transgressions of Ulysses and Guido. Porena and Sapegno offered a broad and comprehensive reading, asserting that the eighth *bolgia* is the region dedicated to the punishment of those who practice deceit in politics, that is, those who are masters of a Machiavellian realpolitik. Nardi's heated interpretive polemic with Fubini about the figure of Ulysses and his fundamental importance to the pilgrim's salvific journey somewhat obscured the question of "fraudulent counsel" for more than two decades, while other scholars investigated the possibility that the *folle volo* ("mad flight," 26.125), Ulysses' attempt to reach Mount Purgatory by boat, constituted the real reason for which he was condemned to Hell. The question of exactly which sin Ulysses and Guido had in common was again addressed in polemical terms by Hatcher who pronounced "fraudulent counsel" a "preposterous misnomer" that could not stand up to careful scrutiny.

In the series of studies that ensued, critics centered on two fundamental points, both of which are restrictive in nature. "Fraudulent counsel" is not a recognized classification of sin in the Middle Ages and is used by Dante very specifically to describe only the evil guidance of Guido. Moreover, Virgil's list of Ulysses' sins—his deployment of the Trojan horse, his persuasion of Achilles to rejoin the war, his theft of the Palladium, his abandonment of his family (26.55–63)—contains no obvious reference to an instance of evil advice. Ahern argues that many of the difficulties associated with an adherence to "fraudulent counsel" would disappear if we were to embrace instead *astutia* as the general rubric for the sin addressed in *Inf.* 26 and 27, while Durling suggests that the sin is that of advising fraudulence in war. Dante's presumably intentional decision to omit a specific term, how-

ever, suggests that the question cannot be fully resolved.

Bibliography

Ahern, John. "Dante's Slyness: The Unnamed Sin of the Eighth Bolgia." *Romanic Review* 73.3 (1982), 275–291.

Durling, Robert M. "Ulysses' Last Voyage." In *The Divine Comedy of Dante Alighieri: Inferno*. Edited and translated by Robert M. Durling. Introduction and notes by Ronald L. Martinez and Robert M. Durling. Oxford, New York: Oxford University Press, 1996, pp. 414–415, 571–573.

Fubini, Mario. *Il peccato di Ulisse e altri scritti danteschi*. Milan, Naples: Ricciardi, 1961.

Hatcher, Anna. "Dante's Ulysses and Guido da Montefeltro." *Dante Studies* 88 (1970), 109–117.

Pagliaro, Antonio. *Ulisse: Ricerche semantiche sulla Divina Commedia*. 2 vols. (especially vol. 1). Messina: D'Anna, 1967, pp. 371–432.

Pertile, Lino. "*Inferno* XXVII. Il peccato di Guido da Montefeltro." *Atti dell'Istituto Veneto di Scienze, Lettere ed Arti* 141 (1982–1983), 147–178.

Musa, Mark. "Filling the Gap with *consiglio frodolente*." *Italian Culture* 3 (1981), 11–21.

Nardi, Bruno. "La tragedia di Ulisse." In *Dante e la cultura medievale*. Bari: Laterza, 1942, pp. 153–165.

Padoan, Giorgio. "Ulisse 'fandi fictor' e le vie della sapienza." *Studi danteschi* 37 (1960), 21–61. Reprinted in *Il pio Enea, l'empio Ulisse: Tradizione classica e intendimento medievale in Dante*. Ravenna: Longo, 1977, pp. 170–199.

Porena, Manfredi. "*Inferno* XXVI." *Lamia lectura Dantis*. Naples: Alfredo Guida, 1932. Reprinted 1934, pp. 87–112.

Sapegno, Natalino. "Ulisse." *Letture Classensi* 7 (1979), 91–98.

Thompson, David. "A Note on Fraudulent Counsel." *Dante Studies* 92 (1974), 149–152.

Michael Papio

Frederick I, Emperor

Born c.1123 to Frederick, Duke of Swabia, and Judith of Bavaria, Frederick *(Federico)* succeeded his uncle, Conrad III, as emperor on March 4, 1152. He was known by the surname Barbarossa ("Redbeard"). Frederick attempted to assert imperial rule in Italy, and spent thirty years in conflict with the Italian communes. In 1189 he joined forces with Richard the Lion-Hearted and Philip Augustus to promote the third crusade, undertaken in response to the capture of Jerusalem by Saladin two years earlier. He strove to create a foundation for a peaceful, united Europe, and his close family links to both Ghibellines and Guelfs made his goal seem achievable. Despite the ultimate failure of Frederick's ambitions, Dante admired him as a strong emperor, known for his courage, prudence, and great political ability, and for his fierce defense of the rights of Empire against Church. He died in 1190.

Dante mentions Frederick, and in particular his punitive destruction of the rebellious cities of Spoleto in 1155 and Milan in 1162, in a warning to the Florentines with regard to their treatment of Henry VII, in *Epist.* 6.20. In the *Commedia,* the Abbot of San Zeno, among the slothful in Purgatory, refers to *lo 'mperio del buon Barbarossa, / di cui dolente ancor Milan ragiona* ("the reign of the good Barbarossa, of whom Milan still speaks with grief," *Purg.* 18.119).

Angela G. Meekins

Frederick II of Swabia

Born on December 26, 1194, Frederick *(Federico)* was the son of Constance of Sicily, the Norman heiress to the Kingdom of Sicily, and Henry VI, the German Holy Roman Emperor. He became the ward of Pope Innocent III when his mother died in 1198. Frederick was raised in the Norman-Sicilian court at Palermo, a city enriched by Arab, Greek, and Latin-Norman political and cultural traditions. Although little is known of his early years, Frederick's adult accomplishments attest to his vigorous intellect and breadth of interests, which included astronomy, agronomy, biology, philosophy, law, and architecture. Frederick knew Latin and Sicilian and some sources claim that he spoke Arabic, Greek, and German as well. His book on falconry reveals a keen interest in scientific method that is unusual in the Middle Ages. During Frederick's reign, the first lay school of poetry in an Italian vernacular, the *Scuola Siciliana,* was established.

Frederick was crowned emperor at Rome in 1220, but because of his failure to keep a crusade vow, he was excommunicated by Pope Gregory IX in 1227. A year later, Frederick went to Jerusalem, negotiated Christian access to holy shrines and,

still excommunicate, he crowned himself King of Jerusalem. On his return to the Kingdom of Sicily, Frederick established a government that has been described as totalitarian. Pope Gregory finally lifted the sentence of excommunication in 1230. Outside the Kingdom of Sicily, Frederick's power was based on political and economic accommodation and outright conflict with the papacy, the independent states of the Italic peninsula, and the German nobles. Despite sporadic diplomatic and military successes, however, Frederick was never able to assert imperial claims in Italy in any enduring way. In 1239 he was excommunicated a second time and Pope Innocent IV deposed him in 1245. Frederick died in 1250, at his castle in Florentina, in Basilicata.

For Dante, Frederick was a model of civility. This is expressed most forcefully in *DVE* 1.12.4: *Siquidem illustres heroes, Fredericus Cesar et benegenitus eius Manfredus, nobilitatem ac rectitudinem sue forme pandentes, donec fortuna permisit, humana secuti sunt, brutalia dedignantes* ("Indeed, those illustrious heroes, the Emperor Frederick and his worthy son Manfred, knew how to reveal the nobility and integrity that were in their hearts; and, as long as fortune allowed, they lived in a manner befitting men, despising the bestial life"). As a leader, Dante hails Frederick as *ultimo imperadore de li Romani* ("last of the Roman emperors") in *Conv.* 4.3.6, and in *Inf.* 13.75 Pier delle Vigne, Frederick's personal secretary and counselor, praises Frederick as a man *d'onor sì degno* ("so worthy of honor"). But in *Conv.* 4.3, referring to him as *Federico di Soave* ("Frederick of Swabia"), Dante advances his own definition of nobility as the product of character by criticizing Frederick's aristocratic conception of nobility based on ancestral wealth together with fine manners. In the *Commedia,* Frederick is found among the damned. He is assigned a silent tomb among the heretics (*Inf.* 10.119), probably because of the Epicurean opinions attributed to him by his enemies. Both his son and his mother, however, achieve a higher position in Dante's judgment: Manfred is found among the late repentants in the Ante-Purgatory (*Purg.* 3), while Constance resides in Paradise with the saved in the sphere of the Moon (*Par.* 3).

Bibliography

Abulafia, David. *Frederick II. A Medieval Emperor.* New York, London: Penguin, 1988.

Kantorowicz, Ernst. *Frederick the Second, 1194–1250.* Translated by E. O. Lorimer. New York: Frederick Ungar, 1957.

Van Cleve, Thomas Curtis. *The Emperor Frederick II of Hohenstaufen. Imperator Mundi.* Oxford: Clarendon Press, 1972.

Vallone, Aldo. "La componente federiciana della cultura dantesca." In *Dante e Roma. Atti del Convegno di Studi.* Rome, 8–20 April, 1965. Florence: Le Monnier, 1965, pp. 348–369.

Laurie Shepard

Frederick II of Aragon

Son of Peter III of Aragon and Constance, and grandson of Manfred. Frederick (1272–1337) was initially ruler of Sicily under his brother James, later in his own right (1296), and he held the titles of King of Trinacria (1302) and King of Sicily (1312). Dante has nothing but contempt for Frederick *(Federigo),* denouncing him as a tyrant, along with Charles the Cripple, King of Naples, in *Conv.* 4.6.20. In *Purg.* 7.119–120, Sordello cites him as one who possesses his father's kingdom but not his virtues, and in *Paradise* as one whose people lament his still being alive. In *DVE* 1.12.5, he is called a new Frederick, and his grandfather Manfred refers to him as the "honor of Sicily" *(Purg.* 3.116). In *Par.* 19.130–134 and 20.63, the Eagle in the Heaven of Jupiter reproaches him for avarice and baseness. The name Trinacria *(Par.* 8.67) might refer to his title. Dante's dislike of Frederick derives from his greater interest in the welfare of Sicily than in the fate of Italy as a whole.

Leslie Zarker Morgan

Free Will

Of all the gifts God bestowed on Adam, Dante says free will was the greatest *(Par.* 5.19–24; cf. *Mon.* 1.12.6). The idea of free will (the terms Dante uses most often in Italian are *libero arbitrio, libero voler,* and *libertate de la volontà;* in Latin, *libertas arbitrii* [*Mon.* 1.12.6]) has a long history; in the second half of the thirteenth century it was the subject of especially intense debate. Dante seems to nod at these controversies in *Mon.* 1.12.2; notwithstanding the assurance with which he states his position there, we find a range of opinions in his works. In a famous lyric, *Rime* 111, "Io sono stato con Amore insieme," Dante denies that within the ambit of amorous passion free will was ever free.

In the *Convivio,* the *Commedia,* and the *Monarchia,* however, Dante argues that the independence of our will is never impaired because the act of pursuing or shunning something always follows an unconstrained judgment, whether or not that object conforms to the good. On this view, however, the freedom of *libero arbitrio* lies in this judgment, not in the will; indeed, this view seems to require that the will obey the dictates of reason. Aquinas in fact had concluded as much in his *De veritate;* Franciscan thinkers, however, who in general thought the will had the power to move itself, disputed this view. Étienne Tempier, the Bishop of Paris, was influenced by Franciscan thought; in 1277 he condemned Aquinas' teaching along with any notion that external forces can compel our action or that human will is only a passive power. In the *Letter to Cangrande* (13.25), Dante identifies the *Commedia*'s allegorical subject as how "man, in the exercise of his free will, becomes liable to the rewards or punishments of justice"; if the letter is indeed his, Dante has asked the Lord of Verona to read his poem within the context of one of the most vexed issues of his time.

Dante treats the question of free will most fully in the *Monarchia* and the *Commedia.* In *Mon.* 1.12.2–4, he says that the first principle of our freedom is freedom of choice; consequently, free will is the freedom of will in judging *(liberum arbitrium esse liberum de voluntate iudicium).* Dante expounds this well-known definition, which comes from Boethius, as follows: "Judgment stands between apprehension and appetite. First a thing is apprehended, then it is judged good or bad, and finally he who has so judged it pursues or avoids it." By judgment Dante means rational knowledge, expressed as a proposition: x is (or is not) good. Apprehending an object is the precondition for producing such a judgment; appetite or the willed movement toward the object is its necessary consequence. From this Dante concludes that "if the judgment of reason altogether sets the appetite in motion, and in no way is anticipated by it, it [appetite, that is, will] is free." Judgment thus takes precedence over appetite; it determines whether an appetible object is good or not, without being in any way anticipated or influenced by desire. In this account, *libero arbitrio* is the freedom of reason from all appetite in deciding if something should be sought.

In the *Commedia,* Dante locates his discussion of free will at the center of the poem. In *Purg.*

F 16.52ff., he asks whether the cause of the evil we do lies in us or in the stars. In response, Marco Lombardo says that if the heavens determined our actions, free will would be destroyed. He explains that the stars only initiate our movements by causing a certain inclination, which is registered as an impression, to use Aquinas' language, "on the sensitive powers that are acts of bodily organs having an inclination for human acts" (*ST* 2.2.95.5). The heavens, in other words, exert their influence on our bodies alone; by exciting the passions, they can incline the will toward something, but in no way can they compel it to pursue it. The technical reason why they cannot compel is that nothing corporeal can directly affect anything incorporeal by nature; in human beings, will is intellectual appetite, not the act of a bodily organ.

But even if our faults cannot be ascribed to the stars, for us to justly bear full responsibility for our actions Dante still must show that human will is free. He does this in *Purg.* 17–18. In 17.91–105, he speaks of natural love, which is for the end or goal; it is each thing's desire for its source or perfection. As such this love is innate and without error; inanimate things invariably seek their proper place, beasts instinctively move to realize their nature. In human beings, the goal of natural love is, from our point of view, perfect happiness; from an objective point of view, it is the complete good which is God. But we are able to apprehend this primal good, Dante says, only in a confused way.

Even though we necessarily seek ultimate happiness, this confusion, strange to say, vouchsafes the freedom of our will in a general sense. If eternal beatitude, which is the only good that is perfect and lacks nothing, is beyond our capacity to comprehend fully, it follows that any end human reason does apprehend as good is not completely good. Consequently, no end we rationally perceive can compel our will to move to it necessarily.

For Dante, an act of human will therefore consists of the movement toward specific objects perceived as sharing in the good as such. In *Purg.* 18.19ff., we learn that since the soul in human beings is disposed by nature to love, the will rouses it into action whenever something appears to offer it pleasure. As in the *Monarchia,* Dante identifies three stages in this process. First, our faculty of perception *(apprensiva)* abstracts an intention or image from some material object; by elaborating and judging this form, reason determines the nature of the object in respect to truth and false-

hood (*Purg.* 18.22–23). The "apprehensive" faculty then presents this intentional object to the soul so that it turns to consider it. The soul forms a judgment of it as good or bad—whether, that is, it offers happiness and pleasure. If it judges it to be good, the will inclines toward it, and such an inclination is love (*Purg.* 18.24–25). Because the disposition of the will toward the good as such is a natural movement, fixed by God who implanted it in human beings, no merit or blame attaches to it. But while the inclination toward the good is necessarily blameless, desiring every appetible object may not be; "although the wax be good," as Dante puts it, "not every seal is good" (*Purg.* 18.38–39). For just as an inferior seal may make a bad imprint on excellent wax, so a base object may cause the good instinct of love to have an improper passion.

In every person, Dante therefore explains, the intellective soul contains a virtue composed of two faculties, intellect and will. Aquinas says that knowing, which is the function of the intellect, has its beginning in a "kind of confused knowledge of all things" (*De veritate* 18.4). This knowledge consists of general principles like being and non-being, whole and part. Where we learn these principles, which Dante calls "first notions" (*Purg.* 18.55–56), no one knows. We accept them as true, though they are not subject to demonstration themselves; they serve as the premises that enable us to know whether a proposition is true or false.

In a similar way, we cannot demonstrate where the will received its beginning, which Dante calls "our love of first desirables" (*Purg.* 18.57). This affection for "first desirables" *(primi appetibili)* is again that natural inclination toward the good in general; under its heading Aquinas includes everything else that belongs to human nature, such as knowledge of truth, which is the particular good of the intellect, the inclination to be and to live, and other natural laws that regard our well-being. These first objects of desire are the end for the sake of which the will moves to obtain any object we perceive as good.

Now just as the plant reveals its inclination to live through its green leaves, we become aware of first notions only when the soul uses them to know, just as we become aware of primal objects of desire only by means of the end or effect of the object we will (*Purg.* 18.52–54). In any act of reason, the intellect avails itself of first principles, which serve as the major premise from which we conclude that a proposition is true or false; reason, however, also makes use of the first objects of desire, from which it constructs a syllogism that enables it to judge whether the inclination toward an object is good or not. With regard to the end, this judgment of reason is thus the operation that allows the will to bring its desire for any appetible object into conformity with "the first desire" for the good as such (*Purg.* 18.61). The comparisons and determinations that comprise the judgment are entirely free; in response to this judgment the will inclines toward the object in love, desires it, and enjoys it. Insofar as we seek its cause, then, the root of liberty, as Aquinas says, is reason (*ST* 1.2.13.1). It is this "power that gives counsel and must guard the threshold of assent" (*Purg.* 18.62–63), a power that for Dante is "the principle that accounts for the cause of merit in you, according as it accepts or winnows good or evil loves" (*Purg.* 18.64–66).

To this point, the good apprehended by the autonomous operations of reason has been considered as the end or goal of the will. For Aristotle, however, the will moves us to act not only with regard to the end but by way of our deliberating about the means to attain it (*Nicomachean Ethics,* 1111b 4ff.). We all will to be healthy, but in willing this we also will a further act, such as exercising or dieting, that makes us healthy. When the will regards the end, it necessarily moves toward it insofar as it is judged good, but when will desires things for the sake of the end, it is free to choose among various means. Free will, in short, is the power of choice. Reason asks what possible acts that lie within our power can gain us the end we desire, and which among them is the most suitable. The will then freely rejects or consents to the acts judged suitable, and selects or abandons the one that has been deemed the best. As a person's power to choose *(vis electiva),* therefore, the root of liberty lies in the will (*ST* 1.2.13.1).

Although it may seem from this account that will and free will are distinct faculties, in Aquinas' reading they are not. Free will's choice of means stands to will's regard for the first objects of desire in the same relation that first principles stand to the rational conclusion we accept on their account. Therefore, Aquinas concludes, and Dante would agree, will and free will are not two powers, but one.

Bibliography

Boyde, Patrick. *Perception and Passion in Dante's Comedy.* Cambridge: Cambridge University Press, 1993.

Donagan, Alan. "Thomas Aquinas on human action." In *The Cambridge History of Later Medieval Philosophy.* Edited by Norman Kretzmann et al. Cambridge: Cambridge University Press, 1982, pp. 642–654.

Harwood-Gordon, Sharon. *A Study of the Theology and the Imagery of Dante's "Divina Commedia": Sensory Perception, Reason and Free Will.* Lewiston, N.Y.: Edwin Mellen Press, 1991.

Korolec, J. B. "Free will and free choice." In *The Cambridge History of Later Medieval Philosophy.* Edited by Norman Kretzmann et al. Cambridge: Cambridge University Press, 1982, pp. 629–641.

Lottin, Odon. *Psychologie et morale aux XIIᵉ et XIIIᵉ siècles* (6 vols. in 7). Louvain: Abbaye du Mont César, 1942–1960.

Miller, Edward G. "Free Will." In *Sense Perception in Dante's Commedia.* Lewiston, N.Y.: Edwin Mellen Press, 1996, pp. 189–230.

Rovighi, Sofia Vanni. "Arbitrio." *Enciclopedia dantesca,* 1:345–348.

Stabile, Giorgio. "Volontà." *Enciclopedia dantesca,* 5:1134–1140.

Warren Ginsberg

Fubini, Mario

A gifted critic who last taught at the Scuola Normale Superiore di Pisa, Fubini (1900–1977) concentrated his attention on Italian authors such as Dante, Parini, Alfieri and, above all, Foscolo (the national edition of whose works he was editor), as well as on French authors such as De Vigny and Racine. He devoted various studies and "lecturae" to Dante in the volume *Due studi danteschi* (1951), which he expanded in *Il peccato di Ulisse e altri studi danteschi* (1966). His essay "Il mito della poesia primitiva in G.B. Vico," in *Stile e umanità di G.B. Vico* (1946; 2nd ed., 1965), is strongly indicative of the originality of his thought. Working in the wake of the theoretical work of Leo Spitzer and Benedetto Croce, he became the most vigorous and discerning representative of the stylistic/aesthetic critical approach. His attention was equally devoted to linguistic features and psychological experience. Croce's particular influence can be noted in his tone as well as in his methodological self-assurance, and in his sense of literary taste.

Bibliography

Marti, Mario. *Giornale storico della letteratura italiana* 95 (1978), 30–51.

F

Vallone, Aldo. *Storia della critica dantesca dal XIV al XX secolo*. Vol. 2. Milan: Vallardi, 1981, pp. 992–994.

Aldo Vallone
(translated by Robin Treasure)

Fucci, Vanni

The contentious Black Guelf leader from Pistoia, whom Dante may have known personally, is graphically remembered for the blasphemous obscene gesture, for which he is punished, of the double fig he makes against God in the opening lines of *Inf.* 25. That he actually appeared on stage and addressed the pilgrim at some length in the previous canto (*Inf.* 24.122–126 and 133–151) is often forgotten. But this is a deliberate effect achieved by the Dante-poet, who contrives to split Vanni's appearance between two cantos and thereby himself have, as it were, the last word in the altercation between Vanni and Dante-pilgrim. Vanni's punishment is to be metamorphosed into dust and ashes as a result of a snakebite, then restored to his original form, an act he repeats for eternity. In *Inf.* 24 the pilgrim shames this illegitimate son of local nobleman Fuccio dei Lazzari by forcing him to confess that what condemned him to spend eternity among the malignant reptiles of the seventh bolgia of the eighth circle was not simply the violence characteristic of his class but a more humiliating act of sneak thievery from the chapel of St. James in the local cathedral, a crime for which someone else had been convicted. By way of revenge, Vanni prophesies the imminent political vicissitudes of northern Tuscany, culminating in the final defeat of the exiled White Guelfs by the forces of Moroello Malaspina in the siege of Pistoia in 1306.

Bibliography

Chapin, D. L. Derby. "Io and the Negative Apotheosis of Vanni Fucci." *Dante Studies* 89 (1971), 19–31.

De Robertis, Domenico. "Lo scempio delle umane proprietadi (*Inf.* XXIV e XXV, con una postilla sul XXVI)." *Bolletino storico pistoiese* 81 (1979), 37–60.

Muresu, Gabriele. "I ladri di Malebolge (*Inferno* XXIV–XXV)." In *I ladri di Malebolge: Saggi di semantica dantesca*. Rome: Bulzoni, 1990, pp. 9–50.

Anthony Oldcorn

Fulcieri da Calboli

Fulcieri da Calboli was the grandson of Rinieri da Calboli. Born sometime during the 1270s, he first appeared on the political scene in 1295 and was then to lead an intense political career, becoming known as a zealous supporter of the papal cause. Fulcieri was chief magistrate of Parma and was elected podestà of Florence in 1303. Through the voice of Guido del Duca on the second terrace of Purgatory, Dante describes Fulcieri, a Black Guelf, as a ferocious persecutor and murderer of the White Guelfs and the Ghibellines in Florence (*Purg.* 14.58–64). There are further indications that Fulcieri's notoriety as a bloodthirsty individual developed during his career particularly when he was podestà of several other cities. He died sometime during 1340.

Bibliography

Bárberi Squarotti, Giorgio. "Il canto XIV del *Purgatorio*." *Letture Classensi* 1 (1966), 23–62.

Quinones, Ricardo. *Foundation Sacrifice in Dante's Commedia*. University Park, P.A.: The Pennsylvania State University Press, 1994, pp. 27–28, 67–68.

Paul Colilli

Furies

Dante's encounter with the three Furies in *Inf.* 9 is part of the complex Christian restaging of classical motifs that occurs in that episode. Alecto, Tisiphone, and Megaera *(Aletto, Tesifón, Megera),* the *tre furie infernal* who appear at the gates of Dis to ward off intruders, are bloodstained creatures resembling women, girt with hydras and coifed with smaller snakes. Virgil identifies them as the ferocious Erinyes *(le feroci Erine),* handmaids *(meschine)* of Persephone, the "queen of eternal weeping."

Virgil's *Aeneid* is in fact one of Dante's main sources for the Furies, Erinyes, Dirae, or Eumenides, as they are also called. Dying Dido invokes them, along with Hecate (Persephone), to curse her fleeing lover (4.609–610). At the gates of Tartarus, Aeneas sees Tisiphone, the avenger, draped in a bloody robe, guarding the entrance, shaking her serpents and calling her cruel sisters (6.555–572). To foment war between the Latins and the Trojans, Juno conjures Alecto from the underworld, who duly takes a viper from her hair and thrusts it into the Latin queen's breast (7.324–329, 345). Megaera, like her sisters "born of night" and entwined with snakes, is sent to enrage Turnus at the epic's conclusion (12.845–848).

Ovid also has Juno call on the "sisters born of Night" who sit before the fortified door of the Stygian city (*Meta.* 4.451–452). He too emphasizes their bloodsoaked appearance and their having snakes entwined about the head and waist (4.474, 481). In *Theb.* 1.52–124, Statius pictures Tisiphone watering her snakes on the banks of the Cocytus when blind Oedipus' appeal for vengeance against his own sons reaches her. In *Phars.* 6.733, Lucan has Erichtho rouse the furies she calls "Stygian dogs" to assist in reviving a corpse—the same *Eritón cruda* who in this canto of the *Inferno* Virgil claims enlisted his necromantic assistance on another occasion (9.22–30).

The Furies of classical mythology were heavily allegorized throughout the Middle Ages. Fulgentius (5th–6th century C.E.) reports that they were servants of Pluto, explaining that Alecto means "unstoppable," that Tisiphone is etymologized as *tuton phone,* or "voice of these same ones," and that Megaera comes from *megale eris,* that is, "great contention." In his commentary on the *Inferno* Boccaccio translates these terms as *senza riposo* ("without rest"), *voce d'ira* ("voice of anger"), *gran litigio* ("great contentiousness"). In the commentary on the *Aeneid* attributed to Bernard Silvester (12th century), the parents of the three Eumenides are made to signify that sorrow (Acheron) begets on ignorance (Night) three sisters—Allecto, or evil thought *(prava cogitatio),* Thesiphone, or evil speech *(sermo scilicet malus),* and Megera, or evil works *(mala operatio).* Bernard's scheme is echoed in the early commentaries of Iacopo, Pietro, Ottimo, Boccaccio, and others who understand the three Furies as three components of all mortal sin—thought, speech, and deed *(mal pensare, mal parlare tenacemente, male operare).* Fulgentius had interpreted the three sisters as stages in a process: "The first stage, therefore, is to create rage without pause; the second, to burst forth into words; the third, to stir up a quarrel" (*Mythologies* 1.7). Dante's alignment of the Furies from right to left— Alecto, Tisiphone, Megaera—can thus be seen to symbolize that sin begins with a mental choice and then breaks out first into words and then into action (as in Pietro and Benvenuto). Sometimes the Furies are said to form a predisposition for obstinacy, symbolized by the Medusa they invoke, or for heresy, addressed explicitly in the following canto. Alternatively they are allegorized as anger, greed, and lust (*ira, cupidità,* and *lussuria*), or as imagination, deliberation, and memory (as in Iacopo and Ottimo). Persephone, their mistress, is said to signify *superbia,* or haughtiness.

Benvenuto da Imola justifies the female sex of the furies by the philosopher's dictum that because women do everything more intensely there is no rage like that of a woman *(nec ira super iram mulieris).* Francesco da Buti simply points to the grammatical gender of what they represent *(mala cogitazione, mala locuzione, mala operazione).* Da Buti also explains that the Furies, standing for a perturbation of the mind, appear at this point in Dante's narrative to mark the distinction between the sins of incontinence punished in the higher circles of Hell and the sins of malice punished below. In the nineteenth century, Giovanni Pascoli similarly claimed that the Furies represent spiritual, as opposed to fleshly or sensual, sins, allegorizing them as *ira, invidia,* and *superbia.* More recently Luigi Pietrobono proposed a political allegory of the whole scene in which the Furies stood for violence, fraud, and betrayal.

Bibliography

Freccero, John. "Medusa: The Letter and the Spirit." *Dante: The Poetics of Conversion.* Cambridge, Mass: Harvard University Press, 1986.

Fulgentius, Fabius. *Mythologies.* In *Fulgentius the Mythographer.* Translated by L. G. Whitbread. Columbus: Ohio State University Press, 1971, pp. 39–102.

Marcazzan, Mario. "Il canto delle furie." *Humanitas* 7 (1952), 1131–1145.

Pascoli, Giovanni. *La mirabile visione.* In *Prose* Vol. 2.1. Milan: Mondadori, 1954, pp. 1283ff.

Pietrobono, Luigi. *Il poema sacro.* Bologna: Zanichelli, 1915, p. 50.

Triolo, Alfred A. "Ira, Cupiditas, Libido: The Dynamics of Human Passion in the *Inferno.*" *Dante Studies* 95 (1977), 1–37.

Alison Cornish

G

Gabriel, the Archangel

In the Bible, the archangel Gabriel *(Gabriello)* functions as God's messenger (see *Conv.* 2.5.4, where Dante cites him as God's *grande legato* or "grand ambassador"). He appears to Daniel as a revelator (Dan. 8:15–27, 9:20–27), to Zachariah to announce John the Baptist's birth (Luke 1:11–20), and to Mary to inform her she will give birth to Jesus (Luke 1:26–38).

Dante depicts Gabriel sculpted on the wall of Purgatory's terrace of the proud in a reenactment of the annunciation to Mary (*Purg.* 10.34–45) and later identifies him as the angel who spoke to Mary (*Par.* 14.36). Beatrice teaches that archangels such as Gabriel only seem to have bodies so that mankind can apprehend them (*Par.* 4.47). Folco describes Nazareth as the place where Gabriel spread his wings (*Par.* 9.138). The archangel appears as *una facella* and *amore angelico* (*Par.* 23.94 and 103, "a torch" and "angelic love") when he encircles the Virgin Mary in the Heaven of the Fixed Stars. In the Empyrean he kneels before her and is described as *quello amor,* then *quell'angel . . . con tanto gioco,* and finally as *quelli che portò la palma / giuso a Maria* ("that love," "that angel . . . with so much joy," and "he who carried down the palm to Mary," *Par.* 32.94, 103, 112–113).

Madison U. Sowell

Gaddo

Gaddo was one of two sons of Count Ugolino who with him and his father's grandsons suffered imprisonment and death by starvation in a tower in Pisa in March 1289 (*Inf.* 33.68). He expired on the fourth day, before his father, his brother Uguiccione, and his nephews Nino and Anselmuccio. He complains not of cruel treatment at the hands of Archbishop Ruggieri, who had imprisoned them, but of abandonment by his father, in words (*Inf.* 33.69) that echo Christ's famous last words in Matt. 27:46.

Roy Rosenstein

Gaeta

City and port in southern Latium on the Tyrrhenian coast. It was traditionally said to have been named by Aeneas in honor of his nurse Caieta, who had died there (*Inf.* 26.92-93; cf. *Aen.* 7.1-4). It was one of the limits of the Kingdom of Naples (*Par.* 8.62), and in *DVE* 1.9.4 its dialect is differentiated from that of Naples.

Claire Honess

Galen

Greek physician and celebrated medical authority, born in Pergamus (Mysia) in the fall of 130 C.E. He began his medical training in Smyrna and studied in Corinth and Alexandria. He lived and practiced in Rome over a number of years: for approximately four years around 163–164; after 168 as physician to Emperor Marcus Aurelius's nine-year-old son, the future emperor L. Aurelius Commodus; and also probably toward the end of the century. He died after 201.

The surviving corpus of Galen's writings consists of eighty-three treatises considered genuine, nineteen doubtful, forty-five spurious, and nineteen fragmentary. Altogether he wrote more than five hundred treatises. Translated into Arabic in the ninth century by Hunain Ben Ishaq, his work became the standard of medical perfection, and his popularity in the Latin Middle Ages derived more from his popularity among Arabic medical writers than from any direct knowledge of his texts.

Dante encounters Galen *(Galieno)* in Limbo *(Inf.* 4.143) in the company of Hippocrates and Avicenna. He mentions him in *Conv.* 1.8.5 as the author of the *Tegni (Ars medica),* and in *Mon.* 1.13.6 quotes his *De cognoscendis curandisque animi morbis* in support of an assertion.

Bibliography

Brock, Arthur J. *Greek Medicine.* New York: AMS Press, 1977.

Castiglioni, Arturo. *A History of Medicine.* Translated by E. B. Krumbhaar. New York: Knopf, 1941.

Massimo Ciavolella

Gallehaut

Dante refers once in the *Inferno* to Gallehaut *(Galeotto),* a character in the Arthurian prose romance *Lancelot du Lac.* A friend of Lancelot, Gallehaut acted as an intermediary between the lovers Lancelot and Guinevere. In *Inf.* 5.137, Francesca tells Dante that the book which she and Paolo were reading acted as a "Galeotto" between herself and Paolo; in other words, the book served as an intermediary between them, just as the character Gallehaut did between Guinevere and Lancelot. As a result of this episode, the word has come to signify "pander" in Italian, although it does not have this sense for Dante.

Maria Ann Roglieri

Ganelon

A traitor to his homeland, Ganelon *(Gano,* also *Ganellone)* betrayed Charlemagne at Roncesvalles, causing the slaughter of the Frankish rearguard, as recounted in the *Chanson de Roland.* Dante refers to this defeat in *Inf.* 31.16–18, and then has Bocca degli Abati point out Ganelon in Antenora, the second zone of the ninth circle of Hell *(Inf.* 32.122).

Alessandro Vettori

Ganges

River in India whose mouth was considered by Dante to be the easternmost point of the inhabitable world *(Questio* 54), in his conception 90° east of Jerusalem. The westernmost point is conceived by medieval thinkers to be indicated by the town of Cadiz in Spain. The Ganges *(Gange)* serves as a marker in geographical and temporal periphrases, as in *Purg.* 2.5, 27.4, and *Par.* 11.51.

Claire Honess

Gano degli Scornigiani

Referred to by Dante as *quel da Pisa* ("he of Pisa") in *Purg.* 6.17. He is mentioned in connection with his father Marzucco, who forgave rather than avenged Gano's murder, which some believe was carried out by Nino della Gherardesca, a grandson of Ugolino (see *Inf.* 33), in 1287.

Molly Morrison

Ganymede

In mythology, Ganymede *(Ganimede)* was a Trojan prince, the son of Tros and Callirhoë. Jupiter, in love with him because of his great beauty, assumed the form of an eagle and snatched him up from Mount Ida to Olympus to be his cupbearer. Dante would have read the story in Ovid, *Meta.* 10.155–161 (and a reference in 11.756), and in Virgil, *Aen.* 5.252–257. He uses the image in recounting his being borne aloft into Purgatory proper by St. Lucy *(Purg.* 9.19–33), an experience of which he is conscious only through a dream in which he imagines that, like Ganymede, he is seized from Mount Ida by an eagle and taken up to the sphere of fire.

Jennifer Petrie

Garamantes

According to the ancients, the southernmost inhabitants of northern Africa, in an area now known as Fezzan. Dante speaks of the Garamantes *(Garamanti)* in *Conv.* 3.5.12 and 3.5.18 as inhabitants of the "first climate," which is so hot that they usually go naked. He notes that Cato saw them when he fled there (Lucan, *Phars.* 4.334; 9.369, 438, 511ff.; Virgil, *Eclogues* 8.44, *Aen.* 6.794), and that they must see the Sun circling directly above like a wheel. In *Mon.* 1.14.6, Dante

G contrasts the law necessary for the Scythians, in their freezing climate, to that for the Garamantes, in excessive heat. Ptolemy (source of Alfraganus, Dante's authority) divided the habitable globe (Northern Hemisphere) into seven climates, the first being nearest the equator.

Leslie Zarker Morgan

Gardner, Edmund Garrat

A dedicated Italianist and Dante scholar, Gardner (1869–1935) taught at the University of Manchester and University College, London, and was editor of the *Modern Language Review* (1911–1935), for which he reviewed numerous Italian works. His many books and articles on Italian literature are wide-ranging. Of particular Dantean interest are *Dante's Ten Heavens: A Study of the Paradiso* (1898; second edition, revised, 1904), *Dante* (1900, revised 1923), *Dante and Giovanni del Virgilio* (1920), with P.H. Wicksteed, and especially *Dante and the Mystics* (1913, reprinted 1968), on the mystical dimension of the *Commedia*.

A. L. Pellegrini

Gemma Donati

Wife of Dante. The daughter of Manetto and Maria Donati and closely related to Corso and Forese Donati, Gemma belonged to one of the most powerful Guelf families in Florence. Records indicate that Manetto had settled her dowry in 1277, which suggests that she was betrothed to Dante in childhood: the year of their marriage is set as 1285, two years after the death of Dante's father. Gemma bore Dante several children: we know of Pietro, Jacopo, and Antonia (probably the same woman who took the name Sister Beatrice at the convent of Santo Stefano dell' Ulivi in Ravenna), and there were possibly others (a 1308 document mentions a Giovanni, "filius Dantis Alagherii"). Unlike her children, Gemma did not join Dante in exile. Her mother's will, dated 1315, left Gemma a modest legacy; she was still alive in 1332, eleven years after Dante's death.

Boccaccio, in the *Trattatello in laude di Dante* (c. 1351–1355), states that "Dante's relatives and friends gave him a wife so that his tears for Beatrice would come to an end"—but asserts further that "once he had left that person who had been granted to him as a consolation for his woes, never did he want to go where she was, nor would he ever allow her to come to him, even though they had borne several children together." Subsequent commentators perpetuated this tradition of an unhappy marriage, but no real evidence confirms it, and it should be remembered that if Gemma had visited her husband, she would probably have fallen under the city's ban against him. Dante's seeming indifference has troubled some biographers, who have from time to time attempted to identify Gemma with the *donna pietosa* of the *Vita Nuova,* the *donna pietra* of the *Rime,* or the character Phyllis in Giovanni del Vergilio's response to an eclogue by Dante (*Egl.* 3.45).

Bibliography

Anderson, William. *Dante the Maker.* London: Routledge and Kegan Paul, 1980.

Barbi, Michele. *Life of Dante.* Translated by Paul G. Ruggiers. Berkeley: University of California Press, 1960.

Boccaccio, Giovanni. *The Life of Dante (Trattatello in Laude di Dante).* Translated by Zin Bollettino. Garland Library of Medieval Literature, vol. 40, Series B. New York: Garland, 1990.

Petrocchi, Giorgio. *Vita di Dante.* Bari: Laterza, 1983.

Kathleen Verduin

Gentucca

Early commentaries maintain that in using the term *Gentucca,* Dante is alluding to *gentuccia,* a pejorative form of *gente,* indicating people of low status (the view of the Anonimo Fiorentino and Lana), and probably his political enemies among the White Guelfs (see the *Ottimo Commento*). Following Buti, modern interpretations regard the murmured utterance (*Purg.* 24.37) as a proper noun referring to a woman of Lucca whose mysterious identity is linked to the prophecy delivered by the poet Bonagiunta (43–48), who appears among the gluttonous souls on the sixth cornice of Purgatory. Bonagiunta says that the lady in question is still unmarried in 1300 and therefore does not wear the fillet (*benda,* 43) that identifies married women. Her exemplary behavior, however, will lead Dante to modify his negative opinion of the Lucchesi (previously expressed in *Inf.* 18.122, 21.37). Historical documentation shows a Gentucca di Ciucchino Morla, wife of Buonaccorso Fondora of Lucca. It is probable that the reference is in recognition of hospitality received by the exiled Dante, though the date of his sojourn in

Lucca is not documented. Unsubstantiated speculation of a romantic liaison between Dante and the lady has been widely rejected. Rather, the image of Gentucca fosters the notion of hospitality and caregiving and shows Dante's appreciation of an act of gracious civility extended to him during his wanderings in exile.

Diana Cavuoto Glenn

Geri di Bello

An important minor figure in *Inf.* 29, Geri is Ruggieri del Bello degli Alighieri, the son of Bello degli Alighieri, who was brother to Dante's grandfather Bellincione. Geri was thus first cousin to Dante's father, Alighiero II, and hence first cousin once removed to Dante himself. He is the first member of Dante's family encountered in the poem, but Dante himself never sees him—he only looks for him (29.4, 14). It is rather Virgil who sees him and reports his actions and gestures to Dante (29.22–30).

A figure of some controversy in understanding the poem, Geri (named in 29.27) is placed among the schismatics, or sowers of discord. Dante does not see him, Virgil explains, because when Geri was nearby, Dante was intent on Bertran de Born, the most famous of the schismatics and among the most memorable figures in the *Commedia.* When Virgil tells Dante that he saw Geri making a menacing gesture in Dante's direction, Dante replies, in lines that are something of a crux, that Geri's unavenged death is what made him *disdegnoso; ond' el sen gio / sanza parlarmi, sì com' ïo estimo: / e in ciò m'ha el fatto a sé più pio* ("full of scorn; therefore he walked away without speaking to me, as I judge, and that has made me more compassionate toward him," *Inf.* 29.34–36). The issue of pity points to the crux.

Virgil has already chided Dante, *Qui vive la pietà quand' è ben morta* ("Here pity lives when it is quite dead," *Inf.* 20.28), and commentators have long wondered what Dante means by the term *pio* in 29.36: for example, does he approve of the blood-feud (the vendetta in Italy as elsewhere in medieval culture being virtually axiomatic)? Consensus is lacking, but it seems reasonable to assume that since Virgil also chides Dante for pausing to look for Geri (29.4–6, 22–24), this episode somehow continues the discourse in *Inferno* against misplaced pity—pity that fails to understand and therefore honor *la ministra / de l'alto Sire infallibil giustizia* ("the minister of the high Lord, infallible Justice," *Inf.* 29.55–56).

R. Allen Shoaf

Germany

For Dante, the country separated from Italy by the Alps and called *Lamagna* (*Inf.* 20.62), a word derived from the Latin *Alamannia* (*DVE* 1.18.5). Geographically, Germany was considered in the Middle Ages and in the Renaissance as a vast expanse of Europe, inhabited by peoples speaking not only Germanic but also non-Germanic languages. In Dante's words, Germany embraced "that whole area that extends from the mouth of the Danube (or the Meotide marshes) to the westernmost shores of England, and which is defined by the boundaries of the Italians and the French, and by the ocean" (*DVE* 1.8.3). Politically, Germany was identified with the Holy Roman Empire, the ideal continuation of the Carolingian state which derived its legitimacy from the transfer of the imperial power to the Germans ("translatio imperii ad Germanos"). Linguistically, Germany was considered a homogeneous area, because the Slavic and Finno-Ugric languages were erroneously considered Germanic by medieval and Renaissance scholars. For this reason, Dante lumps together the vernaculars spoken by "the Slavs, the Hungarians, the Teutons, the Saxons, the English, and several other nations" who "answer in the affirmative" and "say *iò*" (*DVE* 1.8.3). Such vernaculars constitute a linguistic group that Dante distinguishes from the ones spoken by peoples who use *oc, oïl* or *sì*.

1. German Cultural and Political Life in Dante

It is wrong to apply modern national standards to the Middle Ages, when modern nations existed only as potential developments which took many centuries in order to be brought to fruition. Medieval culture was local and universal at the same time. The local culture was expressed mainly by modern languages, while the universal one had its appropriate linguistic vehicle in Latin. Dante ignored the local aspect of German culture, which found its loftiest expression in the Minnesinger poetry of the twelfth and thirteenth centuries. But he was open to the influence of the universal aspect of its culture, which loomed large over theology, the leading discipline of the medieval *cursus studiorum,* thanks to the influential writings of

G Albertus Magnus (1193?–1280). This great theologian, known as the *Doctor Universalis,* is introduced to Dante in the Heaven of the Sun by his pupil, St. Thomas Aquinas (*Par.* 10. 97–99). According to Bruno Nardi, Dante owed to Albertus not his own philosophy, which was original, but his philosophical preparation, characterized by a strong Neoplatonic component. Undoubtedly Albertus is more relevant to Dante studies than is Aquinas, whose influence was magnified for confessional and patriotic reasons.

The modern construct of Dante as the champion of the Italian nation resulted in the paradox (pointed out by Karl Witte) of a writer who paved the way for the resurrection of Italy by advocating "the divinely ordained rights . . . of the Romano-German Empire, not only in a special treatise, but in almost every one of his works." The Hohenstaufen or Swabian house is widely represented in the *Commedia.* Conrad III (c. 1093–1152), the founder of the Hohenstaufen dynasty, appears in Cacciaguida's speech as the leader of the Second Crusade and as the emperor who knighted Dante's ancestor (*Par.* 15. 139–141). Frederick I, called Barbarossa (c. 1122–1190), is mentioned by the Abbot of San Zeno in Verona in connection with the destruction of Milan: "the reign of good Barbarossa, of whom Milan still speaks with grief" (*Purg.* 18.119–120). Giosuè Carducci (1835–1907), who greatly contributed to the legend of Dante the champion of Italy, took exception with such uncompromising praise of the German emperor and, in his sonnet to Dante *(Rime nuove),* bluntly asserted that the "good Barbarossa" deserved to lose his crown. Henry VI (1190–1197) is mentioned by Piccarda in the Heaven of the Moon as "the second wind of Swabia," as Piccarda points out to Dante Henry's wife, "the great Constance," daughter of Roger, king of Sicily. From their marriage was born Frederick II (1194–1250), the "third and last power" of the Swabian house (*Par.* 3.118–120). Frederick II, called *stupor mundi* for his political and intellectual achievements, is punished with the heretics in the sixth circle of Hell (*Inf.* 10.119), while his natural son, Manfred (c. 1231–1266), is a prominent figure of the Ante-Purgatory (*Purg.* 3. 103–145). He will be saved, notwithstanding the fact that he died excommunicate, because Dante feels obliged to make an exception for him, the last chief of the Ghibelline party. The execution of Conradin (1252–1268), the unlucky son of Conrad IV (1228–1254) and the nephew of Manfred, is deplored in the anti-French episode of Hugh Capet (*Purg.* 20.68), which incensed Francis I of France.

Dante was disappointed by the successors of the Hohenstaufen dynasty. He complains about Rudolf of Hapsburg (1218–1291), the negligent emperor who did not care to heal the wounds of Italy (*Purg.* 7.94–95). Compared to Frederick II, Rudolf, Adolf of Nassau (d. 1298), and Rudolf's son, Albert I (c. 1250–1308), appeared to be failures (*Conv.* 4.3.6). In one of his most vehement invectives, Dante scolded Albert for having abandoned Italy, following the example set by his father Rudolf (*Purg.* 6.97–117). Only Albert's successor, Henry VII, count of Luxemburg, who vainly attempted to restore imperial authority in Italy, won Dante's admiration. A great seat surmounted by a crown is reserved in Paradise for "the noble Harry" (*l'alto Arrigo, Par.* 30.137), while the French pope Clement V (1264–1314), who betrayed the German monarch, will join Boniface VIII in the third section of the eighth circle of Hell, where simoniacs meet their eternal punishment (*Par.* 30.133–148).

2. Dante's Reception in Germany

During the sixteenth and seventeenth centuries, Dante was known in Germany as the author of the *Monarchia,* a work that became a Protestant weapon against the Church of Rome in the hands of Matthias Flaccius Illyricus (1520–1575) and Pietro Paolo Vergerio (1498–1564). Even the *Commedia* was considered by Johannes Wolfius (1537–1600) as a mine of anti-Catholic propaganda. Information about Dante was still scarce in the first decades of the eighteenth century, despite the place allotted to the Italian poet in the encyclopedic work *(Dictionnaire historique et critique)* compiled by the French philosopher Pierre Bayle (1647–1706). Bayle's work was translated into German, and its entry on Dante influenced such scholars as Daniel Georg Morhof (1639–1691), Johann Franz Buddeus (1667–1729), Johann Burkhard Mencke (1674–1732), and Christian Gottlieb Jöcher (1694–1758).

The first German-speaking critic who proclaimed the poetic excellence of the *Commedia* was the Swiss Johann Jakob Bodmer (1698–1783), a representative of a pre-Romantic movement who vehemently opposed French rationalism. Yet the negative judgments expressed by Voltaire were mirrored in the translations of the *Commedia* by

Johann Nikolaus Meinhard (1727–1767) and Leberecht Bachenschwanz (1729–1802). Not until 1791 did August Wilhelm von Schlegel (1767–1845) reveal the esthetic relevance of the *Commedia* in an article that marked a turning point in the history of Dante's fame. For the rest of his life, Schlegel continued to work on Dante, devoting important articles to the *Commedia*. Karl Wilhelm Friedrich von Schlegel (1772–1829), August's brother, was a staunch supporter of Dante until his conversion to Catholicism, after which his enthusiasm gave way to misgivings over the antipapal dimension of Dante's writings. Prominent philosophers such as Friedrich Wilhelm Joseph von Schelling (1775–1854) and Georg Friedrich Wilhelm Hegel (1770–1831) called attention to Dante's poetic genius.

The verse translations by Karl Friedrich Ludwig Kannegiesser (1781–1861) and Karl Streckfuss (1778–1844) made Dante accessible to a vast sector of educated German society. The need for more exegetical information was satisfied by Karl Witte (1800–1883) and by King John of Saxony (1801–1873), who used the pseudonym of Philalethes. The latter in 1865 founded the Deutsche Dante-Gesellschaft, the first Dante society to be created outside Italy. Despite a period of decay that followed Witte's death, Dante studies became an essential part of German culture and managed to survive the irrationality of Nazi policy, which caused the flight of outstanding critics such as Leo Spitzer (1887–1960) and Erich Auerbach (1892–1957). Since Dante's cult was not incompatible with fascism, as Ezra Pound's case proves, Germany still retained an uninterrupted tradition of Dante scholarship, highlighted by such distinguished figures as Franz Xaver Kraus (1840–1901), Karl Vossler (1872–1949), Walther Goetz (1867–1958), Ernst Robert Curtius (1886–1957), and Hermann Gmelin (1900–1958).

Bibliography

Caesar, Michael (ed.). *Dante: The Critical Heritage, 1314(?)–1870*. London and New York: Routledge, 1989.

Davis, Charles Till. "Dante and the Empire." In *The Cambridge Companion to Dante*. Edited by Rachel Jacoff. Cambridge and New York: Cambridge University Press, 1993, pp. 67–79.

Federn, Karl. *Dante and His Time*. Introduction by A. J. Butler. New York: Haskell, 1970 (reprint of 1902 ed.).

Friedrich, Werner P. *Dante's Fame Abroad, 1350–1850*. University of North Carolina Studies in Comparative Literature 2. Rome: Istituto Grafico Tiberino, 1950.

Grundmann, Herbert, Otto Herding, and Hans Conrad Peyer. *Dante und die Mächtigen seiner Zeit*. Münchner Romanistische Arbeiten 15. Munich: Max Hueber, 1960.

Lazzarini, Lino (ed.). *Convegno di studi danteschi: Dante e la cultura tedesca*. Padua: Università degli Studi, 1967.

Nardi, Bruno. "Raffronti fra alcuni luoghi di Alberto Magno e di Dante." In *Saggi di filosofia dantesca*. Florence: La Nuova Italia, 1967, pp. 63–72.

Rheinfelder, Hans. "La *Deutsche Dante-Gesellschaft*." In *Comitato nazionale per le celebrazioni del VII centenario della nascita di Dante, Atti del Congresso internazionale di studi danteschi*, vol. 2. Florence: Sansoni, 1966, pp. 31–35.

Roddewig, Marcella. "Deutsche Ausgaben und Übersetzungen der Werke Dantes im zwanzigsten Jahrhundert." In *L'opera di Dante nel mondo: Edizioni e traduzioni nel Novecento, Atti del Convegno internazionale di studi, Roma, 27-29 aprile 1989*. Edited by Enzo Esposito. Ravenna: Longo, 1992, pp. 103–113.

Sofer, Johann. *Dante und Österreich*. Moderne Sprache, Schriftenreihe 10. Vienna: Verband der österreichischen Neuphilologen, 1965.

Toynbee, Paget. "Some Obligations of Dante to Albertus Magnus." In *Dante Studies and Researches*. London: Methuen, 1902, pp. 38–55.

Witte, Karl. *Essays on Dante (Being Selections from the Two Volumes of "Dante-Forschungen")*. Selected, Translated and Edited with Introduction, Notes and Appendices by C. Mabel Lawrence and Philip H. Wicksteed. New York: Haskell, 1970 (reprint of 1898 ed.).

Gustavo Costa

Geryon

The mythic cruel king of an unspecified island, thought by some to be the Balearic Islands, and by others to be Erytheia (perhaps lying in the ocean, in the extreme west). He was slain by Hercules. In the myth he is a man with three bodies. Virgil calls him *tricorporis* ("three-bodied," *Aen.* 6.289) or *tergeminus* ("triform," *Aen.* 8.202). Dante transforms the three bodies into three natures combined in a single body, perhaps inspired by the description of monstrous animals found in Rev. 9:7–10 and in medieval encyclopedias (for example, Bartholomaeus Anglicus, *De rerum proprietatibus*, XVIII, 69, talks about a wolf having *pedem leonis, et faciem hominis et caudam scorpionis*—"a lion's foot, a man's face, and a scorpion's tail"). Dante's Geryon has the face of a just man, the paws of a lion, the bust and trunk of a snake painted with knots and intricate circles, and a bifurcated tail in the shape of scorpion's jaws. This alteration makes of Geryon the embodiment of fraud, the living proof of what is deemed impossible, namely the copresence of different "natures" within a single body. Geryon contains in himself all the branches of the animal kingdom, as if a unique metamorphosis had taken place in which one species is not transformed into another but is added to it. At the symbolic level, this body is a living contradiction: the image of justice on his face contrasts with the sting of his scorpion tail; the strength and nobility of the lion is the antithesis of the deceptive action of the snake. Appropriately, Geryon is the guardian of Malebolge, the circle of the fraudulent. His monstrous triple nature represents a culmination in the

Geryon transporting Dante and Virgil into Malebolge. Opere di Dante Alighieri, *edited by Cristoforo Zapate de Cisneros, Venice, 1757–1758. Giamatti Collection: Courtesy of the Mount Holyoke College Archives and Special Collections.*

Dante and Virgil entering Malebolge. La comedia di Dante Aligieri, *with commentary by Alessandro Vellutello, published by Francesco Marcolini, Venice, 1544. Giamatti Collection: Courtesy of the Mount Holyoke College Archives and Special Collections.*

series of guardians of the previous circles: Minos, the Centaurs, and the Minotaur all have two natures. Like Charon and the Centaurs, Geryon is not merely a guardian but a means of transportation for the damned souls assigned to his circle. This function will also be found in the giants and, to some extent, in Lucifer.

Geryon's presence dominates canto 17: the first line—*"Ecco la fiera con la coda aguzza"* ("Behold the beast with the pointed tail")—and the last—*Si dileguò come da corda cocca* ("Vanished like the notch from the bowstring")—contain the same image of the tail. Indeed, the image of Geryon's poisonous and treacherous tail pervades the canto, motivating part of the action (Virgil must shield Dante against it during the flight down into Malebolge) and, above all, creating a sense of physical horror which numbs the pilgrim. Geryon's presence is a mute one: he utters no word that Dante hears, even when Virgil parlays with him. His presence is not hostile, since he makes no threat nor insult; but it is precisely this silence and this appearance of peace that charge the atmosphere with tension, paralyzing the mental faculties of the pilgrim and leaving him speechless throughout the entire canto. The highest degree of terror occurs when Dante cannot avoid physical contact with the monster, on whose shoulders he must sit in order to descend into the eighth circle. The downward flight in the dark pit separating the two circles is one of the most memorable in the whole *Commedia:* a blind flight, without a sense of time or space, only the air blowing from underneath giving Dante the sense of being propelled. Yet, even if the description of this flight is kept on a purely sensorial—that is, not intellectual—level, its meaning in the salvific design of the *Commedia* is indicated in the comparison between this flight and those of Phaethon and Icarus. The analogy with two other mythic and literary episodes is meant to convey the intensity of the fear Dante experiences: there were no other recorded experiences of flight (Alexander's was little known) to which readers could relate. But readers who were familiar with Phaethon and Icarus because they had read their Ovid (just as Dante did) knew that the outcome was a tragic one for both of them. Phaethon's sin was similar, in a sense, to that of Adam, who defied his father's order, and his flight results, in fact, in a fall. Icarus's flight is similar to Ulysses' *folle volo* ("mad flight"): he quests after freedom, but his wings are not adequate to the task. Dante's flight, by contrast, is in obedience to a celestial call and is directed toward the true God unknown to the pagan world. Of course, the knowledge of the outcome does not prevent the pilgrim from feeling fear and from being disgusted by a monster like Geryon. Indeed, Dante and his journey would be far less credible if he lacked such emotional reactions. *Per aspera ad astra* ("the road to the stars leads through difficulties"), as the ancients put it; and there is little doubt that contending with Geryon is to be considered among the most difficult moments Dante experiences during his journey to the stars.

Bibliography

Barolini, Teodolinda. *The Undivine Comedy: Detheologizing Dante.* Princeton: Princeton University Press, 1992, pp. 58–73.

Cherchi, Paolo. "Geryon's Canto." *Lectura Dantis: A Forum for Dante Research and Interpretation* 2 (1988), 31–44.

Damon, Phillip. "Geryon, Cacciaguida, and the Y of Pythagoras." *Dante Studies* 85 (1967), 15–32.

Friedman, John Block. "Antichrist and the Iconography of Dante's Geryon." *Journal of the Warburg and Courtauld Institutes* 35 (1972), 108–122.

Lanza, Antonio. "L'allegoria della corda nel canto XVI dell'*Inferno.*" *Rassegna della letteratura italiana* 84 (1980), 97–100.

Mercuri, Roberto. *Semantica di Gerione: Il motivo del viaggio nella "Commedia" di Dante.* Rome: Bulzoni, 1984.

Paolo Cherchi

Gherardo da Camino

Captain-General of Treviso from 1283 until his death in 1306. A defender of the White Guelfs, he was known as a protector of poets and writers. Dante cites him in a discussion on the origin of nobility in *Conv.* 4.14.12. Since Dante treats Gherardo as having already died, the passage suggests that the remaining part of the fourth book of the *Convivio* could not have been written before March, 1306. In *Purg.* 16.124, Marco Lombardo cites him as one of three old men who survive to reproach the younger generation.

Leslie Zarker Morgan

Ghibellines

The Ghibellines were a thirteenth-century Italian political faction, the opponents of the Guelfs. From the late twelfth century, local rivalries in the Italian towns consolidated into factions. Then, in the 1240s, local factions gradually formed two party alliances that took sides in the renewed conflict between the German emperors and the Italian popes. The supporters of the efforts of Holy Roman emperors to establish hegemony over northern Italy formed a *pars imperii* or imperial party, in opposition to supporters of the political and territorial ambitions of the papal curia and its allies. The imperial party backed the Italian claims of the Hohenstaufen family, the dynasty holding the imperial crown at the end of the twelfth century. Contemporary chroniclers were fascinated with derivations for the names of the parties: Giovanni Villani wrote of a feud between German barons with castles called Guelfo and Ghibellino (*Cronica,* 6.38). The name probably did derive from a Hohenstaufen castle in Germany called

G Waiblingen, which became a battle cry for the emperor.

Origins

The factions had their roots not in international politics but in rivalries between elite families within the towns. Urban politics were especially volatile in the last decades of the twelfth century. The towns enjoyed rapidly expanding economies and populations. Florence doubled in population in the twelfth century and then doubled again, reaching approximately 105,000 by 1300. Institutions of government were not well established. The emperor Frederick Barbarossa (1155–1190) had failed to establish imperial rule, and towns became effectively independent, often usurping imperial prerogatives. Internally, as older forms of governance faded, rising new families scrambled for control. In *Par.* 15–16 Dante looks back on this period as the sober and honorable time of his ancestor Cacciaguida. In fact, this was a turbulent and creative period of experimentation with new forms of association and governance. Townsmen formed corporations that united people with shared interests, including not only societies of footsoldiers and of knights, but also craft and professional guilds. Many towns, including Florence, came to be precariously ruled by executives who were termed "consuls," in imitation of republican Roman institutions. Consuls represented a town's neighborhoods and its corporate groups, including the major guilds. As consular offices became sources of power and wealth, rising urban families competed to control them, forming networks of political and military alliance to battle for domination in a series of petty civil wars. An alliance of Florentine families that formed in this period became the nucleus of the Ghibelline faction.

The early factional struggles were a mix of familial and political competition. This quality is conveyed by the earliest account of the genesis of the Guelf–Ghibelline rivalry in Florence, contained in a chronicle that was falsely attributed to Dante's teacher, Brunetto Latini. The anonymous author is conventionally known as the Pseudo-Brunetto. He writes that the conflict began in 1215/1216 over a squabble at a banquet celebrating a man's dubbing as a knight (see *Par.* 16.140–141). When a buffoon snatched away a plate shared by Uberto dell'Infangati and Buondelmonte de' Buondelmonti, a scuffle broke out and Buondelmonte wounded Oddo Arrighi with a knife. Oddo consulted his allies and then arranged a peace through the marriage of his Amidei niece with the young Buondelmonte. Buondelmonte consented but then, mocked as a dishonored knight by Gualdrada dei Donati, he repudiated the Amidei girl to marry a Donati. Oddo Arrighi and his Amidei allies avenged the insult by murdering Buondelmonte during his wedding procession.

In the bitter division that ensued, the chronicler tells us, Oddo Arrighi, the Amidei, and their allies formed the Ghibelline faction. In fact, Oddo Arrighi's alliances did form the nucleus of the Ghibelline faction, but this dated back at least to an 1177 civil war. The rivalry between these rising families was rooted in competition for control of urban turf and consular offices. The fourteenth-century chronicler Marchionne di Coppo Stefani, who spoke from experience when he argued that all factional strife was based in *gara d'ufici* ("competition for offices"), was surely correct.

The factions thus are best understood as the coalescence of local networks based on political, social, and economic ties. When the Hohenstaufen Holy Roman Emperor Frederick II (1220–1250) sought to establish working imperial vicariates in northern Italy in opposition to papal interests, local factions linked themselves to his cause. The Florentine name for imperial partisans, Ghibellines, was extended to their allies in other towns. By the 1240s, the factions became sworn associations governed by captains and advisory councils. For a time, when a town made peace with Florence the treaty had to be ratified by the captain of the Ghibellines as well as by the officers of the commune.

Factional politics created complex webs of conflicting loyalties. A man could be forced to choose between his kinsmen and faction, and his city. Bocca degli Abati was a Ghibelline who the Florentines believed betrayed his city to her Ghibelline opponents at the Battle of Montaperti: he cut off the hand of the Florentine standard-bearer to prevent him from rallying the town's troops at a crucial moment in the battle. Dante in the *Inferno* placed Bocca in the darkest pit of Hell for his treason to his city, but the action surely was considered heroic loyalty by his Ghibelline allies and Abati kinsmen.

Ghibelline Rule in Florence

The Florentine Ghibellines dominated the city for two brief periods in the mid-thirteenth century.

Their fortunes were closely tied to imperial success. In 1238 Frederick II was strong enough to claim the right to ratify the choice of a new Florentine podestà. In 1246 he named his illegitimate son, Frederick of Antioch, to the office. Frederick of Antioch was quick to strengthen the connection, rewarding imperial supporters with offices and estates. Internal battles between Guelfs and Ghibellines led to the 1248 exile of the leading Guelfs, and a short-lived Ghibelline regime. When Frederick II died in 1250, Ghibelline rule in Florence was supplanted by a popular regime, the Primo Popolo. In 1258 Florentine Ghibellines, emboldened by the coronation of Manfred, rose in revolt; after they failed, the Ghibelline leaders were exiled from the city and their forts and palaces destroyed.

Two years later, the exiled Ghibellines in alliance with the commune of Siena defeated the Florentine militia at the bloody Battle of Montaperti and captured the city. The tale of Farinata degli Uberti's protection of Florence from destruction after the battle (*Inf.* 10.91–93) is considered true. Manfred had written to the victorious Sienese that the conquering sword should not stop until the city was so thoroughly destroyed that it could never rise again. The Florentine Ghibellines halted the Sienese, but they systematically destroyed the property of the leading Guelf families of the city, razing their towers, shops, and palaces.

Florence returned to Ghibelline rule from 1260 until 1266, when Manfred's death at the Battle of Benevento (see *Purg.* 3) and the cruel execution of his youthful successor Conradin by the Guelf Charles of Anjou in 1268 marked the real failure of the imperial cause in Italy. In 1268 the Guelfs took power in Florence and exiled the Ghibelline leadership, razing their towers and palaces in turn. The presence of bitter factional leaders in exile was destabilizing, and a papal legate, the Dominican Cardinal Latino Malabranca, was sent to reconcile the exiled Ghibellines. Latino was able to establish a bipartisan government in 1279. This was quickly supplanted by a system of guild-based rule that became the Priorate.

Contemporary sources give detailed information about the makeup of the Florentine Ghibelline faction, including records of Ghibelline officeholders and the list of the men who took part in Cardinal Latino's reconciliation. The Ghibelline elite in Florence derived from a handful of noble families that owed their titles and privileges to the German emperor. The research of Sergio Raveggi, however, reveals that the men in high office during the periods of Ghibelline rule did not derive from the older rural nobility but rather from urban families with twelfth-century origins. These were merchant houses like the Abati, ruling in alliance with men drawn from the minor guilds: tavernkeepers, shoemakers, coopers. The powerful Florentine banking houses like the Cerchi were notably excluded, which best explains the failure of these regimes. The Ghibellines are probably best understood as conservatives who sought to return the city to conditions before the innovations of the Primo Popolo.

Ghibellines outside Florence

After the Battle of Montaperti, Tuscany was dominated by Ghibellines until the death of Manfred. A list of towns contributing troops to an anti-Guelf league in 1261 includes the longstanding imperial partisans Pisa and Siena, as well as the smaller towns of Pistoia, Prato, Volterra, San Miniato, and San Gimignano. After the deaths of Manfred and Conradin, Siena and the smaller towns were pressured into submission to Guelf rule. Pisa remained staunchly independent and Ghibelline, a policy shaped by opposition to her commercial rivals Florence and Lucca.

Identification with the Guelf and Ghibelline factions structured politics outside Tuscany from the 1240s, though its importance can be exaggerated. Chroniclers often continued to define local rivalries in terms of fidelity to local families. In Bologna, the Ghibelline faction was termed the *pars Lambertazza* after its Lambertazzi leaders, and their opponents similarly were the *pars Geremei.* In Piacenza, chroniclers spoke of Guelfs and Ghibellines from 1247, but the factions were also termed the *pars Marchiani,* supporters of the Marquis of Este, and the *pars Eccelini,* backing Ezzelino da Romano.

Nevertheless, as Jacques Heers argues, a sort of traditional political map can be sketched. In Emilia, Ghibelline Modena was supported by Rimini in opposition to Guelf Bologna. In Lombardy, Guelf Milan was challenged by the Ghibelline alliance of Monza, Pavia, and Cremona. In the Po Valley, Mantua, Ferrara, and Padua formed a Guelf alliance against Verona. Thus, identification with the two factions persisted but became divorced from any ideological link to the papal or

G imperial cause, serving essentially to identify a local party's foreign allegiances. After 1273 there were imperial claimants supported by the papacy in opposition to local Guelf leadership.

Ghibellines and Cathar Heresy

Ghibellinism came to be linked to the Cathars, a popular heretical religious movement that challenged the authority of the Catholic Church in thirteenth-century Italy. A number of Ghibelline leaders were convicted of heresy after their deaths, including two Uberti, Bruno and Farinata; the latter is depicted in *Inf.* 10. Did their distaste for the politics of the Roman curia actually lead them into heresy? Possibly, but the evidence is unclear because charges of heresy were used as a political weapon: the papacy from the time of Innocent III identified heresy with treason, so that repudiation of papal sovereignty could constitute heresy. The penalty for heresy extended to the third generation: the grandchildren of a convicted heretic could be stripped of civic or ecclesiastical office and real property. The Uberti postmortem heresy condemnations meant that their descendants could be deprived of benefices in the Church.

Ghibellines in the Early Fourteenth Century

By the fourteenth century, then, factional alliances generally were not animated by papal and imperial ideology. The political theorist Bartolo of Sassoferrato wrote a brief treatise on the Guelfs and Ghibellines, probably in 1355. Bartolo points out that membership in the factions was relative: if a tyrant in a town calls himself and his supporters Guelf, then any good man in the town who opposes tyranny will therefore consider himself Ghibelline.

Ghibelline hopes briefly revived with the 1310 Italian expedition of the emperor Henry of Luxemburg, who sought an imperial coronation and the pacification of the peninsula under his imperial rule. As J. K. Hyde has pointed out, Henry's aim to end factional strife in Italy served instead to revive it. In the *Monarchia,* Dante argued for a divinely sanctioned universal imperial rule in this general atmosphere. Henry's death from malaria in 1313 quickly put an end to Ghibelline aspirations. Louis of Bavaria in 1327, and Charles IV in 1354 and 1368, similarly failed to establish imperial rule in Italy.

Bibliography

Historical Texts

Bartolo da Sassoferrato. "De Guelphis et Gebellinis." In *Politica e diritto nel trecento italiano: Il "De Tyranno" di Bartolo da Sassoferrato* by Diego Quaglioni. Florence: Olschki, 1983.

Compagni, Dino. "La Cronica di Dino Compagni." Edited by Isidoro del Lungo. In *Rerum Italicarum Scriptores,* new ed., Città di Castello: 1907–1916, vol. 9, part 2. Translated into English by Daniel Bornstein as *Dino Compagni's Chronicle of Florence.* Philadelphia: University of Pennsylvania Press, 1986.

Latini, Pseudo-Brunetto. "Cronica Florentina." In *I Primi due secoli della storia di Firenze.* Edited by Pasquale Villari. Florence: Sansoni, 1898, vol. 2, pp. 195–269.

Stefani, Marchionne di Coppo. "Cronaca Fiorentina." Edited by Niccolò Rodolico. In *Rerum Italicarum Scriptores,* new edition, Città di Castello: 1903–1955, vol. 30, part 1.

Villani, Giovanni. *Cronica: con le continuazioni di Matteo e Filippo.* Giovanni Aquilecchia (ed.). Turin: Einaudi, 1979.

Critical Texts

Abulafia, David. *Frederick II: A Medieval Emperor.* Oxford: Oxford University Press, 1988.

Bowsky, William. *Henry VII in Italy: The Conflict of Empire and City-State, 1310–1313.* Lincoln: University of Nebraska Press, 1960.

Davidsohn, Robert. *Geschichte von Florenz.* Berlin, 1896–1927. Translated into Italian by Giovanni Battista Klein as *Storia di Firenze.* Florence: Sansoni, 1956–1968.

Fasoli, Gina. "Guelfi e Ghibellini di Romagna nel 1280–81." *Archivio storico italiano,* ser. 5, 94 (1936), 157–180.

Heers, Jacques. *Parties and Political Life in the Medieval West.* Amsterdam and New York: North-Holland, 1977.

Holmes, George. *Florence, Rome and the Origins of the Renaissance.* Oxford: Clarendon Press, 1986.

Hyde, J. K. "Contemporary Views on Faction and Civil Strife in Thirteenth- and Fourteenth-Century Italy." In *Violence and Civil Disorder in the Italian Cities, 1200-1500.* Edited by Lauro Martines. Berkeley and Los Angeles: University of California Press, 1972, pp. 273–307.

Lansing, Carol. *The Florentine Magnates: Lineage and Faction in a Medieval Commune.* Princeton, N.J.: Princeton University Press, 1991.

Ottokar, Nicola. "La condanna postuma di Farinata degli Uberti." *Archivio storico italiano,* ser. 5, 77 (1919), 115–123.

Raveggi, Sergio, Massimo Tarassi, Daniela Medici, and Patrizia Parenti. *Ghibellini, Guelfi e Popolo Grasso: I detentori del potere politico a Firenze nella seconda metà del Dugento.* Florence: La Nuova Italia, 1978.

Toubert, Pierre, and Agostino Paravicini Bagliani (eds.). *Federico II e le città italiane.* Palermo: Selerio, 1994.

Carol Lansing

Ghino di Tacco

The son of Tacco of the noble Della Fratta family of Siena, Ghino became famous as a robber and highwayman in the second half of the thirteenth century. Dante mentions his savage murder of Benincasa da Laterina, the judge who had sentenced Ghino's brother or uncle (or perhaps both) to death (*Purg.* 6.13–14). The Anonimo Fiorentino gives a detailed account of the circumstances surrounding the slaying of Benincasa. For a description of the more flamboyant traits of this outlaw, see both Benvenuto's comments and Boccaccio's incisive portrait in *Dec.* 10.2.

Antonio Illiano

Ghisolabella

Daughter of Alberto Caccianemico dell'Orso of Bologna and sister of Venedico, Ghisolabella was married to Niccolò del Fontana of Ferrara about 1270, but she did not live with him for many years. Her family had helped Obizzo II of Este take Ferrara, but it seems that some Fontanas were exiled from the city in 1270, and the rest in 1273. Ghisolabella returned to her family's home in Bologna. Her relationship with the Marchese of Ferrara is undocumented, though it is the reason for which her brother Venedico is placed in the first bolgia of Malebolge in Hell as a pander, a crime that he admits (*Inf.* 18.55). Early commentators state that she was extremely beautiful, but they are not helpful historically. For example, it is not certain with which marchese she would have had a relationship; Obizzo II (1264–1293) and Azzo VIII (1293–1308) are both suggested. Whether or not she was married at the time is also unclear, as are how, why, and where Venedico was believed to have convinced his sister to concede her favors to the marchese. It would seem most logical to accept Zaccagnini's view that the event occurred when she was in her parents' home while her husband was in exile. General opinion favors Obizzo II as the marchese in question, since he was famous for seducing Ferrarese women (cf. Salimbene, *Cronica,* 1:245, 10–11); Caccianemico mentions his sister by name at *Inf.* 18.55.

Leslie Zarker Morgan

Giacomino da Verona

A Veronese Franciscan who lived and wrote (probably in Venice) during the middle decades of the thirteenth century, Giacomino is the author of two vernacular poems, *De Babilonia civitate infernali* (340 lines in length) and *De Jerusalem celesti* (280 lines), devoted, respectively, to descriptions of Hell and Paradise. Both realms are represented as towns, with some hints at an appalling environs for Hell and a rapturous description of enclosed gardens for Paradise. Intriguing suggestions of an urban vision are likewise to be found in Dante's *Inferno* ("the city whose name is Dis," 8.68ff.), while in the third canticle the image of the empyrean as a heavenly city, though more Rome than Jerusalem, is repeatedly suggested through use of simile and metaphor.

The two poems, consisting of mono-rhymed alexandrine quatrains and written in Old Veronese (a Veneto dialect verging, more then than now, on Lombard), can be regarded, like Bonvesin's *Scripturae,* as thematic and generic precursors of the *Commedia.* In the *Babilonia,* probably composed well before the *Jerusalem,* Giacomino unfolds a narration full of drama and surprise, in which colorful *realia* are eagerly assembled only to be scattered into a vortex of hyperbole and amazement. The reader discovers the comforts and delights of Hell through the "progress" of an exemplary sinner recently arrived and duly persecuted by a gang of resourceful and overzealous devils. Memorable highlights are the professional roasting of the damned wretch, properly spitted and seasoned (*Bab.* 117–136), and the rabid debate between a father and his spoiled son, who, meeting in Hell, aggressively castigate and abuse each other (*Bab.*

G

117–136). Predictably, the *Jerusalem* is less dramatic and more repetitious; its most interesting aspect is perhaps the musical activity carried on in Heaven, with the blessed organized into a kind of church choir whose master is Christ himself (*Jer.* 149–170). Peculiarly enough, the triumph of Mary ends in terms of courtly life. Posing among a group of faithful knights (the Virgins), Mary behaves like a chatelaine at a tournament, graciously bestowing palfreys and standards upon her champions (*Jer.* 253–268).

Ruggero Stefanini

Giacomo da Santo Andrea

Consigned to the second ring of the seventh circle, which punishes the violent, Giacomo (or Iacopo) da Santo Andrea is damned for squandering his goods (*Inf.* 13.115-135). He is one of two "naked and torn"(116) spirits pursued by black bitches through a forest of deformed vegetation. The other is the quick-footed Sienese Lano (killed in battle at Pieve del Toppo in 1288), whom Giacomo maliciously mocks. The *contrapasso* of their sin is manifest: having destroyed their wealth through violent dissipation, the spirits of the two squanderers are "dissipated" or wasted as were their goods. The lacerating dogs, traditionally interpreted as demons, also may symbolize the sinners' guilt, or, possibly, the creditors who pursued them in life. Giacomo and Lano continue even in Hell to leave destruction in their wake. As they seek cover in vain from the dogs, Giacomo despoils a bush, which he uses as a screen. This act of willful destruction emphasizes the violently antisocial nature of this sin: more extravagantly and consciously than the prodigals (*Inf.* 7), the squanderers wreck themselves, others, and society. The poet's use of the popular demonic hunt motif stresses its exemplary quality for the Middle Ages: the black dogs incarnate evil, while the beastliness, desperation, fear, and fury of the episode stress the underlying motif of destructiveness.

The son of Oderico da Monselice, the historic Giacomo has been identified as a member of Padova's Cappella di Santo Andrea family. Having received substantial legacies from both parents, the young heir appears to have squandered them in lavish spending. Among the early commentators, Benvenuto reports that Giacomo was a pyromaniac who set fire to his own properties simply to enjoy the spectacle. Other anecdotes include acts of ordering servants to tear costly silk cloth until the sound made him drowsy enough to sleep, and throwing gold and silver coins to fish in the Brenta River as a pastime. The early commentators note that the despot Ezzolino da Romano (*Inf.* 12) ordered Giacomo da Santo Andrea put to death in 1239.

Fiora A. Bassanese

Giacomo da Lentini

Born in Lentini in Sicily and known as "Il Notaro" ("the Notary"), Giacomo served Frederick II at his court in Palermo and is attested in documents between 1233 and 1240. He is regarded as the founder of the *Scuola Siciliana,* the earliest school of poetry in the Italian vernacular, and is credited with having invented the sonnet. The poetry of the Sicilian School is modeled on the troubadour love lyric, and Giacomo sings accordingly of the joy *(gioia)* and sorrow *(dolore)* the lover experiences in serving his lady. His striking use of the image of the lady as a figure painted within his heart (see *"Meravigliosamente"*) relates to Dante's psychology of love (see *VN* 19.12, *Purg.* 18.22–24). Since the Sicilian poets tended to be notaries, judges, princes, and administrators who lacked musical training, the musical component of the Provençal model was omitted in favor of a new formal complexity.

It is questionable whether Dante knew Giacomo's corpus of nearly forty poems in their original form. Most likely he read them in the Tuscan transliteration. Dante implicitly recognizes Giacomo among the *praefulgentes* ("outstanding ones") of Apulia, citing the canzone "Madonna, dir vi voglio" for praise (without naming its author) in *DVE* 1.12.8. The poet Bonagiunta da Lucca names Giacomo along with Guittone d'Arezzo as a prominent poet of the old style that has been superseded by the *dolce stil novo* (*Purg.* 24.55–57).

Bibliography

Antonelli, Roberto (ed.). *Giacomo da Lentini: Poesie.* Rome: Bulzoni, 1979.

Cesareo, G. A. *Le origini della poesia lirica e la poesia siciliana sotto gli Svevi.* Milan and Palermo: Sandron, 1924.

Folena, Gianfranco. "Siciliani, la poesia degli Siciliani e le origini della tradizione lirica italiana." In *Dizionario critico della letteratura italiana.* Turin: UTET, 1973.

Jensen, Frede (ed. and trans.). *The Poetry of the Sicilian School.* New York: Garland, 1986.

Kleinhenz, Christopher. *The Early Italian Sonnet: The First Century (1220–1321).* Lecce: Milella, 1986.

Panvini, B. *Le rime della scuola siciliana.* Florence: Olschki, 1962.

Roncaglia, Aurelio. "De quibusdam provincialibus translatis in lingua nostra." In *Letteratura e critica: Studi in onore di Natalino Sapegno,* vol. 2. Rome: Bulzoni, 1975, pp. 1–36.

Wilkins, Ernest Hatch. *The Invention of the Sonnet and Other Studies in Italian Literature.* Rome: Edizioni di Storia e Letteratura, 1959.

Laurie Shepard

Gianni de' Soldanieri

A Florentine Ghibelline, Soldanieri betrayed his party by siding with the populace when it rose against Guido Novello and drove him and the Ghibellines from Florence on 11 November 1266. His betrayal made the victory possible, prompting the people to make Soldanieri head of their provisional government while they awaited notification of Pope Clement VII's choice for podestà. The pope did not approve of Soldanieri's appointment because his change of parties was so sudden and dictated by self-interest; he seems then to have left Florence for Prato. Dante places him in Antenora among the political traitors (*Inf.* 32.121).

Pamela J. Benson

Gianni, Lapo

Poet of the Stilnovistic school, identified with the Florentine judge and notary Lapo di Gianni Ricevuti. The register of his notarial acts from 1298 to 1328 is held in Florence's Archivio di Stato. Regarding his poetic production, still extant are eleven *ballate,* three *canzoni,* two *stanze di canzone,* and the sonnet "Amor, eo chero mia donna in domino." He appears to have been a close friend of both Dante and Guido Cavalcanti, as evidenced by a sonnet that Dante addresses to the latter: *Guido, i' vorrei che tu e Lapo ed io* ("Guido, I wish that you and Lapo and I," *Rime* 52). In this wish-fulfillment poem, Dante fantasizes that the three poets are swept away in a boat through enchantment and are endlessly speaking of love in the company of their respective ladies. This sonnet, perhaps uncharacteristic of Dante, is instead suggestive of the musical and refined tone of Lapo Gianni's own *ballate.* In *DVE,* Dante records his appreciation of Lapo Gianni by naming him along with Cavalcanti, Cino, and Dante himself as the only poets who achieved excellence in the vernacular (*vulgaris excellentiam,* 1.13.3) by writing, it appears, in the "sweet new style."

Bibliography
Gianni, Lapo. *Rime: Lapo Gianni.* Francesco Iovine (ed.). Rome: Bagatto, 1989.

Jo Ann Cavallo

Giano della Bella

Florentine nobleman alluded to by Cacciaguida in *Par.* 16.131–132, in a reference to the Marquis Hugh of Brandenburg's coat of arms. Hugh conferred knighthood on six Florentine families (including Giano's), who bore variations of his heraldic symbol. Although a noble himself and one of the Florentine priors, Giano was the principal author of the *Ordinances of Justice* (1293), which introduced various strict reforms against the nobility and excluded them from holding political office. To enforce the ordinances, a new office was created, the *Gonfaloniere di Giustizia,* who was provided with foot-soldiers. The nobility subsequently inflamed the populace against Giano, and he was banished from Florence in 1295.

Molly Morrison

Giants

Greek and Latin literature, mythology, and the figurative arts make copious reference to *gigantes,* the sons of Gaea or Earth, born of the blood of Uranus and conceived in order to vindicate the Titans. Monsters of extraordinary stature, their powerful physical force inspired in them the mad desire to wage open war against the gods on Olympus. With the help of Hercules and other gods, Jove defeats the giants on the plains of Phlegra in Macedonia (or in the Phlegraean fields west of Naples), striking them down with lightning bolts. The smoking bodies of certain giants were buried under nearby mountains and explain the presence of volcanoes in the area. The battle of Phlegra is recalled repeatedly in the *Commedia* (*Inf.* 14.58, *Inf.* 31.45,92, *Purg.* 12.28–33). Poetic tradition places the giants in Tartarus (*Aen.* 6.580–584; *Phars.* 6.665, 8.47; *Theb.* 4.534; *Meta.* 1.151–162). Notable variations

G and frequent contaminations with other stories of rebellion against the gods occur in both Greek and Latin literature. In the Middle Ages, scripture authorized belief in the existence of giants and fostered a tendency to view the giants of classical myth, the Bible, and medieval legend as belonging to the same imaginative world. Genesis 6:4 ("Now giants were upon the earth in those days") lent credibility to the ancient authors' references, as did the obvious parallels between the scaling of Olympus and the construction of the tower of Babel (Gen. 11:1–9).

Nimrod appears, in the chapter preceding the Genesis account of Babel, as the son of Cush, "a mighty hunter before the Lord" (Gen. 10:8–10), which explains the hunter's horn he carries in *Inf.* 31. In the pre-Vulgate Latin translation of Genesis, Nimrod is a *gigas,* and beginning with Augustine, the giant Nimrod has become the instigator and general manager of the building of the Tower of Babel which resulted in the confusion of tongues (*De civitate Dei* 16.3). Dante's account of mankind's display of pride on the plain of Sennaar under the aegis of the giant Nimrod (*DVE* 1.7.4) expands on the brief reference in Genesis and stands out as one of the more original and striking aspects of the philosophy of language expounded in the treatise. According to Dante, construction of the tower resulted in language differentiation rather than in the total confusion that Genesis implies. God in his mercy did not wield the justifiable vengeance merited by the transgression, but rather effected a "memorable and merciful correction." Nimrod is named in the *Commedia* in *Inf.* 31.77, in *Purg.* 12.34, among the exempla of defeated pride, and in *Par.* 26.126, by Adam in connection with the tower.

Ephialtes *(Fialte)* and his twin brother Otus, the offspring of Poseidon and Iphimedeia, attempted to scale Olympus by piling Mount Ossa onto Mount Pelion. Virgil located the brothers in Tartarus (*Aen.* 6.771–774). Briareus or Aegaeon, a monstrous deformity of the human form with fifty heads and fire-breathing mouths, brandished fifty shields and fifty swords in his fight against the Olympian gods (*Aen.* 10.565–568, 778–781). Statius' Briareus, on the other hand, is a decidedly humanoid figure (*Theb.* 2.596). Briareus is named in *Purg.* 12.28–30 among the exempla of overweening pride. Antaeus, the issue of Earth and Poseidon, born too late to participate in the war against Olympus, therefore "unfettered" in Dante's

Dante before the Giants in Cocytus. Opere del divino poeta Danthe, ed. Pietro da Figino, Venice, 1520. Giamatti Collection: Courtesy of the Mount Holyoke College Archives and Special Collections.

text, lived in a cave near the valley of the Bagradas River, where he slew and consumed lions. Hercules defeated him by lifting him from his mother, Earth, who was the source of his strength (*Phars.* 4.593–660). Dante describes the contest between Antaeus and Hercules and the former's chthonic power in *Conv.* 3.3.7, and in *Mon.* 2.8 and 2.10.

Tityus *(Tizio)* and Typhon are mentioned but do not appear in *Inf.* 31. Most classical accounts describe the punishment of Tityus, whose liver was devoured by vultures because of his attempted rape of Latona, mother of Diana and Apollo (*Aen.* 6.789–796; *Meta.* 4.456–458; *Theb.* 4.538). As punishment for his attack on the Olympian gods, Typhon or Typhoeus, whose monstrous form rivals or surpasses that of Briareus, was buried alive under the island of Ischia or, according to some accounts, Etna (*Phars.* 4.593–597; *Theb.* 10.917; *Meta.* 5.321–358). In addition to his having one hundred fire-breathing heads, Typhon's lower body is often composed entirely of snakes. Dante mentions him in connection with Cupid in *Conv.* 2.5.14.

The aforementioned giants appear (or are mentioned) in *Inf.* 31 as massive, speechless, human forms, who serve both as guardians and as transport for Dante and Virgil into the ninth circle of Hell, where treachery is punished. The giants whose upper bodies emerge from the pit of Cocytus are initially perceived by the pilgrim as towers, and although Virgil explains the pilgrim's error, clearly distinguishing the false perception (towers) from the reality (giants—*Inf.* 31.31). The play on giant-towers and towering-giants continues and intensifies by means of both visual and verbal images. The position of the giants around the pit of lower Hell is compared to the ring of towers around Monteriggioni, a thirteenth-century castle; the verb *torreggiare,* "to tower," is coined to describe the giants' stance; Ephialtes' movement is compared to that of a tower shaken by an earthquake; the Garisenda Tower of Bologna is compared to the bending figure of Antaeus; and at the heart of this matrix is the Tower of Babel, evoked in Nimrod, the canto's central figure. The tower functions iconographically in the biblical, classical, and medieval worlds as the visual image of pride, and as such is the appropriate metaphor for the pride of the giants who rebelled against the divinity. The giants may, in addition, represent the infernal equivalent of the angelic choirs in Paradise, and they may recall the towers of contemporary Italy, visually appropriate signs of arrogance and treason in a politically sinister era.

Implicit in most studies of the giants is a line separating those who view them as inanimate automatons, devoid of any trace of humanity and intent only on repeating the empty actions of their former selves (Nimrod's sounding of the trumpet, etc.), and those who detect a frustrated, though not obliterated, humanity in these figures paradoxically both greater and less than human. Most point out that Dante humanizes the forms of the giants, most obviously by having Virgil, author of the *Aeneid* and creator of the monstrous Briareus, correct his description, thereby highlighting Dante's purposeful humanization of the monstrous (*Inf.* 31.97–105). Typhon, unlike the fantastical figure of tradition, is nondescript (*Inf.* 31.124). Critics cite the massive dimensions and inanimate images with which Dante compares the giants as evidence for their subhuman numbness: Nimrod's face is said to be the size of the enormous pine cone situated at that time in St. Peter's Square (now in the Belvedere Courtyard of the Vatican Museum); Antaeus moves like the mast of a ship; Ephialtes' seismic shudder is compared to a tower struck by an earthquake. Others argue, on the contrary, that Nimrod's sounding of the horn and unintelligible utterance represent attempts, albeit ineffectual

ones, to communicate; that Ephialtes shakes with anger and jealousy, human emotions, upon hearing Virgil claim that Briareus has greater ferocity; or that Antaeus is responsive to Virgil's false flattery and to his promise of earthly fame, the all too human desire that drives the denizens of Hell.

The giants' pit is characterized by a pervasive heavy silence, anticipatory of the tomblike silence that dominates *Inf.* 34. Nimrod alone attempts to communicate verbally, and his fundamental inability to do so is vividly manifest in his unintelligible babble (*Inf.* 31.67). Though Virgil claims that Antaeus speaks (*Inf.* 31.101), the information may serve instead to underscore what the reader and pilgrim experience and perceive to be the case—his silence and apparent inability to speak. The hellish pit in which the giants are trapped may be the pit of their own inarticulateness.

Numerous attempts have been made to compute the total number of giants in the pit, the exact measurements of their dimensions (Galileo Galilei estimated their stature at between 20 and 27 meters), and to decipher Nimrod's gibberish, in defiance of Virgil's warning to the contrary (*Inf.* 31.79–81). Others have considered the aloof distancing of the canto attributable to what has been loosely described as either an ironic or comic tone in Dante's presentation of the giants. Irony and comedy are both critical concepts for discussions of the poem at large and, it has been suggested, of this realm of Hell in particular.

Bibliography

Butler, George F. "Giants and Fallen Angels in Dante and Milton: The Commedia and the Gigantomachy in *Paradise Lost." Modern Philology* 95 (1998), 352–363.

Chiari, Alberto. "Canto 31." In *Letture dantesche: Inferno.* Florence: Sansoni, 1965, pp. 597–612.

Corti, Maria. "Dante e la torre di Babele: una nuova *allegoria in factis."* In *Il viaggio testuale.* Turin: Einaudi, 1978, pp. 243–256.

Dronke, Peter. "The Giants in Hell." In *Dante and Medieval Latin Traditions.* Cambridge: Cambridge University Press, 1986, pp. 32–54.

Esposito, Enzo. "Il canto 31 dell'*Inferno.*" In *Inferno: Letture degli anni 1973–1976.* Rome: Bonacci, 1975, pp. 743–757.

Kleinhenz, Christopher. "Dante's Towering Giants: *Inferno* 31." *Romance Philology* 27 (1974), 269–285.

Pézard, André. "Le chant des géants." In *Bulletin de la Societé d'Études Dantesques du Centre Universitaire Méditerranéen* 12 (1959), 53–72.

Stephens, Walter. *Giants in those Days: Folklore, Ancient History, and Nationalism.* Lincoln: University of Nebraska Press, 1989.

Donna Yowell

Gideon

A judge of Israel, Gideon *(Gedeone)* was designated by an angel of God to deliver the Israelites from their oppressors (Judg. 6:11–18). When he had assembled thirty-two thousand men on a hill with the Midianites and their allies encamped in the plain below, the Lord ordered him to reduce his troops to three hundred men by means of two tests. First he dismissed twenty-two thousand who acknowledged their fear; then he divided into two groups those who remained by observing their custom of drinking water (Judg. 7:1–8). In *Purg.* 24.124–126, a voice from a tree names the final group dismissed by Gideon as an example of gluttony. Because they demonstrated by their manner of drinking that they were soft *(molli),* Gideon rejected them as fighting companions. This passage reflects the traditional moral interpretation (of what is, in fact, a problematic text), according to which those who knelt down to drink were less prepared for attack than those who remained standing.

Carolynn Lund-Mead

Gilson, Étienne

Philosopher and historian of theology and philosophy (1884–1978) whose prodigious writings include seminal studies of the relationship between theological and philosophical thought in Dante's works. Born in Paris, Gilson taught first at the Sorbonne and later at the Collège de France. His major contribution to the study of Dante, *Dante and Philosophy,* departs from a critique of Pierre Mandonnet's *Dante le théologien* (1935) and seeks to counter the claim that Dante's conceptions were wholly and exclusively founded on Thomistic theology. Gilson shows that St. Thomas's belief in a single beatitude was not endorsed by Dante, who clearly promoted the principle of "duo ultima," a double end, or two beatitudes: one attained through philosophy and leading to happiness in this life, and the other attained through Christian revelation and leading to happiness in the next life. Gilson points not only to the closing chapter of the *Monarchia*—which explicitly speaks of the separate goals of the pope and the emperor, whose authority is based on holy scripture and philosophical texts respectively (3.15)—but also to the spirit of the *Convivio* and the poetic structures of the *Commedia.* He seeks to show that, for Dante, the domains of philosophy, theology, and politics were interdependent and not dominated by notions of hierarchical subordination, and that each had its proper role in establishing peace on earth. If Dante's thought was not simply a construct of Thomistic tenets in poetic guise, it was also not predicated, even in part, on Averroistic philosophical principles, a position that would pit him against views held by Bruno Nardi. Gilson rejects the idea that Dante ever endorses the Averroist doctrine of a single possible intellect or that of the mortality of the human soul; and he argues that at no point does Dante ever embrace a philosophical concept that is unorthodox, let alone heretical.

Bibliography

Gilson, Étienne. *Dante et Beatrice: Études dantesques.* Paris: J. Vrin, 1974.

———. *Dante et la philosophie.* Paris : J. Vrin, 1939. English version, *Dante and Philosophy.* Translated by David Moore. New York: Harper and Row, 1963 [1949]; reprint of *Dante, the Philosopher.* London: Sheed and Ward, 1948.

———. "Dante's *Mirabil Visione.*" *Cornell Library Journal* 5 (1968), 1–17.

———. "Dante's Notion of a Shade: *Purgatorio* XXV." *Mediaeval Studies* 29 (1967), 124–142.

Richard Lansing

Giotto

Giotto di Bondone, the great Florentine painter, architect, and sculptor, was Dante's friend, according to the commentator Benvenuto da Imola and the biographer Giorgio Vasari. Vasari claims that Giotto visited Dante while the latter was in exile in Ravenna, and that Dante influenced Giotto's painting of the Apocalypse in the Church of Santa Clara in Naples. The two were immediate contemporaries, Dante having been born in 1265 and Giotto probably in 1267. Both were members of the Arte dei Medici e Speziali guild in Florence, and both drew on the *Last Judgment* mosaic in the Florentine Baptistery (San Giovanni) when fashioning their respective iconographies of Hell.

is darkened"). Giotto died on 8 January 1337 in Florence.

Caron Cioffi

Statue of Giotto in Florence. Richard Lansing.

Unlike his teacher Cimabue, whose scenes are represented two-dimensionally, Giotto reconstructed three-dimensional space illusionistically on a two-dimensional surface. Thus, he gave his frescoes a naturalism and a tangibility that were lacking in Byzantine painting. Giotto's rebellion against traditional religious iconography led some early Dante critics to view Giotto's work as too middle-class and progressive for Dante's aristocratic and moral bent. However, recent scholars argue that Giotto's frescoes of the life of St. Francis in the Upper Church at Assisi (dated around 1290–1296) may have influenced Dante's portrayal of the saint in *Par.* 11. More important, critics now acknowledge the influence of Giotto's *Last Judgment* fresco in the Arena Chapel at Padua (completed by 1305) on Dante's descriptions of the punishments of the damned in the *Inferno* (completed by 1314). Dante has Oderisi, the miniaturist, mention Giotto in *Purg.* 11.94–95 as the painter who has surpassed Cimabue: *"Credette Cimabue ne la pittura / tener lo campo, e ora ha Giotto il grido, / sì che la fama di colui è scura"* ("Cimabue believed he held the field in painting, and now Giotto has the cry, so that the fame of the first

Giovanna

According to Dante, Giovanna was a lady loved by Guido Cavalcanti, Dante's closest friend and mentor; he introduces her in the *Vita Nuova,* where Love is followed by *una gentile donna, la quale era di famosa bieltade, e fue già molto donna di questo mio primo amico* ("a gentlewoman, noted for her beauty, who had been the much loved lady of my best friend," 24.3). Giovanna is presented as walking before Beatrice and is given the *senhal* "Primavera" (Spring), a nickname that does not appear in Cavalcanti's poetry. In Dante's poetic language, made more cogent by the order in which the two women are introduced in the poem, the etymology of both Giovanna's name and nickname assumes particular importance in the mind of the poet-narrator Dante. Literally, as John the Baptist preceded Christ the "true Light," Giovanna precedes Beatrice the "true Love." The notion of the Baptist preceding Christ is reinforced by the nickname "Primavera," which is a play on *prima verrà* ("will come first"). On another level, Giovanna, symbolizing Cavalcante's poetry, chronologically precedes Beatrice, symbolizing Dante's poetry.

Pina Palma

Giovanna, Daughter of Nino

The only child of Nino de' Visconti of Pisa and Beatrice d'Este, Giovanna (c. 1291–1339) became fatherless at age five. Soon after Visconti's death, Pisa stripped the girl of much of her substantial inheritance because of his affiliation with the Guelfs. Nevertheless, as heiress to Sardegna, Giovanna was a highly contested bride on the political marriage market. In 1308 she wed Rizzardo da Camino, lord of Treviso, who was assassinated in 1312. Impoverished and childless, Giovanna lived modestly on a subsidy provided by the city of Florence from 1323 until her death. In *Purg.* 8.71, Nino recalls his daughter with fondness as an innocent whose voice is heard in Paradise, exemplifying the continuing bond uniting the living and the dead and the value of prayer in the process of salvation. In contrast to his daughter, her mother is proposed as an image of feminine faithlessness,

G reflected in Beatrice's quick removal of her widow's weeds and subsequent remarriage.

Fiora A. Bassanese

Giovanna, Wife of Bonconte

Mentioned by Bonconte da Montefeltro. Having noted that neither Giovanna nor anyone else cares for him, he points to this neglect as the cause of having to walk in shame among his peers in the Ante-Purgatory (*Purg.* 5.89–90).

Antonio Illiano

Giraut de Bornelh

Considered the master troubadour in Dante's day, Giraut flourished during the twelfth century (career, 1165–1200). Dante identifies him as the exemplary Occitan poet of moral rectitude in *DVE* 2.2.8 (Gerardus de Bornello), thereby aligning himself with the troubadour. But the voice of Giraut, referred to as *quel di Lemosì* ("he of the Limousin"), is rejected in *Purg.* 26.115–120, where Dante links the poet to Guittone d'Arezzo. Critics have attributed Dante's change of heart to the troubadour's profile as a moralist, noting that the spurned Guittone was a poet who also developed moralistic themes in his verse.

Bibliography

Contini, Gianfranco. "Dante come personaggio-poeta della *Commedia*." In *Un'idea di Dante: Saggi danteschi*. Turin: Einaudi, 1976, pp. 33–62.

Barolini, Teodolinda. *Dante's Poets: Textuality and Truth in the Comedy*. Princeton: Princeton University Press, 1984.

Paterson, Linda M. *Troubadours and Eloquence*. Oxford: Clarendon Press, 1975.

Sharman, Ruth Verity. *The Cansos and Sirventes of the Troubadours Giraut de Borneil: A Critical Edition*. New York and Cambridge: Cambridge University Press, 1988.

Laurie Shepard

Glaucus

A fisherman from Boeotia, Glaucus *(Glauco)* is possessed by an uncontrollable urge to plunge into the sea after he consumes the juice of magical grass. According to Ovid *(Meta.* 13.898–968), the sea-divinities transform their new arrival into a deity by purging away his mortal nature in the water of a hundred streams, but Glaucus finds himself unable to remember or articulate the actual moment of deification. Dante likens his own metamorphosis, as he gazes upon Beatrice in *Par.* 1.67–69, to the change the potent grass effects in Glaucus; and, like Ovid's Glaucus, he expresses the impossibility of rendering in words the transformative experience of *trasumanar* ("transhumanizing," *Par.* 1.70).

Bibliography

Brownlee, Kevin. "Pauline Vision and Ovidian Speech in *Paradiso* 1." In *The Poetry of Allusion: Virgil and Ovid in Dante's "Commedia."* Edited by Rachel Jacoff and Jeffrey T. Schnapp. Stanford: Stanford University Press, 1991, pp. 202–213.

Hollander, Robert. *Allegory in Dante's "Commedia."* Princeton: Princeton University Press, 1969, pp. 213–219.

Singleton, Charles. *Dante Studies 2. Journey to Beatrice*. Baltimore: Johns Hopkins University Press, 1958, pp. 28–29.

Jessica Levenstein

Gluttons

Sinners who inhabit both Hell (the third circle, *Inf.* 6) and Purgatory (the sixth terrace, *Purg.* 22.130–24.154). Among the infernal gluttons only Ciacco, an unidentified contemporary and acquaintance of Dante from Florence, converses with the pilgrim. The others remain submerged in a foul-smelling muck, beaten down by an eternal cold rain mixed with hail and dirty snow, while the three-headed watchdog, Cerberus, lacerates and deafens them. Ciacco's prophecy of a Florence torn by discord and bloodshed foreshadows the events leading to Dante's political exile from the city in 1302.

In Purgatory six shades are named, including two poets who address the pilgrim. Their penitence consists of desiring forbidden and inaccessible fruit hanging from an inverted tree whose branches are bathed with refreshing water, likewise inaccessible. Voices within the trees cite examples of temperance from the Old and New Testaments and classical antiquity (*Purg.* 22.130–154), and examples of gluttony from classical mythology and the Old Testament (*Purg.* 24.103–126). The penitents are emaciated almost beyond recognition, their facial features resembling the written word *OMO* (man). They sing the Psalm "Labia mea Domine" ("Open my lips, O Lord," *Ps.* 50.17 [51.15]) as they circle the terrace (*Purg.* 23.10–33).

The first penitent who speaks is Forese Donati (died 28 July 1296), the son of Simone, from a politically prominent Florentine family. Friends and distant kin through Dante's wife, Gemma Donati, he and Dante exchanged insults in a series of six sonnets, the three by Forese being his only extant works. Forese points out other gluttons to the pilgrim and finally prophesies his brother Corso Donati's violent death (*Purg.* 23.85–117, 24.13–25, 70–97). Bonagiunta Orbicciani da Lucca (*Purg.* 24.19–20, 34–63, *DVE* 1.13), the pilgrim's second interlocutor, was a poet and notary of Lucca of the middle-to-late thirteenth century. His thirty-six extant poems represent a significant contribution to Tuscan lyric poetry before Dante; he is considered to be instrumental in bringing the Sicilian style of vernacular poetry to Tuscany. In the *Commedia* Bonagiunta calls forth Dante's statement on the role of inspiration in his creative process. He introduces the term *dolce stil novo* ("sweet new style") as he acknowledges the crucial difference between Dante and certain of his Sicilian and Tuscan predecessors, including Bonagiunta himself (*Purg.* 24.49-63).

The other named gluttons are members of the ecclesiastic aristocracy and the feudal nobility, all with powerful political connections: the French Pope Martin IV (1281–1285) was a close ally of Charles d'Anjou, king of Naples (*Purg.* 24.20–24); Ubaldino da la Pila, a Ghibelline leader of the Tuscan Ubaldini family, the brother of Cardinal Ottaviano degli Ubaldini and of Ugolino d'Azzo, and father of Archbishop Ruggieri, favored destroying Florence after the battle of Montaperti in 1260 (*Purg.* 24.28–29; cf. *Inf.* 10.120, 33.14, and *Purg.* 14.105); Bonifazio dei Fieschi, archbishop of Ravenna (1274–1295), was involved in papal-imperial politics (*Purg.* 24.29–30); and the Marchese degli Argogliosi was a nobleman of Forlì and podestà of Faenza in 1296 (*Purg.* 24.31–33).

Bibliography

Abrams, Richard. "Inspiration and Gluttony: The Moral Context of Dante's Poetics of the 'Sweet New Style.'" *MLN* 91 (1976), 30–59.

Dombroski, Robert S. "The Grain of Hell: A Note on Retribution in *Inferno* VI." *Dante Studies* 88 (1970), 103–108.

Mazzoni, Francesco. *Il canto VI dell'Inferno.* In *Nuove letture dantesche,* vol. 1. Florence: Le Monnier, 1966, pp. 133–181.

Piromalli, Antonio. *Il canto VI dell'Inferno.* In *Lectura Dantis Scaligera: Inferno.* Florence: Le Monnier, 1967, pp. 187–220.

Denise Heilbronn-Gaines

Gluttony

One of the seven capital sins, consisting in a disordered appetite for food and drink. When loved excessively food can become an end in itself, leading the soul away from God. Gluttony is one of the sins of concupiscence or material desire (lust, gluttony, and avarice); the other four sins (sloth, anger, envy, and pride) are spiritual and therefore more serious offenses (see *Purg.* 17.91–137 on Dante's analysis of sin).

Dante classifies sins in the above order of gravity from lust to pride, pride being the worst and the root of them all. In the early Middle Ages there was little consensus as to the exact order of classification. A minority of writers from Cassian (d. 448) to St. Bernard (d. 1153) considered lust to be graver than gluttony, but the majority, among them St. Gregory (d. 604), Hugh of St. Victor (d. 1141), St. Bonaventure (d. 1274), St. Thomas Aquinas (d. 1274), and Brunetto Latini (d. 1294) thought of gluttony as being more serious than lust, and these opinions had firmly established Dante's system by the thirteenth century.

The classification of gluttony as a greater evil than lust reflects a widespread medieval interpretation of Genesis 2.15–17 and 3.6, according to which Adam's sin was literally an excessive love of food and the initial occasion for yielding to the flesh in general. Since the food was offered to Adam by Eve, gluttony has sexual implications that link it causatively to lust—hence the emphasis on fasting as a means to salvation, reflected in medieval edifying literature and various monastic and church practices.

In Dante's *Commedia,* gluttony is punished in the third circle of Hell (*Inf.* 6) and expiated on the sixth terrace of Purgatory (*Purg.* 22.130–24.154). Whereas in Hell the damned gluttons flail about in filthy mud, tortured by Cerberus and howling like dogs (*Inf.* 6.7–21), the penitents in Purgatory joyfully suffer desire for forbidden fruit and flowing water that cover strange upside-down trees, descendants of the tree whose fruit was eaten by

Dante among the gluttonous in third circle of Hell. La comedia di Dante Aligieri, *with commentary by Alessandro Vellutello, published by Francesco Marcolini, Venice, 1544. Giamatti Collection: Courtesy of the Mount Holyoke College Archives and Special Collections.*

Eve (*Purg.* 22.130–141, 24.103–117). The reference to original sin in terms of Eve's role (24.116) evokes the connection between gluttony and lust.

The two principal themes of the gluttony cantos are politics and poetry. The latter informs the purgatorial cantos, whereas politics dominate *Inf.* 6. Here a glutton named Ciacco describes a politically torn Florence. He prophesies future hostilities and bloodshed accompanying the alternate rise and decline of the city's two political factions, thus implicitly forecasting Dante's exile in 1302 (*Inf.* 6.64–72). The political theme, again associated with prophecy, resurfaces in Purgatory when the glutton Forese Donati predicts the violent death of his brother Corso, an important instigator of Florentine factionalism, who as leader of the Black Guelfs was directly responsible for Dante's exile (*Purg.* 24.82–90).

The purgatorial cantos focus on the poetry of praise (cf. *VN* 18) and its opposite, the poetry of vituperation, through two minor thirteenth-century poets. The Florentine Forese Donati and Dante had once engaged in an exchange of personal insults in a series of six sonnets. Their meeting in Purgatory occasions expressions of deep friendship and sorrow for their former life together. Bonagiunta, from Lucca, whose love poetry fell short of the

ideal of praise, elicits Dante's definition of his inspired poetic style (*Purg.* 24.52–54). The verses in which Bonagiunta admits his own and other Italian vernacular poets' failure (*Purg.* 24.55–62) introduce the term *dolce stil novo* ("sweet new style"), later applied to Dante's lyric style.

The common thread that joins the gluttony cantos in the *Inferno* and *Purgatorio* is speech. The rhetorical art of persuasion is closely associated with politics; poets and prophets use rhythmic language. But whereas in the third circle of Hell Ciacco's prophetic voice emerges from a background of inarticulate doglike barking and howling, in Purgatory human voices speak and sing: Dante recognizes his friend Forese by his voice; mysterious voices from the inverted trees cite examples of temperance and gluttony. Furthermore, water, associated elsewhere in Dante with eloquence and poetic inspiration (*Inf.* 1.80; *VN* 19), stagnates in an impure mixture in Hell (*Inf.* 6.10–12) but flows clear in Purgatory (*Purg.* 22.136–138).

The association of gluttony with speech derives from the simple notion that both involve the mouth: food enters, words come out (cf. Matt. 15:11; Isidore of Seville, *Etym.* 11.1.49). The verse sung by the penitents in Purgatory ("Labia mea Domine," *Purg.* 23.11, "Open my lips, O Lord [and my mouth will announce your praise]," Ps. 50:17), confirms the inherent contrast between gluttony and speech, ideally words that praise the Lord.

Bibliography

Dombroski, Robert S. "The Grain of Hell: A Note on Retribution in *Inferno* VI." *Dante Studies* 88 (1970), 103–108.

Moore, Edward. "The Classification of Sins in the *Inferno* and *Purgatorio*." *Studies in Dante,* Second Series. Oxford: Clarendon Press, 1899; reprint, New York: Greenwood Press, 1968, pp. 152–208.

Denise Heilbronn-Gaines

Godfrey of Bouillon

Duke of Lower Lorraine, a charismatic leader of the first Crusade (1096–1099), and self-proclaimed "devotee of the Holy Sepulcher," Godfrey captured the Kingdom of Jerusalem and then governed it from 1099 until his death in 1100. Already legendary in Old French epics, or *chansons de geste,* of the so-called Crusade Cycle, his renown is implicit in Dante's first-name evocation of *'l duca Gottifredi* among the militant spirits, the defenders of the faith exalted in the heaven of Mars (*Par.* 18.47).

Donald Maddox

Gomita, Fra

Fra Gomita had a brilliant but ultimately ignoble career as the deputy of Nino de' Visconti, lord of Gallura in Sardegna. According to medieval commentators, such as the Anonimo Fiorentino, this Sardinian friar, having been entrusted with guarding a number of wealthy prisoners, instead accepted a large bribe and assisted in their escape. Visconti's subsequent investigation led to the hanging of Gomita in 1296. This final misbehavior appears to have crowned a lifetime marked by repeated abuse of power and sale of public offices, perpetrated because of Visconti's unshakable trust in his deputy. In *Inf.* 22.82 Dante presents Fra Gomita as the *vasel d'ogne froda* ("vessel of every fraud"), placing him among the grafters lying in pitch in the fifth bolgia of the eighth circle of Hell, for *barattier fu non picciol, ma sovrano* ("he was not a small barrator, but a champion," *Inf.* 22.87).

Fiora A. Bassanese

Grammar

To Dante, *gramatica* meant essentially two things: first, the art of binding speech by rules that stabilize it and make it fit to express high values; and second, the typical implementation of this process, that is, in Latin and Greek, the grammatical languages *par excellence,* but also in the vernacular, starting with Italian, once this new language has been "illustrated" with grammatical regularity (cf. *DVE* 1.1.2–3). Language, the coupling of sensible signs and meanings to which Dante referred as *razionalità,* finds in grammar the foundation of conventional standards which correct the "natural" mutability, and hence instability, of positive languages (*DVE* 1.3.2).

A detailed application is in *DVE* 2.6, where Dante exemplifies *constructio* or sentence structure. There he blends together language and style, grammar and rhetoric (and logic), and both ancient rhetorical theory and its medieval application, the *ars dictaminis.* Since his aim is to cover all of literature with poetry at its peak, this work is also one of poetics and relates to the medieval *poetriae,* another adaptation of ancient rhetoric. He constantly refers to both Latin (verse and prose) and vernacular composition—and for the latter his examples are mostly poetic, since vernacular prose was then still in its infancy.

Dante's notion of *gramatica* invests the role and nature of the *volgare illustre,* which as a regulated language might replace Latin but which has different formal characteristics. The vernacular is closer to the natural illiterate, unregulated idiom, and therefore it still partakes of the mutability that Latin transcended. We cannot assume that Dante postulated for the *illustre* the same degree of fixedness he claimed for Latin as a "dead language." Furthermore, like some of his contemporaries, Dante felt an intellectual and emotional tension between, on the one hand, the realization of the ephemeral quality of things natural and human, starting with language, and on the other hand, the effort to arrest this inexorable flux and stabilize cultural values. The poet perceived Latin, an artificial and literary language, as derived from the vernaculars, not *vice versa.* The relationship between the two is the linguistic subtext of *De vulgari eloquentia.*

After the classical treatises of Apollonius Dyscolus and Varro, unavailable to the Middle Ages and still partly lost, it was only with Dante that discussion of positive language was once again conducted within a theoretical framework. The only predecessors as far as the vernacular was concerned, the Provençal manuals, were concerned chiefly with the normative description of the *drecha parladura;* perhaps this was undertaken in order to protect the authenticity of the *langue d'oc* when, after the Albigensian war, poetic vitality was declining and threatened at home, and the language had "fallen" into the hands of foreign imitators, primarily in Northern Italy and Catalonia. Dante's new approach leaned not on these precedents but on the examples of scholastic speculation on the *modi significandi,* which he also applied to his new concern with regional realities. Thus, he had to start with a defense of local uses on the basis of the natural necessity of mutability and instability.

In *DVE* 1.9.11, speaking of the work of the inventors of grammar (*inventores gramatice facultatis*), Dante defines *gramatica* as "a certain immutable identity of language in different times and places" (*que quidem gramatica nichil aliud est*

G *quam quedam inalterabilis locutionis idemptitas diversis temporibus atque locis).* Rather than to universal speculative grammar, *idemptitas locutionis* must refer to the stable features of a positive *lingua regulata* that will be stabilized by rules and eloquence, to the point of serving as an effective medium of communication through time and space. Dante is not speaking of *scientia grammatica,* but of a language being used in a regulated way (not a primary concern of the *modistae*), so that we can understand past authors, be understood by posterity, and speak to distant fellow-citizens.

In the youthful *VN* 30.3–4, the notion had first appeared that some peoples, like the Latins and Greeks, had two languages (they were "diglossic"), namely a vernacular and a literary language. Other important statements on the subject occur in the *Convivio,* especially 2.13.10, and in *DVE* 1.2–19 (see 7–8 for theoretical principles). But Dante's last word on linguistics matters came in *Par.* 26.124–138, in the episode of Adam. Here the poet-thinker, through his revelation that Adam's language was not Hebrew and had already disappeared before the Tower of Babel, cast aside all notion of a stable natural language. He managed to leave behind him all the traditional modistic speculation on a theoretical perfect language, while taking his place as the first unequivocal proponent of a thoroughly historicistic view of language change. We realize Dante's originality when we note how the myth of the confusion and corruption of languages as punishment for the building of the Tower of Babel, a sin of pride, was repeated by writers through the end of the eighteenth century. Dante, instead, affirmed change as a "natural," general, and absolute law of language. Although this echoed preceding authorities, he took pride in the "boldness" of his sweeping formulation (*audacter testamur, DVE* 1.9.7). Nor was this for him merely an abstract scientific assertion: it was a solution to crucial sociolinguistic, cultural, and literary problems that were particularly close to his heart, including the legitimization of the vernacular for the highest cultural purposes.

Bibliography

Alessio, Gian Carlo. "La grammatica speculative e Dante." *Letture Classensi* 13 (1984), 69–88.

Corti, Maria. *Dante ad un nuovo crocevia.* Florence: Sansoni, 1981.

Mengaldo, Pier Vincenzo. *Linguistica e retorica di Dante.* Pisa: Nistri Lischi, 1978.

Pagani, Ileana. *La teoria linguistica di Dante: De vulgari eloquentia: discussioni, scelte, proposte.* Napoli: Liguori, 1982.

Scaglione, Aldo. "Dante and the *ars grammatica.*" In *The Divine Comedy and the Encyclopedia of Arts and Sciences: Acta of the International Dante Symposium,* 13–16 Nov. 1983. Hunter College, New York. Edited by G. Di Scipio and A. Scaglione. Amsterdam: John Benjamins, 1988, pp. 27–41.

Aldo Scaglione

Grandgent, Charles Hall

One of the foremost American Dante critics of the early twentieth century. A graduate of Harvard University, receiving his bachelor's degree in 1883, Grandgent (1862–1939) later became Harvard's resident Dante scholar as professor of Romance languages (1896–1932). He thus carried on a venerable university tradition that had already included among its distinguished Dantists such luminaries as Henry Wadsworth Longfellow, James Russell Lowell, and Charles Eliot Norton.

The author of more than twenty books, Grandgent produced four on Dante alone: in *Dante Alighieri* (1916, 1921) he studied the Florentine poet in the context of late medieval culture; *The Ladies of Dante's Lyrics* (1917) treated the interaction between Dante's emotional life and his symbolic art; *The Power of Dante* (1918) dealt with the poet's influence not only on faith and morality but also on poetic craftsmanship and diction; and *Discourses on Dante* (1924) gathered occasional poems and addresses clustered around the sexcentenary year, 1921. He also edited and annotated *The Divine Comedy* (1909; rev. ed. 1933).

Because of these books and his numerous articles, Grandgent became America's premier Dantist in the period from World War I to the outbreak of World War II. His service as president of the Dante Society of America from 1915 to 1932, the longest tenure of any of the Society's presidents, underscores this fact.

Grandgent's approach to the *Commedia* was eclectic. He viewed the poem as many genres blended into one. As he argued in the introduction to his edition of the *Commedia,* the work is first a medieval encyclopedia, "a practical compendium of human knowledge" in the tradition of Pliny's *Natural History* and St. Isidore of Seville's *Etymologies.* But it also falls into the categories of journey literature, in the vein of the *Voyage of St. Brendan;* vision literature, stretching from Virgil's trip to Hades, to St. Paul's vision (2 Cor. 12), to numerous medieval accounts of the otherworld; and even autobiography, calling to mind Augustine and Boethius. Finally, Grandgent often framed Dante's greatest work in light of literature written in praise of women, particularly Provençal lyrics, and as "mystic symbolism [combined] with formal allegory." The last view, emphasizing the allegorical nature of Dante's poem, helped set the stage for the allegorized readings of the *Commedia* that have dominated American Dante scholarship since World War II.

Bibliography

"A Bibliography of Charles Hall Grandgent's Writings." *PMLA* 47 (1932), 911–914.

McKenzie, Kenneth, et al. "Charles Hall Grandgent." *Speculum* 15 (1940), 379–381.

Wilkins, Ernest Hatch. "In Memory of Professor Grandgent." *Italica* 16 (1939), 159–161.

Madison U. Sowell

Gratian

Franciscus Gratianus *(Graziano),* born in Tuscany around 1090, became a Benedictine monk and was considered to have founded the science of canon law as a separate field. His *Decretum* (1140–1150), also called *Concordia Discordantium Canonum,* is a vast compilation of about four thousand *capitula,* presenting authoritative voices from sacred and secular sources. It is held together with summaries and commentaries in which he attempts to demonstrate the harmony between ecclesiastical and secular laws. In the Heaven of the Sun, Aquinas remarks, *"Quell'altro fiammeggiare esce del riso / di Grazïan, che l'uno e l'altro foro / aiutò sì che piace in Paradiso"* ("That next flame comes from the smile of Gratian, who helped the one and the other forum so well that Heaven is pleased," *Par.* 10.103–105); this highlights the importance of the *Decretum* for both civic and religious life.

Jo Ann Cavallo

Greeks

Dante thought of the Greeks as a political and linguistic group inhabiting a region—partly in Europe and partly in Asia (*DVE* 1.8.2)—roughly corresponding to the Balkan Peninsula and Asia Minor. Like the Romans, the Greeks possessed an artificial *gramatica* in addition to their natural, vernacular language (*DVE* 1.1.3). In the *Monarchia,* Dante portrays Greece, along with Carthage, as a nation that unsuccessfully challenged Rome for universal supremacy (2.9.18). The poet was acquainted with ancient Greek figures—both historical and fictional—primarily from their appearance in the works of major Latin authors (Cicero, Virgil, Ovid, Livy, Lucan, Statius) and, to a lesser extent, from medieval redactions, encyclopedias, florilegia, and available translations. In the *Commedia,* the vast majority of these Greek figures are confined to Limbo, the first circle of Hell. There Homer appears as the leader of a "lovely school" of classical poets (*Inf.* 4.86–96), and Aristotle heads a "philosophic family" of great thinkers, most of whom are Greek (*Inf.* 4.131–144). In the *Purgatorio,* Dante uses the encounter with Statius as an opportunity to expand the ranks of Greek literary authors in Limbo to include the playwright Euripides, the lyric poet Simonides, and the tragic poets Antiphon and Agathon (*Purg.* 22.106–108). Also joining Virgil in Limbo is a host of Greek literary characters, including Antigone, Manto, and Deidamia, who are drawn from Statius' *Thebaid* and *Achilleid* (22.109–114).

Notable among the few Greek figures who are more than names in the *Commedia* are the blasphemer Capaneus (*Inf.* 14.43–72), the "false Greek, Sinon of Troy" (*Inf.* 30.98), and, most important, Ulysses. In fact, with his presentation of Ulysses in *Inf.* 26, Dante raises in summary fashion the issue of the relationship between the ancient Greek world and the late European Middle Ages. When the pilgrim expresses his desire to address the "horned flame" containing Ulysses and Diomedes, Virgil responds that the request is a worthy one but that he, not Dante, must be the one to address the sinners: *"Lascia parlare a me, ch'i' ho concetto / ciò che tu vuoi; ch'ei sarebbero schivi, / perch'e' fuor greci, forse del tuo detto"* ("Let me speak, for I have conceived what you wish; for perhaps they would shun, because they were Greeks, your words," 26.73–75). Virgil's emphasis on the cultural (or linguistic) identity of his interlocutors finds its complement in the next canto, when he instructs the pilgrim to address a modern inhabitant of the eighth bolgia, Guido da Montefeltro: *"Parla tu: questi è latino"* ("You speak: this one is Italian," 27.33). Why the Greeks would respond to Virgil but perhaps not to Dante is a question that

G has spawned a vast array of responses, "some ingenious, some absurd, and none of them completely satisfactory" (Bosco and Reggio 386).

The more literal interpretations, favored by many of the early commentators, focus on the actual languages spoken and understood by Dante's characters. According to this line of reasoning, Virgil addresses Ulysses because he, unlike Dante, knows Greek and can therefore converse with the spirit in his native tongue. The Renaissance poet Torquato Tasso, followed by a few later commentators, thinks Virgil actually passes himself off as Homer in order to induce Ulysses to speak. Another critic, Daniel Donno, argues that Dante has Virgil speak Greek based on the myth of the Diomedean birds, Diomedes' transformed comrades who were friendly to Greeks and hostile to all others. The two major objections to these explanations are that, first, it is unclear how Dante would then be able to understand and report the Greek conversation; and, second, that in the next canto Guido identifies a word spoken by Virgil as from *lombardo,* an Italian dialect (27.20), although it is of course possible that Virgil could dismiss Ulysses in one language after first addressing him in another.

Others see a broader cultural issue at stake in Virgil's reference to the Greeks' possible disdain of Dante's speech. Recalling the proverbial haughtiness of the Greeks, some interpret Virgil's injunction to mean that Ulysses would consider Dante an enemy as a descendant of Troy by way of Rome (cf. *Inf.* 15.76–77), whereas Virgil's origins in Mantua (founded by the daughter of Tiresias, a Greek) make the Latin poet an acceptable interlocutor. The current trend of critical opinion follows Benvenuto da Imola's lead in noting that Virgil, as an epic poet of ancient Rome, served as Dante's source for knowledge of the Homeric heroes, even though, as Padoan and others have shown, Virgil actually condemns Ulysses in the *Aeneid.*

Bibliography

Bosco, Umberto, and Giovanni Reggio (eds.). *La Divina Commedia.* Vol. 1, *Inferno.* Florence: Le Monnier, 1979.

Donno, Daniel J. "Dante's Ulysses and Virgil's Prohibition: *Inferno* XXVI, 70–75." *Italica* 50.1 (1973), 26–37.

Fubini, Mario. "ll Canto XXVI dell'*Inferno.*" In *Letture dantesche.* Edited by Giovanni Getto. Vol. 1, *Inferno.* 2nd. ed. Florence: Sansoni, 1968, pp. 511–535.

Lipari, Angelo. "Parla tu, questi è latino." *Italica* 23.2 (1946), 65–81.

Padoan, Giorgio. "Ulisse 'fandi fictor' e le vie della Sapienza." *Studi danteschi* 37 (1960), 21–61.

Pagliaro, Antonino. *Ulisse: Ricerche semantiche sulla "Divina Commedia,"* vol. 1. Messina and Florence: G. D'Anna, 1967, pp. 433–464.

Guy P. Raffa

Gregory the Great

Saint, prefect of Rome in 573, and later pope. Not long after leaving the prefecture, Gregory (c. 540–604) donated all his earthly possessions to the Church, including substantial amounts of inherited property, and dedicated himself to a life of poverty. He became a monk in St. Andrew's monastery, formerly one of his family's estates on the Caeline Hill in Rome. Much against his will, Gregory was made pope in 590. He then initiated sweeping administrative reforms, purging the corrupt from papal offices and redistributing resources to assist the numerous victims of poverty, famine, and warfare (cf. *Epist.* 11.16). His consolidation of power and prestige earned him the reputation of being the most significant architect of the medieval papacy. During Gregory's reign, Christianity made great inroads into Spain, Africa, and England, and even among the Lombards in Italy, with whom there had been constant conflict. Although Gregory was a great proponent of the separation of spiritual and civic authority between papacy and empire, Dante does not mention him in the *Monarchia.* It is the literary Gregory who seems to have been most significant to the poet. The legend of Gregory's intercession in Trajan's redemption—Trajan being recalled to life from Hell in order to experience repentance—is noted twice (*Purg.* 10.73–75, *Par.* 20.106–111), and he is shown to be graceful in the recognition of his errors regarding the hierarchy of the angelic orders (*Par.* 28.133–135, cf. *Conv.* 2.5.5–13).

Bibliography

Evans, G. R. *The Thought of Gregory the Great.* Cambridge: Cambridge University Press, 1986.

Markus, Robert Austin. *Gregory the Great and His World.* Cambridge: Cambridge University Press, 1997.

Straw, C. E. *Gregory the Great.* Berkeley: University of California Press, 1988.

Vickers, Nancy J. "Seeing is Believing: Gregory, Trajan, and Dante's Art." *Dante Studies* 101 (1983), 67–85.

Michael Papio

Griffin

Dante's griffin appears in the procession which he witnesses in the Earthly Paradise, drawing the chariot of Beatrice which it later ties to the tree of Adam (*Purg.* 29.106–114, 32. 37–60). The griffin originated in ancient Egypt and the Middle East as the artistic motif of a lion with the head of a predatory bird. Information about it as a real animal was transmitted from Greek sources (mainly Herodotus in his account of Aristeas of Proconnesus) by Pliny, Solinus, and Virgil (*Eclogue* 8.26–28) to medieval writers and compilers and to some of the bestiaries. The Vulgate Bible includes the griffin among the unclean birds which Moses forbade the Israelites to eat (Lev. 11.13; Deut. 14.12). St. Isidore wrote, "The griffin is a winged animal and a quadruped. This species of wild beast is born in the Hyperborean Mountains. They are lions in every part of their bodies and resemble eagles in their faces and wings, and they are violently hostile to horses. They also tear men up on sight." In the Middle Ages, griffins were thought of as huge, fierce birds which lived in Scythia or India, where they greedily guarded gold or fought for emeralds with a one-eyed race of men called Arimaspians. When interpreted symbolically, they represented avarice (or warnings against it), devils, or tyrants.

Appearing in the procession in the Earthly Paradise, Dante's griffin draws a two-wheeled triumphal chariot yoked to its neck; it has immensely tall wings; and its birdlike parts are gold, the rest white mixed with red (*Purg.* 29.106–114, 30.8). After Beatrice's appearance in the chariot and Dante's confession and repentance, it is described as "the animal that is one person in two natures"; Dante then sees its two *reggimenti* (literally, "governments" or "regimes") miraculously alternating in its reflection from Beatrice's eyes, while the "double beast" remains the same (*Purg.* 31.80–81, 118–126). The griffin then draws the chariot to the bare tree of Adam, where it is praised for not having despoiled the tree with its beak; uttering words on the preservation of justice, it ties the chariot to the tree, which is renewed with leaves and flowers. Dante is lulled by music into an ecstatic sleep, and when he awakes, he is told that the griffin and most of the other processioners are ascending upward with sweeter and more profound song (*Purg.* 32.26–27, 43–60, 89–90, 95–96).

Since the time of the earliest commentators, Dante's griffin has been interpreted as a symbol of Christ (see *Purg.* 31.80–81): its aquiline parts represent Christ's divinity, its leonine parts his humanity; and the alternation of the two, reflected from Beatrice's eyes, is Dante's vision of the mystery of the incarnation. The griffin's tying of the chariot to the tree is seen as Christ's joining of his Church to divine justice, or obedience, or (for some critics) the Roman Empire.

If accepted, this reading must be considered an unprecedented and even unsuitable invention by Dante. It is contradicted by the Bible (including the substitution of the griffin for the lamb in Rev. 5.6), by contemporary beliefs concerning griffins, and by other anomalies, including the subordinate relationship of the griffin to Beatrice in the narrative. Even so, alternative interpretations have been relatively few. They include regarding the binary griffin as a symbol of the union of the two *reggimenti,* the spiritual and the temporal, in the leadership of the Christian community (Aroux, Grieben, Bergmann; see *Purg.* 16.128), or as the combined priestly and kingly powers of the papacy (Didron, Barelli, Fransoni—readings which entirely contradict Dante's doctrine of the separation of the two earthly powers); as the harmony of Dante's own spiritual and sensitive powers (Hardie); as chastity and Dante's *daimon,* guiding his soul (Dronke); or as the union of the divine and the human, the imperial and the popular powers in Dante's conception of ideal Rome, its empire, and its Christlike prince, the agent of the redemption at Christ's birth and death, and the guide to temporal happiness in the Earthly Paradise (Armour).

Bibliography

Armour, Peter. "La spuria fonte isidoriana per l'interpretazione del grifone dantesco." *Deutsches Dante-Jahrbuch* 67 (1992), 163–168.

———. *Dante's Griffin and the History of the World: A Study of the Earthly Paradise ('Purgatorio,' cantos xxix–xxxiii).* Oxford: Clarendon Press, 1989.

G

Bergmann, Frédéric Guillaume. *Dante: Sa vie et ses oeuvres.* 2nd ed., Strasburg: Schmidt, 1881, pp. 317–321.

Chierici, Joseph. *Il grifo dantesco.* Rome: De Luca, 1967.

La Comédie de Dante. Translated and edited by Eugène Aroux. Paris: Renouard, 1856–1857, vol. 1, pp. 561–562, n. 27.

Cristaldi, Sergio. "'Per Dissimilia': Saggio sul Grifone dantesco." In *Arcadia, Accademia Letteraria Italiana, Atti e Memorie,* ser. 3. vol. 9, fasc. 1 *(Studi in onore di Giorgio Petrocchi).* Rome, 1988–1989, pp. 57–94.

Didron, Adolphe Napoléon. *Iconographie chrétienne.* Paris: Imprimerie Royale, 1843, p. 323.

———. *Christian Iconography.* Translated by E. J. Millington. London: Bohn, 1851; repr. New York: Ungar, 1965, vol. 1, p. 317.

Dronke, Peter. "*Purgatorio* XXIX." In *Cambridge Readings in Dante's 'Comedy.'* Edited by K. Foster and P. Boyde. Cambridge: Cambridge University Press, 1981, pp. 114–137.

Hardie, Colin. "The Symbol of the Griffin in *Purgatorio* XXIX.108 and Following Cantos." In *Centenary Essays on Dante.* Oxford: Oxford University Press, 1965, pp. 103–131.

Isidore, St. *Etymologiarum libri XX, XII.2.17.* In *Patrologia latina.* Edited by J.-P. Migne, vol. 82, col. 436.

Mazzoni, Francesco. "Il canto XXXI del *Purgatorio.*" In *Lectura Dantis Scaligera: Purgatorio.* Florence: Le Monnier, 1971, p. 1166.

Oldroyd, Drina. "Hunting the Griffin in Dante's *Purgatorio.*" *Spunti e ricerche* 2 (1986), 46–65.

Peter Armour

Griffolino

This alchemist from Arezzo, placed among the falsifiers in Hell, furiously claws at scabs on his body, while seated back to suppurating back with Capocchio (*Inf.* 29.85). Griffolino speaks less of his alchemy, which places him in the tenth bolgia of Malebolge, than of the act that brought him to the stake: he deceitfully claimed that he could fly and promised to teach a literal-minded Albert of Siena the art. When he could not keep his false promise, Albert had him denounced as a magician and burned alive. In death, his skin seems on fire for his principal act of falsification, that of alchemy.

Roy Rosenstein

Guccio de' Tarlati

The Tarlati family of Pietramala headed the Ghibelline faction in Arezzo. Dante makes no direct reference to them, but early commentators identify a man Dante encounters in the Ante-Purgatory as Guccio, an otherwise unknown Tarlati. Dante says that he drowned while in pursuit of (or being pursued by) enemies; commentators specify that he drowned in the Arno during an engagement with the Bostoli, Guelf exiles from Arezzo (*Purg.* 6.15).

Pamela J. Benson

Guelfs

The Guelfs were a thirteenth-century Italian political faction, the opponents of the Ghibellines. The factions derived from local political rivalries in the late twelfth-century towns. During the period of intense conflict between the papacy and the Holy Roman emperor in the 1240s, local factions gradually joined together to form party alliances. The supporters of the political and territorial ambitions of the papal curia and its allies formed a *pars ecclesiae,* literally a party of the church, in opposition to those who backed the efforts of Holy Roman emperors to establish hegemony over northern Italy. The name "Guelf" derived from one of the rivals for the imperial throne at the end of the twelfth century—Otto of Brunswick, who belonged to the Welf dynasty and was for a time allied with Pope Innocent III against Philip of Swabia of the Hohenstaufen. By 1268, a Guelf alliance that included the papacy, the Angevins, and Tuscan bankers, defeated the Hohenstaufens. The Guelf alliance, with fluctuations, remained dominant for a half-century.

Origins

Factional antagonisms developed in the towns in a period marked by the weakness of outside authority. The late twelfth and thirteenth centuries saw rapid urban growth and the invention of new civic institutions. Rising families competed to control civic offices that gave access to wealth and power. They were quick to resort to violence. The Florentine factions ultimately derived from networks of political and military alliance that formed the basis of a civil war in 1177.

Chroniclers attributed the origins of the Guelfs and Ghibellines in Florence to a vendetta on Easter morning of 1215/1216 over a broken marriage engagement (see *Par.* 16.140–141). In the version written by the Florentine Dino Compagni about 1310, a young noble named Buondelmonte de' Buondelmonti agreed to marry the daughter of Oderigo Giantruffetti. (In earlier versions she is instead called the daughter of an Amidei.) Buondelmonte was coaxed by Aldruda Donati to marry one of her beautiful daughters instead. When he succumbed to temptation and took her advice, Oderigo and his kinsmen and allies, the Uberti, avenged the insult by murdering Buondelmonte on his wedding day. "As a result of this death," Dino wrote, "the citizens became divided, and relatives and allies were drawn in on both sides so that there was no end to this rift, from which many fights and murders and civil battles were born." The Donati and Buondelmonti families were in fact leaders of the Florentine Guelf faction; a century later, it was Corso Donati who led the Black Guelfs and drove Dante and the Whites from Florence.

As the legend of their origins suggests, factional conflicts were a volatile blend of social and political competition. Political and economic interests combined with family hatreds and loyalties. In the mid-thirteenth century, when the two factions became linked with the papal and imperial causes, they retained their roots in neighborhood rivalries. The Guelf chronicler Giovanni Villani described the outbreak of fighting between Guelfs and Ghibellines in Florence in 1248 in terms of "battle points" in the city's parishes. Fighting tended to break out between neighboring families that had been in competition for decades. This element of personal and neighborhood rivalry helps to explain the bitterness of factional struggles. When one side was victorious, they not only took control of civic offices but also sought to eradicate their enemies from the city through exile and destruction of their homes and property.

The Guelf Alliance

The Florentine Guelfs are best understood against the background of international politics. In the first half of the century, the Holy Roman Emperor Frederick II held not only the German empire but also the kingdom of Naples and Sicily, and he was able to expand his effective jurisdiction in northern Italy. After his death, his illegitimate son, Manfred, by 1258 was able to establish control over the southern kingdom of Naples and Sicily. In the 1260s, two French popes sought to counterbalance Hohenstaufen power by importing a French prince to replace Manfred as king of Naples. Charles, count of Anjou and brother of the French monarch Louis IX, agreed to lead a military expedition. The effort was supported by funds borrowed from Florentine bankers, to be repaid with papal revenues from taxation of the clergy in northern France. The plan was made by Urban IV (1261–1264) and pursued by Clement IV (1265–1268). Charles was crowned king of Naples, and with a French army supported by Tuscan Guelf troops led by Count Guido Guerra, he defeated Manfred at the Battle of Benevento (referred to in *Purg.* 3). In 1268, when Charles defeated Manfred's nephew Conradin at the Battle of Tagliacozzo, and then killed the youth, he effectively destroyed the Hohenstaufen cause.

The alliance of the papacy, Tuscan bankers, Naples, and France succeeded in establishing a Guelf hegemony that lasted almost a half-century. The Tuscan cities, with the exceptions of Pisa and Arezzo, became Guelf; Tuscan Guelfs became, as George Holmes writes, the natural bankers of the popes, trading in Naples, northern France, and Flanders as well. Charles of Anjou wielded considerable power from 1267 to 1277 as imperial vicar in Tuscany. Like Frederick II a few decades before, he held power both north and south of the papal state. In effect, from the perspective of the papacy Hohenstaufen had been replaced with Angevin. Some popes began efforts to conciliate the Ghibellines as a counterweight to the Angevins. Angevin power declined precipitously after the 1282 uprising in Sicily known as the Sicilian Vespers (referred to in *Par.* 8.67–75). Tuscany remained predominantly Guelf and under Florentine influence. The Guelf domination of Tuscany set the stage for the expansion of Florentine power in the region in the course of the next century.

Guelf Fortunes within Florence

The Florentine Guelfs suffered two periods of exile. In the 1240s, the rise of imperial influence and the appointment of the Ghibelline podestà Frederick of Antioch led in 1248 to open civil war and Guelf exile, which lasted until Ghibelline rule in Florence was supplanted by a popular regime, the Primo Popolo, in 1250. In 1260, exiled Ghibellines in alliance with Siena defeated

G the Florentine militia at the bloody Battle of Montaperti and captured the city (see *Inf.* 10.85–86). The new Ghibelline regime systematically destroyed the palaces, shops, and towers of the leading Guelf families of the city. A detailed record exists in the *Liber Extimationum,* a list of Guelf claims for compensation for their destroyed and damaged properties.

In 1268, after the military successes of Charles of Anjou and the Guelf alliance, the Guelfs took power in Florence. The Ghibelline leadership was exiled and their towers and palaces demolished. Roughly three to four thousand people were exiled from Florence; many never returned. The Guelf regime lasted for a decade but was unstable owing both to divisions within the Guelf leadership and pressure from the exiled Ghibellines. The papacy had come to view Florence as a bastion of Guelf power and a counterweight to Angevin ambitions, and it was concerned enough over Florentine instability to attempt a factional reconciliation. In 1273, Gregory X personally brought the two factions together to make a peace that did not, however, outlast the papal visit to Florence. In 1279 a papal legate, Cardinal Latino Malabranca, succeeded in replacing Guelf rule with a bipartisan government. It was unstable, and within three years Florentines had replaced it with the Priorate, a system based not in factional but in guild membership, reflecting the real structure of power in the late thirteenth-century city.

When the Dominican preacher Fra Remigio de' Girolami described the factions, he characterized a Ghibelline as a lion and a Guelf as a calf— an unwarlike, sacrificial animal. In fact, the research of Sergio Raveggi and Massimo Tarassi has shown that the Guelf elite like the Ghibellines were lions, if that meant nobles trained in the military. Leaders tended to be landed nobility, including families like the Adimari, Pazzi, and Buondelmonti. The shape of the Guelf party changed significantly after 1260: the list of men exiled from Florence after the Battle of Montaperti included not only the older nobility and consular aristocracy, but also men from recent commercial and banking houses who had been active in the Primo Popolo. Initially most were not papal partisans so much as opponents of the imperial faction. However, many Florentine bankers quickly became intertwined with papal interests: between 1263 and 1265, roughly 146 members of Florentine merchant and banking companies took oaths of obedience to the pope. This meant that the wealthy new class of men involved in the large banks and commercial houses became substantially Guelf.

The Florentine Parte Guelfa

The Guelf party existed from the 1240s as a corporate institution with captains and councils. From 1267 to 1280, the party dominated the commune and civic offices. After the establishment of the Priorate and guild-based rule, it persisted as a private corporate group. The wealth of the party helps to explain its considerable influence: after 1266, the property of the exiled Ghibellines was divided into three parts. One-third went to the commune and one-third to compensate Guelfs for their losses, and the final third went into the keeping of the Guelf Party. After 1280, although the party ceased to be a formal part of Florentine government, it kept control of the money. These substantial resources were loaned to the commune under specific conditions, a practice that enabled the Guelf party to wield political influence. In 1288 the commune owed the Guelf party the enormous sum of thirteen thousand gold florins, probably loaned in support of the war against the Tuscan Ghibellines. Popular efforts to bring the resources of the Parte Guelfa under the control of the civic government failed.

Blacks and Whites

Between 1295 and 1300, two factions within the Guelfs developed and came to be known as Blacks and Whites, names adopted from factions in nearby Pistoia. Their conflict began, according to contemporary accounts, with animosity and social rivalry between the aristocratic Corso Donati, who came to lead the Blacks, and the nouveau-riche banker Vieri dei Cerchi, of the Whites. They represented extreme versus moderate Guelf ideology. The Blacks chose uncompromising fidelity to the Guelf alliance and were strongly supported by Pope Boniface VIII. The Whites tended to be new men who, as Hyde writes, were "no longer dominated by memories of Montaperti and Benevento." Some had economic ties within Ghibelline regions. When Boniface sent Charles of Valois (brother to the French king Philip the Fair) to pacify the city, he instead allowed the Blacks to attack their opponents, which led to the tragic exile of Dante and the White leadership from Florence. In exile, the Whites effectively became identified with the Ghibellines.

Fourteenth-Century Views of the Factions

By the fourteenth century, as J. K. Hyde writes, the Parte Guelfa had become "the censor and guardian of political orthodoxy in Florence," keeping the town loyal to the Church and the Angevins. To be a good Florentine meant to be a good Guelf. Guelfs came to be characterized as the defenders of liberty: the chronicler Matteo Villani wrote that they were opposed to all tyranny. Over time, however, writers recognized that party alliances had lost their ideological meaning. The Lombard Pietro Azarii wrote in the mid-fourteenth century, "I have seen worse things done by Guelfs among themselves than against Ghibellines, and vice versa." If the two factions did not exist, he commented, two worse ones would come into being. When Bartolo da Sassoferrato wrote, around 1355, a treatise "On Guelfs and Ghibellines," he derived the conflict from the twelfth-century struggles between the papacy and Frederick Barbarossa, but he argued that the factions by his own day had become simply names for local rivalries and alliances. A Guelf was someone who adhered to the Guelf party, a choice that had come to be dictated by local allegiances rather than any affection for the Church.

Bibliography

Historical Texts

Bartolo da Sassoferrato. "De Guelphis et Gebellinis." In *Politica e diritto nel trecento italiano: Il "De Tyranno" di Bartolo da Sassoferrato* by Diego Quaglioni. Florence: Olschki, 1983.

Compagni, Dino. "La Cronica di Dino Compagni." Edited by Isidoro del Lungo. In *Rerum Italicarum Scriptores*. New Ed., Città di Castello, 1907–1916, vol. 9, part 2. Translated into English by Daniel Bornstein as *Dino Compagni's Chronicle of Florence*. Philadelphia: University of Pennsylvania Press, 1986.

Latini, Pseudo-Brunetto. "Cronica Florentina." In *I Primi due secoli della storia di Firenze*. Edited by Pasquale Villari. Florence: Sansoni, 1898, vol. 2, pp. 195–269.

Stefani, Marchionne di Coppo. "Cronaca Fiorentina." Edited by Niccolò Rodolico. In *Rerum Italicarum Scriptores*. New ed., Città di Castello, 1903–1955, vol. 30, part 1.

Villani, Giovanni. *Cronica: Con le continuazioni di Matteo e Filippo*. Edited by Giovanni Aquilecchia. Turin: Einaudi, 1979.

Critical Texts

Caggese, Romolo. "Sull'origine della Parte Guelfa e le sue relazioni col comune." *Archivio storico italiano,* ser. 5, 32 (1903), 265–309.

Davidsohn, Robert. *Geschichte von Florenz*. Berlin: E. S. Mittler und Sohn, 1896–1927. Translated into Italian by Giovanni Battista Klein as *Storia di Firenze*. Florence: Sansoni, 1956–1968.

Del Lungo, Isidoro. "Una vendetta in Firenze il giorno di San Giovanni del 1295." *Archivio storico italiano,* ser. 4, no. 18 (1886), 355–409.

Fasoli, Gina. "Guelfi e Ghibellini di Romagna nel 1280–81." *Archivio storico italiano,* ser. 5, 94 (1936), 157–180.

Heers, Jacques. *Parties and Political Life in the Medieval West*. Amsterdam and New York: North-Holland, 1977.

Holmes, George. *Florence, Rome and the Origins of the Renaissance*. Oxford: Clarendon Press, 1986.

Hyde, J. K. "Contemporary Views on Faction and Civil Strife in Thirteenth- and Fourteenth-Century Italy." In *Violence and Civil Disorder in the Italian Cities, 1200–1500*. Edited by Lauro Martines. Berkeley and Los Angeles: University of California Press, 1972, pp. 273–307.

Jordan, Edouard. *Les Origines de la domination angevine en Italie*. Paris: Picard, 1909.

Lansing, Carol. *The Florentine Magnates: Lineage and Faction in a Medieval Commune*. Princeton: Princeton University Press, 1991.

Ottokar, Nicola. *Il comune di Firenze alla fine del Dugento*. 2nd ed. Turin: Einaudi, 1962.

Raveggi, Sergio, Massimo Tarassi, Daniela Medici, and Patrizia Parenti. *Ghibellini, Guelfi e Popolo Grasso: I detentori del potere politico a Firenze nella seconda metà del Dugento*. Florence: La Nuova Italia, 1978.

Carol Lansing

Guido Cavalcanti

Poet and aristocrat, friend of Dante, and ardent Guelf, Cavalcanti was born between 1250 and 1255 and later married a daughter of Farinata degli Uberti. He composed one of the most difficult philosophical poems in the Italian language, the canzone "Donna me prega." Because his death occurred in August 1300, after the fictive date of Dante's vision, he does not appear in the *Commedia*.

G Cavalcanti is described as philosopher and *speculativus . . . auctoritatis non contemnendae in physicis* ("a thinker of no mean authority on the natural sciences") by a tradition that includes Giovanni and Filippo Villani, and by Giovanni Boccaccio as a *filosofo naturale* ("natural philosopher"), an Epicurean, and an unbeliever. In light of Nardi's and Corti's important studies, it is impossible today to deny that Cavalcanti's poetry is rooted in Averroistic philosophy, which spread through Europe beginning in the first half of the thirteenth century. Averroistic philosophy, which influenced Parisian thinkers like Siger of Brabant, Boethius of Dacia, and others active in Bologna, shapes the poetry of Cavalcanti and "Donna me prega" in particular. This poem utilizes tools of logic applied to natural philosophy in order to define the ontology of love, and the extent of its importance for Dante is still an open topic for scholars. It may be assumed, however, that the full meaning of Cavalcanti's work for Dante, initially as an object of fascination and later as representing philosophical views he opposed, is more latent than manifest, particularly in the *Commedia*.

At the beginning of the *Vita Nuova,* Dante depicts Cavalcanti as his *primo amico* ("first friend," 3.14). As Dante indicates, their friendship began when he sent Cavalcanti his poem "A ciascun' alma presa e gentil core," receiving an answer in the sonnet "Vedeste, al mio parere, onne valore." Most significantly, in *VN* 24 Dante analogizes Cavalcanti's lady, Giovanna, called "Primavera," to Giovanni (John the Baptist), "who will come first" *(prima verrà),* suggesting that Giovanna heralds Beatrice as John heralds Christ. The first sign of rupture in their friendship is apparent in Cavalcanti's sonnet "Io vegno a te infinite volte ne lo giorno," probably written shortly after the *Vita Nuova.*

One aspect to be evaluated is Dante's tepid reaction to "Donna me prega," a poem recalled in *De vulgare eloquentia* as a strong example of a *canzone* written in hendecasyllables (2.11.12) rather than of a *canzone illustre,* for which Dante chooses "Poi che di doglia" as an exemplar (2.6.6). Considering that in *DVE* Dante ranks Cino da Pistoia as the most important poet, we may ascribe Dante's tepidity to the break between the two poets. According to some scholars, this break occurred not just for literary or philosophical reasons, but as a result of political positions Dante

took as a member of the Florentine government, which ultimately brought about Cavalcanti's exile from the city, in June of 1300, to Sarzana in Lunigiana, along with other leaders of the White Guelfs. Although the exile was brief, Cavalcanti fell ill during his stay in Sarzana and died shortly before his return to Florence in August.

Whatever the reasons for the break, Cavalcanti has a central place in Dante's *Vita Nuova.* He is also the inspiration for some of the *canzoni* in the *Convivio,* although in these texts we can trace the gradual change from friendship to opposition. In these compositions Dante maintains that mind and body, sense and intellect, are integrated, whereas Cavalcanti, in "Donna me prega" for example, conceives of them as separated and opposing elements. Dante's *Commedia,* whose idea of love is rooted in superior transcendent values, represents a rejection of Cavalcanti's theory of love as determined by the physics of the body.

In *Purg.* 24.52–54, Dante's assertion of his poetics as deeply inspired by a love which *ditta dentro* ("dictates within") appears once more to be related to the poet's need to explain his idea of poetry while establishing a distance between himself and the poetry written before him, specifically that of Cavalcanti. This distance is underscored in two other places in the *Commedia* where Cavalcanti is recalled: in *Inf.* 10, during Dante's conversation with Cavalcanti's father Cavalcante de' Cavalcanti; and in *Purg.* 11.97, where he is mentioned in connection with Guido Guinizzelli. The *gloria della lingua* ("glory of our language") is recalled here in order to announce that just as Guido Cavalcanti has surpassed the glory of Guido Guinizzelli, a third poet is going to surpass both. Whoever the third poet might be, it is evident that Guido Cavalcanti and the *dolce stil novo* ambience in general are here confirmed as important historical references which are nonetheless about to be surpassed. The context in which Cavalcanti is recalled in *Inf.* 10, where his father is portrayed as an "Epicurean" who believed that the soul died with the body (10.15), suggests that philosophical differences motivated the break-up of the two poets.

Bibliography

Barolini, Teodolinda. *Dante's Poets: Textuality and Truth in the Comedy.* Princeton: Princeton University Press, 1984.

Castle at Poppi, a stronghold of the Conti Guidi. Source: Richard Lansing.

Cavalcanti, Guido. *Rime, con le Rime di Iacopo Cavalcanti.* Edited by Domenico de Robertis. Turin: Einaudi, 1986.

———. *The Poetry of Guido Cavalcanti.* Edited and translated by Lowry Nelson, Jr. New York: Garland, 1986.

Corti, Maria. *Dante a un nuovo crocevia.* Florence: Sansoni, 1981.

———. *La felicità mentale.* Turin: Einaudi, 1983.

Nardi, Bruno. "L'Averroismo del primo amico di Dante." In *Dante e la cultura medievale.* Bari: Laterza, 1942; reprint, 1985.

Maria Luisa Ardizzone

Guido Guerra

One of the Conti Guidi, an ancient feudal family of Tuscany whose heads were counts Palatine. Born around 1220, he was a grandson of Count Guido the Elder and a great-grandson of the Florentine Messer Bellincione Berti dei Ravegnani (see *Par.* 15.112–113, 16.94–99). Although he spent his youth at the imperial court, he subsequently became a protagonist of Tuscan Guelfism, principally as a soldier. In 1260 he tried unsuccessfully to dissuade Guelf Florence from marching on Siena. He survived the defeat at Montaperti, took refuge in Romagna, and in 1266 led four hundred knights in the army of Charles of Anjou at Benevento, where his role was decisive in Manfred's defeat. He was thus the restorer of Guelf fortunes in Florence, and he returned there in triumph the following year. He died in 1272.

Guido is placed in Hell among the sodomites (*Inf.* 16.34), although the basis of that collocation is unknown to us. Dante nonetheless has great respect for him: as the *Commedia*'s protagonist, he is told in *Inf.* 16.36 and 39 that Guido was *di grado maggior che tu non creda* ("of higher degree than you think") and that he achieved *con senno assai e con la spada* ("much with wisdom and the sword").

John C. Barnes

Guido II of Romena

One of the Guidi counts (d. 1292), who, along with his brothers Alessandro, Aghinolfo, and Ildebrandino, employed Master Adam to counterfeit

G

the gold florin. He is placed with him in the lowest pit of Malebolge (*Inf.* 30.77).

Donna Yowell

Guido da Castello

Guelf nobleman of the Roberti di Reggio Emilia faction, born between 1233 and 1235 and still living in 1315. He is named by Marco Lombardo in Purgatory, together with Currado da Palazzo and Gherardo da Camino, as one of three old men in whom true nobility is still preserved, a quality for which Dante praises him again in *Conv.* 4.16.6. In calling him *il semplice Lombardo* ("the simple Lombard," *Purg.* 16.126), Marco honors him for his simplicity in the French sense of the word, meaning that he is loyal and unassuming, or candid. Benvenuto suggests that during his exile Dante was once his guest.

Richard Lansing

Guido da Montefeltro

Renowned Ghibelline captain whose astute military and political sense allowed him to dominate much of the Romagna region in the last quarter of the thirteenth century. Dante places him in the eighth bolgia of the eighth circle of Hell, Malebolge, as Ulysses's contemporary counterpart among the fraudulent counselors (*Inf.* 27).

The chroniclers consistently hail Guido as an extraordinarily able strategist, respected statesman, and noble character (see in particular Giovanni Villani, 7.80.44; Dino Compagni 2.33; Salimbene da Parma, ed. Bernini, Scalia, 2, p. 224). Born around 1220, he was in Rome in 1268 as vicar of Corradino, Frederick II's grandson. Having taken charge of the Ghibellines of Romagna after the expulsion of the Lambertazzi (a Ghibelline clan) from Bologna in 1274, Guido first asserted his might in a stunning victory over the Guelf Geremei under Malatestino da Rimini in June 1275 at Ponte San Procolo, between Faenza and Imola. He succeeded in ousting the Malatesta from Cesena with another victory at nearby Raversano in September of that same year. As captain of Forlì in 1276, Guido held the reins of all antipapal power in Romagna. Pope Martin IV laid siege to Forlì in 1282 with a formidable alliance of Angevin and Geremei forces led by the French general Jean d'Eps. Under Guido's shrewd command, the defenders held out at length, scored significant vic-

tories, and exacted heavy casualties among the French troops (*Inf.* 27.43–44). Nonetheless, Forlì eventually fell in 1283 as most of Romagna submitted to papal rule. Guido himself was compelled to accept the authority of Honorius IV three years later and withdraw to Piedmont.

But this apparent defeat merely closed the first chapter on a life of high ambition. As in a more fateful moment later in life, Guido's retreat from worldly affairs in the mid-1280s proved only temporary. Suffering excommunication, he returned to action as captain of the Pisan Ghibellines in 1288 and aided Pisa in its struggles against Florence for the next five years. Master of Urbino in 1292, he successfully warded off the aggressions of Malatestino, then podestà (governor) of Cesena. In hopes of calming hostilities in Romagna and undoubtedly eager to cap the career of an energetic enemy leader, Pope Boniface VIII admitted Guido back into the Church in 1296 so that he could enter the Franciscan order and retreat once and for all, it appeared, from secular pursuits.

The following year Boniface found himself in the grip of a fierce struggle with the powerful Roman Colonna family, who questioned the circumstances surrounding Celestine V's abdication (see *Inf.* 3.60) and thus disputed the legitimacy of Boniface's rule. Excommunicated, they had taken refuge in their hilltop fortress at Penestrino (now Palestrina) about twenty miles southeast of Rome, where they managed to hold out against papal forces until 1298. In September of that year, Boniface called on Guido for advice on how to take the fortress. Guido suggested that Boniface first promise his enemies complete amnesty in order to draw them out of their defensive position and then simply renege on his promise, the fraudulent counsel for which Dante condemns him. Indeed, Villani (8.23) reports that Boniface razed Palestrina immediately after the Colonna's surrender and, according to Buti, he continued to persecute them.

Scholars generally accept the historicity of Guido's false counsel after the studies of Torraca, Parodi, and Massèra. Specifically, a passage from Riccobaldo da Ferrara's *Historiae*, which was written before 1313 and thus not possibly of Dantean extraction, relates the entire episode along with Guido's aphoristic words of wisdom: *Multa promittite, pauca servate de promissis* ("Promise many things, keep few of the things promised"), which anticipate *Inf.* 27.110, *lunga promessa con l'attender corto* ("a long promise with a short keeping").

Ironically, Dante's Boniface was already well-acquainted with the efficacy of hollow promises, for he had penetrated Guido's own wary defenses with just such a strategy. In Dante's scenario, Boniface convinces Guido to overlook his recently donned spirituality by promising him absolution for all future transgressions (*Inf.* 27.101), a promise he evidently could not keep. In *Conv.* 4.28.8, Dante had sung Guido's praises as *lo nobilissimo nostro latino Guido montefeltrano* ("the most noble of our Italians, Guido of Montefeltro") and offered him and Lancelot as illustrations of men who wisely disengaged from human affairs as they approached the end of life's temporal arc: *Bene questi nobili calaro le vele de le mondane operazioni, che ne la loro lunga etade a religione si rendero, ogni mondano diletto e opera diponendo* ("These noble men did indeed lower the sails of their worldly preoccupations and late in life gave themselves to religious orders, forsaking all worldly delights and affairs"). Guido again employs the nautical metaphor to characterize his decision to retire to the convent in *Inf.* 27.79–81.

Dante focuses his poetic lens on the arduously computed second reckoning that brought about Guido's fall, as well as on Guido's own retrospective recognition of his self-deceiving miscalculations (see *Inf.* 27.69 and 84). Employing Ciceronian metaphors (*De officiis* 1.13.41) that will resurface in Machiavelli, Dante's Guido defines his lifetime strategizing as foxlike, not leonine, thus emphasizing the mental industry that underlay his error. (We are told by an anonymous Pisan chronicler that Guido's Florentine adversaries had nicknamed him "the Fox.")

Canto 27 is thus couched, quasiparodically, in the language of syllogistic refinement (see in particular 27.72) climaxing in the wonderfully spiteful triumph of the black cherubim in verses 118–123: *ch'assolver non si può chi non si pente, / né pentere e volere insieme puossi, / per la contradizion, che nol consente. / . . . Forse / tu non pensavi ch'io lóico fossi!* ("for he cannot be absolved who does not repent, nor can one repent and will together, because of the contradiction, which does not permit it. . . . Perhaps you did not think I was a logician!"). This last-minute contest between St. Francis and the dark angel over Guido's soul will undergo parodic reversal in a similar scene involving Guido's son, Bonconte, in *Purg.* 5.

But for all that Guido finds himself victim of a logical and chronological legerdemain, Dante finally uses this figure to represent the perversion of a spatial binary opposition—inside/outside—inherent in the sins of fraud, particularly of fraud perpetrated through clever verbal acrobatics. All of Guido's external dialectical sophistication could not ultimately conceal internal self-interest. Dante casts Guido as master of "hidden ways" (76) by calling attention to the falseness of his Franciscan cord (92–93) and by reminding the reader in the end of his new, eternal robe (129), the *contrapasso* he now shares with Ulysses and Diomedes in the "thieving flame" (127) that forever conceals its true contents. In this, Guido must be emblematic for Dante, in a specifically political key, of so many of the self-promoting lords of Romagna and of his own Tuscany: *O anima che se' là giù nascosta, / Romagna tua non è, e non fu mai, / senza guerra ne'cuor de'suoi tiranni; / ma 'n palese nessuna or vi lasciai* ("O soul hidden down there, your Romagna is not, and never was, without war in the hearts of its tyrants; but no open war did I leave there now," 36–39). So many individual instances of noncorrespondence between interior intent and external appearance had brought Italy to its present turmoil, and thus Dante to the difficulties of exile. For all its signifying richness, Dante's portrayal of Guido ultimately impresses as the poet's indictment of such personal political corruption.

Bibliography

Bàrberi Squarotti, Giorgio. "La voce di Guido da Montefeltro." *Forum Italicum* 21.2 (Fall 1987), 165–196.

Harrison, Robert Pogue. "Comedy and Modernity: Dante's Hell." *MLN* 102.5 (December 1987), 1043–1061.

Markulin, Joseph. "Dante's Guido da Montefeltro: A Reconsideration." *Dante Studies* 100 (1982), 25–40.

Mazzotta, Giuseppe. "The Light of Venus and the Poetry of Dante." In *Magister Regis: Studies in Honor of Robert Earl Kaske*. Edited by A. Groos, E. Brown, Jr. et al. New York: Fordham University Press, 1986, pp. 147–169.

Gary P. Cestaro

Guido da Pisa

Born in Pisa in the second half of the thirteenth century, Guido da Pisa was, to the best of our knowledge, a member of the Carmelite Order. His commentary on Dante's *Inferno* is the most complete explanation of the general and especially the allegorical meaning of Dante's verses to be written in the first dozen years after the poet's death. In spite of its known importance among scholars, the complete critical edition of that important work, entitled *Expositiones et Glose super Comediam Dantis* ("Commentaries and Glosses on Dante's *Commedia*"), was not published until 1974.

Very little is known about this monk, who spent most of his life in Pisa. He may have spent some time in Naples, because in his commentary he makes a reference to the Carmelite Order of Naples; he may actually have died there, but no documentation has been found. His patron was Lucano Spinola of Genoa, to whom his commentary on the *Inferno* is dedicated. There are indications that he wrote this commentary when he was an elderly man; in fact, he is portrayed as such in the illuminated manuscript in Chantilly. In addition to his commentary, he wrote *La Fiorita, I Fatti di Enea,* and the *Declaratio* or *Dichiarazione Poetica dell'Inferno.* He was familiar not only with Dante's *Commedia* but also with the *Convivio* and perhaps other works of Dante. He may have intended to comment also on the *Purgatorio* and the *Paradiso,* but all attempts to find any such continuation have failed.

Guido da Pisa's commentary on the *Inferno* can be dated between 1328 and 1333, which places it among the earliest commentaries, along with those of Jacopo Alighieri (1322), the *Chiose anonime Selmi* (before 1325), Graziolo de' Bambaglioli (1324), Jacopo della Lana (1324–1328), the *Ottimo* (first version, 1334), and Pietro Alighieri (first version 1340–1341).

Bibliography

Guido da Pisa. "Prologue to the Commentary." In *Critical Essays on Dante.* Edited by Giuseppe Mazzotta. Boston: G. K. Hall, 1991, pp. 14–20.

——. *Expositiones et Glose super Comediam Dantis.* Edited by Vincenzo Cioffari. Albany: State University of New York Press, 1974.

Vallone, Aldo. "Guido da Pisa nella critica dantesca nel Trecento." *Critica letteraria* 3 (1975), 435–469.

Vincenzo Cioffari

Guido da Prata

Probably born in Prata (modern Prada, between Faenza and Ravenna), in Romagna, and of humble origin, Guido da Prata was reported to have gained importance through the creation of a family estate. He was very popular in Ravenna, where he held the post of counselor. He is mentioned in many documents between 1184 and 1228; he probably died between 1235 and 1245. Guido del Duca lists him among other noble figures of Romagna on the second terrace of Purgatory (*Purg.* 14.104).

Paul Colilli

Guido del Duca

A nobleman of Bertinoro, in Romagna, Guido del Duca lived between 1170 and 1250 and was associated with the Ghibellines. He was the son of Giovanni del Duca of the Onesti family of Ravenna. This family had as distant relatives St. Romuald, the founder of the Frati Camaldolesi, and Pier Damiano, and they had ties with the Mainardi and the Traversari. Guido's name is found in a document of 4 May 1199, where it is said that he was a judge under the podestà of Rimini. Together with Pier Traversaro, he was expelled from Bertinoro in 1218, escaping to Ravenna. The last known record of his name is his signature on a deed he witnessed at Ravenna in 1229.

On the second terrace of Purgatory, where the envious purge their sinful disposition, Guido is the voice through which Dante laments the moral degradation of Tuscany and Romagna, which Guido describes by means of geographic and climatological imagery (*Purg.* 14.28–72). Guido's rebuke of his homeland is followed by his recollection of better men in better times—of a humane, civil, and chivalric past rooted in Romagna (*Purg.* 14.73–126), expressed in the *ubi sunt* topos. Guido lived during the time of Frederick II, which Dante considered the final epoch of the virtuous tradition. It is not clear why Dante perceived Guido as being guilty of envy, given the scarcity of historical information in this regard, nor is it evident why, though one of the envious, Guido should serve to declare the praise of chivalric virtue. It has been suggested that his envy derives essentially from his fear of being upstaged by others in acts of chivalry. But in Purgatory he manifests the qualities of gentleness and courtesy in recalling a noble and ideal past, and he seems to have atoned for his tendency toward envy.

Paul Colilli

Guido delle Colonne

A judge and poet in the Hohenstaufen court of Frederick II of Sicily in the mid-thirteenth century. Documents attest to his activity between 1243 and 1280. Of the poets of the Sicilian School, Dante favors Guido delle Colonne and cites two of his five surviving *canzoni*, "Ancor che l'aigua per lo foco lassi" and "Amor che lungiamente m'hai menato," in *De vulgari eloquentia*. Dante praises Guido for his metrical excellence, in particular his choice of hendecasyllabic and heptasyllabic verses (*DVE* 2.5.4–6), and for the gravity and elegance of his poetics (*DVE* 1.12.1, 2.6.4–6). In all likelihood Dante also appreciated Guido's extensive use of images borrowed from natural philosophy. The same images were later elaborated by Guido Guinizzelli in "Al cor gentile rempaira sempre amore," the poem that became a kind of manifesto for the *dolce stil novo*. Dante's earlier preference for Guido delle Colonne over the other poets of the Sicilian School is no longer evident in the *Commedia*, where Giacomo da Lentini assumes the position of its leading exponent (*Purg.* 24). Dante makes no mention of Guido's Latin prose work, the *Historia Trojana*.

Bibliography

Barolini, Teodolinda. *Dante's Poets: Textuality and Truth in the Comedy.* Princeton: Princeton University Press, 1984.

Contini, Gianfranco. "Le Rime di Guido delle Colonne." *Bolletino del Centro di Studi Filologici e Linguistici Siciliani* 2 (1954), 178–203.

Dionisotti, Carlo. "Proposta per Guido giudice." *Rivista di Cultura Classica e Medievale* 7 (1965), 452–466.

Jensen, Frede (ed. and trans.). *The Poetry of the Sicilian School.* New York: Garland, 1986.

Marti, Mario. *Con Dante fra i poeti del suo tempo.* Lecce: Milella, 1971.

Laurie Shepard

Guido di Carpigna

Descendant of a family of counts from Montefeltro, Guido died sometime during the 1280s. Well known for his generosity, he was a Guelf allied with the pope against Frederick II. He is mentioned by Guido del Duca on the second terrace of Purgatory as one of the noble figures of Romagnole history (*Purg.* 14.98).

Paul Colilli

Guinevere

A character in the Arthurian romance *Lancelot du Lac,* Guinevere *(Ginevra)* was the wife of King Arthur and the lover of Lancelot. The first reference to Guinevere in Dante's *Commedia* is found in *Inf.* 5.133, where Dante encounters Francesca da Rimini in the circle of the lustful. Francesca tells Dante the story of the love between herself and Paolo Malatesta, implicitly comparing Paolo to Lancelot and herself to Guinevere. In her comparison, however, Francesca reverses the literal events of the amorous encounter. In *Lancelot du Lac,* it is Guinevere who first kisses Lancelot; in Francesca's version, it is Lancelot who first kisses Guinevere. Guinevere's name is mentioned by Dante in *Par.* 16.15, when he alludes to the episode in the romance in which one of Guinevere's ladies-in-waiting (who is also in love with Lancelot) overhears Guinevere's first affectionate words to Lancelot. The lady coughs to inform Guinevere of her knowledge of their amorous secret. Dante compares Beatrice to the lady-in-waiting in that Beatrice stands apart from Dante and laughingly rebukes him as Dante asks Cacciaguida about his ancestors.

Maria Ann Roglieri

Guinizzelli, Guido

Poet, judge, and jurisconsult, and native of Bologna, Guido Guinizzelli (1225?–1276) participated in the political life of his city in the ranks of the Ghibelline party until 1274, when the victory of the opposing Guelf faction forced him into exile. He was the most distinguished Italian poet prior to Dante. In the history of vernacular lyric, Guinizzelli occupies an intermediary position between the Sicilian-Tuscan school of Guittone d'Arezzo and the *dolce stil novo*. In *DVE* 1.15.6 and 2.6.6, Dante praises him for his rejection of the Bolognese vernacular and for his use of the most illustrious style, and he acknowledges him as the mentor of Dante's own generation of poets in *Purg.* 26.112–114. Of the twenty lyrics that are attributed to Guinizzelli with certainty, fifteen are sonnets and five are *canzoni*. Since there is no internal or external evidence of a chronological progression among them, they are customarily grouped according to content and style.

Two sonnets are in the rhetorical tradition of the realistic or jocose mode: one draws the caricature of an ugly old woman, and the other contains the portrait of a spirited and desirable girl. The greater part of Guinizzelli's verse adheres to the manner of the Sicilian-Tuscan school. He employs traditional themes of love's tyrannical domain, the lady's superiority and remoteness, and the lover's distressed state of mind. The images used to objectify the experience of love are the magnet, the panther, the salamander surviving in the fire, the ship tossed about in a stormy sea. To them Guinizzelli adds terms and concepts drawn from the economic, military, and theological realms. A clear proof of Guittone d'Arezzo's influence on him is Guinizzelli's display of *trobar clus:* that is to say, the use of complex hypotactic constructions, frequent wordplays, and a profusion of harsh, rare, identical, and internal rhymes. There are also examples of verse in the gnomic moralizing manner typical of the Tuscan school. Guinizzelli concedes Guittone's mastery by addressing him in a sonnet as "my dear father" and inviting his opinions about and emendations of his verse.

Only one *canzone* and five sonnets foreshadow the content and style of the *stil novo* poetry. Guinizzelli's ability to harmonize abstract theory with resplendent imagery in linear and melodic constructions is at its best here. Furthermore, the lover is no longer perceived as a man conscious of his lineage and social standing; his worthiness is defined exclusively in terms of moral and intellectual excellence. In his poetry the lady acquires a miraculous influence over him, thus becoming the force that actualizes his potential worth as a human being. In the celebrated song "Al cor gentil rempaira sempre amore" ("In the noble heart Love always finds its refuge"), love and moral uprightness are equal and coexist. Their coexistence is illustrated in each stanza by images that become increasingly luminous and comprehensive, culminating in a suggestive parallel between the shining beauty of the lady in her lover's consciousness and the splendor of God always present in the angelic mind. By analogy, the lady is seen as the embodiment of a spiritual force whose ascendancy over the noble heart is instantaneous and total. In the sonnets, she is extolled for her beauty and moral qualities. Likened to flowers and colors, to the bright star of Venus, and to all constellations, she has the capacity of lowering pride, vanquishing evil, and bringing about religious conversion.

In the context of the *Vita Nuova,* Dante's admiration for Guinizzelli is unconditional, while in the *Commedia* Guido's ethics are rejected and the concept of love's irresistible supremacy becomes Francesca da Rimini's illusory justification of a wayward behavior that has gained her eternal damnation (*Inf.* 5). And, although spoken of with admiration, Guinizzelli himself is placed on the seventh terrace of Purgatory to purge his sin of lust.

Bibliography

Barolini, Teodolinda. *Dante's Poets: Textuality and Truth in the Comedy.* Princeton, N.J.: Princeton University Press, 1984.

Bertelli, Italo. *La poesia di Guido Guinizzelli e la poetica del "Dolce stil novo."* Florence: Le Monnier, 1983.

Contini, Gianfranco. *Poeti del Duecento.* Vol. 2. Milan and Naples: Ricciardi, 1960.

Edwards, Robert (ed. and trans.). *The Poetry of Guido Guinizzelli.* New York: Garland, 1987.

Folena, Gianfranco. "Il canto di Guido Guinizzelli." *Giornale storico della letteratura italiana* 154 (1977), 481–508.

Marti, Mario. *Con Dante fra i poeti del suo tempo.* Lecce: Milella, 1971.

Moleta, Vincent. *Guinizzelli in Dante.* Rome: Edizioni di Storia e Letteratura, 1980.

Pasquini, Emilio, and Antonio Enzo Quaglio. *Lo stilnovo e la poesia religiosa.* Bari: Laterza, 1970.

Russell, Rinaldina. *Tre versanti della poesi stilnovistica: Guinizzelli, Cavalcanti, Dante.* Bari: Adriatica, 1973.

Valency, Maurice. *In Praise of Love.* New York: Macmillan, 1961.

Rinaldina Russell

Guiscard, Robert

A Norman of noble extraction, born in 1015, who undertook numerous military conquests against the Saracens in southern Italy and Sicily. Guiscard was count of Apulia (1057–1059), then duke of Apulia, Calabria, and Sicily (1059–1085). In 1084 he captured the city of Rome, rescuing Pope Gregory VII from an attack instigated by Emperor Henry IV. He died the following year. In the simile that opens *Inf.* 28, Dante describes the bloodshed occasioned by his and other battles in southern Italy over the centuries as being an inadequate collective measure of the monstrous carnage meted out to the perpetrators of mayhem and schism in the ninth bolgia (*Inf.* 28.14). In the *Paradiso,* the same *Ruberto Guiscardo* is honored with a place among the militant spirits in the heaven of Mars (*Par.* 18.48).

Donald Maddox

Guittone d'Arezzo

The dominant figure in Tuscan poetry in the second half of the thirteenth century. Midway through his life, Guittone joined the lay order of the Cavalieri di Santa Maria, where he continued his career as a widely respected man of letters. He was the first Italian to grapple extensively with significant political and ethical issues in vernacular verse and letters, and for that reason he was an important model for Dante. Guittone ultimately rejects human for divine love as his source of poetic inspiration, unlike Dante, whose love of Beatrice leads from the human to the divine.

Guittone's poetry is studded with rhetorical figures that tend to obscure the argument: the abundance and elevation of his thought, he claims, demand a highly ornamental style. Such rhetorical choices were admired by the young Dante, but he later rejected them and endeavored to endow his doctrinal poems with a more lucid style and an elegant, clearly articulated structure. Despite Guittone's obvious influence on Dante, or perhaps because of it, the Florentine characterizes Guittone's poetry as "plebeian" in *DVE* 2.6.8, and in the same passage (as well as *Purg.* 26.124–126), Dante scorns those who admire it.

Bibliography

Barolini, Teodolinda. *Dante's Poets: Textuality and Truth in the Comedy.* Princeton: Princeton University Press, 1984.

Boyde, Patrick. *Dante's Style in His Lyric Poetry.* Cambridge: Cambridge University Press, 1971.

Egidi, Francesco. *Le rime di Guittone d'Arezzo.* Bari: Laterza, 1940.

Margeron, Claude. *Recherches sur Guittone d'Arezzo.* Paris: Presses Universitaires de France, 1966.

Picone, Michelangelo (ed.). *Guittone D'Arezzo nel settimo centenario della morte: Atti del Convegno internazionale di Arezzo (22–24 aprile 1994).* Florence: Franco Cesati, 1995.

Segre, Cesare. *Lingua, stile e società.* Milan: Feltrinelli, 1976.

Laurie Shepard

Guy de Montfort

Son of Simon de Montfort, count of Leicester, who led the baronial revolt against his brother-in-law King Henry III of England and who was defeated and killed (and his corpse drawn) at the Battle of Evesham in 1265. Guy avenged his father's death in 1271 by murdering Henry of Cornwall, his own cousin and the king's nephew, at a mass in a church of Viterbo, during an assembly of the cardinals to elect a successor to Pope Clement IV. He is punished among the violent against others in the seventh circle of Hell (*Inf.* 12.118–120). Villani records an account of his brutal murders (*Cronica,* 8.39).

Yolande de Pontfarcy

H

Haakon V of Norway

King of Norway (1299–1319), Haakon *(Acone)* engaged in wars with Denmark. In the heaven of Jupiter *(Par.* 19.139), the Eagle probably alludes to him as *quel . . . di Norvegia* ("he of Norway") when condemning unjust rulers. Since Dante's knowledge of Norwegian kings was limited, some have suggested that the reference may actually be to Haakon IV, Magnus VI, or Erik II.

Molly Morrison

Habit

The Aristotelian word "habit" *(habitus,* from *habere,* "to have") defines a quality permanently inherent in a subject as a second nature. There are both supernatural and natural habits. Grace is a supernatural habit; it is, according to Dante, a "divine light" *(lumen divinum)* that enlightens the human soul and aids it to act supernaturally in order to ascend to the "beatitude of eternal life" *(Mon.* 3.15.8). Humans possess *lo intelletto de le prime notizie* ("[an] understanding of first notions," *Purg* 18.55–56), as a natural habit empowering human reason to know the primary ideas. Natural habits like beauty, ugliness, health, congenital disease, or defects, being naturally inherent in their subjects (i.e., from birth), are not contingent on human freedom and hence deserve neither blame nor praise: *Onde noi non dovemo vituperare l'uomo, perché sia del corpo da sua nativitade laido* ("So we must not blame a man because he was born with an ugly shape," *Conv.* 3.4.6–7).

Humans are responsible, however, for operative habits (acts)—that is, habitual dispositions that affect and determine their intellectual and moral activity. Both good (virtuous) and bad (vicious) habits result from a frequent repetition of an act which generates a state of mind that conditions the subject to behave consistently (and not just occasionally) in a certain way. As one swallow does not make a summer, so one act does not create a habit. Habit can result from practice: *L'abito di virtude, sì morale che intellettuale, subitamente avere non si può, ma conviene che per usanza s'acquisti* ("The habit of virtue, whether moral or intellectual, cannot be had of a sudden, but must be acquired through practice," *Conv.* 1.11.7); or it may result from study: *E uno studio lo quale mena l'uomo a l'abito de l'arte o de la scienza* ("The study that leads a man to acquire the habit of an art or a science," *Conv.* 3. 12. 2). Repetition of acts creates a qualitative condition in an individual, so that the term "habit" refers to both act and condition: *Onde dicemo alcuno virtuoso, non solamente virtute operando, ma l'abito de la virtù avendo* ("And so we call someone virtuous not only when performing a virtuous action but for having the habit of virtue," *Conv.* 3.13.8). Following Aristotle *(Ethics* 2.1, 1103.) and St. Thomas *(In decem libros ethicorum Aristotelis ad Nichomacum expositio,* 2, lectio 1, 246–247), Dante makes a distinction between the habit of knowledge inherent in the intellect (intellectual virtue or science), and the habit of moral acts inherent in the will (moral virtues). Intellectual habits are differentiated according to types of intellectual activity: speculative or practical. The speculative "habit of knowledge" inclines the intellect to inquire after and know universal truths: "The speculative use (of the mind) consists not in our acting but in reflecting upon the works of God and nature" *(Conv.*

4.22.11); in contrast, the practical or moral habit, or *abito eligente* ("habit of choice," *Conv.* 4.17.1), inclines the intellect to judge and choose the mean between the extremes—*E ciascuna di queste virtudi ha due inimici collaterali, cioè vizi, uno in troppo e un altro in poco* ("Each of these virtues has two related enemies, that is, vices, one through excess and the other through shortfall," *Conv.* 4.17.7). Dante's list of eleven moral virtues (*Conv.* 4.17), explicitly taken from Aristotle, defines ideal human activity. The main moral habits that perfect the will are the four cardinal virtues: prudence, temperance, fortitude, and justice.

Bibliography

Aristotle. *Nichomachean Ethics.* In *The Basic Works of Aristotle.* Edited by Richard McKeon. New York: Random House, 1941, pp. 935–1112.

Aquinas, Thomas. *Summa Theologiae,* 1.2.49–54.

Lottin, D. Odon. *Psichologie et morale aux XIIe et XIIIe siècle,* vol. 2, *Problèmes de Morale.* Louven: J. Duculot, 1948.

Tapia, R. G. "Habit." In *New Catholic Encyclopedia.* Toronto and London: McGraw-Hill, 1967, vol. 6, pp. 880–885.

Vasoli, Cesare. "Abito." *Enciclopedia dantesca,* 1:14–15.

Mario Trovato

Haman

On the terrace of Anger in Purgatory, Dante sees three visions of the wrathful punished; the second of these is Haman *(Aman),* the only biblical figure among them (*Purg.* 17.25–30). As reported in the Book of Esther, Haman was the chief minister of Ahasuerus (now identified with Xerxes), who was enraged when the Jew Mordecai (called by Dante *'l giusto Mardoceo*) refused to bow down to him, and decreed that all the Jews in the Persian Empire should be put to death. Through the intervention of Esther and Mordecai, this plot was unraveled and Haman was put to death on the very gibbet he had prepared for Mordecai. Dante's version of Haman's hanging as a crucifixion scene probably derives from the Vulgate's use of the term *crux* for "gibbet"; there is no biblical precedent for his image of Haman dying in scornful pride *(fero e dispettoso)* surrounded by Ahasuerus, Esther, and Mordecai. Haman later became the typological figure of the murderous antisemite.

Rachel Jacoff

Harpies

Mythological creatures, half bird and half woman, who nest in the thorn bushes into which the souls of the suicides have sprouted. The Harpies (*Arpie*), by feeding on the leaves of these bushes, provide both pain and an outlet (literally a window, *finestra*) for that pain, since the suicide-trees can communicate only in the process of being damaged (*Inf.* 13.100–102). Early commentators saw the Harpies either as emblematic of the psychic state of the suicides—for example, of their remorse or despair—or as etymologically traceable to the Greek word for "theft" or "plunder" and therefore relevant either to the specific circumstance of Pier della Vigna (assuming that he was guilty of theft) or to the general situation of souls who metaphorically robbed themselves of their being (see 13.105). Dante's specific source for the Harpies is pinpointed in the lines in which they are introduced into the poem (*Inf.* 13.10–12), where they are called the Harpies who drove the Romans from the Strophades *con tristo annunzio di futuro danno* ("with dire prophecy of their future woe"). The allusion is to *Aen.* 3.253–257, where Celaeno, prophetic leader of the Harpies, proclaims that the Romans will reach their ancestral homeland only after a long voyage, at the end of which they will eat their tables.

The specificity of this allusion may invite a closer look at the ironic fulfillment of this prophecy in the *Aeneid.* When the Trojans arrive at the Tiber, they eat food gleaned from the countryside and then the bread onto which they had piled it, leading Aeneas's son Ascanius to joke that they had eaten their tables (7.112–122). Aeneas recalls Celaeno's prophecy and realizes that they have unwittingly reached the end of their journey: what had seemed a "dire prophecy of their future woe" turns out to be a blessing, the means by which they can identify the success of their mission. This may provide an implicit commentary on suicide as an action which, in arbitrarily curtailing the future, denies the possibility of hope—a matter of some importance to the poet who claims eventually to see exile from Florence as a blessing.

Bibliography

Hollander, Robert. "*Purgatorio* XIX: Dante's Siren/Harpy." In *Dante, Petrarch, Boccaccio: Studies in the Italian Trecento in Honor of Charles S. Singleton.* Edited by Aldo S. Bernardo and Anthony L. Pellegrini. Binghamton, N.Y.:

Medieval and Renaissance Texts and Studies, 1983, pp. 78–88.

Stephany, William A. "Dante's Harpies: 'tristo annunzio di futuro danno.'" In *The Poetry of Allusion: Virgil and Ovid in Dante's Comedy.* Edited by Rachel Jacoff and Jeffrey Schnapp. Stanford: Stanford University Press, 1991, pp. 37–44, 258–261.

William A. Stephany

Harrowing of Hell

Theologically, the Harrowing (the term is from Old and Middle English) of Hell denotes the belief that the soul of Jesus triumphally descended into Hell, or Hades, after the crucifixion and remained there until the resurrection, during which time he brought salvation to those just souls who had awaited his coming. It is described by Dante in *Inf.* 4.52–63.

Dante's sources for the Harrowing of Hell are both theological and biblical/apocryphal. Theologically, the harrowing theme goes back to apostolic times and is reflected in many New Testament passages. At a very early stage (cf. Melito of Sardis, *Hom. Passionis,* 102), the harrowing was infused with triumphal imagery: Christ's descent was seen as a total victory over the powers of Hades, death and Satan, and it was this triumphal imagery that shaped all subsequent Patristic accounts. The Scholastics also described the harrowing; the best known account is that of Aquinas (*ST* 3.52.1–8), who identifies the scene of the harrowing as the *limbus patrum* and describes the salvific activity of Christ there as a total victory over death, sin, and the Devil. Apocryphal sources likewise took up the harrowing theme. Principal among these is the *Evangelium Nicodemi* or *Gospel of Nicodemus,* which relates (chapters 17–27) Christ's descent into the underworld *(Descensus Christi ad inferos)* and describes, among other things, how Christ appears in Hell as the lord of majesty, breaks the bonds of Hell, tramples on death, and surrenders Satan into the power of Hell.

The harrowing was a favorite medieval motif, and the *Evangelium Nicodemi,* as a dramatic embodiment of that motif, enjoyed great authority and prestige. Not only were there summaries of it (cf. Vincent of Beauvais and his widely read *Speculum Maius,* book 7, chs. 40–63; and Jacobus de Voragine, *Legenda aurea,* ch. 54), but the *Evangelium* found its way into many medieval Italian texts and its influence was enormous. In poetry, in prose, on the stage—from *laude* (religious poems, both dramatic and nondramatic, which were sung by lay fraternities throughout Italy) and *sacre rappresentazioni* to religious *cantari* and sermons—the *Evangelium* left its mark on many areas of medieval Italian literature and art (in miniatures, mosaics, manuscript illuminations, ivory carvings, enamel, stained glass, and painting). The tone of all these evocations is always joyous and celebratory.

Both the pervasive influence and the joyful tone of the harrowing are due to its critical significance in salvation history. Not only did Christ become flesh in the incarnation and redeem humankind through his passion; after his death he descended to the dead and into Hell, which had no power over him. The harrowing therefore is a powerful reminder that Jesus has conquered both sin and death, and that over him Satan and Hell have no dominion. Moreover, the harrowing dramatizes the central event in history—the reversal of the fall—and as such it is a victorious and joyous symbol for all humankind of deliverance from sin and death.

Dante was clearly familiar with the harrowing theme in both the theological (Aquinas) and apocryphal sources (the *Evangelium Nicodemi,* and probably its epitome in Vincent of Beauvais and Jacobus de Voragine), but the harrowing as described in *Inf.* 4.52–63 is not the focal point of his Limbo. In fact, in his unusual treatment, Dante evokes the memory of a *limbus patrum* of long ago and presents us with a capsule version of the harrowing that is stripped of its dramatic, agonistic, and triumphal imagery. In *Inf.* 4 Dante is interested primarily not in the souls who were liberated during the harrowing but in the souls of those who were left behind. Accordingly, the description of the harrowing conveys not the joy and jubilation of liberation, but the sadness and melancholy of the souls still in Limbo. As such, Dante's harrowing, though much reduced in scale, still plays a significant role: it reminds us of the tragic fate of the virtuous pagans in Limbo.

The harrowing theme is not limited to *Inf.* 4 but is anticipated in and deferred to other cantos of the poem. In *Inf.* 2, for example, Dante taps the harrowing motif in a far more subtle and profound manner. There the descent of Beatrice into Limbo is presented in lyrical terms reminiscent of the *dolce stil nuovo,* and is delicately modeled on the harrowing of hell. She descends to secure Virgil's aid in order to "harrow" her former lover from the hell of despair that exists in his heart (*Inf.* 2.61–66), and Dante describes this descent as occurring at exactly noon on Good Friday of 1300, thus establishing a temporal correspondence between the descent of Beatrice and that of Christ, albeit centuries before. And in *Inf.* 8 and 9, Dante exploits the harrowing imagery most effectively in the frightful drama before the walls of the City of Dis. The whole episode (the descent of the divine messenger, an obvious analogue of Christ, who scatters the devils and overcomes the Furies and the Medusa in their attempt to block entry into the City of Dis) blends the traditional Christian images of the harrowing with pagan ones drawn from *Aen.* 6. The significance of both *Inf.* 2 and *Inf.* 8 and 9 is the same as that of their archetype. Both celebrate victory over the forces of darkness, whether figurative or literal, and release from the slavery of sin. In addition to Dante's innovative treatment of the harrowing in these episodes, we may cite also the landslide or *ruina* of *Inf.* 12.31–45 as a reminder of the earthquake at the moment of Christ's descent on the cross and descent into Limbo; the same *ruina* in the episode of the barrators in *Inf.* 21–22; and the earthquake *(tremoto)* of *Purg.* 21 and 22, a stock image of the harrowing, which accompanies the deliverance of the soul of Statius from Purgatory.

Dante's treatment of the harrowing theme suggests that Dante considered the descent of Christ *(descensus Christi)* as portrayed in the *Evangelium Nicodemi,* along with *Aen.* 6 and the Exodus story, to be a major narrative model, within which he cast his own pilgrim's journey, especially in the first phase. Much has been written about Dante's use of book 6 of the *Aeneid* and of the Exodus story, although the latter becomes determining only in the Ante-Purgatory. On the other hand, the harrowing paradigm has been almost completely neglected by Dante's critics because, of Dante's three models, the *descensus* is the least authoritative (despite its immense popularity in the Middle Ages). As a narrative model it is overwhelmed by the descent of Aeneas to the underworld. This is already clearly evident in *Inf.* 4. With Dante's brief evocation of the harrowing (46–63), the theological and apocryphal material gives way to the Virgilian. However, if Virgil dictates form, style, and narrative flow in *Inf.* 4 and the *Commedia* as a whole (the *Inferno* in particu-

lar), the harrowing—that is, the Christian model—continues to dictate meaning.

Bibliography

Iannucci, Amilcare A. "The Gospel of Nicodemus in Medieval Italian Literature." *Quaderni d'Italianistica* 14 (1993), 191–220.

———. "Beatrice in Limbo: A Metaphoric Harrowing of Hell." *Dante Studies* 97 (1979), 23–45.

———. "Limbo: The Emptiness of Time." *Studi danteschi* 52 (1978), 69–128.

———. "Dottrina e Allegoria in *Inferno* VIII, 67–IX, 105." In *Dante e le Forme dell'Allegoresi.* Edited by Michelangelo Picone. Ravenna: Longo, 1987, pp. 99–124.

MacCulloch, J. A. *The Harrowing of Hell.* New York: AMS Press, 1983.

Monnier, Jean. *La Descente aux Enfers.* Paris: Librairie Fischbacher, 1904.

Quillet, H. "Descente de Jésus aux Enfers." *Dictionnaire de Théologie Catholique.* Paris: Letouzey et Ane, 1901. Vol. 4, cols. 565–619.

Amilcare A. Iannucci

Hector

Eldest son of Priam and Hecuba, husband of Andromache, and leading Trojan hero. Hector *(Ettore),* who appears together with Aeneas and Julius Caesar in the "noble castle" of Limbo (*Inf.* 4.121–123), was slain by Achilles during the Trojan War. Dante mentions his tomb at Troy in *Par.* 6.68, and in *Epist.* 5.5 he speaks of Henry VII as *Hectoreus pastor* ("the shepherd descended from Hector"), where the descriptor signifies "Trojan" and hence "Roman." He refers to Hector twice in the *Convivio,* as the light and the hope of the Trojans (3.11.16) and indirectly in reference to Misenus (4.26.13), and calls him the equal of Aeneas in *Mon.* 2.3. The passage in *Conv.* 3.11.16, which textually reads *Enea* rather than *Ettore,* reveals the presence of a lacuna in the archetypal manuscript; the Vasoli-De Robertis edition retains the lapse, while both Simonelli and Ageno propose emendations.

Guy P. Raffa

Hecuba

The second wife of King Priam of Troy, Hecuba appears in all Greek and Latin accounts of the

Trojan War in her paradigmatic role as mother bereft of her children and queen become slave. With the fall of Troy, Hecuba witnesses the loss of all she values, including the deaths of her husband and several children. As Ulysses' slave she is helpless to prevent the sacrifice of her daughter Polyxena on the tomb of Achilles, and this death is followed by the discovery of the body of her son, Polydorus, cast up on the seashore. Driven mad by her grief, Hecuba loses her mind and takes revenge on her brother-in-law Polymestor for having killed her son, by blinding him. As she is stoned by vengeful Thracians, Hecuba is transformed into a dog and reduced to howling and barking. According to some mythographers, she then hurls herself into the sea. References in Virgil's *Aeneid,* a lengthy episode in Ovid (*Meta.* 13.404–575), and Seneca's *Troades* are among Dante's major sources for the story.

Hecuba *(Ecuba)* appears indirectly in the *Commedia,* in an extended simile that opens *Inf.* 30 and describes the madness visited on falsifiers of person. Representative of Dante's high or tragic style, the simile recounts two well-known cases of classical insanity—Hecuba of Troy and Athamas of Thebes—establishing a comparison between the archetypal rage and madness of these two women and the far greater rage and madness of two souls damned in the lowest pit of Malebolge: Capocchio and Gianni Schicchi, who are condemned to attack each other viciously for all eternity.

Donna Yowell

Helen of Troy

The wife of a Greek king, Menelaus, she was abducted by a Trojan prince, Paris, an act that indirectly led to the war between the Greeks and Trojans. Helen *(Elena)* is pointed out in the circle of the lustful in Hell as the cause of much ill (*Inf.* 5.64–66). She is obliquely referred to in the *Detto* (*Alena,* v. 197).

Joan M. Ferrante

Heliodorus

Treasurer of the Syrian king Seleucus IV (187–175 B.C.E.), who sent him to steal treasures from the temple in Jerusalem. Upon his arrival there, he was nearly kicked to death by a horse ridden by a man in golden armor, and he was flogged by two men (2 Macc. 3:25–30). Heliodorus (*Eliodoro*) is

included among the examples of avarice in *Purg.* 20.113.

Molly Morrison

Hell

According to Catholic doctrine, Hell is the place where the rebel angels and the souls of humans who perished in mortal sin are eternally punished. In the *Commedia,* Hell is the first realm of the afterlife and the subject of the first *cantica,* the *Inferno.* In his representation of Hell, Dante reveals himself to be both a canny connoisseur of a complex tradition and a radical innovator.

The Hebrew Bible offers a vast abyss, Sheol, "the grave," to which after death the good and the wicked alike descend. In its moral neutrality Sheol parallels the ancient Greek concept of Hades. The concept of retribution for the wicked after death, which begins to manifest itself in the Old Testament, especially in the books of the prophets, is rendered explicit in the gospels of the New Testament. "Three crucial passages in the synoptic Gospels helped form the concept of Hell" (Bernstein 228); these are Mark 9:43–48, Matt. 25:31–46, and Luke 16:19–31. The passage in Mark is the first to identify the fire and the worm of Isa. 66:24 with Hell: "And if thy hand offend thee, cut it off: it is better for thee to enter into life maimed, than having two hands to go into Hell, in the fire that never shall be quenched: where their worm dieth not, and the fire is not quenched" (43–44). In the great eschatological discourse of Matt. 25 ("perhaps the single most important biblical passage for the history of hell," Bernstein 231), Christ predicts the division of the souls at the Last Judgment ("And he shall set the sheep on his right hand, but the goats on his left," 33) and explicitly contrasts eternal fire and punishment to eternal life: "Then shall he say also unto them on the left hand, Depart from me, ye cursed, into everlasting fire, prepared for the devil and his angels" (41), continuing "And these shall go away into everlasting punishment: but the righteous into life eternal" (46).

This doctrine of Hell, based on the symmetry and justice of eternal reward for the good and eternal punishment for the wicked, was challenged in the third century by Origen, who affirmed the medicinal and corrective value of a non-eternal system of punishment which would eventually succeed in restoring all souls to God. However, the eternity of Hell was vigorously defended by

Dante preparing to enter the Gate of Hell. From the 1481 edition illustrated by Baldino after sketches by Botticelli, published in Florence by Nicholo di Lorenzo della Magna. Giamatti Collection: Courtesy of the Mount Holyoke College Archives and Special Collections.

Augustine, who puts the passage from Matthew at the center of his argument, noting that "the sentence of the Lord could not be evacuated of meaning or deprived of its force; the sentence, I mean, that he, on his own prediction, was to pronounce in these words: 'Out of my sight, accursed ones, into the eternal fire which is prepared for the Devil and his angels'" (*City of God* 21.23). Laying the eschatological foundations of the later Middle Ages, Augustine writes in the *Enchiridion* not only of fixed and eternal lots for the bad and the good, but also of degrees of happiness and misery:

> After the resurrection, however, when the final, universal judgment has been completed, two groups of citizens, one Christ's, the other the devil's, shall have fixed lots; one consisting of the good, the other of the bad—both, however, consisting of angels and men. The former shall have no will, the latter no power, to sin, and neither shall have any power to choose death; but the former shall live truly and happily in eternal life, the latter shall drag a miserable existence in eternal death without the power of dying; for both shall be without end. But among the former there shall be degrees of happiness, one being more pre-

eminently happy than another; and among the latter there shall be degrees of misery, one being more endurably miserable than another. (ch. 111)

Both these concepts—fixed, eternal lots and degrees of misery for the wicked proportionate to their sins—are key to Dante's Hell, whose sinners are distributed through nine circles according to the gravity of their sins. The eternity of Hell is solemnly proclaimed by the Gate of Hell itself: *Per me si va ne l'etterno dolore . . . Dinanzi a me non fuor cose create / se non etterne, e io etterno duro* ("Through me the way into eternal sorrow . . . Before me were no things created except eternal ones, and I endure eternal," *Inf.* 3.2, 7–8).

Augustine conceives the wages of sin in terms of loss and alienation—it is "to be lost out of the kingdom of God, to be an exile from the city of God, to be alienated from the life of God" (*Enchiridion* 112). So does Aquinas, who defines sin as, first, "aversion, the turning away from the changeless good" *(aversio ab incommutabili bono)* and, second, as "conversion, the disordered turning towards a changeable good" (*inordinata conversio ad commutabile bono, ST* 1.2.87.4). Aquinas further teaches that aversion from God

Hresults in the *poena damni* or "pain of loss," which corresponds to the loss of the beatific vision, while disordered conversion results in the *poena sensus,* or "pain of sense" (*ST* 1.2.87.4), which corresponds to the torments of hell-fire. These concepts are fundamental to Dante, who holds that sin alienates us from God—"sin alone is that which unfrees" us and renders us "dissimilar from the highest good" (*Par.* 7.79–80)—and who structures his poem around a metaphor (life as a path or journey) that embodies the ideas of *aversio* and *conversio:* at the beginning of the poem, the pilgrim has lost the right path and figures the state of *aversio,* of the sinful soul that has turned away from God, in his case temporarily, but with respect to the sinners of Hell permanently. The notion of sin as *conversio,* as a turning toward the changeable goods of the world, likewise permeates Dante's thought. It is inscribed into the center of the *Commedia,* in *Purg.* 16's depiction of the newborn soul as a female child who, set forth by a happy maker on the path of life, willingly turns toward all that brings delight, only to find itself deceived and seduced by earthly goods: *"Di picciol bene in pria sente sapore; / quivi s'inganna, e dietro ad esso corre, / se guida o fren non torce suo amore"* ("Of some lesser good it first tastes the flavor; there it is deceived and runs after it, if a guide or rein does not turn away its love," *Purg.* 16.91–93). And *conversio* is the centerpiece of the rebuke that Beatrice issues to the pilgrim when they meet at the top of Mount Purgatory, where she compels him to acknowledge that after her death *"Le presenti cose / col falso lor piacer volser miei passi"* ("Present things with their false pleasure turned aside my steps, as soon as your face was hidden," *Purg.* 31.34–35).

While Dante's conceptualizing of sin, and ultimately of Hell, is thus firmly embedded within theological tradition, his representation is frequently idiosyncratic to the point of being heterodox. For instance, there is no theological precedent for creating a vestibule to Hell that houses neutral angels and cowardly souls "who lived without infamy and without praise" (*Inf.* 3.36); nor is there theological justification for putting virtuous pagans into Limbo alongside the unbaptized children, or for claiming that certain traitors are damned before death—their souls sent to Hell while devils inhabit their bodies on Earth (*Inf.* 33). Therefore, although Dante reflects the most informed theological thought on Hell, he is cer-

tainly not constrained by it. By the same token, he is not limited to the high-culture sources from which he explicitly borrows, such as Aristotle's *Nicomachean Ethics,* which he credits as a source for the structure of his Hell, or Virgil's underworld in *Aen.* 6, various of whose characters and features he appropriates and transforms. Rather, Dante's Hell also demonstrates clear links to an established popular iconography of Hell, as well as to popular cultural forms like sermons, visions, and the didactic poetry of vernacular predecessors such as Bonvesin da la Riva and Giacomino da Verona. Dante's representation of Hell is unique, however, in its rich and uninhibited blending of these remarkably heterogeneous constituents into a personal vision: for instance, while Aquinas cites Aristotle in his discussion of sin, and the vision authors knew the Bible, Dante alone brings together traditions as disparate as the *Aeneid* and the *Apocalypse of Paul.*

The scheme of Dante's Hell. La commedia di Dante, Allighieri, *illustrated by Ugo Foscolo and edited by Giuseppe Mazzini (London, 1842). Giamatti Collection: Courtesy of the Mount Holyoke College Archives and Special Collections.*

Dante's Hell is a hollow cone excavated by Lucifer's fall; the displaced matter became Mount Purgatory (see *Inf.* 34.121–126 for this highly original account). Situated under Jerusalem, Hell is made of nine concentric circles that house ever more grievous sinners; it tapers to a point at the Earth's core, where Lucifer, the apex of creaturely sinfulness, is eternally fixed at *lo mezzo / al quale ogne gravezza si rauna* ("the center / toward which all weight collects," *Inf.* 32.73–74). The topography of Hell is extensive and varied, embracing rivers (one of blood), a swamp, a wood, a burning plain, some landslides, an immense waterfall, a frozen lake, the fortified turrets of Dis, and the ditches and bridges of Malebolge. The demography of Hell is likewise extensive, ranging from biblical and classical characters (a true innovation, since, as Morgan points out, classical figures "are totally unrepresented in the earlier medieval texts" [57]) to contemporaries, mainly Italians. Many of the circles have guardians, which again range from classical figures (Charon, Minos) and monsters (the centaurs, Geryon) to contemporary demons. The order of the nine circles and its underlying logic are explained by Virgil in *Inf.* 11, prior to the descent to the seventh circle, using a schema based on Aristotle's *Nicomachean Ethics* (7.1).

Virgil's account makes no mention of the first circle (Limbo) or the sixth (heresy)—both of which involve deficient faith and hence have no place in Aristotle's ethics—and it distinguishes between sins of incontinence and malice. The sins of incontinence (circles two through five) are sins of impulse, brought about by immoderate passion rather than by habit; they are lust, gluttony, avarice (or prodigality), and anger. The sins of malice cause injustice and harm to others, either by force or by fraud (a distinction that Dante finds, as Moore points out, in Cicero's *De officiis* 1.13). Injurious acts achieved by fraud are more sinful because fraud requires the misuse of reason, man's peculiar gift. The seventh circle, then, houses the violent, while the eighth and the ninth circles contain the fraudulent. Violence is divided into three subsets; each subset in turn involves two types of violence: violence against one's neighbor in his person and in his possessions (tyrants, murderers, robbers); violence against the self in one's person and in one's possessions (suicides, squanderers); and violence against God in his person and in his possessions (blasphemers, sodomites, usurers). (Virgil explains that sodomy is violence against

nature, the child of God, while usury is violence against human art, the child of nature.) Fraud too is subdivided. The eighth circle contains those who practiced fraud on the untrusting, distinguished into ten groups: panders and seducers, flatterers, simoniacs, diviners, barrators, hypocrites, thieves, fraudulent counselors, sowers of scandal and schism, and falsifiers. The ninth and lowest circle of Hell contains sinners who practiced fraud on those who trusted them—traitors.

The resulting overlap between the Aristotelian scheme adopted for Hell and the theological scheme that Dante adopts for Purgatory (where the seven terraces corresponding to the seven deadly sins include lust, gluttony, avarice and prodigality, and anger) displays a uniquely Dantesque contamination of Christian and classical paradigms—and of popular with high culture, for Dante is conflating popular religious currents (the seven deadly sins were not part of Church doctrine but were important in confession manuals of the period) with a hyperliterate textual tradition. With respect to Hell, we could say that an arrangement that at first seems to be loosely based on the seven deadly sins is then grafted onto Aristotle, whose distinction between sins of incontinence and sins of malice provides the overarching order. (However, while this system of classification is Aristotelian, the material remains fundamentally Christian, given that "the thirty-seven sins punished in the *Inferno* are essentially the same sins as those traditionally represented in the popular visions of the other world and listed in the confession manuals of the twelfth and thirteenth centuries" [Morgan, 131].) With respect to Purgatory, where the seven deadly sins provide the order, the classical/Christian syncretism can be seen in the theologically unorthodox coupling of avarice with its Aristotelian counterpart, prodigality.

Dante's infernal system of classification is not without its puzzles and inconsistencies (for instance, prodigality occurs as a sin of both incontinence and violence, and theft occurs as a sin both of violence and of fraud). On the whole, however, when one compares the *Inferno* to the previous accounts of Hell in vision literature, one is struck not by its inconsistencies but by the opposite: Dante's *Inferno* stunningly conveys the appearance of a totally inclusive penal system from which no sin is omitted and no sinner can escape. Key to creating such an illusion is the deployment of a system of classification that seems quite logical,

H precise, and rigorous in its definitions and distinctions, and that invokes the immense authority of Aristotle. In the confused and unsystematic earlier visions, where sins and sinners are frequently piled one on the other with minimal differentiation, the reader has no way of distinguishing the first category from the second, third, or fourth, and consequently little incentive to see who comes next. In the *Inferno,* by contrast, we know the order in which sins will be encountered, as well as the moral value that has been assigned to each. As a result, the reader can anticipate the narrative and is thereby induced to proceed, propelled by the subliminal desire to see how cogently the author's rendering will conform to his earlier declarations, as well as by the urge to participate in a possible world that seems to make sense, or that can be challenged if it does not, because its structuring principles have been made known.

Also key to constructing a persuasive representation of Hell is what Dante calls the *contrapasso* ("counter-suffering," *Inf.* 28.142), the principle whereby the punishment fits the crime. For Dante, the *contrapasso* frequently takes the form of literalizing a metaphor: thus, the souls of the lustful are tossed by a Hell-storm as in life they were buffeted by their passions; the schismatics, who in life rent the body politic, now find their own bodies torn. Dante's punishments display remarkable inventiveness and draw from a broad spectrum of sources, from traditional motifs like the graduated immersion of a sinner in a river or a lake (already present in the *Apocalypse of Paul*) to the metamorphosis of man into tree as in *Aen.* 3. Overall, Dante effectively deploys the *contrapasso* to deflect any sense of randomness or arbitrariness and to suffuse his text with a feeling for God's order and justice. In this way, the *contrapasso* is a crucial tool in Dante's attempt to represent Hell in a way that bears out the declaration on its gate—*Giustizia mosse il mio alto fattore* ("Justice moved my high maker," *Inf.* 3.4)—and in a way that reflects its true nature: since Hell is deserved separation from God, punishment is not something inflicted by God but the consequence of the sin itself. Here too, though some of Dante's punishments may seem more fitting than others, and some more transparently suggest the sin being punished, a comparison of Dante's Hell to those of his precursors reveals that he is the first author to deploy an ideology of moral decorum not sporadically, but as a systematic feature of his other world.

Ultimately, of course, what most distinguishes Dante's *Inferno* from other representations of Hell is that he creates sinners so complex and alive that the reader is compelled to sympathize and identify with them, rather than simply to fear their lot and resolve to avoid it. While the lessons of earlier Hells are straightforward—beware, mend your ways, or this will happen to you—the reader of Dante's Hell is drawn into a much more sophisticated dance, in which he or she must sort through the sirens' songs of sinners who are devilishly attractive and tragically human. Only Dante constructs a Hell in which the reader encounters figures like Francesca, Brunetto, and Ulysses, and is thereby induced to engage the challenges not just of death but of life.

Bibliography

Aquinas, Thomas. *Summa Theologiae.* 1a2ae. Question 87: "The Guilt of Punishment." Blackfriars. Vol. 27. Translated by T. C. O'Brien. New York: McGraw-Hill; London: Eyre and Spottiswoode, 1974.

Augustine. *The Enchiridion on Faith, Hope, and Love.* Edited by Henry Paolucci and translated by J. F. Shaw. Washington, D.C.: Regnery Gateway, 1961.

Augustine. *City of God.* Translated by Henry Bettenson. London: Penguin Books, 1972.

Aurigemma, Marcello. "Inferno." *Enciclopedia dantesca,* 3.432–435.

Barolini, Teodolinda. "Minos's Tail: The Labor of Devising Hell (*Inferno* 5.1–24)." *Romanic Review* 87 (1996), 437–454.

Bergin, Thomas Goddard. "Hell: Topography and Demography." In *A Diversity of Dante.* New Brunswick, N.J.: Rutgers University Press, 1969, pp. 47–64.

Bernstein, Alan E. *The Formation of Hell: Death and Retribution in the Ancient and Early Christian Worlds.* Ithaca, N.Y.: Cornell University Press, 1993.

Busnelli, Giovanni. *L'Etica Nicomachea e l'ordinamento morale dell' 'Inferno' di Dante.* Bologna: Zanichelli, 1907.

Gardiner, Eileen (ed.). *Visions of Heaven and Hell before Dante.* New York: Italica Press, 1989.

Hardwick, E. G. "Hell (Theology of)." In *New Catholic Encyclopedia,* vol. 6. New York: McGraw-Hill, 1967, pp. 1005–1007.

Moore, Edward. "The Classification of Sins in the *Inferno* and *Purgatorio.*" In *Studies in Dante:*

Second Series. 1899, reprinted New York: Greenwood Press, 1968, pp. 152–209.

Morgan, Alison. *Dante and the Medieval Other World.* Cambridge: Cambridge University Press, 1990.

Piolanti, Antonio. "Inferno." In *Enciclopedia Cattolica,* vol. 6. Vatican City: Ente per l'Enciclopedia Cattolica e per il Libro Cattolico, 1948–1954, cols. 1941–1949.

Teodolinda Barolini

Hendecasyllable

The Italian hendecasyllable is by definition a verse-line of ten, eleven, or twelve syllables whose last word-accent falls on the tenth syllable. Since most Italian words are accented on the penultimate, most hendecasyllables have eleven syllables; but they can have ten when the last accent is in word-final position, or twelve if it is on the antepenultimate. Dante's poetry contains instances of both ten-syllable and twelve-syllable hendecasyllables, but they are very few; the vast majority have eleven syllables.

How are Dante's hendecasyllables scanned? With certain exceptions, in the Italian hendecasyllable from the thirteenth century on, all groups of adjacent vowels count as one syllable, although each vowel retains some of its distinct articulation. This principle is termed *sineresi* (synaeresis) when it operates within the word, and *sinalefe* (synaloepha) when it operates across word boundaries. When there is a syllable division between adjacent vowels, the term *dieresi* (diaeresis) is used within the word, and *dialefe* (dialoepha) across word boundaries. (*Sineresi* and *dieresi* are sometimes used more strictly, to describe respectively counting as one syllable two vowels that would normally be two syllables, and counting as two syllables two vowels that would normally be one; but the terms are used in their looser acceptance here.) In Dante's practice, as in that of his successors, *sineresi* and *sinalefe* are the normal rule; the latter applies even when a major syntactical division, represented by a punctuation mark in modern editions, separates vowels that would otherwise be adjacent.

There are also, however, a large number of instances of *dieresi* and *dialefe*—more than in Dante's successors from Petrarch on, and applied less systematically. One set of vowel combinations always has diaeresis, and as a result this diaeresis is usually not marked in modern critical editions: *a, e,* or *o* immediately followed by any accented vowel, as in *paura, leone,* or *poeta.* The other main instances of diaeresis (usually marked in modern critical editions) are as follows: imperfect verb forms such as *avëan, dovëa, facëa,* though here synaeresis is the general rule; verbs with an initial *ri-* (from Latin *re-*) followed by a vowel (here diaeresis is the rule); some cases of accented *u* and *i* followed by a vowel, such as *colüi, cüi, süo, disïo, fïa, ïo* (alongside a much greater number of instances of the same forms without diaeresis); and (more consistently) Latinate combinations involving an initial *e, i,* or *u* that preserve the vowel structure of their origins—*empirëo, Enëa, Pegasëa; settentrïon, trïunfo, vïaggio; continüando, intellettüal, perpetüa. Beatrice* sometimes has diaeresis but more often does not. Dante's etymological sense is thus a significant factor in his use of diaeresis: there is always synaeresis on the Italian diphthongs *ie* and *uo* from Latin *e* and *o.*

Dialefe occurs regularly in the *Commedia* after polysyllables that end in an accented diphthong or vowel, and after the great majority of monosyllables, such as *e, io, più, è, noi, da, o,* but not after *di* ("of") or the definite article or proclitic pronouns *(ci, la, le, li, lo, mi, ne, si, ti, vi).* Again, there are a number of exceptions, with no apparent motivation, to the use of *dialefe* after these categories of forms: about one in ten uses *sinalefe* instead. Apart from these categories, there are only about forty instances of *dialefe* in the *Commedia,* after final unaccented vowels in polysyllables, and for the most part there is no discernible reason other than the immediate needs of scansion. Although Dante has a strict sense of the number of syllables in the verse line, as *De vulgari eloquentia* shows, and although there is a high degree of regularity in the way he counts syllables, he uses considerably more license in this respect than his successors from Petrarch on.

A semiconsonantal *i* between two vowels also produces a syllable division (not properly speaking a diaeresis or *dialefe*) either inside or at the beginning of a word, with a very small number of apparently arbitrary exceptions. In the *Commedia, primaio* has both two and three syllables, for instance, and *migliaio* has two, in contrast to *migliaia,* with three.

Italian versification is mainly syllable-based rather than stress-based like English and German, so there is no fixed division of the hendecasyllable

H into accented feet. But from Petrarch on, and from the sixteenth century in a rigidly conventional form, it becomes a requirement for the hendecasyllable to have a middle accent on either the fourth or the sixth syllable in addition to the required accent on the tenth. A break of some degree generally follows the word containing this middle accent, though this is not as marked as the caesura in, for instance, the French Alexandrine. Dante's practice in this respect, as in the matter of the syllable count, is less rigid than that of his successors, though for the most part it is similar.

There are a few lines in the *Commedia* that cannot feasibly be read with an accented fourth or sixth syllable, and must therefore be illegal by later standards; there are also somewhat more that can have such accents only at the cost of a rather eccentric mode of enunciation. Examples of the former group are *con tre gole caninamente latra* (*Inf.* 6.14); *parea che di quel bulicame uscisse* (*Inf.* 12.117); *e vidila mirabilmente oscura* (*Inf.* 21.6); *per lo furto che frodolente fece* (*Inf.* 25.29); *la vipera che Melanesi accampa* (*Purg.* 8.80); *Ogne forma sustanzïal, che setta* (*Purg.* 18.49); *e Cesare, per soggiogare Ilerda* (*Purg.* 18.101); *cotanto glorïosamente accolto* (*Par.* 11.12).

It is thus going too far to maintain, as some have done, that all lines in the *Commedia* can be reduced to three main types, with accents respectively on the sixth and tenth, on the fourth, eighth, and tenth, and on the fourth, seventh, and tenth. Dante's practice is more fluid than that, and there are no signs that such a classification was part of the system of conventions within which he was working. It is true, on the other hand, that in the great majority of hendecasyllables in both the lyric poetry and the *Commedia* there is an accented fourth or sixth syllable with a phrase division, and frequently a clause division as well, at the next word boundary; to a degree, Dante's verse-line, like that of his successors but in a less regular way, can be said to fall into two halves. It is also true that the main word accents in each line tend to fall on even syllables in the *Commedia,* and that more than half the lines in the poem have no prominent accents on odd syllables at all, thus lending it a predominantly even accentual rhythm.

Modern Dante criticism has seen an interesting debate on the function or effect of particular kinds of rhythm in the *Commedia:* for instance, are the many lines with accents on the fourth and seventh syllables associated with a particular kind of content, or with effects of emphasis or intensity? The answer to this must be partly a matter of individual interpretative judgment, but it also requires a truly systematic study, such as does not yet exist, of the accentual rhythms of the poem. It must also be stressed that there is no agreed basis for describing these rhythms, for the good reason that our knowledge of Dante's metrical principles is limited, and there are many possible ways of reading each of his lines.

Bibliography

Baldelli, Ignazio. "Endecasillabo." *Enciclopedia dantesca,* 2:672–676.

Beccaria, Gian Luigi. "Cesura"; "Dialefe"; "Dieresi"; "Ritmo." *Enciclopedia dantesca* 1:928–931; 2:420–424; 2:432–436; 4:985–992.

———. *L'autonomia del significante.* Turin: Einaudi, 1975.

Bertinetto, Pier Marco. *Ritmo e modelli ritmici.* Turin: Rosenberg and Sellier, 1973.

Di Girolamo, Costanzo. *Teoria e prassi della versificazione.* Bologna: Il Mulino, 1976.

Fasani, Remo. "Endecasillabo e cesura." *Studi e problemi di critica testuale* 36 (1988), 5–21.

David Robey

Henry I

Known as "the Fat," Henry was king of Navarre (1270–1274) and the second son of the courtly poet Thibaut IV of Champagne. He inherited both countries on the death of his brother in 1270. He married Blanche, the daughter of Robert, count of Artois and brother of King Louis IX of France. Their only daughter, Jeanne, who was betrothed to the son of Edward I of England and later to the son of the king of Aragon, eventually married King Philip IV of France, who transferred the papal Curia to Avignon and for this and many other reasons is despised by Dante (*Purg.* 7.104–109).

Dante places Henry I in the Valley of the Princes in the Ante-Purgatory, together with other rulers who deferred their repentance (*Purg.* 7.85–136). He describes him, without stating his name, as "kindly in appearance" (*benigno aspetto,* 104).

Yolande de Pontfarcy

Henry II of England

King of England from 1154 to 1189; married Eleanor of Aquitaine. In *Inf.* 28.136, Bertran de

Born refers to the rebellion of Henry's son (*re giovane,* "the young king"), which Dante believes Bertran had encouraged. In this context, Bertran speaks of Henry simply as *il padre* ("the father").

V. Stanley Benfell

Henry II of Lusignan
King of Cyprus, 1285 to 1324. Henry failed in his attempt to retake Acre, the last Christian possession in the Holy Land, which was lost to the Saracens in 1291. The Eagle in the Heaven of Jupiter cites him together with other cruel and corrupt tyrants (*Par.* 19.147).

Pamela J. Benson

Henry III of England
King of England, 1216 to 1272; married to Eleanor, daughter of Raymond Berenger IV, count of Provence. Henry *(Arrigo)* is placed among the negligent rulers in the Ante-Purgatory, where he is described by Sordello as sitting alone. The reason for his isolation is unclear, but it may reflect either the fact that England was not part of the Holy Roman Empire, or his characteristic modesty and simplicity. Sordello characterizes him as *il re de la semplice vita* ("the king who lived simply," *Purg.* 7.130), a phrase that Dante appears to have derived from Villani's description of him as *uomo di semplice vita* ("a man of simple life," *Cronica* 8.39). The praise of Henry's progeny refers to his son Edward I, who was credited with having brought about administrative and legal reforms.

Richard Lansing

Henry of Susa
Enrico Bartolomei (1200–1271), author of a famous commentary on the Decretals and cardinal bishop of Ostia. He is cited by Bonaventura in his eulogy of St. Dominic as an example of a great scholar who sought worldly gain (*Par.* 12.83).

Pamela J. Benson

Henry VI, Emperor
The son of Frederick Barbarossa, Henry VI, with the assistance of the archbishop of Palermo, removed Constance, daughter of Roger of Sicily, from a convent in order to effect a politically advantageous marriage. He is referred to by Piccarda as the *secondo vento di Soave* ("the second wind of Swabia," *Par.* 3.119), the first being his father and the third his son Frederick II, emperor and king of Sicily.

Richard Lansing

Henry, the Young King
Prince Henry of England (1155–1183), son of Henry II and Eleanor of Aquitaine, is referred to as [*il*] *re giovane* ("[the] young king," *Inf.* 28.135) by the troubadour Bertran de Born, who claims responsibility for instigating enmity between father and son (*Io feci il padre e 'l figlio in sé ribelli,* "I made father and son revolt against each other," 28.136), thereby meriting his punishment as a schismatic. Henry's demand of his father that he be given the right to rule either England or Normandy had led to open military conflict between the two.

Richard Lansing

Henry VII of Luxemburg
Henry, count of Luxemburg, (c. 1275–1313), was educated at the French royal court. Holding the County of Luxemburg as a fief of the Holy Roman Empire, Henry was also a vassal of the king of France. In 1294, the latter granted him an annual income in return for support given to Philip the Fair's policies. In 1308, however, Henry was the successful rival of the French candidate, Charles of Valois, for election to the imperial throne. Elected in November 1308, he was crowned at Aix-la-Chapelle on January 6, 1309; six months later he received papal approval and confirmation—although the date set by the pope for his imperial coronation in Rome (February 2, 1312) was almost three years distant. At the time of his election, Henry had been secretly supported by Pope Clement V, who feared that the election of Philip's brother Charles would be "to the detriment of the church's freedom," while Cardinal Niccolò da Prato urged him to support Henry as "the best man in Germany, the most loyal . . . the most Catholic . . . who will accomplish great things" (Villani, *Cronica,* 9.101).

Throughout Henry's life even his enemies recognized his nobility of character and qualities as a just ruler and administrator. He also proved to be an able diplomat by overcoming the hostility of the powerful Habsburgs and by marrying his son John

H to Elizabeth of Bohemia (August 1310), thus greatly increasing the lands under his control. These successes encouraged Henry to plan an expedition to Italy, where he was determined not only to be crowned in Rome but also to pacify the warring factions. The ambassadors dispatched to Piedmont, Lombardy, Veneto, Emilia, Liguria, and Tuscany obtained a mixed reception in the lands that made up the "Kingdom of Italy," which were theoretically subject to the Empire but had enjoyed over half a century of independence. Tuscany was emblematic in providing two fiercely opposing attitudes: in Pisa, the imperial embassy received a royal welcome; in Florence—which had created a military league to defend the interests of the Guelf party, the pope, and King Robert of Sicily—Betto Brunelleschi claimed that the citizens of Florence had never bowed their heads in subjection to any lord.

Henry desperately needed public papal support, which came first with the encyclical *Exultet in gloria* (September 1, 1310). At Lausanne (October 11, 1310), he accepted Clement's conditions that he recognize papal rule over Perugia and the Romagna, as well as the Patrimony of St. Peter in Tuscany. On October 23, Henry arrived at Susa, with a small force of about five thousand men and virtually no funds. Dante now wrote his *Epist.* 5 to all the rulers of Italy, comparing the emperor's mission to that of Moses and greeting the dawn of a new age which was to bring "consolation and peace" to all. Like its successors, the letter is replete with biblical tropes; Henry is even greeted with the messianic title "lion of the tribe of Judah." Two points emerge, both of great significance: the Florentine exile now regarded the Emperor as human by nature but divine by grace, and he felt himself to be invested with a truly prophetic mission. In the flush of enthusiasm caused by Clement's blessing of Henry's mission, Dante refers to the emperor in traditional terms originating in Gen. 1:16 as "the lesser luminary" (*Epist.* 5.10)—a comparison utterly rejected in the central section of the *Commedia,* where pope and emperor are referred to as "two suns" (*Purg.* 16.106–108; cf. *Mon.* 3.4).

Dante may have been present at the ceremony in Milan when Henry assumed the iron crown of Lombardy (January 6, 1311). Despite some early successes and Henry's efforts to be impartial in pacifying both Guelf and Ghibelline exiles, revolt quickly spread. On March 31, 1311, Dante bitterly attacks "the most iniquitous Florentines within the city" (*Epist.* 6), condemning them as the slaves of greed for their rejection of the most sacred laws of the divinely willed empire, in which is found "the essence of true liberty." Once again, the emperor's christological role is highlighted by the application to Henry of Isaiah's prophetic words: "Surely he has himself borne our griefs, and carried our sorrows." Less than a month later (April 17, 1311), Dante addresses Henry directly (*Epist.* 7). Like the prophets of Israel, Dante now chides the emperor for his neglect of Tuscany and for his acceptance of limitations to his imperial sovereignty. Florence is the viper of civil war, the Goliath that must be slain. The second paragraph develops the christological implications as never before, when Dante asserts that on seeing the emperor his spirit had rejoiced and he had repeated St. John's words: "Behold the Lamb of God, behold him who takes away the sins of the world" (Luke 1:47).

The outcome, however, belied all of Dante's deepest hopes and aspirations. Henry lost two-thirds of his small army during the siege of Brescia and was forced to rely more and more on partisan Ghibelline support. On January 24, 1312, Henry declared the Florentines rebels against the empire. Crowned in Rome on June 29, 1312 (but not in St. Peter's, which was controlled by the forces of Robert of Naples), Henry tried to assert his imperial authority. King Philip of France rejoined that the French sovereigns had never recognized any temporal overlord. Far more damaging was the fact that the pope did not address Henry as emperor for some six months, ordered Henry not to invade Robert's kingdom, and prohibited him from returning to Rome and other Church lands. Allied with Frederick of Trinacria, the emperor finally moved against Florence in September, but with a force incapable even of encircling the city. Ill with malaria, Henry was obliged to lift the siege on October 31. Leonardo Bruni states that Dante's love of his native city was such that he refused to be present at the siege. The final act in the drama was played out over ten months. On April 26, 1313, Henry condemned King Robert to death as a rebel. Philip the Fair denounced the emperor. The pope threatened excommunication should Henry attack Robert. The end came with the emperor's death of malarial fever on August 24, 1313.

Unfortunately, the chronology of Dante's writings will always be matter for debate and conjecture. Nevertheless, most scholars see the *Monarchia* as heavily influenced by the immense hopes and disillusionment aroused by Henry's imperial enterprise. The insistence on the complementary but autonomous roles of pope and emperor, the assertion that the emperor's authority is derived solely and directly from God (*Mon.* 3.15)—these cardinal tenets of the third book of Dante's treatise on empire were most likely either inspired or reinforced by Clement's eventual hostility toward Henry. Similarly, the picture of civil war and anarchy rampant in Italy and so vehemently denounced in *Purg.* 6 may well have been painted during or after the Emperor's isolation in 1312. Dante's abhorrence of treachery—which led him to place it in the pit of Hell—inspired the reference in *Par.* 17.82 to the Gascon pope's betrayal of "noble Harry." The same epithet ("high, noble," *l'alto Arrigo*) returns in one of the most astounding scenes in the whole *Commedia,* as Dante strains every poetic nerve in his description of the reality of Heaven, as revealed to him by God, who allows him to see "both the courts of Heaven made manifest" (*Par.* 30.95–96). Never before has Dante's vision been so emphasized, when, in a trinitarian cluster (95–99), the word *vidi* ("I saw") is made to rhyme with itself, a privilege otherwise reserved for the name of Christ. At this most solemn moment, the poet chooses to honor the memory of Henry VII in a unique way. Not only is no modern pope singled out for Heaven by the poet; not only is Dante himself the only other person specifically destined for Heaven (135); but Henry's "great throne," one of the few still empty in Heaven, is the only one reserved for a soul on earth, for "noble Harry . . . [who] will come to straighten Italy before she is so disposed" (133–138). The cause for the Emperor's failure is highlighted in the treachery practiced by Pope Clement (143–144), who, soon after Henry's death, will be imprisoned in the third bolgia of the eighth circle of Hell, while his august victim will receive his true reward for his good stewardship on earth as God's vicar in the temporal sphere.

Bibliography

Bowsky, W. M. *Henry VII in Italy: The Conflict of Empire and City State, 1310–1313.* Lincoln: University of Nebraska Press, 1960.

Capitani, O. "Enrico VII di Lussemburgo, Imperatore." *Enciclopedia dantesca,* 2:683–688.

Davis, C. T. *Dante and the Idea of Rome.* Oxford: Oxford University Press, 1957, pp. 138–194.

John A. Scott

Heraclitus

Greek philosopher of Ephesus (c. 540–480 B.C.E.), placed in Limbo together with the great philosophers of antiquity (*Inf.* 4.138). Heraclitus *(Eraclito)* is known for his theory that fire constitutes the essential principle of all matter in the universe. His only book is lost, except for fragments. Dante would have learned of him in Aristotle's *Physics* and in any of several works by Cicero (*De finibus* 2.5.15; *Academia* 2.27.118; *De natura deorum* 3.14.35).

Robin Treasure

Hercules, Pillars of

According to classical tradition, Mount Abyla in Africa and Mount Calpe in Spain, on either side of the Strait of Gibraltar, marked the limits of the human world. Beyond them lay the Hemisphere of Water, closed to mankind by divine injunction. These symbolic columns, formed by Hercules's sundering of a single mountain, are signposts indicating the limits of humanity's knowable and proper environment. In *Inf.* 26.108, Dante makes use of this classical topos to highlight the folly of Ulysses' voyage through the Strait of Gibraltar— *dov' Ercole segnò li suoi riguardi / acció che l'uom più non si metta* ("that narrow strait which Hercules marked with his warnings so that one should not go further")—into the southern seas and the world of the unknown. By going beyond the pillars, the intrepid but foolhardy Greek hero breaks the prohibition and is doomed. Commentators have also interpreted this tale of trespass as an allegory for the boundaries of pagan achievement, devoid of the benefits of Christian revelation, as well as an act of hubris similar in nature to Adam's trespass against God's injunction not to eat of the Tree of Knowledge.

Fiora A. Bassanese

Heresy

The obstinate belief in doctrines condemned by the Roman Catholic Church, usually involving adherence to a separate group, is a tearing of the unity of the church, often compared to Christ's *tunica*

H *inconsutilis* ("seamless garment," John 19:23). Heresy was seen as distinct from schism, which need not involve theological error, and from error itself, which need not be obstinate. St. Paul had identified and predicted heresies: "For there must be also heresies: that they also who are approved may be made manifest among you" (1 Cor. 11:19; cf. Tit. 3:10), a text focusing especially on denial of the resurrection (1 Cor. 15; see below).

The early history of the church was marked by a series of theological disputes, some of them quite prolonged; most of them were settled at assemblies of bishops (the councils of Nicaea, 325 C.E.; Carthage, 417; Chalcedon, 451; Orange, 529; and the Synod of Arles, c. 473). The more important of the early heresies are as follows: In regard to the persons of the Trinity, Arius and his followers denied that the Son was coequal and cosubstantial with the Father, while Sabellius and his followers taught that the persons of the Trinity were merely different manifestations of God. On the incarnation of Christ, the Docetists and Gnostics taught that Jesus was a mere phantasm, and his death an illusion; Nestorius and his followers held that Christ's divine and human natures remained separate, and the Monophysites that he had but one nature combining divine and human. The Gnostics and Manichaeans taught that evil was eternal and coequal with good, and that the visible world was created not by God but by a lesser deity, or by the devil himself. Pelagius and his followers considered unaided human nature as capable of achieving salvation without divine grace. The Donatists denied the validity of ordinations by bishops who had renounced Christianity during the great persecutions.

In the intervening centuries, although theological disputes arose (and unorthodox beliefs were sometimes persecuted, as in the famous case of the poet Godescalc, c. 808–c. 868), heresy was not regarded as a serious problem by the leaders of the western Church until the late eleventh century. At that time a late descendant of Gnosticism and Manichaeanism, the heresy of the Cathars (perhaps from Greek *katharós,* "pure"), or Albigensians (from the town Albi, a principal center), was imported from the Balkans into southern France and northern Italy, where it spread rapidly. Like other late medieval heresies, this was an essentially popular movement, associated with the growth of cities and the spread of literacy among the laity. In the twelfth century, a wealthy Lyons merchant,

Valdes, gave away his wealth in order to practice radical poverty as a wandering preacher; he attracted a mass following (the "Waldensians," from his name). Originally concerned to remain orthodox, the Waldensians were pushed into extreme positions by the intolerance and rigidity of the Catholic clergy. Several heresies arose out of the Franciscan movement itself. St. Francis had practiced and enjoined radical poverty; after the saint's death, the increasing wealth and corruption of the order led to a split between the so-called Conventual friars, the majority, and the Spirituals, some of whom advocated absolute poverty.

Innocent III (1198–1216) and his successors were the first popes to make the struggle against heresy a central focus of concern, eventually declaring a crusade against the Albigensians. Under papal patronage, the Dominican order (*Ordo praedicatorum,* "Order of Preachers") was founded in 1215 by the Spaniard Dominic of Calaruega with the express purpose of combating the Cathar heresy through the vigorous, well-informed preaching of friars living among the people and sharing their poverty. The Franciscan order (*Ordo fratrum minorum,* "Order of Lesser Brothers"), organized in 1210 with the oral approval of the pope, eventually became equally active. Leaders in preaching and in the study of theology, the two mendicant orders achieved great prominence under direct papal patronage at the University of Paris and also in the papal inquisition established in 1231–1234 by Pope Gregory IX. Their influence was to be incalculable.

Dante celebrates the importance of the Dominicans and Franciscans in the fight against heresy, as well as in the development of Catholic theology, in *Par.* 10–14, where the Dominican Thomas of Aquino and the Franciscan Bonaventura of Bagnoreggio are made leading representatives—as indeed they deserved to be—of the two great currents of Christian theology, intellectualistic and voluntaristic, respectively. Each praises the founder of the other order: Bonaventura particularly stresses the importance of Dominic in the fight against heresy (*Par.* 12.97–104); Aquinas, in answering the pilgrim's doubts, warns against presumption in judgment, stressing the training and subtlety required for a just view of theological questions and mentioning Arius and Sabellius as having egregiously distorted scripture (*Par.* 13.127–129). Bishop Folquet of Marseilles appears in the Heaven of Venus because of his youthful devotion to love (*Par.* 9.67–142); no mention is made of his having been one of the most influential leaders in the Albigensian Crusade.

The most extended treatment of heresy in the *Commedia* is that in *Inf.* 9.106–11.9. An entire circle of Hell, the first within the walls of the City of Dis, is devoted to the heretics; they are enclosed, segregated by belief and with their leaders ("heresiarchs"), in burning sarcophagi whose lids will be closed after the Last Judgment; it is made clear that each heresy occupies a different portion of the circle. Except in *Inf.* 11.8–9, Dante focuses exclusively on the heresy of the Epicureans, "who make the soul die with the body"; his encounter with two members of the older Florentine aristocracy—one a Ghibelline and one a Guelf, the father, in fact, of his friend Guido Cavalcanti—is one of the most richly dramatic parts of the poem. Puzzlement has been caused by Dante's placement of the heretics, by his choice of the Epicureans as exemplary, and by his failure to mention specifically Cathars, Waldensians, or Averroists (radical Aristotelians who interpreted the master correctly as teaching the mortality of the soul; Dante seems to have feared that his friend Guido held that doctrine). The "Apostolic Brethren," one of the offshoots of the Franciscan Spiritual controversy, are identified as schismatics in *Inf.* 28.55–60. Dante's Virgil does not account for the placement of the heretics in Hell, probably because the sin was unknown to pagans; some have sought to explain the placement by the idea that the sin was anomalous because "purely intellectual" (a misconception). The heretics are just inside the walls of Dis, a principal expression of the devils' obstinate resistance to God, because obstinacy in error is a principal trait of heresy. In an overarching analogy of the structure of Hell with that of the human body, heresy is located in what corresponds to the human breast and heart, because the heart is named in countless biblical texts as the seat of wisdom and faith (an important parallel with the placement of the theologians in *Par.* 10–14; see also 13.94–96 and 1 Kings [Vulgate 3 Kings] 3:9; the sun was traditionally the heart of the cosmos).

The choice of the Epicureans as exemplars of heresy is undoubtedly motivated by the major biblical text on the subject, St. Paul's discussions in 1 Cor. 11 and 15, which associate denial of the resurrection with unworthy participation in the Eucharist and denial of Christ in his resurrection, in language often applied to Epicureanism: "If the dead rise not again, let us eat and drink, for tomorrow we die." The heretics are shown abortively imitating the resurrection of Christ, with many references to its iconography. Dante draws also on Augustine's discussion of St. Paul's disputes with Epicurean and Stoic philosophers in Athens (Acts 17:18), in the two contrasting figures of Farinata degli Uberti and Calvalcante de' Cavalcanti. Farinata, who in life seems to have been a Cathar (like Epicureans, the Cathars denied the validity of the Mass), is presented as a parodic version of the famous iconographic motif of the *Imago pietatis*, or "Man of Sorrows," an image of the dead Christ associated with the consecrated Host or Mass wafer; in the fight against heresy, the doctrine of transubstantiation was often used as a key test, and it inspired the establishment of the Feast of Corpus Christi in the 1260s.

Finally, *Inf.* 11.8–9 mentions "Pope Anastasius, whom Photinus drew from the right way." Pope Anastasius II (496–498) seems to be meant, even though he had been canonized; he was perhaps chosen for the irony of his name (meaning "resurrected"), which also associates him with the Epicureans. The identification of Photinus is disputed; in any case, the heresy involved denial of the divinity of Christ.

Dante himself has repeatedly been accused of heterodox opinions. As a result of the ferocious attack on the *Monarchia* by the Dominican friar Guido Vernani, who accused it of Averroism, the work was adjudged heretical and publicly burned by the bishop of Bologna in 1328; it was on the Church's Index of Prohibited Books until the nineteenth century. In 1335 all Dominicans were forbidden to read the *Commedia* by the provincial chapter of the Roman Province. Much puzzlement has been occasioned by the fact that, in the *Paradiso*, Dante includes among the theologians two thinkers accused of heretical views. Siger of Brabant, a leading exponent of radical Aristotelianism and leader of the reaction of the arts faculty in Paris against the theologians, was condemned in 1276 by the bishop of Paris; he insisted that his faith was orthodox and appealed to the pope in Orvieto, where he was imprisoned and, some years later, apparently murdered by a deranged servant. Dante places him among the intellectualist theologians led by Aquinas, who says that he "syllogized invidious truths" (*Par.* 10.138), an obscure line on which interpreters do not agree. The abbot Joachim of Fiore appears among the voluntarist theologians led by Bonaventura, who calls him "endowed with prophetic spirit" (*Par.* 12.140–141); his doctrine of the imminence of the Age of the Holy Spirit, to supersede the Age of the Son, was condemned after his death, partly because of the radical interpretation given to it by some Spiritual Franciscans, several of whom were put to death for maintaining that in the Age of the Spirit the traditional priesthood would be superseded. Dante sympathized deeply with the Spirituals, whose attacks on the wealth of the Church he echoes; he never espouses, however, their most radical views.

Bibliography

Browe, Peter. *Die Verehrung der Eucharistie im Mittelalter.* Munich, 1933.

Cassell, Anthony K. *Dante's Fearful Art of Justice.* Toronto: University of Toronto Press, 1984.

Durling, Robert M. "Farinata and the Body of Christ." *Stanford Italian Review* 2 (1981), 5–35.

Gilson, Étienne. *Dante and Philosophy.* Translated by David Moore. New York: Harper and Row, 1949.

Lambert, Malcolm D. *Medieval Heresy: Popular Movements from the Gregorian Reform to the Reformation.* 2nd ed. Oxford: Blackwell, 1992.

———. *Franciscan Poverty: The Doctrine of the Absolute Poverty of Christ and the Apostles in the Franciscan Order, 1210–1323.* London: SPCK, 1961.

Leff, Gordon. *Heresy in the Later Middle Ages: The Relation of Heterodoxy to Dissent, c. 1250–c. 1450.* 2 vols. Manchester: Manchester University Press; New York: Barnes and Noble, 1967.

Pelikan, Jaroslav. *The Christian Tradition: A History of the Development of Doctrine.* Vol. 1, *The Emergence of the Catholic Tradition (100–600).* Vol. 3, *The Growth of Medieval Theology (600–1300).* Chicago: University of Chicago Press, 1971, 1978.

Peters, Edward. *Heresy and Authority in Medieval Europe.* Philadelphia: University of Pennsylvania Press, 1980.

Reeves, Marjorie. *The Influence of Prophecy in the Later Middle Ages: A Study in Joachimism.* Rev. ed. Notre Dame, Ind.: Notre Dame University Press, 1992.

Robert M. Durling

Heretics

Medieval society's attempts to deal with the problem of heresy were based on the belief that "to err is human, to persevere is diabolical." As Robert Grosseteste asserts: "Heresy is an opinion chosen by human faculties, contrary to Holy Scripture, openly taught, and pertinaciously defended." Dante and his contemporaries learned the term's etymology from, for example, Isidore of Seville's *Etymologies* 8—"*Haeresis* is called in Greek from choice"—but for the orthodox, no choice was possible in matters of faith.

After a period of relative peace, the great wave of Catharism began around 1150 to threaten orthodoxy in large sections of western Europe. As a result, the Fourth Lateran Council (1215) declared it the duty of every Christian to report heretics to the authorities, so that they might be "exterminated," and Emperor Frederick II asserted that heretics "offend the Divine Majesty, which is far worse than offending human majesty," even as he condemned heretics to be burned at the stake in 1224. It is with just irony that Dante places Frederick among the heretics of the sixth circle (*Inf.* 10.119). In 1231, the papal Inquisition was

Dante before the gates of Dis and among the heretics in the sixth circle of Hell. La comedia di Dante Aligieri, *with commentary by Alessandro Vellutello, published by Francesco Marcolini, Venice, 1544. Giamatti Collection: Courtesy of the Mount Holyoke College Archives and Special Collections.*

brought into being through Gregory IX's decretal *Ille humani generis.* A few months later, the pope showed his mettle by having a group of heretics—Cathars or Patarenes (as they came to be known in Italy)—burned in Rome. In 1233, Pope Gregory entrusted the work of the Inquisition to the new Dominican Order (in *Par.* 12.97–105, Dante praises its founder for his vigorous attacks against heretics); it was soon joined in this work by the complementary Franciscan Order. As urban dwellers, both orders, though beset by rivalry, were well fitted for this task.

Scholars have pointed to the fact that heresy is a peculiarly Christian sin, unknown to the pagans Aristotle and Cicero, who provide Dante with the basis for the moral order of the *Inferno.* It once seemed to many that the medieval poet had placed heresy somewhat by chance in the sixth circle. Instead, recent scholarship has rightly pointed to the fundamental truth that heresy divided the City of God by destroying the essential unity of Christ's church on earth. Hence, heretics are placed at the entrance to the devil's city, Dis, where their tombs signify, among other things, the wasteland of death created by their rejection of the vivifying spirit of God's word. Hence, too, Dante chooses to exemplify heretics with two Florentines—the Ghibelline Farinata and the Guelf Cavalcante, intended to illustrate the spirit of faction

Dante with Farinata and Calvalcante. Opere del divino poeta Danthe, *ed. Pietro da Figino, Venice, 1520. Giamatti Collection: Courtesy of the Mount Holyoke College Archives and Special Collections.*

that was destroying the poet's city (cf. Matt. 12.25)—but also with an emperor, a pope, and a cardinal, signifying that even the pinnacles of state and Church are threatened. The tombs or *monimenti* (*Inf.* 9.131: "monuments" that are also a terrible "warning") are a particularly appropriate form of punishment for the two types of heretics encountered: those who, like Epicurus, denied the soul's immortality (*Inf.* 10.13–15); and the solitary example of Pope Anastasius II, who was (wrongly) supposed to have believed that Christ possessed only a human and not a divine nature (*Inf.* 11.7–9). Both groups had seen the tomb as the end of human destiny: their infernal tombs, roasted by fire, are an eternal reminder of their rejection of the doctrine of the resurrection of the body and the soul's immortality. Until the Last Judgment, their tombs will remain open (*Inf.* 10.8–9), the open tomb being a common iconographic symbol indicating Christ's resurrection (cf. *Conv.* 4.22.15, where Christ's open tomb is likewise called a *monimento,* hence a promise of eternal life).

In the *Convivio,* Dante had inveighed against the belief punished in *Inf.* 10, claiming that to deny the soul's immortality is "the most foolish, the basest, and the most pernicious" of bestialities, which, if true, would confirm "an impossibility too horrible even to relate" (*Conv.* 2.8.8–10). In *Inf.* 10, on the other hand, his poetic vision turns away from such "bestiality" in order to focus on the possible coexistence of heresy with a certain greatness of character. In *Inf.* 6.79–84, the pilgrim had placed Farinata first among the Florentines *ch'a ben far puoser li 'ngegni* ("who turned their wits to doing well," 81). The heretics' earthly vision is now revealed as spiritual blindness, and their attempts to find substitutes for the immortality they denied are shattered: for Farinata, in the fact that the Uberti and his party never succeeded in returning to his beloved Florence; and for Cavalcante, in the supposed news of his son's death (*Inf.* 10.77–78, 67–72).

The heretics' punishment will be complete after the Last Judgment, when their tombs will be sealed and their intellects—which had led them to reject and misappropriate God's word—will be made void (*Inf.* 10.100–108). In Hell, heresy is a fitting introduction to the circle of violence that follows. It returns in the apocalyptic nightmare of *Purg.* 32.118–123 under the traditional figure of a fox, routed by Beatrice.

H

Bibliography

Cassell, Anthony K. "Farinata." In *Dante's Fearful Art of Justice*. Toronto: University of Toronto Press, 1984, pp. 15–31.

Durling, Robert M. "Farinata and the Body of Christ." *Stanford Italian Review* 2 (1981), 5–35.

Lambert, Michael. *Medieval Heresy: Popular Movements from the Gregorian Reform to the Reformation*. 2nd ed. Oxford: Blackwell, 1992.

Manselli, Raoul. "Eresia." *Enciclopedia dantesca,* 2:719–722.

Mazzotta, Giuseppe. "The Language of Faith." In *Dante, Poet of the Desert: History and Allegory in the "Divine Comedy."* Princeton: Princeton University Press, 1979, pp. 275–318.

Moleta, Vincent B. "Dante's Heretics and the Resurrection." *Medioevo Romanzo* 7 (1980), 247–284.

Padoan, Giorgio. "Il canto X dell'*Inferno*." *Letture Classensi* 5 (1975), 81–99.

Scott, John A. "Politics and *Inferno X*." *Italian Studies* 19 (1964), 1–13.

———. "*Inferno* X: Farinata as *magnanimo*." *Romance Philology* 15 (1962), 395–411.

John A. Scott

Hermaphrodite

In Greek mythology, Hermaphroditus *(Ermafrodito)* was the son of Hermes and Aphrodite, whose beauty excited the love of the nymph of the fountain of Salmacis. One day while he was bathing in the fountain, she embraced him against his will, praying to the gods that they never be separated. The gods granted her prayer by uniting the two in a single human body of both genders (Ovid, *Meta.* 4.285–388). The adjective "hermaphrodite" generally indicates an individual's possession of both male and female sexual organs. Dante uses it to describe one of the two forms of lust being expiated on the seventh and last terrace of Purgatory. The poet Guido Guinizzelli identifies the group of sinners rushing in the opposite direction as sodomites, but says of his own group, *Nostro peccato fu ermafrodito* ("Our sin was hermaphrodite," *Purg.* 26.82). In this context, he means that their sin was that of illicit or unrestrained heterosexual union. The term is ambiguous, however, and a number of ancient and modern commentators have taken the "hermaphrodite sin" to suggest bisexuality.

Olivia Holmes

Hezekiah

A king of Judah (c.715–687 B.C.E.) and one of the six just rulers who form the eye and brow of the Eagle in the Heaven of Jupiter (*Par.* 20.49–54). Hezekiah *(Ezechia)* is identified by means of an incident in which God, having announced Hezekiah's imminent death from illness through the prophet Isaiah, responded to his prayers by granting him another fifteen years (2 Kings 20:1–6; Isa. 38:1–8). The penitence that Dante attributes to Hezekiah (*morte indugiò per vera penitenza,* "delayed death through true penitence," 51) may be attributed either to his prayer of thanksgiving (Isa. 38:15, 17), or to a subsequent incident in which Hezekiah turned aside the wrath of God from himself and Judah by repentance for his own pride (2 Chron. 32:24–26). Hezekiah is lauded as an eminent ruler in 2 Kings 18, 3, 5, and in Eccles. 49:4. In both passages, as in the brow of Dante's Eagle, Hezekiah is ranked with King David. In Matt. 1:9–10, he is named in the genealogy of Jesus Christ.

Carolynn Lund-Mead

Hippocrates

Greek physician, the most celebrated of the ancient world and considered to be the founder of Western medicine. Ancient sources place his birth on the island of Cos in the year 460 B.C.E., and his death at Larissa, in Thessaly. Many of the sixty works attributed to him in the *Corpus hippocraticum* belong to other authors. Dante encounters him in Limbo (*Inf.* 4.143), together with Avicenna and Galen, and calls him *quel sommo Ipocràte* ("that highest Hippocrates") in *Purg.* 29.137. His most renowned work, the *Aphorisms,* is mentioned in *Conv.* 1.8.5, and in *Par.* 11.4 Dante uses the term *amforismi* ("aphorisms") to denote the study of medicine.

Bibliography

Brock, Arthur J. *Greek Medicine.* New York: AMS Press, 1977.

Castiglioni, Arturo. *A History of Medicine.* Translated by E. B. Krumbhaar. New York: Knopf, 1941.

Massimo Ciavolella

Hippolytus

Cacciaguida begins his prophecy of Dante's unjust exile (*Par.* 17.46–47) by comparing it to that of Hippolytus *(Ippolito)*. Hippolytus was the son of Theseus and the stepson of Phaedra; the latter tried in vain to obtain the young Hippolytus's love and, on failing, accused him of having attempted to seduce her. Believing Phaedra's lies, Theseus unjustly banished his son from Athens and even forced his own father, Neptune (who was bound by a Stygian oath to grant any request of Theseus), to cause the innocent young man's death. Cicero (*De officiis* 1.10.32) cites this story, along with that of Apollo's disastrous promise to Phaethon—alluded to at the opening of *Par.* 17—as examples of the foolishness of making blind promises or commitments to the unknown future. However, Dante also finds a fuller version of Hippolytus's story in Ovid (*Meta.* 15.495–505) and, more briefly, in Virgil *(Aen.* 7.761–782), both of which report a further development. Diana, moved by Hippolytus's innocence and purity, intervened to bring the dead hero back to life as a demigod, arranging that he be given the appearance of an old man and that his name be changed to Virbius, as a measure of protection. Traditional interpretations believed the name to be derived from *vir bis,* or "twice a man," and to indicate Hippolytus's rebirth and the ultimate triumph of his purity over his enemies' perfidy. The imagery and content of Cacciaguida's famous prophecy strongly support the thesis that we are to take Hippolytus not just as the figure of an innocent victim, but, most important, as a figure of death and rebirth whose poetic presence forecasts the final triumph Cacciaguida announces for his great-great-grandson beyond the temporary hardships of his undeserved exile.

Bibliography

Chiarenza, Marguerite. "Hippolytus' Exile: *Paradiso* XVII, vv. 46–48." *Dante Studies* 84 (1966), 65–68.

———. "Time and Eternity in the Myths of *Paradiso* XVII." In *Dante, Petrarch and Others: Essays in the Italian Trecento: Essays in Honor of Charles Singleton.* Edited by Aldo S. Bernardo and Anthony L. Pellegrini. Binghamton, N.Y.: Medieval and Renaissance Texts and Studies, 1983, pp. 133–151.

Schnapp, Jeffrey T. "Dante's Ovidian Self-Correction in *Paradiso* 17." In *The Poetry of Allusion: Virgil and Ovid in Dante's "Commedia."* Edited by Rachel Jacoff and Jeffrey T. Schnapp. Stanford: Stanford University Press, 1991, pp. 214–223, 289–293.

Marguerite Chiarenza

History

Perhaps following Hugh of St. Victor, Dante used the term *istoria* (plur., *istorie*) in a wider sense than that of the standard medieval definition provided by Isidore of Seville. Isidore distinguished between *historia,* events that actually happened, *argumenta,* events that might have happened, and *fabulae,* events that could not have happened (*Etym.* 1.44.5). Hugh of St. Victor, while taking account of Isidore's definition, said that in a wider sense the word *historia* could be used to signify "not only the recounting of actual deeds but also the first meaning of any narrative" (*Didascalicon* 6.4). Dante's usage of *istoria* seems to reflect Hugh's broad approach and even includes the recounting of mythological stories. He employs the word five times in the *Convivio* and three times in the *Commedia.* In *Conv.* 1.1.18, he uses it to refer to the literal narrative level of a piece of writing, as distinct from the allegorical level. In *Conv.* 3.3.7, he uses it to refer to the mythological story told by Ovid about the fight between Hercules and the giant Antaeus. Dante also refers to Ovid's account of the pestilence of Aegina as another *istoria* (cf. 4.27.19). In *Conv.* 4.25.6 and 4.26.9, he calls Virgil's *Aeneid* and Statius's *Thebaid* "histories." In *Purg.* 10.52 and 71, he refers to the representations in stone of David dancing before the ark and Trajan doing justice to the widow before setting out on campaign as "histories." In *Conv.* 4.5.11, he mentions *scritture de le romane istorie, massimamente per Tito Livio* ("writings of Roman history, especially those of Titus Livy"); compare the very similar phrase in *Mon.* 2.3.6, *Titus Livius, gestorum Romanorum scriba egregius* ("Titus Livy, the illustrious chronicler of the Roman deeds"). In these last two passages, the words *istorie* and *gestorum* seem to be used in the same sense. Evidently Dante thought of the word "history" as capable of referring to the deeds themselves as well as to the written accounts of those deeds. Did he, like Hugh of St. Victor, draw a sharp distinction between sacred and secular history? (See Hugh of St. Victor, 5, and the discussion in Mazzotta, especially 66–67.) If so, he regarded not only the experiences of the Hebrews and the church as the stuff of sacred history, but also the experiences of what was for him another chosen people, the Romans: the "histories" of David and Aeneas and their descendants run parallel.

H In Dante's era, the histories of the Roman Empire and the Roman Catholic Church are also closely intertwined, though by no means always to the advantage of either institution. Dante himself seems to have thought that he was living in a period of intense crisis for these institutions, when only a deliverer with a very special mission could save the situation. It is possible that he thought this crisis heralded a final great struggle between the forces of good and those of evil, the eschatological events foretold in the book of Revelation. In any case, there are passages in his works which imply that the last stage of history has already begun. Beatrice, for example, tells Dante that very few seats in the Mystic Rose remain to be filled because the number of the saved is almost complete (*Par.* 30.131–132; cf. *Conv.* 2.14.13).

Dante constructed an impressive, and in part original, theology of history. He also devoted a good many pages to the *istorie* or *gesta* of the Romans and to their alleged place in God's providential plan (for example, *Conv.* 4.4–5, *Mon.* 2, *Par.* 6), but he was certainly no historian in the modern sense, if that means accumulating and verifying data, tracing webs of interaction and causation, and analyzing political, social, and economic institutions. Even according to the more generous standards of his own day, by which Virgil's, Lucan's, and Statius's epics might be regarded as works of history, it would be surprising if Dante viewed his *Commedia* in this light. His poem was at once more personal and more universal than theirs. At the same time, it and some of his other writings contain many historical passages and are filled with historical allusions.

What sources supplied these allusions is not always clear. In addition to his heavy reliance on classical poets and on the Bible for his knowledge of the ancient world, Dante also read at least parts of the works of Livy, though perhaps only in Florus's epitome, perhaps Sallust, in a French or Italian adaptation; Orosius, St. Augustine's *City of God,* and perhaps Paul the Deacon's *Historia Romana.* As for his modern historical sources, he almost never mentions them by name, and they can seldom be determined with any certainty. They no doubt included John of Salisbury's *Policraticus,* Brunetto Latini's *Tresor,* Martin of Troppau's (Martino Polono's) *Chronicon*—perhaps in one of the numerous Italian translations and adaptations containing additional information about Florence—and one or more of Riccobaldo of Ferrara's

historical works. Dante may have also drawn on a Latin chronicle that made Julius Caesar one of the founders of Florence. Composed or written around 1200, this *Chronica de origene civitatis* also attracted adapters and translators. Whether Dante knew this work is uncertain, but he did recall several times in his works the legendary story near its end that Attila or Totila (the names were often confused in early Florentine historiography) had introduced himself by trickery into the city, massacred its inhabitants, and destroyed it (*Inf.* 12.134; 13.149; *DVE.* 2.6.5).

As might be expected, Dante's knowledge of modern as well as of ancient history is fragmentary and inexact. For example, he gets even major thirteenth-century events in the neighboring kingdom of France out of sequence, putting the Capetian acquisition of Provence before that of Normandy. But his knowledge of very recent history is rich, if violently partisan. His great poem is filled with contemporary and recent scandal about important and not-so-important personages on both sides of the Alps. He learned a great deal about the politics of northern Italian cities and courts which he visited during his two decades as a wandering exile. In his earlier public career he had served on the councils and embassies of his own city, a metropolis with commercial, political, and intellectual contacts all over Europe.

No doubt sharpened by anger over his exile, Dante's judgment of his own time was mainly negative. The cities of Italy, he said, were full of tyrants, and the Arno River valley inhabited not by men but beasts (Aretines were dogs, Pisans foxes, and Florentines wolves). "Valor and courtesy" had disappeared from the valleys of the Po and Adige rivers since the rebellion there against Emperor Frederick II (*Purg.* 6.124, 14.29–54, 16.115–117). Dante reproached the emperors-elect Rudolf and Albert with having failed to visit Italy, leaving her at the mercy of her factions; therefore, when Henry VII finally came to rescue her, his attempt failed. In one passage of the *Commedia*, Dante indicated that the attempt had been made too early; in another, too late (*Purg.* 7.94–96, 6.97–105, *Par.* 30.133–138). Florence was now controlled by immigrants, the newly rich. The pope himself was so obsessed with the city's gold florin that he had forgotten St. Peter and St. Paul and had eyes only for the image of St. John the Baptist stamped on that coin (*Par.* 16.49–69, *Inf.* 16.73–75, *Par.* 18.133–136). Alluding to the crusade that Boniface VIII preached against his enemies, the Colonna family of Rome, Dante said he now made war not against Syrians or Jews but against Christians near the Lateran (*Inf.* 27.85–87).

Outside Italy, disorder and strife also prevailed. Most of the kings Dante saw on the mountain of Purgatory represented a past that was gloomy, but not so dark as the present. They knew that they had been bad rulers but that their descendants were worse. Dante was told that King Ottokar of Bohemia, though relegated to the valley of the negligent princes, was a better ruler as a baby than his son Wenceslaus was as a grown man. Philip III of France, though declared to have disgraced the French lilies by his defeat in battle, was weeping in the same valley—not for his own disgrace, but for the misdeeds of his son Philip IV. Also grieving for their degenerate offspring were Charles I of Anjou, king of Naples, whose son was Charles II, and Peter III, king of Aragon and Sicily, whose heirs were James II and Frederick II. The only exception was Henry III of England, sitting apart from the rest, surpassed by his son Edward I (*Purg.* 7.97–132).

Later, in *Purg.* 16, Dante learns the reason why the world has gone astray and has suffered moral and political degeneration. The fault lies not in the stars but in the selfish appetites of men, unbridled by imperial law since the emperor has ceased to be the rider of the human will. Discipline has given way to avarice and lust for power. Cupidity now reigns on earth and exists in its most pernicious form in the Roman Church, which in its craving for earthly wealth and power has rebelled against the supreme temporal authority of the emperor.

This spirit of rebellion is also apparent in particular political entities like cities and monarchies. Florence is for Dante the leading example of the former, and France of the latter. Florence, France, the Roman Church, and the Roman Empire occupy the center of Dante's historical stage, and he treats their history in some detail. All are closely linked; the first three are injurious to the fourth and also to each other.

Florence, for Dante, is the most beautiful and famous daughter of Rome, but she is also the most flagrant and destructive example of rebellion on the part of cities within the "garden" of the Roman Empire, which is Italy (*Purg.* 6.105). Her destructive influence, moreover, extends far beyond her boundaries. The evil flower, the gold florin, of this new Babylon founded by the devil has led the whole world astray and turned into a wolf the pope who should be a shepherd (*Par.* 9.127–132). Her own lust for wealth and power has brought down on her the punishment of factional war and political instability, and Dante believed her rebelliousness against imperial overlordship would eventually destroy her.

Dante put forward a legendary and metaphorical explanation for this rebelliousness and factionalism. He used elements from the stories that had accumulated about his city's origins and early history, to which he made his great-great-grandfather Cacciaguida refer in *Par.* 15.124–126 as the tales of the "Trojans, and Fiesole and Rome." These stories had assumed a grandiose and rigidly schematic form in the *Chronica de origene civitatis.* Fiesole on its crag was supposed to have been the first and noblest city of Europe, distinguished for its healthy climate and its vigorous inhabitants; one of these, Dardanus, founded Troy, the mother of Rome. Then Rome became the mother of Florence, which was founded—in fact as well as in legend—by Roman soldiers. The legend said their commander had been Julius Caesar and connected the founding with a long but finally successful siege of Fiesole, whose defeated citizens were settled along with the Romans in the valley below. Five hundred years later, a barbarian army under Totila destroyed Florence and restored Fiesole. Then Florence was rebuilt with the help of the Romans; subsequently, five hundred years after Totila's sack, it destroyed Fiesole, and again the populations of the two cities were merged.

Dante borrowed details from some of these stories, although he may have read or heard them in a different form. He presented them, in any case, in a more sharply anti-Fiesolan way. He did not say that Dardanus came from the noblest city in Europe, Fiesole, but rather from the noblest province in Europe, Italy. He never praised Fiesole at all, but made it a symbol of barbarism and of unwillingness to submit to the divinely ordained empire of Rome. Writing a letter to the Florentines "within the walls," at the time of Henry VII's expedition, he denounced them as the "most wretched offshoot of Fiesole" and as barbarians about to be punished again. He makes his old friend and master Brunetto Latini denounce the Fiesolans, though he had never done so in his *Tresor,* in the following words: *Faccian le bestie fiesolane strame / di lor medesme, e non tocchin la pianta, / s'alcuna* surge ancora in lor letame, / in cui riviva la sementa santa / di que' Roman che vi rimaser quando / fu fatto il nido di malizia tanta ("Let the Fiesolan beasts make straw of each other, but let them not touch the plant, if any still sprout in their manure, in which may live again the holy seed of the Romans who remained there when that nest of so much malice was built," *Inf.* 15.73–78). This apparently refers to the Roman nobles and soldiers who remained in the city after the Fiesolans came down to join them on the new site. Brunetto calls these Fiesolans quello ingrato popolo maligno / che discese di Fiesole ab antico, / e tiene ancor del monte e del macigno ("that ungrateful, malicious people who came down from Fiesole of old, and still smack of the mountain and the granite," *Inf.* 15.61–63). He is really referring not to the ancient Fiesolans but to the modern Florentines: those Florentines of both factions of whom Dante, the Roman, should beware. Brunetto's use of the term "Fiesolan" is therefore not primarily historical but metaphorical, although it is connected to a historical, or legendary, event.

The only time that Dante uses the term "Fiesolan" in a wholly literal and unmetaphorical sense is in *Par.* 16.121–122. Dante has Cacciaguida, who lived in Florence in the early twelfth century, declare that the noble Fiesolan Caponsacchi family had already settled in Florence during his lifetime. Yet Dante also makes Cacciaguida say that la cittadinanza, ch'è or mista / di Campi, di Certaldo e di Fegghine, / pura vediesi ne l'ultimo artista ("but the population, now mixed with those from Campi, from Certaldo, and from Figline, then was pure to the last artisan," *Par.* 16.49–51). Dante believed that it was immigration from the countryside produced by Florentine expansion, and the consequent factionalism within the city—and not merely the infusion of Fiesolan blood—that destroyed this harmony. "Fiesolan" is therefore, in Dante's mind, a metaphor for "immigrant" as well as "rebel." In *Inf.* 15, Dante's Brunetto was using the name "Fiesolan" to refer to factionalism and to both factions of Guelfs within the city, Whites as well as Blacks, since he went on to say that both sides would feel hunger for Dante. Obviously Dante considered himself to be a part of the old Roman stock that avoided factionalism and defended the common good. This view would seem to be supported by Cacciaguida's remark that Dante, in his exile, would be glad that he had made a party for himself (*Par.* 17.68–69).

So when Dante wrote his *Commedia,* he disliked not only the Florentines inside the walls (the Black Guelfs), but also those Florentines outside the walls (the White Guelfs plus the Ghibellines who had been exiled before them). In a metaphorical sense, practically all were Fiesolans. They represented the spirit of factionalism which Dante thought had been the result of conquering the surrounding territories. Dante applied the same moral to the other cities of Italy in *Purg.* 6.76–126 and said that every rustic who came into town to stir up faction was hailed as a hero. He also made Justinian denounce both the Guelfs and the Ghibellines of Italy as rebels concerned with factional struggles rather than the public good (*Par.* 6.97–108). Analogous to the term *Fiesolani* are the terms "Lombards and sons of Scandinavia," which Dante used to address the rulers of Italy when exhorting them to submit to Henry VII. He equates "Lombards" and "sons of Scandinavia" with barbarism and contrasts them with "Trojan and Latin seed" because they resist the Roman emperor (*Epist.* 5.11–12). Whether that emperor speaks German like Barbarossa or Italian like Frederick II or French like Henry VII does not matter; he is still a Roman. The parallel with the phrase *sementa santa* that Dante made Brunetto use in *Inf.* 15.76 is especially striking.

In later times, the history of Florence was much more closely bound up with that of France and the Roman Church than with that of the Roman Empire. Dante was told by Cacciaguida, who was allegedly a crusader knighted by Barbarossa's uncle Emperor Conrad III, that in his lifetime, Florentine women did not yet have to lie alone in bed because their husbands were trading in France. In Dante's day, however, Florence's chief trading partners were France and the French Kingdom of Naples. A French prince, Philip IV's brother Charles of Valois, would soon come to Florence at the instigation of the pope, in the guise of a peacemaker, and would collaborate with the Black Guelfs in a coup that would make them masters of the city and condemn Dante to exile: *Sanz' arme n'esce e solo con la lancia / con la qual giostrò Giuda, e quella ponta / sì, ch'a Fiorenza fa scoppiar la pancia* ("Unarmed he comes forth, carrying only the lance that Judas jousted with, but this he will aim so that it will burst Florence's belly," *Purg.* 20.73–75).

Charles of Valois is also referred to by Dante in *DVE* 2.6.5 as a second Totila, obviously because the barbarian chieftain, whom Dante usually calls "Attila," was depicted in early Florentine chronicles as having destroyed Florence through treachery. The malign influence of the Capetian house extended, according to Dante's Hugh Capet, beyond France and Italy. He tells Dante, *Io fui radice de la mala pianta / che la terra cristiana tutta aduggia* ("I was the root of the evil plant that overshadows all the Christian lands," *Purg.* 20.43–44). Hugh says that the cities of Flanders would take vengeance on it if they could. He remarks that the avarice of his royal line was completely unrestrained after it acquired "the great dowry of Provence" (a reference to the marriage of Charles I, the first Angevin king of Naples, to Beatrice of Provence in 1246: *Purg.* 20.61). Now Charles's degenerate son, Charles II, was haggling over the bride price of his own daughter, also named Beatrice, with the elderly marquis of Ferrara, Azzo VIII d'Este, and selling her to him (in 1305) as a corsair would sell the flesh of female slaves (*Purg.* 20.80–81). But worst of all was Philip IV, avaricious, brutal, and corrupt, who is never mentioned by name in the *Commedia*. In *Epist.* 11.8, he is said to have played the role of Demetrius, king of Syria, referred to in 1 Macc. 7, who appointed Alcimus, an enemy of Judas Maccabeus, as high priest in Israel. In *Inf.* 19.85–87, Philip IV is cast in the role of Antiochus IV Epiphanes, to whom Jason was obliging in order to be named high priest, just as Clement V was obliging to Philip. Probably Philip IV is the giant in the Earthly Paradise who drags the chariot with the prostitute on top of it away into the forest, since this would seem to represent the removal of the papal curia to Avignon (*Purg.* 32.158–160).

Dante also believed that Clement V betrayed both Church and empire, and especially Dante's own emperor, Henry VII, whose enemies included the kings of Naples and of France (*Par.* 17.82). In more general terms, Dante believed that one of the two great lights or authorities created by God had extinguished the other, since the pope had taken over a function proper to the emperor, that of directing temporal affairs (*Purg.* 16.106–112). If the emperor was no longer allowed to fulfill this function and show mankind the road to earthly beatitude, then the pope, usurping the emperor's authority, was unable to fulfill his own function of showing man the road to Heaven: *Dì oggimai che la Chiesa di Roma, / per confondere in sé due reggimenti, / cade nel fango, e sé brutta e la soma*

("Say then that the Church of Rome, because it has confounded in itself the two governments, falls in the mud and soils both itself and its burden," *Purg.* 16.127–129).

The process by which the Church was corrupted and the empire weakened had been begun, Dante believed, by the first Christian emperor himself. According to the account in that most famous of all forgeries, the Donation of Constantine, that emperor, in gratitude to Sylvester I for having cured him of leprosy, granted to the pope jurisdiction over Rome and the imperial provinces in the West. The forged document attesting to this act was almost universally believed in the Middle Ages to be genuine. Even if the emperor's grant was only intended to be a revocable trusteeship for the pope, it was still, in Dante's opinion, a most unwise and disastrous act by the emperor, since a long succession of pontiffs had been able to assert that it constituted an outright gift. They had not transferred the wealth entrusted to them to Christ's poor as clerics ought to do, but instead had used it to pursue luxury and power. Constantine's Donation had infected the church with a deadly poison from which, over the centuries, its sickness had grown worse and worse. Attempts to reform the clerical church from the inside had failed despite the efforts of the two great champions, St. Francis and St. Dominic, sent by God to rescue and discipline the Church Militant (*Par.* 12.40–45). Their followers had, for the most part, returned to the old, disreputable ways (*Par.* 11.124–132, 12.112–126).

Why did Dante think his world was being ravaged by the wolf of cupidity, a fit symbol for Florence, France, and the Roman Church? Beatrice gives the answer in Paradise: *'n terra non è chi governi* ("on earth there is no one who governs," *Par.* 27.140). There was no Roman emperor, no divinely appointed rider of the human will, able to discipline humanity with Justinian's bridle of Roman law. Rome was now a widow, the papacy a prostitute, and Italy a whorehouse (*Purg.* 6.76–90). Henry VII had tried but failed to conciliate the Italian factions and bring peace to this erstwhile "mistress of provinces." Frederick II and his grandfather Frederick I had met resistance in northern Italy, but Dante evidently believed their influence had been beneficent there (*Purg.* 16.116–117, 18.119). Long before, Charles the Great was able to rescue the church from "the Lombard fang" (*Par.* 6.94). But not since Augustus had the whole

H world been at peace. Then the temporal end of mankind was most fully realized, for, untroubled by wars between greedy and ambitious cities and kingdoms, it could enjoy in tranquility its natural beatitude. At the same time, Christ's birth was opening the way to mankind's supernatural beatitude (*Mon.* 1.16, 3.15.7).

Dante regarded many aspects of God's providence as unsearchable, but not its general historical design. Its Roman dimension seemed to him transparent because of the magnitude of past Roman success. In that success he saw the cooperation of divine providence with human free will. His letter to the rulers of Italy urging them to support Henry VII's expedition, since the Roman prince was God's instrument and vicar, expresses this concept succinctly: *Itaque solis existentibus liberus qui voluntarie legi obediunt, quos vos esse censebitis qui, dum pretenditis libertatis affectum, contra leges universas in legum principem conspiratis?* ("Seeing then, that they only are free who of their own will submit to the law, what do you call yourselves, who, while you make pretense of a love of liberty, in defiance of every law conspire against the prince who is the giver of the law?" *Epist.* 6.23). Dante's vision of God's historical design was an essential element in his ethical views and his political theology. These were bound together into a vision of history at once universal and individual in its application. The pope's attempt to exercise temporal as well as spiritual authority, accepted all too passively by those who had forgotten ancient virtues both pagan and Christian, had deprived the world of rightly ordered governance and turned it into a desert (*Purg.* 16.58–129). For Dante, public and private virtue and vice were closely intertwined. But an avenger, probably an emperor, would come to cleanse the world of cupidity and raise up low Italy; of that Dante seems to have been sure, despite his bleak view of the present (cf. *Inf.* 1.101–111, *Purg.* 33.37–45, *Par.* 27.19–63).

Bibliography

Buck, August. "Dante und die Geschichte." *Deutsches Dante Jahrbuch* 68/69 (1993/1994), 15–30.

Davis, Charles T. *Dante's Italy and Other Essays.* Philadelphia: University of Pennsylvania Press, 1984.

Ferrante, Joan M. *The Political Vision of the Divine Comedy.* Princeton, N.J.: Princeton University Press, 1984.

Hugh of St. Victor. *On the Sacraments of the Christian Faith (De sacramentis).* Translated by Roy J. Deferrari. Cambridge, Mass.: Mediaeval Academy of America, 1951.

Kantorowicz, Ernst H. *Frederick the Second 1194–1250.* Translated by E. O. Lorimer. London: Constable, 1931.

Kaske, R. E. "The Seven *Status Ecclesiae* in *Purgatorio* XXXII and XXXIII." In *Dante, Petrarch, Boccaccio: Studies in the Italian Trecento in Honor of Charles S. Singleton.* Edited by Aldo S. Bernardo and Anthony L. Pellegrini. Binghamton, N.Y.: Medieval and Renaissance Texts and Studies, 1983, pp. 193–214.

Mastrobuono, A. C. *Essays on Dante's Philosophy of History.* Florence: Olschki, 1979.

Mazzotta, Giuseppe. *Dante, Poet of the Desert: History and Allegory in the Divine Comedy.* Princeton, N.J.: Princeton University Press, 1979.

Moore, Edward. *Studies in Dante. First Series: Scripture and Classical Authors in Dante.* Oxford: Clarendon Press, 1969.

Nardi, Bruno. "La 'Donatio Constantini' e Dante." *Studi danteschi* 26 (1942), 47–95. Reprinted in *Nel mondo di Dante.* Rome: Edizioni di Storia e Letteratura, 1944, pp. 107–160.

Parodi, E. G. *Poesia e storia nella "Divina Commedia."* 2nd ed. Vicenza: Neri Pozza, 1965.

Reade, W. H. V. "Dante's Vision of History." *Proceedings of the British Academy* 25 (1939), 187–215.

Reeves, Marjorie. "Dante and the Prophetic View of History." In *The World of Dante.* Edited by Cecil Grayson. Oxford: Clarendon Press, 1980, pp. 44–60.

Renaudet, Augustin. *Dante humaniste.* Paris: Les Belles Lettres, 1952.

Renucci, Paul. *Dante disciple et juge du monde gréco-latin.* Paris: Les Belles Lettres, 1954.

Scott, John A. *Dante's Political Purgatory.* Philadelphia: University of Pennsylvania Press, 1996.

Schnapp, Jeffrey T. *The Transfiguration of History at the Center of Dante's Paradise.* Princeton, N.J.: Princeton University Press, 1986.

Charles T. Davis

Holofernes

According to the apocryphal Book of Judith, Holofernes was the commander of the Assyrian army under King Nebuchadnezzar who laid siege to the Jewish city of Bethulia. Judith, an Israelite widow, gained access to Holofernes's tent by pretending to betray her people, then beheaded him while he slept. When the Assyrians saw the decapitated body of their general, they fled in terror and were slaughtered by the Israelites. Throughout the Book of Judith, the Assyrians in general and Holofernes in particular are depicted as proud and arrogant. The twelfth of the thirteen examples of pride engraved on the marble floor of the first terrace of Purgatory depicts the flight of the Assyrians (*Purg.* 12.58–59) and, according to most commentators, the decapitated head of Holofernes (*Oloferne,* 12.59). Some critics, however, interpret this final line—*e anche le reliquie del martiro* ("and also what remained from the murder")—as a reference not to the head of Holofernes but to his headless trunk; others believe it refers to the bodies of the slain Assyrian soldiers.

Lawrence Baldassaro

Homer

The incomparable epic poet, *poeta sovrano* ("the supreme poet," *Inf.* 4.88), Homer (*Omero;* Latin, *Homerus*) is consistently presented in Dante's works with great admiration, first as *quel signor de l'altissimo canto* ("that lord of highest song," *Inf.* 4.95) and later as *quel greco / che le Muse lattar più ch'altro mai* ("that Greek whom the Muses nursed more than they ever did another," *Purg.* 22.101–102). Although the *Iliad* and the *Odyssey* were both unknown in the original Greek during the Latin Middle Ages, their author's reputation endured in the writings of Virgil, Horace, Ovid, Cicero, Statius, and others whose works were well known to Dante. In Limbo (*Inf.* 4.88) Homer appears, sword in hand, at the head of *la bella scola* ("the lovely school"), a group that expands by the canto's close to include Dante himself. The Greek poet is mentioned several times in Dante's minor works (*VN* 2.8, 25.9, *Conv.* 1.7.15, 4.20.4, *Mon.* 1.5.5, 2.3.9).

Michael Papio

Homicide

Dante defines homicide as violence against one's neighbor, and places those guilty of it in the seventh circle of Hell, which is guarded by the Minotaur and itself divided into three *gironi* (rounds) corresponding to the three types of violence, as Virgil explains in his blueprint for Hell (*Inf.* 11.31–39.)

Violence to others and their possessions is punished in the first of these rounds. In the twelfth canto of the *Inferno,* Dante encounters the homicides submerged in *la riviera del sangue in la qual bolle / qual che per vïolenza in altrui noccia* ("the river of blood, in which are boiling those who harm others by violence," *Inf.* 12.47–48). The homicides are also tormented by centaurs armed with bows and arrows, who shoot at whatever shade attempts to lift itself higher out of the river of blood than its sin permits. The first group pointed out to Dante and Virgil by Nessus, the centaur appointed as their guide, is that of the tyrants, who are submerged up to their brows. The murderers are submerged up to their necks, and Nessus points out one who stands to one side, alone, identifying him thus: *"Colui fesse in grembo a Dio / lo cor che 'n su Tamisi ancor si cola"* ("'That one cleft, in the bosom of God, the heart that still drips blood along the Thames,'" *Inf.* 12.119–120). It is the soul of Guy de Montfort, who murdered his cousin, Prince Henry of Cornwall, in the church of San Silvestro in Viterbo, supposedly while Henry knelt for the elevation of the host. The image of the victim's heart, dripping its unavenged blood into the river

Dante at the edge of the Phlegethon, the river of blood and the first ring of the seventh circle of Hell. La comedia di Dante Aligieri, with commentary by Alessandro Vellutello, published by Francesco Marcolini, Venice, 1544. Giamatti Collection: Courtesy of the Mount Holyoke College Archives and Special Collections.

H

Thames, may refer to the enshrining of the prince's heart in London (either, as Villani claims, atop a pillar on London Bridge or, according to Benvenuto, in the hand of a statue in Westminster Abbey); but the image itself suggestively underscores the *contrapasso* of the homicides, who bathe in the river of blood they themselves have shed.

Bibliography

Ferrante, Joan. *The Political Vision of the Divine Comedy.* Princeton, N.J.: Princeton University Press, 1984.

Moore, E. "The Classification of the Sins in Dante's *Inferno* and *Purgatorio.*" *Studies in Dante. Second Series: Miscellaneous Essays.* Oxford: Clarendon Press, 1899, reprint 1968, pp. 152–209.

Morgan, Alison. *Dante and the Medieval Other World.* Cambridge and New York: Cambridge University Press, 1990.

Varanini, Giorgio. "Omicida." *Enciclopedia dantesca,* 4:148.

Claudia Rattazzi Papka

Horace

Like Virgil, a poet of the so-called Augustan circle (65–8 B.C.E.). By 38 B.C.E. he enjoyed the generous patronage of Maecenas and composed both lyrical and satirical works. Horace (*Orazio;* Latin, *Oratius*) appears in Limbo, together with Homer, Ovid, Virgil, and Lucan, as one of the *bella scola* and the greatest poets of antiquity (*Inf.* 4.89). He is described as *Orazio satiro* ("Horace the satirist"), which may refer to him as author of the *Satires,* but may also mean simply "moralist." Although scholars have identified a large number of indirect allusions to his works, the Latin poet is mentioned by name rather infrequently in Dante's works (*VN* 25.9, *Conv.* 2.13.10, *DVE* 2.4.4, *Epist.* 13.30). It is certain that Dante knew the *Ars poetica,* but most scholars believe he was comparatively—possibly even completely—unfamiliar with Horace's other works.

Michael Papio

Hugh Capet

Duke of the Franks and subsequently (987) founder of the Capetian line of French kings, which lasted until 1328. Dante, foregrounding Hugh among the avaricious in *Purg.* 20.16–123, treats him not as an individual but as an authority on his hereditary dynasty, which by its inveterate greed obstructs the universal, indivisible (and non-hereditary) empire. Like anti-Capetian propagandists before him, the poet locates the origin of the French kings' waywardness at the point where doubt could be cast on their legitimacy—the point at which the Capetians took over the Carolingian succession.

Dante merges Hugh (c. 940–996) with his father, also Hugh, duke of the Franks; and he invokes an anti-Capetian insult, calling him the son of a Parisian butcher (*Purg.* 20.52) and thus undermining his royal status (20.55–56). In fact, the historical Duke Hugh had a perfectly sound claim to the crown and was selected as king by the Frankish barons.

In his vitriolic attack on his progeny (20.43–48, 61–96), Dante's Hugh finds no place for the admirable few, most obviously St. Louis (1214–1270)—in many respects a model Christian king—who is absent from all Dante's writings. Hugh introduces his lineage as *la mala pianta / che la terra cristiana tutta aduggia, / sí che buon frutto rado se ne schianta* ("the evil plant that overshadows all the Christian land so that good fruit is seldom plucked therefrom," 43–45); and after alluding to Philip IV's cruel treatment of Flanders and its count, Guy de Dampierre, in the late 1290s (46–48), he begins a more or less chronological account of his scions' increasing iniquities. His descendants were more worthless than maleficent, he says (61–63), until the union of Provence with France in 1245, which inaugurated a display of violence and fraud leading (64–66) to the seizure of Gascony, Normandy, and Ponthieu in 1294. Three Charleses are censured: Charles d'Anjou (67–69) for murdering Conradin in 1268 and—supposedly—Thomas Aquinas in 1274; Charles de Valois for his ill-starred mission to Italy in 1300–1302, with its disastrous consequences for White Guelf Florence (70–78)—Hugh moves into pseudo-prophetic mode at this point; and Charles the Lame for allegedly selling his youngest daughter in marriage to the lord of Ferrara in 1305 (79–81). The climactic lines (85–93), however, are devoted to Philip IV's imprisonment of Pope Boniface VIII at Anagni in 1303 and his destruction of the Knights Templars in 1307–1312.

John C. Barnes

Hugh of St. Victor

Scholastic theologian (1096–1141) of Germanic origin who entered the Augustinian Abbey of St. Victor just outside Paris around 1120, shortly after it was founded by William of Champeaux. Within two decades he led his school to an extraordinary level of renown as a center of mysticism. He devoted his life to the composition of many works, the two most important being the encyclopedic *Didascalicon* and *De sacramentis Christianae fidei* ("The Sacraments of the Christian Faith"), a summa of Christian theology on the nature of God and the creation of the world. Among his other works are the treatises *De arca Noe Morali, De arca Noe mystica, De vanitate mundi,* and commentaries on the Scriptures and on *De caelesti ierarchia* of Pseudo-Dionysius. Hugh assumed the chair of theology in 1130 and made important contributions to theological dogma. Among his students were Richard of St. Victor (*Par.* 10.131) and Peter Lombard (*Par.* 10.106).

Dante places Hugh in Paradise within the Heaven of the Sun, together with the wise spirits of the second crown, where he is named by St. Bonaventure (*"Ugo da San Vittore," Par.* 12.133). Among Hugh's lesser works whose influence on the *Commedia* (either direct or indirect) is almost certain is *De quinque septenis,* which expounds the spiritual significance of five series of sevens in holy scripture: the seven requests of the Father, the seven gifts of the Holy Spirit, the seven capital sins, the seven virtues, and the seven beatitudes. The numerology of seven serves as the conceptual structure of the *Purgatorio,* in which each of the seven terraces purges one of the seven capital vices, with penitents rejoicing in the beatitude that celebrates the virtue opposite to the vice purged and meditating on sets of historical exempla of both the sin and its opposing virtue.

Bibliography

Hugh of St. Victor. *Soliloquium de arrha animae.* PL 176, col. 951–970.

———. *De quinque septenis seu septenariis. PL* 175, col. 405–414.

———. *Hugh of Saint Victor: Selected Spiritual Writings.* Translated by a Religious of C.S.M.V. New York: Harper and Row, 1962.

———. *Didascalicon: A Medieval Guide to the Arts.* Translated by Jerome Taylor. New York: Columbia University Press, 1961.

Anna Maria Chiavacci Leonardi
(translated by Tamao Nakahara)

Hypocrites

Punished in the sixth pocket of the Malebolge (*Inf.* 23), Dante's hypocrites divide into two groups. The first, exemplified by Catalano dei Malavolti and Loderingo degli Andalò, wear robes that resemble those of Franciscan friars but have a golden exterior that belies the weighty leaden interior that impedes the sinners' movement. Dante punishes these two in particular because of the comfortable lives they led as Frati Gaudenti ("Jovial Friars"). Moreover, as chief magistrates of Florence in 1266, they promoted the Guelf interests of Pope Clement IV rather than maintaining civic peace between Guelfs and Ghibellines, as was their ostensible charge. As they walk, they trample the souls of the other group, including Caiaphas, his father-in-law Annas, and all those high priests and Pharisees who favored a death sentence for Jesus. These souls have been crucified on the ground, their arms and legs pinned not by nails but by posts

CANTO XXIII

The hypocrites in the sixth bolgia of Malebolge. Opere di Dante Alighieri, *edited by Cristoforo Zapate de Cisneros, Venice, 1757–1758. Giamatti Collection: Courtesy of the Mount Holyoke College Archives and Special Collections.*

H in a parody of Christ's own crucifixion, for which Dante holds them responsible.

Dante may have conceived of the punishment for the first group of hypocrites from a false etymology of the Italian *ipocrita,* taken to mean "superauratus," or "golden on the outside." Equally important for him, however, would have been the Gospel of Matthew, where hypocrisy is specifically associated with false piety (Matt. 6:2, 5, 16; 23:14).

Bibliography

Bonora, Ettore. "Gli ipocriti di Malebolge." In *Gli ipocriti di Malebolge e altri saggi di letteratura italiana e francese.* Milan and Naples: Ricciardi, 1953, pp. 3–29.

Maggini, Francesco. "Lettura del canto XXIII dell'*Inferno.*" In *Due letture dantesche inedite (Inf. XXIII e XXXII) e altri scritti poco noti.* Florence: Le Monnier, 1965, pp. 1–22.

Psaki, Regina. "*Inferno* XXIII." In *Dante's "Divine Comedy." Introductory Readings I: "Inferno." Lectura Dantis* 6, Supplement (1990), 297–306.

Sanguineti, Edoardo. *Interpretazione di Malebolge.* Florence: Olschki, 1961.

Tartaro, Achille. "Il canto XXIII dell'*Inferno.*" In *Inferno: Casa di Dante in Roma.* Rome: Bonacci, 1977, pp. 533–558.

Michael Sherberg

Hypsipyle

A mythological character (see Ovid, *Heroides* 6; Statius, *Theb.* 4.740ff., 5.720ff.), Hypsipyle was queen of Lemnos and the daughter of Thoas, king of Lemnos. Dante mentions her in *Inf.* 18.92 when he sees Jason, observing that Jason fooled the one who before had fooled all the rest, a reference to the story of how Hypsipyle was loved and abandoned by Jason and how she saved her father from certain death through trickery. In *Purgatorio,* she is mentioned twice in reference to her life after her escape from Lemnos. Virgil names Hypsipyle *(Isifile)* in *Purg.* 22.112 as a resident of Limbo, referring to her as the one who showed the Greeks the fountain of Langia (*Theb.* 4.740ff.). In *Purg.* 26.94–96, Dante expands his reference to the episode, in which a child in her care, Archemorus, died after being attacked by a serpent after she left him unattended while submitting to the Greek princes' request to show them the fountain. Lycurgus, Archemorus's father, sought to punish Hypsipyle for her lapse, but she was saved from death by her two sons, who appeared suddenly and embraced her (*Theb.* 5.720ff.). Dante draws a parallel between that embrace and his own desire to embrace Guinizzelli. The episode of Archemorus's fate is also alluded to in *Conv.* 3.11.16.

Maria Ann Roglieri

I

Iacopo della Lana

Author of the first complete vernacular commentary on Dante's *Commedia*. Influenced by his academic education in his native Bologna, Lana (c. 1278–c. 1358) approaches the *Commedia* from a Scholastic perspective as a didactic encyclopedia and endeavors to provide readers with extensive information on topics that he considers necessary to a correct understanding of the *Commedia*, but which may not be strictly related to Dante's subject matter. The result is a wide-ranging exegesis, written between 1324 and 1328, which had enormous diffusion owing both to its use of the vernacular and to the quantity of materials it employs. Lana structures his commentaries in two different sections. The first is a *proemio* in which he presents a summary of a canto's narrative action, its most important allegories, and its doctrinal content (philosophy, theology, astronomy, astrology, and science, mainly based on St. Thomas's works and Aristoteles Latinus). In the second part, he gives glosses to the text in which principal situations and characters are highlighted, the literal meanings of a number of expressions are explained, and brief synopses of historical and mythical events are appended. Lana's commentary was not only highly appreciated by his contemporaries (Andrea Lancia based his *Ottimo commento* on Lana's text, and a few of its copies were attributed to Petrarch) but was also the first vernacular commentary on Dante to be printed, though under the name of Benvenuto da Imola (Venice, 1477).

Bibliography

Iacopo della Lana. *Comedia di Dante degli Allagherii col commento di Jacopo della Lana bolognese.* Edited by Luciano Scarabelli. 3 vols. Bologna: Tipografia regia, 1866–1867.

Mazzoni, Francesco. "Jacopo della Lana e la crisi nell'interpretazione della *Divina Commedia*." In *Dante e Bologna nei tempi di Dante*. Bologna: Commissione per i Testi di Lingua, 1967, pp. 265–306.

Parker, Deborah. *Commentary and Ideology: Dante in the Renaissance*. Durham, N.C.: Duke University Press, 1993.

Vallone, Aldo. "Jacopo della Lana, interprete di Dante." In *Dante, Petrarch, Boccaccio: Studies in the Italian Trecento in Honor of Charles S. Singleton*. Edited by Aldo S. Bernardo and Anthony L. Pellegrini. Binghamton, N.Y.: Medieval and Renaissance Texts and Studies, 1983, pp. 151–182.

Luca Carlo Rossi

Icarus

Son of Daedalus, the famous craftsman of classical mythology who contrived feathered wings by means of which he and Icarus *(Icaro)* tried to escape from Crete. Daedalus warned his son not to fly too high or too low, but Icarus approached too near the sun while flying over the sea, so that the wax which held his wings together melted and he fell and drowned (Ovid, *Meta.* 8.183–235). Dante compares the fear experienced by the pilgrim when descending into Malebolge mounted on the back of the monster Geryon to the fear that Icarus must have felt when his feathers fell off in mid-flight (*Inf.* 17.109–114). Although the Icarus legend was frequently interpreted allegorically in the Middle Ages as showing, for instance, the consequences of pride, Dante does not stress its symbolic meaning here, except inasmuch as he implicitly contrasts the pilgrim's eventual ascension to Heaven with Icarus's unsuccessful flight. He also refers to him, as the son of Daedalus, in *Par.* 8.126.

Olivia Holmes

Illuminato da Rieti

An early follower of St. Francis who accompanied him on his mission into Egypt and later became bishop of Assisi in 1273. Illuminato is among the wise souls in the Heaven of the Sun (*Par.* 12.130).

Molly Morrison

Illustrations, Medieval and Renaissance

In imagining his *Inferno, Purgatorio,* and *Paradiso* for his *Commedia* in the first decades of the four-

Dante retreating to the selva oscura, *from the 1564 edition of the* Commedia. Dante, *with commentary by Cristofo Landino and Alessandro Vellutello, published in Venice in 1564 by Marchiò Sessa & fratelli. Giamatti Collection: Courtesy of the Mount Holyoke College Archives and Special Collections.*

teenth century, Dante would have known many of the depictions of the Last Judgment in mosaic and fresco on the walls of the churches in Northern Italy. Among them may have been the *Inferno* mosaic in the ceiling of the Baptistery of Florence (last quarter of the thirteenth century), freer and more animated than those of the Byzantine tradition from which it derives, and, quite likely, the *Last Judgment* of Dante's contemporary and friend Giotto in the Arena chapel in Padua (c. 1304).

The liveliness of the depictions of gruesome punishments in Hell in both renditions seems to have established a painterly tradition that for the next century and a half fed more on itself than on its borrowing from Dante's imagery in the *Commedia*. The major examples of this tradition are the Camposanto frescos in Pisa (Francesco Traini [?], c. late 1340s), the *Inferno* fresco in the Duomo in San Gimignano (Taddeo di Bartolo, 1396), the *Inferno* fresco in San Petronio in Bologna (Giovanni da Modena, c. 1410), and the paintings of Fra Angelico in San Marco in Florence (1432–1433) and Giovanni di Paolo in the Accademia in Siena (1453). These representations of Hell have magnificent verve and inventiveness, but, generally, they are not derived from Dante, though there are unquestionably borrowings in some details, perhaps most in the di Paolo. Questions of the relationships of these works to Dante are handled in Ludwig Volkmann's indispensable *Iconografia dantesca* (English edition, 1899) and in "The Iconography of Hell" (Nassar).

The one fresco that in almost all details attempts a faithful illustration (faithful, that is, to the tonal complexity of Dante's text) of all thirty-four cantos of the *Inferno* is that of Bernardo Orcagna ("Nardo di Cione") in the Strozzi chapel of the church of Santa Maria Novella in Florence, dating from the early 1350s. There are everywhere in the Nardo fresco a mastery and understanding of—and sympathy with—the full range of Dantean attitudes. Curiously, his brother Andrea Orcagna's depiction of Paradise on the facing wall of the chapel, done at the same time, borrows not at all from Dante; it is a thoroughly conventional rendering in the traditional manner, in Volkmann's words, of "Christ and the Madonna on the throne; saints and angels on both sides; underneath, the band of the elect." This is true also of the representations of Paradise in the frescos of the Camposanto, the Duomo in San Gimignano, and San Petronio in Bologna, and the paintings of Fra

Angelico at San Marco in Florence and Giovanni di Paolo in the Accademia in Siena.

The Nardo di Cione fresco, for all its giant size, disposes itself compositionally as a series of smaller paintings, each much like an enlarged "illumination" or "miniature" (small paintings or illustrations in the vellum manuscripts of the time), and it is to the illuminated manuscripts of the *Commedia* that we must turn for Dante illustration in the century and a half (c. 1330–1480) before the age of the printed book in Italy. The entire subject has been brilliantly handled in the collaborative volumes of Peter Brieger, Millard Meiss, and Charles Singleton, *Illuminated Manuscripts of the Divine Comedy* (1969). Hundreds of manuscripts of the *Commedia* are extant, and close to one hundred of these have some illumination or decoration. The reader can view the best of these in the volumes just mentioned, but the following manuscripts merit special attention for their analytical and interpretive power: (1) Chantilly, Musée Condé, MS. 597 (Pisan, c. 1345); (2) Vatican, Biblioteca Apostolica, MS. 4776 (Florentine, c. 1390–1400), perhaps the finest of all the manuscripts, generally influenced throughout by the Nardo di Cione fresco; (3) Paris, Bibliothèque Nationale, MS. it. 74 (Florentine, Bartolomeo di Fruosino, c. 1420), whose frontispiece is a direct borrowing from the Nardo di Cione fresco; (4) Paris, Bibliothèque Nationale, MS. it. 2017 (Lombard, c. 1440), whose depiction of the Hypocrites of *Inf.* 23 ought to be viewed together with the depiction of the same scene in MS. it. 74, as masterpieces of the art of illumination; (5) London, British Museum, Yates Thompson MS. 36 (Sienese, Priamo della Quercia, c. 1442–1450, Giovanni di Paolo and assistant, mid-15th century), a manuscript di Paolo completed by illuminating the *Paradiso;* and (6), finally, not so much for its interpretive power but for the sheer beauty of the Piero della Francesca-like illuminations, Vatican, Biblioteca Apostolica, MS. Urb. Lat. 365 (Ferrara, Guglielmo Giraldi and assistants, c. 1478; illuminations to the *Paradiso* added by a later miniaturist, c. early 17th century).

Botticelli's drawings for the *Commedia* (begun in 1480) date from this transitional period between the last great illuminated manuscript (no. 6 above, 1478) and the advent of the first illustrated printed book of the *Commedia* in Italy (Florence, Nicolò di Lorenzo della Magna, 1481). The Botticelli drawings are in fact the clear model for the copperplate engravings that adorn the first nineteen cantos of the 1481 edition. Botticelli illustrated all one hundred cantos of the *Commedia,* but the drawings for *Inf.* 2–7 and 11 have not survived; seven of the drawings are in the Vatican Library and the others at the Berlin State Museum. The drawings are praised by their early editor, F. Lippmann, as "one of the most significant artistic renderings ever given to poetry, and not the least among the many marvels of the Italian Renaissance," a conclusion with which their recent editor, Kenneth Clark, wholeheartedly agrees. Bernard Berenson, in reviewing Lippmann's edition of the drawings in 1896, calls Botticelli "the greatest master of the single line that our modern Western world has yet possessed," yet he feels that "Botticelli was not the man for the task . . . . Their value consists in their being drawings by Botticelli, not at all in their being drawings for Dante." There are marvelous vignettes everywhere in the details of the drawings, which display an obviously powerful mind and spirit in the artist interpreting the text. There are also details of expression and gesture that seem merely perfunctory. (The drawings are meant to be read as flowing narrative; Dante and Virgil appear more than once in an individual drawing as they move through sequences in the text, a style copied by subsequent illustrators.) It seems apparent that the drawings, at least initially, were conceived by Botticelli as preliminary for what were to be finished paintings, where all details of expression and gesture would be refined. Four of the drawings are in fact colored, and some of them are clearly more finished than others. Lippmann traces the many starts and stops in Botticelli's work on the drawings during his lifetime. Many of Berenson's objections to the drawings as illustration can be traced to their unfinished state, but not all can be. There is perhaps some fundamental hesitation in Botticelli's approach to the punishments of the *Inferno;* both the *Purgatorio* and the *Paradiso* are more congenial to his spirit. There are simply no illustrations to the *Paradiso* that are the equal of Botticelli's, though these are often restricted to the two figures of Dante and Beatrice.

The copperplate engravings of the 1481 Florentine printed book are certainly inferior to the Botticelli drawings on which they are based, but immeasurably better in expressive power than the quite inferior, banal woodcuts (which they influenced) of subsequent printed editions: in 1487

(Brescia, B. de Boninis), 1491 (Venice, B. Benali & M. da Parma), 1491 (Venice, P. Cremonese), 1493 (Venice, M. de Parma), 1497 (Venice, Piero de Zuanne), 1506 (Florence, F. di Giunta), 1512 (Venice, Bernardino Stagnino), and 1555 (Venice, Gabriel Giolito).

The exception is the very interesting Venetian edition of 1544 (F. Marcolini, illustrations reprinted in 1564 in Venice by G. Sessa with a new frontispiece of Dante, the "grand naso" edition). The illustrations in this edition are perhaps more designs than illustrations, but ingenious and often dramatic. In the *Inferno,* the anonymous designer envisions each illustration as a horizontal section of Hell, as Dante and Virgil move ever lower, spiraling downward into circles of ever-decreasing diameter. These are remarkably effective in creating a sense of claustrophobia, and, at the same time, a sense of Dante's awe at the divine architecture of Hell. The *Purgatorio* is a series of designs of ascent up a conical mountain to the apex, and the *Paradiso* of a spreading outward into circles of ever-increasing diameter. These designs are the product of an interesting and original mind.

After the 1544 edition, meaningful book illustration of Dante is dormant for two hundred years, until a Venetian edition of 1757, around the time when interest in Dante reawakened in Italy. One must go back to the beginning of the sixteenth century and the high Renaissance frescos of Luca Signorelli at the cathedral at Orvieto (c. 1499–1504) to view the greatest influence of Dante on the visual arts since the drawings of Botticelli. The frescos demonstrate Signorelli's remarkable ability to draw the human figure, though of the many frescos of the Anti-Christ, the Last Day, the Last Judgment, the Resurrected, the Elect, and the Damned, only one fresco has direct relationship to a scene from the *Inferno:* that of the neutrals or opportunists of canto 3, who are stung by wasps as they pursue a wavering banner, while Charon ferries the damned across the river Acheron to be judged on the other shore by Minos. The Charon–Minos scene is also the one scene in the Last Judgment fresco of Michelangelo in the Sistine Chapel of the Vatican (c. 1540) that is directly related to Dante's poem. In the Michelangelo, Charon whacks the sinners with his oar just as Dante describes, while Minos, in both the Signorelli and the Michelangelo, winds his tail around his body to designate a given sinner's place in Hell, again according to Dante's description.

There is evidence that Michelangelo studied Signorelli's frescos at Orvieto and that both frescos are the products of lifelong devotion to Dante and his *Commedia.* There are many correspondences in both frescos to the earlier painterly tradition mentioned above. Some scholars focus on Signorelli and Michelangelo's interest in the nude form and the New Humanism it implies, or on Michelangelo's giving the head of a personal enemy to Minos and the awakening of the egoistic personality in art that it implies. But their faithfulness to Dante is nevertheless fully evident. The tonalities of Dante's text, its complexity, compassion, faith, and doubt, the sardonic comedy and the poignant tragedy, had never been so awesomely captured as in these masterful frescos.

Signorelli and his assistants also depicted scenes from the first eleven cantos of the *Purgatorio* in the plinths under the great frescos. These are in gray and blue, and although they do not have the wonderful finish of the great frescos, they are among the best illustrations of *Purgatorio* that we have. They carry on Botticelli's technique of multiple vignettes in one painting, with Dante and Virgil appearing two or three times in each (a technique used later by Zuccaro). The entire body of Signorelli's work at Orvieto can best be studied in *Temi danteschi ad Orvieto* (Rotondi, 1965) or in *Signorelli e Dante* (Gizzi, 1991). The Michelangelo fresco of the Last Judgment in the Sistine Chapel was cleaned in the 1990s and can now be studied without the drapery additions of da Volterra, which were intended in part to veil some instances of sardonic sexual imagery, imagery that goes back to Giotto. These and other details in both the Michelangelo and the Signorelli flow from the painterly tradition that began with the Baptistery mosaic and the Giotto, the Camposanto, and the Nardo frescos. These links to past tradition in both artists, and the deep respect that both had for Dante, constitute links of continuity between the late medieval period and the new Humanism of the Renaissance.

There is a hint of Dantean influence in Raphael's *Saint Michael and Satan* in the Louvre (c. 1504), where the city of Dis is in fire and smoke in the background and figures in clerical garb walk in a circle in front of the city walls, reminiscent of the hypocrites in *Inf.* 23. In the later Renaissance–Early Baroque period (c. 1586–1588), we find two comparatively obscure artists in Florence who are independently engaged in a series of drawings to the *Commedia* a full century after Botticelli had begun his series. These drawings, like those of Botticelli, remained unpublished and largely unstudied until the late nineteenth century. The drawings of Federico Zuccari are in the Uffizi, and those of Hans van der Straet (a Fleming from Bruges, called Stradanus) are in the Biblioteca Laurenziana in Florence. Stradanus's drawings appeared in an English edition edited by G. Biagi in 1892; a more comprehensive volume was edited by C. Gizzi in 1994. Zuccari's drawings are finally available in a splendid volume edited by C. Gizzi in 1993. Both artists are too often willing to give Dante's text a journeyman's handling for the most obvious theatrical effects; both are, at the same time, prolific and talented draftsmen working in a time of high standards, so that one can often find excellent detailing of expression and mood in their work.

Stradanus occasionally is able to evoke an elegiac mood of the pathos of Hell and the sinners' sufferings, which seems to reflect a personal expression while remaining true to one aspect of Dante's tonality. The *Inferno* is represented in twenty-five drawings in dark sepia, and the *Purgatorio* in four drawings in green that seem to be by Stradanus. The codex in the Laurenziana also contains twelve drawings for the *Paradiso* in blue and white which seem clearly not up to Stradanus's standards; the expressions of Dante and Beatrice are strikingly vacuous. They are nevertheless interesting compositions, whoever the artist.

Zuccari, often mannered, grotesque, and burlesque, can still be very moving, as with his Earthgiants of canto 31, whose powerful bodies strain in perpetual confinement. The twenty-eight drawings for the *Inferno* are often filled with bombastic architectural and landscape backgrounds and foreground spectacle. In the fifty drawings for the *Purgatorio*, the human scale and focus are more satisfying. Dante and Virgil take part in multiple vignettes in a single drawing, and long quotations from Dante's text are included in the drawings. In the eleven drawings for the *Paradiso*, Zuccari's spirit seems most involved and his designs are quite effective. Zuccari also incorporated Dantean motifs in his cupola frescos in the Duomo in Florence.

The seventeenth century and the first half of the eighteenth saw a slackening of interest in Dante, with very few new editions of his works. No illustrations of the poem worthy of comment appear in the seventeenth century, save for those mentioned above to the *Paradiso* added early in the century to a fifteenth-century manuscript done for the Urbino family and now in the Vatican Library (MS. urb. lat. 365). Volkmann terms these colorful and charming Baroque miniatures the "art of the Epigoni," granting them their obvious technical and compositional skill and their elegance but decrying their lack of force, depth, or power of expression. One can only be less enthusiastic about the illustrations in the 1757 Venetian edition of Dante's complete works (A. Zatta), which is not distinguished in its copperplate engravings by various hands. The landscape of Hell is serene and placid, an ordered place, rather like a Sunday stroll through a great outdoor park. It is an eighteenth-century Age of Reason trip through Hell, Purgatory, and Paradise, not Dante's.

The 1757 edition is incidentally one of the few up to this date to offer any illustrations, albeit quite weak ones, to the *Vita Nuova* or any other of Dante's minor works. The phenomenal revival of interest in Dante, his life and works, the deep complexity of his world-view, and his artistic tonalities is ushered in with the beginnings of Romanticism.

Bibliography

Barricelli, Jean-Pierre. *Dante's Vision and the Artist.* New York: Peter Lang, 1993.

Berenson, Bernard. "Dante's Visual Images, and His Early Illustrators." *Nation* 58 (1 Feb. 1894), 82–83.

Berenson, Bernard. "Botticelli's Illustrations to the *Divina Commedia*." *Nation* 63 (12 Nov. 1896), 363–364.

Bertolini, Licia. *Camposanto monumentale di Pisa: Affreschi e sinopie.* Pisa: Opera della Primaziale Pisana, 1960.

Biagi, Guido (ed.). *Illustrations to the Divine Comedy of Dante, Executed by the Flemish Artist, John Stradanus, 1587.* London: T. F. Unwin, 1892.

Brieger, Peter, Millard Meiss, and Charles Singleton. *Illuminated Manuscripts of the Divine Comedy.* 2 vols. Princeton, N.J.: Princeton University Press, 1969.

Clark, Kenneth. *The Drawings of Sandro Botticelli for Dante's Divine Comedy.* New York: Harper and Row, 1976.

Il Dante Urbinate della Biblioteca Vaticana (Codex Urb. lat. 365). Vatican City, 1965.

Donati, Lamberto. *Il Botticelli e la prime illustrazioni della Divina Commedia.* Florence: Olschki, 1962.

Gizzi, Corrado (ed.). *Giovanni Stradano e Dante.* Milan: Electa, 1994.

———— (ed.). *Federico Zuccari e Dante.* Milan: Electa, 1993.

———— (ed.). *Raffaelo e Dante.* Milan: Charta, 1992.

———— (ed.). *Signorelli e Dante.* Milan: Electa, 1991.

————. *Botticelli e Dante.* Milan: Electa, 1990.

Gronau, Hans. *Andrea Orcagna und Nardo di Cione.* Berlin: Deutscher Kunstverlag, 1937.

Koch, T. W. (ed.). *Catalogue of the Dante Collection.* Ithaca, N.Y.: Cornell University Library, 1898–1900.

Lippmann, Friedrich. *Drawings by Sandro Botticelli for Dante's Divine Comedy.* London: Lawrence and Bullen, 1896.

Michelangelo and Raphael in the Vatican. Vatican City, 1984.

Nassar, Eugene Paul. *Illustrations to Dante's Inferno.* Cranbury, N.J.: Fairleigh Dickinson University Press, 1994.

————. "The Iconography of Hell." *Dante Studies* 111 (1993), 53–105.

Pope-Hennessy, John. *A Sienese Codex of the Divine Comedy (British Museum Yates Thompson MS 36).* London: Phaidon Press, 1947.

Rotondi, P. "Gli affreschi della Cappella di San Brizio e l'arte di Luca Signorelli." In *Temi danteschi ad Orvieto.* Milan: Arti Grafiche Ricordi, 1965.

Volkmann, Ludwig. *Iconografia dantesca.* London: H. Grevel, 1899.

Eugene Paul Nassar

Illustrations, Modern

If by "modern" we mean representation subsequent to the Renaissance, Baroque, and Neoclassical periods, then we must begin a survey of illustrators of the *Commedia* with the late eighteenth century. Prior to the work of John Flaxman, Henry Fuseli, and especially William Blake, artists like Federico Zuccari, Hans van der Straet (Stradano), Cesare Pollini, and Antonio Zatta were hampered by two overarching characteristics of their time: either the pretentious rationalisms of the Cartesian *logos,* or the esthetic of grace, pleasantness, and technical refinement. Fuseli's six wash drawings of the *Inferno* (including a famous one of the Bocca degli Abati scene) and the *Purgatorio* (1774), and several oils (notably a controversial one of Ugolino, 1806), helped begin a reorientation of the Dantean vision by way of a broader and more subjectively expressive mode. Analogously, the sculptor Flaxman's 110 engravings (1793) gave new meaning to line drawing which, though lacking in vigor because of the absence of pronounced sinews and shading, pointed in the direction of abstract or stylized shapes, conveying few emotions beyond agony. See his writhing thieves and attacking snakes (*Inf.* 25), his grotesque Lucifer (*Inf.* 34), his restful Matelda episode (*Purg.* 28), or his exultant Triumph of Christ (*Par.* 23).

Blake emerges as the first great post-Renaissance illustrator. A mystic, he gave his personal stamp to his watercolored drawings (commissioned by the painter John Linnell in 1824), from which some engravings were made. He used Cary's translation of Dante, and gave us what has been called the last legacy of his imagination. Though Blake was hostile to some aspects of the poet's theology (for him, the angry God of the *Inferno,* like his own Urizen who preached punishment more than pardon, was closer to Homer and Aristotle than to the Bible), he was obviously fascinated by the *Inferno,* since most of the 102 pencil sketches and watercolors (seventy-two for *Inferno,* twenty for *Purgatorio*, ten for *Paradiso*) deal with it. He reacted against Beatrice as the "Female Will" and chastity, and against Virgil who, like Homer, extolled military valor; and in the name of the Bible, he questioned Dante's evocation of the Greek Muses. Ultimately, however, Blake subscribed strongly to the Florentine poet's symbolism and praised the power of his imagination, even while trying to superimpose his own vision on Dante's. His illustrations are not accurate visual renderings of the text; they have a private, intellectual content, rendered with stylized fluidity (many of his figures appear effeminate), swirling movements, linear grace, and intense mythological—even dreamlike—emotion; he sometimes incorporates passages of the text in the illustration itself. If not politically, Blake's vision merged spiritually with Dante's. The most famous of these illustrations are his three beasts, Entrance to Hell, Minos, Francesca, Cerberus, Capaneus, the hypocrites, Fucci, Bertran de Born, the angel guardian, the purgatorial fire, the edenic chariot, Christ, the recording angel, and Sts. John, James, and Peter.

Romantic enthusiasm over Dante kept artists, convinced of the poet's painterly value, looking for subjects beyond the poem's account of events: narrations inside the narrative (like Ulysses' voyage or Pia's story), significant images (flowers, landscapes, animals), and metaphors. The works of Carl Vogel von Vogelstein, Alfred Rethal, Giuliano and Francesco da Sangallo, Francesco Nenci, and Giuseppe Bezzuoli come to mind. Favorite topics emerged: Ugolino, for example, was utilized by Luigi Ademollo, Joshua Reynolds, John Dixon, Francesco Pagnoni, J. A. Ramboux, Francesco Scaramuzza, C. C. Condulmieri, and F. Bigioli, to mention but a few artists inspired by the starving count and his sons. Most prolific was Domenico Fabris (500 woodcut vignettes, 1840–1842), who pictured all aspects of the *Commedia*. Another excellent craftsman was Peter Cornelius, a member of the German Romantic Nazarene School: his Dante frescos (1817–1819) for Rome's Villa Massimo in Laterano and for Munich's Ludwigskirche (1840) reveal, through forceful colors, a strong brush at work.

The most admiring of these artists was Joseph Anton Koch, who collaborated with Cornelius on the Villa Massimo project and who could recite whole passages of the poem by heart. From 1800 onward, he illustrated it abundantly in all media; again, the *Inferno* commanded his greatest attention. He illustrated each of its cantos, though he devoted only two illustrations (an oil and a watercolor) to the *Purgatorio*'s ship of souls, two—a drawing and an oil—to the dream of the Golden Eagle, and none to the *Paradiso*. His forms are Classical, and he tones down Dante's horrible dramas, but his use of color is fiery, so that he bridges Classicism and Romanticism. His masterpiece is the fresco of Brunelleschi and the dragon (*Inf.* 25) and of Minos, surrounded by various infernal characters.

The number of artists who lent their talents to the Dantean enthusiasm continued unabated. Among them were Anselm Feuerbach, Peter Cornelius, Philip Veit, Otto Greiner, Carl von Ramohr, Friedrich Prell, Giovan Giacomo Machiavelli, Robert von Langer, Bonaventura Emler, Wilhelm Hansel, Franz Ittenbach, Karl Müller, Eduard Bendemann, Theodor Mintrop, Hugo Freiherr von Blomberg, Carl Begas, Karl F. Lessing, Bonaventura Genelli, Dante Gabriel Rossetti, Edward Bourne-Jones, Heinrich Hess, Antoine Etex, Yan d'Argent, and Franz von Bayros. From Nazarenes to Pre-Raphaelites, from Realism to Art Nouveau, no other work of literature has inspired so many artists as the *Commedia*. Notable is the easel painting by Eugène Delacroix called *Dante's Bark*—the crossing of the Styx (*Inf.* 8)—one of his most famous, with its focus on composition, powerful contrasts, and avoidance of the sentimentalism of many Italian and German illustrators.

Perhaps the most popular of nineteenth-century illustrators was Gustave Doré, whose 1860 woodblock engravings (seventy-five for *Inferno*, forty-two for *Purgatorio*, eighteen for *Paradiso*) demanded three years of study and labor (he worked from Pier Angel Fiorentino's French version). His style exudes hallucinatory awe, and his method of sfumato and chiaroscuro resembles painting more than drawing. Nature looms in both mystery and majesty, stressing his greater interest in creating wonder than understanding. A single canto may receive more than one treatment, depending on the moment Doré chooses (*Inferno*'s canto 1, for example, or the giants of 31). His gift for anatomy and sense of the colossal underscored his popularity. He also did non-woodcut illustrations: *Inferno* 5, 24, 33, and others, variously in watercolor, ink, gouache, and oil. He considered the *Commedia* his major undertaking as an illustrator.

The momentum of Dante illustration carried into the twentieth century. To be singled out among the many illustrators is Amos Nattini, an academic anatomist of the first order, whose stone lithographs—one for each canto, completed in 1929—are dramatic (especially in the *Inferno* [see canto 8] and to some extent the *Purgatorio* [see canto 11]) and realistic, yet suffused with poetic mood and atmosphere (see canto 1) which, through landscape, lighting, and color give the whole production a dreamlike quality. In its draperies and placement of figures, his *Paradiso* is less ethereal than one might expect, and more heavily religious (see canto 12). But as a total representation of the poem, whether because of its literalness or because of its detailed craftsmanship, Nattini's work is more than impressive—a connoisseur's delight on specially hand-laid paper. Nattini also emulated sixteenth-century Humanist fonts to gold-print the text.

Salvador Dalí's one hundred lithographs (one for each canto), in various styles and media, from sketches and anatomical exercises to watercolors and color/wood engravings, with accompanying text, reveal stylistically and conceptually the artist's changing posture before the *Commedia*. Begun in 1951, the whole series appeared in 1960. As an admirer of Freud, Dalí approaches the first canticle in a befittingly surrealistic manner; Hell is full of elongated limbs, melting mandibles, crutch-upheld appendages, and bone-pierced flesh, according to his philosophy of the "paranoiac" process of thought, "delirious phenomena," grotesqueness, and "cannibalistic" or mandibulary subconscious realities (see his cantos 14, 18, 20, 28, and 30 as examples). The *Purgatorio* modulates to a more expressionistic, often poetic manner, with few exceptions (see cantos 19, 31, and 33). Finally—Dalí was a devout Christian—his *Paradiso* becomes genuinely religious, realistic in a modern, stylized sense, and worthy of placement in any church (see his jovial canto 3, festive 25, or reverent 32). His fantasy thrives on sharply lucid details basking in a lyrical light.

Totally different—and personal—is the sociopolitically inspired work of Robert Rauschenberg, who limits himself to the thirty-four cantos of the *Inferno* (1963) as Dore Ashton read it to him from the John Ciardi translation. He worked with rubbings from newsprint images transferred chemically onto paper and touched slightly with such media as pencil, wash, crayon, and gouache. The total effect is monochromatic. With the help of arrows and other devices, one moves from canto to canto through a series of private symbols: for example, Dante is a GI, or everyman; the forest is replaced by oil derricks, because modern man has replaced nature with business (canto 1); Richard M. Nixon is the bad politician in the river of blood (canto 12). These are very frank representations, frequently confounding in their need for interpretation, and totally energetic in their Dante-inspired convictions of man's perpetual injustice to man, who has created his own Hell on earth.

With the increase in translations of the *Commedia* has come a concurrent increase in illustrated editions. They are too numerous to list: more than fifty in the past century, from more than a dozen countries. In 1970, Renato Guttuso brought a Marxist inspiration into play: his fifty-six mostly colored illustrations (thirty-one for *Inferno*, nineteen for *Purgatorio*, six for *Paradiso*) reveal multitudes brutalized by oppressors, emaciated concentration camp sufferers, and perishing Asian boat refugees, all accompanied by telling snippets of the text. Barry Moser, who did pen-and-ink drawings for Allen Mandelbaum's translation

(1980, 1982, 1984) at times took abstruse liberties with the poem, while at other times he remained strikingly faithful to it. Tom Phillips, who both translated and illustrated the *Inferno* (139 pictures, including four for each canto) in 1985, used images or events eclectically in his laser-scanning offset lithographies to open up a world of related visions—mocking, cynical, and serious—to show the human soul in crisis. Dantean scenes and themes were pursued at length by Giorgio De Chirico, Paul Schubring, and Mirko Racki during the first half of the twentieth century, and by Emilio Greco, Vaquero Turcios, and Fernand van Hamme during the second half. Most notable during the century's final decades is the ongoing work of Francis Phillipps, who reads no Italian and uses the Dorothy Sayers translation to probe the poem's many layers, sometimes doing multiple watercolor and oil paintings of the same event in order to arrive at its essence. His expressionistic work is colorful, dramatic, and explosive, and his dedication proves that the painterly richness of the *Commedia* is inexhaustible.

Bibliography

Barricelli, Jean-Pierre. *Dante's Vision and the Artist*. New York: Peter Lang, 1992.

Bassermann, Alfred. *Dantes Spuren in Italien*. Munich: Oldenbourg, 1898.

Blake's Dante. Edited by Milton Klonsky. New York: Harmony, 1980.

Dalí, Salvador. *Dante's Commedia*. Paris: Éditions d'Art Les Heures Claires, 1960.

Doré, Gustave. *The Divine Comedy*. New York: Pantheon, 1948.

Nassar, Eugene Paul. *Illustrations to Dante's "Inferno."* Rutherford, N.J.: Fairleigh Dickinson University Press, 1994.

Nattini, Amos. *La Divina Commedia*. 3 vols. Milan: Edizioni d'Arte à la Chance du Bibliophile, 1953.

Pite, Ralph. "Illustrating Dante." In *The Circle of Our Vision: Dante's Presence in English Romance Poetry*. Oxford: Clarendon Press, 1994, pp. 39–67.

Rauschenberg, Robert. *XXXIV Drawings for Dante's Inferno*. New York: Museum of Modern Art, 1963.

Volkmann, Ludwig. *Iconografia dantesca*. London: Grevel, 1899.

[See also the series of volumes edited by Corrado Gizzi (Pescara: Casa di Dante in Abruzzo, 1981 and after) dealing individually with Dante and various painters.]

Jean-Pierre Barricelli

Imagination

Dante employs the terms *fantasia, imaginazione, imaginativa,* and in a few cases *imagine.* In his lone reference to the act of the imagination in Latin (*Questio* 82), Dante refers to it as *ymaginatio.* It is the power of the mind that forms and stores mental images that derive from sensation as well as those that are suprasensory. His understanding of this human faculty derives from Aristotle's *De anima* and medieval commentaries on it.

The imagination in the *Vita Nuova* is a faculty that operates at the margin, so to speak, of the human being's rational faculties. The majority of uses of the term appear in chapter 23, in which Dante narrates the protagonist's delirium born of his thoughts about Beatrice's mortality. The protagonist's hallucinations are presented as effected by the imagination, which by implication is the power of the mind to apprehend what is not actually present. The imagination is linked to visions (9.3, 24.2, 39.1). The passions, particularly love, are likewise linked to the imagination (2.7, 15.2, 16.2); either one may bring about the other, and both together move the person to action. There is one reference to memory using the imagination (16.2).

Little is said about the imagination in the *Convivio,* although what there is shows a more philosophical understanding of it; for example, Dante says that the imagination is the mental faculty that retains sense images nonmaterially (2.9.4). This silence, in light of the numerous references to the intellect in the *Convivio,* bespeaks a view of the human mind that does not note any significant relation between imagination and intellect, a view consistent with Dante's conception in the *Convivio* of the human intellect as angelic. In such a conception, the imagination is more a hindrance than a help to the intellect (cf. 4.15.15–16). Nevertheless, there is one passage in which Dante alludes to the Aristotelian doctrine that the intellect grasps what it understands in images presented to it by the imagination (3.4.9,11), and he has the reader construct mental images to understand certain points (3.5, 4.6.4). In contrast, the Aristotelian view of the relation between imagination and intellect dominates and shapes the *Commedia:* the few

passages that allude to this teaching in the *Convivio* correspond to a transitional stage in Dante's thinking.

The preceding characteristics of the imagination are all present in the *Commedia.* As in *VN* 23, the imagination is specifically referred to repeatedly in relation to a vision Dante receives (*Purg.* 17.13–18, "O *imaginativa* . . ."; see also *Purg.* 9.32); as in *Conv.* 2.9.4, there is a reference to the manner in which the imagination receives sense data in *Par.* 1.53; and like *Conv.* 3.5, *Par.* 13.1–21 exhorts the reader to use the imagination to construct a particular mental image. The inability of the imagination to retain experiences that surpass the ordinary abilities of the senses is mentioned often in the *Paradiso* (e.g., 10.43–44, 24.25–27, 31.136–138). Two such references deserve special consideration: in one, the imagination is unmistakably linked to the memory in the act of remembering (*nol mi ridice,* "cannot tell it back to me," *Par.* 24.22–24); in the other, it is linked to the intellect in the act of understanding (*Par.* 33.142). The first confirms Dante's conception of the act of remembering in *VN* 16.2. The second echoes *Conv.* 3.4.9, 11, and its meaning is illumined by *Par.* 4.28–48: every act of intellection is accompanied by images taken from the imagination in which image the intellect contemplates its object, an object which is not, properly speaking, sensible. *Par.* 33.142 means that the imagination is powerless to offer to the intellect any image that might in some way reflect insight or knowledge gained by Dante in his vision of the Deity.

The act of the imagination is mentioned four times as the reason for erroneous judgments (*Inf.* 31.21–24, 34.106–108, *Purg.* 29.43–45, *Par.* 1.88–90). *Purg.* 29.49 identifies the faculty which judges on the basis of mental images (presented, it is understood, by the imagination) as the faculty *ch'a ragion discorso ammanna* ("that gives reason the manna for its discourse"; see also *Purg.* 4.68), i.e., the *ingegno* (cf. *Par.* 4.40-42) or the *stimativa* (cf. *Par.* 26.75). The imagination is in effect the instrument of three faculties for their respective operations: it is used by the *ingegno* for judging particular things, by the memory for recalling the past, and by the intellect for thinking.

Bibliography

Baldelli, Ignazio. "Visione, immaginazione e fantasia nella *Vita nuova.*" In *I sogni nel Medioevo.* Edited by Tullio Gregory. Rome, 1985, pp. 1–10.

Bundy, Murry Wright. *The Theory of Imagination in Classical and Mediaeval Thought.* Urbana: University of Illinois, 1927.

Wolfson, Harry Austryn. "The Internal Sense in Latin, Arabic, and Hebrew Philosophic Texts." *Harvard Theological Review* 28 (1935), 69–133.

Paul A. Dumol

Immortality

The word "immortality" *(immortalità, immortalitade)* means a condition of living forever. In classical Latin the word was applied to the gods and, in philosophy influenced by Plato, to the human soul, associating it with the Biblical, credal doctrine of the resurrection of the body. In the Aristotelian philosophy of Dante's time, however, immortality presented problems: according to the radical "Averroist" version of Aristotle influential in Italy, the (immortal) intellect was separate from the personal soul, making personal immortality open to doubt. Disbelief in the immortality of the soul was obviously far from unknown among Dante's contemporaries, as *Conv.* 2.8.8 and *Inf.* 10 make clear. In the former, Dante expresses his extreme revulsion at such a denial, and goes on (*Conv.* 2.8.9–16) to set out a series of arguments in favor of immortality. The first is the consensus of writers and of religious systems. Second, animals are mortal but do not hope for immortality as humans do; if humans were mistaken, they would be less perfect than animals, and moreover through a defect of the ennobling human attribute of reason. Third, Nature would be acting against itself in implanting a false hope of immortality, since this hope can lead people to court physical death. Fourth, dreams and revelations are communicated by immortal beings; since there has to be a correspondence between the communicator and the recipient, some part of the recipient must be immortal. Finally, Christian doctrine asserts immortality, the revelation being given by God who knows our immortality in a way impossible to partly mortal humans.

In *Inf.* 10, the heretics singled out for attention are those who claim that the soul dies with the body; they include not only Christian heretics but also the philosopher Epicurus, who is seen as in some way their master (*Inf.* 10.14–15). The placing of Epicurus here could be accounted for by Dante's first argument in the *Convivio:* he goes against a philosophical and religious consensus among non-Christians.

The defense of immortality in the *Convivio* passage is associated with the specific case of Beatrice, and it is in the *Vita Nuova* that immortality first appears as an important poetic topic. Dante's love survives her death and becomes directed to her immortal soul. This theme is resumed in the *Commedia,* in which immortality is obviously presupposed throughout. As a philosophical and theological topic, it is touched on in *Par.* 7, in which Beatrice explains that everything directly created by God is undying (*Par.* 7.67–69, 142–148).

Jennifer Petrie

In exitu Israel de Aegypto

The opening words of Psalm 114 (113 in the Vulgate), "When Israel went out of Egypt," are sung by the dead souls as they arrive by boat at the base of Mount Purgatory island just before beginning their purgatorial climb of the mountain (*Purg.* 2.46–48). The psalm, recited from early times in the Easter liturgy involving paschal candle ceremonies, recounts the Exodus journey of Moses and the Israelites over the Sinai desert to the holy land. As interpreted by early church fathers, it signifies by tradition the conversion of the soul from sin to grace. The psalm is introduced at a pivotal point in Dante's otherworldly journey. It is sung on Easter Sunday morning, when the poet has emerged with his guide Virgil from the timeless and eternal Hell into a realm of time and change on Mount Purgatory island, situated at the antipodes on the surface of the globular earth opposite Jerusalem.

Dante and Virgil in *Purg.* 2 hear the singing of the psalm as they watch the boat, propelled by an angel, arriving on a desert strand. On a command from Virgil, Dante kneels. The angel ferrying the dead souls makes the sign of the cross. The souls fling themselves upon the land and hurry forward in excitement and disorder. When the band disembarks, Virgil warmly greets them as *peregrin* ("pilgrims"), using this term for the first time in the *Commedia* and including himself and Dante in the reference (*Purg.* 2.63).

The passage has been seminal to allegorical, thematic, and structural interpretations of the *Purgatorio* and sometimes of the entire *Commedia.* Dante, in the company of other souls, has in

Souls of the saved entering Purgatory. Dante, with commentary by Cristoforo Landino and Alessandro Vellutello, published in Venice in 1564 by Marchiò Sessa & fratelli. Giamatti Collection: Courtesy of the Mount Holyoke College Archives and Special Collections.

ney; the allegorical, the redemption of man by Christ; the moral, the conversion of the soul from sin to grace; and the anagogical, the departure of the soul from mortal corruption to eternal glory.

Modern criticism has been divided on how such "allegory" or other possible symbolism should be interpreted. One school of criticism has viewed Dante's Exodus journey in its literal sense as a fiction or a visionary "beautiful lie," an allegory of the poets which has wide-ranging symbolic or allegorical meaning, often embracing medieval meditative traditions. Typological or figural critics, regarding the literal sense as if historically "true" in the manner of theological allegory, have allowed for similarly wide meanings and meditative readings. But these critics have seen Dante's meeting with dead souls singing Psalm 114 as a fulfilled otherworldly reenactment of "true" foreshadowing earthly events involving the Israelites of Exodus, events recorded in the Bible, the "true" medieval book of God's words. The otherworldly meeting has been held to embrace as well a "back reference" to a foreshadowing Exodus biblical figural pattern in Dante's own past earthly life, a pattern that possibly involves the poet's earthly ritualistic acting out of Exodus episodes with others on local pilgrimage stations in Italian round churches and basilicas, or on Franciscan stations on Monte La Verna. The events beyond life have also been seen more widely as a fulfilled type of the foreshadowing earthly landings and meetings of actual palmers who, during the Jubilee pilgrimage of 1300, began a holy journey over the ancient forty-two Exodus pilgrimage stations leading from Egypt over a special Mount Sinai "ring" to the earth's supposed geographic center at Jerusalem—stations presumed to be scored for the instruction of humanity in the iconographic book of God's works and creatures.

general been interpreted as here beginning an Exodus pilgrimage of *conversio* that continues during his ascent of Mount Purgatory, as seven "P's" for *peccata* are removed one by one from his forehead. Some critics also stress "conversio" themes throughout the *Paradiso,* with the first two cantos of the *Inferno* seen as an initial attempted Exodus pilgrimage of conversion that fails. Others find *conversio* and Exodus themes fulfilled and supplanted by redemption typology in Eden, and transfiguration typology in *Paradiso.*

From the time of the early commentaries of Pietro di Dante (c. 1340), Giovanni Boccaccio (c. 1373), Filippo Villani (c. 1400), and the Anonimo Fiorentino (c. 1400), the Exodus themes and typology have been seen as pointing to from three to seven allegorical senses; the weight of early commentary holds to four traditional senses, the pattern discussed by Thomas Aquinas in the *Summa Theologica* (1.1.10.1–3) and by Dante himself in his dedicatory letter to Cangrande della Scala (*Epist.* 10). In this letter, an important document whose authenticity is questioned by some, Dante explicates the literal and allegorical meanings of his poem by reference to the example of Exodus: the literal sense signifies the actual jour-

Bibliography

Armour, Peter. *The Door of Purgatory: A Study of Multiple Symbolism in Dante's Purgatorio.* Oxford: Oxford University Press, 1983.

Auerbach, Erich. "Figura." In *Scenes from the Drama of European Literature: Six Essays.* New York: Meridian Books, 1959 [1944].

Charity, A. C. *Events and Their Afterlife: The Dialectics of Christian Typology in the Bible and Dante.* Cambridge: Cambridge University Press, 1966.

Chydenius, Johan. "The Typological Problem in Dante." In *Societas Scientiarum Fennica*

I

Commentationes Humanarum Litterarum 25 (Helsingfors, 1958), 1–159.

Demaray, John G. *The Invention of Dante's Commedia*. New Haven and London: Yale University Press, 1978.

Freccero, John. *Dante: The Poetics of Conversion*. Edited by Rachel Jacoff. Cambridge, Mass., and London: Harvard University Press, 1986.

Hollander, Robert. *Allegory in Dante's Commedia*. Princeton, N.J.: Princeton University Press, 1969.

Mazzotta, Giuseppe. *Dante: Poet of the Desert: History and Allegory in the Divine Comedy*. Princeton, N.J.: Princeton University Press, 1979.

Pépin, Jean. *Dante et la tradition de l'allégorie*. Montreal and Paris: Institut d'Études Médiévales and Librairie J. Vrin, 1970.

Singleton, Charles. "In Exitu Israel de Aegypto." *Seventy-Eighth Annual Report of the Dante Society* (1960), 1–24.

———. *Dante Studies 1. Commedia: Elements of Structure*. Cambridge, Mass.: Harvard University Press, 1954.

———. *Dante Studies 2. Journey to Beatrice*. Cambridge, Mass.: Harvard University Press, 1958.

Tucker, Dunstan J. "*In Exitu Israel de Aegypto:* The *Divine Comedy* in the Light of the Easter Liturgy." *American Benedictine Review* 11 (1960), 43–61.

John G. Demaray

Incarnation

The Incarnation is the central mystery of the Christian faith, the pivotal concept around which Christian theology is organized. The Incarnation is the union of human nature with divinity in the person of Jesus Christ, the God-man who is the second person of the Trinity, a single individual in whom the two natures (human and divine) are contained while remaining distinct and separate. The doctrine of the Incarnation evolved over a long period before reaching its final formulation. The complexity of the concept gave rise to numerous heretical positions, particularly during the first few centuries of church history. Dante considers it the central mystery of Christianity, and his final vision of God in *Par.* 33.127–138 climaxes in his understanding of this theological point. Dante gives no theoretical, systematic treatment of this topic, but his christological vision of the world and history, which places Christ at the center of time, is a constant reminder of the mystery of the Incarnation.

In *Conv.* 4.5.3–9, Dante refers to the Incarnation as the event conceived by the Trinity to restore salvation after the sin committed by humanity against God, when Adam and Eve ate from the apple of wisdom in the garden of Eden. Dante follows theological doctrine in his conviction that the Incarnation would not have been necessary if humans had not sinned. In the *Convivio,* Dante observes that the Incarnation occurred during the reign of the ideal Roman monarch, Augustus, when a universal peace had been brought to the world. Christ, the Prince of Peace, consequently, was born at the propitious moment when the world was ordered under Roman rule and when peace flourished. In Dante's chronology there is also a perfect temporal correspondence between the foundation of Rome and the Judaic origins of Christianity, traceable to the ancestry of Aeneas and Jesse—from whom descend, respectively, the empire and Christ. The moment of the Incarnation is further underlined by Dante in his account of the Annunciation to Mary, miraculously reproduced in one of the reliefs described in *Purg.* 10.34–54. Dante insists here that it was God's love which caused this miraculous event. The necessity and importance of the Incarnation are further explained to Dante by Beatrice, who in *Par.* 7.19–120 relates the mystery of the event not to the nativity but to the cross. Dante, following theological doctrine, stresses the clear separation of the two natures in the second person of the Trinity, so that if the crucifixion was unjust for the divine nature, it was nevertheless justifiable for the human nature (*Par.* 7.34–45).

Alessandro Vettori

Incontinence

One of the three principal types of sin in the *Inferno, incontenenza* (or *incontinenza*) is less grave than the other two, *forza* (violence) and *frode* (fraud), and so it is placed in upper Hell and outside the city of Dis. Incontinent faults, six in number, show up in four of the first five circles and in an order of increasing gravity, from heterosexual carnality in the second circle, to gluttony in the third, avarice and prodigality in the fourth, and, finally, anger both open and sullen in the fifth circle (*Inf.* 5–8).

The very same sins, with the exception of anger and the addition of sodomy, are discovered on the upper three cornices of Purgatory, but as the

The circles of the incontinent, from Commedia di Dante, *published by Filippo Giunti, Florence, 1506. Reproduced by permission of the John A. Zahm Dante Collection in the Department of Special Collections, University Libraries, University of Notre Dame.*

wayfarer is now ascending rather than descending, they appear in an order of decreasing gravity, from avarice and prodigality, to gluttony, to lust (*Purg.* 19–27). Nowhere else in the poem is there such clear coincidence between the judgments and the ordering of the sins of the damned and the sins of the penitents.

The term *incontenenza,* which Virgil supplies in *Inf.* 11.82–83, does not designate a classification of sin in the *Purgatorio.* Therein, besides the correlation of the seven cornices with the seven capital sins, another moral scheme is deployed— one that apprehends sinful conduct as being based on love that is either misdirected, or deficient, or excessive in degree (*Purg.* 17–18). It is the excessive love of secondary goods, whether of riches, food and drink, or sexual objects, that is the purgatorial reconception and equivalent of infernal incontinence. Sodomy is removed from the category of violence (*Inf.* 11.46–51) and recast as lust, the least of the capital vices; and as a form of excessive love, it is promoted to the topmost ledge, the same level as intersexual erotic excess. Anger, removed from the incontinent category, is downgraded to the third terrace in Purgatory, as the

third worst of the capital vices and as a sin of defective love.

Questions concerning the relative guilt of the incontinent and their location in Hell are raised by Dante the pilgrim in *Inf.* 11, following Virgil's disquisition on violence and fraud (70–84), and he is told to recall *la tua Etica* ("your *Ethics*"), i.e., the *Nicomachean Ethics* (and specifically 7.1.1145a). Virgil ascribes to Aristotle the "doctrine" *(sentenza)* that incontinence is less offensive to God and less blameworthy than the violent and fraudulent *malizia* (malice) of the "wicked spirits" *(felli)* in lower Hell (11.81–90). This judgment is consistent with that of the philosopher that incontinent persons, acting under the sway of appetite or passion, as if asleep or drunk, and without judgment or malice aforethought, are but half-wicked (*N.E.* 7.10.1152a and *passim*). St. Thomas Aquinas makes a similar distinction: between sins committed by a will externally pressured by strong feelings or desire *(ex passione),* and the sins of malice *(ex electione mali)* that are more grievous partly because they are committed with a will unaffected by passion in its choice of evil (*ST* 1.2.78.4).

The punitive situations of the infernal incontinent derive from commonplace metaphors for their habitual appetites or psychological states, such as the turbulence or tempestuousness of passion, hoggish gluttony, the burden of riches, and suffocating or choking with anger. In *Inf.* 5, for example, where *La bufera infernal, che mai non resta,* / *mena li spirti con la sua rapina* ("The infernal whirlwind, which never rests, drives the spirits before its violence," 31–32), the metaphorical tempest has been literalized to serve as the setting, as the agent of punishment, and also as a symbol of passion. The torment of spirits whirled and buffeted by wind is a repetition, a continuation, and a projection into the afterlife of the torments of erotic passion that their psyches knew in this life: there is a sense of restlessness, of being driven, of submitting to an uncontrollable force. The infernal penalty consists of pain that belongs to the experience of sexual desire, so that willingness to indulge in the sin necessarily entails an assent to the concomitant pain.

The misers must roll great weights *(pesi)* with their chests in one semicircular direction, and the prodigals must do the same in the other, until the weights knock together and the sinners turn around and revile each other, shouting *"Perché tiene?"*

e *"Perché burli?"* ("Why do you hold? and Why do you toss?"); this action continues unendingly. Their "shameful meter" *(ontoso metro)* upon meeting (7.30–33) connotes the hostility of competitors for capital; the weight each pushes connotes his attachment to material things; and the heaviness and resistance, the factors that most contribute the punitive misery, signify the burden of riches—not just the physical weight of gold (cf. 7.64–66), but also the psychological weight of possessions—the constant strain and worry of accumulating, increasing, and preserving them.

The sullen who are beneath the water of the Styx and gurgle words to the surface continue from life the painful feeling of choking or suffocating with anger. The clearest case of vice as self-punitive is that of the wrathful, who not merely fight among themselves but are in a perpetual state of rage. So painful is the passion of anger that sin and punishment are one and the same.

Another notion thematized in the Hell of the incontinent is that each soul is determined by its deepest desire. "The carnal sinners, who subject their reason to their lust" (*i peccator carnali, / che la ragion sommettono al talento*, 5.38–39), a desire for *la bella persona* ("the lovely person," 5.101) of another, retain their human shapes, and they can be together always, physically and mentally united, as are Francesca and Paolo. Gluttons, whose punishment is especially loathsome *(sì spiacente),* lie on stinking ground under rain and hail, howl like dogs, and endure the barking and flaying of Cerberus. Those who feasted and fattened on meat—an implicit synecdoche—are reduced to the condition of swine in a sty. The avaricious and their prodigal opposites are not just inseparable from the weights at their breasts—man and matter merging—but are unrecognizable (*ad ogni conoscenza . . . bruni,* 7.54). Their humanity defaced, their individuality obscured, they take on the inorganic properties of the treasure they sought above all else. Hence, the three kinds of appetitive sinners progressively decline on the scale of being, from the still human erotic lovers, to the animalistic gluttons, to the materialistic and materialized hoarders and wasters. The angry remain human because, being outside the magnetic field of desire, their passion is marked by revulsion and reproach rather than by attraction.

The suffering of the souls in Purgatory follows a radically different principle from that of the damned incontinent. Instead of a projection and perpetual continuation of the souls' earthly malfeasance, the pain now is remedial and so terminates upon achieving its goal of purging all traces of former sinful habits and dispositions. The gluttons furnish a good example. In circling their ledge they must twice pass trees with upward-tapering branches, aromatic fruit, and water pouring over them (*Purg.* 22.130–138). Once corpulent, now emaciated, because they "followed their gullets beyond measure, here in hunger and thirst [they] are making themselves holy again" (*per seguitar la gola oltra misura / in fame e 'n sete qui si rifà santa,* 23.65–66). Despite the stimulation of appetite, they choose to fast, willing to do so until restraint makes their hunger disappear, when at last they are purified.

"What avarice does is shown here [on the fifth terrace] in the penance of the converted souls," who lie stretched out prostrate on the ground. So says one such soul, who continues: "Since our eyes, fixed on earthly things, were not raised up, so here justice has sunk them to the earth" (19.115–120). While this may initially look like an extension of the vice, it is something else entirely: it is a purifying process in which the terrestrial phenomena of desire gradually lose all attractiveness, and disgust with matter liberates the desire to be redirected, in full accord with the will, toward the divine. Statius, who underwent the process as a prodigal, tells us as much (21.59–69; 22.35–36). Similar is the regimen of the erotic sinners, both heterosexual and homosexual, who move through the ledge of lust in separate groups and opposite directions, submerged in flames. They had once been inflamed with passion, but this fire purifies (26.148), by being patiently borne until sexual desire finally burns itself out.

Carnal incontinence is the least culpable of all the mortal sins in Hell, and immoderate libidinal love is the least serious of the sinful dispositions extirpated in Purgatory. Yet Dante, in traveling through the two realms, relates to these failings in an extraordinary manner. He swoons "for pity" at the end of Francesca's account of her and Paolo's love and death (*Inf.* 5.139–142), and he endures excruciating pain from the lust-purifying fire as he crosses the seventh cornice (*Purg.* 27.49–54). Both reactions can be explained by the amorous desires the wayfarer himself harbors (31.118–20), for the journey he makes in the first two canticles of the *Commedia* is toward his beloved Beatrice.

Bibliography

Aristotle. *Nicomachean Ethics. Basic Works.* Edited by Richard McKeon. New York: Random House, 1941.

Ciotti, Andrea. "Incontinenza (incontenenza) e incontinenti." *Enciclopedia dantesca*, 3:415–417.

Lansing, Richard H. "Dante's Concept of Violence and the Chain of Being." *Dante Studies* 99 (1981), 67–87.

Moore, Edward. "The Classification of Sins in the 'Inferno' and 'Purgatorio.'" *Studies in Dante.* Second Series. Oxford: Clarendon Press, 1899, pp. 152–209.

Pequigney, Joseph. "Sodomy in Dante's *Inferno* and *Purgatorio.*" *Representations* 36 (1991), 22–42.

————, and Hubert Dreyfus. "Landscape and Guide: Dante's Modifying of Meaning in the *Inferno.*" *Italian Quarterly* 5–6 (1961–1962), 51–83.

Reade, W. H. V. *The Moral System of Dante's "Inferno."* Oxford: Clarendon Press, 1909.

Triolo, Alfred A. "*Ira, Cupiditas, Libido:* The Dynamics of Human Passion in the *Inferno.*" *Dante Studies* 95 (1977), 1–37.

Joseph Pequigney

Indolent

The second of four classes of spirits encountered by Dante and Virgil in the Ante-Purgatory in the second canticle of the *Commedia,* the indolent are the souls of those who died without benefit of the means of penitence provided by the church. Like the excommunicates of the first group, and the victims of violent death and the kings and princes who delayed repentance because of their preoccupation with worldly matters, who comprise the third and fourth classes, respectively, the indolent put off repentance until just before their deaths. The figure of Belacqua serves as exemplar of the indolent soul, and the conditions of his sojourn at the base of the mountain outside Purgatory proper are explained during his dialogue with Dante. In response to Dante's inquiries concerning his status there, Belacqua reveals that God's angel will not allow him to pass through the entrance to the seven purgatorial terraces until he has waited for a period equal to that of his indolence and indifference on earth, though that period may be shortened by sincere, holy prayers on his behalf. *Prima convien che tanto il ciel m'aggiri / di fuor da essa, quanto fece in vita, / per ch'io 'ndugiai al fine i buon sospiri, / se orazïone in prima non m'aita / che surga sù di cuor che in grazia viva* ("First it is necessary for the heavens to turn about me outside here as long as they did in my life, since I delayed my good sighs until the end, unless prayer help me first, which must rise up from a heart that lives in grace," *Purg.* 4.130–134). These terms of detention are repeated later in connection with Provenzan Salvani (*Purg.* 11.127–132) and Forese Donati (*Purg.* 23.83–90), whose presence among the gluttonous on the sixth terrace seems to surprise Dante: *Io ti credea trovar là giù di sotto, / dove tempo per tempo si ristora* ("I thought to find you down there below, where they repay time for time," 83–84). Though the indolent, as exemplified by Belacqua, have acknowledged their sinful negligence and expressed the active virtue of hope by trusting in the help of prayer, their sin survives in the act, though not in the will, and they continue to exhibit signs of their earthly *pigrizia* (*Purg.* 4.111), a laziness that arises from sloth and hinders the mind from action (see St. Thomas Aquinas, *ST* 2.2.54.2).

George D. Economou

Inferno

As the fullest and most imaginatively detailed Hell ever conceived, Dante's *Inferno*—the first canticle of his *Commedia*—transcends all prior descriptions and provides the pattern for many future ones. Surprisingly and revealingly, it contains very little of the *ars moriendi,* the meditations on death that communicate a contempt for life, with the skeletal refrain, "As I am, you shall be." In fact, Dante's poem is marked by high hopes. In the *Inferno,* even sinners are compelled to recall the "bright life," the "sweet light," and the "beauty of the stars," and suicides are blamed for lamenting where they should have rejoiced. Indeed, the larger program of Dante's poem is to restore by means of a necessarily painful journey the original bright promise that had been so sadly waylaid.

Nor does Dante's Hell conduct a survey of the professions, as summarized by the porter to the imaginary Hell's gate in *Macbeth:* "I had thought to let in some of all the professions that go the primrose way to the everlasting bonfire." While, like the porter, we might have expected a line-up of the professions—that is, a largely satiric mode in the manner of the much later *Ship of Fools* or *Praise of Folly*—we are instead presented with the personal and humanized dramas of Dante's time,

Iin figures who, like Macbeth, are charting their own ways to Hell. While some of Dante's characters are reviled in their professional capacities, their real drama exposes their essential moral nature.

Dante's more humanized *Inferno* is thus largely devoid of the hocus-pocus materials of hobgoblins and witchcraft that have their roles in *Macbeth*. Even in cantos 21–22, where the poet indulges in the farcical and grotesque street humor of the medieval mystery play, in the midst of the scurrilities we are reminded of the council's action that led to the death of Christ. To be sure, in the ultimate presentation of Satan in canto 34, the poem reprises some earlier iconographic traditions, particularly one from the great mosaic in the Baptistery of Florence, where the Evil One is shown with extended serpentine heads crammed with sinners; but we begin to gauge the difference of Dante's purpose when we observe that in Dis's jaws the monumental historical figures of Judas, Brutus, and Cassius are suffering. All this points to a distinctly personal purpose as well as a grander moral, political, and religious one in Dante's poem, which must be understood before the *Inferno* itself can be judged.

It is perhaps plausible, in the much larger wake of the Enlightenment, the period that witnessed "the decline of Hell," to object to the *Inferno* by suggesting that Dante sadistically visits chastisement on his victims (a criticism intensified in the aftermath of the moral fervor of the 1960s, where one encounters such phrases as "the scandal of the *Inferno*"). One cannot deny that Dante, like other great writers, can be motivated by severe personal animus; such criticism, however, deflects attention from the larger merits and purposes of the book. If the *Inferno* were simply or even largely a house of horrors, a torture chamber of the imagination, would it have captured the Western world's literary imagination so intently and for so long? To criticize the poem on such grounds is more or less like dismissing *Hamlet* because of the ghost, or *Macbeth* because of the witches. In our own time of representational violence, of "mean streets," of drugged "less than zero" zombies whose artistic methods are almost necessarily defended by the very critics of Dante's poem, can one in any way admonish Dante for showing what messes people can make of their lives, for revealing the terrible finalities of exis-

Chart of Dante's Inferno, from the 1568 edition of the Commedia. Dante, with commentary by Bernardino Daniello da Lucca, published in Venice by Pietro da Fino in 1568. Giamatti Collection: Courtesy of the Mount Holyoke College Archives and Special Collections.

tence, and for exposing atrocity that defies rational explanation?

Such moralizing criticism fails to appreciate the imaginative purposes of the *Inferno* and the larger program of which the pain and punishment are only a part. The *Inferno* is a literary trope, with a moral, political, and religious disposition, and with its own intellectual dimensions, linguistic requirements, and design. Moreover, while thus having its own dispensations, it is still part of a larger whole: the first installment of a great trilogy, whose meaning is completed only by the end of the journey.

To turn to the poem's accomplishments, one can begin by admiring the sheer inventiveness of Dante's genius, the extraordinarily varied roster of categories and figures. Indicating the personal shape and purpose he gave to the trope of Hell, the neutrals in the third canto and the Limbo of virtuous pagans in the fourth canto are dramatic and startling innovations. In addition to the vast number of episodes, categories, and sinners, one can think of the great dramatic moments—the blocking of Virgil at the gate of Dis in canto 9, the descent on Geryon in canto 17, and the accumulation of injury and sociopathic behavior in the lower Hell—all presented with variety, novelty, and unfailing interest. One can see why Dante's *Inferno* is the most structured and systematic Hell ever created. The extraordinary number of characters and incidents brought forward require distinctions if they are to be kept separate and dramatic interest maintained. At the level of fictional inventiveness, Dante's *Inferno* is a world masterpiece.

There is much to admire in the number of episodes and figures that Dante brings into his poem, but even more important is the patterning of Hell as a distinct representation of existence, a particular version of life. Judging by the categories employed in Hell, by the poem's linguistic arsenal, and by its philosophical limitations, Dante fully understood and respected the requirements of Hell and fit them to his purposes. The very categories of offenses tell us much about the scope and matter of the *Inferno*. The disposition of the offenders is not according to the traditional Christian schema of the seven deadly sins, as might have been expected, although it begins this way (second to fifth circles). That program was reserved for the *Purgatorio*, partly because that canticle would allow for occasions that were more introspective, but mainly because it would not permit deployment of the vast scope of representations, nor of the particular patterning, that Dante required for Hell. Dante's *Inferno*, with its multiple divisions and subdivisions, relies on the Aristotelian (and Ciceronian) ethical model of incontinence, violence, fraud, and, within the last, treachery. With his usual seasoned artistry, Dante does not present us with a road map of his *Inferno* until canto 11, when we have already acquired some experience of the terrain. In that canto, he explains the logic of placement for what is to come and for what has already been witnessed. Specifically invoking Aristotle's *Ethics,* Dante justifies a higher placement of the incontinent (in upper Hell) as being less offensive to God because their sins—lust, gluttony, avarice, and wrath—are conceived, following Aquinas, as originating from an excess of a natural human passion *(peccata ex passione).*

Lower Hell (sixth to ninth circles), which begins at the gates of Dis, will punish sins originating from conscious choice *(peccata ex electione).* The heretics in the sixth circle, who rejected the tenets of Christian dogma, are followed in the seventh circle by the violent (with violence distinguished successively as being directed against another, against the self, and against God, the last of which includes blasphemy, sodomy, and usury). The ultimate perversion of man's great faculty of reason is punished in the eighth and ninth circles, filled by those who perpetrated fraud and by those who treacherously betrayed honored obligations.

Not as limited as the Christian one might be, this schema, in its possibility for wider casting, provides the basis for a full presentation of scenes from contemporary life: the usurers, panders, sycophants, diviners, simonists, barrators, thieves, false counselors, impersonators, and many others. These scenes add up to a marvelous portfolio, indeed a human canvas of vast proportions, conveying the language, character, and issues of Dante's time. They are scenes in which Dante took the interest of a novelist—so inordinate an interest, indeed, that in one episode of artistic self-correction (canto 30) he has his own character rebuked by Virgil for being too engrossed in the angry altercation between Master Adam and Sinon. Such scope and variety are permitted by the classical schema. Moreover, this structure is also fitting for a version of life that is unendowed with any higher purposes or principle, in fact, for a process of degradation whereby the secular gives way to the profane, and that in turn to the horrible. Such systemic pejoration has a basis that Dante can expose in its social extent, but not fully explain by the categories and the mind of Hell.

Like Milton, Dante could well assert that decorum is the great masterpiece to observe. In the *Inferno,* this is most true linguistically. Although Dante expresses the wish that he had *le rime aspre e chiocce* ("harsh and clucking rhymes," 32.1) sufficient to describe the last circle of Hell, what he claims is beyond his measure is present in modified form throughout the *Inferno,* which is replete with those raspy, crackling, grappling words appropriate for a universe where physical and material ends predominate. This is a conscious strategy, and as such it differs from the language of the *Purgatorio,* and is justified by the proverb *ne la chiesa / coi santi, e in taverna coi ghiottoni*

INFERNO.
COMMEDIA DEL DIVINO POE
TA FIORENTINO DAN
TE ALIGHIERI
CAPITOLO
·I·

N EL mezo del camin di nostra vita
Mi ritrouai per una selua oscura,
Che la diritta uia era smarrita.
Ah quanto a dir qual era, è cosa dura
Questa selua seluaggia et aspra et forte,
Che nel pensier rinuoua la paura.
Tantè amara, che poco è piu morte.
Ma per trattar del ben, chi ui trouai,
Diro dellaltre cose, chio uho scorte.
I non so ben ridir, comio uentrai,
Tantèro pien di sonno in su quel punto,
Che la uerace uia abbandonai.
Ma po chi fui al pie dun colle giunto
La, oue terminaua quella ualle,
Che mhauea di paura il cor compunto,
Guardai in alto, et uidi le sue spalle
Vestite gia de raggi del pianeta,
Che mena dritto altrui per ogni calle.
Allhor fu la paura un poco queta,
Che nel lago del cor mera durata
La notte chi passai con tanta pietà.
Et come quei che con lena affannata
Vscito fuor del pelago alla riua
Si uolge a lacqua perigliosa, et guata,

Commedia di Dante, *published by Filippo Giunti, Florence, 1506. Reproduced by permission of the John A. Zahm Dante Collection in the Department of Special Collections, University Libraries, University of Notre Dame.*

("in church with the saints, and in the tavern with the gluttons," *Inf.* 22.15–16), as well as by the phrase from canto 32, where he invokes the Muse that helped build the horror city of Thebes (from Statius' *Thebaid,* the true model for the Cocytus): *sì che dal fatto il dir non sia diverso* ("so that the word may not be different from the fact," 32.12).

Philosophically, the *Inferno* also observes its own limits. Not only is the name of Christ not allowed mention, but neither are the larger philo-

sophical, political, and moral bases of Dante's vision permitted entry: they are reserved for the higher places of spiritual advance. This means that any theoretical discourse is of a kind that might be appropriate for the level of Virgil and Dante at the stage of their progress. The longest discourse occurs in canto 7, where Dante through Virgil registers, in another self-correction, his own larger and altered view that Fortune is an agent of the divine will. This newly acquired wisdom will play a dramatic role in Dante's response to Brunetto Latini in canto 15, and it will mark his own spiritual development in accepting the insinuated but as yet unknown disaster of exile heading his way. But the fullest revelation of this predicted event is not yet developed; Virgil defers such explanation until Dante is ready to benefit from the wisdom of Beatrice. Similarly, in canto 19, where the simoniacal popes are punished, Dante will dramatize his views concerning papal power (including a strong denunciation of the disastrous consequences of the so-called Donation of Constantine). These same issues will be dealt with more philosophically in cantos 6 and 16 of the *Purgatorio* and will receive their fullest delineation in book 3 of the *Monarchia,* but they are nevertheless adumbrated dramatically in canto 27, where Boniface VIII is shown to arrogate to himself powers he does not possess. These are shadowy matters, not yet fully explained—as they would be later—but as such they are perfectly suited to the *Inferno*'s level of understanding.

Within these limitations, the *Inferno* is still a poem of dramatic unfoldings. As modern Dante criticism begins to pay attention to the stories within the *Commedia* as well as to the story of the *Commedia,* we are inclined to complete the storylines that Dante himself, with the restraint typical of a classical artist, suggests for the reader but does not draw. In cantos 3, 6, 19, and 27, we can observe that Boniface emerges as the true *bête noire* of the *Inferno,* like Satan himself everywhere present but nowhere to be seen. We can also follow the story of Virgil's real skills as a guide and mentor and his very definite limitations, suggested in canto 2, verified in the drama at the gates of Dis, and again evident in canto 23, when he "marvels" that a leader of the Pharisees should be crucified for what was rational political advice, or when he is staggered by the gratuitous deceit of Malacoda, a "motiveless malignity" that is beyond his own rational calculus. We can follow the series of predictions alluding to the impending exile of Dante in 1302, an event the preparation for which forms one of the major plot-lines of the poem. In cantos 6, 10, 15, and 24, a small drama of spiritual readiness is played out, with Dante, in darkness and in doubt, struggling to achieve the faith required to confront the unknown. In the *Commedia*'s poetic strategy of progressive revelation, Dante's true justification by faith will occur in cantos 15–17 of the *Paradiso* (parallel to the meeting with Brunetto Latini), where the better father Cacciaguida will clearly explain to Dante the bitter meaning of the dark sayings he has heard, at a time when he has fully acquired means for coping with them.

In the *Inferno* Dante has invented the form of the canticle, which allows for dramatic breaks and changes and for new onsets of intensification. One such important break occurs in canto 9 (and it is important to note that similar breaks will occur in the other two books in this approximate area), when the approach to the City of Dis requires an act of grace to overcome the irrational opposition of the demons (an obstacle that Virgil is unable singlehandedly to surmount). Another occurs in cantos 31–32, particularly in the latter, where Dante musters a new invocation as he is about to describe the bottom of the pit. The most decisive break, however, occurs in cantos 16–17, when Dante, aided by Virgil, descends into the Malebolge on the back of the monster Geryon. This extraordinary invention has provoked diverse interpretations, but one thing is clear: the descent into the levels of fraud marks a radical change in the depiction of the sinners and in Dante's attitude toward them. The upper Hell is more humanistic, and Dante expresses some identification with such figures as Francesca, Farinata, Pier della Vigna, Brunetto Latini, and the Florentine political leaders of canto 16 (though in his quest for freedom he also clearly supersedes them and their message). They all reveal traits that are partially redeeming or memorable, and their exchanges with Dante tend to overshadow their punishments, and even to obscure the fact that their attributes and allegiances are still part of the character of Hell. The pilgrim Dante is saddened and even subdued by their inclusion in Hell, since obviously he had at one time shared in some of their attachments, particularly in the devotion to the city of Florence. But after the break, a process of debasement occurs which is facilitated by the adoption of the classical categories of offense. With one major excep-

tion, Dante now indicates not identification with but rather separation from the sinners. In most instances, the grotesqueness of punishment dominates exchange, and fame, the coin current in the upper Inferno, is now shunned. While Dante still wants to carry back a true report, names are only reluctantly revealed; Bocca degli Abati exemplifies this attitude when he responds, to Dante's proffered blandishments of fame, *"ché mal sai lusingar per questa lama"* ("for you flatter badly here in this swamp," 32.96). Among the treacherous, a dead and welcomed silence takes the place of the trumpeting promise of Creation.

So, too, the mode of denunciation increases appreciatively in lower Hell, as Dante, now increasingly detached from his Florentine affiliations, takes into moral survey the cities of central and northern Italy. Bologna, Pistoia, Florence, Siena, Pisa, and Genoa are all roundly vilified, as the individual sinners become representative of a larger moral climate of corruption and decline (the fuller reasons for which will be presented in the *Purgatorio*). Matters become both more localized and more generalized, more pervasive, as the dismal accumulation of death and destruction—Virgil had promised Dante "full experience"—takes its toll, causing weariness and disgust in Dante, and nothing like the appreciation of doomed heroism that would be read into the *Inferno* by Romantic criticism.

In the centrally located canto of the lower *Inferno* (central both physically and spiritually), Dante encounters Ulysses, the one character in the lower realms with whom he shows some identification. If canto 13 (the suicides) is the most integrated of the cantos, and 15 the most poetically accomplished and affecting, canto 26 is the most intellectually synoptic and far-reaching. Here and in canto 5, with Francesca, Dante addresses the two great forces of his culture, love and knowledge; and so powerful are these presentations that again and again throughout the other canticles Dante will feel compelled to confront the important issues there developed. But the presentation of Ulysses will even fly the bounds of the poem and be overtaken by the very forces that Dante had anticipated. As a victim of insidious political conniving that ultimately brought about his exile from Florence, Dante has no reason to admire the contriver of the Trojan horse, Ulysses, the ultimate false counselor, whose cohorts and descendants are so abundantly present throughout lower Hell.

Dante repelled by the three beasts. From the 1481 edition illustrated by Baldino after sketches by Botticelli, published in Florence by Nicholo di Lorenzo della Magna. Giamatti Collection: Courtesy of the Mount Holyoke College Archives and Special Collections.

Nonetheless, he bestows on this intellectually resourceful figure a daring and resolve, an intellectual energy and adventurousness, that will find vindication in the subsequent ages of exploration and discovery. Ulysses will then become the figure of Western man, unrestrained by authority, freely launching himself into the unknown. While fully appreciating this part of himself and of his society, Dante finally condemns it as disintegrative and presents Ulysses as a footloose adventurer whose quest for experience can only be seen as destructive of the means of civilization.

As a mediator and thus interpreter between Dante and Ulysses, Virgil serves his broadest function as a voice of culture and of history. When Virgil intervenes suddenly in canto 1 to save Dante from his disastrous run back down the hill, much more is intended. Poetically, his large epic was the model and source for Dante's poem; its quality of larger representativeness in telling of gods and of men provided Dante with the means and inspiration to transcend more parochial versions of Hell. If Virgil's magisterial book 6 of the *Aeneid,* which Dante knew intimately and incorporated fully into *Par.* 15–17, provides the more transcendent model for Dante's *Inferno,* it is also superseded by Dante's poem. In *Aen.* 6 (as in its model, book 11 of the *Odyssey,* which Dante did not know), the

journey to the underworld is both centrally placed and determining: at the center, the essential and positive values of the respective cultures are revealed. But in Dante's poem, the journey to the underworld is only the necessary first step, and its incompleteness requires the other books of the trilogy. In it Dante does not uncover essential value, but only its absence—he meets the gods that have failed, the anti-types as well as the antimyths of his culture. The *Inferno* is a great negative critique, and its essential emotion cannot be inspiration or admiration, but rather disgust. This also explains the somewhat anticlimactic meeting with Satan in canto 34. Rather than appearing heroically rebellious (even if only falsely so, as in Milton's presentation), this figure bears the sad weight of the world's misery. Dante can devote only a few lines to his description because he has already shown us the effects of Satan's works on human history in the body of the poem.

As we look at the larger import of Dante's *Inferno,* at its own qualities and dispensations and its placement within the larger confines of the *Commedia,* we can see broader human merit and wisdom in his arrangement and values. In the latter decades of the twentieth century, we have gained renewed insight into the human capacity for atrocity—into the radical, even unfathomable nature of human evil. Such discovery can only come as a shock to a post-Enlightenment culture that believes that human nature is not only potentially good but essentially good. Against the bald fact of the Holocaust, such a belief comes crashing to the ground, with only suicidal despair as a consequence, since in it all human nature is condemned. In Dante's arrangement, humans, though potentially good, are quite capable of monstrous acts. Hence, the final dramatic revelation of the *Inferno* is the Ugolino episode, with the deaths of the innocent children. In Dante, as in Shakespeare, the Massacre of the Innocents represents the death of history (*Inf.* 33). But confined to the *Inferno,* this vision is not all-encompassing. Although it might be pervasive and even dominant, both the *Purgatorio* and *Paradiso* are there to emphasize that it is only one version of life. If human good is potential but not essential, this means that human freedom is still intact, and that there may be great examples of individuals and even cultures who have steadfastly resisted temptation. Dante's *Inferno* may be a world monument because in its own quest for justification and faith, it examines with resoluteness the full experience of evil while leading, perhaps even pointing, to other possibilities of existence. Even within its own constraints, it provides an argument in defense of human freedom.

Bibliography

Barolini, Teodolinda. *The Undivine Comedy: Detheologizing Dante.* Princeton, N.J.: Princeton University Press, 1994.

Masciandaro, Franco. *Dante as Dramatist.* Philadelphia: University of Pennsylvania Press, 1991.

Musa, Mark. *Advent at the Gates: Dante's Comedy.* Bloomington: Indiana University Press, 1974.

Pagels, Elaine. *The Origin of Satan.* New York: Random House, 1995.

Quinones, Ricardo J. "The Plot-Line of Myth in Dante's *Inferno*." In *Dante's Inferno: The Indiana Critical Edition.* Translated and edited by Mark Musa. Bloomington: Indiana University Press, 1995, pp. 353–366.

———. *Foundation Sacrifice in Dante's "Commedia."* University Park: Pennsylvania State University Press, 1994.

Russell, Jeffrey. *The Prince of Darkness: Radical Evil and the Power of Good in History.* Ithaca, N.Y.: Cornell University Press, 1988.

Taylor, Daniel P. *The Decline of Hell: Seventeenth-Century Discussions of Eternal Torment.* Chicago: University of Chicago Press, 1964.

Turner, Alice K. *The History of Hell.* New York: Harcourt, Brace, 1993.

Wlassics, Tibor (ed.). *Dante's "Divine Comedy": Introductory Readings: I. Inferno.* Charlottesville: University of Virginia Press, 1990.

Ricardo J. Quinones

Injustice

The noun *ingiuria* occurs three times in the *Commedia,* first at *Inf.* 11.23, during Virgil's discourse on the penal system of Hell, where it denotes "injustice" or "violation of law." It derives from the Latin word of the same meaning, *iniuria*—a combination of *in-* (un-) + *iure* (law) + *-ia* ([ful]ness). *Ingiuria* here is generally glossed as a technical term in Roman law, or as an infraction of divine or of natural or human law.

The word most likely came into *Inferno* directly and specifically from *iniuria* as used in *De officiis* 1.13.41. Here Cicero asserts that "injustice" may be done in two ways, either by force or by fraud, and that while both ways are most improper for man *(homine alienissimum),* fraud *(fraus)* is more heinous *(odio digna maiore)* than force *(vis).* Dante took his own comparative evaluation of violence and fraud from this passage, which he virtually paraphrases in these lines: *D'ogne malizia, ch'odio in cielo acquista, / ingiuria è 'l fine, ed ogne fin cotale / o con forza o con frode altrui contrista. / Ma perché frode è de l'uom proprio male, / più spiace a Dio* ("Of every malice gaining the hatred of Heaven, injustice is the goal, and every such goal injures someone either with force or with fraud. But because fraud is an evil proper to man, it is more displeasing to God," *Inf.* 11.22–26). Injustice thus apprehended is the effect of each and every sin punished in circles seven (violence), eight (simple fraud), and nine (complex fraud, or treachery).

For Cicero and Dante alike, then, violence and fraud are the two sole means toward the end of *ingiuria,* and the term is semantically limited to these two categories of vice. The Christian poet does, to be sure, expand on the pagan prose statement: he adds the religious dimension that the hatefulness of sin offends God rather than men alone; he explains that the greater culpability of fraud is owing to its abuse of human rationality;

and he introduces the notion of *malizia* from Aristotle's *Ethics* (7.1.1145a15). For Aristotle, malice is a reprehensible disposition (see *Inf.* 11.79–83), and it is conceived of by Dante as preceding and leading to the Ciceronian *ingiuria* that harms one or more persons by means of violent or fraudulent acts.

The term *ingiuria* at 11.23 has been translated as "injustice" (Singleton, Sinclair, Mandelbaum, Pinsky, Durling)—and this accords with the annotations regularly found in Italian editions—or else as "injury" (Sayers, Ciardi, Carlyle-Okey-Wicksteed). The latter choice is defensible because *ingiuria* (as *fine*) is finally injurious, and because the Italian word, along with the Latin *iniuria,* can also denote "harm." When the term appears in *Purgatorio* in Virgil's definition of anger (17.121–123), Singleton so translates it (as does Mandelbaum): the angry man "seems so outraged *(par ch'aonti)* by injury *(ingiuria)* that he becomes greedy of vengeance, and . . . must needs contrive another's harm *(male altrui)*"; Durling renders this "and there are those who seem outraged by injury, so that they become greedy for vengeance, and thus they must ready harm for others." Italian editors annotate *ingiuria* in this tercet as an *offesa* or *ingiuria ricevuta,* an angering offense or injury, through words or action, received by someone in whom it triggers thoughts of vengeance.

In *Paradiso* Beatrice, while theologizing in juridical terminology on the Fall and the Redemption, employs *ingiuria* in 7.40–45. Of the punishment *(pena)* suffered by Christ crucified, she says "[none] ever took its toll as justly" *(nulla già mai sì giustamente morse),* from the viewpoint of the guilty human nature he assumed; but from the viewpoint of the divinity of his person, "none was ever so unjust" *(nulla fu di tanta ingiuria).* Italian editors take *ingiuria* in line 43 to signify *ingiustizia* (injustice) rather than "wrong" (Singleton), and rightly so, in part because *tanta ingiuria* is contrastive with *sì giustamente morse.* The norm of justice now pertinent would be found not in Roman law but in the divine will and the moral law.

Joseph Pequigney

Intellect

Dante uses primarily the term *intelletto* in Italian and *intellectus* in Latin, but he also refers to the intellect as *intelligenza* (or *intelligenzia*), *ragione,* *ingegno,* and *mente* (Italian), and as *ratio* and *mens* (Latin).

There are no passages in the *Vita Nuova* on the nature of the intellect, except for one reference to the powerlessness of the intellect to apprehend pure spirits (41.6). The *Convivio,* in contrast, contains a number of explicit references to the nature of the intellect: the intellect is the most perfect, the noblest, and the most excellent part of the soul (3.2.13–19; 4.22.13); through it man participates of the divine nature like an angel; in it the soul is ennobled and stripped of matter, so that the divine light shines in it as in an angel; thus man is called a divine animal (3.2.14; cf. 3.7.6). Angels and human beings arranged according to intellectual power form a continuous scale from the angel with the highest intellect to the human being with the lowest: there is no radical break between the angelic nature and the human soul (3.7.6).

Complementing this conception of the nature of the human intellect as angelic (cf. 3.3.11, 3.4.2, 3.14.8–9) is the conception of its origin (4.21.5). The human intellect, which Dante calls the "possible intellect" (that is, an intellect which passes from a state in which it is merely in potency to think, to one in which it is actually doing so, and vice versa), is infused into the sensitive soul of the fetus by a celestial mover or angel (see also 3.6.5), and it possesses in potency all the universal forms or ideas in its producer, in decreasing degree according to the increasing distance its producer is from God. Dante's account assumes nine angelic orders (2.5.5), all contemplating God and consequently all things as these exist in God (3.6.5), but progressively removed from him (2.5.6–11). God is the cause of the human intellect (2.4.14), but through the mediation of the angelic intelligences (3.14.4). The act of thinking is made possible by an "intellectual light" that comes from God and illuminates the ideas possessed in potency, much as the light of the sun makes things visible (3.12.7).

The *Convivio*'s conception of the human intellect as angelic is rejected explicitly in the *Monarchia* and implicitly in the *Commedia,* a rejection presaged by isolated passages in the *Convivio* (e.g., 2.4.17, 3.4.9, 13.5) that do not square with what Dante says elsewhere in the book regarding the intellect. *Mon.* 1.3.6–7 states unequivocally that the human intellect constitutes a species by itself, distinct from the angel's, precisely because of its characteristic of passing from potency to act, in contrast to the angelic intellect which is always in act. The *Commedia* gives a radically different account of the origin of the intellect: the possible intellect is a faculty of a new spirit created by God and infused by him without angelic intermediaries (cf. *Par.* 7.142–143) into the fetus (*Purg.* 25.61–75). Several passages clearly link the process of intellection to the use of mental images (*Inf.* 11.67–90; *Purg.* 4.67–84, 29.46–49; *Par.* 2.94–96, 4.28–48).

The *Monarchia* distinguishes between a higher and a lower intellect; the former has concepts for its object, and the latter has experience (1.16.5). The two are the speculative intellect and the practical intellect (1.14.7). The speculative and higher intellect is the intellect referred to as such in the *Commedia* and the *Convivio;* the practical and lower intellect is what Dante calls the *ingegno* in many places in the *Commedia* and in a few of the *Convivio,* and which he conceives of as an organic faculty.

The primary influences in the *Convivio* concept of the intellect are certainly the *Liber de causis* and Albert the Great's commentary on Aristotle's *De anima.* The primary influence in the *Commedia* concept is Aristotle's psychology in the *De anima* and *Nicomachean Ethics* 6, through the mediation of Aquinas's commentaries on these works. The *Monarchia* reveals Averroës's commentary on Aristotle's *De anima* to be a secondary but important source of Dante's concept of the intellect.

Paul A. Dumol

Interminei, Alessio

A member of the Lucchese patrician family (also called Interminelli, Antelminelli) which also produced Castruccio Castracani (1281?–1328), ruler (1316) and duke (1327) of Lucca. Since Alessio is documented as still alive in December 1295, he must have died less than five years before the pilgrim's encounter with him in the second bolgia of Malebolge, where he is immersed in excrement as punishment for the sin of flattery (*Inf.* 18.115–126). We know nothing further about him from independent sources. Dante, however, seems to indicate that he knew him personally when, as the *Commedia*'s protagonist, he says *già t'ho veduto* ("I have seen you before") and is able to name him (*Inf.* 18.121–122).

John C. Barnes

Iole

Folco, the troubadour poet placed in the sphere of Venus, compares the ardor of his love for Adelais to that of Hercules *(Alcide)* for Iole, whom Hercules had abducted and fallen in love with (*Par.* 9.102). Hercules's wife Deianira becomes jealous when she learns of his infidelity, but hoping to recover her husband's love for her, she sends Hercules a tunic soaked in the blood of Nessus, which instead brings about his death (see *Meta.* 9.136ff).

F. Regina Psaki

Iphigenia

Daughter of Agamemnon and Clytemnestra, Iphigenia *(Ifigènia, Efigènia)* is mentioned by Beatrice in *Par.* 5.70 in her discourse on vows. Drawing on accounts by Virgil (*Aen.* 2.116–119), Ovid (*Meta.* 12.24–34), and Cicero (*De officiis* 3.25.95), Dante presents her as alluding to Agamemnon's foolish promise to sacrifice the fairest being born that year. Agamemnon had sought to appease Diana, who, angered by his slaying a stag in her sacred grove, sent a plague on the Greek army and a calm on the sea, thus thwarting the Greeks in their attack on Troy. As Agamemnon is about to sacrifice the fair Iphigenia, who bewails the beauty of her face *(onde pianse Efigènia il suo bel volto),* Diana at the last moment takes pity on her and substitutes a hind (although Dante does not mention this part of the myth).

Virginia Jewiss

Iris

Daughter of Thaumas and Electra, Iris *(Iride, Iri)* is the goddess of the rainbow (*Purg.* 21.50) and the handmaid and messenger of Juno (*Par.* 12.12, 28.30).

Virginia Jewiss

Isidore, St.

One of the most influential clerics and scholars of the early Church and one of its major exponents for the reconciling of pagan learning with Christianity. Isidore was closely associated with the Visigothic court, for which he was a leading apologist in its opposition to the establishment in Constantinople. He was born around 570 in Cartagena into a prosperous family, which included a learned brother Leander, also a notable cleric, acquaintance of Gregory the Great, and dedicatee of the *Moralia in Job.* In 599–600 Isidore succeeded Leander, who had provided him with his early clerical education, as bishop of Seville. He died there in 636. His association with this city has led him often to be known as St. Isidore of Seville in addition to the Latin name *Isidorus Hispalensis.* Dante places Isidore *(Isidoro)* in the sphere of the Sun in the general company of other notable doctors of the church, and the specific company of Bede and Richard of St. Victor *(Par.* 10.131).

Isidore is best remembered as the author of numerous works on a wide variety of subjects, including *De natura rerum, De ecclesiasticis officiis,* the *Chronica, De viris illustribus,* and the *Sententiarum sive de summo bono libri tres.* His most influential work was the *Originum seu etymologiarum libri XX* (also known as the *Etymologiae* or *Origines*), a sort of encyclopedia which became a source and model for many subsequent works; it is notable in part for providing a basic knowledge of pagan classics. Among the subjects covered in the *Etymologiae* are the seven liberal arts, medicine, law, theology, poetry, natural history, war, and pagan games.

It is not clear if Dante had any particular work of Isidore in mind when he assigned him his position in the Sun, but it is likely that his activities as encyclopedist stood out in Dante's mind. Nevertheless, despite much critical work, there remains little consensus concerning the extent of Dante's direct acquaintance with the Spaniard's works or even with the *Etymologiae;* Isidore's influence was so extensive that many of Dante's seeming borrowings from his predecessor's works could as easily have been derived from other authors who had made extensive use of the saint's writings. Notable possible mediating texts are Brunetto Latini's *Tresor* and Uguccione's *Derivationes.*

Frank B. Ordiway

Islam and Islamic Culture

Islam, like Christianity and Judaism, is an Abrahamic faith: a monotheistic religion centered on a foundational moment of sacrifice. For Christians, Abraham's willingness to sacrifice his son prefigures the will of the divine Father to offer up his own Son on the cross; for Muslims, who have no comparable belief in original sin, it represents Abraham's *islam,* literally, his "submission" to

God. Unlike Jews and Christians, who hold that the child Isaac was the son offered up by Abraham, Muslims recognize the adult Ishmael as the intentionally submissive victim. The genealogical descent from Ishmael claimed by the Arab tribes was recognized by medieval Christians, who referred to Arabs as "Ishmaelites," as well as "Agarenes" (after Ishmael's mother, Hagar) or, most frequently, "Saracens."

Medieval theologians debated whether to classify Islam as paganism or heresy. The ninth-century Byzantine theologian John of Damascus refutes Islam in his *De Haeresibus,* while in the twelfth century Peter the Venerable states in a letter to Bernard of Clairvaux that he truly does not know whether to refer to Muslims as "heretics" on account of their faith, or as "pagans" on account of their practice (Sahas, Kritzeck). This dichotomy is reflected in medieval literary depictions of Muslims, which portray them either as heretics or schismatics (as does Dante), or as idolatrous polytheists. The latter convention is ubiquitous, especially in the *chansons de geste* and the vernacular romances patterned on them (Daniel, Metlitzki). Muslims are often portrayed worshiping idols arranged in a kind of pagan Anti-Trinity composed of Muhammad, Apollo, and Tervagant.

Misrepresentations of Islam are common even in apparently more objective accounts: medieval biographies of the Prophet stress his lasciviousness and lust for temporal power, and even liken him to the Antichrist himself (Akbari 1997). Such accounts appear in full-length accounts such as the thirteenth-century *Roman de Mahomet,* as well as in summaries in medieval encyclopedias, historical chronicles, saints' lives, mirrors of princes, and even the Anonimo Fiorentino commentary on *Inf.* 28.

Seen in this light, Dante's treatment of Islam appears relatively moderate. His representation of Muhammad as a schismatic is in keeping with theological views of Islam as a form of Christian heresy. Dante's Muhammad *(Mäometto)* is a schismatic, the instigator of a split in the body of the community of Christian believers. His followers are themselves guilty not of creating schism but of heresy (that is, false faith), and they are led into this sin by Muhammad's preaching of a *nuova legge* ("new law") based on Christianity, yet *il contrario* ("contrary" to it), as early commentators such as Jacopo Alighieri and the *Ottimo* put it. For this reason, Ali *(Alì)* alone appears with Muhammad in the circle of schismatics. He is there not on account of his belief in Islam (heresy), but because of his role in the development of the Shi'i movement within orthodox Islam (schism). It is striking that Dante's identification of Ali as a schismatic implies that Islam itself is a form of Christianity, albeit a perverted version of it: only if Islam is, in some sense, still a form of Christianity can Ali's transgression be seen as schism. The *contrapasso* (*Inf.* 28.142) experienced by Muhammad embodies the split in the Christian community caused by schism; the *contrapasso* experienced by Ali embodies the split in the caliphate, or headship of the Muslim community, which resulted from his rule. The image of schism is reiterated as one of the seven major calamities in church history dramatized in the Earthly Paradise, where its affront to Christianity is allegorized as a dragon attacking and dismantling a part of the chariot of the church (*Purg.* 32.130–135).

Early commentators on the *Commedia* display ignorance regarding the theology underlying Dante's treatment of Islam. Several, including Jacopo Alighieri (1322), Jacopo della Lana (1324), the *Ottimo* commentator (1333), and (most elaborately) the Anonimo Fiorentino commentator (1400), repeat the popular story that Muhammad was a Christian cleric who, when frustrated in his effort to achieve the papacy, satisfied his lust for power by founding his own religious sect (d'Ancona). Unaware of the position of Ali in the development of Islam, they ignore him or, at best, like Jacopo Alighieri, refer to him as "one of [Muhammad's] companions named Ali." Not until the nineteenth century do commentators show knowledge of Ali's specific role.

The importance of Dante's treatment of Ali has been largely overlooked by modern commentators on *Inf.* 28, who state that Dante's representation of the Prophet is in keeping with the popular legend of Muhammad as an apostate Christian cardinal. Similarly, the entry under "Maometto" in the *Enciclopedia dantesca* refers to *la leggenda occidentale, a cui esclusivamente D. s'ispirò* ("the Western legend, which was the only source used by Dante"). It is certainly true that the early commentators based their understanding of *Inf.* 28 on "the Western legend"; however, Dante's own treatment of Ali, an enigma to the early commentators, illustrates the poet's more subtle understanding of the theological relationship between Christianity and Islam.

Medieval commentators on the *Commedia* also display ignorance regarding the relationship of Christianity and Islam in their treatment of Saladin, who appears in *Inf.* 4 among the virtuous pagans in Limbo. Sultan Yusuf ibn Ayyub (1138–1193), surnamed Salah ad-Din, reclaimed Jerusalem for the Muslims in 1187 and defended the city against European assaults during the Third Crusade. Dante's commentators recognize that Saladin is a Muslim, or, as the Anonimo Fiorentino commentator puts it, *della legge di Macometto*. They justify his presence in Limbo by focusing on the significance of his physical position: Saladin is said to be *solo, in parte* ("by himself apart"; *Inf.* 4.129). The *Ottimo* commentator explains that this refers to Saladin's special position among other Muslims: *Intra Saraceni fu singulare* ("Among Muslims he was unique"). Benvenuto glosses the phrase similarly, stating that Saladin *fuit singularissimus in virtute temporibus suis* ("was unique in virtue among those of his time"). Jacopo della Lana, however, interprets the reference in the context of the many popular legends of Saladin, in which the Muslim ruler travels throughout the West in disguise. Jacobo states that Saladin, dressed as a pilgrim, *Venne a Parigi solo e passando per una via solo* ("Came alone to Paris, and went his way alone"). Here, the commentator draws on a popular tradition which saw Saladin not only as a model of generosity (as Dante portrays him in *Conv.* 4.11.14), but as a man of the East who could pass unnoticed throughout the West, his identity concealed by his clothing and his mastery of the local language. Such portraits of Saladin appear in Boccaccio's *Decameron* and the *Novellino*, as well as many other vernacular accounts (Paris, Castro, Kirkham).

Saladin's position *solo, in parte* must be understood in the context of Dante's theology regarding Limbo, particularly with regard to the fate of the "virtuous pagan." Efforts have been made recently to articulate Dante's position regarding the fate to be experienced after death by those who, in life, were not members of the Christian church. Yet the treatment of Saladin remains difficult to explain: in her survey of theological treatments of the virtuous pagan, Colish remarks that Dante's inclusion of Saladin and Averroës in Limbo is "peculiar." Iannucci argues that Limbo is populated by those pagans who were "born too early or too far away" to be included in the redemption by Christ; yet such an explanation does not really account for Saladin, whose frequent and often friendly contacts with Christians are attested to in contemporary accounts, some of which go so far as to claim that Saladin had a Christian mother.

Saladin's position among the virtuous pagans in Limbo is liminal in a double sense. Like his companions, he is within Hell and yet outside it; but he is also separated from his companions, aside, alone. In this sense, he is a figure of exile, the heroic equivalent of the narrator himself at the outset of his journey to God. For this reason, Saladin's physical position parallels that of the narrator as he momentarily joins the souls in Limbo: Saladin is named last among the political figures, just as Averroës appears last among the philosophers (*Inf.* 4.144), and Dante himself brings up the rear among the poets (*Inf.* 4.102).

This symmetrical arrangement magnifies the narrator, implicitly comparing him to *Averoìs che 'l gran comento feo* ("Averroës, who made the great commentary," 4.144) and Saladin, unique in his munificence. The coupling of Dante with exemplary Muslims also supports Menocal's argument (1987) that Dante's position with regard to Islamic culture is one of "anxiety." She suggests that Dante's treatment of Muhammad and Ali, his depiction of the pit of Hell as a city full of *meschite* ("mosques," *Inf.* 8.70), and his condemnation of Averroism collectively represent a rejection of Islam, seen by Dante as a religion which elevated the intellect above all else, placing the individual on a level with God. The positioning of the narrator alongside Averroës and Saladin emphasizes the immediacy of the world of Islam, representing it not as a threat located far away on the other side of the world, but rather (in the form of Latin Averroism) as a danger appallingly close to home.

Just as Saladin is distinguished by his munificence, Averroës is distinguished by his intellect. The philosopher ibn-Rushd (1126–1198) was born in Muslim Cordoba, in what is now Spain, and exerted a great influence on Western philosophical thinking during the thirteenth century. Aristotle's *De anima* was known in the West primarily through the Latin translation of Averroës's text with commentary. In *Conv.* 4.13.8, Dante refers to him simply as *lo Commentatore* ("the Commentator"), and he cites Averroës in *Mon.* 1.3.9, *Questio* 12, and *Questio* 46. Yet Averroës's argument that the possible intellect is separate from the individual soul is rejected by Dante in no uncertain terms (*Purg.* 25.61–66); it is essential to

Dante's vision of the afterworld that each human soul continue to exist after death, retaining its individuality (Bynum). Those who follow Averroës in this matter are depicted as heretics by Dante (*Inf.* 10; Corti 1981), and his treatment of Averroism must be understood in the context of his rivalry with Guido Cavalcanti, the poet to whom Dante dedicated the *Vita Nuova* and whom he calls his *primo amico* ("first friend"; *VN* 3.14; Corti 1983). The works of Bruno Nardi remain authoritative regarding Dante's view of Averroism.

Menocal argues that the "anxiety" regarding Islamic culture displayed by Dante in the *Commedia* can be seen most acutely in the structure of the journey to the other world. Dante's position with regard to Islamic eschatology has been, arguably, one of the most profound controversies in Dante criticism during the twentieth century. In 1919, Asín Palacios put forth the thesis that the story of the miraculous journey or *mi'raj* of Muhammad through the circles of Heaven and down into the depths of Hell was a source of the structure of Dante's *Commedia*. This hypothesis was coldly received (Cantarino, Menocal 1996); even after Latin and Old French versions of the *mi'raj* were discovered and edited (Cerulli, Wunderli, Werner), strong resistance to the proposal has not diminished. More recently, however, Corti (1995) has argued that there are several possible ways in which Dante could have known the Latin version of the *mi'raj,* or *Libro della Scala,* and she has examined particularly the possible role of Brunetto Latini in mediating that knowledge. Corti's study, along with a more general willingness to acknowledge non-Western sources and influences on masterworks of Western culture, may lead to a more mature understanding of Dante's relationship to non-Christian, non-Western culture. That indebtedness, especially manifest in the *Convivio* and *Commedia,* includes Dante's deployment of philosophical concepts derived either directly from Islamic philosophers like Averroës, Avicenna, Algazel, and Alpetragius, or indirectly through the mediation of texts by Albert the Great and Thomas Aquinas.

Bibliography

Akbari, Suzanne Conklin. "The Rhetoric of Antichrist in Western Lives of Muhammad." *Islam and Christian-Muslim Relations* 8 (1997), 297–307.

Asín Palacios, Miguel. *La escatologia musulmana en la Divina Comedia.* 1919. Translated and abridged by Harold Sunderland as *Islam and the Divine Comedy.* London: J. Murray, 1926.

Bynum, Caroline Walker. "Faith Imagining the Self: Somatomorphic Soul and Resurrection Body in Dante's *Divine Comedy.*" In *Faithful Imagining: Essays in Honor of Richard R. Niebuhr.* Edited by Sang Hyun Lee, Wayne Proudfoot, and Albert Blackwell. Atlanta: Scholars' Press, 1995, pp. 81–104.

Cantarino, Vincente. "Dante and Islam: History and Analysis of a Controversy." In *A Dante Symposium in Commemoration of the 700th Anniversary of the Poet's Birth (1265–1965).* Edited by William de Sua and Gino Rezzo. North Carolina Studies in Romance Languages and Literatures, 58. Chapel Hill: University of North Carolina Press, 1965, pp. 175–198.

Castro, Americo. "The Presence of the Sultan Saladin in the Romance Literatures." In *An Idea of History: Selected Essays of Americo Castro.* Translated by Stephen Gilman and Edmund L. King. Columbus: Ohio State University Press, 1977, pp. 241–69.

Cerulli, Enrico. *Il "Libro della Scala" e la questione delle fonti arabo-spagnole della Divina commedia.* 1949. Reprinted, Rome: Roma Multigrafica, 1970.

———. *Nuove ricerche sul "Libro della scala" e la conoscenza dell'Islam in Occidente.* Vatican City: Biblioteca Apostolica Vaticana, 1972.

Colish, Marcia L. "The Virtuous Pagan: Dante and the Christian Tradition." In *The Unbounded Community: Papers in Christian Ecumenism in honor of Jaroslav Pelikan.* Edited by William Caferro and Duncan G. Fisher. New York and London: Garland, 1996, pp. 43–77.

Corti, Maria. "La *Commedia* di Dante e l'oltratomba Islamico." *Belfagor* 50 (1995), 301–314.

———. *La felicità mentale: Nuove prospettive per Cavalcanti e Dante.* Turin: Einaudi, 1983.

———. *Dante a un nuovo crocevia.* Florence: Sansoni, 1981.

d'Ancona, Alessandro. "La leggenda di Maometto in Occidente." 1889. Reprinted as *La leggenda di Maometto in Occidente.* Edited by Andrea Borruso. Rome: Salerno, 1994.

Daniel, Norman. *Heroes and Saracens: An Interpretation of the Chansons de Geste.* Edinburgh: Edinburgh University Press, 1984.

Iannucci, Amilcare A. "Limbo: The Emptiness of Time." *Studi danteschi* 52 (1979–1980), 69–128.

Kirkham, Victoria, and Maria Rosa Menocal. "Reflections on the 'Arabic' World: Boccaccio's Ninth Stories." *Stanford Italian Review* 7 (1987), 95–110.

Kritzeck, James. *Peter the Venerable and Islam.* Princeton, N.J.: Princeton University Press, 1964.

Menocal, Maria Rosa. "An Andalusianist's Last Sigh." *La Coronica* 24 (1996), 179–189.

———. *The Arabic Role in Medieval Literary History: A Forgotten Heritage.* Philadelphia: University of Pennsylvania Press, 1987.

Metlitzki, Dorothee. *The Matter of Araby in Medieval England.* New Haven: Yale University Press, 1977.

Morgan, Alison. *Dante and the Medieval Other World.* Cambridge: Cambridge University Press, 1990.

Nardi, Bruno. *Dante e la cultura medievale.* Rome and Bari: Laterza, 1983 [1949].

———. *Saggi di filosofia dantesca.* Florence: La Nuova Italia, 1967 [1930].

Paris, Gaston. "La Légende de Saladin." *Journal des savants* (May–Aug. 1893), 284–299, 354–364, 428–438, 486–498.

Sahas, Daniel J. *John of Damascus on Islam: The "Heresy of the Ishmaelites."* Leiden: Brill, 1972.

Vallone, Aldo. "Oriente-Occidente: La Civiltà Islamica." In *Percorsi medievali e cultura dantesca.* Naples: Accademia di Archeologia, Lettere e Belle Arti, 1994, pp. 13–28.

Werner, Edeltraud. *Liber Scale Machometi: Die lateinische Fassung des Kitab al mi'radj.* Studia Humaniora, 4. Düsseldorf: Droste, 1986.

Wunderli, Peter (ed.). *Le Livre de l'Eschiele Mahomet: Die französische Fassung einer alfonsinischen Übersetzung.* Bern: Francke, 1968.

Suzanne Conklin Akbari

Ismene

Daughter of Oedipus and of his mother Jocasta, and sister of Antigone, Eteocles, and Polynices. Statius's *Thebaid* recounts her numerous sufferings, including her father's self-blinding, her mother's suicide, her fiancé's murder, the mutual slaying of her brothers Eteocles and Polynices, and the fall of Thebes. In *Purg.* 22.111, Statius tells Virgil that she resides with other great pagan women in Limbo.

F. Regina Psaki

Israel

"Israel" is the name given in Gen. 32:27–28 to Jacob, son of Isaac son of Abraham, in view of his becoming father of the progenitors of the twelve tribes of the people known collectively by this name. Dante uses the name "Israel" for Jacob in *Inf.* 4.59, and for the whole Jewish people *(quello popolo d'Israel)* in *Conv.* 2.5.1; *DVE* 1.7.8; *Epist.* 7.19 and 29 and 13.21; and *Mon.* 1.8.3, 1.14.9, 2.7.5, and 8. Dante's references typically reflect the view of the Jews as blind to salvation, even though God had spoken to them through their prophets *(Conv.* 2.5.1–2). In this respect Dante is in line with traditions dominant in the Middle Ages that represented Israel as stubbornly unbelieving in Christ the Messiah. And yet, Israel has symbolic value in the Bible as the promised land—not only the land promised the Jews, but the true and final spiritual home of all human beings. Accordingly, in the Middle Ages Israel was also the symbolic place of redemption, the holy land, as well as the figure of the chosen souls destined for eternal life. This connotation of the name "Israel" as the people and place of promise is conveyed by Dante especially in a phrase *(In exitu Israel de Aegypto)* he quotes from the Psalms on three different occasions, in *Purg.* 2.46, *Conv.* 2.1.6, and *Epist.* 13.21.

In *Purg.* 2.46, Dante quotes *In exitu Israel de Aegypto,* the first verse or "incipit" of Psalm 113 in the Vulgate (= 114 + 115 in the Hebrew and Protestant Bibles), as a way of keying the whole of the second *cantica* in a special way to the Exodus paradigm. Meaning "When Israel went out from Egypt," the verse is sung by the souls as they arrive at the shore of the mountain of Purgatory, ferried by an angel over the sea covering the Southern Hemisphere. Dante quotes only the opening verse but explains that all the souls "were singing all together with one voice, with as much of that psalm as is written thereafter" *(cantavan tutti insieme ad una voce / con quanto di quel salmo è poscia scripto).* The Latinism—*scripto* instead of the Italian *scritto*—calls attention to the fact that this writing is "scriptural." The singing in unison may allude to choral chanting of the psalm in the liturgy. Dante's explanation may also be understood as spelling out a convention whereby psalms were cited by their incipits only, even when the psalm in its entirety was meant—as seems to be the case, for example, in the gospels with Jesus' citation from the Cross of Psalm 22: "My God, my God, why hast thou forsaken me?" Like Psalm 22,

Psalm 113 as a whole celebrates the passage from death to life by grace of the saving act of God, as becomes more explicit in its concluding verses: "The dead praise not the Lord, neither any that go down into silence, but we who live bless the Lord."

The psalm's theme literally is the Exodus, the successful flight of the Hebrews from slavery in Egypt, their passing through the Red Sea (which the psalm conflates with their crossing over the Jordan into the promised land, as recounted in Joshua 3) by the miraculous intervention of God—the founding event of early Israelite, Mosaic religion. The souls' leaving behind the perils of the world and reaching Purgatory, "Israel"—that is, the promised land of Christian salvation—is thereby understood to be a fulfillment of what had been prefigured by the Exodus of the people of Israel from Egypt. In accordance, moreover, with the traditional meaning of the Exodus as prefiguring the Christian's escape from death and passage to resurrected, glorified life, Dante's emergence from Hell and a condition of sin to a state of grace is presented in this light allegorically as an Exodus. As such, the verse becomes a *leitmotif* for Dante's redemptive, paschal poem in its entirety, as brought to focus in the passage to Purgatory set at dawn on Easter morning, 1300. Dante refers to his journey as an Exodus again in a number of places, signally in *Par.* 25.55–56.

Dante takes the Exodus, the most canonical of stories of return from exile, as the paradigm also for his method of interpreting scripture and, by extension, of building spiritual meaning into his own *poema sacro.* He employs the psalm, citing its incipit, as a key illustration in detailed expositions of scriptural allegory, the so-called allegory of the theologians, in *Conv.* 2.1.6–7 and the Letter to Cangrande *(Epist.* 13.20–25). The Exodus event, in fact, serves ideally to illustrate the four different levels of meaning ascribed to texts by the fourfold method of scriptural exegesis that had become canonical in the Middle Ages and that Dante himself adopts. On the first level, the literal, this text designates a historical event: Moses' leading the Israelites out of Egypt, the whole history of which is told in the book of Exodus. Next, the typological level of significance relates this event in Old Testament history to the New Testament, and specifically to its central event, Christ's redemption of humanity. This event, furthermore, has an inner, moral dimension: the freeing of the individual soul from sin, which constitutes the third level of significance of the Exodus event, its so-called tropological or moral sense. Finally, the Exodus signifies an exit of Christian souls from the corruptible world into eternal glory, and this is its anagogical sense.

The meaning of the Exodus was firmly established in the exegetical tradition dedicated to this psalm verse, and more broadly in commentary on the book of Exodus, as a prefiguration of the events of Easter—Christ's resurrection from death, and beyond that, the general resurrection. St. Augustine in his sermons on this psalm says, "When we hear in the psalm, *In exitu Israel de Aegypto,* [etc.], let us not think of past things narrated to us but rather of things future being taught: for those miracles in that people were and indeed are, but not without bearing signification of future things (*sed non sine futurorum significatione gerebantur, Enarrationes in Psalmos* 113.1). According to Peter Lombard, "These miracles are figures of the spiritual mysteries of Christ and the Church, as exposition of the psalm makes clear" (*In psalmis* 113). Hugh of St.-Cher defines the psalm as a sign of victory (*signum victoriae).*

Beyond its role in allegorical exegesis of the Bible, the verse has a life in the church liturgy. As dictated by the Roman Breviary, the psalm is sung regularly—that is, as part of the Ordinary, at Vespers on Sunday. Despite considerable variation, especially of psalms for the Proper (those that change day by day according to the seasons and feasts), it has a prominent role in the Easter liturgy. Furthermore, in the Middle Ages it was sung in the Office of the Dead, accompanying the transport of the deceased to their final resting place, symbolized thereby as an Exodus to the promised land of the afterlife. Certainly its familiarity to Dante in these contexts, as well as its already achieved exemplary status in exegetical tradition, impressed it on his mind and contributed to its becoming a keystone for his reflection.

Bibliography

Armour, Peter. "The Theme of Exodus in the First Two Cantos of the *Purgatorio*." In *Dante Soundings: Eight Literary and Historical Essays.* Edited by David Nolan. Dublin: Irish Academic Press, 1981.

Augustine. *Enarrationes in Psalmos.* Corpus Christianorum, Series Latina, 40. Turnholti: Brepols, 1966.

Demaray, John. "From Egypt to Jerusalem: Spiritual Conversion on Earth and Beyond." In *Dante and the Book of the Cosmos. Transactions of the American Philosophical Society* 77, pt. 5 (1987), pp. 47–60.

Hugh of St.-Cher. *Adnotationes super universam Bibliam.* Lovanio, 1627.

Lombardi, Petrus. *In psalmis.* In *Patrologia Latina* 191, cols. 1017–1026. Edited by J. P. Migne. Paris: Garnier, 1879.

Rondeau, Marie-Josèphe. *Les Commentaires patristiques du Psautier (3–5 siècles).* Rome: Pont. Inst. Studiorum Orientalium, 1982.

Singleton, Charles. *"In exitu Israel de Aegypto."* In *Dante: A Collection of Critical Essays.* Edited by John Freccero. Englewood Cliffs, N.J.: Prentice-Hall, 1965.

William Franke

Italian Language

When Dante speaks of the Italian language, he means the Italian vernacular (*lo volgare italico, Conv.* 1.6.8). The characterization of Italian as vernacular *(volgare)* is predicated on its being the language of the common people *(volgo)* and is intended to distinguish it from Latin, the language of the learned *(litterati).* The Italian vernacular is variously called *la lingua di sì* ("the language of sì," *VN* 25.5), *lo parlare italico* ("the Italian speech," *Conv.* 1.11.14), and *vulgaris Ytaliae* ("the vernacular of Italy," *DVE* 1.10.9); all these terms are synonymous. To understand the essence and evolution of the Italian language in Dante, one needs to comprehend his notion of the Italian vernacular with all its nuances and connotations.

Origin of the Italian Vernacular

Dante notes in the *De vulgari eloquentia* that human discourse was created by God simultaneously with Adam himself, and that this God-given language was highly stable and fully developed from the outset, being lexically, syntactically, and phonetically very sound (*DVE* 1.6.4). He adds that the Adamic language was unchangeable and was passed on as such to all subsequent generations, and that this same language would still be spoken in his own time were it not for the Babelic confusion (*DVE* 1.6.4–5). The construction of the Tower of Babel led to the creation of numerous distinct languages, eliminating forever the linguistic uniformity and stability humankind had previously enjoyed (*DVE* 1.7.6–7). The Babelic confusion contributed not only to the emergence of many diverse languages, but also to the continuous mutation of these languages. Thus, whereas prior to Babel there had been one unchangeable language, after Babel there were numerous languages, each of which (except for Hebrew, which retained the stability of the Adamic language) was marred by intrinsic mutability. That the post-Babel languages should be mutable is logical enough, Dante argues, for, unlike the language of Adam which was the product of God, these languages depend on the discretion *(beneplacitum)* of man, who, as an inconstant and changeable being, produces languages which are themselves inconstant and changeable (*DVE* 1.9.6).

In Europe the post-Babel linguistic mutability manifested itself as a threefold idiom *(ydioma tripharium),* encompassing the "Germanic," "Romance," and "Byzantine" languages. These languages evolved into further linguistic forms. The Romance idiom developed into an *ydioma tripharium* of its own: the languages of *oc* (Provençal/Spanish), *oïl* (French), and *sì* (Italian). And the languages of *oc, oïl,* and *sì* themselves ramified into different linguistic entities. Thus, the language of *sì* evolved into fourteen major vernaculars, each with numerous linguistic derivatives (*DVE* 1.10.7). The intrinsic mutability of the post-Babelic languages did not preclude their having linguistic efficacy; for example, the Romance idioms possessed much expressive power, with French being especially proficient in prose literature, and Provençal and Italian in lyric poetry (*DVE* 1.10.2).

Defense and Potential of the Italian Vernacular

In Dante's time it was common for Italian writers to shun their vernacular in favor of either French or Provençal. For example, Brunetto Latini, Dante's mentor (*Inf.* 15.82–87) and one of the leading intellectuals of thirteenth-century Italy, wrote his masterpiece, the *Tresor,* in French. Believing in the linguistic proficiency of Italian, Dante resented his fellow Italians' rejection of their own vernacular. Thus, in the *Convivio* he chides those individuals who considered the Italian vernacular linguistically inferior to other vulgar tongues, especially the language of *oc.* The contemporary argument that Provençal is superior to the Italian vernacular, Dante argues, is as absurd as the ancient contention—censured by Cicero—that the Greek language was more praiseworthy than Latin

(*Conv.* 1.11.14). That Italian can be as effective a linguistic instrument as Provençal is attested to by the works produced by the good vernacular writers of Italy (*Conv.* 1.11.13).

Dante maintains, again in the *Convivio,* that the Italian vernacular has the ability to express lofty and new matters effectively and gracefully, and that this ability will become apparent in his commentary of the *canzoni* of the *Convivio,* which he had chosen to write in Italian rather than in Latin (1.10.12). Dante argues that the potential to express lofty matters in a cogent and elegant fashion has always been implicit in the Italian vernacular, but that this potential has not been fully realized. His commentary will remedy this deficiency: *io lo fo avere in atto e palese ne la sua operazione* ("I make it express actively and openly through its own proper activity," *Conv.* 1.10.9). Indeed, Dante foretells a day when, on the strength of this commentary, the Italian vernacular will emerge as a respected language, serving as a viable linguistic instrument for the many who have no knowledge of Latin: *Questo sarà luce nuova, sole nuovo, lo quale surgerà là dove l'usato tramonterà, e darà lume a coloro che sono in tenebre e in oscuritade per lo usato sole che a loro non luce* ("This [the Italian vernacular] shall be a new light, a new sun which shall rise where the old sun [Latin] shall set and which shall give light to those who lie in shadows and in darkness because the old sun no longer sheds its light upon them," *Conv.* 1.13.12).

The Italian Vernacular vs. Latin

Dante concludes that, notwithstanding its many linguistic merits, the vernacular is inferior to Latin. At best, the vernacular could approximate the linguistic efficiency of Latin but never equal it, for, as anyone who knows both Latin and the vulgar tongue can attest, Latin has an expressive range far superior to that of the vernacular: *lo latino molte cose manifesta concepute ne la mente che lo volgare far non può* ("Latin expresses many things conceived in the mind which the vernacular cannot," *Conv.* 1.5.12). The superiority of Latin is due to its being an artificial, conventional language, whereas the vernacular is a natural, fluid one: *lo volgare seguita uso, e lo latino arte* ("the vernacular follows usage, while Latin follows art," *Conv.* 1.5.14). In fact, Latin, which Dante characterizes as *gramatica* (*DVE* 1.1.3–4) , came into being as a remedy for the inevitable diversification and instability of the post-Babel languages (*DVE* 1.1.3–4).

It was formulated by learned men *(inventores)* and reduced to rule by the common consent of many peoples (*DVE* 1.1.3-4, 9.11). As such, unlike the vernacular, Latin was immune to individual choices, and therefore immutable in time and space. Being unchangeable, Latin served as a viable linguistic instrument for the peoples of different eras and different countries (*DVE* 1.9.11). Dante's perception of Latin parallels his notion of the Adamic language in the *De vulgari eloquentia,* a notion he was to revise in the *Commedia* (*Par.* 25.124–138); both languages are stable, cosmopolitan, functional, and immune to man's will.

Dante argues that for many centuries Latin had met its intended objectives. However, in recent times its effectiveness has been hampered by a decline in literacy—that is, a decline in the knowledge of Latin language and culture. In Italy the decline in literacy was so profound that fewer than one in a thousand could be considered truly conversant in Latin (*Conv.* 1.9.2). Given the deplorable state of Latin in contemporary times, those who wanted to instruct and enlighten society, a moral responsibility of any sage, as Dante himself acknowledges (*Conv.* 1.1.8–9), had to make use of the vernacular. That is the reason, he argues in the *Convivio,* that he has decided to write this work's commentary in the Italian vernacular. Had he written it in Latin, the moral message implicit in this commentary would have been beneficial only to a few literati, whereas in the vernacular it will benefit a large number of Italians: *manifestamente si può vedere come lo latino averebbe a pochi dato lo suo beneficio, ma lo volgare servirà veramente a molti* ("it may clearly be seen that Latin would have conferred its benefits on few while the vernacular will be of service to many," *Conv.* 1.9.4). The need for an Italian vernacular is reiterated in the *De vulgari eloquentia* (1.1.1), but whereas in the *Convivio* Dante is concerned with the effectiveness of the Italian vernacular in general, in the *De vulgari eloquentia* he concentrates on its quintessence, the illustrious vernacular: *decentiorem atque illustrem Ytaliae venemur loquelam* ("let us hunt for the most respectable and illustrious vernacular that exists in Italy," *DVE* 1.11.1).

Toward the Formulation of an Illustrious Vernacular (Vulgare Illustre)

The illustrious vernacular constitutes one of the most elusive and complex aspects of Dante's thought. It has thus been the object of much speculation and polemic among Dantean scholars. Broadly speaking, Dante's notion of the illustrious vernacular denotes a language that exists potentially in all the regional vernaculars of Italy, but is identifiable with none of them (*DVE* 1.16.1, 4). This language can be brought to fruition by highly learned and divinely inspired poets (*doctores illustres, DVE* 2.1.5–6, 7.7). In formulating the illustrious vernacular, the *doctores illustres* must make use only of grand words *(grandiosa vocabula),* which, by being very perfect *(nobilissima),* are the only ones worthy of the illustrious vernacular (*DVE* 2. 7.1, 4). They must discard "puerile," "feminine," and "rustic" words and concentrate instead on urbane terms. And among the urbane terms they must choose only those which are carded *(pexa)* and hirsute *(yrsuta),* for these alone can be considered grand (*DVE* 2.7.2).

The *doctores illustres* must be equally discriminating in their choice of stylistic norms. They must avoid the incongruous construction and rely instead on the congruous one. And of the various types of the congruous construction—the one without flavor, the one with flavor, the one with flavor and grace—they must make use of its highest form, the lofty construction *(excelsa constructio),* which possesses flavor and grace as well as excellence (*DVE* 2.6.5–6). A language so constructed would have a regularity lacking in the regional vernaculars of Italy. It thus would serve as norm of the many vernaculars of the Italian people: *quo municipalia vulgaria omnia Latinorum mensurantur et ponderantur et comparantur* ("against which the vernaculars of all the cities of the Italians can be measured, weighed, and compared," *DVE* 1.16.6).

The illustrious vernacular assumes characteristics of Latin: it is cosmopolitan; it possesses stability and regularity. However, unlike Latin, whose influence extended to most of Europe, the influence of the illustrious vernacular is limited to Italy. As to its stability and regularity, they are relative rather than absolute, as Dante believes is the case with Latin. By appropriating linguistic elements from the vernaculars of Italy, the illustrious vernacular is in the final analysis a natural language; and stability and regularity, as Dante observes in conjunction with the formulation of Latin (*DVE* 1.9.11), are characteristics peculiar to artificial languages. The illustrious vernacular is in a state of becoming (*DVE* 1.18.1); consequently its effectiveness and endurance are not intrinsic to

I the idiom itself. Rather, they depend on the diligence and ingenuity of its formulators, the *doctores illustres*.

The Language of the Commedia

The language of the *Commedia* is not the illustrious vernacular about which Dante had theorized in the *De vulgari eloquentia*. That language was too rarefied and stylized to suit the linguistic needs of the *Commedia,* which treats a variety of subject matter from the sublime to the trivial. It thus makes use of "grand" words as well as of "puerile," "feminine," and "rustic" ones, with some coarse terms typical of the crudest Italian vernaculars. Even its rhetorical apparatus deviates from the lofty construction he considers fundamental to the illustrious vernacular. Ultimately, the language of the *Commedia* is the idiom of contemporary Florence, enriched with many latinisms, with numerous terms derived from foreign languages and other Italian vernaculars, and with some words coined by Dante himself. However, reliance on the Florentine idiom rather than the illustrious vernacular does not mean that the language of the *Commedia* is regional and inelegant. With a few exceptions, the linguistic form of the *Commedia* is elevated and urbane, and, especially in the *Paradiso,* it meets the criteria of a literary, noble, and learned language.

The Florentine language of the *Commedia,* reinforced by the language of Petrarch and Boccaccio, eventually superimposed itself on the regional idioms of Italy, even as it appropriated linguistic terms from them, becoming (at least in the area of literature) the official language of the country. The very name of this language, which had traditionally been called "Florentine" or "Tuscan," became "Italian." Early in the eighteenth century (1724) the distinguished linguist Anton Maria Salvini (1653–1729) notes that "the common language of Italy, that is, the language the Italians have used in the past and still use now, is Tuscan . . . so one can reasonably call the Tuscan language Italian because all Italians make use of it and write in it when they wish to write for posterity" (288).

Bibliography

Cremona, Joseph. "Dante's Views on Language." In *The Mind of Dante.* Edited by Umberto Limentani. Cambridge: Cambridge University Press, 1965, pp. 138–162.

Dante: De vulgari eloquentia. Edited and translated by Steven Botterill. Cambridge: Cambridge University Press, 1996.

Davis, Charles T. "Dante's Italy." In *Dante's Italy and Other Essays.* Philadelphia: University of Pennsylvania Press, 1984, pp. 1–22.

Mazzocco, Angelo. *Linguistic Theories in Dante and the Humanists: Studies of Language and Intellectual History in Late Medieval and Early Renaissance Italy.* Leiden, New York, and Cologne: Brill, 1993.

Mengaldo, Pier Vincenzo. "Le teorie dantesche sulla lingua." *Enciclopedia dantesca,* 3:656–664.

———. *Linguistica e retorica di Dante.* Pisa: Nistri–Lischi, 1978.

———. "Volgare." *Enciclopedia dantesca,* 5:1127–1129.

Nardi, Bruno. "Il linguaggio." In his *Dante e la cultura medievale: Nuovi saggi di filosofia dantesca.* Bari: Laterza, 1949, pp. 148–175.

Pagani, Ileana. *La teoria linguistica di Dante.* Naples: Liguori, 1982.

Salvini, Anton Maria. "Annotazioni critiche alla *Perfetta poesia italiana* del Muratori." In L.A. Muratori, *Della perfetta poesia italiana.* Milan: Dalla Società Tipografica dei Classici Italiani, 1821, vol. 3, p. 288.

Santangelo, Salvatore. "Il volgare illustre." In *Saggi danteschi.* Edited by Antonio Milani. Padua: CEDAM, 1959, pp. 131–142.

Shapiro, Marianne. *De Vulgari Eloquentia: Dante's Book of Exile.* Lincoln and London: University of Nebraska Press, 1990.

Terracini, Benvenuto. "Natura ed origine del linguaggio umano nel *De Vulgari Eloquentia.*" In his *Pagine e appunti di linguistica storica.* Florence: Le Monnier, 1957, pp. 237–246.

Vinay, Gustavo. "Ricerche sul *De Vulgari Eloquentia.*" *Giornale storico della letteratura italiana* 136 (1959), 236–388.

Wunderli, Peter von. "Dante—ein Linguist?" In *Deutsches Dante-Jahrbuch* 68/69 (1993/1994), 81–126.

Angelo Mazzocco

Italy

According to Dante, Italy—also referred to as *terra latina* ("the Latin land")—extends eastward from Genoa along the arch of the Alps across to the Gulf of Carnaro east of Istria. From the Alps it extends southward to the region of Apulia

(= Puglia, Basilicata, Calabria, and Campania), including the islands of Sicily and Sardinia (*DVE* 1.8.8–9, 10.7; *Inf.* 9.113–114, 20.62–63; *Par.* 8.61–63). Conforming with the chorography of the time, exemplified by the map associated with Pietro Vesconte (1321), Dante's Italy spans the peninsula from west to east. It is crossed by the Apennines, *lo dosso d'Italia* ("the back of Italy," *Purg.* 30.86), which divide it into two sides. On the right Italy borders the Tyrrhenian Sea, and on the left, the Adriatic. Dante seems to believe that these two seas converge in the Straits of Messina; he thus appears to preclude the existence of the Ionian Sea, which he never mentions. The geographic limits of Italy are determined almost entirely by linguistic criteria: they extend to wherever the Italian vernacular is spoken. Indeed, Italy is the *bel paese là dove 'l sì suona* ("the lovely land where *sì* is spoken," *Inf.* 33.80), and the Italians are the ones *qui sì dicunt* ("who say *sì,*" *DVE* 1.8.8) or the ones who speak the *volgare di sì* ("vernacular of *sì,*" *Conv.* 1.10.12). The interconnection between Italy and its vernacular is not only spatial/quantitative, but also cultural/qualitative.

In the *De vulgari eloquentia* (c. 1305), while assessing the linguistic state of the Italian vernacular, Dante concludes that Italy possesses at least fourteen linguistic regions, and each region has linguistic varieties of its own (*DVE* 1.10.7). He notes that part of Apulia, Rome, the Duchy of Spoleto, Tuscany, and the March of Genoa, plus the islands of Sicily and Sardinia, constitute the linguistic areas right of the Apennines; the rest of Apulia, the March of Ancona, Romagna, Lombardy, and the March of Treviso with Venice, plus the regions of Friuli and Istria, are those left of the Apennines (*DVE* 1.10.7–8). The vernaculars of these areas differ from one another qualitatively. Thus, the vernaculars of Sicily and Bologna, being the products of a refined culture, are superior to that of Rome, which is most displeasing, reflecting the unpleasantness of the ambiance in which it is realized: *Dicimus igitur Romanorum non vulgare, sed potius tristiloquium, ytalorum vulgarium omnium esse turpissimum; nec mirum, cum etiam morum habituumque deformitate pre cunctis videantur fetere* ("For what the Romans speak is not so much a vernacular as a vile jargon, the ugliest of all the languages spoken in Italy; and this should come as no surprise, for they also stand out among all Italians for the ugliness of their manners and their outward appearance," *DVE* 1.11.2).

A qualitative discrepancy also exists between most of the Italian vernaculars and the peripheral vernaculars of the peninsula, such as the idioms of Trent, Turin, and Alessandria, which, having evolved outside the linguistic mainstream of Italy, lack the purity needed to be enumerated among its great vernaculars (*DVE* 1.15.8). Notwithstanding their qualitative differences, these vernaculars, by being part of the linguistic patrimony of Italy as a whole, possess elements of a superior, quintessential Italian vernacular, which Dante characterizes as illustrious vernacular *(vulgare illustre)*. The illustrious vernacular could be brought to fruition by highly learned and divinely inspired poets *(doctores illustres)* and could serve as the norm of all the regional vernaculars of Italy: *quo municipalia vulgaria omnia Latinorum mensurantur et ponderantur et comparantur* ("against which the vernaculars of all the cities of the Italians can be measured, weighed, and compared," *DVE* 1.16.6).

In the *De vulgari eloquentia* the argument on the Italian idioms and the illustrious vernacular gives impetus to an equally important, though not so well developed, argument on regional cultures and *Italianitas* ("Italianness"). The linguistic regions of Italy come to signify regional cultural entities with their own language *(locutio),* their own manners *(mores),* and their own customs *(habitus).* Therefore, like the idioms of Italy, these regional cultures differ qualitatively from one another, their quality being determined, like that of the idioms, by the nature of the environment that engenders them. But, being integral parts of the culture of greater Italy, they embody elements of a higher, quintessential culture: *Italianitas.* This *Italianitas,* which bears characteristics peculiar to the illustrious vernacular, could be realized at the court of an Italian monarch and could serve as the standard for Italian culture in general. Dante laments that contemporary Italy lacks a monarch and a court; consequently, it lacks a unified, viable *Italianitas* (*DVE* 1.16.3–5, 18.2–5). However, he believes that Italy has not always been this unfortunate, for there had been a court in Italy where *Italianitas* had flourished. Dante attributes this distinction to the court of Emperor Frederick II (1194–1250) and his son Manfred (c. 1231–1266), who, by living like men rather than brutes, attracted the most gifted and the most virtuous of Italian men to their palace: *Propter quod corde nobiles atque gratiarum dotati inherere tantorum principum maiestati conati sunt* ("On this account, all who were noble of heart and rich in graces strove to attach themselves to the majesty of such worthy princes," *DVE* 1.12.4). Thus, whatever eminent Italian minds accomplished at that time first came to fruition at the royal residence of these great sovereigns: *ita ut eorum tempore quicquid excellentes animi Latinorum enitebantur primitus in tantorum coronatorum aula prodibat* ("so that, in their day, all that the most gifted individuals in Italy brought forth first came to light in the court of these two great monarchs," *DVE* 1.12.4).

The Italy of the *De vulgari eloquentia,* then, is a well-defined geographic entity with a linguistic and cultural, but not political, unity (since Dante believes that political unity is limited to regional autonomies). Indeed, this Italy is capable of producing a language and a culture that are quintessentially Italian and that are brought about, respectively, by divinely inspired poets and a royal court of the type Italy enjoyed during the reigns of Frederick II and Manfred. However, as Charles T. Davis argues convincingly, Dante's conception of Italy undergoes a significant modification beginning with the fourth book of the *Convivio* (4.4.8–13), which was written only a couple of years after the completion of the *De vulgari eloquentia,* and continuing with the *Monarchia* and the *Commedia* as well as some of the letters. It retains its geographic and linguistic uniqueness, but loses its cultural integrity, which becomes considerably less concrete and more generic. To be sure, the Italy of this period is *Europe regione nobilissima* ("the most noble region of Europe," *Mon.* 2.3.17), and it is *'l giardin de lo 'mperio* ("the garden of the Empire," *Purg.* 6.105), but these attributes are not due so much to virtues and values particular to Italy itself. Rather, they flow from Italy's special rapport with the Roman Empire of which it is the origin and heart, by virtue of its being the region where Rome is located. Indeed, it is in the context of the providential mission and universality of the Roman Empire that the Italy of this period finds its raison d'être. When it refuses to submit to the authority of the Roman emperor, it is *di dolore ostello, / nave sanza nocchiere in gran tempesta* ("dwelling of grief, ship without a pilot in a great storm," *Purg.* 6.76–77), but when it bows to imperial guidance, as Dante hopes will happen in the case of the new emperor-elect Henry VII, it rejoices in its justice and peace (*Epist.* 5.5–6, 15–

17). The destiny of Italy is interconnected with that of the Roman emperors, who are German and not Italian, but who are nevertheless judged favorably by Dante, if they carry out the divinely ordained rights of the empire. He thus characterizes Frederick I, called Barbarossa (c. 1122–1190), the Roman emperor most berated by the northern Italian communes, as *il buon Barbarossa* ("the good Barbarossa," *Purg.* 18.119) and sanctions his destruction of Milan (*Epist.* 6.20). By contrast, he diminishes the moral authority of the two most Italian of Roman princes, Frederick II (condemned to Hell as a heretic) and Manfred (consigned to the Ante-Purgatory, where he expiates his excommunication and other horrible sins); these two, unlike later Italian potentates, subscribe to a high moral and cultural standard (*DVE* 1.12.3–5).

The emphasis on the universality of the Roman Empire, of which Italy is but a part, leads Dante to reassess his perception of Rome. Thus, whereas in the *De vulgari eloquentia* he had spoken of a Rome which was incubator of a vile people and culture, in the fourth tractate of the *Convivio* he speaks of a Rome that is home to a *popolo santo* ("sacred people"), endowed with *grandissima e umanissima benignitade* ("the greatest and most humane kindness"), and which therefore is sole inheritor of the empire (*Conv.* 4.4.10–11). And whereas the assessment of the *De vulgari eloquentia* is deduced from concrete historical evidence, that of the *Convivio* is predicated on Virgilian myths and providential dictates: *E in ciò s'accorda Virgilio nel primo de lo Eneida, quando dice, in persona di Dio parlando: "A costoro—cioè a li Romani—. . . ho dato imperio sanza fine* ("Virgil concurs in this in the first book of the *Aeneid* when, speaking in the person of God, he says: 'To these (namely the Romans) . . . I have given empire without end," *Conv.* 4.4.11).

Italy looms large in the later works of Dante, especially in the *Commedia.* All fourteen regions into which Dante divides the Italian peninsula come to life in the *Commedia,* with Lombardy, Romagna, but especially Tuscany being mentioned most often. The *Commedia* captures the physical character of these regions with their ever-changing scenery, their rivers—now calm and limpid, now turbulent and murky—their snow-covered Apennines, their imperious castles, and their turreted towns. More important, the *Commedia* probes the socio-historical essence of the people of these regions. It explores their aspirations, passions, social conflicts, political orientation, intellectual achievements, cultural background, and historical roots, and it judges these attributes favorably or unfavorably, depending on how well they conform to Dante's sense of world order and his precepts of *cortesia e valor* ("courtesy and valor," *Inf.* 16.67), precepts that encapsulate the whole value system of medieval culture. Hence, the Italy of the *Commedia* is an *umile Italia* ("humble Italy") soon to be freed of her cupidity and, therefore, of her numerous endemic travails by a symbolically charged Greyhound (*Veltro, Inf.* 1.100–108); or she is a *dolce terra latina* ("sweet Italian earth") remembered fondly from the depths of Hell (*Inf.* 27.25–30). But she is also a *serva Italia* ("slavish Italy") whose cities *tutte piene son di tiranni* ("are all filled with tyrants," *Purg.* 6.77, 124–125).

The *Commedia's* broad and deeply felt interpretation of physical and spiritual Italy made Dante a major force in the political and cultural life of nineteenth-century Italy, when after centuries of foreign domination and political fragmentation, the Italians undertook to unify the peninsula. Italian patriots glossed over Dante's contradictory rendition of Italy—Italy the unique geographic, linguistic, and cultural entity vs. Italy the integral part of a Roman Empire led by German emperors—and transformed Dante into a champion of Italian unity. Giuseppe Mazzini (1805–1872), one of the architects of the unification of Italy, acknowledges Dante as the prophet of a unified Italian state. By this Mazzini means the whole Italian peninsula, including the city of Rome, which at the time was under the control of the papacy. The yearning for Rome to be a member and the capital of the Kingdom of Italy became an essential element of the nationalistic movement. In a paraphrase of *Purg.* 6. 112–114 that appeared in 1859, the youthful patriot and novelist Raffaello Giovagnoli (1838–1915) has Rome implore the companionship of Victor Emmanuel II, soon to be king of Italy: "Come and see your Rome, lonely, crying widow, who night and day asks, 'My dear Vittorio, why don't you join me?'" (Bellezza, 135). After the formulation of the Italian Kingdom, which took place in 1861, Dante continued to energize those Italian patriots who wished to incorporate northeastern Italy, a region still under foreign control, into the Italian state. These patriots found in Dante's acknowledgment of the Ital-

ian nature of Trent, the Carnaro area, and other communities of this region the validation of their struggle to annex this part, which they characterized as *Italia irredenta* ("unredeemed Italy"). *Italia irredenta* was eventually incorporated into the Italian state with the restructuring of Europe after World War I.

The influence of Dante during the struggle for independence was not limited to the political sphere and the world of the intelligentsia, but extended to the common people as well. Volunteers carried the *Commedia* to war, and political prisoners read it in jail. Its verses were inscribed on medals and buildings, and the name Dante came to denominate many an Italian piazza. The impact of Dante on the Italian consciousness of this period is best expressed by Bernardino Zendrini (1839–1879), who writes: "The *Comedy* was for us, as the Bible was for the Jewish wanderers, the symbol of fatherland and nationality during the years of foreign domination" (Bellezza, 103).

Bibliography

Barbi, Michele. "L'Italia nell'ideale politico di Dante." *Studi danteschi* 24 (1939), 5–37.

Battaglia, Salvatore. "L'idea di Dante nel pensiero di Giuseppe Mazzini." In *Filologia e letteratura* 12 (1966), 113–124.

Bellezza, Paolo. *Curiosità dantesche.* Milan: Hoepli, 1913.

Casella, Mario. "Questioni di geografia dantesca." *Studi danteschi* 12 (1927), 65–77.

Cibele, Francesco. *Il paesaggio italico nella Divina Commedia.* Vicenza: Officina Tipografica Vicentina, 1957.

Davis, Charles T. "Dante's Italy." In his *Dante's Italy and Other Essays.* Philadelphia: University of Pennsylvania Press, 1984, pp. 1–22.

———. "Dante and Italian Nationalism." In *A Dante Symposium.* Edited by William De Sua and Gino Rizzo. Chapel Hill: University of North Carolina Press, 1965, pp. 199–213.

Ferrante, Joan. *The Political Vision of the Divine Comedy.* Princeton, N.J.: Princeton University Press, 1984.

Hay, Denys. "Italian View of Renaissance Italy." In *Florilegium Historiale.* Edited by J. G. Rowe and W. H. Stockdale. Toronto: University of Toronto Press, 1971, pp. 4–17.

Limentani, Umberto. "Dante's Political Thought." In *The Mind of Dante.* Edited by U. Limentani.

Cambridge: Cambridge University Press, 1965, pp. 113–137.

Mazzocco, Angelo. *Linguistic Theories in Dante and the Humanists: Studies of Language and Intellectual History in Late Medieval and Early Renaissance Italy.* Leiden, New York, and Cologne: Brill, 1993.

Revelli, Paolo. *L'Italia nella Divina Commedia.* Milan: Treves, 1922.

Scott, John A. "An Uncharted Phase in Dante's Political Thought." In *Essays in Honour of John Humphreys Whitfield.* Edited by H. C. Davis. London: Saint George's Press, 1975, pp. 41–52.

Vinay, Gustavo. "Ricerche sul *De vulgari eloquentia:* iii Apenini devexione clauduntur." *Giornale storico della letteratura italiana* 136 (1959), 367–382.

Angelo Mazzocco

J

Jacob

Son of Isaac and Rebecca, Jacob is renamed "Israel" by God (Gen. 32:28, 35:10); both names become designations of the nation (*Epist.* 13.21; Ps. 114:1). Virgil names Israel, his father, his children (the twelve ancestors of Israel), and Rachel as being among those led forth from Limbo by Christ (*Inf.* 4.59–60). In the *Paradiso,* Charles Martel (8.130–131) and St. Bernard (32.67–72) refer to Jacob *(Giacobbe, Iacobbe)* as differing from his the twin brother Esau according to God's providential will (Gen. 25:22–27, Mal. 1:2–3, Rom. 9:10–13); St. Benedict (*Par.* 22.70–72) compares the ladder of contemplation (*nostra scala,* line 68) to the ladder reaching into Heaven dreamed by Jacob at Bethel (Gen. 28:12). In *Mon.* 1.13.4, Dante refers to Jacob's deception of his blind father with the false hands of Esau (Gen. 27:22), and, in 3.5.1–2, to Jacob's sons Levi and Judah, as symbolic of the Church and Empire respectively.

Carolynn Lund-Mead

Jacopo di Dante

More generally known as Jacopo di Dante, Jacopo Alighieri was the third son of Dante and perhaps the earliest of the commentators on the *Inferno.* He was the younger brother of Pietro, who became even better known than Jacopo as a commentator on the *Commedia* because Pietro commented on the whole of the poem, whereas Jacopo wrote only on the *Inferno.* Jacopo was born a few years before 1300, accompanied his father into exile, and rose to become a canon of the Church in Verona. He died in 1349, perhaps as a result of the famous plague of 1348.

Within a year of his father's death Jacopo sent to Guido da Polenta his *Divisione,* which is perhaps the earliest analysis of the structure of the great poem. The *Divisione* was followed by another analysis in a poem called *Il Dottrinale,* and that in turn by another short summary called *Il Capitolo.* Finally, Jacopo wrote an actual commentary on the first canticle, entitled *Chiose alla cantica dell'Inferno di Dante Alighieri.* There has been continuing scholarly debate over whether Jacopo ever wrote a commentary on the other two canticles, but the consensus is that he limited himself to the *Inferno.* His commentary has an allegorical tendency and was written before 1325 (and perhaps as early as 1321–1322), making it the earliest Italian commentary. Some scholars maintain that Jacopo's *Chiose* shows traces of Guido da Pisa's Latin *Expositio,* but nothing definite has been proven.

Bibliography

Alighieri, Jacopo. *Chiose all' "Inferno."* Edited by Saverio Bellomo. Padua: Antenore, 1990.

———. *Chiose alla cantica dell'Inferno.* Edited by G. Piccini. Florence: Bemporad, 1915.

Vincenzo Cioffari

Jahrbuch der Deutschen Dante-Gesellschaft

Title of the yearbook of Dante studies published under the aegis of the Deutsche Dante-Gesellschaft and founded by Johann Heinrich Friedrich Karl Witte (1800–1883) in 1865. Its four volumes appeared in the years 1867–1877, under the imprint of the prestigious F. A. Brockhaus Publishing House of Leipzig. Eduard Boehmer

J

(1827–1906), the secretary of the Deutsche Dante-Gesellschaft, coedited the first three volumes with Witte. The *Jahrbuch* became the meeting ground of the most distinguished medievalists of the second half of the nineteenth century.

Among its contributors, we find the author of an important biography of Dante (3rd ed., 1879), Franz Xaver Wegele (1823–1897), who published an article on the Ghibellines (1 [1867]: 21–34); the historian Alfred von Reumont (1808–1887), who offered documented studies on Dante's condemnation and exile (1 [1867]: 375–385), on Dante's family (2 [1869]: 331–353), and on Rome in Dante's times (3 [1871]: 369–422); the Swiss pastor Giovanni Andrea Scartazzini (1837–1901), who contributed articles on the Earthly Paradise (2 [1869]: 99–150), on Dante's spiritual development (3 [1871]: 1–39; 4 [1877]: 143–237), on the correspondence between sins and punishments in the *Inferno* (4 [1877]: 273–354), and on the problem of Matelda (4 [1877]: 411–480); Karl Friedrich Adolf Bartsch (1832–1888), the author of seminal essays on the Provençal sources of Dante (2 [1869]: 377–384) and on Dante's poetics (4 [1877]: 303–367); Theodor Paur (1815–1892), whose essays on Dante's iconography (2 [1869]: 262–330) and the relationship between Dante and Immanuel Romano (3 [1871]: 423–462; 4 [1877]: 667–672) are still useful.

After a long interruption, the yearbook was resurrected in 1920 by Hugo Daffner (1889–1936) under the new title *Deutsches Dante-Jahrbuch,* which it still retains. However, this periodical was quite different from its predecessor, inasmuch as Daffner, a physician turned musicologist turned Dantist, was mainly interested in popularizing the Italian poet. The five volumes that appeared under his editorship (1920–1925) dedicated considerable space to translations at the expense of scholarly research.

Bibliography

Folena, Gianfranco. "La filologia dantesca di Carlo Witte." In *Dante e la cultura tedesca*. Edited by Lino Lazzarini. Padua: Università degli Studi, 1967, pp. 109–139.

Goetz, Walter. "Geschichte der Deutschen Dante-Gesellschaft." In *Dante: Gesammelte Aufsätze.* Münchner Romanistische Arbeiten, 13. Munich: Max Hueber, 1958, pp. 103–142.

Rheinfelder, Hans. "Nascita e sviluppo della Società Dantesca Germanica." In *Dante e la cultura tedesca.* Edited by Lino Lazzarini. Padua: Università degli Studi, 1967, pp. 27–38.

———. "La *Deutsche Dante-Gesellschaft.*" In *Atti del Congresso internazionale di studi danteschi (20-27 aprile 1965).* Florence: Sansoni, 1966, pp. 31–35.

Witte, Karl. *Essays on Dante (Being Selections from the Two Volumes of "Dante Forschungen."* Edited and translated by C. Mabel Lawrence and Philip H. Wicksteed. New York: Haskell, 1970 (reprint of the 1898 ed.).

Gustavo Costa

James II of Aragon

James *(Iacomo)* belongs to the fourth class of the late repentant in the Ante-Purgatory, rulers whose preoccupations with their worldly ambitions detained them from addressing the higher concerns of the spirit (*Purg.* 7.119). Surnamed "the Just" by his subjects, he was king of Sicily from 1285 to 1295 and king of Aragon from 1291 to 1327. On the death of his father Pedro III in 1285, his elder brother Alfonso III became king of Aragon while James himself succeeded to the throne of Sicily. When Alfonso died in 1291, James took over Aragon, leaving Sicily in the hands of his younger brother Frederick II. But soon he agreed to cede Sicily to the Angevin claimant, Charles II of Naples, as he married the latter's daughter Blanche in 1295. Upon learning of this arrangement, the Sicilians gave up their allegiance to James and proclaimed Frederick as their king. James died at Barcelona on November 2, 1327. Dante, through the voice of Sordello, regrets that although Pedro III was a worthy man, his sons did not inherit "the better heritage" of their father; he concludes, "Seldom does human probity rise up through the branches, and this is willed by him who gives it" (*Purg.* 7.121–123).

R. A. Malagi

James, King of Majorca

Second son of James I of Aragon and brother of Pedro III, James *(Iacomo)* came into possession of the Balearic Islands after his father's death in 1276. He is one of the living kings rebuked by the Eagle in the Heaven of Jupiter (*Par.* 19.137). He died in 1311.

R. A. Malagi

James, St., the Apostle

Son of Zebedee and brother of John the Evangelist, called "the Great" to distinguish him from the homonymous Apostle James the Less, son of Alphaeus. James (*Iacopo*) is one of the Apostles in Jesus' innermost circle, together with John and (Simon) Peter (as Dante recalls in *Par.* 25.33), and the only apostle whose martyrdom is recorded in the New Testament (Acts 12:2). The three appear together in the account of the Gospels, called by Christ to serve as witnesses on three specific occasions: at the raising of Jairus's daughter, one of the greatest miracles of Jesus (Luke 8:41–56); at the Transfiguration of Jesus on Mt. Tabor (Matt. 17:1–9); and at the agony of Jesus in the Garden of Gethsemane (Matt. 26:36–46). An exegetical tradition allegorically identified the three Apostles with the three theological virtues of faith (Peter), hope (James), and charity (John).

According to tradition, St. James preached and diffused the Christian Gospel in Spain and died a martyr to the faith in Jerusalem, under the rule of King Herod Agrippa I of Judaea, about 42 C.E. After his death his body was transferred to Santiago de Compostela in Galicia, Spain. His sepulcher became a celebrated shrine and destination for pilgrims, the most important in the Middle Ages after Jerusalem (the sepulcher of Christ) and Rome (the sepulcher of Peter). In *VN* 40 Dante identifies pilgrims destined for Santiago as properly called *peregrini,* as opposed to *palmieri* (palmers) and *romei* (romers).

St. James appears in the Heaven of the Fixed Stars, where he administers an examination to the pilgrim Dante on hope, the second of the three theological virtues (*Par.* 25.25–99). Dante refers to him as the author of the celebrated Epistle of St. James (*Par.* 25.29–30, 77), which today is attributed to James the Less. The Epistle is also cited in *Conv.* 4.2.10, *Conv.* 4.20.6, and *Mon.* 1.1.6.

Bibliography

Busnelli, Giovanni. *Il concetto e l'ordine del Paradiso dantesco.* Città di Castello: S. Lapi, 1911, pp. 118 ff., esp. 151–157.

Conrieri, D. "San Giacomo e la speranza: osservazioni su *Par.* XXV, vv. 13–99." *Giornale storico della letteratura italiana* 148 (1971), 309–315.

Tartaro, Achille. "Certezze e speranze nel XXV del *Paradiso*." *L'Alighieri* 24 (1983), 3–15.

Anna Maria Chiavacci Leonardi
(translated by Tamao Nakahara)

Jason

The son of Aeson, Jason *(Giasone)* built the first ship, the *Argo,* and led the Argonauts to Colchis in quest of the golden fleece. Stopping in Lemnos, Jason seduced and impregnated Hypsipyle, promising to return. In Colchis, with the aid of Medea's magic, he yoked fire-breathing oxen to a plough, and after tranquilizing the dragon guarding it, he successfully obtained the fleece. He then sailed away with Medea, whom he married. He later deserted her to marry Creon's daughter, Creusa, and, in revenge, Medea killed her children by Jason and poisoned his new wife. Dante, whose sources for the story are Ovid (*Meta.* 7.1–158, *Her.* 6, *Her.* 12) and Statius (*Theb.* 5. 403–485; see also Valerius Flaccus, *Argonautica* 2.311–424, and Statius, *Achilleid* 1.25–26), places Jason among the seducers in the eighth circle of Hell (*Inf.* 18.83–99), where Virgil identifies him as a regal figure who captivated Hypsipyle by misusing *parole ornate* ("elaborate words," *Inf.* 18.91). Jason is a crucial figure for Dante in the *Paradiso;* his story appears in *Par.* 2.16–18, where the poet claims that the astonishment of the Argonauts, as they watched Jason yoke the fiery oxen, will be surpassed by the amazement of the *Commedia*'s readers as they follow Dante traversing waters that have never been sailed before. In *Par.* 33.94–96, Dante adduces the voyage of the *Argo* when he describes the oblivion wrought by his vision of the universal form. Moreover, *Par.* 25.7–9 arguably elaborates the parallel between Dante's and Jason's voyages by obliquely figuring Dante as a new Jason, returning from his expedition with a new fleece and a new voice. The *Paradiso* stages a reenactment and revision of the journey of the Argonaut: both the pilgrim and the poet stand as Jasons, cutting new paths and amazing those left in their wake. Jason is also mentioned in *Il Fiore* 8.2, 161.6, and 190.6.

Bibliography

Barolini, Teodolinda. *The Undivine Comedy: Dethe-ologizing Dante.* Princeton: Princeton University Press, 1992, pp. 56–57.

Curtius, Ernst Robert. "The Ship of the Argonauts." In *Essays on European Literature.* Translated by Michael Kowal. Princeton, N.J.: Princeton University Press, 1973, pp. 465–496.

Hollander, Robert. *Allegory in Dante's "Commedia."* Princeton, N.J.: Princeton University Press, 1969, pp. 220–232.

Jessica Levenstein

J

Jason, High Priest

In the Old Testament, second son of the high priest Simon II and brother of the high priest Onias III. He usurped the high priesthood from his brother by promising Antiochus IV Epiphanes, the Seleucid king, a total of 510 talents of silver. Upon his accession, Jason proceeded to do the king's bidding by attempting to hellenize Jewish worship and culture (see 2 Maccabees 4–6). Nicholas III mentions Jason (*Iasón*) in *Inf.* 19.85–87, comparing him and his king to Bertran de Got (Pope Clement V) and Philip the Fair, king of France. Dante alludes to the story, recounted by Villani (*Cronica* 9.80), that Bertran obtained the papacy through the influence of Philip, to whom he promised all the tithes of France for five years.

V. Stanley Benfell

Jerome, St.

Along with St. Augustine, St. Ambrose, and St. Gregory, one of the four major Latin Fathers of the Church. Born in Stridon along the border of Dalmatia and Pannonia in 345, he studied in Rome, where one of his teachers was the grammarian Donatus. Dante associates Jerome *(Ieronimo)* with the theory that the angels existed many ages before the creation of the world (*Par.* 29.37–39), a view not supported by Thomas Aquinas and even more strongly rejected by Dante himself.

Assigned by Pope Damasus I to "straighten out the problem of the Bible," Jerome translated the Greek and Hebrew versions of the Bible and edited the *Vetus Latina,* to produce the *Vulgata,* the authoritative Latin Bible of the western Catholic Church from the fifth century through the sixteenth. Recognized as the most important commentator on the literal level of the Bible, he established standards for philological studies which influenced theories of the translation and editing of ancient texts from late antiquity to the Renaissance. The Bible Dante read and consulted would have been Jerome's *Vulgata.*

In addition to the great task of editing and translating the Bible, Jerome also wrote prefaces to various sections of the Bible which were standard introductions in medieval bibles, one of which Dante cites in *Conv.* 4.5.16. In his numerous commentaries and letters, and in these prefaces, he advances a theory of interpretation and translation based on the work of the great Alexandrian Greek biblical scholar, Origen. Insistent on the need to establish the text on sound philological and historical grounds, Jerome argues nonetheless that interpretation should be threefold, and embrace the literal (or philological) and the historical, as well as the spiritual dimensions of the text. His prejudice in favor of the philological dimension of the text led him into heated disputes with his long-time correspondent, St. Augustine, whom he accused of not understanding the words of scripture. After 386 he resided in Bethlehem, where he founded several convents for nuns; he died there in 419 or 420.

Brenda Deen Schildgen

Jerusalem

The city of Jerusalem was for Dante the central location of the inhabited world. With his contemporaries, he understood it to lie at the midpoint of the Northern Hemisphere of dry land, equidistant from the Ganges (or India) to the east and the Pillars of Hercules at Gibraltar in the west. Where he departed from received notions of geography, however, was in his placement of Purgatory at the antipodes from Jerusalem, on an island mountain rising up from the waters of the uninhabited Southern Hemisphere. Dante reinforces the relationship between Jerusalem and Purgatory by having the two locations share the same horizon (*Purg.* 2.1–3, 4.67–68), with Satan buried equidistant between them (*Inf.* 34.112–126). Here geography does the work of theology: sin and redemption are shown to be understandable only in terms of what took place in Jerusalem.

There is strong biblical warrant for according Jerusalem this central position. In the Old Testament, it is the city of David, home of the temple of the Lord, and source of both celebration and lament. God was believed to have chosen it as his dwellingplace and therefore to have put it in the midst of the surrounding peoples (Ezek. 5:5). For Christians, Jerusalem is also the place where Christ suffered, died, and was resurrected. The Church of the Holy Sepulchre, built by the Emperor Constantine in the early fourth century, marked this site of death and rebirth; it quickly became the most hallowed spot in Christendom, both the destination of pilgrims and an ongoing point of contention with the Muslim powers that largely controlled the Holy Land.

Throughout his works, Dante draws on this body of tradition. According to *Inf.* 34.114–115,

Jerusalem stands at the "zenith" of the Northern Hemisphere and is named in periphrasis as the place where Christ died, *l'uom che nacque e visse senza pecca* ("the man who was born and lived without sin"). This association of the city with Christ is noted elsewhere (*Mon.* 3.9.10, *Purg.* 27.2, *Epist.* 2.5), but Jerusalem is also considered in other contexts: it is the city of David (*Epist.* 11.1) laid waste by the Roman Emperor Titus in 70 C.E. (*Purg.* 23.28–30; see also *Purg.* 21.82–84). In the *Vita Nuova,* Dante uses the much earlier fall of Jerusalem, mourned in the Psalms and in the Lamentations of Jeremiah, to describe the desolation of Florence after the death of Beatrice. In *Epist.* 7.30, moreover, he likens the condition of Florentine exiles like himself to the ancient Jews who were filled with memories of Zion as they bewailed their fate by the waters of Babylon. Finally, in *Par.* 25.55–57, Jerusalem becomes (as in the New Testament) a way of speaking about the heavenly city itself. It is in keeping with Dante's high evaluation of Rome's place in God's providential plan that Paradise is also identified as *quella Roma onde Cristo è romano* ("that Rome of which Christ is a Roman," *Purg.* 32.102), and it is described in *Par.* 31–32 in imperial terms. Dante's City of God unites the world of the Bible with that of Virgil's *Aeneid.*

Bibliography

Demaray, John G. *The Invention of Dante's "Commedia."* New Haven and London: Yale University Press, 1974.

———. "Patterns of Earthly Pilgrimage in Dante's *Commedia:* Palmers, Romers, and the Great Circle Journey." *Romance Philology* 24 (1970), 239–258.

Heilbronn, Denise. "Dante's Gate of Dis and the Heavenly Jerusalem." *Studies in Philology* 72 (1975), 167–192.

McClung, William Alexander. *The Architecture of Paradise: Survivals of Eden and Jerusalem.* Berkeley, Los Angeles, and London: University of California Press, 1983.

Tucker, D. J. "*In Exitu Israel de Aegypto:* The *Divine Comedy* in the Light of the Easter Liturgy." *American Benedictine Review* 11 (1960), 43–61.

Peter S. Hawkins

Joachim of Fiore

Calabrian visionary, famous even in his own lifetime as an eschatological prophet, whom Dante places with Bonaventure in the second circle of the Sun (*Par.* 12.140–141). Born around 1135 in Celico in Calabria and converted during a pilgrimage to the Holy Land around 1167, Joachim *(Gioacchino da Fiore)* joined the monastery of Corazzo around 1171, ultimately becoming abbot in 1177. By 1190 he had established his own monastery, San Giovanni, near Fiore in Calabria, which developed into the Ordo Florensis, whose rule was approved by Celestine III in 1196. Bonaventure's heavenly praise of Joachim, *il calavrese abate Giovacchino / di spirito profetico dotato* ("the Calabrian abbot Joachim, endowed with prophetic spirit," *Par.* 12.140–141) echoes the antiphon to Vespers in which the Florensian Order commemorated his memory: *Beatus Joachim, spiritu dotatus prophetico* ("Blessed Joachim, endowed with prophetic spirit"). Joachim died in 1202. Although his understanding of the Trinity was condemned at the Fourth Lateran Council (1215), Joachim himself was never branded a heretic and was proclaimed orthodox by Honorius III in 1220.

At San Giovanni Joachim wrote his three most important works: the *Liber concordie,* a study harmonizing the Old and New Testaments; the *Psalterium decem chordarum,* a mystical meditation on the growth of spiritual understanding in history; and the *Expositio in Apocalypsim,* which established his reputation as a prophet. The *Liber figurarum,* a fascinating collection of symbolic drawings that reflect Joachim's trinitarian conception of history, is also now usually attributed to Joachim or to an early follower. To modern scholars and theologians, Joachim is best known for his trinitarian understanding of history as unfolding through three overlapping ages associated with God the Father, the Son, and the Holy Spirit. To his contemporaries, however, he was better known for his exegesis of the Apocalypse, and specifically for foreseeing the appearance of Antichrist and the events of the Last Days. His reputation attracted a visit from Richard the Lionhearted on his crusade to the Holy Land.

Because Joachim identified the two witnesses of Apocalypse 11 as representing a new order of "spiritual men," in the thirteenth century he was understood to have prophesied the foundation of the mendicant orders. The Franciscans were particularly influenced by Joachim's exegesis, and the radical Spiritual Franciscans used his works, and later writings mistakenly attributed to him, to develop an apocalyptic eschatology that gave St. Francis a crucial role in salvation history. As they became marginalized within the order, the radical Franciscans increasingly understood themselves as the persecuted remnant who were to play the role of the final witnesses in opposition to a tyrannical Antichrist, whom they identified with a corrupt institutional church and sometimes with the papacy itself. Bonaventure, as minister general of the Franciscans, strongly opposed the radicals, while retaining in his *Legenda Maior* their emphasis on the centrality of St. Francis in the events of the Last Days. Bonaventure is often described as a bitter enemy of Joachim, but their theologies of history share many common elements, as is clear in Bonaventure's combination of mysticism and apocalypticism in his *Collationes in Hexaemeron*. Bonaventure was primarily opposed to the excesses of later Joachimists such as Gerard of Borgo San Donnino, who in his *Liber introductorius* blurred the distinction between the roles of Francis and Christ. Dante's placement of Joachim with Bonaventure may thus reflect the poet's awareness that they shared prophetic interests; on the other hand, it may be Dante's way to reconcile in Heaven two figures who had an enormous influence on the Franciscans—a reconciliation similar to that achieved by placing Siger with Thomas Aquinas in the first circle of the Sun (*Par.* 10.136–138).

It is difficult to assess the extent to which Joachim's apocalyptic and mystical theology of history influenced Dante. In a general sense, Dante's optimistic political hope—expressed in the *Monarchia*—for the establishment of a world government, and his praise of Emperor Henry VII as a new Caesar Augustus in his letter to the princes and people of Italy (1310), may reflect radical Joachimist expectations that a last world emperor would introduce a third age of spiritual *renovatio*. But such political messianism was quite common in Italy at this time and was not limited to Joachimists. Furthermore, although for centuries medieval eschatological scenarios had expected a last world emperor to unify Christendom in preparation for the tribulations of the Last Days, Joachim himself had little faith in political solutions to earthly problems.

It is more likely that Dante was influenced by two sets of figures from Joachim's *Liber Figurarum*. The first set, known as the Tree-Eagles, helps explain Dante's vision of the stars writing *Diligite iustitiam . . . qui iudicatis terram* ("Love

justice . . . you who judge the earth," *Par.* 18.91–93) as they move through heaven and then gather on the final *M,* which is slowly transformed into an eagle (*Par.* 18.106–108). This image resembles Joachim's figures of stylized trees that, when turned upside-down, resemble an *M* with the head of an eagle. A second set, Joachim's figures representing the Trinity as three equal and interlacing circles of three colors, may have influenced Dante's climactic image of the Godhead near the conclusion of the *Commedia* (*Par.* 33.115–120). A third figure, the Tree of the Two Advents, has been compared to Dante's tree in the pageant of the Earthly Paradise (*Purg.* 32); but, given the popularity of tree diagrams in medieval iconography and mysticism, it is difficult to determine specific Joachimist influence here.

Bibliography

Emmerson, Richard K., and Ronald B. Herzman. *The Apocalyptic Imagination in Medieval Literature.* Philadelphia: University of Pennsylvania Press, 1992.

Grundmann, Herbert. "Dante und Joachim von Fiore." *Deutsches Dante-Jahrbuch* 14 (1932), 210–256.

McGinn, Bernard. *The Calabrian Abbot: Joachim of Fiore in the History of Western Thought.* New York: Macmillan, 1985.

Reeves, Marjorie. "Dante and the Prophetic View of History." In *The World of Dante.* Edited by Cecil Grayson. Oxford: Clarendon Press, 1980, pp. 44–60.

———. *The Influence of Prophecy in the Later Middle Ages: A Study in Joachimism.* Oxford: Clarendon Press, 1969.

Reeves, Marjorie, and Beatrice Hirsch-Reich. *The Figurae of Joachim of Fiore.* Oxford: Clarendon Press, 1972.

Tondelli, Leone. *Il Libro delle figure dell'abate Gioachino da Fiore.* 2nd ed. Turin: Società editrice internazionale, 1953.

Richard K. Emmerson

Jocasta

Wife of Laius, king of Thebes, Jocasta *(Giocasta)* unwittingly married his killer, their son Oedipus, and bore him four children: twin boys, Eteocles and Polynices, and daughters, Antigone and Ismene. In *Purg.* 22.56, Virgil, in the presence of Statius, refers to Jocasta's grief over the bitter fratricidal conflict between the brothers for the succession of the crown, as related in Statius's *Thebaid*. Virgil calls it a "double grief" because she loses both sons.

Diana Cavuoto Glenn

John the Baptist, St.

Dante grew up in a city whose patron was John the Baptist *(San Giovanni Battista),* the precursor and cousin of Jesus (Luke 1:3, Matt. 3:4, Mark 1:6, John 1). Like all other Florentines, Dante was baptized in the city's Baptistery, which bore the patron's name. Both building and patron occupied an important place in Dante's imagination, as indicated by the recurrent references to them throughout his works, especially the *Commedia.* His great-great-grandfather, Cacciaguida, recalls his baptism in the "ancient baptistery" *(Par.* 15.134–135). He compares the holes in which the corrupt popes are wedged to the fonts for baptizing priests *nel mio bel san Giovanni* ("in my beautiful St. John"), one of which he says he broke to save a life *(Inf.* 19.16–21). Master Adam recalls that the city's coin, the florin, bore its patron's image ever since it was first minted in 1252 *(Inf.* 30.73–74).

John's name interested Dante. According to Luke's Gospel (1:59–63), it had been chosen through divine inspiration. Jerome interpreted it as meaning "the Lord his grace." In the *Vita Nuova,* Love tells Dante that the first of the women whom he saw in a vision of Beatrice was named *Primavera* (Spring), a word taken to mean *prima verrà* (she will come first); this corresponds to the woman's actual name, Giovanna, the feminine form of Giovanni (John), "who came before the true light, saying 'I am the voice of one crying in the wilderness: prepare the way of the Lord'" (*VN* 24.4; John 1:23)—which is appropriate because this Giovanna is the precursor of Beatrice, herself a figure of Christ. The etymology of *Giovanna* reappears in Bonaventure's life of St. Dominic (*Par.* 12.79–81).

Later Dante saw John as the rival of the city's earlier patron Mars, the Roman god of war, whose temple was thought to have been replaced by the Baptistery. The anonymous suicide says he came from "the city that for the Baptist changed its first patron [Mars]," *Inf.* 13.143–144). Cacciaguida gives these two antithetical patrons as demarcating the much smaller city of the late twelfth century: "between the Baptist and Mars" (*Par.*

16.47)—that is, the area between the Baptistery next to the cathedral, and the surviving fragments of what was believed to be a statue of Mars that had been moved from his temple to the Ponte Vecchio.

Dante came increasingly to see John as the solitary prophet in the desert and as a transitional figure between the Jewish and Christian dispensations. On the terrace of gluttony, the voice from the tree recalls John as living on "honey and locusts" in the desert (*Purg.* 22.151–152). Near the end of the *Commedia,* Bernard of Clairvaux points to him in the heavenly rose as "the great John who, ever holy, suffered the wilderness and martyrdom and then Hell for two years" (*Par.* 32.31–33)—a reference to the rescue of John by Jesus during the Harrowing of Hell.

Dante came to identify with John the Baptist, the herald of Christ and denouncer of contemporary mores. In *Epist.* 7.7, addressed to Henry VII in the spring of 1311, he likens the emperor to Jesus, citing John ("Behold the lamb of God!"), while condemning those who rejected him. This same tone of bitter prophetic denunciation appears often in the *Commedia.* The poem's penultimate, highly concentrated reference to John does not name him. In condemning avaricious popes, rather than saying that they covet money, or florins, the poet sarcastically says that they ignore Peter and Paul because they fix their desire on "the man who wanted to live alone and was brought to martyrdom by leaping [i.e., Salome's dancing]" (*Par.* 18.133–135). In his last years Dante hoped in vain to return one day to *l'ovil di San Giovanni* ("the sheepfold of San Giovanni," *Par.* 16.25), his native Florence, to receive the poet's crown at the font of his baptism (*Par.* 25.1–9).

John Ahern

John, St.

Of Jesus's twelve disciples, St. John, *l'aguglia di Cristo* ("Christ's eagle," *Par.* 26.53)—the sign by which he is represented iconographically in medieval art—is commonly known as the "Beloved Disciple." He appears in *Par.* 26 to interrogate Dante on the nature of love. In medieval painting and sculpture, John is often seen as the disciple who stood at the cross with Mary when Jesus was crucified, an image based on the crucifixion scene that is told only in the Gospel of John (John 19:26–27). Modern biblical scholars are not convinced

J

Gold florin obverse with image of St. John, the patron saint of Florence, dating from 1306. Private collection. Richard Lansing.

Gold florin reverse showing Florentine lily. Private collection. Richard Lansing.

that the John who wrote the Gospel of John was the John identified as one of Jesus's disciples, particularly since the gospel is generally dated around 90 C.E. But in the Middle Ages, it was commonly held not only that the gospel writer was John the disciple, but also that he wrote all the Johannine material in the Bible (the Gospel of John, the Apocalypse of John, and the three Letters of John).

This was the view Dante himself accepted. Identifying John along with Peter and James as the inner group of disciples who were present at the Transfiguration (*Purg.* 32.76), Dante refers to the writer of both the Gospel and Apocalypse of John as the Evangelist John, attributing the vision of the Apocalypse to the Evangelist: *Di voi pastor s'accorse il Vangelista, / quando colei che siede sopra l'acque / puttaneggiar coi regi a lui fu vista* ("Of you shepherds the Evangelist took note, when he saw her who sits upon the waters whoring with the kings," *Inf.* 19.106–108). Furthermore, he affirms the veracity of John's vision against Ezekiel's by making his own vision coincide with that of the Apocalypse: *Giovanni è meco e da lui si diparte* ("John is with me, and departs from him," *Purg.* 29.105). No contemporary biblical scholar believes that the Johannine texts were written by the same person, although the leading John scholar, Raymond Brown *(Community of the Beloved Disciple*; *The Anchor Bible Commentary on the Gospel of John),* has argued that the letters of John were produced in an exclusive Johannine community that continued theological traditions developed in

the Gospel of John. There is no doubt, however, that the Apocalypse was authored by another John, John of Patmos.

Although the Gospel of Matthew had pride of place in the lectionary and in the New Testament itself and is the most quoted gospel from the early church through the Middle Ages, John's gospel was also favored. It had particular appeal to a number of theological writers in the long period from late antiquity to the time of Dante, and both St. Augustine and St. Thomas Aquinas wrote commentaries on it. The themes of God's love and justice were developed in the gospel, and its opening lines, "In the beginning was the Word . . . and the Word was made flesh," were echoed in many medieval texts. The Apocalypse of John, the last book of the Bible and the only thoroughly apocalyptic text of the New Testament, presents a vision of the end of time and God's victory over evil; it was a very popular part of the Bible, inspiring much medieval art. Richard of St. Victor (*Par.* 10.131–132) and St. Bonaventure (*Par.* 12), both important writers for Dante, composed commentaries on the Apocalypse of John. Dante particularly shows both his knowledge of and interest in the Apocalypse in the pageant that comes at the end of the *Purgatorio* (29–32). Moreover, the theme of exile pervading the Apocalypse has profound resonances in the *Commedia*.

The Gospel of John and the Apocalypse share several themes central to the subject of *Commedia*. John's interrogation of the pilgrim Dante on

"... nel mio bel San Giovanni" (Inf. *19.17*). *The Baptistery of Florence, where Dante was baptized. Richard Lansing.*

the nature of love is especially appropriate because John's gospel, more than any other, dwells on love, particularly in the passage "I am the vine and my father is the gardener" (15:1), at the close of which Jesus commands his disciples to "love one another" (John 15:17). Dante integrates the themes of love and gardening in *Par.* 26 (especially in lines 63–66 and in the closing speech of Adam, 109–142). Augustine and Thomas Aquinas had referred to the garden setting for the beginning and end of time (Genesis and the Apocalypse), and John's is the only gospel that sets the central events of Jesus' life in gardens. In *Par.* 26, where both John and Adam appear in the same canto and where God is described as "the eternal gardener" (26.65), Dante connects the main figures from the first and last books of the Bible by deploying the typology of the garden and the themes of love and exile.

Dante quotes from or refers to the books of John on numerous occasions: *Conv.* 2.1.5, 3.14.7; *Mon.* 2.11.2, 3.8.2, 3.9.15–16, 3.14.4; *Epist.* 13.89, 90; and *Fiore* 5.14. He appears among the saved in the top tier of the White Rose in *Par.* 32.127.

Brenda Deen Schildgen

Jordan

River in Palestine. In the Old Testament it constitutes an important boundary, and in the New Testament it is a place of baptism. In *Par.* 22.94–96, St. Benedict asserts his confidence that God will intervene to put an end to the corruption of the Church, with a miracle, like the biblical miracles of the turning back of the waters of the river Jordan *(Iordan),* or the parting of the Red Sea. In *Purg.* 18.135, where it figures in one of the examples of the sin of sloth, the river stands for the Promised Land, which those Israelites who had crossed the Red Sea with Moses were never able to enter, having delayed on their journey through the desert.

Claire Honess

Joseph, St.

Husband of the Virgin Mary. Joseph *(Giuseppe)* is alluded to in *Purg.* 15.91 with the citation of Mary's reproach of Christ when he remained in the temple at Jerusalem (Luke 2:48).

Molly Morrison

J

Joshua

The military leader of the Israelites who succeeded Moses, and under whose command they entered and conquered the Promised Land. Cacciaguida points Joshua *(Iosuè)* out to Dante as the first of the holy warriors in the cross of Mars, where he is paired with another Old Testament hero, Judas Maccabeus *(Par.* 18.37–39). Joshua is also named in *Epist.* 7.7, *Purg.* 20.111, and *Par.* 9.125. In the last passage, Dante makes use of the conventional interpretation of Joshua as a type of Christ.

Mark Balfour

Jovial Friars

Founded officially under Augustinian rule by Loderingo degli Andalò, Gruamonte Caccianemici, Scianca di Reggio, and Raniero degli Adalardi in March 1261 and approved by Pope Urban IV in December of the same year, the Ordo Militiae Beatae Mariae Virginis (Order of the Army of the Blessed Virgin Mary) quickly became known as the *frati gaudenti* (Jovial Friars), primarily because one category of members, the lay knights (the equivalent of a tertiary order), enjoyed the privileges of living in their own homes, marriage, and personal property. Three other categories required greater sacrifice: married brothers and their wives, who often served convents; conventual—but still secular—brothers who took vows of poverty, chastity, and obedience; and regular clerics. All members of the order held noble rank or joined from professional classes, such as jurists, notaries, and apothecaries. At a time when the Church's authority and the noble class were threatened in northern Italian cities by political strife and populist, anti-magnate legislation, the Knights of the Virgin Mary were, like earlier military-religious groups, constituted primarily to aid on the Church's behalf in the resolution of political uprisings that divided the noble families, and, in general, to fight heresy. The diverse political affiliations of the two Bolognese friars most closely associated with the order's early years—Loderingo degli Andalò (Ghibelline) and Catalano di Guido d'Ostia (Guelf)—underscored the Jovials' role as antifactional peacemakers, a devotion clearly spelled out in the letters and later poetry of the order's most important literary figure, Guittone d'Arezzo.

Numerous Jovials appear in the *Commedia,* including Alberico de' Manfredi *(Inf.* 34) and Focaccia de' Cancellieri *(Inf.* 32). But the episode of Loderingo and Catalano in the sixth bolgia of the eighth circle *(Inf.* 23.76–144) reveals that Dante shared his contemporaries' view of the Jovials as hypocrites. For Dante and many Florentines, the defining episode of the two friars' seeming betrayal of their antifactional mission occurs when, after their successful mediation among the warring parties in Bologna (1265), both are sent by Pope Clement IV to Florence in 1266 as podestà (a city governor from another town) to establish a nonpartisan peace. Ultimately both were forced to follow Clement's political agenda of giving the Guelfs exclusive power in the city. By the first half of 1267, the houses of prominent Ghibelline families, including those of the Uberti (in the area called the Gardingo [see *Inf.* 23.108] near the Palazzo Vecchio), were destroyed in Guelf uprisings.

Bibliography

De Stefano, Antonino. "Le origini dei Frati Gaudenti." In *Riformatori ed eretici del Medio Evo.* Palermo: Società siciliana per la storia patria, 1938. Reprint, 1990, pp. 201–255.

Margueron, Claude (ed.). *Guittone d'Arezzo: Lettere.* Bologna: Commissione per i Testi di Lingua, 1990.

H. Wayne Storey

Jubilee Year

On 22 February 1300, Pope Boniface VIII proclaimed in his bull *Antiquorum habet fidem* the availability of a plenary indulgence to all, confessed and penitent, who visited the basilicas of the Apostles Peter and Paul during that centenary year. The vast number of pilgrims who flocked to Rome swelled the coffers of both the church and the people of the city, a fact emphasized by eyewitness accounts. Boniface later referred to 1300 as "this Jubilee year": the Old Testament year of Jubilee, during which debts were canceled and slaves were freed (Leviticus 25), was seen to prefigure the redemptive work of Christ which made possible the remission of the punishment for one's sins, a benefit that was granted to all who received a plenary indulgence. The Florentine chronicler Villani records an eyewitness account of the pilgrimage to Rome in this first Jubilee year *(Cronica* 8.36).

This great pilgrimage to the earthly Rome took place at the same time as Dante's fictional pilgrimage to the heavenly Rome. In *Inf.* 18.24–

33, Dante likens the panders and seducers, circling in opposite directions and marshaled by devils, to the great throng of pilgrims stewarded by Romans across the bridge of Sant'Angelo to and from St. Peter's during the Jubilee Year *(l'anno del giubileo)*. The belief that the Jubilee indulgence extended to the dead lies behind Casella's explanation that for the past three months the angel-boatman has hindered none of the souls waiting at the mouth of the Tiber from boarding his bark to Purgatory *(Purg.* 2.98–99). In the *Paradiso,* Cunizza makes a brief reference to 1300 as the centenary year *(Par.* 9.40). Finally, it has been suggested that the symbolism Dante employs in the episode of the pilgrim's entrance to Purgatory in *Purg.* 9 is informed by the theology of the Jubilee indulgences, and by Dante's critical reaction to a historical event at which he himself may have been present.

Bibliography

Armour, Peter. *The Door of Purgatory.* Oxford: Clarendon Press, 1983, esp. pp. 144–185.

Demaray, John G. *The Invention of Dante's "Comedy."* New Haven and London: Yale University Press, 1974.

———. "Patterns of Earthly Pilgrimage in Dante's *Commedia:* Palmers, Romers, and the Great Circle Journey." *Romance Philology* 24 (1970), 239–258.

Frugoni, Arsenio. *Il giubileo di Bonifacio VIII.* Anagni: Istituto di storia e di arte del Lazio meridionale, Centro di Anagni, 1996.

Mark Balfour

Judah

Son of Jacob, and one of the twelve tribes of Israel. In *Mon.* 3.5.1, Dante refers to the symbolism by which Judah *(Iudas)* and his brother Levi are made to typify the empire and the church, challenging the argument that because Levi is older the church therefore precedes the empire in authority. Dante refers to him in *Epist.* 5.4 ("the strong lion of the tribe of Judah") and implicitly includes him among the Hebrew patriarchs released from Limbo by Christ *(Inf.* 4.59).

Richard Lansing

Judas Iscariot

Apostle and betrayer of Christ. One of the twelve Apostles, Judas Iscariot is portrayed consistently in the gospels as the avaricious traitor who, for thirty pieces of silver, hands Jesus over to be crucified. The "kiss of Judas" came to mean "act of defection" in the early church, emphasizing the centrality of betrayal in Judas's deliverance of Christ.

Dante reserves the worst punishment in the *Inferno* for Judas *(Giuda Scariotto),* who is placed head-first in the central of Satan's three mouths (with Brutus and Cassius occupying the other two). Indeed, as Virgil mentions in *Inf.* 9.27, the final circle of Hell (technically the innermost of its four zones), Judecca, is in fact named after Judas. Dante twice highlights the avaricious motivation of Judas's selling of Christ *(Inf.* 19.96, *Purg.* 21.84), and he further classifies Judas's art as the art of betrayal in *Purg.* 20.73–74. The name of Judas is never mentioned in the *Paradiso.*

Bibliography

Herzman, Ronald B. "Cannibalism and Communion in *Inferno XXXIII.*" *Dante Studies* 98 (1980), 53–78.

Lucifer gnawing on Judas, Cassius, and Brutus. Opere di Dante Alighieri, *edited by Cristoforo Zapate de Cisneros, Venice, 1757–1758. Giamatti Collection: Courtesy of the Mount Holyoke College Archives and Special Collections.*

Klassen, William. "Judas Iscariot." In *The Anchor Bible Dictionary.* Edited by David Noel Freedman. Vol. 3. New York: Doubleday, 1992, pp. 1091–1096.

George Andrew Trone

Judas Maccabeus

In the Heaven of Mars, among the souls of those who fought and died for their religious faith, Beatrice names *l'alto Macabeo* ("the great Maccabee," *Par.* 18.40) with Joshua, Charlemagne, Roland, and others, who appear as lights on a great cross. Judas Maccabeus led the Jewish resistance against the tyrannical rule of Antiochus IV Epiphanes, king of Syria, and his attempts to destroy the Jewish faith in the mid-second century B.C.E. After an important victory, Maccabeus repurified the temple in Jerusalem, which had been profaned by Antiochus three years before. He fell in battle against Bacchides at Elasa in 160 B.C.E., and is remembered in the book of Maccabees as one of the great heroes and warriors of the Jewish faith.

Claudia Rattazzi Papka

Judecca

The fourth and innermost zone of Cocytus, the ninth circle of Hell, and the nadir of the universe, containing the gigantic figure of Satan, at the farthest possible remove from his original seraphic nearness to the divinity as Lucifer. The naming of Judecca *(Giudecca)* clearly centers on Judas, the arch-traitor, whose head and upper torso are eternally gnawed by the mouth in Satan's central face; it also reflects the term *Judaica* or *Iudeca,* which designated the Jewish ghetto of Venice as well as that of other cities and localities associated with Jews in the Middle Ages and later.

Dante's Judecca has a certain uniqueness that sets it off even from the preceding three areas of Cocytus. The majority of its inmates are totally immersed in the ice and therefore completely silent, and not one of them is named. Dante, however, insists on giving them varying positions: some lie prone; others are erect, face up or face down; and still others are arched like a bow (*Inf.* 34.13–15). It has been tempting to see in all of this Dante's desire to subdistinguish, or nuance, the guilt of these lowest of sinners, but efforts such as that of the fourteenth-century commentator Francesco da Buti to formulate differences have

proved fruitless. It is nevertheless true that Dante distinguishes the punishments of Brutus and Cassius, whose faces and torsos are turned outward from the side mouths of Satan, from the fate of Judas, who in plunged head-first into the devil's central orifice.

Globally, the precise definition of the fundamental sin punished here is generally held to be treachery to benefactors, and therefore an extreme form of ingratitude, but its full context is just beyond our grasp. Brutus, Cassius, and Judas—perhaps also those under the ice—ideally and symbolically suggest betrayal on a historico-spiritual scale as against a basically personal one. Their treacheries caused the greatest possible damage *(nocumetum)* to the human community, whose providentially ordained leaders merit the utmost respect. Their sin is near degree zero on the scale of the injustice of mad bestiality.

Bibliography

"Giudecca." *Enciclopedia dantesca,* 3:214–215.

Presta, Vincenzo. "Nota sulla topografia del Cocito." *Convivium* 34 (1966), 353–361.

Triolo, Alfred A. "Matta Bestialità in Dante's Inferno: Theory and Image." *Traditio* 24 (1968), 247–292.

Alfred Triolo

Judgment, Last

The complex and elaborate Christian doctrine of God's last judgment is scripturally based on a passage from Matt. 25:31–46:

> When the Son of Man comes in his glory, escorted by all the angels of heaven, he will sit upon his royal throne, and all the nations will be assembled before him. Then, he will separate them into two groups, as a shepherd separates sheep from goats. The sheep he will place on his right hand, the goats on his left. The king will say to those on his right: "Come. You have my Father's blessing! Inherit the kingdom prepared for you from the creation of the world.". . . Then he will say to those on his left: "Out of my sight, you condemned, into that everlasting fire prepared for the devil and his angels!"

A long-standing argument within theological interpretations of this passage focuses on whether human souls find immediate reward and punishment after death, or whether they lie dormant in the afterworld until the last judgment at the end of human time. These two concepts are known in theology as "particular judgment," the one reserved to each individual soul at death, and "general judgment," the one administered by Christ at the end of the world when bodies are resurrected. The latter event is also known as the Second Coming of Christ (Greek, *Parousia*), his first coming being his life on earth.

At the time of Dante, the Christian Church took a formal stand on this issue. The Second Ecumenical Council of Lyon (1274) decreed the doctrine of the "particular judgment," thereby stating that souls receive their reward and punishment immediately after death. Dante structures the entire poetic work of the *Commedia* on this principle. The condition of souls after the "particular judgment," but before the "general judgment," is known in theology as the "intermediate state." It is at this stage that Dante describes the souls he encounters. In Dante's journey into the afterworld, the souls have already received a particular judgment—a specific place of reward or punishment—and they are now simply awaiting confirmation of that condition at the final (general) judgment. The only souls that will change their condition before the final judgment are those in Purgatory, who are being purged of their sinful dispositions on earth before they are granted access to Paradise. A specific reference to divine judgment occurs in *Inf.* 6.94–111. On Dante's prompting, Virgil outlines the teachings of Scholastic philosophy, which agreed that in the day of "general judgment," the bliss or punishment of each individual soul will be increased. This augmentation of either reward or punishment is caused by the reunification of body and soul. In the broader context of a dialogue between Dante and the divine eagle on the subject of divine justice (*Par.* 19.67–111), the eagle stresses the fact that for human beings the concept of divine judgment is unintelligible. Dante dramatizes the Second Coming allegorically in the Earthly Paradise, where Beatrice's advent is explicitly related in figural terms to Christ's appearance at Judgment Day (*Purg.* 30.13–21). The parallel is apt because Beatrice comes a second time (her first coming being her life on earth), and she comes to judge Dante for his moral lapses (*Purg.* 30.103–145, 31.37–63).

Alessandro Vettori

Judith

Protagonist of a book of the Catholic Old Testament (Jewish Apocrypha), this beautiful and forceful widow saved Israel by infiltrating the enemy camp and killing their leader, Holofernes. Judith (*Iudìt*) was a figure for the church in medieval exegesis. She appears in Dante's celestial rose, on the sixth level of Mary's line (*Par.* 32.10).

Joan M. Ferrante

Julia

Julius Caesar's daughter and Pompey's wife (see Lucan, *Phars.* 1.111–120), Julia (*Iulia*) is found in Limbo among the noble Roman wives: *Vidi . . . Iulia* ("I saw . . . Julia," *Inf.* 4.127, 128).

Rebecca S. Beal

Julius Caesar

First Roman emperor (101–44 B.C.E.), in Dante's view. By crossing the Rubicon in 49 B.C.E., Julius Caesar defied the Roman Senate and consolidated his power to become emperor. A group of conspirators, led by Cassius and Brutus, assassinated him on the steps of the Senate in 44. Dante's placement of Cassius and Brutus in Cocytus, the lowest circle of Hell—indeed in its innermost zone, Judecca—indicates the severity of their crime against the founder of the Roman Empire (cf. *Conv.* 4.5.12). Only Judas, the betrayer of Christ, suffers a worse punishment than the co-conspirators, each of whom dangles headlong from one of Satan's mouths.

Despite his clear position in favor of monarchy and empire, Dante's treatment of Julius Caesar (*Giulio Cesare*) is ambiguous. Not only is Caesar's ally, Curio, condemned in the circle of the sowers of discord (*Inf.* 28.97–99), but Cato, Caesar's enemy, is apparently among the saved (*Purg.* 1). Moreover, Caesar's moral reputation is sullied with accusations of sodomy in *Purg.* 26.77–78. Mostly, however, Dante lavishes praise on Julius Caesar as the emblem of the military might of the Roman Empire. His depiction of Caesar in *Inf.* 4.123 with the other virtuous pagans emphasizes the emperor's martial prowess: *Cesare armato con li occhi grifagni* ("Caesar in armor, with hawk-like eyes"). In *Par.* 11.69 Aquinas refers to him as *colui ch'a tutto 'l mondo fé paura* ("he who terrified the whole world"). Justinian's recall of Julius Caesar's military victories in *Par.* 6.55–72 places

J Caesar's dominance in a broad providential scheme which ultimately results in the world peace under the reign of Augustus.

Bibliography

Davis, Charles T. *Dante and the Idea of Rome.* Oxford: Clarendon Press, 1957.

Ferrante, Joan M. *The Political Vision of the* Divine Comedy. Princeton, N.J.: Princeton University Press, 1984.

Iliescu, Nicolae. "The Roman Emperors in *The Divine Comedy.*" *Lectura Dantis Newberryana* 1 (1988), 3–18.

Renucci, Paul. *Dante: Disciple et juge du monde gréco-latin.* Paris: G. de Bussac, 1954.

Schanzer, Ernest. "Dante and Julius Caesar." *Medium Ævum* 24, 1 (1955), 20–22.

Wigodsky, Michael. "'Nacqui *sub Iulio*' (*Inf.* I, 70)." *Dante Studies* 93 (1975), 177–183.

George Andrew Trone

Juno

In Roman mythology, the daughter of Saturn and Rhea, and sister and consort of Jupiter. Dante treats Juno *(Giunone, Giuno, Iuno, Hera)* as the personification of natural forces, identifying her with the turning of the winds against the Trojans (*VN* 25.9; cf. *Aen.* 1.65, 76–77). In a simile Dante portrays her mad jealousy of Semele, which causes her to drive Athamas, the last king of Thebes, to murder his two sons (*Inf.* 30.1–8; cf. *Meta.* 3.259–309). She is equated with fortune by Pyrrhus, a force Dante says is better identified with divine providence (*Mon.* 2.9.8). At the behest of the more benign Jupiter, she sends Iris forth with the rainbow (*Par.* 12.10–15, 28.31–33).

Sally Mussetter

Jupiter

The sixth planet and heaven in the Ptolemaic system, and the abode of the just souls in the *Paradiso*. It receives its motion, according to *Par.* 28.99–139, from the angelic order of Dominions (or, according to *Conv.* 2.5, from the order of Principalities). In *Conv.* 2.13.25–27, Dante associates Jupiter *(Giove)* with the science of geometry and its handmaid optics.

In *Par.* 18, as soon as Dante has ascended to the Heaven of Jupiter, the spirits present themselves in a flock or chorus that alternately sings and pauses to shape itself into a sequence of thirty-five letters of the alphabet ("five times seven vowels and consonants," 88–89) that spell out the phrase *Diligite iustitiam qui iudicatis terram* ("Love justice, you who rule the world"). These words are taken from the opening verse of the book of the Wisdom of Solomon, whom Dante represents in the Heaven of the Sun as the wisest ruler who ever lived (*Par.* 10.109–114). When the last letter of the phrase has been formed, additional spirits increase the height of the letter's central stroke and the entire figure assumes the shape of an eagle. It is immediately evident, and the *Commedia* soon makes it explicit, that the eagle is the symbol of imperial Rome, the *segno / che fé i Romani al mondo reverendi* ("the emblem that caused the Romans to be revered by the world," 19.101–102). Modern commentators have recognized the letter *M* as standing for the word *monarchia* ("monarchy"). Dante's political tract of the same name, probably written no more than a year before this part of the *Paradiso*, serves as the ever-present subtext for the entire Jupiter episode. The biblical text that becomes the imperial eagle makes it clear that this last great political discussion in the *Commedia* will reinforce the central assertion of Dante's *Monarchia: Imperatorem, sive mundi Monarcham, inmediate se habere ad principem universi qui Deus est* ("that the emperor, or world ruler, is directly dependent on the prince of the universe, who is God," 3.16.2).

In a striking departure from the *Commedia*'s narrative, in which Dante's encounters and exchanges have up to this point been with individual souls, it will be the eagle, not the individual souls that comprise it, who will serve as Dante's interlocutor throughout the episode of the Heaven of Jupiter. After introducing the phantasmagorical scene, the poet pauses to address the muse of song with an invocation that calls attention to the extraordinary contrivance of the entire episode (18.82). Then, when the spectacle has culminated with the appearance of the eagle, the poet intrudes again, this time to prepare for the episode's review of doctrinal questions and exemplary personages by addressing the spirits of the just in prayer.

The poet beseeches the spirits to intercede on behalf of those who have been misled by the *malo essemplo* ("evil example," 18.126) of the popes who pervert the church's sacramental mission by employing their office to amass riches and using excommunication as a means of waging war against enemies. The poet lashes out against John XXII (pope from 1316 to 1334) in a scathing apostrophe which accuses him of having *fermo 'l disiro / sì* ("[his] desire so fixed") upon St. John the Baptist—i.e., upon the gold florin which bore the Baptist's image—that he knows neither *il pescator né Polo* ("the Fisherman [i.e., St. Peter, the first pope] nor [St.] Paul," 133–136). The reference would have been pointed for Dante's contemporaries in that Cangrande della Scala, the imperial vicar so extravagantly praised in the preceding canto, had only as recently as 1317 come under one of John XXII's excommunications, a ban that lasted past Dante's death until Cangrande's own in 1329. Already reminded in the preceding canto of Emperor Henry VII's betrayal by John XXII's predecessor Clement V, the reader contemplates anew the dire contemporary malaise confronting those who would champion the cause of political justice.

In the succeeding canto, the eagle answers Dante's long-standing doubt regarding divine justice: how can a virtuous heathen who has never heard of Christ be justly condemned? The eagle's response is to urge humans to accept the inscrutability of the mind of God and to take unquestioning refuge in the revealed truths of scripture. Although none is saved without belief in Christ, the eagle assures Dante that *"molti gridan 'Cristo, Cristo!' / che saranno in giudicio assai men prope / a lui, che tal che non conosce Cristo"* ("many cry 'Christ, Christ!' who at the judgment will be much less *prope* [near] to him, than someone who does not know Christ," 19.106–08). The eagle then describes the unsealing of the book of the damned and identifies some whose names it will contain. All are infamous for their various depredations, fratricides, treacheries, derelictions, usurpations, and other injustices. The discordance of this motley triumph of arrogant, greedy rulers contrasts sharply with the solemn unity of the heavenly just, who, in the form of the eagle, literally speak with one voice.

The review of unjust rulers is confined mainly to nine tercets (115–141), of which the first three all begin with the letter *L*, the second three with *V*, and the last three with *E*. Some have taken this to be an acrostic for *lue* ("plague"). If so, the acrostic would seem to suggest that, except for Henry VII and his vicar Cangrande, contemporary rulers have been a triple pox on the universal body politic. (A similar acrostic is deployed in *Purg.* 12.) Kindred preciosities mark the use of the same-word rhyme *(Cristo . . . Cristo . . . Cristo)* in 104–108 and the use of Roman numerals to refer to words in 19.127–129. There the eagle says that the Gimp of Jerusalem (Charles II "the Cripple" of Anjou) will have his goodness *segnata con un i . . . / quando 'l contrario segnerà un emme* ("marked with an *I* for his goodness, while an *M* will mark the opposite"). That is, the book of judgment will note that the ratio of King Charles's good works to his bad is one to a thousand. In addition to the literal meaning of the passage, however, the pairing of *I* and *M* as letters wryly insinuates that "*I*USTI-TIA*M*" (as in 18.91) is not to be expected in the "*I*erusale*mme*" of Charles the Cripple. (A similar enigmatic combination of letters is likewise apparently intended in the "DXV" of *Purg.* 33.43–44.)

Having concluded its review of evil rulers and given its constituent spirits an interval for the singing of another ineffable hymn, the eagle resumes its discourse and at last identifies the supremely just rulers. These six spirits form the eagle's eye, with King David as its pupil, and Trajan, Hezekiah, Constantine, William II of Sicily, and Ripheus arrayed in a semicircle to form the brow. Their selection exhibits the *Paradiso*'s predilection for "surprise" salvations (like those of Manfred in Purgatory and Siger of Brabant in the Heaven of the Sun), and it sets the framework for completing and unifying one of the *Commedia*'s most impassioned sections. Constantine's presence

Dante before the Eagle in the Heaven of Jupiter. Opere del divino poeta Danthe, ed. Pietro da Figino, Venice, 1520. Giamatti Collection: Courtesy of the Mount Holyoke College Archives and Special Collections.

among the elect serves to demonstrate how God's justice gives more weight to the motivation of human deeds than to their material consequences. By abandoning (as it was thought) the secular rule of Rome to the church, the emperor (so Dante believed) did incalculable harm, but *ora conosce come il mal dedutto / dal suo bene operar non li è nocivo* ("now he knows how the evil resulting from his good act does not harm him," 58–59). The mention of William II unites the discussion of the just rulers with that of the unjust by contrasting him with his successors (Charles the Cripple and Frederick of Aragon), who are lamented in the previous canto.

The presentation of Trajan and Ripheus, two pagans, renews the question of the apparent contradiction between justice and election that was examined in the previous canto with respect to virtuous heathens. When Dante erupts with a blunt *"Che cose son queste?"* ("What things are these?," 82), the eagle explains how heaven can be swayed *"da caldo amore e da viva speranza"* ("[by] burning love and lively hope," 95) which, far from violating God's purpose, *"vince la divina volontate / . . . perché vuole esser vinta"* ("conquer it [God's will] because it wishes to be conquered," 96–98). Trajan, dead for nearly five centuries, was returned to the flesh in answer to the earnest prayer of St. Gregory and then found sufficient faith that when he died again, he was worthy of salvation.

Ripheus, in recognition of his unqualified love of justice, was granted knowledge of *"la nostra redenzion futura; / ond' ei credette in quella, e non sofferse / da indi il puzzo più del paganesmo"* ("our future redemption, and he believed in it, and suffered no longer the stench of paganism," 123–125). Dante learns that faith, hope, and charity themselves served as his baptism *dinanzi al battezzar più d'un millesmo* ("more than a thousand years before baptizing began," 129). Predestination, the eagle says, cannot be fathomed by human understanding. The sacred bird admonishes mortals that they should therefore refrain from judging, *"ché noi, che Dio vedemo, / non conosciamo ancor tutti li eletti"* ("for we, who see God, do not yet know all the elect," 134–135).

Dante's willing assent to the providential framing of human history in all its perplexity is seen in the added pleasure he takes from the blinking of the eagle's eye that follows the eagle's speech, a blinking that is caused precisely by the scintillating souls of Trajan and Ripheus. With such a sense of lyric arrival and emotional closure, the *Commedia* takes leave of one of its mightiest subjects, the theme of politics. The remaining thirteen cantos will concern themselves almost exclusively with theology and set their sights on the poet's final ecstatic vision.

Todd Boli

Justice

For Dante, as for other medieval thinkers, especially those influenced by Aristotle, justice was one of the four moral virtues, with prudence, fortitude, and temperance (*Conv.* 4.22.12, *Purg.* 29.130–131, 31.103–104), and one of the eleven Aristotelian virtues (*Conv.* 4.17.6), discussed by Aristotle in the *Nichomachean Ethics,* book 5. There Aristotle defines justice as the moral state of doing what is just in both intention and action—that is, in the will and in behavior. Dante echoes this sense when he defines moral virtues as "the fruits which are in the fullest sense ours, since producing them is something that lies totally within our power" (*Conv.* 4.17.2), since justice resides only in the rational part of humans, specifically in the will (*Conv.* 1.12.9). He then defines justice as that moral virtue "which moves us to love rectitude and to realize it in all areas of life" (*Conv.* 4.17.6). Dante planned to end the *Convivio* with an extensive discussion of justice (*Conv.* 1.12.9–12, 4.27.10–11) which was probably to have been based on the *canzone,* "Tre donne intorno al cor mi son venute," but his failure to complete the *Convivio* requires that his idea of justice be looked for in his other works, chiefly the *Commedia* and the *Monarchia*. It is also important to note that it seems to have been only in Dante's years of exile that he fully formulated his concept of justice and raised it to the status of a governing virtue for all human affairs. That is, Dante developed it gradually out of his reading of Aristotle, Aquinas, and Roman law and out of his own political experience and perception of the world around him, making himself, as he said, "a man preaching justice" (*Epist.* 7). It developed in the same way and over the same period as did Dante's conception of the empire.

Dante's justice is "a kind of rightness or straight rule without deviation" (*Mon.* 1.3). The chief obstacle to justice is avarice, or cupidity (*Mon.* 1.11.13), and therefore the emperor should be moved to establish justice by the theological virtue of charity, which is the opposite of avarice (*Mon.* 1.11.13). For Dante, avarice was personally the most pernicious and deep-rooted of sinful desires, and he believed that solely the emperor, who alone was immune to avarice because he possessed everything, could establish justice (*Mon.* 1.11–13), which would put the world in its greatest order (cf. *Purg.* 16.92–96). Here Dante follows Thomas Aquinas, whose Christian reading of Aristotle (who had not considered charity) linked justice with the theological virtue of charity as laid out in 1 Corinthians 13. Aquinas then defined justice as "a habit whereby a man renders to each one his due by a constant and perpetual will" (*ST* 2.2.58.1).

The most elaborate expression of Dante's concept of justice is the speech of the eagle (itself a symbol of justice: *Par.* 6.1) in *Par.* 19.67–90, in which justice is identified with the will of God. Justice among creatures is achieved to the extent that their wills accord with the divine will (*Par.* 19.88). Creatures may reach this state by two means: participation and revelation. Participation in the divine will is achieved by natural law, the link between the Creator and the created. Humans participate in the divine will more perfectly than other creatures because they can do so rationally and voluntarily. Revelation complements participation because it guides humans to their higher goal and is uniquely theirs for that purpose.

Justice may sometimes seem unjust, because human perception is limited; even participation and revelation do not enable humans to perceive divine justice fully (*Par.* 19.60). But humans nevertheless have a responsibility to strive constantly for justice, not only through natural law and revelation, but also through the laws that humans make for themselves in communities, known as "positive law." When human jurisprudence fails to align itself with the natural and divine laws, it perverts justice. In Dante's age, Roman law was considered by jurists and by Dante himself to represent written reason. It was termed the *ius commune,* or "common law" for all Christians under the empire. Dante briefly expressed hope that the arrival of Emperor Henry VII would restore justice to Italy and the Empire (*Epist.* 5 and 7). All lesser laws were *iura propria,* "local laws," which could not challenge the authority of Roman law, as Dante accuses some jurists of trying to do (*Mon.* 2.10) and also accuses the laws of Florence of attempt-

ing (*Epist.* 6). Thus, the achievement of justice among humans required subjection to the emperor, obedience to Roman law, and the alignment of lesser laws with those of Rome.

From the organizing principle of the proper relationship between God and the created order, through the natural and therefore necessary experience of civil society, to the organization and training of the human intellect and will, Dante's concept of justice can be seen to inform all his thought, from theology to logic and moral psychology. It also informs the master plan of the *Commedia.*

The famous Letter to Cangrande della Scala (*Epist.* 13)—which displays an acute understanding of the *Commedia* even though not all scholars agree that Dante is its author—states that the allegorical meaning of the poem is human merit or fault incurred through the exercise of freedom of choice that subjects humans to justice, which rewards or punishes accordingly. By the time he wrote the *Commedia,* justice had emerged as a governing principle in Dante's universe. At the beginning of *Inf.* 1, Dante encounters the wolf of avarice, and in *Par.* 30 the spirit of Henry VII denounces the avarice of the popes that has prevented him from establishing justice during his reign on earth. Injustice brackets the beginning and end of the *Commedia,* although it does not diminish the ideal of justice that governs the universe. Justice moved the great maker of the Gate of Hell (*Inf.* 3), and justice is pronounced by the eagle in *Par.* 19, who has already formed the words, "Love justice, you who rule the earth" (Wisdom 1).

The complexity, versatility, and function of Dante's idea of justice is as good an indication as any of the ways in which Dante's thought and experience turned his poetic powers away from the interests of his life before the exile, and directed them toward the great assessment of the human condition that is the *Commedia.*

Bibliography

Gilbert, Alan H. *Dante's Conception of Justice.* New York: AMS Press, 1965.

Cassell, Anthony K. *Dante's Fearful Art of Justice.* Toronto: University of Toronto Press, 1984.

Peters, Edward. "The Frowning Pages: Scythians, Garamantes, Florentines and the Two Laws." In *The Divine Comedy and the Encyclopedia of the Arts and Sciences.* Edited by Giuseppe Di Scipio and Aldo Scaglione. Amsterdam and

J

Philadelphia: John Benjamins Publishing Company, 1988, pp. 285–314.

Bellomo, Manlio. *The Common Legal Past of Europe, 1000–1800.* Washington, D.C.: Catholic University of America Press, 1995.

Edward Peters

Justinian

Flavius Petrus Sabbatius Justinianus became emperor of Rome on the death of his uncle Justin II in 527, married the theatrical performer Theodora in 523, and ruled until his death in 565. His reign was chronicled several times, once scandalously, by the historian Procopius. Among his achievements were the rebuilding of the city of Constantinople, the reconquest of much of Africa, Italy, and Iberia from their Germanic conquerors, and the codification of Roman law into the *Code,* the *Digest,* the *Institutes,* and the *Novels.* These four together are known as the "Code of Justinian," or Civil Law *(Corpus Iuris Civilis).* It is as a supremely able lawgiver that Justinian appears in *Par.* 6, and that is Dante's chief interest in him.

In *Purg.* 6.88–96, Dante credits Justinian *(Giustiniano, Iustiniano)* with having refitted the bridle (of law) to the great horse of empire, only to complain that his own contemporary emperors have left the saddle empty through their neglect of Italy (cf. *Epist.* 5–8, *Purg.* 16.92–96). Dante frequently refers to Justinian's codification of Roman law (e.g., *Conv.* 1.10.3, 4.6.17, 4.19.4, and especially 4.4–9; also *Fiore* 110.9). Justinian begins to narrate the story of his life to Dante in *Par.* 6 by referring to his revision of Roman law (*Par.* 6.11–12). His correction from heresy to religious orthodoxy by Pope Agapetus represents for Dante the ideal relation between a pope (the perfect religious teacher) and an emperor. Justinian then figuratively recounts the history of the Roman Empire (cf. *Mon.* 2) and complains that in Dante's own lifetime the universal authority of the empire has been made the symbol of a single political faction.

The sixth canto of each of the three *cantiche* of the *Commedia* deals in one way or another with political themes, and Justinian is placed in the Heaven of Mercury ostensibly because he and his fellow spirits have been politically active chiefly for reasons of self-interest, "so that honor and fame might follow them" (*Par.* 6.113–114). But as

Justinian ends his speech by telling the story of Romeo (*Par.* 6.127–138), he graciously expresses generosity and humility in expressing admiration for a much lesser political figure than himself. Justinian and Romeo span the range of the honorable political life.

Bibliography

Ferrante, Joan M. *The Political Vision of the "Divine Comedy."* Princeton, N.J.: Princeton University Press, 1984.

Hollander, Robert, and Albert L. Rossi. "Dante's Republican Treasury." *Dante Studies* 104 (1986), 59–82.

Jacoff, Rachel. "Sacrifice and Empire: Thematic Analogies in San Vitale and the *Paradiso.*" In *Renaissance Studies in Honor of Craig Hugh Smyth.* Edited by Andrew Morrogh, Fiorella Superbi Gioffredi, Piero Morselli, and Eve Borsook. Villa I Tatti, The Harvard University Center for Italian Renaissance Studies, 7. Vol 1: *History-Literature-Music.* Florence: Giunti Barbèra, 1985, pp. 317–332.

Peters, Edward. "The Frowning Pages: Scythians, Garamantes, Florentines, and the Two Laws." In *The "Divine Comedy" and the Encyclopedia of Arts and Sciences.* Edited by Giuseppe Di Scipio and Aldo Scaglione. Amsterdam and Philadelphia: John Benjamins Publishing Company 1988, pp. 285–314.

Raffa, Guy. "Paradiso 6." In *Dante's "Divine Comedy": Introductory Readings III: "Paradiso."* Edited by Tibor Wlassics. *Lectura Dantis* 16–17 (Spring-Fall, 1995). *Special Issue: Lectura Dantis Virginiana,* vol. III, 91–106.

Edward Peters

Juvenal

A Roman satirist (c. 60–c. 140 C.E.), Juvenal (Decimus Junius Juvenalis), the Roman satirist, was a contemporary of Statius, whose *Thebaid* he praised (*Sat.* 7.82–86). As the travelers climb to the sixth terrace of Purgatory, Virgil credits Juvenal *(Giovenale),* upon his arrival in Limbo, with making Statius's affection known to him (*Purg.* 22.13–15). In *Conv.* 4.12.8 Dante cites Juvenal's denunciation of accumulating wealth, and in *Mon.* 2.3.4 he quotes his verse "virtue is the only true nobility" (*Sat.* 8.20) slightly inaccurately.

Guy P. Raffa

L

Lachesis

Together with Clotho and Atropos, one of the Fates, divine agents of human destiny. The term of each mortal's life is represented by an amount of wool placed by Clotho on Lachesis' distaff and spun by her until Atropos severs the thread. Virgil employs a circumlocutory reference to Lachesis in *Purg.* 21.25 to indicate to Statius that Dante is still among the living, despite his presence in the realm of Purgatory.

Diana Cavuoto Glenn

Lady Philosophy

The *donna gentile* or noble lady of the *Convivio* is the principal metaphor in and through which Dante proposes, as an object of contemplation and celebration, his new philosophical concerns following the death of Beatrice (1290) and in the early years of his exile (1301). In this work, she is an allegorical personification of philosophy—that is, of universal knowledge or secular learning in a broad sense. She must, therefore, be interpreted in the context of a continuing commitment (already under way in the *Vita Nuova*) to the reconstruction of his own intellectual itinerary, to a tracing of the main lines of his own development as a poet and philosopher and to the identification of its key moments. The problems generated by this line of interpretation are not so much synchronic as diachronic; they relate not so much to the meaning and function of the *donna gentile* in the *Convivio* itself as to her relationship with the *donna gentile* of the *Vita Nuova* (with whom she is identified in the *Convivio*) and to the reevaluation of what she stands for in the *Convivio,* viewed

from the ampler theological context of the *Commedia.*

The significance of the *donna gentile* image in books 2 and 3 of the *Convivio* is unambiguous, thanks to Dante's own account of it. Dante respects the precedent of Boethius in the *Consolation of Philosophy,* where the principal interlocutor is Lady Philosophy, and proceeds by way of a "poets' allegory" according to which the image functions in respect of the author's true meaning as a "beautiful fiction" (2.1.3); he thus interprets the *donna gentile* in the *Convivio* as the love of wisdom, first and foremost in the mind of God. Philosophy, properly understood, is the self-love and self-intellection of God as he contemplates his own comprehending of every discrete idea in the universe. Characteristically, it is the affective aspect of this definition that is to the fore in Dante's mind; for where the efficient cause of philosophy is truth and its final cause happiness, its formal cause—that by virtue of which it is what it is—is love: the love whereby man, as party only discontinuously to the love of wisdom primarily in God, is drawn into likeness with God. This, in fact, is Dante's leading emphasis in the key chapters 13–15 of book 3 of the *Convivio,* where (in a manner somewhat prejudicial to the general conception of the *Convivio* as a *vademecum* for active people without leisure for contemplation) he insists on the way in which man is made over again in God's likeness, because he shares in the love of wisdom pertaining to God as of the essence. Philosophy thus understood becomes a principle of ontic affirmation—an assurance that humans exist in and through union with God as the first principle of all being (3.2.7). Every other aspect of Dante's discourse relative to philosophy in the *Convivio* turns on this central emphasis. He regards philosophy as a means of man's properly human happiness; as morally remedial; as an aid to faith; as the means to a kind of paradisal ascent of the mind; and as apt to satisfy spiritual yearning, not only of the Christian but also of the Stoic, the Peripatetic and the Epicurean. All these notions presuppose a sense that philosophy belongs primarily to God and that it is active in man's regard by way of assimilation (*Conv.* 3.14.15).

In addition to its function as a metaphor for the love of wisdom primarily in God, the image of the *donna gentile* serves in the *Convivio* to dramatize the crisis of Dante's own development as a poet-philosopher: the crisis of allegiance implicit in his movement away from the "neo-courtly" and stilnovistic spirituality of the *Vita Nuova* toward the more dialectical and at times rationalistic spirituality of the *Convivio*. While the *donna gentile* beckons him to the "more virile" disciplines of the trivium and quadrivium and of natural and moral philosophy (1.1.16), Beatrice continues to summon him to the more esoteric and exclusive spirituality of the vernacular-lyric tradition within which he started out as a lover of wisdom. The drama that Dante conceives takes the form, in the end, of a conflict between his old love for Beatrice and his new love for Lady Philosophy, which ends in the victory of the latter (2.2). The dominant mood, therefore, of Dante's encounter with the *donna gentile,* as rehearsed in book 2 of the *Convivio,* is one of anxiety, pain, and misgiving as the poet contemplates, in and through allegorical projection, the ascendancy of one order of concern over another.

The difficulties surrounding the interpretation of the *donna gentile* in the *Convivio* are, as already noted, diachronic rather than synchronic in character. They relate not so much to what is said in the *Convivio* itself, as to Dante's handling of the image in works he wrote before and after the *Convivio.* The most intractable of these difficulties is the relation between the *donna gentile* of the *Convivio* as a metaphor for the love of wisdom primarily in God, and the *donna gentile* of the *Vita Nuova* as the noble lady of the casement who looked compassionately on Dante in his bereavement after the death of Beatrice. In the *Vita Nuova,* too, the element of psychological conflict is dominant, and leads eventually, in chapter 37 of the *libello,* to Dante's cursing his eyes as instruments betraying

the memory of Beatrice. The problem, however, is that there is nothing in the *Vita Nuova* itself to suggest an esoteric interpretation of the lady of the casement; on the contrary, her function seems to be that of mounting a final challenge to the book's leading notion of love as a matter not so much of acquisition as of disposition, of a state of mind radically independent of the historical presence of *madonna.* To interpret her allegorically as representing philosophy involves a drastic redefinition of the book's *problematica,* of its overt status as a *tractatus de amore* in the neo-Ovidian and Siculo-Tuscan tradition of love speculation within which Dante was working. On the other hand, contesting an author's own account of his meaning is, as Gilson has argued, a hazardous business, even if, as in this case, the author himself provides some reason for doing so (considerations of ideal continuity or of writerly *gravitas*—*Conv.* 2.12.4 and 1.2.16–17, respectively).

A further problem is raised by the reception of the *canzone* "Amor, che ne la mente mi ragiona" in *Purg.* 2. Here, the lingering of the Dante character and Virgil on the plane of the aesthetic (Dante encourages his former acquaintance to sing the *canzone*) is severely reprimanded by Cato; the reprimand may amount simply to a recall to the task in hand, but it may also carry implications relative to Dante's mature evaluation of his former philosophical enthusiasm, which is now qualified by the theologism of the *Commedia.* If so, then this brief episode at the beginning of the *Purgatorio* might be understood to anticipate Dante's more sustained indictment of his earlier philosophism (or at least of its more radical aspects) in the final stages of the canticle.

However we seek to resolve these difficulties, the image of the *donna gentile,* which dominates the central books of the *Convivio,* represents the most sustained, subtle, and carefully elaborated of Dante's allegories outside the *Commedia.* Combining as it does the imaginative and expressive features of his stilnovistic manner with the sterner and more sophisticated intuitions of his intellectual maturity, it witnesses powerfully to both the pain and the passion of his emergence as a new kind of philosopher-poet.

Bibliography

Gilson, Étienne. *Dante and Philosophy.* Translated by David Moore. New York: Harper and Row, 1963 [1949].

Pietrobono, Luigi. "Filosofia e teologia nel *Convivio* e nella *Commedia*." In *Nuovi saggi danteschi*. Turin: SEI, 1954, pp. 69–122.

Shaw, James E. *The Lady "Philosophy" in the Convivio*. Cambridge, Mass.: Dante Society of Cambridge, 1938.

Took, John. *Dante: Lyric Poet and Philosopher: An Introduction to the Minor Works*. Oxford: Clarendon Press, 1990.

John Took

Lancelot

The most celebrated and valorous knight of the court of King Arthur, made famous by Chrétien de Troyes' romance and the later prose romance *Lancelot du Lac*. Lancelot *(Lancialotto, Lancillotto)* is remembered in *Inf.* 5.128 as the lover of Queen Guinevere. In this canto, Dante describes his encounter with Francesca da Rimini and Paolo Malatesta in the circle of the lustful, where Francesca tells Dante the story of the love between herself and Paolo. She recalls the day when, as she and Paolo were reading together from the prose *Lancelot*, Paolo kissed her. In her story, Francesca compares Paolo to Lancelot and herself to Guinevere but reverses the roles of the characters. In the original story, it is Guinevere who kisses Lancelot; in Francesca's retelling, it is Lancelot who kisses Guinevere. (In the Arthurian tradition, the woman first kissed the suitor as an indication that he was welcome to serve the woman in exchange for her love.) Lancelot *(Lancelotto)* is also cited in *Conv.* 4.28.8 as an exemplum of the aged noble soul's retreat from the active life in preparation for death.

Maria Ann Roglieri

Landino, Cristoforo

Florentine humanist who wrote the most influential fifteenth-century commentary on the *Commedia*. In 1481, Landino (1425–1498) presented to the Florentine government his edition of the poem, the first to have been printed in the city of Dante's birth, containing engravings derived from Botticelli and an improved text and a new commentary. Landino freely acknowledged his debt to earlier commentators, especially Pietro Alighieri, Boccaccio, Benvenuto da Imola, and Francesco da Buti, for many of the details of his presentation, but he broke new ground in identifying Dante's classical references. His commentary is most orig-

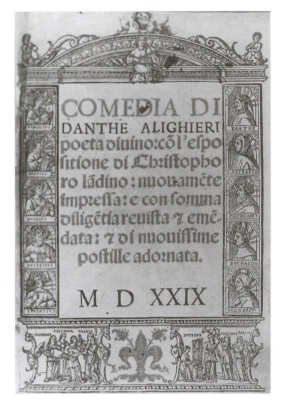

1529 edition of the Commedia *with the Cristoforo Landino commentary, published by Giunta in Venice. Reproduced by permission of the John A. Zahm Dante Collection in the Department of Special Collections, University Libraries, University of Notre Dame.*

inal in developing a systematic interpretive scheme compatible with the Neoplatonic philosophy of his pupil Marsilio Ficino. Landino explains at the beginning of his commentary to *Inf.* 2 that Dante follows Virgil in showing that "wishing to go to paradise, that is to happiness, one must first pass through hell and purgatory, that is, descend into the understanding of the vices, and having understood them, be purged of them; the mind that continues to be purged of them is easily able to arrive at an understanding of heavenly affairs, in which happiness consists." Landino's commentary was reprinted regularly into the sixteenth century, but its fortunes ultimately declined along with those of the Neoplatonism on which it was based.

Bibliography

Landino, Cristoforo. *Comento di Christophoro Landino fiorentino sopra la Comedia di Danthe Alighieri Poeta fiorentino*. Florence: Nicholò di Lorenzo della Magna, 1481.

Commentary of Landino and Vellutello surrounding the opening lines of Inferno *in the 1564 edition of the* Commedia. Dante, *with commentary by Cristoforo Landino and Alessandro Vellutello, published in Venice in 1564 by Marchiò Sessa & fratelli. Giamatti Collection: Courtesy of the Mount Holyoke College Archives and Special Collections.*

Kallendorf, Craig. "'You Are My Master': Dante and the Virgil Criticism of Cristoforo Landino." In *In Praise of Aeneas: Virgil and Epideictic Rhetoric in the Early Italian Renaissance.* Hanover and London: University Press of New England, 1989, pp. 129–165.

Lentzen, Manfred. *Studien zur Dante-Exegese Cristoforo Landinos.* Cologne and Vienna: Böhlau, 1971.

Craig Kallendorf

Lano

Into the wood of the suicides, in the seventh circle of *Inferno,* two souls come running, naked and bleeding, pursued by a pack of hounds: they are the squanderers, who have done violence to themselves with respect to their possessions. The one in front calls on death to free him: *"Or accorri, accorri, morte!"* ("Now hurry, hurry, death!,"

Inf. 13.118). The second soul, Giacomo da Santo Andrea, identifies him when he calls out, *"Lano, sì non furo accorte / le gambe tue a le giostre dal Toppo"* ("Lano, not so nimble were your legs at the jousts at Toppo," *Inf.* 13.120–121). Lano—the commentators identify him as Arcolano di Squarcia Maconi—was a Sienese gentleman who apparently belonged to a group of big spenders calling themselves the *Brigata Spendereccia* ("Spendthrift Club"), with whom he squandered his substantial wealth. Boccaccio recounts Lano's participation in an expedition against Arezzo in 1288, which ended in an ambush at the ford of the Pieve del Toppo, to which the shade of Giacomo refers. Boccaccio writes that Lano could have saved himself but, because of the poverty to which he had reduced himself, he preferred to be killed in the battle, as he was. The story, and the words Lano speaks, underscore the ethical affinity between the two types of violence against oneself punished in the second round of the seventh circle, and make Giacomo's comment bitterly ironic. Some commentators, however, interpret Giacomo's words in a more straightforward manner, and deny any suicidal impulse behind Lano's death.

Claudia Rattazzi Papka

Laomedon

King of Troy, named in Dante's discussion of the nature of true nobility in *Conv.* 4.14.14–15. Laomedon (*Laomedonte*) was a descendant of Dardanus, the mythical ancestor of the Trojans, and father of Priam (see Horace, *Epistulae* 5.24).

Leslie Zarker Morgan

Late Repentant

The inhabitants of Ante-Purgatory who delayed their repentance until the very end of life. They are referred to as the *negligenti* ("the negligent," *Purg.* 4.110), and their sin as *negligenza* ("negligence," 2.121; also *negghienza,* 4.105). Although they have gained salvation, they must postpone their entrance into Purgatory proper for a fixed period of time, according to the nature of their imperfect preparation for the afterlife. Of all the souls in Purgatory they alone experience punishment, which is to remain in detention, deprived of the opportunity of purging their sins. The late repentant fall into four groups: the excommunicate (or contumacious), who, in addition to being guilty of postponing their penance, have been excommunicated by the Church; the indolent; those who died violently, often referred to as the unabsolved or unshriven (although Dante provides no name for them); and the negligent or preoccupied rulers, whose preoccupation with worldly affairs caused them to defer repentance. As they made God wait, so they are now made to wait, unable to begin the ascent of the mountain until their term of detention has expired, unless it is shortened by the prayers of the living (*Purg.* 3.145). The period of delay for the excommunicate is thirty times the period of their disobedience (contumacy), while for the other three classes it is equal to the term that repentance was postponed. Although there are four classes of negligent, they reside in two separate zones in Purgatory. The excommunicate are confined to the shore of the island, whereas each of the other groups of late repentant occupies a different level, called a *balzo* ("ledge," 4.47), of a higher zone on the mountain itself. The negligent rulers are secluded in a *vallea* ("valley," 8.98), an area that is also referred to as a *balzo* (7.88). These attributes are generally understood by critics to define a clear separation between the excommunicate and the other late repentant, so that the total number of moral levels in Purgatory is ten (two in Ante-Purgatory, seven in Purgatory proper, and the Earthly Paradise), thereby maintaining topographical symmetry both with Hell, which has ten circles (the neutrals and the nine circles of sin), and with Paradise, which has ten spheres.

Richard Lansing

Latin Language

Dante's attitudes toward Latin went through several stages. In *VN* 25 he somewhat ambiguously criticizes the Guittoniani for using the vernacular in didactic, scientific compositions. Dante then regarded the poetry of love as the only appropriate genre for the vernacular, because the poets wished to address women, who did not read Latin.

An open defense of the vernacular appears first in the *Convivio*, where Dante decides to do precisely what he had criticized the Guittoniani for (inadequately) attempting to do: to write philosophical compositions in the vernacular, in both poetry and prose. This step was a novelty only on the level of theoretical apologia, since by 1303–1304 Dante had already written several philosophical *canzoni*. Unprecedented, however, was the prolonged composition of a prose treatise in the vernacular, and Dante states that he was moved to do this by three reasons: to avoid the *disordinazione* of appending a Latin commentary to vernacular poems; to cater—shall we say, "democratically"—to the unlearned populace who could not partake of the "banquet" of a Latin philosophical commentary; and to obey the natural love that every man owes his mother tongue.

Even at this stage, Latin still appears to him as a higher medium because of its grammatical precision. He still looks on grammar as the artificial, or "artful," man-chosen rather than God-given foundation of linguistic and cultural stability. In any event, *gramatica* means for him not Latin *tout court,* as most commentators assume, but any *lingua regulata,* Latin or other (cf. *Conv.* 1.11.14). Italian could become a grammatical language too, if his advice and example were followed. He aims at a *vulgare illustre* that would combine *universalitas* and *naturalitas,* as the Adamic language had once done, but Latin no longer does. Yet the "universality" of Italian could only be, if anything, a vague and relative notion, quite remote from the rigor implied in "modistic" speculation, the kind of linguistic theorizing that was then dominant among logicians.

There may be one additional, not quite explicitly articulated reason for Dante's fateful decision in favor of the vernacular in the *Convivio,* despite the demurrers he still accepts at the time; this motive is to defend and "illustrate" his vernacular against the other vernaculars that have already emerged, mainly Provençal and French. In other words, it is in order to detect an element of "national" pride in the position Dante takes in this matter.

There is little agreement on the reasons for Dante's differing statements on the relationship between Latin and the vernacular in the contemporaneous *De vulgari eloquentia* and *Convivio.* In *DVE* 1.1.3–4, he asserts the greater nobility of the vulgar tongue *(nobilior est vulgaris)* on three accounts, namely of chronological priority, universality, and naturalness—*prima fuit humano genere usitata; totus orbis ipsa perfuitur; naturalis est nobis, cum illa potius artificialis existat.* In *Conv.* 1.5.7–14, however, he declares Latin superior to the *volgare* because it is more beautiful, more virtuous, and more noble. These apparently contradictory statements rest on different definitions of nobility, since in the *Convivio* the paramount consideration is stability.

Dante's last remarks on language occur in *Par.* 26.124–138, where Adam contradicts the view that his language, Hebrew, was separated from other languages at the time of the building of the Tower of Babel and was preserved for the Jews as the original uncorrupted language that would be used by Jesus. Instead, Adam avers, his language (not Hebrew and predating Hebrew) was but another of the mutable positive tongues, subject to the same universal law of mutability that characterizes everything done by man. This remarkable anticipation of Saussure's doctrine of the arbitrary nature of the linguistic sign affects Dante's conception of Latin, confirming its definition as one of several cases of an artificial language created by culture in order to ensure stability and a degree of universality.

Dante's three main statements on language—and, explicitly or implicitly, Latin—disclose a high degree of speculation and soul-searching, and they can be reconciled with two considerations. First, "nobility" can be invoked in an absolute or a relative sense: the former is the realization that Latin, like literary Greek or Biblical Hebrew, is a conventional medium artificially made to respond to the highest needs in intellectual and cultural intercourse, to which the natural languages have difficulty adapting; the latter is the "natural" nobility that comes from being the tongue of our parents and our country, and in this sense the *volgare* is "nobler" than Latin. Second, the *volgare* can be raised to the level of Latin, Greek, and Hebrew by being cultivated into a *volgare illustre, aulico, cardinale,* and *curiale,* according to the principles of *De vulgari eloquentia.* The vernacular would then have the same special nobility and excellence as Latin.

This is what Dante proposed to do in order to give Italy a medium of expression that would be adequate for the highest messages. For him the *volgare illustre* was not just a thing of the future: it already existed, corresponding to whatever the highest poets of Italy, of whatever region (starting with the Sicilians), had already composed to date: *doctores illustres qui lingua vulgari poetati sunt in Ytalia* (*DVE* 1.19.2). This "illustrious" language was a question of subject matter, style, and genius: the subjects had to be the highest, the *magnalia,* namely *salus, venus,* and *virtus,* or salvation, love, and rectitude, the sublime themes of religion, emotion, and morality (*DVE* 2.2.8). They require intellectual elevation, doctrine, and genius: *optimae*

conceptiones non possunt esse nisi ubi scientia et ingenium est (2.2.8).

The *Commedia,* however, illustrates what may have been a flaw in Dante's theorizing: the text that delivers the highest message written since the Bible is not written in the *volgare illustre* because it is, precisely, a "comedy" and not a "tragedy" or a *canzone*—the genres he has explicitly reserved for the *illustre* (*DVE* 2.4.5–6, 2.3.8, 2.8.2). The problem remains, even though Dante feels that some mixing of tragic with comic is permissible in a longer poem: this is certainly the case with the *Commedia,* which especially in the *Paradiso* comes close to being pure "tragedy" on the stylistic level. We must then assume that Dante abandoned the relative rigidity of the *De vulgari eloquentia* as soon as he moved on to the conception of the *Commedia,* whose stylistic inclusiveness boldly transcends the traditional doctrine of the separation of styles. Indeed, the Letter to Cangrande (*Epist.* 13) shifts the critical terminology to new ground, and even the title *Commedia* must be explained with reference to the first *cantica,* before Dante can reflect on the full stylistic implications of his great poem in its definitive form.

Bibliography

Auerbach, Erich. *Literary Language and Its Public in Late Latin Antiquity and in the Middle Ages.* Translated by Ralph Manheim. Princeton, N.J.: Princeton University Press, 1993.

Corti, Maria. *Dante a un nuovo crocevia.* Florence: Sansoni, 1981.

Curtius, Ernst R. *European Literature and the Latin Middle Ages.* Translated by W. R. Trask. New York: Harper and Row, 1953.

Jernej, Josip. "Latino e lingue romanze nella concezione di Dante." In *Studien zu Dante und zu anderen Themen der romanischen Literaturen. Festschrift für Rudolf Palgen.* Edited by Klaus Lichem and H. J. Simon. Graz: Hugo Schuchardtschen Malvinenstiftung, 1971, pp. 55–58.

Aldo Scaglione

Latinus

In the *Aeneid,* Latinus is king of Latium and father of Lavinia by Amata, who wishes their daughter to marry Turnus. When an oracle decrees that Lavinia must marry a foreigner, Latinus betroths her to Aeneas. Latinus appears in *Inf.* 4.125 as one of the heroes of antiquity residing in Limbo; Dante also mentions him in *Mon.* 2.3.16 as enhancing Aeneas's nobility by giving him Lavinia in marriage.

Nancy Vine Durling

Latona

Latona (Latin name of Greek Leto) was the daughter of the Titans Coeus and Phoebe. Jove fell in love with her and impregnated her with the twins Apollo and Diana. His jealous consort, Juno, sent the serpent Python to harass her and forbade the earth to grant her refuge for the birth. The free-floating island of Delos at last took her in. To show his gratitude, Jove anchored it to the bottom of the sea with chains.

Apollo and Diana were associated respectively with the sun and the moon. Dante refers to the moon as *la figlia di Latona* ("the daughter of Latona," *Par.* 10.67, 22.139), and to the sun and moon as *li figli di Latona* ("the children of Latona," *Par.* 29.1).

Latona became a powerful goddess. When Niobe claimed for herself the veneration due to Latona, the latter decreed the death of Niobe's children and then transformed her into a perpetually flowing marble fountain. This episode of punished pride, recounted by Ovid in *Meta.* 6.165–316, is recalled by Dante in *Purg.* 12.37–39. Dante also refers to Latona in *Purg.* 20.130–132, noting that the great shaking of the mountain of Purgatory at the liberation of Statius's soul resembles that of Delos when Latona gave birth to *li due occhi del cielo* ("the two eyes of heaven").

Nancy Vine Durling

Lavinia

The third wife of Aeneas and mother of the Roman race (*Mon.* 2.3.16), barely mentioned in Virgil's *Aeneid,* Lavinia becomes an active figure in the story of her courtship in medieval versions. In the *Commedia,* she is seated with her father Latinus in Limbo (*Inf.* 4.125–126), among the pagan souls. She also appears in a vision in the *Purgatorio,* where she is described as lamenting the suicide of her mother Amata (*Purg.* 17.34–39).

Joan M. Ferrante

Law

Dante does not present a unified theory or practical doctrine of law. His general conception of law, both divine and human, reflects current analyses presented by theologians, by the written corpus of Roman law, and by glossators, lawyers, and jurists such as, perhaps, his friend Cino da Pistoia. For Dante, God's law is revealed in the scriptures, and from it human reason can deduce that natural law to which all human law should conform. The human law that most closely reflects natural law and contains the universal principles of law (analogous to the *ius gentium,* the "law of all peoples") is Roman law, enshrined in Justinian's written code and administered by the emperor. From this the laws of particular, sub-universal communities derive, and to it they must conform. Dante's arguments concerning law are crucial to his doctrine of the divine origin of the two supreme universal authorities, the Church and the empire (see *Epist.* 5.27); and given that the medieval conflict between the two was principally a conflict of jurisdictions, Dante's legal and juridical arguments concerning the temporal power form an integral part of his "political" attitude and thought.

Roman or civil law in Dante's time was known generically as the *Corpus Iuris Civilis,* the written collections drawn up by a legal commission entrusted with the reform of Roman law by the Eastern emperor Justinian (527–565). Medieval glossators usually refer to the different sections of the *Corpus:* the *Digest* (in Greek, *Pandects*), the *Institutes,* the *Code,* and the *Novellae* ("New Constitutions"). The *Digest* is divided into three sections: the *Old Digest;* a middle part known from its first word as the *Infortiatum;* and the *New Digest.* Rediscovered in the eleventh century, the *Corpus Iuris Civilis* was widely studied and glossed, and it became the basis of law and jurisprudence in Italy and much of southern Europe.

More specifically, Dante's references to law may be summarized according to the three overlapping and sometimes interchangeable terms which he uses for it: *ius, lex,* and *ragione scritta.*

Ius

Ius denotes the legitimate collective rights through which justice is achieved and practiced at all levels, from God's justice to natural justice to human justice, both universal and particular, to the specific virtue of justice (one of the four Cardinal Virtues), which is defined as "the constant and perpetual will to give to each person his rights" (see *Mon.* 1.11.7; *Epist.* 5.27). The concept of

L infringing legal justice at the social level may underlie Dante's definition of the sins of *malizia* in the *Inferno* as motivated by *ingiuria,* and hence as more hateful to God than the sins of upper Hell (*Inf.* 11.22–24).

Dante's *canzone* on *Drittura* ("Justice"), "Tre donne intorno al cor mi son venute," illustrates how human justice descends, by way of natural justice, from God's. Pietro Alighieri, explaining that the *duo giusti* of *Inf.* 6.73 are the two *iura,* the divine and the natural law, interprets the three ladies of his father's *canzone* as follows: the first is divine and natural law, who is the mother of the second lady, the "law of all peoples" *(ius gentium)*—that is, universal human law—whose daughter is particular legislation *(lex).*

Ultimately, for Dante, *ius* is identical with God's will, and *ius* in practice must be whatever reflects and is consonant with God's will; hence God's operations, revealed in the history of the Roman people, were visible signs which proved that its world jurisdiction (the *imperium*) was acquired not by force but *de iure* (*Mon.* 2.2.4–8). At the human level, he defines *ius* as "a real and personal bond between man and man whose preservation preserves society and whose corruption corrupts it"; in this respect, the goal of *ius* is the common good of the state *(res publica)* and of society (*Mon.* 2.5.1–2, 4). At the universal level, human law *(ius humanum)* is the foundation of the empire as Christ is of the Church, and to destroy the empire is against human law (*Mon.* 3.10.7–9); the emperor's rights are both divine and human, and therefore, according to laws and reason, to God, nature, and universal consent, they must be eternal and immutable (*Epist.* 6.5–7). The monarch is the supreme judge, with universal jurisdiction (a term interpreted in the Middle Ages as the "speaking" or "promulgation" of *ius*), and he joins his judgment and his justice in his function as legislator and executor of the law and of justice (*iudex primus et summus; legis lator; legis executor; executor iustitie, Mon.* 1.10.5, 1.11.12, 1.13.7, 2.10.1).

Lex

Lex (Ital., *legge*), the generic word for "law," again refers to divine law, natural law, and human legislation. God's law laid down the physical order of the created universe (*Conv.* 3.15.16; see Prov. 8:27–29), and governs the whole structure of justice and the souls' situation in the afterlife (*Inf.*

14.21; *Purg.* 1.46, 89-90; 2.106; *Par.* 32.55). In the Empyrean, it operates beyond the natural law, which nature receives from God and imposes on everything produced by its causality in the natural world (*Par.* 30.121–123; see *Mon.* 3.13.2–3). The divine law was revealed in the Old Testament (the law of Moses) and in the New through Christ (*Mon.* 3.13.4; see also 2.7.7); it consists principally in the program for Christian redemption and salvation, which was unknown to pagans such as Virgil (*Inf.* 1.125).

In the sphere of human activity, Dante defines law as a "directive rule of life" (*Mon.* 1.14.5). He applies the term generally to any rational system of beliefs, as of the pagans or adherents of other religions (*Conv.* 2.8.9; 4.15.5; see also *Par.* 15.143). In the moral sense, it is a means of controlling nonhuman or "bestial" appetites (*Purg.* 26.83–84; and see, perhaps, the laws concerning Love in *Detto,* 216–218 and *Fiore,* 183.2, 5); thus, a society is totally corrupted when any carnal desire is made legal, as by a ruler such as Semiramis (*Inf.* 5.56; see also 19.83).

True laws are directed toward the common good and the utility of the many who are subject to them; they are the "bond of human society," distinguishing the good citizen from the bad (*Conv.* 1.8.4; *DVE* 1.16.3; *Mon.* 2.5.3). *Lealtade,* obedience to the laws, is a virtue of youth, for a mature man's will should be identical with justice and law, and an example of law to others; indeed, those who use intellect and reason and who possess the divine gift of liberty are not directed by laws, but rather it is they who direct the laws (*Conv.* 4.26.14; 4.27.10; *Epist.* 13.7). Laws, including the monarch's, exist for the benefit of those subject to them, not for the legislators themselves (*Mon.* 1.12.11–12; and see 3.10.10), and Dante condemns lawyers, among others, who study only to acquire money or honors (*Conv.* 3.11.10; see also *Par.* 11.4).

Roman law originated in the civilized laws of ancient Athens and Sparta (which Dante contrasts with Florence's over-subtle and unstable legislation), and its reform by Justinian was a high task inspired by love of God and by God's love and grace (*Purg.* 6.139–147; *Par.* 6.11–12, 23–24). It is the rule *(regula)* or law *(lex)* governing those matters which are common to the whole human race as it is guided by the emperor toward peace (*Mon.* 1.14.7). The emperor's laws are sacred imitations of the image of natural justice itself (*Epist.*

6.22); he has overall command of human society, as the helmsman commands the crew of a ship; his word is law and must be obeyed by all (*Conv.* 4.4.5–7); his law is the bond of rights, both public and private, of all the subjects of the Empire (*Epist.* 5.20). His laws include such matters as marriage, slaves, armies, and succession rights, to which all are subject and which pertain to the emperor's own specific craft or sphere of action ("arte"); it is not his task, however, to administer laws that follow nature but do not apply to everyone, or to pass judgments (such as defining nobility) that pertain to the role of the philosopher (*Conv.* 4.9.14–16). Nor is it the duty of the emperor to administer the laws of individual cities, since there are necessarily different laws for the inhabitants of frozen climes and for those who live in the tropical heat. Indeed, municipal laws, when defective, need a higher directive, and this is the emperor's law; it is from him that particular princes receive this law, just as the practical intellect derives its premise for action from the speculative, and just as Moses reserved for himself the higher judgments concerning the whole community, delegating the lower and more specific to the leaders of each tribe (*Mon.* 1.14.4–9).

In all this, Dante seems to applying the common distinction between natural law (mediated from God by nature to all creation) and positive, human law, and the division of the latter into the rationally deducible laws required for all human association (the *ius gentium* or "law of all peoples") and the civil law in the strict sense, which consists in particular determinations of universal law by a city. Indeed, only by voluntarily accepting the universal law of the emperor will a rebellious city such as Florence, held by greed under the law of sin, obtain true liberty (*Epist.* 6.22–23). Dante's apparent ambiguity in presenting an ideal of civic freedom under the universal monarch probably derives from the fundamental principle of contemporary legal theory and discussion, which also underlies book 2 of the *Monarchia;* this is the premise that the Roman Republic had conceded or transferred its imperial power to the single prince by means of the royal law *(lex regia),* and that therefore the power with which the emperor is vested was originally the power of the people.

For Dante, law is the bridle with which the king, and above all the emperor, should guide the human race away from greed for earthly things and to within sight of the true city; in the absence of such a minister of the laws, the greed of the papacy has corrupted the world (*Purg.* 16.94–105). Likewise, Justinian's code is the bridle for the control of the Italian territories of the empire (the *regnum italicum* and Rome itself), and it is the usurpation of this law by the church, and its neglect by the emperor-elect, which has led to the shameful, lawless, and fragmented condition of Italy in 1300 (*Purg.* 6.88–96).

Ragione scritta

Ragione scritta ("written right" or "written reason"), the written law, is divided into canon law and civil law, both of which were founded explicitly to oppose greed for wealth (*Conv.* 4.12.9–10; see also the implications of the citation from Lucan in 4.11.3). With regard to the canon law, Dante's attitude is to express reverence for the papal authority of the *Decretals* but to condemn the clergy's obsession with them in the pursuit of benefices and wealth (*Mon.* 3.3.14, *Epist.* 11.16, *Par.* 9.133–35, 12.82–83). Gratian, the author of the *Decretum,* is in Paradise (*Par.* 10.104) for his work in the two forums—probably, the interior forum of the conscience and the forum of public judgment in the church, rather than canon and civil law.

The purpose of the civil law is to preserve equity and discourage iniquity (inequity) in the voluntary actions of humans; it is the "art of good and of equity," which it is the duty of the emperor, the "rider of the human will," to formulate, promulgate, and impose (*Conv.* 4.9.8–9). Dante cites the written Roman law, or glosses on it, on several occasions (*Conv.* 1.10.3, 4.9.8, 4.15.17, 4.19.4, 4.24.2, 15, 17; *Mon.* 2.5.1; with possible echoes also in *VN* 13.4; *Conv.* 1.8.4, 4.11.7, 9; *Mon.* 1.10.1, 1.11.7, 2.10.3; and, perhaps, *Fiore* 110.9–12).

Bibliography

Alighieri, Pietro. *Petri Allegherii super Dantis ipsius genitoris Comoediam Commentarium.* Florence: Piatti, 1845, p. 94.

Armour, Peter. *Dante's Griffin and the History of the World.* Oxford: Clarendon Press, 1989, pp. 130–140, 194–214.

Cancelli, Filippo. "Corpus iuris civilis" and "diritto romano." *Enciclopedia dantesca,* 2:216–218, 472–479.

Chiappelli, Luigi. "Ancora su Dante e il diritto romano." *Il giornale dantesco* 20 (1912), 202–206.

L

———. "Dante in rapporto alle fonti del diritto." *Archivio Storico Italiano,* ser. 5, 41 (1908), 3–44.

Chiaudano, Mario. "Dante e il diritto romano." *Il giornale dantesco* 20 (1912), 37–56, 94–119.

Crosara, Fulvio. "Dante e Bartolo da Sassoferrato: Politica e diritto nell'Italia del Trecento." In *Bartolo da Sassoferrato: Studi e documenti per il VI centenario.* Vol. 2. Milan: Giuffrè, 1962, pp. 107–198.

Ercole, Francesco. "La cultura giuridica di Dante." In *Il pensiero politico di Dante.* Vol. 2. Milan: Alpes, 1927–1928, pp. 7–37.

Fiorelli, P. "Sul senso del diritto nella *Monarchia.*" *Letture Classensi* 16 (1987), 79–97.

Gilbert, Allan H. *Dante's Conception of Justice.* Durham, N.C.: Duke University Press, 1925.

"Legge." *Enciclopedia dantesca,* 3:613–617.

Lumia, Giuseppe. "Legge, diritto e giustizia nel pensiero di Dante." In *Atti del Convegno di Studi su Dante e la Magna Curia.* Palermo: Centro di Studi Filologici e Linguistici Siciliani, 1967, pp. 563–568.

Pazzaglia, Mario. "Tre donne intorno al cor mi son venute." *Enciclopedia dantesca,* 5:709–711.

Solmi, Arrigo. "Dante e il diritto." In *Il pensiero politico di Dante: Studi storici.* Florence: La Voce, 1922, pp. 219–252.

Ullmann, Walter. *Law and Politics in the Middle Ages: An Introduction to the Sources of Medieval Political Ideas,* Ithaca, N.Y.: Cornell University Press, 1975.

Williams, James. *Dante as a Jurist.* Oxford: Blackwell, 1906.

Peter Armour

Lawrence, St.

Deacon of the Church of Rome, supposed native of Huesca, Spain, who suffered martyrdom. He was grilled alive in 258 by Emperor Valerian for refusing to relinquish church treasures, yet remained steadfast, mocking his executioners by asking them to turn his body in order to roast it on both sides. Beatrice mentions Lawrence *(Lorenzo)* as an example of fortitude in *Par.* 4.83–84, along with Mucius.

Molly Morrison

Leah

Leah is the lady *giovane e bella* ("young and beautiful," *Purg.* 27.97) who appears to the sleeping Dante the pilgrim in his third purgatorial dream (*Purg.* 27.94–108), which he has at the dawn (the privileged time for prophetic dreams; see *Purg.* 9.16–18; 27.92–93) of the third Purgatorial day, at the conclusion of his Purgatorial ascent, and just before entering into the Earthly Paradise (*Purg.* 28–33). In the dream Leah is intent on gathering flowers to make herself a garland, and in her song she compares herself to her sister Rachel, who—Leah sings—always sits in front of her mirror (*Purg.* 27.104–105). In the Bible, Leah and Rachel are the elder and younger daughters of Laban and the first and second wives of Jacob, respectively. Primarily because of her fertility (she bore eight sons and a daughter to her husband Jacob), Leah came to symbolize the active life, while Rachel, who is briefly mentioned in *Inf.* 2.102 and 4.60 and whom the pilgrim will behold in the Empyrean (*Par.* 32.8), became the symbol of the contemplative life. Early and contemporary commentators on the *Commedia* accept this ancient and uncontested tradition. Many commentators see Leah as a prefiguration of Matelda, the lady whom the pilgrim first beholds in the Earthly Paradise and who also sings and gathers flowers. For other commentators, however, both Leah and Rachel—that is, both the active and the contemplative life—are represented in Matelda. But here Leah herself prefigures incipient contemplative life in several ways: by her mention of Rachel's gazing at her own image in a mirror, and by her announcement that she herself will become engaged in contemplation (*Purg.* 27.103).

The pilgrim's prophetic dream implicitly likens Dante the seer and wayfarer to Jacob, who received Leah and Rachel as wives from their father while in exile and after seven years of labor. Like the ancient patriarch, Dante the pilgrim departs from his native land on a journey; he labors strenuously to acquire the virtues the two sisters represent; and finally, like Jacob in exile (Gen. 28:10–19), he has a dream and meets Leah and Rachel. Thus the pilgrim's third and last dream represents for the first time along his journey a state of harmony between the seer and the holy appearance.

Dino Cervigni

Leander

A mythological youth whose tragic story was very popular from the time of Augustus on. The tale survives in only two classical works: Ovid's *Heroides* (letters 18 and 19), and a poem by Musaeus, a late Greek author. In the Ovidian account, Leander swims each night from his home in Abydos in Asia Minor to the opposite shore of Sestos in Thrace, where his lover Hero, a priestess of Venus, resides. Although the distance he must swim as he crosses the Hellespont is not great, Leander drowns in a violent storm. Dante refers to the myth in *Purg.* 28.71–74, where he compares his hatred for the stream separating him from Matelda with Leander's hatred of the Hellespont for separating him from Hero: *ma Elesponto . . . / più odio da Leandro non sofferse / per mareggiare intra Sesto e Abido* ("but Hellespont . . . did not suffer more hatred from Leander for its swelling waters between Sestos and Abydos"). Dante may also have been familiar with the interpretation of the story provided by the glossator of the *Ovide moralisé* (4.3587–3731), who states that Leander deserved to drown because he overestimated the value of earthly love. Dante uses the myth to suggest that in this canto he is not like the prelapsarian Adam but rather like Leander, a man plagued by erotic desire and the threat of death even in the Earthly Paradise.

Caron Cioffi

Learchus

Athamas, driven insane by Juno so that he thought his wife Ino and their sons Learchus *(Learco)* and Melicertes were a lioness and two cubs, killed Learchus by dashing his head against a rock (Ovid, *Meta.* 4.512–530). Dante compares the raging fury of the falsifiers of persons in the tenth pouch of Malebolge to that of Athamas in slaying his infant son (*Inf.* 30.1–12).

Olivia Holmes

Lelio

Gaius Laelius, Roman politician, philosopher, and close friend of Scipio Africanus Minor, and after him the best orator of Rome. Known as "the Wise" for his great learning, Laelius *(Lelio)* is the principal interlocutor in the *De amicitia,* Cicero's study of the value of friendship. Dante cites Cicero's consolatory words to him on the death of Scipio (*Conv.* 2.12.3).

Leslie Zarker Morgan

Lethe

The river of forgetfulness in classical literature, and the first of the two streams from which Dante must drink in the Earthly Paradise. In the *Republic* (10.621), Plato mentions Lethe as the river that the soul must imbibe during the process of metempsychosis, the passing of the soul at death into another body. Likewise, Virgil refers to Lethe during Anchises' speech on transmigration in the *Aeneid* (6.713–715). Ovid alludes to the river in *Meta.* 11.602–604, in the course of his description of the cave of Sleep. Statius mentions Lethe as the river of the underworld inaccessible to the shade of Laius (*Theb.* 1.296–298). In Lucan's *Pharsalia* (5.221–222), Apollo pours water from Lethe down the throat of his oracle in order to obliterate her knowledge of the future, while in *De raptu Proserpina* (1.282–283) Claudian also refers to the stagnant, oblivion-bringing waters of Lethe.

Drawing on these pagan sources, Dante retains the association of Lethe *(Letè)* with forgetfulness, but he adds a moral dimension by specifying that it removes only the remembrance of sins rather than all memories of a former life. His Lethe, as glossed by Matelda in *Purg.* 28.121–135,

The Procession at the banks of the river Lethe in the Earthly Paradise. La comedia di Dante Aligieri, with commentary by Alessandro Vellutello, published by Francesco Marcolini, Venice, 1544. Giamatti Collection: Courtesy of the Mount Holyoke College Archives and Special Collections.

L is a branch flowing down one side of the purgatorial mountain and originating from a divine fountain that divides into another branch, Eunoe. Lethe is first mentioned at *Inf.* 14.130–138, where Virgil explains that this is the river in which souls bathe after their repented guilt has been removed by drinking. Although the pilgrim initially experiences Lethe as a negative space separating him from Matelda (*Purg.* 28.70–75), it soon becomes the focal point in the landscape which orients him toward Matelda and turns him toward the east, so that he literally and symbolically faces salvation (29.10–12). In *Purg.* 30, Beatrice elicits from Dante a confession of his personal sins and his heartfelt contrition, processes which are the collective prerequisite for passing and tasting Lethe. Dante's immersion and drinking in Lethe is physically guided by Matelda (*Purg.* 31.92–104).

The allegorical significance of Dante's actions in Lethe is the subject of scholarly debate. Some critics, following Giovanni Pascoli, trace Dante's concept of Lethe to St. Bernard, who speaks of two fountains which issued from Christ's wounds and which remove all sins, save the penitent souls, and perform for them the function that the Eucharist plays in earthly life. Others, like A. E. Quaglio, argue that Lethe represents a fundamental stage in Dante's personal attainment of human perfection and, more generally, a stage in the process of redemption. Finally, Tilde Nardi and Charles Singleton view Lethe as a modified rite of baptism. That is, whereas baptismal water washes away the guilt of original sin, the immersion in Lethe is closer to the sacrament of penance in that it removes personal sin. The crossing of Lethe completes Dante's ritual of absolution, but his drinking from the river is not figurally allied with baptism. Perhaps Dante, who alludes to the sweetness of the waters (*Purg.* 28.133), intends to dramatize his return to Eden by presenting himself as an antitype of Adam, whose expulsion was caused by his eating of the fruit of the Tree of Knowledge. Adam eats, feels guilt, and is exiled; Dante drinks, remembers no sins and so experiences no guilt, and is led to Beatrice, his paradise and his salvation.

Bibliography

Cervigni, Dino S. "The Eunoe or the Recovery of the Lost Good." In *Lectura Dantis Newberryana*. Vol. 2. Edited by Paolo Cherchi and Antonio C. Mastrobuono. Evanston, Ill.: Northwestern University Press, 1990, pp. 59–80.

Donno, Daniel J. "Moral Hydrography: Dante's Rivers." *MLN* 92 (1977), 130–139.

Nardi, Bruno. "Intorno al sito del Purgatorio e al mito dantesco dell'Eden." *Il giornale dantesco* 25 (1922), 289–300.

Nardi, Tilde. *Il Canto XXVIII del Purgatorio.* Lectura Dantis Romana. Nuova serie. Turin: Società Editrice Internazionale, 1963, pp. 5–29.

Pascoli, Giovanni. "L'altro viaggio." In *Sotto il velame: Saggio di un'interpretazione generale del poema sacro.* 3rd ed. Bologna: Zanichelli, 1923.

Quaglio, Antonio Enzo. "Il canto XXVIII del *Purgatorio.*" In *Lectura Dantis Scaligera.* Vol. 2. Florence: Le Monnier, 1966, pp. 1037–1061.

Singleton, Charles. "Rivers, Nymphs and Stars." In *Dante Studies 2. Journey to Beatrice.* Cambridge: Harvard University Press, 1958, pp. 159–183.

Caron Cioffi

Levi

Son of Jacob and Leah. In *Mon.* 3.5.1, Dante refers to the symbolism by which Levi and his younger brother Judah are made to typify the Church and the Empire, challenging the argument that the Church precedes the Empire in authority on the basis that Levi was older. The tribe of Levi, or Levites, who were ministers of the temple, represent the Church in *Purg.* 16.132. Dante, responding to Marco Lombardo's denunciation of the Church for having wrongly appropriated temporal power, says that he understands why they were denied the right of inheritance. Levi is also implicitly included among the Hebrew patriarchs released from Limbo by Christ (*Inf.* 4.59).

Richard Lansing

Light

Light, be it "sensible" or "spiritual," actual or metaphorical, looms large in medieval thought, and Dante's writings are no exception. The entire *Commedia* can be seen as a journey toward the light, as the pilgrim travels from the dark wood and the shadows of Hell to the supernatural brightness of the final visions of Paradise. The words Dante uses for "light" are many and have multiple functions: *luce, lume, raggio, splendore, chiaritade, chiarezza, gloria, lumera, lucerna, luminositade.* The human eye, the human intellect, the sun, the stars,

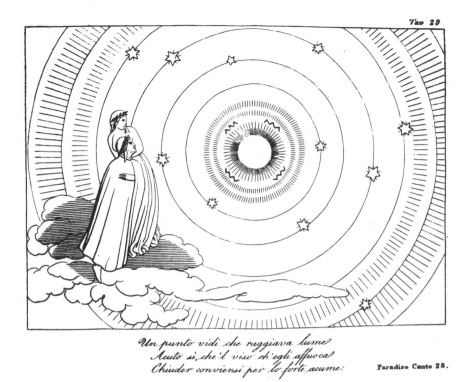

Un punto vidi che raggiava lume
Acuto sì, che 'l viso ch'egli affuoca
Chiuder conviensi per lo forte acume:

Paradiso Canto 28.

Dante and Beatrice contemplating the point of light in the Empyrean. Invenzioni di Giovanni Flaxman sulla Divina commedia, *illustrated by John Flaxman and Beniamino del Vecchio, Rome, 1826. Giamatti Collection: Courtesy of the Mount Holyoke College Archives and Special Collections.*

the planets, the souls of the blessed, the angels, divine grace, glory and power, and God himself are all characterized as light by Dante. For the purposes of this discussion we will divide Dante's use of light into three categories: light symbolism, light metaphysics and cosmology, and the science of optics.

Light Symbolism

Following medieval tradition, Dante makes sensible light a symbol of goodness and intellection. Thus, in the opening scene of the *Commedia,* the lost and fearful pilgrim emerges from the dark wood; the presence of the sun, *che mena dritto altrui per ogne calle* ("that leads us straight on every path," *Inf.* 1.18), quiets his fear. We soon learn that St. Lucy, along with Mary and Beatrice, has interceded on Dante's behalf; it is likely that the poet chose Lucy because of her association with light (*Inf.* 2.100ff.; cf. *Purg.* 9.55ff.). Hell, where goodness and true understanding are lacking, is a dark valley (*Inf.* 12.86), *d'ogne luce muto* ("where all light is silent," *Inf.* 5.28); the absence of light in Hell reflects the Augustinian notion that

evil is merely the privation of good. Judecca, the lowest ring of Hell, is farthest from heaven and darkest of all: *'l più oscuro, / e 'l più lontan dal ciel. (Inf.* 9.28–29). The castle housing the virtuous pagans in Limbo is the one relatively luminous part of Hell: a glowing fire, symbolic of the limited goodness and understanding achieved by those souls, wins out over the hemisphere of shadows (*un foco / ch'emisperio di tenebre vincia, Inf.* 5.68–69).

In Purgatory, the alternation of day and night symbolizes the transitional state of the souls on the path to Heaven. Whereas in Hell the souls generally notice that Dante is not dead because his body has weight, the souls in Purgatory recognize his corporeality because he blocks the rays (*raggi,* 3.18, 5.26, 6.57, 27.65; *lume,* 5.5) of the sun. The progress of the pilgrim and the penitent souls must come to a halt when the sun sets, further emphasizing the association between sensible light and spiritual illumination. Whereas Hell is dark, and Purgatory is illumined by the sun, much of Paradise is inherently luminous. The pilgrim rises through the spheres of the material universe, penetrating the planets, which he imagines to be made of ether and imbued with light. He describes the inside of the moon, for example, as a "shining, dense, solid, clean" cloud (*nube . . . / lucida, spessa, solida e pulita, Par.* 2.31–32). Throughout Paradise, the souls that Dante meets appear to him as shining lights (e.g., *lampe,* 17.5; *lucerne,* 8.19, 23.28; *luci,* 18.49, 20.10, etc.; *lumere,* 5.130, 9.112, 11.16; *lumi,* 8.25, 10.73, etc.).

When the pilgrim reaches the Primum Mobile, the boundary of the material universe, he has his first vision of God, who appears as a point of light surrounded by rings of fire, which are the angels (*Par.* 28.16ff.). This is the first of several successive visions of God, each of which will be figured in terms of light. When Dante leaves behind the material universe, he enters the Empyrean, that heaven which is *pura luce: / luce intellettüal* ("pure light: light intellectual," *Par.* 30.39–40). As the pilgrim moves closer to God, his vision strengthens, and he is able to see God as a river of light (*Par.* 30.61). After Dante bathes his eyes in this river, his sight is further enhanced, and he sees God as an immense, round sea of light (*Par.* 30.100–105). Finally, gazing into this expanse of light, the pilgrim sees the three persons of the Trinity figured as three rings of colored light (*Par.* 33.115–120).

Light Metaphysics and Cosmology

The connection between light and divinity is an ancient one. Plato theorized that the Good in the realm of ideas is similar to the sun in the material world; as the light of the sun is necessary in order for us to see anything with the eye of the body, so is the light of the Good essential if we are to "see" anything with the eye of the intellect (*Republic* 4.508d–509a). This notion proved to be highly influential over the centuries, and later philosophers tended to posit a close relationship between sensible and intellectual light. In the late Middle Ages, the connection between God and light in philosophical and theological texts and in scripture inspired a school of thought called "light metaphysics," according to which creation, cosmology, and theology could all be explained in terms of light. Spearheaded by thinkers such as Robert Grosseteste (c. 1168–1253), this tradition certainly influenced Dante, although scholars disagree to what extent.

Light metaphysicians conceived of creation as the radiation of God's light in the material realm: God created a point of intense light, and its expansion resulted in the whole of creation. While Dante does not speak of such a primeval point of created light, he does describe creation as a radiation of divine light or will (*Par.* 19.89–90, 13.52ff., etc.).

Dante's discussions of the motion and functioning of the universe draw heavily on the branch of light metaphysics in which the entire universe is believed to operate by means of divine and created light. Dante tells us that a ray of divine light strikes the Primum Mobile (*Par.* 30.106–108), which is completely and uniformly diaphanous; in this sphere the divine light is translated into material energy and is transmitted below to the sphere of the fixed stars. Since each star has a unique composition, it receives (from above) and in turn transmits (below) this force differently (*Par.* 2.112–123). In addition, God's light is imparted to the nine orders of angels, each of which conveys this light to the sphere of the material universe in its charge (2.127ff.). Subsequent to God's initial act of creation, and apart from the highest part of each human soul, everything on earth is created and governed by means of the rays of light and power given off by the planets and stars (*Par.* 7.130ff.; 13.52ff.; cf. *Conv.* 2.6.9ff.).

A final branch of light metaphysics that is significant for Dante is based on a notion of God as the archetypal light, thus allowing an understanding of theology in terms of the behavior of sensible light. Dante uses light to explain theological principles several times—for example, the bestowal of divine grace upon the pilgrim in the final vision of the *Paradiso* (33.139ff.), and the idea that God's goodness does not diminish when it is shared (*Purg.* 15.67–75).

While Dante was undeniably influenced by the theories of light metaphysics, scholars disagree as to how strictly Dante adhered to these theories. While some (Nardi, Mazzeo) maintain that Dante falls squarely within the bounds of this tradition, others (Mellone) argue that he was fond of its imagery but used it only metaphorically and did not truly share its beliefs.

Optics

The importance of light in medieval culture, coupled with an abundance of newly translated Greek and Arabic optical treatises, led to an increased study of physical light in late medieval Europe.

Throughout his works Dante demonstrates an awareness of many of the trends of this science, commonly called *perspectiva* (Latin) or *perspettiva* (Italian). For example, in *Purg.* 15, he refers to a fundamental law of optics regarding the reflection of light (i.e., that the angle of incidence equals the angle of reflection, 15.16–21); and in the *Paradiso,* he describes an experiment one can perform involving light and mirrors (2.97–105).

Some of Dante's most scientific discussions of light occur in the *Convivio.* In book 3, he distinguishes among three types or stages of sensible light: *luce, raggio,* and *splendore.* Using *lume* as the generic term for light, he tells us that philosophers call light *luce* "as it exists in its original source" *(in quanto esso è nel suo fontale principio),* as in the sun or in the flame of a candle, *raggio* ("ray" or "radiance") "as it exists in the medium between its source and the first body which it strikes" *(in quanto esso è per lo mezzo, dal principio al primo corpo dove si termina),* and *splendore* "as it is reflected into another place that becomes illuminated" (*in quanto esso è in altra parte alluminata ripercosso, Conv.* 3.14.5). It should be noted that most medieval theorists of light actually delineated four stages of light: the three mentioned by Dante plus *lumen* or *lume,* which was used not as a generic term for light but rather to describe the phenomenon of luminosity, or the collective effect of rays *(raggi)* in the medium. In any case, although Dante makes it clear that he is aware of various scientific distinctions and arguments, he adapts them with varying degrees of precision in his poetry. Thus, whereas *raggio* is generally used by Dante to refer to rays of light or radiance, and *lume* frequently describes luminosity, *splendore* often refers not to reflected light but to radiance, and *luce* is used to describe light in all its stages.

Dante repeatedly calls the eyes *luci* (*Inf.* 29.2, *Purg.* 15.84, etc.) and often speaks of a light *(lume, luce, raggio, splendore)* that shines out of them. Sometimes this light refers to a display of emotion expressed through the eyes; at other times, it refers more specifically to the action of the glance. The idea that the eyes emit a ray of light stems from Platonic visual theories, as Dante is well aware. In *Convivio* (3.9.6–10), he refutes the Platonic theory of visual rays; however, he continues to utilize the concept in his poetry, usually to convey the power of the beloved's glance.

Bibliography

Boyde, Patrick. *Perception and Passion in Dante's "Comedy."* Cambridge: Cambridge University Press, 1993.

———. *Dante: Philomythes and Philosopher.* Cambridge: Cambridge University Press, 1981.

Cantarino, Vincent. "Dante and Islam: Theory of Light in the *Paradiso.*" *Kentucky Romance Quarterly* 15 (1968), 3–35.

Crombie, A. C. *Robert Grosseteste and the Origins of Experimental Science.* Oxford: Clarendon Press, 1962 [1953].

Di Pino, Guido. *La figurazione della luce nella "Divina Commedia."* Florence: La Nuova Italia, 1952.

Durling, Robert, and Ronald Martinez. *Time and the Crystal: Studies in Dante's "Rime Petrose."* Berkeley: University of California Press, 1990.

Lindberg, David. *Theories of Vision from Al-Kindi to Kepler.* Chicago: University of Chicago Press, 1976.

Mazzeo, Joseph Anthony. *Medieval Cultural Tradition in Dante's "Comedy."* Ithaca, N.Y.: Cornell University Press, 1960.

Mellone, Attilio. "Luce: La 'metafisica della luce.'" *Enciclopedia dantesca,* 3:712–713.

Nardi, Bruno. *Dante e la cultura medievale.* Rome: Laterza, 1990 [1942].

Parronchi, Alessandro. "La perspettiva dantesca." *Studi danteschi* 36 (1959), 5–103.

Radcliff-Umstead, Douglas. "Dante on Light." *Italian Quarterly* 9.33 (1965), 30–43.

Rutledge, Monica. "Dante, the Body and Light." *Dante Studies* 113 (1995), 151–165.

Schnapp, Jeffrey. "Injured by the Light: Violence and *Paideia* in Dante's *Purgatorio.*" *Dante Studies* 111 (1993), 107–118.

Dana E. Stewart

Limbo

In Christian theology, Limbo designates an intermediary state or place reserved for those souls who have died and who have experienced neither Christ nor the Church. Dante appropriates and significantly modifies this concept in *Inf.* 4, where it is the first circle of Hell.

The Tradition

By Dante's time, theologians distinguished between two Limbos, the *limbus patrum* and the *limbus puerorum.* The *limbus patrum* (Limbo of the

Fathers) designated the abode of those souls who, while alive, were just, but who lived before the time of Christ (mainly the Old Testament righteous, but sometimes certain just pagans are included) and who were freed from this Limbo when Christ descended there in the so-called Harrowing of Hell. The *limbus puerorum* (Limbo of the Children) was the exclusive domain of those souls who died without baptism—that is, in a state of original sin (the sin inherited by all humankind after the Fall of Adam)—and who nevertheless had committed no personal or mortal sin of their own, since they had not attained the use of reason. Although both Limbos were the products of Scholastic thought, this thought in turn was shaped by earlier and extensive theological reflection.

Neither Limbo is explicitly mentioned in sacred scripture. The theology of the *limbus patrum* grew out of early Church reflection on Christ's descent into Hell (cf. Acts 2:24ff.; Rom. 10:6ff.; Eph. 4:8–10), alternatively identified as Hades, Sheol, or the Bosom of Abraham (cf. Luke 16:22). In the East, this reflection was focused on what happened during Christ's descent (i.e., preaching, baptizing, doing battle with Satan) rather than on where it happened. It was only much later, with the writings of Origen and others, that the geography of Christ's descent was considered. In the West, there are only passing references to a possible division in Hell for the resting place of the Hebrew just (cf. Tertullian and the Ambrosiaster), and the matter does not receive serious attention until Augustine. In his sermons on the Creed (*Sermo* 244 [*PL,* 39, 2195]; *Sermo de Symbolo* [*PL,* 40, 1189–1202]), Augustine maintains that Christ descended into Hell to free "Adam, and the Patriarchs, and the Prophets, and all the just, who were held in that place for original sin." In considering the location of "this place," he concludes that there must be two regions in Hell: one reserved for the damned, and one for the souls of the ancient just.

In a similar way, the *limbus puerorum* was a relatively late theological development. It grew out of reflection on the state of infants who died in a state of original sin—that is, without recourse to the sacrament of baptism, the necessity of which is stressed by sacred scripture (John 3:5). In the East, the Cappadocian Fathers, driven in their theology by the primacy of the Incarnation of the Logos and the ultimate restoration of all things in God, were most benign to such infants. Gregory of

Nyssa (*On the Early Deaths of Infants* [*PG* 46, 179, 183, 191]), for example, says that an unbaptized child who died without personal sin would neither be afflicted with the torments of Hell nor be admitted to the kingdom of Heaven; in this he was followed by Gregory of Nazianzus, who argues along the same lines in a homily he gave at Constantinople on the sacrament of baptism (*Oratio 40 in Sanctum Baptisma* [*PG,* 36, 364 ff.]). In the West, the matter receives scant attention until the Pelagian heresy. Pelagius denied the validity of original sin and downplayed the efficacy of divine grace. In so doing, he was forced to reexamine the role of infant baptism, the absence of which, he concluded, did not deny an infant eternal life with God, albeit not in the full kingdom of God, but in some kind of intermediate eternal state. He was vehemently opposed by Augustine, Bishop of Hippo, who argues (*Serm.* 294, 3 and 4 [*PL,* 38, 1337]) that no intermediate state between damnation and Heaven existed, and so the only alternative for those children who died unbaptized was the fire of Hell. Augustine himself was bothered by his own severity; in another passage (*Enchiridion* 93 [*PL,* 40, 275]) he reasons that the punishment meted out to such infants would be the mildest one of all *(mitissima poena)*. However,

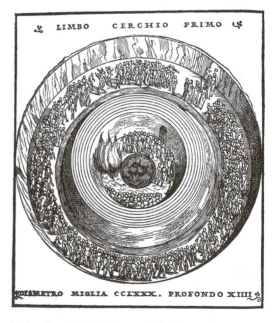

Limbo, from the 1544 edition of the Commedia *with commentary by Vellutello.* La comedia di Dante Aligieri, *with commentary by Alessandro Vellutello, published by Francesco Marcolini, Venice, 1544. Giamatti Collection: Courtesy of the Mount Holyoke College Archives and Special Collections.*

Augustine remained steadfast in his conviction that unbaptized infants who died in a state of original sin would be condemned to Hell for all eternity. This tradition continued to prevail among the later fathers, such as Gregory the Great and Isidore of Seville.

The Scholastics, especially of the twelfth and thirteenth centuries, systematized much of this discussion in their shaping of Limbo along three important lines. First, they brought together the *limbus patrum* and the *limbus puerorum* as separate but adjoining receptacles or repositories of Hell reserved for distinct categories of souls. Honorius of Autun (*Eleucidarium* 3, 4 ff. [*PL, 172*, 1159ff.]) speaks of an upper and a lower Hell, the former being an abode of those just souls who had awaited Christ's descent there and who shared their abode with unbaptized children. Shortly afterward, Albert the Great was the first to assign to this place the name "Limbo" *(limbus),* signifying "hem" or "border" *(Sent.* 4.1.20.1); he argues that Limbo is at the outermost limit of Hell and is divided into two separate Limbos reserved for two different categories of souls: the ancient Hebrew just, and the souls of children who had died unbaptized in a state of original sin (*Sent.* 4, 44, 45). Albert's student, Thomas Aquinas, provides the fullest and most detailed account of Hell of all the Scholastics in his *Commentary on the Sentences of Peter Lombard* (3.22.2.1.2), in which he maintains that Hell has a fourfold division, and that two of those upper divisions are the *limbus patrum* and *limbus puerorum.* Second, although there is considerable Scholastic discussion about which souls (i.e., only the Hebrew righteous, or the Hebrew righteous and certain righteous pagans) were delivered from the *limbus patrum* during the Harrowing of Hell, there is no Scholastic thinker who proposes that any adults are to be found in the *limbus patrum* after the Harrowing of Hell. Third, beginning with Abelard, the scholastics were in total agreement against Augustine that the souls of infants in the *limbus puerorum* experienced no sensible pain of any kind *(poena sensus)* and were subject only to the pain of loss *(poena damni)* as the eternal punishment of original sin, although there was considerable disagreement on whether these infants were truly happy (Aquinas) or shared in some kind of sadness because of the lack of the beatific vision (Bonaventure).

Catholic doctrine, as developed by the Scholastics, thus maintained that there are two Limbos which together form an antechamber on the very border of Hell. The *limbus patrum,* the abode of the souls of the Hebrew righteous, was brought to an end by Christ's Harrowing of Hell. The *limbus puerorum* continues to hold the souls of those infants who died without baptism. Their lot is one not of physical pain, but of privation or loss of the beatific vision.

Dante's Rewriting of Limbo

In *Inf.* 4, Dante shapes a picture of Limbo that constitutes a complete and radical break with the preceding theological tradition. Relentlessly appropriating elements from many diverse theological sources and adapting them to shape his tragedy of the virtuous pagans in Limbo, Dante poetically creates a Limbo that is unique in four details: the location of Limbo, the treatment of the *limbus puerorum* and the *limbus patrum,* and Dante's creation of the Limbo of the virtuous pagans.

Dante's Limbo is not on the border of Hell, nor is it conceived as an antechamber to Hell. Rather, Limbo is the first circle of Hell. And even if Virgil and his fellow Limbo dwellers are not subject to the jurisdiction of Minos (cf. *Minos me non lega,* "me Minos does not bind," *Purg.* 1.77), the location of Dante's Limbo is still beyond the Acheron and, hence, beyond salvation (Padoan, 105).

It is clear that Dante is not all that interested in the *limbus puerorum* (Iannucci, 90). In fact, only one line is devoted to the children in *Inf.* 4 (*d'infanti e di femmine e di viri,* "of infants and of women and of men," 30), and Dante postpones any further mention of their otherworld existence until the very end of *Paradiso* (33.40ff.). What strongly interests Dante, however, is their fate as described in the theological tradition. And, as Dante describes it in *Inf.* 4, it is a fate they share with the adult pagans, a fate brought about by their lack of baptism and consisting not of physical torment but of sighs (*non avea pianto mai che di sospiri,* "there was no weeping except of sighs," 26)—sighs caused by an eternal life of longing without hope (*che sanza speme vivemo in disio,* "without hope we live in desire," 42). Dante therefore appropriates and transfers to the pagan adults of Limbo the afterlife fate of the children as described mainly by the theology of Bonaventure. The children and their fate thus serve merely as the entree to Dante's principal theme in *Inf.* 4: the tragedy of the virtuous pagans.

The most stunning break on Dante's part against the entire theological tradition on Limbo is his placement there of virtuous pagan adults. As we have seen, the *limbus patrum,* according to the theological tradition, was emptied of its inhabitants at Christ's Harrowing of Hell. To be sure, Dante does describe this harrowing (*Inf.* 4.52ff.), but the description, which is not the focal point of Dante's Limbo, is extremely limited and stripped of its triumphal imagery. The emphasis for Dante is not on the souls who were liberated victoriously, but on those sad souls—Virgil and his fellow pagan just—who were left behind. Thus does Dante populate the *limbus patrum* after the harrowing; and, having placed the virtuous pagans in Limbo, Dante assimilates them to the unbaptized children, and their sin to that of the infants. Like the infants, they are blameless (*ei non peccaro,* "they did not sin," 34), but they also died without baptism (*non ebber battesmo,* "they did not receive baptism," 35), which, as Dante reminds us, is an absolutely theological necessity for salvation (*ch'è porta de la fede,* "which is the gateway to the faith." 36). As a result, and not through any personal fault, these souls are lost (*per tai difetti, non per altro rio, / semo perduti,* "because of such defects, not for any other wickeness, we are lost," 40–41) and, neither sad nor happy (*né trista né lieta,* 84), they must live an eternal life of hopeless longing. In such a manner, Dante creates a drama of predestination in which the emphasis is on the virtuous pagans who are denied entry into the kingdom of God and are condemned to Limbo, simply because they lived at the wrong historical moment, "that graceless period between the fall and the incarnation; in the emptiness of time" (Iannucci, 84).

In his representation of Limbo, Dante is not interested in the *limbus puerorum,* the *limbus patrum,* or the Harrowing of Hell. Rather, he is concerned with the *limbus gentilium virtuosum* and the *nobile castello,* which he creates in order to dramatize the tragic consequences of the fall in that unredeemed section of time between Adam and Christ. So Dante encounters the great poets of the *bella scola* and, in fact, is made an honorary member of the group (*sì ch'io fui sesto tra cotanto senno,* "so that I was sixth among so much wisdom," 102). He discusses with them things that are not recorded, but whose focus is undoubtedly Parnassus, and they make their way toward the light that wins out against the surrounding darkness.

They enter the noble castle (clearly modeled on Virgil's Elysian Fields) and within, "on the bright green grass," Dante beholds the great-hearted spirits of antiquity conveniently arranged in groups (121–144): the first ones encompass great-heartedness by action, such as Hector, Aeneas, and Julius Caesar; the next are exemplary by their contemplative lives, such as Aristotle, Socrates, Plato and the great thinkers who followed. The virtuous pagans in Dante's Limbo are left free to pursue their own intellectual interests, and their apartness in the *nobile castello* represents a state of natural bliss which is tempered only, but significantly, by the fact that they have no hope of ever gaining Heaven.

The depiction of the *nobile castello* and its great-hearted spirits has caused modern commentators, for the most part (cf. Mazzoni, 29ff.), to argue that such a depiction reveals Dante's exaltation of pagan philosophy and poetry and constitutes a humanistic *hommage* on Dante's part to pagan antiquity. Such a reading, however, misses the real poetic meaning and the subject of this canto. The subject, emphatically, is not the celebration of pagan poetry and philosophy, but rather the limits of humanism when it is not illuminated by revelation. The virtuous pagans, for all their great personal merits, were left behind because they did not have faith; and the *nobile castello,* while certainly an expression of Dante's humanism, nevertheless also reveals his painful awareness of the limits of humanism alone, and hence of the tragic limits of pagan civilization.

Dante's Limbo, introduced in *Inf.* 4, is not limited to this canto, but resounds as an episode throughout the *Commedia.* Associated with it are the great theological themes that will continue to occupy Dante's mind until the very end of the *Paradiso:* the definition and role of faith in salvation; the place of the church and its sacraments; election by divine grace; and, especially, the relationship between divine justice and the predestination and damnation of individuals who live a just life and yet have no way of knowing God (cf. *Par.* 19.70ff.). Moreover, the tragedy of the virtuous pagans in Limbo, as embodied in the person of Virgil as guide, will be ever before us. It is Virgil's story, in fact, that will resound as a recurrent theme through many key moments (cf. *Inf.* 1–2, 8–9; *Purg.* 1, 3, 6, 7, 21–22) and that will be used by Dante as a key narrative element in the linking of the entire poem. And Virgil's story, whenever encountered, will keep before us not only Dante's bold repositioning of pagan values but also his unique and tragic shaping of the virtuous pagans' destiny—a destiny which, though theologically heterodox in its details, poetically evokes pity and compassion and hence becomes a powerful vehicle for expression of the great theological themes of Dante's *poema sacro.*

Bibliography

Busnelli, Giovanni. "La Colpa del 'non fare' degli infedeli negativi." *Studi danteschi* 23 (1938), 79–97.

Caperan, Louis. "Le problème du salut des infidèles." Reprinted by F. Ruffini as "Dante e il Problema della Salvezza degli Infedeli." *Studi danteschi* 14 (1930), 79–92.

Dyer, George J. *Limbo: Unsettled Question.* New York: Sheed and Ward, 1962.

———. "Limbo: A Theological Evaluation." *Theology Studies* 19 (1958), 32–49.

———. *The Denial of Limbo and the Jansenist Controversy.* Mundelein, Ill.: St Mary of the Lake Seminary, 1955.

Foster, Kenelm. "The Two Dantes (I): Limbo and Implicit Faith." In *The Two Dantes and Other Studies.* London: Darton, Longman and Todd, 1977, pp. 156–189.

Gaudel, A. "Limbes." In *Dictionnaire de Théologie Catholique.* Paris: Letouzey et Ane, 1926, vol. 9, cols. 760–772.

Hollander, Robert. "Tragedia nella 'Commedia.'" In *Il Virgilio Dantesco: Tragedia nella "Commedia."* Florence: Olschki, 1983, pp. 117–154.

Iannucci, Amilcare A. "Limbo: The Emptiness of Time." *Studi danteschi* 52 (1978), 69–128.

Mazzoni, Francesco. "Saggio du un nuovo commento alla *Commedia*": Il Canto IV dell'*Inferno.* *Studi danteschi* 42 (1965), 29–206.

McBrien, Richard P. *Catholicism.* Minneapolis, Minn.: Winston Press, 1989, pp. 1123ff.

Padoan, Giorgio. "Il Limbo Dantesco." *Lettere italiane* 21 (1969), 369–388. Reprinted in *Il pio Enea, l'impio Ulisse.* Ravenna: Longo, 1977, pp. 103–124.

Rahner, Karl. *On the Theology of Death.* New York: Herder and Herder, 1965.

Amilcare A. Iannucci

Linus

Mythical pastoral poet paired by Dante with Orpheus in Limbo (see Virgil, *Ecl.* 6.67): *"Vidi . . . Lino"* ("I saw . . . Linus," *Inf.* 4.140–141). Augustine names him among the first theological poets (*De civ. Dei* 18.14.37).

Rebecca S. Beal

Linus, Pope

Universally listed as immediate successor of St. Peter, the first pope. The *Liber Pontificalis* says that he was martyred under Nero, a tradition followed by Dante in *Par.* 27.41, where Linus *(Lino)* is mentioned by St. Peter along with Cletus, his successor.

Michael Haren

Liturgy

The liturgy of the Catholic Church comprises the set of formularies for the conduct of corporate worship, principally the Missal (containing the order of service for the Mass throughout the year) and the Breviary (containing the constituent parts of the Divine Office for each day, to be recited at the various hours by those in holy orders). Dante would have been acquainted with versions deriving from the revisions of the Franciscan Haymo of Faversham (d. 1244), which changed the course of Western public worship. Since much of the liturgy consists of passages from the Bible, for the present purpose liturgy is understood as the non-biblical elements (hymns, prayers, creeds, and the confession), together with biblical passages that were used at least weekly (mainly the psalms and certain canticles).

Dante had a remarkable familiarity with the liturgy, including that of the Divine Office, which would seem to indicate regular attendance on his part at a collegiate or monastic church. He drew extensively on the liturgy in his writing (primarily in the *Commedia,* though Paola Rigo has argued for a liturgical element in *Epist.* 5), so that one does not read far in the *Purgatorio* or *Paradiso* without detecting a liturgical flavor.

Little use is made of the liturgy in *Inferno,* presumably because Hell is an anti-church, a wrong turning on the ideal path from the Church Militant (on earth) via the Church Suffering (in Purgatory) to the Church Triumphant (in Heaven). The first *cantica*'s most striking allusion to a specific liturgical text involves the hymn *Vexilla Regis* (*Inf.* 34.1), quoted as a means of placing Lucifer in the context of the Cross which vanquished him.

Dante modeled his Purgatory much more obviously on an earthly church than either his Hell or his Heaven, and the *Purgatorio* is the most fertile of the three *cantiche* in its cultivation of liturgical language. This is least surprising in the seven circles of Purgatory proper (cantos 10–27): there the souls' essential business is penance, an important part of which is prayer, and on each *cornice* except one the souls recite an appropriate prayer from the Roman liturgy. Only one of these six prayers (*Purg.* 11.1–21), however, was a prayer, in the narrow sense, in earthly usage: a hymn serves the purpose in *Purg.* 25.121, single verses from the Psalms in *Purg.* 19.73 and 23.11, the *Agnus Dei* in *Purg.* 16.19, and part of the Lenten litany in *Purg.* 13.49–51. Outside the *cornici,* psalms are prominently sung in *Purg.* 2.46–48 and 5.22–24; the evening scene in the Valley of the Princes (cantos 7–8) is full of references to the compline service; there is a connection between Dante-character's encounter with the angel doorkeeper (*Purg.* 9.73–145) and the ritual of public penance; the protagonist's admission to Purgatory proper is accompanied by the singing of the *Te Deum* (*Purg.* 9.140); several psalms are exploited in the Terrestrial Paradise (*Purg.* 29.3, 30.83–84, 31.98, 33.1–3); and Beatrice's appearance is punctuated by references to the Mass (*Purg.* 29.51, 30.19).

Although the six lowest spheres of Heaven are marked by a regular series of liturgical utterances, as in *Par.* 3.121–122 and 8.28–30, with these two exceptions we do not recognize texts from the Roman liturgy: this is a celestial liturgy (e.g., *Par.* 7.1–3). In any case, the poet sometimes declares himself unable to report the experience in full (*Par.* 14.122–126, 19.39). The most interesting of the heavens from the liturgical viewpoint is the eighth (*Par.* 22.106–108, 24.2, 25.38, 27.57). The triumph of the Virgin twice quotes the Litany of Loreto (*Par.* 23.73–74, 92–93) and is completed by the singing of the Marian antiphon *Regina Caeli* (*Par.* 23.128). In his examination on faith, the protagonist quotes or paraphrases both the Nicene and the Athanasian creeds (*Par.* 24.130–132, 139–141), and the choir of the blessed sings a chant taken from the Roman liturgy at the end of each of his three examinations (*Par.* 24.112–114, 25.98, 26.69). The same choir later sings the Lesser Doxology (*Par.* 27.1–2), apparently as a magnificent punctuation mark between Adam's speech and St. Peter's condemnation of the corrupt papacy. The liturgical content of the Empyrean cantos, by contrast, is fairly slim; apart from two references to the Psalms, it all focuses on the Virgin (*Par.* 31.116–17, 32.95, 32.135, 33.1–9).

To some extent, Dante creates a liturgy of his own in the second and third *cantiche.* Much of it consists of texts from the liturgy of this world, but particularly in *Purgatorio* he also draws on other sources for *his* liturgy. For instance, he uses the Beatitudes (e.g., *Purg.* 27.7–9), as well as other biblical phrases (e.g., *Purg.* 27.58, 30.11) and even secular texts (as in *Purg.* 30.21), or he invents pseudo-liturgical texts (*Purg.* 15.39, *Par.* 7.1–3). A particularly remarkable part of this invented liturgy involves the whips and bridles of cornices 2 and 4–7 in the *Purgatorio* (e.g., *Purg.* 20.25–27, 25.127–129).

Bibliography

Barnes, J. C. "Vestiges of the Liturgy in Dante's Verse." In *Dante and the Middle Ages: Literary and Historical Essays.* Edited by J. C. Barnes and C. Ó Cuilleanáin. Dublin: Irish Academic Press, 1995, pp. 231–269. Includes fuller bibliography.

Eisenhofer, L., and J. Lechner. *The Liturgy of the Roman Rite.* Translated by A. J. and E. F. Peeler, edited by H. E. Winstone. Freiburg: Herder; Edinburgh and London: Nelson, 1961.

Fiatarone, J. J. *From "selva oscura" to "divina foresta": Liturgical Song as Path to Paradise in Dante's "Commedia."* Dissertation, University of California, Berkeley, 1986.

Liber Usualis: Missae et Officii pro Dominicis et Festis Duplicibus, cum Cantu Gregoriano. Tournai: Desclée and Lefebvre; London: Breitkopf and Härtel, 1904.

Martimort, A.-G., et al. *L'Eglise en prière: introduction à la liturgie.* 3rd ed. Paris: Desclée, 1965. English translation of the first part of the first (1961) edition, *The Church at Prayer: Introduction to the Liturgy.* Shannon: Irish University Press, 1968.

Rigo, P. "Tempo liturgico nell'epistola dantesca ai principi e ai popoli d'Italia." *Lettere italiane* 22 (1980), 222–231.

Salmon, P. *L'Office divin au Moyen Age: Histoire de la formation du bréviaire du IXe au XVIe siècle.* Paris: Cerf, 1967.

Sources of the Modern Roman Liturgy: The Ordinals by Haymo of Faversham and Related Documents (1243–1307). Edited by S. J. P. van Dijk. 2 vols. Leiden: Brill, 1963.

Tucker, D. J. "Dante's Reconciliation in the *Purgatorio*." *American Benedictine Review* 20 (1969), 75–92.

van Dijk, S. J. P., and J. Hazelden Walker. *The Origins of the Modern Roman Liturgy: The Liturgy of the Papal Court and the Franciscan Order in the Thirteenth Century*. Westminster, Md.: Newman; London: Darton, Longman and Todd, 1960.

John C. Barnes

Livy

Celebrated Roman historian (59 B.C.E.–17 C.E.). His *Ab urbe condita* is a history of Rome from its beginnings to Emperor Augustus, his patron. Of some 142 books, thirty-five have survived; summaries exist of all but two books. Dante's familiarity with Livy is debated. He refers to him in *Inf.* 28.12 as *Livïo . . . che non erra* ("Livy . . . who does not err") and frequently cites him in both the *Convivio* (3.11.3, 4.5.11), the *De vulgari eloquentia* (2.6), and the *Monarchia* (2.3.6, 2.4.5, 2.5.9, 2.5.12, 2.8.8, 2.9.15–16). Despite these references, Dante's real source for his information is on occasion not Livy but Orosius.

Nancy Vine Durling

Lizio da Valbona

A descendent of Nicola da Valbona, Lizio was part of a noble Guelf family that controlled the abbeys of Sant'Ellero di Galeata and Santa Maria dell'Isola. In 1260 Lizio worked for Guido Novello, the chief magistrate of Florence, but later he assisted Rinieri da Calboli in a battle against the Ghibellines of Forlì. He was still alive in 1279. He is cited by Guido del Duca on the second terrace of Purgatory (*Purg.* 14.97) as one of the noble and civilized individuals of Romagna.

Paul Colilli

Loderingo degli Andalò

Noble Ghibelline from Bologna who appears among the hypocrites in the sixth bolgia of Malebolge (*Inf.* 23.103–108). He was a member of the Jovial Friars, or Knights of St. Mary, a religious order of clergy and laymen founded to help preserve peace among feuding political factions. Loderingo and his Guelf colleague Catalano were appointed as governors by Pope Clement IV in 1226 to mediate the peace between the Guelfs and Ghibellines in Florence. Acting strictly under his orders, however, they favored the Guelfs. Later, when the Ghibellines rebelled against the Guelf magistracy, they and their leader Guido Novello were exiled from the city. Their possessions were confiscated and the ruins of their destroyed homes remained visible for years. Loderingo and Catalano ultimately resigned their office and were banished from Florence, being accused of corruption and of acting hypocritically in their mission to reconcile the two factions. The historian Villani (*Cronica* 7.13) also portrays them as hypocrites.

Pina Palma

Longfellow, Henry Wadsworth

Born in Portland, Maine, in 1807, Longfellow was educated at Bowdoin College (1821–1825) and the following year traveled to Europe to perfect his knowledge of modern European languages. It was during this trip that his friend George Washington Greene, later U.S. consul at Rome, introduced him to the work of Dante, who, Longfellow wrote in 1828, "excited [him] more than any other poet." Longfellow later returned to teach at Bowdoin (1829–1854). He died in 1882.

Longfellow helped to promote American interest in Dante with his massive anthology *The Poetry and Poets of Europe* (1845), which included selections from the *Commedia* and Dante's other works: but he was to exert his greatest influence as a translator. His first collection of poems, *Voices of the Night* (1839), included versions of five passages from the *Purgatorio,* which he translated intermittently during the 1840s and 1850s. In 1861, the tragic death by fire of Longfellow's wife caused him to turn for consolation to the *Paradiso,* which he began translating the following year; the entire *cantica* was in draft by 1863. In 1864 he began informal Wednesday night discussions of his translation at his home in Cambridge with friends who shared his interest in Dante: Greene, James Russell Lowell (who had succeeded Longfellow at Harvard), Charles Eliot Norton, and the publisher James T. Fields (the group later included William Dean Howells, and occasionally others). Longfellow's *Inferno* was published in limited edition in time for international celebrations of the sexcentennial of Dante's birth in 1865; the entire *Commedia* was issued by Ticknor and Fields in 1867.

Longfellow himself insisted, "The only merit my book has is that it is exactly what Dante says, and not what the translator imagines he might have said if he had been an Englishman." His translation, in unrhymed tercets, was criticized for excessive literalness, but it also reflects the ear for sound and rhythm with which Longfellow is credited even by his detractors, and Longfellow's status as the unofficial American laureate assured a wide readership. The volumes also represented Longfellow's considerable erudition: though the text was unimpeded by editorial notes, each canticle was followed by a section of "illustrations," essentially small anthologies of Dante scholarship and reception up to Longfellow's own time. The sonnets by Longfellow that precede each canticle have been praised as among his best. Moreover, the interest in Dante generated by his work precipitated the formation of the Dante Society of America at his home in 1881, with the poet himself as first president, and thus established a tradition of American scholarly interest in Dante that is still vital today.

Bibliography

Arvin, Newton. *Longfellow: His Life and Works.* Boston: Little, Brown, 1962.

Cunningham, Gilbert F. *The Divine Comedy in English: A Critical Bibliography.* Edinburgh and London: Oliver and Boyd, 1966.

De Sua, William J. *Dante into English: A Study of the Translations of the Divine Comedy in Britain and America.* Chapel Hill, N.C.: University of North Carolina Press, 1964.

De Vito, Anthony J. "The First Hundred Years of the Dante Society." *Dante Studies* 100 (1982), 99–118.

La Piana, Angelina. *Dante's American Pilgrimage: A Historical Survey of Dante Studies in the United States 1800–1944.* New Haven, Conn.: Yale University Press, 1948.

Mathews, J. Chesley. "H. W. Longfellow's Interest in Dante." *Papers Presented at the Longfellow Commemorative Conference.* Washington, D.C.: National Park Service, 1982, 47–58.

———. "Longfellow's Dante Collection." *ESQ* 68 (1971), 10–22.

Norton, Charles Eliot. *Henry Wadsworth Longfellow: A Sketch of His Life.* Boston: Houghton Mifflin, 1907.

Wagenknecht, Edward. *Henry Wadsworth Longfellow: His Poetry and Prose.* New York: Ungar, 1986.

Wallace, David. "Dante in English." In *The Cambridge Companion to Dante.* Edited by Rachel Jacoff. Cambridge: Cambridge University Press, 1993, pp. 237–258.

Kathleen Verduin

Lotto degli Agli

A Florentine judge, who also acted in numerous political and administrative roles in northern and central Italy between 1266 and 1291. Said to have taken his own life because he had accepted a bribe to pass sentence against an innocent defendant, he is identified by some of the early commentators (Graziolo, Lana, the Anonimo Fiorentino, and Serravalle) as the anonymous suicide whose branches are painfully damaged by Giacomo da Santo Andrea's trying to take refuge among them (*Inf.* 13.133–151). But other commentators give this character a completely different identity, that of Rocco dei Mozzi, while still others abstain from making any identification.

Michael Caesar

Lucan

Roman epic poet consigned to Limbo together with other noble pagan spirits. Born Marcus Annaeus Lucanus in 39 C.E. in Córdoba, Spain, Lucan *(Lucano)* was the nephew of Seneca the Philosopher. Educated in Rome, he rose to early prominence with the sponsorship of Nero on the strength of his precocious poetic gifts. Lucan subsequently fell out of the emperor's favor and, accused of joining the Pisonian conspiracy, was forced to end his own life in 65, at the age of twenty-six. His early biographers attribute to him a variegated output, including an *Iliacon,* a *Saturnalia,* a tragedy entitled *Medea,* fourteen pantomime fables, a book of epigrams, and a work entitled *Catachthonion* (or "Journey to the Underworld"). None of these works survived the late antique period, so Lucan was remembered in Dante's time only as the author of *De bello civili* (also known as the *Pharsalia*), an incomplete epic poem of ten books in hexameters which narrates the history of the war between Julius Caesar and Pompey in fiercely pro-republican and anti-imperial terms. Immensely popular during the Middle Ages, this work was as widely read, studied, and imitated, like Virgil's *Aeneid* and Statius's *Thebaid.*

Dante's enthusiasm for and deep familiarity with Lucan's epic is attested to by the more than fifty quotations, direct references, or allusions scattered throughout his works (e.g., *VN* 25.9; *Conv.* 3.3.7, 3.5.12, 4.11.3, 4.13.12, 4.28.13; *DVE* 1.10.4, 2.6.7; *Mon.* 2.4.6, 2.7.10, 2.8.7–12, 2.9.17; *Epist.* 7.16, 13.63). This debt is especially apparent in the *Commedia,* where Lucan makes a cameo appearance in Limbo as the last member of Dante's *bella scola / di quel signor dell'altissimo canto* ("lovely school of that lord of highest song," *Inf.* 4.94–95), the "lord" being Homer. Lucan is designated as *ultimo* ("last," *Inf.* 4.90) both in the chronological sense—he succeeds Homer (ninth to seventh century B.C.E.), Virgil (70–19 B.C.E.), Horace (65–8 B.C.E.), and Ovid (43 B.C.E.–18 C.E.)—and probably also in a qualitative sense, at least to the degree that Homer was thought by many to be the greatest poet in order of magnitude, Virgil the second greatest (as Homer's Roman successor), Horace the third, and Ovid the fourth. Lucan was considered the last because his epic violates numerous standard Greco-Roman compositional rules. It is built around nearly contemporaneous subject matter (the Roman civil wars had transpired during the past century); it follows a "natural" expository order (beginning *ab ovo,* much like a history book, rather than *in medias res* like the *Aeneid*); and it does not frame the historical events that it describes in terms of the actions of warring gods. This negative value judgment is more apparent than real, because Lucan's position places him closest to the sixth member of Limbo's poetic academy: Dante himself, also an author of a nonstandard epic whose actions also unfold in the historical present.

Lucan's influence is most powerfully felt in the *Inferno* and *Purgatorio.* The lurid descriptions found in *De bello civili* (book 6) of the Thessalian landscape and of an act of conjury performed by the sorceress Erichtho leave their mark on Dante's descriptions of lower Hell and give rise to his extravagant fiction that Virgil had once before embarked on a similar journey: *Ver è ch'altra fiata qua giù fui, / congiurato da quella Eritón cruda / . . . ch'ella mi fece intrar dentr'a quel muro, / per trarne un spirto del cerchio di Giuda* ("It is true that I have been down here once before, conjured by that harsh Erichtho . . . when she made me enter those walls, to bring up a spirit from the circle of Judas," *Inf.* 9.22–30). Similarly, Dante engages in a poetic duel with Lucan in canto 25 of the *Inferno,* claiming that the horrifying descriptions of the deaths of Sabellus and Nasidius (*De bello civili*

9.763–797) are outdone by the metamorphoses undergone by the thieves Cianfa Donati and Agnolo de Brunelleschi (*Inf.* 25.49–78), and by Francesco Guercio de' Cavalcanti and Buoso di Forese Donati (*Inf.* 25.79–138). Perhaps Lucan's most enduring contribution to the *Commedia* comes at the opening of the second canticle, with Dante's portrayal of Cato as guardian of the Ante-Purgatory. Whereas Lucan's protagonists Julius Caesar and Pompey are less heroes than anti-heroes, the Roman poet casts Cato in the role of martyr. Cato embodies the austere virtues of republican Rome and sacrifices his life in the name of freedom. Although Dante's political convictions were decidedly pro-imperial, he borrows Lucan's Cato and transforms him into an emblem of the higher freedom, associated with salvation, that is achieved by the souls who reach the shores of Mount Purgatory.

Bibliography

De Angelis, Violetta. ". . . E l'ultimo Lucano." In Amilcare A. Iannucci (ed.), *Dante e la "bella scola" della poesia: Autorità e sfida poetica.* Ravenna: Longo, 1993, pp. 145–203.

Paratore, Ettore. *Dante e Lucano.* Lectura Dantis Romana. Turin: Società Editrice Internazionale, 1962.

Wetherbee, Winthrop. "'Poeta che mi guidi': Dante, Lucan, and Virgil." In *Canons.* Edited by Robert von Hallberg. Chicago and London: University of Chicago Press, 1984, pp. 131–148.

Jeffrey T. Schnapp

Lucifer

With Dis, Satan, and Beelzebub, Lucifer *(Lucifero)* is one of the four names attributed to the king of Hell. Three—Lucifer, Dis, and Beelzebub—occur once in *Inf.* 34. In addition, Lucifer is also designated by circumlocution: *la creatura ch'ebbe il bel sembiante* ("the creature who had once been beautiful," *Inf.* 34.18), *lo 'mperador de lo doloroso regno* ("the emperor of the dolorous kingdom," 34.28), *vermo reo che 'l mondo fóra* ("the evil worm that gnaws the world," 34.108; see also *Purg.* 12.25–26; *Par.* 9.127–128, 19.46–48, 27.26–27, 29.55–57). In the first line of *Inf.* 34, *Vexilla regis prodeunt inferni* ("The standards of the king of Hell go forth"), parodying a Latin hymn in honor of the Cross and Christ crucified, Virgil refers to Lucifer as "king of Hell." Lucifer is for

CANTO XXXIII.

EXILLA *regis pro-*
deunt inferni
Verſo di noi : però di'nan
Zi mira ,
Diſſe'l Maeſtro mi ; ſe tu'l
diſcerni .
Come quand'una groſſa
nebbia ſpira ,

Dante and Virgil at the center of Hell, from an edition of the
Commedia *published in Brescia in 1487. Reproduced by per-*
mission of the John A. Zahm Dante Collection in the Depart-
ment of Special Collections, University Libraries, University
of Notre Dame.

all eternity planted, thus parodying Christ's cross, in the middle of the frozen lake Cocytus, into which all Hell's rivers flow and which Lucifer himself causes to freeze by endlessly flapping his six batlike wings (*Inf.* 34.49–52).

Created *la somma d'ogni creatura* ("the highest of all creatures," *Par.* 19.47) and nobler than all others (*Purg.* 12.25–26), Lucifer, a seraph angel whose name signifies "light-bearer," is cast down headlong from heaven by the archangel Michael (Isa. 14:12; see also Luke 10:18, 2 Pet. 2:4, Rev. 12:7–9, *Purg.* 12.25–26) for his pride in challenging God: "For thou hast said in thine heart, I will ascend into heaven, I will exalt my throne above the stars of God. . . . Yet thou shalt be brought down to hell, to the sides of the pit" (Isa. 14:13–15,

Inf. 34.35, *Purg.* 12.25–26, *Par.* 19.46–48). In Dante's mythic conception of his fall, Lucifer actually causes both Hell and Purgatory to be created. The surface land that originally covered the Southern Hemisphere retreats to the Northern Hemisphere to avoid any contact with the falling Lucifer, its place being taken by the sea. The internal earth as well recoils from him, creating the abysm of Hell and leaving space for Lucifer to occupy the earth's center, itself rushing to the world's southern surface to form the mass of land that becomes Mount Purgatory (*Inf.* 34.100–132).

In a fitting punishment, Lucifer resides in the nethermost point in the universe, the most remote from God, and at the very center of Judecca, the place where Judas and other betrayers of masters and benefactors are tormented. An antithesis of all he ever was in Heaven before the fall, Lucifer has been turned from "the creature who once was beautiful" (*Inf.* 34.18) into a monster of gigantic proportions and incomparable ugliness. A caricature of his former self, a six-winged seraph hovering at God's throne (Isa. 6:2), Lucifer endlessly flaps his six batlike wings, broader than any ship's sails, thereby engendering the three winds that freeze Cocytus (*Inf.* 34.46–52). Despite having wings, which once moved him around God's throne faster than any other angel (*Par.* 28.98–102), he remains eternally immobile at the center of the frozen lake.

Lucifer is the mirror inverse of God, symbolically reflecting in reverse the divine attributes. The fluttering of his six wings, a form of *spiratio,* a spiration or breathing, is ironic of the life-giving *spiratio* or *processio* of the Holy Spirit from the Father to the Son, according to an eternal mutual exchange and communication that is the Holy Spirit himself. The antithesis of the Trinity, which is presented through the image of three circles with equal circumference and three different colors (*Par.* 33.115–117), Lucifer has one head with three faces of three different colors: the face at the center is vermilion, the right face is between white and yellow, and the left face is black (*Inf.* 34.37–45), perhaps to show that his dominion has spread over the three known parts of the world. The three colors have also been interpreted variously as hatred, impotence, and ignorance; wrath, avarice, and envy; concupiscence, ignorance, and impotence; or, parodying God the Father's power, the Son's wisdom, and the Holy Spirit's love (as inscribed in

LVCIFERO

Dante and Virgil in Judecca. La comedia, *edited by Pietro da Figino, 1491. Giamatti Collection: Courtesy of the Mount Holyoke College Archives and Special Collections.*

Hell's gate, *Inf.* 3.5–6. Lucifer is impotent, speechless, and loveless.

In a grotesque perversion of the two primary functions of the mouth, speaking and eating, Lucifer's three faces eternally cannibalize the three traitors of the two supreme authorities on earth: Judas, who betrayed Christ, founder of the Church; and Brutus and Cassius, whose betrayal and murder of Julius Caesar, the first supreme prince (*Conv.* 4.5.12), represents an act of infamy against the empire.

Engaged as he is in a futile cannibalism that perverts both eating (as an act of physical, spiritual, and intellectual nourishment) and speaking, Lucifer is himself condemned to eternal silence. He is thus the parody of Christ, the Incarnate Word (*Logos* and *Verbum*), as well as of the Trinity. Deprived of speech (the visible manifestation of one's rationality, *DVE* 1.3) and of any other form of external communication, Lucifer gives no sign that he is still a rational being. The text's refusal to respond to any inquiry as to whether Lucifer is endowed with intelligence dramatizes Lucifer's rebellion. Like God, Lucifer is inscrutable, albeit by way of parody and antithesis. In fact, whereas God's inscrutability is an essential attribute of the divinity, the Dantean Lucifer's imperviousness to any satisfactory explanation concerning his rationality becomes the text's signal of his rebellious pride. His cannibalism represents a perversion of the sacrament of the Eucharist, a Christian rite in which Christ offers his body and blood for consummation, as an act of sacrifice that grants the possibility of communion with the divine.

Standing in front of Lucifer, Dante the pilgrim, who has been shielded by Virgil until the latter proclaims *"Ecco Dite"* ("Behold Dis," *Inf.* 34.20), becomes bereft of life and yet he does not die (34.25). "Frozen and hoarse" (34.22), he is thus deprived of what characterizes human beings most uniquely: speech. Finally, the vision of Lucifer causes Dante the pilgrim to experience sin and dread to a greater extent than ever before. In fact, the infernal silence, the frozen waters, and Lucifer's huge mass parody God's creation of the universe and humankind out of the primordial chaos and suggest that pride, hubris, returns everything and everybody to a condition more dreadful and miserable than primordial chaos. Having seen and experienced everything (34.68–69), Virgil, with the pilgrim on his back clasping his neck, climbs down the body of Lucifer. At the very center of the universe, they reverse their position, and, after a brief pause, they begin their climb to the surface of the earth in the Southern Hemisphere, where they finally see the stars (34.139).

Bibliography

Cassell, Anthony K. "The Tomb, the Tower and the Pit: Dante's Satan." *Italica* 56 (1979), 331–351.

Cervigni, Dino S. "The Muted Self-Referentiality of Dante's Lucifer." *Dante Studies* 107 (1989), 45–74.

———. "Dante's Lucifer: The Denial of the Word." *Lectura Dantis: A Forum for Dante Research and Interpretation* 3 (1988), 51–62.

Pagels, Elaine. *The Origin of Satan.* New York: Random House, 1995.

Russell, Jeffrey Burton. *Lucifer: The Devil in the Middle Ages.* Ithaca, N.Y.: Cornell University Press, 1984.

———. *The Devil: Perceptions of Evil from Antiquity to Primitive Christianity.* Ithaca, N.Y.: Cornell University Press, 1977.

Dino Cervigni

Lucilius

Cited in *Conv.* 4.12.8 in a discussion of the evils of riches according to authorities (from Seneca, *Epistulae* 119.9), Lucilius *(Lucillo)* was a friend and correspondent of Lucius Annaeus Seneca and the dedicatee of his *Naturales Quaestiones, De Providentia,* and *Epistulae morales ad Lucilium.*

Leslie Zarker Morgan

Lucretia

Wife of Collatinus, she was raped by Sextus Tarquinius, son of the Roman king. Her subsequent suicide led to a popular uprising and the establishment of the Roman Republic. Dante places Lucretia *(Lucrezia)* among the noble souls of Limbo *(Inf.* 4.128); see also *Par.* 6.41.

Diana Cavuoto Glenn

Lucy, St.

Despite the fact that its chronological precedence has been recently challenged, the tradition of St. Lucy as patron of sight indeed predates the *Commedia:* Lucy's very name, *Lucia,* meaning "light," immediately suggested the connection; her feast day of December 13 was the darkest day in the Julian calendar; and she was and is often depicted with a lamp or with two eyes on a platter. Her association with sight is made, for example, by Pietro da Eboli (c. 1150–1221) in one of the most widely distributed texts of the Middle Ages, *De balneis puteolanis (The Spas of Pozzuoli),* where he describes the *Balneum Sanctae Luciae* ("Spa of St. Lucy") as curative of eye diseases; the spa's construction and nomenclature predate Pietro's description by some years or even centuries.

Although in the original martyrologies Lucy dies from a sword thrust to her throat, fourteenth-century hagiographers concocted an absurd tale "reexplaining" her iconography: to destroy her own beauty and thus permanently safeguard her chastity, she gouged out her eyes with a butcher knife and sent them on a salver to an unwanted suitor.

Lucy appears first in *Inf.* 2.100 in Virgil's account of his commissioning as the pilgrim's guide by a chain of heavenly grace: Lucy descends to Beatrice asking succor for Dante. In *Purg.* 9, the Wayfarer dreams that an eagle has carried him up, Ganymede-like, to the sphere of fire, but as Virgil reveals, in reality St. Lucy has borne him up sleeping to the Gate of Purgatory. Verses 136–138 of *Par.* 32 elucidate Lucy's earlier efforts on the Wayfarer's behalf. Just as in his prophetic dream she was the sharp-eyed eagle who alone can stare at

the sun, she now sits opposite Adam in the Heavenly Rose gazing upward at God; the Wayfarer's sins and "falling down" (in *Inf.* 1.61) are revealed in synechdoche as one with the lowering of his own eyes: *[E] contro al maggior padre di famiglia / siede Lucia, che mosse la tua donna / quando chinavi, a rovinar, le ciglia* ("And opposite that greatest paterfamilias sits Lucy, who sent your Lady when you bent your brow [eyelids] to fall," *Par.* 32.137–39).

That Lucia was Dante's patron saint is a commonplace of commentators beginning with Graziolo de' Bambaglioli (1324): *Beata Lucia, in qua ipse Dantes tempore vite sue habuit maximam devotionem* ("Saint Lucy to whom during his life Dante bore the greatest devotion," ed. Fiammazzo, p. 13). In his *Espositiones* (ed. Cioffari, p. 49), Guido da Pisa interprets Lucy as that prevenient and illuminating grace that enlightened the blinded, then converted, St. Paul on the road to Damascus. The tradition uniting Lucy with Dante's problems with his eyes builds partially on Dante's references to his eyes in his minor works. In *VN* 37–39, the *vanitade* of his eyes is probably not merely a disease but a metaphor of Dante's inconstancy in transferring his attentions from Beatrice to the *donna gentile.* The fact that his eyes should be the organ of sin reflects the tradition that sensuality is biblically "the lust of the eyes." In *Conv.* 3.9.15–16, physical eyestrain is unquestionable, although we cannot rule out further intention or interpretation. That Dante uses the classical vatic and bardic flaw of blindness to bolster his authorial authority cannot be discounted: it connects him to the blind Homer, whom Virgil hails in *Inf.* 4.88 as *"poeta sovrano,"* supreme poet among the lofty geniuses of the Noble Castle in Limbo.

The sight-imagery that consistently surrounds Lucy in the *Commedia* emphasizes that she is, in the allegorical-symbolic sense of the poem, an image of the light of grace "given freely" by God.

Bibliography

Cassell, Anthony K. "Santa Lucia as Patroness of Sight: Hagiography, Iconography, and Dante." *Dante Studies* 109 (1991), 71–88.

Graziolo de' Bambaglioli. *Il commento più antico e la più antica versione latina dell'Inferno di Dante.* Edited by Antonio Fiammazzo. Udine: Doretti, 1892.

Guido da Pisa. *Expositiones et glose super Comediam Dantis;* or, *Commentary on Dante's*

Inferno. Edited by Vincenzo Cioffari. Albany: State University of New York Press, 1974.

Anthony K. Cassell

Luke, St.

Luke the Evangelist *(Luca),* the author of the third Gospel and of Acts, and the companion of Paul. Born in Antioch in Syria, he was a gentile physician and a patron of doctors and artists. In the mystical procession in the Terrestrial Paradise, Luke is represented twice by his writings: his Gospel appears as one of the four beasts surrounding the chariot and the griffin, crowned with green, the color of hope (*Purg.* 29.92); the Acts of the Apostles appear as a venerable elder, a physician, "a familiar of . . . Hippocrates" (*Purg.* 29.133–138). In *Epist.* 7.14 he is referred to by his conventional symbolic identity as an ox (*bos noster evangelizans,* "our evangelizing ox"). He is mentioned or referred to throughout Dante's works: *Purg.* 21.7; *Conv.* 4.5.8, 4.17.10, 4.23.11; *Mon.* 1.16.2 (*scriba mansuetudinis Cristi,* "the evangelist of Christ's gentleness"), 2.8.14, 2.10.6, 2.11.6, 3.9.1, 3.9.19, 3.10.14; *Fiore* 5.13.

The Gospel of Luke is quoted in *Purg.* 10.40 (Luke 1:28), 10.44 (Luke 1:38), 18.100 (Luke 1:39), 20.136 (Luke 2:14), 25.128 (Luke 1:34), 29.85–87 (Luke 1:42); *Par.* 3.121–122 (Luke 1:28), 16.34 (Luke 1:28), 32.95 (Luke 1:28); *Conv.* 4.11.6 (Luke 16:9), 4.17.10 (Luke 10:38ff.), 4.23.11 (Luke 23:44); *Mon.* 1.4.3 (Luke 2:14, 24:36), 3.9.1ff. (Luke 22); and *Epist.* 7.7 (Luke 7:19). The Acts of the Apostles are quoted in *Conv.* 4.20.3 (Acts 10:34), *Mon.* 3.9.19 (Acts 1:1), 3.12.5 (Acts 25:10, 27:24, 28:19); and *Epist.* 5.14 (Acts 9:5).

R. A. Malagi

Lustful, The

One of the seven capital sins, and the least grave sin in Dante's penal system, lust *(lussuria)* characterizes a group of sinners in Hell and a group of penitent in Purgatory. The lustful in Hell are located in the second circle and constitute the first sinners guilty of personal sin. In ordering the moral system of Hell, Dante follows the tripartite categories of sin put forth by Aristotle in his *Nicomachean Ethics* (7.1.1145a), the authority to which Virgil refers in his explanation of the structure of Hell in *Inf.* 11.81–83: *le tre disposizion che 'l ciel non vole, / incontinenza, malizia e la matta bestialitade* ("the three dispositions that Heaven refuses: incontinence, malice, and mad bestiality"). In placing the lustful above the wrathful of the fifth circle, however, Dante differs from Aristotle, who considered anger to be less an affront than lust, gluttony, and avarice. He also diverges from dominant Christian thought. For an important theological perspective, see Aquinas, in particular *De vitio luxuriae* (2.2.153–154).

The souls condemned for lust are punished by darkness and the relentless beating of tempestuous winds. The stormy atmosphere actualizes the passionate emotions which buffeted them in their earthly lives. Woeful laments fill the air, in contrast to the sweet, amorous words the lovers spoke on earth. Lust is a sin of the flesh; like all sins, it constitutes a perversion of love, as Virgil explains in *Purg.* 17. In both the *Inferno* and the *Purgatorio,* lust is formally conceived as an excess of a natural human desire deriving from an improper inversion of appetite over reason that results in an act contrary to reason. Dante specifically defines the lustful as *i peccator carnali, / che la ragion sommettono al talento* ("the carnal sinners, who subject their reason to their lust," *Inf.* 5.38–39). *Inf.* 5 is often called the canto of the queens, for

Dante among the lustful in the second circle of Hell. La comedia di Dante Aligieri, with commentary by Alessandro Vellutello, published by Francesco Marcolini, Venice, 1544. Giamatti Collection: Courtesy of the Mount Holyoke College Archives and Special Collections.

the gathering of the lustful includes Semiramis, Dido, Cleopatra (who is called *lussurïosa,* 63), and Helen, as well as Achilles, Paris, Tristan, and Paolo and Francesca da Rimini. The presence of so many rulers draws politics into the realm of erotics; these figures disastrously neglected their civic duty to attend to their amorous affairs.

The substance of the poet's treatment of lust unfolds through his conversation with Francesca, who is condemned for adultery with her brother-in-law. The female of the couple speaks, in an inversion of convention and of the accepted natural power structure in which the man was the head of the union. Eternally united with her lover, Francesca recounts how she and Paolo fell in love while reading the story of Guinevere and Lancelot. In her reasoning, the book becomes the Gallehaut or go-between which seduces them to their infernal end. Upon hearing the story, the pilgrim faints out of pity; however, the poet implies, in the famous line *quel giorno più non vi leggemmo avante* ("that day we read there no further," *Inf.* 5.138), that the fault lies not in the text but in the readers, who failed to recognize and take responsibility for the wider implications of their intimate actions. Indeed, finishing the book might have shown them the disastrous consequences of adultery, for the love affair of Guinevere and Lancelot leads ultimately to the death of Arthur and the destruction of his court.

It should be noted that in Hell the sin of sodomy is classified as violence against God and nature (*Inf.* 15–16), and the sins of seduction and pandering as fraud (*Inf.* 18).

In Purgatory, Dante groups together the lustful and the sodomites. These penitent shades are purged of their excessive and illicit desires on the seventh and final terrace (*Purg.* 25.109–27.57). As they walk through fires, they sing *Summae Deus clementiae,* a hymn which asks God's help in overcoming temptations of the flesh. In keeping with the didactic structure of Purgatory, they recite examples of chastity and lust. One group of penitents lauds the virtue of chastity by evoking the Virgin Mary and Diana, the goddess of chastity, along with chaste wives and husbands (*Purg.* 25.112–139). Another group of souls remembers the cities and sins of Sodom and Gomorrah, and yet another the bestial appetite of Pasiphae, who hid inside the image of a cow in order to mate with a bull. The groups circle in opposite directions, and when they meet, they greet each other with brief

kisses, a demonstration that they are practicing the proper restraint in the expression of affection. Among the repentants Dante encounters the poets Guido Guinizzelli and Arnaut Daniel, who speaks in Provençal. In this significant metaliterary encounter, Dante offers a critique of the *dolce stil nuovo,* the poetic school which Dante names (*Purg.* 24.57) and of which Guinizzelli was the progenitor, as well as of his own poetic and amorous endeavors in the *Vita Nuova.*

In contrast to the lustful shades, the blessed souls of earthly lovers who overcame lust are found in Paradise, in the realm of Venus, the goddess of love (*Par.* 9 and 10). Here Dante encounters Cunizza da Romano, who glories in her devotion to Venus; Folco, a troubadour love poet who later became a monk and bishop; and Rahab, the biblical prostitute (*Par.* 9).

For specific uses of the term *lussuria* in the *Commedia,* see *Inf.* 5.55; 5.63 *(lussurïosa)*; *Purg.* 7.102, in reference to King Wenceslaus II *(Vincislao)*; *Purg.* 26.42; and *Par.* 19.125, in reference to Ferdinand IV of Castile and Wenceslaus II. See also *Rime* 83.33; *Conv.* 4.6.19 and 4.9.7 *(lussuriare).*

Virginia Jewiss

Lycurgus

King of Nemea in Greece and father of Archemorus; mentioned by Dante in a simile expressing the poet's desire to rush to embrace Guinizzelli (*Purg.* 26.94–96). Archemorus was bitten by a snake and died while Hypsipyle, the king's slave entrusted with his care, told the seven Greek princes who were marching against Thebes the story of her life and capture. Overcome by wrath and anger (*tristizia, Purg.* 26.94) at the death of his son, Lycurgus (*Licurgo*) decided to put the slave to death in retribution, but he was forestalled by the arrival of Hypsipyle's two sons, who rushed to embrace her. Statius relates the story in *Theb.* 4.739–5.753.

Frank B. Ordiway

Lyric Poetry (Dante's)

The corpus of Dante's lyric poetry includes both lyrics that he wrote individually but eventually commandeered for a larger enterprise (e.g., the thirty-one poems that he set into the prose frame of the *Vita Nuova,* and the three poems whose glosses serve as points of departure for three books of the *Convivio*) and lyrics that he left as individual compositions. These latter poems, never pressed into the service of an overarching project or ordered among themselves in any way (although there are inherent groupings of linked or clustered poems, such as the *tenzone* with Forese Donati and the *rime petrose*), are referred to by scholars as the *Rime*. The twentieth century has produced three great editions of Dante's lyrics, each magisterial in its own way. Michele Barbi laid the philological foundation for modern study of the *Rime* in the 1921 edition prepared for the *Opere di Dante* sponsored by the Società Dantesca Italiana. Barbi's commentary was published after his death in two volumes prepared and updated by other scholars: *Rime della 'Vita Nuova' e della giovinezza* in 1956, with Francesco Maggini; and *Rime della maturità e dell'esilio* in 1969, with Vincenzo Pernicone. Gianfranco Contini's *Rime* of 1946 remains unsurpassed for the pithiness and elegance of its formulations (many of which have been copied in recent Italian paperback editions). Particularly useful for its comprehensiveness and for the clarity of the portrait that emerges of the early Italian lyric schools is the edition of Kenelm Foster and Patrick Boyde, *Dante's Lyric Poetry* (1967). While the Barbi-Maggini-Pernicone and Foster-Boyde editions include the poems later included in the *Vita Nuova* and *Convivio,* the Contini edition does not. There are decisive advantages to printing all of Dante's lyric corpus together: not only does it remind us that the poems of the *Vita Nuova* were written prior to insertion in the *libello,* and free of the agenda of the *libello,* but it also allows us to track the stylistic and thematic continuities among the poems chosen for inclusion and those rejected.

In fact, Dante's *Rime* offer a kind of window onto the poet's workshop: they testify to the paths not taken, and they help us see more freshly and vividly when, how, and by what slow process of accretion Dante embarked on the paths he did take. This wonderful collection of eighty-nine poems of definite attribution—sonnets, *ballate,* and *canzoni*—was written over a span of approximately twenty-five years (from c. 1283 to c. 1307–1308), that is, from Dante's teens to after the *Inferno* was already begun. The *Rime* embody the essence of Dante as a poetic adventurer; they remind us that Dante's hallmark as a poet is his never-ceasing experimentalism, his linguistic and stylistic variety.

Because the poems vary so greatly among themselves, editors have found it convenient to order them under rough chronological headings, as follows: very early poems written in the Tuscan manner (e.g., the *tenzone* with Dante da Maiano); early poems experimenting in a variety of manners, from the Sicilian (e.g., the *canzone* "La dispietata mente"), to the playful realism associated with Folgòre da San Gimignano (e.g., the sonnet "Sonar bracchetti"), to the light strains of the Cavalcantian *ballata* (e.g., the *ballata* "Per una ghirlandetta"); poems of the time of the *Vita Nuova,* and—whether or not included in the *libello*—written in the style we associate with the *stil novo* (a style that includes, for instance, the love poems dedicated in the *Convivio* to, but in my opinion not originally written for, Lady Philosophy). Throughout the *stil novo* phase, Dante's poetic agenda is, as Foster and Boyde point out, one of contraction and refinement: former lexical and stylistic choices are eliminated to achieve the refined purity of the high *stil novo.*

The phase of contraction gives way around 1295 to the expansion, both lexical and stylistic, that will characterize the rest of Dante's poetic career. This is pioneered in the following groups of lyrics: the *tenzone* with Forese Donati, written before Forese's death in 1296; the so-called *rime petrose,* or "stony" poems, about a stony, hard, ice-cold lady, *la pietra,* dated internally by "Io son venuto" to December of 1296; moral and doctrinal verse, written most likely between 1295 and 1300, such as the *canzone* on true nobility, "Le dolci rime," and the *canzone* on the esteemed courtly quality of *leggiadria,* "Poscia ch'Amor." Finally, there are the great lyrics that belong to the period of Dante's exile: the *canzone* that treats Dante's own exile, "Tre donne"; powerful late moral verse, such as the *canzone* on avarice, "Doglia mi reca"; and late love poetry, such as the correspondence sonnets exchanged with Cino da Pistoia and the *canzone* "Amor, da che convien."

The *Rime* contain the traces of Dante's stylistic and ideological experimentation. The *tenzone* of scurrilous sonnets exchanged between Dante and his friend Forese Donati, for instance, was long denied a place in Dante's canon because of its vulgar content, considered inappropriate for the "virginal" poet of the *Vita Nuova;* and yet, without it, we would be hard put to trace the passage from the tightly circumscribed world of the *libello* to the all-inclusive cosmos of the *Commedia.* Nor does the *tenzone*'s lowly content obscure the archetypal signs of Dante's poetic mastery, evidenced by the compact vigor and concise force of his diction, and by the effortless energy with which one insult springs from another. Whereas Forese requires a full sonnet to accuse Dante of being a bounder who lives off the charity of others, Dante characteristically packs an insult into each verse of the opening quatrain of "Bicci novel," which tells Forese that (1) he is a bastard, (2) his mother is dishonored, (3) he is a glutton, and (4) to support his gluttony he is a thief: *Bicci novel, figliuol di non so cui / (s'i' non ne domandasse monna Tessa), / giù per la gola tanta roba hai messa, / ch'a forza ti convien torre l'altrui* ("Young Bicci, son of I don't know who [short of asking my lady Tessa], you've stuffed so much down your gorge that you're driven to take from others," 77.1–4). Stylistically, as the example of "Bicci novel" makes clear, the *Rime* demonstrate continuities converging in the *Commedia:* thus, we can discern in the *tenzone* with Forese the seeds of a later vulgar and realistic style associated with the *Inferno.* Ideologically, however, the *Rime* offer fascinating examples of discontinuities: thus, the early and generically stilnovist *canzoni* "E' m'incresce di me" and "Lo doloroso amor" testify to the possibility of an anti-*Vita Nuova,* a Cavalcantian *Vita Nuova,* whose Beatrice brings not life but death. In "Lo doloroso amor" Dante declares, *Per quella moro c'ha nome Beatrice* ("Through her I die, whose name is Beatrice," 68.14)—a scandalous enough assertion for a poet whose career is predicated on the notion that "Through her I live, whose name is Beatrice." And in "E' m'incresce di me," the birth of a lady who possesses *occhi micidiali* ("death-dealing eyes," 67.49) is described in language resonant of the *Vita Nuova: Lo giorno che costei nel mondo venne, / secondo che si trova / nel libro de la mente che vien meno, / la mia persona pargola sostenne / una passïon nova, / tal ch'io rimasi di paura pieno* ("The day that this lady came into the world—as I find it written in the book of the mind that is passing away—my childish body felt a strange emotion so that I was filled with fear," 57–62). From the perspective of the *Vita Nuova* or the *Commedia,* where Cavalcanti has been ideologically discounted, what we find in this canzone is an impossible hybrid, a fusion of elements that in the more canonical texts are kept separate. There are elements typical of the *Vita Nuova:* the treatment of Beatrice's presence, in this

case her birth, as a historically and literally miraculous event; the reference to the protagonist's "book of memory," in which the events of his life have been recorded; his juvenile susceptibility to a *passïon* defined as *nova,* that is, miraculous, unexpected, totally new. But these elements are joined, as they would not be in the *Vita Nuova,* to Cavalcantian stylemes: the book of his mind is passing away, failing, dying, while the *passïon nova* fills the lover with that most Cavalcantian of emotions, fear.

The *Rime* allow us to balance an uncensored version of Dante's poetic development with the ideologically corrected version that Dante's completed texts offer us. For instance, the lyrics in the *Vita Nuova* are chosen with an eye to telling the story of the lover's development, his gradual realization of Beatrice's sacramental significance as a visible sign of invisible grace. At the same time, they also tell an idealized story of the poet's development, tracing Dante's lyric itinerary from his early Guittonianism (see the double sonnets, a Guittonian form, of chapters 7 and 8), through his Cavalcantianism (see the sonnet that begins with the hapax *Cavalcando* in chapter 9; the *ballata*—Cavalcanti's form par excellence—of chapter 12; and the Cavalcantian torments of the sonnets in chapters 14–16), to the discovery—with some help from Guido Guinizzelli—of his own voice in the canzone "Donne ch'avete intelletto d'amore" in chapter 19. The implication of the story told by the *Vita Nuova* is that Guittone and Cavalcanti had been utilized and liquidated by Dante early in his poetic career, never again to function as important influences on his verse; this story is then rendered canonical in the *Commedia,* where Guittone is openly denigrated and Guinizzelli absorbs much of the credit due to Cavalcanti as the primary stylist of the *stil novo.* Yet the *Rime* tell a very different tale: elements of the poetry of the dismissed precursor, Guittone d'Arezzo, reappear in Dante's late moral lyrics, and the supposedly superseded Cavalcanti is present as late as Dante's last *canzone,* "Amor, da che convien."

Thus, Dante cannot be pigeonholed, even by himself. His lyrics are salutary reminders that the dialectical twists of his itinerary cannot be flattened into a straightforward progress. After the *Vita Nuova,* written most likely from 1292 to 1294, we encounter the haunting eroticism and desperate passion of the *rime petrose,* poems that offer a template for the dance of desire—of motion

Title page of a collection of lyrics published in Venice in 1532. Reproduced by permission of the John A. Zahm Dante Collection in the Department of Special Collections, University Libraries, University of Notre Dame.

versus stasis—in the unmoving stone that must be moved, in the *pietra* as the icon of inert unmoving "death" that is unresponsive to the lover's turgid, pressing, all-too-living need. The *petrosa* "Io son venuto" enacts love as death, Eros as Thanatos. For, if the *canzone*'s strophes ring out changes on the topos "it is winter, i.e., death, and yet I love, i.e., live," their rhetoric accomplishes an inversion, whereby the natural death of winter lives and "true" death, so to speak, is associated with the lover. All the pulsating, vibrant verbs of life belong to the dead natural world of the first part of each strophe; when we shift to engage the "I" in the conclusion of each strophe, the living language gives way to the passive static verbs that qualify the lover, whose life/love is more dead than the death of winter.

Nor should we forget the sonnet to Cino da Pistoia, written most likely between 1303 and 1306, and thus a decade or so after the spiritualized love of the *Vita Nuova*. Here Dante characterizes love as a dominating force that controls reason and free will, and he admits to having first experienced such love in his ninth year, that is, vis-à-vis Beatrice: *Io sono stato con Amore insieme / da la circulazione del sol mia nona, / e so com'egli affrena e come sprona, / e come sotto lui si ride e geme* ("I have been together with Love since my ninth revolution of the sun, and I know how he curbs and spurs, and how under his sway one laughs and groans," 111.1–4). As Foster and Boyde comment: "This is the more remarkable in that Dante is now about forty years old and has behind him not only the *Vita Nuova* with its story of an entirely sublimated 'heavenly' love, but also the series of *canzoni* that more or less directly celebrated a love that had its seat in the mind of the intellect" (2: 323). By the same token, Dante's last *canzone* is no tribute to sublimation: "Amor, da che convien pur ch'io mi doglia" is, as the incipit suggests, a Cavalcantian testament to deadly Eros. In this poem, known as the *canzone montanina* because the lover finds himself in the mountains of the Casentino, love works him over, kneading him, reducing him to a pulp: *Così m'hai concio, Amore, in mezzo l'alpi, / ne la valle del fiume / lungo il qual sempre sopra me se' forte: / qui vivo e morto, come vuoi, mi palpi* ("To this state, Love, you have reduced me, among the mountains, in that river's valley along whose banks you have always been powerful over me: here, just as you will, you knead me, both dead and alive," 116.61–64). Does desire control us or do we control it? This question, which runs through Dante's lyric production and is of overriding importance to him, will ultimately require the larger meditational field of the *Commedia* for its resolution. But there are already among the *Rime* poems that frame this issue in a philosophical manner that portends the later work. Chief among these is the *canzone* "Doglia mi reca ne lo core ardire," whose indictment of passion ungoverned by reason inhabits a moral framework that is highly suggestive vis-à-vis the *Commedia*. Commonly referred to as Dante's poem on avarice, "Doglia mi reca" is in fact much more; by grafting a discourse on avarice onto an anti-courtly premise, the *canzone* is an indictment of all forms of misplaced desire. In verses whose irascible energy adumbrates the *Commedia*, Dante depicts the "mad desire" *(folle volere)* that induces a man to run after that which can never afford him satisfaction: *Corre l'avaro, ma più fugge pace: / oh mente cieca, che non pò vedere / lo suo folle volere / che 'l numero, ch'ognora a passar bada, / che 'nfinito vaneggia!*

/ *Ecco giunta colei che ne pareggia:* / *dimmi, che hai tu fatto,* / *cieco avaro disfatto?* / *Rispondimi, se puoi, altro che "Nulla."* / *Maladetta tua culla,* / *che lusingò cotanti sonni invano!* / *Maladetto 'l tuo perduto pane,* / *che non si perde al cane!* / *ché da sera e da mane* / *hai raunato e stretto ad ambo mano* / *ciò che sì tosto si rifà lontano* ("The miser runs, only to be ever further away from peace. O blinded mind, for its insane desire cannot see that the sum which every moment it strives to pass stretches on to empty infinity! See, the one who makes us all equal has come. Tell me, what have you done, blind, undone miser? Answer me—if you can—other than 'Nothing.' Cursed be your cradle which beguiled so many dreams in vain; cursed be the bread you've wasted, that's not wasted on a dog; for evening and morning you have gathered and hoarded with both hands that which so quickly slips from your grasp," 106.69–84). The force and vitality of this passage alert us to the fact that Dante has here tapped into a wellspring of his poetic identity. Indeed, the same miser recurs in *Conv.* 3.15.9, where Dante inveighs against the *avaro maladetto* ("cursed miser"), and he will ultimately surface as the insatiably concupiscent she-wolf of *Inf.* 1. The miser is a figure through whom Dante explores the possibility of expanding the problematic of desire from the courtly and private to the social and public; from this perspective, the *avaro maladetto* of "Doglia mi reca" and the contemporaneous *Convivio* is an emblem of the transition from the enclosed, private courtly world of the *Vita Nuova* to the wide-open, public world of the *Commedia*. The lyrics of Dante's maturity are important steps in his moving toward an ever greater engagement with the social and political and toward a poetic identity that is committed to dealing with the problems of humanity as a whole. Dante's poem of exile, "Tre donne intorno al cor mi son venute" (104), which handles the most intimate and personal tragedy of his life, his exile from Florence, focuses on three allegorical ladies who are also exiled and homeless—Justice and her progeny—thus shifting the locus of concern from the poet's own tragedy to that of all humans inhabiting an unjust world.

In a sonnet addressed to his friend and fellow poet Cino da Pistoia, Dante bids farewell to "this poetry of ours" *(queste nostre rime),* distancing himself from their common enterprise of lyric poetry, and likening himself to a voyager whose ship is headed for deeper waters: *Io mi credea del tutto esser partito* / *da queste nostre rime, messer Cino,* / *ché si conviene omai altro cammino* / *a la mia nave più lungi dal lito* ("I thought, messer Cino, that I had quite abandoned this poetry of ours; for now my ship must hold a different course, being farther from the shore," 114.1–4). This lovely image haunts us with its peculiarly Dantesque sense of self-awareness and transition; the poet knows that he is moving on to new adventures. It also brings us back to Dante the poetic adventurer, and to the *Rime* as the embodiment of that spirit. For, although Dante's lyrics are sometimes valued less than the more monotonal and homogeneous productions of a Cavalcanti or a Petrarch, it is precisely their variety that is the key to Dante's greatness; they are the worthy and necessary prerequisites for a work as infinitely various as the *Commedia.*

Bibliography

Barbi, Michele, and Francesco Maggini (eds.). *Rime della 'Vita Nuova' e della giovinezza.* Florence: Le Monnier, 1956.

Barbi, Michele, and Vincenzo Pernicone (eds.). *Rime della maturità e dell'esilio.* Florence: Le Monnier, 1969.

Barolini, Teodolinda. "Guittone's *Ora parrà,* Dante's *Doglia mi reca,* and the *Commedia*'s Anatomy of Desire." In *Seminario Dantesco Internazionale/International Dante Seminar 1.* Edited by Zygmunt B. Barański. Florence: Le Lettere, 1997, pp. 3–23.

———. *Dante's Poets: Textuality and Truth in the 'Comedy.'* Princeton, N.J.: Princeton University Press, 1984.

Contini, Gianfranco (ed.). *Rime.* 1946. 2nd ed. Milan: Einaudi, 1970.

Boyde, Patrick. *Dante's Style in His Lyric Poetry.* Cambridge: Cambridge University Press, 1971.

Durling, Robert M., and Ronald L. Martinez. *Time and the Crystal: Studies in Dante's 'Rime petrose.'* Berkeley: University of California Press, 1990.

Foster, Kenelm, and Patrick Boyde (eds.). *Dante's Lyric Poetry.* 2 vols. Oxford: Oxford University Press, 1967.

Kleinhenz, Christopher. *The Early Italian Sonnet: The First Century (1220–1321).* Lecce: Milella, 1986.

Teodolinda Barolini

M

Macarius, St.

Macarius does not speak but is declared by St. Benedict to be present among the contemplatives in the Heaven of Saturn alongside Romuald, founder of the Order of Camaldoli or the Reformed Benedictines (*Par.* 22.49). The two figures, whose very names divide the verse into two symmetrical halves, are clearly intended to be emblematic of Eastern and Western monasticism. The Greek adjective *makarios* means "saintly" or "blessed," so it is not surprising that there are several holy men named Macarius among the Desert Fathers. It is, however, probable that Dante was familiar only with the one chronicled by the 13th-century Dominican Jacobus de Voragine in his *Golden Legend.* This account, while mostly apocryphal, nevertheless tends to correspond with what is known of the historical Macarius of Alexandria. This fourth-century Egyptian anchorite and disciple of St. Anthony the Abbot was reputed to have composed a monastic rule, which no doubt explains his pairing with Romuald.

Bibliography

Evelyn-White, Hugh Gerard. *The Monasteries of the Wâdi'n Natrun.* 3 vols. New York: Publications of the Metropolitan Museum of Art, Egyptian Expedition, 1926–1933. Reprint, New York: Arno Press, 1973.

Jacobus, de Voragine. *Legenda aurea. The Golden Legend: Readings on the Saints.* Translated by William Granger Ryan. Princeton, N.J.: Princeton University Press, 1993.

Waddell, Helen. *The Desert Fathers.* London: Constable, 1936.

Anthony Oldcorn

Macaulay, Thomas Babington

Whig politician, essayist, and historian, Macaulay (1800–1859) was the author of the influential five-volume *History of England* (1849–1861), which conceived history in terms of the evolution of the English constitution rather than the actions of great men and events. Long interested in Dante, Macaulay discussed him in many articles he wrote for the influential *Edinburgh Review,* most notably in his "Essay on Milton" (1825) and "Essay on Machiavelli" (1827). Drawn to Dante as a statesman as well as a poet, Macaulay took a historical view, situating him in his time and place. While preferring Milton, Macaulay considered the *Commedia* "the greatest work of imagination which had appeared since the poems of Homer."

Thomas L. Cooksey

Magnanimity

The concept of magnanimity *(magnanimità, magnanimitade)* was reintroduced into western European thought and literature with the rediscovery of Aristotle's writings, in particular his *Ethics* (4.3), where it was regarded as the hallmark of an elite that rightly concerned itself with honor, the greatest of "external goods." Theologians such as Albert the Great and Aquinas did their best to make this pagan, aristocratic virtue consonant with humility, the essential Christian attribute. In his *Summa Theologicae* (2.2.129.3.4), Aquinas claimed that the magnanimous man displays humility in recognizing his own deficiencies while steadfastly refusing to hide under a bushel the outstanding qualities conferred on him by God.

In *Conv.* 1.11, Dante implies that he possesses

M true magnanimity in undertaking the arduous task of writing about philosophy in the Italian vernacular. Again, in *DVE* 2.7.2, he uses *magnanimitatis . . . opera* ("the works of magnanimity") to signify great achievements gained through exemplary prowess. Then, in *Conv.* 4, he gives two very different definitions: one (4.17.5) is purely Aristotelian, whereby magnanimity *è moderatrice e acquistatrice de' grandi onori e fama* ("moderates our desire for great honors and fame"), while a second (4.26.7) makes magnanimity synonymous with the cardinal virtue of fortitude. The same dichotomy had already appeared in Aquinas (*ST* 2.2.128, 129.2, and 129.5) and Brunetto Latini (*Tresor* 2.23 and 2.82). Here, however, magnanimity as fortitude is exemplified by the courage of Virgil's Aeneas in his infernal descent *contra tanti pericoli* ("in the face of so many perils," *Conv.* 4.26.9).

This pregnant parallel impels the reader toward the first of the two occurrences of *magnanimo* in the *Commedia*. In *Inf.* 2.44, the term is applied to Virgil in direct opposition to Dante's pusillanimity, his *viltade . . . la qual molte fiate l'omo ingombra / sì che d'onrata impresa lo rivolve* ("cowardice, which many times so encumbers a man that he turns back from honorable endeavor," 2.45–47). The theme of pusillanimity or *viltade* is then developed in *Inf.* 3—in diametrical contrast to Limbo, where the word "honor" and its derivatives form a sevenfold Aristotelian cluster illustrating the magnanimity of the *spiriti magni* ("the great spirits," 4.119) of the ancient and Islamic worlds.

The second occurrence is found in *Inf.* 10.73, where it is applied to Farinata degli Uberti. Although the Italian text (*quell'altro magnanimo,* "that other great-souled one") may be taken to imply that Farinata and Cavalcante share this quality, it is usually interpreted as a distinguishing mark of the great Ghibelline leader's personality. Just as Dante's pusillanimity had been contrasted with Virgil's magnanimity, so now Farinata's impassive immobility is set off against Cavalcante's physical devastation by his son's supposed death. Farinata *non mutò aspetto, / né mosse collo, né piegò sua costa* ("did not change his expression, nor move his neck, nor bend his side," 10.74–75), his attitude epitomizing the Stoic conception of *magnanimitas* as found, for example, in Cicero and Seneca, and then fused with the Christian virtue of fortitude.

An excess of magnanimity may lead to *praesumptio* (*ST* 2.2.130.2) and *fol hardement* (*Tresor* 2.82.8)—mad, overweening ambition leading to destruction and damnation, as in the case of Ulysses (*Inf.* 26). Excessive self-confidence led Farinata to heresy. Hence, magnanimity's association with pride (Villani, *Cronica* 8.54). Franciscan theologians were especially hostile to this Aristotelian quality, which seemed so irreconcilable with the Christian call to humility. It is therefore all the more remarkable that the saint who appeared to be the very embodiment of humility, the *poverello* ("poor man") from Assisi, should be transformed into an example of magnanimity in *Par.* 11.88–92. There, in contrast to the sources which mention Francis's humble entreaties, Dante emphasizes the saint's lack of *viltà* or pusillanimity in his appeal to the pope: *ma regalmente sua dura intenzione / ad Innocenzio aperse* ("but regally he set forth his harsh intention to Innocent," 91–92)—where Benvenuto glosses "regally, that is to say, magnanimously." This fascination with magnanimity shows how alien the medieval *contemptus mundi* ("contempt of the world") was to Dante the Christian existentialist.

Bibliography

Bosco, Umberto. "Il tema della magnanimità nella *Commedia.*" *L'Alighieri* 15 (1974), 3–13.

Corti, Maria. "Campi semantici mobili: (a) Magnanimità." In *La felicità mentale: nuove prospettive per Cavalcanti e Dante.* Turin: Einaudi, 1983, pp. 44–53.

Forti, Fiorenzo. *Magnanimitade: studi su un tema dantesco.* Bologna: Pàtron, 1977.

———. "Il limbro dantesco e i megalopsicoi." In *Fra le carte dei poeti.* Milan, Naples: Ricciardi, 1965, pp. 9–40.

Gauthier, R. A. *Magnanimità: l'idéal de la grandeur dans la philosophie païenne et dans la théologie chrétienne.* Paris: Vrin, 1951.

Scott, John A. *Dante magnanimo: studi sulla "Commedia."* Florence: Olschki, 1977.

John A. Scott

Malebolge

Malebolge ("evil pouches," or "ditches") is the term coined by Dante (*Inf.* 18.1) to identify the ten concentric ditches of iron-colored stone that constitute the eighth circle of Hell, the circle of simple fraud (*Inf.* 18–30). Sinners condemned to this

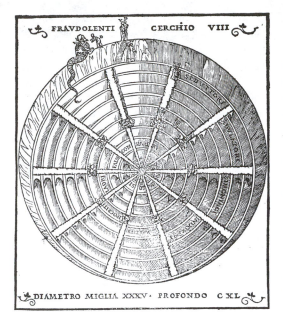

Dante before Geryon at the edge of Malebolge, the eighth circle of Hell. La comedia di Dante Aligieri, *with commentary by Alessandro Vellutello, published by Francesco Marcolini, Venice, 1544. Giamatti Collection: Courtesy of the Mount Holyoke College Archives and Special Collections.*

stone bridges that span the ditch at intervals around its circumference.

Of the thirty-four cantos in the *Inferno,* thirteen are devoted to the eighth circle of Hell, a reminder of the seriousness of fraud within Dante's moral scheme. As Virgil told Dante in his overview of the structure of hell, *perché frode è de l'uom proprio male, / più spiace a Dio* ("because fraud is an evil proper to man, it is more displeasing to God." (*Inf.* 11.25–26). The sinners in the eighth circle, however, are less reviled than those in the ninth and last circle, which contains those who violated the trust placed in them by family, political allies, guests, or benefactors.

Though Dante establishes an architectural unity to Malebolge as a whole, he also provides details that are unique to each bolgia as appropriate to the distinct category of fraudulent sinners assigned to it. Furthermore, there can be no movement from one bolgia to another, either by the sinners or by the demons that punish them. In this way the poet underscores the divisive nature of fraud that breaks down the natural bonds that should hold society together.

As Dante and Virgil walk along the outer bank of the first bolgia they observe two groups of naked sinners moving in opposite directions along the bottom of the ditch and spurred on by horned devils who lash them with whips. The group walking toward Dante and Virgil are pimps, while those moving in the other direction are the shades of the seducers.

In the final thirty-six lines of canto 18 Dante describes the second bolgia, which contains the shades of the flatterers. In one of the crudest episodes in the *Inferno,* Dante describes first the mold-encrusted bolgia itself and, then, the sinners who are submerged in foul-smelling excrement at the bottom of the deep pit. One of these, Thais the whore *(Taide),* is depicted as alternately squatting and standing, and "scratching herself with her shitty nails" (*si graffia con l'unghie merdose,* 18.131).

In the third bolgia (canto 19) Dante finds the simonists, those guilty of selling Church offices for personal gain. Here those who sinned by pocketing money are stuck in "pockets" of stone; the simonists are punished by being buried head first in holes in the floor of the bolgia. Their legs stick out of the holes from the calves up, and flames flicker across the soles of their feet. When Dante notices one shade whose legs quiver more than the others, Virgil carries him down into the bolgia and

circle are guilty of various kinds of fraud, but each of these sins results from an act of malice which the individual sinner has chosen to commit. Dante boldly announces his entrance into this circle in the opening verse of canto 18—*Luogo è in inferno detto Malebolge* ("There is in Hell a place called Malebolge")—so that the canto begins, as it were, part two of *Inferno,* the second of two sets of seventeen cantos (of the total of thirty-four).

Geographically, Malebolge is a microcosm of Hell: an inverted, hollow cone of concentric circles. The eighth circle begins at the foot of the long precipice that descends from the seventh circle and ends at the edge of the deep pit that drops down to the ninth and final circle of Hell. From the base of the precipice, the ten concentric ditches of Malebolge slope down toward the pit at the center of Hell, the circumference of each bolgia being smaller than that of the one above it, so as to resemble an amphitheater in shape.

At the beginning of canto 18 Dante provides an aerial view of Malebolge in which he compares the concentric rings to successive moats surrounding a castle (*Inf.* 18.10–18). And just as the moats are connected to one another by bridges, each bolgia is connected to the next by a series of

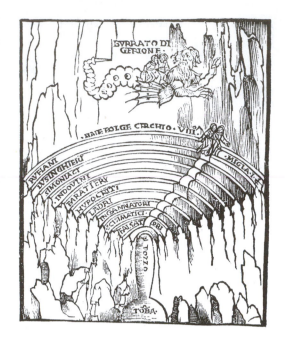

Geryon above Malebolge, from Commedia di Dante, *published by Filippo Giunti, Florence, 1506. Reproduced by permission of the John A. Zahm Dante Collection in the Department of Special Collections, University Libraries, University of Notre Dame.*

to the side of that shade. The sinner identifies himself as Pope Nicholas III, and predicts that two other popes, Boniface VIII and Clement V, will soon join him in his hole.

After Virgil carries him to the summit of the bridge over the fourth bolgia, Dante observes the shades of the sorcerers and soothsayers (canto 20). For their attempt to see into the future they are punished by having their heads twisted 180 degrees on their bodies, so that they are forced to walk backwards.

From the slow and somber mood of the fourth bolgia the pace shifts suddenly to the frenetic action of the fifth bolgia (cantos 21–23.57), where Dante is startled by a black, winged devil who rushes onto the bridge with a sinner slung over his shoulder, then hurls the shade into the bolgia, whose sides and bottom are lined with thick, boiling pitch. In the bolgia itself the shades, who are guilty of barratry, or political graft, are forced to hide beneath the surface of the pitch to avoid being slashed by the long grappling hooks of the guardian devils, known as the Malebranche ("Evil Claws"). In this, the longest episode in Malebolge, sinners and devils play out a constant farcical game of trickery and deception. Even Dante and

Virgil become caught up in the game when Malacoda, the leader of the Malebranche, lies to them by sending a troop of devils to accompany the wayfarers to the next bridge, when in fact the next bridge is broken (as are all the bridges over the sixth bolgia). In a final comic touch, Dante and his guide must scramble down the outer bank of the sixth bolgia to escape the devils who pursue them.

The pace slows again when Dante and Virgil see, in the sixth bolgia, the plodding movement of the weeping hypocrites (23. 58–end), who resemble monks because of the cloaks they wear. The cloaks, however, are an image of the sin itself; gilded and dazzling on the outside, they are lined with lead, forcing the shades to shuffle around the bolgia at a snail's pace.

The seventh bolgia (cantos 24–25) is filled with a great variety of serpents who torment the shades of the thieves. The poet portrays a bizarre series of various kinds of metamorphoses that the sinners undergo: some shades, bitten by serpents, are reduced to ashes and then are restored to their human form; others exchange their forms with serpents who suddenly attack them.

In the eighth bolgia (cantos 26–27) the shades are concealed within flames that move along the floor of the ditch. Here Dante encounters two noble figures, the Greek hero Ulysses (26) and a contemporary military leader turned Franciscan friar, Guido da Montefeltro (27). Though Guido's sin is identified as *consiglio frodolente* ("fraudulent counsel," 27.116), there has been widespread disagreement among scholars as to the precise nature of Ulysses' sin. In canto 11, when Virgil lists the sins of the various circles of hell, he identifies the precise sin in only eight of the ten bolge. The sins in the two remaining bolge (eight and nine) are identified only as *simile lordura* ("like filth," 11.60).

The enigmatic and eloquent Ulysses, who tells the story of his daring but ill-fated journey after the Trojan war, is one of the most extensively analyzed figures in the entire *Commedia,* while the episode of Guido da Montefeltro was made famous among English-language readers by T. S. Eliot, who used lines 61–66 of canto 27 as the epigraph to "The Love Song of J. Alfred Prufrock."

The ninth bolgia (canto 28) contains the shades of the schismatics. These sowers of discord who divided the religious and political institutions of their times are punished by having their shade-bodies split apart by a sword-wielding devil each time they complete a journey around the bolgia.

The monster Geryon. Invenzioni di Giovanni Flaxman sulla Divina commedia, *illustrated by John Flaxman and Beniamino del Vecchio, Rome, 1826. Giamatti Collection: Courtesy of the Mount Holyoke College Archives and Special Collections.*

In the tenth and last bolgia (cantos 29–30) four groups of falsifiers are punished: alchemists (falsifiers of metals), falsifiers of persons, counterfeiters, and liars. Unlike all the other sinners in the Malebolge, whose torments are inflicted by an external source, the falsifiers are racked with disease. The alchemists suffer from leprosy, the falsifiers of persons are mentally deranged and run around the ditch like mad animals, the counterfeiters suffer from dropsy (which swells their bodies to grotesque proportions), and the liars are tormented by a raging fever which makes them stink.

Here, in the lowest of the ten bolge, the predominant imagery of disease suggests the corrosive nature of all the sins of fraud, sins which corrupt the "body politic" from within. Fraud, in other words, is a disease that eats away at the bonds of trust without which a healthy society cannot function. The lies and deceptions depicted in Malebolge make a mockery of the natural bonds of human relationships and turn society into a stony jungle in which cooperation and trust are replaced by self-serving exploitation of others.

Bibliography

Bonora, Ettore. "Gli ipocriti di Malebolge." In *Interpretazioni dantesche.* Modena: Mucchi, 1988, pp. 67–96.

Durling, Robert M. "Deceit and Digestion in the Belly of Hell." In *Allegory and Representation. Selected Papers from the English Institute, 1979, New Series, No. 5.* Edited by Stephen J. Greenblatt. Baltimore, London: Johns Hopkins University Press, 1981, pp. 61–93.

Ferrante, Joan M. "Malebolge (*Inf.* XVIII–XXX) as the Key to the Structure of Dante's *Inferno.*" *Romance Philology* 20 (1967), 456–466.

Muresu, Gabriele. "I ladri di Malebolge *(Inferno* XXIV–XXV)." In *I ladri di Malebolge: Saggi di semantica dantesca.* Rome: Bulzoni, 1990, pp. 9–50.

Sanguineti, Edoardo. *Interpretazione di Malebolge.* Florence: Olschki, 1961.

Tuscano, Pasquale. "Le Malebolge: dai seduttori ai ladri (*Inf.,* canti XVIII–XXV)." In *Dal vero al certo. Indagini e letture dantesche.* Naples: Edizioni Scientifiche Italiane, 1989, pp. 37–74.

Lawrence Baldassaro

M

Malice

Virgil twice employs the word malice *(malizia)* when expounding the plan of Hell in *Inf.* 11. He does so first in lines 22–26, where he defines the nature of malice and its relation to violence and fraud; he does so again in lines 79–83, where he maintains that malice is more culpable than incontinence.

In *Inf.* 11.22–26 malice is said to be hated on high *(odio in cielo acquista)* and to have *ingiuria* (injustice) for its end *(fine);* this unjust end afflicts others *(altrui contrista)* by means of either violence *(forza)* or of fraud *(frode)*. Malice here is to be understood not as action but as a disposition *(disposizion),* just as it is by Aristotle and in lines 81–82 of this same canto, and thus will malice be seen as an iniquitous tendency that aims at and results in unjust activity forcefully or deceitfully committed and harmful to its victims.

Now when Virgil accounts *malizia* in 11.79–83 one of the "three dispositions that Heaven refuses" *(le tre disposizion che 'l ciel non vole),* he specifies *incontenenza* (incontinence) and *la matta bestialitade* (mad bestiality) as the other two. The guide, in the process of impatiently replying to his puzzled pupil's query as to why incontinent wrongdoers are located higher in hell, are deemed less blameworthy, and are punished less severely than the violent and fraudulent damned, urges him to recall "your Ethics." The allusion is to Aristotle's *Nicomachaean Ethics,* and not in the unavailable Greek original but rather in the Latin translation familiar to Dante, wherein the habits to be shunned *(mores fugiendorum)* correspond to Virgil's three dispositions, namely *malitia, incontinentia et bestialitas.* For Aristotle the least bad is incontinence (7.1.1145a15); and further along he argues that the incontinent, because they do not act with malice aforethought, are carried away though not blinded by passion, and for having good purposes and principles are only half-wicked, are less reprehensible than malicious transgressors (7.10.1152a and *passim*).

Verses 82–83 raise the problem of what *matta bestialitade* is and where, if anywhere, it is to be found in the regions of hell. While it has been equated with heresy in circle 6 (by Ferretti) and with treachery in circle 9 (by Triolo), the solution adopted by the majority of the commentators has been to equate it with the violence of circle 7. This move, though, involves Virgil in a glaring inconsistency. Although he had previously included under *malizia* all the violent and fraudulent sins punished in the three lowest circles, now, a mere sixty lines later, he implicitly connects fraud alone with malice and puts violence into a new category, so that the *forza* that before was malicious herewith becomes bestial instead.

A second problem is that virtually no correlation exists between Aristotelian "brutishness" (the term preferred to "bestiality" in most English translations of the *N.E.*) and Dantean violence. Brutish conduct is dehumanized, whether savage or pathological *(matta)*. Among the examples cited in the *Ethics* are the eating of raw meat, or of human flesh, or of dirt, or of a fetus ripped from a woman's womb. No such conduct is represented in *Inferno;* and no sin of violence therein is deemed bestial by Dante, nor, with one exception, by Aristotle either.

That exception is sexual acts between males (7.5.1148b25). But Virgil in *Inferno* clearly classifies sodomy as one of the sins of violence and clearly never places it in a separate class of its own, while in *Purgatorio* sodomy becomes a form of incontinence, in the terms of Aristotle and of *Inferno,* and is elevated to the same level as its heterosexual counterpart.

Finally, some exegetes, among them Lansing, Sapegno, and di Salvo, hold that *matta bestialitade* is not to be found at all among the sins encountered in Dante's moral system. This position saves Virgil from inconsistency, but it brings up another question: in that case why should he even make mention of bestiality? He does so when his purpose is to show that malice is worse than incontinence; and for this purpose he elicits Aristotle, who affirms that not just one but in fact *two* dispositions are worse, these being *bestialitas* as well as *malitia.* This supports what appears to be Virgil's point, clinched with the authority of "the Master of those who know" *(Inf.* 4.131).

St. Thomas Aquinas also follows this master in contending that sins of deliberate malice *(peccata ex certa malitia)* are more grave than sins of passion *(peccata ex passione)*: more grave because the former are more purely willful, while strong emotion or sensual appetite mitigates the latter; the former are more habitually abiding and the latter more intermittent; and the former more fully and dangerously disorient the soul from its natural desire for the good *(appetitum boni),* a desire that the latter sins only occasionally disrupt *(ST* 1.2.78.1, 4).

Whereas Aristotelian thought is expressly introduced into the text, Thomistic influence remains tacit; yet neither the ancient Greek philosopher nor the medieval Catholic theologian judged the malice of fraud to be more heinous than the malice of violence (11.25–27). That assessment comes from Cicero (*De officiis* 1.13.41).

Bibliography

Bufano, Antonietta. "Malizia." *Enciclopedia dantesca* 3:792–793.

Ferretti, Giovanni. *Saggi danteschi.* Florence: Le Monnier, 1950.

Lansing, Richard H. "Dante's Concept of Violence and the Chain of Being." *Dante Studies* 99 (1981), 67–87.

Reade, W. H. V. *The Moral System of Dante's "Inferno."* Oxford: Clarendon Press, 1909.

Triolo, Alfred A. "*Ira, Cupiditas, Libido:* The Dynamics of Human Passion in the *Inferno.*" *Dante Studies* 95 (1977), 1–37.

Joseph Pequigney

Manfred

The illegitimate son of Emperor Frederick II and Bianca Lancia di Monferrato, Manfred *(Manfredi)* was born around 1232. On his father's death, he was made regent of the Sicilian kingdom until Conrad IV, his half-brother, could take the throne. When Conrad died in 1254 Manfred assumed the regency on behalf of the infant Conradin, the kingdom's rightful heir. Having built up and consolidated his power, he took advantage of a false rumor that Conradin had died and had himself crowned king of Sicily in August 1258. Guelf chroniclers, including Brunetto Latini, record the accusation that Manfred murdered his father, his half-brother, and two of his nephews, and also attempted to murder Conradin. The papacy trusted the Ghibelline Manfred as little as it had his father and refused to recognize his authority. Manfred was excommunicated twice, by Alexander IV in 1258 and by Urban IV in 1261. His alliance with the Tuscan Ghibellines, which contributed to their victory at Montaperti, and his frequent incursions into the papal state, exacerbated the papacy's enmity. In 1265 Charles I of Anjou was crowned king of Sicily in St. Peter's and almost immediately led a crusading army into the *Regno*. The treachery of Manfred's soldiers at Ceprano (*Inf.* 28.15–17) allowed Charles to advance to meet the main army at Benevento where, on February 26, 1266, Manfred was defeated and killed. Charles refused the excommunicate Manfred a grave in consecrated ground, having him buried near the battlefield. Later chroniclers repeat the story that the Angevin army filed past, each soldier placing a stone over the grave to form a large cairn.

The Hohenstaufen court remained under Manfred the center of cultural production and exchange that it had been under Frederick II. Manfred was himself a poet and musician. He knew Hebrew and Arabic and wrote a prologue to the Latin translation of the Hebrew *Liber de pomo sive de morte Aristotelis.* In *DVE* 1.12.4, Dante holds up both Manfred and Frederick II as exemplars of the courtly values no longer found among Italy's degenerate rulers. In praising them, he emphasizes their important contribution to the development of Italian literature, in their role as patrons to the "Sicilian school" of poets. Dante's description of Manfred in the *De vulgari eloquentia* as *benegenitus* ("well-born") has been interpreted as a riposte to the emphasis in anti-Hohenstaufen polemics upon Manfred's illegitimacy. Moreover, it is worth noting that Manfred's status as ruler of Sicily is here presented by Dante as unproblematic, with no trace of the accusations of murder and fraudulent usurpation.

Dante may well have perceived Manfred to be a man who at one time had the potential to be Roman Emperor. Certainly, Manfred's Manifesto to the Roman people, dated May 24, 1265, in which he advanced his claims as candidate for the imperial throne, contains many points of similarity to Dante's political philosophy. However, it cannot be proved that Dante knew this document, although it was certainly known in his day, as it is cited in Francesco Pipino's *Chronicon*.

Dante's judgment regarding the Hohenstaufen is considerably modified in the *Commedia*. Frederick II is damned as a heretic (*Inf.* 10.119), while Manfred is located among the excommunicate late-repentant in the Ante-Purgatory (*Purg.* 3.103–145). As with another father and son, Guido and Bonconte da Montefeltro, the damnation of the one adds to the narrative surprise of the other's salvation. Manfred calls out from the group of excommunicate souls, asking the pilgrim whether he recognizes him. Dante describes his appearance (107–108): *biondo era e bello e di gentile aspetto, / ma l'un de' cigli un colpo avea diviso* ("he was blond and handsome and of noble appearance, but one of his brows had been opened by a wound"). When the pilgrim replies that he has never seen him before, Manfred shows him another wound on his breast. Then, smiling, he reveals his name (112–113): *Io son Manfredi, / nepote di Costanza imperadrice* ("I am Manfred, grandson of the Empress Constance"), identifying himself by naming his grandmother, whom Dante will see among the blessed (*Par.* 3.118–120), while passing over his father's name in silence. He asks the pilgrim, when he returns to earth, to make known his true fate to his daughter Constance, the wife of Peter III of Aragon: he explains that after being mortally wounded, he repented with tears and received God's pardon. Confessing that his sins were indeed "horrible," he underlines the doctrine dramatized by his startling presence in Purgatory (122–123): *ma la bontà infinita ha sì gran braccia, / che prende ciò che si rivolge a lei* ("but the infinite Goodness has such open arms that it takes whatever turns to it"). Neither the Archbishop of Cosenza, who disinterred Manfred's bones and cast them out of the *Regno* onto the banks of the Verde, nor Clement IV, who ordered the action, properly understood this doctrine. Their pursuit of vengeance upon Manfred's dead body is rendered futile by his presence in Purgatory. (It is worth noting that the story of Manfred's body being disinterred, like that of his last-gasp repentance, has no historical basis.) The Church's *maladizion* ("curse") cannot prevent salvation, although, as Manfred explains, anyone dying excommunicate must remain in Ante-Purgatory thirty times the length of their excommunication upon earth. The time spent in Ante-Purgatory can be shortened, however, by the prayers of the living, and Manfred ends by repeating his request that the pilgrim inform his daughter concerning his soul's true whereabouts, so that she might pray for him.

The description of Manfred as "blond [. . .] and handsome and of noble appearance" is in accord with contemporary portraits of the Hohenstaufen ruler. Contemporary chroniclers and poets, even those with Guelf sympathies, ascribe to him courtly virtues and great physical beauty. The line also makes an explicit allusion to the biblical description of the young David about to be anointed king by the prophet Samuel: *erat autem rufus, et pulcher aspectu, decoraque facie* ("Now he was ruddy, and withal of a beautiful countenance, and goodly to look at," 1 Sam. 16:12). By linking Manfred to David, Dante draws attention to his status as ruler, and possible representative of the imperial ideal. His appearance is, however, marred by two wounds. The majority of critics have interpreted the wounds as a sign of Manfred's chivalric heroism. He has also been likened to Christ, whose resurrected body bore the marks of crucifixion and who also died as a result of treachery in his thirty-fourth year, or, more generally, to the martyrs whom St. Augustine thought would possibly still carry their scars in heaven (*De civ. Dei* 22.19). A somewhat different interpretation is that the wounds, which were inflicted prior to Manfred's repentance, are signs of sin, indicating a specific criticism on Dante's part of Manfred's actions on earth. They link him to the schismatics of the ninth bolgia, whose punishment consists of an eternal wounding, and in particular to Muhammad and Ali, who are similarly, albeit more seriously, wounded in chest and head. It will be remembered that the wounds were inscribed on his body by a crusading army. The papal justification for that crusade was the accusation of *impium foedus* ("blasphemous alliance"), which resulted from Manfred's toleration of the Saracen colony at Lucera and his employment of Saracen troops. By entering into alliance with the Saracens, Manfred helped to continue the schism begun by Muhammad and Ali which as a western ruler, even possibly a potential Roman emperor, it should have been his task to bring to an end.

Bibliography

Angiolillo, Giuliana. "Il *Manifesto* di Manfredi ai Romani e il III libro della *Monarchia* di Dante." *Studi Romani* 21 (1973), 38–60, rpt. in *Tra 'l vero e lo 'ntelletto: vecchi e nuovi studi su Dante.* Naples: Liguori, 1987, pp. 147–172.

Aurigemma, Marcello. "Manfredi e il problema delle indulgenze." In Umberto Bosco, ed., *Dante nella critica d'oggi: risultati e prospettive.* Florence: Le Monnier, 1965, pp. 540–550.

Balfour, Mark. "'Orribil furon li peccati miei': Manfred's Wounds in 'Purgatorio' III." *Italian Studies* 48 (1993), 4–17.

Bárberi Squarotti, Giorgio. "Lo 'scandolo' di Manfredi." In *L'ombra di Argo: Studi sulla 'Commedia.'* Turin: Genesi, 1988, pp. 147–167.

Cilento, Nicola. "La cultura di Manfredi nel ricordo di Dante." In *Dante e la cultura sveva.* Florence: Olschki, 1970, pp. 3–15.

Frattarolo, Renzo. "Storia dantesca di Manfredi di Svevia." *Esperienze letterarie* 16 (1991), 3–20.

Freccero, John. "Manfred's Wounds and the Poetics of the *Purgatorio*." In *Dante: the Poetics of Conversion*. Cambridge, Mass.: Harvard University Press, 1986, pp. 195–208.

Frugoni, Arsenio. "Il canto III del Purgatorio." In *Nuove letture dantesche,* III. Florence: Le Monnier, 1969, pp. 267–290.

Lansing, Richard. "*Purgatorio* III." *Lectura Dantis* 9 (1991), 54–71.

Nardi, Bruno. "Il canto di Manfredi (*Purgatorio,* III)." In *'Lecturae' e altri studi danteschi,* Quaderni degli "Studi danteschi," 6. Florence: Le Lettere, 1990, pp. 91–103.

Vallese, Giulio. "Teologia e poesia nel canto terzo del Purgatorio." In *Dante e la cultura sveva.* Florence: Olschki, 1970, pp. 251–267.

Vallone, Aldo. "La componente federiciana della cultura dantesca." In *Dante e Roma: Atti del Convegno di Studi a cura della 'Casa di Dante.'* Florence: Le Monnier, 1965, pp. 347–369.

Mark Balfour

Manlius Capitolinus

Marcus Manlius Capitolinus (*Manlio Capitolino*), cited in *Conv.* 4.5.18 and *Mon.* 2.4.7–8 as an example of divine providence working through men to improve the Empire. Awakened by the sacred geese, he rallied others to defend the Capitol from the Gauls (*Aen.* 8.652–656; Livy, *Ab urbe condita* 5.47).

Leslie Zarker Morgan

Manto

There are two characters of the same name in the *Commedia,* one Virgil's Manto, who is seen among the false prophets in Malebolge (*Inf.* 20.55–99), the other Statius's Manto (identified not by name but as the daughter of Tiresias) who, according to Dante's Virgil (*Purg.* 22.113), is in Limbo. Scholars have argued about this apparent confusion and what it means, whether the poet nodded or scribes erred, or whether the contradiction is intentional. If intentional, is Dante giving two versions of the same figure, one pious one impious, or is he distinguishing a fictional Manto (Virgil's) from a historic (Statius's)? Or does Dante distinguish between two fictional characters, condemning one as a sinner and placing the other among virtuous pagans, just as he relegated the creator of one (Virgil) to Limbo, and granted the creator (Statius) of the other salvation? It is not irrelevant that he features each Manto in a canto in which he carefully dissociates himself and Virgil, both prophetic in their poems, from the false prophets they see.

Virgil's Manto is referred to at *Aen.* 10.199 (*fatidicae Mantus,* "prophesying Manto") as one whose son Ocnus named the city he founded after her, but Dante turns her into a grotesque, her head twisted so her hair falls on her breasts; and he has Virgil imply that his earlier version of the origin of Mantua was a lie, that it was in fact built over the bones of Manto, who chose to live and practice her art in a swamp, where no one lived or tilled. In Statius, the daughter of Tiresias is a votary of Apollo but does not herself prophesy. She serves her father in his work, catching in vessels the blood of slaughtered animals, making libations as her father orders, and describing the visions they evoke; it is he who calls on the spirits and goddesses of the underworld and prophesies, interpreting what she has described (*Theb.* 4.443ff). The location of this Manto in Limbo is revealed by Virgil apparently as a compliment to Statius, who is himself saved in part by misreading some of Virgil's lines and reading others as prophetic.

Bibliography

Barolini, Teodolinda. "*Inferno* XX." In *Dante's "Divine Comedy": Introductory Readings. I: "Inferno."* Edited by Tibor Wlassics. *Lectura Dantis VI: Supplement: Special Issue: Lectura Dantis Virginiana, I* (spring, 1990), 262–274.

D'Ovidio, Francesco. "Dante e la magìa." In *Studii sulla Divina Commedia.* Milan, Palermo: Sandron, 1901, pp. 76–112.

———. "Ancora Dante e la magìa." In *Studii sulla Divina Commedia.* Milan, Palermo: Sandron, 1901, pp. 113–149.

Hollander, Robert. "The Tragedy of Divination in *Inferno* XX." In *Studies in Dante.* Ravenna: Longo Editore, 1980, pp. 131–218.

Joan M. Ferrante

Marchese, Messer

"Messere" is a form of address reserved for those of a high social rank, while "marchese" is the Italian form of "marquis." Dante uses both terms to refer to a member of the Argogliosi family of Forlì, who was podestà of Faenza in 1296. He is placed with the gluttons *(golosi)* in the sixth terrace of Purgatory *(Purg.* 24.31) for his excessive consumption of wine. Benvenuto da Imola tells that when this sinner heard that people accused him of doing nothing but drink, he laughingly replied: "And why do they never say that I am always thirsty?"

Jo Ann Cavallo

Marcia

The second wife of Cato of Utica, a hero of republican Rome famous for his stern morality. Cato ceded her to his best friend Hortensius, but immediately after Hortensius's death Marcia implored Cato to take her back so that she might die as his wife. Lucan's version of the story *(Phars.* 2.326–349) accentuates Cato's funereal solemnity in accepting her plea. For Lucan, the story is evidence of Cato's character, his austerity and unselfish devotion to the State rather than to his own desire.

Dante cites Lucan in *Conv.* 4.28.13, where he gives an extended allegorical reading of Marcia's biography as the progress of the noble soul. Her return to Cato signifies that "at the beginning of extreme old age the noble soul turns back to God," with Cato designated as the person most worthy to represent God. In the *Commedia,* Marcia *(Marzia)* is mentioned in Limbo *(Inf.* 4.128) in the catalogue of exemplars of civic virtue, alongside other distinguished Roman wives. In *Purg.* 1, Virgil identifies himself to Cato by saying that he is from the same circle as "your Marcia," remarking on her "chaste eyes" and continued longing for Cato. Virgil's request that Cato assist them for love of Marcia leads to a gruff reproof in which Cato insists on the absolute gap between his prior earthly affections and his current state. Earthly attachments are declared irrelevant to the *legge* ("law," 1.89) which governs his responses in Purgatory.

Rachel Jacoff

Marco Lombardo

One of the wrathful in the third terrace of Purgatory *(Purg.* 16.25–145). He probably lived in the second half of the thirteenth century, but little is known with any certainty of his life, even after many attempts to identify him with one of a number of documented individuals. Early commentators believed that he lived in Venice, although this belief is disputed, as in the meaning of the appellation "Lombardo." There is some consensus that the name indicates his Lombard origin, an area understood in Dante's period to include the entire Marca Trevigiana; other possibilities include the idea that *Lombardo* simply means Italian (as the term was used in France), or that Marco was a member of the Lombardi family of Venice.

Marco Lombardo and his character had become anecdotal even before his appearance in the *Commedia.* He appears, in a story in the *Novellino* (46), as a particularly wise and virtuous man who, although poor, was nevertheless a noble *uomo di corte* ("courtier"). In both he is credited with witty and biting responses to other courtiers who mockingly ask about his poverty. The commentator Buti mentions his generosity, and Villani tells of the time that Marco, upon Ugolino's showing him the grandeur of his court, stated that the count was better prepared to suffer bad fortune than any other lord in Italy, because he lacked nothing other than the wrath of God *(Cronica* 7.121). The commentator Benvenuto relates that once, having been taken captive, Marco asked Rizzardo da Camino to ransom him; upon hearing that the latter was trying to raise money from Lombard nobles for this purpose, Marco replied that he would rather remain in prison than be obliged to such men, thus shaming Rizzardo into paying the ransom himself.

Stories such as these may have suggested Marco to Dante as an appropriate character to discourse on morality and corruption. Marco explains that the cause of the moral corruption of Italy is a result not, as some try to argue, of any malevolent influence of the stars, but rather because of poorly exercised free will, which he discusses at length. He asserts as well that people need the guidance both of the Empire and of the Church, claiming that the hostility between these two, and the Church's assumption of temporal authority, has led to the current moral degeneracy. He cites Lombardy as a particular example of this degeneracy.

Bibliography

Il Novellino. Edited by Guido Favati. Genova: Bozzi, 1970.

Muresu, Gabriele. "La 'sentenza' di Marco Lombardo *(Purgatorio* XVI)." In *I ladri di Malebolge: Saggi di semantica dantesca.* Rome: Bulzoni, 1990, pp. 83–121.

Frank B. Ordiway

Mark, St.

Author of the second canonical gospel. His symbolic representation is the winged lion. Dante quotes the Gospel of Mark *(San Marco)* more infrequently than the other three gospels. It appears in the mystical procession of Earthly Paradise *(Purg.* 29.91–105) as one of the four beasts. In *Conv.* 4.22.14–18 Dante offers a symbolic interpretation of Mark 16:1–8: the three Marys (Mary Magdalene, Mary of James, and Mary Salome), visiting Jesus' tomb after the resurrection and finding it empty (as Jesus has walked ahead to Galilee), represent the three schools of the active life—the Epicureans, the Stoics, and the Peripatetics—as they seek blessedness (Jesus) in the corrupted world (the tomb) and need to be redirected to the realm of contemplation (Galilee). The Gospel of Mark is quoted in *VN* 23.7 (Mark 11:10). Mark is also referred to in *Mon.* 3.9.14.

Bibliography

Dante e la Bibbia. Atti del Convegno Internazionale promosso da "Biblia." Firenze, 26–27–28 settembre 1986. Edited by Giovanni Barblan. Florence: Olschki, 1988.

Kleinhenz, Christopher. "Dante and the Bible: Biblical Citation in the *Divine Comedy.*" In *Dante: Contemporary Perspectives.* Edited by Amilcare Iannucci. Toronto: University of Toronto Press, 1997, pp. 74–93.

Alessandro Vettori

Mars

The Roman god of war, son of Jupiter and Juno, and father of Romulus, the founder of Rome *(Inf.* 24.145, 31.51; *Purg.* 12.31; *Par.* 4.63, 8.132, 22.146). Also, Mars *(Marte)* is the fifth planet and heaven in Dante's Ptolemaic cosmology. Following classical precedent and the belief that the planet exercised a bellicose influence on the earth, Dante sometimes uses the name of the god to mean war and destruction *(Inf.* 24.145, 31.51). Early Florentine chroniclers note that Mars was the patron god of pagan Florence and accept the tradition that the worn fragment of an equestrian statue which stood by the Ponte Vecchio in Dante's time was an image of the god which had once stood in his temple on the site of the present Baptistery. It was at the foot of this statue that Buondelmonte de' Buondelmonti was assassinated in 1216 by the Amidei for having failed to marry a

The Cross in the Heaven of Mars. La comedia di Dante Aligieri, with commentary by Alessandro Vellutello, published by Francesco Marcolini, Venice, 1544. Giamatti Collection: Courtesy of the Mount Holyoke College Archives and Special Collections.

woman of their household, an event which was understood as precipitating the destructive civil wars in Florence between the Guelfs and the Ghibellines *(Inf.* 13.144; *Par.* 16.47, 140–147).

At *Conv.* 2.13.20–24, Dante accepts the belief that the planet exudes a fiery heat which causes objects under its influence to dry up and ignite. The ignition of the vapors which accompany the planet gives it its characteristic red color (see *Par.* 14.86–87). This process also explains the appearance in the sky of meteors, balls of fire, and the like, which signify the deaths of kings and mutations in earthly kingdoms. An example, significant in the context of the Cross—the configuration in which the souls in this planet appear *(Par.* 14.100–102)—is the fiery cross that appeared in the sky at the beginning of Florence's *destruzione* ("ruin"), whatever catastrophic event Dante may mean here *(Conv.* 2.13.22). Mars' ability to attract and ignite vapors, together with its position as the middlemost of the nine spheres and its consequent "beautiful relation" to the others, suggests to Dante the comparison of the heaven of Mars to music—for music *è tutta relativa* ("consists entirely of relations") and draws *spiriti umani* ("human spirits") to itself so that these spirits nearly totally abandon their other operations.

M

Dante and Beatrice in the Heaven of Mars. La comedia, *ed. Pietro da Figino, 1491. Giamatti Collection: Courtesy of the Mount Holyoke College Archives and Special Collections.*

While this comparison is not explicitly restated in the *Paradiso,* Dante's description of his stay in Mars (14.82–18.51) is replete with references to music and poetry, the two being closely allied in Dante's conception. The souls in this sphere sing a hymn which holds Dante bound *con sì dolci vinci* ("with such sweet chains," *Par.* 14.129). Cacciaguida, the principal character in Mars and Dante's great-great-grandfather, describes the other souls who appear there as those who *fuor di gran voce, / sì ch'ogne musa ne sarebbe opima* ("had great fame, so that every Muse would be richly furnished by them," *Par.* 18.32–33). Cacciaguida's soul itself ends the episode by moving among these others in such a way that it shows Dante *qual era tra i cantor del cielo artista* ("what an artist he was among the singers of Heaven," *Par.* 18.51).

The souls who appear in Mars are commonly described as having fought for the faith while alive and include, in addition to the crusader Cacciaguida, noted Jewish and Christian warriors. This collection of souls suggests Dante's *in bono* understanding of the planet's operation. Cangrande is also reported as particularly influenced by this star (*Par.* 17.76–78). The sphere is dominated by Cacciaguida's discourse on his life, Florence in his day, and its subsequent degeneracy (15.169–173, 16.34–154). He also tells Dante of his impending exile and instructs him to report accurately in his poem the things he has seen and heard during his

journey through the afterworld (37–142). The placement of this advice in Mars suggests that Dante's *Commedia* participates in the Christian martial work of the Church Militant in a manner similar to that of the warriors appearing in this sphere.

Frank B. Ordiway

Marsyas

A Phrygian satyr, Marsyas *(Marsia)* challenges Apollo to a musical contest. The Muses declare Apollo the victor and Marsyas is flayed alive, according to Ovid, Dante's authority (*Meta.* 6.382–400; see also Ovid, *Fasti* 6.697–708; Statius, *Theb.* 4.186; Lucan, *Phars.* 3.205–208). At the beginning of *Paradiso,* Dante invokes Apollo with the words *Entra nel petto mio, e spira tue / sì come quando Marsïa traesti / della vagina delle membra sue* ("Do you come into my breast and inspire, as when you drew Marsyas forth from the sheath of his members," *Par.* 1.19–21). Dante entreats Apollo to inspire him with the same poetic prowess that allowed the god to vanquish the satyr. At the same time, Dante transforms the violent image of the removal of Marsyas' skin into a figure for the transcendence of corporeal, or mortal, limitations.

Bibliography

Brownlee, Kevin. "Pauline Vision and Ovidian Speech in *Paradiso* 1." In *The Poetry of Allusion: Virgil and Ovid in Dante's "Commedia."* Edited by Rachel Jacoff and Jeffrey T. Schnapp. Stanford: Stanford University Press, 1991, pp. 202–213.

Hollander, Robert. *Allegory in Dante's "Commedia."* Princeton, N.J.: Princeton University Press, 1969.

Renucci, Paul. "Dante et le mythe de Marsyas." *Bulletin de la société d'études dantesques* 1 (1949), 21–33.

Jessica Levenstein

Martha

The contrast between the sisters Martha and Mary is presented in Luke 10:38–42, where Christ responds to Martha's preoccupation with domestic duties in favor of her sister's absorption in listening to his words. This text underlay the distinction between the active life (Martha) and the contemplative life (Mary), which developed as a legend in the ninth century and was later diffused through Vincent of Beauvais's *Speculum historiale*. Dante invokes Luke in his discussion of the relative merits of the moral and intellectual virtues in *Conv.* 4.17.9–12, reiterating Christ's words to Martha *(Marta)* as an argument for the superiority of the contemplative to the active life. Mary and Martha were frequently compared to their Old Testament prototypes, Rachel and Leah, who appear in Dante's third purgatorial dream *(Purg.* 27.100–108).

Rachel Jacoff

Martin IV

Simon de Brion (or Brie), a native of Montpincé, France, became treasurer of the cathedral of Tours, chancellor of France in 1260, and was made cardinal by Pope Urban IV in 1261. As legate in France for the pope, he was responsible for the election of Charles of Anjou to the throne of Sicily and Naples. When Pope Nicholas III died, Simon de Brion was elected pope, thanks to Charles of Anjou, after a difficult six-month conclave. He became pope on February 11, 1281, with the name of Martin IV, at Viterbo, where the conclave had been held. He could never enter Rome during his pontificate because of the opposition of the Romans to his election. He lived in Orvieto, Montefiascone, Città della Pieve, and Perugia, where he died on March 28, 1285, four years after his election.

In politics, Martin IV always sided with the French. Soon after his election, at the request of Charles of Anjou, he excommunicated the Greek emperor Michael VIII Palaeologus. The excommunication instigated a separation between the Eastern and Western churches which held until 1437. In the course of the Sicilian rebellion against French power—the Sicilian Vespers—in 1282, Martin IV tried in vain to restore Angevin rule by excommunicating Peter III of Aragon.

Following a much-quoted source in contemporary chronicles, Dante sees Martin as having been avaricious and places him on the sixth terrace of Purgatory, among the gluttonous. In *Purg.* 24.20–24, Forese Donati describes him as having a face more emaciated than the rest of the gluttonous (20–21) and as being purged of his sinful passion for eels cooked in vernaccia wine (23–24). Dante adopts this bitterly ironic trait of Martin IV's out of revenge: Dante blamed him for the rein-

statement of Ghibelline power in Italy as well as for his favorable attitude toward Charles of Anjou. The anecdote that Martin IV's death was caused by an indigestion of eels is reported by numerous contemporary chronicles, but it does not appear in the generally reputable *Cronica* by Giovanni Villani (8.58, 106).

Alessandro Vettori

Martyrdom

Isidore of Seville, in his hugely and durably influential seventh-century etymological dictionary, gives the name of *martyres* to those "who have suffered agonies in order to bear witness to Christ" *(Etymologiarum libri* 7.11). As the supremely self-sacrificial act of testimony to the faith, martyrdom has for Dante the extraordinary resonance that it might be expected to have for any Christian believer in the late Middle Ages. Images of individual instances of martyrdom, however, are comparatively rare in his works, being confined—not altogether unexpectedly—to *Purgatorio* and *Paradiso*. Even there, the number of exemplary figures who seem to qualify for their roles in the *Commedia*'s narrative specifically on account of their historical status as Christian martyrs remains relatively, perhaps surprisingly, small. With one important exception—Cacciaguida, discussed below—Dante's martyrological short list consists of individuals well known in the central tradition of Christian history and hagiography.

The terminology Dante uses when dealing with martyrs and martyrdom requires careful attention from the modern reader. The standard terms *martiro* and *martirio* are frequently used by him—as by other medieval authors in various forms of the Italian vernacular—in a much looser sense, to refer to any kind of mental anguish, physical pain, emotional suffering, or practical trouble, often in contexts where to imply that these "sufferings" were specifically Christian acts of martyrdom would at best seem inappropriate and at worst border on the blasphemous. Thus at *Inf.* 5.116 Dante-character is moved to tears by the spectacle of Francesca da Rimini's *martìri*—inflicted, of course, by a just and inappellable judgment of God—while on several occasions in the *Vita Nuova* and the *Rime* the word is used with a sense no stronger than that of "emotional torment inspired by unhappiness in love." Throughout *Inferno,* in fact, the undeniable physical sufferings

M of the damned are repeatedly described as *martìri,* without any possibility of their being confused with the martyrdom in the positive, fully Christian, sense, as undergone by certain outstanding individual believers at the end of their lives on earth.

The fundamental *martiro* in this sense is that of Christ himself, on the cross, as the *Commedia's* own attribution of responsibility for that event to Caiaphas makes clear: *Quel confitto che tu miri / consigliò i Farisei che convenia / porre un uom per lo popolo a' martìri* ("That one staked there at whom you are looking counseled the Pharisees that it was expedient to put one man [Christ] to death for the people," *Inf.* 23.115–117). In this usage the meaning of *martirio* is clearly double, since Christ's sufferings were both real in themselves and also an act of witness to the truth that he embodied. Subsequent instances of *martiro* and *martirio* in the *Commedia* consistently reflect this duality of meaning, usually focusing on particular individuals who had, in their lives, taken the injunction to follow in Christ's footsteps to the logical extreme of being prepared to imitate his self-sacrificial death, and had therefore become, in the Isidorian sense, martyrs for Christ's sake.

These individuals include, almost inevitably, the first and most famous martyr of all, St. Stephen, whose death, recounted at length in the New Testament in the Book of Acts, is vividly represented as one of the examples of meekness that appear as an ecstatic vision to Dante-pilgrim in the third circle of Purgatory, occupied by the penitent irascible (*Purg.* 15.106–114). The angry crowd that stones Stephen to death is heard by Dante to shout, in a significant addition to the Biblical text (Acts 7:57–60), *Martira, martira!* ("Kill, kill!," 108). Another allusion to a celebrated early martyr appears in *Par.* 4.82–83, where the steadfastness of St. Lawrence (d. 258) in the face of torture is cited by Beatrice to rebuke the inconstancy of those who break their vows. Other notable figures connected by Dante with martyrdom include: St. Francis, whose missionary journeys were inspired by *la sete del martiro* ("the thirst for martyrdom," *Par.* 11.100)—although of course such was not, in fact, to be his fate; Boethius, who came to the peace of heaven *da martiro / e da essilio* ("from martyrdom / and exile," *Par.* 10.128–129); and St. Peter, whose passionate denunciation of the moral failings of the papacy of Dante's time is based on his outright statement that it is no longer worthy of the blood shed by him and his immediate successors in the papal line: *Non fu la sposa di Cristo allevata / del sangue mio, di Lin, di quel di Cleto, / per essere ad acquisto d'oro usata; / ma per acquisto d'esto viver lieto / e Sisto e Pïo e Calisto e Urbano / sparser lo sangue dopo molto fleto* ("The bride of Christ was not raised up by my blood, by Linus's, by that of Cletus, to be used for acquiring gold, but to acquire this happy life did Sixtus and Pius and Calixtus and Urban shed their blood after much weeping," *Par.* 27.40–45).

All these actual and potential martyrs—with the possible exception of the slightly obscure early popes—belong firmly to the familiar mainstream of medieval Christian tradition. The most interesting of Dante's exemplary witnesses to the faith, however, is perhaps the only one who does not: his own great-great-grandfather, Cacciaguida (*Par.* 15.28–17.142). Cacciaguida appears in the heaven of Mars as celestial spokesman for a group of the blessed who have in common the fact that their defense of the Christian faith expressed itself in military action: they represent the Church Militant in the most literal sense. He is also assigned the role of spokesman for the moral values associated by Dante with the earliest stages of Florentine history, a pristine state of aristocratic virtue now irremediably sacrificed to the imperatives of a spineless and money-grubbing culture sustained by *la gente nova e' subiti guadagni* ("the new people and the rapid gains," *Inf.* 16.73). The confluence in Cacciaguida of Christian chivalry, Florentine lineage, moral purity, and an admirable death on crusade (*Par.* 15.139–148)—not to mention the personal relationship to Dante that evokes much of his discourse in cantos 16 and 17—make of him the most substantial and psychologically rounded of the *Commedia's* martyr figures, the one whose motivation and understanding of what martyrdom involves are most clearly elaborated, and perhaps the one who is most directly offered to the (male) reader—unlikely as he is to have the stature or the opportunities for self-sacrifice of a Stephen or a Peter—as a model for imitation.

Bibliography

Bowersock, G. W. *Martyrdom and Rome.* Cambridge: Cambridge University Press, 1995.

Bufano, Antonietta. "Martirio." *Enciclopedia dantesca,* 3:848–849.

"Martyrdom." *New Catholic Encyclopedia.* Vol. 9. New York: McGraw-Hill, 1967, pp. 314–415.

Peterson, E. et al. "Martirio e martire." *Enciclopedia Cattolica.* Vol. 8, col. 233–44.

Schnapp, Jeffrey T. *The Transfiguration of History at the Center of Dante's "Paradise."* Princeton, N.J.: Princeton University Press, 1986.

Steven Botterill

Mary, the Virgin

The Gospels, particularly the infancy narratives of Matthew and Luke, are the scriptural sources for the idea that Mary *(Maria)* was the mother of Jesus and that she conceived him without a human father. According to Matthew, "She was found to be with child by the Holy Spirit," thereby fulfilling the prophecy of Isa. 7:14 ("Behold a virgin shall conceive and bear a son"). Luke describes the angel Gabriel's annunciation to Mary and her willing acceptance ("Let it be done to me according to your will") of her role in the Incarnation. Apocryphal texts such as the *Book of James* and the *Gospel According to the Pseudo-Matthew* contributed other elements of the narrative that were to shape her mythic status and iconography. The early church fathers called her "ever-virgin" to affirm her perpetual virginity and wrote of her as the "new Eve" who reversed the consequences of Eve's sinfulness just as Christ was the "new Adam." Debates concerning the relationship between Christ's humanity and divinity led to a doctrinal definition of Mary's significance: the Council of Ephesus (431) declared her *Theotokos* (mother of God).

Mary became increasingly important in Christian piety, particularly in the twelfth century. By the thirteenth century her central role in the economy of salvation was firmly established. Theology, liturgy, and iconography celebrated her unique status as both mother of God and virgin, her exemplary goodness and humility as the vehicle of the Incarnation, and her exaltation as Queen of Heaven. Because Mary was the source of Christ's body, her freedom from sin became a major concern in the emerging ideas of the Immaculate Conception and Bodily Assumption, both of which granted her body a unique status. Her role as mediatrix or intercessor was primary: through her the divine became human and, by means of her intercession, humans gained access to divine grace.

All of these ideas are important in Dante's depiction of Mary. In the *Commedia* Mary's mediation both initiates Dante's journey and brings it to completion. Beatrice explains to Virgil that she has undertaken Dante's rescue at the urging of a heavenly lady: *Donna è gentil nel ciel che si compiange / di questo 'mpedimento ov' io ti mando, / sì che duro giudicio là sù frange* ("There is a noble lady in Heaven, who grieves for this impediment to which I send you, so that she vanquishes harsh judgment there on high," *Inf.* 2.94–96). Commentators now agree that this unnamed lady is Mary, responding to Dante's predicament even before she is asked, as she will be commended for doing in the final canto of *Paradiso*: *La tua benignità non pur soccorre / a chi domanda, ma molte fiate / liberamente al dimandar precorre* ("Your good will succors not only those who ask, but many times freely runs ahead of the asking," *Par.* 33.16–18). Her compassion and its efficacy are noted elsewhere, for example in Buonconte da Montefeltro's last minute appeal to her *(Purg.* 5.101), or in the angels *del grembo di Maria* ("from Mary's bosom," *Purg.* 8.37) who guard the valley of the princes where the Marian hymn *"Salve, regina"* is sung by the penitents *(Purg.* 7.82).

Mary's human perfection is emphasized in *Purgatorio.* On each of the seven purgatorial terraces episodes from her life serve as the first examples of the virtues which are opposed to the sins purged on the terraces. Scriptural allusions provide reminders of her exemplary humility, charity, mildness, alacrity, poverty, temperance, and chastity. For example, her humility in the Annunciation is the subject of the first of the bas reliefs that Dante sees on the terrace of pride. This scene from Mary's life, so beloved in the visual arts of Dante's time, will be recalled again twice in *Paradiso* (23.103–105, 32.93–96, and cf. 14.36). The hymn "Ave Maria," which contains the Angel's greeting to Mary in the Annunciation, is also cited twice, both at the beginning and the end of *Paradiso* (3.121–22 and 32.95).

Mary is *regina* or *agusta,* queen or empress of Heaven in *Paradiso,* implicitly co-regent with her son of *quella Roma onde Cristo è romano* ("that Rome of which Christ is a Roman," *Purg.* 32.102). She appears first in a symbolic triumph in the circle of the Fixed Stars (canto 23) and later in the Empyrean as la *faccia che a Cristo / più si somiglia* ("the face that most resembles Christ," *Par.* 32.85–86). The description of her triumph *(Par.* 23.79–120) invokes several traditional Marian figures: Mary as *la rosa in che 'l verbo divino / carne si fece*

M ("the rose in which the divine Word was made flesh," 73); [il] bel fior ch'io sempre invoco / e mane e sera ("the lovely flower that I ever invoke both morning and evening," 88–89); lo maggior foco ("the greatest fire," 90); la viva stella ("the living star," 92); il bel zaffiro / del quale il ciel più chiaro s'inzaffira ("the beautiful sapphire with which the brightest Heaven is ensapphired," 101–102). She is crowned by the circulata melodia ("circling melody," 109) of "angelic love" that praises her womb as the albergo del nostro disiro ("shelter of our Desire," 105) and honored by the deep love of all the blessed who sing the Easter hymn Regina celi ("Queen of Heaven") to her. The idea of Mary as queen is also present in the Vita Nuova, where she is called regina della gloria ("queen of glory," 5) and quella regina benedetta virgo Maria, lo cui nome fue in grandissima reverenzia ne le parole di questa Beatrice beata ("that blessed queen Virgin Mary whose name was held in great reverence in the words of this blessed Beatrice," 28).

In the heavenly rose Mary is the apex of the line of Old Testament matriarchs. Her role as second Eve is clear in the description that Bernard gives of Eve: La piaga che Maria richiuse e unse, / quella ch'è tanto bella da' suoi piedi / è colei che l'aperse e che la punse ("The wound which Mary closed and anointed, that one who is so beautiful at her feet is she who opened it and pierced it," 32.4–6). St. Bernard is presented as Mary's fedel ("faithful one") and as burning with love for her. His ardent prayer to her at the opening of the final canto foregrounds the key paradoxes of Mariology (virgin mother, daughter of her son, most humble and most exalted), praising Mary's ennobling goodness and her compassion. This prayer shows Mary as the cornerstone of Dante's faith, her intercession as necessary for achievement of the beatific vision as it had been for the initiation of the journey itself.

The importance of Mary in the poem's architecture, the intensity of poetic language she occasions, and the affective tenderness with which she is treated leave no doubt of her centrality to Dante's religious sensibility. Her role as both universal and personal female mediatrix underwrites Beatrice's function in Dante's unique salvific narrative.

Bibliography

Auerbach, Erich. "Dante's Prayer to the Virgin (Paradiso, XXXIII) and Earlier Eulogies." Romance Philology 3.1 (1949), 1–26.

Balthasar, Hans Urs von. Dante. Translated by Giuseppe Magagna. Brescia: Morcelliana, 1973.

Botterill, Steven. Dante and the Mystical Tradition: Bernard of Clairvaux in the "Commedia." Cambridge: Cambridge University Press, 1994, especially pp. 148–193.

Graef, Hilda. Mary: A History of Doctrine and Devotion. 2 vols. New York: Sheed and Ward, 1963.

Johnson, Elizabeth. "Marian Devotion in the Western Church." In Christian Spirituality: High Middle Ages and Reformation. Edited by Jill Raitt. New York: Crossroad, 1989, pp. 392–414.

O'Carroll, Michael. Theotokos: A Theological Encyclopedia of the Blessed Virgin Mary. Wilmington, Del.: M. Glazier, 1982.

Pelikan, Jaroslav. Mary Through the Centuries: Her Place in the History of Culture. New Haven: Yale University Press, 1996.

Warner, Marina. Alone of All Her Sex: The Myth and the Cult of the Virgin Mary. New York: Random House, 1983.

Rachel Jacoff

Mary Magdalen

Pious woman and follower of Christ. She was from Magdala, an ancient town on the western shore of the Sea of Galilee. According to the New Testament, Christ cured her of evil spirits. She was present at his crucifixion, helped with his burial, and was the first to see him resurrected. Dante quotes Mark's account (16:1–7) of her visit, together with Mary the mother of James and Mary Salome, to Jesus' tomb (Conv. 4.22.14–15). He identifies Mary Magdalen (Maria Maddalena) allegorically with the Epicureans, one of the three famous schools of Greek philosophy, while identifying Mary the mother of James with the Stoics and Mary Salome with the Peripatetics. Together they are presented as types of the three schools of the active life.

Molly Morrison

Mary of Jerusalem

According to Josephus (The Jewish War 6.3), during the Roman siege of Jerusalem by Titus (70 B.C.) a Hebrew named Mary was reported to have killed her infant, roasted his flesh, and consumed it. In this gruesome reversal of the maternal, nurturing figure, Dante emphasizes the emaciation of the gluttons on the sixth cornice (*Purg.* 23.30). Mary *(Maria di Eleazaro)* is one of two exempla of the sin of gluttony. The story is also retold by John of Salisbury (*Policraticus* 2.6) and by Vincent of Beauvais (*Speculum historiale* 10.5).

Diana Cavuoto Glenn

Master Adam

A counterfeiter of florins punished in the last bolgia of Malebolge together with the alchemists, impersonators, and liars guilty of defrauding society (*Inf.* 30.49). He is most commonly identified with Adam of Brescia or of England, an employee of the Guidi counts of Romena caught passing bad gold florins and burned at the stake in 1281. Like so many of Dante's other great sinners, he forces himself on our attention, crying out to the pilgrim in words used by Jerusalem to cry out for a savior (Lam. 1:12). He thinks himself different from the crowd of jokesters and disreputable fools surrounding him. He is dignified if pathetic, pitiable if self-obsessed (he refers to himself in the first person eleven times in thirty-three lines). Like his biblical namesake, he has "fallen" from an earthly "Eden" at the evil instigation of men jealous of the wealth of Florence. For all his claim on our sympathy, he is grossly misshapen by disease—his hydropic form so distended with a "liquid that it ill converts" that he can neither move nor even see over his belly. After telling Dante-pilgrim his story, he is drawn into a pointless exchange of insults with the liar Sinon, quite possibly a palinodic allusion to the series of shameful verses that Dante once exchanged with Forese Donati (*Rime* 73–78).

Master Adam is one of Dante's more complex characters: an anti-type of the cosmic Smith (*Par.* 2.128), an anti-type of the Adam who fell and rose with Christ, an ever-corrupt failed experiment of the Divine Alchemist, and a bloated embodiment of the "body politic, economic, and spiritual" that his falsification of the coin, Caesar's and God's, created.

Bibliography

Contini, Gianfranco. "Sul XXX dell'*Inferno*." *Paragone* 44 (1953), 3–13.

Dragonetti, Roger. "Dante et Narcisse ou les Faux-Monnayeurs de l'Image." *Revue des Études Italiennes* 11 (1965), 85–146.

Durling, Robert M. "Deceit and Digestion in the Belly of Hell." *Allegory and Representation.* Selected Papers from the English Institute, 1979–1980, New Series, No. 5. Edited by Stephen J. Greenblatt. Baltimore and London: The Johns Hopkins University Press, 1981, pp. 61–93.

Heilbronn, Denise. "Master Adam and the Fat-bellied Lute." *Dante Studies* 101 (1983), 51–65.

Iannucci, Amilcare. "Musical Imagery in the Mastro Adamo Episode." In *Da una riva e dall'altra. Studi in onore di Antonio D'Andrea.* Edited by Dante Della Terza. Florence: Edizioni Cadmo, 1995, pp. 103–118.

Livi, Giovanni. "Un personaggio dantesco." *Giornale dantesco* 24 (1921), 265–270.

Mussetter, Sally. "*Inferno* XXX: Dante's Counterfeit Adam." *Traditio* 34 (1978), 427–435.

Shoaf, R. A. *Dante, Chaucer, and the Currency of the Word.* Norman: Pilgrim Books, 1983, especially pp. 39–48.

Vivaldi, Fulberto. "Fantasie del lettore solingo (*Inf.* XXX.75–78)." *L'Alighieri* 1 (1960), 49–56.

Sally Mussetter

Matelda

The tutelary female spirit of the Earthly Paradise, first encountered by Dante as she gathers flowers by a stream (*Purg.* 28.40) and later seen surrounded by four nymphs, Beatrice's handmaids, who represent the Cardinal Virtues (*Purg.* 31.104–8). Matelda's function is to administer the water of the two streams Lethe and Eunoe to all souls who reach the top of the purgatorial mountain. In keeping with his tendency to classicize the landscape of Eden, Dante presents Matelda not as an angel but as a pagan nature deity, weaving garlands of flowers on the bank of Lethe. As C. Singleton rightly points out, she also corresponds to the classical figure Astraea, the virginal goddess of justice who lived among men during the Golden Age. Accordingly, Matelda approaches Dante *non altrimenti / che vergine che li occhi onesti avvalli* ("not otherwise than a virgin who lowers her modest eyes," *Purg.* 28.56–57). Dante also compares her to the pagan goddesses Proserpina (*Purg.* 28.49–51), Venus (*Purg.* 28.64–66), and, obliquely, the priestess Hero (*Purg.* 28.71–74). Matelda's prelapsarian innocence and rectitude make her the fitting character to lead Dante into Eden proper and to supervise his ritual purification in Lethe and Eunoe. Her name appears only once in the text, spoken by Beatrice (*Purg.* 33.119).

Dante also draws on the medieval lyrical genre of the pastorella, consisting of a brief dialogue in which a gallant tries to seduce a shepherdess. In *Purg.* 28 Dante specifically recalls Guido Cavalcanti's pastorella "In un boschetto," which culminates in the sexual embrace of the narrator and his rustic maiden. Like Cavalcanti's lady, Matelda is *una donna soletta* ("a lady solitary," *Purg.* 28.40), who is "singing like a lady in love" (*Purg.* 29.1). Just as Cavalcanti's speaker believes that he has seen the god of love, so the pilgrim likens Matelda's shining eyes and smile to those of Venus when Cupid made her love Adonis (*Purg.* 28.64–66). Dante evokes Cavalcanti's pastorella to demonstrate that the pilgrim perceives Matelda as an erotic object: he desires her in a physical sense, just as Pluto desired Proserpina, Venus desired Adonis, and Leander desired Hero.

What is the meaning of Dante's desire? Most critics agree that Matelda's innocence is not questioned here. As Robert Hollander emphasizes, she is a woman before sin and death entered the world, the unfallen Eve, and she resides in an Eden which shall never suffer the Fall again. The network of literary allusions suggests the pilgrim is not yet free of lust. C. Singleton, refusing to accept the literal implications of Dante's sensuality, allegorizes it as man's longing for primal justice. Other critics, such as Emerson Brown, affirm the literal level and argue that Dante dramatizes his limits in understanding Matelda and the residue of eroticism in his own soul. In their reading, Dante's response to Matelda demonstrates that he cannot fully comprehend or recapture the original purity of Eden.

Although, as Virgil remarks, Dante's will is rightly ordered (*Purg.* 27.140–142), as a result of the Fall the structure of his mind distorts what he sees. Not until the "baptism" in Lethe and Eunoe is the pilgrim's purification from lechery completed. Through Matelda's bidding, Dante finally achieves an inner life that mirrors the harmonious aspects of the Earthly Paradise (*Purg.* 33.143–144). As Franco Masciandaro aptly observes, Matelda's overall role is to affirm for Dante certain truths, namely, the original good of all creation, the permanent perfection of the garden, and human culpability for the expulsion from Eden.

Many other critical interpretations of this enigmatic figure have been put forth. The early commentators, including Jacopo della Lana, Pietro Alighieri, Francesco da Buti, and Landino view Matelda as a symbol of the active life because of her association with Leah (*Purg.* 27.97–108). Modern critics have assigned her several more precise meanings. G. Busnelli sees Matelda as signifying the operations of the virtuous human will;

Matelda. Invenzioni di Giovanni Flaxman sulla Divina commedia, *illustrated by John Flaxman and Beniamino del Vecchio, Rome, 1826. Giamatti Collection: Courtesy of the Mount Holyoke College Archives and Special Collections.*

similarly, V. Barelli interprets her as industrious charity. G. Scartazzini, following the early commentator F. da Buti, believed that Matelda symbolizes the ministry of the Church; to S. Bastiani and V. Botta, she embodies Christian doctrine. G. Pascoli presents the interesting hypothesis that she is an emblem of art in the Thomistic sense, i.e., a function of the practical intellect. C. H. Grandgent identifies Matelda as pastoral beauty and pleasure. According to M. Porena, she represents the perfect earthly life which combines action (gathering flowers; *Purg.* 28.41–142) with contemplation of God's works (singing the hymn *Delectasti; Purg.* 28.80). F. D'Ovidio, N. Sapegno, T. Nardi, A. E. Quaglio, B. Nardi, and R. Dragonetti agree with Porena's basic reading.

Other critics associate Dante's Earthly Paradise with human happiness prior to original sin, and hence they take Matelda to be a symbol of primal innocence. They include A. Graf, N. Scarano, D. Bianchi, and, as previously noted, C. Singleton. A. Pézard points to Matelda's image as a "paranymph"—a goddess of purifying waters—who reunites the soul with God by helping it to remember its divine nature. In a similar vein, Torraca argues that Matelda signifies sanctifying grace, which frees the soul from sin and results in the spiritual regeneration of man.

Yet another interpretive approach focuses on Matelda's role as guide and teacher. G. Rossetti sees her as the embodiment of royal authority and administration presiding over a reunited and harmonious Italy. In other words, Matelda reflects Dante's political ideal of a functional Roman Empire. C. F. Goeschel interprets her as the personification of philosophy; following him, R. Forniciari glosses Matelda as the Christian knowledge to rule and govern which completes the pagan erudition of Virgil and Statius. L. Pietrobono argues that she personifies Old Testament wisdom, and M. Campodonico interprets her as the active life that is governed by doctrinal learning, and that leads to the Earthly Paradise. More generally, U. Fresco presents Matelda as the emblem of human sagacity reconciled with God. For R. B. Harrower, she is the intellect of man before original sin, just as Virgil is the intellect of postlapsarian man. M. Casella perceives Matelda as the exegetical learning necessary to understand the allegorical meanings of the Scriptures, and of Dante's poetry as well. Others like N. Zingarelli and G. Natali compare Matelda with the *donna gentile* ("gentle lady") in

the *Vita Nuova* and conclude that both symbolize wisdom pointing to the apex of the temporal life. More recently, Peter Armour views Matelda as a reworking of Lady Philosophy in the *Convivio*.

A number of scholars reject the moralized readings in favor of a purely secular interpretation. B. Croce is perhaps the most influential. He views Matelda as Dante's exquisite embodiment of the beautiful, youthful, and enticing lady that was typically found in contemporary Provençal and Italian lyrics. L. Mascetta-Caracci also notes the debt to the genre of pastorella, specifically the poem by Cavalcanti, and argues that Dante uses the erotic love motif allegorically, to symbolize the vain desire to possess Adam's innocence in the form of the lovely Matelda. U. Bosco, noting that the *Purgatorio* climaxes with the appearance of Beatrice, who is preceded or preannounced by Matelda, reads the last six cantos as a reworking of the *Vita Nuova* (24), where Beatrice is preceded by the gentle lady Primavera ("Spring" in the Italian), her beautiful friend who literally comes first (*prima verrà;* i.e., "she who comes first") just as St. John the Baptist preceded Christ. Matelda is thus a persistent lyric fantasy of Dante's imagination. So, too, N. Sapegno reads Matelda as the product of the poet's Stilnovistic sentiments. S. Battaglia summarizes the aesthetic dimension by celebrating *Purg.* 28 as the first great example of idyllic poetry in Italian literature.

The fact that Dante calls the "fair lady" Matelda only once, at the end of *Purgatorio* (33.119), invites the symbolic interpretations thus far delineated. But why name her at all? Could she be a specific historical figure, just as Beatrice and Virgil are? Many theories concerning a "real life" Matelda have been advanced, though none of them are very convincing. All of the early commentators, including Benvenuto da Imola, Jacopo della Lana, and Pietro Alighieri, identify her as the Countess Matilde of Canossa (1046–1115), who supported the Church (specifically allying herself with Pope Gregory VII) by funding the construction of numerous basilicas. The anonymous Florentine remarks that Matilda, after her parents' deaths, married a Guelf Duke and that, finding herself barren, rejected carnality and energetically devoted herself to pious works. This line of interpretation was unbroken until the end of the nineteenth century, when critics began to reject the prevailing interpretation. Another reading, first mentioned by A. Lubin (1860) and later endorsed by F. D'Ovidio (1906), linked Matelda to Mechtildis of Hackeborn, a mystic who lived in a convent in Sassonia and who died in 1298. E. Boehmer (1871) suggested St. Mechtildis of Magdeburg (1207–1282), author of a poem entitled "Fliessendes Licht der Gottheit" ("The Flowing Light of the Godhead"), the Latin translation of which Dante supposedly knew. It may be that Matelda, like Beatrice, is a person from Dante's private biography, and also that the poet transforms Matelda, as he does Beatrice, into a larger allegorical symbol, perhaps that of prelapsarian justice and innocence, as Singleton has claimed. Allegory, however, allows the possibility of more than one meaning, so that Matelda may represent both a historical figure and an abstract idea.

Bibliography

Armour, Peter. *Dante's Griffin and the History of the World: A Study of the Earthly Paradise.* Oxford: Clarendon Press, 1989.

———. "Matelda in Eden: The Teacher and the Apple." *Italian Studies* 34 (1979), 2–27.

Boehmer, E. "Matelda." *Jahrbuch der deutschen Dante–Gesellschaft* 3 (1871), 101–178.

Bosco, Umberto. "Il canto della processione." In *Dante Vicino.* Rome: Sciascia, 1966, pp. 274–296.

Brown, Emerson. "Proserpina, Matelda, and the Pilgrim." *Dante Studies* 89 (1971), 33–48.

Cioffi, Caron Ann. "'Il cantor de' bucolici carmi': The Influence of Virgilian Pastoral on Dante's Depiction of the Earthly Paradise." In *Lectura Dantis Newberryana.* Vol. 1. Edited by Paolo Cherchi and Antonio C. Mastrobuono. Evanston, Ill.: Northwestern University Press, 1988, pp. 93–122.

Del Popolo, Concetto. "Matelda." *Letture Classensi* 8 (1979), 121–134.

Dronke, Peter. "Dante's Earthly Paradise: Towards an Interpretation of *Purgatorio* 28." *Romanische Forschungen* 82 (1970), 470–478.

Ferrante, Joan. *The Political Vision of the "Divine Comedy."* Princeton, N.J.: Princeton University Press, 1984, pp. 244–248.

Harrower, Rachel. *A New Theory of Dante's Matelda.* Cambridge: Cambridge University Press, 1926.

Hawkins, Peter S. "Watching Matelda." In *The Poetry of Allusion: Virgil and Ovid in Dante's "Commedia."* Edited by Rachel Jacoff and Jeffrey T. Schnapp. Stanford, Calif.: Stanford University Press, 1991, pp. 181–201.

Hollander, Robert. *Allegory in Dante's "Commedia."* Princeton, N.J.: Princeton University Press, 1969, pp. 152–158.

Masciandaro, Franco. *Dante as Dramatist: The Myth of the Earthly Paradise and Tragic Vision in the "Divine Comedy."* Philadelphia: University of Pennsylvania Press, 1992. Especially chap. 6, "The Earthly Paradise and the Recovery of Tragic Vision."

Nardi, Bruno. "Il mito dell'Eden." In *Saggi di filosofia dantesca.* 2nd ed. Florence: La Nuova Italia, 1967, pp. 311–340.

Nardi, Tilde. "Matelda." *L'Alighieri* 3 (1962), 29–34.

Natali, Giulio. "Il Paradiso terrestre e la sua custode." *Siculorum Gymnasium* 8 (1955), 198–210.

Pecoraro, Marco. "L'ora di Citerea (Una interpretazione della Matelda dantesca)." *Critica letteraria* 40 (1983), 419–444.

Pézard, André. "Nymphes platoniciennes au Paradis terrestre." In *Medioevo e Rinascimento: Studi in onore di Bruno Nardi.* Vol. 2. Florence: G. C. Sansoni, 1955, pp. 543–594.

Quaglio, A. E. "Il canto XXVIII del *Purgatorio*." In *Lectura Dantis Scaligera: Purgatorio.* Florence: Le Monnier, 1967, pp. 1039–1061.

Singleton, Charles S. *Dante Studies 2. Journey to Beatrice.* Cambridge, Mass.: Harvard University Press, 1958, pp. 204–221.

Caron Cioffi

Matthew, St.

Author of the first canonical gospel, Matthew *(San Matteo)* has been identified with the son of Alphaeus, Levi, who was the tax-collector called by Jesus to become his disciple. It is supposed that his gospel was written around 70 C.E. in Aramaic and later translated into Greek. St. Matthew's symbol is an angel and he is iconographically represented with a spear, possibly the instrument of his martyrdom. In the Middle Ages Matthew's Gospel was referred to with much greater frequency than any of the others, and granted greater authority. Dante, too, makes extensive reference to the Gospel of Matthew both in exact quotations and in indirect references. Together with the other three gospels, the Gospel of Matthew appears in the mystical procession of Earthly Paradise as one of the four beasts (*Purg.* 29.92).

Bibliography

Dante e la Bibbia. Atti del Convegno Internazionale promosso da "Biblia." Firenze, 26–27–28 settembre 1986. Edited by Giovanni Barblan. Florence: Olschki, 1988.

Kleinhenz, Christopher. "Dante and the Bible: Biblical Citation in the *Divine Comedy*." In *Dante: Contemporary Perspectives*. Edited by Amilcare Iannucci. Toronto: University of Toronto Press, 1997, pp. 74–93.

Alessandro Vettori

Medea

Princess of Colchis, from Greek mythology, with whose magical help Jason secured the Golden Fleece. Jason married Medea, but afterward abandoned her for Creusa, daughter of Creon. In revenge Medea murdered Creusa and her own two children by Jason. The pilgrim Dante encounters Jason among the seducers in Malebolge. Virgil describes Jason's sin as the seduction of Hypsipyle, and seems to mention Medea only as an afterthought: *e anche di Medea si fa vendetta* ("also for Medea vengeance is taken," *Inf.* 18.96). She is cited as an example in *Fiore* 161.6 and 190.5. Dante's source is Ovid, *Meta.* 7.1–424.

Olivia Holmes

Medusa

In classical mythology, one of three sisters known as the Gorgons, daughters of Phorcys and Ceto. The figure of Medusa would have been known to Dante from Ovid's *Metamorphoses* and from medieval legend. References would also have been found in Virgil's *Aeneid* (6.289, 7.341, and 8.435–438). Ravished by Neptune in a temple dedicated to Minerva, Medusa subsequently gives birth to Pegasus. But Minerva is offended by the violation of her temple and transforms the young girl into a monstrosity whose face and reptilian hair have the power to turn those who look upon her to stone.

In *Meta.* 4.793–803, Ovid concentrates upon the figure of Perseus, who defeats Medusa with the aid of a reflecting shield given to him by Minerva. Carrying Medusa's severed head as he flies over the Libyan desert, drops of blood fall on the sand and produce the snakes for which the region is notorious. In the *Metamorphoses,* this episode immediately follows the episode transformation of Cadmus and his wife into serpents, which Dante draws upon in *Inf.* 25. Here Dante claims to outdo Ovid in the description of transformation, and he also challenges Lucan, who in the *Pharsalia* speaks of the snakes that infest the Libyan desert. (In medieval legend the Medusa myth circulated as an example of pride whereby the transformation of Medusa was seen as a punishment visited upon her by Minerva for the pride she took in her own beauty.)

In the *Inferno,* reference is made to Medusa at an important turning point in the ethical and poetic program of the canticle. In *Inf.* 9, Dante-pilgrim, having moved through the circles of incontinence, is brought to a halt before the walls of the City of Dis, the region of Hell in which sins of malice are punished. Emphasis is placed here upon the inability of Virgil to secure Dante's entry into the city and correspondingly upon the paralysis of will that the protagonist suffers: only the *messo da ciel* ("[one] sent from Heaven") can open the gates of Dis on Dante's behalf; until he does, Dante is confronted with the threat that the call of the Furies will summon Medusa, the sight of whom will turn him to stone and deprive him of all power either to advance further on his journey or retrace his steps back to Earth.

This episode—structured around internal parallels between the action of Medusa and the *messo da ciel* and rich in external parallels between Dante and Perseus, Minerva and Beatrice—is one which invites allegorical explication, as the author himself suggests in canto 9. Some early commentators, like Pietro di Dante and Guido da Pisa, associate the name "Medusa" with the word terror and "Gorgon" with oblivion; others such as Jacopo della Lana (and, among modern critics, Padoan) speak of Medusa as a figure for heresy and for the conscious resistance of evil to the evidence of revelation. Such interpretations are consistent with the fact that Virgil, often read as representing human reason, cannot effect an entry into the City of Dis by his own powers alone: the crisis which Dante here confronts is one in which the very faculties of rational thought that have so far allowed him to advance toward salvation are not only paralyzed but may also be the source of sins such as those that are punished within the walls of Dis. Other interpretations link Medusa to sensuality (Boccaccio), cupidity (Benvenuto), obstinacy (Buti), and doubt (Scartazzini). This latter attitude becomes, in its extreme form, despair, specifically despair of the mercy of God, a sin defined by the Church as having no remedy because it cuts off the possibility of hope, in which rests the possibility of salvation. St. Thomas,

M defining despair *(desperatio)* in one sense as the ultimate of sins, refers to Isidore's comment that "To commit a crime is to kill the soul, but to despair is to fall into hell" (*De Summo Bono* 2.14), while St. Gregory states that despair "cuts off the way of return [to God]" (*Moralia* 8.18.34).

Following Auerbach's reading, it is also important to see the Medusa episode as one in which Dante as author consciously engages, through allusion, with the culture of the classical world. Though less explicitly than in *Inf.* 25, to which this canto is related by virtue of its Ovidian allusion, Dante here vies with the classics in point of narrative virtuosity. At the same time, since literary and moral questions are inevitably connected in Dante's poetry, the literary and cultural contest which is joined here also reveals a subtext in which the moral standing of contemporary vernacular literature is also at issue. On this level, the figure of Medusa is closely connected via the common denominator of stone with the motif of city walls and the corresponding questions of inclusion and exclusion within such walls. The experience of exile lies behind the episode; Medusa threatens the very remedy for exile which Dante is constructing, since her gaze would destroy the capacity for independent motion and thought which allows Dante to convert his exile into a pilgrimage and a narrative of pilgrimage.

The petrification theme which emerges in this episode is one that Dante also broaches in love poems devoted to the Stony Lady, the *rime petrose* where, admitting no possibility of freedom or conversion, he explores conditions of spiritual frustration and sterility. Extrinsically, the parallels here point to Dante's continuing attempt to define and redefine the nature of freedom which began in the *Vita Nuova* when the poet first dissociated himself from the tendency evident in Guido Cavalcanti's poetry to emphasize the malign rather than the beatific effects of love. Significantly, *Inf.* 8 contains a reminiscence of Guido's poetry which Dante puts in the mouth of Filippo Argenti, and in that episode the emphasis falls upon physical motion—and also upon the motions of narrative procedure—as it does throughout the Medusa episode: Filippo Argenti must "remain" as Dante exultantly proclaims. Yet such "remaining" must also apply implicitly to classical and vernacular poets alike who are incapable of perceiving the possibility of conversion and providential advance which Dante reflects in his own narrative.

But the episode also carries self-critical implications. The Medusa legend, in speaking of the divine power of Minerva, alerts the attention of the reader to the parallels to be drawn between *Inf.* 9 and *Inf.* 2. The Beatrice who was invoked in *Inf.* 2 by the ladies of Heaven to ensure that Dante should begin his salvific journey is parodically called to mind by the Medusa and the attendant Furies of *Inf.* 9. For a brief moment the narrative as well as the journey is in danger of betraying its own first principles.

Bibliography

Auerbach, Erich. *Literary Language and its Public in Late Latin Antiquity and in the Middle Ages.* Translated from the German by Ralph Manheim. New York: Pantheon Books, 1965.

Freccero, John. "Medusa: The Letter and the Spirit." In *Dante and the Poetics of Conversion.* Cambridge, Mass.: Harvard University Press, 1986, pp. 119–135.

Kirkpatrick, Robin. *Dante's Inferno: Difficulty and Dead Poetry.* Cambridge: Cambridge University Press, 1987, pp. 120–141.

Padoan, Giorgio. "Il canto X dell'*Inferno.*" *Letture Classensi* 5 (1976), 81–100.

Suther, Judith D., and R.V. Griffin. "Dante's Use of the Gorgon Medusa in *Inferno* IX." *Kentucky Romance Quarterly* 27 (1980), 69–84.

Robin Kirkpatrick

Megaera

Daughter of Night and Pluto or Acheron and first named of the three Furies threatening Dante at the gates of Dis: *"Quest'è Megera dal sinistro canto"* ("This is Megaera on the left," *Inf.* 9.46). Classical sources for the passage include Virgil (*Aen.* 12.845–848), Statius (*Theb.* 1.712ff, 4.636, 11.60), and Lucan (*Phars.* 1.577, 6.730).

Rebecca S. Beal

Meleager

An Argonaut, Meleager *(Meleagro)* was fated to live as long as a brand on the fire remained unconsumed. To save his life, his mother, Althaea, extinguished and preserved the wood. As an adult, Meleager slew the Calydonian boar and gave its hide to Atalanta. When his uncles seized it, Meleager killed them, thus grieving Althaea, who vengefully threw the fateful brand into the fire. Far from home, Meleager felt a flame scorch his innards and, as the brand burned, he died, according to Ovid (*Meta.* 8.445–525), Dante's source. On the terrace of gluttony, Virgil explains to Dante how incorporeal penitents grow lean by adducing the invisible link between Meleager's body and the burning wood (*Purg.* 25.22–24).

Jessica Levenstein

Melissus

Greek philosopher of Samos cited by St. Thomas in *Par.* 13.125, together with Parmenides, his mentor, and Bryson, as lacking competency in the art of reasoning. Dante, refuting arguments validating the subordination of the authority of the Empire to that of the Church, again invokes the examples of Melissus *(Melisso)* and Parmenides in *Mon.* 3.4.4 as bad thinkers, citing Aristotle's claim that "They adopt false premises and use invalid syllogisms" (*Physics,* 1.3.186a6).

Richard Lansing

Memory

Dante employs two terms for memory: *memoria* and, occasionally, *mente* (or Latin *mens*). The *Vita Nuova* opens with an explicit reference to memory, from which its nature as understood by Dante may be inferred: it is that part of the mind in which the past, together with the intellect's judgment regarding its significance, is preserved (1.1, 2.10). In 16.2 Dante distinguishes memory from the imagination, with memory making use of the imagination to represent the past. The implications of this distinction are developed in the *Commedia,* and in passages of the *Vita Nuova* (21.8 and 34.4, 6) which imply that the memory's preserved images must be read with this distinction in mind. Memory makes prudence possible, although passion may lead one to disregard it (15.2, 16.4).

The references to memory in the *Convivio*— e.g., an allusion to Galen's teaching (2.2.4) and the use of the technical philosophical term *corruzione* ("corruption," 4.4.10) for forgetfulness—reveal a familiarity with medieval theories of memory. Dante refers to the usefulness of a gift as the stamping of the memory of its receiver with an image of the gift (1.8.12), recalling the teaching of medieval Aristotelian philosophers regarding the difference between the memory and the imagination: the imagination preserves and stores information that originates from sense perception, whereas memory preserves the nonsensible

aspects of things. In 2.15.8 and 4.27.5 (as in *VN* 15.2 and 16.4) a relation is drawn between memory and virtue, particularly the virtue of prudence.

All these threads are woven together in the *Commedia.* Of the various characteristics of memory mentioned in this work one stands out, particularly in the *Paradiso:* the limitations of the act of memory. The song of the angels (*Purg.* 31.97–99), Beatrice's appearance (*Par.* 3.14.81), her eyes (*Par.* 18.11), the songs of the blessed (*Par.* 20.10–12), Dante's ecstasy in the sphere of the fixed stars (*Par.* 23.43–45), Beatrice's smile (*Par.* 30.25–27), and details of Dante's vision of God (*Par.* 33.5–57) are said to escape his memory's grasp. In all these instances Dante recalls having had an experience he cannot reconstruct, calling attention to the two components of the act of memory: the representation of the thing recalled (specifically a function of the imagination) and the apprehension of the thing recalled as having been sensed, or understood, in the past (specifically a function of the memory). Dante compares memory in the *Commedia* to a written record (*Inf.* 2.8 and *Purg.* 33.76). He contrasts it with the imagination (*Purg.* 33.76), comparing the latter to a painting. The obvious point is that the memory does *not* preserve sense data, hence the need for Dante to flesh out memories in order to reconstruct his voyage in the otherworld in the reader's mind. What is also obvious is that the imagination preserves *only* sense data, that is, sense data apprehended as sense data, not as data of this or that particular thing, hence the possibility of turning to it for images to flesh out an experience (e.g., *Par.* 14.103). The record of the past that memory preserves is constituted by the relationship between the person remembering and what is remembered: memory preserves only the *intenzioni* of particular things (see *Purg.* 18.23: *intenzione* in *Purg.* 18.23 is sometimes misleadingly translated as "image"). It is thus the first component of memory, the representation of the thing recalled, with which Dante has difficulty: in effect, the limitations of the act of memory with regard to sense experiences are traceable to the limitations of the imagination.

Dante's memory cannot relate what his intellect saw in its vision of God (*Par.* 1.4–9). This is explained in part by the Aristotelian doctrine that human beings cannot think without mental images, which are what the memory actually retains. Once again, the limitation of memory that Dante speaks of implies an incapacity on the part of the imagination, to which inability Dante precisely alludes at the end of the *Paradiso* (33.142). Beatrice mentions the act of remembering as *per concetto diviso* ("because of divided concepts," *Par.* 29.81) and notes that the angels, unlike humans, have no need of memory because they possess direct and continuous knowledge. Humans, on the other hand, see and know things sequentially, since they are unable to know simultaneously all the things that they know.

In Purgatory Statius serves as a vehicle to introduce a disquisition on the nature of the soul in life and after the death of the body. He observes that memory, together with intelligence and will, is sharper than ever immediately after death, in contrast to the other powers of the soul (*Purg.* 25.83–84). That this is so of intelligence and will is not surprising, considering that Dante conceives of them as non-organic powers (cf. *Par.* 1.120); in light of his insistence on the limitations of memory, however, and its immediate influence on feelings (*Inf.* 3.130–132 and *Purg.* 14.126), it is difficult to say that he conceives of the memory similarly. Likewise, Dante does not include memory among the faculties that characterize rational beings in *Par.* 1.120. He also does not explain how memory can operate without an organ, but it is clear why it does so immediately after death even before the soul has formed a body for itself from the surrounding atmosphere: without memory the soul would not know the concrete reasons for its being in Heaven, Hell, or Purgatory. It is, in short, an exigency of divine justice.

Paul A. Dumol

Mendicant Orders

The unobtrusive foundation, rapid growth, and eventual diffusion throughout Europe of the two great orders of friars—Franciscans and Dominicans, members of both of which were often called "mendicants" because they were forbidden to own property and sometimes had to beg for food—constituted perhaps the most significant development in the institutional history of the Christian Church during the twelfth century, and both the work of the orders and the ideals they claimed to represent impinged on Dante's life and writing in several interesting and complex ways.

The Franciscan order began to gather around Francis of Assisi at the end of the first decade of the thirteenth century; before Francis's death in 1226 it had already spread throughout Western Europe, including distant England. Francis's canonization in 1228 spurred the ever more rapid expansion of the Order, aiming to spread its founder's evangelical message of poverty, renunciation, service, and purity of heart. By the third quarter of the century, however, the Franciscan order had also become a potent institutional force within the church, providing prelates, theologians (Alexander of Hales, Bonaventure), and at least one pope—and for some dissident members this greatly elaborated role, with its inevitable compromise of the spiritual simplicity of Francis's own teaching, proved unacceptable. The order thus divided along sharply partisan lines into an "Official" (or "Conventual") wing, which accepted the more recent adaptation of the Franciscans' role with what looked to the dissidents suspiciously like enthusiasm, and a "Spiritual" group that urged—in often violently extremist terms—summary rejection of all temporal entanglements and immediate return to the pristine letter of Francis' Rule. The bitter mutual hostility between the two groups, which did not stop short even of bloodshed, characterized the situation of the order during most of Dante's lifetime, and by the 1320s the survivors among the defeated Spirituals were being persecuted as heretics.

The Dominicans' contemporary history was less dramatic. Founded as a body of preachers and teachers by a Spanish Augustinian canon, Dominic Guzman, in the second decade of the thirteenth century, the order spread almost as rapidly as the Franciscans—whom Dominic expressly took as an organizational model—but in a very different context. Its appeal was especially great in university towns and among intellectuals; it encouraged the creation of new centers of learning, and already by mid-century it had produced outstanding thinkers of the caliber of Albertus Magnus and Thomas Aquinas. This educational mission was in the forefront of Dominican activity until well into the fourteenth century, although by then the order had also begun to undertake a leading role in the development of the investigative practices associated with the notorious Inquisition.

Dante's involvement with both orders was clearly of great significance, though its exact contours are often hard to determine. According to the *Convivio* (2.12), during his early infatuation with the *donna gentile* of philosophy, he frequented *le scuole de li religiosi e . . . le disputazioni de li filosofanti* ("the schools of the religious orders and . . . the disputations held by the philosophers"), and this very probably refers to his attendance at two Florentine schools or *studia,* the Franciscan house at Santa Croce and its Dominican counterpart at Santa Maria Novella, in the early 1290s. (Interestingly enough, among the teachers at Santa Croce in precisely these years were two of the most famous Spiritual Franciscans, Pietro di Giovanni Olivi and Ubertino da Casale, while Santa Maria Novella was home to a major Dominican thinker, Remigio de' Girolami.) Certainly the *Commedia* gives ample evidence of Dante's indebtedness to the respective intellectual traditions of Franciscanism and Dominicanism, although, as is not entirely unexpected given the histories of the two orders, the Dominican thinking of such as Albertus and Thomas seems to have been more influential on him than that of Bonaventure or any of his fellow Franciscans.

Individuals, episodes, and even symbolism connected with the two orders appear throughout the *Commedia,* which presents them in both positive and negative contexts (such as that of Guido da Montefeltro's backsliding in *Inf.* 27). Most controversially, the mysterious episode of the *corda* ("cord") that Dante-character gives to Virgil to be thrown into the abyss as a summons to Geryon (*Inf.* 16.106–114) has often been interpreted as signalling the historical Dante's affiliation with the Franciscans as a tertiary, or lay, member. But the most sustained and elaborate treatment of the mendicant orders is reserved for Paradise, and specifically for the great eulogies of Francis and Dominic themselves uttered by Thomas Aquinas and Bonaventure in *Par.* 11–12.

Many critics have observed that the structural principle of this episode is parallelism and chiasmus. In canto 11, Thomas Aquinas (significantly appearing alongside Albertus Magnus) describes the complementary stature of the mendicant orders' founders, the one (Francis) *tutto serafico in ardore* ("all seraphic in his love," 37), the other (Dominic) *per sapienza . . . di cherubica luce uno splendore* ("in wisdom . . . a splendor of cherubic light," 38–39). He goes on to offer a heartfelt biographical tribute to Francis (40–117), before concluding with a denunciation of the failure of his own, Dominican, order to live up to the standards set by its founder (118–139). In canto 12, meanwhile, the Franciscan Bonaventure likewise praises Dominic in effusive terms (31–105) before denouncing the condition of the contemporary Franciscans and their deviation from the path laid down by Francis himself (106–126).

Dante is clearly offering here, through two chosen mouthpieces of unimpeachable authority, his own vision of the mendicant orders and their relationship to their own professed ideals. It is often observed that he seems more interested in, and knowledgeable about, the Franciscans than the Dominicans. If this is indeed the case, it may be because the Franciscan order was much more deeply in crisis at the time of *Paradiso*'s composition than its Dominican counterpart and rival, rather than (or at least as much as) for any reason connected with personal commitments of his own. Through Bonaventure's speeches, rich in rhetorical fervor and sometimes startling metaphor, Dante presents the unmistakable image of an order hopelessly divided against itself, one group (the Officials, or Conventuals) relaxing Francis's Rule to an unacceptable degree, and the other (the Spirituals) applying it with excessive force (12.121–126). As a corrective, *Par.* 12 proposes the middle way associated with the historical Bonaventure himself, the symbol of a phase in the order's history (roughly 1250–1275) when it was still possible for a Franciscan luminary to hold high office and remain true to Francis's ideals. Bonaventure's resonant declaration *Io son la vita di Bonaventura / da Bagnoregio, che ne' grandi offici / sempre pospuosi la sinistra cura* ("I am what lives of Bonaventure of Bagnoreggio, who in my great duties always subordinated the left-hand cares [treated temporal responsibilities as less important],"12.127–129) makes him Dante's standard-bearer of true Franciscanism, a moderate doctrine able to combine the essence of Francis's radical message with a proper sense of duty toward the secular world, and the embodiment of Dante's vision of what the mendicant order to which he seems most personally attached had once been, and might one day still be.

Bibliography

Davis, Charles T. *Dante's Italy and Other Essays.* Philadelphia: University of Pennsylvania Press, 1984.

Foster, Kenelm. *The Two Dantes and Other Studies.* London: Darton, Longman & Todd, 1977.

Manselli, Raoul. "Dante e l'Ecclesia Spiritualis." In *Dante e Roma.* Florence: Le Monnier, 1965, pp. 115–135.

Mellone, Attilio (ed.). *Dante e il francescanesimo (Lectura Dantis Metelliana)*. Cava de' Tirreni: Avagliano, 1987.

Petrocchi, Giorgio. *Vita di Dante*. Bari: Laterza, 1983.

Steven Botterill

Mercury

The Roman god of traders and commerce and the messenger of the gods, as well as the second planet and heaven in Dante's cosmology. Dante mentions Mercury *(Mercurio)* in his role as the gods' messenger at *Mon.* 2.6.10 and *Epist.* 7.17, and he twice refers to the god in the *Commedia* (*Par.* 4.61–63, 22.144), both times as a way of referring to the planet of the same name. Pietro Alighieri suggests that the messenger from heaven at *Inf.* 9.80–103 is to be identified with Mercury, although this identification has found little support.

Dante seems to have considered himself a "child" of Mercury (see *Par.* 5.97–99). He states that he was born under Gemini, one of the "houses" of that planet, and that he owes to those stars his poetic genius (*Par.* 22.106–123). The question of his natal horoscope is raised by the first of the so-called "stony rhymes," probably written in the 1290s.

The planet Mercury was considered to be the smallest of the seven known to the medieval world. This characteristic, together with the fact that it is so close to the sun that the latter's rays conceal it from our sight more than they do any other planet, led Dante to compare it to dialectic; for Dante, Dialectic comprises a smaller body of knowledge than the other sciences, and is more *velata* ("concealed") in its procedure than they are because of its sophistical and hypothetical manner of argumentation (*Conv.* 2.13.11).

But there is no overt reference to this comparison in the *Paradiso,* and in the sphere of Mercury Dante encounters *i buoni spirti, che son stati attivi / perché onore e fama li succeda* ("good spirits who were active so that honor and fame might follow them," *Par.* 6.113–114). Their motivation, while not preventing their salvation, does, however, represent a failing of some sort, since it caused *i raggi del / vero amore* ("the rays of the true love," 116–117) to rise to heaven less strongly. There is little critical agreement concerning the underlying moral or theological principle governing Dante's decision to have this class of souls

Dante with Justinian in the Heaven of Mercury. Opere del divino poeta Danthe, *ed. Pietro da Figino, Venice, 1520. Giamatti Collection: Courtesy of the Mount Holyoke College Archives and Special Collections.*

appear in the second heaven other than what Dante himself explicitly provides. Justinian and Romeo di Villanova are the only two named souls in this heaven.

Dante's stay in Mercury (*Par.* 5.88–7.148) is dominated by Justinian's and Beatrice's speeches to Dante. Justinian speaks for the entirety of *Par.* 6, describing his life and his law-code (the supposed activity undertaken for the fame and honor it would bring), as well as providing a brief summary of the history of Rome up to Dante's time (told as the history of the Roman eagle), and narrating the story of Romeo. In the seventh canto, Beatrice resolves certain doubts which this speech raises in Dante's mind concerning God's justice, and also speaks of the body's resurrection.

Bibliography

Costa, Gustavo. "Dialectic and Mercury (Education, Magic and Religion in Dante)." In *The "Divine Comedy" and the Encyclopedia of Arts and Sciences.* Edited by Giuseppe di Scipio and Aldo Scaglione. Amsterdam and Philadelphia: J. Benjamins, 1988, pp. 43–64.

Durling, Robert M., and Ronald L. Martinez. *Time and the Crystal: Studies in Dante's "Rime petrose."* Berkeley and Los Angeles: University of California Press, 1990.

Frank B. Ordiway

Meridian

Sacrobosco's medieval textbook definition, probably known to Dante, states: "The meridian is a circle passing through the poles of the world and through our zenith, and it is called 'meridian' because, wherever a man may be and at whatever time of year, when the sun with the movement of the firmament reaches his meridian, it is noon (*meridies*) for him. For like reason it is called the 'circle of midday.'. . . If two cities have the same meridian, then they are equally distant from east and from west" (*Sphere* 2, p. 126). In the *Commedia,* Dante introduces the term *(meridiano, merigge)* in this sense without explanation (*Purg.* 2.2) and often uses it or its equivalent to indicate the time of day (*Purg.* 2.57, 4.138, 25.2, 33.104). Dante also has Folco use the technical concept to describe the length of the Mediterranean (*Par.* 9.86). Finally, the Virgin Mary is said to be a *"meridïana face / di caritate"* ("noon-bright torch of love," *Par.* 33.10) because she is as bright as the sun, and possibly as well because of her placement on the central axis of the Mystic Rose.

Bibliography

The "Sphere" of Sacrobosco and Its Commentators. Edited and translated by Lynn Thorndike. Chicago: University of Chicago Press, 1949.

Buti, Giovanni, and Renzo Bertagni. "Meridiano." *Enciclopedia dantesca,* 3:912.

Richard Kay

Messo celeste

A term used to refer to the "heavenly messenger" figure who intervenes in *Inf.* 9 to open the gates of Dis that had been shut in Virgil's face. Although momentarily disconcerted by the obstinacy of the devils, Dante's guide knows that help is on the way even before it appears, and assures the pilgrim that already, on this side of the upper gate of Hell, *discende l'erta, / passando per li cerchi sanza scorta, / tal che per lui ne fia la terra aperta* ("there comes down the slope, passing through the circles without a guide, such a one that by him the city will be opened to us," *Inf.* 8.128–130). This divine aid arrives accompanied by "the crashing of a fearful sound" as the *messo* treads dry-shod over the waves of the Styx, "from his face . . . moving that greasy air" (82). The phrase *da ciel messo* (85) can mean simply that he was "sent from Heaven" or that he is a "heavenly messenger," in the sense of an angel, as more strongly indicated by the manuscript variant *del ciel messo* ("messenger of/from heaven"). With his *parole sante* ("holy words," 105) this personage disdainfully rebukes the citizens of Dis, who flee before him. While Dante, following Virgil's direction, bows down before him, he opens the gate with a *verghetta* ("little wand," 89), and then returns by the way he came, looking otherwise preoccupied (*Inf.* 9.79–105).

Among the early commentators, Ottimo and Boccaccio took the *messo* for an angel, as have most modern readers. Yet Pietro Alighieri and, later, Benvenuto da Imola rejected this assumption, recognizing instead the pagan deity, Mercury, by his unmistakable little staff, caduceus or *virga,* with which he guides the dead. It is under this aspect of psychopomp that Statius depicts Mercury flying down into Hades to fetch the shade of Laius, a description in turn modeled on Virgil's episode of Mercury's descent to goad Aeneas (*Theb.* 2.1–6; *Aen.* 4.238–258; cf. Martianus Capella *The Marriage of Philology and Mercury* 1.9).

Sometimes called the *nuntius deorum,* Mercury is the messenger and interpreter *(interpres)* of the gods, sent to the depths from on high to expedite divine wishes. Augustine etymologized his name as *sermo medius currens,* or "speech running between," as indicative of his role as the carrier of God's pronouncements (*City of God* 7.14). Mercury boasts special competence in eloquence, prudence, and slyness *(astutia).* Moreover, as god of commerce, he represents skills apparently necessary to descend into the nether regions of Hell. Early commentators also commonly noted that Mercury was the second planet, having influence on men's eloquence, industry, cleverness, and even fraudulence. Pietro remarked that this "promiscuous" planet can be an omen of good fortune when it is in the company of benign stars, but can be an evil influence when found in a malevolent sign.

Other suggestions for this character's identity have included Hercules, Aeneas, Caesar, Moses, Aaron, Saint Peter, Henry VII of Luxemburg, a devil, and even Christ. Pasquazi elaborated a theory that the *messo* was an angel, possibly the archangel Michael, especially assigned to Limbo. More recently, critics have seen the *messo celeste* as a figure alluding to a specific typological event or to a complex of classical allusion. Musa interprets it as a re-enactment of the First Coming, when Christ descended into Hell. Quint instead

M

views the episode as a critical recasting of important epic motifs: the trip to the underworld and the descent from Heaven.

Like angelic mediators, Mercury delivers messages and pronouncements to men; like Mercury, angels can also be depicted with a small wand indicative of their communicative mission. The ambiguous identity of the *messo celeste* is symptomatic of Dante's effort to synthesize classical topoi within a Christian framework. The *messo* might therefore best be described as an angel in disguise, seen under the aspect of a pagan god, as befits the infernal perspective.

Bibliography

Greene, Thomas. *The Descent from Heaven: A Study in Epic Continuity.* New Haven, London: Yale University Press, 1963.

Heilbronn, Denise. "Dante's Gate of Dis and the Heavenly Jerusalem." *Studies in Philology* 72 (1975), 167–192.

Iannucci, Amilcare. "Dottrina e allegoria in *Inferno* VIII, 67–IX, 105." In *Dante e le forme dell'allegoresi.* Edited by Michelangelo Picone. Ravenna: Longo, 1987, pp. 99–124.

Mazzotta, Giuseppe. *Dante: Poet of the Desert.* Princeton, N.J.: Princeton University Press, 1979, pp. 275–318.

Musa, Mark. *Advent at the Gates.* Bloomington: Indiana University Press, 1974.

Pasquazi, Silvio. "Messo celeste." *Enciclopedia dantesca,* 3:19–21.

Quint, David. "Epic Tradition and *Inferno* IX." *Dante Studies* 93 (1975), 201–207.

Alison Cornish

Metellus

A tribune, Lucius Caecilius Metellus *(Metello)* unsuccessfully defended the Roman treasury—kept in the temple of Saturn on the Tarpeian Hill—against Caesar in 49 B.C.E. When Caesar threw open the temple doors, the hill resounded (Lucan, *Phars.* 3.153–155). Dante claims that the roar of the doors of Purgatory surpasses the grating of Tarpea's temple doors (*Purg.* 9.133–138).

Bibliography

Armour, Peter. *The Door of Purgatory: A Study of Multiple Symbolism in Dante's "Purgatorio."* Oxford: Clarendon, 1983.

Jessica Levenstein

Metrics and Versification: The Minor Works

Poetry, Dante believed, was an art that required both knowledge and skill, in the vernacular as in Latin; the poet must possess *cautio* ("caution") and *discretio* ("discernment"), which can never be acquired *sine strenuitate ingenii et artis assiduitate scientiarumque habitu* ("without exertion of the intellect, dedicated study of technique, and immersion in knowledge," *DVE* 2.4.10). More specifically, according to the *Convivio,* the art of poetry combines three skills, those of the grammarian, the rhetorician, and the musician (2.11). Metrics and versification belong, in Dante's thinking, to the last category. Poetry is language *per legame musaico armonizzata* ("harmonized according to the rules of poetry," 1.7.14), not just because in Dante's time it was often sung, but because he saw the metrical form—rhyme, rhythm and *lo numero regolato* (1.10.12), the regulated structure of lines and syllables—as governed by essentially musical laws.

The *De vulgari eloquentia* develops this general position with a more specific discussion of the verse structure of lyric poetry in the vernacular, but it contains, incomplete as the book is, only a partial treatment of the subject (most of the argument is in any case concerned with matters of language and style), and has very little to say on other kinds of poetry. As a result, its bearing on the *Commedia* is limited, very limited as far as metrics and versification are concerned. Of the three principal lyric forms, the *canzone,* the *ballata,* and the sonnet, the first is the most "excellent" (2.3.3), and is suited to the "illustrious" vernacular, the subject with which the *De vulgari eloquentia* as we have it is principally concerned. The *canzone* is also associated with the highest, "tragic" level of style and the most noble subjects: arms, love, and virtue. The *ballata* is less excellent for a number of reasons, one being that it needs dancers to accompany it, while it is generally accepted, Dante maintains, that the *ballata* is superior to the sonnet. Dante proposed to deal with the *ballata* and the sonnet in the fourth book of the *De vulgari eloquentia,* which he did not write, and which was also to deal with the less illustrious, middle level of language.

The *De vulgari eloquentia*'s treatment of the *canzone* is largely a description of established practice, including Dante's own. The form is defined (2.8) as series of "equal" stanzas *(stantiae)* in the highest, "tragic" style with a single subject and without a refrain (which characterizes the *ballata*). "Equal" stanzas means stanzas each with the same rhyme scheme, though not necessarily the same rhymes, and the same sequence of line-types, mainly 11- and 7-syllable; when sung, plainly, the melody for each stanza is the same. There follows an account (2.9–11) of the internal divisions of the stanza, which may either have a single melody or involve a repetition and change of melody. In the latter case there may either be a single *frons* with an initial melody, followed by a new melody repeated in two or more *versus* (or *volte* in the vernacular); or, alternatively, there may be an initial melody repeated in two or more *pedes,* followed by a new melody in a single *cauda* (or *sirma*), or repeated in two or more *versus.* Because they correspond to a repetition of the melody, each of the *pedes* or *versus* must contain the same sequence of line types and the same rhymes, or at least the same rhyme scheme (2.13).

Of the line types used by Italian poets, the hendecasyllable (11-syllable line) is the best because of its capacity for elevated style and subject matter (2.5). However, a mixture with 7-syllable lines can further increase its splendor, and 5-syllable lines are also occasionally acceptable; other odd numbered lines are much less acceptable, while even numbered lines are, Dante maintains, scarcely ever used. The poet should generally avoid excessive repetition of the same rhyme *(rithimi repercussio),* "equivocal" rhymes involving the repetition of the same word form with different meanings *(inutilis equivocatio),* and an excess of rough sounds *(asperitas)* in rhyme position; but rough mixed with softer sounds *(lenitas)* add distinction to the verse (2.13). The *De vulgari eloquentia* breaks off (2.14) at the point at which Dante begins to discuss the number of lines in the stanza and the number of syllables in the line— though he has earlier said something about the relative dimensions of *frons, cauda, pedes,* and *versus,* which are allowed to vary considerably. Nothing is therefore proposed about rhythm in the sense of accentual structures, or about the rules for counting syllables—which may also reflect the fact that the practice of Dante and his contemporaries in these matters was far less strictly rule bound than that of their successors.

All the lyric poems firmly attributed to Dante belong to the three categories he refers to in the *De vulgari eloquentia*: sixteen are *canzoni,* plus two in the special *canzone* form of the *sestina* and two single stanza *canzoni*; fifty-six are sonnets, plus three "double" sonnets; and six are *ballate.* In the

canzone, the number of stanzas varies from one (the single stanza *canzoni*) to seven (in *Doglia mi reca*), and, as the convention requires, each stanza of the poem repeats the same rhyme scheme and the same distribution of 11-syllable, 7-syllable, or, in one case (*"Poscia ch'Amor"*), 5-syllable lines. Except in the case of the *sestine,* the stanzas all begin with two *pedes* with the same rhymes (for instance *abbc abbc;* occasionally the order is inverted), and then continue with a *cauda* or *sirma.* The first rhyme of the *cauda,* which marks the *diesis* or change of melody and is known as the *verso chiave,* usually repeats the last rhyme of the *pedes* (*DVE* 2.13); and in all cases but one the *cauda* concludes with a rhyming couplet. Most of the *canzoni* end with a *congedo,* a shorter stanza often addressed to the poem itself, with a rhyme scheme and line structure that in most cases repeat those of the preceding *sirma.* In all these aspects of the *canzone* Dante follows the common practice of his contemporaries, though with an exceptional degree of variety, and with a pronounced taste for weighty and complex stanza structures.

The *sestina* form was borrowed by Dante from the Provençal poet Arnaut Daniel. The first of Dante's poems in this mode ("Al poco giorno") follows Arnaut's model closely. It consists of six stanzas of six hendecasyllables, each employing the same six rhyme words. Each stanza repeats the rhyme words of the stanza before as follows: line 1 that of the previous stanza's line 6, line 2 that of line 1, line 3 that of line 5, line 4 that of line 2, line 5 that of line 4, and line 6 that of line 3 (*abcdef, faebdc,* etc.). There is a 3-line *congedo* containing all six rhyme words, three at the end and three in the middle of the line. Dante's second *sestina* ("Amor, tu vedi ben") embodies a more elaborate scheme (*abaacaaddaee, eaeebeeccedd,* etc.), with five stanzas and five rhyme words, each stanza consisting of twelve lines. Lines 3, 4, 6, 7, and 10 in each stanza use the same rhyme word as the first line; lines 8 and 9 share another rhyme word, as do lines 11 and 12. The first rhyme word in each stanza is the same as that of the last two lines of the stanza before, each of the five rhyme words occupying this position in turn; the remaining rhyme words appear in the same order as in the stanza before, but in different positions, each one place further down in the scheme. There is a 6-line *congedo* in which the five rhyme words appear in the opposite order to that of the preceding stanza (*aeddcb*). The extreme formal complexity of this

M poem is exceptional in Dante's work, but by outdoing Arnaut Daniel in such a way he illustrates strikingly the importance he attaches to technical skill in poetry. Referring to the poem in the *De vulgari eloquentia* (2.13.13), he speaks of it as something new and untried *(novum aliquid atque intentatum artis),* comparable to the feats of prowess attempted by a newly dubbed knight.

Dante's *ballate* and sonnets also generally follow the practice of his contemporaries. The *ballate* use 11-syllable, 7-syllable, and in one case ("Per una ghirlandetta") 9-syllable lines in varying combinations, in a scheme determined by the movements of the dance: an initial refrain of three or four lines, followed by one or more stanzas, each consisting of two *pedes* and a *versus* like those of the *canzone* stanza, the *versus* ending with the last rhyme of the refrain. Dante's sonnets almost all consist of hendecasyllables in two quatrains each with the same two rhymes—either alternating (the larger number: *abab*) or enclosed (*incrociate* in Italian: *abba*)—followed by two tercets each with the same two or three rhymes in a variety of orders: *cdc, dcd; cdd, dcc; cdc, cdc; cde, cde; cde, dce; cde, edc.* Three sonnets are "double" (*doppio* or *rinterzato*), a form apparently invented by Guittone d'Arezzo: an additional line of seven syllables is added after lines 1, 3, 5, 7, 10, and 13 of the normal sonnet scheme, each one repeating the rhyme of the line that precedes it. The 232 sonnets of the *Fiore,* which may or may not be by Dante, follow the same scheme as eleven of Dante's lyric poems: *abba, abba, cdc, dcd.*

In accordance with the practice of some of his contemporaries, a small number of Dante's lyric verse lines do not rhyme: the first line of some of the *ballate,* the first line of the *congedo* of some of the *canzoni,* and (exceptionally) lines 8 and 11 of each stanza and lines 1 and 3 of the *congedo* of "Lo doloroso amor." On the other hand at least one poem ("Poscia ch'Amor," which also contains the only 5-syllable lines in Dante's work) has two lines in each stanza with an internal rhyme on the second and third syllables, a practice to which Dante refers in *DVE* 2.12.

Bibliography

Boyde, Patrick. *Dante's Style in His Lyric Poetry.* Cambridge: Cambridge University Press, 1971.

Foster, Kenelm, and Patrick Boyde (eds.). *Dante's Lyric Poetry.* 2 vols. Oxford: Oxford University Press, 1967.

Pazzaglia, Mario. *L'armonia come fine: conferenze e studi danteschi.* Bologna: Zanichelli, 1989.

David Robey

Michael, the Archangel

Mentioned in the Old Testament (Dan. 10 and 12) as a guardian of the Israelites and in the New Testament (Rev. 12) as having fought against "the great dragon . . . that old serpent, called the Devil, and Satan, which deceiveth the whole world" and as having cast the Devil or Satan "out into the earth." In *Inf.* 7.11–12, Virgil reminds Plutus of how the rebellion of the bad angels in Heaven was defeated by the loyal angels when, chastising Plutus for attempting to block his and Dante's way, he assures him that Dante's journey through Hell is willed in Heaven *là dove Michele / fé la vendetta del superbo strupo* ("where Michael avenged the proud onslaught"). In *Purg.* 13.51, Michael is among those whose intercession is invoked by the envious to help speed their purgation. In *Par.* 4.22–63, Beatrice explains to Dante how sacred scripture *condescende / a vostra facultate* ("condescends to your faculties," 43) by representing God with hands and feet and giving *aspetto umano* ("human shape," 47) to *Gabriel e Michel . . . e l'altro che Tobia rifece sano* ("Gabriel and Michael . . . and the other [Raphael] who cured Tobias," 46–48). According to some critics, Michael is also the angel-like figure *da ciel messo* ("sent from Heaven") of *Inf.* 9.64–103. In the Book of Jude, where Michael is called an archangel, he is also mentioned as having contended with the devil for the body of Moses, a tradition which affords Dante the pattern for the twin episodes of the angel and the devil who make rival claims for the soul and bodies of Guido da Montefeltro and Buonconte da Montefeltro (*Inf.* 27.112–120, *Purg.* 5.104–108).

Todd Boli

Michal

The daughter of Saul, Michal *(Micòl)* disdainfully observes King David, her husband, dancing before the ark (2 Sam. 6:16). She rebukes him and is consequently punished with sterility. Dante depicts the scene of her scornful stare on a marble wall on the terrace of pride, where David stands as an example of humility (*Purg.* 10.67–69).

Jessica Levenstein

Microcosm

The term refers to a small world (Gr. *mikròs kósmos*) or model of the universe, great world, or macrocosm (Gr. *makròs kósmos*). The microcosm is characteristically represented by man or a work of art. Such a conception has existed in many, perhaps most, cultures; for the European Middle Ages the concepts and correspondences handed down in the Platonic and Neoplatonic traditions (see Plato; Neoplatonism) were particularly important, partly because of the enormous influence exerted on all schools of thought in antiquity by Plato's late dialogue *Timaeus (Timeo),* partly because the *Timaeus* was the only Platonic dialogue widely known in the Latin West (in the incomplete translation and commentary by the third- or fourth-century Christian bishop Calcidius).

According to the creation myth set forth in the *Timaeus,* the world is a living creature directly fashioned by a divine craftsman (demiurge); its body expresses the nature of its soul, which combines the two spiritual motions of the Same or of Identity (corresponding, in the world's body, to the regular diurnal motion of the heavens from east to west) and of the Other or Different (corresponding, in the world's body, to the diverse contrary motions of the seven planets from west to east along the zodiac—monthly for the Moon, annual for the Sun, shorter or longer for the other five). The soul and body of the world, because made directly by the demiurge, are immortal and perfect, perfect in shape (spherical) and in motion (circular). Man's immortal soul is modeled on this world; the human body, however, is made out of the lower elements by the lesser deities (i.e., the stars and planets) and is therefore mortal and not self-sufficient. For this reason the spherical head, shaped to house the same spiritual motions as the heavens, must be supported by the rest of the body, whose construction Plato likens to that of an elaborate garden.

Transmitted in numerous ancient texts influenced by the *Timaeus,* such as Seneca's *Natural Questions,* Macrobius' *Commentaries on the Dream of Scipio,* Boethius' *Consolation of Philosophy,* as well as in Calcidius' incomplete version, these ideas elicited an upsurge of interest in the twelfth and thirteenth centuries, reflected in the works of Bernard Silvester, Alain of Lille, Hildegard of Bingen, and others. Pope Gregory the Great (590–604) had made a formulation that was widely echoed (for instance by John Scotus Erigena and Robert Grosseteste) that "we share being with the stones, life with the plants, sensation with the animals, and intellection with the angels": man thus mirrors all creation, and parallels were frequently drawn between the atmosphere and the breath, the veins of the body and the rivers of earth, the belly or the feet and the earth, and so forth.

Microcosmic thinking had many varieties and was extremely flexible. Perhaps the most obvious variety is the one, derived from the *Timaeus,* which correlates the human soul with the World Soul, the spherical head with the heavens raining down influence, and the rest of the body with animals, plants, and Earth with its rivers and minerals. The first of Dante's *rime petrose* ("stony rhymes") poems, "Io son venuto al punto de la rota," carries out such parallels in great detail. The *Commedia* also draws upon the notion, though less obviously, for after the descent through Hell, correlated with the body of death, *Purgatorio* and *Paradiso* imply an ascent through the breast (rectification of the will) into the (spherical) head.

Microcosmic thinking can be applied to society, which is seen as a human being writ large or as a model of the cosmos. The idea of the body politic in its various versions also goes back to Plato, who in the *Republic* developed the idea that a social structure mirrors the characteristic personality structure of its members. The medieval conception of the body politic often involved a detailed parallelism between classes and parts of the body; John of Salisbury's *Policraticus,* for instance, correlated the king with the head, the heart with the senate, the stomach and intestines with tax-gatherers and treasurers, and the hands and feet with soldiers, merchants, and laborers. The idea of the Church as the body of Christ developed out of the classical idea of the body politic. From it obviously derive such conceptions as the personified justice of the eagle of *Par.* 18–20, formed by myriad souls, as well as the overall body analogy in *Purgatorio* and *Paradiso,* which represent a "growing up into the head, which is Christ" (Eph. 4:15). The *Inferno* exploits in great detail the idea of Hell as the body of Satan.

Regarding society as an analogue of the cosmos, the Church could be considered a second creation of the world. Book 13 of Augustine's *Confessions* is devoted to an allegory of Gen. 1 developing the idea in detail: the Bible corresponds to the firmament, its authority spread over all mankind, the clergy to the heavenly bodies shaping all below, and the laity to the sublunar. Dante draws on this and similar conceptions in the *Paradiso,* most notably in his life of St. Francis of Assisi (*Par.* 11), according to which St. Francis was a sun shedding light and warmth and formative influence (*virtute,* line 57). The parallel between secular rulers and heavenly bodies (especially the Sun) underlies Virgil's exposition of Fortune in *Inf.* 7, and informs the expectation of Henry VII's descent into Italy, which is described as "the rising of a long-awaited Sun" (*Epist.* 7.1).

Closely related is the extended analogy drawn in *Conv.* 2.12–14 between the nine heavens (including the Empyrean) and the seven liberal arts plus metaphysics and theology. Dante's conception is explicitly astrological as well as microcosmic—he lists three "similarities" between the sciences and the heavens: (a) both revolve about what is subject to them; (b) both shed light on what is below; and (c) both induce perfection. Thus the philosophical writings of Cicero and Boethius, because of their rhetorical power (the third heaven corresponds to rhetoric), have affected him like heavenly bodies, shaping him and inducing perfection in him, specifically the love of wisdom.

If either a book or its writer may serve a role analogous to that of the heavenly bodies, influencing or shaping their readers, so too can the processes whereby the heavens shape the sublunar be compared with the activity of a human craftsman, an idea that also goes back to the *Timaeus.* Dante's fullest exposition of this notion appears in *Par.* 2.112–148, according to which the Intelligences governing the heavenly spheres take from above the form they impose on the sublunar; the spheres themselves correspond to the hammer of the smith, governed by conscious art.

All these patterns of microcosmic analogy come together in the traditional idea that the work of art itself may be a model of the universe. An important tradition of ancient thought regarded works of human art as normatively microcosmic, and there is much evidence of conscious imitation of the cosmos in both the content and the form of literary works, from the famous descriptions of Achilles' shield (*Iliad* 16) and certain of Plato's dialogues, through Virgil's *Eclogues* and *Aeneid* and Seneca's *Natural Questions,* to Boethius' *Consolation of Philosophy,* not to speak of many ancient architectural monuments (such as the Pantheon in Rome, which Dante undoubtedly visited). The Gothic cathedrals were microcosmic in representing all reality and all history (for the universe itself is God's temple) as well as the glory of the next world and the structure of the human body; the famous account of the building of the abbey church of St. Denis by Abbot Suger (1081–1151) explicitly relates the light-centered design of the new style with Neoplatonic light-metaphysics.

Like the "petrose," the *Commedia* accounts for the relation of the protagonist to all history and all creation. In content the *Commedia* is a representation of the cosmos, particularly in the *Paradiso,* and is thus a microcosm. The structure of the entire poem is based on the principle of the Neoplatonic return of the universe to God, so that the formal principles that account for the poem, like those that account for the universe—the origins or causes of both poem and universe—are revealed in the *Paradiso:* the Omega (goal) of poem and universe is revealed to be their Alpha (cause). Like that of the Pantheon or the abbey church of St. Denis, the microcosmic structure of the *Commedia* emphasizes the formal causality of light—both that of the visible heavenly bodies and the "uncreated light" or glory of the Creator, which permeates all things.

In many formal respects as well, the *Commedia* mirrors the universe, as in its 100 cantos (embodying the square of the "perfect" number 10) and its rhyme-scheme, *terza rima* ("triple rhyme"), which, like the cosmos itself, bears the imprint of the triune being of its creator, the trinity of Father, Son, and Holy Ghost.

Bibliography

Allers, Rudolf. "Microcosmus: From Anaximander to Paracelsus." *Traditio* 2 (1944), 319–407.

Barkan, Leonard. *Nature's Work of Art: The Human Body as Image of the World.* New Haven: Yale University Press, 1975.

Cornford, F. M. *Plato's Cosmology: The "Timaeus."* London: Routledge & Kegan Paul, 1937.

Coulter, James. *The Literary Microcosm: Theories of Interpretation of the Later Neoplatonists.* Leiden: Brill, 1976.

Durling, Robert M., and Ronald L. Martinez. *Time and the Crystal: Studies in Dante's "Rime petrose."* Berkeley, Los Angeles: University of California Press, 1990.

Miller, James L. *The Cosmic Dance in Classical and Christian Antiquity.* Toronto: University of Toronto Press, 1986.

Panofsky, Erwin (ed.). *Abbot Suger: On the Abbey Church of St. Denis and Its Art Treasures.* Princeton, N.J.: Princeton University Press, 1946.

Rico, Francisco. *El pequeño mundo del hombre: Varia fortuna de una idea en las letras españolas.* Madrid: Editorial Castalia, 1970.

Robert M. Durling

Midas

Rewarded by Bacchus for caring for the god's companion, Silenus, Midas *(Mida),* king of Phrygia, requested the power to turn all he touched into gold. When he found that even food and drink became inedible metal, Midas begged the god to revoke the favor. He was instructed to bathe in the river Pactolus, which thenceforth bore gold. Afterwards, when judging a musical contest between Pan and Apollo, Midas chose Pan, and was forced by Apollo to wear ass's ears. He concealed them from all but his barber, who whispered the secret into a hole in the ground. Reeds covering the hole murmured the buried words. Dante, who follows Ovid, *Meta.* 11.100–193, mentions Midas in *Purg.* 20.106–108, where the penitents shout his name as an example of avarice, and in *Egl.* 4.50–53, where Alphesibeus alludes to the reeds whispering Midas's secret.

Jessica Levenstein

Minerva

The Roman name of Pallas Athena, the goddess of wisdom and of many arts and sciences. As patroness of Athens she bestowed invaluable benefits on her city. Minerva *(Minerva, Pallade)* is depicted in the marble frieze on the first terrace of Purgatory in the act of punishing pride, once explicitly, in helping to defeat the giants' rebellion (*Purg.* 12.31), and once implicitly, as the force behind Arachne's punishment for insolently claiming to surpass Minerva at weaving (*Purg.* 12.43–45). When Arachne hanged herself, Minerva in pity turned her into a spider (see Ovid's *Meta.* 6.1–140).

She is associated with wisdom in *Conv.* 2.4.6, and in *Purg.* 30.68, where Beatrice's head is said to be crowned with her olive. The story of her naming of Athens is alluded to in *Purg.* 15.98, and her visit to Helicon to inquire about the Hippocrene fountain is referred to in *Epist.* 13.3 (*Epistle to Cangrande*).

F. Regina Psaki

Minos

In Greek and Roman mythology, Minos *(Minòs)* was the son of Zeus and Europa. He became ruler of ancient Crete and was renowned for his sense of justice. Following Virgil's example (*Aen.* 6.432–433), Dante assigns to Minos the role of judge of Hell, but transforms him into a monstrous figure with a long tail and a bestial voice. Located at the entrance to the second circle (*Inf.* 5), which is the first circle of personal sin, he serves as its guardian and sits in judgment of all the souls condemned to Hell. One by one they appear before him and confess their sins. He then announces his judgment by wrapping his tail around himself a number of times equal to the number of the circle to which the sinner is condemned. When he catches sight of Dante, he warns him to be careful whom he trusts once inside Hell (*Inf.* 5.16–20), but Virgil warns Minos not to attempt to thwart Dante's divinely ordained journey. Additional references to Minos appear in *Inf.* 13.94–96, 20.35–36, 27.124–127, 29.118–120, and in *Purg.* 1.77.

Lawrence Baldassaro

Minotaur

The monstrous offspring of a bull and queen Pasiphae, wife of Minos of Crete, the Minotaur was immured by Minos in a labyrinth designed by Daedalus and was fed with Athenian youth until

Dante with the Minotaur and Centaurs. Opere del divino poeta Danthe, ed. Pietro da Figino, Venice, 1520. Giamatti Collection: Courtesy of the Mount Holyoke College Archives and Special Collections.

M it was slain by Theseus with Ariadne's help. Called by Dante *l'infamïa di Creti . . . che fu concetta ne la falsa vacca* ("the infamy of Crete . . . conceived in the false cow," *Inf.* 12.12–13), the hybrid beast appears stretched out on the ruin separating the sixth from the seventh circles of Hell. Dante's primary source is Ovid (*Meta.* 8.152ff.; *Ars amatoria* 1.289–316, 2.24; see also *Aen.* 6.25–26), but Dante differs from his predecessors both in implying that his monster has a bull's body and human head and in connecting the beast with violence. Thus, a simile comparing the monster's thrashing to that of a bull (12.22–25; see *Aen.* 2.223–224), and Dante's manner of presenting the other monster-guardians of the seventh circle as human-headed with bestial bodies, would hint at the Minotaur's having a beast's body. Virgil's identification of the Minotaur as *quell'ira bestial* ("that bestial anger," *Inf.* 12.33) suggests its emblematic connection with the sin of wrath and hence the seventh circle, although some scholars question the appropriateness of linking the monster too closely with the complex sin of violence.

Bibliography

Tartaro, Achille. "Il Minotauro, la 'matta bestialitade' e altri mostri." *Filologia e critica* 17 (1992), 161–186.

Rebecca S. Beal

Momigliano, Attilio

Distinguished Dante scholar trained in Turin by Arturo Graf and in Florence by Pio Rajna, Momigliano (1883–1952) owes his lasting reputation to the annotated edition of the *Commedia* he published in 1946–1948 (Florence, Sansoni), when, after suffering racial persecution, he was reinstated in his Florentine chair. The actual achievement of Momigliano's commentary (which, owing to the cogency and elegance of its prose, can be considered a literary work in its own right) lies in a masterfully charted rediscovery of the *Commedia* as a poetic unit and continuum. In Dante, Momigliano does not seek the theologian or the scientist, and not even the well-read author thriving on sources and reminiscences. What he looks for instead are the new ways by which the poet incessantly strives to express the emotions and the awareness of a common humanity. Momigliano's sensitive, insightful analysis involves every aspect and every layer of the text: metrics,

narrative pace, contrasts and analogies, landscapes and atmospheres, images, special effects (light, music, silences) and, to be sure, diction and lexicon. Momigliano's lesson, evident in his well-known essay "Il paesaggio della *Divina Commedia*" (contained in *Dante, Manzoni, Verga*), is, difficult as it may be to reenact today, still an effective antidote against the trend of mistaking the poem for a glorified tract or a well-knit cento or a lyric anthology of disconnected fragments.

Bibliography

Momigliano, Attilio. *Dante, Manzoni, Verga.* Messina: D'Anna, 1944, pp. 3–31.
Petrocchi, Giorgio. "L'eleganza di Momigliano." In *La selva del protonotario: Nuovi studi danteschi.* Naples: Morano, 1988, pp. 201–211.

Ruggero Stefanini

Monarchia

Sometime during the last seven years of his life, Dante completed the three books of this work on the relationship between the papacy and the empire. We know this from an affirmation in *Mon.* 1.12.6, found in all manuscript versions, that Dante had completed at least up to the fifth canto of the *Paradiso* (where he speaks of free will, *della volontà la libertate,* at verse 22) before finishing the *Monarchia:* "This freedom (or this principle of freedom) is the greatest gift given by God to human nature—as I have already said in the *Paradiso* of the *Comedy.*" As recent critics have noted, we must not treat the information, as earlier editors and critics did, as a mere scribal intervention, but accept it as the only concrete evidence that we have for a dating of the *Monarchia* after 1314.

Perhaps from his reading of the dispassionate writings of St. Thomas Aquinas, in the *Monarchia*—as all the manuscript versions and *editio princeps* attest, and as Michele Barbi insisted, the title is *Monarchia* or *Liber Monarchiae,* not *De Monarchia*—Dante achieved a certain aloofness unreflective of the stress and strife of his times. Leaving the earlier intense, political *Epistles,* written in support of Henry VII's descent into Italy during the period 1310–1313—Henry was crowned Holy Roman Emperor in Rome in 1312—the reader approaching this treatise is struck by the poet's tactic of shrouding any reference to immediate contemporary affairs. The passionate patriot of the letters has disappeared. Dante does not identify himself; nor does he discuss any contemporary cause célèbre. In the *Monarchia*, Dante still tacitly refuses to recognize the inevitable decline of the Empire so unsuited to the temper of those times of independent city states and growing national kingdoms. He instead manipulates his reader's sense of a text discarnate, striving to create the impression of a message beyond time, derived from man's divine reason and inspired by God's revelation. The difficulty historians and critics have had in dating the treatise is therefore a result of the author's own strategy.

The other characteristic of the treatise, and one that is both subversive within the tradition of the "rule" or "mirror of princes" tradition of the Middle Ages, is its dependence, especially in Book 2, not so much upon the Bible but most firmly upon the classical version of pagan history given by Roman poets and historians, between whom, curiously, he makes no distinction. The *Monarchia* quietly omits any mention of the Jews being the chosen people in the times before Christ and argues that God's attention and will manifested itself temporally in the Romans' pursuit of dominion. Dante turns Augustine's negative interpretation of history in *The City of God* against itself. Whereas those writing in the early Christian tradition, like the Bishop of Hippo, his predecessors and followers, such as Lactantius and Paulus Orosius, had used pagan history as a series of negative *exempla* "against the pagans," seeing in Roman dominion over the known world only *latrocinia magna*, or "a great piracy," Dante records his own change of mind in *Mon.* 2.1.2: "For my own part, I used once to be amazed that the Roman people had set themselves as rulers over the whole world without encountering any resistance, for I looked at the matter only in a superficial way and I thought that they had attained their supremacy not by right but only by force of arms. But when I penetrated with my mind's eye to the heart of the matter and understood through unmistakable signs that this was the work of divine providence, my amazement faded. . . ."

Dante considers Roman history as a divine, not human, institution, one capable, as Augustine had affirmed, of human "valid inference" (*De doctrina christiana* 2:32), observable by men and recorded so that they might interpret God's actions in history and thus learn and teach the truth of God's plan: history is, for the poet, a record of God's *positive* intervention to bring peace to the world in the fullness of time and thus it is central to the project of the *Monarchia*. Christ put his seal upon Rome's authority by his enrollment in the Roman census at his birth. As Dante said in the *Epistle to the Italian Cardinals* (*Epist.* 8.2): "Rome . . . after so many triumphs and glories, Christ by word and deed confirmed the empire of the world." With Charles Till Davis we can concur that "[Dante] did not merely value the ancient city for itself; he used it as an *exemplum* which could compel humility, rather than arrogance" (32).

Dante's Forensic Procedure

The rediscovery of Aristotle after the twelfth century had given the West a complete outline of all known areas of knowledge. Aristotle was "the master of Philosophers" (*Conv.* 4.8.15). Consequently, for Dante and his contemporaries, Aristotle's syllogistic logic was equivalent to logic itself. The *Monarchia* is an outstanding example of Aristotelian thought, proceeding from a first principle (each of the three books proceeds thus) discussed in a concatenation of syllogisms that lead to conclusions often odd or surprising to the modern, uninitiated reader. The most important effect of the Aristotelian conquest in logic was the institution and habit of litigation on any issue of importance. In every field, debates became acrimonious and polemicists scored points by attending to abstractions divorced from concrete experience. The controversy that engaged Dante, and, after Dante's death, passionately enthralled his severe censors, such as the Dominican Guido Vernani (in his *Reprobation of Dante's Monarchia*), was certainly no exception.

The Contents of the **Monarchia**

Each of the books of the treatise deals with a specific problem following the order outlined in *Mon.* 1.2.3: first, whether a sole world governor is necessary for the good of the world; second, whether the Roman people appropriated the office of monarchy to itself *de jure;* third, whether the authority of monarchy depends directly upon God or on some other minister or vicar of God.

Book 1 of the treatise argues that the human race is best governed by a single world ruler. This monarch is necessary for the total function of the intellect—not the intellect of one particular man, but of all those upon earth in some future time when all thought and will shall be one. Nor is Dante Averroistic here, despite possible miscomprehension of

M DANTIS

A L I G H E R I I
F L O R E N T I N I
MONARCHIA.

C O L O N I Æ A L L O B R O G U M,

Apud HENR. ALBERT. GOSSE & SOC.

M D C C X L.

Title page of the Monarchia *published by Gosse in 1740. Reproduced by permission of the John A. Zahm Dante Collection in the Department of Special Collections, University Libraries, University of Notre Dame.*

his terminology and his allusion to the heretical commentator of Aristotle's treatise *On the Soul* (*Mon.* 1.4.9). Dante foresees a time when the world would be one under the sway of one ruler within the realm of time. The poet's concepts deal explicitly with "those things which are measured by time" (*Mon.* 1.2.2), that is, within temporality, not within the hereafter, and are thus divorced from any heretical concept of the individual's soul subsumed into a total world soul in eternity, as Averroës had taught. The peace and beatitude attainable in this life would pertain only to those alive at some future time in which the right functioning of temporal rule is achieved. God, through nature ("God's art"), creates for a purpose—he creates nothing in vain. The human "possible intellect," the highest part of the human intellect, which has possibilities, potentialities, and capabilities beyond

what it may presently be putting into effect, must achieve its fullness of function. Therefore, the poet believes, that divine purpose must and will be fulfilled.

To be unified, mankind, Dante believes, needs a single governor. The human race can only achieve the fulfillment of the possible intellect when mankind acts as one. Dante argues this from the firmness of tradition, for the monad (the one, unity) had always meant holiness, peace, and concord, while the dyad (plurality, the many) signified division and disintegration. Dante depends upon this numerological abstraction to give a divine dimension to his argument; humanity best resembles God when it is one and united.

Étienne Gilson declared, "Dante was able to raise up a universal Monarch vis-á-vis to the universal Pope only by imagining this monarch himself as a kind of Pope" (179). While there is much truth and logic in this, and while we can agree that Dante saw the analogy clearly, his reasoning for a unique monarch has further and far older bases. The poet, in fact, argues for the singleness of the emperor based not merely upon the contemporary analogy of a unique spiritual vicar of Christ, but directly, upon the ancient analogy of a unique godhead. His argumentation for world monarchy belongs to a tradition that stretches back to early Christianity and exactly reverses and parallels that used by the early apologists who had pleaded for monotheism by basing their reasoning on the rule of an existing single Roman Emperor. That a king stood in the same relation as God stood to the world had been common in Hellenistic political philosophy as well as in Pythagorean–Platonic traditions, and we find it echoed not only in Lactantius in a reversal of its intent, but in Stabs (C.E. fifth century), in Ambrosiaster, and John of Salisbury; even St. Thomas had used the analogy in his *De regno ad regem Cypri* (*On Princely Government,* 51). Moreover, Dante bases his argument against the validity of the "Donation of Constantine" (*Mon.* 3.10)—a document that Lorenzo Valla would prove a forgery in 1440—on Lactantius' reasoning of a single God (*Divine Institutes* 1.3).

Book 2 of the *Monarchia* is at once the most original, most problematic, and, perhaps, to modern readers, the most unconvincing of the three. In essence Dante makes a synthesis between the two Western currents of opinion on the origin of earthly government: that is, not only the Aristotelian but the Augustinian. The essential Christian doctrine came primarily from Augustine's great treatise *The City of God,* wherein the Bishop of Hippo excoriated the Romans for their idolatry and obsessive pursuit of worldly glory through war and bloodshed: in a famous passage (4.4), he cited the tale of Alexander and the brigand, where empires were revealed as no more than robber baronies or brigandage. Yet, at the same time, Augustine saw God's providence as the origin of all empire, for even unjust rulers are a God-sent chastisement for the sins of subjects. Augustine was thus remarkably ambiguous about the Roman Empire, vituperating its paganism on one side while giving divine origin to it on the other. It is the latter view of Augustine that Dante adopts, that of the Augustine who proclaimed in *The City of God:* "The Roman Empire is ordained by God, from whom every power is derived, and by whose providence all things are governed" (5.21).

Dante's adoption of the concept of *disceptatio,* meaning "divine revelation through the decision or outcome of a contest," owes much to Augustine's treatise. For both writers, "The time and the outcome of wars depend on the will of God" (*City of God* 5.22). In Book 2 Dante forsakes human reason to claim a direct intervention of the Deity in human affairs: no longer is human reasoning required here, but faith in the judgment of the supernatural. First, he lists what he sees as miracles showing a direct intervention of God's hand in history's events: Numa and the fall of the divine buckler from the heavens; the cackling of the goose that saved the Capitol; the defeat of Hannibal by a hailstorm; and the wondrous escape of Cloelia during Porsenna's siege. The appeal is to the reader's faith, not to his logic.

Second, Dante's argument from the *certamen* ("putting-to-the-test") of Roman victory as an athletic contest and then as a duel between rival champions again depends on this direct intervention of the Deity. Finally, he deals with the argument of Christ's birth in the fullness of time, again adducing the direct intervention by God himself.

Book 3 of the *Monarchia* deals with the analogical reasonings of the papal curia and the correcting of its rhetorical abuses. Dante brings nine arguments to bear: six are scriptural (three each in biblical order, from the Old and New Testaments) and three historical and rational. Most revealing of the typical cast of Dante's thought is the process by which, even as he must refute false conclusions, he cannot escape the system in which

those conclusions were reached. For him analogical reasoning must be refuted by analogical disputation. First, in *Mon.* 3.4.1–22, he attacks the centuries-old hierocratic commonplace of the "two luminaries" based on Gen. 1:14–19: the temporal ruler receives his power from the pope just as the Moon receives all its light from the Sun. Dante first attacks it on the grounds of biblical exegesis. Citing Augustine's *City of God* 16.2 and *On Christian Doctrine* 1.36–37 concerning the imposition of spiritual meanings into a text where none exist, he complains of the error of those who twist the meaning of the inspired writer of Exodus, and thus the meaning of the Holy Spirit, to a sense never intended. Dante proceeds to denounce the analogy's soundness on the grounds of chronological order, for the ruling powers of man are "accidents" or qualities of man: the two offices of the two guides of mankind were founded far later than the "great lights" to which they are compared, and were necessitated by man's later Fall into "the infirmity of sin." God had created the Sun and Moon on the fourth day of Creation, two days before mankind on the sixth day (Gen. 1:14–19, 26–27): citing for his procedure Aristotle's *On Sophistry* 18, 176b29, he confutes as false and inconceivable the assumption that God would create the "accidents," that is, sinfulness and its necessitating the cure of the two powers and their symbols, before the substantial subject, man (*Mon.* 3.4.13–17).

In the second part of his argument, however, we feel the power of Christian symbolic and exegetical tradition as he turns to re-admit the original analogy with a modification. The Moon does not depend upon the Sun either for its being or for its light (its "power" or *virtus*), for (as Dante unscientifically alleges, remarking on the moonglow in eclipses) God alone created it and it has "some light of its own" (*Mon.* 3.4.18): like the Moon the temporal power derives its being and power from God, but it receives an increase in its ability to function from the grace of the pope's blessing. Thus, ironically, he permits the mighty simile of the "luminaries" to persist. The second papalists' error, dealt with in *Mon.* 3.5.1–5, consists in their adducing the primogeniture of Levi, the founder of priesthood, over that of Judah, the founder of kingship among the Jews (Gen. 29:34–35), to prove the superiority of the spiritual power over the temporal. Dante argues that the case of Jacob's sons does not apply because the papal syllogism involves four terms instead of the allowed three,

M for the equation of "birth" with "authority" is untenable: many who are younger hold positions of power over those who are older. Thirdly, Dante maintains that in order to prove that the pope has the power to grant and take away temporal power, it is wrong to assert the precedent of Samuel (1 Kings 8:11–31, 10:1, 15:23), who raised Saul to the throne and then deposed him, for Samuel did not act as "vicar of God" as the pope does. On the contrary, like a hammer in the hands of a smith, Samuel acted only with the direct order of God and the limited power of an ad hoc nuncio, unable to take independent action or act on his own authority.

With the Old Testament analogies concluded, for the fifth error Dante turns to papal analogies from the New. Defenders of hierocratic hegemony err when they equate the authority of Christ, who received both spiritual and temporal authority in the figure of the Magis' gift of frankincense and gold, with that of the pope. The assertion of coequality of Christ and his vicar is untenable, for a vicar never enjoys the same power as he who sends him, "for no vicariate, human or divine, can be equivalent to the primary authority" (3.7.4). Although the next two arguments assailed are far more traditional, and thus, persistent, Dante shows his expertise in dialectic in confuting them. They are, in fact, known under their symbolic names "the keys," and "the two swords": St. Peter as "keeper of the keys of heaven" and his supposed possession of the "two swords of spiritual and temporal authority." "Thou art Peter . . . And I will give you the keys of the kingdom of Heaven. And whatsoever thou shalt bind upon Earth, it shall be bound also in Heaven; and whatsoever thou shalt loose on Earth, it shall be loosed also in Heaven." These words of Christ to Peter, in Matt. 16:19, hierocrats had interpreted as Christ's endowing the first of the Apostles with the limitless prerogative to abolish or impose binding laws and decrees in the temporal sphere. Dante insists that the limit and extension of meaning of Christ's term "whatsoever" pertains not to limitless dominion but only to those things restricted within Peter's office. Christ referred only to the Apostle's role as keeper of the keys, that is, only in spiritual affairs: "And thus the universal sign which is contained in 'whatsoever' is limited in its reference by the office of the keys of the kingdom of heaven" (3.8.10). If "whatsoever" signified limitless power, then Peter and his successor the pope would be able to per-form even forbidden or impossible acts such as divorcing a wife from a man and marrying her to someone else while her husband is still living, or forgiving the sins of those unrepentant. Dante then (3.9.1) turns to the question of the interpretation of Peter's words to Christ—"here are two swords" (Luke 22:38)—as implying that the Apostle and his successors possessed both temporal and spiritual powers. First, it was the hasty, sometimes confused and simple-mannered Peter who spoke of the swords, not Christ, and, secondly, in context, the Savior was speaking of the numerous swords that the disciples needed to spread the faith. The two swords, therefore, mean not realms of authority, but the "works and words" of the Apostles.

The last paragraph of 3.16, the very end of the *Monarchia,* has received a diversity of interpretations and much incomprehension. Within it Dante returns to the traditional analogy of the two luminaries, but is mindful of his own twist on it, that the Moon, the Empire, has light of its own: "But the truth concerning this last question should not be taken so literally as to mean that the Roman Prince is not in some sense subject to the Roman Pontiff, since this earthly happiness is in some sense ordered towards immortal happiness. Let Caesar therefore show that reverence towards Peter which a firstborn son should show his father, so that, illumined by the light of paternal grace, he may the more effectively light up the world, over which he has been placed by Him alone who is ruler over all things spiritual and temporal."

The emperor gives reverence in exchange for the paternal grace of the pope in a spiritual guidance beyond the competence of the temporal power. In the *Monarchia,* Dante maintains the separation of the power of the empire from that of the papacy as central and he retains that contention throughout his works. The realms of the temporal and spiritual, however, although separate from one another, must aid and respect each other on earth. In other words, Dante does not write the *Monarchia* to demonstrate a Ghibelline superiority or precedence of the empire over the papacy; he writes to restore a balance in mutuality between the two powers. No thinker of Dante's time could have denied, neither would or could Dante deny, the superiority of spirit over matter, of soul over body, of the transcendent over the immanent and thus of the spiritual over the temporal, or deny that the spiritual is the ultimate end of man beyond any temporal or temporary goal.

Despite A. P. d'Entrèves and Marjorie Reeves's contention that this ending vitiates the arguments of the rest of the treatise, *Mon.* 3.16.17–18 is really no such aberration; it is both a Christian and Aristotelian conclusion. In fact, Dante carefully prepares for his ending in several earlier passages of the treatise, especially in *Mon.* 3.4.20, where he tackled the traditional analogy of the two governing powers to the two great luminaries: "Thus I say that the temporal realm does not owe its existence to the spiritual realm, nor its power (which is its authority), and not even its function in an absolute sense; but it does receive from it the capacity to operate more efficaciously through the light of grace which in Heaven and on Earth the blessing of the supreme pontiff infuses into it." Their functions are of different purpose and different derivation: the Moon even has its own fainter light. However, to fulfill its function more effectively the Moon receives greater light from the Sun as the emperor receives the fatherly blessing of the pope.

Dante insists that the addition of this benediction bestows the light of grace and increases the efficacy of the emperor's power received directly from God—the passage prepares for the ending of the treatise. Dante's position throughout the *Monarchia* and in its last words does not differ substantially from the statements of the imperial position that preceded him. Ghibelline apologists, such as Giovanni Brancazoli of Pavia in his *On the Beginning and Origin and Power of the Emperor and the Pope* of 1313, claimed that the emperor's oath sworn to the pontiff during the coronation signified not vassalage but reverence and devotion. Traditionally *reverentia* or *reverenza* was not equated with *obedientia* and signified, rather, the very circumscribed duties of a son in full maturity toward his father. In return the father would grant love, instruction, and example. The son would regard his parent as a man, not as an authority (Sistrunk, 95–112; Di Scipio, 267–284). Dante sets forth the perfect relationship between the Church and Empire, just as he was to do in *Par.* 6 where the emperor Justinian recounts how Pope Agapetus removed him from the error of monophysitism and led him to accept God's grace. With the aid of God, Justinian reformed Roman law and brought it into line with God's law. Dante thus gives a concrete example of the ideal cooperation of two powers directly ordained by God for mankind's gaining the goal of earthly peace and justice on the way to the goal of the blessedness of the next life. For Dante, natural law, the reasonable ordering of the world, is the basis for all his claims for the empire: he recognizes the dignity of the natural sphere of rational and ethical values—original sin did not blot that out nor will God's last judgment annihilate it. Spiritual power does not replace or delete the earthly. Dante's vision of reciprocal aid and the increase of effectiveness of the emperor through the grace of the pontiff's blessing fulfills St. Thomas's dictum: *Gratia non tollit naturam sed perficit* ("Grace does not abolish Nature but perfects it"). Man, says Dante, is of a dual nature, mortal and divine. He is, therefore, to enjoy two kinds of beatitude: the blessedness of this life, insofar as he is mortal, and the blessedness of the eternal life, insofar as he is immortal. The beatitude of this life consists in the *operatio proprie virtutis* ("operation of one's own virtue"), by which Dante means the exercise of the highest human faculties. The blessedness of the eternal life consists in the *fruitio divini aspectus* ("fruition of the divine aspect").

The *Commedia* is in perfect accordance with this scheme. The empire was established before the church: Aeneas's descent to the underworld in *Inf.* 2.6–7 is a favor of the Deity, parallel to Paul's rapture to the third heaven. The event set the stage for the founding of Rome and the Empire, and, consequently, prepared the seat of the papacy. The chronology here is identical to the *Monarchia:* the empire is God-founded and was established prior to the see of Rome. In the *Commedia,* the arrival at personal justice and temporal blessedness is symbolized by the Earthly Paradise; the attainment of eternal blessedness by the Heavenly Paradise. The guidance of philosophy (understood as all human wisdom) allows man to achieve temporal blessedness through the practice of the moral and the intellectual virtues, although progress toward earthly felicity occurs simultaneously with the gaining of eternal blessedness through revelation and the practice of the theological virtues (faith, hope, and charity). Human reason makes known the nature of temporal blessedness and the means of attaining it through philosophy, yet it is aided by grace in the pursuit of eternal blessedness, and the means of attaining both are made available by the Holy Spirit, operating directly and through intercession, through the prophets, through Scriptures and sacred writers, through Christ, and his disciples. By the government of the emperor man attains temporal blessedness; eternal blessedness

M he attains under the leadership of the pope. In the *Commedia,* Virgil, exemplifying the limitations of classical philosophy (though he is Virgil, tragically damned yet chosen divinely as a guide and no mere personification), leads Dante-pilgrim to the Earthly Paradise to both "crown and mitre" him over himself (*Purg.* 27.142); and Beatrice (Dante's beloved, now in glory, but likewise in some sense typifying theology and revelation) guides him on from there, through the nine heavens, to the Empyrean, to St. Bernard, and thence the sight of God. The near-parity of the two beatitudes, however, as Dante asserts them in the *Monarchia,* is unprecedented: St. Thomas, like those before him, had treated the blessedness of this life as merely ancillary to eternal blessedness; for him, as for Augustine, true beatitude, in fact, could not be had in this life. Dante, of course, recognized, more clearly, perhaps, than anyone, the far greater importance of eternal blessedness. The logic that underlies his scheme in the *Monarchia* is forensic, political, and corrective.

Early Manuscripts and Fortune

Boccaccio informs us in his *Trattatello in laude di Dante* that the *Monarchia* was "scarcely known" before the coronation of Ludwig of Bavaria in 1328, when it became a major pamphlet in Ludwig's quarrel against the papacy. At about the same time the treatise was assailed by several censures, the most notable being the *Reprobatio Monarchiae Dantis,* by an obscure Dominican, Guido Vernani of Rimini. The manuscript tradition of the early years, that of the first two generations of copies, is mostly lost because of the proscription by Cardinal Poujet, the nephew of Pope John XXII, ordering all copies of the *Monarchia* to be burned as heretical in 1329. Manuscripts were hunted out and burned publicly, though no official, posthumous charge of heresy against Dante was ever made to the curia. The prohibition was continued with the *Monarchia*'s inclusion on the Index in Venice and then on the list of Paul IV. Only in 1881 did the church remove it from the *Index librorum prohibitorum.* Thus the earliest manuscripts are found without the author's name, with false ascriptions, or with false titles. Taking advantage of its brevity, scholars had copies bound amid collections of works of a different kind. Only in 1559 did the editio princeps of the original Latin appear—in Lutheran Basel, and the first publication on Italian soil had to wait for the edition published in Venice in 1758 by Zatta. Yet Marsilio Ficino had made an elegant Italian translation of it in the fifteenth century that was very popular (published first in Florence in 1839, edited by Pietro Fraticelli), and abundant glosses in the early manuscripts show that the work was avidly read by friends and foes alike.

The tradition of reliable early texts is meager. Pier Giorgio Ricci counted only nineteen extant manuscripts when he made his edition for the Società Dantesca published by Mondadori in 1965. Many more copies surely remain to be discovered in libraries and archives. Prudence Shaw is preparing a new critical edition of the *Monarchia;* she has recently published an *editio minor* with translation and notes. Richard Kay's edition and commentary, which has just appeared, is the most recent.

Bibliography

Primary Works

Aquinas, St. Thomas. *De regno ad regem Cypri.* In *Selected Political Writings.* Edited by A. P. d'Entrèves. Translated by J. G. Dawson. Oxford: Blackwell, 1948.

Dante Alighieri. *Monarchia.* Edited and translated, with commentary, by Richard Kay. Toronto: Pontifical Institute of Medieval Studies, 1998.

———. *Monarchia.* Edited and translated by Prudence Shaw. Cambridge: Cambridge University Press, 1995.

———. *Monarchia.* In *Opere minori.* Vol. 5/2. Edited by Bruno Nardi. Milan, Naples: Ricciardi, 1979.

———. *Dantis Alagherii Epistolae.* Edited by Paget Toynbee. Revised by Colin Hardie. 2nd ed. Oxford: Clarendon Press, 1966.

———. *Monarchia.* Edited by Pier Giorgio Ricci. Edizione Nazionale delle opere di Dante Alighieri a cura della Società Dantesca Italiana. Milan, Rome: Mondadori, 1965.

———. *Monarchia.* Edited and translated by Donald Nichol, with notes by Colin Hardie. London: Weidenfeld and Nicolson, 1954.

Vernani, Guido. *Il più antico oppositore politico di Dante: Guido Vernani da Rimini. Testo critico del Reprobatio Monarchiae Dantis a cura di Nevio Matteini.* Padua: CEDAM, 1958.

Secondary Works

Barbi, Michele. "L'Italia nell'ideale politico di Dante." *Studi danteschi* 24 (1939), 5–27.

———. "L'ideale politico religioso di Dante." *Studi danteschi* 23 (1938), 46–77.

Capitani, Ovidio. "*Monarchia,* il pensiero politico." In *Dante nella critica d'oggi.* Edited by Umberto Bosco. Florence: Le Monnier, 1965, pp. 722–738.

Davis, Charles Till. *Dante and the Idea of Rome.* Oxford: Clarendon Press, 1957.

d'Entrèves, A. Passerin. *Dante as a Political Thinker.* Oxford: Clarendon Press, 1952.

Ercole, Francesco. *Il pensiero politico di Dante.* 2 vols. Milan: Terragni e Caligari, 1927–1928.

Gilson, Étienne. *Dante and Philosophy.* New York, Evanston, London: Harper Torch Books, Harper and Row, 1963.

Di Scipio, Giuseppe. "Dante and Politics." In *The Divine Comedy and the Encyclopedia of Arts and Sciences: Acta of the International Dante Symposium, 13–16 November 1983, Hunter College, New York.* Edited by Giuseppe Di Scipio and Aldo Scaglione. Amsterdam, Philadelphia: John Benjamins Publishing Company, 1988, pp. 267–284.

Kay, Richard. "The Intended Reader of Dante's *Monarchia.*" *Dante Studies* 110 (1992), 37–44.

———. "Roman Law in Dante's *Monarchia.*" In *Law in Medieval Life and Thought.* Edited by Edward B. King and Susan J. Ridyard. Sewanee Medieval Studies 5. Sewanee, Tenn.: The Press of the University of the South, 1990.

Maccarrone, Michele. "Il terzo libro della *Monarchia.*" *Studi danteschi* 33, no. 1 (1955), 5–142.

———. "Teologia e diritto canonico della *Monarchia* III, 3." *Rivista di Storia della Chiesa in Italia* 5 (1951), 7–42.

———. "La teoria ierocratica e il canto XVI del *Purgatorio.*" *Rivista di Storia della Chiesa in Italia* 4 (1950), 359–398.

Nardi, Bruno. "Dal Convivio alla Commedia." In *Dal Convivio alla Commedia. (Sei saggi danteschi).* Rome: Nella sede dell'Istituto, 1960. Reprinted in *Dal Convivio alla Commedia (Sei saggi danteschi).* Nuovi Studi Storici 18. Rome: Istituto Storico Italiano per il Medio Evo, 1992, pp. 37–150.

———. "Di un'aspra critica di Fra Guido Vernani a Dante." *L'Alighieri: Rassegna bibliografica dantesca* 6 (1965), 42–47. Reprinted in *Saggi e note di critica.* Milan, Naples: Ricciardi, 1966.

———. "Filosofia e teologia ai tempi di Dante in rapporto al pensiero del poeta." In *Saggi e note di critica dantesca.* Milan, Naples: Ricciardi, 1966, pp. 3–109.

———. *Saggi e note di critica dantesca.* Milan, Naples, 1966.

———. "Di un'aspra critica di Fra Guido Vernani a Dante." *L'Alighieri: Rassegna bibliografica dantesca* 6 (1965), 42–47. Reprinted in *Saggi e note di critica dantesca.* Milan, Naples: Ricciardi, 1966, pp. 377–385.

———. "Intorno ad una nuova interpretazione del terzo libro della *Monarchia* di Dante." In *Dal Convivio alla Commedia,* pp. 152–314. Rome: Nella sede dell'Istituto, 1960.

Reeves, Marjorie. "Marsiglio of Padua and Dante Alighieri." In *Trends in Medieval Political Thought.* Edited by Beryl Smalley. Oxford: Blackwell, 1965.

Shaw, Prudence. "Sul testo della Monarchia." *Studi danteschi* 53 (1981), 187–217.

———. "Il volgarizzamento inedito della *Monarchia.*" *Studi danteschi* 47 (1970), 59–224.

Sistrunk, Timothy G. "Obligations of the Emperor as the Reverent Son in Dante's *Monarchia.*" *Dante Studies* 105 (1987), 95–112.

Took, John F. "The *Monarchia.*" In *Dante: Lyric Poet and Philosopher.* Oxford: Clarendon Press, 1990, pp. 147–173.

Vinay, Gustavo. *Interpretazione della "Monarchia" di Dante.* Florence: Le Monnier, 1962.

Anthony K. Cassell

Monasticism

Withdrawal from society and dedication to the spiritual struggle to achieve perfection of the self. The term monasticism derives from the Greek *monos,* "one, alone," and *monachos,* "solitary one." The monastic life, which promotes asceticism, contemplation, and service for the glory of God, signifies living either in absolute solitude (eremitism, from the Greek *eremites,* "desert," or anchoretism, from the Greek *anachoresis,* "withdrawal") or in communities (cenobitism, from the Latin *coenobita,* "conventual," "living together"). The aim of monasticism originated not so much from a rejection of the world in itself as from a desire to love God more intensely by separating the self from the attractions of the world.

The phenomenon has taken various forms in different cultures and religions. If one accepts the discoveries of the Dead Sea Scrolls, one could probably trace Christian monasticism to the religious community of Qumran. It is certain, however, that monasticism was practiced in early Christian communities. It grew out of the words of Christ, which established both its object (perfection) as well as its manner of operation: "Be perfect just as your heavenly father is perfect" (Matt. 5:48), and "If you wish to be perfect, go, sell what you have and give to the poor, and you will have treasure in heaven; then come, follow me" (Matt. 19:21). These words were interpreted by many Christians as advocating the practice of celibacy, poverty, obedience, austerity, prayer, and the separation of the self from the other faithful.

Christian monasticism can be divided into Eastern and Western monasticism. Eastern monasticism was founded by St. Anthony, whose retreat into the Egyptian desert dates from c. 285. Historically, we can trace the first form of Western monasticism to Rome and the year 340, when St. Athanasius (c. 295–373), author of the *Life of Anthony,* visited the city accompanied by two Egyptian monks, Ammon and Isidore, who were disciples of St. Anthony. Roman monasticism followed the Egyptian model, and this new format spread to Gaul through the work of Martin of Tours, who established a monastery near Poitiers in 362. The true founder of Western monasticism, however, is considered to be St. Benedict of Nursia, despite the import of earlier influence from the East. St. Benedict (480–543) was the first to give rules to his monks *(Regula Sancti Benedicti)* and to stress as an underlying principle of their pursuit the belief that *Operi Dei nihil praeponatur* ("nothing must be put before the work of God"). Departing from the practices of Eastern monasticism, he established an abbot who functioned as the father in a family (from the Hebrew *abbas,* "father"), and also imposed the rule of fixed residency (*Regula,* Cap. IV; see *Par.* 22.50–51), which favored collective work. He taught above all the importance of detachment from self-will and the praise of God's will through contemplation and prayer. St. Benedict's rules were largely accepted in Western Europe. Written at Monte Cassino during the decade preceding his death (c. 550), they were observed even when, through the evolution of monasticism, other institutions were established under different names: Cistercians, Cluniacs, Carthusians, and Camaldolese, for example. Generally these names derive from the places where monasteries were built. Since the primary goal of

the monk was asceticism and the contemplative life (a direct "conversation" with God), emphasis was given not only to prayer but to manual labor as well: *Ora et labora* ("pray and work") became the motto established by St. Benedict. The skills developed were necessary for the good of the monastic communities: architectural skills to build monasteries, agricultural skills for sustenance, and literacy skills to help preserve the chronicles of their time. Missionary fervor was also developed, to promote the spread of the faith to areas that were still pagan.

Monasticism served as a major vehicle for preserving and passing on, from generation to generation, the classical culture of antiquity as well as technological skills and social and economic accomplishments. From this monastic culture emerged trained popes, leaders, and great minds of the Middle Ages. Among the most important developments of Dante's time were the great revival of monasticism during the seventh century with the Venerable Bede (c. 672–735), the Carolingian Renaissance with Alcuin (735–804), the spread of classicism with Rabanus Maurus (776–856), and the founding of Scholasticism with Anselm of Canterbury (c. 1033–1109).

Monasticism, however, diversified according to the spiritual needs of the places where it took root. During Dante's time there were various forms of monasticism, but all of them had, as their primary goal, the direct communication with God without any mediation: prayer, and, therefore, the contemplative life (*Par.* 21.117, 22.47). Dante had written in his *Convivio:*

> We must know, however, that we may have two kinds of happiness in this life, according to two different paths, one good and the other excellent, which lead us there. One is the active life, the other the contemplative life; and although by the active, as has been said, we may arrive at a happiness that is good, the other leads us to the best happiness and state of bliss, as the Philosopher proves in the tenth book of the *Ethics.* Christ affirms this with words from his own lips in the Gospel of Luke, when speaking to Martha and replying to her: "Martha, Martha, you are distressed and trouble yourself about many things; truly one thing alone is necessary," namely, what you are doing. He adds: "Mary has chosen the best part, which shall not be taken from her." As made clear in the verses just preceding

these words of the Gospel, Mary, who was sitting at the feet of Christ, showed no concern for domestic affairs, but simply listened to the words of the Savior. The moral sense of these words is that our Savior sought thereby to show that the contemplative life was the best, even though the active life was good. This is evident to anyone who considers well these words of the evangelist. (*Conv.* 4.17.9–11)

A few chapters later, Dante reinforces his point: "Contemplation is more imbued with spiritual light than anything else found here below" (*Conv.* 4.22.17). J. M. Leclercq, a scholar of monasticism and a monk himself, wrote: "Wherever the Gospel is lived, ascetics or monks are found who wish to live out its message so fully and logically that they freely renounce certain kinds of human activity. Far from forbidding these activities, the Gospel sanctifies them; yet they can still be obstacles to the uninterrupted pursuit of higher activities, especially prayer. It is this last word that gives us the secret of the whole monastic movement: prayer, which is oriented towards union with God, is 'the' reason for monasticism. This union or clinging to God, soon came to be called *pure*" (11). This is precisely the concept that is captured in Dante's writings, and especially in his presentation of the contemplative spirits in the sphere of Saturn. In *Par.* 21 and 22, the poet assigns the value of contemplation to monasticism and to the monk Peter Damian and St. Benedict in particular. Later, as he approaches God in the highest reaches of Heaven, it is St. Bernard, a Cistercian monk, who replaces Beatrice as his third and final guide (*Par.* 32.139). Dante, therefore, clearly identifies monasticism with the highest degree of the perfection of life to which the human mind can aspire. Dante portrays it in the symbol of the golden ladder seen by Jacob, as in Gen. 28:12 (*Par.* 22.71–72). A pervasive image in Christian writings, the golden ladder is mentioned in the writings of the very two figures whom Dante encounters on the ladder. St. Benedict refers to it in Ch. VII of the *Regula,* while St. Peter Damian, in his *Laus eremiticae vitae,* praises it with the words *Tu scala illa Jacob, quae homines vehis ad coelum . . . Tu via aurea, quae homines reducis ad patriam* ("You are that Jacob's ladder that conveys men to heaven . . . You are the golden way that leads them back to the fatherland," *PL* 145, 248). In his *Paradiso* Dante places the souls of the contemplatives on the heaven of Saturn, the seventh and the last of the planetary heavens, the planetary sphere farthest from earth and closest to God, and the one which was traditionally associated with the love of solitude. In it, the souls, stepping on the golden ladder which like Jacob's reaches into heaven, perform three tasks in silence (*Par.* 21.37–39) that can be identified with the three actions of the contemplative life recorded in *De gratia contemplationis seu Beniamin maior* by Richard of St. Victor (*PL* 196, lib. I, cap. V).

The poet places in the planet Saturn only figures taken from the monastic life, both Eastern monasticism, in the person of St. Macarius (*Par.* 32.49), who was a disciple of St. Anthony, and Western monasticism, in the person of St. Benedict. He does, however, emphasize Western monasticism by presenting not only its founder, St. Benedict, but also two of its reformers: St. Romuald (*Par.* 22.49), who reinstituted the strict interpretation of the Benedictine rule by founding the new order of the Camaldolese, and St. Peter Damian, a monk at Santa Croce di Fonte Avellana who reluctantly became a cardinal—only as a sign of his obedience to the pope—and tried to shame and reform the prelates of his time by preaching the value of the monastic life. For Dante, therefore, monasticism represents the pinnacle of human perfection, and the contemplative life the supreme human activity.

The presentation of the ideal, however, does not obscure Dante's awareness of its corruption over time and the need for correcting the moral and disciplinary abuses of the clergy (*Par.* 21.113–125, 22.73–96), which awareness attests to his advocacy, manifest throughout the *Commedia,* of the renewal and purification of the Church.

Bibliography

Constable, Giles. *Medieval Monasticism: A Select Bibliography.* Toronto, Buffalo: University of Toronto Press, 1977.

Hawkins, Peter S. "'By Gradual Scale Sublimed': Dante's Benedict and Contemplative Ascent." In *Monasticism and the Arts.* Edited by Timothy Gregory Verdon. Syracuse, N.Y.: Syracuse University Press, 1984, pp. 255–269.

Kay, Richard. "Saturn." In *Dante's Christian Astrology.* Philadelphia: University of Pennsylvania Press, 1994, pp. 218–242.

Leclercq, Jacques. "Monasticism and St. Benedict." *Monastic Studies* 1 (Berryville, Virginia) (1963), pp. 9–23.

Louis La Favia

Montaperti

A castle just southeast of Siena, near the Arbia River. On September 4, 1260, Montaperti was the site of a major battle pitting the Florentine Guelfs and their allies against the banished Florentine Ghibellines, the Sienese, and imperial (that is, German) forces. The massacre of the Guelfs (contemporary chronicles put the number of Guelf deaths at 2,500–10,000) destroyed the government of the *primo popolo,* the first democratic government, in Florence and ended attempts to unify north-central Italy as an autonomous region free of imperial domination.

Dante directly mentions this battle in *Inf.* 32.76–123 (and refers to it in *Inf.* 10.85–87). The pilgrim and Virgil there meet Bocca degli Abati, to whose treachery the Guelf defeat at Montaperti was attributed. During medieval battles, flags allowed combatants to locate their comrades and gauge the success of their units. Bocca, while serving in the Florentine Guelf cavalry along with others of secret Ghibelline sympathies, is said by the chronicler Giovanni Villani to have attacked his own unit's flagbearer, causing the flag to fall and throwing the cavalry into panic and retreat. The Bocca of *Inf.* 32 infers that the pilgrim kicks him in the face as vengeance for this betrayal.

Susan Noakes

Moon

The first planet and heavenly sphere in Dante's Paradise, based on the Ptolemaic cosmological model which provides for seven such heavens, arranged as concentric spheres or shells, each of which carries with it a planet, called a *stella* ("star"). Classical mythology associated the Moon with the deity Diana, who possesses several names (Trivia, *Par.* 23.26; Delia, *Purg.* 29.78; Phoebe, *Mon.* 1.11.5) and is referred to periphrastically as *la figlia di Latona* ("the daughter of Latona," *Par.* 10.67) and as *Caino e le spine* ("Cain and his thorns," *Inf.* 20.126). The Moon is conceived as the sister of the Sun (*Purg.* 23.120), Diana and Apollo having been born as twins (*Purg.* 20.130–132). In Hell, time is determined according to the phases of the Moon, and Hecate *(Ecate),* who is also identified with the planet, is the queen of Hell, *la donna che qui regge* ("the lady who reigns here," *Inf.* 10.80).

The Moon's revolution around the earth in twenty-nine days (*Conv.* 2.14.16) results from three separate movements, which are governed by the lowest order of angels. The Moon occupies the slowest of all the spheres (*la spera più tarda, Par.* 3.51) to move around the earth, because it is the sphere located farthest from the Empyrean. The only planet to exhibit any apparent blemish, it is described as *lucida, spessa, solida e pulita* ("shining, dense, solid and clean," *Par.* 2.31–32), reflecting light like a diamond, and is called the *eterna margarita* ("eternal pearl," *Par.* 2.34). Its chief distinctive feature, however, consists of its spots, its *segni bui* ("dark marks," *Par.* 2.49), a property that the pilgrim innocently attributes to the presence of matter of varying density, *corpi rari e densi* ("rare and dense bodies," *Par.* 2.60). Beatrice refutes this theory, once sustained by Dante himself in an earlier work and derived from Averroës (*Conv.* 2.13.9). As one proof in her argument that the moonspots result from the differing quality or "virtue" of the lunar material rather than the thickness or thinness of uniform matter, she meticulously details steps in an experiment based on the positioning of three mirrors with respect to a beam of light. Her conclusion, that the light reflected from the two more distant mirrors shines in a degree equal (*igualmente, Par.* 2.105) to that reflected in the nearer mirror, even if the image is not as large (*Par.* 2.103), has been judged by modern critics as fundamentally illogical, and, alternatively, as entirely feasible (see, for example, Boyde). Nevertheless, Dante's primary interest is to explain apparent irregularities in the heavens not as material defects but as wholly good differences in celestial virtue or power.

Following tradition, which associated the moon with the feminine sex, Dante makes this sphere the temporary residence of nuns who have failed to keep their sacred vows. Here Dante encounters Piccarda Donati, who tells little about the actual event of her violent abduction from a convent at the hands of her brother, Corso Donati. The brightest splendor of the Moon and the only other inhabitant who is named is Constance, wife of the emperor Henry VI. Their religious infidelity is associated with the influence of the Moon, which, because of its phases, has been a traditional symbol of inconstancy in human affairs. Imperfection is characteristic not only of the Moon, however, but also of the succeeding two planets, Mercury and Venus, which, like the Moon, bear the imprint of the earth's shadow, which symbolizes residual terrestrial weakness (*Par.* 9.118).

Dante and Beatrice in the Heaven of the Moon. La comedia, ed. Pietro da Figino, 1491. Giamatti Collection: Courtesy of the Mount Holyoke College Archives and Special Collections.

These first three heavens have therefore been interpreted to define a pattern of symbolism that associates the souls appearing in each heaven with a deficiency of one of the three theological virtues, faith, hope, and charity, with the souls in the Moon representing inadequate and marred faith.

Dante always conceives of the Moon in a symbolic or allegorical guise, though he adopts different models in different works. In *Conv.* 2.13, it is associated with Grammar, the first subject in the Scholastic trivium. In *Mon* 3.4.3, 17–18, the Sun and Moon serve as an allegorical analogue to the temporal and spiritual realms. Dante rejects here the argument that because the Moon takes its light entirely from the Sun the Empire must therefore derive its authority from the Church, claiming that the Moon generates some of its own light independently of the Sun.

Bibliography

Boyde, Patrick. "L'esegesi di Dante e la scienza." In *Dante e la scienza*. Edited by Patrick Boyde and Vittorio Russo. Ravenna: Longo Editore, 1995, pp. 9–23.

Carroll, John S. *In Patria: An Exposition of Dante's Paradiso*. London, New York: Hodder and Stoughton, 1911; reprinted, Kennikat Press: Port Washington, 1971.

Lansing, Richard H. "Piccarda and the Poetics of Paradox: A Reading of *Paradiso* III." *Dante Studies* 105 (1987), 63–77.

Ordiway, Frank B. "In the Earth's Shadow: The Theological Virtues Marred." *Dante Studies* 100 (1982), 77–92.

Mazzotta, Giuseppe. "Teologia ed esegesi biblica (*Par.* III–V)." In *Dante e la Bibbia*. Edited by G. Barblan. Florence: Olschki, 1988, pp. 95–112.

Nardi, Bruno. "La dottrina delle macchie lunari nel secondo canto del *Paradiso*." In *Saggi di filosofia dantesca*. Florence: La Nuova Italia, 1967, pp. 3–39.

Stocchi, Manlio Pastore. "Dante e la luna." *Lettere italiane* 33 (1981), 153–74.

Richard Lansing

Moore, Edward

Distinguished British textual critic whose scrupulous work with manuscript variants earned him recognition in Italy as well as in the English-speaking world. Moore (1835–1916) was Principal of St. Edmund Hall at Oxford University (1903–1912) and Canon of Canterbury (from 1903). He founded the Oxford Dante Society in 1876 and held several Lectureships on Dante. In 1889 he published *Contributions to the Textual Criticism of the "Divina Commedia,"* and his *Textual Criticism of the "Convivio"* was published posthumously in the fourth volume of his *Studies in Dante*. Among his other important contributions were his defense of the authenticity of the *Questio de aqua et terra* and of the *Epistle to Cangrande*. His most important essays are collected in the four volumes of *Studies in Dante* (1896–1917). Moore was a problem-solver with a great range of interests (geography, astronomy, history, numerology) whose work on Dante remains of value. His friend Edward Armstrong noted that Moore had "a romantic, almost passionate love for Beatrice, and nothing would rouse him more than scepticism as to her reality."

Bibliography

Alighieri, Dante. *De monarchia*. Edited by Edward Moore. Oxford: Clarendon Press, 1916.

———. *Tutte le opere di Dante Alighieri*. Edited by Edward Moore. Oxford: Stamperia Dell' Università, 1894.

Armstrong, Edward. "Edward Moore." In *Studies in Dante First Series*, pp. ix–xxii. Oxford: Clarendon Press, 1969. Reprinted from *Proceedings of the British Academy*, vol. 7 (1915–1916).

Lindon, John. "Gli apporti del metodo di Edward Moore nei primi decenni della Società Dantesca Italiana." In *La Società Dantesca Italiana 1888–1988*. Edited by Rudy Abardo. Milan, Naples: Ricciardi, 1995, pp. 37–53.

Moore, Edward. *Studies in Dante. First Series: Scripture and Classical Authors in Dante.* Oxford: Clarendon Press, 1896. Reprinted by Haskell House, New York, 1968, and by Greenwood Press, New York, 1968.

———. *Studies in Dante. Second Series: Miscellaneous Essays.* Oxford: Clarendon Press, 1899. Reprinted by Haskell House, New York, 1968, and by Greenwood Press, New York, 1968.

———. *Studies in Dante. Third Series: Miscellaneous Essays.* Oxford: Clarendon Press, 1903. Reprinted by Haskell House, New York, 1968, and by Greenwood Press, New York, 1968.

———. *Studies in Dante. Fourth Series: Textual Criticism of the "Convivio" and Miscellaneous Essays.* Oxford: Clarendon Press, 1917. Reprinted by Haskell House, New York, 1968.

———. *The "DXV" prophecy in the Divina Commedia (Purg. XXXIII. 37–45).* Oxford, 1901.

———. *Dante and His Early Biographers.* London: Rivingtons, 1890.

Toynbee, Paget Jackson. "Edward Moore." In *Dictionary of National Biography 1912–1921.* Edited by H. W. C. Davis and J. R. H. Weaver. London, New York: Oxford University Press, 1980, pp. 383–384.

Rachel Jacoff

Mordecai

Foster father and uncle of Esther, Dante describes Mordecai the Jew as *'l giusto Mardoceo* ("the just Mordecai," *Purg.* 17.29) because he saved the Jews from being destroyed by Haman, counselor of King Ahasuerus of Persia. Haman is presented as an exemplum of wrath, punished on the third terrace of Purgatory for his rage against the sacred race of the Jews (see Esth. 5:6).

R. A. Malagi

Mordred

Condemned to Caina among the traitors to kin, Mordred (*Inf.* 32.61) was nephew and son to King Arthur by his sister Morgan le Fay. Run through by Arthur's lance and left with a gaping wound so large that a ray of sunlight passed through his chest, he gave Arthur, his father-uncle, his own death blow before dying. These events are referred to by Camiscion de' Pazzi. Dante's source for the reference is the prose *Mort le roi Artu (The Death of King Arthur),* which concludes the Vulgate cycle.

Roy Rosenstein

Moroello Malaspina

Since several members of the aristocratic Malaspina clan were called Moroello, it is not entirely clear which of these is connected with Dante and his works. A case has been made for Moroello di Obizzino of Villafranca, but the likeliest identification is with his Welsh uncle, Marquis Moroello di Manfredi of Giovagallo. Both belonged to the "Spino Secco" side of the family.

The latter Moroello was a cousin of Conrad II (*Currado, Purg.* 8.65, 8.118) and a grandson of Conrad I (*Purg.* 8.119). He married Alagia de' Fieschi, the niece of Pope Hadrian V praised in *Purg.* 19.142–145. Scion of a Guelf branch of the family, he appears to have captained the Florentines in their 1288 campaign against Ghibelline Arezzo. He was captain general of Bologna's Guelf troops in their 1297 war against Azzo of Este, and in the following year became Bologna's podestà. In 1299 he led the Milanese troops in their operations against the Marquis of Montferrat. During the opening decade of the new century he was constantly fighting on behalf of Tuscany's Black Guelfs. After conquering the Whites of Pistoia in 1306 as leader of Lucca's Blacks, in alliance with those of Florence, he was appointed *capitano del popolo* of Pistoia, and in 1307 became head of the Tuscan Guelf League. He died in or around 1315 with a distinguished record of military valor and political wisdom. Dante may have met Moroello in 1288, in Florence; and he was certainly staying in Lunigiana at one of the Malaspina castles (though not necessarily Moroello's) in October 1306 (cf. *Purg.* 8.133–139). It was perhaps during this stay that Moroello received from Cino da Pistoia the sonnet "Cercando di trovar minera in oro," in which Cino complains that he has been pricked by the *mala spina* ("evil thorn") of an unhappy new love. Dante replied on Moroello's behalf, using the rhymes of Cino's sonnet, in "Degno fa voi trovare ogni tesoro." Presumably in 1307–1308, now in Casentino, Dante evidently addressed *Epist.* 4 to Moroello, apologizing for apparent negligence in the Marquis's service, the reason being a passionate love that had overwhelmed him—the love described in the canzone "Amor, da che convien pur ch'io mi doglia," which accompanied the letter. A passage in *Inf.* 24 contains a dramatic reference to Moroello's defeat of Pistoia in either 1302 or 1306: he is a *vapor . . . di torbidi nuvoli involuto* ("hot wind wrapped in roiling clouds") who will cause a *tempesta impetuosa e agra* ("impetuous, bitter violence," 145–147) on Campo Piceno.

The unreliable Boccaccio reports that while Dante was staying with Moroello the first seven cantos of *Inferno* (which Boccaccio implausibly says the poet had written before his exile) were sent to the Marquis, who persuaded Dante to continue the poem. Perhaps influenced by the eulogy of the Malaspina family in *Purg.* 8, Boccaccio is also the source of the unfounded tradition that Moroello is the dedicatee of *Purgatorio*.

John C. Barnes

Mosca de' Lamberti

Instigator of the murder of Buondelmonte de' Buondelmonti in 1215, who after having promised to marry a lady of the Amidei family, appeared on his wedding day with a bride from the Donati family (see *Par.* 16.140). When the Amidei gathered to devise a way to avenge the insult, it was Mosca who, in preference to giving Buondelmonte a beating or a wound in the face, advised them to deal a fatal blow, saying *cosa fatta capo ha* ("a thing done is done"). Following his counsel, the Amidei assaulted and stabbed Buondelmonte to death at the foot of the pillar on which stood the statue of Mars. This originated the bitter feud between the two families that later expanded into the conflict between the Guelfs and the Ghibellines in Florence. A passionate Ghibelline, Mosca and his family were banished from the city and never allowed to return. Since he brought bloodshed to Florence, he is found handless and befouled with his own blood in the ninth bolgia of Malebolge, where he finds himself damned among the Schismatics (*Inf.* 28.106). Mosca is one of the five Florentines about whom Dante inquires of Ciacco in the third circle of Hell (*Inf.* 6.79–85).

R.A. Malagi

Moses

Leader of the Israelites out of Egypt (Exodus) who received the tablets of the Law (the Ten Commandments) at Mt. Sinai (c. thirteenth century B.C.E.). He was thought to have authored the Pentateuch (the first five books of the Old Testament), the principal source for his story. Prophet and lawgiver, Moses *(Moisè)* was considered in Dante's time to be both the founder of Judaism and a figure for Christ *(figura Christi)*.

By leading the Israelites out of oppression and slavery in Egypt, Moses prefigured Christ's leading His faithful from perdition to salvation; both were seen as agents of God's redemption of his chosen people. Like Christ, he was to have been killed with all the male infants, but was hidden and survived; Pharaoh's daughter found him floating at the river's edge in a basket made of rushes, and rescued him and secretly cared for him. God worked various miracles (the plagues of Egypt, the parting of the Red Sea, manna from heaven) as Moses later attempted to lead his unruly people out of Egypt and into a righteous and independent state. Delivered out of Limbo by Christ (*Inf.* 4.57), he occupies a high position in the hierarchy of Dante's heaven and is named among the souls in the white rose (*Par.* 32.130–132).

Mediator between God and humanity, the figure of Moses typically has a powerfully legitimating effect in the *Commedia* and in the *Monarchia*. In these texts, which purport to gloss the divine will with regard to humankind, Dante invokes Moses regularly with an eye to shoring up his own prophetic authority (*Purg.* 32.80; *Par.* 4.29, 24.136, 26.41, and above; *Mon.* 1.14.9, 2.4.2, 2.11.4, 3.4.11, 3.4.16, 3.5.1, 3.14.5; *Epist.* 5.4).

F. Regina Psaki

Mucius

Gaius Mucius Scaevola, legendary Roman hero who attempted to kill the Etruscan king Porsenna during the latter's siege of Rome (6th century B.C.E.). He accidentally stabbed Porsenna's secretary and was subsequently apprehended and condemned to be burned alive. Mucius then thrust his right hand into a nearby sacrificial fire and held it there without flinching. Porsenna was so impressed with his fortitude that he spared Mucius's life. He was henceforth known as Scaevola ("left-handed").

M

Dante mentions Mucius (*Muzio;* Latin, *Mutius*) in connection with this episode, along with St. Lawrence, as a model of fortitude in keeping religious vows in *Par.* 4.84. Dante also refers to this incident in *Conv.* 4.5.13 and, with a reference to Livy, in *Mon.* 2.5.14.

Molly Morrison

Muhammad

In *Inf.* 28, the figure of Muhammad *(Mäometto)* emerges as Dante's personification of schism, specifically of the great schism within monotheism instigated by the prophet during the seventh century. Muhammad (570–632) announced his prophetic mission in Mecca in 611, thus founding the religion of Islam. At the time of his death he had achieved religious and political sovereignty from the Euphrates River to the Red Sea. Medieval polemics against Islam falsely declared that Muhammad was an apostate Christian, a cardinal whose thwarted ambitions for the papacy led to his separation from the Church. Although Dante does not utilize this legend in the *Commedia,* he does depict Muhammad as the instigator of schism in the Christian church. Muhammad is placed in the ninth bolgia of the eighth circle of Hell, among the sowers of discord. Like other souls in this bolgia, he is punished by being hacked by a devil's sword each time he appears before the demon. Muhammad's unhealing wound reflects both the general nature of the sin punished—the disruption of the constituted moral or social order—and the ugliness of his particular evil. He is split open from chin to anus, his intestines spilling out. When he encounters Dante-pilgrim he opens and displays his chest cavity to him, declaring himself *storpiato* ("mangled," *Inf.* 28.31). His wounds are a literal embodiment of the mutilation of the unified body of Christianity by the schism of Islam.

Bibliography

D'Ancona, Alessandro. "La leggenda di Maometto in Occidente." 1889. In *La leggenda di Maometto in Occidente.* Edited by Andrea Borruso. Reprint, Rome: Salerno, 1994.

Al-Sabah, Rasha. "The Figure of Muhammad." *Yale Italian Studies* 1 (1977), 147–161.

Fiora A. Bassanese

Muses, the

The nine sister divinities of Greek mythology, daughters of Zeus and Mnemosine, who had the responsibility of inspiring and protecting the arts, music, and, in particular, poetry. Each muse was soon associated with a specific literary genre or activity: Calliope, the muse of epic poetry; Clio, the muse of history; Erato, the muse of lyric poetry; Euterpe, the muse of music; Melpomene, the muse of tragedy; Polyhymnia, the muse of sacred song and dancing; Terpsichore, the muse of choral song and dance; Thalia, the muse of comedy; Urania, the muse of astronomy. The god Apollo was their guardian and leader. The allegorical tradition commonly represented them as the power of poetic inspiration and as the very activity of the poet. The Latin poets often referred to them according to their place of origin in Greece (Pieria). Hence they are called the Pierides, a term Dante uses in his exchange of eclogues with Giovanni del Virgilio (*Egl.* 4.55–56).

Dante invokes the Muses at the beginning of each canticle. In *Inf.* 2.7, he invokes them collectively: *O Muse, o alto ingegno, or m'aiutate* ("O Muses, O high wit, help me now!"). In *Purg.* 1.7–9, he invokes Calliope especially as the muse of epic poetry: *ma qui la morta poesì resurga, / o sante Muse, poi che vostro sono, / e qui Caliopè alquanto surga* ("But here let dead poetry rise up again, O holy muses, since I belong to you; and here let Calliope arise somewhat"). In *Par.* 1, since the aid of the Muses, which he invokes in verses 16–18, is insufficient for the final poetic undertaking, Dante invokes the god Apollo as well (*O buono Appollo,* 1.13). Explicit references to the Muses in the *Commedia* occur throughout the poem: *Inf.* 32.10–11; *Purg.* 22.58 *(Cliò),* 102; 29.37 (*sacrosante Vergini,* "O most holy Virgins"), 41 *(Urania); Par.* 12.7; 15.26 (*nostra maggior musa,* "our greatest Muse," referring to the poetry of *Aeneid* and its author Virgil); 18.33, 82; 23.56 (*Polimnìa con le suore,* "Polyhymnia and her sisters").

Dante took most of his information about narrative myths relating to the Muses from Ovid's *Metamorphoses.* As the Muses represented divine assistance to the poet, they were invoked by convention at the beginning of long poems, but also whenever the poet considered the act of creativity particularly demanding or the subject matter especially important.

Ernesto Livorni

Music

Dante's conception of music is based on medieval music theory, in particular the three classes of music, *musica mundana* ("worldly music"), *musica humana* ("human music") and *musica instrumentalis* ("instrumental music"), defined by Boethius in the second chapter of the first book of *De institutione musica*. The first of these classes, *musica mundana,* was considered to be the music of the universe, depicting the harmony of the planets, the stars, the four elements, and the four seasons. The second type of music, *musica humana,* was the music of human nature and represented the human soul and body. To the final classification, *musica instrumentalis,* belonged all the musical sounds produced by the human voice (a natural instrument), and artificial instruments such as strings, winds, and percussion. Another aspect of medieval music theory central to Dante's own conception of music was *armonia,* which, unlike our modern conception of harmony, was based on a carefully structured composition of words and music. In the *Paradiso,* Dante describes this intricate relationship between music and words with an analogy: music is to words as an object is to its reflection in a mirror (*Par.* 28.4). In the *De vulgari eloquentia,* Dante similarly notes this relationship when he defines song as *fictio rethorica musicaque poita* ("a verbal invention composed according to the rules of rhetoric and music," 2.4.2). Also crucial to the medieval and Dantean theory of *armonia* are the concepts of order and sweetness; these concepts are directly related to each other in that the more ordered the composition, the sweeter it is (*Conv.* 1.7.14).

The preceding theoretical framework concerning medieval and particularly Dantean conceptions of music allows a clear consideration of the presence of music in the *Commedia*. All three medieval classes of music are present in the *Commedia,* but only in *Purgatorio* and *Paradiso;* music is absent in *Inferno*. Key phrases in Dante's text emphasize this lack of music in the *Inferno* by noting the lack of words, order (described as time), harmony, and sweetness. The first indication that *Inferno* is devoid of music is found in the opening canto where Dante describes the *selva oscura* ("dark wood") as the place *dove il sol tace* ("where the sun is silent," *Inf.* 1.60). The next indication comes soon thereafter, when Dante describes the *dis*harmony and the lack of order of the souls passing through the gates of Hell: *Quivi sospiri, pianti ed alti guai / risonavan per l'aer senza stelle, / per-ch'io al cominciar ne lagrimai. / Diverse lingue, orribili favelle, / parole di dolore, accenti d'ira, / voci alte e fioche, e suon di man con elle / facevano un tumulto, il qual s'aggira / sempre in quell'aura sanza tempo tinta, / come la ren quando turbo spira* ("There sighs, weeping, loud wailing resounded through the starless air, for which at the outset I shed tears. Strange languages, horrible tongues, words of pain, accents of anger, voices loud and hoarse, and sounds of blows with them, made a tumult that turns forever in that air darkened without time, like sand when a whirlwind blows," *Inf.* 3.22–30). Instead of singing, only sighs and screams "resound." Instead of ordered time, there is a lack of time "in the air." Instead of sweetness and harmony, there is tumult. The general infernal disharmony is later described as the "noise" of the suicides: *similemente a colui che venire / sente il porco e la caccia alla sua posta, / ch'ode le bestie e le frasche stormire* ("like one who hears the boar and the hunt approaching his post, who hears the beasts, and the branches breaking," *Inf.* 13.112–114). Finally, instead of poetry, we hear only *le rime aspre e chiocce* ("harsh and clacking rhymes," *Inf.* 32.1).

Though there is no music per se in the *Inferno,* Dante uses a limited amount of musical imagery to describe the sadness and horrors of Hell, and the characters he encounters. There are a few references to singing: the lustful cry *come gru van cantando lor lai* ("as the cranes go singing their lays," *Inf.* 5.46); the diviners are silent and weeping, advancing *al passo / che fanno le letane in questo mondo* ("at the pace taken by litanies in this world," *Inf.* 20.8–9); and Virgil parodies a liturgical hymn traditionally sung during Holy Week in honor of the Cross as he proclaims the presence of Lucifer: *Vexilla regis prodeunt inferni* ("the standards of the king of Hell go forth," *Inf.* 34.1).

Dante also uses musical instruments to describe the characters he encounters. For example, Master Adam, a counterfeiter of gold florins, is described in terms of two musical instruments: his swollen body, which is afflicted by dropsy, appears in the form of a lute (*Inf.* 30.49), then, when his stomach is struck by another sinner, it makes a sound like a drum (*Inf.* 30.103). The counterfeiter first *appears* as what he is not, a superior instrument associated with perfection and the sign

M of the cross, a lute. When his body is actually sounded, however, it produces the disharmonious sounds of an inferior instrument, a drum. In another example, Dante says that Barbariccia, a devil torturing the barrators, *avea del cul fatto trombetta* ("of his ass had made a trumpet," *Inf.* 21.139). Nimrod, meanwhile, is portrayed as a babbling idiot who blows a horn which is louder than a thunderclap and more ominous than Roland's horn at Roncesvalles, the horn which proclaimed the defeat of Charlemagne's army (*Inf.* 31.10–18). Finally, the teeth of the traitors chatter *mettendo i denti in nota di cicogna* ("playing the tune of the stork with their teeth," *Inf.* 32.36).

In *Purgatorio*, music is heard on every terrace. When Dante enters Purgatory proper, he hears the souls singing *Salve, Regina* (*Purg.* 7), while on the second terrace he hears them singing *Te deum laudamus* (*Purg.* 8). At one point during his journey, Dante exclaims *Ahi quanto son diverse quell foci / da l'infernali! ché quivi per canti / s'entra, e là giù per lamenti foci* ("Ah, how different are these passageways from those of Hell! for here one enters with singing, down there with fierce laments!" *Purg.* 12.112–114).

Music serves three functions in *Purgatorio*: it is used to soothe the mind, as an act of worship, and as a teaching tool. An example of the first function, soothing the mind, is found in *Purg.* 2, where Casella sings a love poem which serves to *consolare* ("console," *Purg.* 2.109) Dante's soul. So sweet is the love song Casella sings that the sweetness still sounds within Dante after the song ends (*Purg.* 2.113–114). The second function, worship, is fulfilled as part of the purification process, when the souls sing a hymn or antiphon from the liturgy. Generally, these songs highlight the virtue which is the antithesis of the particular sin being purged from the souls on each given terrace. For example, in *Purg.* 23.10–12, the gluttonous sing *Labia mea Domine* ("O Lord, open thou my lips," Ps. 51:15). While in life the sin of the gluttonous was to use their mouths to overeat and drink to excess, in Purgatory, they use their mouths to praise God. The last function, teaching, is demonstrated in two songs, the song of the Siren and the song of Leah. In the first song (*Purg.* 19.19–24), the Siren tells Dante how she led men astray by granting them sexual satisfaction. In the second song (*Purg.* 27.100–108), Leah describes a different kind of satisfaction: a Christian spiritual satisfaction found through action and contemplation.

These three functions of music are achieved only through a particular kind of *musica instrumentalis* ("instrumental music"), as demonstrated in Cato's rebuke of the souls who listen to Casella's song. Cato administers his rebuke because of the lack of ethical and spiritual content in the words and tune of Casella's song, a song which is the only profane music in the *Purgatorio*. Casella's song, in this light, does not inspire the pilgrims to love God, but rather distracts them from this love with its sweet sound (see Iannucci, 1990). The only acceptable forms of *musica instrumentalis,* then, are sacred hymns, hymns that will help the souls to direct their minds to the *musica humana* ("human music") so that they can ultimately hear the *musica mundana* ("worldly music"), *la dolce sinfonia di Paradiso* ("the sweet symphony of Paradise," *Par.* 21.59).

The music of *Purgatorio* culminates in the Earthly Paradise. The birds sing *con piena letizia* (*Purg.* 28.13–21), Matelda sings *come donna innamorata* ("like a lady in love," *Purg.* 29.1), the forest resounds with *una melodia dolce* ("a sweet melody," *Purg.* 29.22), the twenty-four elders sing *Benedicta tue / nelle figlie d'Adamo, e benedette / sieno in etterno le bellezze tue!* ("*Benedicta* [Blessed] be you among the daughters of Adam, and blessed in eternity be your beauties!" *Purg.* 29.85–87), and the three theological virtues and the four cardinal virtues sing *alternando / or tre or quattro dolce salmodia* ("alternating their sweet psalmody, now by three, now by four," *Purg.* 33.1–2).

Because music conveys the nature of God's love in *Paradiso,* it is crucial to the context of this canticle. In the first canto of *Paradiso,* Dante hears the harmony of the spheres *(l'armonia),* which God tunes and for which God determines the pitch (*Par.* 1.78). Dante also notes *la novità del suono* ("the wonder of the sound," *Par.* 1.82); he hears this new music, *la dolce sinfonia di Paradiso* ("the sweet symphony of Paradise," *Par.* 21.59) everywhere in *Paradiso* except for the heaven of the contemplatives.

In two instances Dante indicates that the heavenly music of Paradise surpasses earthly music. First he describes the heavenly song he hears as superior to the songs of human poetry and music (*Par.* 12.7–8). Later he claims that the sweetest melody on earth would seem like thunder compared to the sound of the heavenly lyre: *Qualunque melodia più dolce sona / qua giù e più a sé l'anima tira, / parrebbe nube che squarciata tona, / com-*

parata al sonar di quella lira / onde si coronava il bel zaffiro / del quale il ciel più chiaro s'inzaffira ("Whatever melody down here sounds sweetest and most draws the soul, would seem a shattered cloud thundering, compared with the sounding of the lyre that crowned the beautiful sapphire with which the brightest Heaven is ensapphired," *Par.* 23.97–102).

Not surprisingly, this superior music is beyond human comprehension. The eagle in Jupiter informs Dante that just as its notes are beyond comprehension, so is eternal justice: *Quali / son le mie note a te, che non le 'ntendi, / tal è il giudicio etterno a voi mortali* ("Such as my notes are to you, who cannot understand them, so is the eternal judgment to you mortals," *Par.* 19.97–99).

Dante attempts to describe this heavenly music using musical terms common to earthly music, including musical instruments, polyphonic song, movement and dance. Instruments found in Paradise include the harp, lyre, viol, trumpet, lute, and flute. One example of Dante's use of instruments in the *Paradiso* is found in canto 14, where the melody produced by the cross formed by the lights in the sphere of Mars vibrates *come giga e arpa, in tempra tesa / di molte core, fa dolce tintinno* ("as a viol and harp, stretched and tuned, make a sweet sound of many strings to one who cannot distinguish the melody," 14.118–119). In the next canto, Dante notes that God tunes with his right hand the chords of the *dolce lira* ("sweet lyre") formed by the souls of the cross (*Par.* 15.4). Later, the voice of the Eagle is described as the music of a lyre and then of a flute (*Par.* 20.22–24). Gabriel's singing, meanwhile, is described in terms of a heavenly lyre (*Par.* 23.100). Finally, Dante claims that his own trumpet is insufficient to herald the heavenly beauty of Beatrice (*Par.* 30.34–36).

Dante also describes the music of Paradise in terms of polyphonic performance. In *Par.* 23.109–110, for example, Gabriel's song to the Virgin Mary is described as a circular melody. In *Par.* 12.6, the first singing circle of theologians is joined by a second circle which matches the motion and song of the first circle. Moreover, the apostles Peter, James, and John, who appear as three burning flames, spin in a concentric motion and sing such that Dante hears *il dolce mischio / che si facea nel suon del trino spiro* ("the sweet blend made by the sound of its triple breath," *Par.* 25.131–132).

Finally, heavenly music is characterized by dance, in the Earthly Paradise where the three theological virtues (*Purg.* 29.121 and 31.132) and the four Cardinal Virtues dance about the chariot (*Purg.* 31.104), and in Celestial Paradise, where many of the saved spirits are presented as singing and dancing. In particular, Justinian and the souls sing and dance (*Par.* 7.8–9) while the saints dance courtly round dances, or *carole,* which are also sung (*Par.* 24.16–19). These dances in *Paradiso* are often circular and generally occur in groups of three: the singing lights circle around Dante three times (*Par.* 10.64–81) and St. Peter sings and circles Dante three times (*Par.* 24.151–154). The triple repetition of the dance reflects the fact that ternary rather than binary rhythm was central to thirteenth-century polyphony.

Bibliography

Bonaventura, Arnaldo. *Dante e la musica.* Livorno: R. Giusti, 1904.

Einstein, Alfred. "Dante, On the Way to the Madrigal." *Musical Quarterly* 25 (1939), 142–155, 507–509.

Freccero, John. "Casella's Song (*Purg.* II, 112)." *Dante Studies* 101 (1973), 73–80.

Haar, James. *Essays on Italian Poetry and Music, 1350–1600.* Berkeley: University of California Press, 1986.

Heilbronn, Denise. "Concentus musicum: the Creaking Hinges of Dante's Gate of Purgatory." *Rivista di studi italiani* 2 (1984), 1–15.

———. "Master Adam and the Fat-Bellied Lute (*Inf.* XXX)." *Dante Studies* 101 (1983), 51–65.

Iannucci, Amilcare A. "Musical Imagery in the Mastro Adamo Episode." In *Da una riva e dall'altra. Studi in onore di Antonio D'Andrea.* Edited by Dante Della Terza. Florence: Edizioni Cadmo, 1995, pp. 103–118.

———. "Casella's Song and the Tuning of the Soul." *Thought: A Review of Culture and Idea* 65, No. 256 (March 1990), 29–46.

Monterosso, Raffaello. "Problemi musicali danteschi." *Cultura e scuola* 4 (1965), 207–212.

———. "Musica." *Enciclopedia dantesca,* 3:1061–1065.

———. "Musica e poesia nel *De Vulgari Eloquentia.*" In *Dante: Atti della giornata internazionale di studio per il VII centenario. Ravenna, 6–7 marzo 1965.* Faenza: Fratelli Lega, 1965, pp. 83–100.

Pestalozza, Luigi (ed.). *La musica nel tempo di Dante: Ravenna, Comune di Ravenna, Opera di Dante, Musica/Realtà, 12–14 settembre 1986.* Milan: Edizioni Unicopli, 1988.

Picchi, Alessandro. "La musicalità dantesca nel quadro delle metodologie filosofiche medioevali." *Annali dell'istituto di studi danteschi* 1 (1967), 155–194.

Pirrotta, Nino. "Dante Musicus: Gothicism, Scholasticism, and Music." *Speculum* 43 (1968), 245–257.

Spitzer, Leo. *Classical and Christian Ideas of World Harmony.* Edited by Anna Granville Hatcher. Baltimore, Md.: The Johns Hopkins Press, 1963.

Stevens, John. "Dante and Music." *Italian Studies* 23 (1968), 43–61.

Maria Ann Roglieri

Myrrha

A falsifier punished among the fraudulent in the eighth circle of Hell (*Inf.* 30.37–41). Driven by an illicit passion for her father, King Cinyras of Cyprus, Myrrha *(Mirra)* disguises herself in order to lay with him. Upon being discovered, she flees to Arabia, gives birth to Adonis and is turned into a myrrh tree (Ovid, *Meta.* 10.298–513; *Ars amatoria* 1.285–288). Dante compares Florence to Myrrha in *Epist.* 7.24, rebuking the city's unnatural desire to align itself with the papacy while abandoning support of the emperor, her legitimate "spouse."

Virginia Jewiss

Mysticism

A religious or philosophical tendency which believes in spiritual apprehension of truths beyond the understanding, and which exists in all cultures and religions, including Christian theology, where it plays an important role.

Western mysticism has its origins in Plato's theory of ideas and forms, and in his concept of the individual soul, both of which were later expanded into a mystical, philosophical system by Neoplatonists, especially Plotinus and the Alexandrian School. The early Christians found much in Neoplatonism that was compatible with Christian belief, including the idea of a symbolic universe which needed to be interpreted to reveal, indirectly, its creator. Christian mystics, however, sought knowledge of God through direct and personal experience of the divine, rather than through the use of reason or analogy alone, believing that the union of the soul and mind with God was a possible and achievable goal during their lifetime.

Mystical union with God is attained by following a series of steps or stages, which vary according to the mystic's own system. The process generally requires that, before the goal can be achieved, the mystic's entire intellect and will be directed toward God, until he or she obtains virtue as a natural state, thereby coming into harmony with God and sharing in His will. Mystical union does not consist simply of increased understanding through a spiritual state, but is rather a merging with the divine which is often described by those who experience it in terms of love and desire, and even marriage: in this way the mystic both becomes more godlike and comes to "know" God.

Paradoxically, the mystic is unable to describe the experience of mystical union with God, because human language is inadequate. In any case, the moment of union is also a moment of loss: the human mind and memory being incapable of retaining such a high and exquisite experience, as Dante explains at the beginning of *Paradiso*: *Nel ciel che più de la sua luce prende / fu'io, e vidi cose che ridire / né sa né può chi di là sù discende; / perché appressando sé al suo disire, / nostro intelletto si profonda tanto, / che dietro la memoria non può ire* ("In the heaven that receives most of his light have I been, and I have seen things that one who comes down from there cannot remember and could not utter; for as it draws near to its desire, our intellect goes so deep that the memory cannot follow it," *Par.* 1.4–9). Those who have written about such experiences are able, therefore, to describe the journey, or series of stages leading to the union of the soul with God, only up to the moment of achieving their goal. They are unable, however, to recount the details of the culmination of their experience. Like the mystics, in the *Commedia,* Dante describes the details of the pilgrim's journey right up to the moment of union; but then, at the point of supreme understanding, he claims that, on account of the limitations of his human mind and memory, he cannot remember or find words adequate to describe the ultimate experience of the divine. Faced with the problem of how to depict the third realm of the afterlife, Dante chose to present the whole of Paradise as a metaphor for the Empyrean (we learn from Beatrice in *Par.* 4.28–39 that all the souls in Heaven inhabit the Empyrean, and not the spheres in which they appear to the pilgrim); and his presentation of the Empyrean itself is merely another approximation of what Paradise really is like, human memory and intellect being unable to retain more than a shadow of the highest vision.

While there are mystical elements in Dante's other works (his love for Beatrice in the *Vita Nuova,* and his love of philosophy in the *Convivio*), the pilgrim's turning away from sin and his submission to the process of purgation in the *Inferno* and the *Purgatorio* are representative of stages identified by mystics as being essential preparatory steps to communion with God. The descent through the various circles of Hell can also been seen as a perversion of the stages of mystical ascent. Similarly, the climb from terrace to terrace on Mount Purgatory, arriving at last in the Earthly Paradise, has a prefigurative function. It foreshadows the pilgrim's rising through the spheres in the *Paradiso,* which has been compared to the mystical journey culminating in union with God.

Several centuries of Christian mysticism meant that by the late medieval period a whole tradition had been established with its own customs for writing about mystical experience, including the use of specific technical terms, formulae, and allusions. Dante would certainly have been familiar with some mystical writings (for example, St. Bonaventure's *Itinerarium mentis in Deum* [The Soul's Journey to God]). He was also clearly aware of the conventions of writing about direct human experience of God, and utilized many of these when he wrote the *Paradiso.* In fact, the *Paradiso* has many stylistic features characteristic of mystical writing. Writers of mystical works were dependent on the use of symbolism and imagery because of the problems inherent in writing about their experiences, which were considered to be inexpressible directly and which often were remembered only as transcendental, emotive, and abstract sensations and perceptions. Like biblical writers, they sought to express their experiences using imagery that would be easily understood, for example, describing the joy and exaltation of partaking of spiritual experience in terms of eating and drinking, tasting, and sweetness. The language of the mystics, rich in the use of metaphor and symbolism, had much in common with poetic language. Dante, in the third realm of the afterlife, chose to restrict the visual portrayal of characters and landscape to degrees and qualities of light (characteristic features of some mystical writing), and to employ much more symbolic imagery and language than in *Inferno* or in *Purgatorio.* In the disputed letter to Cangrande, its author refers both to biblical sources and to mystical writings of St. Augustine, St. Bernard, and Richard of St. Victor as authorities to justify the mystical content of the *Paradiso* (*Epist.* 13.28). Whether or not he was the author of the letter to Cangrande, Dante's presentation of the experiences of the pilgrim throughout the third *cantica,* and especially at the climax of the *Paradiso,* has demonstrable similarities to other accounts of mystical union with God.

In the Heaven of the Sun, St. Bonaventure, a Franciscan mystical theologian and representative of Christian Neoplatonism, is paired with St. Thomas Aquinas, a Dominican and the chief proponent of Christian Aristotelianism (*Par.* 10–14): together they represent the two main currents of Scholastic thought. Dante scholarship has long debated the extent of the relative influences of Christian Aristotelianism and Christian Neoplatonism on Dante. Whereas in the nineteenth century Dante was seen as essentially Thomist, in the first part of this century Bruno Nardi demonstrated that Neoplatonism, Albertus Magnus, and Averroës were also important influences on the poet. Modern research reveals Dante to be a complex, individual, and eclectic thinker; and it is now becoming increasingly apparent that he was much more sympathetic to Christian Neoplatonism and mysticism than was previously thought to be the case. Aquinas is nowadays likewise seen as much more Neoplatonic than formerly.

The wise souls in the Heaven of the Sun include the pseudo-Dionysius, Richard of St. Victor, and Hugh of St. Victor, who were authors of important and influential mystical writings (*Par.* 10.115–117, 131–132, 12.133). St. Francis, whose story is told by Thomas Aquinas in *Par.* 11, and who founded an order of mystics, and St. Augustine, who was instrumental in integrating Neoplatonism with Christianity, are seen in the Celestial Rose (*Par.* 32.34–36). Other contemplatives, including Peter Damian and St. Benedict, appear in the Heaven of Saturn (*Par.* 21–22), and are seen ascending and descending a ladder, an image often used to represent the stages of mystical contemplation. Of course, in choosing St. Bernard of Clairvaux, a mystic *che 'n questo mondo, / contemplando, gustò di quella pace* ("who in this world, contemplating, had tasted of that peace," *Par.* 31.110–111), as the pilgrim's guide in the momentous final stages of his journey, Dante is making obvious his debts to the mystical tradition.

M

Bibliography

Barański, Zygmunt G. "Dante's Signs: An Introduction to Medieval Semiotics and Dante." In *Dante and the Middle Ages: Literary and Historical Essays.* Edited by John C. Barnes and Cormac O'Cuilleanain. Dublin: Irish Academic Press, 1995, pp. 139–180.

———. "Dante commentatore e commentato: riflessioni sullo studio dell'*iter* ideologico di Dante." *Letture Classensi* 23 (1994), 135–158.

Barbi, Michele. "Razionalismo e misticismo in Dante." In *Problemi di critica dantesca. Seconda serie.* Florence: Sansoni, 1964, pp. 1–86.

Botterill, Steven. *Dante and the Mystical Tradition. Bernard of Clairvaux in the* Commedia. Cambridge: Cambridge University Press, 1994.

Butler, Cuthbert. *Western Mysticism: The Teaching of Saints Augustine, Gregory, and Bernard on Contemplation and the Contemplative Life.* New York: Dutton, 1924.

Colombo, Manuela. *Dai mistici a Dante: Il linguaggio dell'ineffabilità.* Florence: La Nuova Italia, 1987.

Gardner, Edmund G. *Dante and the Mystics.* London and New York: Dent, 1913.

Jallonghi, Ernesto. *Il misticismo bonaventuriano nella Divina Commedia.* Padua: CEDAM, 1935.

Mazzeo, Joseph A. *Structure and Thought in the Paradiso.* New York: Greenwood Press, 1968.

———. *Medieval Cultural Tradition in Dante's Comedy.* Ithaca, N.Y.: Cornell University Press, 1960.

Mazzotta, Giuseppe. *Dante's Vision and the Circle of Knowledge.* Princeton, N.J.: Princeton University Press, 1993.

Nardi, Bruno. *Dante e la cultura medievale.* 1942. Bari: Laterza, 1983.

———. *Saggi di filosofia dantesca.* 2nd ed. Florence: La Nuova Italia, 1967.

Pertile, Lino. *"Paradiso:* A Drama of Desire." In *Word and Drama in Dante.* Edited by J. C. Barnes and J. Petrie. Dublin: Irish Academic Press, 1993, pp. 143–180.

Underhill, Evelyn. *Mysticism: A Study in the Nature of Man's Spiritual Consciousness.* New York: Dutton, 1911. Reprinted London, Methuen, Totowa, N.J.: Rowman and Littlefield, 1977.

Angela G. Meekins

N

Napoleone degli Alberti

Son of Alberto (*Inf.* 32.57) and father of Count Orso (*Purg.* 6.19), Napoleone degli Alberti butts heads like a billy goat with his brother Alessandro in Caina (*Inf.* 32.41–60). More deserving of being jellied in Hell than all other traitors to kin, according to Camiscion de' Pazzi—who is also punished in the ninth circle of Hell—these Ghibelline and Guelf rivals killed each other while quarreling over their father's possessions.

Roy Rosenstein

Narcissus

Dante's Ovidian Narcissus narrative comes from *Meta.* 3.339–510. When Narcissus *(Narciso)* reaches his sixteenth year, his beauty causes many to fall in love with him, but because of his great pride he rejects them all, including the nymph Echo. Hurt by his rejection, she pines away until only her voice remains. When another of his scorned would-be lovers prays that the disdainful Narcissus be punished by himself falling in love with an unattainable object, the goddess of vengeance, Nemesis, responds. One day after hunting, the exhausted Narcissus lies down next to a clear pond and sees his own reflection, with which he immediately falls in love, thinking that it is another being under the water. When he finally realizes the paradoxical truth of his impossible situation, his unsatisfiable longing causes him to waste away until he dies. His body is transformed into the flower that still bears his name.

The *Commedia*'s first overt mention of Narcissus occurs in *Inf.* 30.128, when, during the argument between Sinon the lying Greek and Maestro Adamo the counterfeiter, the latter taunts the former about the eternal punishment that makes him unceasingly yearn for water, referred to by the periphrasis *lo specchio di Narciso* ("the mirror of Narcissus"). Virgil rebukes Dante for having become too absorbed in the spectacle of this infernal dispute, telling him to look away. Implicit references to Narcissus occur in the thirtieth cantos of both the other two canticles. In *Purg.* 30.76–78, Dante is implicitly presented as a corrected Narcissus, as he lowers his eyes after Beatrice's first reproach and sees himself reflected in the *chiaro fonte* ("clear spring") of Lethe, from which he immediately turns away. Furthermore, the extended simile that introduces Dante's first penitential tears, comparing them to melting snow and wax (*Purg.* 30.85–90), recalls the double simile used by Ovid to describe the final wasting away of Narcissus' body (*Meta.* 3.487–490). In *Par.* 30.85–87, there may be a further evocation of Narcissus when Dante, following Beatrice's instructions, bends over the River of Light in order to make *migliori spegli* ("better mirrors") of his eyes.

The *Commedia*'s second and final overt reference to Narcissus occurs in *Par.* 3.17–18, as Dante looks into the sphere of the moon and mistakes the faint figures he sees there for reflections of people standing behind him, thus committing—as the text specifies—an error of perception exactly contrary to that of Narcissus, who had taken his own reflection to indicate the presence of another person.

Bibliography

Brownlee, Kevin. "Dante and Narcissus (*Purg.* 30.76–99)." *Dante Studies* 96 (1978), 201–206.

N

Dragonetti, Roger. "Dante et Narcisse ou les faux-monnayeurs de l'image." *Revue des Études Italiennes* n.s. 11 (1965), 85–146.

McMahon, Robert. "Satan as Infernal Narcissus: Interpretative Translation in the *Commedia*." In *Dante and Ovid: Essays in Intertextuality.* Edited by Madison U. Sowell. Binghamton, N.Y.: Medieval Texts and Studies, 1991, pp. 65–86.

Picone, Michelangelo. "Dante e il mito di Narciso: Dal *Roman de la Rose* alla *Commedia*." *Romanische Forschungen* 89 (1977), 382–397.

Shoaf, R. A. *Dante, Chaucer, and the Currency of the Word.* Norman: University of Oklahoma Press, 1983.

Kevin Brownlee

Nardi, Bruno

One of the most important Italian critics of the twentieth century, Nardi (1884–1968) was an individual of prodigious learning whose work on philosophic and theological influences in Dante's thought remains vitally important, even if his claim that an Averroist strain of heterodoxy informed his early works is now generally deemed exaggerated.

Although Nardi's individual essays number more than four hundred, it is his numerous collections that merit special attention: *Saggi di filosofia dantesca* (1930; 2nd ed., 1967); *Dante e la cultura medievale: Nuovi saggi di filosofia dantesca* (1942; 2nd ed., 1983); *Nel mondo di Dante* (1944); *Dal "Convivio alla Commedia": Sei saggi danteschi* (1960); *Saggi e note di critica dantesca* (1966); the critical edition of the *Monarchia* in the Ricciardi edition of Dante's works (*Opere,* vol. 2, 1979, pp. 239–503). Finally, his *lecturae Dantis* have been collected in a posthumous volume entitled *Lecturae e altri saggi danteschi* (1990).

Nardi was predominantly preoccupied with the philosophic Dante of the Middle Ages, an interest that was principally historical and philological in nature. His research focused on questions concerning the origin and nature of Dante's political thought and on the importance of the Neoplatonic strain in his thought, combating the tendency to see Dante as exclusively Thomistic; he did groundbreaking work on the question of Averroism in the *Commedia*. His interpretive spirit was always governed by the quest for original sources, by his belief in the inseparability of poetry and structure, and by a general hostility to critics whose interpretations were predisposed toward accommodating patterns of allegory and the enigmatic in general. He entered critical debates with polemic vigor (against, for example, G. Busnelli, M. Maccarrone, and P. G. Ricci), always seeking to distinguish the multiple cultural layers of medieval thought in Dante's texts.

Bibliography

Garin, Eugenio. "Ricordo di B.N." *Studi danteschi* 45 (1969), 5–28.

Gregory, Tullio. "Gli scritti di Bruno Nardi." In Bruno Nardi, *"Lecturae" e altri studi danteschi.* Florence: Le Lettere, 1990, pp. 285–312.

———. "Bruno Nardi." *Giornale storico della letteratura italiana* 47 (1968), 469–501.

Gregory, Tullio, and Paolo Mazzantini. "Gli scritti di Bruno Nardi." *L'Alighieri* 9.2 (1968), 39–58.

Vallone, Aldo. *Storia della critica dantesca dal XIV al XX secolo.* Vol. 2. Milan: Vallardi, 1981, pp. 890–893.

Vasoli, Cesare. "B.N. dantista." In *Letteratura italiana: I critici.* Vol. 3. Milan: Marzorati, 1970, pp. 2023–2051.

Aldo Vallone
(translated by Robin Treasure)

Nathan

Hebrew prophet (2 Sam. 7:1–17) and chronicler (1 Chron. 29:29; 2 Chron. 9:29). Nathan reproved David for plotting the death of Uriah the Hittite in order to make Bathsheba his wife (2 Sam. 12:1–15), and he was instrumental in having Solomon crowned David's successor (1 Kings 1). St. Bonaventure points out *Natàn profeta* ("Nathan the prophet") among the great wise spirits of the second crown in the Heaven of the Sun (*Par.* 12.136).

Carolynn Lund-Mead

Navarre, King of

The trouvère, Thibaut IV, count of Champagne, referred to by Dante in the *De vulgari eloquentia* as *Rex Navarre,* ruled in Navarre from 1234 to 1253. His canzone, *De fin amor si vient sen et bonté,* is cited in *DVE* 1.9 3 and 2.5.4, and another poem (actually by Gace Brulé) is erroneously attributed to him in *DVE* 2.6.6. Thibaut is the only lyric poet of the *langue d'oïl* mentioned by Dante.

Laurie Shepard

Nebuchadnezzar

Chaldean king of Babylonia who besieged and captured Jerusalem, deporting its people (597 and 589 B.C.E.). In *Par.* 4.13–15 and *Epist.* 13.81, reference is made to a dream Nebuchadnezzar had but could not recall (Dan. 2). In the *Paradiso* passage, Beatrice is compared to Daniel, who through God's revelation disclosed the dream and its interpretation, thus saving the lives of the wise men whom Nebuchadnezzar *(Nabuccodonosor)* had condemned to death for their inability to divine the mystery. Beatrice, who sees all things in God, reveals and explains Dante's unspoken doubts and so brings him peace. In *Epist.* 13.81 Dante names Nebuchadnezzar *(Nabuchodonosor)*, as one who despite his unlikely candidacy was nevertheless the recipient of divine revelation.

Carolynn Lund-Mead

Negligent Rulers

Dante and other medieval political theorists set extremely high standards for those who wielded political authority, and some of his harshest criticism was directed at rulers who failed to live up to those standards because of idleness or negligence. This strand in medieval political thought underlies the well-known French expression of the seventeenth century, *roi faineant* (lazy king). Dante's chief discussion of negligent rulers is in *Purg.* 7, in which the negligent princes must delay beginning the process of purgation because they have failed in their royal responsibilities.

Dante did not invent this concept. Gratian's *Decretum,* the standard textbook of medieval canon law, contained a text from Pope Gregory VII (1073–1085) that stated a pope could depose a king because of royal "uselessness," and in 1245, Pope Innocent IV suspended King Sancho II of Portugal from his royal duties on the grounds that the king possessed neither the power nor the will to act responsibly. Canon law also contained extensive provisions dealing with the negligence or incapacity of ecclesiastical officials, and much of the thought about royal incapacity was colored by the canonists' discussions of prelatal incapacity. In 1294, Celestine V resigned the papacy because of his admitted incapacity to rule the Church, and in 1298, Adolf of Nassau was deposed as emperor on the same grounds. During Dante's exile and the writing of the *Commedia,* King Henry II of Cyprus (1285–1324) was suspended from governance from 1306 to 1310 on the grounds of negligence, a case that was widely known and discussed throughout Europe.

Dante's concern with negligent rulership focuses on the Empire in his own lifetime. He introduces the theme in *Purg.* 6.91 in a bitter denunciation of emperors who failed to use the spur after having "put your hand to the bridle" of the Empire, and who, like Albert and Rudolf of Habsburg, are deflected by greed and ignore their imperial responsibilities in Italy and permit chaos and violence to reign. In *Purg.* 7, Sordello provides a catalogue of negligent rulers who occupy a valley of flowers, beginning with Rudolf of Habsburg, who *fa sembianti / d'aver negletto ciò che far dovea* ("has the expression of one who has neglected what he should have done," *Purg.* 7.91–92), and followed by Ottakar of Bohemia, Philip III of France, Henry I of Navarre, Pedro III of Aragon, Charles I of Naples, Henry III of England, and William VII, marquis of Monferrat. Dante's primary concern is with emperors who neglected Italy during their reigns, but he includes kings as well—even a still-living king, Ottakar's son Wenceslaus II, "who feeds on lust and idleness" (*Purg.* 7.102). They constitute the fourth and last group of late repentants in the Ante-Purgatory.

With the exception of his primary focus on the Empire and his denunciations of Habsburg greed, Dante's condemnations of negligent rulers reflect conventional medieval political and psychological theory. Rulers might fail to perform their duties—just as other men, including clergy, might—because of mental incapacity or illness, age, sloth, boredom, or lust. The last three of these are vices, however, over which Christians (including Christian rulers) were expected to exercise control. When they did not, they sinned. Such sins were greater in the case of rulers, because they were responsible for the peace and prosperity of their kingdoms, which they were supposed to rule with love, justice, and energy. What makes Dante's depiction of the negligent princes original is his locating them together within the structure of Purgatory and his linking of imperial negligence to that of lower-ranking rulers.

Dante was familiar with the conventional medieval distinction among the tyrant, the wicked ruler, and the just king, but the extraordinary range and sensitivity of his political thought also led him to consider the equally dangerous problem of the negligent ruler and to provide a memorable

N catalogue of instances of royal negligence in which he condemns some of his contemporaries and offers a dramatic and stern example of the dangers of royal negligence.

Bibliography

Bowra, C. M. "Dante and Sordello." *Comparative Literature* 5 (1953), 1–15.

Ferrante, Joan. *The Political Vision of the "Divine Comedy."* Princeton, N.J.: Princeton University Press, 1984.

Masciandaro, Franco. *Dante as Dramatist: The Myth of the Earthly Paradise and Tragic Vision in the "Divine Comedy."* Philadelphia: University of Pennsylvania Press, 1991. See chapter 5.

Scott, John A. *Dante's Political Purgatory.* Philadelphia: University of Pennsylvania Press, 1996.

Edward Peters

Nella

A collateral target of Dante's acerbic poetic exchanges with her husband Forese Donati, who he suggests was an impotent husband to her (*Rime,* 73). In an exchange in which the pilgrim repudiates those unkind verses, the poet makes amends to her by having Forese attribute his progress through Purgatory to Nella's prayers for him (*Purg.* 23.85). Moreover, Dante subtly contrasts her to the shameless women of Florence and aligns her with the virtuous Beatrice. Early commentators praise her devout prayers for her dead husband, probably on the basis of this passage. (The authenticity of the *tenzone,* however, has recently been called into question by Mauro Cursietti.)

Bibliography

Cursietti, Mauro. *La falsa tenzone di Dante con Forese Donati.* Anzio: De Rubeis, 1995.

F. Regina Psaki

Neologisms

A neologism is a word coinage: a creation of a new word from other words already existing in the same language, or the borrowing of a word or words from a foreign language to make a new word in the speaker's or writer's language. In Dante's *Paradiso,* the poet introduces many neologisms which he invents by combining already existing words from his maternal language. Creating mostly reflexive verbs, Dante generally combines a preposition (like *in, di,* or *tra,* "in," "of," "between") with another part of speech such as a noun (*cielo, giglio, zaffiro,* "heaven," "lily," "sapphire"), a pronoun (*lui, mi,* or *lei,* "him," "me," her"), an adjective (*uno, cinque, tre,* "one," "five," "three"), or an adverb (*meglio, forse, dove,* "better," "perhaps," "where"). Specific examples include *inzaffirarsi* ("to ensapphire itself," 23.102), *immegliarsi* ("to in-better itself," 30.87), *imparadisare* ("to imparadise," 23.3), and *trasumanare* ("to go beyond being human," 1.70).

Dante does not create these words purely to experiment with language. His use of neologisms is directly related to the literary purposes of the *Commedia,* in which he seeks to approach God if not to overcome the separation between man and God. Word coinages are one of the literary mechanisms Dante employs to overcome the dichotomies between words and things, mind and body, and God and mankind which were brought into existence by the Fall. (See *Par.* 26.109–142 for Adam's discussion of the fragility and corruptibility of human language.) Some neologisms (*incielare,* "to inheaven"; *infuturarsi,* "to infuture itself") convey entrance into a time and place beyond ordinary understanding. Others, such as those based on numbers (e.g., *intrearsi,* "to in-three oneself"), are used to approximate the mysteries of the Trinity and of infinity. Thus, in the *Paradiso* these words signify more than their part of speech, their place in the sentence, and their dialectic. While disrupting conventional syntactic expectations and thwarting normal word order, Dante attempts to express the inexpressible. Such neologisms demonstrate the poet's paradoxical attempt to transcend language while declaring that it is not possible to do so.

In the Middle Ages, grammarians and rhetoricians repudiated the use of neologisms because Cicero and Donatus had rejected them as "barbarisms." Their grammatical warning is repeated by St. Isidore *(Etymologies),* Hugh of St. Victor *(Didascalicon),* John of Salisbury *(Metalogicon),* and Matthew of Vendôme *(Art of Versification),* among others. But there were circumstances in which neologisms could be introduced, and the tradition justifying their use is as old as the one that proscribed it. Cicero *(De oratore)* had argued that since the Greeks had invented new words to express new philosophical phenomena, Latin, the medium into which Greek works were to be translated, could make use of invented words. Similarly

Horace had suggested that neologisms were at times necessary to express obscure material. In translating the Bible from Greek into Latin, St. Jerome employs the same argument, arguing that holy scripture was expressive of "new realities," and that consequently new words were needed to articulate the essence of new spiritual and religious truths. But even though these writers allow for the invention of words, they caution against excess. Dante's lexical rule-breaking finds its justification in this Latin rhetorical tradition, but Dante, far from exercising restraint, seems to revel in a linguistic inventiveness that joyously attempts to say something while also conveying that it is not possible to say it in any language that exists.

Bibliography

Di Pretoro, P. A. "Innovazioni lessicali nella 'Commedia.'" *Atti della Accademia Nazionale dei Lincei* 25 (1970), 263–297.

Ferrante, Joan. "Words and Images in the *Paradiso:* Reflections of the Divine." In *Dante, Petrarch, Boccaccio: Studies in the Italian Trecento in Honor of Charles S. Singleton.* Edited by Aldo S. Bernardo and Anthony L. Pellegrini. Binghamton, N.Y.: Medieval and Renaissance Texts and Studies, 1983.

Schildgen, Brenda Deen. "Dante's Neologisms in the *Paradiso* and the Latin Rhetorical Tradition." *Dante Studies* 107 (1989), 101–119.

Brenda Deen Schildgen

Neoplatonism

The term refers in the first instance to the philosophy of Plotinus (204–270 C.E.), and in the second instance to the countless pagan, Muslim, Jewish, and Christian thinkers influenced in turn—directly or indirectly—by Plotinus's thought (among Christians, virtually every patristic and medieval thinker of any importance). It can be hard to draw a distinction between Neoplatonism and other forms of Platonism (especially "Middle Platonism," the term covering the period between Plato's immediate successors—the Old Academy—and Plotinus), particularly when it concerns doctrines that were widely shared. In addition to the pagan classical sources (the most widely read being Porphyry, Proclus, Macrobius, Martianus Capella, and Servius the Grammarian), one may distinguish at least three currents of Neoplatonic thought that influenced Dante's period. All derive ultimately from Plotinus, though they are influenced as well by Middle Platonism: the Latin current, including both Augustine and Boethius; the Greek current, mainly deriving from the mystical theology of the Pseudo-Dionysius; and the Arab current.

Plotinus postulated the emanation (the term refers to a flowing forth or radiation) of all things from the utterly transcendent, absolute One, which is beyond all essence or knowledge, and about which only negative statements can be made. This emanation resulted in three successive levels of being: absolute Mind *(noûs),* which contains the principles or essences of all possible things—the Platonic Ideas—by knowing them; Soul *(psyché),* a development of Plato's World Soul, capable of producing and animating bodies in space; and material things. Each successive principle adheres in love to the one just above it—Mind to the One, Soul to Mind—and radiates its own influence downward. Plotinus created a powerfully original simplification and systematization of what in Plato was often confused or inconsistent, always insisting that he was merely the master's faithful interpreter. In cosmology the important text by Plato was the *Timaeus,* readily fitted into Plotinus's scheme asserting one spherical cosmos governed by planetary deities. For Plotinus the human soul is divine and immortal, participating in the nature of Soul, and happy in the direct contemplation of Mind until falling of its own accord into bodily existence, from whose bondage it can gradually free itself by the ascetic discipline of philosophy, which leads it eventually to "enter the sanctuary" of mystical contemplation of the divine (here the most important Platonic texts are the *Phaedo,* the *Phaedrus,* and the *Republic).* From late antiquity on, the *Timaeus* was the only dialogue of Plato to circulate at all widely in the Latin West (in the incomplete translation and commentary by Calcidius), and Plotinus was directly known only in part; a critical understanding of Plato's own thought did not become possible until the modern period.

Plato's interest in elaborate myths as vehicles of philosophical ideas (such as the myths of the Cave in *Republic* VII, or the chariot of the soul in the *Phaedrus)* helps to account for the Neoplatonists' intense development of allegorical approaches to literary and philosophical texts. They were particularly drawn to the heuristic of microcosm–macrocosm correspondences: Porphyry, for instance, read the description of the

Cave of the Nymphs in *Ody.* 13 as a symbolic representation of the cosmos; Proclus applied the principle to the relation of part to whole in texts. The notion of man as microcosm, central to Plato's *Timaeus,* gained great currency through the Neoplatonists' adaptations.

Plotinus's Neoplatonism was itself heir to "Middle Platonism," whose most influential representatives included Cicero, Apuleius, Calcidius, and Philo of Alexandria. The Book of Wisdom in the Old Testament, and the Epistles of St. Paul (d. c. 65) and the Gospel of St. John (d. c. 90) in the New show the influence of Middle Platonic ideas. Plotinus was apparently a fellow student in Alexandria with Origen, one of the greatest Christian Platonic theologians, and may have been influenced by him and other Christians. As Christianity spread among Greek-speaking intellectuals, its theology acquired an increasingly Platonic character. The emphasis in the Gospel of St. John on the divinity of the Word (Logos), "through [whom] all things were made," led inevitably to an adaptation of the Platonic theory of ideas that made the Logos the bearer, within the triune godhead, of the ideas or essences of all things. Influenced by Plotinus's conception of Mind, though by the Christians made coequal with God the Father, this conception was shared by virtually all patristic and medieval Christian thinkers.

Other philosophical issues entered Christian thought via the Platonic/Neoplatonic tradition. The question of the preexistence of the soul was seriously debated by both Origen and Augustine; both left the question open, though they argued strongly that the union of soul and body was not the result of any fall (least of all the Fall of Man), but rather a good. Other Neoplatonic Christians, like Gregory of Nyssa and Erigena, regarded the physical body and the division of mankind into sexes negatively, as the proleptic result of the Fall, but the central tradition strenuously fought that view.

A major influence on all later Christian thinkers, including Dante, was the sixth-century Pseudo-Dionysius, so called because his works circulated under the name of the Athenian judge converted by St. Paul (Acts 17:34), an attribution that lent them almost apostolic authority; they were actually written under the influence of the last great pagan Neoplatonist, Proclus (411–485). Though strongly creationist, the Pseudo-Dionysius followed Origen and Proclus in making central to his thought the procession of all things from God as a kind of radiation of light, and their return to him through the mediation of Christ. This pattern also governed the literary structure of his *On the Divine Names* by determining the order and emphasis with which the various names of God (Being, Good, Life, Light, and so forth) are treated. The Pseudo-Dionysius' works also strongly influenced the twelfth-century interest in optics and "light metaphysics," to which the new Gothic style of architecture owed so much.

Arab thought developed Neoplatonism to new complexities, especially in the work of Al-farabi (d. 950), Avicenna (980–1037), and Averroës (1126–1198), though Averroës consciously attempted to eliminate the Neoplatonic element in his interpretation of Aristotle. Avicenna's Plotinian-Proclan synthesis attributed the existence of the world to a radiation of the One into the successively lower hypostases and secondary causes in such a way that God was excluded from the direct fashioning of anything other than first (i.e., formless) matter; man's body and soul were left to the fashioning of the Intelligences (angels) governing the heavenly spheres. Avicenna's system became known in the West at about the same time as the influential *Liber de causis,* for a long time attributed to Aristotle, but in fact, as Aquinas eventually realized, an Arabic epitome of Proclus's *Elements of Theology;* together with Averroës's Neoplatonic version of Aristotle, which assigned an equally important role to the Intelligences, they occasioned much discussion. Arab and Western interest in astrology was considerably strengthened by the Arab philosophical tradition, which seemed to provide it with a scientific foundation.

One of the chief issues was the status of human intellection. According to the more radical Arab positions, intellection was possible exclusively through an illuminating Intelligence and was thus unconnected with the individual personality; Averroës correctly understood the similar grounds on which Aristotle had denied the immortality of the soul, the "form," or actualizing principle, of the body. Thinkers like Albert the Great, Aquinas, and Duns Scotus appealed to the strongly creationist Augustinian and Pseudo-Dionysian versions of Neoplatonism against the emanationist theories of Proclus and Avicenna. They asserted the unity of the individual soul, including intellect.

Dante was deeply influenced by Neoplatonism as early as the *Vita Nuova.* In that early work, Dante's Neoplatonic reading seems restricted to

Boethius's *Consolation of Philosophy* (see *Conv.* 2.12.2), but both the *Convivio* and the *Commedia* reflect a much wider acquaintance, including the Pseudo-Dionysius and the *Liber de causis,* which Dante almost certainly read with Albertus Magnus's and Aquinas's commentaries, and Avicenna and Averroës (perhaps via Albertus's *De causis et processu universi*). In his long and complicated development, the effort to assimilate and adapt Neoplatonic ideas is a major thread; he was aware of the currents just enumerated and took a characteristically independent position on a number of the issues. (Dante's highly original treatment of allegory and of the idea of the microcosm are discussed in separate entries.)

Like most other Christians, Dante accepted the Augustinian identification of Plotinus's principle of Mind with the Logos, the second person of the Trinity. The intuition of the Logos as the principle that contains and creates all things by knowing them is the first level of the pilgrim's vision of the godhead: he first sees a "simple light" revealing the "universal forms" uniting "substances and accidents" (*Par.* 33.85–95). As this and countless other passages reveal, Dante's conception of the intellectual ascent to God is based on the Neoplatonic conflation of logical categories and procedures (especially *division,* which descends from genera to species to individuals, and *collection* or classification, which ascends the ladder) with metaphysical ones.

The problem of deriving the multiplicity of things from the unified—or triunified—light of God's creative power informs all the cosmological passages in the *Paradiso,* along with the classic Neoplatonic problem of the secondary causes: *Dentro dal cielo de la divina pace / si gira un corpo ne la cui virtute / l'esser di tutto suo contento giace* ("Within the heaven of God's peace there turns a body within whose power lies the being of all it contains," *Par.* 2.112–14). Referring to the Primum Mobile, this means, quite literally, that it imparts both existence and power to everything within it. Strictly speaking, then, lines 113–114 express an emanationist conception of the relation of the successive heavens that is inconsistent with the idea that the heavens were directly created as formed (see below). It is true that the lines can be taken to mean that once created, the universe is sustained in existence by this transfer of "being and power" downward through all the spheres (in either case, the notion is Neoplatonic):

"Lo ciel seguente, c'ha tante vedute, / quell' esser parte per diverse essenze, / da lui distratte e da lui contenute" ("The next heaven, which has so many sights, divides that being among different essences, separated by it, yet contained by it," *Par.* 2.115–117). The sphere of the fixed stars (*tante vedute,* "so many sights") is, then, the first step in the derivation of multiplicity from the "simple light" of God's power. In containing all the multiplicity of the universe virtually, the sphere of the fixed stars follows a pattern similar to that attributed to the Logos, but here there is a material embodiment of the power, which descends through the cosmos from high to low in the mediation characteristic of medieval Neoplatonism: *Li altri giron per varie differenze / le distinzion che dentro da sé hanno / dispongono a lor fini e lor semenze. / Questi organi del mondo così vanno, / come tu vedi omai, di grado in grado, / che di sù prendono e di sotto fanno* ("The other spheres through various differences dispose the distinctions held within them to their goals and to their sowings. These organs of the world thus descend, as you can now see, by degrees, for they take from above and fashion below," *Par.* 2.118–123).

So far Beatrice's account has mentioned only the heavenly spheres and their contents. Now she brings in the angelic Movers of the spheres: *"Lo moto e la virtù d'i santi giri, / come dal fabbro l'arte del martello, / da' beati motor convien che spiri; / e 'l ciel cui tanti lumi fanno bello / de la mente profonda che lui volve / prende l'image e fassene suggello"* ("The motion and the power of the holy spheres, as the art of the hammer from the smith, must necessarily proceed from the blessed movers; and the heaven that so many lights make beautiful takes the image from the profound mind turning it and makes itself its seal," *Par.* 2.127–132). In lines 127–129, the angelic Intelligences direct the motions of the heavens on the model of an artisan using an already formed tool; lines 130–132, however, assert that the Heaven of the Fixed Stars takes form from the mind of its angelic Mover. This may be understood to mean that the form to be imposed below, derived from the mind of the Mover, is conveyed in the light of the fixed stars (cf. *Par.* 22.112–114), but it is very close to the Avicennan or Averroist view in which the spheres and planets take their forms from the Movers. Implied through the entire passage is the further idea that each fixed star and planet has a unique formal principle—that while all light shares a

N common generic nature, each source of light produces a formally unique species of light (explicit in line 147; cf. Aquinas, *ST* 1.70.1). Although in lines 127–129 Dante seems to avoid the language used by thinkers, such as Witelo, who speak of the light of the heavenly bodies containing and carrying down the forms to be imposed on the sublunar world, the idea is not far from the surface.

Beatrice comes close to the Neoplatonic idea of the World Soul, too, in calling the heavens "organs of the world" (line 121), analogous to the organs produced by the human soul to carry out its functions. *"E come l'alma dentro a vostra polve / per differenti membra e conformate / a diverse potenze si risolve, / così l'intelligenza sua bontate / moltiplicata per le stelle spiega, / girando sé sovra sua unitate. / Virtù diverse fa diversa lega / col prezïoso corpo ch'ella avviva, / nel qual, sì come in voi, si lega"* ("And just as the soul within your dust is distributed through different members shaped appropriately for different powers, so the intelligence unfolds its goodness, multiplied through the stars, turning itself about its unity. Different powers make different alloys with the precious bodies they vivify, in which, like life in you, they bind themselves," *Par.* 2.133–141).

The notions that the angels are united with the heavenly spheres they govern, and that the heavens are their "organs" rather than their "instruments" was one of the theses condemned as heretical in 1277 by the archbishop of Paris (H. Denifle and E. Chatelain, *Chartularium Universitatis Parisiensis,* Paris, 1889, 1, 549). Modern critics such as Nardi, Sapegno, and Chiavacci Leonardi seek to minimize the heterodoxy of *Par.* 2, but at the very least Dante is skirting dangerous possibilities.

In such passages Dante's struggle to synthesize creationist and emanationist views is evident. *Par.* 29.10–48 sets forth Dante's adaptation— unique to him—of the Neoplatonic doctrine of the role in creation of secondary causes, that is, the angelic Intelligences. The passage is creationist in attributing the creation to God's desire to share the happiness of being with his creatures (lines 13–15; cf. *Timaeus,* 29D–30A, and Boethius's *Consolatio,* 3.m.9), but it limits God's direct act of creation (apart from that of Adam and Eve) to "form and matter, combined and separate" (*forma e matera, congiunte e purette,* line 22): that is, the angels are pure form; first matter is pure matter, pure poten-tiality without form—what would become, under the shaping influence of the heavens, the earth, and all sublunar things; and the heavens are shaped matter, form and matter combined. These three are described as radiating forth simultaneously, on the model of light (lines 25–30), reflecting back to the Creator his own brightness (lines 10–12; cf. *Par.* 1.1–9, 13.52–66). Based in part on Augustine's interpretation of Gen. 1:1, this conception assigns the entire process of shaping the sublunar world to the influence of the heavenly bodies governed by the angelic Intelligences. Except for Adam's and Eve's bodies, which were fashioned directly by God (Gen. 2:7, 21–22), it applies also to the fashioning of all human bodies.

The question of the part played by the secondary causes in the fashioning of human beings preoccupies Dante from the *Convivio* onward. He ultimately accepts the Dominicans' refutations of Averroës's central Aristotelian doctrines of the separation of intellect and the mortality of the soul (*Purg.* 25.61–66), but he rejects Aquinas's theory of the repeated miraculous discontinuities of fetal development in favor of Albertus Magnus's more naturalistic one, which limits God's intervention to the single act of infusion of the active intellect.

The passage in *Conv.* 4.21 on the production of the human soul documents an important moment in the evolution of Dante's thought, and it reveals very clearly its Neoplatonic origins. The development of the fetus, Dante says, is governed ɔy three factors: the generative power in the seed, derived from the father; the power of the heavens; and the power of the elements assimilated into the fetus to form its "complexion." The power of the heavens "produces the living soul" from "the potentiality of the seed": *La quale [l'anima], incontanente prodotta, riceve da la vertù del Motore del cielo lo intelletto possibile; lo quale potenzialmente in sé adduce tutte le forme universali, secondo che sono nel suo produttore, e tanto meno quanto più dilungato dalla prima Intelligenza è* ("As soon as it [the soul] is produced it receives from the virtue of the celestial mover [literally, "the mover of the heaven"] the possible intellect, which draws into itself in potentiality all the universal forms as they are found in its maker, to an ever lesser degree the more it [i.e., the mover of the heaven producing the soul] is removed from the primal [literally, "the first"] Intelligence [most probably, the Intelligence that moves the Primum Mobile]," 4.21.5). Although not fully spelled out, the idea is clear enough that the various angelic Movers of the spheres are more or less distant from the First Intelligence (whether the Mover of the Primum Mobile, as in *Par.* 29, or God himself) according as they govern lower or higher planetary heavens. The possible intellect received from the Mover of the sphere of the Moon will be less pure than that received from the Mover of Saturn, and consequently its possessor will have more difficulty in achieving the most abstract understanding.

It is clear that the roots of this passage lie in the Avicennan/Averroist version of the emanation of the angels and the heavens and their power over human beings. It is an unusually technical variant of the popular astrological doctrine of the children of the planets, according to which the planet that "rules" a nativity has a preponderant influence on the native, to the extent of determining the occupation to which he or she will be drawn, as well as the temperament, a principle that Dante uses as a fundamental doctrine and chief organizing principle of the entire *Commedia. Purg.* 25.37–78, Statius's account of human embryology, avoids specifying the role of the angelic Intelligence, though it is clear that the entire process is governed by "nature" (the three "powers" of *Conv.* 4.21) and must be understood in connection with the other passages we have discussed, as well as *Par.* 8.97–148. How far Dante has moved from the *Convivio* is not at all clear.

Finally, in addition to the procession of all things from God—whether by creation or emanation—there is the great Neoplatonic theme of their return to him, especially that of the human soul, of course in Christian guise. This is fundamental to the *Vita Nuova* and the *Commedia,* and recurrent in the "petrose" poems and the *Convivio.* In both completed works, understanding the modes of procession—the intellectual ascent—is a major aspect of the return. The great turning point of the *Vita Nuova,* the canzone "Donne ch'avete intelletto d'amore," is an elaborate experiment enacting the patterns of procession and return, as its "division" allows us to grasp (Durling and Martinez 1990).

When beginning his ascent through the spheres, the pilgrim marvels at his "transcending these light bodies" (*com'io trascenda questi corpi levi, Par.* 1.99), and Beatrice gives an explanation (lines 103–142) that is overtly Aristotelian insofar as it draws on Aristotle's explanation of the motion of sublunar, elemented things as caused by the tendency of the elements to return each to its proper level (*Physics,* book 5), the pilgrim's "proper place" being Heaven. But the Aristotelian terminology is put to the service of a conception entirely foreign to Aristotle, who denied the possibility of the separate existence of the soul, as well as its descent from or return to a spiritual realm (the crossing of the Neoplatonic ascent of the soul with Aristotle's terminology goes back to Augustine's *Confessions,* book 13). As so often in thirteenth-century texts, the outward clothing of Aristotelian terminology masks the more fundamental allegiance to the Platonic/Neoplatonic tradition.

Although detailed discussion is beyond the scope of this article, mention should be made of the important influence that Ficinian Neoplatonic interpretations of the *Commedia* had during the Renaissance, especially via the widely read commentary by Cristoforo Landino (Florence, 1481).

Bibliography

Armstrong, A. H. (ed.). *The Cambridge History of Later Greek and Early Medieval Philosophy.* Cambridge: Cambridge University Press, 1967.

Chenu, M.-D. *Nature, Man, and Society in the Twelfth Century.* Selected, edited, and translated by J. Taylor and L. K. Little. Toronto: University of Toronto Press, 1997.

D'Ancona Costa, Cristina. *Recherches sur le Liber de causis.* Paris: Vrin, 1995.

Dillon, John. *The Middle Platonists: A Study of Platonism 80 B.C. to A.D. 220.* London: Duckworth, 1977.

Durling, Robert M., and Ronald L. Martinez. *Time and the Crystal: Studies in Dante's "Rime petrose."* Berkeley and Los Angeles: University of California Press, 1990.

Leaman, Oliver. *An Introduction to Medieval Islamic Philosophy.* Cambridge: Cambridge University Press, 1985.

Gersh, Stephen. *Middle Platonism and Neoplatonism: The Latin Tradition.* 2 vols. Notre Dame: University of Notre Dame Press, 1986.

Gilson, Étienne. *Dante and Philosophy.* Translated by David Moore. New York: Harper and Row, 1963.

———. *History of Christian Philosophy in the Middle Ages.* New York: Random House, 1955.

Gregory, Tullio. *Mundana sapientia: Forme di conoscenza nella cultura medievale.* Rome: Storia e Letteratura, 1992.

———. *Platonismo medievale: Studi e ricerche.* Studi storici, 26–27. Rome: Istituto Storico Italiano per il Medio Evo, 1958.

N Nardi, Bruno. *Saggi di filosofia dantesca.* 2nd ed. Florence: La Nuova Italia, 1967.

———. *Studi di filosofia medievale.* Rome: Storia e Letteratura, 1960.

Rorem, Paul. *Pseudo-Dionysius: A Commentary on the Texts and an Introduction to Their Influence.* New York and Oxford: Oxford University Press, 1993.

Wallis, R. T. *Neoplatonism.* London: Duckworth, 1972.

Robert M. Durling

Neptune

In Roman antiquity, Neptune *(Nettuno)* was the god of seas, known by the Greeks as Poseidon. The son of Chronos and Rhea, he lived in a castle at the bottom of the sea with his wife Amphitrite. He was greatly honored and feared by seafarers because of his dominion and power over the waters. He is generally depicted as holding a trident. In *Inf.* 28.83 Dante uses the name "Neptune" as a hyperbolic image of the world known to his contemporaries. Among the sowers of scandal and schism, Dante says that between Cyprus on the east and Majorca on the west, the Mediterranean, or Neptune, had never witnessed such a cruel action as Malatestino's betrayal of Guido del Cassero and Angiolello di Carignano (*Inf.* 28.76–90). In *Par.* 33.94–96, Dante recalls Neptune's surprise at witnessing the *Argo* course across his seas. His defeat by Athena over the right to name the capital of Cecropia, later Athens, is alluded to at *Purg.* 15.97.

Alessandro Vettori

Nessus

The centaur who fell in love with Hercules' wife, Deianira, and attempted to rape her, but was killed by Hercules' poisoned arrow. As he died, however, he gave Deianira his own blood-soaked (and thus poisoned) shirt, telling her that it would guarantee her husband's faithful love. When Deianira, worried about Hercules' faithfulness, gave it to her husband, she unwittingly caused his death. Dante's probable source for these monsters possessing the body of a horse and the trunk and head of a man was Ovid (*Meta.* 9.98–133). In the *Inferno,* Nessus *(Nesso)* appears as one of the three centaurs watching over those who were violent against their neighbor (seventh circle, first ring). Virgil tells Dante Nessus' story (*Inf.* 12.67–69) and requests

that Chiron, the leader of the centaurs, provide them with an escort. To this task Chiron assigns Nessus, who carries Dante across the Phlegethon and points out the sinners immersed to varying depths in the river.

V. Stanley Benfell

Neutrals

The neutrals are the first of the lost souls encountered by the pilgrim Dante in Hell (*Inf.* 3.22–69). Unnamed by the poet, these spirits, who technically escape being numbered among the damned, are also known in English translations as the indecisive, the lukewarm, the opportunists, the trimmers (individuals who make changes for reasons of expediency), the cowards, and the futile. Italian critics prefer the designations *pusillanimi* ("the cowardly" or "the faint-hearted") or *ignavi* ("the slothful"). They inhabit the vestibule to Hell proper, an ambiguous space in the netherworld between the gates of Hell and the Acheron, the river that defines the outer border of Hell and the place from which all sinners are ferried to their eternal abodes. This spatial designation reflects the neutrals' inability to choose good or evil and characterizes their propensity for indecision and spiritual inertia. Because they did not choose good or evil, they are deserving of eternal residency in a kind of no-man's-world, neither Hell nor Heaven; they are guilty of no personal sin and can equally make no claim to glory for any act of goodness. The poet dismisses them as *sciagurati, che mai non fur vivi* ("wretches, who never were alive," *Inf.* 3.64), and Virgil tells the pilgrim that they merit no attention: *"non ragioniam di lor, ma guarda e passa"* ("let us not speak of them, but look and pass on," 51). The neutrals' companions include those angels who became unworthy of Heaven because they took no side in Lucifer's rebellion against God. The vestibule to Hell, often referred to in criticism as the *Antinferno* ("Ante-Hell"), in parallel with "Ante-Purgatory," houses those humans and angels who preferred to avoid any commitment that would compromise issues of self-interest.

The presentation of the neutrals functions as a prelude to the visual and auditory phenomena of Hell, and as an introduction to the law of *contrapasso,* in which the punishment prescribed mirrors the nature of the sin. The neutrals circle furiously around in their area, rushing to follow an

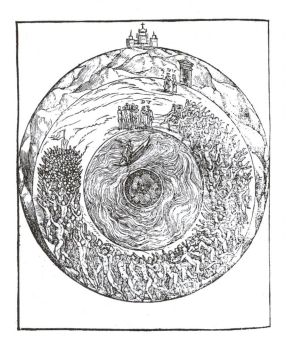

Dante among the neutrals in the antechamber of Hell. La comedia di Dante Aligieri, *with commentary by Alessandro Vellutello, published by Francesco Marcolini, Venice, 1544. Giamatti Collection: Courtesy of the Mount Holyoke College Archives and Special Collections.*

unidentified banner, spurred to action after a life of inaction and indecisiveness. They are also tormented by hornets and wasps that buzz about, sting, and suck blood from their wounds. Persistent irritants that reflect the pettiness of their self-centered lives, the insects are also stinging reminders of the neutrals' earthly life, which was untouched by any stimulus. The insects' bites, which produce the blood, tears, and pus that mingle and trickle to the ground where they become food for maggots and worms, are illustrative of the neutrals' moral decay and spiritual insignificance.

Dante's contempt for the neutrals owes much to his unshakable belief in the value of the *vita attiva* ("active life") and in each individual's need to serve the ends of society. As he remarks in the *Convivio,* following Aristotle's dictum, man is a *compagnevole animale* ("social animal," 4.4.1); without participating in a community to foster its culture and provide for its defense, man cannot achieve earthly happiness. The neutrals join no group and in turn are rejected by both the powers of good (Heaven) and evil (Hell). Despite the lack of theological basis in scripture for assigning individuals to an area outside either of these realms, commentators cite Apoc. 3:14–16 as a description

of their essence: "But because thou art lukewarm and neither cold nor hot, I am about to vomit thee out of my mouth." Even recognized souls are unacknowledged—a sign of their insignificance to both mankind and God. Only one is referred to—*colui / che fece per viltade il gran rifiuto* ("h[e] who in his cowardice made the great refusal," 3.60)—and by a circumlocution that preserves the individual's anonymity. The neutrals are as anonymous in death as they were in life.

Scholars and commentators have attempted for centuries to argue the identity of the "great coward." Candidates include biblical, historical, and contemporary figures. The two most often cited are the contemporary Celestine V, the pope who renounced the papacy within months of his election in 1294, and the Roman Pontius Pilate, who washed his hands of responsibility for Christ's fate. Others include Esau, Diocletian, and Julian the Apostate. The identification of Celestine is primarily based on the ascension of Pope Boniface VIII after the renunciation; throughout the *Commedia* Dante employs Boniface as a symbol of the Church's spiritual corruption and political interference in the affairs of the Empire. Because Celestine retired to a hermit's life of prayer and contemplation, leading to his canonization in 1313, some scholars reject this identification. Just how indeterminate the question must remain can be deduced from the commentary of Pietro di Dante, the poet's eldest son, who identifies the figure as Diocletian in one edition and as Celestine in another. Similarly, there is a long-standing critical debate surrounding the relationship of the neutrals' sin to *accidia* (sloth). Commentators dating from the fourteenth century generally reject the association with sloth on the grounds that these spirits are equally distant from both good and evil. Many modern critics, however, distinguish two types of *accidia,* the second of which is represented and punished in the Ante-Hell.

Bibliography

Freccero, John. "Dante and the Neutral Angels." *Romanic Review* 51 (1960), 3–14; reprinted in *The Poetics of Conversion.* Edited by Rachel Jacoff. Cambridge, Mass.: Harvard University Press, 1986, pp. 111–118.

Mazzoni, Francesco. "Il canto III dell'*Inferno*." In *Saggi di un nuovo commento alla "Divina Commedia."* Florence: Sansoni, 1967, pp. 314–455.

N Nardi, Bruno. "Gli angeli che non furon ribelli né fur fedeli a Dio." In *Dal "Convivio" alla Commedia."* Rome: Istituto storico italiano per il Medio Evo, 1960, pp. 331–350.

———. "Dante e Celestino V: 'L'ombra di colui che fece per viltà il gran rifiuto." In *Dal "Convivio" alla Commedia."* Rome: Istituto storico italiano per il Medio Evo, 1960, pp. 315–330.

Padoan, Giorgio. "Il canto III dell'*Inferno.*" In *Nuove letture dantesche,* vol. 1. Florence: Le Monnier, 1966, pp. 47–71.

Petrocchi, Giorgio. "Dante e Celestino V." In *Itinerari danteschi.* Bari: Adriatica, 1969, pp. 54–74.

Sapegno, Natalino. "Il canto III dell'*Inferno.*" In *Lectura Dantis Scaligera: Inferno.* Florence: Le Monnier, 1967, pp. 51–76.

Vazzana, Steno. "Chi sono gli ignavi?" *L'Alighieri* 30 (1989), 3–14.

Fiora A. Bassanese

Niccolò of Siena

Mentioned by the sinner Capocchio as an example of a "frugal Sienese," but ironically, since he was reputed to be a member of the so-called Spend-thrift Club of Siena, one who *"la costuma ricca / del garofano prima discoverse / ne l'orto dove tal seme s'appicca"* ("first discovered the rich custom of cloves, in the garden where that seed takes root," *Inf.* 29.127–129). Like his brother Stricca, Niccolò was probably a son of Giovanni Salimbeni da Siena. There is no agreement about the meaning of the phrase "the rich custom of cloves," but the commentator Benvenuto thinks it referred to the practice of roasting pheasants over fires made of cloves (*expensa maxima vanissima, novissime adinventa,* "the grossest and most wasteful expense, and a practice of incredible novelty").

R. Allen Shoaf

Nicholas III, Pope

Son of the Roman senator Matteo Rosso Orsini and Perna Caetana, Giovanni Gaetano Orsini was born between 1220 and 1230 into one of the most powerful families of the Roman nobility. He is one of several popes whom Dante damns in Hell for the sin of simony. Neither a learned theologian nor a canonist, he probably did not receive a formal university education. Created cardinal deacon of San Nicola in Carcere Tulliano by Innocent IV in 1244, he became an expert in international policy during his more than forty years of activity, beginning with the final years of Emperor Frederick II's reign. He played a decisive role in calling Charles of Anjou into Sicily. In 1262 Pope Urban IV appointed him head of the Inquisition. Elected pope at Viterbo on 25 November 1277, after six months of bitter struggle between the Italian and the French-Angevin factions in the college of cardinals, he took the name of the patron of his church. He continued Gregory X's policy of papal independence from Charles of Anjou, king of Naples and Sicily, whose terms of office as imperial vicar of Tuscany and as senator of Rome he refused to extend by renewal in 1278.

Soon after his election to the papacy, Nicholas resumed negotiations with Rudolf of Habsburg, the German king, asking him to come to Rome to be crowned emperor and demanding cession to him of Romagna. The territories under the control of the papacy now reached as far north as Bologna and Ferrara. Despite Nicholas's attempts to reconcile the Greek and Latin churches against the firm resistance of the clergy and people of Byzantium, his achievements in the field of international politics were rather limited. As far as internal problems of the Church were concerned, his main success was probably the compromise between the moderates and the radicals (Spirituals) of the Franciscan Order concerning the issue of poverty, which he brought about by his bull "Exiit qui seminat" of 14 August 1279.

Nicholas's personality has always been a matter of controversy. Tolomeo of Lucca, on the one hand, praises his personal integrity, his high moral standards, his care for the poor, and his qualities as a preacher. On the other hand, he and other contemporaries also criticize his excessive nepotism; Villani (*Cronica* 8.54) accuses him of simony as well as nepotism. Among the new cardinals he created, three were relatives, and other relatives were given high positions in the government of the papal state. Still, modern historians observe that this kind of nepotism contributed to a more efficient governing of the papal territories. Dante is Nicholas's severest critic, placing the Orsini Pope, "the son of the she-bear" supporting "her cubs" (*figliuol dell'orsa, / cupido sì per avanzar li orsatti*) in the eighth circle of Hell among the simoniacs, condemned for buying and selling ecclesiastical offices (*Inf.* 19.70–71). Nicholas died in 1280 near Viterbo and was buried in St. Peter's in Rome.

Bibliography

Herde, Peter. *Storia della Chiesa*. Vol. 11. Diego Quaglioni (ed.). Milan, 1994, pp. 35–45.

Levillain, Philipe (ed.). *Dictionnaire historique de la papauté*. Paris: Fayard, 1994.

Peter Herde

Nicholas, St.

Bishop of Myra in Lycia, Asia Minor, supposed to have died around 350. According to legend, Nicholas *(Niccolò)* prevented an impoverished nobleman from prostituting his three daughters by furnishing dowries for them. He is the patron saint of virgins, travelers, merchants, thieves, and children. Hugh Capet cites him as an example of generosity in *Purg.* 20.31–33.

Molly Morrison

Nimrod

Biblical figure associated in the Middle Ages—based on the authority of St. Augustine (*De civ. Dei* 16.4)—with the building of the Tower of Babel. In the Bible, Nimrod *(Nembrotto)*, the first king of Babylonia, is called "a mighty hunter

". . . la pina di San Pietro a Roma" (*Inf. 31.59*). *The bronze pine cone to which Dante compares the face of the giant Nimrod. Richard Lansing.*

before the Lord," and he is not directly associated with the building of the Tower of Babel (see Gen. 10:9–10). Dante first mentions Nimrod in the *De vulgari eloquentia* (1.7.4–5), where he is portrayed as the instigator of the Tower of Babel, a significant event because it led to the corruption of Hebrew, a language that God himself had created incorruptible.

Nimrod appears three times in the *Commedia*, first in the *Inferno* as one of the giants guarding the entrance to Cocytus (31.46). Many critics have attempted to decipher his mysterious single line of speech, *Raphèl maí amècche zabí almi* (67), though none of the proposed solutions has been accepted by a majority of scholars; his utterance is best understood, therefore, as symbolic of man's inability to communicate after Babel. Virgil explicitly says that Nimrod can be understood by no one but himself. Nimrod also appears as an example of fallen pride on the first terrace of Purgatory (*Purg.* 12.34–36), and he is mentioned by Adam in his discourse on language in *Par.* 26.124–126. Adam's speech proves significant because Dante uses it to revise the views concerning Hebrew that he sets forth in the *De vulgari eloquentia*.

V. Stanley Benfell

Niobe

Daughter of Tantalus and wife of Amphion, king of Thebes, who demanded for herself the worship her people gave to Latona, mother of Apollo and Diana. Vainly proud of her seven sons and seven daughters, she disparaged Latona for having only two. Latona complained to her children, however, and they punished Niobe's pride, Apollo killing her sons and Diana her daughters. The grief caused by the loss of her children transformed her into a weeping marble stone (see *Meta.* 6.146–309). Niobe *(Nïobè)* appears as an exemplary tomb sculpture on the floor of the terrace of pride, one of a series of tableaux depicting the hideous nature of that sin and of its punishments (*Purg.* 12.37).

F. Regina Psaki

Nisus

Trojan companion of Euryalus who was slain together with him after a nocturnal raid on the Rutulian camp (*Inf.* 1.108; see *Aen.* 9.176–449). Their mutual devotion came to symbolize true friendship. Dante cites Nisus *(Niso)* and his friend as heroes who died in the cause of founding Italy.

Richard Lansing

Noah

Because he was a righteous man, Noah was singled out of his generation to be saved, along with his family, when God sent a flood to destroy all flesh (Gen. 6). In *Inf.* 4.56, Virgil names Noah *(Noè)* among those whom Christ drew out of Limbo. After God dried up the waters, he renewed his covenant with Noah and his descendants, the sign of which was the rainbow, indicating that never again would a flood destroy the earth (Gen. 9:8–17; Isa. 54:9). In *Par.* 12.17–18, Dante alludes to this covenant in his simile of a double rainbow, describing the relationship of Franciscans and Dominicans. In *DVE* 1.7.8, Dante names Noah's son Shem as the progenitor of the minority who retained the sacred Hebrew language (because they did not participate in building the tower of Babel), from whom rose the Israelites.

Carolynn Lund-Mead

Noble Castle

Dante's treatment of Limbo in *Inf.* 4 is theologically unique. The theological tradition taught that there were two Limbos, or afterlife abodes, reserved for souls who had died without faith, and that these two, adjacent but apart, were situated at the very edge of Hell. The *limbus patrum* (Limbo of the Fathers) held the souls of those Hebrew righteous who had awaited their deliverance by Christ during the Harrowing of Hell, at which time the *limbus patrum* was stripped of its adult inhabitants and left empty. The *limbus puerorum* (Limbo of the Children) was the exclusive domain of souls of infants who had died unbaptized, but free from personal sin since they had not attained the age of reason. Dante's Limbo, by contrast, is the first circle of Hell, beyond the Acheron and hence beyond salvation. Moreover, Dante collapses the two Limbos into one; he places beside the children adult virtuous pagans, whom he describes as absolutely blameless except for their lack of faith, and assigns to these pagans the same fate that theology had assigned to the children alone—an eternal life characterized not by sensible pain of any sort, but by exclusion from God's kingdom and hopeless longing for it. The purpose of Dante's unique treat-

ment of Limbo is to develop his tragedy of the virtuous pagans, a tragedy of Christian predestination that underscores the insufficiency of human reason in salvation and bases the pagans' poignant fate on one fact alone: they lived at the wrong historical moment, in that graceless section of history between the fall of Adam and the incarnation of Jesus Christ.

The centerpiece of both Dante's treatment of Limbo and his tragedy of the virtuous pagans is the *nobile castello* or Noble Castle of *Inf.* 4.106–147. After Dante is welcomed into the company of *la bella scola* (the "lovely school") of the great poets of antiquity, they all walk toward a bright light which vanquishes the surrounding "hemisphere of shadows." They reach the base of a "noble castle" which is "seven times encircled by high walls" (107) and surrounded by a "lovely little stream" (108). They ford the stream, traverse the seven portals, and reach "a meadow of fresh green" (111). There they draw aside to a space

Dante and Virgil with Homer, Horace, Ovid, and Lucan. Opere di Dante Alighieri, *edited by Cristoforo Zapate de Cisneros, Venice, 1757–1758. Giamatti Collection: Courtesy of the Mount Holyoke College Archives and Special Collections.*

"open, bright, and high" (116), and from this vantage point they look down on the great-hearted spirits of antiquity who are assembled "on the bright green grass" (118). These souls are arranged by Dante in groups: the first of those who expressed great-heartedness by action, such as Hector, Aeneas, and Julius Caesar; the following are exemplary by their contemplative lives, such as Aristotle, Socrates, Plato, and the great thinkers who followed. Dante's overall presentation of the *nobile castello* is, as has often been observed, modeled on the ancient poets' depiction of the Elysian Fields, especially Virgil's in book 6 of the *Aeneid*. In fact (see Padoan, 117–118), echoes of Virgil's Elysian Fields resound throughout the depiction of the *nobile castello* and individual descriptive elements, such as its light (*la lumera*, cf. *Aen.* 6.640–641), its defensive position with its own stream (*d'un bel fiumicello*, cf. *Aen.* 6.635–636), its verdant meadow (*di fresca verdura*, cf. *Aen.* 6.638–639), and the high vantage point within it (*in loco aperto, luminoso e alto*, cf. *Aen.* 6.752–755). All these are traceable to *Aen.* 6, as is the inclusion of heroes who are Trojan-Roman, with no Greeks, in the catalogue of the great-hearted spirits, and the catalogue's expansive encompassing of different types, such as poets and philosophers.

The entire episode of the Noble Castle is grounded in a complex allegory that has generated diverse interpretations (see Mazzoni, 156–168). The castle itself has been identified variously as fame, philosophy, and science. The fair stream encircling it may represent either, positively, the disposition of the human intellect toward study which leads to knowledge and virtue, or, negatively, worldly riches and preoccupations that the wise individual must avoid. Depending on one's primary interpretation of the castle itself, its walls, seven in number, may represent the seven virtues, moral and intellectual, so well known to the ancients, the seven constitutive parts of philosophy, or the seven liberal arts of the trivium (grammar, rhetoric, logic) and the quadrivium (arithmetic, geometry, music, astronomy). Finally, the high open space of the meadow and its bright light may be a reference to the illuminating role of the philosophers, poets, and scientists who have provided a *lumen naturale,* or light of reason, in their works across the ages.

The allegory of the Noble Castle as a whole, however, is not an autonomous image existing independently of the rest of Limbo. It is not sim-

Dante in Limbo. La comedia, *ed. Pietro da Figino, 1491. Giamatti Collection: Courtesy of the Mount Holyoke College Archives and Special Collections.*

ply a *tempio* ("temple") that Dante erects in the middle of his Christian poem to celebrate pagan culture and civilization, pagan poetry and philosophy, pagan wisdom and knowledge, pagan nobility and intelligence. Nor is it a tribute to the unaided powers of the human intellect. To be sure, the Noble Castle with its privileged position and its great-hearted inhabitants is an expression of Dante's humanistic acknowledgment of the achievements of the past, but is also an expression of his awareness of the limits of human intellect alone (see Iannucci 1978, 99–114). Although the Noble Castle occupies a privileged position in Dante's lower world, segregated as it is from the rest of Hell, it is an image not only of segregation but also of containment. For all their achievements and good works, the virtuous pagans, unbaptized as they are, are not in the Celestial Rose, the Heavenly Jerusalem, the city of the blessed, but are entrapped for all eternity within a castle-city which is locked within the confining and hopeless circularity of Christian Limbo: *sanza speme vivemo in disio* ("without hope we live in desire," 42). As an image of the extent to which humankind can recover Eden without divine aid, the Noble Castle expresses both the dignity and the frailty of humankind, both the conquests of humanism and its shortcomings, both the achievements of pagan culture and its limits. In the image of the Noble Castle is grounded the tragedy of the virtuous pagans.

The image of the *locus amoenus* or "pleasant place," as provided by the *nobile castello,* is not limited to *Inf.* 4, but resonates as a *topos* throughout the *Commedia*. In fact, Dante's *nobile castello* is only a pale image of paradise as conceived by Virgil, and it is no surprise that Dante should save Virgil's Elysian imagery and apply it much more comprehensively elsewhere, to places more pleasant than Limbo and more representative of foreshadowed or actual supernatural bliss, such as the Valley of the Princes in *Purg.* 7–9, the Earthly Paradise of *Purg.* 28, and the Celestial Rose of *Par.* 31.

Bibliography

Grabher, Carlo. "Il Limbo e il Nobile Castello." *Studi danteschi* 29 (1950), 41–60.

Iannucci, Amilcare A. "Inferno IV." *Lectura Dantis* 6 (1990), 42–53.

———. "Limbo: The Emptiness of Time." *Studi danteschi* 52 (1978), 69–128.

Mazzoni, Francesco. "Saggio du un nuovo commento alla 'Commedia': Il Canto IV dell'*Inferno*." *Studi danteschi* 42 (1965), 29–206.

Padoan, Giorgio. "Il Limbo Dantesco." *Lettere italiane* 21 (1969), 369–388. Reprinted in *Il pio Enea, l'impio Ulisse,* Ravenna: A. Longo Editore, 1977, pp. 103–124.

Pertile, Lino. "Il Nobile Castello, Il Paradiso Terrestre e L'Umanesimo Dantesco." *Filologia e critica* 5 (1980), 1–29.

Amicare A. Iannucci

Norton, Charles Eliot

Born in Cambridge, Massachusetts, Norton (1827–1908) was the son of the prominent Unitarian clergyman and Harvard Divinity School professor Andrews Norton. Both his father and mother were serious readers of European and especially of Italian literature, having translated, respectively, Manzoni's *I promessi sposi* and Pellico's *Le mie prigioni*. After graduating from Harvard, Norton began a career in business, traveling to India, but in 1855 he decided to devote himself to literary work and quickly gained a reputation for artistic discrimination. He was intimate with a number of prominent English writers and artists, including Rossetti, Morris, Carlyle, and especially Ruskin (who describes his meeting with Norton in *Praeterita*). Editor of the *North American Review* from 1864 to 1868, among the founding editors of

the *Nation,* and appointed professor of the history of art at Harvard in 1874, Norton was well placed to shape American cultural taste in the decades following the Civil War.

A lifelong friend of Longfellow, to whose courses at Harvard he credited his love of Dante, Norton was among the initial members of the "Dante Club" that met at Longfellow's home during the 1860s to discuss Longfellow's translation of the *Commedia*. Norton's translation of the *Vita Nuova* was published in 1859 and reissued in 1867, with three critical essays by Norton, as a companion to Longfellow's *Divine Comedy*. In 1891–1892 Norton published his own translation of the *Commedia,* the first complete prose version in English.

Norton's importance for American Dante studies lies primarily in his role as an active propagandist. Convinced that the dissemination of high culture was crucial to the preservation of democracy, he lectured widely on Dante and promoted contemporary Dante scholarship and translation in influential reviews. In 1877, succeeding James Russell Lowell, he began teaching Dante at Harvard and became, in the words of La Piana, "the spiritual father of the new generation of American Dantists." He played a leading part in the establishment of the Dante Society of America, which after its historic first meeting at Longfellow's home in 1881 met regularly in Norton's home in Cambridge. Serving as president of the society from 1892 until his death, Norton promoted, edited, or endorsed native and European Dante scholarship, arranged the publication of important texts (such as the Latin commentary of Benvenuto da Imola and the Dante concordance), and supervised acquisition of the Dante collection at Harvard. As Kermit Vanderbilt observes, Norton was "the primary influence in stimulating excitement for Dante studies in America, an influence felt by T. S. Eliot and which, through him, has been transmitted to scores of young poets down to the present day."

Bibliography

Cioffari, Vincenzo. "C. E. Norton's Corrections on Nannucci." *Dante Studies* 100 (1981), 159–167.

Cunningham, Gilbert S. *The Divine Comedy in English: A Critical Bibliography.* 2 vols. Edinburgh and London: Oliver and Boyd, 1965, vol. 1, pp. 158–164.

De Vito, Anthony. "The First Hundred Years of the Dante Society." *Dante Studies* 101 (1982), 99–132.

La Piana, Angelina. *Dante's American Pilgrimage: A Historical Study of Dante Studies in the United States, 1800–1944*. New Haven, Conn.: Yale University Press, 1948.

Thayer, William Roscoe. "Professor Charles Eliot Norton." *Annual Report of the Dante Society* 28 (1909), 1–6.

Vanderbilt, Kermit. *Charles Eliot Norton: Apostle of Culture in a Democracy*. Cambridge, Mass.: Belknap Press of Harvard University Press, 1959.

Kathleen Verduin

Numa Pompilius

Second king of Rome, 715–673 B.C.E., known for his piety and wisdom. Dante cites him *(Numa Pompilio)* incorrectly as a contemporary of Pythagoras *(Conv.* 3.11.3) and lists him as the second king of Rome *(Conv.* 4.5.11). In *DVE* 1.17.2, he and Seneca are cited as examples of well-taught men who taught well. In *Mon.* 2.4.5–6, Dante recalls the fall of a shield from Heaven as a sign of the gods' favor of Rome during Numa's reign, citing Livy as his source *(Ab urbe condita* 1.20).

Leslie Zarker Morgan

Numerology

For the Middle Ages, and Dante in particular, number symbolism was virtually a sacred science. Medieval thinkers attached extraordinary significance to the idea that numbers had the power to reveal the hidden truths of God's creation, and consequently they sought in their writings to show precisely how the structure of the universe and the course of human events through time displayed the presence of God's shaping hand. In the Bible, numbers were mystical signs that both pointed to eternal truths and at the same time served to disclose to the intelligent mind the perfection and order of God's plan (Isidore, *Liber numerorum, PL,* 83, 179ff.). A compelling form of allegoresis or symbolism, numerology, in reality more an art than a science, had the power to induce the experiences of delight in the divine creation and belief in its creator's purpose. Theologians cited the Bible itself in support of the notion that numbers symbolized eternal truths, the fundamental passage in this regard being Wisdom 11:21: *omnia in mensura et numero et pondere disposuisti* ("you have ordered all things in measure, number, and weight"). Augustine, who did more to endorse the acceptance of numerology in the West than any other theologian, adverts to these verses approvingly in *De civ. Dei* 11.30. By the high Middle Ages, number science had become fully established by the Biblical exegesis of numerous theologians—foremost among them Hugh of St. Victor, who defined the symbolic computational properties of numbers in *Exegetica* 15 (*PL* 175.22)—and by the arithmology of Martianus Capella *(De nuptiis),* Isidore of Seville *(Liber numerorum),* and Rabanus Maurus *(De numero).* Dante is well informed of this numerological tradition.

While all numbers have the power of possessing symbolic meaning, some more than others acquire special and enduring significance, to the extent that their symbolic properties become conventional among medieval philosophers and theologians. Indeed, by Dante's day the symbolic significance of the numbers one through ten is virtually universal, with 1, 3, 7, 8, and 10 having special value. The primal number 1 signifies unity, which is God the creator; 3 signifies the Trinity; 7 is the number of creation and by extension life and the world itself, thereby symbolizing completeness and perfection, because God created the universe in seven days; 8 is the number of resurrection and salvation, because it goes one beyond the number of terrestrial life; and 10 is the number of perfection, because it is the base on which all numbers are built.

If the Creator ordered his universe according to numerical patterns, the writer can express and endorse these truths in writing by imitating his procedure. Numbers have not simply an aesthetic import but a philosophical and theological significance: they have the power to convey hidden truths. Hence, all aspects of the form of a literary work have potential meaning: the number of books in a work, verses in a stanza, characters in a scene, the relation of any part to the whole, the time that events take place, and so on. Number symbolism works by the processes of analogy, symmetry, and association, and consequently identifying the presence of a numerical feature in a literary work has the power to invoke a full set of ideas and ethical values.

Dante's love of numbers begins with his love for Beatrice. The *Vita Nuova* establishes her

N identity with the number 9, the square of 3. The poet repeatedly discovers that important moments in her life and their relationship are related to the number 9. The poet-lover first sees her when both are in their ninth year; he does not see her again until another nine years have passed by; she dies in 1290, the ninth decade of the century. In chapter 29, Dante discloses that she is related to the number 9 because she is related to the harmony of the Creation itself, which has nine heavens, and to the Trinity, which is *fattore per sé medesimo del nove* ("the sole factor of nine," *VN* 29.3). This association, which makes her a *miracolo* ("miracle"), affiliates her directly with the divinity. The term *miracolo* should be understood in its theological sense, as an external demonstration or sign of divine revelation. The root of the number 9 is, moreover, a structural feature of the book's compositional form. As Charles Eliot Norton noticed more than one hundred years ago, the placement of thirty-one poems of the *Vita Nuova* reveals a conscious pattern based on the number 3. There are three and only three complete *canzoni,* so arranged that the second occupies the precise numerical center of the work and defines a chiastic ordering of all the poems: ten poems, first *canzone,* four poems, second *canzone,* four poems, third *canzone,* ten poems. This symmetrical arrangement, which places the poet's vision of Beatrice's death at the poetic center, thematically relating it to Christ's death and resurrection, turns on the number 3, the number of the Trinity. This pattern underwent some refinement in the hands of Charles S. Singleton, who argued that it was better to view the first set of ten poems as 1+9 and the last set as 9+1, and the center panel of four poems, the second canzone, and four succeeding poems as a 9. His eventual pattern, 1+9+1+9+1+9+1, had its own elegance and suggestiveness, but the logic for such a division lacks the kind of strong internal evidence that one finds in Norton's pattern. The point of such numerological patterning is, of course, that Beatrice's relation to Christ as the divinity is inescapable, and is the work of the divinity itself, not the poet. There can, however, be no serious discussion about the significance of the number of chapters into which the *Vita Nuova* is divided. Dante never divided his work into chapters; that division would occur only under the editorship of Boccaccio, who also took the liberty of omitting Dante's remarks pertaining to how each poem was divided into its constituent parts.

The *Convivio* appears to be little indebted to number symbolism, although its structure is clearly governed by the number 5 and its multiple 15. There were to be fifteen *trattati* (treatises, or books); following the first, which serves as an introduction, the second and third *trattati* both have fifteen chapters, and the fourth thirty, clearly divided into two halves of fifteen. But it is in the *Commedia* that we find numerological principles as signs of symbolic import. Its one hundred cantos, symbolizing the totality and perfection of the universe (the perfect number 10 multiplied by its own perfection), break down into three major parts, or canticles *(Inferno, Purgatorio, Paradiso),* which in turn divide into cantos equally distributed among them (34+33+33). Critics traditionally view the slightly greater number of cantos in *Inferno* as 1+33, the first canto being a prologue or introduction recounting events that take place before the journey through the other world has begun. Indeed, its last line, *Allor si mosse, e io li tenni dietro* ("Then he moved, and I followed after him," 1.136), seems to define the moment of departure. Further support for isolating the first canto is the fact that the invocation to the Muses, which is placed in the first canto of each of the other two realms, appears only in canto 2 of *Inferno* (2.7–9), thereby creating a precise numerical correspondence among the three realms.

The number 33 which invests the formal structure of the cantos reappears in the next lower level of poetic division, in *terza rima,* the stanzaic form based on a triple rhyme that binds each and every one of the 14,233 hendecasyllabic verses of the poem. The *Commedia's* constituent parts, then, privilege the numbers 3 and 33, signs of the Trinity and one of its most important multiples, since Christ died at the age of thirty-three. The poem marks in every succeeding *terza rima* the presence of the death of Christ, a death that signals the possibility of resurrection and eternal salvation. The poem's length, the 14,233 verses, itself records the presence of Christ's sacrifice in the last two digits. Dante even divides his *Epistle to Cangrande,* conceived as an introduction to *Paradiso,* into thirty-three sections.

Dante's poem begins *in medias res,* in the middle of the road of life, *nel mezzo del cammin di nostra vita* (*Inf.* 1.1). In a literal sense, that moment occurs at the arc of life, in the thirty-fifth year, half of the three score and ten which the Bible identifies as the norm for human life (Ps. 90:10;

Isa. 38:10). In Dante's reasoning it was therefore proper that Christ should die in his thirty-fourth year, before reaching the point of perfection: "Christ had a perfect nature and desired to die in the thirty-fourth year of his life, because it would not have been fitting for a divinity to enter into such a decline as [represented by passing beyond maturity into old age]" (*Conv.* 4.23.10). By a stroke of numerological luck, Dante happens to be precisely in his thirty-fifth year of life at the time he undertakes his journey through the otherworld. His journey, then, takes Christ as its model, which is the model of imitation for all who would be saved, an analogy further reinforced by the date assigned for the journey, Good Friday 1300.

Number symbolism governs not only the overall formal structure of the poem but the structure of the otherworld realms as well. Critics are not entirely in agreement about how the three realms divide into parts and subsections. Several models have been proposed, and it is possible that to an extent these models can coexist. All seem to agree that each realm divides into three major parts, by which each realm mirrors and corresponds to the others, although how and where such divisions occur have occasioned disagreement. For some, Hell separates into the Ante-Inferno (the neutrals), upper Hell, and lower Hell (the city of Dis). For others, the three categories of sin—incontinence, violence, and fraud—define the division. Purgatory divides into the Ante-Purgatory (balancing the Ante-Inferno), Purgatory proper, and the Earthly Paradise. Paradise divides its ten heavens into either 3 (lower Heaven, virtue deficient) +6 (higher Heaven, virtue proficient) +1 (Empyrean), or 7 (planetary) +2 (heavens of glory) +1 (Empyrean). In every pattern, however, 3 is the operative number.

Each realm simultaneously divides into ten subdivisions. Hell has nine circles of sinners plus one for the neutrals; Purgatory has two levels in Ante-Purgatory, seven terraces on which sinful disposition is purged, and the Earthly Paradise, for a total of ten; and Paradise has nine physical heavens and a tenth that lies beyond time and space (Empyrean). Other critics stress 9 as the proper number of circular divisions, however, discounting the Ante-Inferno altogether as lying outside Hell proper, defining the Ante-Purgatory as an undivided area, and excluding the Empyrean because it is beyond the claims of time and space. The fact that the number of circles, terraces, or

spheres in the three realms can be counted as nine or ten probably owes to the fact that originally there were ten orders of angels (10 being a perfect number), until Lucifer and the rebellious angels fell, leaving nine orders until man was created to make up the perfect ten (Bonaventure, *Sentences* 2.9.7). In *Conv.* 2.5.12 Dante associates the number of the heavens with the angels: *Li numeri, li ordini, le gerarchie narrano i cieli mobili, che sono nove, e lo decimo annunzia essa unitade e stabilitade di Dio* ("The moving heavens, which are nine, declare the numbers, the orders, and the hierarchies, and the tenth proclaims the very unity and stability of God," *Conv.* 2.5.12). Because the number 10 symbolizes perfection (*lo perfetto numero*, "the perfect number," *VN* 29.1) and the law (the Ten Commandments), one beyond, 11, came to signify transgression of the law and hence sin (Augustine, *De civ. Dei*, 15.20). It appears therefore significant that Dante should present his blueprint of the moral structure of sin in *Inf.* 11 and expressly give the ninth and tenth pouches of Malebolge at the bottom of Hell circumferences of precisely twenty-two and eleven miles respectively (*Inf.* 29.9 and *Inf.* 30.86). If each verse of the poem figures forth the number of sin in its eleven syllables, Christ, whose number is 33, might be said to redeem that sin in each *terza rima* (33 syllables) through his sacrifice.

Numerology is one means by which Dante establishes Hell as the symmetrical inversion of Paradise. Just as all goodness derives from a triune God (the Trinity), so evil, being but a perversion of that goodness, echoes the number 3 in its forms. Dante is attacked by three beasts *(lonza, leone, lupa)* in the dark wood; three ladies (Mary, Lucy, Beatrice) set his journey into motion; his journey is challenged by a three-headed Cerberus, the three Furies, and a tripartite Geryon; there are three categories of sin, three rivers feeding into Cocytus, three faces of Lucifer, and three arch-traitors. The three attributes of the Deity inscribed on the Gate of Hell—*divina potestate, somma sapienza, primo amore* ("divine power, highest wisdom, primal love," *Inf.* 3.5–6)—find their inversion in the negative attributes of Lucifer, the colors of whose three faces symbolize impotence, ignorance, and malice. The symbolism of 3 attaches to Purgatory (the subdivision into three areas; the three steps at St. Peter's gate, *Purg.* 9; the three nights spent there) as well as to Paradise, where, in addition to the overwhelming presence of the Trinity throughout

N (especially in the sphere of the Sun), the final image of the divine essence is a triple rainbow: *tre giri / di tre colori e d'una contenenza* ("three circles of three colors and one circumference," *Par.* 33.116–117). And Beatrice herself is seated in the third tier of the Celestial Rose (*Par.* 32.7–9).

The most sacred number, 7, is for virtually all medieval theologians the number of humanity, the fullness and wholeness of life on earth, and universality. It is the number of man, as the sum of the soul and body (3+4), and the number of time, because God created the universe in six days, resting on the seventh. While 6 also symbolizes time, it is traditionally taken to represent the number of distinct historical eras from Adam and Eve to the present. At the close of the *City of God* Augustine posits a final, future era of peace and tranquility on earth, a seventh age, which in turn heralds the age of eternal repose in the afterlife. Consequently, 7 symbolizes the fullness or completeness of earthly life. There are the seven days of the week, the seven ages, the seven planets, the seven tones of the Gregorian mode, the seven diurnal canonical hours (lauds, prime, tierce, sext, nones, vespers, compline), and the seven sciences (trivium and quadrivium). The moral structure of Purgatory is based on the traditional opposition between the seven virtues and the seven capital vices. The seven virtues are balanced by the seven gifts of the Holy Spirit and the seven beatitudes. So significant is the mysterious power of 7 that Peter Lombard, at the suggestion of Hugh of St. Victor and Roland of Parma, established in his *Sentences* that the holy sacraments should be seven because 7 was a mystical number (La Monte 395). Among modern critics, Charles Singleton has argued that Dante contrived to feature the number 7 at the very center of the *Commedia,* by arranging the length of the central canto and of the three cantos on either side of it so as to create a pattern of chiasmus. The fact that the central canto, *Purgatorio* 17, containing 139 verses, was preceded by cantos of 151, 145, and 145 verses, and followed by cantos of precisely 145, 145, and 151 verses, seemed to him part of a conscious design to image the idea of "conversion," since chiasmus reverses the previous order of things, and to disclose a correspondence with the seven terraces of Purgatory. Moreover, Singleton believed that summing the digits of these verse numbers held further significance: the framing cantos' 151 number broke down into 1+5+1=7, highlighting the number 7 yet

again, while 145 became 1+4+5=10, where 10 is the perfect number. But it should be observed that taking into account all canto lengths, from the shortest (the 130 verses of *Inf.* 7) to the longest (the 160 verses of *Purg.* 32), summing the digits produces only four different numbers—4, 7, 10, and 13—and that each of these numbers, with the exception perhaps of 4 (which occurs only four times), can be viewed as possessing symbolic meaning (13 being conceived, following tradition, as 10+3). In the last analysis, because summing the digits virtually always produces an inevitable number, this kind of calculation may not be of special importance. Furthermore, symmetrical patterns like the one Singleton noted can be found elsewhere in the poem (e.g., *Purg.* 3–9: 145, 139, 136, 151, 136, 139, 145).

Because 7 symbolized the fullness of life on earth, the succeeding number 8 came to express the idea of resurrection and salvation, as being one beyond 7; Christ's resurrection took place on an eighth day of the week, which is why Sunday became "the Lord's Day," and all major feasts are celebrated for eight days. It is also the number of baptism, because that rite establishes the possibility of the resurrection of the soul. Consequently, a large majority of baptismal fonts in Europe are octagonal in shape. On the closing page of the *City of God,* as noted earlier, Augustine speaks of a final eighth day of eternal rest in the otherworld following the seventh age in this world. The number 8 was seen to express the idea of renewal in music as well, where the eighth tone renewed the first at the octave. In mathematics, the symbol for infinity, ∞, called the lemniscate, is the number 8 placed on its side; it was chosen because of the association between eternity and infinity, as well as because one could trace the number in writing continuously *ad infinitum* without lifting pen from paper. (The first documented use of this symbol is by the mathematician John Wallis, *Arithmetica infinitorum* [1656].) Significantly, Dante's Earthly Paradise, the garden on the summit of Purgatory which was the original site of the Garden of Eden where man fell, now the locus of redemption, is placed on the eighth tier of the mountain. In Paradise, the eighth sphere, that of the Fixed Stars, is the heaven in which the triumph of Christ and the Church Triumphant are manifested, thereby establishing a symmetrical correspondence with the appearance of the Church Militant in the procession in the Earthly Paradise.

Numbers may possess inherent, culturally assigned symbolic properties, as the previous examples illustrate. But Dante also creates his own numerical symbolism on at least one salient occasion: his prophetic reference to the coming of the slayer of the "Anti-Christ" of his day, the papacy prostituted at the hands of the French king, Philip the Fair, who removed the papal court from Rome to Avignon. This mysterious figure is known only by the code name of *cinquecento diece e cinque* (*Purg.* 33.43), or 515, a number formulated to echo in reverse the number of the Anti-Christ, 666, the beast of the Book of Revelation (13:18). Despite a wealth of proposed solutions, some reasonable and others far-fetched, the identity of Dante's political redeemer remains shrouded in mystery. Or perhaps it would be better to say that while the identity of Dante's hero is widely believed to be Henry VII of Luxemburg, no one is quite able to prove it numerologically. It has been suggested that the number expressed in Roman numerals, DXV, signifies Henry because those letters, rearranged, spell out the Latin word for "leader" (DUX, where V in Latin is the letter U). Edward Moore's suggestion—which relies on gematria, or the numerical values of the letters in the Hebrew alphabet, to generate the name *Arrico* (a variant of *Arrigo,* or Henry)—may be the most ingenious, but it has not proved any more convincing than other interpretations. In fact, no attempt at decoding the 515 conundrum can be said to have gained overwhelming favor: its significance remains a mystery.

Bibliography

Butler, Christopher. *Number Symbolism.* London: Routledge and Kegan Paul, 1970.

Curtius, Ernst. "Numerical Composition." In *European Literature and the Latin Middle Ages.* Translated by Willard R. Trask. New York: Harper and Row, 1953, pp. 501–509.

Gorni, Guglielmo. *Lettera nome numero: L'ordine delle cose in Dante.* Bologna: Il Mulino, 1990.

Guzzardo, John. J. *Dante: Numerological Studies.* New York: Peter Lang, 1987.

Hardt, Manfred. "Dante and Arithmetic." In *The Divine Comedy and the Encyclopedia of Arts and Sciences.* Edited by Giuseppe Di Scipio and Aldo Scaglione. Amsterdam: Benjamins, 1988, pp. 81–94.

———. "Zur Zahlenpoetik Dantes." In *Dante Alighieri 1985: In memoriam Hermann Gmelin.* Edited by R. Baum and W. Hirdt. Tübingen, 1985, pp. 149–167.

———. *Die Zahl in der "Divina Commedia."* Frankfurt: Athenäeum, 1973.

———. "I numeri e le scritture crittografiche nella *Divina Commedia.*" In *Dante e la scienza.* Edited by Patrick Boyde and Vittorio Russo. Ravenna: Longo Editore, 1995, pp. 71–90.

Hopper, Vincent Foster. *Medieval Number Symbolism: Its Sources, Meaning, and Influence on Thought and Expression.* New York: Columbia University Press, 1938.

La Monte, John. *The World of the Middle Ages: A Reorientation of Medieval History.* New York: Appleton-Century-Crofts, 1949.

Moore, Edward. "The DXV Prophecy." In *Studies in Dante, Third Series: Miscellaneous Essays.* 1903. New York: Haskell House, 1968, pp. 253–283.

MacQueen, John. *Numerology.* Edinburgh: Edinburgh University Press, 1985.

Sarolli, Gian Roberto. *Analitica della "Divina Commedia."* Bari: Adriatica, 1974.

Singleton, Charles S. "The Poet's Number at the Center." *MLN* 80 (1965), 1–10.

Richard Lansing

O

Oderisi da Gubbio

An illuminator of manuscripts, Oderisi was born in Gubbio in the duchy of Urbino (Umbria) and lived during the second half of the thirteenth century. He is the second of three penitents representing the sin of pride in Purgatory (*Purg.* 11.79). He spent some years in Bologna and Rome and died in Rome in 1299. The dialogue between the pilgrim and the shade of Oderisi in the *Purgatorio* characterizes artistic evolution in terms of mutable human nature and cautions against excessive pride in the making of art. A note of humor may be detected as Oderisi retains a measure of honor for himself and his art within the larger discussion of pride (*Purg.* 11.82–84). Dante's fascination with the visual arts is well attested. The poet was probably in the Padua area following his expulsion from Florence in 1302, and the composition of the *Inferno* coincides roughly with the execution of Giotto's *Last Judgment* in the Scrovegni Chapel of that city. The *Commedia* also contains numerous allusions to painting and the mixing of colors. Dante proclaims Nature a painter (*Purg.* 7.79) and extols God's artistry in similar terms in *Par.* 18.109–110.

Bibliography

Fallani, Giovanni. *Dante e la cultura figurativa medievale.* Bergamo: Minerva Italica, 1971, pp. 81–100.

Marks, Herbert. "Hollowed Names: *Vox* and *Vanitas* in the *Purgatorio*." *Dante Studies* 110 (1992), 135–178.

Marianne Shapiro

Old Man of Crete

A statue described by Virgil in *Inf.* 14.94–120 and introduced by way of explaining an apparently marginal detail, the origin of Phlegethon, the stream of boiling blood. As Dante the pilgrim begs Virgil to satisfy his thirst for knowledge, his guide depicts the mythical figure of the Old Man (*gran veglio, Inf.* 14.103) who resides inside Mt. Ida on the island of Crete (cf. *Aen.* 3.104–106). One of the minor local allegories of the *Commedia,* this episode symbolizes the moral decline of mankind through the ages. Borrowing the iconographical features of the statue in Nebuchadnezzar's dream from the book of Daniel (2:31–35) and charging them with Ovid's allegory of the ages (*Meta.* 1.89–150), Dante portrays a head of gold, a chest and arms of silver, and a lower trunk of brass. The left leg, fashioned of malleable iron, and the right leg, composed of porous clay, upon which it rests more than the other, have traditionally been seen as symbolizing the Empire and the Church respectively. Tears drip forth through a crack that makes its way through all of the figure's parts, except for the head of gold, and collect into a stream that seeps into the earth, eventually forming the rivers that run through Hell. The Old Man faces to the west, and therefore toward Rome, center of the new civilization and locus of the two universal authorities, the Empire and the Church. It is worth noting that the pilgrim does not inquire of Virgil as to the significance of this narrative. The poet likewise leaves to the reader the task of deciphering its allegorical meaning.

The image of decadence may also connect to

The Old Man of Crete, Inferno *14. Invenzioni di Giovanni Flaxman sulla Divina commedia, illustrated by John Flaxman and Beniamino del Vecchio, Rome, 1826. Giamatti Collection: Courtesy of the Mount Holyoke College Archives and Special Collections.*

Paul's concept of the "old man" vs. "new man." The stone of the statue, in St. Paul's allegorical reading of Daniel, is Christ, the new man who replaces Adam, the old man. Thus, Dante, aided by the erudite exegesis of such writers as Richard of St. Victor, may be alluding to St. Paul's notion of Jesus as the new man, the new Adam, through whose death and sacrifice humanity reacquires life.

Bibliography

Cassell, Anthony K. *Dante's Fearful Art of Justice.* Toronto: University of Toronto Press, 1984, chap. 5.

DuBois, Page. *History, Rhetorical Description and the Epic from Homer to Spenser.* Cambridge, England: D. S. Brewer, 1982, pp. 52–70.

Mazzotta, Giuseppe. *Dante, Poet of the Desert: History and Allegory in the Divine Comedy.* Princeton, N.J.: Princeton University Press, 1979, pp. 14ff.

Giuseppe Di Scipio

Olivi, Petrus Johannis

Peter of John Olivi (1248–1298) entered the Franciscan Order in 1259 or 1260, studied in Paris, and taught in southern France and (for several years) in Florence. A wide range of his doctrines was censured by a commission set up by the order in 1283. He was rehabilitated in 1287 and appointed lector at the Franciscan *studium* of Santa Croce until 1289, when he was transferred to Montpellier. His writings on poverty (*Quaestiones de perfectione evangelica,* 8–10, and *Tractatus de usu paupere*), together with his Apocalypse commentary *(Lectura super apocalypsim)* helped set the ideological agenda for the "Spiritual" Franciscans and their radical followers (especially in Provence and central Italy) during Dante's time.

Olivi's opinions could have been transmitted to Dante through Santa Croce, which was one of the "schools of the religious" the latter may have frequented (*Conv.* 2.12.7). Unlike his younger contemporary and follower, Ubertino of Casale, he is never mentioned in Dante's work. This may, however, be one of the poet's "most explicable silences," as Manselli remarks (1965, 122). Olivi's ideas continued to shape radical thinking about the Church during the early fourteenth century, and the influence of his apocalypse commentary has been identified behind several of Dante's anti-papal pronouncements in the *Commedia* (Davis 226–227; Manselli 1965, 124–125, 133).

Bibliography

Burr, David. *Olivi and Franciscan Poverty.* Philadelphia: University of Pennsylvania Press, 1989, chap. 4.

Davis, Charles T. *Dante and the Idea of Rome.* Oxford: Clarendon Press, 1957.

Manselli, Raoul. "Dante e l' *Ecclesia spiritualis*." In *Dante e Roma.* Florence: Le Monnier, 1965, pp. 115–135.

———. *Spirituali e beghini in Provenza.* Rome: Istituto Storico Italiano per il Medio Evo, 1959, pp. 35, 154–155, 173–176, 181, 195–205.

Olivi, Pierre Jean. *De usu paupere: The quaestio and the tractatus / Petrus Ioannis Olivi.* Edited by David Burr. Florence: Olschki; Perth: University of W. Australia Press, 1992.

Nicholas Havely

Omberto Aldobrandeschi

Of an ancient Ghibelline family, Omberto undergoes purgation for the sin of pride in ancestral nobility on the first terrace of Purgatory (*Purg.* 11.47). He was count of Santafiora in the Maremma (cf. *Purg.* 6.111). The Aldobrandeschi lost a great part of their territory to Siena at the close of the thirteenth century, and in 1259 Omberto was killed by Sienese troops at his stronghold of Campagnatico, a victim of his hubris in taking on "an invincible number of adversaries" (Scott 144). Benvenuto da Imola says that the Aldobrandeschi boasted of having as many forts as there are days in the year and adds that they had become nearly extinct in his day. Extolling the idea of humanity's common heritage, Omberto nevertheless reminds the pilgrim that he was born of a *gran Tosco* ("great Tuscan," *Purg.* 11.58).

Bibliography

Scott, John. *Dante's Political Purgatory.* Philadelphia: University of Pennsylvania Press, 1996.

Marianne Shapiro

Opizzo II da Este

Guelf nobleman (1247–1293) who fought against Manfred with the army of Charles of Anjou. As marquis of Ferrara and of the March of Ancona, Opizzo was known for his pitiless cruelty. Dante consequently places him among the tyrants in the first round of the seventh circle of Hell, among the homicides and plunderers, where he is pointed out to the pilgrim by the centaur Nessus (*Inf.* 12.111). It was rumored that Opizzo was killed by his own son, Azzo VIII, referred to by Nessus as the *figliastro* (12.110–112). Literally meaning "stepson," this title may indicate the unnaturalness of his crime, or it may be an allusion to Azzo's illegitimacy as the son of Giacomina Fieschi, Opizzo's first wife. Opizzo, rather than Azzo, may be *il Marchese* referred to by Venedico Caccianemico, damned among the panders, as the intermediary who arranged the seduction of Ghisolabella (*Inf.* 18.55–57).

Robin Treasure

Optics

During the Middle Ages, the discipline now known as optics was designated *perspectiva* in Latin (Italian, *perspettiva*). This science took as its subject the study of the nature and propagation of light and color, the function of the eye, the operation of vision, the properties of mirrors and refracting surfaces, image formation by reflection and refraction, and meteorological phenomena involving light. Roger Bacon deploys the term *perspectiva* in the *Opus maius* to introduce his theory of optics, thereby establishing the roots of the science in Western culture. On the authority of Aristotle, *perspectiva* belongs to the category of *visus,* that is, to the visual instruments of sight. As a science, *perspectiva* involves the study of heavenly and earthly phenomena, which includes, according to Ptolemy and other astronomers, the study of the heavenly bodies as well as phenomena generated in the air, such as comets and rainbows.

Dante's knowledge of this science is evident in a number of his works. In *Conv.* 2.13.27–28, *perspectiva* is related to the disciple of geometry. In *Conv.* 3.9.15–16, Dante's discussion of how vision takes place relies on the principles of *perspectiva* derived from Aristotle's teaching on the subject in *De anima* 2.5 and in *De sensu et sensato,* which Dante had probably read in the commentaries of Thomas Aquinas and Albert the Great. Dante introduces here the Aristotelian theory of the diaphanous or transparent medium through which the forms of the objects become visible.

In *Conv.* 3.9, Dante recalls and refutes Plato's extramissionist theory of optics, which claims that vision occurs by means of rays emanating from the eye, in order to support the mediumistic-intromissional theory propounded in *De sensu et sensato*. *Conv.* 2 and 3 reveal that Dante conceives of optics as a *scientia media* between physics and mathematics (in accordance with the principles of thirteenth-century optics). His remarks show that theories of optics underlay poetic conceptions in Italian poetry from its beginnings. Notions of *perspectiva* are evident in some of the work of such Sicilian poets as Giacomo da Lentini; in Guido Guinizzelli's "Al cor gentile rempaira sempre amore"; and in several of Cavalcanti's poems, including the canzone "Donna me prega." In the *Vita Nuova,* Dante employs notions of *perspectiva* in describing his relation to Beatrice—for instance, in chapter 5, where the *donna schermo* ("screen lady") is suggested as a medium for Beatrice rather than as an element of substitution. Here Dante uses technical expressions like *mezzo* ("medium"), *retta linea* ("straight line"), and *terminasse* ("terminate"), which are drawn from optical theory. The appearance of references to optics in the *Rime,* and in particular in the "petrose" poems, suggests that the so-called Stilnovist poets and the *fedeli d'amore* had knowledge of the new science, which they would have derived through Aristotle and his medieval commentators as well as such Arabic sources as Alhazen (965–1039), whose *Perspectiva* and *De aspectibus* were fundamental texts. The *Commedia*'s consistent utilization of the science of *perspectiva* suggests that Dante may have had knowledge of the mathematical optics that first entered into the Western world through Robert Grosseteste and was later disseminated by Roger Bacon and Dante's contemporaries John Peckham and Witelo. More recently, however, it has been argued that Dante's sources derive almost exclusively from paraphrases and commentaries of Aristotle's works on nature (Gilson 54). In the *Paradiso,* Dante closely relates mathematical optics to his theory of light and its diffusion, a theory which from Grosseteste onward is determined by the physical property of matter, where "determined" means that geometry is ruled by the laws of physics. It is still not fully understood how this teaching became known to Dante. Some of his knowledge of optics, however, may derive from his study at Santa Croce, where he may have heard lectures by the Franciscan Pier Giovanni Olivi, who was well acquainted with Grosseteste's work on optics.

Dante's knowledge of notions of optics and meteorology is evident, however, from his earliest works. While the *Inferno* reveals Dante's utilization of the dramatic power of darkness, a power described by Alhazen in *Optics* 2.3 ("Darkness causes beauty to appear"), the *Purgatorio* makes use of another aspect of optics, which Alhazen defines, in book 3, as *deceptiones* ("errors of vision"). Dante's description of the false appearance of the seven candelabras of gold as trees in *Purg.* 30.43–50 seems indebted to Alhazen: "Objects standing on the surface of the ground, such as palms, trees and columns, provide an example of how sight may err in inference regarding distance" (3.7.2). In *Par.* 3.13–15, Dante's mistaken belief that the souls he sees before him are reflections, an example of the so-called white-on-white effect (Parronchi 16–17), may be indebted to a another passage in Alhazen: "Error may also occur in regard to *transparency* on account of its excessiveness. For suppose that behind a transparent and pure white body a second body is stuck to it which is of weak transparency but has a strong and bright color: sight will perceive two such bodies as if they were one" (*Optics* 3.7.175). Examples of indebtedness to the tradition that dealt with the phenomena of reflection are evident in *Purg.* 15.16–22, in the experiment of the three mirrors described by Beatrice in *Par.* 2, and in the *rosa mistica* in the Empyrean, containing the souls of the saved, which is created by the light of God reflected off the convex surface of the Primum Mobile. Dante's Paradise appears to reflect a first-hand knowledge of notions of optics gleaned from Grosseteste (such as the representation of God as a point of light in *Par.* 28) and of Bacon (for the mirror experiment). All these examples make clear the fact that the theory of optics was intimately related to the theory of light, for Dante as for all philosophers of the period.

Bibliography

Alhazen (Ibn al-Haytham). *The Optics of Ibn Al-Haytham.* 2 vols. Translated, with introduction and commentary, by A. I. Sabra. London: Warburg Institute, 1989.

O ———. *Opticae thesaurus.* Edited and introduced by David C. Lindberg. New York and London: Johnson Reprint Corporation, 1972.

Boyde, Patrick. "Perception of Light and Colour." In *Perception and Passion in Dante's "Comedy."* Cambridge and New York: Cambridge University Press, 1993, pp. 61–92.

Gilson, Simon A. "Dante's Meteorological Optics: Refraction, Reflection, and the Rainbow." *Italian Studies* 52 (1997), 51–62.

Lindberg, David C. *Roger Bacon and the Origins of Perspective in the Middle Ages: A Critical Edition and English Translation of Bacon's Perspectiva with Introduction and Notes.* Oxford: Clarendon Press, 1996.

———. *Studies in the History of Medieval Optics.* London: Variorum Reprints, 1983.

———. *Theories of Vision from Al-Kindi to Kepler.* Chicago and London: University of Chicago Press, 1976.

Parronchi, Alessandro. *Studi su la dolce prospettiva.* Milan: Aldo Martelli, 1964.

Rutledge, Monica. "Dante, the Body and Light." *Dante Studies* 113 (1995), 151–165.

Maria Luisa Ardizzone

Orestes

The spoken words *"I' sono Oreste"* ("I am Orestes," *Purg.* 13.32) constitute the second example of charity in the "Whip" on Purgatory's terrace of envy. When Orestes was being sought for execution for the crime of killing his mother, Clytemnestra, his friend Pylades offered to die in his place by making this false confession. Either Pylades's assertion or Orestes's rejection of it (which would be made in the same words), or both, would represent an act of charity. Dante's probable source for the anecdote, though it was available in several other Latin sources, was Cicero's *De amicitia* 7.24.

William A. Stephany

Orlando

The nephew of Charlemagne, Orlando signaled that he was surrounded by Saracens at Roncesvalles by blowing on his horn so forcefully that his temples burst. Dante, who probably knew the story from the *Chanson de Roland,* claims that Nimrod's horn blast rivals Orlando's (*Inf.* 31.16–18); he places Orlando among those who fought for faith, in the Heaven of Mars (*Par.* 18.43–45).

Bibliography

Hauvette, Henri. *La France et la Provence dans l'oeuvre de Dante.* Paris: Boivin, 1929.

Jessica Levenstein

Orosius, Paulus

Historian and Spanish priest who lived between the fourth and fifth centuries C.E. He fled to North Africa shortly after the Vandal invasion in 414 and there became well acquainted with St. Augustine, who urged him to compose a historical defense of Christianity. He completed his most famous work, *Historia adversus paganos (A History against the Pagans),* around 417–418. Dante refers to it directly in *Conv.* 3.11.3, *Quest.* 54, and *Mon.* 2.3.13, 2.8.3, 2.8.5, and 2.9.15. It is worthwhile to note that Orosius strongly believed in the necessity of the monarchic form of government for the welfare of mankind. Although not generally considered to be an exemplary model of rhetoric, Orosius, together with Livy, Pliny, and Frontinus, is described by Dante in *DVE* 2.6.7 as one of those *qui usi sunt altissimas prosas* ("who have used the highest prose").

Orosius *(Paolo Orosio)* dwells in the Heaven of the Sun along with the other doctors of the Church and is introduced by St. Thomas as *"quello avvocato de' tempi cristiani"* ("that advocate of Christian times," *Par.* 10.119). Some early commentators assert that the reference is not to Orosius but to Ambrosius—a marginal nineteenth-century hypothesis even suggests it is to Lactantius—but modern critics have expressed little doubt. One critic, however, has revisited the argument, noting that the reading *templi* ("temples") in place of *tempi* ("times"), found in a majority of manuscripts, points more to Ambrose than to Orosius (Lieberknecht). In the past hundred years, scholars have identified numerous instances of Orosius' influence throughout almost all of Dante's mature work.

Bibliography

Davis, Charles T. *Dante and the Idea of Rome.* Oxford: Clarendon Press, 1957, especially pp. 40–73.

Lieberknecht, Otfried. "'L'avvocato de' tempi cristiani' (*Par.* 10.118–120): Ambrose of Milan Reconsidered." *EBDSA* (1996).

Moore, Edward. *Studies in Dante. First Series: Scripture and Classical Authors in Dante.*

Reprinted, New York: Haskell House, 1968 [1896], especially pp. 279–282.

Toynbee, Paget. "Dante's Obligations to Orosius." *Romania* 24 (1895), 385–398.

Michael Papio

himself was killed, probably out of revenge, by his cousin Alberto, son of Alessandro. Dante believed that, unlike his father and uncle, Orso repented *in extremis* and thus gained access to Purgatory.

Antonio Illiano

Orpheus

According to myth, Orpheus was the son of the muse Calliope, and he gained fame as the inventor of poetic song. He played so well on his lyre that he charmed not only people but also animals, rocks, and trees. Dante may have known about him through accounts in Ovid's *Metamorphoses* (10.1–85, 11.1–85) and Virgil's *Georgics* (4.454–527). Both Latin poets tell portions of the story of the death by snakebite of Orpheus's wife, Eurydice. Upon learning of her demise, Orpheus travels to the underworld to beg for her restitution, which he obtains by dint of his musical charms. However, he fails to abide by the conditions for her release, turning back to gaze at her before they have left the underworld, and thus he loses her again, this time forever. Ovid tells that he is later beheaded by Thracian women angry at his rejection of women in favor of young boys.

In the *Commedia,* Dante does not mention Orpheus's trip to the underworld at the point when he refuses to compare his own journey to that of two other famous travelers, Aeneas and Paul (*Inf.* 2.32). Rather, he locates the Thracian among the poets of Limbo (*Inf.* 4.140). In *Conv.* 2.1.3, he recalls Orpheus's extraordinary talents as part of a discussion of allegory.

Bibliography
Friedman, John Block. *Orpheus in the Middle Ages.* Cambridge, Mass.: Harvard University Press, 1970.

Michael Sherberg

Orso, Count

Orso degli Alberti della Cerbaia, one of the late repentants in the Ante-Purgatory who died violently and who besiege the poet with requests of prayers from the living (*Purg.* 6.19). Historically, he was the son of Count Napoleone degli Alberti, who is fixed, together with his brother Alessandro, in Caina, the first zone of the frozen lake of Cocytus (*Inf.* 32.40–60). Napoleone and Alessandro had killed each other over matters of inheritance. Orso

Otherworld Journeys

Tales of otherworld journeys appear in most cultures and civilizations and are not necessarily connected with the fate of the traveler in the afterlife according to his or her conduct on earth. They can be part of rituals of spiritual initiation (for example, in shamanism or Mithraism); rituals of fertility like that attached to the underworld visit of Innanna, the Sumerian goddess of fertility, or her Greek counterpart Demeter in the Eleusinian Mysteries; or initiations into kingship, the warrior class, adulthood, and so on. These journeys may be expressed as a search for a loved one, or a bride, or royal talismans or magic objects (such as the vessel of plenty, archetype of the Grail), or a quest for knowledge or immortality, as in the Babylonian/Assyrian epic of Gilgamesh. They are the subjects of dramas or ritual enactments, and many epics, romances, and folk stories (see Patch). Their sources lie in the idea of death and rebirth as a dynamic force.

Where is the otherworld? It may be part of this world, present and unseen: it may appear when a mist falls or dreams occur; it may be far beyond the ocean or only on the other side of a river, a forest, a mountain; it may be an island in a sea or a lake, or lie under water or hills. Such an otherworld, coexistent with mundane geography, is found in the ancient Irish tradition (see Patch, Seymour). The *Voyage of St. Brendan,* which recounts the seven-year voyage of the saint to find the Promised Land among the islands of the ocean, is the Christianized version of this belief.

Ascent to heaven may be the natural expression of a search for spiritual transcendence (as in the case of shamans and Mithraic initiates), and may also have resulted from a vertical vision of the world inherited from Babylonian astrology. Ascents to heaven are therefore found in apocalyptic visions *(Apocalypse of Paul),* in many otherworld journeys (such as those of Fursa and Adomnán), and in the heavenly journey of the Prophet Muhammad. The holy mountain is a corollary of this ascension. In the *Apocalypse of Peter,* for example, the vision occurs when Jesus

O invites the twelve disciples to come and join him in prayer on the mountain. The intellectual effort to match Christian cosmogony and eschatology with a vertical universe appears in the *Book on the Order of Creatures,* by an anonymous Irish author of the seventh century who awkwardly tries to integrate the spiritual otherworld (the kingdom of God, angels and demons, celestial and terrestrial paradise and a place of waiting; and places of eternal and temporary torments) into a descending system of celestial spheres.

The descent into the underworld, however, is the most familiar form of otherworld voyages. The custom of burial and the observation of the setting of the sun (as if on its way to the nether regions) may have led people to believe that underneath the earth was the kingdom of the dead. Consequently, caverns, grottoes, hollow hills, and craggy mountains were seen as entrances to the otherworld, and volcanoes were thought to be the doors of Hell (Gregory the Great). From the twelfth century to the early sixteenth century, the entrance to the beyond was believed to be in Ireland, precisely on Station Island, Lough Derg (Co. Donegal), in an underground passage called St. Patrick's Purgatory. This was visited by many pilgrims from all over Europe, who recounted in writing their going to and coming back from the beyond (see Haren and Pontfarcy).

As for the nature of the otherworld, one can oppose the gloomy concept of the old Mesopotamian underworld, like the Sheol of the Psalmist (Job 10:21–22) or the Homeric Hades in *Odyssey* 11, to the happy Irish otherworld with its *Mag Mell* "Plain of Delights," *Tír na nÓg* "Land of the Young," *Tír na mBeo* "Land of the Living," and so on. Very early, in Egyptian, Indian, Persian, and Greek religions, otherworld journeys were described not only to characterize the kingdom of the dead, but also as a warning of what might be in store for one after death. In the Hebrew religion, this may have been introduced after the Babylonian captivity and influenced by contact with Mazdaism and Greek eschatological conceptions (see James, chaps. 9 and 12). Inferior locations (often underground) tend to be the abode of the wicked, and superior locations (in Heaven) of the righteous (see Plato, *"Vision of Er," Republic* 10); similarly, darkness and light are contrasted. In the underworld visited by Aeneas, the Elysian fields are somehow situated in the air (*Aen.* 6); St. Paul is brought to the third heaven and then back to earth

(at the end of the ocean beneath the place where the sun sets) to visit Hell, a land of darkness; and if in the *Vision of Fursa* the purgatorial fire is in the air, it is nevertheless inferior to the place of bliss. With the development of eschatological interest, the significance of otherworld journeys appears to be in the effort to localize the different places of punishment for those who commit sins that are redeemable and those whose sins are unforgivable, and the different places of bliss, playing on St. Augustine's quadripartition of the otherworld (*Enchiridion* 29.110) while finding a way to accommodate the idea of two judgments, one after death and one Last Judgment. Each vision creates an imaginary space (the most elaborate of which are found in the *Vision of Adomnán* and the *Vision of Tnugdal*) that is at the same time realistic enough to support the narrative of a spiritual and cosmic journey. This leads progressively toward the well-known tripartition: Hell, Purgatory, and Paradise (see Le Goff, Pontfarcy). The otherworld journey is also the discovery of an inner space, so the experience involves the whole person—even if his carnal envelope stays behind as if dead—and it transforms the traveler's life (Fursa, Drycthelm, Tnugdal, Owein, Alberic, to name only a few of these travelers). These otherworld journeys are also aimed at changing the world and its ways, so specifying the presence in the underworld of many great laymen and even clerics may have been a powerful political weapon for their critics *(Book of Enoch, Vision of Charles the Fat, Vision of Tnugdal).*

After the twelfth century, a different spirit appears in otherworld journeys. They tend to be written in the vernacular as opposed to Latin (the *Vision of Adomnán* excepted) and are more allegorical and consciously literary: parodical and satirical like *Le Songe d'Enfer* of Raoul de Houdenc, or intellectual like Brunetto Latini's *Il Tesoretto.*

Dante inherited much from this complex tradition of otherworld journeys—the classical, Near Eastern, apocalyptic, and Islamic traditions—to which are added the medieval eschatological visions, particularly Irish ones, and the intellectual influence of the vernacular thirteenth-century visions (see Dods and Smith).

Bibliography

Boswell, Charles Stuart. *An Irish Precursor of Dante: A Study on the Vision of Heaven and*

Hell Ascribed to the Eighth-Century Saint Adamnán, with Translation of the Irish Text. London: David Nutt, 1908. Reprint, New York, 1972.

Cicero. *De re republica, De Legibus.* Edited and translated by C. W. Keyes. The Loeb Classical Library. London: Heinemann, 1928. *Somnium Scipionis,* pp. 260–283.

Dods, Marcus. *Forerunners of Dante: An Account of Some of the More Important Visions of the Unseen World, from the Earliest Times.* Edinburg: T. and T. Clark, 1903.

Dinzelbacher, Peter. *Vision und Visionsliteratur im Mittelalter.* Monographien zur Geschichte des Mittelalters, 23. Stuttgart: Anton Hiersemann, 1981.

Gregory the Great. *Dialogues.* Translated by Odo John Zimmerman. Washington, D.C.: The Catholic University Press, 1959. Vol. 2, p. 35: Vision of Benedict; vol. 4, p. 37, Vision of Stephen.

Gregory of Tours. *History of the Franks.* Translated by L. Thorpe. Harmondsworth and Baltimore: Penguin, 1974. *Vision of St. Salvius,* vol. 4, p. xxxiii.

Haren, Michael, and Yolande de Pontfarcy (eds.). *The Medieval Pilgrimage to St. Patrick's Purgatory: Lough Derg and the European Tradition.* Enniskillen: Clogher Historical Society, 1988.

Himmelfarb, Martha. *Ascent to Heaven in Jewish and Christian Apocalypses.* New York: Oxford University Press, 1993.

———. *Tours of Hell: An Apocalyptic Form in Jewish and Christian Literature.* Philadelphia: University of Pennsylvania Press, 1983.

Kappler, Claude, et al. (eds.). *Apocalypses et voyages dans l'au-delà.* Paris: Editions du Cerf, 1987.

Le Goff, Jacques. *The Birth of Purgatory.* Translated from the French by Arthur Goldhammer. London: Scholar Press; Chicago: University of Chicago Press, 1984.

Morgan, Alison. *Dante and the Medieval Other World.* Cambridge: Cambridge University Press, 1990.

O'Meara, John Joseph (trans.). *The Voyage of St. Brendan: Journey to the Promised Land.* Dublin: Dolmen Press, 1976.

Patch, Howard Rollin. *The Other World According to Descriptions in Medieval Literature.* Cambridge, Mass.: Harvard University Press, 1970.

Plutarch. *Moralia.* Edited and translated by Phillip H. de Lacy and Benedict Einarson. The Loeb Classical Library. London: Heinemann, 1959. Vol. 7, "On the Delays of the Divine Vengeance," part 22–33, Vision of Thespesius.

Pontfarcy, Yolande de. "The Topography of the Otherworld and the Influence of the Twelfth-Century Irish Visions on Dante." In *Dante and the Middle Ages.* Edited by John C. Barnes and Cormac O'Cuilleanáin. Dublin: Irish Academic Press, 1995, pp. 93–115.

Saint Patrick's Purgatory. Translated by Jean-Michel Picard with an introduction by Yolande de Pontfarcy. Dublin: Four Courts Press, 1985. [Translation of the long version of the *Tractatus de Purgatorio Sancti Patricii,* and bibliography].

Silverstein, Theodore. *Visio sancti Pauli: The History of the Apocalypse in Latin Together with Nine Texts.* London: Christophers, 1935.

Smith, Forrest S. *Secular and Sacred Visionaries in the Late Middle Ages.* New York and London: Garland, 1986.

The Vision of Tnugdal. Translated by Jean-Michel Picard with an introduction by Yolande de Pontfarcy. Dublin: Four Courts Press, 1989.

William of Malmesbury. *Chronicle.* Translated by John Sharpe. Edited and revised by J. A. Giles. London: H. G. Bohn, 1847. *The Vision of Charles the Fat,* pp. 102–105.

Zaleski, Carol. *Otherworld Journeys: Accounts of Near-Death Experience in Medieval and Modern Times.* New York and Oxford: Oxford University Press, 1987.

Yolande de Pontfarcy

Ottaviano, Cardinal

In Hell's sixth circle of the heretics, the Ghibelline Farinata satisfies Dante the pilgrim's curiosity by identifying, after Frederick II, only one other soul: 'l Cardinale (*Inf.* 10.120, "the Cardinal"). All ancient commentators of Dante agree that this Epicurean cardinal can only be Ottaviano degli Ubaldini (c. 1210–1273), a member of a powerful Tuscan Ghibelline clan and uncle of the nefarious Archbishop Ruggieri degli Ubaldini of Hell's ninth circle (*Inf.* 33.14). Thus, members of the same family and imperial political faction who opposed the Guelfs—the papal party which Dante's ancestors supported—subtly frame the opening and closing of Lower Hell.

Ottaviano was made bishop of Bologna in 1240 and was elevated to the cardinalship by Innocent IV at the Council of Lyons only four years later. He served as papal legate in Lombardy, enjoying a lavish lifestyle. Notwithstanding his lofty ecclesiastical office, he favored the imperial or Ghibelline party, for whose cause he is reputed to have said "If the soul exists, I have lost mine more than a thousand times for the Ghibellines." (See, for example, the commentaries of Benvenuto da Imola and Jacopo della Lana for this famous saying.)

With sardonic wit, Dante portrays the cardinal's soul as indeed existing and, like Farinata's, as lying "with more than a thousand" other souls in fiery tombs (*Inf.* 10.118). Farinata's reference to more than a thousand souls echoes the cardinal's claim to have lost his soul more than a thousand times.

Madison U. Sowell

Ottimo Commento

The first Florentine commentary on the *Commedia,* dating from the period 1333–1340 and written in the vernacular by an anonymous contemporary of Dante. Its title, which means "the very best," was conferred on it by the Accademia della Crusca in the early seventeenth century because its members considered this work superior to all the preceding commentaries. Its author has been identified with Ser Andrea di Ser Lancia, a Florentine notary. Although he relies heavily on the commentaries of Jacopo della Lana and Graziolo de' Bambaglioli, he at times asked Dante himself for elucidations, so that his commentary represents a serious attempt to comment on Dante in the poet's own words. There are three versions of the commentary extant: two written in 1333, and one prepared between 1337 and 1340.

Bibliography

De Medici, Giuliana. "Le fonti dell'Ottimo commento alla *Divina Commedia.*" *Italia Medievale e umanistica* 26 (1993), 71–123.

Jenaro-MacLennan, Luis. *The Trecento Commentaries on the "Divina Commedia" and the Epistle to Cangrande.* Oxford: Clarendon Press, 1974, pp. 22–58.

L'Ottimo Commento della Divina Commedia, testo inedito d'un contemporaneo di Dante citato dall'Accademia della Crusca. Edited by A. Torri. Pisa: N. Capurro, 1827–1829.

Mezzadroli, Giuseppina. "Rassegna di alcuni commenti trecenteschi alla *Commedia.*" *Lettere italiane* 44 (1992), 130–173.

Robert C. Melzi

Ottokar II, King of Bohemia

Reigned from 1253 to 1278. Refusing to accept the election of Rudolph as emperor, Ottokar *(Ottachero)* was defeated and subsequently killed in the war waged against him by Rudolph. Dante places him among the negligent rulers in the Ante-Purgatory and has Sordello point to him as he "comforts" his old enemy. Sordello takes the opportunity of praising Ottokar by declaring that, even as an infant, Ottokar was of far greater worth than his grown son Wenceslaus, who feeds on lust and sloth (*Purg.* 7.97–102).

Antonio Illiano

Ovid

Publius Ovidius Naso (43 B.C.E.–8 C.E.) is the Latin poet who, after Virgil, figures most significantly in Dante's works as a canonical author. The *Metamorphoses* is by far the most important Ovidian text for Dante and is central to his repeated presentation of Ovid as *auctor.* The earliest such presentation occurs in *VN* 25.9, where Ovid *(Ovidio)* is named along with four other authoritative poets (Virgil, Lucan, Horace, and Homer), although here, uniquely in Dante's oeuvre, as the author of the *Remedia amoris.* In *DVE* 2.6.7, the "Ovid of the *Metamorphoses*" appears (along with Virgil, Statius, and Lucan) as one of the four Dantean *regulati poetae* ("poets who respect the rules"). In *Conv.* 4.27, *Ovidio* is twice named in connection with the *favola* of Cephalus and Aeacus (*Meta.* 7.474ff.), which Dante uses to illustrate the third stage of human life, old age, in a sequence (*Conv.* 4.25–28) in which passages from Statius, Virgil, and Lucan illustrate the other three stages. The *Metamorphoses* is referred to as *Ovidio Maggiore* (a standard medieval designation) in *Conv.* 3.3.7, where Ovid is grouped with Lucan and *altri poeti* as a source for the story of Hercules and Antaeus (*Meta.* 9.183–184).

In the *Commedia,* Ovid is named only twice: as a character in Limbo (*Inf.* 4.90) with Homer,

Horace, and Lucan, who, along with Virgil, constitute the *bella scola* (*Inf.* 4.94); and as author in *Inf.* 25.97, where his accounts of the transformations of Aretheusa (*Meta.* 5.572ff.) and Cadmus (*Meta.* 4.570ff.) are deemed inadequate by Dante the author in an apostrophe which links Ovid with Lucan as models surpassed by the poetry of the *Inferno*. Ovid as author also seems to be invoked implicitly in the references to the phoenix (*Inf.* 24.106–110; *Meta.* 15.392–402), to Aegina (*Inf.* 29.63; *Meta.* 7.523–657), and to the Golden Age (*Purg.* 28.139–141; *Meta.* 1.89–112).

Comparisons between Ovidian characters and Dante as poet or as pilgrim extend throughout the *Commedia*. Dante's descent on Geryon's back is compared to the falls of Phaeton (*Inf.* 17.106–108; *Meta.* 2.178–200) and of Icarus (*Inf.* 17.109–111; *Meta.* 8.223–230). In *Purg.* 1.9–12, Dante's opening invocation contains a self-presentation as a corrected version of the Pierides (*Meta.* 5.294–678). About to enter the wall of fire on the seventh terrace of Purgatory, Dante the pilgrim (*Purg.* 27.37–39) is compared to Pyramus (*Meta.* 4.55–166), while his encounter with Matelda in the Earthly Paradise recalls the rape of Proserpina (*Purg.* 28.49–51; *Meta.* 5.397ff.), Venus and Adonis (*Purg.* 28.64–66; *Meta.* 10.525–32), and Leander and Hero (*Purg.* 28.70–75; *Her.* 18–19). Dante's falling asleep in the Earthly Paradise evokes Argus and Syrinx (*Purg.* 32.65–66; *Meta.* 1.682–721). In *Par.* 1, Dante the poet's invocation of the "good Apollo" (1.13) remotivates the Ovidian Daphne (1.13–15, 28–33; *Meta.* 1.452–567) and Marsyas (1.19–21; *Meta.* 6.382–400), while Dante the protagonist's transformation (1.67–69) evokes Glaucus (*Meta.* 13.904–959). *Par.* 2.10–18 presents the proper readers of the third *cantica* as analogous to Jason's Argonauts (*Meta.* 7.100–158); *Par.* 3.17–20 presents Dante's initial perception of the first heaven with a contrastive reference to Narcissus (*Meta.* 3.416–473). During his encounter with Cacciaguida, Dante is compared to Phaeton (*Par.* 17.1–6; *Meta.* 1.755–761) and to Hippolytus (*Par.* 17.46–48; *Meta.* 15.497–498). Beatrice in the seventh heaven (*Par.* 21.4–6) compares Dante to Semele (*Meta.* 3.253–315). In the Empyrean, Dante's direct vision of God evokes Neptune's wonder at Jason's *Argo* (*Par.* 33. 94–96; *Meta.* 6.721; 8.302).

The most important Ovidian characters to appear at the level of the *Commedia*'s plot are Tiresias (*Meta.* 3.316–338) among the diviners in *Inf.* 20.40–45, and Myrrha (*Meta.* 10.298–513) among the falsifiers in *Inf.* 30.37–41. There is also the centaur Nessus (*Inf.* 12.67–69; *Meta.* 9.101ff.), who takes Dante across the river Phlegethon.

Numerous references to Ovidian loci are made by various characters in the *Commedia*, as well as by Dante the poet. In the *Inferno* are mentioned Daedalus (*Inf.* 29.116; *Meta.* 8.183ff.); Athamas and Ino (*Inf.* 30.4–12; *Meta.* 4.511ff.); Hecuba (*Inf.* 30.15–21; *Meta.* 13.404ff.); and Narcissus (*Inf.* 30.128). Ovidian *exempla* evoked on the terraces of Purgatory are almost all negative: on the first terrace, Niobe (*Purg.* 12.37–39; *Meta.* 6.182ff.) and Arachne (*Purg.* 12.43–45; *Meta.* 6.140ff.) figure pride; on the second terrace, Aglauros (*Purg.* 14.139; *Meta.* 2.708ff.) figures envy; on the third, Procne (*Purg.* 17.19–20; *Meta.* 6.609ff.) figures anger; on the fifth, Midas (*Purg.* 20.106–108; *Meta.* 11.100ff.) and Polymestor (*Purg.* 20.114–115; *Meta.* 13.429ff.) figure avarice; on the sixth, the centaurs in their fight with the Lapithae and Theseus at Pirithous's and Hippodamia's wedding (*Purg.* 24.121–123; *Meta.* 12.210–231) figure gluttony; on the seventh, Diana's expulsion of Helice (the only positive Ovidian *exemplum* on the Mountain; *Purg.* 25.130–132; *Meta.* 2.453ff.) figures chastity, and Pasiphae (*Purg.* 26.41–42; *Meta.* 8.131–137; the last purgatorial *exemplum*) figures lust. Other Ovidian references in the *Purgatorio* include Philomela (*Purg.* 9.14–15; *Meta.* 6.412–764), Ganymede (*Purg.* 9. 23; *Meta.* 10.155–161), Iris (*Purg.* 21.50; *Meta.* 14.14.845), Latona at Delos (*Purg.* 20.130–132; *Meta.* 6.185ff.), Erysichthon (*Purg.* 23.25–27; *Meta.* 8.738ff.), Meleager (*Purg.* 25.22–24; *Meta.* 8.511ff.), Pasiphae (*Purg.* 26.85–86), Argus (*Purg.* 29.95–96), Phaeton (*Purg.* 29.118–119), and Pyramus (*Purg.* 33.69). Beatrice (*Purg.* 33.46) compares her "DXV" prophecy to that of Themis (*Meta.* 1.379–394) and the Sphinx (*Meta.*7.759–760). Ovidian references in the *Paradiso* include Alcmaeon (*Par.* 4.105; *Meta.* 9.407ff.), Typhoeus (*Par.* 8.67–70; *Meta.* 5.346–353), Echo (*Par.* 1.2.14–15; *Meta.* 3.356ff.); Ariadne (*Par.* 13.13–15; *Meta.* 8.174–182), Hyperion (*Par.* 22.142; *Meta.* 4.192), Europa (*Par.* 27.84; *Meta.* 2.833–875), and Helice (*Par.* 31.32–33; *Meta.* 2.496–530).

In addition, Ovid is cited by name in *Conv.* 2.1.3 for his Orpheus narrative (*Meta.* 9.1ff.),

O

which illustrates how allegorical truth is derived from poetic fiction; in *Conv.* 2.5.14 for Venus's characterization of Cupid in *Meta.* 5.365; in *Conv.* 2.14.5 for the *favola* of Phaëthon at the beginning of *Meta.* 2 (esp. 2.293–300); in *Conv.* 4.15.8 for Prometheus and the creation of man (*Meta.* 1.78–83); in *Conv.* 4.23.14 for the four horses of Apollo's chariot (*Meta.* 2.153–154); in *DVE* 1.2.7 for the Pierides in *Meta.* 5.294–299, characterized as figurative rather than literal; in *Mon.* 2.7.10 for the fight between Hercules and Antaeus (*Meta.* 9.183–184) and the race between Atalanta and Hippomene in *Meta.* 10.560–161; and in *Mon.* 2.8.4, where *Meta.* 4.58 and 88 (identified as "in the Pyramus episode") are cited to show the limits of the Assyrian Empire under Semiramis and Ninus. *Epist.* 3.4 refers to Ovid as "Naso," citing *Meta.* 4.192 to evoke the passion of Apollo (called "Hyperion's son") for Leucothoe.

Bibliography

Brownlee, Kevin. "Dante and the Classical Poets." In *The Cambridge Companion to Dante.* Edited by Rachel Jacoff. Cambridge: Cambridge University Press, 1993, pp. 100–119.

Hawkins, Peter S. "Transfiguring the Text: Ovid, Scripture and Dante's Dynamics of Allusion." *Stanford Italian Review* 5 (1985), 115–139.

Jacoff, Rachel, and Jeffrey T. Schnapp (eds.). *The Poetry of Allusion: Virgil and Ovid in Dante's Comedy.* Stanford: Stanford University Press, 1991.

Moore, Edward. "Dante and Ovid." In *Studies in Dante, First Series: Scriptural and Classical Authors in Dante.* Oxford: Clarendon Press, 1896, pp. 206–228.

Picone, Michelangelo. "L'Ovidio di Dante." In *Dante e la "Bella Scola" della Poesia: Autorità e sfida poetica.* Edited by Amilcare A. Iannucci. Ravenna: Longo, 1993, pp. 107–144.

Sowell, Madison U. (ed.). *Dante and Ovid: Essays in Intertextuality.* Binghamton, N.Y.: Medieval and Renaissance Texts and Studies, 1991.

Kevin Brownlee

Oxford Dante Society

Founded in 1876 by Edward Moore, restricted to twelve members (though for a time there were fifteen), and consisting of both amateurs and specialists in Dante studies, the Society originally met once a term to "read papers and discuss subjects connected with Dante; to encourage mutual enquiry as to critical, historical and other points relating to his works; to interchange information as to new books, reviews, monographs, etc., and generally to stimulate and forward the study of the *Divina Commedia,* and other works of Dante and his age," and to dine. Eminent Dantists belonging to the Society have included, in addition to Moore himself, Paget Toynbee, Colin Hardie, and Cecil Grayson.

John Took

P

Pallas

Young son of Evander, king of the Arcadian colony of Pallanteum and ally of Aeneas in the conquest of Latium. He is killed by Turnus (*Aen.* 10.479–489), and the sight of the young man's plundered war belt so enrages Aeneas that when Turnus begs for mercy on the battlefield, the prayer is savagely denied (*Aen.* 12.940ff.). According to Justinian (*Par.* 6.35–36), the imperium passed by right to Aeneas "from the hour when Pallas [*Pallante*] died to give it rule," a point of inheritance law that Dante cites again in *Mon.* 2.9.12–14, but not in the corresponding passage of *Conv.* 4.5.10.

Sally Mussetter

Panders and Seducers

Naked and driven forward by the ever-present whips of horned demons in the first bolgia (ditch) of the eighth circle of Hell (*Inf.* 18.22–99), the panders *(ruffiani)* and seducers *(seduttori)* represent the first sinners Dante encounters in Malebolge, where—according to *Inf.* 11.54—those who have used simple fraud are punished. This initial episode also serves as Dante's introduction to the circle's unique landscape of sloping terrain, ditches, and footbridges, which will span just over thirteen cantos (*Inf.* 17.121–30.148).

From one side of the footbridge over the bolgia, Dante espies among the panders Venedico Caccianemico, the Guelf Bolognese noble whose political aspirations and greed led him to sell his sister's favors to the marquis of Ferrara, Obizzo II d'Este. From Venedico's rapid confession Dante learns that many Bolognesi inhabit the bolgia (18.58–63). Moving on, Dante positions himself on the bridge to search the faces of the seducers, who proceed at a faster pace in the direction opposite that of the panders. Among them he sees the classical hero Jason, who *con segni e con parole ornate* ("with tokens and elaborate words," 91) seduced and abandoned Hypsipyle and Medea.

While Venedico's notorious pandering of Ghisolabella breaks both familial and political bonds, the seductions of the ancient hero Jason, who marches stoically with regal demeanor (*Inf.* 11.83–85), are punished in the same *bolgia,* underscoring the uniform application of divine justice: *tal colpa a tal martiro lui condanna* ("such guilt condemns him to this punishment," 18.95). In spite of his epic exploits, the proud hero, like the nefarious Venedico, has fraudulently violated "the bond of love that Nature makes" (*Inf.* 11.56).

Bibliography

Salsano, Fernando. "Ruffiani e seduttori nell' 'Inferno.'" *Enciclopedia dantesca* 4:1053–1055.

Storey, H. Wayne. "*Inferno* XVIII." In *Dante's Divine Comedy, Introductory Readings, I: Inferno.* Edited by Tibor Wlassics. Charlottesville: University of Virginia Press, 1990, pp. 235–246.

H. Wayne Storey

Paolo Malatesta

Little is known of this third son of Malatesta da Verrucchio, lord of Rimini, Dante's so-called *mastin vecchio* ("old mastiff," *Inf.* 27.46). First mentioned in a papal letter of 1263–1264, in 1269 he married Orabile Beatrice, daughter of the count of Ghiacciuolo, and together they had two sons. One of these, Uberto, was murdered in 1324 by his uncle. Historians presume that Paolo Malatesta was politically active in his hometown, where he would have been a defender of Guelf interests. In 1282–1283 he was present in Florence as *capitan del popolo,* where his principal duty was to ensure civic peace. Dante, who would have been seventeen at the time, may have met him there.

Paolo's legacy is linked foremost to that of his sister-in-law Francesca da Rimini. The two were murdered around 1283–1285 by his elder brother, her husband, Gianciotto Malatesta, who discovered them together. Dante introduces the lovers in *Inf.* 5 as part of the *bufera infernal* ("infernal whirlwind") of the lustful. While Francesca, deploying impressive rhetorical skill, recounts the tale of their love and demise, Paolo weeps and does not speak, nearly disappearing behind the force of her personality.

Michael Sherberg

Papacy

The office of bishop of Rome, so called from the term *papa* (a diminutive of "father") applied to the incumbent. Important for its political location, the see's status was particularly enhanced by the tradition of the martyrdom at Rome of St. Peter and St. Paul. The traditional burial place of St. Peter at the Vatican lent a special prestige. Accordingly, Rome came peculiarly to be entitled the "apostolic see." This and "Roman Church" rather than "papacy" were the normal medieval designations of the popes for the institution. The title "supreme pontiff" was inherited from pagan religion. As with other bishoprics, the papacy was elective—from 1059, in theory, by the cardinals alone.

Two texts emphasizing the importance of St. Peter were of prime significance: Matt. 16:18–19, where Peter is presented as the foundation of the Church and promised the keys of the kingdom of heaven, and John 21:16–17, a mandate to feed the Lord's sheep. Key-bearer, with its implication of power to include and exclude, and supreme pastor became recurring metaphors of the papal function. By the mid-third century, the bishop of Rome is known to have claimed primacy by virtue of the Petrine commission.

The popes' administrative role grew with the decline of Byzantine imperial authority in Italy from the later sixth century, as did their importance in the West in the face of increasing divisions between the Greek and Latin worlds. The papal creation of Charlemagne as emperor in 800 was the culmination of a long political process. The development provided the popes with a protector but also threatened them with a new master. Conflict between empire and papacy is a dominant feature from the mid-eleventh century to the early twelfth and again from the later twelfth to the mid-thirteenth. By Dante's time, the papacy had evolved into a complex judicial and administrative structure affecting every part of western Europe. Territorial rights in central Italy were justified by the Donation of Constantine, a forgery dating from perhaps the years 753–754. Difficulties with the French king, Philip IV, led in 1309 to the papacy's establishment at Avignon (cf. *Purg.* 32.158–160), where it remained until 1377.

Dante treats the papacy as an institution in book 3 of the *Monarchia,* where he considers the relationship of the two great luminaries, the Roman pontiff and the Roman monarch or emperor. The issue is whether the authority of the latter derives from the former or from God alone. Dante accepts from the papal theorists the terms "vicar of God, successor of Peter" (*Mon.* 3.6.6) and "vicar of God, universal bishop" (*Mon.* 3.6.2), and he uses "Peter" as shorthand for the papal office (*Mon.* 3.15.18). However, he rejects the argument from the Old Testament prophet Samuel's deposing Saul, on the grounds that Samuel was a legate or nuncio, specially mandated by God, rather than a vicar (*Mon.* 3.6.6). He slyly equates the transfer of empire to Charlemagne and the deposition of Pope Benedict V by Emperor Otto I (964) as a usurpation that does not constitute a right (*Mon.* 3.10.20). Christ before Pilate expressly rejected earthly rule, and Peter was instructed to follow Christ (*Mon.* 3.14.5). The papacy's role is pastoral (*Mon.* 3.14.3; cf. *Par.* 6.17). The emperor should show Peter the reverence due from first-born son to father (*Mon.* 3.15.18). While the sentiment invites comparison with the discourse on obedience in *Conv.* 4.24 and on reverence in *Conv.* 4.8.1, the context in the *Monarchia* implies respect rather than submission, an attitude consonant with *Inf.* 19.100–102 and *Purg.* 20.87. Dante's works refer or allude to about twenty-five individual popes, often in critical terms. Only one pope besides Peter is seen in the *Paradiso. Inf.* 11.8–9 evinces the prevailing assumption that a pope might be heretical.

Bibliography

Barraclough, Geoffrey. *The Medieval Papacy*. London: Thames and Hudson, 1968.

John, Eric. (ed.). *The Popes: A Concise Biographical History*. London: Burns and Oates, 1964.

Partner, Peter. *The Lands of St. Peter: The Papal State in the Middle Ages and Early Renaissance*. London: Methuen, 1972.

Southern, Richard W. *Western Society and the Church in the Middle Ages*. Harmondsworth: Pelican, 1970.

Ullmann, W. *A Short History of the Papacy in the Middle Ages*. London: Methuen, 1972.

———. *The Growth of Papal Government in the Middle Ages*. 2nd ed. London: Methuen, 1962.

Waley, Daniel. *The Papal State in the Thirteenth Century*. London: Macmillan, 1961.

Michael Haren

Paradise

Topographically, the journey through Paradise which Dante describes in the *Paradiso* can be divided into five major phases. The first phase (*Par.* 1–9) begins on the summit of Mount Purgatory and depicts the ascent of Dante-pilgrim through the first three of the planetary spheres identified by medieval astronomers—those of the Moon, Mercury, and Venus. These three heavens are situated within the cone of shadow which the Earth casts into the universe. In the second phase (*Par.* 10–22), the protagonist passes through the remaining four planetary spheres, the Sun, Mars, Jupiter, and Saturn. The third phase (*Par.* 23–27) is set in the Heaven of the Fixed Stars, at the outer limit of the created universe, where the stellar bodies are "fixed" in the sense that, unlike the planets, they do not "wander" in the sky but maintain an unchanging relation to the other stars in any particular constellation. By the end of *Par.* 27, Dante has passed to the fourth phase, which continues through cantos 28 and 29 and is set in the sphere of the Primum Mobile or Unmoved First Mover, the source of all movement in planetary time and space: *Non è suo moto per altro distinto, ma li altri son mensurati da questo* ("Its motion is not marked by another's, but the others are measured by this one," *Par.* 27.115–116). In canto 28, Dante discovers that the physical revolutions of the planetary heavens are caused by angelic intelligences who initiate and sustain the cycles by which all things come to be and cease to be. Finally, he

passes beyond space and time to enter the direct presence of God. This last region is the Empyrean, which Dante describes—in a profound synthesis of Aristotelian and Neoplatonic language—as the heaven that "has no other *where* than the mind of God, in which is kindled the love that turns it and the power that it rains down. Light and love enclose it with one sphere, as this does all the others, and that girding only he who girds it understands" (*Par.* 27.109–114).

The map that Dante depicts in the *Paradiso* is significantly indebted to Aristotelian cosmology but also draws on Neoplatonic notions of emanation, and, momentarily in *Par.* 22, on Cicero. The Aristotelian view envisages a universe in which an immobile Earth is surrounded by the movements of the heavenly bodies. The luminaries are composed of ethereal substance and are set in concentric spheres of aether. It is the property of aether to move in a circle, so the heavens are in continual circular motion, though the velocity of the orbit differs from one heaven to another. The ethereal sphere of the Primum Mobile "regulates," as Dante puts it in *Conv.* 2.14.15–17, "the daily revolution of all the others, by which every day they all receive and transmit here below the virtue of all their parts. . . . [Without the Primum Mobile], there would be no generation here below, either of animal or of plant life; there would be no day or night, or week or month or year, but rather all the universe would be disordered, and the movement of the other heavens would be in vain."

Here Dante's profoundly Aristotelian concern with "causes" as the proper object of knowledge is immediately apparent: "We think we know something when we know its primary causes and first principles right back to its elements" (Aristotle, *Posterior Analytics* 1.2. 71b 9–12). But when Dante speaks of regions beyond the physically moving heavens—as in discussing of the place of angels in his cosmology—he maintains a clear connection not only with Aristotelian thought but with traditions of Neoplatonic philosophy as well. Angels, from the *Vita Nuova* onwards, occupy a place of particular importance in Dante's thought. But his developed conception, which persists in the cosmology of the *Paradiso,* is nurtured by Aristotle's understanding that the specific motion of any given sphere is determined by the action of purely intelligent beings, the angels, which are separate from the spheres on which they act. This notion in the *Paradiso* is associated (though not

P

Image of Paradise. Dante, with commentary by Bernardino Daniello da Lucca, published in Venice by Pietro da Fino in 1568. Giamatti Collection: Courtesy of the Mount Holyoke College Archives and Special Collections.

to the point of abandoning notions of a personal creator) with Neoplatonic theories of emanation, where creation is seen as an emanation or shining out from the One, producing many different degrees of intellectual existence (Boyde 196). Although Dante, like Aristotle, takes great interest in the theoretical physics of the universe, he is also concerned, in the *Paradiso* as in the *Convivio,* with questions of practical astronomy. Furthermore, he goes beyond Aristotle in accepting, as did Arabic astrologers and Scholastic philosophers, that stars exert an influence on the generation of beings in the lower cosmos. Thus, on arriving in the constellation of Gemini, his own birth sign, Dante can attribute all that he has of genius—*tutto, qual si sia, il mio ingegno*—to the influence of these stars (*Par.* 22.114). It is consistent with this position that Dante should associate the various heavens through which he passes in the *Paradiso* with various degrees and kinds of virtue, as, for instance, in the connections he draws between inconstancy and the Moon, prudence and the Sun, or fortitude and Mars.

In imaginative terms, the spatial and temporal coordinates of Dante's narrative in the *Paradiso* are no less significant than they are in the first two canticles of the *Commedia.* Detailed analysis reveals that the five phases of the last canticle produce strongly contradistinguished modes of diction, imagery, and narratological plan while at the same time evincing thematic cross-references to parallel sequences in the *Inferno* and the *Purgatorio:* for instance, Dante uses the image of the shadow of the Earth to produce a contrast within the *Paradiso* between the supra-solar virtues of prudence, fortitude, justice, and temperance and the apparent weaknesses—which miraculously can still be reconciled with divine order—of human inconstancy, ambition, and desire within the infra-solar regions. The same shadow points to connections with the early subdivisions of the *Inferno* and *Purgatorio* that Dante develops to deal with the subtly indeterminate states of Limbo and penitential waiting or patience.

The specific plan of the *Paradiso* reflects and develops the characteristic principles of Dante's thought. It is by no means obvious that Dante need have pursued a cosmological scheme, still less an Aristotelian scheme, in providing a representation of Paradise. Some early Christian thinkers, for instance, had thought of an Edenic (and quasi-terrestrial) garden of delights as the appropriate resting place for souls who were awaiting the ultimate resurrection of the body. Dante, though acutely conscious of questions concerning Judgment and the Resurrection, prefers to use the notion of an Earthly Paradise to confirm his understanding of the possibility of beatitude in this temporal life under the guidance of a just emperor. But his cosmological conception of Paradise is in one aspect consistent with a continuing concern with the competence of rational procedure. Here as throughout his career Dante envisages a God who wishes to be known in and through his creation by those who are moved, in intellectual love, to admire the wisdom of God's creation. In large part, the topography of the *Paradiso* reveals the heavens as they would appear to the mind that was able to see rationally and clearly into the wisdom of God's design. In this aspect, the canticle is a final expression of the concerns that are particularly evident in the *Convivio;* when at *Par.* 10.7–9 Dante invites readers to raise their eyes along with the poet himself to the "high wheels" of the heavens, he repeats a motif that was first heard at the conclusion of *Conv.* 3.5, where Dante excoriates those who are blind to the "ineffable wisdom" that created the order of the cosmos and who keep their eyes fixed "in the mire of stupidity." It is compatible with this emphasis that each of the heavens should be associated with one of the liberal arts, as in *Conv.* 2.13.9, where Dante declares that "to the first seven heavens correspond the seven sciences making up the Trivium and the Quadrivium, namely, Grammar, Dialectic, Rhetoric, Arithmetic, Music, Geometry and Astronomy. To the eighth sphere, namely the Starry Heaven, corresponds natural science, which is called Physics, and the first science, which is called Metaphysics; to the ninth sphere corresponds Moral Science; and to the still heaven corresponds Divine Science, which is called Theology."

The Christian rationalism inherent in the plan of the *Paradiso* is compatible with Dante's decision in the *Inferno* to build his moral geography around categories chosen from the classics and Cicero, and his invention in the second canticle of a Purgatory which demands from the penitent a renewed attention to the temporal and spatial schemes of the natural world. However, the originality of Dante's conception extends beyond this reaffirmation of rationalism to an understanding, unique to the *Paradiso,* that the categories of space and time may indeed be usable for narrative and exemplary purposes, but only if they are recognized to be provisional and relative to modes of understanding that dispense with spatial and temporal coordinates. The effect this position has on any conception of Paradise *as a place* is best illustrated by close analysis of narrative scene in the canticle and of the pressures under which spatio-temporal language operates in the *Paradiso;* an instance is found in the opening lines of *Par.* 13, where Dante invites readers to construct for themselves a model of what he has seen in Paradise by selecting fifteen of the brightest stars in the sky and recomposing them in a new imaginary constellation; he finally declares that even then the reader will "almost"—and only "almost"—possess "the shadow" of the true image that lies beyond human conception. But the reader is alerted to these particular aspects of the narrative by at least three explicit features of the plan of the third canticle. First, in the opening cantos of the work, Dante not only insists that *trasumanar significar* per verba / *non si porìa* ("to signify transhumanizing *per verba* [through words] is impossible," *Par.* 1.70); he also sees the laws of physics and spatial logic collapse as one body merges with another (*Par.* 2. 37–39). Again, and yet more explicitly, at *Par.* 4. 40–45, the poet makes it clear that what is seen and described in the *Paradiso* is no more than a show—comparable to the metaphorical ascription in biblical texts of hands and feet to God—

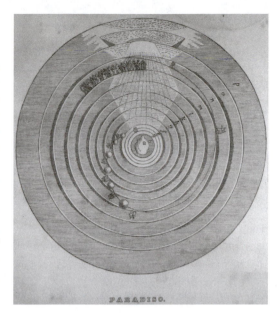

The ten heavens of Paradise. La commedia di Dante Allighieri, *illustrated by Ugo Foscolo and edited by Giuseppe Mazzini (London, 1842). Giamatti Collection: Courtesy of the Mount Holyoke College Archives and Special Collections.*

designed by God to allow human beings a preliminary understanding of God in terms appropriate to the workings of the human mind. Third, at *Par.* 22.60, Dante pursues the logic of his statement in *Par.* 4 and stresses that the final vision which he will enjoy in Paradise will lie beyond space and time in a region of pure light, where the object of his attention will no longer be the circling heavens or patterns of light but the faces of the blessed seen in their recognizably human lineaments.

In all these passages, Dante admits that the cosmic system, as discovered by reason, may be used as a reliable source of information and imagery in dealing with God. But beyond space, our understanding will be shaped by a direct intuitive response to the human face itself, seen in terms of pure intellectual light. Thus, the final vision of God in canto 33 allows that the mind moves toward God in and through an orderly perception of geometric circles and circulations. Yet finally the vision of God's human face defeats not only language but all conceptions of space which are geometrically definable: *Qual è 'l geomètra che tutto s'affige / per misurar lo cerchio, e non ritrova, / pensando, quel principio ond' elli indige: / tal era io a quella vista nova* ("Like the geometer who is entirely intent to measure the circle and cannot find, for all his thought, the principle he

P lacks: such was I at that marvelous sight," *Par.* 33.133–136).

The notion of an Empyrean region determined purely by light and love has, then, to be taken seriously as a determining factor in Dante's narrative conception of the place of Paradise. And connected with the final vision of God "face to face" is Dante's constant concern in the third canticle not only with astral space but also with those spaces between persons which are traversed by words and smiles. It is these spaces which are ultimately revealed in the "precinct of love and light." But, at other points in the *Paradiso,* Dante anticipates this revelation by speaking consistently of paradisal space as analogous to that of the small, personal community of a court or a city. Despite Dante's theoretical concern with world empire in the *Monarchia,* he constantly asserts that the small community is the arena in which individuals can be justly recognized for what they are and where the excellence of individuals can be truly praised. Thus, when Dante speaks of the reception he desires for the *Commedia,* he imagines that it may win him readmission to his own city and acknowledgment in the eyes of his Florentine compatriots (*Par.* 25.1–9). Notably, in passages such as this, the spaces of the heavens are imaginatively elided with those of the temporal world, as they are also in reference to natural phenomena, which occur more frequently in this canticle than in either of the other two. At the same time, Dante is aware that it is precisely in a court that one will seek *sollazzo* ("solace") in the company of those—and particularly in the company of the Lady—who are truly friends "of virtue." The Empyrean is the apotheosis of such a court, where the act of looking from face to face and finally to the face of God is orchestrated and directed by St. Bernard: *vedi Beatrice con quanti beati / per li miei prieghi ti chiudon le mani* ("see how Beatrice and so many blessed souls are folding their hands to pray with me," *Par.* 33.38–39).

In anticipation of this moment, Dante throughout speaks of Paradise as the place which defines and is defined by Beatrice's presence. This emphasis can be understood in two ways. First, since the opening chapters of the *Vita Nuova,* where Dante establishes Beatrice's age by reference to the movement of the stellar heaven, he has been concerned to see Beatrice rationally in the perspective of the cosmic order; and the function of the *Paradiso* is in part to place Beatrice as the supreme excellence in the rational scheme of creative wisdom. But the final evocation of space in the *Paradiso* imagines a distance which dissolves all logical geometry or optics. Thus, when Dante witnesses the smiles of Beatrice as she stands in the eternal rose, the incalculable distance between the two positively enhances the clarity of his perception: *Da quella regïon che più sù tona / occhio mortale alcun tanto non dista, / qualunque in mare più giù s'abbandona, / quanto lì da Beatrice la mia vista; / ma nulla mi facea, ché süa effige / non discendëa a me per mezzo mista* ("From the region that thunders highest up, no mortal eye is so distant, not one that is lost deepest in the sea, as was my gaze from Beatrice there; yet it deprived me of nothing, for her image was not descending to me affected by any medium," *Par.* 31.73–78).

Bibliography

Boyde, Patrick. *Dante Philomythes and Philosopher: Man in the Cosmos.* Cambridge: Cambridge University Press, 1981.

Foster, Kenelm. *The Two Dantes and Other Studies.* London: Dartman, Longman and Todd, 1977.

Kay, Richard. *Dante's Christian Astrology.* Philadelphia: University of Pennsylvania Press, 1994.

Kirkpatrick, Robin. *Dante's "Paradiso" and the Limitations of Modern Criticism: A Study of Style and Poetic Theory.* Cambridge: Cambridge University Press, 1978.

Morgan, Alice. *Dante and the Medieval Other World.* Cambridge: Cambridge University Press, 1990.

Nardi, Bruno. *Dal Convivio alla Commedia.* Rome, 1960.

Ordiway, Frank B. "In the Earth's Shadow: The Theological Virtues Marred." *Dante Studies* 100 (1982), 77–92.

R. Kirkpatrick

Paradiso

The third and final canticle of the *Commedia, Paradiso* represents the narrative and poetic climax of Dante's journey through the otherworld. Divided into thirty-three cantos like *Purgatorio,* it traces the pilgrim's ascent, first through the nine celestial spheres of Dante's Ptolemaic cosmos, and then into the Empyrean: the site of the celestial rose where the angels, saints, and beatified souls repose, basking in the radiance of God for all eternity. *Paradiso*'s theme, as described in the *Epistle to Cangrande della Scala* (which purports to dedicate the work to the lord of Verona), is the *status animarum beatarum post mortem* ("state of beatified souls after death," *Epist.* 13.33). The canticle, composed late in the course of Dante's exile from his native Florence, was probably completed by 1318, although some have assigned it to his final years (1319–1321).

Whereas the crossing over into Hell transpires in only three cantos and the climb into Purgatory proper requires nine, *Paradiso* is largely dedicated to the elaborate preparations that are necessary for a mere mortal to partake in a vision that, by definition, surpasses human cognitive capabilities and understanding. Its task is to move the pilgrim from seeing God "through a glass darkly" to encountering him "face to face" (1 Cor. 13:12). Thirty entire cantos are devoted to these preparations; during them, Beatrice and Dante traverse the heavens one by one, from the Moon to Mercury, Venus, the Sun, Mars, Jupiter, Saturn, the Fixed Stars, and the Crystalline Heaven. Souls descend into each of these heavens *non perchè sortita / sia questa spera lor, ma per far segno / de la celestïal* ("not because this sphere is allotted to them, but to signify that level of Heaven," *Par.* 4.37–39)—that is, not because they inhabit these spheres, but in order to illustrate the precise degree of beatitude which they have been assigned in the Empyrean. Actually residing in the celestial rose, they "condescend" to greet and to enlighten the pilgrim at every step of the way in the heaven most closely associated with their earthly existence. In the Heaven of the Moon, for instance, Dante encounters spirits who were unable to uphold their monastic vows, in keeping with the Moon's association with inconstancy. In the Heaven of Mars, linked to the Roman god of war, he encounters the Crusader Cacciaguida, his great-great-grandfather, who followed Emperor Conrad into battle *incontro alla nequizia / di quella legge il cui popolo usurpa, per colpa d'i pastor, vostra giustizia* ("against the wickedness of that law [Islam] whose people usurp, through fault of your shepherds, what is justly yours," *Par.* 15.142–144). In the Heaven of Saturn, associated with contemplation, he encounters St. Benedict, the author of the corpus of laws—the Benedictine rule—that governed most Western monastic communities. In each of these encounters, the reader is introduced not just to an exemplary Christian personage, but also to the ways in which his or her presence among the saved sheds light on the Creator's universal plan. This yields a cast of characters in which, predictably, theologians (Bonaventure, Thomas Aquinas), emperors (Justinian, Trajan), apostles (Peter, James, and John), and saints (Peter Damian, Francis of Assisi, and Dominic) abound. But it also leads to some notable surprises: for example, the presence of Ripheus in the eyebrow of the eagle formed by the beatified spirits that appear in the Heaven of Jupiter. An insignificant character from the *Aeneid,* Ripheus is called *iustissimus unus* (the "most just [of the Trojans]," *Aen.* 2.426) by Virgil, who dismisses his premature death with the Stoic tag line *dis aliter visum* ("the gods saw it otherwise," *Aen.* 2.428). By elevating Ripheus to the sixth heaven and placing him on a par with exalted figures like King David and Emperor Trajan, Dante reverses a pagan "gods' will," and with it Virgil's Stoic vision of man's subjection to fate's seemingly capricious logic. Similarly, the joyous appearance of Cunizza in the Heaven of Venus defies the reader's expectations. Married four times, the mistress of several other men (including the poet Sordello), she feels no sense of shame. On the contrary, Cunizza proclaims *"lietamente a me medesma indulgo / la cagion di mia sorte, e non mi noia"* ("joyfully I forgive myself the cause of my fate, and it does not harm me," *Par.* 9.34–35), underscoring the fact that love, even excessive carnal love, can be part of God's plan. The gesture is characteristic of *Paradiso* as a whole, which is a canticle built around the twin principles that the workings of divine justice are so mysterious as to transcend human understanding, and that only in a Christian universe can humble figures, like the "most just of the Trojans," receive their just desserts.

Dante-pilgrim's encounters with beatified spirits are only half the story, for *Paradiso* is the canticle of Beatrice. At the summit of Mount Purgatory, Beatrice had returned from the dead only to be revealed as a kind of personalized Messiah, as the Christ-event in Dante's biography. Just as Christ is to human history, so Beatrice is to Dante (at least, such is the poet's claim). This clarification of Beatrice's nature sets the stage for her assuming the leading role in explaining complex Church doctrines, like those concerning grace, predestination, the nature of the Trinity, the Crucifixion, and baptism. Throughout *Paradiso* Beatrice's role is that of guide and teacher. Her aim is to strengthen and sharpen the intellectual vision of her charge so that he will be able to pass an examination on the

P

The beginning of the third canticle. Opere del divino poeta Danthe, ed. Pietro da Figino, Venice, 1520. Giamatti Collection: Courtesy of the Mount Holyoke College Archives and Special Collections.

cardinal virtues of faith, hope, and charity, administered by Peter, James, and John in the Heaven of the Fixed Stars (*Par.* 24–25) and, having passed this exam, proceed onward and upward. This implies that, like her predecessor Virgil, Beatrice is fated to disappear once she accomplishes her mission. Virgil's task was to lead the pilgrim down through Hell and up Mount Purgatory; hers is to lead him from Eden to the Empyrean. Having done so, she will return to her seat in the Celestial Rose (*Par.* 30), leaving Dante under the guidance of Bernard of Clairvaux, who is responsible for interceding on Dante's behalf with the Virgin Mary (*Par.* 33.1–39) in order to ensure that the final face-to-face vision with the Deity is granted. In pointed contrast with the departure of Virgil in *Purg.* 30, this separation is a joyous one because it is only momentary. Beatrice will be there seated among the blessed, happily awaiting Dante's return. All that stands between them is the remaining portion

of the poet's mortal existence and the immense challenge which Cacciaguida had already placed upon his shoulders: to compose a poem which "puts aside all falsehood" and "makes manifest all [the] vision," irrespective of the sacrifices entailed or the personal cost (*rimossa ogne menzogna, / tutta tua visïon fa manifesta, Par.* 17.128–129)— the *Commedia* itself.

The fact that Beatrice serves as spokesperson for Christian theology might lead one to conclude that the third canticle is concerned with abstract ideas and not with politics or love. Nothing could be further from the truth. Dante's vision of the decisive role assigned to the Roman Empire within Christian salvation history is laid out by numerous characters, among them Emperor Justinian, who appears in the Heaven of Mercury and recounts the march of Rome's *sacrosanto segno* ("sacrosanct emblem," *Par.* 6.32), the imperial eagle, across the world map. Programmatic rebukes of the corruption of the papacy also continue, reaching their peak in canto 27, when St. Peter, the founder of the church, denounces Dante's nemesis Pope Boniface VIII for having made *del cimitero mio cloaca / del sangue e de la puzza; onde 'l perverso / che cadde di qua sù, là giù si placa* ("my burial place into a sewer of blood and stench; hence the perverted one [Satan] who fell from up here is pleased down there," *Par.* 27.25–27). As regards love, Dante collapses the distinction between thinking and loving from the canticle's opening to its closing verse. In the course of the journey, we learn that the overflowing love that binds together Creator and creatures "makes the world go round": literally so, inasmuch as love causes the nine orders of angels—Seraphim, Cherubim, Thrones, Dominations, Virtues, Powers, Principalities, Archangels, and Angels—to spin furiously around God and, in so doing, to turn the nine heavenly spheres (*Par.* 28). Love is also the force that drives the blessed to descend in order that the pilgrim may ascend, that prompts them to share their stories, and that inspires them to create harmonious constellations in the form of concentric circles in the Sun (*Par.* 10–13), a cross in Mars (*Par.* 14–18), an eagle in Jupiter (*Par.* 19–20), and a ladder in Saturn (*Par.* 21–22). Last but not least, it is precisely this same purified and intellectualized form of love that serves as *Paradiso*'s system of propulsion. In *Inferno* the pilgrim's motion spiraled downward, and little more was required of him than to give in to his fallen body's natural tendency to gravitate "geocentrically" toward Satan and sin. In *Purgatorio* he had struggled to undo the effects of original sin and to transform this pull into levitation towards God. In *Paradiso* the transformation is complete, and, like the Apostle Paul in 2 Cor. 12:2 "rapt to the third heaven," Dante can no longer tell whether he journeys inside or outside of his body. But what is certain is that the celestial Paradise is a realm in which "theocentric" levitation is the law. It thus suffices for Dante to gaze into the radiant eyes of his beloved, eyes in which the vision of every upcoming heaven is reflected, and the effect is sudden. They rise up rapturously, as if disembodied, to the next heaven, inexorably and effortlessly drawn toward their creator, the true center of the universe.

Paradiso's concluding cantos offer a preview of the state of the blessed at the end of time (*Par.*

Dante and Beatrice leaving the Earthly Paradise and entering the Heavenly Paradise. La comedia di Dante Aligieri, with commentary by Alessandro Vellutello, published by Francesco Marcolini, Venice, 1544. Giamatti Collection: Courtesy of the Mount Holyoke College Archives and Special Collections.

30–32), followed by a brief though poetically dazzling account of the pilgrim's final vision (*Par.* 33). Upon his arrival in the Empyrean, Dante undergoes a final baptism, dipping his brow into a river of light (*Par.* 30), after which a vast amphitheater in the form of a *rosa sempiterna* ("eternal rose," *Par.* 30.124) comes into view. This *sicuro e gaudïoso regno, frequente in gente antica e novella* ("secure and joyous kingdom, abounding with ancient and recent people," *Par.* 31.25–26) is of vast dimension (*Par.* 30.129) yet remains perfectly visible; so much so that when Beatrice regains her seat, Dante is able to see not just her, but also Mary, the kingdom's empress, and Lucy *che mosse la tua donna / quando chinavi a rovinar le ciglia* ("who sent your lady when you bent your brow to fall," *Par.* 32.137–138). Beatrice and Lucy are seated at the rose's opposite points, so that the reader now becomes aware that the acts of intercession (described in *Inf.* 2) that led to the pilgrim's survival in the poem's prologue required Lucy to traverse the entire expanse in order to summon Beatrice, who summoned Virgil. The point is that time and space are irrelevant in this purely supernatural realm. But they are far from irrelevant for *Paradiso*'s readers, who are invited to note that heaven's seats are *sì ripieni, / che poca gente più ci si disira* ("so full that few people are still lacking," *Par.* 30.132). Dante thought that the hour of Judgment was approaching and that his task was to spread the word.

The final vision crystallizes much of what is distinctive about *Paradiso*. It offers furtive glimpses of a divinity—in the form of a single volume in which everything dispersed in leaves throughout the universe is bound together (*Par.* 33.85–90), of three tricolor circles (*Par.* 115–120), and of *la nostra effige* ("our image," *Par.* 33.130–132) inscribed within the second circle—a divinity that necessarily exceeds the powers of human language and imagination. In accordance with the Western mystical tradition, the poet's emphasis is twofold: on stretching the expressive capabilities of language through recourse to neologism, metaphor, Latinisms, and extravagant analogies, and on emphasizing language's breakdown through repeated assertions of incapacity and ineffability. This twofold poetic enterprise makes *Paradiso*, despite its weighty theological and doctrinal monologues, the most experimental of the *Commedia*'s three canticles. Brimming with coinages such as *intuarsi* (to "in-you") and *immiarsi* (to "in-me"), abounding in enigmatic or lushly synesthetic imagery—like the Empyrean's *lume in forma di rivera / fulvido di fulgore, intra due rive / dipinte di mirabil primavera* ("light in the form of a river, as radiant as gold, between two banks painted with wondrous springtime," *Par.* 30.61–62)—*Paradiso* stands as Dante's *ultimo lavoro* ("last labor," *Par.* 1.13): "last" in the sense of presenting the greatest poetic challenge, but "last" also in sense of marking Dante's literary coming of age, the completion of his poetic apprenticeship under the tutelage of Virgil and other predecessors.

Bibliography

Botterill, Steven. *Dante and the Mystical Tradition.* Cambridge: Cambridge University Press, 1994.

Busnelli, Giovanni. *Il concetto e l'ordine del Paradiso dantesco.* 2 vols. Città del Castello: Lapi, 1911–1912.

Ferrante, Joan M. "Words and Images in the *Paradiso*: Reflections of the Divine." In *Dante, Petrarch, Boccaccio: Studies in the Italian Trecento in Honor of Charles S. Singleton.* Edited by Aldo S. Bernardo and Anthony L. Pellegrini. Binghamton, N.Y.: Medieval and Renaissance Texts and Studies, 1983, pp. 115–132.

Freccero, John. "Introduction to the *Paradiso.*" *Dante: The Poetics of Conversion.* Edited by Rachel Jacoff. Cambridge, Mass.: Harvard University Press, 1986, pp. 209–220.

Gardner, Edmond. *Dante and the Mystics.* London: J. M. Dent, 1913.

———. *Dante's Ten Heavens.* London: J. M. Dent and Sons, 1904.

Gilson, Étienne. *Dante and Philosophy.* Translated by David Moore. New York: Harper and Row, 1963.

Jacoff, Rachel. "'Shadowy Prefaces': An Introduction to *Paradiso.*" In *The Cambridge Companion to Dante.* Edited by Rachel Jacoff. Cambridge: Cambridge University Press, 1993, pp. 208–225.

Mazzeo, Joseph Anthony. *Structure and Thought in the Paradiso.* Ithaca, N.Y.: Cornell University Press, 1958.

Mineo, Niccolò. *Profetica e apocalittica in Dante.* Catania: Università di Catania, Facoltà di Lettere, 1968.

Nardi, Bruno. *Saggi di filosofia dantesca.* 2nd ed. Florence: La Nuova Italia, 1967.

Orr, M. A. *Dante and the Early Astronomers.* London: Wingate, 1913.

Schnapp, Jeffrey T. *The Transfiguration of History at the Center of Dante's Paradise.* Princeton, N.J.: Princeton University Press, 1986.

Toynbee, Paget. *Dante Studies and Researches.* London: Methuen, 1902.

Jeffrey T. Schnapp

Paris

Son of Priam and Hecuba, Paris (*Parìs; Paride* in modern Italian) is obliged to decide whether Hera, Athena, or Aphrodite is the fairest goddess. He chooses the goddess of love in exchange for Helen, whose subsequent abduction incites the Trojan War. Dante places him among the lustful, after Achilles and Helen and before Tristan (*Inf.* 5.67). Identifications of Dante's Paris with the hero of the French romance *Paris et Vienne* have largely been dismissed.

Bibliography

Renucci, Paul. *Dante disciple et juge du monde gréco-latin.* Paris: Les Belles Lettres, 1954.

Toynbee, Paget. "Paris and Tristan in the *Inferno* V 67." In *Dante Studies and Researches.* London: Methuen, 1902.

Jessica Levenstein

Parmenides

Greek philosopher, born at Elea in Italy in 515 B.C.E., and cited by St. Thomas in *Par.* 13.125, together with his pupil Melissus and Bryson, as an incompetent logician. Dante again refers to Parmenides *(Parmenide)* as a bad thinker, along with Melissus, in *Mon.* 3.4.4, in his refutation of arguments validating the subordination of the authority of the Empire to that of the Church, citing Aristotle's claim, "They adopt false premises and use invalid syllogisms" (*Physics,* 1.3.186a6).

Richard Lansing

Parnassus

A lofty mountain in central Greece north of the Gulf of Corinth, situated primarily in ancient Phocis. According to classical mythology, Parnassus was sacred to the Muses and to Apollo, whose oracle at Delphi was at the foot of the mountain to the south. Just above Delphi, deep within Parnassus' caverns, is the Castalian spring, the water of which was thought to be a source of poetic inspiration.

For this reason, the Muses are often referred to metonymically as *Castaliae sorores* ("the Castalian sisters") in pagan verse. Parnassus has two peaks, which Ovid (*Meta.* 1.316–317) and Lucan (*Phars.* 5.75–78) mention as the only dry land remaining during the Flood. The taller peak, Cirrha, was said to be the seat of Apollo, whereas the shorter one, Nisa, was dedicated to Bacchus (*Phars.* 1.63–65).

For Dante, Parnassus is an important symbol of poetry, artistic aspiration, and the power of the human imagination. When Statius, citing Virgil's Fourth Eclogue, credits the latter with his salvation, he does so in terms that bring together aesthetic creativity and divine enlightenment: *"Tu prima m'inviasti / verso Parnaso a ber ne le sue grotte, / e prima appresso Dio m'alluminasti"* ("You first sent me to Parnassus to drink from its springs, and first lit the way for me toward God," *Purg.* 22.64–66). Drawing again on the legend of the Muses and their spring, Virgil speaks of Homer as having been nourished by them, and that mountain, *"che sempre ha le nutrice nostre seco"* ("that forever holds our nurses," 104–105). Dante's ascent up the purgatorial mountain to its summit, Eden, is thus figuratively allied with the quest for Parnassus: both are pastoral oases where artistic genius and divine illumination are attained. The Eden–Parnassus link is overtly stated by Matelda in *Purg.* 28.139–141: *"Quelli ch'anticamente poetaro / l'età de l'oro e suo stato felice, / forse in Parnaso esto loco sognaro"* ("Those who in ancient times wrote in their poetry of the age of gold and its happy state, perhaps in Parnassus dreamed of this place").

Dante twice uses allusions to Parnassus in the context of the problems that confront him as a poet. After he has been immersed in Lethe and has seen divinity reflected in Beatrice, he compares his difficulty in writing down the vision to that of any other dedicated poet (*Purg.* 31.140–142). Similarly, to indicate the arduousness of composing the third canticle, Dante invokes Apollo for Delphic inspiration (*Par.* 1.16–18).

Caron Cioffi

Pasiphae

The wife of king Minos of Crete, Pasiphae developed an unnatural passion for a white bull, a passion brought on as a punishment by Poseidon, who had requested that the bull be sacrificed. Pasiphae confided her desire to Daedalus, who fashioned a wooden cow covered in hide to enable the queen to consummate her lust. From this union the Minotaur, half man and half bull, was born, to be housed in the Labyrinth devised by Daedalus (see *Inf.* 12.13). The penitent lustful souls on the seventh cornice of Purgatory recall the deed of Pasiphae *(Pasife)* as an example of their rejection of bestiality and unnatural sexual practices (*Purg.* 26.41, 86–87).

Diana Cavuoto Glenn

Paul, St.

Born of Jewish parents at Tarsus, Cilicia (now in Turkey), at the beginning of the Christian era (c. 3–62) and a descendant of the tribe of Benjamin, Paul was trained and educated in strict observance of the Jewish law. His teacher, the learned Rabbi Gamaliel the Elder, was honored by Jews and Christians alike for his spirit of equity. Paul, whose original name was Saul, earned a living as a tentmaker. He was absent from Jerusalem when Jesus preached and died there, but he must have returned soon after that, since he was present at the martyrdom of Stephen (Acts 7:57). The major event of his life was his conversion on the road to Damascus, after which he became an apostle for Christ. His missionary journeys to the Gentiles ended with his beheading in Rome, under Emperor Nero, in A.D. 67, according to tradition. As a Jew of the Diaspora, he spoke and wrote Greek, the language of his Epistles.

St. Paul is the most important personality in the history of the Church. As such, he is considered a theologian of Christianity for the Epistles attributed to him (some have been questioned), which lay the foundation for subsequent Christian theology. Dante was much influenced not only by Paul's theology but also by his life of tribulation. One of the fundamental concepts of Pauline theology underlying Dante's *Commedia* is the belief that the true Christian is reborn in Christ even in this life, and that this new life, *vita nuova,* which is no longer of the flesh but of the spirit, originates with baptism in Christ. Paul is by example a personal guide to Dante in his journey through the three realms of the afterlife, even though he is not physically present, as Virgil is. Aeneas and St. Paul, the chosen vessel, are the two exemplary *personae* who successfully undertook this journey, underscoring the fusion of the two as symbols of Rome and the Church into a new Aeneas and new

Paul—the pilgrim Dante—whose mission it is to reassert and remind humanity of God's providential plan of redemption through Rome as site first of the Empire and later the Church as well (*Inf.* 2.10–36). The thought of assuming the role of Paul as well as of Aeneas initially instills doubt in the pilgrim, causing him to hesitate to accept the undertaking proposed by Virgil: *"Ma io perchè venirvi? o chi 'l concede? io non Enëa, io non Paulo sono; / me degno a ciò né io né altri 'l crede"* ("But I, why come there? Or who grants it? I am not Aeneas, I am not Paul; neither I nor others think me worthy of that," 2.28–33). Nevertheless, it is a role that he later comes to understand and exemplify.

The Pauline *raptus* and the events surrounding Paul's conversion are echoed in the *Commedia* (*Par.* 1–2, 26, 30, 33) and serve as a model for Dante's own journey toward the final vision. While the pilgrim Dante does meet face to face three major apostles, Peter, James, and John (*Par.* 24–26), he never speaks with Paul. He does nevertheless register Paul's presence as the elder bearing a sword in the mystical procession of the Earthly Paradise (*Purg.* 29.139–141). Throughout the *Commedia,* Dante refers to the most important aspect of St. Paul's life and mission: his being rapt to the third heaven, *Inf.* 2.28, *Par.* 28.139; his status as author of the Epistles, *Purg.* 29.139–141; his martyrdom and his teaching, *Par.* 18.131–132, 136; his simple life and his gifts as a vehicle of the Holy Ghost, *Par.* 21.127–128; and his role as a primary theologian of the Church and as a guide for salvation, *Par.* 24.61–66.

References to Paul's life as narrated in the Acts and the Epistles, and quotations from them, are found throughout Dante's opus: *Conv.* 2.5.1 (Heb. 1), 4.5.16, 4.13.9 (Rom. 12:3), 4.21.6 (Rom. 11:3), 4.22.6 (1 Cor. 9:24), 4.28.10 (Rom. 2:28–29); *Mon.* 1.16.2 (Gal. 4:4), 2.10.8 (1 Tim. 4:8), 2.12.2 (Rom. 5:12), 2.12.3 (Eph. 1:5–8), 3.1.3 (1 Thess. 5:8), 3.10.7 (1 Cor. 3:11), 3.13.15 (Acts 25:10, 27:24, 27:19), 3.13.6 (Phil. 1:23); *Epist.* 2 (Rom. 8:4, Gal. 4:29), *Epist.* 6 (Rom. 7:23, 2 Cor. 7:9–10, Heb. 11:3), *Epist.* 11 (Eph. 6:11, 1 Cor. 15:8–11), *Epist.* 13 (Eph. 4:10, 2 Cor. 12:2–4); *Quest.* 77 (Rom. 11:3); *VN* 2.6 (Tim. 2:2); 12.6 (Rom. 12:3); 26.2, 6 (Col. 3:2).

Bibliography

Di Scipio, Giuseppe. *The Presence of Pauline Thought in the Works of Dante.* Lewiston, N.Y.: Edwin Mellen Press, 1995.

Hollander, Robert. *Dante and Paul's "Five Words with Understanding."* Binghamton, N.Y.: Medieval and Renaissance Texts and Studies, 1992.
Petrocchi, Giorgio. "San Paolo in Dante." In *La selva del protonotario: Nuovi studi danteschi.* Naples: Morano, 1988, pp. 65–82.

Giuseppe Di Scipio

Pazzo, Rinier

Rinier Pazzo (d. 1280) was a Florentine highwayman from the noble family of the Pazzi di Valdarno. Outlawed and excommunicated along with his descendants, he boils in the river of blood with the homicides beside a fellow robber and eponymous hothead, Rinier da Corneto (*Inf.* 12.137).

Roy Rosenstein

Penance. *See* Confession

Penthesilea

Queen of the Amazons, she fought for Troy until she was killed by Achilles. In Limbo she is paired with Camilla (see Virgil, *Aen.* 11.661–663)—*Vidi Cammilla e la Pantasilea* ("I saw Camilla and Penthesilea," *Inf.* 4.124)—and associated with heroes who helped establish Rome (*Aen.* 1.490–493).

Rebecca S. Beal

Peraldus, William

Biographical data for Peraldus (Guillaume Peyraut, or Peyraud) are meager and often approximate. Born around 1200 in Peyraud, near Vienne in the French department of Ardèche, he entered the Dominican Order between 1236 and 1240. Though he is often called Guillelmus Parisiensis (or simply Parisiensis), his association with Paris is undocumented. His activity was centered mainly in Lyons, where he served as prior of the Dominican house several times (he was never archbishop of Lyons nor auxiliary bishop, as has been claimed). An industrious theologian, moralist, and preacher who appeared on the scene just after the Fourth Lateran Council (1215), Peraldus's efforts, like those of other figures of his generation such as Raymund of Peñafort, were directed to carrying out the Council's directives in terms of doctrinal exposition and guidance for confessors and laity. The chronicler Salimbene of Parma, who met Peraldus in Vienne in 1249, describes him as very short in stature, humble and courteous, and a magnificent preacher.

Peraldus is best known for his *Summa de vitiis* (or *vitiorum*), perhaps completed by 1236, and the *Summa de virtutibus,* written before 1248. The two were subsequently considered a single work, *Summa de vitiis et de virtutibus.* The *Summa* achieved enormous fame and diffusion in Europe over the following three centuries and beyond, in translation, adaptation, reduction, and expansion. Its influence extended into the domain of literature, given the great popularity of the theme of the seven capital or deadly sins and allied topics, enhanced by Peraldus's insertion of exemplary stories, classical, scriptural, and patristic quotations, proverbs, similes, and images, and by his attractive Latin style. Four other works of his are extant: *Sermones de dominicis et festis, Expositio professionis monachorum, De eruditione religiosorum,* and *De eruditione principum.* Peraldus died in Lyons after early 1261 or, as some hold, around 1271.

Peraldus's contribution to Dante in terms of images, motifs, and other stylistic features seems significant and has been the object of some attention, albeit fragmentary. Perhaps his most conspicuous distinction lies in providing Dante with his way of theorizing the system of the seven capital sins in the *Purgatorio,* which emerges clearly from the studies of Siegfried Wenzel. While Dante adopts the widely accepted Gregorian ordering (pride, envy, wrath, sloth, avarice, gluttony, lust), Peraldus prefers a different one in his *Summa de vitiis et de virtutibus.* But when Peraldus arrives at his treatment of pride (located after wrath and envy), he sets forth his general theory, and this is what passes down to Dante, directly or indirectly. Underlying his analysis is the Augustinian view of misdirected love as the root of all evil. Peraldus first divides disordered love into two main categories: love directed to the neighbor's evil or harm, and defective love of a (legitimate) good. Straightforward perverted love *(alieni malo)* is then subdivided into three categories: the proud person (characterized by *superbia*) takes pleasure in his own self-elevation and the abasement of his neighbor *(sui exaltationis et proximi deiectionem);* the envious person desires the other's evil lest the latter become his equal *(vult malum alterius ne ille*

sibi parificetur); and the wrathful individual desires the other's harm because he was injured by him *(vult ei malum, quia malum ab eo recipit).* Defective love of a good breaks down into two unsymmetrical parts: sloth, the insufficient love of an important good *(parvus amor magni boni);* and gluttony, lust, and avarice, the disordered love of exterior goods, deemed trifling *(amor parvi boni inordinatus).* These and other inner details of Peraldus's analysis, different from those of other thirteenth-century theologians, are closely inscribed in Dante's treatment in *Purg.* 17.91–139, and enriched by the poet.

Bibliography

Corti, Maria. "Le fonti del *Fiore* di virtù e la teoria della 'Nobiltà' nel Duecento." *Giornale storico della letteratura italiana* 136 (1959), 1–90.

Dondaine, Antoine. "Guillaume Peyraut, vie et oeuvres." *Archivium Fratrum Predicatorum* 18 (1948), 162–236.

Mancini, Franco. "Un' 'Auctoritas' di Dante." *Studi danteschi* 45 (1968), 95–119.

Shoaf, R. A. "Dante and Peraldus: The *aqua falsa* of Maestro Adamo (A Note on *Inferno* 30, 64–69)." *Quaderni d'Italianistica* 10 (1989), 311–313.

Triolo, Alfred A. "Purgatorio XVIII." In *Dante: Divine Comedy, Introductory Readings 11: Purgatorio* 12. *Lectura Dantis Virginiana,* special issue (1993), 259–278.

Wenzel, Siegfried. "The Continuing Life of William Peraldus' *Summa vitiorum.*" In *Ad Litteram: Authoritative Texts and Their Medieval Readers.* Notre Dame: University of Notre Dame Press, 1992, pp. 135–163.

———. "The Seven Deadly Sins: Some Problems of Research." *Speculum* 18 (1968), 1–22.

———. "Dante's Rationale for the Seven Deadly Sins (*Purgatorio* XVII)." *Modern Language Review* 60 (1965), 529–533.

———. *The Sin of Sloth: Acedia in Medieval Thought and Literature.* Chapel Hill: University of North Carolina Press, 1960.

Alfred Triolo

Perillus

Ingenious craftsman from Athens who made a brazen bull for Phalaris, tyrant of Agrigentum, to serve as an instrument of torture. The victim was shut inside the machine and a fire set beneath it.

When the brass became red-hot, the prisoner's cries would issue from the mouth like roarings of a real bull. Phalaris decided that the first person to test the apparatus should be its maker, Perillus *(Perillo)*, who thus became its first victim. Perillus's bull, about which Dante could have read in Ovid, Orosius, and Valerius Maximus, is mentioned in *Inf.* 27.7–15 to evoke the way in which the voice of the fraudulent counselor Guido da Montefeltro issues from the flame that envelops him. Placed at the beginning of the canto, it anticipates the exemplary destiny of Guido, who, like Perillus, by using his intelligence without moral restraint unwittingly brought about his own punishment in the form of eternal damnation.

Lino Pertile

Peripatetics

The school and followers of Aristotle. The name signifies "walking about" and was traditionally attributed to Aristotle's practice of pacing back and forth while teaching; it actually derives, however, from the *peripatos* ("covered walkway") at the house provided by Aristotle's disciple Theophrastus. With the Stoics and the Epicureans, the Peripatetics comprise the chief schools of ancient philosophy. Dante compares them, in an allegorical paradigm, to the three Marys who found the angel at the empty tomb of Christ (*Conv.* 4.22.14–15). Drawing on the works of Aristotle, and the authority of Cicero's *Academica* 1.4.17, Augustine's *City of God* 8.12, and John of Salisbury's *Policraticus* 7.6, Dante considered the Peripatetics the most authoritative of the philosophic schools.

Thomas L. Cooksey

Persius

Aulus Persius Flaccus (34–62 C.E.), Roman satirist admired by his contemporaries not only for his poetic skill but also for his commitment to Stoic ideals. Six of his satires have survived. Dante knew his work only indirectly. Virgil refers to Persius *(Persio)* in *Purg.* 22.100 as one of the Roman authors residing in Limbo.

Nancy Vine Durling

Peter the Comb-Seller

A humble seller of combs, apparently of the decorative type used as adornment, and native of the town of Campi, northeast of the city of Siena where he died, apparently in his nineties, in December 1289. He was revered in Siena for his piety and for his uncommon business scruples—he reputedly refused to sell any merchandise that was less than perfect. He was, according to Franciscan sources and early Dante commentators, a member of the Third Order of St. Francis, a layman devoted especially to the principles of the order's Spiritual faction (to which Dante seems also to have been attracted). Within a month of his death, the Sienese *comune* allocated a large sum to fund construction of a tomb within the city's Franciscan church for a figure whom they seem to have regarded as an uncanonized saint. In *Purg.* 13.128, his fellow-citizen Sapia cites Peter *(Pier Pettinaio)* for his prayers on her behalf as the reason for her surprising presence on the terrace of envy, rather than lower on the mountain where her late repentance would be expected to have consigned her. As such, Peter plays a role in establishing the efficacy of prayers by the living on behalf of souls in Purgatory.

William A. Stephany

Peter Comestor

"Peter the Eater" *(Pietro Mangiadore),* so named because of his insatiable appetite for books, was born in the first half of the twelfth century; he became a priest and later was made dean of the cathedral of Troyes in France. He was appointed canon of St. Victor in 1164 and chancellor of the University of Paris in 1179. Upon his death in 1179 he left all his possessions to the poor. Dante places him with Hugh of St. Victor and Petrus Hispanus in the Heaven of the Sun, among the doctors of the Church named by St. Bonaventura (*Par.* 12.134). His most famous work was *Historia scholastica,* professed to be a history of the Church from the creation to the apostolic days.

R. A. Malagi

Peter Lombard

Theologian, born in Lumellogno in Lombady. After studying in Bologna, he traveled to Paris in 1133 (with recommendations from Bernard of Clairvaux), where he was to become professor of theology at the school of Notre Dame. He was appointed canon around 1144, and in 1148 he participated actively at the Council of Rheims. By 1159, one year before his death, he had become bishop of Paris. He is best known for his *Sentences* (*Libri Quatuor Sententiarum,* most likely composed 1155–1158), a comprehensive attempt to reconcile apparently contradictory or incongruous biblical and/or patristic teachings. In form, the *Sentences* seems to have been influenced by Abelard and others who had already juxtaposed conflicting points of Church doctrine, but Peter Lombard was among the very first to attempt a rational resolution of the discrepancies. The work was remarkably popular from its first appearance and, indeed, was the most widely read handbook of theology in universities until the sixteenth century. Dante places Peter Lombard *(Pietro Lombardo)* among other intellectually and spiritually enlightened figures in the sphere of the Sun (*Par.* 10.106–108), where he is pointed out to the pilgrim by Thomas Aquinas, perhaps the most famous of the hundreds of commentators of the *Sentences.* He is cited again specifically, in relation to the nature of baptism, in *Mon.* 3.7.6.

Bibliography

Colish, Marcia L. *Peter Lombard.* 2 vols. Leiden: Brill, 1994.

Da Carbonara, Michele. *Dante e Pier Lombardo.* Città di Castello: Lapi, 1897.

Lombard, Peter. Complete works in J.-P. Migne (ed.), *Patrologia Latina,* vols. 191–192.

Michael Papio

Peter of Spain

Born in Lisbon between 1210–1220, Petrus Hispanus *(Pietro Ispano)* became Pope John XXI in September 1276, succeeding Adrian V; he died eight months later when a ceiling collapsed in the papal palace at Viterbo. Peter studied medicine at Salerno, and then philosophy and theology at the University of Paris with Albertus Magnus. He also studied with the Franciscan John of Parma. He taught medicine at Siena (1247–1252) before taking up theological appointments in Lisbon, Vermuy, and then Braga. In 1273 he was made cardinal bishop of Tusculum by Gregory X. He was elected pope after the death of Adrian V.

As pope, he attempted to restore unity between the Greek and Roman churches, and acted as conciliator between Rudolph of Habsburg and Charles of Anjou, and between Alfonso X of Castile and Philip III of France, with variable success. He ordered an investigation into heretical (Averroistic and Aristotelian) doctrines at the University of Paris, which led to the condemnation of 219 propositions. His hopes of bringing peace to Italy through the coronation of the emperor, as well as his plans for a crusade, were thwarted by his sudden death.

Better known for his works as a scholar than for his achievements as pope, Peter produced important texts on medicine, philosophy, and theology. His best-known work, the *Summulae logicales,* was a compendium in twelve parts of formal logic, both Aristotelian and Scholastic. This became the major text on logic throughout the Middle Ages and the Renaissance. That Dante was familiar with the *Summulae logicales* is particularly evident in the *Monarchia.*

Dante would no doubt have approved of Peter's role as conciliator during his papacy. He places Peter in the Heaven of the Sun, among the theologians, where he is named by Bonaventure, who also refers to his *Summulae logicales: "Pietro Spano, / lo qual giù luce in dodici libelli"* ("Peter of Spain, who shines down there in twelve books," *Par.* 12.134–135). He is the only contemporary pope to be placed in Heaven by Dante.

Angela G. Meekins

Peter, St.

Gospel accounts of the apostles always list Peter first (cf. Matt. 10:2, Mark 3:16, Luke 6:14), pointing to his preeminence as God's vicar. Jesus called Peter, originally a fisherman, to the discipleship (Mark 1:16–17; Luke 5:10) and conferred upon him the keys of the kingdom of Heaven (Matt. 16:19). After Jesus' death, resurrection, and ascension, Peter acted as head of the Christian community in Jerusalem (Acts 1:15, 2:14) and traveled to Antioch (Gal. 2:11), Corinth (1 Cor. 1:12), and Rome (see 1 Pet. 5:15, where "Babylon" appears to be a code name for the Roman capital). According to Catholic tradition, which Dante would have known and embraced, Peter became the first bishop of Rome (i.e., the first pope) and suffered martyrdom in that city.

Dante refers in his writings to many of these events and at numerous points invokes Peter by his

PVRGATORIO

St. Peter's gate in Purgatory. La comedia di Dante Aligieri, with commentary by Alessandro Vellutello, published by Francesco Marcolini, Venice, 1544. Giamatti Collection: Courtesy of the Mount Holyoke College Archives and Special Collections.

Italian or Latin names or via various periphrastic expressions, including these: *Pietro* (*Purg.* 13.51, 21.54, 32.76; *Par.* 9.141, 11.120, 18.131, 25.12, 32.133); *Pier* or *Piero* (*Conv.* 4.22.14 and 16; *Inf.* 2.24, 19.94; *Purg.* 9.127; *Par.* 22.88); *Petrus* (*Mon.* 2.8.1, 3.1.5, 3.7.5, 3.8.1 ff., 3.9.1 ff., 3.15.4; *Epist.* 6.3, 11.3); *san Pietro* (*Inf.* 1.134 and 19.91, referring to the man); *Santo Pietro* or *San Pietro* (*Inf.* 18.32 and 31.59, referring to the basilica at Rome); *Cefàs* (*Par.* 21.127, "Cephas"); *pescator* (*Purg.* 22.63 and *Par.* 18.136, "fisherman"); *Archimandrita* (*Mon.* 3.9.17, "head of the fold"); *Barone* (*Par.* 24.115, "Baron"); *santo Padre* (*Par.* 24.124, "holy father"); *padre vetusto / di Santa Chiesa* (*Par.* 32.124–125, "ancient father of Holy Church"); *alto primipilo* (*Par.* 24.59, "high commander"); *primizia / che lasciò Cristo d'i vicari suoi* (*Par.* 25.14–15, "first harvest that Christ left of his vicars"); *Dei vicarius (Epist.* 5.30, "God's vicar"); *luce etterna del gran viro / a cui Nostro Segnor lasciò le chiavi* (*Par.* 24.34–35, "eternal light of the great hero with whom our Lord left the keys"); *colui che tien le chiavi* (*Par.* 23.139, "he who holds the keys"); *un foco sì felice* (*Par.* 24.20, "a fire so joyful"); *foco benedetto* (*Par.* 24.31,

"blessed fire"); *luce* (*Par.* 24.54, "light"); *amore acceso* (*Par.* 24.82, "burning love"); *luce profonda* (*Par.* 24.88, "deep light"); *appostolico lume* (*Par.* 24.153, "apostolic light"); and *quella* [*face*] *che pria venne* (*Par.* 27.11, "that one [torch] that had come first").

Peter, James, and John respectively represent faith, hope, and charity, both in medieval biblical exegeses of episodes when the three are alone with Jesus (e.g., on the Mount of Transfiguration and in Gethsemane) and in Dante's so-called examination cantos (*Par.* 24–26). Peter examines Dante on the subject of faith (*Par.* 24), denounces papal corruption (*Par.* 27), and sits in the Celestial Rose immediately to the right of the Virgin Mary (*Par.* 32). Functioning in the *Commedia* as the authority figure par excellence, Peter charges Dante-pilgrim in the Primum Mobile with the task of calling corrupt popes to repentance when he returns to Earth (*Par.* 27.64–65), a charge that reveals a central purpose of the poem.

Bibliography

Di Gregorio, F. "Il canto XXIV del *Paradiso:* La fede tra 'ansia' e letteratura." *L'Alighieri* 30/1 (1989), 15–44.

Di Scipio, Giuseppe C. "*Paradiso* XXIV." *Lectura Dantis* 16–17 (1995), 352–370.

Fallani, Giovanni. "L'esame teologico." In *Dante poeta teologo.* Milan: Marzorati, 1965, pp. 274–287.

Favati, Guido. "San Pietro in Dante." In *Psicoanalisi e strutturalismo di fronte a Dante,* vol. 2, *Letture della Commedia.* Florence: Olschki, 1972, pp. 327–354.

Getto, Giovanni. "Il canto XXIV del *Paradiso.*" *Letture Classensi* 1 (1966), 83–108.

Madison U. Sowell

Peter III of Aragon

King of Aragon (1276–1285) and the son and successor of James I the Conqueror. Through his marriage to Constance, the daughter of King Manfred, Peter acquired a legitimate right to the crown of Sicily, and, in spite of Charles of Anjou's strong opposition, he reigned as king of Sicily from 1282 until his death in 1285.

Dante places him among the negligent rulers in the Ante-Purgatory and observes him as he sings in harmony with his ancient enemy, Charles of Anjou (*Purg.* 7.112–113). The poet, who held

Peter in high esteem, has Sordello praise Peter's moral character by stating that he "wore the belt of all knightly worth" and that his virtue would have passed from father to son if the youth now sitting behind him had remained on the throne, which cannot be said of James and Frederick, his other heirs, since they possess only the kingdoms of their father and not his heritage (*Purg.* 7.114–120). Some commentators identify the youth as Alfonso III, who succeed Peter but reigned for only six years; others surmise that the poet is referring to Peter's youngest son, Pedro, who never reigned.

Antonio Illiano

Petrarch

The greatest Italian lyric poet and, together with Dante and Boccaccio, one of the "three crowns" of late medieval Italian literature. The influence of Dante on Petrarch (1304–1374), if we are to believe the latter, was neither early nor profound. In fact, Petrarch is curiously silent concerning Dante. Writing to Boccaccio in response to a gift of the *Commedia* (*Familiares* 21.15), he tells his friend that he had avoided close reading of Dante's works in his youth in order to avoid unwitting imitation; now, praising the vernacular Dante over the Latin author, he records his regret concerning the nature of the reception that an uncultured audience has accorded the *Commedia*.

It is certain nonetheless that the young Petrarch could hardly have escaped Dante's influence. Dante's political prominence was considerable, in part through his pronouncements on the fate of Italy and of the Florence from which he was exiled. Petrarch, whose father had been exiled from that city in the same year as Dante, records an early childhood memory of an encounter with the great man. By the time Petrarch initiated his literary career during his period of study in Bologna, Dante was the acknowledged master of the still fledgling Italian love lyric; the younger poet's assimilation of the lessons of the vernacular poetic tradition in general, and of troubadour poetry in particular, was marked profoundly by Dante's earlier response.

Petrarch's apparent near-indifference to Dante is moreover belied, as recent studies have amply demonstrated, by numerous reminiscences in his Latin works—in his epistolary collections as well as in the unfinished epic *Africa*—and by the overwhelming evidence of his own vernacular poetry.

Statue of Petrarch in Florence. Richard Lansing.

Both the *Rime sparse* ("Scattered Rhymes") or *Canzoniere* and the *Trionfi* ("Triumphs") bear testimony to an extraordinary familiarity with the *Vita Nuova,* the *Commedia,* and the *rime petrose.* While it has been suggested that many of the echoes of Dante's poems in Petrarch's works are unconscious—a function of involuntary reminiscence, of a memory informed by his vast reading in the classics and vernacular poets alike—many recent studies demonstrate that they are both deliberate and strategic, designed to provoke the reader's recognition of an extraordinarily complex intertextual relationship in which the experience of Dante as recorded in the *Vita Nuova,* the *rime petrose,* and the *Commedia* serves as essential referent.

We have no record of Petrarch's mention of the *Vita Nuova,* but the example of Dante's *libello* is a pervasive presence in the collection of his own vernacular lyrics both in content and in form. Although Petrarch's new poet's "story" is assembled without the connective tissue of narrative that

Pties together and explains the lyrics of the *Vita Nuova,* it repeatedly recalls the poetic and affective experience recorded in Dante's youthful work, and with identical outline: love for an unattainable lady, poetic evolution through attempts to praise her, loss of her to death, and poetic and spiritual renewal *in morte di madonna.*

Petrarch's collection of *Rime sparse* extends the first-person lyric "story" to an entire lifetime, and it engages in dialogue not only with the *Vita Nuova* but also with the *Commedia,* which, in retrospect, appears as its fulfillment. Petrarch almost certainly first read the *Commedia* too during his student days in Bologna. Although his own poetic language is quite restricted in comparison with the rich linguistic experimentation of the *Commedia,* volumes have been devoted to the Dantean presence, to echoes that are both thematic and stylistic, sometimes subtle but often insistent. Certain episodes of the *poema sacro,* notably *Inf.* 5 and *Purg.* 6 and 30–31, have been identified as privileged sources.

Petrarch's record of love and bereavement in the *Rime sparse* differs from Dante's both in the roles attributed to the lady and, as a consequence, in the unresolved tension between earthly and heavenly attachment. His Laura, bound to his search for poetic laurels through her name and through a mythic subtext recalling Apollo's thwarted pursuit and subsequent celebration of a nymph transformed into a laurel plant *(lauro),* is also a sensuous creature sensuously portrayed. Her inaccessibility, sometimes attributed to a resolute chastity, is also on occasion read as coldness or as cruelty; she plays vengeful Diana to his fearful Acteon or, as Medusa, threatens him with petrification. It is here that the impact of Dante's *rime petrose* is readily discernible: Petrarch's formulations of frustrated passion and of Laura's cold indifference resonate with Dante's "hard rhymes" for the unyielding, even cruel lady known as Petra. It is noteworthy that the only direct textual citation of Dante in the *Rime sparse* is from one of the *petrose:* in a canzone in which verses from a variety of earlier poets are incorporated as the closing lines of stanzas recapitulating the speaker's own experience, Dante's verse *Così nel mio parlar voglio esser aspro* ("So in my speech I wish to be harsh") closes a stanza combining complex echoes of several of the *petrose.*

In a more exalted vein, recalling the portrayal of Beatrice in the *Vita Nuova,* Petrarch in the *Rime* also calls his lady a "miracle," and the triumphant itinerary of the lover who found in Beatrice an intimation of the divine is repeatedly evoked. Even following the death of Laura, however, the sensuous recall of her earthly beauty is insistent, confirming the instability both of the poet's fantasy and of his will as a central issue in the collection—a fragmentation of the self mirrored in the fragmentation or "scattering" of his collected rhymes.

The exemplary itinerary toward *caritas* that Dante traces from the *Vita Nuova* to the *Commedia,* never fully realized in the *Rime sparse,* is recast in Petrarch's *Trionfi.* In the form of a dreamvision adopting the *Commedia's* meter of *terza rima*—the most ambitious example of that meter to follow the *Commedia* itself—the *Trionfi* rewrites the story of love and loss in a resolutely edifying key. Here the lover is readily converted to the virtuous rereading of their love urged on him by the lady. Beginning with the *Triumph of Love,* the work proceeds steadily through the succession of triumphs—of chastity, death, fame, time, and

Prose antiche di Dante, Petrarcha, et Boccaccio, *published by Doni in 1547. Reproduced by permission of the John A. Zahm Dante Collection in the Department of Special Collections, University Libraries, University of Notre Dame.*

finally eternity—to which the poet is witness. In this didactic enterprise, the ambiguities of the presentation of Laura central to the *Rime sparse* are resolved in favor of a lady who assumes a role of spiritual guide almost identical to that assigned by Dante to Beatrice in the *Commedia*.

Was Petrarch's reluctance to acknowledge his massive debt to Dante a sign of an intensely felt rivalry, of an anxiety at the core of his own urgent poetic self-definition? Or does it reflect rather a difference of temperament, attested also in his conviction of the superiority of Latin over the vernacular as a poetic language, the attitude that led him to disparage the significance of his own Italian poems? It is in any case as a vernacular poet of love that he twice records Dante's name in his own vernacular works: in the *Trionfo d'Amore* he includes Dante, in the company of Beatrice, among the vernacular poets of love; in *Rime* 287, addressed to fellow-poet Sennuccio del Bene, he asks his recently deceased friend to greet on his behalf, in the third sphere of Heaven, a band of poets among whom Dante is included. Boccaccio, a fervent admirer of both Dante and Petrarch, was to include Petrarch along with Dante in that same band, "contemplating things beyond our understanding" (Boccaccio, *Rime* 126).

Bibliography

Foster, Kenelm. "Beatrice or Medusa." In *Italian Studies Presented to E. R. Vincent*. Edited by C. P. Brand, K. Foster, U. Limentani. Cambridge, England: W. Heffer, 1962, pp. 41–56.

Sturm-Maddox, Sara. *Petrarch's Laurels*. University Park: Pennsylvania State University Press, 1992.

———. *Petrarch's Metamorphoses: Text and Subtext in the Rime sparse*. Columbia: University of Missouri Press, 1985.

Vickers, Nancy. "Re-membering Dante: Petrarch's 'Chiare, fresche, e dolci acque.'" *MLN* 96 (1981), 1–11.

Warkentin, Germaine. "The Form of Dante's 'Libello' and its Challenge to Petrarch." *Quaderni d'italianistica* 2 (1981), 160–170.

Sara Sturm-Maddox

Petrocchi, Giorgio

Italian philologist and literary critic (1921–1989) whose critical edition of Dante's *poema sacro* is the established standard on which all other modern editions and translations are now based. Entitled *Commedia secondo l'antica vulgata,* the edition was developed under the auspices of the Società Dantesca Italiana and published by Mondadori in 1966–1967, in four volumes. A second, revised edition was published in 1994 (Florence: Le Lettere). This work is the result of the most systematic analysis of the manuscript tradition of the poem ever undertaken, and it marks a high point in the history of the new school of Florentine philology headed by Gianfranco Contini. Given the impossibility of reviewing the more than six hundred extant manuscripts, Petrocchi focused on the *antica vulgata* ("ancient vulgate")—that is, on the twenty-seven early manuscript versions that had achieved the widest diffusion (with special emphasis on the Trivulziano 1080 ms. of 1337). His decision to base his critical edition on the early manuscripts from the north of Italy, which he regarded as superior to the Tuscan and Florentine ones, has recently come under attack by Antonio Lanza.

Although his name is often associated primarily with his ground-breaking philological work, Petrocchi's interest and considerable expertise in Dante was remarkably extensive and diverse. He produced several works of literary and biographical criticism, including *Itinerari danteschi* (1969), *Politica e letteratura nella vita giovanile di Dante* (1974), and *Vita di Dante* (1983). He was general editor of the *Enciclopedia dantesca* (1970–1976), under the direction of Umberto Bosco.

Bibliography

Alighieri, Dante. *La Commedìa: Nuovo testo critico secondo i più antichi manoscritti fiorentini.* Edited by Antonio Lanza. 2nd ed. Anzio: De Rubeis, 1996.

———. *La Commedia secondo l'antica vulgata.* Edited by Giorgio Petrocchi. 4 vols. 2nd ed., revised. Florence: Le Lettere, 1994.

Andreotti, Serena, with Antonietta Bufano and Marisa Cimino. "Bibliografia dei contributi di Giorgio Petrocchi su Dante, Tasso, Foscolo, Manzoni, Pascoli." *Letteratura italiana contemporanea* 11 (1990) 29, 195–207.

"Bibliografia degli scritti." In Giorgio Petrocchi, *Saggi sul Rinascimento italiano*. Edited by Antonietta Bufano and Eugenio Ragni. Florence: Le Monnier, 1990.

"Ricordo di Giorgio Petrocchi." *L'Alighieri* 31.1 (1990), 27–53. Essays by Salvatore Accardo,

Ignazio Baldelli, Vincenzo Cappelletti, Luigi Gui, Silvio Pasquazi, and Aldo Vallone.

Vallone, Aldo. *Storia della critica dantesca dal XIV al XX secolo.* Vol. 2. Milan: Vallardi, 1981, pp. 880–882.

Aldo Vallone
(translated by Robin Treasure)

Petrose Poems

Four *canzoni* apparently written by Dante at about the same time (dated by the first of them, it is generally agreed, in December 1296). Their theme is the poet's frustrated love for a young woman who is compared in each of them to a precious stone, either because of her beauty or because of her cruel power over him.

1. "Io son venuto al punto de la rota" ("I have come to the point on the wheel," *Rime* 100) has five 13-line stanzas (*piedi* ABC.ABC, *sirma* CDEeD*FF*—here and in the following, italics in a rhyme scheme indicate repetition of the entire word), with a seven-line *congedo* repeating the scheme of the *sirma*. Each of the stanzas describes the effects of the stars of winter on the cyclical events in a realm of nature: (1) the stars (the astronomical position both dates the poem and seems to be a significant inversion of what Dante thought of as his natal horoscope; see Durling and Martinez 1990); (2) the atmosphere; (3) birds and other animals; (4) trees and plants; (5) waters and the Earth. Beginning with the tenth line of each stanza, the fiery desire of the speaker is contrasted with the frozen immobility of the rest of nature. The *congedo* imagines the reversal of the situation in the spring, when, if the lady is still cruel, the lover will be turned to stone. Among the many formal refinements of the poem is that the six rhyme-words are chiastically arranged (*petra* "stone," *donna* "lady," *tempo* "time," *sempre* "always," *dolce* "sweet," *marmo* "marble").

In describing the seasonal cycles in this descending order, in each case a half-cycle (night; gathering of clouds and storm; departure of birds and deadening of other animals' desire; death of leaves and flowers; floods and freezing), the observer's gaze imitates the spiraling descent of the Sun toward the winter solstice. This elaborate representation of the cosmos and the forces arrayed, like the lady, against the lover, also involves a sustained parallel with the human body (traditional in a large number of texts known to

Dante; see Microcosm): the heavens : head; atmosphere : breath; desires of birds and animals : heart; life in plants : heart; flooding rivers and frozen ground : belly and genitals.

2. "Al poco giorno e al gran cerchio d'ombra" ("To the short day and the great circle of shadow," *Rime* 101) is a sestina (a form invented by the troubadour Arnaut Daniel, altered by Dante so that all the lines are hendecasyllables). Six rhyme words appear in each of six 6-line stanzas, with their position varied according to *retrogradatio cruciata* ("crossed retrograde motion"): 1. *A* (*ombra* "shadow"), *B* (*colli* "hills"), *C* (*erba* "grass, herb"), *D* (*verde* "green"), *E* (*petra* "stone"), *F* (*donna* "lady"); 2. *FAEBDC*; 3. *CFDABE*; and so on (in a seventh stanza, the original order would recur). The three-line *congedo* includes two rhyme-words in each line.

The form of this poem again imitates the Sun, this time the Sun's combination of direct and retrograde motion. (The former motion is diurnal, from east to west, and is represented in the stanza by three of the rhyme-words appearing in "direct" order with reference to the preceding stanza (i.e., in stanza 2 above, *A, B,* and *C*); the latter is annual, from west to east through all the signs of the Zodiac—the motion that produces the season—and is represented in the stanza by three of the rhyme-words appearing in "retrograde" order (i.e., in stanza 2 above, *F, E,* and *D*). Both in form and in theme, the poem invokes the heliotrope, the flower that turns to follow the sun, and the precious stone that can cause invisibility.

Though still situated in winter, the sestina broadens the theme to embrace the imagined succession of seasons, against which are set the beauty and unchanging resistance of the lady. The circling recurrence of the rhyme-words expresses the obsessively circling meditation of the lover, culminating in a fantasy of her returning his love in the springtime (stanza 5), followed by the recognition of its impossibility (stanza 6). Like the *congedo* of "Io son venuto," the *congedo* imagines the death of the lover, in a veiled reference to the power of the heliotrope stone, when coupled with a certain herb, to cause one to disappear.

3. "Amor, tu vedi ben che questa donna" ("Love, you see well that this lady," *Rime* 102) is often incorrectly called a double sestina because it also employs rhyme-words exclusively, in this case five (*donna, tempo* "time," *luce* "light," *freddo* "cold," *petra*), in five 12-line stanzas (*piedi:*

ABA.ACA, sirma: ADD.AEE), followed by a six-line *congedo;* the order is varied by using the *E*-word of each stanza as the *A*-word of the next, shifting the others downward (stanza 2: *EAE.EBE:ECC.EDD).* In each stanza, then, one rhyme-word predominates (in most cases, in a pattern of gradually increasing frequency), with the central third stanza dominated by the rhyme-word *freddo.* The *congedo* presents the rhyme-words in the order of their predominance in the stanzas— *AED.DCB,* where the emphatic repetition of *freddo* at the center explicitly identifies it as the means of the production of the poem's novel form. The form imitates the coming to dominance at the winter solstice of the sign of Capricorn and the cold planet Saturn, the influences that produce the severe winter, and their giving way as the Sun moves on toward spring.

Thematically, the poem is microcosmically centered on the lover, subjected both to winter and to the cold influence of the lady, threatening him with death. It is an apostrophe to the god of love, anaphorically structured: stanza 1, *Amor, tu vedi* ("Love, you see"); stanza 3, *Segnor, tu sai* ("Lord, you know"); stanza 5, *Però, virtù* ("Therefore, power"), begging for his help. He is gradually revealed, especially in stanza 5, as the Christian creator—indeed, as Christ, to whom the lover appeals against the cruelty that is killing him. Diachronically imitating the passage of time and the production of the seasons, synchronically the poem is a crystal centered on the principle of cold.

4. "Così nel mio parlar voglio esser aspro" ("So in my speech I would be harsh," *Rime* 103) turns away from representation of the cosmos to the metaphorics of combat, and from rigid imitation of cosmic cycles in its form to a much more flexible and varied stanza, without rhyme-words. It comprises six 13-line stanzas (*piedi:* ABbc.ABbC, *sirma:* CDdEE), with a five-line *congedo* repeating the scheme of the *sirma.* The new flexibility—indeed, a violent breaking of the rigidities—leads to the introduction of new topics in the *sirma* of the stanzas rather than their *piedi.*

The "harsh speech" announced in the first line (involving especially multiple consonants, particularly in rhyme, as in *aspro* "harsh"), mirrors the violent theme. The lover and lady are represented, at first, as engaged in combat at a distance (bows and arrows : glances); all her arrows strike home, but his are blunted or deflected by her armor. The second half of the poem reveals what has gradually become clear in the other poems: that the death that threatens the lover is the expression of his own self-destructive side. The combat has become his hand-to-hand struggle with the god of love, who has thrown him to the ground and stands over him with the sword of Dido's suicide (line 36). At the moment when a last, mortal blow is to fall, an upsurge of resistance redirects it toward the heart of the lady: so might Love cleave her heart. The rest of the poem imagines her in love, culminating in a violent description of the act of love as the gradual transformation of hand-to-hand combat into reconciliation and peace; the violence, close to that of rape, is disturbing. The *congedo* returns to the "real" situation, sending the poem to be an arrow to pierce the lady's heart and gain her love.

The *petrose* are closely connected in three respects unprecedented in Dante's earlier poetry: the imagery of precious stones—one (marble, heliotrope, crystal, jasper) is mentioned or implied in each; violence of feeling, harshness of language, and difficulty of syntax; and, in the first three, the technique of rhyme-words (and the specific rhyme-words, a number of which are used several times), the exploitation of the form of the *canzone* to imitate the solar cycles thematized in each poem, and the introduction of natural descriptions and scientific conceptions concerning the microcosmic relation between the lover, the cosmos as a whole, and the forms of the poems.

Whatever the order of composition of the four poems, their traditional arrangement is well founded: "Io son venuto" stands to the others as programmatically setting up the situation governing all of them and as initiating the technique of rhyme-words developed with increasing intensity first in "Al poco giorno" and then in "Amor, tu vedi ben," mirroring the psychological theme, which reaches a kind of impasse at the end of "Amor, tu vedi ben." "Così nel mio parlar" is appropriate as the final poem because it is a violent shattering of both the psychological impasse and the rigid forms.

Critical responses to the poems have differed widely. At the turn of the twentieth century, it was fashionable to regard them as allegorical representations of Dante's relations with the city of Florence or with the papacy, in either case after his exile. Gianfranco Contini directs attention to the daring stylistic experimentation as preparation for the *Commedia,* but treats the sexual theme as a

P

mere pretext. The fullest study (Durling and Martinez, 1990) restores the astrology and the sexual problematic as central, identifies and explores the remarkable microcosmic themes and formal techniques embodied in the poems, and stresses their thematic and formal links with the *Commedia,* in addition to the stylistic importance of the works as the first emergence of Dante's "microcosmic poetics."

The *petrose* have had great influence on later Italian poetry, beginning with Petrarch, who made them the basis of his entire poetics, though diluting their intensity; his output included eight sestinas and one double sestina.

Bibliography

Angelitti, Filippo. "Sulle principali apparenze del pianeta Venere . . . dal 1290 al 1309." *Atti della Reale Accademia di Scienze, Lettere e Belle Arti di Palermo* 6 (1901), 3–24.

Blasucci, Luigi. "L'esperienza delle petrose e il linguaggio della *Divina Commedia.*" *Belfagor* 12 (1957), 403–431.

Durling, Robert M., and Ronald L. Martinez. *Time and the Crystal: Studies in Dante's "Rime petrose."* Berkeley and Los Angeles: University of California Press, 1990.

Fenzi, Enrico. "Le rime per la donna Pietra." In *Miscellanea di studi danteschi.* Genoa: Bozzi, 1966, pp. 229–309.

Perugi, Maurizio. "Arnaut Daniel in Dante." *Studi danteschi* 51 (1978), 59–152.

Robert M. Durling

Pézard, André

Distinguished French critic and translator (1893–1984) whose prolific studies of Dante stressed the importance of a philological and stylistic analysis of the poet's works within their historical context. He is most remembered for his original and provocative study *Dante sous la pluie de feu (Enfer, chant XV),* in which he argues that the sodomites in the seventh circle of Hell are not in fact guilty of sodomy, but rather of blasphemy. Central to this interpretation is his assertion that Brunetto Latini's sin consists of his having written his encyclopedic *Tresor* in French, thereby abandoning his native Tuscan vernacular. This reading was immediately met with skepticism, but it succeeding in generating, over time, similar studies of a polemical nature. Pézard wrote numerous essays

on a wide range of topics, dealing with all Dante's works, including *lecturae* on individual cantos of the *Commedia.* On the seventh centenary of Dante's birth, he published a single-volume translation of the poet's complete works into French, with commentary.

Bibliography

Alighieri, Dante. *Oeuvres complètes.* Translation and commentary by André Pézard. Paris: Gallimard, 1965.

Pézard, André. *"La rotta gonna": Gloses et corrections aux textes mineurs de Dante.* 3 vols. Florence: Sansoni antiquariato; Paris: M. Didier, 1967–1979.

———. *Dans le sillage de Dante.* Paris: Societé d'Études Italiennes, 1975.

———. *Dante sous la pluie de feu (Enfer, chant XV).* Paris: J. Vrin, 1950.

Richard Lansing

Phaëthon

The Ovidian Phaëthon narrative utilized by Dante in the *Commedia* comes from *Meta.* 1.750–776 and 2.1–366. Stung by the accusation that he is not the son of Apollo, Phaëthon complains to his mother Clymene, who affirms his divine paternity and sends him to visit his father, the sun god, for further confirmation. Upon arriving at Apollo's palace, Phaëthon obtains from his father the promise to grant him whatever proof he chooses to demonstrate the truth of his exalted lineage: when Phaëthon insists on being allowed to drive the Sun's chariot for a day, the deeply reluctant father is constrained by his oath to allow his son this dangerous privilege. Ascending into the heavens, Phaëthon quickly loses control of the horses of his father's chariot, and the destructive scorching heat that results causes Earth to pray for relief to Jupiter, who strikes Phaëthon from the sky with a thunderbolt, so that he falls to his death in the river Po.

Phaëthon is explicitly referred to five times in the *Commedia.* Twice, Dante-protagonist is compared directly to the Ovidian character: first, in *Inf.* 17.106–108, as Dante is about to begin his infernal descent on Geryon's back; and second, in *Par.* 17.1–6, as he prepares to ask Cacciaguida about his future exile. The other three explicit references to Phaëthon occur in *Purg.* 4.71–75, as Virgil explains to Dante the position of the Sun in the

Southern Hemisphere's sky; in *Purg.* 29.115–120, as part of the presentation of the superlative status of the triumphal chariot pulled by the griffin; and in *Par.* 31.124–129, as Dante begins his vision of Mary, Queen of Heaven, seated in the Empyrean. Phaëthon is mentioned by name in *Inf.* 17.107; *Purg.* 4.72; *Par.* 31.125.

In *Conv.* 2.14.5, Dante opines that the *favola* ("fable") of Phaëthon in Ovid's *Meta.* 2 engenders the Pythagorean view of the origin of the Milky Way (which he situates in the eighth heaven). In *Epist.* 11.5, Dante charges the Italian cardinals with corruption for having deviated from the right path, misguiding the Church in a manner analogous to Phaëthon's disastrous handling of Apollo's chariot.

Bibliography

Brownlee, Kevin. "Phaëthon's Fall and Dante's Ascent." *Dante Studies* 102 (1984), 135–144.

Chiarenza, Margaret Mills. "Time and Eternity in the Myths of *Paradiso* XVII." In *Dante, Petrarch, Boccaccio: Studies in the Italian Trecento in Honor of Charles S. Singleton.* Edited by Aldo S. Bernardo and Anthony L. Pellegrini. Binghamton, N.Y.: Medieval and Renaissance Texts and Studies, 1983, pp. 133–150.

Kevin Brownlee

Pharisees

The predominant sect or religious party among Jews at the time of Christ, the Pharisees were distinguished by minute observance of the Hebrew law as defined by both written and oral tradition. Unlike the priestly Sadducees, who accepted only the written law of the Pentateuch, they believed in such doctrines as the resurrection of the body and the existence of angels. After the destruction of the Temple of Jerusalem (70 C.E.), they were the most influential group among the Jews and are credited with upholding the law and traditions in the Diaspora. The authors of the Gospels record a number of debates between Jesus and the Pharisees, in most of which they are criticized for legalism or literalism (see especially Matt. 23:1–36). But there are counterindications of more positive attitude in Luke (13:31) and the Acts of the Apostles (5:34) that reveal an underlying ambivalence. Contemporary theologians acknowledge that the Gospel narratives reflect the judaizing crisis of the early Church and thus shape the portrayal of the Pharisees in terms of their own agendas. Dante uses the term "Pharisee" *(fariseo)* negatively as a synonym for "hypocrite" (*Inf.* 23.116), but it is interesting that he uses it most visibly to describe the relationship of Pope Boniface VIII to the papal curia (*Inf.* 27.85).

In *Epist.* 8, addressed to the Italian cardinals of Florence, Dante makes the greed of the ancient chiefs of the Pharisees, which in his view brought about the destruction of Jerusalem, the basis of his attack on the avarice of the contemporary Church.

Rachel Jacoff

Philip III

King of France (1270–1285), known as Philip the Bold *(Filippo)*, and referred to by Dante as *quel nasetto* ("that small-nosed one," *Purg.* 7.103). He was the second son of King Louis IX and Margaret of Provence and became heir to the throne in 1260 upon the death of his brother. He married Isabella of Aragon and had four sons: Louis, who died in 1276; Philip, who succeeded as Philip IV; Charles, count of Valois; and Robert, who died in infancy. After Isabella's death, he married Mary of Brabant. Their children were Louis, count of Evreux; Margaret, wife of King Edward I of England; and Blanche, wife of Rudolph III, duke of Austria. Philip III enlarged the royal domain by acquiring the countship of Toulouse, Poitou, and Auvergne upon the death without posterity of his uncle, Alphonse of Poitiers, husband of Joan of Toulouse, but he gave the Comtat Venaissin to Pope Gregory X. He married his son Philip IV (the Fair) to Jeanne, the daughter of Henry I of Navarre, but failed in his campaign against Peter III of Aragon, whose crown was promised to him for his son by Pope Martin IV. Philip died during the retreat.

Dante places him in the Valley of the Princes in the Ante-Purgatory, together with other rulers who deferred their repentance (*Purg.* 7.85–136).

Yolande de Pontfarcy

Philip IV, the Fair

King of France from 1285 to 1314. Born in 1268, Philip, the second son of Philip III, was king of France from 1285 to 1314. His reign was marked by repeated, often successful, efforts to bring about the territorial expansion of France, and by his consolidation of the political authority of the French monarchy. He acquired Champagne and Navarre through marriage in 1284; Lille, Douai, and Béthune in 1305; and the region around Lyon in 1302, though his bid to annex Flanders was thwarted at Courtrai in 1302. His delegation of authority to legists adept in Roman law centralized monarchic control while lessening aristocratic influence at court.

Although Philip's vigorous political initiatives considerably advanced the fortunes of France, they brought him into profound conflicts on several fronts. In opposition to papal taxation of clergy by Pope Boniface VIII, he convened the first Estates General in 1302 and had the pontiff arrested the following year. This quarrel culminated in the election, in 1305, of a French pope, Clement V, the first of seven pontiffs to reside in Avignon during the so-called Babylonian Captivity, which lasted until 1377, when Pope Gregory XI returned to Rome. In order to cope with the onerous financial burdens incurred by his militant statesmanship, Philip resorted to regular taxation, imposing particularly harsh levies on Jews and Lombards, in some cases confiscating their assets. He also proclaimed various monetary devaluations. Coveting the immense wealth that had been amassed by the crusading order of the Knights Templar, he obtained the order's suppression by Clement V (1312), had certain of its leaders burned at the stake (1314), and seized its liquid assets.

Philip's innovative conceptualization of a sovereign polity and his aggressive exploitations of political and religious institutions in order to further its cause were clearly at odds with Dante's own commitment to the idea of productive coexistence binding papacy and empire. At several junctures in the *Commedia,* Dante alludes—only indirectly, though always with acute disfavor or hostility—to Philip the Fair: for abetting abuses of papal power by Clement V (*Inf.* 19.85–87); for Philip's seizure of Boniface VIII, a "Vicar of Christ" (*Purg.* 20, 86–87; see also *Purg.* 32.152–156 and 33.45); for invasive territorial conquests (*Purg.* 20.46–47, 64–66); for the destruction of the Knights Templar (*Purg.* 20.91–93); and for ruinous devaluations of currency (*Par.* 19.118–119). Animosity of a more personal nature plausibly stems from the role of Philip's brother, Charles of Valois, in exiling from Florence some six hundred partisans of the White Guelfs (Bianchi), among them Dante himself (*Purg.* 20.70–75).

In sum, Dante's more general negative qualification of Philip, uttered by the persona of Sordello in *Purg.* 7.109–110, as the *mal di Francia / . . . la vita sua viziata e lorda* ("the plague of France / . . . his vicious, filthy life") was clearly conditioned by a considerable variety of grievances, religious, political, and personal. These find expression in no single, devastating portrait of the monarch, but rather in a number of sporadic, vitriolic evocations scattered throughout the *Commedia.*

Donald Maddox

Philosophy

It is within the Noble Castle of Limbo (*Inf.* 4. 130–144) that Dante encounters the great philosophers of the past and thereby identifies his preferred philosophical *fontes.* These consist of Aristotle, Plato, Socrates, a number of minor Greek thinkers who were hardly more than names to Dante, Cicero, Seneca, Avicenna, and Averroës.

Philosophically, Dante was influenced by Aristotle more than by any other philosopher. On the one hand, this is hardly surprising, given that Dante lived during and immediately after the period in which much of the wisdom of ancient Greece, especially that of Aristotle, reappeared through the intermediary influence of Arabic translations and confronted Western Latin philosophy (cf. Nardi, 166ff.). On the other hand, what is surprising is the depth and breadth of Dante's familiarity with Aristotle, an intellectual achievement described by Moore as "astonishing" (94). There seem to be few Aristotelian works with which Dante was unfamiliar (the *Poetics* is an exception, as Moore points out [93], but this text was not generally available before the mid-1500s), and Aristotle is quoted repeatedly throughout Dante's works as a supreme philosophical authority. He is, as Dante says prosaically, *il maestro de li filosofi* ("the master of philosophers," *Conv.* 4.8.15), or, according to the poetic depiction of the *Commedia, il maestro di color che sanno* ("the master of those who know," *Inf.* 4.131). Aristotle's philosophical influence on Dante and his literary output reigns supreme. In fact, taking all his writings together, Dante quotes or refers to Aristotle's works more than any other authoritative text save the Bible, and in the *Commedia* Aristotle is surpassed only by the Bible, Virgil, and Ovid (Moore, 321ff.).

Dante, of course, did not know Aristotle in the original Greek; as he himself tells us in *Conv.*

2.14.7, he used two Latin translations of Aristotle, which he calls the "new" and the "old." Moore (307–318) traces the latter to the Arabic-into-Latin versions of Aristotle and the former to the Greek-into-Latin versions now known as the "Antiqua Translatio." Armed with these translations, Dante immersed himself completely in the Stagirite's works. In the *Commedia,* the resultant influence of Aristotle is everywhere to be seen. Four examples will suffice. First is the distinction between sins of incontinence *(incontenenza)* and sins of vicious habit *(malizia)* which Dante makes in *Inf.* 11.82 and which he bases on the same distinction in Aristotle's *Nichomachean Ethics* (7.1.1145a), as he expressly states in *Inf.* 11.80. Second is the odd collocation by Dante in the punishment of certain categories of sinners, such as the suicides and the spendthrifts in *Inf.* 11.43–44, or the sodomites and the usurers in *Inf.* 11. 49–51, which can be traced to the influence of Aristotle (cf. *Nic. Eth.,* 4. 1.120a and *Phys.,* 2. 2. [194a.21]). Third is Dante's awareness of the good for humankind of society, represented by the speech of Charles Martel in *Par.* 8.115–120—an awareness voiced by Aristotle in *Politics* 1.1.2 (he is expressly acknowledged in *Par.* 8.120). Last, there is the long speech of Statius on the development of the embryo which occupies most of *Purg.* 25 and which mirrors Aristotle's theory in his *Generation of Animals;* not only is the vocabulary derivative, but the entire presentation is closely modeled on Aristotelian ideas, such as the underlying argument of the four digestions, the initial development of the soul, and the importance of the heart for the life of the embryo.

Therefore, front and center in Dante's philosophical thought stands Aristotle, who, as *magister sapientium* ("master of those who know," *DVE* 2.10.1), is *degnissimo di fede e d'obbedienza* ("most worthy of faith and obedience," *Conv.* 4.6.7). Interestingly enough, this close relationship between Aristotle and Dante has served as the touchstone for Dantean philosophical studies of the twentieth century. Scholars in the earlier part of the century, most notably Cornoldi and Busnelli, posited that Dante was in essence a Thomist and therefore also an Aristotelian. This belief came under heavy fire in the mid-twentieth century from a number of scholars, primarily Bruno Nardi. Nardi tried to situate Dante within a much more dynamic world of thought than is suggested by the simple catch-phrases "Thomist" or "Aristotelian," and he sought to unravel the complex series of philosophical thought patterns at work in Dante's output. His important conclusion was that Dante's ideas are a mixture of Neoplatonic, Averroistic, and Avicennistic elements, so that they cannot be possibly traced to the sole influence of one particular source, Aristotle or otherwise. For Nardi, therefore, Dante is essentially a Neoplatonist whose philosophical world is highly eclectic. More recently, however, the pendulum has begun to swing in the opposite direction. As Kenelm Foster points out, although there is not much to be said for calling Dante a Thomist/Aristotelian, and although there are clear signs of Neoplatonic influence in Dante's thought, Aristotle is nevertheless not to be forgotten. In his view, Dante's world when "analysed philosophically . . . turns out to be a rather uneasy synthesis of Neoplatonist and Aristotelian elements" (57). Most recently, in an engaging study of Dante and Christian Aristotelianism, Patrick Boyde explores the processes of "creation" and "generation" as Dante knew them and shows how Dante has fused them in his theory of human embryology. In this endeavor Boyde emphasizes the primary importance of Aristotle, who is not only regarded as " 'the master of human life,' precisely because he had shown us the goal of our existence" (294), but who is also responsible for driving Dante in his last years to elaborate the two ends, the earthly and the heavenly, and hence the two human natures that are the consequences of mankind's two efficient causes, generation and creation—the former supplied by Aristotle, the latter by Christianity (294–295). Therefore, although Neoplatonic influences are everywhere to be seen in Dante, they in no way diminish the pivotal importance that Aristotle held in Dante's conception of the universe and of humankind's place in it.

Grouped next to Aristotle, but possessing far less philosophical significance for Dante's thought, are Socrates and Plato, respectively the precursor and the founder of the Academy. Socrates (cf. Delhaye) was the teacher of Plato, as Dante was well aware, but he seems to be afforded his privileged place in Limbo (next to Aristotle and in front of all the rest) because, as Dante remarks in *Conv.* 3.14.8, he is representative of those who have subjugated all other human pleasures to the pursuit of ideas. This singular honor aside, Socrates is treated in a brief and fragmentary manner in Dante's works, being seen merely as a precursor or as the one who inaugurated that search for moral truth which was perfected and found its fullest expression in the genius of Aristotle (*Conv.* 4.6.15), who is regarded by Dante as *maestro e duca de la ragione umana* ("the master and leader of human reason," *Conv.* 4.6.8). Socrates is thus cast into the shadows by Dante, who notes that Socrates, "because in his philosophy no affirmative statements were made" (*Conv.* 4.6.14), did not even leave his name to his followers. In a similar manner, Plato is treated by Dante most summarily (cf. Moore 156–164, and Cristiani). He is noted in the *Convivio* as the friend of Aristotle and as the founder of the Academy (*Conv.* 3.14.8, 4.6.14). In two other passages of the same work, Dante relies on more legendary evidence to add that Plato was the son of a king (3.14.8) and that his lifespan of eighty-one years is a perfect embodiment of the natural existence of human beings (4.24.6). But of Plato's works Dante, like his contemporaries, seems to have had limited knowledge, relying almost exclusively on a fifth-century Latin translation and commentary of the *Timaeus* by Calcidius. Moreover, with respect to this work Dante seems to be decidedly negative in the *Commedia*. In *Purg.* 4.1–16, he attacks the "error" (*Purg.* 4.5) of Plato, who Dante thought espoused in the *Timaeus* a belief in the plurality of souls, refuted by Aristotle in *De anima* 3.9. Furthermore, in *Par.* 4.22ff., the pilgrim's seeing the souls of Piccarda and Costanza within the Moon raises doubt about the belief expressed in the *Timaeus* that the creator of the universe had assigned the souls to stars and that they, at death, returned to their originating star. This belief is then vehemently attacked by Beatrice, who points out that all souls in reality inhabit the Empyrean, and that they appear to Dante in the different spheres only to demonstrate for his mortal eyes the degrees of their beatitude. Beatrice intensifies her attack on this Platonic doctrine by calling it "insidious" (*Par.* 4.27), precisely because it suggests an overpowering influence of the stars on human actions and therefore threatens the critical Dantean doctrine of free will (cf. *Purg.* 16.67–81). Thus, while allowing himself the use of a Platonic construct to stage the placement of souls throughout the heavens, Dante resolutely denies the underlying doctrine. Dante, in fact, seems almost anti-Platonic in the *Commedia,* and there is no celebration of Platonic ideas for their affinity with Christianity, a belief particularly dear to Augustine (cf. *De civ. Dei,* 8.5.8 and 10).

For Dante, however, as for medieval culture in general, Platonism was not limited to Plato proper; rather, it was an odd combination of many elements, including Aristotelian, Platonic, Neoplatonic, and Averroistic-Avicennistic ideas (Nardi and Gilson). For Dante's times it can be defined as a meetingplace, not only between Eastern and Western philosophy, but also between ancients and moderns and between these and everything that lay between. Plato, Aristotle, Plotinus, Porphyry, Augustine, Avicenna, Averroës: all these thinkers are subsumed under the heading of Platonism; all were available to Dante either directly or through various intermediaries, and all contributed to the shaping of his thought. Many ideas in Dante are thus not direct borrowings from Plato but from Neoplatonic elements. Nardi points to ideas such as the role of the angels in the formation of the sublunary world (245–250), human nature as a creation to restore the ruin of the fallen angels (250–253), and creation of the sensible world (253–262). Moreover, the influence of the last two philosophers listed in *Inf.* 4, the Arabs Avicenna and Averroës, appears to have been substantial, as Nardi (209ff.), Gilson (257ff.), and others (cf. Giacon, Vasoli) have shown. Thus, Dante's view in *Conv.* 4.21 of the soul's three resident powers or virtues (*la vertù formativa, la vertù celestiale,* and *la vertù del motore del cielo*) and especially his treatment of the role of *la vertù celestiale* (the influence of the heavenly bodies) as the active principle in the soul's passage from potency to act, offer clear references not only to Aristotle and Neoplatonism but also to Avicenna and Averroës (cf. Nardi 209–223). Dante's doubt, expressed in *Conv.* 4.1.8, about whether the primal matter of the elements was contained within God—a doubt that lingers in the *Commedia* (cf. *Par.* 29.22–24)—reflects the view held by Avicenna in his *Metaphysics* (*ST* 1.15.3.3; cf. Nardi 248–253); Dante's theory of a possible intellect, unique and separate for humankind, is directly inspired by Averroës, as he expressly tells us in *Mon.* 1.3.9. The Arabs, therefore, represent for Dante the new or modern learning at its best (signified by their placement, which occurs last in the list of *Inf.* 4 and parallels the placement of the contemporary Saladin in the preceding list of great-hearted individuals of action); they contribute in a major way to Dante's philosophical thought. In sum, Dante's Platonism includes a broad spectrum of philosophical thought that results from a synthesis of many disparate elements.

Next to Aristotle, Cicero exercises the greatest influence on Dante's philosophical thought (cf. Moore 258–273; Ronconi). Surprisingly, it is not as a supreme orator but as a philosopher that Cicero is retrieved and presented by Dante. Of Cicero's rhetorical works Dante seems scarcely aware (cf. Moore, 258 ff.), and Cicero is explicitly absent from the catalogue of writers listed by Dante in *DVE* 2.6.7 as masters of the high prosaic style *(qui usi sunt altissimas prosas)*. Cicero's philosophical works, however, are quoted extensively in Dante's works; more than half of the Ciceronian citations come from *De officiis* or *De senectute,* and after these *De amicitia* and *De finibus* (Moore 258). Dante has a special affection for Cicero, referring to him in *Inf.* 4 and elsewhere as "Tully." In *Conv.* 2.12.3, Dante lays bare the formative influence of Cicero in his philosophical growth: it was a reading of Boethius's *De consolatione philosophiae* coupled with Cicero's *De amicitia* that consoled Dante after Beatrice's death and that led him to the study of philosophy.

In the *Commedia* Cicero's influence is evident on a number of fronts, although he is never expressly acknowledged. First among these is Dante's distinction between sins of violence and sins of fraud (*Inf.* 11.22ff.), which accords closely with Cicero's distinction between the same vices in *De officiis* (1.13.41). In addition, though there is no actual quotation, Dante's depiction in *Purg.* 19.22 of the Sirens as having turned Ulysses aside may derive from his reading of *De officiis* 5.18.49, where Cicero implies that Ulysses had been trapped by the Sirens and traces this entrapment to a desire for knowledge, a fact in perfect conformity with Dante's depiction of Ulysses in *Inf.* 26 (cf. 97–99, 112–120). Furthermore, the Cacciaguida episode that spans the central cantos of the *Paradiso* may involve echoes of Cicero's *Somnium Scipionis* (cf. Raffa). Finally, in addition to these borrowings, Dante seems to have used Cicero as his meeting point with the minor Greek thinkers of *Inf.* 4—Democritus, Diogenes, Empedocles, Zeno, Thales, Anaxagoras, and Heraclitus, all of whom are discussed by Cicero and by Dante in a similar manner.

As it is not Cicero the orator but Cicero the philosopher who influences Dante, so it is Seneca the philosopher *(Seneca morale)* and not Seneca the tragedian who is recalled by Dante in *Inf.* 4 (cf. Paratore and Verbeke). Seneca figures in Dante's list of those who have sacrificed their lives for knowledge (*Conv.* 3.14.8), and he, along with Numa Pompilius, is described as *illustre* ("illustrious") because of his example or teaching *(DVE* 1.17.2). Thus, Seneca, by virtue of both his epithet *morale* and Dante's prose references to him, stands out for the poet as an *exemplum* of those concerned with moral truth and as a continuator, in Latin, of what Dante considered to be the hallmark of Greek speculative thought: the science of morality. In the *Commedia* there are only slight traces of Seneca. Seneca's description of Alexander of Pherae as *latro gentiumque vastator* ("robber and devastator of nations," *De beneficiis* 1.13.3) may provide support for the latter's identification as the person intended in *Inf.* 12.107. More certain is that Seneca's description of Ulysses' voyage as *extra notum nobis orbem* ("beyond the world known to us," *Epistolae morales* 88.6) and of the hero's placement among those *sapientes laboribus et contemptores voluptatis et victores omnium terrarum* ("who are wise for their labors, contemptuous of pleasure and victors over all the earth," *De constantia sapientis* 2.1) contributed to Dante's account of the Homeric figure. Finally, although commentators draw attention to the Virgilian influence (*Aen.* 6.470–471 and 10. 693ff.) in the poet's admonition to the pilgrim to persevere and stand *come torre ferma, che non crolla / già mai la cima per soffiar di venti* ("firm as a tower, which never bends its top, however hard the winds may blow," *Purg.* 5.14–15), it may well be that this is a rendering of Seneca's *quemadmodum proiecti quidam in altum scopuli mare frangunt . . . ita sapientis animus solidus est* ("As projecting crags are not affected by the beating of the deep sea, so too the soul of the wise man is ever constant," *De const. sap.* 3.5).

Thus does Dante lay bare his canon of preferred philosophical *fontes* in *Inf.* 4. By staging his encounter with them within the Noble Castle in Limbo, Dante is also revealing not only his attitude toward pagan knowledge in general, but also, and more important, the difference in attitude between the author of the *Convivio* and the author of *Commedia*. For all these philosophers, like the pagan poets before them, are condemned to a "life of hopeless longing" in Limbo. Although Dante acknowledges and even praises their contributions

P to rational thought by constructing the Noble Castle for them, he nevertheless locates that castle in Limbo, thereby denying them the true destiny of humankind. Thus, Dante's philosophers, though representative of value, do not represent the truest value, because their words are not imbued with the Word of God. They are condemned precisely because, whether they lived before or after the time of Christ, they did not believe in him. It is because of this great deficiency of theirs that Dante in the *Commedia* revisits his earlier flirtation with the *donna gentile* of philosophy of the *Convivio.* Now everything is focused on following the true path, and anything that diverges from that true path is seen as error. It is for this reason that Beatrice charges the pilgrim in *Purg.* 31 with infidelity: in veiled language, she intimates that at her death he was distracted by the comforts offered not only by other women but also, and more insidiously, by Lady Philosophy. Thus, the poet of the *Commedia* realizes and acknowledges his earlier stumbling. Dante's attitude toward philosophy in the *Commedia,* therefore, is a revision of an earlier attitude expressed in the *Convivio,* and such a revision highlights perfectly the complex relationship between these works. For, more than a simple continuation of his earlier literary efforts and more than a simple palinode, the *Commedia* represents a total rethinking and a total reworking of previously held ideas and views, all of which are now judged in the light of faith. As a result, the pagan learning celebrated for its own sake in the *Convivio* now is seen in the *Commedia* as leading to nothing more than a life of "fruitless longing" (cf. *Purg.* 3.40–45).

Bibliography

Boyde, Patrick. *Dante Philomythes and Philosopher: Man in the Cosmos.* Cambridge: Cambridge University Press, 1981.

Busnelli, Giovanni. *Cosmogonia e antropogenesi secondo Dante Alighieri e le sue fonti.* Rome: Civiltà Cattolica, 1922.

Cristiani, Marta. "Platone." *Enciclopedia dantesca* 4:547–550.

Delhaye, Philippe. "Socrate." *Enciclopedia dantesca* 5:283–284.

Foster, Kenelm. *The Two Dantes and Other Studies.* London: Darton, Longman and Todd, 1977.

Giacon, Carlo. "Avicenna," *Enciclopedia dantesca* 1:481–482.

Gilson, Étienne. *Dante and Philosophy.* New York: Harper, 1963.

Mazzotta, Giuseppe. *Dante's Vision and the Circle of Knowledge.* Princeton, N.J.: Princeton University Press, 1993.

Moore, Edward. *Studies in Dante, First Series: Scripture and Classical Authors in Dante.* New York: Greenwood Press, 1968.

Nardi, Bruno. *Dante e la cultura medievale.* Bari: Laterza, 1985.

Paratore, Ettore. "Seneca." *Enciclopedia dantesca* 5:156–159.

Placella, Vincenzio. "Filosofia." *Enciclopedia dantesca* 2:881–885.

Raffa, Guy. "Enigmatic 56's: Cicero's Scipio and Dante's Cacciaguida." *Dante Studies* 110 (1992), 121–134.

Ronconi, Alessandro. "Cicerone." *Enciclopedia dantesca* 1:991–997.

Simonelli, Maria. "Convivio." *Enciclopedia dantesca* 2:193–204.

Vasoli, Cesare. "Averroè." *Enciclopedia dantesca* 1:473–479.

Verbeke, Gérard. "Stoici." *Enciclopedia dantesca* 5:448–449.

Amilcare A. Iannucci

Phlegethon

Dante's *Flegetonta* (from the Greek, meaning "flaming, fiery"), the third river of Hell (*Inf.* 12; first named in 14.116), originates, like all the rivers of Dante's hydrographic system in the *Inferno,* from tears flowing from a crack in the statue of the Old Man of Crete. The Phlegethon consists of boiling-hot blood, which probably symbolizes the blood of victims of violent death. The stream forms the first ring *(girone)* of the seventh circle, in which the sinners of violence against others are immersed at various depths corresponding to the severity of their crimes against their fellow men. Along its banks centaurs armed with bows and arrows see to it that the sinners maintain their proper places. An offshoot of the river cuts across the second and third rings of the circle *(fiumicello, rigagno,* 14.77, 121); its waters finally cascade over a cliff into the lake of Cocytus. The figure of the fiery river has a rich background from Homer to Virgil (*Aen.* 6.550–551) and beyond.

A. L. Pellegrini

Phlegyas

A mythological figure, son of Mars, variously said to be king of the Lapiths and eponym of the barbarous peoples of Thessaly. In *Aen.* 6.618–620, he is condemned within the gates of Tartarus for setting fire to the temple of Apollo at Delphi (Statius concurs in *Theb.* 1.712–715). Dante, however, does not have Phlegyas *(Flegiàs)* so punished. In *Inf.* 8.19–24, he ferries the pilgrim and Virgil across the Styx to the gates of Dis and, angry himself, serves as guardian of the wrathful who are condemned to reside in the slimy bog.

Sally Mussetter

Pholus

A centaur mentioned by Virgil (*Georgics* 2.456; *Aen.* 8.294), Statius (*Theb.* 2.564), Ovid (*Meta.* 12.306), and Lucan (*Phars.* 6.391). According to Ovid, whose account Dante would certainly have known, Pholus participated in the war resulting from the rape of the women of the Lapiths by another centaur named Euritus. Pholus *(Folo)* is pointed out in company with Nessus and Chiron in *Inf.* 12.67–72, and there, as in Statius, he is said to be "full of anger."

Sally Mussetter

Photinus

Fifth-century deacon of Thessalonica who accepted Acacius's heretical denial of the divinity of Christ, asserting instead that Christ was begotten only as a mortal being. Photinus *(Fotino)* was sent to Pope Anastasius II, who attempted a peaceful reconciliation by allowing Photinus to take communion. For this act, Anastatius was himself seen as agreeing with the heresy. Dante places Photinus among the heretics in the sixth circle of Hell: *Anastasio papa guardo, / lo qual trasse Fotin de la via dritta* ("I hold Pope Anastasius, whom Photinus drew from the straight way," *Inf.* 11.9).

Pina Palma

Pia, La

The late-repentant who identifies herself in *Purg.* 5.133 as *la Pia* receives no description in the poem and is introduced only as the third of the spirits who urge their stories on Dante. Her words, like those of her two companions, Jacopo del Cassero and Buonconte da Montefeltro, recall the sudden, violent death that destined her to a sojourn among the late-repentant in the second division of Dante's Ante-Purgatory. From the earliest commentaries, but without known evidence, she has been identified as Pia Tolomei, of the noble family whose house in Siena now bears the inscription from Dante's poem; this Pia was killed in the Maremma by her husband, an important civic figure in Tuscany. Although she has one of the briefest speaking parts in the *Commedia,* her movingly restrained speech has provoked a response in readers out of proportion to its brevity. Not only does she preface her request with a compassionate anticipation of Dante's weariness when he returns to the world of the living; unlike the many other souls in this canto who are eager to tell their stories in order that Dante may carry news of them back to the world of the living, she asks only that Dante himself not forget her: *Ricorditi di me, che son la Pia* ("Remember me, I am Pia," 5.133).

Sara Sturm-Maddox

Piccarda Donati

Daughter of Simone Donati of Florence, sister of Corso and Forese Donati, and a relation of Dante by his marriage to Gemma Donati. Devoting her life to poverty, she chose to become a nun and entered the convent of Santa Chiara at Monticelli just outside Florence, joining the Order of the Minors founded by Chiara Sciffi, a follower of St. Francis, not long after 1212. Between the years 1283 and 1288, she was forcibly abducted from the convent by her brother Corso, who had arranged to marry her to Rossellino della Tosa in order to secure a politically advantageous alliance. Shortly after her marriage she fell ill and died. Early commentators diffused the story that her sudden death resulted from God's having granted her petition to escape an involuntary marriage in order to preserve her chastity.

Despite the fact that she was an innocent victim of political intrigue, Dante, by placing her in the Heaven of the Moon, calls attention to the weakness of her commitment to her sacred vow (*Par.* 3.34). Piccarda herself, in fact, informs the pilgrim Dante of her shortcomings and accepts responsibility for not resisting her fate and attempting to return to her conventual life. She is fully aware that by failing to return force against

Dante and Beatrice among the inconstant nuns. La comedia, ed. Pietro da Figino, 1491. Giamatti Collection: Courtesy of the Mount Holyoke College Archives and Special Collections.

force, she allowed her will to abet the force applied against her (*Par.* 4.80). If her will was weak in life, however, it is strengthened in the afterlife by the knowledge that God's will is her will. She repeatedly invokes variants of the word for "will"—*volontà* (70), *voler* (84), *voglia* (80) *voglie* (81), *'nvoglia* (84)—a series that culminates in what some have called the finest line of poetry in the *Commedia: E 'n la sua volontade è nostra pace* ("And in his will is our peace," 85). Although she inhabits the lowest and the slowest sphere, her joy and love of God are not thereby diminished, nor does she dwell on the events of her past. Transcending earthly affairs, she says little of a specific nature regarding her abduction or of what followed: *Iddio si sa qual poi mia vita fusi* ("God alone knows what my life was afterwards," 3.108).

Piccarda, the first soul Dante encounters in Paradise and the only soul in the Heaven of the Moon to appear (although Constance, daughter of Roger II of Sicily, is referred to), manifests a limited degree of perfection with respect to the souls in the higher heavens. She preserves a measure of her human outline, lacks exceptional brightness, sings alone, and moves with linear simplicity (3.123). She is, moreover, unable to express her joy collectively by joining with others to create a symbolic form greater than the self; because she abandoned the convent, such forms of community are beyond her capacity, and consequently in the Moon an aura of solitude prevails. Although Dante identifies her failing only as an abandoned vow, some critics have suggested that the souls in the Moon, together with those in the two subsequent heavens, Mercury and Venus, symbolize, respectively, a deficiency of each of the three theological virtues, faith, hope, and charity (Carroll). And in a kind of symmetry that extends across the three canticles, Dante appears to treat the theme of inadequate faith and failed will synchronically in each of the third cantos of each realm. It has been argued that the Moon is a kind of Ante-Paradise whose souls share with the neutrals of Ante-Inferno as well as with the late-repentants of Ante-Purgatory an inclination toward negligence (Russo); more recently, it has been argued that the neutrals in Hell and the excommunicate in Purgatory share with the inconstant nuns of the Moon a deficiency of faith and "delineate various degrees of human passivity in the face of political events demanding personal commitment" (Lansing, 71). Celestine V's abdication of the papacy, Manfredi's excommunication from the Church (with which he never sought reconciliation), and Piccarda's abandoned vow define a hierarchy of faith found wanting.

Dante shows a special interest in the first souls he encounters in each of the three otherworld realms (Francesca in Hell and Casella in Purgatory), but Piccarda is a figure for whom Dante reveals an unusual sympathy. In Purgatory he even asks her brother Forese about her fate (*Purg.* 24.10). One reason for this may be that he shares with her a personal tragedy of a similar kind. As Piccarda was driven from her convent, so Dante was driven from his native city Florence into exile—each instance, ironically, a result of her brother Corso Donati's political intrigue.

Bibliography

Battaglia Ricci, Lucia. "Piccarda, o della carità: Lettura del terzo canto del *Paradiso.*" *Critica e filologia* 14 (1989), 27–67.

Carroll, John S. *In Patria: An Exposition of Dante's Paradiso.* Reprinted, Port Washington, N.Y.: Kennikat Press, 1971 [1911].

Lansing, Richard H. "Piccarda and the Poetics of Paradox: A Reading of Paradiso III." *Dante Studies* 105 (1987), 63–77.

Levi, Ezio. *Piccarda e Gentucca: Studi e ricerche dantesche*. Bologna: Zanichelli, 1921.

Marti, Mario. "Lettura di *Paradiso* III." In *Letture scelte sulla Divina Commedia*. Edited by Giovanni Getto. Florence: Sansoni, 1970, pp. 937–948.

Russo, Vittorio. "*Pg.* IV: Belacqua e il suo tipico." *MLN* 102 (1987), 14–31.

Stefanini, Ruggero. "Piccarda e la luna: *Paradiso* III." *Lectura Dantis* 11 (Fall 1992), 26–41.

Richard Lansing

Pier da Medicina

Sower of discord punished in the ninth bolgia of Malebolge, where he displays a head and throat hacked in several places (*Inf.* 28.73). Although Piero's historical identification is uncertain, Dante appears to have known him personally (*Inf.* 28.71–72). The commentator Benvenuto da Imola, who claims they had met at Medicina, a town near Bologna, may be a reliable source of information.

Piero tells Dante (74–90) to warn Guido del Cassero and Angiolello di Carignano that they will be treacherously drowned by the *tiranno fello* ("wicked tyrant") *che vede pur con l'uno* ("who sees with only one eye"), Malatestino of Rimini. Having fomented strife, as Benvenuto relates, between Malatestino's father Malatesta and Guido da Polenta, Piero is an appropriate mouthpiece for such a prophecy.

Like his fellow sufferers, Piero is horribly mangled. Muhammad says that he and the sinners Dante sees with him *seminator di scandalo e di scisma / fuor vivi, e però son fessi così* ("were sowers of scandal and schism while they were alive and therefore are they cloven in this way," 35–36). Each scandalmonger is mangled differently, as though to suggest an exact fitting of the punishment to the sin in every case. Bertran de Born (118–142), who carries his severed head *a guisa di lanterna* ("like a lantern"), remarks, *Così s'osserva in me lo contrapasso* ("Thus you observe in me the counter-suffering," 142). Piero has his throat pierced, his nose cut off, and only one ear. The reader is invited to ponder the symbolic meaning of these details as they relate to the iniquity of one whose nose for scandal led him to use his ears and voice against the cause of peace.

Todd Boli

Pier della Vigna

Chief minister of Emperor Frederick II (Petrus de Vineis, or Vinea) and the main character with whom Dante-pilgrim interacts in *Inf.* 13. There, he is one of the suicides whose souls are represented in the form of gnarled, fruitless thorn bushes. Born at Capua around 1190, he studied civil and canon law at the University of Bologna, and in 1220 or 1221 he began a career of civil service as notary and scribe in Frederick's court. By 1225 he was appointed judge of the Magna Curia (the great court), a title he retained until 1247, although his duties and responsibilities exceeded those expected of one in that office. He seems to have been chief compiler of the *Liber Augustalis*, the revision of the imperial legal code that was completed in 1231; and from 1239 he was, with another judge, Taddeo da Sessa, de facto codirector of the imperial bureaucracy and judiciary. On Taddeo's death in 1247, Pier's status was acknowledged with the creation of the Byzantine-influenced title, "Protonotary of the Imperial Court and Logothetes of Sicily," but soon thereafter, in February 1249, he was removed from office, arrested, imprisoned, and blinded. A few months later, while a prisoner, Pier committed suicide—thereby preventing an apparently inevitable trial and execution—by rushing headlong into a stone wall, according to a story told by most of the *Commedia*'s early commentators.

In the poem, Pier is placed in the second ring of the seventh circle of Hell (*Inf.* 13.31–108). Here he emphasizes the concepts of justice and fidelity (forms of the words *fede* and *credere* recur throughout his presentation), concepts related to his judicial and administrative responsibilities while alive. He asserts his loyalty as one who remained ever faithful to his "glorious office" (62) and swears "by the strange new roots of this tree" (i.e., by his soul) never to have broken faith with his lord (73–75). He recalls the mannered rhetoric of the imperial chancery on several occasions, for example in casting blame for the collapse of his fortune on a conspiracy at the imperial court instigated by envy: "The whore that never turns her sluttish eyes away from Caesar's dwelling . . . inflamed against me all spirits; and those inflamed inflamed Augustus" (64–68). In response to this injustice, he says, he killed himself: "My spirit, at the taste of disdain, believing by death to flee disdain, made me unjust against my just self" (70–72).

Pier's narrative leaves Dante unable to speak—*tanta pietà m'accora* ("such pity weighs on my heart," 84), he tells Virgil—perhaps overcome by compassion for the suffering of one so magnanimous as Pier or by the injustice of his fate. From the fourteenth century, the most common response to the episode has been to take Pier's words at face value and see him sympathetically as victim of injustice. During the past quarter century, however, especially in North America, Dante scholars have increasingly viewed the words of souls in Hell in a rigorously ironic light, Pier's included. Such a view presupposes a gap between the sympathy expressed by the character Dante and Pier's infernal situation, which provides the unalterable evaluation of his life by the poet and, in the fiction of the poem, by God. Pier's case is complicated by the implicit correspondence between his experiences and Dante's: both were poet-rhetoricians who devoted their talents to civil service, and both claim to have been unjustly condemned by the governments they had served, making Pier the first of the poem's several mirrors of the exiled Dante—characters such as Brunetto Latini, Romeo da Villanova, and Boethius.

The narrative of Pier's downfall which evokes such sympathy is, of course, a self-representation, specifically his response to Virgil's invitation that he use Dante's unique status as infernal sojourner to revise history's evaluation of him. Anthony Cassell's convenient summary of the historical evidence demonstrates that Pier's official improprieties, both financial and judicial, render his protestations of loyalty irrelevant or deceptive. In addition, several recent studies (including those by Mazzamuto, Cassell, Chiampi, Stephany, and Biow, all in various ways indebted to the magisterial reading of Spitzer) emphasize a parodic rhetorical strain in the episode's echoing of both classical and biblical texts. The reference to Frederick as Caesar and as Augustus recalls the affectation of classical Roman imperial vocabulary at Frederick's court. Court documents also conventionally punned on Pier's name (literally, Peter of the Vineyard), speaking of him as both the St. Peter of the imperial church and as the vineyard whose fruits are his fellow courtiers. In the poem, his boast of controlling both keys to Frederick's heart parodically recalls the keys of St. Peter, and his soul has become a parodic vineyard. In such a view, Pier della Vigna's apology boomerangs to become an inadvertent self-condemnation. This interpretation, though increasingly widespread, is by no means universal. For recent essays congruent with the traditional sympathetic reading, see those by Higgins and by Scaglione.

Bibliography

Biow, Douglas. "Pier della Vigna, Dante, and the Discourse of Virgilian Tragedy in the *Commedia*." *Stanford Italian Review* 11 (1992), 131–144.

Cassell, Anthony K. "Pier della Vigna's Metamorphosis: Iconography and History." In *Dante, Petrarch, Boccaccio: Studies in the Italian Trecento in Honor of Charles S. Singleton.* Edited by Aldo S. Bernardo and Anthony L. Pellegrini. Binghamton, N.Y.: Medieval and Renaissance Texts and Studies, 1983, pp. 31–76.

Chiampi, James P. "*Consequentia Rerum:* Dante's Pier della Vigna and the Vine of Israel." *Romanic Review* 25 (1984), 162–175.

Fengler, Christie K., and William A. Stephany. "The Capuan Gate and Pier della Vigna." *Dante Studies* 99 (1981), 145–157.

Higgins, David H. "Cicero, Aquinas, and St. Matthew in *Inferno XIII*." *Dante Studies* 93 (1975), 61–94.

Huillard-Bréholles, Alphonse. *Vie et correpondence de Pierre de la Vigne.* Paris: Plon, 1895.

Maresu, Gabriele. "Vinea vs. Silva? In margine al canto XIII dell'*Inferno*." *Critica letteraria* 23 (1995), 97–107.

Mazzamuto, Pietro. "L'epistolario di Pier della Vigna e l'opera di Dante." In *Atti del convegno di studi su Dante e la Magna Curia.* Palermo: Centro di studi filologici e linguistici siciliani, 1967, pp. 201–225.

Olschki, Leonard. "Dante and Peter de Vinea." *Romanic Review* 31 (1940), 105–111.

Paratore, Ettore. "Analasi 'retorica' del canto di Pier della Vigna." *Studi danteschi* 42 (1965), 281–336.

Petrocchi, Giorgio. *La selva del protonotario.* Collana di linguistica e critica letteraria 6. Naples: Morano, 1988, pp. 83–100.

Ringger, Kurt. "Pier della Vigna o la poesia del segno." *Medioevo romanzo* 5 (1978), 85–99.

Scaglione, Aldo. "*Inferno XIII*." In *Dante's "Divine Comedy": Introductory Readings. I: "Inferno."* Edited by Tibor Wlassics. *Lectura Dantis* 6: Supplement (Spring 1990), 163–172.

Spitzer, Leo. "Speech and Language in *Inferno XIII*." *Italica* 19 (1942), 81–104.

Stephany, William A. "Pier della Vigna's Self-Fulfilling Prophecies: The 'Eulogy' of Frederick II and *Inferno* 13." *Traditio* 38 (1982), 193–212.

Villa, Claudia. "'Per le nove radici d'esto legno.' Nicola della Rocca (e Dante): Anamorfosi e riconversione di una metafora." *Strumenti critici* 6 (1991), 131–144.

William A. Stephany

Pier Traversaro

A descendant of a powerful Ghibelline family from Ravenna of Byzantine origin, born around the mid-twelfth century (c.1145–1225). He became a figure of major importance in his lineage, as well as in the city of Ravenna, where he was podestà (chief magistrate) on several occasions. Pier is mentioned by Guido del Duca in the second terrace of Purgatory, along with other noble and civilized individuals from Romagna (*Purg.* 14.98).

Paul Colilli

Pierre de la Brosse

Chamberlain of Louis IX, king of France, and minion of Philip III, his son, Pierre fell victim to bitter court rivalries. Jealous of the influence of Queen Mary of Brabant and her partisans, he spread rumors that she had poisoned Louis, the eldest son of Philip by his first marriage. He then found himself falsely accused of having exchanged treasonable letters with Alphonse X of Castille, with whom the king was at war, and of having caused the failure of the army in Gascony. He was quickly sentenced to death and hanged in 1278.

Dante sees Pierre *(Pier da la Broccia)* among other late-repentants in the Ante-Purgatory who died violently without last rites (*Purg.* 6.22). Deeming him innocent of the charges of treason, the poet admonishes Mary, who was thought to have falsely accused Pierre of trying to seduce her, against conduct that would send her soul to Hell (6.22–24).

Yolande de Pontfarcy

Pietro Bernardone

Wealthy wool merchant of Assisi, father of St. Francis. He had little sympathy for his son's desire to become a disciple of Lady Poverty. In *Par.*

11.89, Thomas Aquinas refers to the fact that St. Francis, in humility, called himself *fi' di Pietro Bernardone* ("the son of Pietro Bernardone").

Molly Morrison

Pietrobono, Luigi

Major Italian critic of the first half of the twentieth century, and friend and disciple of Giovanni Pascoli, who, like the poet, had a particular interest in deciphering Dante's allegory. Pietrobono (1863–1960) pursued his Dantean studies in Rome, organizing *lecturae* at the Casa di Dante and founding and directing several Dantean journals, including the early *L'Alighieri* (1890–1893), the *Giornale dantesco,* which he directed from 1921 to 1943, and the new *L'Alighieri* (founded in 1960), which continues to be published under his name.

As a persuasive and insightful scholar whose influence is still evident in Italian schools, he produced a commentary on the *Divina Commedia* (1918) as well as numerous critical studies of Dante's poem: *La teoria dell'amore in Dante Alighieri* (1887), *Il poema sacro* (1915), *Dal centro al cerchio* (1923), *Saggi danteschi* (1936), and *Nuovi saggi danteschi* (1954). In these works he sought to counter the Crocean principle that allegory had nothing to do with art by insisting that Dante's *Commedia* derived its meaning in large measure from a detailed understanding of allegorical images and events and the process by which polysemous forms revealed their hidden significance.

Bibliography

Vallone, Aldo. *Storia della critica dantesca.* Vol. 2. Milan: Vallardi, 1981, pp. 932–939.

———. "Luigi Pietrobono tra Dante e Pascoli con lettere inedite." In *Percorsi danteschi.* Florence: Le Lettere, 1991, pp. 131–147.

Zennaro, Silvio. "Scritti di L. P." *L'Alighieri* 1 (1960), 37–46.

Aldo Vallone
(translated by Robin Treasure)

Pilgrimage

The word "pilgrim" is etymologically derived from the Latin *peregrinus,* originally meaning "stranger" or "anyone who finds himself in a foreign land." Visits to holy places in the early Middle Ages were generally undertaken by the sick, who believed religious relics possessed curative properties (cf. *Fiore* 67.12–14, 224.3–4), and by the healthy, who regarded the hardships of the journey itself as an efficient means of spiritual cleansing and penance for sins. By the eleventh century, pilgrimages were widely considered the most efficient means of increasing one's chances of salvation. In response to the ever-increasing popularity of pilgrimages, the Church officially regulated the practice early in the thirteenth century, requiring pilgrims to dress humbly (cf. *VN* 9.3 and 9.9.4) and to carry a staff in order to be more easily recognized. Boniface VIII declared 1300, the year in which the *Commedia* is set, as the Golden Jubilee Year and granted plenary indulgences to all those (as many as 100,000, according to Villani) who visited certain churches or beheld the *sudarium,* or "Veronica" (the veil that Christ used to wipe his brow as he climbed to Calvary and that retained the image of his face; *Par.* 31.103–108), in St. Peter's Basilica in Rome (cf. *Inf.* 18.28–33). The common conception of the pilgrim as a sincerely devoted and deeply meditative traveler is central to the theme of the sonnet "Deh peregrini che pensosi andate" (*VN* 40) and to the simile of *Purg.* 23.16–21. Dante, following contemporary tradition, defined the term "pilgrim" in its general, secular sense as *chiunque è fuori de la sua patria* ("one who is traveling outside of his own country") and delineated its specific sense into three parts (*VN* 40.6-7): *chiamansi palmieri in quanto vanno oltremare, là onde molte volte recano la palma; chiamansi peregrini in quanto vanno a la casa di Galizia; . . . chiamansi romei in quanto vanno a Roma* ("They are called 'palmers' who cross the sea to the Holy Land and often bring back palms; they are called 'pilgrims' who travel to the house of Galicia . . . [cf. *Par.* 25.17–18]; they are called 'Romers' who travel to Rome" [cf. *VN* 40]).

Although Dante does indeed use the term "pilgrim" in its secular meaning (*Par.* 6.135, *DVE* 1.18.3, *VN* 41.5, *Rime* 100.15), it appears far more often in a metaphorical sense. Beginning with the commentary of Iacopo della Lana (1342), exegetes regularly have focused on the poet/pilgrim dichotomy in their examinations of various texts. The obvious parallels between the difficulties inherent in the travels of pilgrims and exiles lend themselves easily to a poetic fusion of the terms (*Conv.* 1.3.4): *per le parti quasi tutte a le quali questa lingua si stende, peregrino, quasi mendi-*

cando, sono andato ("I have wandered like a stranger, almost like a beggar, through virtually all the regions to which this tongue of ours extends"—cf. also *Conv.* 4.12.15; *Purg.* 8.1–6, 27.109–114; *Par.* 1.49–54).

Of even more profound significance, however, is Dante's use of pilgrim imagery and allegory in his representation of the otherworldly journey of the *Commedia,* a literary treatment which is firmly rooted in the scriptural tradition of perceiving life as a pilgrimage to God (2 Cor. 5:6–8; Eph. 2:19; Heb. 11:13, 13:14; 1 Pet. 2:11). In several early medieval and patristic texts, such as Gregory's *Moralia* (8.52.92), the anonymous *Epistle to Diognetus,* and Augustine's *De doctrina christiana* (1.4), the figure of the pilgrim, whether *viator* or *peregrinus,* serves as a metaphor for the Christian who travels through life on his way to Heaven, his most desired destination and true home. The pilgrim was charged in these writings with the onerous task of completing a hazardous journey while constantly beset by physical and spiritual adversity. Indeed, the successful voyage of Ulysses was often selected as the allegorical example of choice, a fact which interestingly complicates Dante's adaptation of the tale in *Inf.* 26. St. Thomas contributed to this motif in his discussion (*ST* 3.15.10) on the transformation of the *homo viator* (traveler) into the *homo comprehensor* (enlightened man), a conversion purposefully applicable to that of the *Commedia*'s protagonist (whom, on account of these intentional affinities, scholars often identify as the "pilgrim").

Dante elaborates his allegorical conception of earthly pilgrimage (*Epist.* 11.5, 11.26) throughout the *Commedia* in such a way as to underscore the correlation between the well-established doctrinal system described above and the literary depiction of the sinner who journeys through each of the three realms of the afterlife on his way to eventual enlightenment. Hence, the allegorical pilgrimage becomes the cornerstone of the transformation of the Bonaventurian journey to God into a momentous Christian epic. The word *peregrino* is first used in the *Commedia* by Virgil: *Voi credete / forse che siamo esperti d'esto loco; / ma noi siam peregrin come voi siete* ("You believe perhaps that we know this place, but we are strangers here, as you are," *Purg.* 2.61–63). When Dante, on the terrace of the envious in Purgatory, asks whether any of the shades there are from Italy, Sapia replies, *O frate mio, ciascuna è cittadina / d'una vera città;*

ma tu vuo' dire / che vivesse in Italia peregrina ("O my brother, each of us is citizen of one true city; but you mean to say 'who lived in Italy as a pilgrim,' " *Purg.* 13.94–96). All souls there had been pilgrims on Earth in that their "true city" is the City of God. The true destination of all pilgrim souls is Heaven, known also figuratively by the names of earthly places of pilgrimage such as *quella Roma onde Cristo è romano* ("that Rome in which Christ is a Roman," *Purg.* 32.102) and the Celestial Jerusalem (*li è conceduto che d'Egitto / vegna in Ierusalemme per vedere, / anzi che 'l militar li sia prescritto* ("it is granted him that from Egypt he come to Jerusalem to see before his warfare has been concluded," *Par.* 25.55–57). The church's prescription for the medieval pilgrimage to the Holy Land was consciously molded to reflect the departure of the children of Israel from Egyptian bondage, and the poet conflates the Exodus tradition with that of the palmer, emphasizing the salvific nature of the arrival in Jerusalem. In *Purg.* 33.76–78, Beatrice explains to Dante the purpose of his otherworldly experience: *voglio anco, e se non scritto, almen dipinto, / che 'l te ne porti dentro a te per quello / che si reca il bordon di palma cinto* ("I wish, too, that you carry it back within you, if not written, at least depicted, for the reason that pilgrims bring their staffs back wreathed with palms"). The artistic climax of the motif comes in the beautiful verses of *Par.* 31.43–48 as the pilgrim stands gazing upon the celestial rose, shortly before Beatrice takes her place among the heavenly host: *E quasi peregrin che si ricrea / nel tempio del suo voto riguardando, / e spera già ridir com'ello stea: / su per la viva luce passeggiando, / menava ïo li occhi per li gradi, / mo sù, mo giù, e mo recirculando* ("And like a pilgrim who refreshes himself, gazing, in the temple of his vow, and hopes, later, to relate what it is like: strolling with my eyes through the living light, I directed them along the tiers, now up, now down, and now circling back").

Bibliography

Basile, Bruno. "Il viaggio come archetipo: Note sul tema della 'peregrinatio' in Dante." *Letture Classensi* 15 (1986), 9–26.

Demaray, John G. *The Invention of Dante's Commedia.* New Haven, Conn.: Yale University Press, 1974.

———. "Patterns of Earthly Pilgrimage in Dante's *Commedia:* Palmers, Romers, and the Great Circle Journey." *Romance Philology* 24:2 (1970), 239–258.

Singleton, Charles S. " 'In Exitu Israel de Aegypto.' " In *Dante: A Collection of Critical Essays.* Englewood Cliffs, N.J.: Prentice-Hall, 1965, pp. 102–121.

Michael Papio

Pisistratus

A tyrant of Athens, Pisistratus *(Pisistrato)* responded to his wife's demand to punish a boy who embraced their daughter with an argument for clemency. He stands as an example of gentleness on the terrace of wrath (*Purg.* 15.94–105), where Dante paraphrases Valerius Maximus's version of the story (*Fact. Dict. Mem.* 5.1. ext. 2).

Jessica Levenstein

Pius I, Pope

Second-century pope, the exact dates of whose pontificate are uncertain but generally taken as c. 142–155. (The first redaction of the *Liber Pontificalis,* following the fourth-century Liberian Catalogue, places him after Pope Anicitus, whereas the second redaction places him before. This latter ordering accords with other evidence.) The tradition of his martyrdom, absent from the earliest sources, was established by the ninth-century author Ado of Vienne. It is followed by Dante (*Par.* 27.44), who makes St. Peter contrast the faithful witness of Pius *(Pio)* and other early popes with the degeneracy of their successors in the poet's time.

Michael Haren

Plato

Athenian philosopher, 428–348 B.C.E., founder of the Academy, teacher of Aristotle, and author of philosophic dialogues. Only one of Plato's dialogues was widely known in the medieval Christian West: the late cosmogony *Timaeus,* in an incomplete Latin translation by the fourth- or fifth-century Christian bishop Calcidius. However, some of his other teachings were known indirectly through Cicero, Seneca, and the Latin Neoplatonists (Servius, Macrobius, Augustine, Boethius, and others), and, eventually, through the critiques included by Aristotle in his own works, especially the *Physics, Metaphysics,* and *De anima.* His influence thus permeates medieval Christian thought.

P

Mentioned by name (as *Platone* or *Plato*) fifteen times in the *Convivio* (2.4, 2.13, 3.5, 3.9, 3.14, 4.6, 4.15, 4.21, 4.24), Plato is included in Dante's lists of the virtuous pagan philosophers in *Conv.* 4 and in *Inf.* 4, where he is ranked below Aristotle. In *Par.* 4.49–63, Beatrice cites Plato's doctrine (in the *Timaeus*) that souls return to their stars at death, giving it a favorable interpretation, "not to be derided," as referring to astrological causality, for which the soul's stars are to be praised or blamed. Dante's conception of the relation between microcosm and macrocosm also seems to have been influenced by the *Timaeus*. In his writings, Dante regularly employs the terminology of Plato's theory of vision (according to which the eye emits a beam of light), although, as he himself points out in *Conv.* 4.9, it had been conclusively refuted by Aristotle.

Robert M. Durling

Plautus

Early Roman playwright (c. 255–184 B.C.E.), born in Sarsina, Umbria, and known for his comedies, of which Dante had no direct knowledge. The poet Statius asks Virgil whether Terence, Caecilius, Plautus *(Plauto),* and Varius are among the damned and, if so, in which area of Hell (*Purg.* 22.98–99). Virgil replies that they, together with Persius, join Homer (and Virgil himself) in Limbo.

Guy P. Raffa

Polycletus

Celebrated sculptor of ancient Greece (c. 452–412 B.C.E.), acclaimed by Aristotle, Cicero, and others as unsurpassed in carving images of men (just as his contemporary Phidias was regarded as unsurpassed in carving images of the gods). Polycletus *(Policleto)* was frequently cited in the Middle Ages as an exemplar of artistic perfection. Dante mentions him in connection with the reliefs carved into the cliff-wall on the first terrace of Purgatory (that of pride), which he says would have put to shame not only Polycletus, but Nature too (*Purg.* 10.31–32). Dante viewed human art as an imperfect imitation of Nature, which in turn imitated God's eternal ideas; fashioned directly by God, these carvings surpass even the work of his finest imitators.

Olivia Holmes

Polydorus

Entrusted by his father Priam to the care of Polymnestor, the Thracian king, together with an abundant treasure, Polydorus is slain by his guardian and the money seized (Ovid, *Meta.* 13.429–438, 533–575). Dante recalls the murder of Polydorus *(Polidoro)* in *Purg.* 20.115. The passage *Inf.* 30.18 recounts the grief of his mother Hecuba, who discovers her son's corpse. Virgil's image (*Aen.* 3.22–48) of Polydorus transfixed with spear-shafts that have sprouted into saplings—which, when uprooted by Aeneas, ooze blood—serves as a model for the punishment of the suicide Pier delle Vigne, who is transformed into a bush (*Inf.* 13.22–51).

Diana Cavuoto Glenn

Polymnestor

A Thracian king entrusted with Priam's son Polydorus during the Trojan War, Polymnestor *(Polinestore)* kills his charge after the Trojans are defeated for the treasure the boy has brought to Thrace (Ovid, *Meta.* 13.429–438; Virgil, *Aen.* 3.49–57). He is named as an example of avarice on the fifth terrace of Purgatory (*Purg.* 20.114–115), and the incident is referred to in the description of Hecuba's madness (*Inf.* 30.16–21).

Jessica Levenstein

Polynices

Son of Oedipus, Polynices *(Polinice)* and his twin brother, Eteocles, killed each other in battle over the Theban throne, thus doubly saddening their mother, Jocasta (*Purg.* 22.55–57). Their abiding antagonism is manifested by the forked flame of their joint funeral pyre, mentioned by Dante in *Inf.* 26.52–54, and detailed in Statius, *Theb.* 429–432, and Lucan, *Phars.* 1.549–552. In *Conv.* 4.25.6, Polynices' lion skin elicits reverence in Adrastus, whose awe illustrates Dante's definition of modesty.

Jessica Levenstein

Polyxena

Daughter of Priam and Hecuba, she was taken captive and sacrificed on the tomb of Achilles after Troy's fall. She is alluded to (*Inf.* 30.17) in an extended simile that describes Hecuba's madness after seeing the bodies of Polyxena *(Polissena)* and Polydorus, a passage that has been praised as exemplifying a tragic style. See Ovid, *Meta.* 13.404–571.

Rebecca S. Beal

Pompey

Roman general and statesman, Gnaeus Pompeius Magnus (Pompey the Great), born 106 B.C.E., served with Julius Caesar and Crassus in the first triumvirate (60 B.C.E.). Caesar's increasing power led to dissension and, in 49 B.C.E., to the defeat of his armies. After fleeing first to Brindisi and later to Greece, Pompey *(Pompeo)* was slain in Egypt in 48 B.C.E. Pompey's early victories against Marius are cited by Justinian in the Heaven of Mercury (*Par.* 6.53) as progress, under the Roman eagle, toward the formation of the Empire.

Richard Lansing

Pound, Ezra

American poet born in Hailey, Idaho, where his father was working for the U.S. government on mining. Pound (1885–1972) spent most of his youth in Philadelphia, attending first the University of Pennsylvania and later graduating from Hamilton College, where he studied Provençal and Dante under W. P. Shepard. It was here that he first voiced his intention of writing a modern epic that would in some way resonate against the *Commedia.*

After being dismissed from Wabash College on his first teaching job, Pound removed himself to Europe for most of the rest of his life, living in London until after World War I, in Paris from 1921 to 1924, and in Italy, usually Rapallo or Venice.

Around 1912, he founded the Imagist movement with Hilda Doolittle and Richard Aldington, always crediting Dante as a prime inspiration because of his verbal precision. During World War I, he began to write his epic, *The Cantos,* although he was not clear about the form it would take. He knew only that the modern world did not want rigid distinctions between the *Inferno, Purgatorio,* and *Paradiso,* but an intermixing of the three.

However, the early cantos (1–30) have a hellish cast, especially those dealing with London (14–15), and the central cantos (31–70) show the activities of purgatorial builders, usually bankers, Chinese emperors, and good presidents like Jefferson

and Adams. With the onset of World War II, Pound made the mistake of broadcasting for Benito Mussolini; after the war he was apprehended by American military police, placed in a detention camp at Pisa (where he wrote the *Pisan Cantos,* his most famous later poetry), and finally remanded to St. Elizabeth's Hospital in Washington, D.C., where he spent thirteen years but avoided a charge of treason. He was freed in 1958 and spent most of his final years in Italy; he is buried in Venice.

Dante is cited or played off throughout Pound's work, from chapter 7 of *The Spirit of Romance* (1910) to the last cantos, "The Fragments," some of which were written not long before his death. To Pound, Dante was always the moral barometer of the modern world.

Bibliography

Dasenbrock, Reed Way. *Imitating the Italians: Wyatt, Spenser, Synge, Pound, Joyce.* Baltimore and London: Johns Hopkins University Press, 1991.

Pound, Ezra. *The Cantos.* New York: New Directions, 1970.

———. *The Spirit of Romance.* New York: New Directions, 1968.

Sicari, Stephen. *Pound's Epic Ambition: Dante and the Modern World.* Albany: State University of New York Press, 1991.

Wilhelm, James J. *Dante and Pound: The Epic of Judgement.* Orono: University of Maine Press, 1974.

James J. Wilhelm

Poverty

The topic of poverty (*povertà,* Lat. *paupertas*) takes several forms across the spectrum of Dante's writing, from the *Convivio, Fiore, Monarchia, Epistles,* and *Rime* to the *Commedia.* The basic sources on which he drew are outlined in *Conv.* 4.12–13. These are, in the order he lists them there: Boethius, *Consolation* 2. pr. 5 and met. 5; Cicero, *Paradoxa Stoicorum* 1 and 6; Proverbs, Ecclesiastes, and Psalms; Seneca, *Ad Lucilium* 17; Horace, *Satires* 1.1; Juvenal, *Satire* 10.22; and also, more generally, *la verace Scrittura* ("the truthful Scriptures")—which would include Gospel texts, such as Matt. 6:19–34 and 19:24, and Luke 16:19–31—and Lucan (*Phars.* 5.527–531).

Medieval views of poverty have been usefully outlined in such general histories as those by Mollat (see especially chapter 7), Geremek (see especially chapters 1.1 and 2.1), and Little. Geremek characterizes the medieval "ethos of poverty" in terms of "a conflict between two incompatible ideals: the heroic life of renunciation on the one hand, and the duty to help the poor on the other" (20). Drawing on Little, he also notes that by Dante's time, wealth was "no longer the result of privileges conferred by power, land ownership and military conquests" but was "based on money and expressed solely in money" (22). Compare Dante's comments on "new money" in *Inf.* 16.73–75 (*sùbiti guadagni,* "rapid gains") and *Par.* 16.49–72, and his concern with avarice (often symbolized by the figure of the *lupa* or "she-wolf") and usury throughout the *Commedia.*

Geremek identifies "the theme, frequent in Italian literature of the fourteenth century, of the moral vices which [poverty] engenders" as reflecting "the trend to reject poverty as a moral value" (31). This negative view is evident in Dante's reworking of the *Roman de la rose* in the sonnets of *Il Fiore* (especially nos. 71, 83, 85, 107, 114, 115, 117, 153, 160, 169) and, more personally, in his references to poverty as a condition of exile (see *Conv.* 1.3.3 and 5; *Epist.* 2.7, 13.88; *Par.* 17.55–60). Yet even in the latter conditions, poverty comes paradoxically to be valued. Justice *(Drittura),* the leading figure among the *tre donne* of *Rime* 104, describes herself as outwardly *povera* ("poor," 36), leading Dante to conclude that in such company exile is to be held an honor (76); while in his letter of 1314 to the Italian cardinals, he ironically equates the exile's poverty with the authority to prophesy (*Epist.* 11.9).

In both the *Convivio* and the *Monarchia,* the theme of poverty is also bound up with the questioning of authority, wealth, and power. In *Conv.* 4.10–13, Dante is pursuing his dispute with an emperor (Frederick II) on the subject of nobility and inherited wealth, and he argues that riches *non possono causare nobilitade perché sono vili* ("cannot be the cause of nobility because they are base," *Conv.* 4.10.7). At the end of this argument (*Conv.* 4.13.12), Dante stages an encounter between another ruler (Julius Caesar) and another pauper (Amyclas the fisherman), drawing on a scene from Lucan's *Pharsalia* (5.519ff.) which he uses again to illustrate the security of poverty in *Par.* 11.67–69. In *Mon.* 2.5.8–11, poverty in the form of austerity is identified as a virtue of republican Rome, and the consul Gaius Fabricius Luscinus (third

century B.C.E.) is cited as *altum . . . exemplum avaritie resistendi* ("a lofty example of resisting avarice"), as he is also in *Purg.* 20.25–27. At the opening of book 3 of the *Monarchia,* Dante takes on a prophetic role (much as he does in *Epist.* 11.9), to dispute the Church's claim to temporal wealth and power; and at the end of *Mon.* 3.10 (14–17) he cites one of the key Gospel texts on apostolic poverty (Matt: 10:9–10) to support his assertions that the Church is *omnino indisposita . . . ad temporalia recipienda* ("utterly unsuited . . . to receiving temporal things") and that the pope should, like the apostles, act merely as the guardian and administrator of the Church's patrimony *pro Ecclesia pro Christi pauperibus* ("for the Church and for Christ's poor").

In the *Commedia,* the theme emerges chiefly as a concern with apostolic poverty and as a critique of avarice, particularly in Florence and the clergy (above all the papacy). Dante thus seems mainly preoccupied here with what Gerhoh of Reichersberg had earlier defined as "the [voluntary] poor with Peter," rather than "the [involuntary] poor with Lazarus" (Mollat 103–104; Geremek 24), although the situation of the latter is alluded to in the process of criticizing the former, for instance in *Par.* 12. 88–96.

Clerical and papal avarice *(avarizia)* is explicitly addressed early in the *Commedia* (*Inf.* 7.37–48). It is the sin of which the simonist Nicholas III and his fellow "pastors" are accused by Dante-pilgrim (*Inf.* 19.104), and the one which is confessed and expiated by Adrian V (*Purg.* 19.112–114). The dependence of the Avignon papacy on Florentine financiers is emphasized at the end of *Par.* 9 (127–142), and the greed of the popes is linked there to that of Florence's *gente nuova* through the image of the "accursed florin" that has "turned the shepherd into a wolf"—thus also recalling the poem's initial image of the wolf as symbol of cupidity (*Inf.* 1.94–102). A similarly satirical point is made at the end of *Par.* 18 (133–136), where John XXII's devotion to the image of John the Baptist on the florin is said to render him oblivious to the apostolic examples of Peter and Paul.

Apostolic example and the ideal of voluntary poverty lie behind such criticisms, as the voices of Peter Damian (*Par.* 21.124–42) and St. Peter himself (*Par.* 27.40–60) make clear. Such ideals had (as Dante would have known) been associated with St. Bernard and the Cistercians, and during the late twelfth and early thirteenth centuries the imitation of the poverty of Christ had become an important issue for a variety of groups, from academics (Peter of Blois, Alanus of Lille) to radicals such as the Waldensians and the new mendicant orders, especially the Franciscans (see Mollat, 106–134).

The Franciscan ideal of apostolic poverty is most directly reflected in Dante's allegory of St. Francis's devotion to Lady Poverty in *Par.* 11.58–114—a tradition shaped by Thomas of Celano (*Vita Secunda* 55, dated 1246/47), by the anonymous *Sacrum Commercium sancti Francisci cum domina Paupertate* (dated between 1227 and 1270), and by Ubertino of Casale (*Arbor vitae*, p. 426a-b, dated 1305). The first beatitude, *Beati pauperes spiritu* ("Blessed are the poor in spirit"), accompanies Dante's ascent from the first terrace of Purgatory (*Purg.* 12.110), to which he has been admitted by an angel of Franciscan appearance (*Purg.* 9.115–120); and the concern with Franciscan poverty is signaled at a number of other points in the *Commedia* (see Petrocchi 51–52). The debate between the "Spiritual" and the "Conventual" Franciscans over the interpretation and observance of poverty as part of the Rule was in a particularly acrimonious phase during Dante's lifetime and the period of the *Commedia*'s composition (see especially Leff, chaps. 1–2, and Lambert), and the role of Ubertino in the conflict is directly referred to in *Par.* 12.121–126. Several of the popes whom Dante represents as betrayers of the apostolic ideal (Nicholas III, Clement V, and John XXII) actively intervened in the dispute, and Petrus Johannis Olivi, lector at Santa Croce in Florence from 1287 to 1289, was the leading exponent of the rigorist views on poverty associated with the Spirituals. The degree of Dante's own sympathy with the Spirituals' views on poverty and other issues cannot be precisely ascertained (see Davis), but his appropriation of Franciscan discourse on this subject suggests awareness of the contemporary debate.

Bibliography

Davis, Charles T. "Poverty and Eschatology in the *Commedia*." In *Dante's Italy and Other Essays*. Philadelphia: University of Pennsylvania Press, 1984.

Geremek, Bronislaw. *Poverty: A History*. Translated by A. Kolakowska. Oxford: Blackwell, 1994.

Havely, Nicholas. "Poverty in Purgatory: From *Commercium* to *Commedia*." *Dante Studies* 114 (1996), 229–244.

Lambert, Malcolm. *Franciscan Poverty: The Doctrine of the Absolute Poverty of Christ and the Apostles in the Franciscan Order, 1210–1323*. London: SPCK, 1961.

Leff, Gordon. *Heresy in the Later Middle Ages*. 2 vols. Manchester: Manchester University Press, 1967.

Little, Lester K. *Religious Poverty and the Profit Economy in Medieval Europe*. Ithaca, N.Y.: Cornell University Press, 1978.

Mollat, Michel. *The Poor in the Middle Ages: An Essay in Social History*. Translated by A. Goldhammer. New Haven, Conn.: Yale University Press, 1986.

Petrocchi, Giorgio. "Dante and Thirteenth-Century Asceticism." In *From Time to Eternity: Essays on Dante's 'Divine Comedy.'* Edited by Thomas G. Bergin. New Haven, Conn.: Yale University Press, 1967.

Nicholas Havely

Prayer

For most modern theologians, prayer is the conscious attempt by a believer to conform all of his or her life to the entire will of God. Christian prayer recognizes three distinct aspects: invocation, adoration, and petition. Although the popular idea of prayer sees the third aspect as the principal purpose for seeking union with the Deity, the first two (if recognized at all) being but preparation for the making of requests to the bounty of divine grace, Church doctrine gives equal weight to all three, even though its practice has often tended to favor the first two at the expense of the third. However, it should be noted that until well into the Middle Ages—perhaps even into the sixteenth century—the popular, petitionary understanding of prayer was by far the most widespread among theologians and ordinary believers alike, and for that reason it was probably the most influential in Dante's thinking on the subject.

The stress on invocation and adoration stems from the Christian belief that prayer is based entirely on the initiative of God, his "prevenient grace," given to faith in the redeeming mission, death, and resurrection of Jesus Christ. Thus, prayer begins with invocation, the "calling out" of God's name—not one's own, as would be the case if the Deity were aloof and its powers needed prodding. Adoration follows, as the Christian believer realizes that God's aid is there prior even to the

P invocation of his name. And just as adoration follows naturally on invocation, so then does petitionary prayer follow. God's initiative in grace, for which the believer is thankful and offers praise and love, moves the believer to ask for the shape his or her life must now take, the deeds he or she ought to do, and (only then) for the things needed to carry out the divine will. In this last phase, the believer's life is conformed to the providence of God initiated in the new life wrought by Christ. Accordingly, despite its predominance in the religious thought of the Middle Ages, the popular belief that prayer is above all a request that God fulfil our immediate wishes (stave off hardship, ensure good luck, provide worldly treasures, etc.) is an absurdity to true Christian prayer. Rather, one asks for only those earthly goods necessary for the success of the personal mission which, by its very nature, is intended to mirror the arduous and self-sacrificing mission of Christ.

The basic question asked of the prayerful remains even when the moment of petition is correctly understood: "Why ask God for anything if the initiative, the goal, and the means are entirely in his providence?" The doctrinal answer to this question (which Dante poses and answers in *Par.* 20–21, following the classic response given by St. Augustine in book 5 of the *City of God*) is clear: the priority of God's will in all things, his "predestination," is not the same as fate or predeterminism. The mere fact that God knows the future events in a man's or a woman's life does not mean that the actual execution of these events is not a result of the person's free will. In other words, predestination is about what God knows (future events, his and ours); it is about his powers of knowing, which so transcend ours that he can know what we will quite freely do.

It follows, then, that for the divine mind, human free will is a cause in the whole plan for creation. In prayer, the believer seeks to play the part, in love and service and in knowing that it pleases God to give him or her what is needed in the full fellowship of invocation and adoration. Petitions not made in the spirit of prayer are seen as instances of supreme vanity. One notices that in the *Commedia* all the petitions to Heaven are only for those gifts the pilgrim Dante will need to fulfil his epic and complete his poem (e.g., *Par.* 33.1–37). Indeed, the whole pilgrimage, so fraught with doubt, reflection, trial and error—that is, with free will—can be said to be an answer to the prayer of

the three ladies from Heaven for the lost soul of Dante (*Inf.* 2.52–112). This complex relationship between human and divine desire is dramatized in Purgatory, where the prayers of those who are still alive can shorten the period that the saved must spend to complete their penance. Manfred of Sicily, who is under a divine decree that requires him to delay his entrance into Purgatory proper for thirty times the number of years he spent as an excommunicate, beseeches Dante the pilgrim to ask his daughter Constance to pray for him, because *"ché qui per quei di là molto s'avanza"* ("for here we gain much from those back there," *Purg.* 3.145). Dante's position is accepted doctrine, based on 2 Macc. 12:42, 45–46. As St. Thomas makes clear, prayer can help to diminish the degree of punishment but cannot alter the state of happiness or unhappiness (*ST* 3, Suppl., 71.2). Prayers cannot benefit those who are condemned to Hell (71.5), only those in Purgatory (71.6). The prayers of the pagans, as Virgil explains in *Purg.* 6.34–48, can have no access to God and therefore fail, a point that dispels Dante's doubt that the souls in Purgatory cannot benefit from the power of intercession, a doubt that had arisen from his reading of *Aen.* 6.376.

In the *Commedia* there are frequent instances of prayer to the classical Muses and deities who inspire poetry and music, usually in the form of an invocation (e.g., *Inf.* 2.7–10, 32.10–13; *Purg.* 1.7–12; *Par.* 1.13–43). Dante believed that the entire classical dispensation was part of the Christian God's plan for history. But the greatest use of prayer is Christian, occurs in Purgatory, and is liturgical in nature. In all but three areas of Purgatory, each group of souls recites a specific prayer, taken from either the Psalms or church hymns, which are appropriate to the process of their particular spiritual renewal. Souls that have just entered the gate of Purgatory sing *Te deum laudamus* ("We praise thee lord," 9.140), and *Gloria in excelsis Deo* ("Glory to God on high," 20.136) upon leaving the realm after their spirits have been entirely cleansed, as the example of Statius makes clear. In the Ante-Purgatory, neither the excommunicate nor the indolent make prayers, while the unabsolved recite *Miserere* ("Have mercy," 5.24; Ps. 50:1) and the negligent rulers both *Salve regina* ("Hail, Holy Queen," 7.83; a hymn sung after Vespers) and *Te lucis ante* ("Before the ending of the day," 8.13; a Compline hymn). The proud recite a version of the Lord's Prayer in Italian (11.1–24;

Matt. 6:9–13); the envious cry out the Litany of the Saints (13.50–51; a petition commonly heard at the Easter Vigil); the wrathful recite *Agnus Dei* ("The Lamb of God," 16.19; John 1:29, 36); the slothful are the third group without a prayer, which links them appropriately to the indolent; the avaricious and prodigal recite *Adhaesit pavimento anima mea* ("My soul has cleaved to the dust," 19.73; Ps. 118:25); the gluttonous, *Labïa mëa, Domine* ("O Lord, open thou my lips," 23.11; Ps. 50:15); the lustful, *Summae Deus clementïae* ("God of supreme mercy," 25.121; a hymn sung on Saturday morning). And finally, in the Earthly Paradise, the souls sing *Delectasti* ("O Lord, how great are thy works," 28.80; Ps. 91:5). But the most remarkable prayer of the *Commedia* is reserved for the stupendous hymn in praise of the Virgin Mary which opens the last canto of *Paradiso, "Vergine Maria, figlia del tuo figlio"* ("Virgin mother, daughter of your Son," 33.1), delivered by St. Bernard, in which he beseeches her to grant his request that Dante gain access to the beatific vision of God. Although it draws on traditional concepts and phrases, and is particularly to the style of St. Bernard, this is the only prayer entirely of Dante's own making.

William Wilson

Pride

One of the seven capital sins, pride was universally viewed by theologians in Dante's day as the worst and most common human failing, and the root of all sin (Eccles. 10:15). Pride occupies a founding place in the history of sin: it first induced Lucifer to rise up against his creator, and led Eve to sin and to beguile Adam into sinning. A failure to respect the divine hierarchy, an appropriation to oneself of privileges not one's own, an overestimation of one's own merits and desserts, pride results in sinful acts that earn retribution in the afterlife. Although pride is divisible into several distinct types (including arrogance, vainglory, and presumption), it is always a discernible substratum of the defective human will.

The *Commedia* opens with the pilgrim's prideful attempt to save himself, to climb the mountain, to catch the leopard, on his own; the journey begins when he humbly asks for help. Indeed, pride is ubiquitous in Hell rather than localized, as Musa notes: "The key to the sins in Lower Hell is the 'evil will,' that is, an

Dante among the proud in Purgatory. La comedia, ed. Pietro da Figino, 1491. Giamatti Collection: Courtesy of the Mount Holyoke College Archives and Special Collections.

active willing of evil ends; and of all the capital sins, only pride and envy could cause such a will to evil" (228). The disorder, corruption, violence, chaos, and fraud portrayed in Lower Hell result from an arrogant rejection of the natural order, of fortune's natural reverses, and of the natural bond among all human beings (and particularly among family and compatriots). At the very bottom of Hell the poet places proud Lucifer, once fair and now hideous, gnawing the worst traitors and rebels in human history. At the bottom of Purgatory proper he positions pride, the gravest and also the archetypal sin, used to gloss for the reader the new laws governing this realm. He describes pride as the besetting sin of the pilgrim, for which he will do penance far longer than for envy (*Purg.* 13:133–138).

This said, however, it is clear that Dante as pilgrim and poet has an intricate and ambivalent relationship with pride. The entire pretext of the *Commedia* indicts him for it: he claims to have been singled out for sanctifying grace, uniquely rescued by a chain of intercession reaching from the Virgin Mary herself, and escorted by Virgil through all three realms of the afterlife, for the express purpose of saving his own soul from certain damnation. He claims that his journey was willed above, *dove si puote ciò che si vuole* ("where what is willed can be done," *Inf.* 3.95–96), and that for him alone the entire mechanism of retribution, restitution, and reward has been un-veiled—and crowned with the beatific vision. These claims necessarily foreground pride in our reading of the *Commedia;* the pilgrim may purport to have explained it away in claiming impenetrable divine grace, but the poet knows that the question is far from resolved. Indeed, despite his rhetoric of conscious sinfulness, the pilgrim retains title to a certain civic righteousness which puts him in a position to judge the many characters he encounters in the afterlife (e.g., *Inf.* 7, 19, 32).

Even more problematic is the issue of pride for the poet. If we accept the edifice of the *Commedia* as he presents it—as a true vision vouchsafed to him, not invented by him—we allow him to dictate, to a certain extent, our evaluation of his righteousness. This we may not be willing to do. But even if we do, what remains over and above the content of his vision is his formulation of it, his articulation of it in poetry, and that articulation is a matter of considerable pride to him. He works, reworks, polishes, and perfects the *Commedia;* at times he reveals a heightened consciousness of the poeticity of his creation and revels in ostentatiously disciplined rhetorical pyrotechnics (e.g., the transformations of the thieves in *Inf.* 25, the marble sculptures that seem to speak in *Purg.* 10), which betray nothing if not pride.

The terrace of pride episode (*Purg.* 10–12) has traditionally been read, rather literally, as Dante's own oblique confession to the sin of pride and an overcoming of it. In *Purg.* 10 the pilgrim encounters the souls of the prideful, so crushed as to look like corbels, the dignity of the upright human stance entirely lost. *Purg.* 11 presents Oderisi da Gubbio as an example of one who discredits excessive pride in artistic achievement and equates the claim for personal renown with vainglory, whose reward is empty and transitory. But in the middle of this intricately wrought masterpiece, the question the poet attributes to Oderisi rings false: *"Che voce avrai tu più, se vecchia scindi / da te la carne, che se fossi morto / anzi che tu lasciassi il 'pappo' e 'l 'dindi,' / pria che passin mill' anni?"* ("What more acclaim will you have if you strip off your flesh when it is old, than if you had died before you left off saying 'pappo' and 'dini,' before a thousand years have passed?," *Purg.* 11.103–106). If Dante endorsed this position he could only fall silent, or, rather, he would never have begun his undertaking. In *Purg.* 12, the pilgrim studies the floor reliefs which portray over-

The terrace of the proud. La comedia di Dante Aligieri, *with commentary by Alessandro Vellutello, published by Francesco Marcolini, Venice, 1544. Giamatti Collection: Courtesy of the Mount Holyoke College Archives and Special Collections.*

weening arrogance of many kinds—religious, political, personal, aesthetic, parental, and more—which destroys every realm and relationship of human life, in a poetic acrostic which spells *vom* (= *uomo,* "man"). The first of the seven P's (standing for *peccatum,* "sin") is erased from his forehead, and he climbs more easily; we are to understand, then, that he has been cleansed of his pride.

Whatever pilgrim and poet say about pride, the artistic achievement of the *Commedia* implies, and sometimes explicitly claims, a place for pride in human endeavor. Because the poem as artifact exists in its perfection only because of its maker's pride in it; because it claims that its magnificence is subordinated to the greater good and to God's loving intentions for humankind; and because the poem aims to be worthy of, not to rival, its divine source, Dante the poet in effect clears a space for a kind of pride which is not sinful, which is in fact righteous. The pride in our works and our being which Dante legitimates has a double basis: its harmony with the divine realm, and its integrity and usefulness in the human realm. Here again Dante valorizes the *beatitudo huius vitae* ("beatitude of this world," *Mon.* 3.16.7), making it clear that for him humankind has *duos fines* ("two ends," *Mon.*

3.16.7), and making it difficult to read the *Commedia* as solely "divine."

Bibliography

Barolini, Teodolinda. *The Undivine Comedy: Detheologizing Dante.* Princeton, N.J.: Princeton University Press, 1992, pp. 122–142.

Chiarenza, Marguerite Mills. *The Divine Comedy: Tracing God's Art.* Twayne's Masterwork Studies, No. 25. Boston: Twayne Publishers, 1989, pp. 56–92.

Forti, Fiorenzo. "Superbia e superbi." *Enciclopedia dantesca,* 5:484–487.

Mazzotta, Giuseppe. *Dante, Poet of the Desert.* Princeton, N.J.: Princeton University Press, 1979, pp. 227–274.

Shapiro, Marianne. "*Purg.* 11." In Tibor Wlassics (ed.), *Introductory Readings II: Purgatorio. Lectura Dantis* 12, Supplement (Spring 1993), 158–168.

Vickers, Nancy J. "Seeing is Believing: Gregory, Trajan, and Dante's Art." *Dante Studies* 100 (1982), 67–85.

F. Regina Psaki

Primum Mobile

The Primum Mobile is the ninth sphere in Dante's cosmology. The largest in size and swiftest in motion, it contains the other eight lower spheres and sweeps them along in its daily revolution around the Earth. As Dante explains in *Conv.* 2.3, Aristotle believed there were eight heavens, but his thesis did not account for the second, very slightly regressive, motion in the revolution of the stars. It was Ptolemy who surmised that the daily revolution around the Earth to which all the heavenly bodies were subjected could only be explained by the existence of a ninth, entirely transparent sphere that carried all the others with it. The ninth heaven was posited not just to explain the complex motion of the fixed stars but also to respond to the philosophical need to trace all movements to one simple motion. Consequently, this sphere was called the Primum Mobile, meaning "the first moving thing" (it was also called "Crystalline," because of its transparency). The Primum Mobile, then, was surmised, partly on philosophical grounds, as the beginning of all motion. Furthermore, being transparent in all its parts, its physical presence is not perceived but rather deduced from the motion of the other spheres. No other part of Dante's universe is so speculative in character. Its existence is postulated not because such a sphere can be seen but because it must exist if certain principles are to be upheld. We explain the same phenomenon with the rotation of the Earth, a hypothesis the science of Dante's age had excluded.

Dante's treatment of the ninth sphere is far more complex in the *Commedia (Par.* 27.100–148; 28; and *passim*) than in the *Convivio,* although its essential nature is the same. Contained only by the mind of God, it contains all physical creation, or space. Furthermore, unchanging in its perpetual motion, it provides the structure within which all change is framed: the means of measuring time by counting years, days, and hours. Its motion is ever even and ever the same, and it is so uniform that its parts are identical throughout its entire extension. The rest of the universe reflects the infinite aspects of God's bounty, the Primum Mobile its unified totality. And yet it is from this immense uniformity that all diversity derives, for this sphere is not only the outermost limit of the universe, it is also the beginning of creation. In fact, all the diversity fragmented into the millions of stars in the eighth sphere and from there distributed throughout the universe is contained in seed in this sphere's uniformity.

Because the Primum Mobile represents the beginning and end of creation, it is during the pilgrim's visit to it that Dante explores two fundamental principles of the physical universe: the derivation of physical motion from the spiritual motion of intention or love, and the theocentric message of the geocentric cosmos. It is, in fact, in the Primum Mobile that he has a vision of the circling of the nine orders of angels around a luminous center *(Par.* 28.12–40). The angels' circling is the spiritual motion of their love for God, and this love actually turns the spheres; that is, love is the direct cause of their motion. In this vision the pilgrim recognizes the model of the physical universe, but the copy seems backward, because the most brilliant and fastest moving circles in the universe are the largest, while here they are the smallest. Beatrice explains *(Par.* 28.58–78) that the spiritual greatness of the love of the angels closest to God is reflected in the universe by the greatness of the size and speed of the Primum Mobile. Just so, the love of the other orders of the angels, which although still great decreases as their rank decreases, is reflected in the other spheres, which become smaller and slower as they revolve closer

P

to the Earth. This correspondence of spiritual greatness and intensity to physical size and speed makes the universe's hierarchy an appropriate copy of that of the angels. The vision of an inside-out universe, at the edge of space, foreshadows the final stage of the pilgrim's journey, in which he will transcend space itself by moving into the spiritual dimension of the Empyrean, where all things revolve around the stability of God's love.

Marguerite Chiarenza

Priscian

Priscian (fl. first half of the sixth century C.E.), a major Latin grammarian, is placed by Dante in the circle of the sodomites (*Inf.* 15.109). Born at Cesarea in Mauretania, he taught grammar in Constantinople and wrote what was to become the most famous medieval Latin grammar, the *Institutiones grammaticae,* which was long used as a standard textbook in medieval schools. As is the case with Brunetto Latini, there seem to have been no references to Priscian as a sodomite prior to Dante's placement of him in this circle of Hell. The fact that Priscian was not a known sodomite has led some commentators over the centuries to suggest that Dante was referring instead to Priscillian, a fourth-century heretical bishop who, along with his followers, was accused of engaging in the practice of magic and had a reputation for promiscuity and sexual perversity. Other scholars have maintained that Dante was referring to a "magister Prisianus," a professor of grammar at the University of Bologna in the late thirteenth century, and a colleague of Francesco d'Accorso, who is mentioned in the following verse. However, the majority of critics agree that Dante was, in fact, referring to Priscian. Some scholars have theorized that Priscian's sin was not merely sexual. Pézard argues that Priscian's sodomy was grammatical in nature. Vance, citing a medieval legend which stated that Priscian renounced his religion in order to sign his name to his work, argues that Priscian's sodomy must be viewed as an idolatry of the text. Most modern scholars accept the interpretation of the fourteenth-century commentators, who suggested that Priscian was placed in this circle as a representative of teachers of grammar. The argument the early commentators cite is *pedagogus ergo sodomiticus* ("teacher, therefore sodomite"): it was widely believed in the Middle Ages that the close student-teacher relationship in seminaries, schools, and colleges often led to sodomy. Teachers of grammar were seen as especially prone to this practice.

Bibliography

Curtius, Ernst Robert. *European Literature and the Latin Middle Ages.* Translated by Willard R. Trask. Princeton, N.J.: Princeton University Press, 1973 [1948].

Pézard, André. *Dante sous la pluie de feu.* Paris: J. Vrin, 1950.

Schizzerotto, Giancarlo. "Uguccione da Pisa, Dante e la colpa di Prisciano." *Studi danteschi* 43 (1966), 79–83.

Vance, Eugene. "The Differing Seed: Dante's Brunetto Latini." In *Vernacular Poetics in the Middle Ages.* Edited by Lois Ebin. Kalamazoo, Mich.: Medieval Institute Publications, 1984, pp. 129–152.

Dana E. Stewart

Prodigality

In the fourth circle of the Inferno (*Inf.* 7), the pilgrim Dante encounters two groups of sinners, the prodigal and the avaricious, who repeatedly heave great boulders against each other while exchanging insults, then turn away, roll the stones back around in a semicircle, and clash again. This penalty probably derives in part from one witnessed by Aeneas in his visit to the underworld (*Aen.* 6.616), as well as from the mythical punishment of Sisyphus. The prodigal appear on the pilgrim's right hand, a somewhat less onerous collocation than that of the avaricious on the left, although the form of the punishment and the fact that the two groups are punished together suggest that Dante—following Aristotle *(Nicomachean Ethics)*—understood hoarding and squandering as opposite forms of the same sin, and virtue as a mean between two extremes. Both vices involve an endless, excessive, and ultimately fruitless concern with worldly goods, symbolized by the sinners' wasted energy in moving the boulders. The image of the circle traced by each pair of sinners is also related to the concept of Fortune's wheel. As Virgil explains at the end of the same canto, Fortune is God's obedient minister in charge of administering the world's riches. The avaricious and the prodigal are thus punished for vainly trying to resist the divinely ordained revolutions of Fortune by eternally turning in circles.

The prodigal are punished together with the avaricious again on the fifth terrace of Purgatory (*Purg.* 19), where they are found weeping with their faces to the ground. Only the avaricious are mentioned here, but we learn that the prodigal were on the same terrace three cantos later, when Virgil asks Statius how he could have found room in his heart for avarice. Statius replies that, on the contrary, avarice was too far removed from him, and he was guilty of the opposite form of excess (*Purg.* 22.22–36). A special category of prodigals, the spendthrifts or profligates, also appears in *Inf.* 13 in the Wood of the Suicides.

Bibliography

D'Andrea, Michele. "Dinamica della pena di avari e di prodighi." In *Il volo cosmico di Dante.* Rome: Ateneo, 1985, pp. 169–190.

Olivia Holmes

Prometheus

Son of the Titan Iapetus and the Oceanid Clymene, Prometheus *(Prometeo)* is traditionally represented as the creator of humankind, whom he fashioned from earth and water. He is also remembered for granting the gift of fire. Dante, in *Conv.* 4.15.8, alludes to Prometheus's identity as the son of Iapetus and confirms his status as humanity's creator (cf. Ovid, *Meta.* 1.78–83).

Diana Cavuoto Glenn

Prophecy

In the Middle Ages prophecy was associated not only with the prophetic books of the Hebrew Bible, such as Daniel, Ezekiel, Isaiah, and Jeremiah, but also with other Old Testament figures, such as Moses, who was considered the greatest of the prophets, and David, whose Psalms were interpreted as prophecies of the birth and sufferings of Christ. The prophetic tradition continued into New Testament times and included such figures as John the Baptist, the voice crying in the wilderness; John the Revelator, author of the Apocalypse; and Paul, whose Epistles warned of the Last Days, and who was reputed to be the author of the *Visio Pauli,* a popular otherworldly vision that focused on the punishment of the damned in Hell. Biblical prophecy, therefore, is one source of Dante's prophetic vision, as is evident in the very beginning of the *Commedia.* Isaiah 38:10 ("In the midst of my days I shall go to the gates of Hell") is alluded to in the poem's first line: *Nel mezzo del cammin di nostra vita* ("In the middle of the journey of our life," *Inf.* 1.1).

In the medieval tradition, prophecy was not limited to biblical figures; this gift of grace could be shared by Christian martyrs and other saints, later contemplatives, and hermits, as well as earlier classical oracles like the sybils, and pagan poets like Virgil, whose Fourth Eclogue was widely interpreted as predicting the birth of Christ. Even the fictional character Aeneas, whose underworld journey allowed him to glimpse his descendants' future, could play a prophetic role. Dante's seemingly humble comparison of himself to Aeneas and Paul at the beginning of the poem— *Io non Enëa, io non Paulo sono; / me degno a ciò né io né altri 'l crede* ("I am not Aeneas, I am not Paul; neither I nor others think me worthy of that," *Inf.* 2.32–33)—is the first indication that he implies a prophetic role for himself as pilgrim and poet, since he calls attention to the fact that he is about to undertake an otherworldly pilgrimage similar to theirs.

By the time Dante meets his great-great-grandfather, Cacciaguida, in the central cantos of the *Paradiso* (14–18), the poet's self-identification as a prophet has become explicit. Like the Old Testament prophets who were commissioned by God to speak out against the abuses of their times, Dante is given a direct commission by his crusading ancestor: *rimossa ogne menzogna, / tutta tua visïon fa manifesta; / e lascia pur grattar dov'è la rogna* ("putting aside every falsehood, make manifest all your vision, and just let them scratch where the itch is," *Par.* 17.127–129). Dante would seem to have become a second John the Baptist, his voice crying like the wind against the mightiest: *Questo tuo grido farà come vento, / che le più alte cime più percuote* ("This cry of yours will be like a wind that hardest strikes the highest peaks," *Par.* 17.133–134). This heavenly injunction received by the pilgrim as he nears the summit of his otherworldly journey is the basis for the prophetic voice adopted by the poet throughout the *Commedia,* particularly for his condemnation of Florentine politics. Speaking out against the evils of his time is a "forthtelling" that is as important to prophecy as is the "foretelling" usually associated with prophets. Here, both the daunting difficulty of Dante's tasks and the tone of uncompromising righteousness that he takes in addressing the spiritual and temporal leaders of his time mark him as a worthy successor to the great Old Testament prophets—perhaps especially to Jeremiah, whose exile can be seen as a foreshadowing of Dante's own.

Dante's zealous denunciation of Church corruption similarly receives prophetic justification in Heaven, this time from St. Peter, who, after condemning *"In vesta di pastor lupi rapaci"* ("In shepherd's clothing rapacious wolves," *Par.* 27.55), tells Dante to speak out: *e tu, figliuol, che per lo mortal pondo / ancor giù tornerai, apri la bocca, / e non asconder quel ch'io non ascondo* ("and you, my son, who because of the weight of your mortality will go back down again, open your mouth, and hide not what I do not hide," *Par.* 27.64–66). This commission from the first pope allows the poet to condemn the simoniac popes whom the pilgrim meets in *Inf.* 19. Here Nicholas III is stuffed upside-down in a rock while flames burn his feet, an apt parody both of Pentecost, when Peter and the other disciples received the gift of prophecy from the Holy Spirit, and of the humble crucifixion of Peter.

The canto of the simoniac popes includes both foretelling and forthtelling. The foretelling is put in the mouth of the proud Nicholas, who expects two further popes, Boniface VIII and Clement V (*Inf.* 19.52–54, 82–84), to follow him in this hellish papal succession as they followed him in earthly papal simony. The forthtelling comes from Dante the poet, who frames the canto with two denunciations of Church corruption and its root cause in material, rather than spiritual, wealth. The first identifies the popes as the *miseri sequaci* ("wretched followers," *Inf.* 19.1) of Simon Magus, the Early Church opponent of Peter who sought to purchase the Holy Spirit (Acts 8:14–24), and who, in medieval tradition, was understood to be a type of Antichrist expected to deceive the faithful in the Last Days. The second denunciation condemns the Donation of Constantine, traditionally the historical justification for the papacy's immense material wealth and political power: *Ahi, Constantin, di quanto mal fu matre, / non la tua conversion, ma quella dote / che da te prese il primo ricco patre!* ("Ah, Constantine, not your conversion, but that dowry which the first rich father took from you, has been the mother of so much evil!" *Inf.* 19.115–117). These condemnations and other allusions throughout the canto identify the simoniac popes as contemporary types

of Antichrist. While these condemnations are in the voice of the poet, Dante the pilgrim also takes on a prophetic role in this canto, as his position becomes analogous to that of the Two Witnesses (Apoc. 11:3) who were expected in the Last Days to oppose the bestial Antichrist. In medieval exegesis the witnesses were identified as Enoch and Elijah. In opposing the contemporary type of Antichrist, Dante becomes a type of Elijah, the prophet who was taken up into heaven in a fiery chariot, and Virgil a type of Enoch, the virtuous patriarch who lived before the age of the law.

Dante's prophetic voice is further supported by his understanding of history *sub specie aeternitatis:* his pilgrimage has given him the perspective of eternity, so that he can look upon individuals and historical events within the context of salvation history, running from Creation to Doomsday. Such a prophetic view of history is particularly evident in the apocalyptic visions Dante receives in the Earthly Paradise, as detailed in the concluding cantos of the *Purgatorio,* which draw on the imagery of Ezekiel, Daniel, and the Apocalypse. The various ages of salvation history are symbolically recapitulated in *Purg.* 29, and the tribulations suffered by the Church are presented allegorically in *Purg.* 32. Prophetic history is then explained by Beatrice in *Purg.* 33, where she takes on the role of angelic interpreter, explicating the mysteries of the heavenly procession much as an angel explains Daniel's enigmatic dreams to the Old Testament visionary and John's visions in the Apocalypse. Once again, in the midst of Beatrice's highly charged prophecy, Dante the pilgrim is given a prophetic commission: *Tu nota; e sì come da me son porte, / così queste parole segna a' vivi / del viver ch'è un correre a la morte* ("Do you take note, and just as they come from me, write these words to those who live the life that is a race to death," *Purg.* 33.52–54).

Much prophecy in the *Commedia* is *ex eventu*—that is, spoken after the fact. In Dante's fiction his pilgrimage is set in 1300, which allowed him to place "prophecies" in the mouths of his characters which would soon be fulfilled. According to Farinata, although the damned cannot know the present on Earth, they can see the future (*Inf.* 10.100–108); thus, unlike the false prophets and soothsayers whose suffering is described in *Inf.* 20, these hellish prophets are to be believed. Once again, the prophecies are political in nature. Ciacco the glutton, for example, foretells the bloody violence that will shake Florence, divide the Whites from the Blacks, and give Boniface VIII and Charles of Valois the opportunity to intervene on the side of the Blacks (*Inf.* 6.64–72). This intervention led to the downfall of the Whites, the party of Dante, and thus to his exile from Florence.

Dante's exile and the political machinations surrounding it are regular themes of such *ex eventu* prophecies. They may be brief allusions, such as Farinata's enigmatic warning about the "art" of returning from exile: *Ma non cinquanta volte fia raccesa / la faccia de la donna che qui regge, / che tu saprai quanto quell' arte pesa* ("But not fifty times will be rekindled the face of the lady who reigns here, before you will know how much that art weighs," *Inf.* 10.79–81). Or they may be lengthy, such as Cacciaguida's extensive foretelling of Dante's life in exile (*Par.* 17.49–99). But if they vary in length and intensity, they do not vary in truth. On the one hand, Cacciaguida speaking from the perspective provided by Heaven calmly compares Dante to a classical hero wrongly exiled from Athens: *Qual si partio Ipolito d'Atene / per la spietata e perfida noverca, / tal di Fiorenza partir ti convene* ("As Hippolytus left Athens, because of his pitiless, treacherous stepmother, so you must leave Florence," *Par.* 17.46–48). On the other hand, Vanni Fucci, in a bitter outburst, details the historical events leading to the defeat of the Whites at the Battle of Campo Piceno: *Pistoia in pria d'i Neri si dimagra; / poi Fiorenza rinova gente e modi. / Tragge Marte vapor di Val di Magra / ch'è di torbidi nuvoli involuto; / e con tempesta impetüosa e agra / sovra Campo Picen fia combattuto; / ond' ei repente spezzerà la nebbia, / sì ch'ogne Bianco ne sarà feruto* ("Pistoia first thins itself of Blacks; then Florence makes new its laws and people. Mars draws from Val di Magra a hot wind wrapped in roiling clouds, and with impetuous, bitter violence they will fight above Camp Piceno; and he will suddenly break the cloud, so that every White will be stricken by it," *Inf.* 24.143–150). The historical events are masked by the elliptical language of prophecy, which often uses meteorological as well as animal and numerological symbolism. In giving Vanni Fucci these words, Dante reveals his familiarity with the esoteric form of contemporary political prophecy.

Dante's prophetic view of history also tempted him to pronounce some genuine prophecies, which, unlike the *ex eventu* prophecies, went unfulfilled. He was convinced that the contempo-

rary descendants of Rome had a providential role to play in salvation history, just as the Pax Romana established by Caesar Augustus in Virgil's time had been crucial in establishing world peace in anticipation of the birth of Christ. Dante's hope for an imperial intervention into the tangled politics of Florence and the rest of Italy led him to place great faith in Emperor Henry VII, and, in his letter to the princes and people of Italy (1310), Dante praised him as a new Caesar Augustus. This suggests that the poet may have thought of himself as Henry's Virgil, as a prophet of the new age. If so, Dante was quickly disappointed, although he may also have hoped another would do what Henry failed to accomplish.

In the *Commedia,* genuine prophecy is much more difficult to decipher than that based on recent Florentine politics. At the very beginning of Dante's visionary pilgrimage, Virgil predicts the coming of a *Veltro* ("Greyhound," *Inf.* 1.101), who, nourished on wisdom, love, and virtue, will overcome the rapacious enemy and be the instrument of Italy's salvation, driving back into Hell the she-wolf who threatens Dante (*Inf.* 1.101–111). Beatrice foresees a similarly unidentified future savior, whom she designates with a numerical code common in medieval apocalyptic as well as political prophecies: *un cinquecento diece e cinque / messo di Dio* ("a five hundred ten and five, messenger of God," *Purg.* 33.43–44). This time the prophetic fury will be directed not against the she-wolf but against the enemies of the Church, the harlot and giant whom Dante has witnessed in his apocalyptic vision. The identification of the *Veltro* and DXV remains unclear, as does the question of whether at this point in his life Dante expected human or supernatural agents of salvation, despite critical attempts to identify both agents with Henry VII. But whatever the exact meaning of these two enigmatic prophecies, they are definitely associated with Dante's prophetic vision of Italy's political future and the role of the descendants of the Romans within salvation history.

Bibliography

Charity, A. C. *Events and Their Afterlife: The Dialectics of Christian Typology in the Bible and Dante.* Cambridge: Cambridge University Press, 1966.

Davis, Charles T. *Dante and the Idea of Rome.* Oxford: Oxford University Press, 1957.

Dronke, Peter. *Dante and Medieval Latin Traditions.* Cambridge: Cambridge University Press, 1986.

Emmerson, Richard K., and Ronald B. Herzman. *The Apocalyptic Imagination in Medieval Literature.* Philadelphia: University of Pennsylvania Press, 1992.

Kaske, Robert E. "Dante's *Purgatorio* XXXII and XXXIII: A Survey of Christian History." *University of Toronto Quarterly* 43 (1974), 193–214.

———. "Dante's 'DXV' and 'Veltro.'" *Traditio* 17 (1961), 185–254.

Nardi, Bruno. "Dante profeta." In *Dante e la cultura medievale.* 2nd ed. Bari: Laterza, 1949, pp. 336–416.

Reeves, Marjorie. "Dante and the Prophetic View of History." In *The World of Dante.* Edited by Cecil Grayson. Oxford: Clarendon Press, 1980, pp. 44–60.

Schnapp, Jeffrey T. *The Transformation of History at the Center of Dante's Paradiso.* Princeton, N.J.: Princeton University Press, 1986.

Richard K. Emmerson
and Ronald B. Herzman

Prose

In *Conv.* 1.10.12–13 Dante maintains that the beauty and power of a language can be better seen in prose than in verse, as the beauty of a woman can be more surely assessed when she is unadorned. This interesting line of reasoning calls attention to the stylistic care with which he composed five major works in prose, to wit: *Vita Nuova, Convivio* (these two being a mixture of vernacular prose and verse), *De vulgari eloquentia, Monarchia,* and *Epistles,* in addition to the *Questio de Aqua et Terra* (these last four all in Latin). This was also his way of bringing the Italian vernacular up to a high cultural level. While he was confident that Italian, thanks to him and his best predecessors, had equaled Provençal and French in poetic expression, he felt that he could also produce the most mature and sophisticated prose in any living language.

His contrastive assessment of the Romance languages of *oc, oïl,* and *sì*—namely Provençal, French, and Italian (here, in *DVE* 1.8, called the idioms of the *Yspani, Franci,* and *Latini*)—is important for Dante's notion of grammar. In *DVE* 1.6.3 he admits that *plerasque nationes et gentes delectabiliori atque utiliori sermone uti quam Latinos* ("most other countries enjoy a more pleasing and handy language than the Italians")—somehow echoing Brunetto's judgment of French as *la*

langue la plus commune et la plus délitable ("the most widespread and pleasing language"). Then in *DVE* 1.10.2–3 he cites the French claim to primacy in vernacular (narrative) prose: *Allegat ergo pro se lingua oïl, quod propter sui faciliorem ac delectabiliorem vulgaritatem quicquid redactum sive inventum est ad vulgare prosaycum, suum est* ("French can boast that because of its easy and pleasing diffusion whatever has been redacted and invented in vernacular prose rightfully belongs to it")—and gives, as second example, the *Arturi regis ambages pulcerrime* ("King Arthur's beautifully meandering tales"). Provençal, he writes, had the first vulgar poets, thanks to its greater perfection and sweetness *(tamquam in perfectiori dulciorique loquela).* Yet he believes that Italian can justly claim superiority over the others, not so much for the relative merit of being close to Latin at least in having *sì* for *sic,* or for its closeness to a rational philosophical grammar *(gramatica comunis—DVE* 1.10.4), but, more concretely, because its poets (i.e., mainly Cino da Pistoia and Dante) have added to the sweetness of Provence the rational, intellectually and philosophically grounded depth of the *stil nuovo: qui dulcius subtiliusque poetati vulgariter sunt, hii familiares et domestici sui* [i.e., of the Italian vernacular] *sunt puta Cynus pistoriensis et amicus eius* (ibid).

Medieval consciousness of linguistic and stylistic structures relied on the classical rhetorical tradition, as interpreted in the medieval *artes poetriae* and *artes dictaminis:* the former codified the rules for poetic or verse genres; the latter, flourishing in the centers of legal training, concentrated on the writing of formal letters. The *ars dictaminis* adapted the classical *clausulae* in the form of *cursus,* both being particular rhythms, especially at sentence ends. It is clear that Dante practiced the *cursus* methodically in his Latin prose, but some have denied the relevance of searching for it in his vernacular or that of other authors. Nevertheless, at least in the *Vita Nuova* he seems to have adopted the most common types of *cursus,* namely, the *planus,* the *velox,* and the *trispondaicus,* with limited use of the least common type, the *tardus.* Examples of these are, respectively: *lóro priéghi; mirábile Beatríce; pensáva duraménte;* and *maggióri parágrafi.* Regular use of the *cursus* is evident in the *De vulgari eloquentia, Monarchia, Questio de Aqua et Terra,* and especially *Epistole* I–XII. Examples are *ostèndere veritàtes* (*velox,* the most elegant and most frequent); *ingurgitàta*

refùndens (planus); and *occùlta et ùtiles (tardus)*—
all in *Mon.* 1.1.

Syntactically, one notes radical shifts from the
Vita Nuova, dominated by para-hypotaxis (a narrative and discursive style that blurs the distinction
between coordination and subordination: subordi-
nating conjunctions may be used as coordinating
ones), to the *Convivio,* where the periodic style
reaches unprecedented sophistication and logical
firmness. For both vernacular and Latin prose his
declared models were the Latin classics of Livy,
Pliny, Frontinus, and Paulus Orosius but also, even
for prose, the poetry of Virgil, Ovid, Statius, and
Lucan (*DVE* 2.6.7). This was because of Dante's
emphasis on the rhythmic and musical elements of
art prose, in line with the medieval habit of stressing rhetorical patterns and rhythms (poetry is language *musica poita,* "ruled by music"—*DVE* 2.4.2).

Dante's made-up examples of excellent prose
style in *DVE* 2.6 (the second in order, i.e., the
gradus sapidus constructionis, and the fourth and
last one, the *gradus excelsus,* befitting the canzone
and the tragic style) are indicative of his taste for
rhetorical figures supported by intellectual and
emotive commitment. They are the following: *piget
me, cunctis pietate maiorem, quicumque in exilio
tabescentes patriam tantum somniando revisunt*
("it makes me, who am second to none in the
capacity to feel pity for human misfortunes, sorry
to think of whoever, rotting in exile, can afford to
see his country only in his dreams"); *ejecta maxima
parte florum de sinu tuo, Florentia, nequicquam
Trinacriam Totila secundus adivit* ("Charles of
Valois, the new Totila, succeeded in casting out of
thy bosom the greatest part of thy flowers, oh Florence, but then he failed in his assault on Sicily").

Bibliography

Baldelli, Ignazio. "Lingua e stile delle opere in volgare di Dante." *Enciclopedia dantesca,* Appendice, 55–114.

Di Capua, Francesco. "Appunti sul *cursus* o ritmo
prosaico nelle opere latine di Dante Alighieri."
In *Scritti minori* I. Rome, New York: Desclée,
1959, pp. 564–585. Originally published in 1919.

Guerrieri Crocetti, Camillo. "Divagazioni sul *De
vulgari eloquentia.*" *Nel mondo neolatino.* Bari:
Adriatica, 1969, pp. 361–377.

Lindholm, Gudrun. *Studien zum mittellateinischen
Prosarhythmus. Seine Entwicklung und sein
Abklingen in der Briefliteratur Italiens.* Stock-
holm: Almqvist and Wiksell, 1963.

Lisio, Giuseppe. *L'arte del periodo nelle opere volgari di Dante Alighieri e del secolo XIII.*
Bologna: Zanichelli, 1902.

Scaglione, Aldo. "Dante and the Rhetorical Theory
of Sentence Structure." In *Medieval Eloquence:
Studies in the Theory and Practice of Medieval
Rhetoric.* Edited by James J. Murphy. Berkeley,
Los Angeles, London: University of California
Press, 1978, pp. 259–269.

Schiaffini, Alfredo. *Tradizione e poesia nella prosa
d'arte italiana dalla latinità medievale al Boccaccio.* 2d ed. Rome: Edizioni di Storia e Letteratura, 1969.

Segre, Cesare. "La sintassi del periodo nei primi
prosatori italiani." In *Lingua, stile e società.*
Milan: Feltrinelli, 1963, pp. 79–270. Revised in
1974.

Vallone, Aldo. *La prosa del* Convivio. Florence: Le
Monnier, 1967.

Zitarosa, Gerardo Raffaele. "La lingua italiana nel
Convivio e nel *De vulgari eloquentia.*" *Aspetti
letterari* 28 (1968), 19–30.

Aldo Scaglione

Proserpina

In Ovid's *Meta.* 5.346–571 the story of Proserpina
(Persephone in Greek), daughter of Jupiter and
Ceres, is told by the muse Calliope. As the king
of the underworld (Dis or Pluto) wanders in Sicily,
he is shot by Venus and Cupid and thus falls in love
with the innocent and chaste Proserpina, who is
gathering spring flowers near Enna in a grove
where *perpetuum ver est* ("spring is everlasting,"
Meta. 5.391). Wild with love, Dis seizes the terrified girl and carries her off to Tartarus, as Proserpina cries out to her absent mother. When Ceres
learns that her daughter is gone, she searches in
vain for her throughout the world, finally returning
to Sicily, where she discovers the place of Proserpina's disappearance. In her grief and rage Ceres
suspends Sicily's famous fertility until the nymph
Arethusa informs her that she has seen the sad and
fearful Proserpina reigning as queen of the underworld. In response to Ceres' poignant complaint to
him, Jupiter decrees that Proserpina can return
only if she has eaten nothing while in Hades. The
discovery that she has consumed seven infernal
pomegranate seeds prompts Jupiter to decide on a
compromise which changes Proserpina's sorrow
to joy: she will spend half of every year with her
husband, and the other half with her mother.

P

In *Inferno* Proserpina's identity as queen of the underworld is twice alluded to. In *Inf.* 9.44, the Furies on the walls of Dis are called the handmaidens of the *regina de l'etterno pianto* ("queen of eternal weeping"). In *Inf.* 10.80, Farinata predicts the coming of Dante's exile by means of a time reference that mentions *la donna che qui regge* ("the lady who reigns here")—a simultaneous allusion, it would appear, to Proserpina and to the Moon (and, perhaps, to Hecate as subsuming both).

The only time Proserpina is mentioned by name in the *Commedia* is in *Purg.* 28.50. Having entered the Earthly Paradise and reached the river Lethe, Dante sees a beautiful lady (not identified as Matelda until *Purg.* 33.119) gathering flowers and singing on the opposite bank. In his request that she move closer so that he can understand the words of her song, Dante states that she makes him remember *dove e qual era / Proserpina nel tempo che perdette / la madre lei, ed ella primavera* ("where and what Proserpina was, in the time when her mother lost her and she the spring," *Purg.* 28.49–51). While many commentators follow Lana in taking *primavera* to indicate the "spring flowers" that Proserpina drops as she is kidnaped, Buti's interpretation—that the word signifies simply the eternal springtime prevailing in Proserpina's idyllic grove, which, from Dante's point of view, would thus function as an (ultimately inadequate) figuration of Eden—is ultimately more convincing and more satisfying.

Bibliography

Armour, Peter. "Matelda in Eden: The Teacher and the Apple." *Italian Studies* 34 (1979), 2–27.

Brown, Emerson, Jr. "Proserpina, Matelda, and the Pilgrim." *Dante Studies* 89 (1971), 33–48.

Dronke, Peter. "Dante's Earthly Paradise: Towards an Interpretation of *Purgatorio* XXVIII." *Romanische Forschungen* 82.4 (1970), 467–487.

Hawkins, Peter. "Watching Matelda." In *The Poetry of Allusion: Virgil and Ovid in Dante's 'Commedia.'* Edited by Rachel Jacoff and Jeffrey T. Schnapp. Stanford, Calif.: Stanford University Press, 1991, pp. 181–201.

Pizzorno, Patrizia Grimaldi. "Matelda's Dance and the Smile of the Poets." *Dante Studies* 112 (1994), 115–132.

Kevin Brownlee

Provenzan Salvani

This Sienese Ghibelline, who remained faithful to his party, counterbalances the Ghibelline turncoat Aldobrandeschi among the political figures expiating the sin of pride on the first terrace in Purgatory (*Purg.* 11.121). He held many elected positions in Siena, worked with the populace for a fair system of taxation, and supported Frederick II and his sons Manfred and Conradin. As the most important Ghibelline general in Tuscany after the battle of Montaperti (1260), Provenzan was captured and put to death by the Florentines in 1269. According to Villani (*Cronica* 7.31), his head was cut off and carried about on a lance, fulfilling the prophecy that it would be higher than all others (which prophecy he had taken to signify victory). Since he had intended to destroy Florence, Dante's willingness to purge him seems to further a political evenhandedness in *Purg.* 11. However, Provenzan's action of humbling himself in the service of others may have been an unusually strong motivating factor: in order to raise the ransom for a friend held by Charles of Anjou, he sat in a public square and begged of the passers-by until he had collected the necessary sum. Commentators have pointed out that Provenzan could have procured the money by force, and they suppose that his charitable gesture atoned for his many acts of presumption.

Marianne Shapiro

Psalms

A collection of 150 hymns, prayers, poems, and lamentations found in the Writings, that part of the Hebrew Bible which includes such poetical works as Ecclesiastes and the Canticles. The word "psalm" comes from the Greek, where it indicates a poem sung to the accompaniment of a stringed instrument. In Hebrew, the collection is called "hymns" or "prayers," and only the ending of individual psalms suggests instrumental accompaniment. Patristic writers believed that David authored the Book of Psalms, and Dante seems to share this opinion, calling David *il cantor de lo Spirito Santo* ("the singer of the Holy Spirit," *Par.* 20.38) and identifying the more generic "psalmist" with David (*Purg.* 10.65, *l'umile salmista*, "the humble psalmist"; *Mon.* 1.13.5). For "psalmist" alone, see *Conv.* 2.3.11, 2.5.12, 4.23.8; *Mon.* 1.15.3, 3.14.6; and *Questio* 77. For the author of

Psalms as prophet, see *Conv.* 3.4.8 and *Mon.* 2.1.5, 3.3.12.

The early church used the Book of Psalms in worship; early commentaries suggest that the book was also used for private devotion. Christ's comment that "all things must be fulfilled that are written in the Law of Moses and the Prophets and the Psalms concerning me" (Luke 24:44) not only reflects the Jewish division of the Hebrew Bible into the Law, the Prophets, and the Writings but also suggests how Christians assimilated the Hebrew Bible, including Psalms, to their understanding of Christ as Messiah. Dante follows the precedent of St. Luke in treating the triad ("Moses and the Prophets and the Psalms," *Par.* 24.136) as comprehending the entire Old Testament. *"Moïse"* signifies the books of the Pentateuch, *"profeti"* the historical and prophetic books, and *"salmi"* the poetic and sapiential books.

The importance of Psalms to Christians throughout the Middle Ages is reflected in the popularity of Psalters, which included the text of Psalms and of the Pater Noster, Ave Maria, Gloria, Credo, and other formulas used for private and liturgical worship. For Dante, "Psalter" is interchangeable with "Psalms": thus *salmo* (*Conv.* 4.19.7; *Mon.* 2.9.1); *psalmo* (*Epist.* 13.62); *Salterio* (*Conv.* 1.7.15); *Saltero* (*Conv.* 3.4.8). In the *Commedia,* "Psalms" predominates (*Inf.* 31.69; *Purg.* 2.48, 28.80; and *Par.* 24.136 are examples, but see *tëodia* in *Par.* 25.73). The book is symbolized by one of the twenty-four elders in the mystical procession of the Earthly Paradise in Purgatory.

Dante quotes individual psalms frequently in the minor works (see, for instance, *Conv.* 2.3.11, 2.5.12, 3.4.8, 4.19.7, 4.23.8; *Mon.* 1.13.5, 7 and 1.15.3), usually in the Vulgate translation. That Dante knew other translations is attested by his citing an Italian translation of Ps. 9:11 in *Par.* 25.73–74. Like other medieval Christians, Dante experienced Psalms as both an oral and a written text. The Book of Psalms figures prominently in the liturgy, especially the Divine Office—originally organized so that all 150 psalms were recited during a week of devotions—but also in the prayers, antiphons, and responsories of the Mass. Dante's understanding of Psalms as an oral, liturgical text is most obvious in *Purgatorio,* where the psalms not only appear most frequently but are usually sung (2.46–47 [Ps. 113:1]; 5.24 [Ps. 50:3]; 19.73 [Ps. 118:25]; 23.11 [Ps. 50:17]; 28.80 [Ps. 91:5];

29.3 [Ps. 31:1]; 30.83–84 [Ps. 30:2–9]; 31.98 [Ps. 50:9]; 33.1–3 [Ps. 78:1]), often at a time corresponding to their hour in the Divine Office. Direct citations and more indirect allusions occur as well in *Inferno* (1.65; 7.76; 21.131 [see Ps. 50:3; 103.2; 34.16]) and *Paradiso* (22.94–95 [Ps. 113:3, 5]; 25.38 [Ps. 120:1]; 25.73–74, 98 [Ps. 9:11]; 32.12 [Ps. 50:3]). Dante probably used Psalms in private devotional practice as well: from the thirteenth century on, books of hours included at least seven penitential psalms and fifteen gradual psalms.

Medieval scholars citing Psalms follow the Vulgate translation because its numbering differs from that of other translations.

Rebecca S. Beal

Ptolemaic Universe

The term refers loosely to the geocentric models of the cosmos that prevailed in the West between the time of Aristotle and Copernicus. More narrowly it refers to the specific planetary system proposed by the Alexandrian mathematician Claudius Ptolemaeus in the second century. Dante's view of the universe is clearly Ptolemaic in the broadest sense of the term. But whether he accepts the details of Ptolemy's system, or is even fully aware of them, is less certain.

Ptolemy's most celebrated work is his treatise on astronomical motion, the *Almagest.* An immensely influential work, it was employed as a standard textbook throughout Europe until the latter half of the sixteenth century. The broad assumptions of the *Almagest* correspond on many points with those of earlier Greek science and, in particular, the cosmology of Aristotle. Thus, in the *Almagest,* Earth is pictured as a solid sphere fixed at the center of a series of concentric spheres. On the vast outermost sphere are arrayed the Fixed Stars, and on the inner spheres are positioned each of the seven planets: the Moon, Mercury, Venus, the Sun, Mars, Jupiter, and Saturn. All celestial motion is held to consist of circles and compound circles.

Ptolemy does, however, depart from Aristotle on a number of specific points and, more substantially, in his aims and emphasis. Aristotle's main purpose is identifying the causes of astronomical phenomena rather than providing a thorough description of planetary motion. Thus while his model of the heavens explains the very broadest features of the planets' movements, it does not allow for precise predictions that can be tested against observation. In the *Almagest,* these priorities are reversed. Apart from a brief introductory chapter in which Ptolemy sets out his assumptions about the physical universe, the *Almagest* is almost entirely concerned with the technical tasks of measurement and calculation. Ptolemy offers advice on the construction of astronomical instruments, tabulates observations made by previous astronomers, and presents a set of detailed models designed to fit those observations. Ptolemy's models allow him not only to predict eclipses—something that Hipparchus had already achieved—but also to account in a rigorous fashion for the retrograde motion of the outer planets and their periodic brightening.

Several mathematical devices are critical to Ptolemy's calculations and have, as a consequence, become associated with his name even though some were introduced by earlier astronomers. The most prominent of these is the epicycle—the only "Ptolemaic" device explicitly mentioned by Dante. To explain the observed variations in the planets' speeds and their varying brightness, Ptolemy postulates that each planet travels along two circles: one large circle (the deferent) whose center, roughly speaking, is Earth, and a smaller circle (the epicycle) whose center lies along the path of the first circle. Other devices include the eccentric and the equant, both of which allow the astronomer to account for observed irregularities in the movements of the various planets.

Though widely embraced for their predictive power, Ptolemy's constructions nonetheless provoked resistance, especially among close followers of Aristotle. The main point of contention was the physical status of the various mathematical devices that Ptolemy employed in his calculations. Were the epicycle and equant real, or were they merely convenient fictions? The skepticism of Averroës, who sits in the company of both Aristotle and Ptolemy in Dante's Limbo, is fairly typical. "Ptolemy," he notes, "was unable to see astronomy on its true foundations. . . . The epicycle and the eccentric are impossible. We must, therefore, apply ourselves to a new investigation concerning that genuine astronomy whose foundations are the principles of physics."

Dante certainly honors Ptolemy in the *Commedia* and elsewhere in his writings. In addition to Ptolemy's appearance among the virtuous pagans in *Inf.* 4, he is repeatedly named as an authority in the *Convivio* and in the *Questio de Aqua et Terra*

on matters both astronomical and astrological. Ptolemy is cited, for example, in Dante's discussions of the origin of the Milky Way (*Conv.* 3.14) and the nature of Mars's fiery influence (*Conv.* 2.13). The most pointed allusion comes in *Conv.* 2.3, where Dante sides with Ptolemy against Aristotle on the subject of stellar motion and the order of the spheres. In early Greek astronomy, the stars, alone among the heavenly bodies, were thought to complete a single perfectly regular motion, and it was therefore conventional to assign them a single sphere. This simple model, which Aristotle endorsed, was subsequently troubled by Hipparchus' discovery of a second stellar motion—the slow drift of the stellar sphere against the ecliptic (a motion that has come to be called "the precession of the equinoxes"). Ptolemy incorporates Hipparchus' discovery into his system, and so Dante comes to credit Ptolemy for correcting Aristotle.

This apparently technical matter has significant consequences because it leads to a renumbering of the spheres, a renumbering that Dante again credits to Ptolemy but that is in fact a much later embellishment. In the version of Ptolemy's system that Dante inherits and endorses, the sphere of the Fixed Stars is not the outermost sphere of the physical universe, nor is its proper motion the swift daily rotation with which it had previously been associated. The source of the diurnal rotation of the sphere of the Fixed Stars is attributed instead to a ninth, invisible sphere—the Primum Mobile—while the source of its slow precessional rotation is attributed to the sphere of the fixed stars itself.

Conv. 2.3 also contains Dante's fullest description of an epicycle. It is a significant reference on two counts: first, because Dante seems to treat the epicycle as an actual part of the physical universe and not merely a mathematical device; and, second, because he fails to describe the epicycle's function. Though elsewhere in the *Convivio* Dante exhibits a keen interest in connecting astronomical models with actual observations, he makes no effort in *Conv.* 2.3 to explain how epicycles might account for the retrograde motion of Venus and the other planets.

The planetary system of the *Commedia* is often referred to as "Ptolemaic," but this claim is accurate only in the very broadest sense of the term. Indeed, apart from the numbering of the spheres, Dante's system seems shaped more by Aristotle's influence than by the *Almagest.* Only once does a Ptolemaic term of art enter the poem:

Solea creder lo mondo in suo periclo / che la bella Ciprigna il folle amore / raggiasse volta nel terzo epiciclo ("The world used to believe, to its peril, that the lovely Cypriote, turning in the third epicycle, radiated mad desire," *Par.* 8.1–3).

This passage clearly echoes *Conv.* 2.3. Again, it is specifically Venus's epicycle that Dante chooses to point out. This time, however, Dante goes on to link epicycles with retrograde motion. Venus, he notes in a subsequent *terzina,* is *la stella / che 'l sol vagheggia or da coppa or da ciglio* ("the star that woos the sun, now at his nape, now at his brow," *Par.* 8.11–12). And yet if this passage seems an endorsement of Ptolemy's system, it is a decidedly ambiguous one. For alongside Ptolemy's theory of erratic motion, Dante alludes to another kind of planetary error: the erroneous pagan association of the planets with the gods. The main verb—*solea creder*—obviously governs the misidentification of the planets as divinities, but it also potentially governs the clause *volta nel terzo epiciclo.* It is, as a consequence, impossible to say for certain whether Ptolemy is being accepted or refuted in *Par.* 8—whether Dante is endorsing the epicycle as real or construing it as yet another dangerous pagan myth.

Bibliography

Boyde, Patrick. *Dante Philomythes and Philosopher: Man in the Cosmos.* Cambridge: Cambridge University Press, 1981.

Grant, Edward. *Planets, Stars, and Orbs: The Medieval Cosmos.* Cambridge: Cambridge University Press, 1994.

Moore, Edward. "The Astronomy of Dante." In *Studies in Dante. Third Series: Miscellaneous Essays.* Oxford: Clarendon Press, 1903, pp. 1–108.

Orr, M. A. *Dante and the Early Astronomers.* London: Wingate, 1913.

Taub, Liba. *Ptolemy's Universe.* Chicago: Open Court, 1993.

Toomer, G. J. *Ptolemy's Almagest.* New York: Springer-Verlag, 1984.

John Kleiner

Ptolemy

The most famous astronomer of classical antiquity, whom Dante places in Limbo, the first circle of Hell. Claudius Ptolemy in fact perfected and systematized the principal applications of mathematics, not only to astronomy and astrology but also to geography, optics, and music. Little is known of his life, except that he worked in Egypt—almost certainly at Alexandria—where he was active from 127 to about 170 C.E. His most famous work, the *Almagest,* as it came to be known, provided a mathematical model that largely accounted for the observed motions of heavenly bodies and hence had high predictive value. Dante seems to have known it only at second hand, perhaps from the epitome by Alfraganus (c. 850). The *Almagest,* together with several lesser treatises, provided the basis for the Ptolemaic system that dominated astronomy until Copernicus (1473–1543).

Ptolemy's major works on geography, optics, and musical theory were not available to Dante in Latin translation, though their indirect influence was nonetheless considerable. He also provided the theoretical basis for the astrolabe and may be regarded as its inventor. Of all Ptolemy's works, Dante probably had firsthand knowledge only of the *Quadripartitum* (Greek = *Tetrabiblos*), a textbook of astrology. Ptolemy himself considered astrology as astronomy in the service of medicine (*Quad.* 1.3), and for that reason it would seem that Dante appropriately placed Ptolemy between the geometer Euclid and the physician Hippocrates in the Noble Castle (*Inf.* 4.142). He also cites him in *VN* 29; *Conv.* 2.3, 13, 14; *Quest.* 21; and *Fiore* 170.7.

Bibliography

Carmody, Francis J. *Arabic Astronomical and Astrological Sciences in Latin Translation: A Critical Bibliography.* Berkeley, Los Angeles: University of California Press, 1956; Latin translations listed on pp. 15–21.

Kay, Richard. *Dante's Christian Astrology.* Philadelphia: University of Pennsylvania Press, 1994; bio-bibliography on pp. 261–263.

Ptolemy (Claudius Ptolemaeus). *The Almagest.* Translated by R. Catesby Taliaferro. In *Great Books of the Western World.* Edited by Robert M. Hutchins and Mortimer J. Adler. Vol. 16. Chicago: Encyclopaedia Brittanica, 1952, pp. ix–477.

———. *Tetrabiblos.* Translated by F. E. Robbins. Loeb Classical Library. Cambridge, Mass.: Harvard University Press, 1940.

Toomer, G. J. "Ptolemy." *Dictionary of Scientific Biography,* 2:186–206.

Volpini, Enzo. "Tolomeo." *Enciclopedia dantesca,* 5:620–621.

Richard Kay

P

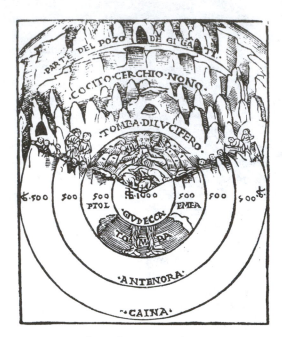

In tutti quefti difegni (come uoi hauete potute no
tare) manno molte cofe, & molte ce ne fono pofte
quafi (come uulgarmente fi dice) alla burchia
rifpecto alla fcarfita delli fpatii & alla impoffi
bilita della

The last circle of Hell, from Commedia di Dante, *published by Filippo Giunti, Florence, 1506. Reproduced by permission of the John A. Zahm Dante Collection in the Department of Special Collections, University Libraries, University of Notre Dame.*

Ptolomea

The third zone of Cocytus in the ninth circle of Hell, Ptolomea *(Tolomea)* is reserved for traitors of the guest-host relationship *(Inf.* 91–157). The precise allusion inherent in its name constitutes a minor exegetical conundrum. One possibility, now less in favor, is that it refers to Cleopatra's brother Ptolemy XII (51–47 B.C.E.), who ordered the assassination of his guest Pompey, whom he had reason to honor as an ally and benefactor when Pompey sought refuge in Egypt after his defeat at Pharsalus (48 B.C.E.)—Lucan for one bitterly denounces him for his violation of *fides* ("trust") and *pietas* ("piety"). The more favored view posits that it refers to the Ptolemy of 1 Maccabees, murderer of his father-in-law, Simon Maccabee, high priest and ethnarch in Israel and brother of Judas Maccabee, chief founder of the Hasmonean dynasty (exalted as *alto Maccabeo,* fighter for the faith in *Par.* 18.40–42). It should be added that Simon is credited with having renewed the Jewish alliance with the Romans, first made by Judas, in a letter from the consul Lucius Metellus enjoining the people to obey Simon, cited in 1 Macc. 15:17–18. Thus in the cases of both Ptolomeys there is a strong Roman thematic tie, alluding to the period shortly before the founding of the Roman Empire, and consequently it is also possible Dante meant to allude to both.

The guest-host relationship constitutes a deep and sacred value in ancient cultures, involving a kind of special family nexus, enhanced by a special trust within the context of a meal or banquet. It is clear that Dante takes it with the utmost seriousness. He has the Ptolomeans positioned with their heads thrown back such that their tears are frozen in their eye sockets. The chief exemplar in *Inf.* 33 is Fra Alberigo Manfredi, a noble Guelf of Faenza and a Jovial Friar, who out of resentment and avarice had his cousin treacherously killed at a banquet meeting at his villa, arranged in order to effectuate a reconciliation among the quarreling factions of Faenza—and he surely induced his guest to the meal by dint of an oath, which he then violated. This is an example of special perjury and an infraction of the virtue of *veritas* ("truth telling"). The result of treachery of this type, as Dante has it, is the immediate descent of the soul of the sinner into Ptolomea, while the devil-controlled body remains on Earth for its allotted time. The second inmate cited is Branca d'Oria, of the prominent family of Genoa. Branca slew his father-in-law, Michele Zanche, governor of Logodoro, at a banquet in Sardinia to which he had invited him. Branca seems to have lived on to at least 1325. To be noted is that in both cases there is an accumulation of close relationships, which contributes to the gravity of the crime.

Bibliography

"Tolomea." *Enciclopedia dantesca,* 5:617–618.

Triolo, Alfred A. "*Inferno* XXXIII: Fra Alberigo in Context." *L'Alighieri* 11 (1970), 39–70.

———. "Matta Bestialità in Dante's *Inferno:* Theory and Image." *Traditio* 24 (1968), 247–292.

Alfred Triolo

Puccio Sciancato

One of five Florentines placed among the thieves in Malebolge, and the only spirit among them who does not undergo corporeal transformation *(Inf.* 25.148). A member of the Galigai family of Florence, he was banished with his children in 1268 as a Ghibelline. In 1280, together with others, he entered into a peace pact with the Guelfs. He is reported to have "committed beautiful and graceful thefts" and said to have been a "mannerly thief" who stole by day. His nickname *Sciancato* means "lame."

R. A. Malagi

Purgatorio

The passage from time to eternity; the overcoming of sin; the redemptive potential of poetry, imagination, and art; the Bible as model book; the advent of Beatrice; God's salvific plan and the role of the Roman emperor: these are the great themes of Dante's second canticle.

Having reached the shores of Mount Purgatory after his lengthy detour through Hell, Dante-pilgrim now successfully realizes the ascent that he failed to complete in the opening canto of *Inferno*. The ascent consists in a step-by-step process of purification whose destination is the Garden of Eden, the Earthly Paradise, where man was created in the image of God. If sin may be compared to the layers of soot and varnish that, over time, diminish the beauty of an artistic masterpiece, then purgation strips away these accretions and restores the human image to its original divine splendor. This restorative process is literalized in the case of Dante-pilgrim. He begins the climb with the letter "P" traced seven times on his forehead (9.112), standing for the wounds of sin borne by all human beings after the Fall. As he clears each of the seven terraces, one mark is erased. He ends the climb as a blank slate, a double of the prelapsarian Adam. Freed from sin's disfigurements, baptized in the Edenic rivers of Lethe and Eunoe, he is reborn and ready to undertake the journey narrated in *Paradiso*.

Purgation assumes the form of a time-bound, dynamic process. Souls in Purgatory are on the move, and their mobility accounts for the tone of urgency set by Cato in canto 2: *Correte al monte* ("Run to the mountain," *Purg.* 2.122), the Roman patriot urges the laggard spirits, reminding them that time is precious here. For Dante-pilgrim time is precious because he has been granted only a three-day stay (*Purg.* 23.5–6). For souls undergoing purgation time is precious inasmuch as they have been assigned a sentence in exact proportion to the sins they have committed. Once they have "served their time" on a given terrace, they must

PVRGATORIO.

P ER correr miglior acqua alza le uele
Homai lanauicella del mio ingegno,
Che lascia retro a se mar si crudele.
Et cantero' di quel secondo regno,
Oue lhumano spirito si purga,
Et di salir al ciel diuenta degno.
Ma qui la morta poesia resurga
O sante Muse poi che uostro sono,
Et qui Caliope alquanto surga.
Seguitandol mio canto con quel sono,
Di cui le piche misere sentiro
Lo colpo tal, che disperar perdono,
Dolce color doriental zaphiro,
Che saccoglieua nel sereno aspetto
Del aer puro infin al primo giro,
A gliocchi miei ricomincio' diletto,
Tosto chi usci fuor de laura morta,
Che mhauea contristati gliocchi elpetto.
Lo bel pianeta che ad amar conforta,
Faceua tutto rider loriente
Velando i pesci, cherano in sua scorta.
I mi uolsi a man dextra, & posi mente
A laltro polo, & uidi quattro stelle
Non uiste mai, fuor che a la prima gente.
Goder pareua al ciel di lor fiammelle.
O settentrional uedouo sito,
Poi che priuato se di mirar quelle.
Come i da loro sguardo, fui partito
Vn poco me uolgendo a laltro polo
La, ondel carro gia era sparito,
m

Commedia di Dante, published by Filippo Giunti, Florence, 1506. Reproduced by permission of the John A. Zahm Dante Collection in the Department of Special Collections, University Libraries, University of Notre Dame.

press on to the next one, gaining freedom only when they have finished paying off their debt to God.

Purgatory's pilgrims measure out their sentences in the same units that mortals do their lives: units defined by the circling of the stars and planets. This explains why astronomical references abound in Dante's account of his spiral ascent as nowhere else in the *Commedia*. A few are symbolic, like the constellations that appear in cantos 1 (vv. 23–24) and 8 (vv. 89–90), representing the four cardinal and the three theological virtues. Most mark the relation between Dante-pilgrim's position on the mountain and the movements of the Sun, playing upon liturgical traditions that

P associate the Sun with divine guidance, sunrise with resurrection, and nightfall with death. The Sun serves as a literal guide up the slopes of Mount Purgatory, since *andar sù di notte non si puote* ("we cannot ascend by night," *Purg.* 7.44) because, without its rays, *ben si poria con lei tornare in giuso* ("one can of course descend [by night]," *Purg.* 7.58). Daytime is for circling and climbing; nighttime is for sleep.

Sleeping is associated with dreaming, and Dante's three-day sojourn on the mountain yields three interlocking dreams, described in cantos 9, 19, and 27. Of decisive importance to *Purgatorio's* meditation on the perils and powers of images, these dreams are deceptive to the degree that their content is either mythic or imaginary. Thanks to subsequent decoding, however, each can be shown to contain a truth. The first involves the myth of Jove's rapture/rape of Ganymede. Dante imagines that he too was *ratto al sommo consistoro* ("carried off to the highest consistory," *Purg.* 9.24), like the most beautiful of mortal youths. This fantasy turns out to be doubly true. It is true first because, as he was sleeping, Lucy had lifted him up to Purgatory's door. But it is also true because to this first rapture will correspond a second: the flight into the Empyrean, described in the final canto of *Paradiso,* where he will encounter the Christian Jove. The protagonist of the second dream also comes from the world of myth. She is a *dolce serena* ("sweet Siren," *Purg.* 19.19). Transformed by the dreamer's imagination from a hag into a seductress, she is unmasked by Virgil as an emblem of corruption. The unmasker furnishes a gloss: *Vedesti . . . quell'antica strega / che sola sovr' a noi omai si piagne* ("You saw . . . that ancient witch who is the only thing they weep for now above us," *Purg.* 19.58–59). The siren/hag reveals the essence of the sins purged on the next three terraces: avarice, gluttony, and lust all are expressions of an unbridled love for evanescent goods. The third dream is of biblical derivation. Its subject is Leah and Rachel, traditional representatives of, respectively, the active and the contemplative virtues. Dreaming of these two Old Testament figures, Dante hints at the nature of the two ladies he will encounter in Eden: Matelda and Beatrice. Broadly concerned with the psychology of love and with the role of female intercessors, this tripartite sequence forms a crescendo. Moving from Greco-Roman myth to biblical typology, it sets up and prefigures the action of succeeding cantos, while dividing up the narrative action of *Purgatorio* into three discrete temporal units.

Reunion is another of *Purgatorio's* great themes: the reuniting of individuals with God as well as the mending of broken families and communities. Old friends and lovers are rejoined on the mountain slopes: friends like Dante and Casella (canto 2), lovers like Dante and Beatrice (canto 30). The citizens of cities rent by civil wars embrace one another as brothers, such as Virgil and his fellow Mantuan Sordello in canto 6. Bitter political enemies like Rudolf I (1218–1291) and Ottokar II forge eternal friendships (see canto 7). Warring polities make their peace. And the codes of civility which render harmonious coexistence possible are reborn. The political, moral, and spiritual rebirth carried out in Purgatory finds its highest earthly expression in the ideal of the Roman Empire—an ideal that shapes the whole of Dante's poem. Hopes for an imperial resurgence had suffered a blow with the condemnation for heresy in *Inf.* 10 of Frederick II. But, as is often the case in *Purgatorio,* when a father must be damned, a son is spared so as to imply the survival of the father's hopes. So the dream of empire lives on in Manfred, Frederick's son. An ugly wound across Manfred's brow suggests that the dream has been humbled (*Purg.* 3.108). Nonetheless, it remains alive: Manfred greets the pilgrim with a beaming smile (*Purg.* 3.112). Similar hopes are raised anew in Dante's famed invective on Italy's enslavement in canto 6 (vv. 76–151). They persist throughout the second canticle, coming to a head in Beatrice's mysterious prophecy that a *cinquecento diece e cinque* ("five hundred, ten, and five," *Purg.* 33.43)—a *DXV* or *DUX* (Latin for "leader")—will right all of history's wrongs.

As indicated by Dante's emphasis upon political matters throughout the *Commedia,* poetry has a key role to play in civilization's renewal—and nowhere more so than on Mount Purgatory's slopes, where the rebuilding of the body politic coincides with the reuniting of the Latin literary family. First the ancient Latin poets Virgil and Statius are brought together, followed by their vernacular successors: Dante, Guido Guinizzelli, Bonagiunta da Lucca, and Arnaut Daniel—all writers instrumental in the rebirth of literary language during the High Middle Ages. In this setting the theme of rebirth takes on an ever broader meaning. More than the rise of a new vernacular Latinity, more than the regeneration of individuals

Diagram of Purgatory, from the 1568 edition of the Commedia. *Dante, with commentary by Bernardino Daniello da Lucca, published in Venice by Pietro da Fino in 1568. Giamatti Collection: Courtesy of the Mount Holyoke College Archives and Special Collections.*

or communities, it refers to all human art. *Qui la morta poesì resurga* ("But here let dead poetry rise up again," *Purg.* 1.7), Dante intones in the canticle's opening verses. The descent into Hell entailed the death of poetry. Poetry "died" by becoming implicated in crimes against morality, nature, and the social order and, moreover, by being denied the full range of its expressive powers. Faced with the task of capturing the horror of a soulless, truly dead world, it is reduced to babbling of the sort that issues forth from the mouths of Plutus (*Pape Satàn, pape Satàn aleppe! Inf.* 7.1) and the giant Nimrod (*Raphèl maì amècche zabì almi, Inf.* 31.67). In *Purgatorio,* this trajectory is reversed. Poetry, the imagination, the arts—all come back to life. They rise again in the service of the restoration of values such as beauty, truth, morality, and community. They are reborn by becoming instruments of salvation, sparks that kindle other sparks.

The shift is already signaled in canto 2, where the cacophony of Hell gives way to the harmony of sacred song: "In exitu Israel de Egypto" ("When Israel went out of Egypt," *Purg.* 2.46; Ps. 113). Sung by souls who are themselves embarked on an exodal journey from the world of the living into Purgatory's promised land, Ps. 113 is the first in a long series of biblical and liturgical texts that will be heard as Dante and Virgil head toward the summit. The *Miserere* (Ps. 50) is chanted in canto 5 (v. 24); in canto 8 (v. 13) the Compline hymn "Te lucis ante" is sung; the "Te Deum laudamus" rings out as the pilgrim passes through Peter's gate (*Purg.* 9.140); Dante-poet translates the Lord's Prayer in the opening tercets of canto 11; and the Beatitudes are intoned on every terrace as an antidote to the sin to which they correspond. Biblical materials form the backbone of Purgatory's program to turn sinners against sin. Every terrace—whether in the form of bas-reliefs (pride), disembodied voices (envy), ecstatic visions (wrath), running spirits (sloth), prostrate souls (avarice), voices in a tree (gluttony), or singing (lust)—accomplishes its restorative work by presenting its denizens with examples to be imitated and counterexamples to be shunned. The lead example is always furnished by Mary.

The prominence granted to sacred materials in Dante's second canticle does not point to a rejection of secular or non-Christian poetry and art. On

P the contrary, the sacred and secular are viewed as complementary. Hence the inclusion of nonbiblical literary exempla within Purgatory's image bank. Hence also the many this-worldly creators encountered in Purgatory: musicians like Casella, illuminators like Oderisi of Gubbio, poets like Sordello and Bonagiunta. Their very number indicates that Dante viewed art as a pursuit with a built-in transcendental potential. Their current state of spiritual imperfection, however, underscores the fact that, no matter how ennobling, art alone is not enough. In order to fulfill their salvific potential, artworks and artists must find a point of anchorage in the sacred Word.

The supreme example of art's powers and limitations is Dante's guide. In cantos 21 and 22 the Latin poet Statius bears witness to the salvific power of Virgil's poetry, declaring that it was by reading the *Aeneid* that he was cured of the sin of prodigality (*Purg.* 22.37–45). Statius' reading might just as well be designated a misreading, because where Virgil had denounced avarice (*Aen.* 3.56–57), Statius heard instead a call to curb his excess spending. He then goes on to recount that his poetic apprenticeship coincided with his conversion to Christianity, thanks to Virgil's Fourth *Eclogue* (*Purg.* 22.64–73). The tale of Statius' conversion is of Dante's devising. Its purpose is to prove that even non-Christian poetry can spiritually enliven and enlighten. Poetry can provide models of moral rectitude. Poetry can prophesy events like the coming of Christ and can bring about the salvation of future readers. But this salvific effect cannot ensure an author's salvation, regardless of his actual faith. As a result, the *Commedia* insists that the divine Virgil walks in the darkness even as his creations light the way for future generations of readers. Blind to his own message of hope, he is the sole outsider of the second realm.

Virgil's tragedy is fundamental to the second canticle's ruminations on the nature of art. Virgil's role was defined as transitional from the outset. His task was to guide his charge to another guide. The mission is completed at the mountain's summit, where Dante-pilgrim's will is pronounced *libero, dritto e sano* ("free, upright and whole," *Purg.* 27.140). Until this juncture Virgil's guidance had been indispensable to the pilgrim's progress. Now it has reached its term, and Virgil can discern no further. The *occhi belli* ("beautiful eyes," *Purg.* 27.136) of Beatrice are required if the journey is to proceed.

The shift from Virgil's once discerning gaze to Beatrice's beautiful eyes crowns the ascent of Mount Purgatory. In a very real sense, it also stands as the central action of the entire *Commedia,* encapsulating the poem's overall movement from time to eternity, from nature to the supernatural, from poetic apprenticeship to poetic mastery, and from Latin cultural models to a vernacular Christian poetics. The transfer is carried out by means of three retrospective glances: the first suggesting the powers of Virgil's art; the second, its limitations; and the third, Dante's movement beyond Virgilianism toward a new, specifically Christian concept of literary art.

The first retrospective glance occurs at the close of canto 28 when Matelda reveals that the Earthly Paradise is not only the seedbed of the universe but also the true Parnassus. Matelda asserts that such was the model toward which Virgil had unwittingly reached out in the form of a poetic dream when composing his *Eclogues*. A smile flashes back and forth between Dante, Virgil, and Statius (*Purg.* 28.145–147) because poets had been denounced as traffickers in lies ever since Plato. But in a universe like Dante's where God himself is a poet, even blatant fictions like the myth of the Golden Age participate in sacred truths.

If the first retrospective glance underscores the continuity between human and divine artistry, the second adds a caveat: namely, that while poetic "lies" or "dreams" may indeed lead you to the Garden's edge, they cannot help you to cross over into Eden proper, unless illumined by the Christian truth. The message is brought home by means of an apocalyptic procession. Preceded by a candelabra that paints the heavens with the colors of the rainbow, the whole of the Bible parades before the poets' eyes, book by book. Scripture's triumph confirms what the programmatic use of biblical materials in cantos 1–27 had already implied: that, despite (or because of) its humble style, the Holy Book is the only absolute source of literary authority. The disclosure drives a subtle wedge between Dante and Virgil. Viewing the spectacle from within the Earthly Paradise, the former feels *d'ammirazion pieno* ("full of amazement," *Purg.* 29.55), while the latter, standing outside, appears *carco di stupor non meno* ("no less charged with stupor," *Purg.* 29.57; my translation). A pointed contrast lurks beneath the parity implied between the terms of comparison: Dante is "full," Virgil is "burdened"; Dante admires, Virgil is stupefied;

Dante is about to be included in the spectacle, Virgil is being abandoned.

What eludes Virgil in the Edenic pageant can be summed up in two words: "Beatrice" and "Christ"—two words that in a sense are one, since the procession celebrates the advent of Beatrice *as* Christ. Dante's identification of his beloved from the *Vita Nuova* with the Son of God may surprise the modern reader, given that Beatrice is no canonized saint. Audacious as it is, such a claim is grounded in Christian typological thought, which holds that beneath the apparently random surfaces of human history, there lies a deeper providential logic. This logic so thoroughly shapes historical events and human experiences that everything and everyone, no matter how humble or exalted, participates in its unfolding. It binds the past, present, and future together into an intelligible whole, saturated with forward and backward interconnections pivoting around the Christ-event. To fully live the Christian life is to participate in these interconnections, even to the point of "becoming" Christ. Yet such a metamorphosis does not entail relinquishing one's individuality; rather, one becomes a Christ-type, a double being, both Christ-like and unlike Christ.

Dante's Beatrice is such a being. When she strolled the streets of thirteenth-century Florence, the typological links to Christ were hidden to all except a young poet. He alone could read a deeper meaning into signs like the mysterious 9s that accompanied her earthly existence. Atop Mount Purgatory, those signs are made public. Beatrice is revealed as a kind of personalized Messiah, as the Christ-event in Dante's biography. Just as Christ is to human history, so Beatrice is to Dante. The connection is spelled out in an elaborate succession scene. Three Latin verses mark Beatrice's second coming. The first, *Veni, sponsa, de Libano* ("Come from Lebanon, my bride," *Purg.* 30.11), cited from the Song of Songs, looks forward to the arrival of a woman, conventionally allegorized as the Church, coming to be crowned. The second inverts this implicit allegory, identifying Beatrice not with the bride but with the *bridegroom,* or Christ. Shouted out by the throng gathered in Eden at the moment of Beatrice's epiphany, it reshapes the mocking cry heard as Christ enters Jerusalem to be crucified—*Benedictus qui venit in nomine Domini* ("Blessed is he who comes in the name of the Lord," Matt. 21:9)—into a more direct but no less masculine cry of celebration: *Benedictus qui venis* ("Blessed are you [i.e., a male] who come," *Purg.* 30.19). To this shift from feminine to masculine, from bride to bridegroom, Dante adds a full verse from *Aen.* 6, whose meaning as well as gender it reverses: *Manibus, oh, date lilïa plenis* ("O, scatter lilies with full hands," *Purg.* 30.21). Pronounced at the moment of greatest sadness in Virgil's epic—the moment at which the tragic price to be paid to found Rome has come fully into view—the verse had originally referred to the scattering of lilies over the corpse of the young Marcellus. Marcellus was the most promising of the Romans, so Virgil makes of his untimely death a symbol of the sacrifices that history imposes upon humankind. Dante asks his reader to revisit this verse from the perspective of the Crucifixion, showing how Christ's sacrifice transforms irony into allegory, classical tragedy into Christian comedy, Virgilian despair into Dantean hope. Beatrice returns from the dead to what were once the funerary flowers of Marcellus. These are now revealed as the eternal lilies of the Virgin Mary: flowers that signify the resurrection of the dead for all eternity.

Such is the context within which the pilgrim-poet casts a final backward glance at Virgil (*Purg.* 30.43–45). But Virgil is gone, and Beatrice has come: Beatrice, who will name him for the first and only time in the entire *Commedia* (*Purg.* 30.55); Beatrice, who will guide him on his journey through the heavens; Beatrice, who embodies both his poetic beginnings and his destiny as the founder of a new vernacular poetics—a Christian poetics fusing the exalted with the humble, the ancient with the modern.

Bibliography

Armour, Peter. *The Door of Purgatory: A Study of Multiple Symbolism in Dante's Purgatorio.* Oxford: Clarendon Press, 1983.

Auerbach, Erich. *Dante, Poet of the Secular World.* Translated by Ralph Manheim. Chicago: University of Chicago Press, 1961.

Barolini, Teodolinda. *Dante's Poets: Textuality and Truth in the Comedy.* Princeton, N.J.: Princeton University Press, 1984.

Fergusson, Frances. *Dante's Drama of the Mind: A Modern Reading of Purgatorio.* Princeton, N.J.: Princeton University Press, 1953.

Freccero, John. "Manfred's Scar." In *Dante: The Poetics of Conversion.* Edited by Rachel Jacoff. Cambridge, Mass.: Harvard University Press, 1986, pp. 195–208.

Hollander, Robert. *Allegory in Dante's Commedia.* Princeton, N.J.: Princeton University Press, 1969.

Lewis, C. S. "Dante's Statius." *Medium Aevum* 25 (1957), 133–139.

Mazzotta, Giuseppe. *Dante, Poet of the Desert: History and Allegory in the Divine Comedy.* Princeton, N.J.: Princeton University Press, 1979.

Moore, Edward. *Studies in Dante. First Series: Scripture and Classical Authors in Dante.* Oxford: Clarendon Press, 1896.

Schnapp, Jeffrey T. "Injured by the Light: Violence and Paideia in Dante's *Purgatorio.*" *Dante Studies* 111 (1993), 107–118.

———. "Dante's Sexual Solecisms: Gender and Genre in the *Commedia.*" In *The New Medievalism.* Edited by Kevin Brownlee, Marina S. Brownlee, and Stephen J. Nichols. Baltimore: Johns Hopkins University Press, 1991, pp. 201–225.

Singleton, Charles. *Dante Studies 1. Commedia: Elements of Structure.* Cambridge, Mass.: Harvard University Press, 1954. Reprinted Baltimore: Johns Hopkins University Press, 1977.

———. *Dante Studies 2. Journey to Beatrice.* Cambridge, Mass.: Harvard University Press, 1977.

Jeffrey T. Schnapp

Purgatory

In the *Commedia,* Purgatory is the second realm of the afterlife and the subject of the second *cantica, Purgatorio.* It is the place of temporary waiting and punishment for the souls of those who, by dying repentant of all mortal sins, have avoided damnation to the eternal punishments of Hell but who still need to be purified of the debt of temporal punishment which remains due to their sins before they can be admitted to Paradise.

The doctrine of Purgatory is not explicitly defined in the Bible but was evolved from what were seen as the implied meanings of a series of texts: those which stated that less serious sins would be tested, punished, or canceled by fire on the Day of Judgment; Christ's words on baptism by fire and the Parable of Dives and Lazarus; and in particular St. Paul's statement that each person who has built upon the foundation of Christ—whether of gold, silver, precious stones, wood, hay, or straw—will be tested by fire on the Last Day: "If the work he has built remains, he will receive his reward; if his work is burnt, he will suffer injury, but he will be saved, yet even so as if through fire" (1 Cor. 3:11–15; see also Ps. 16:3; Isa. 12:1; Ezek. 33:11–20; Mic. 7:8–9; Matt. 3:11; 5:22, 25–26; 12:31–32; Mark 3:28–29; Luke 3:16; 12:10, 58–59; 16:19–31; 1 John 5:16). The wood, hay, and straw were interpreted by St. Augustine as the loves of earthly things, which are burned away by sorrow; and for St. Gregory purgatorial punishment after death restored the power of love which had not been strong enough to cancel the sins. This punishment or fire came to be described with the adjective "purgatorial" *(purgatorius)* until the noun "Purgatory" *(Purgatorium)*—denoting a place in the afterlife—was introduced in the late twelfth century, alongside the account by Henry (or Hugh) of Saltrey of the Purgatory of St. Patrick, a hole in the ground on an island in Lough Derg in Ireland, where pilgrims doing penance could be purged of their sins. Though sometimes presented as a dungeon or cold place where the souls await the Last Judgment, Purgatory was more generally conceived of as a fire, or sometimes as a river of fire, located close to Hell and even an upper part of Hell itself. Whereas the fire of Hell is eternal, however, that of Purgatory is temporal (*Purg.* 27.127).

Closely bound up with the doctrine of Purgatory was the belief in the *suffragia mortuorum*—the masses, prayers, alms, and pious works by which the living could assist the souls of the dead and free them from their purgatorial pains. This doctrine was based upon the episode in which, when some of his soldiers slain in battle were discovered to be wearing idolatrous objects beneath their tunics, Judas Maccabeus made offerings for their sins, so demonstrating his belief that they would rise again to grace and that "it is a holy and wholesome thought to pray for the dead so that they may be loosed from their sins" (2 Macc. 12:40–46; see also 2 Tim. 1:18). The custom of praying for the dead on the anniversaries of their deaths was known to Tertullian, and the *Memento* of the dead was incorporated into the Canon of the Mass, probably from the time of St. Gregory.

The validity of prayers to release souls from Purgatory apparently conflicted with those texts which stated that they would remain there until the Last Day, and this formed part of a theological divergence between the Latin and the Greek churches concerning the fate of souls immediately after death. In a letter of March 6, 1254, to his cardinal legate to the Greeks in Cyprus, Pope Inno-

The mountain of Purgatory. La commedia di Dante Allighieri,
*illustrated by Ugo Foscolo and edited by Giuseppe Mazzini
(London, 1842). Giamatti Collection: Courtesy of the Mount
Holyoke College Archives and Special Collections.*

cent IV expounded the points of contact between
the two sides in that the Greeks held that, after
death, souls can make up for penances left unper-
formed and are purified of venial sins and small
defects by "transitory fire"; and for the Second
Council of Lyons in 1274, the Greek emperor
accepted a profession of faith which included the
doctrine of Purgatory while avoiding defining it
as a place and omitting the distinction between
venial and mortal sins: "That if those who are
truly repentant die in charity before they have
made satisfaction for their sins of commission or
omission with worthy fruits of penance, their
souls . . . are purged after death by purgatorial or
purifying punishments; and in the lifting of these
punishments they are assisted by the suffrages of
the living faithful, that is, by the sacrifices of
Masses, prayers and alms and other works of piety
which have customarily been performed by the
faithful for other faithful, according to the precepts
of the Church." This doctrine was incorporated,
after further debate, into the decree of union with
the Greek Church at the Council of Florence
(1439), and after it was rejected by the Protestant
Reformers, the Council of Trent reaffirmed the
need for temporal punishment after death, the existence of Purgatory, and the validity of masses and
prayers for the dead (1547, 1562, 1563).

The crucial concept underlying the doctrine of
Purgatory is that of the obligation to make satisfaction for sins after they have been forgiven. When
a sinner repents, God removes the guilt *(culpa)* and,
in the case of mortal sins, the obligation to eternal
punishment in Hell, but the debt of temporal punishment *(poena)* remains and must be paid off by
penances, namely, acts of satisfaction: those
imposed by the priest in confession, voluntary
penances, and the acceptance of sufferings sent by
God. Purgatory is the place where the punishments
not yet paid off in life are paid off after death, and
in the case of unrepented venial sins (which do not
carry the obligation to eternal punishment in Hell),
Purgatory removes the guilt too, as well as the punishments: "From the conclusions we have drawn
above. . . , it is sufficiently clear that there is a Purgatory after this life. For if the debt of punishment
is not paid in full after the stain of sin has been
washed away by contrition, nor again are venial
sins always removed when mortal sins are remitted,
and if justice demands that sin be set in order by
due punishment, it follows that one who after contrition for his fault and after being absolved, dies
before making due satisfaction, is punished after
this life. Wherefore those who deny Purgatory
speak against the justice of God. . . ." (Aquinas, *ST*
3, Suppl., Appendix 2.1). For St. Thomas, the pain
of Purgatory is twofold: "the pain of loss *(poena
damni),* namely the delay of the divine vision, and
the pain of sense *(poena sensus),* namely punishment by corporeal fire." The souls accept their satisfaction voluntarily as a way of obtaining good,
and, knowing they will be freed, they often ask for
prayers. Their torments are not administered by
demons or angels, but it is possible that "they take
them to the place of punishments." The severity of
the punishments in Purgatory is proportional to the
guilt, the duration to "the disposition of the person
punished," the submission of the affections to
venial sins, and "the firmness with which sin has
taken root in the subject." For Thomas, Purgatory
is situated close to Hell, although souls may be
punished elsewhere, "either that the living may
learn, or that the dead may be succored, seeing that
their punishment being made known to the living

P may be mitigated by the prayers of the Church," and he states that Purgatory remits the debt of punishment, venial sins, and the remains of sin, "and consequently the pain of fire only is ascribed to Purgatory, because fire cleanses and consumes" (*ST* 3, Suppl., Appendix 1.2, 2.2).

The process of making satisfaction for the punishment due to sins was thus twofold and continuous—by penances in life and by Purgatory after death—and the theology of Purgatory was also closely connected with that of "pardons" (indulgences), to which Dante alludes three times (*Purg.* 13.42, 62; *Par.* 29.120). By the power of the keys, opening the treasury of superabundant merit, the Church could commute a person's duty of penance into the performance of certain acts, such as praying at specified churches or shrines, participating in crusades, or giving money for spiritual causes. By helping to pay off the debt in life, indulgences reduced what remained to be paid in Purgatory after death; in the case of plenary indulgences, such as that of the year 1300, the punishment was entirely canceled for those who were contrite and had confessed their sins. Indulgences were often presented, incorrectly, as remitting the *culpa* as well as the *poena* of sins, and they were expressed in terms of periods of time, sometimes wildly exaggerated, of release from Purgatory; the falsification and selling of indulgences led to the rejection of the doctrine, alongside that of Purgatory, by the Protestant Reformers.

For Dante, Purgatory is the realm of the afterlife where the souls suffer contentedly in their preparation to go to Paradise (*Inf.* 1.118–120; *Purg.* 1.4–6, 65–66). He locates it on an island-mountain at the antipodes of Jerusalem, in the ocean of the Southern Hemisphere, where it was formed when the land there fled from Lucifer at the time of his fall (*Inf.* 34.112–126; *Purg.* 2.1–3; see also *Par.* 17.20, 137); and Dante's spiral journey up the mountain is a corrective unwinding of his spiral journey down the conical pit of Hell. Access to Purgatory was forbidden to the pagan Ulysses, for it was opened only at the Redemption as the place of purification for Christians who die repentant of their sins; its punishments will come to an end on the Day of Judgment (*Inf.* 26.133–142; *Purg.* 1.130–132, 7.4–6, 10.109–111).

The souls of the saved assemble at the mouth of the Tiber, and Dante indicates that, before they are ferried in the angel's boat to the shore of Purgatory, some are subject to an initial period of delay but that this has been reduced by the plenary indulgence of 1300 (*Purg.* 2.91–105; see also 25.85–87). The lower slopes of Dante's Purgatory are conventionally called Ante-Purgatory, and there the souls of the excommunicates, the lazy, those who repented at the moment of violent death, and the negligent rulers are excluded for statutory periods of time from entry through the door to the punishments of Purgatory proper (cantos 3–9; see 4.127–129). The lesson is that, while contrition and God's forgiveness (with or without the sacrament of confession) are essential preconditions for access to the whole mountain, those who did not perform acts of penance in life must make up time with time before they can start the active process of paying the debt of punishment in Purgatory after death.

Dante uses the noun *purgatorio* twice, both times with reference to the seven cornices of the mountain above the door (*Purg.* 7.39, 9.49). These constitute the realm for the remission of the temporal punishments which remain due to the seven capital sins (pride, envy, wrath, sloth, avarice and prodigality, gluttony, and lust) (cantos 10–27). Following contemporary beliefs, Dante may also be implying that the guilt as well as the punishment of venial sins in the seven categories is remitted here too. Overemphasizing this latter function of Purgatory, Jacques Le Goff incorrectly concludes that Dante neglects the teachings of theologians by structuring his Purgatory according to mortal sins (1984, 341).

Dante's Purgatory is the place where the souls pay the debt of satisfaction to God, so untying the "knot" which holds them back from going to Heaven (*Purg.* 9.126; 10.108; 11.88, 125–126; 16.24; 19.91–92, 140–141; 23.15; see also 30.142–145). The moral structure of the seven cornices is based on the doctrine of the redirection of the souls' power of love away from desiring evil for others, from defective love of good, and from excessive love of earthly goods and of the souls' realignment with their innate love of God, the Supreme Good and their Creator; in this way they regain true freedom of the will (*Purg.* 17.91–139, 18.19–75). The *poenae,* represented by the seven tracings of the letter "P," are removed progressively by a series of punishments appropriate to each sin, by liturgical prayers, and by the study of moral exempla, the "whips" and "bridles" (*Purg.* 13.37–42, 14.143–147). The punishments are inspired by the love shown by Christ on the cross and are both painful and joyful (*Purg.* 23.70–75, 86). Only on the first cornice is it implied that the severity of a soul's punishment is proportional to the gravity of the sin (*Purg.* 10.136–139); otherwise, the souls remain for long periods of time on the cornices pertaining to their particular sins before their purified wills sense the power to fulfill their simultaneous desire to ascend (*Purg.* 21.61–66). At each "pass of pardon" between one terrace and the next (*Purg.* 13.42), an angel erases one "P" of the seven, and one of the Beatitudes is sung (Matt. 5:3–9). In Dante's case, the removal of each "P" lightens the burden of his body and makes his climb easier (*Purg.* 12.115–126).

Throughout his presentation of Purgatory, and particularly in relation to the souls on the lower slopes, Dante adheres to the associated doctrine that the suffrages, especially the prayers, of the living who are good can commute the debt of satisfaction which the dead owe to God's justice and so can help them to pay it off; indeed, it is a duty of relatives to pray for their dead (*Purg.* 3.140–145; 4.133–135; 5.70–72; 6.25–42; 11.31–36; 13.125–129; 23.85–90; 26.130–132, 147; *Par.* 15.95–96).

Dante's conception of Purgatory is firmly based on the recently evolved theological doctrine concerning the existence of a place for the remission of temporal punishment after death, but upon this he constructs a highly original poetic world and logically structured scheme—not of a place merely of waiting or of punishment exclusively by fire but of a journey up a mountain through a series of different and appropriate punishments, expressing a process which is both negative (the payment of a debt) and positive (the curing of the will and the redirection of its love toward God). As a whole, Purgatory above the door presents a lesson on the path of penance each Christian should embark upon in life in order to reduce the debt to be paid in Purgatory; and, by providing an image of a truly penitential community, guarded by the angel doorkeeper, the vicar of St. Peter (*Purg.* 9.127–129, 21.54), and traveling to salvation, it stands also as a polemical warning to the corrupt Church on Earth and a model for its moral and spiritual reform.

Dante's location of Purgatory establishes a figural relation between the place of Christ's death on the cross, the process of purification from sin through the infinite merits of Christ's act of satisfaction, and the Garden of Eden (the Earthly Paradise), where Adam and Eve committed the first sin by eating the fruit of the forbidden tree. He situates the Earthly Paradise on the summit of the mountain, where it acts as the goal of the ascent, through purification, to liberty, original innocence, and earthly happiness as a prelude to the ascent to the Heavenly Paradise (cantos 28–33).

Bibliography

Armour, Peter. *The Door of Purgatory: A Study of Multiple Symbolism in Dante's "Purgatorio."* Oxford: Clarendon Press, 1983.

Augustine, St. *Enarratio in Psalmum CIII,* 5, and *Enchiridion,* chapter 68, in *Patrologia latina.* Edited by J.-P. Migne. Vol. 37, col. 1363; vol. 40, cols. 264–265.

Aurigemma, Marcello. "Purgatorio." *Enciclopedia dantesca,* 4:745–750.

Bastian, Ralph J. "Purgatory." *New Catholic Encyclopedia.* New York: McGraw-Hill, 1967, vol. XI, pp. 1034–1039.

Denziger, Heinrich (ed.). *Enchiridion Symbolorum, Definitionum et Declarationum de rebus fidei et morum.* 32nd ed. Revised by Adolf Schönmetzer. Barcelona: Herder, 1963, pp. 271–272, 276, 331, 380, 409, 411, 418–419.

Gregory, St. *In primum Regum expositiones,* II, 3, 26, in *Patrologia latina.* Edited by J.-P. Migne. Vol. 79, col. 123.

Le Goff, Jacques. *La naissance du Purgatoire.* Paris: Gallimard, 1981. *The Birth of Purgatory.* Translated by A. Goldhammer. Chicago: University of Chicago Press, 1984.

Morgan, Alison. *Dante and the Medieval Other World.* Cambridge: Cambridge University Press, 1990, pp. 144–165.

Piolanti, Antonio. "Purgatorio." *Enciclopedia cattolica.* Vatican City: Ente per l'Enciclopedia Cattolica e per il Libro Cattolico, 1948–1954, vol. 10, cols. 330–339.

Schnapp, Jeffrey T. "Introduction to *Purgatorio.*" In *The Cambridge Companion to Dante.* Edited by Rachel Jacoff. Cambridge: Cambridge University Press, 1993, pp. 192–207.

Thomas Aquinas, St. Appendix I, Question 2, and Appendix II ("Two Articles on Purgatory"). In *The "Summa Theologica" of St. Thomas Aquinas.* Translated by Fathers of the English Dominican Province. Third Part (Supplement) [tome 3]. London: Burns, Oates and Washbourne, 1922, pp. 224–235, 236–240.

Wolter, Hans, and Holstein, Henri. *Lyon I et Lyon II.* Paris: L'Orante, 1966, pp. 166–168, 276–278.

Peter Armour

P

Pygmalion

Son of King Belus of Tyre, brother of Dido, and nephew of Dido's husband Sychaeus. Pygmalion killed Sychaeus in hopes of acquiring his wealth, but Dido eluded the murderer and took her husband's treasure with her to Africa, where she founded Carthage. In *Aen.* 1.340–164, Venus tells Aeneas of Pygmalion's treachery, parricide, and frustrated theft. Pygmalion *(Pigmalïone)* is included among the examples of punished avarice which are enumerated by Hugh Capet in *Purg.* 20.103–105. Hugh calls Pygmalïon *traditore e ladro e paricida* ("traitor and thief and parricide") and attributes Pygmalion's crimes to *la voglia sua de l'oro ghiotta* ("his gluttonous desire for gold").

Todd Boli

Pyramus

In *Meta.* 4.55–166 Ovid recounts the tragic tale of Pyramus *(Piramo)* and Thisbe *(Tisbe),* ancient Babylonian lovers at the time of Queen Semiramis. Forbidden to marry, the youths decide to rendezvous outside the city walls at the tomb of Ninus under a white mulberry tree. Thisbe arrives first, is frightened by a lioness, and flees, dropping her cloak, which the lioness smears with the blood of previous prey. Pyramus arrives, spies the bloody cloak and lion prints, and concludes that Thisbe has been devoured. Despairing, he stabs himself, and his spurting blood bathes the mulberry, changing its fruit from white to crimson. Thisbe returns and in horror calls out to her beloved, using her own name. At the name of Thisbe, Pyramus opens his eyes one last time and expires, after which, overcome by grief, Thisbe slays herself.

Medieval allegories of Ovid, such as Pierre Bersuire's *Ovidius Moralizatus,* interpret Pyramus as a Christ figure, and the bloodstained mulberry as a type of the Cross. With such an allegorical tradition likely in mind, Dante alludes in a simile to Pyramus by name in *Purg.* 27.38, comparing the dying youth to Dante-pilgrim, who stands before the purifying fire that will kill the "old man" of sin (cf. Rom. 6:6), and likening the sorrowful Thisbe to Beatrice, whose name inspires Dante to enter the flames. *Purg.* 33.69 compares the darkening effect of Dante-pilgrim's vain thoughts on his mind to Pyramus' bloodstains on the mulberry. A pass-ing reference to Pyramus also occurs in *Mon.* 2.8.4, but only in relation to the story of Ninus and Semiramis.

Bibliography

Lansing, Richard. *From Image to Idea: A Study of the Simile in Dante's "Commedia."* Ravenna: Longo, 1977, pp. 89–92.

Lorch, Maristella, and Lavinia Lorch. "Metaphor and Metamorphosis: *Purgatorio* 27 and *Metamorphoses* 4." In *Dante and Ovid: Essays in Intertextuality.* Edited by Madison U. Sowell. Binghamton, N.Y.: Medieval and Renaissance Texts and Studies, 1991, pp. 99–122.

Madison U. Sowell

Pyrrhus

Either the son of Achilles, who is reported by Virgil (*Aen.* 2.469–559) to have first brutally killed the aged Priam and then his son Polites, and, finally, to have sacrificed his daughter Polyxena to the shade of Achilles (*Inf.* 30.17); or the king of Epirus (c. 318–272 B.C.E.), who made war against the Romans but was finally defeated in 275 B.C.E. While Boccaccio favors Pyrrhus' identification with the son of Achilles, Benvenuto prefers the king of Epirus, as "the most powerful and most violent." Pyrrhus *(Pirro)* is punished among the homicides in the first ring of the seventh circle of Hell (*Inf.* 12.135).

R. A. Malagi

Pythagoras

Greek philosopher who lived c. 582–c. 506 B.C.E. He left no writings. Dante's knowledge derives from the works of Aristotle, Cicero, and St. Augustine. Most relevant to Dante's works are Pythagoras' theories of numbers, deemed the essence of all things, and of cosmology (fire is the center of the universe and its edge; in between, various planets revolve in ten concentric orbits; the antichthon [ἀντίχθων] protects Earth from the central fire). Pythagoras *(Pittagora)* is cited to define his era (*Conv.* 3.11.3); he is celebrated as inventor of the term "philosophy" (*Conv.* 3.11.4–5, 2.15.12; from Cicero *Tusculanae quaestiones* 5.3 and Augustine, *De civ. Dei,* 8.2). Dante cites his number theory (*Conv.* 2.13.17–18; from Aristotle, *Metaphysica* 1.5). Pythagorean cosmology is mentioned (*Conv.* 3.5.4–5; from Aristotle, *De caelo,* 2.13). Dante cites his theory that all souls are equally noble—not only human but also animal and plant souls and the forms of minerals (*Conv.* 4.21.3). In *Conv.* 4.1.1, Dante says he quotes Pythagoras, but he actually quotes from Cicero, *De officiis* 1.17. Dante also refers to his theory of fundamental oppositions—Plurality and Evil in one column versus Unity and Good in another (*Mon.* 1.15.2; from Aristotle, *Metaphysica* 1.5)—and further cites him in *Egl.* 3.34 as the "prophet of Samos."

Leslie Zarker Morgan

Q

Questio de aqua et terra

Informed by a militancy transcending the eminently speculative nature of the matter in hand, the *Questio,* along with the more or less contemporary eclogues, testifies eloquently to Dante's disposition as a poet-philosopher in the last years of his life. Delivered in the presence of the intellectual elite of Verona on January 20, 1320, the *Questio* has ostensibly to do with the problem of the apparently irregular relationship of earth (dry land) and water in an ideally concentric universe—the difficulty here being the standing proud of the former in respect of the latter in the inhabited part of the world. The question had enjoyed a good airing in Dante's time—most conspicuously, in the Augustinian Giles of Rome (Egidio Colonna)—and, in scrupulous obedience to the demands of quodlibetal intervention, Dante duly reviews the countertheses. Any attempt to resolve this question, he says, involves one or the other of two hypotheses: either the spheres of the earth and of the water are not perfectly concentric (which raises a problem as to the precise location of the center of the universe) or, while remaining perfectly concentric, they each bear about them a hump *(gibbus)* apt to account for the emergence of the earth in the inhabited part of the world (which overlooks the fact that water, left to itself, invariably settles on an even plane). Having offered various objections to these hypotheses, Dante then advances his own view to the effect that the elevated character of dry land in the inhabited world is a divine provision designed by way of a commingling of the elements to ensure the possibility of complex creatures like ourselves, creatures of an organic and psychosomatic constitution. The efficient cause of this situation, he maintains, is the starry heaven or firmament, which, by way of the constellations visible from this part of the world, bring about its rising up—though why this part of the world and no other should be so privileged is inexplicable. It is a matter of God's hidden wisdom and purposes for man and for Creation generally.

But, as this concluding providentialism suggests, there is here a hidden order of concern; for what is at issue in the *Questio* is Dante's reputation and, perhaps more fundamentally, his sense of self as a philosopher-poet (1) equal to the demands of properly Scholastic inquiry and yet (2) as committed as ever to his undertaking as a poet in the allegorical and prophetic manner of the *Commedia.* The first aspect of this—Dante's sense of himself as equal to the rigor of properly Scholastic debate—is evident, not only in the (at times excessively scrupulous) dialectical care with which his argument is developed and in his systematic citing of philosophical authority, but also in the repeated affirmation, both explicit and implicit, of his own status as philosopher, as one accomplished in the ways of inductive reasoning; so, for example, the concluding *Determinata est hec phylosophia dominante invicto domino, domino Cane Grandi de Scala pro Imperio sacrosancto Romano, per me Dantem Alagherium, phylosophorum minimum, in inclita urbe Verona* . . . ("This philosophical discourse was made by me, Dante Alighieri, least of philosophers, in the time of the lordship of the illustrious Cangrande della Scala, governor in the name of the Holy Roman Empire, in the city of Verona. . . ," 87) or the opening concern for the integrity of his text: *Et, ne livor multorum, qui,* absentibus viris invidiosis, mendacia confingere solent, post tergum bene dicta transmutent, placuit insuper in hac cedula meis digitis exarata quod determinatum fuit a me relinquere, et formam totius disputationis calamo designare ("And in order that what has been carefully argued might not be distorted, behind his back, by the malice of those who, envious in respect of one no longer present, are given to the invention of falsehood, it was my pleasure to leave behind, in pages I have myself copied out, a record of my findings, thus indicating in written form the course of the argument," 3). But underlying these gestures of philosophical prowess and constituting the deep reason for his intervention in Verona is a concern, in circumstances of more or less greater hostility, for self-affirmation as poet of the *Commedia*. For this is not the first time that Dante had turned his attention to cosmography and the distribution of the elements. A passage in *Inferno* (34.121–126) had given an account of how it came about that there was a rising up of dry land in the Northern Hemisphere in consequence of Lucifer's fall to the center of the universe, this in turn precipitating a voiding of the earth in the north in favor of Mount Purgatorio's emergence in the south. The explanation was nothing if not theological, but it stood in need now of fresh accommodation. And this, cleverly, is what Dante achieves in the *Questio,* for while on the one hand he offers a naturalistic explanation for the topography of the globe as it stands, he nonetheless sets the whole discourse within the context of God's inscrutable providence. In an impassioned passage toward the end of the work (77), Job, the Psalmist, Isaiah, Paul, and Christ himself are called as witnesses to the notion that God's ways are above our ways and that little in the universe is reducible to the merely ratiocinative. The indictment of philosophical hubris is absolute—and, with it, Dante's confidence in the *sermo humilis* of his *Commedia*.

No manuscripts of the *Questio* have survived. The *editio princeps,* published by the Augustinian Giovanni Benedetto Moncetti and dedicated to Cardinal Ippolito d'Este, dates from 1508. The authenticity of the *Questio,* although contested by Bruno Nardi (the single most important commentator on its cultural circumstances), is nonetheless accepted by the majority of scholars. The critical edition established by Giorgio Padoan in 1968 bears the revised title *De situ et forma aque et terre.*

Bibliography

Alighieri, Dante. *Questio de aqua et terra.* Edited by Francesco Mazzoni. Critical edition of Emenegildo Pistelli. In *Opere minori. Tomo 2.* Milan, Naples: Ricciardi, 1979.

———. *De situ et forma aque et terre.* Edited by Giorgio Padoan. Florence: Le Monnier, 1968.

Freccero, John. "Satan's Fall and the *Quaestio de aqua et terra.*" *Italica* 38 (1961), 99–115.

Ghisalberti, Alessandro. "La cosmologia nel Duecento e Dante." *Letture Classensi* 13 (1984), 33–48.

Mazzoni, Francesco. "Il punto sulla *Quaestio de aqua et terra.*" *Studi danteschi* 39 (1962), 39–84.

———. "La *Quaestio de aqua et terra.*" *Studi danteschi* 34 (1957), 163–204.

Moore, Edward. "The Genuineness of the *Quaestio de aqua et terra.*" In *Studies in Dante. Second Series: Miscellaneous Essays.* New York: Greenwood Press, 1968 (1899), 303–357.

Nardi, Bruno. *La caduta di Lucifero e l'autenticità della Quaestio de aqua et terra.* Turin: SEI, 1959.

Padoan, Giorgio. "La *Quaestio de aqua et terra.*" In *Dante nella critica di oggi.* Edited by Umberto Bosco. Florence: Le Monnier, 1965, pp. 758–767 (with bibliography).

Took, John F. *Dante, Lyric Poet and Philosopher: An Introduction to the Minor Works.* Oxford: Clarendon Press, 1990.

John Took

Quadrivium

The quadrivium, along with the trivium, forms the seven liberal arts. While the trivium (which includes grammar, rhetoric, and logic or dialectic) represented the intellectual foundation for subsequent professional education, the quadrivium (which includes arithmetic, geometry, music, and astronomy) represented the basis for advanced study in philosophy. Underlying this was an intellectual framework derived from St. Augustine, who envisioned a unified core education—focusing on language, music, and mathematics—that reflected the divine order. The components of the quadrivium were not seen as autonomous disciplines but as an intellectual progression of increasing abstraction and philosophical idealization. In practical terms, the curriculum drew on Boethius' *De institutione arithmetica* and *musica* for the study of arithmetic and music, on Euclid's *Elements* for geometry, and on Ptolemy's *Tetrabiblos* and Aristotle's *De caelo et mundo (Concerning Heaven and Earth)* for astronomy.

The term "quadrivium" first appeared in the work of Boethius, and the four disciplines became a part of the liberal arts curriculum in the work of Martianus Capella and Alcuin of York. It was later synthesized with theology by St. Bonaventure in *De reductione artium ad theologiam* and by Aquinas in his *Commentary on the De Trinitate of Boethius*. The underlying principles, however, derived ultimately from Pythagoras' concept of quantity. For Pythagoras quantities were either discrete (that is, countable things or numbers) or continuous (that is, lines). Arithmetic was therefore an examination of discrete quantities. Music extended this notion, looking at the ratio of discrete quantities. Geometry, on the other hand, looked at fixed continuous quantities such as the figures of plane geometry, while astronomy looked at continuous quantities in motion. In this way, the student of philosophy moved up a hierarchy of abstraction, turning from knowledge predicated on sense perception to knowledge predicated on pure reason— a knowledge in harmony with the divine mind. Thus by liberating themselves from the realm of sense perception, the students turned toward God.

Central to Dante's understanding of the liberal arts is their typology and correspondences with the physical and moral order. Thus, in the second book of the *Convivio,* he argues that the orders of knowledge represented by the seven liberal arts correspond to the first seven heavens. In the quadrivium, arithmetic is related to the Sun, music to the planet Mars, geometry to Jupiter, and astronomy to Saturn. He explains this by suggesting that each planet shares two corresponding properties with its representative order of knowledge. First, Dante says, the Sun is the source of light for all other stars. Second, the eye cannot look on the light because of its brightness. By analogy, arithmetic, the study of numerical properties, is the foundation of all other analytical sciences. Similarly,

since numbers are infinite, the human intellect cannot see or comprehend the fundamental principles. Mars is characterized by its proportional relationship with the other stars—as midway—forming a series of ratios with them. In addition, Dante understands Mars to be hot (thus the red color), causing it to dry things. In a similar fashion, music involves ratios and harmonies and has the power to dry and elevate the vapors of the heart by its beauty. The planet Jupiter is characterized by following an antithetical path between Mars and Saturn and by its white appearance, because of its purity, which Dante attributes to its being covered with silver. These also, for Dante, are the properties of geometry, which describes the relationship between the most basic figure, the point, and the most perfect and complete figure, the circle, and stands antithetical to each. Similarly, geometry is the discipline most free from error. Finally, Saturn is the slowest and the highest of the planets. In a similar fashion, astronomy requires the most time to master and was therefore the highest of the sciences.

Bibliography

Alberson, Paul. *The Seven Liberal Arts: A Study in Mediaeval Culture.* New York: Columbia University Press, 1906.

Curtius, Ernst Robert. *European Literature and the Latin Middle Ages.* Translated by Willard R. Trask. Princeton, N.J.: Princeton University Press, 1953.

Di Scipio, Giuseppe, and Aldo Scaglione (eds.). *The "Divine Comedy" and the Encyclopedia of Arts and Sciences.* Amsterdam, Philadelphia: Benjamins, 1988.

Gualazzini, Ugo. *Trivium e quadrivium.* Mediolani: Giuffrè, 1974.

Masi, Michael (ed.). *Boethius and the Liberal Arts.* Berne: Peter Lang, 1981.

Wagner, David L. (ed.). *The Seven Liberal Arts in the Middle Ages.* Bloomington: Indiana University Press, 1983.

Thomas L. Cooksey

R

Rabanus, Maurus

Encyclopedist, theologian, pedagogist, biblical exegete, poet, archbishop of Mainz. Born in Mainz in 776 (764?), Rabanus (Hrabanus, Rhabanus, Magentius) entered the Benedictine monastery of Fulda. At Tours he studied liberal arts and theology under Alcuin, the architect of the Carolingian Reform of Studies. From Alcuin he received the name of Maurus, borrowed from one of St. Benedict's disciples. In 803 he returned to Fulda, where he was elected the director of the monastic school, which under him excelled and became one of the most esteemed schools in Germany, combining sacred studies and classical culture. Ordained priest in 814 and elected abbot of Fulda in 822, he contributed to the temporal, intellectual, and spiritual prosperity of his subjects; collected books for the library and treasures of art; and worked to provide education to the illiterates. He was called "Praeceptor Germaniae." In the dispute between Louis the Pious and his sons, Rabanus sustained the legitimate dynastic successor and chose exile after Louis the German defeated Lothair, the oldest son of Louis the Pious. He returned from exile in 841 and a year later retired to Petersberg, dedicating himself to the contemplative life. Nevertheless in 847 he was elected archbishop of Mainz, and as such he condemned the monk Gottschalk of Orbais for his doctrine on predestination. He died at Winkel, near Mainz, in 856. Rabanus left numerous works and was considered one of the most learned men of his time.

Dante places Rabanus among the twenty-four spirits of the fourth heaven (*Par.* 12.139), the wise men who enlighten the world. Rabanus *(Rabano)* is the eleventh spirit of the second garland guided by St. Bonaventure. In Dante's time Rabanus was well known as an encyclopedist, theologian, and biblical exegete. Rabanus' many and varied cultural interests may have spurred Dante to place him among those who "enlightened" the world; not only his encyclopedic knowledge encompassing his love for the classics but also his political views, his doctrine on predestination, and his dedication to the contemplative life as reflected in his writings certainly could have influenced Dante to place Rabanus within the second garland.

Louis La Favia

Rachel

The wife for whom Jacob served fourteen years in Genesis, daughter of Laban, and mother of Joseph and Benjamin. Rachel became in medieval exegesis a figure for the contemplative life, while her sister Leah became a figure of the active life. In Dante's dream before he enters the Earthly Paradise he sees the two sisters in those roles: Leah gathering flowers and speaking to the poet, Rachel only contemplating herself in the mirror (*Purg.* 27.100–108). Rachel is also mentioned in both *Inferno* and *Paradiso* sitting beside Beatrice (*Inf.* 2.102; *Par.* 32.8–9), where she is on the third level of Mary's line. She is the only woman named in Limbo among the Jews whom Christ led out in the harrowing of Hell (*Inf.* 4.60).

Joan M. Ferrante

Rahab

A prostitute in the City of Jericho who provided a hiding place for Joshua's spies. In return, she was

R guaranteed her safety when Jericho fell to the Israelites—her house being distinguished by a scarlet cord displayed in the window (Josh. 2 and 6). In the New Testament she is listed among the ancestors of Christ (Matt. 1:5) and is cited as an example both of faith (Heb. 11:31) and of justification by works (James 2:25). In patristic and medieval exegesis, Rahab is a type of the Church drawn from the Gentiles, spared by Jesus Christ (Joshua) from the destruction of this world and eternal death (Jericho), her salvation effected by Christ's blood (the scarlet cord).

Rahab ("Raab") is the last soul the pilgrim sees in the Heaven of Venus (*Par.* 9.109–126). Folquet of Marseilles explains that she was the first among those whom Christ harrowed from Hell to arrive in the third heaven. Her presence in Heaven is a sign of *l'alta vittoria / che s'acquistò con l'una e l'altra palma* ("the great victory acquired by his two palms," 123), a reference to both Joshua's defeat of Jericho, accomplished through prayer, and Christ's death on the cross—the one prefiguring the other. Rahab's status as type of the Church adds considerable force to Dante's polemical comparison between her love for God, which prompted her to help Joshua to victory, and the Pope's neglect of the Holy Land (see also *Par.* 9.127–138).

Mark Balfour

Reason

As a cognitive power, reason (*ragione;* Latin *ratio*) is the faculty that produces the discursive process by which humans know. Dante associates it with both "mind" *(mente)* and "intellect" *(intelletto)*. Its operations, combined with those of the will, constitute the life of the intellective soul. The faculty of reason has as its proper end or goal knowledge, and its ultimate proper end is the *ben de l'intelletto* ("the good of the intellect," *Inf.* 3.18), which is God. Like Aristotle, however, Dante believes that rational knowledge originates in sensory experience; to understand reason, one must first understand the role the inner and outer senses play in knowing.

Both Albert the Great and Thomas Aquinas, the most important Scholastic influences on Dante, claimed that material things act as objects of sensation and, ultimately, knowledge. When we know a thing via sensation, however, we do not know it as it actually exists, as a form united with its mat-ter. Rather we know it by means of an "intention" (cf. *Conv.* 3.9.7), which is an image of the material object that its form produces in the sense organ. The first level of sensation thus involves the generation of the intention through the abstraction of the sensible form from the matter of an existing thing. We do not sense the stone itself but a likeness of it, which, in Aquinas' words, is not stony.

The next stage of knowing occurs in the internal senses. The common sense enables us to be aware that we hear and see; it also allows us to compare sounds to textures, scents to sights. The imagination, also called the phantasy, forms and stores images called phantasms. Like the images of the outer senses, phantasms are the forms of sensible objects; unlike the outer senses, however, the imagination is able to retain its image of a sensible object even when the latter is no longer present. Phantasms therefore are a second grade of abstraction; they are the forms that the intellective faculties of the soul use to arrive at rational knowledge. There are two other internal senses: the estimative or cogitative power, and memory. In animals the estimative sense perceives phantasms that are not directly known to the external senses, and it moves animals to instinctive judgments; it causes sheep, for example, to sense danger in the presence of a wolf and to flee from it. Aquinas calls this sense in humans the cogitative power, since it makes some rational comparisons among intentions and acts. Finally, memory stores all this information for reference to past time. Because all the internal senses make use of intentions abstracted from sensible things even when those things are no longer present, they all utilize some form of memory.

The operations of the sensitive soul share a structure that is continuous with and analogous to the operations of reason, which begins with the abstracting of a second phantasm from the form of the object the imagination had produced. The imagination's phantasm is still of a form individualized by matter; it presents one image of Rover, another of Spot. The intellect, however, bears upon the universal; from the particulars produced in sensation it therefore abstracts the essential form—that which makes Rover and Spot both dogs.

The faculties that allow this activity to take place are the passive and the active intellects. The active intellect illuminates the particular thing which is represented in the phantasm and renders it intelligible by abstracting its essential form from the matter and the conditions that individuate it. The resulting universal likeness, called the "intelligible species," is then impressed on the passive intellect, which in response forms its own likeness of the abstracted nature. This is the *verbum mentis,* the universal concept in the full sense. This abstract concept, expressed by a single word, determines how we know anything with respect to its nature.

Because human beings, however, are a compound of body and soul, the universal concept is not, in and of itself, the object of cognition; rather it is the means by which we come to know the material object, which is the proper goal of human understanding. Knowing something with respect to its nature alone is not enough, for if understanding stopped here, one could not know anything particular. To comprehend a thing as it exists therefore requires that the soul return to the phantasms *(se convertere ad phantasma),* armed, as it were, with the abstracted concept, through which it can now form a judgment of the discrete object as true or false. This judgment takes the form of a proposition: not a single word, such as "human," but the concept embedded in a statement of the form a = b, such as "Socrates is a man." For Aquinas, reason therefore was a synthesizing act of apprehension that culminated in the production of language.

This description of the nature of cognition and the role reason plays in it mostly follows Aquinas; it is important, however, to note that these issues were vigorously debated in the Middle Ages. Dante's epistemology is neither exclusively Thomistic nor entirely consistent; it develops and changes from work to work. In the *Monarchia,* for instance, Dante seems to side with Averroës when he says that the passive intellect, whose possession is what distinguishes people from all other creatures, can be completely actualized only in the whole of mankind, not in each human being (*Mon.* 1.3.6 ff.). In the *Convivio,* Dante subscribes to the notion that the passive intellect possesses ideas in potency, like seeds, which enter the mind only with divine aid and burgeon when they are illuminated by a divine light that comes from God (*Conv.* 3.12.7; cf. *Purg.* 16.75); this Neoplatonic theory—formulated by Augustine and championed by Franciscan thinkers like Bonaventure—is one that Aquinas rejected.

Nevertheless, it is true to say that by incorporating Scholastic theories of knowing into their accounts of love, poets of the "sweet new style" (*Purg.* 24.57) distinguished their verse from that of their contemporaries: Dante's first poem in this manner, "Donne ch'avete intelletto d'amore," certainly takes as its subject a far different conception of understanding (see *VN,* 18–19; *Purg.* 24.49ff.) from that which informs earlier works like *The Romance of the Rose* (and the *Fiore,* a partial translation of it, perhaps by Dante), in which Reason appears as a personification of ethical principles the Lover is urged to embrace instead of physical pleasure. Dante felt this impulse to allegorize reason as well; he personified it in some early poems (e.g., *Gentil pensero, Vita Nuova,* 38), and the ancient commentators on the *Commedia* often followed suit by identifying Virgil as Reason. Boccaccio, for instance, says Virgil is "the reason God granted us, wherefore we are called rational animals" (*Esposizioni,* Canto I (ii):150). But just as Dante was not concerned with reconciling opposing philosophical views of reason, so his desire to explore the limits of human intellect and its relation to faith kept him from reducing reason to any static, allegorical gloss. Because understanding relied on sense knowledge, its grasp of the pure intelligible nature of eternal things was inherently limited. Moreover, Christian revelation made claims the truth of which no human science could hope to comprehend. These propositions, both of which Dante often defends in various works, inform his dynamic conception of the roles Virgil and Beatrice play as guides in the poem.

After Virgil has discussed the origin and operation of love in fine Scholastic fashion in the central cantos of *Purgatorio,* Dante responds to his master's account by saying that it seems neither to our credit nor to our blame if our love is well or badly directed. Virgil answers: "As far as reason sees here, I can tell you; beyond that, wait for Beatrice, for it is a matter of faith" (*Purg.* 18.46–48). These and other passages (e.g., *Purg.* 13.20, 15.76) have produced a controversy in Dante criticism: if one grants that some truths are ascertained only through belief, the dignity of reason clearly is beneath that of faith. Does it follow from this subordination that faith therefore has jurisdiction over all matters that properly fall within the province of rational understanding, as Aquinas held? Dante seems to disagree; even in *Paradiso* Aristotle continues to be quoted, which suggests that his authority within the sphere of reason remains unimpaired. Philosophy is beneath faith; Virgil gives way to Beatrice. When Virgil disappears at the summit of Mount Purgatory, Dante draws attention to the defects in the love and poetry that he represents. But just before they enter the Garden of Eden, Virgil "crowns and mitres" Dante by his own authority; within its own realm, reason remains autonomous, yet never independent from, revealed truth.

Bibliography

Boyde, Patrick. *Perception and Passion in Dante's Comedy.* Cambridge: Cambridge University Press, 1993.

Cristiani, Marta. "Ragione." *Enciclopedia dantesca,* 4:831–841.

Gilson, Étienne. *Dante and Philosophy.* Translated by David Moore. New York: Harper and Row, 1949, pp. 122–130, 152–159.

Mahoney, Edward. "Sense, Intellect, and Imagination in Albert, Thomas, and Siger." In *The Cambridge History of Later Medieval Philosophy.* Edited by Norman Kretzmann et al. Cambridge: Cambridge University Press, 1982, pp. 602–622.

Nardi, Bruno. *Dal Convivio alla Commedia.* Rome: Istituto Storico Italiano per il Medio Evo, 1960.

———. *Dante e la cultura medievale.* Bari: Laterza, 1942.

Owens, Joseph. "Faith, ideas, illumination, and experience." In *The Cambridge History of Later Medieval Philosophy.* Edited by Norman Kretzmann et al. Cambridge: Cambridge University Press, 1982, pp. 440–459.

Steneck, Nicholas. "Albert on the Psychology of Sense Perception." In *Albertus Magnus and the Sciences: Commemorative Essays.* Edited by James Weisheipl. Toronto: Pontifical Institute of Medieval Studies, 1980, pp. 263–290.

Warren Ginsberg

Rebecca

Wife of Isaac, chosen by Abraham's servant under the assumption that she had been appointed by God (Gen. 24). The mother of the twins Jacob and Esau, Rebecca proposed and directed a plan for Jacob, her favorite, to take from his elder brother the position of primary heir (Gen. 27). In *Par.* 32.10, Bernard points out Rebecca's place among the foremost Hebrew women in the Celestial Rose. In lines 67–69, her womb is identified as the locus of the initial conflict between her unborn twins

brought about by God, as proof of his preference of Jacob over Esau (Rom. 9:10–13).

Carolynn Lund-Mead

Reginaldo de' Scrovegni

The progenitor of the Paduan Scrovegni family, Reginaldo (or Rinaldo) established the family's economic dominance through usury and raised it socially by marrying into a noble family. After his death in 1288 or 1289, an enraged mob assaulted his house, and a huge fire destroyed the family's properties. He is probably to be identified with the usurer holding a white bag with a blue sow, the family symbol, in the third ring of the seventh circle of Hell (*Inf.* 17.64). The only non-Florentine usurer, he rudely addresses Dante, urges him to report the names of his fellow damned so their reputations will be ruined, and predicts the arrival of the Florentine usurer Gianni Buiamonte.

Pamela J. Benson

Regulus, Marcus Attilius

Roman consul 267 and 256 B.C.E., died 247 B.C.E.; cited in *Conv.* 4.5.14 *(Regolo)* as one moved by divine nature to give his government advice contrary to his personal well-being. In 255, the Carthaginians defeated his force and took him prisoner. A legend says he returned to Rome to plead for peace and an exchange of prisoners while under oath to return to Carthage. Instead, he spoke against the peace and exchange, returned to Carthage, and was tortured to death. Dante's sources appear to be Cicero, *De officiis* 1.13.39, and St. Augustine, *De civ. Dei* 2.23.

Leslie Zarker Morgan

Rehoboam

Successor to his father, Solomon, as king of Israel, Rehoboam precipitated the division of the kingdom ("So Israel has been in rebellion against the house of David to this day," 1 Kings 12:19). When the assembly of Israel requested that Rehoboam reduce the forced labor imposed upon them by Solomon, he rejected the advice of the elders who had advised his father in favor of the advice of the young men who had grown up with him, declaring that he would add to the Israelites' already grievous yoke. Rehoboam *(Roboàm)* is depicted in the pavement of the first terrace of Purgatory among the examples of pride brought low, as he escapes in a chariot from the Israelites who are stoning his taskmaster (*Purg.* 12.46–48; 1 Kings 12:18; 2 Chron. 10:18). Rehoboam fled to Jerusalem, where he ruled over Judah, while Israel chose Jeroboam to rule in the north.

Carolynn Lund-Mead

Renouard

According to several Old French epics widely diffused in Italy, most prominently *Aliscans,* Renouard *(Rinoardo)* was a giant pagan convert who fought alongside William of Orange, his brother-in-law, on behalf of the Franks. Dante places him with William, among those who fought for faith, in the Heaven of Mars (*Par.* 18.46–48).

Bibliography

Foglia, Giuseppe. "Guiglielmo e Rinoardo della croce di Marte." *Giornale dantesco* 22 (1914), 1–9.
Hauvette, Henri. *La France et la Provence dans l'oeuvre de Dante.* Paris: Boivin, 1929.

Jessica Levenstein

Resurrection

The resurrection of the flesh signifies the bodily raising of the dead at the end of time so that they may live eternally in union with God. It is an article of Christian faith present in the Apostles' Creed from its earliest formulation: *credo carnis resurrectionem* ("I believe in the resurrection of the flesh"). This doctrine is based on Christ's Resurrection on the third day after his burial, an event central to the very birth of the Church and to all Christian teaching. It has its broadest biblical formulation in 1 Cor. 15, where the rising up of the dead at the blast of God's trumpet is proclaimed and where the new characteristics of the resurrected bodies, likened to Christ in his Resurrection, are suggested. No longer subject to the laws of matter, but rather transfigured and glorified, "It is sown a natural body; it is raised a spiritual body. There is a natural body, and there is a spiritual body" (1 Cor. 15:42–44). St. Thomas (*ST* 3, Suppl. 82.1), following Paul, describes with greater precision the four principal characteristics of these bodies: impassibility, subtlety (permeability), agility, and clarity (luminosity).

Belief in the resurrection of the body is central to Christianity and distinguishes it from most other organized religions. Not surprisingly, therefore, it undergirds Dante's poem of the afterlife. Dante's otherworld is, in fact, a world of bodies, not of spirits, and this is not simply the result of poetic licence. The characters that throng the pages of *Inferno* and *Purgatorio* have a bodily materiality entirely similar to what they possessed on Earth. Despite this appearance, however, their bodies are, as Dante explains in *Purg.* 25, only aerial projections of the spiritual reality of each individual. These bodies are only temporary, given to the souls so that they can endure physical torment (in Hell) or complete the process of penance (in Purgatory). At the Last Judgment, however, all souls will be *rivestiti* ("clothed again") in their true flesh (see *Inf.* 6.94–99, 13.103–105). Only by virtue of this article of faith, which grants the human body immortal life outside of time, do the individuals of the first two canticles take on an extremely vital reality—as does indeed the landscape in which they dwell. Their manner of existence, composed of gestures and looks—the damned in Hell furious and violent, the penitents of Purgatory affectionate and mild—is familiar to us because it is similar to our own and, by contrast, quite different from the pallid shades that inhabit, for example, the pagan underworld of Virgil's Elysium.

The theme of the bodily resurrection is a recurring leitmotif in the *Commedia.* As early as *Inf.* 6 we are told that at the end of the world, at the sound of the *angelica tromba* ("the angelic trumpet," 95), each of the damned will return to his tomb to retrieve *sua carne e sua figura* ("his flesh and his shape," 98). Further below in Hell, Pier della Vigna warns ruefully that the suicides, returning like the others to recover their own *spoglie* ("remains," 13.103), will not be permitted to reclothe themselves, because they despised and rejected their bodies when alive. But if this serves as a gloomy reminder in Hell, it becomes a reason for exultation in Purgatory, where Virgil will rejoice in the knowledge that Cato will reacquire his body at Judgment Day: *la vesta ch'al gran dì sarà sì chiara* ("the raiment that will be so bright on the great day," *Purg.* 1.75). In Paradise the saved do not possess aerial bodies, because they have no torture or purgation to endure. It is strangely ironic that the only "true" bodies of the entire poem (aside from that of Dante the pilgrim) should appear in the heavenly rose, which entirely transcends physical, corporeal reality; in the white rose, where the blessed are gathered in their *bianche stole* ("white stoles," *Par.* 30.129)—an image taken directly from John's vision of the Apocalypse (Rev. 7:9). These stoles, or garments, are an image of human bodies in a state of glory, and they possess an extraordinary luminosity. Their intensity is heralded in *Par.* 14, where Dante refers to the doctrine of the resurrection of the flesh (43–60).

The strongly human desire to perceive with one's senses, to communicate with another person through the body, is expressed at other points in the canticle: in canto 22, when Dante asks St. Benedict to be allowed to see him *con imagine scoverta* ("see your countenance openly," 60); in canto 25, when he tries to look through the light that entirely envelops John the Apostle, in order to make out the body which according to one tradition had ascended into Heaven immediately after death. But every body other than those belonging to Christ and the Virgin Mary still lies buried in the ground. This deep desire to perceive the resurrected body will finally be fulfilled in the *ultima spera* ("the last sphere," 22.62), as St. Benedict says, where the faces of the innumerable blessed appear as they will after Judgment Day. Among them is the mother of Mary, Anna, who, while singing Hosanna with the others, does not remove her gaze from her daughter's face (22.133–135).

Dante, to whom nothing human seems unfamiliar—from the deepest experiences to the most fleeting emotions—could not but be the great poet of the resurrection of the flesh, for he believed that man is not really himself unless clothed in two stoles, both the body and the soul. It is only through the body that he is able to see those whom he loves.

Bibliography

Aquinas, St. Thomas. *Summa contra gentiles.* Notre Dame, Ind.: University of Notre Dame Press, 1975 [1955–1957], book 4, chapters 79–86.

Augustine, St. *The City of God.* New York: The Modern Library, 1950, book 22, chapters 19–21.

Bernard of Clairvaux, St. *On loving God.* Edited by Hugh Martin. Westport, Conn.: Greenwood Press, 1981 [1959], chapters 10–11.

Bynum, Caroline Walker. *The Resurrection of the Body in Western Christianity, 200–1336.* New York: Columbia University Press, 1995.

Chiavacci Leonardi, A. M. "'Le bianche stole': il tema della resurezione nel *Paradiso*." In *Dante e la Bibbia. Atti del Convegno internazionale*

promosso da "Biblia." Edited by Giovanni Barblan. Florence: Olschki, 1986, pp. 249–271.

Anna Maria Chiavacci Leonardi
(translated by Susan Gaylard)

Revelation

"Revelation" in its broadest sense refers to the way in which God communicates to humans. In his Epistle to the Romans, Paul speaks of Creation itself as a kind of general revelation, such that all humans are able to come to a knowledge of God through a knowledge of his Creation (Rom. 1:18–20). In the Middle Ages, the idea of revelation certainly included this general communication, but also, and more typically, it referred to the specific communication that God made, first with his chosen people, the Hebrews; and then through the life, death, and Resurrection of Jesus Christ; and finally through the church established by Christ as the conduit of his saving actions. The Bible, which tells the story of all these communications, was considered a revealed document, a text authored by God and under the care of his church. Moreover, the Bible was considered in connection with another text, since the universe itself was also considered a book authored by God. Thus the Bible was a revealed document which provided the key to help understand the book of the universe.

As Dante himself tells us in the *Monarchia*, revelation is necessary because "there are some judgments of God to which human reason, even if it cannot arrive at them by its own unaided efforts, can nonetheless be raised with the help of faith in those things which are said to us in the Scriptures" (*Mon.* 2.7.4). In an important passage from the same work, Dante contrasts revelation with reason as two distinct ways of knowing: "Now these two kinds of happiness must be reached by different means, as representing different ends. For we attain the first through the teachings of philosophy, provided that we follow them putting into practice the moral and intellectual virtues; whereas we attain the second through spiritual teachings which transcend human reason, provided that we follow them putting into practice the theological virtues, i.e. faith, hope, and charity" (*Mon.* 3.16.8).

This same distinction between reason and revelation is often applied to the figures of Dante the pilgrim's first guides in the *Commedia*, Virgil and Beatrice. In the tradition of personification allegory present in so many of the early commentaries,

Virgil was in fact equated with reason, and Beatrice with revelation. Insofar as Virgil both leads to and yields to Beatrice, it can be inferred that revelation builds on reason, that grace builds on nature. But in the economy of the *Commedia*, these equations don't totally or adequately cover the relationship between these two guides or their function within the poem. For one thing, Virgil has a far more complex function in the poem than simply as a representative of reason. Though he comes to lead Dante on the first stage of his journey, he himself has been placed among the damned in the first circle in *Inf.* 4, the circle of the virtuous pagans, and this clearly can be seen as an especially striking example of the limits of reason. But it also needs to be said that he comes to the pilgrim only because a special revelation has been granted to him, a revelation mediated through the intercession of the three blessed ladies of *Inf.* 2: Mary, Lucy, and Beatrice (*Inf.* 2.94–105). Moreover, it is surely more accurate to see Virgil as an embodiment of—a particularly eminent representative of—the whole weight of classical culture, rather than simply of reason. To be sure, the classical tradition emphasizes reason, but in the Middle Ages it was not limited to it. For one thing, Virgil's fourth eclogue was widely interpreted as a prediction of the birth of Christ, and so not surprisingly Virgil plays a prophetic role within the *Commedia*. One especially strong example of this is the role he plays as the means of salvation for his fellow poet Statius, a story told beginning with canto 20 of *Purgatorio*.

In the *Convivio* Dante speaks about the prophetic perception to be found sometimes in dreams as a kind of revelation (*Conv.* 2.8.13). That God revealed truths through dreams was well established by scriptural authority, as is evident in the dreams of Joseph (Gen. 37, 40, 41) and Daniel in the Old Testament. At Pentecost the newly established Christian Church is promised the gift of prophecy, which is also linked to dream experience (Acts 2:17). Later, Peter changes his attitude toward the Gentiles as a result of his dream about unclean beasts (Acts 10:9–16), which was a new visual revelation that significantly overturned the old written law. The vision of John the Revelator was also often understood as a dream in the Middle Ages; he is sometimes shown in illustrated Apocalypse manuscripts as sleeping on the Isle of Patmos when the angel approaches him at the start of his visionary revelation. Illustrated manuscripts

of the *Visio Pauli*—which the Middle Ages attributed to Paul, whom Dante cites as a model for his own otherworldly journey (*Inf.* 2.32)—also show the apostle asleep, as if dreaming before his vision.

Sometimes Dante's pilgrimage in the *Commedia* is described as if the poet too had been dreaming, for at the beginning of the poem Dante mentions that when he discovers himself in the dark wood, it is as if he has been sleeping (*Inf.* 1.1–12). But Dante's "sleep" has been his sinful waking life (cf. Rom. 13:11–12), so that his pilgrimage vision is not so much a dream as an awakening into divine revelation. Dante thus experiences revelation in an immediate way, while awake, which, according to Augustine (*De Genesi ad litteram* 12.18), is a higher form of divine perception. Medieval theology sometimes associates this more immediate revelation with mystical experience. Interestingly, the most important medieval model of such contemplative mysticism is Bernard of Clairvaux, *un sene / vestito con le genti gloriose* ("an old man clothed like the glorious ones," *Par.* 31.59–60), who takes over from Beatrice as Dante's guide in the concluding cantos of the poem (*Par.* 31.102).

Dante clearly values both reason and revelation, and although his beatific vision at the conclusion of *Paradiso* is the result of a privileged revelation, not reason, his description of this experience uses an image drawn from classical geometry (*Par.* 33.133–145), suggesting the value of reason even here at the pinnacle of his pilgrimage, just as revelation is valued in *Inferno* when Virgil is his guide. At the place where reason is definitively superseded, reason is necessary to describe its own limitations and to point beyond itself. Thus reason and revelation are not in conflict but are supportive of one another and perfectly united in divine wisdom (*Conv.* 3.12.12–13). That Dante gave Thomas Aquinas—who sought to reconcile Aristotelianism with the truths learned from divine revelation—an authoritative voice in Heaven (*Par.* 10.99) underscores the poet's belief in the value of both means of gaining knowledge. Throughout his pilgrimage, what Dante learns through reason is supported by what he learns through revelation. Perhaps the best example of this close linking of reason and revelation is the great symbolic pageant of Church history that concludes *Purgatorio*. The pageant clearly relies on images drawn from the cosmic revelations to the prophet Ezekiel in the Old Testament and to John the Revelator in

R the New Testament, and its subject is revelation itself; but to understand its significance, it is necessary to use reason, informed by the particulars of Church history. Dante's earlier concern with history and the intellectual search for its meaning is here placed within the perspective of eternity through a unique revelation granted by Beatrice to him as a contemporary prophet.

Bibliography

Botterill, Steven. *Dante and the Mystical Tradition: Bernard of Clairvaux in the Commedia*. Cambridge: Cambridge University Press, 1994.

Gilson, Étienne. *Dante the Philosopher*. Translated by David Moore. London: Sheed and Ward, 1948.

Kruger, Steven F. *Dreaming in the Middle Ages*. Cambridge: Cambridge University Press, 1992.

Took, John F. *Dante, Lyric Poet and Philosopher: An Introduction to the Minor Works*. Oxford: Clarendon Press, 1990.

Richard K. Emmerson
and Ronald B. Herzman

Richard of St. Victor

Scholastic philosopher and theologian (d. 1173). Few historical details are known of this influential member of the Victorine school who studied with Hugh of St. Victor. Perhaps of Scottish origin, Richard of St. Victor *(Riccardo da San Vittore)* arrived at the monastery of St. Victor in Paris probably in the early 1150s. He was elected subprior in 1159 and prior in 1162, which position he held until his death.

His works include doctrinal and mystical tracts, such as *De trinitate, De gratia contemplationis, sive de arca mystica, sive Benjamin maior,* and *De præparatione animi ad contemplationem, sive duodecim patriarchis, sive Benjamin minor.* His mystical writings on contemplation most certainly influenced Bonaventure's *Itinerarium mentis in Deum.*

Richard is placed among the *sapienti* ("the wise") in the sphere of the Sun. In *Par.* 10.131–132 Richard is introduced to the pilgrim in the same verse as Isidore and Bede. Furthermore, testifying to Richard's stature as a master of contemplative methods, Aquinas describes Richard in the next verse as the one *che a considerar fu più che viro* ("who was more than man in contemplation"). The technical resonance of *considerar* links Richard,

as in *Epist.* 13, to Bernard's *De consideratione*. Richard's placement in the Heaven of the Sun (with the wise) instead of the Heaven of Saturn (with the contemplatives) emphasizes Dante's appraisal of Richard as more a teacher of contemplation to others and less an experienced mystic himself. Attesting to the loss of memory characteristic of mystical experiences, Dante cites Richard's *De contemplatione (Benjamin minor)* in the *Letter to Cangrande* (*Epist.* 13.80) along with Bernard's *De consideratione* and Augustine's *De quantitate animae.*

Bibliography

Richard of St. Victor. *The Twelve Patriarchs. The Mystical Ark. Book Three of the Trinity.* Translated by Grover A. Zinn. The Classics of Western Spirituality. New York: Paulist Press, 1979.

Colombo, Manuela. "Il XXIII Canto del *Paradiso* e il *Benjamin Major* di Riccardo da San Vittore." In *Dai mistici a Dante: Il linguaggio dell'ineffabilità.* Florence: La Nuova Italia, 1987, pp. 61–71.

Dumeige, Gervais. "Le mysticisme surnaturel chez Richard de Saint-Victor." In *Lectura Dantis Mystica.* Florence: Olschki, 1969, pp. 85–99.

Maggioni, M. Julie. "The *Paradiso* and Richard of St. Victor." *Romance Notes* 7 (1965), 87–91.

Nolan, Barbara. "The *Vita Nuova* and Richard of St. Victor's Phenomenology of Vision." *Dante Studies* 92 (1974), 35–52.

George Andrew Trone

Rime. *See* Lyric Poetry (Dante's)

Rinaldo d'Aquino

Poet of the Sicilian school who wrote canzoni in both the high and medium style, and famous for the woman's lament *"Già mai non mi conforto"* ("I shall never be consoled"). He is mentioned by Dante in *DVE* 2.5.4, who cites his canzone "Per fino amor vo sì letamente" ("I go so happily for true love's sake").

Rinaldina Russell

Rinier da Corneto

Notorious robber baron who had his hold near Corneto in the Maremma district and frequented the roads leading into Rome. He is punished in the first ring of the seventh circle (*Inf.* 12.137).

R. A. Malagi

Rinieri da Calboli

A descendant of the Paolucci, a powerful Guelf family, Rinieri was born in Forlì in the first half of the thirteenth century. His political career began in 1247, when he was elected podestà of Faenza. He held positions of prestige in Parma (1252), in Cesena (1255), and Ravenna (1265). Taking advantage of his friendship with Lizio di Valbona and of the alliance linking the Florentine and the Bolognese Guelfs, he failed in an attempt to take Forlì from Guido da Montefeltro in 1276. After Romagna became part of the Papal States in 1279, Rinier was able to regain some prestige among the Guelfs, but he returned to Forlì only in 1284. In 1288, he was captain of the Modena, and in 1292 he took forced control of Forlì but was expelled in 1294. In 1296 he succeeded in entering the city while the Forlì militia led by Scarpetta degli Ordelaffi were besieging the Calboli castle, but he was killed in battle. He is paired with the Ghibelline Guido del Duca, both of whom undergo penance on the second terrace of Purgatory to purge themselves of envy (*Purg.* 14.88). Guido praises Rinier while disparaging his grandson Fulcieri da Calboli, whose vicious character he delineates (14.58–65).

Paul Colilli

Ripheus

Ripheus *(Rifeo)* is one of the special souls who form the eye of the Eagle in the Heaven of Jupiter (*Par.* 20.67–72, 100–106, 118–138). Dante's only source for Ripheus is a short passage in Virgil's *Aeneid* (2.339, 394, 426–428), where the hero, described simply as "the most righteous *(iustissimus unus)* of the Trojans," is said to have fallen and died in battle. However, the most significant part of the Virgilian passage is, in the context of the *Commedia,* its bitter three-word ending: *dis aliter visum* ("The gods willed otherwise"). With these words Virgil questions whether the gods, who allow the untimely death of even the best men, can care at all for human virtue, to which they seem to offer no reward. A similar question—concerning the apparently unfair exclusion from salvation of those souls who, although they live in justice, have no access to the word of Christ—is addressed by the Eagle here in the Heaven of Jupiter. In answer to the pilgrim's doubts about this, the Eagle states unequivocally that no soul can go to Heaven without believing in Christ,

either as the Messiah to come or as the Savior already come. Yet, to the pilgrim's astonishment, two of the privileged souls forming its eye, Trajan and Ripheus, are indeed pagan. The Eagle soon explains that, despite what might seem to be the historical facts, both Trajan and Ripheus were Christians, thanks to a miracle of God's mercy: Trajan was raised from the dead and converted to Christianity, while Ripheus knew Christ through a vision that was granted to him because of his great virtue. While Trajan's conversion thanks to Pope Gregory's prayers is a well-known medieval legend, that of Ripheus is entirely Dante's invention.

The discussion surrounding these two pagans deals with one of the most important and poignant questions raised by the *Comedy,* that of the exclusion from salvation of the pagans, and with them Virgil. Theologians of Dante's time spoke of the possibility of the salvation of good souls whose ignorance of Christ was beyond their control. There was, for instance, the concept of "implicit faith," meaning faith in the natural manifestations of God available even to a pagan, whereby it was speculated that the virtuous heathen might be saved. The Eagle's words do not deny such a possibility, but they deny the possibility of any full understanding of the mystery of how and to whom such implicit faith is granted by God. The question, then, is why has Dante made a point of including pagans here and, in particular, of including a very minor character who appears only in Virgil's *Aeneid*—almost as if to call our attention to Virgil's own absence. Ripheus represents a powerful demonstration that God is not indifferent to human merit and, furthermore, that his means of dealing justly with it are beyond all human comprehension; but it is also supremely ironic that Virgil is excluded from God's grace, while the character through whom he expressed his frustration at the gods' indifference is miraculously included. Critics disagree on whether the irony of Ripheus' presence in this exalted position should be seen as an unstated condemnation of the despair expressed in Virgil's poetry or as an answer to that despair.

Bibliography

Chiarenza, Marguerite Mills. "Boethian Themes in Dante's Reading of Virgil." *Stanford Italian Review* 3, No. 1 (Spring) (1983), 25–35.

Picone, Michelangelo. "La *viva speranza* di Dante e il problema della salvezza dei pagani virtuosi.

R

Una lettura di *Paradiso* 20." *Quaderni d'Italianistica* 10, Nos. 1–2 (Spring–Fall) (1989), 251–268.

Marguerite Chiarenza

Robert of Anjou

Robert of Anjou was born in 1275 as third son of Charles II and Mary of Hungary. After the death of his two elder sons Charles II declared him the heir of the Kingdom of Naples with the approval of Pope Boniface VIII in 1297, ignoring the rights of his grandson Charles Robert, son of his eldest son, Charles Martel. Crowned twelve years later in Avignon, by Pope Clement V, Robert ruled for four decades (1309–1343) and faced many challenges to his authority. Although he successfully resisted the attempts by Henry VII and Louis of Bavaria to restore the imperial power in Italy, he failed to capitalize on this and to strengthen the Angevin position in northern Italy. Instead he wasted the revenues and forces of his kingdom in eight unsuccessful military campaigns for the reconquest of the Island of Sicily. His reign saw a continuous increase of the power of the nobility, which instigated various rebellions against the king in the Kingdom of Naples and consequently paved the way for the anarchy during the reign of his granddaughter Joanna. His financial policies were more successful because he succeeded in paying off the debts of his father to the Curia. Robert's greatest merit lies in his support of culture, because he surrounded himself with poets like Barbato da Sulmona and stood on good terms with Petrarch and Boccaccio. He steadily increased the Angevin Library and wrote various literary works, especially sermons, himself. A great impediment to his reign was the question of succession to the throne after the death of his son Charles of Calabria. By nominating his young and inexperienced granddaughter Joanna as heiress and brushing aside the pretensions of the Hungarian collateral line, he created the conditions for the dynastic struggles which made the Regno the battlefield for the different collateral Angevin dynasties. Although the Kingdom of Naples once again displayed an ephemeral splendor during Robert's reign, in reality the power of the state experienced a continuous decline. The king, who was more an intellectual than a vigorous ruler, died on January 19, 1343, in Naples.

Dante's judgment of Robert is unredeemably negative and severe, mainly for two reasons: he regards Robert as a usurper at Charles Robert's expense (the son of Charles Martel so highly esteemed by Dante) and as the stubborn adversary of the emperor Henry VII, who thereby shattered Dante's dream of the restoration of the imperial power and a universal monarchy with lies and deception. At one point Dante alludes explicitly to Robert's usurpation of the Angevin crown by fraudulent means (*Par.* 9.2: *li 'nganni*). Elsewhere Dante attacks Robert's greed—a commonplace accusation by many authors of the fourteenth century, although it is historically unfounded: the king surrounded himself with the avaricious Catalans who exploited their subjects. It is probably an allusion to Diego della Ratta, a confidant of Robert, who was active as a *marescallus* and *capitaneus* in Tuscany in the years from 1305 to 1318, supporting the Black Guelfs and organizing the resistance against Henry VII; or it may allude to King James II of Aragon, Robert's brother-in-law, who tried to come to terms with Florence at the beginning of the fourteenth century because he needed the support of the city for his planned conquest of Sardinia.

According to Dante the king and his counselors have overloaded the Angevin "ship of state" with taxes and financial burdens to the point of sinking it. Robert—contrary to the generous nature *(natura larga)* of Charles Martel—is therefore forced to seek help from characters similar to his own, who help him to extort his subjects (*Par.* 8.76–84). In the *Monarchia* there may be several other general allusions to Robert (2.2.1, 3.3.18), but one must bear in mind that the date of origin of the *Monarchia* is still subject to discussion. Dante even ridicules Robert's love for culture, calling him a *re ... da sermone* ("a king ... that should be a preacher," *Par.* 8.147), thereby emphasizing that the Angevin was more suited to be a priest or scribe than a king.

Bibliography

Arnaldi, G. "La maledizione del sangue e la virtù delle stelle. Angioini e Capetingi nella *Commedia* di Dante." *La Cultura* 30 (1992), 47–74, 185–216.

Caggese, R. "Dante e Roberto d'Angiò." In *Studi per Dante*. Vol. 3. Edited by A. Solmi. Milan: Hoepli, 1935, pp. 67ff.

————. *Roberto d'Angiò e i suoi tempi.* 2 vols. Florence: Bemporad and Figlio, 1922, 1930.

Goetz, W. *König Robert von Neapel (1309–1343). Seine Persönlichkeit und sein Verhältnis zum Humanismus.* Tübingen: Mohr, 1910.

Kiesewetter, A. "Das Geburtsjahr König Roberts von Anjou und Fürst Philipps I. von Tarent." *Quellen und Forschungen aus italienischen Archiven und Bibliotheken* 74 (1994), 664ff.

Léonard, E. G. *Les Angevins de Naples.* Paris: Presses universitaires de France, 1954, pp. 209ff.

Pézard, A. *Il canto VIII del Paradiso.* Bologna: Cappelli, 1953, pp. 15ff.

Siragusa, G. B. *L'ingegno, il sapere e gl'intendimenti di Roberto d'Angiò.* Palermo: Clausen, 1891.

Andreas Kiesewetter

Roland

Nephew of Charlemagne and one of the twelve peers, Roland *(Orlando)* is the protagonist of the *Chanson de Roland.* Dante mentions him together with other champions and defenders of the Faith (including Charlemagne, Renouard, William of Orange, Godfrey of Bouillon, and Robert Guiscard), who appear in the shining cross in the Heaven of Mars (*Par.* 18.43). In *Inf.* 31.16–18 the bugle sound the pilgrim hears upon entering Cocytus, the last circle of Hell, is compared to the sound that Roland's horn made when he desperately attempted to recall Charlemagne and his troops to Roncesvalles.

Michelangelo Picone
(translated by Robin Treasure)

Romanticism

The importance of Romanticism in the unfolding reception and appropriation of Dante in Western literary culture can be conveniently summarized by comparing the critical reactions of two of the greatest men of letters of their times, Voltaire in the eighteenth century and Matthew Arnold in the nineteenth. For Voltaire, who both spoke for and represented the literary values of his day—and these were values accepted even by Dante's defenders—Dante's poem was a "salmagundi," a kind of hodge-podge of grotesque imbalance and poor taste, the product of a barbarous age before poetic refinement and the social advancements brought about by the dawning philosophy of enlightenment were in place. For Matthew Arnold—and that this is a major English critic demonstrates Dante's emergence from the confines of Italian criticism into a kind of European universality—Dante ranks with the Greek tragedians, with Homer, and with Shakespeare in giving expression to that "high and excellent seriousness" that is the touchstone of all great literature.

What happened in between was something that could be called Romanticism but may be considered the third stage in the developing fortunes of Dante as a poet. If the first stage is represented by the extraordinary commentaries of the fourteenth century that treated the *Commedia* as a more or less contemporary event (but one still requiring elaborate explication), the second stage originated with the criticism of Cardinal Bembo, when Dante, along with Petrarch and Boccaccio, became a model of imitation for the writers of the sixteenth century. Following the *secolo senza poesia* ("age without poetry"), broadly understood, writers of the sixteenth century were urged to find in their own national past the classics of their language. In time, this classicizing impetus was overtaken by its own critical progressivism, and Dante began to be faulted by the same *renascence des lettres* that he had helped initiate throughout Europe. This relegation of Dante to obscure Gothic mists was completed in the attitudes of Voltaire, but even Giuseppe Baretti, who wrote contra Voltaire, was obliged to accept his standards of refinement and taste. While defending the *Inferno* against charges of effeminacy, he still laments the crudities of language, which he attributes to the impure literary tastes of Dante's epoch: "That spirit of method and geometry that hath taken possession, for more than an age, of the poetry of the principal nations, and hath been the consequence of rigid observation and exact criticism, could not be found in the time of Dante, as he was the first great poet and great writer" (quoted in Corrigan, 41).

The development of the third phase of Dantean criticism obviously predated the boundaries of Romanticism, strictly conceived. In fact, in the midst of full classicism and enlightenment, Giambattista Vico initiated the first major reevaluation of Dante. In his *New Science* and in his introduction to the publication of an ancient commentary on the *Commedia,* Vico was struck by one fact: Homer, who by then had superseded Virgil as the greatest poet of the classical world, wrote

R before the critical principles of either Aristotle or Longinus were established. In this sense a historical parallel exists between Homer and Dante, since Dante's own powerful performance also predated the reintroduction of classical standards and rules. From this poetic fact, Vico derived a conclusion of great cultural importance—that poetic wisdom and poetic creation may require a faculty which is antithetical to philosophical wisdom and the creation of philosophy: "In the very nature of poetry it is impossible for anyone to be at the same time a sublime poet and a sublime metaphysician . . . metaphysics soars up to the universals, and the poetic mind must plunge deep into particulars" (quoted in Quinones, 191).

Vico's approach bore two crucial implications for the coming new age of Dantean criticism. One was historical: Dante had to be understood in relation to his times (for Vico, this meant a Dante who possessed some of the concrete historical powers of the precedent age of barbarism; that is, Dante himself was a historical poet). The other was the legacy of "two Dantes"—a Dante who would have been a greater poet had he not been so interested in philosophy. These two issues help establish the positions of Ugo Foscolo and Francesco De Sanctis in the nineteenth century.

Given the somewhat self-confident, certainly blithe rhetorical criticism of the eighteenth century, which led to smug dismissals on the most impressionistic bases, the historical purpose of the nineteenth century can be attributed to motives of critical generosity. Its critical practitioners wished to understand and even judge a work in regard to the particular events and ideas of its own time. In two review articles appearing in the *Edinburgh Review* in 1818, Foscolo wrote of his discovery of the *terra incognita* of Dantean criticism. His main insight was that Dante must be understood in relation to the events, ideas, personalities, and language of his time. This led to a still useful esthetic principle: history is not only the background of Dante's poem; it is also the foreground, making up the substance of much of the action. The kind of interests that Foscolo represented led to the great accumulation of positive historical data crucial to any understanding of Dante, as well as to valuable philological and textual readings.

In a more general sense Romantic criticism devoted attention to poetic creations agitated by great passions. New terms of value that came to the front were "dramatic energy" and "compas-

sion." A post-Napoleonic generation was infatuated by the throes of a doomed heroism and consequently became committed to retrieving the rejected. While in Shakespearean criticism this meant a vindication of Richard III and Richard II, of Falstaff and Shylock; or in regard to Milton an inordinate attachment to Satan in *Paradise Lost;* in parallel fashion, in Dantean criticism this new transformation of values involved an extraordinary amount of attention paid to the *Inferno,* including passionate critical justifications of its dominant characters: Francesca, Farinata, Brunetto Latini, Ugolino, et al. The age of Romantic criticism was largely (but not exclusively) the age of the *Inferno.*

While more a postromantic than a Romantic, Francesco De Sanctis gave fullest expression to all these motivations. Moving beyond both rhetorical as well as historical criticism, he wished to recapture the great human drama of Dante's poem. By means of intensely personal re-creation his criticism seeks to force dramatic encounters with Dante's characters in their essential human natures. Francesca is not a depraved person but a woman who, "in the weakness and distress of her struggle, preserves inviolate the essential qualities of womanhood—purity, modesty, gentleness, exquisite delicacy of feeling; [who], even if guilty, we feel to be part of ourselves, of our common nature, and she arouses the highest interest, draws tears from our eyes, and makes us fall . . . 'like a dead body' " *Inf.* 5.143 (quoted in Rossi and Galpin, 41). Citing the subaltern nature of scholarly background information, his critical aim is to find in the poetry enduring human situations. For instance, the history of Dante's involvement with the Cavalcanti may be useful, yet it lies esthetically inert. But when the old father asks Dante about his son, the poetic situation is eternal: "The poetry here derives its value, its interest, and its accessory ideas from human nature, immortal and ever young, and it preserves thus its freshness even when the impressions, feelings and facts that inspired the poet have vanished" (77).

For De Sanctis, the absolute validity of Dante's poetry comes from this power to present living images of human nature. Francesca is "the first real, flesh-and-blood woman to appear on the poetical horizon of modern times" (36). With the imperious figure of Farinata, "Man appears for the first time on the modern poetical horizon" (66). Like Matthew Arnold, De Sanctis places Dante alongside Homer in the ancient world, alongside

Shakespeare in the modern world, by virtue of his prodigious ability to recreate classical situations of abiding emotional appeal. It is for this reason that Dante could be called a "classic." But, as with Shakespeare, Dante has the added glory of being the first among the moderns to bring forward as enduring types the men and women of his age. Dante, the first classic of the modern world, has replenished the repertoire of modern myth.

While like Vico, like Foscolo, De Sanctis himself has made essential contributions—contributions that are still valid—to our understanding of Dante, he has also perpetuated the critical problem of the *two* Dantes. This division is based upon such false dichotomies as abstraction *versus* human reality; dogma or doctrine *versus* poetry or passion; poetry *versus* structure. Such oppositions are related to the essential romantic faith that beneath a surface appearance there lies a deeper truth; beneath the conventional there lies the genuine. This leads to the illusion that historical knowledge, philosophical ideas, even architectonics are separable from and even irrelevant to our apprehension of the genuine poetry; and to the even greater illusion that emotional response may be pure and hence separable from the contents of the mind.

Unlike Dante's fortunes among the French critics, his reputation among the English has had a bountiful history. Geoffrey Chaucer could be regarded as Dante's greatest English follower in the fourteenth century, and with the coming of the Reformation, Dante's antipapal attacks found eager reception among English reformers (particularly with John Milton). But the age of Romanticism in England, as in Italy, was the beginning of the age of Dante. Prior to 1782 there is no record of any translation in English of even a canto of Dante. But from that date through 1900, there were some forty translations—certainly abundant evidence of Dante's growing appeal. The greatest translation was that of Henry Cary, who "Englished" the *Commedia* (he at first called it *The Vision*) into blank verse. His rendering of the *Inferno* appeared in 1804 and that of the entire poem in 1814, but it was only when Foscolo reviewed it in the *Edinburgh Review* in 1818 and Samuel Taylor Coleridge used it as the standard text of Dante's poem in his course of lectures of 1818 that Cary's version began to have the success that was its due.

Coleridge stands as a critical figure in Dante's fate among the English Romantics. In his course of lectures, all eleven quotations and references made to Dante's poem come from the *Inferno*. But in other ways he differs from the Italian critics and thus reflects the different conditions of England as a growing economic powerhouse. From that perspective Dante was not the product of a divided culture; nor did his works reflect any such division. In contrast to his own country's economic liberalism, Coleridge could admire in Dante's Florence the reconciliation of the commercial spirit with the "nobler principles of social polity." "It [the commercial spirit] tended there to union and permanence and elevation,—not as the overbalance of it now in England is doing, to dislocation, change and moral degradation" (quoted in Corrigan, 68). Furthermore, himself an heir of the Reformation, he did not see in Dante any gaping division between the classical and the Christian. In fact, ". . . Dante was the living link between religion and philosophy; he philosophized the religion and christianized the philosophy of Italy" (69). Perhaps because Coleridge perceived such unity and promise in Dante's culture and in its philosophical and religious purposes, he was able to anticipate much twentieth-century criticism in emphasizing Dante's poetic performance. For instance, he praises Dante's style, "the vividness, logical connection, strength and energy of which cannot be surpassed" (72); in fact, on this point he regards Dante as superior to Milton. He praises Dante's "images" which "are ever conjoined with the universal feeling received from nature, and therefore affect the general feelings of all time" (73). In "picturesqueness" Dante surpasses all poets ancient and modern, as Coleridge goes on to single out the topographic reality of Dante's Hell, admiring its sheer inventiveness.

Obviously, Coleridge shared many of the Italian Romantic attitudes toward Dante—particularly their praise of the poet's high patriotism, which established him in their mind as a precursor of the Risorgimento. But while his own evaluations reveal the different economic, political, and religious conditions of England in the nineteenth century, like that of his Italian compeers Coleridge's criticism elevated Dante's work to the status of world classic—a preeminence that it maintains to the present.

Bibliography

Brandeis, Irma. *Discussions of the "Divine Comedy."* Garden City, N.Y.: Anchor Books, 1962.

R

Corrigan, Beatrice. *Italian Poets and English Criticism, 1755–1859*. London, Chicago: University of Chicago Press, 1969.

Cunningham, Gilbert F. *The "Divine Comedy" in English, 1782–1800*. New York: Barnes and Noble, 1965.

De Sanctis on Dante. Edited and translated by Joseph Rossi and Alfred Galpin. Madison: University of Wisconsin Press, 1957.

Pite, Ralph. *The Circle of Our Vision*. Oxford: Clarendon Press, 1994.

Quinones, Ricardo J. *Dante Alighieri*. New York: Twayne Macmillan, 1979.

Ricardo J. Quinones

Rome

For Dante Rome was more than a city; indeed he seems to have been little interested in the contemporary commune. She was rather the symbol of the universal empire and of the universal church. Dante even pictured the Old Man of Crete, representing humanity in its various historical stages, looking toward the city as toward his mirror (*Inf.* 14.103–105). She was the *patria* of all Italians. It was the earthly *patria* of Christ, who enrolled himself in the census decreed by Augustus. The temporal peace established by that emperor was not only a unique contribution to human happiness but also could symbolize the eternal peace enjoyed in the heavenly *patria* of which Beatrice told Dante they would be citizens forever: *quella Roma onde Cristo è romano* ("that Rome in which Christ is a Roman," *Purg.* 32.102).

Dante and the Physical City

Dante is generally thought to have visited the city at least twice, although this is not certain. He describes the crowds crossing the Tiber in two directions over Ponte Sant'Angelo in a way that suggests that he was a participant in the papal Jubilee of 1300 (*Inf.* 18.28–33). He was listed by the contemporary chronicler Dino Compagni as one of three Florentine ambassadors sent to Pope Boniface VIII in 1301 (*Cronica* 2.25). Dante characterizes the citizens of contemporary Rome—as was often done by medieval writers—in a satirical and disparaging fashion, calling their dialect the basest in Italy, but a good match for their manners and morals. He speaks of the stones and site of Rome as hallowed in *Conv.* 4.5.22–24, but he does not describe many of her monuments. He refers to Rome's appearance in general terms when he says the view from the Uccellatoio, a hill overlooking Florence, now surpasses that from Montemalo (Monte Mario), a hill overlooking Rome (*Par.* 15.109–111). He describes the awe of the barbarian beholding the Lateran, when it stood above all mortal things, probably using the name metonymically to designate the whole city of Rome (*Par.* 31.31–37). He refers to the size of the great bronze pine cone in the atrium of St. Peter's as comparable with the size of the giant Nimrod's face (*Inf.* 31.58–60). He also refers to the stone needle or obelisk standing beside the same basilica and to the image of Christ's face on the veil of St. Veronica kept within it (*Conv.* 4.16.6; *Par.* 31.104; *VN* 40.1). He mentions the Tarpeian rock, whose treasury was plundered by Julius Caesar, and the Aventine rock, under which Cacus had his lair (*Purg.* 9.137–138; *Inf.* 25.25–27). But some of these references are probably only literary. He is much more concerned with Rome's history and prehistory and with demonstrating that God predestined it to be the seat of both imperial and ecclesiastical authority. The history of Troy was the prehistory of Rome; Aeneas, who brought his band of Trojans to Latium, was, according to Dante and Virgil, the father of the Romans. In regard to the other journey of Aeneas that Virgil had recounted—that to the world of the shades—Dante told Virgil that this journey was the reason behind the successful completion of the other one, because on it Aeneas *intese cose che furon cagione / di sua vittoria e del papale ammanto* ("understood things that were the cause of his victory and of the papal mantle," *Inf.* 2.26–27). Dante also told Virgil that it should not seem inappropriate to a rational person that Aeneas was allowed to make this journey while he was still alive, for he had been chosen in the Empyrean to be the father of Rome and the Empire, that is, of the monarchy or universal temporal rule, ordained by God for Rome, and for Rome alone. Rome was also ordained as the place where St. Peter's successors should sit, and their spiritual responsibility was correspondingly universal. Rome was thus given two suns, one to light the way of men toward earthly beatitude, the other toward heavenly beatitude; one was supposed to teach men virtue through law, the other revealed truth through imitation of Christ's life. Dante lamented that instead the spiritual light, in its eagerness to dominate everything, had put out the temporal one, and as a result could not function properly itself (*Purg.* 16.106–111).

Prehistory and Empire

Dante read about the prehistory and imperium of Rome mainly in Virgil, Livy, Lucan, Orosius, St. Augustine, John of Salisbury, Brunetto Latini, and perhaps Paul the Deacon. Rome's prehistory began for Dante inauspiciously, with the Trojans' denial of hospitality to the Argives (the Argonauts) when on their voyage to bring back the Golden Fleece (*Epist.* 5.24). He must have read in Brunetto Latini's *Tresor* (1.28.32) that the Trojan King, angry because the Greeks had killed his uncle, had closed his gates to Jason, Hercules, and their companions. This denial of entrance was, according to Dante, the first "tiny spark" of the great fire of predestination by which God had ordained that the Roman people should win the imperium. The "sacred standard," the eagle, "the bird of God," started its flight to Latium from Troy after that proud city was humbled and destroyed by the Greeks. Aeneas' "victory" over the Latins started the process by which Rome gained a prize never won before. These wars culminated in the defeat of Pyrrhus and his Greeks and Hannibal and his Carthaginians. At this point, Rome had won what Dante calls the "crown of the whole world" (*Mon.* 2.9.19; cf. *Inf.* 1.74–75; *Par.* 6.1–51).

The Roman people gained this crown by law or right since their victory was so spectacular that it was evidently part of God's providential plan. Their right, Dante seems to be saying, was based not on might but on God's will. It was, however, revealed by might, by the success of the military force through which they won their victories. Force was the instrument, and God's will, which is identical with justice, was the cause. Therefore, all Rome's wars were righteous, and all her conquests were just. Only the stupid or perverse, Dante says, could fail to see this, though Dante confessed that he himself had failed to see it for a time (*Mon.* 2.1–2). Then perhaps he was under the influence of St. Augustine's less sympathetic view of Roman history. Augustine had praised the exploits of Rome and her heroes, but in an ironic way, saying that they were the result of ambition and pride (*De civ. Dei* 5.17–18). But by 1307–1308, when he wrote *Conv.* 4.4–5, Dante thought that Rome's successes were part of God's provident plan. Probably, as Ulrich Leo has suggested, this was the result of rereading Virgil.

This establishment of world rule through wars decided by God is also described in *Mon.* 2 and in *Par.* 6; in the *Paradiso* passage, where Justinian is Dante's mouthpiece, the Roman victories do not end with Scipio's, as they do in *Mon.* 2.9.18. Justinian also describes exultantly and at length the campaigns—extending from the Rhine to the Red Sea—of the first two emperors to bear the sacred standard: Julius Caesar and Augustus. Their triumphs made possible the Augustan peace, under which, Dante remarks, mankind was happier than it had ever been or would ever be.

The overwhelming success of the sacred standard clearly revealed divine predestination. This by itself seems to have been Dante's principle argument, perhaps on the model of the analogous contention so favored by Christian Fathers, that the spread of Christianity was the supreme miracle which validated all other miracles. But Dante, perhaps uncomfortable with the starkness of this single argument—a starkness that may have seemed to him almost Augustinian—was not content to stop here. Following and developing Virgilian, Livian, Ciceronian, and Orosian themes he tried also to justify Rome's imperium on other grounds. The competition between Rome and its rivals might be viewed as a race for a prize or a kind of judicial duel entered into without greed or anger but for the sole purpose of discovering God's will. God's predestination of the Romans was also apparent from the miracles that authoritative writers like Livy, Virgil, and Lucan had attested to as occurring in pagan times. These indicated that the Romans, like the Jews, were a chosen people. To reinforce this concept, Dante took from the encyclopedia of his old master Brunetto Latini the information that the arrival of Aeneas in Latium coincided with the birth of King David, the ancestor of Christ. This obviously foreshadowed the future coincidence between Christ's birth and the Augustan peace. Dante said, moreover, following Orosius, that Christ had chosen to be born at a time when he could be enrolled as a Roman in the Augustan census, and therefore tacitly recognized the legitimacy of Roman rule. But the Roman authorities had executed a guiltless man at the instigation of the Jews. Orosius said that the Romans, through Titus' subsequent sack of Jerusalem, had punished the Jews justly. Dante followed him in advancing this theory. But Dante also advanced, in connection with Christ's death, a sweeping and original theory of his own. He made

Justinian say that all the achievements of the Eagle up to and after the reign of the third caesar (Tiberius), and afterward throughout the world subject to it, seemed small in comparison with what it wrought under him. Then it was given the privilege of exacting vengeance for the ancient sin, that is, of executing Christ as a penalty for Adam's Fall (*Par.* 6.82–93). By submitting to Pilate, Christ recognized the earthly authority of Rome. Dante maintained that if the jurisdiction of Rome had not been universal and based on justice, Christ's death could not have redeemed mankind (*Mon.* 2.11). Therefore pagan Rome was indispensable not only to man's earthly beatitude but to his heavenly beatitude as well.

These events in the life of the Messiah were part of the revealed truth contained in the Scriptures and were additional signs that God had predestined the Romans to win and exercise world monarchy. Why had he done so? This question could be answered, at least in part, on rational grounds. The Romans could be said to have won the prize of imperium because they demonstrated such a high degree of acquired moral virtue. Dante did not use this technical term, but he agreed with a theologian like Aquinas that the moral and intellectual virtues were real and praiseworthy, even though they did not suffice for salvation (*Mon.* 2.7.4). Dante even thought that man could reach his ultimate temporal end through natural reason and virtue—or, more precisely, through following philosophical teachings while practicing the moral and intellectual virtues (*Mon.* 3.15.8).

In describing the moral virtues of the Romans that made them especially fitted to rule, Dante found the ideas of pagan apologists like Virgil, Cicero, and Livy very helpful. Their imperium might appropriately be called, as Cicero had said in his *De officiis,* a *patrocinium,* for the Romans were willing to sacrifice their own interests to the common good and gave conquered nations peace with liberty—that true liberty which, according to Dante, consisted in obedience to legitimate authority. It is evident from various passages in his works that while he thought resistance to Rome was permissible until it had won the prize of empire, after that the rebel who refused to submit to Rome's sacred laws was not free but a slave, subjecting reason to selfish appetite.

As for the *patrocinium,* Dante does not discuss its nature in any detail but illustrates it somewhat obliquely by eulogizing the famous heroes of the republic. In some cases the same heroes accused of ambition and self-love by St. Augustine are praised by Dante for sacrifice and altruistic love for their *patria.* Such virtue, Dante affirmed, was a natural attribute of the Latin race—*e massimamente [di] quello popolo santo, nel quale l'alto sangue troiano era mischiato, cioè Roma* ("and especially of that sacred people in whom was mingled the lofty blood of the Trojans, namely Rome"). No other people, said Dante, had been or ever would be better at getting, keeping, and exercising rule than the *gente latina,* or Latin race. Therefore God had chosen them for this task (*Conv.* 4.4.10–11).

So far God's choice might be considered a recognition of natural virtue. But for Dante that choice involves an infusion of celestial virtue as well. Dante believes that this was necessary to enable the Romans to fulfill their historical mission. He says that Rome was *essaltata non co[n] umani cittadini, ma co[n] divini, ne li quali non amore umano, ma divino era inspirato in amare lei. Certo e manifesto esser dee . . . non sanza alcuna luce de la divina bontade, aggiunta sopra la loro buona natura, essere tante mirabili operazioni state* ("exalted not with human but with godlike citizens whose love of her was inspired not by a human but a divine love . . . Surely it must be evident . . . that these wondrous events took place, not without some light of the divine goodness over and above their own natural goodness," *Conv.* 4.5.12, 17).

Dante does not use the technical terms employed by theologians like Aquinas to differentiate between "infused" and "acquired" virtues, though he seems clearly aware of the distinction. Aquinas says that the theological virtues of faith, hope, and charity are always infused; the moral virtues may be either infused or acquired. The former must be infused by divine grace; the latter can be infused by grace or acquired by human effort. At times Dante seems to draw a sharp line between these sets of virtues, as when he says at the end of *Monarchia* that while the moral virtues help man attain temporal happiness, the theological virtues help him attain eternal happiness. But in *Mon.* 1.11.13 Dante says that the emperor should possess charity, and it is surely charity that Dante is talking about in *Conv.* 4.5 when he speaks of the intense love of their *patria* infused in the Romans by God. Dante sees the evidence of such love in their extreme temperance and fortitude and in their willingness to sacrifice wealth or life for their *patria.*

Dante's heroes in *Conv.* 4.5 possessed *caritas*, but there is no evidence that any of them—except perhaps Cato, whom we find as guardian of purgatory in Dante's *Comedia*—possessed that faith in Christ without which Dante believed salvation is impossible. The good Emperor Trajan and the Trojan hero Ripheus had such faith but only because of divine aid. Dante followed the celebrated legend which told how God acceded to Pope Gregory I's prayer and allowed Trajan to leave Hell and return to his own body so that he could believe in Christ. This kindled such a fire of love in him for God that he was able to obtain salvation. Dante created his own legend for Ripheus, whom he knew only from the brief passage in the *Aeneid* that pictured him as meeting his death in the last battle for Troy, and called him "the most just of the Trojans" (*Aen.* 2.426–428). According to Dante, God's grace enabled him to set all his love on right (*drittura*). Successive gifts of grace from God allowed him to see man's future redemption and to hate and condemn the stench of paganism, so that he was permitted to possess the theological virtues of faith, hope, and charity and receive from them his baptism into the Christian faith long before the coming of Christ (*Par.* 20.100–129).

Neither Trajan nor Ripheus seems to have taken the initiative in his conversion. God's fulfilment of Gregory's hope allowed Trajan to possess faith and charity. God's grace infused such an exceptional love of *drittura* in Ripheus that it led to the subsequent infusions of the theological virtues, so that when Ripheus died, he was already a Christian. Was it the extraordinary degree to which Trajan and Ripheus possessed the natural virtue of justice that attracted God's grace? One may think so, but Dante does not say so.

Among Christian emperors Dante saves Constantine, Justinian, and Charlemagne and sees a great throne awaiting Henry VII in Paradise (*Par.* 20.55–57, 6.10, 18.43, 30.133–138). The only emperor he damns is Frederick II—condemned to a fiery tomb because he did not believe in immortality (*Inf.* 10.118–119)—but he praises Frederick and his son Manfred for making their court the center of literary brilliance in Italy and for living nobly and generously (*DVE* 1.12.4). After Frederick's death in 1250 and after the interval of Henry VII's ill-fated expedition to Italy between 1310 and 1313, Rome lived, Dante thought, deprived of her imperial husband (*Purg.* 6.112–114). Also left alone in misery was Italy, of whose civilization Rome was the origin and head (*Epist.* 11.22–23).

Papal Rome

Dante's version of ecclesiastical history is told brilliantly, if sometimes enigmatically, by the pageant he describes in the final cantos of *Purgatorio*. The pageant includes many figures and symbols representing episodes in the history of the Church, and it often uses imagery taken from the Book of Revelation, which was widely supposed to contain prophecies of that history. The symbol for the Church is a chariot or triumphal car, which Dante describes as more glorious than any prepared for Scipio Africanus or Augustus—those two Romans who stood at the culminating points of secular history. Scipio won the prize of world monarchy for Rome by defeating Hannibal, and Augustus established the universal peace. This chariot is preceded by twenty-four elders representing the books of the Old Testament and surrounded by the symbols of the Evangelists and the four cardinal moral and the three theological virtues, dancing in their respective groups at the left and right wheels. The chariot is followed by figures indicating the other books of the New Testament. On the chariot appears Beatrice, at once Dante's personal saint and, on the allegorical level, the symbol of divine grace and revelation transmitted through the Church.

The chariot is drawn by a griffin, half eagle and half lion. Its two natures, representing Christ's, are reflected in Beatrice's eyes. It draws the chariot toward a great barren tree, the tree of divine justice despoiled by Adam. The tree begins to blossom after the griffin has attached the chariot's pole (the Cross) to it—an act that represents Christ's atonement for Adam's sin. Then the griffin and his entourage ascend to Heaven, leaving Beatrice and the chariot below. She descends from it and sits on the root of the great tree.

The chariot now suffers a series of attacks. After the Eagle (representing imperial persecutions of Christians) strikes the tree and the chariot, a fox (probably heresy) jumps into the chariot but is put to flight by Beatrice. Then comes a second descent by the Eagle which leaves its feathers on the chariot—without doubt a reference to the so-called Donation of Constantine, a forged document indicating that the first Christian emperor had given control over Rome and the western provinces to the pope.

Next, a dragon (a devilish infusion of hypocrisy and luxury within the Church?) pulls off part of the bottom of the chariot with its tail. Meanwhile the chariot sprouts seven heads and ten horns and becomes the seat of a prostitute (probably representing the corruption and cupidity of the modern papacy). Then a giant appears (Antichrist? Phillip IV, king of France, as a precursor of Antichrist?) and first embraces and then beats the whore. Finally, the giant drags her and the chariot off into the forest (the transfer of the papacy to Avignon?). Beatrice tells Dante that the Eagle that dropped its feathers on the chariot will not always be without an heir and that a messenger of God, "a five hundred ten and five" (a Roman emperor?) will come and kill the giant and the prostitute.

Much of the interpretation suggested above is traditional and generally accepted. Some of it, however, has provoked vigorous dissent. A recent and highly original example of such dissent is Peter Armour's attack on the identification of the griffin as Christ. Armour says that the griffin was reputed to be much too ferocious an animal to be used for this purpose and that no examples of this interpretation have been found in medieval writing or art. Instead, he believes the griffin represents an idealized Rome, its aquiline nature reflecting the empire, and its leonine nature the commune. But the rapid succession of three contrasting symbols for Rome is not very plausible. It is hard to conciliate the ascent of a griffin representing imperial and civic Rome with the drama of the monstrous interaction of imperial Rome, the descents of the Eagle, and ecclesiastical Rome (the whore and transformed chariot) down below.

A woman very similar in appearance to the prostitute of *Purg.* 32 is referred to in *Inf.* 19. There she is specifically identified with papal Rome and with the Great Whore of Apoc. 17. Finding the simoniac pope Nicholas III (reigned 1278–1280) stuck upside down in a burning hole in Hell, Dante addresses him in the following terms: *Di voi pastor s'accorse il Vangelista, / quando colei che siede sopra l'acque / puttaneggiar coi regi a lui fu vista; / quella che con le sette teste nacque, / e da le diece corna ebbe argomento, / fin che virtute al suo marito piacque* ("Of you shepherds the Evangelist took note, when he saw her who sits upon the waters whoring with the kings; she who was born with seven heads, and took strength from her ten horns as long as virtue pleased her husband," *Inf.* 19.106–111).

John the Evangelist in the Book of Revelation describes a prostitute sitting above the waters and on a beast with seven heads and ten horns, though it is sometimes difficult to determine from St. Jerome's translation whether she and the beast were two creatures or one and, if two, which has the heads and horns. St. John is told that the Whore is Babylon the great city; that the waters are peoples, nations, and languages; that the seven heads are seven hills on which she sits, or seven kings; and that the ten horns are ten kings, who first connive with the Whore and then rebel against her. The Whore holds in her hand a golden vase containing the filth of her fornications with the kings of Earth, and she is drunk with the blood of the saints, of the followers of Christ. Obviously she is the new Babylon: pagan Rome.

After the conversion of Constantine and the rise to power of the Christian Church, this interpretation of the Whore was less relevant. Most orthodox exegetes used the metaphor of the Great Whore to describe wickedness within the Church and identified her not with external persecutors but with the whole mass of the reprobate. In the thirteenth century, the symbol came more and more frequently to be interpreted again in a historical way and was often referred to Rome, but this time especially to the new Rome of the popes.

Even if an exegete did not attack the papacy specifically, he might, like the great scriptural commentator Joachim of Fiore, refer to a particular and contemporary period of corruption within the Church. It would be misleading to call Dante a follower of the famous abbot, though he did say that Joachim was *di spirito profetico dotato* ("endowed with prophetic spirit," *Par.* 12.141). Joachim's influence touched the radical wing of the Franciscan movement—for example, the head of the so-called Spiritual faction of the order, Petrus Johannis Olivi, and through him, his disciple Ubertino da Casale.

Olivi and Ubertino were both teaching at the great convent of Santa Croce in Florence between 1287 and 1289, very close to the time when Dante said he began to attend the schools of the religious orders. Olivi identified the figure of the Great Whore with Rome, singling out both the Rome of the pagan persecutors and the papal Rome of his own day (*Postilla in Apocalipsim,* extract edited by Tocco, 39). His friend and disciple, Ubertino da Casale, went further: he identified particular popes with monsters from the Apocalypse, declaring that

Boniface VIII was the beast coming out of the sea and that his successor, Benedict XI, was the beast coming from the land; together they represented the mystical Antichrist (*Arbor vite crucifixae Jesu,* Venice, 1485, v. viii, ff. 232b–235a; cf. Apoc. 13).

Dante follows Olivi in coupling the persecutions of pagan emperors and contemporary popes, and he follows Ubertino in applying apocalyptic imagery to particular popes. Perhaps Dante's choice of Nicholas III as the simoniac pope he meets in *Inf.* 19 was inspired by another apparently Franciscan text: the anonymous *Vaticinia de summis pontificibus.* It contains pseudo-prophecies of corrupt popes from Nicholas III down at least to Boniface VIII, sparing only Celestine V, the hermit-pope who protected radical Franciscans. Dante selects Boniface VIII and Clement V (the pope who transferred the Curia to Avignon) as the companions in simony who Pope Nicholas reveals will replace him at the top of his hole. Dante also links John XXII to his predecessor, Clement V, as one of those new persecutors coming to drink the blood of the saints.

Dante seems to have agreed with Olivi and Ubertino and the author of the *Vaticinia* that the corruption of the Roman Church had increased greatly in the late thirteenth and early fourteenth centuries. But he went back further than they to find the origin of ecclesiastical decadence: the Donation of Constantine. This was the event that in his opinion had confused the functions of the imperial and papal authorities, weakening the former and corrupting the latter. In this he was closer to the heretical tradition of the Waldensians and Albigensians than to the Spiritual Franciscans.

Dante's theory of the Donation is an indispensable key to understanding his conception of the course of Church history. It is also indispensable to understanding the meaning of his descriptions of the Whore. When she appears on the chariot of the Church and is embraced by the giant, she is already a prostitute. The effects of her wealth and luxury are apparent, not only in her appearance and behavior but also in the chariot of the Church, which has been "Romanized" in a political and secular sense by her greed and ambition. Her dalliance with the giant and the subsequent beating he gives her seem to reflect the fornications of the Whore with the kings of Earth described in the Apocalypse and their subsequent attack upon her. She represents papal Rome in its most corrupt stage.

The lady of *Inf.* 19 resembles her closely in the phase in which Dante says the Evangelists saw her fornicating with the kings. But she was not always a prostitute. She was born like Rome, with seven heads, and she had aid from the ten kings, Dante says, as long as "virtue" (strength, rule, probably the exercise of world imperium) pleased her husband (surely here the emperor). But after Constantine gave her other husband, Pope Sylvester I, the dowry of the western provinces and made him *il primo ricco patre* ("the first rich father," *Inf.* 19.115–117), the period of wealth, corruption, and fornication with the kings began. Constantine ceased to be Roman and made himself Greek, together with the laws and the Eagle. Constantine did not suffer for this, but the world did (*Par.* 20.55–60).

Dante must have believed that Justinian had arrested but not reversed this process. He certainly seems to have thought, together with the Spiritual Franciscans, that ecclesiastical decadence had reached a climax in his own time. So Rome and the western provinces had become "papalized" in a temporal rather than a spiritual sense, with the popes trying to be earthly rulers rather than guides to the beatitude of Heaven.

During the interregnum between the pontificates of Clement and John, Dante wrote a public letter (May or June 1314) to the Italian cardinals in the conclave, telling them that Rome was now like ruined Jerusalem. He quoted the passage from Lamentations: *Quomodo sola sedet civitas plena populo! facta est quasi vidua domina gentium* ("How doth the city sit solitary that was full of people! She is become as a widow that was great among the nations," *Epist.* 11.1–2) He said that Rome was now bereft of both her lights and in a state to be pitied even by Hannibal (*Epist.* 11.21). Dante urged the cardinals to remember their duty to the "country of the illustrious Scipios" (*Epist.* 11.25) and elect an Italian pope: . . . *si unanimes omnes qui huiusmodi exorbitationis fuistis auctores, pro Sponsa Christi, pro sede Sponse que Roma est, pro Ytalia nostra, et ut plenius dicam, pro tota civitate peregrinante in terris* . . . (". . . if you all, who were the authors of this deviation from the track, with one accord shall fight manfully for the Spouse of Christ, for the seat of the Spouse, which is Rome, for our Italy, and, to speak more at large, for the whole body politic now in pilgrimage on earth. . . ," *Epist.* 11.26). But no Italian was elected. In August 1316, Jacques Duese of

Cahors was chosen, and Dante is certainly referring to him as well as to Clement V when he makes St. Peter say that Gascons and Cahorsines were preparing to drink his blood.

John XXII did not bring the papacy back to Rome, but Dante evidently did not despair of the possibility of future Church reform. He probably believed that this reform would be initiated by a lay ruler, perhaps an emperor, as is indicated by Beatrice's linking of "the five hundred ten and five" with a new heir of the Eagle. Moreover, St. Peter himself after his tirade asserts that providence will soon bring succor: *Ma l'alta Provedenza, che con Scipio / difese a Roma la gloria del mondo, / soccorrà tosto* ("But the high Providence that with Scipio defended for Rome the glory of the world [the imperium] will come to our aid soon," *Par.* 27.61–63). Therefore Dante's tragic vision of Rome's destiny is not ultimately pessimistic, despite his somber view of the course that Christian times had followed after the loss of "the good world that Rome made" (*Purg.* 16.106).

Bibliography

Armour, Peter. *Dante's Griffin and the History of the World.* Oxford: Clarendon Press, 1989.

Dante e Roma: Atti del Convegno di Studi. Florence: Le Monnier, 1965.

Davis, Charles T. *Dante and the Idea of Rome.* Oxford: Clarendon Press, 1957.

Graf, Arturo. *Roma nella memoria e nelle immaginazioni del medio evo.* 2 vols. Turin: Loescher, 1882–1883.

Hollander, Robert, and Albert L. Rossi. "Dante's Republican Treasury." *Dante Studies* 104 (1986), 59–82.

Kantorowicz, Ernst H. *The King's Two Bodies.* Princeton, N.J.: Princeton University Press, 1957.

Kay, Richard. "The *mentalité* of Dante's *Monarchia.*" *Res Publica Litterarum* 9 (1986), 183–191.

Lenkeith, Nancy. *Dante and the Legend of Rome.* London: Warburg Institute, 1952.

Leo, Ulrich. "The Unfinished *Convivio* and Dante's Reading of the *Aeneid.*" *Medieval Studies* 13 (1951), 41–64.

Manselli, Raoul. "L'Anticristo Mistico: Pietro di Giovanni Olivi, Ubertino da Casale e i papi del loro tempo." *Collectanea Franciscana* 47 (1977), 5–25.

Nardi, Bruno. *Saggi di filosofia dantesca.* 2nd ed. Florence: La Nuova Italia, 1967.

Olivi, Petrus Johannis. *Postilla in Apocalipsim* (extract). Edited by F. Tocco. *Lectura Dantis: il canto XXXII del Purgatorio.* Florence: Sansoni, 1902, pp. 37–52.

Padoan, Giorgio. *Il pio Enea, l'empio Ulisse: Tradizione classica e intendimento medievale in Dante.* Ravenna: Longo, 1977.

Renucci, P. "Dante et les mythes du millenium." *Revue des Études Italiennes* 11:1–3 (1965), 393–421.

Scott, John A. "La contemporaneità Enea-Davide (*Convivio,* IV V 6)." *Studi Danteschi* 49 (1972), 129–134.

Thompson, David. "Dante's Virtuous Romans." *Dante Studies* 96 (1978), 145–162.

Zingarelli, Nicola. *Dante e Roma.* Rome: Loescher, 1895.

Charles T. Davis

Romeo di Villanova

The historical figure of Romeo is remarkably different from the character developed in *Par.* 6.127–142. Born around 1170 and identified by Pispisa (600) as a Catalan, Romeo was a keenly adept minister and political advisor for Raymond Berenger IV (1198–1245), the last count of Provence before the Angevin inheritance of the region through the marriage of Raymond's daughter Beatrice to Charles I of Anjou in 1246. Romeo's extraordinary political skills are cited by Dante in the "great and beauteous work" (6.129), in the advantageous marriages which Romeo arranged for Raymond's four daughters and future queens (Margaret, to Louis IX of France [1234]; Eleanor, to Henry III of England [1236]; Sancha, to Richard of Cornwall [1243]; and Beatrice, to Charles) in vv. 133–135, and in the mercantile description of Romeo's expansion of Raymond's political power (v. 138). Bigi (1032) reports that Raymond left Romeo "the sole conveyor of his land and daughters." However, much of Dante's episode turns on the poet's probable utilization of a late-thirteenth-century legend, preserved in Villani's fourteenth-century *Cronica* (7.90), in which the savvy politico is transformed into an exemplum of the wise, religious, industrious, yet modest and poor counselor who wins Raymond's trust through his prodigious increase of the count's wealth and power. The legendary Romeo becomes the victim of false accusations of political treachery brought by jealous barons. Disheartened by such injustice, the legendary Romeo calls Raymond ungrateful (*ovra grande e bella mal gradita,* "great and beauteous work . . . ill received"), requests only the few belongings with which he came to court, and vanishes to a life of begging (*Par.* 6.139–141; in Villani's later version: "you are hardly grateful; I came to your court a poor Rome-bound pilgrim [*romeo;* cf. *VN* 40.7], and have lived here honorably. Let me have the little mule, the staff, and the poor little bag I came here with"). A notarial document of December 15, 1250, places a still active Romeo in Provence, where he died shortly thereafter.

Critical response to Dante's Romeo has concentrated on parallels with Dante's own life of dedication to justice rewarded with unjust exile and wandering. Other scholars have attempted to incorporate this parallel of the "just man" (6.137) and the poet in the larger context of Justinian's narrative of his earthly establishment of heavenly justice and the history of the imperial Eagle, the "sacred emblem" (6.32). In response to the second of Dante's two questions at the close of *Par.* 5.127–128 ("I do not know . . . why . . . you occupy [this] sphere"), Justinian explains that the star Mercury "is adorned by good spirits who were active so that honor and fame might follow them" (*Par.* 6.112–114; cf. *Conv.* 2.13.11). The rhetorical artifice with which Justinian announces Romeo (*luce la luce di Romeo,* "shines the light of Romeo," 128) recalls the subtext for the canto (Matt. 5:16, *sic luceat lux vestra . . .*) and supplies the scriptural context for Romeo's presence as a legendary exemplum (Matt. 5:10–12). Romeo's light shines forth so that mankind "may see your good works" (Matt. 5:16) as a reflection of God's glory and the justice and reward of Heaven (Matt. 5:10–12). The legend of Romeo's good works and saintly character defines the active good spirits which the sphere contains beyond the example of Justinian's good works (in his laws and his Christian victories). Romeo's political virtues are not just Christian but saintly in their humble reflection of the glory of divine justice seemingly thwarted on Earth (but note *Par.* 6.130–132).

Bibliography

Bellomo, Saverio. "Contributo all'esegesi di *Par.* VI." *Italianistica* 19 (1990), 9–26.

Pispisa, Enrico. "Beringhieri, Ramondo." *Enciclopedia dantesca,* 1:599–600.

H. Wayne Storey

Romuald, St.

Of the Onesti family of Ravenna, St. Romuald (*Romoaldo;* c. 950–1027) founded the order of the Camaldoli, or reformed Benedictines, and established a number of hermitages, including a famous monastery in the Casentino near Florence. The members of his order (which received papal sanction from Alexander II in 1072) were directed to live a life of pure contemplation, and the monastic habit was changed from the Benedictine black to white. His life is recorded in St. Peter Damian's "Life of St. Romualdus." Dante places him, coupled with St. Macarius, among the spirits of the contemplatives in the Heaven of Saturn, where he is pointed out by St. Benedict (*Par.* 22.49).

Olivia Holmes

Romulus

Legendary founder of Rome, whose origins were so humble that the Romans ascribed his paternity to the god Mars. He is referred to in *Par.* 8.131 by his name Quirinus (*Quirino*) as an example of how heredity does not predetermine character, and in *Conv.* 4.5.11 (*Romolo*), where he is cited as the first of the Seven Kings of Rome.

Richard Lansing

Rudolph I

Son of Albert IV, count of Habsburg, and the father of Emperor Albert I, Rudolph (*Rodolfo;* 1218–1278) was elected emperor of the Roman Empire in 1272. Dante places him among the negligent princes in the Ante-Purgatory and observes him as he is "comforted" by his former foe, Ottokar of Bohemia (*Purg.* 7.94). In pointing him out to Dante, Sordello reproaches him for having neglectfully forgone the opportunity to heal Italy's wounds. See also *Par.* 8.72, where Charles Martel refers to him as his father-in-law, and *Conv.* 4.3.6, where Dante speaks of him disparagingly as a non-Roman emperor, because he was never crowned emperor in Rome.

Antonio Illiano

Ruggieri, Archbishop

Son of Ubaldini della Pila (*Purg.* 24.28) and nephew of Cardinal Ottaviano degli Ubaldini (*Inf.* 10.120), Ruggieri degli Ubaldini was Ghibelline archbishop of Pisa from 1278 to 1295

R (*Inf.* 32.125). He is found among the traitors to their guests in Antenora, home of those who betrayed their country or political party, at the border with Ptolomea, where he might be expected to be found. There his skull is gnawed upon by the turncoat Guelf Count Ugolino della Gherardesca, whom he had imprisoned and starved to death along with his sons and grandsons.

Roy Rosenstein

Rusticucci, Iacopo

A wealthy Guelf member of Florence's minor nobility, his family having only recently entered the aristocracy at the time of his birth. Documented as an adult between 1237 and 1269, Iacopo was eminent as a politician and a diplomat; in the latter capacity he was particularly active in 1254, when Florence subjected the Ghibelline cities of Pistoia, Siena, and Pisa in quick succession. He and Tegghiaio Aldobrandi were neighbors and worked together for their city-state on at least one occasion. In 1258 Iacopo was *capitano del popolo* of Arezzo.

He is one of the five notable Florentines of the past who *a ben far puoser li 'ngegni* ("put their minds to doing well") and about whom Dante inquires during his conversation with Ciacco (*Inf.* 6.79–82); and later he is one of the bearers of *onorati nomi* ("honored names," *Inf.* 16.59) encountered in the *girone* of the sodomites—indeed he is their spokesman (*Inf.* 16.44). His line *"la fiera moglie piú ch'altro mi nuoce"* ("my fierce wife harms me more than anything else," *Inf.* 16.45), now objectively impenetrable, was taken by early commentators to mean that his wife was so shrewish as to have driven him to homosexuality.

John C. Barnes

Ruth

Protagonist of a book of the Old Testament, a Moab, she chose to remain with and follow her Jewish mother-in-law, Naomi, after her husband's death and became a symbol of loyalty and a figure for the church of the Gentiles in medieval exegesis. Dante places her in the rose in the Empyrean Heaven, on the seventh level of Mary's line, describing her as the great-grandmother of the singer (David) who sorrowed for his sin (*Par.* 32.11–12).

Joan M. Ferrante

S

Sabellius

Roman cleric of the third century *(Sabellio)* who rejected the doctrine of the Trinity. He emphasized the view, deemed heretical by Dionysius of Alexandria (d. c. 264), that the Son did not have an individual divine existence, and that the Father, Son, and Holy Ghost were modes or aspects of the divine Unity, not individual persons. He is referred to in the Heaven of the Sun by St. Thomas Aquinas along with another heretic, Arias *(Par.* 13.127). None of his works survives.

Richard Lansing

Sabellus

In Lucan's *Pharsalia,* a soldier in the army of Cato of Utica who, when bitten by a seps (a tiny serpent of the Libyan desert), disintegrates while still alive into a little pool of decomposed matter *(Phars.* 9.761–788). His grotesque metamorphosis provides Dante with a descriptive model to emulate in *Inf.* 25.95, where in the mutual transformation of Francesco Cavalcanti and a certain Buoso, Sabellus *(Sabello)* vaunts his own imaginative superiority. Lucan's description of Sabellus' death may have provided a model for the torment of Vanni Fucci as well *(Inf.* 24.97–120).

Sally Mussetter

Saints

In a loose sense, all the characters who appear in *Paradiso* might be said to be saints, since they all enjoy the condition of complete celestial beatitude that is the eternal reward of those who have died at peace with God and passed in due time through the refining fires of Purgatory. But if the term is applied in its strict technical sense, as referring to deceased individuals who have been officially declared by the Church to have already entered into glory, and for whom the observance of a public cult throughout the whole Church is ordained—who have undergone the process commonly known as "canonization"—its relevance to the *Commedia* seems much more limited. Dante's "official" saints are a small and somewhat conservatively chosen body, and many of the most interesting and substantial characters in *Paradiso* (and elsewhere in the poem) are not among them.

It is worth remembering that canonization itself was a relatively recent development in Dante's time and that the complex and time-consuming process by which the contemporary Church makes decisions of this kind was not yet in existence. Exemplary individuals, particularly martyrs, had been venerated by the Christian community since its earliest days, and the practice of regionally circumscribed devotions to individuals famous within a particular diocese had become fairly widespread in the early Middle Ages, generally being subject to the authority of the local bishop; but the first attempt by central ecclesiastical authority, in the form of the pope, to regulate such practices by making official proclamation of the saintly status of a given individual dates only from the late tenth century, and only in the mid–thirteenth century Decretals of Pope Gregory IX (promulgated in 1234) did this assertion of the papacy's unique authority to confer the honors associated with canonization enter canon law. The elaboration of the canonization process to its modern complexity was the work of subsequent centuries.

The saints who make their appearance (or are invoked by name) in the text of the *Commedia* fall into three main groups, which might be defined as biblical, patristic, and modern. The biblical saints are figures whose fame rests on the account of their lives and witness given in the text of the New Testament; most of them are also venerated—usually on the authority of extrabiblical legend—as martyrs. This group includes John the Baptist; Stephen (whose prototypical act of self-sacrifice is evoked at *Purg.* 15.106–114); Paul (whose textual presence is surprisingly, and interestingly, scanty, being limited to a handful of references of which the most crucial is at *Inf.* 2. 28–32); Thomas the Apostle (*Par.* 16.129); Peter (frequently invoked but most palpably present in *Par.* 24–27); James (*Par.* 25); and John the Evangelist (*Par.* 25–26). Many interpreters also see biblical saints—most of the above plus Matthew, Mark, and Luke—among the personnel of the procession in the Earthly Paradise, in *Purg.* 29.

The patristic saints, on the other hand, are drawn from the early, but post-biblical, period of Christian history—through the mid–twelfth century—and are mostly individuals celebrated for their learning and the pertinence or authority of their doctrine; several of them were already, by Dante's time, being venerated as Church fathers or doctors. Augustine (though he is also seen as the founder of a religious order, *Par.* 32.35); John Chrysostom (*Par.* 12.136–137); Jerome (*Par.* 29.37); Gregory the Great (*Par.* 20.108, 27.133); Benedict, Macarius, and Romualdus (*Par.* 22.40, 49); Anselm (*Par.* 12.137); and Bernard of Clairvaux (*Par.* 31–33) all belong with this group, as does Dante's own personal patron, Lucy, the fourth-century martyr of Syracuse (*Inf.* 2.97; *Purg.* 9.55; *Par.* 32.137).

The "modern" saints are thirteenth-century figures, belonging to a historical generation only one or two before Dante's own, and mainly connected with the rivalry and internal disputes afflicting the Franciscan and Dominican orders—Francis (canonized in 1228 by Gregory IX) and Dominic (canonized in 1234, also by Gregory IX) above all (*Par.* 10–12). Bonaventure too, of course, appears in this connection, but he, not having been canonized until 1482, belongs to an interesting group of celebrated Christians who are, in the offi-

cial sense, saints for us but not for Dante, because they were not so honored during his lifetime. Most strikingly, this group includes none other than Thomas Aquinas, one of Dante's most influential intellectual mentors, who was only canonized in 1323; but his status is also shared by Albertus Magnus (*Par.* 10.98; canonized as late as 1931), Isidore of Seville (*Par.* 10.131; canonized in 1598), and Peter Damian (*Par.* 21.121; canonized in 1828).

Many more of the exemplary Christians who appear in *Paradiso* were never, of course, canonized in the official sense at all, and it should perhaps be pointed out that the text of the *Commedia* makes little if any distinction between the stature of the canonized and that of the uncanonized souls among the blessed. Implicit in this appealingly democratic approach, perhaps, is the soundly orthodox idea that canonization and all that it entails may possibly be important from a strictly human perspective, since it involves judgments and definitions made by mortal, fallible beings and aimed at the edification of the faithful in their lives on Earth, but that from God's viewpoint—which *Paradiso* consistently strives to present—it is sainthood in the looser sense, as shared by *all* the inhabitants of the celestial rose (*Par.* 32), that is the only kind that counts.

Steven Botterill

Saladin

Saladin (c. 1138–1193) was the skillful and powerful Muslim general who, after the death of Nur al-Din in 1174, consolidated the military and political forces of Islam in the Near East. In 1187 his army successfully routed the crusaders at the battle of Hittin and retook Jerusalem. In contrast to the crusaders' ruthless sack of the city in 1099, Saladin's victory was marked by an unusual magnanimity toward the defeated Christians. Dante places him on the list of liberal leaders in *Conv.* 4.11.14 and in Limbo near the heroes of Troy and Rome (*Inf.* 4.129): *e solo, in parte, vidi 'l Saladino* ("and alone, to the side, [I saw] Saladin"). His isolation is most likely meant to portray his lack of connection with classical civilization. His reputation for generosity is recalled in several tales of the anonymous *Novellino* and in the *Decameron*.

Michael Papio

Salterello, Lapo

In the Heaven of Mars, Dante's ancestor, Cacciaguida, contrasts the Florence in which he lived with the current, corrupt and degenerate, one: *Sarìa tenuta allor tal maraviglia / una Cianghella, un Lapo Salterello, / qual or sarìa Cincinnato e Corniglia* ("A Cianghella, then a Lapo Salterello would have been thought as much a wonder as now Cincinnatus or Cornelia," *Par.* 15.127–129). That Salterello should be paired with the notoriously vain and arrogant Florentine woman, Cianghella, as a paragon of the evils of Dante's Florence is particularly interesting in light of the fact that he shared Dante's own fate as a White Guelf banished from Florence by the decree of March 10, 1302. Lapo, a prominent Florentine lawyer, judge, and politician, incurred the wrath of Pope Boniface VIII and of his Black supporters with his repeated championing of the legislative and juridical autonomy of the commune in the face of papal incursions. Indeed, Boniface leveled a charge of heresy against Salterello, claiming that he thus denied the power given the successors of Peter. While the Whites were in power in Florence, Salterello was protected, but in 1301, sensing the imminent crisis of White power, Salterello betrayed his party and its trust in him by convincing some members to entrust themselves to Charles of Valois, who held them hostage for the Blacks. But this self-serving betrayal did not save him, and he died in poverty and exile in Sardinia, reviled even by the party whose major spokesman he had been—as is confirmed not only by Dante in Cacciaguida's lamentation but also by the negative views of the early commentator Ottimo and the Florentine chronicler Dino Compagni.

Claudia Rattazzi Papka

Salvation

Salvation signifies an infusion of grace in an individual soul, conditioned by its faith, a divine act that brings the soul into a state of eternal bliss after death. This Christian doctrine—which explains how a triune God delivers humans from the power and consequences of sin and restores them to communion with God through the person of Christ and presence of the Holy Spirit—is a major concern of Dante's *Commedia*.

Medieval writers concerned with soteriology, or salvation, begin with original sin, which is characterized in Scholastic philosophy by two elements: *concupiscence* (the disordering of human faculties; the tendency to evil affecting human sensual desires and especially evidenced in human sexuality) and *deprivation*. Augustine introduced the identification of original sin with concupiscence; Anselm of Canterbury concentrated on the resulting break in relations between the divine and human (Fairweather). Sin—a result of Adam and Eve's choosing to disobey God (*Purg.* 33.52–63; *Par.* 26.115–117)—is the condition in which humans radically distort the image of God in which they were created and commit themselves instead to actions contrary to the will of God. Persistent sinful action in the absence of repentance results in the damnation of the soul upon death. Salvation, by contrast, is the process by which God graciously chooses to adopt sinners as his children and transform them into the image of Christ, with their participation. God saves all souls who turn to him. The nature of sin explains the necessity of the Incarnation of Christ. Reparation is necessary to restore the image of God and to repair the breach between the divine and the human. Since an equal balance between sin and satisfaction is not available to humans, only Christ—fully God and fully man—is able, through his death, to make just reparation for Adam's sin (original sin) and satisfy the demands of mercy and justice.

Baptized Christians have begun the process of salvation: through baptism, the soul is incorporated into Christ, made part of the church, and involved in working out its own salvation. Sin interrupts the salvific enterprise. In the sacrament of penance, the repentant sinner receives absolution after confessing and displaying sorrow for sin (contrition); nevertheless, the penitent must still perform works of satisfaction either in this life or in Purgatory, because such satisfaction prepares the soul for the perfect happiness of the vision of God (see Aquinas, *De quolibet* 2.8.2). Dante's *Purgatorio* reflects teachings concerning penitential satisfaction; unlike the souls in Hell, whose suffering reflects the effects of sin, the pains of the purgatorial sinners involves satisfaction as preparation for the blessed vision of the Empyrean.

But how do those born before Christ and those who lived virtuous lives without knowing Christ fit into this scheme? Dante understands that the Jewish patriarchs born before Christ escaped sin through observing the Law of Moses, through belief in the coming Messiah, and through the rite of circumcision, which was conceived as an early and imperfect form of baptism (*Par.* 32.79–82). Moreover, through their historical participation in the Incarnation of Christ (the Virgin Mary is born from the lineage of David and the house of Jesse [*Conv.* 4.5.5–6]), the Hebrew worthies participate intimately in salvation. Thus in the celestial rose, divided between believers of the Old and New Covenants, Dante brings believers from before and after Christ into harmony.

The virtuous pagans present a knottier problem, especially for Dante, who views Rome as having a providential role to play in the history of salvation (see especially *Par.* 6.34–93). Limbo—appropriated by Dante for the virtuous pagans in ways which alter traditional understandings of it as the abode of unbaptized infants or of Old Testament saints awaiting deliverance (Iannucci)—for some raises the question of God's justice. The fate of Virgil intensifies the difficulty, and some recent critics (Allan, Iliescu) have again argued the minority view that Virgil is to be found among the saved, against the traditional view that he resides in Limbo with the virtuous pagans (Barolini). But despite critical disagreement of this kind, Dante's poem adheres to orthodoxy: salvation is brought about by God's will, and his will can work in mysterious ways. It is the providential and unfathomable grace of God which saved the pagans Ripheus and Trajan (*Par.* 20.46–48, 67–72), and without which no one can be saved.

Bibliography

Allan, Mowbray. "Does Dante Hope for Virgil's Salvation?" *MLN* 104:1 (1989), 193–205.

Barolini, Teodolinda. "Q: Does Dante Hope for Virgil's Salvation? A: Why Do We Care? For the Very Reason We Should Not Ask the Question." *MLN* 105:1 (1990), 138–144.

Fairweather, Eugene R. *A Scholastic Miscellany: Anselm to Ockham.* New York: Macmillan, 1970.

Fallani, Giovanni. "Salvezza." *Enciclopedia dantesca,* 4:1092–1096.

Iannucci, Amilcare. "*Inferno* IV." *Lectura Dantis* 6: Supplement (1990), 42–53.

Iliescu, Nicolae. "Will Virgil Be Saved?" *Mediaevalia* 12 (1989, for 1986), 93–114.

Rebecca S. Beal

Samaritan

After the quake on the fourth terrace of Purgatory and just before the appearance of Statius, whose resurrection caused it, Dante associates his "natural thirst" for knowledge with that of the Samaritan woman, *la femminetta / samaritana* ("the Samaritan woman," *Purg.* 21.2–3), who asked Christ at a well for the "living water" of truth he offered (John 4:13–15).

Rebecca S. Beal

San Zeno, Abbot of

Nothing is known of the Abbot of San Zeno, though he has been identified with a certain Gherardo II, who was abbot at the church and monastery at Verona and who died in 1187. He is placed on the terrace of the slothful in Purgatory, where he is the lone penitent whom Dante meets (*Purg.* 18.118). The fourth-century church and monastery were both restored in the twelfth century.

R. A. Malagi

Sapia

On the ledge of envy in *Purgatorio,* where the souls have their eyelids sewn shut with iron wires, Dante meets Sapia, who answers his request to speak to any Italians that may be there by declaring, *"Io fui sanese"* ("I was Sienese," *Purg.* 13.106). Scholars have identified her as Sapia of the Sienese Salvani family, born c. 1210, the wife of Ghinibaldo Saracini, and the aunt of Provenzan Salvani, whom Dante has already met on the ledge of pride; but in order for the story she tells to be understood as an example of the sin of envy, only her self-identification as Sienese is needed. She defines her sin thus: *. . . fui de li altrui danni / più lieta assai che di ventura mia* ("I rejoiced at others' harms much more than at my own good fortune," *Purg.* 13.110–111); and the senselessness of her envy (she calls it *folle* [*Purg.* 13.113]) is made clear when she relates that she so rejoiced at the defeat of her own countrymen at the battle of Colle (1269), in which her nephew, Provenzan Salvani, died, that she uttered a blasphemous oath to God: *Omai più non ti temo* ("Now I fear you no more," *Purg.* 13.122). The indications of treason, at least in thought, and of blasphemy in act, suggest the gravity of Sapia's transgressions, but she tells Dante that at the end of her life she repented, and that she was helped by the prayers of one Pier

Pettinaio, a Franciscan hermit known to have been living in Siena during Sapia's lifetime. She calls Pier Pettinaio's prayers a form of *caritate* ("charity," *Purg.* 13.129), and since documents survive chronicling her foundation of a hospital in Siena with her husband and her donations to it before her death, Sapia's exemplification of envy may also be a demonstration of the power of charity, with which envy is countered in Dante's *Purgatorio.* The passage is considered by many critics to constitute one of Dante's most masterful psychological portraits.

Claudia Rattazzi Papka

Saracens

During the Middle Ages, Christians referred to Muslims as "Ishmaelites," "Agarenes" (after Hagar, the mother of Ishmael), or, most frequently, "Saracens." The ninth-century Byzantine theologian John of Damascus traces the origin of the term to Gen. 16:8. Although it connotes both religious and ethnic difference (that is, both Muslim and Arab), the term is never used to refer to Christian Arabs. Dante refers explicitly to *saracini* in *Inf.* 27.87, where Guido da Montefeltro condemns Pope Boniface VIII for persecuting the Colonna family, making war against Christians *e non con Saracin né con Giudei* ("and not with Saracens or with Jews"). Dante also alludes to *saracine,* or Saracen women, in the context of the lascivious displays of flesh by Florentine women (*Purg.* 23.103), invoking the popular association of Islam with lust and lechery (see "Islam"). In the sphere of Mars, the poet meets his ancestor Cacciaguida, who recounts how he was martyred during the Second Crusade by the Muslims, that *gente turpa* ("base folk," *Par.* 15.145). It is noteworthy that Dante includes Renouard (*Rinoardo, Par.* 18.46), a converted Saracen featured in the Guillaume d'Orange cycle of *chansons de geste,* in his list of fictional and historical warriors for Christ: this suggests that, for Dante, the Saracens are *gente turpa* only as long as they resist conversion. In *Conv.* 2.8.9, Dante notes that *Saracini,* along with Jews and Tartars, are among those peoples who believe in the immortality of the soul. In *Epist.* 5.11.4, Dante describes the Saracen persecution of Christians along with the biblical Egyptian persecution of Israelites in order to draw an analogy with the political situation of his own day.

Suzanne Conklin Akbari

Sarah

Wife of Abraham and mother in old age of Isaac in Genesis, Sarah *(Sarra)* was a figure for the New Covenant and the heavenly Jerusalem in Gal. 4:22–26 and appears in Dante's celestial rose in the Empyrean Heaven, on the fourth level of Mary's line (*Par.* 32.10).

Joan M. Ferrante

Sassol Mascheroni

Florentine lord of the Toschi family who killed his ward and cousin or nephew, the only son of his uncle or brother (or alternately the brother himself) for his inheritance. Tortured and beheaded for this crime against kin, he is punished in the ninth circle of Hell by being locked in the ice of Caina along with the fratricides and patricides. The Anonimo Fiorentino (the Anonymous Florentine commentator) states that Sassol's story was so well known that all Tuscany retold it—a fact made clear by fellow sinner Camiscion de' Pazzi, who remarks that if Dante is a Tuscan he will certainly recognize his name (*Inf.* 32.65).

Roy Rosenstein

Satan

One of four names attributed to the king of Hell in the *Inferno,* the others being Beelzebub, Dis, and Lucifer. The name of Satan *(Satàn)* is the first to appear, and it is proclaimed twice by one of Lucifer's minions, Pluto, in a barely intelligible exclamation (*Inf.* 7.1). The word "Satan," in Hebrew, means "messenger," "enemy," or "adversary."

Dino Cervigni

Saturn

The father of Jupiter, as well as the seventh planet and heaven in Dante's cosmology. In Dante's works, the god Saturn *(Saturno)* was king of Crete and later of Italy, whose reign was considered to be the Golden Age. (See *Inf.* 14.95–96; *Purg.* 22.70–71, 28.139–140; *Par.* 22.26–27, 22.145; *Mon.* 1.11.1.) The planet was thought to exert a cold influence on Earth. In his *Rime petrose,* especially in the first ("Io son venuto al punto de la rota"), Dante draws on the lore of Saturn in connection with his own temperament.

Because it was the highest of the seven planets and the slowest to revolve around Earth, Dante compares Saturn to astronomy, which he considered to be the highest of the sciences and the one

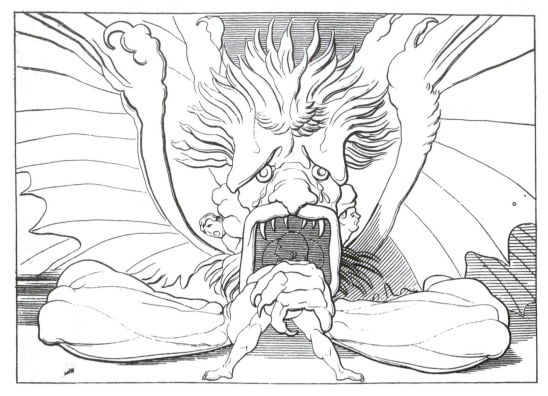

Lucifer, emperor of Hell. Invenzioni di Giovanni Flaxman sulla Divina commedia, *illustrated by John Flaxman and Beniamino del Vecchio, Rome, 1826. Giamatti Collection: Courtesy of the Mount Holyoke College Archives and Special Collections.*

which required the longest time to learn competently (*Conv.* 2.13.28–29). Dante makes no overt reference to this comparison in the *Paradiso.* Instead, because of a prevalent medieval notion that Saturn's influence disposed a person to solitude and contemplation, Dante places in Saturn those souls who on Earth had been *contemplanti uomini* ("contemplative men," *Par.* 22.46–47), in a particularly monastic understanding of this disposition. These men are sometimes thought to exemplify an extraordinary form of temperance.

Most of Dante's stay in this sphere is taken up by the speeches of Peter Damian and Benedict concerning their lives and works, predestination, and the degeneracy of the clergy and monastic orders. The dominant image is that of Jacob's ladder, which perhaps symbolizes the contemplatives' mystical ascent to God.

Bibliography

Durling, Robert M., and Ronald L. Martinez. *Time and the Crystal: Studies in Dante's "Rime petrose."* Berkeley, Los Angeles: University of California Press, 1990.

Kay, Richard. *Dante's Christian Astrology.* Philadelphia: University of Pennsylvania Press, 1994.

Klibansky, Raymond, Erwin Panofsky, and Fritz Saxl. *Saturn and Melancholy: Studies in the History of Natural Philosophy, Religion, and Art.* London: Warburg Institute, 1964.

Frank B. Ordiway

Saul

The first king of Israel, who was lifted up and later, after disobeying God's command, cast down by divine judgment revealed to him through the prophet Samuel (1 Sam. 15; *Mon.* 2.7.8, 3.6.1; *Epist.* 7.19). Saul *(Saùl)* appears among the examples of pride abased (*Purg.* 12.40–42), carved in the pavement of the first terrace of Purgatory, transfixed by his own sword in his final battle with the Philistines. Dante's description captures not only Saul's tragic end (1 Sam. 31.4; 1 Chron. 10.4) but also David's elegy over Saul and his son Jonathan in which he utters a curse of drought on Mount Gilboa, where they died (2 Sam. 1.21).

Carolynn Lund-Mead

Sayers, Dorothy Leigh

Born in Oxford, England, and educated at Oxford University, where she earned First Class Honors in medieval and modern literature, Sayers (1893–1957) established a reputation as a writer of detective fiction (the Lord Peter Wimsey series), a Christian apologist, and a writer of religious drama. In August 1944, after reading with excitement *The Figure of Beatrice* by her friend Charles Williams, she took a copy of the Temple Classics *Inferno* with her into an air-raid shelter and thus began an engagement with Dante that absorbed the rest of her life. Though plans for collaboration with Williams on a Dante handbook were terminated by his death in 1945, Sayers contracted with the recently initiated Penguin Classics series to produce her own translation of the *Commedia*. The first volume, *Hell,* was published in 1949, selling 50,000 copies the first three months; *Purgatory* appeared in 1955. Sayers's version of *Paradiso* was unfinished at her death, but the final thirteen cantos were completed by her friend Barbara Reynolds, Lecturer in Italian at Cambridge University, and the volume was issued in 1962. During her last decade Sayers lectured frequently on Dante: these talks have been published in the three volumes by Sayers listed below.

As an Anglican Christian, Sayers affirmed the relevance of Dante's "drama of the soul's choice" for a postwar culture; a popular novelist herself, she aimed her translation and commentary at what she termed "the common reader," actively opposing traditional views of the *Commedia* as, in her words, "permeated from end to end by Awful Sublimity and unmitigated Grimth" and stressing instead Dante's humor and skill as a storyteller. Her lively rendering of Dante's *terza rima,* a form usually rejected by translators as too difficult in English, has been deprecated for "slickness and brashness," but as her biographer Reynolds notes, Sayers "brought Dante within the reach of thousands of readers for whom he would otherwise have remained unintelligible." Sayers's discussions of Dante's allegory (in her preferred phrase, "symbolic images") are particularly lucid; readers should note, however, that her interpretation is heavily influenced by the often idiosyncratic theology of Williams, to whom she dedicated her translation.

Bibliography

Brabazon, James. *Dorothy L. Sayers: A Biography.* New York: Scribner's, 1981.

Dunlap, Barbara J. "'Through a Dark Wood of Criticism': The Rationale and Reception of Dorothy L. Sayers' Translation of Dante." In *As Her Whimsey Took Her: Essays on the Work of Dorothy L. Sayers.* Edited by Margaret P. Hannay. Kent, Ohio: Kent State University Press, 1979, pp. 133–149.

Perry, Anne. "Dorothy L. Sayers and Dante." In *Dorothy L. Sayers: The Centenary Celebration.* Edited by Alzina Stone Dale. New York: Walker, 1993, pp. 109–121.

Reynolds, Barbara. *The Passionate Intellect: Dorothy L. Sayers' Encounter with Dante.* Kent, Ohio: Kent State University Press, 1989.

———. "Dorothy L. Sayers and the Penguin Dante." *Studies in Medievalism* 2, no. 3 (Spring 1983): 29–39.

———. "Dorothy L. Sayers, Interpreter of Dante." In *As Her Whimsey Took Her: Essays on the Work of Dorothy L. Sayers.* Edited by Margaret P. Hannay. Kent, Ohio: Kent State University Press, 1979, pp. 123–132.

Sayers, Dorothy L. *The Poetry of Search and the Poetry of Statement.* London: Victor Gollancz, 1963.

———. *Further Papers on Dante.* London: Methuen, 1957.

———. *Introductory Papers on Dante.* London: Methuen, 1954.

Verduin, Kathleen. "Sayers, Sex, and Dante." *Dante Studies* 111 (1993), 223–234.

Kathleen Verduin

Schicchi, Gianni

A member of the Cavalcanti family of Florence (died before 1280) and noted mimic, Gianni Schicchi is punished among the falsifiers of persons in the tenth pouch of Malebolge (*Inf.* 30.25–45) by being afflicted with raving fury. While the pilgrim Dante is conversing with the alchemists Capocchio and Griffolino, two pale and naked shades appear and run around biting, like rabid animals. One of them sinks his teeth into Capocchio's neck and drags him off. Griffolino then identifies that *folletto* ("goblin" or "elf," but also the diminuative of *folle,* "madman") as Gianni Schicchi, and the other as the classical figure of Myrrha. He explains that Myrrha, pretending to be someone else, committed incest with her father, whereas Gianni disguised himself as Buoso Donati so as to dictate a will for the dead man and to gain for himself *la donna della torma* ("the queen of the herd"). This incident is recounted in more detail, although in somewhat differing versions, by a number of Dante's early commentators. From them we learn that Schicchi conspired with Simone Donati, nephew (in some versions, son) of the wealthy Buoso; Simone concealed Buoso's death and engaged Gianni to impersonate him in bed and to dictate a will in Simone's favor. Gianni took the opportunity to bequeath on himself Buoso's prize mare (in some versions, she-mule). The fact that this story shows up later in the *novellistica* tradition has caused some critics to speculate whether the episode might be a fictional commonplace, attributed to Gianni Schicchi by Dante because of the historical Schicchi's friendship with Simone Donati and his notorious talent as mimic (we are told by the Anonimo Fiorentino that Gianni's son Guiduccio was nicknamed Scimmia, or "Ape"— perhaps in allusion to his father's gift). But most critics consider the episode factual (or, at least, authentically legendary), and research into contemporary documents has confirmed the historicity of the persons involved. Gianni Schicchi later became the burlesque hero of Puccini and Forzano's homonymous comic opera (1918).

Bibliography

Barbi, Michele. "A proposito di Buoso Donati ricordato nel canto XXX dell' 'Inferno.'" In *Problemi di critica dantesca: Prima serie (1893–1918)*. Florence: Sansoni, 1934, pp. 305–322.

Bosco, Umberto. "I due stili della decima bolgia dantesca." *Romanic Review* 62 (1971), 167–182.

Contini, Gianfranco. "Sul XXX dell' *Inferno* dantesco." In *Varianti e altra linguistica*. Turin: Ricciardi, 1970, pp. 447–457.

Frankel, Margherita. "Juno among the Counterfeiters: Tragedy vs. Comedy in Dante's *Inferno* 30." *Quaderni d'Italianistica* 10.1–2 (1989), 173–197.

Olivia Holmes

Schismatics

Often generically labeled the makers of discord, the schismatics and scandalmongers occupy the ninth ditch of Malebolge, and Dante's encounter with them fills all of *Inf.* 28. The sin is identified succinctly by one of the sinners, Muhammad, who groups all of them under the heading *seminator di scandalo e di scisma* ("sowers of scandal and schism," 28.35). These sinners suffer extreme mutilation of their bodies at the hands of punitive devils: one is cleft from chin to anus, while another lacks arms, and a third has no tongue. Their punishment is cyclical: as the souls complete their circular path around the ditch, their wounds heal, and the devils then reopen them. Thus while Dante emphasizes the visual spectacle of these mangled bodies, he also stresses the act of corporeal disunion as an important aspect of the punishment, a perfect reflection of the acts of disunion these men performed on others while alive. Among the schismatics are Muhammad and his son-in-law Ali, the former punished as an agent of Christian disunity, the latter for breaking with Muhammad's sect and creating one of his own. Muhammad prophesies the future arrival of Fra Dolcino, leader of the heretical sect of the Apostles, who will not die until 1307 (28.55). Four other schismatics—Pier da Medicina, Curio, Mosca, and Bertran de Born— display their wounds and speak to the pilgrim, but modern criticism of this episode has focused on the latter sinner. Punished for having encouraged Prince Henry of England to rebel against his father, Henry II, Bertran here carries his head like a lantern, holding it up in order to speak. Dante had already praised Bertran for his martial poetry in *DVE* 2.2.9, and for his generosity in *Conv.* 4.11.14. His purpose in including Bertran here has been the subject of debate. While one reader (Shapiro) has seen Dante as punishing Bertran's poetry as well as the poet, another (Picone) has read the encounter as being about religion more than poetry. Yet another critic (Barolini) has found political implications in their meeting.

Dante has Bertran give voice to the word *contrapasso* ("countersuffering," 28.142)—the type of retributive justice that underlies the punishments in Hell and the mode of penance in Purgatory. Bertran offers himself as an example of the logic of *contrapasso: Perch' io parti' così giunte persone, / partito porto il mio cerebro, lasso!, / dal suo principio ch'è in questo troncone* ("Because I divided persons so joined, I carry my brain divided, alas! from its origin which is in this trunk," *Inf.* 28.139–140).

Bibliography

Barolini, Teodolinda. *Dante's Poets: Textuality and Truth in the* Comedy. Princeton, N.J.: Princeton University Press, 1984.

Fubini, Mario. "Il canto XXVIII dell'*Inferno.*" In *Lectura Dantis Scaligera.* Florence: Le Monnier, 1962, pp. 7–29.

Paratore, Ettore. "Il canto XXVIII dell'*Inferno.*" In *Inferno: Letture degli anni 1973–76.* Edited by Silvio Zennaro. Rome: Bonacci, 1977, pp. 683–704.

Parker, Mark. "XXVIII." In *Dante's* Divine Comedy. *Introductory Readings I:* Inferno. *Lectura Dantis* 6: Supplement (1990), pp. 363–372.

Picone, Michelangelo. "I trovatori di Dante: Bertran de Born." *Studi e problemi di critica testuale* 19 (1979), 71–94.

Shapiro, Marianne. "The Fictionalization of Bertran de Born (*Inf.* XXVIII)." *Dante Studies* 92 (1974), 107–116.

Michael Sherberg

Sciarra Colonna

Sciarra Colonna (c.1270–1329) was a bitter enemy of Pope Boniface VIII. The hostility between Boniface and the Colonna family is recalled in Guido da Montefeltro's report of Boniface's request for advice on how to overthrow their opposition (*Inf.* 27.102). Hugh Capet refers to his infamous attack on the pope in September 7, 1303 (*Purg.* 20.86–90). On the eve of his excommunication, Sciarra joined William of Nogaret (with the political backing of Philip the Fair) and stormed into Anagni with armed troops, taking the pope prisoner. Two days later the townspeople liberated Boniface, but he died less than three months later. Hugh Capet, in a reference to Matt. 27:38, calls the two *vivi ladroni* ("living thieves," *Purg.* 20.90).

Michael Papio

Science

Far more than most poets, Dante delves into areas that, by modern measures at least, count as science. Embryology, meteorology, geography, astronomy, principles of optics, and theories of motion all feature in his works, and not merely in the form of passing allusions. His discussion of moonspots in *Par.* 2, for instance, occupies nearly an entire canto, features a detailed analysis of competing accounts of the phenomenon, and includes instructions for performing an experiment. In the *Questio de Aqua et Terra,* Dante lectures at length on the possible causes of oceans and dry land. And in the *Convivio,* he devotes several chapters to the Sun's motion, picturing it as it might appear from various points on Earth's surface. There is, moreover, a strong critical tradition praising Dante for his scientific acumen: Landino labels him the equal of any natural philosopher; Galileo admires the mathematical precision of his Hell; contemporary physicists credit him with intuiting the principles of non-Euclidean geometry.

At the same time, however, it may be anachronistic to claim that the category of science, as it is currently understood, figures centrally in Dante's writings. Certainly the term *scienza* does not—in his work or in the Middle Ages more generally—have the specific associations it has today. For while modern usage tends to associate "science" with the protocols and topics of the physical sciences, Dante uses the term much more broadly to refer to any kind of systematic knowledge. His expansive understanding of the term is perhaps best reflected in *Conv.* 2.13. Glossing his canzone "Voi, che 'ntendendo il terzo ciel movete," Dante fits eleven different sciences into a single system modeled on the order of the heavens. These eleven sciences include not only the mathematical disciplines of the quadrivium but also the liberal arts, ethics, metaphysics, and theology.

The elaborate allegory of *Conv.* 2.13 is revelatory in other ways as well. It betrays, for example, an insistently systematic and hierarchical approach to the ordering of the sciences. As the spheres of the Moon, Mercury, and Venus lie closer to Earth than those of the Sun, Mars, Jupiter, and Saturn, so the liberal arts represent a lower order of knowledge than the arts of the quadrivium. Each science is accorded its own level, and theology—identified with the tenth sphere of the Empyrean—is placed firmly at the top. Though Dante may be the first person to propose precisely this analogy, the ordering impulse behind it is widely reflected in other allegorical systems and, perhaps even more pertinently, in the educational programs put forth throughout the medieval period. Boethius, Cassiodorus, Isidore, and Hugh of St. Victor are just a few of the authors to propose elaborate classificatory systems organized in strictly hierarchical terms. The point of such systems, much like the point of Dante's system, is to establish the distinct stages in which an education should proceed and, at the same time, to demonstrate the mutual compatibility of the sciences. Harmony is established, as it often is during the Middle Ages, by postulating a neatly tiered system

S in which one kind of power or authority is clearly subjugated to another.

In contrast to these theoretical models, in which the sciences are faultlessly ordered and happily compatible, the actual study of science in the Middle Ages often proved extremely divisive. There were sharp disagreements over the relative standing of logic and grammar, over the role played by mathematics, and over the autonomy of the various disciplines and their methods. Particularly vexed was the critical distinction between theology and the natural sciences. For though there was general agreement that theology was preeminent—the queen of the sciences—there was considerable divergence as to how exactly that preeminence actually applied in practice. Some, like Siger of Brabant and Boethius of Dacia, argued that science should be pursued independently of theology and that it would be possible to conduct a legitimate, rational inquiry that would lead to conclusions that contradicted articles of faith. (Such conclusions were, it was admitted, false, but still a valid object of investigation.) Others, like Albertus Magnus and Thomas Aquinas, argued that philosophy, when properly pursued, could never yield conclusions contrary to faith. And still others, like Bonaventure, argued that natural philosophy could not be relied upon to reach conclusions consonant with the revealed truths of Christian Scripture and that it therefore should be practiced only within very strict limits.

These disagreements provoked institutional crises at several points in the thirteenth century. In 1210, a council of bishops issued to the faculty of arts at the University of Paris a sternly worded prohibition against "any public and private reading, under penalty of excommunication, of the Books of Aristotle on natural philosophy and their commentaries." Similar, though less comprehensive bans were issued in 1215 and 1231 with the support of Pope Gregory IX. In 1270 and 1277, further bans were issued against specific doctrines, including thirteen that had been taught by Siger and his followers. Dante was well aware of these debates, incorporating them into the *Commedia* and indeed into his vision of Heaven itself. In the sphere of the Sun, Siger and Aquinas circle side by side, even though on Earth Aquinas had lobbied actively against Siger's controversial teachings.

The thirteenth-century debates over the proper role of natural philosophy were as much debates about the role of ancient learning as they were debates about the competing claims of reason and revelation. For while it might have been possible in the abstract to imagine a Christian physics or geometry, natural philosophy in the Middle Ages was based overwhelmingly on pagan texts. Indeed, the history of scientific speculation in the period is very largely a story of successive generations of translators and commentators gradually rediscovering the works of ancient philosophy.

Plato is the first pagan philosopher to have a direct and substantial impact. Indeed, he remained a continual, if intermittent, influence in the Latin West throughout the Middle Ages. For while nearly all of Plato's works were lost, one work—the *Timaeus*—survived in the form of a partial translation and commentary by Calcidius. In this least Platonic of Platonic dialogues, Plato discourses on a variety of topics ranging from planetary motion, to the structure of the human body, to the nature of vision and reflected images. Most critical of all is his extended discussion of the world's creation out of formless matter by a Demiurge. The efforts of figures like Bernard of Chartres and William of Conches to reconcile this creation myth with Genesis produced in the early twelfth century a curious kind of natural philosophy that combined numerological speculation with allegorical exegesis. Dante alludes several times to the *Timaeus* and engages the work at length in *Par.* 4. There Beatrice both faults Plato for suggesting that human souls shall return to the stars and opens the possibility that this Platonic doctrine might, under the guise of allegory, convey a substantial truth. Plato may also have exerted a less direct influence on Dante through the mediating influence of the Oxford philosopher Grosseteste. Drawing on the *Timaeus,* on Neoplatonic theories of emanation, on Aristotle, as well as on Islamic optical treatises, Grosseteste founded a metaphysical science of light with strong affinities to the *Paradiso*.

Aristotle's scientific writings reached the West later than the *Timaeus* but ultimately had a more decisive impact on the medieval curriculum and the debates about natural philosophy. They arrived, for the most part circuitously, having been translated first from Greek into Arabic and then from Arabic into Latin. In *Inf.* 4, Dante portrays two of the most celebrated Islamic translators and commentators—Avicenna and Averroës—sitting in Limbo alongside their *maestro* ("master"). The commentaries of these Islamic philosophers provided the lens through which Aristotle's philosophy was viewed in the Latin West, and their ideas were largely incorporated into the extensive commentaries and translations produced by Albertus Magnus and Aquinas. The influence of this tradition on Dante's conception of natural philosophy is too extensive to be easily isolated and discussed. Indeed, it is probably only a slight exaggeration to say that natural philosophy is, for Dante, essentially Aristotle's philosophy as it was variously interpreted by his Islamic and Christian commentators.

Dante draws explicitly on Aristotelian texts such as *De Caelo, De Meteoris, De Generatione Animalium,* and *Physica* throughout his works. He borrows from them theories about very specific natural phenomena such as lightning, comets, and the growth of embryos, but perhaps more importantly he appropriates a whole style of analysis. When Dante describes, for example, his ascent through the sphere of fire in *Par.* 1, he is clearly borrowing an Aristotelian idea about the disposition of matter in the universe. Even more telling than any particular debt to *De Caelo* is the whole procedure by which Dante expresses his puzzlement and by which Beatrice resolves it. As they fly upward to the Moon—a movement that might in the work of another poet represent high fantasy—they carefully consider the scientific ramifications of this flight. Aristotle's doctrine appears contradicted by the ascent, and so that ascent must be shown to be consistent with a revised account of that doctrine. Aristotle's science provides, in short, the problems, the terminology, and the rules for what counts as a solution.

A less central but still important influence on Dante's science are the various encyclopedias and epitomes that circulated during the Middle Ages. Dante's knowledge of Ptolemaic astronomy derives, for example, not from the *Almagest* directly but from Roman, Arabic, and finally Italian summaries in which the Greek mathematician's work is both simplified and elaborated upon. It is from compilers like Isidore of Seville and Brunetto Latini that Dante acquires much of his geographical lore, his zoology, and his astrology. And it is from such compilers that Dante may conceivably draw his sense of science's place in his own encyclopedic project. The science of the *Commedia*—which seems so often casual, incidental, and opportunistic—clearly reflects the sensibility of Brunetto's *Tesoretto,* even as it aspires to a grander synthesis.

Perhaps the hardest influence on Dante's science to gauge accurately is that of nature itself. Certainly Dante's forays into natural philosophy match in large measure the bookishness of most of his contemporaries; a treatise like the *Questio,* which proposes to explain the total absence of dry land in the Southern Hemisphere in terms of the asymmetric action of astral influences, clearly reflects a fairly cloistered approach to the study of nature. And yet there are also in Dante's writings hints of empiricism, hints of the kind of direct experimentation that is intermittently recorded in the writings of Bacon, Grosseteste, and the Bolognese Averroists. The moonspot discussion of *Par.* 2 appears to offer the best evidence of this empirical bent. To disprove a hypothesis about the cause of moonspots that Dante had championed in *Conv.* 2.13 and that he had borrowed from Averroës, Beatrice asks Dante to imagine performing an actual experiment involving three mirrors and a lamp. She even champions *esperienza* as the *fonte ai rivi di vostr' arti* ("the source for the streams of all your arts," *Par.* 2.96). But while this is a strikingly Baconian pose, one needs to be cautious about accepting it at face value. "Experience" is a conventional rallying cry even among the most bookish of natural philosophers. It is easy to overestimate the depth of Dante's commitment, something that the path-breaking empiricists of the Accademia Fiorentina appear to have done when they took their motto *Provando e Riprovando* ("Proving and Refuting") from the first lines of *Par.* 3. The phrase does not in fact urge the careful testing and retesting of hypotheses but instead recommends the proof-and-reproof method of Scholastic philosophy.

Bibliography

Boyde, Patrick. *Dante: Philomythes and Philosopher.* Cambridge: Cambridge University Press, 1981.

Boyde, Patrick. *Perception and Passion in Dante's "Comedy."* Cambridge: Cambridge University Press, 1993.

Di Scipio, Giuseppe, and Aldo Scaglione (eds.). *The Divine Comedy and the Encyclopedia of Arts and Sciences.* Amsterdam: Benjamins, 1988.

Grant, Edward. *A Source Book in Medieval Science.* Cambridge, Mass.: Harvard University Press, 1974.

Lindberg, David. *The Beginnings of Western Science.* Chicago: University of Chicago Press, 1992.

Kay, Richard. *Dante's Christian Astrology.* Philadelphia: University of Pennsylvania Press, 1994.

Mazzotta, Giuseppe. *Dante's Vision and the Circle of Knowledge.* Princeton, N.J.: Princeton University Press, 1992.

Nardi, Bruno. "La dottrina delle macchie lunari." In *Saggi di filosofia dantesca.* Florence: La Nuova Italia, 1967, pp. 3–39.

Steenberghen, Fernand Van. *Aristotle in the West.* Louvain: E. Nauwelaerts, 1955.

Weisheipl, James. "Classification of the Sciences in Medieval Thought." *Medieval Studies* 27 (1965), 54–90.

Wetherbee, Winthrop. *Platonism and Poetry in the Twelfth Century.* Princeton, N.J.: Princeton University Press, 1972.

John Kleiner

Scipio

Publius Cornelius Scipio Africanus (235–183 B.C.E.), Roman general, victor over Hannibal and the Carthaginians at Zama in 202 B.C.E. Scipio is cited in *Conv.* 4.5.19 as the agent of providential history and in *Mon.* 2.9.18, where Dante gives Livy as his source for the war-ending duel between Scipio and Hannibal. Scipio's victory makes him "heir of glory" in *Inf.* 31.115–117; the triumph accorded him in Rome is compared in splendor to the pageant of the chariot in *Purg.* 29.115–117; and his "young" bearing of the Roman banner assures his place in Justinian's imperial history in *Par.* 6.52–53.

Sally Mussetter

Scot, Michael

A renowned philosopher, scientist, occultist, author, and learned cleric, Michael Scot (c. 1175– c. 1235) was born in Scotland, lived and studied in Spain, taught astronomy in Paris, and spent many years at the imperial court of Frederick II in Palermo. There he served as court astrologer, performed magic tricks, and with other scholars translated Aristotle and Averroës into Latin. Michael also addressed to Frederick II an untitled, tripartite series on the occult: *Liber introductorius, Liber particularis,* and *Liber physiognomiae.*

Dante places Michael *(Michele Scotto),* who was best known for his occult learning and pre-sumed supernatural powers, in the eighth circle of Hell, fourth pouch, where diviners, astrologers, and magicians have their heads twisted backward. The single tercet describing Michael's appearance, however, emphasizes not his head but his spare ribs: *Quell'altro che ne' fianchi è così poco, / Michele Scotto fu, che veramente / de le magiche frode seppe 'l gioco* ("That other who is so slender in the flanks was Michael Scot, who truly knew the game of magic frauds," *Inf.* 20.115–117).

In the *Liber physiognomiae* Michael himself propounds that leanness of flanks can indicate a man who is *malum* ("bad" or "evil"). Since no contemporary accounts survive that describe Michael's actual physique, Dante probably drew on the occultist's own treatise for a physical detail that would iconographically capture the sinner's inner psychological state or spiritual degeneracy.

Bibliography

Kay, Richard. "The Spare Ribs of Dante's Michael Scot." *Dante Studies* 103 (1985), 1–14.

Thorndike, Lynn. *Michael Scot.* London: Nelson, 1965.

Madison U. Sowell

Screen Lady

Screen ladies figure twice in the narrative of the *Vita Nuova.* One day in church onlookers mistakenly identified a woman standing between Dante and Beatrice as his beloved and the addressee of his love poetry (*VN* 5–6). Dante encouraged this misconception by circulating poems addressed to this woman: "Voi che per la via d'amore passate" (7), a lost epistle on her leaving the city (6, 2), and the sonnet "Guido, io vorrei." Thus this woman became his *schermo* ("screen," 7). The screen lady served to conceal the name of the beloved from others, as Andreas Cappellanus in the late twelfth century had enjoined in *De arte honeste amandi (The Art of Courtly Love)*—a text familiar to Dante and his peers. Although Dante claimed to have feigned love for this screen lady, onlookers found his performance completely convincing. Subsequently he wrote poems to this screen lady and also poems to Beatrice which he knew would be misread as referring to the screen lady. When this first screen lady left Florence, Dante wrote her a poem as was expected in these circumstances (7). Later when he had to travel to the place where she was staying, he had a vision of the Lord of Love, who told him that he was carrying Dante's heart to another lady who would be his new screen or defense (9). Dante's performance as poet-lover of this second screen lady compromised her reputation and thus violated the rules of courtly love. In response Beatrice, apparently unaware of Dante's ruses, stopped greeting him (10), provoking a great crisis for him as lover and poet.

Bibliography

De Robertis, Domenico. *Il libro della Vita Nuova.* 2nd edition. Florence: Sansoni, 1970, chapter 3.

John Ahern

Semele

Daughter of Cadmus, king of Thebes, and Harmonia in classical mythology. The Semele narrative to which Dante refers in the *Commedia* comes from Ovid's *Meta.* 3.259–315. Juno's anger upon learning that her husband's mortal lover, Semele, is pregnant by Jupiter leads her to a carefully planned revenge. Disguising herself as Semele's aged nurse, Juno convinces the young girl that she must oblige her divine lover to give her a particular proof of his true identity. Thus when the lovers next meet, Semele, following Juno's deceitful suggestions, tricks Jupiter into giving his oath that he will come to her as he does to his wife, in all his divine splendor. Unable to change Semele's mind, Jupiter attempts to protect his lover by mediating his divine form as much as possible. This attempt proves futile, however, for even the mediated view of the god of thunder and lightning causes Semele's merely mortal body to burn up, though not before Jupiter seizes their unborn son and places the fetus in his own thigh. When Bacchus issues from his father's body, he is thus known as the *bis genitus* ("twice born"). In *Par.* 21.4–21, Beatrice explains to Dante that he is not yet strong enough to bear a more nearly complete revelation of her smile in the eighth heaven, saying that the exposure of his limited mortal capacities to such heavenly beauty would destroy him the way Semele *(Semelè)* was destroyed by Jupiter.

The *Commedia*'s only other explicit reference to Semele compares Juno's continuing anger against the family of Thebes (because of Semele's love affair) with the greater madness of the falsifiers of persons in the tenth bolgia of Malebolge (*Inf.* 30.1–3). At issue in Dante's text is Juno's punishment of Ino (Semele's sister) by first causing her husband, Athamas, to go mad. Mistaking his wife and two sons for a lioness and her two cubs, Athamas kills one (Learchus), before Ino herself goes mad and drowns herself and their other son (Melicerta) in the sea. The story comes from *Meta.* 416–530.

In *Epist.* 3.4, Dante uses the periphrasis *semen Semeles* ("seed of Semele") to refer to Bacchus, in an evocation of the story of Minyas' three daughters. They deny that Jupiter was the father of Bacchus and refuse to worship him, preferring to tell each other stories as they weave together (*Meta.* 4.1–42).

Bibliography

Brownlee, Kevin. "Ovid's Semele and Dante's Metamorphosis: *Paradiso* XXI–XXIII." *MLN* 101 (1986), 147–156.

Yowell, Donna. "*Inferno* XXX." In *Dante's "Divine Comedy": Introductory Readings. I: "Inferno." Lectura Dantis 6:* Special Issue: *Lectura Dantis Virginiana* I (1990), 388–399.

Kevin Brownlee

Semiramis

Queen of Assyria mentioned in ancient and medieval histories, she inspired both negative and positive traditions—on the one hand, as a figure of uncontrollable lust who committed incest with her son and, on the other, as a queen who ruled effectively and extended the boundaries of her kingdom by conquest. Dante accepts the negative tradition, placing her among the lustful in Hell and adapting Orosius's Latin play on words (*quod libitum esset liberum fieret, Historiae* 1.4.8) to Italian: *A vizio di lussuria fu sì rotta / che libito fé licito in sua legge* ("So broken was she to the vice of lust that in her laws she made licit whatever pleased," *Inf.* 5.55–56), but acknowledging the extent of her power in calling her the "empress over many languages" (*Inf.* 5.54).

Joan M. Ferrante

Seneca

Lucius Annaeus Seneca (d. 65 C.E.)—the leading Stoic philosopher of Rome, tutor to the emperor Nero, and author of tragedies, moral epistles, and treatises on moral and scientific subjects—is mentioned as *Seneca morale* ("moral Seneca") in *Inf.* 4. Seneca's *Natural Questions* influenced both

Dante's treatment of scientific matters and his conception of microcosmic literary form as early as the *rime petrose*. Dante's Ulysses (*Inf.* 26) owes something to Seneca's *Epistle to Lucilius* 85, which argued that Ulysses must have traveled beyond the known world. It has not been conclusively established whether or not Dante knew Seneca's tragedies.

Dante praises Seneca's probity as a magistrate (*DVE* 1.17.2), his philosophical courage in the face of death (*Conv.* 3.14.8), and his contempt for wealth (*Conv.* 4.12.8); he cites him on gifts (*Conv.* 1.8.16) and omens (*Conv.* 2.14.22). Two other references (*Epist.* 3.5.8 and *Mon.* 2.5.3) are actually to works by an early medieval writer, Martinus Dumensis, often confused with Seneca.

Bibliography

Mezzadroli, Giuseppina. *Seneca in Dante. Dalla tradizione medievale all'officina dell'autore.* Florence: Le Lettere, 1990.

Robert M. Durling

Sennacherib

King of Assyria whose military campaigns against Hezekiah, king of Judah, ended in disaster. To punish Sennacherib's pride and blasphemy, "the angel of the Lord" (Isa. 37:36–38) utterly destroyed his army of 185,000 men in one night. Sennacherib fled back to his city of Nineveh but was killed by his own sons Adrammelech and Sharezer as he worshiped in a temple. His sacrilegious arrogance makes him exemplary of the sin of pride, punished on the first terrace of Purgatory (*Purg.* 12.53).

F. Regina Psaki

Sestina

Through imitation of the Occitan poet Arnaut Daniel, Dante introduced the sestina to Italian literature. This metrical form, often referred to as *coblas retrogradadas* or *retrogradatio cruciata,* is composed of six strophes of six hendecasyllables, each in a different rhyme, which then change their position according to an intricate fixed permutation:

abcdef faebdc cfdabe ecbfad deacfb bdfeca

at the end of which the series would be ready to begin once again. The short seventh stanza, or *congedo (commiato, envoi),* is composed of three verses in which all six rhymes reappear, two per verse, also according to a regular pattern. In *De vulgari eloquentia* 2.10.2 Dante cites the sestina as a special example of a canzone that has a single melody for each strophe with no internal division *(diesis)* and refers to the troubadour Arnaut as a major practitioner of this metrical form, as well as to his own poem, "Al poco giorno e al gran cerchio d'ombra." Later in that treatise (2.13.2) he again mentions his sestina and a similar poem (but not a sestina) by Arnaut as examples of a canzone stanza without rhyme.

Because they are repeated throughout the poem, the six rhyme words are—or at least should be—extremely important to its meaning. In his sestina "Al poco giorno," the second of the *rime petrose,* Dante focuses attention on the following words and their meaning, both specific and general: *ombra, colli, erba, verde, petra, donna.* Two of these words (*petra* and *donna*) are also found as the paired rhymes that conclude two of the strophes in the first of the *petrose* "Io son venuto al punto de la rota." In this way, we see how the essence of this poetic experience is directly carried over into the next poem of the cycle; indeed, we could say that it generates it. Similarly, the so-called double sestina, "Amor, tu vedi ben che questa donna," repeats two of the sestina's rhymes: *donna* and *petra.* Dante structures this metrical tour de force on only five rhyme words (the other three being *tempo, luce,* and *freddo*) and varies the pattern over the five stanzas according to the following scheme:

abaacaaddaee eaeebeeccedd etc.

Unlike the sestina, the double sestina displays the normal division of the strophe into *fronte* (and *piedi*) and *sirma.* Dante is well aware of his metrical innovation, for he notes this fact both in *DVE* 2.13.13 and in the poem itself: *si' ch'io ardisco a far per questo freddo / la novità che per tua forma luce, / che non fu mai pensata in alcun tempo* (vv. 64–66).

Dante's experimentation with the sestina form would be continued by Petrarch, who composed nine of them, including one true example of the double form (i.e., twelve stanzas of six verses based on six rhyme words and a three-line *congedo*).

Bibliography

Baldelli, Ignazio. "Sestina, sestina doppia." *Enciclopedia dantesca,* 5:193–195.

Battaglia, Salvatore. *Le rime "petrose" e le sestina (Arnaldo Daniello, Dante, Petrarca)*. Naples: Liguori, 1964.

Cremante, Renzo, and Mario Pazzaglia (eds.). *La metrica*. Bologna: Il Mulino, 1973.

Durling, Robert M., and Ronald L. Martinez. *Time and the Crystal: Studies in Dante's Rime petrose*. Berkeley: University of California Press, 1990.

Fubini, Mario. *Metrica e poesia: Lezioni sulle forme poetiche italiane*. Milan: Feltrinelli, 1970.

Pazzaglia, Mario. *Il verso e l'arte della canzone nel De vulgari eloquentia*. Florence: La Nuova Italia, 1967.

Shapiro, Marianne. *Hieroglyph of Time: The Petrarchan Sestina*. Minneapolis: University of Minnesota Press, 1980.

Spongano, Raffaele. *Nozioni ed esempi di metrica italiana*. Bologna: Pàtron, 1974.

Christopher Kleinhenz

Sesto

Sextus Pompeius Magnus, son of Pompey the Great, who, after suffering defeat in a battle against Julius Caesar at Munda in 45 B.C.E., became a pirate, conducting raids along the coast of southern Italy. He was defeated by Augustus' forces under Agrippa and was soon after taken prisoner and executed under Antony's authority. Dante places Sesto among the robbers and plunderers in the first ring of the seventh circle, where the sins of violence are punished (*Inf.* 12.135). The Battle at Munda is alluded to in *Par.* 6.71–72. Dante took his information about Sesto from Lucan (*Phars.* 6.420–423) and Orosius (*Hist.* 6.18.19).

Richard Lansing

Sexuality

Historians point out that there is no equivalent in medieval Latin for the word "sexuality." "Concupiscence" and "lust" were the key terms in Scholastic theology's discussion of sexual behaviors that were analyzed under the rubric of temperance—the virtue which is their opposite. The presence of lust in human nature was theorized as a direct consequence of the Fall, and it was seen as both the cause and the perpetuation of original sin. The sole sexual relation regarded as legitimate was heterosexual intercourse for the purpose of procreation and only within marriage. All other sexual relations (fornication, adultery, sodomy, incest, bestiality) were regarded as sinful to varying degrees. Chastity was praised as a difficult victory over lust, and virginity was prized above all. These values often entailed problematic if not negative attitudes toward women and toward the body, which have been the subject of many recent studies.

Dante writes about sexuality most explicitly in his treatment of lust and of sodomy, but in both cases sexual issues are connected with other transgressions. The second circle of *Inferno* is the place of the *peccator carnali, / che la ragion sommettono al talento* ("carnal sinners, who subject their reason to their lust," 5.38–39). Lust is the first sin in the category of sins of incontinence which Dante specifies later (11.82), sins that are said to offend God less than those of malice. The lustful are punished by being buffeted by a *bufera infernal* ("infernal whirlwind," 5.31), their restlessness and lack of peace an image of their sin. Dante first presents a (largely female) catalogue of famous figures *ch'Amor di nostra vita dipartille* ("whom Love parted from our life," 5.69). This association of adulterous love and death is reiterated throughout the canto. Dante's major interlocutor is Francesca da Rimini, who speaks about love as an overwhelming and irresistible force. Current readings of Francesca emphasize her inability to admit her responsibility in giving way to passion and the role of literature in creating the dangerous illusions within which she both acts and speaks.

In *Inferno* sodomy is not treated as a species of lust but rather as a sin of violence against nature and therefore against God, from whom *Natura lo suo corso prende* ("Nature takes its course," 11.99). Because sodomy is nonprocreative, it was regarded as unnatural. Like the lustful, the sodomites are in constant motion, but they are running under huge flakes of fire on a sandy desert. Their fiery domain alludes to the biblical account of the destruction of Sodom by fire. Critics disagree about the meaning of Brunetto Latini's placement in the circle of sodomy, and there have been attempts to read sodomy as a figure for a nonsexual sin. Critics also disagree about whether Dante's praise of Brunetto is ironic or sincere. Brunetto says that all the others in his group were clerks and distinguished men of letters, implying a relationship between sodomy and these professions. In the following canto, however, Dante

S

meets with another group of sodomites who were all Guelf political figures and who are unusual in their infernal camaraderie.

Although the lustful and the sodomites are separated in the moral scheme of *Inferno,* in *Purgatorio* the terrace of the lustful contains both heterosexual and homosexual penitents, and there are equal numbers of both categories. This has recently led critics to question whether Dante's attitudes toward sodomy changed over the course of writing the poem. Once again the lustful are seen in motion; they are divided into two groups that circle the terrace in opposite directions, members exchanging a kiss of peace as they meet. Each group shouts out phrases that indicates the particular nature of its vice. The homosexuals name Sodom and Gomorra, while the heterosexuals speak of Pasiphae's bestialization of herself in order to mate with the bull. The heterosexuals are compared to beasts because they followed their appetites rather than observing *umana legge* ("human law," 26.83). It is striking that none of the named penitents are women, in contrast with the strong female presence in *Inf.* 5.

The examples of the virtue opposed to lust include the Virgin Mary's response to the angel Gabriel's announcement that she will give birth *Virum non cognosco* ("I know no man," *Purg.* 25.128), and the goddess Diana. The final examples of virtue are unnamed *donne / . . . e mariti che fuor casti / come virtute e matrimonio imponne* ("wives . . . and husbands who were chaste, as virtue and marriage require of us," *Purg.* 25.132–135).

As the lustful were the first of the incontinent sinners in *Inferno,* so they are the last category in *Purgatorio.* Sexual sins are by implication less grave than all other sins. In both cases, too, the pilgrim's clear identification with the sinners makes us aware that lust was a serious issue for him. As in *Inferno* the relation between lust and literature is established by the presence of the literary figures (the poets Guido Guinizzelli and Arnaut Daniel) who are Dante's interlocutors on the terrace of lust.

Although lust is sinful, sexual desire has the potential for positive transformation, as the Heaven of Venus (*Par.* 8–9) shows. The three examples of saved carnal lovers—Cunizza, the poet Folquet of Marseilles, and the biblical Rahab—represent three conversion stories. In each case the propensity for erotic experience which

marked the character's early life was renounced and transformed into a form of service of the divine. Folquet's story (he was a troubadour love poet who gave up poetry and became a crusading bishop) refigures the complicity of poetry and sexual desire seen in the poem's other treatments of lust.

Dante represents the power of sexual passion in a group of four poems (the *rime petrose*) which express the poet's unrequited passion for an idolized stony lady. In "Così nel mio parlar voglio esser aspro" ("So in my speech I would be harsh") the lover's frustration gives way to a fantasy of erotic violence and possession as he imagines taking vengeance on the lady's unresponsiveness.

The redemptive potential of eros is a central theme of Dante's poetry. His idealization of his youthful sexual attraction to Beatrice made her beauty a lure to higher things. Even though his love for her is chaste, it is represented in language that acknowledges its erotic origins and power. Dante is a poet of sublimation rather than renunciation. He gives a positive value to desire (cf. *Purg.* 17.91–105, 18.19–39) and is concerned with the choice of the object of desire and the quality of love for it.

Bibliography

Bernardo, Aldo S. "Sex and Salvation in the Middle Ages: From the *Romance of the Rose* to the *Divine Comedy.*" *Italica* 67 (1990), 305–318.

Boswell, John. *Christianity, Social Tolerance and Homosexuality: Gay People in Western Europe from the Beginning of the Christian Era to the Fourteenth Century.* Chicago: University of Chicago Press, 1980.

Brundage, James A. *Law, Sex, and Christian Society in Medieval Europe.* Chicago: University of Chicago Press, 1987.

Durling, Robert M., and Ronald L. Martinez. *Time and the Crystal: Studies in Dante's "Rime Petrose."* Berkeley: University of California Press, 1990.

Jacquart, Danielle, and Claude Thomasset. *Sexuality and Medicine in the Middle Ages.* Translated by Matthew Adamson. Princeton, N.J.: Princeton University Press: 1988.

Kleinhenz, Christopher. "Texts, Naked and Thinly Veiled: Erotic Elements in Medieval Italian Literature." In *Sex in the Middle Ages: A Book of Essays.* Edited by Joyce E. Salisbury. New York: Garland Publishing, 1991, pp. 83–109.

Payer, Pierre J. *The Bridling of Desire: Views of Sex in the Later Middle Ages.* Toronto: University of Toronto Press, 1993.

Pequigney, Joseph. "Sodomy in Dante's *Inferno* and *Purgatorio.*" *Representations* 36 (1991), 22–42.

Radcliff-Umstead, Douglas. "Erotic Sin in the *Divine Comedy.*" In *Human Sexuality in the Middle Ages and the Renaissance.* Edited by Douglas Radcliff-Umstead. Pittsburgh: University of Pittsburgh Center for Medieval and Renaissance Studies, 1978, pp. 41–96.

Salisbury, Joyce E. *Medieval Sexuality: A Research Guide.* New York: Garland Publishing, 1990.

Rachel Jacoff

Shelley, Percy Bysshe

An English romantic poet, Shelley (1792–1822) was drawn more to the idea of Dante as the poet of freedom and love than to the real historical figure. Although an avowed atheist, Shelley admired the *Purgatorio* and especially the *Paradiso.* While rejecting Dante's politics and theology, he drew on his imagery for a number of works, including *Prometheus Unbound, The Triumph of Life,* and *Epipsychidion.* In *A Defense of Poetry,* Shelley characterized Dante as a Platonist whose poetry transcended his historical particularity to express universal truth. He also saw Dante as the first modern poet.

Thomas L. Cooksey

Sibyl

In the final canto of the *Paradiso,* Dante compares his faded memory of his beatific vision to the scattering of the leaves on which the oracles of the Sibyl *(Sibilla)* were recorded *(Par.* 33.65–66). In Greco-Roman religion, the term *Sibyl* was used to refer to a sort of prophetess who, by merit of her possession or inspiration by a god, was capable of divining future events. Although classical tradition reported as many as ten Sibyls, in his works Dante refers only to the Cumaean Sibyl, located at Cumae near Naples. His description of her derives from Virgil's *Aeneid,* books 3 and 6, where she functions as Aeneas' guide to the underworld. He remembers her in this role also at *Conv.* 4.26.9.

At *Aen.* 3.441–452, Helenus, the son of Priam of Troy, tells Aeneas of the Cumaean Sibyl's manner of writing her prophecies on leaves, which she then arranges in proper order and stores in her cave. When the opening door to the cave creates a breeze, they are scattered, and she makes no effort to put them back in order, thus leaving the prophecies largely unintelligible to any who would consult them.

Frank B. Ordiway

Sicilian School

A group of about thirty poets, not all of whom were of Sicilian origin, who flourished around 1230 to 1250 at the court of Emperor Frederick II Hohenstaufen in Palermo and who were the first to write verse in a literary Italian vernacular. The most important figures are Pier della Vigna, Giacomo da Lentini, Stefano Protonotaro, Rinaldo d'Aquino, and Guido delle Colonne. Unlike the Provençal troubadours whose themes and poetic forms they borrowed, they were not professional minstrels but were administrators of the imperial court, notaries, judges, and jurists for whom poetry was a refined avocation kept apart from the commitments of politics and administration. Their influence on the poets of the Tuscan school led by Guittone d'Arezzo, on the Bolognese group headed by Guido Guinizzelli, and on the *dolce stil novo* poets was paramount in matters of language, style, and form. Their achievement is recognized by Dante in *DVE* 1.12.2–6 and has earned them their rightful place at the beginning of Italian literary history.

The social and academic background of the Sicilian poets is reflected in the way they adapted and interpreted the Provençal tradition. Except for a few compositions of moral and didactic content, their verse is entirely dedicated to love and eschews political or military themes. The traditional homage to the lady is not generally expressed in terms of vassalage to an overlord but rather under the guise of allegiance to an absolute form of love whose effects on the lover are gauged, analyzed, and illustrated. Their language is elevated, modeled on Latin and Provençal; their construction tends toward hypotactical development and conceptual complexity. The best examples of this high-tone manner are the canzoni of Pier della Vigna, Guido delle Colonne, and Stefano Protonotaro. Their description of love is highly intellectualized and generally free of any reference to personal circumstances or topical situations. However, the many images drawn from medieval bestiaries and the natural sciences for illustrative purposes take on a precious and mesmerizing quality.

The distinction of founder and leader of the school goes to Giacomo da Lentini for the quality and quantity of his works as well as his many technical achievements. Advocating a logical congruence between subject and literary form, Giacomo set the pattern for the canzone, the *canzonetta,* and the *discordo;* he is also the reputed inventor of the sonnet. In the Sicilian form, which is the archaic one, the sonnet is a stanza of fourteen hendecasyllabic lines, divided into octave and sestet, and linked by the following rhyme scheme:

abababab + cdecde or *cdcdcd*

This pattern invites a two-part structure of thought that progresses from the sestet toward a concluding tercet or couplet. Some sonnets were sent to fellow poets and proposed a theme to be developed or a problem to be solved. A notable example of these exchanges is the *tenzone,* or debate, on the nature of love among Giacomo da Lentini, Jacopo Mostacci, and Pier della Vigna. A genre of extraordinary verbal and technical virtuosity is the *discordo,* a song of unequal stanzas that depicts the soul-rending experience of love by means of jarring contrasts of sounds and motifs. Quite distinguishable from the high-toned canzone is the *canzonetta,* a song written in the middle style, with short lines and melodious stanzas. It originates several thematic subgenres by dramatizing feelings drawn from real-life situations: a lover's anguish over his separation from his beloved, in the *canzone di lontananza;* a lover's bereavement over his lady's death or a girl's consuming desire to be married or a woman's distress over the impending departure of her lover on a crusade, in the distinctive forms of the *lamento.* The conventions of the so-called realistic or popular poetry are followed in "Rosa fresca aulentissima," a well-known *contrasto* by Cielo d'Alcamo that presents a lively parody of courtly love in the form of a debate between a girl and her suitor.

The poetry of the Sicilians is accessible today almost entirely in transcriptions from the original Sicilian dialect into a variety of Tuscan, made by scribes in Tuscany. One of the few examples of a poem in the Sicilian original is Stefano Protonotaro's "Pir meu cori alligrari."

Bibliography

Cesareo, Giovanni A. *Le origini della poesia lirica e la poesia siciliana sotto gli Svevi.* 2nd. ed. Milan: Sandron, 1924.

Contini, Gianfranco. *Poeti del Duecento.* Vol. 1. Milan, Naples: Ricciardi, 1960.

Jensen, Frede (ed. and trans.). *The Poetry of the Sicilian School.* New York: Garland Publishing, 1986.

Kleinhenz, Christopher. *The Early Italian Sonnet: The First Century (1220–1321).* Lecce: Milella, 1986.

Panvini, Bruno (ed.). *Le rime della scuola siciliana.* Florence: Olschki, 1962.

Pasquini, Emilio, and Antonio Enzo Quaglio. *Le origini e la scuola poetica siciliana.* Bari: Laterza, 1971.

Pirrotta, Nino. "I poeti della scuola siciliana e la musica." *Yearbook of Italian Studies* 4 (1980), 5–12.

Roncaglia, Aurelio. "Le corti medievali." In *Letteratura italiana.* Edited by Alberto Asor Rosa. Vol. I: *Il letterato e le istituzioni.* Turin: Einaudi, 1982, pp. 33–147.

Russell, Rinaldina. *Generi poetici medievali.* Naples: Società Editrice Napoletana, 1982.

Valency, Maurice. *In Praise of Love.* New York: Macmillan, 1961.

Rinaldina Russell

Siger of Brabant

Thirteenth-century Scholastic philosopher whose teachings at the University of Paris were controversial and conflicted with the more orthodox doctrines espoused by St. Thomas Aquinas. In the *Paradiso,* Dante places Siger next to St. Thomas in the Heaven of the Sun as one of the twelve souls configuring the second garland of eminent doctors of the Church, creating thereby an image of transcendental reconciliation. A document of August 27, 1266, describes Siger as the violent head of a group of students from the province of Picardy in northern France dedicated to promoting doctrines of radical Aristotelianism. Deemed heretical by his opponents, these doctrines are manifest in three unquestionably authentic works: *Quaestiones in tertium "De anima"* (1269), *De aeternitate mundi* (1272), *De anima intellectiva* (1274). In these works Siger analyzes Aristotelian psychology and gnoseology under the aegis of Averroës' commentary on *De anima,* from which he seldom deviates. Arguing against the Thomistic thesis affirming that "soul comes from outside as a subject of three different powers" (namely, the vegetative, the sensitive, and the intellective), Siger promotes an Aristotelian-Averroistic theory according to which humans are endowed with two souls: one intrinsic—the sensitive soul—and the other the intellective soul. This intellective soul is an immaterial substance endowed with two powers, the possible and the active intellect; it is not personal in nature but rather is common to the whole human race. Only during the process of cognizance does the intellective join the organic soul. Through the active intellect, the soul has the power to turn the individual sensitive forms into intelligible universal concepts and transmit them to the possible intellect. The corollaries of this doctrine all contrasted sharply with both traditional philosophy and teachings of the Church. Among the 219 heterodox theses condemned in 1277 by Étienne Tempier, bishop of Paris, are found several articles relating to Sigerian philosophy. Central among these heterodox theses was the notion that the subject of knowledge resides not in the individual self but in a universal intellect. Deprived of a personal intellect, human beings are dominated, like irrational beings, by a coercive necessity determined either, as Dante says in *Purg.* 16.81, by *ciel* ("heaven," or astral influence) or *piacere* ("pleasure," or one's own desire). In *De anima intellectiva,* Siger modifies his Averroistic dualism: he borrows the traditional image of the ship guided by the divine pilot to describe the relationship between the sensitive soul (ship) and the intellect (the pilot), without the pilot and ship ever becoming a substantial unity. In this model, each individual is able to contemplate the quiddity of all things in the light of the divine intellect. Only this philosophical activity can guarantee earthly perfection and beatitude. In his *Quaestiones super librum de causis,* Siger explicitly rejects all Averroistic theses and converts to the orthodox doctrine.

Nevertheless his unorthodox views, considered fundamentally heretical, led to his persecution and excommunication from the Church. Siger appealed to the pope, went to Rome, and died while awaiting his trial. Consequently his presence in the Heaven of the Sun has itself generated controversy as well as a diversity of interpretation. Dante clearly rejects the theoretical foundation of Averroism. In his exposition of the creation of the rational soul in *Purg.* 25.61–66 he incorporates St. Albert the Great's doctrine that the vegetative and sensitive soul develops from the father's seed and, contrary to Siger, that the rational soul, infused directly by God, subsumes the vegetative and sen-

sitive faculties into its own substantial unity, which becomes one single soul *(fassi un'alma sola),* endowed with three different powers. This unified soul is personal and constitutes the proper human virtue. Taking this textual evidence into account, some critics believe that Dante's celebration of Siger has less to do with the issue of his Averroism than it does with his admiration for Siger's methodological reading of Aristotle. Despite the theological conflict between the two interpreters of Aristotle, Dante makes St. Thomas recognize the value of Siger's commentary. In *Par.* 10, therefore, Dante portrays the two opponents in harmony with one another, with St. Thomas celebrating Siger as a theologian whose scientific methodology made him the object of envy, as one who *silogizzò invidiosi veri* ("demonstrated invidious truths," 138) and persecution—perhaps even, in Dante's view, unjustly.

Bibliography

Foster, Kenelm. *The Two Dantes and Other Studies.* London: Darton, Londman, and Todd, 1977.

Gilson, Étienne. *Dante and Philosophy.* Translated by David Moore. New York: Harper and Row, 1949.

Mazzotta, Giuseppe. "Dante's Siger of Brabant: Logic and Vision." In *Dante: Summa Medievalis. Proceedings of the Symposium of the Center for Italian Studies, SUNY Stony Brook.* Edited by Charles Franco and Leslie Morgan. Stony Brook, N.Y.: Forum Italicum, 1995, pp. 40–51.

Nardi, Bruno. *Sigieri di Brabante nel pensiero del rinascimento italiano.* Rome: Edizioni Italiane, 1945.

———. "L'origine dell'anima umana secondo Dante." In *Studi di Filosofia Medievale.* Rome: Edizioni Storia e Letteratura, 1945.

Putallaz, X. François. "La Connaissance de soi au Moyen Age: Siger de Brabant." *Archives d'Histoire Doctrinale et Littéraire du Moyen Age* 59 (1992), 89–157.

Ryan, Christopher. "Man's Free Will in the Works of Siger de Brabant." *Mediaeval Studies* 45 (1981), 155–199.

Van Steenberghen, Fernand. *Maître Siger de Brabant. Philosophes Médiévaux* XXI (1977), 9–444.

Vasoli, Cesare. "Sigieri di Brabante." *Enciclopedia dantesca,* 5:238–242.

Mario Trovato

S Simile

One of the most distinctive and characteristic rhetorical devices employed in the *Commedia,* the Dantean simile stands out for its remarkable power to communicate clear, vivid images of the real world and to express complex ideas and concepts. The poem contains more than 600 similes, ranging in length from one to twenty-seven verses, but in referring to the "Dantean simile" critics generally mean the extended simile, which has its origins in the classical simile of the Homeric and Virgilian epics. Dante's use of the simile—in particular, the longer or extended simile—is unparalleled in medieval literature, and it contravenes the conventions set down by the rhetoricians of the period, such as Geoffrey of Vinsauf and Matthew of Vendôme, who considered this form of narrative amplification obsolete and advised that it be used sparingly if at all. But their views derived from a longstanding antipathy to simile that began with Aristotle (*Rhetoric* 3.4.1406b), who promoted the use of metaphor instead (Quintilian, *Istitutio oratoria* 8.6.4; Cornificius, *Ad Herennium* 4.45–48). For Dante, simile *(similitudine)* is a means of establishing an analogy between one thing, experience, or phenomenon and another; and analogy is the basis both for understanding the nature of the real world—of the here and now—and for comprehending the relationship between the present world and the world of the afterlife. Simile is, therefore, like allegory and symbolism, metaphor and comparison, one of several devices used to express analogy. For Dante, it is the characteristic and most evident of all linguistic tropes.

Formally, a simile is a figure of speech that defines or describes a likeness shared by two things or events which are normally conceived to be different. Similes are commonly introduced by the term "like" or "as." The most common terms used by Dante are *come . . . così* and *quale . . . tale,* but similes are also introduced by the terms *similemente* or *non altrimenti* and *quanto . . . tanto;* and similes of the shorter variety frequently begin with *a guisa di* and *quasi.* It is customary, following I. A. Richards's practice, to refer to the two halves of a simile as the vehicle (the figure used to illustrate the basic narrative reality) and the tenor (the object being compared or described). The tenor and the vehicle point to a shared likeness, called the *tertium comparationis.* In the *Commedia* the vehicle almost always precedes the tenor, and the two parts, in the majority of examples, are balanced in length, having the same number of verses. For medieval rhetoricians, similes take one of two forms: similes can be short, *per brevitatem;* or they can be long, *per collationem* (i.e., where the tenor and the vehicle are collated or placed, as it were, "side by side," which is to say that the two parts are placed one after the other). Examples of the short simile in Dante would include, for example, the description of Dante's fainting before Francesca: *e caddi come corpo morto cade* ("and I fell as a dead body falls," *Inf.* 5.143); or that of Geryon's swift departure after ferrying Dante into the pit of Malebolge: *si dileguò come da corda cocca* ("disappeared like the notch from the bowstring," *Inf.* 17.136); or his portrayal of his own fear: *e stetti come l'uom che teme* ("and stood like one who is afraid," *Inf.* 13.45). The description of the solicitude of the gluttons in expiating their sin in Purgatory typifies the *per collationem* simile: *Come li augei che vernan lungo 'l Nilo / alcuna volta in aere fanno schiera, / poi volan più a fretta e vanno in filo: / così tutta la gente che lì era, / volgendo 'l viso, raffrettò suo passo, / e per magrezza e per voler leggera* ("As the birds that winter along the Nile sometimes flock in the air, then fly with more haste and form a file: so all the people there, turning their faces, hastened their pace, made light by both their leanness and their desire," *Purg.* 24.64–69). The term "extended simile," however, is usually reserved for especially long similes, of what is called the Homeric variety, where the length of the vehicle is so great that it creates a virtually separate and secondary narrative which threatens to destabilize, if only temporarily, the main narrative. Typical examples include the oft-mentioned and analyzed *villanello* simile at the opening of *Inf.* 24, or the clock simile in *Par.* 10.139–148.

Until recently the principal purpose of Dante's similes was deemed to be their ability to make the reader visualize more clearly the narrative scene. Similes were not disposable ornaments but were designed, in T. S. Eliot's words, "to make reality more real" (24). Dante's similes, of course, *do* present vivid images of scenes taken from the everyday world and from the world of nature, but they also do much more as well. One of their essential functions is to underscore the theological tenet that the seen (the *visibilia*) demonstrates the existence and nature of the unseen reality (the *invisibilia*): "For the invisible things of him from the creation of the world are clearly seen, being understood by the things that are made, even his eternal power and Godhead" (Rom. 1:20). The language of simile partakes of the language of signs, which informs the modes of allegory and symbolism that lie at the heart of Dante's realism. Visual reality is a sign pointing to a higher, unseen spiritual reality. This ontological model is highly dependent on orthodox conceptions whose best expression is found in St. Thomas's thought. In effect, the reality of the earthly world and the truer reality of the otherworld bear an analogical relationship not unlike that of the vehicle and the tenor of a simile, which is a relationship of likeness, not identity. Dante's similes continually remind the reader that cognition of reality depends on sense perception (cf. *Par.* 4.41–42); hence they dramatize the mode of the learning process. Consequently the purpose of many similes is not so much to make the reader see the scene more clearly, as an end in itself, but to heighten the reader's awareness of the process of discovery of meaning. Similes obligate the reader to look for similarity in the nature of things, to discover likenesses and to extrapolate from likenesses the true nature of reality. Such a process argues against conceiving of Dante as a mystical poet.

The burden of meaning in Dante's similes, then, has often more to do with thematic and symbolic concerns than with pictorial considerations. For example, the *pecorelle* simile (*Purg.* 3.79–87) that introduces the first group of souls in Purgatory—the excommunicates, as sheep timidly following one after the other, almost blindly and without knowing why *(lo 'mperché non sanno)*—defines their moral identity and spiritual condition by means of a common image taken from the natural world. The meaning of the analogy requires interpretation on the part of the reader, because there is no direct authorial statement by the poet. The image of the sheep conveys a sense of restraint and modesty, of humility and deference, which stands in marked contrast with the excommunicates' earthly pride and arrogance, and so it reveals the degree to which these individuals have learned to reject their sinful earthly nature. Indeed, the simile's content evokes the traditional image of Christ as shepherd who leads his obedient and trusting flock of sheep to salvation. The simile's symbolism gives rise to the idea of reconciliation and redemption, which is the central moral lesson of Purgatory. As this example makes clear, no less important is the fact that Dante requires the reader

to extrapolate this meaning from the image: to borrow a phrase from Wayne Booth, Dante is a poet who shows rather than tells, who dramatizes the learning process.

Often similes structure the meaning of the narrative and the way in which meaning is apprehended by characterizing an individual's moral identity, by describing his or her initial appearance before Dante the pilgrim. For example, Statius's appearance, perceived to be like that of Christ on the road to Emmaus, serves to identify Statius as a *figura Christi,* as a figure of Christ Arisen (*Purg.* 21.7–11); Beatrice's appearing like the rising sun establishes her likewise as a *figura Christi* (*Purg.* 30.22–33); Cacciaguida's affection upon meeting Dante in Heaven is analogous to that of Anchises when he meets his son in the Elysian Fields, a comparison that reinforces, by extension, Dante's role as an Aeneas figure (*Par.* 15.22–27). But similes often have as well a thematic as opposed to a symbolic purpose, and a power to establish richly allusive correspondences of a conceptual order that go beyond the announced *tertia comparationum.* The simile of the *bue cicilian,* or Sicilian bull (*Inf.* 27.7–15), for example, ostensibly purports to compare the sound of the device of torture made by its victim to the sound of the flame of fire that contains the false counselor Guido da Montefeltro. But the important connection is not so much the similarity of the two sounds, or the flames of fire in each instance, but rather a submerged correspondence that becomes evident only later in the canto's narrative. The real point of the analogy is the irony that underlies the fates of both the Sicilian bull's inventor, Perillus, and Guido da Montefeltro. For just as Perillus became the victim of his own invention, so too Guido—who discovers that the strategy he recommends to Boniface VIII backfires on him with disastrous results. When Guido recommends that the pope defeat his enemy by promising more than he intends to deliver (*lunga promessa con l'attender corto,* "a long promise with a short keeping," *Inf.* 27.110), little does he suspect that he will become a victim of precisely this very kind of promise. For when Boniface absolves him in advance of his act of fraud in assisting him (*finor t'assolvo,* "henceforth I absolve you," 101), promising him that his soul will be saved in spite of his evil (*Lo ciel poss' io serrare e diserrare,* "Heaven I can lock and unlock," 103), he makes a large promise that cannot be delivered. Guido's sins are not absolved, and

S consequently his soul ends in Hell. The simile underscores in advance the theme of ironic reversal, for each deceiver is deceived, in effect, by his own doing. The stated analogy, the likeness of sounds, then, does not contain the simile's primary meaning; indeed, it serves only as a springboard for more important associations of a thematic order. And visualizing the scene—it is almost needless to point out—is not in this instance the simile's principal function.

In their most powerful form, Dante's similes have an extraordinary capacity for suggesting multiple points of analogy between tenor and vehicle as a way of integrating thematic and conceptual associations within the narrative framework. This is not to deny or undervalue the fact that many similes have a more immediate and limited purpose, that of simply describing a simple image or action with such precision and detail that they convey a sense of a human experience with which we are all familiar. The firefly simile (*Inf.* 26.25–33), or the tailor simile (*Inf.* 15.20–21), for example, appear more visually than symbolically oriented (although the latter simile is strongly suggestive of sexual connotations). But the most striking examples have the power of creating narrative and thematic coherence and of delineating complex patterns of meaning. A prime example is the poem's initial simile of the shipwrecked swimmer (*Inf.* 1.22–27), used to describe the plight of Dante the pilgrim as he escapes the *selva oscura* ("dark wood"). Critics have detected in it numerous thematic and symbolic allusions to contexts of failure or initial lapse, both inside and outside the poem. The image of shipwreck recalls Aeneas' shipwreck in the early stage of his voyage from sacked Troy in search of a new world, thereby linking Dante to Aeneas, whose epic actions and heroic purpose he manifestly imitates (despite the pilgrim's own protestations to the contrary: *Io non Enëa . . . sono,* "I am not Aeneas," *Inf.* 2.32). Since Fulgentius and Bernardus Silvestris find in Aeneas' shipwreck the allegory of the birth of the hero's soul (the waters being an analogue for the amniotic fluid of parturition), Dante's simile may likewise be said to illustrate symbolically the idea of spiritual rebirth. For Singleton and Freccero (1966), the simile's waters associate Dante the pilgrim with the waters of the Red Sea and the story of Exodus. Freccero (1975) and Lansing perceive a meaningful affinity between the figure of the shipwrecked swimmer and the fate of Ulysses, whose

shipwreck results in death and damnation. What is remarkable in this simile, as in many others, is Dante's ability to suggest multiple and richly allusive meanings and to compress them into a small space: a concise and simple image gives rise to a complex network of ideas. The simile is, throughout the poem, a fundamental stylistic device for defining the nature of reality and expressing the meaning inherent in the poet's vision of the otherworld.

Bibliography

Allavena, Oreste. *Stile e poesia nelle similitudini della Divina Commedia.* Savona: Priamar, 1970.

Applewhite, James. "Dante's Use of the Extended Simile in the *Inferno.*" *Italica* 41(1964), 294–309.

Baldelli, Ignazio. "Lingua e stile delle opere in volgare di Dante." *Enciclopedia dantesca,* Appendice, 55–114.

Brandeis, Irma. *The Ladder of Vision: A Study of Dante's Comedy.* Garden City: Anchor Books, 1962.

Chiarenza, M. M. "Hippolytus' Exile: *Paradiso* XVII, 46–48." *Dante Studies* 89 (1966), 65–68.

Cuomo, Luisa Ferretti. *Anatomia di un'immagine (Inferno 2.120–132). Saggio di lessicologia e di semantica strutturale.* New York: Peter Lang, 1994.

Economou, George D. "The Pastoral Simile of *Inferno* XXIV and the Unquiet Heart of the Christian Pilgrim." *Speculum* 51 (1976), 637–646.

Eliot, T. S. *Dante.* London: Faber and Faber, 1929.

Franciosi, Giovanni. *Dell'evidenza dantesca nelle metafore, nelle similitudini e nei simboli.* Modena, 1872.

Freccero, John. "The River of Death: *Inferno* II, 108." In *The World of Dante: Six Studies in Language and Thought.* Edited by S. B. Chandler and J. A. Molinaro. Toronto: University of Toronto Press, pp. 25–42.

———. "Dante's Ulysses: From Epic to Novel." In *Concepts of the Hero in the Middle Ages and the Renaissance.* Edited by Norman T. Burns and Christopher J. Reagan. Albany: State University of New York Press, 1975, pp. 101–119.

Lansing, Richard H. *From Image to Idea: A Study of the Simile in Dante's Commedia.* Ravenna: Longo, 1977.

Lewis, C. S. "Dante's Similes." In *Studies in Medieval and Renaissance Literature.* Cambridge: Cambridge University Press, 1966 [1940].

Mallin, Eric S. "The False Simile in Dante's *Commedia.*" *Dante Studies* 102 (1984), 15–36.

Pagliaro, Antonino. "Similitudine." *Enciclopedia dantesca,* 5:253–259.

Rabuse, G. "Dantes Bilder und Vergleiche." *Orbis Litterarum* 15 (1960), 65–94.

Singelton, C. S. "In Exitu Israel de Aegypto." *78th Annual Report of the Dante Society* (1960), 1–24.

Sowell, Madison U. "A Bibliography of the Dantean Simile to 1981." *Dante Studies* 101 (1983), 167–180.

Venturi, Luigi. *Le similitudini dantesche ordinate, illustrate e confrontate.* Florence: Sansoni, 1889.

Richard Lansing

Simon Magus

Simon Magus *(Simon mago)* appears in the New Testament as a sorcerer or magician ("magus," in the Vulgate) from Samaria who, having heard the preaching of Philip, was converted and baptized. When Simon saw that Peter and John were able to confer the Holy Spirit through the laying on of hands, however, he offered the apostles money for that power. Peter rebuked him severely for his request (see Acts 8:9–24). In the apocryphal *Acts of Peter and Paul,* the two apostles meet Simon, now the emperor Nero's magician, in Rome and have a magic contest before the emperor; Simon flies through the air, but when St. Peter makes the sign of the cross, he falls headlong. "Simony," the trafficking in things sacred, takes its name from this Simon Magus. It is thus appropriate that Dante opens *Inf.* 19 (which deals with those who practice simony—the inhabitants of the third bolgia of the eighth circle) with an apostrophe to Simon Magus and his *miseri seguaci* ("wretched followers") and that the simonists are punished upside down. Beatrice also refers to Simon in her final speech to Dante *(Par.* 30.147).

V. Stanley Benfell

Simonides

Greek lyric and elegiac poet (c. 556–467 B.C.E.), famous especially for the epigrams he wrote for tombstone inscriptions. Only fragments of his poetry survive. Virgil tells Statius that Simonides *(Simonide)* is one of the Greek poets in Limbo *(Purg.* 22.107); in *Conv.* 4.13.8, Dante cites Aris-

totle's criticism of Simonides while advocating attainment to the divine.

Nancy Vine Durling

Simonists

Those who attempt to buy or sell sacred things, most frequently Holy Orders, commit simony and are, therefore, called simonists. Dante places the simonists in the third bolgia, or pouch, of the *Inferno*'s eighth circle; whereas the practice of simony was spread throughout the Church, Dante portrays only simonist popes in *Inf.* 19 (Nicholas III, and by anticipation Clement V and Boniface VIII). He describes the simonists as spiritual panders, since they sell the sacred goods of the Church, which should be the spouse of Christ, to others. The simonists' inversion of spiritual priorities is made concretely literal by Dante through the canto's *contrapasso:* the simonists are placed head first into holes in the floor of Hell, thus revealing where their true interests lie. Their appearance, moreover, satirizes the procedure of papal succession, as pope upon pope makes his appearance in this bolgia. Nicholas, who is already in Hell, predicts the damnation of both Boniface and Clement, who are both still alive at the time of Dante's otherworld journey.

Dante describes both the buying and the selling of spiritual goods with reference to two of the three simonist popes mentioned. Nicholas tells the pilgrim that his eagerness to advance his family led him to pursue wealth (through the selling of spiritual things—see *Inf.* 19.70–72). Nicholas prophesies that Clement V, on the other hand, will "buy" the papacy from the French king Philip the Fair, much like the biblical high priest Jason (see 2 Macc. 4–6). The poet vigorously censures Nicholas on his simony in a kind of sermon, citing the appropriate biblical passages, thereby reversing the traditional roles of pastor and parishioner. Ultimately Dante accuses the simonist popes of corrupting the entire Church; he rewrites a portion of Apocalypse (Rev. 17) so as to argue that John the Revelator foresaw not pagan Rome but the simonist popes as the great persecutors of the Church (see *Inf.* 19.106–111). His condemnation of the Donation of Constantine as a source of simony—which marks the peroration of the pilgrim's words of reprimand (*Inf.* 19.115–117)—takes on a special force in light of Boniface's claim, in the bull *Unam Sanctam,* that the

Donation authorized the Church to possess temporal powers, including the right to acquire wealth and territory.

V. Stanley Benfell

Simony

Broadly speaking, simony *(simonia)* is the buying and selling of spiritual things. The term takes its name from the biblical figure Simon Magus, who attempted to purchase the power of conferring the Holy Spirit from the apostles (see Acts 8:9–24) and became a subject of reform in the eleventh century. Dante uses the term only once, at *Inf.* 11.59, when listing the sins punished in the eighth circle: *falsità, ladroneccio e simonia* ("falsifying, thievery, and simony"), but he also employs the verb formed from the noun, *simoneggiando,* at *Inf.* 19.74.

The practice of simony was virtually unknown in early Christian history and became a problem only after Christianity was declared the official state religion of the Roman Empire, as Church officials began to adopt the common late imperial practice of offering bribes and gifts to secular officials. Long before Dante's own day, simony had become rampant, despite intermittent efforts at reform. The most common form of simony was the sale of Holy Orders, which proved lucrative because of the degree to which feudal institutions had become intertwined with Church practice. The ordination to the priesthood, for example, was often accompanied by the conferral of a benefice—a permanent income associated with an ecclesiastical office. Benefices were often sold for the income they generated.

Dante devotes the third bolgia, or pouch, of the *Inferno*'s eighth circle to simony. He chooses not to emphasize the widespread buying and selling of things sacred but instead focuses on the corruption at the top of the Church; the sinner Dante encounters, Nicholas III, and those mentioned by Nicholas as destined for damnation, are all popes. There was some debate as to whether popes could be simonists, to the extent that Aquinas, in *ST* 2.2.100, felt compelled to refute the objection that "the pope cannot commit simony." In Dante's view, the papal practice of simony infects and contaminates the rest of the Church: *la vostra avarizia il mondo attrista* ("your avarice afflicts the world," *Inf.* 19.104).

Dante among the simonists. La comedia, *ed. Pietro da Figino, 1491. Giamatti Collection: Courtesy of the Mount Holyoke College Archives and Special Collections.*

Dante portrays simony throughout *Inf.* 19 as a corruption of the divinely ordained relationship between God, the Church, and the world. Combining the common medieval metaphor of the Church as the bride of Christ with the frequent Old Testament portrayal of a straying Israel as an adulterous spouse, Dante describes simony as a kind of spiritual pandering (see *Inf.* 19.1–6, 55–57). And through the canto's *contrapasso,* he literally represents the papal inversion of spiritual priorities. Ultimately, for Dante, simony is simply idolatry; the popes of *Inf.* 19 worship gold and silver rather than God.

Bibliography

Brezzi, Paolo. "Il canto XIX dell'*Inferno*." In *Nuove Letture Dantesche.* Vol. 2. Casa di Dante in Roma. Florence: Le Monnier, 1968, pp. 161–182.

Fallani, Giovanni. "Il canto dei simoniaci." In *Poesia e teologia nella Divina Commedia. I. L'Inferno.* Milan: Marzorati, 1959, pp. 77–93.

Kelly, J. N. D. *The Oxford Dictionary of the Popes.* Oxford, New York: Oxford University Press, 1986, pp. 201–202, 208–210, 212–214.

Lynch, Joseph H. *Simoniacal Entry into Religious Life from 1000 to 1260.* Columbus: Ohio State University Press, 1976.

Petrocchi, Giorgio. "La prosapia del Mago Simone di Samaria." *Studi danteschi* 51 (1978), 255–269.

V. Stanley Benfell

Singleton, Charles Southward

The leading American Dantist (1909–1985) from the 1950s to his death. Except for an initial appointment at the University of Missouri and a nine-year interval at Harvard (1948–1957), he spent his academic career at the Johns Hopkins University from 1939 until his retirement. After early studies on Florentine pageantry, Renaissance carnival songs, and an edition of Boccaccio's *Decameron* (1955), Singleton turned his attention to Dante, publishing *An Essay on the Vita Nuova* (Harvard University Press) in 1949, following it with his seminal studies on the *Commedia: Dante Studies 1. Elements of Structure* (Harvard University Press, 1954) and *Dante Studies 2. Journey to Beatrice* (Harvard University Press, 1958). His prose translation and substantial commentary on the poem appeared in six volumes between 1973 and 1975 from Princeton University Press in the Bollingen Series. His revision of Paget Toynbee's *A Dictionary of Proper Names and Notable Matters in the Works of Dante* appeared in 1968, and the following year he joined Peter Brieger and Millard Meiss in editing *Illuminated Manuscripts of the Divine Comedy,* also published in the Bollingen Series.

Decisively anti-Crocean, Singleton's critical position was much influenced by the work of Michele Barbi, Erich Auerbach, Ernst Robert Curtius, and Leo Spitzer, and by the theological studies of Jean Daniélou and Étienne Gilson. His hermeneutic method anticipated to a certain extent that of Hans Robert Jauss and the Konstanz school in its insistence upon understanding the work of art in its historical context. Singleton saw that medieval theology was, along with the Latin classics, essential to Dante's inspiration, language, and poetics. Holding that the *Epistle to Cangrande* and its discussion of the fourfold structure of allegory was authentic, Singleton showed that the matrical structure of the *Commedia* was that of the biblical Exodus, the event which, in turn, prefigured the central Christian facts of the spiritual journey of escape from sin: conversion, redemption, the Last Judgment, and eternal glory. Rejecting the view that the poem was merely a poetic allegory (the Romantic and Crocean view), Singleton claimed that Dante was "imitating God's way of writing" through historical events and their spiritual significance. Despite criticisms that he gave exaggerated stress to theology or even mysticism, Singleton's approach has become fundamental for his leading students and followers; most scholars, even if they disagree with his tenets and findings, value the significance of his contribution to and influence on the history of Dantean studies.

While his major focus was on Dante, Singleton never abandoned his interest in the Renaissance. His translation of Castiglione's *The Book of the Courtier* appeared in 1959, and his revision of the John Payne translation of the *Decameron* was published in 1982.

Bibliography

Della Terza, Dante. "Charles S. Singleton: An Appraisal." *Dante Studies* 104 (1986), 9–25.

Mazzotta, Giuseppe. "Dante e la critica americana di Charles Singleton." *Letture Classensi* 18 (1989), 195–209.

Pellegrini, Anthony L. "The Publications of Charles S. Singleton." *Dante Studies* 104 (1986), 3–8.

Anthony K. Cassell

Sinon

Greek warrior and protagonist of a critical episode of the Trojan War, Sinon figures in the *Aeneid* and the *Commedia* as the paradigmatic liar. In accordance with the Greek strategy, Sinon is wittingly captured by the Trojans, whom he convinces with his persuasive tale and false tears to receive inside the walls of Troy the infamous horse from which the Greek warriors emerge to defeat the Trojans (*Aen.* 2.57–198). Dante places Sinon in the tenth pouch of the eighth circle among the falsifiers of words, condemned to suffer eternal fever (*Inf.* 30.91–148). The vulgar altercation between Sinon and the counterfeiter, Master Adam, is representative of Dante's most comic, realistic style in the *Commedia* and evokes the *tenzone,* or debate, poems, which Dante himself composed as a young poet. Critics disagree as to whether the passage and the poetry it evokes represent attempts to repudiate, reorient, or redeem Dante's earlier poetic experiments (see *"Tenzone"*). Likewise, readers debate the appropriateness of the pilgrim's response to the bickering and Virgil's uncharacteristically harsh reprimand, in light of the base poetics of the *Inferno* and its attendant sensationalism.

Donna Yowell

Siren

The siren who sings her sweet song to the pilgrim Dante in *Purg.* 19 has both dramatic and symbolic significance. The central figure of the second of Dante's two dreams on Mount Purgatory, she appears first as a hideous creature, deformed and stammering. The pilgrim's gaze effects her transformation into a beautiful woman and readies her tongue, and she begins a seductive song whose theme is its own irresistible attraction. She it is, *dolce sirena* ("sweet siren"), who leads mariners astray, she who fulfills all desires of those who submit to her enchantment.

The example of which she boasts, that of having turned aside Ulysses from his course, has given rise to considerable critical speculation: does Dante conflate the siren and the enchantress Circe, or is the siren to be understood to be lying in her claim, which does not conform to known sources? The pilgrim himself is in any case mesmerized, unable to turn his attention from her until a lady *santa e presta* ("holy and quick") appears at his side and rebukes Virgil for his failure to intervene. Dante's guide responds wordlessly by tearing away the clothes of the siren, from whose belly emerges a stench so powerful that it brings his dream to an end.

The dream of the siren links the central lesson in human love pronounced by Virgil in the preceding canto of the *Purgatorio* and the experience of the final terraces of the mountain that remain to be crossed. The pilgrim's enthralled response to the siren's song illustrates the innate human response to the stimulus of pleasure, while the holy lady's intervention underlines the need for vigilance in determining between base and praiseworthy objects of love. As they resume their ascent, Virgil tells Dante that he has seen *quell'antica strega* ("that ancient witch") for whom penance is done on the terraces above by those who have sinned through misdirected love, and he explains as well how one frees oneself from her hold—which, as the dream dramatizes, is through alert and unbewitched moral vision.

The siren is not only the antithesis of the saintly lady through whose intervention she is unmasked. In the larger structure of the *Commedia,* she has been termed both a "false Beatrice" and an anti-Beatrice, offering promises of happiness that she cannot fulfill. Beatrice herself, reunited with the pilgrim, will insist on recalling his past errors so that in time to come, *udendo le serene* ("hearing the Sirens"), he may be more strong (*Purg.* 31.45).

Bibliography

Cervigni, Dino. *Dante's Poetry of Dreams.* Florence: Olschki, 1968, chapter 4.

Hollander, Robert. *Allegory in Dante's Commedia.* Princeton, N.J.: Princeton University Press, 1969, pp. 136–144.

Norton, Glyn P. "Retrospection and Prefiguration in the Dreams of *Purgatorio.*" *Italica* 47 (1970), 351–365.

Shapiro, Marianne. *Woman Earthly and Divine in the Commedia of Dante.* Lexington: University Press of Kentucky, 1975, pp. 89–97.

Sara Sturm-Maddox

Sloth

One of the seven deadly sins. The sin of sloth *(accidia)* is addressed in both the *Inferno* and the *Purgatorio.* In the *Inferno,* the slothful are anonymous and characterized only as a group. In the *Purgatorio,* they are represented by individual examples. Not only is the *Purgatorio's* treatment of the sinners more personal and more dramatic, but its psychological and ethical perspective on the sin is also different.

In *Inf.* 7, when Virgil and Dante have arrived at the swamp Styx and see the wrathful damned striking and mutilating one another in the mud, Virgil hastens to inform Dante that submerged beneath the marsh's surface are other souls whose attempt at speech makes the water bubble. According to Virgil, the souls try to say that they were *tristi* ("gloomy") in the world's open air and sunshine, carrying inside them *accidioso fummo* ("fumes of sullenness"), and that now their gloom continues in the black sludge (121–124).

Dante's placement of the slothful alongside the wrathful was doubtless suggested by authorities who treated sloth as a form or consequence of wrath. For Aristotle, wrath and sloth are both extremes of the irascible appetite. St. Thomas Aquinas notes how Aristotle's *Ethics* divides the irascible into three categories: the acute, the bitter, and the difficult. Aquinas says in *ST* 2.2.158.5 that *amari habent iram permanentem propter permanentiam tristitiae, quam inter viscera tenent clausam* ("the bitter have a permanent wrath on account of the permanence of the gloom they keep closed within them"); St. Bonaventure says in *Breviloquium* 3 that *Ira, cum non potest se vindicare, tristatur, et ideo ex ea nascitur accidia* ("Wrath, when it cannot avenge itself, turns sullen, and thus from it is born sloth"); and Brunetto Latini, similarly, remarks that *In ira nasce e posa / accidia nighittosa* ("In wrath neglectful sloth is born and abides," *Tesoretto* 2683–2684).

For Dante's authorities, gloominess and sloth were one and the same. According to St. Thomas (*ST* 1.63.2): *Acedia vero est quaedam tristitia, qua homo redditur tardus ad spirituales actus propter laborem corporalem* ("Sloth in fact is a sort of gloom which renders a person slow to spiritual deeds because of bodily effort"). Dante's decision to locate the slothful in Styx was most likely prompted by authorities like Servius and Isidore who interpreted the swamp's name as meaning sad or gloomy (cf. *tristo ruscel,* "sad stream," 7.107). The *Inferno* does not name the sin of the submerged, and opinion as to its identity has not been unanimous. But the majority view, from Dante's sons forward, has held it to be sloth.

Unlike the *Inferno*'s suggestive and oblique treatment of sloth, the *Purgatorio*'s is explicit and analytical. In *Purg.* 17, Virgil and Dante arrive at the threshold of the fourth circle just as day ends, and they lose the power to go farther. Dante asks what sin is purged there, and Virgil answers by giving a short definition of sloth: *l'amor del bene, scemo / del suo dover* ("The love of the good, falling short of what is right," i.e., insufficient love of the good, 85–86). Then Virgil proceeds to explain more fully so that Dante can derive *alcun buon frutto di nostra dimora* ("some good fruit from our delay," 90). The following discussion occasions an exhaustive analysis of sins in general, which in turn explains the order in which the seven deadly sins are expiated. Thus, by having night fall exactly as the poets arrive at the threshold of the circle in which sloth is purged, the *Commedia* artfully creates in the *Purgatorio*'s central canto a convenient pretext for expounding the canticle's overall physical arrangement and moral system.

All sins, Virgil explains, derive from love: perverted love, excessive love, or, as in the case of sloth, deficient love. Thus, love is the *sementa . . . d'ogne virtute / e d'ogne operazion che merta pene* ("the seed . . . of every virtue and of every action that deserves punishment," 104–105). Humans sin, Virgil goes on to explain, by loving their neighbor's misfortune; or loving a lesser good too much; or, again in the case of sloth, if in loving the good, *lento amore a lui veder vi tira / o a lui acquistar*

("If slack love draws you to see it or to acquire it," 130–131). The *Purgatorio*'s notion of sloth is thus fundamentally different from the *Inferno*'s: *lento amore* ("slow love"), not the *lenta ira* ("slow wrath") with which the Renaissance commentator Bernardino Daniello identified the *accidioso fummo* of the *Inferno*. The focus of Dante's reading of St. Thomas has shifted from the permanent wrath of the sullen to a comprehensive account of human motivation, which allows the poet to set sloth in a spiritually dynamic context: *Amor enim est prima radix omnium passionum* ("Love is surely the source of all the emotions," *ST* 1.2.46.1; see also 1.2.27.4). The *Inferno*'s suffocated wrath admits of no possibility of change, but the *Purgatorio*'s torpid love is, as it must be, open to correction.

Dante's questioning then leads Virgil to a discussion of love and free will. Virgil's reasoning leaves Dante in wonderment, but his reverie is broken by the sudden approach of the penitent slothful who hurry through the night. The two spirits in front cry out examples of dispatch: the Virgin Mary, who made haste to visit Elizabeth; and Caesar, who hurried to subdue Spain. Those who follow urge one another on so as not to lose time *per poco amor* ("through lack of love," 18.104).

Virgil asks the spirits where Dante can ascend when day returns, and he is answered by one spirit who in life had been abbot of St. Zeno's in Verona. Pietro Alighieri's commentary asserts that *vitium accidiae multum inter claustrales frequentatur* ("the sin of sloth is very common among cloistered monks"). The abbot complains of the monastery's current abbot and predicts that the lord (Alberto della Scala) who has put his unworthy son (Giuseppe) in the place of St. Zeno's *pastor vero* ("true shepherd," 18.126) will soon die and be punished for the abuse. The abbot's prophecy may be no more than a parenthesis in which Dante discharges his personal indignation, for he had observed the situation in Verona firsthand. Nevertheless, Alberto's clumsy and selfish intrusion on the prerogatives of the Church stands in stark contrast with Mary's busying herself with the work of God and Caesar's attending to the future of the Empire.

Following the abbot and the rest of the penitent are two spirits who bring up the rear. Like the two spirits in front, they invoke a pair of examples—one sacred and one profane—but here, appropriate to their coming behind, the examples they cite are of sloth: the recalcitrant Israelites who failed to reach the Promised Land and the Trojans who deserted Aeneas before he reached the site of Rome. The examples show how sloth is antithetical to the providential purposes of both church and empire, and thus the *Purgatorio* concludes its treatment of sloth by setting the sin in its universal context.

Bibliography

Wenzel, Siegfried. *The Sin of Sloth: "Acedia" in Medieval Thought and Literature.* Chapel Hill: University of North Carolina Press, 1967.

Todd Boli

Società Dantesca Italiana

The Italian Dante Society was officially founded in Florence in 1888, in the "Sala di Leo X" in the Palazzo Vecchio, where Pietro Torrigiani, mayor of Florence, became first provisional and later honorary president of the society. Its most important founding members—including Giosue Carducci, Alessandro D'Ancona, Isidoro Del Lungo, Guido Mazzoni, Ernesto Monaci, and Pio Rajna—sought to ensure that the mission of the society would be national and not local in character. Among its earliest projects were the plan for a critical edition of the *Commedia* and the *Opere minori* (under the direction of Adolfo Bartoli, D'Ancona, and Del Lungo) and the publication of a monthly *Bullettino* devoted to research on Dante's life and works (the first issue appeared in 1890 under the directorship of Michele Barbi). E. G. Parodi assumed the directorship from 1906 through 1928, when it ceased publication. But the society's most distinguished early Dantist, Michele Barbi, went on to found *Studi danteschi,* in 1920, which ultimately became the official research organ of the society. After Barbi's death in 1941, the journal was directed in succession by Mario Casella (from 1948 through 1956), Gianfranco Contini (from 1957 through 1981), and Francesco Mazzoni (1982 to the present).

From the beginning the society sought to spread interest in Dante and his works among the general public. Guido Mazzoni presented the society's first public lecture on the *Commedia,* in April 1899, in the Orsanmichele Hall—a room later called "Dante's Hall" and where the presentation of public lectures designated "Lecturae Dantis"

would eventually become a tradition, as it would not only in Florence but throughout Italy. These efforts were complemented by an intense philological scrutiny of Dante's corpus of works, promoted by the extraordinary expertise and scholarship of Michele Barbi, who, together with Parodi, published a complete edition of Dante's works in Florence in 1921 *(Le Opere di Dante: Testo critico della Società Dantesca Italiana).* Since then, the society has continued to work on the *Edizione Nazionale* ("National Edition") of Dante's works, with the publication of modern critical editions of each text. The enormous project regained some of its vigor under the presidency of Mario Casella in the 1950s and received further stimulus under that of Gianfranco Contini in the 1960s, but it has yet to be completed.

The society made its first home in the Riccardiana Library (1890), and since 1904 it has resided in the Palagio dell'Arte della Lana, where it maintains a large library and continues to be the center of the society's activity. Since 1968 Francesco Mazzoni has served as the president of the society.

Palagio dell'Arte della Lana, home of the Società Dantesca Italiana since 1904. Richard Lansing.

Bibliography

Mazzoni, Francesco. "La Società Italiana Dantesca dalle origini ad oggi." In *Società Dantesca Italiana 1888–1988: Convegno internazionale.* Edited by Rudy Abardo. Milan: Ricciardi, 1995, pp. 13–35.

Richard Lansing

Socrates

Renowned Athenian philosopher (c. 469–399 B.C.E.), referred to several times in the *Convivio,* admired in the *Fiore* (43.12, 44.1), and placed with Aristotle and Plato among the virtuous heathen in Limbo (*Inf.* 4.133–135). Although Socrates left no writings of his own, he was known in the Middle Ages through the works of Plato, Xenophon, and others as a righteous pagan martyr and for having been the first philosopher to make a connection between knowledge and virtue. Hugh of St. Victor, for example, speaks of him as *ethicae inventor* ("the inventor of ethics," *Didascalicon* 3.2). Socrates *(Socrate, Socrato)* is cited by Dante with regard to his theory of the soul's "substantial generation" in *Conv.* 2.13.5, praised for his selflessness in *Conv.* 3.14.8, and noted for his personal integrity and belief in the immortality of the soul in *Conv.* 4.24.6, 4.6.13.

Michael Papio

Sodomites

Sodomites are males who have committed the sin of Sodom, or homosexuality, and in the *Commedia* they occupy two locations. The impenitent, in the third ring of the seventh circle of Hell, are punished by having to move in different groups upon sterile sand under a falling fire (*Inf.* 14–16). The penitent, on the seventh terrace of Purgatory, expiate their guilt as all of them together move through an engulfing flame (*Purg.* 26). The elements common to their situations—fire and perpetual motion—connote two aspects of their erotic passion: its heat and unrest.

Eight of the sodomites in Hell, but none in Purgatory, are identified by name, and of these all but one (Priscian) are Florentines. The pilgrim converses with two: first with ser Brunetto Latini, his revered and beloved benefactor, at their unexpected reunion (*Inf.* 15.24–120), and afterwards with Iacopo Rusticucci, known to him before only by reputation (16.28–72). The latter appears with

Dante with the sodomites. Opere del divino poeta Danthe, ed. Pietro da Figino, Venice, 1520. Giamatti Collection: Courtesy of the Mount Holyoke College Archives and Special Collections.

two associates, Guido Guerra and Tegghiaio Aldobrandi—all three having played significant roles in the political and/or military affairs of their city. One other member of their troop is spoken of: the exemplary Guiglielmo Borsiere. Brunetto—author of the *Tresor,* an encyclopedic work in French that he refers to as *il mio Tesoro* ("my *Treasure*") at line 119, and also of a didactic poem in Italian, the *Tesoretto*—belongs to a band consisting of "clerks, and great men of letters and of great fame" (15.106–107). He signals out three among these for mention: Francesco d'Accorso, a jurist; an unnamed bishop who is Andrea de' Mozzi; and Priscian, the great Latin grammarian of late antiquity. The only man linked to sodomy in *Purgatorio* is Julius Caesar; that once he was called *Regina* ("Queen") for indulging in the fault serves to identify the sin of the purgatorial sodomites (26.76–78).

Members of different professions, such as scholars and writers or those engaged in politics and warfare, apparently make up the separate sodomitical groups in Hell. The sinners there, under threat of severe penalties, must follow two rules: never to pause and never to mingle with a group other than one's own. These rules give rise to two athletic tropes—one drawn from the foot race, one from the wrestling match—that bear on the conception of sodomy as male-male sexuality.

When Brunetto at the close of canto 15 saw others approach "with whom [he] must not be," he darted off "and seemed one of those who at Verona race [naked, according to Boccaccio] for the green cloth across the fields, and of those he seemed the one who wins, not the one who loses." In the following canto the three Florentine leaders, wanting to speak with Dante but required to keep moving, "wheeled," in order to direct their faces toward him while rotating their bodies, and did so "As is the custom of wrestlers, naked and oiled, spying out their holds and their advantage" before making physical contact (16.22–27). These figurative athletes are explicitly naked, and they engage in a sport where men hold and hug each other. The daring and witty comparison captures the affinity and contrast between wrestling and sodomy. A message of these two similes is that masculine games, even when the players wear no clothes, are normal if informed by a competitive spirit and not by erotic desire.

Joseph Pequigney

Sodomy

Neither the word "sodomy" *(sodomia)* nor the word "sodomites" *(sodomiti)* appears in the *Commedia*. Dante designates the sin with references to Sodom *(Soddoma),* the city razed by fire from above in Gen. 19. He does so in *Inferno* at 11.50, and in *Purgatorio* at 26.40, where the name of Gomorrah is added, and at 26.79. The sin so signified is that of sexual relations between men. Although in the Middle Ages the term "sodomy" could signify certain noncarnal sins or the diverse noncoital sexual behaviors also deemed to be "contrary to nature," Dante's particularized notion conforms with that of St. Thomas Aquinas (*ST* 2.2.154.11, 12) and that of St. Albert the Great; and yet he departs from these theologians in showing no awareness of female sodomy and in never indicating that he conceives of male sodomy specifically in terms of anal intercourse (Boswell 316ff.; Pequigney 22–23).

The *Commedia* treats of the sin of Sodom in cantos 14–16 of *Inferno,* where the guilty are eternally punished as far down as the seventh circle, and in canto 26 of *Purgatorio,* where those saved through repentance suffer a terminable expiation on the seventh and uppermost ledge of the mountain. In both places the souls must move continuously and endure tormenting fire. Perpetual motion

is ascribed to all the types of erotic offenders in the afterlife, be they heterosexual or homosexual, to connote the restlessness of passion, the agitation of fleshly desire. The fire connotes libidinal ardor, though with a different character and import at each site. The descending fire in Hell, analogous to that which rained on the Cities of the Plain, educes the biblical representation of divine vengeance (Gen. 19:24–25). In Purgatory a dense mass of excruciating flame shoots out across the ledge to submerge the spirits, but it refines rather than scorches or disfigures them and has the interior effect of cleansing them of lustful dispositions. The hellfire is, by contrast, externally searing and serves as a purely penal effect. Both of these fires symbolize passion—passion as a driving force for the damned who would not give it up, but passion to be endured until it burns itself out in penitence for those who chose to turn from it.

In *Inferno* sodomy is a sin of violence. Virgil so classifies it in canto 11—and as an act of violence of the worst kind, that directed against God himself. This transgression violates the Deity by means of *spregiando natura e sua bontade* ("scorning Nature and its goodness"), whose course is divinely ordained (*Inf.* 11.48, 98–99). Contempt of nature is manifested by the willful omission of the sole lawful purpose of sexual acts, which is procreation. That idea is implicit in the infernal locale. The fire there is denatured in that it falls rather than rises; descends like snow but with burning, orange flakes; and forces the sodomites to tread incessantly upon "a plain that removes every plant from its bed" (*Inf.* 14.8–9, 28–30). While blasphemers and usurers also occupy the inner ring of the seventh circle, the sodomites are the most numerous, and their sin seems to determine the design of the landscape. The torrid, arid, self-sterilizing sand and the falling flames of fire serve to signify the exclusion of fertility from intermale sexual engagements assumed to be *peccata contra naturam* ("sins against nature"). The judgment is Thomistic and that of Catholic moral theology generally.

Even so, the attitude taken toward homosexual activity in *Inferno* is anomalous insofar as Dante condemns the sin but can still admire the sinners guilty of it. All of the sodomites identified, with but one exception, are unusually estimable and accomplished individuals, such as the three noble Florentines encountered in canto 16 and, above all, Brunetto Latini. The dramatic meeting between the wayfarer and his admiring and admired old friend in canto 15 is so affectionate and moving as to have prompted some scholars, most notably André Pézard and Richard Kay, to seek to exonerate Brunetto from the shame of sexual perversion by defining his violation of nature as something else. Others have joined this endeavor, though no two ever agree on what that something else should be; the vast majority of the commentators, however, continue to regard the sodomitical sin as homoerotic.

The conception, categorization, and appraisal of sodomy undergo radical alteration in the *Purgatorio*. In canto 26 the homosexually oriented souls go through the fire of the highest terrace in order to purge lust, the least of the seven capital sins. Marching in the opposite direction through the same fire are the heterosexual lustful. Every other trespass is more serious than these male-male and male-female sexual faults. In the seventh infernal circle sodomites had been put a full five circles below the "natural" venereal sinners, with whom they are now on a par; and they have now been elevated over all other incontinent wrongdoers, who were above them in Hell, so that here they are accounted less culpable than misers or spendthrifts or gluttons.

The capital sins basic to purgatorial organization are complemented by another ethical criterion, the one supplied by Virgil, in *Purg.* 17: he expounds the universal moral order and the coordinated tripartite plan of the seven terraces on the basis of love. Love is blameworthy when for an evil object or when deficient or inordinate in pursuit of a good object. The souls of the upper three ledges lavished inordinate love on secondary goods, such as wealth or food or persons of either sex passionately desired (*Purg.* 17.91–99, 136–137). Sodomy, viewed in this scheme as an excess of male erotic love for a male, is never in the *Purgatorio* deemed unnatural, nor can it be, for Virgil terms the very inclination of the mind to love what pleases it "nature" (18.19–27; cf. 17.91–94).

Purgatorial sodomy is conceived of, then, as at the top of the seven gradations of sinfulness ascending from most to least serious; as on a level with heterosexual lust and less grave than other forms of incontinence; as extravagant love; no longer as violence against God, or as unnatural, or in terms of a reproductive telos; and even as attributable to the illustrious Julius Caesar (*Purg.* 26.76–78). These positions on homoerotic love strikingly deviate from those that were dominant at the time—those not only intellectualized by Scholastic theologians but also adopted by Dante himself in the *Inferno*. That the first two canticles present such contrasting conceptualizations of homosexuality has generally gone unrecognized in the commentary tradition.

Bibliography

Ahern, John. "*Nudi Grammantes:* The Grammar and Rhetoric of Deviation." *Romanic Review* 81 (1990), 466–486.

Boswell, John. *Christianity, Social Tolerance, and Homosexuality.* Chicago: University of Chicago Press, 1980.

———. "Dante and the Sodomites." *Dante Studies* 112 (1994), 63–76.

Harris, John. "Three Dante Notes (1. Brunetto the Sodomite . . .)." *Lectura Dantis: A Forum for Dante Research and Interpretation* 2 (1988), 73–78.

Kay, Richard. *Dante's Swift and Strong: Essays in "Inferno" XV.* Lawrence: Regents Press of Kansas, 1978.

Pequigney, Joseph. "Sodomy in Dante's *Inferno* and *Purgatorio.*" *Representations* 36 (1991), 22–42.

———, and Hubert Dreyfus. "Landscape and Guide: Dante's Modifying of Meaning in the *Inferno.*" *Italian Quarterly* (1961–1962), 51–83.

Pézard, André. *Dante sous la pluie de feu.* Paris: Vrin, 1950.

Joseph Pequigney

Soldan

The soldan, or sultan, of Egypt, signifying Muslim sovereign. Egypt, often called "Babylon" in the Middle Ages, was confused with the ancient Kingdom of Babylon ruled by Semiramis. In *Inf.* 5.60 Dante thus erroneously refers to the latter's dominion as *la terra che il Soldan corregge* ("the lands the Sultan governs now"); and in *Inf.* 27.90, Egypt is called *terra di Soldano.* One of the most renowned sultans, Saladin, the founder of the Ayubite dynasty, is placed with the wise pagans in Limbo (*Inf.* 4.129) and celebrated for his generosity in *Conf.* 4.11.14. Other references are made to the sultan in 1300 (*Inf.* 5.60), the sultan in 1297 (*Inf.* 27.90), and the sultan in 1219 (*Par.* 11.101).

Robin Treasure

S

Solomon

When Solomon *(Salomone),* the son of David, was about to inherit his father's kingdom, he asked God only for the wisdom to be a good king. God so approved of Solomon's humble request that he granted him not only the greatest wisdom a king might ever have but also the greatest wealth (3 Kings 2:4–14). Consequently, Solomon's wisdom and his wealth became proverbial. But the later years of his reign were marred by lust (he was said to have had a thousand concubines) and even idolatry. Dante quotes him frequently in the *Convivio,* most often from Wisdom and Ecclesiastes (which the Middle Ages attributed to Solomon), as a source of wisdom and an example of kingly virtue. In the *Commedia,* it is especially Solomon the lover and the poet of the Canticle of Canticles who is celebrated, both when the Canticle's voice is chosen to greet Beatrice at her arrival in Eden *(Purg.* 30.10–18) and when Solomon himself is introduced as the brightest soul in the Heaven of the Sun: *La quinta luce, ch'è tra noi più bella, / spira di tale amor, che tutto 'l mondo / là giù ne gola di saper novella: / entro v'è l'alta mente u' sì profondo / saver fu messo che, se 'l vero è vero, / a veder tanto non surse il secondo* ("The fifth light, loveliest among us, breathes from such love that the whole world down there is greedy to have news of it: within it is the lofty mind where such deep wisdom was placed that, if truth is true, no second ever rose to see so much," *Par.* 10.109–114). The words with which Solomon is introduced allude not only to his proverbial wisdom but also, and first, to his unrestrained love and to the controversy, because of that love, over his salvation. In fact, while earlier theologians, including St. Augustine, believed the excesses of the great king, partially reflected in the Canticle, had cost him his place in Heaven, some later ones argued for his salvation. Dante's position in the controversy is clearly in favor of Solomon and no doubt reflects the importance Dante gave to the religious love poetry of the Canticle of Canticles.

Still in the Heaven of the Sun, St. Thomas gives a long explanation of how his words—*a veder tanto non surse il secondo* ("no second ever rose to see so much")—should not be taken to mean that Solomon rivaled Adam or Christ but merely that his wisdom as a king was unmatched *(Par.* 13.37–111). Finally, at the end of the same episode, Solomon is chosen to answer the pilgrim's questions about the important subject of the res-urrection of the flesh and to confirm the glory of the risen bodies of the blessed as the final consummation of their beatitude *(Par.* 14.36–63).

Marguerite Chiarenza

Solon

Mentioned at *Par.* 8.124 as a type for lawgivers or political men and at *Conv.* 3.11.4 as one of the Seven Sages of Greece. Solon *(Solone)* is remembered primarily for his reformation of the Athenian legal code, which is referred to at *Purg.* 6.139–141. He lived c. 630–c. 560 B.C.E.

Frank B. Ordiway

Song of Songs

The Song of Songs, or Canticle of Canticles, is a book of the Old Testament composed of a series of often explicitly erotic love poems. Both its fragmentary form and its erotic content have contributed to making it problematic to interpreters from all periods. In the Christian Middle Ages, it was believed to have been written by Solomon, and its songs were believed to constitute a unified story celebrating a marriage—a marriage which was, however, almost universally understood to be allegorical and to stand for the mystical union of God with the human soul or with the collectivity of human souls comprised by the Church. In the late Middle Ages it was sometimes seen to celebrate, in the figure of the bride, the exquisite spiritual features of the Virgin Mary. Commentaries expounding on the spiritual meaning of Solomon's song abound from Origen's in the third century to Bernard of Clairvaux's in the twelfth century—to name only the most famous. In the Heaven of the Sun, Dante not only celebrates Solomon but also includes among the wise three authors of well-known commentaries of the Song of Songs: Isidore, Bede, and Richard of St. Victor.

Dante quotes the Song of Songs briefly several times in the *Convivio* and in the *Monarchia*—always in relation to the medieval commonplace of the Church's role as bride of Christ. More interestingly, in the *Vita Nuova,* when he speaks of Beatrice's name as spontaneously inspired to many who did not know what else to call her *(VN* 2) and of her special place in a list of sixty beautiful women *(VN* 6), he seems to be recalling a passage in the Song of Songs where the bride is said to be unique among the king's sixty wives and to have been proclaimed "most blessed" *(beatissima)* by his daughters (SS 6:7–8). Whether in the *Vita Nuova* Dante already thought of Beatrice in relation to the bride of the Song of Songs or not, it is certain that this relation had developed in his mind by the time he composed the *Purgatorio,* where Beatrice's arrival in the Earthly Paradise is hailed, by the figure in the procession representing the Book of the Song of Songs, with the words from that book: *Veni, sponsa, de Libano* ("Come from Lebanon, my spouse," *Purg.* 30.11; SS 4:8). The whole scene of Dante's reunion with Beatrice is, in fact, strewn with images echoing the Song of Songs.

Recent criticism suggests that the poetry of the Song of Songs—representing eternal, spiritual love through the allegory of earthly, carnal love—is much more important as a model for the *Commedia*'s allegorical love story than had previously been suspected. This thesis is strengthened by the important role played by Solomon in the Heaven of the Sun. Solomon is, in fact, spoken of as the most beautiful of the souls of the wise, not just for his wisdom but, first of all, for the very love that has caused the world to wonder about his eternal destiny (*Par.* 10.109–111). Because of the excesses of Solomon's later years, his salvation had, in fact, been placed in doubt by St. Augustine and by others. In the *Paradiso,* however, Dante seems to be saying that it is that very earthly love that reverberates with its true meaning in the spiritual brightness that sets Solomon above the other souls of the wise.

Bibliography

Astell, Ann W. *The Song of Songs in the Middle Ages.* Ithaca, N.Y., London: Cornell University Press, 1990.

Matter, Ann E. *The Voice of My Beloved: The Song of Songs in Western Medieval Christianity.* Philadelphia: University of Pennsylvania Press, 1990.

Priest, Paul. "Dante and *The Song of Songs.*" *Studi danteschi* 49 (1972), 79–113.

Scherillo, Michele. *Alcuni capitoli della biografia di Dante.* Turin: Ermanno Loescher, 1896, pp. 293–311.

Marguerite Chiarenza

Sonnet

In his discussion of the hierarchy of poetic forms in *De vulgari eloquentia* (2.3.5–6), Dante notes that the canzone is the most noble, followed by the *ballata,* which is in turn followed by the sonnet. Moreover, he says that these two "inferior" forms will be treated in the fourth book of his treatise, where the "middle level of the vernacular" will be discussed (2.4.1). Unfortunately this fourth book was never written, and thus we may only speculate about Dante's reluctance to consider the sonnet as a noble metrical form. Perhaps his reasons lie in the brevity of the form itself or in the fact that it had become a very popular vehicle for the expression of all sorts of arguments in the course of the thirteenth century.

The sonnet was probably invented in the early thirteenth century by Giacomo da Lentini, a notary attached to the imperial court of Frederick II of Hohenstaufen in Sicily. The fourteen-line form (all hendecasyllables) resulted from the fusion of two eight-line *strambotti* (the latter in reduced form) or from an imitation of the strophic structure of the canzone. The earliest sonnets had two quatrains in alternate rhyme (*abab abab*) and two tercets in a variety of rhyme schemes (generally *cde cde* or *cdc dcd*). In the course of the thirteenth century a marked preference for the *rima incrociata* scheme for the quatrains—*abba abba,* perhaps introduced by Guittone d'Arezzo—develops into the rhyme scheme of choice by most later poets. Numerous patterns were devised for the tercets, such as *cde edc, cdc cdc, cde dce,* etc. From its invention among the poets of the Sicilian school the sonnet was used as the means for poetic correspondence in *tenzoni,* the exchange of sonnets among two or more poets in which questions on amorous, moral, or political topics were posed and answered. The sonnet was also the basic strophic unit in sonnet cycles *(corone di sonetti),* as, for example, the cycle on the days of the week or the months of the year by Folgore da San Gimignano.

Dante wrote at least 59 sonnets and perhaps as many as 291, if we attribute to him the 232 sonnets that form the elaborate series of *Il Fiore,* the greatly abbreviated version of the Old French *Roman de la rose.* Of the 59 sonnets, 25 are found in the *Vita Nuova* and thus assume special importance and meaning because of their selection for and integral position in that work. Approximately one-fourth (14) of the 59 sonnets are part of *tenzoni* with other poets and lose thereby a certain degree of spontaneity and freedom of expression. In a few of his early sonnets Dante follows the stylistic models and techniques of the Sicilian,

Siculo-Tuscan, and Guittonian schools of poetry, in his use of the archaic alternating rhyme scheme for the quatrains and of equivocal and composite rhymes. He also followed the experimental lead of other poets and wrote three *sonetti doppi* (or *rinterzati*), i.e., sonnets that have six heptasyllabic lines inserted after the first and third verses in the quatrains and after the second verse in each of the tercets; thus, "O voi che per la via d'Amor passate" (*VN* 7) has the following pattern: *AaBAaB AaBAaB CDdC DCcD*. In most of his sonnets, however, Dante uses the more "modern" *abba abba* rhyme scheme for the quatrains, just as Guido Cavalcanti, Cino da Pistoia, and Petrarch would also do. In the first sonnet of the *Vita Nuova* ("A ciascun'alma presa e gentil core") Dante asks other poets to send him their interpretation of his vision; among those who responded, *tenzone*-fashion, were Dante da Maiano, Cino da Pistoia (or Terino da Castelfiorentino), and Guido Cavalcanti. Over the years Dante participated in *tenzoni* with Dante da Maiano, Cino da Pistoia, and Forese Donati.

It is apparent from his writings—both theoretical and practical—that Dante preferred, and was expert in, the longer and, in his view, more elegant and noble poetic form of the canzone. Nevertheless, he was, to a certain degree, also a master of the sonnet form, as the following few examples attest: "Tanto gentile e tanto onesta pare" and "Vede perfettamente onne salute" (*VN* 26), "Oltre la spera che più larga gira" (*VN* 41), "Guido, i' vorrei che tu e Lapo ed io" (*Rime* 52), "Sonar bracchetti, e cacciatori aizzare" (*Rime* 61), and "Due donne in cima de la mente mia" (*Rime* 86).

Dante's sonnets are heterogeneous, both in style and in subject matter, and it is in this great variety that we can gain some perspective on the entire range of his literary apprenticeship and insights into his amorous, intellectual, and poetic development. For example, through the sonnets of the *Vita Nuova* we can observe how he passes from imitating the models furnished by Guittone, Cavalcanti, and Guinizzelli to charting of his own individual literary style. For Dante the sonnet represented an ideal, initial proving ground, and some sonnets do appear to be sketches or rough drafts for longer works. Most of his sonnets were written in the early stages of his literary career, in that necessary training period when he experimented with traditional forms and ideas. These traditional elements he ultimately rejected or substantially reworked in his quest for and attainment of poetic excellence. Dante's sonnets are important signposts along the literary *iter* that would culminate in the writing of the *Commedia*.

Bibliography

Antonio da Tempo. *Summa Artis Rithimici Vulgaris Dictaminis*. Edited by Richard Andrews. Bologna: Commissione per i Testi di Lingua, 1977.

Beltrami, Pietro G. *Metrica, poetica, metrica dantesca*. Pisa: Pacini, 1981.

Biadene, Leandro. "Morfologia del sonetto nei sec. XIII e XIV." In *Studi di filologia romanza* 4 (1889), 1–234. Reprinted Florence: Le Lettere, 1977.

Boyde, Patrick. *Dante's Style in His Lyric Poetry*. Cambridge: Cambridge University Press, 1971.

Cremante, Renzo, and Mario Pazzaglia (eds.). *La metrica*. Bologna: Il Mulino, 1973.

Fubini, Mario. *Metrica e poesia: Lezioni sulle forme poetiche italiane*. Milan: Feltrinelli, 1970.

Kleinhenz, Christopher. *The Early Italian Sonnet: The First Century (1220–1321)*. Lecce: Milella, 1986.

Pazzaglia, Mario. *Il verso e l'arte della canzone nel De vulgari eloquentia*. Florence: La Nuova Italia, 1967.

Spongano, Raffaele. *Nozioni ed esempi di metrica italiana*. Bologna: Pàtron, 1974.

Wilkins, Ernest Hatch. *The Invention of the Sonnet and Other Studies in Italian Literature*. Rome: Edizioni di Storia e Letteratura, 1959.

Christopher Kleinhenz

Soothsayers

A cornerstone of pagan religious practice, soothsaying is the act of determining future events through the interpretation of signs. Soothsayers, or diviners, claimed to be able to read the future through a variety of portents, ranging from dreams and oracles to the behavior of birds, stars, weather patterns, animal entrails, and human sneezes.

The Christian church, however, roundly condemned divination, on the grounds that only God and true prophets could see events before they occur and that humans gained access to knowledge solely through divine revelation. Soothsayers, on the other hand, maintained that their understanding was exhaustive of the truth, asserting that areas of knowledge unavailable to others were accessible to them. This desire to know the unknowable proved profoundly disturbing to Christian thinkers: divination appeared to push human knowledge beyond its limit, encroaching on territory thought to belong to revelation alone. The claims of soothsayers conflicted with several other central tenets of Christian doctrine as well: the notion of divination disregards the possibility of human free will and divine liberty. The actions of God are made to conform to the rational classifications of the human intellect—as if he could be made knowable to man through scientific systemization—and belief in his capacity to provide for the good government of individual souls is severely challenged. Moreover, diviners were thought to promote the erroneous conviction that divine decisions were somehow flexible and could be evaded or altered if known in advance. The medieval public, however, regarded divination with as much enthusiasm as trepidation, and the medieval Christian church appeared to tolerate its practice even as it prohibited it. St. Thomas Aquinas, for example, followed ecclesiastical tradition by denouncing the arts of soothsayers as the work of demons, but he legitimated some forms of divinatory practice by expressing belief in both natural divination, e.g., conclusions drawn on the basis of astral influence or meteorological observation, and true divination, e.g., the words of the prophets of the Old Testament (*ST* 2.2.171–178).

In *Inf.* 20, Dante and Virgil encounter the soothsayers condemned to the fourth bolgia of the circle of the fraudulent in Malebolge. The bodies of the sinners are twisted in such a way that their faces are directed behind them and they are forced to walk backward, *perché 'l veder dinanzi era lor tolto* ("since seeing forward was taken from them," *Inf.* 20.15). A fitting *contrapasso* to the sin of propelling human knowledge into the future, the punishment of the soothsayers turns their heads backward, prohibiting them from looking forward. Confronted by their contorted bodies, Dante weeps, for which he is harshly chastized by Virgil, who asks him: *Ancor se' tu de li altri sciocchi?* ("Are you still one of the other fools?," *Inf.* 20.27). Proceeding to name many of the diviners present, Virgil points out the classical figures Amphiaraus, Tiresias, and Aruns and then, identifying Manto (who bafflingly is said in *Purg.* 22.113 to reside in Limbo), pauses for a lengthy digression on her and the origin of Mantua, which conspicuously contradicts the account found in Virgil's own

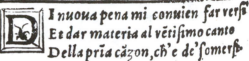

Dante among the soothsayers. Opere del divino poeta Danthe, ed. Pietro da Figino, Venice, 1520. Giamatti Collection: Courtesy of the Mount Holyoke College Archives and Special Collections.

Aeneid (10.198–200). Finally, after indicating Eurypylus, Virgil's roster of soothsayers concludes with brief references to several diviners more contemporary to Dante: Michael Scot, Guido Bonatti, Asdente, and a group of nameless women.

As Dante recounts the experiences of the pilgrim and his guide in the fourth bolgia of the *Commedia,* he exhibits a literary self-consciousness striking enough to provoke particular critical interest. Beginning the canto with a reference to the divisions of the poem—it is the *ventesimo canto / de la prima canzon* ("the twentieth song in the first canticle," *Inf.* 20.2–3)—Dante goes on to direct the reader to *prender frutto / di tua lezione* ("take profit from your reading," 20.19–20) and has Virgil complete his account of the founding of Mantua with a vexing *terzina* that appears to allow Virgil to distance himself from the material of the *Aeneid* at the same time that it unequivocally aligns the *Commedia* with veracity: *Però t'assenno che, se tu mai odi / originar la mia terra altrimenti, / la verità nulla menzogna frodi* ("Therefore I advise you, if you ever hear any other origin given for my city, that you let no lie defraud the truth," 20.97–99). This attention to metaliterary concerns underscores the literary nature of prophecy—diviners read and interpret signs—and,

S as Barolini has shown, suggests that the issue of textual verity is at the center of the canto's concerns. Moreover, given the proliferation of medieval legends associating Dante's guide with sorcery, Virgil's self-contradiction regarding the origin of his birthplace and his emphatic condemnation of the soothsayers provide Dante with the opportunity of correcting and exculpating his precursor.

Dante's emotional response to the fate of the diviners, however, indicates a stake in their circumstances that seems rooted less in his interest in exonerating the poet of the *Aeneid* and more in his desire to link his own poem with divine truth. The puzzling *terzina* that concludes Virgil's monologue on Manto demonstrates that the *verità* ("truth") communicated by the *Commedia* distinguishes it from other poems, which are all purveyors of *menzogne* ("lies"), meant to defraud their readers, in much the same way as the false texts of the soothsayers delude their trusting public (see *Inf.* 11.52–60). The *Commedia,* then, which occasionally crosses the unstable boundary between poetry and prophecy, seems to posit itself as the voice of a true prophet. Indeed, Dante's letter to the Florentines further reinforces that position: Dante refers to his *presaga mens* ("prophetic soul"), capable of reading the future through truth-telling omens (*Epist.* 6.17). As Hollander has suggested, the pilgrim's passionate weeping at the sight of the soothsayers, then, may reveal the poet's sense of kinship with the sin of divination and his profound ambivalence about his audacious poetic stance.

Bibliography

Barolini, Teodolinda. "True and False See-ers in *Inferno* XX." *Lectura Dantis* 4 (1989), 42–54.

D'Ovidio, Francesco. "Dante e la magia" and "Ancora Dante e la magia." In *Studii sulla Divina Commedia*. Milan, Palermo: Sandron, 1901, pp. 76–112, 113–149.

Flint, Valerie J. *The Rise of Magic in Early Medieval Europe*. Princeton, N.J.: Princeton University Press, 1991.

Hollander, Robert. "The Tragedy of Divination in *Inferno* XX." In *Studies in Dante*. Ravenna: Longo, 1980, pp. 131–218.

Mineo, Nicolò. *Profetismo e apocalittica in Dante*. Catania: Università di Catania, 1968.

Nardi, Bruno. "Dante profeta." In *Dante e la cultura medievale: Nuovi saggi di filosofia dantesca*. 2nd ed. Bari: Laterza, 1949, pp. 336–416.

Paratore, Ettore. "Il canto XX dell'*Inferno*." *Studi danteschi* 52 (1979–1980), 149–169.

Thorndike, Lynn. *A History of Magic and Experimental Science*. Vol. 2. New York: Macmillan, 1923.

Jessica Levenstein

Sordello

One of the first and the most celebrated Italian poets to cultivate the troubadour lyric in Provençal, Sordello was born at Goito near Mantua in the early years of the thirteenth century. The son of a poor knight, he frequented in his youth the courts of Lombardy, where we first find traces of him in the mid-1220s. In 1229, however, he became deeply implicated in certain scandals, including the kidnaping and possible seduction of Count Ricciardo di San Bonifazio's wife, Cunizza (*Par.* 9.22–66). Thereupon he fled Italy for Provence and then for the courts of Roussillon, Castile, and Toulouse. Scott (111) writes that "some time before 1233, he took up residence at the court of Raymond Berenger, Count of Provence, where his signature is found as that of a witness on various important documents (often next to that of Romeo de Villeneuve, cf. *Par.* 6.127–42)." From 1241 to 1269 Sordello was a court functionary. When in 1265 Charles of Anjou first undertook his extensive military campaign in Italy, Sordello, now a knight, was able to return there. It is presumed that he died in or about 1269.

Sordello's known compositions number forty-three in all. The majority, including the *cansos* and *sirventes,* date from the 1230s and early 1240s. Dante remembers him for his "Ensenhamen d'onor," a long didactic poem on courtly virtue, and above all for the *planh-sirventes* in memory of a Provençal nobleman, Blacatz, which comprises a trenchant critique of the present-day kings and princes of western Europe. These leaders, Sordello claims, are so devoid of courage and virtue that they ought to eat of the dead man's heart in order to become fit rulers. The poem generated several imitations and led Dante to consider Sordello a fit spokesman for his ideas of princely conduct and probity. The impressive figure Dante created for *Purg.* 6–8, who is placed in Ante-Purgatory and thus temporarily excluded from the process of purgation, leads the pilgrim and Virgil through the Valley of the Princes. Eight recent political figures pass in review, including two emperors (*Purg.* 7.91–136). Sordello has the rare privilege of being able to move within his province like the heroes of Elysium in the *Aeneid,* and he greets Virgil as a fellow Mantuan, exemplifying in this gesture the fraternal unity Dante might have desired for Italy (*Purg.* 6.74–75). Dante compares Sordello to a lion (*Purg.* 6.66), which Benvenuto da Imola considers evidence of his greatness of soul. In the *De vulgari eloquentia* Dante praises Sordello for the desertion of his local dialect; the *Commedia* similarly stresses the language he shares with Virgil.

The question of why Sordello is placed in Ante-Purgatory is a matter of controversy. Bowra held that Sordello is "one of the late repentant who have died violent deaths" (4), a much-seconded view which, however, does not explain how his life showed the negligence common to that of all the shades in the Ante-Purgatory. That information is so far lost to us, but the absence of indications in Dante's text cannot support the allegation that he is negligent (of his native language) because he composed in Provençal.

Bibliography

Barolini, Teodolinda. *Dante's Poets: Textuality and Truth in the "Comedy."* Princeton, N.J.: Princeton University Press, 1984.

Boni, Marco (ed.). *Sordello: le poesie.* Bologna: Libreria antiquaria Palmaverde, 1954.

Bowra, C. M. "Dante and Sordello." *Comparative Literature* 5 (1953), 1–15.

Ferrante, Joan M. *The Political Vision of the "Divine Comedy."* Princeton, N.J.: Princeton University Press, 1984.

Scott, John A. *Dante's Political Purgatory.* Philadelphia: University of Pennsylvania Press, 1996, pp. 96–127.

Marianne Shapiro

Soul

Dante employs two terms for soul: *anima* (Italian and Latin) and occasionally *alma* (Italian). *Alma* in Dante's works always refers to the human soul, but *anima* may refer as well to the souls of plants or animals.

The *Vita Nuova* introduces certain basic characteristics of the human soul that remain constant throughout the works of Dante: in the separation of the soul from the body consists the death of the human being (8.1, 23.8, 29.1); the human soul is immortal (23.10; see also *Conv.* 2.8.6–16); the act of thinking is an act of the soul (4.1; see also 38.5, 7); the soul suffers emotions such as love (2.7) or sorrow (31.1); the human soul is a spirit, impossible for the intellect of the living to apprehend when it is separated from the body (41.6).

While Dante's concept of the soul in the *Vita Nuova* does not differ from the popular notion of the soul in medieval Europe, except for the point he makes in 41.6, his concept of the soul in the *Convivio* is impossible to understand without a knowledge of Aristotle's teaching on matter and form, act and potency, and cause and effect. The soul is conceived of in the *Convivio* above all as a substantial form (3.2.3–4), and references to it as form (that is, an intrinsic ontological principle by which a thing is what it is) abound: 2.7.6; 2.8.6; 3.2.6; 3.3.5; 3.6.5, 6, 12; 3.7.5, 6; 3.8.1. The relation of soul to body is that of act (*act* is a fundamental and undefinable Aristotelian concept referring to actual existence) to what is in potency to it: the soul is the cause of the living body as living body (3.6.11–12) and is therefore the principle of its life. It organizes the body (3.8.1), and to it is attributed the growth and development of the body (4.24.2).

There are three kinds of souls: vegetative, sensitive, and human. The vegetative soul (or soul of plants) possesses powers (e.g., of life, growth, reproduction) found as well in the sensitive soul (or soul of animals) and the human soul; the sensitive soul in its turn possesses powers (e.g., sensation, locomotion) from which it takes its name and which it does not share with the vegetative soul, but shares with the human soul; the human soul possesses some powers (e.g., reason, speech, etc.) exclusive to it (3.2.11–15). Dante thus speaks of the human soul as having three natures (or principles of operations) joined within it: the vegetative, the sensitive, and the intellective (3.8.1). Nevertheless, the human soul is a single substance (3.3.5).

Dante describes the human soul as free of matter in one part (the rational part) and consequently as resembling angels and impeded by matter in another (the sensitive part) and consequently resembling the soul of beasts (3.7.5). The sensitive part of the human soul (1.11.3) uses corporal organs (2.4.17, 2.13.24, 3.8.1, 4.25.11). Its rational part (1.11.3) participates in the divine intelligence (3.2.14). The intellect is the noblest part of the human soul (3.2.16), and knowledge its ultimate perfection (1.1.1). The human soul naturally desires to know (1.1.1; cf. 2.14.20). Nevertheless, because of certain infirmities that deprive the soul or the body of its soundness, the mind of certain individuals (those who suffer from arrogance of disposition, weak-mindedness, capriciousness of mind, or physical deformities) may be hindered from knowing truth (4.15.12–17).

The production of the human soul comprises two moments for Dante: the production of a sensitive soul from the matter in the womb to which the semen has united (4.21.4) and, occurring immediately after, the infusion of the possible intellect (see "Intellect") into the sensitive soul (4.21.5). The production of the sensitive soul is attributed to the *vertù celestiale* ("celestial virtue") in the natural heat of the semen (2.13.5); the infusion of the possible intellect is attributed to the *vertù del Motore del cielo* ("virtue of the celestial mover" [4.21.5]), often mistakenly identified as God, following *Purg.* 25.70 (*lo motor primo,* "the First Mover"), but almost certainly the angelic mover of a heavenly sphere, following Dante's description of angels as *spezialissime cagioni* ("the most specific cause") of the human form (3.6.5).

Human souls differ individually in their intelligence and goodness (or nobility [4.21.1])—differences which are ultimately traceable to the *puritade* ("purity") of the sensitive soul initially produced in the individual (4.21.7–8). (Dante does not explain what he means by the "purity" of the sensitive soul, but it would seem to involve the matter which individuates it [cf. 3.6.6 and 4.20.8].) The pure sensitive soul receives a superior intellectual power and is consequently endowed with a greater share in the divine goodness (4.21.8). The gift of goodness is the source of desire in the human soul (4.22.4–18), which desire has God for its object, insofar as God is the source of the divine gift of goodness (3.2.7–9; see also 4.12.14). This divine gift takes root in the various powers of the human soul, directing them to their perfection up to the moment of death, when the divine gift returns to God with the rational part of the soul (4.23.3).

References to the soul in general or to the soul as such of plants, animals, or human beings are much fewer in the *Commedia* than in the *Convivio.* Some of these repeat a number of ideas presented in the *Vita Nuova* and the *Convivio* (e.g., *Inf.* 16.64–65, 27.73; *Purg.* 10.124–125; *Par.* 2.133–135). *Purg.* 18.19–75 presents in greater detail a discussion of the constitution of the human soul: it possesses *prime notizie* ("first notions," 56) and *de' primi appetibili l'affetto* ("our love of first desirables," 57). It also has a faculty *che consiglia / e de l'assenso de' tener la soglia* ("that counsels and must guard the threshold of assent"), viz., free will (see also *Purg.* 4.11).

In *Purg.* 25.67–75 and *Par.* 7.139–144 we have a conception of the origin of the human soul that differs radically from *Conv.* 4.21.5: the human soul is created directly by God and assumes into itself the sensitive soul that initially animates the fetus. This conception complements the point made in *Purg.* 16.70–81 that the human being is not determined in his acts by stellar influence. The verses which follow the two passages above—*Purg.* 25.79–108, on the body that the formative power of the soul forms from the air in the otherworld; and *Par.* 7.145–148, on the resurrection from the dead—underscore the nature of the soul as a form created specifically to animate a particular body and therefore its imperfection while separated from the body. *Par.* 14.43–60 is a paean to the perfect existence of the human being once soul is reunited to body. Nothing could be further removed from the *Convivio,* in which the body is described as a prison of the soul (2.4.17); the sensitive soul (whether of the human being or beasts) as being contained in matter (3.7.5); and the human soul's existence after death as existence in a more than human nature (2.8.6) with all its implications of superiority. The human soul in the *Convivio* is an animal soul made rational (cf. *DVE* 2.10.1); in the *Commedia* it is a substantial form specifically created as such by God.

The sources of Dante's concept of the human soul have been the object of much discussion, with some scholars claiming Thomas Aquinas as Dante's source and others proposing Albert the Great in particular. At present, most critics agree that the source of Dante's account of the production of the sensitive soul of the fetus is not Thomas but rather Albert the Great. Corti in particular presents passages from Albert's commentary on Aristotle's *De anima* that argue for that work of Albert's as Dante's direct source. The *Liber de causis* must be cited as the primary source of Dante's concept (and Albert's in his commentary) of the human soul in the *Convivio* as created by God with intelligences (angels) as intermediaries (3.14.4). Dante's concept of the human soul in the *Commedia,* however—with its strong emphasis on the imperfect existence of the human soul separated from the body—points to Thomas Aquinas as Dante's source.

Bibliography

Albert the Great. *Opera omnia*. Vol. 7: *De anima*. Edited by Clemen Stroick. Monasterium Westfalorum: Aschendorff, 1968.

Bettoni, Efrem. "Anima." *Enciclopedia dantesca,* 1:278–285.

Boyde, Patrick. *Dante: Philomythes and Philosopher.* Cambridge: Cambridge University Press, 1981.

Corti, Maria. *La felicità mentale.* Turin: Einaudi, 1983.

Gilson, Étienne. *The Philosophy of St. Thomas Aquinas.* Translated by Edward Bullough. St. Louis, Mo.: B. Herder, 1941.

Liber de causis. Edited by Adriaan Pattin. Louvain: Uitgave van "Tijdschrift voor Filosofie," n.d.

Nardi, Bruno. *Dante e la cultura medievale.* New ed. Bari: Editori Laterza, 1985.

———. *Saggi di filosofia dantesca.* 2nd ed. enl. Florence: "La Nuova Italia" Editrice, 1967.

———. "L'origine dell'anima umana secondo Dante." In *Studi di Filosofia Medievale.* Rome: Edizioni di Storia e Letteratura, 1960, pp. 9–68.

Pegis, Anton Charles. *St. Thomas and the Problem of the Soul in the Thirteenth Century.* Toronto: Pontifical Institute of Mediaeval Studies, 1934. Reprinted 1976.

Shapiro, Marianne. "The Twofold Representation of the Soul." In *Dante and the Knot of Body and Soul.* New York: St. Martin's Press, 1998, pp. 161–197.

Thomas Aquinas. *Opera omnia. Iussu impensaque Leonis XIII P.M. edita.* Vol. 5: *Summa theologiae: Prima pars: A quaestione 50 ad quaestionem 119.* Rome: Typographia Polyglotta, 1889.

Paul A. Dumol

Spendthrifts

The name usually applied to the group of souls presented in a sudden and brief episode in the wood of the suicides (*Inf.* 13.109–129). In *Inf.* 11.31–33, Virgil, following the dictum of Roman law that one's goods are an extension of one's person, had proclaimed that one can commit violence either against persons or against their possessions. These souls, by having squandered their possessions in ostentatious and wasteful displays, have committed an act of violence destructive to the self and hence akin to physical suicide. Since their acts are deliberate, they are punished more severely than the prodigals in the fourth circle (*Inf.* 7) whose sin results from weakness and not from willfulness. Dante here encounters two of these souls, one of whom—subsequently identified as Giacomo da Santo Andrea of Padua—identifies the other as Lano of Siena. Dogs chase them through the woods, overtake Giacomo, tear him apart, and carry the pieces off in their mouths, perhaps in a grotesque *contrapasso* of the way they had destroyed themselves through the scattering of their possessions. Because of their precipitous flight through the woods, they also interact in symbiosis with the suicides—snapping off thorny branches even as they are themselves torn by them. Early commentators on Dante's poem identified Lano as a member of the so-called *brigata spendereccia,* the "Spendthrifts' Club," a group of wealthy young men (also mentioned in *Inf.* 29.125–132) who impoverished themselves through contests of public consumption.

William A. Stephany

Spitzer, Leo

Born in Vienna, Spitzer (1887–1960) was a student of the great romance philologist Wilhelm Meyer-Lübke in Vienna. He published his first, forty-six-page article on Dante, *Bermerkungen zu Dantes 'Vita Nuova'* ("Remarks on Dante's *Vita Nuova*"), at the University of Istanbul in Turkey, where he spent his first three years of exile after being compelled by Nazi Germany's racial laws to leave the University of Marburg in 1933. The article, a remarkable synthesis of intelligence and philological erudition, advances a series of original and often persuasive theses inspired by a synchronic vision of Dante's entire poetic activity. Not all of those critics who have admired the brilliance of his arguments have agreed, however, with his conclusions. (Harry Levin, an admirer of Spitzer's, describes him as "a secular Talmudist, almost a Kabbalist.") Is it plausible, for example, that the verb *obumbrare* ("to overshadow"), which occurs at *VN* 11.3, really is an anticipation, as Spitzer maintains, of the passage in *Par.* 30 where the mystical concept of "divine darkness" derived from Dionysius the Areopagite is translated into the radiation of brilliant light "in the shadow" of the

S Divinity? Among Spitzer's more notable excursions into Dante criticism—published for the most part in the American periodical *Italica* during his lengthy tenure at the Johns Hopkins University—are "Speech and Language in *Inferno* XIII" (1942), which describes with great subtlety and originality Dante's mimesis of the arboreal speech of Pier della Vigna; "The Addresses to the Reader in the *Commedia*" (1955), a reply to an article by Auerbach in which Spitzer uses Dante's asides to the reader to construct a portrait of the ideal reader the poet has in mind; and "The Ideal Typology in Dante's *De vulgari eloquentia*" (1955), where he suggests that Dante's dismissal of the various literary dialects of Italy is a rhetorical ploy designed to identify himself as the true inventor of the "illustrious vernacular."

Bibliography

Contini, Gianfranco. "L. S." *Paragone Letteratura* 12 (1961), 3–12.

Della Terza, Dante. *Da Vienna a Baltimora: La diaspora degli intellettuali europei negli Stati Uniti d'America.* Rome: Editori Riuniti, 1987.

Hytier, J. "La méthode de M. L. S." *Romanic Review* 41 (1950), 42–59.

Levin, Harry. "Two *Romanisten* in America: Spitzer and Auerbach." In *The Intellectual Migration: Europe and America, 1930–1960.* Edited by Donald Fleming and Bernard Bailyn. Cambridge, Mass.: Harvard University, 1969, pp. 463–484.

Vallone, Aldo. "Gli studi danteschi di L. S." In *La critica dantesca nel Settecento e altri saggi danteschi.* Florence: Olschki, 1961, pp. 211–227.

Wellek, René. "The Scholar-Critics in the Romance Literatures: Leo Spitzer." In *A History of Modern Criticism: 1750–1950.* Vol. 7: *German, Russian, and Eastern European Criticism, 1900–1950.* New Haven, Conn.: Yale University Press, 1991, pp. 134–153.

Dante Della Terza

Statius

The Latin epic poet Publius Papinius Statius was born in Naples c. 45 C.E. and died in Rome c. 96. In *Purg.* 21, however, Dante's Statius *(Stazio)* presents the "facts" of his life such as they were generally accepted in the Middle Ages, identifying himself as *Tolosano,* perpetuating the then-common identification of him with the rhetorician Lucius Statius, born in Toulouse early in the reign of Nero (c. 58). Statius also identifies himself as author of the *Thebaid,* an epic poem about the fratricidal conflict between Oedipus' sons Eteocles and Polyneices of Thebes, and of the *Achilleid,* a fragmentary epic about Achilles' involvement in the Trojan War, a work left uncompleted at his death (*Purg.* 21.91–93). He cites Virgil's *Aeneid* as his great inspiration and model—as the sparks which ignited him, the seeds which germinated in him, as his poetic mother and nurse—and, in one of the poem's most shocking moments, says he would gladly spend another year on the mountain to have had the privilege of living when Virgil did. Had he lived then, of course, he would have been disqualified from entry into Purgatory, rendering moot the question of length of time to be spent there; and when he learns that it is Virgil who stands before him, he reinforces the indecorousness of his words by attempting to embrace Virgil's feet.

In *Purg.* 22, Statius introduces details about his life which Dante seems to have invented to suit the purposes of his own narrative. The apparently excessive homage at the end of the previous canto becomes more comprehensible through Statius' claims that Virgil served as more than a literary model: his works saved Statius, first from vice and then from paganism, and Statius expresses his indebtedness to Virgil in the famous summary line: *per te poeta fui, per te cristiano* ("through you I was a poet, through you a Christian," 22.73). Virgil is surprised by this, given the apparently pagan nature of Statius' poetry, but Statius explains that he was a *chiuso Cristian* ("a secret Christian," 22.90), afraid to proclaim his faith in a time of persecution (a "tepidness" which required four centuries of atonement on the terrace of sloth).

A variety of rhetorical devices in the poem reinforces the notion that Statius is *Purgatorio*'s most important character after Virgil, Beatrice, and the pilgrim himself. His entry into the poem is heralded at the conclusion of *Purg.* 20 by the mysterious earthquake and by the responsorial shout of "Gloria in excelsis Deo" from the mountain's repentant souls—events which connect his arrival with both the death and the birth of Christ. His appearance to Virgil and Dante in *Purg.* 21 is compared to Jesus' post-Resurrection appearances to his disciples in Luke 24. Statius is granted the privilege of explicating for the pilgrim (and thereby for

Statius with Dante in the Earthly Paradise. La comedia, *ed. Pietro da Figino, 1491. Giamatti Collection: Courtesy of the Mount Holyoke College Archives and Special Collections.*

the poem's readers) two of the controlling fictional premises of the poem: the *religïone de la montagna* (the rule by which souls feel prepared to abandon their regimen of purgation and move onward toward Heaven, *Purg.* 21.40–72) and the nature of shade bodies (*Purg.* 25). And Statius is the only character in the poem who leaves behind his terrain to join Dante on his journey through the rest of Purgatory. In this fellowship of poets, Statius acts as a foil to both Virgil and Dante: he is a writer of classical epic like Virgil and a Christian like Dante, and in various ways the text establishes parallels and contrasts with each poet. At the level of plot, he stands guard with Virgil over the sleeping Dante on his last night on the mountain (27.76–87); with Virgil, he smiles in response to Matelda's "corollary" in tribute to the prescience of classical writers (28.134–148); and with Virgil, he is witness to the biblical pageant of *Purg.* 29. But Statius also remains after the arrival of Beatrice and the disappearance of Virgil in canto 30, and he is presumably witness to her reproof of Dante and to Dante's remorse in cantos 30 and 31 and to the transformations of the chariot of the Church in canto 32. He is defined—by contrast with the absent Virgil—as "the sage who remains" (*'l savio che ristette*) at the beginning of canto 33, and in the final episode in *Purgatorio*'s narrative (just before the concluding address to the reader) he is summoned by Matelda to join Dante in the crossing of the Eunoè (33.130–135).

The reason for Statius' privileged status is that the poem's invented biography makes him its primary model of conversion. He exemplifies all three of the nonliteral senses of Ps. 113, offered in the *Letter to Cangrande* (*Epist.* 13.7) as the paradigm for the poem's methodology and meaning. His conversion to Christianity exemplifies the allegorical significance of Exodus (in the words of the *Letter,* "the redemption that Jesus worked for all humanity"); his rejection of vice dramatizes his moral or tropological Exodus ("the conversion of the soul from the grief and misery of sin to the state of grace"); and the completion of his purgatorial process and transition to Paradise makes him the poem's exemplar of an anagogical Passover ("the exodus of the soul from the servitude of this corruption to the liberty of eternal glory"). His conversion is effected, moreover, through his reading of the poems of Virgil, and in this respect Statius' experience parallels that of Dante, rescued through the intervention of Virgil in *Inf.* 1.

For all of Virgil's importance in this process, however, the Statius episode is insistent on reasserting Virgil's limitations. Statius is saved from his vice by the description of the murder of Polydorus in *Aen.* 3, and he is converted to Christianity by a passage from the *Fourth Eclogue,* taken to predict the birth of Jesus; but neither passage is of spiritual use to Virgil. In the *Aeneid,* the Polydorus episode laments the effects of greed, but Statius reads it as pertaining to his own vice of prodigality. Through this creative misreading, Statius makes the text serve his moral needs, in a sense inverting Francesca's action in *Inf.* 5, where she projects onto the *Lancelot* a meaning unintended by its author which serves her emotional need to vindicate her behavior. The *Fourth Eclogue*'s prediction, meanwhile, is clear only in retrospect: if it predicted the birth of Christ, as widely believed in the Middle Ages, then its significance was fulfilled nineteen years after Virgil's death—beyond a time when Virgil could have understood the significance of what he had written. As Statius says, Virgil was like one who walks by night carrying a lantern behind him, benefitting others but not himself (*Purg.* 22.67–69). The beginning of Statius' exodus and the permanence of Virgil's exile are both affirmed by the same Virgilian texts. Finally, Statius serves as a foil for Dante as well, not just positively, as a poet converted through reading Virgil's poem, but negatively as well, as one who concealed that

S conversion from the world out of fear. As such, he offers a "negative exemplum," a warning to Dante against behavior to be avoided. The episode's focus on a salvific role for reading implies a reciprocal role for writing, and Statius' refusal to reveal his faith to the world stands in contrast to Dante's acceptance of his responsibility as a writer, the public proclamation of faith represented in the *Commedia*'s narrative.

Bibliography

Brugnoli, Giorgio. "Statius Christianus." *Italianistica* 17 (1988), 9–15.

Cecchetti, Giovanni. "The Statius Episode: Observations on Dante's Conception of Poetry." *Lectura Dantis (Virginiana)* 7 (1990), 96–114.

Franke, William. "Resurrected Tradition and Revealed Truth." In *Dante's Interpretive Journey*. Chicago: University of Chicago Press, 1996, pp. 191–232.

Hawkins, Peter. "Resurrecting the Word: Dante and the Bible." *Religion and Literature* 16 (1984), 59–71.

Heilbrun, Denise. "The Prophetic Role of Statius in Dante's *Purgatory*." *Dante Studies* 95 (1977), 53–67.

Kleinhenz, Christopher. "The Celebration of Poetry: A Reading of *Purgatorio* XXII." *Dante Studies* 106 (1988), 21–41.

Lewis, C. S. "Dante's Statius." *Medium Aevum* 25 (1956), 133–139.

Martinez, Ronald. "Dante and the Two Canons: Statius in Virgil's Footsteps (*Purgatorio* 21–30)." *Comparative Literature Studies* 32.2 (1995), 151–175.

Picone, Michelangelo. "*Purgatorio* XXII." *Lectura Dantis (Virginiana)* No. 12: Supplement (Spring 1993), 321–335.

Shoaf, R. A. "'Auri sacra fames' and the Age of Gold (*Purg.* XXII, 40–41 and 148–150)." *Dante Studies* 96 (1978), 195–199.

Stephany, William A. "Biblical Allusions to Conversion in *Purgatorio* XXI." *Stanford Italian Review* 3 (1983), 141–162.

William A. Stephany

Stephen, St.

According to the Book of the Acts of the Apostles (6–7, in the New Testament), St. Stephen was stoned to death by Hellenistic Jews for his decision to join the followers of Jesus. The drama of the account is underscored (and made quite poignant for Christians) by the fact that the execution was directed by Saul of Tarsus, later to be named Paul, the last of the Twelve Apostles. The Church counts Stephen "the first of the martyrs."

Dante mentions him *(Stefano)* on the third terrace of Purgatory, where wrath is purged, as an example of Christian humility and steadfastness in the face of trial and tribulation (*Purg.* 15.106–114).

William Wilson

Stephen Urosh II of Serbia

Second son of Stephen Urosh I and Queen Helena, known as Milutin, reigned 1282–1321. He is one of the wicked Christian kings named by the eagle in the sphere of Jupiter as "he of Rascia" after the medieval designation of Serbia. Stephen counterfeited the Venetian grosso or matapan to the detriment not only of Venice but also of other cities in Italy (*Par.* 19.140–141). The Venetian *Libro d'oro* twice decreed that money changers were to take the false coins out of circulation (March 3, 1282, and May 3, 1306).

Sally Mussetter

Stricca

Mentioned (*Inf.* 29.125–126) by the sinner Capocchio as an example of a "frugal" Sienese, but ironically, because he was reputed to be a member of the so-called Spendthrift Club of Siena and had wasted his entire patrimony. His exact identity is impossible to establish, but he is probably the son of Giovanni Salimbeni da Siena and the brother of Niccolò, who is mentioned in the following verse (127).

R. Allen Shoaf

Styx

One of the five rivers of the ancient underworld, Dante's *Stige* (*Inf.* 7.106), the second of four rivers in Hell, first appears in the fourth circle as a boiling spring that descends to the fifth (*Inf.* 8–9), where it becomes a filthy swamp. Here are immersed the sinners guilty of wrath, among whom Dante-pilgrim is ferried in the bark of Phlegyas across to the Gate of Dis. Its definition as a *tristo ruscel* ("sad stream," *Inf.* 7.106)—recalling Servius' etymology of the river's name (commenting on *Aen.* 6.134)—links it to sadness. Virgil speaks of it as marsh (*Aen.* 6.323). The Styx, like all the rivers of Dante's hydrographic system in the *Inferno,* originates in the tears emanating from a crack in the great statue of the Old Man of Crete.

Anthony L. Pellegrini

Suicide

One of the three categories of violence described by Virgil in *Inf.* 11.28–51. The souls of the suicides form *Inf.* 13's pathless wood—thorn bushes in whose branches Harpies make their nests. Pier della Vigna, speaking as a member of this group, describes their *contrapasso* (93–108) in words implying the violence and, perhaps, the randomness of their deaths: the soul of the suicide is said to "uproot itself" from its body—a metaphor consonant with the infernal representation of the souls—after which Minos condemns it to this circle, where it lands and sprouts "wherever chance hurls it" (literally, wherever fortune "crossbows" it, *là dove fortuna la balestra,* 98). The souls, so "planted," grow up into bushes, and the Harpies, by feeding on the leaves, simultaneously provide the souls—who are capable of expressing themselves only when broken—both with pain and with a "window" for the pain.

At the beginning of the canto, Dante erroneously believes that souls are hiding behind the bushes, since he cannot imagine that the trees are themselves the source of the laments he hears. At Virgil's request, he breaks off a twig from the bush that turns out to be Pier della Vigna and is horrified when words and blood hiss out of the fracture together. (Perhaps the suggestion is that in life, too, such souls were unable to communicate except through physical violence.) In *Purg.* 25, Statius explains the nature of the shade body as the result of the soul's "informing" power. As an essence created directly by God, its instinct for expressing form is so intense that when separated from the body at death, it shapes the surrounding air into the perfect expression of its inner reality. When viewed from this perspective, the nonhuman representation of these souls may thus be explained as an expression of the reality of their willful decision to separate their souls from the human form into which God had breathed it. So absolute is this separation that even after the Last Judgment the resurrected bodies of the suicides—rather than reuniting with their souls in accord with religious orthodoxy—will hang from their tree-souls eternally signifying this willful division, for, in the final proclamation of the judge Pier della Vigna, "it is not just to have what one has taken from oneself" (105).

Dante's attitudes about suicide are somewhat complicated by his admiration for the writers of classical Rome who often sanctioned suicide in the face of extreme suffering or of disgrace. Dante's Christian tradition, however, was absolute on the matter. (See Daniel Rolfs for a discussion of Dante's ambiguities about the conflicting attitudes of these two traditions.) The most important discussion of suicide in the early Christian tradition is found in St. Augustine's *City of God* (e.g., 1.20 and 19.4), a text—written in the pluralistic world of the early-fifth-century Roman Empire—which specifically addressed the claims of opposing philosophical and religious groups in the ancient world. Augustine addresses in detail difficult cases which Dante also engages in *Inferno.* He criticizes the republican Roman matron Lucretia for killing herself after her rape by King Tarquinius (Dante includes her, among other suicides from the pre-Christian world, in Limbo), and he criticizes Cato, for whom Dante invents a surprisingly privileged afterlife. St. Thomas Aquinas cites Augustine as a major source in his article "Is it legitimate for somebody to kill himself?" (*ST* 2.2.64.5), arguing that there are three reasons why suicide is invariably sinful: it is against the law of nature by which anything seeks self-preservation; it damages the community by removing one of its members; and it usurps divine authority over life and death. Most tellingly for the nature of Pier della Vigna's argument, Thomas argues that one may not kill oneself to escape any of life's miseries, since to do so is to take on a greater evil to escape a lesser.

At the end of the canto, Dante and Virgil encounter an anonymous Florentine suicide whose branches have been torn by the onrushing hounds and souls of the spendthrifts. After characterizing Florence as a city continuously afflicted by Mars, the Roman god of war, this character concludes, "I made a gibbet for myself of my houses." Early commentators proposed possible specific identities for the figure, but the lack of conclusive evidence suggests that it is probably best to see him as intentionally unnamed. The reference to *case*— to houses in the plural—combined with the assertion of the general influence of Mars on the commune as a whole, suggests to many that this suicide should be seen as representative of the City of Florence, with the civil war, of which Dante himself was victim, implicitly a type of urban suicide.

Bibliography

Aquinas, Thomas. *Summa Theologiae*. Latin text and English translation. Vol. 38. New York: McGraw-Hill; London: Eyre and Spottiswoode, 1975.

Biow, Douglas. "From Ignorance to Knowledge: The Marvelous in *Inferno* 13." In *The Poetry of Allusion: Virgil and Ovid in Dante's Commedia*. Stanford, Calif.: Stanford University Press, pp. 45–61.

Paratore, Ettore. "Analasi 'retorica' del canto di Pier della Vigna." *Studi danteschi* 42 (1965), 281–336.

Pietrobono, Luigi. "Il canto XIII dell' *Inferno*." *Lectura Dantis Romana*. Turin: SEI, 1962, pp. 3–26.

Rolfs, Daniel. "Dante, Petrarch, Boccaccio and the Problem of Suicide." *Romanic Review* 57 (1976), 200–225.

Spitzer, Leo. "Speech and Language in *Inferno* XIII." *Italica* 19 (1942), 81–104.

William A. Stephany

Sun

Usually referred to as *il sole,* but Dante's allusions to the Sun frequently make use of periphrasis: *dolce lume* ("the sweet light," *Inf.* 10.69; *Purg.* 13.16); light's chariot (*Purg.* 4.59); the world's lamp (*Par.* 1.38); *lo ministro maggior de la natura* ("the greatest minister of nature," *Par.* 10.28); *padre d'ogne mortal vita* ("father of every mortal life," *Par.* 22.116). Classical traditions account for Dante's identification of the Sun with mythical figures: e.g., Delius (*Epist.* 6.8), Titan (*Epist.* 5.3, 7.5; *Egl.* 4.2), Apollo (*Par.* 29.1), and, perhaps, Bacchus (Martinez, 137), but the poet understands these in light of medieval and Christian traditions. He derives the phrase *sub sole* (under the Sun) from Ecclesiastes's description of the human condition (*Conv.* 2.10.10; *DVE* 1.6.2); understands homiletic and liturgical traditions identifying Christ as the Sun of righteousness *(sol justiciae),* the rising Sun *(sol oriens)* in birth and the setting Sun *(sol occidens)* in death and the victorious Sun *(sol invictus)* in the Resurrection (Bufano, 296; Kleiner, 12); and alludes to the myth of the eagle's

renewing itself by looking into the Sun (*Par.* 1.46–54, 20.31–33).

The Sun is the fourth planet in the Ptolemaic system (*Conv.* 2.3.4–7). Dante relates the Sun allegorically to the science of arithmetic (*Conv.* 2.13.15), computes its diameter (*Conv.* 4.8.7), and describes its revolutions (*Conv.* 3.5.2–21). Following Pseudo-Dionysius, Dante conceives of the Sun's light as generative (*Conv.* 3.14.3; *Mon.* 1.9.1).

In the *Commedia* the Sun's movement or position is often cited to indicate the passage of time: years (*Inf.* 6.68; *Purg.* 21.101; *Par.* 26.119–120), seasons (*Inf.* 24.1–2, 26.26–27), hours (*Par.* 26.142); and the Sun's placement in the sky orients the pilgrim as to his temporal location on his pilgrimage, especially in *Purgatorio* (*Purg.* 2.1–3 is the first of many loci in this canticle, but see also *Inf.* 34.96; *Par.* 27.86). Temporal references emphasize its light, which symbolizes the power of the Divinity; when Sordello informs the pilgrims that no one can proceed after the Sun has set (*Purg.* 7.54; see also 27.66–68), a parallel is drawn between sunlight and the grace of God. In *Paradiso,* the Sun's position can indicate terrestrial location (St. Dominic's birthplace, 12.49–51; see also 23.11–12), but the Sun appears more frequently as a symbol of God and as God's reflection in the souls of the blessed. As the fourth sphere of *Paradiso* (cantos 10–14), the Sun has been the subject of numerous critical studies of its inhabitants—the souls of Church doctors, including Thomas Aquinas and Bonaventure—and of its iconographic significance (Beal, Freccero, Mazzeo), its structural importance to the canticle (Castellani, Kleiner), and its value as a paradigm of Dante's textuality (Barolini).

The Sun's presence and influence, which are always grounded in observation and expressed according to precise astronomical calculation, carry both narrative and symbolic significance throughout the poem. Thus the Sun is invoked at important junctures in the *Commedia*. At the beginning, its rising above a mountain over the pilgrim's dark valley prefigures the entire pilgrimage (Singleton), even as its appearance in the constellation of Aries evokes God's creation and restoration through the Redemption—a theme reiterated in the fourth heaven (compare *Conv.* 4.20.8). The Sun is a physical and moral guide (*Inf.* 1.17–18; *Purg.* 1.107–108, 13.16–21); the pilgrim's human guides are also "suns": Virgil (*Inf.* 11.91), Cato (*Purg.* 1.39), and Beatrice (*Purg.* 30.22–33; *Par.*

30.75), who is symbolically crowned in the Heaven of the Sun (*Par.* 10). Not surprisingly, then, the pope and emperor who guide civilization are suns (*Purg.* 16.106–108; compare *Mon.* 3.4.3, 17–21). The saints who image God are suns or mirrors of the Sun: Beatrice, the spirits in the Sun (*Par.* 10.76), St. Francis (*Par.* 11.50), Cacciaguida (*Par.* 15.76, 17.123), and Mary (*Par.* 32.108). The image of sunrise typically symbolizes the moment of revelation, as in the examples of Beatrice (*Purg.* 30.22–33) and Mary (*Par.* 31.118–129), who are thereby associated with the coming of Christ. The Sun also symbolizes the journey's end: Christ (*Par.* 10.53, 23.29; see also *Conv.* 3.12.6–8) and God (*Purg.* 7.26, the first instance of many), are both suns. In the last line of the poem, *l'amor che move il sole e l'altre stelle* ("the Love that moves the sun and the other stars," *Par.* 33.145), Dante fixes his thematic goal at the structural end of the poem.

Bibliography

Barolini, Teodolinda. "Dante's Heaven of the Sun as a Meditation on Narrative." *Lettere italiane* 40 (1988), 1–36.

Beal, Rebecca S. "Beatrice in the Sun: A Vision from Apocalypse." *Dante Studies* 103 (1985), 57–78.

Bufano, Antonietta. "Sole." *Enciclopedia Dantesca*, 5:296–297.

Castellani, Victor. "Heliocentricity in the Structure of Dante's Paradiso." *Studies in Philology* 78 (1981), 211–223.

Freccero, John. "*Paradiso* X: The Dance of the Stars." *Dante Studies* 86 (1968), 85–111.

Kay, Richard. *Dante's Christian Astrology*. Philadelphia: University of Pennsylvania Press, pp. 98–136.

Kleiner, John. "The Eclipses in the *Paradiso*." *Stanford Italian Review* 9 (1990), 5–32.

Martinez, Ronald L. "Ovid's Crown of Stars (*Paradiso* 13.1–27)." In *Dante and Ovid: Essays in Intertextuality*. Edited by Madison U. Sowell. Binghamton, N.Y.: Medieval and Renaissance Texts and Studies, 1991, pp. 124–138.

Mazzeo, Joseph. "Dante's Sun Symbolism and the Visions of the Blessed." In *Structure and Thought in the Paradiso*, 1958, chapter 6. Reprinted New York: Greenwood Press, 1968.

Singleton, Charles S. "In Exitu Israel de Aegypto." In *Dante: A Collection of Critical Essays*. Edited by John Freccero. Englewood Cliffs, N.J.: Prentice-Hall, 1965, pp. 102–121.

Rebecca S. Beal

Sylvester, St.

An early disciple of St. Francis, St. Sylvester (*Silvestro*) is mentioned, along with St. Giles, by St. Thomas in his account of the rise of Francis and his order (*Par.* 11.83).

William Wilson

Sylvester I, Pope

On the evidence of the fourth-century chronology known as the Liberian Catalogue, his pontificate is dated from January 31, 314, until December 31, 335. It corresponds broadly to the reign of Emperor Constantine I (312–337), under whom Christianity was officially tolerated and lavishly patronized. The lengthy article devoted to Sylvester in the *Liber Pontificalis* consists largely in fact of a list of Constantine's foundations during the period, and it is this aspect, as reworked by legend, that is Sylvester's prime significance for Dante. The legend had diverse expression. It is represented in a brilliant mid-thirteenth-century series of frescoes in the convent of the Church of Santi Quattro Coronati, Rome. Its chief literary expression is in the late-thirteenth-century *Legenda Aurea* of Jacobus de Voragine. An important pseudo-legal source was the Donation of Constantine, a forgery dating probably from the mid–eighth century. According to legend, Sylvester was supposed to have fled Rome to Mt. Soracte to escape persecution by Constantine. But Constantine recalled him in order to be baptized and then cured of leprosy by him (*Inf.* 27.94–95), in return for which Constantine ceded to Sylvester Rome and the western empire—thereby making the pope, with what Dante regarded as perverse effects, *il primo ricco patre* ("the first rich father," *Inf.* 19.117)—before his own withdrawal to the newly founded capital of the Greek half of the empire, Constantinople (*Par.* 20.57). In *Mon.* 3.10, Dante disputes both Constantine's power to make the gift and Sylvester's authority to receive it.

Michael Haren

Symbolism

Ever since the Romantic period of the late eighteenth and the early nineteenth centuries, critics have commonly defined symbolism by contrasting it with allegory. The Romantic poets (Goethe and Coleridge being the most notable examples) disparaged allegory as an artificial comparison, while praising the symbol as a more organic form of figurative language. In this Romantic view, the allegorical narrative has no necessary relationship to its figurative meaning; the author simply imposes it on the narrative. A symbol, on the other hand, has a *necessary* relationship to its figurative meaning. Several scholars, drawing on the Romantic distinction, have termed Dante a "symbolist" poet rather than an allegorical one; they contrast the *Commedia*'s vivid, historical characters with the "allegorical rubbish" (in Gilson's phrase) presented in personification allegories such as the *Roman de la rose*. Thus, Dozon, in a recent psychological attempt to understand symbolism in Dante, paints allegory as a univocal, unambiguous form of figurative language—the meaning of an allegory being simply what is intended by the author. Symbols, however, are "archetypal images" that evoke the "profound relations of the psyche to metaphysical problems."

The medieval allegorical readings applied to Scripture and Dante's own allegorical method in the *Commedia,* however, militate against such a rigid distinction between allegory and symbol; for, it will be recalled, medieval scriptural allegories depend upon the assumption that the allegorical narrative is true and has a real existence while also referring to something else. Or, more accurately, a scriptural allegory refers to a real event or thing, and that event or thing in turn refers to *other* events or things. Furthermore, the distinction between symbol and allegory posited since the Romantics is not a distinction Dante himself seems to have made. Dante never uses the word *simbolo* in any of his works, nor does it appear in any literary text before the late Renaissance.

Some critics have attempted to distinguish allegory from symbolism in a way that medieval writers could have accepted. The most influential of these attempts is that of Charles Singleton, who proposes a way of separating symbol and allegory while admitting that "Dante's own terminology . . . did not provide for this distinction" (19). Drawing on the common medieval belief in God's two books—the Bible and the Book of Nature—Singleton suggests that "symbolism is Dante's imitation of the structure of the real world, and allegory is his imitation of the structure of God's other book, Holy Scripture" (29). This notion of symbolism depends upon the medieval sense of a world whose creation and development were not accidental but "written" by God. The things of the world, therefore, are not only things but also signs that lead us to God.

Many scholars define symbolism in a way that accords with this medieval conception of a symbol as a "sign" that points beyond itself. Dante, in fact, occasionally uses the word *segno* ("sign") in this sense. Beatrice informs Dante in Paradise, for instance, that the souls he sees in the lowest heaven do not truly reside in that heaven but appear there solely for Dante's benefit, *per far segno / de la celestïal c'ha men salita. / Così parlar conviensi al vostro ingegno, / però che solo da sensato apprende / ciò che fa poscia d'intelletto degno* ("to signify that level of Heaven which is least exalted. It is necessary to speak thus to your intellect, for it takes from sense perception alone that which later it makes worthy of intellection," *Par.* 4.38–42). While Beatrice goes on to compare this type of symbolism to the figural language of the Bible, this statement can also be taken to refer to Dante's use of symbols or signs in the poem. He uses concrete, sensuous symbols to make comprehensible that which would otherwise be ineffable. Ugolino thus manifests his hatred for Archbishop Ruggieri not through words but through a *bestial segno* ("bestial sign"; see *Inf.* 32.133). In this view, then, Dante's symbolism is found in the concrete and sensuous details of the poem, which Dante uses not only for themselves but also for their value as signs, for their ability to point beyond themselves.

Perhaps the most common way of studying Dante's symbolism is to examine the imagery or iconography of the *Commedia*. John Freccero's study of the imagery of *Inf.* 1.29–30—*ripresi via per la piaggia diserta, / sì che 'l piè fermo era 'l più basso* ("I took my way again along that deserted slope, so that my halted foot was always the lower")—serves as an example of the symbolism of Dante's imagery. In the Christian tradition, the feet are compared to the faculties of the soul; the right foot symbolizes the intellect, while the left foot connotes the will. When Adam fell, however, both his will and his intellect were wounded, but especially his will, which can be healed only by an act of divine grace. Man, therefore, limps since the Fall. As Freccero shows, this left foot is the "halted" one; it is heavy because it is weighed down by appetites and avarice. Thus, as Dante attempts to approach the light, he can only drag his will along, attempting to force it to accord with his intellect.

Freccero's study reveals an approach common to many examinations of Dante's symbolism. Since images were signs for the medieval writer, they possessed a figurative meaning, one that is, for the most part, lost to modern readers. Critics such as Freccero attempt, therefore, to uncover the meanings ascribed to certain images in the Middle Ages in order to elucidate the symbolism of Dante's images, which has become obscure over time. (Kaske's *Medieval Christian Literary Imagery* provides a valuable guide for the study of medieval symbolism.) Thus, scholars may study the figurative meaning which medieval writers associated with the Sun and investigate how Dante exploits that meaning in his Heaven of the Sun in *Par.* 10–13.

Other scholars follow this same historical method but apply it to the numbers of the poem, drawing on the medieval belief that attached mystical meanings to numbers. Dante himself provides a good example of this kind of analysis in the *Vita Nuova* (29). After observing that Beatrice was frequently associated with the number 9, Dante concludes that, by *similitudine* ("analogy"), *questo numero fue ella medesima* ("this number was she herself"). Since 3 is the number of the Trinity and 9 is simply three times itself, Dante concludes that *ella era nove, cioè uno miracolo, la cui radice, cioè del miracolo, è solamente la mirabile Trinitade* ("she was a nine, or a miracle, whose root, namely that of the miracle, is the miraculous Trinity itself"). Taking Dante's lead, scholars have examined the symbolic value of numbers throughout the *Commedia* (see "Numerology").

The *Commedia*'s very structure is symbolic, as are the punishments and rewards meted out in its three canticles. This "moral symbolism" finds its justification in the remarks Dante makes in *Inf.* 19.10–11 concerning the "artistry" of the structure of Hell: *O somma sapïenza, quanta è l'arte / che mostri in cielo, in terra e nel mal mondo* ("O highest Wisdom, how great is the art you show in the heavens, on earth, and in the evil world!"). Dante thus implies that the symbolism of the natural world—of the Book of Nature—finds a parallel in the punishments of his own "evil world." The punishment of Satan, for example, is symbolic of God's art of justice. Satan hoped to become like God, and he has attained his wish: he is a horribly perverted negation of God's image and identity. Satan has become a hideous kind of triune creature—his three faces being separate and yet joined

to a single head (*Inf.* 34.38). In addition, his head, trunk, and bat-like wings form a cross-like image that reminds the reader of the Crucifixion of Christ, the second member of the Trinity. At the center of this "cross," however, is not Christ but Judas, his betrayer, eaten by Satan. And whereas the Christian Trinity "spirates" love, which is often symbolized by the color red, Satan's central face is also red, suggesting a perversion of Christian love—most likely hate. And thus the "art" of Dante's Hell symbolizes God's justice.

This study of Dante's moral symbolism can likewise be applied to the purging torments of the souls in the *Purgatorio* and of the blessed in the *Paradiso*. For example, in the sixth sphere of Heaven—the sphere of Jupiter and of justice—the numerous souls act in concert, using the luminosity of their spirits to form shapes: first a Latin phrase, and then the outline of an eagle. The souls, as the eagle, also speak in unity. The eagle—a unity formed out of diverse souls—symbolizes the justice and spiritual unity that prevails in Paradise and should prevail on Earth, but that are instead sadly lacking in Dante's own Italy.

The souls who form letters and spell out a message for Dante point to the prominence of the symbolism of writing and the book in Dante's works, especially in the *Vita Nuova* and the *Commedia*. Dante, for example, opens the earlier work with a metaphor that compares his memory to a book, a metaphor that he repeats in *Inf.* 2.8: *o mente che scrivesti ciò ch'io vidi* ("O memory that wrote down what I saw"). The book comes to symbolize many things in Dante's poem, but the culmination of this symbolism occurs at the end of the poem, where Dante compares the Trinity itself to a large book that encompasses the dispersed pages of the entire universe. As Dante's vision rests on the eternal light, he sees all things: *Nel suo profondo vidi che s'interna / legato con amore in un volume / ciò che per l'universo si squaderna* ("In its depths I saw internalized, bound with love in one volume, what through the universe is scattered quires," *Par.* 33.85–87). In the *Commedia,* a book can symbolize either Dante's memory or the Godhead, depending on Dante's use of it.

The expressive power of symbols is thus almost infinitely flexible and varied, a characteristic that Dante himself refers to in the *Vita Nuova* when, following his explanation of the significance of Beatrice's association with the number 9, he states that someone could perhaps find a *più sottile*

S *ragione* ("more subtle explanation"). In Dante's mind, then, symbols possess surplus meaning. Dante lived in a world which he believed to be authored by God and therefore free from accidental details; everything in it had meaning. He attempted to create a poem that would mirror the structure of the world—that would, in all its parts, have meaning beyond itself and point toward God. The structure of the poem, its imagery, and its characters were, in Dante's mind, not only things but signs, and as signs they served an indispensable function. Dante did not envision literary critics reading his poem so much as fellow Christians, who would be aware that it continually points beyond itself. His symbolism is not simply a "literary" feature of the *Commedia:* it forms an integral part of its message. For, as Dante well knew, mortals limited by a materialist vision can only see immaterial truth through a tangible symbol.

Bibliography

Barański, Zygmunt G. "Dante's Signs: An Introduction to Medieval Semiotics and Dante." In *Dante and the Middle Ages*. Edited by John C. Barnes and Cormac Ó Cuilleanáin. Dublin: Irish Academic Press, 1995, pp. 140–180.

Boyde, Patrick. *Dante Philomythes and Philosopher: Man in the Cosmos*. Cambridge: Cambridge University Press, 1981.

Cassell, Anthony. *Dante's Fearful Art of Justice*. Toronto: University of Toronto Press, 1984.

Curtius, Ernst Robert. "The Book as Symbol." In *European Literature in the Latin Middle Ages*. Princeton, N.J.: Princeton University Press, 1953, pp. 302–347.

Dozon, Marthe. *Mythe and Symbole dans la Divine Comédie*. Florence: Olschki, 1991.

Dronke, Peter. "The *Commedia* and Medieval Modes of Reading." In *Dante and Medieval Latin Traditions*. Cambridge: Cambridge University Press, 1986, pp. 1–31.

Dunbar, H. Flanders. *Symbolism in Medieval Thought and Its Consummation in the Divine Comedy*. New Haven, Conn.: Yale University Press, 1929.

Durling, Robert M., and Ronald L. Martinez. *Time and the Crystal: Studies in Dante's "Rime Petrose."* Berkeley, Los Angeles: University of California Press, 1990.

Fletcher, Jefferson B. *Symbolism of the Divine Comedy*. New York: Columbia University Press, 1921; New York: AMS Press, 1966.

Freccero, John. "The Firm Foot on a Journey without a Guide." In *Dante: The Poetics of Conversion*. Edited by Rachel Jacoff. Cambridge, Mass.: Harvard University Press, 1986, pp. 29–54.

Gilson, Étienne. "Concerning Two Families of Dantesque Symbols." In *Dante and Philosophy*. Translated by David Moore. 1949. New York, Evanston, and London: Harper and Row, 1963, pp. 289–297.

Green, Richard. "Dante's 'Allegory of Poets' and the Medieval Theory of Poetic Fiction." *Comparative Literature* 9 (1957), 118–128.

Hollander, Robert. *Allegory in Dante's "Commedia."* Princeton, N.J.: Princeton University Press, 1969.

Kaske, Robert E., with Arthur Groos and Michael W. Twomey. *Medieval Christian Literary Imagery: A Guide to Interpretation*. Toronto: University of Toronto Press, 1988.

Mazzeo, Joseph Anthony. "Dante's Sun Symbolism." *Italica* 33 (1956), 243–251.

Pagliaro, Antonino. "Simbolo e allegoria nella Divina Commedia." *L'Alighieri* 4 (1963), 3–35.

Pépin, Jean. "Allégorie, symbolisme, typologie." In *Dante e la tradition de l'allégorie*. Montreal: Institut d'études médiévales, 1970, pp. 15–51.

Sarolli, Gian Roberto. *Prolegomena alla "Divina Commedia."* Florence: Olschki, 1971.

Singleton, Charles S. "Allegory" and "Symbolism." In *Dante Studies 1. Commedia: Elements of Structure*. Cambridge, Mass.: Harvard University Press, 1954, pp. 1–17, 18–44.

V. Stanley Benfell

T

Tarquin

Last of the seven Roman kings. He murdered his predecessor, Servius Tullius, and Servius' friends. His reign of terror included his son's rape of Lucrezia, wife of a cousin. Tarquin was finally expelled from Rome by the people, who abolished the monarchy and proclaimed the republic, making Lucius Junius Brutus the first consul. Tarquin is remembered by Dante in *Inf.* 4.127—*Vidi quel Bruto che cacciò Tarquino* ("I saw the Brutus who drove Tarquin out")—and referred to in *Conv.* 4.5.12.

Pina Palma

Tebaldello

A member of the Ghibelline Zambrasi family of Faenza, also called Tribaldello. His name had become a byword for villainy, and it is reported that the disastrous affair with his people was caused by a quarrel about a couple of pigs. In order to avenge his private grudge against members of the Lambertazzi family—Ghibellines of Bologna who had taken refuge in Faenza after their expulsion from Bologna in 1274—he treacherously opened the gates of the city in the early morning of November 13, 1280, to the Geremei of Bologna, their Guelf opponents, allowing them to rush in upon their enemy while the whole city slept. For this act of treachery he is punished in Antenora, the second ring of the ninth circle of Hell (*Inf.* 32.122).

R. A. Malagi

Tenzone

An Italian poetic form representing a debate between two poets, especially one that is often polemical in nature and sometimes filled with invective. The debate, or expression of opposing views, is carried out by means of an exchange of poems. Like other Italian poetic forms of the Middle Ages, such as the canzone, the *lauda,* or the sonnet, the *tenzone*'s content was shaped by the genre's history and traditions.

The Italian *tenzone* derives ultimately from the *tenso,* a poetic form developed in southern France from about the beginning of the twelfth century. Writing in the medieval language of that region, Old Provençal, such poets as Marcabru, Ugo Catola, and Cercamon created witty verbal conflicts, jousts in rhyme, which embodied some form of "tension" between them. Sometimes these Provençal poets seem to have worked together, creating a poem in which each of the two authors wrote alternating stanzas. At other times, the *tenso* seems rather to have been a form of rhymed correspondence, with each of the two parties writing a poem, then sending it off to the other and awaiting his response. In still other instances, it seems likely that an entire *tenso* might well have been written by a single poet who attributed to a colleague the position opposed to his own. The Provençal *tenso* usually treated autobiographical, amorous, moral, or political themes, and its tone varied from serious to ironic to outright satirical.

The Sicilian school of poetry took up the *tenso* in the early thirteenth century. For the Sicilians, the *tenso* retained its content but changed its form in an important way. Some members of the Sicilian school adapted the sonnet to the *tenzone,* so that it became an exchange of sonnets. Because the sonnet often already had some form of conflict or at least a marked change built into its structure,

T this integration of the two forms made the Sicilian *tenzone* generally somewhat more complex than the *tenso,* because it was composed of conflicts and changes embedded within an overall larger structure of "tension."

In Tuscany and nearby regions later in the thirteenth century, the *tenzone* drew upon both Old Provençal and Sicilian models. Among its most able practitioners were not only Guittone d'Arezzo but also Dante himself. His "*Tenzone* with Forese [Donati]"—consisting of a set of six sonnets, three by each poet, initiated by Dante (*Rime* 73–78)—presents a conflict over masculine and family honor in bitterly comic terms. Some scholars also consider as a *tenzone* Dante's exchange of sonnets with Dante da Maiano *(Tenzone del "Duol d'amore"),* but this debate about the relative degrees of suffering to be experienced in love, carried out in five sonnets (*Rime* 41–45), seems more an old-fashioned scholastic debate, lacking the combative edge which gives such power to the "*Tenzone* with Forese." Critics also speak of two other occasions of an exchange of sonnets by the two poets (*Rime* 39–40, 46–47).

Some scholars have seen in the three sonnets Dante contributed to his exchange with Forese an anticipation of the *terzina* he employs to such great effect in *Inferno.* The rhythm and concision of his syntax in the "*Tenzone*" is suggestive of the style he will adopt to express moral issues with a comic edge in many episodes of the *Commedia.* More recently, however, Mauro Cursietti has argued that the "*Tenzone* with Forese" was not written by Dante at all but is a deliberate falsification composed in Florence, c. 1400, in an elaborate homosexual slang unknown in Dante's time but widely practiced in the later period.

Bibliography

Barbi, Michele. "La tenzone di Dante con Forese." In *Problemi di critica dantesca. Seconda serie (1920–1937).* Florence: Sansoni, 1941, pp. 87–188. Reprinted in 1975; essay originally published in 1924.

Cursietti, Mauro. *La falsa tenzone di Dante con Forese Donati.* Anzio: De Rubeis, 1995.

Lanza, Antonio. *Polemiche e berte letterarie nella Firenze del primo Quattrocento.* Rome: Bulzoni, 1971.

Stefanini, Ruggero. "Tenzone sì e tenzone no." *Lectura Dantis* 18–19 (1996), 111–128.

Susan Noakes

Terence

Roman comic playwright (195–159 B.C.E.) who, as Virgil reports in answer to Statius' question about his fate, resides in Limbo with Homer and other classical authors (*Purg.* 22.97–108) and who provided Dante with an example of comedy defined as a narrative with a happy ending (*Epist.* 13.10). It is unlikely that Dante had direct knowledge of the works of Terence *(Terenzio),* but his name would be familiar to him from his reading of Augustine's *De civitate Dei* (2.12) and Horace's *Epistles,* Book 2, 1.56–59.

Bibliography

Barański, Zygmunt. "Dante e la tradizione comica latina." In *Dante e la "bella scola" della poesia: Autorità e sfida poetica.* Edited by Amilcare A. Iannucci. Ravenna: Longo, 1993, pp. 225–245.

Guy P. Raffa

Terza rima

A verse form consisting of stanzas of three lines, called "tercets," in which the first and third lines rhyme with each other while the second line rhymes with the first and third lines of the succeeding tercet. *Terza rima* is a fundamental constituent of the *Commedia* both thematically, because of its Trinitarian associations, and structurally. It seems to have been Dante's own invention. Possible sources have been identified in the *serventese,* a mode of discursive poetry that derived from the Provençal *sirventes* and assumed a variety of forms in Italy; and in one of the rhyme schemes for the last six lines of the sonnet, the two alternating rhymes *(cdcdcd)* used by Dante in nineteen of his fifty-six regular versions of this form, as well as throughout the *Fiore* (if Dante is the author of this work). But *terza rima* differs from this last scheme in a very important respect: each canto begins and ends with a pair rather than a trio of alternating rhymes

aba bcb cdc, . . . wxw xyx yzy z

so that each also concludes with a single isolated line. Not only does this structure give a strong sense of closure to the end of the canto, but it also imparts a strong forward movement to the verse, by ensuring that each group of three lines, or *terzina,* is linked by rhyme both to the group before and to the group after. Beginning each canto with two trios of alternating rhymes, as in the sonnet model, would have broken up the flow of the verse into discrete six-line units

ababab cdcdcd efefef

with an effect more akin to that of the later *ottava rima.*

The *terzina* is also fundamental to the *Commedia's* structure in the way in which it determines the poem's syntax. The vast majority of the poem's lines are end-stopped; the opposite feature of *enjambement* is comparatively rare, and only a minute number of sentence breaks (nineteen in the whole poem in the authoritative Petrocchi edition) occur in the middle of a line. More distinctively, the major syntactic divisions regularly fall at the end of the three-line unit; in the whole poem only about one in thirty sentence endings fall at the end of the first or second lines of the *terzina,* if one excepts the obligatory single line at the end of each canto. At this level, therefore, the rhythm of the poem is remarkably regular. It is worth noting that the few sentence breaks at the end of the first and second lines are about twice as frequent in *Inferno* as in either *Purgatorio* or *Paradiso,* and that the number of sentences encompassing two or more *terzine* increases markedly from one canto to the next; there are 290 in *Inferno,* 334 in *Purgatorio,* and 432 in *Paradiso.* The rhythm becomes slower and more even as the poem proceeds.

The range and difficulty of Dante's rhymes also lend force to the *terzina* structure. The ten most common rhymes in Dante's lyric poetry are *-ore* (152), *-ia* (82), *-ate* (81), *-ente* (74), *-are* (64), *-ui* (57), *-ato* (43), *-ura* (35), *-ita* (35), and *-osa* (34), out of a total of only 2,417 rhyming lines. The ten most common rhymes of the *Commedia* are *-ura* (153), *-io* (140), *-ente* (133), *-etto* (131), *-ia* (121), *-ai* (118), *-enti* (111), *-era* (108), *-ore* (108), and *-one* (101), out of the far greater total of 14,233 rhyming lines. Thus, while similar kinds of grammatical or suffixal endings dominate in both categories of work, as one might expect, the figures show how much less space they occupy, proportionately, in the *Commedia,* and how much Dante has expanded his range of rhymes.

The total number of different rhymes in the *Commedia* is 753; of these, 240 occur only once: 214 in tercets and 27 in couplets at the beginning or end of a canto. While each of the second two *cantiche* is slightly longer than the one before, in each case the number of different rhymes is reduced, though not by much; the effort toward variety in rhyme seems to decline slightly from one *cantica* to the next. The same development can be seen in somewhat different terms when we consider the number of different rhymes exclusive to each *cantica:* this declines from 117 to 84 between *Inferno* and *Purgatorio* and then rises slightly to 88 in *Paradiso.* But what is most striking here is the way in which substantial numbers of new rhymes are introduced as the poem progresses. Dante was an extraordinarily inventive rhymer— much more so than his later rivals in this respect, Pulci and Tasso.

Some small development can be detected in the distribution of the accented vowels in rhymes from one *cantica* to the next: there is an increase in the front vowels *e* and *i* in accented position in rhymes from *Inferno* to *Purgatorio* and from *Purgatorio* to *Paradiso,* and a slightly greater number of accented back vowels *o* and *u* in rhyme in *Inferno* than in the other two *cantiche.* This to some extent corresponds to a long-held view about the iconic values of these sounds in the different parts of the *Commedia* (front vowels expressing light and joy, back vowels expressing darkness and gloom, etc.). A comparable development may also be detected in the use of consonants in rhyming syllables. It is noteworthy first that the total number of consonants in the rhymes of each *cantica* drops noticeably from *Inferno* to *Purgatorio* and then remains at the same (lower) level in *Paradiso.* An added dimension appears in this pattern when the consonants are broken down by manner of articulation; taken together, the proportion of liquids and nasals in rhyme increases; and the proportion of alveolar, plosive, and sibilant consonants in rhyme decreases by some 5.5 percentage points. These are only minor observations, but they provide an interesting gloss on the association that Dante himself makes (*Inf.* 32.1) of *rime aspre* with the bottom of *Inferno.*

The vast majority of Dante's rhymes in both the lyric poetry and the *Commedia* are paroxytonic (with the accent on the penultimate), as in the succeeding Italian tradition. Only a very small number have the accent on the final syllable (*-à, -è, -ì, -ò, -ù;* but never a final syllable ending in a consonant) or on the antepenultimate *(-argini, -endere, -evole, -olica, -abile, -irano).* A number of rhymes are irregular by later standards. There are some cases of "Sicilian" rhyme, reflecting the phonology of the language of early Italian poetry:

in the lyric poems -*etto* rhymes with -*itto*, -*onto* with -*unto*; in the *Commedia* -*esse* rhymes with -*isse*, -*ui* with *oi*, -*ugna* with -*ogna*, -*oso* with -*uso*, -*ome* with -*ume*, -*utto* with -*otto*, and -*uri* with -*ori*. In both the lyric poetry and the *Commedia* there are a number of imperfect rhymes: -*orto* with -*olto*, *morra'ti* with -*ati*, *rife'mi* with -*emi*, *acco'lo* with -*olo*, and similar combinations; and composite rhymes such as *par l'à* and *par là* with -*arla*, *seguer de'* with -*erde*, *pur lì* with -*urli*, *oh me* with -*ome*, *non ci ha* with -*oncia*, *ne la* with -*ela*, *Almen tre* with -*entre*, *per li* with -*erli*, *sol tre* with -*oltre*, *dì dì* with -*idi*, and *ne lo* with -*elo*. Finally, there is the famous broken rhyme in *Par.* 24.16: *così quelle carole, differente- / mente danzando . . .* ("so those carols, differently dancing"). As in his use of rhythm and meter, Dante could allow himself a degree of license in rhyme which was common in his time but which later generations found less acceptable.

Contrary to Dante's stricture in *De vulgari eloquentia,* there are numerous (eighty-four) instances of equivocal rhyme (combining the same word forms with different meanings) in the *Commedia,* and a few cases in the lyric poetry, in addition to the obligatory repetitions of the sestina form. In the *Commedia* there are also some simple repetitions (without equivocation) of words in rhyme: the ironic threefold *per ammenda* in *Purg.* 20, the dramatic threefold *vidi* of *Par.* 30, and the exclusive rhyming of *Cristo* with *Cristo* (*Par.* 12, 14, 19, 32).

But what is most striking, distinctive, and powerful in Dante's use of rhyme is his choice of vocabulary in rhyme position, including some notable metaphors such as the following: *e questo basti de la prima valle / sapere e di color che 'n sé* assanna ("let this be enough to know about the first ditch and those it grinds in its teeth," *Inf.* 18.98–99); *né . . . / valse a le guance nette di rugiada / che, lagrimando, non tornasser* atre ("nor did . . . suffice to prevent my cheeks, though cleansed with dew, from turning dark with tears," *Purg.* 30.52–54); *onde si coronava il bel* zaffiro / *del quale il ciel più chiaro* s'inzaffira ("that crowned the beautiful sapphire with which the brightest Heaven is ensapphired," *Par.* 23.101–102). The first circle of Malebolge sinks its fangs into *(assanna)* the sinners in it; Dante's cheeks become "dark" *(atre)* with tears; the Virgin is a sapphire *(zaffiro)* that bejewels *(inzaffira:*

"en-sapphires") Heaven. A large proportion of the forms used in rhyme position in the *Commedia* do not appear at all in other positions in the line—substantially more, it can be shown, than the comparable figures for later poets such as Pulci, Ariosto, and Tasso, as well as for Dante's own lyric poetry; some forms, indeed, are the poet's invention, such as the *inluia* and *immii* ("enter[s] into him/me") of *Par.* 9.73 and 81. Dante used greater liberties than his successors in his choice of rhyme words and rhymes, not just for the sake of technical difficulty but also for effects of vigor, emphasis, and surprise.

Bibliography

Baldelli, Ignazio. "Rima," "Terzina." *Enciclopedia dantesca,* 4:930–949, 5:583–594.

Beltrami, P. G. *Metrica, poetica, metrica dantesca.* Pisa: Pacini, 1981.

Parodi, Ernesto Giacomo. "La rima e i vocaboli in rima nella *Divina Commedia.*" In *Lingua e letteratura.* Edited by G. Folena and P. V. Mengaldo. Venice: Neri Pozza, 1957, pp. 203–284. Essay originally published in 1896.

Robey, David. "The *Fiore* and the *Comedy:* Some Computerized Comparisons." In *The "Fiore" in Context: Dante, France, Tuscany.* Edited by Zygmunt Barański and Patrick Boyde. Notre Dame, Ind.: University of Notre Dame Press, 1997.

Tatlock, J. S. P. "Dante's Terza Rima." In *American Critical Essays on the Divine Comedy.* Edited by Robert J. Clements. New York: New York University Press, 1967, pp. 26–36. Reprinted from *PLMA* 51 (1936), 895–903.

David Robey

Tesauro de' Beccheria

A native of Pavia, Tesauro de' Beccheria was the abbot of Vallombrosa and the papal legate to Tuscany under Alexander IV. In 1258 Beccheria was accused by the Florentines of conspiring against the city, together with the Ghibelline exiles. He was beheaded in Piazza di Sant'Apollinare after being tortured. His death led to a seven-year excommunication of all Florentines for sacrilege. Although according to Villani (*Cronica* 7.65) he was not universally believed to have been guilty of treachery, Dante thought otherwise, for Beccheria is placed in the ninth and lowest circle of Hell, in the zone of Antenora, among the traitors to country or party. In *Inf.* 32.119 he is ignominiously pointed out to Dante the pilgrim by a fellow traitor, Bocca degli Abati. Like the other damned in Antenora, Beccheria is encased in ice up to his erect head.

Fiora A. Bassanese

Tesiphone

Daughter of Night and Pluto or Acheron and the last named of the three Furies threatening Dante at the Gate of Dis: *Tesifón è nel mezzo* ("Tisiphone is in the middle," *Inf.* 9.48). Dante's description parallels Statius' account of Tesiphone in *Theb.* 1.100ff.; see also Lucan (*Phars.* 6.730ff.), Ovid (*Meta.* 4.480–481), and Virgil (*Aen.* 6.555, 571, 10.761).

Rebecca S. Beal

Thaddeus

Taddeo d'Alderotto, renowned Florentine physician (d. 1295) who is said to have founded the school of medicine at the University of Bologna. He is cited by Bonaventura in his eulogy of St. Dominic as an example of a great scholar who sought worldly gain (*Par.* 12.83). In *Conv.* 1.10.10, Dante calls him Thaddeus the Hippocratist and speaks of his translation of Aristotle's *Ethics* from the Latin. Some scholars, however, believe the reference in *Paradiso* is to Taddeo Pepoli, a celebrated canonist of the day.

Richard Lansing

Thais

Athenian courtesan of the fourth century B.C.E. whose name in literature symbolized the social degradation associated with prostitution. A character in Terence's *Eunuchus* (III, 391–392), she receives a flattering gift from Gnatho. Dante, relying upon an ambiguous passage in an intermediary text, Cicero's *De amicitia* (26.98) or John of Salisbury's *Policraticus,* portrays Thais *(Taide)* as the flatterer and consigns her to the second bolgia of Malebolge (*Inf.* 18.133). His depiction of Thais as "filthy . . . with disordered hair" in the fetid world of the flatterers derives from the fable *De Iuvene et Thaide,* contained in Waltherio Anglico's *Liber Aesopi.*

Pina Palma

Thales

The founder of the Ionian school of natural philosophy and one of the Seven Wise Men, born in Miletus c. 640 B.C.E. He advanced the theory that all things are sustained by the element water, believing that Earth floated on water, and asserted that the world could be comprehended through reason alone. Thales *(Tale, Talete)* is found in Limbo with the wise pagans (*Inf.* 4.137). Dante omits his name from the list of the Seven Wise Men in *Conv.* 3.11.4, possibly because of a corrupt textual source.

Richard Lansing

Thebes

The city of Cadmus and Oedipus whose history in ancient poetry comprises a chain of horrific events of violence. *Inferno* invokes this history: Jove's destruction of the invader Capaneus (14.49–72); the fatal duel of the sons of Oedipus (26.52–54); the infanticide of the mad King Athamas (30.1–12). Preparing to describe Cocytus, Dante recalls Amphion's walling in of Thebes (32.10–11); reflecting on the fate of Ugolino and his sons, he calls Pisa *novella Tebe* ("new Thebes," 33.89).

In *Purgatorio,* though Statius acknowledges having sung of Thebes (21.92) and Virgil recalls Jocasta's "double sorrow" (22.56), Theban history is nearly absent. The activeness of the once-slothful souls of the fourth terrace is compared to the frenzied Theban worship of Bacchus (18.91–96). Dante's Thebes is the classic example of a state riven and barbarized by faction.

Winthrop Wetherbee

Theology

In the sphere of the Sun (*Par.* 10–12) Dante highlights the Christian theologians to whom he is most indebted for the conceptual and intellectual structure of the *Commedia*. Although the list of the *spiriti sapienti* ("wise spirits") who configure themselves as two holy crowns of twelve souls each is not exclusive, it does include two of the major and most of the minor theological sources most favored by Dante. The two most prominent are St. Thomas Aquinas and St. Bonaventure, who are depicted not as members of rival religious orders, Dominican and Franciscan, but as harmonious souls, each eager to praise not only the

T founder of the other's order but also those thinkers—namely, Siger of Brabant and Joachim of Flora—whom they had criticized severely in life (Gilson, 256–277). Aquinas and Bonaventure are thus the focus of the encounter. They serve to introduce their fellow spirits, all of whom are relegated to the background, and only they are afforded speaking roles (*Par.* 10.83–138, 12.31–145).

While there can be no doubt that Aquinas was a major theological source for Dante (Foster 1986; 1977, 66ff., 156ff.), caution must be exercised in pinpointing both the extent and the nature of the poet's use of the Angelic Doctor. The earlier and simplified position espoused by Busnelli and Mandonnet that Dante was, in essence, a Thomist has been successfully challenged and refuted by Nardi and Gilson. In their respective ways they have demonstrated that Dante's world includes elements opposed to Thomistic teaching, such as the doctrines of the original creation of a *prima materia* devoid of form, of the close involvement of angels in the workings of the heavenly bodies, and of man's two separate but related goals of temporal and eternal happiness. But it also lacks many distinctive features of Thomas's metaphysics and anthropology, such as the distinction between essence and existence in creatures and the notion of *intellectus agens*. As Kenelm Foster has observed, "Doctrinally there is not much to be said for calling Dante a Thomist" (61). Dante's world is, in fact, a synthesis of many eclectic theological influences. Moreover, not only is Dante not a Thomist, but neither can the framework of the *Commedia* be said to be essentially Thomistic. Mastrobuono has argued against the long-held belief first advocated by Singleton (88) that Aquinas supplied Dante with the major theological apparatus for his concept of the journey of the pilgrim in grace as involving two moments, namely, a state of preparation for sanctifying grace, represented by Virgil's role as guide, and the actual reception of this grace, represented by the appearance of Beatrice atop Mount Purgatory (x–xii and 42ff.). Mastrobuono maintains that Singleton has thoroughly misinterpreted Aquinas, who asserts that the infusion of grace takes place in an instant (*ST* 1.2.113.7), and has totally confused Thomas's key distinction that justification is a process in the order of nature (cause and effect), and not a process in the order of time (before and after). He argues that the process of justification,

rather than involving two moments, takes place in an instant in the Prologue scene (*Inf.* 1). This reading has provided a necessary corrective to Singleton's mistaken interpretation of justification in Aquinas.

Nevertheless, while Dante and his work cannot be said to be singularly Thomistic, Thomas and his *Summa theologicae* are of paramount significance for Dante in the area of dogmatic theology. Despite his critique of Singleton's Thomistic reading of Dante, Mastrobuono deems Thomas's influence on Dante fundamental and argues for a resolutely Thomistic Dante (against Freccero—cf. below). And Gilson (117) remarks that Dante had a profound love for Thomas, who exercised over the poet a major cultural hold to the extent that Dante's "doctrinal affinities were with the school of Aquinas rather than with any other" (Foster 1986, 76). Countless episodes and themes in the *Commedia* bear witness to Thomas's supremacy as a theological source, such as the theology of love that inspires Beatrice's descent into Hell in *Inf.* 2; the general law of *contrapasso*—a term which appears in *Inf.* 28.142 and which is almost certainly a translation of Thomas's *contrapassum* (*ST* 2.2.61.4); the doctrines of love, free will, and responsibility in *Purg.* 16 and 17; and the very experience of the vision of God in *Par.* 33. On the other hand, however, Dante is at times quite independent in his use of Thomas and does not hesitate to diverge from the teachings of the Angelic Doctor when his poetic ends and faith convictions so warrant. In his portrayal of the souls of those in Limbo (*Inf.* 4.22ff.), for example, Dante rejects Aquinas' position that the souls of unbaptized children suffer no pain whatsoever (*De Malo* 5.2.1, 2, 3; 5.3.3) in favor of Bonaventure's view that such children, while suffering no physical pain, do experience the pain of loss and so live in a midway point between the election of grace and the condemnation of sin (*Sent.* 2.33, 3.2). It is, in fact, the latter's theological view of the fate of unbaptized children that Dante appropriates and daringly transfers to the virtuous pagans in order to confer a poignancy to their eternal lot. Likewise, in his portrayal of the eternal beatitude of those infants who have been saved (*Par.* 32.40ff.), Dante for visual effect not only leaves the infants as infants (Grandgent, 915), against all medieval theological opinion which claimed that the elect would rise after the Resurrection in the aspect of the prime of life (*ST* 3 Suppl. 81.1), but also, in his assigning to them of different ranks, rejects Aquinas' position that there can be no difference in degree of beatitude among the infants in Heaven (*ST* 3 Suppl. 69.8). While Aquinas remains the chief theological point of reference for the *Commedia,* Dante subjects him, as he does all his other theological references, to ongoing debate and revision.

Similarly, the theology of Bonaventure is of critical importance for Dante (cf. Rivighi, Jallonghi, Bottagisio). Bonaventure's mystical theology, in fact, underlines the very journey of the pilgrim, his *Itinerarium mentis in deum* not only providing the predominant metaphor for Dante's twofold *itinerarium,* or journey to God (Singleton, 4: "a journey there, through Hell and Purgatory and Paradise, and a journey here, an event in this 'our life'"), but also lending a much needed contemplative touch to Dante's personal entry into the presence of the Godhead. It is thus for his superior contemplative knowledge that Bonaventure is esteemed by Dante; and just as he had found in Aquinas the ideal Dominican, that is, a great thinker and teacher (Foster, 61ff.), so he found in Bonaventure the ideal Franciscan, that is, one of those *che ne' grandi offici / sempre pospuosi la sinistra cura* ("who in my great duties always subordinated the left-hand cares," *Par.* 12.128–129; that is, who always favored the spiritual over the temporal side). It is this spiritual concern and equilibrium that Dante undoubtedly prized in Bonaventure, for it was an equilibrium as divorced from the laxity of Matthew of Acquasparta as it was from the harshness of Ubertino da Casale, both of whom were locked in a bitter battle for supremacy of the Franciscan order after Bonaventure's death (*Par.* 12.121ff.). Moreover, apart from his influence as a mystical theologian, individual episodes in the *Commedia* (e.g., the Limbo episode of *Inf.* 4) are heavily Bonaventurian (cf. Bottagisio), as pointed out above.

In addition to the special influence of Aquinas and Bonaventure, the encounter with the two crowns also dramatizes many of those minor theological sources that Dante calls upon and appropriates in the composition of the *Commedia:* Albertus Magnus, primarily for his Neoplatonic representation of the world and secondarily for his systematic theology; Peter Lombard, for the *Sentences,* his compendium of doctrinal excerpts from the Church Fathers; Paulus Orosius, for his theologically guided universal history; Siger of Brabant, for his Averroistic reading of theology;

Richard of St. Victor, the *magnus contemplator;* Hugh of St. Victor, for his mystical theology; Anselm, for his intellectually grounded theology; and Joachim of Flora, for his spiritualism.

Two other sources who do not appear in the two crowns of *Par.* 10–12 but who constitute along with Aquinas and Bonaventure Dante's main theological *fontes* are St. Augustine and, more especially, St. Bernard of Clairvaux. St. Bernard is accorded the singular honor of being chosen to be the last guide of Dante who leads the pilgrim unto the divine vision (*Par.* 31.58ff.). This distinction is very probably based on Dante's long familiarity with Bernard's works and on the influence they exerted on him (cf. Botterill, Mazzoni). While Dante does not cite Bernard's works directly, there are numerous parallel loci in Dante and Bernard (cf. Mazzoni), and the poet repeatedly turns to the saint's works for images, situations, concepts, and structural suggestions: the *De consideratione,* for example, may have served as the allegorical basis for the pilgrim's upward ascent to God, culminating in the divine vision. Bernard's theological influence in Dante's intellectual life was therefore considerable (cf. Vecchi, 190, who has argued that the bond between Dante and St. Bernard is strongly autobiographical). The fundamental reason for Bernard's preeminence in the last stages of the *Commedia* is attributable to several factors: he is the great Christian mystic, the devotee of Mary (the *alumnus familiarissimus Dominae nostrae*), a preacher of incomparable eloquence *(doctor melifluus)* whose theology is rooted in a firm grasp of the Scriptures, a thinker of penetrating and engaging insight into the theological controversies of his times (to wit, his acerbic theological struggle with Peter Abelard), and one whose faith was firmly founded on the transcendent nature of God's being and revelation. Thus Bernard and Dante share a privileged relationship, shaped in equal parts by their belief in a "transhumanizing" faith and by their mystical approach to the Godhead.

Augustine also has a place among Dante's theological sources (Pincherle, Chioccioni), but his influence is not equal to that of the other three, a fact underscored by his not having a speaking role in the *Commedia* and his limited appearance toward the very end of *Paradiso,* where his place in the celestial rose is described by St. Bernard as being fourth in descent from that of John the Baptist (*Par.* 32.35). It is probable that Dante was familiar with certain writings of Augustine, such as the *Confessions* and, especially, *The City of God*. From the latter work he not only appropriates for the *Commedia* its predominant paradigm of the two cities—the celestial city founded on God's love and enduring forever, and the terrestrial city founded on self-interest and enduring but a moment; but he also radically revises it by projecting an image of the earthly Rome, not so much in the Augustinian sense, as a source of sin and confusion (in short, as a reborn Babylon), but rather as a celestial abode conflated with the heavenly Jerusalem—*quella Roma onde Cristo è romano* ("that Rome in which Christ is Roman," *Purg.* 32.102)—and with which he contrasts his native infernal Florence. But this borrowing aside, Augustine does not seem to have been a major theological source for Dante. In fact, attempts to emphasize Augustine's influence on Dante have, by and large, failed. So Freccero (1–2), who sought to impose on the *Commedia* the Augustinian model of conversion, has been countered by Mastrobuono's argument that Augustine lacks a metaphysics and approaches conversion only as a moral problem, ignoring its metaphysical dimension (212ff.). It would rest with Aquinas to develop such a metaphysical dimension in his profound awareness of being—God's being signifying the eternal present and God's immanence in his creatures being the cause of their being. The *Commedia* makes abundantly clear the importance of its metaphysical claims and how the meaning of life is shaped not so much by an Augustinian antinomy of eternity and mutability (Augustine's "Eternity, it is the very substance of God") but by a Thomistic conception of being (Thomas's "God is his own act-of-being"). Scholars like Chioccioni who lament that Augustine is not accorded in the *Commedia* a more significant role fail to understand the limited use that Dante makes of him. Augustine's thinking is present more by reflection in the thought of theologians closer to Dante's own time than it is as a direct source. Thus, even though it appears that Dante is resolutely Augustinian in his emphasis on the primacy of faith and baptism as absolute conditions for salvation, it is just as likely that Dante received these Augustinian notions from a theologian like St. Bernard, who stressed these positions forcefully in his fierce debate with Peter Abelard, a debate much more proximate to Dante than Augustine's with Pelagius. Moreover, in individual episodes (e.g., Limbo) Dante flies repeatedly in the theological

face of Augustine, refusing to condemn the innocent infants (and the virtuous pagans, for that matter) to a fiery afterlife of torment. Dante clearly refuses to accept the view that there can be no such thing as a virtuous pagan, and he rejects Augustine's negative evaluation of both the Roman Empire and pagan culture in general.

Why then is Augustine to be included as a member of Dante's theological canon? The answer lies in Dante's understanding of the working of the will of God, an understanding central to his unique treatment of the virtuous pagans in Limbo and an understanding which has as its raison d'être a doctrine particularly dear to Augustine. This is the stern doctrine of predestination to which Dante clings in *Inf.* 4 and to which he returns in *Par.* 20 (130ff.) and 32 (40ff.) to justify not only the salvation of the Roman pagans Trajan and Ripheus but also the condemnation of Virgil, his fellow virtuous pagans, and the unbaptized children as well. No theological influence, in fact, seems more important than that of Augustine in the shaping of the poet's development of the tragic fate of the virtuous pagans and unbaptized children along theologically predestined lines, although elsewhere in the poem Dante approaches predestination in a Thomistic sense (cf. *Par.* 17.36–42). It is the Augustinian doctrine of predestination that drives Dante's poetic account of Limbo and lends it such poignant intensity. But, apart from predestination, it seems that Augustine and his theology were not quite congenial to Dante's overall humanistic bias, which places a higher value on human virtue and accomplishment outside the Christian dispensation than does Augustine.

In melding his theological sources Dante achieves in the *Commedia* a consummate fusion of theology and poetry. The poet's use of theology, however, has been studied by modern scholars chiefly from the perspective of the poem's truth claims and Dante's supposed application of the allegory of the theologians, a claim registered in the disputed *Letter to Cangrande*. The central issue here has been the question of the poem's ontological status, which has been interpreted variously as a *visio* ("vision"), a divinely revealed *verità* ("truth"; for Guido of Pisa, Pascoli, Pietrobono, and especially Nardi), or a *fictio* ("fiction"), that is, a *bella menzogna,* or "beautiful lie" (for most of the early commentators and more recently for Auerbach, Charity, Singleton, and Freccero). On this issue Dante's role has tended to be seen primarily as either the work of a *theologus* (Hollander) or of a *poeta* (Barolini). By and large this debate has resulted in an adversative approach toward the relationship between poetry and theology, one that perceives each as mutually hostile to the other and that lays claims to the primacy of one over the other—poetry pitted against theology, the allegory of the theologians pitted against the fictive nature of the narrative. But such a dichotomy is viewed by some as entirely artificial, since the question of whether Dante regarded himself primarily as *poeta* or *theologus,* as *fabbro* or *propheta,* can never truly or effectively be resolved. The radical claims of Croce, who argued that the theology in the *Commedia* virtually suffocates the poetry, or of Mazzotta, who contends that the poetry subsumes the theology, constitute the poles at either side. The majority view holds, rather, that each is intimately bound with the other—theology being the very source of the poetry and poetry being the ultimate expression of theological truth—although a more detailed investigation of the subject remains to be undertaken.

Bibliography

Barolini, Teodolinda. *The Undivine Comedy: Detheologizing Dante.* Princeton, N.J.: Princeton University Press, 1992.

Bottagisio, Tito. *Il limbo dantesco.* Padua: Tipografia e letterarii Antoniana, 1898.

Botterill, Steven. *Dante and the Mystical Tradition: Bernard of Clairvaux in the Commedia.* Cambridge: Cambridge University Press, 1994.

Busnelli, Giovanni. *Cosmogonia e antropogenesi secondo Dante Alighieri e le sue fonti.* Rome: Civiltà Cattolica, 1922.

Charity, A. C. *Events and Their Afterlife: The Dialectics of Christian Typology in the Bible and Dante.* Cambridge: Cambridge University Press, 1966.

Chioccioni, Pietro. *L'agostinismo nella Divina Commedia.* Florence: Olschki, 1952.

Contini, Gianfranco. *Un'idea di Dante.* Turin: Einaudi, 1976.

Croce, Benedetto. *La poesia di Dante.* Bari: Laterza, 1966.

Foster, Kenelm. *The Two Dantes and Other Studies.* London: Darton, Longman and Todd, 1977.

———. "Tommaso d'Aquino." *Enciclopedia dantesca,* 5:626–649.

Freccero, John. *Dante: The Poetics of Conversion.* Edited by Rachel Jacoff. Cambridge, Mass.: Harvard University Press, 1986.

Gilson, Étienne. *Dante and Philosophy.* New York: Harper and Row, 1963.

Grandgent, Charles H. *La Divina Commedia.* Cambridge, Mass.: Harvard University Press, 1972.

Hollander, Robert. "Dante Theologus-Poeta." *Studies in Dante.* Ravenna: Longo, 1980, pp. 39–89.

Iannucci, Amilcare A. "*Paradiso* XXXI." *Lectura Dantis* 16–17 (Spring-Fall 1995), pp. 470–485.

Jallonghi, Ernesto. *Il misticismo bonaventuriano nella Divina Commedia.* Città di Castello: CEDAM, 1935.

Mandonnet, Pierre. *Dante le théologien.* Paris: Desclee, de Brouer, 1935.

Mastrobuono, Antonio C. *Dante's Journey of Sanctification.* Washington, D.C.: Regnery Gateway, 1990.

Mazzoni, Francesco. "San Bernardino e la visione poetica della *Divina Commedia.*" *Seminario Dantesco Internazionale: International Dante Seminar 1.* Edited by Zygmunt G. Barański. Florence: Casa editrice le lettere, 1997, pp. 171–241.

Mazzotta, Giuseppe. *Dante's Vision and the Circle of Knowledge.* Princeton, N.J.: Princeton University Press, 1993.

Nardi, Bruno. *Dante e la cultura medievale.* Bari: Laterza, 1985.

Pascoli, Giovanni. *La mirabile visione: Abbozzo d'una storia della Divina Commedia.* Bologna: Zanichelli, 1913.

Pietrobono, Luigi. *La Divina Commedia di Dante Alighieri commentata da Luigi Pietrobono.* 3 vols. Turin: Società editrice internazionale, 1924–1930.

Pincherle, Alberto. "Agostino." *Enciclopedia dantesca,* 1:80–82.

Rivighi, Sofia Vanni. "Bonaventura." *Enciclopedia dantesca,* 1:669–673.

Singleton, Charles. *Dante Studies 2. Journey to Beatrice.* Cambridge, Mass.: Harvard University Press, 1958.

Vecchi, Alberto. "Dante e San Bernardo." *Benedictina* 7.2 (1953), 181–190.

Amilcare A. Iannucci

Theory and Criticism (Contemporary)

If by contemporary criticism we wish to designate the sequence of theoretical trends that has defined what readers do with texts, largely since the end of the Second World War—American New Criticism, structuralism, reader response theory, semiotics, post-structuralism and deconstruction, Marxist critique, psychoanalysis, feminism, race and gender studies, queer theory—we are, at least at first glance, struck by the apparent impenetrability of institutional Dante studies by these larger trends. Such resistance is all the more puzzling when we consider the centrality of Dante's texts in the work of earlier critics such as Benedetto Croce, T. S. Eliot, and Erich Auerbach, who might all somewhat reductively be said to represent the kind of esthetic reading to which so much of contemporary theory responds in its defining gesture. As we know, however, Dante criticism as an institutional practice predates even T. S. Eliot. Perhaps the birth and steady, independent growth of a centuries-old commentary tradition on the *Commedia* has lent Dante studies a confidence that allows *dantisti*, unperturbed by current fashion and keenly aware of the many who have gone before them, to remain focused on the quasi-fetishistic, hermeneutical unfolding of that single text.

But surely, to assert that Dante studies has proceeded untouched by contemporary theory would be an exaggeration. A degree of interaction between contemporary theory and Dante studies has come to pass in three relatively distinct genres. In the first instance, there exist very few attempts to engage directly one or another school of contemporary theory and apply that theory to Dante's text. Secondly, there are several American and European *dantisti* whose work, while not aggressively or systematically engaging contemporary theory, nonetheless reflects one or more of its basic tenets and makes casual use of its strategies. Finally, there are many illustrious theorists from outside the world of professional *dantisti* for whom Dante has been an occasional focus of attention.

The first class can be dispensed with in brief. In *Dante's Inferno: Difficulty and Dead Poetry* (1987), Robin Kirkpatrick offers a reading of *Inferno* which sees in Dante's continual focus on the functions and misfunctions of language an anticipation of contemporary theoretical concerns. In *Dante and Difference: Writing in the Commedia* (1988), Jeremy Tambling evokes the central Derridean category of *écriture* to resist traditional allegorical interpretations and characterize the *Commedia*, in classic deconstructive form, as a text ultimately interested in its own fragmented textuality. In *Timely Readings: Between Exegesis and Interpretation* (1988), Susan Noakes inherits

Paul de Man's fascination with temporality and the reading process in an attempt to offer models of reading from Dante to Baudelaire. More recently, Giuliana Carugati's *Dalla menzogna al silenzio: La scrittura mistica della Commedia di Dante* (1991) takes a declaredly post-structuralist approach to the representation of mystical experience in the *Commedia*.

Among Dante scholars whose work often reflects, though seldom directly cites, contemporary theory, one might first turn to Charles Singleton himself. Singleton's quasi-mystical emphasis on form and number reflects American New Critical attitudes, as well as a certain structuralism (despite his occasional disavowal of that movement). One need only think of the title of his groundbreaking *Dante Studies 1. Commedia: Elements of Structure* (1954; rpt. 1977). In many ways, John Freccero inherited Singleton's concern for the *Commedia*'s underlying form. Freccero's essays (collected in *Dante: The Poetics of Conversion,* 1986) explore the Augustinian paradigm of conversion as it inheres in the temporal unfolding of the poem. Directly engaged with contemporary theory is Freccero's eventual de Manian focus on the rhetorical figure of irony (see, for example, "Infernal Irony: The Gates of Hell").

Indeed, much of contemporary theory might fall under the general rubric of rhetorical criticism, concerned as it is with literary discourse as power and the complex ways in which literary texts deploy language to create authority. Many of Singleton's and Freccero's scholarly heirs pursue variations on these themes in their readings of Dante. Giuseppe Mazzotta's essays frequently ponder and problematize the relation between sign and referent in language indebted to both semiotics and deconstruction (see *Dante, Poet of the Desert: History and Allegory in the Divine Comedy,* 1979, and *Dante's Vision and the Circle of Knowledge,* 1993). In "Models of Literary Influence in the Comedy" (*Medieval Texts & Contemporary Readers,* edited by Laurie A. Finke and Martin B. Shichtman, 1987), Rachel Jacoff has considered the complex dynamics of intertextuality in the *Commedia*. Robert Pogue Harrison's reading of the *Vita Nuova* in *The Body of Beatrice* (1988) traces the phenomenological function of Beatrice's body in ways that implicate contemporary discussions of the linguistic sign. Albert Russell Ascoli has analyzed the rhetorical construction of authority in the *Convivio* ("The Vowels of Authority:

Convivio IV.vi.3–4" in *Discourses of Authority in Medieval and Renaissance Literature*, edited by Kevin Brownlee and Walter Stephens, 1989, pp. 23–46) and *De vulgari eloquentia* ("Neminem Ante Nos: Historicity and Authority in the *De vulgari eloquentia*," *Annali d'Italianistica* 8 [1990]). In *The Undivine Comedy: Detheologizing Dante* (1992), Teodolinda Barolini has challenged the ways in which the *Commedia*'s rhetorical strategies entrap the reader within its author's theological worldview.

With specific reference to psychoanalysis, Roger Dragonetti invoked Lacan to explicate "The Double Play of Arnaut Daniel's Sestina and Dante's *Divina Commedia*" in *Literature and Psychoanalysis: The Question of Reading: Otherwise,* edited by Shoshana Felman (1982). While predominantly historical and philological, Maria Corti's work nonetheless betrays her ardent interest in contemporary semiotics: see *Il viaggio testuale: Le ideologie e le strutture semiotiche* (1978); *La felicità mentale: Nuove prospettive per Cavalcanti e Dante* (1983); and *Dante a un nuovo crocevia* (1982). Though unconcerned with theoretical (French) feminism, Joan M. Ferrante in *Woman as Image in Medieval Literature: From the Twelfth Century to Dante* (1975) and Victoria Kirkham in "A Canon of Women in Dante's *Commedia*," *Annali d'Italianistica* 7 (1989) have analyzed the role of women in the *Commedia*. Somewhat more provocative is Joy Potter's essay on Beatrice's mute disempowerment, "Beatrice, Dead or Alive: Love in the *Vita Nuova*," *Texas Studies in Literature and Language* 32.1 (1990). The larger realm of gender studies is exemplified by Rachel Jacoff, "Transgression and Transcendence: Figures of Female Desire in Dante's *Commedia*," *Romanic Review* 79 (1988), and Jeffrey T. Schnapp, "Dante's Sexual Solecisms: Gender and Genre in the *Commedia*" *Romanic Review* 79 (1988), as well as by Madison U. Sowell, "Dante's Poetics of Sexuality," *Exemplaria* 5.2 (1993). Extraordinary interest in the figure and function of Brunetti Latini has developed recently among readers attentive to issues of medieval sexuality and queer theory; see, for example, Joseph Pequigney, "Sodomy in Dante's *Inferno* and *Purgatorio*," *Representations* 36 (1991).

Finally, we must not overlook the many, albeit often brief, references to Dante found in the pages of seminal works of contemporary theory. These sometimes casual citations can nonetheless pro-

vide wonderfully suggestive and truly new conceptual modes of thought to the serious Dante scholar. They can begin to help us recognize the myriad connections that exist between our efforts and interests and those of the larger world of cultural studies.

Mikhail Bakhtin's early materialist emphasis on language in its social context includes Dante among its many sources of literary reference. See in particular Bakhtin's exploration of vertical and horizontal form in relation to historical temporality in the *Commedia* in "Forms of Time and of the Chronotope in the Novel: Four Essays" in *The Dialogic Imagination,* edited by Michael Holquist (1981). (For an attempt to read Dante's Renaissance commentators in light of Bakhtin's concept of dialogism and Hans Robert Jauss's reception theory, see Deborah Parker, *Commentary and Ideology: Dante in the Renaissance,* 1993.) While defying easy categorization, Kenneth Burke foreshadows contemporary theoretical discourse by emphasizing the rhetorical priority of language to thought or objective reality (see, for instance, his comments on the relations among the unconscious, the *De vulgari eloquentia,* and D. H. Lawrence in *A Rhetoric of Motives,* 1950). On Dante and the New Critics, see Frederic Jameson, *The Prison-House of Language: A Critical Account of Structuralism and Russian Formalism* (1972), where he also uses Dante's *Paradiso* as a sample text to mount a critique of Formalist and Structuralist procedures.

Within structuralism, Dante's name was frequently on the lips of the participants at the seminal 1966 Johns Hopkins University symposium recorded in *The Structuralist Controversy* (1972), edited by Richard Macksey and Eugenio Donato. Reader response theory is at the heart of the exchange of ideas on authorial intention instigated by Singleton with, among others, Georges Poulet and René Girard. Poulet takes the *Commedia* as his point of departure in *Les Métamorphoses du Cercle* (1961). For a reading of Dante on the cusp between structuralism and poststructuralism by a central protagonist of French theory, see Phillipe Sollers, "Dante et la traversée de l'écriture," *Tel Quel* 23 (1965). For a review of structuralism's influence on Italian Dante criticism, see David Robey, "Literary theory and critical practice in Italy: formalist, structuralist and semiotic approaches to the *Divine Comedy*," *Comparative Criticism* 7 (1985).

Among archetypal and psychoanalytic critics, Northrop Frye cites Dante throughout *Anatomy of Criticism* (1957): *Inferno* depicts an archetypal image of nightmare, while *Purgatorio* resonates with primal forms of the myth of rebirth. A more recent attempt at archetypal criticism is found in Marthe Dozon, *Mythe et Symbole dans la Divine Comédie* (1991). Harold Bloom has repeatedly used Dante to explicate his Oepidal theory of literary influence: see in particular *Ruin the Sacred Truths: Poetry and Belief from the Bible to the Present* (1989). On Bloom and Dante, see Paul Colilli's "Harold Bloom and the Post-theological Dante," which provides as well a useful bibliography and the most extensive overview of contemporary theoretical issues in Dante criticism to date, as does David Robey's "Dante and Modern American Criticism: Post-structuralism," both in *Annali d'Italianistica* 8 (1990). Among those taking up the Lacanian deconstructive model, Lacan himself offers an occasional, always enigmatic allusion to Dante: Paola and Francesca's kiss, for example, encapsulates the notion of fatal identification that arises from his musings on "Aggressivity in Psychoanalysis" in *Ecrits* (1977). Julia Kristeva's post-structuralist explorations of pre-subjective being have drawn her attention to medieval mysticism on more than one occasion. In *Powers of Horror: An Essay on Abjection* (1982), Kristeva hears echoes of the fearful jouissance that lies beyond the ego in the joyful laughter of the souls of *Paradiso* as they rejoice, at long last, in a "successful incest"; see also "Motherhood According to Bellini" in *Desire in Language: A Semiotic Approach to Literature and Art,* edited by Leon S. Roudiez (1980), and Kristeva's comments on the *De vulgari eloquentia* in *Language—the Unknown: An Initiation into Linguistics* (1989). In the vein of post-structuralist psychoanalytic feminism, there is Gayatri Chakravorty Spivak's reading of the *Vita Nuova,* "Finding Feminist Readings from Dante to Yeats" in *American Criticism in the Post-Structuralist Age* (1981).

On Dante and nationalism from a postcolonial perspective, one might begin with James Snead's brief remarks in "European pedigrees/African contagions" in the volume *Nation and Narration,* edited by Homi K. Bhabha (1990), and Edward W. Said's *Culture and Imperialism* (1993).

Gary P. Cestaro

Theseus

Son of Aegeus and king of Athens. Theseus *(Teseo)* appears three times in the *Commedia,* always in confrontation with monstrous or demonic powers. The Furies complain of not having avenged his invasion of the underworld (*Inf.* 9.54) when, with Pirithoüs, he sought to abduct Proserpina (and according to Virgil, *Aen.* 6.617–618, remained eternally imprisoned in Hades). Virgil recalls Theseus' slaying of the Minotaur at *Inf.* 12.16–20. In *Purg.* 24.121–123, gluttony is exemplified by the Centaurs, whose drunken violence at Pirithoüs' wedding was resisted by Theseus. In all these episodes, as in his intervention in the Theban war of Statius' *Thebaid* as allegorized by commentators, Theseus can perhaps be viewed as a figure of Christ in his redemptive role.

Winthrop Wetherbee

Thetis

Daughter of Nereus and Doris and mother of Achilles by Peleus, the semi-divine Thetis is one of the fifty Nereids who attend Neptune. Thetis *(Teti)* is first referred to in *Purg.* 9.37 when Dante parallels his confusion upon awakening in Ante-Purgatory to that of Achilles awakening in his mother's arms as she carries him to safety from the Trojan War. Later, in *Purg.* 22.113, we learn in Virgil's response to a question posed by Statius that Thetis resides in Limbo with the Latin and Greek poets and heroines from Statius' own poems (the *Thebaid* and the *Achilleid*).

Maria Ann Roglieri

Thieves

Dante places thieves in the seventh section of the circle of fraud, the Malebolge, thereby defining their crime as the taking of other's property by deceptive means; this is in contrast to robbers, who are placed in the circle of violence, and reverses the Thomistic ordering of the two kinds of crime, which holds robbery worse than theft because it involves physical harm to the victim. Dante considers deception worse because it betrays the natural trust between people and thus undermines the social structure. The kinds of theft he has in mind, presumably, are dubious financial dealings, not simple usury, which is relegated to the circle of violence.

Dante among the thieves. La comedia, *ed. Pietro da Figino, 1491. Giamatti Collection: Courtesy of the Mount Holyoke College Archives and Special Collections.*

Among the souls Dante sees in the two cantos devoted to thieves, *Inf.* 24 and 25, are members of major merchant-banking families, the Brunelleschi, Cavalcanti, and Donati. The thieves undergo continuous metamorphoses to and from serpents, the emblem of deception. The words Dante uses for the changes—*converte, trasmutò, cambiar*—may have been intended to suggest the lucrative practice of money-changing, the Arte del Cambio being one of the three major guilds in Florence.

Since Dante chooses this place in his poem to make his strongest statement of challenge to his poetic rivals, Ovid and Lucan, from whom he draws heavily in his descriptions of the metamorphoses, he may also be presenting himself as a thief of poetry, who steals from others—he acknowledges the debt to Ovid and Lucan here, but not to Virgil, whose words he uses covertly— even if he puts their goods to a better purpose.

Bibliography

Beal, Rebecca. "Dante among Thieves: Allegorical Soteriology in the Seventh Bolgia (*Inferno* XXIV and XXV)." *Medievalia* 9 (1986 for 1983), 101–123.

Ferrante, Joan M. "Good Thieves and Bad Thieves: A Reading of *Inferno* XXIV." *Dante Studies* 104 (1986), 83–98.

Skulsky, Harold. "Thieves and Suicides in the *Inferno:* Metamorphosis as the State of Sin." In *Metamorphosis: The Mind in Exile.* Cambridge, Mass., London: Harvard University Press, 1981, pp. 114–128, 232–234.

Terdiman, Richard. "Problematical Virtuosity: Dante's Depiction of the Thieves (*Inf.* XXIV–XXV)." *Dante Studies* 91 (1973), 27–45.

Joan M. Ferrante

Thisbe

The earliest extant literary version of the dire story of Thisbe, the Babylonian maiden whose marriage to Pyramus is forbidden by their parents, appears in *Meta.* 4.55–166. This Ovidian tale constituted a poignant and influential account of the love-death theme for medieval authors.

Dante refers to Thisbe *(Tisbe)* only once by name, in *Purg.* 27.37, in a simile comparing a fearful Dante-pilgrim, who is inspired by the name of Beatrice to enter the purifying flames atop Mount Purgatory, to the moribund Pyramus, who revives briefly at the name of Thisbe (see *Purg.* 27.37–39). Dante-poet, in likening Beatrice to Thisbe, emphasizes not only the power of a woman's name (and the inspiration the female represents) but also the distance between the pagan Thisbe, who can revive but not rescue, and the Christian Beatrice, who can both inspire and save.

Madison U. Sowell

Timaeus

Plato's cosmological dialogue, the *Timaeus (Timeo),* was known in the medieval period through the incomplete fourth-century translation and commentary of Calcidius. Though the rediscovery of Aristotle's physics exposed the unscientific character of Plato's cosmology, his mythical cosmic model remained influential. The "happiness" of the *motor primo* of *Purg.* 25.70–71, clearly Aristotle's "prime mover," may also recall the creator of *Timaeus* 37C, who rejoices in the power of the created world to emulate its divine exemplar. In *Par.* 4, Beatrice finds the idea that "the soul returns to its star" after death (*Timaeus* 42B; *Par.* 4.22–24, 49–54; *Conv.* 4.21.2) sufficiently attractive to redeem it through allegory (55–60). Conversely, at *Conv.* 3.5.6 Plato's claim that Earth rotates about its center (*Timaeus* 40B) is refuted by Aristotle's notion of a wholly immobile Earth (*De coelo et mundo* 2.13–14).

Dante may not have known the *Timaeus* directly. He knew Boethius' *Consolation of Philosophy* (3, metr. 9), a brilliant distillation of Plato's ideas. The affirmation of divine benevolence in *Par.* 7.64–66, which recalls *Timaeus* 29E, is verbally closer to *Cons.* 3, metr. 9.6–7. But Beatrice seems to consider tone as well as substance in Timaeus' comments on the destiny of the soul: *come dice, par che senta* ("it appears that he means what he says literally," *Par.* 4.51), suggesting a firsthand knowledge of the text.

Winthrop Wetherbee

Tiresias

Dante sees Tiresias *(Tiresia)* punished in the fourth pouch of the Malebolge (*Inf.* 20.40–45), among the classical diviners, each of whom is represented more negatively by Dante than by the epic poems that were Dante's sources. Although Theban Tiresias was a famous prophetic figure in antiquity, the only part of his story that Dante retells is the bizarre episode from *Meta.* 3.322–338 in which Tiresias undergoes gender metamorphosis. He was changed into a woman when he struck a stick between two copulating serpents, and then seven years later he changed back into a man by reenacting the same gesture. In Ovid this allows Tiresias to be the arbiter of an argument between Juno and Jove about whether men or women have more pleasure in lovemaking; when Tiresias agrees with Jove that women have more pleasure, he is punished with blindness by Juno and then rewarded with the gift of prophecy by Jove. Some critics have claimed that Dante's negative portrayal of Tiresias owes something to his reading of the *Thebaid*, in which Tiresias is associated with necromancy, but Dante's brief description of Tiresias makes no reference to any of his activities as a prophet.

Bibliography

Hollander, Robert. "The Tragedy of Divination in *Inferno XX*." In *Studies in Dante*. Ravenna: Longo, 1980, pp. 173–184.

Rachel Jacoff

Tithonus

Tithonus *(Titone)* is a mortal granted eternal life, but not eternal youth, by his wife, Aurora, the goddess of the dawn. In a critically disputed modification of Virgil, who designates daybreak by describing Aurora's departure from her husband's bed (*Aen.* 4.584–585, 9.459–460; *Georg.* 1.446–447), Dante depicts sunrise with a portrayal of Tithonus' mistress leaving her lover's bed (*Purg.* 9.1–6). Prevalent opinion holds that the awakening of Tithonus' mistress signifies either the time of the lunar dawn or the time in Purgatory at the hour of the Italian solar dawn.

Bibliography

Moore, Edward. *The Time-References in the Divina Commedia*. London: D. Nutt, 1887.

Jessica Levenstein

Titus

Son of Vespasian and Roman emperor from 79 to 81 C.E. Titus *(Tito)* is referred to by Statius on the fifth terrace of Purgatory (*Purg.* 21.82) and mentioned by Emperor Justinian in the Heaven of Mercury (*Par.* 6.92). Dante, following Orosius (*Hist.* 7.3.8, 9.9), holds that the destruction of Jerusalem by Titus was God's punishment of the Jews for the Crucifixion of Christ (see *Par.* 7).

R. A. Malagi

Tityus

Giant who tried to rape Latona, for which crime he was killed by her children, Apollo and Diana, and flung into Hades, where he lies stretched over a very large area while vultures eternally prey on his liver. Tityus *(Tizio)* belongs to the classical canon of mythological sufferers in the underworld. Dante places him, coupled with Typhon, among the giants who tower around the pit of Cocytus (*Inf.* 31.124).

Olivia Holmes

Tomyris

Scythian queen of the Massagetae whose army ambushed the Persian tyrant Cyrus after his treacherous murder of her son. Decapitating her enemy, she threw his head into a vessel filled with human blood and mocked his bloodlust (Orosius, *Hist.* 2.7.6). Tomyris *(Tamiri)* is shown, in the marble pavement of the first terrace of Purgatory, as the avenger of Cyrus' act of pride in having rejected her appeal to release and spare her son (*Purg.*

12.56). In *Mon.* 2.8.6, Dante contrasts the divinely instituted Roman Empire with Cyrus' failure to carry out his plan of conquest.

Diana Cavuoto Glenn

Torquatus

A Roman general and consul of the republic, Titus Manlius Torquatus forbade his troops from engaging in single combat with the Latins. According to Livy (*Ab urbe condita* 8.7), his son disobeyed and, although victorious, was consequently condemned to death by his father. In *Conv.* 4.5.14, Dante adduces Torquatus' military fortitude in the face of paternal sentiment as testimony of divine involvement in the fortune of Rome. In *Par.* 6.46, Dante names Torquatus *(Torquato)* among those who carried the sign of the eagle against the enemy.

Jessica Levenstein

Toynbee, Paget Jackson

An active Dante scholar in England, Toynbee (1855–1932) prepared an index to the "Oxford Dante" (1894; works) edited by Edward Moore, which he expanded into the ever useful *Dictionary of Proper Names and Notable Matters in the Works of Dante* (1898; revised by Charles S. Singleton, 1968). Other works of Dantean interest are *Dante in English Literature from Chaucer to Cary* (1909), important for comparative studies; many articles collected in *Dante Studies and Researches* (1902; Italian version published in Bologna, 1899–1904) and in *Dante Studies* (1921); an important edition of Dante's *Epistolae* (1920, second edition, 1966); and an exhaustive bibliographical survey for the 1921 Dante centenary, *Britain's Tribute to Dante in Literature and Art* (1921).

A. L. Pellegrini

Tragedy

The term *tragedia* occurs infrequently in Dante's works and is usually employed in its classically rhetorical connotation rather than in reference to a work of drama or dramatic performance. Dante mentions *tragedia* in *DVE* 2.4.5–7, 2.8.8, and 2.12.3, 6, 8, 12; in *Conv.* 1.5.8; in *Inf.* 20.113; and in *Epistle to Cangrande* 13.10 (if Dante is its author). Dante's main source for the concept of tragedy is Horace's *Ars poetica,* which he quotes in *DVE* 2.4.4 (*Ars poetica,* vv. 38–40); in *Conv.* 2.13.10 (vv. 70–71); in *Vita Nuova* 25.9 (vv. 141–142); and in *Epistle to Cangrande* 13.10 (vv. 93–96). In *DVE* 2.4.5–7, Dante opposes the nobility of the tragic style to its lowly counterpart, the comic, while relegating the elegiac style to the lowest position of all: *Per tragediam superiorem stilum indicimus; per comediam inferiorem; per elegiam stilum intelligimus miserorum . . . Stilo equidem tragico tunc uti videmur, quando cum gravitate sententie tam superbia carminum quam constructionis elatio et excellentia vocabulorum concordat* ("By 'tragic' I mean the higher style, by 'comic' the lower, and by 'elegiac' that of the unhappy. . . . The tragic style is clearly to be used whenever both the magnificence of the verses and the lofty excellence of construction and vocabulary accord with the gravity of the subject matter"). Hence, Dante designates Virgil's *Aeneid* as a tragedy, having Virgil himself, a character in the *Commedia,* refer to his own work as *l'alta mia tragedìa* ("my high tragedy," *Inf.* 20.113). In *Inf.* 1.87 Virgil is identified by Dante as the author who taught him the *bello stilo* (the beautiful or tragic style of his poetry), for which Dante was so famed in his youth. Further on in *DVE* (2.8.8, 2.12.3), in his analysis of the canzone form, Dante cites his own canzone from the *Vita Nuova,* "Donne ch'avete intelletto d'amore," as an example of the tragic style. This poem is the first work in any European vernacular language in the Middle Ages to be associated by its author with the tragic style (Kelly). Further references to the tragic style occur in *DVE* 2.12.3, 6, 8, 12 with regard to meter. Explaining, in *Conv.* 1.5.8, why he chose the vernacular rather than Latin for his canzoni, Dante further clarifies the difference between the nobility of Latin and the impurity of the vernacular. In *Epistle to Cangrande* 13.10, the opposition between "comedy" and "tragedy" is spelled out in terms of contrasting subject matter and inverse development of plot: while comedy delineates the movement from conflict to a happy resolution, tragedy moves from happiness to misery. Dante may have derived his definition of these two terms from Uguiccione da Pisa's *Magnae derivationes.*

Bibliography

Baldelli, Ignazio. "Sulla teoria linguistica di Dante." *Cultura e scuola* 13–14 (1965), 710–713.

Hollander, Robert. "Tragedy in Dante's *Comedy.*" In *The Classical Heritage: Vergil.* Edited by Craig

Kallendorf. New York: Garland Publishing, 1993, pp. 253–269.

Jacomuzzi, Stefano. "La 'fantasia' tragica della *Commedia*." *Letture Classensi* 20–21 (1992), 185–194.

Kelly, Henry A. *Ideas and Forms of Tragedy from Aristotle to the Middle Ages.* Cambridge: Cambridge University Press, 1993.

Rajna, Pio. "Il titolo del poema dantesco." *Studi danteschi* 4 (1921), 6–9.

Alessandro Vettori

Traitors

When the configuration of Hell is described by Virgil, we learn that traitors are punished in the lowest circle: *nel cerchio minore, ov'è 'l punto / de l'universo in su che Dite siede, / qualunque trade in etterno è consunto* ("in the smallest circle, at the point of the universe where Dis is enthroned, whoever is a traitor is eternally consumed," *Inf.* 11.64–66). Dante links traitors to the sin of fraud, which is the abuse of trust, but distinguishes traitors from the fraudulent by specifying that while the latter betray only the bond of human nature, the former betray that bond as well as an additional trust. When Dante arrives at the ninth and final circle of Hell, he discovers that it is divided into four sections, based on which additional trust the souls have betrayed.

The first section, Caina, holds those who have betrayed members of their families and is named for Cain, who in the Old Testament slew his brother Abel. The second section, Antenora, holds those who have betrayed their countries or their political parties and is named after the Trojan Antenor, who, in medieval versions of the story of the fall of Troy, was held responsible for betraying the Trojans to the Greeks. The third section, Ptolomea, holds those who have betrayed friendship or the guest-host relationship and is named either after Ptolemy XII, king of Egypt and murderer of Pompey (first century B.C.E.), or after Ptolemy, the captain of Jericho, who murdered Simon the Maccabee at a banquet he hosted for Simon and his sons. And the last section, Judecca, reserved for traitors against benefactors, is named after Judas Iscariot, the apostle who betrayed Jesus Christ. While the sources for these divisions and the ethical distinctions behind them have not been definitively identified, some early commentators (including Jacopo and the *Ottimo Commento*) point

out that Dante, in keeping with his particularly social conception of sin, condemns the betrayers of social bonds (hospitality, friendship, gratitude) more forcefully than he does the betrayers of the more "natural" bonds (kinship, patriotism)—because, as Joan Ferrante puts it, the former "are the quintessential social relations and cannot be denied without destroying society itself" (190).

The traitors' punishment is eternal immersion in a lake formed by the waters of the river Cocytus *(Cocito),* which are frozen by the frigid wind generated by the beating wings of Lucifer, who stands immobile at the center of Judecca, the ultimate traitor: the angel who rebelled against God. He, too, is fixed in the ice, but he also executes the special punishment destined to the three greatest traitors among mortals: Judas, who betrayed Christ; and Brutus and Cassius, who betrayed Julius Caesar. The soul of each of these three men is chewed by one of Lucifer's three mouths. Brutus and Cassius are eaten feet first, while Judas' head and upper body have disappeared inside, and the rest of his body is being brutally scratched, so that he is *quell'anima . . . c'ha maggior pena* ("the soul . . . who has the greatest punishment," *Inf.* 34.61).

Just before reaching Lucifer, Dante encounters many Italian traitors connected to the hostili-

Dante and Virgil approaching Cocytus, the last circle of Hell. Dante, with commentary by Cristofo Landino and Alessandro Vellutello, published in Venice in 1564 by Marchiò Sessa & fratelli. Giamatti Collection: Courtesy of the Mount Holyoke College Archives and Special Collections.

Dante pulling the hair of the traitor Bocca degli Abati. Opere del divino poeta Danthe, ed. Pietro da Figino, Venice, 1520. Giamatti Collection: Courtesy of the Mount Holyoke College Archives and Special Collections.

Ferrante, Joan. *The Political Vision of the Divine Comedy.* Princeton, N.J.: Princeton University Press, 1984.

Giacomelli, Marco. "L'ordinamento penale nell' *Inferno* dantesco." In *Dante in the Twentieth Century.* Boston: Dante University of America, 1982, pp. 90–98.

Moliterno, Gino. "Mouth to Mandible, Man to *lupa:* The Moral Lesson of Cocytus." *Dante Studies* 104 (1986), 145–161.

Moore, Edward. "The Classification of the Sins in Dante's *Inferno* and *Purgatorio.*" *Studies in Dante. Second Series: Miscellaneous Essays.* Oxford: Clarendon Press, 1899 (reprinted in 1968), pp. 152–209.

Morgan, Alison. *Dante and the Medieval Other World.* Cambridge, New York: Cambridge University Press, 1990.

Reade, W. H. *The Moral System of Dante's "Inferno."* Oxford: Oxford University Press, 1909, pp. 354–366.

Scott, John A. "Treachery in Dante." In *Studies in the Italian Renaissance: Essays in Memory of Arnolfo B. Ferruolo.* Edited by G. P. Biasin et al. Naples: Società Editrice Napoletana, 1984, pp. 27–42.

Triolo, Alfred A. "Matta Bestialità in Dante's *Inferno:* Theory and Image." *Traditio* 24 (1968), 247–292.

Claudia Rattazzi Papka

ties between Guelfs and Ghibellines, including, in the second zone, Bocca degli Abati, the Florentine Guelf whose betrayal caused the bloody defeat at Montaperti and whose hair Dante violently tears from his head. He and his companion sinner Fra Alberigo suffer a special and unusual punishment for their heinous acts of evil: even before they have died on Earth, both find their souls placed in Hell and their bodies possessed by devils. As Fra Alberigo announces to Dante: *Cotal vantaggio ha questa Tolomea, / che spesse volte l'anima ci cade / innanzi ch'Atropòs mossa le dea* ("Ptolomea has this advantage, that often the soul falls here before Atropos cuts it off," *Inf.* 33.124–126). The rule of Ptolomea, whose severity is imaginative but theologically unorthodox, appears to derive from popular tradition, but it finds some basis in the New Testament ("Then Satan entered into Judas," Luke 22:3). In the previous zone, Antenora, Dante encounters one of the most memorable figures of the *Commedia,* Count Ugolino della Gherardesca, frozen in ice along with the man who betrayed him, the archbishop of Pisa, Ruggieri degli Ubaldini, on whose head Ugolino, still trapped in his earthly hatred, eternally gnaws.

Bibliography

Cassell, Anthony. *Dante's Fearful Art of Justice.* Toronto: University of Toronto Press, 1984.

Trajan

Marcus Ulpius Traianus, born in 53 C.E., Roman emperor from 98 to 117. Trajan was renowned for his moral rectitude and his dedication to justice in government affairs. In his *Life of Pope Gregory the Great,* written at the end of the eighth century, Paul the Deacon recorded a legendary act of humility on the part of Trajan. When a widow appealed to him that justice be done for her son who had been unjustly slain, Trajan delayed his departure for war in order to reestablish the law and grant the woman her wish. The episode is presented on the terrace of the proud as an example of humility (*Purg.* 10.73–93). Here the scene, carved out on the stone wall of the mountain, is perhaps the most charming of the series: the widow *(vedovella)* holds back the emperor, amid the crowd of armed cavalry, flags flying in the wind. In the brief, intense dialogue, her insistence wins Trajan's heart, and he finally yields to her appeal: *giustizia vuole e pietà mi ritiene* ("justice demands it and compassion holds me here"). The same event is recalled in the Heaven of the Just Rulers in *Par.* 20.43–45, where Dante surprisingly places Trajan *(Traiano)*, together with another pagan, Ripheus, in Paradise, as great examples of justice. The salvation of Trajan was theologically problematic for the culture of the period: How could a pagan enter Heaven? Did not Church doctrine insist that baptism and faith in Christ were necessary for that end to be achieved? Dante followed tradition in accepting the legend that Trajan's soul went to Hell upon his death but that the prayers of Gregory the Great (stirred by Trajan's act of compassion and justice) brought him back to life so that he might have knowledge of and believe in Christ and thereby, after a second bodily death, be granted salvation. As a result of Paul the Deacon's eighth-century and John the Deacon's late-ninth-century lives of Gregory, the event was frequently recited in the Middle Ages (in the compilation entitled *Fiore di filosofi* and in Vincent of Beauvais' *Speculum historiale*) and ultimately became accepted as a miracle by theologians (see Aquinas, *ST* 3 Suppl. 71.5). Trajan's appearance among the Just Rulers in Paradise, together with that of Ripheus, constitutes an answer to Dante's question about how the righteous and good who never had the opportunity of knowing Christ can justly be damned for eternity (*Par.* 19.69–78). The first explicit reply, articulated in the words of the holy eagle that represents divine justice, summarizes a Christian theological position that has its roots in the teaching of St. Paul: man should not presume to judge God's actions, which infinitely transcend human reason; and man must surrender himself to God through faith (Rom. 10:14–21; Augustine, *In Ioannis Evangelium* 26.2). But the presence of the two pagans among the saved suggests as well another answer, one that had the endorsement of eminent theologians from Albert the Great to St. Thomas: God has the power to reveal the truth of Christ's being to the righteous who are ignorant of it, either directly, through angels or other intermediaries, or by unknown means (see Albert the Great, *Sent.* d. 25 B a. 2; Aquinas, 4 *Sent.* d. 27, q. 1. a. 4). This theological rationale underlies the Trajan episode in *Paradiso,* whose conceptual and emotional essence centers on the gospel quotation of Matt. 11:12 which Dante introduces in Latin and then translates: *Regnum cælorum vïolenza pate / da caldo amore e da viva speranza / che vince la divina volontate* ("*Regnum celorum* suffers the violence of burning love and lively hope, which conquer God's will," *Par.* 20.94–96).

Bibliography

Chiavacci Leonardi, A. M. "Un uom nasce a la riva." In *Dante Alighieri, Commedia*. Vol. 3. Milan: Mondadori, 1997, pp. 546–548.

Graf, Arturo. *Roma nella memoria e nelle immagini del Medioevo*. Turin: Loescher, 1882–1883.

Paratore, Ettore. "Il canto XX del *Paradiso*." In *Tradizione e struttura in Dante*. Florence: Sansoni, 1968, pp. 281–314.

Paris, Gaston. *La légende de Trajan*. Paris: Imprimerie nationale, 1878.

Paul the Deacon. *S. Gregorii Magni vita*. PL 75, cols. 59–242.

Vickers, Nancy. "Seeing Is Believing: Gregory, Trajan, and Dante's Art." *Dante Studies* 101 (1983), 67–85.

Whatley, Gordon. "The Uses of Hagiography: The Legend of Pope Gregory and the Emperor Trajan in the Middle Ages." *Viator* 15 (1984), 25–63.

*Anna Maria Chiavacci Leonardi
(translated by Susan Gaylard)*

Translations in English

The Divine Comedy

Ever since Chaucer, English poets have read and imitated Dante and even translated brief passages, but only in 1782 did Charles Rogers provide English readers with the first translation of a complete work, the *Inferno,* in blank verse. Three years later Henry Boyd provided another *Inferno,* in rhymed six-line stanzas. But it was Henry Francis Cary's first complete translation of the *Commedia* in 1805–1806 with facing Italian text that opened Dante's poem to English-speaking readers. Cary (1772–1844), an accomplished translator of Greek and French poetry, cast the *Commedia* into large Miltonic verse paragraphs of unrhymed verse in the lexicon of English poetry, obscuring the tercet structure of the original and the integrity of individual verses. Initially he intended to publish the *Inferno* in Italian; an English translation was an afterthought. In 1815 he published his translation of the complete poem whose new title, *The Vision of Dante,* made it appear a traditional English long poem. High printing costs made the inclusion of the Italian original impossible this time. This minuscule edition with barely legible type attracted scant attention until favorable mention by Coleridge and Foscolo in 1818 launched its long career, bringing Dante to readers such as Blake and Keats. Cary's restrained, almost monotonous diction conveys little of the poem's tension and energy, but nonetheless this is the only nineteenth-century version to combine accuracy and some poetic merit. Throughout the nineteenth century and into the twentieth it saw many editions, often with illustrations by Blake, Flaxman, and Doré.

Four decades later the American poet Henry Wadsworth Longfellow (1807–1882), a professor of romance languages at Harvard, published the second great nineteenth-century verse translation. Beginning in the 1840s, he read his translation aloud at weekly meetings of the Dante Society in his Cambridge home. From 1865 to 1867, when the complete *Commedia* appeared, many of his friends acclaimed it, while others voiced reservations. W. D. Howells observed that Longfellow had rendered Dante's poem not into the English language but into the English dictionary. Another reviewer noted that it was not really in verse but in "poetic prose in a tripartite arrangement." Longfellow had in fact adopted the happy innovation of another translator, W. F. Pollock (1854), of arranging the unrhymed verse in tercets. Longfellow's translation exhibited the virtues and vices of his own verse: homespun simplicity, sentimentality, and a certain glibness. His heavy use of cognate and Latinate words rendered some passages barely comprehensible. While the translation was criticized as too literal, Longfellow's defenders cited his modest intention of translating "the words not the meaning." More literal than Cary's, his version was of greater use to would-be readers of the Italian. None of the ten or more versions in unrhymed verse in the nineteenth century won the large audiences that Cary and Longfellow enjoyed.

The first prose translation appeared only in 1849, when John Aitken Carlyle (1801–1879), brother of Thomas, published a well-received, lively rendition of the *Inferno* remarkable for its heavy use of capitalization and eccentric punctuation. (Prose translations had already appeared in Germany and France in the eighteenth century.) He too conceived of the ideal reader as a lover of poetry who needed help in tackling Dante's Italian. He positioned the Italian text at the top of the page, followed by the translation and notes, which often included a freer, clearer translation.

By the end of the nineteenth century the *Commedia* was reaching a broader and better-informed public in part because of the large number of translations. Forty translators had provided a total of more than eighty versions of individual *cantiche*. Strong traditions of Dante scholarship had begun in Italy, England, and the United States. In 1889 Edward Moore (1835–1926), for example, published his monumental *Contributions to the Textual Criticism of the Divina Commedia*. Better texts became available, such as Moore's own Oxford edition of Dante's complete Italian and Latin works (1894). Most of Dante's minor works had by then been translated (see below). The *Commedia* had become a classic, and its author had been defined as the "central man of all the ages" (Ruskin). From these changed circumstances two important translations were to emerge.

In 1891–1892 another Harvard professor, Charles Eliot Norton (1827–1908), published a prose translation in large paragraphs of the *Commedia* based on Moore's correction of Witte's text and fortified with a modicum of useful notes. Longfellow's verse rhythms reverberated through his disciple's more literally accurate prose revision. Although Howells found this mildly archaic version "literal with a difference," others deemed it pedestrian and too literal. Of the three *cantiche*, most readers preferred Norton's *Inferno*, whose vitality owed something to Carlyle's rendition. After a careful revision in 1902, Norton's version, like Cary's and Longfellow's, continued to be reprinted well into the twentieth century.

The second important translation to appear in this period was a collaborative effort. Its guiding spirit, Philip Wicksteed (1844–1927), launched the Temple Classics series in 1899 with his own edition of the Italian text and with his own translation and notes. He modestly defined what became one of the most influential English translations of Dante as having been conceived "for the sole purpose of enabling the publisher to bring out a cheap edition of the text, accompanied by an English version." He produced the series for the general public and also readers who, as T. S. Eliot later noted, "can follow the Italian even gropingly." Its six slim, pocket-size, blue volumes, at two shillings apiece, contained the *Commedia* (in English and Italian) and all the minor works, and appeared in short order (1899–1904). Like its competitors, it sought literal accuracy in dignified literary language. Extensive inversion and archaism, including pseudo-Elizabethan neologisms, reduced somewhat the lucidity to which Wicksteed aspired. The layout's Bible-like versets reflected Dante's original tercets. Wicksteed's prose, like Norton's, had a tendency to lapse into blank verse. He prefaced each canto with an essay-like introduction, or "argument," which he coordinated with his extensive notes, diagrams, tables, and appendices, whose length and quality distinguished the series from its competitors. In 1900 Carlyle's *Inferno,* as revised by Wicksteed and Thomas Okey, appeared in the series, followed in 1903 by Okey's own translation of the *Purgatorio,* edited and annotated by Hermann Oelsner but with Wicksteed's "arguments." This was the edition most used by poets in English throughout the world until the 1960s, when it went out of print. Nothing comparable replaced it. (The Pléiade series in France published André Pézard's one-volume translation of Dante's complete works in 1965.)

The Temple Dante reigned unchallenged until 1939, when John Dickinson Sinclair (1865–1921), dissatisfied with Wicksteed's translation, began publishing a new prose translation with facing Italian in three volumes, which he completed in 1946. A theologian rather than a scholar or medievalist— a minister, in fact, of the Church of Scotland—Sinclair had devoted a lifetime to study of the poem. His up-to-date, scholarly commentary, in the form of short essays following each canto, were an improvement on Wicksteed's brief notes. He abandoned late-nineteenth-century literary English for a neutral tongue that was neither contemporary nor colloquial and that avoided inversion, archaism, and oddity. As with his predecessors, literal accuracy came at the price of diminished intensity. Well received by the general public, Sinclair's translation became the preferred text in college and university courses in the English-speaking world.

Between 1971 and 1975 the leading American *dantista,* Charles S. Singleton (1909–1985), published an important edition of the *Commedia* with the support of the Bollingen Foundation. Volumes 1, 3, and 5 contained Petrocchi's text with minor modifications along with his prose translation. Volumes 2, 4, and 6 provided the longest commentary to date in English, notable for generous citation of primary sources in the original language, followed by translations. Singleton cast his version in language close to that of Sinclair, Wicksteed, and Norton, whom he corrected and revised. Widely respected, Singleton's edition became a preferred academic version, although without displacing Sinclair.

In 1996 Robert Durling, an American Dante scholar who had made the first English translation of Petrarch's *Rerum vulgarium fragmenta,* published his translation of the *Inferno,* the first volume in a projected complete *Commedia.* His Italian text, like Singleton's, followed the Petrocchi critical edition, with occasional differences. Durling's prose translation offered a fresh rendering from the Italian rather than a revision of earlier versions. It followed the order of Dante's often complex syntax and was arranged in versets that match the original *terzine.* Trenchant, informative notes by Durling and another American Dante scholar, Ronald Martinez, synthesized the critical tradition on many key issues.

Beginning in 1843 there were also many translations in *terza rima.* In the nineteenth century, eight triple-rhymed versions of the entire *Commedia* had appeared, as had several of the *Inferno.* Suffering from the constrictions of triple rhyme in rhyme-poor English, these early translations often degenerated into paraphrase and doggerel and had little impact. In the twentieth century, in reaction to the dullness of unrhymed and prose translations, five notable *terza rima* versions appeared. In 1921 the twenty-year labor of Melville Best Anderson (1851–1933) won critical favor for its accuracy and polish. Three years later another American, Louis How (1873–1947), produced an ill-received version full of colloquialisms, Americanisms, and nonliterary language.

The most important *terza rima* versions came from Great Britain. The poet and historian of Asian art, Laurence Binyon (1869–1943), published his version with facing Italian text between 1934 and 1943. Ezra Pound, who served as his close advisor, observed that its archaism, inversions, and language "never spoken on land or sea" were not necessarily inappropriate for a fourteenth-century poem. He pronounced it the most interesting English Dante and thought it would replace the Temple version. Another poet translator, Robert Fitzgerald, subsequently admired its accuracy, clarity, and fluency. In the oft-reprinted *Viking Portable Dante* (1947) Binyon's version (without the Italian text) enjoyed a broad public for many decades in the United States.

Partly in reaction to Binyon, the British writer Dorothy Sayers (1893–1957) published a *terza rima* rendition which sought to capture the poem's "speed, humor and flexibility." Her success in rendering the poem's narrative drive led to sales of 50,000 copies of the *Inferno* in its first six months (1949) in the new Penguin series. Some criticized this exuberant translation for boldly mixing the colloquial and the archaic and found its lively notes slick and brash. C. S. Lewis praised its "cheerful energy" but thought, as did others, that Sayers, who presented herself as neither an Italianist or Dante scholar, had misheard Dante's meter. Many thought that she found humor in Dante where there was none. Barbara Reynolds completed the final thirteen cantos of the *Paradiso* after Sayers's death. In the postwar years, Sayers's and Binyon's versions gained a wider reading public for Dante than ever before.

Perhaps the most painstaking version in triple rhyme was that of Geoffrey Bickersteth (1884–1974), a British professor of English and a philologist, who had previously translated Leopardi and Carducci. He first published a translation of the *Paradiso* in 1932 and then the entire *Commedia* in 1955 with minimal notes. Later editions and revisions (1965, 1972, 1981) included the Italian. He too wanted a text that could stand on its own as an English poem but that could also be read with the Italian. He composed his very accurate version in a contemporary English that was, however, not free of instances of inversion and archaism.

Three Americans produced versions in "defective *terza rima*," a rhyme scheme developed a century and a half earlier by August Wilhelm von Schlegel, in which the middle line remains unrhymed, affording the translator greater freedom while preserving much of the effect of the original form. In 1931 the American professor Jefferson Butler Fletcher (1865–1946) unwittingly, it seems, rediscovered this rhyme scheme in a translation which critics found less distorted than that of Anderson. Two decades later the American poet John Ciardi (1916–1986) used this meter for a loosely rhymed, colloquial version (1954–1970) which some found crude. Ciardi at times rendered Dante into fewer lines than the original and ignored the poem's division into tercets. The freedom of his version makes it a poor "pony" to Dante's original. In 1994 Robert Pinsky (1940–) published his translation with facing-page Italian. Its strong versification and contemporary but not overly colloquial language found critical and popular acclaim. His cantos, like Ciardi's, often contain fewer lines than Dante's do, nor do his tercets

always match Dante's. The notes, based in part on Longfellow's, include short essays by Pinsky and the American Dante scholar John Freccero.

In two instances groups of poets have combined their efforts and produced collective translations. John Heath-Stubbs, Vernon Watkins, and others first read their cantos on the BBC Third Programme, subsequently publishing their collective *Inferno* in 1966. Thirty years later in New York, Seamus Heaney, Amy Clampitt, and Richard Wilbur and others, after presenting their translations in public readings, issued a complete *Inferno* (1996). In these enterprises the poets embraced the usual solutions: unrhymed verse; *terza rima,* both whole and defective; and free verse. Those poets without Italian in effect created paraphrases based on existing prose translations. The level of literal accuracy was uneven. Great differences in tone and rhetoric between one canto and another resulted in a work whose unity and coherence were compromised.

After the success of Cary and Longfellow in the nineteenth century, no important English translations in blank verse appeared until the last third of the twentieth century. Beginning in the 1960s a new generation produced readable versions of literary classics in contemporary idiom, consciously following Pound's strictures against archaism and inversion. Three complete versions won large publics.

The Italianist Mark Musa (1934–) published a complete translation with extensive notes (1971–1981) with Indiana University Press, which was issued later in a Penguin paperback edition. Allen Mandelbaum (1926–), a poet and translator of Homer, Virgil, Ovid, and twentieth-century Italian poets, published his translation with facing-page Italian (1980–1982) with the University of California Press and also as a mass-market paperback (Bantam). It reappeared in a one-volume Everyman Library edition (1995), without the Italian text, together with notes by the British scholar Peter Armour. The British poet and translator of Virgil and Lucretius, C. H. Sisson (1914–) also published a single-volume edition in 1980, later with an introduction and extensive notes by the British scholar David Higgins (1981).

Translations of individual *cantiche* also appeared, such as Nicholas Kilmer's *Inferno* (1985) and James Torrens's translation of the *Paradiso* with commentary (1994). The British artist Tom Phillips (1937–) published a translation of the

Inferno with his own illustrations, iconographical notes, and commentary on the illustrations, but without the traditional notes (1985). A translation of the whole *Commedia* by Thomas Bergin (1904–1987), the American Italianist, into paragraphs of blank verse with some untranslated portions in prose summaries, appeared in 1969. (The individual *cantiche* had appeared between 1949 and 1954.) The American poet and scholar James Finn Cotter (1929–) published a complete translation in 1987 in unrhymed verse arranged as tercets with basic notes and introduction that offered a spiritual reading of the poem.

The approximately two hundred *cantiche* rendered by over ninety translators in the past two centuries testify to Dante's enduring popularity but also to dissatisfaction with the translations which created that popularity. No translation in English has attained the classic status of Mikhail Lozinsky's Russian version (1939–1945). From Cary on, inspired perhaps by Dante's powerful language, most translators have provided literal renderings that could stand on their own and also aid in construing the Italian. Translators have consequently relied on three fundamental, recurrent features in their English-language translations of the *Commedia,* each of which serves to direct the reader's attention to the Italian, whether or not he or she is able to decode it: inclusion of the Italian text, preservation of tercet structure in both verse and prose, and extensive notes.

These translations constitute a system of interrelated texts. Some readers consult several translations, such as a prose and a *terza rima* rendering. In addition, some translations, particularly influential ones, engender new ones. Thus Norton improved on Longfellow, and Sinclair rewrote Wicksteed as Singleton revised Norton, Wicksteed, and Sinclair. This interdependence produces at times an echo chamber effect as one moves from translation to translation. Different translators bring different credentials to their work. The ninety-odd translators of the *Commedia* include inspired amateurs, ill-prepared dilettantes, university professors, practicing poets, clerics, and theologians. Some with no or rudimentary Italian have relied on previous translations. Others with good Italian have lacked sufficient philological preparation to register and then render the text's levels of meaning; they have consequently tended, like Longfellow, to render the words rather than the meaning. The best versions—prose, verse, and rhymed—all share a high level of literal accuracy. No version, however, succeeds entirely in capturing the poem's remarkable mix of diverse stylistic registers, the infinite variation of its many voices, and its compelling verbal and narrative tension.

Minor Works

Interest in the author of the *Commedia* had become so strong by mid–nineteenth century that the public was ready for the minor works, all of which appeared in English translation by the century's end—some, more than once. The enterprise began in 1846 with the first English *Vita Nuova* and concluded in 1897 with the translation of the *Questio de aqua et terra.* Unlike the translators of the *Commedia,* most of the translators of the minor works were British, divided between amateurs and scholars. A second wave of translations, both English and American, appeared in the second half of the twentieth century.

The botanist Charles Lyell (1746–1849) made the first translation of the verse of the *Vita Nuova* and the *Convivio* (1835, reprinted in 1842). An anthology of Duecento verse by the poet and artist Dante Gabriel Rossetti (1828–1882), *Dante and His Circle* (1874), included a selection of Dante's poetry in rhymed translation as well as the *Vita Nuova* (reprinted in 1981). It provided generations of readers, such as Pound and Eliot, with access to most of Dante's verse in its literary context and in sensitive poetical versions in Pre-Raphaelite language. Six other verse translations of Dante's *Rime* appeared: E. H. Plumptre, *Commedia and Canzoniere,* in two volumes (1886); Lorna de' Lucchi, *Minor Poems* (1926); H. S. Vere-Hodge, *Odes* (1963); Patrick Diehl, *Dante's "Rime"* (1979); and Joseph Tusiani, *Dante's Lyric Poems* (1992), which included the Latin *Egloge. Dante's Lyric Poetry,* in two volumes (1967), by Patrick Boyde and Kenelm Foster, stands in a category by itself for its scrupulous prose versions and extensive scholarly commentary.

Four years after Lyell's version of the *Rime,* Joseph Garrow, an Anglo-Indian, published in Florence the first English translation of the entire *Vita Nuova.* In these same years (1842), at the urging of Margaret Fuller, Ralph Waldo Emerson, using principally the "castigated" Sermartelli edition (1576), made a version that saw publication only in 1960. In the nineteenth and early twentieth centuries the dominant translations were those of Charles Eliot Norton (1859) and Dante Gabriel

Rossetti (1861). There were also versions by Theodore Martin (1862) and Charles Stuart Boswell (1890). The rendering of Okey and Wicksteed in the Temple Classics (1899) enjoyed wide popularity in the first half of the twentieth century. The next major translation appeared in 1957, when Mark Musa published a version in contemporary English (a heavily revised second edition appearing in 1973). In England Penguin published a version by William Anderson (1964) and another by Barbara Reynolds (1969), which, like Musa's, has often been reprinted. In 1995 Dino S. Cervigni and Edward Vasta published their translation with facing Italian text and extensive concordances, glossaries, and indices, omitting division of the texts into numbered chapters, which had been standard since Barbi's edition of the Italian text in 1907.

At the end of the nineteenth century two English women made the first translations of the *Convivio* into English: Elizabeth Sayer (1887) and Katherine Hillard (1889). The Temple Classics published the version by Philip Wicksteed in 1903, and Clarendon Press published W. W. Jackson's six years later in 1909. The year 1910 saw the appearance of William Michael Rossetti's *Dante and His Convito: A Study with Translations,* which included translations and paraphrases of extensive selections. At the end of the twentieth century two scholarly translations in contemporary idiom were published almost simultaneously: one by the British scholar Christopher Ryan, *The Banquet* (1989), and another by the American scholar Richard Lansing, *Dante's Il Convivio (The Banquet)* (1990). Both were based on Maria Simonelli's critical edition of the original text (1966).

A. G. Ferrers Howell produced the first English version of the *De vulgari eloquentia* in 1890, which he revised for the Temple *Latin Works* (1904). This was the only English version until Robert S. Haller's in his *Literary Criticism of Dante Alighieri* (1973). In 1981 two versions appeared: Sally Purcell, *Literature in the Vernacular*—and Warman Welliver, *Dante in Hell: The "De Vulgari Eloquentia."* The American scholar Marianne Shapiro included her own translation in her critical study *De vulgari eloquentia: Dante's Book of Exile* (1990). Six years later, the British scholar Steven Botterill published a new translation, *Dante: "De vulgari eloquentia,"* which includes the Latin original in facing-page format.

The first English translation of the *Monarchia,* by F. J. Church, appeared in *Dante: An Essay* by R. W. Church (1879). The year 1904 saw the publication of two translations: one by Aurelia Lee and another by Wicksteed in the Temple *Latin Works.* In 1954 Donald Nicholl presented a new English version in his *Monarchy and Three Political Letters,* published in London in 1954, in New York one year later, and reprinted again in New York in 1972. H. W. Schneider published his literal version as *On World Government* (1957). In 1995 the British scholar Prue Shaw published her edition and translation, *Dante: "Monarchia,"* which includes the Latin original on the facing page, together with an extensive introduction. Even more recent is Richard Kay's translation with commentary, *Dante's Monarchia* (1998).

In 1891 C. S. Latham made available the first English version of Dante's surviving epistles, *A Translation of Dante's Eleven Letters.* Philip Wicksteed published his translation in the Temple *Latin Works* (1904). In 1920 Paget Toynbee translated these letters in his critical edition of the Latin text: *Dantis Alagherii Epistolae, The Letters of Dante: Emended Text.* Donald Nicholl included English versions by Colin Hardie of Epistles 5, 6, and 7 in his translation of the *Monarchia* (1954). Robert Cogan included versions of 5, 6, 7, and 8 in *Babylon on the Rhone: A Translation of the Letters by Dante, Petrarch and Catherine of Siena on the Avignon Papacy* (1984). A translation of the *Epistle to Can Grande della Scala* by Robert S. Haller appeared in his *Literary Criticism of Dante Alighieri* (1973).

Five translations exist of Dante's only Latin verse, his exchange of *Eclogues* with Giovanni del Virgilio: one by E. H. Plumptre in his *Commedia and Canzoniere* (1886); a better one by Wicksteed and Edmund G. Gardner in *Dante and Giovanni Del Virgilio* (1902), reprinted in the Temple *Latin Works* (1904); and Wilmon Brewer's verse rendition in his *Dante's Eclogues, The Poetical Correspondence between Dante and Giovanni del Virgilio* (1927, reprinted in 1961). Robert Haller's version of the First Eclogue appears in his *Literary Criticism of Dante Alighieri.* Joseph Tusiani's versions appeared in his translation of Dante's Italian poems (see above).

The five translations of the *Questio de aqua et terra* all appeared at the turn of the twentieth century. Shortly after C. H. Brombly made the first translation (1897), Alain C. White provided the

Latin text along with his English version in volume 21 of the *Annual Report of the Dante Society* (1902), reprinted in book form the following year. Wicksteed's rendering appeared in the Temple *Latin Works*. S. P. Thompson included his translation in the facsimile of the Editio princeps published by Olschki in Florence (1905). C. L. Shadwell's version appeared in 1909.

Two works in the vernacular, *Il Fiore,* an early fourteenth-century sequence of Italian sonnets based on *The Romance of the Rose,* and *Il Detto d'Amore,* appeared in English this year for the first time, in a translation by Santa Casciani and Christopher Kleinhenz, published by the University of Notre Dame (2000).

Bibliography

Ahern, John. "L'aquila fra gli indiani: le traduzioni americane di Dante." *Letture Classensi* 18 (1989), 211–234.

Boitani, Pietro. "Il potere e la croce: le traduzioni novecentesche di Dante in Gran Bretagna." In *L'opera di Dante nel mondo: edizioni e traduzioni nel Novecento.* Edited by Enzo Esposito. Ravenna: Longo, 1992, pp. 95–101.

Cachey, Theodore, J. "Between Hermeneutics and Poetics: Modern American Translation of the *Commedia.*" *Annali d'Italianistica* 8 (1990), 144–164.

Cunningham, Gilbert F. *The Divine Comedy in English: A Critical Bibliography 1901–1966.* Edinburgh, London: Oliver and Boyd, 1966.

———. *The Divine Comedy in English: A Critical Bibliography 1782–1900.* Edinburgh, London: Oliver and Boyd, 1965.

De Sua, William J. *Dante into English: A Study of the Translation of the Divine Comedy in Britain and America.* Chapel Hill, University of North Carolina Press, 1964.

Fitzgerald, Robert. "Mirroring the *Commedia:* An Appreciation of Laurence Binyon's Version." *Paideuma* 10 (1981), 489–501. Reprinted in *Dante in America: The First Two Centuries.* Edited by A. Bartlett Giamatti. Binghamton, N.Y.: Medieval and Renaissance Texts and Studies, 1983, pp. 390–410.

Friederich, Werner Paul. *Dante's Fame Abroad, 1350–1850.* Chapel Hill: University of North Carolina Press, 1950.

Koch, Theodore Wesley. *Dante in America: A Historical and Bibliographical Study.* Boston: Ginn, 1896.

La Piana, Angelina. *Dante's American Pilgrimage: A Historical Survey of Dante Studies in the United States, 1800–1944.* New Haven, Conn.: Yale University Press, 1948.

Reynolds, Barbara. *The Passionate Intellect: Dorothy L. Sayers' Encounter with Dante.* Kent, Ohio: Kent State University Press, 1989.

Wallace, David. "Dante in English." *The Cambridge Companion to Dante.* Edited by Rachel Jacoff. Cambridge: Cambridge University Press, 1993, pp. 237–258.

John Ahern

Treachery

This sin, *tradimento,* is Dante's equivalent for the Latin *proditio.* The traitor *(traditore)* is assigned to the ninth and lowest circle of the Inferno, Cocytus, as set forth in *Inf.* 11.64–66. Just prior to this passage Virgil formulates the basic definition of treachery as part of his twofold division of malicious injustice: violence and fraud, the latter being *dell'uom proprio male* ("an evil proper to man" *Inf.* 11.22). Fraud may be perpetrated on two levels: (1) against someone who invests no specific trust in us, which violation involves a sundering of only that bond *(vinco)* or love which nature creates within humanity; and, (2) against someone in whom there exists an additional *(quel ch'è aggiunto)* love-bond, which builds a special trust *(fede spezial).* Such trust violated by fraud against a closely associated person *(che 'n lui fida,* "who trusts in him") constitutes the special case of treachery.

The simple and compounded "natural" love can be taken to be a distillate of Aristotle's *philia,* loving friendship *(Nicomachean Ethics* 8–9), which runs parallel with natural justice, and Cicero's *caritas* (*De officiis* 1.16ff.). Thus antiquity provided Dante with a "natural" substratum for Christian *caritas.* It supposes the existence of a universal human community (derived from Stoicism) instituted by God's handmaiden Nature, and it possesses a clearly religious-political character. Treachery then denotes the basest conceivable human crime and sin. Dante discriminates four subdivisions of his ninth circle: treachery (1) against kinsmen (Caina); (2) against political party, but ultimately against the patria (Antenora); (3) against guests, and very probably also against hosts (Ptolomea); (4) against benefactors, personal ones, but finally against heroes of the greater historico-political and spiritual commonweal (Judecca).

For what both underlies and clarifies this conception Dante had at hand a series of powerful theoretical tools: (1) the *summae,* or *maximae, iniuriae* ("the gravest injustices"), best articulated in Aristotle's *Rhetoric* 1.13–14, as expanded in the Latin translation of Averroës' commentary and that of Giles of Rome (Aegidius Romanus). These flesh out the *magnum augmentum malitiae* ("the extraordinary increase in malice") which, in the view of some critics, Dante takes to represent mad bestiality, the third Aristotelian disposition of *Ethics* 7, introduced by Virgil in his discussion in *Inf.* 11.81–82; (2) the opposites of Cicero's "natural virtues associated with justice," from *De inventione* (his early treatise on rhetoric) 2.53.161, and broadly developed by Thomas Aquinas, *ST* 2.2.81–120. These tally nicely with the Aristotelian *summae iniuriae.* In Cicero they are six (St. Thomas adds a seventh, Aristotle's inequity), the chief among them being *impietas* and *ingratitudo.* Impiety in the classical sense covers the offenses found in Caina and Antenora and, partially, those found in Ptolomea (wherein the guest-host relationship creates a very special tie—special, because chosen). Ingratitude, which Dante names alongside treachery in *Conv.* 1.12.10, covers Ptolomea in part and Judecca, together with the violation of *observantia* (special respect). We may say in general that it is a question of sins against *domus* (hearth and family), *vicinia* (associated neighborhood), *civitas* (city) and *regnum* (kingdom), which entities Dante stresses as crucial in *Mon.* 1.5 and in *Conv.* 4.4.1–4. But it extends beyond, and beneath, to excessively cruel punishment (against *vindicatio*) and lying when bound by special oath (against *veritas*). It is important to note that in *Par.* 17.64–67 Dante will locate the terms *empia* and *ingrata* on either side of *matta* to specify the *bestialità,* the treachery, which he ascribes to his erstwhile White Guelf associates in exile. In sum, such a hate-filled, quasi-diabolic temper inheres in all the denizens of the ninth circle, and it culminates in Brutus and Cassius, betrayers of Caesar, and in Judas—each of them masticated by Satan in separate mouths. Moreover, this characterization, it has been argued, is consistent with the glosses of Albertus Magnus and Thomas Aquinas with respect to the "brutish" or "bestial" man treated by Aristotle in *Politics* 1. The great Scholastics describe him as one capable of the greatest harm *(nocumentum)* which may be perpetrated on the human community because man possesses the significant "weapon" of intellect, whose right use he can and does pervert—to the most inhuman and inhumane degree when it is allied to malevolence and power (*Inf.* 31.55–57).

Bibliography

Mazzoni, Francesco. "Canto XI." *Lectura Dantis Neapolitana: Inferno.* Naples: Loffredo, 1986, pp. 167–209; especially pp. 190–207.

Triolo, Alfred A. "Ira, Cupiditas, Libido: The Dynamics of Passion in the *Inferno.*" *Dante Studies* 95 (1977), 1–37; especially pp. 20–23, 28–33.

———. "*Inferno* XXXIII: Fra Alberigo in Context." *L'Alighieri* 11 (1970), 39–70.

———. "Matta Bestialità in Dante's *Inferno:* Theory and Image." *Traditio* 24 (1968), 247–292.

Alfred Triolo

Trinity

The central affirmation of Christianity is "one God in three Persons." Although there is New Testament warrant for this notion of God—in Christ's commission to baptize "in the name of the Father, and of the Son, and of the Holy Spirit" (Matt. 28:19); in St. Paul's invocation of "the grace of our Lord Jesus Christ, and the love of God, and the fellowship of the Holy Spirit" (2 Cor. 13:13)—Trinitarian doctrine itself is the product of centuries of theological development, culminating in the fourth-century creeds formulated at Nicaea (First Council, 325) and Constantinople (First Council, 381). St. Augustine's *De Trinitate* was the most important influence on the theology of the Western Church, as can readily be seen in the Scholastic thought of Peter Lombard, Albertus Magnus, Aquinas, and Bonaventure. Trinitarian controversy continued well into Dante's own day and remained a sticking point in relations with the Eastern Church.

In *Par.* 24, Dante shows himself to be well versed in his theology. When asked to give an account of what he believes, he answers St. Peter in the precise language of the orthodox creeds: *Io credo in uno Dio / solo ed etterno* ("I believe in one God, sole and eternal"), who is revealed *in tre persone etterne* ("in three Persons"), *e queste / credo una essenza sì e sì trina* ("and these I believe to be one essence"). The Trinity, he says, is the spark that ignites the "living flame" of his Christian faith.

T Earlier in the *Paradiso,* in the Heaven of the Sun (*Par.* 10–14), the poet also reflects a highly sophisticated understanding of "one God in three." *Par.* 10 opens with a meditation on two Trinitarian doctrines: the Father's "generation" of the Son and the "spiration" of the Holy Spirit by *l'uno e l'altro* ("the One and the Other"). Later on, in *Par.* 13.26–27, the souls of the theologians sing the praises of both the Trinity and the Incarnation, of *tre persone in divine nature, / e in una persona essa e l'umana* ("three Persons in the divine nature and in one Person the divine and the human nature").

But the Trinity is not only the subject of meditation and praise; it is also the object of Dante's whole journey and the final vision of the last canto. The promise of the beatific vision is the sight of God "face to face"; but what Dante sees in the end is an image of *tre giri / di tre colori e d'una contenenza* ("three circles of three colors and one circumference") that may recall the Trinitarian imagining of Joachim of Fiore's *Liber figurarum.* Contemplating these equal but distinct circles, Dante comes to see that the central one, representing the Son, *mi parve pinta de la nostra effige* ("seemed painted with our image," 131). He wants to understand how the Trinity and the Incarnation can possibly "fit" together, but learns in the end that God in three Persons and made flesh cannot be understood: he can only be revealed, as Dante learns in the poem's final moment, by an act of divine grace.

The culmination of Dante's journey in the beatific vision properly belongs to Paradise. Yet the Trinity is made manifest throughout the poem in a variety of indirect revelations. The tripartite structure of the three canticles, as well as the *terza rima* verse form of interlocking triple rhymes (*aba bcb cdc,* etc.) reflect a Trinitarian consciousness. So too does Hell itself, whose "high maker" is named in the traditional terminology of the divine Persons, *LA DIVINA POTESTATE, / LA SOMMA SAPIËNZA E 'L PRIMO AMORE* ("DIVINE POWER, HIGHEST WISDOM, AND PRIMAL LOVE," *Inf.* 3.5–6). At the deepest point of Hell, the Trinity is also represented, albeit through parody, in Satan's grotesque form. The one who wanted to be God's equal is given his wish for eternity, with *tre facce a la sua testa!* ("three faces on his head," *Inf.* 34.38).

Bibliography

Priest, Paul. *Dante's Incarnation of the Trinity.* Ravenna: Longo, 1982.

Reeves, Marjorie. *The Influence of Prophecy in the Later Middle Ages: Studies in Joachism.* Oxford: Oxford University Press, 1969.

Swing, T. K. *The Fragile Leaves of the Sibyl: Dante's Master Plan.* Westminster, Md.: Newman Press, 1962.

Peter Hawkins

Tristan

A courtly knight and nephew of King Mark of Cornwall, Tristan is the eponymous hero of numerous Old French romances reflecting antecedent Celtic written and oral traditions. Tristan and Mark's fiancée, Iseut, are united in an intense, ultimately tragic love affair after they mistakenly consume the magic potion that had been prepared for the king and his bride. Surviving twelfth-century texts include fragments by Béroul and Thomas and variant versions of the *Folie Tristan,* all in verse. The tradition was reworked in the vast thirteenth-century *Prose Tristan* cycle. In *Inf.* 5.67, Dante places Tristan (*Tristano*) among the carnal sinners. He may well have associated Paolo's and Francesca's deaths at the hands of her jealous husband—an episode evoked in the latter part of the canto (5.106–107)—with the story of King Mark's murder of his nephew in the *Prose Tristan.*

Donald Maddox

Trivium

The trivium, along with the quadrivium, forms the subject matter of the seven liberal arts. It includes grammar, rhetoric, and logic, or dialectic; and the quadrivium continues with arithmetic, geometry, music, and astronomy. In the medieval system of education, the trivium represented the intellectual foundation (thus the expression "grammar school") for subsequent professional studies in medicine, law, or theology. Grammar focused on Latin and the Latin classics, examining both grammar in the conventional sense and literature. The standard texts were those of Priscian and Donatus. Rhetoric pertained to Latin composition in verse and prose and typically included rhetorical works by Cicero and the *Institutio Oratoria* of Quintilian. Logic, or dialectic, involved the study of formal logic and argumentation, though occasionally dialectic included more informal modes of argumentation as well. The logical works of Aristotle, Porphyry, and, from the eleventh century, Gilbert de la Porée's *De sex principiis* were the basis of instruction.

The prototype of the trivium occurs in the writings of Plato and the fourth-century-B.C.E. rhetorician Isocrates, who developed a course of study to prepare students for philosophy. It entered medieval thought in the seven liberal arts described in *The Marriage of Philosophy and Mercury* (439 C.E.) by Martianus Capella and the *Etymologies* of Isidore of Seville (560–635), which focused on the trivium as preparatory for theological studies. Central to Dante's understanding of the trivium and the quadrivium were their structural and symbolic correspondences with the world. Works such as the *Didascalion* of Hugh of Saint-Victor (d. 1141), *The Metalogicon* of John of Salisbury (d. 1180), and *The Marriage of the Seven Arts and the Seven Virtues* of Jean le Tentrier sought to explain and defend the typological relationship between the curriculum and the moral and physical orders. Of particular importance to Dante were the *Il Tesoretto (The Little Treasure)* and *Li livres dou tresor (The Book of the Treasure)* of his mentor, Brunetto Latini (d. 1292). Influenced by the School of Chartres, Latini advocated a reintegration into a higher order based on Platonic cosmology. He further taught that rhetoric and politics were the noblest pursuits of the citizen.

Dante offered an extended discussion of the typology and correspondences of the trivium and quadrivium in the second book of the *Convivio.* Defining "heaven" allegorically as "knowledge" *(scienza),* he explained that the seven orders of knowledge corresponded with the seven heavens. Thus the first seven heavens related to liberal science (the matter of trivium and quadrivium). The eighth heaven, the sphere of the Fixed Stars, corresponded to natural science (physics and metaphysics), the ninth to moral philosophy, and the last to theology.

Turning to the trivium, Dante explains that the Moon is linked to grammar because each shares two properties. Thus as shadow and varying degrees of luminosity depend on the lunar density and the presence of the Sun, so the light of reason is either reflected or obscured by the surface structure of language (*Conv.* 2.8.9, 10). The planet Mercury is linked with dialectic by virtue of being the smallest "star" and having the most hidden course. This, for Dante, corresponds to dialectic, since that body of knowledge is the most compact, contained

in a volume or two, and its arguments are the most subtle and difficult to follow. Finally, Dante compares Venus to rhetoric—first, because of its brightness and, second, because it appears in the sky in both the morning and the evening. In a similar fashion, rhetoric is characterized by its brightness and sweetness, since indeed for Dante *la Rettorica è soavissima di tutte le altre scienze* ("Rhetoric is the sweetest of all the sciences," *Conv.* 2.8.14). In addition, rhetoric is like the morning star when the rhetorician speaks directly to an audience, and it is like the evening star when he speaks at a step removed, through the written word. This kind of artificial, contrived allegory will give way to the more elaborate and sophisticated model employed in the *Paradiso,* which associates the heavens with various virtues, but it reveals nonetheless Dante's habit of investing the order of the universe with fundamental meaning.

Bibliography

Alberson, Paul. *The Seven Liberal Arts: A Study in Mediaeval Culture.* New York: Columbia University Press, 1906.

Curtius, Ernst Robert. *European Literature and the Latin Middle Ages.* Translated by Willard R. Trask. Princeton, N.J.: Princeton University Press, 1953.

Di Scipio, Giuseppe, and Aldo Scaglione (eds.). *The "Divine Comedy" and the Encyclopedia of Arts and Sciences.* Amsterdam, Philadelphia: John Benjamins Publishing, 1988.

Gualazzini, Ugo. *Trivium e quadrivium.* Mediolani: Giuffrè, 1974.

Masi, Michael (ed.). *Boethius and the Liberal Arts.* Berne: Peter Lang, 1981.

Wagner, David L. (ed.). *The Seven Liberal Arts in the Middle Ages.* Bloomington: Indiana University Press, 1983.

Thomas L. Cooksey

Trojans

The inhabitants of the ancient city of Troy (also known as Ilium). On the eastern shores of the Mediterranean Sea, Troy was the site of the legendary war between Greeks and Trojans over the abduction of Helen, wife of the Greek king Menelaus, by the Trojan Paris. The story of the fall of Troy is recounted in Homer's *Iliad* and was transmitted to the Middle Ages through various Latin sources, the most important of which, for

Dante, was Virgil's *Aeneid.* The Greeks won the war by tricking the Trojans with the "gift" of the giant wooden horse—filled with Greek warriors who thus entered the city walls. When Dante encounters the Greeks Ulysses and Diomed in the infernal circle in which the fraudulent counselors are punished, the treachery of the Trojan horse is recast as *l'agguato del caval che fé la porta / onde uscì de' Romani il gentil seme* ("the deceit of the horse that made the gate to send forth the noble seed of the Romans," *Inf.* 26.59–60).

Throughout his works, Dante displays the conviction that the Trojans and the fate of Troy form an integral part of Roman history and, therefore, of the history of salvation. The role of Virgil in the *Commedia* is predicated on this conviction, and Virgil himself draws attention to the intersecting histories of Troy and Rome by citing his *Aeneid* immediately upon meeting Dante at the beginning of *Inferno: cantai di quel giusto / figliuol d'Anchise che venne di Troia, / poi che 'l superbo Ilion fu combusto* ("I sang of that just son of Anchises who came [to Italy] from Troy when proud Ilion was destroyed by fire," *Inf.* 1.73–75). The fall of Troy and the arrival of Aeneas on the shores of Italy are seen, by Dante as by Virgil, as the providential beginning of the Roman Empire, which Dante, particularly and explicitly in the *Convivio* and the *Monarchia,* and implicitly in the *Commedia,* posits as the necessary context for the incarnation of the Redeemer, Christ. Dante further interconnects the messianic and imperial designs by making the Trojan arrival in Italy contemporaneous with the birth of David in Palestine: *E tutto questo fu in uno temporale che David nacque e nacque Roma, cioè che Enea venne di Troia in Italia, che fu origine de la cittade romana, sì come testimoniano le scritture. Per che assai è manifesto la divina elezione del romano imperio per lo nascimento de la santa cittade, che fu contemporaneo a la radice de la progenie di Maria* ("All this occurred at one point in time: David was born when Rome was born—that is, when Aeneas came to Italy from Troy, which was the origin of the Roman city, according to written records. As a result the divine choice of the Roman Empire is made manifest by the birth of the Holy City which was contemporaneous with the root of the family of Mary," *Conv.* 4.5.6).

The Trojan role in the divine plan of salvation was realized when Christ was born during the *pax augusta,* under the rule of Augustus, the first emperor of the Roman Empire. The nobility of the Roman people which made them worthy to rule the world and to judge and condemn Christ for the salvation of the world is also for Dante in part a function of the admixture of *l'alto sangue troiano* ("the lofty blood of the Trojans," *Conv.* 4.4.10). An example of this nobility is found in the figure of the Trojan Ripheus, to whom Dante grants a place in the Heaven of Jupiter (*Par.* 20.68) despite the fact that he was a pagan, on the basis that, following Virgil, he was *iustissimus* ("most just," *Aen.* 2.426). The role of Virgil himself as Dante's guide through *Inferno* and *Purgatorio* underscores his position as the quintessentially Roman bridge between pagan (Trojan) past and Christian present. Dante's sense of his own role in synthesizing these two traditions, and these two Romes, is suggested when, faced with Virgil's declaration of the nature of the journey upon which he is about to embark, the pilgrim remarks: *Io non Enea, io non Paulo sono* ("I am not Aeneas, I am not Paul," *Inf.* 2.32).

Dante refers to Dardanus, the mythical founder of Troy and remote ancestor of the Romans and ultimately of the Italians as well, in *Conv.* 4.14.14 and *Mon.* 2.3.11.

Bibliography

Battistini, Andrea. "*Rifeo troiano* e la riscrittura dantesca della storia (*Paradiso XX*)." *Lettere italiane* 42 (1990), 26–50.

Birns, Nicholas. "The Trojan Myth: Postmodern Reverberations." *Exemplaria* 5, 1 (1993), 45–78.

Claudia Rattazzi Papka

Troy

Troy *(Troia)* was important to Dante not only as a focal point of the legendary prehistory of the ancient world but also as the center from which the divinely ordained mission of the founding of Rome had been launched. The burning of the proud ancient city (*superbo Iliòn, Inf.* 1.75)—for Dante an archetype of the punishment of pride (*Purg.* 12.61–63; cf. *Inf.* 30.13–15)—and the removal to "humble Italy" (*umile Italia, Inf.* 1.106) had been the subject of Virgil's *Aeneid,* as summarized in *Inf.* 1.73–75, and Virgil had stressed the role of destiny in his story. Passages from the long prophetic exchange between Venus and Jupiter on the future glories of Rome (*Aen.* 1.227–296) appear in several of Dante's writings (234–236 in *Mon.* 2.8.11; 278–279 in *Conv.* 4.4.11; 286–288 in *Epist.* 7.13), and the implications for world history of the link between Troy and Rome are elaborated with continual reference to Virgil in *Mon.* 2.3.

Dante translates the Virgilian emphasis on Rome's unalterable destiny into providential terms. *Conv.* 4.5.6 asserts that Aeneas' coming to Italy, which marks the foundation of the "Holy City" of Rome, coincided with the birth of David, "the root of the family of Mary." The treachery whereby the Trojans were induced to open their walls to the Greeks' gift of the wooden horse was providential in that it prepared *la porta / onde uscì de' Romani il gentil seme* ("the gate to send forth the noble seed of the Romans," *Inf.* 26.59–60). Rome is a *popolo santo* ("holy people") to whom God has entrusted the government of the world (*Conv.* 4.4.10), and their Trojan origins are asserted repeatedly (*Inf.* 26.59–60, 28.7–12; *Par.* 6.4–6; *Conv.* 4.4.10; *Epist.* 7.13). In *Purg.* 18.133–138, those Trojans who elected to remain in Sicily rather than endure further voyaging with Aeneas (*Aen.* 5.604–640) are compared with the Israelites who refused to follow Moses through the desert after crossing the Red Sea (*Num.* 14:1–39). Ripheus (*Rifëo Troiano*), an obscure figure whom Virgil had nonetheless declared "the most just of the Trojans" (*Aen.* 2.426–427) appears among the blessed pagans in *Par.* 20.68. In *Epist.* 5.11 Dante urges the peoples of Italy to repudiate barbarism and acknowledge the primacy of "the seed of the Trojans and Latins," and Cacciaguida recalls a time when housewives would tell tales of "the Trojans, of Fiesole, and of Rome" (*Par.* 15.126).

Winthrop Wetherbee

Turnus

Rutulian king and Aeneas' rival for the hand of King Latinus' daughter Lavinia, as told in Virgil's *Aeneid*. Because Aeneas killed Turnus in a duel (*Aen.* 12.887–952), Dante in *Mon.* 2.10.13 ascribes to Rome the right to rule the world (in *Mon.* 2.3.16, the poet refers to Turnus' appeal to Aeneas to spare his life). *Inf.* 1.106–108 names Turnus (*Turno*) as one who, along with fellow Italian Camilla and Trojans Euryalus and Nisus, gave his life fighting for *quell'umile Italia* ("that humble Italy") whose well-being Dante's poem promotes.

Todd Boli

Tuscany

Medieval Tuscany (*Toscana*) occupied part of what had once been the Roman province of Etruria; its name derives from the Latin adjective *tuscus,* which in turn is related to the Roman name for the inhabitants of the region (*Tusci*). In Dante's time, as today, the region was triangular in shape, with two sides formed by the Mediterranean to the west and the Apennines and the regions of Emilia and Liguria to the north. The southeast frontier bordered the regions of Umbria and Latium. However, there is evidence to suggest that some among Dante's contemporaries, or those who lived soon after, believed Tuscany to extend as far southward as the bank of the Tiber in Rome (see Giovanni Villani, *Cronica* 1.43; Fazio degli Uberti, *Dittamondo* 3.6.13–24; Boccaccio, *Esposizioni* 10.21–26). That this was not Dante's perception is demonstrated by *DVE* 1.10.5, where he divides the right-hand side of Italy into regions; there Tuscany (*Tuscia*) is clearly distinct from Rome and the Duchy of Spoleto (*Ducatus*). *Tuscia* is also mentioned as Dante's home region in *DVE* 1.6.3; in *Par.* 9.90 Dante refers to the river Magra as the border between Tuscany and Liguria and other brief references to *Toscana* as region are found in *Conv.* 4.11.8, *Inf.* 24.122, *Purg.* 11.110, and *Purg.* 13.149.

Elsewhere in the *De vulgari eloquentia,* Dante surveys the "municipal vernaculars" (*municipalia vulgaria*) of Tuscany, in what composes a list of virtually all the region's principal cities: Florence, Pisa, Lucca, Siena, and Arezzo (1.13.1–4). Here and elsewhere (1.10.9) Dante notes that Tuscan, like other vernaculars, varies from city to city, yet the inference is that he understands Tuscany to be constituted primarily in linguistic terms: it is defined as the place where Tuscan is spoken. Several souls in the *Commedia*'s first two *cantiche* identify the pilgrim as Tuscan by his speech: Farinata (*Inf.* 10.22–27), Ciampolo (*Inf.* 22.99), Catalano (*Inf.* 23.76, 91), and Marco Lombardo (*Purg.* 16.137). It is true that Farinata proceeds to identify Dante more narrowly as a Florentine, and he is also identified as such by his clothing (*Inf.* 16.8–9), yet, although in the *Commedia* a greater emphasis is placed upon Dante as Florentine, nevertheless it is evident that he also thought of himself as a "Tuscan": in *Par.* 22.117, for instance, he writes of having felt *l'aere tosco* at his birth.

That Dante primarily defines Tuscany in terms of language is, possibly, symptomatic of the region's lack of coherence as a political entity. It ceased to be a marquisate in 1115, when the Countess Matilda died and left her lands, including Tuscany, to the Church. The ensuing contest for possession of the region was accompanied by the emergence of the city communes, a process which greatly accelerated in the thirteenth century. Thus, although at the time of the *Commedia* Tuscany was part of the Regnum Italicum, and therefore theoretically part of the Empire, in reality it consisted of a number of independent city-states in various positions of alliance and conflict. When Mosca, in the bolgia of the schismatics and sowers of discord, admits the evil which he, the "originator" of the struggle between Guelfs and Ghibellines, has brought to *la gente tosca* ("the Tuscans," *Inf.* 28.108), Dante underlines the extent to which this conflict affected the whole of Tuscany. However, it must also be emphasized that this ostensibly ideological conflict cannot be separated from abiding local enmities such as those between Pisa and Lucca, Florence and Pistoia, or Siena and Arezzo.

In the thirteenth century, the most coherent attempt to impose imperial rule upon Tuscany (along with the Regno and the papal state) was made by Manfred, son of the Hohenstaufen Emperor Frederick II. From his base in Sicily, Manfred forged an alliance with Tuscan Ghibellines. The ensuing campaign enjoyed its greatest success at the Battle of Montaperti (1260), which saw total defeat for the Tuscan Guelfs and the subsequent exile of many of their number (including Brunetto Latini). With papal backing, Charles of Anjou launched a crusade against Manfred, partly funded by Tuscan bankers and in which many Tuscans took the cross. At the Battle of Benevento in 1266 Manfred was defeated and killed, and, by 1270, Charles held the lordship of most of the towns of Tuscany, remaining imperial vicar of the region until 1277. The Guelf-Ghibelline conflict continued in its various forms, a watershed of which was the Battle of Campaldino (1289), at which the Florentine Guelf army (Dante among them) inflicted a heavy defeat upon a Ghibelline force made up of Aretines and exiles from other Tuscan cities.

The papacy continued to assert its own claims in Tuscany, particularly during the pontificate of Boniface VIII, whose crusade against the Colonna cardinals and war against the Aldobrandeschi mixed papal with (Caetani) family ambitions. Of most consequence for Dante was the campaign of Charles of Valois, whom Boniface VIII invited to Italy to be, inter alia, "pacifier of Tuscany": Charles's entry into Florence in 1301 restored propapal, Black Guelf rule and led to the exile of the White Guelfs, including Dante. The imperial expedition of Henry VII of Luxembourg (1310–1313) was accompanied by a resurgence of Tuscan Ghibellinism, although Henry made little military impact upon Tuscany. Indeed, his inattention to the region, and to the "rebellious" city of Florence in particular, provoked Dante to write a letter to him, aligning himself with *universaliter omnes Tusci qui pacem desiderant* ("all the Tuscans everywhere who desire peace," *Epist.* 7.1). In the letter Dante argues in the strongest terms that Tuscany is rightly part of the Roman Empire. After Henry's death Tuscany remained a battleground, with Popes Clement V and John XXII, Robert of Naples (confirmed as Imperial Vicar in 1317), and the Guelf League ranged against the Ghibelline alliance, which had Pisa and Lucca as its focal point.

The almost continual disorder in Tuscany during the thirteenth and fourteenth centuries took place alongside not only the development of strong, republican government but also tremendous economic growth. The manufacture of textiles may have been the principal and most successful industry of medieval Tuscany, but the main production of wealth lay in the realms of trade and finance. Tuscan merchants (from Lucca, Siena, Pistoia, and Florence) were to be found trading throughout western Europe and beyond, while Florentine companies held a prime position as creditors for European princes and courts and as bankers for the papacy. Indeed, through banking and commerce, "Tuscany between 1250 and 1300 quickly became the leading trade and financial power in Italy and Europe" (Jones, 292). During this period, the major cities of the region experienced considerable growth in population, with Florence, the largest, nearly doubling in size to over 90,000 inhabitants.

Tuscan people and places feature prominently in the *Commedia;* for example, invectives against several of the major Tuscan towns and cities appear in the later cantos of *Inferno*—Lucca (21.37–42), Pistoia (25.10–15), Siena (29.121–132), and Pisa (33.79–90)—and cantos 5 and 6 of *Purgatorio* are noticeable for their concentration of references to the region's bloodied landscape in the late thirteenth century. The poem's most extended polemic against the region as a whole is found in *Purg.* 14.25–54, where Guido del Duca laments the degeneracy of the inhabitants of settlements along the river Arno who have undergone a Circean transformation; those from the Casentino and Arezzo (both of which had escaped such intense censure in *Inferno*), have become *brutti porci* ("ugly swine") and *botoli* ("curs"), whereas the Florentines and Pisans are now *lupi* ("wolves") and *volpi* ("foxes"), respectively.

In *Paradiso* specific references to Tuscan towns are largely absent, with the notable and important exception of the Heaven of Mars, where Cacciaguida mentions many small towns around Florence whence came its "new" families—and with them, the corruption of what Dante believed to have once been an ideal earthly city. These cantos confirm what is evident elsewhere in the poem: Dante's remarkably detailed knowledge of Tuscan topography and historical events.

Bibliography

Catto, Jeremy. "Florence, Tuscany and the World of Dante." In *The World of Dante: Essays on Dante and His Times*. Edited by Cecil Grayson. Oxford: Clarendon Press, 1980, pp. 1–17.

Holmes, George. *Florence, Rome and the Origins of the Renaissance*. Oxford: Clarendon Press, 1986.

Jones, Philip. *The Italian City-State: From Commune to Signoria*. Oxford: Clarendon Press, 1997.

Larner, John. *Italy in the Age of Dante and Petrarch 1216–1380*. London, New York: Longman, 1980.

Mengaldo, Pier Vincenzo. "Toscana [language]." *Enciclopedia dantesca*, 5:667–668.

Savino, Giancarlo. "Toscana [region]." *Enciclopedia dantesca*, 5:666–667.

Toynbee, Paget. "Toscana." In *A Dictionary of Proper Names and Notable Matters in the Works of Dante*. Revised by Charles Singleton. Oxford: Clarendon Press, 1968, p. 616.

Waley, Daniel. *The Italian City-Republics*. 3rd ed. London, New York: Longman, 1988.

Mark Balfour

Tydeus

Greek king of Calydon and father of Diomedes who accompanied Adrastus, king of Argos, in the expedition against Thebes. In the war he was mortally wounded by the Theban Menalippus, whom he too managed to slay in turn. Dante compares Ugolino gnawing on the head of Archbishop Ruggieri in the ninth circle of Hell to Tydeus (*Tidëo*) gnawing on the head of Menalippus (*Inf.* 32.130), following Statius' description in *Theb.* 8.739–762, where Tydeus furiously seizes and gnaws Menalippus' skull; there is a strong suggestion that he eats the eyes. Tydeus is also referred to in *Conv.* 4.25.6, 8.

R. A. Malagi

Typhon

Sometimes described as a hundred-headed monster or dragon, Typhon (*Tifo*), or Typhoeus (*Tifeo*), is one of the mythological giants, children of Earth, who attempted to storm Heaven but were cast out by Jupiter and imprisoned underground. Typhon was quelled with a thunderbolt. Dante mentions him, coupled with Tityus, among the giants who tower around the pit of Cocytus (*Inf.* 31.124), and again when Charles Martel explains that the eruptions of Mount Etna are not caused by the struggles of Typhoeus to free himself (*Par.* 8.67). He is also mentioned in *Conv.* 2.5.14, in a citation of *Aen.* 1.664–665, which Dante mistranslates.

Olivia Holmes

U

Ubaldino della Pila

A member of the powerful Ghibelline family of the Ubaldini, which included his brother Cardinal Ottaviano degli Ubaldini (*Inf.* 10.120), his nephew Ugolin d'Azzo (*Purg.* 14.105), and his son Archbishop Ruggieri of Pisa (*Inf.* 33.14). Ubaldino, who died about 1291, inhabits the sixth terrace of Purgatory, where he expiates his sin of gluttony, for which he was apparently known (*Purg.* 24.29). Benvenuto da Imola attests to his reputation in his commentary on the passage, noting Ubaldino's habit of always ordering more delicacies to add to his cook's already rich menus. Ubaldino is pointed out to Dante by Forese Donati among the other gluttons who are reduced by the ledge's penitential fast to "chewing the air for hunger" (*Purg.* 24.28).

Claudia Rattazzi Papka

Ubertino da Casale

Along with Angelo of Clareno, Ubertino (1259–c. 1341) was the most prominent and articulate of the Spiritual (strict-observant) Franciscans in Italy during Dante's time. He entered the order in 1273 and studied at Paris. He was in Florence from 1285 to 1289, where, like his older fellow-Spiritual, Olivi, he may well have taught at S. Croce while Dante was frequenting "the schools of the religious" (*Conv.* 2.12.7). A period of preaching the Spiritual Franciscan message in Tuscany and Umbria was followed by enforced retirement at La Verna (c. 1305), during which he wrote his visionary *Arbor vitae crucifixae Jesu.* The Prologue of this work (pp. 4a–6b) is the source for information about Ubertino's earlier life. His diplomatic activities in Italy (1307) and his role as spokesman for the Spirituals at the Avignon inquiry of 1309–1312 relate quite closely to some of Dante's political concerns, and he was during this time a protégé of Cardinal Napoleone Orsini, whom Dante addresses in *Epist.* 11. Pope John XXII transferred Ubertino from the Franciscan order in 1317 and, having accused him of heresy, unsuccessfully ordered his arrest in 1325, after which little is known of him for certain.

Ubertino's career and ideas intersect with Dante's in some respects. Dante's only explicit reference to him is as an excessively rigid interpreter of the Franciscan Rule (*Par.* 12.124–126), but *Par.* 11.70–72 reveals a possible indebtedness to Ubertino's representation of poverty (*Arbor vitae,* p. 426a–b). The *Arbor vitae* was not widely circulated until later in the century, but its apocalyptic vision of St. Francis, poverty, and ecclesiastical history, like Olivi's, converges with the *Commedia* at a number of points.

Bibliography

Davis, Charles. "Poverty and Eschatology in the *Commedia.*" In *Dante's Italy, and Other Essays.* Philadelphia: University of Pennsylvania Press, 1984, especially pp. 51–52, 59–69.

Havely, Nicholas. "From Assisi to Avignon." *Journal of the Institute of Romance Studies* 3 (1994), 43–53.

Potestà, Gian Luca. *Storia ed escatologia in Ubertino da Casale.* Milan: Università Cattolica, 1980.

Ubertino da Casale. *Arbor vitae crucifixae Jesu.* With an introduction and bibliography by Charles T. Davis. Turin: Bottega d'Erasmo, 1961 (reprint of the 1485 edition).

Nicholas Havely

Ugolin d'Azzo

A descendent of the Ubaldini of Tuscany, the son of Azzo da Senno. He lived in Romagna and died in 1293. According to other sources, he represented Faenza in the battle for the peace of Constantinople in 1183. He is mentioned by Guido del Duca on the second terrace of Purgatory as one of the noble figures of Tuscany (*Purg.* 14.105).

Paul Colilli

Ugolin de' Fantolini

A nobleman of Romagna born in the early thirteenth century, remembered by Guido del Duca on the second terrace of Purgatory as a just and upright man, and a Guelf of Faenza. In his celebration of the past glory and his lamentation of the current degeneracy of the men of Romagna, Guido remarks: *O Ugolin de' Fantolin, sicuro / è 'l nome tuo, da che più non s'aspetta / chi far lo possa, tralignando, scuro* ("O Ugolin de' Fantolini, your name is safe, no one can be expected who could darken it by his degeneration," *Purg.* 14.121–123). The "safety" of which he speaks is meant to suggest that his name could not be besmirched by his offspring, since both his sons were killed not long after his own death, which occurred in 1278.

Claudia Rattazzi Papka

Ugolino della Gherardesca

A prominent figure in Pisan and Tuscan politics, Ugolino was born in the first half of the thirteenth century into the powerful Ghibelline Gherardesca family of Pisa. His name appears in historical records first in 1252 as vicar of the imprisoned King Enzo and again in 1257 as a participant in Pisa's victorious expedition against Sant'Igia, after which he held a prominent position in the Sardinian Kingdom of Cagliari. After Manfred's defeat and death at Benevento in 1266 and a Guelf expansion that threatened all of Tuscany, Ugolino transferred his political affiliations to the Guelf party. Between 1274 and 1275, with the aid of his son-in-law, Giovanni Visconti, he attempted but failed to establish a Guelf government in Pisa, was consequently imprisoned, and finally was exiled along with other Guelfs. In 1276, Ugolino returned to Pisa with his grandson, Nino Visconti, and regained favor among the Pisans. He led the Pisan fleet against Genoa in 1284 and, though defeated, was subsequently elected to the position of podestà, in great part because of support from the Florentine Guelfs. During his four years in power Ugolino attempted to neutralize the internal party strife that consumed his city, enlisting as "captain of the people" his grandson, Nino Visconti.

In order to break the newly formed political pact which allied Genoa, Lucca, and Florence against an isolated Pisa, in 1285 Ugolino ceded several minor Pisan castles to Lucca (Viareggio and Ripafratta) and Florence (Pontedera). The cession of the castles provoked strong reactions in Pisa and created a rift between Ugolino and Nino which culminated in a party schism. Consequently, Ugolino aligned himself more closely with the Ghibellines, headed by Archbishop Ruggieri and supported by the powerful Lanfranchi, Gualandi, and Sismondi families, who demanded exile for Nino Visconti. The orders were carried out in 1288, possibly by Ugolino himself, who then retired to his castle at Settimo. The fourteenth-century historian Giovanni Villani maintains that Ugolino also had his sister's son, Anselmo di Capraia, poisoned for opposing him politically.

The traitor was betrayed shortly thereafter when, in an attempt to win public approval and support, Archbishop Ruggieri condemned Ugolino for having deeded Pisa's castles to her enemies and incited the Pisans against him. Under the guise of negotiating a new agreement, he summoned Ugolino to the city, where on July 1, 1288, a mob attacked his palace, killing one son and one nephew and capturing Ugolino with two sons (Gaddo and Uguiccione) and two grandsons (Anselmo and Brigata)—all adults, with the exception of Anselmo. Imprisoned, they died the following year, in March 1289.

According to Villani, whose account clearly validates the suggestion that Ugolino earned his reputation as a traitor, Ugolino betrayed his country, his party, and both his grandson and his nephew, and he abused the power invested in him by allegedly bestowing lavish wealth and political office on family members (*Cronica* 8.47ff.)

Ugolino resides in Antenora, the second ring of Cocytus, in the ninth circle of Hell, where traitors to country and political party weep bitter cold tears and where he alone gnaws with ferocity the cranium of his cohort in Hell, Archbishop Ruggieri. Sociopolitical interpretations of the episode point to Ugolino's voracity and savagery as extensions of his political self and to all of Cocytus as representative of the boundless, destructive greed that passes, at its worst, for politics. Far more often, however, readers, like Ugolino himself, focus on the personal rather than the political—a false dichotomy, it has been argued. Rather than provide the details of his and others' political treachery (most likely known to the pilgrim), Ugolino—the most aggrieved and most loquacious of all the sinners in *Inferno* (he holds forth for seventy-two continuous lines, the lengthiest uninterrupted monologue delivered by any sinner)—recounts the heretofore mysterious occurrences in the dark tower where he was imprisoned and died along with his children (*Inf.* 32.123–139, 33.1–90).

The story that Ugolino recounts has been called the most human and the most inhuman of the *Commedia* as critics proffer readings that vehemently support or deny Ugolino's right to clemency and defend or defame his character, his paternity, his very humanity. Cannibalism—the horrific taboo graphically dramatized in the text in Ugolino's undeniable devouring of the archbishop in Hell and perhaps more horrifically suggested in the possibility of Ugolino's cannibalism of his children in the tower—is the subject of most studies of the episode. Certainly one of the most disturbing and provocative, it is also one of the most ambiguous episodes of the *Commedia*. Like all others in the poem, the Ugolino narrative invites interpretation; perhaps more than any other, it requires and resists it.

The statement with which Ugolino concludes his tale—*Poscia, più che 'l dolor, potè 'l digiuno* (*Inf.* 33.75; literally, "Then fasting [hunger] had more power than grief")—allows for the either/or interpretation that most readers, with good reason, refuse to entertain: either "fasting (hunger) killed me where sorrow could not" or "fasting (hunger) overcame grief and induced me to feed on my children." Controversy over the correct interpretation of the verse began in the first century of the poem's exegesis and continues as critics, pro- and anticannibal, offer arguments—the vehemence with which they maintain their positions speaking eloquently to the importance of clarity in matters such as these. Since Lana raised the question in the years immediately following the poet's death, the following arguments have been put forth as support for the cannibalistic reading: the bestial repast of Ugolino in Hell; a preexisting topos in the well-known thirteenth-century *chanson de geste* enti-

tled *Amis et Amiles;* Christological echoes in the episode which suggest a parodic reenactment of the Eucharist; further biblical references in Jer. 19:8–9 which propose cannibalism as an inversion of the heavenly banquet on Earth; and Ugolino's literal-mindedness and inability to interpret spiritually his children's offer (likened to that of the critic who reads only death in Ugolino's final words). Those who oppose the cannibalistic reading argue that Dante wants to arouse pity and not horror in his reader; that the employment of *digiuno* ("fasting") rather than *fame* ("hunger") precludes the interpretation; and that it is too revolting. Certain of those who oppose a cannibalistic reading paradoxically allow for that possibility, awaiting conclusive extraliterary documentation. Hollander has compiled an exhaustive bibliography of studies and an accompanying chart of those in favor of and opposed to a cannibalistic reading.

In efforts to either avoid or answer the episode's nagging question—Did he, or didn't he?—numerous studies have examined Ugolino's masterful rhetoric of the self; his adoption of the tactics of the courtroom attorney in an attempt at exculpation; the sophisticated interplay of narrative levels in the episode; the significance of the account in the greater context of Cocytus; autobiographical echoes (for purposes of comparing or contrasting the fates and characters of Ugolino and the poet); a semantic study of the term *dolor* in light of its medieval resonances; scriptural language and allusions in the episode; classical and biblical passages which suggest themselves as the thematic backdrop to Ugolino's drama; the exegesis (self and other) of Ugolino's dream; the exact nature of the treachery which condemns Ugolino to Antenora—if not the cession of the Pisan castles, about which the poem expresses reservations (*Inf.* 33.85–86); and the function of the *contrapasso*. Recent studies have turned attention from Ugolino's first-person obsession, and the riveting story that it engenders, to the children's narrative—the story Ugolino conceals and the only one that elicits a response from the poet in the fiery invective against Pisa that concludes the episode (*Inf.* 33.85–87). Alongside the reader's struggle to arrive at a satisfying interpretation of Ugolino's final words in the text, they point to the children's desperate and futile attempts to interpret their father's look (*Inf.* 33.51), his gesture, (33.58), and his silence in the tower.

The narrative blanks which punctuate the episode, more than 600 years of heated debate on the significance of Ugolino's closing remarks, and an "innocent" first reading of the canto should reassure the reader of one thing—that nothing is clear about Dante's treatment of Ugolino's suggested? possible? undeniable? cannibalism of his children and that the text requires the reader's unease with the ambiguity it generates.

Bibliography

Bàrberi Squarotti, Giorgio. "L'orazione del conte Ugolino." In *L'Artificio dell'Eternità*. Verona: Fiorini, 1972, pp. 283–332.

Boitani, Piero. "*Inferno* 33." In *Cambridge Readings in Dante's Comedy*. Edited by Patrick Boyde and Kenelm Foster. Cambridge: Cambridge University Press, 1981, pp. 70–89.

Cioffari, Vincenzo. "Il canto 33." In *Inferno: Letture degli anni 1973–76*. Rome: Bonacci, 1976, pp. 785–801.

Ciotti, Andrea. "Il canto 33 dell'*Inferno*." In *Lectura dantis romana*. Turin: Casa di Dante, 1965.

Contini, Gianfranco. "Filologia ed esegesi dantesca." In *Varianti ed altra linguistica. Una raccolta di saggi (1938–1968)*. Turin: Einaudi, 1970, pp. 407–432.

Cook, William, and Ronald Herzman. "*Inferno* 33: The Past and the Present in Dante's Imagery of Betrayal." *Italica* 56 (1979), 377–383.

De Sanctis, Francesco. "L'Ugolino." In *Nuovi saggi critici*. Naples: A. Morano, 1901, pp. 51–77.

Di Pietro, Robert. "*Inferno* 33." *Lectura Dantis* 6 (1990), 419–427.

Frattini, Alberto. "Il canto 33 dell'*Inferno*." In *Lectura dantis romana*. Turin: Società Editrice Internazionale, 1965.

Freccero, John. "Bestial Sign and Bread of Angels (*Inf.* 32–33). *Yale Italian Studies* 1 (1977), 53–66.

Herzman, Ronald B. "Cannibalism and Communion in *Inferno* 33." *Dante Studies* 98 (1980), 53–78.

Hollander, Robert. "Ugolino's Supposed Cannibalism: A Bibliographical Note." *Quaderni d'italianistica* 6/1 (1985), 64–81.

———. "*Inferno* 33.37–74: Ugolino's Importunity." *Speculum* 59/3 (1984), 459–555.

Moliterno, Gino. "Mouth to Mandible, Man to Lupa: The Moral and Political Lesson of Cocytus." *Dante Studies* 104 (1986), 145–161.

Pasquini, Emilio. "Il canto 33 dell'*Inferno*." *Letture Classensi* 9/10 (1982), 191–216.

Perotti, Pier Angelo. "Il conte Ugolino." *L'Alighieri* 32 (1991), 39–50.

Russo, Vittorio. "Il *dolore* del conte Ugolino." In *Sussidi di esegesi dantesca*. Naples: Liguori, 1966, pp. 147–181.

Sansone, Mario. "Il canto 33 dell'*Inferno*." *Nuove letture dantesche* 3 (1969), 143–188.

Shapiro, Marianne. "Addendum: Christological Language in *Inferno* 33." *Dante Studies* 94 (1976), 141–143.

Yowell, Donna L. "Ugolino's *bestial segno:* The *De vulgari eloquenti* in *Inferno* 32–33." *Dante Studies* 104 (1986), 121–143.

Donna Yowell

Uguccione da Lodi

Author of two lengthy religious poems, *Il Libro* and (much more questionably) *La Istoria*. Uguccione is to be considered alongside Bonvesin and Giacomino as a major voice in thirteenth-century Lombard literature and a minor precursor of Dante for his vivid images of Hell and Paradise. A deep religious involvement and a pessimistic slant lend to his didacticism a passionate, mournful tone. Uguccione shuns the mono-rhymed alexandrine quatrain—a standard form in Lombard poetry—tending to prefer mono-rhymed stanzas of varying length in which alexandrines and hendecasyllables freely alternate (in *Il Libro*), and assonanced couplets of nine-syllable lines (in *La Istoria*.)

Bibliography

Bonvesin da la Riva. *Volgari Scelti / Selected Poems*. Edited and translated by Ruggero Stefanini and P. S. Diehl. Bern, New York: Peter Lang, 1987, pp. 203–209.

Ruggero Stefanini

Uguccione de' Bagni

Uguccione de' Bagni of Pisa (Latin name, Huguitio), a twelfth-century grammarian and author of a dictionary, the *Magne derivationes* (full title, *Liber de derivationibus verborum,* or *Huguitionis Pisani magnae derivationes sive dictionarium etymologicum*). He was a professor of canon law at Bologna and bishop of Ferrara from 1190 to his death in 1210. Dante cites the *Derivationes* in *Conv.* 4.6.5 in his discussion of Uguccione's derivation of the word *autore* ("author") from the Greek *autentin*. Noting that this word means "worthy of faith and obedience" in Latin, Dante concludes that "'authority' is nothing but 'the pronouncement of an author.'" Uguccione may also be the source for Dante's use and definitions of *Protonoè* ("Primal Mind," *Conv.* 2.3.11), *Galassia* ("Galaxy," *Conv.* 2.14.1), *allegoria* ("allegory," *Epist.* 13.7), and *hypocrita* (for the *contrapasso* of the hypocrites in the eight circle of Hell, *Inf.* 23.61). It is certain that Dante—if he is the author of the *Epistle to Cangrande*—took his definitions of tragedy and comedy (*Epist.* 13.10) from Uguccione's discussion under the entry *oda* ("ode," "song").

Richard Lansing

Uguccione della Faggiuola

Renowned Ghibelline leader, born in 1250. At various times he was podestà of Arezzo, Gubbio, and Pisa; *capitano del popolo* (Captain-General) of various cities, including Cesena and Pisa; and ruler of Lucca. He achieved his greatest military victory in 1315 at the Battle of Montecatini, where he destroyed the Guelf forces. He was a vigorous supporter of Henry VII of Luxembourg, who made him ruler of Pisa, and late in life he placed himself in the service of Cangrande della Scala. He died in battle in 1320. His possible links to Dante are several, although most appear to be more legendary in nature than real. Boccaccio added his weight to the story that the poet dedicated his *Inferno* to Uguccione, presumably because, it is said, early in his exile he hosted Dante at one of his castles (*Trattatello* 1.193). One critic (Carlo Troya) has even advanced the theory that the *veltro* of *Inf.* 1.101—the prophesied destroyer of the *lupa* ("she-wolf")—is to be identified with him. But historical records (Villani) show that he was not only tyrannical, brutal, and power-hungry but also avaricious, and therefore an unlikely candidate for the solution to the problem of greed represented by the she-wolf.

Richard Lansing

Uguiccione della Gherardesca

Son of Ugolino and Margherita de' Pannocchieschi, Uguiccione (*Uguiccione, Inf.* 33.89) was imprisoned by Archbishop Ruggieri in the Gualandi tower at Pisa in 1288—together with his father, brother Gaddo, and Ugolino's grandsons Anselmuccio and Nino—where they were starved

to death. Although Dante portrays Uguccione as a child (*Inf.* 33.48, 87), he was an adult at the time of his imprisonment.

Richard Lansing

Ulysses

The Greek hero whose adventures while returning home from Troy are sung by Homer in the *Odyssey,* Ulysses figures in canto 26 of Dante's *Inferno,* where he is placed among the fraudulent counselors, engulfed by a flame in the eighth pit of the eighth circle of Hell. Ulysses' story was not known to Dante through Homer, whose poems were not yet available to the Christian West in Dante's time; if Dante knew the various medieval retellings of the story, both Latin and vernacular, which relate Ulysses' return to Ithaca and (in a total departure from Homer) his death at the hands of Telegonus, he shows no signs of it. Rather, Dante's Ulysses is pieced together from a pastiche of classical Latin sources—especially Virgil, Statius, Ovid, Horace, Cicero, and Seneca. From these and other authors the Middle Ages inherited a bifurcated Ulysses, both negative and positive. The negative Ulysses is portrayed in Book 2 of Virgil's *Aeneid,* where he is labeled *dirus* ("dreadful," 2.261) and *scelerum inventor* ("deviser of crimes," 2.164). Virgil's portrayal came to dominate the Latin and later the medieval tradition, producing the conventional stereotype of a treacherous and sacrilegious warrior that leads directly to Dante's fraudulent counselor, who is punished in one flame with his comrade-in-arms Diomedes, since *insieme / a la vendetta vanno come a l'ira* ("together they go to punishment as they went to anger," *Inf.* 26.56–57).

However, Dante's Ulysses is a complex creation that goes far beyond the negative stereotype. Dante borrowed also from the positive rendering of Ulysses that was preserved mainly among the Stoics, for whom the Greek hero exemplified heroic fortitude in the face of adversity. Horace praises Ulysses in the Epistle to Lollius for his discernment and endurance and especially for his ability to withstand the temptations—*Sirenum voces et Circae pocula* ("Sirens' songs and Circe's cups," *Epistles* 1.2.23)—that proved the undoing of his companions. From the *Ars Poetica,* where Horace cites the opening verses of the *Odyssey,* Dante learned that Ulysses *mores hominum multorum vidit et urbes* ("saw the wide world, its ways and cities all," 142). And, most suggestively, Cicero celebrates the mind's innate love of learning and of knowledge, the *discendi cupiditas,* in *De finibus* 5.18.49, using as his exemplary lover of wisdom none other than Ulysses. Cicero reads Homer's Sirens as givers of knowledge and Ulysses' response to their invitation as praiseworthy, for "It is knowledge that the Sirens offer, and it was no marvel if a lover of wisdom held this dearer than his home."

Dante's reconfiguring of Ulysses is a remarkable blend of the two traditional characterizations that also succeeds in charting an entirely new and extremely influential direction for this most versatile of mythic heroes. For Dante invents a new story, never heard before; his Ulysses departs from Circe straight on his new quest, pulled not by the desire for home and family but by the lure of adventure, by the *ardore / ch'i' ebbi a divenir del mondo esperto / e de li vizi umani e del valore* ("the ardor that I had to gain experience of the world and of human vices and worth," *Inf.* 26.97–99). As Stanford points out, "In place of [Homer's] centripetal, homeward-bound figure Dante substituted a personification of centrifugal force" (181), claiming further that "Next to Homer's conception of Ulysses, Dante's, despite its brevity, is the most influential in the whole evolution of the wandering hero" (178).

On the one hand, Dante's placement of Ulysses among the sinners of fraud, and specifically among the fraudulent counselors, depends heavily on the anti-Greek pro-Trojan propaganda of imperial Rome: the sentiment Dante found in the *Aeneid.* Aeneas, Virgil's choice as mythic founder of Rome, is a Trojan, and Virgil's Ulysses reflects the tone of the second book of the *Aeneid,* in which Aeneas recounts the bitter fall of Troy to its Greek conquerors: a fall that occurred, after ten long years of war, not because of military superiority but because of the stratagem—the Ulyssean stratagem—of the Trojan horse. The Virgil who guides Dante through Hell recites a list of Ulyssean "crimes" in *Inf.* 26 that are fully consonant with the *scelera* of which Ulysses is the *inventor* in *Aen.* 2. He is guilty first and foremost of the Trojan horse, *l'agguato del caval che fé la porta / onde uscì de' Romani il gentil seme* ("the deceit of the horse that made the gate to send forth the Romans' noble seed," 59–60), but also of the trick by which Achilles was lured to war and the theft of the Palladium, *l'arte per che, morta, / Deïdamìa*

Dante and Virgil before the flame of Ulysses. Opere di Dante Alighieri, *edited by Cristoforo Zapate de Cisneros, Venice, 1757–1758. Giamatti Collection: Courtesy of the Mount Holyoke College Archives and Special Collections.*

ancor si duol d'Achille, / e del Palladio pena vi si porta ("the art that makes Deidamia, though dead, still grieve for Achilles; and there they bear the punishment for the Palladium," 61–63).

On the other hand, despite this damning recital, countless readers have felt compelled to admire Ulysses' stirring account of his journey beyond the Pillars of Hercules, in other words—like the European explorations of the Atlantic that were just beginning in Dante's day—beyond the markers of the known world. In order to persuade his old and tired companions to undertake such a *folle volo* ("mad flight," 125), Ulysses deploys his forceful eloquence in an *orazion picciola* ("little oration," 122) that has, rightly or wrongly, moved generations of readers and (quite divorced of its infernal context) achieved proverbial status in Italy: *"O frati,"* dissi, *"che per cento milia / perigli siete giunti a l'occidente, / a questa tanto picciola vigilia / d'i nostri sensi ch' del rimanente / non vogliate negar l'esperïenza, / di retro al sol, del mondo sanza gente. / Considerate la vostra semenza: / fatti non foste a viver come bruti, / ma per seguir virtute e canoscenza,"* ("O brothers," I said, "who through a hundred thousand perils have reached the West, to this so brief vigil of our senses that remains, do not deny the experience, following the Sun, of the world without people. Consider your sowing: you were not made to live like brutes, but to follow virtue and knowledge," *Inf.* 26.112–120). While this oration exemplifies fraudulent counsel, since through it Ulysses leads his companions to their destruction, it also powerfully evokes the authentic spirit of the Ciceronian *discendi cupiditas.*

Dante's Ulysses is an adventurer who dies while adventuring—indeed after embarking on his ultimate quest. Sailing into the uncharted waters of the uninhabited Southern Hemisphere, he sees a mountain in the distance, the highest he has ever seen. However, from this *nova terra* ("new land," *Inf.* 26.137) a whirlwind arises that hits his ship and sinks it, bringing his exploration of the new world he has seen on the horizon to a sudden and tragic end. The shore that Ulysses cannot attain is the shore of Mount Purgatory, a shore that does not yield its secrets lightly to human daring; it is a *lito diserto, / che mai non vide navicar sue acque / omo, che di tornar sia poscia esperto* ("the deserted shore, which never saw any man sail its waters who afterwards experienced return," *Purg.* 1.130–132). It is a shore that Dante-pilgrim will reach, for Dante's transgressive journey through the afterworld is willed by God, while Ulysses' is undertaken alone, a solitary enterprise without divine sanction: *ma misi me per l'alto mare aperto / sol* ("but I put out on the deep, open sea alone," *Inf.* 26.100–101).

Dante criticism has been divided on the subject of Ulysses essentially since its inception. Among the fourteenth-century commentators, Buti takes a moralizing position critical of the Homeric hero, while Benvenuto sees him as exciting Dante's admiration. We could sketch the positions of various modern critics around the same polarity. There is a pro-Ulysses group, spearheaded by Fubini, who maintains that Dante feels only admiration for the *folle volo,* the desire for knowledge it represents, and the oration that justifies it (Fubini's supporters include Sapegno, Pagliaro, Forti). Then there is a less unified group that emphasizes the Greek hero's sinfulness and seeks to determine the primary cause for his infer-

nal abode (rendered less clear by Dante's avoidance of the eighth pit's label until the end of the encounter with Guido da Montefeltro in the next canto). This second group could be divided into those who see the *folle volo* itself as the chief of Ulysses' sins and those who concentrate instead on the sin of fraudulent counsel as described by Guido and on Ulysses' rhetorical deceitfulness as manifested in the *orazion picciola* (Padoan, Dolfi). Most influential in the first category has been the position of Nardi, who argues that Dante's Ulysses is a new Adam, a new Lucifer, and that his sin is precisely Adam's, namely, *il trapassar del segno* ("the going beyond the mark," *Par.* 26.117). Ulysses is thus a transgressor, whose pride incites him to seek a knowledge that is beyond the limits set for man by God, in the same way that Adam's pride drove him to a similar transgression, also in pursuit of a knowledge that would make him Godlike. Ulysses rebels against the limits marked by the Pillars of Hercules, and his rebellion is akin to that of Lucifer and the rebel angels.

To account for Ulysses' heroic stature within the *Commedia,* Nardi posits a split within Dante himself, whereby the poet is moved by what the theologian condemns. Nardi's reading has much in common with that of an earlier critic, Valli, who also considered Ulysses deeply embedded within the symbolism of the *Commedia* and representative of the perilous pride that besets mankind. Valli too sees the sin of Dante's Ulysses as akin to Adam's eating of the tree of knowledge, as a *trapassar del segno* analogous to the original sin. The key difference between the two is that Valli relates the figure of Ulysses to Dante's sense of a peril within himself, rather than arguing for an unconsciously divided poet; indeed, Valli goes so far as to invoke Dante's encyclopedic prose treatise, *Convivio,* as an example of Dante's own propensities toward intellectual pride, thus anticipating the positions of such critics as Freccero, Thompson, and Corti.

We can consider the positions of Dante scholars within the Ulysses *querelle* along a continuum, with extreme positions at either end: at one extreme are those critics, like Fubini, who maintain that Dante feels only admiration for Ulysses' voyage and that it has nothing whatever to do with his damnation; at the other are those critics, like Cassell, who deny Ulysses any special importance, telling us that the poet feels nothing but scorn for his creature and to see anything else at work in the canto is to read it through anachronistic romantic eyes. Both these readings rob the episode of its tension and deflate it of its energy—on the one hand, by making the fact that Ulysses is in Hell irrelevant and, on the other, by denying that this particular sinner means more to the poem than do his companions. Fubini's simple admiration fails to deal with the fact that Dante places Ulysses in Hell; Cassell's simple condemnation fails to take into account the structural and thematic significance that the Greek hero bears for the *Commedia* as a whole.

The positions of the two major critical schools—the one that posits Ulysses' sinfulness primarily in the *folle volo* and the other that defends the voyage and sees his sinfulness primarily in his fraudulent counsel—can reflect the complex integrity of Dante's creation only when they are themselves integrated. It is not possible to divorce the idea of fraudulent counsel from this hero's later behavior, since the speech with which Ulysses persuades his companions to undertake their last voyage exemplifies it. At the same time, Dante's great addition to the story of Ulysses— precisely the mad journey beyond the Pillars of Hercules—cannot be overlooked in a balanced assessment of Ulysses' role in the poem. There is much to be said for Nardi's linking of Ulyssean trespass to Adamic trespass. Dante himself uses Ulyssean language in describing Adam's sin: in *Par.* 7 he calls it *follia* ("madness," 93), and in *Par.* 26, as we saw, he describes it as *trapassar* ("trespass" or "transgression"). Contemporary readers of the *Commedia* responded to the linguistic and thematic correspondences Dante drew between Ulysses and Adam: Boccaccio conflates the *Paradiso*'s Adamic *trapassar del segno* with the description of the purgatorial shore from *Purg.* 1 to characterize Ulysses as one who *per voler veder trapassò il segno / dal qual nessun poté mai in qua reddire* ("in his desire to see trespassed the boundary from which no one has ever been able to return," *Amorosa visione,* redaction A, 27.86–87). For Petrarch, too, Ulysses *desiò del mondo veder troppo* ("desired to see too much of the world," *Triumphus fame* 2.18). Far from being anachronistic, as charged by his critics, Nardi is reviving a contemporary insight when he associates Dante's Ulysses with Adam: with primal trespass, with a mad assumption of limitless and unchecked further adventure—further knowledge.

The least convincing aspect of Nardi's reading is his formulation of an unconsciously divided poet. It seems far more likely that Ulysses reflects instead Dante's conscious concern for himself. The perception of a profound autobiographical alignment between the poet and his creation seems also to have had early roots: Bosco shows that Dante's intransigence in not accepting Florentine terms for repatriation despite the suffering of his family elicited contrasting reactions from Boccaccio, who defended him, and Petrarch, whose criticism implicitly brands him a Ulysses. Moreover, the Dante who is implicated in the figure of Ulysses is not solely the Dante of the *Convivio,* a Dante of the past, but also the Dante of the *Commedia.* And, within the *Commedia,* Ulysses is reflected not only by Dante-pilgrim, who, as Scott and others have shown, is related to Ulysses as an inverse type, his negative double, but also, as Barolini demonstrates, by Dante-poet, who has embarked on a poetic voyage that transgresses the boundary between life and death, between God and man. Asking "To what do we owe the tragic weight of [the Ulysses] episode?" Borges replies: "I think there is one explanation, the only valid one, and that is that Dante felt, in some way, that he was Ulysses. I don't know if he felt it in a conscious way—it doesn't matter. In some tercet of the *Commedia* he says that no one is permitted to know the judgments of Providence. We cannot anticipate them; no one can know who will be saved and who condemned. But Dante has dared, through poetry, to do precisely that. He shows us the condemned and the chosen. He must have known that doing so courted danger. He could not ignore that he was anticipating the indecipherable providence of God. For this reason the character of Ulysses has such force, because Ulysses is a mirror of Dante, because Dante felt that perhaps he too deserved this punishment. Writing the poem, whether for good or ill, he was infringing on the mysterious laws of the night, of God, of Divinity" (24).

A further textual sign of Ulysses' irreducibility, of the fact that he is not just any sinner, is his sustained presence in the poem: he is named in each canticle, not only in *Inf.* 26 but also in *Purg.* 19, where the siren of Dante's dream claims to have turned Ulysses aside from his path with her song, and in *Par.* 27, where the pilgrim, looking down at Earth, sees the trace of *il varco / folle d'Ulisse* ("the mad leap of Ulysses," 82–83), in a stunning reminiscence of the original episode's

U *folle volo.* As *folle volo* and *varco folle* indicate, Ulysses embodies and dramatizes the poem's most fundamental trope: voyage. Specifically, he is linked to the *Commedia*'s metaphorization of desire as flight, a metaphor embedded in the verse in which Ulysses conjures the wild exuberance he had solicited from his aged crew by saying *de'remi facemmo ali al folle volo* ("of our oars we made wings for the mad flight," *Inf.* 26.125). Ulysses and his surrogates, other failed flyers like Phaëton and Icarus, are connected to one of the *Commedia*'s most basic metaphorical assumptions: if we desire sufficiently, we fly. In other words, if we desire sufficiently, our quest takes on wings; if we desire sufficiently, we vault all obstacles, we cross all boundaries. Thus we have the passage in *Purgatorio* in which the narrator overtly establishes the metaphorical identity between desire and flight, saying that in order to climb the steep grade of lower Purgatory one needs to fly with the wings of desire: *ma qui convien ch'om voli; / dico con l'ale snelle e con le piume / del gran disio* ("but here one must fly, I mean with the swift wings and the pinions of great desire," *Purg.* 4.27–29).

Dante-pilgrim flies on the *piume del gran disio,* and the saturation of the *Commedia* with flight imagery—with imagery that the poem codes as Ulyssean flight imagery—reflects the importance of desire as the impulse that governs all questing, all voyaging, all coming to know. Desire and the search for understanding are intimately linked, indeed ultimately one, for desire is spiritual motion, as Dante tells us: *disire, / ch' moto spiritale* ("desire, which is spiritual motion," *Purg.* 18.31–32). This equivalence—desire equals spiritual motion—crucially recasts in the metaphorical language of voyage and pilgrimage the Aristotelian precept that stands on the *Convivio*'s threshold, where we already find articulated the link between desire and knowledge, *desiderio* and *sapere: tutti li uomini naturalmente desiderano di sapere* ("all men by nature desire to know," *Conv.* 1.1.1). The treatise's abstract conceptual pairing returns in the *Commedia*'s metaphorical copulae: the winged oars, the plumage of great desire. Desire—Ulyssean *ardore*—is the motor propelling all voyage: both right voyages, conversions, and those that, like Ulysses' own, tend toward the left (the *lato mancino* of *Inf.* 26.126), toward perdition. The complex and polysemous character of Ulysses is conceived and written in

such a way as to tap into the deepest wellsprings of the *Commedia*'s energy, for Ulysses holds up a mirror to the poem's principal voyager, Dante himself, whose ambitions were no less grand.

Bibliography

Avalle, D'Arco Silvio. "L'ultimo viaggio di Ulisse." In *Modelli semiologici nella "Commedia" di Dante.* Milan: Bompiani, 1975.

Barolini, Teodolinda. *The Undivine "Comedy."* Princeton, N.J.: Princeton University Press, 1992.

Boccaccio, Giovanni. *Amorosa visione.* Edited by Vittore Branca. *Tutte le opere di Giovanni Boccaccio.* Vol. 3. Verona: Mondadori, 1974.

Boitani, Piero. *The Shadow of Ulysses: Figures of a Myth.* Oxford: Clarendon Press, 1994.

Borges, Jorge Luis. *Seven Nights.* Translated by Eliot Weinberger. New York: New Directions, 1984.

Bosco, Umberto. "La 'follia' di Dante." 1958. Reprinted in *Dante vicino.* 2nd ed. Caltanissetta: Sciascia, 1972, pp. 55–75.

Cassell, Anthony K. *Dante's Fearful Art of Justice.* Toronto: University of Toronto Press, 1984.

———. "*Ulisseana:* A Bibliography of Dante's Ulysses to 1981." *Italian Culture* 3 (1981), 23–45.

Cicero. *De Finibus Bonorum et Malorum.* Translated by H. Rackham. Loeb Classical Library. Cambridge, Mass.: Harvard University Press; London: Heinemann, 1971.

Corti, Maria. *Dante a un nuovo crocevia.* Florence: Libreria Commissionaria Sansoni, 1981, pp. 85–97.

Dolfi, Anna. "Il canto di Ulisse: occasione per un discorso di esegesi dantesca." *Forum Italicum* 7–8 (1973–1974), 22–45.

Forti, Fiorenzo. "'Curiositas' o 'fol hardement'?" In *Magnanimitade: Studi su un tema dantesco.* Bologna: Pàtron, 1977, pp. 161–206.

Freccero, John. "Dante's Ulysses." 1975. Reprinted in *Dante: The Poetics of Conversion.* Edited by Rachel Jacoff. Cambridge, Mass.: Harvard University Press, 1986.

Fubini, Mario. "Il peccato d'Ulisse" and "Il canto XXVI dell'*Inferno.*" In *Il peccato d'Ulisse e altri scritti danteschi.* Milan: Ricciardi, 1966, pp. 1–76.

Horace. *Satires, Epistles, and Ars Poetica.* Translated by H. Rushton Fairclough. Loeb Classical Library. London: Heinemann; Cambridge, Mass.: Harvard University Press, 1970.

Nardi, Bruno. "La tragedia di Ulisse." 1937. Reprinted in *Dante e la cultura medievale*. 2nd. ed. rev. Bari: Laterza, 1949, pp. 153–165.

Padoan, Giorgio. "Ulisse 'fandi fictor' e le vie della sapienza." 1960. Reprinted in *Il pio Enea, l'empio Ulisse*. Ravenna: Longo, 1967, pp. 170–199.

Pagliaro, Antonino. "Ulisse." In *Ulisse: Ricerche semantiche sulla "Divina Commedia."* 2 vols. Messina: D'Anna, 1967. Vol. 1, pp. 371–432.

Petrarca, Francesco. *Triumphi*. Edited by Marco Ariani. Milan: Mursia, 1988.

Sapegno, Natalino. "Ulisse." *Letture Classensi* 7 (1979), 93–98.

Scott, John A. "L'Ulisse dantesco." In *Dante magnanimo*. Florence: Olschki, 1977, pp. 117–193.

Seriacopi, Massimo. *All'estremo della "prudentia": l'Ulisse di Dante*. Rome: Zauli Arti Grafiche, 1994.

Shankland, Hugh. "Dante *Aliger* and Ulysses." *Italian Studies* 32 (1977), 21–40.

Stanford, W. B. *The Ulysses Theme: A Study in the Adaptability of a Traditional Hero*. 2nd ed. Ann Arbor: University of Michigan Press, 1968.

Thompson, David. "Dante's Ulysses and the Allegorical Journey." 1967. Reprinted in *Dante's Epic Journeys*. Baltimore: Johns Hopkins University Press, 1974.

Valli, Luigi. "Ulisse e la tragedia intellettuale di Dante." *La struttura morale dell'universo dantesco*. Rome: Ausonia, 1935, pp. 26–40.

Virgil. *Aeneid*. Translated by H. Rushton Fairclough. Loeb Classical Library. 2 vols. Cambridge, Mass.: Harvard University Press; London: Heinemann, 1974.

Teodolinda Barolini

Urban I, Pope

Pope from 222 to 230 and martyr to the faith, Urban *(Urbano)* is cited, along with Popes Sixtus I, Pius I, and Callistus I, as an example of sacrificial devotion to the Church, in St. Peter's denunciation of the corrupt papacy in the Heaven of the Fixed Stars (*Par.* 27.44).

Richard Lansing

Usury

Usury becomes the focus of Virgil's description of the moral structure of Hell in *Inf.* 11 when the pilgrim fails to comprehend how it is a sin of violence, in particular, a sin of violence against *la divina bontade* ("God's goodness," 94–96). Virgil's explanation gives rise to a genealogical account of the three general categories of violence against God: direct offense (blasphemy); violence against nature, God's progeny (sodomy); violence against art or human industry (usury). To explain this last form of violence, twice removed from God, Virgil first calls on the authority of Aristotle's *Physics* to establish the idea that art follows nature (*ars imitatur naturam,* 2.2.194). He then discloses the sinful nature of usury by reminding the pilgrim of God's harsh words to Adam for having disobeyed his command not to eat from the tree of knowledge of good and evil in the Garden of Eden: *in laboribus comedes ex ea [terra] cunctis diebus vitae tuae* ("in toil you shall eat of it [earth] all the days of your life," Gen. 3:17).

The notion that fallen man must live "by the sweat of his brow" (Gen. 3:19), combined with Christ's exhortation to his followers to "lend, expecting nothing in return" (Luke 6:35), gave the Christian Middle Ages a firm foundation from which to condemn the lending of money at interest. In his *Summa theologiae,* Thomas Aquinas marshals a variety of sources, from biblical passages and Aristotle's writings to Roman law and contemporary statutes, to prove that usury, defined as "not merely the restoration of some equivalent but also a charge for its use," is indeed a sin (2.2.78.1). According to Aquinas, the biblical passages apparently permitting usury—e.g., Deut. 23:19 and Luke 19:23—are not only countered by biblical injunctions against usury (Exod. 22:25, Ps. 15:5) but are also ineffective on their own terms as arguments in favor of the economic activity of lending at interest. In the first case, God's permission to charge interest to foreigners no longer applies, since all people are exhorted to treat one another as neighbors in the "epoch of the Gospel." And in the Gospel example itself, Aquinas interprets Christ's statement that he has come to collect "with interest" metaphorically to mean that God expects "a natural increase of spiritual goods."

However, in a move that helps to shape Dante's view, Aquinas depends mostly on Aristotle to put forth his argument against usury. Beginning from the premise that money should be used as a "middle term," a way to measure the relative values of goods and services by some single

U

Dante among the usurers. La comedia, *ed. Pietro da Figino, 1491. Giamatti Collection: Courtesy of the Mount Holyoke College Archives and Special Collections.*

standard (*Nicomachean Ethics,* 5.5), Aristotle argues in the *Politics* (1.10.1258b) that to charge interest on a monetary loan is "absolutely contrary to nature" *(maxime praeter naturam)*. Aquinas' gloss on this characterization of usury has a direct bearing on Dante's presentation of the usurers in the third ring of the circle of violence: "Thus a kind of birth takes place when money grows from [other] money. For this reason the acquisition of money is especially contrary to Nature, because it is in accordance with nature that money should increase from natural goods and not from money itself" (*Exp. Polit.* 1.8.134). The "unnatural birth" resulting from usury thus stands in ironic contrast to the sterile desert landscape in which the usurers are punished (*Inf.* 17)—the same barren terrain that is home to the sodomites, the sinners whose acts were most consistently perceived as *contra naturam* in the medieval theological imagination. In fact, usury in Dante's day was associated with heresy as well as with sodomy in canon law and the denunciations of the inquisition (Boswell, pp. 269–276).

By positioning his usurers toward the inner edge of the seventh circle, Dante suggests a close relationship between the sin of usury and the sins of fraud punished below, in the eighth circle, as well as the other forms of violence with which Virgil groups usury in *Inf.* 11 (Ferrante, 344–356). To emphasize the relationship of usury to fraud, Dante frames his brief presentation of the usurers in

canto 17 with descriptions of Geryon, the *sozza imagine di froda* ("filthy image of fraud," 17.7) whom Virgil calls up from the abyss (16.106–136, 17.1–30) in order to transport the travelers down to the eighth circle (17.79–136). Geryon's painted hide (17.16–18) and the usurers' colorful purses (17.55–65) bring to mind the leopard of the opening canto (1.31–33), whose "spotted hide" *(pelle dipinta)* is recalled as a prelude to Geryon's arrival (16.108). While Virgil requests Geryon's assistance, the pilgrim goes off by himself to gain "full experience" of the third and final ring of the circle of violence. By this structuring of scenes, Dante seems to suggest that while usury is technically a sin of violence—because as St. Thomas says it is performed openly *(manifeste)*, unlike fraud, which is performed by deception *(occulte)*—it is nevertheless virtually a kind of fraud.

The usurers are all Florentines except for the Paduan who rudely addresses the pilgrim and abruptly ends the encounter with a lewd gesture: *Qui distorse la bocca e di fuor trasse / la lingua, come bue che 'l naso lecchi* ("Here he twisted his mouth and stuck out his tongue, like an ox licking its snout," 17.74–75). The bovine image is a fitting emblem of this "mournful people" (45) who are distinguished only by their family coats of arms, each of which contains an animal (lion, goose, sow). Defending themselves from the flakes of fire like dogs that bite and scratch when assailed by fleas or flies (47–51), the usurers are now forced to use the hands that they neglected to use in the service of industrious labor while alive (Getto, 342–343). A more straightforward aspect of Dante's *contrapasso* for the usurers is their seated position, since this is how they would most likely have conducted their business.

On an autobiographical note, Forese Donati (*Purg.* 23–24), in an exchange of insulting sonnets with Dante, alleges that Dante's father was himself a usurer or moneychanger (*Rime* 74 and 78).

Bibliography

Aquinas, Thomas. *Summa theologiae* (Latin text and English translation). Blackfriars Edition. New York: McGraw-Hill, 1964–1981.

———. *In octo libros Physicorum Aristotelis Expositio.* Edited by P. M. Maggiòlo. Turin, Rome: Marietti, 1954.

———. *In libros Politicorum Aristotelis Expositio.* Edited by R. M. Spiazzi. Turin, Rome: Marietti, 1951.

Aristotle. *Physics: Books I and II.* Translated by W. Charlton. Oxford: Oxford University Press, 1970.

———. *Nichomachean Ethics.* Translated by Martin Ostwald. Indianapolis, New York: Liberal Arts Press, 1962.

Boswell, John. *Christianity, Social Tolerance, and Homosexuality.* Chicago, London: University of Chicago Press, 1980.

Capitani, Ovidio. "Il *De peccato usurae* di Remigio de' Girolami." *Studi medievali* 6.2 (1965), 537–662.

Ferrante, Joan M. *The Political Vision of the Divine Comedy.* Princeton, N.J.: Princeton University Press, 1984.

Freinkel, Lisa. "*Inferno* and the Poetics of *Usura.*" *MLN* 107.1 (1992), 1–17.

Getto, Giovanni. "Il canto XVII dell'*Inferno.*" In *Letture dantesche.* Vol. 1: *Inferno.* 2nd ed. Florence: Sansoni, 1968, pp. 333–352.

McLaughlin, T. P. "The Teaching of the Canonists on Usury in the 12th, 13th and 14th centuries." *Medieval Studies* 1 (1939), 81–147.

Noonan, John T. *The Scholastic Analysis of Usury.* Cambridge, Mass.: Harvard University Press, 1957.

Shoaf, R. A. *Dante, Chaucer, and the Currency of the Word.* Norman, Okla.: Pilgrim Books, 1983.

Soldati, Paolo. "Canto XVII." In *Lectura Dantis Scaligera: Inferno.* Florence: Le Monnier, 1967, pp. 563–577.

Guy P. Raffa

Varius

Lucius Varius Rufus, Roman poet of the first century B.C.E. and close friend of Horace and Virgil. Quintilian considered his tragedy, *Thyestes,* comparable to the best Greek tragedies. The emperor Augustus appointed Varius to help oversee the posthumous publication of Virgil's *Aeneid.* Dante mentions Varius *(Varro)* in *Purg.* 22.98, when Statius asks Virgil about the fate of several Roman poets.

It has been suggested that the *Varro* mentioned by Dante is the Latin poet Publius Terentius Varro Atacinus (b. 82 B.C.E.). The spelling "Varro" for "Vario" was common, however, and Virgil's close friendship with Varius makes it probable that he is the one to whom Dante refers.

Nancy Vine Durling

Vatican

The hill on the right bank of the Tiber in Rome, traditional burial place of St. Peter and site of the Constantinian basilica dedicated to him. Though protected after the mid–ninth century by the Leonine wall, the Vatican complex was not the normal residence of the early medieval popes—whose church as bishops of Rome was San Giovanni in Laterano—and "Vatican" was not a synonym for "papacy." The word is used only once in the *Commedia,* by the troubadour poet Folco (*Par.* 9.139–142), who prophesies the freeing of the Vatican from the adultery of the simoniacal popes. The Vatican became the principal residence of the pope only after the papacy returned to Rome from Avignon in France, where it had been during the years from 1309 to 1377.

Michael Haren

Vellutello, Alessandro

A Lucchese intellectual active in Venice from c. 1515, Alessandro Vellutello (dates of birth and death unknown) published his commentary to the *Commedia* in 1544. Printed by Francesco Marcolini and dedicated to Pope Paul III, the commentary contains some of the most beautiful illustrations to the poem of the Renaissance.

Although there exists little biographical information on Vellutello, we can glean some sense of his literary sensibilities from his polemical *proemio,* in which he criticizes Landino's commentary and earlier Renaissance editions of the poem. Vellutello does not share Landino's preference for Boccaccio's rather romantic biography of Dante, finding Leonardo Bruni's life of the poet more historically accurate. Vellutello also criticizes Landino's calculations of *Inferno*'s dimensions. Both commentators' desire to offer a precise account of Hell's topography reflects the Renaissance interest in cartography and exploration. Vellutello's sharpest criticisms are directed at Aldus Manutius' 1502 edition of the poem, *Le terze rime di Dante.* The title of this production, which emphasized the poem's metrical form, was likely bestowed by the editor, Pietro Bembo. While Bembo is not singled out by name, he is undoubtedly implicated as the *datore* ("giver") of false authority.

Vellutello did not share Bembo's emphasis on purity of diction. The commentary contains few observations concerning Dante's language and style. Vellutello seeks primarily to clarify the poem's literal meaning. He provides a far more detailed explication of the poem's historical allusions than Landino. Francesco Sansovino pub-

LA COMEDIA DI

DANTE ALIGIERI

CON LA NOVA ESPOSITIONE
DI ALESSANDRO
VELLVTELLO.

CON GRATIA ET PRIVILEGIO.

IN VENETIA,
Appresso Francesco Rampazetto.
M D LXIIII.

1564 edition of the Commedia *with the Alessandro Vellutello commentary, published by Rampazetto in Venice. Reproduced by permission of the John A. Zahm Dante Collection in the Department of Special Collections, University Libraries, University of Notre Dame.*

lished Vellutello's and Landino's commentaries together in a sumptuous edition in 1564. The two commentaries complement one another well: Vellutello's attention to history and the poem's literal significance balances Landino's philosophical expositions. Sansovino's edition was subsequently reprinted in 1572 and 1596.

Bibliography

Belloni, Gino. "Un eretico nella Venezia del Bembo: Alessandro Vellutello." *Giornale storico della letteratura italiana* 97 (1980), 43–74.

Bigi, Emilio. *Forme e significati nella "Divina Commedia."* Bologna: Capelli, 1981.

Parker, Deborah. *Commentary and Ideology: Dante in the Renaissance.* Durham, N.C.: Duke University Press, 1993.

Vallone, Aldo. *Storia della critica dantesca dal XIV al XX secolo.* Padua: Vallardi, 1981.

Deborah Parker

Veltro

In *Inf.* 1.101, Virgil predicts the coming of *[i]l Veltro* ("the greyhound"), who will chase the she-wolf of concupiscence out of the communes of Italy "back into Hell, whence envy first sent her forth" (1.110–111). The crux of the meaning here hinges upon whether Dante intended his prophecy as a real prophecy in the mode of the Old Testament or Apocalypse (in which case the identity would be known only to God) or, as occurs in so many instances in the poem, as a *vaticinium ex eventu* or *post factum* (in which case he would have had a specific individual or entity in mind).

The early commentators (beginning with Graziolo de' Bambaglioli, c. 1324, who saw in it a reference to Christ's Second Coming) preferred the first, eschatological option, hesitating to perceive in the *veltro* any specific person; modern interpreters, however, have often followed the second, seeking a precise identification among contemporary emperors, popes, or military leaders. Regardless of their position, almost all scholars have believed that the key to the *veltro*'s identity was to be found in the line *e sua nazion sarà tra feltro e feltro* (1.105).

Jacopo di Dante (1322)—followed, more elaborately, by Jacopo della Lana (c. 1324–1328), Giovanni Boccaccio (1373), Francesco da Buti (1385–1389), and Cristoforo Landino (1481)—was the first to give an astrological explanation of the line: *tra feltro e feltro* meant *tra cielo e cielo* ("among the heavens"), since redemption would come from the stars. Della Lana, in turn followed by the Ottimo (1333), also saw the image as astrological but, in construing *feltro* as "felt," saw the word as a symbol of poverty and, thus, of the humble birth of the redeemer to come. Some modern scholars (Kaske and Friedman, for example) have seen *feltro* as a specific reference to the humble garments of the mendicant orders and thus have theorized that Dante anticipated reform from the Franciscans. Boccaccio frankly confessed his incomprehension of the prediction while rebutting then-current views: the verse referred neither to the Second Coming of Christ nor to the coming of some Tartar emperor (despite the fact, as Boccaccio explains, that the Khans were customarily buried in felt wrappings). The Anonimo Fiorentino rejected the explanation that *tra feltro e feltro* signified either base birth or that it referred to the two cities of Feltre and Montefeltro; he returned to the conventional idea that it meant the "supernal

V

constellations" that would drive avarice from the world. Pietro di Dante gave more complex and eclectic exegeses in the three versions of his *Commentarium* (1340–1341, 1350–1355, c. 1358): "felt" was a vile, matted cloth "not duly woven," signifying the bastardy of the future redeemer who would be a *vir virtuosus et dux* ("a virtuous man and leader") who (in the Ottobonian version) would become not only leader of Italy but governor of the whole world; the prophecy referred both to a future emperor and to Christ. In the Ashburnham version Pietro suggested the Veltro's identity with the Pseudo-Methodius' prediction of a last emperor who would vanquish the Muslims and herald Christ's Second Coming. In all three versions of his commentary Pietro compared the prediction with the coming of the *novus homo* ("new man") of Alain de Lille's *Anticlaudianus:* both Alain's and Dante's heroes were to combat avarice and restore the world. In Pietro's later two versions the *veltro* is specifically identified with the *cinquecento diece e cinque* prophecy ("five hundred ten and five") of *Purg.* 33.43.

Guido da Pisa (1327–1328), taking cues from the *Monarchia,* saw in the greyhound the primacy and "the nobility of the Roman people" embodied in some coming emperor in the mold of Scipio Africanus (cf. *Par.* 27.55–63) and, anagogically, in Christ at his Second Coming. Guido is followed by the Anonimo Selmiano (1337) and the "falso Boccaccio" (1375), and by the author of the *Codice Cassinese* (c. 1330): "Veltrus, id est Christus" ("the *veltro,* that is, Christ"). Benvenuto da Imola, like Guido da Pisa and Pietro di Dante, viewed the prophecy as an imitation of Virgil's *Eclogue* IV and a dual prediction, first of a future Roman prince who would curtail the greed of prelates and, second, of Christ to come; he ridiculed the geographical interpretation of Feltre and Montefeltro but accepted the astrological *tra cielo e cielo.*

Vellutello (1544) seems to have been the first to give written testimony of the identity of the *veltro* as Cangrande della Scala (with the *cinquecento diece e cinque* ["five hundred ten and five"] of *Purgatorio* regarded as Henry of Luxembourg, the future Emperor Henry VII), an interpretation taken up by Magalotti in his commentary of 1665. Among many modern critics, Auerbach proposed Cangrande and the Great Khan or the Phoenix; and more recently, Hollander has suggested the joint identification of Cangrande and Christ.

Gentile and Mazzoni have supported the interpretation of the *veltro* as symbolizing Henry VII, with Arezio even proposing in support an unlikely etymology of *veltro* from the German *Weltherr* ("world ruler"). Troya, in a long essay of 1826 (published in 1932), suggested Uguccione della Faggiola, and more recently Ferrante has supported Ludwig of Bavaria.

Pietrobono understood the prophecy more generally as predicting an emperor who would restore society. In a similar vein Nardi (1963) saw in the *veltro*'s pursuit of the wolf the coming of a universal monarch who would rescind the Donation of Constantine and restore the ideal of poverty to the Church. Sarolli identified the *veltro* with the *cinquecento diece e cinque* prophecy, understanding them both as two "Christomimetic symbols" to be embodied in a Holy Roman Emperor springing from the people.

In 1921, Regis suggested that *tra feltro e feltro* referred to the felt linings of ballot boxes (*bossoli foderati di feltro*) used to deaden the sound of the lead ball, *pallotta* ("ballot"), as it dropped within: many Italian communes indeed employed this form of election; however, there is no evidence that the German imperial electors used the system. *Nazion* signifies "birth," "nation," "race," "stock," "lineage," or perhaps "clan" or "people"—all things, surely, impossible to change through any subsequent vote.

Contrasting with these "neo-Ghibelline" interpreters are the "neo-Guelf" supporters who have held that Earth's restoration would be undertaken by a pope (among others, for example, Porena, 1946–1948). Pope Benedict XI especially found supporters among many nineteenth-century critics and, in the twentieth century, in Renucci (1954). The identification, however, is unconvincing, since it would assume an impossibly early date for the completion of the *Inferno:* Benedict died in 1304. Dante's attitude to contemporary popes is clearly expressed in *Par.* 27.55–63 where he has St. Peter denounce them as rapacious wolves ready to drink the blood of saints. It is clear that he did not believe any redemption of "humble Italy" would come from them.

Other more speculative identifications have also been made. In several studies Della Torre defended the proposal of interpreting the *veltro* as Dante himself; he was followed in this by several scholars, the most important being Olschki. Having interpreted the words *tra feltro e feltro* in his

Myth of Felt as a reference to the felt caps of Castor and Pollux, the twins of the zodiac, Olschki published a second short treatise in 1953 in which he claimed that the poet himself was the longed-for messiah, born under the sign of Gemini. Getto also espoused this view. On the other hand, Hardie, following the lead of Crescimanno (1905), developed the thesis that the *veltro* was the *Commedia* itself.

The interpretation of the enigmatic verse 105 has continued to be divided mainly between the geographical and the anagogical even in modern times. The controversial capitalization of the words "Feltro e Feltro" as place names in the 1921 edition of the Società Dantesca Italiana garnered converts to the identification with Cangrande, despite the fact that those two cities did not delimit the boundaries of the Scaligera realm. Petrocchi's edition returned the capitals to lowercase; Singleton (1970) translated v. 105 as "his birth shall be *between felt and felt*," thus preserving the mystery.

The apocalyptic writings of the great Cistercian seer Gioachino da Fiore (c. 1132–1202) have also played a large role in the interpretations of the prophecy. In 1929 Dempf asserted that the *Commedia* itself was "a Joachite apocalypse." In 1911, Filomusi-Guelfi, in a well investigated but ultimately unconvincing chapter, identified the *veltro* with the Holy Spirit expected by the Joachite Franciscan Spirituals. His contention was ably rebutted by Foberti, Barbi, and Tondelli (1940). Tondelli himself, however, retained the belief in the prophecy's Joachite inspiration but saw the *veltro* as signifying an order of monks. Later studies have refuted the exaggerated beliefs of Joachite influence on the *Commedia,* holding that such influence is, on the contrary, rather slim (Reeves).

Following the interpretation reported but rejected by Boccaccio, A. Bassermann (1901) and H. Matrod (1914) argued that the *veltro* prophecy signified the coming of the Great Khan of the Tartars—the distinction and chronic wars between Mongols and Tartars generally having been ignored until C. Emiliani's intelligent article of 1993. Emiliani concludes: "What Dante may have had in mind was a leader with the virtues of the Great Khans of the orient, as reported by Marco Polo, but without their lust for land and riches" (151).

We can only conclude that Dante devises the *veltro* enigma in the mode of true biblical prophecy, in the mode of true *vaticinium;* he creates a purposeful obscurity to give the widest possibility for its eventual fulfillment. The author presents himself as a prophet, like Moses, unknowing, yet certain of a propitious outcome. Dante's faith, the substance of his hopes that had been so often raised and dashed—especially by the early success, then failure and sudden death of Emperor Henry VII in 1313—led him several times to modify the expression of his temporal expectations, and these modifications he reflected in the various prophecies of his "sacred poem." That of the *veltro* pronounced, significantly, through the mouth of Virgil *vates,* has the effect almost of a credo upon the reader. If the historical Virgil had failed to believe his own prophecy of Christ's birth in *Eclogue* 4 (as the Middle Ages believed), Dante seems to allow the ancient poet of the Empire—damned for "not having faith"—to make some amends here, professing hope in an inevitable justice to come in the restoration of imperial rule.

The prophecy of *Inf.* 1.100–114 constitutes possibly the most vexed and overtreated of any crux in the *Commedia*. A complete bibliography on the *veltro* up to 1988 may be found in Cassell; see also Davis. (Omitted here are such ludicrous efforts as those identifying the *veltro* with Luther, Garibaldi, Mussolini, Hitler, et al.)

Bibliography

Arezio, Luigi. "Il 'Veltro' e 'il Cinquecento diece e cinque' nel Poema dantesco." *Giornale dantesco* 32, n.s. 2 (1931), 3–58.

Auerbach, Erich. *Dante als Dichter der irdischen Welt.* Berlin, Leipzig: De Gruyter, 1929. Translated by Ralph Manheim. *Dante, Poet of the Secular World.* Chicago, London: University of Chicago Press, 1961.

Barbi, Michele. "L'Italia nell'ideale politico di Dante." *Studi danteschi* 24 (1939), 5–37.

Bassermann, Alfred. "Veltro und Gross-Chan." *Deutsches Dante-Jahrbuch* 11 (1929), 173–182.

———. "*Veltro,* Gross-Chan und Kaisersage." *Neue Heidelberger Jahrbücher* 11 (1901), 28–75.

Cassell, Anthony K. "Il Veltro." In *Lectura Dantis Americana: Inferno I.* Philadelphia: University of Pennsylvania Press, 1989, pp. 94–113.

Davis, Charles T. "Il problema del Veltro nell'*Inferno* di Dante. *Enciclopedia dantesca,* 5:908–912.

Della Torre, Ruggiero. *Commento letterale al primo Canto della "Divina Commedia": ricostruzione*

V

logica dell'antefatto o proemio. La volontà. Lo spazio e il tempo. Turin: Carlo Clausen, 1898.

———. Sistema dell'arte allegorica nel Poema dantesco. Cividale: Tipografia Fulvio Giovanni, 1892.

———. Tra feltro e feltro: Nota dantesca. Cividale: Tipografia Fulvio Giovanni, 1891.

———. Poeta-veltro. 2 vols. Cividale: Tipografia Fulvio Giovanni, 1887–1890.

Dempf, Alois. Sacrum Imperium: Geschichte und Staatsphilosophie des Mittelalters und der Renaissance. Munich, Berlin: Oldenbourg, 1929.

Emiliani, Cesare. "The Veltro and the Cinquecento diece e cinque." Dante Studies 101 (1993), 149–152.

Ferrante, Joan. The Political Vision of the Divine Comedy. Princeton, N.J.: Princeton University Press, 1984.

Filomusi-Guelfi, Lorenzo. Nuovi studi su Dante. Città di Castello: S. Lapi, 1911.

Foberti, F. "Questioni dantesche e storia francescana (Veltro—Gioachinismo—Ubertino da Casale)." Miscellanea francescana 39 (1939), 153–171.

Gentile, Giovanni. "La profezia di Dante." In Frammenti di estetica e letteratura. Lanciano: R. Carabba, 1921, pp. 253–296.

Getto, Giovanni. "Il canto 1 dell'Inferno." Lectura Dantis Scaligera. Florence: F. Le Monnier, 1960. Reprinted in Aspetti della poesia di Dante. Florence: Sansoni, 1966, pp. 1–16.

Hardie, Colin. "The 'Veltres' in the Chanson de Roland." Deutsches Dante-Jahrbuch 41–42 (1964), 158–172.

Hollander, Robert. Allegory in Dante's "Commedia." Princeton, N.J.: Princeton University Press, 1969.

Kaske, Robert Earl. "Dante's DXV and Veltro." Traditio 17 (1961), 185–254.

Magalotti, Lorenzo. Commento sui primi cinque Canti dell'Inferno di Dante, e quattro Lettere del conte Lorenzo Magalotti [1637–1712]. Milan: Imp. Regia Stamperia, 1819.

Matrod, H. "Le Veltro de Dante et son DXV: Khan e Can." Études Franciscaines [Tamine: Belgique] 31 (January 1914), 61–81.

Mazzoni, Francesco. Saggio di un nuovo commento alla "Divina Commedia": Inferno—Canti I–III. Quaderni degli "Studi Danteschi" 4. Florence: Sansoni, 1967.

Nardi, Bruno. "Il preludio alla Divina Commedia." Alighieri 4, 1 (1963), 3–17. Reprinted in Lectura Dantis Romana. Turin: SEI, 1964.

Olschki, Leonard. The Myth of Felt. Berkeley, Los Angeles: University of California Press, 1949.

———. Dante, "Poeta Veltro." Florence: Olschki, 1953.

———. "Tra feltro e feltro." Nuova antologia, anno 87 (1952), 386–398.

Pézard, André. Tant que vienne le veltre: Enfer I:100–101. Paris: Chez Tallone Editeur-imprimeur, 1978.

Pietrobono, Luigi. Il canto I dell'Inferno presentato alla Casa di Dante a Roma il 5 febbraio 1925. Lectura Dantis Romana. Turin: SEI, 1925. Reprinted in 1959.

Porena, Manfredi. "Il Veltro." In La Divina Commedia. Edited by M. Porena. Vol. 1: Inferno. Bologna: Zanichelli, 1946–1948. Reprinted in 1951, pp. 17–18.

———. "Una nuova chiosa alla profezia dantesca del Veltro liberatore." Atti della Accademia Nazionale dei Lincei: anno CCCL (1953), serie VIII, Rendiconti: classe di scienze morali, storiche e filologiche, vol. 8, fasc. 5–6 (maggio–giugno 1953), 230–237.

Regis, Aurelio. "E sua nazion sarà tra feltro e feltro." Studi danteschi 4 (1921), 85–97.

Renucci, Paul. Dante disciple et juge du monde gréco-latin. Paris: Société d'Edition "Les Belles Lettres," 1954.

———. "Dante et les mythes du Millenium." Revue des Études Italiennes n.s. 11 (1965), 393–421.

Sarolli, Gian Roberto. "Dante 'scriba Dei.'" Convivium 31 (1963), 385–671. Reprinted in Prolegomena alla "Divina Commedia." Biblioteca dell'Archivum Romanicum, Serie 1, vol. 112. Florence: Olschki, 1971.

Troya, Carlo. Del veltro allegorico di Dante [1826] e altri saggi storici. Edited by Costantino Panigada. Bari: Giuseppe Laterza e figli, 1932.

Anthony K. Cassell

Venus

In Roman mythology, daughter of Jove and Dione, mother of Cupid (Par. 8.7–8; linked metonymically with Dione Par. 22.144). Born in Cyprus, she was hence known as la bella Ciprigna ("the lovely Cyprian," Par. 8.2). Goddess of sensual love, she plays an important role in classical literature; in Virgil's Aeneid her role as Aeneas' mother underlies the Roman claim to divine origin. Dante gives her less distinction. In the Fiore, she is Venus

(18.14, 27.12, 221.1, 225.1) or *Venusso* (17.1, 12; 18.2; 216.9; 217.1; 218.2, 12; 220.1; 222.1; 223.1), an allegorical figure representing erotic love who enables the Lover to attain his desires—first a kiss (17–18), and later, more violently, complete destruction of the rose's defenses (216–225; see also *Veno* in the *Detto* 300–306, 474).

Although alluded to in terms of her classical identity (*Venere, Purg.* 25.132, 28.65), Venus appears more prominently as a planet (see *Conv.* 2.2.1, 8; 2.3.1, 7, 12, 16–18; 2.4.1; 2.5.13, 16–17; 2.6.1; 2.12.9; 2.13.1, 2; 2.14.16), the star of love (*Purg.* 1.19) set between Mercury and the Sun as the third heaven of *Paradiso*, which is associated with rhetoric (*Conv.* 2.13.13, 2.14.21). In this heaven of lovers, which spans cantos 8–9, Dante is concerned to dispel pagan myths that the planet's influence spreads mad sensual love (see also *Conv.* 2.5.13–14). Charles Martel, who receives Dante into the sphere, discourses on the nature of heredity, after whom his companion souls, Cunizza da Romano and Folco of Marseille, appear and present, in sequence, a denunciation of earthly evils followed by a prophecy. This heaven is also the residence of Rahab, the harlot of the Old Testament, who ranks highest among these souls. The sphere is presided over by the angelic hierarchy of the principalities (*Par.* 28.124–126), although in the *Convivio* the thrones are said to be its rulers. Venus is the last planet to which the shadow of Earth extends when Earth is positioned between it and the Sun (*Par.* 9.124), a feature that defines it as the highest heaven in the lowest region of Paradise.

Bibliography

Kay, Richard. *Dante's Christian Astrology.* Philadelphia: University of Pennsylvania Press, 1994, pp. 66–97.

Mazzotta, Giuseppe. "The Light of Venus." In *Dante's Vision and the Circle of Knowledge.* Princeton, N.J.: Princeton University Press, 1993, pp. 56–74.

Rebecca S. Beal

Vernani, Guido, O.P.

Of the origin of this author of the first "reprobation" of Dante's *Monarchia,* no notice appears in any civic or Dominican archive; he appears first c. 1310 as a lecturer at the Studium, or University of Bologna (despite the claim of one scholar, Fra Guido was never its chancellor). After c. 1320, Vernani spent his later life in Rimini, where he executed wills and managed property sales. In 1325 he was given the charge of explaining publicly, in the Cathedral of St. Colomba, Pope John XXII's excommunication of Ludwig of Bavaria and Castruccio Castracane degli Antelminelli. We hear no more of Vernani after the Black Death of 1348.

Well-schooled in Aristotelian thought, he penned three commentaries on the philosopher (on the *Nicomachaean Ethics,* the *De Anima,* and the *Rhetoric*); two works on the temporal power of the popes (*De potestate summi Pontificis* [On Papal Power]) and a commentary on the papal bull *Unam Sanctam;* and a treatise on ethics, the *Liber de virtutibus* (The Book of Virtues). The *De potestate* and the *Reprobation* were first published together in 1746; none of his other works have appeared in print.

Vernani's treatise on papal power of 1327 expounds typical papal hierarchical theories that he was to find invaluable for his caustic refutation of the *Monarchia,* probably begun in the same year and published in 1329. Dedicating the *Reprobation* ironically to Graziolo de' Bambaglioli, author of the first commentary on the *Commedia,* the narrow-minded Dominican is a surprisingly patronizing and derisive opponent, scorning Dante, whom he never calls by name, as a "vessel of the Devil": *quidam fuit multa fantastice poetizans et sophista verbosus . . . qui . . . non solum egros animos, sed etiam studiosos conducit fraudulenter ad interitum salutifere veritatis* ("a certain man who wrote many fantastic things in poetry, a palaverous sophist . . . who . . . fraudulently seduces not only sickly minds, but even zealous ones to the destruction of salutary truth"). Later he charges Dante with "bombastic rhetoric," and "smug ignorance," and even accuses him of Averroistic heresy.

Vernani's rebuttals range from the cogent to the absurd, but the inflexibility of his thought and the inelegance of his Latin style compare most unfavorably with those of his deceased victim.

Bibliography

Matteini, Nevio. *Il più antico oppositore di Dante: Guido Vernani da Rimini: Testo critico del "De reprobatione Monarchiae."* Padua: CEDAM, 1958.

Anthony K. Cassell

Vernon, William Warren

English Dante scholar (1834–1919). Relying chiefly on the commentary of Benvenuto da Imola, Lord Vernon published many and varied studies on the works of Dante, collecting them largely in six volumes of *Readings on the Divine Comedy* (*Inferno* 1894–1906; *Purgatorio,* 1889–1897; *Paradiso,* 1900–1909), which follow the commentary format. Though of a popularizing cast, the studies contain a number of interesting exegetical insights. Vernon served for many years as corresponding member of the prestigious Accademia della Crusca. For his considerable Italianist activities, he was decorated by Queen Margherita of Italy.

A. L. Pellegrini

Veronica, The

One of the most treasured relics in the basilica of St. Peter's is an image of the face of Christ called "The Veronica." Present in Rome since the late tenth century, it was venerated throughout the Middle Ages as *pictura Domini vera* ("true picture of God"), or *vera icon.* It was also associated with a woman, known as Veronica, thought to be among the earliest followers of Jesus. Tradition varies as to how the picture came to be. One of the earliest accounts has it that Jesus miraculously transferred his own image to a piece of cloth to honor Veronica's request for a picture of him. Later versions report that Jesus made the impression in blood when he wiped his own face during his night of agony in the Garden of Gethsemane; still others have it that the imprint was taken on his way to Calvary.

Popes during the thirteenth century made the Veronica the object of great veneration, displaying it with candles and incense and occasionally carrying it in solemn procession. They also created massive indulgences for those faithful pilgrims who came to Rome to see the "Holy Face." John XXII (1316–1334), for instance, offered an indulgence of 10,000 days in Purgatory for those who made their devotions before the holy image.

It is precisely this context of pilgrimage that Dante draws upon in his two references to the relic. In *VN* 40.1, the poet describes his city as a stopping point for pilgrims on their way to Rome, *per vedere quella imagine benedetta la quale Iesu Cristo lasciò a noi per essempio de la sua bellissima figura* ("to see that blessed image which Jesus Christ left to us as an example of his own beautiful face"). Later, in *Par.* 31.103–108, when he finds himself in that heavenly Rome *onde Cristo è romano* ("of which Christ is a Roman," *Purg.* 32.102), Dante names the Veronica explicitly. In order to describe the intense gaze he focuses on the face of St. Bernard, he likens himself to a pilgrim from Croatia who has finally come to Rome and succeeded in looking upon *la Veronica nostra* ("our Veronica"). Dante evokes the devotion of someone whose hunger for the image is not satisfied by a simple look, but rather lingers in astonishment as he asks himself, *Segnor mio Iesù Cristo, Dio verace, / or fu sì fatta la sembianza vostra?* ("My lord Jesus Christ, true God, was your face indeed like that?" *Par.* 31.107–108).

Peter S. Hawkins

Vico, Giambattista

Vico (1668–1744) is commonly credited with the merit of having discovered Dante despite the fact that the first decades of the eighteenth century were rather indifferent to the *Commedia.* This view of Vico's unmatched contribution to the revival of Dante's fame is founded on the premise that Vico did not propose a deterministic view of poetry, according to which the sublime can exist only under primitive conditions of sociocultural life. Those who do not accept such a premise, such as Fausto Nicolini and Mario Fubini, are inclined to view the "discovery of the true Dante" (a pseudo-Vichian label) as a construct of Crocean critics. Judged from this viewpoint, Vico's opinions about Dante, though relevant to the interpreters of Vichian philosophy, appear by and large to be of little use to Dante scholars. This conclusion, consistent with textual evidence, carries more weight than any plea for Vico's relevance in Dante criticism.

Unquestionably, Vico insists on the creativity of barbaric ages and points out their exclusive capacity to produce sublime poetry which is the fruit not of individual genius but of primitive society, as appears from his "discovery of the true Homer" (*New Science,* Book III). Such creativity, in his view, tends to diminish with the progress of civilization and, at a certain stage, completely disappears. In the *Universal Law* (*De Constantia Philologiae* XII.21 [46]), Vico shows his admiration for Dante by asserting that he was a barbaric poet: Dante appeared when the history of Italy had reached the climax of barbarism (*in summa Italo-*

rum barbarie), when no models of poetry were available. In the first, second, and third editions of the *New Science* (1725, 1730, 1744), Vico simply homologizes Homer and Dante, who becomes "the Tuscan Homer." Vico holds an uncompromisingly primitivistic view of poetry which he applies to a very general assessment of the *Commedia.* According to Vico, Dante's knowledge of theology and Latin made him unfit to compete successfully with a poet of Homer's caliber. A similar reservation about Dante's culture appears in the second and third editions of the *New Science,* where Vico states that Dante was "learned in the loftiest esoteric knowledge" (*NS,* 817). Yet Vico also asserts that Dante "filled the scenes of his *Commedia* with real persons and portrayed real events in the lives of the dead," a typical manifestation of "barbarism, which for lack of reflection does not know how to feign" (817). Under this aspect, the *Commedia* can be considered the Italian counterpart of the *Iliad.* This Homer-Dante parallel rests on Vico's primitivistic view of poetry, which is sublime inasmuch as it is produced by savages unable to think in rational terms. He could not accept a middle position, since he sought to maintain his distance from Gianvincenzo Gravina, the author of the *Ragion poetica* (1718), who also viewed Dante as a kind of Italian Homer but who stressed the sophisticated learning of both poets. Vico's regard for Gravina's astute assessment of Dante (*Ragion poetica,* Book II, 1–13) no doubt reveals an anxiety of influence, and consequently his view represents something of an overreaction. In any case, Vico was not the only person in Naples who showed an interest in the Italian poet. An acquaintance of Vico's, Lorenzo Ciccarelli (Cellenio Zacclori), published an edition of the *Commedia* in Naples in 1716.

In order to make Vico more consistent with Crocean criticism, interpreters such as Fubini did not hesitate to exaggerate the relevance of the minor writings composed for the sake of public relations, namely, the letter Vico addressed to Gherardo Degli Angioli (1725) and the preface (1729) to Pompeo Venturi's commentary on the *Commedia,* which appeared only in the year 1818. The letter is but a well-turned compliment to an untalented former pupil who entertained literary ambitions—destined to remain unfulfilled—while the preface is an attempt to promote the *New Science* by jumping on the bandwagon of an incipient renewal of interest in Dante. Both writings are basically self-serving and show a cavalier attitude toward the intellectual history of the Middle Ages, which reflects the shortcomings of the *New Science,* Book V, which is dedicated to the "recourse of human institutions which the nations take when they rise again." The preface is a more serious attempt to reconcile traditional views (the *Commedia* "as a source of Tuscan speech") with the basic tenets of the *New Science* (the *Commedia* "as a history of the period of barbarism in Italy" and "as an example of sublime poetry"). But it is not much more than a sketch, jotted down between 1728 and 1730, which Vico did not care to develop later or include in the final edition of his *New Science.* One can safely say that, on the basis of Vico's published record, his familiarity with Dante's masterpiece was superficial. The Neapolitan philosopher was not an interpreter of the *Commedia,* let alone the discoverer of it.

Bibliography

Caesar, Michael (ed.). *Dante: The Critical Heritage, 1314(?)–1870.* London, New York: Routledge, 1989, pp. 352–355.

Cambon, Glauco. "Vico and Dante." In *Dante's Craft: Studies in Language and Style.* Minneapolis: University of Minnesota Press, 1969, pp. 146–160.

Fubini, Mario. "Il mito della poesia primitiva e la critica dantesca di G. B. Vico." In *Stile e umanità di Giambattista Vico.* 2nd ed. Milan, Naples: Ricciardi, 1965, pp. 147–174.

Pietropaolo, Domenico. *Dante Studies in the Age of Vico.* Ottawa: Dovehouse, 1989, pp. 63–92.

Vico, Giambattista. *Il Diritto universale.* Edited by Fausto Nicolini. Bari: Laterza, 1936.

———. *New Science/Giambattista Vico.* Translated by David Marsh. London: Penguin Books, 1999.

———. *Opere.* Edited by Andrea Battistini. Milan: Mondadori, 1990.

———. *Opere.* Edited by Fausto Nicolini. Milan, Naples: Ricciardi, 1953.

Gustavo Costa

Vico, Manfredi da

An example of one pretending to nobility by virtue of his ancestry (*Conv.* 4.29.2). Scion of a powerful family who were hereditary prefects of Rome, Manfredi succeeded to the prefecture in 1304 and died in 1337.

Leslie Zarker Morgan

Villani, Filippo

Florentine historian (1325–1405) whose commentary of the first canto of *Inferno,* written in Latin, stressed the importance of allegory. He studied law in Florence and molded his civic humanism on the example of his teacher Coluccio Salutati. His *Liber de origine civitatis Florentiae et eiusdem famosis civibus* (1381–1388 and 1395–1397), or treatise on the origin of Florence and its most prominent citizens, expresses great reverence for Dante for his having elevated poetry in Florence to the same level enjoyed by Latin poetry in classical Rome. His biography of Dante is contained in his *Vita Dantis, Petrarche et Boccacci,* which is preserved in a Barberini codex. He was appointed by the Commune of Florence to succeed Boccaccio as *lettore* (professor) of Dante, a position that he held from 1391 until 1404, the commonly supposed year of his death. His unbound admiration for the author of the *Commedia* is evident in the only one of his lectures that has survived, namely the commentary, in Latin, to the first canto of the *Inferno.* Here Villani affirms that Dante is a *"scriba Dei,"* a writer inspired directly by God, and argues that Virgil's *Aeneid* should be read as Christian allegory. It cannot be established whether Villani had read Dante's *Epistle to Cangrande,* but he accepts and applies Dante's prescription there for reading the *Commedia* according to the traditional theological model for reading a text on four levels, namely the literal, the allegorical, the moral, and the anagogical.

Bibliography

Aurigemma, Marcello. *Studi sulla cultura letteraria fra Tre e Quattrocento Filippo Villani, Vergerio e Bruni.* Rome: Bulzoni, 1976.

Basile, Bruno. "Il Commentario di Filippo Villani al Canto I della *Commedia.*" *Lettere italiane* 23 (1971), 197–224.

Hollander, Robert. "Dante and his Commentators." In Rachel Jacoff (ed.), *The Cambridge Companion to Dante.* Cambridge: Cambridge University Press, 1993, pp. 228–229.

———. *Allegory in Dante's "Commedia."* Princeton, N.J.: Princeton University Press, 1969, pp. 290–296.

Villani, Filippo. *Expositio seu Comentum super "Comedia" Dantis Alighieri.* Edited by Saverio Bellomo. Florence: Le Lettere, 1989.

———. *Il commento al primo canto dell'"Inferno" pubblicato e annotato da Giuseppe Cugnoni.* Città di Castello: S. Lapi, 1876.

———. *Liber de civitatis Florentiae famosis civibus.* Edited by a C. G. Galletti. Florence: Mazzoni, 1847.

Robert C. Melzi

Villani, Giovanni

A Florentine merchant, public administrator, and diplomat who wrote an important chronicle of Dante's world, the *Nuova cronica.* Born into a merchant family, no later than 1276, he initially worked in the Peruzzi company, first as an employee and soon as a partner. He was in the company's Bruges branch for much of the years from 1302 to 1307 (but was based in Florence from 1308 until his decease in the Black Death in 1348). He left the Peruzzi and in 1322 became a partner in the Buonaccorsi company, which went bankrupt twenty years later; Villani represented it

Statue of Giovanni Villani, Florence. Richard Lansing.

in subsequent negotiations with creditors, and in 1346 he spent a period in the debtors' prison. A moderate Black Guelf, he was three times prior between 1316 and 1328 and (especially between 1322 and 1331) was appointed to numerous administrative positions, with responsibility for such sectors as the mint, the city walls, and taxation. His public service gave him access to statistical information and official documents which provided valuable material for his chronicle.

The *Nuova cronica,* which includes the earliest biography of Dante (10.136), also has many other sources, including earlier chronicles of Florence and elsewhere, as well as Villani's own wide experience. Although the spotlight falls primarily on Florence, it is a history of the known world from the Tower of Babel onwards (1280 is not reached until Chapter 56 of Book 8), in thirteen books of increasing length. Villani, who displays a respectable classical education and a considerable knowledge of the Bible, is archaic in his superstition and his providential view of history but progressive in his concern with causes and effects and in his attention to practical details, for example, financial matters; and 12.94 contains a famous statistical account of Florentine society in the year 1339. Despite the occurrence of major disasters in the narrative, his is an optimistic story of Florentine prosperity and greatness.

It is unlikely that Dante knew Villani's chronicle, which was probably not begun until about 1322. Villani revised it, apparently after 1332, and continued to extend it until his death. Modern editions print the revised version, which (among other changes) drastically shortens the Dante biography and eliminates a number of quotations from the *Commedia* (though Villani is increasingly influenced by some of Dante's attitudes). Evidently two decades after the poet's death a conservative writer closely identified with the Florentine state still felt obliged to distance himself from the most outspoken critic of the basis of that state's prestige.

Bibliography

Aquilecchia, Giovanni. "Introduzione" to his (abridged) edition of G. Villani, *Cronica, con le continuazioni di Matteo e Filippo.* Turin: Einaudi, 1979, pp. vii–xxv (pp. vii–xviii).

———. "Dante and the Florentine Chroniclers." *Bulletin of the John Rylands Library* 48 (1965–1966), 30–55.

Bec, Christian. "Sur l'historiographie marchande à Florence au XIVe siècle." In *La Chronique et l'histoire au Moyen-Age.* Edited by Daniel Poirion. Paris: Presses de l'Université de Paris-Sorbonne, 1984, pp. 45–72. Also published as Chapter 5 of Bec's *Florence 1300–1600: histoire et culture.* Nancy: Presses Universitaires de Nancy, 1986, pp. 129–153.

Cherubini, Giovanni. "La Firenze di Dante e di Giovanni Villani." *Atti dell'Accademia peloritana dei Pericolanti, Classe di lettere filosofia e belle arti* [Messina] 254 (1984), 5–26.

Davis, Charles T. "Topographical and Historical Propaganda in Early Florentine Chronicles and in Villani." *Medioevo e Rinascimento* 2 (1988), 33–51.

Green, Louis. *Chronicle into History: An Essay on the Interpretation of History in Florentine Fourteenth-Century Chronicles.* Cambridge: Cambridge University Press, 1972, pp. 9–43, 155–169.

Luzzati, Michele. *Giovanni Villani e la compagnia dei Buonaccorsi.* Rome: Istituto della Enciclopedia Italiana, 1971.

Mehl, Ernst. *Die Weltanschauung des Giovanni Villani: Ein Beitrag zur Geistesgeschichte Italiens im Zeitalter Dantes.* Leipzig, Berlin: Teubner, 1927.

Varanini, G. "Villani, Giovanni." In *Dizionario critico della letteratura italiana.* Edited by Vittore Branca et al. 3 vols. Turin: UTET, 1974, III, 633–635.

Villani, Giovanni. *Nuova cronica.* Edited by G. Porta. 3 vols. Parma: Fondazione Pietro Bembo/ Guanda, 1990–1991.

John C. Barnes

Violence

One of the three major categories of sin in *Inferno, forza* ("violence") is more grave than incontinence but less so than *frode* ("fraud"). This judgment on the relative gravity of the two worst kinds of sin derives not from Aristotle or Aquinas but instead from Cicero (*De officiis* 1.13.41). Both violence and fraud are species of *malizia* ("malice"), which has *ingiuria* ("injustice") for an end; this is an end that afflicts another *(altrui contrista)* or, more broadly, maltreats or destroys the person or goods of someone else or oneself. The means adopted—of force by the violent and guile by the

V fraudulent—is what differentiates the two forms of malice (*Inf.* 11.22–27).

Those sent to Hell for violence occupy the seventh circle (cantos 12 through 17). The circle subdivides into three *gironi* ("rings") in conformity with the three branches of violence, those distinguished in Virgil's exposition of the plan of Hell in terms of the person afflicted; that is, violence (*forza* or *vïolenza*) may be done *A Dio, a sé, al prossimo* ("To God, to one's self, and to one's neighbor," *Inf.* 11.31). At least seven distinct types of sin are classified as violent. These include, in an ascending order of seriousness, such malefactions as homicide and plundering, punished in the first *girone;* suicide and squandering, in the second; and blasphemy, sodomy, and usury, in the third.

Located inside the wall that surrounds the City of Dis and Lower Hell, this circle has settings significantly different from anything seen before. Before the landscape had been Earth-like and familiar, whether the green and pleasant fields of Limbo or the wind, rocks, water, hail, and mud of circles 2–5. Now the landscape turns surreal, with a river of seething blood, then a thicket where broken twigs bleed and talk, and finally with fire exotic in that it falls rather than rises and in flakes of flame on combustible sand. Besides, mythic creatures of intermixed species populate the circle: on the approach to it lies the hybrid Minotaur produced by the bestial union of Pasifaë and the Cretan bull; human-equine centaurs police the culprits steeped in blood; and human-faced, aviary harpies infest the wood of suicides. That these eerie locales and preternatural figures are represented in conjunction with the practitioners of violence must needs convey something about this class of sins.

The incontinent, residing outside the wall, transgressed out of weakness or passion and overindulged normal appetites and feelings. Their circles in Upper Hell, accordingly, present phenomena cognate with nature's. Those who engage in violence, by contrast, do so deliberately and malevolently; and the element of willfulness initiated with and by them can be dangerous to others and proves detrimental to themselves. The distortions of their abodes are external correlatives of inward and psychological distortions.

In some mysterious way the violent chose to tamper with their normal mechanisms of response. Each group repudiated an impulse or inclination native to humankind—whether love of neighbor

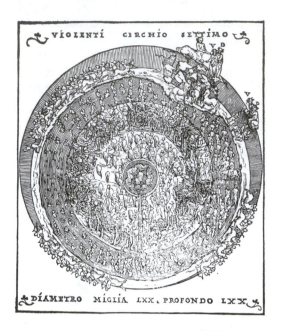

Dante at the entrance to the seventh circle of Hell containing three rings of violent sinners. La comedia di Dante Aligieri, with commentary by Alessandro Vellutello, published by Francesco Marcolini, Venice, 1544. Giamatti Collection: Courtesy of the Mount Holyoke College Archives and Special Collections.

(those brutal to others), the instinct for self-preservation (suicides, squanderers), reverence toward godhood (blasphemers), the heterosexual/procreative drive (sodomites), or the labor imperative (usurers). Rejection is only half the psychological story, however, the other half being substitution. The violent also had to educe new goals, and they did so by projecting a pseudo-attractiveness onto an object or by projecting onto behavior of some special kind a satisfaction it does not naturally provide. Self-murder and same-sex desire are clear examples of substituted dispositions oriented toward violence (see Aquinas, *ST* 1.2.6.4.3).

Another example is the ferocious aggression that in its perpetrators displaced neighborly love, which Virgil calls, at 11.56, *lo vinco d'amor che fa natura* ("the bond of love that Nature makes"). Elsewhere Dante writes of *la naturale amistade,* the "natural friendship" whereby each of us is friendly toward everyone else (*Conv.* 3.11.7; cf. 1.1.8). Whoever *per vïolenza in altrui noccia* ("by violence injures others") is in these terms unnatural, for having deflected such friendship in favor of *cieca cupidigia e ira folle* ("blind cupidity and mad rage," 12.48–49). The various crimes against neighbors discernible in canto 12 include killing them, whether one or many; wounding them; and robbing them or demolishing their possessions.

The punitive agent for the violent here is *la riviera del sangue* ("the river of blood"), which boils and sullies them, and in which degrees of guilt determine the depth of submersion. The guiltiest, the tyrants, *che dier nel sangue e ne l'aver di piglio* ("who put their hands to blood and to others' goods"), are the deepest, up to their eyebrows in blood (12.103–105); the least violent—say robbers who do their victims little if any bodily harm—are having just their feet cooked. In patrolling the banks the centaurs provide the only action of the scene. The sinners, whose lives had been so full of fierce energy and activity, are depicted as immobilized and speechless in the gory river. Its *bollor vermiglio* ("red boiling") makes them shriek in pain and also connotes the heated temperament that underlies their malicious deeds and the spilt blood that results. The symbolism of the river visually manifests the guilty as hot-blooded and blood-stained.

In the pathless wood that composes the second ring, inhabited by the violent against themselves, the sinners are inseparable from the setting. The gnarled, thorny, fruitless, dusky-leafed bushes *are* the suicides. They suffer this rooted, vegetative condition for preferring the extinction of the self-moving human body to its preservation. They must have recoiled from the physical pain of the suicidal act, and yet welcomed the escape it offered and the dramatic means of self-expression or protest. Now, in Hell, they can vent sorrow or rage only by hissing forth blood and speech upon being broken. They formerly broke themselves, but now they are torn by hounds rushing though the brush or harpies feeding on their leaves. These souls continue in the afterlife, as before, to be passive, unable to affect their environment.

Also in the wood of suicides are the reckless squanderers, in human form. Like their ring-mates they proved self-destructive, not in discarding their bodies but in dissipating their wealth, for possessions are presumed a necessity for sustaining life; and they likewise have in Hell something they had, even if unconsciously, sought. As wastrels of their property they had courted their own ruin, which now they painfully undergo through the agency of hounds that chase them and tear them apart.

The worst violence of all, punished by the fire dropping upon the sand of the third *girone,* is that against God, and it admits of further gradations.

Deity may be violated directly through blasphemy—this being, curiously, the least heinous way—or else indirectly through sodomy and, worse yet, usury. The latter two are expressly conceived of as sins against Nature, which *lo suo corso prende / dal divino 'ntelletto e da sua arte* ("takes its course from the divine intellect and its art," 11.109–110). Usury, further, contemns the human "art" (crafts, industry) that follows nature *come 'l maestro fa 'l discente* ("as a disciple does the master") and hence *a Dio quasi è nepote* ("is almost God's grandchild," 11.99–105). Sodomy, then, affronts God indirectly by scorning *Natura,* his daughter, as usury does so by offenses against both Nature and her dependent, art.

Of the blasphemers, lying supine, the single one met with is Capaneus, one of the seven kings against Thebes, who still keeps raging at Jove. Reverence for divinity is a trait so universal and innate to human nature that all irreverence is perverse—toward pagan gods no less than toward the Trinity.

The homosexual sin associated with Sodom is contrary to nature specifically for precluding reproduction, the one licit end of volitional sexual acts. That idea, which Dante could assume was familiar to his readers, is alluded to only in the description of the hot sand as self-sterilizing: *una landa / che dal suo letto ogne pianta rimove* ("a plain that removes every plant from its bed," 14.8–9). Sodomites far outnumber the others here, and their sin determines the design of the landscape. The falling fire derives from, and is meant to recall, that which rained on Sodom and Gomorrah (Gen. 19). This fire is a symbol at once of God's wrath and, with its denatured properties, of the passion that inflamed these sodomitic souls, while their incessant motion suggests another facet of passion—its agitation.

The usurers sit on the edge of the *girone* and, facially unrecognized or unrecognizable, must be identified by the coat of arms on pouches hanging from their necks. They committed violence against human industry both by exploiting workers and by eschewing work, commanded by the God of Genesis (3.17–19); they preferred to make interest-bearing loans so that the money alone, by increasing and multiplying in an unnatural kind of reproduction, would earn them a living.

Of the sins in the category of *forza* in *Inferno,* we would ordinarily think of some but not all of them as violent. Only the crimes of the first ring

V

that use weapons and force against victims and some forms of suicide would nowadays be accounted instances of violence. And in *Inferno* the amount of harm caused by the violence is not—except among the sinners within the first ring—a measure of the gravity of the sin. Moreover, the one violent sin in circle 7 to be recognizably introduced into *Purgatorio* is that of Sodom; but there, in canto 26, the conception and judgment of homoerotic love have been radically revised.

Bibliography

Ciotti, Andrea. "Violenza e violenti in Dante." *Enciclopedia dantesca,* 5:1028–1030.

Lansing, Richard H. "Dante's Concept of Violence and the Chain of Being." *Dante Studies* 99 (1981), 67–87.

Moore, Edward. "The Classification of Sins in the *Inferno* and *Purgatorio.*" *Studies in Dante. Second Series: Miscellaneous Essays.* Oxford: Clarendon Press, 1899.

Pequigney, Joseph, and Hubert Dreyfus. "Landscape and Guide: Dante's Modifying of Meaning in the *Inferno.*" *Italian Quarterly* 5–6 (1961–1962), 51–83.

Reade, W. H. V. *The Moral System of Dante's "Inferno."* Oxford: Clarendon Press, 1909.

Joseph Pequigney

Virgil

The Roman poet who is the basis of the fictional *Virgilio,* whom Dante takes as his guide through Inferno and Purgatory as far as the Earthly Paradise and who, Dante says, resides eternally in Limbo along with the other pagan poets and philosophers whose only fault was lack of faith.

The historical Virgil was born in 70 B.C.E. not far from Mantua; he began his poetic career with the publication of his *Eclogues* c. 37 B.C.E. These were followed by the *Georgics* some seven years later. The *Aeneid,* begun perhaps in 30 B.C.E., occupied him until his death in 19 B.C.E. It was his wish that the work, not brought to the degree of completion that he insisted on, be destroyed. It was preserved through the intervention of no less a personage than the emperor Augustus himself.

Dante's involvement with the works of Virgil is one of Western literature's most renowned and most complex examples of the way in which a later writer appropriates the texts of a precursor. It is

difficult to conceive of a major literary text that might be as closely involved with an earlier masterwork as is the *Commedia* with the *Aeneid,* with the major exception of the involvement of Virgil's epic with those of Homer. Dante's early works, however, show little special, or more than conventional, admiration either for Virgil or for classical poetry in general. In his first work, the *Vita Nuova,* the single gesture in the direction of classical poetry (*VN* 25) reveals a concern on the young writer's part to relate his work to a tradition of writerly excellence in the lofty style of classical antiquity. This stance is also evident in the *De vulgari eloquentia,* as is perhaps only to be expected in a work dealing with contemporary poetry in the vernacular, a work written by a poet who wants to put his contemporaries and himself (especially himself) on something like an equal footing with glorious antecedents. The case of the *Convivio* is more complicated. Its first three treatises are written more or less in a similar spirit, revisiting classical sources in a nearly perfunctory way. In the fourth treatise, however, we find a major change, as was first noted by Ulrich Leo in a justly celebrated article. Virgil and some other classical writers now become important more for what they are saying than for the nobility of their expression. The case of the *Monarchia* is a complicated one. The question of its date is essential and difficult to resolve. If the work is composed after the *Commedia* was begun, the thickness of the allusions in the second book to Virgil (*divinus poeta noster,* "our divine poet," 2.3.6) would indicate a similar lofty view of Virgil as *auctor,* while the total absence of Virgilian citation in the concluding third book (see Kay on this point) might seem to show a surprising lack of classicizing interest on Dante's part. The sudden shift, however, is more likely to indicate rather a change in strategy (discussing theological matters, he will resort only to theologically valid texts) than a change of heart with regard to the Latin poet. One must also be aware of the indisputably Virgilian spirit—essentially one of imitation of his *Eclogues*—found in Dante's own Latin *Eclogues,* composed late in his career. Concerning the minor works composed before the *Commedia,* one may say that, with the exception of the last book of the *Convivio* (which should probably be understood as having been composed at a moment of considerable pressure and of a consequent change in direction toward a new writerly identity), there is little by way of a

Virgil rescuing Dante from the three beasts. La comedia di Dante Aligieri, *with commentary by Alessandro Vellutello, published by Francesco Marcolini, Venice, 1544. Giamatti Collection: Courtesy of the Mount Holyoke College Archives and Special Collections.*

deeply involved reading of classical text evident in the texts of Dante.

If one considers the question from a later vantage point, however, one can hardly overestimate the importance of Virgil for Dante. Here is the evaluation of Curtius: "The conception of the *Commedia* is based upon a spiritual meeting with Virgil. In the realm of European literature there is little which may be compared with this phenomenon. The 'awakening' of Aristotle in the thirteenth century was the work of generations and took place in the cool light of intellectual research. The awakening of Virgil by Dante is an arc of flame which leaps from one great soul to another. The tradition of the European spirit knows no situation of such affecting loftiness, tenderness, fruitfulness. It is the meeting of the two greatest Latins" (358). There can be no doubt that Virgil plays an essential role in almost every aspect of Dante's compo-

sition of his great poem—and probably with his very decision to write an "epic" poem, leaving incomplete his two treatises, the *Convivio* and the *De vulgari eloquentia,* in order to attach himself firmly to the great Latin tradition of writing about serious things in verse. As has frequently been pointed out, Virgil's example may be found as seminal for many aspects of Dante's poetic strategies in the *Commedia:* to write a poem that prominently features a visit to the underworld, celebrates the Roman concept of political order as exemplified in the Empire, and is narrated by a poet who has been lent prophetic powers.

As one of the principal characters in Dante's poem (Toynbee, in the entry "Virgilio," offers a convenient listing of all his appearances), Virgil's presence as guide in this most Christian of poems is something of a scandal. It is at least possible that puzzlement about Dante's reasons for choosing him for this role is at the root of the early commentators' tactic of treating the poem not as the "history" of an actual experience that Dante claims it to be (with a consequent treatment of Virgil as the historical figure he is so clearly meant to be taken as) but as an allegorical fiction. While in fact the introductory information processed in the poem (*Inf.* 1.67–75) makes Virgil entirely and recognizably historical (Mantuan parents, approximate dating of birth and career, authorship of the *Aeneid*), commentators responded (and, sometimes, still respond) by making Virgil "Reason" or some related allegorical characteristic of the human psyche. The poem that is created by such interpretation is thus meant to be considered the record of an internal struggle in a threatened Christian soul, as represented by the contending forces of appetite (whose role is supposedly played by the character Dante) and those of reason (personified in Virgil). While Virgil's *Aeneid* itself was subjected to such readings by interpreters like Fulgentius and Bernard Silvester, it seems clear that Dante himself—at least not when he was composing the *Commedia*—did not read Virgil's poem in this manner nor write the *Commedia* with such criteria in mind. Dante's treatment of the greatest Latin poet makes his own Virgil a problematic character for the earliest interpreters of the *Commedia*. Yet there are other problems, not of a commentator's devising, that afflict our attempt to come to grips with Dante's choice of Virgil as the guide in his poem. And these problems arise from Dante's own troubled perception of his pagan poetic hero. One tradition of Christian reception of Virgil, which is at least as old as the emperor Constantine, held that Virgil's much-discussed fourth *Eclogue* actually foretold the coming of Christ. Had Dante so believed, his choice of Virgil might have been less burdensome. However, we may be certain from *Mon.* 1.11.1 that Dante knew that Virgil's "Virgin" was not the blessed Mary but Astraea, or "justice." Any number of passages within the *Commedia* make it plain that Dante did not consider the Roman a Christian *avant-la-lettre*. We must conclude that Dante willfully chose a pagan as his guide. In recent years a growing number of Dante's interpreters have taken the view that Dante deliberately undercuts his guide, showing that both in some of his decisions as guide and in some of his own actual texts he is—from Dante's later and Christian vantage point—prone to error. If this is the case, we must nevertheless not forget that Dante at the same time is intent upon glorifying Virgil. And then we might further consider the proposition that Dante's love for Virgil, genuine and heartfelt, needed to be held at arm's length and gently but firmly chastised, perhaps revealing to a pagan-hating reader that Dante knows full well the limitations of his Virgil. Yet he could not do without him. Virgil is the guide in Dante's poem because he served in that role in Dante's life. It was Virgil, and not Aristotle or Aquinas, who served as model for the poem; it was Virgil who, more than any other author, helped make Dante Dante.

In the 14,233 verses of this theologized epic, verses of Virgil make themselves heard with greater frequency than any other sources except for the Bible and the texts of Aristotle (see Moore; for the most recent "census" of Virgilian text in the *Commedia,* see Hollander 1993). In the opening action of the first two cantos, Dante carefully and unobtrusively interlaces strands from the first book of the *Aeneid* into his narrative fabric (see Hollander 1969). This pattern of quotation—while not as persistent later in the text (roughly one-fifth of all Dante's citations of Virgil occur in the first five cantos of the poem)—runs through its entirety, even after Virgil leaves the poem as a character in *Purg.* 30. We are therefore not surprised when Dante has his character Virgil inform us that the younger poet knows his master's poem by heart (*Inf.* 20.114). The medieval Virgil, a figure of legend and a subject of tales of magic that pleased the popular imagination (as has been documented by

Comparetti), is essentially missing from the highly literary focus of Dante's reading of Virgilian text. Whatever Virgil meant for Dante, it was the fact that he was a poet that seems to have meant the most.

Bibliography

Auerbach, Erich. "Dante und Virgil." *Das Humanistisches Gymnasium* 42 (1931), 136–144.

Barolini, Teodolinda. *Dante's Poets.* Princeton, N.J.: Princeton University Press, 1984, especially pp. 188–269.

Comparetti, Domenico. *Virgil in the Middle Ages.* Translated by E. F. M. Benecke. Hamden, Conn.: Archon Books, 1966 [1872].

Consoli, Domenico. *Significato del Virgilio dantesco.* Florence: Le Monnier, 1967.

———. "Virgilio Marone, Publio." *Enciclopedia dantesca,* 5:1030–1044.

Curtius, Ernst Robert. *European Literature and the Latin Middle Ages.* Translated by W. R. Trask. New York: Harper and Row, 1963 [1948].

Davis, Charles Till. *Dante and the Idea of Rome.* Oxford: Oxford University Press, 1957.

Enciclopedia virgiliana. Rome: Istituto della Enciclopedia Italiana, 1984.

Hollander, Robert. *Il Virgilio dantesco: tragedia nella "Commedia."* Florence: Olschki, 1983.

———. *Allegory in Dante's "Commedia."* Princeton, N.J.: Princeton University Press, 1969, especially pp. 80–92.

———. "Le opere di Virgilio nella *Commedia* di Dante." In *Dante e la "bella scola" della poesia: Autorità e sfida poetica.* Edited by Amilcare A. Iannucci. Ravenna: Longo, 1993, pp. 247–343.

Jacoff, Rachel, and Jeffrey T. Schnapp (eds.). *The Poetry of Allusion: Virgil and Ovid in Dante's "Commedia."* Stanford, Calif.: Stanford University Press, 1991.

Kay, Richard. "The *Mentalité* of Dante's *Monarchia.*" *Res publica litterarum* 9 (1986), 183–191.

Lenkeith, Nancy. *Dante and the Legend of Rome.* London: Warburg Institute, 1952.

Leo, Ulrich. "The Unfinished *Convivio* and Dante's Rereading of the *Aeneid.*" *Mediaeval Studies* 13 (1951), 41–64.

Marigo, Aristide. "Le *Georgiche* di Virgilio fonte di Dante." *Giornale dantesco* 17 (1909), 31–44.

Moore, Edward. *Studies in Dante. First Series: Scripture and Classical Authors in Dante.* Oxford: Oxford University Press, 1969 [1896].

Renaudet, Augustin. *Dante humaniste.* Paris: Société d'édition les belles lettres, 1952.

Renucci, Paul. *Dante disciple et juge du monde gréco-latin.* Paris: Société d'édition les belles lettres, 1954.

Ronconi, Alessandro. *Interpretazioni grammaticali.* Padua: Liviana, 1958.

———. "Echi virgiliani nell'opera dantesca." *Enciclopedia dantesca,* 5:1044–1049.

Shapiro, Marianne. "Virgilio." In *Dante and the Knot of Body and Soul.* New York: St. Martin's Press, 1998, pp. 87–110.

Toynbee, Paget. *A Dictionary of Proper Names and Notable Matters in the Works of Dante.* Edited by Charles S. Singleton. Oxford: Clarendon Press, 1968 [1898].

Whitfield, J. H. *Dante and Virgil.* Oxford: Basil Blackwell, 1949, especially pp. 61–106.

Robert Hollander

Virgilio, Giovanni del

A scholar, sometime poet, and renowned professor of literature at the University of Bologna in the early 1320s. He is known primarily for the series of Latin verse letters he exchanged with Dante in the years 1319–1320, and for the epitaph he composed for Dante's tomb as cited in Boccaccio's *Vita di Dante.* Precise biographical data are few. He was born sometime before the year 1300 of a father named Antonio, probably of Paduan origin. Del Virgilio was a nickname (not a proper surname) earned for his devotion to the Roman poet. He was an ardent student of and inspired lecturer on classical poetry. But he was equally admiring of the works of the two men who were for him the most significant literary figures of his day: Albertino Mussato (who, along with his teacher Lovato Lovati, made of fourteenth-century Padua the most significant center of proto-humanist thought) and Dante Alighieri. Giovanni was well-liked by his students in Bologna. Indeed, it was at the students' request that the city of Bologna offered Giovanni a stipend to lecture on Virgil, Statius, Lucan, and Ovid in the year 1321. Giovanni spent the years 1324–1325 in Cesena, a period during which he composed the eclogue to Mussato, his longest poem, which he nevertheless did not send him until 1327. We lose all trace of Giovanni after this date.

Dante had been the guest of Guido Novello da Polenta at Ravenna for several years when, in 1319, Giovanni initiated a poetic correspondence by sending him a *carmen* in Latin hexameters. Giovanni praises Dante for his erudition and skill while expressing dismay at his decision to write the *Commedia* in the vernacular and thus for a more popular audience. Giovanni warns that the vernacular public is unworthy of Dante's effort and exhorts him to compose in Latin for the learned readers who eagerly await his work. He invites Dante to Bologna where he promises to present him to the scholarly community and honor him by placing the laurel crown upon his head (a revived ancient ceremony signifying supreme poetic achievement that Mussato had undergone in Padua in 1315).

Giovanni's correspondence to Dante has come down to us in a manuscript once owned and largely copied by Boccaccio, the so-called Zibaldone Boccaccesco or Zibaldone Laurenziano, which dates from around 1348 (ms. 29.8 of the Laurentian Library). In addition to the four letters, commonly referred to as eclogues among critics, the manuscript contains three of Dante's other epistles *(epistolae),* as well as several of Giovanni's other works: the lengthy eclogue to Mussato *(Tu modo Pieriis),* two verse epistles to other addressees (one anonymous, the other to the physician Guido Vacchetta), and 43 hexameters of an epic poem.

In addition to these writings, Giovanni is author of the famous epitaph cited by Boccaccio, a poetic correspondence with one ser Nuzio marchigiano known as the *Diaffonus,* a brief commentary on Virgil's *Georgics* 1.432 (mentioned by Benvenuto da Imola), two commentaries on Ovid (the *Allegorie* and the *Esposizioni*), and a brief *Ars dictaminis* discovered in a Naples manuscript and published by Paul O. Kristeller. According to Gian Carlo Alessio, Giovanni's written lectures at Bologna reflect the influence of speculative grammar.

Bibliography

Alessio, Gian Carlo. "I trattati grammaticali di Giovanni del Virgilio." *Italia medioevale e umanistica* 24 (1981), 159–212.

Kristeller, Paul Oskar. "Un'*Ars dictaminis* di Giovanni del Virgilio." *Italia medioevale e umanistica* 4 (1961), 181–200.

Dante's First Eclogue to Giovanni Del Virgilio. Translated by Joseph Tusiani. In *Italian Quarterly* 29 (1988), No. 111, pp. 77–79.

Dante's Second Eclogue to Giovanni Del Virgilio.

Translated by Joseph Tusiani. In *Italian Quarterly* 29 (1988), No. 111, pp. 80–83.

Wicksteed, Philip H. and Edmund G. Gardner. *Dante and Giovanni del Virgilio.* Westminster: A. Constable, 1902. rpt. New York: Haskell House Publishers, 1970.

Gary P. Cestaro

Virtues and Vices

Virtue is a quality of character that enables an individual to perform good actions and to act according to defined standards of morality. Vice, conceived as the opposite of virtue, results from reprehensible actions that are evil in nature and that contravene the established standards of morality. Two of Dante's works in particular, the *Convivio* and the *Commedia,* define and illustrate, if in different ways, traditional conceptions of both vice and virtue, and it is possible to trace the development of the various stages of the poet's thought by examining these two works.

By the author's own definition in the *Letter to Cangrande*—if this letter was in fact written by him—the *Commedia* is concerned above all with moral activity and ethics (*morale negotium, sive ethica, Epist.* 13.40). As a visual representation in which the pilgrim's journey through the otherworld coincides with his mental journey toward God, the *Commedia* constitutes the most successful of the *Summae virtutum ac vitiorum,* or encyclopedias of virtue and vice, that the Middle Ages ever produced. Singleton's assertion should be kept in mind: Dante has the vision of a poet (not a philosopher or a moralist) whose art represents an image of centuries of theological and philosophical thought.

In the *Convivio* (and to some degree in the *Monarchia*), the treatment of the virtues is both less complex and more philosophical than religious in nature, since there Dante is concerned principally with the moral and intellectual virtues, which are often linked to one another (*Conv.* 4.16.10, 4.19.5, 4.17.11–12) and which are defined according to the Aristotelian model: *fine de la vertù* [è] *la nostra vita essere contenta* ("the end of life is to make ourselves content," *Conv.* 1.8.12); *nostra beatitudine . . . prima trovare potemo quasi imperfetta ne la vita attiva, cioè ne le operazione de le morali virtudi, e poi perfetta quasi ne le operazioni de le intellettuali virtudi* ("we are able to find our blessedness . . . imperfectly, as it were, in the active life, that is, in the exercise of the moral virtues, and later almost perfectly in the exercise of the intellectual virtues," *Conv.* 4.22.18). In the hierarchic association of the seven liberal arts with individual heavens set forth in the *Convivio,* moral philosophy corresponds to the Primum Mobile, and only theology transcends it, represented by the Heaven of the Empyrean (2.14.14–21). Although he confirms the supremacy of the science of theology, Dante nevertheless gives decisive importance to moral philosophy, a science that all mankind has access to through the power of human reason. For Dante, the moral and intellectual virtues are the natural fruit of one's *nobilitade,* one's nobility of spirit, a topic he explores in the fourth and last book of the *Convivio.* The topic of nobility had particular currency, given the emergence of a new urban class of bourgeois origin and the growing intellectual lay public to which the *Convivio*—written in the vernacular to reach a broad audience—was directed. Dante defines nobility as implicitly containing the seed of every virtue (*Conv.* 4.16.10, 4.20.9) and as a gift from God. Although he was convinced of the superiority of the contemplative life over the active life, each of which was an end of nobility (*Conv.* 4.17.11), the poet names first and substantively discusses only the moral virtues, because, as he says, these virtues were both more common and more sought after and because the individuals Dante was addressing—who were preoccupied by daily civic duties—wished nevertheless to legitimize their earthly existence and achieve human perfection by means of the "loving use of knowledge" (*Conv.* 3.12.12).

According to Aristotle's definition, the active life is characterized by eleven moral virtues (*Eth.* 2.7.1107b, 1108a, 1108b; *Conv.* 4.17.2ff.): courage, temperance, liberality, munificence, magnanimity, love of honor, gentleness, affability, truth, good disposition, and justice. Recent studies on Dante have focused particular attention on his concept of the virtue of magnanimity, considered in antiquity to be among the most important virtues. In her examination of the few but significant vernacular occurrences of the terms *magnanimitade* ("magnanimity") and *magnanimo* ("magnanimous," meaning "great-souled person") in the *Convivio* and the *Commedia,* Maria Corti has stressed the great impact that the newly received philosophy of Aristotle had on Dante. And Fiorenzo Forti has been able to show that the *spiriti magni* ("great spirits," *Inf.* 4.119) of Limbo derive their identity from Aristotle's concept of magnanimity. While assigning them a privileged status in the *Commedia*, in contrast to Christian tradition, Dante nevertheless exiles the great philosophers and poets of antiquity (including Virgil and Aristotle, who represent the summit of virtue and human knowledge) by placing them in Hell and forever denying them the possibility of salvation. In moving from the *Convivio* to the *Commedia* Dante clearly devalues the virtue of magnanimity. As Corti points out, the epithet "magnanimous" occurs only twice in the poem, and both times it refers to the damned.

Justice, another moral virtue that stands out consistently in Dante's thought, is correlated with prudence, temperance, and courage in discussions on the practical use of the soul (*Conv.* 4.12.11). These are the traditional four cardinal virtues, which are sometimes presented together with the three theological virtues of faith, hope, and charity. In the *Convivio,* however, Dante founds the theory of virtue primarily on the Aristotelian model, which is not entirely consistent with the system of the four cardinal virtues. When Dante finds himself at the intersection of diverse traditions, he tends to act independently. He explicitly departs from Aristotle in considering prudence a moral, rather than an intellectual, virtue, because, in his view, prudence is *conduttrice de le morali virtù* ("the guide of moral virtues," *Conv.* 4.17.8)— virtues that could not exist in the absence of prudence.

Dante assigns some of the moral virtues, and a number of others related to them, to the four periods, or ages, of life which are allegorized in *Conv.* 4. Thus, obedience, sweetness, sense of shame, and loveliness of being (4.24.11) correspond to adolescence *(adolescenza);* temperance, courage, magnanimity (4.26.7), loyalty (4.26.14), courtesy, and love (4.26.15) correspond to maturity *(gioventute);* prudence, (4.27.5), judgment (4.27.10), generosity (4.27.12), and affability, or the ability "to speak of what is good and to hear it spoken of willingly" (4.27.16), are the exemplary virtues of old age *(senettude).* Dante specifies no virtues for the last age of life, senility *(senio),* defining it as a period during which the soul withdraws from the active life and prepares its return to God (*Conv.* 4.28.2–3).

In the *Convivio* the concept of vice is defined as the mirror opposite of virtue. Following Aristotle (*Conv.* 3.8.17–20), Dante distinguishes between the innate vices, which derive from an instinctive predisposition within the human soul, and the habitual vices, brought about by repeated actions, which are nevertheless rectifiable through the repetition of acts contrary to those in question, with the resulting acquisition of the opposite virtue as habit. In fact, each of the moral virtues "has two related enemies, that is, vices, one through excess and the other through shortfall" (4.17.7). In Aristotelian terms, virtue is thus the mean between two extremes.

The intellectual virtues, unlike the moral virtues which promote the active life, sustain and fortify the contemplative life. Dante again follows the Aristotelian model, identifying them as the scientific, the ratiocinative or deliberative, and the inventive and judicial virtues (*Conv.* 3.2.15).

The purpose and goal of the *Convivio* is to "lead men to knowledge and virtue" (1.9.7), because, according to Aristotle, "Happiness is activity in accordance with virtue in a perfect life" (4.17.8; cf. 3.15.12). The utility of the moral and intellectual virtues is reconfirmed in *Mon.* 3.15.8, which posits that earthly happiness, symbolized by the Earthly Paradise, is achieved through both the study of philosophical texts and the practice of these virtues. These virtues are not, however, sufficient for the attainment of man's supernatural end, which is embodied in Heavenly Paradise. As Virgil himself knows (*Purg.* 7.34–36), one cannot attain salvation without possessing the theological virtues of faith, hope, and charity—even if one has practiced the moral and intellectual virtues to perfection (see also *Mon.* 2.7.4–5). Unlike the moral and intellectual virtues, the theological virtues are received by the soul as gifts from God and cannot be acquired simply through human activity. They require a knowledge of Christ; that is, possession of these three virtues derives from baptism into the Christian faith. Even in *Conv.* 3.14.15, if only by implication, Dante affirms the necessity of faith, hope, and charity. In accord with those critics who detect a change in cultural orientation in the fourth book of the *Convivio* (and a fairly clear convergence with the *Monarchia*), Dante outlines a sharp distinction between human knowledge (reason) and revealed knowledge (revelation), identifying our supreme happiness with the vision of God. Nevertheless, he does maintain, in accord with Aquinas, that the speculative use of the human intellect, although limited, can understand God *per li suoi effetti* ("by means of his effects"), which is to say by means of the phenomena of the natural world perceived through the senses. The difference between the ethical and philosophical perspectives of the *Convivio* and those of the *Commedia*—which proposes to *removere viventes in hac vita de statu miserie et perducere ad statum felicitatis* ("to remove those living in this life from a state of misery, and bring them to a state of happiness," *Epist.* 13.39)—are therefore substantial and manifest. Mankind reaches the second end, eternal salvation, by means different from those required to achieve only an earthly happiness, not through the natural virtues but through the theological virtues (*Mon.* 3.15 [16]).

The specification of diverse goals for the cardinal and the theological virtues is characteristic of Dante's works written after the *Convivio,* as we have already seen to some extent. The classification and correlation of these virtues had become canonical with St. Thomas, who drew upon two traditions: the classical (from Plato to Cicero) and the Christian (Augustine, Ambrose, and Gregory the Great). The role of the cardinal and theological virtues predominates in *Purgatorio* and *Paradiso.* In the second canticle the theological virtues span the pilgrim's journey up Mount Purgatory. The four stars of the cardinal virtues, "never seen except by the first people," brightly illuminate the face of Cato, the pagan custodian of Purgatory (*Purg.* 1.37–39). According to Freccero, these stars embody original justice, only fully possessed by Adam at the time of Creation. This perfection of primitive human nature is manifest in the fullness of the cardinal virtues—prudence, justice, courage, and temperance—which correspond respectively to the powers of the soul, that is, reason, will, irascible appetite, and concupiscible appetite. Moreover, Singleton identifies Matelda, who undoubtedly symbolizes happiness in the Earthly Paradise, with the perfection of natural justice, forever lost after the Fall. As the pilgrim passes through Ante-Purgatory, the four stars give way to the three lights of the theological virtues, which appear at the threshold of the true Purgatory (*Purg.* 8.89). Finally, in the Earthly Paradise (*Purg.* 30.106–135), the cardinal and theological virtues—personified in the form of seven dancing nymphs—guide Dante into the presence of Beatrice. If the cardinal virtues, which are subordinate to the theological virtues, have been assigned to serve as Beatrice's handmaidens before her descent into the world, only the theological virtues

have the power to bring the poet's vision to its consummation.

Yet according to E. G. Parodi's studies, the presence of the cardinal and theological virtues in *Paradiso* is even more significant, because they determine both its moral topography and its structural framework. Parodi has argued that an ethical principle informs the spheres of *Paradiso.* Although in some respects incomplete, his conception nevertheless indicates the importance that Dante wished to attribute to the moral virtues, which are embodied in and represented definitively by the four cardinal virtues. One clearly recognizes the virtue of prudence in the Heaven of the Sun, courage in the Heaven of Mars, and justice in the Heaven of Jupiter. Though somewhat less evident, temperance is, according to Parodi, the virtue characteristic of the contemplatives in the highest planetary heaven, Saturn.

While some of the details of this picture may be strained, the role assigned to the theological virtues in *Paradiso* is unquestionable. Dante is examined on the nature of the three theological virtues in the Heaven of the Fixed Stars in three consecutive cantos (*Par.* 24, 25, 26), by the apostles who best represent these virtues in the Gospel. St. Peter, the rock *(pietra)* and foundation of the Church and its first pope, conducts the examination on faith, which is the first and fundamental theological virtue which prepares the way for the succeeding two. St. James examines Dante on hope, and St. John conducts the exam on charity. The examination on faith (*Par.* 24.64–66) is defined by an expression that is directly taken from St. Paul (Heb. 11:1). Likewise, the definition of hope follows a formulation already widely diffused by Scholastic texts commented on by St. Thomas Aquinas and Peter Lombard (*Libri IV Sententiarum* 3.26). Finally, Dante's discourse on charity (*Par.* 26.16–18) alludes to St. John's passage in 1 John 4:8, which defines God's existence as *caritas.* It should be noted here that St. Paul was the first to group the three virtues together (1 Cor. 13:13).

As is evident from the structure of an ethical system dependent upon the cardinal and theological virtues, the relationship and definition of vice and virtue in the *Commedia* are never independent of the moral structure of Dante's narrative. It would therefore be improper to consider them abstractly, purely from a general or theoretical perspective. This consideration is especially relevant for the *Commedia,* which is the pinnacle of Dante's poetic and intellectual experience, and where, as many critics have argued (among them Auerbach, Lotman, Freccero, Chiavacci, and Le Goff), it is absolutely impossible to separate the pilgrim's physical journey from the soul's spiritual journey toward God. In this poetic text, whose purpose is—as the poet himself explicitly states in the *Letter to Cangrande (Epist.* 13.15)—the advancement of human morality in the light of God's judgment, the ethical system completely informs the topography of the other world. With regard to fact that only in *Inf.* 11 are we provided with any explanation of the ethical structure of the afterlife, Chiavacci accurately observes: "The *Commedia* is not, in fact, a treatise, but a poem whose doctrine and dogma are presented in a complementary and subsidiary, rather than a primary, manner." In other words, Dante's poetry tends to reveal the nature of good and evil more by visual demonstration than by exposition, more by the presentation of images that require interpretation than by direct discourse.

Each canticle relies upon a different ethical conception rather than on a single universal definition, a fact that may at first seem surprising. This difference is most pronounced in the *Paradiso,* for as a place Paradise occupies a space beyond the terrestrial domain and, as a text, it takes as its subject the contemplation of spiritual truths. But the other two canticles likewise reveal noteworthy differences. The classification of the vices in the *Inferno* derives from Aristotelian thought. As Freccero notes in an erudite essay, sin resides only in the will. The classic, three-part division of the appetite into the rational will (*appetitus rationalis,* or *voluntas*) and the two parts of the *appetitus sensitivus* (the irascible and the concupiscible), a formulation accepted by theologians, permits Dante to structure and categorize the sins of Hell almost entirely in Aristotelian terms, which he has access to through the mediation of St. Thomas. The disorder of the human appetite in its three parts is reflected, according to Freccero, in the three major categories of sin in Hell, namely malice, bestiality, and incontinence, respectively. The conceptual schema for the moral system of the *Inferno* is, then, fundamentally Aristotelian (*Inf.* 11.79–83) as described by Virgil: *Non ti rimembra di quelle parole / con le quai la tua Etica pertratta / le tre disposizion che 'l ciel non vole, / incontenenza, malizia e la matta / bestialitade* ("Do you not remember the words with which your Ethics treats the three dispositions which Heaven wills not: incontinence, malice and mad bestiality").

Virgil's reference to Aristotle (*Eth.* 8.1.1145a) pinpoints the general model for the classification of vices in the *Inferno,* even if the category of bestiality remains problematic. In the view of many critics, Dante, freely adapting the *Ethics* to his *Inferno,* makes it coincide with the sins of violence. In other instances as well Dante presents elements that are incongruous with the Aristotelian model, either out of necessity or poetic license. For example, Dante places the sin of heresy after incontinence and before violence and fraud. Heresy, according to Freccero a sin of the intellect and not of the will, is conceivable only within the Christian system, since the sin is completely foreign to Aristotelian ethics.

Each of the three conceptual categories of incontinence, violence, and fraud incorporates in turn a whole subset of specific vices. Incontinence comprises the lustful, the gluttonous, the avaricious and prodigal, the wrathful and sullen. Violence divides into three species, according to the person injured (neighbor, self, God), and comprises the murderers and tyrants, the suicides and the squanderers, and the blasphemers, sodomites, and usurers. Ordinary fraud, punished in the eighth circle of Hell, is exemplified by the panders and seducers, the flatterers, the simonists, the diviners, the barrators, the hypocrites, the thieves, the fraudulent counselors, the sowers of scandal, and the falsifiers. Finally, treacherous fraud, punished in the ninth and last circle, is divided into four classes: the traitors to kin, to homeland or party, to guests, and to benefactors.

This complex schema of division and subdivision, which enumerates a total of twenty-four discrete areas of sin, may not have been Dante's original conception for his moral system. As has been often noted, the sins of incontinence reveal the presence of part of another important schema: the seven deadly, or capital, sins. This originated in the West with John Cassian (d. 435), was modified by Pope Gregory the Great (d. 604), and became canonical with St. Thomas Aquinas. Wenzel offers the hypothesis that after canto 7 Dante changed the moral system of *Inferno,* after having unsuccessfully attempted to link heterogeneous ethical structures, including the schema of the seven deadly sins. Whether or not this is the case, Dante's final system reveals an extraordinary logicality and complexity in the classification of vice.

V

The moral system of *Purgatorio,* however—articulated by a series of the gradations or discrete levels along the journey up the mountain—classifies the vices and virtues in relation to their birth and growth within the human soul, which is governed by free will *(libero arbitrio),* rather than on the basis of specific acts. Man's free will is an obviously crucial concept in Dante's texts, being the foundation of personal responsibility for acts of virtue and vice. But free will is literally central to the meaning of the second canticle, where it is dealt with in the central cantos (16–18). The moral system of this canticle is based on the schema of the seven deadly sins, with the gravest sin at the bottom and the least grave sin at the top. According to Bloomfield's classic study, Dante follows the canonical order established by Gregory the Great, which was known by the medieval acronym *siiaagl,* for *superbia, invidia, ira, accidia, avarizia, gola, lussuria* (pride, envy, wrath, sloth, avarice, gluttony, and lust). It should be observed that within the terrace of avarice, Dante also punishes the related vice of prodigality, in keeping with the Aristotelian model.

Dante maintains the preeminence of pride even though, according to Lester Little, economic and social changes in his time resulted in the classification of avarice as the root of all evil, in a modification of traditional Christian teaching. The poet does, however, identify avarice as an increasingly pernicious vice that underlies the corruption and collapse of society's most important institutions, in particular, the Church. In fact, avarice is the sin most frequently addressed in the *Commedia* by way of allegorical reference, metaphor, and apostrophe. The power of the *lupa* ("she-wolf") that initially blocks Dante's way in the opening canto of *Inferno*—a figure traditionally interpreted as representing avarice—is repeatedly recalled throughout the poem (*Inf.* 6.74, 19.104; *Purg.* 20.10; *Par.* 19.130). It underpins the more serious sins like simony, and it informs the spirit that moved the papacy to defend its claim to temporal power. The cure for what Dante perceives as a rampant social disease can be found only in the example of St. Francis, who represents a new model for the religious life (*Par.* 11), one in which the virtue of poverty—based on the renunciation of all earthly goods—replaces humility (a virtue that had previously been predominant as the opposite of the worst of all vices, pride).

The moral system of Purgatory is based on a polarity between each principal vice and its complementary virtue, a procedure that had already been employed by Hugh of St. Victor in his *De quinque septenis seu septenariis.* Pride is overcome by humility *(umiltà);* envy, by fraternal love *(carità);* wrath, by gentleness *(mansuetudine);* sloth, by zeal *(sollecitudine);* avarice, by poverty *(povertà);* gluttony, by temperance *(temperanza);* and lust, by chastity *(castità).* On each terrace the penitent soul not only expiates a vice by examining its major exempla but also is rehabilitated by the study of exempla of the opposite virtue. In each instance Dante selects as the first exemplum of virtue an event from the life of the Virgin Mary, drawing on a pattern employed in the *Speculum Beatae Mariae Virginis,* a work widely diffused in the Middle Ages by the Franciscan Conrad of Saxony (see Girotto). Finally, a benediction based on a beatitude *(beatitudine)* is pronounced as the pilgrim prepares to ascend to the succeeding terrace. These benedictions are taken from the Book of Psalms or from the hymns of the church, and they number seven (in ascending order): *Beati pauperes spiritu, Beati misericordes, Beati pacifici, Beati qui lugent, Beati qui sitiunt, Beati qui esuriunt, Beati mundo corde.*

By the second half of the thirteenth century—in the wake of the influence of Albert the Great, St. Bonaventure, and St. Thomas Aquinas—the seven capital vices were considered to result from a misdirected love, a disorder of the will *(voluntas),* and were thus linked, as has been noted, to the soul's faculties. The preeminent source for Dante's conception of disordered love *(amor inordinatus),* which assigns a place to each of the seven capital vices, is William Peraldus' *Summa de vitiis et virtutibus,* which divides these sins into three conceptual groups. An individual may err by choosing to love the wrong object *(malo obietto),* which is perverted love, or by choosing to love the right object in the wrong degree, either by excess or deficiency *(per troppo o per poco di vigore,* 17.96). Love of the wrong object comprises the sins of pride, envy, and wrath. Love of the right object by excess comprises avarice, gluttony, and lust; deficient love of the right object leads to sloth. The moral system of Dante's Purgatory, therefore, reveals an extraordinary conflation of multiple models found in Scholastic discourse which organize virtue and vice in a coherent, logical, and didactic manner. His originality here lies less in the formulation of the existing models themselves than the way in which he uses them to create a harmonious whole whose unity depends upon the single and fundamental concept of Christian love.

Bibliography

Alighieri, Dante. *Commedia: Inferno.* Edited by Anna Maria Chiavacci Leonardi. Vol. 1. Milan: Mondadori, 1991, p. 337.

———. *Commedia: Purgatorio.* Edited by Anna Maria Chiavacci Leonardi. Vol. 2. Milan: Mondadori, 1994, pp. xiv–xxiii.

Bloomfield, Morton W. *The Seven Deadly Sins: An Introduction to the History of a Religious Concept, with Special Reference to Medieval English Literature.* 2nd ed. Michigan State University Press, 1967, pp. 72, 89, 157ff.

Corti, Maria. *La felicità mentale: nuove prospettive per Cavalcanti e Dante.* Turin: Einaudi, 1983, pp. 38–53.

Delcorno, Carlo. *Exemplum e letteratura: tra Medioevo e Rinascimento.* Bologna: Il Mulino, 1989, pp. 183, 199.

Forti, Fiorenzo. "Il limbo dantesco e i megalopsichoi dell'Etica nicomachea." *Giornale storico della letteratura italiana* 138 (1961), 329–340.

Freccero, John. "The Firm Foot on a Journey without a Guide." In *Dante: The Poetics of Conversion.* Edited by Rachel Jacoff. Cambridge, Mass.: Harvard University Press, 1986, pp. 29–54.

Girotto, Samuele. *Corrado di Sassonia predicatore e mariologo del sec. XIII.* Florence: Studi francescani, 1952, pp. 205–216.

Little, Lester K. "Pride Goes before Avarice: Social Change and the Vices in Latin Christendom." *The American Historical Review* 76 (1971), 17–49.

Mancini, Franco. "Un'*auctoritas* di Dante." *Studi danteschi* 45 (1968), 95–119.

Moore, Edward. "Unity and Symmetry of Design in the Purgatorio." In *Studies in Dante. Second Series: Miscellaneous Essays.* Oxford: Clarendon Press, 1899, pp. 246–268. Reprinted New York: Haskell House, 1968.

Nardi, Bruno. *Dal "Convivio" alla "Commedia."* Rome: Istituto storico italiano per il Medio Evo, 1960, p. 82.

Parodi, Ernesto G. "La costruzione e l'ordinamento del Paradiso dantesco." In *Poesia e storia nella "Divina Commedia."* Venice: Neri Pozza, 1965, pp. 363–586.

Reade, William H. V. *The Moral System of Dante's Inferno.* Oxford: Clarendon Press, 1909. Reprinted Port Washington, N.Y.: Kennikat Press, 1969.

Scott, John A. *Dante magnanimo: studi sulla Commedia.* Florence: Olschki, 1977.

Singleton, Charles. *Dante Studies 1. Commedia: Elements of Structure.* Cambridge, Mass.: Harvard University Press, 1954.

———. *Dante Studies 2. Journey to Beatrice.* Cambridge, Mass.: Harvard University Press, 1958.

Wenzel, Siegfried. *The Sin of Sloth: Acedia in Medieval Thought and Literature.* Chapel Hill: University of North Carolina Press, 1967, pp. 108, 128, 130–134, 200–202.

———. "Dante's Rationale for the Seven Deadly Sins ('Purgatorio' XVII)." *Modern Language Review* 60 (1965), 528–533.

———. "The Seven Deadly Sins: Problems of Research." *Speculum: A Journal of Medieval Studies* 63 (1968), 1–22.

Giuseppina Mezzadroli
(translated by Robin Treasure)

Virtuous Heathen

The salvation of virtuous pagans has been one of the most discussed issues in theology. At the heart of the debate is the tension between the universal salvific will of God by which, as 1 Timothy (2:4–6) proclaims, God wills the salvation of all humankind and the historical reality that many virtuous individuals either lived before the coming of Christ or, if afterwards, are in geographical areas where the Gospel is not preached.

In the early Church the issue was fiercely debated. In the East theologians were driven by texts such as 1 Timothy and by a love for Greek learning. Hence, they opted for a universalistic theology of salvation which extended grace and eternal life with God to the upright pagans of the past. Justin Martyr (*Apol.* 46.3) early argued that not only the Hebrew just but certain pagan righteous such as Socrates and Heraclitus had received seeds of the Logos in advance and were saved. He was followed by Clement of Alexandria, who had such respect for Greek philosophy that he argued (*Eclogae* 20 [*PG* 9, 707]; cf. *Stromata* 1.5 [*PG* 8, 717–728]) that philosophy was for the Greeks what the

V Law was for the Jews—a pedagogue leading to Christ. The Western fathers, on the contrary, offered a much more limited view of salvation for virtuous pagans. The fourth-century Bishop Philastrius (*Diversarum haereson liber* 27 [*PL* 77, 870]), for example, condemned as heretics those, such as Clement and Origen, who had extended Christ's liberation to both Jews and pagans; and Augustine (*De civ. Dei* 7.32; 10.25, 32), following Philastrius, flatly denied that anyone could win salvation without belief in Christ, the one mediator between God and man.

The Scholastics were likewise divided, and the acrimony which the issue produced can be seen clearly in the debate between Abelard (who maintained that certain virtuous gentile philosophers were saved by virtue of their natural reason, which led them to God) and Bernard of Clairvaux (who vociferously attacked the position that anyone can come to a knowledge of God by reason alone)—a debate which ended in Abelard's condemnation in 1140. Of all the Scholastics Aquinas is the most comprehensive. He discusses the issue in a number of passages that develop three key ideas on which the official theological position of Dante's time was based. In the *Summa Theologiae* (2.2.10.1) Thomas makes a clear distinction between positive infidelity (open opposition to the faith) and negative infidelity (simple unbelief) and argues that only the former constitutes a sin. However, Aquinas elsewhere (*De veritate* q. 28, a.3, ad. 4) finds it impossible to imagine a completely virtuous pagan or negative infidel: upon attainment, therefore, of the age of reason one is either damned or saved. And in the *Summa contra Gentiles* (3, 159ff.) the Angelic Doctor reasons that, even though God offers his grace to all, one can, in free will, become an impediment to that grace by not taking the appropriate steps to secure salvation. In so doing, one is culpable and is guilty of a grave personal sin of omission (*De veritate* q. 24, a. 12, ad. 2).

In *Inf.* 4 Dante adopts a theological position on the salvation of virtuous pagans which is unique (Iannucci, 73–74). First, he places his adult virtuous pagans alongside the children in Limbo (*d'infanti e di femmine e di viri,* "of infants and of women and of men," 4.30). The theological tradition, however, had reasoned that the harrowing of Hell had stripped the *limbus patrum* of all its adults and was in agreement that the *limbus puerorum* was the exclusive domain of unbaptized children, except for those with mental disabilities. Second,

Dante is insistent that his pagans are not only meritorious (*hanno mercedi,* "have merits") but guiltless of all personal sin (*ei non peccaro,* "they did not sin") and are condemned (*perduti,* "damned," *sospesi,* "suspended") in Limbo for no reason other than their lack of faith (*perché non ebber battesmo, / ch'è porta de la fede,* "for they did not receive baptism, which is the gateway to the faith," 4.35–36), as Virgil explains. Such a position is extraordinarily radical and pits Dante against Aquinas on two fundamental theological arguments, namely, the impossibility of a completely virtuous positive infidel and the impossibility of being damned for only not having faith. Dante bars the gates of Heaven to the virtuous pagans; he shuts the gates of Limbo upon them instead. He imprisons the exceptional men and women of antiquity—or, more precisely, all virtuous negative infidels, whether B.C.E. or C.E.—in a Limbo that resembles more that of the infants than that of the adults. Their expectation is not one of hope like that of the Hebrew fathers of the *limbus patrum* but one of hopeless desire like that of the children: *sanza speme vivemo in disio* ("without hope we live in desire," 4.42).

Dante adopts this unique theological stand to develop and underscore the tragedy of the virtuous pagans. These pagans were all born under the shadow of one sin, original sin, and it is with original sin that Dante associates the drama of predestination. The tragic players in this drama are the virtuous pagans of Limbo who simply lived at the wrong historical moment, in the graceless section of history between the Fall and the Incarnation, and who, because of their lack of faith, are forever excluded from eternal life with God.

The theological issues of predestination, grace, loss, and justice, introduced in *Inf.* 4, are kept before us throughout the *poema sacro.* Throughout the first two *cantiche,* in fact, Virgil's story, as emblematic of the tragedy of the gracelessness and loss of the virtuous pagans, resonates repeatedly (*Inf.* 1, 2, 8, 9, 26; *Purg.* 1, 3, 7, 21, 22). And the great theological issues of grace, predestination, and divine justice reach their ultimate climax in the eagle episode of *Par.* 19–20, an episode that finally resolves Dante's dilemma regarding the negative infidels' damnation: divine justice and the will of God are synonymous, the virtuous pagans are suspended in Limbo because God willed it, and human reason is totally inadequate to explain the just will of God and must accept it on faith.

God's ways, however, are mysterious, so that to be born in an age of ignorance is not an absolute bar to salvation. God may, at his discretion, extend grace even to those born in the midst of an unenlightened world. In the *Commedia* Dante offers three examples of pagans who have been snatched from Limbo and saved outright: Cato, Trajan, and Ripheus. Cato was one of the many souls liberated during the harrowing of Hell. Trajan and Ripheus, it is made clear, were saved by explicit acts of faith in Christ. Although theology clearly distinguished between explicit and implicit faith (a faith in Christ and God existing unconsciously in the hearts of infidels) and argued that both could lead to salvation, Dante does not make use of implicit faith, either in the case of Trajan and Ripheus or in that of his virtuous pagans. Dante thus seems to underscore two points, namely, that explicit faith is required for salvation and that such faith is possible for anyone, provided that God wills that person to possess it. The salvation of these three pagans thus reaffirms the unfathomable mystery of grace and reinforces the tragedy of the virtuous pagans, who were born in an age when grace was scarce.

Bibliography

Busnelli. "La Colpa del 'non fare' degli infedeli negativi." *Studi danteschi* 23 (1938), 79–97.

Caperan, Louis. "Le problème du salut des infideles." Reprinted by F. Ruffini in "Dante e il Problema della Salvezza degli Infedeli." *Studi danteschi* 14 (1930), 79–92.

Foster, Kenelm. "The Two Dantes (I). Limbo and Implicit Faith." *The Two Dantes and Other Studies.* London: Darton, Longman and Todd, 1977, pp. 156–189.

Harent, S. "Infideles (Salut de)." *Dictionnaire de Theologie Catholique.* Paris: Letouzey et Ane, 1922, vol. 7, cols. 1726–1930.

Hollander, Robert. "Tragedia nella 'Commedia.'" *Il Virgilio Dantesco: Tragedia nella "Commedia."* Florence: Olschki, 1983, pp. 117–154.

Iannucci, Amilcare A. "Limbo: The Emptiness of Time." *Studi danteschi* 52 (1978), 69–128.

Mazzoni, Francesco. "Saggio di un nuovo commento alla *Commedia.* Il Canto IV dell'*Inferno.*" *Studi danteschi* 42 (1965), 29–206.

Padoan, Giorgio. "Il Limbo Dantesco." *Lettere italiane* 21 (1969), 369–388. Reprinted in *Il pio Enea, l'impio Ulisse.* Ravenna: A. Longo Editore, 1977, pp. 103–124.

Amilcare A. Iannucci

Visconti, Nino de'

A major political figure of Pisa in the late thirteenth century, Nino de' Visconti (c. 1265–1296) was a grandson of Count Ugolino della Gherardesca. Visconti participated actively in the heated communal struggles of his city, leading one of its Guelf factions and becoming his grandfather's partner in governing Pisa for a short period. Notwithstanding considerable friction between their camps, grandfather and grandson jointly held the position of podestà (mayor) until Count Ugolino drove Nino and his followers into exile in 1288 in order to quell discontent and check the growing Ghibelline threat. As a warrior in the Guelf party, Nino led the Pisan exiles against their city, closely associating himself with Pisa's enemies, Florence and Lucca. One of his campaigns, the siege of Caprona (1289), is mentioned in *Inf.* 21.94–96. Eventually, Nino was made captain general of the party. By birthright, he was also the lord of Gallura, one of the four judicial districts of Sardinia: thus his title of "judge," synonymous with "governor." After peace was concluded with Pisa in 1293, he departed for Sardinia, where he eventually died. He requested that his heart be buried in Lucca, the stronghold of the Guelf party.

In *Purg.* 8, Dante the pilgrim encounters Nino "among the great shades" (44) in the Valley of the Princes. His placement is reinforced by Dante's joy in seeing "noble Judge Nino . . . not among the damned!" (53–54). Given Nino's ties to Florence, Dante very likely had opportunities to have met him. In their reunion in Ante-Purgatory no mention is made of Nino's turbulent existence and partisan politics. What the poet stresses in this episode is the acceptance of God's will and the importance of human ties: friendship, paternity, and marriage. The crepuscular atmosphere of the canto forms an appropriate backdrop to the conversation and Nino's recollection of distant loved ones, whose only relationship to the deceased consists of memory and prayer. Like other souls, Nino asks to be remembered in the prayers of his loved ones, so his journey toward God may be expedited.

Nino's fond remembrance of his innocent daughter Giovanna contrasts with the criticism of his wife, Beatrice, who appears to have forgotten him. In point of fact, after Nino's death Beatrice d'Este married Galeazzo Visconti of Milan (no relation to Nino). It is a marriage, Nino foretells, she is destined to regret. As the daughter of Obizzo II, lord of Ferrara, the historical Beatrice was pressured to remarry to provide a political alliance for her family. In Nino's view, however, such haste to put aside her widow's weeds is proof of feminine inconstancy in love: a form of infidelity to himself and to his noble house.

Fiora A. Bassanese

Vita Nuova

Even as Dante's earliest work, the *Vita Nuova* (New Life) gives evidence of the author's ideological and poetic maturity. The work is a balanced synthesis of the preceding romance tradition in terms of lyricism and narration because it offers a definitive solution to that tradition's central problem, which is love. In fact, the poet-pilgrim of the *Commedia* is given the privilege of journeying to the otherworld precisely because he has resolved the mystery created by love (*Inf.* 1.85–87).

From this perspective, the *Vita Nuova* can be considered a treatise on the nature of love, a new *liber de amore* in the style of Andreas Capellanus. It is therefore no coincidence that the book opens with a mysterious vision in which the god of Love gives the narrator's heart to Beatrice for her to eat (3). It closes, likewise, in a final epiphany, with another vision of Beatrice and the revelation of the divine nature of the narrator's love (41). Between these two moments lies a series of explanations concerning the phenomenon of love (see 13, 20, and 24), which in part foreshadow the final revelation. The ensemble of these attempts to explain the nature of love, progressing from uncertainty to conviction, not only characterizes the narrator's love life (which progresses from the sensual love evident in the image of the eating of the heart to the spiritual love embodied in his *facie ad faciem* vision with Beatrice) but also characterizes the poetic tradition in the vernacular, which passes from the troubadours to the Stilnovist poets before reaching Dante.

The *Vita Nuova* is presented to the reader as a kind of songbook, a collection of lyrical poems organized not by a copyist (as were all previous songbooks, such as those in Provençal, French, and Italian) but rather by the author himself. By compiling the lyrics composed during his amorous youth, Dante intended to prove himself a modern *auctor,* comparable to the classical *auctores* (Virgil, Lucan, Horace, and Ovid), who are cited in chapter 25 as absolute paradigms of poetic writing. In order to achieve that objective, the *scriba*

who copies the lyrics from the book of his memory (1) must be aware that he is both commentator and compiler of his own poetic creation. By explicating his poems and their formal division into parts, he intends to make manifest the deeper meaning of his poetic inventions. He also intends to select and organize his lyrics within the corresponding prose passages in a way that conveys a coherent and unified narrative, one that reconstructs his exemplary love story as a work of art. If the lyrics reveal the presence of themes and motifs of the romance tradition (the *celar,* or motif of hiding the amatory experience from others; the praise of woman; the *gab,* or motif of mocking one's love; the *iter amoris,* or stages of love), the prose commentary links those topical situations in a narrative sequence that recounts the poetic and spiritual formation of the narrator. The songbook thus becomes the author's amatory autobiography.

The alternation between poetry and prose gives the *Vita Nuova* qualities of a *prosimetrum,* a form inspired not so much by Boethius' *De Consolatione philosophiae* (which instead served as a model for the *Convivio*) as by the songbooks of Provence, where the poems of a single troubadour were preceded by a *vida* (life) and, at times, accompanied by *razo* (explication) in prose. Above all, however, the form was inspired by the poetic works of the classical *auctores,* particularly Ovid's *Remedia amoris* with a Christian commentary in prose. On the other hand, the book illustrates an autobiography that is to be understood neither in a realistic sense (the recording of actual events dealing with the narrator's love life) nor in a strictly historical-cultural sense (the narrator's love life as a metaphor for his poetic and intellectual formation), but in a poetic context (the narrator's love life as the typological realization of the preceding poetic tradition). The *Vita Nuova*'s autobiographical reading, which wholly dominates today's criticism (owing principally to De Robertis's studies), has reshaped the biographical and hagiographic reading sponsored earlier by critics like Schiaffini, Singleton, and Branca, among others, who argued that the book recounted the life, death, and miracles of Beatrice and could thus be considered a *Legenda sanctae Beatricis* ("Legend of St. Beatrice"). Yet this interpretative hypothesis is hindered by the fact that Beatrice is not a character who can be the basis for a story, given the divine perfection that already defines her in her first apparition (2.8); her name ("she who blesses")

VITA NVOVA
DI DANTE
ALIGHIERI.

Cón xv. Canzoni del medeſimo.

E la vita di eſſo Dante ſcritta da Giovanni Boccaccio.

CON LICENZA, E PRIVILEGIO.

IN FIRENZE,
Nella Stamperia di Bartolomeo Sermartelli.
MDLXXVI.

Vita Nuova. *Title page of the Sermartelli edition of 1576. Reproduced by permission of the John A. Zahm Dante Collection in the Department of Special Collections, University Libraries, University of Notre Dame.*

already identifies her ideological and narrative function, which is to show the narrator the path he should pursue to discover love's truth and thus renew himself on a spiritual and literary level.

As a book of poetry that speaks of poetry, the *Vita Nuova* is dedicated to Guido Cavalcanti, who is considered the best lyrical poet prior to Dante. This dedication is underscored in further refrains throughout the book. Under the circumlocutory phrase "first friend," Cavalcanti is summoned at crucial moments in the narration: at the beginning, when he is said to explain the meaning of Dante's first sonnet in an exchange sonnet (3.4); in the middle, when he is described allegorically as John (the Baptist) who preceded the True Light, thus as the precursor to Dante-Christ (24.4); and finally near the end, when he is called to the scene to endorse the author's decision to write the book in

the vernacular and not in Latin (30.3). The dedication, however, initially disguises the fact that Dante has taken another side in the debate at hand. Although Cavalcanti stands at the apex of Love's faithful subjects—the privileged audience for whom the work is written—he has proved incapable of fully comprehending the phenomenon of love because his investigation focuses wholly on its sensory nature and fails to probe its rational dimension. This is apparent even in the interpretation he gives of the *Vita Nuova*'s initial sonnet: Cavalcanti, by declaring that death is the meaning behind the image of Beatrice's eating of the narrator's heart, remains separated from truth, from the *verace giudicio* ("true judgment") which *ora è manifestissimo a li più semplici* ("is completely clear even to the least sophisticated," 3.15). Dante's final, dazzling vision essentially reveals the true meaning of the initial vision: a meaning not of death but of life and transfiguration.

The book contains thirty-one lyrics, primarily sonnets (twenty-five, two of which are double sonnets), together with three canzoni, two stanzas of a canzone (one of which is double), and a ballad. Their composition extends across a period of time whose initial moment can be determined with precision: the opening sonnet "A ciascun' alma presa e gentil core" (3.10–12) was written when the poet was 18 years old, in the spring of 1283. The dating of the final lyric, however, remains uncertain. In fact, the last poem whose date is certain is the sonnet that marks the one-year anniversary, on June 8, 1291, of Beatrice's death (34). The duration of the events referred to in the following lyrics—from the crisis of the *donna gentile* to the final vision—while uncertain, cannot have been very long. The pilgrims' *transitus,* described in a sonnet (40), most likely points to Holy Week of 1292. For this reason, the celestial encounter with Beatrice in the last sonnet (41) could coincide, given the pentecostal nature of the revelation it portrays, with the second anniversary of Beatrice's death, thereby completing a perfect temporal cycle begun nine years earlier in their earthly encounter.

The span of time outlined by the *Vita Nuova*'s lyrics is circular, given the parallelism that is established between the first and the last composition. The geometric image that best represents the time frame of the prose passages is that of a single point, or more precisely, the central point of a circle around which the lyrics themselves are deployed (as in 12.4). The prose language

V

originates at the same moment in which Dante intuits the full meaning of his youthful love life and conceives of a unity and systematic nature to the poems he had previously composed. This point coincides with the final vision of Beatrice held in reverence; it is the time frame of the narrative "prose present," as opposed to the time frame of "lyric past" (cfr. 3.15). This is Dante's privileged time, in which he not only understands his past as a lover but also becomes aware of his future as an author: *io spero di dicer di lei quello che mai fue detto d'alcuna* ("I hope to write of her that which has never been written of any other woman," 42.2).

The arrangement of the thirty-one lyrics, besides being the vehicle of ideological and narrative meaning, defines the structural coherence of the book's internal divisions. The work's present division into forty-two chapters does not reflect the original form of the text, which was not divided into numbered chapters, but rather is a format implemented by nineteenth-century editors and endorsed by those of the twentieth century (Barbi in particular), designed to make the text more accessible to a modern readership. Critics have recently begun to question this editorial practice (especially Gorni, along philological lines) and have promoted reinstating the divisions identified in the oldest manuscript tradition, whose thirty-one paragraphs are distinguished by decorated capital initials. The number of paragraphs, then, is the same as the number of lyrics, although not every paragraph contains a lyric (for example, three paragraphs contain two lyrics while three others contain none). The lyrics therefore act as gravitational centers which draw together individual themes and motifs, making them clearly identifiable.

The metric forms of the lyrics also have an organizing role, which is particularly discernible in the opposition established between the long forms—the canzone—and the short forms, which include the sonnet, the stanza of a canzone (comparable to the sonnet in morphology and genealogy), and the ballad. In fact, the three canzoni are employed as supporting columns for the entire structure of the work. If the first (19) and the third (31) canzoni mark decisive turns in the narration—these turns being, respectively, the transition from the early theme of the *saluto* ("greeting") to the new theme of *lode* ("praise"), and from the

rhymes of Beatrice's life to those of her death—the central canzone (23), which is the sixteenth component in the sequence, constitutes the supporting axis on which the entire work pivots, just as Beatrice's death (which is announced here) is the focal event of the narrative. The short metric forms are distributed on each side of the three canzoni: ten (nine sonnets and a ballad) precede the first canzone, and ten (nine sonnets and a double stanza of a canzone) follow the last canzone. The central canzone is flanked on either side by four short components (all of which are sonnets, excepting the last, which is the stanza of a canzone). It is therefore possible to identify a structural outline underlying the book's composition which can be represented by the following numeric formulation:

$$10\,(1+9) \,//\, I - 4 - I - 4\,(3+1) \,//\, I - 10\,(9+1)$$

The Arabic numbers indicate the short components, and the Roman numerals represent the longer components. Numbers within parentheses indicate a further subdivision, denoting not only the alternation between different metric forms (sonnet and not sonnet) but also the position of the different component; finally, the double bars signal a change in theme. As first worked out by Norton and later perfected by Singleton, this schema calls attention not only to sacred numbers that refer to the divinity (3 and 1, symbolizing the Trinity, which is already adumbrated in the total number of lyrics) but also to the number 9, the number symbolic of Beatrice's perfection, as glossed in chapter 29.

The tripartite structure of the *Vita Nuova* is made salient not only by the placement of the metric forms but also by the text itself. The separation between the first and second parts, found in chapter 17, is marked by the change of theme from greeting to praise: . . . *a me convenne ripigliare matera nuova e più nobile che la passata* ("I felt forced to find a new theme, one nobler than the last," 17.1). In turn, in chapter 27, the dramatic interruption of a canzone in praise of Beatrice, immediately followed in the succeeding chapter's first line by the citation of a verse from Jeremiah's Book of Lamentations, denotes the beginning of the third part, the arrival of another new theme (*nuova materia,* 30.1), the theme of Beatrice's glory. The three parts thus describe the three most important aspects of significance that Beatrice assumes for the narrator in the course of his love journey. The passage from one part to another is achieved when the nature of the relationship with the beloved Beatrice is thrown into crisis by a epiphanic event, which propels the narrator toward a reformulation of that relationship.

The first part (2–16) tells the beginning of the story: the protagonist's encounter with and immediate enamorment of Beatrice. The fact that the lady is so closely associated with her own gesture of greeting ensures that their relationship is established on the level of the senses (vision and hearing). This form of relationship, whose secrecy from public awareness requires the participation of a screen lady, is thrown into crisis when Beatrice withholds her greeting from the narrator and then derides him in public, revealing the inadequacy of his amorous conduct and his need to elevate his love to a higher level.

The second part (17–27) describes his attempt to overcome the amorous and cognitive impasse which threatened to destroy their relationship. Now the protagonist announces his desire to establish contact with his beloved not on an exterior but on an interior basis; he passes from dependence on her greeting, which can be denied, to seeking something that cannot fail him: the words themselves that praise his lady (18.4–6). Dante abandons his habit of speaking *to* her (*dire a lei*, 17.1) in order to give himself over to speaking exclusively *about* her (*parlare di lei*, 18.1); that is, he establishes communication with his lady on the level of the internal senses (fantasy and imagination). Yet even praise is placed in a crisis when Beatrice dies, for with her death an interior contemplation of her beauty is no longer possible. Although this crisis is more dramatic than the preceding one, it is nevertheless overcome; death is not to be considered the end of love but, rather, the transition into a still higher form of love.

The third part (27–42) recounts the conclusion of the story. Here, Beatrice's full significance, which had already been declared in the first paragraph of the book ("the *glorious* lady of my mind," 2.1), is finally realized. This revelation is wholly intellectual, and it guides the poet along a path that leads from the earthly to the divine. After venting his sadness and lamenting Beatrice's departure, the protagonist encounters a *donna gentile* who appears to share his grief. This episode represents the third and final moment of crisis in the story: such an encounter as this has the potential to weaken his fidelity to Beatrice and provoke a lapse back into the web of earthly passion. The constancy of reason, or rational knowledge, prevails nonetheless, compelling the poet to identify Beatrice with the glory of God once and for all. In fact, as Dante observes a group of pilgrims arriving in Rome to view the image of Christ imprinted on the Veronica, he, too, is compelled to make a *peregrinatio* whose terminus is not earthly but celestial. His journey ("Beyond the sphere that makes the greatest round," 41.10), recorded in the last poem "Oltre la spera che più larga gira," comprises the ascent of the most spiritual part of his being—his "pilgrim spirit," into the Empyrean, where it can contemplate the absolute perfection of God in the perfect mirror of Beatrice.

A prefatory and a concluding paragraph frame the three parts in the book. In the preface (1) the *auctor* of the *Vita Nuova* announces his plan for the writing at hand, which was to record in the book before us the allegorical meaning of the words (both lyrics and recollections) which he finds registered in the *libro de la mia memoria* ("the book of my memory"). In the epilogue (42), on the other hand, the *auctor* announces his plan for the composition of a future text, a book (apparently the *Commedia*) recounting a *mirabile visione* ("miraculous vision") in which the final vision of Beatrice in the *Vita Nuova* is brought to fruition. His first and youthful work forms, therefore, the initial stage of a love story whose full meaning is developed and completed only in his last and most mature work.

Bibliography

Alighieri, Dante. *Vita Nuova.* Edited by Guglielmo Gorni. Turin: Einaudi, 1996.

———. *Vita Nuova.* Edited by Dino S. Cervigni and Edward Vasta. Notre Dame, London: University of Notre Dame Press, 1995.

———. *Vita Nuova.* Vol. 1, part 1. Edited by Domenico De Robertis. Milan, Naples: Ricciardi, 1980.

———. *La Vita Nuova.* Critical edition edited by Michele Barbi. Florence: Bemporad, 1932.

Branca, Vittore. "Poetics of Renewal and Hagiographic Tradition in the *Vita Nuova*" [1966]. In *Lectura Dantis Newberryana.* Edited by Paolo Cherchi and Antonio C. Mastrobuono.

V

Evanston, Ill.: Northwestern University Press, 1988, pp. 123–152.

De Robertis, Domenico. *Il libro della "Vita Nuova."* Florence: Sansoni, 1961.

Gorni, Guglielmo. "Paragrafi e titolo nella *Vita Nuova.*" *Studi di filologia italiana* 51 (1993), 203–222.

Harrison, Robert Pogue. *The Body of Beatrice.* Baltimore, London: Johns Hopkins University Press, 1988.

Hempfer, Klaus W. "Allegoria e struttura del racconto nella *Vita Nuova.*" *Lingua e stile* 17 (1982), 209–232.

Mazzoni, Francesco. "Nota introduttiva." In Dante Alighieri, *Vita Nuova.* Alpignano: Tallone, 1965, pp. xiii–xxxi.

Moleta, Vincent (ed.). *"La gloriosa donna de la mente." A Commentary on the "Vita Nuova."* Florence: Olschki, 1994.

Picone, Michelangelo. "Songbook and Lyric Genres in the *Vita Nuova.*" *The Italianist* 15 (1995), Supplement n. 2, 158–170.

———. "La *Vita Nuova* fra autobiografia e tipologia." In *Dante e le forme dell'allegoresi.* Edited by M. Picone. Ravenna: Longo, 1987, pp. 59–70.

———. *"Vita Nuova" e tradizione romanza.* Padua: Liviana, 1979.

Schiaffini, Alfredo. "Lo Stilnuovo e la *Vita Nuova.*" In *Tradizione e poesia nella prosa d'arte italiana dalla latinità medievale al Boccaccio.* Rome: Edizioni di Storia e Letteratura, 1969, pp. 89–112.

Singleton, Charles S. *An Essay on the "Vita Nuova."* Cambridge, Mass.: Harvard University Press, 1949.

Wallace, David (ed.). *Beatrice Dolce Memoria, 1290–1990: Essays on the "Vita Nuova" and the Beatrice-Dante Relationship.* Special issue of *Texas Studies in Literature and Language* 32, no. 1 (1990).

Wehle, Winfried. *Dichtung über Dichtung. Dantes "Vita Nuova": die Aufhebung des Minnesangs im Epos.* Munich: Fink, 1986.

Michelangelo Picone

Vitaliano

Early commentaries identify Vitaliano del Dente as a notable of Padua and podestà of the city in 1307, known to Dante through patrons, including Bartolomeo della Scala and Gherardo da Camino. Vitaliano's arrival among the usurers in the seventh circle is anticipated by Reginaldo degli Scrovegni, a Paduan from a moneylending family identified only by a visual emblem (*Inf.* 17.68). This is the first instance in which an infernal soul names a future inhabitant of Hell to ensure that his sin is relayed back to the living. Dante's silence throughout the episode indicates his rejection of usury, a practice well established in commercial centers such as Florence and Padua.

Diana Cavuoto Glenn

Vossler, Karl

Distinguished early twentieth century romance linguist, literary critic, and student of Dante. Vossler (1872–1949) studied in Tübingen, Geneva, Strasbourg, and Rome and completed his Habilitation (the German examination for the *venia legendi*) in Heidelberg in 1906. He became professor of Romance literature first in Würzburg (1909) and then in Munich, where he settled for the rest of his life. Vossler did scholarly work in all branches of the Romania, i.e., in French, Italian, Spanish, and Portuguese literature. Two particular approaches characterize his dealing with literature. He always focused on the formal and esthetic aspects of a literary work and attempted to comprehend its particular poetic unity. This approach has some resemblance to North American New Criticism but is more closely related to Benedetto Croce's rigorous and narrow concept of poetry. The other approach is marked by his keen interest in language—poetic language in particular—and found expression in a number of books such as *Positivismus und Idealismus in der deutschen Sprachwissenschaft* (1904), *Sprache als Schöpfung und Entwicklung* (1905), *Frankreichs Kulturleben im Lichte seiner Sprachentwicklung* (1913), *Gesammelte Aufsätze zur Sprachphilosophie* (1923), and *Geist und Kultur in der Sprache* (1925). His main work in Dante criticism is *Die göttliche Komödie: Entwicklungsgeschichte und Erklärung* (1907–1910), translated as *Mediaeval Culture: An Introduction to Dante and His Times*. His work on Dante shows his close relationship to Benedetto Croce's *La poesia di Dante* (1920). In 1921 Vossler published his *Dante als religiöser Dichter,* and in 1942 his translation of the *Commedia* appeared.

Bibliography

Klemperer, Victor. "Vosslers Verhältnis zu Dante." *Deutsches Dante-Jahrbuch* 29/30 (1951), 1–18.

Vossler, Karl. *Mediaeval Culture: An Introduction to Dante and His Times.* Translated by William Cranston Lawton. 2 vols. New York: Ungar, 1958.

Wellek, René. *A History of Modern Criticism: 1750–1950.* Vol. 7: *German, Russian, and Eastern European Criticism, 1900–1950.* New Haven and London: Yale University Press, 1991, pp. 93–97.

Ernst Behler

W

Water

One of the four sublunar elements in Aristotle's physics, water unites the primary qualities cold and wet. It is the second heaviest of the elements and therefore finds its proper place above the level of earthy matter and below the level of aerial matter. Like the other three elements, water is mutable. If

heated, it can be transformed from a cold-wet element into hot-wet element. Water can, in other words, evaporate into air. The pure elements air and water are not identical with the air and water that we breathe and drink, but the behavior of air and water are nonetheless to be understood in the same terms. Springs are generated on mountaintops, not from water rising but from the condensation of vapor—an aerial body. The nature of water is one of the principal subjects of the *Questio de aqua et terra*. In that treatise Dante tries to accommodate within Aristotelian theory the anomalous appearance of dry land in the Northern Hemisphere. Since the proper place of water is higher than Earth, one would expect on the basis of Aristotle's physics that the surface of Earth should be uniformly covered by water. In the *Questio de aqua et terra* Dante entertains several possible explanations before finally invoking astral influences. Stars in the northern celestial hemisphere have drawn up the earthy matter of the continents.

John Kleiner

Wenceslaus II of Bohemia

Wenceslaus (1270–1305) was the son and successor of Ottokar II, who reigned from 1278 to 1305, and the brother-in-law of Emperor Albert I. He is mentioned by Sordello, who, in identifying his father among the negligent rulers, reveals that Ottokar was by far more worthy than his "bearded" son even as an infant (*Purg.* 7.100–102). Wenceslaus *(Vincislao)* is also featured among the Christian rulers who are scrutinized by the Eagle in the Heaven of Jupiter. Referring to him as *quel di*

Boemme ("him of Bohemia"), the Eagle states that he lacked both the knowledge of worthiness and a desire for it, while rebuking him for his lechery and sybaritism (*Par.* 19.125).

Antonio Illiano

White Rose

The image used to describe the residence of the blessed souls in the Empyrean, whose queen is Mary: *In forma dunque di candida rosa / mi si mostrava la milizia santa / che nel suo sangue Cristo fece sposa* ("In the form, then, of a white rose the holy army was shown to me which Christ married with his blood," *Par.* 31.1–3). The term *rosa* had been first used to designate Mary as that flower in which the divine word had become flesh (*Par.* 23.73–74). The tradition of the white rose as the flower of Paradise—in its purity, beauty, chastity, and perfection and in its association with the Virgin Mary—is rich and is seen in contrast to the red rose, symbol of earthly love. The red rose, however, also symbolizes Jesus and his Passion, his charity, and his martyrdom on the cross— which is why Dante says, "which Christ married with his blood." The image of Mary as a white rose is introduced to us, among others, by the very guide of these last cantos, St. Bernard, who had said that Mary is a white rose because of her virginity, whereas Eve is a thorn (*PL* 184, col. 1020). The floral imagery, which began in canto 23, where Mary is also called *bel fior* ("fair flower," 78) and the apostles *gigli* ("lilies," 74), flourishes in canto 31, where the blessed souls are the petals of this white rose and the angels descend into it as bees into flowers, then returning to their fountain of love, God (1–12). In this majestic spectacle of pure light, *luce intellettüal, piena d'amore* ("intellectual light, full of love," 30.40), the poet envisages a huge rose in order to provide both a structural and a symbolic representation of Paradise and its most exemplary inhabitants.

The White Rose, which is formed of the light of God reflected from the outer surface of the Primum Mobile (*Par.* 30.106–114), is unfolded in *Par.* 32. It is divided into two major vertical sectors: a row of women on the one side—on whose first tier is Mary—and a row of men, headed by John the Baptist, on the other, delineating a wall separating the elect of the Old and the New Testaments. Eve sits on the second tier below Mary, for she opened the wound that Mary healed. Mary is in effect the figural fulfillment of Eve, as Jesus is the new Adam. Mary as mother of all the living is also a figure of the Church, as are all those women positioned downward below her—Rachel, Sara, Rebecca, Judith, Ruth, and others—whom Dante places not chronologically but according to their degree of merit. These women are *figurae Ecclesiae,* and while they provide the dividing line, on the one side, between the Old and New Laws, they also provide the unity and the link that binds the two laws. The Church is the ultimate manifestation of their figurative meaning: all of them are connected to the House of David, with the exception of Judith, who nevertheless became the glory of Israel by delivering the nation from peril.

On the other side of the semicircle, the dividing line consists of John the Baptist, Christ's precursor, of whom Jesus said: "I tell you this: never has there appeared on earth a mother's son greater than John the Baptist" (Matt. 11:11). Directly below John are Francis of Assisi, Benedict, and Augustine, founders of religious orders. They may represent the perfect imitation of Christ (St. Francis), contemplation (St. Benedict), and theology (St. Augustine), and as such they are figures, or fathers, of the Church. They as well are placed according to merit rather than historical chronology. Dante's present guide, St. Bernard, famous for his ardent devotion to Mary, points out that the lower rows of this rose are reserved for infants who

Dante among the saved in the White Rose. Opere del divino poeta Danthe, *ed. Pietro da Figino, Venice, 1520. Giamatti Collection: Courtesy of the Mount Holyoke College Archives and Special Collections.*

were not saved by their own merit; rather, through the "perfect baptism of Christ" (32.40–48), each of them received God's grace in its diversity according to his own will. The structure of the White Rose is completed with the assignment of seats to those who are the "roots" of the flower: Adam, who sits to Mary's left, and Peter, who sits to her right. Next to Peter is seated John the Evangelist, and next to Adam is Moses. The last two are considered types of Christ. Peter and John are the foremost apostles—the first, as Christ's vicar; the latter, as the disciple whom Jesus loved the most, the author of a Gospel and the Apocalypse. The last two positions on either side of John the Baptist are filled by Anna and Lucia. Anna (whose Hebrew name, Hannah, means grace) sits diagonally across from Peter and is so content to admire her daughter Mary that she sings hosannas and does not move her eyes. She also is a *typus Ecclesiae.* Lucia, the Syracusan martyr who had come to the poet's rescue in *Inf.* 2, where she is described as *nimica di ciascun crudele* ("enemy of all cruelty," 100), is a *typus Christi.* While she may represent faith whose consummation is charity, she assuredly represents justice, as implied by Dante's own description of her.

From the center of the rose, *nel giallo de la rosa sempiterna* ("into the yellow of the sempiter-

The souls of the saved in the White Rose. La comedia, *ed. Pietro da Figino, 1491. Giamatti Collection: Courtesy of the Mount Holyoke College Archives and Special Collections.*

nal rose," 30.124), the pilgrim Dante is able to observe the magnitude of this realm in which Mary is the empress. In its image and structure this white rose suggests a correspondence with the rose windows of Gothic cathedrals, most of which were built in honor of Mary. As E. Panofsky points out, the Gothic cathedral "sought to embody the whole of Christian knowledge, theological, moral, natural and historical." Similarly Dante's rose assembles the summation of this knowledge with the two laws and with the personae who contributed to this knowledge. The numerical symbolism must also be noted. There are eight figures on the first topmost tier: Mary, Peter, John the Evangelist, Lucy, John the Baptist, Anne, Moses, Adam. Eight is the number of baptism and eternal life. Eight is also an architectural component of most baptismal fonts and baptisteries, including Dante's own "bel San Giovanni" in the city of Florence, which has eight sides. In Dante's representation of the flower of Paradise one can discern, within its geometric circularity, the union of the cross with the image of the rose, symbol of the highest love.

"... in forma di candida rosa ..." *The souls of the saved in the petals of the White Rose.* La comedia di Dante Aligieri, *with commentary by Alessandro Vellutello, published by Francesco Marcolini, Venice, 1544. Giamatti Collection: Courtesy of the Mount Holyoke College Archives and Special Collections.*

Bibliography

Apollonio, Mario. "Candida rosa." *Enciclopedia dantesca,* 2:786–787.

Di Scipio, Giuseppe. *The Symbolic Rose in Dante's Paradiso.* Ravenna: Longo, 1984.

Joret, Charles. *La Rose dans l'Antiquité et au Moyen Age.* Paris: Emile Bouillon, 1892.

Leyerle, John. "The Rose Wheel Design and Dante's *Paradiso.*" *University of Toronto Quarterly* 46, no. 3 (1977), 280–308.

Panofsky, Erwin. *Gothic Architecture and Scholasticism.* New York: New American Library, 1957.

Giuseppe Di Scipio

Wife of Potiphar

In the tenth pouch of Malebolge, Master Adam, responding to Dante-pilgrim's inquiry, identifies two sinners by his side, Sinon the Greek and *la falsa ch'accusò Gioseppo* ("the false woman who accused Joseph," *Inf.* 30.97). The wife of the Egyptian official Potiphar, she tried to seduce her Hebrew servant Joseph (son of Jacob) but then accused him of trying to rape her when he rejected her advances (Gen. 39:7–20). She is punished with stinking and burning fever, among the falsifiers of words.

Olivia Holmes

Wilkins, Ernest Hatch

Ernest Hatch Wilkins (1880–1966) was a scholar of Dante and Petrarch and past president of the Dante Society of America. After obtaining the doctorate at Harvard University and subsequently holding teaching positions at Amherst, Harvard, and the University of Chicago, where he also served as dean of the college (1923–1926), he became president of Oberlin (1927–1946), from which he retired to his native Massachusetts, commuting regularly to Widener Library at Harvard for his remaining and most active years of scholarship. Trained in the largely historical school of criticism, Wilkins became noted for his authoritative studies in Italian literature of the Middle Ages and Renaissance. For a generation, he was the dean of Petrarch studies, his goal being a detailed account of Petrarch's life and the evolution of his works based on original sources. A Dante scholar too, as president of the Dante Society of America (1954–1959), he much revivified the organization; he also served as president of the Modern Language Association (1946) and of the Medieval Academy of America (1957–1960). During his long professional career Wilkins received many honorary degrees and other national and international decorations and citations. Apart from his numerous articles, many of which reappeared in subsequent volumes, some selected books of Dantean and Petrarchan interest are *Dantis Alagherii operum latinorum concordantiae,* with E. K. Rand (1912); *A Concordance to the Divine Comedy . . .* (general editor, 1965); *The Making of the "Canzoniere" and Other Petrarchan Studies* (1951); *Studies in the Life and Works of Petrarch* (1955); *The Invention of the Sonnet and Other Studies in Italian Literature* (1959); *Life of Petrarch* (1961); *A History of Italian Literature* (1954, revised by T. G. Bergin, 1974).

A. L. Pellegrini

Will

In the medieval Scholastic model, the will *(appetitus rationalis)* is one of the three faculties of the soul, together with the intellect or reason *(intellettus)* and the sensitive appetite *(appetitus sensitivus).* In Italian, Dante uses several terms—primarily *voglia, volontà,* and *volere*—and in Latin, *voluntas* and *velle.* The operations of the will and the intellect formed the intellectual life of the rational soul. Although Dante frequently speaks of God's will, this article addresses only human will. It is the part of the soul responsible for human action, and, consequently, it is conceived to be the source of either virtuous or sinful acts.

From what Dante says in *Mon.* 1.12.2, he seems to have followed, with some irritation, the disputes about free will that preoccupied Franciscans, Latin Averroists, Dominicans, and others in the second half of the thirteenth century; these controversies, which themselves originated in ancient philosophy, inevitably were concerned with the larger question of the relation of the will itself to the intellect. Since Dante's conception of will generally coincides with that of Aquinas, the following description draws mostly from Thomas's elaboration of ideas found in Aristotle. Dante, however, was aware of other theories of the will. He knew that Augustine, in contrast to Aquinas, thought the will was not a distinct faculty of the soul but that which brought its other parts, intellect and memory, into act (*On the Trinity* 15.21.41; cf. *Purg.* 25.83–84). Ultimately, Dante could agree with the Franciscans that the will was the whole soul as loving, but he differed from them in his

Wanalysis of its operations, and he rejected any position that finally subordinated reason to will.

Aristotle had defined the will as appetite made rational (*On the Soul*, 3.9.432b 5–7). In contrast to sensitive appetite, whose concupiscible and irascible powers incline a person toward or away from a material object, the will moves toward an object only after reason, having determined its true nature, judges that object in relation to the good in general. That is to say, our sensory powers incline us toward an apple because it tastes good; our will turns toward it because reason has determined that eating it will make us healthy, so that obtaining an object will be a movement toward happiness. As Aquinas says, "the will means rational appetite" (*appetitus rationalis, ST* 1.2.6.2).

In *Purgatorio* (17–18), Dante fleshes out this condensed account of the operations of the will by considering it in relation to love. Virgil first tells Dante that neither God nor any creature was ever without natural love or intellectual love ("love of the mind," *Purg.* 17.91–93). Natural love in a being has as its end or goal the desire for its proper place and the realization of its own perfection. As such it is without error; inanimate things invariably seek their proper place, and beasts instinctively move to realize their nature. In human beings, natural love has as its end or goal the complete good which is God. We are able to apprehend this primal good, however, only in a confused way; because eternal beatitude is beyond our capacity to comprehend fully, the human will consequently consists of the movement toward specific objects perceived as sharing in the good as such.

In *Purg.* 18.19ff., Virgil therefore explains how something in particular causes the will to enter into act. Since the soul in human beings is disposed by nature to love, the will rouses it into action whenever something offers it pleasure. There are three stages in this process. First, our faculty of perception *(apprensiva)* abstracts an intention or image from some material object. The "apprehensive" faculty then presents this intentional object to the soul *(animo)* so that it turns to consider it. The soul judges whether it is beautiful *(piacer)* and offers happiness and pleasure. If it does, the will inclines toward it, and such an inclination is called love *(amor)*.

Aquinas defines this love as the complacency that arises in the will from the adaptation (*co-aptatio*, a "fitting together") which the appetible object, having undergone rational perception, is able to bring about in the rational appetite. That is to say, the intention of a particular object that appears good to the rational appetite generates a change in that appetite such that it takes pleasure in the object as something like it. In this technical sense, love is thus an alteration in the will that takes the form of an inclination toward an object. Love becomes desire when the will is moved by the object to obtain it; for this reason Dante calls desire a "spiritual motion" (*Purg.* 18.32). Finally, desire turns into joy when the soul rests in possession of the object.

The pivotal event in these unfoldings of will occurs when the soul determines whether an object is good or bad. How the soul comes to form this judgment is complex; it is the source of free will, and therefore treated under that heading. Insofar as the will in general is concerned, however, it is important to note that once this judgment has been made—once the soul has judged that an object participates in the good in general—the inclination toward it is part of the will's very nature *(voluntas ut natura)* and therefore a necessary act on its part. But, as Virgil explains, the will can err by loving things of lesser merit and thereby can cause the individual to engage in sin.

According to this theory of appetition, human will is not autonomous but a passive potency that enters into activity only when and if the soul apprehends some external object. This seems to imply that rational appetite is not voluntary, since the principal cause of our acts of will appears to come from outside us. We should note, however, that to this point we have considered the will with respect to its end, which is the good as such. Even though the will is bound to seek its happiness, because we are able to apprehend such happiness only in a confused manner, this subjection does not impede its freedom. Since eternal blessedness is the only good that is complete and lacks nothing, it follows that no end that reason can apprehend as good is completely good. Consequently, no end we rationally conceive can compel our will to move to it necessarily. Moreover, the will is free to act on the respective values of several different goods which the intellect has delineated, just as it can choose the means to obtain what it desires. (Although these operations are fully acts of will, they more appropriately fall under the rubric of free will and are discussed there.)

Critics from the earliest commentators to the present day have argued that Dante allegorizes the faculties of the soul in his poem. Perhaps the most dramatic allegorization of the will in the *Commedia* is Dante's "limp" in the prologue scene. As he inches toward his encounter with the leopard, lion, and wolf, Dante says his "halted foot was always the lower" (*Inf.* 1.30). Freccero has shown that in this scene Dante draws on a long tradition that pictured the *affectus,* or appetite, as the left foot of the soul. This foot was lamed by the wound of concupiscence when Adam sinned in the Garden of Eden.

Bibliography

Boyde, Patrick. *Perception and Passion in Dante's Comedy.* Cambridge: Cambridge University Press, 1993.

Freccero, John. "Dante's Firm Foot and the Journey without a Guide." In *Dante: The Poetics of Conversion.* Edited by Rachel Jacoff. Cambridge, Mass., London: Harvard University Press, 1986, pp. 29–54.

Warren Ginsberg

William of Nogaret

William of Nogaret (c. 1260–1313) rose from relatively humble origin, through his reputation as a lawyer, to highest service and acquired wealth under King Philip IV of France. From 1302 he was principal agent in the king's dispute over jurisdiction with Pope Boniface VIII. Nogaret, accompanied by Sciarra Colonna and an armed party, entered Boniface's City of Anagni, southeast of Rome, on September 7, 1303, to serve notice of a French appeal against the pope to a general council and to prevent the pope's imminent excommunication of Philip. Boniface suffered detention and considerable indignities, dying soon after the incident. Dante records this event in *Purg.* 20.86–90, where Hugh of Capet refers prophetically to William and Sciarra as *vivi ladroni* ("living thieves"), equating them with the two thieves crucified with Christ.

Michael Haren

William of Orange

The hero of a series of *chansons de geste* well known in Italy, the *Cycle de Guillaume,* William *(Guiglielmo)* battled the Saracens for the Franks alongside Renouart. Dante places them both in the Heaven of Mars, among those who fought for faith (*Par.* 18.46–48).

Bibliography

Foglia, Giuseppe. "Guiglielmo e Rinoardo della croce di Marte." *Giornale dantesco* 22 (1914), 1–9.

Hauvette, Henri. *La France et la Provence dans l'oeuvre de Dante.* Paris: Boivin, 1929.

Wathelet-Willem, Jeanne. "La pénétration en Italie de la legende de Guillaume vue à travers l'onomastique." *Cultura neolatina* 21 (1961), 155–163.

Jessica Levenstein

William II of Sicily

Of the Norman House of Hauteville and known as "William the Good"—in contradistinction to his father, William I, "the Bad"—William II *(Guiglielmo)* reigned as king of Sicily and Puglia in southern Italy (the Kingdom of Sicily) from 1166 to 1189. He established a flourishing court at Palermo, and despite his cultivation of courtly refinement and pleasure—perhaps even with a certain Oriental coloration reflecting Arab domination in preceding centuries—he was very positively evaluated by chroniclers of the period. Dante, his customary rigor against worldliness notwithstanding, follows suit and places him among the exemplary just rulers—including Constantine, Trajan, Hezekiah, Ripheus, and David—around the eye of the eagle, emblem of empire, that dominates, even as speaker, the Heaven of Jupiter (*Par.* 20.61–66).

What the eagle says about William II, beyond mantling him in the splendor of a generic love of heaven for just princes, is that he is sorely missed by the territories that "now" languish under the misrule of his tyrannical successors, Charles II of Anjou and Frederick II of Aragon, rulers of Sicily and Puglia, respectively, in Dante's own time, and unrelentingly vituperated by him (see also *Par.* 19.127–135): *E quel che vedi ne l'arco declivo / Guiglielmo fu, cui quella terra plora / che piagne Carlo e Federigo vivo* ("And the one you see in the lower arch was William, whom the land mourns that weeps for Charles and Frederick being still alive," *Par.* 20.61–63). Dante's placing William II in the lower arc of the eagle's brow perhaps alludes to his being the end of the line of Norman kings in Sicily.

William II's reign represents the climax of Norman rule in southern Italy, which began with Robert Guiscard, who in 1061—five years before the Norman Conquest of England—invaded Sicily and won it back from Saracen dominion, under which it had fallen during the attacks against the Byzantine Empire in the ninth century. William died childless and was succeeded by his aunt, *la gran Costanza,* who married Frederick Barbarossa's son, Henry VI of Swabia, and gave birth to Frederick II, "its [the House of Swabia's] third and last power," as Dante puts it (*Par.* 3.118–120). The "last of the Roman emperors" (*Conv.* 4.3.6) was thus produced by a mixing of the House of Hauteville's Norman blood with that of Hohenstaufen in the Swabian line, which makes William a forebear of the imperial dynasty, so supremely important in Dante's view.

Among William II's achievements still appreciable today is the Cathedral of Monreale near Palermo, chief monument of Norman architecture in Sicily. The sarcophagi of William II and his father are to be found there, in the south transept.

Bibliography

Moore, Edward. "Dante and Sicily." In *Studies in Dante, Second Series: Miscellaneous Essays.* Oxford: Clarendon Press, 1899, pp. 269–302.

William Franke

William VII of Monferrat

William *(Guiglielmo),* marquis of Montferrat, is placed in the lowest position by Dante in the valley of the negligent princes in Ante-Purgatory: *Quel che più basso tra costor s'atterra, / guardando in suso, è Guiglielmo marchese, / per cui e Alessandria e la sua guerra / fa pianger Monferrato e Canavese* ("The one that lower down sits on the ground among them, looking, is the marquis William, for whom Alexandria and its war make Monferrato and Canavese weep," *Purg.* 7.133–136). William, born in 1254, reached the apogee of his power around 1280, when he controlled nine Piedmontese and Lombard cities—including Milan, Turin, and Alessandria—constituting a powerful Ghibelline league. When, in 1282, several of these cities seceded and joined the Guelfs, William regained them by force, but when Alessandria, incited by Asti, rose against him, he was captured and imprisoned. He was put on display in his cell until, after seventeen months, on February 6, 1292, he died. His son—from his second marriage, to Beatrice, the daughter of Alfonso X of Castile—sought to avenge his father's humiliation and death by declaring war against Alessandria. Not only did William's son fail to defeat the City of Alessandria, but he furthermore failed to stop its troops from capturing several towns within the territory of Monferrat—the cause of the mourning to which Dante alludes. Contemporary accounts stress William's excessive political ambition and his cruelty, while Dante's placement of him in the valley of flowers emphasizes his neglect of duty because of the lure of worldly things—represented in the valley by the nightly appearance of a serpent.

Claudia Rattazzi Papka

Witte, Karl

Karl Witte (1800–1883) was a jurist who early in his life aroused attention because of his extraordinary learning capacity. At age 10 he enrolled at the University of Leipzig; there he wrote a Latin thesis on the Greek mathematician Nicodemus and obtained his Ph.D. at the University of Giessen at age 14. His attempt to do his Habilitation (an examination required in Germany for university teaching) failed because the university refused to give him access to it owing to his young age. The Prussian minister of culture therefore gave him a grant to go on a trip for study and research, and Witte went to Italy for two years, where he studied law, art history, and Italian literature. In this context he discovered Dante. In 1823 he was appointed professor of law, first at the University of Breslau and later at the University of Halle. He published several books on legal problems and, parallel to these activities, became the most advanced Dante scholar of his time. He edited the first scholarly and annotated edition of the *Divina Commedia* (Berlin, 1862), which he also translated into German (Berlin, 1865). Witte then edited Dante's *Monarchia* (Vienna, 1874) and *La Vita Nuova* (Leipzig, 1876). His two-volume *Dante-Forschungen* appeared in 1862 (Halle) and in 1879 (Heilbronn). Witte collaborated with Philalethes, i.e., King Johann Nepomuk of Saxony, who used this pseudonym for his work on Dante. Under his protection Witte founded the *Deutsche Dante-Gesellschaft* (1865) and in the same year the *Jahrbuch der Deutschen Dante-Gesellschaft* (first issued in 1867). He also edited the fifth edition of Ludwig Kannegiesser's popular translation of the *Göttliche Komödie* in 1873.

Bibliography

Witte, Johann Heinrich Friedrich Karl. *Essays on Dante* [containing selections from the two volumes of *Dante–Forschungen*]. Selected, translated, and edited with introduction, notes, and appendices by C. Mabel Lawrence and Philip H. Wicksteed. New York: Haskell House, 1970.

Ernst Behler

Women

While in some ways Dante seems to have a traditional view of the roles of women in his work, in others he is quite unusual. There are echoes of ancient and medieval misogyny, particularly in *Inferno,* but there are also corrections of such misogyny in *Purgatorio* and *Paradiso* and an attempt to establish a place for women in his ideal world. And there is evidence as early as the *Vita Nuova* that Dante's relations with women went beyond the narcissism of the poet-lover, not only in his worship of Beatrice but also in his acceptance of criticism from women friends and his acknowledgment that that criticism moves him in a new direction. He finds that new direction, finally, in the *Commedia,* as the instrument of women: the Virgin Mary and her messenger, Beatrice.

Attitudes toward women in the Middle Ages were complicated and varied. Misogynist attacks arguing the inferiority of women and blaming them for the destruction of men from Eve and Delilah to contemporary seducers and shrews—drawing authority from Paul, Tertullian, Jerome, and a host of others down to Jean de Meun—are certainly a part of medieval culture, but there is another side. Women played important roles in medieval life, not only in the religious sphere as powerful abbesses, mystics, and reformers but also in the secular, as rulers, regents, and consorts. Women were often the instigators of texts—religious and historical as well as literary—by asking questions, making requests, or giving commissions; and many of them exerted an influence as friends and/or patrons of churchmen and intellectuals. There are medieval texts supporting women's political roles, or asserting the superior devotion of women to Christ, as well as courtly lyrics in which women may be silent objects of worship or anger or may be articulate debaters unmasking male postures. And there is literature by women, religious and secular, asserting their needs and expressing their views.

It is impossible to know how much of this material, historical or literary, Dante knew or was aware of—perhaps very little. What one can say is that his work reflects most of the medieval attitudes toward women, negative and positive, and that he finally comes out on the positive side. There were many women in Dante's literary life, and presumably in his real life as well. The love lyrics in the *Rime* are addressed to a variety of named (Fioretta, Violetta, Lisetta) and unnamed ladies, some of whom may be Beatrice or perhaps the lady at the window in the last part of the *Vita Nuova.* There is also a *pargoletta* and a "stone lady," cold and cruel, who inspired Dante's so-called *rime petrose,* or "stony poems." The *Vita Nuova* makes a revisionist attempt to explain away some of the early ones as shields Dante used to hide his love for Beatrice. In one poem no longer extant about sixty ladies of Florence, Beatrice's name was ninth; Dante interprets that as significant for her symbolic meaning, but the fact remains that he once put eight other names before hers. Though the *Vita Nuova* was written apparently to explain the significance Dante has come to see in Beatrice—her role as a Christ figure in his life—it is impossible for him to conceal altogether the feelings he had for a number of other women. He was apparently so embarrassed by the woman he turned to for comfort after Beatrice's death—the *gentile donna* at the window, who showed compassion for his suffering—that he constructed an elaborate allegory in the *Convivio* to explain her as Lady Philosophy.

But women were not only objects of Dante's love; many were also friends, whom he addressed in the *Rime,* talking to them about his love, asking their comfort, or warning them against bad men. In the narrative of the *Vita Nuova,* women friends are even more important. They are sensitive to but not always indulgent of his moods—comforting him when he is ill or grieving, making fun of him when he plays the swooning lover—and by their critical perceptions, they turn his poetry in a new direction. One friend *(amica persona)* takes him to a gathering of lovely women (a wedding reception) for his pleasure, but Beatrice's presence makes him tremble, and they laugh at him; when, on the other hand, he grieves with them for Beatrice over the death of her father, they notice the change in him (*VN* 22). Dante enjoys the conversation of women, drawn by their *molto leggiadro parlare* ("very lively [or elegant] speech," *VN* 18), and their perceptive questions and comments force him to see himself and his poetry in a new light (*VN* 18.2), to recognize that he has been talking about himself when he should have been talking about Beatrice, and to seek a new mode in which to praise her. He decides to address a poem about her to women who understand love ("Donne ch'avete intelletto d'amore"), a poem in which Heaven expresses its desire for Beatrice, and it is this poem which Bonagiunta cites in *Purg.* 24 to identify Dante with a "sweet new style." After Beatrice's death, Dante prefers to address his poems to the ladies he had addressed while she was alive (*VN* 31). The final poem quoted in the *Vita Nuova,* "Oltre la spera," in which Dante's sigh has a vision of Beatrice in Heaven—an adumbration of the *Commedia,* whether intentional or not—was written at the request of two noble women, for whom he wished to do something new (*cosa nuova, VN* 41).

Dante sees women not just as love objects or the lover's friends but as potential lovers, on whom the effects of courtly love can work as they work on men (*e simil face in donna omo valente, VN* 20). It is clear from the women's comments in the *Vita Nuova* about Dante's poetry that they are part of his literary audience. Women continue to be included in Dante's audience in the *Convivio,* which though "tempered and virile" is meant to be useful to all noble people, men and women (1.9.5), and in the *Commedia* (messages to them in *Purgatorio* and the address to *bella Clemenza, Par.* 9.1). Though Dante once said that Adam must have been the first to speak—too important an action for a woman to initiate (*DVE* 1.4.2–3)—he respects the judgment of his women friends and acknowledges the roles of other women for good in human life. And though statistically he concentrates on men in the *Commedia,* because of their role in history as he knew it, he makes a real effort to balance the roles of women in *Purgatorio* and to suggest a balance of numbers in the rose, which is the final end of mankind.

Dante begins *Inferno* by associating women with lust and deception (fraud) and presenting sinful men as effeminate, like any medieval misogynist, but that is not all he does. He also shows women as victims of male violence and deception. Lust is indeed dominated by women, the queens Semiramis, Dido, Cleopatra—women in male roles, just as lust casts men in female roles—and the adulterers, Helen and Francesca, whose husbands responded with war and murder. Hypsipyle and Medea are not in Hell, but the man who seduced and deceived them, Jason, is. The women had deceived others, but to save those they loved; the man did it to indulge himself. Dante does not condemn prostitutes per se—the flatterer Thais, a prostitute, is condemned for abuse of language—instead he focuses on the men who seduce and sell women. Women are found among the false prophets and the falsifiers, but the rest of fraud is dominated by men, just as most of Hell (gluttony, avarice, wrath, violence) is dominated by men.

There are no women among the betrayers and traitors in the lowest circle of Hell, whereas in the first circle, Limbo, there are a good many women among the virtuous pagans. Indeed, Dante seems to correct Virgil's male-centered view of Roman history (the women in the *Aeneid* are driven by uncontrolled passions) with a list of women heroes: Camilla and Penthesilea, who died fighting for Italy and Troy (Dante's Virgil names Camilla first among those who died for Italy, in *Inf.* 1.106–107, though she fought against Turnus); Electra and Lavinia, mothers of the Trojan and Roman people; and Lucretia, Julia, Marcia, and Cornelia. Later Virgil testifies in *Purgatorio* to the presence of many more women in Limbo—many of them characters from Statius's *Thebaid,* another poem much more positive about women than its model, the *Aeneid* (*Purg.* 22).

There are female monsters in Hell—the Furies at the Gate of Dis, the Harpies who feed on the suicides, Geryon (who has, however, the face of a just man, the part that lures its victims)—but there is no more reason to derive an attitude toward women from them than to derive one toward men from Cerberus, Pluto, the Minotaur, the centaurs, or the giants. Dante may even be commenting on the way men project their desires onto women and then blame the women for deceiving them in the episode of the *femmina balba* ("stuttering female") in *Purgatorio.* Grotesque as she clearly is, she becomes beautiful under Dante's gaze until a holy lady rouses Virgil to reveal the stink beneath (*Purg.* 19). Dante himself goes through Purgatory blaming Eve for all he and mankind have lost, until the procession in the Earthly Paradise reminds him of Adam.

The presence of women is strong throughout *Purgatorio* and largely positive. There are women from Heaven: the Virgin Mary is the first example of the appropriate virtue on every ledge and the source of salvation to whom souls turn in death (*Purg.* 5.101) and in purgation (7.82, 13.50); Lucy appears to help Dante at moments of transition; Beatrice is the voice of authority Virgil refers Dante to when he cannot answer his questions, and the inspiration that draws him through the final purging fire; and the virtues are personified as stars in Heaven, women on Earth. Earthly women are invoked as family, wives and daughters whose life is a source of comfort to the souls and whose prayers helped them enter Purgatory. Manfred identifies not with his emperor father (who is in Hell) but with his grandmother (in Heaven) and his daughter (on Earth); Forese credits his wife's prayers with shortening his time in Ante-Purgatory, praises his sister in Heaven, and condemns the actions of his brother destined for Hell. Pope Hadrian remembers his good niece as all that is left to him (19.142–145). And Bonagiunta, the poet who identifies Dante by his poem to women ("Donne ch'avete"), tells him about a woman who will be good to him in his exile (*Purg.* 24.43–51).

This is not to say there are no bad women in Purgatory: Judge Nino is distressed that his wife remarried, though his daughter is loyal; Forese contrasts the virtue of his widow with the mores of other Florentine women. Some women are examples of vices: Niobe and Arachne, of pride; Aglauros, of envy; Amata, of wrath; Sapphira, of greed; Pasiphaë, of lust. But if Michal's pride is condemned in contrast to David's humility, it is the widow's correction that evokes Trajan's humility; Lavinia is the innocent victim of Amata's wrath, and Esther is the means by which the Jews are saved from Haman's wrath.

Two women appear among the souls of Purgatory: Pia, who alludes to her husband's crime but does not seek revenge, and Sapia, who acknowledges the mediating effect of a man's prayers on her situation (the one example of a man effectively praying for a woman, but enough to make the point that it should work both ways). One woman appears as the inhabitant—and ruler?—of the Earthly Paradise: Matelda. If the early commentators are right in their identification of this woman with Countess Matelda of Tuscany—a woman still remembered in contemporary Italian chronicles as a mediator between reform popes and her cousin, the emperor; a woman who inherited and ruled her own lands in northern Italy—it is hard to imagine

a better guardian for this place posited by Dante in the *Monarchia* as the home of mankind restored. A woman who supported reform in the Church and a proper balance of power between church and state takes the place of both emperor and pope—functions left vacant or worse on Earth by the failures of both.

Beatrice appears behind the biblical procession in the Earthly Paradise as Christ figure, as admiral on the ark of the Church, as priest who confesses Dante, as messenger from Heaven who gives him his mission and prophesies future reform; but she also appears as the woman he loved and still responds to physically, the woman he must be reunited with to enter Paradise. In *Paradiso* Beatrice is his guide, leading him through the successive heavens and teaching him theology (another priestly function) as she goes. She is the dominant woman in Paradise until they reach the upper spheres, where Mary rules as queen of Heaven.

Dante does not see many women souls during his journey, except in the Moon and Venus. In the Moon he sees women who wanted to be nuns but were forced out of the convent by men in their families to make advantageous marriages; their desires never wavered, but their courage failed, and they bowed to male violence. Now they are examples of peaceful acceptance of God's will and of their place in God's scheme (one of them gave birth to the emperor, Frederick II), but they also allude to a woman higher in Heaven who did not fail: Clare, the founder of their order, the only human whose life is called "perfect" in the *Commedia* (*Par.* 3.97–98). The women in Venus are examples of lust, but with a positive twist. Cunizza rejoices in having been "overcome" by "the light of this star" (*mi vinse il lume d'esta stella, Par.* 9.32–33), perhaps because she was also known for her great charity; Rahab is the biblical prostitute who "joined with our order [and] is its highest seal" (*Par.* 9.116–117) because she helped Joshua take the Holy Land.

If Dante does not meet other women, neither does he forget them. In the Moon, we hear of two who were victims of their fathers' bad vows, Jephthah's daughter and Iphigenia; and we hear of women who played roles in Roman history (the Sabines, Lucretia, Cleopatra, among those active for fame in Mercury) or in the history of saints (Dominic's mother, godmother, and nurse, in the Sun). It is perhaps surprising that there are no women among the martyrs in Mars when the stories of women martyrs were so popular in the Middle Ages, but Dante is more interested in fighters who spread the faith than in courageous victims who were persecuted for it (and he does have Cacciaguida praise the virtuous women of earlier Florence). There are no women rulers in Jupiter, but Trajan is identified by the widow who instructed him (*Par.* 20.44–45), as though men might need the guidance of women even at the height of power.

There is, however, a woman ruler in the rose; Mary is empress (Augusta) and the *regina, che puoi ciò che tu vuoli* ("queen, for you have the power to do that which you will," 33.34–35), whose power moved Dante through his journey. Said early on to be among those who see most deeply into God (4.29–30), Mary appears first at the center of angels and souls in Heaven of the Fixed Stars (*Par.* 24). As the mother of Christ, the one who most resembles him (32.85–86), the one who gave him his human features, it is she who can enable Dante to see Christ in the final vision of the Trinity, as Beatrice enabled him to see Christ in life. Mary presides over the rose of saved souls, sitting at the top of a line of biblical women named before any of the other souls: Eve, Rachel, Sarah, Rebecca, Judith, and Ruth. Mary's mother, Anna, sits opposite Peter, the father of the Church; Lucy is opposite Adam; and Beatrice sits beside Rachel. Though Dante may have identified many more men as he progressed through Heaven, he names more women in the rose, as if to suggest that, in its final state, mankind will achieve equity for the sexes.

Bibliography

Ferrante, Joan M. *Dante's Beatrice: Priest of an Androgynous God.* Binghamton, N.Y.: SUNY Press, 1992. CEMERS Occasional Papers, 2.

———. *Woman as Image in Medieval Literature from the Twelfth Century to Dante.* New York: Columbia University Press, 1975.

Kirkham, Victoria. "A Canon of Women in Dante's *Commedia.*" *Annali d'Italianistica* 7 (1989), 16–41.

Jacoff, Rachel. "Transgression and Transcendence: Figures of Female Desire in Dante's *Commedia.*" *Romanic Review* 79 (1988), 129–142.

Schnapp, Jeffrey. "Dante's Sexual Solecisms: Gender and Genre in the *Commedia.*" *Romanic Review* 79 (1988), 143–163.

Waller, Marguerite. "Seduction and Salvation: Sexual Difference in Dante's *Commedia* and the Difference it Makes." In *Donna: Women in Italian Culture.* Edited by Ada Testaferri. *University of Toronto Studies* 7 (1989), 225–243.

Joan M. Ferrante

Wrath

One of the seven capital sins, wrath is punished as a sin in the fifth circle of Hell, where it is classified as one of the sins of incontinence. As a disposition it is corrected on the third terrace of Purgatory. As the English translation of the term *ira* or *iracondia,* it carries negative connotations not present in the word "anger." While anger is an antagonistic emotion or irascible passion of the sensitive appetite which may be either just or sinful, wrath implies an excess of intensity or duration, thus becoming a settled disposition. Dante had at his disposal both classical and ecclesiastic texts on the matter. Aristotle considers anger to be

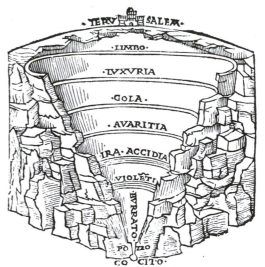

Wrath with the other sins of Incontinence, from Commedia di Dante, *published by Filippo Giunti, Florence, 1506. Reproduced by permission of the John A. Zahm Dante Collection in the Department of Special Collections, University Libraries, University of Notre Dame.*

a natural and appropriate sentiment when exercised within reason: "The man who is angry at the right things and with the right people, and, further, as he ought, when he ought, and as long as he ought, is praised." Conversely, one errs through excess if one is angry "with the wrong persons, at the wrong things, more than is right, too quickly, or too long" (*Ethics* 4.5). The contrasting virtue does not consist in a complete lack of anger, which for Aristotle signals a deficiency, but in a "good temper," which, although tending more toward the deficiency, is the mean state between the two extremes. In the Latin tradition, Cicero's *Tusculan Disputations* and Seneca's *De ira* present the negative aspects of irascibility. Aquinas follows Aristotle in condemning both the excess and the deficiency of anger, and he states that anger is sinful only when it is against reason and not accompanied by a sense of justice (*ST* 1.2.46–48, 74; 2.2.157–158). Following Aristotle and Aquinas, Dante also distinguishes sinful wrath from righteous anger, using the term *ira mala* (*Purg.* 17.68–69) to refer to the former and the terms *dritto zelo* ("righteous zeal," *Purg.* 8.83) and *buon zelo* ("good zeal," *Par.* 22.9) for the latter.

While anger characterizes the emotional state of many of the shades in Hell as well as of their guardians, those punished specifically for the sin of wrath are to be found in the fifth circle (*Inf.* 7.100–8.63). In Christian terms, anger becomes sinful when it overpowers the intellectual faculties of will and reason. Dante underscores this in *Inferno* by situating wrath along with other sins of incontinence and by referring to the wrathful as *Color cui vinse l'ira* ("those whom anger vanquished," *Inf.* 7.116). Moreover, although anger is not in itself necessarily malevolent, it becomes sinful when it causes one to seek revenge without considering the circumstances, thus leading to violations of justice and charity. Dante focuses on this aspect of the vice in *Purgatorio* by considering wrath, along with pride and envy, as a sin that shows the intent to harm one's neighbor (*Purg.* 15.85–17.39). In each canticle, the *contrapasso* reveals just how complementary these two aspects are: in Hell the wrathful continue to exhibit their intent to harm their neighbors by beating one another with their hands, heads, chests, and feet and tearing at each other's naked bodies with their teeth. In Purgatory, the penitent wrathful are reminded of the absence of reason and insight that

accompanied their sin by a dense smoke that now encircles and literally blinds them.

Jo Ann Cavallo

Wrathful, The

The *iracondi,* those who experience vehement and long-lasting anger or who are consistently and readily excited to violent and uncontrolled anger in the face of obstacles, frustration, injury, or insult. In *Ethics* 4.5, Aristotle distinguishes among the "hot-tempered," who "get angry quickly and with the wrong persons and at the wrong things and more than is right"; the "choleric," who are "ready to be angry with everything and on every occasion"; the "sulky," who are "hard to appease, and retain their anger long"; and the "bad-tempered," who are "angry at the wrong things, more than is right, and longer, and cannot be appeased until they inflict vengeance or punishment." While the above-mentioned types are to be blamed for their excess, Aristotle equally condemns those who err through deficiency, although he does not find a name for this vice: "the deficiency, whether it is a sort of 'inirascibility' or whatever it is, is blamed. For those who are not angry at the things they should be angry at are thought to be fools."

In *Inf.* 7, although Dante refers to the wrathful generically as the souls of those who were overcome by anger (*Color cui vinse l'ira, Inf.* 7.116), he may have intended some differentiation. As pilgrim and guide pass by the wrathful, who are immersed in the bog, Virgil explains that there are other shades who are completely submerged, their presence indicated only by their sighs, which reach the surface and create bubbles. They state their sin and *contrapasso* in a bitter and nostalgic gurgling chant, referring to their sadness while on Earth and to "the fumes of sullenness" (*accidioso fummo,* 7.123) which they harbored within. Critics disagree as to whether this group is distinguished by a different form or degree of wrath or whether it represents a different sin altogether (that of *accidia*). By Aristotle's standards, these sinners are rather akin to the "sulky," in contrast to Filippo Argenti, who will prove to be "hot-tempered."

As Dante and Virgil cross the river Styx, they encounter the Florentine Filippo Argenti (*Inf.* 8.31–63). After Dante's angry words, the shade takes hold of the boat, perhaps in a futile attempt

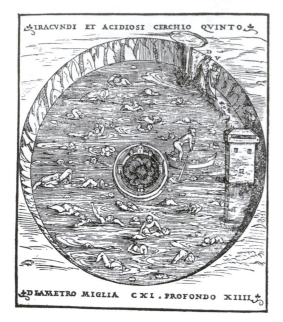

Dante among the wrathful immersed in the Styx, the fifth circle of Hell. La comedia di Dante Aligieri, *with commentary by Alessandro Vellutello, published by Francesco Marcolini, Venice, 1544. Giamatti Collection: Courtesy of the Mount Holyoke College Archives and Special Collections.*

to capsize it, and is immediately thrust away by Virgil, who commends Dante for his outburst of anger. Virgil then seconds Dante's expressed desire for retaliation, acknowledging the just pleasure to be derived from the ensuing scene, in which Filippo Argenti is attacked by the other shades and bites himself. Borgese remarks on the savagery of this episode, arguing that wrath characterizes not only the boatsman Phlegyas, the chorus of rioting devils, and the damned souls but even Virgil and the pilgrim Dante, who experiences here for the first time an outburst of violent passion. Dante's motives for cursing Filippo may be, as biographical accounts by early commentators suggest, personal and political. Most critics, however, have maintained that the episode, in Aristotelian fashion, is meant to offer a contrast between the sinful anger of the shades and the righteous anger of Dante and Virgil. Dante's anger would not be in this case a personal desire for revenge but rather the just zeal of one who wishes to see God's punishment of the unrepentant damned.

On the third terrace of Purgatory, the penitent wrathful, enveloped in a dense smoke, *d'iracun-*

dia van solvendo il nodo ("are untying the knot of wrathfulness," *Purg.* 16.24), with the *contrapasso* and metaphor combining to suggest a transformative process in which anger is released from the sinners into the air around them in the form of smoke. Dante encounters Marco Lombardo, a thirteenth-century Venetian courtier. While earlier Dante treated Filippo Argenti with contempt, here the pilgrim enters into a lengthy conversation with the Venetians on the present evils of the world and the decline of Italy. It has been suggested that Marco's lament reveals a lingering tendency toward irascibility. At the same time, however, Marco's attitude could be intended to present a positive manifestation of anger in the form of moral indignation, i.e., the reaction of the conscience against what is wrong or evil. Thus the burden of exhibiting righteous anger would be transferred in this case from the pilgrim to the penitent sinner.

Following Aristotle's description of the good-tempered individual (*Ethics* 4.5), in the *Convivio* Dante defines the virtue opposing *ira* not as meekness but as the mean between the extremes of excessive anger and excessive patience: *mansuetudine . . . modera la nostra ira e la nostra troppa pazienza contr'a li nostri mali esteriori* ("gentleness . . . regulates our wrath and our excessive patience with regard to evils that confront us," *Conv.* 4.17.5). In Purgatory, the virtue represented as the opposite of wrath is likewise gentleness, or forbearance. A series of visions illustrating the virtue represent the Virgin Mary upon finding the boy Jesus in the temple, Pisistratus after learning that a youth had kissed his daughter, and the Christian martyr Stephen upon being stoned to death (*Purg.* 15.85–114). A further series of visions illustrates the vice of wrath by underscoring its potentially disastrous consequences for the subject: Procne's murder of Itys and subsequent metamorphosis into a nightingale, Haman's hanging for his persecution of the Jews, and Amata's suicide after the death of Turnus (*Purg.* 17.19–39). These three visions thus present an aspect of wrath also suggested in the final gesture of Filippo Argenti: its tendency to lead ultimately to self-destruction.

Bibliography

Bloomfield, Morton W. *The Seven Deadly Sins.* East Lansing: Michigan State College Press, 1952.

Borgese, G. A. "The Wrath of Dante." *Speculum* 13 (1938), 183–193.

Busnelli, Giovanni. *L'etica nicomachea e l'ordinamento morale dell'*Inferno *di Dante.* Bologna: Zanichelli, 1907.

Reade, William H. V. *The Moral System of Dante's Inferno.* Oxford: Clarendon Press, 1909. Reprinted Port Washington, N.Y.: Kennikat Press, 1969.

Jo Ann Cavallo

X

Xerxes

King of Persia and son of Darius, Xerxes *(Serse)* set out to invade Greece in 480 B.C.E. with an immense host, crossing the Hellespont on a bridge of boats. His forces were defeated, however, and the bridge on the Hellespont was shattered by winter storms, forcing him to cross back over in a tiny fishing skiff. Already in classical antiquity Xerxes had become an emblem of excessive pride and thirst for power, which makes a man forget his own limits and destines him for divine punishment.

Dante recalls this tradition when he compares the stream that divides him from Matelda in the Earthly Paradise with *Ellesponto, là 've passò Serse, / ancora freno a tutti orgogli umani* ("Hellespont—where Xerxes passed, a bridle still on all human pride," *Purg.* 28.71–72). Recalling Lucan (*Phars.* 2.672–673), Dante cites the failed attempt in *Mon.* 2.8.7. Charles Martel also mentions him in the Heaven of Venus as an exemplum of a military general or warrior (*Par.* 8.124).

Olivia Holmes

Z

Zanche, Michele

Though he never appears in person in the *Commedia,* we have it on the hearsay evidence of the hapless Navarrese whom the early commentators call Ciampolo that *donno Michel Zanche / di Logodoro* (*Inf.* 22.88–89) is another of the shades submerged in the boiling pitch of the third bolgia of the eighth circle of Hell, in which the barrators (or corrupt holders of public office) are punished. He is reported to consort there with fellow islander Frate Gomita, former deputy "judge" or governor of the northeastern Sardinian judicature of Gallura and *vasel d'ogne froda* ("vessel of every fraud," 22.82), reminiscing indefatigably about their native Sardinia. Dante's text in canto 22 devotes only three lines to Michele Zanche and does little more than name him. He is named again, however, in *Inf.* 33.144—this time not as perpetrator but as victim—by Frate Alberigo, who confirms his confinement "Up in the ditch of the Evil Claws, there where the sticky pitch is boiling" (*Inf.* 33.142–143). The soul of Michele's traitorous son-in-law, the Genoese Branca Doria, on the other hand, who violated the rights of hospitality (and kinship) by assassinating the wealthy and powerful Michele Zanche at a banquet in his honor, lies considerably below him, frozen face up in the ice of Ptolomea—although his body, now inhabited by a demon, continues, like that of Frate Alberigo, to go through the motions of life on Earth: *e mangia e bee e dorme e veste panni* ("and he eats and drinks and sleeps and wears clothes," *Inf.* 33.141). Additional biographical details concerning Michele Zanche are supplied by the early commentators, although his alleged marriages to the mother of Emperor Frederick II's illegitimate son Enzo and to the same King Enzo's repudiated Sardinian wife, Adelasia, and even his vicariate as governor of the northwestern judicature of Logodoro (also called Torres), appear to be apocryphal. The historical Michele Zanche belonged to one of the wealthiest and most influential feudal families of Sassari. Caught up in the conflict for hegemony in Sardinia between that maritime republic and Pisa, they were exiled in 1234 to Genoa. Michele himself was probably born around 1210. Surprisingly, even the approximate date and place of his violent death are not ascertainable from historical sources. Historians have, however, posited a political as well as economic motive for his assassination by a member of the ruling Genoese Doria family, suggesting that Michele may in the course of time have betrayed the Genoese cause and gone over to the Pisan side. Jacopo della Lana claims (somewhat fancifully) that Michele succeeded Frate Gomita as deputy in Gallura of Dante's friend Judge Nino Visconti, a Pisan exile eventually granted Genoese citizenship, who—some modern commentators have speculated—may have been Dante's privileged source for these allusions.

Bibliography

Boscolo, A. "Michele Zanche nella storia e nella leggenda." *Studi sardi* 10–12 (1952), 337–385.

Anthony Oldcorn

Zeno

Greek philosopher born in Citium on Cyprus (c. 335–263 B.C.E.). Zeno *(Zenone)* studied in Athens with the Cynic philosopher Crates and later founded the Stoic school. Only fragments of

Z his works survive. Dante praises his devotion to truth in *Conv.* 3.14.8 and mentions his role as founder of the Stoic school in *Conv.* 4.6.9 and 4.22.4, but he rejects (in the latter two chapters) Zeno's notion of the end of human life based on restrained emotions in preference for Aristotle's moral philosophy. In *Inf.* 4.138, Zeno is cited as one of the ancient philosophers residing in Limbo.

Nancy Vine Durling

Zodiac

A belt around the heavens that includes about 9 degrees on either side of the ecliptic. The ecliptic is the great circle on the celestial sphere that lies in the plane of the Sun's apparent orbit. The apparent paths of the Sun, the Moon, and the major planets all fall within this zone. The zodiac is divided into twelve equal parts of 30 degrees each, called signs. All signs are named after a constellation, and many of them have animal names such as Aries ("Ram"), Taurus ("Bull"), Pisces ("Fishes"), etc. The zodiac provides a convenient means of indicating the position of the heavenly bodies, but it is also of fundamental importance in astrology. The place occupied by the Sun in the zodiac during its daily path is believed to be of great relevance in human life.

Dante mentions the zodiac both in the *Convivio* (2.3.15ff.) and in the *Questio de aqua et terra* (55–73), where the reference is of a scientific nature. In *Conv.* 4.11.4–5 Dante underscores the influence exercised by the heavenly bodies in the formation of the human soul. In the *Vita Nuova* Beatrice is seen as the most perfect soul because at the time of her birth "all nine of the moving heavens were in perfect relationship to one another" (*VN* 29.2). In *Purgatorio* Dante mentions the zodiac in a group of tercets that can be considered as a lesson in astronomy on the geographic

Dante and Beatrice under the sign of the Ram, from Paradiso, *in the Bartholomeo de Zanni da Portese edition of the Com-* media, Venice, 1507. *Reproduced by permission of the John A. Zahm Dante Collection in the Department of Special Collections, University Libraries, University of Notre Dame.*

coordinates of Jerusalem in relation to Mount Purgatory (*Purg.* 4.61–75). The zodiac is also alluded to in a passage of *Paradiso* in which Dante refers to its obliquity or inclination in relation to the plane of the celestial equator, which, as we know from *Conv.* 3.5.13–14, is 23 degrees 30 minutes. This inclination guarantees the planets' optimal degree of influence on Earth and on the activities of human beings (*Par.* 10.7–25).

Gino Casagrande

A Chronology of the Life of Dante Alighieri

During Dante's lifetime, the new year in Florence began on March 25 and ended on the following March 24. This chronology uses the conventional calendar year, beginning on January 1, for reasons of convenience.

1260–64	Dante's grandfather Bellincione exiled with Guelfs from Florence.
1264	Death of Ghibelline leader Farinata degli Uberti (*Inf.* 10).
1265, late May	Dante born in Florence.
1266, March 26	Baptized in San Giovanni.
1266	Guelfs return to Florence after Ghibellines are defeated at Benevento.
1270–75	Mother Bella (probably degli Abati) dies.
1274, May	First encounter with Beatrice.
1277 ca.	Studies with local professional teachers.
1277	Engaged to Gemma Donati.
1280	Father's cousin Geri del Bello assassinated (*Inf.* 28–29).
1281 or 1282 (1283?)	Death of father Alaghiero.
1283	Second recorded encounter with Beatrice; first poems; friendship with Guido Cavalcanti.
1285 or 1290	Marries Gemma.
1286, summer, to early 1287	Resides in Bologna (?).
1287 (1290?, 1295?)	Son Pietro is born.
1289, June 11	Distinguishes himself as horse soldier in the Battle of Campaldino (*Purg.* 5.85–129).
1289, August 16	Takes part in the expedition against Caprona.
1290, June	Beatrice dies.
1290, July to November	Guido da Polenta the Elder podestà of Florence.
1290 (1292?, 1297?)	Son Jacopo is born.
1294 (1293 or earlier?)	Brunetto Latini dies (*Inf.* 15).
1294	Friendship with Charles Martel of Anjou, king of Hungary and heir to the throne of Naples (*Par.* 8–9).
1294	Abdication of Pope Celestine V and election of Pope Boniface VIII.
1294 (1292?)	Writes the *Vita Nuova*.
1295 (?)	Enrolls in the Guild of Physicians and Apothecaries ("Arte dei Medici e Speziali") in order to qualify for political office.
1295, November, to April 1296	Member of the Council of Thirty-Six ("Consiglio dei Trentasei del Capitano del Popolo").
1296	Member of the Council of the Hundred ("Consiglio dei Cento").
1296, December	Writes the four *petrose* poems.
1299	Daughter Antonia (later Suor Beatrice) born.
1300	May Day disturbance, causing the Guelfs to separate into two factions, the Blacks and Whites, led, respectively, by the Donati and Cerchi families.
1300, April 22	Pope Boniface VIII proclaims the Jubilee Year.
1300, May 7	Ambassador to San Gimignano on behalf of the Guelfs.

1300, June 15 to August 15	Elected to the Council of Priors, Florence's six-member executive board.
1300, June	Signs the warrant sending Guido Cavalcanti into exile.
1301, April 1 to September 15	Once again member of the Council of the Hundred.
1301, June 19	Opposes Pope Boniface VIII's request to send troops to the Maremma to fight the Santafiora.
1301, October	Diplomatic mission to Pope Boniface VIII in Rome.
1301, November	Charles of Valois enters Florence; White Guelfs fall from power.
1302, January 27	Expelled from Florence for two years and fined 5000 florins.
1302, February	In Gargonza with exiled White Guelfs.
1302, March 10	Banned from Florentine territory under pain of death.
1302, June	At San Godenzo in the Mugello with exiled White Guelfs.
1302, autumn	In Forlì as guest of Scarpetta degli Ordelaffi.
1303, May to March 1304	In Verona as guest of Bartolomeo della Scala (*Par.* 17).
1303, October 11	Death of Pope Boniface VIII.
1303–04	Writes the *De vulgari eloquentia* (left incomplete).
1304	Still active as leader of exiled White Guelfs.
1304, April	Writes *Epistola* 1 to Niccolò da Prato; leaves Verona with hope of helping Whites to re-enter Florence.
1304, April to August	In Arezzo; advises exiled Whites, then separates to make "a party unto [him]self" (*Par.* 17.69).
1304, May–June	Writes *Epistola* 2 lamenting death of Alessandro da Romena, head of White Guelfs.
1304, July 20	Allied White Guelfs and Ghibellines suffer disastrous defeat at La Lastra outside Florence (Dante not present).
1304–06	In Treviso (as guest of Gherardo da Camino), Venice, Padua, and vicinity.
1304–05	Meets Giotto in Padua (*Purg.* 11).
1304–07	Writes the *Convivio* (left unfinished).
1304–08	Conception of the *Inferno*.
1305, June 5	Election of Pope Clement V.
1306 (1302–04?)	Writes *Epistola* 3 to Cino da Pistoia.
1306, autumn, to 1307	In Lunigiana as guest of Moroello Malaspina.
1306–09	Execution and versification of the *Inferno*.
1307	In the Casentino as guest of Guido Salvatico and Guido di Battifolle; writes *Epistola* 4 to Moroello Malaspina.
1308, early, to March 1309	In Lucca (with wife and children?), befriended by "Gentucca" (*Purg.* 24); intense work on the *Inferno*.
1308–12	Plans and writes the *Purgatorio*.
1309, March	Florentine exiles expelled from Lucca.
1309	Pope Clement V moves the papacy from Rome to Avignon.
1309–10	In Paris (according to Villani, Boccaccio, Buti, and other early authorities).
1310	Writes *Epistola* 5 exhorting Italy to receive Henry VII as emperor.
1310, October, to January 1311	In Turin, Asti, Vercelli, and Milan accompanying Emperor Henry VII.
1311, January, to late 1311	In the Casentino again as guest of Guido di Battifolle; works on the *Purgatorio*.
1311, March 31	Writes *Epistola* 6 criticizing Florence's refusal to accept Henry VII as emperor.
1311, April 17	Writes *Epistola* 7 to Henry VII exhorting him to enter Florence.

1311, April–May	*Epistole* 8, 9, and 10 congratulating Henry VII's wife on her husband's campaign, written for Guido di Battifolle's wife Gherardesca.
1312, March–April	In Pisa; meets the young boy Petrarch.
1312, May, to 1318	In Verona as guest of Cangrande della Scala (*Par.* 17).
1313, August	Henry VII dies.
1314, April 20	Death of Pope Clement V.
1314 (May?)	Writes *Epistola* 11 to Cardinals imploring them to return the papacy to Rome.
1314, late	Publishes the *Inferno*.
1315, summer	Writes *Epistola* 12 to a friend, announcing his rejection of Florence's conditions for amnesty and return.
1315, October	Exile from Florence and death sentence reconfirmed and extended to family members.
1315, autumn	Publishes the *Purgatorio*.
1315–18	Writes *Paradiso* 1–17.
1316	Writes explanatory *Epistola* 13 dedicating the *Paradiso* to Cangrande.
1317	Writes the *Monarchia*.
1318, early, to September 1321	In Ravenna as guest of Guido Novello da Polenta; joined by children Pietro, Jacopo, and Antonia (Suor Beatrice).
1319–20	Exchanges *Egloge* with Giovanni del Virgilio.
1320, January 20	Reads his *Questio de aqua et terra* to a learned audience in Verona.
1321	Completion of the *Paradiso*; diplomatic mission to Venice on behalf of Ravenna.
1321, September 13	Dies in Ravenna; buried in the church of San Pier Maggiore (now San Francesco).

Popes, 33–1334 C.E.

The list includes all popes who lived before or during Dante's lifetime. **Boldface** indicates those he mentions or alludes to in his works.

33 – 67	**Peter**	418 – 422	Boniface I	686 – 687	Conon
67 – 76	**Linus**	422 – 432	Celestine I	687 – 701	Sergius I
76 – 88	**Anacletus [Cletus]**	432 – 440	Sixtus III	701 – 705	John VI
88 – 97	Clement	440 – 461	Leo I	705 – 707	John VII
97 – 105	Evaristus	461 – 468	Hilary	708 – 708	Sisinnius
105 – 115	Alexander I	468 – 483	Simplicius	708 – 715	Constantine
115 – 125	Sixtus I	483 – 492	Felix III (II)	715 – 731	Gregory II
125 – 136	Telesphorus	492 – 496	Gelasius I	731 – 741	Gregory III
136 – 140	Hyginus	496 – 498	**Anastasius II**	741 – 752	Zachary
140 – 155	**Pius I**	498 – 514	Symmachus	752 – 752	Stephen II
155 – 166	Anicetus	514 – 523	Hormisdas	752 – 757	Stephen II (III)
166 – 175	Soter	523 – 526	John I	757 – 767	Paul I
175 – 189	Eleutherius	526 – 530	Felix IV (III)	768 – 772	Stephen III (IV)
189 – 199	Victor I	530 – 532	Boniface II	772 – 795	**Adrian I**
199 – 217	Zephyrinus	533 – 535	John II	795 – 816	Leo III
217 – 222	**Callistus I**	535 – 536	**Agapetus I**	816 – 817	Stephen IV (V)
222 – 230	**Urban I**	536 – 537	Silverius	817 – 824	Paschal I
230 – 235	Pondian	537 – 555	Vigilius	824 – 827	Eugenius II
235 – 236	Anterus	556 – 561	Pelagius I	827 – 827	Valentine
236 – 250	Fabian	561 – 574	John III	827 – 844	Gregory IV
251 – 253	Cornelius	575 – 579	Benedict I	844 – 847	Sergius II
253 – 254	Lucius I	579 – 590	Pelagius II	847 – 855	Leo IV
254 – 257	Stephen I	590 – 604	**Gregory I**	855 – 858	Benedict III
257 – 258	Sixtus II	604 – 606	Sabinian	858 – 867	Nicholas I
259 – 268	Dionysius	607 – 607	Boniface III	867 – 872	Adrian II
269 – 274	Felix I	608 – 615	Boniface IV	872 – 882	John VIII
275 – 283	Eutychian	615 – 618	Deusdedit	882 – 884	Marinus I
283 – 296	Gaius	619 – 625	Boniface V	884 – 885	Adrian III
296 – 304	Marcellinus	625 – 638	Honorius I	885 – 891	Stephen V (VI)
308 – 309	Marcellus I	640 – 640	Severinus	891 – 896	Formosus
309 – 310	Eusebius	640 – 642	John IV	896 – 896	Boniface VI
311 – 314	Miltiades	642 – 649	Theodore I	896 – 897	Stephen VI (VII)
314 – 335	**Sylvester I**	649 – 655	Martin I	897 – 897	Romanus
336 – 336	Marcus	654 – 657	Eugenius I	897 – 897	Theodore II
337 – 352	Julius I	657 – 672	Vitalian	898 – 900	John IX
352 – 366	Liberius	672 – 676	Adeodatus II	900 – 903	Benedict IV
366 – 384	Damasus I	676 – 678	Donus	903 – 903	Leo V
384 – 399	Siricius	678 – 681	Agatho	904 – 911	Sergius III
399 – 401	Anastasius I	682 – 683	Leo II	911 – 913	Anastasius III
401 – 417	Innocent I	684 – 685	Benedict II	913 – 914	Landus
417 – 418	Zosimus	685 – 686	John V	914 – 928	John X

928 – 928 Leo VI	1045 – 1046 Gregory VI	1187 – 1187 Gregory VIII
928 – 931 Stephen VII (VIII)	1046 – 1047 Clement II	1187 – 1191 Clement III
931 – 935 John Xl	1047 – 1048 Benedict IX	1191 – 1198 Celestine III
936 – 939 Leo VII	1048 – 1048 Damasus II	1198 – 1216 **Innocent III**
939 – 942 Stephen VIII (IX)	1049 – 1054 Leo IX	1216 – 1227 **Honorius III**
942 – 946 Marinus II	1055 – 1057 Victor II	1227 – 1241 Gregory IX
946 – 955 Agapetus II	1057 – 1058 Stephen IX (X)	1241 – 1241 Celestine IV
955 – 964 John XII	1059 – 1061 Nicholas II	1243 – 1254 **Innocent IV**
963 – 965 **Leo VIII**	1061 – 1073 Alexander II	1254 – 1261 Alexander IV
964 – 966 **Benedict V**	1073 – 1085 Gregory VII	1261 – 1264 Urban IV
965 – 972 John XIII	1086 – 1087 Victor III	1265 – 1268 **Clement IV**
973 – 974 Benedict VI	1088 – 1099 Urban II	1271 – 1276 Gregory X
974 – 983 Benedict VII	1099 – 1118 Paschal II	1276 – 1276 Innocent V
983 – 984 John XIV	1118 – 1119 Gelasius II	1276 – 1276 **Adrian V**
985 – 996 John XV	1119 – 1124 Callistus II	1276 – 1277 **John XXI**
996 – 999 Gregory V	1124 – 1130 Honorius II	1277 – 1280 **Nicholas III**
999 – 1003 Sylvester II	1130 – 1143 Innocent II	1281 – 1285 **Martin IV**
1003 – 1003 John XVII	1143 – 1144 Celestine II	1285 – 1287 Honorius IV
1004 – 1009 John XVIII	1144 – 1145 Lucius II	1288 – 1292 **Nicholas IV**
1009 – 1012 Sergius IV	1145 – 1153 Eugenius III	1294 – 1294 **Celestine V**
1012 – 1024 Benedict VIII	1153 – 1154 Anastasius IV	1294 – 1303 **Boniface VIII**
1024 – 1032 John XIX	1154 – 1159 Adrian IV	1303 – 1304 **Benedict XI**
1032 – 1044 Benedict IX	1159 – 1181 Alexander III	1305 – 1314 **Clement V**
1045 – 1045 Sylvester III	1181 – 1185 Lucius III	1316 – 1334 **John XXII**
1045 – 1045 Benedict IX	1185 – 1187 Urban III	

Roman and Holy Roman Emperors

The list includes the Roman emperors mentioned or alluded to by Dante and the complete line of Holy Roman Emperors in the West, with those he refers to in his works in **boldface**.

Roman Emperors

Augustus	B.C.E. 27–C.E. 14
Tiberius	14–37
Nero	54–68
Titus	79–81
Domitian	81–96
Trajan	98–117
Constantine	306–337
Justinian	527–565

Holy Roman Emperors

Carolingian dynasty

Charlemagne (Charles I)	800–814
Louis I	814–840
(*Civil War*)	840–843
Lothair I	843–855
Louis II	855–875
Charles II	875–877
(*Interregnum*)	877–881
Charles III	881–887
(*Interregnum*)	887–891

House of Spoleto

Guy (Guido di Spoleto)	891–894
Lambert (Lamberto di Spoleto)	894–898

Carolingian dynasty

Arnulf of Carinthia	896–899
Louis III	901–905

House of Franconia

Conrad I	911–918

Carolingian dynasty

Berengar (Berengario I)	915–924

House of Saxony (Liudolfings)

Henry I	919–936
Otto I	936–973

Otto II	973–983
Otto III	983–1002
Henry II	1002–1024

Salian dynasty

Conrad II	1024–1039
Henry III	1039–1056
Henry IV	1056–1106

Rival claimants

Rudolf (Rudolf of Swabia)	1077–1080
Hermann	1081–1093
Conrad	1093–1101
Henry V	1111–1125

House of Supplinburg

Lothair II	1125–1137

House of Hohenstaufen

Conrad III	1138–1152
Frederick I (Barbarossa)	1152–1190
Henry VI	1190–1097
Philip	1198–1208

Welf dynasty

Otto IV	1198–1214

House of Hohenstaufen

Frederick II	1215–1250

Rival claimants

Henry (VII)	1220–1235
Henry Raspe	1246–1247
William of Holland	1247–1256
Conrad IV (Conradin)	1250–1254
Great Interregnum	
Richard	1257–1272
Alfonso (Alfonso X of Castile)	1257–1275

House of Habsburg

Rudolf I	1273–1291

House of Nassau		*House of Habsburg*	
Adolf	1292–1298	Frederick (III)	1314–1326
House of Habsburg		*House of Wittelsbach*	
Albert I	1298–1308	Louis IV	1314–1346
House of Luxembourg			
Henry VII	1308–1313		

Musical Settings of the *Commedia*, arranged by year of composition

Year	Composer	Life	Nationality	Title of Work	Type of work	Dante Reference
1562	Montanari, Giovanni Battista		Italian	(title unknown)	madrigal	Inf. I.1–3
1570	Galilei, Vincenzo	1520–1591	Italian	Lamento del Conte Ugolino	song	Inf. XXXIII
1576	Luzzaschi, Luzzasco	1545–1607	Italian	Quivi sospiri	madrigal	Inf. III.22–27
1576	Renaldi, Giulio		Italian	Quivi sospiri	madrigal	Inf. III.22–27
1578	Mosto, Giovanni Battista	–1596	Italian	Quivi sospiri	madrigal	Inf. III.22–27
1580	Courtoys, Lambert			Quivi sospiri	madrigal	Inf. III.22–27
1581	Soriano, Francesco	1549–1621	Italian	Quivi sospiri	madrigal	Inf. III.22–27
1581	Micheli, Domenico	1575–1659	Italian	Quivi sospiri	madrigal	Inf. III.22–27
1584	Vinci, Pietro	1531–1584	Italian	Quivi sospiri	madrigal	Inf. III.22–27
1586	Balbi, Lodovico		Italian	Stavvi Minos orribilmente e ringhia	madrigal	Inf. V4
1604	Merulo, Claudio	1533–1604	Italian	Vergine Madre, figlia del tuo figlio	madrigal	Par. XXXIII
1796	Dittersdorf, Carl Ditters von	1739–1799	Austrian	Ugolino	opera	Inf. XXXIII
1805	Zingarelli, Nicola	1752–1837	Italian	Canto XXXIII di Dante	song	Inf. XXXIII
1806	Morlacchi, Francesco	1784–1841	Italian	Inferno XXXIII	cantata	Inf. XXXIII
1818	Rossini, Giacchino	1792–1868	Italian	Otello	opera	Inf. V.121–123
1820	Confidati, Luigi	1772–1847	Italian	Iscrizione su la porta dell'Inferno	song	Inf. III.1–9
1820	Confidati, Luigi	1772–1847	Italian	Episodio di Francesca da Rimini	song	Inf. V.70–142
1820	Confidati, Luigi	1772–1847	Italian	La morte del Conte Ugolino	song	Inf. XXXIII.1–78
1821	Seyfried, Ignaz Xever	1776–1841	Austrian	Ugolino, oder Der Hungerturm	opera	Inf. XXXIII
1825	Carlini, Luigi		Italian	Francesca da Rimini	opera	Inf. V
1828	Donizetti, Gaetano	1797–1848	Italian	Canto XXXIII della Divina Commedia	song	Inf. XXXIII.1–78
1829	Mercadante, Saverio	1795–1870	Italian	Francesca da Rimini	opera	Inf. V
1829	Quilici, Massimiliano	1799–1889	Italian	Francesca da Rimini	opera	Inf. V
1829	Generali, Pietro	1773–1832	Italian	Francesca da Rimini	opera	Inf. V
1831	Staffa, Giuseppe		Italian	Francesca da Rimini	opera	Inf. V
1832	Morlacchi, Francesco	1784–1841	Italian	L'Ugolino di Dante	song	Inf. XXXIII
1832	Manna, Ruggiero		Italian	Francesca da Rimini	opera	Inf. V
1832	Fournier-Gore, Giuseppe		Italian	Francesca da Rimini	opera	Inf. V
1835	Tamburini, Giuseppe		Italian	Francesca da Rimini	opera	Inf. V
1835	Orsini, Luigi	1810–1881	Italian	La Pia de' Tolomei	opera	Purg. V
1836	Borgatta, Emanuele		Italian	Francesca da Rimini	opera	Inf. V
1836	Morlacchi, Francesco	1784–1841	Italian	Francesca da Rimini	opera	Inf. V
1837	Liszt, Franz	1841–1886	German	Après une lecture de Dante	sonata	Inf., Purg., Par.
1837	Donizetti, Gaetano	1797–1848	Italian	Pia de' Tolomei	opera	Purg. V
1837	Donizetti, Gaetano	1797–1848	Italian	Ave Maria	song	Par. XXXIII

Year	Composer	Life	Nationality	Title of Work	Type of work	Dante Reference
1838	Serafini, Giacomo cor.		Italian	Francesca da Rimini	ballet	Inf. V
1840	Nordal, Eugen			Francesca da Rimini	opera	Inf. V
1840	Maglioni, Antonio		Italian	Francesca da Rimini	opera	Inf. V
1841	Bellini, DeVasini, Meiners		Italian	Francesca da Rimini	opera	Inf. V
1842	Cannetti, Francesco		Italian	Francesca da Rimini	opera	Inf. V
1843	Brancaccio, Antonio		Italian	Francesca da Rimini	opera	Inf. V
1843	Donizetti, Gaetano	1797–1848	Italian	Amor che a nullo amato	song	Inf. V
1843	Donizetti, Gaetano	1797–1848	Italian	O anime affanate	song	Inf. V
1844	Donizetti, Gaetano	1797–1848	Italian	Ave Regina	song	Par. XXXII
1844	Rolland, Enrico		Italian	Francesca da Rimini	opera	Inf. V
1847	Pappalardo, Salvatore		Italian	Francesca da Rimini	opera	Inf. V
1848	Rossini, Giacchino	1792–1868	Italian	Farò come colui che piange e dice	song	Inf. V
1852	Carrer, Paolo	1829–1896		Dante e Beatrice	opera	
1855	Ruggieri, Pietro		Italian	Francesca da Rimini	opera	Inf. V
1856	Pinelli, Pietro		Italian	Francesca da Rimini	opera	Inf. V
1856	Coppini, Antonio cor.	1806–1888	Italian	Francesca da Rimini	ballet	Inf. V
1856	Ronzani, Domenico	1800–1868	Italian	Ugolino della Gherardesca	ballet	Inf. XXXIII
1857	Franchini, Giovanni		Italian	Francesca da Rimini	opera	Inf. V
1857	Platania, P.	1828–1907	Italian	Piccarda Donati	opera	Par. III
1860	Zescewich, Francesco		Italian	Francesca da Rimini	opera	Inf. V
1860	Marchisio, Antonio	1817–1875	Italian	Piccarda Donati	opera	Par. III
1863	Pacini, Giovanni	1796–1867	Italian	Sinfonia Dante	symphony	Inf., Purg., Par.
1863	Liszt, Franz	1811–1886	German	Eine Symphonie zu Dantes Divina Commedia	symphony	Inf., Purg., Par.
1863	Moscazza, Vincenzo		Italian	Piccarda Donati	opera	Par. III
1865	Noseda, Gustavo Adolfo	1837–1866	Italian	Meditazione su Dante dal canto XXXIII	sinfonia	Inf. XXXIII
1865	San Fiorenzo, Cesare	1834–1909	Italian	La Divina Commedia	piano piece	Inf., Purg., Par.
1865	Gilson, Paul	1865–1942	Belgian	Francesca da Rimini	opera	Inf. V
1865	Mabellini, M. Teodulo	1817–1897	Italian	Lo spirito di Dante	song	Inf., Purg., Par.
1865	San Fiorenzo, Cesare	1834–1909	Italian	Tre illustrazioni drammatico-musicali della Divina Commedia		Inf., Purg., Par.
1865	Ruta		Italian	Brano del 1 Canto dell'Inferno		Inf.
1865	Pincherle		Italian	Omaggio a Dante		Purg. VIII
1866	Boullard, J. Marius		French	Francesca da Rimini	operetta	Inf. V
1866	Granados, Enrique	1867–1916	Spanish	Dante e Virgilio	symphonic poem	Inf. V/91–138
1866	Campana, Fabio	1819–1882	Italian	Dante a Beatrice	song	
1868	Massa, Alexandre		French	Le Dante	opera	
1868	Bantock, Granville	1868–1946	English	Dante and Beatrice	symphonic poem	
1870	Marcarini, Giuseppe	1832–1905	Italian	Francesca da Rimini	opera	Inf. V

Year	Composer	Life	Nationality	Title of Work	Type of work	Dante Reference
1873	Dall'Olio, Cesare	1849–1906	Italian	Inferno, Purgatorio, Paradiso	sinfonia descrittiva	Inf., Purg., Par.
1876	Tchaikovsky, Peter	1840–1893	Russian	Francesca da Rimini	symphonic poem	Inf. V
1877	Moscuzza, Vincenzo		Italian	Francesca da Rimini	opera	Inf. V
1877	Goetz, Hermann	1840–1876	German	Francesca da Rimini	opera	Inf. V
1877	Chaumet, William		French	Dante au tombeau de Beatrice	song	
1878	Cagnoni, Antonio		Italian	Francesca da Rimini	opera	Inf. V
1879	Moreno, Pons			Les Malatesta	opera	Inf. V
1880	Verdi, Giuseppe	1813–1901	Italian	Padre Nostro	song	Par. XXXIII
1880	Verdi, Giuseppe	1813–1901	Italian	Ave Maria volgarizzata da Dante	song	Par. XXXIII
1883	Strepponi, Feliciano		Italian	Francesca da Rimini	opera	Inf. V
1885	Graziani-Walter, Carlo	1851–1927	Italian	Paolo e Francesca	opera	Inf. V
1885	Raff, Joseph Joachim	1822–1882		Introduzione e allegro scherzoso op. 87		
1890	Godard, Benjamin	1849–1895	French	Dante et Beatrice	opera	Inf., Purg., Par.
1890	Bazzini, Antonio	1818–1897	Italian	Francesca da Rimini	symphonic poem	Inf. V
1890	Foote, Arthur	1853–1937	American	Francesca da Rimini	prologo sinfonico	Inf. V
1892	Woyrsch, Felix von	1860–1944	German	Symphonic Prologue	symphonic prologue	Inf., Purg., Par.
1892	Bridge, John Fredrick	1844–1924	English	The Lord's Prayer	song	Purg. XI
1898	Verdi, Giuseppe	1813–1901	Italian	Laudi alla Vergine Maria	song	Par. XXXIII
1899	Zandonai, Riccardo	1883–1944	Italian	Canto XXXIII	cantata	Inf. XXXIII
1899	Zandonai, Riccardo	1883–1944	Italian	Canto V	cantata	Inf. V
1899	Ollone, Max d'	1875–1959	French	La Visione de Dante	symphonic poem	Inf., Purg., Par.
18-?	Schumann, Robert	1810–1856	German	Canzone della Sera or Abenlied	song	Purg. VIII.1–6
18-?	Marchetti, Filippo	1831–1902	Italian	La Pia	song	Purg. V
18-?	Ponchielli, Amilcare	1834–1886	Italian	Noi leggevamo insieme	aria da camera	Inf. V
18-?	Di Giulio, Angelo	1800's	Italian	Il conte Ugolino	song	Inf. XXXIII
18-?	Sanzone	1800's	Italian	La Francesca di Dante, Ballata in chiave di Sol	ballet	Inf. V
18-?	Rondanina, A.	1800's	Italian	Francesca da Rimini		Inf. V
18-?	D'Arcais, Francesco	1800's	Italian	Francesca da Rimini		Inf. V
18-?	Conti, Claudio	1836–1878	Italian	Amor		Inf. V
18-?	Silveri, Domenico	1800's	Italian	Francesca da Rimini		Inf. V
18-?	Podestà, Carlo	1800's	Italian	Francesca da Rimini		Inf. V
18-?	Rebbora	1800's	Italian	Ugolino	song	Inf. XXXIII
18-?	Gaggi, Adauto	1800's	Italian	Inferno I	song	Inf. I
18-?	Palminteri, Antonio	1800's	Italian	La Pia	song	Purg. V
18-?	Auteri-Manzocchi, Salvatore	1800's	Italian	title unknown	song	Purg. VIII
18-?	Cimoso, Guido	1804–1878	Italian	Sinfonia a Dante	sinfonia	
18-?	von Bulow, H.	1830–1894	German	Pia		Purg. VIII

Year	Composer	Life	Nationality	Title of Work	Type of work	Dante Reference
18-?	Vianesi, Enrico	1837–1908	Italian	Dante	piano piece	
18-?	Mattiozzi, Rodolfo	1832–1871	Italian	Un pensiero a Dante	marcia	
18-?	Marchetti, Filippo	1831–1902	Italian	La Pia	song	Purg. V.130–136
18-?	Roberti, Giulio	1800's	Italian	L'ora che volge il desio	song	Purg. VIII
18-?	Fodale, Paolo	1818–1896	Italian	Dodici scene drammatiche tratte dalla Divina Commedia		
1900	Vannini, Pietro	1800's	Italian	Sordello		
18-?	Massa, Duca di	1800's	Italian	Dante		
18-?	Sala, Alessandro	1800's	Italian	Bice Alighieri		
1901	Brunel, Raoul	1848–1921	French	La Visione de Dante	sym. poem	Inf., Purg., Par.
1901	Mancinelli, Luigi		Italian	Pater Noster	song	Purg. XI
1902	Gerli, Giuseppe		Italian	L'apparizione de Beatrice a Dante	song	Purg. XXX
1902	Napravnik, Eduard	1839–1916	Bohemian	Francesca da Rimini	opera	Inf. V
1906	Rachmaninov, Sergey	1873–1943	Russian	Francesca da Rimini	opera	Inf. V
1906	Foulds, John	1880–1939	English	The Vision of Dante	opera	Inf., Purg., Par.
1907	Mancinelli, Luigi	1848–1921	Italian	Paolo e Francesca	opera	Inf. V
1909	Gastaldon, Stanislao	1861–1939	Italian	Dante	opera	
1911	Tentarelli, F.			A Trip to Dante City	trio	
1912	Abranyi, Emil	1882–1970	Hungarian	Paolo e Francesca	opera	Inf. V
1913	Leoni, Franco	\1864–1938	Italian	Francesca da Rimini	opera	Inf. V
1913	Zandonai, Riccardo	1883–1944	Italian	O padre nostro che nei cieli stai	song	Purg. XI
1914	Nougues, Jean	1875–1932	French	Dante	opera	Inf., Purg., Par.
1914	Zandonai, Riccardo	1883–1944	Italian	Francesca da Rimini	opera	Inf. V
1915	Del Campo, Conrado	1879–1953	Spanish	Paolo e Francesca	opera	Inf. V
1915	Fokine, Michel	1880–1942	Russian	Francesca da Rimini	ballet	Inf. V
1916	Ollone, Max d'	1875–1959	French	Les Amantes de Rimini	opera	Inf. V
1918	Puccini, Giacomo	1858–1924	Italian	Gianni Schicchi	opera	Inf. XXX
1919	Klenau, Paul von	1883–1946	Danish	Paolo und Francesca: Dante-Phantasie	symphony	Inf. V
1920	Haydon, Claude		American	Paolo and Francesca	opera	Inf. V
1920	Hernried, Robert	1883–1951	American	Francesca da Rimini	opera	Inf. V
1921	Graziani-Walter, Carlo	1851–1927	Italian	Dante e Beatrice meditazione	song	
1923	Castelnuovo-Tedesco, Mario	1895–1968	American	La Sera	song	Purg. VIII.1–6
1924	Geddes, Norman-Bel	1893–1958	American	The Divine Comedy of Dante Alighieri	20th cent. theatre	Inf., Purg., Par.
1928	Sicuriani, F.		Italian	La Pia	opera	Purg. V
1930	Dobici, Cesare	1873–1944	Italian	Vergine Madre	song	Par. XXXIII
1932	James, Dorothy	1898–1982	American	Francesca da Rimini	opera	Inf. V
1932	Scalero, Rosario		Italian	La divina foresta	sym. poem	Purg.
1935	Migot, George	1891–1976	French	Trois nocturnes dantesques pour piano	piano piece	

Year	Composer	Life	Nationality	Title of Work	Type of work	Dante Reference
1937	Langgaard, Rued	1893–1952	Danish	Flammekamrene	sonata/phantasy	Inf. XXV
1937	Lichine, David cor.	1910–1972	French	Francesca da Rimini	ballet	Inf. V
1938	Lockwood, Norman	1906–	American	O Our Father Who Art In Heaven	song	Purg. XI.1–24
1940	Ashton, Frederick	1904–1988	English	Dante Sonata	ballet	Inf.
1951	Langgaard, Rued	1893–1952	Danish	Dante's Helvede	organ piece	Inf. V
1955	Blacher, Boris	1903–1975	German	Francesca da Rimini: Fragment aus Dantes	song	Inf., Purg., Par.
1955	Herrmann, Hugo	1896–1967	German	Trilogie nach Dantes Göttlicher Kömodie	symphony	Inf. V
1956	Leclair, Andre cor.		French	Francesca da Rimini	ballet	Inf. V
1958	Lifar, Serge	1905–1986	French	Francesca da Rimini	ballet	Inf. V
1959	Creston, Paul	1906–1985	American	The Celestial Vision	song	Par. XXVII, XXXII
1959	Ross, Herbert cor.	1927–		Dark Songs	ballet	Inf. I
1961	Dobrievich, Pierre			Francesca da Rimini	ballet	Inf. V
1962	Dallapiccola, Luigi	1904–1975	Italian	Ulisse	opera	Inf. XXVI
1963	Klusak, Jan	1934–	Czech	Five Fragments from the Divine Comedy for alto and piano		
1965	Pistoni, Mario cor.		Italian	Francesca da Rimini	ballet	Inf. V
1966	Jachino, Carlo	1887–1971	Italian	Santa Orazione alla Vergine Maria	20th cent.	Par. XXXIII.1–21
1967	Norgaard, Per	1932–	Danish	The Labyrinth	opera	Inf., Purg., Par.
1967	Newberry, Stirling Scott	1967–	American	Sketches from Dante: L'amor che move le sole e le altre stelle		Par.
1968–69	Castiglioni, Niccolò	1932–1996	Italian	Sinfonia in C	sinfonia	Inf., Purg., Par.
1973	Barraud, Henry	1900–	French	La Divine Comédie	cantata	Inf. V.121–138
1973	Rodriguez, Robert Xavier	1946–	American	Canto I	cantata	Inf. XXXIV
1973	Lidholm, Ingvar	1921–	Swedish	a riveder le stelle	a cappella	Inf., Purg., Par.
1973	Bayle and Parmegiani		French	La Divine Comédie d'après Dante	ballet	Inf. XVII.61–75
1974	Gaburo, Kenneth	1926–1993	American	Subito: theater for 4 instruments	20th cent.	Inf. II.1–9
1974	Bois, Robert du	1934–	Dutch	Inferno	20th cent.	Par. I, XXIV, XXXIII
1974	Martino, Donald	1931–	American	Paradiso Choruses	opera	Inf. VI.1–12
1975	Furtwangler, Giese		German	Dante Sinfonie	ballet	Inf. III.1–3
1976	Gaburo, Kenneth	1926–1993	American	Dante's Joynte	20th cent. electronic	Inf., Purg., Par.
1976	Gilbert, Amy		Canadian	Cette étoile ensigne à s'incliner	20th cent. electronic	
1976	Biagi, Vittorio cor.		Italian	La divine comédie	ballet	
1977	Frumerie, Gunnar de	1908–1987	Swedish	Dante	song	
1977	Helmschrott, Robert M.	1938–	German	Entelechiae: Riflessioni su Dante per orchestra		
1979	Vivier, Claude	1948–1983	Canadian	Lettura di Dante	20th cent.	Par. XXXIII.67–145
1979	Thorne, Francis	1922–	American	La luce eterna	20th cent.	Inf.
1979	Laman, Wim		Dutch	Canto infernale	20th cent.	

Year	Composer	Life	Nationality	Title of Work	Type of work	Dante Reference
1980	Charpentier, Jacques	1933–	French	Mais déjà le soleil touchait à l'horizon	symphony	Purg. II.2
1980	Walter, Erich cor.	1915–	German	Francesca da Rimini fantasy	ballet	Inf. V
1980–82	Hanus, Jan		Czech	Labyrinth. Dance meditations on the motifs of Dante's Divine Comedy	ballet	
1981	Sciarrino, Salvatore	1947–	Italian	La Voce dell'Inferno	20th cent.	Inf. I
1981	Paola, Ennio		Canadian	Cantica III, canto XXXIII: Dante beholds the universe	piano piece	Par. XXXIII
1982	Hartway, James	1944–	American	The Ninth Circle	20th cent.	Inf. XXXIV
1982	Hillborg, Anders	1954–	Swedish	Variations	20th cent.	
1982	Kunad, Rainer	1936–	German	Pro novo: Für gemischten chor a capella conatum	a cappella	Par. I.76–84
1982	Terzakis, Dimitri	1922–	Russian	Für Willis Dologlou (four Monologues)	song	Inf. III.46–51
1983	Bibalo, Antonio		Italian	Cantico for mezzo soprano and prepared tape	cantico	Inf. V
1983	Standford, Patric	1939–	English	Symphony #3: Toward Paradiso	symphony	Purg., Par.
1984	Norton, James		American	From Dante's Inferno	chorus	Inf. V. 25–39
1985	Nordheim, Arne	1931–	Norwegian	Aurora	20th cent. electronic	Par. XXXIII.115–145
1986	Fulkerson, Christopher		American	E io etterno duro	20th cent.	
1986	Pehkonen, Ellis	1942–	English	Russian Requiem	requiem	Inf. III
1987	Sciarrino, Salvatore	1947	Italian	La Divina Commedia	20th cent.	
1988	Sciarrino, Salvatore	1947–	Italian	Per i cerchi concentrici	20th cent.	Inf., Purg., Par.
1989	Wiprud, G. Theodore		American	Refining Fire	quartet	Purg. XXV–XXVII
1989	Aracil, Alfredo	1954–	Spanish	Francesca	opera	Inf. V
1989	Wiprud, Theodore		American	Il Racconto di Francesca	song	Inf. V
1989	Hultqvist, Anders	1955–	Swedish	E l'altre stelle	song	Par. XXXIII
1989	Kokoro Dance		Canadian	Zero to the Power	ballet	
1990	Hoecke, Micha van		Dutch	Dante Symphonie	ballet	
1990	Back, Sven-Erik	1919–1994	Swedish	Musik till Dantes Divina Commedia, I: Inferno	20th cent.	Inf. I
1991	Darasse, Xavier	1934–	French	Organum VII	song	Purg. II
1991	Miranda, Regina		Brazilian	Divina Comedia	ballet	Inf., Purg., Par.?
1991	Allik, K. and Mulder, R.		American	Electronic Purgatory	20th cent. electronic	Purg.
1992	Abbinanti, Frank	1949–	American	Come una forza di luce	oratorio	Inf., Purg., Par.
1992	Wuorinen, Charles	1938–	American	The Mission of Virgil	ballet	Inf. I
1992	Radulescu, Michael	1943–	Rumanian	Versi/Dante		
1992	Rea, John		American	Canto di Beatrice		
1992	Veldhuis, Jacob ter	1951–	Dutch	Paradiso I for mixed choir	choir	Par. I
1993	Carlson, Carolyn	1943–	American	Commedia	ballet	Inf., Purg., Par.

Year	Composer	Life	Nationality	Title of Work	Type of work	Dante Reference
1994	Veldhuis, Jacob ter	1951–	Dutch	Paradiso II for baritone and orchestra		Par. XXX, XXXIII
1994	Vlijmen, Jan van	1935–	Dutch	Inferno: cantate per tre gruppi vocali e quattro gruppi strumentali		Inf.
1994	Wettstein, Peter	1939–	Swiss	Un giro immortale. Totentanz	20th cent.	
1994	Wuorinen, Charles	1938-	American	The Great Procession	ballet	Purg. XXIX–XXXII
1994	Denniston, David	1957–	American	Moto Dante	20th cent. electronic	
1994	Veldhuis, Jacob ter	1951-	Dutch	Sempre l'amor	20th cent.	Par. XXX
1995	Veldhuis, Jacob ter	1951–	Dutch	Sempre l'amor II	20th cent.	Par. XXX
1995	Pluers, Sussman, Bordeaux		American	Inferno	musical	Inf.
1995	Edlund, Lars	1922–	Swedish	Paradiso: tre canti	choral work	Par.
1995	Dun, Tan	1957–	Chinese	Marco Polo	opera	
1995	Koolmees, Hans		Dutch	Lilywhite	20th cent.	
1995	Bjurling, Bjorn	1966–	Swedish	Si traviato è 'l folle mi' desio	choral work	
1996	Felder, David	1953-	American	Three Pieces for Orchestra	20th cent. orchestral	Par. XXI
1996	Wuorinen, Charles	1938-	American	The River of Light	ballet	Par. III
1996	Saij, Anita		Danish	Acid Cirq	ballet	Inf. I
1997	Hippler, Dietmar		German	Inferno		Inf.
19-?	Vissarronovich, Aleksei	1921–	Russian	Francesca da Rimini	ballet	Inf. V
19-?	Buchtger, F.	1903–1978	German	Dante		
19-?	Rytel, Piotr	1884-1970	German	Dante's dream		
19-?	Machover, Todd		American	Three Hyperstring Works	20th cent.	Inf., Purg., Par.
19-?	Curchack, Fred		American	The Underworld, Purgatory and Paradise performance art	20th cent.	Inf. V
19-?	Chichinadze, Aleksei	1921–	Italian	Francesca da Rimini	ballet	Inf. V
18?	Battista, Vincenzo		Italian	Francesca da Rimini		
18?	Bozzano, Emilio		Italian	Inferno III		
18?	Bozzano, Emilio		Italian	Francesca da Rimini		
18?	Magazzari, Agostino		Italian	Francesca da Rimini		
18?	Maza, Francesco		Italian	Francesca da Rimini		
18?	Viceconte		Italian	Francesca da Rimini		
18?	Benventui, T.		Italian	Ugolino		
18?	Lucilla, Domenico		Italian	Ugolino		
18?	Palminteri, Antonio		Italian	Pia de' Tolomei		
18?	Fabiani		Italian	Pia de' Tolomei		
18?	Auteri-Manzocchi, Salvatore		Italian	La sera		
18?	Sala, Marco		Italian	La sera		
18?	Sinico, Giuseppe		Italian	Pater Noster		

Year	Composer	Life	Nationality	Title of Work	Type of work	Dante Reference
18?	Silveri, Domenico		Italian	Purgatorio XVI e XXVIII		
18?	Anichini, Francesco		Italian	A Dante		
18?	Bicchierai, Luigi		Italian	Al sepolcro di Dante		
18?	Cacchiatelli, Adele		Italian	Ricordo della Pia de' Tolomei		
18?	Cerezzano		Italian	I giuochi puerili di Dante e Bice		
18?	Cianchi, Emilio		Italian	Il genio di Dante		
18?	Cortesi, Francesco		Italian	Il ritorno di Dante		
18?	Dechamps, E.		Italian	A Dante		
18?	Favi, S.		Italian	Laudi a Dante		
18?	Felici, R.		Italian	Il Veltro		
18?	Gamucci, Baldassare		Italian	A Beatrice		
18?	Gialdini, Gialdino		Italian	Il centenario di Dante		
18?	Giovannini, Alberto		Italian	Inno a Dante		
18?	Holmes, Augusta		Italian	Inno alla Pace, in onore della Beatrice di Dante		
18?	Lucchetti, M.		Italian	L'addio di Dante a Firenze		
18?	Luzzi, Fortunato		Italian	Nel sesto centenario della nascita di D.A.		
18?	Manzini		Italian	Inno a Dante		
18?	Magazzari, Agostino		Italian	Il vessillo d'Italia		
18?	Mariotti, Olimpo		Italian	Preghiera a Dante		
18?	Palloni, Gaetano		Italian	Inno pel monumento a Dante		
18?	Romani, Carlo		Italian	Inno a Dante		
18?	Ronzi, P.		Italian	Dante		
18?	Scudo, Paolo		Italian	Dante		
18?	Ivancich, Alessandro		Italian	Dante, walzer per pianoforte		
18?	Del Lungo, A.		Italian	Dante, Marcia		
18?	Paggi		Italian	Francesca per pianoforte		
18?	Piatti, V.		Italian	Scene dantesche, poesie per pianoforte		
18?	Burali-Forti		Italian	Piccarda Donati		
1872	Casilini, Andrea		Italian	Il Re Manfredi		
1872	Montuoro, Achille		Italian	Il Re Manfredi		
1884	Stessa, Carlo		Italian	Il Re Manfredi		
1856	Buzzi, Antonio		Italian	Sordello		
1843	Canetti, Francesco		Italian	Francesca da Rimini		
18?	Zezevich, Andrea		Italian	Francesca da Rimini		
18?	Giotti, Napoleone, cor.		Italian	Ballo dantesco		

Recorded Musical Settings of the *Commedia*

Composer	Title	Type	Label name	Issue	Year
Bantock, Granville	The Cyprian goddess, Helena, Dante and Beatrice	CD	Hyperion Records	CDA66810	1995
Barraud, Henry	La Divine Comédie	LP	Ades	Ades 14.019	1980
Blacher, Boris	Francesca da Rimini	LP			1993
Blak, Kristian	Antiphonale (L'incontro di Dante ed Offenbach nell'altro mondo)	CD	Tutl	HJF 20	1993
Charpentier, Jacques	Symphonie no. 6	LP	Erato	STU 71509	1983
Dallapiccola, Luigi	Ulisse	CD	Stradivarius	STR 1006	
Donizetti, Gaetano	Pia de' Tolomei	CD	Melodrama MRF Records	Mel 37017	1988
Donizetti, Gaetano	Pia de' Tolomei	LP	Celebrity Records	EJS 412	
Foote, Arthur	Francesca da Rimini	LP		LS 754	1976
Godard, Benjamin	Le Dante	LP	Victor	GDA 211*	
Godard, Benjamin	Le Dante	LP		VIC 87508*	
Granados, Enrique	Dante e Virgilio	LP	First edition records		1971
Lidholm, Ingvar	Fyra kadenser for violincell och orkester [a riveder le stelle]	LP	EMI Odeon	EMI4E 061-355161	1976
Lidholm, Ingvar	a riveder le stelle	CD	Chandos Digital	CHAN 8963	1991
Lidholm, Ingvar	a riveder le stelle	CD	Phono Suecia	PSCD 35	1986
Lidholm, Ingvar	a riveder le stelle	LP	His Master's Voice	4E06135161	1976
Liszt, Franz	Dante Symphony	LP	Hungaroton	SLPX 11918	1978
Liszt, Franz	Dante Symphony	LP	SPA Records	SPA 44	1953
Liszt, Franz	Dante Symphony	LP	London	SXDL 7542	1982
Liszt, Franz	Dante Symphony	LP	Decca	DL 98670	1953
Liszt, Franz	Dante Symphony	CD	Erato	ECD 88162	1986
Liszt, Franz	Dante Symphony	CD	Musical Heritage Society	W52275757	1991
Liszt, Franz	Dante Sonata	LP	Lyrichord Discs	LL 14	1972
Liszt, Franz	Busoni and his circle [Après une lecture de Dante]	CD	Pearl	GEMM Cd 9014	1993
Liszt, Franz	Liszt an Italian Recital [Dante sonata]	CD	Virgin Classics	VC 7 59222 2	1992
Liszt, Franz	Klaviersonate h-Moll; Après une lecture du Dante	LP	Deutsche Grammophon	2531 271	1981
Liszt, Franz	De Vienne a Bayreuth [Après une lecture du Dante]	LP	Lyrinx	LYR 8004-021	1983
Liszt, Franz	Après une lecture de Dante	LP	Bourg	BG 3006	1983
Liszt, Franz	Années de pelerinage [Après une lecture de Dante]	LP	Odean	PALP 1987	1963
Liszt, Franz	Dante sonata	LP	Qualiton	LPX 1020	1962
Liszt, Franz	Années de pelerinage [Après une lecture de Dante]	CD	Philips	420 169-2	1987
Liszt, Franz	Après une lecture de Dante	Cassette	Philips	7337 273	1983
Liszt, Franz	Après une lecture de Dante	CD	Delos	D/CD 3022	1985
Liszt, Franz	Ranki plays Liszt [Après une lecture de Dante]	CD	Denon	C37-7547	1985
Martino, Donald	Paradiso	LP	Golden Crest	NEC 114	1974

Composer	Title	Type	Label name	Issue	Year
Nordheim, Arne	Aurora	LP	Aurora	AR 1902	1986
Nordheim, Arne	Wirklicher Wald (Aurora)	CD	Norwegian Composers	NCD4910	1986
Pacini, Giovanni	Sinfonia Dante	CD	Bongiovanni	GB 2059-2	1988
Ponchielli, Amilcare	Noi legevamo insieme	LP	Sipario Dischi	CS 13	1986
Puccini, Giacomo	Gianni Schicchi	LP	Capitol EMI	SGAR 7179	1986
Puccini, Giacomo	Gianni Schicchi	LP	Cetra-Soria	50.028	1950
Puccini, Giacomo	Gianni Schicchi	LP	Angel	34048	1986
Puccini, Giacomo	Gianni Schicchi	CD	Eurodisc	RC77512	1988
Radulescu, Michael	Ephiphaniai [Dante]	CD	Deutsche Harmonia Mundi	HM 1075-2	1993
Rodriguez, Robert	Canto	LP	Orion	ORS 74138	1973
Ruders, Poul	Dante Sonata	LP	Odeon	MOAK30010	1970
Tchaikovsky, Peter	Francesca da Rimini	LP	Musical Heritage Society	MHS 4135	1979
Tchaikovsky, Peter	Francesca da Rimini	CD	Sony Classical	SMK 47633	1993
Tchaikovsky, Peter	Francesca da Rimini	LP	Deutsche Grammophon	2532069	1982
Tchaikovsky, Peter	Francesca da Rimini	LP	Philips	6500643	1974
Tchaikovsky, Peter	Francesca da Rimini	LP	London	CS6841	1974
Verdi, Giuseppe	Quattro pezzi sacri	LP	His Master's Voice	SXLP 30508	1980
Verdi, Giuseppe	Quattro pezzi sacri	Cassette	EMI	TC-ASD 1435724	1983
Verdi, Giuseppe	Quattro pezzi sacri	LP	His Master's Voice	S36125	1980
Verdi, Giuseppe	Quattro pezzi sacri	CD	EMI	CDC 7470662	1983
Verdi, Giuseppe	Quattro pezzi sacri	LP	Stimme Seines Herrn	1 C06500016	1963
Verdi, Giuseppe	Quattro pezzi sacri	LP	Decca	DL9661	1952
Verdi, Giuseppe	Quattro pezzi sacri	LP	London	OS 26176	1970
Verdi, Giuseppe	Quattro pezzi sacri	CD	Erato	ECD 88170	1986
Vivier, Claude	Lettura di Dante	LP	Radio Canada International	RCI 411	1975
Woyrsch, Felix	Symphonic Prologue	CD	MDG Gold	MDG 329 0588-2	1995
Zandonai, Riccardo	Francesca da Rimini	CD	First edition records		1975
Zandonai, Riccardo	Francesca da Rimini	CD	Decca	DECC 0436301 2da	1993
Zandonai, Riccardo	Francesca da Rimini	CD	RCA	RCA 40902661 2362	1992

Reference Works

Bibliographies

Evola, Niccolò Domenico. *Bibliografia dantesca (1920–1930)*. Florence: Olschki, 1932.

Wieruszowski, Hélène. *Bibliografia dantesca (1931–1937)*. In *Giornale dantesco* 39 (1938), 341–410.

———. *Bibliografia dantesca (1938–1939 e supplemento 1937)*. In *Giornale dantesco* 41 (1940), 219–250.

Vallone, Aldo. *Gli studi danteschi dal 1940 al 1949*. Florence: Olschki, 1950.

Esposito, Enzo. *Bibliografia analitica degli scritti su Dante 1950–1970*. Florence: Olschki, 1990.

Compendia

The following reference works include concordances, dictionaries, encyclopedias, and inventories of artists' illustrations:

Brieger, Peter, Millard Meiss, and Charles S. Singleton. *Illuminated Manuscripts of the Divine Comedy*. 2 vols. Princeton: Princeton University Press, 1969.

Bosco, Umberto (dir.). *Enciclopedia dantesca*. 6 vols. Rome: Istituto dell'Enciclopedia Italiana, 1970–1978.

Gordon, Lewis H. *Supplementary Concordance to the Minor Works of Dante*. Cambridge, Mass.: Harvard University Press, 1936.

Lovera, Luciano (ed.). *Concordanza della Commedia di Dante Alighieri*. 3 vols. Turin: Einaudi, 1975.

Nassar, Eugene Paul. *Illustrations to Dante's "Inferno."* Rutherford-Madison-Teaneck, New Jersey: Fairleigh Dickinson University Press, 1994.

Toynbee, Paget. *A Dictionary of Proper Names and Other Notable Matters in the Works of Dante*. Revised by Charles S. Singleton. Oxford: Clarendon Press, 1968.

Rand, Edward Kennard, and Ernest Hatch Wilkins (eds.). *Dantis Alagherii Operum Latinorum Concordantiae*. Oxford: Clarendon Press, 1912.

Roglieri, Maria Ann. *Dante and Music*. Aldershot, Eng.: Ashgate Press, 2000.

Sheldon, E. S., and A. C. White (eds.). *Concordanza delle Opere Italiane in Prosa e del Canzoniere di Dante Alighieri*. Oxford: Oxford University Press, 1905.

Taylor, Charles H. and Patricia Finley. *Images of the Journey in Dante's "Divine Comedy."* New Haven and London: Yale University Press, 1997.

Wilkins, Ernest Hatch, and Thomas G. Bergin (eds.). *A Concordance to the "Divine Comedy" of Dante Alighieri*. Cambridge, Mass.: Harvard University Press, 1966.

Journals

The following journals currently publish annual issues devoted exclusively to Dante criticism:

Dante Studies, edited by Christopher Kleinhenz and published for the Dante Society of America by Fordham University Press.

Deutsches Dante-Jahrbuch, edited by Marcella Roddewig and published by Böhlau Verlag (Cologne).

L'Alighieri, edited by Aldo Vallone and published by Longo Editore (Ravenna).

Letture Classensi, published by Longo Editore (Ravenna)

Studi danteschi, edited by Francesco Mazzoni and published by the Società Dantesca Italiana.

Electronic Resources

The following resources are available on-line and may be accessed via the Internet:

The American Dante Bibliography: www.brandeis.edu/library/dante/

The Dartmouth Dante Project: www.princeton.edu/~dante

Digital Dante: www.ilt.columbia.edu/projects/dante/

EBDSA (Electronic Bulletin of the Dante Society of America): www.princeton.edu/~dante

Italica: www.italica.rai.it/3d/4livello/facolta/dante/
f_dante.htm

Otfried Lieberknecht's Homepage for Dante Studies:
members.aol.com/lieberk/welcome.html

The Princeton Dante Project: www.princeton.edu/
~dante

Renaissance Dante in Print (1472-1629):
www.italnet.nd.edu/Dante/

The World of Dante: jefferson.village.virginia.edu/
dante/

Index of Italian and Latin Proper Names in Dante's Works

This index lists all Italian and Latin proper names appearing in Dante's works. Entries reflect spellings as they appear in the original texts (in the editions cited in the Preface), not modern usage. It includes many, if not all, indirect or implied references. The citation of loci is selective and is not exhaustive. All major and primary occurrences are cited, including at least one occurrence from each canticle of the *Commedia* and at least one from each of the minor works. Accents serve to indicate the syllable accented in pronunciation and are not part of the normal spelling of the term, unless the accented vowel is terminal. Unaccented words have their stress on the penultimate syllable, as is the norm in Italian. Parentheses are used to indicate alternative forms, including the Latin form of an Italian name. Brackets are used to indicate the main locus of an entry in this index.

Aghinolfo da Romena one of the Conti Guidi, encouraged Maestro Adamo to counterfeit the florin; *Inf.* 30.77

Aggregazioni de le stelle, Libro de l' the *Elementa astronomica* of Alfraganus; *Conv.* 2.5.16

Aglàuro Aglauros, daughter of Cecrops, king of Athens; *Purg.* 14.139

Agli, Lotto degli Florentine judge who hanged himself after delivering an unjust judgment; perhaps referred to in *Inf.* 13.151

Agnèl (Agnolo, Agnolello, Agnello) Agnello Brunelleschi, Florentine damned among the thieves in Malebolge; *Inf.* 25.68

Agnus Dei prayer, part of the Mass ("Lamb of God") *Purg.* 16.19

Agòbbio Gubbio, town in central Italy; *Purg.* 11.80

Agostino [Augustino]

Aguglión castle in the Val di Pesa Valley in Tuscany; *Par.* 16.56

Aiace Ajax, Homeric hero, son of Telamon; *Conv.* 4.27.20

Alagherius [Alighieri]

Alàgia dei Fieschi daughter of Niccolò dei Fieschi of Genoa; *Purg.* 19.142

Alagna Anagni, town in Latium forty miles SE. of Rome; *Purg.* 20.86; *Par.* 30.148

Alamània Germany; *Inf.* 20.62

Alamanni (Alamani) Germans; *DVE* 1.8.9

Alardo Érard de Valéry, counselor to Charles I of Anjou; *Inf.* 28.18

Alba Alba Longa, oldest town in Latium; *Par.* 6.37

Albani Albans, inhabitants of Alba Longa; *Conv.* 4.5.18; *Mon.* 2.3.16

Albano Alban; *Mon.* 2.9.15

Alberichi ancient noble family of Florence; *Par.* 16.89

Alberigo di Ugolino dei Manfredi, frate Friar Alberigo, one of the Jovial friars of the Manfredi family; *Inf.* 33.109

Àlbero (Alberto) da Siena son or protégé of a bishop of Siena; *Inf.* 29.109

Alberti, counts of Mangona [Alberto, Alessandro, Napoleone, Orso degli Alberti]

Alberti, frati plural of proper name "frate Alberto"; *Rime* 99.10

Alberto tedesco Albert I of Austria, son of Rudolf I of Habsburg; *Purg.* 6.97; *Par.* 19.115; *Conv.* 4.3.6

Alberto Camiscione dei Pazzi [Camiscìon dei Pazzi]

Alberto da Casalodi [Casalodi]

Alberto d'Agimoro friar, considered hypocritical; *Fiore* 88.13

Alberto degli Alberti count of Mangona; *Inf.* 32.57

Alberto della Scala lord of Verona; *Purg.* 18.121

Alberto Magno (Alberto de la Magna, Alberto di Cologna) Albertus Magnus (or Albert of Cologne), Domenican philosopher, master of St. Thomas; *Par.* 10.98

Albi [Bianchi]

Àlbia the river Elbe, N. of Bohemia; *Purg.* 7.99

Albuino (Alboino) de la Scala lord of Verona; *Conv.* 4.16.6

Albumasàr Albumazar, Arab astronomer; *Conv.* 2.13.22

Alcide Alcides, i.e., Ercule (Ercole) Hercules; *Par.* 9.101; *Epist.* 7.20

Àlcimus high priest appointed by Demestrius I, king of Syria; *Epist.* 11.8

Alcithoè daughter of Minyas of Boeotia; *Epist.* 3.7

Alderotto [Taddeo di Alderotto]

Aldighiero [Alighieri]

Aldobrandeschi ancient and powerful Ghibelline family [**Guiglielmo, Omberto, Santafiora**]

Aldobrandi, Tegghiàio Florentine Guelf of the powerful Adimari family; *Inf.* 6.79

Aldobrandino de' Mezzabati [Ildebrandinus Paduanus]

Alena [Èlana]

Alepri Florentine family; *Par.* 16.127

Alessàndria town in Piedmont on the Tanaro; *Purg.* 7.135

Alessandro da Romena Alexander I, count of Romena *Inf.* 30.77

Alessandro da Romena Alexander II, count of Romena *Epist.* 2.1

Alessandro degli Alberti son of Alberto degli Alberti; *Inf.* 32.57

Alessandro di Fere in Tessàglia Alexander, tyrant of Pherae; possibly referred to at *Inf.* 12.107

Alessandro Magno Alexander the Great of Macedon; *Inf.* 14.31; *Conv.* 4.11.4; *DVE* 2.1.2; *Mon.* 2.8.8; possibly referred to at *Inf.* 12.107

Alessandro Novello bishop of Feltre; *Par.* 9.53

Alèssio Interminei (Interminelli) noble of Lucca; *Inf.* 18.122

Aletto Alecto, one of the three Furies; *Inf.* 9.47

Alexis shepherd adapted from Virgil's *Eclogues; Egl.* 3.8, 56

Alexander [Alessandro]

Alfagrano Alfraganus, Arab astronomer; *Conv.* 2.13.11

Alfonso III king of Aragon, placed in the Ante-Purgatory; *Purg.* 7.116

Alfonso VIII king of Castile, an example of liberality; *Conv.* 4.11.14

Alfraganus [Alfagrano]

Algazèl Arab philosopher and theologian; *Conv.* 2.13.5

Alì Ali, fourth of the Caliphs or successors of Muhammad; *Inf.* 28.32

Alichino one of the ten demons in the fifth bolgia of Malebolge; *Inf.* 21.118

Alighieri family name of Dante; *Par.* 15.138; *Epist.* 2; *Quest.* 1.87

Alighiero I son of Cacciaguida and Dante's great-grandfather; *Par.* 15.91

Alighiero II (Alaghieri) Dante's father; *Rime* 74.8

Almeone Alcmaeon, son of Amphiaraus; *Purg.* 12.50; *Par.* 4.103

Alpe the Alps, mountain chain in northern Italy; *Inf.* 20.62; *Par.* 6.51

Alpe the Apennine mountains; *Inf.* 16.101; *Rime* 116.61

Alpetràgio Alpetragius, al-Bitrudiji Nur al-Din Abu Ishak, Arab philosopher; *Conv.* 3.2.5

Alphesibeus Alphesiboeus, shepherd from Virgil; *Egl.* 4.7

Altaforte Hautefort, Bertram de Born's castle in the Limousin; *Inf.* 29.29

Alvèrnia [Petrus de Alvèrnia]

Amalèch Amalek, ancestor of the Amalekites; *Epist.* 7.19

Amàn Haman, minister of Ahasuerus; *Purg.* 17.26

Amata wife of Latinus, king of Latium; *Purg.* 17.35; *Epist.* 7.24

Ambròsius Ambrose, saint; *Epist.* 11.16

Amicìtia, De Cicero's treatise *On Friendship; Conv.* 1.12.3

Àmiclas (Amiclate) Amyclas, renowned for poverty in Lucan's *Pharsalia; Par.* 11.68; *Conv.* 4.13.12

Amidei noble Florentine family at the heart of early civil strife in Florence; *Par.* 16.136

Amos father of the prophet Isaiah; *Epist.* 7.7

Amphitrite daughter of Oceanus and wife of Neptune; *Epist.* 7.12; *Quest.* 31

Amore Love, i.e, Cupid; *VN* 25.1; *Conv.* 2.5.14

Anagni [Alagna]

Analỳtica Priora the *Prior Analytics,* treatise of Aristotle; *Mon.* 3.7.3

Ananìa (1) Ananias, husband of Sapphira (Safira), example of avarice; *Purg.* 20.112

Ananìa (2) Ananias, disciple of Christ at Damascus who healed Paul's blindness; *Par.* 26.12

Anassàgora Anaxagoras, Greek philosopher of the Ionian school; *Inf.* 4.137

Anastagi noble Ghibelline family of Ravenna; *Purg.* 14.107

Anastàsio Pope Anastasius II, placed among the heretics in Hell; *Inf.* 11.8

Anchise Anchises, father of Aeneas, *Inf.* 1.74; *Purg.* 18.137; *Par.* 15.25; *Conv.* 4.26.9; *Mon.* 2.6.9

Anco Ancus Marcius, fourth king of Rome; *Conv.* 4.5.11; *Par.* 6.41

Ancona [Màrchia Anconitana]

Anconitani inhabitants of the March of Ancona; *DVE* 1.10.8

Andalò, Loderingo degli [Loderingo]

Andolfo Adolf of Nassau, emperor 1292–1298; *Conv.* 4.3.6

Andrea de' Mozzi bishop of Florence and then Vicenza; *Inf.* 15.112

Andrea III Andrew III, king of Hungary; *Par.* 19.142

Andròmache daughter of Eetion; *Mon.* 2.3.14

Anfiarao Amphiaraus, prophet and hero of Argos *Inf.* 20.31; *Par.* 4.104

Anfione Amphion, son of Jupiter, helped build the walls of Thebes; *Inf.* 32.11

Àngeli angels, the lowest order of angels, who preside over the Heaven of the Moon; *Conv.* 2.5.6; *Par.* 28.126

Àngeli neutral fallen angels; *Inf.* 3.37

Àngeli rebellious fallen angels; *Inf.* 7.11; *Conv.* 3.12.9

Àngeli the nine hierarchies of angels or Angelic Intelligences; *Par.* 28.212; *Conv.* 2.5.5 [Angeli, Arcangeli, Troni, Dominazioni, Virtuti, Principati, Potestati, Cherubini, Serafini]

Angiò Anjou [Beatrice, Carlo I, Carlo II, Roberto]

Angiolello di Carignano nobleman of Fano; *Inf.* 28.77

Angiolieri [Cecco Angiolieri]

Ànglia [Inghilterra]

Ànglici [Inghilesi]

Ànglicum mare the English channel; *DVE* 1.8.9

Anibàl (Anibale) Hannibal, Carthaginian general; *Inf.* 31.117; *Par.* 6.50

Ànima, De Aristotle's treatise *On the Soul; Conv.* 2.8.9; *Mon.* 1.3.9

Ànime, De Quantitate Augustine's *On the Capacity of the Soul; Epist.* 13.80

Animali, De li Aristotle's books on animals, quoted in *Conv.* 2.3.2, 2.8.10

Animàlium, De Generatione Aristotle's treatise *On the Generation of Animals; Quest.* 28

Anna St. Anne, mother of the Virgin Mary; *Par.* 32.133

Anna Annas, father-in-law of Caiaphas; *Inf.* 23.121

Anselmo, Sant', d'Aosta St. Anselm, archbishop of Canterbury 1093-1109; *Inf.* 33.50; *Par.* 12.137

Anselmùccio grandson of Count Ugolino della Gherardesca of Pisa, *Inf.* 33.50

Antandro Antandros, city of Mysia; *Par.* 6.67

Antenora second of the four divisions of Cocytus; *Inf.* 32.88

Antenori [Padovani]

Anteo Antaeus, giant son of Neptune and Terra; *Inf.* 31.100; *Mon.* 2.7.10; *Conv.* 3.3.7

Antheus [Anteo]

Anticthona Antichthon, i.e., the "counter-earth," corresponding sphere opposite Earth according to Pythagoras; *Conv.* 3.5.4

Antifonte Antiphon, Greek tragic poet; *Purg.* 22.106

Antìgone daughter of Oedipus; *Purg.* 22.110

Antìoco Antiochus IV Epiphanes, king of Syria; *Inf.* 19.87

Antònio, Sant' St. Anthony the Great, Egyptian hermit, founder of monastic institutions; *Par.* 29.124

Anubis Egyptian divinity identified with Mercury by Romans; *Epist.* 7.17

Aonides [Muse]

Aònius Aonian; *montes Aonii,* the range of Mt. Helicon in Boeotia; *Egl.* 2.28

Apennino the Apennine mountains, in Italy; *Inf.* 16.96; *Purg.* 5.96

Apocalisse the Apocalypse or Revelation of St. John; *Inf.* 19.106; *Purg.* 29.143; *Epist.*13.90

Apollo son of Jupiter and Latona; *Purg.* 12.31; *Par.* 1.13

Apòstoli the twelve apostles; *Purg.* 22.78; *Par.* 24.137

Àpuli [Pugliesi]

Apùlia [Pùglia]

Aqua et terra, Questio de [Questio de aqua et terra]

Aquàrio Aquarius, constellation and eleventh sign of the Zodiac; *Inf.* 24.2

Aquilegienses inhabitants of Aquileia in Venetian territory; *DVE* 1.10.8

Aquilone Aquilo, the N. wind; *Purg.* 4.60

Aquino [Renaldus de Aquino]

Aquino, Tommaso d' [Tommaso]

Àrabi [Cartaginesi]

Aràbia Arabia, country above the Red Sea; *Inf.* 24.90; *Par.* 6.79; *VN* 29.1

Arcàdia country in the Peloponnesus; *Egl.* 2.11

Aragne Arachne, i.e., "spider," excelled in weaving, challenged Minerva; *Inf.* 17.18; *Purg.* 12.43

Aragona Aragon, one of the old kingdoms of Spain; *Purg.* 3.116

Aragones inhabitants of Aragon; *Mon.* 1.11.12

Aratòr [Uguccione della Faggiuola]

Àrbia small stream of Tuscany; *Inf.* 10.86

Arca, De l' Florentine family; *Par.* 16.92

Àrcade Arcas (Boote), son of Helice and Jupiter, constellation of the Little Bear; *Par.* 31.33

Arcàngeli Archangels, second lowest order of the celestial hierarchies; *Conv.* 2.5.6; *Par.* 28.125

Archades inhabitants of Arcadia; *Egl.* 3.21

Archiano tributary of the Arno in Tuscany; *Purg.* 5.95

Archimoro Son of Licurgo; *Purg.* 26.94; *Conv.* 3.11.16

Arcippe [Leucippe]

Ardinghi ancient noble family of Florence; *Par.* 16.93

Aretini Aretines, inhabitants of Arezzo; *Inf.* 22.5

Aretusa Arethusa, one of the Nereids; *Inf.* 25.97

Arezzo city in southeast Tuscany; *Inf.* 29.109

Argenti, Filippo one of the Cavicciuli branch of the Adimari family of Florence; *Inf.* 8.32

Argi Argives, inhabitants of Argos; also Argos, the city; *Epist.* 5.24

Argia daughter of Adrastus, king of Argos; *Purg.* 22.110

Argo the ship *Argo* built by Argus and sailed by Jason; *Par.* 33.96

Argo Argus, son of Arestor, having one hundred eyes; *Purg.* 29.95

Argòlico *gente argolica,* meaning the Greeks; *Inf.* 28.84

Argonàuti Argonauts, sailors of the *Argo*

Arianna Ariadne, daughter of Minos and Pasiphae, fell in love with Theseus; *Inf.* 12.20; *Par.* 13.14

Aries fluvialis [Montone]

Ariete Aries, the Ram, constellation and the first sign of the Zodiac; *Par.* 28.117; *Conv.* 3.5.13; *Rime* 100.41

Àrio [Àrrio]

Aristòtele [Aristòtile]

Aristòtile Aristotle, the Greek philosopher; *Conv.* 1.1.1; *Inf.* 4.131; *DVE* 2.6.2; *Mon.* 1.1.4; *Quest.* 24

Arli Arles, town in Provence; *Inf.* 9.112

Arnaldo Daniello Arnaut Daniel, Provençal poet; *Purg.* 26.142; *DVE* 2.2.8

Arnaut [Arnaldo Daniello]

Arno principal river of Tuscany; *Inf.* 13.146; *Purg.* 5.126; *Par.* 11.106

Aronta Aruns, Etruscan soothsayer; *Inf.* 20.46

Arpie Harpies, avian monsters; *Inf.* 13.10

Arrigo unknown Florentine; *Inf.* 6.80

Arrigo Prince Henry, second son of Henry II of England; *Inf.* 28.135

Arrigo Henry II, King of England; *Inf.* 28.136

Arrigo Prince Henry of Cornwall; *Inf.* 12.119

Arrigo I di Navarra Henry I of Navarre, the "Fat," father-in-law of Philip the Fair; *Purg.* 7.104

Arrigo II di Sassonia Emperor Henry II of Saxony; *Conv.* 3.4.8

Arrgio II Henry II of Lusignan, king of Cyprus; *Par.* 19.147

Arrigo III d'Inghilterra Henry III of England; *Purg.* 7.131

Arrigo VI Emperor Henry VI of Swabia, son of Frederick Barbarossa; *Par.* 3.119

Arrigo VII (Henricus) Henry VII of Luxemburg; *Par.* 17.82, 30.137; *Epist.* 5.5;

Arrigo Mainardi nobleman of Bertinoro (Romagna), referred to by Guido del Duca; *Purg.* 14.97

Arrigucci ancient noble family of Florence; *Par.* 16.108

Àrrio Arius, originator of the Arian heresy; *Par.* 13.127

Arte Vecchia e Nuova Ars vetus and *Ars nova,* dialectical treatises by Aristotle; *Conv.* 2.13.12

Arzanà the Arsenal shipyard at Venice; *Inf.* 21.7

Artù Arthur, mythical king of Britain; *Inf.* 32.62; also as Arturus; *DVE* 1.10.2

Ascànio Ascanius, son of Aeneas and Creusa; *Conv.* 4.26.11; *Epist.* 7.18

Ascesi Assisi, town in Umbria; *Par.* 11.53

Asciano [Càccia d'Asciano]

Àscoli [Cecco d'Àscoli]

Asdente shoemaker of Parma and soothsayer; *Inf.* 20.118

Àsia continent, *DVE* 1.8; *Mon.* 2.3.8

Asiani (Asiàtici) Asiatics, inhabitants of Asia, *Mon.* 3.14.7

Asopo Asopus, river in Boeotia; *Purg.* 18.91

Assàracus king of Troy, son of Tros, grandfather of Anchises; *Mon.* 2.3.10

Assiri Assyrians, people of Asia Minor; *Purg.* 12.59

Assisi [Ascesi]

Assuero Ahasuerus, king of Persia; *Purg.* 17.25

Astrea Astraea, daughter of Jupiter and Themis; *Mon.* 1.11.1; *Purg.* 22.71

Atamante Athamas, king of Orchomenus in Boeotia; *Inf.* 30.4

Atene Athens, capital of Attica; *Purg.* 6.139; *Par.* 17.46

Athalanta Atalanta, Boeotian maiden; *Mon.* 2.7.10

Athlantis Electra, daughter of Atlas; *Mon.* 2.3.11

Athlas Atlas, son of Iapetus and Clymene; *Mon.* 2.3.11; *Conv.* 4.29.4

Atiopia [Etiopia]

Atropòs Atropos, one of the three Fates; *Inf.* 33.126

Àttila king of the Huns; *Inf.* 12.134; *Inf.* 13.149 **[Totila]**

Augustino (Augustinus) St. Augustine, greatest of fathers of the Latin Church; *Par.* 10.120; *Conv.* 1.2.14, 4.28.9; *Mon.* 3.3.13; *Epist.* 13.80

Augustino Augustine, one of the first disciples of St. Francis; *Par.* 12.130

Augusto (Augustus) Gaio Julio Cesare Ottaviano, Emperor Augustus; *Inf.* 1.71; *Purg.* 7.6; *Par.* 6.73; *Epist.* 5.24; *Mon.* 1.16.1

Àulide Aulis, port in Boeotia; *Inf.* 20.111

Aurora goddess of dawn; *Purg.* 2.8; *Par.* 30.7

Ausònia ancient name for Italy in general, and in particular for the area comprising the kingdom of Naples (Campania, Puglia, Calabria); *Par.* 8.61; *Mon* 2.11.8

Auster [Austro]

Àustria [Osterlicchi]

Àustro Auster, southern wind; *Purg.* 31.72

Aventino Mt. Aventine, one of the seven hills of Rome; *Inf.* 25.26

Avellana, Fonte Benedictine monastery of Santa Croce di Fonte Avellana; *Par.* 21.110

Averroè [Averoìs]

Averoìs Averroës, celebrated Arab scholar, commentator of Aristotle; *Inf.* 4.144; *Purg.* 25.63; *Conv.* 4.13.8; *Quest.* 12

Avicenna Arab philosopher and physician of Ispahan in Persia; *Inf.* 4.143

Azzo, Ugolìn d' native of Tuscany, resident of Faenza; *Purg.* 14.105

Azzo da Esti Azzo VIII of Este, son of Obizzo II; *Inf.* 12.112; *Purg.* 5.77

Azzolino Ezzelino II da Romano, father of Ezzelino III; *Par.* 9.31

Azzolino Ezzelino III da Romano, son of Ezzelino II and Adeleita degli Alberti di Mangona; *Inf.* 12.110; *Par.* 9.29

Babèl the tower of Babel; *Purg.* 12.34; *Par.* 26.125

Babilòn kingdom of Babylon; *Par.* 23.135

Babilònii (Babilonesi) Babylonians; *Epist.* 6.8

Bacchiglione river of N. Italy; *Inf.* 15.113; *Par.* 9.47

Bacco (Baco) Bacchus, god of wine; *Inf.* 20.59; *Purg.* 18.93; *Par.* 13.25

Bagnacavàl Bagnacavallo, town in Romagna; *Purg.* 14.115

Bagnorègio Bagnorea, village in Italy near Lake Bolsena; *Par.* 12.128

Bàlaam prophet, son of Beor, saved by his speaking ass; *DVE* 1.2.6; *Epist.* 11.18

Baldo d'Aguglione politician, prior of Florence; *Par.* 16.56

Barbàgia mountainous region in central Sardinia; *Purg.* 23.94

Barbarìccia leader of the ten demons in the fifth bolgia of Malebolge; *Inf.* 21.120

Barbarossa [Federigo I]

Barga village near Lucca; *Fiore* 156.13

Bari town of S. Italy in Apulia; *Par.* 8.62

Barone, il gran [Ugo di Brandeburgo]

Bartolomeo de' Folcacchieri [Abbagliato]

Bartolomeo della Scala [Lombardo, gran]

Bartolomeo Mocati [Minus Mocatus]

Bartolomeo Pignatelli Archbishop of Cosenza; *Purg.* 3.124

Barucci Florentine family; *Par.* 16.104

Batifolle (Battifolle), Gherardesca di Countess G[herardesca] di Battifolle, in whose name Dante addressed three letters to Empress Margherita di Brabante; *Epist.* 8.1, 9.1, 10.1

Batista [Giovanni Battista]

Batisteo baptistery of San Giovanni at Florence; *Inf.* 19.17; *Par.* 15.124

Beatrice Beatrice Portinari, Dante's inspiration; *Inf.* 2.70; *Purg.* 30.124

Beatrice d'Angiò daughter of Charles II of Naples, married Azzo VIII; *Purg.* 20.80

Beatrice d'Este wife of Nino Visconti of Pisa and later of Galeazzo Visconti of Milan; *Purg.* 8.73

Beatrice di Provenza daughter of Raymond Berenger IV, count of Provence; *Purg.* 7.128; *Par.* 6.133; *Par.* 6.134

Beccheria Tesauro di Beccheria, abbot of Vallombrosa and legate in Florence; *Inf.* 32.119

Beda the Venerable Bede, English theologian; *Par.* 10.131

Belàcqua probably Ducio di Bonavia, a Florentine lutenist; *Purg.* 4.98

Belenoi [Belnui]

Belisàr Belisarius, celebrated general of the Emperor Justinian; *Par.* 6.25

Bella [Giano della Bella]

Bellinciòn Berti de' Ravignani Florentine citizen; *Par.* 15.112

Bello Geri del Bello degli Alighieri, grandson of Alighiero I; *Inf.* 29.27

Bellondi [Pùccio Bellondi]

Belluzzo Bello di Bellincione, Dante's paternal uncle; *Rime* 76.11

Belnui [Namericus de Belnui]

Belo Belus, king of Tyre, father of Dido; *Par.* 9.97

Beltramo dal Bòrnio [Bertràm dal Bòrnio]

Belzebù Beelzebub **[Lucìfero]**

Benaco Lacus Benacus, Latin name for Lake Garda; *Inf.* 20.63

Bene [Sennùccio del Bene]

Benedetto V Benedict V, pope, 964; *Mon.* 3.9.3

Benedetto XI Benedict XI (Niccolò Boccasini), elected pope 1303; *Epist.* 11.25

Benedetto, San St. Benedict of Nursia, founder of the Montecassino monastery; *Par.* 22.28; *Conv.* 4.28.9

Benevento town near Naples in Campania; *Purg.* 3.128

Benincasa da Laterina jurist avenged by Ghino di Tacco; *Purg.* 6.13

Benivento [Benevento]

Bentivenga [Matteo d'Acquasparta]

Berengario IV [Beringhieri, Ramondo]

Bergamaschi (Pergamei) Bergamates (Bergamese), inhabitants of Bergamo; *Inf.* 20.71; *DVE* 1.11.4

Bergamo [Pergamum]

Beringhieri, Ramondo Raymond Berenger IV, last count of Provence; *Par.* 6.133

Bernardin di Fosco citizen of Faenza, defended the city against Emperor Federico II; *Purg.* 14.101

Bernardo da Bologna Bernard of Bologna; *Rime dubbie,* 10.1

Bernardo da Quintavalle Bernard of Quintavalle of Assisi, disciple of St. Francis; *Par.* 11.79

Bernardo (Bernardus) di Chiaravalle, San St. Bernard of Clairvaux, French monk and theologian; *Par.* 31.59

Bernardone Pietro Bernardone, father of St. Francis; *Par.* 11.58

Berta Bertha, first name used to indicate a woman of modest disposition; *DVE* 2.6.5; *Par.* 13.139

Berti [Bellincion Berti]

Bertinoro [Brettinoro]

Bertràm dal Bòrnio (Bertramus de Bòrnio, Beltramo) Bertran de Born, Provençal poet; *Inf.* 28.118

Bianca Blanche, perhaps Bianca Giovanna, daughter of count Guido Novello; *Rime* 106.153

Bianchi "the Whites," Guelf political faction headed by the Cerchi in Florence; *Inf.* 6.6, 24.143

Biante Bias of Priene, sage from Priene in Ionia; *Conv.* 3.11.4

Bìbbia (la Scrittura, le Scritture, Bìblia, Scripturae, Sacrae Lìtterae) the Bible, the Old and New Testaments; *Conv.* 4.5.16; *Par.* 4.43

Bicci [Forese]

Bice abbreviated form of Beatrice; *Rime* 21.9; *VN* 24.8

Bilància, la [Libra]

Bindo masculine first name, common in Florence; *Par.* 29.103

Bisenzo (Bisènzio) the Bisenzio, tributary of the Arno; *Inf.* 32.56

Bismàntova mountain in the Apennine range S. of Reggio Emilia; *Purg.* 4.26

Bocca degli Abati Florentine citizen who betrayed the Guelfs; *Inf.* 32.106

Boemme (Boèmia) Bohemia, region in Europe; *Par.* 19.125 **[Vincislao]**

Boèzio (Boètius) Boethius (Anicius Manlius Severinus), Roman senator and philosopher; *Conv.* 1.2.13; *Par.* 10.125; *Mon.* 1.9.3; *Epist.* 13.33

Bologna (Bonònia) city; *Inf.* 18.61; *Purg.* 14.100

Bolognese, Franco Franco of Bologna, illuminator mentioned by Oderisi; *Purg.* 11.83

Bolognesi (Bononienses) the Bolognese, inhabitants of Bologna; *Inf.* 18.58; *DVE* 1.15.6

Bolsena lake near Viterbo; *Purg.* 24.24

Bonaccolsi [Pinamonte Bonaccolsi]

Bonagiunta Orbicciani degli Overardi notary and poet of Lucca; *Purg.* 24.19

Bonatti Guido Bonatti, famous astrologer and soothsayer of Forlì; *Inf.* 20.118

Bonaventura da Bagnorègio, San St. Bonaventura (Giovanni Fidanza) Franciscan monk and theologian; *Par.* 12.127

Bonconte da Montefeltro Buonconte da Montefeltro, son of Guido, one of the heads of the Ghibelline faction; *Purg.* 5.88

Bondelmonte [Buondelmonte]

Bondelmonti Florentine family; *Par.* 16.66

Bonifàzio dei Fieschi archbishop of Ravenna 1274–1294; *Inf.* 19.53; *Purg.* 24.29

Bonifàzio I marquis of Montferrat; *Conv.* 4.11.14

Bonifàzio VIII Boniface VIII (Benedetto Caetani), elected pope in 1294; *Inf.* 19.53; *Purg.* 20.87; *Par.* 30.148

Bonifàzio de' Morubaldini [Fàzio Morubaldini]

Bonònia [Bologna]

Bononienses [Bolognesi]

Bonsignori [Niccolò de' Bonsignori]

Bonturo Dati leader of the popular faction in Lucca; *Inf.* 21.41

Boote [Àrcade]

Bòrea Boreas, wind that blows from the north; *Par.* 28.81

Borgo Borgo Santi Apostoli, district in Florence; *Par.* 16.134

Borgo San Felice [Burgum Sancti Felicis]

Borneilh (Bornello) [Giraut de Borneilh]

Bòrnio [Bertràm dal Bòrnio]

Borsiere Guglielmo Borsiere, Florentine placed among the sodomites; *Inf.* 16.70

Bostichi noble Florentine family; *Par.* 16.93

Bougie [Buggea]

Brabante Brabant, ancient duchy of the Netherlands; *Purg.* 6.23

Brabante, Maria di Marie of Brabant, second wife of Philip III; *Purg.* 6.23

Branca d'Òria nobleman from Genova; *Inf.* 33.137

Branda, Fonte fountain at Siena near church of San Domenico; *Inf.* 30.78

Brandeburgo [Ugo di Brandeburgo]

Brandìzio Brindisi (Brundusium), town on the Adriatic in Puglia; *Purg.* 3.27

Brenno Brennus, commander of the Senonian Gauls; *Par.* 6.44

Brenta river of Upper Italy; *Inf.* 15.7; *Par.* 9.27

Brèscia (Brixia) town in Lombardy; *Inf.* 20.68

Bresciani (Brixienses, Brixiani) Brescians, inhabitants of Brescia; *Inf.* 20.71; *DVE* 1.14.5

Bretinoro (Bertinoro) city in Romagna; *Purg.* 14.112

Briareo Briareus or Aegaeon, son of Uranus and Earth; *Inf.* 31.98; *Purg.* 12.28

Brigata, il nickname of Nino della Gherardesca; *Inf.* 33.89

Brìndisi [Brandìzio]

Brisso Bryson, Greek philosopher and mathematician; *Par.* 13.125

Brixia [Brèscia]

Brixienses, Brixiani [Bresciani]

Bròccia, Pier da la Pierre de la Brosse, French surgeon; *Purg.* 6.22

Bròmius "the noisy one," surname of Bacchus; *Egl.* 4.53

Brùggia Bruges, city in Flanders; *Inf.* 15.4; *Purg.* 20.46

Brunèl, de [Giraut de Borneilh]

Brunelleschi [Agnèl Brunelleschi]

Brunetto perhaps Brunetto Brunelleschi, gentleman and ambassador of Florence; *Rime* 99

Brunetto Latino (Brunettus Florentinus) Florentine Guelf; *Inf.* 15.30

Bruto Lucius Junius Brutus, led the revolt against Tarquinius Superbus; *Inf.* 4.127; *Conv.* 4.5.12

Bruto Marcus Junius Brutus, headed the conspiracy against Caesar; *Inf.* 34.65; *Par.* 6.74

Bucciola Ugolino (Ugolinus) Bucciola, Guelf, member of Manfredi family; *DVE* 1.14.3

Bucòlica (Bucòlica carmina) the *Bucolics* or *Eclogues* of Virgil; *Purg.* 22.57

Buggea (Bougia, Bougie) Algerian city; *Par.* 9.92

Buiamonte, Giovanni Florentine usurer of the Becchi family; *Inf.* 17.72

Bulicame hot springs near Viterbo; *Inf.* 14.79

Buonconte [Bonconte]

Buondelmonte Buondelmonte dei Buondelmonti, Florentine whose death sparked conflict between the Guelfs and the Ghibellines; *Par.* 16.140

Buondelmonti [Bondelmonti]

Buoso di Forese di Vinciguerra Donati a thief in Malebolge; *Inf.* 25.35, 26.4

Buoso Donati Florentine son of Vinciguerra di Donato del Pazzo, uncle of Gianni Schicchi; *Inf.* 30.44

Buoso da Duera Ghibelline of Cremona; *Inf.* 32.106

Burgum Sancti Felicis (Borgo San Felice) quarter of Bologna; *DVE* 1.9.4

Càccia d'Asciano Caccianemico, of the Scialenghi Cacciaconti of Siena, member of the "Spendthrift Club"; *Inf.* 29.131

Cacciaguida Dante's great-great-grandfather; *Par.* 15.19

Caccianemico [Càccia d'Asciano]

Caccianemico, Venèdico Venedico dei Caccianemici dell'Orso, son of Alberto de' Caccianemici; *Inf.* 18.50

Caccume mountain near Frosinone; *Purg.* 4.26

Caco Cacus, satyr son of Vulcan; *Inf.* 25.17

Càdice [Gade]

Cadmo Cadmus, founder of Thebes; *Inf.* 25.97

Caetani inhabitants of Gaeta; *DVE* 1.9.4

Cagioni, Di [Causis, De]

Cagnano small river than runs into the Sile near Treviso; *Par.* 9.49

Cagnazzo "Dogface," one of ten demons of Malebolge; *Inf.* 21.119

Cahors [Caorsa]

Càifa (Càyphas) Caiaphas, high priest of the Hebrews; *Inf.* 23.111; *Mon.* 2.11.6

Caina region of the Inferno that takes its name from Cain; *Inf.* 5.107

Caino Cain, son of Adam and Eve, murderer of his brother Abel; *Inf.* 20.126; *Par.* 2.51

Càiro, Il [Caro, il]

Caïster the Caÿster, river of Asia Minor; *Egl.* 4.18

Càlabri (Calabresi) the inhabitants of Calabria; *DVE* 1.10.6

Calaroga Calaruega, village in Old Castile; *Par.* 12.52

Càlboli [Fulcieri, Rinièr]

Calcabrina one of the ten demons of the fifth bolgia of Malebolge; *Inf.* 21.118

Calcanta (Calcante) Calchas, Greek priest and prophet who accompanied Greeks to Troy; *Inf.* 20.110

Calfucci Florentine family; *Par.* 16.106

Calisto I Calixtus I, bishop of Rome and martyr; *Par.* 27.44

Calliopè Calliope, Muse of epic poetry; *Purg.* 1.9

Camàldoli, Eremo di monastery in the Casentino; *Purg.* 5.96

Camisciòn de' Pazzi, Alberto Alberto (Uberto) Camiscione, member of Ghibelline family of Valdarno; *Inf.* 32.52

Camillus [Cammillo]

Cammilla Camilla, queen of the Volsci; *Inf.* 1.107

Cammillo (Camillus), Marco Furio M. Furius Camillus, Roman patrician; *Conv.* 4.5.15

Camino, Gherardo da captain-general of Treviso, citizen of Padua; *Purg.* 16.124; *Conv.* 4.14.12

Camino, Rizzardo da son of Gherardo da Camino, whom he succeeded as lord of Treviso; *Par.* 9.50

Cammino [Camino]

Camònica [Val Camònica]

Campagnàtico castle belonging to the Aldobrandeschi family; *Purg.* 11.66

Campaldino plains in the Casentino; *Purg.* 5.92

Campi part of Florentine countryside in the Bisenzio valley; *Par.* 16.50

Campidòglio (Capitòlium) the Capitol at Rome; *Conv.* 4.5.18; *Mon.* 2.4.7

Campo di Siena principal piazza of the city; *Purg.* 11.134

Campo Piceno district in Pistoia; *Inf.* 24.148

Canavese region in Piedmont; *Purg.* 7.136

Cancellieri Guelf family of Pistoia; *Inf.* 32.63

Cancro Cancer ("the Crab"), constellation of the Zodiac; *Par.* 25.100; *Conv.* 3.5.14

Cangrande della Scala (Canis Grandis de la Scala, or de Scala) lord of Verona; *Par.* 17.76; *Quest.* 87; *Epist.* 13

Cànticum Canticorum Canticle of Canticles or Song of Solomon; *Mon.* 3.10.8; *Purg.* 29.83

Caorsa Cahors, French city where usury was particularly common; *Inf.* 11.50

Caorsini Cahorsines, inhabitants of Cahors; *Par.* 27.58

Capaneo Capaneus, one of the seven kings who besieged Thebes; *Inf.* 14.46

Capetingi (Capeti) Capetian dynasty of French kings; *Purg.* 20.43

Capitòlium [Campidòglio]

Capòcchio "Blockhead," alchemist of Siena; *Inf.* 29.124

Caponsacchi [Caponsacco]

Caponsacco, il founder of the Florentine family Caponsacchi; *Par.* 16.121

Cappelletti (Capelletti) Guelf party of Cremona; *Purg.* 6.106

Capràia Tyrrhenian island facing the Tuscan coast; *Inf.* 33.82

Capricorno Capricorn, constellation of the Zodiac; *Purg.* 2.56; *Par.* 27.68; *Conv.* 3.5.14

Caprona castle belonging to Pisa; *Inf.* 21.95

Cardinale, il Cardinal Ottaviano degli Ubaldini; placed among the heretics; *Inf.* 10.120

Cariddi Charybdis, part of the Straits of Messina; *Inf.* 7.22

Carignano [Angiolello da Carignano]

Carìnthia [Chiarentana]

Carlino de' Pazzi betrayed the Bianchi family, destined to be punished in Caina; *Inf.* 32.69

Carlo Charles I, king of Naples and Sicily, count of Anjou and Provence; *Inf.* 19.99; *Purg.* 7.113

Carlo Charles II, king of Naples; *Purg.* 5.69; *Par.* 6.106; *Conv.* 4.6.20; *DVE* 1.12.5

Carlo di Lorena Charles, duke of Lorraine, last of the Carolingian line; *Purg.* 20.54

Carlo di Valois Charles of Valois, count from Provence, brother of Philip the Fair, king of France; *Purg.* 20.71

Carlo Magno (Càrolus Magnus) Charlemagne (Charles the Great), restorer of the Empire in the West; *Inf.* 31.17; *Par.* 6.96

Carlo Martello Charles Martel, son of Charles II of Naples and Anjou; *Par.* 8.31

Carlo Roberto Charles Robert (Carobert), son of Charles Martel and king of Hungary, 1308-42; *Par.* 8.67

Carnaro (Quarnaro) Gulf of Quarnero at head of Adriatic sea; *Inf.* 9.113

Caro, il Cairo, city in Egypt; *Detto* 432

Carolingi Carolingian line of French kings (751–987); *Purg.* 20.53

Caron (Caronte) Charon, divinity of the pagan afterlife and infernal demon; *Inf.* 3.83

Carpigna, Guido di one of the counts of Montefeltro; *Purg.* 14.98

Carraresi Carrarese, inhabitants of Carrara; *Inf.* 20.48

Carro, il the Wain, constellation otherwise known as *Ursa Major; Purg.* 1.30; *Par.* 13.7

Cartàgine Carthage, African city on Mediterranean coast; *Conv.* 4.5.14; *Epist.* 11.25

Cartaginesi (Affricani, Arabi, Cartaginenses, Peni) Carthaginians, inhabitants of Carthage; *Par.* 6.49

Casale city in Montferrat (Piedmont); *Par.* 12.124

Casalodi Guelf family of Mantua; *Inf.* 20.95

Càscioli (Càsoli) small town in the Abruzzi; *DVE* 1.11.3

Casella musician of Florence; *Purg.* 2.76

Casentinesi (Casentinenses) inhabitants of Casentino; *DVE* 1.22.6; *Purg.* 14.43

Casentino district in Tuscany; *Inf.* 30.65; *Purg.* 5.94

Càssero, Guido del nobleman of Fano killed by order of Malatestino of Rimini; *Inf.* 28.77

Càssero, Jàcopo del member of the della Berarda family of Fano; *Purg.* 5.64

Cassino site of the first Benedictine monastery; *Par.* 22.37

Càssio (Caio Càssio Longino) Gaius Cassius Longinus, helped head the conspiracy against Caesar; *Inf.* 34.67; *Par.* 6.74

Castàlia spring on Mt. Parnassus; *Purg.* 22.65

Castèl, Guido da nobleman of Reggio; *Purg.* 16.125

Castèl Sant'Àngelo Castle of St. Angelo, the mole of Hadrian; *Inf.* 18.32

Castella (Castìglia) Castile, region in Spain; *Par.* 12.46

Castellana Civitas Civita Castellana, town in province of Viterbo; *DVE* 1.13.2

Castìglia [Castella]

Càstore Castor, twin brother of Pollux; *Purg.* 4.61

Castra Florentine poet; *DVE* 1.11.3

Castrocaro, conti di noblemen of Romagna; *Purg.* 14.116

Catalano dei Malavolti friar Godente of Bologna; *Inf.* 23.104

Catalogna Catalonia (Cataluña), region in Spain; *Par.* 8.77

Catellina Cataline (Lucius Sergius Catilina), Roman conspirator; *Inf.* 25.12; *Conv.* 4.5.19

Catellini noble family of Florence; *Par.* 16.88

Cato [Catone]

Catona village in the most distant part of Calabria; *Par.* 8.62

Catone (Marcus Porcius Cato) Cato the censor (Cato the Elder), Roman patrician; *Conv.* 4.21.9

Catone (Marcus Porcius Cato Uticensis) Cato the Younger, Roman patrician who killed himself so as not to live through the end of the Roman Republic; *Inf.* 14.15; *Purg.* 1.31; *Conv.* 4.27.3

Càtria Mount Catria between Gubbio and Pergola in the Marches; *Par.* 21.109

Cattòlica, La city on the Adriatic coast south of Ancona; *Inf.* 28.80

Càucasus (Caucaso) Mt. Caucasus in Asia; *Epist.* 6.12; *Egl.* 4.22

Caudine Furce Forche Caudine, the Caudine Forks near Caudium; *Mon.* 2.9.17

Càusis, De (Di Cagioni, De le Cagioni) *On Causes,* a work by Proclus attributed to Aristotle; *Conv.* 3.2.4; *Mon.* 1.11.17; *Epist.* 8.57

Cavalcante Cavalcanti Florentine nobleman, father of Guido Cavalcanti; *Inf.* 10.53

Cavalcanti [Cavalcante, Francesco, Guido, Gianni Schicchi]

Càyphas [Càifa]

Cecìlio Cecilius Statius, Roman writer of comedies; *Purg.* 22.98

Cècina river of Tuscany; *Inf.* 13.9

Cèfalo Cephalus, king of Athens; *Conv.* 4.27.17

Cefàs Cephas, Syriac word for "rock," name given by Christ to Simon; *Par.* 21.127

Celesti Hierarchia, De treatise *On the Celestial Hierarchy* by the pseudo-Dionysius the Areopagite; *Epist.* 13.60

Celestino V Celestine V (Pietro da Morrone), elected pope in 1294; *Inf.* 3.59

Celo et Mundo, De (De Caelo, De Coelo) Aristotle's treatise *On the Heavens*; *Conv.* 2.3.4; *Quest.* 25

Celo, De treatise of Albert the Great, known as *De caelo et mundo*; *Conv.* 2.3.5

Centàuri centaurs, mythological creatures that are half man, half horse; *Inf.* 12.56

Ceperano (Ceprano) place on the Liri where the nobles of Puglia betrayed Manfredi; *Inf.* 28.16

Cephàs [Cefàs]

Cèrbero Cerberus, mythological doglike monster with three heads; *Inf.* 6.13

Cecerone (Cicerone, Citerone) mountain in Greece, Venus's throne; *Fiore* 215.8, 217.3

Cerchi Florentine family heading the white Guelfs; *Par.* 16.65

Cèrere Ceres, goddess of the harvests and mother of Proserpina; *Purg.* 28.51

Certaldo town in the Florentine countryside; *Par.* 16.50

Cèrvia village in Romagna; *Inf.* 27.42

Cèsare, Caio Giùlio Julius Caesar, born 102 or 100 B.C.; *Inf.* 4.123; *Purg.* 26.77; *Par.* 6.57

Cèsare Ottaviano [Augusto]

Cesena city in Romagna; *Inf.* 27.52

Cherubini (Cherubi) Cherubim, second highest order of the Angelic Hierarchy; *Par.* 28.98; *Conv.* 2.5.6

Chiana river in the region of Arezzo; *Par.* 13.23

Chiara d'Assisi, Santa St. Clare, founder of the Clarisse religious order; *Par.* 3.98

Chiaramontesi ancient noble family of Florence; *Par.* 16.105

Chiarentana Carinthia, region in the Eastern Alps; *Inf.* 15.9

Chiaro Davanzati Florentine lyric poet; *Rime dubbie* 20–23

Chiàscio (Chiassi) stream in Umbria; *Purg.* 28.20; *Par.* 11.43

Chiassi (Classe) Roman Classis, ancient harbor of Ravenna; *Purg.* 28.20

Chiàveri (Chiavari) city on the coast of Liguria; *Purg.* 19.100

Chilon one of the Seven Sages of Greece; *Conv.* 3.11.4

Chirone (Chyron) Chiron, centaur; *Inf.* 12.65; *Purg.* 9.37

Chiusi ancient Clusium, Etruscan city; *Par.* 16.75

Chremes (Cremete) old man in some Latin comedies; *Epist.* 13.30

Christus [Cristo]

Chyron [Chirone]

Ciacco one of Dante's Florentine contemporaries; *Inf.* 6.38

Ciampolo di Navarra courtier of King Thibaut II of Navarre; *Inf.* 22.32

Cianfa Donati Florentine thief; *Inf.* 25.43

Cianghella Florentine, daughter of Arrigo della Tosa; *Par.* 15.128

Ciappetta, Ugo Hugh Capet, king of France 987–996; *Purg.* 20.49

Cìcero (Tùllio, Tùllius) Marcus Tullius Cicero, Roman writer, philosopher, and statesman, born 106 B.C.; *Inf.* 4.141; *Conv.* 1.11.14; *Mon.* 2.5.2; *Epist.* 13.49

Cicìlia (Sicìlia) island of Sicily; *Inf.* 12.108; *Purg.* 3.116; *Conv.* 4.26.11; *DVE* 1.8.6

Ciciliani Sicilians; *Inf.* 27.7

Ciclopi (Ciclopes) mythological giants; *Inf.* 14.55; *Egl.* 4.27

Cieldàuro Saint Peter's basilica of Ciel d'Oro ("Golden Cieling") in Pavia; *Par.* 10.128

Cimabue, Giovanni Cenni di Pepo, known as Giovanni Cimabue, Florentine painter; *Purg.* 11.94

Cincinnato Lucius Quinctius Cincinnatus, Roman dictator; *Par.* 6.46; *Conv.* 4.5.15; *Mon.* 2.5.9 [Quinzio]

Cìnira (Cìnyras) king of Cyprus; *Inf.* 30.39; *Epist.* 7.24

Cino da Pistoia (Cinus Pistoriensis, Cynisu Pistoriensis, Cinus de Pistorio, messer Cin) lyric poet; *DVE* 1.10.4; *Rime* 96; *Epist.* 3

Ciolus Ciolo degli Abati, one of the Florentines condemned to exile; *Epist.* 12.6

Ciotto, il [Carlo II d'Angiò]

Cipri (Cipro) Cyprus, Mediterranean island; *Inf.* 28.82

Ciprigna Cypriot (i.e., of Cyprus), name used by Dante for the planet Venus; *Par.* 8.2

Cipro [Cipri]

Circe enchantress Circe, daughter of Sole and Perse; *Inf.* 26.91; *Purg.* 14.42

Ciriatto one of ten demons of Malebolge; *Inf.* 21.122

Ciro (Cyrus) Cyrus the elder, founder of Persian Empire; *Purg.* 12.56

Cirra Cirrha, one of the two buttresses of Mt. Parnassus; *Par.* 1.36

Citerea Cytherea, epithet for Venus; *Purg.* 27.95

Cìvitas Castellana [Castellana Cìvitas]

Civitate Dei, De St. Augustine's work *City of God*; *Mon.* 3.4.7

Clèlia Cloelia, Roman maiden given over to King Porsenna; *Mon.* 2.4.10

Clemente IV Guy Foulquois, elected pope Clemente IV in 1265; *Purg.* 3.125

Clemente V (Clemens) Bertrand de Got, elected pope Clement V in 1305; *Inf.* 19.82; *Par.* 17.82; *Epist.* 5.30

Clemenza Clemence, either widow or daughter of Charles Martel of Hungary; *Par.* 9.1

Cleobulo Cleobulus, one of Seven Sages of Greece; *Conv.* 3.11.4

Clèofa Cleophas, Christ's disciple; *Purg.* 21.8

Cleopatra (Cleopatràs) Cleopatra VII, queen of Egypt; *Inf.* 5.63; *Par.* 6.76

Cleto St. Cletus, pope and martyr; *Par.* 27.41

Climenè Clymene, mother of Phaethon by Phoebus; *Par.* 17.1

Cliò Clio, muse of epic exploits and history; *Purg.* 22.58

Cloto Clotho, one of the three Fates; *Purg.* 21.27

Clugnì (Cluny) city in Burgundy; *Inf.* 23.63

Cocito Cocytus, frozen lake, the ninth circle in Hell; *Inf.* 14.119

Colchi Colchians, inhabitants of Colchis; *Inf.* 18.87

Colco (Colchide) Colchis, country in W. Asia; *Par.* 2.16

Colle Colle di Val d'Elsa, town in Tuscany; *Purg.* 13.115

Collina, porta [Porta Collina]

Cologna (Colònia) Cologne, German city; *Par.* 10.99

Colonna [Egìdio, Iàcopo, Pietro, Sciarra]

Colonne, Guido delle writer and judge of Messina; *DVE* 2.5.4

Colonnesi Colonna family of Rome; *Inf.* 27.85

Colossenses, Epìstola ad Colossians, epistle of St. Paul; *Mon.* 3.1.3; *Conv.* 4.24.17

Columpnis, Iudex de [Colonne, Guido delle]

Comedìa the *Comedy*, title Dante gives to his poem; *Inf.* 16.128, 21.2; *Epist.* 13.11

Comestor, Petrus [Pietro Mangiadore]

Commentatore (Commentator, Comentator) the Commentator, i.e., Averroës [Averoìs]

Confessioni, Le the *Confessions* of St. Augustine; *Conv.* 1.2.14

Cònio, Cunio, castle near Imola; *Purg.* 14.116

Consideratione, De treatise of St. Bernard, *On Consideration*; *Epist.* 13.80

Consolatione, De (la Consolazione) *De Consolatione philosophiae* (*On the Consolation of Philosophy*) work by Boethius; *Conv.* 4.12.4; *Epist.* 13.89

Constantinòpolis Constantinople, capital of Eastern Empire founded by Constantine the Great (A.D. 330); *Par.* 6.5; *Mon.* 3.10.18

Constantinus [Costantino]

Contemplatione, De treatise of Richard of St. Victor *On Contemplation; Epist.* 13.80

Contessa [Bianca]

Contra Gentiles (Contra-li-Gentili), Summa contra Gentiles work by St. Thomas Aquinas; *Conv.* 4.15.12; *Mon.* 2.4.1

Convìvio the *Banquet*, philosophical treatise in verse and prose; *Conv.* 1.1.2

Corìnthios, Ad (Epìstola ad Corìnthios) St. Paul's Epistle to the Corinthians; *Mon.* 3.10.7; *Epist.* 13.79; *Conv.* 4.22.6

Cornèlia [Cornìglia]

Corneto, Rinièr da infamous highway robber, placed in Hell; *Inf.* 12.137

Corneto Tarquinia, city in Latium bordering the Maremma; *Inf.* 12.137

Cornìglia (Cornèlia) Cornelia, Roman matron, daughter of Scipio Africanus; *Inf.* 4.128; *Par.* 15.129

Coro (Caurus) Caurus, (or Corus), NW. wind; *Inf.* 11.114

Corona constellation of the Crown; *Par.* 13.13

Corradino, Corrado [Curradino, Currado]

Corsi Corsicans, inhabitants of Corsica; *Purg.* 18.81

Corso Donati head of the Donati family and leader of the Black Guelfs in Florence; *Purg.* 24.82; *Par.* 3.106

Corydòn Virgilian pastor; *Egl.* 3.57

Cosenza town in N. Calabria; *Purg.* 3.124

Costantino (Constantinus) Constantine the Great, Roman emperor; *Inf.* 19.115, 27.94; *Par.* 6.1, 20.55; *Mon.* 3.10.1

Costantinòpoli [Constantinòpolis]

Costanza di Altavilla Constance, wife of Emperor Henry VI; *Purg.* 3.113; *Par.* 3.118

Costanza Constance, daughter of Manfred, king of Naples; *Purg.* 3.115

Crasso Marcus Licinius Crassus, Roman citizen known for his wealth and greed; *Purg.* 20.116

Cremona town in S. Lombardy; *DVE* 1.15.2

Creta (Creti) Crete, eastern Mediterranean island; *Inf.* 12.12

Creusa daughter of Priam and Hecuba; *Par.* 9.98

Crisippus Chrysippus, Stoic philosopher; *Mon.* 2.7.12

Crisòstomo St. John Chrysostom, celebrated Greek father of the Church; *Par.* 12.137

Cristallino, Cielo (Primo Mòbile, Primum Mòbile) ninth heaven from Earth; *Conv.* 2.3.7; *Par.* 30.107

Cristo (Iesus Christus, Iesu Cristo, del il Figliuol di Dio, il Salvatore) Jesus Christ; *Purg.* 20.87; *Par.* 6.14

Croàzia Croatia, region in Europe; *Par.* 31.103

Cunizza da Romano daughter of Ezzelino II; *Par.* 9.32

Cupìdo (Amore) Cupid, son of Venus and god of love; *Purg.* 28.66; *Par.* 8.7

Curiazi (Curiàtii) the three Alban brothers who fought against the Roman Horatii; *Par.* 6.39; *Mon.* 2.9.15

Cùrio (Mànio Cùrio Dentato) Manius Curius Dentatus, Roman consul; *Conv.* 4.5.13

Cùrio (Càio Curione) Gaius Scribonius Curio, Roman tribune; *Inf.* 28.102

Curradino (Corradino di Svevia) Conradin, son of Emperor Conrad IV; *Purg.* 20.68

Currado Conrad III of Swabia, king of Germany; *Par.* 15.139

Currado da Palazzo Conrad, nobleman from Brescia; *Purg.* 16.124

Currado Malaspina, il vecchio Conrad, father of Federico I of Villafranca; *Purg.* 8.119

Currado Malaspina, il giovane Conrad, son of Federico I of Villafranca; *Purg.* 8.65

Cyrus [Ciro]

Da Camino [Gaia, Gherardo, Rizzardo]

Dafne Daphne, daughter of the Thessalian river-god Peneus; *Par.* 10.32

Damascenus (San Giovanni di Damasco) St. John of Damascus, eminent theologian of the early Greek Church; *Epist.* 11.16

Damiano, Pietro St. Peter Damian, proclaimed doctor of the Church; *Par.* 21.43

Damiata Damietta, Egyptian city on the delta; *Inf.* 14.104

Daniele [Daniello]

Danielis, Arnaldus [Arnaldo Daniello]

Daniello, Arnaldo [Arnaldo Daniello]

Daniello (Daniel) prophet Daniel; *Purg.* 22.146; *Par.* 4.13; *Epist.* 13.81

Danòia the river Danube (Danubio); *Inf.* 32.26; *Par.* 8.65

Dante (Dante Alleghier, Alighier, Dantes, Dantes Alagherii, Dantes Alagherius) Dante Alighieri; *Purg.* 30.55; *Epist.* 12.8; *Quest.* 1

Dante da Maiano poet and friend of Dante; *Rime* 4.39

Danùbio (Danùbius, Danoia, Hyster) the river Danube; *Inf.* 32.26; *Par.* 8.65; *DVE* 1.8.4

Dardànide sons of Dardanus, i.e., the Trojans; *VN* 25.9

Dardano (Dardanus) Dardanus, son of Jupiter and Electra; *Conv.* 4.14.14; *Mon.* 2.3.11

Dàrio (Dàrius) Darius I, king of the Persians 521-486 B.C.; *Mon.* 2.8.7

Dati [Bonturo Dati]

Davanzati [Chiaro Davanzati]

Davìd (il Salmista, Psalmista, Propheta) King David, succeeded Saul as second king of Hebrews; *Inf.* 4.58; *Purg.* 10.65; *Par.* 20.37

Davus servant's name; *Egl.* 1.9

De Ànima; De Celo; etc. [Ànima, De; Celo, De; etc.]

Deci the Decii, famous Roman family; *Par.* 6.47; *Mon.* 2.5.16

Dècius, Pùblius Publius Decius Mus, first of the three Decii who sacrificed their lives for their country; *Mon.* 2.5.16

Decretali (Decretales) the Decretals, i.e., the papal decrees or epistles; *Par.* 9.134; *Epist.* 9.16

Dèdalo Daedalus, created the labyrinth in Crete; *Inf.* 17.111; *Par.* 8.125

Deianira wife of Hercules; *Inf.* 12.68

Deïdamia daughter of Lycomedes, king of Scyros; *Inf.* 26.62; *Purg.* 22.114

Deifilè Deipyle, daughter of Adrastus, king of the Argos; *Purg.* 22.110

Del Bello [Bello, Geri del]

Delia surname of Diana; *Purg.* 29.78

Dèlius surname of Apollo; *Epist.* 6.8

Delo island of Delos where Latona gave birth to Apollo and Diana; *Purg.* 20.130

Demètrius Demetrius I, king of Syria; *Epist.* 11.8

Demòcrito Democritus, Greek philosopher; *Inf.* 4.136; *Conv.* 3.14.8

Demofoonte Demophon or Demophon, son of Theseus and Phaedra; *Par.* 9.101

Dente [Vitaliano del Dente]

Derivazioni the dictionary *Magnae derivationes* of Uguiccione da Pisa; *Conv.* 4.6.5

Desidèrius (Desidèrio) last of the kings of the Longobards (Lombards); *Par.* 6.94

Dialèttica dialectic, one of the liberal arts (Trivium); *Conv.* 2.13.8

Diana (Dèlia, Phebe, Trìvia) daughter of Latona and Jupiter; *Purg.* 25.131; *Par.* 10.67

Diana subterranean river beneath Siena; *Purg.* 13.153

Dido (Helyssa Didone) Dido (or Elissa), daughter of Belus and widow of King Sichaeus of Tyre; *Inf.* 5.61; *Par.* 8.9

Digesto (Digestum) the *Digest* or *Pandects*, collection of decisions made by Roman jurists, part of Justinian's *Corpus iuris civilis; Conv.* 4.9.8

Dino Perini [Melibeus]

Dio (Iddio, Deus, Deo, EL, Elì, I, Padre) God; *Inf.* 1.131; 3.103; *Purg.* 28.74; *Par.* 20.138; *Mon.* 1.3.2; *DVE* 1.4.2

Diogenès, Diògene Diogenes, Greek philosopher, called the Cynic; *Inf.* 4.137

Diomede Diomedes, Homeric hero, son of Tydeus and Deipyle; *Inf.* 26.56

Dione mother of Venus by Jupiter; *Par.* 8.7

Dionìsio Dionysius the Elder, tyrant from Syracuse; *Inf.* 12.107; *Par.* 10.115

Dionìsio (Dionỳsius) Dionysius the Areopagite; *Par.* 10.115; *Epist.* 11.16

Dionìsio Diniz (Dionysius Agricola), king of Portugal, 1279–1325; *Par.* 19.139

Dionìsio Accadèmico Dionysius the Academician; *Conv.* 2.13.5

Dioscòride Pedanius Dioscorides, Greek philosopher and doctor; *Inf.* 4.140

Dite Dis, name given by Romans to Pluto; division of Dante's Hell; *Inf.* 9.44; *Purg.* 28.50

Doàgio (Douai) Douai (formerly Douay), town in N. of France; *Purg.* 20.46

Dolcìn, fra' Dolcino de' Tornielli, head of the heretical sect of the Apostolici; *Inf.* 28.55

Domènico, San St. Dominic, founded the religious order that bears his name; *Par.* 10.95

Dominazioni Dominions, order of the Angelic Hierarchy; *Par.* 28.122; *Conv.* 2.5.6

Domiziano, Tito Flavio Domitian, Roman emperor; *Purg.* 22.83

Donati ancient noble family of Florence; *Par.*16.95 **[Buoso, Cianfa, Corso, Forese, Gemma, Gualdrata, Piccarda, Ubertino]**

Donàtio Constantini the Donation of Constantine, document; *Inf.* 19.115; *Mon.* 3.10.1

Donato Aèlius Donatus, Roman grammarian; *Par.* 12.137

Donato dei Chiaramontesi Florentine who changed the measurement for salt out of greed; *Purg.* 12.105

Dòria [Branca d'Òria]

Douai [Doàgio]

Draghignazzo one of ten demons in Malebolge; *Inf.* 21.121

Drìades (Drìadi) Dryads, forest nymphs; *Egl.* 4.56

Drusi distinguished plebeian Roman family; *Conv.* 4.5.14

Duca, Guido del [Guido del Duca]

Ducatus duchy of Spoleto; *DVE* 1.10.5

Duera, Buoso da [Buoso da Duera]

Durante protagonist in the *Fiore; Fiore* 82.9, 202.14

Durazzo Dyrrachium, the ancient Apidamnus, seaport in Greek Illyria; *Par.* 6.65

DXV "five hundred, ten, and five," cryptic name of Dante's prophesied savior; *Purg.* 33.43

Eàcide (gli Eàcidi) the Aeacidae, mythological descendants of Aeacus; *Mon.* 2.9.8

Èaco Aeacus, king of Aegina, son of Jupiter and the nymph Aegina; *Conv.* 4.27.18

Ebrei (Giudei, Iudei, Hebrei, Israel) the Hebrews, people of Israel; *Purg.* 4.83; *Mon.* 3.15.5; *DVE* 1.6.6; *Epist.* 7.19

Ebro (Ibero) the river Ebro in Spain; *Purg.* 27.3; *Par.* 9.89

Ecclesiaste (Ecclesiastes) Book of Ecclesiastes in the Old Testament; *Conv.* 2.10.10

Ecclesiàstico (Ecclesiàsticus) the Book of Ecclesiasticus; *Conv.* 3.8.2; *Epist.* 13.62

Eco nymph Echo, daughter of Air and Earth; *Par.* 12.14

Ècuba Hecuba, wife of King Priam of Troy; *Inf.* 30.16

Edipo (Edippo) Oedipus, son of King Laius of Thebes; *Purg.* 33.49

Edoardo Edward I, king of England 1272–1307; *Purg.* 7.132; *Par.* 19.122

Edoardo Edward II, king of England 1307–1327; *Par.* 19.122

Efialte [Fialte]

Egìdio Aegidius of Assisi, one of St. Francis of Assisi's first followers; *Par.* 11.83

Egìdio Colonna Aegidius Romanus Eremita, theologian; *Conv.* 4.24.9

Egina Aegina, Greek island; *Inf.* 29.59

Egìptii (Egiptius, Egiziani) Egyptians, inhabitants of Egypt; *Epist.* 5.4

Egitto (Egiptus, Aegyptus) Egypt, region in Africa; *Inf.* 5.60; *Par.* 25.55; *Mon.* 2.8.5

Egiziani [Egìptii]

Ègloghe the Latin *Eclogues* of Dante

Ègloghe the Latin *Eclogues* or *Bucolics* of Virgil; *Purg.* 22.57; *Mon.* 1.11.1

El (Elì) name used by Dante for God; *Par.* 26.133

Elba [Àlbia]

Èlena Helen, wife of King Menelaus of Sparta; *Inf.* 5.64; *Detto,* 197

Eleonora daughter of Count Raymond Berenger IV; *Par.* 6.133

Elettra (Electra) Electra, daughter of Atlas; *Inf.* 4.121; *Mon.* 2.3.11

Elì [El]

Elia (Elyas) Jewish prophet Elijah; *Inf.* 26.35; *Purg.* 32.80

Èlice Helice or Callisto, one of Diana's nymphs; *Purg.* 25.131; *Par.* 31.32

Elicona (Nisa) Helicon, buttress on Mount Parnassus sacred to the Muses; *Purg.* 29.40

Eliodoro Heliodorus, treasurer of King Seleucus IV of Syria; *Purg.* 20.113

Eliòs name used by Dante for God; *Par.* 14.96

Eliseo Cacciaguida's brother; *Par.* 15.136

Eliseo prophet Elisha; *Inf.* 26.34

Eliso (Campi Elisi) Elysium, place in the pagan afterlife; *Par.* 15.27

Ellesponto the Hellespont, Greek name for the straits of Dardanelles; *Purg.* 28.71

Eloquèntia, De Vulgari (*Volgare Eloquenza*) Dante's treatise *On Eloquence in the Vernacular*; *Conv.* 1.5.10

Elsa tributary of the Arno; *Purg.* 33.67

Elyas [Elia]

Ema tributary of the Arno; *Par.* 16.143

Emilis Terra (Emìlia) Italian region; *Egl.* 4.68

Empedoclès (Empèdocle) philosopher from Agrigento; *Inf.* 4.138

Empìreo, Cielo (empỳreum celum) Empyrean, heaven of pure light beyond time and space enclosing all heavens; *Inf.* 2.21; *Par.* 4.34; *Conv.* 2.3.8

Èmpoli town in Tuscany; *Inf.* 10.91

Enea (Eneas) Aeneas, Trojan hero; *Inf.* 1.74; *Purg.* 18.137; *Par.* 6.3; *Mon.* 2.6.9; *Epist.* 7.17

Enèide (*Eneida, Enes*) the *Aeneid* of Virgil; *Purg.* 21.97; *Conv.* 1.3.10; *Mon.* 2.3.6

Enotrii [Oenotri]

Enrico [Arrigo]

Enrico da Susa (Ostiense, Ostiensis) commentator on the *Decretali; Par.* 7.83; *Epist.* 11.16

Èolo Aeolus, god of the winds; *Purg.* 28.21

Eoo Eous, one of the four horses of the Sun chariot; *Conv.* 4.23.14

Ephèsios, Epìstola ad St. Paul's Epistle to the Ephesians; *Mon.* 2.11.3; *Epist.* 13.76

Epicurei (Epricùrii) Epicureans, followers of Epicurus; *Conv.* 4.6.12

Epicuro Epicurus, Greek philosopher; *Inf.* 10.14

Epìstole Pauline the Pauline Epistles; *Purg.* 29.134

Era river of France; *Par.* 6.59

Eràclito Heraclitus, philosopher from Ephesus; *Inf.* 4.138

Ercolano Maconi [Lano]

Èrcole (Èrcule, Hercules, Alcide, Alcides) Hercules, half-god, son of Jupiter and Alcmena; *Inf.* 25.32; *Par.* 9.101

Erìdanus Latin poets' name for the Po river; *Epist.* 7.11

Erìfile Eriphyle, wife of Amphiaraus the seer; *Purg.* 12.50; *Par.* 4.104

Erine the Erinyes, Eumenides, or Furies, who dwell in the depths of Hell; *Inf.* 9.38

Erisìttone Erysichthon, son of Thessalian King Triopas; *Purg.* 23.26

Eritòn Erichtho, Thessalian sorceress; *Inf.* 9.23

Ermo, l' the Hermitage, e.g., the monastery of Camaldoli; *Purg.* 5.96

Erode Herod, Antipas, son of Herod the Great; *Mon.* 2.7.6; *Par.* 18.135

Esaù Esau, eldest son of Isaac and Rebekah; *Par.* 8.130

Esopo Aesop, Greek author of *Aesop's Fables; Inf.* 23.4

Este [Esti]

Estensis of Este, the marquis of Este; *DVE* 2.6.5

Ester Ester the Jewess, wife of Ahasuerus, king of Persia; *Purg.* 17.29

Esti now Este, town in NE. Italy from which Este family took their name; *Purg.* 5.77

Eteocle Eteocles, son of Oedipus; *Inf.* 26.54; *Purg.* 22.56

Ètica (Èthica ad Nicòmacum) the *Nicomachean Ethics* of Aristotle; *Inf.* 11.80; *Conv.* 1.9.9; *Mon.* 1.3.1; *Quest.* 21

Ethna [Etna]

Etiopi Ethiopians, in sense of "heathen"; *Purg.* 26.21; *Par.* 19.109

Etiòpia Ethiopia, ancient country in NE. Africa; *Inf.* 24.89

Etna Mt. Etna; *Par.* 8.67

Eton Aethon, one of four horses that drew the chariot of the sun; *Conv.* 4.23.14

Èttore Hector, eldest son of Priam; *Inf.* 4.122; *Par.* 6.68

Euclide (Euclides) Euclid, Greek mathematician; *Inf.* 4.142; *Mon.* 1.1.4

Ëufratès Euphrates, river of SW. Asia; *Purg.* 33.112

Eünoè invented name for one of rivers of the Earthly Paradise; *Purg.* 28.133

Eurìalo (Eurìalus) Euryalus, Trojan youth who accompanied Aeneas to Italy; *Inf.* 1.108; *Mon.* 2.7.11

Eurìpide Euripides, Greek tragic poet; *Purg.* 22.106

Eurìpilo Eurypylus, augur, consulted oracle of Apollo prior to Greeks' departure from Troy; *Inf.* 20.112

Èuro Eurus, ancient name for the E. or SE. wind; *Par.* 8.69

Europa daughter of Agenor, king of Phoenicia; *Par.* 27.84

Europa continent of Europe; *Purg.* 8.123; *Par.* 6.5; *Mon.* 2.3.11; *DVE* 1.8

Eva Eve, the first woman; *Purg.* 8.99, 12.71; *Par.* 7.148; *DVE* 1.4.2; *Mon.* 1.16.1

Evander Arcadian son of Mercury and a nymph; *Mon.* 2.3.2

Evangèlio (Vangèlio) the Gospel; *Purg.* 22.154; *Par.* 9.133; *Conv.* 2.1.5

Evangèlio the Gospel of St. John; *Conv.* 3.14.7

Èxodus the Book of Exodus; *Purg.* 2.46; *Conv.* 2.1.6; *Epist.* 5.4, 13.21

Ezechias Hezekiah, king of Judah; *Par.* 20.49

Ezechièl Ezekiel, third and last of the prophets; *Purg.* 29.100

Ezzelino [Azzolino]

Fabbro de' Lambertazzi Ghibelline of Bologna; *Purg.* 14.100

Fabi the Fabii, ancient patrician family at Rome; *Par.* 6.47

Fabrìzio Gaius Fabricius Luscinus, famous Roman hero; *Purg.* 20.25

Fabrùtius Fabruzzo di Tommasino de' Lambertazzi, Bolognese poet; *DVE* 1.15.6

Faentini [Faventini]

Faenza town in Emilia near Ravenna; *Inf.* 27.49; *Purg.* 14.101

Falàride Phalaris, Greek tyrant of Acragas (Agrigentum), Sicily; *Inf.* 27.7

Falterona on of the central peaks of Tuscan Apennines; *Purg.* 14.17

Famagosta Famagusta, seaport on Eastern coast of Cyprus; *Par.* 19.146

Fano town in Marches; *Inf.* 28.76; *Purg.* 5.71

Fantolìn, Ugolìn de' Ugolino de' Fantolini, nobleman of Faenza; *Purg.* 14.121

Faraone [Phàrao]

Farfarello one of the ten demons in the fifth bolgia of Malebolge; *Inf.* 21.123

Farinata degli Scornigiani name associated by early commentators with one referred to as *quel da Pisa*; *Inf.* 6.17 [*see* **Gano degli Scornigiani**]

Farinata degli Uberti leader of the Ghibellines of Florence, damned among the heretics; *Inf.* 6.79, 10.32

Farisei Pharisees, whose avarice was said to have caused the destruction of Jerusalem; *Inf.* 23.116, 27.85; *Epist.* 11.1

Faro, Capo [Peloro]

Farsàlia Pharsalia, district in E. Thessaly; *Par.* 6.65; *Epist.* 5.10

Farsàlia the *Pharsalia* or *De bello civili*, Lucan's epic poem; *Conv.* 4.28.13

Faventini inhabitants of Faenza; *DVE* 1.9.4

Fàzio dei Morubaldini turncoat lawyer from Signa; *Par.* 16.56

Federigo I Barbarossa Emperor Frederick I, "Redbeard," second emperor of the Hohenstaufen line; *Purg.* 18.119

Federigo II di Soave Emperor Frederick II of Swabia, son of Emperor Henry VI and Constance of Sicily; *Inf.* 10.119; *Purg.* 16.117; *DVE* 1.12.4; *Conv.* 4.3.6

Federigo II d'Aragona Frederick II of Aragon, king of Sicily, third son of Pedro III of Aragon

and Constance; *Purg.* 3.116; *Par.* 19.131; *Conv.* 4.6.20

Federigo Novello one of the Conti Guidi; *Purg.* 6.17

Federigo Tignoso nobleman of Rimini; *Purg.* 14.106

Fedra Phaedra, daughter of Minos and Pasiphae; *Par.* 17.47

Fegghine Figline Valdarno, town in Tuscany; *Par.* 16.50

Felice Felix de Guzmán, Spanish nobleman; *Par.* 12.79

Feltro Feltre, town in N. Italy, above Treviso; *Inf.* 1.105; *Par.* 9.52

Fenice the Phoenix, mythical Arabian bird; *Inf.* 24.107

Fenìcia Phoenicia, ancient maritime country on coastland in Syria; *Par.* 27.83

Ferdinando IV Ferdinand IV, king of Castile and León; *Par.* 19.125

Ferrarienses inhabitants of Ferrara; *DVE* 1.10.9

Festus Porcius Festus, procurator of Judea; *Mon.* 3.13.5

Fetonte (Pheton) Phaethon, son of Phoebus Apollo and Clymene; *Inf.* 17.107; *Purg.* 4.72; *Par.* 31.125; *Epist.* 11.5

Fialte Ephialtes the giant, son of Neptune and Iphimedia; *Inf.* 31.94

Fiamminghi Flemings, inhabitants of Flanders; *Inf.* 15.4

Fidùcio de' Milotti [Alphesibeus]

Fieschi [Alàgia dei Fieschi]

Fiesolani inhabitants of Fiesole; *Inf.* 15.73

Fièsole Roman Faesulae, city of Tuscany; *Inf.* 15.62; *Par.* 6.53

Fifanti noble family of Florence; *Par.* 16.104

Figline Valdarno [Fegghine]

Filattiera, Gherardino da member of the Malaspina family; *Epist.* 11.15

Filippeschi Ghibelline family of Orvieto; *Purg.* 6.107

Filippi noble family of Florence; *Par.* 16.89

Filippi Philips, kings of France of the Capetian line; *Purg.* 20.50

Filippo III Philip III, the Bold, king of France 1270–1285; *Purg.* 7.109

Filippo IV Philip IV, the Fair, king of France 1285–1314; *Inf.* 19.87; *Par.* 19.118

Filippo Argenti [Argenti, Filippo]

Filistei [Philistei]

Fìllide [Rodopèa]

Filomela Philomela, daughter of Pandion, king of Athens; *Purg.* 9.15

Filosofia, la Prima First Philosophy, e.g., Aristotle's *Metaphysics; Conv.* 1.1.1; *Mon.* 3.12.1

Filòsofo the Philosopher (i.e., Aristotle)

Fìnibus, De Cicero's treatise; *Conv.* 1.11.14; *Mon.* 2.5.10

Fiorentini the Florentines; *Inf.* 17.70; *Par.* 16.86; *DVE* 1.9.4

Fiorenza Florence; *Inf.* 10.92; *Purg.* 6.127; *Par.* 15.97

Fioretta woman mentioned in Dante's lyrics, probably Violetta *Rime* 56.12

Firenze [Fiorenza]

Fìsica the *Physics* of Aristotle; *Inf.* 11.101; *Conv.* 2.1.13; *DVE* 2.10.1; *Epist.* 13.70

Flaccus [Oràzio]

Flegetonta Phlegethon, one of the rivers of Hell; *Inf.* 12.47

Flegiàs Phlegyas, son of Mars and Chryse; *Inf.* 8.19

Flegon Phlegon, one of the four horses that drew the chariot of the sun; *Conv.* 4.23.14

Flegra Phlegra, scene of the battle in which Jupiter defeated the Giants; *Inf.* 14.58

Florèntia the Latin name for Florence; *DVE* 1.6.3; *Epist.* 1.1.9; *Quest.* 1

Florentini [Fiorentini]

Focàccia nickname of Vanni de' Cancellieri of Pistoia; *Inf.* 32.63

Focara lofty headland on the Adriatic; *Inf.* 28.89

Foco Phocus, son of Aeacus, king of Aegina; *Conv.* 4.27.20

Folcacchieri, Bartolomeo de' [Abbagliato, l']

Folchetto di Marsiglia [Folco]

Folco di Marsiglia Folquet de Marseille, Provençal troubadour; *Par.* 9.37

Folo Pholus, one of the centaurs; *Inf.* 12.72

Folquetus da Marsìlia [Folco]

Fonte Avellana [Avellana, Fonte]

Fonte Branda [Branda, Fonte]

Forese Donati Florentine nobleman, brother of Corso and Piccarda; *Purg.* 23.48

Forlì town in Emilia; *Inf.* 16.99; *Purg.* 24.32

Forlivienses inhabitants of Forlì; *DVE* 1.14.3

Fortuitorum Remèdia the *Liber ad Galionem de remediis fortuitorum* of Martinus Dumiensis, which Dante believed to be a work by Seneca; *Epist.* 3.5

Fortuna Fortune, guide appointed by God to reign over the sublunar world; *Inf.* 7.67; *Mon.* 2.9.8

Fortuna Maggiore the "greater fortune" of the art of geomancy; *Purg.* 19.4

Fortunate Ìnsule [Ìnsule Fortunate]

Forum Ìulii Friuli, formerly an independent duchy; *DVE* 1.10.7

Fosco, Bernardìn di [Bernardìn di Fosco]

Fotino Photinus, deacon of Thessalonica; *Inf.* 11.9

Fractenses inhabitants of Fratta; *DVE* 1.11.6

Francesca Francesca da Rimini, daughter of Guido Vecchio da Polenta; *Inf.* 5.116

Franceschi (Franci) Frenchmen; *Inf.* 27.44; *Purg.* 16.126; *DVE* 1.8.5

Francesco Alighieri half-brother of Dante, son of Alighiero di Bellincione and Lapa Cialuffi; *Rime* 76.10

Francesco d'Accorso [Accorso, Francesco]

Francesco d'Assisi St. Francis of Assisi; *Inf.* 27.112; *Par.* 11.35

Francesco Cavalcanti thief punished in the seventh bolgia of Malebolge; *Inf.* 25.151

Francesi [Franceschi]

Francia France; *Inf.* 19.87; *Purg.* 7.109; *Par.* 15.120

Franco Bolognese [Bolognese, Franco]

Frati Godenti Jovial Friars, popular name of the knights of a military and conventual order; *Inf.* 23.103

Frati minori Minor Friars, name borne by the Franciscans; *Inf.* 23.1

Friges Phrygians, term used by Dante in imitation of Virgil; *Epist.* 5.24

Frìgia Phrygia, ancient country of NW. Asia Minor; *Mon.* 2.3.10

Friuli [Forum Ìulii]

Frontinus Sextus Julius Frontinus, Roman statesman and writer; *DVE* 2.6.7

Fucci, Vanni natural son of Guelfuccio di Gerardetto dei Lazzari, noble family of Pistoia; *Inf.* 24.129

Fulcieri da Càlboli member of illustrious Guelf family of that name at Forlì; *Purg.* 14.58

Furce Caudine [Caudine, Furce]

Fùrie the Furies or Erinyes; *Inf.* 9.38

Gabriele (Gabriello) the Archangel Gabriel, angel of the Annunciation; *Purg.* 10.34; *Par.* 4.47

Gaddo della Gherardesca son of Count Ugolino della Gherardesca of Pisa; *Inf.* 33.68

Gade Gades, modern Cadiz, seaport on SW. coast of Spain; *Par.* 27.82

Gaeta ancient Caieta, seaport of central Italy; *Inf.* 26.92; *Par.* 8.62

Gaetana Alighieri Dante's half-sister; *Rime* 76.10

Gàia da Camino daughter of Gherardo da Camino of Treviso; *Purg.* 16.140

Galàssia the Galaxy or Milky Way; *Par.* 14.99

Galasso da Montefeltro first cousin of Guido da Montefeltro; *Conv.* 4.11.14

Galathea Galatea, a sea nymph, one of the Nereids; *Egl.* 4.78

Galeazzo Visconti son of Matteo Visconti of Milan; *Purg.* 8.79

Galehaut [Galeotto]

Galeno [Galieno]

Galenus [Galieno]

Galeotto Gallehault, go-between in *Lancelot du Lac;* *Inf.* 5.137

Galieno Galen, celebrated physician from Asia Minor; *Inf.* 4.143; *Mon.* 1.13.6; *Conv.* 1.8.5

Galigàio Galigàio dei Galigai, member of a noble family of Florence; *Par.* 16.101

Galilea Galilee, northernmost of the three provinces into which the Holy Land was divided; *Conv.* 4.22.14

Galìzia Galicia, region and ancient kingdom in NW. Spain; *Par.* 25.18

Galli noble family of Florence; *Par.* 16.105

Galli the Gauls; *Mon.* 2.4.7 **[Franceschi]**

Gallura name of one of the four judicial districts of Sardinia; *Inf.* 22.82; *Purg.* 8.82

Gallus Pisanus Gallo or Galletto of Pisa, poet of school of Guittone d'Arezzo (1250-1300); *DVE* 1.13.1

Galluzzo village of Tuscany; *Par.* 16.53

Gand [Guanto]

Ganellone Ganelon, traitor who brought ruin to Charlemagne's rearguard; *Inf.* 32.122

Gangalandi Florence family; *Par.* 16.128

Gange the river Ganges in India; *Purg.* 2.5; *Par.* 11.51

Ganimede Ganymede, one of the forefathers of Aeneas; *Purg.* 9.23

Gano degli Scornigiani Gano or Giovanni, referred to by Dante as *quel da Pisa; Purg.* 6.17

Gano di Maganza [Ganellone]

Garamanti the Garamantes, an ancient people of interior of Africa; *Conv.* 3.5.12

Garda town in on the E. shore of Lake Garda; *Inf.* 20.65

Gardingo name of part of Florence near Palazzo Vecchio; *Inf.* 23.108

Garigliano [Verde]

Garisenda a leaning tower at Bologna; *Inf.* 31.136

Gaville village in Tuscany; *Inf.* 25.151

Gedeòn Gideon, son of Joash the Abiezrite, one of the judges of Israel; *Purg.* 24.125

Gelboè Gilboa, mountain in NE. Palestine; *Purg.* 12.41

Gemelli Gemini ("the Twins"), constellation and third sign of the Zodiac; *Par.* 22.152

Gemma Donati Dante's wife

Generatione Animàlium, De [Animàlium, De Generatione]

Generatione et Corruptione, De Aristotle's treatise *On Generation and Corruption; Conv.* 3.10.2

Genesì (Genesis) Book of Genesis; *Inf.* 11.107; *DVE* 1.4.2; *Mon.* 3.4.7

Genovesi the Genoese; *Inf.* 33.151; *DVE* 1.13.6 **[Ianuenses]**

Gentiles, Summa contra Against *the Heathen,* treatise of Thomas Aquinas on the Catholic Faith; *Conv.* 4.15.12

Gentili Gentiles, as opposed to Christians; *Par.* 20.104; *Conv.* 4.15.6

Gentucca name of a lady from Lucca mentioned by Bonagiunta; *Purg.* 24.37

Gerardus de Brunèl Giraut de Borneil, troubadour *Purg.* 26.120; *DVE* 1.9.3

Geremia the prophet Jeremiah; *VN* 7.7; *Epist.* 11.3

Geri del Bello [Bello, Geri del]

Geriön Geryon, monster with three bodies, symbol of fraud and guardian of Malebolge; *Inf.* 16.131; *Purg.* 27.23

Germània [Lamagna]

Germano, San *Fiore* 159.2, 203.7

Geròlamo [Ierònimo]

Gerusalèm [Ierusalem]

Gesù Jesus; *Par.* 25.33; *Mon.* 3.9.10; *Epist.* 11.9 *VN* 40.1

Gherardesca [Anselmùccio, il Brigata, Gaddo, Ugolino, Uguiccione, Batifolle]

Gherardino da Filattiera [Filattiera, Gherardino da]

Gherardo II [Zeno, San]

Gherardo da Camino [Camino, Gherardo da]

Ghibellini Ghibellines, political party, enemies of the Guelfs; *Inf.* 10.47; *Purg.* 11.113; *Par.* 6.103

Ghin di Tacco famous highwayman, son of Tacco di Ugolino; *Purg.* 6.14

Ghisilèrius (de Ghisilèriis), Guido Guido Ghisilieri, Bolognese poet of school of Guido Guinizzelli; *DVE* 1.15.6

Ghisolabella dei Caccianemico daughter of Alberto de' Caccianemici of Bologna; *Inf.* 18.55

Giacobbe [Iacòb]

Giàcomo da Lentini (Iàcopo) poet, commonly called "Il Notaro" (The Notary); *Purg.* 24.56; *DVE* 1.12.8

Giàcomo da Santo Andrea nobleman of Padua, damned as a squanderer; *Inf.* 13.133

Giàcomo d'Aragona [Iàcomo II]

Giàcomo di Maiorca [Iàcomo]

Gianciotto Malatesta [Malatesta, Gianciotto]

Giandonati Florentine family; *Par.* 16.128

Gianfigliazzi Florentine family; *Inf.* 17.59

Gianni [Giovanni]

Gianni [Lapo Gianni]

Gianni [Presto]

Gianni de' Soldanieri Florentine Ghibelline, traitor placed in Antenora; *Inf.* 32.121

Gianni Schicchi Florentine of the Cavalcanti family, damned as a falsifier; *Inf.* 30.25

Giannìn [Giovanni Quirini]

Giano Janus, Roman god; *Par.* 6.81

Giano, messer unknown person; *Rime* 99.14

Giano della Bella Florentine tribune who instituted the Ordinances of Justice of 1293 *Par.* 16.131

Giapeto [Iàpeto]

Giasòn [Iasone]

Gibilterra, Stretto di Strait of Gibraltar; *Inf.* 26.107

Giganti giants; *Inf.* 31.95; *Purg.* 12.33

Ginevra Guinevere, wife of King Arthur; *Par.* 16.15

Gioacchino [Giovacchino, Ioacchino]

Giobbe [Iob]

Giocasta [Iocasta]

Giordàn [Iordan]

Giordano, Monte hill on the left bank of the Tiber; *Inf.* 18.33

Giosafàt [Iosofàt]

Gioseppe [Giuseppo]

Giosuè [Iosuè]

Giotto Giotto di Bondone, Florentine artist; *Purg.* 11.95

Giovacchino da Fiore Joachim of Floris, Calabrian abbot; *Par.* 12.140

Giòvane, il Re [Arrigo]

Giovanna wife of Buonconte da Montefeltro; *Purg.* 5.89

Giovanna daughter of Nino Visconti of Pisa and Beatrice of Este; *Purg.* 8.71

Giovanna mother of St. Dominic; *Par.* 12.80

Giovanna beloved of Guido Cavalcanti, called *Primavera* by Dante; *VN* 24.8

Giovanna lady mentioned in Dante's canzone "Doglia mi reca," *Rime* 106.153, also called Bianca and Contessa, and possibly the sister of Federigo Novello, one of the Conti Guidi (see *Purg.* 6.17)

Giovanna Jeanne (or Joan) of Navarre, daughter of Henry, King of Navarre, and wife of Philip the Fair; *Par.* 19.143

Giovanni (Gianni) John, proper name used to signify "someone"; *Conv.* 1.8.13

Giovanni John the Evangelist, one of the twelve apostles; *Purg.* 29.105; *Par.* 4.29; *Mon.* 2.11.3; *Epist.* 13.89; *Conv.* 3.14.7; *Quest.* 80

Giovanni di Lussemburgo (Iohannes) first son of Henry VII; *Epist.* 7.18

Giovanni I (Iohannes) marquis of Montferrat; *DVE* 1.12.5

Giovanni XXI [Ispano, Pietro]

Giovanni XXII John XXII (Jacques d'Euse or Duèse), succeeded Clement V as pope, 1334; *Par*. 27.58

Giovanni Battista St. John the Baptist, son of Zacharias and Elisabeth, cousin of Jesus; *Purg*. 22.152; *Par*. 4.29

Giovanni Buiamonte [Buia-monte, Giovanni]

Giovanni Crisòstomo [Crisò-stomo]

Giovanni del Virgìlio poet of Bologna (Mopsus); author of *Egl*. 1 and 3

Giovanni Quirini Venetian poet, supposed correspondent of Dante; *Rime dubbie* 8.12

Giove (Iùppiter) Jove or Jupiter, supreme deity of Roman gods; *Inf*. 14.52; *Purg*. 12.32; *Par*. 4.62; *Epist*. 13.63

Giove Jupiter, the planet and Heaven of Jupiter; *Par*. 16.95; *Conv*. 2.3.7

Giove Jove, name applied to God by Dante; *Purg*. 6.118

Giovenale (Iuvenalis) Juvenal, Roman satirist; *Purg*. 22.14; *Conv*. 4.12.8; *Mon*. 2.3.4

Giraut de Borneilh [Gerardus de Brunèl]

Giròlamo [Ierònimo]

Giuba [Iuba]

Giubileo Jubilee, year of religious festivity instituted by Boniface VIII, first celebrated in 1300; *Inf*. 18.28; *Purg*. 2.98

Giuda forefather of the Florentine family Giudi; *Par*. 16.123

Giuda Jude, or Judas, the Apostle; *Purg*. 29.142

Giuda [Iudas]

Giuda Maccabeo [Maccabeo]

Giuda Scariotto Judas Iscariot, betrayer of Christ; *Inf*. 9.27; *Purg*. 20.74

Giudea the land of Judaea; *Conv*. 2.1.6

Giudecca Judecca, last zone of Cocytus, the ninth circle of Hell, named after Judas Iscariot; *Inf*. 34.117

Giudei the Jews; *Inf*. 23.123; *Par*. 7.47; *Conv*. 2.4.9

Giùdice Nino [Nino Visconti]

Giuditta [Iudìt]

Giùlia [Iùlia]

Giuliano, Monte San modern Monte Pisano, mountain in Tuscany; *Inf*. 33.29

Giunone (Iunone, Giuno, Iuno, Hera) the goddess Juno, daughter of Saturn and Rhea; *Inf*. 30.1; *Par*. 12.12; *Conv*. 2.4.6; *Mon*. 2.9.8

Giuochi noble family of Florence; *Par*. 16.104

Giuseppe (Giuseppo) della Scala illegitimate son of Alberto della Scala *Purg*. 18.124

Giuseppe (Giuseppo), San Joseph, husband of the Virgin Mary; *Purg*. 15.91; *Rime* 77.11

Giuseppe (Gioseppo) Joseph, son of patriarch Jacob and his wife Rachel; *Inf*. 30.97

Giustiniano Justinian I, emperor of Constantinople; *Purg*. 6.89; *Par*. 6.10

Glàuco Glaucus, fisherman of Anthedon in Boeotia; *Par*. 1.68

Godenti, frati [Frati Godenti]

Goffredo di Buglione [Got-tifredi]

Golias Goliath, giant of Gath, fought for Philistines; *Mon*. 2.9.11; *Epist*. 7.29

Gomita, frate Sardinian friar placed among the barrators in Hell; *Inf*. 22.81

Gomorra Gomorrah, ancient city of Palestine; *Purg*. 26.40

Gorgòn Gorgon Medusa, mortal daughter of Phoreys and Ceto; *Inf*. 9.52

Gorgona small island in the Ligurian Sea; *Inf*. 33.82

Gottifredi, duca Duke Godfrey (Godefroy de Bouillon), French crusade leader; *Par*. 18.47

Gottus Mantuanus Gotto of Mantua, poet and contemporary of Dante; *DVE* 2.13.4

Governo (Govèrnolo) town in Lombardy; *Inf*. 20.78

Graffiacane one of the ten demons of the fifth bolgia of Malebolge; *Inf*. 21.122

Grai [Greci]

Graziano Gratian (Franciscus Gratianus), founder of science of canon law; *Par*. 10.104

Greci the Greeks; *Inf*. 26.75; *Purg*. 9.39; *Par*. 5.69; *Mon*. 2.3.11

Greci noble family of early Florence; *Par*. 16.89

Grècia Greece; *Inf*. 20.108

Gregòrio I St. Gregory I, called Gregory the Great, elected pope in 590; *Purg*. 10.75; *Par*. 20.108

Griffolino d'Arezzo alchemist of Arezzo; *Inf*. 29.109

Gualandi noble Ghibelline family of Pisa; *Inf*. 33.32

Gualdo village of Gualdo Tadino in Umbria; *Par*. 11.48

Gualdrada daughter of Bellincion Berti de' Ravignani of Florence; *Inf*. 16.37

Gualdrada Donati wife of Forese de' Donati; *Par*. 16.141

Gualterotti noble family of Florence; *Par*. 16.133

Guanto Ghent, Belgium, capital of East Flanders; *Purg*. 20.46

Guaschi Gascons, natives of Gascony; *Par*. 27.58

Guascogna Gascony, region in SW. France; *Purg*. 20.66; *Par*. 20.66

Gùbbio [Agòbbio]

Gùccio dei Tarlati one of the Tarlati of Pietramala in Arezzo; *Purg*. 6.15

Guelfi Guelfs, supporters of the Church, enemies of the Ghibellines; *Par*. 6.107

Guglielmo [Guiglielmo]

Guglielmo di Nogaret [Guiglielmo di Nogaret]

Guicto Aretinus [Guittone]

Guidi, Conti powerful family of Tuscany and Romagna; *Par*. 16.64 **[Aghinolfo da Romena, Alessandro da Romena, Federigo Novello, Guido da Romena, Guido Guerra, Uberto da Romena]**

Guido Bonatti [Bonatti, Guido]

Guido Cavalcanti Florentine poet; *Purg.* 11.97; *Rime* 51.1

Guido da Castèl (Castello) [Castèl, Guido da]

Guido da Prata native of Romagna; *Purg.* 14.104

Guido da Romena one of Conti Guidi involved in counterfeiting the florin; *Inf.* 30.77; *Epist.* 2

Guido del Càssero [Càssero, Guido del]

Guido del Duca gentleman of Bertinoro in Romagna; *Purg.* 14.10

Guido delle Colonne [Colonne, Guido delle]

Guido di Carpigna [Carpigna, Guido di]

Guido di Montfort Guy de Montfort, son of Simon de Montfort, earl of Leicester; *Inf.* 12.118

Guido Ghisilèrius (de Ghisilèriis) [Ghisilèrius, Guido]

Guido Guerra one of the Conti Guidi of the Dovadola line; *Inf.* 16.34

Guido Guinizelli (Guinizzelli) poet of Bologna; *Purg.* 11.97; *Conv.* 4.20.7; *DVE* 1.9.3; *VN* 20.3

Guido Montefeltrano Guido, count of Montefeltro, Ghibelline captain; *Inf.* 27.4; *Conv.* 4.28.8

Guido Novello da Polenta one of the Conti Guidi; *Par.* 16.64

Guiglielmo Guillaume d'Orange, William of Orange, hero in Carolingian epics; *Par.* 18.46

Guiglielmo, Mastro Guglielmo di Sant'Amore, teacher of Parisian studies; *Fiore* 92.1

Guiglielmo II William II, the Good, king of Sicily and Naples (1166–1189); *Par.* 20.62

Guiglielmo VII William VII, marquis of Montferrat and Canavese, 1254–1292; *Purg.* 7.134

Guiglielmo Aldobrandesco count of Santafiora in the Sienese Maremma; *Purg.* 11.59

Guiglielmo Borsiere [Borsiere, Guiglielmo]

Guiglielmo di Nogaret French knight who assailed Boniface VIII, referred to, with Sciarra Colonna, by Hugh of Capet; *Purg.* 20.90

Guinizelli, Guido [Guido Guinizelli]

Guiscardo, Ruberto Robert Guiscard, duke of Apulia and Calabria; *Inf.* 28.14; *Par.* 18.48

Guittone d'Arezzo (Guittone del Viva) poet of Arezzo; *Purg.* 24.56; *DVE* 1.13.1

Guizzante medieval port of Wissant in what was formerly part of Flanders; *Inf.* 15.4

Hadrianus [Adrianus]

Hautefort [Altaforte]

Heber patriarch Eber, great-grandson of Sem, son of Sale; *DVE* 1.6.5

Hebrei the Hebrews, so called from Heber; *DVE* 1.6.5

Hebreos, Epìstola ad Paul's epistle to the Hebrews; *Mon.* 2.7.5

Hector [Èttore]

Hectòreus Pastor [Arrigo VII]

Helene Sacellum church of St. Helen in Verona; *Quest.* 87

Helyssa [Dido]

Henricus [Arrigo VII]

Hera [Giunone]

Hèrcules [Alcide, Èrcole]

Herodes Herod the tetrarch; *Mon.* 2.11.6

Hespèria Greek name for Italy; *Mon.* 2.3.12; *Epist.* 6.12

Hèsperus the evening star, the planet Venus; *Mon.* 1.11.5

Hieremias [Geremia]

Homerus [Omero]

Honestus Bononiensis Onesto Bolognese, Bolognese poet of school of Guido Guinizzelli; *DVE* 1.15.6

Hostìlius Tullus Hostìlius, third legendary king of Rome (673–641 B.C.); *Mon.* 2.9.15

Hydra the Lernaean monster with 100 heads; *Epist.* 7.20

Hyster [Danùbio]

Iacòb patriarch Jacob, grandson of Abraham and younger son of Isaac; *Inf.* 4.59; *Par.* 8.131 [Israèl]

Iacobi, Epìstola *Epistle of St. James the Apostle*, written by St. James the Less; *Par.* 25.29; *Mon.* 1.1.6

Iacobi, Maria Mary of James, i.e., Mary the mother of James; *Conv.* 4.22.14

Iàcobus James the Less, son of Alphaeus and Mary, sister of the Virgin Mary; *Conv.* 4.22.14; *Par.* 25.29

Iàcomo II James II, the Just, king of Sicily; *Purg.* 7.119

Iàcomo James, second son of James I of Aragon and brother of Pedro III; *Purg.* 3.116; *Par.* 19.137

Iàcomo da Sant'Andrea [Giàcomo da Santo Andrea]

Iàcopo James the Apostle, also known as St. James the Great and St. James of Compostela; *Purg.* 32.76; *Par.* 25.17; *Conv.* 2.14.1; *Mon.* 3.9.11

Iàcopo Colonna son of Oddo Colonna and cardinal; *Epist.* 11.24

Iàcopo da Lentino [Giàcomo da Lentini]

Iàcopo del Càssero [Càssero, Iàcopo del]

Iàcopo Gaetano Stefaneschi [Transtiberinus]

Iàcopo Rusticucci Florentine, placed among the sodomites; *Inf.* 16.44

Iano [Giano]

Ianuenses the Genoese; *DVE* 1.8.7

Iàpeto Iapetus, one of the Titans, son of Uranus (Heaven) and Gaea (Earth); *Conv.* 4.15.8

Iarba Iarbas or Hiarbas, son of Jupiter Ammon, king of the Gaetulians; *Purg.* 31.72

Iasòn (Giasone) Jason, leader of the Argonauts on expedition to Colchis; *Inf.* 18.86; *Par.* 2.18

Iasòn Jason, obtained office of high priest from Antiochus Epiphanes; *Inf.* 19.85

Ibero the river Ebro in NE. Spain; *Purg.* 27.3

Ìcaro Icarus, son of Daedalus; *Inf.* 17.109; *Par.* 8.126

Ida Mt. Ida, highest mountain in Crete; *Inf.* 14.98

Ida Mt. Ida, mountain in Phrygia and Mysia, home of the gods; *Purg.* 9.22

Iddio [Dio]

Ieptè Jephthah the Gileadite, judge of Israel; *Par.* 5.66

Ieremias the prophet Jeremiah; *Epist.* 11.3

Ierònimo St. Jerome, one of the four doctors of the Church; *Par.* 29.37; *Conv.* 4.5.16

Ierusalèm Jerusalem, Holy City of the Jews; *Purg.* 2.3; *Par.* 19.127; *Epist.* 2.5; *Mon.* 3.9.10

Ierusalemme, il Ciotto "the Cripple of Jerusalem," Charles II of Naples; *Par.* 19.127

Iesse Jesse (or Isai), father of David; *Conv.* 4.5.6; *Epist.* 7.29

Iesu, Iesus [Cristo]

Ifigènia Iphigenia, daughter of Agamemnon and Clytemnestra; *Par.* 5.70

Ildebrandinus Paduanus Aldobrandino de' Mezzabati of Padua, judge of Padua; *DVE* 1.14.7

Ilerda modern Lèrida, capital of the province of same name in Spain; *Purg.* 18.101

Ilìade Homer's *Iliad; VN* 2.8; *Conv.* 4.20.4; *Mon.* 1.10.6, 2.3.9

Iliòn Ilion or Ilium, citadel founded by Ilus, son of Tros; *Purg.* 12.62

Iliòneus Trojan soldier; *Mon.* 2.3.8

Illuminato Illuminato da Rieti, one of earliest followers of St. Francis of Assisi; *Par.* 12.130

Ìmola town in modern region of Emilia; *Inf.* 27.49

Imolenses [Ymolenses]

Importuni noble family of Florence; *Par.* 16.133

Ìndia India; *Inf.* 14.32

Indo Indian, inhabitant of India; *Purg.* 32.41; *Par.* 29.101

Indo the river Indus in N. India; *Par.* 19.71

Infangato name, in singular, to designate the Infangati family; *Par.* 16.123

Inferno Hell; *Inf.* 1.110; *Purg.* 1.129; *Par.* 6.74; *Conv.* 4.26.9; *Epist.* 13.31

Inferno the first canticle of the *Commedia; Inf.* 20.3; *Epist.* 13.31

Inforzato, Infortiatum the *Infortiatum,* one of three parts of the *Digest* of Roman law; *Conv.* 4.15.17

Inghilese Edward I of England; *Par.* 19.122

Inghilesi the English; *DVE* 1.8.4; *Conv.* 1.7.13

Inghilterra (Ànglia) England; *Purg.* 7.131; *DVE* 1.8.4

Innocèntius IV Sinibaldo de' Fieschi, Pope Innocent IV; *Epist.* 11.16

Innocènzio III Giovanni Lotàrio de' Conti, Pope Innocent III; *Par.* 11.92

Ino daughter of Cadmus of Thebes and Harmonia, wife of Hathamas; *Inf.* 30.5

Ìnsule Fortunate the Fortunate Islands, or Isles of the Blessed; *Mon.* 2.3.13

Intellectu, De (Intelletto, De lo) *On the understanding,* treatise of Albertus Magnus; *Conv.* 3.7.3

Intelligenze [Àngeli]

Interminei, Alèssio [Alèssio Interminei]

Inventione, De Cicero's *De inventione* (called *Prima* or *Nova Rethorica*); *Mon.* 2.5.2; *Epist.* 13.49

Ioacchino Joachim, first husband of St. Anne and father of the Virgin Mary; *Conv.* 2.5.2

Iob the patriarch Job; *Mon.* 3.4.2

Iob the Book of Job; *Quest.* 77; *Purg.* 29.83

Iocasta Jocasta, wife of Laius, king of Thebes; *Purg.* 22.56

Iohannes [Giovanni Evangelista]

Iohannes John of Luxemburg, son of Emperor Henry VII; *Epist.* 7.18

Iohannes John I, the Just, marquis of Monferrat; *DVE* 1.12.5

Iohannis Vìsio the Book of Revelation of St. John; *Epist.* 13.33

Iohannis [Giovanni]

Iole daughter of Eurytus, king of Oechalia; *Par.* 9.102

Iollas a shepherd, one of characters in Virgil's *Eclogues; Egl.* 4.95

Iordàn the river Jordan in Palestine; *Purg.* 18.135; *Par.* 22.94

Iosafàt the Valley of Jehoshaphat (Kidron); *Inf.* 10.11

Iosuè Joshua, successor of Moses; *Purg.* 20.111; *Par.* 9.125; *Epist.* 7.7

Iosuè, Liber the Book of Joshua; *Purg.* 20.109; *Par.* 9.116; *Epist.* 7.7

Iovis [Giove]

Iperione Hyperion, the father of the Sun; *Par.* 22.142; *Epist.* 3.7

Ipocràte Hippocrates, famous physician of antiquity; *Inf.* 4.143; *Purg.* 29.137

Ippòcrate [Ipocràte]

Ippòlito Hippolytus, son of Theseus by Hippolyte, queen of Amazons; *Par.* 17.46

Ìride (Iri) Iris, daughter of Thaumas and Electra, personified the rainbow; *Par.* 33.118; *Purg.* 21.50

Isacco Isaac, son of patriarch Abraham and Sarah; *Inf.* 4.59

Isai [Iesse]

Isàia the prophet Isaiah; *Par.* 25.91; *Epist.* 7.7

Isara the Isère, river of SE. France; *Par.* 6.59

Isidoro St. Isidore of Seville, writer and theologian; *Par.* 10.131

Isìfile Hypsipyle, daughter of Thoas, king of Lemnos; *Inf.* 18.92; *Purg.* 22.112

Ismenè Ismene, daughter of Oedipus by his incestuous marriage with this mother Jocasta; *Purg.* 22.111

Ismeno Ismenus, river in Boeotia; *Purg.* 18.91

Isopo [Esopo]

Ispagna [Spagna]

Ispani (Yspani) Spaniards; *Par.* 29.101; *DVE* 1.8.6

Ispano, Pietro Petrus Hispanus, elected pope under title of John XXI in 1276; *Par.* 12.134

Israèl (Israele) Israel, national name of the twelve Hebrew tribes; *Inf.* 4.59; *Purg.* 2.46

Israèl [Iacòb]

Ìstria peninsula on the NE. coast of Adriatic; *DVE* 1.10.7; *Inf.* 9.113

Istriani (Ystriani) inhabitants of Istria; *DVE* 1.10.8;

Ìtali [Ytali]

Itàlia Italy; *Inf.* 1.106; *Purg.* 6.76; *Par.* 21.106; *Conv.* 1.5.9; *DVE* 1.8.8

Itàlico Italian; *Par.* 9.26; *Conv.* 1.6.8;

Iuba Juba I, king of Numidia, son and successor of Hiempsal II; *Par.* 6.70

Iudea the land of Judaea; *Epist.* 13.21

Iudei the Jews; *Mon.* 3.13.5; *Epist.* 11.4

Iudas the patriarch Judah; *Mon.* 3.5.1; *Epist.* 5.4

Iudex de Columpnis [Colonne, Guido de le]

Iùdicum, Liber the Book of Judges; *Purg.* 24.124; *Par.* 5.66

Iudìt Judith, daughter of Meraris, heroine of the Book of Judith; *Par.* 32.10

Iudìt, Liber the Book of Judith; *Purg.* 12.58

Iùlia Julia, daughter of Julius Caesar and Cornelia; *Inf.* 4.128

Iùlius [Cèsare, Caio Giùlio]

Iulus son of Ascanius and grandson of Aeneas; *Epist.* 7.17

Iuno, Iunone [Giunone]

Iùppiter [Giove]

Iuvenalis [Giovenale]

Iuventute et Senectute, De Aristotle's treatise *On Youth and Old Age*; *Conv.* 4.28.4

Iuventute et Senectute, De Albert the Great's treatise *On Youth and Old Age*; *Conv.* 4.23.12

Julia [Iùlia]

Julio [Iùlius]

Lacedèmona Lacedaemon or Sparta, capital of ancient Laconia; *Purg.* 6.139

Làchesis Lachesis, one of the three Fates; *Purg.* 21.25

Laerte Laertes, king of Ithaca, father of Ulysses; *Inf.* 26.95

Làgia the beloved of Lapo Gianni; *Rime* 52.9, 45.6

Lamagna Germany; *Inf.* 20.62; *Conv.* 3.5.12; *DVE* 1.18.5

Lambertazzi, Fabbro de' [Fabbro]

Lamberti noble family of Florence; *Par.* 16.110

Lamberti, Mosca de' [Mosca de' Lamberti]

Lamone small river of N. Italy near Ravenna; *Inf.* 27.49

Lancialotto (Lancelotto) Lancelot, hero of the romance *Lancelot du lac; Inf.* 5.128; *Conv.* 4.28.8

Lanfranchi noble Ghibelline family of Pisa; *Inf.* 33.32

Langìa name of a fountain near Nemea in the Peloponnesus; *Purg.* 22.112

Lano gentleman of Siena; *Inf.* 13.120

Laomedonte Laomedon, king of Troy, great-great-grandson of Dardanus; *Conv.* 4.14.14; *Epist.* 5.24

Lapo (Lapus Florentinus) Lapo Gianni, Florentine notary and lyric poet; *Rime* 52.1; *DVE* 1.13.3

Lapo Salterello Florentine lawyer and judge; *Par.* 15.128

Laterano Palazzo del Laterano, in Rome, residence of the pope until 1309; *Inf.* 27.86; *Par.* 31.35

Latini the inhabitants of Latium, as distinguished from the Romans; *Mon.* 2.5.16; the subjects of Latinus, king of Latium; *Epist.* 7.18

Latini the Latins, ancient Romans (e.g., Virgil); *Purg.* 7.16; *Epist.* 5.2; *Conv.* 1.10.12, 4.4.10

Latini (Làtii, Ỳtali) the Italians; *Inf.* 29.91; *DVE* 1.8.4, 2.5.2; *Epist.* 9.1; *Conv.* 4.13.13

Latino the Latin language; *Par.* 10.120; *VN* 25.1; *Conv.* 1.5.7

Latino Italian, inhabitant of Italy; *Inf.* 22.65; *Conv.* 4.28.8

Latino (Latinus) king of Latium; *Inf.* 4.125; *Mon.* 2.3.16

Latona the Greek Leto, mother of Apollo and Diana by Jupiter; *Purg.* 20.131; *Par.* 10.67

Lavagna small river of Liguria; *Purg.* 19.101

Lavina Lavinia, daughter of Latinus, king of Latium; *Inf.* 4.126; *Purg.* 17.37; *Par.* 6.3

Latium Latium; *DVE* 1.10.4

Làzzaro Lazarus of Bethany; *Conv.* 4.7.4

Leandro Leander, Greek youth of Abydos; *Purg.* 28.73

Learco Learchus, son of Athamas, king of Orchomenus; *Inf.* 30.10

Leda daughter of Thestius, wife of Tyndareus, king of Sparta; *Par.* 27.98

Lèlio Gaius Laelius Sapiens, Roman statesman and philosopher; *Conv.* 2.12.3

Lemosì Limoges, town of W. central France; *Purg.* 26.120

Lenno Lemnos, island in the N. Aegaean Sea; *Inf.* 18.88

Lentino, Iàcomo da [Giàcomo da Lentini]

Leone Pope Leo VIII; *Mon.* 3.11.3

Lèrice Lerici, town in Liguria near La Spezia; *Purg.* 3.49

Lèrida [Ilerda]

Letè Lethe, one of the two rivers of the Earthly Paradise; *Inf.* 14.131; *Purg.* 1.40

Leucippe daughter of Minyas of Boeotia; *Epist.* 3.7

Leuconoe daughter of Minyas of Boeotia; *Epist.* 3.7

Leucothoe daughter of Orchamus, king of Babylonia, and his wife Eurynome; *Epist.* 3.7

Levì the patriarch Levi, son of Jacob and Leah; *Purg.* 16.132; *Mon.* 3.5.1

Leviti the Levites, members of the tribe of Levi; *Purg.* 16.132; *Mon.* 3.13.8

Levìticus the Book of Leviticus; *Mon.* 2.7.5; *Purg.* 29.83

Lia Leah, first wife of Jacob; *Purg.* 27.101

Lìbanus (Lìbano) Lebanon; *Purg.* 30.11

Lìbia Libya; *Inf.* 14.14

Libicocco one of ten demons in the fifth bolgia of Malebolge; *Inf.* 21.121

Libra the Balance, constellation and seventh sign of Zodiac; *Purg.* 2.7.3; *Par.* 29.3; *Conv.* 3.5.13

Libri Regnum the Books of Kings (comprising the two books of Samuel and the two books of Kings of the Vulgate); *Par.* 13.93; *Conv.* 4.27.6; *Mon.* 3.6.1; *Epist.* 7.7

Liceus (Liceo) mountain in Arcadia; *Egl.* 3.25

Lìgures inhabitants of Liguria; *Epist.* 7.2

Ligurgo Lycurgus, king of Nemea; *Purg.* 26.94

Lilla Lille, capital of medieval Flanders, later city of France; *Purg.* 20.46

Lìndio of Lindos, town on E. coast of Rhodes; *Conv.* 3.11.4

Lino St. Linus, pope; *Par.* 27.41

Lino Linus, mythical Greek poet of ambiguous origin; *Inf.* 4.141

Lippo an unidentified friend of Dante; *Rime* 48.1

Liri [Verde]

Lisetta unidentified lady in one of Dante's sonnets; *Rime* 118.1

Lìvio Livy (Titus Livius), Roman historian; *Inf.* 28.12; *Conv.* 3.9.3; *Mon.* 2.4.5

Lìzio Lizio da Valbona, nobleman of Bertinoro; *Purg.* 14.97

Loderingo degli Andalò one of the Frati Godenti; *Inf.* 23.104

Logodoro Logudoro or Torres, district of Sardinia; *Inf.* 22.89

Lombardi Lombards, inhabitants of Lombardy; *Inf.* 1.68; *DVE* 1.19.1

Lombardia Lombardy; *Inf.* 28.84; *DVE* 1.10.7; *Purg.* 16.115

Lombardo, il gran most likely Bartolomeo della Scala, lord of Verona; *Par.* 17.71

Lombardo, il semplice [Castèl, Guido da]

Lombardo, Marco [Marco Lombardo]

Lombardo, Pietro [Pietro Lombardo]

Londra London; *Inf.* 12.120

Longobardi Longobards or Langobardi, later called Lombards; *Mon.* 3.11.1; *DVE* 1.15.3; *Epist.* 5.11

Lorenzo St. Lawrence, deacon of Church of Rome; *Par.* 4.83

Lotto degli Agli [Agli, Lotto degli]

Luca Luke the Evangelist, the author of the Gospel bearing his name; *Purg.* 21.7; *Conv.* 4.5.8; *Mon.* 2.8.14

Lucano Lucan (Marcus Annaeus Lucanus), Roman epic poet; *Inf.* 4.90; *DVE* 2.6.7; *VN* 25.9; *Conv.* 3.3.7; *Mon.* 2.4.6; *Epist.* 13.63

Lucca town in Tuscany; *Inf.* 18.122; *Purg.* 24.20

Lucchesi [Lucenses]

Lucenses inhabitants of Lucca; *DVE* 1.13.1

Lucia name given by Dante to an imaginary city; *Conv.* 3.5.9

Lucia St. Lucy, Christian virgin and martyr of Syracuse; *Inf.* 2.97; *Purg.* 9.55; *Par.* 32.137; *Conv.* 3.9.14

Lùcifer the morning star; *Mon.* 1.11.5; *Rime dubbie* 7.7

Lùcifero Lucifer, traditional name for Satan; *Inf.* 31.143; *Purg.* 12.25; *Par.* 9.127; also called Belzebù (Beelzebub, *Inf.* 34.127), Luciferus (*Epist.* 13.76), Satàn (*Inf.* 7.1), Satanas (*Mon.* 3.9.10)

Lucillo scribal error for Lucìlio, Lucilius Iunior; *Conv.* 4.12.8

Lucrèzia Lucretia, wife of Lucius Tarquinius Collatinus; *Inf.* 4.128

Luigi kings of France of the Capetian line; *Purg.* 20.50

Luna the Moon, as planet *Inf.* 7.64; *Purg.* 10.14; *Par.* 2.34; *Conv.* 2.3.6

Luna, Cielo de la the Heaven of the Moon; *Par.* 16.82, *Conv.* 2.3.4; *Epist.* 13.71

Lunensis Pontifex bishop of Luni, namely Gherardino da Filattiera; *Epist.* 11.15

Luni Etruscan Luna, ancient port town near Sarzana; *Inf.* 20.47; *Par.* 16.73

Lunigiana district of NW. Tuscany near the Ligurian border, referred to as the Val di Magra; *Inf.* 24.145; *Purg.* 8.116

Maccabeo Judas Maccabaeus, the great Jewish warrior; *Par.* 18.40

Maccabei the Books of the Maccabees; *Inf.* 19.86; *Purg.* 20.113; *Epist.* 11.8

Maccàrio St. Macarius, placed by Dante among the contemplatives; *Par.* 22.49

Macra the Magra, small river in the Lunigiana region of NW. Tuscany; *Par.* 9.89

Maddalena, Maria Mary Magdalen; *Conv.* 4.22.14

Madiàn Madian (Midian), ancient region of NW. Arabia; *Purg.* 24.126

Maghinardo Pagani [Mainardo Pagano]

Magi the Magi, wise men from the East; *Mon.* 3.7.1

Magister Sex Prinicipiorum title given to Gilbert de La Porrée; *Mon.* 1.11.4

Magna, La [Lamagna]

Magnae Derivationes [Derivazioni]

Màia mother of Mercury by Jupiter; *Par.* 22.144

Mainardi family of Bertinoro; *Purg.* 14.113

Mainardo (Maghinardo) Pagano head of the Pagani family; *Inf.* 27.50; *Purg.* 14.118

Maiòlica Majorca, largest of the Balearic Islands; *Inf.* 28.82

Malacoda "Evil-tail," name of chief devil in the fifth bolgia of Malebolge; *Inf.* 21.76

Malaspina noble family of the Lunigiana region; *Inf.* 24.145; *Purg.* 8.119; *Epist.* 4 **[Currado, Moroello]**

Malatesta lords of Rimini; *Inf.* 27.46 **[Gianciotto, Pàolo]**

Malatesta da Verrùcchio eldest son of Giovanni Malatesta; *Inf.* 27.46

Malatestino lord of Rimini, eldest son of Malatesta da Verrucchio; *Inf.* 27.46, 28.81

Malavolti, Catalano de' [Catalano]

Malebolge "Evil-pouches," name given by Dante to the eighth circle of Hell; *Inf.* 18.1

Malebranche "Evil-claws," collective name given to the demons in the fifth bolgia of Malebolge; *Inf.* 21.37

Malehaut, Dama di the Lady of Malehaut, companion to Queen Guinevere; *Par.* 16.14

Malvicini Ghibelline counts of Bagnacavallo in Romagna; *Purg.* 14.115

Manardi [Mainardi]

Manfredi (Manfredus) Manfred, natural son of Emperor Frederick II by Bianca; *Purg.* 3.112; *DVE* 1.12.4

Manfredi da Vico hereditary prefect of Rome; *Conv.* 4.29.2

Mangiadore, Pietro [Pietro Mangiadore]

Mangona, conti di the Alberti, counts of Mangona; *Inf.* 32.55

Mànlius Marcus Manlius Capitolinus, Roman consul; *Mon.* 2.4.7

Manto daughter of Tiresias, soothsayer and priestess; *Inf.* 20.55; *Purg.* 22.113

Màntova Mantua, town in Lombardy south of Lake Garda; *Inf.* 20.93; *Purg.* 6.72

Maometto Muhammad, Arabian prophet and founder of the Islamic religion; *Inf.* 28.31

Marca [Màrchia]

Marcabò castle near Ravenna at the mouth of the Po river; *Inf.* 28.75

Marcèl (Marcello) Gaius Claudius Marcellus, Roman consul and follower of Pompey; *Purg.* 6.125

Marchese Azzo VIII, marquis of Este; *Inf.* 18.56; *DVE* 1.12.5

Marchese Messer Marchese, nobleman of Forlì and one of the gluttonous; *Purg.* 24.31

Marchese di Monferrato Boniface I (II?), marquis of Montferrat; *Conv.* 4.11.14

Marchese, Guiglielmo [Guiglielmo VII]

Màrchia Anconitana the March of Ancona, former province of Italy; *DVE* 1.10.7; *Purg.* 5.68

Màrchia Januensis the March of Genoa; *DVE* 1.10.7

Màrchia Trivisiana the March of Treviso, former province of Italy; *DVE* 1.10.7; *Epist.* 1.1; *Purg.* 16.115

Marchiani inhabitants of the March of Ancona; *DVE* 1.12.7

Marco Mark the Evangelist; *Purg.* 16.46; *Conv.* 4.22.14; *Mon.* 3.9.14; *VN* 23.7

Marco Lombardo Lombard (or Venetian) nobleman placed among wrathful; *Purg.* 16.46

Mardoceo Mordecai, saved the Jews from the destruction planned by Haman; *Purg.* 17.29

Mare Adriàtico [Adriano, mare]

Mare Ànglicum the English Channel; *DVE* 1.8.9

Mare di Tiberìade the Sea of Tiberias or Sea of Galilee; *Par.* 24.39

Mare Mediterràneo the Mediterranean Sea; *Inf.* 14.94; *Par.* 8.63

Mare Ocèano the ocean whose waters were believed the encircle the earth; *Conv.* 3.5.12; *Par.* 9.84

Mare Rosso the Red Sea; *Inf.* 24.90; *Purg.* 17.134; *Par.* 22.95

Mare Tirreno [Tirrenum mare]

Maremma marshy region in SW. Tuscany; *Inf.* 13.9; *Purg.* 5.134

Margarita Margaret of Brabant, wife of Henry VII of Luxemburg; *Epist.* 8.1, 9.1, 10.1

Margherita Margaret, daughter of Raymond Berenger IV and wife of Louis IX, king of France; *Par.* 6.133

Margherita di Borgogna Margaret, second wife of Charles I, king of Naples and Sicily; *Purg.* 7.128

Maria the Virgin Mary; *Purg.* 3.39; *Par.* 3.122, 33.1; *VN* 28.1; *Conv.* 2.5.2

Maria Mary of Eleazar; *Purg.* 23.30

Maria Mary of Bethany, sister of Martha and Lazarus; *Conv.* 4.17.10

Maria name given to an imaginary city placed at North Pole; *Conv.* 3.5.18

Maria di Brabante [Brabante]

Maria Iacobi [Iacobi, Maria]

Maria Maddalena [Maddalena, Maria]

Maria Salomè name by which Dante describes woman mentioned in Mark 16:1; *Conv.* 4.22.14

Maria in Porto, Santa [Nostra Donna, casa di]

Maro [Virgìlio]

Marocco [Morrocco]

Màrsia Marsyas, a satyr of Phrygia; *Par.* 1.20

Marsìlia Marseilles, city of SE. France; *Purg.* 18.102; *Par.* 9.92

Marta Martha, sister of Mary of Bethany; *Conv.* 4.17.10

Marte (Mars) Roman god of war; *Inf.* 13.144; *Purg.* 12.31; *Par.* 4.63

Marte the planet Mars; *Purg.* 2.14

Marte the Heaven of Mars; *Par.* 18.28; *Conv.* 4.13.20

Martello, Carlo [Carlo Martello]

Martino Martin, common name for the average person; *Par.* 29.103; *Conv.* 1.8.13

Martino IV Martin IV (Simon di Brie or Brion), pope; *Purg.* 24.20

Màrzia Marcia, second wife of Cato of Utica; *Inf.* 4.128; *Purg.* 1.79; *Conv.* 4.28.13

Marzucco degli Scornigiani nobleman of Pisa; *Purg.* 6.18

Mascheroni, Sassòl Florentine, member of the Toschi family; *Inf.* 32.65

Matelda Matilda, Dante's guide through the Earthly Paradise; *Purg.* 28.40

Matia Matthias the Apostle, elected to fill the place of Judas Iscariot; *Inf.* 19.94; *Mon.* 2.7.9

Matteo (Matheus) Matthew the Evangelist; *Conv.* 4.16.10; *Mon.* 3.3.13; *Epist.* 13.80

Matteo Bentivenga d'Acquasparta monk of the Franciscan order; *Par.* 12.126

Mattia [Matia]

Medea daughter of Aeetes, king of Colchis, abducted by Jason; *Inf.* 18.96

Medicina, Pièr da sinner placed among the schismatics; *Inf.* 28.73

Mediolanenses, Mediolani Milanese, inhabitants of Milan; *DVE* 1.9.4; *Epist.* 7.20

Mediterràneo [Mare Mediterràneo]

Medusa one of the three Gorgons; *Inf.* 9.52

Megera Megaera, one of the three Furies; *Inf.* 9.46

Melano Milan, the capital of Lombardy; *Purg.* 18.120

Melchisedèch Melchizedek, priest and king of Salem; *Par.* 8.125

Meleagro Meleager, son of Oeneus, king of Calydon, and Althaea; *Purg.* 25.22

Melibeus pastoral name of a character in the Latin *Eclogues*; *Egl.* 2.4

Melicerta Melicerta or Melicertes, son of Athamas, king of Orchomenus in Boeotia; *Inf.* 30.5

Melisso Melissus, philosopher of Samos; *Par.* 13.125; *Mon.* 3.4.4

Menalippo Menalippus or Melanippus, son of Astacus; *Inf.* 32.131

Mènalus Maenalus, mountain range in Arcadia; *Egl.* 2.11

Mèncio Mincio, river which flows from Lake Garda; *Inf.* 20.77

Meo dei Tolomei [Meùccio]

Meotidis Paludes Lake Maeotis (Palus Maeotis), gulf opening from N. shore of the Euxine Sea in the Crimea; *DVE* 1.8.4

Mercùrio Mercury, son of Jupiter, messenger of the gods; *Par.* 4.63; *Mon.* 2.6.10

Mercùrio the planet Mercury; *Conv.* 2.13.7; *Par.* 5.96

Mercùrio the Heaven of Mercury; *Par.* 5. 93; *Conv.* 2.3.7

Messana city of Messina in Sicily; *DVE* 2.5.4

Metamorfòseos the *Metamorphoses* of Ovid; *DVE* 1.2.7; *Conv.* 4.15.8; *Epist.* 3.7

Metaphỳsica the *Metaphysics* of Aristotle, called the "First Philosophy" (*Prima Filosofia*); *Conv.* 1.1.1; *Mon.* 3.12.1; *VN* 41.6; *Epist.* 13.14

Metàura (De Metauris) the *Meteorologica* of Aristotle; *Conv.* 2.14.6; *Quest.* 14

Metàura, de la the *De meteoris* of Albert the Great; *Conv.* 2.13.22

Metello Quintus Caecilius Metellus, the Roman tribune; *Purg.* 9.138

Meùccio one of Dante's friends; *Rime* 63.1

Mezzabati, Ildebrandino de' [Ildebrandinus Paduanus]

Michael Michael I, Rhangabe, emperor of Constantinople; *Mon.* 3.11.1

Michèl Zanche Michael Zanche of Logodoro in Sardinia, placed among barrators; *Inf.* 22.88

Michele the Archangel Michael; *Inf.* 7.11; *Purg.* 13.51; *Par.* 4.47

Michele Scotto Michael Scott, philosopher and astrologer, punished as a soothsayer; *Inf.* 20.116

Micòl Michol (Michal), daughter of Saul, king of Israel; *Purg.* 10.68

Mida Midas, king of Phrygia; *Purg.* 20.106; *Egl.* 4.53

Minerva Roman goddess, identified with Greek Pallas Athene; *Purg.* 15.98; *Par.* 2.8; *Conv.* 2.4.6; *Epist.* 13.3

Miniato, San church of San Miniato al Monte, one of the oldest Florentine churches; *Purg.* 12.101

Minoi [Minos]

Minòs Minos, king of Crete, lawgiver; *Inf.* 5.4; *Purg.* 1.77; *Par.* 13.14

Minotàuro the Minotaur, mythological monster,

guardian of the seventh circle of Hell; *Inf.* 12.12

Minus Mocatus Bartolomeo Mocati, Sienese poet; *DVE* 1.13.1

Mira, la small town between Padua and Venice; *Purg.* 5.79

Mirmidoni the Myrmidons, people of southern Thessaly; *Inf.* 29.64

Mirra Myrrha, daughter of Cinyras, king of Cyprus; *Inf.* 30.38; *Epist.* 7.24

Miseno Misenus, son of Aeolus, Trojan hero who drowned on journey to Italy; *Conv.* 4.26.13; *Mon.* 2.3.9

Mòbile, Primo [Cristallino]

Mocatus, Minus [Minus Mocatus]

Modarette Mordred, traitorous nephew of King Arthur; *Inf.* 32.61

Mòdena town of N. Italy; *Par.* 6.75

Moisè Moses, the prophet and lawgiver of the Hebrews; *Inf.* 4.57; *Purg.* 32.80; *Par.* 4.29

Molta the Moldau river in SW. Bohemia; *Purg.* 7.98

Monaldi Guelf family of Orvieto; *Purg.* 6.107

Monarchìa Dante's political treatise in Latin; *Mon.* 1.1.5

Monferrato Montferrat, former marquisate of NW. Italy; *Purg.* 7.136

Mongibello ancient name of Mt. Etna; *Inf.* 14.56

Montagna de' Parcitade (Parcitati) head of Ghibelline party in Rimini; *Inf.* 27.47

Montagne Rife the Riphaean mountains; *Purg.* 26.43

Montaperti village in Tuscany near Siena, site of the battle of 1260; *Inf.* 10.85

Monte, il [Giordano]

Monte Aventino [Aventino]

Monte Cassino [Cassino]

Montecchi Ghibelline family of Verona; *Purg.* 6.106

Monte di San Giuliano [Giuliano, San, monte di]

Montefeltro, Buonconte da [Bonconte]

Montefeltro, Guido da [Guido Montefeltrano]

Montemalo modern Monte Mario; *Par.* 15.109

Montemurlo castle situated between Prato and Pistoia; *Par.* 16.64

Montereggiòn Monteriggioni, fortified castle near Siena; *Inf.* 31.41

Monte Veso Monviso, mountain in Piedmont, source of the Po river; *Inf.* 16.95

Montfort [Guido di Montfort]

Montone [Ariete]

Montone river of N. Italy; *Inf.* 16.94

Monviso [Monte Veso]

Mopsus pastoral name by which Dante addresses Giovanni del Virgilio in his *Eglogues; Egl.* 2.6

Moroello Malaspina [Malaspina, Moroello]

Moronto brother of Dante's great-great-grandfather Cacciaguida; *Par.* 15.136

Morrocco Morocco, in NW. Africa; *Inf.* 26.104; *Purg.* 4.139

Mosca de' Lamberti member of Lamberti family of Florence; *Inf.* 6.80

Mosè [Moisè]

Motore Primo [Dio]

Moyses [Moisè]

Mozzi [Andrea de' Mozzi]

Mùcius [Mùzio]

Muse the nine Muses, daughters of Zeus and Mnemosyne; *Inf.* 2.7; *Purg.* 1.8; *Par.* 2.9; *Egl.* 4.65

Musica one of the four arts of the Quadrivium; *Conv.* 2.13.20

Mutinenses inhabitants of Modena; *DVE* 1.15.1

Mùzio Gaius Mucius Scaevola, Roman citizen; *Par.* 4.84; *Conv.* 4.5.13; *Mon.* 2.5.14

Myrrha [Mirra]

Nabuccodònosor Nabuchadnezzar II, Chaldean king of Babylon; *Par.* 4.14; *Epist.* 13.81

Naiade Naiads or river nymphs; *Purg.* 33.49

Namericus de Belnui Aimeric de Belenoi, Provençal troubadour; *DVE* 2.6.6

Namericus de Peculiano Aimeric de Preguilhan, Provençal troubadour; *DVE* 2.6.6

Napoleone degli Alberti son of Alberto degli Alberti, punished in Caina; *Inf.* 32.41

Napoleone Orsini [Ursus]

Nàpoli Naples, capital of old kingdom of Naples; *Purg.* 3.27

Napoletani [Neapolitani]

Narcisso Narcissus, beautiful Greek youth enamoured of his own image; *Inf.* 30.128; *Par.* 3.18

Nasetto, il "the small-nosed one," term applied to Philip III of France; *Purg.* 7.103

Naso [Ovìdio]

Nasìdio Nasidius, Roman soldier belonging to Cato's army in Africa; *Inf.* 25.95

Nasuto, il "the large-nosed one," term applied to Charles I of Naples; *Purg.* 7.124

Natàn Nathan, the Hebrew prophet who rebuked David; *Par.* 12.136

Natura de' luoghi e de le proprietadi de li elementi, De la Dante's title for Albert the Great's treatise *De Natura Locorum* ("On the Nature of Places"); *Conv.* 3.5.12

Naturali Auditu, De the treatise "On Physical Discourse," one of Dante's title for the *Physics* of Aristotle; *Mon.* 1.9.1

Navarra Navarre, kingdom on either side of the Pyrenees; *Inf.* 22.48; *Par.* 19.143; *DVE* 1.9.3

Navarrese the one from Navarre, referring to the barrator Ciampolo; *Inf.* 22.121

Nàyas Naiad, referring to the nymph of the river Savena, signifying Bologna; *Egl.* 4.85

Nazarette (Nazaret) Nazareth, site of the Annunciation; *Par.* 9.137

Nazzaro, Santo exemplary family of Pavia and Casale, later of Naples; *Conv.* 4.29.3

Neapolitani Neapolitans, inhabitants of Naples; *DVE* 1.9.4

Nella wife of Forese Donati; *Purg.* 23.87

Nembròt Nemrod (Nimrod), supposed builder of the Tower of Babel; *Inf.* 31.46; *Purg.* 12.34; *Par.* 26.126

Nemesis [Rhamnusia]

Neottolemo [Pirro]

Nèreus sea god, father of the Nereids; *Egl.* 4.21

Neri the "Blacks," a faction of the Guelf party; *Inf.* 24.143

Nerli noble family of Florence; *Par.* 15.115

Nerone Nero, Roman emperor; *Mon.* 3.13.5; *Conv.* 4.9.16

Nesso Nessus, one of the centaurs; *Inf.* 12.67

Nettuno Neptune, god of the sea; *Inf.* 28.83; *Par.* 33.96

Niccola Acciaioli [Acciaioli, Niccola]

Niccolò, San St. Nicholas, bishop of Myra in Lycia; *Purg.* 20.32

Niccolò da Prato [Nicholaus]

Niccolò dei Bonsignori [Niccolò de' Salimbeni]

Niccolò dei Salimbeni reputed member of "the Spendthrift" club of Siena; *Inf.* 29.127

Niccolò III Pope Nicholas III (Giovanni Gaetano Orsini); *Inf.* 19.70

Nicholaus Niccolò da Prato, cardinal; *Epist.* 1.1

Nichòmacum, Ad [Ètica]

Nicosia town on island of Cyprus, used to refer to Henry II of Lusignan, king of Cyprus; *Par.* 19.146

Nilo the river Nile; *Inf.* 34.45; *Purg.* 24.64; *Par.* 6.66

Ninfe nymphs; *Purg.* 29.4; *Epist.* 3.7; *Egl.* 4.58

Nino Ninus, mythical founder of the Assyrian empire; *Inf.* 5.59

Nino Visconti a judge of Gallura in Sardinia; *Purg.* 8.53

Nìobè Niobe, daughter of Tantalus and Dione and wife of Amphion, king of Thebes; *Purg.* 12.37

Nisa [Elicona]

Niso Nisus, Trojan youth who accompanied Aeneas to Italy; *Inf.* 1.108

Noarese Novarese, inhabitant of Novara; *Inf.* 28.59

Nocera town in province of Perugia; *Par.* 11.48

Noè the patriarch Noah; *Inf.* 4.56; *Par.* 12.17

Nogaret, Guiglielmo di [Guiglielmo di Nogaret]

Noli town in Liguria; *Purg.* 4.25

Normandia Normandy, northern region of France; *Purg.* 20.66

Norvègia Norway; *Par.* 19.139

Notaro, il "the Notary," common name of Sicilian poet Giacomo da Lentini; *Purg.* 24.56

Novarese [Noarese]

Novello [Alessandro, Federico Novello]

Numa Pompìlio Numa Pompilius, second king of Rome; *Conv.* 4.5.2; *DVE* 1.17.2; *Mon.* 2.4.6

Nymphe [Ninfe]

Obertus de Romena Uberto, one of the Conti Guidi of Romena; *Epist.* 2

Òbizzo da Esti [Òpizzo da Esti]

Obriachi Florentine family; *Inf.* 17.62

Ocèano the ocean; *Conv.* 3.5.9; *Mon.* 1.11.12; *DVE* 1.8.4; *Epist.* 7.12

Octo (Ottone) Otto or Otho I, duke of Saxony and king of Germany; *Mon.* 3.11.3

Oderisi da Gùbbio manuscript illuminator, placed on the first terrace of Purgatory; *Purg.* 11.79

Oenotri Oenotrians, inhabitants of ancient Oenotria in S. of Italy; *Mon.* 2.3.12

Offici, de li (Offìtia) the *De officiis*, Cicero's treatise on morality; *Conv.* 4.8.2; *Mon.* 2.5.7

Ognissanti All Saints' Day; *Rime* 69.2

Olimpo Olympus, the home of the pagan gods, or heaven; *Purg.* 24.15

Oloferne Holofernes, the general of Nabuchodonosor's armies; *Purg.* 12.59

Omberto Omberto Aldobrandesco, count of Santafiora, placed on the first terrace of Purgatory; *Purg.* 11.67

Omero (Homerus) the poet Homer; VN 2.8, 25.9; *Inf.* 4.88; *Purg.* 22.101; *Conv.* 4.20.4; *Mon.* 1.5.5

Onesto degli Onesti [Honestus Bononiensis]

Onòrio III Pope Honorius III (Cencio Savelli); *Par.* 11.98

Òpizzo II d'Esti marquis of Ferrara and of the March of Ancona, placed in the first ring of the violent in Hell; *Inf.* 12.111

Oràtii the Horatii, three Roman brothers who fought with three Curiatii of Alba Longa; *Par.* 6.39; *Conv.* 4.5.18; *Mon.* 2.9.15

Oràzio (Horàtius) the poet Horace; *Inf.* 4.89; *VN* 25.9; *Conv.* 2.13.10; *DVE* 2.4.4; *Epist.* 13.30

Orbicciani [Bonagiunta]

Orbivieto [Orvieto]

Ordelaffi family alluded to by Dante as rulers of Forlì; *Inf.* 27.45

Oreste Orestes, son of Agamemnon and Clytemnestra; *Purg.* 13.32

Orfeo Orpheus, mythical Greek poet; *Inf.* 4.140; *Conv.* 2.1.3

Òria, Branca d' [Branca d'Òria]

Oriaco modern Oriago, village in Venezia Euganea; *Purg.* 5.80

Orlando Roland, nephew of Charlemagne and epic hero; *Inf.* 31.18; *Par.* 18.43

Ormanni noble family of Florence; *Par.* 16.89

Oròsio, Pàulo Paulus Orosius, Spanish priest and historian; *Par.* 10.119; *DVE* 2.6.7; *Conv.* 3.11.3; *Mon.* 2.3.13

Orsa, Orsatti [Orsini]

Orsa Maggiore e Minore Great and Little Bear, constellations; *Purg.* 4.65; *Par.* 2.9

Orsini Roman family; *Inf.* 19.70

Orsini, Napoleone [Ursus]

Orso degli Alberti Count Orso di Mangona, son of Count Napoleone degli Alberti, placed among the late repentant in the Ante-Purgatory; *Purg.* 6.19

Ortènsio Quintus Hortensius Hortalus, Roman orator and leader; *Conv.* 4.28.14

Orvieto [Urbs Vetus]

Osterlicchi Austria; *Inf.* 32.26

Ostiense belonging to Ostia, village in Latium; *Par.* 12.83

Ottàchero Ottokar II, king of Bohemia 1253-78; *Purg.* 7.100

Ottaviano [Augusto]

Ottaviano degli Ubaldini [Cardinale, il]

Ottobono de' Fieschi [Adriano V]

Ottocaro II [Ottàchero]

Ovìdio Roman poet Ovid; *Inf.* 4.90; *VN* 25.9; *Conv.* 2.1.3

Ovìdio Maggiore "the Greater Ovid," Dante's term for Ovid's *Metamorphoses; Conv.* 3.3.7

Oza Uzzah, one of Abinadab's sons; *Purg.* 10.57; *Epist.* 11.9

Pachino modern Cape Passero, ancient Pachynus Promontorium of SE. Sicily; *Par.* 8.68

Pactolis of the Pactolus, river in Lydia; *Egl.* 4.53

Pado the Po river in northern Italy; *Par.* 15.137

Pàdova Padua, city near Venice; *Par.* 9.46

Padovani Paduans, inhabitants of Padua; *Inf.* 15.7; *Purg.* 5.75

Paduani [Padovani]

Pagani [Gentili]

Pagani noble Ghibelline family of Faenza; *Purg.* 14.118

Palazzo, Currado da [Currado da Palazzo]

Palermo capital of Sicily; *Par.* 8.75

Palestina Palestine; *Purg.* 18.135; *Par.* 9.125

Palestrina [Penestrino]

Pàllade Pallas Athena; *Purg.* 12.31; *Epist.* 13.3; *Conv.* 2.4.6

Pallàdio the Palladium, statue of Pallas Athena; *Inf.* 26.63

Pallante Pallas, son of Trojan Evander; *Par.* 6.36; *Mon.* 2.9.14

Pània [Pietrapana]

Pantasilea Penthesilea, daughter of Mars and queen of the Amazons; *Inf.* 4.124

Pàolo (Pàulus) Paul the Apostle; *Inf.* 2.28; *Par.* 18.131; *Conv.* 4.5.16; *Mon.* 1.4.4; *Epist.* 11.3

Pàolo Malatesta [Malatesta, Paolo]

Pàolo Oròsio [Oròsio, Pàolo]

Papia [Pavia]

Papienses inhabitants of Pavia; *DVE* 1.9.7

Paradiso the third canticle of the *Commedia; Epist.* 13.11

Paradiso Heaven; *Purg.* 1.99; *Par.* 3.89; *Conv.* 3.8.5; *Mon.* 3.16.7; *Epist.* 13.51

Paradiso the Earthly Paradise at the top of Purgatory; *Par.* 7.38; *DVE* 1.4.2; *Mon.* 3.16.7

Paradoxo, De Cicero's *Paradoxa Stoicorum,* the *Paradoxes of the Stoics; Conv.* 4.12.6

Paralipòmenon the Books of Chronicles; *Mon.* 2.7.8; *Purg.* 29.83

Parche, le tre [Atropòs; Cloto; Lachesis]

Parcitati, Montagna de' [Montagna de' Parcitade]

Pàride [Parìs]

Parigi Paris, capital of France; *Purg.* 11.81; *Par.* 10.137

Parìs Paris (Alexander) of Troy, son of Priam and Hecuba; *Inf.* 5.67

Parisi [Parigi]

Parma town in Emilia; *Conv.* 4.16.6

Parmènide Parmenides, Greek philosopher; *Par.* 13.125; *Mon.* 3.4.4

Parmenses inhabitants of Parma; *DVE* 1.15.4; *Epist.* 6.19

Parnaso Parnassus, mountain in Greece; *Purg.* 22.65; *Par.* 1.16; *Epist.* 13.87

Pasife Pasiphae, daughter of Helius and nymph Persa; *Inf.* 12.13; *Purg.* 26.41

Passo d'Arno [Ponte Vècchio]

Pàulo, Pàulus [Pàolo]

Pavesi [Papienses]

Pavia town in Lombardy; *Conv.* 4.29.3; *Epist.* 7.22

Pazzi noble family of Tuscany; *Inf.* 32.68

Pazzo, Rinièr da robber, punished in the first ring of the seventh circle of Hell; *Inf.* 12.137

Peana Paean, hymn of triumph or praise; *Par.* 13.25

Peccatòr, Pietro [Damiano, Pièr]

Peguilhan, Aimeric de [Namericus de Peculiano]

Peire d'Alvernhe [Petrus de Alvèrnia]

Pèleo (Pèleus) father of Achilles; *Inf.* 31.5; *Conv.* 4.27.20; *Epist.* 13.30

Peloro Pelorus, promontory at NE. extremity of Sicily; *Purg.* 14.32; *Par.* 8.68

Peneys Daphne, daughter of Peneus; *Par.* 1.32; *Egl.* 2.33 **[Dafne]**

Penelopè wife of Ulysses; *Inf.* 26.96

Penestrino Palestrina, fortress of the Colonna family; *Inf.* 27.102

Peni Phoenicians, i.e., Carthaginians; *Mon.* 2.4.9

Pentesilea [Pantasilea]

Pera, de la noble family of Florence; *Par.* 16.124

Pèrgama citadel of Troy; *Epist.* 6.15

Pergàmei inhabitants of Bergamo; *DVE* 1.11.4

Pèrgamum Bergamo, town in Lombardy; *Epist.* 7.22

Periandro Periander, son of Cypselus; *Conv.* 3.11.4

Perillo Perillus, inventor of the brazen bull in which Phalaris roasted his victims; *Inf.* 27.7

Perini, Dino [Melibeus]

Peripatètici the peripatetics, or Aristotelian school of philosophers; *Conv.* 3.14.15, 4.6.15–16

Perse Persians, inhabitants of Persia; *Par.* 19.112; *Mon.* 2.8.6

Pèrsio Persius (Aulus Persius Flaccus), Roman satyrist; *Purg.* 22.100

Perùgia town in N. Umbria; *Par.* 6.75

Perùsium Latin name for Perugia; *DVE* 1.13.2

Pescatore, il "the fisherman," i.e., Peter; *Purg.* 22.63; *Par.* 18.136

Peschiera town and fortress at SE. shore of Lake Garda; *Inf.* 20.70

Pesci Pisces ("the Fishes"), constellation and last of the twelve signs of the Zodiac

Petra [Pietra]

Petramala Pietramala, village at foot of N. slopes of Etruscan Apennines; *DVE* 1.6.2

Petrus name of an imaginary person; *DVE* 2.8.4

Petrus [Pietro, San]

Petrus Comestor [Pietro Mangiadore]

Petrus de Alvèrnia Peire d'Alvernha, Peter of Auvergne, troubadour poet; *DVE* 1.10.3

Pettinaio, Pièr Peter the combmaker of Siena, hermit of Franciscan order; *Purg.* 13.128

Phàrao Pharaoh, king of Egypt; *Mon.* 2.4.2

Pharisei Pharisees; *Epist.* 11.1

Pharsàlia [Farsàlia]

Pharsàlia [Farsàlia]

Phebe [Diana]

Phebus [Apollo, Sole]

Pheton [Fetonte]

Philistei, Philistini [Filistei]

Phylòsophus the Philosopher, title by which Aristotle was known; *Mon.* 1.3.1; *Epist.* 11.5; *Quest.* 4

Phỳsica (Fisica, De Naturali Auditu) the *Physics* or *Physical Discourse* of Aristotle; *Inf.* 11.101; *Conv.* 2.1.13; *DVE* 2.10.1; *Epist.* 13.70; *Quest.* 21; *Mon.* 1.9.1

Pia, la Sienese lady placed among the late repentant in the Ante-Purgatory; *Purg.* 5.133

Piacentini [Placentini]

Piava the Piave, river of N. Italy; *Par.* 9.27

Piccarda daughter of Simone Donati, placed in the Heaven of the Moon; *Purg.* 24.10; *Par.* 3.49

Piceno, Campo [Campo Piceno]

Piche, le the Magpies, i.e., the Pierides, the nine daughters of Pierus; *Purg.* 1.2; *DVE* 1.2.7

Pièr dalla Broccia [Bròccia, Pièr da la]

Pièr da Medicina [Medicina, Pièr da]

Pièr Damiani [Damiano, Pièr]

Pièr d'Aragona [Pietro III]

Pièr degli Onesti [Pietro degli Onesti]

Pièr de la Brosse [Bròccia, Pièr de la]

Pièr della Vigna Petrus de Vineis, minister of Emperor Frederick II; *Inf.* 13.32

Pièridi Pierides, the nine daughters of Pierus; *Purg.* 1.2; *DVE* 1.2.7

Piero [Pietro]

Pièr Pettinaio [Pettinaio, Pièr]

Pièr Traversaro Ghibelline nobleman from Ravenna; *Purg.* 14.98

Piètola town near Mantua where Virgil was born; *Purg.* 18.83

Pietra (Petra) the "stony" lady, subject of Dante's *Rime petrose* (e.g., *Rime* 103)

Pietramala [Petramala]

Pietrapana name of mountain mentioned in connection with ice of Cocytus; *Inf.* 32.29

Pietro St. Peter the Apostle; *Inf.* 1.134; *Purg.* 9.127; *Par.* 9.141; *Conv.* 4.22.14; *Mon.* 2.8.1

Pietro Colonna son of Giovanni Colonna and cardinal; *Epist.* 11.24

Pietro Lombardo Peter Lombard, theologian and bishop born near Novara; *Par.* 10.107

Pietro III Pedro III, king of Aragon; *Purg.* 7.112

Pietro Bernardone [Bernardone, Pietro]

Pietro Damiano [Damiano, Pietro]

Pietro degli Onesti monk of Ravenna, founded monastery of Santa Maria in Portofuori; *Par.* 21.122

Pietro Ispano [Ispano, Pietro]

Pietro Mangiadore Petrus Comestor, French theologian; *Par.* 12.134

Pietro Peccatore [Damiano, Pietro]

Pietro, San St. Peter's basilica in Rome; *Inf.* 18.32; *Conv.* 4.16.6

Pigli noble family of Florence; *Par.* 16.103

Pigmalione Pygmalion, son of Belus, king of Tyre; *Purg.* 20.103

Pignatelli, Bartolomeo archbishop of Cosenza; *Purg.* 3.124

Pila, Ubaldìn da la Ubaldino degli Ubaldini of La Pila, member of a powerful Ghibelline family of that name; *Purg.* 24.29

Pìlade Pylades, son of Strophius, king of Phocis; *Purg.* 13.32

Pilato (Pilatus) Pontius Pilate, Roman procurator of Judaea who tried Christ; *Purg.* 20.91; *Mon.* 2.11.5; *Epist.* 5.28

Pinamonte Pinamonte dei Bonacolsi lord of Mantua; *Inf.* 20.96

Pio Pius I, pope; *Par.* 27.44

Pìramo Pyramus, lover of Thisbe; *Purg.* 27.38; *Mon.* 2.8.4

Pirenei the Pyrenees, mountain range between France and Spain; *Par.* 19.144; *Epist.* 6.12; *Egl.* 4.66

Pirro Pyrrhus, king of Epirus, perhaps referred to in *Inf.* 12.135

Pirro Pyrrhus or Neoptolemus, son of Achilles and Deidamia; *Inf.* 12.135; *Par.* 6.44

Pirroi Pyroeis, one of the four horses which drew the chariot of the sun; *Conv.* 4.23.14

Pisa city of Tuscany; *Inf.* 33.79; *Purg.* 6.17

Pisani inhabitants of Pisa; *Inf.* 33.30

Pisanus, Gallus [Gallus Pisanus]

Piscitelli family of Naples; *Conv.* 4.29.3

Pisìstrato Pisistratus, tyrant of Athens, an example of the meek in Purgatory; *Purg.* 15.101

Pistòia town in Tuscany; *Inf.* 24.126

Pittàgora Pythagoras, Greek philosopher; *Conv.* 2.13.18; *Mon.* 1.15.2

Pittagòrici Pythagoreans, followers of Pythagoras; *Conv.* 2.15.5

Placentini inhabitants of Piacenza; *DVE* 1.10.9

Platone Plato, Greek philosopher; *Inf.* 4.134; *Purg.* 3.43; *Par.* 4.24; *Conv.* 3.5.6; *Epist.* 13.29

Plàuto Plautus, Roman comic poet; *Purg.* 22.98

Plìnius Pliny the Elder, Roman naturalist and historian; *DVE* 2.6.7

Pluto name given by Dante to guardian of the fourth circle of Hell; *Inf.* 6.115

Po the Po river (the Roman Padus); *Inf.* 5.98; *Purg.* 14.92; *Par.* 6.51; *Conv.* 4.13.13; *Epist.* 7.23; *Egl.* 2.67

Podestadi the Powers, an Angelic Hierarchy; *Conv.* 2.5.6; *Par.* 28.122; *Conv.* 2.5.6

Poètria the *Ars poetica* of Horace; *VN* 25.9; *Conv.* 2.13.10; *Epist.* 13.30; *DVE* 2.4.4

Pola sea-port in Istria; *Inf.* 9.113

Polenta castle near Bertinoro in Emilia; *Inf.* 27.41

Policleto Polycletus, Greek sculptor; *Purg.* 10.32

Polidoro Polydorus, son of Priam, king of Troy; *Inf.* 30.18; *Purg.* 20.115

Polimnia Polyhymnia, Muse of lyric poetry; *Par.* 23.56

Polinestor Polymestor, king of Thracian Chersonese; *Purg.* 20.115

Polinice Polynices, son of Oedipus; *Purg.* 22.56

Poliphemus one of Cyclopes in Sicily; *Egl.* 4.75

Polìssena Polyxena, daughter of Priam, king of Troy; *Inf.* 30.17

Politica (De Polìticis, Politici libri) the *Politics* of Aristotle; *Conv.* 4.4.5; *Mon.* 1.3.10

Polluce Pollux, son of Jupiter and Leda, twin brother of Castor; *Purg.* 4.61

Polo popular form of Paolo; *Par.* 18.136

Pompeo Pompey the Great, Roman politician and general; *Par.* 6.53

Pompeo [Sesto Pompeo]

Pompìlio [Numa Pompìlio]

Ponte Vècchio bridge over Arno in Florence; *Inf.* 13.146; *Par.* 16.46

Ponti Ponthieu, former district of France; *Purg.* 20.66

Pòppii, Castrum Poppi castle, in the Casentino; *Epist.* 10.6

Porciano stronghold of the Conti Guidi in the Casentino; *Purg.* 14.43

Porsenna Lars Porsena, king of Etruscan town of Clusium; *Mon.* 2.4.10, 2.5.14

Porta Collina gate in Rome; *Mon.* 2.9.17

Porta Peruzza one of minor gates of city of Florence; *Par.* 16.125

Porta San Piero one of gates of ancient Florence; *Par.* 16.94

Porta Sole one of gates of Perugia; *Par.* 11.47

Portinari, Beatrice [Beatrice]

Portinari, Folco father of Beatrice Portinari; *VN* 22.1

Portinari, Manetto a brother of Beatrice Portinari; *VN* 32.1

Portinari, Ricòvero a brother of Beatrice Portinari; *VN* 32.1

Portogallo Portugal; *Par.* 19.139

Potestadi [Podestadi]

Praga Prague, capital of Bohemia; *Par.* 19.117

Prata now Prada, village in Romagna; *Purg.* 14.104

Pratenses inhabitants of Prato; *DVE* 1.11.6

Prato town in Tuscany; *Inf.* 26.9

Pratomagno mountain-ridge in Tuscany; *Purg.* 5.116

Predicamenta the *Categories* of Aristotle; *Mon.* 3.15.9

Pressa, Della noble family of Florence; *Par.* 16.100

Presto the priest Gianni, legendary eastern monarch of the Christian faith; *Fiore* 126.12

Prìamo (Prìamus) Priam, king of Troy at time of Trojan war; *Inf.* 30.15; *Mon.* 2.3.10

Prieneo Prieneus; *Conv.* 3.11.4

Prima Phylosophia [Phylosophia Prima]

Primo Mòbile [Cristallino, Cielo]

Primavera "Spring," nickname of Giovanna, beloved of Guido Cavalcanti; *VN* 24.3

Principati Principalities, Angelic Hierarchy; *Par.* 28.124; *Conv.* 2.5.6

Prisciano Priscian (Priscianus Caesariensis), celebrated Latin grammarian; *Inf.* 15.109

Proenza [Provenza]

Progne Procne, daughter of Pandion, king of Athens; *Purg.* 17.19

Promèteo Prometheus, son of the Titan Iapetus and Clymene; *Conv.* 4.15.8

Proprietadi de li elementi, De le Albert the Great's treatise *De Proprietatibus Elementorum* ("On the Properties of the Elements"); *Conv.* 3.4.12

Prosèrpina Proserpine, daughter of Jupiter and Ceres; *Inf.* 9.44

Protëusso (Pròteo) Proteus, the sea god; *Fiore* 100.2

Provenza Provence, former province of France; *Purg.* 7.126; *Par.* 8.58

Provenzali Provençals, inhabitants of Provence; *Par.* 6.130; *DVE* 1.8.9

Provenzàn Salvani prominent Ghibelline of Siena; *Purg.* 11.121

Proverbi (Provèrbia) Book of Proverbs of Solomon; *Conv.* 3.11.12; *Purg.* 29.83

Provinciales [Provenzali]

Psalmi [Salmi]

Psalmista [Salmista]

Ptolomeus [Tolomeo]

Pùblius Dècius [Dècius, Pùblius]

Pùccio Bellondi Italian vernacular poet; *Rime dubbie* 24

Pùccio Sciancato "Puccio the lame," member of Galigai family of Florence; *Inf.* 25.35

Pùglia Apulia, region in SE. Italy; *Inf.* 28.9; *Purg.* 5.69; *Par.* 8.61

Pugliesi Apulians, inhabitants of Apulia; *Inf.* 28.17; *DVE* 1.10.8

Pùnico (Bello pùnico) Livy's history of the Second Punic War in *Ab urbe condita*; *Mon.* 2.4.9

Purgatòrio Purgatory, realm of the penitent; *Purg.* 7.39

Purgatòrio the second canticle of the *Commedia*; *Purg.* 33.140

Putifarre, mòglie di Potiphar's wife, placed among the Falsifiers; *Inf.* 30.97

Pyerides [Muse]

Pyreneus Pyreneus; *Egl.* 4.66

Pyrrhus [Pirro]

Pythàgoras [Pittàgora]

Quadrìvio the Quadrivium, comprising four of the seven liberal arts, i.e., music, arithmetic, geometry, and astronomy; *Conv.* 2.13.8

Quantitate Ànime, De [Ànime, De Quantitate]

Quarnero [Carnaro]

Quàtuor Virtùtibus, Liber de (Libro de le quattro vertù cardinali) treatise of Martinus Dumiensis *On the Four Cardinal Virtues*; *Conv.* 3.8.12; *Mon.* 2.5.3

Quèstio de Aqua et Terra Dante's treatise on the relative levels of water and land

Quìnzio Quinctius, i.e., Lucius Quinctius Cincinnatus; *Par.* 6.46; *Conv.* 4.5.15

Quirini, Giovanni [Giovanni Quirini]

Quirino Quirinus, name given to Romulus after his death and subsequent elevation to divinity; *Par.* 8.131

Raàb Rahab, harlot of Jericho; *Par.* 9.116

Rabano Màuro Rabanus Maurus Magnentius, author of the *De institutione clericorum*; *Par.* 12.139

Rachele Rachel, younger daughter of Laban, second wife of Jacob; *Inf.* 2.102, 4.60; *Purg.* 27.104; *Par.* 32.8

Raffaele the Archangel Raphael; *Par.* 4.48

Raimondo V [Tolosa, conte di]

Ramondo Berlinghieri [Berlinghieri, Ramondo]

Ràscia name of the kingdom of Serbia in the Middle Ages; *Par.* 19.140

Ravenna town in Romagna on Adriatic; *Inf.* 5.97; *Par.* 6.61

Ravennates inhabitants of Ravenna; *DVE* 1.9.4

Ravignani noble family of Florence; *Par.* 16.97

Re Giòvane, il [Arrigo]

Re Militari, De the treatise *On the Art of War* of Flavius Vegetius Renatus; *Mon.* 2.9.3

Rëa Rhea, or Cybele, ancient goddess, daughter of Heaven and Earth; *Inf.* 14.100

Rebecca Rebekah, daughter of Bethuel and sister of Laban; *Par.* 32.10

Reggiani [Regiani]

Reggimento de' Prìncipi, De lo Dante's title for the *De regimine principum* (*On the Government of Princes*) of Egidio Colonna Romano *Conv.* 4.24.9

Reggio town of N. Italy near Parma; *Conv.* 4.14.6

Regi Antichi [Carolingi]

Regiani inhabitants of Reggio; *DVE* 1.15.4

Regina Austri [Saba, regina di]

Reginaldo degli Scrovegni nobleman from Padova, damned as a usurer; *Inf.* 17.64

Regno, il the Kingdom (of Sicily); *Purg.* 3.131

Règolo Marcus Atilius Regulus, famous hero of Roman history; *Conv.* 4.5.14

Regum libri (libro de li Regi) [Libri Regum]

Remèdio d'Amore Ovid's *Remedia Amoris* (*The Remedies of Love*); *VN* 25.9; *Inf.* 31.5

Renaldus de Aquino Rinaldo d'Aquino, poet of Sicilian school; *DVE* 2.5.4

Reno river of N. Italy; *Inf.* 18.61; *Purg.* 14.92

Reno the Rhine river; *Par.* 6.58

Renoardo Renouard, French epic hero, placed among the crusaders in the Heaven of Mars; *Par.* 18.46

Rerum Transformatione or Transmutatione one of Dante's titles for Ovid's *Metamorphoses*; *Mon.* 2.7.10; *Epist.* 3.7

Rethòrica, Prima (Nova) Cicero's *De inventione rhetorica*; *Epist.* 13.49; *Mon.* 2.5.2

Rettòrica (Rethòrica) Aristotle's *Rhetoric*; *Conv.* 3.8.10; *Epist.* 13.44; *Mon.* 1.9.11

Rettòrica rhetoric, one of the three arts of the Trivium; *Conv.* 3.11.9; *VN* 25.7.10

Rhamnùsia name applied to Nemesis; *Epist.* 3.8

Rïalto the bridge in Venice, used by Cunizza for Venice itself; *Par.* 9.26

Riccardo da San Vittore (Riccardus) Richard of St. Victor; *Par.* 10.131; *Epist.* 13.80

Ridolfo [Rodolfo]

Rife, Montagne [Montagne Rife]

Rifeo Ripheus (occasionally spelled Rhipeus), Trojan hero slain during sack of Troy; *Par.* 20.68

Rime title used for Dante's collected lyrics

Rìmini town of N. Italy in SE. Emilia; *Inf.* 28.86

Rìmini, Francesca da [Francesca]

Rinaldo d'Aquino [Renaldus de Aquino]

Rinièr da Càlboli member of Guelf family of that name at Forlì; *Purg.* 14.88

Rinièr da Corneto [Corneto, Rinièr da]

Rinièr Pazzo [Pazzo, Rinièr]

Rizzardo da Camino [Camino, Rizzardo da]

Roberto Robert, king of France; *Purg.* 20.59

Roberto d'Angiò Robert, king of Naples; *Par.* 8.77

Roberto [Ruberto]

Roboàm Rehoboam, son of Solomon, an example of pride in Purgatory; *Purg.* 12.46

Rocco de' Mozzi [Mozzi]

Ròdano the Rhone, a principal river of France; *Inf.* 9.112; *Par.* 6.60

Rodolfo (Ridolfo) d'Asburgo Rudolf I, emperor; *Purg.* 7.94; *Par.* 8.72; *Conv.* 4.3.6

Rodopèa Phyllis, daughter of the king of Thrace; *Par.* 9.100

Roma Rome, city on the Tiber; *Inf.* 1.71; *Purg.* 21.89; *Par.* 6.57; *VN* 25.9; *Conv.* 3.5.10

Romagna (Romaniola) former province of N. Italy; *Inf.* 27.37; *Purg.* 5.69; *Epist.* 1.1

Romagnuoli (Romandioli) Romagnoles, inhabitants of Romagna; *Inf.* 27.28; *Purg.* 14.99; *Conv.* 4.3.6; *DVE* 1.10.8

Romani Romans, inhabitants of Rome; *Inf.* 15.77; *Par.* 6.44; *Conv.* 3.11.3; *DVE.* 1.9.2; *Mon.* 2.3.16

Romano, colle di hill in the March of Treviso; *Par.* 9.28

Romanos, Epìstola ad St. Paul's Epistle to the Romans; *Conv.* 4.28.10; *Mon.* 2.2.8; *Epist.* 5.23

Romena village in the Casentino; *Inf.* 30.73

Romeo di Villanova the minister of Raymond Berenger IV; *Par.* 6.128

Romoaldo degli Onesti St. Romualdus, founder of order of Camaldoli or Reformed Benedictines; *Par.* 22.49

Ròmolo Romulus, mythical founder of Rome; *Conv.* 4.5.10; *Par.* 8.131

Rosso, Mare [Mare Rosso]

Rubaconte old name for the Ponte alle Grazie, bridge in Florence; *Purg.* 12.102

Ruberto Guiscardo [Guiscardo, Ruberto]

Rubicante one of ten demons in the fifth bolgia of Malebolge; *Inf.* 21.123

Rubicone the Rubicon, small river of N. Italy flowing into the Adriatic near Rimini; *Par.* 6.62

Ruggieri degli Ubaldini the Ghibelline archbishop of Pisa, damned as a traitor in Antenora; *Inf.* 33.14

Rusticucci, Iàcopo [Iàcopo Rusticucci]

Ruth Moabitish wife of Boaz and great-grandmother of David; *Par.* 32.10

Rùtuli Rutulians, ancient people of Italy; *Mon.* 2.7.2; *Epist.* 7.18

Saba, Regina the queen of Sheba; *Epist.* 13.3

Sabèllio Sabellius, heretic; *Par.* 13.127

Sabello Sabellus, Roman soldier, cited in Lucan's *Pharsalia; Inf.* 25.95

Sabine Sabine women; *Par.* 6.40

Sabini Sabines, ancient people of central Italy; *Par.* 6.40; *Mon.* 2.9.16

Sacchetti noble family of Florence; *Par.* 16.104

Safira Sapphira, wife of Ananias, both examples of avarice; *Purg.* 20.112

Saguntum ancient town of Spain near Valencia; *Epist.* 6.18

Saladino, il Saladin, sultan, placed in Limbo; *Inf.* 4.129; *Conv.* 4.11.14

Salamone [Salomone]

Salimbeni, Niccolò de' [Niccolò]

Salmi (Psalmi, Psaltèrio, Saltèrio) the Book of Psalms; *Inf.* 31.69; *Purg.* 2.48; *Par.* 14.136; *Conv.* 4.19.7; *Mon.* 2.9.1; *Epist.* 13.62; *Quest.* 77

Salmista (Psalmista) the Psalmist David; *Purg.* 10.65; *Conv.* 2.3.2; *Mon.* 1.15.3; *Quest.* 77

Salomè "the mother of Zebedee's children" and sister of Mary; *Conv.* 4.22.14

Salomone Solomon, king of Israel; *Purg.* 30.10; *Par.* 10.109; *Conv.* 2.5.5; *Mon.* 3.1.3

Salterello, Lapo [Lapo]

Saltèrio (Saltero) [Salmi]

Salvagnone literary name for a thief; *Fiore* 31.14

Salvani, Provenzàn [Provenzàn Salvani]

Sàmius Vates [Pittàgora]

Sammaritana, la woman from Samaria, in New Testament; *Purg.* 21.3

Samnites inhabitants of Samnium; *Mon.* 2.9.16

Samuèl Samuel, the prophet and last judge of Israel; *Par.* 4.29; *Mon.* 2.7.8

San Benedetto de l'Alpe mountain in Etruscan Apennines; *Inf.* 16.100

San Gal (Santa Maria a San Gallo) hospital in Florence; *Rime* 76.1

San Giovanni [Giovanni]

San Giuliano, monte di [Giuliano, San, monte di]

San Leo [Sanleo]

San Miniato a Monte [Miniato, San]

San Pietro [Pietro]

San Pietro in Ciel d'Oro [Cieldàuro]

San Simone church in Florence near city's principal jail; *Rime* 75.5

San Vittore abbey of Saint-Victor, near Paris; *Par.* 12.133

San Zeno [Zeno, San]

Sància Sanchia, daughter of Raymond Berenger IV; *Par.* 6.133

Sanesi (Senenses) the Sienese; *Inf.* 29.134; *Purg.* 11.65; *DVE* 1.13.2

Sanleo San Leo, town of mountainous district of Montefeltro; *Purg.* 4.25

Sannella, De la noble family of Florence; *Par.* 16.92

Sanniti Samnites, inhabitants of Samnium; *Conv.* 4.5.13; *Mon.* 2.9.16

Santafiòr Santafiora, county and town in Sienese territory; *Purg.* 6.3

Sant'Amore [Guiglielmo de Sant'Amore]

Sant'Andrea [Giàcomo da Santo Andrea]

Sant'Elena [Helene sacellum]

Santerno small river in N. Italy; *Inf.* 27.49

Santo Nazzaro [Nazzaro, Santo]

Santo Volto "Holy Face," the name of crucifix preserved in the Basilica of San Martino in Lucca; *Inf.* 21.48

Sapia wife of Ghinibaldo Saracini, Sienese noble, and

aunt of Provenzàn Salvani; *Purg.* 13.109

Sapienza (Sapièntia) the Book of Wisdom, or the Wisdom of Solomon; *Conv.* 3.15.5; *Epist.* 13.6;

Sara Sarah, wife of Abraham and mother of Isaac; *Par.* 32.10

Saracini (Saraceni) Saracens, term used in Middle Ages to designate Arab and Muhammadan races; *Inf.* 27.87; *Purg.* 23.103; *Epist.* 5.5

Sardanapalo Sardanapalus, last of the great Assyrian kings; *Par.* 15.107

Sardegna [Sardigna]

Sardi Sards (Sardinians), inhabitants of Sardinia; *Inf.* 26.104; *Purg.* 18.81; *DVE* 1.10.6

Sardigna (Sardìnia) the island of Sardinia; *Inf.* 22.89; *Purg.* 23.94; *DVE* 1.10.5

Sarnus Latin name Dante uses, incorrectly, for the Arno river; *DVE* 1.6.3; *Epist.* 4.2; *Egl.* 2.44

Sàrpina [Sàvena]

Sassòl Mascheroni [Mascheroni, Sassòl]

Sàssoni, Sassònia [Sàxones, Saxònia]

Satàn (Satanàs) [Lucìfero]

Saturno Saturn, pagan god, father of Jupiter; *Inf.* 14.96; *Par.* 22.145

Saturno Saturn, the heaven and planet; *Purg.* 19.3; *Par.* 21.26; *Conv.* 2.3.7

Saùl Saul, first king of Israel; *Purg.* 12.40

Sàvena (Sàrpina) small river of N. Italy; *Inf.* 18.61; *Egl.* 4.41

Savi d'Egitto Wise Men of Egypt; *Conv.* 2.14.1

Savi, Sette Seven Sages of Greece; *Conv.* 3.11.4

Sàvio small river of N. Italy near Ravenna; *Inf.* 27.52

Sàxones inhabitants of Saxony; *DVE* 1.8.4

Saxònia Saxony, medieval duchy in central Germany; *Mon.* 3.11.3

Scala, Della the Della Scala (or Scaliger) family of Verona; *Par.* 17.72; *Epist.* 13.1 **[Alberto, Albuino, Bartolomeo, Cangrande, Giuseppe]**

Scandinàvie Soboles [Lombardi]

Scariotto, Giuda Judas Iscariot; *Inf.* 34.62; *Purg.* 20.74

Scarmiglione one of demons in the fifth bolgia of Malebolge; *Inf.* 21.105

Scèvola Mùzio [Mùzio]

Schiavoni [Sclavones]

Schicchi, Gianni [Gianni Schicchi]

Schiro Scyros, island in the Aegean Sea; *Purg.* 9.37

Sciancato, Pùccio [Pùccio Sciancato]

Sciarra della Colonna desecrator of Boniface VIII at Anagni; *Purg.* 20.90

Scipione (Scìpio) Publius Cornelius Scipio Africanus Major, Roman general, later consul *Inf.* 31.116; *Purg.* 29.116; *Par.* 6.53; *Conv.* 4.5.19; *Epist.* 11.25; *Mon.* 2.9.18

Scipione Publius Cornelius Scipio Aemilianus Africanus Minor; *Conv.* 2.12.3; *Epist.* 11.25

Scipiones the Scipios, i.e., Scipio Africanus Major and Minor; *Epist.* 11.25

Sciro [Schiro]

Scirocco the Scirocco or Sirocco, SE. wind; *Purg.* 28.21

Scithe the Scythians, nomadic tribes inhabiting regions to the N. of the Black Sea; *Mon.* 1.14.6

Sclavones Slavonians, inhabitants of Slavonia; *DVE* 1.14.6

Scornigiani [Farinata, Gano, Marzucco]

Scòrpio Scorpio, the constellation and eighth sign of the Zodiac; *Purg.* 25.3

Scotto inhabitant of Scotland; *Par.* 19.122

Scotto, Michele [Michele Scotto]

Scrittura, Scriptura Holy Scripture; *DVE* 1.4.2; *Mon.* 3.3.14; *Par.* 4.43

Scrovegni, Reginaldo degli [Reginaldo degli Scrovegni]

Sem Shem, eldest son of Noah; *DVE* 1.7.8

Semelè Semele, daughter of Cadmus, king of Thebes; *Inf.* 30.2; *Par.* 21.6

Semiramìs Semiramis, queen of Assyria; *Inf.* 5.58

Sèneca Lucius Annaeus Seneca, Roman philosopher and tragedian; *Conv.* 1.8.16; *Inf.* 4.141; *Epist.* 13.10

Senectute, De (De la Vegliezza) Cicero's treatise *On Old Age*; *Conv.* 2.8.9

Senenses [Sanesi]

Senna the Seine, prinicipal river of France; *Par.* 6.59

Sennaàr "land of Shinar," Babylonia, where the tower of Babel stood; *Purg.* 12.36; *DVE* 1.7.4

Sennacherìb king of Assyria, example of pride in Purgatory; *Purg.* 12.52

Sennùccio del Bene poet and contemporary of Dante; *Rime dubbie* 6.1

Senòcrate [Zenòcrate]

Senso e Sensato, Libro del (Sensu et Sensato, De) Aristotle's treatise *On Sense and Sensibles*; *Conv.* 3.9.6

Serafini, Serafi (Seraphin) Seraphim, highest order of angels; *Par.* 4.28, 28.99; *Conv.* 2.5.6; *Mon.* 3.1.3

Sèrchio river of Tuscany; *Inf.* 21.49

Serene [Sirene]

Sergestus character in the *Aeneid*; *Egl.* 4.30

Serse (Xerxes) Xerxes, son of Darius, king of Persia; *Purg.* 28.71; *Par.* 8.124; *Mon.* 2.8.7

Sesto Sestos, town in Thrace; *Purg.* 28.74; *Mon.* 2.8.7

Sesto probably Sextus Pompeius Magnus, son of Pompey, punished in Hell as a robber; *Inf.* 12.135

Sestri [Siestri]

Setta Ceuta, city in Morocco; *Inf.* 26.111

Sex Principiorum (Liber Sex Principiorum) *Mon.* 1.9.4

Settentrïone the constellation of the Plough (the Wain); *Purg.* 30.1; *Mon.* 2.8.13

Settentrïone the northern region; *Purg.* 4.83

Sfinge Sphinx, the Theban she-monster; *Purg.* 33.47

Sibìlia Seville, city of Spain; *Inf.* 20.126

Sibilla the Cumaean Sibyl or prophetess of Cumae; *Par.* 33.66

Sicani name for the Sicilians; *Egl.* 4.30

Sicheo Sychaeus, wealthy Phoenician of Tyre; *Inf.* 5.61; *Par.* 9.97

Sicìlia [Cicìlia]

Siciliani [Ciciliani]

Sìculi inhabitants of Sicily; *DVE* 1.12.6

Siena city in central Tuscany; *Inf.* 29.109; *Purg.* 5.134

Siestri Sestri Levante, town in Liguria on Riviera di Levante; *Purg.* 19.100

Sigieri di Brabante Siger of Brabant, professor of philosophy at the University of Paris; *Par.* 10.136; *Fiore* 92.9

Signa village of Tuscany; *Par.* 16.56

Sile small river in the Venetian region; *Par.* 9.49

Sillogismo Simplìciter, De [Analỳtica Priora]

Silvestro St. Sylvester, an early follower of St. Francis of Assisi; *Par.* 11.83

Silvestro (Sylvester) Pope Sylvester I; *Inf.* 27.94; *Par.* 20.57; *Mon.* 3.10.1

Sìlvio Silvius, son of Aeneas by Lavinia; *Inf.* 2.13

Simifonti fortress in the Valdelsa; *Par.* 16.62

Simoenta the Simois, one of chief rivers of the Troad; *Par.* 6.67

Simòn Mago Simon Magus, the sorcerer of Samaria; *Inf.* 19.1; *Par.* 30.147

Simònide Simonides, Greek lyric poet; *Purg.* 22.107

Simplíciter Ente, De the treatise *On Simple Being*, Dante's title for Aristotle's *Metaphysics*; *Mon.* 1.12.8

Sinigàglia Senigallia (ancient Sena Gallica), city on the Adriatic near Ancona; *Par.* 16.75

Sinone Sinon, dishonest Greek soldier, placed among the falsifiers in Malebolge; *Inf.* 30.98

Siòn name of one of two hills upon which Jerusalem is situated; *Purg.* 4.68

Siratti modern Monte Soratte (Soracte), hill N. of Rome; *Inf.* 27.95

Sirene the Sirens; *Purg.* 19.19, 31.45; *Par.* 12.8; *Epist.* 5.13

Sìria Syria, name for Holy Land generally; *VN* 29.1; *Conv.* 4.5.9

Siringa Syrinx, nymph of Arcadia; *Purg.* 32.65

Sismondi noble Ghibelline family of Pisa; *Inf.* 33.32

Sisto Sixtus I, bishop of Rome; *Par.* 27.44

Sivìglia [Sibìlia]

Sìzii noble family of Florence; *Par.* 16.108

Soave (Svèvia) Swabia, ancient duchy of SW. Germany; *Par.* 3.119; *Conv.* 4.3.6

Sòcrate Socrates, Greek philosopher; *Inf.* 4.134; *Conv.* 3.14.8

Sòddoma Sodom, ancient city of Palestine; *Inf.* 11.50; *Purg.* 26.40

Soldanieri noble family of Florence; *Par.* 16.93

Sole (Sol) the Sun; *Inf.* 1.38; *Purg.* 1.39; *Par.* 1.47; *Conv.* 2.3.4; *Mon.* 1.9.1; *Rime* 90.2; *Epist.* 3.7; *Quest.* 54; *Egl.* 4.2

Sole, Cielo del the Heaven of the Sun; *Par.* 10.49; *Conv.* 2.3.7

Solone Solon, celebrated Athenian legislator, one of Seven Sages of Greece; *Par.* 8.124

Soratte, Monte [Siratti]

Sophìsticis Elenchis Aristotle's treatise *On Sophistical Refutations*; *Mon.* 3.4.4

Sordello (Sordellus) Italian troubadour; *Purg.* 6.74; *DVE* 1.14.2

Sorga the Sorgue, small river of France; *Par.* 8.59

Spagna Spain; *Inf.* 26.103; *Purg.* 18.102; *Par.* 6.64

Spagnuoli [Ispani]

Sparta [Lacedèmona]

Spèculum the *Speculum legatorum* and the *Speculum iudiciale*, treatises on civil and canon law by Guillelmus Durandus (Guillaume Durand); *Epist.* 11.16

Speusippo Speusippus, Athenian philosopher; *Conv.* 4.6.14

Spirito Santo the Holy Spirit; *Purg.* 20.98; *Par.* 3.53

Spoletani inhabitants of Spoleto; *DVE* 1.10.6

Spoletum Spoleto, city near Perugia; *Epist.* 6.20

Stagirite Stagirite, native of Stagira (town of Macedonia); *Conv.* 4.6.15

Stàzio Roman poet Statius, most eminent poet of the Silver Age; *Purg.* 21.91; *Conv.* 3.8.10; *DVE* 2.6.7

Stefaneschi [Iàcopo Gaetano Stefaneschi]

Stèfano, Santo St. Stephen, first Christian martyr; *Purg.* 15.107

Stèfano Uròsio II Stephen Ouros II, king of Rascia; *Par.* 19.140

Stellato, Cielo Starry Heaven, Heaven of the Fixed Stars; *Conv.* 2.3.5; *Par.* 2.64

Stelle Fisse the Fixed Stars (Cielo Stellato); *VN* 2.2; *Conv.* 2.3.3; *Par.* 20.6

Stige Styx, river of ancient Arcadia; *Inf.* 7.106

Stòici the Stoic school of philosophers; *Conv.* 2.8.9

Stòria Tebana [Thebàidos]

Strami, Vico de li the Rue du Fouarre in Paris; *Par.* 10.137

Stricca supposed member of Spendthrift Club of Siena; *Inf.* 29.125

Stròfade the Strophades, two small islands in Ionian Sea; *Inf.* 13.11

Subàsio, Monte mountain in Umbria; *Par.* 11.45

Substàntia Orbis, De Averroës' treatise *On the Substance of the World*; *Quest.* 46

Sùmmulae Logicales a manual of logic compiled by Petrus Hispanus; *Par.* 12.135

Susa, Enrico da [Enrico da Susa]

Svèvia [Soave]

Tacco, Ghin di [Ghin di Tacco]

Taddeo d'Alderotto physician and founder of the school of medicine in Bologna; *Par.* 12.83; *Conv.* 1.10.10

Tagliacozzo town near Aquila, in the Abruzzi; *Inf.* 28.17

Tagliamento river of N. Italy, boundary of the March of Treviso; *Par.* 9.44

Taïdè Thais, name of a courtesan, punished as a flatterer in Malebolge; *Inf.* 18.133

Talamone small sea-port on the Tyrrhenian Sea; *Purg.* 13.152

Tale Thales, philosopher and one of Seven Sages; *Inf.* 4.137

Tambernicchi name of a mountain (perhaps the Tambura, in the Alpes); *Inf.* 32.28

Tamiri (Tamiris) Tomyris, queen of Massagetae; *Purg.* 12.56; *Mon.* 2.8.6

Tamisi the Thames river; *Inf.* 12.120

Tana [Gaetana Alighieri]

Tànaï river Don (also called the Tana) in heart of Russia; *Inf.* 32.27

Tarlati, Gùccio de' [Gùccio de' Tarlati]

Tarpea the Tarpeian hill at Rome; *Purg.* 9.137

Tarquini the Tarquin kings of Rome; *Conv.* 4.5.2

Tarquino (Tarquìnio) Lucius Tarquinius Superbus, seventh and last king of Rome; *Inf.* 4.127

Tàrtari the Tartars; *Inf.* 17.17

Taumante Thaumas, son of Pontus and Ge; *Purg.* 21.50

Taurinum Turin, city of N. Italy; *DVE* 1.15.8

Tàuro Taurus (the Bull), constellation and second sign of the Zodiac; *Purg.* 25.3; *Par.* 22.111

Tebàide (Tebana Istòria, Thebàidos) [Thebàidos]

Tebaldello de' Zambrasi (Tribaldello) member of Ghibelline Zambrasi family of Faenza; *Inf.* 32.122

Tebaldo Thibaut IV, count of Champagne, later Teobaldo I, king of Navarre; *DVE* 1.9.3

Tebaldo Thibaut V, count of Champagne, later Teobaldo II, king of Navarre; *Inf.* 22.52

Tebani Thebans; *Inf.* 20.32; *Purg.* 18.93

Tebe Thebes, capital of Boeotia; *Inf.* 14.69; *Purg.* 21.92

Tedeschi Germans; *Inf.* 17.21; *Conv.* 1.7.13; *DVE* 1.8.9 [Alamanni]

Tegghiàio [Aldobrandi, Tegghiàio]

Tegni, Li Galen's *Methodus medendi* (or *Ars parva*), "Art of Healing"; *Conv.* 1.8.5

Tèlamon (Telamone) supposed son of Aeacus and father of Ajax; *Conv.* 4.27.20

Telèmaco Telemachus, son of Ulysses and Penelope; *Inf.* 26.94

Tèlephus son of Hercules; *Epist.* 13.30

Temi Themis, daughter of Uranus (Heaven) and Ge (Earth); *Purg.* 33.47

Terènzio (Terèntius) Terence (Publius Terentius Afer), Roman comic poet; *Purg.* 22.97; *Epist.* 13.29

Terra the Earth, the terrestrial globe; *Conv.* 2.6.10; *Purg.* 19.3; *Par.* 22.134

Terra Santa the Holy Land; *Par.* 9.125

Tervisina Màrchia [Màrchia Trivisiana]

Tesàuro di Beccheria [Beccheria]

Tèseo Theseus, son of Aegeus, king of Athens; *Inf.* 9.54; *Purg.* 24.123

Tesifòne Tisiphone, one of the Furies; *Inf.* 9.48

Tesoro the *Tresor* of Brunetto Latini; *Inf.* 15.119

Tesoro title Dante uses to refer to Peter Lombard's *Liber sententiarum*; *Par.* 10.108

Tessa Forese Donati's mother; *Rime* 77.2

Tessàglia [Thessàlia]

Testamento Nuovo (novum Testamentum) the New Testament; *Par.* 5.76; *Mon.* 3.3.12

Testamento Vècchio (vetus Testamentum) the Old Testament; *Purg.* 29.83; *Par.* 5.76; *Mon.* 3.3.12

Teti Thetis, one of the Nereids; *Purg.* 9.37

Teutònici Teutons; *DVE* 1.8.3

Tèucros (Tèucri) one of the names of the Trojans; *Mon.* 2.3.11

Tèver, Tevero (Tìberis) the Tiber, river on which Rome sits; *Inf.* 27.30; *Purg.* 2.101; *Par.* 11.10; *Mon.* 2.4.10; *Epist.* 7.23

Thebàidos the *Thebaid* of Statius; *Conv.* 3.11.16, 4.25.6 **[Tebana Storia]**

Theòphilus name of a person addressed by St. Luke in his Gospel; *Mon.* 3.9.19

Thessàlia Thessaly, region of Greece; *Epist.* 5.10

Thessalonicenses, Epìstola ad St. Paul's epistle to the Thessalonians; *Mon.* 3.1.3

Thimòtheum, Epìstola ad St. Paul's epistle to Timothy; *Mon.* 2.9.19

Thomàs d'Aquino [Tommaso d'Aquino]

Tiberìade [Mare di Tiberìade]

Tibèrio (Tibèrius) Tiberius Claudius Nero, Roman emperor, A.D. 14-37; *Par.* 6.86; *Mon.* 2.11.5; *Epist.* 5.28

Tideo Tydeus, son of Oeneus, king of Calydon; *Inf.* 32.130

Tifeo (Tifo) Typhoeus or Typhon, monster with a hundred heads; *Inf.* 31.124; *Par.* 8.70

Tignoso, Federigo [Federigo Tignoso]

Tigri Tigris, river of Asia; *Purg.* 33.112

Timbreo Thymbraeus, epithet of Apollo; *Purg.* 12.31

Timeo Plato's *Timaeus*; *Par.* 4.49; *Conv.* 3.5.6

Timòtheum, Epìstola ad St. Paul's Epistle to Timothy; *Mon.* 2.9.19

Tiralli the Tyrol, mountainous district between Italy and Austria; *Inf.* 20.61

Tirèsia Tiresias, soothsayer of Thebes; *Inf.* 20.40; *Purg.* 22.113

Tirrenum Mare the Tyrrhenian Sea; *DVE* 1.10.7

Tisbe Thisbe, maiden of Babylon; *Purg.* 27.37

Tisirìn primo the first month of the Syrian calendar; *VN* 29.1

Titan the Titan, i.e., the Sun; *Egl.* 4.2; *Epist.* 5.3

Tito Titus, son and successor of Vespasian, Roman emperor; *Par.* 6.92

Tito Lìvio [Lìvio]

Titone Tithonus, son of Laomedon; *Purg.* 9.1

Tìtyrus the name Dante uses for himself in his eclogues to Giovanni del Virgilio; *Egl.* 2.6

Tìzio Tityus, one of the Giants; *Inf.* 31.124

Toante Thoas, son of Jason and Hypsipyle; *Purg.* 26.95

Tobia Tobias, who was healed of blindness by the angel Raphael; *Par.* 4.48

Tolomea the third division of Cocytus, the ninth circle of Hell; *Inf.* 33.124

Tolomei, Pia de' [Pia, la]

Tolomeo Ptolemy (Claudius Ptolemaeus), mathematician, astronomer, and geographer; *Inf.* 4.142; *Conv.* 2.3.5

Tolomeo Ptolemy XII, king of Egypt; *Par.* 6.69; *Mon.* 2.8.9; *VN* 29.2

Tolosa, Conte di Raimondo V, count of Toulouse; *Conv.* 4.11.14

Thomas (Tommaso da Faenza) poet of Faenza; *DVE* 1.14.3

Thomas [Tommaso d'Aquino]

Tommaso, San St. Thomas the Apostle; *Par.* 16.129

Tommaso d'Aquino Thomas Aquinas, theologian and philosopher; *Purg.* 20.69; *Par.* 10.99; *Conv.* 2.14.14; *Mon.* 2.4.1

Topino [Tupino]

Toppo, il name of a ford near Arezzo; *Inf.* 13.121

Torino [Taurinum]

Toro [Tàuro]

Torquato, Tito Mànlio Titus Manlius Torquatus, Roman hero; *Par.* 6.46; *Conv.* 4.5.14

Torquato, Lucio Mànlio Lucius Manlius Torquatus, supporter of Pompey; War; *Conv.* 4.6.12

Torso Tours, capital of the old province of Touraine; *Purg.* 24.23

Tosa, Della [Cianghella, Tosinghi]

Toscana (Tùscia) Tuscany, region of N. Italy; *Inf.* 24.122; *Purg.* 11.110; *Par.* 22.117; *Conv.* 4.11.8; *DVE* 1.10.7; *Epist.* 1.1

Toscani (Toschi) Tuscans; *Inf.* 10.22

Tosinghi noble Florentine family; *Par.* 16.112

Tòtila last Ostrogothic king of Italy (used to refer to Charles of Valois); *DVE* 2.6.4

Traiano Trajan, Roman emperor; *Purg.* 10.76; *Par.* 20.44

Transtiberinus Trasteverine, across the Tiber; used to refer to Jacopo Gaetano Stefaneschi; *Epist.* 11.25

Traversara, casa the Traversari family, Ghibellines of Ravenna; *Purg.*14.107

Trentino pastore bishop of Trent; *Inf.* 20.67

Trento Trent on the Adige; *Inf.* 12.5

Trespiano village in Tuscany N. of Florence; *Par.* 16.54

Tridentum Trent on the Adige; *DVE* 1.15.8

Trinàcria Sicily; *Par.* 8.67; *DVE* 1.12.3; *Egl.* 4.71

Tristano Tristan, hero of French romance; *Inf.* 5.67

Trìvia "the goddess at the three ways," name for the goddess Diana; *Par.* 23.26

Trìvio the Trivium, three of the seven liberal arts, namely grammar, dialectic (logic), and rhetoric; *Conv.* 2.13.8

Trivisiana, Màrchia [Màrchia Trivisiana]

Trivisiani inhabitants of town and March of Treviso; *DVE* 1.10.7

Tròade the Troad, territory of Troy; *Par.* 6.6, 67

Tròia city of Troy; *Inf.* 1.74; *Purg.* 12.61; *Mon.* 2.3.2 [Iliòn, Pèrgama, Ylìaca urbs]

Troiani Trojans; *Inf.* 13.11; *Purg.* 18.136; *Par.* 15.126

Troni Thrones, one of the Angelic Hierarchies; *Conv.* 2.5.6; *Par.* 9.61, 28.104

Tronto river of central Italy; *Par.* 8.63

Tùllius (Tùllio) [Cìcero]

Tullo Tullus Hostilius, third king of Rome; *Conv.* 4.5.11; *Mon.* 2.9.15

Tupino stream in N. of Umbria; *Par.* 11.43

Turbia village in Liguria; *Purg.* 3.49

Turchi Asiatic Turks; *Inf.* 17.17

Turni followers of Turnus; *Epist.* 7.18

Turno Turnus, king of the Rutulians at time of Aeneas' arrival in Italy; *Inf.* 1.108; *Mon.* 2.3.16

Tuscani, Tusci [Toscani, Toschi]

Tùscia [Toscana]

Tyrenum Mare [Tirrenum Mare]

Ubaldìn da la Pila [Pila, Ubaldìn da la]

Ubaldini Ghibelline family of Tuscany

Ubaldini, Ottaviano degli [Cardinale, il]

Ubaldini, Ruggieri degli [Ruggieri degli Ubaldini]

Ubaldo Baldassini bishop of Gubbio; *Par.* 11.44

Uberti Ghibelline family of Florence; *Conv.* 4.20.5; *Par.* 16.109

Ubertino da Casale Ubertino d'Ilia da Casale, leader of the Spirituals in Franciscan order; *Par.* 12.124

Ubertìn Donato member of the Donati family of Florence who married a daughter of Bellincione Berti; *Par.* 16.119

Uberto [Obertus de Romena]

Ubriachi [Obriachi]

Uccellatoio hill outside Florence; *Par.* 15.110

Ughi noble family of Florence; *Par.* 16.88

Ugo Ciappetta [Ciappetta, Ugo]

Ugo da San Vittore Hugh of St. Victor, mystic and theologian of the 12th century; *Par.* 12.133

Ugo di Brandeburgo Marquis Hugh of Brandenburg, conferred knighthood on six Florentine families; *Par.* 16.128

Ugolìn d'Azzo [Azzo, Ugolino d']

Ugolìn de' Fantolìn [Fantolìn, Ugolìn d']

Ugolino, Conte Count Ugolino della Gherardesca, head of the Guelf party in Pisa; *Inf.* 32.125

Ugolinus Bucciola [Bucciola, Ugolinus]

Uguccione della Faggiuola great Ghibelline captain; referred to as *arator* (ploughman) in *Egl.* 1.27

Uguiccione della Gherardesca Uguiccione della Gherardesca, fifth son of Count Ugolino; *Inf.* 33.89

Uguiccione da Pisa Uguiccione de' Bagni of Pisa, grammarian; *Conv.* 4.6.5

Ulisse Ulysses of Ithaca, son of Laertes; *Inf.* 26.56; *Purg.* 19.22; *Par.* 27.83

Umberto [Omberto]

Ùngari Hungarians, *DVE* 1.8.4

Ungheria (Ungaria) Hungary; *Par.* 19.142

Uranìe Urania, the Muse of heavenly things; *Purg.* 29.41

Urbano Urban I, bishop of Rome; *Par.* 27.44

Urbino town in Romagna; *Inf.* 27.29

Urbisàglia ancient city Urbs Salvia, near Ancona; *Par.* 16.75

Urbs Vetus Orvieto, town in Umbria; *DVE* 1.18.2

Uròsio [Stèfano Uròsio]

Ursus name by which Dante addresses Cardinal Napoleone Orsini; *Epist.* 11.24

Ùtica city in N. Africa near Carthage; *Purg.* 1.74

Vaio [Pigli]

Val Camònica valley in NE. Lombardy; *Inf.* 20.65

Valdarno valley of the Arno; *Purg.* 14.30

Valdichiana valley of the Chiana in Tuscany; *Inf.* 29.47

Valdigrieve valley of the Greve in Tuscany; *Par.* 16.66

Val di Magra valley of the Magra; *Inf.* 24.145; *Purg.* 8.116

Val di Prado valley of the Po; *Par.* 15.137

Vallatrensis of Velletri, town SE. of Rome; *Epist.* 1.1

Vangèlio (Vangelo) [Evangèlio]

Vangèlio di Luca the Gospel of St. Luke; *Conv.* 4.17.10; *Mon.* 2.8.14

Vangèlio di Marco the Gospel of St. Mark; *Conv.* 4.12.14

Vangèlo di santo Matteo (Evangèlium) the Gospel of St. Matthew; *Conv.* 4.16.10; *Mon.* 2.3.5

Vanna [Giovanna]

Vanni dei Cancellieri [Focàccia]

Vanni Fucci illegitimate son of Fuccio de' Lazzari; *Inf.* 24.97

Varo the Var, river of S. France; *Par.* 6.58

Varro probably for Vario, Lucius Varius Rufus, Roman poet of Augustan age; *Purg.* 22.98

Vascones Gascons; *Epist.* 11.26

Vaticano the Vatican hill in Rome; *Par.* 9.139

Vècchio, Del noble family of Florence; *Par.* 15.115

Vegètius Flavius Vegetius Renatus, author of *Art of War*; *Mon.* 2.9.3

Vegliezza, De la Dante's title for Cicero's *De senectute*; *Conv.* 2.8.9

Vèglio (il veglio di Creta) the old man of Crete, statue within mountain on Crete; *Inf.* 14.103

Veltro the greyhound, allegorical figure of prophesied savior of Italy; *Inf* 1.101

Venceslao [Vincislao]

Venèdico Caccianemico [Caccianemico, Venèdico]

Vènere (Ciprigna, Citerea) Venus, Roman goddess of love; *Purg.* 25.132; *Par.* 8.2; *Conv.* 2.5.14; *DVE* 2.2.8; *Fiore* 17.1

Vènere (Citerea, Ciprigna, Hèsperus) the planet Venus; *Conv.* 2.2.1; *Purg.* 1.19; *Par.* 18.12

Vènere the Heaven of Venus; *Conv.* 2.13.13; *Par.* 8.38

Vèneti [Viniziani]

Venèzia [Vinègia]

Veneziani [Viniziani]

Veno, Venùs, Venusso [Vènere]

Vercelli town of N. Italy; *Inf.* 28.75

Verde (Liri) river of S. Italy; *Purg.* 3.131; *Par.* 8.63

Verna mountain between the Arno and Tiber valleys; *Par.* 11.106

Verona city of N. Italy; *Inf.* 15.122; *Purg.* 18.118 *DVE* 1.15.2

Veronenses the Veronese, inhabitants of Verona; *Inf.* 20.68; *DVE* 1.14.3

Verònica, La name of veil of St. Veronica bearing the image of Christ; *Par.* 31.104

Verrùcchio castle and village near Rimini; *Inf.* 27.46

Vesoges ancient king of Egypt; *Mon.* 2.8.5

Via Lattea [Galàssia]

Vicentini [Vigentini]

Vicenza town near Verona in NE. Italy; *Par.* 9.47

Vico de li Strami [Strami, Vico de li]

Vico hereditary castle of family of Vico near Spoleto; *Conv.* 4.29.2

Victòria fortress in Parma built by Emperor Frederick II; *Epist.* 6.19

Vigentini inhabitants of Vicenza; *DVE* 1.14.4

Vigna, Pier della [Pier della Vigna]

Vìncislao Wenceslaus II, king of Bohemia ("quel di Boemme"); *Purg.* 7.101; *Par.* 19.125

Vinègia (Venètie) Venice; *Par.* 19.141; *DVE* 1.10.7

Viniziani (Vèneti) the Venetians; *Inf.* 21.7; *DVE* 1.10.8

Vìoletta lady in Dante's poetry; *Rime* 58.1

Virgìlio (Virgìlius) the Roman poet Virgil; *Inf.* 1.79; *Purg.* 2.61; *Par.* 17.19; *Conv.* 2.5.14; *Mon.* 1.11.1; *DVE* 2.6.7; *Epist.* 7.13; *Eg.* 1.36 (Maro)

Virgìlio, Giovanni del grammarian of Bologna (as Mopsus); *Egl.* 1.6

Virgo [Astrea]

Visconti di Milano Ghibelline family of Milan; *Conv.* 4.20.5; *Purg.* 8.80

Visconti di Pisa Guelf family of Pisa; *Purg.* 8.53

Visdòmini noble Florentine family; *Par.* 16.112

Vìsio Iohannis [Iohannis Vìsio]

Viso [Monte Veso]

Vitaliano del Dente name of a Paduan placed among the usurers; *Inf.* 17.68

Vita Nuova (Vita nova) Dante's autobiographical book *The New Life*; *VN* 1.1; *Conv.* 1.1.16; *Purg.* 30.115

Vitèrbium Viterbo, town of central Italy; *DVE* 1.8.2; *Inf.* 12.119

Vulcano Vulcan, Roman god of fire; *Inf.* 14.57; *Conv.* 2.4.6

Xerxes [Serse]

Ylìaca urbs [Tròia]

Ymolenses inhabitants of Imola; *DVE* 1.15.1

Yperiòn Hyperion, the father of the Sun; *Epist.* 3.7; *Par.* 22.142

Ypòmenes Hippomenes, greatgrandson of Neptune; *Mon.* 2.7.10

Ystria Istria, region bordering NE. Italy; *DVE* 1.10.7

Ystriani inhabitants of Istria; *DVE* 1.10.8

Ytali inhabitants of ancient Italy; *Mon.* 2.9.18

Ytali Italians, or inhabitants of modern Italy; *DVE* 1.8.4; *Epist.* 2.1

Zama city in Numidia; *Conv.* 4.5.19; *Inf.* 31.115

Zambrasi, Tebaldello de' [Tebaldello]

Zanche, Michèl [Michèl Zanche]

Zebedeus Zebedee, father of apostles James and John; *Mon.* 3.9.2

Zèfiro western wind; *Par.* 12.46; *Par.* 12.47

Zeno, San church and monastery of San Zeno at Verona; *Purg.* 18.118

Zeno, Zenone Zeno, founder of the Stoic school of philosophy; *Inf.* 4.138; *Conv.* 3.14.8

Zenòcrate Xenocrates, philosopher; *Conv.* 4.6.15

Zita, Santa patron saint of Lucca; *Inf.* 21.38

Zodìaco the Zodiac; *Purg.* 4.64; *Par.* 10.14

General Index

Page numbers in **boldface** refer to the main entry on the subject. Page numbers in *italics* refer to illustrations.

Alberigo, Fra (Alberigo Manfredi), **10**, 542, 823
  traitor of the guest-host relationship, 722
Albero da Siena, **10**, 12
Albertazzi, Giorgio, 283
Albert I, 5, **10–11**, 434, 488
Alberto degli Alberti, **11–12**
Alberto della Scala, **12**
Alberto di Casalodi, **12**
Albert of Cologne. *See* Albert the Great
Albert the Great (*Alberto,* Albert of Cologne, Albertus Magnus), **11**, 62, 64, 312, 314, 434
  and astronomy, 69
  in the *Commedia,* 760
  on contemplation, 217
  and Dante's concept of intellect, 519
  De aetate sive de iuventute et senectute, 8
  and human embryology, 115
  on the human soul, 642, 796
  influence on Dante's reason, 738
  as intermediary to classical authors, 173
  light metaphysics, 39
  on Limbo, 567
  and magnanimity, 583
  on sodomy, 788
  on study of science, 768
  as theological source, 813
  Thomas Aquinas and, 56
Albertus Magnus. *See* Albert the Great
Albigensians. *See* Cathars
Albumassar (*Albumasar,* Abā Ma'shar), **12**, 67
Alcabitius, 67
alchemists, 587
  Capocchio, 141, 369
  as falsifiers, 456
  Griffolino, 369, 456
alchemy, **12–13**
Alcmeon, 135
"Al cor gentile rempaira sempre amore" ("In the noble heart Love always finds its refuge") (Guinizzelli), 37, 465, 466
  use of optics in, 661
Alcuin, 736
  Carolingian Renaissance, 624
  Rabanus and, 737
Aldine Press, 202
Aldington, Richard, 705
Aldobrandesco, Guiglielmo, **13**
Aldobrandesco, Omberto, 13
Aldobrandi, Tegghiaio, **13**, 758, 787
Alecto (*Aletto*), **14**, 428

Alessandro da Romena, 9, **14**
Alessandro degli Alberti, 11, **14**, 135, 637, 663
Alessandro Novello, **14**
Alessio, Gian Carlo, 865
Alexander IV (pope), 365
Alexander of Aphrodisias, 62
Alexander of Hales, 120
Alexander of Pherae, 15
Alexander the Great, **15**
Alexandrian school, and mysticism, 634
al-Farabi, 15, 642
Alfonso I (Este), 60
Alfraganus (*Alfragano,* Abā 'l-'Abbas Ahmad ibn Muhammad ibn Kathir al-Farghani), **15**, 69, 721
  and fixed stars, 383
Algazel (Abā Hamid Muhammad ibn Muhammad al-Tusi al-Ghazali), **15**
  Destruction of Philosophers, 79
Alhazen
  De aspectibus, 661
  Perspectiva, 661
Ali (*Alì,* Ali ibn Abu Talib), **15**
  Dante's treatment of, 521
  as schismatic, 520–521, 766
Aligheri, L' (journal), 701
Alighieri, Antonia (Sister Beatrice), 23, 432
Alighieri, Dante, **15–20**
  accused of barratry, 85
  biographical links with Francis of Assisi, 415–416
  as champion of Italian unity, 434, 531
  and Charles Martel, 159
  and Dominican order, 313
  Donation of Constantine accepted as authentic by, 216
  and drawing, 250
  epitaph for tomb written by Giovanni del Virgilio, 865
  as Franciscan tertiary, 415
  house of, 23
  knowledge of history, 488
  plays based on his characters, 321–322
  plays based on his life, 319–320
  plays based on his works, 320–321
  popularized in English-speaking world, 180
  portraits, *16, 17, 182*
    by H. Robinson, *399*
  as prior of Florence, 105
  schooling, 253
  seen as patriotic citizen in 15th century, 272
  statue, *345*

  See also Dante-pilgrim; Dante-poet
Alighieri family, **21–24**
Alighieri, Giovanni, 23
Alighieri, Jacopo. *See* Jacopo di Dante
Alighieri, Pietro, **20–21**, 24, 432
  Commedia commentator, 207
  commentary on sloth, 785
  identifying Matelda with Matilde of Canossa, 601
  on Matelda, 600
  on Mercury, 608
  on *messo celeste* as Mercury, 609
  influence on Cristoforo Landino, 553
  on "Tre donne intorno al cor mi son venute," 558
Aliscans, 741
"Alla sua donna" (Leopardi), 270
allegory, **24–34**
  of active and contemplative life, 4
  allegorical reading of Dante rejected by Croce, 238–239
  allegorical realism in Dante, 194–195, 197
  in the *Commedia*
    allegorical presentation of the Bible, 102
    Dante's actions in Lethe, 562
    discussion by Schlegel, 267
    of the Furies, 429
    Inferno, 288
    of Medusa, 603
    of Noble Castle episode, 651
    three beasts and, 288
  in *Convivio,* 226
  defined, 194
  distinguished from symbolism, 803, 804
  donna gentile as philosophy, 317
  and fourfold method of interpretation, 376
  functioning illustrated in *Epistle to Cangrande,* 350
  Neoplatonism and, 641
  and *petrose* poems, 689
  relation to history in Dante, 267
  of the theologians, 524
Allen, Judson, 29
Allgemeines Gelehrtenlexikon (Joecher), 265
Allgemeines historisches Lexikon (Buddeus), 265
alliteration, **34–35**
Almagest (Ptolemy), 719, 720, 721
Alpetragius (*Alpetragio,* Abu Ishak Nur al-Din al-Bitrudji), **35–36**, 43

"Al poco giorno e al gran cerchio d'ombra" ("To the short day and the great circle of shadow") (Dante), 140, 611, 688, 689
and sestina form, 772
"Altra notte mi venne una gran tosse, L'" (Forese Donati), 22, 23
"Ambition" (Gauthier), 260
Ambrosiaster, 618
Ambrosius, 662
American Dante Bibliography (ADB) (Lansing, ed.), 286, 287
American New Critics, 219
Amerigo di Narbona, 46–47
Amert, Susan, 278
Ameto (Boccaccio), 113
Amezúa, Agustín de, 279
Amis et Amiles, 840
"Amor che lungiamente m'hai menato" (Guido delle Colonne), 465
"Amor, che movi tua virtù da cielo" (Dante), 140
"Amor che ne la mente mi ragiona" (Dante), 19, 140, 148, 227, 228, 552
set to music by Casella, 251
"Amor, da che convien pur ch'io mi doglia" (Dante), 354, 579, 580, 581, 629
Amorosa visione (Boccaccio), 113–114
Amoroso convivio di Dante, L', 231
"Amor, tu vedi ben che questa donna" ("Love, you see well that this lady") (Dante), 140, 611, 688–689
and sestina form, 772
Amphiaraus *(Anfiarao),* **36,** 793
Anacletus (pope). *See* Cletus (pope)
Anagni, Treaty of, 159
Anastasius II *(Anastasio)* (pope), **36,** 483, 485
anathema, doctrine of, 361
Anatomy of Criticism (Frye), 818
Anaxagoras *(Anassagora),* **36**
Anchises *(Anchise),* **36**
"Ancor che l'aigua per lo foco lassi" (Guido della Colonne), 465
Anderson, Melville Best, 827
translation of the *Commedia,* 826
Anderson, William, 829
Andrea dei Mozzi, Bishop, **36**
as sodomite, 787
Andreas Capellanus, **37,** 237, 874
De amore, 236
De arte honeste amandi (The Art of Courtly Love), 770

Andreoli, Raffaele, 203
Andreotti, Giulio, 170
Angelico, Fra, 498
Angelo of Clareno, 838
angels, **37–45**
angelic influence, 41–42
and distinction of active and contemplative life, 4
importance of, for Dante, 671
messo celeste as, 609
and motion of spheres, 643, 644, 711
nature of human intellect as angelic, 518
neutral, 44, 190, 297, 646
number and hierarchy, 42–43, 192
rebels, 297
Saint Jerome's theory on, 536
Saint Matthew symbolized by, 602
Angevin dynasty, **45–46**
Angiolello da Carignano, **46,** 296, 699
Angiolieri, Cecco, **46–47,** 111
Anleitung zur Poesie (an.), 265
Annales (Ennius), 34
annals, Florentine, 167–168
Annas, 47
Anna, Saint, 47
in White Rose, 882
Annotationes (Vergerius), 263
Annotationi (Gabriele), 211
Annual Report of the Dante Society, with Accompanying Papers, 286
Annunciation of the Death of the Virgin (Duccio), 250
Anonimo Fiorentino, **47–48,** 208
on Belacqua, 96
on Casella, 142
on Exodus theme, 507
on fraudulent counsel, 422
knowledge of Compagni's *Cronica,* 213
on Matelda, 601
on murder of Benincasa da Laterina, 441
on Sassol Mascheroni, 763
on treatment of Muslims, 521
on *veltro,* 851–852
Anonimo Latino, **48,** 207
Anonymous Latin Commentary on Dante's Commedia. See Anonimo Latino
Anselm of Canterbury, Saint *(Anselmo),* 43, **48–49**
in the *Commedia,* 760
on original sin, 761
and Scholasticism, 624
as theological source, 813
Anselm of Havelberg, 52
Anselmuccio, **49**

Antaeus *(Anteo),* **49,** 444
as transportation for Dante-pilgrim, 421
Antenor, 49, 822
Antenora, 1, **49–50,** 109, 131, *179, 190,* 421
as part of Cocytus, 179, 190
traitors against country or party, 822, 830
Ante-Purgatory, **50–51,** 191, 730, 873
Bonconte in, 121
excommunicates in, 361
indolent in, 511
late repentant in, 554
Sordello in, 794
Anthony, George, 321
Anthony, Saint, 624
antica lupa (ancient she-wolf), 242, 870
metaphor for avarice, 76, 85
Anticlaudianus (Alain de Lille), 852
Antigone *(Antigonè),* **51**
antimagnate laws, 393
Antinferno (Ante-Hell). *See* Hell: vestibule to
antipeponthòs, 220
Antiphon *(Antifonte),* **51**
Antiquorum habet fidem (bull), 542
Antonius de Firimo, 200
Anziani, 392
Aphorisms (Hippocrate), 486
Apocalypse, **51–53**
commentary by Olivi, 659
Middle Ages interest in, 540
preoccupation of Franciscans, 101
procession in Earthly Paradise based on, 332, 753
Apocalypse of John, 540
Apocalypse of Paul, 663
Apocalypse of Peter, 663–664
apocalyptic procession. *See* Earthly Paradise: procession
apocalyptic visions
and ascents to heaven, 663
received in Earthly Paradise, 714
Apollo, **53–55**
identified with Sun, 802
as name for intelligences moving spheres, 54
Apollonius of Perga, 347
Apostles, 766
Apostles' Creed, 741
Apostolic Brothers, 311
crusade against, 239
identified as schismatics in *Commedia,* 483
apostolic poverty
in *Commedia,* 706–707
as heretical doctrine, 399

appetite *(appetito;* Lat. *appetitus),*
55–56
sensitive, 883
"Appressamento della morte"
(Leopardi), 270
appropriateness, principle of, 294
Après une lecture de Dante (Hugo),
260
Apuleius, 642
Aquinas, Saint Thomas, **56–58,** 62,
147
and alchemy, 12
on angels, 37, 39, 41
on avarice, 75, 76
and baptism, 82
Beatrice and, 92
on blasphemy, 108
and chain of being, 155
classification of sins, 449, 509,
588, 869
in the *Commedia,* 760
depicted in Heaven of the Sun,
811–812
on Dominican order, 313–314,
482
on mendicant orders, 607
on Saint Francis and the Franciscan Order, 312, 314, 415
*Commentary on the
Nichomachean Ethics,* 308
*Commentary on the Sentences of
Peter Lombard,* 567
on contemplation, 217
contrapasso, 220
on despair, 603–604
*De unitate intellectus contra
Averroistas,* 62
division of habits according to,
468
on fantasy, 370
and Fortune, 405
and fraud, 420
on Hell, 473–474
and human embryology, 116,
644
influence on Dante's philosophical thought, 738
as intermediary to classical
authors, 173
on justice, 213, 219, 549
and magnanimity, 583, 584
moving of the spheres, 41
on prayer, 708
on Purgatory, 729–730
and Scholasticism, 11
on sodomy, 788
on soothsayers, 793
as source of Harrowing of Hell,
470
as source on Dante's view of the
human soul, 642, 796, 797
on study of science, 768
on suicide, 801

Summa contra Gentiles, 65, 872
Summa theologiae, 872
on efficient cause, 148
as theological source for Dante,
812
on virtuous pagans, 872
and will, 883
on wrath, 891
Arab thought
contribution to Dante's philosophical thought, 694–695
Neoplatonism in, 641, 642
search for *Commedia*'s Arabic
roots, 182
Arachne *(Aragne),* **58**
Aragon and Valencia, Kingdoms of,
159
Arbor vitae crucifixae Jesu
(Ubertino da Casale), 838
Archangels, 42
architecture, Dante and, 250
Archivum romanicum (Auerbach),
70
"Arco della vita, L'" (Nardi), 9
Arcolano di Squarcia Maconi, 554
Arethusa *(Aretusa),* **58**
Arezio, Luigi, 852
Argenti, Filippo, **58–60,** *59,* 86,
604, 891–892
in *Decameron,* 113
Argent, Yan d', 503
Argia, 2, 5, **60**
Arias, 759
Ariosto, Ludovico, **60–61**
Aristotle, **61–65,** 832
as *auctor,* 73
Averroës's commentaries on, 79
and chain of being, 155
and classification of sins, 509,
513
in the *Commedia*
in Noble Castle, 651, 692
Dante's knowledge of, 227,
692–693
Dante's references to, 172, 173
Dante's use of theories, 769
and definition of nobility, 229
on distinction of active and contemplative life, 4
division of habits according to,
468
and fraud, 420
and hierarchy of being, 228
influence on *Commedia*'s planetary system, 720–721
influence on Dante's structure of
Paradise, 671
on irascible appetite, 784
Metaphysics, 40
and four causes, 149
Monarchia as example of Aristotelian thought, 617
and natural philosophy, 768–769

on number of "intelligences," 42
and optics, 660
as philosophic authority in the
Convivio, 227
physics, 10
Poetics, 144
as source of classification of sinners in Hell, 513
as source on Heraclitus, 481
Thomas Aquinas's commentaries
on, 57
on time, 357
on universe, 719
on wrath, 890–891
See also De anima
arithmetic identified with the Sun,
736, 802
Arius *(Arrio, Ario),* **65,** 482
Armour, Peter, 827
on identification of griffin, 754
on Matelda, 601
Armstrong, Edward, 627
Arnaut Daniel, **65–66,** 293, 403,
578, 611
in *Purgatorio,* 724
and sestina, 772
Arnold, Matthew, 748
on Dante, 747
Arnolfo di Cambio, 250, *400*
statue of Boniface VIII, *123*
Aroux, Eugène, 260
Arrigo Mainardi, **66**
Ars dictaminis (Giovanni del Virgilio), 35
Ars grammatica (Donatus), 34
Ars maior (Donatus), 316
Ars medica (Galen), 431
Ars minor (Donatus), 316
Ars poetica (Horace), 494
Dante's references to, 173
quoted in *Vita Nuova,* 175
source for the concept of tragedy,
821
Ars versificatoria (Matthew of
Vendôme), 34
art
limitations of, 726
transcendental potential of,
according to Dante, 726
Arte dei Medici e Speziali guild,
446
Arthurian romance, Dante's knowl-
ege of, 408
arts, Dante and the, **250–252**
Aruns *(Aronta),* **66,** 793
Ascoli, Albert Russell, 816
Asdente (Maestro Benvenuto), **66,**
120, 793
Ashton, Dore, 504
"Ash-Wednesday" (Eliot), 337
astrology, **66–68**
and explanation of the *veltro,* 851
importance in Paradise, 672

in *petrose* poems, 688–689, 690
Ptolemy and, 721
zodiac, 896
astronomy, **68–69**
astronomical references in *Commedia*, 183
astronomical references in *Purgatorio*, 723
in Dante's works, 767
Greek, 69
importance in Paradise, 672
Saturn linked to, 736, 763
and time of the journey, 289
See also Fixed Stars
Athanasian creed, 570
Athanasius, Saint, 624
Athenaeum (periodical), 267
Atropos *(Atropòs)*, **70**
Attila, **70**
Auden, W. H., 257
Auerbach, Erich, 25, **70–71**, 162, 378, 379, 435, 816
and Dante's allegory, 29
on Dante's use of vernacular, 271
"Figura," 269, 375
figural interpretation, 195
Curtius and, 243
influence of Croce on, 238
influence on Singleton, 783
on Medusa episode, 604
on *veltro*, 852
Augias, Corrado, 283
Augustalis libellus (Benvenuto da Imola), 97
Augustine, Friar *(Agostino)*, **71**
Augustine of Dacia, 25
Augustine, Saint, 25, **71–72**, 872
ambiguous about the Roman Empire, 619
on Apocalypse, 52
on avarice, 76
on blasphemy, 108
and Book 3 of *Monarchia*, 619
on Cato, 147
in the *Commedia*, 760
no speaking role, 813–814
in the White Rose, 635, 881
on contemplation, 217
Dante following Augustine's theology of the Fall, 367–368
Dante's references to, 173
as Dante's source on Roman history, 751
De ordine, 233
on eternity of Hell, 473
on *In exitu Israel de Aegypto*, 525
and figuralism, 376
as historical source, 488
mystical writings
and *Paradiso*, 635
and Neoplatonism, 641, 694
on non-existence of Limbo, 566–567

and numerology, 653
on original sin, 761
on pre-existence of soul, 642
and Saint Jerome, 536
sermons on the Creed and Limbo, 566
on she-wolf, 87
as source for Dante's theology, 813
three types of vision for seeing God, 325
on will, 883
works studied by Dante, 18
See also City of God, The; Confessions
Augustus *(Augusto)*, **72**
author *(autore;* Lat. *auctor, autor)*, 73
authority *(autorità, autoritade;* Lat. *auctoritas)*, **72–75**
autobiography
autobiographical narrative of Dante, 222–223
autobiographical reading of the *Vita Nuova*, 874
Commedia as, 453
Autumn Sequel (MacNeice), 257
avarice *(avarizia)*, **75–77**, 163, 706, 870
Charles II of Anjou as epitomizing, 407
as chief obstacle to justice, 548–549
Crassus as example of, 238
cupidity and, 242
effect on the body, 117
Heliodorus as example of, 472
and love of the right object by excess, 870
Polymnestor as example of, 704
Pygmalion, 732
as root of all sin, 299
as sin of incontinence, 508
symbolized by she-wolf, 76, 85
avaricious and prodigal, the, **77–79**, *78*, 190, 869
Adrian V (pope), 5, 78
avaricious
in Hell, 510
Hugh Capet among, 494
in Purgatory, 510
contrapasso, 222, 509–510
in Hell, 510
Hugh Capet, 78
spendthrifts distinguished from prodigal, 797
"Avegna ched el m'aggia più per tempo" (Cino da Pistoia), 171, 237
Averroës *(Averois,* Ibn-Rushd), 38, 61, **79**, 522, 642
Dante's treatment of, 521–522
Colish on, 521

Destruction of Algazel's Destructions, The, 79
influence on Dante, 643, 694
notion of passive intellect, 739
interpretation of Aristotle's *De anima*, 62
and natural philosophy, 768–769
in Noble Castle, 692
skeptical of Ptolemy's universe, 720
and treachery, 831
Averroistic thinking
in Cavalcanti's poetry, 460
in the *Convivio,* 230
Avicenna (Abā Ali al-Husain ibn Abd-Allah ibn Hasan ibn Ali ibn Sina), 15, 41, 61, **80,** 642
influence on Dante, 643, 694
and natural philosophy, 768–769
in Noble Castle, 692
Avignon papacy, 177, 670, 692
Epistle to the Italian Cardinals, 19, 354, 617, 691, 755
Azarii, Pietro, 459
Azzagnini, 441
Azzolino. *See* Ezzelino III da Romano

B
Babele (television program), 283
Babel, Tower of
De vulgari eloquentia on, 526–527
as epitomy of the corruption of human nature, 368, 421
and language differentiation, 444
Nimrod and, 649
Babylon on the Rhone: A Translation of the Letters by Dante, Petrarch and Catherine of Siena on the Avignon Papacy (Cogan), 829
Bacchus, identified with Sun, 802
Bachenschwanz, Leberecht, 435
first complete translation in German prose, 266
Bacon, Roger
and alchemy, 12
and optics, 661
use of term *perspectiva* in *Opus maius,* 660
Bakhtin, Mikhail, 817
Balbo, Cesare, 274
Baldassarre da Gabiano, 259
Baldino (illustrator), *516*
Dante at gates of Hell, *473*
ballata, **81,** 610, 612
in *Vita Nuova,* 875
Balzac, Honoré de, 261
Balzo, Carlo del, 320

Bambaglioli, Graziolo de', **81–82**
Boccaccio and, 109
Latin exegesis on *Inferno,* 206
and *Ottimo Commento,* 666
on Saint Lucy as patron saint of
Dante, 576
on *veltro,* 851
banks. *See* finance
Banquet, The (Ryan), 829;
(Lansing), 829
baptism, **82–83**
eight as number of, 656
Barbato da Sulmona, 746
Barberini Codex, 858
Barbi, Michele, **83–84,** 130, 184,
204, 229
on Aldine edition of the *Commedia,* 202
and dating of the *Convivio,* 226
influence on Singleton, 783
on *Monarchia,* 616
on *princeps* editions of the *Commedia,* 201
on *Rime,* 579
and *Studi danteschi,* 786
on *veltro,* 853
Bardi family
Edward I and, 343
Bardi, Simone dei, 89
Barelli, V., 601
Baretti, Giuseppe, 747
Barolini, Teodolinda, 794, 817
on Dante's Ulysses, 845
barrators *(baratti),* **84–85,** 190,
420, 513, 869
barratry, sin of *(baratteria),* 84, 586
Ciampolo, 169
Bartholomeo de Zanni da Portese,
896
Bartoli, Cosimo, 203
Bartolomeo della Scala, 19
Bartsch, Karl Friedrich Adolf,
534
Barzizza, Guiniforte, 208, 210
Bassermann, Alfred, 853
Bastiani, S., 601
Battaglia, S., 601
Battagli, Marco, 410
Baudelaire, Charles
and Dante, 261
on Delacroix, 296
Bayle, Pierre, 434
on Dante, 264–265
Bayros, Franz von, 503
beasts, the three, **85–89,** *86, 195,*
288, *516, 863*
Beatie, Bruce A., 278
Beatitudes, **89,** 870
in *Purgatorio,* 570, 725
Beatrice, 6, **89–95,** *90, 92,* 237
announced by the third dream in
Purgatory, 724
on archangels, 430

and Boethius's Lady Philosophy,
118
as Christ figure, 164, 727, 889
on Christian doctrine of the Fall,
367
on Daniel, 246
and Dante's confession, 562
descent into Limbo, 470–471
equated with revelation, 743
example of figuralism in *Commedia,* 378
explaining apparent violations to
doctrine of elements in
Commedia, 336, 381, 645,
769
explaining Incarnation, 508
faulting Plato, 694, 768
as guide and teacher in *Paradiso,*
675–676
in Heaven of Mercury, 608
and Neoplatonic idea of the
World Soul, 644
numbers identified with,
653–654
placement in the White Rose,
677
on Primum Mobile, 711
prophecy of the DXV, 408
See also Portinari, Beatrice
"Beatrice, Dead or Alive: Love in
the *Vita Nuova*" (Potter),
817
Beatrice degli Uberti, 150
Béatrice, visage d'un mythe (televi-
sion program, Belgium), 284
Beatrix (Balzac), 261
Beaumarchais, Pierre-Augustin
Caron, 260
Beccaria de' Beccari, 200
Becchi family, 130
Bec, Christian, 262
Beckett, Samuel, 257, 258, 319
Bede the Venerable, Saint *(Beda),*
95–96
De schematibus et tropis, 34
and revival of monasticism, 624
Bédier, Joseph, 218
Beelzebub *(Belzebù),* **96,** 573
See also Lucifer; Satan
Begas, Carl, 503
Belacqua (Duccio di Bonavia), **96**
indolent, 511
bella scola, 568, 650
Horace part of, 494
Bellincione, Alaghiero di, 23
Bello, Messer Geri del (character),
22
Bellum Iugurthinum (Sallust),
233–234
"Beloved Disciple." *See* Saint John
Bembo, Pietro, 212
condemnation of Dante's lan-
guage, 272

on Dante, 747
edition of the *Commedia,* 200,
202, 850
Prose della volgar lingua, 60,
211, 272
Terze rime di Dante, Le, 202
Bendemann, Eduard, 503
Benedict, Saint *(Benedetto),* **96–97,**
625
building temple on Mount
Cassino, 143
in the *Commedia,* 625, 760
in Heaven of Saturn, 635, 764
in the White Rose, 881
on contemplation, 217
founder of Western monasticism,
624
Benedict XI (pope), 19
identified with *veltro,* 852
Benevento (town), **97**
Benevento, Battle of, 104, 392,
407, 439, 457
death of Manfred at, 157, 589
Guido Guerra at, 461
Benigni, Roberto, 283–284
Benincasa da Laterina, **97**
murdered by Ghino di Tacco,
441
Benoit de Saint Maure, 49
Benvenuto da Imola, 65, 66, **97–98,**
173, 454
about Esau among neutrals, 356
on Andrea dei Mozzi, 36
on Belacqua, 96
on Casella, 142
Comentum, 87, 207
and concept of magnanimity, 584
on Dante's treatment of Saladin,
521
on Dante's Ulysses, 844
on Eunoe, 357
on fraudulent counsel, 422
on Furies, 429
on Giacomo da Santo Andrea,
442
on Giotto's friendhip with Dante,
446
glosses revised by Serravalle, 208
on glutton of Argogliosi family,
592
on identification of Pyrrhus, 732
influence on Cristoforo Landino,
211, 553
on Marco Lombardo, 592
on Matelda, 601
on meaning of "rich custom of
cloves," 648
on rejecting *messo celeste* as
Mercury, 609
on Omberto Aldobrandeschi, 660
on Pier da Medicina, 699
on Sordello being compared to a
lion, 795

Bodmer, Johann Jakob (*cont.*)
on poetic excellence of the *Commedia,* 434
body, human, **115–118**
nature of the shade body, 801
usefulness of, in Dante, 116
Body of Beatrice, The (Harrison), 816
body politic
concept of, 613
individual bodies inseparable from, 117
Boehmer, Eduard
and *Jahrbuch der Deutschen Dante-Gesellschaft,* 533
on Matelda, 602
Boethius (*Boezio;* Ancius Manlius Severinus Boethius), **118–119,** 596
and classificatory system of sciences, 767
Dante's references to, 172, 173
De institutione musica
definition of the three classes of music, 631
as inspiration for Fortune, 405
as mirror of the exiled Dante, 700
and Neoplatonism, 641
translations of Aristotle, 61
See also Consolation of Philosophy
Boethius of Dacia, 230, 460
on study of science, 768
Böhme, Jacob, 107
Boker, George Henry, 322
Bolgia, **119**
Bologna
factions in, 439–440
University of, 20
Bonaccorsi, Francesco, 230, 231
Bonaccorsi, Giovanni, 198
Bonagiunta da Lucca, **119–120,** 449, 888
in the *Commedia*
encounter with Dante-pilgrim, 308, 309
on Gentucca, 432
on Giacomo da Lentini, 442
on Guittone d'Arezzo, 442
introduction of the term *dolce stil novo,* 308, 449, 450
in *Purgatorio,* 724
Bonatti, Guido, 67, **120,** 793
Bonaventure, Saint (Giovanni Fidanza), 18, 26, **120–121,** 418
on angels, 42
attack on Aristotle, 62
and baptism, 82
in the *Commedia,* 760
criticizing Franciscans, 58, 418, 482

depicted in Heaven of the Sun, 811–812
on Joachim of Fiore in *Paradiso,* 537
on mendicant orders, 607
narrating life of Saint Dominic, 312, 314, 415
placed with Joachim of Fiore, 538
on Saint Dominic, 312
commentary on the Apocalypse of John, 540
on contemplation, 217
importance as Dante's source of theology, 812–813
influence of Richard of St. Victor, 744
and Joachim of Fiore, 538
Journey of the Mind to God, 28
on order of gravity of sins, 449
on sloth, 784–785
on study of science, 768
Bonconte da Montefeltro, **121–122**
Boniface, Archbishop (Bonifazio dei Fieschi), **122,** 449
glutton, 313
Boniface VIII (pope) (*Bonifazio;* Benedetto Caetani), 105, **122–124,** 151, 407
as *bête noire* of Dante, 514
Charles II of Anjou and, 158
and Corso Donati, 232
criticized by Guido da Montefeltro, 3
crusade against Colonna, 488–489
and Donation of Constantine, 315
and Guido da Montefeltro, 462
and Jubilee Year, 19, 239, 542
opposed by the Spirituals, 18
Philip IV's opposition to papal taxation of clergy, 692
Sciarra Colonna as enemy of, 767
and simony, 78, 586, 755
statue by Arnolfo di Cambio, *123*
and Tuscany, 836
and war of the Sicilian Vespers, 159–160
Bonnefoy, Yves, 262
Bonturo Dati, 85, **124**
Bonvesin da la Riva, **124–125**
Opere volgari, Le, 219
as source for Dante's structure of Hell, 474
Book of Daniel, 52
Book of Gomorrah (Peter Damian), 245
Book of Healing, The (Kitab al-Shifa) (Avicenna), 80
Book of James, 597

Book of Judith, 492, 493
"Book of Memory," 243
Book of Revelation. *See* Apocalypse
Book of the Cosmos *(volume),* 233
Book of the Courtier, The (Castiglione), 783
Book of the Ladder of Muhammad, 220
Book of the Three Scriptures, The (Bonvesin da la Riva), 124, 125
Book of the World, 346
Book on the Order of Creatures, 664
Booth, Wayne, 779
Borgese, G. A., 892
Borges, Jorge Luis, 845
Borghini, Vincenzo, 198, 202
Borsiere, Guiglielmo, **125,** 787
in *Decameron,* 113
Bosco, Umberto, 687
on Dante's Ulysses, 845
on Matelda, 601
Bosom of Abraham, 566
Boswell, Charles Stuart, 829
Botta, V., 601
Botterill, Steven, 349
Dante: "De vulgari eloquentia," 829
Botticelli, Sandro (Alessandro di Mariano Filipepi), **125–126,** 499, *516*
Dante at gates of Hell, *473*
illustrations of the *Commedia,* 208, 210
Bourne-Jones, Edward, 503
Bowra, C. M., 795
Boyde, Patrick, 407, 579
on Dante's conversion of astronomy to poetry, 69
Dante's Lyric Poetry, 828
on Dante's lyric poetry, 581
on Dante's use of alliteration, 35
on influences on Dante, 693
Boyd, Henry, 824
Brakhage, Stan, 249
Branca d'Oria, 10, **126**
traitor of the guest-host relationship, 722, 895
Branca, Vittore, 874
Brancazoli, Giovanni, 621
Breareus (Aegaeon), 444
Brehme, Christian, 264
Breviario di estetica (The Essence of Aesthetics) (Croce), 238
Breviary, 569
Brewer, Wilmon, 829
Briareus *(Briareo),* **126**
Briccio, Giovanni, 319
Brieger, Peter, 499, 783
Brigata, Il (Ugolino (Nino) della Gherardesca), **126–127,** 431

Brignone, Guido, 248
Brockhaus, F. A., Publishing House, 533
Brombly, C. H., 829
Brown, Emerson, 600
Brownlee, Kevin, 254
Brown, Raymond, 540
Brugnoli, Giorgio, 353
Brunelleschi, Betto, 480
Brunetta, Gian Piero, 249
Brunetto Latini, 2, 16, 42, **127–129**, 438
  in the *Commedia,* 7
    denouncing Fiesolans, 489–490
    reason for placement among sodomites, 690, 773
    as sodomite, 787, 788
  concept of earth, 329
  and Dante's scientific knowledge, 769
  as Dante's source on Roman history, 751
  on Dionysius the Elder, 305
  and Florentine culture, 396
  and knowledge of *mi'raj,* 522
  on *lonza,* 87
  on magnanimity, 584
  on Manfred, 589
  as mirror of the exiled Dante, 700
  on order of gravity of sins, 449
  and queer theory, 817
  on sloth, 785
  and study of rhetoric in Florence, 253
  See also Livres dou Tresor, Li; Tesoretto
Bruni, Leonardo, 22, 480
  on Dante's drawing, 250
  Life of Dante, 352
    dissemination in France, 259
    Vellutello on, 211, 850
brutishness, 831
Brutus, Lucius Junius *(Bruto),* **129**
Brutus, Marcus Junius *(Bruto),* **129–130,** *543, 545*
Bryson *(Brisso),* **130**
Bucciola, Ugolino, 10
Buck, August, 300
Buddeus, Johann Franz (Johannes Franciscus), 265, 434
Bufera e altro, La (Montale), 275
Buffet, Bernard, 262
Buiamonte, Giovanni (Gianni di Buiamonte de' Becchi), **130,** 740
Bulgakov, Mikhail, 278
Bullettino degli Studi Danteschi, 84, 204, 786
Buonconte da Montefeltro, 697
  appeal to Mary, 597

Buondelmonte dei Buondelmonti, 104, **130,** 438, 457
  murder of, 391, 629
Buoso, 1, **130–131**
Buoso da Duera, 49, **131**
Buoso Donati, **131**
  Buoso character in *Inf.* identified with, 130
Burgofranco, Jacob del, *17, 137, 189, 211*
Burke, Kenneth, 817
  on allegory, 32
Burton, Tim, 249
Busnelli, Giovanni, 693
  on Dante as Thomist, 812
  edition of the *Convivio,* 231
  on Matelda, 600
Butzbach, Georg, 202
Butzbach, Paul, 202
Buzzati, Dino, 319
Byron, George Gordon Lord, 256

C
Cabiria (film, Pastrone), 248
Caccia di Diana (Boccaccio), 113
Cacciaguida, **132–133**
  and chivalry, 163
  in the *Commedia,* 21, 22
    on Cangrande della Scalla, 137
    as exemplary witness to the faith, 596
    on Guelf-Ghibelline conflict, 104
    in Heaven of Mars, 594
    implicating papacy in Dante's exile, 123
    references to Fiesole in *Paradiso,* 374–375
    welcoming Dante in Heaven, 6, 7
  origin of Dante's family name, 21
Caccianemici, Gruamonte, 542
Caccianemico dell'Orso, Alberto, 133
Caccianemico, Venedico, 133
  among panders, 669
Cacus *(Caco),* **133,** 298
Cadmus *(Cadmo),* **134**
Caecilius Statius *(Cecilio),* **134**
Caetani, Benedetto. *See* Boniface VIII
Cahors, France *(Caorsa),* **134**
Caiaphas *(Caifa), 134,* **134,** 363, 495
Cain, **134–135**
Caina, 12, 14, 50, **135,** *179,* 190, 421
  as part of Cocytus, 179, 190
  traitors to kin in, 822, 830
Caius Julius Caesar Octavianus *(Ottaviano). See* Augustus *(Augusto)*

Calaynos (Boker), 322
Calchas *(Calcanta),* **135–136**
Calcidius, 703
  and microcosm, 613
  Middle Platonism of, 642
Calixtus I *(Calisto)* (pope), **136**
Calliope *(Calïopè; Calliopè),* **136,** 630, 663
Caltabellotta, Treaty of, 158, 160, 239
Camaldoli, Order of (reformed Benedictines), 583, 624, 757
Cambridge, University of, 417
Camilla, **136,** 680
  in Limbo, 888
Camillus, Marcus Furius *(Cammillo),* **136**
Camiscion de' Pazzi (Alberto Camicio), 12, 135, **136,** 142, 637
  on Focaccia, 403
  on Sassol Mascheroni, 763
Campaldino, **136**
Campaldino, Battle of, 18, 47, 104, 136, 836
  Bonconte at, 121
  Corso Donati at, 232
Campello, Pompeo di, 320
Campodonico, M., 601
Camposanto frescos in Pisa, 498
Camus, Albert, 262
Cancellieri family, 104, 105
Cancellieri, Vanni de'. *See* Focaccia
Cangrande della Scala, **136–137**
  in the *Commedia*
    as candidate for prophesied savior, 382
    identified with *veltro,* 852
  Dante at court of, 20
  in *Decameron,* 113
  influenced by Mars, 594
cannibalism, 840
canonization. *See* Saints
canon law, 559
canon lawyers. *See* decretalists
Canon of Medicine, The (al-Qanun fi al-Tibb) (Avicenna), 80
"Canon of Women in Dante's *Commedia,* A" (Kirkham), 817
Cante de' Gabrielli, 105
Canterbury Tales (Chaucer), 162
cantica (canticle), **137–138**
  form invented in *Inferno,* 515
Canticle of Canticles. *See* Song of Songs
"Canticle of the Creatures" (Francis of Assisi), 415
canto *(cantus),* **139–140**
canto of the queens, 577–578
Cantos, The (Pound), 705
  and Dante, 257
Cants from Natural History Works (film, Gary Adkins), 249

classical tradition, Dante and the, **252–255**

Claudel, Paul, 261–262

Clemence of Habsburg, **176**

Clement IV (pope), **176–177,** 407
and Angevin dynasty, 45
and Catalano, 144
Charles I of Anjou and, 157
and French intervention in Italy, 457

Clement of Alexandria, 871
on neutral angels, 297

Clement V (pope) *(Clemente),* **177–178,** 692
betrayal of, 491
crowning Robert of Anjou as king of Naples, 746
and Henry VII of Luxemburg, 479
and simony, 78, 586, 755
treachery of, 481

Cleobulus *(Cleobulo),* **178**

Cleopatra *(Cleopatràs),* **178,** 578
and lust, 86

Clericis laicos (bull), 122

Cletus (pope) *(Cleto,* Anacletus), 99, **178**

Clio *(Clió),* **178,** 630

Clotho *(Cloto),* **178**

Cluniacs, 624

Clymene, **178**

Cocytus *(Cocito),* 49, **178–180,** 190, 306, 421, 822, *822*

Code, 550, 557

Codice Cassinese, 852

Cogan, Robert, 829

cogitative power, 738

Coleridge, Samuel Taylor, **180**
on Cary's translation, 825
on Dante, 749
and Dante's allegory, 30

Colilli, Paul, 818

Colish, Marcia L.
on Dante's treatment of Averroës, 521
on Dante's treatment of Saladin, 521

Collationes in Hexaemeron (Bonaventure), 538

Collingwood, R. J., 238

Colombo, Manuela, 305

colors
of the face of Lucifer, 574
linked to Beatrice, 90

Comedìa delle ninfe fiorentine (Boccaccio), 113

Comedia di Dante Aligieri, La,
with commentary by A. Vellutello, published by Francesco Marcolini, 1544 edition, *40, 50, 78, 90, 165, 179, 328, 331, 332, 333, 341, 436, 450, 484, 493,*
500, 561, 566, 577, 585, 593, 647, 677, 684, 710, 860, 863, 882, 892

Comedia di Dante, published in 1506 by Philippo Giunti, *586*

Comedia di Danthe Alighieri poeta divino, with commentary by Cristoforo Landino, published by Jacob del Burgofra(n)co, 1529 edition, *17, 137, 189, 211*
illustrated by Sandro Botticelli, 125

Comedia, La (Pietro da Figino, ed., 1491), *288, 575, 594, 627, 651, 698, 709, 782, 799, 819, 848, 882*

Comedieta de Ponça (Santillana), 280

comedy, **180–181**
definition, 185

Comentum (Benvenuto da Imola), 87, 207

Commedia, **181–213**
and the ages of life, 8–9
aim of societal reform, 220–221
allegory and realism, 30, **194–197**
apostolic poverty, 706
and astrology, 67
authority in, 75
as autobiography, 453
based on the principle of "particular judgment" in Last Judgment, 545
Bible, correspondences with, 138
bodies of the souls, 741, 801
and Catholic baptismal theology, 82
celebration of Solomon in, 790
characters
appearing in the *Decameron,* 113
historical life of, 376–377
classical canon in, 173, 175, 695
conception of origin of human soul different from *Convivio,* 796
and crusade, 239
Dante dissociating himself from the *dolce stil nuovo,* 182
Dante on Hohenstaufen in, 589
and Dante's devotion to Christ, 164
Dante's position on Eve in, 360
Dante's views on papacy in, 514
dark wood as dream, 324
Decameron's parallels with, 113
defense of immortality in, 506
delight in, 296–297

different ethical and philosophical perspective than *Convivio,* 868
disregard for the Angevins, 46
division in cantos, 139
and doctrine of elements, 336
earth in the, 329
empireo mentioned in, 341–342
encounter with great poets of antiquity, 175
and England, 342
epicycle mentioned in, 721
episode of Adam and language, 452
episode of the *corda,* 607
Epistle to Cangrande used for interpretation of, 349
evocation of Apocalypse in, 52–53
exile necessary precondition to writing the, 364
Exodus as theological counterbalance to classical epic, 365
extensive immediate Italian attention to, 270–271
on fantasy, 370
free will in, 425–426
greatness recognized by Chaucer, 161
Greek figures in, 453
historical figures as personification of abstractions
Hohenstaufen (Swabian) house in, 434
ideas of the *Convivio* developed in, 230
illustrating traditional conceptions of vice and virtue, 866
imagery from Apocalypse, 53
imagination in, 505
importance of title as means to understanding poem, 184
Incarnation in, 508
influence of Aristotle on, 64, 693
influence of Boethius's *Consolation,* 118
influence of Cicero on, 695
influence of *De quinque septenis* (Hugh of St. Victor) on, 495
influence of Neoplatonism in, 643
influence of Virgil's *Aeneid,* 7
influence on *Orlando furioso* (Ariosto), 60
and intellect, 518, 519
interpretation by Dante Gabriel Rossetti, 260
introduction to, **181–184**
itinerary of Dante-pilgrim, 183
and Jubilee Year, 543
legitimating effect of Moses on, 629

commentaries on the *Commedia*,
(*cont.*)
by Vellutello, **850–851**
by Villani, 208
*Commentaries on the Dream of
Scipio* (Macrobius), 613
Commentarium (Pietro Alighieri),
21
*Commentary on the De Trinitate of
Boethius* (Aristotle), 736
*Commentary on the Nichomachean
Ethics* (Thomas Aquinas),
308
*Commentary on the Sentences of
Peter Lombard* (Albert the
Great), 567
commerce
in Florence, 388
in Tuscany, 836
commutative justice, **213**
Compagni, Dino, 48, 168,
213–214, 397
chronicles, 208
on Corso Donati, 394
Cronica, 320
on Dante ambassador to Rome,
750
on Dante's absence at time of
exile condemnation, 362
on Giano della Bella, 393
on origins of Guelfs, 457
as prior, 395
on Salterello, 761
*Compendium Alexandrinum (Liber
Ethicorum),* 64
Compilatio Tertia (Innocent III), 294
*Compositions from the Divine
Poem of Dante* (Flaxman),
384
*Concordance of the Divina Com-
media* (Fay), 286
*Concordance to the Divine Com-
edy, A* (Wilkins and Bergin),
286, 883
*Concordanza delle opere italiane
in prosa e del canzoniere di
Dante Alighieri* (Sheldon
and White), 286
*Concordia Discordantium
Canonum* (Gratian). *See
Decretum* (Gratian)
concupiscence, sins of, 773
gluttony as one of the, 449
Con Dante e coi suoi interpreti
(Barbi), 84
Condulmieri, C. C., 503
confession, **214–215**
Confessions (Augustine), 71
and autobiographical voice, 223,
225
and microcosm, 613–614
theological source for Dante,
813–814

confraternities, 399–401
Confraternity of the Knights of the
Blessed Virgin Mary, 144
Conrad I the Elder *(Currado),* **215**
Conrad II the Younger *(Currado),*
216
Conrad III *(Currado),* **216**
in *Commedia,* 434
Conradin *(Curradino),* **216**
Charles I of Anjou and, 157
in *Commedia,* 434
execution of, 439
Conrad of Saxony, 870
Speculum, 192
*Consolation of Philosophy (De
consolatione philosophiae)*
(Boethius), 30, 118
in *Convivio,* 253
Dante and, 170, 225, 551
impact on *Vita Nuova,* 253
and microcosm, 613
possible source of Dante's
knowledge of *Timaeus,*
820
Consolations chrétiennes (La
Touche-Loisi), 259
Consolations, Les (Sainte-Beuve),
261
Constance *(Costanza),* **216,** 626
Constance, Council of, 262
Constantine the Great *(Costantino),*
216–217
among supremely just rulers,
547–548
in Paradise, 316
See also Donation of Constantine
*Constantini M. Imp. Donatio Sylve-
stro Papae Rom. inscripta*
(M. Freher), 264
consuls, 438
contemplative life, **217–218,**
624–625
associated with Saturn, 675
in *Convivio,* 4, 624–625
and intellectual virtues, 4, 229,
867
Mary symbolizing, 594
as opposed to active life, 3
Rachel symbolizing, 560, 737
superiority of, 866
Conte Ugolino, Il (film), 247
Conte Ugolino, Il (Semproni),
319
Conti, Federico de', 202
Conti Guidi, 461
Castle at Poppi, *461*
Contini, Gianfranco, 120, **218–219,**
579, 687
on authorship of *Detto d'Amore,*
300
on authorship of *Fiore,* 380
on *petrose* poems, 689–690
and *Studi danteschi,* 786

contrapasso, 190, 195, **219–222,**
476
of Ali, 521
explained by Bertran de Born,
766
importance of Thomas Aquinas,
812
of incontinent, 509–510
introduced with the neutrals,
646–647
of Muhammad, 521
of the thieves, 586, 819
for wrath, 891
*Contributions to the Textual Criti-
cism of the "Divine Com-
media"* (Moore), 204, 627,
825
Convenevole da Prato, 396
convenientia, sense of, 196
Conventuals (Franciscans), 482,
606
conversion, **222–224**
Commedia as pilgrimage of,
507
pagans undergoing, 255
of Ripheus, 255, 745, 753
of Statius, 799
of Trajan, 255, 745, 753
Convivio, **224–232**
on active life, 4
on act of artist and act of God,
250
and the ages of life, 8–9
and allegory, 26, 28, 226
analogy between heavens and
liberal arts, 614
and angels, 38, 42
Apollo in, 54
appetite in, 55–56
Aristotelian model of virtue,
867
Aristotle in, 63
on art of poetry, 610
Augustine in, 71
Avicenna mentioned in, 80
Beatrice mentioned in, 94
Bertran de Born in, 100, 766
Boethius mentioned in, 118
Cato in, 146–147
Cavalcanti inspiration for, 460
chain of being explained in, 155
classical canon in, 172, 175,
695
condemnation of desire for
wealth, 241–242
on contemplative life, 4,
624–625
dating, 225–226
David in, 290
on *De amicitia* (Cicero), 253
on *De consolatione philosophiae*
(Boethius), 253
defense of immortality in, 506

defense of Italian vernacular, 526, 555
delight in, 296, 297
Derivationes cited in, 841–842
different ethical and philosophical perspective than *Commedia,* 868
and doctrine of elements, 336
donna gentile in, 317, 551
  and crisis of Dante's own development as a poet-philosopher, 552
  as love of wisdom, 551
dreams as kind of revelation, 743
earth described in, 328
1529 edition, Niccolo di Aristotile detto Zoppino, *225*
embryology, 644
on the Empyrean, 341
envy treated as denigration, 343–344
and Epicureans, 347
epicycle, described, 720
on exile, 362–363
on fantasy, 370
on Guido da Montelfetro, 463
Hector referred to in, 471
on human soul, 795
  on denying the soul's immortality, 485
illustrating traditional conceptions of vice and virtue, 866, 867
Incarnation in, 508
influence of Averroës, 694
influence of Avicenna, 694
influence of Neoplatonism, 643
and intellect, 518
istoria, use of term in, 487
on justice, 308, 548
on language, 452, 555
light discussed in, 565
Livy cited in, 571
on magnanimity, 583–584
on Mars, 593
and memory, 605
Moon in, 627
and music, 252
nobility discussed in, 148
optics discussed in, 660–661
Ovid in, 667–668
on passive intellect, 739
Phaëton in, 691
Plato mentioned in, 704
poverty, 706
praise of Seneca, 772
Primum Mobile, 711
on prose, 716
and psychological aspects of avarice, 76
Ptolemy named as authority in, 720
references to Christ, 164

on Rome, 530
Saladin in, 760
on schools of the religious orders, 606–607
Scipio cited in, 770
Socrates referred to in, 787
Song of Songs quoted in, 790
statement on language differing from *De vulgari eloquentia,* 555
structure, 227–229
on Sun's motion, 767
translations
  English, 828, 829
  of odes by La Touche-Loisi, 259
on virtue opposing wrath, 892
writing of, 19
zodiac mentioned in, 896
Coppola, Francis Ford, 249
Corbinelli, Iacopo, 259
Corinne (de Staël), 260
Cornelia *(Corniglia),* **232**
  in Limbo, 888
Cornelius, Peter, 503
Coronación, La (Mena), 281
Corpus Areopagiticum (Dionysius the Areopagite), 304
Corpus hippocraticum, 486
Corpus iuris civilis (Code of Justinian), 550, 557
Corso Donati, 105, 106, **232,** 457, 458
  in *Decameron,* 113
  exile, 395
  seen as threat by the *popolo,* 394
  supported by Boniface VIII, 122
Corti, Maria, 80, 817
  on Aristotle's impact on Dante, 866
  on Cavalcanti, 460
  on Dante's sources for human soul, 796
  on Dante's Ulysses, 844
  and dating of the *Convivio,* 226
  on influence of *mi'raj* on Dante, 522
  on magnanimity, 866–867
"Così nel mio parlar voglio esser aspro" ("So in my speech I would be harsh") (Dante), 141, 689, 774
Cosmas Indicopleustes, 234
Cosmico, Niccolò Lelio, 208
Cosmographia (Bernard Silvester), 98
cosmology, **232–235**
  light and, 564
Costa, Orazio, 320
Costa, Paolo, 203
Cottafavi, Vittorio, 283
Cotter, James Finn, 828

counterfeiters. *See* falsifiers of coinage
courage, 229, 866
  associated with Mars, 193, 233, 868
  as cardinal virtue, 867
Courcelle, Pierre, 25
courtesy *(cortesia/gentilezza),* 163
courtly love, **235–238**
  Detto d'Amore as expression of the ideology of, 299
cowards. *See* neutrals
Crassus, Marcus Licinius *(Crasso),* **238**
Crawford, Francis Marion, 321
creationism *versus* emanationism, 644
crime
  against kin
    Sassol Mascheroni, 673
  against neighbors, 860–861
Cristoforo Zapate de Cisneros, *843*
Critica, La (journal), 238
criticism
  and *Epistle to Cangrande,* 349
criticism of the abuses of the times
  Dante commissioned by Cacciaguida, 713
Critische Abhandlung von dem Wunderbaren in der Poesie (Bodmer), 265
Critische Betrachtungen über die poetischen Gemälde der Dichter (Bodmer), 265
Croce, Benedetto, **238–239,** 267, 268, 275, 427, 816
  and Dante, 257
  on Matelda, 601
  opposed by Barbi, 84
  Poesia di Dante, La, 878
  and Vossler, 878
Cromwell (Hugo), 260
Cronaca malatestiana, 410
Cronica (Compagni), 320, 397
Cronica (G. Villani), 48
Cronica (Paolino Pieri), 397
Cronica delle cose occorrenti ne' tempi suoi (Compagni), 208, 213
crusades, **239–241**
  against the Cathars, 145, 312, 313, 398, 482
    Folco of Marseilles and, 403
  second
    preached by Saint Bernard, 99
  third
    Frederick I and, 424
    Saladin and, 521
Culture and Imperialism (Said), 818
Cunizza da Romano, 80, **241,** 578, 889
  on Alessandro Novello, 14
  on Cangrande della Scala, 136

Donation of Constantine (*cont.*)
  denounced as forgery by Valla,
    216, 315
  dismissed by Dante as invalid
    transaction, 340
  justifying papal territoral rights
    in Italy, 670
  Sylvester I and, 803
Donatists, 482
Donato, Eugenio, 817
Donatus, **316**
  Ars grammatica, 34
  on neologisms, 640
  texts used in Trivium, 832
Doni, A. F., 353
Donna gentile of the *Vita Nuova,*
  316–318, 877
"Donna me prega" (Cavalcanti),
  459
  Dante's reaction to, 460
  use of optics, 661
"Donna pietosa e di novella etate"
  (Dante), 140
"Donne ch'avete intelletto
  d'amore" ("Ladies that have
  intellect of love") (Dante),
  140, 308, 580, 645, 888
  conception of understanding in,
    739
  example of tragic style, 821
  parallel between ladies and
    angels, 37
Donno, Daniel, 454
Don Quijote (Cervantes), 282
Doolittle, Hilda, 705
Doré, Paul Gustave, **318,** 503
  illustration of Cary's translation,
    825
  inspiration for silent film, 247
  use of illustrations in *Dante,*
    uomo e poeta (television
    documentary), 283
Dottrinale, Il (Jacopo di Dante), 533
"Double Play of Arnaut Daniel's
  Sestina and Dante's *Divina*
  Commedia, The" (Dra-
  gonetti), 817
doubt, Medusa as figure for, 603
D'Ovidio, Francesco
  on authorship of *Il Fiore,* 380
  on *Epistle to Cangrande,* 353
  on Matelda, 601, 602
Dozon, Marthe, 818
  on Dante's symbolism, 804
Dragonetti, Roger, 817
  on Matelda, 601, 602
dramatic arts, **319–324**
dramatic breaks, 515
Draughtsman's Contract, The (film,
  Greenaway), 249
dreams, **324–326**
  dark wood as oneiric image, 288
  function in *Commedia,* 324–325

of Leah, 331, 560, 724
in *Purgatorio,* 218, 325, 724
Rachel in, 724, 737
Siren in, 724, 784
Dronke, Peter
  on Dante's allegory, 27
  on *Epistle to Cangrande,* 353
Drowning by Numbers (film,
  Greenaway), 249
Dubliners (Joyce), 257
Due studi danteschi (Fubini), 427
Duff, Howard, 284
Dumas, Alexandre, 260
Dumensis, Martinus, 772
Duns Scotus, John, 642
Duplessis-Mornay, Philippe, 259
Durantis, Wilhelmus, 295
Durling, Robert, 67
  on allegory, 33
  on fraudulent counsel, 423
  on translation of *ingiuria,* 518
  translation of the *Inferno,* 826
Duse, Eleonora, 321
"Dvenadsat" ("The Twelve")
  (Blok), 277
DXV. *See* five hundred ten and five

E
eagle *(aguglia, aquila),* **327–328,**
  328, 547, 745, 753
  about William II of Sicily, 885
  as Dante's interlocutor, 546
  and justice, 83, 549, 613, 805
  princes condemned by the, 304
  as symbol of imperial Rome, 546
  theological issues in eagle
    episode, 872
earth, element, **330**
earth, globe, **328–330,** *329*
Earthly Paradise, 183, **330–334,**
  331, 332, 333, 677
  different from Genesis, 358
  Matelda tutelary female spirit of,
    599
  music in, 632, 633
  procession in, *561,* 726–727
    allegory of the Second Com-
      ing, 545
    Dante's version of ecclesiasti-
      cal history, 753–754
    explained by Beatrice, 714
    and griffin, 455
    imagery from Book of Revela-
      tion, 332, 753
    linking of reason and revela-
      tion in church history,
      743–744
    Saint Luke represented by his
      writings, 577
    Saint Mark in, 593
Eastern monasticism, 624
Ecclesiastical Hierarchy (Dionysius the Areopagite), 305

Eclogues (Dante), **334–335**
  Boccaccio and, 110
  translations, 829
Eclogues (Virgil), 862
Eden, garden of. *See* Earthly Par-
  adise
Edinburgh Review, 180, 273, 406,
  583, 748, 749, 825
editions
  Commedia, **201–206**
    annotated by Momigliano, 616
    Boccaccio, 112
    critical by Petrocchi, 687
    critical by Scartazzini, 268
    first printed French, 259
    scholarly edition by Witte,
      268, 886
    small edition by Scartazzini,
      268
  of the *Convivio,* 231
  Edizione Nazionale (National Edi-
    tion), 204–205, 687
    Contini and completion of,
      218–219
    and Società Dantesca Italiana,
      786
education
  Dominicans and, 606
  in Florence, 16, 396
  Quadrivium, **735–736**
  television programs on Dante,
    285–286
  Trivium, **832–833**
Educational Filmstrips and Video,
  285
Edward I (England), 342–343
  Accorso and, 2
efficient cause. *See* causes, the four
Egypt *(Egitto),* **335–336**
8½ (film, Fellini), 248
eight, symbolism of, 653, 656, 882
Electra *(Elettra),* **336**
  in Limbo, 888
Electronic Bulletin of the Dante
  Society of America
  (EBDSA), 287
Elementa astronomica (Alfraganus), 15
elements, **336**
  air, 10
  earth, **330**
  fire, **381**
  water, **880**
Elements (Euclid), 357, 736
Elements of Theology (Proclus),
  642
Elijah *(Elia),* **336–337**
Eliot, George, 258
Eliot, T. S., 107, **337,** 816
  and Dante, 257
  and episode of Guido da Monte-
    feltro, 586
  on simile, 778

Elisha *(Eliseo)*, **338**
Ellero, 320
Elwert, Wilhelm Theodor, 269
Elysium *(Elisio, Eliso)* (Elysian
 Fields), **338**, 664
 as model for Noble Castle, 651
embryology, human
 Aristotle source of, 693
 in Dante's works, 644, 767
 in *Purgatorio,* 115
Emerson, Ralph Waldo, 828
Emiliani, Cesare, 853
"E' m'increscce di me" (Dante), 580
Emler, Bonaventura, 503
Empedocles, **338**
empire, **338–341**
 relationship with papacy, 616,
 620–621, 670
 Rome as symbol of universal
 empire, 750
empiricism, Dante and, 769
Empyrean, 192, 193, 233, **341–342**,
 671, 674
 aligned with theology, 228
 point of light in the, *563*
 vision of God as river of light,
 564
 White Rose in, *341*
Enchiridion (Augustine), 473
Enciclopedia dantesca
 on Maometto, 521
 Petrocchi general editor of, 687
Enciclopedia dantesca (Scartaz-
 zini), 268
encyclopedia
 Commedia as, 452
 Convivio as, 224
*Enfer, avec les dessins de G. Doré,
 L',* 318
Enfer de Dante, L' (Buffet), 262
England, **342–343**
 Dante in, **255–259**, 749
Enguerrand de Marigny, 160
Ennius, 34
"Ensenhamen d'onor" (Sordello),
 794
"Entdeckung Dantes in der Roman-
 tik" (Auerbach), 269
Entrèves, A. P. d', 621
envy *(invidia)*, 163, **343–344**
 Aglauros, 9
 Arrigo Mainardi, 66
 Cain as example of, 134
 contrapasso, 222
 and love of the wrong object,
 870
 in Purgatory, 191
 Rinieri da Calboli, 745
 Sapia and, 762
Ephemeris belli troiani (Dictys of
 Crete), 49
Ephesus, Council of, 597
Ephialtes *(Fïalte)*, **344**, 444, 445

epic poetry, **344–346**
Epicureans *(Epicurei)*, **346–347**,
 682
 Mary Magdalen identified allegorically with, 598
 representing heresy in *Commedia,* 483
Epicurus *(Epicuro)*, 255, **347**
 and mortalism, 506
epicycle, **347–348**, 720
 description in *Convivio,* 720
 mentioned in *Commedia,* 721
Epipsychidion (Shelley), 258, 775
Epistles, 19, **352–355**
 and avarice, 76
 Boccaccio as source of, 110
 cursus in, 716
 *Epistle to Henry VII of Luxem-
 burg (Epistle 7),* 480
 Dante identifying with John
 the Baptist in, 539
 Epistle 4 to Moroello, 629
 Epistle to the Florentines
 (Dante), 794
 *Epistle to the Italian Cardinals
 (Epistle 8),* 19, 755
 on opposition of cupidity and
 charity, 241
 reference to Pharisees, 691
 on Rome, 617
 *Epistle to the Princes and
 Peoples of Italy (Epistle 5),*
 19, 480, 492, 538
 forgeries, 353
 See also Epistle to Cangrande
Epistles of Saint Paul, 642, 742
Epistle to Cangrande, 53, **348–352**
 on application of the allegory of
 the theologians, 814
 authenticity of, 181, 350–351
 Moore defending, 627
 Singleton on, 783
 citing *De consideratione*
 (Bernard), 744
 citing *De contemplatione*
 (Richard of St. Victor), 744
 citing *De quantitate animae*
 (Augustine), 744
 classical poets mentioned in, 254
 on comedy *versus* tragedy, 183,
 821
 defined by Uguccione de'
 Bagni, 842
 on the *Commedia*
 allegorical meaning of the
 Commedia, 549, 799
 concern with moral activity
 and ethics, 866
 subject of the *Commedia,* 271,
 425
 and theme of *Paradiso,*
 674–675
 critics on, 28

discussion of allegory in, 26–27,
 28
 division into 33 sections, 654
 on Empyrean, 341
 evocation of Saint Augustine in,
 71
 on the fourfold interpretation
 reserved for Scripture, 102,
 507
 and *In exitu Israel de Aegypto,*
 524
 on language, 556
 on modes of writing, 180
 translation of, 829
*Epitome bibliothecae Conradi Ges-
 neri* (Simler)
 on Dante, 263
Erard de Valéry, **355**
Erato, 630
Erichtho *(Eritòn)*, **355–356**
Erigena, John Scotus, 305, 613,
 642
Erinyes. *See* Furies
erotic sinners. *See* carnal sinners
error, as distinguished from heresy,
 482
Erysichthon *(Erisittone)*, **356**
Esau, **356**
 as "great coward," 647
Espinette amoureuse (Froissart),
 259
*Esposizioni sopra la Comedìa di
 Dante* (Boccaccio), 47, 85,
 114, 207
 on the three beasts, 85
Essais sur les moeurs (Voltaire),
 259
"Essay on Machiavelli"
 (Macaulay), 583
"Essay on Milton" (Macaulay), 583
*Essay on the Genius and the Writ-
 ings of Pope* (Warton), 266
Essay on the Vita Nuova, An (Singleton), 286, 783
Este, Ippolito d', 60
*Estetica come scienza dell' espres-
 sione e linguistica generale
 (Aesthetics)* (Croce), 238
Esther *(Estèr)*, **356**
Eteocles *(Eteocle)*, **356–357**, 704
eternal rose. *See* White Rose
eternity, **357**
Etex, Antoine, 503
ethics
 four causes as foundation of, 150
 identified with Primum Mobile,
 288, 866
Ethics (Aristotle)
 and classification of sinners in
 Hell, 513
 and concept of magnanimity, 583
 source of notion of malice, 518
 on types of wrathful, 891

Etymologies (Isidore of Seville), 34, 179, 452, 520
  used in Trivium, 833
Euclid *(Euclide),* **357**
Eumenides. *See* Furies
Eunoe *(Eünoè),* **357–358,** 562
  Matelda and, 599
Eunuchus (Terence), 811
Euripides *(Euripide),* **358**
Europa, **358–359**
Europäische Literatur und lateinischen Mittelalter (European Literature and the Latin Middle Ages) (Curtius), 243
Europe *(Europa),* **359**
  language in, according to Dante, 526
European Literature and the Middle Ages (Curtius), 269
"European pedigrees/African contagions" (Snead), 818
Euryalus *(Eurialo),* **359,** 649
Eurypylus *(Euripilo),* 135, **359–360,** 793
Eusebius of Cesarea, 216, 217
Euterpe, 630
Evangelium Nicodemi (Gospel of Nicodemus), 470, 471
Eve *(Eva),* **360**
Evgenii Onegin (Eugene Onegin) (Pushkin), 276
excommunicates, 50, **360–362**
  in Ante-Purgatory, 191, 590, 730
  of Manfred, 589
  placed among late repentant, 554
exemplar Pariensis, 101
Exiit qui seminat (bull), 648
exile, **362–365**
  Farinata warning Dante-pilgrim of future exile, 373
  of Guelfs, 392, 439, 457–458
  of Whites, 160, 395
Exodus, **365**
  allegory, 524
  early commentators on, 507
  and fourfold method of scriptural exegesis, 524
  importance of theme in Dante, 363
  interpretations of theme of, 507
Expositio (F. Villani), 208
Expositio in Apocalypsim (Joachim of Fiore), 537
Expositiones et Glose super Comediam Dantis ("Commentaries and Glosses on Dante's *Commedia*") (Guido da Pisa), 199, 350, 414, 463–464
  influence on Francesco da Buti, 414

possible influence on Jacopo di Dante's *Chiose,* 533
  on Saint Lucy, 576
Exposition on the Song of Songs (Gregory the Great), 33
Extravagantes (Clement V), 294
Exultet in gloria (encyclical), 354
  in support of Henry VII of Luxemburg, 480
eyes
  emitting a ray of light, 565
    theory refuted by Dante in *Convivio,* 661
  and St. Lucy as Dante's patron, 576
Ezekiel *(Ezechiele),* **365**
Ezzelino III da Romano *(Azzolino),* **80, 365–366**
  and Giacomo da Santo Andrea, 442

F
Fabbri, Edoardo, 321
Fabbro de' Lambertazzi, **367**
Fabricius (Gaius Fabricius Luscinus, *Fabrizio*), **367**
Fabricius, Joannes Albertus, 265
Fabris, Domenico, 503
factions, 439–440, 458
  expansion of Florence as cause of, 490
  link with heresy, 372
  origins, 438
Faerie Queene (Spenser), 229
faith, 193
  Dante-pilgrim examined by St. Peter on, 193, 384, 684, 868
  Dante's use of liturgy, 570
  deficiency linked with Heaven of the Moon, 627
  as theological virtue, 867
"Fall of Hyperion, The" (Keats), 258
fall of man, **367–369**
"False Boccaccio," 207
  on *veltro,* 852
falsifiers, 190, **369,** 420, 587, 869
  falsifiers of coinage, 369, 587
    Master Adam, 599
  falsifiers of person, 369, 587
    Learchus, 561
    Myrrha, 634
    Schicchi, Gianni, 131, 765–766
  falsifiers of words, 369, 587
    Sinon, 783
Familiares (Petrarch), 353
Fanger, Donald, 277
fantasy, 291, **370**
farcical elements in *Inferno,* 301
Farinata degli Uberti, 22, 104, 151, **370–373,** *371, 485*
  as Cathar, 146
  and magnanimity, 584

  at Montaperti, 392
  protecting Florence after Battle of Montaperti, 439
  punished as heretic, 145
  representation in *Commedia,* 483
Farinelli, Arturo, 279
Fates, 70
  Clotho, **178**
  Lachesis, **551**
Fatti di Enea, I (Guido da Pisa), 464
Faunus (Boccaccio), 110
Fauriel, Claude-Charles
  and Dante scholarship, 260
Favolello (Little Fable) (Brunetto Latini), 128
Fay, E. A., 286
fear of flying, 437
  recalling Icarus, 497
Febrer, Andreu, 184
Federico Novello, **373–374**
Federigo Tignoso, **374**
Felicità mentale, La: Nuove prospettive per Cavalcanti e Dante (Corti), 817
Fellini, Federico, 248
Feltro, **374**
Ferdinand IV of Castille, **374**
Ferrante, Joan, 817, 822
  on *veltro,* 852
Ferrari, Paolo, 320
Ferrers Howell, A. F., 829
Ferrigni, Mario, 320
Feuerbach, Anselm, 503
Feuilles d'automne, Les (Hugo), 260
Ficino, Marsilio, 208, 553
  influence on interpretations of the *Commedia,* 645
  Italian translation of *Monarchia,* 622
Filocolo (Boccaccio), 113
Fidanza, Giovanni. *See* Bonaventure, Saint
Fields, James T., 571
Fieshi, Bonifazio dei. *See* Boniface, Archbishop
Fieschi, Ottobono de'. *See* Adrian V (pope)
Fieschi, Sinibaldo, 295
  See also Innocent IV
"Fiesolan" as term, 490
Fiesole, **374–375**
"Figura" (Auerbach), 70, 269, 375
figuralism, **375–379**
Figure of Beatrice, The (Williams), 765
Filelfo, G. M., 353
Filipepi, Alessandro di Mariano. *See* Botticelli, Sandro
film, Dante and, **246–250**
Filomusi-Guelfi, Lorenzo, 853
Filostrato (Boccaccio), 110, 113

G

Gabriele, Trifone, 210, 211, 246
  Annotationi, 211
  on Dante's language, 272
Gabriel Giolito de Ferrari, *16*
Gabriel, the Archangel *(Gabriello)*, **430**
Gaddo, **430**
Gaeta, **430**
Gaido, Domenico, 247
Galen *(Galieno)*, **430–431**
Galilei, Galileo, on Dante's scientific acumen, 767
Gallehaut *(Galeotto)*, **431**
Ganelon *(Gano, Ganellone)*, 408, **431**
Ganges *(Gange)*, **431**
Gano degli Scornigiani, **431**
Ganymede *(Ganimede)*, **431**
Garamantes *(Garamanti)*, **431–432**
Garatori da Imola, Jacopo dei, 21
García y Tássara, Gabriel, 282
Gardner, Edmund Garrat, **432**
  Dante and Giovanni del Virgilio, 829
Garrow, Joseph, 256, 828
Garzoni, Tommaso, 264
Gassman, Vittorio, 283
Gates of Hell (Rodin), 261
Gautier, Théophile, 260
Gelli, Giovan Battista, 212
gematria, process of, 382
Gemma Donati, **432**
Genelli, Bonaventura, 503
Gentile da Cingoli, 63
Gentile, Giovanni, 852
gentleness, 866, 892
  overcoming wrath, 870
gentleness, virtue of, 229
Gentucca, **432–433**
Gentucca di Ciucchino Morla, 432
Geoffrey of Vinsauf
  Poetria nova, 34–35
  and simile, 778
geography
  Dante's locating of France, 409
  in Dante's works, 767
  limits of Italy, 529
  medieval, 328
George, Stefan, 269
Georgics (Virgil), 862
  source for Orpheus, 663
Gerard of Borgo San Donnino, 538
Gerard of Cremona (Geraldo da Cremona)
  translation of Alfraganus's astronomical treatise, 15
  translation of Avicenna's *Canon of Medicine*, 80
Geremek, Bronislaw, 706
Geri di Bello (Ruggieri del Bello degli Alighieri), **433**

German Dante Society. *See* Deutsche Dante-Gesellschaft
Germany *(Lamagna)*, **433–435**
Germany, Dante in, **262–269**, 434–435
Gerstenberg, Heinrich Wilhelm, 265
Geryon, 32, 190, 298, **435–437**, *436*, *586*, *587*, 848, 888
  allegorical figure of fraud, 420, 436
  Dante on back of, 515
Gesammelte Aufsätze zur romanischen Philologie (Auerbach), 269
Gesta Florentinorum (Sanzanome), 167, 397
Getto, Giovanni, 853
Gherardo da Camino, **437**
  praised by Marco Lombardo, 242
Gherardo II, identified as Abbot of San Zeno, 762
Ghibellines, 104, **437–441**
  defeated at Campaldino, 18
  Florence civil war absorbed in conflicts of, 391
  formation of, 338
  Manfred's alliance with Tuscan Ghibellines, 589
Ghino di Tacco, 97, **441**
  in *Decameron*, 113
Ghisolabella, **441**, 669
Giacomino da Verona, **441–442**
  as source for Dante's structure of Hell, 474
Giacomo da Lentini "Il Notaro," 309, **442–443**, 465
  inventor of the sonnet, 791
  notions of optics in poetry of, 661
  and Sicilian School, 775, 776
Giacomo da Pistoia, 63
Giacomo da Santo Andrea, **442**, 554, 572, 797
Giamboni, Bono, 127
Giambullari, Pier Francesco, 212
Giangula, Nicolo, 266
Gianni de' Soldanieri, 49, **443**
Gianni, Lapo, 17, **443**
Gianni Schicchi (Puccini), 323
Giano della Bella, 18, 393, **443**
giants, 49, 86, 126, **443–446**, *444*
  Antaeus *(Anteo)*, **49**, 421, 444
  in Cocytus, 190
  Ephialtes *(Fïalte)*, **344**
  Tityus *(Tizio)*, **820**
  Typhon *(Tifeo)*, **837**
Giardini, Pietro, 114
Giavagnoli, Raffaello, 531
Gideon *(Gedeone)*, **446**

Gielgud, John, 284, 285
Giles of Rome (Aegidius Romanus), 734
  as intermediary to classical authors, 173
  and treachery, 831
Gilliam, Terry, 284
Gilson, Étienne, 57, 74, 224, **446**
  and *Bibliografia dantesca*, 262
  on Dante as Thomist, 812
  Dante et la philosophie, 267
  and Dante's allegory, 30
  on Dante's idea of single world ruler, 618
  on Dante's love of philosophy, 230
  and *donna gentile* in *Convivio*, 552
  on influence of Avicenna and Averroës on Dante, 694
  influence on Singleton, 783
"Ginestra, La" (Leopardi), 270
Giolito, Gabriele, *16*, 182, 184, *185*
Giordano da Pisa, 313, 398
Giornale dantesco (journal), 701
Giotto di Bondone, 170, 250, **446–447**
  in *Decameron*, 113
  statue, *447*
Giovanna, **447**, 460
Giovanna, daughter of Nino, **447–448**, 873
Giovanna, wife of Bonconte, **448**
Giovanni di Paolo, 498
Girard, René, 817
Giraut de Borneilh (Gerardus de Bornello), 293, **448**
Girolami, Remigio de', 398, 607
  Dante and teaching of, 313
  on Florentine factions, 458
  teaching at Santa Maria Novella, 18, 63
Giudici, Giovanni, 320–321
Giunti, Filippo, *306, 329, 509, 514, 586, 722, 723, 890*
Gizzi, Corrado, 501
Glaucus *(Glauco)*, **448**
Gloria in excelsis Deo, 708
gluttons, 190, **448–449**, *450*
  Boniface dei Fieschi, Archbishop, 122, 313
  Ciacco, 169
  contrapasso, 222
  Forese Donati among, 403
  guarded by Cerberus, 154
  in Hell, 510
  in Purgatory, 191, 510
  Ubaldino della Pila, 838
gluttony, **449–450**
  centaurs as examples of in Purgatory, 153–154
  effect on the body, 117

gluttony (*cont.*)
  and love of the right object by
    excess, 870
  as sin of incontinence, 508
Gmelin, Hermann, 269, 435
Gnostics, 482
God
  as archetypal light, 564
  claimed as model by Dante, 187
  Lucifer as mirror inverse of,
    574
  symbolized by Sun in *Paradiso,*
    802
  as *Auctor,* 73
  vision of, 193, 677
    influenced by Joachim of
      Fiore, 538
    as point of light, 564
    as a sea of light, 564
    and Thomas Aquinas, 812
    Trinity, 166, 832
  will identical with *ius,* 558
Godfrey of Bouillon, **450–451**
God's Tree (Foster), 407
Goeschel, C. F., 601
Goethe, Johann Wolfgang von
  and Dante, 265–266
  on Flaxman, 385
  Sorrows of Young Werther, 406
Goetz, Walter, 435
  and Deutsche Dante-
    Gesellschaft, 300
Goggi, Loretta, 283
Gogol, Nikolai, 276–277
Golden Legend (Legenda Aurea)
    (Jacobus de Voragine), 583,
    803
Golenishchev-Kutuzov, I. N., 276
Gomita, Fra, 85, **451**
Gonfaloniere di Giustizia, 443
good disposition, virtue of, 229,
    866
good manners *(belli costumi),* 163
Gordon, L. H., 286
*Gospel According to the Pseudo-
    Matthew,* 597
Gospel of John, 540
  Middle Platonism of, 642
Gospel of Luke, Dante's quotations
    from, 577
Gospel of Matthew, 540
  hypocrisy associated with false
    piety, 496
Gospel of Nicodemus, 331
*Göttliche Komödie, Die: Entwick-
    lungsgeschichte und Erk-
    lärung* (Vossler), 268, 878
*Göttliche Komödie, Die: Kommen-
    tar* (Gmelin), 269
Gottschalk of Orbais, 737
Gottsched, Johann Christoph, 265
Graf, Arturo, 616
  on Matelda, 601

grammar *(gramatica),* 292,
    451–452, 555
  linked to Moon, 627, 833
  as part of Trivium, 832
Grandgent, Charles Hall, **452–453**
  on Matelda, 601
Grangier, Balthasar, 259
Gratian (Franciscus Gratianus,
    Graziano), **453**
  See also Decretum
Gravina, Gianvincenzo, 857
Grayson, Cecil, 668
Grazie, Le (The Graces) (Foscolo),
    406
Great Commentaries (Averroës),
    79
"great coward," 647
great spirits, Aristotle as, 64
Great Whore, metaphor of, 754
Greco, Emilio, 504
Greeks, **453–454**
Greenaway, Peter, 249
  and Dante, 248
  A TV Dante, 284
Greene, George Washington, 571
Gregory IX (pope)
  and canonization of Dominic,
    312
  and excommunication of Freder-
    ick II of Swabia, 424
  on papacy and canonization,
    759
Gregory of Nazianzus, 566
Gregory of Nyssa, 642
  on contemplation, 217
  on unbaptized children, 566
Gregory the Great (Saint Gregory),
    454–455
  Beatrice and, 92
  in the *Commedia,* 760
  on contemplation, 217
  on despair, 604
  Dialogues, 143
  Exposition on the Song of Songs,
    33
  and microcosm, 613
  on order of gravity of sins, 449
  and seven deadly sins, 869, 870
  and Trajan, 824
Gregory VII (pope), 639
Gregory X (pope), 458
Greiner, Otto, 503
greyhound. *See Veltro*
griffin, 333, **455–456,** 753
  as image of Christ, 166
Griffolino d'Arezzo, 369, **456**
  and Albero da Siena, 10
  and alchemy, 12, 13
Gröber, Gustav, 243
Grosseteste, Robert, 64, 613
  on heresy, 484
  and light metaphysics, 564, 768
  and optics, 661

*Grossmütiger Rechtsgelehrter oder
    Sterbender Aemilius Paulus
    Papinianus* (Gryphius),
    264
Gryphius, Andreas, 264
Guccio de' Tarlati, **456**
Guelfo Taviani, 47
Guelfs, **456–459**
  1248 exile of, 439
  Florence civil war absorbed in
    conflicts of, 391
  origins, 338, 456–457
  See also Blacks and Whites
Guerra, Guido, 787
guides in the *Commedia,* 181, 187,
    676
  Beatrice, 675–676
  Saint Bernard, 342, 625, 635,
    743, 813, 881
  Saint Paul by example, 679
  Virgil as, 8, *385,* 863
Guido Cavalcanti, 106, 291, 309,
    459–461, 522, 604, 792
  ballate of, 81
  and causal relationship, 148
  Dante's comparing himself to,
    182
  in *Decameron,* 113
  exile, 19, 395
  friendship with Dante, 17, 63,
    151
  Giovanna and, 447
  love theory of, 413, 460
  and T. S. Eliot, 337
  and use of optics, 661
  Vita Nuova dedicated to, 875
Guido da Castello, **462**
  praised by Marco Lombardo,
    242
Guido da Montefeltro, 2, 419,
    462–463, 586
  Bonatti astrologer of, 120
  in the *Commedia,* 419
  and confession, 215
  referring to the fall of Acre, 3
Guido da Pisa, 350, **463–464**
  Declaratio, 199
  on fraudulent counsel, 423
  glosses in Latin on *Inferno,*
    206–207
  on Medusa, 603
  on *veltro,* 852
  See also Expositiones
Guido da Polenta, 533
  patron of Dante, 334
Guido da Prata, **464**
Guido da Romena, 9, 14
  Dante's epistle to, 353
Guido del Cassero, 46, 699
Guido del Duca, 66, 87, **464**
  in the *Commedia*
    on Bernardin di Fosco, 98
    on Federigo Tignoso, 374

mentioning Fabbro de' Lambertazzi, 367
Rinieri da Calboli and, 745
Guido delle Colonne, **465**
and Sicilian School, 775
Guido di Carpigna, **465**
Guido Guerra, 457, **461**
Guido II of Romena, **461–462**
"Guido, io vorrei" (Dante), 770
guilds, 386, 389–390, 390–391
and Florentine Priorate, 458
political role of, 393–394
guileful, the, 420
Guillaume de Lorris, 25, 379, 380
Guillaume de Machaut, 251
Guinevere *(Ginevra)*, **465**
Guinizzelli, Guido, 17, 119, 291,
309, 460, 465, **465–466,**
578, 580
"Al cor gentil," 37
in *Commedia*, 486
Dante's comparing himself to,
182
influence of Sicilian school on,
775
in *Purgatorio*, 724
school of, 237
Guiscard, Robert *(Ruberto Guiscardo)*, **466–467**
Guittone d'Arezzo, 16, 140, 255,
309, **467**, 580
influence on Guinizzelli, 466
as member of the Jovial Friars,
542
practitioner of *tenzone*, 808
and sonnet, 791
and Tuscan School, 775
Gulag Archipelago, The (Solzhenitzyn), 278
Gumilev, Nikolai, 277
Guttuso, Renato, 504
Guy de Montfort, 467
Guzmán, Fernán Pérez de, 280

H

Haakon V of Norway *(Acone)*, **468**
habit *(habitus)*, **468–469**
Hades, 472, 566, 664
Hallam, Arthur, 256
Haller, Robert S., 829
Haly, 67
Haman *(Aman)*, **469**
Hamme, Fernand van, 504
*Handlexikon oder kurzgefasstes
Wörterbuch der schönen
Wissenschaften und freien
Künste* (Gottsched), 265
Hansel, Wilhelm, 503
Hardie, Colin, 829
on *Epistle to Cangrande*, 353
and Oxford Dante Society, 668
on *veltro*, 853
Hardouin, Jean, 259

"Harold Bloom and the Post-
theological Dante" (Colilli),
818
Harpies *(Arpie)*, 298, **469–470,**
860, 888
Harrison, Robert P., 223, 816
Harrower, Rachel B.
on Matelda, 601
Harrowing of Hell, **470–471**
Harsdörffer, Georg Philipp, 264
Hatcher, Anna, 423
Haymo of Faversham, 569
Heaney, Seamus, 827
and Dante, 258
Heath-Stubbs, John, 827
heavenly messenger. *See messo
celeste*
heavens, 230, 232–233
associated with virtues, 672, 833
corresponding to seven orders of
knowledge, 672–673, 736,
833
numerology and structure of, 655
and planets, 192
Hecate *(Ecate)*, 626
Hector *(Ettore)*, **471**
in Noble Castle, 651
Hecuba *(Ecuba)*, **471–472**
Hederich, Benjamin, 265
Heers, Jacques, 439–440
Hegel, Georg Wilhelm Friedrich,
435
Lectures on Aesthetics, 267
Helen of Troy *(Elena)*, **472,** 578
Heliodorus *(Eliodoro)*, **472**
Helios of Velletri, 247
Hell, 190, 343, **472–477,** *474, 512*
absence of light, 563
avaricious and prodigal in, 712
center of, *574*
characterized as a place of exile,
363
Dante at gates of, *473*
death of poetry in, 725
difference between sinners in
Upper Hell and Lower Hell,
515
gluttons in, 448, 449
last circle, *722*
Limbo as part of, 567, 650
lustful in, 577
numerology and structure of, 655
organization of, 183
painterly tradition, 498
seventh circle, *860*
sins of incontinence in, 508, *509*
sodomites in, 787
surreal landscape in lower part,
860
as symmetrical inversion of
Heaven, 655
time determined according to the
phases of the Moon, 626

typographical symmetry with
Purgatory, 555
vestibule to, 646
wrathful in, 891
hendecasyllable, **477–478,** 611
Henry II of Cyprus, 639
Henry II of Lusignan (king of
Cyprus), **479**
Henry I, "the Fat" (King of
Navarre), **478**
as negligent ruler, 639
Henry IV of Swabia, 886
Henry II of England, 342, **478–479**
Henry III of England *(Arrigo)*, **479**
as negligent ruler, 639
Henry (or Hugh) of Saltrey, 728
Henry of Susa (Enrico Bartolomei),
295, **479**
Henry, the Young King, **479**
Henry VI, Emperor, **479**
Henry VII of Luxemburg, 20, 338,
434, **479–481**
as the number DXV (515), 657
as candidate for prophesied savior, 382–383
Dante on, 488
Dante's epistles to gather support
for, 354
Epistle to Henry VII, 480, 539
*Epistle to the rulers of Italy
(Epistle 5)* in support of,
480, 492
expedition to Italy, 440, 836
identified with *veltro*, 852
Philip IV's opposition to, 408
Robert of Anjou and, 746
supported by Cino da Pistoia, 171
supported by Uguccione della
Faggiuola, 842
Heraclitus *(Eraclito)*, **481**
Hercules, Pillars of, **481**
heresy, **481–484,** 869
Islam and, 520
link with faction, 372
matta bestialitade equated with,
588
Medusa as figure for, 603
Peter of Spain and investigation
of, 683
heretics, 191, *484,* **484–486,** 513
in city of Dis, 307
and doctrine of Incarnation, 508
Farinata degli Uberti, 145,
371–372
Frederick II of Swabia, 424
Ottaviano, 665
Photinus, 697
Herlihy, David, 106
Hermaphrodite *(Ermafrodito)*, **486**
Heroides (Ovid), 561
Herold, Basilius, 263
Herzen, Aleksandr, 276
Hesiod, 154

Iphigenia *(Ifigènia, Efigènia)*, **519**
Ireland, entrance to underworld, 664, 728
Iris *(Iride, Iri)*, **519**
Isagoge (Porphyry), 61
Ishmaelites. *See* Saracens
Isidore of Seville, Saint *(Isidoro; Isidorus Hispalensis)*, 95, 358, **519–520**
  and allegory, 25
  and classificatory systems of sciences, 767
  in the *Commedia*, 793
  concept of earth, 329
  and Dante's scientific knowledge, 769
  and definition of *istoria*, 487
  on despair, 604
  Etymologies (Etymologiae), 34, 179
  and etymology of exile, 362
  and etymology of heretic, 484
  and etymology of *martyres*, 595
  on the griffin, 455
  on *lupa*, 87
  on neologisms, 640
  and numerology, 653
Islam and Islamic culture, **520–523**
Ismene, **523**
Israel, **524–525**
  Jacob renamed, 533
Istoria, La (Uguccione da Lodi), 841
Italianitas (Italianness), 529
Italian language, **525–528**
  defended in book 1 of *Convivio*, 227–228
  De vulgari eloquentia on, 529–530
  versification, 477–478
Italian literature, Dante in, **269–276**
Italica (periodical), 798
Italienische Dichtung und deutsche Literatur (Elwert), 269
Italy, **528–532**
  connection with England, 343
  crusades in, 239
  Dante as champion of Italian unity, 434
  French invasion of
    and dissemination of Dante's works in France, 259
  geographic limits determined by linguistic criteria, 529
Itinerari danteschi (Petrocchi), 687
Itinerarium mentis in Deum (Journey of the Mind to God) (Bonaventure), 28, 121
  important source for Dante, 813
  influenced by Richard of St. Victor, 744
Ittenbach, Franz, 503
ius, 557–558

ius commune. *See* Roman law
Ivanov, Vyacheslav, 277

J
Jackson, W. W., 829
Jacob *(Giacobbe, Iacobbe)*, **533**
  called Israel, 524
  Dante-pilgrim likened to, 560
Jacobi, Johann Georg, 266
Jacobus de Voragine, 583, 803
Jacoff, Rachel, 816, 817
Jacopo del Cassero, 697
Jacopo della Lana. *See* Iacopo della Lana
Jacopo di Dante (Jacopo [Iacopo] Alighieri), 24, 162, 432, **533**
  on Beatrice, 91–92
  Boccaccio and, 114
  on Dante's treatment of Muslims, 521
  on fraudulent counsel, 422
  on Paolo and Francesca episode, 410
  on title of the *Commedia*, 186
  on *veltro*, 851
Jacopo Mostacci, 776
Jacques le fataliste (Diderot), 260
Jahrbuch der Deutschen Dante-Gesellschaft, 301, **533–534**
  Witte and, 886
James II of Aragon *(Iacomo)*, **534,** 746
James, King of Majorca *(Iacomo)*, **534**
Jameson, Frederic, 817
James, Saint, the Apostle *(Iacopo)*, **535**
  in *Commedia*, 760
Jason *(Giasone)*, **535**
  among seducers, 422, 669
  Dante-pilgrim's encounter with, 603
Jason, High Priest *(Iasòn)*, **536**
Jauss, Hans Robert, 783
Jean de Meun, 25, 379, 380
Jenseitsvorstellungen vor Dante und die übrigen Voraussetzungen der Divina Commedia, Die: Ein quellenkritischer Kommentar (Rüegg), 269
Jerome, Saint *(Ieronimo)*, 25, **536**
  Beatrice and, 92
  in the *Commedia*, 760
  on neologisms, 641
Jerusalem, 157, **536–537**
Jews
  called Israel, 524
  Jewish apocalyptic writings, 52
  Judecca reflecting name of ghettos, 544
  as legitimate crusade enemy, 240
  salvation of patriarchs, 762

Joachim of Fiore *(Gioacchino da Fiore)*, 18, 52, 53, 121, 151, 418, **537–538,** 754
  in the *Commedia*, 484
  depicted in Heaven of the Sun, 812
  influence on Dante, 538
  role in interpretation of *veltro*, 853
  as source for Dante's theology, 813
Joachim of Flora. *See* Joachim of Fiore
Joanna, 746
Jocasta *(Giocasta)*, **538–539**
Jöcher, Christian Gottlieb, 265, 434
John of Damascus
  De Haeresibus, 520
  on origin of term Saracen, 763
John of Garland, 173
John of Parma, 683
John of Patmos, 540
John of Salisbury, 618
  and *Aeneid*, 6
  as historical source, 488, 751
  on Mary of Jerusalem, 599
  Metalogicon, The, 833
  on neologisms, 640
  Policraticus, 5
John of Saxony. *See* Philalethes
John of Seville, 15, 67
John of Sweden, 11
John, Saint, **539–541,** *540*
John the Baptist, Saint *(San Giovanni Battista)*, **539**
  in *Commedia*, 760, 881
John the Deacon, 824
John the Evangelist, 760, 882
John XXII (pope), 756
  condemnation of alchemy and alchemists, 13
  native of Cahors, 134
Jordan *(Iordan)*, **541**
Jordan of Saxony, 312
Joseph, Saint *(Giuseppe)*, **541**
Josephus, 598
Joshua *(Iosuè)*, **542**
journey of the *Commedia*, 453
  chronological setting, 183
  determined by astronomical references, 289
  as a journey toward the light, 562
  life as a journey metaphor
    and ideas of *aversio* and *converso*, 474
  as one of mystical contemplation, 218
  parallel between Dante's and Jason's, 535
  parallel between pilgrim's journey and mystic's journey, 634–635

matta bestialitade, 588
Matteo d'Acquasparta, 418, 813
Matthew of Vendôme
Ars versificatoria, 34
on neologisms, 640
and simile, 778
Matthew, Saint *(San Matteo),*
602–603
on Mary, 597
Matthias Flaccius Illyricus, 434
Matual, D., 278
Mazzeo, Joseph, 29
Mazzini, Giuseppe, 203, 274, *399,
474,* 531, *673, 729*
Mazzoni, Francesco
on *Epistle to Cangrande,* 351
and *Studi danteschi,* 786
on *veltro,* 852
Mazzoni, Guido, 786
Mazzotta, Giuseppe, 816
on allegory, 31
on Cato, 148
Commedia as journey of exodus,
365
and two Dantes, 815
on Ugolino's story, 197
Mazzuoli da Strada, Giovanni, 109
Mazzuoli, Zanobi, 109
measure *(misura),* 163
Mechtildis of Hackeborn, 602
Mechtildis of Magdeburg, Saint,
602
Medea, **603**
Media Centre at the University of
Toronto, 285
*Mediaeval Culture: An Introduction
to Dante and His Time*
(Vossler), 878
Medici e speziali (Physicians and
Apothecaries) guild, 18
Medieval Academy of America,
883
Medium Commentaries (Averroës),
79
Medusa, 298, **603–604**
"Medusa: The Letter and the
Spirit" (Freccero), 31
Megaera *(Megera),* 428, **604**
Meinhard, Johann Nikolaus, 266,
435
Meiss, Millard, 499, 783
Mejlax, M. B., 278
Meleager *(Meleagro),* **604–605**
Melissus *(Melisso),* **605**
Melpomene, 630
memory *(memoria, mente),*
605–606, 738
Mena, Juan de, 280–281
on Santillana, 281
Mencke, Johann Burkhardt, 434
Mendelssohn, Moses, 266
mendicant orders, **606–608**
in Florence, 398

Joachim of Fiore's prophecy of,
537
tertiaries, 399
See also Dominicans; Francis-
cans
Mendoza, Iñigo López de. *See* San-
tillana, Marqués de
Mengaldo, PierVincenzo, 39
Menke, Johann Burckhard, 265
Menocal, María Rosa, 522
Mercanzia, 395–396
Mercury *(Mercurio),* **608**
aligned with dialectic, 228, 833
holiness marred by ambition,
233
messo celeste as, 609
Mercury, Heaven of, *608,* 671
Berenger, Raymond IV in, 98
meridian *(meridiano, merigge),* **609**
Meshekoff, Michael, 284
Messer, **591–592**
Messer Bellincione Berti dei
Ravegnani, 461
"Messer Brunetto, questa pulzelletta" (Dante), 128
reference to Fra Alberto similar
to that in *Fiore,* 379
Messerschmid, Georg Friedrich,
264
messo celeste (heavenly messenger), **609–610**
Michael as, 612
parallel with Medusa, 603
messo da ciel. See messo celeste
Metalogicon, The (John of Salisbury), 833
Metamorphoses (Ovid)
Dante and, 173, 666
on Hecuba, 472
on Hippolytus, 487
on Jason, 535
on Lethe, 561
on Medusa, 603
on the Muses, 630
on Orpheus, 663
on Proserpina, 717
on Semele, 771
on tale of Pyramus, 732
on Tiresias, 820
Métamorphoses du Cercle, Les
(Poulet), 817
metaphor
contrapasso as literalizing
metaphor, 476
in Dante, 30
Metaphysics (Aristotle), 40
Dante's references to, 173
and four causes, 149
Metellus, Lucius Caecilius
(Metello), **610**
meteorology in Dante's works, 767
metrics and versification: the minor
works, **610–612**

Meyer-Lübke, Wilhelm, 797
Michael, the Archangel, **612**
Michael VIII Palaeologus, 595
Michal *(Micòl),* **612**
Michelangelo, 500
microcosm, **613–615**
in *petrose* poems, 688–689, 690
Seneca's influence on Dante, 772
Midas *(Mida),* **615**
Middle Ages
allegorical tradition, 24–26, 32
allegorization of Furies, 429
motif of being lost in the
woods, 287
attitudes toward women, 887
belief in the existence of giants,
444
classical rhetorical tradition,
716
Harrowing of Hell favorite
medieval motif, 470
idea of revelation in, 742
important role of women, 887
music theory in, 631
political theory in, 639
poverty, view of, 705–706
prophecy in, 713
relationship with ancient Greek
world, 453
and Saint John, 540
study of science in, 768
symbolic meaning of griffins,
455
treatment of Eve during, 360
and use of neologisms, 640
Milan, Edict of (313), 216
Milano Films, 247
Milton, John, 513
influence of *Commedia* on, 256
knowledge of Daniello's commentary, 246
Min, D. E., 276
Minerva *(Minerva, Pallade),* **615**
Minnesinger poetry, 433
Minnis, A. J., 73
on *auctor,* 74
Minor Poems (Lucchi), 828
Minos *(Minòs),* 298, **615**
Minotaur, *615,* **615–616,** 860
Mintrop, Theodor, 503
Mirabile visione, La (film), 247
Mirra. *See* Myrrha
mirrors, experiment of the three,
661, 769
Miserere, 708, 725
Misericordia (confraternity), 400
misers and spendthrifts. *See* avari-
cious and prodigal
Missal, 569
"Mito della poesia primitiva in
G.B. Vico, Il" (Fubini), 427
*Mitteilungsblatt der Deutschen
Dante-Gesellschaft,* 301

"Models of Literary Influence in the *Comedy*" (Jacoff), 816
Modern Language Association
  and Dante Society, 287
  Wilkins and, 883
Modern Language Review, 432
modesty, Deiphyle example of, 295
modi scribendi (modes of writing)
  comedy, 180–181
  Commedia and, 185
Mollat, Michel, 705–706
Momigliano, Attlio, **616**
Monachelli, 320
Monaci, Ernesto, 204
  and Società Dantesca Italiana, 786
Monarchia, **616–623**
  Aeneid as major authority in, 253
  and allegory, 26, 30
  angelology in, 38
  and Aristotle's *Ethics,* 63
  and astrology, 67
  and authority, 75
  and avarice, 76
  Cato in, 146
  chain of being and growth of intelligence, 155
  critical edition by Nardi, 638
  critique of in Germany, 263
  cursus in, 716
  Daniel in, 246
  David mentioned in, 289, 290
  and delight, 297
  Dido in, 303
  on Donation of Constantine, 315
  earth described in, 328
  evocation of Saint Augustine in, 71
  free will, 425
  Greece in, 453
  Hector in, 471
  ideas of *Convivio* developed in, 230
  on Index of Prohibited Books, 263, 483, 622
  influenced by Henry VII of Luxemburg's enterprise, 481
  on intellect, 518–519, 739
  Latin edition by Oporinus, 263
  legitimating effect of Moses on, 629
  Livy cited in, 571
  Moon in, 627
  on necessity of revelation, 742
  pairing of Apollo and Moon, 54
  on papacy in, 514, 670
  political vision, 46, 242, 339
  poverty, 706
  references to Christ in, 164
  and Robert of Anjou, 746
  Scipio cited in, 770
  Song of Songs quoted in, 790
  title page of 1740 edition, *618*

translations
  English, 829
  by Herold, 263
  on universal imperial rule, 440
  used as Protestant weapon in Germany, 434
  Vernani's "reprobation," 38, 82, 483, 855
  Virgil and, 862
  Witte's edition of, 268, 886
  writing of, 20
Monarchy and Three Political Letters (Nicholl), 829
monasticism, **623–625**
  Benedict and, 97
  Eastern, 583
Moncetti, Giovanni Benedetto, 735
Monitore (journal), 406
Monologion (Anselm of Canterbury), 48
Monroe, Harriet, 337
monsters
  female, 888
  in Hell, 190
Montale, 275
Montaperti (castle), **626**
Montaperti, Battle of, 1, 13, 49, 104, 392, 438, 439, 458, 836
  Abati, Bocca degli, at, 109
  and Angevin intervention, 46
Montecatini, Battle of, 842
Montfort, Simon, 403
Moon, **626–627**
  aligned with grammar, 228, 833
  and holiness marred by inconstancy, 233
Moon, Heaven of the, 172, *627,* 671, 675
  nuns who have failed to keep their vows, 626, *698,* 889
  parallel with ante-Inferno, 698
  parallel with ante-Purgatory, 698
moonspots, 626
  discussed in *Paradiso,* 767
  explanation of, 769
Moore, Edward, 40, **627–628**
  on 515, 382, 657
  Contributions to the Textual Criticism of the Divina Commedia, 204, 825
  on Dante's epistles, 354
  on Dante's knowledge of Antiquity, 172
  on Dante's references to Aristotle, 173, 692
  and Dante's references to Cicero, 170
  edition of the *Commedia,* 825
  on *Epistle to Cangrande,* 353
  on manuscripts of the *Commedia,* 199
  and Oxford Dante Society, 668

moral habits, 469
  See also cardinal virtues
moral philosophy. *See* ethics
Mordecai, **628**
Mordred, 135, **628**
Moreollo III, 353–354
Morhof, Daniel Georg, 434
  on Dante, 264
Moroello di Manfredi of Giovagallo, 628
Moroello di Obizzino of Villafranca, 628
Moroello Malaspina, 111, **628–629**
Morpurgo, Salomone, 204, 299
Morrone, Pietro da. *See* Celestine V
mortalism
  Epicurus condemned as heretic because of, 347
  heretics singled out because of, 506
Mort le roi Artu (The Death of King Arhtur)
  source on Mordred, 628
Mosca de' Lamberti, **629**
Moser, Barry, 504
Moses *(Moisè),* **629**
  in White Rose, 882
"Motherhood According to Bellini" (Kristeva), 818
motion, theories of, 767
"Mr. Longfellow's Dante Club," 286
Mucius (Gaius Mucius Scaevola; *Muzio;* Lat. *Mutius),* **629–630**
Muhammad *(Mäometto),* **630**
  contrapasso, 521
  heavenly journey of, 663
  as schismatic, 520, 766
Müller, Karl, 503
munificence, 229, 866
  of Alexander the Great, 15
murderers and tyrants. *See* tyrants and murderers
Musaeus, 561
Musa, Mark, 827
  on identity of *messo celeste,* 609
  translation of the *Vita Nuova,* 829
Musenalmanach (journal), 266–267
Muses, the, **630**
  Calliope, **136**
  Clio, **178**
music, **631–634**
  Dante and, 251–252
  musical instruments describing characters in *Commedia,* 631–632
  related to Mars, 594, 736
  musical adaptations based on Dante, 322–323
Muslims, Seee Saracens
Mussato, Albertino, 865

Myrrha *(Mirra)*, **634,** 667, 765
  as falsifier of person, 369
  and lust, 86
mystery play, *Commedia*'s plan
  resembling, 319
Mystical Theology (Dionysius the
  Areopagite), 304
mysticism, **634–636**
  and contemplative life, 217
  and language used in *Paradiso,*
    677–678
  tradition within Franciscan order,
    416
*Mythe et symbole dans la Divine
  Comédie* (Dozon), 818
Myth of Felt (Olschki), 853

N

Naples
  Charles of Anjou crowned king
    of, 457
  naval battle of, 158
  Robert of Anjou king of, 746
Napoleone degli Alberti, 11, 14,
    135, **637,** 663
Narcissus *(Narciso)*, **637–638**
Nardi, Bruno, 42, 57, 224, 269,
    329, 446, **638**
  attacked by Barbi, 84
  on authenticity of *Questio,* 735
  on Cavalcanti, 460
  on Dante as Thomist, 812
  on Dante's allegory, 27, 30
  on Dante's love of philosophy,
    230
  on Dante's Ulysses, 844, 845
  on Dante's view of Averroism,
    522
  on *donna gentile,* 317
  on *Epistle to Cangrande,* 351,
    353
  on fraudulent counsel, 423
  on heterodoxy in *Paradiso,* 644
  on influence of Albert the Great
    on Dante, 9, 11, 434
  on influence of Avicenna on
    Dante, 80
  on influence of Platonism on
    Dante, 694
  on influences on Dante, 635,
    693
  on Matelda, 601
  on the three beasts, 86
  on *veltro,* 852
Nardi, Tilde
  on allegorical significance of
    Dante's immersion in Lethe,
    562
  on Matelda, 601
Nassar, Eugene Paul, 498
Natali, Giulio, 601
Nathan, **638**
Nation, 652

National Edition. *See Edizione
  nazionale*
Nattini, Amos, 503
natural habits, 468
Natural History (Pliny), 452
natural law, 557, 621
Natural Questions (Seneca), 771
  and microcosm, 613
Navarre, King of *(Rex Navarre)*, **638**
Nebuchadnezzar *(Nabuc-
  codonosor)*, **639**
Negative Theology, 305
negligent. *See* late repentant
negligent rulers, 50, **639–640**
  among late repentant, 555
  in Ante-Purgatory, 191, 730
  Charles I of Naples, 639
  Ferdinand IV of Castille, **374**
  Henry III of England, 479
  Ottokar as, 666
  Peter III of Aragon among, 684
  Rudolph I as, 757
  William II of Monferrat, 886
Nella, **640**
Nel mondo di Dante (Nardi), 638
Nenci, Francesco, 503
neologisms, **640–641**
Neoplatonism, **641–646**
  Dante and, 11
  human being defined by, 115
  Landino's commentary and, 211,
    553, 645
  notions of emanation, 671
  and theories of emanation, 672
  See also Platonism
Neptune *(Nettuno)*, **646**
Nereids, 818
Nessus *(Nesso)*, 493, **646,** 667
  Deianira loved by, 295
"Ne s temi ja, kto brosil zemlju"
  ("Not with Those Who
  Have Abandoned the Land
  Am I") (Akhmatova), 278
Nestorius, 482
Neue Dantestudien (Auerbach), 269
Neue Kritische Briefe (Bodmer), 265
neutrals, *152,* 183, 190, 221,
    646–648, *647*
  as innnovation, 512
New Philology *(Nuova Filologia),*
    83
New Science (Vico), 747–748, 857
Nibia, Martino Paolo, 208
Nicaea, Council of (325), 65
Niccolò da Prato
  Dante's epistle to, 353
  and Henry VII of Luxemburg,
    479
Niccolò of Siena, **648**
Nicene creed, 570
Nicholas III (pope), 393, **648–649**
  criticized by Dante, 102
  and simony, 78, 586, 755, 782

Nicholas IV (pope), 2
Nicholas, Saint *(Niccolò)*, **649**
Nicholl, Donald, 829
  *Monarchy and Three Political
    Letters,* 829
Nicholo di Lorenzo della Magna,
    473, 516
Nicolini, Fausto, 856
Nicomachean Ethics (Aristotle), 64
  and concept of intellect in *Com-
    media,* 519
  Dante's references to, 173, 253
  eleven virtues discussed in, 548
  influence on Dante's classifica-
    tion of sins, 190–191, 577
  and malice, 588
  as source for Dante's structure of
    Hell, 474, 475
Nidobeato, 210
Nimrod *(Nembrotto)*, 445, **649**
  and corruption of language,
    421
  and Tower of Babel, 368, 444
Nino della Gherardesca. *See*
  Brigata, Il
Nïobè, **649**
Nisus *(Niso)*, **649–650**
Noah *(Noè)*, **650**
Noakes, Susan, 816
nobility *(nobiltà),* 163
  defined, 228–229, 866
  as subject of book 4 of *Convivio,*
    228–229
Noble Castle, *650,* **650–652**
  and great-hearted spirits of
    Antiquity, 568
  philosophers of the past in, 692
Nogaret, Guillaume de, 122
North American Review, 652
Norton, Charles Eliot, **652–653,**
    825, 826, 828
  Essay on and translation of *Vita
    Nuova,* 256–257, 828
  and Longfellow, 571
  and numerology in *Vita Nuova,*
    876
  on pattern of three in *Vita
    Nuova,* 654
  president of the Dante Society,
    286
Notitia auctorum antique media
  (Hederich), 265
Notre-Dame de Paris (Hugo), 260
Novellae, 557
Novellino, 397
  Francesco d'Accorso in, 2
  Marco Lombardo in, 592
  Saladin in, 521, 760
Novello da Polenta, Guido, 120,
    144, 373
  Dante and, 137
  patron of Dante, 20
Novels, 550

Numa Pompilius *(Numa Pompilio),* **653**
number theories of Pythagoras, 732
Numeister, Johann, 201
numerology, 26, 52, **653–657**
  Beatrice and, 90
  in the *Commedia,* 187, 189
    structure different from classical epic, 346
  in Dante, 30
  Hugh of St. Victor and, 495
  and interpretations of the ordered universe, 233
  and methods of interpretation of 515 prophecy, 382
  numbers associated with Christ, 164–165
  and *Vita Nuova,* 876
  in White Rose, 882
Núñez de Arce, Gaspar, 282
nuns in Heaven of the Moon, 626, *698, 889*
Nuova cronica (G. Villani), 168, 858, 859
Nuova filologia e l'edizione dei nostri scrittori da Dante al Manzoni, La (Barbi), 83
Nuovi saggi critici (De Sanctis), 291
Nuovi saggi danteschi (Pietrobono), 701

O

Obbizo II d'Este. *See* Opizzo II d'Este
Oberto da Romena, 353
obstinacy, Medusa as figure for, 603
oc, language of, 409, 451, 526, 716
Oddo Arrighi, 438
Oderisi da Gubbio, 250, 447, **658, 710**
Odes (Vere-Hodge), 828
Oelsner, Hermann, 826
Oeuvres complètes de Dante (Rhéal), 261
Of Reformation (Milton)
  references to Dante's anti-papal invective, 256
oïl, language of, 409, 526, 638, 716
  Thibaut poet of, 638
Okey, Thomas, 826
  translation of the *Purgatorio,* 826
  translation of the *Vita Nuova,* 829
Old Man of Crete, **658–659,** *659,* 750
  Phlegethon and, 696
  and Styx, 801
Olearius, Johann Gottfried, 263
Olivi, Petrus Johannis (Peter of John Olivi), 101, 418, 607, **659–660,** 707

identification of the Great Whore, 754
  knowledge of optics, 661
  as lector at Santa Croce, 18, 398
Olschki, Leonard, 852
"Oltre la spera che più larga gira" (Dante), 877, 888
Omberto Aldobrandeschi, **660**
On Divine Omnipotence (Peter Damian), 245
one, symbolism of, 653
"On Guelfs and Ghibellines" (Bartolo da Sassoferrato), 440, 459
On Sophistry (Aristotle), 619
On the Beginning and Origin and Power of the Emperor and the Pope (Brancazoli), 621
"On the Boundaries of Art" (Ivanov), 277
On the Divine Names (Pseudo-Dionysius), 642
On World Government (Schneider), 829
Opera Omnia (Albert the Great), 11
Opere del divino poeta Danthe, published by Bernardino Stagnino da Trino de Monferra, 1512 edition, *132, 288*
Opere del divino poeta Danthe, edited by Pietro da Figino, 1520 edition, *86, 92, 210, 485, 547, 608, 615, 676, 787, 793, 823, 881*
Opere di Dante Alighieri, edited by Cristoforo Zapate de Cisneros, 1757–1758 edition, *59, 147, 154, 182, 195, 436, 444, 495, 543, 650, 843*
  on illustrations, 500, 501
Opere di Dante, edited by M. Barbi, 1921 edition, 579
Opere volgari, Le (Bonvesin da la Riva), 219
Opitz, Martin, 264
Opizzo II da Este, **660,** 669
Oporinus, Joannes, 263
opportunists. *See* neutrals
optics *(perspettiva;* Lat. *perspectiva),* 564–565, **660–662**
  in Dante's works, 767
Orcagna, Andrea, 498
Orcagna, Bernardo (Nardo di Cione), 498, 499
Order of Penitents, 399
Order of the Friars Preachers (Ordo Predicatorum, OP). *See* Dominicans
Ordinamenti di giustizia. See Ordinances of Justice
Ordinances of Justice, 18, 106, 393–394

Giano della Bella principal author of, 443
Ordo Florensis, 537
Ordo Militiae Beatae Mariae Virginis (Order of the Army of the Blessed Virgin Mary). *See* Jovial Friars
Orestes, **662**
Origen, 25
  and Christian Platonism, 642
  on Hell, 472
  Jerome and, 536
  and Limbo, 566
  on prexistence of soul, 642
  and scriptural interpretation, 376
  on spiritual meaning of Songs of Songs, 790
Origines (Isidore of Seville). *See Etymologiae* (Isidore of Seville)
Originum seu etymologiarum libri XX (Isidore of Seville). *See Etymologiae* (Isidore of Seville)
Orlandi, Lemmo, 251
Orlando. *See* Roland *(Orlando)*
Orlando furioso (Ariosto), 60–61
Orosius, Paulus *(Paolo Orosio),* 253, **662–663,** 771, 820
  Dante's references to, 172
  as historical source, 15, 488, 571, 751
  as language model for Dante, 717
  on Sesto, 773
  as source for Dante's theology, 813
Orpheus, **663**
Orsanmichele, 401
Orsini, Giovanni Gaetano. *See* Nicholas III
Orso, Count (Orso degli Alberti della Cerbaia), **663**
Orvieto Cathedral, 250
Oshima, Nagisha, 284
otherworld journeys, **663–665**
"Otravlen khleb i vozdukh vypit" ("The Bread Has Been Poisoned and the Air Drunk Up") (Mandelstam), 278
Ottaviano, Cardinal, **665–666**
Ottaviano degli Ubaldini, 665, 757, 838
Ottimo Commento, 207, **666**
  based on Della Lana's commentary, 497
  on Dante's treatment of Muslims, 521
  on Dante's treatment of Saladin, 521
  on *messo celeste* as angel, 609
  on Paolo and Francesca episode, 410

on Salterello, 761
on the *veltro,* 851
Otto, Henry, 247
Ottokar II, King of Bohemia
    (Ottachero), **666,** 880
    as negligent ruler, 639
    Rudolph I and, 757
Otus, 444
Ovid (Publius Ovidius Naso,
    Ovidio), 650, **666–668**
    appearance in *Commedia, 175*
    as authority for ages of man,
        173, 175
    on Cacus, 133
    on Cadmus, 134
    on centaurs, 153–154
    on Cerberus, 154
    in *Commedia,* 254
    Dante's references to, 172, 173
    Dante's use of rhetorical arti-
        fices, 173
    on the Furies, 429
    on Lethe, 561
    listed as classical author in *De
        vulgari eloquentia,* 175
    listed as classical author in *Vita
        Nuova,* 175
    source of mythology in *Comme-
        dia,* 174, 254
*Ovidio Maggiore. See Metamor-
    phoses* (Ovid)
*Ovidius moralizatus (Ovide moral-
    isé)* (Pierre Bersuire)
    and allegory, 26
    Dante and, 561
    on tale of Pyramus, 732
"O voi che per la via d'Amor pas-
    sate" (Dante), 792
"Oxford Dante" (Moore, ed.), 821
Oxford Dante Society, 627, **668**
Oxford, University of, 417
Ozanam, Frédéric, 260

P
Padoan, Giorgio, 735
Padovan, Adolfo, 247
Padrón, Juan Rodríguez del, 280
"Paesaggio della *Divina Comme-
    dia,* Il" (Momigliano), 616
Pagano, Bartolomeo, 248
Pagnoni, Francesco, 503
painting
    allusions to in the *Commedia,*
        658
    Dante and, 250
Palacios, Asín, 522
Palazzo Vecchio (Florence), 250
Palgen, Rudolf, 67
Pallas, **669**
Pallavicini, Uberto, 131
panders and seducers, 190, 420,
        513, 578, 585, **669,** 869
    Caccianemico, Venedico, 133

contrapasso, 221
    Jason as seducer, 535
Panofsky, E., 882
Paolo and Francesca (Delacroix),
    296
Paolo and Francesca episode. *See*
    Francesca da Rimini
    episode
Paolo e Francesca (film), 247
Paolo Malatesta (Paolo il Bello),
    409, **669–670**
papacy, **670–671**
    alliance with Guelf bankers, 392
    and Angevin intervention in
        Italy, 45
    in the *Commedia*
        avarice denounced, 706
        corruption denounced, 53,
            676
    and crusade, 239
    Dante's views on, 514
    ecclesiastical role strengthened
        by Clement IV, 177
    Guelfs as party of, 104
    as obstacle to restoration of
        empire, 339
    relationship with empire
        in *Monarchia,* 616, 620–621
    and Tuscany, 836
papal curia
    analogical reasonings of, 619
    Damian and, 245
    and she-wolf emblem, 87
Paradise, **671–674,** *672, 673, 677*
    imperfection characteristic of
        first three heavens, 626
    inherently luminous, 563
    moral structure of, 4
    no *contrapasso* in, 222
    organization of, 183–184
    situation of the blessed related to
        their behavior on Earth,
        220, 222
Paradise Lost (Milton), 256
Paradiso, **674–678,** *676*
    allegorical structure of, 32
    allusion to zodiac in, 896
    Apollo in, 54
    and Beatrice, 674
    Beatrice citing Plato, 704
    Bernard, Saint, as character, 99
    biblical allusions in, 101
    Bonaventure in, 120
    causal link between planets and
        angels, 41
    Dante's ideal of the empire
        explained by Justinian, 340
    dedicated to Cangrande, 137
    features of mystical writing, 635
    Francis in, 415
    illustrations of Doré, 318
    Jason crucial figure in, 535
    language theory in, 368–369

life of Francis of Assisi as alle-
    gorical marriage, 30
Mary as queen of Heaven, 597
modeled on Ptolemaic system,
    192
music in, 632–633
and name of Christ, 166
neologisms in, 640
references to the Veronica, 856
on relationship between music
    and words, 631
role of theological virtues in, 868
sources of mystical contents, 635
statement on language, 556
sun as symbol of God, 802
Thomas Aquinas in, 57
Paradiso (1507 edition), *896*
Paradiso (film by Psiche), 247
Paradiso/Dante's Dream (film,
    David E. Simpson), 249
*Paralipomeni della Batra-
    comiomachi* (Leopardi),
    270
Paris *(Parìs; Paride),* **678**
Paris et Vienne, 678
Paris, Gaston, 236
Paris, University of, 417
Parker, Alan, 249
parlare italico, lo. See Italian lan-
    guage
Parlement of Fowles (Chaucer),
    162
Parmenides *(Parmenide),* 605,
    678
Parnassus, **678–679**
Parodi, Ernesto Giacomo, 184
    directorship of *Bullettino,* 786
    edition of the *Convivio,* 231
    on virtues determining moral
        topography of *Paradiso,*
        868
Parodi, Marco, 283
parody, use of Dante material in,
    248
par(h)omoeon (paranomeon). See
    alliteration
Pascoli, Giovanni
    on allegorical significance of
        Dante's actions in Lethe,
        562
    on the Furies, 429
    on Matelda, 601
    Pietrobono and, 701
Pasiphae *(Pasife),* **679**
Pasolini, Pier Paolo, 248–249
Pasquazi, Silvio, 609
Pastoralis Cura (bull), 177
pastorella, 600
Pastrone, Giovanni, 248
Patarines. *See* Cathars
Paterini. *See* Cathars
"Patriarch of Western Monasticism,
    The." *See* Benedict, Saint

Paul, Saint, **679–680**
  and allegory, 25
  and choice of Epicureans as
      exemplars of heresy, 483
  in the *Commedia*, 760
  concept of "old man" *versus*
      "new man," 659
  conversion, 223
Paul the Deacon
  as historical source, 488, 751
  Life of Pope Gregory the Great,
      823, 824
Paur, Theodor, 534
Pazzi, Jacopo Nacca de', 1
Pazzo, Rinier, **680**
peace
  attainable under single ruler, 339
  Dante and, 163, 339
Peccato di Ulisse e altri studi dan-
    teschi, Il (Fubini), 427
Peck, Bob, 284, 285
Peckham, John, 661
Pelagius, 482
  on unbaptized children, 566
Pellegrini, Anthony L., 287
Pellegrini, Flaminio, 231
Pellico, Silvio, 321
penance
  rehabilitative and remedial in
      Purgatory, 191, 220
  retributive and eternal in Hell,
      220
  sacrament of, 761
  See also confession; salvation
Penthesilea, **680**
  in Limbo, 888
Pépin, Jean
  and Dante's allegory, 28
  on Phaëton as allegory, 31
Pequigney, Joseph, 817
Peraldus, William (Guillaume
      Peyraut or Peyraud; Guillel-
      mus Pariensis), **680–681**
  Summa de vitiis et de virtutibus,
      192, 870
  and order of vices and virtues,
      229
Perillus *(Perillo)*, **681–682**
Perini, Dino, 114
Peripatetics, 61, **682**
Pernicone, Vincenzo, 579
Perpetual Almanac of Prophatius, 69
Perse, Saint-John (Marie-René
      Léger), 262
Persius (Aulus Persius Flaccus,
      Persio), **682**
  as *auctor* of satire, 180
  in Limbo, 254
personification, 25, 30
  as distinguished from other kinds
      of allegories, 28
perspectiva. See optics
Perspectiva (Alhazen), 661

Peter, Saint, 596, **683–684**, *684*
  in *Commedia*, 760, 882
  importance of for papacy, 670
Peter II of Aragon, 157
Peter III of Aragon, **684–685**
  as negligent ruler, 639
Peter Abelard, 304
  influence on Peter Lombard, 683
  on Limbo, 567
  Sic et Non, 74
  as source for Dante's theology,
      814
  and virtuous pagans, 872
Peter Comestor *(Pietro Man-*
      giadore), **682**
Peter Lombard *(Pietro Lombardo)*,
      682–683
  and baptism, 82
  on *In exitu Israel de Aegypto*,
      525
  as source for Dante's theology,
      813
  student of Hugh of St. Victor,
      495
  and symbolism of seven, 656
Peter of Spain (Petrus Hispanus;
      Pietro Ispano), 682, **683**
  See also John XXI (pope)
Peter the Comb-Seller *(Pier Petti-*
      naio), 419, **682**
  and prayers for Sapia, 419,
      762–763
Peter the Venerable, 520
Petrarch, 28, 75, *685*, **685–687**
  Boccaccio and, 110, 112, 271
  Chaucer's knowledge of the writ-
      ings of, 160
  on Cino da Pistoia, 171
  and Dante, 271–272
  on Dante, 354, 845
  influence of petrose poems on,
      690
  Pietro Alighieri and, 21
  Rerum memorandarum libri, 137
  Rerum vulgarium fragmenta,
      826
  Rime, 144
  Robert of Anjou and, 746
  and versification, 478
Petrocchi, Giorgio, **687–688**, 826
  on Dante's sojourns in Verona,
      137
  edition of the *Commedia*, 184,
      200, 268
  on manuscripts of *Commedia*,
      199
  "National Edition" of the *Com-*
      media, 198, 204
  and television series on *Comme-*
      dia, 283
petrose poems, 140, 141, 579,
      580–581, **688–690**
  and lore of Saturn, 763

and petrification theme in
    Medusa episode, 604
  and power of sexual passion, 774
  references to optics in, 661
  women and, 887
Pettine, Giovanni, 247
Pézard, André, **690**
  and *Bibliografia dantesca*, 262
  on Matelda, 601
  on presence of Priscian among
      the sodomites, 712
  on sodomy of Brunetto Latini,
      789
Phaëthon, **690–691**
Pharisees *(fariseo)*, **691**
Pharsalia (Lucan), 9, 49, 146, 572
  Dante's knowledge of epic
      poetry, 345
  description of Antaeus, 421
  as historical poem, 254
  on Lethe, 561
  on Medusa, 603
  on Sabellus, 759
  on Sesto, 773
  source of Mediterranean geogra-
      phy, 174
Philalethes (King John of Saxony),
      435
  collaboration with Witte, 268, 886
  patron of the Deutsche Dante-
      Gesellschaft, 300
  translation of Dante, 267
Philastrius, Bishop, 872
Philip Augustus, 424
Philip III (Philip the Bold, *Filippo*)
      (France), **691**
  as negligent ruler, 639
Philip IV, the Fair (France),
      691–692
  and Clement V, 177
  denounced in the *Commedia*,
      407–408, 491, 494
  and Henry VII of Luxemburg,
      480
  William of Nogaret and, 885
Phillipps, Francis, 504
Phillips, Stephen, 321
Phillips, Tom, 284, 286, 504
  illustrations to the *Inferno*,
      827–828
Philo of Alexandria
  and allegory, 24
  Middle Platonism of, 642
philosophers
  Guido Cavalcanti described as,
      460
  in Limbo, 255
philosophical allegory
  in *Convivio*, 226–227
  influence on Dante, 181
philosophy, **692–696**
  advanced study of, in Florence,
      397–398

Polynices *(Polinice)*, 3, 5, 356, **704**
Polyxena *(Polissena)*, **704–705**
Pompey (Gnaeus Pompeius Magnus; *Pompeo)*, 146, **705**
Pontius Pilate, as "great coward," 647
popular iconography and Dante's structure of Hell, 474
"Popule mee" (Dante), 19
Porena, Manfredi
   on fraudulent counsel, 423
   on Matelda, 601
Porphyry, 641–642, 694
   Isagoge, 61
   texts used in Trivium, 832
Portinari, Beatrice, 16–17
   death, 18
   See also Beatrice
Portinari, Folco, 89, 402
Portrait of the Artist, The (Joyce), 257
"Portrait, The" (Gogol), 277
"Poscia ch'Amor del tutto m'ha lasciato" (Dante), 140, 579
Postel, Christian Heinrich, 265
Posterior Analytics (Aristotle), 62
Potter, Joy, 817
Poulet, Georges, 817
Pound, Ezra, **705**
   and Dante, 257
   and Eliot, 337
   and translations of the *Commedia,* 826
poverty *(povertà;* Lat. *paupertas),* **705–707**
   Council of Vienne on, 399
   overcoming avarice, 870
Powell, Phyllis W., 278
Power of Dante, The (Grandgent), 452
Powers (angels), 42
Powers of Horror: An Essay on Abjection (Kristeva), 818
praise, poetry of, 450
prayer, **707–709**
   for the dead, 728, 731
   invocation to the Muses, 630
   sung by souls in Purgatory, 725
predestination, 814
   in *Commedia,* 872
Prell, Friedrich, 503
pride, 163, **709–711**, 870
   Arachne, 58
   Briareus, 126
   Cacciaguida, 22
   Capaneus as epitome of, 141
   contrapasso, 221–222
   Cyrus, example of, 243
   and love of the wrong object, 870
   magnanimity associated with, 584

in Purgatory, *14,* 101–102, 191, *709, 710*
   Oderisi da Gubbio, 658
   Omberto Aldobrandeschi, 660
   Provenzan Salvani, 718
   Rehoboam *(Roboàm),* 741
   Sennacherib, 772
   Saul as example of, 764
   symbolized by lion, 85
primo popolo, 392, 439, 457
Primum Mobile, 68, 192, 193, 233, 383, 671, **711–712**
   aligned with moral philosophy (ethics), 228, 866
   Ptolemy and, 720
   vision of God as point of light, 564
Principalities (Dominions), 42, 43
   moving Heaven of Venus, 546, 855
Principi di una scienza nuova d'intorno alla commune natura della nazioni (Vico), 269
printing
   of the *Commedia* in Venice, 210
   and value of commentaries, 208
Priscian, 2, **712**
   as sodomite, 787
   texts used in Trivium, 832
Priscillian, 712
Prison-House of Language, The: A Critical Account of Structuralism and Russian Formalism (Jameson), 817
Problemi di critica dantesca: Prima serie (1893–1918) (Barbi), 84
Problemi di critica dantesca: Seconda serie (1920–1937) (Barbi), 84
Problemi fondamentali per un nuovo commento della Divina Commedia (Barbi), 84
Proclus, 642
Procne, 135
Procopius, 550
prodigal and miserly. *See* avaricious and prodigal
prodigal, avaricious and. *See* avaricious and prodigal
prodigality, 75, **712–713**
   as sin of incontinence, 508
   See also avaricious and prodigal, the
Prohemio (Santillana), 280
Prolegomeni della Divina Commedia (Scartazzini), 268
Prometheus *(Prometeo),* **713**
Prometheus Unbound (Shelley)
   Dante imagery in, 775
   influence of Dante on, 256
prophecy, **713–716**
   prophecies in the *Commedia,* 67, 316, 514–515, 794

Corso Donati's violent death, 449
Dante presented as prophet, 207
   of Dante's exile by Cacciaguida, 486
   ex eventu, 714–715
   of final defeat of White Guelfs by Vanni Fucci, 428
   five hundred ten and five (DXV), **381–383,** 408
   genuine prophecies, 715
   political, 169
"Prophecy of Dante, The" (Byron), 256
Proscrits, Les (Balzac), 261
prose, **716–717**
Prose antiche di Dante, Petrarcha, et Boccaccio, 686
Prose della volgar lingua (Bembo), 60, 272
   influence on commentators of the *Commedia,* 211
Prose Lancelot, 408
Proserpina, **717–718**
Prose Tristan cycle, 832
prosopopeia. *See* personification
prostitutes, 888
Protestantism's view of Dante, 263
Proust, Marcel, 261
Provençal language
   Dante on, 716
   Dante's familiarity with literature, 16
   Italian writers writing in, 526
   tenso, 807
   tradition adapted by Sicilian School, 775
Provenzan Salvani, **718,** 762
prudence
   associated with Sun, 193, 233, 868
   as cardinal virtue, 867
Prudentius, 25
Prufrock and Other Observations (Eliot), 337
Psalms, **718–719**
Psalterium decem chordarum (Joachim of Fiore), 537
Psalters, 719
Pseudo-Brunetto Latini, 438
   and Florentine Chronicle, 167
Pseudo-Dionysius. *See* Dionysius the Areopagite
Psiche, 247
Psychomachia (Prudentius), 25
Ptolemaic universe, **719–721**
Ptolemy (Claudius Ptolemaeus), 67, 68, 719, **721**
   concept of earth, 329
   Dante's references to, 173
   and fixed stars, 383

Romuald, Saint *(Romoaldo),* 583, 625, **757**
  in the *Commedia,* 760
Romuleon, 97
Romulus *(Romolo),* **757**
"Rosa fresca aulentissima" (Cielo d'Alcamo), 776
roses, symbolism of, 881
Rossetti, Dante Gabriel, 503
  Dante and His Circle, 828
  interpretation of the *Commedia,* 260
  on Matelda's role as guide and teacher, 601
  Norton and, 652
  translation of the *Vita Nuova,* 256, 828–829
Rossetti, William Michael, 829
Rubbi, Andrea, 319
Rubini, Rubino, 283
Rudolph I *(Rodolfo),* 434, 488, **757**
  avarice of, 77
  as negligent ruler, 639
  Nicholas III and, 648
Rüegg, August, 269
Ruggieri, Archbishop (Ruggieri degli Ubaldini), 665, **757–758,** 823, 838, 839
Ruin the Sacred Truths: Poetry and Belief from the Bible to the Present (Bloom), 818
Rule of Saint Benedict *(Regula Monachorum),* 97
ruler, single world, 617–618
rulers, just
  Constantine among, 216
  review by Eagle, 547
  William II of Sicily among, 885
rulers, negligent. *See* negligent rulers
rulers, unjust
  Haakon V of Norway, 468
  review by Eagle, 547
rulers who deferred their repentance
  Henry I (Navarre), 478
  Philip III, 691
Ruskin, John
  and Dante, 257
  Norton and, 652
Russell, Ken, 249
Russia, Dante in, **276–279**
Russian Modernism, 277
Rusticucci, Iacopo, **758**
  in the *Commedia*
    on Borsiere, Guiglielmo, 125
    introducing Aldobrandi, Tegghiaio, 13
    as sodomite, 787
Rutebeuf, 355
Ruth, **758**
Ryan, Christopher, 829

S
Sabellius *(Sabellio),* 482, **759**
Sabellus *(Sabello),* **759**
Sachs, Hans, 264
Sacred Wood, The (Eliot), 257
Sacrum Commercium sancti Francisci cum domina Paupertate, 707
Saggi critici (Critical Essays) (De Sanctis), 291
Saggi danteschi (Pietrobono), 701
Saggi di filosofia dantesca (Nardi), 638
Saggi e note di critica dantesca (Nardi), 638
Saggio critico sul Petrarca (De Sanctis), 291
Said, Edward W., 818
Sainte-Beuve, Charles Augustin, 261
Saint Michael and Satan (Raphael), 500
Saints, **759–760**
  Saint Lucy as patron saint of Dante, 576
Saladin (Yusuf ibn Ayyub, Salah ad-Din), **760,** 789
  Dante's treatment of, 521–522
Salimbene of Parma, 681
Sallust
  Bellum Iugurthinum, 233–234
  as historical source, 488
Salò (film, Pasolini), 249
Salomone da Lucca, 370
Salterello, Lapo, **761**
Salvani, Provenzan, 511
salvation, **761–762**
  Cato, 148, 873
  Mary's role in economy of, 597
  pilgrimages and, 702
  Ripheus, 548, 745, 762, 824, 873
  structural-ideological paradigm of *Commedia,* 187
  Trajan, 548, 745, 762, 824, 873
Salve Regina, 632, 708
Salvini, Anton Maria, 528
Salvini, Tommaso, 320
Samaritan, **762**
Sämtliche Werke (Schlegel), 267
Sand, George, 260
Sangallo, Francesco da, 503
Sangallo, Giuliano da, 503
Sanguineti, Edoardo, 320
San Pier Martire of Santa Maria Novella (Confraternity), 400
Sansovino, Francesco, 212, 850
Santa Croce
  as example of Mediterranian Gothic, 250
  Franciscan school, 398, 415, 417, 607, 754
  and optics, 661
  Olivi teaching at, 659

Santa Maria Novella, *314,* 387
  Dominican school at, 313, 398, 417, 607
Santillana, Marqués de, 280
Santi, Zilberto, 21
San Zanobi (confraternity), 400
San Zeno, Abbot of, 424, **762,** 785
Sapegno, Natalino
  on fraudulent counsel, 423
  on heterodoxy in *Paradiso,* 644
  on Matelda, 601
  on *matta bestialitade,* 588
Sapelli, Luigi, 247
Sapia, 419, **762–763**
  in Purgatory, 889
Sapiens Stultitia (Wise Foolishness) (Messerschmid), 264
Saracens, **763**
  as heretics, 520–521
  as legitimate crusade enemy, 240
Sarah *(Sarra),* **763**
Sarolli, Gian Roberto
  on 515 prophecy, 382
  on *veltro,* 852
Sassoferrato, Bartolo of
  on Dante, 263
  treatise on Guelfs and Ghibellines, 440, 459
Sassol Mascheroni, 135, **763**
Satan *(Satàn),* 573, **763**
  body constituted by the damned, 117
  See also Beelzebub, Lucifer
satire, 180
  as middle style of writing, 180
Saturn *(Saturno),* **763–764**
  aligned with astrology, 228
  aligned with astronomy, 736
  associated with temperance, 193, 233, 868
Saturn, Heaven of, 671, 675
  Benedict in, 97
  and figures taken from monastic life, 625
  Macarius in, 583
  Romuald in, 757
Saul *(Saùl),* **764**
Saussure, Ferdinand, 556
Sayer, Elizabeth, 829
Sayers, Dorothy Leigh, **765**
  translation of the *Commedia,* 504, 826–827
S. Bonaventurae opera omnia, 121
scala naturae. See chain of being
scandalmongers. *See* schismatics
Scaramuzza, Francesco, 503
Scarano, N., 601
Scarpetta degli Ordelaffi, 745
Scartazzini, Giovanni Andrea
  and *Jahrbuch der Deutschen Dante-Gesellschaft,* 534
  on Matelda, 601

Siger of Brabant, 57, 62, 230, 460, **776–777**
  in the *Commedia,* 483
    depicted in Heaven of the Sun, 812
    as wise saint, 64
    as source for Dante's theology, 813
    on study of science, 768
sight, Saint Lucy associated with, 576
Signorelli e Dante (Gizzi), 500
Signorelli, Luca, 500
sì, language of, 409, 526, 716
simile *(similitudine),* **778–781**
  use of, in *Commedia,* 188
Simler, Josias, 263
Simon de Brion (Brie). *See* Martin IV
Simone Donati, 131, 766
Simone Fidati da Cascia, 399
Simonelli, Maria, 829
  on *Convivio,* 471
  first critical edition of the *Convivio,* 231
Simonides *(Simonide),* **781**
simonists, 190, 420, 513, 714, **781–782,** *782,* 869
Simon Magus *(Simon mago),* **781,** 782
simony *(simonia),* 77, 585–586, **782**
  barratry compared to, 84
  Boniface VIII and, 123
  Clement V, 78, 177–178, 586, 755
  Donation of Constantine as root of, 315
  name derived from Simon Magus, 781
  Nicholas III, 648
Simpson, David E., 249
Sinclair, John Dickinson, 286, 826, 828
Singleton, Charles Southward, 499, **783,** 816, 817, 826, 828
  Commedia
    allegorical significance of Dante's immersion in Lethe, 562
    as encyclopedia of vice and virtue, 866
    as journey of exodus, 365
    Matelda, 599, 600, 601, 602, 868
    on root of Eunoe, 358
    on *veltro,* 853
  conversion as key topic in Dante, 222
  on Dante and symbolism of number seven, 656
  on Dante as Thomist, 812
  and Dante's allegory, 28, 29, 30, 804

  on Dante's use of simile, 780
  on *Epistle to Cangrande,* 350
  on translation of *ingiuria,* 518
  Vita Nuova
    and conversion, 223
    criticism of, 874
    Essay on the "Vita Nuova," 286
    numerology in, 654, 876
Sinon, 33, 369, 599, **783,** 883
sins
  capital, 869
    and organization of Purgatory, 730
    Peraldus's influence on Dante's system, 681
    wrath as one of, 890
  classification
    influence of Aristotle, 693
    influence of Cicero on, 695
    by order of gravity, 449
  classification in Hell, 419
    not according to seven deadly sins, 513
  classified as violent, 860
  as consequence of misdirected love, 785, 789
  despair as, 298–299
  effect on the body, 117
  original sin and salvation, 761
  pride as root of all sin, 709
  seven capital sins, 89
  social and political consequences of, 420
  spiritual, 449
siren, **783–784**
  dream of, 724
Sismonde de Sismandi
  translation of Ugolino episode in *terza rima,* 260
Sisson, C. H., 827
sleeping, function in *Commedia,* 324–325
sloth *(accidia),* **784–786**
  Abbot of San Zeno, 762
  contrapasso, 222
  and deficient love of the right object, 870
  effect on the body, 117
  purged in Purgatory, 191
"Slyshu, slyshu rannij led" ("I Hear, I Hear the Early Ice") (Madelstam), 278
Snead, James, 818
social concerns in the *Commedia* stressed by Ruskin, 257
Società Anonima Ambrosio, 247
Società Dantesca Italiana, 84, 204, 219, 687, **786–787**
  and canon of Dante's epistles, 353
  Contini president of, 218

Palagio dell'Arte della Lana, *786*
Socrates *(Sòcrate, Socrato),* 693–694, **787**
  in Noble Castle, 651, 692
Sodom *(Soddoma),* 788
sodomites, 86, *787,* **787–788,** 861, 869
  Accorso, Francesco d', 2
  Aldobrandi, Tegghiaio, 13
  Andrea dei Mozzi, Bishop, 36
  Brunetto Latini, 127, 128, 690, 773
  Guido Guerra, 461
  as guilty of blasphemy, 690
  in Hell
    Borsiere, Guglielmo, 125
  Julius Caesar and accusations of sodomy, 545
  Latini, Brunetto, 2
  Pézard on, 690
  Priscian, 2, 712
  in Purgatory, 578
sodomy, **788–789**
  in Hell
    sin of violence against God and nature, 773, 860, 861
  in Hell, as sin of violence against God and nature, 578
  in Purgatory, 509
"Sodomy in Dante's *Inferno* and *Purgatorio*" (Pequigney), 817
Sofonisba (Trissino), 319
Soldan, **789**
Sollers, Phillipe, 817
Solomon *(Salomone),* 790, **790**
  and definition of nobility, 228–229
Solon *(Solone),* **790**
Solzhenitsyn, Aleksandr, 277, 278
Somnium Scipionis (Macrobius), 233
Songe d'Enfer, Le (Raoul de Houdenc), 664
Song of Songs, **790–791**
sonnet, 610, 612, **791–792**
  Giacomo da Lentini as inventor of, 776
  and *tenzone,* 807–808
  in *Vita Nuova,* 875
soothsayers, 190, 513, **792–794,** *793,* 869
  Amphiaraus, 36
  Aruns, 66
  Asdente, 66
  Bonatti, 120
  Calchas, 135
  Eurypylus *(Euripilo),* 359–360
  and magicians, 420
  Scot with, 770
  shades of the, 586
  Tiresias among, 820